PRACTICAL HANDBOOK OF
CIVIL ENGINEERING

[*Ready Reference for Practising Engineers*]

Er. C.S.D. Singhal

Edited by
Vineet Kumar

KHANNA PUBLISHERS
Operational Office
4575/15, Onkar House, Ground Floor,
Darya Ganj, New Delhi 110 002
Phones : 011-23243042, 011-23243043 & Mob. 09811541460
email : contactus@khannapublishers.in

Published by :

Romesh Chander Khanna & Vineet Khanna
for **KHANNA PUBLISHERS**
2-B, Nath Market, Nai Sarak
Delhi- 110 006 (India)

Website : www.khannapublishers.in

Hologram & Description

To all readers of our books, from yourself if being defrauded by pirates to prevent, please make sure that there is an Hologram on the cover of our books with the below specifications. If you find any book without Hologram and Description, please mail us at **contactus@khannapublishers.in**

Thanking you

ISBN No. 978-81-7409-246-5

***First Edition :* 2010**
***First Reprint :* 2016**

***Price :* ₹ 649.00**

PREFACE

In the present book an effort has been made to collect all useful data and site information which is must for a civil engineer working on project sites in different organisations in our volume for their ready reference.

This single volume can be replaced by a number of books which are required for reference at work sites. This collection is also usefull for the contractors at the time of tendering for analysing of rates of different items of works and thereafter execution of base works accordingly as per specifications.

Design engineers will also find sufficient data required at the time of preparing detailed designs. The students who are preparing for their examination and practice projects are also benefited.

The aim of this book is not to supply detailed designs for big projects, which is done in the design office specialised for the job, but for normal works all designs can be done at the work sites by the site engineer by the help of this book and works can be carried out according to specifications.

The book contains all field tests, site proceedings, planning , casting and estimating of works on the basis of Indian and IRC standards on modern technology.

A great care has been taken to express the contents of the book tothe point in a simple language, yet there may be several mistakes and errors, which may arise in such big volume and I will be grateful of such ommissions and errors brought to my knowledge. Any suggestion will be coordially acknowledged with thanks.

C.S.D. SINGHAL

CONTENTS

Chapter		Pages
1. GENERAL INFORMATION	...	**1—31**
1·1. Symbols and Formulae used in Engineering	...	1
1·2. Units	...	4
1·3. Values of Mathematical Functions	...	16
1·4. General—Tables and Appendices	...	17
2. APPLIED MATHEMATICS	...	**32—65**
2.1. Geometry	...	32
2·2. Important Problems	...	35
2·3. Formulae in Trignometry	...	39
2·4. Formulae in Differential and Integral Calculus	...	41
2·5. Some well known Curves	...	43
2·6. Formulae in Plane and Solid Mensuration	...	44
2·7. Dynamics and Statics	...	53
2·8. Plane Coordinate Geometry	...	54
2·9. Solid Geometry (Co-ordinate—three dimensions)	...	60
2·10. Statistics and Graphics	...	61
3. ESTIMATING AND COSTING	...	**66—102**
3·1. Requirement of Materials in Different Items of Works	...	66
3·2. Working Capacities	...	73
3·3. Measurements of Works	...	78
3·4. Costing of Works	...	85
3·5. Area Definition in Building Work (IS : 3861)	...	91
4. THEORY AND DESIGN OF STRUCTURE	...	**103—160**
4·1. Elastic Theory	...	103
4·2. Timber Structures : (A) Timber Beams and Posts	...	120
(B) Flitched or Composite Beams	...	124
(C) Designing Timber Columns and Struts	...	125
(D) Roof Truss in Wood	...	126
(E) Wooden Stairs	...	128
4·3. Masonry Dams	...	129
4·4. Retaining Walls and Walls	...	133
4·5. Foundations	...	141
4·6. Fasteners : (A) Riveted Joints	...	148
(B) Welded Joint	...	154

5. SURVEYING	...	**161—209**
5·1. Printing of Alphabet	...	161
5·2. Conventional Signs used in Topographical Maps	...	162
5·3. Scales (*a*) Diagonal Scale	...	163
5·4. Chain Survey	...	164
5·5. Obstacles in Chaining	...	169
5·6. Levelling	...	170
5·7. Telescope used in Survey Instruments	...	173
5·8. Theodolite and Compass Survey	...	175
5·9. Contouring	...	181
5·10. Adjustment of levelling instruments	...	182
5·11. Adjustment of Theodolites	...	185
5·12. Techeometric Survey	...	187
5·13. Plane Tabling	...	190
5·14. Capacity of Survey Work (I.D.U.P.)	...	194
5·15. Curves	...	194
5·16. Minor Survey Instruments	...	198
5·17. Astronomical Terms	...	206
6. BUILDING MATERIALS	...	**210—307**
6·1. Stones	...	210
6·2(*a*). Nomenclature of Stones	...	210
6·2(*b*). Bricks	...	217
6·3. Lime	...	222
6·4. Timber	...	224
6·5. Ferrous metals	...	239
6·6. Non-Ferrous Metals	...	244
6·7. Bituminous Materials	...	247
6·8. Paints	...	249
6·9. Miscellaneous Materials	...	252
6·10. Aggregates	...	269
6·11. Concrete	...	281
6·12. Field Engineering Materials and Devices : Shoring, Shuttering, Scaffolding and Underpinning	...	295
7. BUILDING CONSTRUCTION	...	**308—395**
7·1. Denotations or Notations in Drawings	...	308
7·2. Stone Walls	...	309
7·3. Technical Terms (Stone masonry and walls)	...	310
7·4. Technical terms (Brickwork)	...	311

7·5. Rules for Bonding in Masonry Work with Bricks ... 318
7·6. Arched Roofs ... 320
7·7. Technical Terms (Arch work) ... 320
7·8. Wall Lining (Cladding) ... 323
7·9. False Ceilings ... 325
7·10. Damp-Proofing in Buildings ... 326
7·11. Lightening Conductors on Buildings ... 330
7·12. Anti Termite Treatment—(Protection against white ants) ... 331
7·13. Sound Proofing of Buildings ... 333
7·14. Fire Resistance ... 337
7·15. Plastering, Pointing and White Washing ... 340
7·16. Flooring ... 342
7·17. Ventilation ... 345
7·18. Door and Window Opening ... 347
7·19. Roofs ... 349
7·20. Forms of Carpentry Joints ... 369
7·21. Building Bye Laws ... 373
7·22. Colony Planning ... 388
7·23. Air Conditioning ... 391

8. CONCRETE TECHNOLOGY ... 396—505

8·1. Cement ... 396
8·1·1. Storing of Cement ... 396
8·1·2. Detoriation of Cement ... 396
8·1·3. Contamination of Cement ... 396
8·1·4. Tests for Cement ... 397
8·1·5. Types of Cement ... 404
8·1·6. Strength of Portland Cement with Age (From date of pouring) ... 407
8·1·7. Different types of Cement as Classified by the Bureau of Indian Standards ... 407
8·1·8. Admixtures ... 408
8·2. Aggregates ... 409
8·2·1. Charateristics of a Good Aggregate ... 409
8·2·2. Coarse Aggregates ... 409
8·2·3. Fine Aggregate (Sand) ... 414
8·2·4. Fineness Modulus of Aggregates ... 417
8·3. Water for Concrete ... 422
8·3·1. Water Hydration ... 422
8·3·2. Test ... 422
8·3·2. Requirement of Water in Concrete ... 423

8·4. Reinforcement Steel (Re bars) ... 423
8·4.1. Reinforcement ... 423
8·4.2. Grades of Steel–TOR-50 ; TOR-55 and TOR-60 (TORKARI) ... 426
8·4.3. Thermo Mechanical Treatment (TMT) ... 427
8·4.4. Bending, Binding and Placing of Re-bars ... 429
8·4·5. Gas Pressure Welding for Jointing Re-bars ... 433
8·4·6. Protection of Reinforcement against Corrosion ... 435
8·4·7. Bar Bending Schedules ... 435
8·4.8. Fixers ... 437
8·5. Centering and Shuttering (Form Work) ... 439
8·5·1. Form work and Scaffolding Systems ... 439
8·5·2. Modern Shuttering Materials and Devices ... 442
8·5·3. Moving Scaffolds for High Rise Buildings ... 443
8·5·4. Custom built Steel Shuttering, Centering and Scaffolding ... 443
8·5·5. Wedge Lock type of Scaffolds ... 444
8·5·6. Stay-in-place Concrete Formwork for Deck Slabs of Girder Bridges ... 444
8·5·7. Stripping time for Formwork ... 445
8·6. Cement Concrete ... 446
8·6·1. Batching of Concrete ... 446
8·6·2. Mixing of Concrete ... 446
8·6·3. Mechanical Mixing ... 446
8·6·4. Transporting of concrete ... 448
8·6·5. Laying of Concrete ... 451
8·6·6. Compaction of Concrete ... 452
8·6·7. Curing of Concrete ... 453
8·6·8. Concrete under special situations ... 454
8·6·9. Shortcomings in Concrete ... 455
8·6·10. Concrete Deterioration ... 458
8·6·11. Durability of Concrete ... 458
8·6·12. Joints in Concrete Structures ... 459
8·6·13. Fire Resistance ... 461
8·6·14. Tests for Concrete ... 463
8·6.15. Factors influencing Workability ... 471
8·6·16. Factors influencing Strength of Concrete ... 472
8·6·17. General Tables regarding Cement Concrete ... 472
8·6·18. Concrete Mix Design ... 473
8·6·20. Protection to Reinforcement ... 487
8·6·21. Strengthening of RCC Beams in Bridges ... 490
8·6·22. Special Preparation of Concrete ... 490
8·6·23. Sound proofing in Concrete ... 495
8·6·24. Concrete Surface Finishing ... 496
8·6·25. Water Proofing of Concrete ... 497

9 (A) REINFORCED CONCRETE STRUCTURE (SIMPLE STRESS) ... 506—567

9A.1. Principles of Design ... 506
9A.2. Provision of Shear Reinforcements ... 507
9A.3. Bending Moment in Slabs and Beams ... 507
9A.4. Basic rules for the Design of Beams and Slabs ... 508
9A.5. General data of RC Structures ... 511
9A.6. Check for Bond ... 517
9A.7. Temperature or Distribution Reinforcement ... 518
9A.8. Two-way Reinforced or Doubly Reinforced Beams ... 518
9A.9(A). Design of Four-way Supported Slabs ... 519
9A.9(B). Circular and Elliptical Slabs ... 521
9A·10. Water Pipes ... 526
9A.11. Design of Columns ... 527
9A·12. Design of T-Beam ... 537
9A.13. Stairs ... 541
9A.14. Walls ... 544
9A.15. Load on Lintels ... 545
9A.16. Design of RC Water Tanks ... 548
9A.17. Reinforced Brick Work ... 553
9A.18. Design of Prestressed Concrete beams ... 556
9A·19. Technical terms used in RCC ... 563

9(B). LIMIT STATE DESIGN IN RCC ... 568—681

9B·1. Design of Singly Reinforced Sections ... 572
9B·2. Design of Doubly Reinforced Beams (Limit State Design) ... 574
9B·3. Design of T-Sections ... 576
9B·4. Shear in Beams ... 578
9B·5. Columns ... 580
9B·6. Design of Beams ... 582
9B·7. Design Table ... 584
9B·8. Design Tables for Slabs ... 608
9B·9. Design Tables for Columns ... 637
9B·10. Crack Width Calculations ... 650
9B·11. Design Data for Reference ... 652

10. STEEL STRUCTURES (AS PER BIS CODE : IS 800 : 2007 INDIAN STANDARDS) ... 682—766

10·1. General ... 682
10·1·1. Technical Terms ... 682
10·1·2. Units ... 688
10·1·3. Convention for Member Axes ... 688

10·2. Materials ... 688
10·2·1. Structural Steel ... 689
10·2·2. Properties ... 689
10·2·3. Connections ... 689
10·3. General Design Requirements ... 692
10·3·1. Methods of Design ... 692
10·3·2. Loads and Forces ... 692
10·3·3. Erection Loads ... 692
10·3·4. Temperature Effects ... 692
10·3·5. Load Combinations ... 693
10·3·6. Geometrical Properties ... 693
10·3·7. Types of Elements ... 695
10·3·8. Maximum Effective Slenderness Ratio ... 696
10·3·9. Resistance to Horizontal Forces ... 696
10·3·10. Expansion Joints ... 697
10·4. Structural Analysis ... 698
10·4·1. Non-sway and Sway Frames ... 698
10·4·2. Rigid Construction ... 698
10·4·3. Semi-rigid Construction ... 698
10·4·4. Simple Construction ... 698
10·4·5. Base Stiffness ... 698
10·4·6. Notional Horizontal Loads ... 699
10·4·7. Elastic Analysis ... 699
10·4·8. Plastic Analysis ... 699
10·4·9. Restraints ... 700
10·5. Limit State Design ... 700
10·6. Design of Tension Members ... 705
10·6·1. Tension Members ... 705
10·6·2. Design Strength Due to Yielding of Gross Section ... 705
10·6·3. Design Strength Due to Rupture of Critical Section ... 705
10·6·4. Design Strength Due to Block Shear ... 707
10·7. Design of Compression Members ... 707
10·7·1. Design Strength ... 707
10·7·2. Effective Length ... 717
10·7·3. Eccentric Beam Connection ... 717
10·7·4. Compression Members in Trusses ... 717
10·7·5. Angle Struts ... 717
10·8. Columns ... 720
10·8·1. Column bases ... 720
10·8·2. Gusseted Bases ... 721
10·8·3. Slab Bases ... 721
10·8·4. Laced Columns ... 722

10·8·5. Design of Lacings ... 723
10·8·6. Battened Columns ... 724
10·8·7. Design of Battens ... 728
10·9. Members Subjected to Bending ... 728
10·9·1. Effective Span of Beams ... 728
10·9·2. Factored Design Moment ... 729
10·9·3. Holes in the Tension Zone ... 729
10·9·4. Shear ... 731
10·9·5. Stiffened Web Panels ... 731
10·9·6. Design of Beams and Plate Girders with Solid Webs ... 731
10·9·7. Sectional Properties ... 734
10·9·8. Flanges ... 734
10·9·9. Flange Splices ... 734
10·9·10. Connection of Flanges to Web ... 735
10·9·11. Bolted/Riveted Construction ... 735
10·9·12. Welded Construction ... 735
10·9·13. Webs ... 735
10·9·14. Stiffner Design ... 735
10·10. Connections ... 736
10·10·1. Location Details of Fasteners ... 736
10·10·2. Minimum Spacing ... 736
10·10·3. Maximum Spacing ... 736
10·10·4. Edge and End Distances ... 736
10·10·5. Tacking Fasteners ... 737
10·10·6. Countersunk Heads ... 737
10·10·7. Bearing Type Bolts ... 737
10·10·8. Shear Capacity of Bolt ... 737
10·10·9. Bearing Capacity of the Bolt ... 738
10·10·10. Tension Capacity ... 738
10·10·11. Welds and Welding ... 739
10·10·12. Size of Weld ... 739
10·10·13. Effective Throat Thickness ... 740
10·10·14. Effective Length or Area of Weld ... 740
10·15. Intermittent Welds ... 741
10·10·16. Weld Types and Quality ... 741
10·10·17. Butt Welds ... 741
10·10·18. Stresses Due to Individual Forces ... 741
10·10·19. Combined bearing, bending and shear ... 742
10·10·20. Lug Angles ... 742
10·11. Working Stress Design ... 743
10·11·1. General Design Requirements ... 743
10·11·2. Tension Members ... 743
10·11·3. Compression Members ... 743

10·12. Design and Detailing for Earthquake Loads	...	744
10·12·1. Steel Frames	...	744
10·12·2. Load and Load Combinations	...	744
10·12·3. Response Reduction Factor	...	744
10·12·4. Connections, Joints and Fasteners	...	744
10·12·5. Columns	...	744
10·13. Testing	...	745
10·13·1. Types of Test	...	745
10·14. Durability	...	748
10·14·1. Requirements for Durability	...	748
10·14·2. Exposure Condition	...	748
10·14·3. Abrasion	...	749
10·14·4. Exposure to Sulphate Attack	...	749
10·14·5. Corrosion Protection Methods	...	749
10·14·6. Surface Protection	...	749
10·15. Fire Resistance	...	750
10·16. Determination of Effective Length of Columns	...	755
10·17. Determining Effective Length for Stepped Columns	...	757
10·18. Connections (Splices)	...	761
11. SOIL MECHANICS	**...**	**789—820**
11·1. Types of soils	...	789
11·1·1. Classification of Soil according to their Mode of Deposition	...	789
11·1·2. Classification of Soil according to Engineering Purposes	...	789
11·2. Soil Properties	...	791
11·3. Field test for Soil Identification	...	797
11·4. Compaction of Earthen Embankments	...	806
11·5. Use of Geogrids for Ground Improvements	...	808
11·6. Soil Nailing	...	810
11·7. Facing	...	813
11·8. Drainage	...	815
11·9. Soil improvement by Stone Columns, Chemical Grouting and Geotextiles	...	815
11·10. Geotextiles	...	817
11·11. Tunnelling	...	818
11·11·1. Geotechnical classification of Tunnelling Projects	...	818
11·11·2. Construction Methodology	...	818
11·11·3. Classification according to Progress Achieved	...	819
12. HYDRAULICS	**...**	**821—1048**
12·1. Atmospheric Pressure	...	821
12·2. Orifices	...	827
12·3. Loss of Head due to change of Sec. of Flow	...	828

12·4. Mouth Pieces	...	829
12·5. Notches and Weirs	...	830
12·6. Flow through Pipes	...	832
12·7. Flow through Open Channels	...	834
12·8. Measurements of Flow in Open Channels (Discharge)	...	836
13. IRRIGATION ENGINEERING	**...**	**866—1048**
13·1. Irrigation Terms	...	867
13·2. Canal Irrigation	...	868
13·3. Losses in Canals	...	869
13·4. Suitability of Canal Water for Irrigation	...	870
13·5. Silt in Canals	...	870
13·6. Velocity in Channels	...	871
13·7. Design of Channels on Kennedy's Silt Theory for Alluvial Soils	...	872
13·8. Design of Channels on Lacey's Theory	...	874
13·9A. Design of Channel Dimensions by Garrett's Diagrams	...	875
13·9B. Design of Channels by Lacey's Diagrams	...	882
13·10. Best Sections of max. Discharge	...	886
13·11. Allowable Curves in Channels—Unlined Canals	...	886
13·12. Standards of Canal Cross-sections in metres	...	888
13·13. (a) Bed-slopes	...	888
(*b*) Stage Discharge Curves	...	889
(*c*) Berms	...	889
(*d*) Dowla Section	...	889
13·14. Design Criteria of Channels and Masonary Works (Bridges) IDUP	...	892
13·15. Dams	...	896
13·15·1. Earthen Dams	...	896
13·16. River Training Works	...	940
13·16·1. Marginal Embankment or Bunds	...	940
13·16.2. Guide Banks	...	941
— Spurs	...	942
— Groynes	...	943
13·17. Foundations of Hydraulic Works	...	943
13·17·1. Design Principles	...	943
13·17·2. Bligh's Creep Theory	...	945
13·17·3. Reforms of Khosla over Bligh's Theory	...	946
13·17·4. Hydraulic Jump	...	961
13·18. Canal Masonry and Cross Drainage Works	...	968
13·18·1. Canal Head Works	...	968
13·18·2. Components of Diversion Headworks	...	970
13·18·3. Design of Sarda Type Fall	...	984
13·18·4. Head and Cross Regulators of Channels	...	987

13·18·5. Contraction of Water Way ... 989
13·18·6. Syphons ... 990
13·18·7. Outlets ... 991
13·18·8. Design for Cross Drainage works ... 994
13·18·9. Canal Navigation ... 1002
13·18·10. Joints in RCC work ... 1002
13·19. Sub-Soil Water Irrigation ... 1006
13·19.1. Well-Irrigation ... 1006
13·19·2. Acquifiers ... 1006
13·19·3. Tube Wells ... 1009
13·19·4. Types of Pumps used ... 1011
13·19·5. Discharge from Tube Wells ... 1013
13·19·6. House hold Pump Strainer ... 1014
13·20. Hydrology of Floods ... 1016
13·21. Water and Power Resources ... 1037
13·22. Major Components of Hydroelectric Scheme ... 1044
13·23. Hydraulic Turbines ... 1047

14. BRIDGES AND FOUNDATION ... 1049—1109

14·1. Bridges ... 1049
14·1·1. Waterway ... 1049
14·1·2. Depth of Foundation ... 1049
14·1·3. Afflux ... 1051
14·1·4. Freeboard or Vertical Clearance ... 1052
14·1·5. Clear Roadway ... 1052
14·1·6. Abutments and Piers ... 1053
14·1·7. Approach slabs ... 1053
14·1·8. Earth Cushion ... 1054
14·1·9. Wings ... 1054
14·1·10. Parapets and Railings ... 1055
14·1·11. Drain Holes and Drainage of Roadway ... 1055
14·1·12. Approaches ... 1055
14·1·13. Bearings ... 1055
14·1·14. Loads to be taken in Design of Bridges ... 1056
14·1·15. Types of bridges ... 1058
14·1·16. Economic Span in Bridges ... 1062
14·1·17. Technical Terms ... 1063
14·1·18. Reference Tables ... 1063
14·2. Bearing Capacity of Soils ... 1066
14·3. Bridge Foundations ... 1074
14·3·1. Well Foundation ... 1074

14·3·2. Laying of Well Curb ... 1077
14·3·3. Verticality of the bore holes ... 1085
14·4. Piles ... 1089
14·5. Other Types of Piles ... 1100

15. ROADS ... 1110—1222

15·1. Technical Terms ... 1110
15·2. Classification of Non-urban Roads in India ... 1111
15·2·1 Express Ways ... 1112
15·2·2. Design Standards ... 1112
15·2·3. Safety Barriers on Expressways ... 1114
15·2·4. Rest Areas ... 1115
15·2·5. Standard of Roads ... 1116
15·2·6. Cross-sectional Standards of Roads ... 1120
15·2·7. Lateral and Vertical Clearance ... 1123
15·2·8. Design Control of Roads ... 1125
15·2·9. Paved Surfaces ... 1130
15·2·10. Low Cost Roads ... 1131
15·2·11. Low volume roads ... 1133
15·2·12. The CBR method of design ... 1133
15·2·13. Super elevation ... 1135
15·2·14. Curves in highways ... 1138
15·2·15. Hair Pin Bends ... 1141
15·2·16. Lives of Roads ... 1142
15·3. Road Binding Materials ... 1143
15·3·1. Filler ... 1147
15·3·2. Penetration ... 1147
15·3·3. Viscosity ... 1147
15·3·4. Softening Point ... 1148
15·3·5. Specific Gravity ... 1149
15·3·6. Ductility ... 1149
15·3·7. Brittleness ... 1149
15·3·8. Heat Stability ... 1149
15·3·9. Comparative Properties of Tar and Bitumen ... 1150
15·3·10. Emulsions ... 1150
15·3·11. Guideline for the selection of a Bituminous Binder (According to Physical Conditions) ... 1151
15·3·12. Tar ... 1152
15·3·13. Modified Binders ... 1154
15·3·14. Rubberised Tar and Bitumen ... 1154
15·3·15. Field application of Bitumen ... 1155
15·3·16. Premix Carpets ... 1156

15·3·17. Built up Spray Grout (BUSG) ... 1158
15·3·18. The specification as recommended by IRC ... 1158
15·4. Water Bound Macadam Roads (W.B.M.) ... 1158
15·4·1. Sub Grade ... 1158
15·4·2. Base ... 1160
15·4·3. Screening and Blending ... 1161
15·4·4. Grouting and Painting of Water Bound Roads ... 1162
15·4·5. Salient points on Water Bound Macadam Roads (W.B.M.) ... 1162
15·5. Bitumen Bound Macadam Roads ... 1163
15·5·1. Pre-coated Grit Carpetting ... 1164
15·5·2. Bituminous Concrete Pavements or Premix Coating 6 to 12 cm thick laid in two layers ... 1165
15·6. Cement Concrete Roads ... 1167
15·6·1. Cement Sandwiched Macadam ... 1167
15·6·2. Collodial Concrete Roads ... 1167
15·6·3. All Concrete Roads ... 1167
15·6·4. General considerations for a Concrete Slab for Roads ... 1168
15·6·5. Reinforced Cement Concrete Roads ... 1168
15·6·6. Joints in Concrete Roads ... 1169
15·6·7. Concrete Mix Design ... 1170
15·7. General ... 1172
15·7·1. Faults in roads ... 1172
15·7·2. Output of 8-10 tonne Three Wheeled Roller per day ... 1172
15·7·3. Material required for Patch Repairs of Roads ... 1173
15·7·4. Gabions or G.I.wire Crates ... 1173
15·7·5. Crack Repair Methodology for Renovation of a Runway or Road Pavement ... 1174
15·8. Preparation of Rubber Bitumen Mixture ... 1177
15·8·1. Road Construction Machinery ... 1178
15·8·2. Road Maintenance Machines ... 1184
15·9 Road Signs ... 1186
15·9·1. Classes of Signs ... 1186
15·9·2. Traffic Signals ... 1188
15·9·3. Road Markings ... 1189
15·9·4. Word Messages ... 1195
15·9·5. Safety during Construction ... 1195
15·9·6. Traffic Impact Attenuators ... 1196
15·9·7. Roadside Rest Areas ... 1198
15·9·8. Highway Safety Appurtenances ... 1198
15·10. Planning of a Road Project ; Route Surveys & Drainage ... 1201
15·10·2. Planning of a Hill Road ... 1203
15·11. Aboriculture—Road side Plantation ... 1203
15·11·1. Curves ... 1207
15·12. Hill Roads ... 1208

15·13. Traffic Control ... 1209
15·14. Use of Fly-ash and Steel Plant Slag in Road-work ... 1210
15·14·1. Use of steel plant slags in road construction and cement ... 1210
15·14·2. Physical and Chemical properties of slags ... 1210
15·14·3. Compaction and Permeability Study of a Soil Stabilised with Flyash, Lime and Na_2CO_3 ... 1212
15·14·4. Laboratory Investigation ... 1212
15·14·6. Engineering Properties of Soil-flyash Mixture ... 1214
15·14·5. Effect of Addition of Lime on Soil-flyash Mixture ... 1215

16. RAILWAYS ... 1223—1269

16·1. Gauges on Indian Railways ... 1223
16·2. Corrugation in Rails ... 1227
16·3. Rail Joints ... 1231
16·4. Coning of wheels ... 1234
16·5. Creep of rails ... 1236
16·6. Sleepers ... 1237
16·7. Ballast ... 1241
16·8. Rail Fixers and Fasteners ... 1243
16·9. Railway Track Geometrics ... 1250
16·10. Super Elevation ... 1253
16·11. Points and Crossings ... 1256
16·12. Signalling ... 1263
16·13. Technical Terms—Railways ... 1266
16·14. Miscellaneous ... 1268

17. WATER SUPPLY ... 1270—1356

17·1. Harmful Constituents in Water and their Tests ... 1270
17·2. Purification of Water ... 1274
17·3. Requirement of Water ... 1281
17·4. Conduits (Pipes) in Water Supply System ... 1286
17·5. Appurtenances in the Water Supply Distribution System ... 1314
17·6. Distribution System of Water Supply ... 1321
17·7. Distribution Reservoirs ... 1325
17·8. Pumps to Lifting Water ... 1348
17·9. Planning of Water Supply Project ... 1354

18. SEWAGE ... 1357—1446

18·1. Collection of Sewage ... 1357
18·2. Sewer Construction and Appurtenances ... 1373
18·3. Decomposing of Sewage ... 1384

18·4. Disposing of Sewage	...	1402
18·5. Domestic Sanitation and its Appliances	...	1410
18·6. Septic Tanks	...	1425
18·7. Air Pollution	...	1430
18·8. Technical Terms	...	1431
19. EARTHQUAKE ENGINEERING—(ENGINEERING SEISMOLOGY)	**...**	**1447—1508**
19·1. Causes of Earthquakes	...	1447
19·2. Earthquake Damage and Intensity	...	1449
19·3. UNESCO Intensity Scale	...	1449
19·4. Geology and Foundation Engineering (Remedial measures of Earthquakes)	...	1453
19·5. Indian Standards on Earthquake Engineering	...	1461
19·6. Earthquake Ground Motion and Codal Provisions	...	1464
19·7. Concepts of Seismic Design and Configuration	...	1467
19·8. Seismic Design and Detailing of Masonry Buildings Including Code Provisions	...	1472
19·9. Seismic Design and Detailing of Steel Structures	...	1484
19·10. Concentrically Braced Frames	...	1485
19·11. Typical damage to Elements subjected to Bending	...	1486
19·12. Increasing Capacity	...	1488
19·13. Construction Chemicals	...	1491
19·14. Earthquake Mechanism	...	1492
19·15. Seismology	...	1501
APPENDIX-I : Design of Steel Structures—General	**...**	**1509—1535**

1

General Information

1·1. Symbols and Formulae used in Engineering

(a) Roman Numericals

English fig.	*Roman fig.*	*English fig.*	*Roman fig.*
1	I	60	LX
2	II	70	LXX
3	III	80	LXXX
4	IV	90	XC
5	V	100	C
6	VI	200	CC
7	VII	300	CCC
8	VIII	400	CD
9	IX	500	D
10	X	600	DC
20	XX	700	DCC
30	XXX	800	DCCC
40	XL	900	MD
50	L	1000	M

Example 1325 = 1000 + 300 + 25 = MCCCXXV

(b) Greek Alphabet

Alpha	A	α	Nu	N	ν
Beta	B	β	Xi	Ξ	ξ
Gamma	Γ	γ	Omicron	O	ο
Delta	Δ	δ	Pi	Π	π
Epsilon	E	ε	Rho	P	ρ
Zeta	Z	ζ	Sigma	Σ	σ
Eta	H	η	Tau	T	τ
Theta	Θ	θ	Upsilon	Y	υ
Tota	I	ι	Phi	Φ	ϕ
Kappa	K	κ	Chi	X	χ
Lambda	Λ	λ	Psi	Ψ	ψ
Mu	M	μ	Omega	Ω	ω

(*c*) **Chemical Symbols of elements**

Name of Element	*Symbol*	*Atomic no.*	*Atomic wt.*	*Melting point, °C*
Aluminium	Al	13	26·97	660
Calcium	Ca	20	40·08	850
Carbon	C	6	12·01	3700
Chlorine	Cl	17	35·457	(–) 101
Copper	Cu	29	63·54	1083
Gold	Au	79	197·2	1063
Hydrogen	H	1	1·008	(–)259
Iodine	I	53	126·92	114
Iron	Fe	26	55·85	1539
Lead	Pb	82	207·21	327
Magnesium	Mg	12	24·32	650
Manganese	Mn	25	54·93	1260
Mercury	Hg	80	200·61	(–) 39
Nickel	Ni	28	58·69	1455
Nitrogen	N	7	14·008	(–) 210
Oxygen	O	8	16·00	(–) 219
Phosphorous	P	15	30·98	—
Potassium	K	19	39·096	63
Silver	Ag	47	107·88	961
Sodium	Na	11	22·997	98
Sulphur	S	16	32·066	—
Tin	Sn	50	118·70	232
Uranium	U	92	238·07	1133
Zinc	Zn	30	65·38	420

(*d*) **Chemical Symbol and Formulae of Common Engineering Materials**

Lime, quick lime (oxide of calcium)	CaO
Slacked lime (Hydraulic oxide of calcium)	$Ca(OH)_2$ or $CaOH_2O$
Cement or lime stone (calcium carbonate)	$CaCO_3$
Water	H_2O
Carbon dioxide	CO_2
Carbon monoxide	CO
Potassium Permangnate	K_2MnO_8
Sulphate of manganese	$MnSO_4$
Oxalic acid	$C_2H_2O_4$
Sulphate of Potassium	K_2SO_4
Sulphuric acid	H_2SO_4

Table contd...

Table contd...

Silica		SiO_2
Alumina		Al_2O_3
Iron oxide		Fe_2O_3
Iron Ore :	Magnetite	Fe_2O_3
	Haemotite	Fe_3O_4
	Limonite	$2Fe_2O_3\,3H_2O$
	Sidorite	$FeCO_3$
	Basic ferric carbonate	$Fe(OH)CO_3$
	Hydrated ferric oxide	$Fe(OH)_3$
Aluminium :	Bauxite double floride of aluminium and sodium	$AlF_3 3NaF$
Copper :	Copper glance	Cu_2S
	Copper pyrites	$CuFeS_2$
	Malachite	$CuCO_3CuO_2H_2$
	Azurite	$2CuCO_3CuO_2H_2$
Lead :	Galena (lead sulphide)	PbS
Tin :	Tin stone or	SnO_2
Zinc :	Zucite	ZnO
	Calamine	$ZaCO_3$
	Zinc blend	ZnS
Gypsum		$CaSO_4.2H_2O$
Plaster of Paris :	(dehydrated gypsum)	$CaSO_4$
	Common salt	$NaCl$
Paints :	Lead acetate	$Pb(CH_3COO)_2$
	Manganese sulphate	$MnSO_4$
	Verdigris (copper acetate)	$Cu(CH_3COO)_2$
	Vermilion (sulphate of mercury)	HgS
	Zeolite	$Na_2Al(SiO_3)$
	Salammoniac (Aluminium chloride)	NH_4Cl

(*e*) **Abbreviations used in measure**

Length	*l*	*Time*	*t*	*Weight*	(wt.)
Inch	(″) in.	Hour	(Hr)	Stone	(st)
Foot	(′) Ft.	Minute	(′) min.	Grain	(gr.)
Yard	(yd)	Second	(″) sec.	Ounce	(oz)
Millimetre	(mm)	**Volume**	(Vol.)	Pound	(lb)
Centimetre	(cm)	Gallons	(galls)	Quarter	(qr)
Metre	(m)	Gram	(grm)	Hundred wt.	(cwt)
Kilometre	(km)	Imperial	(Imp)	Ton	(T)

Table contd...

Square	(sq)	United States	(US)	Maund	(Md)
Cubic	(Cu)	British	(Br)	Seer	(sr.)
Average	(av)	Pint	(pt)	Chhatak	(Chh.)
Acre	(a)	Liquid	(Liq.)	Avoirdopois wt.	(avoir avp.)
Hectare	(ha)	Fluid	(Fl.)	Apothecarius wt.	(ap)
				Troy wt.	(tr)
				Gram	(gm)
				Metric tonne	(MT)
				Millier	(t)
				Quintal (100 kg)	(q)
				Myria gram (10 kg)	mg

(*f*) **Abbreviations used in indices**

Deca	(dk)	10^1	Desi	(d)	10^{-1}
Hecto	(h)	10^2	Centi	(c)	10^{-2}
Kilo	(K)	10^3	Milli	(m)	10^{-3}
Mega	(M)	10^6	Micro	(μ)	10^{-6}
Giga or	(G).		Nano or	(η)	
Kilog mega	KM	10^9	Millimicro	(Mμ)	10^{-9}
Tera or	T		Pico or	(P)	
Mega-mega	(MM)	10^{12}	Micro-micro	(MM)	10^{-12}
Pela	P	10^{15}	Fento	(f)	10^{-15}
Exa	E	10^{18}	Atto	(a)	10^{-18}

(*g*) **Abbreviations used in mathematics**

Plus	(+)	Minus	(−)	Infinity	(∞)
Multiplication	(× or .)	Division	(÷)	Square root	$\sqrt{}$
Equal to	(=)	Not equal to	(≠)	Angle	(∠)
Greater than	(>)	Lesser than	(<)	Sum of	(Σ)
Parallel	(‖)	Not parallel	(∦)	*n* root	$\sqrt[n]{}$
Because or since	(∵)	Rt. angle	⊥	Therefore/hence	(∴)
Area of triangle	Δ	Ratio, is to	(:)	So as	(::)

1·2. Units

(A) Unit Systems

(1) C.G.S. System

Basic Units

Quantity	*Unit*	*Symbol*
Mass	Gram	gm.
Length	Centimetre	cm.

Table contd...

Quantity	Unit	Symbol
Time	Second	sec.
Temperature	Centigrade	°C
Electric current	Ampere	A
Luminous intensity	Candela	Cd.
Force	Dyne	dyne

(2) **M.K.S. System**

Quantity	Unit	Symbol
Mass	Kilogram	kg
Length	Metre	m
Time	Second	sec.
Temperature	Centigrade	°C
Electric current	Ampere	A
Luminous intensity	Candela	Cd.

(3) **S.I. System (International system)**

	Quantity	Unit	Symbol
Basic Units :	Mass	Kilogram	kg
	Length	Metre	m
	Time	Second	sec.
	Temperature	Kelvin	K
	Electric current	Ampere	A
	Luminous intensity	Candela	Cd.
	Force	Newton (kg.m/sec^2)	N
Derived units :	Area	Sq. m.	m^2
	Volume	Cubic metre	m^3
	Density	K. gm per cubic metre	kg/m^3 or per m^{-3}
	Speed and velocity	metre/sec.	m/s or ms^{-1}
	Acceleration	metric/sec./sec.	m/s^2 or ms^{-2}
	Momentum	Kg metre per sec.	kgm/sec or kgms^{-1}
	Work and energy	Joule	J
	Power	Watt	W
	Pressure	Pascal	Pa

Unit of force : Force = mass × acceleration

1 Newton = 1 kg × 1 m/sec^2 or 1 N = 1 kg m/sec^2

1 kgf (kg force) = 9·807 N

One Newton (N) is defined as the force required to move a body of mass equal to 1 kg as to generate in it an acceleration equal to 1 m/sec^2.

Unit of Stress or Pressure. Stress or pressure is the force per unit area. S.I. unit of pressure is Newton/m^2 (N/m^2) and is known as **Pascal (Pa)**.

1 kg/cm^2 = 98·07 kN/m^2 or 100 KPa = 1·02 kg/cm^2

Unit of Energy. When the applied force of 1 Newton displaces a body by 1 m in the direction of application of force, the work done is said to be equal to 1 Newton metre (1 N-m), called 1 Joule (J) and has the dimension of N.m *i.e.* kg.m/sec^2.m.

$$1 \text{ Joule} = 1 \text{ Nm} = 1 \text{ kg m}^2/\text{sec}^2$$

$$1 \text{ kg m of energy} = 9{\cdot}807 \text{ Joule}$$

Unit of Power. Power is the rate of doing work *i.e.* energy per sec. Its M.K.S. unit is kg.m/sec. (kgfm/sec). The S.I. unit is Joule/sec (J/sec) or Nm/sec and this called as watt.

$$1 \text{ watt} = 1 \text{ J/sec} = 1 \text{ Nm/sec}$$

$$1 \text{ kg/sec} = 9{\cdot}807 \text{ W}$$

For convenience 1 kg may be taken equal to 10 Newton *i.e.* 0·01 kN.

$$1 \text{ N/mm}^2 = 10^6 \text{ Pascals} = \text{MPa (Mega Pascal)}$$

$$1 \text{ H.P. (metric)} = 75 \text{ kg.m/sec} = 75 \times 9{\cdot}807 \text{ W} = 735 \text{ watts}$$

$$1 \text{ H.P. (F.P.S.)} = 550 \text{ H lb/sec} = 550 \times 0{\cdot}138 \times 9{\cdot}807 \text{ watts} = 746 \text{ watts}$$

Unit of temperature. In S.I. units, it is Kelvin (K) and is equal to temperature interval corresponding to 1°C (C + 273° = K).

(4) **F.P.S. System**

Mass	Pound	lb
Length	Foot	ft.
Time	Second	sec.
Temperature	Fahrenheit	°F
Electric current	Ampere	A
Luminus intensity	Candela	Cd.
Force	Poundal	Pdl.

(B) **Units of Measure**

Length

English or U.S.		*Metric*	
12 in	= 1 ft.	10 mm	= 1 centimetre
3 ft.	= 1 yard	10 cm	= 1 decimetre
5½ yard	= 1 rod, pole or perch	10 d.m.	= 1 metre
220 yds	= 1 Furlong	10 metre	= 1 deca metre
8 Furlong	= 1 mile (statute)	1 dkm.	= 1 hecta metre
1 mile (statute)	= 5280 ft.	1 h.m.	= 1 kilometre
1 Nautical mile	= 1/3 league = 6075·5 ft.	10 km	= 1 myria metre
1 Fathom	= 6 ft.	1852 m	= 1 Nautical mile
120 Fathom	= 1 Cable	1·83 m	= 1 Fathom
Nautical mile is an arc of one min. at equator of longitude at sea surface. International mile = 6076·12 ft., 1 knot = speed of one nautical mile/Hr.		0·22 km	= 120 Fathom

Table contd...

Table contd...

English or U.S.		*Metric*	
Surveyor's measure (land)			
7·92 in	= 1 link	1 Engineer link	= 12″
25 links	= 1 pole	100 links	= 1 Engineer's chain
100 links	= 1 chain (66 ft Gunter)	1 Cheshin pole	= 8 yards
10 Gunter's chain	= 1 Furlong	2027 yds	= 1 Admiralty km
8 Furlong	= 1 Mile	69·04 Miles	= 1° lat. at equator
3 miles	= 1 League	69·16 Miles	= 1° long. at equator

Area

English or U.S.		*Metric*	
30·25 sq. yds	= 1 sq. rod, pole, perch	100 sqm	= 1 Arc
40 sq. rods	= 1 rood	100 Arc	= 1 hectare
4 roods	= 1 Acre (4840 sq. yds)	100 hectare	= 1 sq. km.
	= 10 sq. chains of 66 ft.		
640 Acres	= 1 sq. mile		
5 Acres	= 8 Bighas		
20 invansi	= 1 kachvansi		
20 kachvansi	= 1 Bisvansi		
20 Bisvansi	= 1 Biswa		
20 Biswa	= 1 Bigha (English) (55 yds × 55 yds)		

Volume (Capacity)

English		*U.S.*		
1 litre	= 1·76 Pints (Imp.)	**Dry—**	2 Pints	= 1 quart
	= 0·22 gallons (Imp.)		3 quart	= 1 Peck
2 Pint	= 1 quart		4 pecks	= 1 Bushel
4 quart	= 1 gal (Imp.)		1 Barrel	= 7056 in^3
2 gallons	= 1 pack			
4 Packs	= 1 Bushel (1284 cft.)			
8 Bushels	= 1 quarter			
1 Barrel	= 31·5 gallons (Imp.)			
	= 42 U.S. gallons (for Petroleum)			
1 Ferkin	= 1·444 cft.	**Liquid—**	60 minims	= 1 dram
1 U.S. gallon	= 3·785 litres		8 dram	= 1 ounce

Table contd...

Table contd...

English		*U.S.*	
1 Imp. gallon	= 1·2 U.S. gallon	4 ounces	= 1 gill
	= 8 Pints	4 gills	= 1 pint
	= 160 Fluid ounces		
	= 10 lb of water		
	= 4·546 litres		
1 cft.	= 6·24 Imp. gal		
	= 7·48 U.S. gal		
	= 28·32 litres		
	= 62·3 lb of water		
60 minims	= 1 dram (draehm)		
8 dram	= 1 ounce (Eng. fluid)		
20 ounces	= 1 Pint (0·568 lits.)		
	= 4 gills		
One tea spoon full	= 1/8 Fluid ounces		
One glass full	= 12 fluid ounces		

Angle

1 Degree	= 60 minutes = 0·0175 radians = π/180 rad.
1 min.	= 60 seconds
1 Rad	= 57·2960 = 180/π Degrees ; 180° = π radians
100 grades	= 90^{σ} (French)

Note : 1 radian is defined as the angle between two radii of a circle which cut off on the circumference an arc equivalent to length of the radius of the circle.

Money

New—	1 Rupee	= 100 paise	**Old—**	Rupee	= 16 Annas
	1 Pound English (£)	= 12 Shilling		1 Anna	= 12 pies (4 Paise old)
	1 Shilling	= 8 Pens		1 Paisa old	= 2 Dhelas = 4 Chhadams

Weight

English		*Metric*	
(*a*) **Avoirdupois Units** (for common use)			
27·344 gram	= 1 dram	1 gm (wt. of 1 cm^3 of water at 4°C)	= 1000 m. gm.
16 drams	= 1 ounce	1 kg	= 1000 gm
	= 0·911 ounce troy	10 kg	= 1 myria gm
16 ounces	= 1 lb	10 myria gm	= 1 quintal
	= 1·215 lb troy	10 qunital	= 1 tonne (Millier)
	= 14·583 ounces troy	200 milli gms	= 1 metric carat (c)
	= 7000 grains	1 kg	= 2·2046 pounds (avp)
28 lb	= 1 quarter		

Table contd...

Table contd...

English		Metric	
4 qr	= 1 hundred weight (cwt)		
20 cwt	= 1 ton		
14 lbs	= 1 stone		
Note : One shipping (merchandise) is 42 cft. in Britain and 40 cft. in U.S.			
(*b*) **Troy Units** (use out of date)		**Carat Weight**	
		(used for weighing precious metal)	
480 grams	= 1 ounce = 1·097 oz.avp	1 carat (metric)	= 3·086 grains
12 ounces	= 5760 grains = 1 pound		= 0·200 gram
	= 13·166 oz (avp)	**Note :** It has different values at different places. It is also used to express the purity of gold. Pure gold is known as 24 carat fine standard gold is 22 carat.	
	= 0·823 lb (avp)		
175 lbs	= 140 lbs (avp)		
100 lbs	= 82 lbs (avp)		
Note : An avp pound is heavier than troy and avp ounce is lighter than troy.			
(*c*) **Apothecary Units** (used for compounding medicines)		**Old Indian** (Out of date)	
20 grains	= 1 scuple (scr)	8 Rattis	= 1 masha
3 scuples	= 60 grains	12 mashas	= 1 tola
	= 1 drachm	5 tola	= 1 chhatak
	= 2·194 dram (avp)	16 chhatak	= 1 seer
8 drachms	= 480 grams	40 seers	= 1 Mound
	= 1 ounce	1 Mound	= 0·373242 quintal
12 ounces	= 5760 grains	9 lbs	= 350 tola (exact)
	= 1 pound	1 Tola	= 11·6638 grams
(*d*) **U.S. Units**			
1 U.S. cwt.	= 100 pound (avp)		
20 U.S. cwt.	= 1 U.S. ton (short)		
1000 pounds avp	= 1 Kip		
1 U.S. quintal	= 0·4536 metric quintal		
Note : U.S. ton is called as short ton			
Br. ton is called as long ton			
1 U.S. ton	= 0·9072 metric tonne		
	= 0·8929 Br. Ton.		

Density

English or U.S.		Metric	
(*a*) **Linear or superficial**			
lb ft.	(lb.ft.)	Kg metre	(kg.m)
or lb ft. squared	(lb ft^2)	Kg metre squared	(kg m^2)

Table contd...

Table contd...

English or U.S.		*Metric*	
(*b*) **Cubical**			
lb ft. cubed	(lb.ft^3)	Kg m cubed	(kg.m^3)
Moment of Inertia			
(*a*) **Dynamical**			
lb.ft squared	(lb ft^2)	Kg metre squared	(kg.m^2)
(*b*) **Geometrical**			
$Foot^4$	(ft^4)	$metre^4$	(m^4)
Modulus of section			
Ft. cubed	(ft^3)	metre cubed	(m^3)
Bending Moment			
Foot-pound	ft.lb	Kilogram-metre	(kg-m)
Stress Pressure or Head			
1 Atmosphere	= 14·696 lb/m^2	1 Atmosphere	= 1·0333 kg/cm^2
	= 29·921 in of mercury		= 760 mm of mercury
	= 34 ft. of water		= 10 metre of water
1 lb/sq. ft.	= 6·944 × 10^{-3} lb/sq in	1 gm/sq cm^2	= 10 kg/sq m.

Force

English or U.S. :

Poundal—A force applied to a body of mass one pound develops an acc. of one ft./sec^2 (g)

Pound force—A force applied to a body of mass one pound develops an acc. of 32·17 ft/sec^2 (g)

1 pound force = 32·17 poundal

Metric :

Dyne (dyn)—A force applied to a body of mass one gram develops an acc. of 1cm/sec^2.

Sthene (Sn)—A force applied to a body having a mass of one tonne develops with an acc. of one metre/sec^2 = 10^8 dynes.

Newton—A force applied to a body having a mass of one kg. develops in it an acc. of one metre/sec^2 = 10^5 dynes.

Kilogram force—A force applied to a body having a mass of one kg. gives an acc. of 9·80 metre/sec^2 = 980 dynes.

Work Power and Energy

British System

Foot Poundal—Work done when point of application of one poundal is displaced by one foot in the direction of the force applied.

Metric

Erg—Work done when point of application of one dyne is displaced by one centimetre in the direction of the force applied (1 erg = 10^{-7} joule = 1 dyn-cm.)

Joule—Work done when point of application of one newton is displaced by one metre in the direction of force applied.

Table contd...

Table contd...

English or U.S.		*Metric*	
1 British H.P.	= 550 ft lbs/sec	1 Metric H.P.	= 75 kg m/sec
	= 33000 ft lbs/min	1 KW/sec	= 737·56 ft lb/sec
	= 1·014 metric H.P.	Power	$= \frac{\text{Work}}{\text{Time}}$
	= 10·70 kg cal/min	1 watt	= 1 joule/sec
	= 76·040 kg/m/sec	1 K.W.h	= 3600 kilo joules
	= 42·44 B.Th.units/min		= 3,67,098 kg m
	= 746 watts		= 2,654,200 ft lbs
	= 0·746 Kilo watts		= 8,54,29000 ft. poundal
1 H.P./Hr.	= 550 × 60 × 60	1 M.H.P./Hr.	= 2,70,000 kg m
	= 19,80,000 ft lbs = 641·19 kg cal		= 6,32,527 kg cal
	= 2,73,745 kg m		= 0·7355 kWH
	= 6,37,05,000 ft. poundal		
	= 2,544 B.Th. Us		

Heat

English System

1 B.Th.U—Quantity of heat required to raise the temperature of one pound of water by one degree Fahrenheit at N.T.P.

1 B.Th.U = 251·9960 Calories

Metric System

Calorie—Quantity of heat required to raise the temperature of one gram of water by one degree centigrade at N.T.P. (Normal temperature and pressure).

Illumination

English System		*Metric System*	
Foot candle	= 1 lumen/sq. ft.	Lux (lx)	= one lumen/m^2
lumen is luminous flux incident		Phot	= one lumen/cm^2
		1 phot	= 10^4 lux

Brightness

Brightness is the luminous intensity of unit area. The international unit of brightness is "stilb" (Sb).

A **stilb** is a luminance of one Candela/cm^2

A Lambert is the brightness of a perfectly diffusing surface giving out one lumen/cm^2

1 stilb	= 3·1416 lambert
1 lambert	= 0·3183 stilb
1 ft lambert	= 1 lumen/ft^2
1 candela/in^2	= 452·390 ft. lambert
1 ft. lambert	= 0·002210 candela/in^2.

Table contd...

(C) **Conversion Factors**

Metric to British		*British to Metric*	
Length			
1 cm	= 0·39371 in	1 in	= 2·539998 cm
	= 0·0328 ft.	1 ft	= 0·3048 m
1 meter	= 39·370113 in	1 yard	= 0·9144 m
	= 3·280843 ft. = 1·0936 yds	1 furlong	= 0·2012 km
	= 0·1988 rod	1 mile	= 1·609343 km
1 km	= 0·621372 mile		= 0·869 nautical mile
(app. 5/8 mile)	= 1093·6110 yds	1 nautical mile	= 1·852 km
	= 0·539 nautical mile	1 mile U.K.	= 1·0006 nautical mile
1 nautical mile	= 1·1508 mile	1 rod	= 5·0292 mile
	= 0·9994 nautical mile (U.K)		
Area of superficial			
1 sq. cm.	= 0·15500 sq in	1 sq. in.	= 6·451589 sq. cm.
1 sq. meter	= 10·763929 sq. ft.	1 sq. ft.	= 0·092903 sq. m.
	= 1·195992 sq. yd.	1 sq. yd.	= 0·836126 sq. m.
1 sq. km.	= 0·386103 sq. mile	1 sq. mile	= 2·589984 sq. km.
1 Hectare	= 2·471058 acres	1 acre	= 0·404685 hectare
	= 11959·920720 sq. yd.		= 4,046 sq. m.
Volumetric or Cubical (capacity)			
1 c. cm	= 0·061024 c. in	1 cu. in	= 16·387021 c. cm.
	= 0·0352 fluid oz U.K.	1 cu. ft.	= 0·028317 c.m.
	= 0·0338 fluid oz U.S.		= 28·3161 litre
1 c.m.	= 35·31475 c.ft.	1 cu. yd.	= 0·764553 c.m.
	= 1·307954 c. yd.	1 acre ft.	= 0·1233 ha.m.
	= 27·4962 bushel U.K.	1 imp. gal	= 4·545963 lit.
	= 28·3774 bushel U.S.	1 U.S. gal	= 3·7878 lit.
	= 6·2898 barrel U.S. liquid	1 imp. gal	= 0·004546 c.m.
	= 219·973823 imp gal	1 pint	= 0·568245 lits.
1 lit	= 0·219974 imp gal (or 2·2 lb of water)	1 quart	= 1·136491 lits.
		1 U.S. bushel	= 0·1590 cu. m. (liquid)
	= 0·264 U.S. gal		
	= 0·0353147 c ft.	1 U.K. gill	= 0· 1421 lit.
	= 1·759803 pints	1 U.S. gill	= 0·1183 lit.
	= 0·879902 quarter	1 U.S. fluid oz.	= 29·5737 cu. cm.
1 hectare metre	= 8·1071 acre ft.		
Weight or Mass			
1 gm	= 15·432356 grains	1 gram	= 0·064799 gm
	= 0·035274 oz	1 oz	= 28·349527 gm

Table contd...

Table contd...

1 kg	= 2·204622 lbs	1 Pound	= 0·453592 kg
1 tonne (milliar)	= 0·984206 ton	1 ton	= 1·016047 tonne
	= 2204·62 lbs		= 984·206 kg
Density			
1 gm/cu.cm	= 0·0361 lb/c in	1 lb/cu. in.	= 27·6799 gm/c. cm.
	= 62·4280 lbs/c.ft.		= 2·7680 × 10^4 kg/cm
1 kg/cu.m	= 0·0624 lbs/c.ft.	1 lb/c.ft.	= 16·0185 kg/c.m^3
	= 3·6127 × 10^{-5} lb per cu in		= 0·0160 g/m^3
Stress, pressure and load			
1 gm/sq.cm.	= 2·0481 lb/sq.ft.	1 lb/ft^2	= 0·4875 gm/cm^2
1 kg/sq. m.	= ·2048 lb/sq. ft.		= 4·8804 kg/m^2
	= 14·2230 lb/sq. in.	1 lb/m^2	= 0·070307 kg/cm^2
1 tonne/m^2	= 0·0914 ton/ft^2	1 ton/m^2	= 1·5749 kg/mm^2
1 kg/sq. mm	= 0·6350 ton/m^2	1 ton/ft^2	= 1·0937 kg/cm^2
1·6 m head of water	= 0·01421 lb/m^2	1 tonne head of water	= 0·0025 kg/cm^2
1 cm head of mercury	= 0·19299 lb/m^2	1 tonne head of mercury	= 0·0343 kg/cm^2
Power, Work and Energy			
1 kg m/sec	= 7·2330 ft.lb/sec	1 ft.lb/sec	= 0·1383 kg.m/sec
1 kW	= 737·5620 ft.lb/sec	1 H.P.	= 76·0402 kg.m/sec
	= 1·3410 H.P.		= 1·0139 metric H.P.
1 M.H.P.(75 kg m/sec)	= 542·4760 ft.lb./sec		= 0·7457 kw
	= 0·9863 H.P. (British) (550 ft. lbs/sec)	1 Poundal	= 14·10 dynes (g = 980·7 dynes)
1 kg.m	= 7·2330 ft.lbs		= 13826 dynes
1 kW.H	= 1·3410 H.P.-Hr (kW.-H)	1 British H.P.	= 1·014 metric H.P.
1 Joule	= 0·7376 ft. lbs	1 kW	= 1·341 metric H.P.
1 dyne	= 1·020 × 10^{-3} × g poundals (g = 0·0709 poundals)		
	= 7·2330 × 10^{-5} poundals		
Metric to British		*British to metric*	
Moment of Inertia			
(*a*) **Dynamic**			
1 kg m^2	= 23·7304 lb.ft^2	1 lb.ft^2	= 0·0421 kg.m^2
	= 3417·17 lb.m^2	1 lb.m^2	= 0·000293 kg.m^2
(*b*) **Geometrical**			
1 cm^4	= 0·0240 in^4	1 in^4	= 41·6231 cm^4
1 m^4	= 115·8620 ft^4	1 ft^4	= 0·086 m^4

Table contd...

Table contd...

Section Modulus			
1 cm^3	= 0·0610 m^3	1 in^3	= 16·3871 cm^3
1 m^3	= 35·3147 ft^3	1 ft^3	= 0·283 m^3
Bending Moment			
1 kg.m	= 7·2330 ft.lb	1 ft.lb	= 0·1383 kg-m
1 kg.cm	= 0·0723 ft.lb		= 13·8255 kg-m
	= 0·8680 in.lbs	1 in-lb	= 1·1521 kg-cm
Velocity			
1 m/sec	= 3·28 ft./sec	1 ft/sec	= 0·348 m/sec
	= 2·2369 mile/hr		= 1·0973 km/hr
1 km/hr	= 0·9113 ft/sec	1 mile/hr	= 0·4470 m/sec
	= 0·6214 m.p.hr.		= 1·6093 km/hr
1 nautical mile/hr (U.K.)	= 1·1508 m.p.hr	1 nautical mile	= 1·0006 mile/hr (U.K.)
(International)	= 0·9994 m.p.H.		= 1·8532 mile/hr (International)
Discharge			
1 cumec	= 35·1348 cusec	1 cusec	= ·0283 cumec
	= 220 Imp.gal/sec		= 28·317 lits/sec
	= 264 US gal/sec		= 375 gals/min
Viscosity			
1 poise (dyne sec/cm^2)	= 2·083 × 10^{-3} ft. units	1 ft. unit	= 479 poise lb.sec/ft^2
Kinemetric Viscosity			
1 stoke cm^2/sec	= 1·076 ft.unit	1 ft. unit	= 929 stokes ft^2/sec
Heat and Temperature			
1 k cal	= 3·968 B.Th.u	1 B.Th.u	= 0·252 k cal
1 m.kg	= ·00929 B.Th.u	1 B.Th.u	= 107·6 m.kg
1 k cal/m^2	= ·3683 B.Th.u/ft^2	1 B.Th.u/ft^2	= 2·7126 k cal/m^2
T°C = 5/9 (T°F – 32°)		T°F = 9/5 T°C + 32	
T°A – 273 = C°		= 9/5 (T°A – 273) + 32	
Fuel Consumption			
1 lit./km	= 0·3540 Imp. gal/mile	1 Imp. gal/mile	= 2·8247 lit/km
1 km/lit.	= 2·8247 mile/Imp. gal	1 mile/Imp. gal	= 0·3540 km/lit.
Illumination			
1 Lux	= 0·0929 ft. candle	1 ft. candle	= 10·7639 lux
1 Phot	= 929·0304 ft. candle		= 0·001076 phot
Brightness			
1 Lambert	= 2·0536 cd/sq.in	1 candela/m^2	= 0·4870 lambert
	= 929·0304 ft. lambert		= 0·1550 stilb (sb)
1 Stilb (sb)	= 2918·6500 ft.lambert	1 ft. lambert	= 0·001076 lambert
	= 6·4516 cd/m^2		= 0·000343 stilb

(D) **Convertion Tables** (Minor)

Inches to Decimal of Ft.

In.	1″	2″	3″	4″	5″	6″	7″	8″	9″	10″	11″	12″
Ft.	0·0833′	0·1666′	0·250′	0·3333′	0·4166′	0·500′	0·5833′	0·6666′	0·750′	0·8333′	0·9166′	1·000′

Inches to mm

Inch	**1/16**	**1/8**	**3/16**	**1/4**	**5/16**	**3/8**	**7/16**	**1/2**
mm	1·587	3·175	4·762	6·350	7·937	9·525	11·112	12·70
Inch	**9/16**	**5/8**	**11/16**	**3/4**	**13/16**	**7/8**	**15/16**	**1**
mm	14·20	15·87	17·46	19·05	20·64	22·22	23·81	24·40

Inch	0·01	0·02	0·03	0·04	0·05	0·06	0·07	0·08	0·09	0·10
mm	0·254	0·508	0·762	0·016	1·270	1·524	1·778	2·032	2·286	2·540

°C to °F $\quad {}^\circ F = \frac{9^\circ C}{5} + 32 \quad {}^\circ C = \frac{5({}^\circ F - 32)}{9}$

°C	°F	°C	°F	°C	°F	°C	°F
35·0	95·0	37·1	98·8	39·2	102·6	41·3	106·3
35·1	95·2	37·2	99·0	39·3	102·7	41·4	106·5
35·2	95·4	37·3	99·1	39·4	102·9	41·5	106·7
35·3	95·5	37·4	99·3	39·5	103·1	41·6	106·9
35·4	95·7	37·5	99·5	39·6	103·3	41·7	107·1
35·5	95·9	37·6	99·7	39·7	103·5	41·8	107·2
35·6	96·1	37·7	99·9	39·8	103·6	41·9	107·4
35·7	96·3	37·8	100·0	39·9	103·8	42·0	107·6
35·8	96·4	37·9	100·2	40·0	104·0	42·1	107·8
35·9	96·6	38·0	100·4	40·1	104·2	42·2	108·0
36·0	96·8	38·1	100·6	40·2	104·4	42·3	108·1
36·1	97·0	38·2	100·8	40·3	104·5	42·4	108·3
36·2	97·2	38·3	100·9	40·4	104·7	42·5	108·5
36·3	97·3	38·4	101·1	40·5	104·9	42·6	108·7
36·4	97·5	38·5	101·3	40·6	105·1	42·7	108·9
36·5	97·7	38·6	101·5	40·7	105·3	42·8	109·0
36·6	97·9	38·7	101·7	40·8	105·4	42·9	109·2
36·7	98·1	38·8	101·8	40·9	105·6		
36·8	98·2	38·9	102·0	41·0	105·8		
36·9	98·4	39·0	102·2	41·1	106·0		
37·0	98·6	39·1	102·4	41·2	106·2		

Note :
1. Normal temp. of human body = 98·4 °F = 37°C
2. Boiling point of pure water = 100°C = 212°F
3. Melting point of ice = 0°C = 32°C
4. Water has max. density at 4°C

Fractions, Decimals and Percentage

Fractions	1	7/8	3/4	2/3	5/8	1/2	3/8	1/3	1/5	1/8	1/10	1/40	1/80	1/240
Decimals	1·00	0·875	0·750	0·66	0·625	0·5	0·375	0·3333	0·20	0·125	0·1	0·025	0·0125	0·004
Percentage	100	87·5	75	66·66	62·5	50	37·5	33·33	20·0	12·5	10·0	2·5	1·25	0·416

1·3. VALUES OF MATHEMATICAL FUNCTIONS

(*a*) *Exponential values of e*		(*b*) *Functions of Log*	
e	= 2·71828	$\log_e 2$	= 0·693147
e^2	= 7·38905	$\log_e 3$	= 1·098612
$e^{1/2}$	= 1·64872	$\log_e 10$	= 2·302585
e^{π}	= 23·14069	$\log_e \pi$	= 1·144729

(*c*) **Functions of π**

π	= 22/7 = 3·14159265358979323846264338327950		
π^2	= 9·869604	$180/\pi$	= 57·296
$\sqrt{2}\,\pi$	= 4·44288	$1/\pi^2$	= 0·1013212
$\sqrt{(2/\pi)}$	= 0·7978846	$1/\pi^3$	= 0·032252
$\pi/180$	= 0·01745328	$\pi/\sqrt{2}$	= 2·2214415
$\sqrt{(\pi/2)}$	= 1·2533	π^3	= 31·006277
$1/\sqrt{\pi}$	= 0·5651896	$\sqrt{\pi}$	= 1·7725
$\sqrt[3]{\pi}$	= 1·464022	$\log \pi$	= 0·4971499
$\sqrt{2}/\pi$	= 0·4501582		

(*d*) **Roots of Nos.**		**Cube Roots of Nos.**		**Reciprocal of Nos.**	
$\sqrt{2}$	1·414213	$\sqrt[3]{2}$	1·2599	1/2	0·50
$\sqrt{3}$	1·732050	$\sqrt[3]{3}$	1·4422	1/3	·33333
$\sqrt{4}$	2·000	$\sqrt[3]{3}$	1·5874	1/4	·250
$\sqrt{5}$	2·2361	$\sqrt[3]{5}$	1·7100	1/5	2·000
$\sqrt{6}$	2·4495	$\sqrt[3]{6}$	1·8171	1/6	·16667
$\sqrt{7}$	2·6458	$\sqrt[3]{7}$	1·9129	1/7	·14286
$\sqrt{8}$	2·8284	$\sqrt[3]{8}$	2·000	1/8	·12500
$\sqrt{9}$	3·000	$\sqrt[3]{9}$	2·0801	1/9	·1111
$\sqrt{10}$	3·162217	$\sqrt[3]{10}$	2·544	1/10	·1000

Table contd...

Table contd...

(*e*) **Functions of g (acc. due to gravity) Standard at Madras**

	F.P.S.		*Metric*	
g	32·2	m/sec^2 (32·1740′/sec^2)	9·81	m/sec^2 (9·80665 m/sec^2)
$\sqrt{g}$	5·6745	sec^2	3·1321	sec^2
$\sqrt{2g}$	8·025	sec^2	4·4295	sec^2
log g	1·50786	sec^2	0·99167	sec^2
log 2g	1·80889	sec^2	1·2927	sec^2
g^2	1036·84	sec^2	96·236	sec^2
log $\sqrt{g}$	0·75393	sec^2	0·49583	sec^2
log $\sqrt{2}\,g$	0·90444	sec^2	0·64635	sec^2
1/g	0·031056	sec^2	0·10194	sec^2
1/2 g	0·15528	sec^2	0·050967	sec^2
1$\sqrt{g}$	0·17622	sec^2	0·31928	sec^2
$1/\sqrt{2}\,g$	0·12461	sec^2	0·22575	sec^2
g^3	33386·248	sec^2	944·08	sec^2

1·4. GENERAL—Tables and Appendices

(*a*) **Table of Daily Wages**

Rs./month	*28 day*	*29 days*	*30 days*	*31 days*
0·25	0·01	0·01	0·01	0·01
0·50	0·02	0·02	0·02	0·02
0·75	0·03	0·03	0·03	0·02
1·0	0·04	0·03	0·03	0·03
2·0	0·07	0·07	0·07	0·06
3·0	0·11	0·10	0·10	0·10
4·0	0·14	0·14	0·13	0·13
5·0	0·18	0·17	0·17	0·16
6·0	0·21	0·21	0·20	0·18
7·0	0·25	0·24	0·23	0·23
8·0	0·29	0·28	0·27	0·26
9·0	0·32	0·31	0·30	0·29
10·0	0·36	0·34	0·33	0·32
15·0	0·54	0·52	0·50	0·48
20·0	0·71	0·69	0·67	0·68
25·0	0·89	0·86	0·83	0·81
30·0	1·07	1·03	1·00	0·97
35·0	1·25	1·21	1·17	1·13
40·0	1·43	1·38	1·33	1·29

Table contd...

Table contd...

Rs./month	*28 day*	*29 days*	*30 days*	*31 days*
45·0	1·61	1·55	1·50	1·45
50·0	1·79	1·72	1·67	1·61
55·0	1·96	1·90	1·83	1·77
60·0	2·14	2·07	2·00	1·94
65·0	2·32	2·24	2·17	2·10
70·0	2·50	2·41	2·33	2·26
75·0	2·68	2·52	2·50	2·42
80·0	2·86	2·76	2·67	2·58
85·0	3·04	2·93	2·83	2·74
90·0	3·21	3·10	3·00	2·90
95·0	3·39	3·28	3·17	3·06
100·0	3·57	3·45	3·33	3·23
200·0	7·14	6·90	6·67	6·45
300·0	10·71	10·34	10·00	9·68
400·0	14·29	13·80	13·33	12·96
500·0	17·86	17·24	16·67	16·13
600·0	21·43	20·69	20·00	19·36
700·0	25·00	24·14	23·33	22·58
800·0	58·58	27·60	26·67	25·80
900·0	32·14	31·02	30·00	29·03
1000·0	35·71	34·48	33·33	32·26

Appendix 1-A

Conversion Table

Metres to Feet and Inches

Metres→	*0*	*1*	*2*	*3*	*4*	*5*	*6*	*7*	*8*	*9*
	ft. in. 0	*ft. in.* 3 3	*ft. in* 6 7	*ft. in* 9 10	*ft. in* 13 1	*ft. in* 16 5	*ft. in* 19 8	*ft. in* 23 0	*ft. in* 20 3	*ft. in* 29 0
Metres→ ↓	*0*	*10*	*20*	*30*	*40*	*50*	*60*	*70*	*80*	*·90*
	ft. in.	*ft. in.*	*ft. in.*	*ft. in.*	*ft. in.*	*ft. in.*	*ft. in.*	*ft. in.*	*ft. in.*	*ft. in.*
0	0	32 10	05 7	98 5	101 3	164 1	196 10	229 8	202 6	295 3
100	328 1	360 11	393 8	426 6	459 4	492 2	524 11	557 9	590 7	623 4
200	656 2	689 0	721 9	754 7	787 5	820 3	853 0	885 10	918 8	951 6
300	984 3	1017 1	1049 10	1082 8	1115 6	1148 3	1181 1	1213 11	1246 9	1279 6
400	1312 4	1345 2	1377 11	1410 9	1443 7	1476 5	1509 2	1542 0	1574 10	1607 7
500	1040 5	1673 3	1706 0	1738 10	1771 8	1804 6	1837 3	1870 1	1902 11	1935 8
600	1468 6	2001 4	2034 1	2066 11	2090 9	2132 7	2165 4	2198 2	2231 0	2203 9
700	2296 7	2329 5	2362 2	2395 0	2427 10	2460 8	2493 5	2526 3	2559 1	2591 10
800	2624 8	2637 6	2690 3	2723 1	2755 11	2788 9	2821 6	2854 4	2887 2	2919 11
900	2952 9	2985 7	3018 4	3051 2	3084 0	3116 10	3149 7	3182 5	3215 3	3248 0
1000	3280 10	3313 8	3346 5	3379 3	3412 1	3441 11	3477 8	3510 6	3543 4	3576 1

Illustrative Example. To find the equivalent of 276 metres in feet and inches, obtain first the equivalent of 270 metres in feet and inches which is 885 feet 10 inches given at the intersection of the row corresponding to 200 metres and column corresponding to 70 metres. Then obtain the eqivalent of 6 metres in feet and inches which is 19 feet 8 inches at the intersection of the first row and column corresponding to 6 metres. The equivalent of 276 metres in feet and inches is obtained by adding these two equivalent *i.e.* 885 ft. 10 in. + 19 ft. 8 in. = 905 ft. 6 in.

Yards, Feet and Inches to Metres

Yards→ ↓	*0*	*1*	*2*	*3*	*4*	*5*	*6*	*7*	*8*	*9*
	m	*m*	*m*	*m*	*m*	*m*	*m*	*m*	*m*	*m*
0	0	0·914	1·829	2·743	3·658	4·572	5·956	6·401	7·315	8·230
0	9·144	10·058	10·973	11·887	12·802	13·710	14·630	15·545	16·459	17·374
20	18·288	19·202	20·117	21·031	21·946	22·860	23·774	24·689	25·693	26·518
30	27·432	28·346	29·261	30·175	31·099	32·004	32·918	33·833	34·747	35·862
40	36·576	37·490	38·405	39·319	40·234	41·148	42·062	42·977	43·891	44·806
50	45·720	46·034	47·549	48·463	49·378	50·292	51·206	52·121	53·035	53·950
60	54·864	55·778	58·645	57·607	58·522	59·436	60·350	61·265	62·179	63·094
70	64·008	64·922	65·837	66·751	67·666	68·580	69·494	70·409	71·323	72·238
80	73·152	74·066	74·981	75·895	76·810	77·724	78·638	79·553	80·467	81·882
90	82·298	83·210	84·125	85·039	85·954	86·808	87·782	88·697	89·611	90·526
100	91·440	92·354	93·269	94·183	95·098	96·012	96·926	97·841	98·755	99·670

Inches→ Feet ↓	0	1	2	3	4	5	6	7	8	9	10	11
	m	m	m	m	m	m	m	m	m	m	m	m
0	0	0·025	0·051	0·076	0·102	0·127	0·152	0·178	0·203	0·229	0·254	0·279
1	0·305	0·330	0·350	0·381	0·406	0·432	0·457	0·483	0·506	0·533	0·559	0·584
2	0·610	0·635	0·660	0·686	0·711	0·737	0·762	0·878	0·813	0·838	0·864	0·889

Illustrative Example. To find the metre equivalent of 57 yards 2 feet and 6 inches, obtain first the metre equivalent of 57 yards, which is 52·121 given at the intersection of the row corresponding to 50 yards and the column corresponding to 7 yards. Then obtain the metre equivalent of 2 feet and 6 inches which is 0·762 given at the intersection of the row corresponding to 2 feet and the column corresponding to 6 inches. The metre equivalent of 57 yards 2 feet and 6 inches is obtained by adding the two metre equivalents thus obtained *i.e.*, 52·121 m + 0·762 m to 52·883 m.

Kilometres to Miles and Furlongs

Kilo-metres→	*0*	*1*	*2*	*3*	*4*	*5*	*6*	*7*	*8*	*9*
	M f	*M f*	*M f*	*M f*	*M f*	*M f*	*M f*	*M f*	*M f*	*M f*
	0	*0 5*	*1 2*	*1 7*	*2 4*	*3 1*	*3 6*	*4 3*	*5 0*	*5 5*

Kilo-metres→	*0*	*10*	*20*	*30*	*40*	*50*	*60*	*70*	*80*	*90*
	M f	*M f*	*M f*	*M f*	*M f*	*M f*	*M f*	*M f*	*M f*	*M f*
0	0	6 2	12 3	18 5	24 7	31 1	37 2	43 4	49 6	55 7
100	62 1	68 3	74 5	80 6	87 0	93 2	99 3	105 5	111 7	118 0
200	124 2	130 4	136 6	142 7	149 1	155 3	161 4	167 6	174 0	180 2
300	186 3	192 5	198 7	205 0	211 2	217 4	223 6	229 7	236 1	242 3
400	248 4	254 6	261 0	267 2	273 3	279 5	285 7	292 0	298 2	304 4
500	310 5	316 7	323 1	329 3	335 4	341 6	348 0	354 1	360 3	366 5
600	372 7	379 0	385 2	391 4	397 5	403 7	410 1	416 3	422 4	428 6
700	435 0	441 1	447 3	453 5	459 7	466 0	472 2	478 4	484 5	490 7
800	497 1	503 2	509 4	515 6	522 0	528 1	534 3	540 5	546 6	553 0
900	559 2	565 4	571 5	577 7	584 1	590 2	596 4	602 6	609 0	615 1
1000	621 3	627 5	633 6	640 0	646 2	652 4	658 5	664 7	671 1	677 2

Illustration Example. To find the equivalent of say 545 kilometres in miles and furlong, obtain 1st the equivalent of 540 kilometres in miles and furlong which is 335 miles and furlongs given at the intersection of the row corresponding to 500 kilometers and column corresponding to 40 kilometres. Then obtain the equivalent of 5 kilometres which is 3 miles/furlong given at the intersection of the 1st row and the column corresponding to 5 kilometres. The equivalent of 545 kilometres in miles and furlongs is obtained by adding these two equivalent *i.e.* 335 miles 4 furlongs + 3 miles/furlong = 338 miles 5 furlongs.

Miles and Furlongs to Kilometres

Miles→ ↓	*0*	*1*	*2*	*3*	*4*	*5*	*6*	*7*	*8*	*9*
	km *0*	*km* *1·609*	*km* *3·219*	*km* *4·828*	*km* *0·437*	*km* *8·047*	*km* *9·656*	*km* *11·265*	*km* *12·875*	*km* *14·484*
Miles→ ↓	*0*	*10*	*20*	*30*	*40*	*50*	*60*	*70*	*80*	*90*
	km	km	km	km	km	km	km	km	km	km
0	0	16·093	32·187	48·280	64·374	80·467	96·561	112·654	128·748	144·841
100	160·934	177·028	103·121	209·215	225·398	241·402	257·495	273·588	289·682	305·775
200	321·869	337·962	354·056	370·149	386·243	402·336	418·429	434·523	450·616	466·710
300	482·803	498·897	514·990	531·084	547·177	563·270	579·364	595·457	611·551	627·644
400	643·738	659·831	675·924	692·018	708·111	724·205	740·298	756·392	772·485	788·579
500	804·672	820·765	836·859	852·952	869·046	885·139	901·233	917·326	933·420	949·513
600	965·606	981·700	997·793	1013·887	1029·980	1046·074	1062·167	1078·260	1094·354	1110·447
700	1126·541	1142·634	1158·728	1174·821	1190·915	1207·008	1223·101	1239·195	1255·288	1271·382
800	1287·475	1303·569	1319·662	1335·756	1351·849	1367·942	1384·036	1400·129	1416·223	1482·316
900	1448·410	1464·503	1480·596	1496·690	1512·783	1528·877	1544·970	1561·664	1577·157	1593·251
1000	1609·344	1625·437	1641·531	1657·694	1673·718	1689·811	1705·905	1721·098	1738·092	1754·185
Fur-longs→	*0*	*1*	*2*	*3*	*4*	*5*	*6*	*7*	*8*	
	km 0	km 0·201	km 0·402	km 0·604	km 0·805	km 1·006	km 1·207	km 1·408	km 1·609	

Illustrative Example. To find the kilometre equivalent to say 475 miles 6 furlongs obtain 1st the kilometre equivalent of 470 miles which is 756·392 given at the intersection of the row corresponding to 400 miles and column corresponding to 70 miles. Then obtain the kilometre equivalent of 5 miles which is 8·047 given at intersection of the 1st row and column corresponding to 5 miles. Lastly obtain the kilometre equivalent of 6 furlongs which is 1·207 given at the intersection of the last row and the column corresponding to 6 furlongs. The kilometre equivalent of 475 miles and 6 furlongs is obtained by adding the three kilometre, equivalent thus obtained *i.e.* 756·392 km + 8·047 km + 1·207 km = 765·646 km.

Sq. Feet and Sq. Yards to Sq. Metres (Area)

IS : 1020—1957

Sq. Ft. →	*0*	*1*	*2*	*3*	*4*	*5*	*6*	*7*	*8*	*9*
	sq. m *0*	*sq. m* *0·09*	*sq. m* *0·19*	*sq. m* *0·28*	*sq. m* *0·37*	*sq. m* *0·46*	*sq. m* *0·56*	*sq. m* *0·65*	*sq. m* *0·74*	*sq. m* *0·84*
Sq. Yds→	*0*	*1*	*2*	*3*	*4*	*5*	*6*	*7*	*8*	*9*
	sq. m *0*	*sq. m* *0·84*	*sq. m* *1·67*	*sq. m* *2·51*	*sq. m* *3·34*	*sq. m* *4·18*	*sq. m* *5·02*	*sq. m* *5·85*	*sq. m* *6·69*	*sq. m* *7·53*
Sq. Yds→ ↓	0	1	2	3	4	5	6	7	8	9
	sq. m	sq. m	sq. m	sq. m	sq. m	sq. m	sq. m	sq. m	sq. m	sq. m
0	0	8·36	16·72	25·08	33·45	41·81	50·17	58·53	66·89	75·25
100	83·61	91·97	100·34	108·70	117·06	125·42	133·78	142·14	150·50	158·86
200	107·23	175·59	183·95	192·31	200·67	209·03	217·39	225·75	234·12	242·48
300	250·84	259·20	267·56	275·92	284·28	292·84	301·01	309·37	317·73	326·09
400	334·45	342·81	351·17	359·53	367·90	376·26	384·62	392·98	401·34	409·70
500	418·06	426·42	436·79	443·15	451·51	459·87	468·23	476·59	484·95	443·32
600	501·68	510·04	518·40	526·76	535·12	543·48	551·84	560·21	568·57	576·93
700	585·29	593·63	602·01	610·37	618·73	627·10	635·46	643·82	652·18	660·54
800	668·90	677·26	685·62	693·99	702·35	710·71	719·07	727·43	735·79	744·15
900	752·51	760·88	769·24	777·60	785·96	794·32	802·68	811·04	819·40	827·77
1000	836·13	844·49	852·85	861·21	869·57	877·93	886·30	894·66	903·02	911·38

Illustrative Example. To find the sq. m. equivalent of say 444 sq. yards and 5 sq. ft., obtain 1st sq. m. equivalent of 440 sq. yards which is 3670·90 given at the intersection of row corresponding to 400 sq. yards and column corresponding to 40 sq. yards. Then obtain the square metre equivalent of 4 sq. yards which is 3·34 given in the column corresponding to 4 sq. yards. Lastly obtain the square metre equivalent of 5 sq. feet wherein 0·46 given in the column corresponding to 5 sq. ft. The square metre equivalent of 446 sq. yards 5 sq. ft. is obtained by adding then three equivalent *i.e.* 369·69 sq. m + 3·34 sq. m + 0·46 sq. m = 371·70 sq. metre.

Square Metres to Sq. Yards and Sq. Feet

Sq.→ Metre	*0*	*1*	*2*	*3*	*4*	*5*	*6*	*7*	*8*	*9*
	sq. sq. yd. yd.	*sq. sq. yd. yd.*	*sq. sq. yd. yd.*	*sq. sq. yd. yd.*	*sq. sq. yd. yd.*	*sq. sq. yd. yd.*	*sq. sq. yd. yd.*	*sq. sq. yd. yd.*	*sq. sq. yd. yd.*	*sq. sq. yd. yd.*
	0 0	*1 2*	*2 4*	*3 5*	*4 7*	*6 0*	*7 2*	*8 3*	*9 5*	*10 7*
Sq.→ Metre	*0*	*10*	*20*	*30*	*40*	*50*	*60*	*70*	*80*	*90*
	sq. sq. yd. ft.	*sq. sq. yd. ft.*	*sq. sq. yd. ft.*	*sq. sq. yd. ft.*	*sq. sq. yd. ft.*	*sq. sq. yd. ft.*	*sq. sq. yd. ft.*	*sq. sq. yd. ft.*	*sq. sq. yd. ft.*	*sq. sq. yd. ft.*
0	0	12 0	23 8	35 8	47 8	59 7	71 7	83 6	95 6	107 6
100	119 5	131 5	143 5	155 4	167 4	179 4	191 3	203 3	215 3	227 2
200	239 2	251 1	263 1	275 1	287 0	299 0	311 0	322 8	334 8	346 8
300	358 7	370 7	382 6	394 6	406 6	418 5	430 5	442 5	454 4	466 4
400	478 4	490 3	502 3	574 2	526 2	538 2	550 1	562 1	574 1	586 0
500	598 0	610 0	621 8	633 8	645 8	657 7	669 7	681 0	693 0	705 6
600	717 5	720 3	741 5	753 4	765 4	777 4	789 3	801 3	813 2	825 2
700	837 2	849 1	861 1	873 1	885 0	897 0	909 0	920 8	932 8	944 7
800	956 7	968 7	980 6	992 6	1004 6	1016 5	1028 5	1040 5	1052 4	1064 4
900	1076 4	1088 3	1100 3	1112 2	1124 2	1136 2	1148 1	1166 1	1172 1	1184 0
1000	1196 0	1208 0	1219 8	1231 8	1243 7	1255 7	1267 7	1279 6	1291 6	1303 6

Illustrative Example. To find the equivalent of say 423 sq. m in sq. yds. and sq. ft., obtain 1st the equivalent of 420 sq. m. in sq. yds. and sq. ft. which is 502 sq. yds., 3 sq. ft. given at the intersection of the row corresponding to 400 sq. metres and column corresponding to 20 sq. metres. Then obtain the equivalent of 38 sq. metres, which is 3 sq. yds., 5 sq. ft. given at the intersection of the 1st row and the column corresponding to 3 sq. metres. The equivalent of 423 sq. m. in sq. yds and sq. ft. is obtained by adding these equivalents *i.e.* 502 sq. yds. 3 sq. ft. + 3 sq. yds. 5 sq. ft. = 505 sq. yds., 8 sq. ft.

Acres to Hectares

Acres→	*0*	*1*	*2*	*3*	*4*	*5*	*6*	*7*	*8*	*9*
	ha 0	*ha* 0·4	*ha* 0·81	*ha* 1·21	*ha* 1·62	*ha* 2·02	*ha* 2·43	*ha* 2·83	*ha* 3·24	*ha* 3·64
Acres→ ↓	0	10	20	30	40	50	60	70	80	90
	ha	ha	ha	ha	ha	ha	ha	ha	ha	ha
0	0	4·05	8·09	12·14	16·19	20·23	24·28	28·33	32·37	36·42
100	40·47	44·52	48·56	52·61	56·66	60·70	64·75	68·80	72·84	76·89
200	80·94	84·98	89·03	93·08	97·12	101·17	105·22	109·27	113·31	117·36
300	121·41	125·45	129·50	133·55	137·59	141·64	145·69	149·73	153·78	157·83
400	161·87	165·92	169·97	174·01	178·06	182·11	186·16	190·20	194·25	198·30
500	202·34	206·39	210·44	214·48	218·53	222·58	226·62	230·67	234·72	238·76
600	242·81	246·86	250·91	254·95	259·00	263·05	267·09	271·14	275·19	279·23
700	283·28	287·33	291·37	295·42	299·47	303·51	307·56	311·61	315·66	319·70
800	323·75	327·80	331·84	335·89	339·94	343·98	348·93	352·08	356·12	360·17
900	364·22	368·26	372·12	376·36	380·40	384·45	388·50	392·55	396·59	400·64
1000	404·69	408·73	412·78	416·83	420·87	424·92	428·97	433·01	437·06	441·11

Illustrative Example. To find the hectare equivalent of say 684 acres, obtain first the hectare equivalent of 680 acres which is 275·19 given at the intersection of the row corresponding to 600 acres and column corresponding to 80 acres. Then obtain the hectare equivalent of 4 acres, which is 1·62 given inthe first row in the column corresponding to 4 acres. The hectare equivalent of 684 acres is obtained by adding these two equivalents, *i.e.*, 275·19 ha + 1·62 ha = 276·81 ha.

Hectare to Acres and Square Yards

Sq.→	0		1		2		3		4		5		6		7		8		9	
Metre	Acre	sq. yd.	Acre	sq. yd.	Acre	sq. yd.	Acre	sq. yd.	Acre	sq. yd.	Acre	sq. yd.	Acre	sq. yd.	Acre	sq. yd.	Acre	sq. yd.	Acre	sq. yd.
	0	0	2	2284	4	4560	7	2000	9	4280	12	1770	14	3999	17	1439	19	3719	22	1159
Sq.→	0		10		20		30		40		50		60		70		80		90	
Metre	Acre	sq. yd.	Acre	sq. yd.	Acre	sq. yd.	Acre	sq. yd.	Acre	sq. yd.	Acre	sq. yd.	Acre	sq. yd.	Acre	sq. yd.	Acre	sq. yd.	Acre	sq. yd.
0	0	0	24	3439	49	2030	74	637	98	4076	123	2675	148	1274	172	4713	197	3312	222	1911
100	247	510	271	3949	296	2548	321	1147	345	4586	370	3185	395	1784	420	383	444	3822	469	2421
200	494	1020	518	4459	543	3058	568	1657	593	256	617	3693	642	2294	667	893	691	4332	716	2931
300	141	1530	766	129	790	3568	845	2167	840	766	864	4203	889	2804	914	1403	939	2	963	3441
400	988	2040	1013	639	1037	4078	1062	2617	1087	1276	1111	4715	1136	3314	1161	1913	1186	512	1210	3951
500	1235	2850	1260	1149	1284	4588	1309	3187	1334	1786	1359	385	1383	3824	1408	2423	1433	1022	1457	4461
600	1482	3060	1507	1659	1532	258	1556	3697	1581	2296	1606	893	1630	4334	1655	2933	1680	1532	1705	131
700	1729	3570	1754	2169	1779	768	1803	4207	1828	2806	1853	1405	1878	4	1902	3443	1927	2042	1953	641
800	1976	4080	2001	2679	2026	1278	2050	4717	2075	3316	2100	1915	2125	574	2149	3953	2974	2552	2199	1151
900	2223	4590	2248	3189	2273	1788	2298	387	2322	3826	2347	2425	2378	1024	2396	4463	2421	3062	2446	1661
1000	2471	280	2495	3699	2520	2293	2545	897	2569	4336	2594	2935	2619	1534	2644	133	2668	2572	2693	2171

Illustrative Example. To find the equivalent of say 854 hectares in acres and sq. yds. obtain first the equivalent of 850 hectares and column. Corresponding to 50 hectares. Then obtain the equivalent of 4 hectares which is 9 acres 4280 sq. yds. given at the intersection of the first row and column corresponding to 4 hectares. The equivalent of 854 hectares in acres and sq. yds. is obtained by adding these two equivalents *i.e.* 2100 acres 1915 acres 1915 sq. yds. + 9 acres 4280 sq. yds. = 2110 acres 1355 sq. yds.

Ounces to Grams

Pounds→	0	1	2	3	4	5	6	7	8	9
	g	g	g	g	g	g	g	g	g	g
0	0	28·350	56·694	85·049	113·398	141·748	170·097	198·447	226·796	155·146
110	283·495	311·845	340·194	368·544	396·893	425·243	453·592			

Pounds to Kilograms

Pounds→ ↓	0	1	2	3	4	5	6	7	8	9
	kg	kg	kg	kg	kg	kg	kg	kg	kg	kg
	0	0·454	0·907	1·361	1·814	2·268	2·722	3·175	3·629	4·082
10	4·536	4·990	5·443	5·897	6·350	6·804	7·257	7·711	8·165	8·618
20	9·072	9·529	9·979	10·433	10·886	11·340	11·793	12·247	12·701	13·154
30	13·608	14·061	14·515	14·969	15·422	15·876	16·329	16·783	17·286	17·690
40	18·144	18·597	19·051	19·504	19·958	20·412	20·865	21·319	21·772	22·225
50	22·680	23·133	21·587	24·040	24·494	24·948	25·401	25·855	25·038	26·762
60	27·216	27·669	28·123	28·576	29·030	29·483	29·937	30·391	30·844	31·298
70	31·751	32·205	32·659	33·112	33·566	34·019	34·473	34·927	35·380	35·834
80	36·287	36·741	37·195	37·648	38·102	38·555	39·009	39·463	39·916	41·370
90	40·823	41·277	41·730	42·184	42·638	43·091	43·505	43·998	44·452	44·906
100	45·359	45·813	46·266	46·720	47·174	47·627	48·081	48·534	48·980	49·442
110	49·894	50·349	50·802							

Illustrative Example. These conversions can be read directly from the corresponding tables. For example 13 ounces is equivalent to 368·544 grams and is given in the table for ounces to grams at the intersection of the corresponding row to 10 ounces and column corresponding to 3 ounces. Similarly 92 pounds is equivalent to 41·730 kilograms given in the table for pounds to kilograms at the intersection of the row corresponding to 90 pounds and column corresponding to 2 pounds.

Kilograms to Pounds and Ounces

Kilo-grams→	0	1	2	3	4	5	6	7	8	9
	lb oz	lb oz	lb oz	lb oz	lb oz	lb oz	lb oz	lb oz	lb oz	lb oz
	0	2 3	4 7	8 19	8 13	11 0	13 4	15 7	17 10	19 13
Kilo-Metre→	0	10	20	30	40	50	60	70	80	90
	lb oz	lb oz	lb oz	lb oz	lb oz	lb oz	lb oz	lb oz	lb oz	lb oz
0	0	22 1	44 1	66 .2	88 3	110 4	132 4	154 5	176 6	198 7
100	220 7	242 8	264 9	286 10	308 10	330 11	352 12	374 13	396 13	418 14
200	440 15	463 0	485 0	507 1	529 2	551 2	573 3	595 4	617 5	639 5
300	661 6	683 7	705 8	727 8	749 9	771 10	793 11	815 11	837 12	859 13
400	881 14	903 14	925 15	948 0	970 0	992 1	1014 2	1036 3	1058 4	1080 4
500	1102 5	1124 6	1146 6	1168 7	1190 8	1212 9	1234 9	1256 10	1278 11	1300 12
600	1322 12	1344 13	1366 14	1388 15	1410 15	1433 0	1455 1	1477 2	1499 2	1521 3
700	1543 4	1565 4	1587 5	1609 6	1631 7	1653 7	1675 8	1697 9	1719 10	1741 10
800	1763 11	1785 12	1807 13	1829 13	1851 14	1873 15	1896 0	1918 0	1940 1	1962 2
900	1984 3	2006 3	2028 4	2050 5	2072 6	2094 7	2116 7	2138 8	2160 8	2182 9
1000	2204 10	2226 11	2248 11	2270 12	2292 13	2314 14	2236 14	2358 15	2381 0	2403 1

Illustrative Example. To find the equivalent of say 597 kilograms in pounds and ounces, obtain first the equivalent of 590 kilograms in poiunds and ounces which is 1300 pounds 12 ounces given at the intersection of the row corresponding to 500 kilograms and column corresponding to 90 kilograms. Then obtain the equivalent of 7 kilograms which is 15 pounds 7 ounces given at the intersection of the first row and column corresponding to 7 kilograms. The equivalent of 597 kilograms in pounds and ounces is obtained by adding these two equivalents, *i.e.* 1300 pounds 12 ounces + 15 pounds 7 ounces = 1316 pounds 3 ounces.

Hundred weights to Kilograms and Tons to Metric Tonnes

Hund-red → weights	*0*	*1*	*2*	*3*	*4*	*5*	*6*	*7*	*8*	*9*
	kg	*kg*	*kg*	*kg*	*kg*	*kg*	*kg*	*kg*	*kg*	*kg*
0	0	50·802	101·605	152·407	203·209	254·012	304·814	355·616	406·419	457·221
10	508·024	558·826	609·628	660·43	711·233	762·035	812·838	863·640	914·442	965·245
20	1016·047									

Tons to Metric Tonnes

Tons→ ↓	0	1	2	3	4	5	6	7	8	9
	Tonnes	Tonnes	Tonnes	Tonnes	Tonnes	Tonnes	Tonnes	Tonnes	Tonnes	Tonnes
	0	1·016	7·032	3·048	4·064	5·080	6·096	7·112	8·128	9·144
10	10·160	11·177	12·193	13·209	14·225	15·241	16·257	17·273	18·284	19·305
20	20·321	21·337	22·353	23·369	24·385	25·401	26·417	27·433	28·449	20·465
30	30·481	31·498	32·514	33·530	34·546	35·562	36·578	37·594	38·610	39·626
40	40·642	41·658	42·674	43·690	44·706	45·722	46·738	47·754	48·770	49·786
50	50·802	51·818	52·834	53·850	54·867	55·883	56·899	57·915	58·931	59·947
60	60·963	61·979	62·495	64·011	65·027	66·043	67·059	68·075	69·491	70·107
70	71·123	72·139	73·155	74·171	75·187	76·204	77·220	78·236	79·252	80·208
80	81·284	82·300	83·316	84·332	85·348	86·364	87·380	88·396	89·412	90·428
90	91·444	92·460	93·476	94·492	96·508	96·524	97·541	98·557	99·573	100·584
100	101·605	102·621	103·687	104·653	105·669	106·683	107·701	108·717	109·733	110·749

Illustrative Examples. These equivalent can be read directly from the corresponding tables. For example 15 hundred weights is equivalent to 762·035 kilograms and is given in the table for hundred weights to kilograms at the intersection of row corresponding to 88·396 metric tonnes and is give in the table for tons to metric tonnes at the intersection of the row corresponding to 80 tons and column corresponding to 7 tons.

Metric Tonnes to Tons and Hundred Weights

Tonnes→ ↓	*0*		*1*		*2*		*3*		*4*		*5*		*6*		*7*		*8*		*9*	
	tons	*cwt*	*tons*	*cwt*	*tons*	*cwt*	*tons*	*cwt*	*tons*	*cwt*	*tons*	*cwt*	*tons*	*cwt*	*tons*	*cwt*	*tons*	*cwt*	*tons*	*cwt*
	0		1	0	1	19	2	19	3	18	4	18	5	18	6	18	7	17	8	17
10	9	17	10	17	11	16	12	16	13	16	14	15	15	15	16	15	17	14	18	14
20	19	14	20	13	21	13	22	13	23	12	24	12	25	12	26	11	27	11	28	11
30	29	11	30	10	31	10	32	10	33	9	34	9	35	9	36	8	37	8	38	8
40	38	7	40	7	41	7	42	6	43	6	44	6	45	5	46	5	47	5	48	5
50	49	4	50	4	51	4	52	3	53	3	54	3	55	2	56	2	57	2	58	1
60	59	1	60	1	61	0	62	0	63	0	63	19	64	19	65	19	66	19	67	18
70	68	18	69	18	70	17	71	17	72	17	73	16	74	16	75	16	76	15	77	15
80	78	15	79	14	80	14	81	14	82	13	83	13	84	13	85	13	86	12	87	12
90	88	12	89	11	90	11	91	11	92	10	93	10	94	10	95	9	96	9	97	9
100	98	8	99	8	100	8	101	7	102	7	103	7	104	7	105	6	106	6	107	6

Illustrative Example. To find the equivalent of say 63 metric tonnes in tons and hundred weights, turn to the row corresponding to 60 metric tonnes and column corresponding to 3 metric tonnes. The intersection of the row and column gives the figure 62 tons 0 hundred weight which is the equivalent of 63 metric tonnes.

Tolas to grams (weight) IS : 1020-1957

Tolas→	*0*	*1*	*2*	*3*	*4*	*5*	*6*	*7*	*8*	*9*
	g	*g*	*g*	*g*	*g*	*g*	*g*	*g*	*g*	*g*
0	0	11·664	23·328	34·991	46·655	58·319	69·983	81·647	93·310	104·974
10	116·638	128·302	139·966	151·629	163·293	174·957	186·621	198·285	209·948	221·613
20	233·276	244·940	256·604	268·267	279·931	291·595	303·259	314·923	326·587	338·250
30	349·914	361·578	373·242	384·906	396·569	408·233	419·897	431·581	443·225	454·888
40	466·552	478·216	489·881	501·544	513·207	524·871	536·535	548·199	559·863	571·526
50	583·190	594·854	806·518	618·182	629·845	841·509	653·173	664·837	676·501	688·164
60	699·828	711·492	723·156	734·820	746·483	758·147	769·811	781·473	793·139	804·802
70	816·466	828·130	839·794	851·458	863·121	874·783	886·449	848·113	909·777	921·441
80	933·104									

Tolas→	*1/2*	*1/4*	*1/8*	*1/16*	*1/32*	*1/64*
	g 5·832	*g* 2·916	*g* 1·458	*g* 0·724	*g* 0·364	*g* 0·182

Illustrative Example. To find oiut the gram equivalent of say 68¼ tolas, first obtainb 84 gram equivalent of 68 tolas, which is 793·139 given at the intersection of the row corresponding to 60 tolas and column corresponding to 8 tolas, then obtain the equivalent of ¼ tola, which is 2·916 grams given under ¼ tola. The given equivalent of 68¼ tolas is obtained by adding the two gram equivalents *i.e.* 793·139 grams to 2·916 grams = 796·055 grams.

Gallons (IMP) to Litres (Capacity) IS : 1020—1957

Gallons →	*0*	*1*	*2*	*3*	*4*	*5*	*6*	*7*	*8*	*9*
	l	*l*	*l*	*l*	*l*	*l*	*l*	*l*	*l*	*l*
0	0	4·546	9·092	13·838	18·184	22·730	27·276	31·822	36·368	40·914
10	45·460	50·006	54·552	59·097	63·643	68·189	72·735	77·281	81·827	86·373
20	90·919	95·465	100·011	104·5571	109·103	113·649	118·195	122·741	127·287	131·833
30	136·379	140·925	145·471	150·017	154·563	154·109	163·655	168·201	192·746	177·292
40	184·838	186·384	190·930	105·476	200·022	204·568	209·114	213·660	218·206	222·252
50	227·298	231·844	230·390	240·936	225·482	250·028	254·574	259·120	263·886	268·212
60	272·750	277·304	281·850	286·395	290·941	295·407	300·033	304·579	308·125	313·671
70	318·271	322·763	327·304	331·855	376·401	340·947	345·493	350·034	354·588	359·131
80	363·677	368·223	372·769	377·315	381·861	388·407	390·953	395·499	400·044	404·590
90	409·136	413·682	418·228	428·774	427·320	431·866	436·412	440·958	445·504	450·050
100	454·596	459·142	463·688	468·234	472·78-	477·326	481·873	486·418	490·964	495·510

Illustrative Example. To find the litre equivalent of say 67 gallons, turn to the row corresponding to 60 gallons and coloumn corresponding to 7 gallons. The intersection of the row and column gives the figure 304·574, which is the litre equivalent of 67 gallons.

Litres to Gallons (Imp) and Pints

Litres→ ↓	*0*		*1*		*2*		*3*		*4*		*5*		*6*		*7*		*8*		*9*	
	gal.	*pints*	*gal.*	*pints*	*gal.*	*pints*	*gal.*	*pints*	*gal.*	*pints*	*gal.*	*pints*	*gal.*	*pints*	*gal.*	*pints*	*gal.*	*pints*	*gal.*	*pints*
0	0	0	0	2	0	4	0	5	0	7	1	1	1	3	1	4	1	6	2	0
10	2	2	2	3	2	5	2	7	0	1	3	2	3	4	3	6	4	0	4	1
20	4	3	4	5	4	7	5	0	5	2	5	4	5	6	6	0	6	1	6	3
30		5	6	7	7	0	7	2	7	4	7	6	7	7	8	1	8	3	8	5
40	8	6	9	0	9	2	9	4	9	5	9	7	10	1	10	3	10	4	10	6
50	11	0	11	2	11	4	11	5	11	7	12	1	12	3	12	4	12	6	13	0
60	13	2	13	3	13	5	13	7	14	1	14	2	14	4	14	6	15	0	15	1
70	15	3	15	5	15	7	16	0	16	2	16	4	16	6	17	0	17	1	17	3
80	17	5	17	7	18	0	18	2	18	4	18	6	18	7	19	1	19	3	19	5
90	19	6	20	0	20	2	20	4	20	5	20	7	21	1	21	3	21	4	21	6
100	22	0	22	2	22	3	22	5	22	7	23	1	23	2	23	4	23	6	24	0

Illustrative Example. To find out the equivalent of say 47 litres to gallons (Imp) and pints, turn to the row corresponding to 40 litres and the column corresponding to 7 litres. The intersection of the row and column gives the fig 10 gallons 3 pints, which is the equivalent of 47 litres in gallons and pints.

Appendix 1-B (Mathematical Tables)

Table 1. Powers, Roots and Reciprocals

n	n^2	n^3	$\sqrt{n}$	$\sqrt[3]{n}$	$\sqrt{10\,n}$	$\sqrt[3]{10\,n}$	$\sqrt[3]{100\,n}$	$\frac{1}{n}$
1	1	1	1	1	3·1623	2·1544	4·6416	1
2	4	8	1·4142	1·2599	4·4721	2·7144	5·8480	·50000
3	9	27	1·7321	1·4422	5·4772	3·1072	6·6943	·33333
4	16	64	2·000	1·5874	6·3246	3·4200	7·3681	·25000
5	25	125	2·2361	1·7100	7·0711	3·6840	7·9370	·20000
6	36	216	2·4495	1·8171	7·7460	3·9149	8·4343	·16667
7	49	343	2·6458	1·9129	8·3666	4·1213	8·8790	·14286
8	64	512	2·8284	2·000	8·9443	4·3089	9·2832	·12500
9	81	729	3·000	2·0801	9·4868	4·4814	9·6549	·11111
10	100	1000	3·1623	2·1544	10·000	4·6416	10·0000	·10000
11	121	1331	3·3166	2·2240	10·4881	4·7914	10·3228	·090909
12	144	1728	3·4641	2·2894	10·9545	4·9324	10·6266	·083333
13	169	2197	3·6056	2·3513	11·4018	5·0658	10·9139	·076923
14	196	2744	3·7417	2·4101	11·8322	5·1925	11·1869	·071429
15	225	3375	3·8730	2·4662	12·2474	5·3133	11·4471	·066667
16	256	4096	4·000	2·5198	12·6491	5·4288	11·6961	·062500
17	289	4913	4·1231	2·5713	13·0384	5·5397	11·9348	·058824
18	324	5832	4·2426	2·6207	13·4164	5·6462	12·1644	·055556
19	361	6859	4·3589	2·6684	13·7840	5·7489	12·3856	·052632
20	400	8000	4·4721	2·7144	14·1421	5·8480	12·5992	·05000
21	441	9261	4·5826	2·7589	14·4912	5·9439	12·8058	·047619
22	484	10648	4·6904	2·8020	14·8324	6·0368	13·0059	·045455
23	529	12167	4·7958	2·8439	15·1658	6·1269	13·2001	·043478
24	576	13824	4·8990	2·8845	15·4919	6·2145	13·3887	·041667
25	625	15625	5·000	2·9240	15·8114	6·2996	13·5721	·04000
26	676	17576	5·0990	2·9625	16·1245	6·3825	13·7507	·038462
27	729	19683	5·1962	3·0000	16·4317	6·4633	13·9248	·037037
28	784	21952	5·2915	3·0366	16·7332	6·5421	14·0946	·035714
29	841	24389	5·3852	3·0723	17·0294	6·6191	14·2604	·034483
30	900	27000	5·4772	3·1072	17·3205	6·6943	14·4225	·033333
31	961	29791	5·5678	3·1414	17·6068	6·7679	14·5810	·032258
32	1024	32768	5·6569	3·1748	17·8885	6·8399	14·7361	·031250
33	1089	35937	5·7446	3·2075	18·1659	6·9104	14·8881	·030303
34	1156	39304	5·8310	3·2396	18·4391	6·9795	15·0369	·029412
35	1225	42875	5·9161	3·2711	18·7083	7·0473	15·1829	·028571
36	1296	46656	6·000	3·3019	18·9737	7·1138	15·3262	·027778
37	1369	50653	6·0828	3·3322	19·2354	7·1791	15·4668	·027027
38	1444	54872	6·1644	3·3620	19·4936	7·2432	15·6049	·026316
39	1521	59319	6·2450	3·3912	19·7484	7·3061	15·7406	·025641
40	1600	64000	6·3246	3·4200	20·000	7·3681	15·8740	·02500
41	1681	68921	6·4031	3·4482	20·2485	7·4290	16·0052	·024390
42	1764	74088	6·4807	3·4760	20·4939	7·4889	16·1343	·023810
43	1849	79507	6·5574	3·5034	20·7364	7·5478	16·2613	·023256
44	1936	85184	6·6332	3·5503	20·9762	7·6059	16·3864	·022727
45	2025	91125	6·7082	3·5569	21·2132	7·6631	16·5096	·022222
46	2116	97336	6·7823	3·5830	21·4476	7·7194	16·6310	·021739
47	2209	103823	6·8557	3·6088	21·6795	7·7750	16·7507	·021277
48	2304	110592	6·9282	3·6342	21·9089	7·8297	16·8687	·020833
49	2401	117649	7·000	3·6593	22·1359	7·8837	16·9850	·020408
50	2500	125000	7·0711	3·6840	22·3607	7·9370	17·0998	·02000

Powers, Roots and Reciprocals (contd.)

n	n^2	n^3	$\sqrt{n}$	$\sqrt[3]{n}$	$\sqrt{10n}$	$\sqrt[3]{10n}$	$\sqrt[3]{100n}$	$\frac{1}{n}$
51	2601	132651	7·1414	3·7084	22·5832	7·9896	17·2130	·019608
52	2704	140608	7·2111	3·7325	22·8035	8·0415	17·3248	·019231
53	2809	148877	7·2801	3·7563	23·0217	8·0927	17·4351	·018868
54	2916	157464	7·3485	3·7798	23·2379	8·1433	17·5441	·018519
55	3025	166375	7·4162	3·8030	23·4521	8·1932	17·6517	·018182
56	3136	175616	7·4833	3·8259	23·6643	8·2426	17·7581	·017857
57	3249	185193	7·5498	3·8485	23·8747	8·2913	17·8632	·017544
58	3364	195112	7·6158	3·8709	24·0832	8·3396	17·9670	·017241
59	3481	205379	7·6811	3·8930	24·2899	8·3872	18·0697	·016949
60	3600	216000	7·7460	3·9149	24·4949	8·4343	18·1712	·016667
61	3721	226981	7·8102	3·9365	24·6982	8·4809	18·2716	·016393
62	3844	238328	7·8740	3·9579	24·8998	8·5270	18·3709	·016129
63	3969	250047	7·9373	3·9791	25·0998	8·5726	18·4691	·015873
64	4096	262144	8·000	4·000	25·2982	8·6177	18·5664	·015625
65	4225	274625	8·0623	4·0207	25·4951	8·6624	18·6626	·015385
66	4356	287496	8·1240	4·0412	25·6905	8·7066	18·7578	·015152
67	4489	300763	8·1854	4·0615	25·8844	8·7503	18·8520	·014925
68	4624	314432	8·2462	4·0817	26·0768	8·7937	18·9454	·014706
69	4761	328509	8·3066	4·1016	26·2679	8·8366	19·0378	·014493
70	4900	343000	8·3666	4·1213	26·4575	8·8790	19·1293	·014286
71	5041	357911	8·4261	4·1408	26·6458	8·9211	19·2200	·014085
72	5184	373248	8·4853	4·1602	26·8328	8·9628	19·3098	·013889
73	5329	389017	8·5440	4·1793	27·0185	9·0041	19·3988	·013699
74	5476	405224	8·6023	4·1983	27·2029	9·0450	19·4870	·013514
75	5625	421875	8·6603	4·2172	27·3861	9·0856	19·5743	·013333
76	5776	438976	8·7178	4·2358	27·5681	9·1258	19·6610	·013158
77	5929	456533	8·7750	4·2543	27·7489	9·1657	19·7468	·012987
78	6084	474552	8·8318	4·2727	27·9285	9·2052	19·8319	·012821
79	6241	493039	8·8882	4·2908	28·1069	9·2443	19·9163	·012658
80	6400	512000	8·9443	4·3089	28·2843	9·2832	20·0000	·012500
81	6561	531441	9·0000	4·3267	284605	9·3217	20·0830	·012346
82	6724	551368	9·0554	4·3445	28·6356	9·3599	20·1653	·012195
83	6889	571787	9·1104	4·3621	28·8097	9·3978	20·2469	·012048
84	7056	592704	9·1652	4·3795	28·9828	9·4354	20·3279	·011905
85	7225	614125	9·2195	4·3968	29·1548	9·4727	20·4083	·011765
86	7396	636056	9·2736	4·4140	29·3258	9·5097	20·4880	·011628
87	7569	658503	9·3274	4·4310	29·4958	9·5464	20·5671	·011494
88	7744	681472	9·3808	4·4480	29·6648	9·5828	20·6456	·011364
89	7921	704969	9·4340	4·4647	29·8329	9·6190	20·7235	·011236
90	8100	729000	9·4868	4·4814	30·000	9·6549	20·8008	·011111
91	8281	753571	9·5394	4·4979	30·1662	9·6905	20·8776	·010989
92	8464	778688	9·5917	4·5144	30·3315	9·7259	20·9538	·010870
93	8649	804357	9·6437	4·5307	30·4959	9·7610	21·0294	·010753
94	8836	830584	9·6954	4·5468	30·6594	9·7959	21·1045	·010638
95	9025	857375	9·7468	4·5629	30·8221	9·8305	21·1791	·010526
96	9216	884736	9·7980	4·5789	30·9839	9·8648	21·2532	·010417
97	9409	912673	9·8489	4·5947	31·1448	9·8990	21·3267	·010309
98	9604	941192	9·8995	4·6104	31·3050	9·9329	21·3997	·010204
99	9801	970299	9·9499	4·6261	31·4643	9·9666	21·4723	·010101
100	10000	1000000	10·000	4·6416	31·6228	10·000	21·5443	·0100

Table 2. Degrees to Radians

Degrees	0′ 0°·0	6′ 0°·1	12′ 0°·2	18′ 0°·3	24′ 0°·4	30′ 0°·5	36′ 0°·6	42′ 0°·7	48′ 0°·8	54′ 0°·9	*Mean Difference* 1	2	3	4	5
0	·00000	00175	00349	00524	00698	00873	01047	01222	01396	01571	29	58	87	116	145
1	·01745	01920	02094	02269	02443	02618	02793	02967	03142	03316	29	58	87	116	145
2	·03491	03665	03840	04014	04189	04363	04538	04712	04887	05061	29	58	87	116	145
3	·05236	05411	05585	05760	05934	06109	06283	06458	06632	06807	29	58	87	116	145
4	·06981	07156	07330	07505	07679	07854	08029	06203	08378	08552	29	58	87	116	145
5	·08727	08901	09076	09250	09425	09599	09774	09948	10123	10297	29	58	87	116	145
6	·10472	10647	10821	10996	11170	11345	11519	11694	11868	12043	29	58	87	116	145
7	·12217	12392	12566	12741	12915	13090	13264	13439	13614	13788	29	58	87	116	145
8	·13963	14137	14312	14486	14661	14835	15010	15184	15359	15533	29	58	87	116	145
9	·15708	15882	16057	16232	16406	16581	16755	16930	17104	17279	29	58	87	116	145
10	·17453	17628	17802	17977	18151	18326	18500	18675	18850	19024	29	58	87	116	145
11	·19199	19373	19548	19722	19897	20071	20246	20420	20595	20769	29	58	87	116	145
12	·20944	21118	21293	21468	21622	21817	21991	22166	22340	22515	29	58	87	116	145
13	·22689	22864	23038	23213	23387	23562	23736	23911	24086	24260	29	58	87	116	145
14	·24435	24609	24784	24958	25133	25307	25482	25656	25831	26005	29	58	87	116	145
15	·26180	26354	26529	26704	26878	27053	27227	27202	27576	27751	29	58	87	116	145
16	·27925	28100	38274	28449	28623	28798	28972	29147	29322	29496	29	58	87	116	145
17	·29671	29845	30020	30194	30369	30543	30718	30892	31067	31241	29	58	87	116	145
18	·31416	31590	31765	31940	32114	32289	32463	32638	32812	32987	29	58	87	116	145
19	·33161	33336	33510	33685	33859	34034	34208	34383	34558	34732	29	58	87	116	145
20	·34907	35081	35256	35430	35605	35779	35954	36128	36303	36477	29	58	87	116	145
21	·36652	36826	37001	37176	37350	37525	37699	37174	38048	38223	29	58	87	116	145
22	·38397	38572	38746	38121	39095	39270	39444	39119	39794	39968	29	58	87	116	145
23	·40143	40317	40492	40666	40841	41015	41190	41364	41539	41713	29	58	87	116	145
24	·41888	42062	42237	42411	42586	42761	42935	43110	43284	43459	29	58	87	116	145
25	·43633	43808	43982	44157	44331	44506	44680	44855	45029	45204	29	58	87	116	145
26	·45379	45553	45728	45902	46077	46251	46426	46600	46775	46949	29	58	87	116	145
27	·47124	47298	47473	47647	47822	47997	48171	48346	48520	48695	29	58	87	116	145
28	·48869	49044	49218	49393	49567	49742	49916	50091	50265	50440	29	58	87	116	145
29	·50615	50789	50964	51138	51313	51487	51662	51836	52011	52185	29	58	87	116	145
30	·52360	52524	52709	52883	53058	53233	53407	53582	53756	53931	29	58	87	116	145
31	·54105	54280	54454	54629	54803	54978	55152	55327	55501	55676	29	58	87	116	145
32	·55851	56025	56200	56374	56549	56723	56898	57072	57247	57421	29	58	87	116	145
33	·57596	57770	57945	58119	58294	58469	58643	58818	58992	59167	29	58	87	116	145
34	·59341	59516	59690	59865	60039	60214	60388	60563	60737	60912	29	58	87	116	145
35	·61087	61261	61436	61610	61785	61959	62134	62308	62483	62657	29	58	87	116	145
36	·62832	63006	63181	63355	63530	63705	63879	64054	64228	64403	29	58	87	116	145
37	·64577	64752	64926	65101	65275	65450	65624	65799	65973	66148	29	58	87	116	145
38	·66323	66497	66672	66846	67021	67195	67370	67544	67719	67893	29	58	87	116	145
39	·68068	68242	68417	68591	68766	68941	69115	69290	69464	69639	29	58	87	116	145
40	·69813	69988	70162	70337	70511	70686	70860	71035	71209	71384	29	58	87	116	145
41	·71558	71733	71908	72082	72257	72431	72606	72780	72955	73129	29	58	87	116	145
42	·73304	73478	73653	73827	74002	74176	74351	74526	74700	74875	29	58	87	116	145
43	·75049	75224	75398	75573	75747	75922	76096	76271	76445	76620	29	58	87	116	145
44	·76794	76969	77144	77318	77793	77667	77842	78016	78191	78365	29	58	87	116	145
45	·78540	78714	78889	79063	79280	79412	79587	79762	79936	80111	29	58	87	116	145

Degrees to Radians (contd.)

Degrees	0′ 0°·0	6′ 0°·1	12′ 0°·2	18′ 0°·3	24′ 0°·4	30′ 0°·5	36′ 0°·6	42′ 0°·7	48′ 0°·8	54′ 0°·9	*Mean Difference* 1	2	3	4	5
45	·78540	78714	78889	79603	79238	79412	79587	79762	79936	80111	29	58	87	116	145
46	·80285	80460	80634	80809	80983	81158	81332	81507	81681	81856	29	58	87	116	145
47	·82030	82205	82380	82554	82729	82903	83078	83252	83427	83601	29	58	87	116	145
48	·83776	83950	84125	84299	84474	84648	84823	84998	85172	85347	29	58	87	116	145
49	·85521	85696	85870	86045	86219	86394	86568	86743	86917	87092	29	58	87	116	145
50	·87266	87441	87616	87790	87965	88139	88314	88488	88663	88837	29	58	87	116	145
51	·89012	89186	89361	89535	89710	89884	90059	90234	90408	90583	29	58	87	116	145
52	·90757	90932	91106	91281	91455	91630	91804	91979	92153	92328	29	58	87	116	145
53	·92502	92677	92852	93026	93201	93375	93550	93724	93899	94073	29	58	87	116	145
54	·94248	94422	94597	94771	94946	95120	95120	95470	95644	95819	29	58	87	116	145
55	·95993	96168	96342	96517	96691	96866	97040	97215	97389	97564	29	58	87	116	145
56	·97738	97913	98088	98262	98437	98611	98786	98960	99135	99309	29	58	87	116	145
57	·99484	99658	99833	1·00007	1·00182	1·00356	1·00531	1·00706	1·00880	1·01055	29	58	87	116	145
58	1·01229	01404	01578	01753	01927	02102	02276	02451	02625	02800	29	58	87	116	145
59	1·02974	03149	03323	03498	03673	03847	04022	04196	04371	04545	29	58	87	116	145
60	1·04720	04894	05069	05243	05418	05592	05767	05941	06116	06291	29	58	87	116	145
61	1·05465	06640	06814	06989	07163	07338	07512	07687	07861	08036	29	58	87	116	145
62	1·08210	08385	08559	08734	08909	09083	09258	09432	09607	09781	29	58	87	116	145
63	1·09956	10130	10305	10479	10654	10828	11003	11177	11352	11527	29	58	87	116	145
64	1·11701	11876	12050	12225	12399	12574	12748	120923	13097	13272	29	58	87	116	145
65	1·13446	13621	13795	13970	14145	14319	14494	14668	14843	15017	29	58	87	116	145
66	1·15192	15366	15541	15715	15890	16064	16239	16413	16588	16763	29	58	87	116	145
67	1·16937	17112	17286	17461	17635	17810	17984	18159	18333	18508	29	58	87	116	145
68	1·18682	18857	19031	19206	19381	19555	19730	19904	20079	20253	29	58	87	116	145
69	1·20428	20602	20777	20951	21126	21300	21475	21649	21824	21999	29	58	87	116	145
70	1·22173	22348	22522	22697	22871	23046	23220	23395	23569	23744	29	58	87	116	145
71	1·23918	24093	24267	24442	24617	24791	24966	25140	25315	25489	29	58	87	116	145
72	1·25664	25838	26013	26187	26362	26536	26711	26885	27060	27234	29	58	87	116	145
73	1·27409	27584	27758	27933	28107	28282	28456	28631	28805	28980	29	58	87	116	145
74	1·29154	29329	29503	29678	29852	30027	30202	30376	30551	30725	29	58	87	116	145
75	1·30900	31074	31249	31423	31598	31772	31947	32121	32296	32470	29	58	87	116	145
76	1·32645	32820	32994	33169	33343	33518	33792	33867	34041	34216	29	58	87	116	145
77	1·34390	34565	34739	34914	35088	35263	35438	35612	35787	35961	29	58	87	116	145
78	1·36136	36310	36485	36659	36834	37008	37183	37351	37532	37706	29	58	87	116	145
79	1·37881	38056	38230	38405	38579	38754	38928	39103	39277	39452	29	58	87	116	145
80	1·39626	39801	39975	40150	40324	40499	40674	40448	41023	41197	29	58	87	116	145
81	1·41372	41546	41721	41895	42070	42244	42419	42593	42768	42942	29	58	87	116	145
82	1·43117	43292	43466	43641	43815	43990	44164	44339	44513	44688	29	58	87	116	145
83	1·44862	45037	45211	45386	45560	45735	45910	46084	46259	46433	29	58	87	116	145
84	1·46608	46782	46957	47131	47306	47480	47655	47829	48004	48178	29	58	87	116	145
85	1·48353	48528	48702	48877	49051	49226	49400	49575	49749	49924	29	58	87	116	145
86	1·50098	50273	50447	50622	50796	50971	51146	51320	51495	51669	29	58	87	116	145
87	1·51844	52018	52193	52367	52542	52716	52891	53065	53240	53414	29	58	87	116	145
88	1·53589	53764	53938	54113	54287	54462	54636	54811	54985	55160	29	58	87	116	145
89	1·55334	55509	55683	55858	56032	56207	56381	56556	56731	56905	29	58	87	116	145

Table 3. Areas of Circles (diameters advancing by tenths)

Diameter	0·0	0·1	0·2	0·3	0·4	0·5	0·6	0·7	0·8	0·9
0	0·0	0·0078	0·0314	0·0706	0·1256	0·1963	0·2827	0·3848	0·5027	0·6362
1	0·78540	0·95033	1·1310	1·3273	1·5394	1·7671	2·0106	2·2698	2·5447	2·8353
2	3·1416	3·4636	3·8013	4·1548	4·5239	4·9087	5·3093	5·7255	6·1575	6·6052
3	7·0686	7·5477	8·0425	8·5530	9·0792	9·6211	10·179	10·752	11·341	11·946
4	12·566	13·0202	13·854	14·522	15·205	15·904	16·619	17·349	18·096	18·857
5	19·635	20·428	21·237	22·062	22·902	23·758	24·630	25·518	26·421	27340
6	28·274	29·225	30·191	31·172	32·170	33·183	34·212	35·257	36·317	37·393
7	38·0485	39·592	40·715	41·854	43·008	44·179	45·365	46·566	47·784	49·017
8	50·266	51·530	52·810	52·106	55·418	56·745	58·088	59·447	60·821	62·211
9	63·617	65·039	66·476	67·929	69·398	70·882	72·382	73·898	75·430	76·977
10	78·540	80·118	81·713	83·323	84·949	86·590	88·247	89·920	91·609	93·313
11	95·033	96·769	98·520	100·29	102·07	103·87	105·68	107·51	109·36	111·22
12	113·10	114·99	116·90	118·82	120·76	122·72	124·69	126·68	128·68	130·70
13	132·73	134·78	136·85	138·93	141·03	143·14	145·27	147·41	149·57	151·75
14	153·94	156·14	158·37	160·61	162·86	165·13	167·41	169·72	172·03	174·37
15	176·71	179·08	181·46	183·85	186·26	188·69	191·13	193·59	196·07	198·56
16	201·06	203·58	206·12	208·67	211·24	213·82	216·42	219·04	221·67	224·32
17	226·98	229·66	232·35	235·06	237·79	240·53	243·28	246·06	248·85	251·65
18	254·47	257·30	260·15	263·02	265·90	268·80	271·72	274·65	277·59	280·55
19	283·53	286·52	289·53	292·55	295·59	298·65	301·72	304·80	307·91	311·02
20	314·16	317·31	320·47	323·65	326·85	330·06	333·29	336·53	339·79	343·07
21	346·36	349·67	352·99	356·33	359·68	363·05	366·43	369·84	373·25	376·68
22	380·13	383·60	387·08	390·57	394·08	397·61	401·15	404·71	408·28	411·87
23	415·48	419·10	422·73	426·38	430·05	433·74	437·43	441·15	444·88	448·63
24	452·39	456·17	459·96	463·77	467·59	471·43	475·29	479·16	483·05	486·95
25	490·87	494·81	498·76	502·73	506·71	510·71	514·72	518·75	522·79	526·85
26	530·93	535·02	539·13	543·25	547·39	551·55	555·72	559·90	564·10	568·32
27	572·56	576·80	581·07	585·35	589·65	593·96	598·28	602·63	606·99	611·36
28	615·75	620·16	624·58	629·02	633·47	637·94	642·42	646·92	651·44	655·97
29	660·52	665·08	669·66	674·26	678·87	684·49	688·13	692·79	697·46	702·15
30	706·86	711·58	716·31	721·07	725·83	730·62	733·41	740·23	745·06	749·91
31	754·77	759·64	764·54	769·45	774·37	779·35	784·27	789·24	794·23	799·23
32	804·25	809·28	814·33	819·40	824·48	829·58	834·69	839·82	844·96	850·12
33	855·30	860·49	865·70	870·92	876·16	881·41	886·68	891·97	897·27	902·59
34	907·92	913·27	918·63	924·01	929·41	934·82	940·25	945·69	951·15	956·62
35	962·11	967·60	973·14	978·68	984·23	989·80	995·38	1000·98	1006·6	1012·2
36	1017·9	1023·5	1029·2	1034·9	1040·6	1046·3	1052·1	1057·8	1063·6	1069·4
37	1075·2	1081·0	1086·9	1092·7	1098·6	1104·5	1110·4	1116·3	1122·2	1128·1
38	1134·1	1140·1	1146·1	1152·1	1158·1	1164·2	1170·2	1176·3	1182·4	1188·5
39	1194·6	1200·7	1206·9	1213·0	1219·2	1225·4	1231·6	1237·9	1244·1	1250·4
40	1256·6	1262·9	1269·2	1275·6	1281·9	1288·2	1294·6	1301·0	1307·4	1313·8
41	1320·3	1326·7	1333·2	1339·6	1346·1	1352·6	1359·2	1365·7	1372·3	1378·8
42	1385·4	1392·0	1398·7	1405·3	1412·0	1418·6	1425·3	1432·0	1438·7	1445·4
43	1452·2	1459·0	1465·7	1472·5	1479·3	1486·2	1493·0	1499·9	1506·7	1513·6
44	1520·5	1527·4	1534·4	1541·3	1548·3	1553·3	1562·3	1569·3	1576·3	1583·4
45	1590·4	1597·5	1604·6	1611·7	1618·8	1626·0	1633·1	1640·3	1647·5	1654·7
46	1661·9	1669·1	1676·4	1683·6	1690·9	1698·2	1705·5	1712·9	1720·2	1727·6
47	1734·9	1742·3	1749·7	1757·2	1764·6	1772·0	1779·5	1787·0	1794·5	1802·0
48	1809·6	1817·1	1824·7	1832·2	1839·8	1847·4	1855·1	1862·7	1870·4	1878·0
49	1885·7	1893·4	1901·2	1908·9	1916·6	1924·4	1935·2	1940·0	1947·8	1955·6
50	1963·5	1971·0	1979·2	1987·1	1995·0	2003·0	2010·9	2018·9	2026·8	2034·8

Areas of Circles (contd.)

Diameter	0·0	0·1	0·2	0·3	0·4	0·5	0·6	0·7	0·8	0·9
51	2042·8	2050·8	2058·9	2066·9	2075·0	2083·1	2091·3	2099·3	2107·4	2115·6
52	2123·7	2131·9	2140·1	2148·3	2156·5	2164·7	2173·0	2181·3	2189·6	2197·9
53	2206·2	2214·5	2222·9	2231·2	2239·6	2248·0	2256·4	2264·8	2273·3	2281·7
54	2290·2	2298·7	2307·2	2315·7	2324·3	2332·8	2341·4	2350·0	2358·6	2367·2
55	2375·8	2384·5	2393·1	2401·8	2410·5	2419·2	2428·0	2436·7	2445·4	2454·2
56	2463·0	2471·8	2480·6	2489·5	2498·3	2507·2	2516·1	2525·0	2533·0	2542·8
57	2551·8	2560·7	2569·7	2578·7	2587·7	2596·7	2605·7	2614·8	2623·9	2633·0
58	2642·1	2651·2	2660·3	2669·5	2678·6	2687·8	2697·0	2706·2	2715·5	2724·7
59	2734·0	2743·2	2752·5	2761·8	2771·2	2780·5	2789·9	2799·2	2808·6	2818·0
60	2827·4	2836·9	2846·3	2855·8	2865·3	2874·7	2884·3	2893·8	2903·3	2912·9
61	2922·5	2932·1	2941·7	2951·3	2960·9	2970·6	2980·2	2989·9	2999·6	3009·3
62	3019·1	3028·8	3038·6	3048·4	3058·1	3068·0	3077·8	3087·6	3097·5	3107·4
63	3117·2	3127·1	3137·1	3147·0	3157·0	3166·9	3176·9	3186·9	3196·9	3206·9
64	3217·0	3227·1	3237·1	3247·2	3257·3	3267·4	3277·6	3287·7	3297·9	3308·1
65	3318·3	3328·5	3338·8	3349·0	3359·3	3369·6	3379·8	3390·2	3400·5	3410·8
66	3412·2	3431·6	3442·0	3452·4	3462·8	3473·2	3483·7	3494·1	3504·6	3515·1
67	3525·7	3536·2	3546·7	3557·3	3567·9	3578·5	3589·1	3599·7	3610·3	3621·0
68	3613·7	3642·4	3653·1	3663·8	3674·5	3685·3	3696·1	3706·8	3717·6	3728·4
69	3739·3	3750·1	3761·0	3771·9	3782·8	3793·7	3804·6	3815·5	3826·5	3837·5
70	3848·5	3859·4	3870·5	3881·5	3892·6	3903·6	3914·7	3925·8	3936·9	3948·0
71	3959·2	3970·3	3981·5	3992·7	4003·9	4015·1	4026·4	4037·6	4048·9	4060·2
72	4071·5	4082·8	4094·2	4105·5	4116·9	4128·2	4139·6	4151·1	4162·5	4173·9
73	4185·4	4196·9	4208·3	4219·9	4231·4	4242·9	4254·5	4266·0	4277·6	4289·2
74	4300·8	4312·5	4324·1	4335·8	4347·5	4359·2	4370·9	4382·6	4394·3	4406·1
75	4417·9	4429·6	4441·5	4453·3	4465·1	4477·0	4488·8	4500·7	4512·6	4524·5
76	4536·5	4548·4	4560·4	4572·3	4548·3	4596·3	4608·4	4620·4	4632·5	4644·5
77	4656·6	4668·7	4680·8	4693·0	4705·1	4717·3	4729·5	4741·7	4753·9	4766·1
78	4778·4	4790·6	4802·9	4815·2	4827·5	4839·8	4852·2	4864·5	4876·9	4889·3
79	4901·7	4914·1	4926·5	4939·0	4951·4	4963·9	4976·4	4988·9	5001·4	5014·0
80	5026·6	5039·1	5051·7	5064·3	5076·9	5089·6	5102·2	5114·9	5127·6	5140·3
81	5153·0	5165·7	5178·5	5191·2	5204·0	5216·8	5229·6	5242·4	5255·3	5268·1
82	5281·0	5293·9	5306·8	5319·7	5332·7	5345·6	5358·6	5371·6	5384·6	5397·6
83	5410·6	5423·6	5436·7	5449·8	5462·9	5476·0	5489·1	5502·3	5515·4	5528·6
84	5541·8	5555·0	5568·2	5581·4	5594·7	5607·9	5621·2	5634·5	5647·8	5661·2
85	5674·5	5687·9	5701·2	5714·6	5728·0	5741·5	5754·9	5768·3	5781·8	5795·3
86	5808·8	5822·3	5835·8	5849·4	5863·0	5876·6	5890·1	5903·7	5917·4	5931·0
87	5944·7	5958·3	5972·0	5985·7	5999·5	6013·2	6027·0	6040·7	6054·5	6068·3
88	6082·1	6096·0	6109·8	6123·7	6137·5	6151·7	6165·3	6179·3	6193·2	6207·2
89	6221·1	6235·1	6249·1	6263·1	6277·2	6291·2	6305·3	6319·4	6333·5	6347·6
90	6361·7	6375·9	6390·0	6404·2	6418·4	6432·6	6446·8	6461·1	6475·3	6489·6
91	6503·9	6518·2	6532·5	6546·8	6561·2	6575·6	6589·9	6604·3	6618·7	6633·2
92	6647·6	6662·1	6676·5	6691·0	6705·5	6720·1	6734·6	6749·1	6763·7	6778·3
93	6792·9	6807·5	6822·2	6836·8	6851·5	6866·1	6880·8	6895·6	6910·3	6925·0
94	6939·8	6954·6	6969·3	6984·1	6999·0	7013·8	7028·7	7043·5	7058·4	7073·3
95	7088·2	7103·1	7118·1	7133·1	7148·0	7163·0	7178·0	7193·1	7208·1	7223·2
96	7238·2	7253·3	7268·4	7283·5	7298·7	7313·8	7329·0	7344·2	7359·4	7374·6
97	7389·8	7405·1	7420·3	7435·6	7450·9	7466·2	7481·5	7496·9	7512·2	7527·6
98	7543·0	7558·4	7573·8	7589·2	7604·7	7620·1	7635·6	7651·1	7666·6	7682·1
99	7697·7	7713·2	7728·8	7744·4	7760·0	7775·6	7791·3	7806·9	7822·6	7838·3
100	7854·0	7869·7	7885·7	7901·2	7919·9	7932·7	7948·5	7964·3	7980·1	7996·0

2

Applied Mathematics

2·1. GEOMETRY

Important Theorems

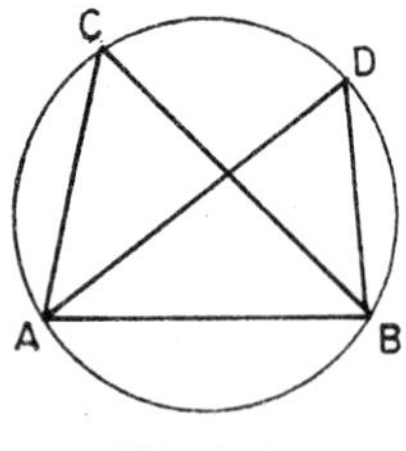

Fig. 2·1.

1. Angles in the same segment of a circle are equal

$\angle ACB = \angle ADB$

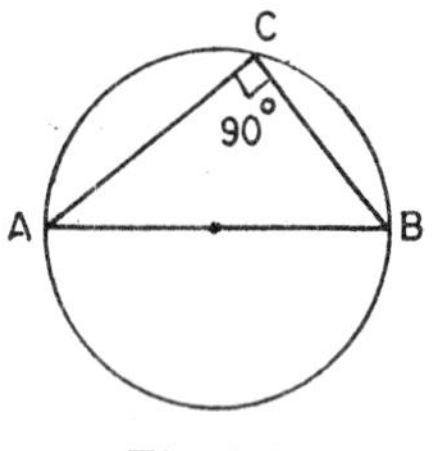

Fig. 2·2.

2. The angle in a semi circle is a right angle

$\angle ACB$ = a right angle

3. The opposite angles of a cyclic quadrilateral are supplementary

$\angle BAD + \angle BCD$ = 2 right angles

$\angle ADC + \angle ABC$ = 2 right angles

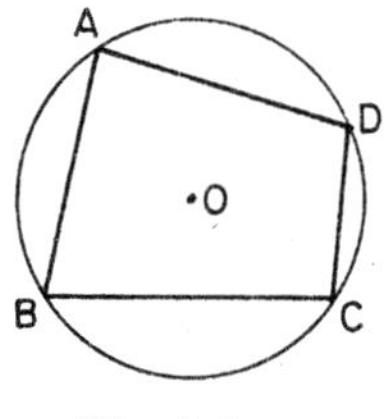

Fig. 2·3.

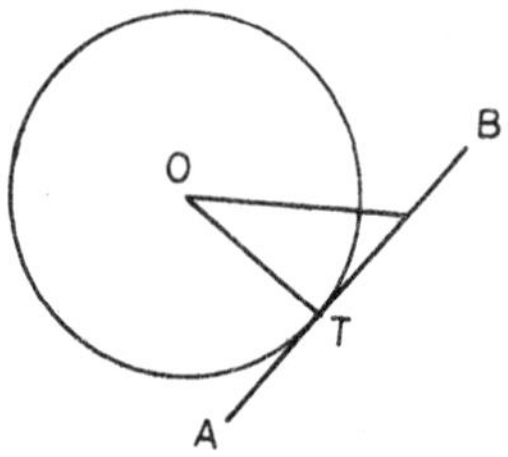

Fig. 2·4.

4. The straight line drawn perpendicular to a radius of a circle at its extremity is a tangent to the circle

If angle OTB = right angle than AB is a tangent on the circle at a tangent point T.

5. If two circles touch one another, the centres and the points of contact are in one straight line.

OTO' are in one straight line

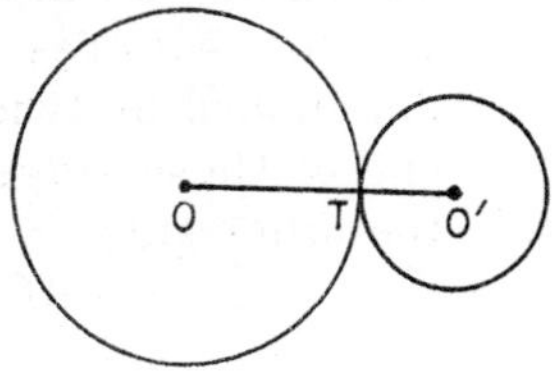

Fig. 2·5.

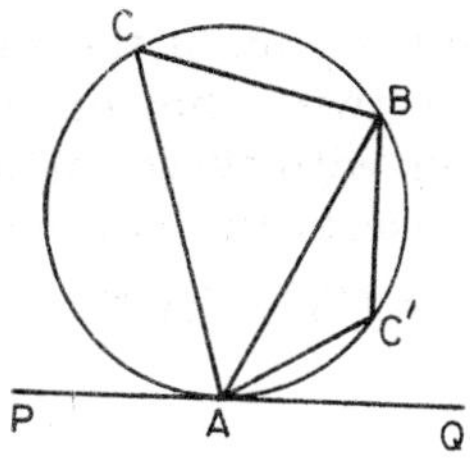

Fig. 2·6.

6. The angles which a tangent to a circle makes with a chord drawn from the point of contact are respectively equal to the angles in the alternate segments of the circle.

$\angle BAQ = \angle ACB$

$\angle BAP = \angle AC'B$

7. If two chords of a circle intersect at a point within the circle the rectangle contained by the segments of one is equal to the rectangle contained by the segments of the other

$Ax.xB = Dx.xC$

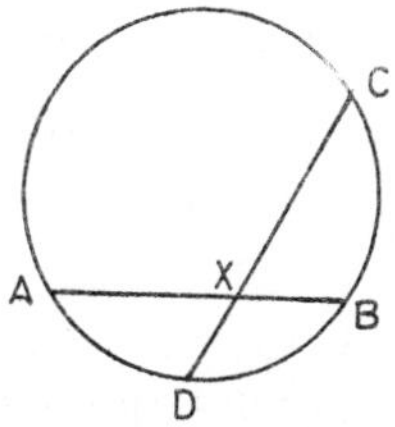

Fig. 2·7.

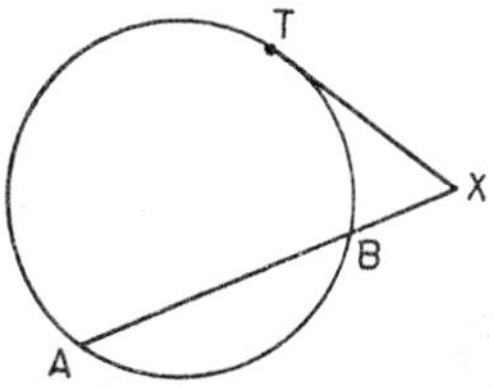

Fig. 2·8.

8. If from a point without a secant and a tangent to the circle are drawn, the rectangle contained by the whole secant and the segment of it without the circle is equal to the square of the tangent

$AX{\cdot}XB = XT^2$

9. In a right angled triangle, the square on the hyp is equal to the sum of the squares on the other two sides

$AC^2 = AB^2 + BC^2$

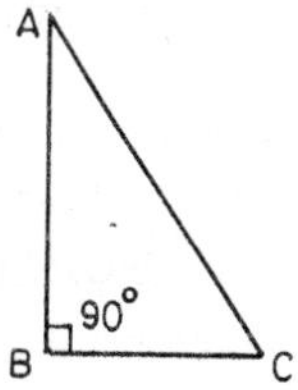

Fig. 2·9.

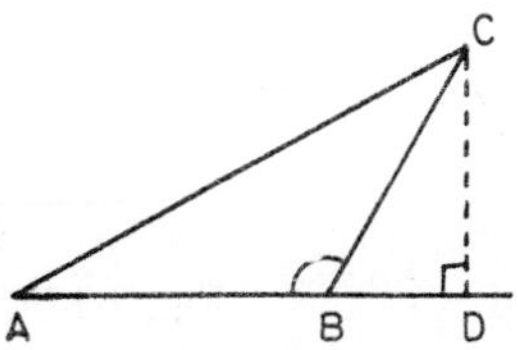

Fig. 2·10.

10. In the obtuse-angled triangle, the square on the side subtending the obtuse angle is equal to the sum of the squares on the other two sides together with twice the rectangle contained by one of these sides and the projection on it of the other.

$AC^2 = AB^2 + BC^2 + 2AB.BD$

11. In every triangle the square on the side subtending an acute angle is equal to the sum of the squares on the other two sides diminished by twice the rectangle contained by one of these sides and the projection on it of the other side.

$$AC^2 = AB^2 + BC^2 - 2AB.BD$$

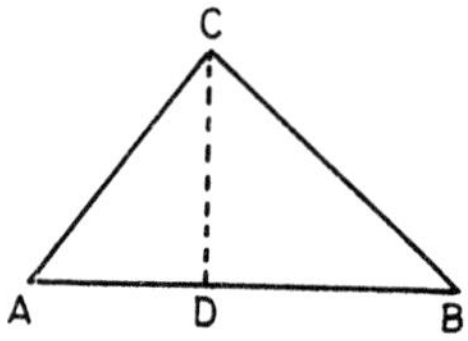

Fig. 2·11.

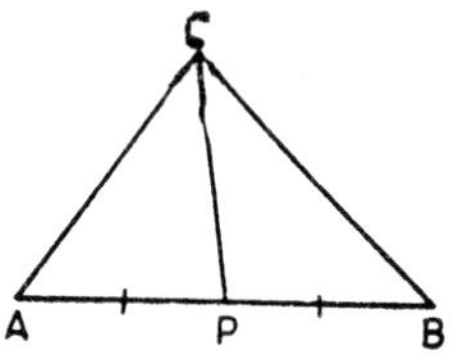

Fig. 2·12.

12. In any triangle the sum of the squares on two sides is equal to twice the square on half the 3rd side together with twice the square on the median which bisects the 3rd side.

$$AC^2 + CB^2 = 2AP^2 + 2PC^2$$

13. A straight line drawn parallel to one side of a triangle cuts the other two sides, or those sides produced proportionally.

$$AB : AC = AC : AF$$

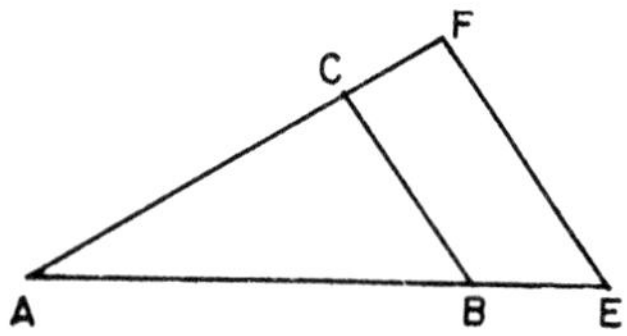

Fig. 2·13.

14. If the vertical angle of a triangle is bisected internally or externally, the bisector devides the base internally or externally into segments which have the same ratio as the other sides of the triangle.

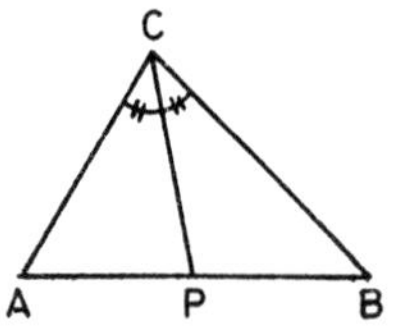

Fig. 2·14 (*a*)

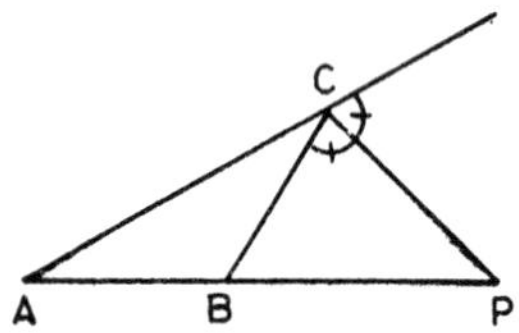

Fig. 2·14 (*b*).

$$AP.PB = CA.CB.$$

15. In a right angled triangle of a perpendicular is drawn from the right angle to the hyp., the triangles on each side of it are similar to the whole triangle and to one another.

ΔABC is similar to ΔACP and BCP

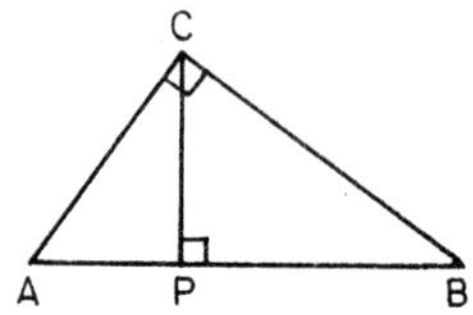

Fig. 2·15.

16. The areas of similar triangles are proportional to the squares on corresponding sides.

$$\Delta ABC : \Delta EFG = AB^2 : EF^2$$

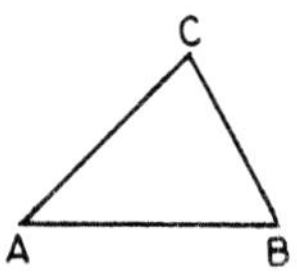

Fig. 2·16 (*a*)

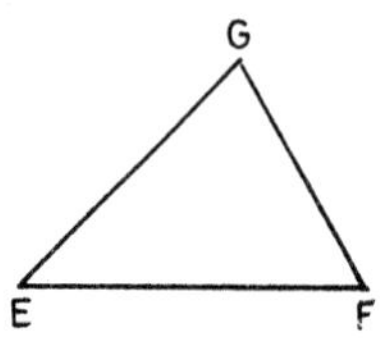

Fig. 2·16 (*b*).

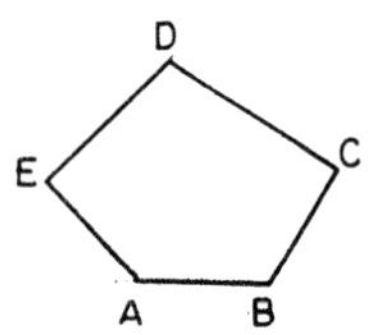

Fig. 2·17 (*a*)

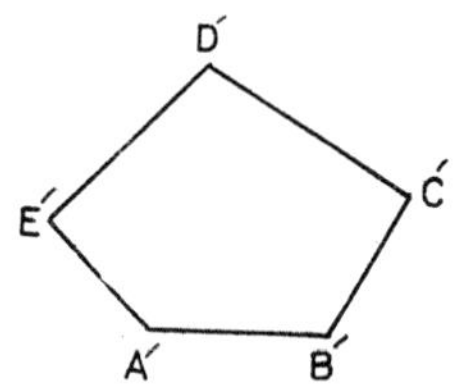

Fig. 2·17 (*b*).

17. The areas of similar polygons are proportional to the squares on the corresponding sides.

$$ABCDE : A'B'C'D'E' = AB^2 : A'^2\, B'^2$$

2·2. Important Problems

1. To inscribe, circumscrib and escribe a circle in a given triangle

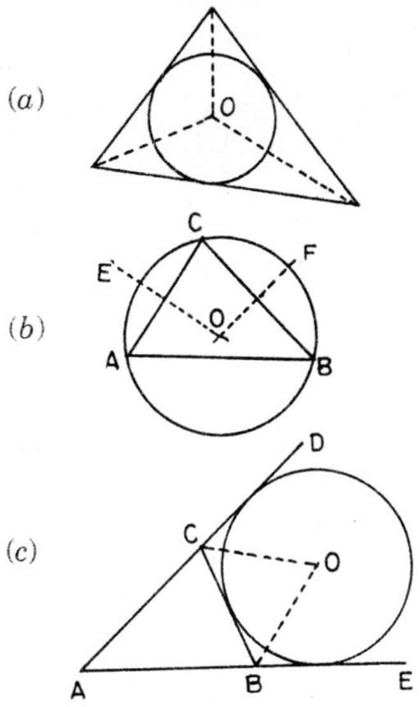

Fig. 2·18.

Const. : Bisect the angles ABC by the straight line which intersect at O, then O will be the centre of the inscribed circle and called, incentre and the bisecting lines as bisectors.

Const. : Bisect AC and BC at right angles at E and F which meets O, then O will be the centre of the circumscribed circle and called circumcentre.

Const. : Bisect angles DCB and EBC by lines which meets at O. Then O will be the required centre of the escribed circle.

2. To draw a common tangent to two circles A and B

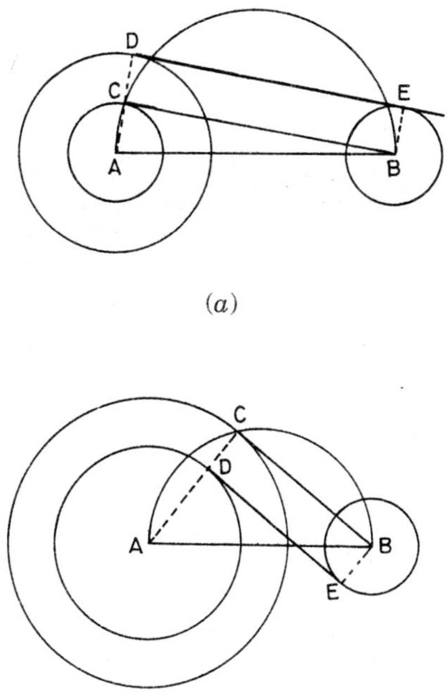

Fig. 2·19.

Const. : With centre A and radius equal to the difference of the radii of the given circles describe a circle and draw BC to touch it by drawing a semi circle on BA which cuts the inner circles at C the tangent point, join AC and produce it to meet the circle A at D.

Through B draw the radius BE parallel to AD in the same sense. Join DE, DE is the common tangent to the given circle.

Length of tangent DE

$$= \left\{d^2 - (r - r_1)^2\right\}^{1/2}$$

$$d = AB$$

r and r_1 are radii of circles.

Note : Other tangent can also be drawn in the manner shown below :

Const. : Adopt same procedure and notation except the circle which was drawn with difference of radii should be drawn with sum of the radii of the circles with centre A.

Length of tangent DE

$$= \left\{d^2 - (r + r_1)^2\right\}^{1/2}$$

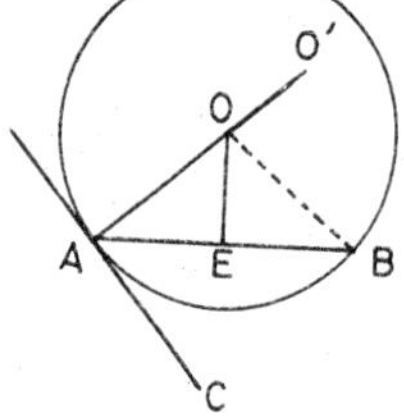

Fig. 2·20.

3. On a given straight line describe a segment of a circle containing an angle equal to a given angle *C*.

Const. : At on the given line *AB* draw an angle *BAC* equal to *C*. From *A* draw *AO'* perp. to *AC*. Bisect *AB* at the point *E* and draw perp. on *E* meeting the line *AO'* on *O*. Then *O* is the centre of the segment required.

4. To draw a square equal in area to a given triangle.

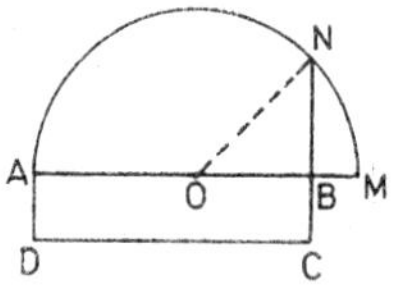

Fig. 2·21.

Const. : Produce *AB* to *M* making *BM* = *BC* on *AM* draw a semicircle and produce *CB* to meet the circumference at *N*. Then *BN* is a side of the required square.

5. To divide a straight line internally, externally in a given ratio say *m* : *n*.

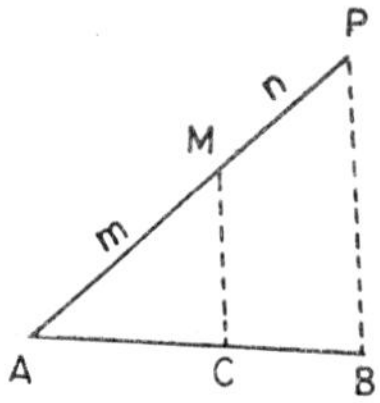

Fig. 2·22.

Const. : From *A* draw a line *AP* at any convenient angle. Divide *AP* in *m* + *n* divisions of any scale join *PB* and draw *MF* parallel to *PB*. The *AC* : *CB* = *m* : *n*.

6. To find mean proportional between two given straight lines.

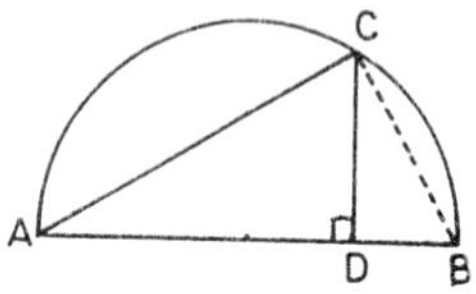

Fig. 2·23.

Const. : Let *AD* & *BD* are the two lines of given length. Place *AD* and *BD* in a line so as to make a line *ADB*. On *AB* describe a semi circle *ABC*, from *D*. Draw *CD* right angle to cut the circumference at *C*. The *DC* is the mean proportional of *AD* and *DB*.

7. On a given side *A'B'*, to draw a fig. similar to a given fig. *ABCD*.

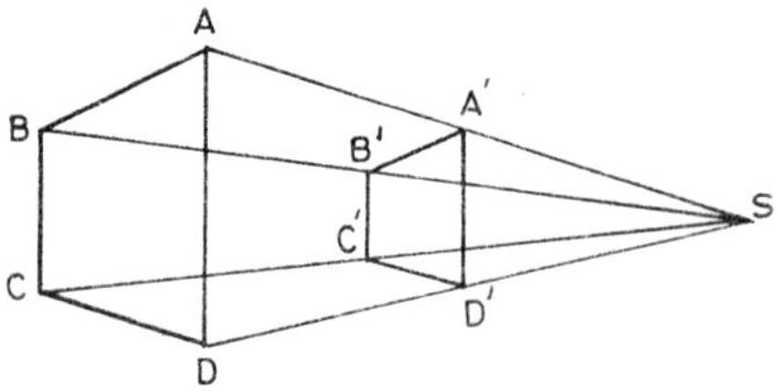

Fig. 2·24.

Const. : Place *A'B'* par to *AB* and join *AA'BB'* by lines meeting at *S*. Join *SC*, *SD*. Through *B'* draw *B'C'* par to *BC* to meet *SC* at *C'*. Through *C'* draw *C' D'* par to *CD* to meet *SD* at *D'*, join *A' D'*. The *A' B' C' D'* is the required fig.

8. To draw a fig. similar to a given rectineal fig. and equal to a given fraction of it in area (say fraction =3/4)

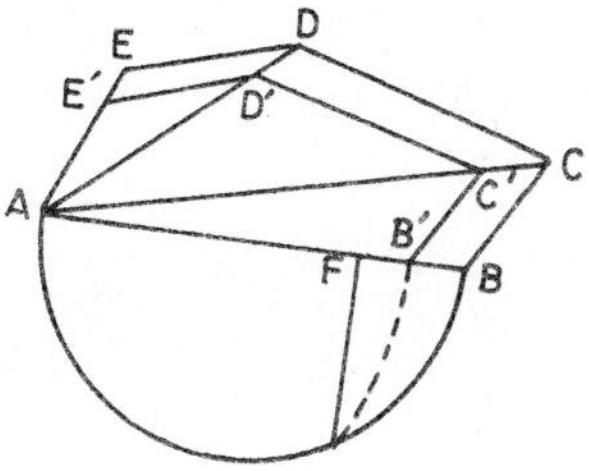

Fig. 2·25.

Const. : Mark AF 3/4 of AB. From AB cut off AB' the mean proportional between AF and AB (Problem 6). On AB' draw the fig. $AB'C'D'E'$ similar to the fig. $ABCD$. Then the fig. $AB'C'D'E'$ = 3/4 of the Fig. $ABCDE$.

9. To draw a square, pentagon, hexagon, septagon and octagon of side "*a*".

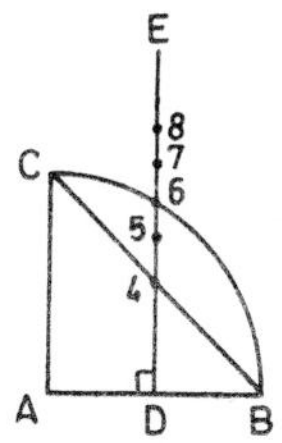

Fig. 2·26.

Const. : Draw a line AB equivalent to given side a. Draw a perp. DE from the point D mid of AB. Draw a quadrent CB taking AB as radius passing through the point 6 on the perp. line DE. Join BC which cuts the perp. line DE at 4. Divide 4, 6 at a point 5. Draw point 7 at a distance of 5-6. Point 8 at a distance 6-7. Now 4 is centre of a square circle, 5 is the centre of pentagon, 6 for hexagon and so on.

Draw circle of rad. A to 4, 5, 6, 7 or 8, for square, pentagon, hexagon septagon or octagon. On the circumference of the circle so obtained draw lines starting AB as one side by a divider of rad. a, which gives the required polygon.

10. To draw incentre, centroid, circumcentre and ortho-centre of a triangle.

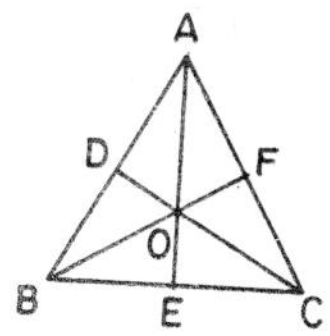

(*a*)

Lines DC bisect the angle C, BF and B and AE angle A. The lines DC, BF and AE are called Bisectors and the point O the intersection point of lines is called in centre.

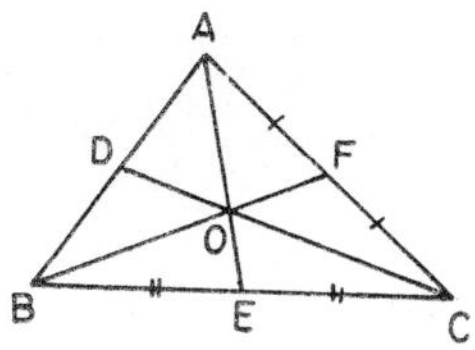

(*b*)

Lines DC, BF, and AE bisects the lines AB, BC and AC respectively. The lines are called medians and the point of intersection O is called the centroid which is 1/3 AE or 1/3 BF or 1/3 DC.

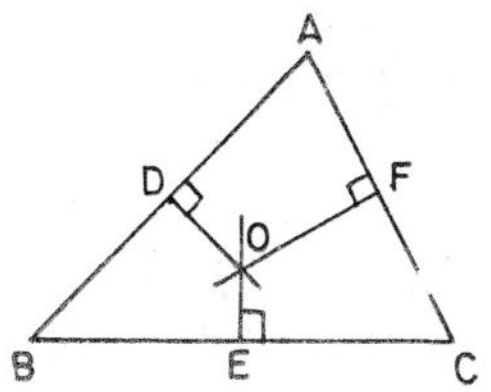

(*c*)

Lines DO, EO and FO are the perp. from the mid points of lines AB, BC and CA respectively and are called the right bisectors and the point of intersection O is called the circumcentre.

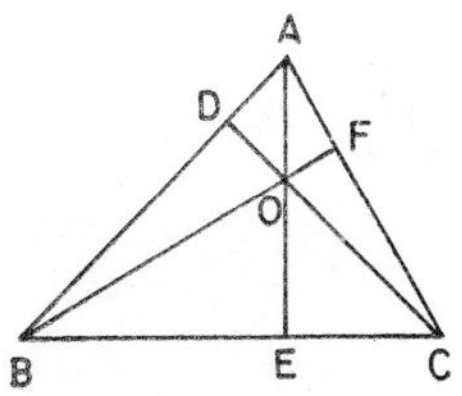

(*d*)

Lines DC, BF and AE are perp. from the opposite vertices C on AB ; B on AC and A on BC and are called altitudes and the point O is called the ortho centre.

Fig. 2·27.

2·2. Algebra

Quadratic Equation : If $ax^2 + bx + c = 0$. Then $x = \dfrac{-b \pm \sqrt{b^2 - 4ac}}{2a}$.

Cubic Equation : If $x^3 + ax + b = 0$. Then $x = \left(-\dfrac{b}{2} + \sqrt{\dfrac{a^3}{27} + \dfrac{b^2}{4}}\right)^{1/3} + \left(-\dfrac{b}{2} - \sqrt{\dfrac{a^3}{2} + \dfrac{b^2}{4}}\right)^{1/3}$

Factors :

$$a^2 - b^2 = (a + b)(a - b)$$

$$(a + b)^2 = a^2 + 2ab + b^2 \; ; \; (a - b)^2 = a^2 - 2ab + b^2$$

$$(a + b + c)^2 = a^2 + b^2 + c^2 + 2bc + 2ca + 2ab$$

$$a^3 + b^3 = (a + b)(a^2 - ab + b^2)$$

$$a^3 - b^3 = (a + b)(a^2 + ab + b^2)$$

$$(a + b)^3 = a^3 + 3a^2b + 3ab^2 + b^3$$

$$(a - b)^3 = a^3 - 3a^2b + 3ab^2 - b^3$$

Binomial Theorem :

$$(1 \pm x)^n = 1 \pm \left[\frac{nx}{\underline{|1}} + \frac{n(n-1)}{\underline{|2}}x^2 + \frac{n(n-1)(n-2)}{\underline{|3}}x^3 + \ldots\ldots\ldots\right]$$

$(\underline{|2} = 1 \times 2,\ \underline{|3} = 1 \times 2 \times 3$ and so on$)$

$${}^nC_r = \frac{n(n-1)(n-2)(\ldots\ldots)(n-r+1)}{\underline{|r}}$$

Maclaurin's Theorem : $f(x) = f(0) + \dfrac{x\,f'(0)}{\underline{|1}} + \dfrac{x^2 f''(0)}{\underline{|2}} + \ldots\ldots\ldots$

Taylor's Theorem : $f(x + h)\dfrac{f(x) + hf'(x)}{\underline{|1}} + \dfrac{h^2 f''(x)}{\underline{|2}} + \ldots\ldots$

Theory of indices : $a^m \times a^n = a^{m+n}$; $a^m \div a^n = a^{m-n}$

$$(a^m)^n = a^{mn},\ a^0 = 1,\ a^{-n} = \frac{1}{a^n},\ \frac{a}{0} = \infty,\ a \times 0 = 0$$

Cross-multiplication :

$a_1x + b_1y + c_1 = 0$ we get $\dfrac{x}{b_1c_2 - b_2c_1} = \dfrac{y}{c_1a_2 - c_2a_1} = \dfrac{1}{a_1b_2 - a_2b_1}$

$a_2x + b_2y + c_2 = 0$

If $x + y = s$ and $xy = P$. Then $x = \dfrac{s + \sqrt{s^2 - 4P}}{2}$; $y = \dfrac{s - \sqrt{s^2 - 4P}}{2}$

Logarithms :

$a^x = N$. Then $\log_a N = x$ $\qquad \log \pi = 0{\cdot}49715$

$\log MN = \log_a M + \log_a N$ $\qquad \log_{10} e = 0{\cdot}43429$

$$\log M/N = \log_a M - \log_a N$$

$$\log M^N = N \log_a M$$

$$\log_a N = \log_{10} N \times \log_e 10$$

$$= \log_{10} N \times 2{\cdot}32058$$

(To convert hyperbolic logarithms from common multiply by 2·30258)
(Common log mean, log of base 10)

$$\log_e 10 = 2{\cdot}30254$$

$$\log_e a = \frac{1}{\log_a e}$$

$$\log 4375{\cdot}8 = 3{\cdot}6410575$$

$$\log {\cdot}43758 = \bar{1}{\cdot}6410575$$

$$e^x = 1 + x + \frac{x^2}{\underline{|2}} + \frac{x^3}{\underline{|3}} + \frac{x^4}{\underline{|4}} \ldots\ldots$$

$$e^x = 2{\cdot}718 \; ; \; \log_e e = 1$$

$$a^x = \left(e^{\log a}\right)^x = 1 + x \log a + \frac{(x \log a)^2}{\underline{|2}} + \ldots\ldots$$

Hyperbolic Functions :

$$\sinh x = \frac{e^x - e^{-x}}{\underline{|2}} = x + \frac{x^3}{\underline{|3}} + \frac{x^5}{\underline{|5}} \ldots\ldots \qquad \cosh x = e^x + e = 1 + \frac{x^2}{\underline{|2}} + \frac{x^4}{\underline{|4}} + \ldots\ldots$$

$$\tanh x = \sinh x \cosh x \qquad \sinh 2x = 2 \sinh x \cosh x$$

$$\coth x = \cosh x \sinh x \qquad \cosh 2x = \cosh^2 x + \sinh^2 x$$

$$\text{sech}\, x = \frac{1}{\cosh x} \qquad \cosh h^2 x - \sinh^2 x = 1$$

$$\text{cosech}\, x = 1/\sinh x \qquad \cosh^{-1} x = \log\left(x + \sqrt{x^2 - 1}\right)$$

$$\log(1 + x) = x - \frac{1}{2}x^2 + \frac{1}{3}x^3 + \frac{1}{4}x^4 + \ldots\ldots \qquad \sinh^{-1} x = \log\left[x + \sqrt{x^2 + 1}\right]$$

$$\tanh^{-1} x = \frac{1}{2} \log \frac{1 + x}{1 - x} \qquad \coth^{-1} x = \frac{1}{2} \log \frac{1 - x}{1 + x}$$

2·3. Formulae in Trignometry

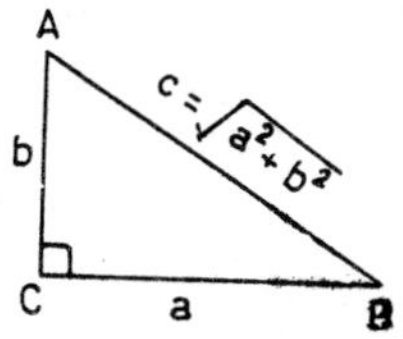

Fig. 2·28.

1. $\sin^2 A + \cos^2 A = 1$
2. $1 + \tan^2 A = \sec^2 A$
3. $1 + \cot^2 A = \text{cosec}^2 A$
4. $\sin(A \pm B) = \sin A \cos B \pm \sin B \cos A$;
   $\cos(A \pm B) = \cos A \cos B \mp \sin A \sin B$;
   $\tan(A \pm B) = (\tan A \pm \tan B)/(1 \mp \tan A \tan B)$
5. $\sin 2A = 2 \sin A \cos A = \dfrac{2 \tan A}{1 + \tan^2 A}$; $\cos 2A = \cos^2 A - \sin^2 A = 1 - 2\sin^2 A$;
   $\tan 2A = \dfrac{2 \tan A}{1 - \tan^2 A}$ $\qquad = 2\cos^2 A - 1 = \dfrac{1 - \tan^2 A}{1 + \tan^2 A}$
6. $\sin 3A = 3 \sin A - 4 \sin^3 A$; $\cos 3A = 4 \cos^3 A - 3 \cos A$
   $\tan 3A = \dfrac{3 \tan A - \tan^3 A}{1 - 3 \tan^2 A}$
7. $\sin A/2 = \pm\sqrt{\dfrac{1 - \cos A}{2}}$; $\cos A/2 = \pm\sqrt{\dfrac{1 + \cos A}{2}}$;

$\tan A/2 = \dfrac{\sin A}{1 + \cos A}$; $\qquad \cot A/2 = \dfrac{\sin A}{1 - \cos A}$

8. $\sin A + \sin B = 2 \sin \dfrac{A+2}{2} \cos \dfrac{A-B}{2}$; $\qquad \sin A - \sin B = 2 \cos \dfrac{A+2}{2} \sin \dfrac{A-B}{2}$;

$\cos A + \cos B = 2 \cos \dfrac{A+B}{2} \cos \dfrac{A-B}{2}$; $\qquad \cos A - \cos B = -2 \sin \dfrac{A+B}{2} \sin \dfrac{A-B}{2}$;

9. $2 \sin A \cos B = \sin(A+B) + \sin(A-B)$; $2 \cos A \sin B = \sin(A+B) - \sin(A-B)$;

$2 \cos A \cos B = \cos(A+B) + \cos(A-B)$; $2 \sin A \sin B = \cos(A-B) - \cos(A+B)$

10. If $s = \dfrac{a+b+c}{2}$ and s = area of Δ.

$\sin A = \dfrac{2}{bc}\sqrt{s(s-a)(s-b)(s-c)}$; $\qquad \sin \dfrac{A}{2} = \sqrt{\dfrac{(s-b)(s-c)}{bc}}$

$\cos A = \dfrac{b^2 + c^2 - a^2}{2bc}$; $\qquad \cos \dfrac{A}{2} = \sqrt{\dfrac{(s)(s-a)}{bc}}$

$\tan A = \dfrac{4\sqrt{s(s-a)(s-b)(s-c)}}{b^2 + c^2 - a^2}$; $\qquad \tan \dfrac{A}{2} = \sqrt{\dfrac{(s-b)(s-c)}{s(s-a)}}$

11. $\dfrac{\sin A}{a} = \dfrac{\sin B}{b} = \dfrac{\sin C}{c} = \dfrac{2\Delta}{abc} = 2R$; $\qquad a^2 = b^2 + c^2 - 2bc \cos A$

R = rad. of ascribed or circumscribed circles.

r = rad. of inscribed circle.

$\sin 15° = \dfrac{\sqrt{3} - 1}{2\sqrt{2}}$, $\cos 15° = \dfrac{\sqrt{3} + 1}{2\sqrt{2}}$; $\qquad \sin 18° = \dfrac{\sqrt{5} - 1}{4}$, $\cos 36° = \dfrac{\sqrt{5} + 1}{4}$

If $\sin \theta = \sin \alpha$. Then $\theta = n\pi + (-1)^n \alpha$

If $\cos \theta = \cos \alpha$. Then $\theta = 2n\pi \pm \alpha$

$\sin x = x - \dfrac{x^3}{\lfloor 3} + \dfrac{x^5}{\lfloor 5} - \dfrac{x^7}{\lfloor 7} \ldots\ldots$; $\qquad \cos \alpha = -\dfrac{x^2}{\lfloor 2} + \dfrac{x^4}{\lfloor 4} - \dfrac{x^6}{\lfloor 6} \ldots\ldots$

$\sin A = \dfrac{\text{perp.}}{\text{hyp.}}$, $\qquad \cos A = \dfrac{\text{base}}{\text{hyp.}}$

$\tan A = \dfrac{\text{perp.}}{\text{base}} = \dfrac{\sin A}{\cos A}$, $\qquad \cot A = \dfrac{\text{base}}{\text{perp.}} = \dfrac{\cos A}{\sin A}$

$\sec A = \dfrac{\text{hyp.}}{\text{base}} = \dfrac{1}{\cos A}$, $\qquad \text{cosec } A = \dfrac{\text{hyp.}}{\text{perp.}} = \dfrac{1}{\sin A}$

vers. $A = 1 - \cos A$, $\qquad$ convers. $A = 1 - \sin A$

Signs of Functions $\qquad$ **Functions of angles.**

Quadrant	*1st*	*2nd*	*3rd*	*4th*	$-A$	$\frac{\pi}{2} \pm A$	$\pi \pm A$	$\frac{3\pi}{2} \pm 1$	$n\, 2\pi A$
sin	+	+	–	–	– sin A	+ cos A	± sin A	- cos A	± sin A
cos	+	–	–	+	+ cos A	μ sin A	– cos A	± sin A	+ cos A
tan	+	–	+	–	– tan A	μ cos A	± tan A	μ cos A	± tan A
cot	+	–	+	–	– cot A	μ tan A	± cot A	μ tan A	± cot A
sec	+	–	–	+	+ sec A	μ cosec A	– sec A	μ cosec A	– sec A
cosec	+	+	–	–	– cosec A	+ sec A	μ cosec A	– sec A	± cosec A

Functions 0 to 360°

	sin	*cos*	*tan*	*cot*	*sec*	*cosec*	*verse*
0	0	1	0	∞	1	∞	0
30	$1/2$	$\sqrt{3}/2$	$1/\sqrt{3}$	$\sqrt{3}$	$1/\sqrt{3}$	2	$2-\sqrt{3}$
45	$1/\sqrt{2}$	$1/\sqrt{2}$	1	1	$\sqrt{2}$	$\sqrt{2}$	$\frac{\sqrt{2}-1}{\sqrt{2}}$
60	$\sqrt{3}/2$	$1/2$	$\sqrt{3}$	$1/\sqrt{3}$	2	$2/\sqrt{3}$	$1/2$
90	1	0	∞	0	∞	1	1
120	$\sqrt{3}/2$	$-1/2$	$-\sqrt{3}$	$-\frac{1}{\sqrt{3}}$	-2	$2/\sqrt{3}$	$3/2$
135	$1/\sqrt{2}$	$-1/\sqrt{2}$	-1	-1	$\sqrt{2}$	$\sqrt{2}$	$\frac{\sqrt{2}+1}{\sqrt{2}}$
150	$1/2$	$-\sqrt{3}/2$	$1/\sqrt{3}$	$-\sqrt{3}$	$-2/\sqrt{3}$	2	$\frac{2+\sqrt{3}}{\sqrt{2}}$
180	0	-1	0	∞	-1	∞	2
270	–	0	∞	0	∞	-1	1
360	0	1	0	∞	1	∞	0

2·4. Formulae in Differential and Integral Calculus

1.	$y = x^n$	$dy/dx = nx^{n-1}$	$\int x^n\,dx = \frac{x^{n+1}}{n+1} (x \neq -)$
2.	$y = \sin\theta$	$dy/d\theta = \cos\theta$	$\int \cos\theta\,d\theta = \sin\theta$
3.	$y = \cos\theta$	$dy/d\theta = -\sin\theta$	$\int \sin\theta\,d\theta = -\cos\theta$
4.	$y = \tan\theta$	$dy/d\theta = \sec^2\theta$	$\int \sec^2\theta\,d\theta = \tan\theta$
5.	$y = \cot\theta$	$dy/d\theta = -\text{cosec}^2\theta$	$\int \text{cosec}^2\theta\,d\theta = -\cot\theta$
6.	$y = \sec\theta$	$dy/d\theta = \tan\theta\sec\theta$	$\int \tan\theta\sec\theta\,d\theta = \sec\theta$
7.	$y = \text{cosec}\,\theta$	$dy/d\theta = \cot\theta\,\text{cosec}\,\theta$	$\int \cot\theta\,\text{cosec}\,d\theta = -\text{cosec}\,\theta$
8.	$y = \sin^{-1} x/a$	$dy/dx = \frac{1}{\sqrt{a^2-x^2}}$	$\int \frac{dx}{\sqrt{a^2-x^2}} = \sin^{-1} x/a$
9.	$y = \cos^{-1} x/a$	$dy/dx = -\frac{1}{\sqrt{a^2-x^2}}$	$\int \frac{-dx}{\sqrt{a^2-x^2}} = \cos^{-1} x/a$
10.	$y = \tan^{-1} x/a$	$dy/dx = \frac{a}{a^2-x^2}$	$\int \frac{a\,dx}{a^2+x^2} = \cot^{-1} x/a$

11. $y = \cos^{-1} x/a$ $\quad dy/dx = -\dfrac{a}{a^2 + x^2}$ $\quad \displaystyle\int \frac{a\,dx}{x\sqrt{x^2 - a^2}} = \sec^{-1} x/a$

12. $y = \sec^{-1} x/a$ $\quad dy/dx = \dfrac{a}{x\sqrt{x^2 - a^2}}$ $\quad \displaystyle\int \frac{-a\,dx}{x\sqrt{x^2 - a^2}} = \text{cosec}^{-1} x/a$

13. $y = \text{cosec}^{-1} x/a$ $\quad dy/dx = \dfrac{a}{x\sqrt{x^2 - a^2}}$ $\quad \displaystyle\int e^x = e^x$

14. $y = e^x$ $\quad dy/dx = e^x$ $\quad \displaystyle\int a^x\,dx = a^x/\log a$

15. $y = a^x$ $\quad dy/dx = a^x \log a$ $\quad \displaystyle\int e^{ax}\,dx = e^{ax}/a$

16. $y = e^{ax}$ $\quad dy/dx = a\,e^{ax}$ $\quad \displaystyle\int \frac{dx}{x} = \log x$

17. $y = \log x$ $\quad dy/dx = 1/x$ $\quad \displaystyle\int \sinh x\,dx = \cosh x$

18. $y = \log_a x$ $\quad dy/dx = \dfrac{1}{x \log a}$ $\quad \displaystyle\int \cosh x\,dx = \sinh x$

19. $y = \text{verse}^{-1} x$ $\quad dy/dx = \dfrac{1}{\sqrt{(2x - x^2)}}$ $\quad \displaystyle\int \sec^2 h\,x\,dx = \tan h\,x$

20. $y = \text{coverse}^{-1} x$ $\quad dy/dx = -\dfrac{1}{\sqrt{(2x - x^2)}}$ $\quad \displaystyle\int \frac{dx}{\sqrt{a^2 + x^2}} = \sin^{-1} x/a$ or $\log \dfrac{x + \sqrt{a^2 + x^2}}{a}$

21. $y = \sinh x$ $\quad dy/dx = \cosh x$ $\quad \displaystyle\int \frac{dx}{x^2 - a^2} = \cosh^{-1} x/a$ or $\log \dfrac{x + \sqrt{a^2 - x^2}}{a}$

22. $y = \cosh x$ $\quad dy/dx = \sinh x$ $\quad \displaystyle\int \frac{dx}{a^2 - x^2} = \frac{1}{a}\tanh^{-1} x/a = \frac{1}{2a} \log \frac{a + x}{a - x}$

23. $y = \tanh x$ $\quad dy/dx = \text{sech}^2 x$ $\quad$ Integral by Parts

24. $y = \coth x$ $\quad dy/dx = -\text{cosech}^2 x$ $\quad y = \displaystyle\int u\,dv = uv - \int v\,du$

25. Diff. coeff. of a constant = 0

$y = c$ $\quad dy/dx = 0$

26. Diff. coeff. of a product of a coeff. and a function = coeff. × diff. coeff. of the function,

$y = a\,f(x)$ $\quad dydx = a\,d\dfrac{f(x)}{dx}$

27. Diff. coeff. of a sum = Sum or diff. coeff. of functions

$y = f_1(x) + f_2(x) + f_3(x) + \ldots\ldots$ $\quad dy/dx - d\,f_1\dfrac{(x)}{dx} + \dfrac{d\,f_2(x)}{dx} + \ldots\ldots$

28. Diff. coeff. of product of two functions = 1st function × diff. coeff of the 2nd + 2nd functions × diff. coeff. of the 1st.

$$y = uv \qquad \frac{dy}{dx} = \frac{v\,du}{dx} + u\frac{dv}{dx}$$

29. Diff. coeff. of quotioent of two functions

$$= \frac{(\text{Diff. coeff. of Nr})\text{Denominator} - (\text{Nr}) \times (\text{diff. coeff. of Denor.})}{\text{sq. of denominator}}$$

$$y = \frac{u}{v} \qquad \frac{dy}{dx} = \frac{\frac{v\,du}{dx} - u\frac{dv}{dx}}{v^2}$$

$$\text{Velocity} = \frac{ds}{dt}, \quad \text{acceleration} = \frac{dv}{dt}$$

s = distance, v = velocity and t = time.

2·5. Some well known Curves

1. Cubical parabola

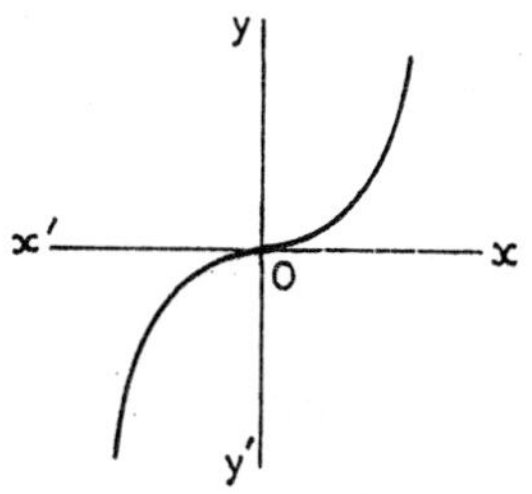

$a^2y = x^3$

Fig. 2·29.

2. Semi-cubical parabola

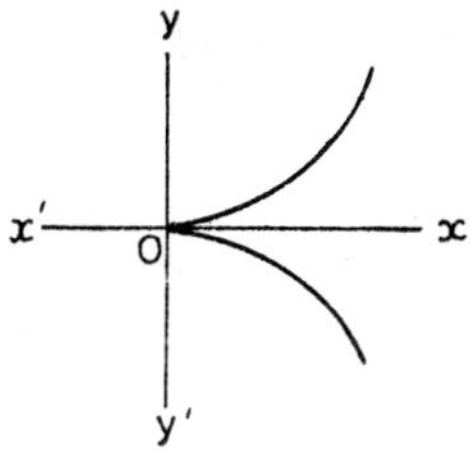

$a^2y = x^3$

Fig. 2·30.

3. Cardiod

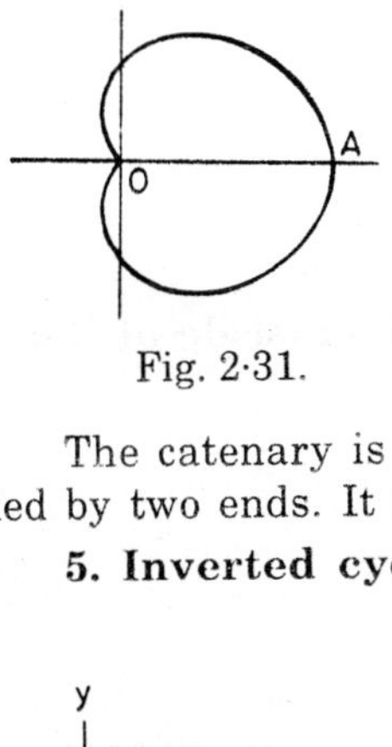

$r = a(1 + \cos\theta)$

Fig. 2·31.

4. Calenary

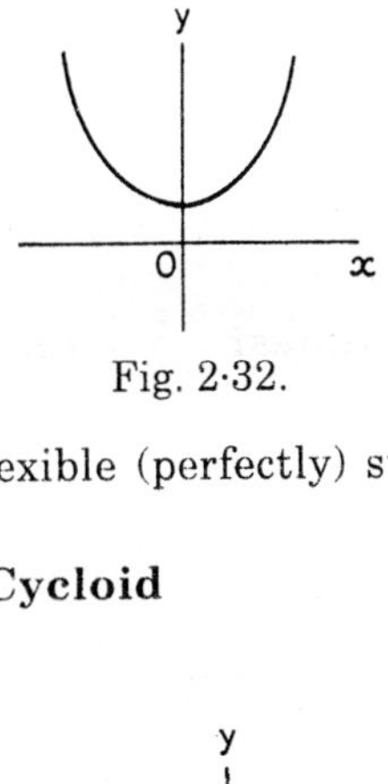

$y = a\cosh {x}/{a}$

Fig. 2·32.

The catenary is a curve in which a heavy flexible (perfectly) string hangs when suspended by two ends. It is also called chainette.

5. Inverted cycloid

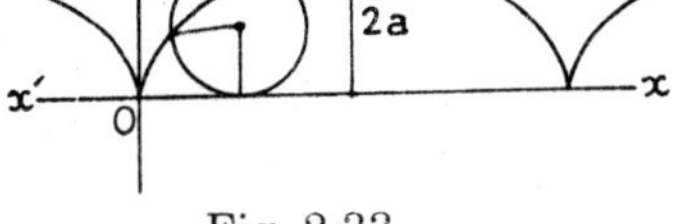

Fig. 2·33.

$$x = a\,\text{verse}^{-1}\,{y}/{a} - \left(2ay - y^2\right)^{1/2}$$

6. Cycloid

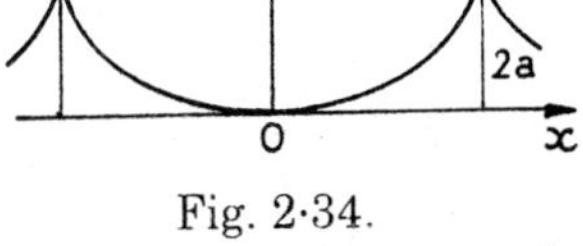

Fig. 2·34.

$$x = a\,\text{verse}^{-1}\,{y}/{a} + \frac{x}{\left(2ay - y^2\right)^{1/2}}$$

The cycloid is a curve which is traced by the locus of a point on the circumference of a circle which rolls without shading along a straight line.

$x = a(\theta - \sin\theta)$; $y = a(1 - \cos\theta)$

$x = a(\theta + \sin\theta)$; $y = a(1 - \cos\theta)$

7. The logarithmic or equiangular spiral

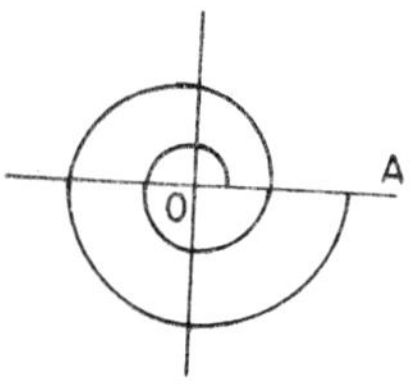

$$r = a\,e^{mg}$$

Fig. 2·35.

The angle θ between the rad. vector and the tangent is const. for this curve hence the name.

8. Spiral of archimedes

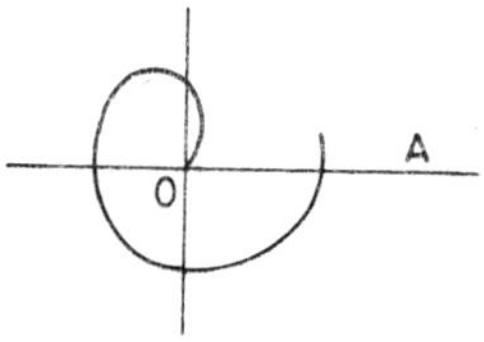

Fig. 2·36.

9. Erolute of an ellipse

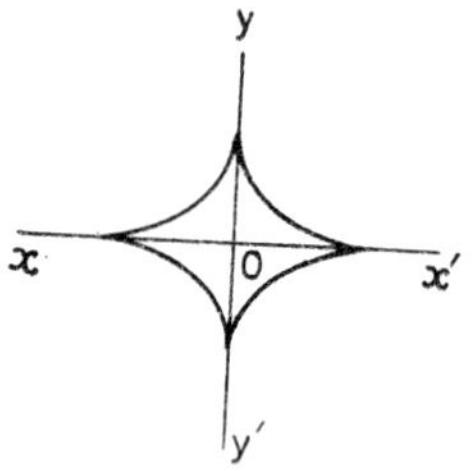

Fig. 2·37 (*a*).

$$(ax)^{2/3} + (by)^{2/3} = (a^2 - b^2)^{2/3}$$

10. Astroid

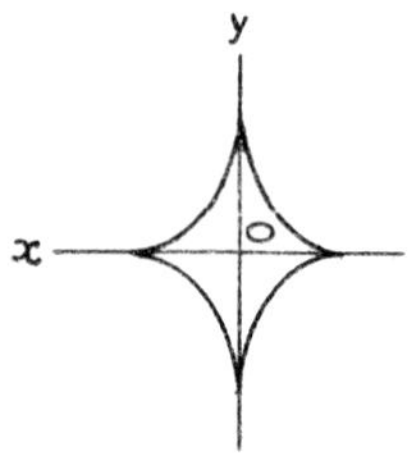

Fig. 2·37 (*b*).

$$x^{2/3} + y^{2/3} = a^{2/3}$$
$$x = a\cos^2\theta$$
$$y = a\sin^2\theta$$

11. Wilch of Agnesi

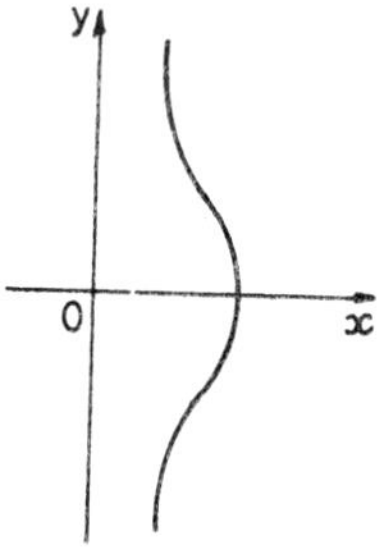

Fig. 2·38.

$$xy^2 = 4a^2(2a - x)$$

12. Cissoid of Diodor

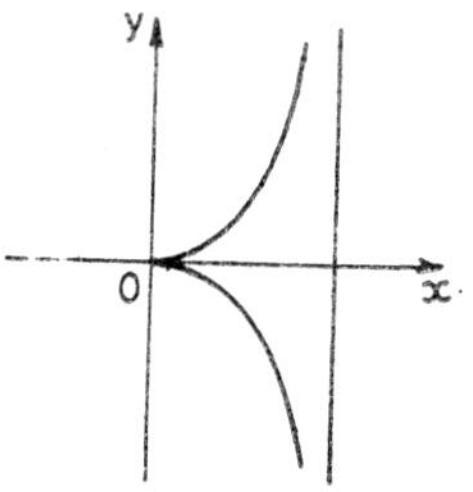

Fig. 2·39.

$$y^2 = (2ax - x) = x^2$$

13. Lamiscale of Bernauli

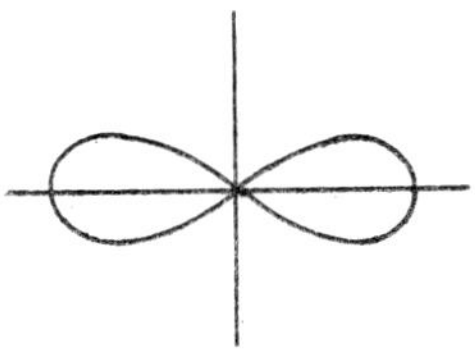

Fig. 2·40.

$$r^2 = a^2\cos 2\theta$$

2·6. Formulae in Plane and Solid Mensuration

Plane mensuration : Area of Planes

1. **Square :** $A = a^2$ where a = side and A = area

2. **Rectangle :** $A = ab$ where a and b are the sides

3. **Parallelogram :** $A = ab \sin \alpha$

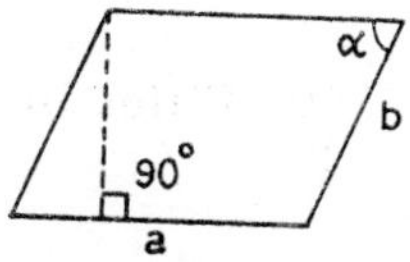

Fig. 2·41.

4. **Triangle :** If $s = 1/2\ (a + b + c)$, Area $= \dfrac{a^2 \sin B \sin C}{2 \sin A}$

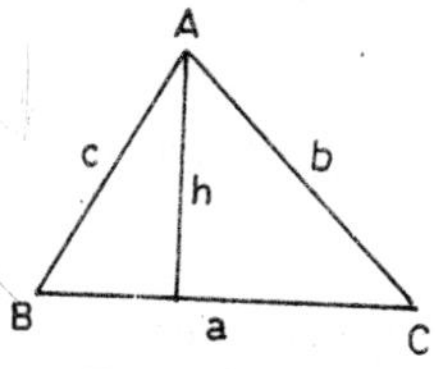

Fig. 2·42.

$$= \frac{1}{2} b.c. \sin A$$

$$= \sqrt{s(s-a)(s-b)(s-c)}$$

$$= \frac{ch}{2} \text{ where } h \text{ is the height.}$$

Right angled Triangle : Area $= \dfrac{1}{2}$ base × height

Obtuse angled Triangle : Area $= \dfrac{c}{2}\sqrt{a^2 - \left(\dfrac{b^2 - a^2 - c^2}{2c}\right)^2}$ where angle B is obtuse

Acute angled Triangle : Area $= \dfrac{c}{2}\sqrt{a^2 - \left(\dfrac{a^2 + c^2 - b^2}{2c}\right)^2}$

5. **Trapezium :** $A = \dfrac{(a+b)h}{2}$

6. **Quadrilateral :** $A = \dfrac{(H+h)a + bh + ch}{2}$

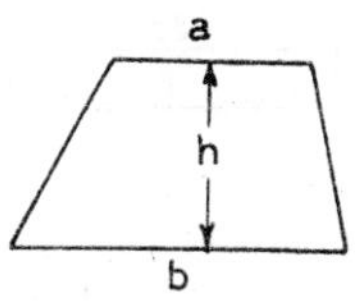

Fig. 2·43.

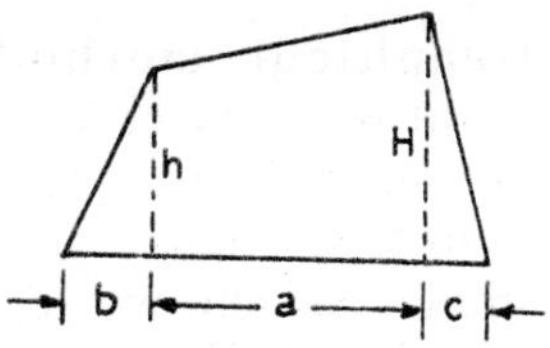

Fig. 2·44.

7. **Regular Polygon :** n = no. of sides, r = rad. of inscribed circle
R = rad. of circumscribe circle.
a = length of a side.

$$\text{area} = \frac{nar}{2} = \frac{na}{2}\sqrt{R^2 - a^2/4}$$

Sum of the angles contained = 2 n – 4 right angles.

8. **Circle :** Area = πr^2 where r = rad. ; circumference = $2\pi r$

9. **Sector of a circle :** Area $= \dfrac{1}{2} rl = \dfrac{1}{2} r^2\,\theta$; where, l = length of arc of sector and θ = angle contained at the centre, r = rad. of circle.

10. **Fillet or spendril :** Area $= r^2 \left(1 - \pi/4\right) = c^2/2 \left(1 - \pi/4\right)$

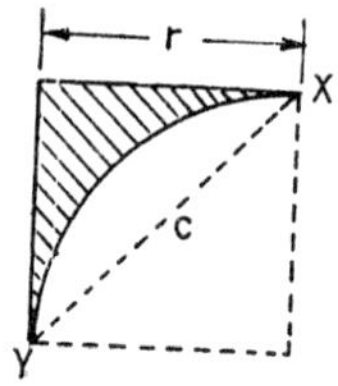

Fig. 2·45.

11. **Segment of a circle :** Area $= \frac{4}{3}h\left(\frac{1}{4}c^2 + \frac{2}{5}h^2\right)^{1/2} = \frac{h^3}{2c} + (2c \times h)$

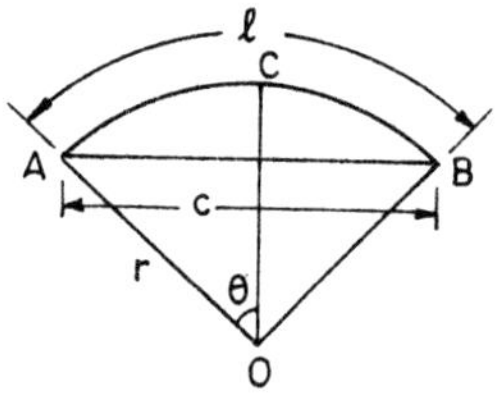

Fig. 2·46.

$$= \frac{1}{2}\left[rl - c(r-h)\right] = 2\sqrt{h(2r-h)}$$

$$r = \frac{c^2 + 4h^2}{8h} \; ; \; h = r - \frac{1}{2}\left(4r^2 - c^2\right)^{1/2}$$

12. **Parabola :** Area $= \frac{2}{3} \times$ base $\times$ altitude

13. **Ellipse :** Area $= \frac{\pi}{4}$ Major axis $\times$ Minor axis

Perimeter $= \frac{\pi}{2}$ Major axis $\times$ Minor axis

14. **Cycloid :** Area = 3 × area of the generating circle.

(Ref. curves) Cycloid is a curve which is traced by the locus of a point on the the circumference of a circle which rolls without sliding along a straight line.

15. Reg. octagon of side $a = 2a^2\left(1 + \sqrt{2}\right)$.

16. **Channel sections :**

(*a*) **Graphical method :** By counting squares in the section plotted on a graph sheet. Counting more than half square as one while leaving less than half.

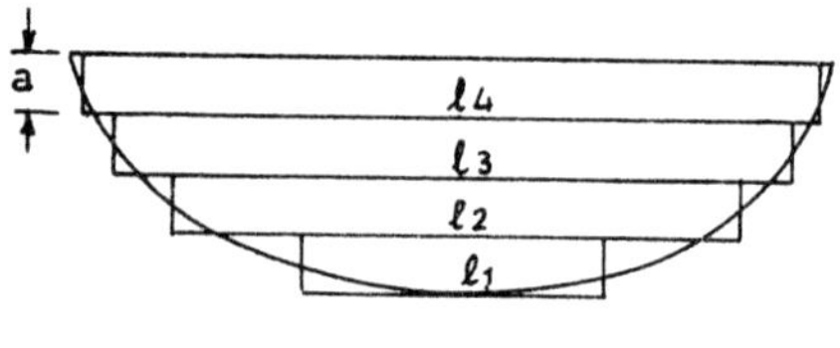

Fig. 2·47.

(*b*) **By dividing the section into trapezoids :**

Area $= a(l_1 + l_2 + l_3 + l_4 \ldots)$

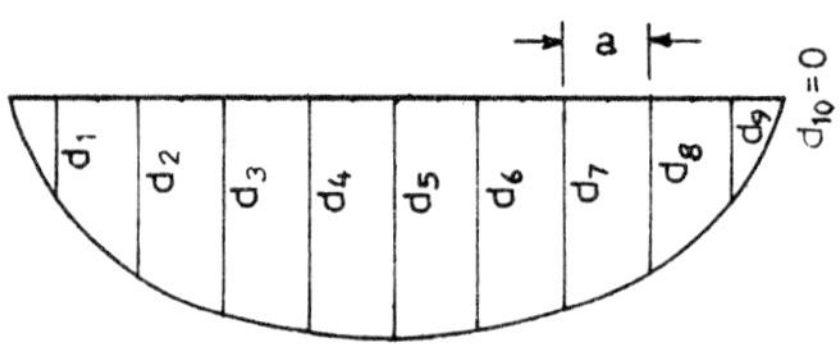

Fig. 2·48.

(*c*) **By trapezoidal method :**

$$\text{area} = \left(\text{sum of all the depths} - \frac{\text{1st + last depth}}{2}\right) \text{common distance}$$

$$= a\left(d_1 + d_2 + d_3 + d_4 + d_5 + d_6 + d_7 + d_8 + d_9 + d_{10} + d_{11} + d_{12} - \frac{d_1 + d_{12}}{2}\right)$$

In this case $d_{12} = 0$

Note : If the last section falls short than the common distance a it should be added separately by calculating the area of the last fig. (see such case in case f).

(d) **By mid ordinate rule :** Area = Sum of all mid ordinates × common distance

$$= a(d_1 + d_2 + d_3 + d_4 + d_5 + d_6 + d_7 + d_8 + d_9 + d_{10})$$

Note : If in the last section common distance in less than the common distance d, the area of the fig. should be added separately. (see case f)

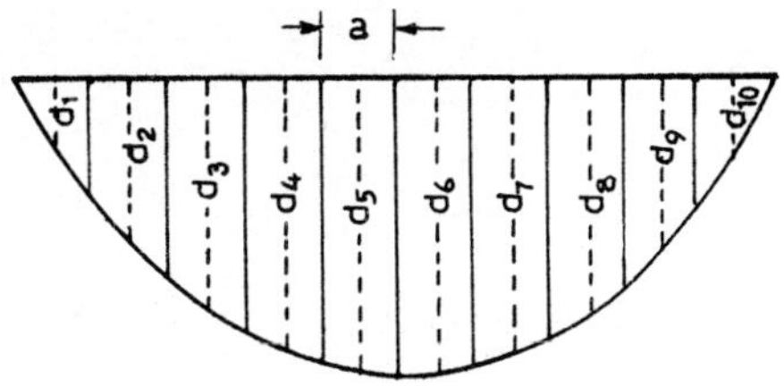

Fig. 2·49.

(e) **By Simpsons rule :** Divide the area in even no. of spaces or odd no, of offsets.

$$\text{Area} = \frac{\text{common distance}}{3}\left\{\begin{matrix}\text{1st + last depth} + 2(\text{sum of all odd depths}) + 4 \\ (\text{sum of all even depths})\end{matrix}\right\}$$

$$= \frac{a}{3}\{(d_1 + d_n) + 2(d_3 + d_5 + d_7 \ldots\ldots) + 4(d_2 + d_4 + d_6 \ldots\ldots)\}$$

where 1st and last depths are taken on the ends.

(f) **When the end compartment is of smaller length than the common length**

Area = area of all the compartments except last smaller one + area of the last smaller compartment calculated separately.

$$A = \left(\begin{matrix} d_1 + d_2 + d_3 + d_4 + d_5 + d_6 + d_7 + d_8 + d_9 \\ + d_{10} + d_{11} + d_{12} + d_{13} - \dfrac{d_1 + d_{13}}{2}\end{matrix}\right)a + \frac{d_{13} + 0}{2} \times b$$

In this case d_1 and d last is zero.

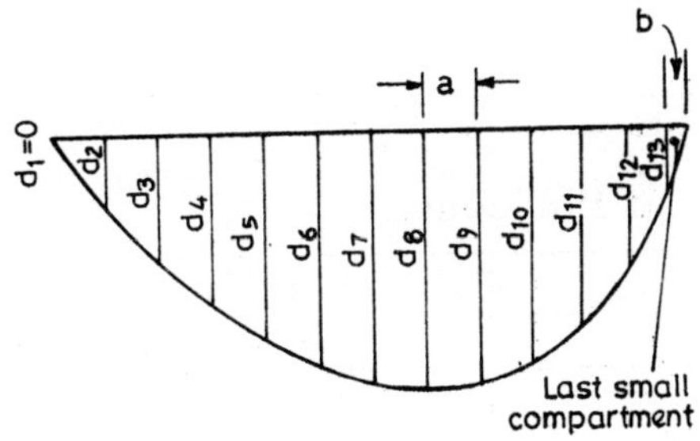

Fig. 2·50.

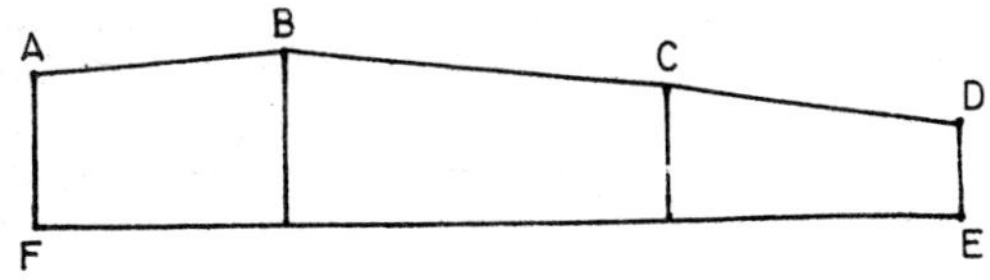

Fig. 2·51.

(g) **By coordinate method :** Let the coordinates of the fig. above are tabulated as below, taking F as origin.

	A	B	C	D	E	F
x	x_1	x_2	x_3	x_4	x_5	x_6
y	y_1	y_2	y_3	y_4	y_5	y_6

Here we see that the values of x, x_6 ; y_5 & y_6 = 0

The corrdinates are arranged in the form of determinants as below :

$$\frac{y_1}{x_1} \times \frac{y_2}{x_2} \times \frac{y_3}{x_3} \times \frac{y_4}{x_4} \times \frac{y_5}{x_5} \times \frac{y_6}{x_6} \times \frac{y_1}{x_1}$$

$$\sum P = y_1x_2 + y_2x_3 + y_3x_4 + y_4x_5 + y_5x_6 + y_6x_1$$

$$\sum Q = x_1y_2 + x_2y_3 + x_3y_4 + x_4y_5 + x_5y_6 + x_6y_1$$

Now area $A = \frac{1}{2}\left(\sum P - \sum Q\right)$ in the units in which the coordinates are taken.

(*h*) **Calculations by dividing the figure into regular geometric figures :** The area is divided into regular geometric figures and the area of each figure is calculated separately and the total of these areas is the area of the figure.

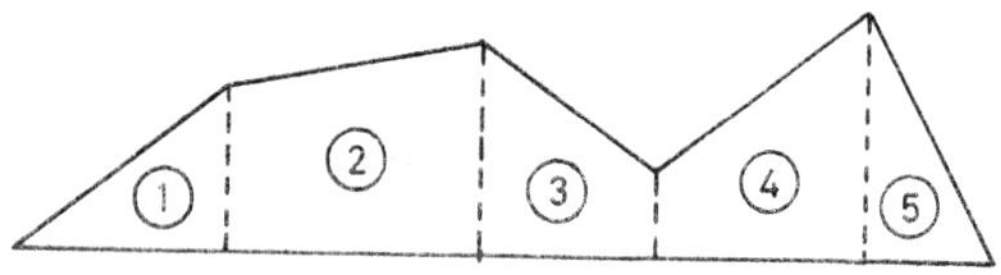

Fig. 2·52.

$$A = (1) + (2) + (3) + (4) + (5)$$

(*i*) **When the land transverse to the centre line is sloping in slopes of r_1 and r_2 on either side from centre line :**

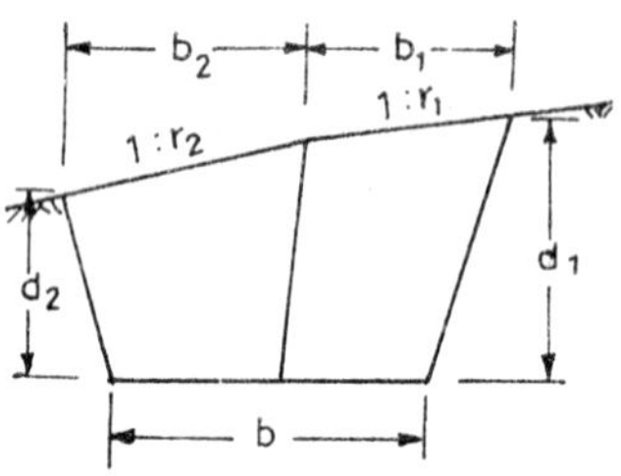

Fig. 2·53.

$$\text{Area} = b/2 \times d(b_1 + b_2) + 1/4\,(d_1 + d_2) \qquad \text{...}(A)$$

where b_1 and b_2 are the width of cutting on right and left side of the centre line respectively, d_1 and d_2 are the height of cutting at right and left side of the centre line.

Now
$$b_1 = \frac{r_1 n}{r_1 - n}\left(d + \frac{b}{2n}\right);\quad b_2 = \frac{r_2 n}{r_2 + r}\left(d + \frac{b}{2n}\right) \qquad \text{...}(B)$$

$$d_1 = \left(d + \frac{b_1}{r_1}\right);\quad d_2 = \left(d + \frac{b_2}{r_2}\right) \qquad \text{...}(C)$$

Properties of Polygons

Name of polygon	*No. of sides*	*Angle degree*	*Area = S^2 ×*	*R = S ×*	*Side = R ×*	*r ×*	*r = S ×*
Triangle	3	60	0·433	0·577	1·732	3·4646	0·289
Tetragon	4	90	1·000	0·707	1·414	1·000	0·500
Pentagon	5	108	1·721	0·851	1·176	1·454	0·688
Hexagon	6	120	2·598	1·000	1·000	1·555	0·866
Octagon	8	135	4·828	1·307	0·765	0·828	1·207
Sectagon	10	144	7·694	1·618	0·618	0·650	1538
Dodecagon	12	150	11·196	1·932	0·517	0·543	1·866

Angle = Angle between two adjecant sides, S = side of polygon, R = Radius of circumscribe circle, r = rad. of inscribe circle.

Theorem of Pappin or Guldin

(1) If an arc of a plane curve revolves about an axis in its plane (the axis not intersecting the curve) the surface generated is equal to the length of the arc multiplied by the length of the path described by the c.g. of the arc.

Volumes and Surfaces of Solids

V denote volume, S = Total surface, C = curved surface L = Lateral surface, l = slant height, h = height and r = radius.

1. **Rectangular Prism or Parallelopiped :**

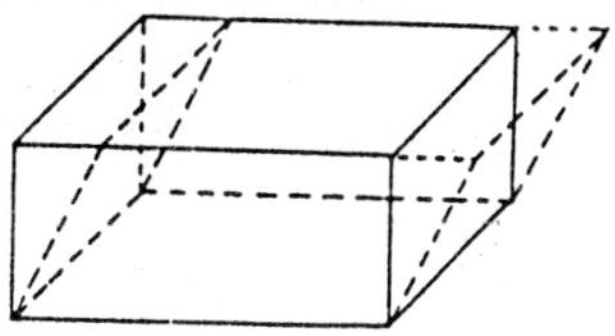

Fig. 2·54.

$V = abc$ (c is height) or $abc \sin \alpha \sin \beta$

$S = 2(ab + bc + ca)$ or $2(ab \sin \alpha + bc \sin \beta + ca \sin \gamma)$

where α, β, γ are the angles in three planes.

2. **Prism :** V = area of end × h

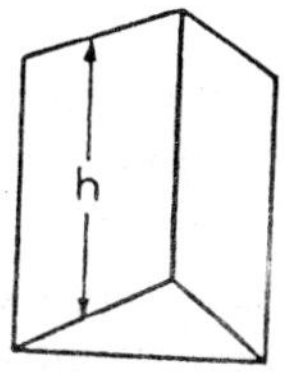

Fig. 2·55.

S = 2 area of end + hx, where x is the perimeter of end (Base may be of any polygon).

3. **Pyramid :** $V = \frac{1}{3} h \times$ area of base

$S = \frac{1}{2} l \times$ perimeter + area of base

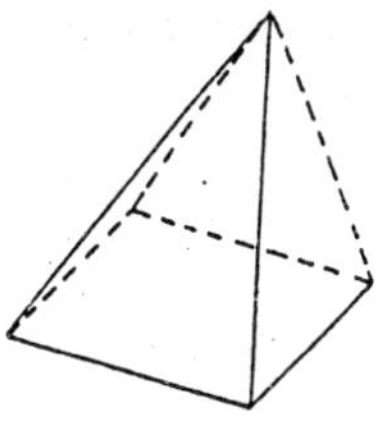

Fig. 2·56.

Regular tetrahedron has four equal sides.

$$V = \frac{2\sqrt{2}}{3} l^3, \quad h = \frac{2\sqrt{2}}{3} l; \quad S = \sqrt{3}(2l)^2$$

4. **Frustum of a pyramid (Prismoid) :**

A_1 = area of top (may be any polygon)

A_2 = area of base

P_1 = perimeter of top

P_2 = perimeter of base

A_m = area of mid section

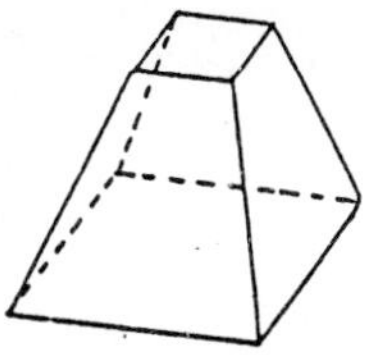

Fig. 2·57.

$$V = \frac{h}{3}\left(A_1 + A_2 + \sqrt{A_1 A_2} = \frac{h}{6}(A_1 + A_2 + 4\,A_m)\right)$$

S = sum of the area of all faces, bed and top.

5.(*a*) **Wedge on rectangular base :**

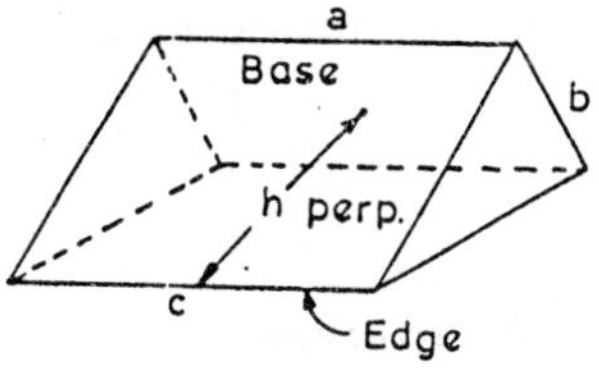

Fig. 2·58.

$$V = \frac{(2a + c)}{6} bh$$

a, b and c are edges of the wedge.

(*b*) **Wedge on trapezoidal base :** or frustum of a triangular prism

$V = \frac{A(l_1 + l_2 + l_3)}{3}$ where l_1, l_2 and l_3 are the lengths of three parallel sides.

and A = area of the triangular section perp. to the base.

6. **Cylinder**

$$V = \pi r^2 h, \quad S = 2\pi r^2 + 2\pi r h$$

Cylindrical ring or Torus

$$V = 2\pi^2 R r^2$$

where R = outer and r is inner rad.

$$S = 4\pi^2 R r$$

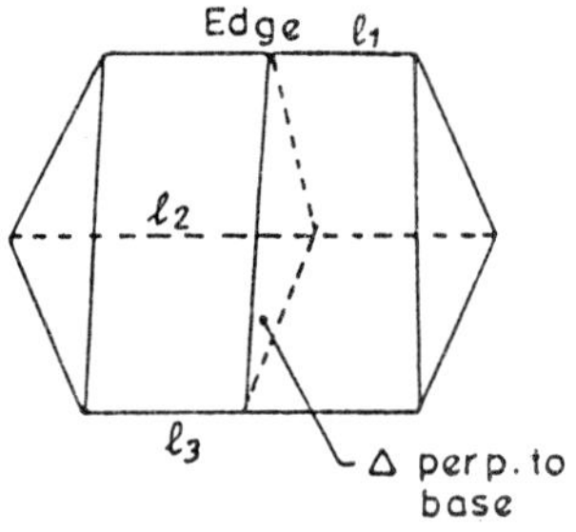

Fig. 2·59.

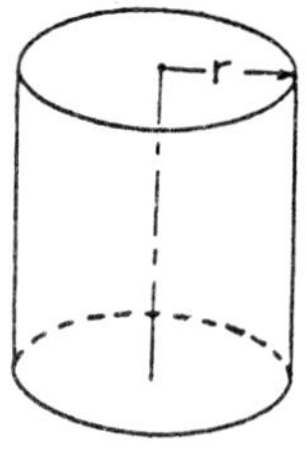

Fig. 2·60.

7. **Frustum of a cylinder :**

(a) $V = \dfrac{\pi r^2 (h_1 + h_2)}{2} \quad C = \pi r(h_1 + h_2)$

(b) $V = \dfrac{2}{3} a^2 \pm b \times \text{area } ABC \times \dfrac{h}{r} \pm b$

$$c = (2ar \pm b \times \text{Arc } ABC) \times \frac{h}{r} \pm b$$

use +ve where base is larger and –ve where less than half of the base circle.

Note : Area of base and top are to be calculated separately as circle or segment of a circle for base and ellipse or segment of an ellipse for top.

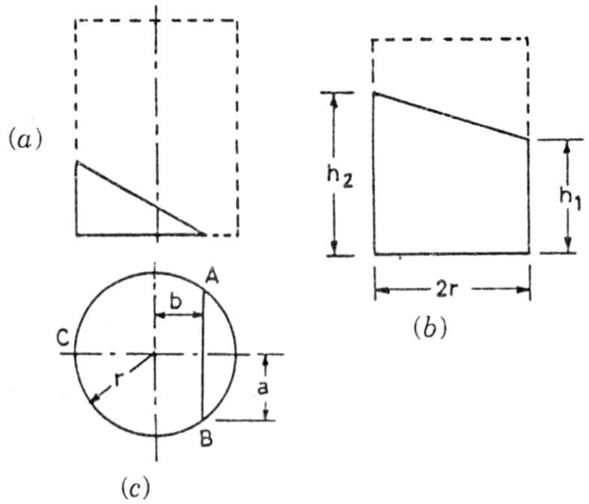

Fig. 2·61.

8. **Cone :**

$$V = \frac{\pi r^2 h}{3} \; ; \qquad c = \pi r l$$

$$S = \pi r^3 (l + r) \; ; \qquad l = \left(h^2 + r^2\right)^{1/2}$$

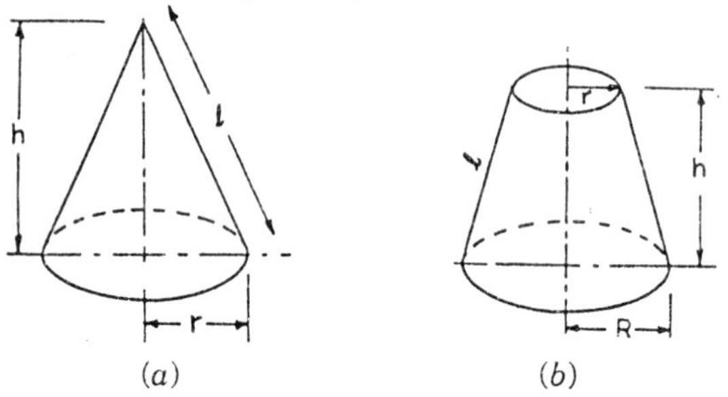

Fig. 2·62.

9. **Frustum of a cone :**

$$V = \frac{1}{3}\pi h\left(R^2 + r^2 + Rr\right) \; ; \qquad C = \pi l(R + r) \; ; \qquad S = \pi\left[R^2 + r^2 + (h + r)l\right]$$

10. **Sphere :**

$$V = \frac{2}{3}\pi r^2 h \qquad S = 4\pi r^2$$

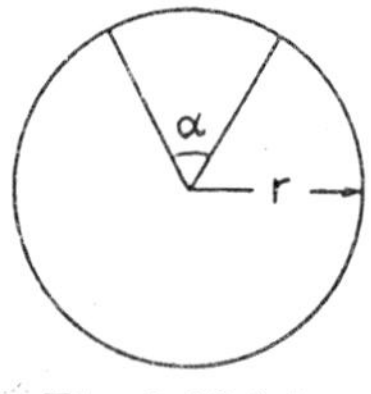

Fig. 2·63 (a).

11. **Spherical wedge :**

$$V = \frac{\alpha}{360}\left(\frac{4}{3}\pi r^3\right)$$

12. **Spherical segment :**

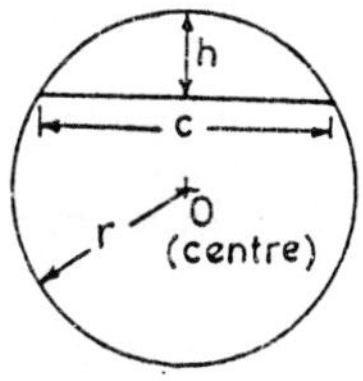

Fig. 2·63 (*b*).

$$V = \frac{1}{16}\pi h\left(\frac{3}{4}c^2 + h^2\right) \qquad c = 2\pi r h = \pi\left(r + h^2\right)$$

$$= \pi h^2\left(r - \frac{h}{3}\right) \qquad S = \pi\left(2rh + \frac{1}{4}c^2\right)$$

$$r = \frac{c^2 + 4h^2}{8h} \qquad c = 2\sqrt{h(2r - h)}$$

13. **Spherical sector :**

$$V = \frac{2}{3}\pi r^2 h \qquad S = \pi r\left(2h + \frac{1}{2}c\right) \qquad c = 2\sqrt{h(2r - h)}$$

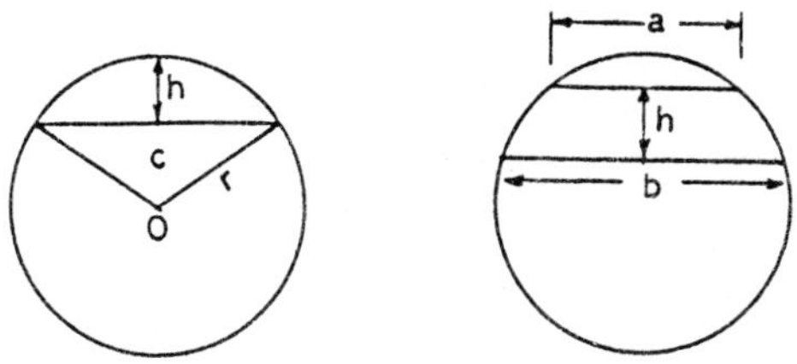

(*c*) (*d*)

Fig. 2·63.

14. **Spherical zone :**

$$V = \frac{1}{6}\pi h\left(\frac{3}{4}a^2 + \frac{3}{4}b^2 + h^2\right) \quad C = 2\pi rh$$

$$S = 2\pi r h + \frac{1}{4}\pi a^2 + \frac{1}{4}\pi b^2$$

15. **Paraboloid :** Solid generated by revolving of parabola on its base.

$$V = \frac{1}{2} \text{ vol. of circumscribing cylinders.}$$

16. If the sphere flattens at poles it is known as **spheroid** (It is formed by the revolution of an ellipse.) If it rotates around minor axis the solid so obtained is **oblate** like orange. If it rotates around major axis, solid so obtained is **Prolate** like tomato. If $2a$ be major axis and $2b$ be minor axis.

$$\text{Oblate } V = \frac{4}{3}\pi a^2 b \qquad C = 2\pi a^2\left[1 + \frac{1 - e^2}{2e}\log\frac{1 + e}{1 - e}\right]$$

$$\text{Prolate } V = \frac{4}{3}\pi a b^2 \qquad C = 2 \text{ area of ellipse} \times \left[\sqrt{1 - e^2} + \frac{\sin^{-1} e}{e}\right]$$

where e is the eccentricity of ellipse.

17. **Theorem of Pappin or Guldin :**

(1) If a closed plane curve is revolved around an axis in its plane (The axis not intersecting the curve), the volume of the solid generated is equal to the area of the curve multiplied by the length of the path described by the centre of gravity of the area.

18. Centre of gravity of Plane figures : (Also refer Appendices in Chapter 8-C Limit State Design)

1. **Semi-circle :** from dia. = $\frac{4r}{3\pi}$ = 0·424 r
   where r = rad. of the circle.

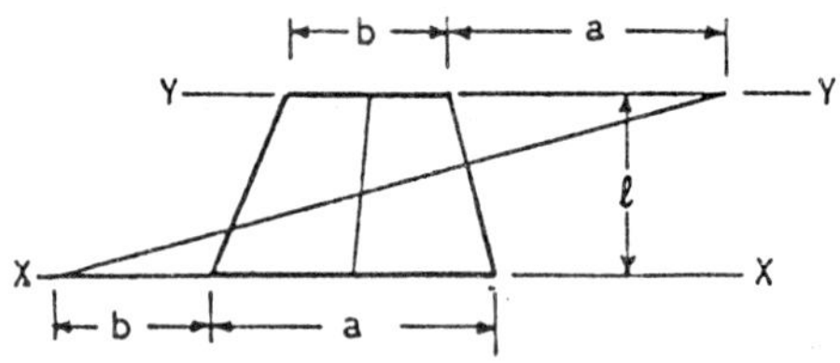

Fig. 2·64 (*a*).

2. **Semi circular arc :** from dia. $\frac{2r}{\pi}$

3. **Triangle** : from base = $\frac{1}{3}$ or medium

4. **Trapezium :**

   (*a*) From x-x = $\frac{a+2b}{a+b} \cdot \frac{e}{3}$

   (*b*) From y-y = $\frac{2a+b}{a+b} \cdot \frac{e}{3}$

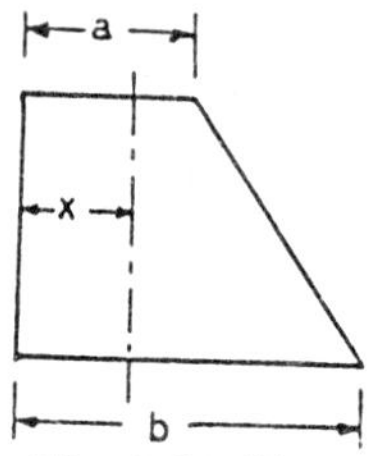

Fig. 2·64 (*b*).

   (*c*) c.g. of Trapezium (by area moment method)

   $A \times 2/3\ a + B.(a + b/2) + C \times (a + b + c/3)$
   $= (A + B + C)\ \bar{x}$

   where $\bar{x}$ = the distance of the c.g. from the origin of YY'

   From vertical face

$$= \frac{a^2 + ab + b^2}{3(a+b)} = x$$

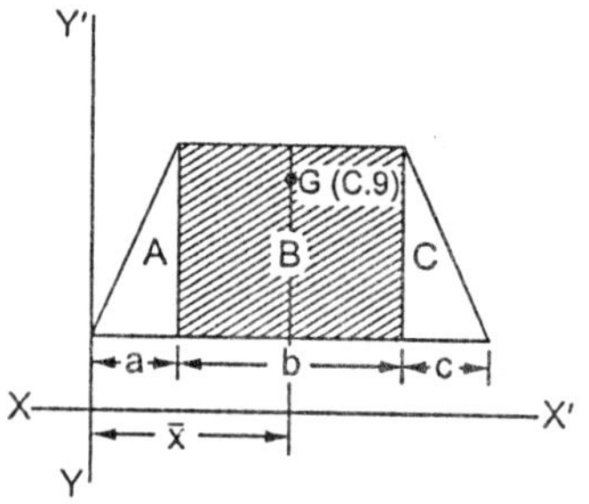

Fig. 2·64 (*c*).

5. **Surface of a hemisphere** :

   From dia. = $\frac{r}{2}$

6. (*a*) **Parabola :** from base AB = $\frac{2}{3}h$

   (*b*) **Semi parabola :** $\frac{3}{5}$ length of the axis from the vertex and $\frac{3}{8}$ of the semi base from the axis.

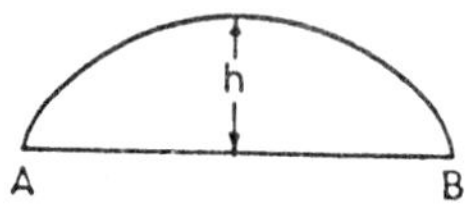

Fig. 2·65.

7. **Ellipse :** Crossing of major and minor axis in the 1st quadrant. Co-ordinates of c.g. are $\frac{4a}{3\pi}, \frac{3b}{3\pi}$ for the ellipse

$$\frac{x^2}{a^2} + \frac{y^2}{b^2} = 1$$

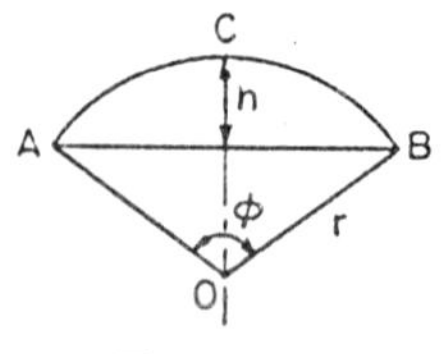

Fig. 2·66.

8. **Sector :** from centre O at a distance of $\frac{2}{3}r + \frac{c}{l}$ or $\frac{2}{3}r\ \frac{\sin\phi}{\phi}$ on the line OC where the point C is the apex of sector.

9. **Segment :** from centre O at a distance of $\frac{c^3}{12A}$ where A = area of the segment.

10. **Fillet :** from dia. of the semi circle = $\frac{2r}{\pi}$.

11. **Surface of hemisphere :** from dia. = $\frac{r}{2}$.

2·7. Dynamics and Statics

Dynamics : $V = v + ft.$ where v = initial velocity

$s = vt + \frac{1}{2} ft^2$ V = final velocity

$V^2 = v^2 + 2fs$ f = acceleration

t = time taken and s = distance

Moment of a body about a point = mr ; Force = $m \times f$
where m is the mass, r = distance of the mass from the point.

$$\text{Kinetic energy} = \frac{1}{2}mV^2, \text{ Potential energy} = mgh$$

where, h is the height of the body.

$$\text{Impulse} = Ft = mV - mv$$

where, F is the force

$$m_1V_1 = m_2V_2 = m_1v_1 + m_2v_2$$

where, m_1 and m_2 are the masses of the bodies

Motion of a connected body over a pulley

$$f = \frac{m_1 - m_2}{m_1 + m_2} ; \quad T = \frac{2m_1 m_2}{m_1 + m_2} g$$

where, T is the tension in the string.

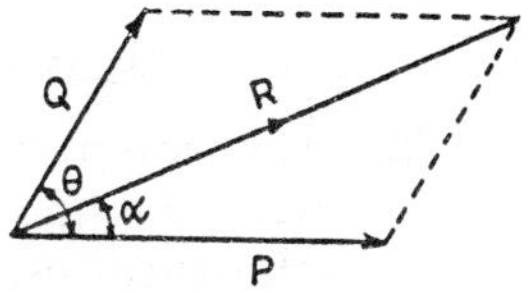

Fig. 2·67.

Statics : $R = \sqrt{P^2 + Q^2 + 2PQ \cos \theta}$

$$\tan \alpha = \frac{Q \sin \theta}{P + Q \cos \theta}$$

where, P and Q are forces and R = Resultant.

Lami's Theory : $\frac{P}{\sin \alpha} = \frac{Q}{\sin \beta} = \frac{R}{\sin \gamma}$

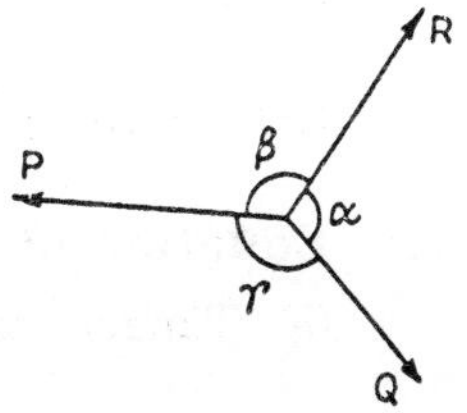

Fig. 2·68.

Friction :

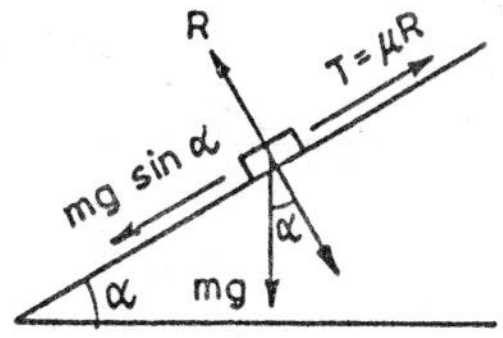

(Inclined surface)
Fig. 2·69 (*a*).

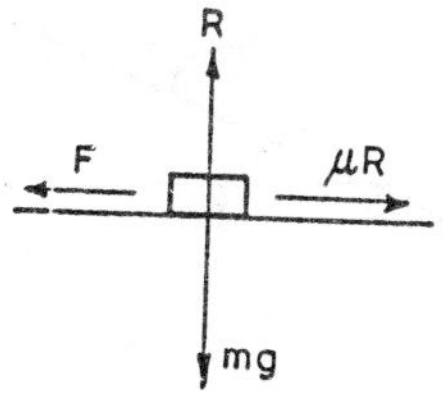

(Plane surface)
Fig. 2·69 (*b*).

$\mu = \frac{F}{R}$ μ = coefficient of friction F = force applied and R = reaction

$\mu = \tan \alpha$; α = angle of friction m = wt. of the body

Theorem. Three forces acting on a body, keeping it in equilibrium, meets in a point.

Theorem of moments. The sum of the moments of all the forces about a point say A left or right is zero, provided that the body is at rest. Taking clockwise direction as +ve and anticlockwise as –ve.

Then $P_1a_1 + P_2(a_1 + a_2) + P_3(a_1 + a_2 + a_3) - R_2(a_1 + a_2 + a_3 + a_4)$ (Refer Fig. 2·7 (*b*)).

$$\text{Vel. ratio} = \frac{\text{Distance through which force acts}}{\text{Distance moved by the resistance}}$$

$$\text{Efficiency} = \frac{\text{Mech. advantage}}{\text{Vel. ratio}}; \text{ mech. advantage} = \frac{w}{P}$$

w = weight and P = force applied.

Moment of a couple = $P \times AB$

where P is the force and AB is the arm of the couple.

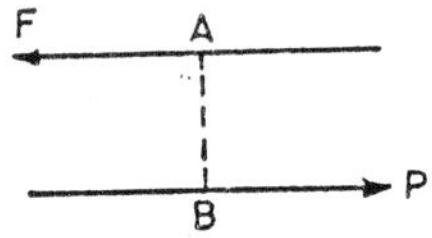

Fig. 2·70.

2·8. Plane Coordinate Geometry

Straight line (1) Relation between rectangular (Cartesian) and polar coordinates.

$$x = r\cos\theta,\quad y = r\sin\theta,\quad r = \sqrt{x^2 + y^2},\quad \theta = \tan^{-1} y/x$$

(2) Distance between two points x, y and

$$x_2 y_2 = \sqrt{(x_2 - x_1)^2 - (y_2 - y_1)^2}$$

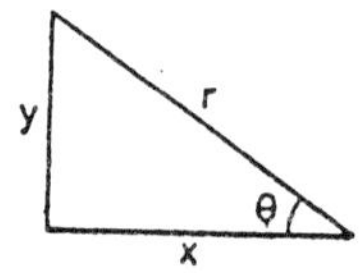

Fig. 2·71.

(3) Co-ordinates of the points which divide the line joining $x_1\,y_1$ and $x_2\,y_2$ in the ratio $m_1 : m_2$ internally and externally.

Internally $\dfrac{m_1x_2 + m_2x_1}{m_1 + m_2}$, $\dfrac{m_1y_2 + m_2y_1}{m_1 + m_2}$

Externally $\dfrac{m_1x_2 - m_2x_1}{m_1 - m_2}$, $\dfrac{m_1y_2 - m_2y_1}{m_1 - m_2}$

Fig. 2·72 (*a*).

(4) **Equation of Straight line :**

(*a*) Tangent from $y = mx + c$

(*b*) Intercept form $\dfrac{x}{a} + \dfrac{y}{b} = 1$

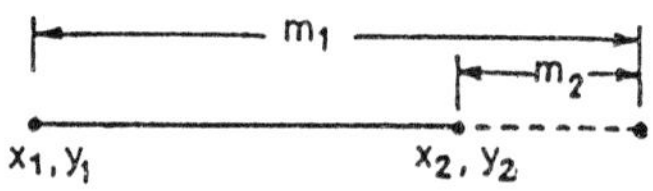

Fig. 2·72 (*b*).

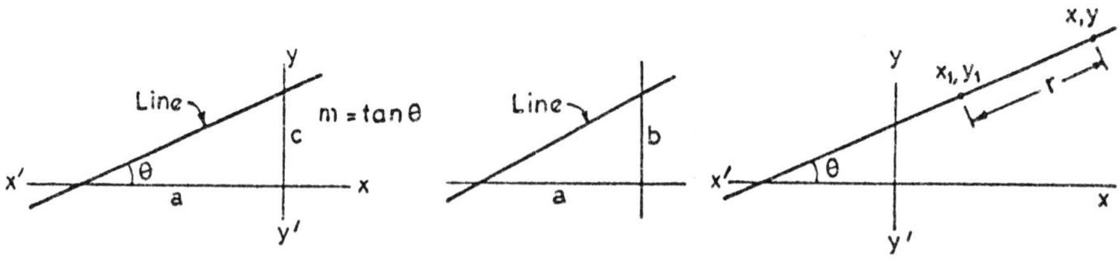

(*a*) (*b*) (*c*)

Fig. 2·73.

(*c*) Passing through a point x_1y_1, $y - y_1 = m(x - x_1)$

(*d*) Parametric form $\dfrac{x - x_1}{\cos\theta} = \dfrac{y - y_1}{\sin\theta} = r$

x_1y_1 is a point on the line, r is the distance between xy and x_1y_1 and θ is the angle which the line makes with the x-axis.

(e) Two point form $\dfrac{y - y_1}{y_1 - y_2} = \dfrac{x - x_1}{x_1 - x_2}$

(f) Perp. form $x \cos \alpha + y \sin \alpha = P$

P = length of perp. drawn from the origin on the line and α is the angle which the perp. makes with x-axis.

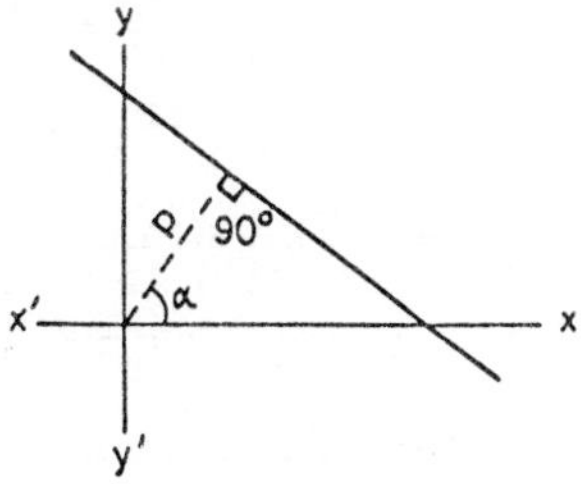

Fig. 2·73 (d).

(5) **Perp. distance of point $P\ x_1\ y_1$ from the line $A_x + B_y + C = 0$**

$$= \pm \frac{A_{x_1} + B_{y_1} + C}{\sqrt{A^2 + B^2}}$$

(6) (a) The equation of a line parallel to $ax + by + c = 0$ is $ax + by + K = 0$

(b) The equation of a line perp. to $ax + by + c = 0$ is $bx - ay + K = 0$

(c) Slope of a line $PQ\ x_1\ y_1\ ;\ x_2\ y_2 = \dfrac{y_2 - y_1}{x_2 - x_1}$

(7) The angle between two lines $y = m_1x + c_1 = 0$ & $y = m_2x + c_2 = 0$ is given by

$$\tan \theta = \pm \frac{m_1 - m_2}{1 + m_1 m_2}.$$

Lines are parallel if $m_1 = m_2$ and perp. if $m_1m_2 = -1$.

(8) Any line passing through the point of intersection of lines $ax + by + c = 0$ and $px + qy + r = 0$ is given by $(ax + by + c) + \lambda(px + qy + r) = 0$

(9) Equation of two lines passing through the origin

$ax^2 + 2\,hxy + by^2 = 0$ where h is a constants

(10) The angle between the straight lines given by

$ax^2 + 2hxy + by^2 = 0$ is $\tan^{-1} \dfrac{2\sqrt{h^2 - ab}}{a + b}$

if $a + b = 0$ lines are perp.

if $h^2 = ab$ lines are coincident

(11) Equation of the bisectors of angles between the lines

$ax^2 + 2hxy + by^2 = 0$ is $\dfrac{x^2 - y^2}{a - b} = \dfrac{xy}{h}$

(12) Equation $ax^2 + 2hxy + by^2 + 2gx - 2fy + c = 0$ represents two straight lines if,

$abc + 2fgh - af^2 - bg^2 - ch^2 = 0$

Circle :

(1) The equation of the circle whose centre is $h\ k$ and radius is r is $(x - h)^2 + (y - k)^2 = r^2$

(2) The general equation of the circle is $x^2 + y^2 + 2gx + 2fy + c = 0$

then centre is $-g, -f$ and radius is $\sqrt{g^2 + f^2 - c}$

(3) The tangent to the circle

$$x^2 + y^2 + 2gx + 2fy + c = 0 \text{ at } x_1y_1 \text{ is}$$

$$x\,x_1 + y\,y_1 + g(x + x_1) + (y + y_1) + c = 0$$

(4) The straight line $y = mx + c$ is tangent to the circle $= x^2 + y^2 = r^2$ if

$$c = \pm\, r\sqrt{1 + m^2}$$

(5) The normal to the circle $x^2 + y^2 + 2gx + 2fy + c = 0$ at x_1y_1 is

$$\frac{x - x_1}{x_1 + g} = \frac{y - y_1}{y_1 + f}$$

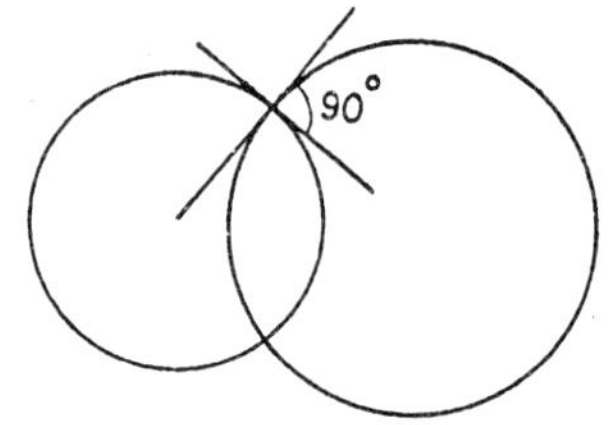

Fig. 2·74.

(6) **Orthogonal circles :** Two circles are said to be orthogonal if the tangent at their point of inter section are at right angles.

(7) **Pole and Polar :** The polar of a point P with respect to a circle or conic is the locus of the point of intersection of tangents drawn at the intersection of the chord through P. The Point P is called the Pole. Through P (the pole) draw a chord cutting the circle at R and Q. Let the tangents at Q and R intersect at T, the locus of T is Polar of P.

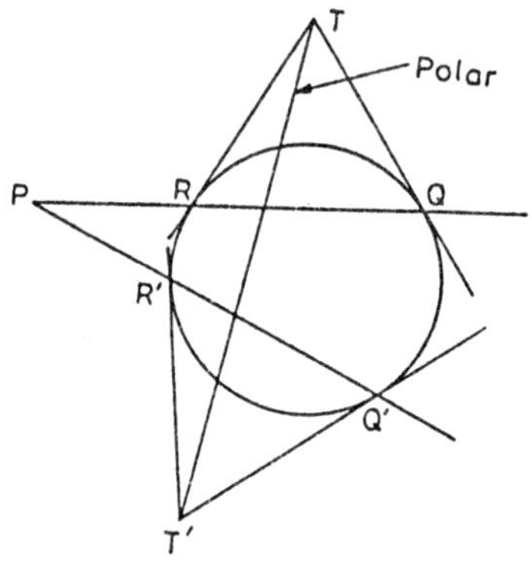

Fig. 2·75.

(8) **Chord of contact :** From P draw PQ, PR tangents to a circle (or a conic) touching the circle at Q and R. The straight line PQ is called the chord of contact of tangents from P.

(9) **Conjugate lines :** Two lines such that Pole of each lies on the other are called conjugate points.

Conic : A conic is a locus of a point which moves in such a way that its distance from the fix point (called focus and denoted by S) always bears a constant ratio (known as eccentricity and is denoted by e) to its distance from a fix line called the directrix. These curves are obtained by the sections of a cone in difference positions (not passing through the apex) hence called conic sections or conic. If $e = 1$ the fig. is called **Parabola,** $e < 1$ the fig. is **ellipse** and if $e > 1$ the fig. is called **hyperbola.**

The sections obtained by the inter section of a right circular conic by a plane in difference positions relative to the axis of the cone are given below.

1. When the sec. plane is inclined to the axis and cut all the generators of the surface on one side of the apex. This section is called ellipse.

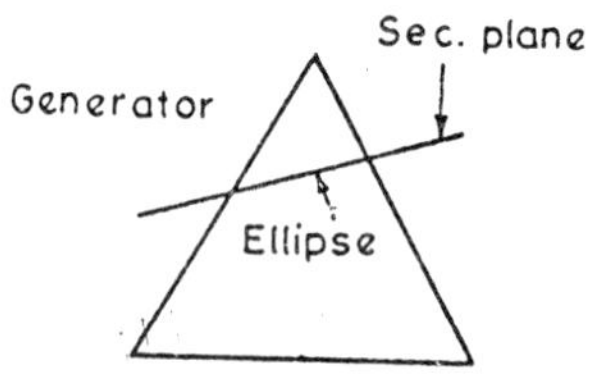

Fig. 2·76 (a).

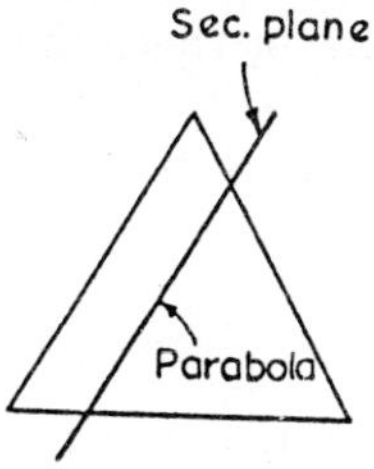

Fig. 2·76 (b)

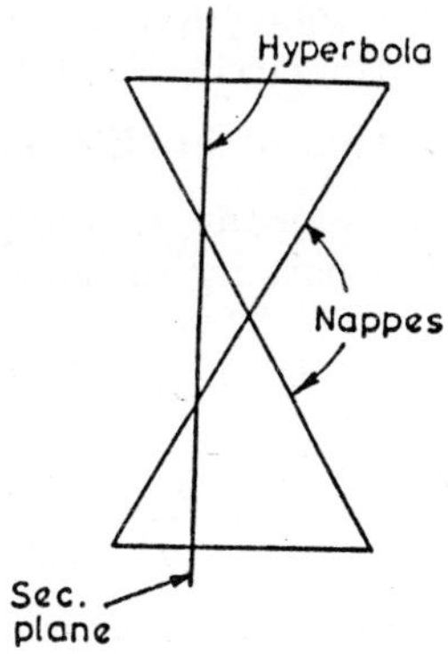

Fig. 2·76 (c).

2. When the sec. plane is inclined to the axis and is parallel to one of the generators of the surface. The sec. is a parabola.
3. When the sec. plane cuts both the nappes of the cone. The section is hyperbola.

Note : (1) Generators : These are the lines flowing the vertex to the circular base.

(2) Nappes : These are two cones on either side of the vertex.

Ellipse : The equation of the Ellipse is $\frac{x^2}{a^2}+\frac{y^2}{b^2}=1$

When foci are $\pm ae$, 0, major axis = $2a$, minor axis = $2b$.

Vertices are $(-a, 0)$ and $(a, 0)$, centre is 0,0 and $e=\sqrt{1-\frac{b^2}{a^2}}$

Equations to the directrices are $x=-\frac{a}{e}$ and $\frac{a}{e}$

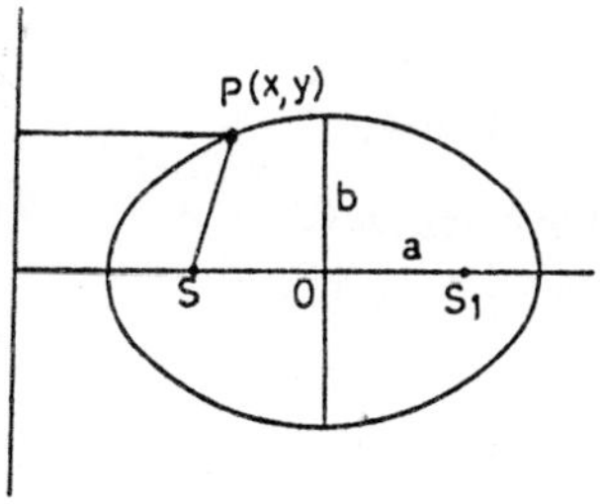

Fig. 2·77.

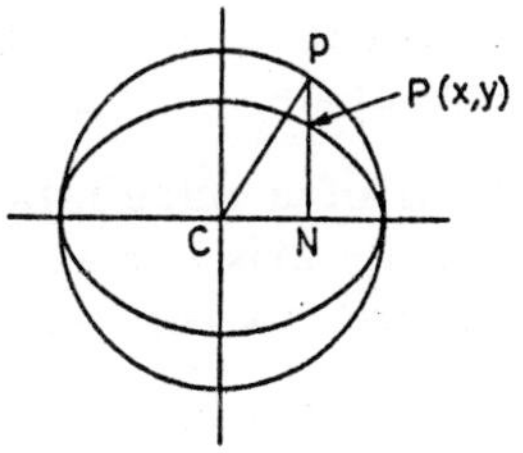

Fig. 2·78.

Length of latus rectum = $\frac{2b^2}{a}$

Tangent to the ellipse= $\frac{x^2}{a^2}+\frac{y^2}{b^2}=1$ is $\frac{xx_1}{a^2}+\frac{yy_1}{b^2}=1$ and normal $\frac{x-x_1}{x_1/a^2}=\frac{y-y_1}{y_1/b^2}$

Auxilliary circle and eccentric angles : The auxilliary circle is a circle which is described on the major axis as dia. Let P be the point xy. Draw PN perp. on the axis. Produce P to p on the circle. Then PCN is the ecc. angle θ.

Properties of an Ellipse :

1. Locus of the middle points of a system of parallel cords of an ellipse is a straight line passing through the origin *i.e.* centre of the ellipse.
2. Equation of the chord of an ellipse $\frac{x^2}{a^2}+\frac{y^2}{b^2}=1$ where middle point is x_1y_1

$$\frac{xx_1}{a^2}+\frac{yy_1}{b^2}=\frac{x_1^2}{a^2}+\frac{y_1^2}{b^2}$$

3. Tangent at a vertex of a diameter of an ellipse is parallel to the chords bisected by the diameter.
4. Normal at any point of an ellipse bisects the angle between the focal distances of the point.

Drawing an ellipse at site :

1. Take a cord (thread) equal in length $2a$ (the length of major axis)
2. Draw axis and mark position of the centre O (length of axis = $2a$)
3. Draw perpendicular OC from the centre O equal to minor axis b.
4. Pick up middle point of the thread and mark point P_1 and P_2 on major axis by putting middle point of thread on the top B of minor axis. These points P_1 and P_2 are foci.
5. Pin both ends of thread on the foci P_1 and P_2 and move the pencil or arrow point tightening the thread all round. Staring from the point A of major axis. Curve so obtained by the pencil or arrow point is the required ellipse.

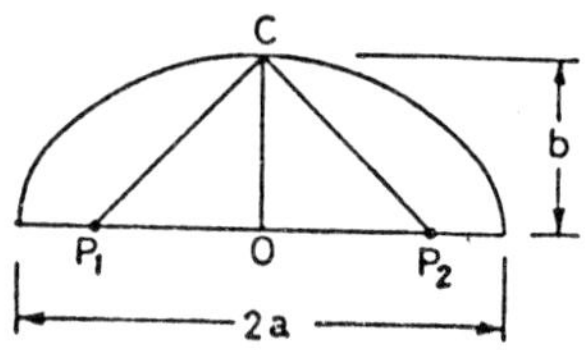

Fig. 2·79.

Parabola :

P is the point, S the focus and MN directrix

$AS = AZ = a$, A is called vertex.

Latus rectum is the length of the chord from the focus S and right angle to the axis of x and is equal to $4a$.

Equation of a parabola. $y^2 = 4ax$ where its vertex A is 0, 0 and its axis is x-axis. Here latus rectum is $4a$ and equation of directrix is $x + a = 0$.

Focal distance of the point xy on the parabola $y = 4\ ax$ is $a + x$.

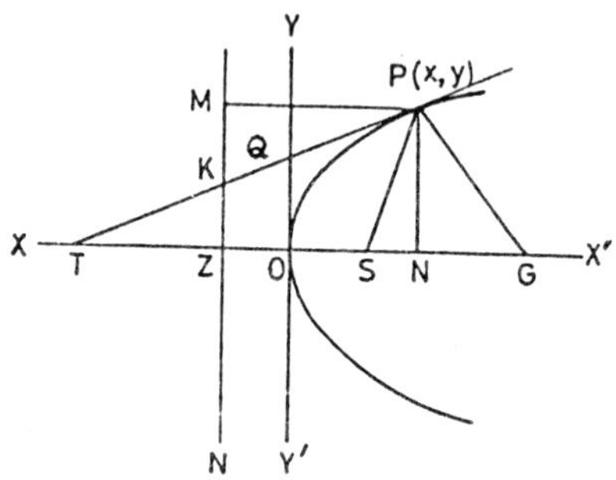

Fig. 2·80

The equation of the tangent to the parabola $y^2 = 4ax$, at x_1y_1 is $yy_1 = 2a\ (x + x_1)$.

The straight line $y = mx + c$ is a tangent to the parabola $y^2 = 4ax$, if $c = \frac{a}{m}$ and normal if $c = 2\ am - am^3$.

Pole of the line $lx + my + n = 0$ with respect to the parabola $y^2 = 4ax$ is $\left(\frac{n}{l}, \frac{-2m}{l}\right)$.

Polar of the point ($P\ x_1y_1$) with respect to the parabola $y^2 = 4ax$

$$yy_1 = 2a\ (x + x_1)$$

If PT is the tangent, PG is normal, TH is sub-tangent and NG is sub-normal.

Properties of a parabola :

1. Sub tangent at any point on a parabola is bisected at vertex.
2. Sub·normal at any point on a parabola is constant and is equal to half of latus rectum.
3. Middle points of a system of parallel chords of a parabola, all lies in a straight line which is parallel ato x axis.

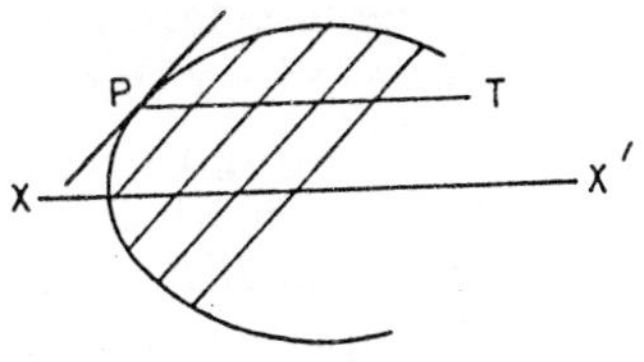

Fig. 2·81.

4. A tangent PT of a parabola $y^2 = 4\ ax$ is intercepted between its points of contact and the axis is bisected by the tangent at vertex at Q *i.e.* $PQ = QT$.
5. If tangent at point P meet the directrix in K then KSP is a right angle where S is the focus.
6. If SM be perp. to the focus to the tangent at P, then M lies on the tangent at the vertex and $SM^2 = AS - SP$ where A is the vertex.

Hyperbola :

$CA = CA' = a$; $CS = ae$; $cz = a/e$

Co-ordinates of foci are $\pm\ ae$, 0

Equation of directrix $x = \pm \dfrac{a}{e} = 0$

Equation of latus rectum $x = \pm\ ae$

Length of latus rectum $= \dfrac{2b^2}{a}$

Latus rectum is the chord of a hyperbola drawn from the focies and perp. to the **transverse** axis AA'. Transverse axis is axis AA' and its length is $2a$ and BB' is the conjugate axis and its length = $2b$.

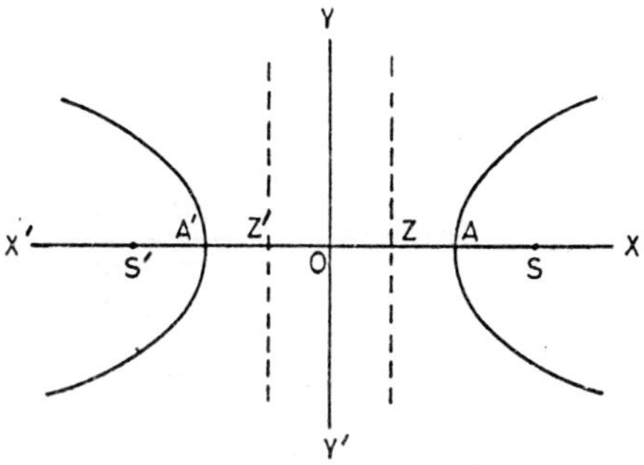

Fig. 2·82.

Equation of the hyperbola is $\dfrac{x^2}{a^2} - \dfrac{y^2}{b^2} = 1$ where $b^2 = a^2\left(e^2 - 1\right)$

Properties of hyperbola :

1. Distance of the focal distance of any point on a hyperbola is constant and equal to its transverse axis = $2a$.
2. The point (a sec θ, b tan θ) lie on hyperbola for all values of θ.

Asymptotes of a parabola : An asymptote is a straight line which meets the hyperbola in two coincident points at infinity but not wholly at infinity ; $y = \pm$

$\frac{b}{a}x$ is required asymptot. Equation of an asymptote differs from hyperbola by a constant.

Rectangular or equilateral hyperbola : It is the hyperbola in which asymptotes are right angles. Its equation is $x^2 - y^2 = a^2$.

Conjugate hyperbola : It is hyperbola in which AA' is the conjugate axis and BB' is the transverse axis. It's equation differs from the equation of asymptote by a constant equation of conjugate hyperbola is $\frac{x^2}{a^2} - \frac{y^2}{b^2} = -1$.

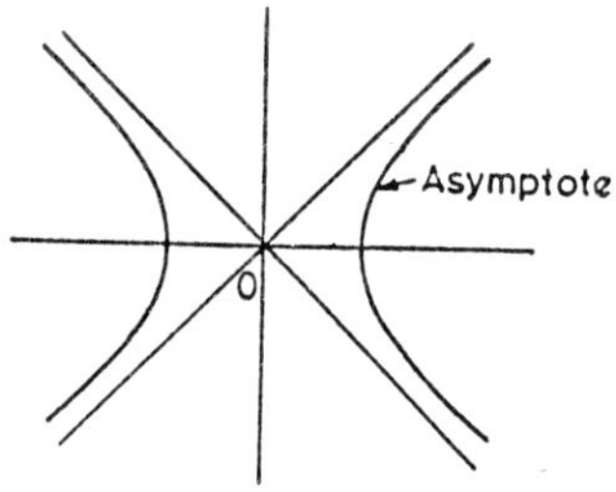

Fig. 2·83.

Note : Equation of an asymptote differs from the equation of a hyperbola by a constant and the equation of the conjugate hyperbola from the equations of the asymptote by the same constant. Equations of rectangular hyperbola referred to asymptotes as axis

$$\left(\frac{y+x}{\sqrt{2}}\right)^2 - \left(\frac{y-x}{\sqrt{2}}\right)^2 = a^2 \text{ or } xy = \frac{a^2}{2} \text{ or } xy = c^2 \text{ where } c = \frac{a^2}{2}$$

2·9. Solid Geometry (Co-ordinate—three dimensions)

1. Distance between two points PQ x_1, y_1, z_1 ; x_2, y_2, z_2 ; x_3, y_3, z_3

$$PQ = \left\{(x_2 - x_1)^2 - (y_2 - y_1)^2 - (z_2 - z_1)^2\right\}^{1/2}$$

2. Co-ordinates of a point which divides the line PQ in ratio $m : n$.

Internally : $\frac{m_1x_2 - m_2x_1}{m_1 + m_2}$; $\frac{m_1y_2 + m_2y_1}{m_1 + m_2}$; $\frac{m_1z_2 + m_2z_1}{m_1 + m_2}$

Externally : $\frac{m_1x_2 - m_2x_1}{m_1 - m_2}$; $\frac{m_1y_2 - m_2y_1}{m_1 - m_2}$; $\frac{m_1z_2 - m_2z_1}{m_1 - m_2}$

Direction cosine. It is the cosine of the angle which a line makes with +ve direction of the axes.

Direction cosine of x-axis are 1, 0, 0
y-axis are 0, 1, 0
z-axis are 0, 0, 1

If $OP = r$ and direction cosines of OP are l, m, n. Then the co-ordinates of P are lr, mr, and nr and $l^2 + m^2 + n^2 > 1$.

Direction ratios. The direction ratios of the line joining $P(x, y, z)$ and $Q(x_2\ y_2\ z_2)$ are $x_2 - x_1$, $y_2 - y_1$ and $z_2 - z_1$.

Angle between two lines whose direction cosines are

$l_1m_1n_1$ and $l_2m_2n_2$ is given by $\cos\theta = l_1l_2 + m_1m_2 + n_1n_2$

or $\sin\theta = \left\{(l_1m_2 - l_2m_1)^2 + (m_1n_2 - m_2n_1)^2 + (m_1l_2 - m_2l_1)^2\right\}^{1/2}$

where θ is the angle between the lines.

Projection of line joining $x_1y_1z_1$ and $x_2y_2z_2$ on another line whose direction cosines are $l_1m_1n_1$ is $(x_2 - x_1)l + (y_2 - y_1)m + (z_2 - z_1)n$.

Plane :

1. General equation of 1st degree in xyz of a plane

$$ax + by + cz + d = 0$$

2. Intercept form $\frac{x}{a} + \frac{y}{b} + \frac{z}{c} = 1.$

3. Normal form $\frac{ax}{\sqrt{a^2+b^2+c^2}} + \frac{by}{\sqrt{a^2+b^2+c^2}} + \frac{cz}{\sqrt{a_2+b^2+c^2}} + \frac{d}{\sqrt{a^2+b^2+c^2}} = 0.$

Angle between two planes :

$$A_1x + B_1y + C_1z + D = 0 \text{ and } A_2x + B_2y + C_2z = 0$$

$$\cos\theta = \frac{A_1A_2 + B_1B_2 + C_1C_2}{\left\{(A_1^2 + B_1^2 + C_1^2)(A_2^2 + B_2^2 + C_2^2)\right\}^{1/2}}$$

Equation of sphere :

(1) $x^2 + y^2 + z^2 = r^2$ centre is 0, 0, 0 and radius r

(2) $(x - a)^2 + (y - b)^2 + (z - c)^2 = r^2$ centre is abc and radii r

(3) $x^2 + y^2 + z^2 + 2ux + 2vy + 2wz + d = 0$ centre is $-u, -v$ and $-w$ and rad. $= (u^2 + v^2 + w^2 - d)^{1/2}$.

2·10. Statistics and Graphics

Frequency. Suppose there are 30 students in a class and the marks obtained by them in an examination are as below :

75	35	41	41	16	28	75	45	55	25
41	45	37	28	75	82	55	61	75	19
75	61	19	28	19	61	28	75	16.	16

The above data !s called as raw data is arranged as below :

16	16	16	19	19	19	25	25	28	28	28	28	35	37	41
41	41	45	45	55	55	55	61	61	61	75	75	75	75	82

This data is called as arranged data. To make it more informative it can be rearranged as below :

Marks obtained	*No. of students*	*Marks obtained*	*No. of students*
16	3	41	3
19	3	45	2
25	2	55	2
28	4	61	3
35	1	75	5
37	1	82	1

Frequency distribution. Let us present the above data in the form below :

Range of marks	*No. of students*	*Range of marks*	*No. of students*
16-25	8	56-65	3
26-35	5	66-75	5
36-45	6	76-80	1
46-55	2		

Cumulative frequency. Let us take frequency of electric bills of a firm :

Bill Rs.	*Frequency*	*Cumulative frequency*
150-225	4	4
225-300	3	4 + 3 = 7
300-375	7	4 + 3 + 7 = 14
375-450	7	4 + 3 + 7 + 7 = 21
450-525	0	4 + 3 + 7 + 7 = 21
525-600	1	4 + 3 + 7 + 7 + 1 = 22
600-675	1	4 + 3 + 7 + 7 + 1 + 1 = 23
675-700	2	4 + 3 + 7 + 7 + 1 + 1 + 2 = 25
Total	**25**	

Graphical representation of statistical data

(*a*) Bar charts—vertical and horizontal (*b*) Histogram (*c*) sPie chart

(*d*) Graphical : (*i*) On simple scale

(*ii*) On log scales : Log scales are used in graphs for reducing the large figures to smaller figures in order to adjust it size of paper.

Graphics

Bar Chart

Bar chart of expenditure of a company (vertical representation)

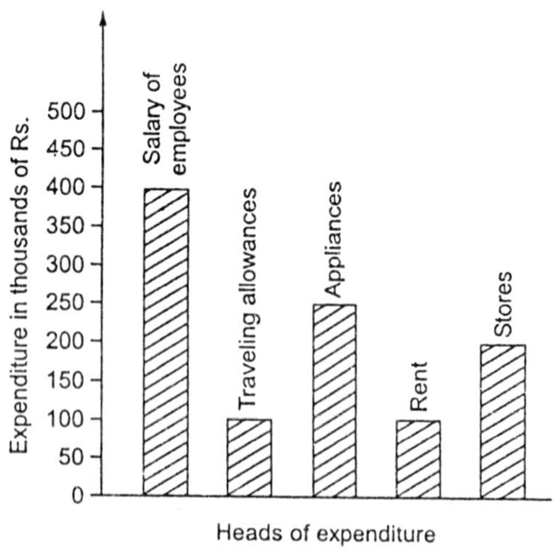

(*a*)

Histogram

Cost of Living Index during 2001-2002 of a city

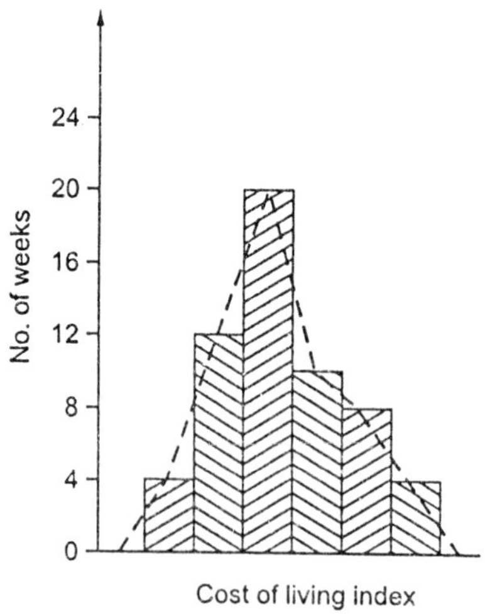

(*b*)

Temperature time chart

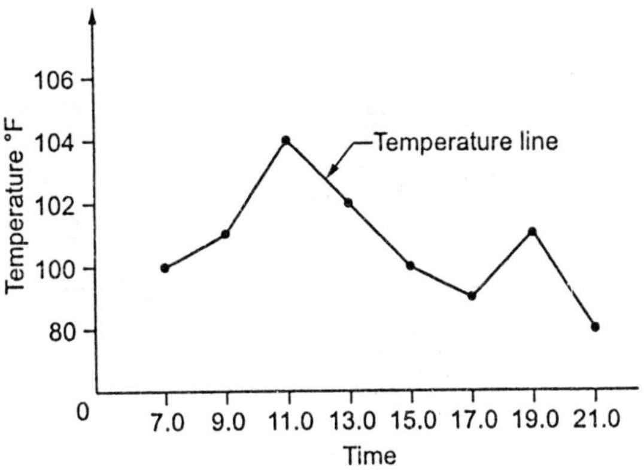

(c)

Pie chart of an election

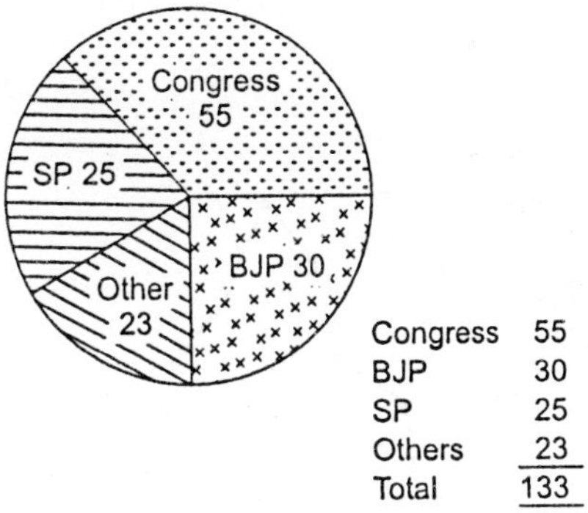

(d)

Bar chart of the construction programme of a building (Horizontal representation)

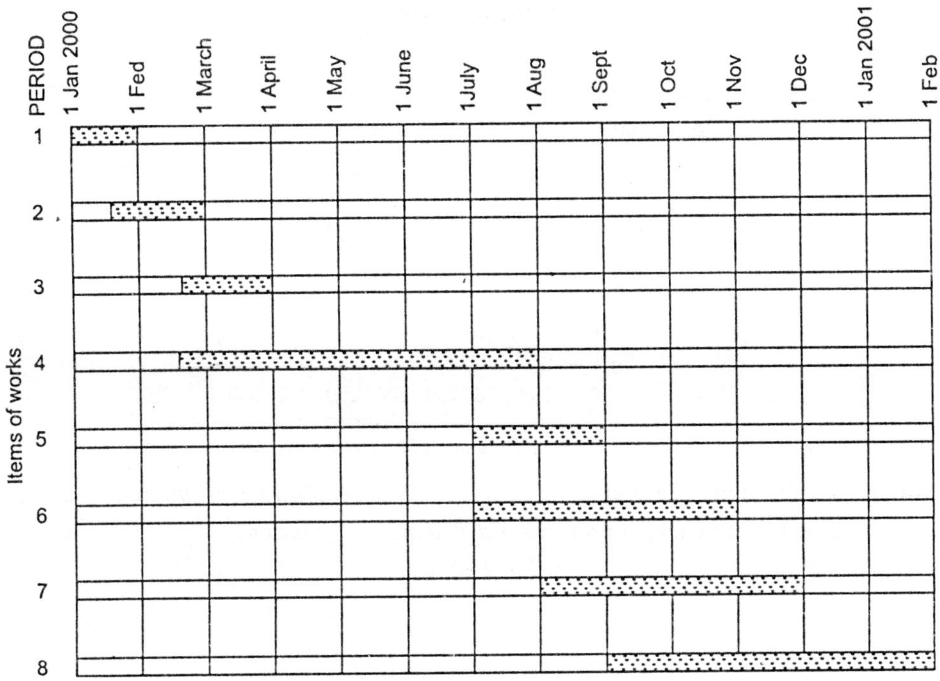

Note : The achievements are marked on the programme chart.

(e)

* **Items of works**

1. E.W. in foundation
2. Foundation concrete
3. Brick work upto plinth
4. Super structure with floor slabs
5. Roofing
6. Plastering, flooring and wood work
7. Colour washing and painting etc.
8. Sanitary and electric fittings.

Frequency Polygon : Simultaneous Equation

Scale : 1 cm = 5 units
on the y-axis

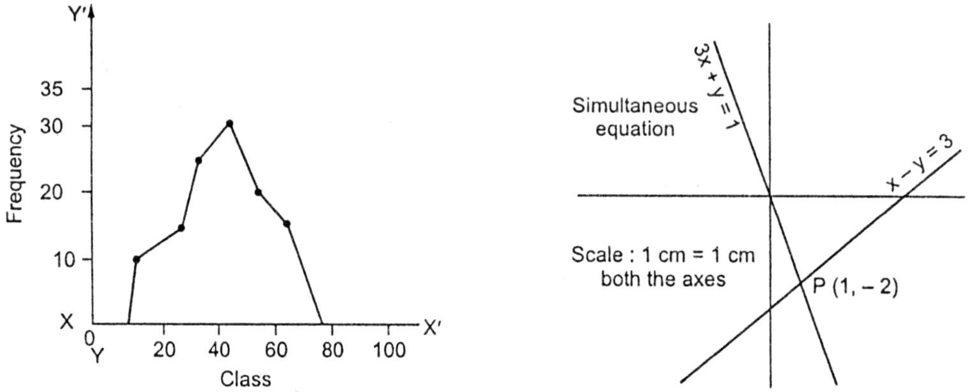

(f) (g)

Fig. 2·84.

Simple Scale

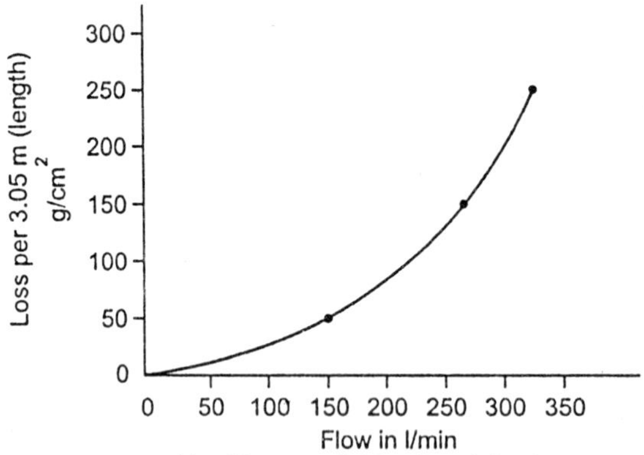

Head loss per 3.05 m length in pipe

Note : 1. A straight line represents a proportional relation $x = ky$ where k is a constant.

2. A smooth curve represents a mathematical relation.

Fig. 2·85 (a).

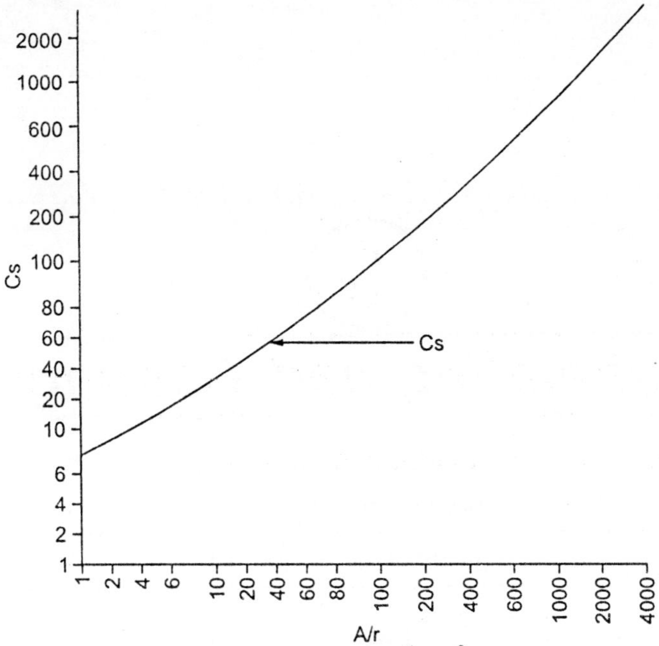

For use in $k = \frac{1}{Csv} \cdot \frac{\theta}{\mu}$

Note : 1. Log scale may be on either axis, or on both the axes.

2. The common ratio of scales may be same or may be different.

Fig. 2·85 (*b*). Conductivity coefficients for some spherical flow in saturated strata through partially penetrating cylinderical test wells.

3

Estimating and Costing

3·1. Requirement of materials in different items of works.

Lime-concrete Mix

S. No.	Type	Mix Ratio	*British units*						*Metric units*					
			Unit	*White lime*	*Surkhi*	*Kankar lime*	*Sand*	*Ballast*	*Unit*	*White lime*	*Surkhi*	*Kankar lime*	*Sand*	*Ballast*
						c.ft						*cu.m.*		
1.	Lime-sand	1 : 1	*% c.ft*	28·5	—	—	28·5	100	*per cu.m.*	0·285	—	—	0·285	1·0
2.	Lime-surkhi sand	1 : 1 : 1		19·0	19·0	—	19·0	100		0·19	0·19	—	0·1919	1·0
3.	Lime-surkhi sand	1 : 1 : 2		14·2	14·2	—	28·3	100		0·142	0·142	—	0·283	1·0
4.	Lime-surkhi	1 : 2		19·0	38·0	—	—	100		0·19	0·38	—	—	1·0
5.	Lime-sand	1 : 2		19·0	—	—	38·0	100		0·19	—	—	0·38	1·0
6.	Lime-sand	1 : 3		14·2	—	—	42·8	100		0·142	—	—	0·428	1·0
7.	Lime-ash sand	1 : 1 : 1		19·2	19·0	—	18·0	100		0·19	0·19	—	0·180	1·0
8.	Kankar lime	—		—	—	40	—	100		—	—	0·40	—	1·0

Cement-concrete Mix

Mix Ratio	*British units % c.ft.*						*Metric units, per cu.m.*					
	Natural agg.			*Crushed agg.*			*Natural agg.*			*Crushed agg.*		
	Cement Bags No.	*Sand c.ft.*	*Bal. c.ft.*	*Cement Bags No.*	*Sand c.ft.*	*Bal. c.ft.*	*Cement Bags No.*	*Sand cm*	*Bal. cm*	*Cement Bags No.*	*Sand cm*	*Bal. cm*
1 : 1 : 2	30·0	37·5	75	31·0	39·0	78	10·67	0·375	0·75	11·1	0·39	0·78
1 : 1½ : 3	21·0	40·0	80	12·0	41·5	83	7·68	0·40	0·80	7·9	0·41	0·83
1 : 2 : 3	20·0	50·0	75	21·0	52·0	78	7·12	0·50	0·75	7·56	0·52	0·78
1 : 2 : 4	16·0	40·0	80	17·0	42·5	85	5·69	0·40	0·80	6·1	0·42	0·85
1 : 2½ : 5	13·7	43·0	86	14·4	45·0	90	4·71	0·43	0·86	5·2	0·45	0·90
1 : 3 : 6	11·5	43·0	86	12·0	45·0	90	4·07	0·43	0·86	4·3	0·45	0·90
1 : 4 : 8	9·0	45·0	90	9·3	46·5	93	3·22	0·45	0·90	3·4	0·46	0·93
1 : 5 : 10	7·0	44·0	88	7·5	47·0	94	2·50	0·44	0·88	2·7	0·47	0·94
1 : 6 : 12	6·0	46·0	90	6·5	49·0	98	2·13	0·45	0·90	2·35	0·49	0·98
1 : 8 : 16	4·7	47·0	94	5·0	50·0	100	1·17	0·47	0·94	1·8	0·50	1·0

Note : 1 bag of cement (50 kg) contains 0·034 m^3 or 1·23 ft^3 of dry cement. It may also (0·35 m^3 or 1·25 c.ft.) practically.

Ballast Breaking

Size of ballast	*Quantity of Bal.*	*Quantity of stone*
$\frac{3}{4}$" (2 cm) or below	100 c.ft. (1 m^3)	110 c.ft. (1·1 m^3)
Above $\frac{3}{4}$" (2 cm)	100 c.ft. (1 m^3)	100 c.ft. (1·0 m^3)

Consumption of material per m^3 of conc. in kg.

S. No.	*Material*	*Grade of conc.*				
		M-150	*M-200*	*M-250*	*M-300*	*M-350*
1	Water	171·0	173·5	114·0	175·5	178·5
2	Cement	300·0	354·0	396·0	438·5	482·5
3	Sand	540·0	520·0	507·0	491·0	482·5
4	Coarse aggr. 10 mm	450·0	442·5	435·5	430·0	410·0
5	Coarse aggr. 20 mm	870·0	850·0	831·5	824·0	796·0

Requirement of material per unit of cement

S. No.	*Grade of conc.*	*Unit*	*Material*			*Coarse aggregate*	
			Water	*Cement*	*Sand*	*10 mm*	*20 mm*
1.	M-150	wt.	0·57	1	1·80	1·50	2·90
		vol.	0·79	1	1·54	1·30	2·47
2.	M-200	wt.	0·49	1	1·47	1·25	2·40
		vol.	0·68	1	1·26	1·14	2·05
3.	M-250	wt.	0·44	1	1·28	1·10	2·10
		vol.	0·61	1	1·10	1·06	1·74
4.	M-300	wt.	0·40	1	1·12	0·98	1·88
		vol..	0·56	1	0·96	0·90	1·60
5.	M-350	wt.	0·37	1	1·00	0·85	1·65
		vol.	0·51	1	0·86	0·78	1·41

Remark : The ingradients mentioned in the table are based on usual conventional practice. Since the size grading, strength and density of aggregates have an important bearing on water and cement requirements, it is therefore recommended that in important works involving large quantities of conc., the concrete mix may be designed taking above factors into consideration after laboratory investigations.

Pitching

Type	*British units % c.ft.*	*Metric units per cu.m.*
Dry Bricks	1650 nos. with no joint	580 Nos. with no joint
Dry Stone	105 c.ft. tightly packed stones with no voids	1 cu.m. tightly packed stones

Quantities of different ingradients ı equired/m^3 of compacted mortar and conc.

Nominal mix			*Water*		*Cement*			
Cement	*Fine aggr.*	*Coarse aggr.*	*w/c ratio*	*Water/50 kg bag of cement litres*	*kg*	*Bag nos.*	*Sand in litres*	*Broken ballast in litres*
1	1	—	0·25	12·5	1051	20·3	710	—
1	1·5	—	0·28	14·0	815	16·3	855	—
1	2	—	0·30	15·0	687	13·75	963	—
1	2·5	—	0·35	17·0	585	11·7	1023	—
1	3	—	0·40	20·0	505	10·1	1060	—
1	4	—	0·53	26·0	325	7·9	1106	—
1	6	—	0·70	35·0	285	5·7	1197	—
1	8	—	0·90	45·0	220	4·4	1232	—
1	1	2	0·30	15·0	560	11·2	392	784
1	2	2	0·42	21·0	480	8·6	602	602
1	1·5	3	0·42	21·0	395	7·4	414	828
1	1·66	3·5	0·48	24·0	363	7·25	419	833
1	2	3	0·50	25·0	385	7·7	539	898
1	2	3·5	0·53	26·5	330	6·6	462	808
1	2	4	0·55	27·5	310	6·2	434	863
1	2·5	3·5	0·57	28·5	305	6·1	534	748
1	2·5	4·0	0·60	30·0	285	5·7	499	798
1	3·0	4·0	0·65	32·5	265	5·3	556	742
1	2·5	5·0	0·65	32·5	255	5·1	446	892
1	3	5	069	34·5	240	4·8	504	840
1	3	6	0·75	37·5	215	4·3	452	904
1	4	8	0·95	47·5	165	3·3	462	924

Note : (1) This table is based on the assumption that the voids in sand and in broken ballast (stone) are 40 and 45% respectively.

(2) For gravel aggregates decrease cement by 5%, in coarse sand by 2% and coarse aggregate in proportion to fine aggregate in mix otherwise the figures given in the table are only for purpose of estimate.

(3) No allowance has been made in the table for bulk and wastage.

Cement conc. flooring 1½″ or 3·5 thick (IPS) with floating coat of cement.

Mix ratio	*British units % sq. ft.*			*Metric units per sq. m.*		
	Cement no. of bags	*Sand c.ft.*	*Stone ballast max. size 3/4″ graded c.ft.*	*Cement no. of bags*	*Sand cu.m.*	*Stone ballast max. size 20 mm graded cu.m.*
1 : 2 : 4	2·25	5·5	11	0·227	0·015	0·30
1 : 3 : 6	1·60	6·0	12	0·161	0·016	0·032

Note : Base 3″ (7·5 cm) thick is provided in cc 1 : 4 : 8 extra.

Brick flooring

Type of floor	*British units % sq. ft.*		*Metric units per sq. m.*	
	No. of bricks	*Sand or wet mortar*	*No. bricks*	*Sand or wet mortar*
Flat Bricks 3″ thick	350	7 c.ft.	38	0·0213 m^3
Brick on edge 4½″ thick	540	10·5 c.ft.	58	0·03195 m^3

Remarks : Size of brick 9 × 4$^3/_8$″ × 2$^3/_4$″ and thickness of joint 3/8″ or 9·5 mm.

For different size of briciks and mortar joints :

Flat brick flooring $M = \dfrac{1{\cdot}3\,t(ld + db + bl)}{(l+1)(b+1)}$; $N = \dfrac{1{\cdot}1}{(l+t)(b+1)}$

M = Quantity of mortar or sand, l = length, b = breadth and d = depth of brick and t = thickness of mortar joint per unit area.

N = No. of bricks per unit area.

Quantity of cement will be as per ratio of mortar.

1 Bag of cement = 1·23 c.ft. = 0·35 m^3 or 50 kg.

Mosaic Pavement 12·5 mm or ½″ thick.

British units % sq. ft.			*Metric units per sq. m.*		
Cement bags	*Marble chips*	*Marble powder*	*Cement bags*	*Marble chips*	*Marble powder*
3 Nos.	4·0 c.ft.	0·5 c.ft.	0·27 Nos.	0·01 m^3	0·0013 m^3

Note : (1) Glass strips according to the requirement based on size of mesh.

(2) Thickness of floor increases with increased gauge of marble chips more than normal of 3 mm and the ingradients will vary accordingly.

Ironite flooring—12·5 mm thick (or 1/2″ thick) over 3·5 mm IPS floor).

British units % sq. ft.				*Metric units per sq. m.*			
Cement bags	*Stone bal. 5-10 mm (1/4-3/8²)*	*Coarse sand*	*Iron grains*	*Cement bags*	*Stone bal. 5-10 mm*	*Coarse sand*	*Iron grains*
3·0 Nos.	3 c.ft.	1·5 c.ft.	0·6 c.ft. (120 kg)	0·27 Nos.	0·008 m^3	0·004 m^3	11 kg

Note : For details refer flooring in building constructions.

Brick work in cement mortar or in mud. (CDD, ID, UP)

	British units % c.ft.			*Metric units per m^3*		
Mix	*Cement Nos.*	*Sand c.ft.*	*Bricks Nos.*	*Cement bags Nos.*	*Sand cu.m.*	*Bricks Nos.*
1 : 3	7·3	27·5	1300	2·6	0·275	460
1 : 4	5·5	27·5	1300	2·0	0·275	460
1 : 5	4·4	27·5	1300	1·6	0·275	460
1 : 6	3·8	27·5	1300	1·35	0·275	460
1·3 (RB)	4·9	36·0	1150	3·5	0·36	405
Mud	—	30 (Mud)	1250	—	0·30 (Mud)	450

Note : (1) The size of bricks is 9″ × $4^3/_8$″ × $2^3/_4$″ (23 × 11 × 7 cm) and thickness of joint 3/8″ or 9·5 mm.

(2) For lime mortar the quantity of lime = Quantity of sand.

(3) If the size of bricks or thickness of joint is different the requirement of sand and bricks may be worked out as under

$$\underset{\text{(cu.m.)}}{\text{Sand}} = 1{\cdot}10\left\{\frac{\dfrac{St}{V} + 0{\cdot}10}{\dfrac{St}{V} + 2{\cdot}0}\right\} = M, \quad \underset{\text{per cu.m.}}{\text{No. of bricks}} = \frac{2{\cdot}06}{\left\{\dfrac{St}{V} + 2{\cdot}0\right\}^{V}} = N$$

Cement in bags = $(m/R) \times 28{\cdot}72$

where S = total surface area of one brick t = thickness of joint

V = total volume of one brick neglecting frog.

R = ratio of mortar mix 1 : R

R.B.—The min. thickness of vertical joint should be as follows :

6 to 8 min dia. bars = 20 mm
9 to 11 mm dia. bars = 23 mm
12 to 14 mm dia. bars = 26 mm
16 mm dia. bars = 28 mm

} Thickness of horizontal joint = 10 mm.

If the size of brick is different, the quantity of ingradients in RB 1 : 3 will be as follows :

No. of bricks $N = \dfrac{1{\cdot}04}{(L+T)(D+T)\times B}$; Sand $M = \dfrac{0{\cdot}05}{\dfrac{BT(L+T+D)+0{\cdot}01+TLD}{(L+T)(D+T)B}}$

where L, B D are length, breadth and depth of one brick and T the thickness of the joint (vertical).

Stone masonry in cement mortar

Type	*British units % c.ft.*				*Metric units per m³*			
	Mortar c.ft.	*Cement bags Nos.*	*Sand c.ft.*	*Stone c.ft.*	*Mortar m^3*	*Cement bags Nos.*	*Sand m^3*	*Stone m^3*
Random Rubble 1 : 4	45	9·0	45	100	0·45	3·2	0·45	1·0
Random Rubble 1 : 3	45	12·0	45	100	0·45	4·3	0·45	1·0
Coarsed Rubble 1 : 3 (dressed stone)	33	8·8	33	105	0·33	3·15	0·33	1·05

Note : In practice generally 1-4 bag/m³ is allowed for RR 1 : 6.

Cement pointing—Ruled, Struck or Flush

Mix ratio	*British units % sq. ft.*		*Metric units per sq. m.*		*Remarks*
	Cement bags No.	*Sand c.ft.*	*Cement bag No.*	*Sand m^3*	
1 : 2	0·5	1·2	0·005	0·0036	33% extra for store work
1 : 3	0·33	1·2	0·035	0·0036	

Cement Plaster 1/2² or 1·25 cm thick

Mix ratio	*British units % sq. ft.*		*Metric units per sq. m.*		*Remarks*
	Cement bags No.	*Sand c.ft.*	*Cement bag No.*	*Sand c.ft.*	
1 : 3	1·3	5	0·140	0·015	33% extra for stone work
1 : 4	1·0	5	0·110	0·015	
1 : 5	0·88	5·5	0·095	0·0165	
1 : 6	0·73	5·5	0·079	0·0165	

Cement Mortars

Mix ratio	*Unit*	*Cement bag*	*Sand*	*Remarks*
1 : 1	1 m^3	20·4 Nos.	0·71 m^3	1. Find sand needs more sand than coarse. Graded sand needs least quantity of sand.
1 : 2	1 m^3	11·6 Nos.	0·95 m^3	2. For producing 1 m^3 of wet mortar about 1·2 to 1·4 m^3 of dry material will require. With fine sand mortar required is more.
1 : 3	1 m^3	10·2 Nos.	1·05 m^3	3. 1 m^3 of cement produces about 0·87 m^2 of cement paste.
1 : 4	1 m^3	7·6 Nos.	1·05 m^3	
1 : 5	1 m^3	6·2 Nos.	1·05 m^3	
1 : 6	1 m^3	5·0 Nos.	1·05 m^3	
1 : 7	1 m^3	4·4 Nos.	1·05 m^3	
1 : 8	1 m^3	4·0 Nos.	1·05 m^3	

Lime Mortars

Mix Ratio	*Material*	*British units % c..ft.*		*Metric units per m^3*	
		White lime	*Surkhi, sand or cinder*	*White lime*	*Surkhi, sand or cinder*
1 : 1	White slacked lime Surkhi sand or cinder	70 c.ft.	70 c.ft.	0·700 m^3	0·700 m^3
1 : 2	White slacked lime Surkhi sand or cinder	47·5 c.ft.	95 c.ft.	0·475 m^3	0·950 m^3
1 : 3	White slacked lime Surkhi sand or cinder	35·7 c.ft.	107 c.ft.	0·375 m^3	1·07 m^3

For producing 1 m^3 of wet mortar about 1·4 m^3 of dry materials (Total of all) is required.

Cement Lime Mortars

Mix	*Materials*	*Cement bag*	*Lime*	*Sand*
1 : 1 : 3	Cement : White slacked lime sand	8·2 Nos.	0·284 m^3	0·852 m^3
1 : 1 : 6	Cement : White slacked lime sand	5·0 Nos.	0·170 m^3	1·020 m^3
1 : 1 : 7	Cement : White slacked lime sand	4·4 Nos.	0·153 m^3	0·071 m^3
1 : 1 : 8	Cement : White slacked lime sand	3·8 Nos.	0·132 m^3	0·056 m^3
1 : 1 : 9	Cement : White slacked lime sand	3·4 Nos.	0·263 m^3	0·062 m^3

White Washing

Type	*No. of coats*	*British units % sq.ft.*		*Metric units per m^2*	
		White line lbs	*Other glue etc. lbs*	*White lime kg*	*Other glue etc.*
Old work	1	2	0·08	0·098	40 gm
Old work	2	3	0·16	0·147	80 gm
New work*	3	6	0·25	·0·294	120 gm

Note : In glue : Rice marh, Bahool gond or Saresh may be used. Neel (Indigo) should be mixed according to the tint required in final coat.

* 1st coat 0·110 kg white unslacked lime is needed.

2nd coat 0·200 kg white unslacked lime is needed.

3rd coat 0·294 kg white unslacked lime is needed.

Zinc powser about 1/4 of the quantity of lime should be need for better shining.

Distempering

No. of coats	*British units % sq.ft. Quantity*	*Metric units per m^2 Quantity*
1st coat	2·5 lb	0·1225 kg
2nd coat	1·5 lb	0·0735 kg

Colour Washing

In the final coat of white washing, required colouring pigments may be mixed according to the darkness of shade required.

Materials and man power required for Residential Buildings.

(In the following expressions "*A*") is the plinth area in sq. m.

Material and man power	*Unit*	*Single Story*	*Double Story*
Bricks	100 Nos.	2·56 *A* + 66·8	2·15 *A* + 63
Cement	Tonnes	0·153 *A* + 0·57	0·145 *A* + 0·54
Steel	kg	21·3 *A* – 314	21·47 *A* – 305
Sand	m^3	0·47 *A* – 7	0·376 – 56
Coarse aggr.			
(*a*) 20 mm or below	m^3	0·176 *A* – 0·21	0·178 *A* – 0·21
(*b*) 40 mm or below	m^3	0·145 *A* – 1·5	0·075 *A* + 0·78
Brick aggr.	m^3	0·113 *A* – 0·83	0·56 – 0·42
Timber frames	m^3	0·019 *A* – 0·23	0·019 *A* + 0·23
Timber shutters	m^3	0·0042 *A*	0·0042 *A*
Ballies	m^3	0·504 *A*	0·504 *A*
Lime	Quintal	0·145 *A* – 0·35	0·073 *A* – 0·17
Surkhi	m^3	0·052 *A* – 0·37	0·026 *A* – 0·18
Bitumen	kg	1·836 *A* – 9	0·918 *A* – 4
Glass	m^2	0·084 *A* – 0·73	0·684 *A*
Primer	lit.	0·068 *A*	0·068 *A*
Paint	lit.	0·108 *A* + 1·27	0·108 *A* + 0·27
Mason	Days	1·335 *A* + 28	0·335 *A* + 26
Carpenter	Days	1·84 *A* – 9	1·194 *A* – 9
Painter	Days	0·089 *A*	0·089 *A*
Blacksmith	Days	0·269 *A* – 4	0·274 *A* – 4
Mazdoor	Days	4·769 *A* + 32	4·91 – 33

Covering Capacities of Paints and Varnishes per lit.

1. Lead priming paint on wood	9 to 11 m^2
2. Lead priming paint on metal	9 to 13 m^2
3. Flat under coating	10 to 12 m^2
4. Glass paint	9 to 13 m^2
5. Enamel paint	9 to 13 m^2
6. Varnish 1st coat	11 to 13 m^2
7. Varnish 2nd coat	13 to 18 m^2
8. Water paints and distemper covers app. 688 m^2/kg and require about one lit. of Renifying liquid or water as the case may be to 4·5 kg of body colour.	688 m^2/kg
9. Extra area of corrugations in corrugated sheets for painting etc.	
(*a*) Corrugated iron sheets	14%
(*b*) Corrugated AC sheets	20% large corrugation with big size
(*c*) Semi corrugated AC sheets	10%

2. Working Capacities

Carrying capacities of Bullock cart or a six wheeler truck

S.No.	*Name of material*	*Bullock cart*		*Truck*
		Pucca road	*Kachcha road*	*metalled road*
1.	Bricks 9″ × $4^{3/8}$″ × $2^{3/4}$″	250 Nos.	225 Nos.	2000 Nos.
2.	Coal	20 Mds (7·5 quintal)	18 Mds (6·75 quintal)	200 Mds (175 quintal)
3.	Steel	20 Mds (7·5 quintal)	18 Mds (6·75 quintal)	200 Mds (175 quintal)
4.	Cemement	15 bags of 50 kg	14 bags	100 bags
5.	Sand or earth	16 c.ft. (0·5 m^3)	145 c.ft. (0·4 m^3)	160 c.ft. (5 m^3)
6.	Brick rora	25 c.ft. (0.75 m^3)	22·5 c.ft. (0·65 m^3)	250 c.ft. (7·5 m^3)
7.	Brick ballast	25 c.ft. (0·75 m^3)	22·5 c.ft. (0·65 m^3)	250 c.ft. (7·5 m^3)
8.	Stone ballast	18 c.ft. (0·55 m^3)	16 c.ft. (0·5 m^3)	180 c.ft. (5·5 m^3)
9.	Stone	18 c.ft. (0·55 m^3)	16 c.ft. (0·5 m^3)	180 c.ft. (5·5 m^3)
10.	Kankar	25 c.ft. (0·75 m^3)	22·5 c.ft. (0·65 m^3)	220 c.ft. (7·5 m^3)
11.	Lime	22 c.ft. (0·6 m^3)	20 c.ft. (0·6 m^3)	220 c.ft. (6·0 m^3)
12.	Surkhi	22 c.ft. (0·6 m^3)	20 c.ft. (0·6 m^3)	220 c.ft. (6·0 m^3)

Quantity of material equal to one tonne.

1.	Bricks (9″ × $4^{3/8}$″ × $2^{3/4}$″)	= 330 Nos.
2.	Cement bags	= 20 Nos.
3.	Sand	= 22·5 c.ft. (0·650 m^3)
4.	Brick rora	= 33 c.ft. (0·94 m^3)
5.	Brick ballast	= 33 c.ft. (0·94 m^3)
6.	Stone ballast	= 25 c.ft. (0·75 m^3)
7.	Stone	= 25 c.ft. (0·73 m^3)
8.	Kankar	= 33 c.ft. (0·94 m^3)
9.	Lime (Kankar lime)	= 30 c.ft. (0·85 m^3)
10.	Surkhi	= 30 c.ft. (0·85 m^3)

E.W. capacity of average worker per day

1.	Dry earth work in foundations, roads, canals etc. within 30 m (100′) lead and 1·5 m (5′) lift in domat soil.	2·8 m^3 (100 c.ft.)
2.	In domat soil wet earth work in capillary fringes with lead and lift as above	2·5 m^3 (90 c.ft.)
3.	Wet under spring in domat soil wet earth work in capacillery fringes with lead and lift as above	2·0 m^3 (70 c.ft.)
4.	Silt clearance in domat soil wet earth work in capillary fringes with lead and lift as above	3·5 m^3 (125 c.ft.)
5.	Dry earth work in mar and kabar in domat soil wet earth work in capillery fringes with lead and lift as above	2·5 m^3 (90 c.ft.)
6.	Dry earth work with chharri in mar and kabur in domat soil wet earth work in capillery fringes with lead and as above	2·3 m^3 (80 c.ft.)
7.	Extra for compaction and dressing	(10% as above)
8.	Extra for lead beyond initial of 30 m (100′) for every 10 m each	10% of above
9.	Extra for lift above initial of 1·5 m (5′) of every 0·3 m each	3·5% of above

Capacity per unit of works

Name of work	Unit	Labour requirement/day				Capacity per man per day	Total rate including 12·5 % Contractors profit	Remarks
1	2	3	4	5	6	7	8	9
1. **Brick work**								Wages per day
(a) B.W. in mud upto 3 m height and 60 m lead of materia	m^3	0·71	1·42	·088	0·88	1·41	Rs.(2A + 4B + 1/4C+1/4D)·04	1. Mason = Rs. A
(b) B.W. in cement or lime upto 3 m height and 60 m lead of material	m^3	0·88	1·76	1·76	0·088	1·13	Rs(2·5A + 5B + 1/2C + 1/4D)·04	2. Labour =Rs. B 3. Bhisti = Rs. C
(c) Uncoursed rubble masonry or R.R. masonry upto 3 m height and 60 m lead of material	m^3	0·88	1·76	1·76	0·088	1·13	Rs(2·5A + 5B + 1/2C + 1/4D)·04	4. Mistri = Rs. D 5. Carpenter=Rs. E
(d) Coursed rubble masonry upto 3 m height and 60 m lead of material	m^3	1·24	1·76	1·76	0·088	0·79	Rs(3·5A + 5B + 1/2C + 1/4D)·04	6. Blacksmith Rs. F 7. Rent of material Rs. G
(e) Extra for every 1·5 m above 3 m with sea folding	m^3	—	0·35	—	0·176	—	Rs(B + 1/2D)0·4	
(f) Extra for load of 30 m beyond 60 m	m^3	—	1·76	—	—	—	Rs(1/2B)0·4	Item 1.d. does not includes dressing of stone.
2. **Arch work**								
(a) Brick arch work	m^3	1·24	2·12	·176	0·088	0·79	Rs(3·5A + 6B + 1/2C + 1/4D)·4	Item 4.d. The rate includes smoothening of surface.
(b) Stone arch work	m^3	1·76	2·12	·176	0·088	0·56	Rs(5A + 6B + 1/2C + 1/4D)·4	
(c) Centering and shuttering	m^2	—	0·53 (carpenter) + 1·76 (Labour) + 0·176 (Mistri) including rent of material				Rs(5B + 1/2D + $1^1/_2$E)·4	
3. **Cement or Lime concrete**								
(a) Cement or lime conc. in foundations including lead and lift	m^3	0·35	1·42	0·35	—	2·83	Rs(A + 4B + C)·4	
(b) Cement or lime conc. in foundation including lead and lift in roof	m^3	0·35	3·88	0·35	0·088	2·83	Rs(A + 11B + C+1/4D)0·4	
(c) Extra for lead of 30 m and lift of 1·5 m	m^3	—	0·176	—	—	—	Rs 1/2B × 0·4	
4. **Flooring and Pitching**								
(a) Flat brick flooring	m^2	0·054	0·054	—	—	18·6	1/2 (A + B) 0·12	
(b) Brick on edge flooring	m^2	0·081	0·081	—	—	12·3	3/4 (A + B) 0·12	
(c) Brick on stone pitching	m^3	0·162	0·216	—	—	1·9	($1^1/_2$A + 2B) 0·4	
(d) Cement conc. flooring over conc. upto 4 cm	m^2	0·324	0·54	0·054	0·027	3·1	(3A + 5B + 1/2C + 1/4D) 0·12	

Table contd....

Name of work	Unit	Labour requirement/day				Capacity per man per day	Total rate including 12·5 % Contractor's profit	Remarks
1	2	3	4	5	6	7	8	9
5. **RB and RCC**								
(*a*) Bending lending, cutting and placing of bars	quintal	1·5 (blacksmith) + 2·0 labour				—	(3/4*F* + *B*) 2·25	
(*b*) RB labour only excluding reinforcement and and shuttering etc.	m^3	1·06	2·12	0·35	0·088	0·94	(3/4*A* + *B*) 2·25	
(*c*) Centering ande shuttering for RB	m^2	0·324 (carpenter) + 1·4 Labour + 0·54 (Mistri)				—	(3*E* + 13*B* + 1/2*D*) 0·12	
(*d*) RCC excluding reinforcement centering and shuttering	m^3	0·71	2·82	0·71	0·088	1·41	(2*A* + 8*B* + 2*C* + 1/4*D*) 0·4	
RCC excluding reinforcement centering and shuttering (mech. mixing)	m^3	0·71	2·82	0·71	0·088	1·41	(2*A* + 8*B* + 2*C* + 1/4*D* + *G*) 0·4	
(*e*) Centering and shuttering for RCC	m^2	0·43 (Carpenter) + + 0·08 (Mistri) + 1·86 labour without material				—	(4*E* + 1·7*B* + 3/4*D*) 0·12	
6. **Painting and Plastering**								
(*a*) Cement plastering on B.W.	m^2	0·108	0·216	0·054	—	9·3	(*A* + 2*B* + 1/2*C*) 0·12	
(*b*) Cement plastering on stone work	m^2	0·108	0·324	0·081	—	9·3	(*A* + 2*B* + 3/4*C*) ·012	
(*c*) Cement pointing flush over B.W.	m^2	0·108	0·108	0·027	—	9·3	(*A* + *B* + 1/4*C*) 0·12	
(*d*) Cement pointing struck deep on B.W.	m^2	0·162	0·108	0·027	—	6·1	(*A* + 1½*B* + 1/4*C*) 0·12	
(*e*) Cement pointing flush over stone	m^2	0·108	0·216	0·027	—	9·3	(*A* + 2*B* + 1/4*C*) 0·12	
(*f*) Cement pointing over stone struck deep or raised	m^2	0·162	0·216	0·027	—	6·1	(1½*A* + 2*B* + 1¼*C*) 0·12	
(*g*) Extra for every 1·5 m above 3m	m^2	—	0·027	—	—	—	(1/4*B* × 0·12)	
7. **Dismentling**								
(*a*) Dismentling B.W., stone work or lime conc.	m^3	0·176	1·42	including rent of tools			(1/2*A* + 4*B*) 0·4	
(*b*) Dismentling B.W. or stone masonry in mud	m^3	—	1·06	including rent of tools			3*B* + 0·4	

Rate of carriage by Bullock Cart

1. Time for loading — 15 minutes
   Unloading — 10 minutes
   Miscellaneous — 5 minutes
   Total — 30 minutes
2. Time for carriage one km. both sides 30 minutes
   Rate of wages per day—one cart without driver @ Rs. A per day
   one Beldar @ Rs. B per day
   one Driver @ Rs. B per day
   Total $(A + 2B)$
   Contingencies = 12·5%
3. No. of trips per day of 8 hrs. $= N = 8\Big/\left(\frac{30\,L}{60}+\frac{1}{2}\right) = L$ = lead in km.

Rate of carriage per bullock cart per trip for a lead of L km.

$$= R = 1{\cdot}125\,\frac{(A+2B)}{N} = \frac{1{\cdot}125}{8}(A+2B)(1/2\,L+1/2)$$

$$= 0{\cdot}14(A+2B)(1/2\,L+1/2)$$

Note : This rate is for return empty journey. If the return jounrey is not empty, the rate should be reduced to 60%.

Rate of carriage per truck of 5 tonne

1. Cost of variables
   (*a*) Cost of truck exclusive of tyres = Rs. A
   Repair charge of 60% over life time = Rs. $0{\cdot}6\,A$
   Life of truck in hrs. = 12,000
   Life of truck in km. assuming speed of 5 km./hr. = 12,000
   Hence depreciation and repair charges of truck/km. $= \frac{1{\cdot}6\,A}{12{,}000}$ per km.
   (*b*) Cost of tyres of and tubes = Rs. B
   Repair and casualties = Rs. $0{\cdot}2\,B$
   Life of tyres = 24,000 kms
   Hence depreciation of tyres and tubes $= \frac{1{\cdot}2\,B}{24{,}000}$ per km.
   (*c*) Cost of operation material per km.
   (*i*) Cost of fuel per lit. = Rs. C
   km. covered in one lit. = 5 km.
   Hence cost of fuel per km. = Rs. $C/5$ per km.
   (*ii*) Cost of mobil oil per lit. = Rs. D
   km. covered in one lit. = 150 km.
   Hence cost of fuel per km. = Rs. $D/150$ per km.
   (*iii*) Other lubricaants and stores. Same as per mobil oil = Rs. $D/150$ per km.
   Ttotal cost of operation materials per km. $= \left(\frac{C}{5}+\frac{2D}{150}\right)$

2. Cost of constants per day of 8 hours

(a) Cost of staff per day of 8 hours — Driver @ Rs. E per day, Cleaner @ Rs. F per day

and 25% for idle days — at Rs. $(E + F)$ 1/4 per day

(b) Cost of labour per day of 8 working hours for loading and unloading etc.

(i) Labour required per day 6 Nos. — @ Rs. G per day

(ii) Cost of labour per day — Rs. 6 G per day

(iii) Cost of accounts and taxes etc. — Rs. H per day

Total per day — = Rs. $5/4\,(E + F) + 6G + H$

3. No. of trips per day — $= N = 8\Big/\frac{2L}{5} + \frac{3}{4}$

where L = lead in km. (one side). — = lead in k.m. (one side)

H = no. of trips in a day of 8 working hours

S = average speed of truck in km. per hour

3/4 = loading and unloading time.

4. Contractors profit on the rate calculated as above — = 12·5%

Rate of carriage of one tonne material by truck both ways included on mettled road for a load of L k.m.

$$= \text{Rs.}\,0{\cdot}225\left[2L\left\{\frac{1{\cdot}6A}{12{,}000\,S} + \frac{1{\cdot}2\,B}{24{,}000} + \frac{C}{5} + \frac{2\,D}{150}\right\} + \frac{5}{4}\,\frac{(E+F)+6G+H}{N}\right]$$

where L = lead in k.m. one side.

S = average speed in k.m. per Hr. can be taken as follows :

Upto 5 km.	15 km. per hour
Upto 25 km.	25 km. per hour
Upto 30 km.	30 km. per hour
above 30 km.	40 km. per hour
Cost of truck excluding tyres and tubes	= Rs. A
Cost of tyres and tubes	= Rs. B
Cost of diesel per lit.	= Rs. C
Cost of mobil oil per lit.	= Rs. D
Daily wages of driver per day	= Rs. E
Daily wages of cleaner per day	= Rs. F per day
Daily wages of labour per day	= Rs. G per day
Average tax per day	= Rs. H per day

No. of trips per day of 8 working hours $= N = 8\Big/\frac{2L}{5} + \frac{3}{4}$

Notes : (1) The rate is inclusive of empty rempty return journey. If the return journey is not empty, the rate may be reduced to 60%.

(2) (a) The above rate is for metalled roads in planes.

(b) Rough metalled, gravel, kankar (small stones) or canal service roads, the rate should be enhanced by 15%.

(c) Kachcha roads, rates should be enhanced by 30%.

(d) Hill smooth metalled roads, rate to be enhanced by 30%.

(e) Hill rough metalled roads, rate to be enhanced by 40%.

3·3. Measurements of Works

Measurements for doors and windows for painting etc.

	Description of works	*Factor*	*Remarks*
1.	Doors and windows		
	(*a*) Panelled or framed and braced, legged and battened	$1^1/_8$ for each side	Measured flat (not girthed) including chaukhats or frames edges, chacks, cleats etc. shall be deemed to be included
2.	Fully glazed or gauged	1/2 for each side	Measured flat (not girthed) including chaukhats or frames edges, chacks, cleats etc. shall be deemed to be included
3.	Partially penelled and partly glazed or gauged	1 for each side	Measured flat (not girthed) including chaukhats or frames edges, chacks, cleats etc. shall be deemed to be included
4.	Flush	1 for each side	Measured flat (not girthed) including chaukhats or frames edges, chacks, cleats etc. shall be deemed to be included
5.	Fully venationed or louered miscellaneous items	$1^1/_2$ for each side	—do—
	(1) Boarding with cover fillet and match boarding	$1^1/_2$ for each side	Measured flat not girthed
	(2) Roof battons (Tile and slate) (for painting overall)	3/4 for each side	Measured flat over all. No deduction shall be made for openings
	(3) Wood roofing (each side)	$1^1/_8$ for each side	Measured flat not girthed
	(4) Trellies, jaffri work one way or two way (Painting overall)	2 for each side	Measured overall. No deduction shall be made for openings.
	(5) Balustrade, gratings, railing, grills, expended metal, guard rails, jalis etc.	1 for painting over all	Measured overall. No deduction shall be made for openings.
	(6) Steel rolling shutters (each side)	$1^1/_4$ for painting over all	Measured flat over all, jali, guards, bottom rails and locking arrangements etc. shall be deemed to be included in the items.
	(7) Covered or enriched work	2 for each side	Measured flat
	(8) Corrugated surfaces		
	(*a*) Corrugated iron sheets	114%	Measured flat not girthed and area increased to cater for corrugations.
	(*b*) Corrugated AC sheets with large corrugations (Big six sheets)	20%	Measured flat not girthed and area increased to cater for corrugations.
	(*c*) Semi corrugated AC sheets (Trafford type)	10%	Measured flat not girthed and area increased to cater for corrugations.

Note : Painting upto 15 cm width or gerth is measured in running metres. Painting on eaves, gutters, steel pipes etc. are all measured in running metres stating the size and girth. Painting or polishing furniture is taken in nos. with full description of size etc. Painting of small items utp say 0·1 m^2 is taken in nos. with description.

Measurements of Plastering and Pointing

Deductions (IS specifications)

1. For end of joists, beams, posts etc. and opening not exceeding 0·5 m^2, no deductions are made. For reveals, jambs, sills, etc. no additions are made.

2. For openings exceeding 0·5 m^2 but not exceeding 3 m^2 each, deductions are made for one face only and the other face is allowed for jambs, soffits and sills each which will not be measured. When two faces are plastered with different mortar or if one side is plastered and the other painted, deductions will be made on the side of chaukhat of door and windows or which the width of jambs or reveals is less than that on the side. Normally deductions are made for the other side only.

3. If the area of the opening is more than 3 m^2 each, deductions is made for both faces of the opening and the jambs, soffets and sills are measured separately and added. In taking measurements of jambs, soffets and sills, chaukhat if any shall be neglected and the whole face should be measured.

4. In cases of plaster or pointing on old surfaces, the racking of old joints is included in the item.

5. Cornices and mouldings when not taken as separate item are girthed and included in the wall measurements.

Measurements of Masonry

Arches (masonry) —Segmental : Span × rise × 2/3 × length of arch

—Semicircular : Span × rise × 3/4 × length of arch

Measurements of Circular pillars

Masonry $= \frac{\pi d^2}{4} l$ where d is the dia and l is the length of pillar.

Plaster $= 2p\ d/2 \times l$

Cornices — (a) mercury $= b \times d \times l$

plaster $= 2b + 2d$

— (b) masonry $= b \times d \times l$

plaster $= (2b + d)\,l$

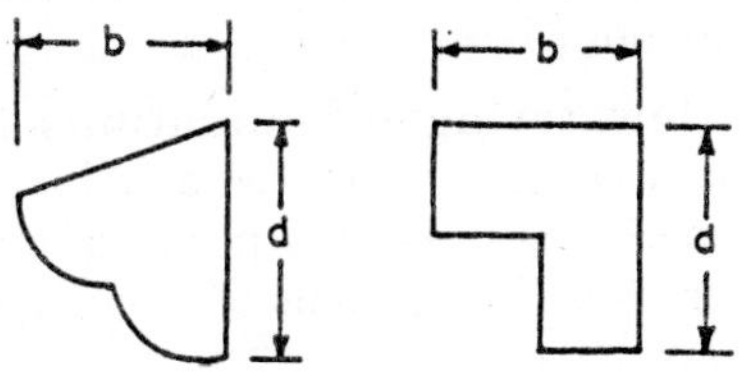

Fig. 3·1.

Note : For calculating masonry no deductions are made for the followings :

1. Opening upto 0·1 sq. m. in section

2. Bearing of beams, ports, rafters, purlins etc. upto ·05 sq. m. in section.

3. Bed plate, wall plate, bearing of chhajja etc. upto 10 cm depth.

4. Bearing of roof slabs are not deducted.

Quantity of masonry in walls can be calculated either by centre line method or by short and long wall method.

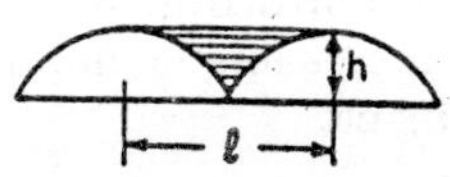

Fig. 3·2.

Sectional area of spendril of arches $= \frac{h+0}{2} \times l$

Measurements of fire places chimneys (IS)

Brick work is assumed as solid if air flues do not exceed 0·25 m^2 in sectional area. No deductions are made for flues and no extra is made for projections and cornices in flue. They are measured in cu.m. when the flues exceed 0·25 m^2 in sectional area deductions should be made for the cone opening and para-getting and coring of flues are taken separately in running metre stating the size of flue.

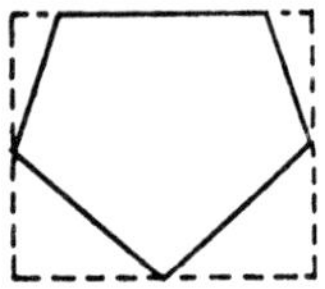

Fig. 3·3.

Estimate of a truss : Rivets bolts and nuts may be taken 5% by wt. of the truss or by actual wt. by calculating nos., multiplied by wt. of each.

Gusset plates : Can be taken as 10% of the wt. of truss by wt. or can be calculated individually taking the area as a rectangle leaving the porters as a waste.

Electric fittings (IS) : Electric wiring is measured in points such as light points, fan points, plug points etc. Brackets, lamps, holders, shades, sockets, outlets, fans, regulator, call bells, fuses, main switch boards etc. are measured in Nos. stating sizes and specifications etc.

If length of wiring is upto 3 m length is called a short point, 3 m to 6 m length is a medium, 6 to 10 m length is a long point and exceeding 10 m is a special point.

The length of wiring from main switch board to sub main board, and the insulated cables are measured in metres while the base cable in kg.

Wiring by different systems such as touch rubber sheated (TRS) on battons, vulcanized insulated rubber (VIR) in casing or capping or in conducit etc. should be fully described and taken separately. Wiring systems are further classified according to the size of cables used nos. of wires and size in the cable should be described under each classification.

Point wiring includes all necessary work in complete wiring such as switch ceiling rose wood and metal blocks, switch boards, battens, clips, nails, screwing joint and junction boxes, bulk head fittings and earth wiring etc.

Pole and struts for over-head lines should be taken in nos., describing the type, sectional size, diametric and the total length, cross arms, clamps, steel brackets etc. fixed to poles and struts should be fully described and taken in nos, in separate items. Earthing poles and service connections should be taken in nos. and should have full details regarding earth electrode, packing charcoal or earth wire etc.

Dewatering of foundations. If seepage water is entering in the foundation pit, its pumping is required. It is measured as a lumpsum item of small foundation area or by running hours of pumps specifying the horse power of pumps. In large trenches where the dewatering operating is long, such as in foundations of a barrage in a river bed, it can be measured on the basis of electric power consumed.

Pile foundations. Sheet pile : it is paid on the base of the wt. of the piles driven or in sq. meters specifying the thickness.

Wood piles. They are paid in metres stating the section of the pile. Shoes and caps are paid extra in nos. according to their wt.

Concrete piles. They are paid in m^3 or in running metre stating the section of the pile. Shoes and caps are paid extra according to their wt.

Well sinking. Well sinking is paid in length of depth (different rates for different depths and sizes increasing on depth) stating the size of the well. Rate includes all operations of dredging and loading etc.

Expansion joints are paid in running metric or in sq. m., if wider stating the thickness or other details of material etc.

Road metal thickness. Consolidated thickness is measured and not the spreaded (loose thickness)

Moulding and cornices. String course, cornices, corbels and drip courses etc., are measured in running metre stating details or shape etc.

Lightening conductors. Are measured in running metres stating width, gauge or thickness etc. including metal method of fixing socket attachments and rods are enumerated with full details.

Pavements and floors. They are measured in sq. metre stating thickness and type of floors and mortars. Surface finishing, rubbing and polishing is included in the item. Base concrete or sand filling is measured separate in m^3 until and otherwise stated.

Roof covering. Measured in m^2 and no allowance is given for overlaps however the size of the overlap is stated. Openings upto 0·4 m^2 are not deducted. The thickness and type of the roofing is also stated. It includes all cost of fasteners and nails etc. Ridges, caves and hips are measured in running metres stating size and lap etc.

Estimate for wood in a standing tree

Sapling for wood = $1/16\, c^2L$ cft (1) where c is the girth circumference

Sapling for fuel = $3/2 \times 1/16\, c^2L$ (2) at a height of 4′ from ground and L = length of bole

Note : In formula (1) use metric units, the volume so obtained is in m^3.

In formula (2) sapling for fuel = $20 \times 1/16\, c^2L$ quintal if metric units are used.

Quantity of fuel for burning :

Brick burning. For one lac bricks about 20 tonnes coal, 20-30 tonnes of fuel wood is required. Quantity varies with climate, type of soil, type of kiln, moisture in soil and air, type of fuel wood and height of water table.

Type of fuel. Wood or coal (wood is Temrind or Imli, Kikar or Babool) Mahua Khali is used as a flux.

Lime burning. 0·36 tonnes of coal for 1 cu m of lime.

Charcoal. After burning about 20 to 25% coal is released from wood.

Earth work classification

(*a*) **Excavation.** E.W. in different type of soils such as soft, hard, kankar mixed, soft rock or hard rock etc. should be classified separately and measured accordingly. The disposal of the earth should also be specified along with its mode of consolidation and dressing.

(*b*) **Filling.** E.W. in embarkments and road fillings is measured on profile basis. Original cross section of the ground are taken and proposed sections are marked on it by which the filled section is calculated. A suitable settlement allowance is given for consolidation which varies 10% to 5% depending on the type of soil. Mode of consolidation is also stated along with dressing of the finished surface.

Lead and lift. Initial rate for earth is usually taken for lead of 30 m and a lift of 1·5 m from centre of cutting to centre of filling. Extra rate is given for every lead of 15 m and lift of 0·5 m beyond and above that of initial.

Shoring, centring and shuttering. Shoring is done by planks in foundations to check the slip of earth by seepage etc. and shuttering is done for concrete etc. and is measured in sq. m.centring is support for shuttering.

Damp-proof course. It is measured in sq. m. stating the thickness and type of material used.

Wood work. Wood work in door *chaukhats* trusses, rafters and purlins is measured in m^3

stating type of wood including cost of all nails, screws and spikes etc. The section lost in rebolts and tenons etc. is not deducted.

Wood work in *door shutters* is measured in sq. m. Stating type of wood thickness and cost of all nails, screws and spikes etc. The cost of fittings like tower or slide bolts and hinges etc. is measured separately in nos. stating the size and nature of metal along with their cost of labour in fixing with cost of nails or screws etc.

Glass Panes are measured in nos. stating the size, thickness and type of glass.

Earth-work calculations. In order to find out the quantity of E.W. in a road, canal or dam project, we take x-sections oi the existing land across the proposed centre line. The proposal are marked with red lines on the x-sections. The areas of the cross-sections are computed as follows :

(1) **When the land transverse to the centre line is level plane.**

$$\text{Area of } x\text{-sec. } A = (b + nd)\, d \qquad ...(1)$$

where A = area of x-sec., b is the bed or formation width, d is the depth of earth on the centric line $n : 1$ is the slope of cutting.

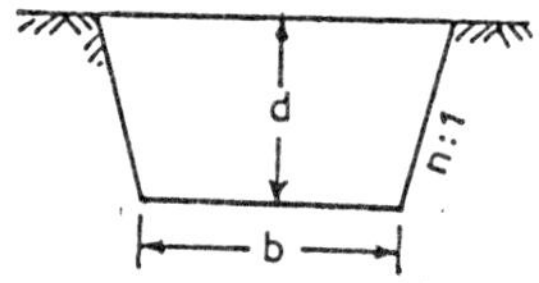

Fig. 3·4 (a)

(2) **When the land transverse to the centre line is sloping $r : 1$.**

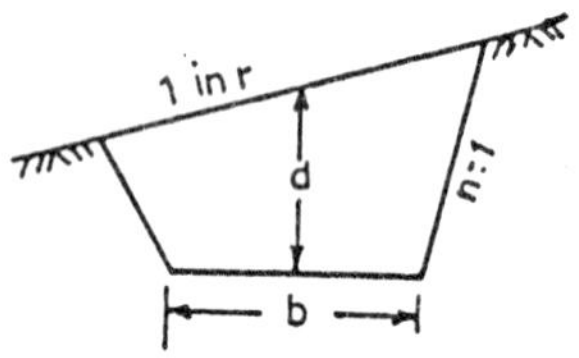

Fig. 3·4 (b).

$$A = \frac{n\left(b/2\right)^2 + r^2bd + r^2\,nd}{(r^2 - n^2)} \qquad ...(2)$$

(3) **When the land transverse to the centre line is sloping 1 in r and the earth involves cutting and filling both.**

$$A_1 = \frac{1}{2}\left\{\frac{(b/2 + rd)^2}{r_2 - n}\right\} \qquad ...(3A)$$

$$A_2 = \frac{1}{2}\left\{\frac{(b/2 - rd)^2}{r_2 - n}\right\} \qquad ...(3B)$$

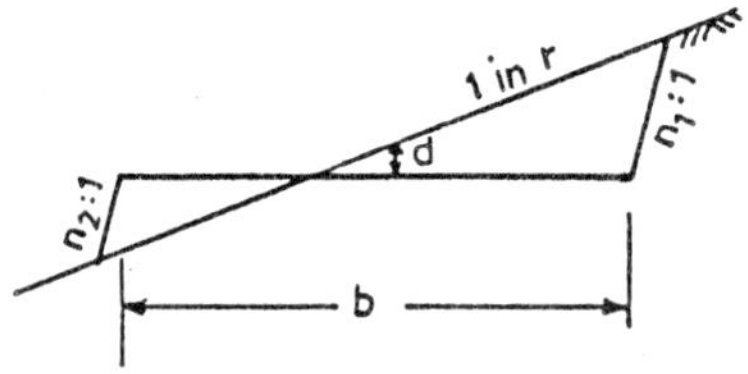

Fig. 3·4 (c).

A_1 = area of cutting (larger), $n_1 : 1$ is side slope of cutting,

A_2 = area is filling (smaller), $n_2 : 1$ is the slope of filling.

(4) **When the land transverse to the centre line, slopes in two slopes 1 in r_1 and 1 in r_2 and slope changes on centre line.**

$$A = b/2\, d(b_1 + b_2) + 1/4\,(d_1 + d_2) \qquad ...(4)$$

where b_1 and b_2 are the width of cutting on right and left side of centre line respectively. d_1 and d_2 are the heights of cutting on right and left side of the centre line

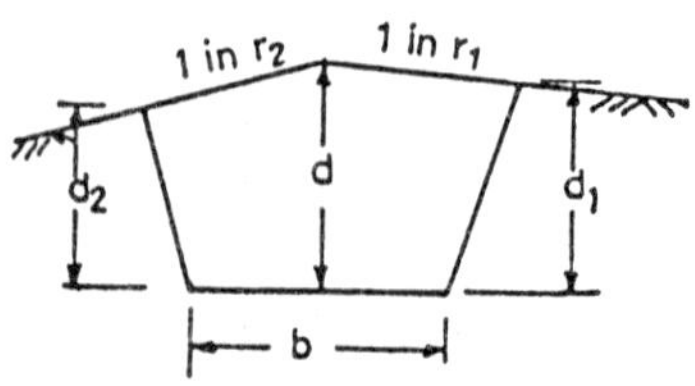

Fig. 3·4 (d).

$$b_1 = \frac{r_1\, n}{r_1 - n}\left(d + \frac{b}{2n}\right); \quad b_2 = \frac{r_2\, n}{r_2 + n}\left(d + \frac{b}{2n}\right) \qquad ...(4A)$$

$$d_1 = \left(d + \frac{b_1}{r_1}\right);\ d_2 = \left(d - \frac{b_2}{r_2}\right) \quad \text{...(4B)}$$

(5) **Multilevel section :**

(*A*) **By graphical method.** Plot the topography of the land transverse to the centre line by a levelling instrument or by stepping according to the accuracy desired. Plot it on graph paper and mark the proposed section on it. The area of cutting or filling can be obtained by counting square of the graph.

(*B*) **By coordinate method.** Field notes should be recorded as follows in the form of coordinates.

y-coordinate	$+D_2$	$+D_1$	$+d$	$+d_1$	$+d_2$	$+d_3$
x-coordinate	$-B_2$	$-B_1$	0	$+b_1$	$+b_2$	$+b_3$
Point	*H*	*G*	*F*	*E*	*D*	*C*
	left		Centre		Right	

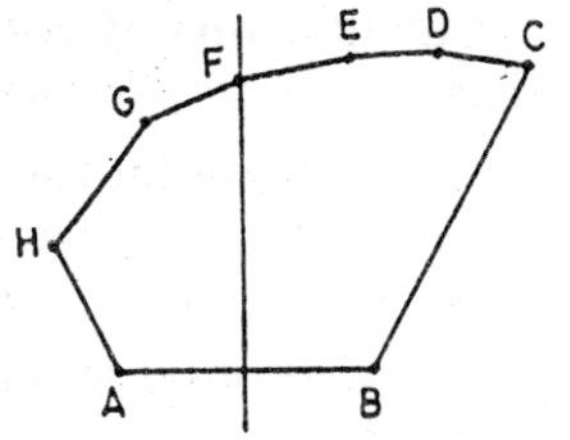

Fig. 3·5

y-coordinates above the formation level are shown as +ve while the coordinates below the formation level are shown –ve. The middle point of the formation width is taken as origin *x*-coordinates left of origin are shown –ve while right shown as +ve. Write the above in the determinant form starting from point *AHGFEDCB*

$$\pm\frac{0}{b/2} \pm\frac{D_2}{B_2} \pm\frac{D_1}{B_1} \pm\frac{d}{0} \pm\frac{d_1}{b_1} \pm\frac{d_2}{b_2} \pm\frac{d_3}{b_3} \pm\frac{0}{b/2}$$

$$0 \times d_1 + b_1 d_2 + b_2 d_3 + b_3 \times 0 + 0 \times D_1 + B_1 \times D_2 + B_2 \times 0 = \Sigma A \text{ (say)}$$

$$d \times b_1 + d_1 \times b_2 + d_2 \times b_3 + d_3 \times b/2 + d \times B_1 + D_1 B_2 + D_2 \times b/2 = \Sigma B \text{ (say)}$$

The area $A = 1/2\,(\Sigma A - \Sigma B)$

(*C*) **By geometrical method.** Divide the figure in the number of triangles and trapeziums. Calculate the area of each and add them all.

Note : Average natural slopes of earth in excavation :

Gravel 48°	Shingle loose 39°	Compact earth 50°
Dry sand 33°	Rubble 45°	Day wet 27°
Sand wet 26°	Vegetable earth 28°	Clay well drained 45°

Calculation for areas of cutting : (another method)

(1) When the ground is level

$$A = \left[b + (S_1 + S_2)\right]h/2$$

(2) When the slopes of the ground does not cut the formation level.

$$A = \frac{1}{2}\left\{b/2\,(h_1 + h_2) + h(S_1 + S_2)\right\}$$

(3) When the slope of the ground cuts the formation level, one part is in filling, while the other in cutting.

$$\text{Cutting} = BTR = \frac{1}{2}\left\{\left(\frac{b}{2n} + h\right)(S_1 + mh) - \frac{b}{2n}\left(b/2 + mh\right)\right\}$$

$$\text{Filling} = ATC = \frac{1}{2}\left\{\left(\frac{b}{2n} - h\right)(S_2 - mh) - \frac{b}{2n}\left(b/2 - mh\right)\right\}$$

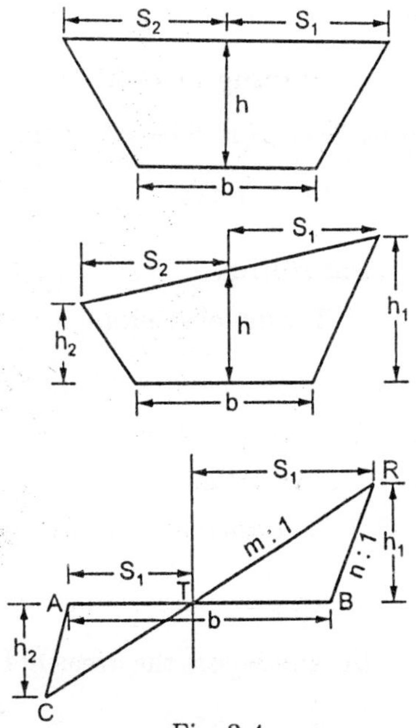

Fig. 3·4.

Width of earth work. It is required to calculate the land width :

(1) Level land with $w = b + nd$: denotations as above.

(2) Land having transverse slope : use formula 4A.

(3) In case of filling and cutting both (havving more cutting) land in transverse slope

$$b_1 = b/2 + \frac{rn_1}{r - n_1}\left(d + \frac{b}{2r}\right); \quad b_2 = b/2 + \frac{rn_2}{r - n_2}\left(\frac{b}{2r} - d\right)$$

Calculations of volume. The cross sectional areas as determined above will be used to determine the volumes by the following rules :

(1) **Trapezoidal formula (average end area rule).** If A_0, A_1, A_2, A_3 ... A_n are the cross sectional areas starting from zero chainage at an interval of a and let Q be the volume. Then $Q = a/2\ (A_0 + 2A_1 + 2A_2 + 2A_3 + \ldots A_n)$.

(2) **Prismoidal formula.** (For three sections) $Q = a/3\ (A_0 + 4A_1 + A_2)$.

$Q = a/3(A_0 + 4A_1 + 2A_2 + 4A_3 + 2A_4 + \ldots A_n)$

or $Q = a/6(A_1 + A_2 + 4A_m)$ (for two sections A_1 and A_2), A_m = mean area of sec. A_1 and A_2.

It is seen that in the prismoidal formula no. of cross sections should be odd. If these are even then leave the last x-section and then volume of the remaining sections should be calculated b the prismoidal formula and the volume of the last section should be calculated separately and should be added. For calculating the area of the last section average of the dimensions (not of the area) of the two end sections should be taken as its area should be calculated. Now for the last section, we have three sections (last, last but one and the middle average sections) by which the volume of the last sections can be calculated.

If in the end of the length of interval is less than the common interval, iot should be calculated separately either by trapezoidal formula or by prismoidal formula as obtained above.

Prismoidal correction. When the prisoidal formula is used for calculating volume a correction is applied which is as follows :

(*a*) **Level section.** $P_C = a/3\ (d - d')^2$ where P_C is prismoidal corrections and d and d' are the depth of cutting in two respective sections.

(*b*) **Sloping ground.** $P_C = \frac{a}{6S}(b_1 - b_1')(b_2 - b_2')$ where b_1 and b_2 are width of section at formation level, S is slope of cutting.

(*c*) **For cutting.** $P_C = \frac{a}{12S}(b_1 - b_1')\{(b/2 + rd) - (b/2 - r'd')\}$

For filling. $P_C = \frac{a}{12S}(b_2 - b_2')\{(b/2 - rd) - (b/2 - r'd')\}$

(*d*) **Transverse slope** has two grades 1 in r_1 and 1 in r_2

$$P_C = \frac{a}{12}(d - d')\{(b_1 + d') - (b_1' - b_2')\}$$

(Dash over a notation means the dimension of the next successive sections.)

Capacity of reservoir

(1) **By contour interval method**

(*a*) Trapezoidal formula $Q = \sum\left\{\frac{a}{2}(A_1 + A_2)\right\}$

(A_1 and A_2 are the areas of two consecutive contours)

(*b*) Prismoidal formula $Q = \sum\left\{\frac{a}{6}(A_1 + 4A_m + A_2)\right\}$

where A_m is the middle area of the two successive contours

$$Q = \sum \frac{a}{3}(A_1 + 4A_2 + A_3) \quad \text{(For three sections)}$$

(2) **By cross-section method.** x-sections are taken at regular interval in the reservoir area and the full reservoir level is marked over them. Calculate the areas of the x-sections (see area of plane figures) and calculate the capacity either by prismoidal or by trapezoidal method.

(3) **By Planimeter.** The areas of cross sections or of contours can be found by the use of plantimeter.

Note : The prismoidal correction is so small that practically it need not to apply, however in important cases can be applied as above.

3·4. Costing of Works

Provisional Sum. It is the amount provided in an estimate of work which is proposed to be done by a specialist firm and whose details are not known at the time of preparing estimate, like installation of a batching or a crushing plant for which full in formation and details may not be known at the time of preparing estimate and entering into contract, a reasonable amount is provided in the estimate as a provisional sum. The amount paid to the contractor will not necessarily be the exact amount of provisional sum. Any other item of work such as actual quantity of earth to be dug, a lump-sum provisions are made. Such lump-sum provisions are known as provisional sum.

In the same way for certain item of works in which detailed quantities can not be worked out at the time of preparing estimates a **provisional quantity** is provided which are known as Provisional qualities.

Prime Cost. It is the actual cost of articles at shop and refers to the supply of articles only and not to the execution of works. At the time of preparing estimates it is not possible to specify the actual size and type to be used such as sanitary fittings or water supply fittings etc. on actual execution of the work which may be according to the choice of the engineer incharge or the house owner. In such cases a reasonable amount is kept in the estimate as prime cost and the same is provided in the bill of quantities of the contract.

Capital cost. It is the total cost of a work including all expenditure incurred from beginning to the completion of construction. Capital cost includes the cost of preliminary works, miscellaneous items supervision charges and cost of land etc. In major projects it includes total cost of the whole project including buildings and external services etc.

External Services. Digging, filling of land, approach roads, sewerage works, water supply works such as storage tanks, pumps service pipes etc. It costs about 10 to 20% of the cost of work.

Scrap Value. It is the value at the expiry of the life of a building or a work obtained from its dismantled material such as bricks, steel or timber etc. after selling in the market. The cost incurred in labour for distmantling is deduced from the cost so obtained from the scrap. In case of a machine the cost obtained by selling the parts or the scrap metal in the market after deducting the dismantling charges of the machine is known as the scrap value. If the dismantling charges are more than the cost of scrap in market the scrap value is negative.

Salvage value. When the utility period of a building is expired or the working of a machine becomes uneconomical, it is sold without dismantling and the cost so obtained is the salvage value of the building or of the machine.

Market Value. The market value of a property is an amount which can be obtained at any particular time from the open market by sale. The market value differs from time to time according to demand and supply and the means of transportation as available with cost of materials etc.

Book Value. Book value is the cost of a work or machine as shown in the account book after deducting the necessary depreciations. The book value of a property at a particular year is the original cost minus the amount of depreciations upto the previous year. After expiry of the life of the building the book value decreases only upto equal the scrap value or the book value remains equal to the scrap value at the end of the utility period.

Raleable Value. Raleable value is the net annual letting value of the property which is obtained after deducting the amount of yearly repairs from the gross income. Municipal and other taxes are charged at a certain percentage on the raleable value of the property.

Obsolescene. When the design of a building is out of fashion or the design of a machine is old even if the building is strong still or the machine is in working order, its value in the market goes down due to its being obsolate. It is known as obsolescene.

Capitalized value. It is the amount of property whose annual interest at the highest prevailing rate of interest will be equal to the net income from the property. To find out the capitalized value of a property it is required to know the net income of the property and the highest prevailing rate of interest.

Capitalized value = Net annual income × Year's purchase

Note. The income from the property is taken as the income of the rent.

Years purchase. It is defined as the capital sum required to be invested in order to receive an annuity of Rs. 100 at certain rate of interest. For 4% interest per annum, to get Rs. 4·00 it is required to deposit Rs. 100·00 in a bank. To get Rs. 1·00 per year it is required to deposit 100/4 = Rs. 25·00.

Thus years purchase = 100/rate of interest = $1/l$ (where l is the rate of interest in decimals)

$= \dfrac{1}{l+S}$ (where S = Sinking fund to replace Re. 1·00 at the end of the given period.)

Sinking Fund. The fund which is gradually accumulated by way of periodic or annual deposite in compound interest for the replacement of the building or structure at the end of its useful life is known as sinking of fund. The sinking fund may be created by taking a sinking fund policy with an insurance company. The calculation of sinking fund depends on the life of the building and scrap value (deducted) of the building for the cost of old materials. The cost of land is not taken into account in calculating sinking fund as land remains intact. Sinking fund may also be required for payment of loan known as **Annuity Payment.** The amount of annual instalment of the sinking fund may be found out by the formula $I = \dfrac{Si}{(1+i)^n - 1}$ where S = total amount of sinking fund to be accumulated, n = no. of years required to accumulate the sinking fund, i = rate of interest in decimal (*i.e.* for 5% = 0·05) and I = annual instalment.

Example. An old building purchased at Rs. 50,000·00, scrap value of the cost is 10% of the purchase value, rate of interest is 5%, life of building is 20 years. Cost of land is not included in cost 50,000. Then $n = 20$, $i = 0{\cdot}5$, $S = 50{,}000 \times \dfrac{9}{100} = 45{,}000$ from which I can be calculated by the formula given above.

Depreciation. It is gradual decrease of the usefulness of a property. Its decrease in value may be taken as annual. The depreciation is low at beginning and gradually increases during later years. The various methods of calculating depreciation are as follows :

(1) **Straight line method.** A fixed amount of the original cost is deducted every year, so that at the end of the utility period only the scrap value is left.

$D = \dfrac{C-S}{n}$ where D = annual depreciation, C = original cost, S = scrap value, n = useful life in years.

Book value = C – N.D. (after n years).

(2) **Constant percentage method, Declining balance method.** It is assumed that the building is depreciating by a constant percentage of its value at the beginning of every year

$$D = 1 - \left(\frac{S}{C}\right)^{1/n}$$ where D, S, C and n are as above (The formula is not rated for $S = 0$).

(3) **Sinking fund method.** The depreciations of a property is assumed to be equal to the annual sinking fund plus the interest on the fund for the year, which is supposed to be inverted on interest bearing investment. If A is annual sinking fund and b, c, d etc. represent interest on the sinking fund for subsequent years and c = total original cost then

At the end of year	*Depreciation*	*Total depreciation*	*Book value*
1st year	A	A	$c - A$
2nd year	$A + b$	$2A + b$	$c - (2A + b)$
3rd year	$A + c$	$3A + b + c$	$c - (3A + b + c)$
4th year	$A + d$	$4A + b + c + d$	$c - (4A + b + c + d)$

So on ...

(4) **By the formula**

$$D = P\left(\frac{100 - rd}{100}\right)^n$$ where D = Depreciation value, P = Present market value rd = rate of depreciation which can be taken as follows.

1 for 100 yr. life 1·3 for 75 yr. life, 2 for 50 yr. life, 4 for 25 yr. life.

The present value can be calculated as actual calculations adding cost of sanitary fittings, electric charges and cost of land etc.

(5) **Quantity survey method.** By actual assessment of depreciations on the basis of wear, tear and obsolescence etc. on logical grounds.

Valuation of works. It is calculated on the following basis.

(1) **On Rental Value.** The cost is calculated on the basis of the rent earned after deducting all out going on the gross rent, the capitalized value can be calculated. The rent may be as taken as prevailed in the area or from enquiries.

Outgoings. (1) **Taxes.** Municipal tax Property tax, Wealth tax. The taxes are fixed on the rental value of the property.

(2) **Repairs.** Annual repairs taken as 10 to 15% of the gross rent, 1 to 1½ months rent for a year or 1 to 1·5% of the total cost of the construction.

(3) **Management and collection charges.** Expenditure incurred for sweeper, guard, clerks or accountant etc. It may be taken as 5 to 10% of the gross rent. For small buildings it can be neglected.

(4) **Sinking fund.** A certain amount of gross rent is set aside annually as sinking fund to cope with the cost of building when the life is over.

(5) **Loss of rent.** An allowance for unoccupied portion is given in the gross rent.

(6) **Miscellaneous.** It may include electric or water charges etc.

(2) **Cost of similar buildings in the area** which can be assessed on the recent sale deeds in the locality. In such cases the capitalized value of the property is fixed by direct comparison with capitalized value of similar property in the locality.

(3) **Based on profile.** This method is suitable for commercial building such as hotels and cinemas etc. The capitalized value is based on net profit obtained by deducting out groups from gross profits. The net profit is multiplied by year's purchase (Y.P.) to get the capitalized value. In such cases valuation may be higher than the cost of construction.

(4) **Based on cost.** The actual cost incurred in constructing the building or in possessing the property is taken and the necessary depreciation is deducted to determine the value of property. The points of obsolescence is also considered.

(5) **Based on development.** This method is applied for the properties which are either developed or are in developing stage, such as planning a colony in an area or for a building which is to be modified or renovated by making additions and alternations. The valuation of the property may be worked out from the anticipated future net income multiplied by the year's purchase (Y.P.) which will give the capitalized anticipated value of the property. The total expenditure incurred in renovations plus the original cost should be compared with anticipated capitalized value and should be decided whether the investment in renovation is justified or not.

(6) **Based on depreciation.** The depreciation cost of the building can be found out by the method described under depreciation. The present value of electric, sanitary and water supply is added to the depreciated value to arrive at the total valuation of the property.

The average life of the works may be taken as under :

Masonry	(1)	Brick or stone work in cement or line	100 years
		Brick or stone work in mud	75 years
		Sun dried brick work	50 years
	(2)	Flooring IPS or Mosaic	50 years
		Brick floor	40 years
	(3)	Roofind RCC or RB	75 years
		Wood roofs	50 years
		Country wood	15 years
		Tiled roofs	25 years
		G.I. Sheet roofing	50 years
	(4)	Doors and windows sal and teak	40 years
		Country wood	25 years

(7) **Valuation Tables.** Valuation tables are used as a ready reckoner to save time and labour. Miram's valuation tables are generally used.

(8) **Plinth area based.** Cost calculated as a cost per unit area of plinth in the vicinity.

(9) **Based on demand in the area.**

Rent Fixation. It is done on the basis of certain percentage of annual interest on the capital cost and all possible annual expenditure as outgoings., The capital cost includes the cost of construction, cost of electric water supply and sanitary fittings. The cost of land and additions and alterations if any is also added in the capital cost. The capital cost divided by the year's purchase gives the net income. If capital cost is not known, it can be worked out by the methods of valuations as already dealt before. The owner expects 2% extra higher rate than the prevalant to cover his risk in investments. All possible expenditure as outgoings is added to this net income, get the gross annual income.

Gross rent or income = net rent or income + outgoings.

The rent worked out per annum is known as the standard rent. The actual rent may be higher or lower to this depending on the site situations. The rate of interest varies from 6 to 8%.

Rates of works at the cost of the materials of the year 1990

1. **Plinth area rates of the buildings**

(*a*) Residential buildings 1st class	1500/- m^2
(*b*) Residential buildings 2nd class	1300/- m^2
(*c*) Residential buildings 3rd class	1100/- m^2
Annual repairs	1% of the cost

(2) **Roads** (*a*) New, formations width 3·7 m with overburnt bricks metalling and two coats of bitumen painting.

Carpetting and earthwork etc.	@ Rs. 8 lacs per km.
(*b*) Metalling 3·7 m wide road with stone ballast ...	@ Rs. 1,20,000 per km
(*c*) Metalling 3·7 m wide road with kankar ballast	@ Rs. 65,000 per km
(*d*) One layer of over burnt soiling	2 Rs. 60,000 per km
(*e*) Cost of bitumen painting 1st coat...	@ Rs. 35,000 per km
2nd coat	@ Rs. 21,000 per km
(*f*) Cement concrete roads 3·7 m wide	@ Rs. 2,70,000 per km.
(3) **Road Culverts.** Culvert on village road	@ Rs. 17,000 per m of span
District road bridges	@ Rs. 50,000 per m of span
Provincial road bridges and National bridges	@ Rs. 75,000 per m of span
(4) Cost of septic tank for 5 users Rs. 1500	
Cost of overhead tank of RCC 12·5 m high	@ Rs. 3/- per lit. of capacity
Cost of tube wells 75 mm G.I. pipe, 90 m deep	Rs. 25,000

Cost of materials in Jan. 90 in Northern India

Bricks :	1st class	Rs. 700 per thousand at kiln.
	2nd class	Rs. 600 per thousand at kiln
	3rd class	Rs. 400 per thousand at kiln
Brick rora		Rs. 150 per cu.m.
Brick ballast		Rs. 175 per cu.m.
Stone ballast	40 mm	Rs. 200 per cu.m.
	20 mm	Rs. 225 per cu.m.
	12 mm	Rs. 250 per cu.m.
Cement 50 kg bag		Rs. 80 per bag
Coarse sand, Badarpur or chambal etc.		Rs. 150 per cu.m.
Local Sand		Rs. 60 per cu.m.
White Lime		Rs. 175 per quintal
Kankar Lime		Rs. 150 per quintal
Surkhi		Rs. 10 cu. ft.
Wood :	Shisham	Rs. 16000 per m^3
	Sal	Rs. 16,000 per m^3
	Teak	Rs. 20,000 per m^3

	Mango	Rs. 3000 per m^3
	Local	Rs. 1500 per m^3
	Cheer	Rs. 8000 per m^3
	Kail	Rs. 10,000 per m^3
	Deodar	Rs. 15,000 per m^3
Labour :	Beldar	@ Rs. 60/- per day
	Coolie	@ Rs. 55/- per day
	Mason	@ Rs. 100/- per day
	Carpenter	@ Rs. 100/- per day
	Joinier	@ Rs. 110/- per day
	Electric man	@ Rs. 90/- per day
	Blocksmith	@ Rs. 90/- per day
	Welder	@ Rs. 90/- per day
	Fitter	@ Rs. 90/- per day
	Plumber	@ Rs. 90/- per day
	Tiler	@ Rs. 90/- per day
	Painter	@ Rs. 90/- per day
	Bar bender	@ Rs. 90/- per day
	Bhisti	@ Rs. 80/- per day

Note : The present costs can be calculated according to the rise in the price index.

Rough estimate for the cost of buildings

Name of items	*Percentage of total cost*
1. Labour	30-35%
2. Cost of material	65-70%
3. Foundation upto plinth	15-20%
4. Super structure	80-85%
5. 1st floor	70-85% of ground floor
6. (*a*) Direct on overall	85%
(*b*) Overhead due to establishment	15%
7. Sanitations and electrification	
(*a*) Sanitation and water supply	7-9%
(*b*) Electric installation without fans	7%
(*c*) Electric fans	5%
8. Cost of different parts	
(*a*) Earth work	1/2 to 1%
(*b*) Foundation conc.	4 to 6%
(*c*) Damp proof course	0·1%
(*d*) Brick work	3·4%

Table contd...

Table contd...

Name of items	*Percentage of total cost*
(*e*) Roofing	20%
(*f*) Doors and windows	16%
(*g*) Painting and plastering	10%
(*h*) White, colour washing and painting etc.	2%
(*i*) Miscellaneous	4%
(9) Cost of material and labour	
(*a*) Bricks	25%
(*b*) Cement	10%
(*c*) Steel	10%
(*d*) Timber	15%
(*e*) Lime	5%
(*f*) Labour	30%
(*g*) Miscellaneous	5%
(10) Material for single storey on plinth area basis	
(*a*) Bricks	500 Nos. per m^2 of plinth area
(*b*) Cement	1·5 bag per m^2 of plinth area
(*c*) Steel	12 kg per m^2 of plinth area
(*d*) Coal for burning bricks	150 kg per m^2 of plinth area
(11) Annual repair and maintenance	1 to 1½% of capital cost.

3·5. Area Definition in Building Work (IS : 3861)

Plinth area or covered area. It is the area covered at any storey taken separately of a building. It covers the external dimensions of building any offset at the plinth line. It includes the followings :

(1) Areas of rooms, verandah including wall thickness.

(2) Sanitary provision such as baths and lavatory etc. (Subject to max. of 2 m^2 in external area)

(3) Air conditioning ducts and lifts etc.

(4) Area of Barasati or mumti at terrace level.

(5) Area of porches which are supported on columns.

It does not include the followings :

(1) Internal sanitary fittings more than 2 m^2 in area.

(2) Cantilevered balconies (unsupported)

(3) Area of lift, towers domes projecting above the terrace level and which do not make a part of the storey.

(4) Sun shades, chhajjas or box louvers projecting out.

Floor area. It is the inside floor area of a building exclusing thickness of walls. It includes area of rooms, verendahs, corridors, staircase, entrance, latrins, baths, kitchens and stores etc. (sills of openings are not included). It may be taken as plinth area minus area of walls. The following should be deducted from the floor area.

(*a*) Fire place projecting beyond the face of the wall (*b*) oven projecting from wall face in kitchens.

Circulation area. It is area of verandahs, balcony, entrance, Porch corridors, staircase and lift shafts etc. This area is used only for air movement in the buildings.

(*a*) **Horizontal circulation area.** It is the area used for horizontal movement such as verandah, corridor and gallery etc.

(*b*) **Vertical circulation area.** It is the area used for vertical movements such as staircases and lifts etc.

Carpet area. It is the area used for dwelling purposes excluding sanitary area such as toilet and bath etc. verandahs, corridors, gallery, porches, staircase, lift shafts, sheds (covered) and garrage etc. (Floor area – circulation area).

Note : (1) Above areas should be calculated for each storey separately.

(2) **Single line plan of a building.** This plan is shown by a single line mentioning inner clear dimensions of the spaces in the building.

Floor area ratio (F.A.R.). The quotient obtained by dividing the total covered area (plinth area) on all floors by the area of the plot.

$$\text{F.A.R.} = \frac{\text{Total covered area of all floors}}{\text{plot area}}$$

Table 3.4. Average Weight of Materials (kg/m^3 or other wise stated if gives in m^2). Also Refer Appendices in Chapter (8C)

Name of material	*Wt. inkg / m^3 (or m^2)*	*Wt. in lbs / ft^3 (or ft^2)*
1	*2*	*3*
Building materials		
Stone ballast 15 mm	1600-1920	100-120
Stone ballast 40 mm	1440	90
Bricks common	1600-1920	100-120
Brick refractory	1760.2000	110-125
Brick ballast	1200	75
Brick surkhi	1010	63
Sand stone	2242·8	140
Lime stone	2643·3	165
Granite stone	2443·3	165
Slate	2883·6	180
Earth compacted	2200	140
Sand or earth	1441·8-1762·2	90-110
Rubbish	1400	88
Puddle clay	2162·7	135
Asphalt	1120	70
Bitumen	849·1	5·3
Cement normal	1440	90
Cement loose	1280	80
Cement in bags	1344	84
Cement in mortar	2080	130
Glass sheets	2600	162
Timber	640-960	40-60
Fire wood choped	1400	87

Table contd...

Table contd...

Name of material	*Wt. inkg / m^3 (or m^2)*	*Wt. in lbs / ft^3 (or ft^2)*
1	2	3
Wire wood choped	400	25
Ash	640	40
Coke	520	32
Coal solid	1300	810
Coal crushed	850	53
Charcoal	300	18
Wheat	830	52
Straw	290	17
Paper in rolls	70044	
Slag wool	270	17
Gravel loose	1600	100
Gravel rammed	1920	120
Water	1000	62·5
Snow fallen	85	5·1
Compact	240-320	15-20
RCC 1% steel	2307	140
2% steel	2371	148
5% steel	2515·1	157
10% steel	2723·4	170
Plane conc. in stone Bal	2240	143
Plane conc. in Bk. Bal	1920	121
Breeze conc.	1120-1180	71-74
Lime concrete	1920	120
Saw dust conc.	1120	70
Aerated conc.	260	16·5
Reinforced brick work	2002·5	125
Masonry-Granite ashlar	6400	403
Granite RR	2400	151·2
Dry RR	2080	131·0
Lime stone ashlar	2560	161·0
Sand stone masonry	2240	143
Brick-work in cement	1920	120
Brick-work in lime	1760	111
Brick-work in mud	1500	95
Mortar : Lime	1760	111

Table contd...

Table contd...

Name of material		*Wt. inkg / m^3 (or m^2)*	*Wt. in lbs / ft^3 (or ft^2)*
1		2	3
	Cement	2080	131
	Plaster of Paris	1200	75
Floors :	25 mm thick Terrozo	60 kg/m^2	12 lb/ft^2
	20 mm wood hard in mastic	22 kg/m^2	44 lb/ft^2
Roofing :	Thatah in bottons	35/m^2	7/ft^2
	Country tiles with battons (single layer)	70/m^2	14/ft^2
	Country tiles with battons (double layer)	120/m^2	24/ft^2
	Allahabad tiles with battons single layer	85/m^2	17/ft^2
	double layer	160/m^2	32/ft^2
A.C. sheet roofs		49/m^2	95/ft^2
G.C.I sheet roofs		20/m^2	6/ft^2
Jack arch roofs with 85 mm conc. fill over crown and 85 mm mud insulation		730/m^2	146/ft^2
Timber truss and purlins		12/m^2	2·6/ft^2
5 mm thick bitumen macadem roof		11/m^2	2·5/ft^2
Metals :	Aluminium (cast)	2650	165
	Wrought iron	2700	178
	Copper	8800	550
	Steel	7850	490
	Lead (cast)	11,340	710
Al-Copper allows-(Al 10% cast + Cu 90%)		7690	480
	(Al 3% + Cu 97%)	8680	542
Metal sheets-	Al. 1 mm thick	2·8 kg/m^2	0.56 lbs/ft^2
	Copper 1 mm thick	8·69 kg/m^2	1·74 lbs/ft^2
	Lead 1 mm thick	11·0 kg/m^2	2·2 lbs/ft^2
	Steel 1 mm thick	7·9 kg/m^2	1·58 lbs/ft^2
Glass	1·3 mm thick	3·4 kg/m^2	0·68 lbs/ft^2
	2·0 mm thick	5·0 kg/km^2	1·0 lbs/ft^2
	2·6 mm thick	6·6 kg/m^2	1·32 lbs/ft^2
	3·2 mm thick	8·0 kg/m^2	1·6 lbs/ft^2
	4·0 mm thick	10·0 kg/m^2	2·0 lbs/ft^2
	6·4 mm thick	17·0 kg/m^2	3·4 lbs/ft^2

Weight of Timber and their bending stress

Timber	*Bending stress*		*Weight*	
Cheer	1874 kg/m^2	1190 lb/ft^2	576·7 kg/m^3	36 lb/ft^3
Deodar	2274 kg/m^2	1450 lb/ft^2	560·7 kg/m^3	35 lb/ft^3
Sal	3780 kg/m^2	2400 lb/ft^2	817·0 kg/m^3	51 lb/ft^3
Siso	3370 kg/m^2	2140 lb/ft^2	785·0 kg/m^3	49 lb/ft^3
Teak	3055 kg/m^2	1940 lb/ft^2	624·0 kg/m^3	39 lb/ft^3

Weight of 16 B.G. gauge (1·588 mm) thick sheets of different metals in kg/m^2

Cast iron	*W.I.*	*Steel*	*Brass*	*Copper*	*Lead*	*Zinc*	*Aluminium*
11·74	12·20	12·55	13·37	13·08	18·10	11·42	4·26

Steel barbed wires

S. No.	*Length per hundred kg*			*Nominal dia. of wire mm*		*Nominal distance between two barbs mm*
	Normal m	*Min. m*	*Max. m*	*Line wire*	*Point wire*	
1	1000	936	1066	2·50	2·24	75
2	1134	1066	1200	2·50	2·24	150
3	1576	1440	1668	2·24	2·24	75
4	1890	1778	2000	2·24	2·24	150

App. quantity of steel in RCC

Industrial buildings 70 kg/m^3

Residential buildings 50 kg/m^3

Moderate traffic bridges 70 kg/m^3

Medium traffic bridges 80 kg/m^3

Heavy traffic bridges 100 kg/m^3

Weight of steel structures

1. Average wt. of structure = wt. of sections + 10% for rivet, bolts and cleats etc. 10% wastage in cutting take extra for field work.
2. Average wt. of beam = wt. of sections and cleats + 2·5% for rivets
3. Average wt. of stanchion = wt. of sections and cleats + 5% for rivets
4. Average wt. of plate girder = wt. of sections and cleats + 10% for rivets
5. Average wt of steel stair (·91 m wide industrial) = wt. of sections and cleats + 167 kg/r.m.

Method of finding the wt. of metals (1 cft of steel = 490 lbs)

Wt. of metal in lbs/yard = area in sq. inches × 10

Example 1. Wt. of 1^2 dia round bar/yd.

area = ·7854 sq. inch ; wt./yard = 7·854 (·7854 × 10)

Example 2. Wt. of 7′ 40″ × 4″ × ½″

area = (4 + 4)½ – $(½)^2$ = 3·75 sq. inches ; wt./yd = 3·75 × 10 = 37·5 lb/yard.

Wt. of steel strips : Width in mm × thickness in mm = 127 kg per m.

Wt. of sheet lead and its thickness

Wt./ft.² lbs	*Decimal thickness in inch*	*Fraction of in.*	*Recommended position*
3	0·051	1/20	Soakers
4	0·068	1/10	Cover fastenings, over doors and windows, cavity walls
5	0·085	1/13	fastenings and aprons
6	0·101	1/10	ridges, hipps etc. small gutters
7	0·118	1/9	roofs, flats, large gutters,
8	0·135	1/8	cisterns and tanks.
9	0·152	1/7	
10	1·00	1	

Note : 1 cft. of lead weights 710 lbs.

Wt. of lead pipes

Bore	*Wt. of pipe in lbs/yd. run*											
	1/2"		*3/4"*		*1"*		*1¼"*		*1½"*		*2"*	
	From	*To*	*From*	*To*	*From*	*To*	*From*	*To*	*From*	*To*	*From*	*To*
Light	3	5	5	8	7	11	9	14	14	18	16	24
Medium	4½	7	7	12	10½	10	14	21	16	27	18	33
Heavy	6	9	9	16	12	21	16	28	18	36	24	48

Note : Light pipes are used for waste, overflows and ventilating pipes *i.e.* pipes with open ends.

Medium pipes are used for services from cisterns

Heavy pipes are used for main service from the Authority Supply.

½" to 1" pipes are supsplsied in 15′ length and coils 20 yd.

1¼" to 2" pipes are supplied in 12′ length and coils of 12 yd.

Lead, Waste, soil and ventilation pipes (wt. per 10 ft. length)

Internal dia.	*6 lb lead or 0·101 in thick*	*7 lb lead or 0·118 in thick*	*8 lb lead or 0·0135 in thick*
2½"	41 lb	48 lb	55 lb
3"	49	57	66
3½"	57	67	76
4"	65	76	87
4½"	73	85	97
5"	80	94	107
6"	94	112	128

Wt. of sheet metals per sq. ft.

Gauge No./ Thickness (in)	Brass lb	Copper lb	Gauge No./ Thickness (in)	Brass lb	Copper lb	Gauge No./ Thickness (in)	Brass lb	Copper lb
6/·192	8·93	9·40	10/·128	6·18	6·50	18/·048	2·04	2·15
7/·176	8·25	8·70	12/·104	4·81	5·08	20/·036	1·69	1·78
8/·160	7·54	7·90	14/·080	3·43	3·60	22/·028	1·37	1·45
9/·144	6·86	7·20	16/·064	2·75	2·90	24/·022	1·10	1·16

Wt. of heavy copper pipes for screwing

Bore in inch	*Thickness of metal in inch*					
	1/16" lb/ft	1/8" lb/ft	1/16" lb/ft	1/4" lb/ft	5/16" lb/ft	3/8" lb/ft
1/2	0·43	0·95	1·56	2·27	3·08	3·97
3/4	0·62	1·32	2·13	3·03	4·02	5·11
1	0·80	1·70	2·70	3·78	4·97	6·24
1¼	0·99	2·08	3·26	4·54	5·91	7·38
1½	1·18	2·46	3·83	5·30	6·86	8·51
2	1·56	3·22	4·97	6·81	8·75	10·78
2½	1·94	3·98	6·10	8·33	10·54	10·78
3	2·32	4·73	7·24	9·74	13·59	15·33

Zinc guages, wt. per ft. supper

E.Z. guage	*Wt. in lb-oz*	*V.M. gauge*	*Wt-lb-oz*
6	0-6 9/10	6	0-6 2/3
7	0-7 3/4	7	0-7 3/4
8	0-9	8	0-8 9/10
9	0-10 1/4	9	0-10 1/3
10	0-11 1/3	10	0-11 2/5
11	0-13 1/2	11	0-13 2/3
12	0-15 1/8	12	0-15 1/8
13	1-3/4	13	1-9/10
14	1-2 1/2	14	1-2 3/4
15	1-5 3/4	15	1-5 3/4
16	1-9	16	1-8 3/4
17	1-13	17	1-11 2/3
18	1-15	18	1-14 2/5

Property of corrugated Asbestos sheets (IS : 277) (A.C. Sheets)

Type	*Thickness in mm*	*Pitch of corrugation mm*	*Depth of corrugation mm*	*Overall width mm*	*Effective width mm*	*Remarks*
Corrugated	6	146	48	1050	1010	Available lengths
	7	146	48	1050	1010	1·5, 7·5, 2·0, 2·25
Semi corrugated	6	338	45	1100	1014	2·5, 2·75 and 3·0 m
	7	338	45	1100	1014	

Thickness of plywood boards

No. of Ply	*Thickness available in mm*
3	3 4 5 6
5	5 6 8 9
7	9 16 16
9	13 19 19
11	19 25 25
above 11	According to requirement.

Wt. of galvanised corrugated iron sheets/m² (IS : 277)

B.S. (gauges) *Thickness (mm)*	*16* *1·6*	*18* *1·25*	*20* *1·00*	*22* *0·80*	*24* *0·63*	*26* *0·50*	*28* *0·40*
Class I	13·31	10·56	8·60	7·02	5·70	4·65	3·20
Class II	13·16	10·41	8·45	6·88	5·55	4·50	3·75
Class III	13·01	10·26	8·30	6·72	5·40	4·35	3·60
Class IV	12·94	10·19	8·22	6·66	5·32	4·27	3·52

Class I. Extra heavy coating of zinc (spelter) Nominal 750 gm/m² both sides inclusive

Class II. Heavy coating of zinc nominal 600 gm/m² both sides inclusing

Class III. Medium coating of zinc nominal 450 gm/m² both sides inclusive.

Class IV. Light coating of zinc nominal 375 gm/m² both sides inclusive.

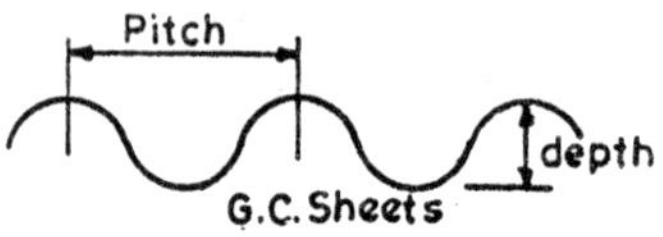

Fig. 3·7.

Note : 1. The depth of corrugation = 18 mm and pitch = 75 mm.

2. The corrugations are 8 to 10 nos. per sheet.

3. Available widths are 90 cm and 75 cm and length 1·8 m, 2·2 m, 2·5 m, 2·8 m and 3·2 m.

4. Area of sheet as taken above is the area of before corrugations in plane.

5. 750 mm wide sheet reduces to 660 mm width while 900 mm wide sheet reduces to 800 mm on corrugation.

Wt. of standard size of of black sheets per m²

B.G. gauges	28	26	24	22	21	20	19	18	17	16
Thickness (mm)	0·40	0·50	0·63	0·80	0·90	1·00	1·12	1·25	1·40	1·60
Wt. kg/m²	3·15	3·90	4·95	6·30	7·05	7·85	8·80	4·80	11·00	12·55
B.G. gauges	15	14	13	12	11	10	9	8	7	
Thickness (mm)	1·80	2·00	2·24	2·50	2·80	3·15	3·55	4·00	4·50	
Wt. kg/m²	14·15	15·70	17·60	19·60	22·0	24·73	27·85	31·40	35·30	

1. B.G. is Birmingham guage, the no. represents no. of sheets in 1″ thickness.
2. Steel sheets in odd gauges *i.e.* 27, 25, 23 etc. are not generally prepared.
3. Standard lengths : 1·8, 2·0, 2·2, 2·5, 2·8, 3·0, 3·2, 3·6, 4·0 and 4·5 m.
4. Standard width are 0·6, 0·75, 0·90, 1·00, 1·10, 1·20 and 1·25.
5. Weight is calculated on the basis of steel weights 7·85 kg/m^2 per mm thickness or 7·85 gms/m^3.

Wt. of standard size of steel strips (kg/m/10 mm width)

B.G. (gauges)	16	16	14	13	12	11	10	9
Thickness (mm)	1·6	1·8	2·0	2·24	2·50	2·80	3·15	3·55
Wt. kg/m 10 mm	′0·126	0·141	0·157	0·176	0·196	0·220	0·248	0·279
B.G. (gauges)	8	7	6	4	2	0		
Thickness (mm)	4·0	4·5	5·0	6·0	8·0	10·0		
Wt. kg/m/10 mm	0·314	0·353	0·392	0·471	0·628	0·785		

Standard widths = 100, 125, 160, 200, 250, 320, 450, 500, 650, 800, 950, 1050, 1150, 1250, 1300, 1450 and 1550 mm.

Wt. of Standard Steel Plates

Thickness (mm)	5	6	7	8	9	10	11	12	13	14
Wt. kg/m²	39·25	47·10	62·80	78·50	94·20	109·40	125·60	141·30	157·0	172·70
Thickness	25	28	32	36	40					
Wt. kg/m²	196·25	219·80	251·20	282·60	314·00					

Standard widths = 0·9, 1·00, 1·10, 1·20, 1·25, 1·40, 1·50, 1·60, 1·80, 2·0, 2·20 and 2·5 m.

Standard lengths = 2·0, 2·2, 2·5, 2·8, 3·2, 3·6, 4·0, 4·5, 5·0, 5·6, 6·3, 7·1, 8·0, 9·0, 10·0, 11·0, 12·50 m.

Weight of chequered plates

Thickness in mm	9	10	12
wt/m² in kg	61·1	84·6	100·3

Dimensions of wire gauge (IS : 1560 : 1960)

Gauge	*Width of aperture (mm)*	*Dia. of wire (mm)*	*Remarks*
16 G	1·60	0·950	Suitable for fly proof screws
140 G	1·40	0·710	
120 G	1·20	0·600	Suitable for mosquito-proof screws
100 G	1·00	0·600	**Note :** Gauges 160 G to 70 G may be made from galvanized miled steel wire, brass wire or bronze wire. Gauge Nos. 50, 40 and 60 G are made from bronze or brass wires.
85 G	0·84	0·560	
80 G	0·79	0·530	
70 G	0·71	0·450	The gauge indicates apperture size of sq. opening in deca microns *i.e.* a gauge of 160 G means that the width of the opening is approximately 1·60 mm. The length of the wire gauge is 15 m or 30 m and the width 0·3, 0·45, 0·6, 0·9 and 1·20 m.
60 G	0·59	0·425	
50 G	0·50	0·355	
40 G	0·42	0·280	

Wire and Sheet Metal Gauges

No.	*Dia. or thickness (mm)*			No.	*Dia. or thickness (mm)*			No.	*Dia. or thickness (mm)*		
	SWG	*BG*	*B & S or AWG*		*SWG*	*BG*	*B & S or AWG*		*SWG*	*BG*	*B & S or AWG*
7/0	12·700	16·93	—	13	2·337	2·240	1·83	32	0·274	0·249	0·202
6/0	11·786	15·88	—	14	2·032	1·994	1·63	33	0·254	0·221	0·180
5/0	10·973	14·94	—	15	1·829	1·755	1·45	34	0·234	0·196	0·160
4/0	10·160	13·76	11·68	16	1·626	1·588	1·29	35	0·213	0·175	0·143
3/0	9·449	12·70	10·40	17	1·422	1·412	1·15	36	0·193	0·155	0·127
2/0	8·839	11·31	9·27	18	1·219	1·257	1·02	37	0·173	0·137	0·113
0	8·230	10·07	8·25	19	1·016	1·118	0·91	38	0·152	0·122	0·101
1	7·620	8·971	7·35	20	0·914	0·996	0·81	39	0·132	0·109	0·090
2	7·010	7·493	6·54	21	0·813	0·886	0·72	40	0·122	0·098	0·080
3	6·401	7·122	5·83	22	0·711	0·794	0·64	41	0·112	0·087	—
4	5·893	6·350	5·19	23	0·610	0·707	0·573	42	0·102	0·078	—
5	5·383	5·652	4·62	24	0·559	0·629	0·511	43	0·091	0·069	—
6	4·877	5·032	4·11	25	0·508	0·560	0·455	44	0·081	0·061	—
7	4·470	4·481	3·67	26	0·457	0·498	0·405	45	0·071	0·055	—
8	4·064	3·988	3·76	27	0·417	0·443	0·361	46	0·061	0·049	—
9	3·658	3·551	2·91	28	0·376	0·397	0·321	47	0·051	0·043	—
10	3·251	3·175	2·59	29	0·345	0·353	0·286	48	0·041	0·039	—
11	2·946	2·827	2·30	30	0·315	0·312	0·253	49	0·030	0·034	—
12	2·642	2·517	2·05	31	0·295	0·279	0·227	50	0·025	0·030	—

Thickness gauge	12	13	14	15	16	17	18	19	20			
B.G. No.	21	22	23	24	25	26	27	28	29	30	31	32

The actual thickness of B.G. No. 12 = 1 inch/12 and so on.

Note : 1. Gauge No. or size 1/0, 2/0, 3/0 and so on is also written as 0·00, 000 etc.

2. SWG is Imperial (English) standard wire gauge and is used for wires and sheets.

3. BWG is Birmingham wire gauge (also called Birmingham Gauge), is used for strips, sheets, bands, hoops and wires. Stubbs steel wire gauge (SSWG) is nearly equal to BWG.

4. B & S or AWG is Brown and Sharpe (American).

5. BG is Birmingham Gauge and is used for Sheets, hoops and plate thickness.

6. BSWG is Whitworth Standard Wire Gauge and is used mainly for threads of bolts, nuts and screws.

7. Zinc gauge is different and is used for zinc sheets.

8. "Gauge measures" are available made of thin iron plates of flat, circular or oblong shapes in which gauge thickness are cut at the edges.

Size and Weight of Expanded Metal (XPM) Sheets

Size of mesh in mm		*Dimensions of strands mm*		*Weight/sq.m kg*	*Size of sheet normally in metres*
SWM	*LWM*	*Width*	*Thickness*		
100	250	6·25	3·15	3·082	2·50 × 3·75
100	250	5·00	3·15	2·470	
100	250	3·25	3·15	1·599	
75	200	6·50	3·15	4·282	
75	200	5·00	3·15	3·294	
75	200	3·25	3·15	2·141	
40	115	6·50	3·15	8·023	
40	115	5·00	3·15	6·172	
40	75	5·00	3·15	6·172	
40	75	3·25	2·24	2·854	Fig. 3·8 (*a*).
40	115	3·25	3·15	4·007	
40	75	3·25	3·15	4·007	2·50 × 3·75
40	115	3·25	1·60	2·039	1·25 × 3·75
40	75	3·25	1·60	2·039	
25	75	3·25	3·15	6·423	2·50 × 3·75
25	75	3·25	2·24	4·564	
25	75	3·25	1·60	3·262	2·50 × 3·75
25	75	3·25	1·25	2·548	1·25 × 3·75
20	60	3·25	3·15	8·023	
20	50	3·25	3·15	8·023	2·50 × 3·75
20	60	3·25	2·24	5·709	
20	50	3·25	2·24	5·709	2·50 × 3·75
20	60	3·25	1·60	4·078	1·25 × 3·75
20	50	3·25	1·60	4·078	
20	60	2·50	1·25	2·447	
20	50	2·50	1·25	2·447	
12·5	50	3·25	1·60	6·525	
12·5	40	3·25	1·60	6·525	
12·5	50	2·50	1·60	5·019	
12·5	50	2·50	1·25	3·921	2·50 × 2·75
12·5	40	2·50	1·25	3·921	1·25 × 2·75
12·5	50	2·50	1·00	3·137	
12·5	40	2·50	1·00	3·137	
10	40	3·25	1·60	8·150	
10	40	2·50	1·25	4·901	

Size of mesh in mm		*Dimensions of strands mm*		*Weight/sq.m kg*	*Size of sheet normally stocked in metres*
SWM	*LWM*	*Width*	*Thickness*		
10	40	2·50	1·00	3·921	2·80 × 1·75
6	25	3·25	1·60	13·591	1·25 × 1·75
6	25	2·50	1·25	8·164	
6	25	2·50	1·00	6·533	
5	20	2·50	1·00	7·843	
3	15	1·50	1·00	7·843	2·50 × 1·25

SWM is shorter way mesh, LWM is longer way of mesh.

When ordering XPM sheets, it is necessary to specify which dimension refers to SWM or LWM.

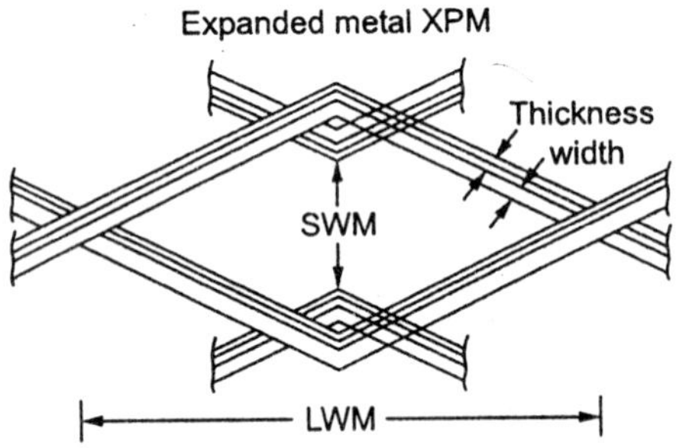

Fig. 3·8(*b*).

4

Theory and Design of Structures

4·1. Elastic Theory

Elastic Limit. Greatest stress on a material upto which the strain remains in proportion to it or the ratio stress : Strain is a constant and the strain in the member disappears after the removal of the external force to which it is subjected and the member comes to its original state.

Yield Point. Above elastic limit plastic deformation takes place and the strain in the member does not disappear totally after the removal of the external force. In this region strain increases rapidly with a slight increase in the stress or even without applications of any load after it. This point of stress is known as yield point and is a bit above the elastic limit. It is also known as **proof stress** point.

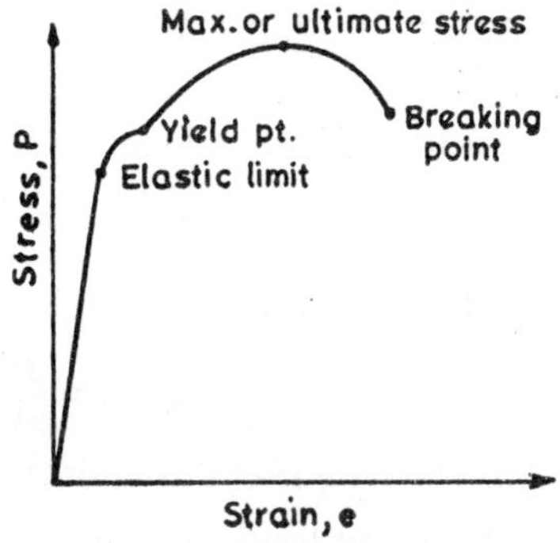

Fig. 4·1.

Ultimate or max. stress. It is max. stress to which a member can be sustained and local yielding takes place and the specimen forms a **waste.** At this stage the load necessary to break the member (Breaking stress) is less than max. or ultimate stress.

Permanent set. When the member is loaded beyond the elastic limit it passes in a plastic range and the deformation does not completely vanish on removal of the external load. This residual deformation is called the permanent set.

Hook's law. Stress is proportional to strain or stress/strain = constant (in elastic limit). This constant is known as Young's Modulus and is denoted by E in engineering (Tension members).

E = stress/strain ; N = shear stress/shear strain where N is the shear modulus or Modulus of rigidity ; K = stress/volumetric strain, K is bulk modulus.

Poisson's ratio. When the elastic material is subjected to an axial push, it is elongated in the logitudinal directions along with a contraction in the transverse direction.

$$\text{Then poisson's ratio} = \frac{\text{transverse contraction}}{\text{longitudinal extension}} = \frac{1}{m}$$

$$E = 2N\left(1 + \frac{1}{m}\right) = \frac{9\,KN}{3K + N}$$

$$\textbf{Factor of safety} = \frac{\text{Ultimate load or strength at failure}}{\text{Permissible stress, allowed or working stress}}.$$

Modulus of rupture. It is max. stress at which the member is subjected to failure in bending and the stress at which failure takes place is known as the rupture stress or the flexural (bending) strength.

Skin stress. The bending stress at the outer edge of the section.

Tensile stress. Force applied per unit area of a section on a member in tension (axial pull) ; $p = P/A$ = Load/Area.

Compressive stress. Force applied per unit area of a section on a member in compression (internal push).

Shear stress. Force applied per unit area of a section on a member which tends to the particles to slide over those which are adjacent to them.

Fatigue. It is diminishing strength of a member to failure after long continuous use at different stress.

Static load. A load applied gradually and is stationery is known as static load.

$$p = P/A \text{ or stress} = \text{Load/Area}.$$

Sudden load. A load applied suddenly.

$$\text{Stress} = \frac{2\text{ load}}{\text{Area}} = \frac{2P}{A} = p$$

Impact load. A sudden loading, such as below of a hammer

$$p = \frac{P}{A} + \sqrt{P^2/A^2 + \frac{2\,PhE}{Al}}$$

where h is the height of fall and Al is the volume of the member.

Dynamic load. A load applied in motions.

Load factor or factor of safety $= \dfrac{\text{Load causing failure}}{\text{Working load}}$.

Resisting moment. The max. bending moment which a body can take or resist.

Temperature stress. (*a*) **Homogeneous sections** : $e = \alpha\, t$, $p = E\,\alpha\, t$ when end do not yield, $e = \dfrac{\alpha t.l - \delta}{l}$, $p = \dfrac{E(\alpha t.l - \delta)}{l}$ when ends yield by δ.

(*b*) **Composite sections.** $p_2\,(A_1) = \alpha_2\,(A_2)$; $e_1 + e_2 = t(\alpha_1 - \alpha_2)$

p, A, e, α are stress, area of X-sec., strain and coefficient of expansion and t is the change in temperature.

Strain Energy. It is the energy absorbed or stored by a member when work is done on it to deform it and is equal to

$$\frac{p^2}{2E}\left\{\text{Volume of loaded member in cm}^3\right\}\text{kg cm}$$

p = Stress in kg/cm^2 and E = mod. of elasticity in kg/cm^2.

Resilience or Strain Energy is energy in an elastic member for which it can be strained without fracture repeatedly. It is the work done per unit volume of a material in producing strain. Max. strain energy without permanent strain is **Proof resilience.**

Shear Force. It is unbalanced vertical force at a particular section of a beam, considered either from the left or right of the section.

Bending Moment. The bending moment at a cross-section of a beam is the algebraic sum of the moments of the forces to the right or left of the sections.

Note : (*a*) The rate of change of shear force at a x-section is equal to the rate of loading at the section or $\dfrac{dF}{dx} = -w$.

(b) The rate of change of bending moment is equal to the shear force at the cross sections

or $\dfrac{dM}{dx} = F$.

Table 4·1. E.N. and 1/m (Poisson's ratio) for different materials.

S.No.	*Material*	*E*	*N*	*1/m*
1.	Aluminium	7×10^5	$2{\cdot}59 \times 10^5$	
2.	Brass	$1{\cdot}09 \times 10^6$	$4{\cdot}34 \times 10^5$	0·33
3.	Bronze	$1{\cdot}05 \times 10^6$	$3{\cdot}92 \times 10^5$	
4.	Manganese	$1{\cdot}12 \times 10^6$	$4{\cdot}2 \times 10^5$	
5.	Cast copper	$1{\cdot}05 \times 10^6$	$3{\cdot}92 \times 10^5$	0·33
6.	Drawn copper	$1{\cdot}19 \times 10^6$	$4{\cdot}48 \times 10^5$	0·33
7.	Cast iron	$1{\cdot}05 \times 10^6$	$4{\cdot}2 \times 10^5$	0·25
8.	Malleable iron	$1{\cdot}54 \times 10^6$	$6{\cdot}16 \times 10^5$	0·25
9.	Wrought iron	$1{\cdot}89 \times 10^6$	$7{\cdot}56 \times 10^5$	0·25
10.	Steel	$2{\cdot}1 \times 10^6$	$8{\cdot}4 \times 10^5$	0·25
11.	Zinc	$8{\cdot}4 \times 10^3$		
12.	Wood	$1{\cdot}05 \times 10^5$		
13.	Concrete	$2{\cdot}1 \times 10^5$		0·08 to 0·16
14.	Glass			0·24

Elasticity. It is the property of a material by virtue of which it regains the original shape and size after the removal of external force.

Plasticity. It is the property of a material by virtue of which it does not regain its original shape and size after the removal of external force.

Bending Moment and Shear Force by Graphical Method.

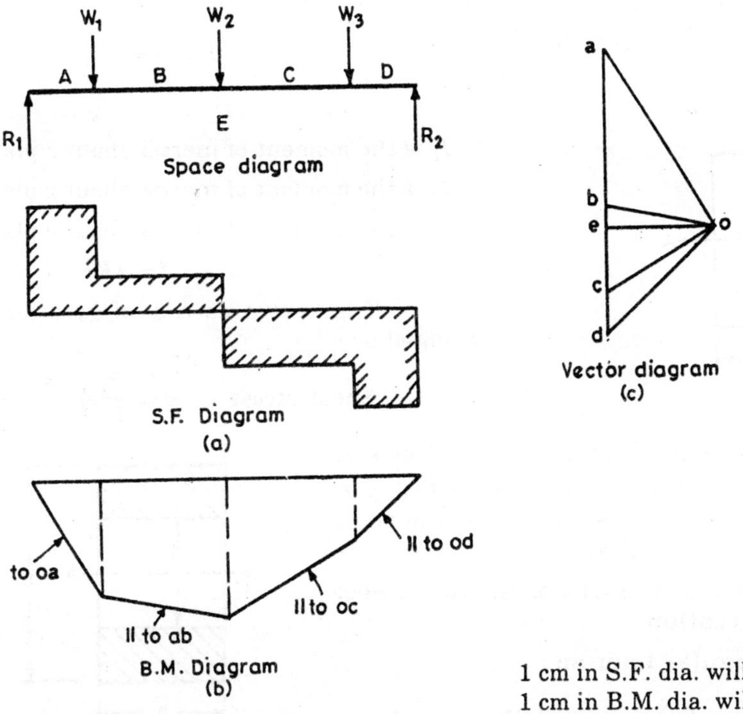

1 cm in S.F. dia. will indicate q kg S.F.
1 cm in B.M. dia. will indicate pqh kg-m of B.M.

Fig. 4·2.

Select a pole O at a convenient distance h from the vector line ad. The vector line is drawn as below :

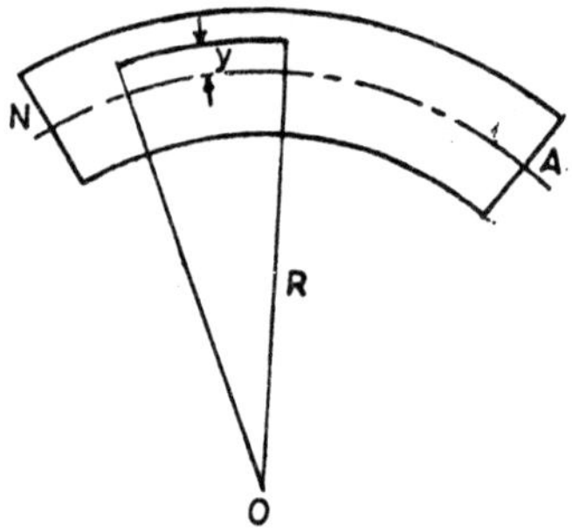

Fig. 4·3.

Take 1 cm = p metre in the space dia. and 1 cm = q kg in vector diagram.

In vector diagram draw ab showing the wt. W_1 AB and similarly draw bc, cd and dc to show W_2, W_3 and R_2 (R_1 and R_2 being reactions at end supports) in magnitude and direction. de will represent the reaction R_2. For convenience O is joined to e in vector dia. Draw $S.F.$ and $B.M.$ dia. as in figure above with the help of vector dia.

Bending of a beam

$$\frac{dM}{dx} = F \; ; \; \frac{dF}{dx} = W, \qquad ...(1)$$

where M represents B.M. and F represents S.F.

Flexural formula,

$$\frac{M}{I} = \frac{p}{y} = \frac{F}{R} \qquad ...(2)$$

$$Z = I/y \qquad ...(3)$$

$$I = Ig + Al^2 \qquad ...(4)$$

where I = moment of inertia about a section, Ig = moment of inertia about $N.A.$ or $c.g.$, A = area of sec. and l = the distance from the point at which moment of inertia is required to the point of $c.g.$ or $N.A.$

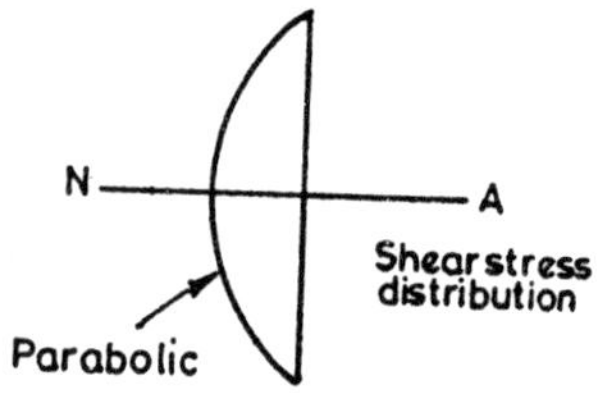

Fig. 4·4.

p = working stress

y = distance from sec. to the N.A.

R = rad. of curvature of N.A. on bending.

I = moment of inertia about NA of the sec.

Z = sec. modulus.

$$I_z = I_x + I_y \qquad ...(5)$$

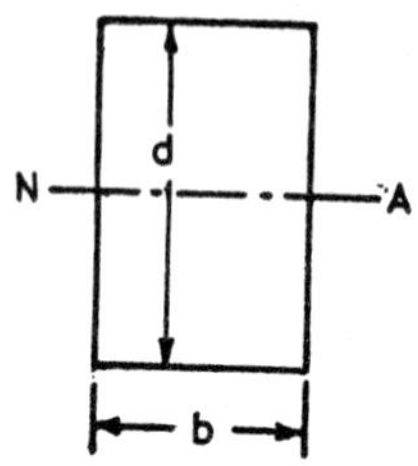

Fig. 4·5 (a).

I_z is the moment of inertia about z plane.

I_x is the moment of inertia about x plane.

I_y is the moment of inertia about y plane.

$$I = AK^2 \qquad ...(6)$$

K is known as rad. of gyration and is denoted by r.

Shear stress $$q = \frac{F}{I_z} A\bar{y} \qquad ...(7)$$

where F = shear force at the sec., I mt. of Inertia of the sec. about N.A., z = width of the sec. at the point concerned, $\bar{y}$ = distance of N.A. (neutral axis) of the area above the point concerned from the N.A. of the total sec.

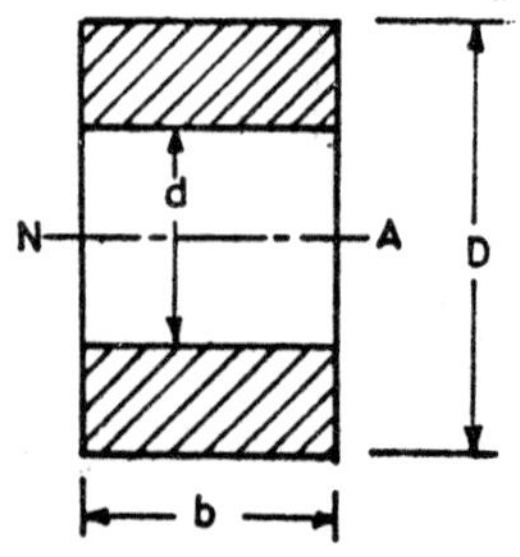

Fig. 4·5 (b).

Moment of Inertia of Figures or Sections, Sec. Modulus and Rad. of Gyration

(1) **Plane Rectangular Lamina :**

(a) about N.A. : $I_{NA} = \dfrac{bd^3}{12}$; $Z_{NA} = \dfrac{bd^2}{6}$; $K_{NA} = \dfrac{d}{3{\cdot}45}$

(b) about base : $I_b = \dfrac{bd^3}{3}$; $Z_b = \dfrac{bd^2}{3}$; $K_b = \dfrac{d}{\sqrt{3}}$

(c) Hollow lamina : $I_{NA} = \dfrac{b\left(D^3 - d^3\right)}{12}$; $Z_{NA} = \dfrac{b\left(D^3 - d^3\right)}{6D}$; $r_{NA} = \left\{\dfrac{D^3 - d^3}{12(D - d)}\right\}^{1/2}$

(2) **Plane Triangular Lamina :**

(a) About N.A. : $I_{NA} = \dfrac{bh^3}{36}$; $Z_{NA} = \dfrac{bh^2}{24}$; $r_{NA} = \dfrac{h}{\sqrt{18}}$

(b) About base : $I_b = \dfrac{bh^3}{12}$; $Z_b = \dfrac{bh^2}{12}$; $r_b = \dfrac{h}{\sqrt{6}}$

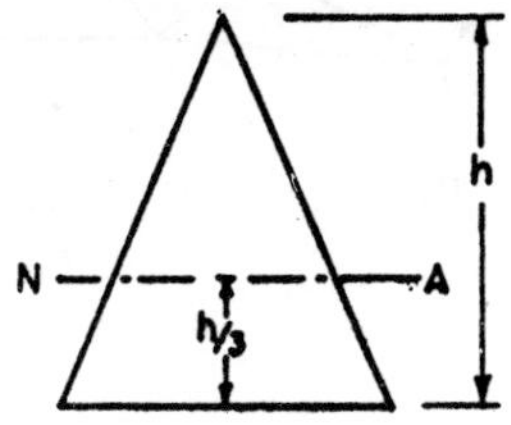

(c)

(c) About vertex : $I_r = \dfrac{bh^3}{4}$; $Z_V = \dfrac{bh^2}{4}$; $r_V = \dfrac{h}{\sqrt{2}}$

(3) **Plane Circular Lamina :**

(a) About xx : $I_{xx} = \dfrac{\pi D^2}{64}$; $Z_{xx} = \dfrac{\pi D^3}{32}$; $r_{xx} = \dfrac{d}{4}$

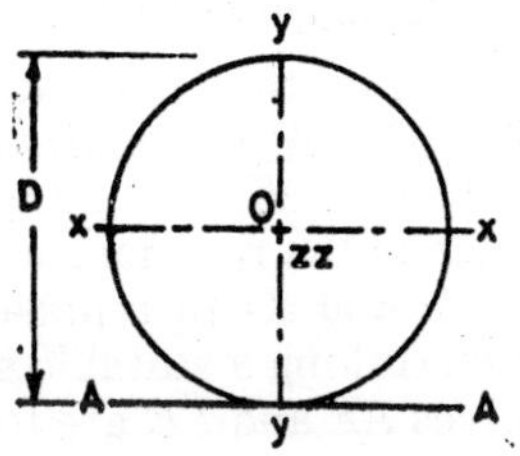

(d)

(b) About hollow section : $I_{xx} = \dfrac{\pi\left(D^4 - d^4\right)}{64}$

$$Z_{xx} = \frac{\pi\left(D^4 - d^4\right)}{32d} \; ; \; r_{xx} = \frac{\sqrt{D^2 + d^2}}{4}$$

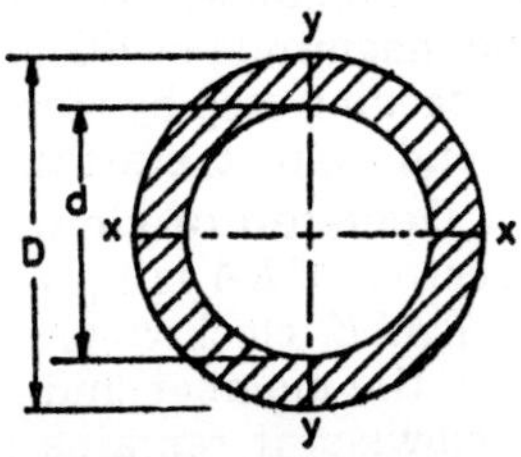

(e)

(c) About AA : $I_{AA} = \dfrac{5}{64}\pi D^4$

(d) About Z-axis (perp. to xx) : $I_{zz} = \dfrac{\pi D^4}{32}$

(e) Semi circle about c.g. : $I_{c.g.} = \dfrac{\pi D^2}{457}$

Semi circle about base : $I_b = \dfrac{\pi r^2}{8}$

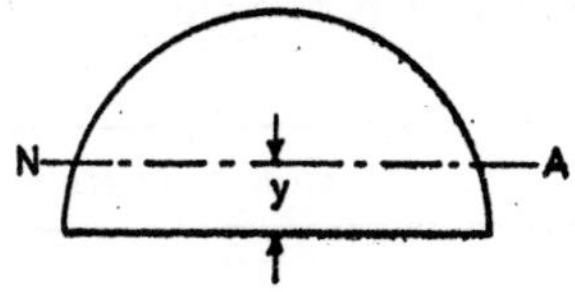

(f)

D = dia., r = radius, $y = 4r/3\pi$.

(4) **Trapezium about c.g. :** $I_{c.g.} = \dfrac{\left(a^2 + b^2 + 4ab\right)d^3}{36(a + b)}$

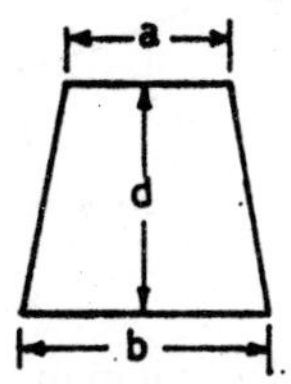

(g)

Fig. 4·5.

a = smaller parallel side

b = larger parallel side

d = distance between parallel sides.

Note : For sections which are not symetrical about NA, sec. modulus of tension and compression zones are calculated separately.

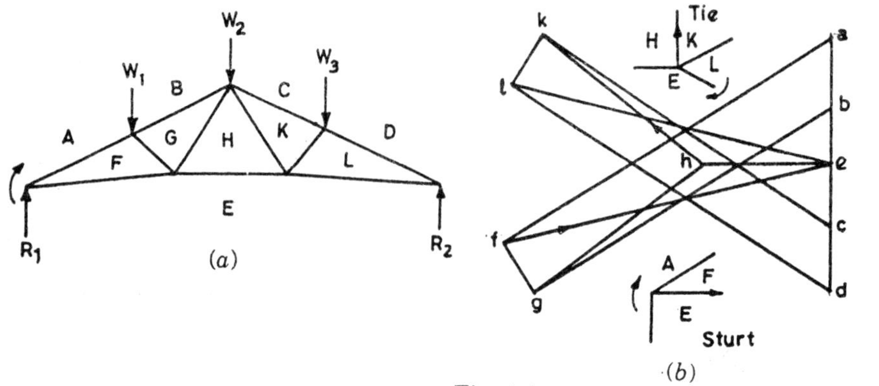

Fig. 4·6.

Analysis of stress in a Truss Frame (refer Fig. 4·6(*a*) and (*b*)

Draw the truss under study as shown in space dia. (scale say 1 cm = *pm*) with forces *AB* (W_1), *BC* (W_2) and *CD* (W_3) acting vertically down at its joint points. Find out the reactions R_1 (*EA*) and R_2 (*DE*) by taking moments about the support points taking separately. In the present case each of the reactions are half the total sum of the loads being the truss symmetrical. Draw *ab*, *bc*, *cd*, *de* and *da* to represent weights *AB*, *BC*, *CD* and reactions *DE* and *EA* in magnitude and direction (taking a suitable scale say 1 cm = *q* kg). Staring from the joint of left support *EA* is known and forces *AF* and *FE* are to be found out. Draw lines *af* and *ef* in vector dia. parallel to *AF* and *EF* in space dia., meeting a point *f* in space dia. Now the distance *af* and *fe* represents the faces *AF* and *FE*. Now proceed to another point in forces *AB*, *BG*, *GF* and *FA.FA* and *AB* are known while *BG* and *GF* are unknown. Draw lines *bg* and *fg* parallel to *BG* and *FG* meeting at a point '*g*' which will give the magnitude of *BG* and *GF* proceeding to points *FG*, *HE*, *GH* and *HE* can be solved. In this way proceeding step by step whole of the stress diagram *abcdefghkl* can be solved (After computing the left end support, start the Right hand support from the end point as is done for left hand support).

Decision of tie or strut. Consider the point (left hand support) EAF as we know that the direction of *EA* is upward so in the vector dia. *ea* is a correct order (not *ae*) and order in the joint is *EAFE* (clockwise) and hence the order for the next member is *fe* (not *ef*) which produces thrust in the member and so the member is a tie. Now when the order has once been fixed clock or anticlowise) it remains the same for other joints. Now consider the joint *HKLE*, the correct order is *HKLE* (not *ELHK*). In the stress dia. the directions *hk* represents a pull and hence the member *HK* is a tie.

Suspension Bridges

Concentrated loads, W

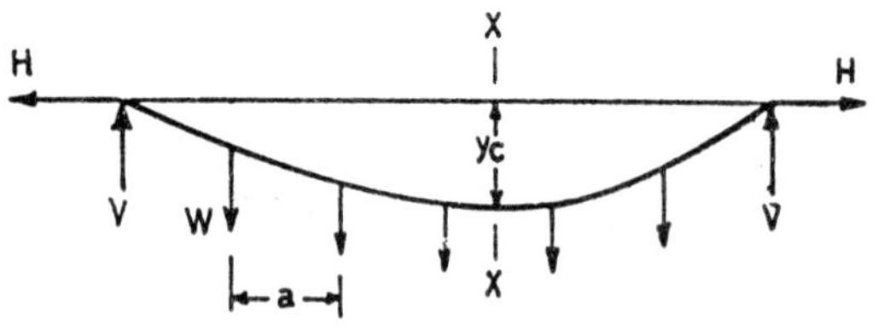

Fig. 4·7 (*a*).

Taking moments about *A* through a sec. *xx*.

Centre of span,

a = distance apart of loads

$H.y_C = W{\cdot}a + W{\cdot}2a + W{\cdot}3a$

y_C = central dip.

Distributed Loads, w/unit length

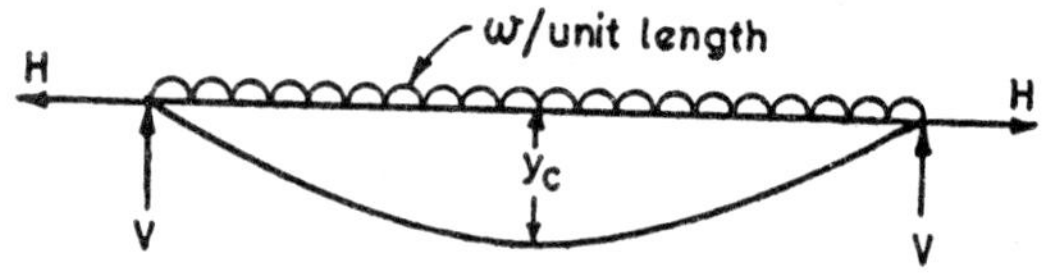

Fig. 4·7 (*b*).

$$H = \frac{wl^2}{8\,y_C}\ ;\ V = \frac{wl}{2}\ ;\ y_C \text{ is central dip.}$$

$$T_{max} = \left(V^2 + H^2\right)^{1/2},\ A = \frac{T_{max}}{f}$$

where f = permissible stress for rope material

A = sec. area of rope

Concentrated loads, W

$H = \dfrac{W.6a}{y_C}$, $V = 3W$

$T_{max} = \left(V^2 + H^2\right)^{1/2}$; $A = \dfrac{T_{max}}{f}$

A = sec. of rope and
f = permissible stress for rope material

Length of the cable by measurement of the polygon.

To draw the funicular polygon

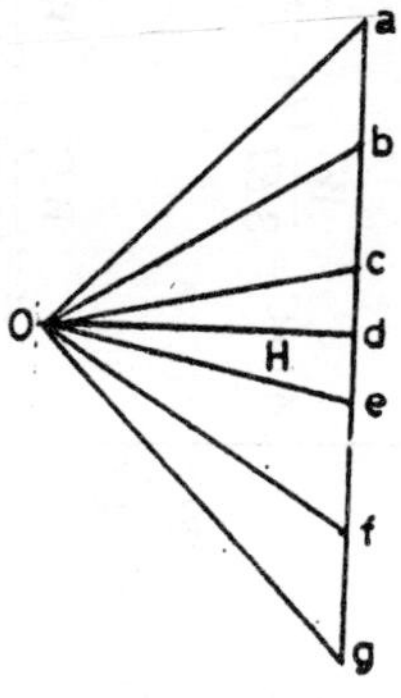

Fig. 4·7 (*c*).

1. Draw *abcdefg* to scale for the loads *W*.

2. Take a pole *O* at a distance *H* from *d* and join *Od*. Draw *Oa, Ob, Oc, Oe, Of* and *Og* in the funicular polygon, which will give the shape of the chord by drawing parallel lines.

Cable at different Levels

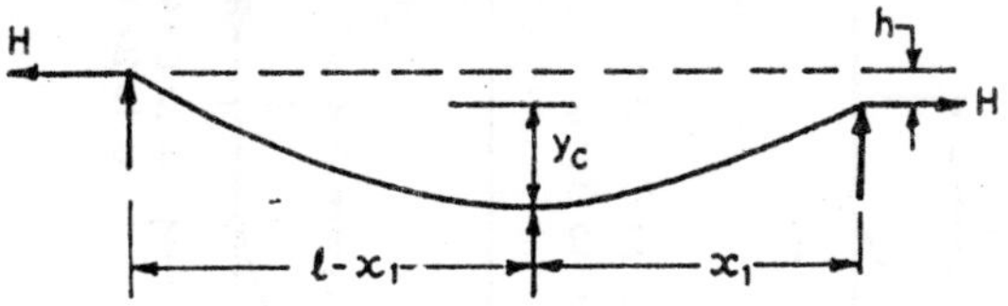

Fig. 4·7 (*d*).

$$H = \frac{Wx_1^2}{2y_C} = \frac{W(l - x_1)^2}{2(h + y_C)} \qquad \text{...(1)}$$

$$V_1 = \frac{W}{2} + \frac{H.h}{l} = \frac{Wl}{2} + \frac{Hh}{l}$$

$$V_2 = \frac{W}{2} - \frac{H.h}{l} = \frac{Wl}{2} - \frac{Hh}{l}$$

$$L = CA + CB$$

$$= l + \frac{2}{3} y_C^{\,2} + \frac{2}{3}\frac{\left(h + y_C^{\,2}\right)}{x_1}$$

$$T_{max} = 2\sqrt{V_1^2 + H^2}$$

Distributed Loads, w/unit length

$$\text{Length of the cable} = l + \frac{8}{3}\frac{(y_C)^2}{l}$$

$$\text{At a point } X, \quad H = \frac{wx^2}{2g} = \frac{Ma_x}{y_C}$$

where M_{max} = Max. B.M. at centre of rope.

$$\delta y_C = \frac{3}{16}\,\alpha t\,\frac{l^2}{y_C}$$

where δy_C is the extension in the central dip due to temperature, α = coefficient of expansion of the rope material and t is the change in temperature.

Suspension cable

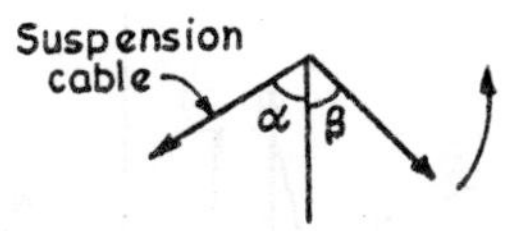

Fig. 4·7 (*e*).

The vertical pressure on the pier

$= V_P = T\cos\alpha + T\cos\beta$

$T = T_1$ where the friction on the pulley is neglected.

B. M. at the base of pier

$= M = H.P. \times h$

where h = height of the pier.

$H.P.$ = hor. pressure

$= T\sin\alpha - T\sin\beta$.

Eccentric Loads due to Wind Pressure on Walls and Columns.

Consider per unit length of a wall and intensityof wind pressure = p per unit area. Density of wall masonry = ρ, w = wt. of masonry = ρbH acting vertically down from centre of wall, p_0 = stress due to vert. load

$$= W/A = \rho bH/b = \rho H \qquad \text{...(1) in strip of width } b.$$

H = Height of wall and P = wind pressure = pH acting at $H/2$ of wall.

So moment on base due to $P = PH/2 = \dfrac{pH^2}{2}$ = M

Z for the base section $= \dfrac{1}{6} 1.b^2 = \dfrac{b^2}{6}$, Z is sec. modulus

pb the stress on base due to wind pressure

Table 4·2. Properties of Cantilevers and beams under loading. (also refer Appendices Chapter (8C)

Sl. No.	Mode of loading	Shear Force	Bending Moment	Deflection Max. Position	Deflection Max. Magnitude	At distance x
1.	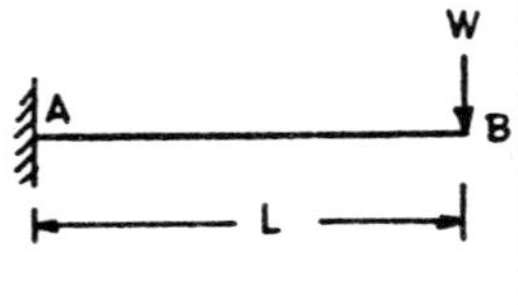 Fig. 4·1-1	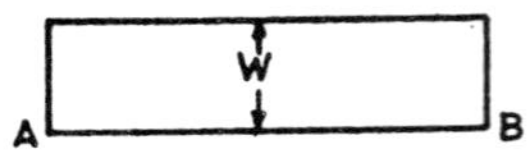	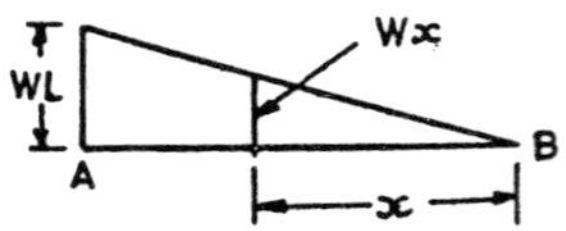	Free end	$WL^3/3\,EI$	$\frac{W}{EI}\left\{\frac{L}{2}(L-x)^2-\frac{(L-x)^3}{6}\right\}$
2.	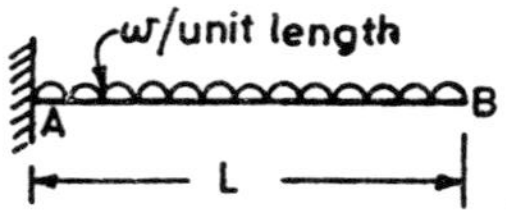 Fig. 4·1-2	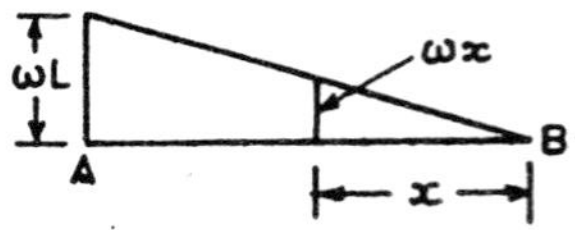	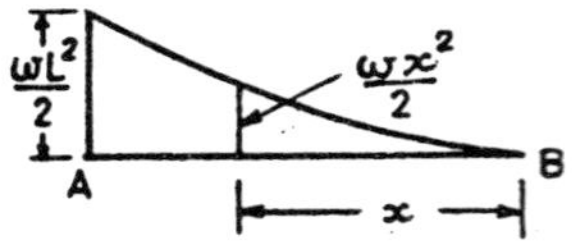	Free end	$WL^4/8\,EI$	$\frac{W}{EI}\left\{\frac{x^4}{24}+\frac{L}{6}(L-x)-\frac{L^4}{24}\right\}$
3.	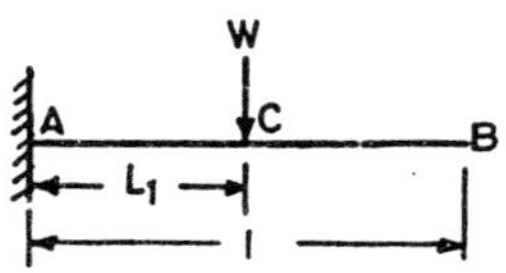 Fig. 4·1-3	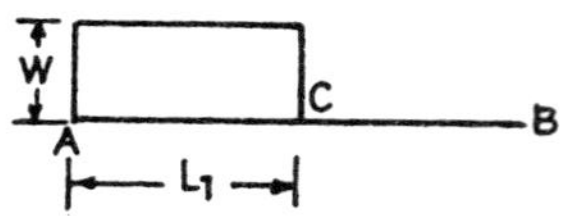 A to C = W C to B = 0	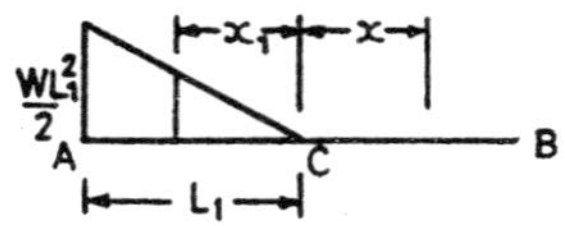 A to $C = Wx_1$ C to $B = 0$	Free end	$\frac{WL_1^3}{3\,EI}+(L-L_1)\frac{WL_1^2}{2\,EI}$	A to $C=\frac{W}{3\,EI}(L_1-x_1)^3$ C to $B=\frac{WL_1^3}{3\,EI}+x\frac{WL_1^2}{2\,EI}$
4.	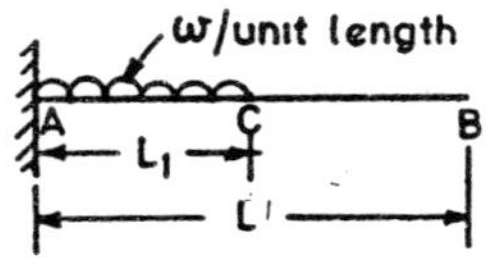 Fig. 4·1-4	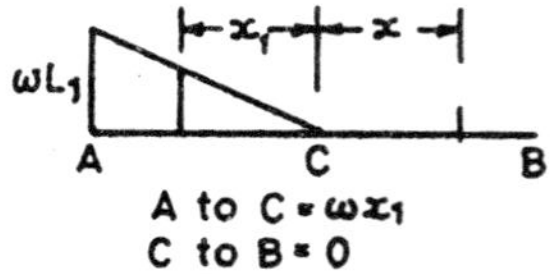	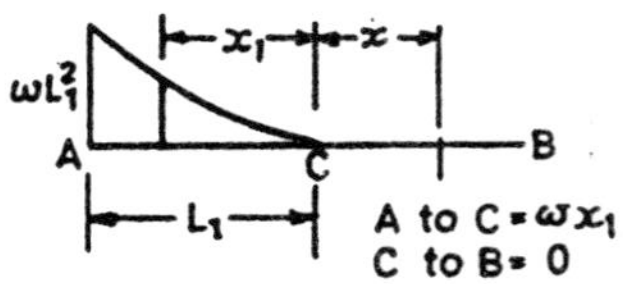	Free end	$\frac{WL_1^4}{8\,EI}+(L-L_1)\frac{WL_1^3}{6\,EI}$	A to $C=W\frac{(L_1-x_1)^4}{8\,EI}$ C to $B=\frac{WL_1^4}{8\,EI}+\frac{xWL_1^3}{6\,EI}$

Sl. No.	Mode of loading	Shear Force	Bending Moment	Deflection Max. Position	Deflection Max. Magnitude	At distance x
5.	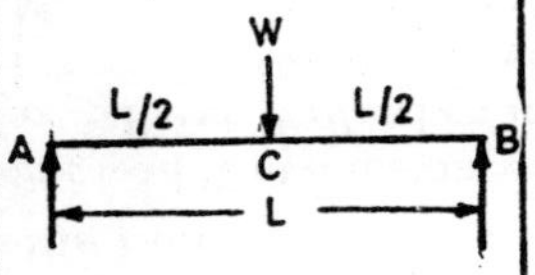 Fig. 4·1-5	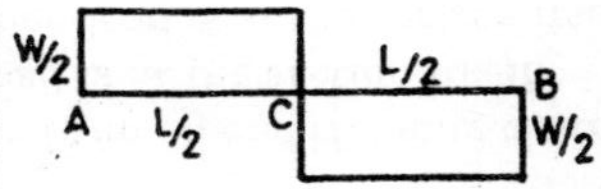	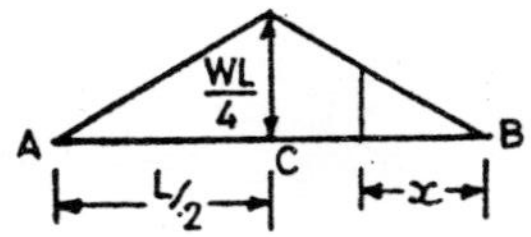	Centre C	$\frac{WL^3}{48\,EI}$	B to C or A to C $\frac{W}{EI}\left\{\frac{L^2}{16}x - \frac{x^3}{12}\right\}$ x means used from A or B or $AC = BC$
6.	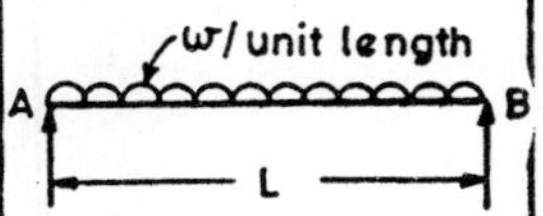 Fig. 4·1-6	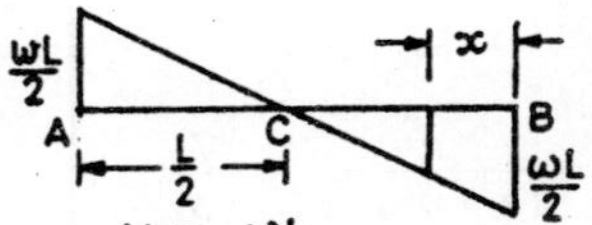 At x, $\frac{\omega L}{2} - \omega x$ At $x = WL/2 - Wx$	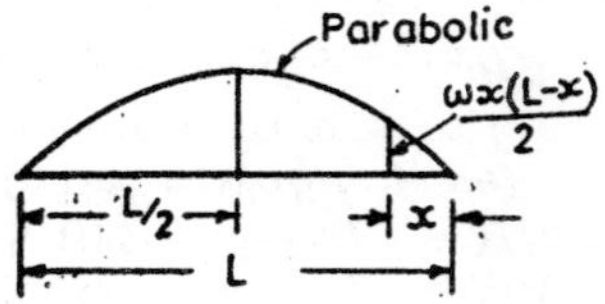 $Wx\frac{(L-x)}{2}$	Centre C	$\frac{5}{384}\;\frac{WL^4}{EI}$	B to C or A to C $\frac{Wx}{EI}\left\{\frac{l^3}{24} + \frac{x^3}{24} - \frac{Wlx^2}{12}\right\}$ x measured from A or B
7.	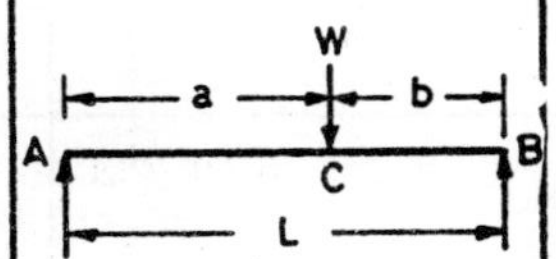 Fig. 4·1-7	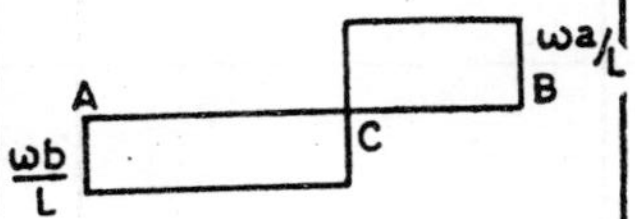	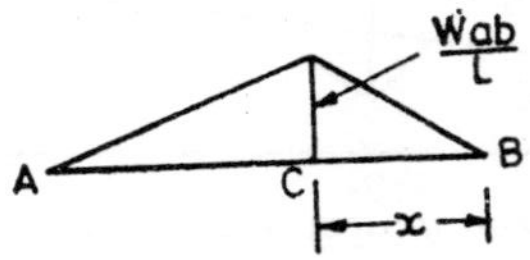 C to B Wax/L x measured from support C to A Wbx/L x measured from A	1 m large span at $\left(\frac{a^2 + 2ab}{3}\right)^{\frac{1}{2}}$ from A	$Wb\,\frac{\left(a^2 - 12\,ab\right)^{\frac{3}{2}}}{a\sqrt{3}\,EIL}$	$Wbx\frac{\left(L^2 - b^2 - x^2\right)}{6\,EIL}$ x measured from support A
8.	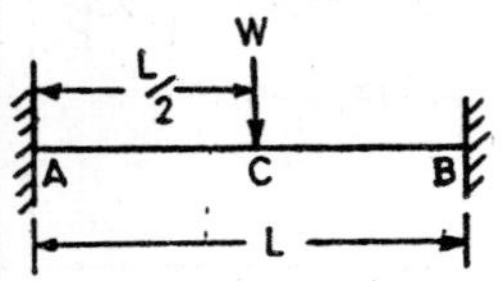 Fig. 4·1-1	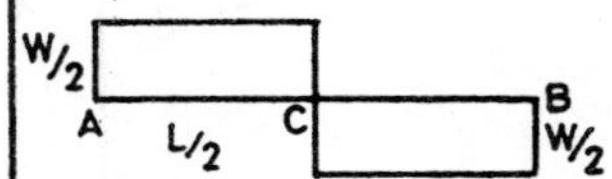	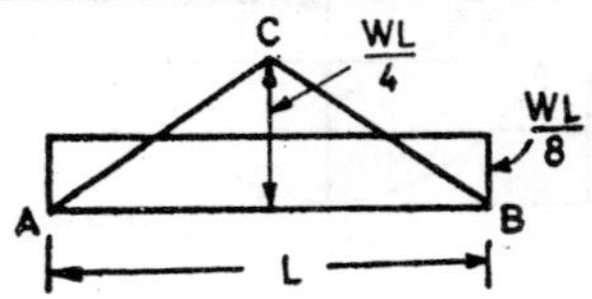 $\frac{WL}{8} - \frac{Wx}{2}$ x measured from A or B	At C	$\frac{WL^3}{192\,EI}$	$\frac{WLx^2}{16} - \frac{Wx^3}{12}$ x measured from A or C

Sl. No.	Mode of loading	Shear Force	Bending Moment	Deflection Max.		At distance x
				Position	Magnitude	
9.	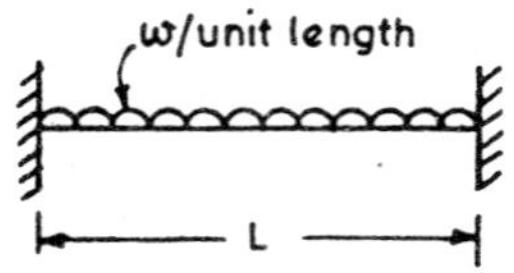 Fig. 4·1-9	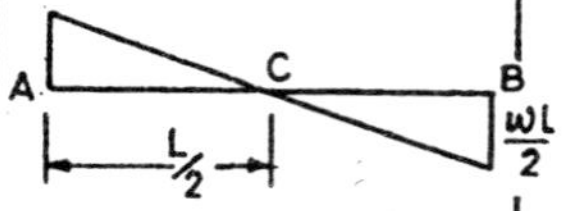	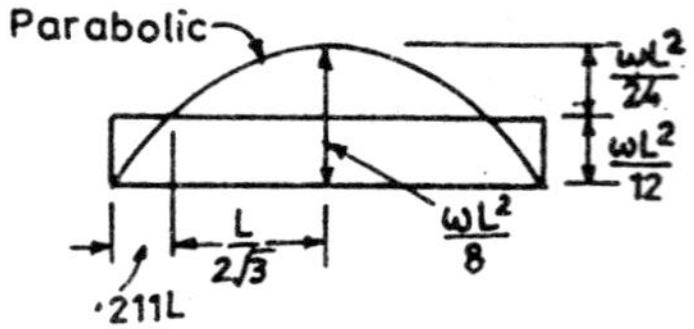 $\frac{WL^2}{12}-\frac{Wx^2}{2}-\frac{WLx}{x}$ x measured from A or B	At C	$\frac{WL^4}{384\,EI}$	$\frac{Wx^4}{24}-\frac{Wl^2x^2}{24}-\frac{Wlx^3}{12}$ x meausred from A or C
10.	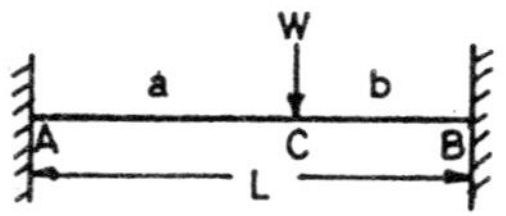 Fig. 4·1-10	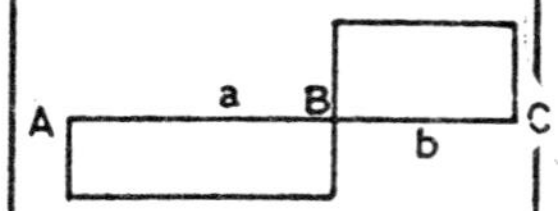 B to C = $\frac{Wa}{L}+\frac{Wab(a-b)}{L^3}$ A to C = $\frac{Wb}{L}+\frac{Wab(a-b)}{L^3}$	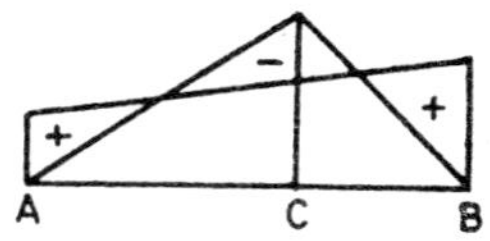 At A BM = $Wab^2/L^2 = MA$ At B BM = $Wa^2b/L^2 = MB$ At C BM = Wab/L (– ve) x measured from A to C $Wab^2/L^2 + Wab\,(a-b)\,x/L^3 - Wbx/L$ $Wa^2/L + Wab(a-b)(L-x) - Wax/L$ x measured from B or C	**Note :** 1. Integral of curvature $1/R$ gives slope and integral of slope gives deflection. 2. Integral of B.M. divided by EI gives slope and integral of slope gives deflection. $\frac{d^2y}{dx^2}=\frac{M}{EI}$		

Moving Loads

1. Point load W at a distance x from an end (L being clear span)

   Max. S.F. +ve Wx/L when load is at the section itself.

   –ve $W/L\,(L-x)$ when load is at the section itself

   B.M. $Wx\,(L-x)/L$ when load is at the section itself

   Absolute max. S.F. = W and B.M. = WL/A at mid span.

2. Continuous load larger than span at a distance x from an end, S.F. +ve $Wx^2/2L$ when head of load is at section itself. B.M. $Wx(L-x)/L$

   –ve $W(L-x)/2L$ when tail of load is at section itself. (entire span is loaded

   Absolute S.F. = $WL/2$ } entire span is loaded
   Absolute M.B. = $WL^2/2$ }

$$= \frac{M}{Z} = \frac{pH^2}{2} + \frac{b^2}{6} = \frac{3pH^2}{b^2} \quad ...(2)$$

On base $\quad p_{max} = p_0 + p_b = (1) + (2)$

$$= \rho H + \frac{3pH^2}{b^2}$$

$$p_{min} = p_0 - pb = (1) - (2)$$

$$= \rho H - \frac{3 \times pH^2}{b^2}$$

p_{max} < bearing capacity of the soil.

For cylinderical shafts if p_n = normal intensity of pressure, then $p = 2/3\ p_n$, where p is assumed to act on the dia. width, so total pressure = $p.dh$.

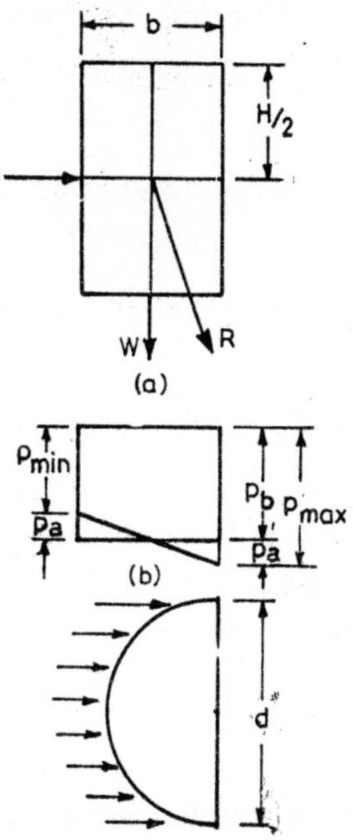

Fig. 4·8.

Eccentric Loaded Foundations on Restrained Property Lines

$$p_1 = \frac{w}{b}\left(\pm \frac{6e}{b}\right)$$

e = eccentricity of load or $c.g.$ of load to the $c.g.$ of the supporting base area

If eccentricity = $b/6$ then p_2 becomes zero and if it is still greater p_2 becomes –ve which is undesirable for masonry, hence the $c.g.$ of load should pass between middle 3rd of the base area.

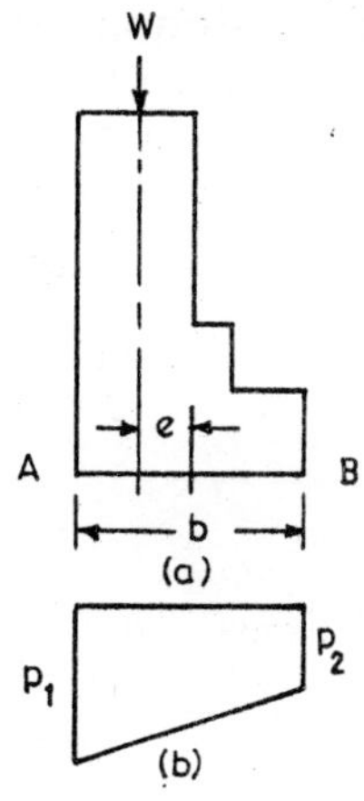

Fig. 4·9.

Wind Loads. $p = KV^2$ where p = normal intensity of wind pressure in lbs/ft^2

V = vel. of wind in miles/hr.

Angle α	60°	45°	30°
Value of K			
Wind ward side	(+) 0·0034	(+) 0·0028	(+) 0·0015
Lee ward side	(–) 0·0032	(–) —	(–) 0·0022

Values for K for walls opened both sides for wind.

It is zero for Leeward side

Duchenim formula $\quad P_n = \frac{P \sin \alpha}{1 + \sin^2 \alpha}$

P_n = pressure normal to slope and α is the inclination of the roof to the horizontal.

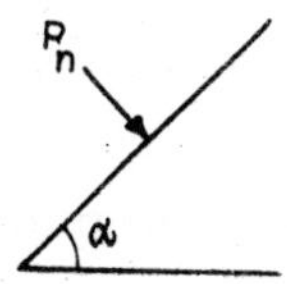

Fig. 4·10.

Comparative Economy in Sections for Strength of the Same Sectional areas or wts. taking I-sec. as Unity

I	*Channel*	*Unequal ∠*	*Equal ∠*	*T-equal*	*T-unequal*
1·0	0·9	0·5	0·4	0·4	0·2

Comparative Economy in Strength Depending on end Positions

(*a*) Simply supported beam :	(*a*) Uniform load	1·0
	(*b*) Concentrated load	0·5
(*b*) Beams fixed at both ends :	(*a*) Uniform load	1·5
	(*b*) Concentrated load	1·0
(*c*) Cantilever supported at end :	(*a*) Uniform load	1·0
	(*b*) Concentrated load	0·6
(*d*) Cantilever fixed one end :	(*a*) Uniform load	0·25
	(*b*) Concentrated load	0·12

Comparative Relations of Depth and Defections of Beams to Span

deflection Ý1/325 of span, depth of beam Ý1/24 of span, for simply supported beams Û1/24. For shock and vibration, bearing beams it must be 1/16 of span, in light floors it is 1/18 while in heavy beams the ratio is 1/15 and deflection Ý1/480. For distributed loads, the ratio of width to span Ý1/20 while in concentrated loads Ý 1/13.

Plate girders should be provided for depths more than 40 cm.

Camber. For beams having span more than 30 m a camber in middle span is given. It can be given equal to the deflection expected or emperically 1·5 mm for every 3 m of span. Rolled sections over 380 mm depth are given with cold cambering.

Provision of Stiffners for Lateral Stability. When the ratio of span to the width of flange is increased by 1/40, stiffners are provided. Stiffners are also provided if the ratio of thickness of web to its depth is increased by 1/85. They are also provided on concentrated loads and at ends of beam. The ratio for cantilevers (flange-width to span) is limited to 1/25.

Permissible Stress for Common Steel Sections in kg/cm^2

1. Direct axial tension,	(*a*) Rolled *I* and channel sections	1500
	(*b*) Flats, Bars (round and square) angle, tee etc. upto 20 mm	1500
	over 20 mm	1420
2. Tensile and compressive stresses in bending		
	(*a*) Rolled *I* and channel sections	1650
	(*b*) Plate flats, bars round and square, angle and tee etc upto 20 mm	1650
	over 20 mm	1575
3. Bending stress for slab, beams, all slabs		1890
4. Bearing stress as net area of contact		1890
5. Max. shear for any part of member		1100
6. Max. equivalent stress due to combined bending, bearing and shearing stress upto 20 mm		2285
over 20 mm		2205
7. Direct stress in axial compression or from sections of axially loaded compression members like columns and struts (steel compressing to IS–1962)		

Table 4·3 (a)

l/K	*kg/cm²*	*l/K*	*kg/cm²*	*l/K*	*kg/cm²*	*l/K*	*kg/cm²*
0	1250	70	1075	140	531	210	243
10	1246	80	1007	150	474	220	219
20	1239	90	928	160	423	230	199
30	1224	100	840	170	377	240	181
40	1203	110	723	180	336	250	166
50	1172	120	671	190	350	260	109
60	1130	130	597	200	270	270	76

l = effective length and K = least rad. of gyration.

Note : (1) Net area = gross area – holes

(2) For untested steel take compressive and tensile stress as 1260 kg/cm² instead of 1650 kg/cm², in shear as 800. kg/cm² instead of 1100 kg/cm². Old steel should be taken as untested. For high tensile steel take 30% extra stresses.

(3) For seismic and wind loads take 33% less in allowable loads.

Table 4·3 (*b*) Compressive Members. Allowable stress in axial compression in kg/cm².

l/k	*M.S.*	*High tension 31*	*High tension 36*	*High tension 42*
0	1225	1537	1785	2083
20	1239	1520	1762	2055
40	1203	1465	1685	1946
60	1130	1347	1522	1710
80	1007	1155	1255	1352
100	840	920	960	1005

Design Procedure for a beam. Take the bending moment at a sec. of max. B.M. and obtain its sec. modulus by dividing the B.M. by the safe allowable bending stress. Locate a section from the steel tables which may suit this section modulus. Check the section for shear. Span to width ratio and diffection as per criteria given in this chapter. For *I*-sections shear force is checked for web only. Some trials will give a suitable section. For particular span and beam, deflection can be calculated. Some tables give the section direct for a given loading and span.

Thickness of Steel Metal. (1) Where it is directly exposed to weather and is liable for cleaning and painting, it must not be less than 6 mm in thickness.

(2) Where it is exposed to wéather and not liable to painting and cleaning the min. thickness should be 8 mm. (This thickness is not applicable for webs and packings.)

(3) When it is not directly exposed to weather, the thickness for main members shoiuld not be less than 6 mm and for secondry members 4·5 mm.

Table 4·3 (*c*) Max. Slenderness Ratio of Compression Members

S.No.	*Type of Loading*	*Max. l/K*
1.	Members subjected to dead and superimposed loads	180
2.	Members subjected to dead and wind loads	250
3.	Ties and roof truss	350
4.	Cast iron columns	80

Note : It is subjected that for main members l/K should be exceed 150 and for secondary members 200. l is effective length and K is the least rad. of gyration.

Loads on Columns

Short Columns. $P = fcA$ where fc = crushing strength of the column material, P = ultimate load on the column and A = area of the col. sec.

Long Columns. $p_e = \frac{\pi^2 EI}{l^2} = P/A = p = \frac{\pi^2 E}{(l/K)^2}$ (Euler's formula) for both ends hinged. For other mods. of end conditions take length of column as below as effective length.

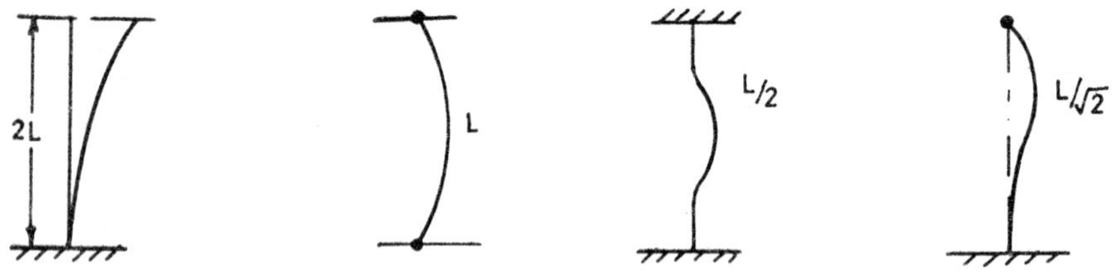

l/k = Slenderness ratio, K = min. rad. of gyration
I should be least for weakest sec.

One end fixed other free, $l/K = 40$ | Both ends hinged, $l/K = 80$ | Both ends fixed, $l/K = 160$ | One end fixed other hinged, $l/K = 113$

Fig. 4·11.

Moderate, long as well as short columns. Rankin's formula

$$P = \frac{f_C A}{1 + \frac{f_C}{\pi^2 E}(l/K)^2} \qquad \frac{f_C}{\pi^2 E} \text{ is a constant say "}a\text{" for column material}$$

where f_C = safe comp. stress of steel or material

A = sectional area of column

l = effective length of column

K = least rad. of gyration

P = load on column

L = actual length of column in between lateral supports.

Long Columns. Which fail due to buckling

or $$\frac{\text{effective length}}{\text{least lateral dimension}} > 15 \text{ or } \frac{\text{effective length}}{\text{least rad. of gyration}} > 50 \text{ (long columns)}$$

Short Columns. Which fail by crushing

or $$\frac{\text{effective length}}{\text{least lateral dimension}} < 15 \text{ or } \frac{\text{effective length}}{\text{least rad. of gyration}} < 15 \text{ (long columns)}$$

Eccentric Load on Columns. Load due to eccentric load = $\frac{P}{A} \pm \frac{M}{Z}$ where $Z = \frac{I}{y}$; y = distance of the point from N.A.

where P = load, e = eccentricity.

I = moment of inertia along a plane which does not have the ecc. point *i.e.* I is taken along yy

$$= \frac{BD^3}{12}.$$

p_0 = P/A intensity due to central load

p_b = intensity due to ecc. load, additive at the load side and substructure on the opp. side. Failure takes place when $p_0 + p_b$ reaches the ultimate crushing strength of the material or $p_0 - p_b$ reaches the ultimate tensile strength of the material.

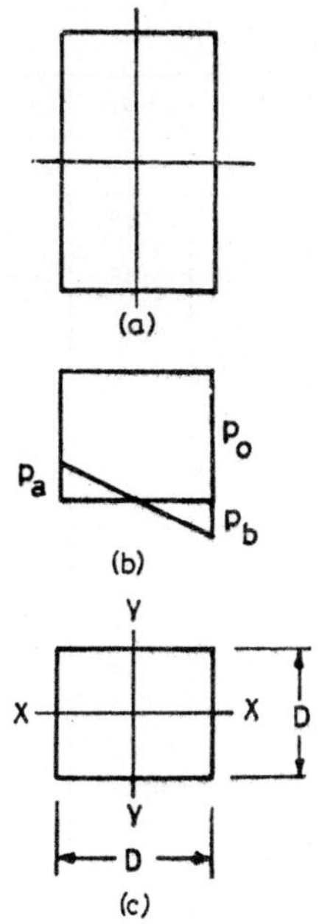

Fig. 4·12.

Shear Stress in Webs. The average shear stress f_S on the gross sections of the web shall not exceed the values of f_S given in the table "Allowable average shear stresses f_S in unstiffened webs".[(Table 4·4 (*a*)] The gross sec. of the web shall be as follows :

(1) Rolled *I*-beams and channels. The depth of the beam × web thickness.

(2) Plate girder. Depth of the web × web thickness.

Table 4·4(*a*) Allowable Average Shear Stress in Unstiffened Webs

Type of steel	*Rolled I-beam fs in kg/cm²*	*Plate girders and single channels fs in kg/cm²*
(1) IS : 226–1962 upto and including 20 mm thickness	945	945
(2) IS : 962–1962 upto and including 45 mm thickness	945	865
over 45 mm thickness	—	1100
(3) IS : 961–1962 HTW grade upto and including 32 mm	1340	1260
over 32 mm	—	1100

Value of d and t as discussed above are being given below : (Table 4·4 (*b*)

(*a*) Webs without horizontal stiffners :

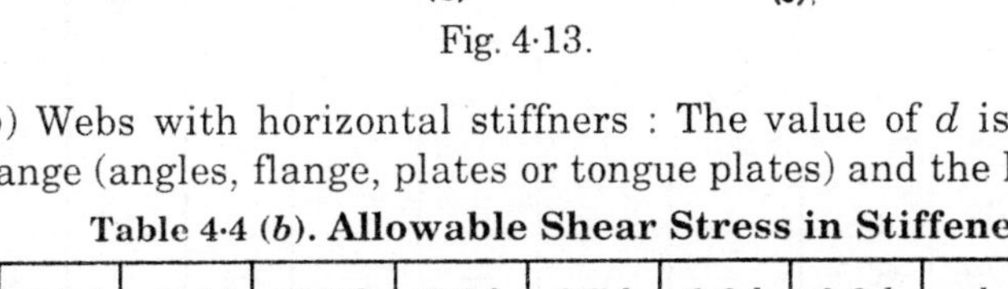

$d = d_1 - 2d_2$ or $d_1 = 8{\cdot}2t$ whichever is less

Fig. 4·13.

(*b*) Webs with horizontal stiffners : The value of d is the clear distance between the tension flange (angles, flange, plates or tongue plates) and the horizontal stiffners.

Table 4·4 (*b*). Allowable Shear Stress in Stiffened Webs in kg/cm²

d/t	*0·3d*	*0·4d*	*0·5d*	*0·6d*	*0·7d*	*0·8d*	*0·9d*	*d*	*1·1d*	*1·2d*	*1·3d*	*1·4d*	*1·5d*
		Steel confirming IS : 226–1962 and ST 440–1962											
85		945	945	945	945	945	945	945	945	945	945	945	945

Table contd...

Table contd...

d/t	*0·3d*	*0·4d*	*0·5d*	*0·6d*	*0·7d*	*0·8d*	*0·9d*	*d*	*1·1d*	*1·2d*	*1·3d*	*1·4d*	*1·5d*
		Steel confirming IS : 226–1962 and ST 440–1962											
90		945	945	945	945	945	945	945	945	945	945	945	945
100		945	945	945	945	945	945	945	945	945	937	928	920
110		945	945	945	945	945	945	945	934	920	907	893	888
120		945	945	945	945	945	939	926	907	891	879	868	858
130		945	945	945	945	931	913	901	880	865	849	838	827
140		945	945	945	931	917	890	876	854	836	821	806	795
150		945	945	945	920	910	885	850	827	808	791	776	765
160		945	945	921	888	861	841	825	800	780	762	746	734
170		945	943	902	868	839	817	800	773	751	782	717	702
180		945	926	882	846	816	792	775	746	724	704	687	672
190		945	909	863	825	794	769	—	—	—	—	—	—
200		945	893	844	803	770	745	—	—	—	—	—	—
210		934	876	825	783	748	—	—	—	—	—	—	—
220		920	858	806	761	724	—	—	—	—	—	—	—
230		907	843	786	740	—	—	—	—	—	—	—	—
240		893	825	767	718	—	—	—	—	—	—	—	—
Steel confirming IS : 961—1962													
75	1340	1340	1340	1340	1340	1340	1340	1340	1340	1340	1340	1340	1323
80	1340	1340	1340	1340	1340	1340	1340	1340	1340	1340	1323	1307	1307
90	1340	1340	1340	1340	1340	1340	1340	1340	1307	1291	1276	1260	1244
100	1340	1340	1340	1340	1340	1340	1307	1291	1260	1244	1228	1213	1197
110	1340	1340	1340	1340	1323	1291	1276	1244	1213	1197	1165	1150	1134
120	1340	1340	1340	1340	1291	1260	1228	1197	1165	1150	1118	1102	1087
130	1340	1340	1340	1291	1244	1213	1181	1165	1118	1102	1071	1055	1024
140	1340	1340	1323	1260	1213	1165	1134	1118	1071	1039	1024	992	926
150	1340	1340	1291	1228	1181	1134	1102	1071	1024	992	961	945	913
160	1340	1340	1260	1197	1134	1087	1055	1024	976	945	913	882	866
170	1340	1323	1228	1165	1102	1055	1008	976	929	898	860	835	803
180	1340	1291	1213	1134	1071	1008	976	945	882	850	810	787	756
190	1336	1276	1181	1087	1024	976	926	—	—	—	—	—	—
200	1323	1244	1150	1055	992	929	882	—	—	—	—	—	—
210	1307	1213	1118	1024	945	882	—	—	—	—	—	—	—
220	1276	1197	1087	992	913	850	—	—	—	—	—	—	—
230	1260	1165	1055	961	882	—	—	—	—	—	—	—	—
240	1244	1150	1024	929	835	—	—	—	—	—	—	—	—

Note : (1) Intermediate values may be obtained by linear interpolation .

(2) The average value of stress shown in the table 4·4 (*a*) for "Average shear stresses" should not be exceeded.

Design of an Axially Loaded Compression Member or Column. For design of a compression member the followings should be determined :

(1) **Effective length (l).** It has already been discussed before in article of "loads on columns". The actual length is measured between centre of the effective lateral supports or bottom of pedastals to top of capitals. For battened struts the effective legnth l should be increased by 10%.

(2) **Max. Slenderness Ratio.** The ratio of effective length l to the rad. of gyration r of a compression member is also given in previous articles.

(3) **Max. Deflection.** The max. horizontal deflection should be 1/325 L. L being the actual length of the column.

(*a*) **Thickness of Elements.** (*a*) Thickness of an outstanding leg of any member in compression unless the leg is stiffened shall not be less than 1/16 of the outstand. This limit is 1/20 of outstand for stiffened outstands.

(*b*) Unless effectively stiffened the unsupported width of plate forming any part of a member primarily in compression, measured between adjacent lines of rivets, bolts or welds connecting the plates to other parts of the section small not exceed the followings.

90t for steel confirming to	IS : 226–1962	t is the thickness of single
80t for steel confirming to	IS : 962–1962	Plate or the total thickness

of two or more plates effectively tacked together.

(5) Effective Sectional Area. It is the gross area of the comp. member. Deduction for the holes carried or filled by rivets, bolts or pins should not be done. However if the holes are not provided with any fastener the area of the hole is deducted.

(6) The Safe Carrying Capacity of a Compression Member is determined as below for a known member :

(*a*) The effective length for the given end condition can be computed.

(*b*) Calculate the min. rad. of gyration by the formula $r_{min.} = \left(\frac{I_{min}}{A}\right)^{1/2}$

(*c*) Calculate the slenderness ratio $l/r_{min.}$

(*d*) Allowable compressive stress (f_C) in direct compression can be computed corresponding to the max. slenderness ratio from the table Allowable stress f_C in axial compression.

(*e*) Safe load carrying capacity P of the member is determined from the formula $P = f_C.A$ (A = sec. area of the member).

Procedure for design. (1) Allowable axial stress in comp. is assumed for the member as follows :

Rolled Steel Sections :

l/R	*Allowable working stresses*
70 to 90 (struts)	1000 kg/cm^2
110 to 113 (struts)	600 kg/cm^2

Builtup Compression Members :

(1) Assuming the suitable compression stress (f_C) as above. Calculate the sectional area $A = P/f_C$.

(2) From the steel section tables locate a suitable section of the area desired as above for largest rad. of gyration possible.

(3) From the geometrical properties, compute the slenderness ratio for the section so selected and allowable f_C is found out from the table "Allowable Compressive Stress (f_C) in direct comp.". (Table 4·3 (*b*)

(4) Load carrying capacity is found out by multiplying the area to the allowable compressive stress f_C as above, which must be more than the actual load. If it is less than test another sections for a larger area.

Design Procedure for Steel Stanchion by Rankin's Formula. Assume a suitable section from steel tables.

Calculate the stress it can take by the formula $p = \dfrac{f_C}{1 + \left\{ \dfrac{f_C}{\pi^2 E} \times (l/K)^2 \right\}}$.

Area required = $P/p = A$(say) P = load as given.

Select a sec. again of this area A from steel tables and check its suitability. In two or three trials a suitable sections will be achieved.

4·2. TIMBER STRUCTURES : (A) Timber Beams and Posts

Design of Timber Beams

Effective Span. Centre of bearing to other centre of bearing for simply supported beams. For continuous beams it is measured from centre of support. For fixed beams it is clear span.

Lateral Support. When the depth to breadth ratio is more than 3 or the span exceeding 25 times its breadth lateral restraints are provided to safe against twisting or buckling and the distance between such restraints shall not exceed 25 times the breadth of the beam.

Ratio of Breadth to Depth. 5/7 for the strongest sections, but due to some restrictions and availability the width can vary 0·6 to 0·75 of depth.

Ratio of Width to Span. 1/24 for normal section, for deep beams it must not be more than 1/25. When lateral supports are used it must not be more than 1/40.

Note : The strength of a circular beam is 3/5th to that of square.

Bending moment (say M) : $M = \dfrac{wl^2}{8}$, w = uniform load and l = effective span.

$= fZ = f \times 1/6\, bd^2$

where f is the allowable bending stress of the timber in tension, b and d being width and depth of beam respectively.

Decide the ratio of b/d from above criteria from which the only unknown d can be calculated.

Deflection. It must not be more than 1/360 of span for brittle roofing materials like slate, AC sheets, gypsum ceilings or tiles etc. For other flexural members it must not be more than 1/240 of span. For cantilever members it must not be more than 1/150 of span.

Shear. (*a*) Max. horizontal shear stress in rectangular beams (H).

$$H = \frac{1{\cdot}5wl}{A} \quad \text{where } l = \text{span and } A = \text{Area of beam section}$$

Note : (1) Notches must not be deeper than d/S and must not be located in the middle 2/3rd of span. Holes must not be greater than $d/4$ in diametre and must not be located in the middle 2/3rd. The area A for H must be taken at the notched or Bored sec. S is span.

(2) In the formula $H = \dfrac{1{\cdot}5wl}{A}$ for distributed load l is taken as span-$2d$. For concentrated

loads the formula is $H = \frac{1{\cdot}5w}{A}$ in which all concentrated loads near the supports may be reduced as given in the table below.

Table 4·5 (*a*)

S. No.	*Distance of the load from the nearest support*	*Percentage reduction*
1.	1·5 *d* or less	60%
2.	2*d*	40%
3.	2·5*d*	20%
4.	3*d* or more	Nil

(3) Builtup beam sections vertically should be firmly bolted or glued together. Bolts must be staggered and spaced longitudinally not further apart than 4*d* (*d* is depth of beam).

Bearing. (*a*) Should be supported in recess for ventilations and should not be enclosed.

(*b*) Beams supported directly on masonry must not have its bearing less than 7·5 cm.

(*c*) Members supported on corbels or offsets etc. should have a wall plate not less than 7·5 × 4·0 cm.

(*d*) Timber joints must not be supported on the bottom flange of a beam of steel unless the bearing stress calculated on the net bearing as shaped to fit the beam, is not greater than permissible compressive stress perp. to the grains.

(4) **Bearing Stress.** Permissible comp. stress perp. to the grains may be multiplied by the coefficients given in the table below for bearings less than 15 cm and located 7·5 cm or more from the end of a member. For bearing stress under a washer or a smaller plate. The same coefficient may be taken for a bearing with a length equal to the dia. of the washer or the width of small plate.

Table 4·5 (*b*)

Length of bearing in cm	*Factor of increase in stress*
1·25	1·75
2·50	1·38
3·80	1·25
5·00	1·19
7·50	1·13
10·0	1·10
15·0	1·00

when the direction of stress is at an angle θ to the directions of grain in any member, then the permissible stress in bearing in that member is calculated by the following formula :

$$S_b = \frac{S_{C_1} \times S_{C_2}}{S_{C_1} \sin^2 \theta \times S_{C_2} \cos^2 \theta}$$

S_b = permissible bearing stress in the direction of the time of action of load

S_{C_1} = Permissible comp. stress parallel to the grain

S_{C_2} = Permissible comp. stress perp. to the grain.

(5) **Form Factor for Bending Members.** In beam or box sections of wood, the reduction in the amount of timber near the N.A. curtails the restraint given to the highly stressed outer fibres in the timber of the comp. flange and these fibres have a greater tendency of buckle. The

effective length of the beam is thereby reduced. With such sections the permissible stress is obtained by multiplying the safe working stress by a factor "Form factor".

Table 4·5 (*c*)

Ratio b_1/b	Ratio d_1/d — Form factors									Remarks
	0·1	0·15	0·2	0·25	0·30	0·35	0·40	0·45	0·50	
0·1	0·65	0·68	0·71	0·74	0·77	0·81	0·84	0·88	0·90	b = overall width
0·2	0·69	0·72	0·74	0·77	0·80	0·83	0·86	0·88	0·91	b_1 = Thickness of web of I sec. or total thickness of two webs of a box sec.
0·3	0·73	0·75	0·77	0·80	0·82	0·85	0·87	0·89	0·92	d = over all depth
0·4	0·77	0·79	0·81	0·83	0·85	0·87	0·89	0·91	0·93	d_1 = depth of flange in comp.
0·5	0·81	0·82	0·84	0·85	0·87	0·89	0·91	0·93	0·95	
0·6	0·85	0·86	0·87	0·88	0·90	0·91	0·93	0·94	0·96	
0·7	0·88	0·89	0·90	0·91	0·92	0·94	0·95	0·96	0·97	
0·8	0·92	0·93	0·93	0·94	0·95	0·96	0·96	0·97	0·98	
0·9	0·96	0·96	0·97	0·97	0·98	0·98	0·98	0·98	0·99	
1.0	1·00	1·00	1·00	1·00	1·00	1·00	1·00	1·00	1·00	

Note : For solid circular x-sec. the form factor is 1·18 and for solid square sections where the load is in the direction of a diagonal it is taken as 1·414.

Table 4·5 (*d*). Factor of Safety to be Applied to Basic Stress to obtain Safe Working Stress

	Particulars	Standard grade		
		Inside	Outside	Wet location
1.	Max. fibre stress in beam for broad leaved species	5	6	7·5
2.	Max. fibre stress for beams in conifers	6	7	8·5
3.	Shear along grains	7	7	7
4.	Hor. shear in beams	10	10	10
5.	Max. Comp. stress along grain	4	4·5	5·5
6.	Comp. stress across grain	1·75	2·25	2·75
7.	Modulus of elasticity for calculating allowable deflection in beams	1·25	1·75	2·0

(1) Safe working stress for timber of select grade for bending shear and compression shall be 7/6 of the safe working stress for timber of standard grade.

(2) Safe working stress for timber of common grade, for bending, shear and compression shall be 5/6 the safe working stress for timbers of standard grade.

Table 4·5 (*e*). Safe load in kg in a verandah post

Sec.(mm)	Height of Post in mm metre				
	1·8	2·1	2·4	3·0	3·7
100 × 100	3,500	3,200	3,000	2,400	1,900
125 × 125	6,400	6,000	5,600	4,900	4,200
150 × 150	10,000	9,600	9,100	8,200	7,300

Table 4·5 (*f*). Safe Working Stresses for Indian Timbers (IS : 883–1961)

S.No.	Name of timber	Coef. for Def. L/360	Coef. for Strength wL/8	Wt. in kg/m^3 12% moisture	Mode of elasticity all grades, Et/cm^2	Bending & tension along grain extreme stress			Shear stress all locations		Compressive Parallel to grain			Stress perp. to grain			Durability grade	Remarks
						Inside location	Outside location	Wet location	Hor	Along grain	Inside location	Outside location	Wet location	Inside location	Outside location	Wet location		
1	2	3	4	5	6	7	8	9	10	11	12	13	14	15	16	17	18	19
1.	Andman badam			625	90	118	98	78	8·8	12·6	72	64	52	30	23	19	III	
2.	Babool (Kikar)	1·27	1·61	835	108	182	154	124	15·4	22·2	112	102	80	65·5	50·5	41·5	III	
3.	Benleak	1·27	1·17	675	110	138	112	92	9·2	13·0	88	78	64	41·5	32·5	26·0	I	
4.	Black siris			735	136	186	154	126	15·4	21·8	134	120	94	72·5	56·0	46·5	I	
5.	Blue pine	0·8	0·58	515	68	66	56	50	5·6	8·0	52	46	38	17·0	13·5	10·5	III	
6.	Chir	1·13	0·72	575	98	84	70	60	6·4	9·2	64	56	46	21·5	17·5	14·0	III	
7.	Deodar	1·07	0·88	560	95	102	88	70	7·0	10·2	78	70	56	26·5	21·0	17·0	I	
8.	Fir (Partal)	1·07	0·66	465	94	78	66	56	6·0	8·4	60	52	42	16·0	12·5	10·5	III	
9.	Haldu	1·07	1·17	675	91	138	112	92	9·4	13·4	84	74	64	36·5	28·0	23·0	III	
10.	Jaman			850	112	152	126	102	11·6	16·6	92	84	66	57·5	45·0	36·5	II	
11.	Jarul			640	88	120	102	80	8·4	12·0	78	66	56	41·5	32·5	26·5	II	
12.	Kail	0·8	0·58	575	68	66	56	50	5·6	8·0	52	46	38	17·0	13·5	10·5	III	
13.	Mango			655	91	124	102	80	9·4	13·8	74	66	52	31·0	24·0	19·5	III	
14.	Oak			865	125	148	124	98	12·0	16·8	92	80	66	45·5	35·5	29·0	II	
15.	Sal	1·47	1·44	850	127	168	140	112	9·4	13·4	106	94	78	45·5	35·0	29·0	I	
16.	Spruce	1·07	0·66	480	92	78	66	52	6·0	8·4	56	50	42	17·0	18·5	10·5	III	
17.	Sisso			770	89	152	126	102	11·6	16·8	94	84	66	46·5	36·0	29·5	II	
18.	Teak	1·07	1·22	625	96	140	116	94	9·8	14·0	88	78	64	40·0	31·0	25·5	I	
19.	Walnut	1·07	1·00	575	91	116	94	78	8·4	12·0	66	60	50	23·0	18·5	15·0	III	
20.	White siris			625	90	134	112	88	9·8	14·0	84	28	64	43·0	33·5	27·5	II	

Note : (1) The value of horizontal stress to be used for only beams.

(2) In all other cases stress along grain are to be used.

Table 4·5 (g). Sizes of Posts for Timber Framed Buildings

No. of Storey		Max. Height, m	Size mm × mm	Dia, m
1. Single storeyed building		3·0	125 × 125	150
2. Double storeyed building	1st storey	3·0	150 × 150	175
	2nd storey	3·0	125 × 125	150
3. Triple storeyed building	1st storey	3·0	175 × 175	210
	2nd storey	3·0	150 × 150	175
	3rd storey	3·0	125 × 125	150
4. Four storeyed building	1st storey	3·0	200 × 200	240
	2nd storey	3·0	175 × 175	210
	3rd storey	3·0	150 × 150	175
	4th storey	3·0	125 × 125	150

Table 4·5 (f). Size of Roof Purlins in mm

Span (m)	Max. slanted distances apart in m		
	1·8	2·3	2·75
1·5	1115 × 75	125 × 75	150 × 75
2·4	150 × 75	175 × 75	175 × 75
3·0	175 × 75	175 × 100	200 × 100
3·65	225 × 100	223 × 115	225 × 125
4·25	225 × 125	250 × 115	250 × 100
5·0	250 × 100	250 × 125	250 × 150

(B) Flitched or Composite Beams. It is wooden beam reinforced (sandwitched) by steel plate between two wooden sections symmetrically (a particular case) and the three parts being fastened together by bolts so that the composite member deforms as if it were a single piece.

The deformation or strain in the wooden and steel sections is the same at one level.

Now let M be the resisting moment of the composite-section and M_W and M_S are for wood and steel respectively.

Then $$M = M_S + M_W \quad ...(1)$$

The strain say 'e' at the edge of steel plate in steel is the same as in wood at level of edge of steel in wooden section.

So, $$e = \frac{p_W}{E_W} = \frac{f_S}{E_S} \quad ...(2)$$

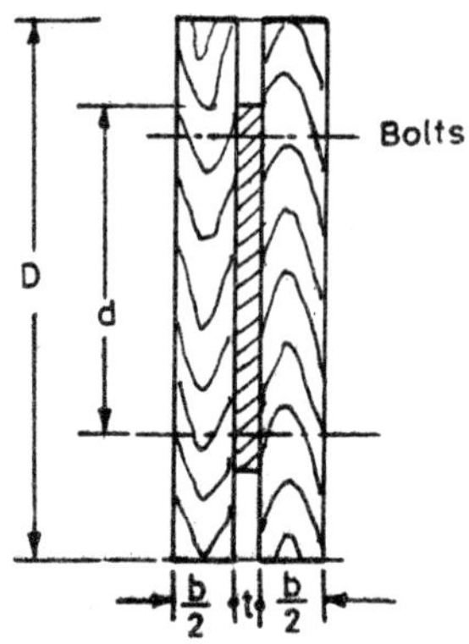

Fig. 4·14.

where p_W and f_S are the bending stress in wood and steel at the edge of steel plate.

E_W and E_S are the modulus of elasticity of wood and steel sec. or $f_S = \frac{p_W \times E_S}{E_W} = \frac{E_S}{E_W} \times \frac{d}{D} \times f_W$ since $p_W = d/D \times f_W$ where f_W is the max. bending stress in wood at its edge.

or $$f_S = m \times \frac{d}{D} \times f_W \qquad ...(3)$$

m = modulus ratio of steel and wood.

Now from equation (1) $$M = M_S + M_W = f_W . \frac{1}{6} BD^2 + f_S \times \frac{1}{6} td^2 \qquad ...(4)$$

By the above relations a composite section can be designed for a given thickness of steel and wood plates. The depth of wood D can be determined from the ratio d/D, if depth of steel plate is known.

Stress in Composite Sections due to External Loads

$$P_1 + P_2 = P \; ; \; p_1 A_1 + p_2 A_2 = P \; ; \; e_1\, l_1 = e_2\, l_2$$

(elongation in one = elongation in 2nd material)

Solving above equations p_1 and p_2 can be calculated $p_1\ A_1\ e_1\ l_1$ belong to material (1) which $p_2\ A_2\ e_2\ l_2$ belong to material (2).

Table 4·6(*a*) Distributed Safe loads in kg (25 mm wide beam) Simply Supported (Deflection taken to consideration)

Depth d in mm	*Clear span in m (A)*											*Remarks*
	1·2	*1·5*	*1·8*	*2·1*	*2·4*	*2·7*	*3·0*	*3·4*	*3·7*	*4·0*	*4·3*	
75	124	80	56	41	31	23	20	16	14	11	10	1. The loads are for 25 mm wide beam. Actual beam width in multiples of 25 mm should be multiplied by the load figures.
100	300	192	133	97	75	59	48	39	33	28	24	
125	584	372	260	191	146	115	93	77	65	55	47	
150	1012	648	450	330	253	200	162	133	112	95	82	
175	1604	1029	714	525	401	317	257	213	178	158	131	
200	2400	1536	1066	783	600	474	384	317	266	277	196	
230	3416	2184	1578	1130	856	675	546	451	379	323	279	
250	4684	3000	2083	1171	926	750	619	520	443	382		2. For end beams partially fixed with B.M. *WL*/10. Table *A* should be multiplied by 2·5 and *B* by 1·25. The table is for coeff. For other class of wood multiply the load by the coeff. given in table 4·5 (*f*) of working stresses in Indian Timber col. 4.
	Designed for strength (*B*)											
75	202	162	135	115	101	90	81	73	67	62	57	
100	360	288	240	205	180	160	144	130	120	110	102	
125	562	450	375	321	281	250	225	204	187	173	160	
150	810	648	540	462	405	360	324	294	270	249	231	
175	1102	715	683	630	531	490	441	401	367	340	315	
200	1440	1152	960	823	720	640	576	523	480	443	325	
230	1822	1458	1215	1041	911	810	729	662	607	561	50	
250	2250	1800	1500	1285	1125	1000	900	818	750	692	642	

(C) Designing Timber Columns and Struts

(*a*) **Short Column.** When l/d ratio does not exceed 11.

l = Unsupported length in cm and d = least cross dimension of col. in cm.

$P/A = C$, P = total load on column in kg, A = cross sectional area in cm^2 and C = allowable unit stress in comp. kg/cm^2.

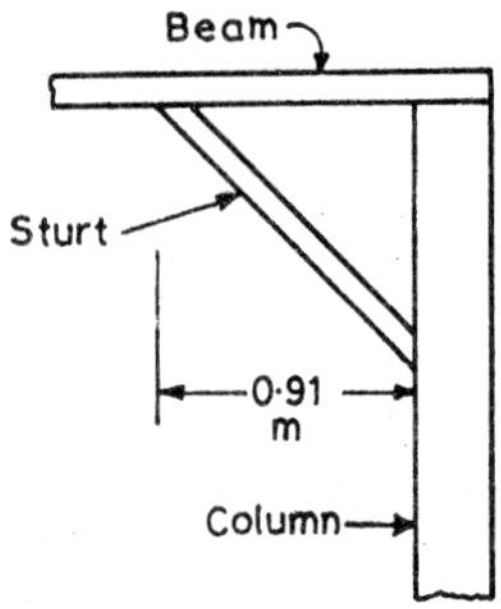

Fig. 4·15.

(*b*) **Intermediate Column.** When *l/d* ratio lies between 11 and *K*.

K = a constant depending on E and C of timber $= 0{\cdot}702\sqrt{E}/C$

E = mod. of elasticity

$$P/A = C\left\{1 - \frac{1}{3}(l/Kd)^4\right\}$$

(*c*) **Long Columns.** When *l/d* is more than *K*.

$$P/A = \frac{0{\cdot}329\,E}{(l/d)^2}$$

Note : (1) The safe working stress are taken in comp. parallel to grain. Multiply the working stress by coefficients given below for different slenderness ratio (effective span/least rad. of gyration)

Table 4·6 (*b*)

l/d	1 to 15	18	21	24	27	30	33	36	39	42	45
Coeff.	1·0	0·9	0·8	0·7	0·6	0·5	0·4	0·3	0·2	0·1	0

(2) In case of solid columns of timber *l/d* ratio should not exceed 50.

(3) Safe load on circular columns should not exceed that permitted for a square column of an equivalent cross sectional area.

(4) The corner column should be bigger in size than intermediate ones. The top of the end corner should be strutted upto 0·91 m in beams on either side. (m is metre)

(5) *l/d* ratio for tapered columns must be measured at 1/3rd or the height from top, but it must be not more than 1½ of dimension at top.

(6) Take 7/8th load for chamfered corners and 0·77 for circular columns having the dia. equal to the width of column.

(7) The compression members should not be notched or holed.

(8) The induced stress at top of tapered section should not exceed the permissible compressive stress in the direction of grains.

(9) Builtup sections should be glued, screwed or bolted together.

(10) If the comp. member is bored or notched. The local stress must be calculated which must be within permissible limits. The distance from the edge of the hole to edge of member should not be less than 1/4 of the width of force.

(D) Roof Truss in Wood

Weights of Covering Materials of Roofs. (1) These weights are vertical wt. normal to the roof surface, should be obtained multiplying by the cosine of the roof angle to horizontal.

(2) Weight due to dead wt. of truss with purlins and rafters etc. may be taken at 2·5 kg/m^2 for normal roofs and 3·0 kg/m^2 for heavy roof.

Wt. of Roofing Materials

1.	Corrugated galvanised iron sheets	18 B.G.	13 kg/m^2
		32 B.G.	8·5 kg/m^2
		24 B.G.	7·3 kg/m^2
2.	Asbestos corrugated sheets 6 mm thick		16 kg/m^2
	plane		11 kg/m^2
3.	Wood boards 25 mm thick		15 kg/m^2
	20 mm thick		10 kg/m^2

4. Bitumin roofing tiles 7·5 kg/m^2
5. Slates supported with battons 34 kg/m^2
   boards 25 mm thick 60 kg/m^2
6. Thatches with frames 25 mm thick 50 kg/m^2
   15 mm thick 30 kg/m^2
7. Single Allahabad tiles with battons 85 kg/m^2
   Double Allahabad tiles with battons 160 kg/m^2
   Manglore tiles with flat tiles set in mortar 105 kg/m^2
   Manglore tiles with ballons tiles set in mortar 70 kg/m^2
   Country tiles with single battons 105 kg/m^2
   Country tiles with double battons 115 kg/m^2

Design Procedure with Wooden Roof Truss Member

Battons : Min. size 25 × 32 mm and spacing 30 cm c/c. For soft wood mm size is 32 × 38 mm. Fix the span of battons according to the available size of boarding and loads on roof.

Common Rafter : $\frac{\text{Spacing of rafters span}}{4} + 14$ cm; span of rafter = Span/2 sec ϕ (max. 2·5 m) where ϕ is the angle of the roof. Span means span of truss. They are considered as partly fixed as they are spiked to ridge and purlins. The load is taken normal to the rafter and is designed for deflection as in beams.

Purlin : They are designed as simply supported beams and not for deflection. As they have tangential force acting along the roof slope. Cleats are provided under purlins to check this load.

Ties : Loads are taken normal to the roof. Tension = $\frac{wL}{4H}$ with a min. of 65 × 25 mm where L is the span in m and H is the height of truss. $W = wLD \sec \phi$ where W = wt. of roof including live load normal to the roof, ϕ = angle of roof, D = spacing of rafters.

(1) Tie should have a min. bearing of 20 cm on wall or pier.

(2) Ties supported with ceilings above 3·6 m span, should be calculated for a deflection of $L/480$.

(3) The beams are given with a camber of $l/240$.

(4) King posts are used for spans upto 6 to 9 m.

Queen posts are used for spans upto 9 to 13·5 m.

Table 4·7. Sections for Members of a King Post Truss Wooden (with iron King Rod)

Span in m	*Principal rafter mm*	*Struts mm*	*Tie beam with ceiling mm*	*Tie beam without ceiling, mm*	*King rod dia. mm*	*Remarks*
			Roof load 220 kg/m^2			
4·25	100 × 125	100 × 75	100 × 125	100 × 100	20	Spacing of trusses 3·0 m and slope of roof at 30°
5·00	100 × 125	100 × 75	100 × 125	100 × 100	20	
5·50	100 × 150	100 × 75	100 × 125	100 × 100	20	
6·00	100 × 150	100 × 75	100 × 125	100 × 100	22	
6·50	100 × 175	100 × 100	100 × 150	100 × 125	25	
7·50	100 × 200	100 × 100	100 × 150	100 × 125	25	
8·00	100 × 200	100 × 100	100 × 150	100 × 125	25	
8·50	100 × 200	100 × 125	100 × 200	100 × 175	40	

Table contd...

Roof load 170 kg/m²						
4·25	100 × 100	75 × 75	100 × 125	75 × 75	16	
5·00	100 × 125	100 × 75	100 × 125	75 × 100	16	
5·50	100 × 125	100 × 75	100 × 125	100 × 100	16	
6·00	100 × 150	100 × 75	100 × 125	100 × 100	20	
6·50	100 × 150	100 × 75	100 × 125	100 × 100	20	
7·50	100 × 175	100 × 75	100 × 125	100 × 100	20	
8·00	100 × 175	100 × 100	100 × 150	100 × 125	25	
8·50	100 × 175	100 × 100	100 × 170	100 × 150	25	
Roof load 120 kg/m²						
4·50	100 × 75	75 × 75	100 × 125	75 × 100	12	
5·00	100 × 100	75 × 75	100 × 125	75 × 100	12	
5·50	100 × 100	100 × 75	100 × 125	75 × 100	16	
6·00	100 × 100	100 × 75	100 × 125	75 × 100	16	
6·50	100 × 125	100 × 75	100 × 125	75 × 100	20	
7·50	100 × 125	100 × 75	100 × 125	100 × 100	20	
8·00	100 × 125	100 × 75	100 × 150	100 × 100	22	
8·50	100 × 150	100 × 100	100 × 150	100 × 125	25	

(1) Principal rafters are kept usually 2·5 m c/c and common rafters at 0·7 m c/c.

(2) ± 25% variation in span will no change in span.

(3) The spans should be reduced by 75 percent for heavy loads.

(4) The spacing between timber trusses are kept between 2·5 m to 3·0 m.

(5) Beyond span of 7·6 m steel trusses are preferred.

(6) For soft wood sectional area is increased by 75%.

Economical span of truss (spacing of trusses) in m	3	4	4·5	5·5	6·0
Span of purlin L in m	6	12	18	24	30

Economical span of purlin

$$L = \sqrt[3]{\frac{0.384\,EI}{w}}$$

w = twice of dead load + live loads + wind loads/cm lengths of purlin

(E) Wooden Stairs

Newel post : The lower most post of sufficient strength on which the hand rail rests or a post on the junction of flight.

Scotia : It is moulding provided under using to beautify the elevation of step.

Winders : Tapering steps which are provided for changing the direction of stair.

Flier : Rectangular steps of uniform width.

Baluster : Vertical posts supporting the hand rail.

Stringer : The inclined members generally two, which supports boards having risers and treads for stairs

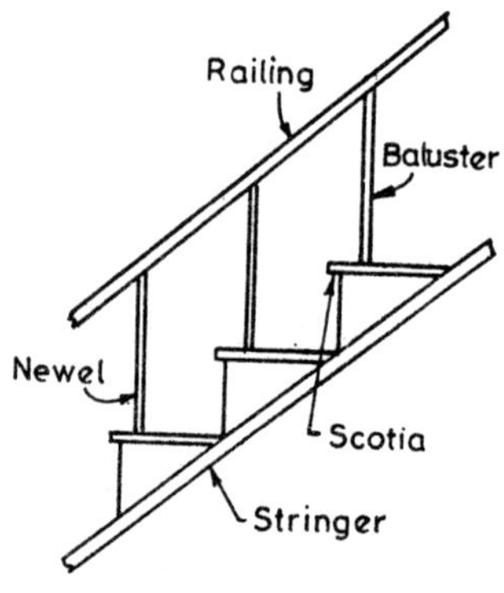

Fig. 4·16.

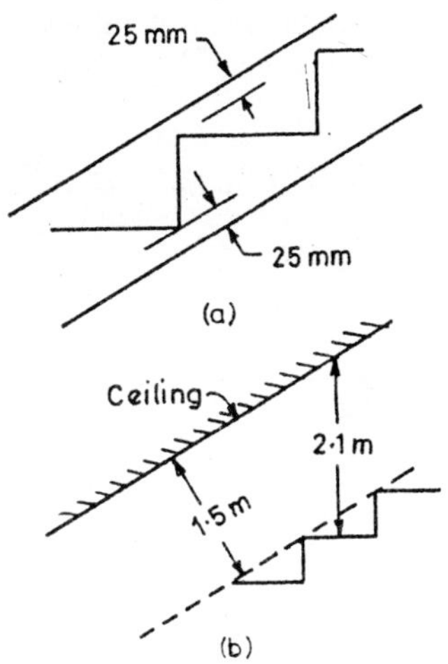

Fig. 4·17.

upto 1·2 m wide. For wider they may be three upto 2·5 m and four beyond 2·5 m width. The width of the end stringer is such that it may project 25 mm above and 25 mm below the edge of riser with a min. thickness of 40 mm for 1·2 m wide step. The thickness will increase by 5 mm for each extra width of 15 mm.

The intermediate stringers (carriage pieces) are kept 100 mm high and 50 mm thick fixed with angles to support stairs. For 15 step flight the steps are either housed or wedged to the stringers. In housing the step is housed to a hole in stringing and in wedge it is supported on a wedge fixed to the stringer.

Treads and Risers : The min. thickness of tread is 32 mm and riser 25 mm upto 1·2 m width of steps. The thickness increases by 3 mm for every increase in width of 15 cm (refer building construction for more details).

General Rules : Head room : Min 2·1 m from pitch line to the ceiling or soffit vertically and also 1·5 m min. clearance at Right angles to the line.

Pitch : Min. 25° Max. 45°.

Going : Min. 20 cm.

Tread : Min. width 22 cm. with nosing.

Flight length : Max. nos. should be 13 (risers) in a flight.

Height of Hand Rail : Pitch line to top of sloping hand rail measured vertically. Min. 75 cm., Max. 85 cm.

Floor level to horizontal hand rail min. 90 cm.

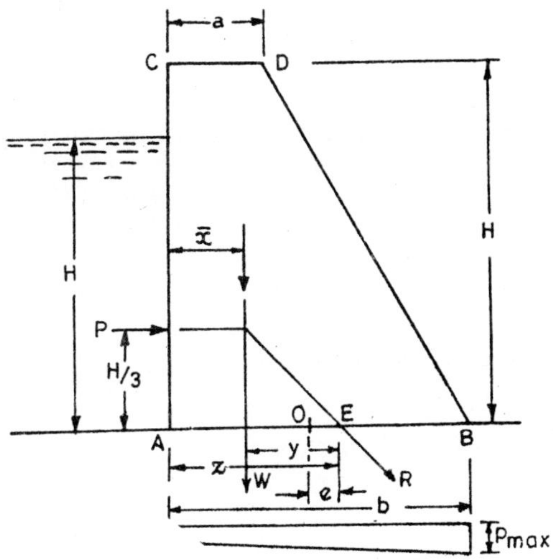

Fig. 4·18.

4·3. Masonry Dams

(a) **Water Face Vertical**

(1) Water pressure

$$= P = \frac{wH^2}{2}$$

acting at $H/3$ from base horizontally.

(2) Wt. of masonry W

$$= \rho\frac{a+b}{2} \times H_1$$

acting vertically at $\bar{x} = \dfrac{a^2 + ab + b^2}{3(a+b)}$ from vertical force.

a = top and b = bottom width

w = density of water, ρ the density of dam masonry.

(3) p_{max} (max. pressure) at base = $W/b\ (1 + 6\ e/b)$ where e = eccentricity OE, O being the mid point of base.

p_{min} = (Min. pressure at base)

$$= W/b\left(1 - \frac{6e}{b}\right)$$

Theory of Design of Structures

If $e = b/6$, then max. pressure at toe = 2 (comp.) and min. = 0 at heel. So it follows that if tension is to be avoided the eccentricity (e) should not exceed $b/6$ on either side of the centre or the resultant should pass through middle 3rd of the base (b).

Taking moments about A the heel $-P \times \frac{H}{3} + W\bar{x} = W_z$, $z = y + \bar{x}$ or $b^2 + ba = a^2 + \frac{W}{\rho}.H^2$ where b is min. or $z = \frac{2b}{3}$. ...(A)

Knowing other factors, z the position of point where resultant crosses the base is determined.

Stability of Masonry Dams

(1) Stability against sliding for which $P < \mu W$, where μ is the coeff. of friction between soil and masonry of dam. A factor of safety of 1·5 to 2·0 is taken against sliding.

(2) The resultant of P and W must pass through middle 3rd of base to avoid overturning and tension in base beyond its safe working capacity.

(3) The max. compressive stress induced in base must be less than the permissible working stress of masonry of dam.

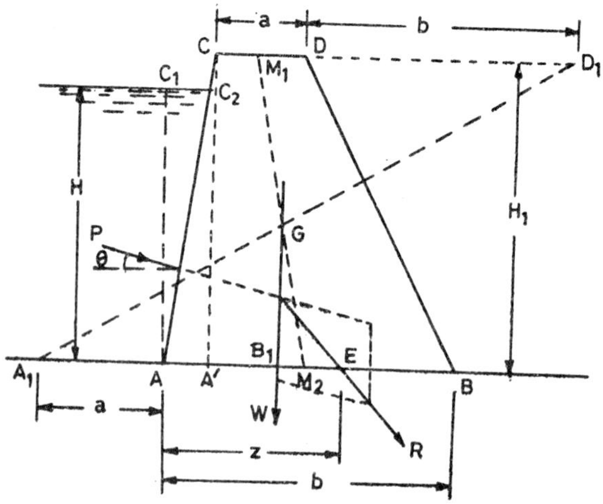

Fig. 4·19.

(4) The min. base width for stability is achieved when the resultant of P and W just passes through the middle 3rd of the base, and is given by the equation, $P \times \frac{H}{3} + W\bar{x} = Wz$, where $P = \frac{WH^2}{2}$; $z = \frac{2}{3}b$; $\bar{x} = \frac{a^2 + ab + b^2}{3(a+b)}$ and W = wt. of masonry/unit length, so b can be calculated from the expression (A), $b^2 + ba = a^2 + \frac{W}{\rho}.H^2$.

(b) **Water Face Slanting**

(1) The water pressure

$P = wH\,l/2$ where l = face AC_2 and acts at $AC_2/3$ normal to face.

(i) Horizontal component of water pressure

$Ph = wH^2/2$ acting at $H/3$ from base on vertical face AC_1 ...(1)

(ii) Vertical component P_V

$$\text{Wt. of water wedge } C_1AC_2 = w \times C_1A \times \frac{C_2C_1}{2} \quad ...(2)$$

acting at $\frac{C_2C_1}{3}$ from face AC_1.

(2) Wt. W of masonry $ABCD = \frac{a+b}{2} \times H_1\rho$ acting at c.g. of sec. ...(3)

Note : Centre of gravity of dam sec. can be determined graphically as below. Take $AA_1 = a$; $DD_1 = b$, M_1M_2 are the mid points of base and top. Then c.g. is the point which is obtained by the intersection of M_1M_2 to A_1D_1.

Analytically : Vertical from the point A (discussed in chapter 2) c.g. of trepezium. Fig. 2·84 (*c*). Component V = wt. of water wedge (2) + wt. of masonry (3) (considering an unit width of dam section).

Let z be the distance from A of the point of intersection of R on the base then ecentricity $e = (z - b/2)$.

$$P_{max} = p_0 \times \left(1 + \frac{6e}{b}\right) \text{ at } B \text{ and } p_{min} = p_0 \times \left(1 - \frac{6e}{b}\right) \text{ at } A \text{ ; } p_0 = \frac{V}{b}.$$

Take moments about A and calculate z the point where resultant of P_h, P_v and W cuts the base, which should be in the middle 3rd as is done in case (*a*).

Graphical Method for determining the position of the point where the resultant cuts the base.

1. Draw the dam section to a scale. Calculate the water pressure normal to the face AC $= wH\frac{l}{2}$ which acts at $l/3$ normal to face from base. Mark it on dam section to a scale.

2. Determine the position of c.g. of the section as determined above and mark the weight of the dam section to a scale passing vertically from c.g. Draw the resultant line which can locate the point where R cuts the base.

(*c*) **Curved Surface of Masonry.** Assume that the dam is full of water (refer the figure 4·20). Consider the section line *bb* as the base of the dam. G_1 be its centre of area above *bb* and W_1 as its weight. P_1 be the water pressure above *bb* acting at 1/3 of height above *bb*. Find the point at which the resultant will pass. Now again consider the whole section of dam above *cc*. This gives a new centre of area G_2, new wt. W_2 and a new pressure P_2. Find the point on *cc* at which resultant of W_2 and P_2 cuts the line *cc* (The procedure of locating this point is discussed above) and so on W_3 and W_4.

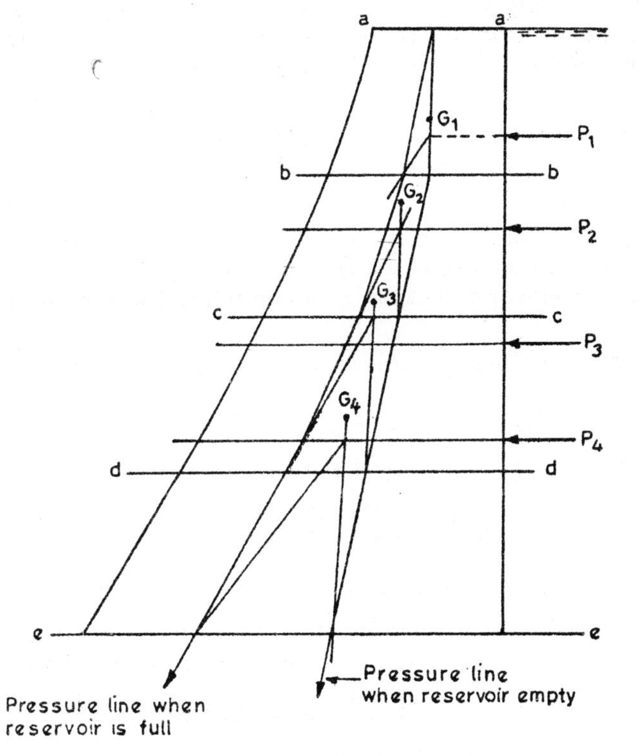

Fig. 4·20.

Repeat this considering the whole section above *dd* and *ee* in turn. Mark clearly the points at which each resultant cuts its own section line and draw a smooth curve through these points. This curve is known as the line of pressure when the dam is full.

Now assume the reservoir empty. In this case only weight of the masonry acts. The point at which it cuts the base section is located and a curve is drawn for this whole sec. This curve is known as pressure curve when the reservoir is empty. Both the curves should pass through the middle 3rd of each sections.

Curved Water Face. The total water pressure and its point of application can be obtained by considering the equilibrium of the volume of water ABC. Consider a unit length of surface in a direction perpendicular to the plane of the figure.

(1) The pressure on vertical $BC = P = wH^2/3$ acting at $H/3$ from the base B.

(2) Weight of volume of water ABC acting at its *c.g.* say $C_1 = W$.

(3) R = Total reaction of fluid pressure of surface AB.

The three forces PW and R maintain the fluid ABC in equilibrium will intersect at a common point "*a*".

Choosing a convenient scale draw ab to represent P and ac to represent W, then diagonal ad gives the resultant force on the surface R. The line of action on the surface AB is at e, the point at which the line of action of R cuts the surface.

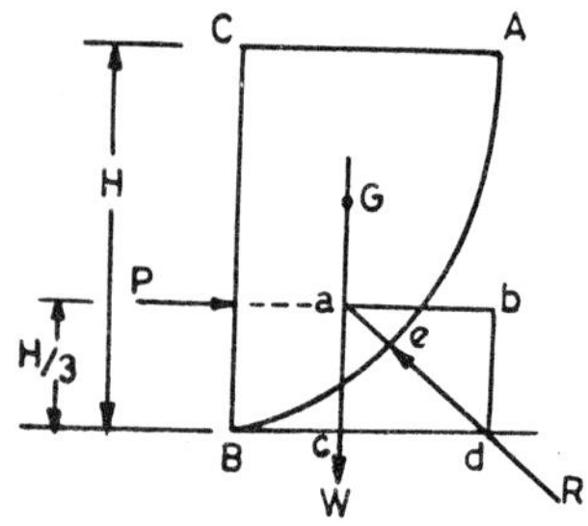

Fig. 4·21.

'High' and 'Low' Gravity Dams. A 'low' gravity dam is one in which, when the resultant passes through the lower middle third point, the maximum compressive stress at the toe does not exceed the permissible limit. A 'high' gravity dam is one in which the maximum permissible compressive stress would be exceeded if the resultant were to pass through the middle third point. To avoid excessive stresses the resultant must be maintained still nearer the centre of the base for which purpose. The down stream slope has to be flattened and the up-stream face also provided with a batter.

In case of high gravity dams it is necessary to proceed with the design of the section step by step. A tentative profile having been assumed, it is divided into a number of zones by horizontal planes and the stress conditions and safety against sliding analysed at the base of each zone. The computation required for complete stability check of a straight gravity dam by the two dimensional method may be summarised as below for at least two main conditions *viz.* reservoir full and reservoir empty.

To locate the point where the resultant R cuts the base, draw the dam section, P, W and R (Pressure of water, wt. of the dam masonry and their resultant) to scale then $\tan\theta = P/W$

Other forces acting on the gravity dams

Uplift Pressure. Some water seeps into foundation of dam causes uplift pressure say P_u. This balances part of vertical load W of the dam and thus reduces the stability. It is used to assume uplift pressure corresponding to head H of water depth at heel and full tail water depth at toe.

Sometimes drainage galleries are also provided in the body of the dam which releases the uplift.

The uplift pressure at heel, $P_e = wH$, (H = u/s head of water)

at toe, $P_e = wH'$ (H' = d/s head of water)

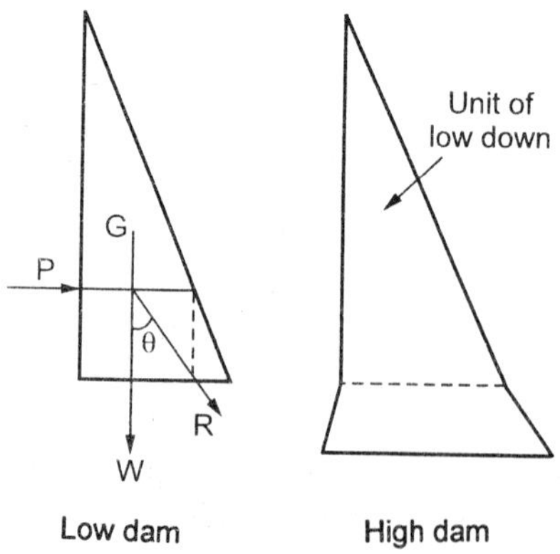

Fig. 4·21.

Uplift pressure acts at c.g. of the uplift pressure diagram.

Pressure due to earthquake (P_e)

$P_e = 0{\cdot}555\ WH^2 \times g/10$ where g is acceleration due to gravity and acts at $\dfrac{4H}{3\pi}$ above the base.

The increase of earthquake pressure is instantaneous. The vertical effect of earthquake is not much damaging and effects only in vertical direction which sometimes increases the weight of the dam while it decreases the weight at the other time.

Ice Pressure (P_i). Its magnitude varies from 25 kg/cm² to 15 kg/cm² depending upon the temperature. An average value is 5 kg/cm².

Wave Pressure (P_w). It is equal to $2wh_w^2 \cdot \frac{t}{m}$ where h_w is the height of waves between trough and crest. The force acts at a distance $\frac{3}{8}\, h_w$ above the reservoir surface. (refer earthen dams in Irrigation Chapter).

4·4. Retaining Walls and Walls

(A) Retaining Walls :

Earth Pressure on Retaining Walls (Rankine formula) :

(1) **Earth Face Vertical and Filled upto Top**

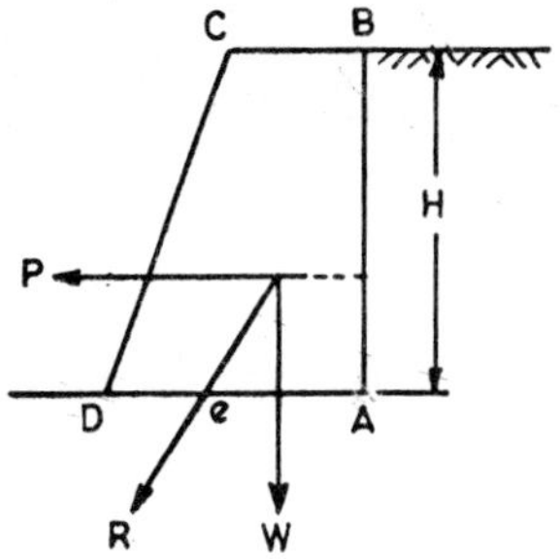

Fig. 4·22.

$$P = \frac{w_1 H^2}{2} \times \frac{1-\sin\phi}{1+\sin\phi}$$ Backfill is considered to be perfectly dry.

acting horizontally $H/3$ from base.

w_1 = wt. of soil and ϕ is angle of repose of soil,

W is the weight of wall masonry at its *c.g.* acting downward.

(2) **Earth Face Vertical and Filled upto Top with an Uniformly Distributed Load on Top as K kg/m.**

Let H = height of earthfill at the base of the wall.

H' = imaginary height of earthfill equivalent to distributed load in metres K/w_1, w_1 being the density of soil so $H + H' = H_1$ (say).

Then $$P = \frac{1}{2} w_1 (H+H')^2 \times \frac{1-\sin\phi}{1+\sin\phi} \text{ acting at } \frac{H+H'}{3}$$ from base ...(2)

Another way :

$$P = \frac{1}{2} w_1 H(H+2H') \times \frac{1-\sin\phi}{1+\sin\phi} \text{ acting at } \frac{1}{3} H \times \frac{H+3H'}{H+2H'} \quad ...(3)$$

when the superimposed load is beyond $H/2$ from the vertical of the heel on the top surface, it is not considered, (refer Fig. 4·25) for more safety it may be considered upto angle $45° + \frac{\phi}{2}$ (refer Fig. 4·25).

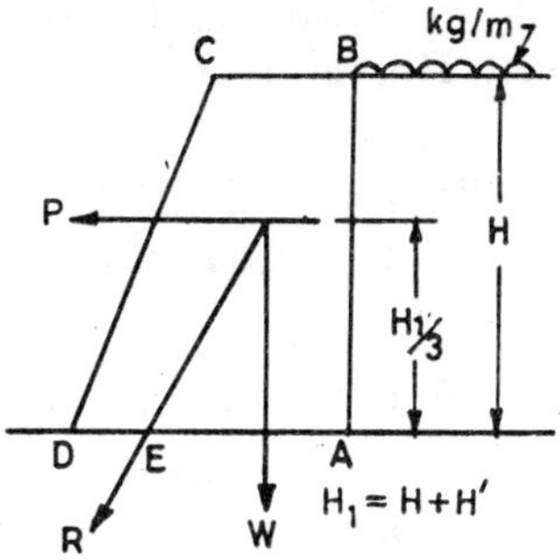

Fig. 4·23.

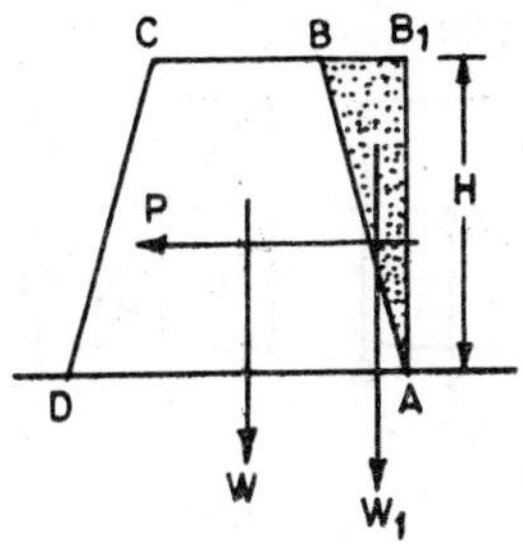

Fig. 4·24.

(3) **Earth Face is Slanting and Filled upto Top.**

$$P = \frac{w_1 H^2}{2} \times \frac{1-\sin\phi}{1+\sin\phi} \text{ acting } H/3 \text{ from base horizontally} \quad ...(4)$$

W_1 = vertical load of the soil triangle sec. acting downward at a distance BB_1 1/3 from

$$AB_1 = BB_1 \times \frac{H}{2} W_1$$

W = wt. of masonry acting vertically down and passing from *c.g.* of the section = $\frac{a+b}{2} \times H \times \rho$ (*c.g.* can be located as in the case of dams), ρ is the density of the masonry.

(4) **Earth Face is Slanting and Filled upto Top together with an Uniformly Distributed Load.**

Convert the distributed load to equivalent load in earth height as above in case 2.

$P = \frac{w_1 H_1^2}{2} \times \frac{1 - \sin\phi}{1 + \sin\phi}$ as expression (2) in case (2) (where $H_1 = H + H'$ and acts at $H_1/3$ horizontally, w_1 = density of soil.

Vertical loads are :

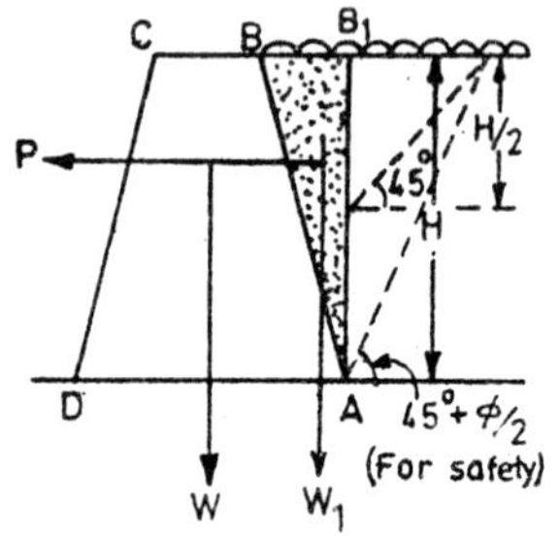

Fig. 4·25.

(1) Wt. of soil triangle $w_1 \times (AB, B) = \frac{H \times BB_1}{2} \times w_1$ and acts at $\frac{BB_1}{3}$ from AB_1.

(2) Wt. of distributed load $BB_1 = \frac{K.BB_1}{w_1}$ at $\frac{BB_1}{2}$ from AB_1.

(3) Wt. of masonry $= \frac{a+b}{2} \times H \times \rho$ and acts at *c.g.* of wall.

5. Face Slanting Earth Surcharged at an angle α with Horizontal

$$P = \frac{w_1 H^2}{2}\left(\cos\alpha \frac{\cos\alpha\sqrt{\cos^2\alpha - \cos^2\phi}}{\cos\alpha + \sqrt{\cos^2\alpha - \cos^2\phi}}\right) = \frac{w_1 H'^2}{2} \cos\phi$$

when $\alpha = \phi$ ...(5)

acting at $H'/3$ from base parallel to face of surcharge.

W_1 = vertical earth load due to triangle AB_1B acting at $BB_1/3$ from face AB_1.

W = wt. of masonry acting downward at its *c.g.*

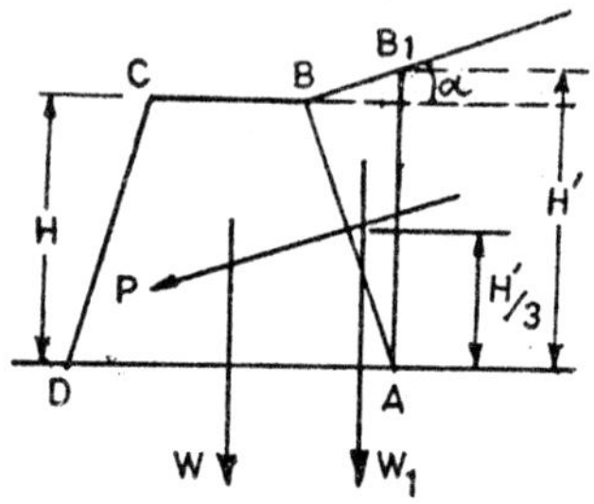

Fig. 4·26.

The vertical component of the inclined thrust P is added with the wt. of the wall when back is inclined

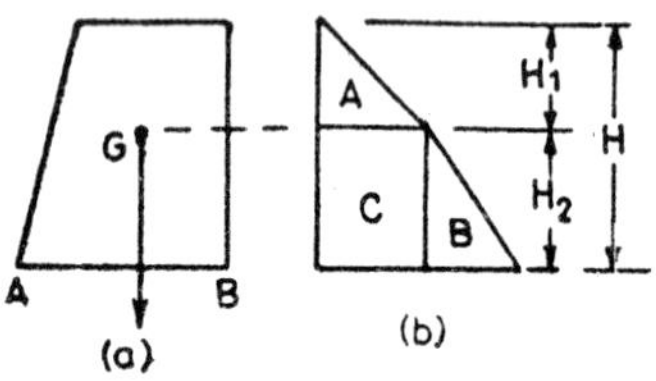

Fig. 4·27.

6. The back fill is Saturated with Water

(*a*) **Saturated upto Top.**

$$P = \frac{w_2 H^2}{2}\left(\frac{1 - \sin\phi}{1 + \sin\phi}\right) + \frac{wH^2}{2} \quad ...(6)$$

(where w_2 is the wt. of saturated soil under water and w is the wt. of water per unit).

$$w_2 = \text{wt. } w_1 \text{ of soil in air} + \left(\frac{\text{Percentage of voids in soil}}{100} \times \text{water wt. } w\right) - \text{wt. of water}$$

(*b*) **Saturated upto height H_2.**

$$P = \underset{(A)}{w_1 H_1^2 \times \frac{1 - \sin\phi}{1 + \sin\phi}} + \underset{(B)}{\frac{w H_2^2}{2}} + \underset{(C)}{w_2 H_2^2 \frac{1 - \sin\phi}{1 + \sin\phi}} \text{(Horizontal)} \quad ...(7)$$

A = Pressure due to dry soil in height H_1 acting at $H_2 + H_1/3$ from base (Hor.)

B = Water pressure in height H_2 acting at $H_2/2$ from base (Hor.)

C = Pressure due to saturated earth acting at $H_2/3$ from base.

Note : (1) W = Vertical load of masonry acting down from *c.g.* of sec. of wall (knowing) the horizontal and vertical loads, take moments about A and locate the point where resultant cuts the base. This point should lie within middle 3rd of the base, as in case of masonry dams.

(2) For the safe guide and against sliding, horizontal force $P = \mu$ total vertical load W as in case of masonry dams. μ being the safe coefficient of friction between the wall and ground. A factor of safety of 1·5 to 2·0 is to be taken.

Properties of Soil under Water

Material	*Angle of repose in water*	*wt. of material in water*
Sand	27°	960 kg/m^3
Sand mixed clay	18°	1040 kg/m^3
Clay	16°	1280 kg/m^3
Gravel	27°	960 kg/m^3
Gravel mixed clay	18°	1040 kg/m^3
Gravel sand and clay	18°	1040 kg/m^3
Soil	16°	1120 kg/m^3
In earthen dam it may be upto		1600 kg/m^3

Coefficient of Friction between different surfaces

Surfaces	*Coeff. of friction*
Masonry–Sand	0·40
Masonry–dry clay	0·50
Masonry–moist clay	0·33
Masonry–Gravel	0·60
Masonry–Rock	0·75
Cement conc.–clay	0·20
Cement conc.–sand	0·40
Cement conc.–gravel	0·40
Wood–wood	0·48

Counter Forts and Buttresses. Long walls are generally provided with counterforts at suitable distance apart depending on the pressure behind it.

Their width at top is about 60 cm thickness of the wall at top which increases at base depending on the load.

The back of the wall is either sloped or provided with steps to have a better friction.

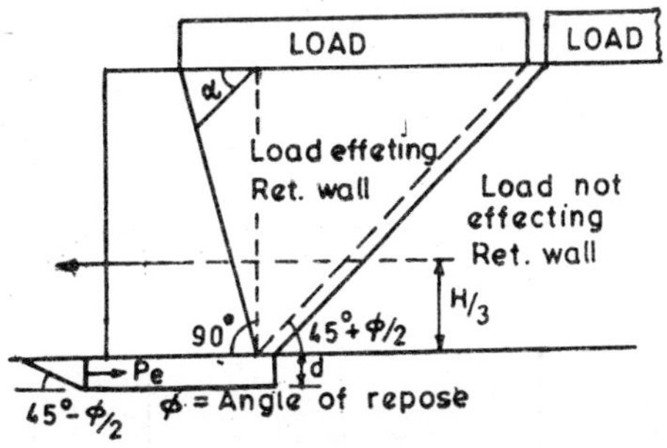

Fig. 4·28.

Front faces are battered 1 : 12 to 14 to have a better stability. The bottom width varies 1/3 to 1·0 of the height of wall and should be sloped down (1 : 8) from toe at right angle from outer face of the wall (refer Fig. 4·29)

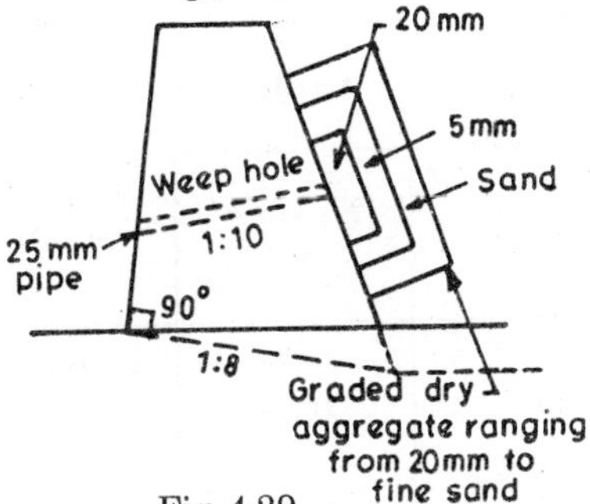

Fig. 4·29.

Draining of Retaining Walls

Weep Holes. Weep holes are provided at regular intervals. The dia. of weep hole pipe and its spacing depends on the pressure of water behind it. A filter of graded material is provided behind weep holes. So that fines of the soil may not pass with water through weep holes.

Table 4·8 (*a*). Weight and Angle of Repose of Different Soils

Type of soil	*Angle of repose degrees*	*Wt. lb/c.ft.*	*Wt. kg/m^3*
Sand dry and loose	30-37	100	1600

Table contd...

Table contd...

Type of soil	*Angle of repose degrees*	*Wt. lb/c.ft.*	*Wt. kg/m³*
Sand consolidated	35	120	1900
Sand damp	35	104-112	1650-1800
Sand very wet	26	120	1900
Dry clay	29	110	1760
Damp clay	45	115	1840
Saturated clay	15	120	1900
Clay with gravel	38	132	2100
Gravel	48	110-115	1760-1840
Gravel with sand	26	120	1900
Shingle loose	29	115	1840
Veg. earth dry	29	90	1450
Veg. earth moist	48	100	1600
Veg. earth wet	17	105	1660
Veg. dry consolidated	50	100	1600
Loamy earth	40	90	1450
Mud	40	90	1450
Ashes	40	40	640

In formula $P = \frac{wh^2}{2} \times \cos\alpha \, \frac{\cos\alpha - \sqrt{\cos^2\alpha - \cos^2\phi}}{\cos\alpha + \sqrt{\cos^2\alpha - \cos^2\phi}} = K.\frac{wh^2}{2}$ (refer expression (5))

P = earth pressure on slanting faces with surcharge, $P_H = P\cos\alpha$ and $P_V = P\sin\alpha$.

(α = angle of surcharge and ϕ is angle or repose of soil.) Vertical component of the inclined thrust P is taken with weight of the wall when back fill is inclined.

Table 4·8 (*b*). Value of *K*

$\alpha°/\phi°$ → ↓	15	20	25	30	35	40	45
10	0·70	0·57	0·46	0·37	0·29	0·23	0·17
20			0·54	0·42	0·32	0·25	0·19
25				0·49	0·37	0·27	0·21
30					0·44	0·32	0·23
35						0·39	0·27
40							0·34

Table 4·8 (*c*). Coefficient for Calculating Earth Pressure

Angles repose of soil (φ) in deg.	$\frac{1-\sin\phi}{1+\sin\phi}$	$\cos\phi$	$\frac{1+\sin\phi}{1-\sin\phi}$	$\cos^2\phi$	$\left(\frac{1-\sin\phi}{1+\sin\phi}\right)^2$	$\left(\frac{1+\sin\phi}{1-\sin\phi}\right)^2$
15	0·59	0·966	1·7	0·933	0·35	2·88
17	0·55	0·956	1·82	0·914	0·30	3·33
20	0·49	0·940	2·04	0·883	0·24	4·22
25	0·41	0·906	2·46	0·821	0·16	6·07
26	0·39	0·896	2·56	0·810	0·15	6·56
28	0·35	0·891	2·88	0·794	0·12	8·30
30	0·33	0·860	3·00	0·740	0·11	9·00
31	0·32	0·857	3·12	0·735	0·10	9·76

Table contd...

Table contd...

Angles repose of soil (ϕ) in deg.	$\frac{1-\sin\phi}{1+\sin\phi}$	$\cos\phi$	$\frac{1+\sin\phi}{1-\sin\phi}$	$\cos^2\phi$	$\left(\frac{1-\sin\phi}{1+\sin\phi}\right)^2$	$\left(\frac{1+\sin\phi}{1-\sin\phi}\right)^2$
32	0·30	0·848	3·26	0·720	0·09	10·59
33	0·29	0·839	3·40	0·704	0·09	11·50
34	0·28	0·829	3·53	0·680	0·08	12·51
35	0·27	0·819	3·69	0·671	0·07	13·62
36	0·26	0·809	3·87	0·655	0·07	14·82
37	0·25	0·798	4·02	0·638	0·06	16·18
38	0·24	0·788	4·20	0·621	0·06	17·67
39	0·23	0·777	4·43	0·603	0·05	19·64
40	0·22	0·766	4·60	0·588	0·05	21·16
41	0·21	0·755	4·81	0·570	0·04	23·40
42	0·20	0·743	5·04	0·552	0·04	25·40
43	0·19	0·731	5·29	0·532	0·04	27·98
44	0·18	0·791	5·55	0·509	0·03	30·84
45	0·17	0·707	5·83	0·500	0·03	33·94
46	0·16		6·12		0·03	37·43
47	0·15		6·43		0·02	41·34
48	0·14		6·78		0·02	45·97
49	0·13		7·16		0·02	51·27
50	0·12		7·54		0·02	56·85

6. Walls : Slenderness ratio for wall = $\frac{\text{effective height or length whichever is less}}{\text{Effective thickness of wall}}$

$$\text{Slenderness ratio for column} = \frac{\text{effective length}}{\text{least rad. of gyration or least lateral width}}$$

The slenderness ratio raises from 12 to 24 according to the mortar.

Effective height : It is as follows :

(1) Walls without lateral support at top = 1·5 of actual height.

(2) Walls with lateral support at top = 0·75 of floor to floor height.

(3) Column without lateral support at top = 2 of actual height.

(4) Column with lateral support at top = actual height between lateral supports.

Height of wall is measured from plinth level to top excluding parapets.

Effective length of Walls. It is distance between the centres of two peir buttress or intersecting walls.

Thickness of Walls. It must not be less than the total load divided by the safe crushing strength of the masonry of the wall. The buckling tendency is less in walls than peirs.

Table 4·9 (*a*). The compressive stress for load bearing should be reduced as follows for long walls and columns.

Slenderness ratio	1	2	4	6	8	10	12	14	16	18	21	24
Factor	1·0	·96	·88	·80	·70	·60	·50	·40	·35	·30	·25	·20

Long Walls or Columns. When ratio of effective height to the least lateral dimension is more than 15 or the ratio of effective height to the least radius of gyration is more than 50 the wall or the column is known as long.

Effective Thickness of Walls. For solid walls, the effective thickness is the actual thickness. Walls stiffened by intersecting walls, piers or buttresses at regular intervals, the effective thickness for calculating slenderness ratio is obtained by multiplying its actual thickness by a coefficient given in the table below.

Table 4·9 (*b*). Effective Thickness of Walls, Stiffened by Piers or Intersecting Walls

Piers spacing c/c	*Effective thickness of piers / Wall thickness*			
	$t_p/t_w = 1$	$t_p/t_w = 2$	$t_p/t_3 = 3$	*Remarks*
6	1·0	1·4	2·0	
8	1·0	1·3	1·7	t_p^*/t_w =
10	1·0	1·2	1·4	*Pier thickness* /
15	1·0	1·1	1·2	*Wall thickness*
20 or more	1·0	1·0	1·0	

Linear interpolation between the values given can be done but not the extra polation outside the limits. Modifications incorporated in the table should not be done when the slenderness ratio is based on the effective length of the wall.

Table 4·9 (*c*). Maximum Permissible Compressive Stresses on Masonry with Slenderness ratio as Unity

Mortar mix by vol.			*Age in days after*	*Max. stress in kg/cm² corresponding to units of bricks and blocks with a crushing strength in kg/cm² of*								*Remarks*
Cement	*Lime*	*Sand*	*finish*	*35*	*70*	*105*	*210*	*280*	*350*	*530*	*700*	*IS B or C class lime*
1	—	3	7	3·5	7·0	10·5	15·0	17·5	25·5	36·0	46·5	-do-
1	0–1/4	4	14	3·5	7·0	10·0	13·5	16·0	18·5	24·5	24·5	-do-
1	1	6	14	3·5	7·0	10·0	13·5	16·0	18·5	24·5	24·5	-do-
1	2	9	14	3·5	5·5	8·5	12·0	15·0	17·5	24·5	24·5	-do-
1	—	6	14	3·5	5·5	8·5	12·0	15·0	17·5	24·5	24·5	-do-
1	3	12	14	2·5	5·0	7·0	9·0	12·0	14·0	14·0	14·0	-do
—	1	2	14	2·5	5·0	7·0	9·0	12·0	14·0	14·0	14·0	IS *A* class lime
—	1	2·3	28	2·5	4·0	5·5	7·0	7·0	7·0	7·0	7·0	IS *B* & *C* class lime

Note : (1) All stresses are for concentric loads and slenderness ratio as unity.

(2) Linear interpolation can be done if crushing strength are intermediate between those given, but interpolation should not be used for mortars of composition intermediate between those specified.

(3) When slenderness ratio exceeds one, the permissible stress will be the product of stress permitted for slenderness ratio of unity as above multipled by the factor given in the table 4·9 (*a*) given before.

(4) The values given in the table are suitable, when the units are bricks or similar proportion, but may be unnecessarily low for units whose ratio of height to thickness is greater than that of bricks.

In case of conc. blocks or other blocks of that type with a height of not less than twice the thickness, the stresses will be increased by doubling the factor given in Table 4·9 (*a*). The factors thus obtained must not be more than one.

Buttresses or Piers in Compound Walls. The following relation should hold good

(1) bd^2 must not less than $(L - b)(d - t)$ or $(L - b) \times a^2$.

(2) L should not be more than $15t$ for lime mortar, $20t$ for cement 1 : 4 and $10t$ for mud mortar.

(3) d must be less than b.

(4) b must not be less than L/b.

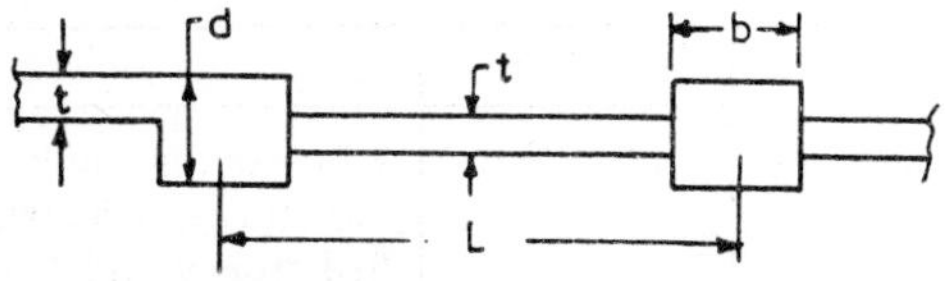

Fig. 4·30.

Table 4·9 (*d*). Thickness of Walls for Residential Building in Brick and Stone Masonry

Height above plinth	*Length between lateral support*	*Thickness of wall*		*Mud mortar*
		Cement mortar 1 : 3 or 1 : 4	*Lime mortar 1 : 6*	
1	2	3	4	5
Upto 3 m	any	1 brick	1 brick	1·5 brick
3-4 m	any	1 brick	1·5 brick	1·5 brick
4·5-6 m	10 m	1 brick	1·5 brick for bottom 3 m 1·0 brick for top 3 m	2 brick for bottom 3m 1·5 bricks for top 3m
4·5-7·5 m	10 m	1 brick for whole heigh (double storey) 1·5 brick for bottom 3 m and 1 brick for remaining	1·5 brick for 1st storey 1·0 brick for remaining 2 bricks for bottom 3·5 m 1·5 brick for remaining (single storey)	2 bricks upto 1st storey 1·5 brick for remaining
	above 10 m	1·5 brick for the height of 1st storey and 1 brick for remaining.	1·5 brick for the full height if double storey. 2 bricks for a height of 3·5 m and 1·5 brick for remaining height (single storey)	
7·5-9 m	upto 7·5 m	1 brick for the whole height (double storey) 1·5 bricks at base of single.	1·5 bricks for the height of 1st storey and 2nd storey and 1 brick for the remaining.	2 bricks for the height of 1st and 2nd storey 1·5 bricks for the remaining.
	7·5-10·5 m	1·5 bricks for the height of 1st storey and 1 brick for the remaining.	2 bricks for the height of 1st storey and 1·5 bricks for the remaining.	2 bricks for the height of 1st and 2nd storey 1·5 bricks for the remaining.
	above 10·5 m	1·5 bricks for the height of 1st and 2nd storey and 1 brick for the remaining.	2 bricks for the heigh of 1st storey and 1·5 bricks for the remaining.	2 bricks for the height of 1st and 2nd storey 1·5 bricks for the remaining.
9-12 m	upto 10·5 m	1·5 bricks for the height of 1st and 2nd storey and 1 brick for the remaining.	2 bricks for the height of 1st storey. 1·5 bricks for the height of 2nd storey and 1 brick for the remaining	2·5 bricks for the height of 1st storey. 2 bricks for 2nd storey and 1·5 bricks for the remaining.
	above 10·5 m	2 bricks for the height of 1st storey, 1·5 bricks for the 2nd storey, 1·5 for 3rd storey and one brick for remaining height	2·5 bricks for the height of 1st storey, 2 for for 2nd and 1·5 for the remaining height.	2·5 bricks for the height of 1st storey. 2 bricks for 2nd storey and 1·5 bricks for the remain-

Table contd..

Table contd...

1	2	3	4	5
12-15 m	upto 7·5 m	2 bricks for the height of 1st storey, 1·5 for 2nd and 3rd storey and 1 brick for the remaining.	2 bricks for the height of 1st storey, 1·5 for 2nd and 3rd storey and 1 for the remaining.	
	7·5 to 10·5 m	2 bricks for the height of 1st storey, 1·5 for 2nd and 3rd storey and 1 brick for the remaining.	2 bricks for the height of 1st and 2nd storey, 1·5 for the remaining.	
	10·5 to 14 m	2 bricks for the height of 1st storey and 2nd storey. 1·5 for the remaining.	2·5 brick for the height of 1st storey. 2 bricks for 2nd storey and 1·5 for the remaining.	
	above 14 m	2·5 bricks for 1st storey 2 bricks for 2nd storey 1·5 bricks for 3rd storey	2·5 bricks for 1st and 2nd storey. 2 bricks for 3rd storey. 1·5 bricks for remaining.	
15-18 m	upto 10·5 m	2 bricks for 1st and 2nd sto-ey 1·5 bricks for all storeys but last 1 brick for top storey	2·5 bricks for 1st storey 2·0 bricks for 2nd storey 1·5 bricks for remaining.	
	above 10·5 m	2·5 bricks for 1st storey 2·0 bricks for 2nd and 3rd storey. 1·5 bricks for remaining.	2·5 bricks for 1st and 2nd storey. 2 bricks for next storeys but top 1·5 bricks for top storey.	
18-21 m	upto 12 m	2·5 bricks for 1st storey 2·0 bricks for 2nd and 3rd storey. 1·5 bricks for remaining	2·5 bricks for 1st and 2nd storey. 2 bricks for next storeys but top 1·5 bricks for top storey.	
	above 12 m	2·5 bricks for 1st storey 2·0 bricks for 2nd and 3rd storey. 1·5 bricks for remaining.	3 bricks for 1st storey 2·5 bricks for 2nd storey 2 bricks for next storey but top 1·5 bricks for top storey.	

Note : (1) Random rubble masonry is kept 33% extra in width to brick walls in cement or lime or mud mortar.

(2) Thickness of 1/2 brick is increased for vibrations due to machines etc.

Table 4·9 (*e*). Thickness of Walls of Public Building, Warehouse and Industrial Buildings

Height of wall	*Length of wall*	*Thickness of wall at base*	
		Cement mortar	*Lime mortar*
Upto 4·5 m	Any	1·5 bricks	1·5 bricks
4·5 to 7·5 m	Any	1·5 bricks	2 bricks
7·5-9 m	Upto 14 m	1·5 bricks	2 bricks
	above 14 m	2 bricks	2·5 bricks

Table contd...

Table contd...

Height of wall	*Length of wall*	*Thickness of wall at base*	
		Cement mortar	*Lime mortar*
9-12 m	Upto 9 m	1·5 bricks	2 bricks
	9-14 m	2 bricks	2·5 bricks
	14-18 m	2·5 bricks	2·5 bricks
	above 18 m	2·5 bricks	3 bricks
12-15 m	Upto 9 m	2 bricks	2·5 bricks
	9-18 m	2·5 bricks	3 bricks
	above 18 m	3 bricks	3·5 bricks
15-18 m	Upto 9 m	2·5 bricks	—
	9-14 m	3 bricks	—

4·5. Foundations

Depth of Foundation below G.L. (Rankine's Formula) : $h = \frac{W}{A_w}\left(\frac{1-\sin\phi}{1+\sin\phi}\right)^2$

where W = total vertical load including dead, live, wall masonry and found conc. etc.

A = area of base which is L in case of unit strip.

L = width of foundation, w = wt. of soil per unit.

and ϕ is the angle of repose of soil.

Knowing all, h can be calculated which is the depth of bottom of conc. from G.L.

Min. depth is 0-9 m or 3′. It can also be founded on firm strata. For chimney and towers h is increased by 1/3 and bearing capacity of soil is taken 0·75 the normal.

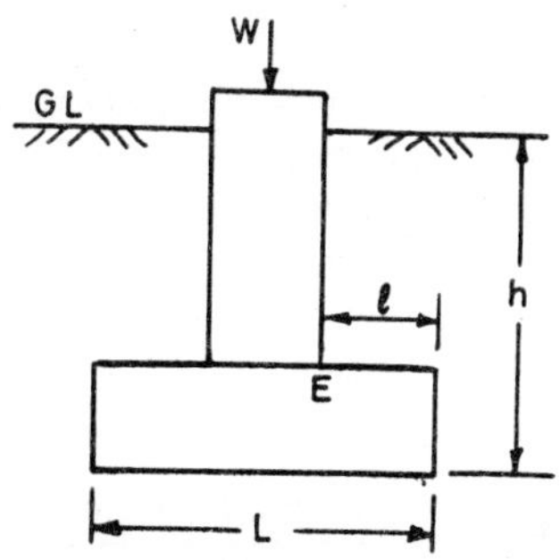

Fig. 4·31.

Base Width. When load is axial

$$\text{Width of conc.} = \frac{\text{Total load on walls and foundation conc. including dead and live}}{\text{Bearing capacity of soil}}$$

Thickness of Conc. (say *t*). *B.M.* at the point $E = \frac{pl^2}{2}$, p = bearing capacity of soil, l is the projection of conc. from face of wall.

Moment of Inertia of conc. sec. $= \frac{bt^3}{12} = \frac{t^3}{12}$, b being unity.

$$\frac{M}{I} = \frac{p}{y} \text{ or } \frac{pl^2}{2} \times \frac{12}{t^3} = \frac{1}{t^2} \text{ or } \frac{6pl^2}{t^3} = \frac{2}{t} \text{ or } \frac{6pl^2}{t^2} = 2 \text{ or } t = \sqrt{3pl^2}$$

Secondly : by the formula $\frac{0}{t} = \left(\frac{f}{3p}\right)^{1/2}$

where 0 = l in this case, p being the bearing capacity of soil and f safe permissible stress in concrete. (for 1 : 4 : 8 conc/may be taken as 100 tonnes/m^2)

Thirdly : $t = p \times k$ where k for different values of p is given below :

Bearing capacity of soil in tonnes/m^2(p)	5	10	15	20	25
Values of k	0·55	0·77	0·95	1·1	1·2

Thickness of conc. should not be less than 30 cm or the projection of the conc. beyond footing.

Stone templates must not have its thickness less than 1/4th to the max. size of the template or 1·5 times the projection whichever is less.

Punching Shear. Footings should be checked for punching and for diagonal shear (for detail refer RCC footings).

Eccentric Loads. It may be due to arches, trusses or **wind** etc. Say it is P acting horizontally at $H/2$ on the wall. H being the height of wall W is the load on wall including its own weight. Taking moment about A

$$W(t + t/6) = W \times t/2 + P\,H/2,$$

t being thickness of the wall

or $$Wt/2 + Wt/6 = W.t/2 + P\,H/2$$

or $$t = \frac{3PH}{W} = \frac{3pH^2}{WHt} \text{ or } t = \sqrt{\frac{3pH}{W}} \quad ...(1)$$

If t is less than this value, there is tension in base at point A and if t is according to formula (1), the whole base of the wall will under comp. or when the resultant at the 1/3rd point. The pressure on the heel of the wall is zero and on the toe it is twice the average *i.e.* $2W/A$.

where A = area of the sec. (1 m strip)

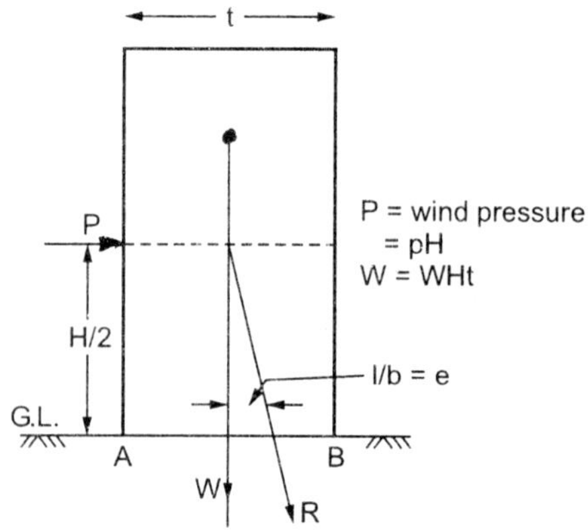

Fig. 4·31 (*b*).

Factor of safety = Resting moment/over turning moment. It may be 1/6 t to 5/12 t

$$M = \text{bending moment} = We \ (e \text{ is eccentricity}).$$

Spread Foundations. In order to spread the load on wider area or to bring the resultant pressure line within the middle 3rd footings are provided.

Safe Permissible Loads on masonry and Conc. (Tonnes/m^2)

1.	Brick work 1 : 3 in cement mortar	100 T/m^2
2.	Brick work 1 : 4 in cement mortar	88 T/m^2
3.	Brick work 1 : 6 in cement mortar	50 T/m^2
4.	Brick work lime in cement mortar	44 T/m^2
5.	Ashlars masonry 1 : 3 cement mortar	170 T/m^2
6.	Rubble	100 T/m^2
7.	Rubble masonry in lime mortar	40 T/m^2
8.	Cement conc. 1 : 1½ : 3 (M-200)	510 T/m^2
9.	Cement conc. 1 : 2 : 4 (M-150)	440 T/m^2
10.	Cement conc. 1 : 3 : 6 (M-100)	280 T/m^2
11.	Cement conc. 1 : 4 : 8	110 T/m^2
12.	Lime concrete	60 T/m^2

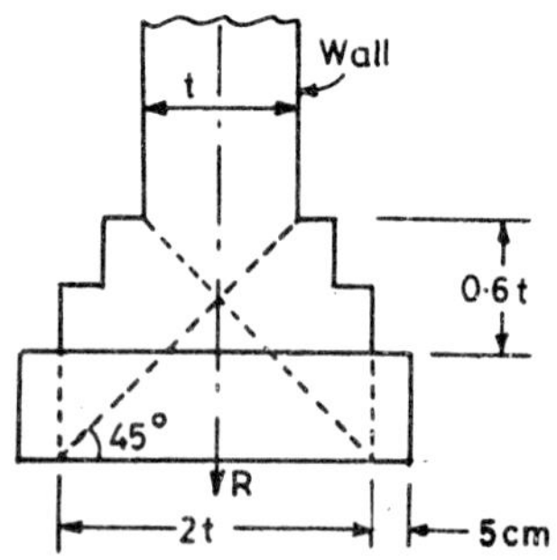

Fig. 4·32.

Table 4·10. Safe Bearing Capacities of Soils in Tonnes/m²

1. Soft clay, alluvial deposit or river beds	2–3·75 T/m²	9. Compact sand	22-32 T/m²
2. Black cotton soil	5–7·5 T/m²	10. Compact sand (confined)	44 T/m²
3. Alluvial soil	5–7·5 T/m²	11. Kankar	33 T/m²
4. Alluvial loam	7·5–16 T/m²	12. Compact gravel	45-55 T/m²
5. Moist clay	10–18 T/m²	13. Mooram	22-44 T/m²
6. Ored clay and clay mixed sand	22 T/m²	14. Mar and kabar	65 T/m²
7. Hard clay with sand	32–44 T/m²	15. Soft rock	80–85 T/m²
8. Loose sand	22 T/m²	16. Ord. rock	110 T/m²
		17. Hard rock	200 and above

Bearing Capacity Improving Devices (also refer chapter on Soil Mechanics and Foundation Engineering)

1. Increasing depth of foundation.
2. Improving drainage of the area, saturated soil has low bearing capacity.
3. Granular material like sand, gravel or crushed stone blended in the natural soil by ramming.
4.(*a*) By piling (*b*) sand piling—sand is filled in the drilled holes in soil and compacted.

Foundation on Loose, Wet or on Undesirable Soils like black cotton soil

1. Loose material is removed upto cracks in soil and foundation is rammed.
2. Ramming sand, mooram, Brocken stone or brick bats on the loose or bad soil so that foundation may not in the direct contact of bad soil.
3. **Cement Grouting.** Cement is blown under pressure in the pores of the foundations soil. Fine sand needs some chemical or bituminous emulsion treatment.
4. **Lean concrete (mud matting).** A lean conc. mix say 1 : 6 : 12 is laid over the soil in thickness of about 15 cm. So that the foundation may not be in the direct touch of the bed soil. It also makes a good surface for raft foundations.
5. **Pile Drawing.** It may be of wood, concrete or sheet piles (For details see Soil Mechanics and Foundation Engineering).

Testing Bearing Capacity of Soil for Foundation

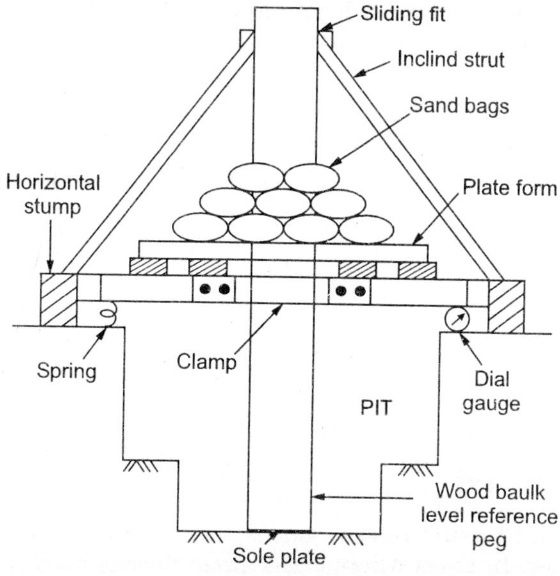

Fig. 4·33.

1. Dig a pit upto the required depth on which the foundation is to be laid 15 times the size of the sole plate). Dig another smaller pit inside the bigger, a bit more than the size of the sole plate.

2. Fix a steel plate (sole plate) 30 cm sq. and 25 mm thick (for sandy and silty soils the plate may be 60 cm sq. and for gravel beds it should be 75 cm sq.).

3. Take a timber baulk 30 cm² and 1·25 to 2·5 m long with flat edges. The bottom edge is fitted with the steel sole plate and is kept vertical by four inclined struts connected to a **sliding fit** coller provided near the top of the baulk and are prevented from sliding by a system of horizontal struts provided at their bottom or bases.

4. A plateform for loading is made by cross wood battons and sleepers and is loaded gradually by sand bags on the sliding fit clamp.

5. To commence the test the plate shall be preloaded with a load of 70 kg/cm^2 and released. Then load is increased in steps of 200 kg or 1/5th of the probable ultimate load whichever is less till about 1·5 times the probable ultimate load is reached. The settlement is recovered accurately by a dial gauge 0·02 mm. The settlement is observed for each increase of load after an interval of 1, 4, 10, 20, 40 and 60 minutes and hourly after it. A time settlement curve with loadings upto the load which indicates 70 to 80% of probable ultimate settlement is drawn on a sudden settlement is observed.

Let load on this sudden settlement is noted to be W.

Then ultimate bearing capacity of soil

$$= \frac{W}{\text{area of sole plate}}$$

Safe bearing capacity of soil

$$= \frac{W}{\text{area of sole plate} \times \text{factor of safety}}$$

Note : Refer testing bearing capacity of soils in chapter of soil mechanics.

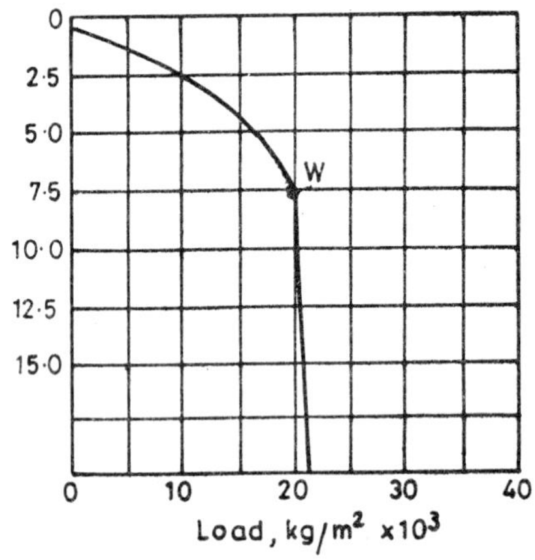

Fig. 4·34.

Heavy Foundations on Bad Soils

Raft : It is considered and designed as follows :

1. The entire area of foundation is covered by a slab supported on columns or walls invertly. The pressure of the soil acts upward and hence the main reinforcement is taken on top.

2. The entire area for foundation is covered by inverted T-beam and slabs in which soil pressure acts upward and so designed for this load.

3. In such cases the centre of gravity of the soil under foundation should be in the vertical line of the centre of gravity of the loads on the structure (dead and live). If it is eccentric the load on the comp. to tension side will vary and hence unequal settlement towards comp. side may take place.

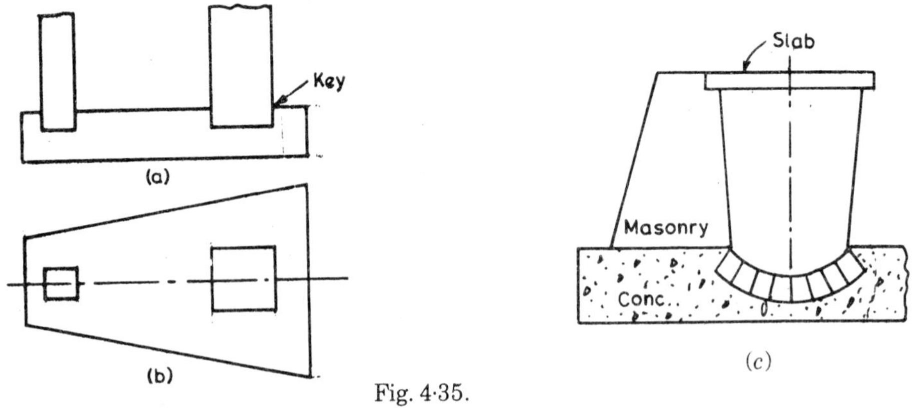

Fig. 4·35.

4. **For Rafts below Spring Level.** Pressure release valves should be provided in the raft to get rid off uplift due to subsoil water. In cases where water proof floor is needed these

valves are not provided and the raft is designed to meet with this pressure. Such foundations are known as **floating foundations**. The uplift pressure of water is equivalent to the head of water (difference of level in spring level to the bed of foundations).

5. **Combined Footing.** A common raft is laid for several footings.

6. **Inverted Arch.** An inverted arch is provided below piers or wall which bear uplift due to soil and water under the foundation.

Grillage Foundations. The large wide and deep foundations such as in large stanchians etc., grillage foundations are used to economise depth and width, by the use of two or more tieres of steel joists, set in conc. The practical requirements are that all joists of a tier should be placed sufficiently far apart to allow of concrete being well rammed between them, say 10 t0 12 cm between flanges. The joists are kept in position by cast iron separates or by bolts passing through steel tubes about 2·5 cm in dia. Concrete about 30 cm in thickness is provided below the joist. The resistance of the joist in bending and shearing must be considered. The joists must not be placed too far apart to provide sufficient shearing resistance in their webs. Usually 3 or 4 joists are provided in 1st tier in one direction. Let W be the total load on the stanchian, so distributed load is W/L per unit width upward. So bending moment in the cantilever $\left(\frac{L-l}{2} \text{ equal to overhang}\right)$.

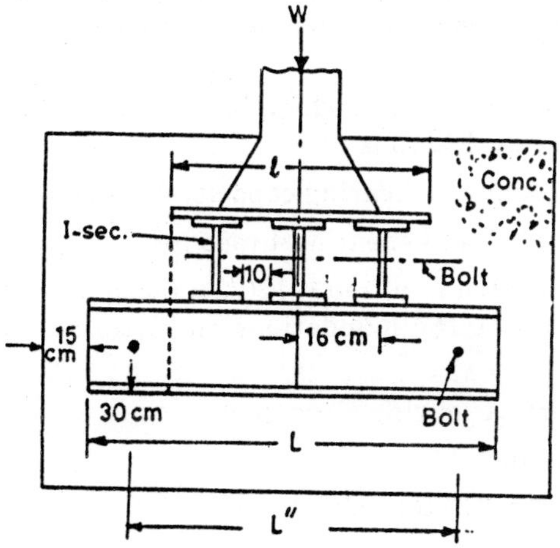

Fig. 4·36 (*a*).

$$= \frac{1}{8} WL(L-l)^2 \qquad ...(1)$$

If the bending of the base due to its flexibility is considered, it will bend like a beam and the max. B.M. at centre will be

$$\frac{1}{2} W.\frac{1}{4} L - \frac{1}{2} W.\frac{1}{4} l = \frac{1}{8} W(L-l) \qquad ...(2)$$

If the base is rectangular use L, L_1 and l, l_1 and calculate B.M. in both directions.

$$\text{The max. S.F.} \quad = \frac{1}{2} W \frac{(L-l)}{L} \qquad ...(3)$$

acting at the point D the point of overhang of joist.

Design Procedure. The max. B.M. $M = \frac{1}{8} W(L-l)$ from (2) l being the base width of stanchion.

Area of the base = W/bearing capacity of foundation. Decide a square or rectangular foundation area taking appropriate sides and then decide length L or L_1 of the sides of foundation (L in case of square or L_1 for rectangular base).

From the width of foundation decide number of I-sections about 10 to 15 cm. Say it is n in number.

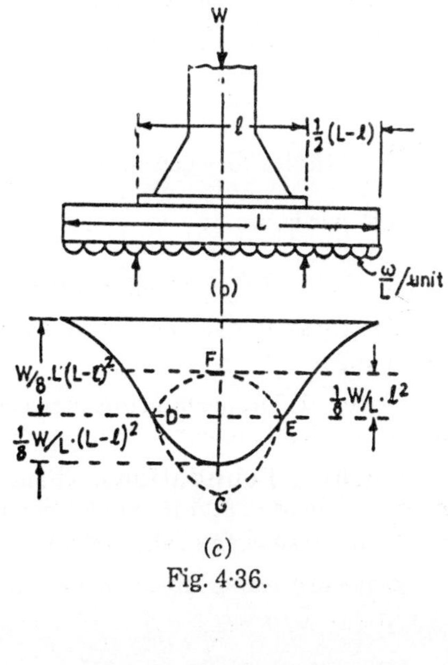

Fig. 4·36.

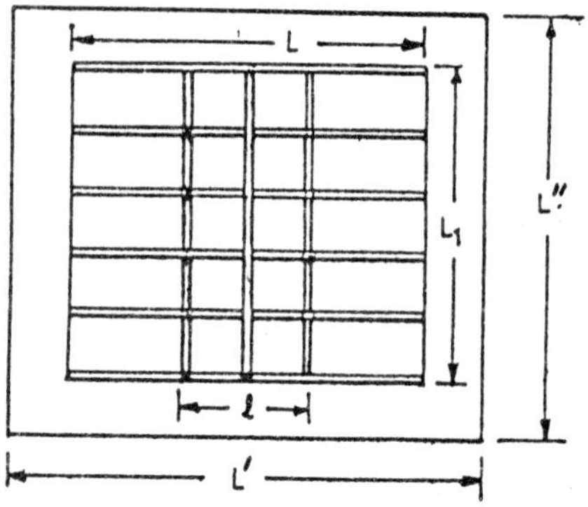

Fig. 4·36 (d).

The B.M. on each section will be M/n. From the steel section tables select a suitable sections fulfilling this requirement for B.M. M/n.

Check the S.F. from formula (3) $= \frac{1}{2} W \frac{(L-l)}{L}$

and for one joist it is $\frac{1}{n} \frac{1}{2} W \frac{(L-l)}{L}$. It must be under allowable limits (For this section only web is considered). For the upper tier the no. of I-sec. will be reduced according to the width of the stanchion say it is n_1. Then B.M. on each sections will be M/n_1 and S.F. $= F/n_1$.

Example. Stanchion base = 30 in. sq. ; Direct load = 120 tons

Allowable pressure on foundation = 2 tons/ft^2 (may be bearing capacity of soil)

Allowable bending stress in flanges = 7·5 tons/in^2 and shear as 4 tons/in^2.

Taking web area = Thickness × depth of I-sec. Area required = 120/2 = 60 sq. ft. of conc., take 8′ × 8′ size of conc. As the stanchion base is square the foundations may also be square. Provide 7′ long I-sec. leaving 6″ on each side of conc.

For the lower tier use 8 nos. of I sec. 12″ apart c/c leaving 6″ on sides.

Then $(L - l) = 84 - 30 = 54$ inch.

Max. S.F. from equation (2) $= 1/8 \times 120 \times 54 = 810$ ton-in.

Mod. section per beam $= \frac{810}{8} \Big/ 7{\cdot}5 = 13{\cdot}6 \text{ m}^3$ (7·5 = bending stress).

Referring from table selected section is 12, 8 × 4 with a mod. 13·92 suiting to it.

The S.F. per beam $= 0{\cdot}28 \cdot \frac{1}{8} \times \frac{1}{2} \times 120 \times \frac{54}{84} = 4{\cdot}82$ tons.

The allowable S.F. per beam $= 0{\cdot}28 \times 8 \times 4 = 9{\cdot}3$ tons.

(0·28″ is thickness of web 8″ its depth).

For upper tier take three joists. The modulus of section required per I sec.

$$= \frac{1}{3} \times \frac{810}{7{\cdot}5} = 36 \text{ inch}^3$$

From tables for section modulus 36 inch^3, the suitable section is 20′/2 × 5

S.F. per beam $= \frac{1}{3} \times \frac{1}{2} \times 120 \times \frac{54}{84} = 129.$

Allowable S.F. per beam is $0{\cdot}35 \times 12 \times 4 = 16{\cdot}8$ (safe).

The three flanges occupy 5 × 3 = 15 in. leaving 15 in. for two spaces each 7·5 in. clear between flanges.

Note : (1) The permissible stress in steel may be exceeded by 33·3% and 50% for wind, seismic or erection loads in case of grillage beams. In poor soils even one layer of joists can be used.

Machine Foundations. Though there is different idea of loads on machines, yet it is designed for a load of 600 to 900 kg per BHP + wt. of machine and the depth should be kept 5 to 6 times of the base of the cylinder for large and medium machines.

Bolts are either fixed in position while concreting or pockets are left in the concrete.

Some times anchor plates and bolts are also provided at the time of casting concrete. When the pockets are left, there must be 6 mm clearance around the bolt, so that it may be grouted properly. The holes in the bed plates should be 3 mm larger than bolt dia. upto 22 mm bolts. 6 mm for 25 to 63 mm dia. and 10 mm for larger size bolts. The following precautions to minimise the effect of vibrations are taken. (Also refer chapter on foundation engineering)

(1) A packing of rubber, filt or timber is provided between bed plate and foundations block. At high temperature (more than 50°C) rubber must not be used. It must also be kept away from oils.

(2) A rubber or lead sheet can be provided between foundation conc. block and lower soil.

(3) By filling sand or sand dust around the foundation block and side soil.

(4) Metal springs between machine and bed plate can be provided.

Back Filling of Foundations. It is preferable to back fill the foundations by a lean concrete. But it is not economical. According to the importance of the structure it must be filled by coarse sand and gravel with sufficient ramming in layers.

Note : The pockets should not be shuttered by solid blocks of wood, as it will be difficult to remove them afterwards.

Dewatering of Foundations. When the foundations are laid in sub soil water, it is necessary to drain off this water. For doing this a trench is cut deeper than the bottom of foundation at its periphery at a distance of about one metre from the edge of the foundations. Sumps are cut in this trench so deeper as to accommodate foot valve in full emersion in water. The number of sumps may be dug according to the requirement and water is pumped from the sumps. If it is unavoidable to dig a sump in the foundation area, it must be filled with lean conc. after use.

Sometimes it is necessary to keep the foundation perfectly dry as in case of sumps surface water carryies cement with it causing the mix to make weaker. For avoiding this **strainer wells** are bored at suitable distances (preferable one metre beyond the periphery of the foundation trench). If they are bored in the foundation area, they mustbe plugged with cement grout at least upto the bottom of the foundation by force grout machine. The depth of this grout can be judged either by the quantity of grout or by the pressure required to force the grout to reach the required depth, taking it equivalent to the head of water at the foundation level. The depth is grouted a bit more than the foundation level to attain a safety factor. Another way of closing or plugging the bore pipe is by pouring a rich mix of small grade aggregate concrete with accelerating agents in stagnent water of the tubewell pipe which is higher than the water table. The depth of conc. in the pipe can be judged by lowering a wt. in the tube. After the concrete in the tube has been set extra height of the tube can be cut by gas flame.

The cavity under the tube can be filled by breaking the bail plug by a long jumper. The strainer used for this job are of a temporary nature. Thin slotted sheet tubes wrapped with jute or coconut mattings can be used. The strainer must be kept below the bottom of concrete. In place of slotted tubes skeleton made by welding m.s. bars (6 to 8 mm dia.) on round sockets can be used on which the coconut cordage can be wrapped.

Precautions. While water is being dewatered care must be taken that the speed is so adjusted that fine particles of sand may not come with water otherwise a cavity around the strainer is formed causing settlement due to hollow under the raft. This action is known as **piping or quick sand.** Quick sand is a process and not a type of sand. When the layer under foundations bed is impervious a wider boring is done in which a strainer of lesser dia. is lowered and pea gravel shrouding is provided around it. By doing so a wider area for dewatering is obtained.

Shrouding also helps to disallow the entry of the fine particles in the strainer tube under permeable strata.

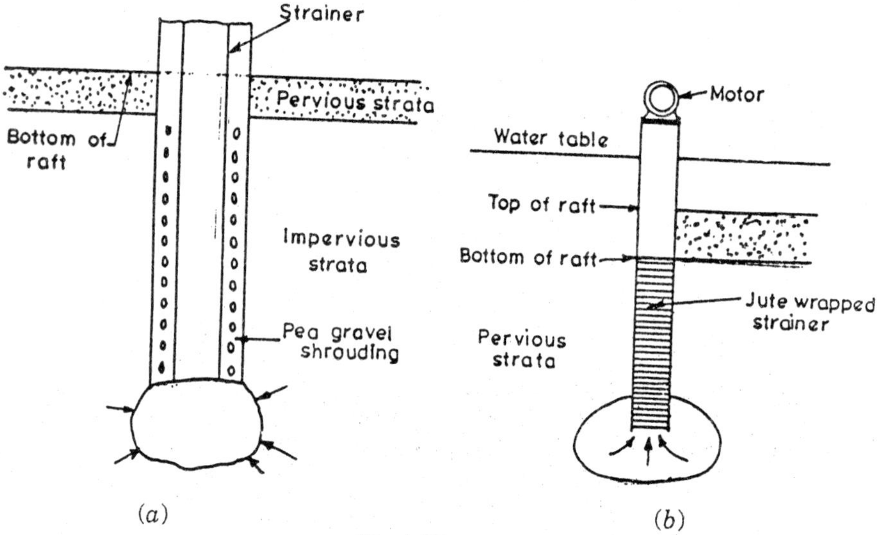

Fig. 4·37.

4·6. Fasteners : (A) Riveted Joints :

Rivets. Before rivetting a structure, the whole structure is assembled and connected by bolts and nuts. Single headed rivets are available in market. These rivets are heated red and replaced in place of bolts one by one. After fixing each rivet red hot the other head is beated by a rivet headed hammer operated by compressed air. The mass in the projected portion of the rivet (x) is just sufficient so as to make rivet head after beating on cooling the rivet contracts in length and keeps the plates tightly in contact.

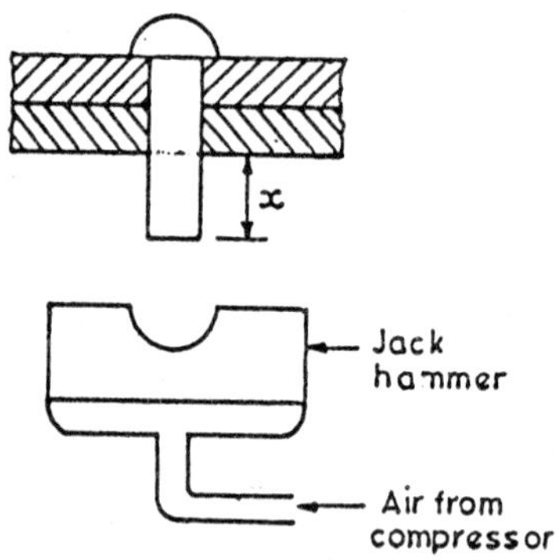

Fig. 4·38.

Joints. (1) **Lap joint :** Subjected to single shear

(2) **Butt joint :** Subjected to double shear.

Dia. of Rivet. Empirical formula given by UnWin the for the dia. of the rivet say d, then $d = 1{\cdot}2\sqrt{t}$, where t is the thickness of the plate (thinnest plate). In metric units $d = 1{\cdot}91\sqrt{t}$.

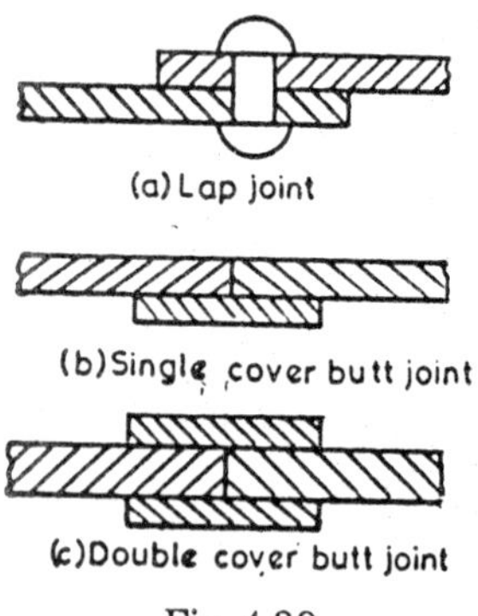

Fig. 4·39.

Another empirical formula : $d = \frac{T}{8} + \frac{5}{8}$ inch. Where T is the total thickness of plates in inches. It is also known as the net dia. of the rivet.

or $$d = 2{\cdot}55\ t \text{ for single shear ;}$$

$$d = 1{\cdot}27\ t \text{ for double shear.}$$

Thickness of Cover Plates. The thickness of the cover plates should be min. (t be the thickness of main plate to be jointed) and can be taken upto $1^1/_8\ t$ for safety in single shear. The thickness should be $t/2$ (can be taken upto 5/8 t for safety) for each plate to be jointed in double shear or cover.

Edge Distance from the Rivet. It can be taken as 1½ d (dia. of rivet) from the edge to the centre of rivet.

Table 4·11 (*a*). IS : 800—1956 for Edge Distance

Dia.		Min. edge distance from centre of rivet in mm and inches					
inch	*mm*	*Sheared edge*		*Rolled edge*		*Rolled beam, T or channel*	
		inch	*mm*	*inch*	*mm*	*inch*	*mm*
1/2	12·7	1	25	3/4	19	3/4	19
5/8	15·9	$1^1/_8$	29	1	25	7/8	22
3/4	19	$1^1/_4$	32	$1^1/_8$	29	1	25
7/8	22·2	$1^1/_2$	38	$1^1/_4$	32	$1^1/_8$	29
1	24·4	$1^3/_4$	44	$1^1/_2$	38	$1^1/_4$	32
$1^1/_8$	27·6	2	50	$1^3/_4$	44	$1^1/_2$	38
$1^1/_4$	30·8	$2^1/_4$	57	2	50	$1^3/_4$	44

Note : When two or more parts are connected together it must not be more than 37 mm + 4*t* where *t* = thickness of thinner plate in mm. In case of work not exposed to weather this may be increased to 12 *t*.

Dia. of Rivet Hole. It is kept 1/16 in or 1·6 mm larger than the dia. of rivet upto 25 mm rivets and 2·0 mm for rivets above 25 mm.

Types of Rivets. (*a*) Normally head is round and is called is **button head.**

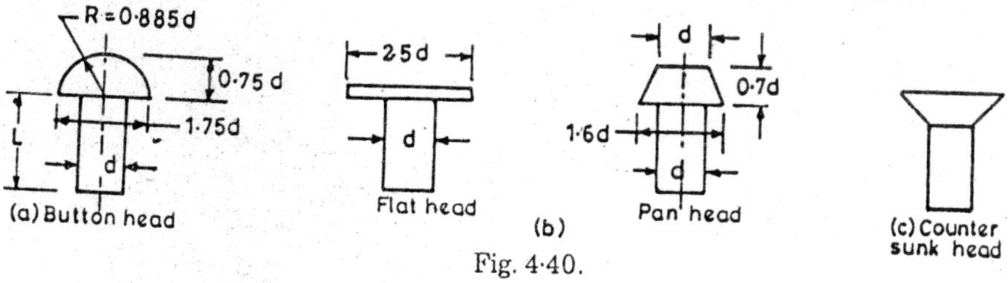

Fig. 4·40.

(*b*) **Flattened Head.** It is used when the clearance is limited.

(*c*) **Counter Sink Head.** Counter sink head is used when the surface is flush. In this case the hole in the plate is cut according to ends.

Pitch. IS Standard 800—1956.

min. Pitch. The distance between the centres of the rivet holes should not be less than 2·5 times the dia. of the hole.

Nominal dia. of rivet (inch)	1/2	5/8	3/4	7/8	1
Pitch in inch	$1^3/_4$	2	$2^1/_2$	3	$3^1/_2$

Max. Pitch for Parts in Tension. 16*t* or 200 mm (8 inch) whichever is less.

Max. Pitch for Parts in Compression. 12*t* or 200 mm (8 inch) whichever is less.

where forces are transferred thorugh butting faces it should not exceed 4·5 times the dia. of rivets for a distance from the abutting faces equal to 1·5 times the width of the member.

Max. Pitch for Parts in Tension or Compression. 32*t* or 300 mm (12″) whichever is less. *t* = thickness of the thinner plate.

The distance between cnetres of any two consecutive rivets in a line adjacent and parallel to an edge of an outside plate shall not exceed 100 mm + 4*t* or 200 mm whichever is less in compression or tension members. Where rivets are staggard at intervals and the gauge does not exceed 75 mm, the specified distances of min. pitch between centres of rivets may be increased by 50 percent.

Table 4·11 (*b*). Permissible Stresses in Rivets, Bolts and Tension Rods.

Type of stress	*Rivets*			*Bolts*			Tie rods	*Remarks*
	Power driven		*Hand driven*	*Turned or fitted*	*Bolts Black*	*High Strength*		
	Shop	*Field*						
Shear or gross area (f_s)	6·5 (1025)	6·0 (945)	5·0 (785)	6·5 (1025)	5·5 (865)	11·2 (1760)		1. Gross area = Area of hole 2. Net area = Area of rivet
Bearing or gross area (f_b)	15·0 (2360)	13·5 (2125)	10·0 (1575)	15·0 (2360)	13·0 (2045)			3. In F.P.S. stress are in tons/m^2.
Tension or gross area of rivets and net area of bolts	5·0 (785)	4·0 (630)	4·0 (630)	over 1½" dia. (38 mm) 8·0 (1260) 3/4" – 1½" dia. (20-38 mm) 6·2 (945) Below 3/4" (120 mm) 5·0 (785)			8·0 (1260)	4. In M.K.S. stress are in kg/cm^2 written under brackets.

Note : (1) For effect of wind and seismic loads permissible stresses may be exceeded by 25%.

(2) Working permissible stress for hand driven rivets is only 4/5th of the machine driven rivets.

Design of Riveted Joint

***Pt* = (*P* – *d*)*t ft* :** Load taken in tension by plate where *ft* is the tensile strength of plate per unit sq., *t* = thickness of plate and *P* is pitch (distance c/c of the rivets) of the rivets.

Ps* = *n*(π*d*²/4) × *fs* :** (for single shear). Where *fs* is the shearing stress of the rivet material and *n* = no. of rows of rivets = **2*n*(π*d*²/4) × *fs (for double shear).

Pb = *ndt.fb*, where *Pb* = comp. strength of rivet material.

Taking the no. of rows of rivets as one.

Pt_1 = Pull on plate per pitch length for tearing of plate.

Ps_1 = Pull on plate per pitch length for shearing of rivet.

Pb_1 = Pull on plate per pitch length for crushing of rivet.

The least of Pt_1, Ps, and Pb_1 is known as the **rivet value** at which the failure will take place.

Procedure. Determine the dia. of rivet by the Un Win's formula $d = 1{\cdot}91\sqrt{t}$.*t* = thickness of plate known, round off the calculated *d* to the available sizes (12, 14, 16, 18, 20, 22, 24, 27, 30, 33, 36, 39, 42 and 48 mm). The most nominal dia. are 16, 18, 20 and 22 mm.

Dia. *d* of the rivet can also be computed by equating *Ps* = *Pb* or $\frac{\pi d^2}{4}.fs = ndt\,fb$ where *fs* and *fb* which are allowable shear and compressive stresses of the rivet material is known.

$$\text{No. of rivets (say } n) = \frac{\text{Total load } P \text{ (say)}}{\text{rivet value}}$$

If the joint is butt the same no. of rivets will be required on the other side.

Arrange the rivets as per site requirements and check the strength at the weakest section which is given ahead.

The pitch *p* can be determined by the formula $Pt = (p - d)t\,ft$. *Pt* must be greater than or equal to Ps_1 or Pb_1 whichever is less.

$$\text{Efficiency of riveted joint} = \frac{\text{Least of } Pt_1,\ Ps_1 \text{ or } Pb_1}{ft\ p.t}$$

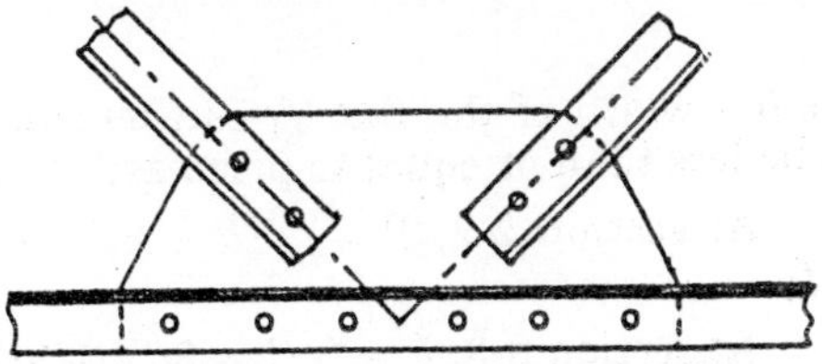

(c)

Note : (1) For members carrying load, no. of rivets should be min. 2.

(2) Centre line of members should meet at a point and the rivet line should be on the centre line.

(3) Tension members should be weakened by least possible extent.

(4) Loose fillers should be avoided.

(5) For eccentric loads the members should be made extra strong to resist the moment.

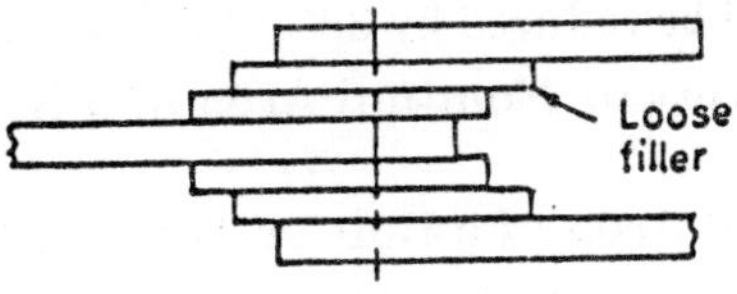

(b)

Fig. 4·41.

Eccentric loads :

$$P_2 = \frac{M \times r_1}{\Sigma r^2}$$

where P_2 = Force in the rivet due to bending moment M. (W_e) developed due to eccentricity e.

Σr^2 = Sum of squares of the perpendicular distances of all the rivets from the c.g. of the rivet group.

r_1 = Distance of the rivet in which the force P_2 is developed due to eccentric load from the c.g. of the rivet group.

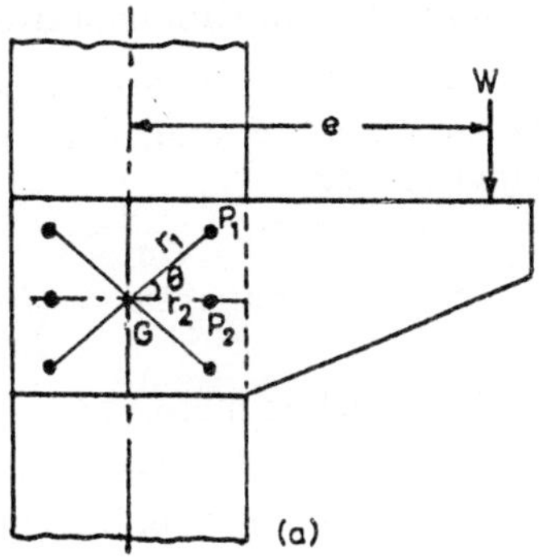

Fig. 4·42.

$$\text{Direct load } P_1 = \frac{\text{Total force}(W)}{\text{No. of rivets}}$$

$$\text{Max. resultant force in the rivet, } P_V = \left(P_1^2 + P_2^2 + 2P_1 P_2 \cos\theta\right)^{1/2}$$

where θ = angle between the forces P_1 and P_2, P must not exceed the rivet value for rivet most severly loaded.

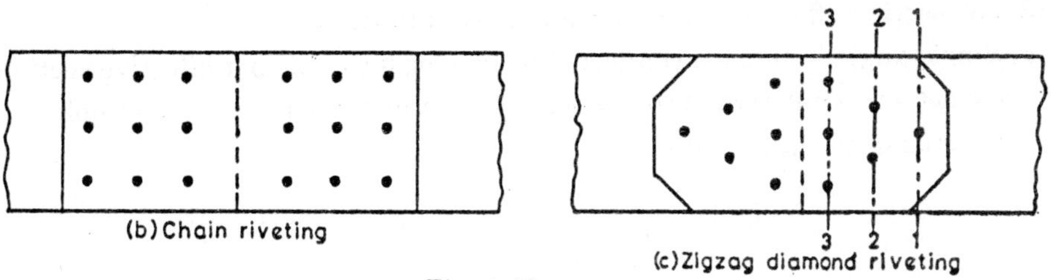

Fig. 4·42.

Checking Strength of a Structural Member

Total load taken by one rivet = P/n.

At section 1-1 which is the weakest and where the no. of rivets is one $P = f_1(b - 1.d)t$

where b = width of the flat. f_1 can be calculated knowing b, d and t for load P. f_1 so obtained must be less than or equal to permissible stress ft.

At section 2-2, $P = f_2 (b - 2d)t + P/n$ from which f_2 can be calculated it will be less than f_1.

At section 3-3, $P = f_3 (b - 3d)t + 3P/n$ from which f_3 can be calculated which will be less than f_2.

Counter Sink Heads. 1/2 of the depth of the counter sinking shall be neglected in calculating the length of rivet in bearing. For rivets in tension with counter sink heads the tensile value shall be reduced by 33%. No reduction is required in shear.

Gross or Nominal Area of a Bolt or Tension Rod. Actual area of the sections of bolt or rod.

Net Area of a Bolt or Tension Rod. Area at the root of the thread of the bolt or rod.

Dia. of a hole of Bolt etc. Nominal dia. + 1·6 mm unless or otherwise specified.

The nominal dia. of the Rivet is the dia. of the cold material.

The gross dia. of the Rivet is the dia. of the hole.

Deduction in the area due to Rivet Holes for Tension Members

(1) (*a*) Deduction of area in section of the tension members for zigzag or diagonal chain of holes as per formula given below :

$$\text{Net sectional area} = \left\{b - (nd) - n'\frac{p^2}{4g}\right\}t$$

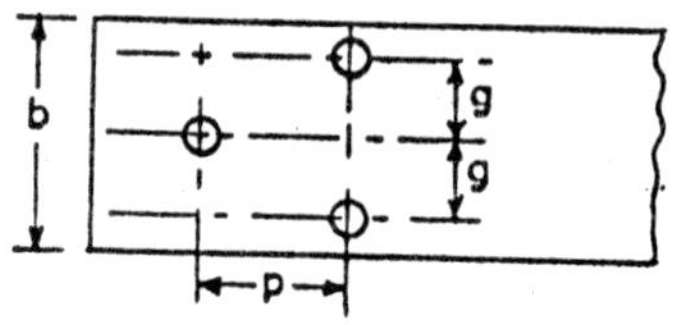

Fig. 4·43.

where b = width of plate.

p = The distance between any two consecutive rivets measured parallel to the direction of the stress in members.

g = The distance (gauge) between any two consecutive rivets measured perpendicular to the direction of stress in member.

n = no. of rivets in one chance (3 in the case shown in Fig. 4·43)

n' = no. of gauge distances which is 2 in case shown in Fig. 4·43)

t = thickness of plate.

In angle sections where the holes are made in both the legs the gauge shall be measured along the centre of the thickness of angle.

(*b*) Deduction of area for hand driven rivets = t (d + 3 mm) where d = dia. of rivet, for machine driven rivets = t (d + 1·5 mm)

(2) Net section effective for angles and tees in tension :

(*a*) Single angle in tension connected by one leg only, the net effective section = $a + bK$.

where a = net sectional area of connected leg after deduction of the rivet hole.

b = area of the outstanding leg.

$$K = \frac{1}{1 + \dfrac{0{\cdot}35\,b}{a}}$$

(*b*) Pair angles placed back to back (or a single tee) in tension connected by only one leg of each angle (or by the flange of tee) to the same side of a gusset, the net effective area is = $a + bK$.

a = area (net after deduction of rivet hole) of connected legs (flange of the Tee), b = area of the outstanding legs (web of Tee)

$$K = \frac{1}{1 + \frac{0.2\,b}{a}}$$

(*c*) Double angles or Tees in direct tension and placed back to back and connected to each side of a gusset or to each side of a rolled sections.

Net sectional area = Gross area – area of holes.

Note : If the angles are not tacked together, they are designed as an independent single piece.

Long Grip Rivets. Where the grip of rivets carrying calculated loads exceeds the 6 times the dia. of hole, the number of rivets required by normal calculations shall be increased by not less than 1% for each additional 1·6 mm of grip, but the grip should not exceed 8 times the dia. of hole.

The Length of Rivet Shanks : Snap heads : $L = t + t/8 + 1{\cdot}5d$

For counter sink heads : $L = t + t/p + d$

when two or more parts are connected together, a line of rivets or holes shall be provided at a distance of not more than 37 mm + $4t$ from the nearest edge, where t is the thickness in mm of the thinner outside plate. In the case of work not exposed to weather this may be increased by $12t$.

Where bolts have to be used instead of rivets, these shall be provided with washers not less than 6 mm thick. Where there is risk of nuts becoming loose due to vibrations or reversal of stresses, these shall be secured from slacking by the use of lock nuts, spring washers, cross cutting or hammering down of threads into deformation (blurred).

Cutting of Loose Rivets. When a loose rivet is removed it may loosen adjoining rivets. For cutting out of loose rivets the head or point must be divided into four by means of two cross cuts, before it is cut off side ways and rivet shank cut out.

Making Holes for Rivets. (1) Drilling (2) Punching (3) Punching and reaming.

(1) Drilling is done by a drill machine to the required width.

(2) Punching is done by a nail, it injures the hole and leads to inaccuracy. It is done in holes and thin plates.

(3) Punching and reaming. The hole is first punched 3 mm less in dia. and thin reamed (with a drill) to the required size.

Area in sq.cm to be deducted for each rivet hole/mm thickness of metal

Rivet dia. (mm)	12	14	16	18	20	22	24
Rivet hole dia. (mm)	13·5	15·5	17·5	19·5	21·5	23·5	25·5
Rivet hole area (cm^2)	0·135	0·155	0·175	0·195	0·215	0·235	0·255
Rivet dia. (mm)	27	30	33	36	39	42	48
Rivet hole dia. (mm)	29·0	32·0	35·0	38·0	41·0	44·0	50·0
Rivet hole area (cm^2)	0·290	0·320	0·350	0·380	0·410	0·440	0·500

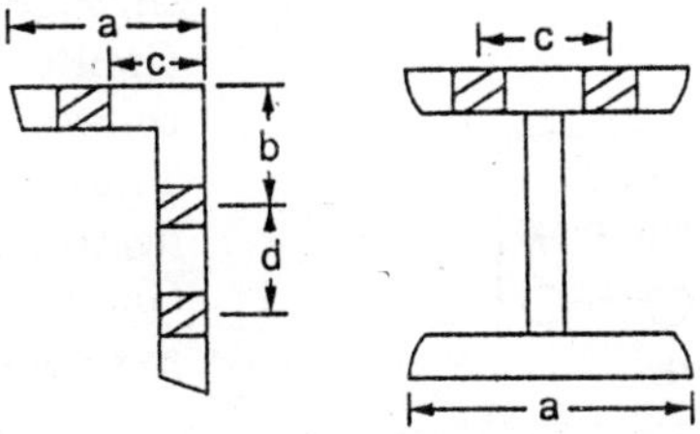

Fig. 4·43.

Table 4·11 (*c*). Spacing of Holes and Size of Rivets in Indian Standard Steel Sections

Leg *a*	Leg *c*	Rivet size		Double row of rivets *b*	*d*
20	12				
25	15				
30	17				
35	19				
40	21	12	Single row of rivets		
45	25	12			
50	28	16			
55	30	20			
60	35	22			
65	35	22			
70	40	24			
75	40	24			
80	45	27			
90	50	27			
95	55	27			
100	60	12	Double row	40	40
110	65	12		45	45
115	70	12		45	55
125	75	20		45	55
130	80	20		50	55
150	90	20		55	65
200	115	27		75	85

Width of flange *a*	*c*	Rivet size
50	30	6
60	30	6
75	35	12
80	40	12
90	50	12
100	55	16
110	60	20
125	65	22
140	80	22
150	90	22
165	100	24
170	100	24
180	100	27
190	100	32
200	100	32
210	140	24
225	140	32

Sizes given for angles apply to channel and size for beam apply to tees.

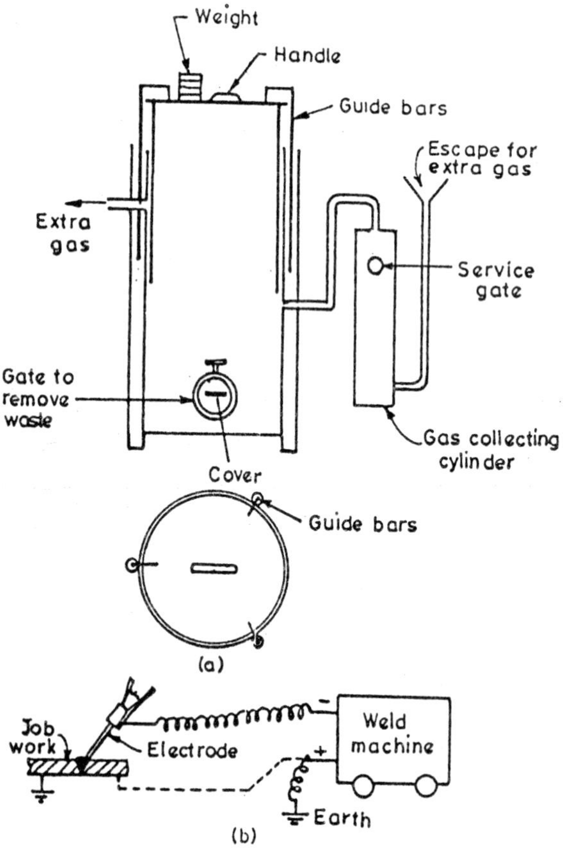

Fig. 4·44.

(B) Welded Joints : Weldings are of the following types :

(1) **Forge or Black Smith Welding.** The two pieces are heated red and are beated by hammer by giving a lap. Flux in the form of borax is sprinkled on the surface.

(2) **Oxyacetylene or Gas Welding.** Mixture of oxygen and acetylene or L.P. gas (acetylene is locally known as D.S.) are burned through a torch giving an intense heat.The welding material is placed on the joint which is welded by the intense heat of the flame.

Oxygen and D.S. cylinders are available in the market. Sometimes acetylene is prepared at site. In a closed vessel water is poured on carbide pieces and the gas produced is collected through a pipe. Carbide (calcium carbide) should be stored in a store away from combustible or in-flamm-able articles. The waste carbide dust should be destroyed by water in an open space. L.P. Gas (cooking gas) is available in town gas agencies.

(3) **Electric Arc Welding.** A metal electrode is connected to the –ve

terminal of the welding machine through a wire conductor. The +ve terminal of the machine is connected to the work by a metal conductor or by earth if the distance is long. When the electrode is brought near the jointing point the electric circuit passes with an arc which fuses the electrode and deposits its fused metal on the joint.

Forms of Welded Joints. (1) **Fillet Weld.** They are generally made triangular in shape having side angles of 45°. The outer convex or concave surface is known as reinforcement, which should not be more than 1/8″.

Weld Size. It is the length of either of the two legs containing the right angle. (Refer Fig. 4·45 (*a*) & (*b*))

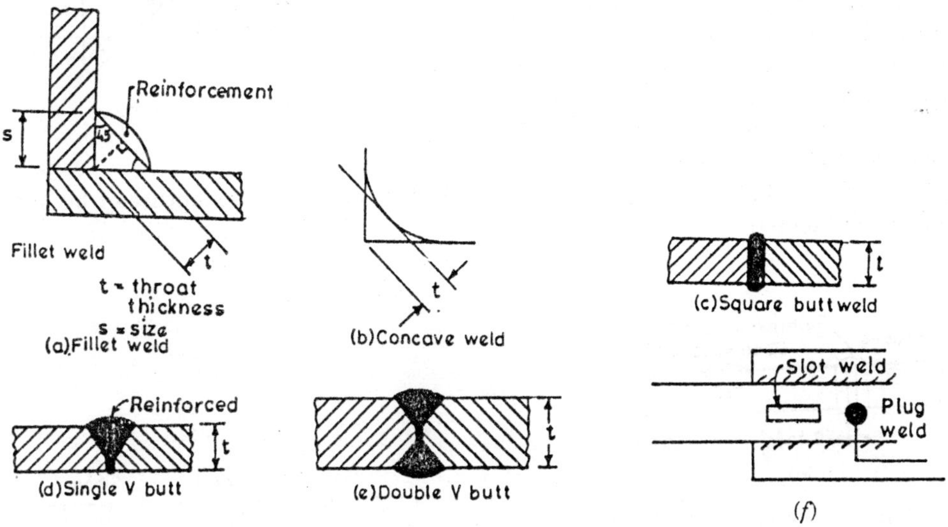

Fig. 4·45 (*c*).

Throat Thickness. It is measured by the perpendicular drawn from the intersection of the two legs on the hypotenuse. It is also simply denoted by throat or the thickness. If it is denoted by t and size by S then

$$t = \frac{1}{\sqrt{2}} \times S = 0{\cdot}707\, S$$

The Throat Section or Throat Area. It is the product of the throat thickness and the length of the weld.

(2) **Butt or Groove Weld.** The size of the weld in butt weld is t_1, the thickness of the plate. The angle of the V should not be less than 70° and the edge of the plate should be left square at about 1/16″. The gap between the plates may be 1/16″ for plates 3/8″ thick and under 1/8″ for thicker plates. No V is used for plates under 1/8″.

The outer extrimity of the weld is reinforced *i.e.* made convex so that the area is about 10% greater than that of the plate.

(3) **Plug or Slot Weld.** In order to give extra strength to a welded joint a plug or slot weld is used. These are generally used where it is not possible to provide the required weld area by butt or fillet, and an additional area is required, then the slots or holes are filled. They are called as plug weld. (refer Fig. 4·45 (*f*)

Classification of Welds according to the Position. Flat, horizontal vertical or over head etc. (refer Fig. 4·45 (*c*) to (*f*), 4·46 and 4·47)

Butt Welds. Types of butt joints are :

(1) **Square butt :** (*a*) Welded one side (*b*) Welded both sides

(2) **Open square :** (*a*) Welded one side (*b*) Welded both sides

(3) (*a*) Single *V* weld one side, weld both sides

(*b*) Double *V* (angle min. 75°)

(*c*) Single *V* with backing strip.

(4) Bevel single weld one side angle 45° min. in horizontal 25° in other position

(5) Single U butt weld one side.

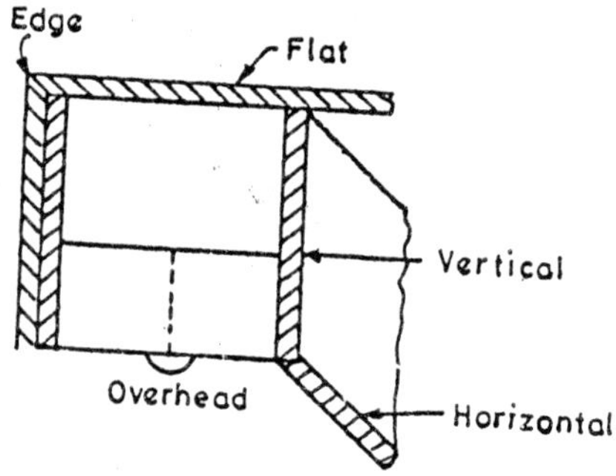

Fig. 4·46.

Square butt joints are used where thickness of the plate is less than 3/8″. The throat thickness is generally taken for the thinner member and reinforcement is ignored. Thickness where the penetration of the joint is not in full thickness is taken for the penetrated depth. In case of single *V*, single bevel or single U as 5/8 of the thinner plate. For full penetration depth design is not required. Full penetration depth can be obtained by providing a backing strip.

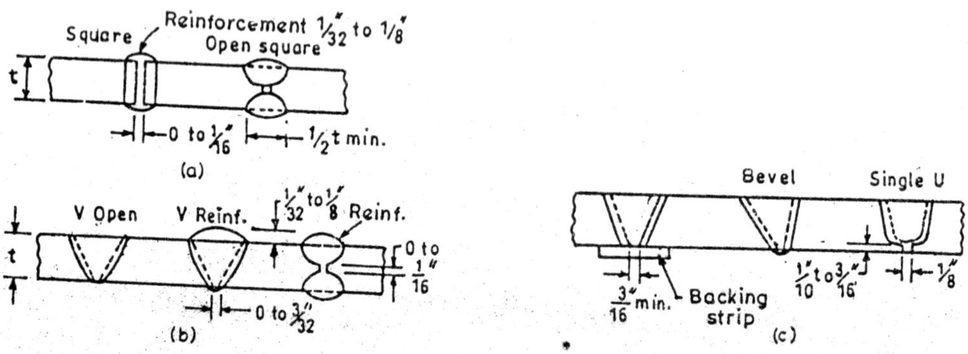

Fig. 4·47.

Intermediate Butt Welds. Intermediate butt welds shall only be used to resist shear and the effective length of any such weld shall not be less than 4 times the long space between the effective lengths of welds and not more than 12 times the thickness of the thinner plate. (Refer Fig. 4·47 (*c*)).

Design of Butt Weld. (1) When penetration of weld metal is full, weld is treated like the parent metal, with thickness equal to that of parts joined and need no design.

(2) When the welded joints are constructed with mild steel of IS : 226—1995 as the parent metal and electrode confirming to IS : 814—1957, the allowable stress will be as under :

Tension or comp. throat of a butt weld =9·0 t/in^2 or 14·2 kg/cm^2.

Fibre stress in bending in comp. and tension = 9·0 t/in^2 or 14·2 kg/cm^2.

Shear on section through throat butt weld 6·5t/m^2 or 1025 kg/cm^2.

Note : (1) For site welds the above stress are taken 80% for wind and seismic load considerations the stress is reduced by 25%.

(2) Incomplete penetration can be taken where there are no dynamic, repeating, alternating or eccentric loads. The effective throat thickness of such weld is the min. thickness of weld metal common to the parts jointed excluding reinforcement.

(3) When the thickness of the plates are different the thicker plate may be tapered by a slope not exceeding 1 : 5. This taper must be done where difference of the thickness is more than 25% of the thinner plate or 1/8″ (3 mm), when it is not convenient to taper, and there are no dynamic, alternating or eccentric loads, the taper may be omitted, but the size of the weld to thicker part should be 25% greater than that for the thinner plate.

Fillet Welds. Lap, Tee or Corners are commonly jointed by this type of welds. Normally the side containing the right angle are equal, but if sides are unequal the lesser side of the triangle is taken as the size of the weld.

Fillet welds if are thin in size are welded in single pass. If the size is more than mutli passes are used. In such case each weld is cooled and the flux (material of rod coating deposited on surface of weld) should be removed by slight hammering of the weld.

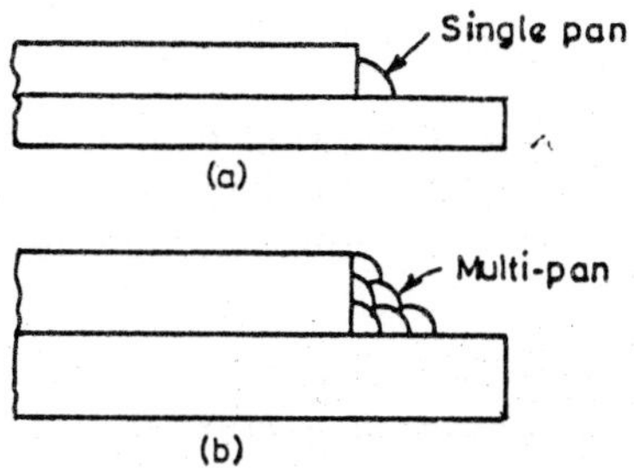

Fig. 4·48.

Table 4·12 (*a*). Sizes of the Fillet Weld

Weld in inch	3/16	1/4	5/16	3/8	1/2	5/8
Thickness of pass in inch	1/2	3/4	1¼	2	6	over 6

Subject to min. of 1/16″ (less than the thickness of edge for square edges and 3/4 of the thickness of rolled edges).

Design of Fillet Weld. These welds are designed for the shear stress at the min. sections of the weld which is known as the throat area.

Table 4·12 (*b*). The Throat Thickness for Different Angles, $t = K$ size of the throat S or $t = KS$

Angle between faces	60°-90°	90°-100°	100°-106°	106°-113°	113°-120°
constant, K	0·70	0·65	0·60	0·55	0·50

Design Steps. (1) Effective length of the fillet weld = overall length $2S$

(2) The effective length should not be less than $4S$. If the effective length is less than the effective size of the weld, it should be taken as $L/4$. (L = overall length of the weld)

(3) On the drawing only effective length is shown and the additional length required as above should be provided by the welder.

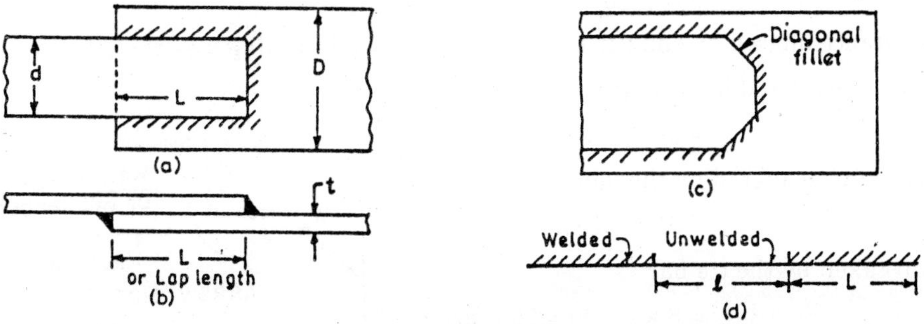

Fig. 4·49.

(4) IS : 816—1956 recommended that length of each fillet weld should be kept more than the perpendicular distance between them. $L > d$.

(5) Transverse distance between the welds should be kept less than 16 times the thickness of the thinner plate, unless end transverse weld. Intermediate plug or slot welds are employed. $L < 16\,t$ where t is the thickness of the thinner plate.

(6) Overlap of the plates should not be less than $5t$; $L > 5t$.

(7) Clause 6·23 of IS : 816—1956. The max. size of a fillet weld of a square edge should be (1/16″) less than the thickness of the plate. Size of a fillet weld along toe of the angle or a rounded edge of a flange should not exceed 3/4 of the thickness of the angle leg or the flange.

When the larger sizes of fillets are required, the size of the fillet welds may be taken equal to the thickness of the plate provided that no injury to the present section should be done by the welder.

(8) $f_S = P/KLS$ where P = load taken by plate = sec. of plate area × tensile strength of plate, K = constant depending on angle of weld which is generally right angle, S = size of the weld.

f_S for end fillets may be taken 6·5 t/in^2 or 10·25 kg/cm^2

f_S for side fillets may be taken $5t/\text{in}^2$ or 787·5 kg/cm^2

f_S for diagonal fillets may be taken $6t/\text{in}^2$ or 906·2 kg/cm^2.

Tensile strength for plate section = $9t/\text{in}^2$ or 1420 kg/cm^2.

(9) Eccenetric loads, wind, seismic and load due to moment caused by the loads should be accounted for.

(10) **Slot Welds.** The periphery of the slot is taken as the length of the weld.

Plug Welds. The area of the hole is taken as the resisting area. This area multiplied by shearing stress gives the stress borne by the plug weld.

Example. 4″ × ½″ tension member is to be jointed by another member by a fillet weld calculate lap lengths.

Working stress in steel = 8 t/in^2, in shear = 7 t/in^2 for end fillet as 5 t/in^2 (for side fillet).

Let l be the lap length.

The throat thickness = $\dfrac{S}{\sqrt{2}} = \dfrac{0\cdot25}{\sqrt{2}}$ = 0·176 taking 0·25 as the size (S)

The resistance offered by end fillets = $7 \times 2 \times 4 \times t = 56\,t$ taking 2 as the effective length

The resistance offered by side fillets

$$= 5 \times 2 \times l \times t = 10\,lt$$

Total resistance offered by the joint

$$= 56\,t + 10\,lt \quad (1)$$

The pull taken by the tie bar

$$= 8 \times 4 \times ½ = 16 \text{ tons} \quad (2)$$

or $56\,t + 10\,lt = 16$ or $l = 3\cdot355^2$ (t being 0·176″)

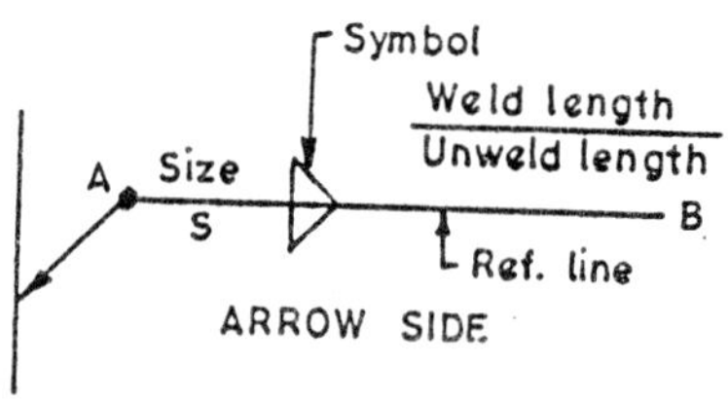

Fig. 4·50.

Welding Symbols and their way of Notations

	Form of weld	*Shape of sec.*	*Notation or symbol*
(*a*)	Fillet Single Butt		Refer Fig. 4·51 (*a*)
(*b*)	Square Butt		Refer Fig. 4·51 (*b*)
(*c*)	Single V Butt		Refer Fig. 4·51 (*c*)
(*d*)	Single U Butt		Refer Fig. 4·51 (*d*)
(*e*)	Double U Butt		Refer Fig. 4·51 (*e*)
(*f*)	Single bewell		Refer Fig. 4·51 (*f*)
(*g*)	Double bewell		Refer Fig. 4·51 (*g*)
(*h*)	Single J		Refer Fig. 4·51 (*h*)
(*i*)	Double J		Refer Fig. 4·51 (*i*)
(*j*)	Stud		Refer Fig. 4·51 (*j*)

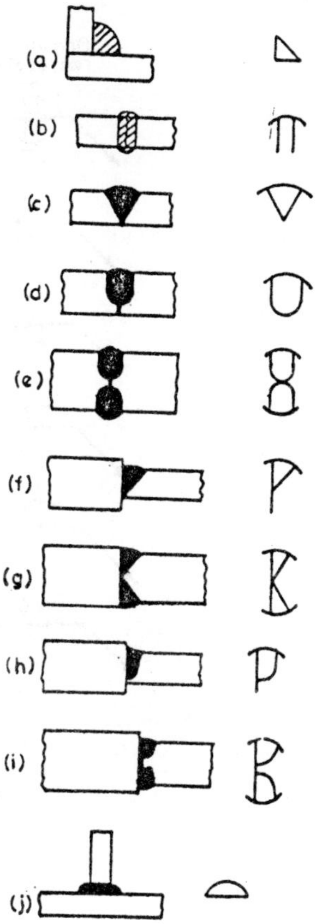

Fig. 4·51.

Way of Showing Welding types and Position. Line AB is the reference line. Symbols of the weld (say double fillet) is marked on the right of A. Size of the weld is marked on the left of symbol on reference line. For intermittent weld figures are written on the right side of the symbol showing the weld length starting from top.

Figures written towards acute angle of the arrow head shows the face towards the arrow head and figures written towards the obtuse angle of the arrow head indicate the position for the other side of arrow heads.

Elbow of the junction of arrow head with the reference line denoted by a fillet small circle denotes plug weld, while infilled circle shows a weld inside a circle with a slot weld around. A circle with centred dot shows the weld to be filled at the time of erection at field.

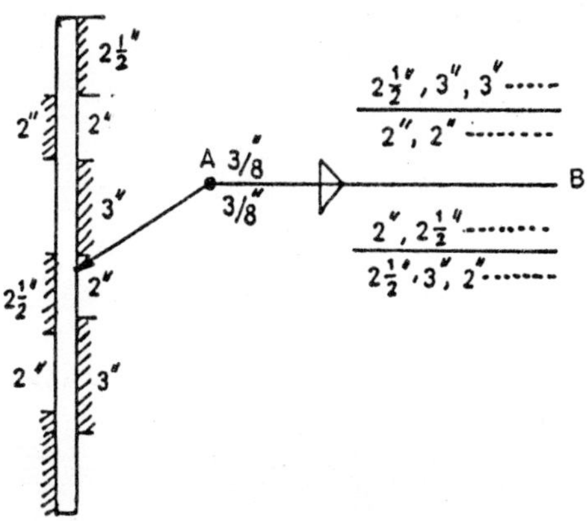

Fig. 4·52.

Other types of symbols are as follows :

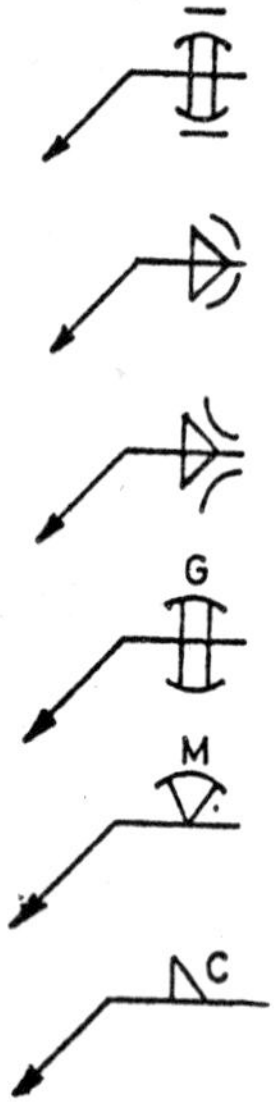

Drawing representation	Symbol	Serial	*Form of contour*
	—	(a)	Surface finish
	)	(b)	Convex finish
	(	(c)	Concave finish
	G	(d)	Grinding finish
	M	(e)	Machine finish
	C	(f)	Chipping finish

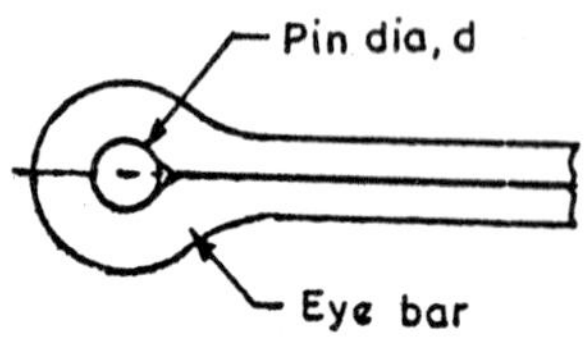

Fig. 4·53. Pin jointed connection.

5

Surveying

DRAWING

5·1. Printing of alphabet

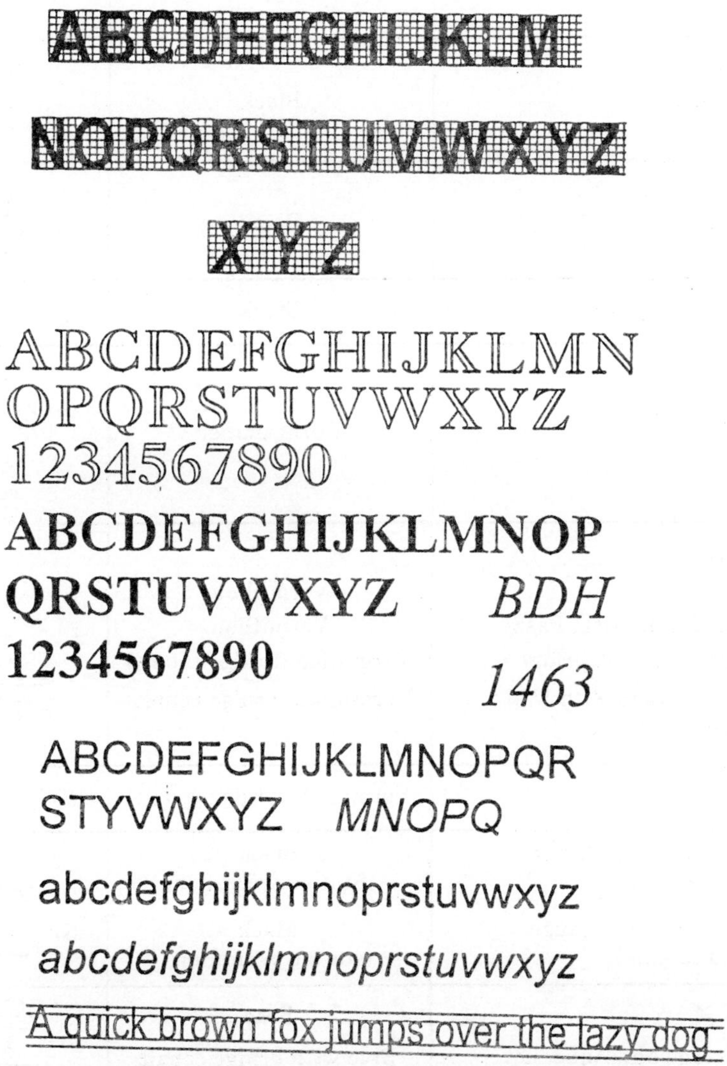

Fig. 5·1. Printing of alphabet.

Table 5·1. Conventional Signs used in Topographical Maps

Items	*Colour*	*Symbol (Refer Fig. 5·2)*
1. Abadi	Vermillion	(a) 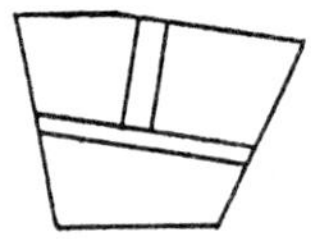
2. Ruined or deserted Abadis	Vermillion	(b) 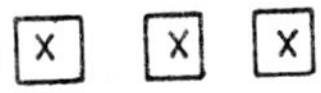
3. Walls masonry	Centre cobalt and out lines vermillion	(c) 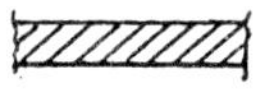
4. Walls kachcha	-do-	(d) 
5. Temple or Pagoda	Black	(e) 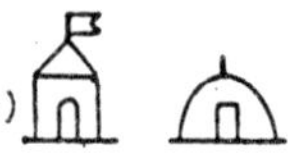
6. Mosque or Church	Black	(f) 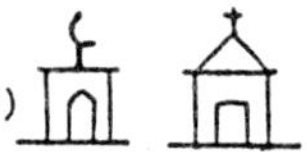
7. Telegraph line with posts	Black	(g) 
8. Contour with value	Burnt umber	(h) 
9. Unmetalled road (*a*) Foot path (*b*) Mule path, Bridle path, Pass (*c*) Village cart road with bridge Metalled or pucca road with K.M. stones and avenue of trees	 Vermillion Vermillion Vermillion (bridge cobalt) Vermillion (bridge cobalt)	(i) 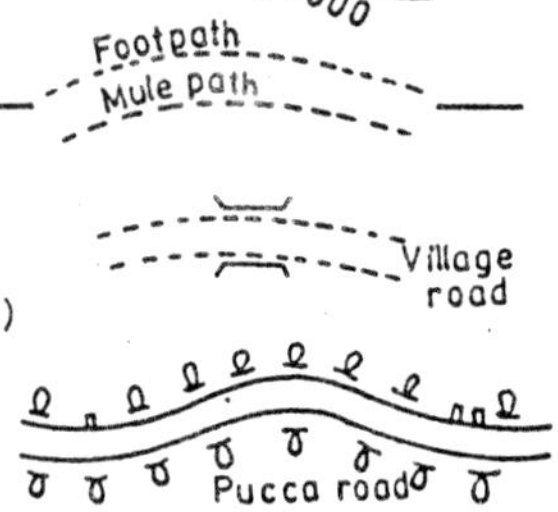
10. Canal road	Vermillion (bridge cobalt)	(j) 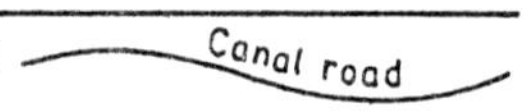
11. Railway line double with gauge (with station and k.m.) Railway line single with gauge (with station and k.m.)	Black (Station vermilion) Black (station vermilion)	(k) 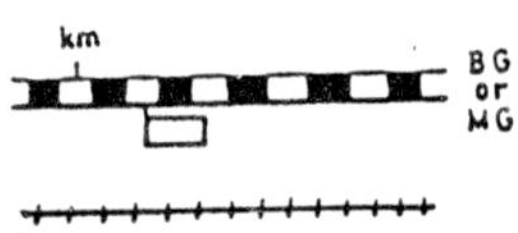
12. Canal with K.M. Canal with Bridge and Aqueduct	Blue Blue with bridge cobalt	(l) 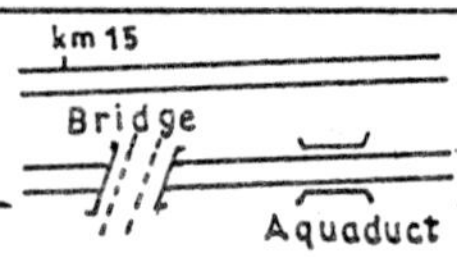

Items	*Colour*	*Symbol*
13. River with Dam	Blue, Dam vermillion	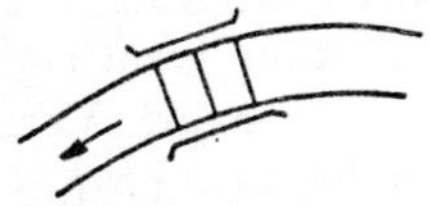 (m)
14. Cutting	Black	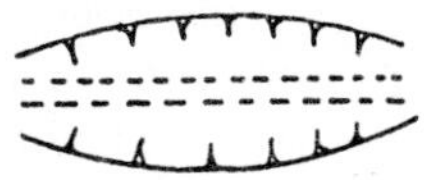 (n)
15. Embankment	Black	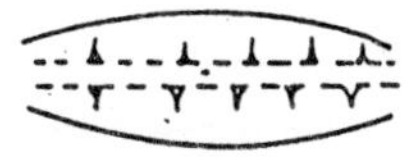 (o)
16. Swamp or marsh	Black	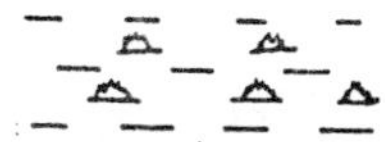 (p)
17. Drain or nala	Blue	 (q)
18. Pond	Blue	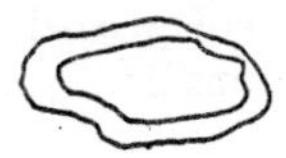 (r)
19. Tree	Black	 or  (s)
20. Fence with hedge	Black	----x----x----x----x---- (t)
21. Building	Vermillion	 (u)

Fig. 5·2.

5·3. SCALES (*a*) Diagonal Scale.

(*b*) Vernier Scale. It consists of a small scale called the vernier scale, graduated edge of which slides along the graduated edge of the main scale. The zero is marked with an arrow on the vernier scale. The scale may be straight or curved to read angles etc.

If it is required to read $1/n$th part of the main scale, smallest division then $(n - 1)$ or $(n + 1)$ division are taken and divided into n-equal parts on the vernier scale (say d = linear or angular value of smallest division of main scale, v = linear or angular value of smallest division of vernier scale.)

Then $1/n\ d$ = least count of the scale).

Reading of the Vernier Scale. Note the main graduation which are full beyond and on which the index of the vernier scale lies. Now observe the division of the vernier which coincides exactly with some division on the main scale. The number of the coinciding vernier division must be multiplied by the least count, gives the fractional part which is to be added to the 1st observed reading with reference to the zero mark.

Note : The readings of the main and vernier scales are graduated in the same direction either from right to left or left to right. Verniers are of the following types :

(*i*) **Direct Vernier.** *n dw* of main scale in equal to (*n* – 1) div. of vernier scale and graduations of both the scales are in the same direction. It is easier to use and is generally used.

(*ii*) **Retrograde Vernier.** *n* div. of main scale is equal to (*n* + 1) div. of vernier scale and the graduations of main and vernier scales are in opposite in directions.

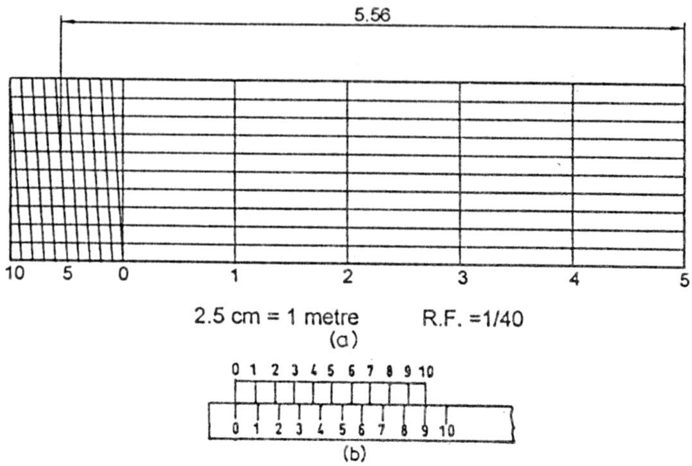

Fig. 5·3.

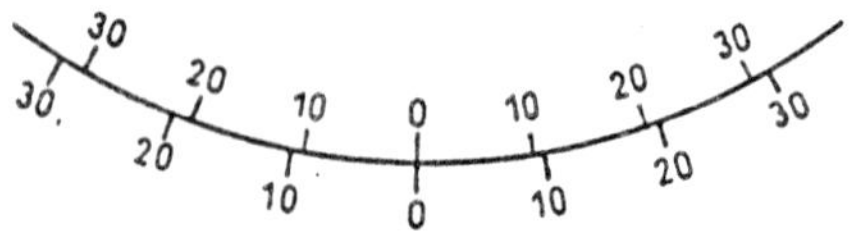

Fig. 5·4.

Double main Vernier. The graduations on the scale is marked on both the directions with common zero, the vernier is also marked in both directions with common zero in order to facilitate to take readings in both the directions.

(*iii*) **Extended Vernier.** When the available length of vernier is small and it is required to have a smaller least count without having the vernier division too closer together, these types of verniers are used in Abney level and in astronomical sexent.

In these verniers (2*n* – 1) main scale division are equal to *n* division on the vernier scale. Least count in such verniers = $\frac{1}{n}d$. For example eleven spaces of main scale graduated to 1° are divided to 6 divisions on the vernier scale, so least count is 1/6 × 60′ = 10′.

(*iv*) **Double folded vernier.** These are also used to minimise space in small transits and compasses. It has two rows of graduations on the vernier. For angles read in clock wise direction use lower row of Fig. on left hand vernier for less than 15′ and the upper row of Fig. on the right hand vernier for more than 15′. For angles read in anticlockwise direction use *vice-versa*.

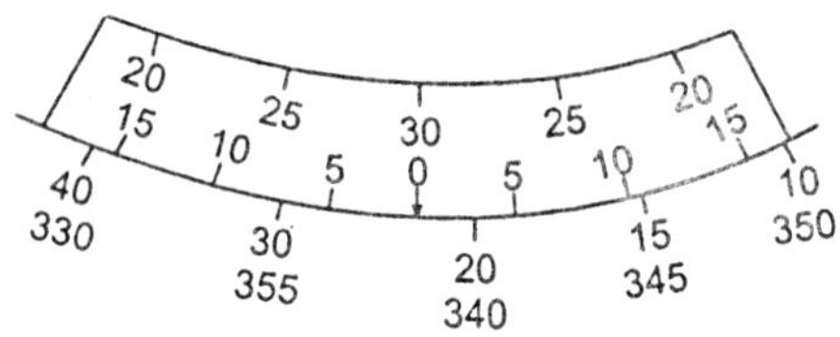

Fig. 5·5.

5·4. Chain Survey

Indirect or Reciprocal ranging. It is used when points in between two points are ranged, specially when the two points or stations say *A* and *B* are not directly visible. Select two points *C* and *D* such that both are visible from *A* and *B*. Range *C* between *A* and *D* to a point C_1. Again range *D* to a new point D_1 in line C_1B. Repeat C_1 to point C_2 in line with D_1A and so on till the points *ABCD* are in one line. Refer Fig. 5·6 (*a*) and (*b*)

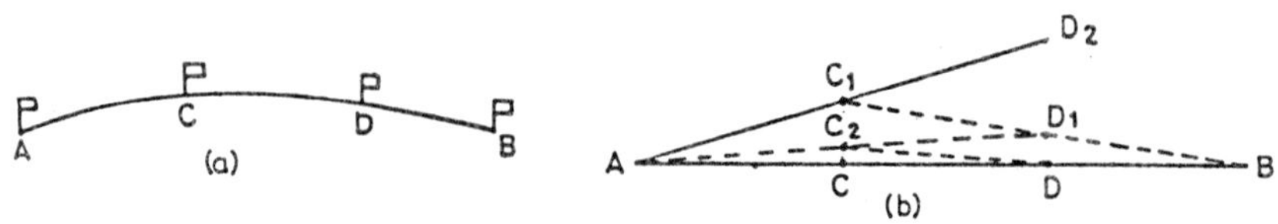

Fig. 5·6.

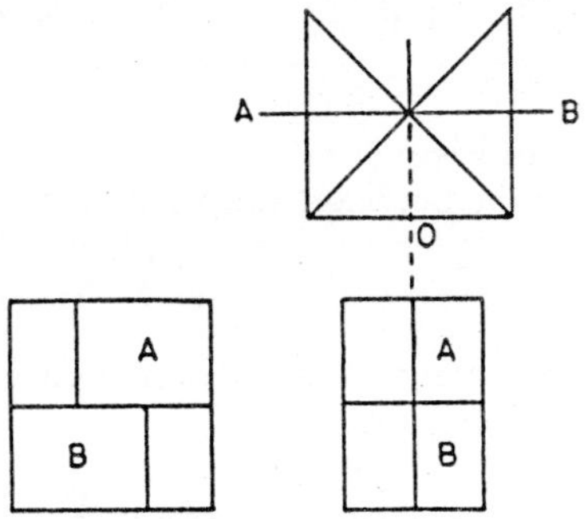

Fig. 5·7.

Line ranger. It is used to range a point in between two points. It consists of two right angled isosceles triangular prisms placed one above the other as shown in Fig. In order to establish a point O in between two stations A and B move backwards and forwards with the line ranger till the images on both the prisms are in one straight line. Since the reflected rays from both the prisms coinside only when the point O is in line with A and B.

Reading angle of a slope of ground by clinometer. In its simplest form clinometer consists of a semi-circular disc having two pins a and b at its two ends of diameter of base for sighting. A plumb is suspended from the centre. On the station A the staff is marked at the height of observer's eye which is ranged by the observer from the point B. An assistant adjusts the clinometer edge by moving till the edge of dia. ab is inline with A and B. Angle on the disc is read by the plumb line on the circumference of the semi circle disc.

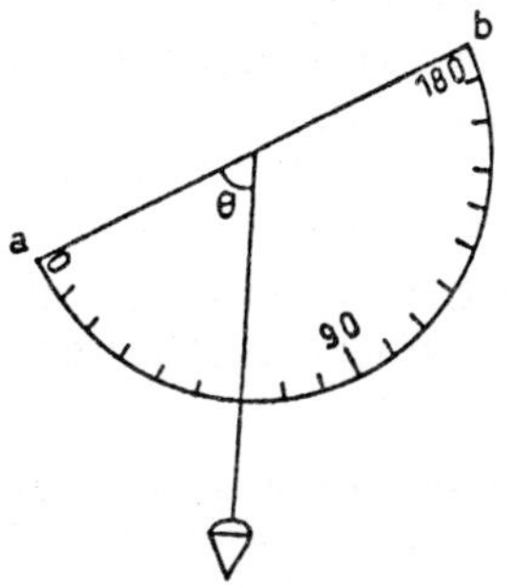

Fig. 5·8.

Corrections in Measuring Distances

(1) Correction for absolute length.

$$Ca = \frac{LC}{l}$$

where Ca = correction for absolute length
L = measured length
l = length of tape
C = correction to a tape

The sign of the correction Ca will be the same as C. Units of measure being the same.

(2) **Correction for Temperature**

$Ct = a(T_m - T_o)\,L$ where
Ct = correction for temperature
a = coef. of thermal expansion of the tape material
T_m = mean temperature during measurement.
T_o = temperature at which the tape is standardise
L = Measured length.

The sign of the correction is in plus or minus according as T_m is greater or less than T_o. The coeff. of expansion of steel varies from 0·0000055 to 0·0000070 per degree Ferenheit, inver 0·00000022 per deg. F. The average coefficient of tape material if not known may be taken as 0·0000063.

(3) **Correction for Pull or Tension**

$$Cp = \frac{(P - P_o)L}{A.E}$$ where Cp is the correction for pull.

P = pull applied during measurements in lbs.
P_o = pull for which the tape is standardised in lbs.
L = measured length in ft.
A = cross sectional area of tape section in sq. inches
E = mod. of elasticity of steel.

The sign of the correction in plus.

(4) **Correction for Sag**

$$C_S = \frac{l_1(wl_1)^2}{24\,P^2}$$ where

C_S = correction for sag.
t_1 = distance between supports in ft.
w = wt. of the tape in lbs/ft.
P = applied pull in lbs.

The correction is substractive.

(5) **Correction for Normal Tension.** It is the tension or pull given to the tape which just neutralises the combined effect of pull and sag.

$$P_n = \frac{0{\cdot}204\, w\sqrt{AE}}{\sqrt{(P_n - P_o)}}$$

P_n = Normal tension in lbs.
w = wt. of length of tape between supports in lbs.

(The value of P_n may be determined by trial and error.)

(6) **Correction for Slope**

$C_{Sl} = l - l \cos \theta$ and is –ve. when slopes are of uniform length l (slantings) and θ is the angle of slope with horizontal.

C_{Sl} = correction for slope.

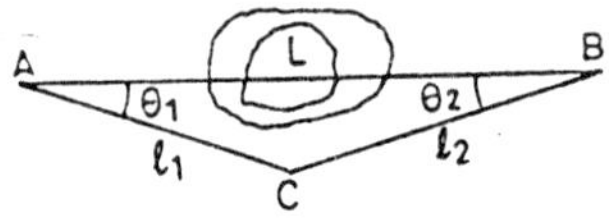

(7) **Correction for Alignment.** By improper alignment the length of line is apparently increased.

The true length $L = l_1 \cos \theta_1 + l_2 \cos \theta_2$

Chain Survey Traversing

Base Line. Longest survey line joining the controlling points in a chain survey is known as base line such as *AB*, *BC*, *CD* and *AD*. Details of features are located by line along it.

Tie Lines. These are lines tieing base lines and are taken to fill up further details which can not be covered from base line.

Check Lines. These lines are taken in order to check the survey accuracy such as *BD* or *Ce*. These can also be used as tie lines.

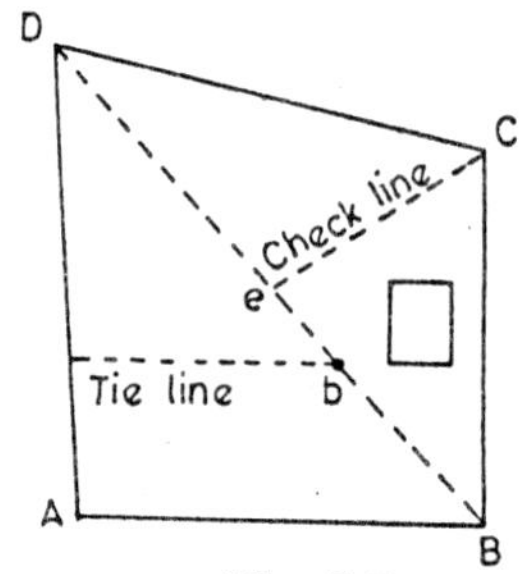

Fig. 5·9.

Field notes :

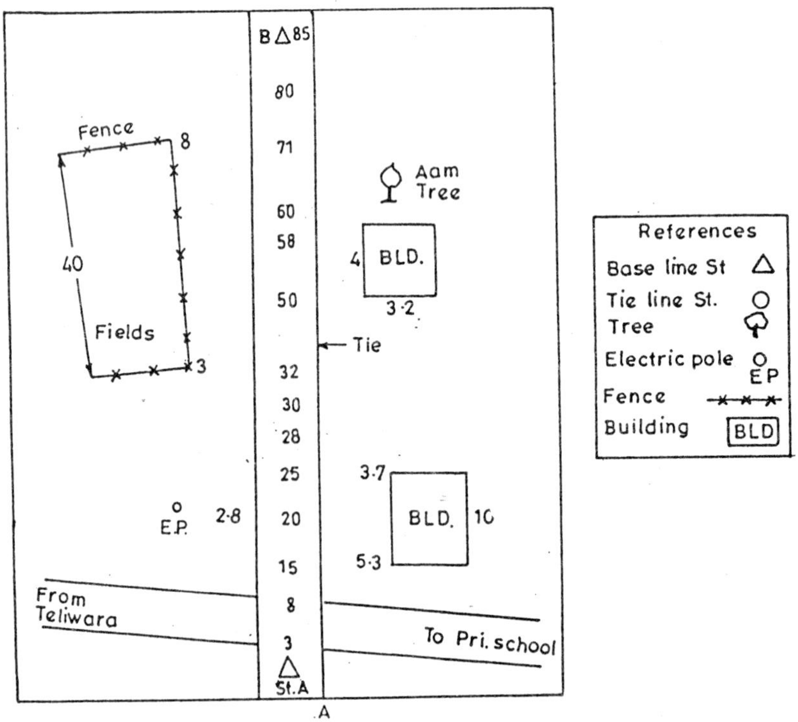

Fig. 5·10 (A).

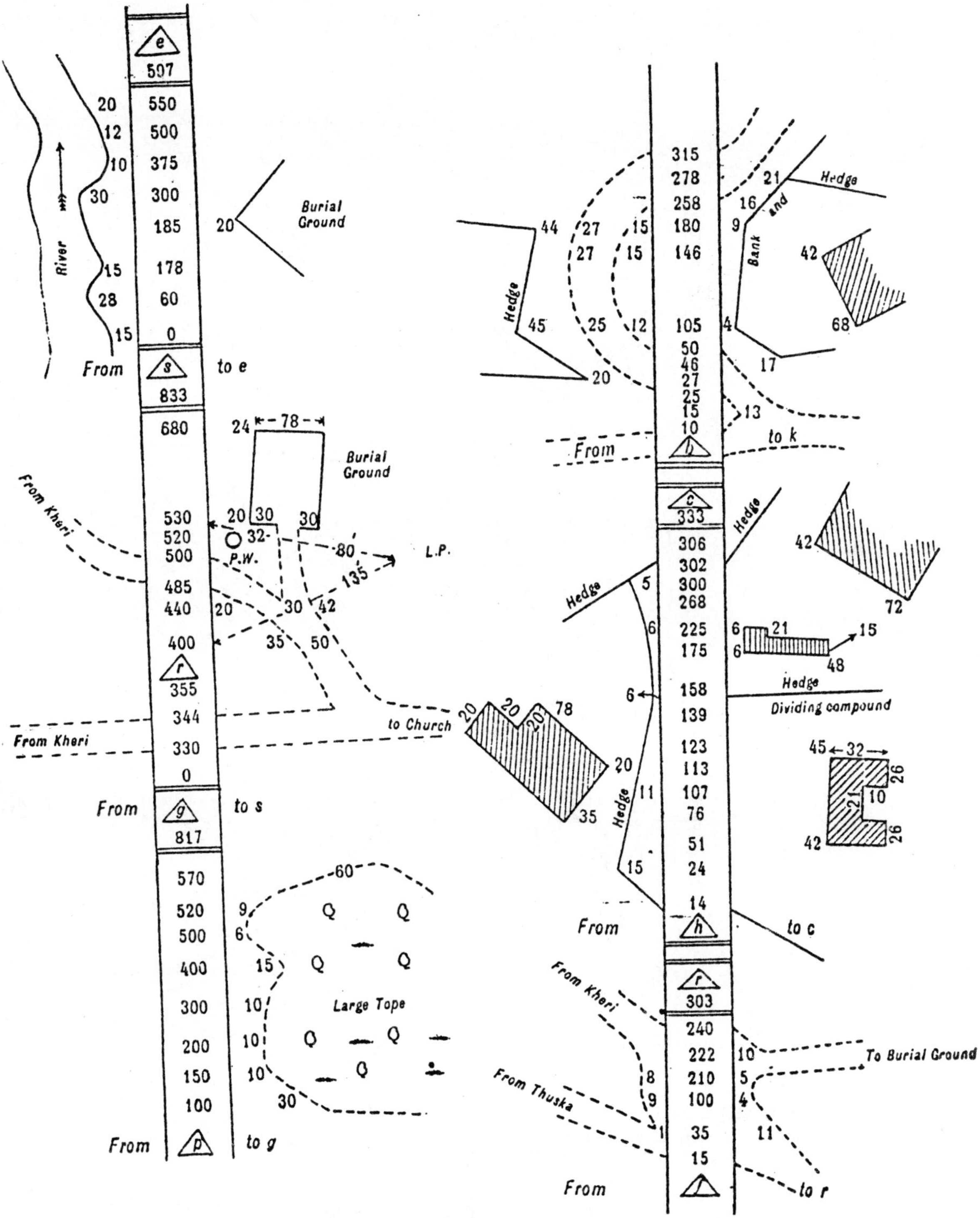

Fig. 5·10(B). A field book of Chain Survey

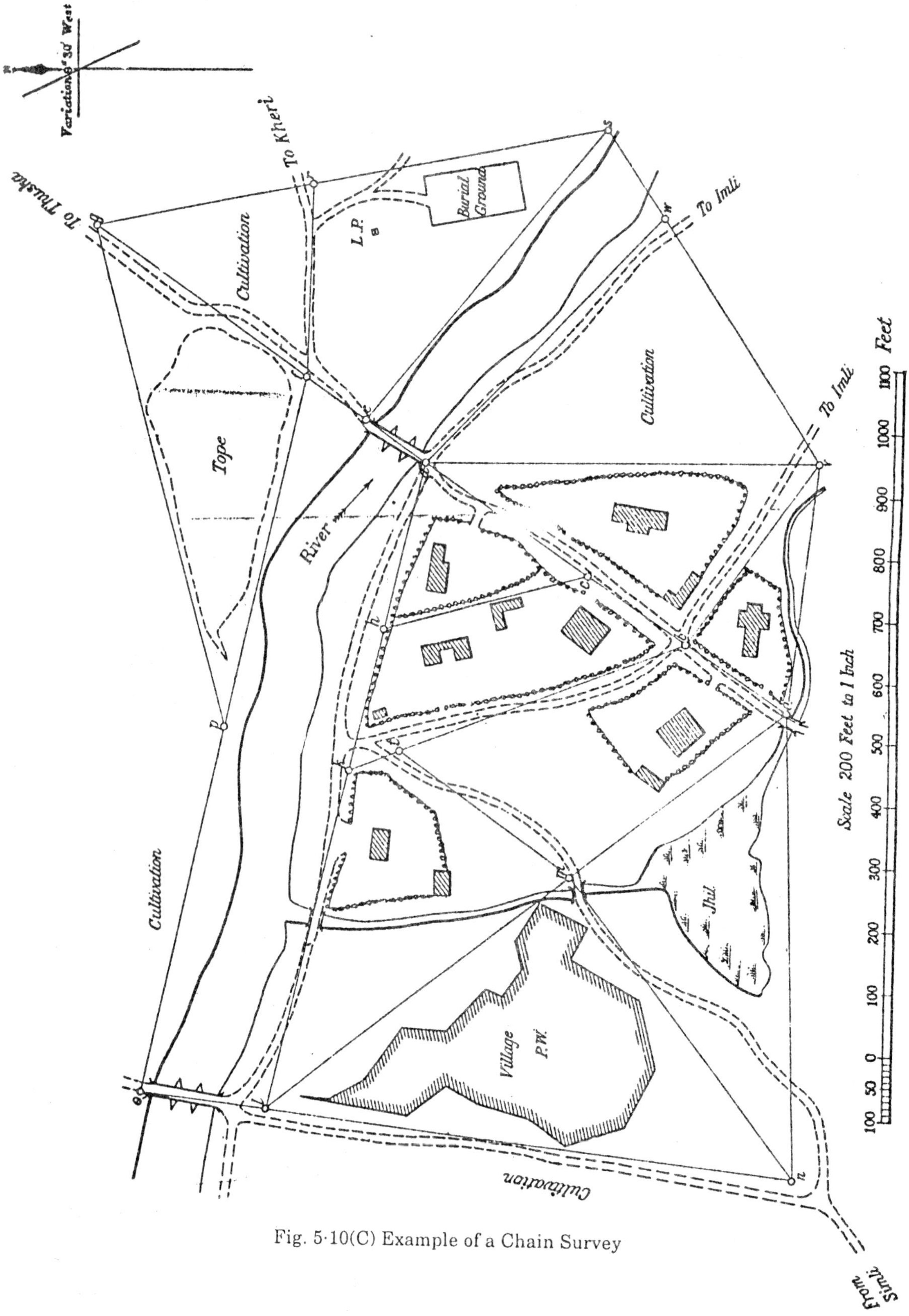

Fig. 5·10(C) Example of a Chain Survey

5·5. Obstacles in Chaining

(1) Obstacle can be seen across but can not be chained across even by rounding off the obstacle such as a river.

(*a*) Let AB be the line

Take a line COC' right angle to AB.

Set $CO = OC'$

Set out a line $C'D'$ right angle to CC' upto D' such that in $D'OD$, D is a point on the line AB on the other bank of the obstacle. Then $CD = D'C'$.

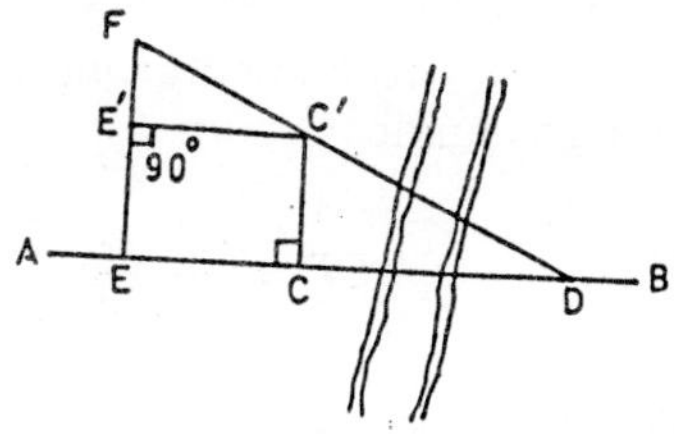

Fig. 5·11 (*a*).

(*b*) Set $OC = C'O$ roughly parallel to the bank. $\angle AOC$ is any convenient angle

$$OD' = OD \sqrt{OC^2 + DC^2}$$

This type of problem is met with when the line crossing the rivet is oblique.

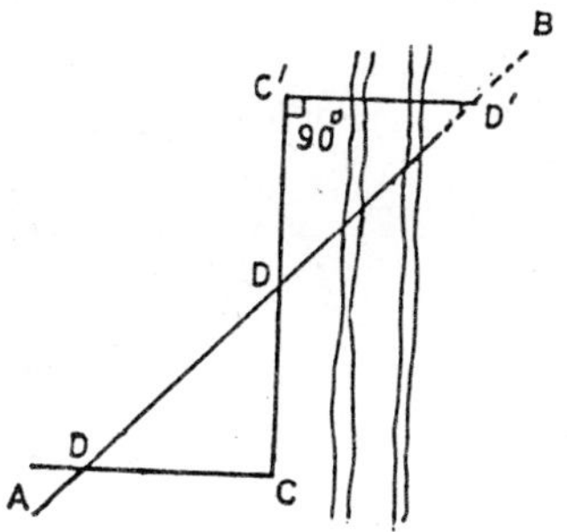

Fig. 5·11 (*b*)

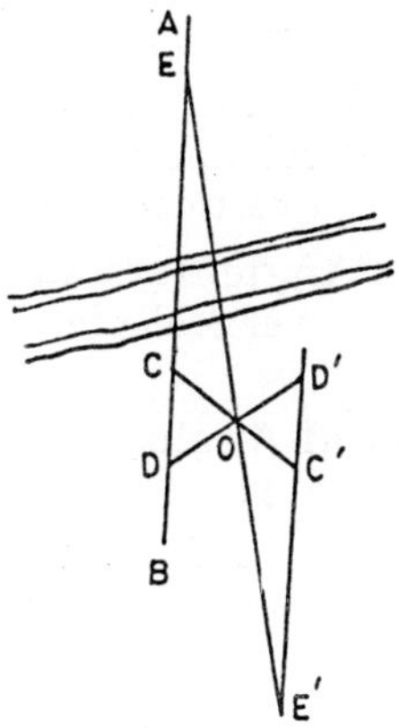

Fig. 5·11 (*c*)

(*c*) Let the line is AB. Take E a point on one bank and CD on the other bank. Take a point O conveniently. Set out $DO = D'O$

$OC = OC'$ and produce DC' to E'

E' must be such that on producing EO it may cut E'. Now $C'E' = CE$.

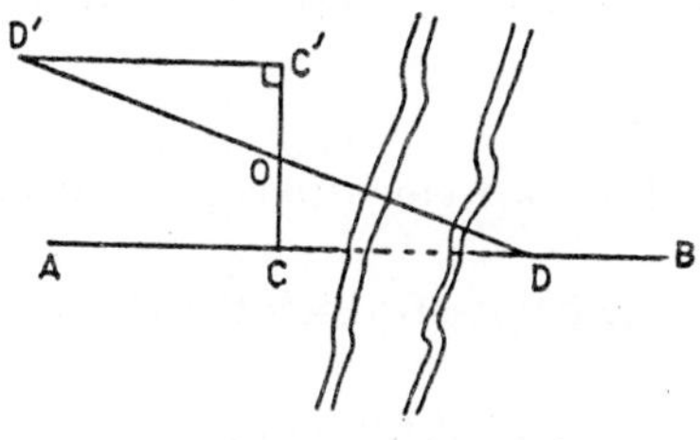

Fig. 5·11 (*d*).

(*d*) On the line AB, set two perp. lines EF and CC' such that in $FC'D$, D will be the point on the other bank. Join $C'E$ parallel to AB. Then $\frac{EC'}{CD} = \frac{EF}{CC'}$. From which CD can be calculated.

(2) To determine the length of two points when both are in accessible.

(*a*) Let the inaccessible distance is AB. Take a point C on the accessible side. Take a point A' on CA. Measure CA'. Take another point B' such that $CB' = \frac{CA' \times CB}{CA}$. (The length CA and CB being determined by the methods explained above).

Then $AB = \frac{A'B' \times AC}{CA'} = \frac{A'B' \times CB}{CB'}$

(*b*) The perp. distance of C from AB.

Set out a perpendicular on $A'B'$ at D' such that $\angle A'D'C$ = right angle.

Then $CD = \frac{CD' \times CA}{CA'} = \frac{CD' \times CB}{CB'}$

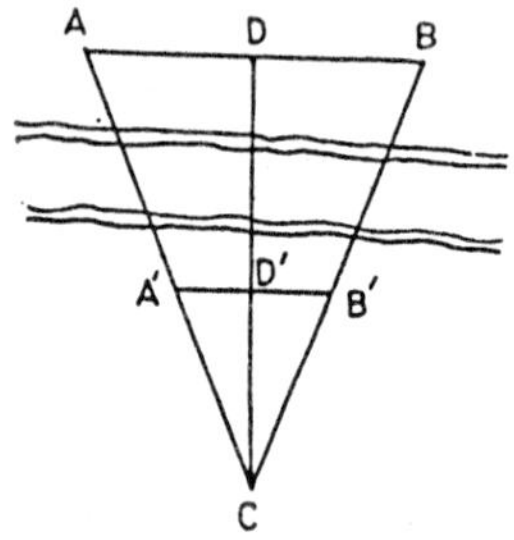

Fig. 5·12.

5·6. Levelling

Terms used in levelling

(1) **Level Surface.** It is a surface parallel to the mean spheroidal surface of the earth. For example a still lake since the earth is an oblate spheroid, a level surface is a curve surface. Every point on a level surface is equidistant from the centre of the earth. It is normal to the plumb line at all points. A level line is therefore normal to plumb line at all points.

(2) **Horizontal Plane.** It is a plane tangential to the level surface at a point on the level surface. It is perp. to the plumb line.

Horizontal Line. It is a line lying on the horizontal plane. It is a straight line tangential to a level line. A vertical line at any point is a line normal to the level surface through that point. A plumb line is a vertical line.

(3) **Vertical Angle.** It is an angle between two intersecting lines in a vertical plane one in which is a horizontal line.

(4) **Horizontal Angle.** It is an angle between two lines in a horizontal plane.

(5) **Difference in Elevation.** It is a vertical distance between the two level surfaces passing through the two points.

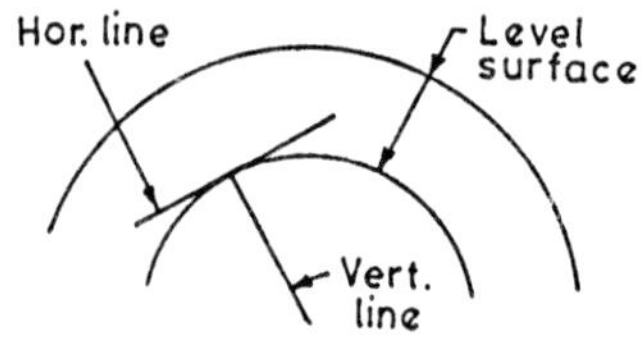

Fig. 5·13.

(6) Line of collimation or line of sight is line joining the intersection of the cross hair to the optical centre of the object glass and its continuation.

(7) **Axis of the Telescope.** Line joining the optical centre of the object glass to the centre of the eye piece.

(8) **Axis of the Level Tube.** (Bubble tube)—A line tangential to the curve of the bubble tube at its middle point. It is also called as bubble line. It is horizontal when the bubble is in centre.

(9) **Vertical Axis.** Centre line of the axis of rotation.

(10) **Back Sight.** Sight observed on the point of known elevation. It is also called the plus sight.

(11) **Fore Sight.** Sight observed on the staff of the point of which the elevation is to be determined.

(12) **Intermediate Sight.** Sight observed on the points of unknown elevations prior to the fore sight on which the instrument is shifted.

(13) **Change point or the Turning point.** A point on which the fore reading is taken and the instrument is shifted to new place. On this point back sight is taken for the next position of the instrument for further levelling.

(14) **Height of Instruments.** It is the elevation level of the line of collimation when the instrument is levelled.

(15) **Parallax.** It is the apparent movement of the image relative to the cross hair when the image formed by the objective does not fall in the plane of the diaphragm. It is removed by

adjusting the eye piece in or out of the telescope tube and by adjusting to focussing screw till the image appears fixed to the cross hair, if the eye is moved up and down.

Correction due to Curvature = $0{\cdot}667\ D^2$ ft. or $0{\cdot}08\ D_1^2$ meter where D and D_1 are the distance in miles or kilometers respectively from the level to the staff and is substractive or the true staff reading is obtained by substracting correction from the observed reading.

Correction due to Refraction = $0{\cdot}095\ D^2$ ft. or $0{\cdot}0114\ D_1^2$ m. and is additive to the staff reading.

Combined Correction due to Curvature and Refraction = $0{\cdot}57\ D^2$ F or $0{\cdot}068\ D_1^2$ m and is substractive to the staff reading.

Reciprocal Levelling. This system of levelling is usual when the distance between the two points (such as a deep valley or a river lies in between them) is considerable and obstacled. In this levelling the error due to refraction curvature and collimation (line of collimation not being parallel to the bubble line) is eliminated. In reciprocal levelling for determining difference of level between two points proceed as follows.

Set up the instrument near to one station (say A) and take the staff reading (If too much close than by the eye piece of the instrument) and then take the reading of the staff on the other station (say B). Calculate the difference of level by the two staff readings say it is 'd_1'. Next set up the instrument near the station B and take the staff readings on station B and A. Calculate the difference of level say it is d_2. Then the true difference of level is the mean of the two differences so obtained $\dfrac{d_1 + d_2}{2}$.

Note : Two instruments of perfect adjustments can be used simultaneously on the two stations to obtain the readings at the same instant to avoid any atmospheric changes that causes refraction.

Barometric Levelling. Atmospheric pressure is inversely proportional to the height of the place. On high altitudes the pressure goes on diminishing. This effect is utilised to determine the altitudes (roughly in reconnaissance survey) with reference to the atmospheric pressure of the place. A formula for this is given below :

$$H = 60158{\cdot}6\,(\log h_1 - \log h_2)\left(\frac{1 + T_1 + T_2 - 64}{900}\right) \quad ...(1)$$

where

H = diff. in elevation in ft. between two stations.

h_1 = barometeric reading in inches at the lower station

h_2 = barometeric reading in inches at the higher station

T_1 = temperature in deg. Fehrenheit at lower station

T_2 = temperature in deg. Fehrenheit at higher station

T_1 and T_2 measured by detached thermometers.

Correction for the readings taken by mercury thermometer.

$h = h'\{1 + a(t_1 + t_2)\}$; h = the corrected height.

h' = observed height of the stations, t_1 and t_2 are the readings on mercury thermometer.

Now place the corrected values of h_1 and h_2 in formula (1)

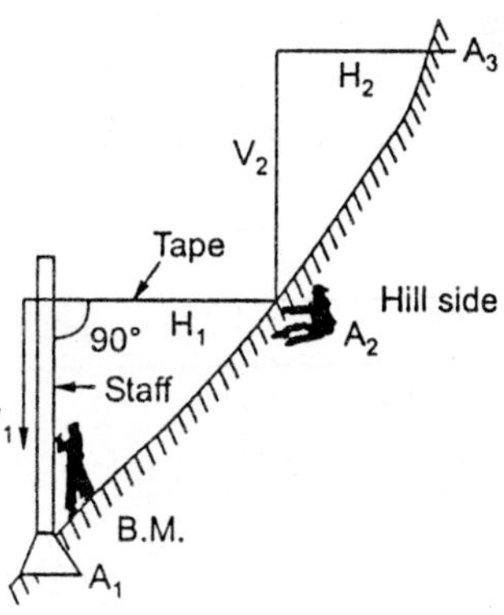

Heights V(m)	Distance D(m)
0	0
3M	2·11
3M	1·92
3M	2·17
3M	2·01
3M	2·13

Fig. 5·13 (A).

Step Levelling. In steep slopes or in hills it is difficult to level with levelling instrument. In such cases process of step levelling is used conveniently. In this operation a level staff, a plumb bob and a measuring tape is used. A staff man keeps the staff on the station of a B.M. whose R.L. is known in a vertical position by the help of a plumb hung on the side of the staff say it is station A_1.

For convenient working the vertical height is fixed and ring of the tape is tied to the staff at that height. The tape is kept perpendicular to the staff by eye estimation. However for correct alignment a stick is tied to the staff at Right angle and the tape is aligned at Right angle to the staff with the help of this rod. The tape man is then marks a point on the hill side slope and reads the horizontal distance. This station is marked as A_2. The procedure is proceeded step by step till the destination station is reached. The vertical and horizontal readings are recorded in a tabular form. The R.L. of the points A_1, A_2, A_3 ... can be computed by adding the heights. It is not necessary that the height point is fixed, it may be taken as convenient at site on each setting.

Level Book—Canal Pattern **Height of instrument method**

X-section No. L_1

Levels from B.M. No. 2 Village Nagla to B.M. No. 4 Village Mant Page 25

No.	*Distance in km.*	*Bearing*		*Reading*			*Height of Instru -ment*	*Reduced Levels*	*Remarks*
		Back	*Fore*	*Back*	*Int.*	*Fore*			
0	0·320	260		4·46			884·70	880·24	Top of B.M. No. 2 Village Nagla R.L. 980·24
1	280·321	261	80	5·21		2·27	887·64	882·43	
2	388·261	260	80	2·97		3·06	887·55	884·58	
3	420·310	240	81	4·62		4·33	887·84	883·22	
		290	60		3·22			884·62	Top of B.M. No. 3 Village Tajpur R.L. 884·60
4	570·112	291	110	3·86		5·77	885·93	882·07	
5	610·101	202	110	6·23		2·11	890·05	883·82	
6	701·210		22		7·20			883·03	Top of B.M. No. 4 Village Mant R.L. 883·00

Arithmatic check 27·35 24·56
24·56
(+) 2·79

Closing error 883·03
883·00
0·03 Reasonable

Sd/- Ram Das J.E.
8.4.2005

X-section No. 4

Level from B.M. No. 2 Village Nagla to B.N. No. 4 Village Mant

Rise and fall method

Sl. No.	*Chainage km.*	*Bearings*		*Readings*			*Rise (+)*	*Fall (–)*	*Reduced levels*	*Remarks*
		Back	*Fore*	*Back*	*Int.*	*Fore*				
0	0·320	260		4·46					880·24	Top of B.M. No. 2 Village Nagla R.L. 880·24
1	280·321	261	80	5·21		2·27	2·19		882·43	
2	288·261	260	80	2·97		3·06	2·15		884·58	
3	420·310	240	81	4·62		4·33		1·36	883·22	
			60		3·22		1·40		883·62	Top of B.M. No. 3 Village Tajpur R.L. 884·60
4	570·112	291	110	3·86		5·77		1·15	882·07	
5	610·101	202	110	6·23		2·11	1·75		883·82	
6	707·210		22			7·02		0·79	883·03	Top of B.M. No. 4 Village R.L. 883·00

Arithmatic check (–) 27·35 24·56 6·09 3·30
24·56 3·30
(+) 2·79 2·79

Sd/- Ram Das, J.E.
8.4.2005

Theodolite. A theodolite in its simplest form consists of the followings :

(1) **A levelling Block.** It consists of two circular parallel plates at a small distance apart. The lower (called trivet) is fixed by a ball and socket arrangement or by a clamping arrangement to the tripod for standing the instrument at suitable position, while the other upper one (called tribrack), is fitted with three levelling foot screws. The lower plate has an aperture in the centre from which the plumb hole can be suspended or the station point can be seen through optical plummet. In the centre of the tribrach two spindles of the upper vernier and lower graduated plate passes. Clamping and the slow motion tangent screws (for lower graduated plate motion) are also fixed in it. Clamping and slow motion tangent screws are provided on the upper vernier scale for its motions.

Sighting Block. A telescope is axeled on the two standards which are rigidly fixed on the upper vernier plate. A bubble tube is also fixed on the vertical vernier arm. A vertical graduated circle for measuring vertical angle is also fixed in axle of the telescope. This vertical circle slides along the vertical vernier arm.

Vernier Scale or Optical Micrometer are fixed for reading angles for a shorter magnitude. Separate verniers are provided for horizontal and vertical angles, while the vertical and horizontal angles are read only by the one optical micrometer marked with '*V*' for vertical and *H* for horizontal.

Plumb or Optical Plummet. For centering the instrument, a plumb hole is provided. In advanced instruments optical plummet is provided by which the station point is visible on a diaphragm having cross wires for centering.

5·7. Telescope used in Survey Instruments

A telescope consists of the following parts :

(1) **Main body.** It consists of two tubes, one is fixed in which other slides by a focussing screw operated by a rack and pinion arrangement and is called as a slide or a focussing tube. In external focussing instrument object glass is fixed in the slide and the outer tube carries the diaphragm and eye piece. In internal focussing instruments eye piece and the diaphragm is fixed in the slide and the object glass is fixed in end of the outer tube.

(2) **Object Glass or Objective.** It is compound lens to eliminate the combined effect of spherical aberration and chromative aberration and is called an achromative lens. When focussed the image of the object after passing through the objective is formed in the plane of cross hairs *viz.* the diaphragm, which is real and inverted.

(3) **Eye Piece.** It is also a combination of lenses which magnifies both the image and the cross hair. The image is seen inverted but in some type of eye pieces the image is converted from invert to erect. The eye piece is adjusted according to the observers eye sight by moving in or out by hand.

(4) **Diaphragm.** It consists of a brass ring fixed with cross hair which appear magnified by the eye piece. The cross hair is either of spider web lines on glass or fine platinum wire in the shape as desired including studia wires. Diaphragm can be adjusted vertically or horizontally by four nuts provided outside the rim of the telescope tube by loosening the one and tightening other in opposite of it for setting permanent adjustments of the instruments.

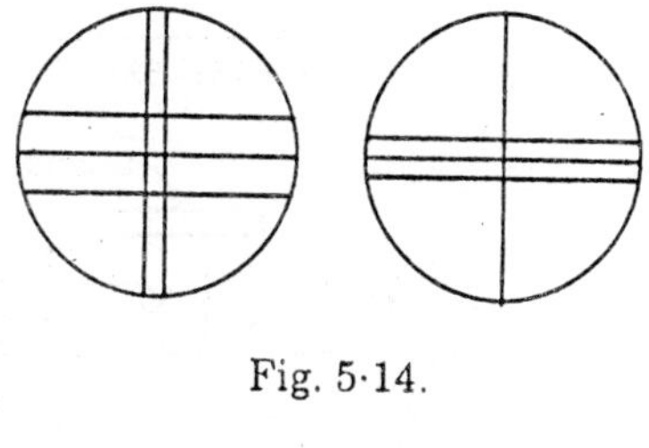

Fig. 5·14.

Subsidiary Parts of the telescope are ray shade or dust cap which slides over object glass to save it from Sun and dust and is drawn in when the instrument is not in use for cutting off extraneous light.

Types of Telescope. (1) **External Focussing Type.** As shown in Fig. 5·15 (*a*) in these instruments the slide tube carries the object glass. The disadvantage of this instrument is that its length is increased and the sliding tube is dusted when in use as a part of it remains out.

(2) **Internal Focussing Type.** As shown in Fig. 5·15 (*b*) that the sliding tube carries double concave lense operated by rack and pinion arrangement while the object glass is fixed at the end of the outer tube. The main advantage of this telescope is this that its length is limited

and fixed and the internal parts remain out of touch of the outer dust. The disadvantage of this type is that the slide carries a double concave lense which makes the image on the diaphragm and due to this extra lense, the brilliancy of the image is reduced.

External Focussing Type

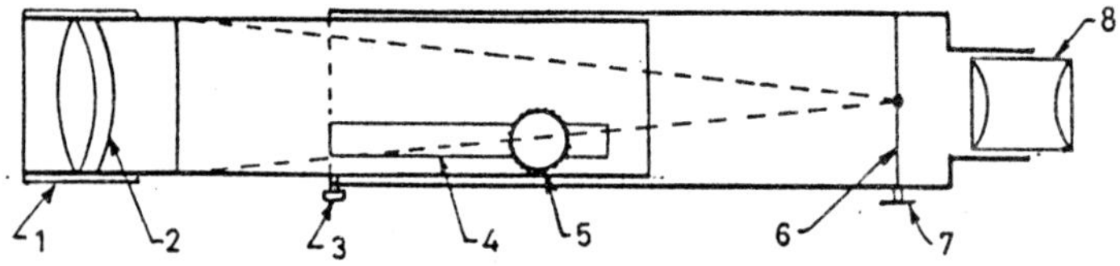

(1) Ray or dust cap	(2) Object glass	(3) Stops	(4) Rock and Pinion
(5) Focussing screw	(6) Diaphragm	(7) Diaphragm screw	(8) Eye piece

Fig. 5·15 (*a*).

Internal Focussing Type

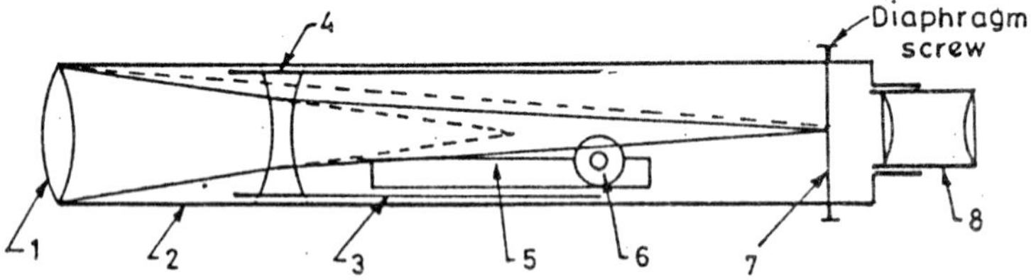

(1) Object glass	(2) Outer tube	(3) Slider	(4) Double concave lense
(5) Rack and pinion	(6) Focussing screw	(7) Diaphragm	(8) Eye piece

Fig. 5·15 (*b*).

Optical Micrometer

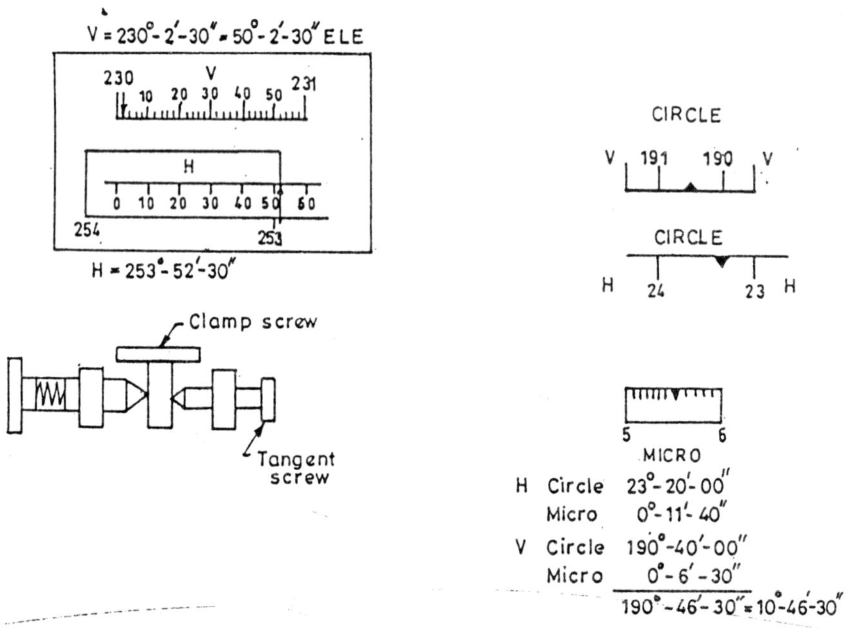

Note : Vertical angle or elevation reading 180
Depression reading 180°

Fig. 5·16.

Theodolite Section

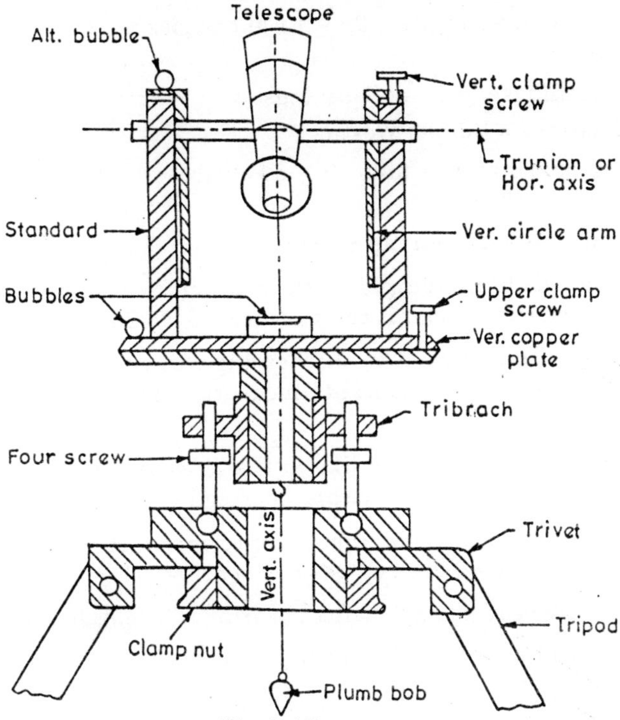

Fig. 5·17.

5·8. Theodolite and Compass Survey

(A) Terms used in Theodolite Survey

(1) **Centering.** Setting of the Theodolite over the station point.

(2) **Transisting, Plunging or Reversing.** It means turning the telescope on its horizontal axis in the vertical plane through 180°.

(3) **Swinging the Telescope.** Moving the telescope in horizontal plane. Swing left means counter clockwise and swing right clockwise motion.

(4) **Changing Face.** To change the position of the vertical circle from right to left or from left and right.

(5) **Face Left.** When the vertical circle is on the left of the observer.

(6) **Face Right.** When the vertical circle is in the right of the observer.

(7) **Telescope Normal.** Bubble up, face left. It is also known as telescope direct.

(8) **Telescope Inverted.** Bubble down, face right, also known as telescope indirect.

(9) **Changing Pivots.** The telescope is lifted from its supports and placed again by turning in through 180°.

(10) **Standards.** The uprights cast in one piece with upper plate.

(B) Terms used in Traversing

(1) **Latitude.** The distance measured north or south = $L = (l) \times$ cos reduced bearing, l = length of the line.

(2) **Departure or Longitude.** The distances measured east or west ward, D = length sine reduced bearing.

(3) **Northings.** The distances measured towards North, Southings, Eastings and Westings are distances measured towards South, East and West respectively.

In a closed traverse the following conditions should be fulfilled.

(*a*) Sum of all included angles = $2n - 4$ right angles

where n = no. of sides.

(*b*) Sum of Northings = Sum of Southings.

(*c*) Sum of Eastings = Sum of Westings.

In observing bearings the following condition should be fulfilled.

Fore Bearing ~ Back Bearing = 180°

W.C.B. Whole Circle Bearing. It is the bearing from North line to line in the clockwise direction. It can vary from 0° to 360°.

R.B. (Reduced Bearing). It is the bearing reckond from North or South line in respective quadrants measured separately. It varies from 0 to 90°.

Fore bearing. The bearing of a line in the direction of the progress of survey is called the fore or forward bearing.

Back Bearing. The bearing of line in the reverse direction of the progress of survey is called back or reverse bearing.

In Figure α = Fore bearing and β = Back bearing of the line AB

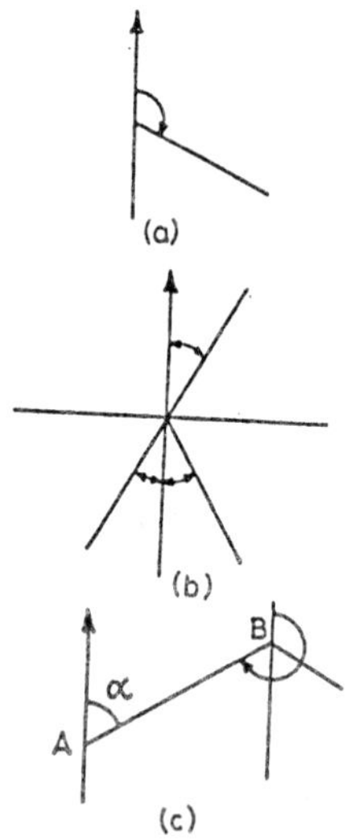

Fig. 5·18.

Balancing of the Error in Traverse

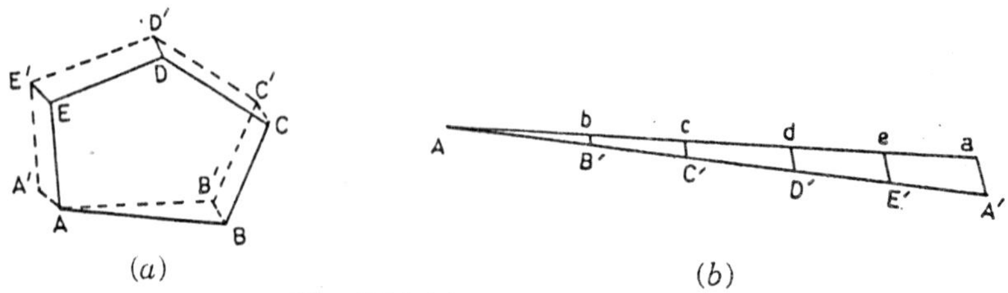

Fig. 5·18 (*c*)

If in a closed traverse $ABCDEA$, the last point does not meet at the same point A as shown by AA' in the fig. due to some error in chaining etc. This error AA' is closed proportionality as follows graphically. This can also be adjusted in the proportion of length mathematically in the direction of error.

Graphical Method. Draw a line $AB'\ C'\ D'\ E'\ A'$ *as measured on site. Draw* A' a parallel to AA' in the drawn plan. Join Aa. Draw parallels $E'C$, $D'd$, $C'c$ and $B'b$. Now in the polygon drawn take points $BCDE$ and A parallel and equal to $B'b$, $C'c$, $E'e$ and $A'a$ respectively.

The plan $ABCDEA$ is the corrected plan.

Reduction of bearings to Centre. In a traverse surveying it is some times needed to set up the instrument exactly over or under the signal which has been observed from other station points. In such cases the instrument is set up near the signal at a satellite station and the observed angles reduced to the centre. The problem can be solved by the following example.

Let B and C are two stations of which observed from the satellite station O as below.

Bearing of OB = 121°-56′ ; OW = 37·325 = d and log d = 1·5720

Bearing of OC = 144°-54′ ; log WB = 5·2393

Bearing of OW = 0′-0′ ; log WC = 5·2316

log WB and WC can be measured at site

The angle WBO is obtained by the sine formula $\frac{\sin A}{a} = \frac{\sin B}{b} = \frac{\sin C}{c}$; $\log \sin WBO = \log a + \log \sin 121°\text{-}56' - \log WB$ and $\log \sin WCO = \log d + \log \sin 144°\text{-}54' - \log WC$.

log sin 121°-56′	= $\bar{1}$·9287	log sin 144°-54′	= $\bar{1}$·7597
	= 1·5007		= 1·3317
log WB	= 5·2393	log WC	= 5·2316
log sin WBO	= $\bar{4}$·2614	log sin WCO	= $\bar{4}$·1001
or WBO	= 37°-66″	or WCO	= 25°-97″

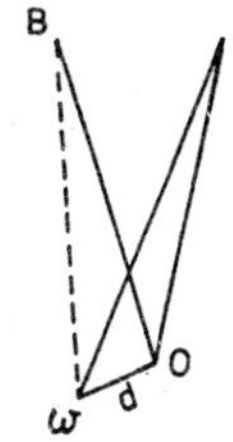

Fig. 5·20.

The correction both are (+ve) and must be added to the bearing B and C from O to obtain the bearings of those point from the true station W

(C) **Prismatic Compass.** It consists of a cylinderical box 2½ to 6″ in dia., in the centre of which on an agate bearing a balanced circular disc, graduated to single degrees to 30′ or even 20′, is attached to a magnetic needle. To prevent undue wear, the disc can be raised off its bearing when not in use, and a small knob is also provided for damping the movement and quickly bringing the needle to rest. At one edge of the box, it carries a cross hair line sight which is a hinged frame that may be folded down over the dial when not required, while diametrically opposite to this is a prism, which may also fold over on the outside edge of this box. The graduations of the scale on the dial are reflected from the hypotenuse side of this prism to the eye and are slightly magnified owing to the shorter sides of the prism being made a little convex. By means of a spring near the hinge of the hair line frame, the needle is automatically raised from its pivot whenever the frame is folded over the dial. The top of the box is covered with a glass lid so that the dial is visible. A metal cover is provided over all except the small parts under the prism.

Sometimes dark glasses are provided for sighting luminous objects and in some instruments a mirror which can be adjusted to any angle in a vertical plane is fitted to slide on the frame which carries the hair line sight. This enables an object of considerable elevation or depression to be sighted by reflection when it would be otherwise difficult to intersect, because as the needle must be allowed to swing quite freely, the instrument cannot be tilted to any great extent. A tripod is also provided for holding the instrument in position. The dial is treated with either a luminous paint or with a radium compound to have a luminosity to work in night time.

To determine the bearing of a line AB from a station A, the eye piece is fixed to the slit in the prism holder and the prism is raised or lowered on its slide untill the dial graduations which are reflected in the prism are clearly seen. The hair line is ranged to the object B and the disc is allowed to swing freely into the meridian. The box is hold horizontal as possible over the station point A. The object B and the graduations can be seen simultaneously and the reading with which the hair line appears to coincide gives the bearing of AB. When the bearing of AB is due North, the reading under prism should 360°, so that in consequence the 360° graduation is at the South end of the needle. Similarly when AB lies due East, the prism would lie on the Western side of the dial during the observations and should be over 90° graduation of the disc.

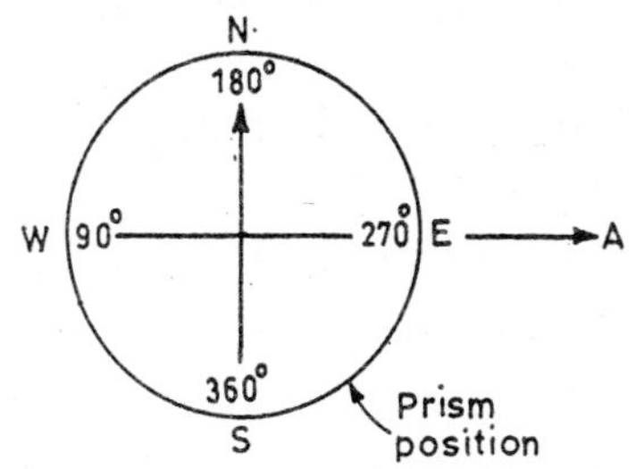

Fig. 5·21.

Free or Loose Needle Method of Measuring Angles. In this method compass or theodolite is set up at each of the successive stations and the bearing of each line is taken with reference to the magnetic meridian and not with reference to the adjacent line (see 1st operation of taking bearing of line *AB* in fast needle method).

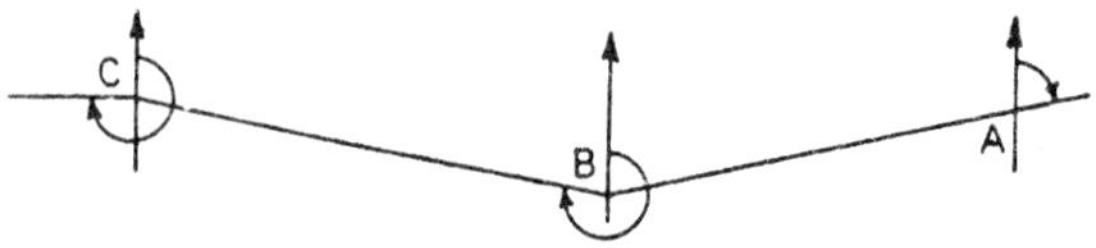

Fig. 5·22.

Fast Needle Method of Measuring Angles. In this method a theodolite is used for measuring bearings of a line. The theodolite is set up at *A* and bearing of *AB* (say α) is taken. For doing this set the instrument at *A*, while the vernier is clamped to coincide with the zero of the scale. The line of sight is then rotated about the vertical axis until the 360° graduation of the scale *N* the central division of a trough compass lies immediately below the north end of the the needle, that is to say that the line of sight is directed along the magnetic meridian and the vernier reads zero.

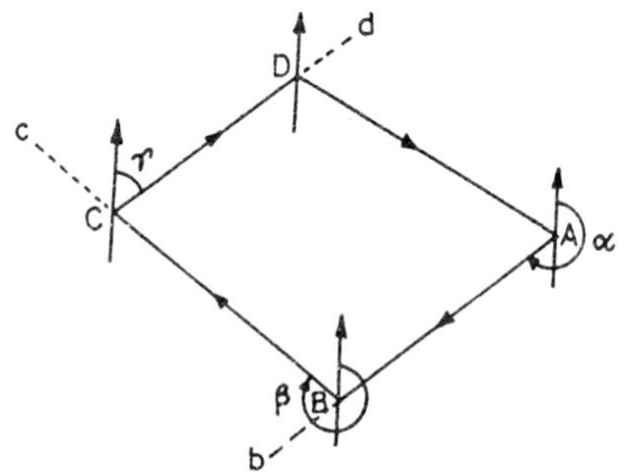

Fig. 5·23.

The vernier is now unclamped and the line of sight is directed towards *B*, exact coincidence is obtained with the upper clamp and tangent screw and the reading on the dial is taken, which is the bearing of *AB* (say α)(It is the operation of taking bearing by loose needle method). The bearing of the last line *AD* is also taken as a check if the traverse is a "closed".

Keeping the vernier still clamped at angle α and change the instrument at *B* and set it. Direct the telescope back to *A* and in exact coincidence by lower clamp and tangent screw. Transit the telescope so that the line of sight is directed along the direction of *AB* produced *i.e.* *Bb* while the vernier is still reading the angle α.

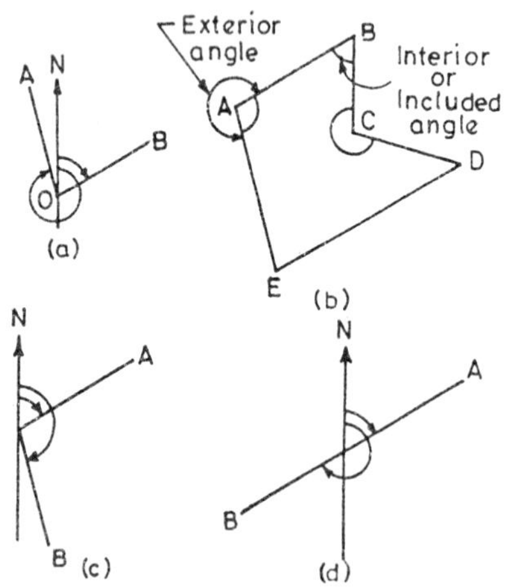

Fig. 5·24.

If therefore the upper clamp is loosened and the telescopic rotated in a horizontal plane through an angle α in the counter clockwise direction *i.e.* untill the vernier reading is zero, the telescope will lie along a meridian *Bb*, parallel to the 1st meridian *Aa*, consequently when the telescope is directed to *C* the vernier reads angle *b*, *BC* which is the bearing β of *BC*. proceed so on.

Included Angle Method. For measuring angles by compass as case-I

(*a*) $\angle AOB$ = bearing *A* + bearing of *B*

(*b*) $\angle AOB$ = bearing of *B* – bearing *A*

(*c*) $\angle AOB$ = bearing of *B* – bearing *A*.

Note : If the difference of bearings of line *AB* is more than 180° then deduct it from 360° if the angle is interior and is less than 180°.

In case when the interior angle is more than 180° then it is not required to deduct it from 360°

(D) **Angles by Theodolite.** Repetition method—set and level at the instrument at A, clamp the vernier at zero for exact concidence use clamp and tangent screw. Unclamp the lower plate and direct the telescope to point B for exact coincidence use lower clamp and tangent screw. Turn the telescope to point C by unclamping upper plate and make the exact coincidence with clamp and tangent screw of upper plate. Read the angle which is the angle α. Repeat the process by loosening of the lower clamp and directing towards B again and then to C as before. Take average of the two readings so obtained.

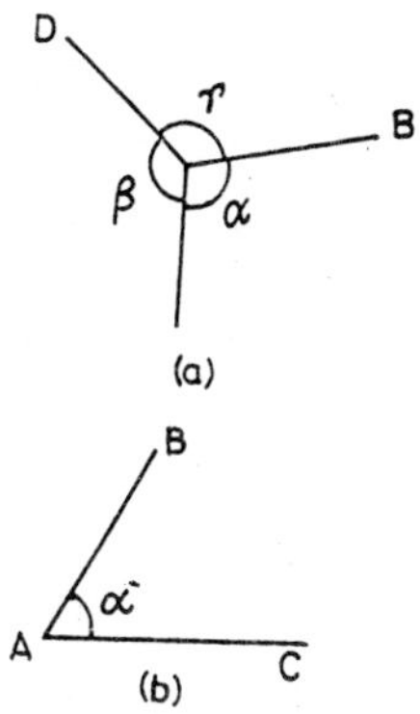

Fig. 5·25.

Reiteration Method. It is used when several angles are taken from one station say A. Set up instrument at the station A and level it. Make the vernier of the upper plate in coincidence with zero of the lower plate and exact coincidence by the upper clamp and tangent screw. Loose the lower plate and direct it to B and make it in exact coincidence with lower clamp and tangent screw (it may be directed to any other selected stations say O) Loosen the upper clamp and direct to point C and to exact coincidence by upper clamp and tangent screw. Read the reading at C, then the angle BAC = difference of the readings at B and C ; Now unclamp the upper clamp screw and direct the telescope to D and read after actual coincidence by clamp and tangent screw. Now the difference of the reading at D and C is the angle CAD (β). Proceed further in the same way.

The procedure may be repeated by taking anticlockwise observations. The average of the readings obtained by above two operations is the correct angle (angles observed by clockwise direction and angles observed by anticlockwise direction). Face left and face right observations can also be taken as a check.

(E) **Determination of the Height of Objects Trigonometrically**

(1) **When the base of the object is accessible.** It may be a case of a parapet of a wall

$$H = D \tan \alpha + h$$

Height from $B.M. = D \tan \alpha + h'$

H = height from ground to object

h = reading on staff at foot of object

h' = reading on staff on B.M.

D = distance from instrument to the foot of object.

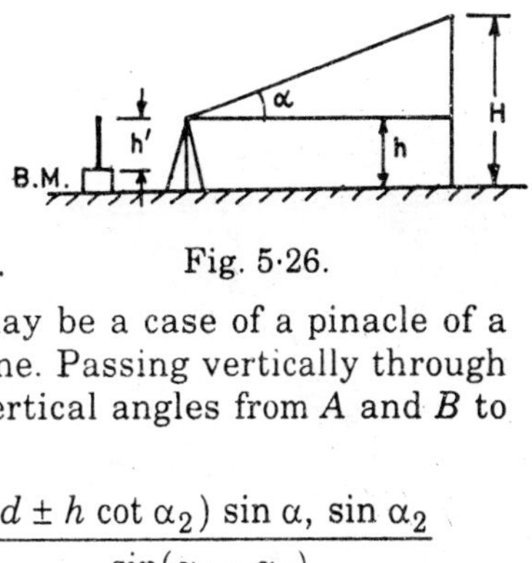

Fig. 5·26.

(2) **When the base of the object is inaccessible.** It may be a case of a pinacle of a Dome. Select two stations A and B on a fair level ground in a plane. Passing vertically through the object O. Measure the horizontal distance accurately. Read vertical angles from A and B to the object point say these are α_1 and α_2.

$$D = \frac{(d \pm h \cot \alpha_2 \tan \alpha_2)}{\tan \alpha_1 - \tan \alpha_2} \quad ; \quad h_1 = \frac{(d \pm h \cot \alpha_2) \sin \alpha, \sin \alpha_2}{\sin(\alpha_1 - \alpha_2)}$$

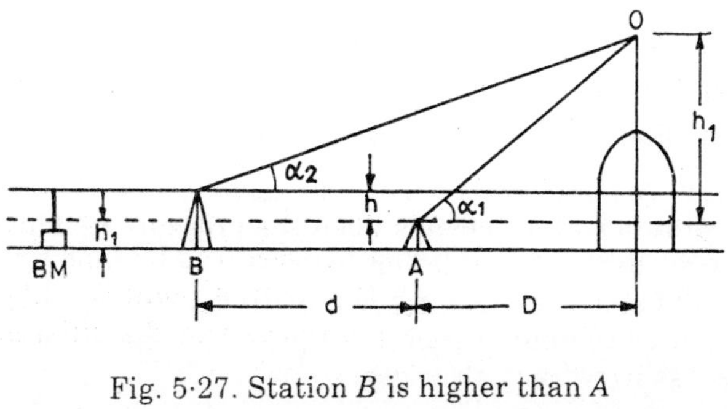

Fig. 5·27. Station B is higher than A

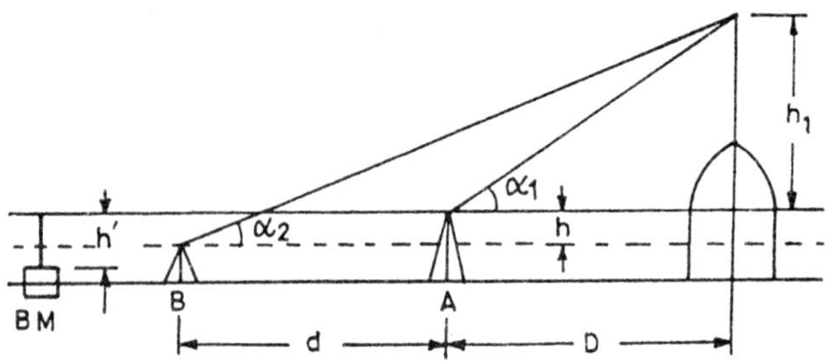

Fig. 5·28. Station B is lower than A

Height from B.M. = $h + h$

where h_1 = Height of object from the H.I. of instrument at A

h = difference of heights of instruments at A and B.

h' = Reading on the staff at BM from the instrument at A

D = Distance from the stations point A to vertical foot of point O

d = horizontal distance between A and B.

Note : Use plus sign when the height of the instrument at B (farther station from O) is higher than A and minus when lower than A.

(3) **When the object is inaccessible and the points A and B on ground are not in the same vertical plane with the object O.**

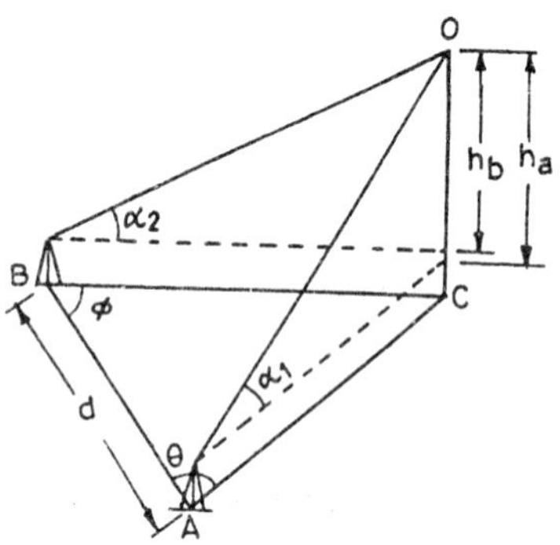

Fig. 5·29.

Take angle of elevation of the object O from the two stations A and B which are not in the same vertical plane with the object O, say these are α_1 and α_2 respectively.

Let C be the foot of the object O, and the horizontal angle BAC, ABC be θ and ϕ respectively.

Note : The oblique triangle ABC is reduced to horizontal triangle.

$$h_a = \frac{d \sin \phi \tan \alpha_1}{\sin(\pi - (\theta + \phi))}$$

The height of instrument can be reduced by connecting with a $B.M.$

$$h_b = \frac{d \sin \phi \tan \alpha_2}{\sin(\pi - (\theta + \phi))}$$

where h_a = Height of the object O from the height of the axis of instrument at A.

h_b = Height of the object O from the height of the axis of instrument at B.

d = Horizontal distance between station A and B.

(F) **Hypsometry.** A liquid boils when its vapour pressure is equal to the atmospheric pressure. The boiling point of water depends upon the pressure to which it is subjected. It goes down as the pressure goes down. The relation between the boiling points and the atmospheric pressure is given in tables. Thus knowing the boiling point h_y, hypsometer corresponding atmospheric pressure can be computed from the tables and the difference of level by the graph given as atmospheric pressure versus altitudes.

(G) **Sensitiveness of the Bubble Tube**

(1) Set up the instrument at B and level it with the bubble in the centre of it's run take the reading on staff A.

(2) By the foot screw under the telescope move the bubble for several say n divisions and again take the reading on the staff at A and find the difference of the two staff readings.

(a) $R = \dfrac{nl\,D}{d}$

where R = rad. of the bubble tube

l = length of one division of bubble say 2 mm or 0·10 inch etc.

n = no. of divisions by which bubble moved.

D = distance apart of A, B.

d = difference of two staff readings.

(In all cases units of measure are the same)

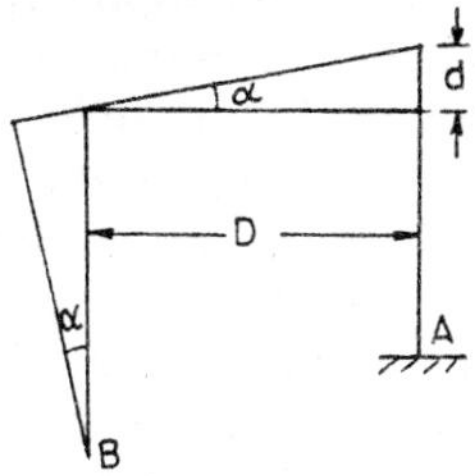

Fig. 5·30.

(b) Angular value of one division of tube in secs. $= \dfrac{d}{D_n \sin 1''}$

(c) Sensitiveness of the bubble tube $= \dfrac{R}{\sin 1''} = \dfrac{R}{206265}$ = travel of the bubble in length corresponding to 1 sec. change of the arc. If in a certain operation bubble travels 4 mm for a change of inclination of 30 secs. sensitiveness of the tube $= \dfrac{4}{30} = 0{\cdot}13$ mm.

5·9. Contouring

Interpolation of Contour. The following methods are used:

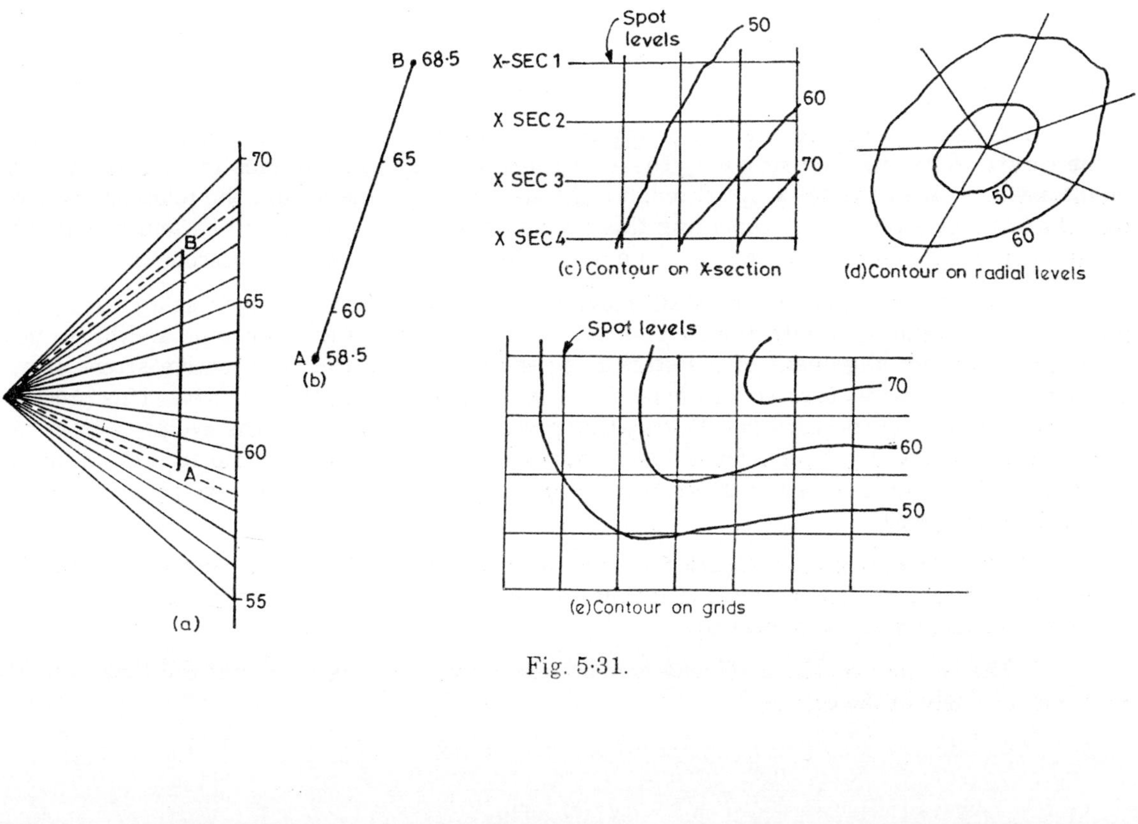

Fig. 5·31.

(1) **By estimation of the position.** The position of the contour is estimated between two spot levels proportionally.

(2) **By Arithmatic proportioning.** Suppose two spot levels 48·0 and 54·0 is available and the contour of 50 is sought to be located in between. Divide the portion between the point 48·0 and 54·0 in the ratio of 2 : 4.

(3) **Graphical Method.** (*a*) On a tracing paper draw parallel lines taking every tenth line as bold line. Suppose that the spot levels of points *A* and *B* are 58·5 and 68·5 and the contour of 60·0 and 65·0 are to be located. Mark the lines on tracing paper from 55·0 to 70·0 taking every line at an interval of 0·5. Fix the point *A* (58·5) on the level line of 58·5 and move the tracing paper till the point *B* (68·5) is in coincidence with the line of level 68·5 on the tracing paper. Prick the point of contour 60 and 65 on the level sheet, between the point *A* and *B*. (*b*) Trace on a tracing paper radial lines having every 10th line as a bold line. Mark at the end the points representing different levels at an interval of 0·5 (say). It may be at any other convenient interval. Move the tracing paper on the map sheet till the points *A* and *B* are in coincidence with the required level of 58·5 and 68·5. Prick on the sheet the points of contours 60 and 65.

Locating Grade Line of a Route on a Contour Map. Suppose a gradient of 1 : 20 is to be marked on a contour, starting from a level of 50 onwards going down. Fix the starting point say *A* on the contour of 50 at the required place. Now take a distance of 20 units on the divider and mark the point say *B* on the contour of 30 and proceed further so on.

5·10. Adjustment of levelling instruments

Setting up of a Dumpy Level or Temporary Adjustments of it.

1. Remove the level from the box, noting at the same time the position in which it was placed so that it may be easily put back in the box in it's proper position.

2. Screw the instrument on the stand and spread the legs of the stand so that the eye piece of the telescope is just at the height of your eye.

3. Bring the bubble of the circular level to the central position approximately by the stand legs and accurately by the foot screws (if such device of circular bubble is provided with).

4. Keep the telescope parallel to any two foot screws and bring the longitudinal bubble to the centre of its run by using only these two foot screws. Your thumbs must go in or out simultaneously. Turn the telescope through right angle in azimuth so that the telescope is now over the 3rd foot screw. After repeating this process twice or thrice, it will be found that the longitudinal bubble remains in the central position for all positions of the telescope in azimuth.

5. Turn the telescope to the staff, move the eye piece, till the cross wires appear sharp and clear. Focus the staff with the help of the focussing screw of the telescope and bring the cross wires in exact alignment of the staff using the clamp and the slow motion screw. If by focussing the cross wires become dull make it again clear by moving the eye piece. This process is known as removing the parallax. During this process avoid taking out the eye piece from its holder, otherwise the slight particles of dust or finger prints will scratch out and spoil the delicate diaphragm glass which is rather difficult to clear and rectify. To move the eye piece in or out push it in or out gently.

6. When the level is so adjusted an allowance is made to bring the longitudinal bubble at rest. If there is any displacement of it from the centre, bring it to its central position by the foot screw which is under the telescope.

7. The reading on the staff may now be taken after making sure that the longitudinal bubble is precisely in the centre.

Permanent Adjustments of a Dumpy Level

1st Adjustment. To make the axis of the bubble at right angle to the vertical axis of the instrument. It is necessary that this adjustment is made before proceeding for the next of the virtual line of site.

1. Adjust the instrument and level it as mentioned above keeping telescope over one foot screw.

2. Reverse the position of the telescope end for end or through 180°. Any deviation of the bubble (say n divisions) will be twice the real error of perpendicularity.

3. Correct half of the deviation ($n/2$) of the longitudinal bubble by the nuts provided at the ends of the bubble tube by loosening one and tightening other as required and half $n/2$ divisions by the foot screw under the telescope. Repeat till perfect.

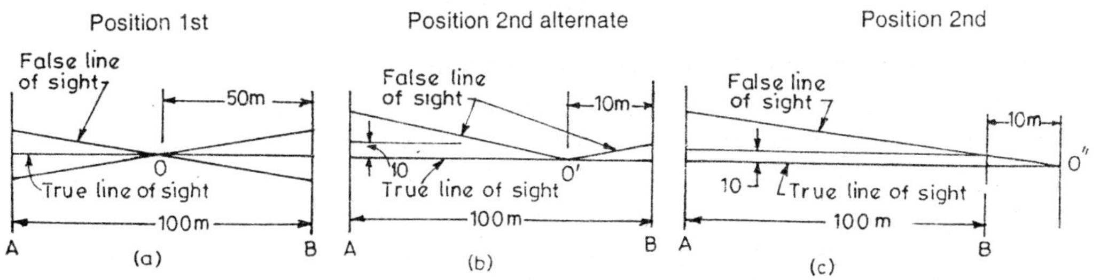

Fig. 5·32.

2nd Adjustment. To make the line of sight parallel to the axis of the bubble.

1. Set up the instrument mid way say O between two pegs A and B at a distance which is convenient say 100 M on a fair level piece of ground. Since the instrument is set up in the centre the difference of the level of the two pegs is say 1·00 M is the true difference of level, as any of instrumental error is cancelled off.

2. Shift the instrument near the peg B in line of the two pegs either in between O'or beyond the pegs at O'' 10 M beyond B. Adjust the level and take the reading of staff on the peg A and B and calculate the difference of level say it is 1·10 M (If the adjustment were correct the difference ought to be 1·00) so error = 1·10 – 1·00 = 0·10. This error is for the distance AB = 100 M, so for distance 110 M ($O''A$) the error will be $x = \frac{110}{100}(1{\cdot}10 - 1{\cdot}00) = \frac{110}{100} \times 0{\cdot}10 = 0{\cdot}110$ (from similar triangles). If O'' is beyond AB.

3. Raise or lower the diaphragm by the diaphragm screws (provided near the eye piece) so as to make the reading on A (far off staff) increased or decreased by 0·110 of the reading taken 1st from the station O' or O'' *i.e.* new reading on A = 1st reading when the instrument was on O' or O'' $\mp 0{\cdot}110$. Use (+) when the difference is decreased by the true difference taken from position I and (–ve) when the difference is increased by the true difference taken from position I (In the above example use (–) as the difference of level is increased from 1·00 to 1·10.

4. If the diaphragm is fixed and can not be adjusted, the adjustment is done by the collimating screws fitted below the telescope. The screws are lowered or raised till the horizontal wire gives the same reading on the staff as required. By doing so the bubble tube will be disturbed which should be brought to the centre of its run by the nuts provided below it.

5. Check the reading on the peg B which should be = 1st reading on B when the level is set up on O'' or O' $\mu \frac{0{\cdot}110}{100/10} = 0{\cdot}01$.

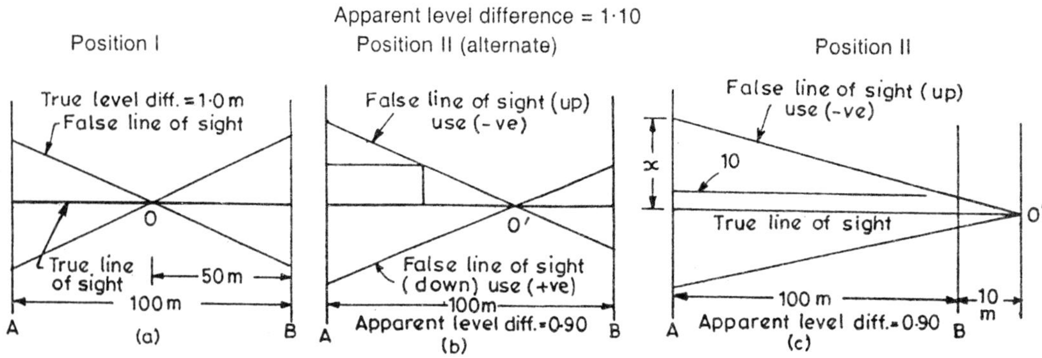

Fig. 5·33.

Setting up of *I.O.P.* level or Temporary Adjustments of it.

1. Remove the level from the box, noting at the same time the position in which it is placed, so that it may be easily put back in the box in its proper position.

2. Screw the instrument on the stand and spread the legs of two stand so that the eye piece of the telescope is just at the height of your eye.

3. Bring the bubble of the pile box to its central position approximately by the stand legs and accurately by the foot screws. Before fitting the level on the stand it must be seen that the foot screws are approximately in their central position.

4. Bring the micrometer screw below the telescope to read zero.

5. Turn the telescope towards the staff and bring the longitudinal bubble to its central position by looking through the prism by micrometer screw.

6. Focus the staff and record the reading after removing parallax if any by the help of eye piece.

7. While looking at other station from this setting the longitudinal bubble should be checked for its central position and if it has been deviated from its position bring it to centre by the micrometer screw at every reading.

Permanent Adjustment of IOP level

1. Set up the instrument mid way with one foot screw on the line joining two pegs fixed in the ground which is fairly levelled.

2. Set the micrometer to zero and level up the instrument by the foot screws and by means of the one foot screw on the line joining the pegs and bring the longitudinal bubble to the centre of its run.

3. Take the reading of the staff held on one of the pegs.

4. Reverse direction of the telescope and bring the longitudinal bubble again to its central positions by means of the same foot screw and read the staff on the other peg.

One of the higher pegs may be tapped down till the reading on both the pegs is the same. Otherwise read the difference of levels. This is a true difference of level of the pegs even if the instrument is out of adjustment.

5. Remove the instrument and set up close to one peg so that a staff placed on the peg will pass about an inch from the eye piece or the staff is just to miss the eye piece. One foot screw must be in the line of the pegs.

6. Level up the instrument (keeping the micrometer screw to read zero) by the foot screws and take a reading to the staff on the near peg through the object glass or by measuring the staff through the centre of the eye-piece.

7. Read the staff to the farther peg and if the reading does not show the same difference of level, make it to read the same difference of level by means of the foot screw under the telescope.

8. The level of the longitudinal bubble so disturbed must be centralise by means of the screws below the longitudinal bubble tube.

5·11. Adjustment of Theodolites

Setting of a Theodolite or Temporary Adjustments of it.

1. The instrument is placed more or less over the station point. It is approximately levelled up by means of the legs of it. It is next carefully centred over the point of station by means of the plumb bob and slight motion of the instrument over the stand by centering plate.

2. The levelling operations of the instrument is more or less is the same as for the dumpy level keeping the upper plate fixed and lower loose. The vertical circle is also kept damped during levelling operation. The levelling is done with reference to the plate bubble.

3. Removing parallax and focussing operation is also the same as dumpy level.

4. Make the verniers of the upper plate and of vertical circle to read zero and clamp them. For exact coincidence use upper clamp and tangent screw.

5. Direct the telescope to the station mark keeping the lower plate loose and proceed further as required.

Permanent Adjustments of a Theodolite. Since certain adjustments will upset others hence the adjustments are to be made in order in which they are stated.

Preliminary Adjustment. To make the diaphragm truely erect. The aim of this adjustment is to ensure that the cross hair are truely horizontal and vertical.

1. Level up the instrument and sight a distant well defined point such as the top of a spire and with both motions clamped rotate the telescope in azimuth by means of one of the tangent screws. If the horizontal cross-wire remain in contact with the point, the adjustment is correct. For vertical cross hair test move the telescope vertically and if the verticl hair remain in contact with the point the adjustment is correct. If not loosen the diaphragm screws and rotate the diaphragm ring. Repeat the test and adjustment till perfect.

First Adjustment. To make the axes of the plate levels perpendicular to vertical axis.

1. Set up the instrument and level it by means of plate longitudinal level and foot screws as is done in temporary adjustment.

2. Keep the telescope over one foot screw or right angle to other two foot screws and level it by means of 3rd foot screw.

3. Turn the telescope through 180° in azimuth. If there is any deviation say $2n$ divisions correct half *i.e.* n divisions by means of the Capston headed nuts underthe longitudinal bubble of the plate and half by the 3rd foot screw. Repeat till perfect. Reason for adjusting by one screw is to avoid unequal motion of the two screws by hand turning.

Alternate Adjustment. If more precision is required, the upper level is also adjusted. For this proceed as follows :

1. Adjust the instrument temporarily as before and bring the vertical level under the 3rd foot screw and level it by the antagonistic screw. (Clip or vertical circle tangent screw)

2. Turn the telescope through 180° end for end in azymuth if there is any deviation say $2n$ divisions correct half (n divisions) by antagonistic screw and half by the 3rd foot screw. Repeat it till perfect.

3. Bring the level parallel to the other two foot screws and if there is any deviation correct it by these two foot screws only.

4. If there is any deviation arise in the lower level correct it by the Capstan headed screws attached to the bubble.

2nd Adjustment. To make the line of sight or collimation to coincide with the optical axis of the telescope or to place the intersection of the cross hair in the optical axis of the telescope.

For this there are two adjustments. 1st for the horizontal cross hair and 2nd for the vertical cross hair.

Adjustment for the Horizontal Hair

1. Drive two pegs A and B say about a distance of 100 meters and a point O at about 10 meter from the point A.

2. Set up the theodolite at O and level it, take the readings at A and B say these are a_1 and b_1 with the telescope direct.

3. Transite the telescope and swing through 180° and set the reading on point A to read as before *i.e.* a_1.

4. Again read the staff held on B if the adjustment is correct the reading will be the same *i.e.* b_1 if not, then error is to be corrected, let the new reading be b_2.

5. To correct the error take the mean of the readings b_1 and b_2 or $\frac{b_1 + b_2}{2}$ and say it is b. Now bring the horizontal hair vertical diaphragm screws to read the reading b on the staff B. Repeat till perfect.

Adjustment for Vertical Hair

1. Set up the instrument on a fairly level ground say at O and level it.

2. Cross the vertical hair at a distant point A about 100 M from O (Conveniently a peg).

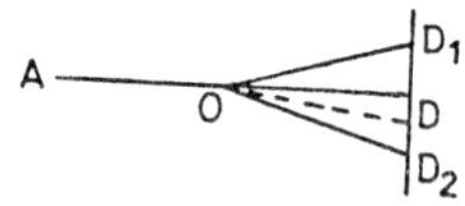

Fig. 5·34.

3. Plung the telescope and fix a point D at a distance 100 M from O.

4. Unclamp the upper plate and swing through 180° and again bisect A.

5. Transite the telescope at the point D again. If it coincides, the adjustment is correct if not then fix a peg at the new point D_2.

6. Make a point D such that D_2O = ¼ D_1D_2 and move the diaphragm such that the vertical hair bisect the point D repeat till perfect.

Fig. 5·35.

3rd Adjustment. To make the horizontal axis perpendicular to the vertical axis.

1. Set up the instrument under a tall building having a sharp pinacle, lightening conductor or a flag mast about 10 m from it and level it carefully. Let O be such point on the building.

2. Sight the point O and with both plates clamped, depress the telescope and make a point say A_1 on the ground.

3. Unclamp, reverse the telescope and swing it through 180°.

4. With this inverted positions of the telescope sight the point O again depress it and make a point A_2 on the ground.

5. If the adjustment were correct the point A_2 must coincide A_1 if not make a point A_0 midway A_1 and A_2.

6. Sight the point A_0, raise the telescope by clamping the upper plate. Now the line of the sight will not coincide with O.

7. Raise or lower the trunion or the horizontal axis by means of the screws provided on the standards of the theodolite for the purpose till the line of sight coincides or passes through the point O. Repeat till perfect.

A levelling staff may be used on the ground in place of marking points A_1 and A_2.

4th Adjustment. To make the axis of the telescope level parallel to the line of sight.

This adjustment is done similar to the two peg method of dumpy level.

1. Proceed with operations as described for two peg method of dumpy level and calculate correct readings for the pegs A and B.

2. Bring the horizontal hair to read the corrected reading on staff B (distant staff) by means of the tangent screw of the vertical circle.

3. Now bring the bubble of the telescope level to its central position by means of the Capstan headed screws below the level tube by loosening one and lightening other.

4. Sight the staff to the nearer peg B and test that it reads the calculated corrected reading for it. Repeat till perfect.

5·12. Techeometric Survey

$$D = \frac{f}{i} S + (f + d)$$

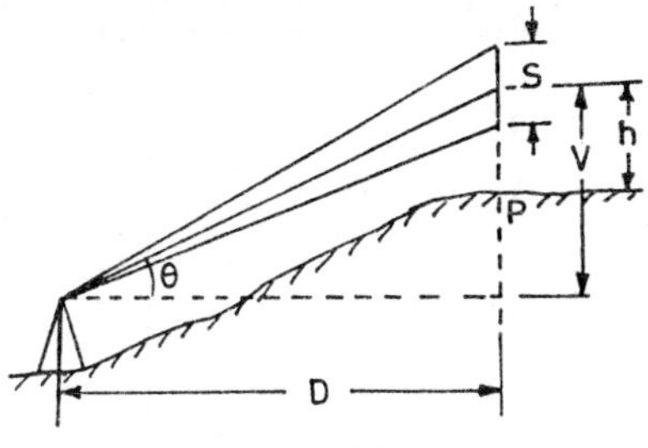

Fig. 5·36 (*a*).

where D = distance of a point from the instrument station.

f = focal length of the object glass

i = vertical distance between the horizontal hair

S = intercept by the two wires at the staff

d = distance between optical axis to the vertical axis of Techeometre.

f/i = constant for an instrument generally kept 100 by the makers or as mentioned by the maker. It is known as multiplying constant.

$(f + d)$ = additive constant. It is also mentioned by the maker. In an instrument fixed with anallatic lens it is zero.

Note : The additive and the mutlplying constants can also be determined for an instrument by applying formula for two or three stations of known distance *i.e.* by measuring the distance D by tape and reading the intercept S. The unknown (f/i) and $(f + d)$ can be computed.

Inclined Sites

D = horizontal distance $= \frac{f}{i} S \cos^2 \theta + (f + d) \cos \theta$ ...(1) Staff held vertical

V = vertical distance $= \frac{f}{i} S \frac{\sin 2\theta}{2} + (f + d) \sin \theta$

$= \frac{f}{i} S \sin\theta \cos\theta + (f + d) \sin\theta$ ...(2)

(*a*) When the observed vertical angle is an angle of elevation (+)

H.I. + elevation of instrument station = Elevation of instrument axis

Elevation of station (staff) P = Elevation of the instrument axis +V-axial reading h.

(*b*) When the vertical angle is an angle of depression (–).

Elevation of staff station P = Elevation of instrument axis –V-axial reading.

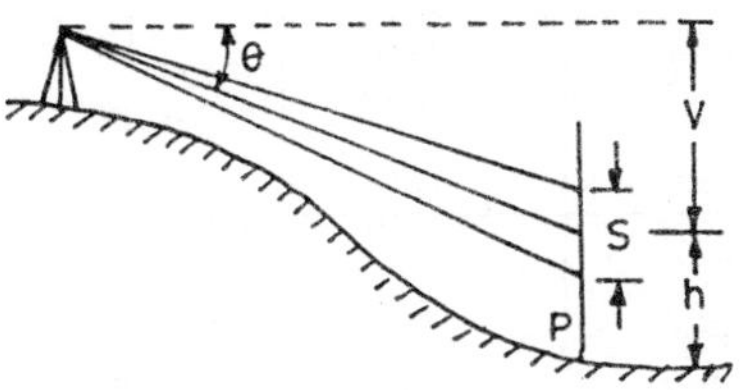

Fig. 5·36 (*b*)

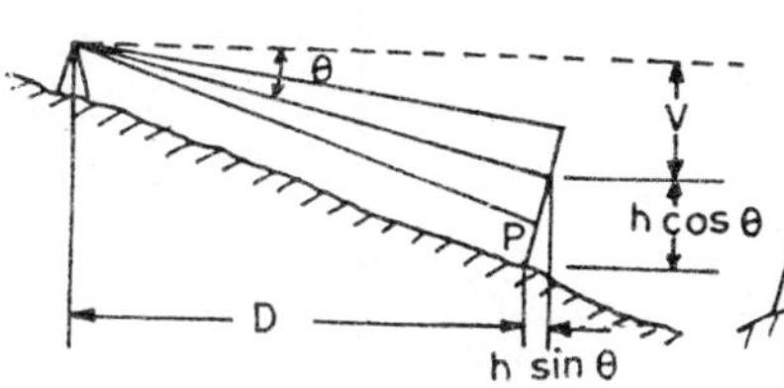

Fig. 5·36 (*c*)

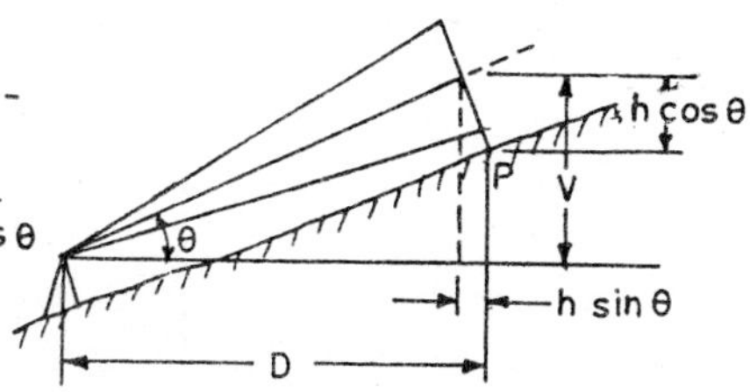

Fig. 5·36 (*d*)

When the line of Collimation is inclined to the horizontal and **staff held normal to the line of Collimation :**

$$D = \text{horizontal distance} = \frac{f}{i} S \cos \theta + (f + d) \cos \theta + h \sin \theta \quad ...(3)$$

Techeometric Field Book

Instrument station	*Staff Station*	*Ht. of instrument axis*	*Azimuth*	*Vertical angle θ*	*Stadia reading*	*Distance along line of collimation*	*Hor. distance (h)*	*Vert. components, y*	*Axial reading*	*Rise*	*Fall*	*R.L. Inst. axis*	*R.L. Staff station*	*Remarks*
1	2	3	4	5	6	7	8	9	10	11	12	13	14	15
A	1	5·01	65°-30′	43°-28′	5·22 / 2·00	322·4	322	19·50	3·61	15·89		70·71	86·60	
	2		2°-14′	0°-0′	3·87 / 1·00	288	288	0	2·43		2·43		68·28	
	3		16°-48′	–2°-36′	6·74 / 3·00	374·6	374	–16·30	4·87		21·86		48·85	
	4		198°-20′	+4°-18′	5·28 / 2·00	328	327	24·60	3·64	20·06			41·67	
B		4·82	18°-20′	–4°-24′	7·28 / 4·00	328	327	–25·16	5·64				65·69	

Trignometrical Functions used in Tachometry

Angle θ, deg.	*sin θ*	*cos θ*	*cos² θ*	*Angle θ, deg.*	*sin θ*	*cos θ*	*cos² θ*
(1)	(2)	(3)	(4)	(1)	(2)	(3)	(4)
0	0	1·0	0	47	·731	·682	·465
5	·087	·996	·992	49	·755	·656	·430
7	·122	·993	·986	51	·777	·633	·401
9	·156	·988	·976	53	·798	·602	·362
11	·191	·982	·964	55	·819	·574	·329
13	·225	·974	·949	57	·839	·545	·297
15	·259	·966	·934	59	·857	·515	·266
17	·292	·956	·914	61	·875	·485	·235
19	·326	·946	·895	63	·891	·454	·206
21	·358	·934	·870	65	·906	·423	·180
23	·391	·921	·848	67	·921	·391	·153
25	·423	·906	·821	69	·936	·358	·128
27	·454	·891	·794	71	·946	·326	·106
29	·484	·875	·766	73	·956	·292	·085
31	·513	·857	·735	75	·966	·259	·067
33	·545	·839	·704	77	·974	·225	·049
35	·574	·819	·671	79	·982	·191	·036
37	·602	·799	·638	81	·988	·156	·024
39	·629	·777	·603	83	·992	·122	·014
41	·656	·755	·567	85	·996	·087	·010
43	·682	·731	·532	87	·999	·052	·003
45	·701	·707	·500	90	1·0	0	0

$D = S\frac{f}{i}\cos^2\theta$; $V = S\frac{f}{i}\sin\theta\cos\theta$ when the mutlplying constant is usually 100 and the additive constant is zero in anallatic lenses, this table can be used to compute D and V without involving in heavy calculations.

V = vertical distance (from axis of instt. to the staff reading of central wire at station P)

$$= \frac{f}{i} S \sin 2\theta + (f + d) \sin \theta \qquad ...(4)$$

h = the axial reading or the reading of centre wire.

(a) When observed vertical angle is angle of elevation (+).

Elevation of staff station P = Elevation of instrument axis + $V - h \cos \theta$.

(b) When the observed vertical angle is angle of depression (–).

Elevation of staff station P = Elevation of instrument axis – $V - h \cos \theta$.

When θ is small $h \sin \theta$ may be neglected and $h \cos \theta$ taken equal to h.

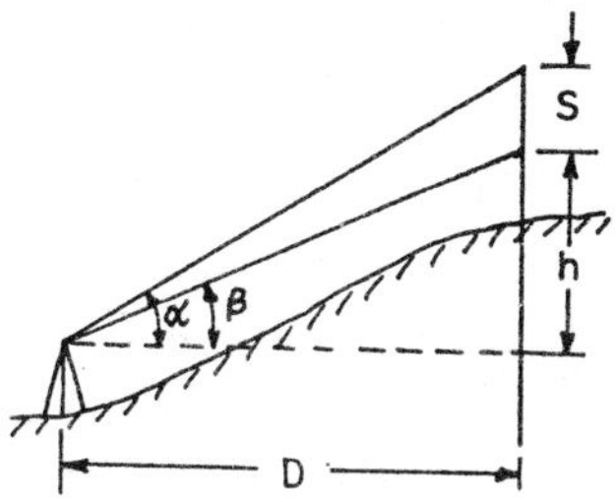

Fig. 5·37

Tangential method :

$$D = \frac{S}{\tan \alpha - \tan \beta}$$

$$V = \frac{S \tan \beta}{\tan \alpha - \tan \beta}$$

Direct reading of horizontal distances and vertical heights by techeometer which are provided with this facility.

$$D = S\frac{f}{i}\cos^2\theta \;;\; V = S\frac{f}{i}\,\frac{\sin 2\theta}{2} = S\,\frac{f}{i}\,\sin\theta\cos\theta$$

neglecting the additive constant $(f + d) \cos\theta$ or $(f + d) \sin\theta$ f/i is usually 100.

The special scales represent the quantity 100 (1 – $\cos^2 \theta$) which is the amount to be substracted from 100 to give 100 $\cos^2 \theta$ and 100 $\sin \theta \cos \theta$. The values corresponding to the reading for θ on the ordinary vertical circle of the instrument.

In some cases the Beaman Arcs form a separate attachment fitted externally to a normal instrument. In other cases the instrument is so designed as to incorporate special scales in the 1st place, the scales being arranged parallel to the normal vertical circle scales.

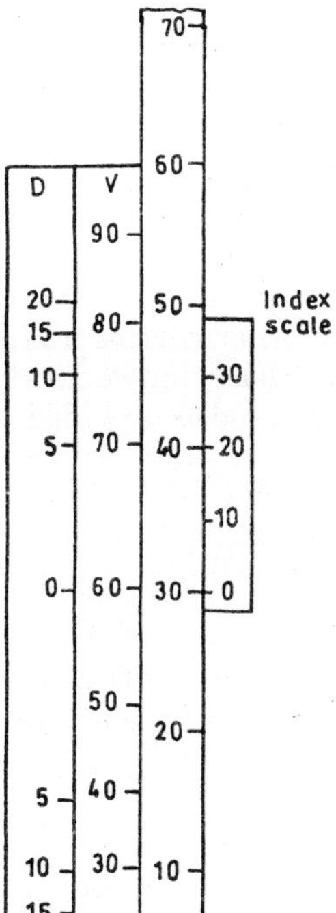

Fig. 5·38.

In the adjoining Fig. 5·38 the zero for vertical angles is 30°, that for V scale is 50 and for D scale is 0.

Example : *For the V divisions 70 (say) D divisions are 4. The reading on the staff is say 3·95 (central) 1·22 and 6·88 for the two stadia wires giving an intercept of 5·46.*

$$D = 5{\cdot}46\,(100 - 4) = 546 - 21{\cdot}8 = 524 \text{ units}$$

$$V = (70 - 50)5{\cdot}46 = 109{\cdot}2 \text{ units}$$

(50 being the value on the V scale corresponding to zero on the index scale. 30° being the vertical scale reading corresponding to zero of the index scale for which it is set.)

The central web reading is 3·95 so that the height of the staff point above the instrument axis is 109·2 – 3·45 = 105·2 units (app.). The vertical angle on vertical scale is 41°-48′

corresponding to 70 on V scale. So the true angle of elevation = 41°-48′-30° = 11°-48′. 30° being the vertical scale setting to zero of the index scale. Thus $V = 100\ S \sin\theta \cos\theta = 50 \times 5{\cdot}46 \sin 2\theta$.

$$= 273 \sin 23°36' = 109{\cdot}3 \text{ units}$$

In another instrument which has a glass circle diaphragm in which direct readings are taken. The angle of elevation or depression is seen in the circle diaphragm. Say at a reading of 24°, the corresponding V reading = 12·8 and D reading as 16·54.

So $D = (100 - 16{\cdot}54) \times S$ (difference in stadia wire reading)

$V = 12{\cdot}8 \times S$ (difference in stadia wire reading)

$100\,(1 - \cos^2 24°) = 16{\cdot}54\ ;\ (50 - 37{\cdot}16) = 12{\cdot}8$

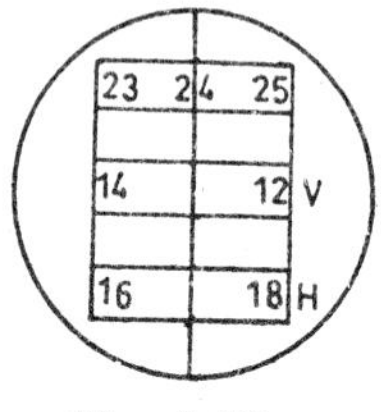

Fig. 5·39.

It is usually preferable to set V scale to a whole number and read the corresponding values of θ and H.

The rays of light from the scales are reflected through 90° by means of a 45° prism to enable readings to be made with the reading microscope located at the top of the instrument.

Note : There are different types of instruments which give direct readings for horizontal and vertical distances and their way of reading is described by the makers.

Techeometric Tables. Tables are prepared which give direct computations of vertical and horizontal distances for different vertical angles.

5·13. Plane Tabling

1. **Drawing Board.** It is of well seasoned pine or teak wood and it varies in size 16″ × 12″ to 30″ × 20″. It is mounted on a tripod in such a way that it can be levelled and revolved about a vertical axis and clamped to any desired position. It is either fitted with levelling screws in a head over tripod or is provided with a ball and socket-arrangement.

Alidade. It consists of brass, gun metal or wood straight edge ruler about 18″ long. The levelling or ruling edge of the alidade is known as **fiducial edge**. It may be plane or telescopic according whether it is fitted with sight vane at both ends or fitted with a telescope. In sight vane type one of the two vanes is provided with a fine slit, while the other carries a cross hair or wire. In some alides (as in the case of a prismatic compass) the vane carrying vertical bars is provided with dark glass to sight luminous points. An inclined mirror is also provided to sight objects at different levels. The telescope type is provided with a level tube and a vertical circle to read angles. It is fitted with cross and stadia hair also. A pill box bubble or two bubble tubes at right angle to each other are attached to the alidade for levelling the table. The fiducial edge is also graduated to form a scale for measuring and is always parallel to the line of sight (line joining the sight slit to the vertical hair of the next vane.)

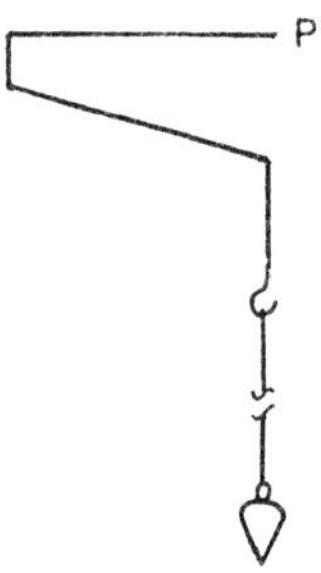

Fig. 5·40.

Trough Compass. A trough compass is also provided with the accessories of a plane table for marking magnetic north-south line.

Plumbing Fork. Or U frame with a plumb bob for centering the table is also provided with.

Centering of Table. (1) By means of legs of tripod, the board of the table is kept at a suitable height according to surveyor.

(2) A point on the sheet paper should be so chosen for the station at which the table is placed so that all the area to be surveyed may be covered. By using U frame point P should be coinciding with the station point on the paper and the table is moved such that the plumb point should coincide with the point of the station on ground.

(3) Table is then levelled either by the levelling screws provided under it or by two levels fitted at right angles in the alidade by 1st levelling with the help of one level tube and than by the other right angle to it with adjusting legs of the tripod.

Orientation of the Table. (1) **Orientation by Compass.** When the table is centred at 1st station, a north point is marked on one side of the paper (generally top middle) with the help of a compass. This north south line is used for orienting the table on other stations. For doing this the compass is placed along the north side line with north on the point marked on the map and the board is then turned until the ends of the needle are on the zero marks of the scale and the board is clamped.

(2) **Orientation by Back Sight.** Suppose *A* and *B* are two points at site which have their corresponding position on map as a and *b* and in table station is *C* of which the position as paper is *c*. Place the fiducial edge of the alidade along *ca*, loose the clamp of the table and move it such that the alidade on *ca* is in alignment with station point *A*. The plane table is then is in orientation.

Method of Plane Tabling—(1) **Radiation Method.** The table is centred and oriented at a station say *A*. Ray from the object point say *O* keeping the alidade pivoted with the station point *a* is drawn. The distance from *A* to *O* is measured at site and this measured distance should be scaled on the map from '*a*' to locate '*o*' the position of object point '*O*' on the paper.

(2) **Intersection Method.** This method is used when the chaining across the points is not accessible due to some obstacle.

Two points *A* and *B* are so selected which are accessible and can be chained and can cover all the area to be survey by vision. Measure the distance of *AB*. Draw this line *AB* (called the base line) in the map at a suitable location so that all the area can be covered on the sheet of paper. Centre the table on the station *A* and orient the table by keeping the alidade on *ab* and ranging *B* by loosing the table. When orientation is done the table is clamped. Proceed as follows :

(*i*) Pivot the alidade on a and range the point say *P* with table at station *A* draw a ray which can approximately cover the position of *P* on paper.

(*ii*) Shift the table on *B* and centre and orient it. Now pivot the alidade on *b* and range the station *P* and draw the line by the fiducial edge of the alidade. The crossing of this line to the line drawn from station *A* is the position *p* of the station *P* on paper.

(3) **Resection Method—Back ray Method.** Let *R* be the station of which the position *r* is to be marked on the sheet. Let two stations *A* and *B* where positions are marked on the sheet as *a* and *b* at a measured distance from *A* to *B*.

(*i*) Centre the table at *A* and orient it from station *B* as discussed before keeping alidade with line *ab* and ranging the station *B*. Clamp the table.

(*ii*) Table at *A*, alidade pivoted at '*d*' range a line to station *R* (ranged at *R*) and mark the positions of *R* on sheet as *r* by estimation.

(*iii*) Shift the table at *R*, centre and orient it from station *A* alidade on the *ra* and ranging *A* and *R*.

(*iv*) Pivot the fiducial edge of the alidade along the pivot '*b*' on sheet and range it from the point *B*. Draw a ray which will cut the ray *P* to *R* at *r*, then *r* will be the location of the point *R* on the sheet.

Two Point Problem. Let *A* and *B* are two points which are inaccessible and whose position on sheet is *ab*. *O* is the point to be located as *o* on the sheet. Take another point *C* such that the angle *ACB* may not be too acute.

(1) Set up the table on station at *C* and roughly orient it with compass or by making *ab* parallel to *AB* by estimation. Clamp the table.

(2) Rays are drawn through '*a*' in the direction *Aa* and through *b* in the direction of *Bb*. The point of intersection locates the position of *C* approximately say it is C_1.

(3) Through C_1 draw a ray $C_1 O_1$ in the direction $C_1 O$.

(4) Transfer the table to the station O. Level and orient it from C. Keeping the rule along the line O_1C_1 and rotating the table until this is in range with C. Clamp the table.

(5) Draw the ray through b towards B which intersect the line $C_1 O_1$ in a point O'. Next draw a ray from O' towards A. If the orientation of the table at C was correct the point a on the paper should be bisected. If not the intersection of $O'A$ with ac_1 fixes another point a_1, to represent A.

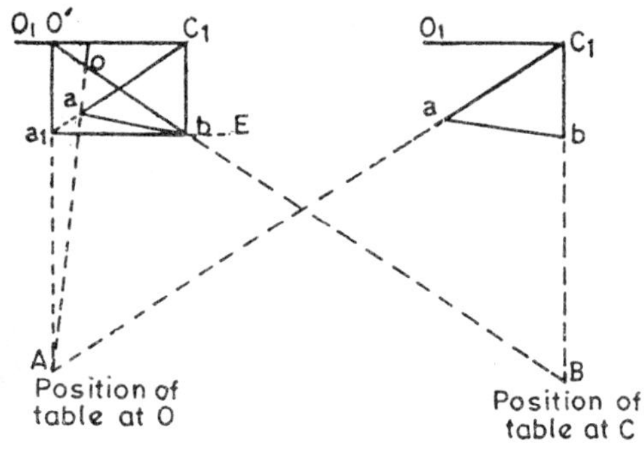

Fig. 5·41.

That is to say a, b, c, o represent $ABCO$ assuming 1st orientation at C, but the true position of AB is ab so that the assumed orientation is incorrect by the quantity shown by the angle ba. For estimating it proceed as follows.

(6) Place the alidade along a_1b_1 and fix a ranging rod E at a distant place, in the line a_1b_1 produced.

(7) Place the alidade along ab and turn the table until the ranging rod E is bisected. Now the orientation of the table is correct.

(8) Now pivot the alidade on 'a' and range A. Draw a ray through 'a'. Similarly from b range B and draw a ray through b. The intersection of the two will give the correct position of O as o on sheet.

3. Three Point Problem. Let ABC are three points, the position of whom on plan is located as ab and c. The position of a point O at site is to be located on the plan.

(1) **Tracing Paper Method.** A sheet of a tracing paper is streched over the plane table and the position of point O on it is roughly estimated as o_1. Table set up at O and oriented roughly by compass.

Alidade pivoted on o_1 and sighting A, B and C draw rays Ao_1, Bo_1 and Co_1 which meet at o_1.

Shift the tracing paper such that the three lines Aa, Bb and Cc passes simultaneously through the point a, b and c on the plan. Prick the point o_1 on the plan which is the true location of O on plan.

For testing the accuracy the line Aa Bb and Cc must be sighted by pivoting the alidade at a, b and c by back ray method. If they are concurrent the point p is correct if not repeat the above operation till correct.

(2) **Graphical Method—**(*a*) **Bessel's Method.** This method can be used even if the North-South line is not marked on the plan or there is any local attraction.

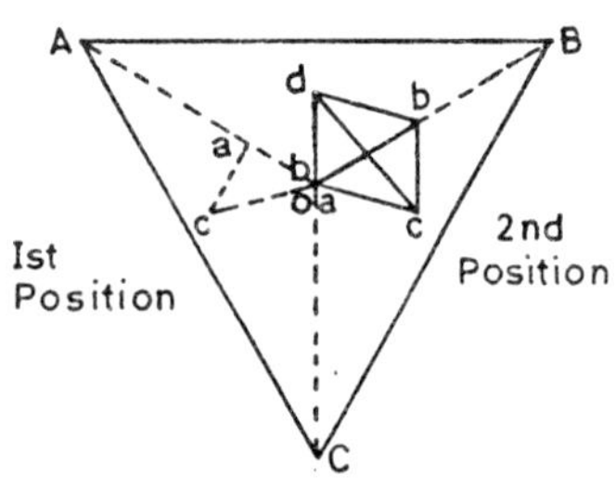

Fig. 5·42.

The point b is placed over the station point o_1. The alidade edge along line ba (pointing a towards A) table is rotated till ba is in the range with A. The table is clamped and a ray bd drawn on the paper through b in the direction Cb produced. The point a is next placed over the point O. ab directed towards B (b being towards B) and the ray ad drawn in the directions Ca produced, intersecting the ray previously drawn through b in d. dc is joined and the table rotated until dc and C are in the same line. The table is now oriented.

Draw a ray *Aa Bb* and *Cc* and produce them to meet in a common point which is location of *O* on the plan as *o*. If these lines are not concurrent, repeat the above operation till correct.

(*b*) Refer the figures given below Fig. 5·43 (*a*)—*ae* is drawn right angle to *ab* and by fixing the edge of the alidade along *ae* the table is rotated till *ea* is in range with *A* (*a* being towards *A*) ; a ray *be* is drawn through *b* in the direction *Bb* intersecting *ae* in *e*.

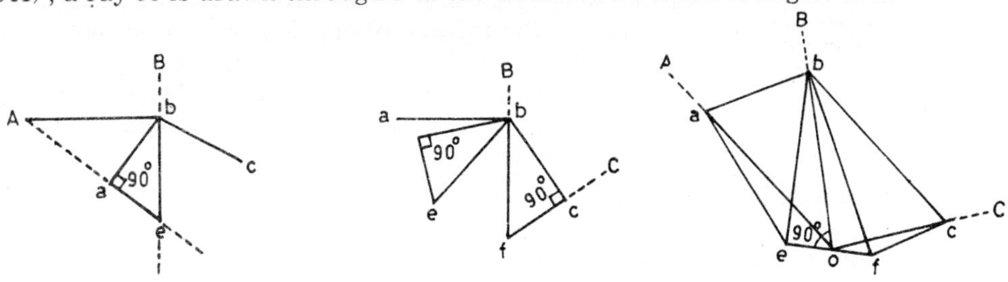

(*a*) 1st position (*b*) 2nd position (*c*) 3rd position.

Fig. 5·43.

Fig. (*b*)—In the same way *fc* is drawn at right angles to *bc* and is ranged with *C* (keeping *C* towards *C*) and *bf* is drawn in the direction *Bb* intersecting *Cf* in *f*.

Fig. (*c*)—*ef* is joined and *bo* is drawn at right angle to *ef*, *o* then represents the position of *O* on plan. The table may be oriented by ranging *Ob* to *B*. As a check the ray *Aa* and *Cc* must also pass through *O* if not repeat the process till correct.

(3) **By Trial and Error Method.** The table being set up and levelled is oriented approximately by eye or by compass draw rays *Aa Bb* and *Cc* by back ray method (resection method) as the orientation is not perfect the three lines will not be concurrent and will form a triangle which is known as '**triangle of error**'.

It is assumed that the observer is facing the station points and left and right directions are determined accordingly. The triangle formed by the station points *A*, *B* and *C* is known as great triangle and the circle passing through *A*, *B* and *C* is great circle. The position of the point *O* on the plan is determined by the following rule (Lehmann's Rule).

Lehmann's Rule : (1) The distance of the point sought from each of the rays *Aa*, *Bb* and *Cc* is proportional to the distance of *A*, *B* and *C* from *O* respectively or corresponding to plotted distance.

(2) Looking in the directions of station points *A*, *B* or *C* the point sought *O* is on the same side *i.e.* either right or left of each of the lines *Aa*, *Bb* or *Cc*.

(3) If the plane table station *O* is outside or inside the great triangle *ABC*, the point sought *o* is outside or inside the triangle of error.

(4) When the station *O* is outside the great triangle, the point sought *o* is always on the same side of the rays drawn to the most distant object as the intersections *e* of the other two rays.

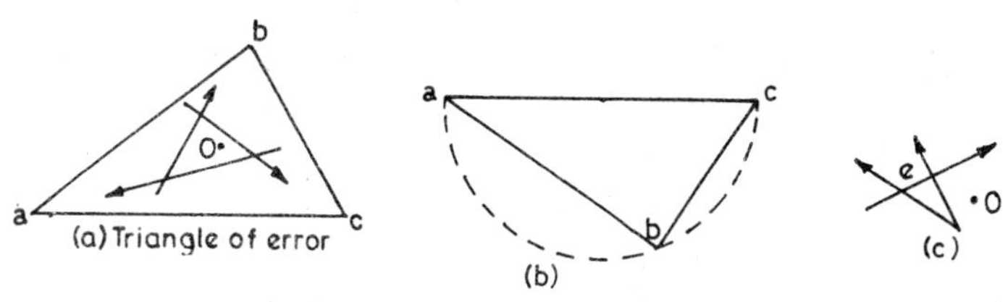

Fig. 5·34.

(5) When the station *O* is outside the great triangle and inside the great circle *i.e.* with in one of the three segments of the great circle, the ray drawn towards the middle point lies between the point sought *O* and intersection of other two rays. Having located the position of point *O* by above rule the alidade edge is placed on *Oa* and sighted towards *A* for orienting

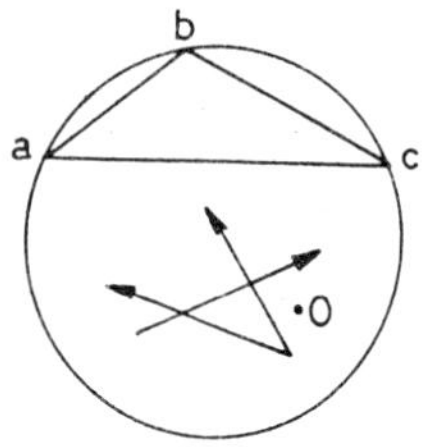

Fig. 5·45.

the table. If the point O is correctly located then the lines Aa, Bb and Cc will be concurrent if not try again till correct.

Failure of Fix. If the station point O lies on the circumference of the great circle ABC the rays Aa, Bb and Cc will be concurrent even if the table is not correctly oriented. It is known as the **failure of fix**. For other position of O either a triangle of error will form or two parallel lines will be cut by the 3rd. In such cases the accuracy of fixing the position of O varies with different positions of o relatively to A, B and C. The accuracy of fix is called the strength of fix.

Strength of Fix. It is good (1) when o is with in the triangle ABC (2) the middle station is much nearer than the other two stations (3) of the two angles subtended at o one is small and other is large provided the distance between two stations subtending a small angle not very acute.

The strength of fix is poor if (1) Both the angle subtended at O are too acute (2) O is near the great circle.

5·14. Capacity of Survey Work (I.D.U.P.)

(1) **Single Levelling**

(*a*) In Plane country—5 km/Surveyor/day or 75 km/Surveyor/Month

(*b*) In Revinous country—3·5 km/Surveyor/day or 52 km/Surveyor/Month

(*c*) In Hilly country—2·5 km/Surveyor/day or 37 km/Surveyor/Month.

(2) **Double Levelling.** 2/3 by a party of two surveyors *i.e.* 1/3 for a single man's share.

(3) **Contour Survey**

(*a*) In plane country = 0·6 sq. km/Surveyor/day or 90 sq. km/Surveyor/Month.

(*b*) In Revinous country = 0·4 sq. km/Surveyor/day or 46 sq. km/Surveyor/Month.

(*c*) In Hilly country = 0·25 sq km/Surveyor/day or 3·75 km/Surveyor/Month.

(4) Detail contour survey—Half of contour survey with contour interval of 33 metre.

(5) **Plane Tabling**

(*A*) Scale RF = 1/5000

(*a*) In Plane country = 0·12 sq. km/Party/day or 1·8 sq. km/Party/Month

(*b*) In Revinous country = 0·06 sq. km/Party/day or 0·9 sq. km/Party/Month

(*c*) In Hilly country = 0·04 sq. km/Party/day or 0·6 km/Party/Month.

(*B*) Scale R.F. 1/1000—Half of above.

5·15. CURVES

Degree of curve. It is the angle at the centre in degrees subtended by a chord of 100 ft. length. (30·48 metres)

Notations for Circular Curves

1. **Tangents**—Lines AB and IC are called the tangents or straights.

The tangent AB which is measured in the direction of the progress of survey is called the 1st tangent, rear or back tangent. The line IC is called the 2nd or forward tangent.

2. **Tangent Points**—The points T_1 and T_2 at which the tangents touch the curve. T_1 is also known as point of curve while T_2 is known as point of tangency.

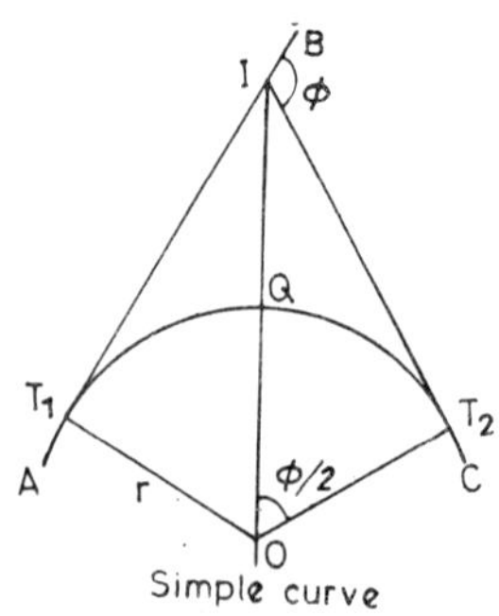

Fig. 5·46.

3. **Point of Intersection**—The point I at which the tangents cut each other.

4. When the curve deflects to the sight of the directions of survey it is called as **right hand curve** and when it deflects to the left it is called as **left hand curve**.

5. **The Angle of Intersection**—The angle AIC at which the tangents intersect towards the curve.

6. **Angle of Deflection**—The angle BIC by which the forward tangent is deflected from the rear tangent and denoted by ϕ. It is equal to triangle subtended by the tangent points T_1 and T_2 at the centre.

7. **Tangent Length**—The distance T_1I and T_2I measured from the tangent points to the point of intersection I.

8. **Long Chord**—The chord joining the tangent points T_1 and T_2.

9. **Length of Curve**—The length of arc $T_1QT_2 = \pi r\phi/180$, r is radius of curve

10. **Apex**—The point Q which is the mid point of the arc T_1QT_2.

11. **Apex Distance**—The distance from the apex Q to the point of intersection I.

12. **Versed Sine**—The distance PQ from the middle point P of long chord to the middle point Q of the curve or apex.

13. **Simple Curve**—Curve having arc of one circle only.

14. **Compound Curve**—Curve having arcs of two circles of different radii.

15. **Transition Curve**—A curve between two curves, or a curve and a straight line or two straight lines.

$r = \dfrac{1719}{D}$ app. where r = radius and D = degree of curve $= \dfrac{15}{\sin D/2}$ (correct)

Angle $AIC = \dfrac{30\,\phi}{D}$.

Setting Out of Curves

1st Method. By chain and tapes (offsets from long chord)

1. Intersect both tangent lines say at I and measure the deflection ϕ.
2. Cut off tangent length from the point I at point of tangents T_1 and T_2.

(Tangent length $= r \tan \phi/2$)

Now T_1T_2 = long chord say of length $= l = 2r \sin \phi/2$.

3. Taking mid point P of the long chord as origin. Calculate co-ordinates x, y by the formula.

$$y = x\frac{(l-x)}{2r}$$

where r = rad. of the curve A for different values of x plot y which will give the curve points.

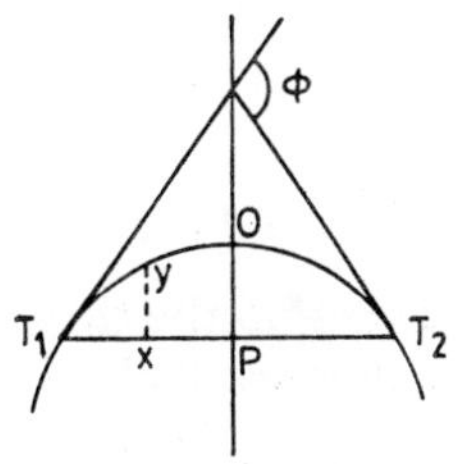

Fig. 5·47.

2nd Method. By offsets from the tangents.

Case I : When the centre of the curve is accessible.

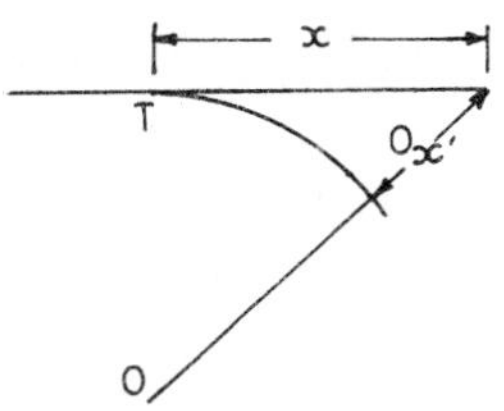

Fig. 5·48.

radial offset $O_x = \sqrt{r^2 + x^2} - r$(exact) or $\dfrac{x^2}{2r}$(app.)

Case II : When the centre of the curve is not accessible, offset perpendicular to the tangent

$$O_x = r\sqrt{r^2 - x^2}\,(\text{exact})$$

or $$\frac{x^2}{2r}(\text{app.})$$

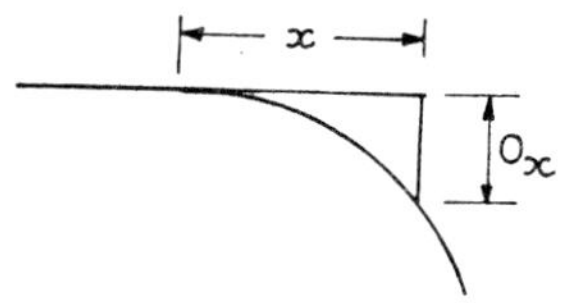

Fig. 5·49.

3rd Method. By offset from chords produced. a_1, a_2, a_3 ... are the length of chords (taking $a_2 = a_3 = a_4$ = (certain length of chain)

$$O_1 = \text{1st offset} = \frac{a_1^2}{2r}$$

$$O_2 = \text{2nd offset} = a_2\frac{(a_1 + a_2)}{2r}$$

$$O_3 = \text{3rd offset} = a_3\frac{(a_2 + a_3)}{2r}(\text{since } a_2 = a_3 = a_4) = \frac{b_2^2}{r}$$

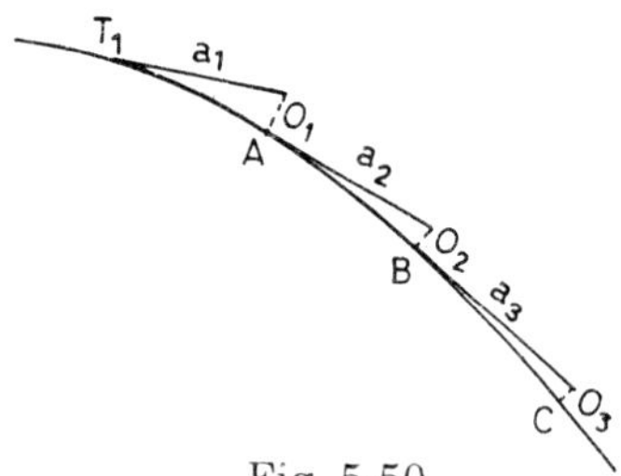

Fig. 5·50.

From the tangent point T_1 measure chord length a_1 and swing the offset O_1 and mark A. Now produce T_1A and mark distance a_2 from A swing a_2 with offset O_2 and mark the point B. Produce AB to length a_3 and so on, till closing the curve.

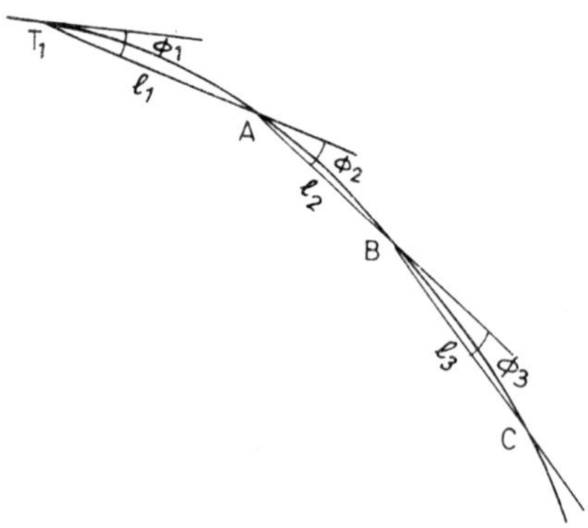

Fig. 5·51.

4th Method. Method of tangencial or deflection angles.

Let ϕ_1, ϕ_2, ϕ_3, ϕ_4 ... are the deflection angles in minutes.

l_1, l_2, l_3, l_4 ... the length of chords.

Then $\phi = 1719\frac{l_1}{r}$; $\phi_2 = 1719\frac{l_2}{r}$; $\phi_3 = 1719\frac{l_3}{r}$ ... (In minutes)

Since $l_2 = l_3 = l_4$ of any length of chain $Q_2 = Q_3 = Q_4$ ...

(**Note :** A_1 the 1st chord may be shorter as some point of it may be measured in the straight line of the chain).

(1) Set up the theodolite at the tanagent point T_1, measure angle ϕ_1 and cut off the chord $T_1A = l_1$ and mark point A.

(2) Now deflect the angle to $Q_1 + Q_2$ and measure $AB = l_2$ and mark point B.

(3) Deflect the angle to $\phi_1 + \phi_2 + \phi_3$ and measure $BC = l_3$ and mark point C. Proceed till the end of curve.

Note : The last length of the chord may be shorter of the common chords hence calculate ϕ for it and mark accordingly at site.

If the degree of curve say D is given the deflection angle for 100 ft. chain = $D/2$ Degrees and for chords of lengths l_1, l_2, l_3 etc.

$$\phi_1 = \frac{l_1 D}{200}\ ;\ \phi_2 = \frac{l_2 D}{200}\ ;\ \phi_3 = \frac{l_3 D}{200}\ \ldots\ \ldots\ \ldots$$

5th Method—Techeometric Method. In this method angles of deflection and length of chords both are measured by the techeometer. Let the additive angle of deflection be

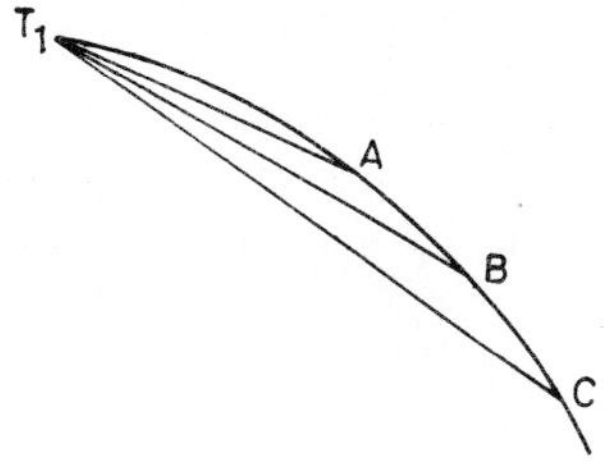

Fig. 5·52.

$\Phi_1 = \phi_1$; $\Phi_2 = \phi_1 + \phi_2$; $\Phi_3 = \phi_1 + \phi_2 + \phi_3$

Length $T_1A = 2r \sin \Phi$; $T_1B = 2r \sin \Phi_2$;

$TC = 2r \sin \Phi_3$ etc.

Read T_1A ; T_1B ; T_1C etc. by techeometer and proceed.

Note : For measuring techeometric distances see chapter on techeometry.

Compound Curves. It is composite of two simple curves. T_1T and T_2T having a common tangent point T. Known as the point of compound curvature. The radius of 1st curve is r_1 with origin O_1 and 2nd of rad. r_2 with origin O_2.

Tangent T_1B is known as smaller tangent say T_S and tangent BT_2 is known as greater tangent Tl (say).

ϕ = deflection angle of the tangents T_1B and BT_2, where α and β are the deflection angles of the tangents of the curves of radius r_1 and r_2 respectively. t_S = tangent length of curve of radius r_1 ; t_C = tangent of the curve or radius r_2.

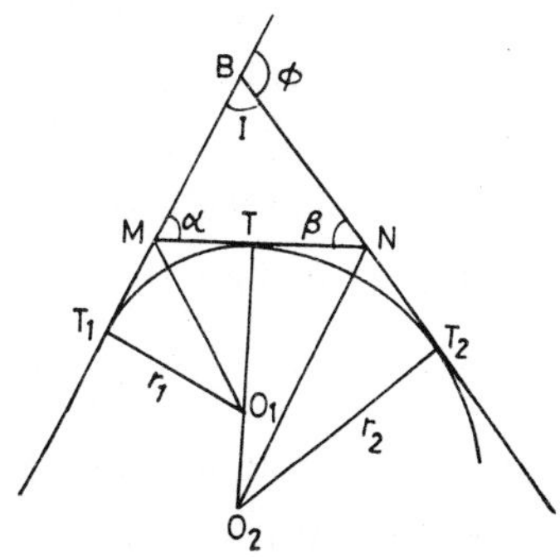

Fig. 5·53.

Elements of the Compound Curves

(1) $\phi = \alpha + \beta$ (2) $MN = t_S + t_L = r_1 \tan \alpha/2 + r_2 \tan \beta/2$

(3) $T_S = t_S + \dfrac{(t_S + t_C)\sin \beta}{\sin \phi}$ (4) $T_L = t_C + \dfrac{(t_S + t_C)\sin \alpha}{\sin \phi}$

$$= r_1 \tan\frac{\alpha}{2} + \left(r_1 \tan\frac{\alpha}{2} + r_2 \tan\frac{\beta}{2}\right)\frac{\sin \beta}{\sin \phi} \; ; \quad r_2 = \tan\frac{\beta}{2} + \left(r_1 \tan\frac{\alpha}{2} + r_2 \tan\frac{\beta}{2}\right)\frac{\sin \alpha}{\sin \phi}$$

Substituting values of t_S and t_C, set out both the curves as simple curves as discussed in simple curves.

Transition Curves. It is a curve by which two curves, one straight and other curve or two straight lines are joined by a smooth curve having different radii. It is also known as an easment curve.

Super Elevation. $h = \dfrac{bv^2}{gr}$(on roads) $= \dfrac{Gv^2}{gr}$(on rails)

where h = super elevation, b = width of road, G = gauge of rails, v = velocity of vehicle.

Length of transition curve :

(1) By arbitrary gradient ; $L = nh$, L = length of curve, h = super elevation and n = rate of canting (values of n varies from 300 to 1200)

(2) By the time rate – $L = \dfrac{hv}{a}$; a = time rate (varies from 1″ to 2″ per sec.).

(3) By rate of change of radial acceleration $L = \dfrac{V^3}{R} = 8\sqrt{R}$ where the rate of gain of radial acc. = 1 ft./sec^3 which is max. that will pass unnoticed by the passengers comfortably.

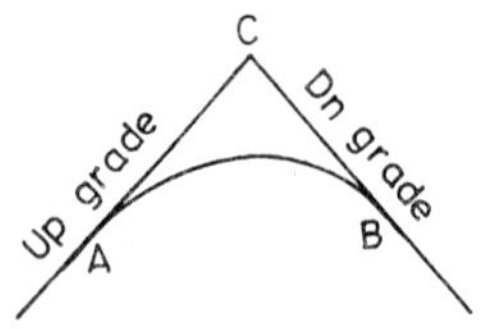

Fig. 5·54.

Vertical Curves. Upgrade (+), D_n grade (–)

1st method for laying curve—By tangent correction grade denoted by S_1, S_2 and S_3 etc. in %. Tangent correction also called as tangent offsets denoted by C. If x and y are the coordinates of a curve.

$$C = \frac{S_1 - S_2}{4n} \text{ when } n = \text{no. of chains}$$

$$y = Cx^2$$

Chainage of A = chainage of C – 100 n where 100 = length of chain and n = no. of chain

Chainage of B = chainage of C + 100

Elevation of A = elevation of $C - nS_1$

Elevation of B = elevation of $C - nS_2$

Thus knowing position and length of points of tangents, curve can be laid for different values of x, obtaining y from the formula $y = Cx^2$, knowing $C = \frac{S_1 - S_2}{4n}$.

Length of curve = $(S_1 - S_2)$/rate of change of grad. = L

No. of chains = length of curve/length of chain = n.

(Rate of change of grade may be as ·1% then place ·1 in the denominator).

Equivalent Inclinations

Slope	*Angle*	*Tan.*	*Sine*	*Radian*	*Slope*	*Angle*	*Tan.*	*Sine*	*Radian*
1 in 30	1°-55′	·0333	0·333	0·0333	1 : 8	7°-8′	0·125	0·1242	0·1245
1 : 25	2°-17′	·0400	·0400	0·0400	1 : 7	8°-8′	0·1429	0·1415	0·1419
1 : 20	2°-52′	·0500	·0500	0·0500	1 : 6	9°-28′	0·1666	0·1645	0·1652
1 : 18	3°-11′	·0555	·0554	0·0555	1 : 5	11°-19′	0·2	0·1926	0·1975
1 : 16	3°-35′	·0625	·0624	0·0625	1 : 4	14°-2′	0·25	0·2425	0·2444
1 : 14	4°-5′	·0714	·0712	0·0713	1 : 3	18°-26	0·3333	0·3162	0·3217
1 : 12	4°-46′	·0833	·0831	0·0832	1 : 2	26°-34′	0·5	0·4472	0·4637
1 : 10	50°-43′	0·1	0·0996	0·0997	1 : 1	45°-0′	0·1	0·7071	0·7854
1 : 9	6′-21′	0·1111	0·1103	0·09105					

5·16. Minor Survey Instruments

1. **Box Sexent.** It is a reflecting type of instrument capable of measuring angles upto 120° in the plane of observer and objects. It can also be used as an **optical square**. It more or less works on the principle of an optical square. It consists of the followings :

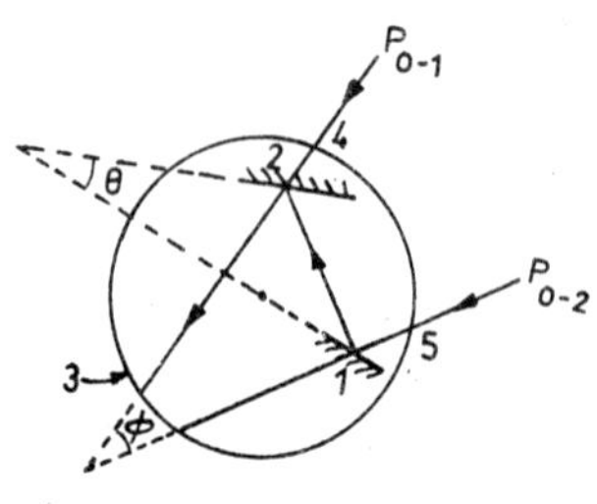

Fig. 5·55.

(1) It is a cylinderical box 3″ in dia and 1½″ deep provided with a cover fitted with a handle.

(2) The principle under lying is that the angle between the two object points is twice the angle between the two mirrors, 1 and 2 *i.e.* $2\theta = \phi$.

(3) Mirror 2 is the horizon mirror lower half of which is unsilvered while the upper is silvered and is fixed within the frame, mirror 1 is the index glass which is wholly silvered and can be moved by a pinion arrangement.

(4) An eye hole (pin hole) provided with a sliding cover is marked 3 and is provided for looking the object.

(5) O_1 and O_2 are two object points the angle of which is sought to be measured.

(6) 4 and 5 are the windows for sighting objects, It may be one continuous window.

Observing angle between the two stations.

(1) Handle the instrument on the station O at which the angle of the two objects is to be sought.

(2) Adjust the index arm of the vernier to read zero. If there is any zero error horizon mirror can be adjusted by a screw to coincide the zero of the graduated arc to the vernier.

(3) Range the object O_1 through the unsilvered part of the horizon mirror.

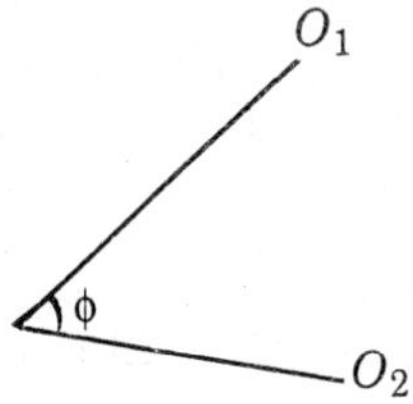

Fig. 5·56.

(4) Move the index mirror—1 by the rack and pinion arrangement operated by a screw till the image of object-2 as seen from the silvered part of horizon mirror-2 is in coincidence with the object 0-1 as seen directly from unsilvered part of horizon glass.

(5) Read the angle by the help of graduated arc and vernier arrangement.

Note (1) **:** For taking vertical angles the box sexent can be handled vertically.

(2) For minimising the error due to parallax, the more distant object should be viewed by reflection.

(3) Correction for the angle if the points O_1 and O_2 does not lie in the same horizontal plane as O, the point of observation

$$\cos\phi = \frac{\cos\phi' - \sin\alpha_1 \sin\alpha_2}{\cos\alpha_1 \cos\alpha_2}$$

where ϕ = the corrected angle between the two objects O_1 and O_2 in the horizontal plane of O.

ϕ^1 = observed angle between the two objects O_1 and O_2.

α_1 = observed angle of elevation of object O_1 from O.

α_2 = observed angle of elevation of object O_2 from O.

Permanent Adjustment of a Sexent

(1) To make the horizontal mirror perp. to the plane of instrument (The index mirror is permanently fixed by the maker at right angle to the plane of instrument).

(*a*) Sight a distant object like spire of a church (set the zero of the vernier with the zero of the scale).

(*b*) If there is any vertical displacement between the direction and reflected image vision, the above adjustment is needed.

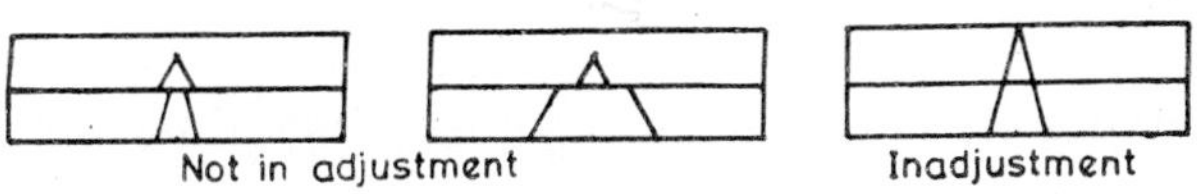

Fig. 5·57.

It is adjusted by eleminating the displacement by a square headed screw on the top of instrument by a key.

(2) To make the index and horizon glass parallel when the vernier reads zero (It is also known as removing index error.)

Set up the instrument as before and make the vernier to read zero and observe a distant object as before if there is any horizontal (lateral) displacement if needs adjustment. For adjusting the above a square headed screw at side of box is moved by a key till perfect.

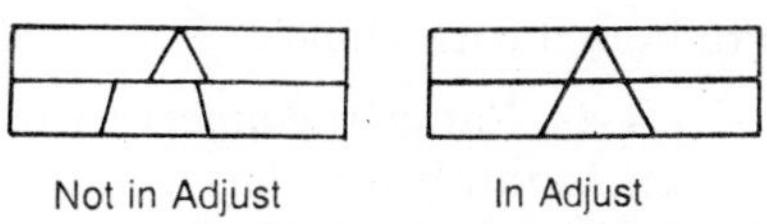

Fig. 5·58.

Bonning rods. In its simplest form **Bonning rods** are three in number in a set. These are wooden T-shaped frames of about 2 cm thick and 7·5 cm wide. The length of the top flange is about 30 cm and height of the vertical leg is about 70 cm to 90 cm. The bottom of the vertical leg is provided with an iron shoe, by the help of which the rod can be fixed in the ground. These rods are used to give a required grade in the pavements.

Use. Insert two rods at a certain distance apart say 30 m. The tops of these two rods are so fixed so that they may be in the required grade. The third rod is then fixed at a distance of 30 metres further apart, the top of which is aligned with the tops of the previous fixed two rods by raising or lowering by tapping down the rod. The fresh rod is then taken further by 30 meter and its top is aligned with the remaining two rods fixed in the pavement. The process is proceeded till reaching the desired point. The Bonning rods are the most handy and practicable process of fixing grades.

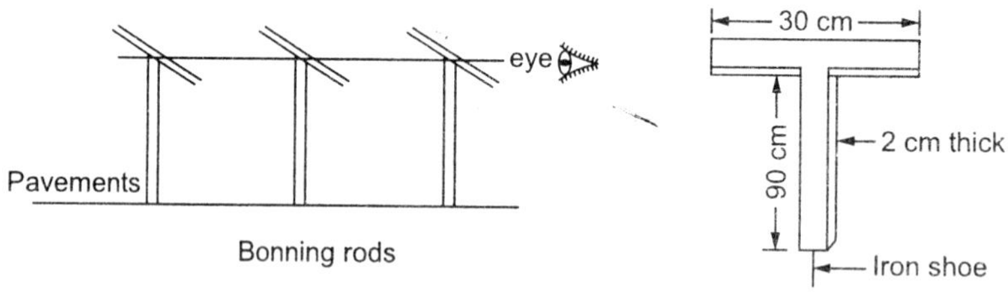

Fig. 5·58 (*a*).

Hand Level. It is used in rough levelling and for reconnaissance and preliminary survey. It consists of a sighting tube circular or rectangular in section. 4″ to 6″ long having a pin hole at the sighting end and a cross hair on the other for ranging. A bubble tube on the top. Immediately below the bubble tube is an opening in the sighting tube through which the bubble can be seen refelected by a mirror fixed at 45° in side the tube which is half silvered. From the silvered portion bubble can be seen while from the unsilvered portion object can be seen.

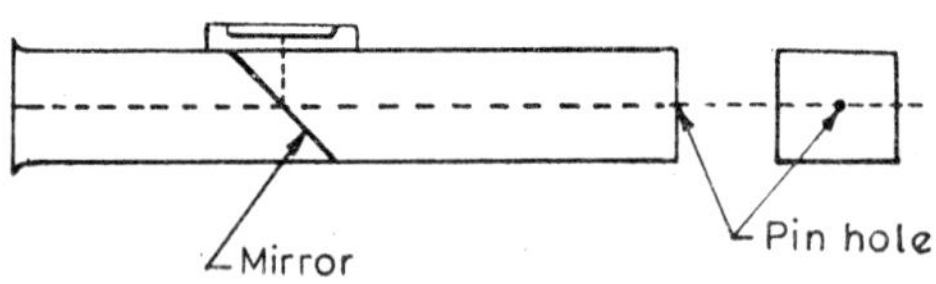

Fig. 5·59.

Line joining the pin hole to the cross hair makes the line of sight. It is horizontal when the cross wire bisects the image of the bubble.

Use. (1) Hold the instrument in hand and range the staff at the object point.

(2) Raise or lower the forward end of the tube till the image of the bubble is bisected by the cross hair.

(3) Note the reading.

Clinometer. A simple form of clinometer has been discussed in a paragraph for Chaining.

Abney Level. It is a type of clinometer with a hand level. It consists of a hand level with an eye piece at one end and the cross hair on the other. A bubble tube, the image of which can be seen through an opening at the top of tube after reflecting through a mirror which is placed at 45° inside the tube half of which is unsilvered for ranging the object. This bubble is fixed with the vernier arm which can be rotated by means of a milled wheel.

A semi-circular graduated arc having zero at the middle to 90° on either end. Inner rim of the arc is graduated with slopes.

Use. Range the object through eye piece and cross hair simultaneously, make the bubble tube image to be bisected by the cross hair behind the mirror for making the bubble tube in level. Read the angle on the arc with the help of the vernier.

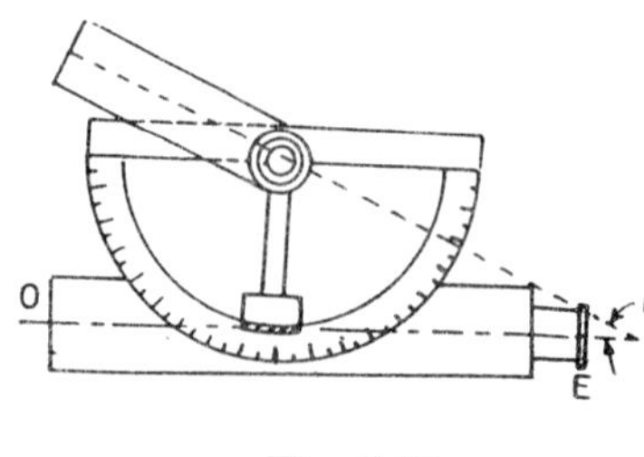

Fig. 5·60.

Abney level is generally used for rough levelling for taking angle of elevation or depression, setting out grades. It is much use full for making reconnaissance. It is light and handy instrument generally used in hill surveys.

Indian Pattern Clinometer. This instrument is also called as tangent clinometer and is generally used for determining elevations or depressions of distant objects.

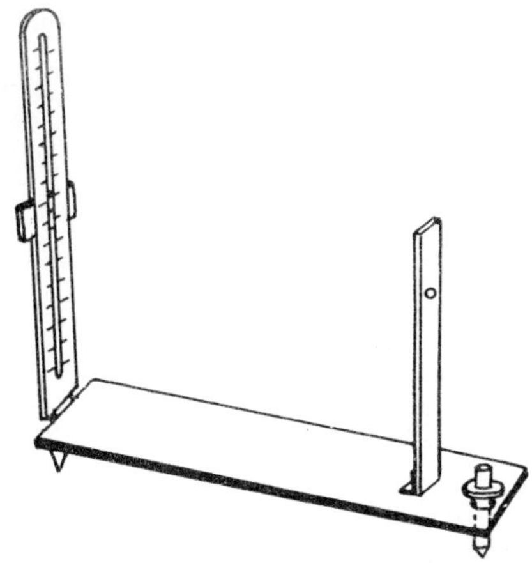

Fig. 5·61.

In its simplest form it consists of a base plate resting on three ivory point so that it may not soil the plane table paper while moving over it. It carries two vertical folding vanes one is longer about 7 in having a sliding cross hair while the other is shorter with a pin hole. (eye hole). The longer vane carries graduations of degree on one side and grades on the other, above the central zero mark to read elevations or upgrades while graduations below zero mark read depressions or down grades. The cross hair can move up or down by a milled head screw provided near the base plate end. A sprit level is also attached to the base plate to make the instrument in level.

Use. The cross hair at zero gives horizontal line with the eye hole. Move the cross hair up or down as required for taking elevations or depressions or grades and range a sight vane at a height of the eye hole from the ground by raising or lowering it. The foot of the sight vane then will be the required grade point or the angle of elevation or depression.

Ceylon Ghat Tracer. It is hand instrument for setting out grade contour in preliminary survey or road surveys.

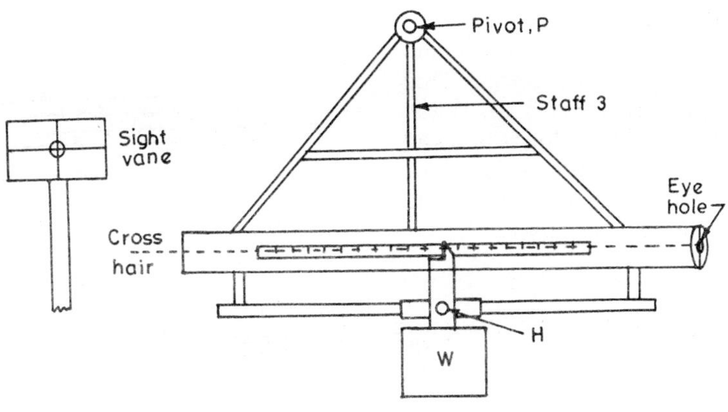

Fig. 5·62.

It consists of a hollow brass sighting tube fitted with an eye hole at one end and a cross hair on the other as in case of a hand level. The tube is suspended through a bracket to a pivot point P in a upright staff.

A horizontal racked bar is provided parallel to the sighting tube on which a wt. W is moved by the milled head H on a rack and pinion arrangement.

The flat side of the sighting tube is marked with slope graduations 1 in 20 to 1 in 6 on either side of the middle zero point. The line joining the pin hole to the cross hair is line of sight.

Use. Pivot the ghat tracer on the staff at the pivot *P*. Adjust the load *W* on the rack bar till the pointer attached in the weight reads the desired slope. A sight vane at the height equal to the height of line of sight from the ground is fixed in a ranging staff which is moved up or down till the line of sight crosses the horizontal line of sight vane, which is a point on the desired slope.

Enlarging or Reducing Plans

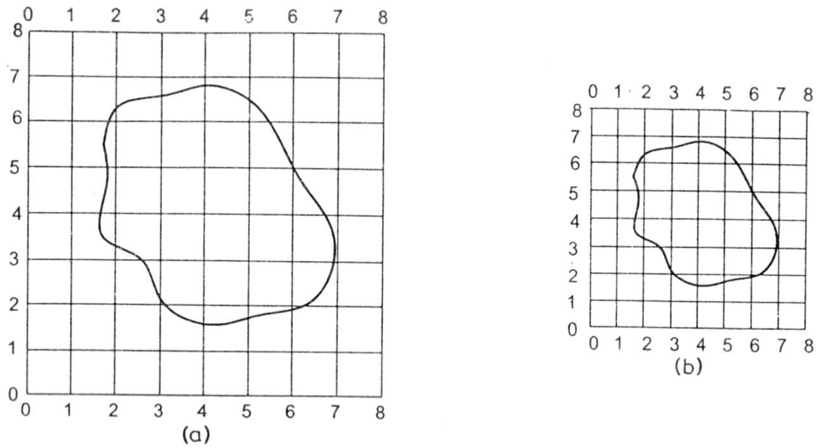

Fig. 5·63

(1) **Graphical Method.** Divide the given plan in the squares on a suitable scale size say ¼′ by a light soft pencil and number it as shown in Fig. 5·63 (*a*) (The squares may be drawn on a tracing paper mounted in the given plan in order to avoid spoiling of the map).

Next on the sheet at which the reduced plan is to be drawn, draw similar squares of the reduced size (say half as needed) and number accordingly.

Draw the plan on the reduced squares in accordance to the given plan.

Proportional Compass. It consists of two slotted and double pointed brass arms clamped with a milled head screw together. This screw slides in the slot and carries an index mark on it, on the left face of the slot is marked linear ratios say $^1/_2$, $^2/_3$, $^3/_4$ etc. while on the right scale of lines say 2, 3, 4, 5. On the other side scale of plans and scale of solids is marked.

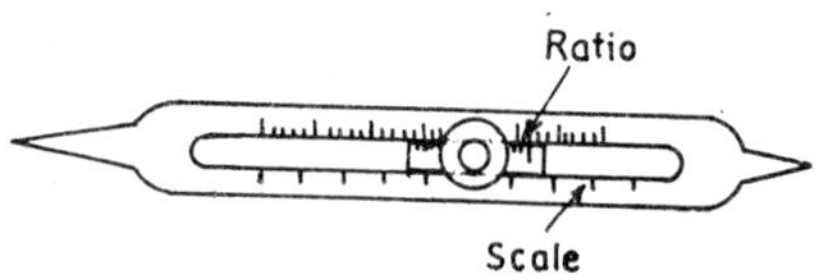

Fig. 5·64.

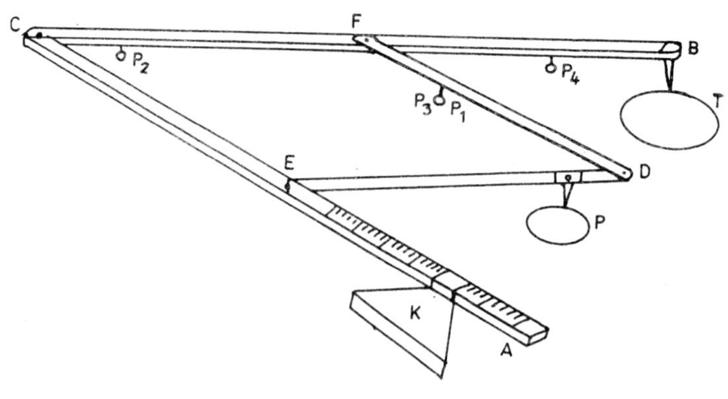

Fig. 5·65.

Use. Close the instrument so as both the arms look as one. Loose the screw and set the index mark on the desired ratio and then open the arms after tighting the screw. Measure the distances from the existing plans by one limb and plot by the other as desired on the paper meant for the purpose according as reduction or enlargement as needed.

Pantagraph. It consists of four bars or arms rectangular in section. Arm *AC* and *BC* is pivoted at the point *C* while the arm *FD* and *ED* is pivoted at *D*, *E* and *F* so as to form *CFDE* as a parallelogram having equal sides in every position of the instrument. The instrument is supported on several castors or small rollers $p_1 p_2$; $p_2 p_3$ or p_4 etc. So as to keep the arms parallel to the paper and for easy movement of the parts. The arms *EA* and *ED* carries marks of ratio as $^1/_2$, $^1/_3$, $^1/_4$, $^1/_5$ etc. according to the ratios of reduction or enlargement. Tubular arms on the arms *CB, ED* and *EA* is provided with index points and vertical axes carrying the tracing point *T*. The pencil point *P* and the fulcrum point *K* with clamping screws. The fulcrum *K* has a heavy triangular weight. So that the instrument may not disturb while in use. The pencil point *P* and the fulcrum point *K* is fixed on the desired ratio of reduction say 1/2. The tracing point *T* is moved along the plan to be reduced and by the pencil point *P* the reduced plan is obtained on a paper under it. If the plan is to be enlarged the position of tracing point and the pencil point is interchanged. It should be seen that when the insturment is adjusted for a reduction factor the points *T*, *P* & *K* should be in a straight line. A cord is also move on the frame *CBE* for moving the arms properly. The pencil point is lifted by a cord on the points which are not continuous.

Eidograph. It consists of three square brass bars *AB*, *BC* and *AD*. A point of support weight *W* having three pin points by which it can remain steady on the paper. A pin in centre of the weight *W* which makes the fulcrum and is connected with a sliding bar through which the bar *AB* slides and can be adjusted on any desired position and can be clamped with a screw. Other two bars *BC* and *AD* are connected to the ends *A* and *B* remain parallel in all positions. The bars *BC* and *CD* slides in the boxes which are fixed in pulley wheels which may be adjusted on any desired position and can be clamped.

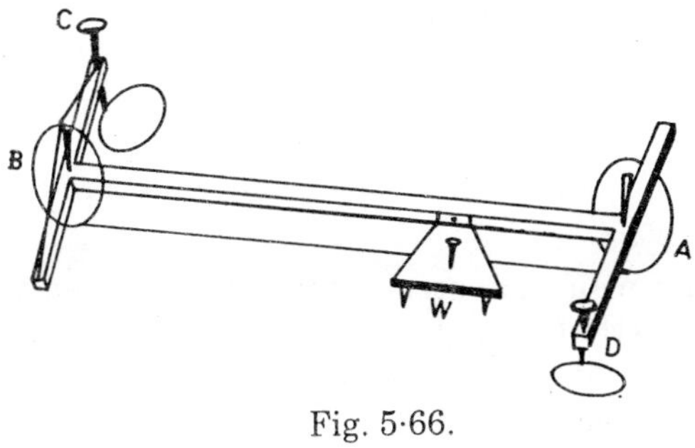

Fig. 5·66.

Bar *BC* carries a tracing point at end *C* and the other *AD* a pencil point at the end *D*. The pencil point can be raised from the paper when the continuity of the line breaks with a lever attached to a cord passing over the instrument to the tracing point. All the three bars are divided in 200 parts of graduations. By means of vernier on sliding boxes reading upto 1/10th point can be adjusted. Lead weight can be applied on the arm *AB* to keep it in balance.

When the instrument is adjusted the arms *BC* and *CD* remain parallel and the tracing fulcrum and pencil points are in one line.

Use. The number *n* to which the three arms are adjusted is obtained by the formula

$$n = \frac{\text{diff. of the fractional term of the proportion}}{\text{sum of the fractional term of the proportion}} \times 100$$

e.g. let it is required to reduce 1/5th then

$$n = \frac{5-1}{5+1} \times 100 = \frac{400}{6} = 66{\cdot}6$$

This number so found (66·6) is to be set on the arms of the eidograph. On the arm *AB* the fulcrum point should be set at 66·6 on the pencil side while the tracing point should be lengthened to the point 66·6 on the arm *BC* and pencil point should be shortened to the point 66·6 on the arm *AD*. Now the instrument is set and will reduce the plan 1/5th.

If the plan is enlarged the fulcrum point should be fixed on the number 66·6 towards the tracing point while the tracing point arm should be shortened on the point 66·6 and the pencil point should be lengthened to the point 66·6.

Plani Meter. It consists of two arms (1) and (2) pivoted or hinged at a point (3) The arm (1) is of fixed length and is called as anchor arm. At its one end it carries a pin point(5) called the anchor point. It is kept in position by a removable weight (4).

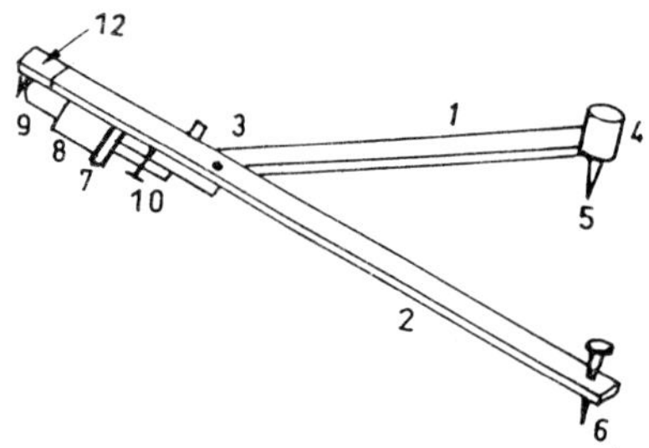

Fig. 5·67.

The other arm (2) is a tracing arm of adjustable length and at one of its end it carries a tracing point (6) which is made to move along the periphery of the area. The total normal displacement is measured by the wheel roller (7) having its axis parallel to the tracing arm (2). This wheel may be between the tracing point and pivot point or beyond pivot. This wheel carries a graduated cylinder (8) which is divided in 100 parts while tenth of each point is further measured to 10th part by vernier (9) with a clamp (12). Every revolution of wheel or roller is measured by the counting disc or dial (10) which is geared to the wheel. The disc is divided in 10 parts, every part counts one revolution of the wheel. This one revolution of disc counts 10 revolutions of the wheel. Every complete reading is a figure of four digits. Units being read on counting disc or dial, 10th and 100th on wheel and drum and thousandth by vernier.

The planimeter rests on three points, one the anchor point, 2nd the tracing point and 3rd the wheel. The wheel may partly rotates or partly slips without advancing the reading. The amount of rotation of wheel measures the area of the wheel.

Use. (1) Set up the index mark (11) on the levelled edge of the disc to the scale to which the plan is drawn.

(2) Fix the anchor point inside or outside of the plan to be measured according to whether it is small or large. Weight it so that it may not shift during use. Mark a point in the periphery of the plan to start with and forward in the clockwise direction by moving the tracing point always in clockwise direction. Also note whether the wheel is rotating in forward or backward directions. The anchor point shoiuld be so placed that the tracing point may approach along the whole periphery of the plan. If convenient divide the plan in a number of smaller plans and add the individual area of each to obtain total.

(3) Read the reading of disc wheel, drum and vernier to obtain the initial reading which is recorded in note book. It is not desirable to bring the whole measuring system to read zero initially. When the circuit is closed note the final reading. Note the number of times by which the disc or dial is revolved.

Now the area of the plan say A is calculation by the following formula

$$A = M(F.R. - I.R. \pm 10\,N + C) \quad ...(1)$$

where M = The no. of units of area per revolution of the roller or wheel which is marked on the tracing.

$F.R.$ = Final reading

$I.R.$ = Initial reading

N = No. of revolutions of the disc around the index mark

C = Constant marked on the top of the tracing arm just abov the scale on.

Use (+) when the zero of the dial passes across the index clockwise *i.e.* 6, 7, 8, 9, 0, 1, 2 and (–) when anticlockwise *i.e.* 6, 5, 4, 3, 2 ... .

The constant C is only added if the anchor point is within the figure.

Note : When the anchor point is inside the plan a confusion of –ve or +ve results may arise. In the case of clockwise rotation, the net rotation of the wheel is always forward if the area of the plan is greate than the zero circle (discussed ahead) otherwise if the area of the zero circle is more than the area of the plan, the motion of the wheel is backward.

Precautions. (1) Check the area by starting at different points.

(2) Rough calculations by figure measurements should also be taken to avoid any blunder.

(3) The surface of the paper should be smooth and horizontal.

Zero Circle. Zero circle or the circle of correction is a circle along the circumference of which if the tracing point is moved the wheel will not roll, it will only slide without effecting the reading. This position comes when the plane of the wheel passes from the anchor point or the line joining the anchor point to the wheel is at right angle to the line joining wheel to the tracing point.

The anchor is the centre of the zero circle with distance of the anchor point to the tracing point as radius. This area is added with the anchor point is inside the plan since the planometer record the area of the annular space between the plan and the zero circle.

Formula for the area of zero circle

(1) When the wheel is placed beyond the hinge away the tracing point

Area of zero circle = $\pi (L^2 + 2LL_1 + R^2) = \pi R_1^2$

where L = length of the tracing arm hinge to the tracing point.

L_1 = Distance from hinge to the wheel plane.

R = Length of the anchor arm from long hinge to the anchor point.

(2) When the wheel is between the hinge and the tracing point.

Area of zero circle = $\pi R_1^2 = \pi(L^2 - 2LL_1 + R^2)$

(3) Area of zero circle = $M \times C$ (Values of M and C are given in equation (1) before.

(4) By measuring the radius of zero circle—Draw two lines WT and WA at right angles. Taking W as point of wheel mark T and A on the lines WT and WA to the anchor and tracing points. Measure the distance A to T which is the required radius R_1.

Area of zero circle = $\pi A_1^2 = \pi TA^2$

(5) By Planometer—(*a*) Take a plan whose area is already known say it is A. Measure the area of this plan by planometer (taking anchor point inside the plan). Say it is = A_1 and let the area of zero circle = A_0. Then $A_0 + A_1 = A$.

(*b*) Measure the area of the plan keeping the anchor point inside of the plan and then outside the plan then the difference of the two will give the area or the zero circle.

Note : In order to have simplicity of working set the tracing arm to the natural scale of the plan and hence the area obtained will be in the same unit at which the plan is drawn. Say if the plan is given in metres then the area of site will be obtained by multiplying the $R.F.$ of the plan.

Example. Scale of the plan 1″ = 8′ Anchor point inside the plan

On natural scale $IR = 6{\cdot}752$; $FR = 4{\cdot}868$

$N = 1$; $C = 22{\cdot}080$; as the area is calculated.

1st on natural scale then $M = 10$. Motion of the wheel is reverse.

$A = M(F.R. - I.R. - 10\,N + C)$ Taking –ve as the anchor point is inside the Plan.

$= 10(4{\cdot}808 - 6{\cdot}725 - 10 + 22{\cdot}080)$

$= 10 \times 10{\cdot}196 = 101{\cdot}96$ sq in.

Since the scale is 1″ = 8′ or 1 sq. in. = 64 sq. ft.

So the area of the plot $= 101{\cdot}96 \times 64 = 6525{\cdot}44$ sq. ft.

Determination of the meridian (Geographical north-south line)

The Chief methods are given below :

(1) **By direction of Sun's shadow.** Let O be the foot of a vertical pole or a plumb line, Mark the end of the shadow of the top of the vertical pole at equal interval of time before and after noon on the plateform at which the pole O is fixed. With pole as centre a number of concentric circles are drawn and on these points a_1 a_2, b_1 b_2, c_1 c_2, a, b, c are taken as their mid points on their respective circles. From O to the mean position of a, b, c etc. a line is drawn which will be the meridian of the place at which the observations are taken.

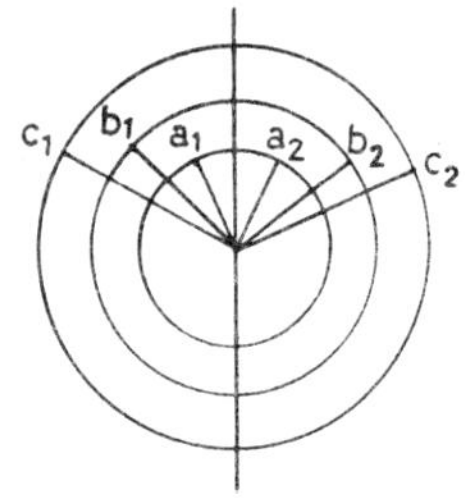

Fig. 5·68.

Note : If O, a, b, c are not in a perfect line, take mean position for locating the meridian.

(2) **By Magnetic Compass.** The direction of the magnetic north-south line can be located by a compass. Then the geographical north-south line can be obtained by giving proper allowance for the magnetic declination of the place which can be found in declination tables for different places.

(3) **By Observation of the Pole Star.** Drive a peg A and mark a fine point on it from which suspend a plumb line. Suspend another plumb line B approximately south of A on the exact time of culmination of pole star (on meridian). Locate the position of B in range of point A and the pole star. The line AB is the meridian of the place.

Note : For this purpose the time of culmination of pole star at that place should be known from tables.

5·17. Astronomical Terms

Celestial Sphere. To an observer upon the earth the fixed star seem to be dotted over the surface of a vast sphere which is known as the celestial sphere at the centre of which the earth is apparently situated.

Ecliptic. It is plane upon the celestial sphere forming a great circle and is inclined at 23°-27′ to the horizon.

Horizon. It is great circle traced on the celestial sphere and is tangencial to the observer on the earth surface or is perp. to zenith-Nadir line.

Zenith-Nadir. It is a straight line at an observer on the earth surface drawn upwards in the direction of force of gravity upto junction of celestial sphere. It is known as the zenith of the observer *i.e.* zenith is a point on the celestial sphere immediately over head.

If the straight line is produced down wards through the centre of gravity of earth, the other intersection of the line to the celestial sphere is termed as Nadir.

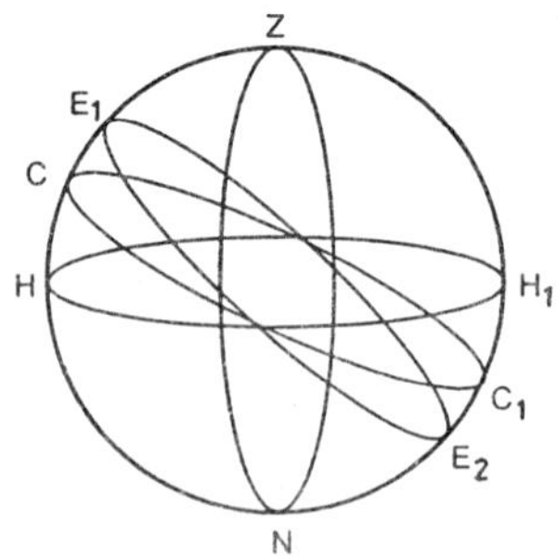

Fig. 5·69.

Z-Zenith HH_1 = Horizon

N-Nadir CC_1 = Ecliptic

PP_1 = Celestial poles and polar axis

E_2EE_1 = Equator

E and W = East and West points at junctions of Horizon and Prime vertical

Meridian. It is a great circle formed on the celestial sphere by intersection of a plane passing through the two celestial poles with Zenith and Nadir.

Latitude. Latitude is an angular distance measured from the equatorial plane towards the nearer pole along the meridian of the place. Latitude at equator is zero while at poles it is 90°. Other lies in between 0 and 90°.

Longitude. Longitude of a place is the angular distance which the meridian of a place makes with some standard meridian and is measured from 0° to 180° either towards east or west.

Declination. Position of heavenly bodies on the celestial sphere. It is the angular distance from the equator to the star measured along the celestial meridian, while co declination is the remainder of the quadrant.

Right Asscention. It is the angular distance between the meridian of the star and the standard meridian. It is measured west towards east and is expressed in hours minutes and seconds. Twenty four hour represents 360°. The standard meridian is first point of Aries. (It is point at which elyplic plane crosses the equatorial plane through which sun passes from south to north, vernal or spring equinox.)

Vernal equinox — on march 21 (or spring equinox)

Autumnal equinox — on Sept. 23

Summer solstice — on June 21

Winter solstice — on Dec. 22

Altitude. It is the angular distance from the plane of horizon measured along the great circle or vertical which passes through the body and the Zenith and Nadir of the observer.

Co-altitude. It is remainder of the quadrant of the angle of altitude.

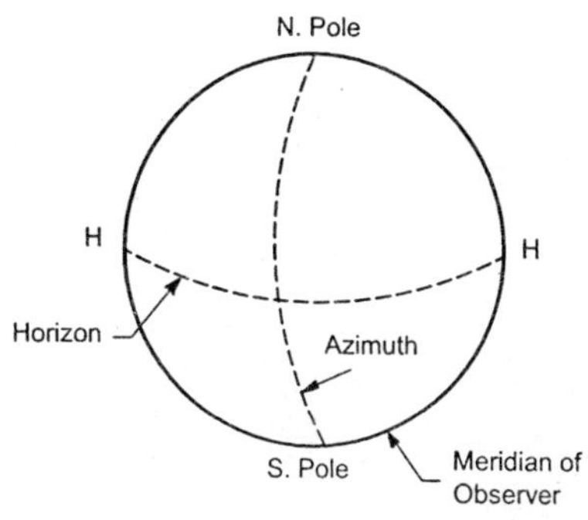

Fig. 5·70.

Azimuth. Azimuth of a point is the angle between the plane of the meridian and the vertical plane passing through the point *i.e.* it is the spherical angle at the Zenith-Nadir and the poles. The arc of the horizon intercepted between these two planes is a measure of azimuth of the point.

Culmination or Elongation. Each of the fixed star appears to describe a circle round the earth and to cross the meridian twice in 24 hrs. *i.e.* when the fixed star is on the middle meridian, it is said to be a culmination or on transit. The line of culmination is fixed for the star. The upper culmination is the time for Zenith and lower culmination is the time for Nadir.

Time

Greenwich Mean Time (GMT). It is measured from the lower transit of the Greenwich meridian by the mean sun *i.e.* Greenwich mean mid night 0 hrs to 24 hrs.

Local Mean Time (LMT). It is measured from the lower transit of the place meridian by the mean sun *i.e.* 0 hrs to 24 hrs.

Conversion of mean time. The successive time interval between two lower transits is 24 hrs. corresponding to 360°. Hence a change of 1° of longitude will effect the local time by

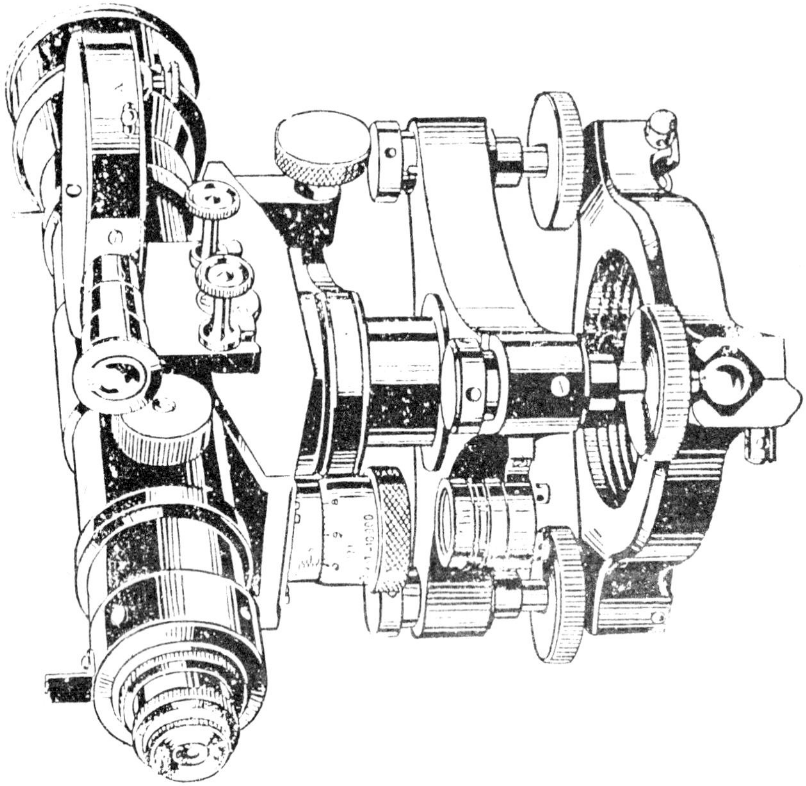

India Office Pattern Level
Fig. 5·71 (*b*).

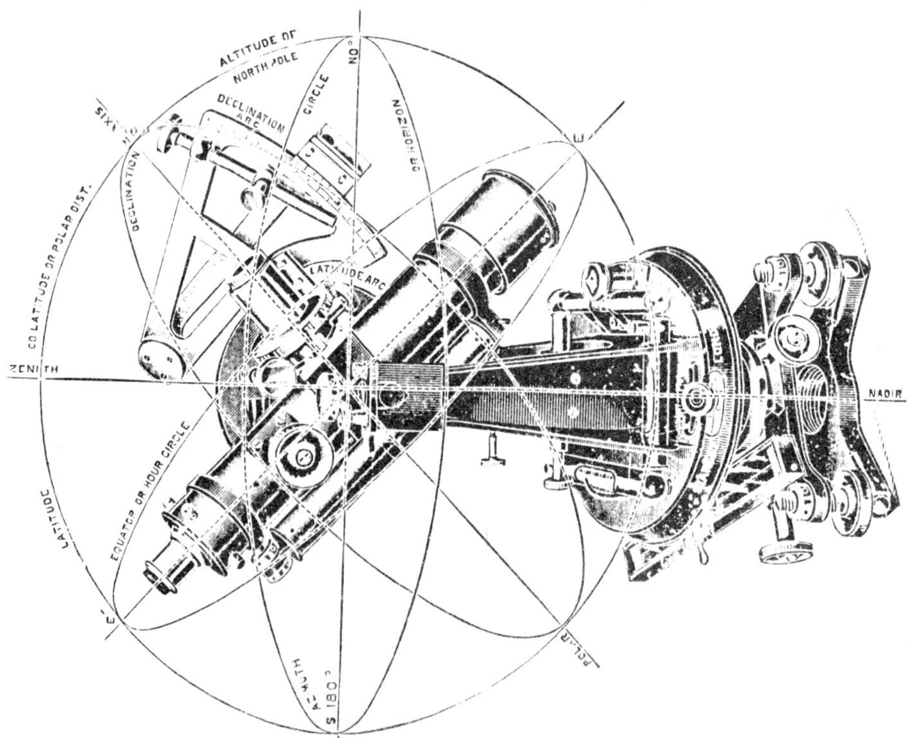

Theodolite
Fig. 5·71 (*a*).

$\frac{24}{360} = \frac{1}{15}$ Hr. or 4 min. If the place is west of Greenwhich the mean mid night will occur later and if in east it will occur earlier.

Example. What will be the G.M.T. corresponding 2H LMT of *B* on April 15 on longitude 56°E ?

56° long expressed in time = 56 × 4 = 224 min = 3 H, 44 m, 0 s

But as the longitude is *E*, the clock at Greenwich is behind the clock at *B*. Therefore at Greenwich time is 24 + 2 – 3H, 44 m, 0 s = 22 H, 16 m, on April 15 – 1 = April 14.

6

Building Materials

6·1. Stones

Classification of Rocks (Stones)

(1) **Geological Classification.** Based on geological formation.

Igneous Rocks or Stones. Primary or Igneous rocks are formed after consolidation of magma. Magma is a molten rock material found below the crust of the earth.

Igneous rocks are divided into three main classes based on silica contents.

(*a*) **Acid rock**—when amount of silica in rock is more than 66% such as Granite, Granodiorite, Rhyolite and Pitch stone etc.

(*b*) **Basic rock**—When amount of silica is between 45 to 55% such as Basalt, Dolerite and Gabbro etc.

(*c*) **Ultra basic rocks**—When amount of silica is less than 45% with few exceptions such as periodolite and pickrite etc.

Sedimentary Rocks. After formation of original crust, water and atmosphere come in existence and begin to disintegrate primary rocks. This disintegrated debris material and material in solution are transported by water and wind and deposited into the hollow crust. This process is known as sedimentation. The deposited sediments finally cemented by heat, mechanical or chemical activity and form hard rocks which are known as sedimentary rocks. Such as sand stones etc.

Metamorphic Rocks. Igneous or sedimentary rocks finally subjected to earth movement and carried down to depths in the crust where they are acted upon by heat and pressure by which these rocks are reconstituted, their original characters are also partly or wholly changed and new rock is formed. These newly formed rocks are known as metamorphic rocks.

Such type of rocks are lime stone and marbles etc.

(2) **Physical Classification according to Size.**

Boulders—rounded by rolling in rivers more than 150 mm

Gravel—rounded by rolling in rivers, 80 to 150 mm

Aggregate—less than 80 mm.

6·2(*a*) Nomenclature of Stones

Granite. It is a very hard, strong, durable and unstratified stone. It takes a fine polish. Its main constituents are quartz and felspar mixed with particles of mica. The colour is due to the presence of felspar. It is mainly obtained in grey, bluish or in reddish colours. It is crystalline and lusturious. On account of its hardness it is used where great strength and durability is required, such as in wheel kerbs, plinths and pedestals etc. Its sp. gravity varies from 2·4 to

2·75 and crushing strength is 770 to 1300 kg/cm^2. It is mainly obtained in Bundelkhand and Southern districts, Dalhousie and Kangra in Himalyan hills.

Basalt and Trap. It is very hard and difficult to work, hence it is generally used as a road metal. It is generally found in central India, Bombay, Bihar, Rajasthan, Dehradun, Poona and Western ghats. Its sp. gravity is 2·96, crushing strength varies from 1530 to 1890 kg/cm^2 and tensile strength is 100 kg/cm^2.

Marble. It is a metamorphosed shape of lime stone. It is hard and takes fine polish. It is generally found in white colour, but some of its varieties are also found in yellow, pink or black in colour. In India it is generally found in Rajasthan near Jaipur. Being costly it is generally used in ornamental works and statues etc. Marble is now also being sawed in slabs by diamond rotating cutters. Its specific gravity is 2·65, crushing strength is 720 kg/cm^2 and tensile strength is 50 kg/cm^2.

Lime Stone. There are great varieties of this stone from pure carbonate of lime to magnesian lime stones which is half carbonate of lime and half carbonate of magnesia. It is generally found with combination of clay. Being weathered with atmosphere lime stone exposures are generally irregular. The colour is generally grey, white, dark blue yellow or mottled. Compact lime stone consisting pure carbonate of lime is burnt to produce white lime. If it contains a considerable quantity of clay (kankar) produce hydraulic lime when burnt. It is also used as a road metal under light traffic. It is effected by acids. Compact lime stone is also used as a flux in blast furnace and for bleaching. Harder varies are also used for building purposes where atmosphere is not acidic. It is also a main raw material for manufacturer of cement. Its sp. gravity varies from 2·0 to 2·75 and crushing strength is 550 kg/cm^2. It is generally found in all hilly regions of India.

Slate. It is a metamorphic clay rock, originally formed as sedimentary rock and converted into slate by intense heat and pressure. It can be splitted into thin sheets. It is hard and impervious and found in a varieties of colours, generally black, blue, grey or green. Being impervious generally used in roofs and metal pieces etc. Slates are generally found in Himalyas, East Punjab, Andhra and Madhya Pradesh in India. Its sp. gravity is 2·89, crushing strength varies from 770 to 2110 kg/cm^2 and tensile strength is 90 kg/cm^2.

Gneiss and Schist. These are metamorphic rocks which have similar constituents as granite. It can easily be separated in thin slabs hence generally used in street paving. It is found in Tamil Nadu, Andhra, Mysore and Bihar States. Its sp. gravity is 2·69 and crushing strength is as 200 kg/cm^2.

Sand Stone. It is a sedimentary rock containing grains of sand or quartz cemented together by lime, magnesia, alumina or oxide of iron etc. Sand stones are found in great varieties of colours such as white, red, grey, blue, black or yellow. The finer the grain, the easier the carving. The coarser grain stone are usually very hard. It is used in roofs, floors and paving sets etc. It is also used as road metal and ashlar masonry. It is found in hills, Fatehpur Sikri near Agra, Madhya Pradesh, Andhra, Bihar, Himanchal and Madras etc. Its sp. gravity is 2·65 to 2·95, crushing strength 650 kg/cm^2 and tensile strength is 90 kg/cm^2.

Quartzite. It is a form of silacius sand stone containing quartzite grains cemented with silica. It is hardest and strongest among stratified rocks. Compact and dense. It is brown red to yellowish white. It is used as road metal and in walls.

Shale. It is compressed and laminated clay. It is also hard as clay and can be splitted into slates.

Flint. Rock consisting of fine crystalline silica and showing remains of spongy and other organism. It has a conchoidal glassy fracture.

Mica Schist. It is a metamorphic composition of mica and quartz, crystalline and fine grained in texure having a grey, greenish, yellow or brownish black colour. It can be used as a road metal.

Mooram admixure. It is a distintegrated granite or trap produced by weather action 20 mm max. size with clay admixture. It is of deep red colour and is used for spreading in yards and blinding road metal in road work.

Pumice. It is "Lava froth" highly vesicular, formed by escaping gases. It is a light stone which can float on water. Pumica is used in light weight concrete preparations and for scrubbing concrete floors.

Field Tests for Strength of Stones

(1) **Structure.** Some pieces of stone under test are kept under water in a bottle of glass for about one hour after which the bottle is shaked and allowed to rest. If the water becomes muddy, the stone particles are poor in cementation to each other.

(2) **Hardness.** A scratch by a pen knife must not leave any impression on a hard stone.

(3) **Toughness.** A sample can be tested by hammer. A tough stone will need a harder blow to break.

(4) **Porosity.** A good stone must not absorb more than 5% of water by weight of its own.

(5) **Crushing Test.** The crushing strength of stone cubes can be tested in a crushing machine used for conc. test.

(6) **Acid or Weather test.** Small test pieces are kept in 1% solution of HCl (Hydrochloric acid) for seven days and is kept well stirred, after which if the edges are still sharp the stone will oppose the weather well. If it shows effervescence by dropping acid on stone, the presence of chaulk (lime) is there in stone.

Tests of Stones (Laboratory)

(1) **Compressive Strength (resistance to rupture)**

Sample. Samples weighing at least 25 kg of unweathered strata that appear to vary in colour, structure and texture should be collected from quaries or field stones. The test piece should be cut from the sample and core drills, in the form of cube, square, prism or cylinder. The diameter of lateral dimension should not be less than 50 mm and ratio from height to dia. or lateral dimension should not be less than 1 : 1. Finish the faces by rock cutting saws, grinding polishing wheels or abrasive powder. Immerse specimen in water for 72 hours for wet testing. For the dry test the specimen should be dried at 105 ± 5°C for 24 hours in oven and cool to room temperature 20 to 30°C in a desicator.

Procedure. The specimen should be put in compression testing machine and a load is applied uniformly and gradually. Increase the load at a rate of 14 N/mm^2 per minute. The max. load applied and type of failure is recorded. Three specimen parallel and perpendicular to the rift should be tested.

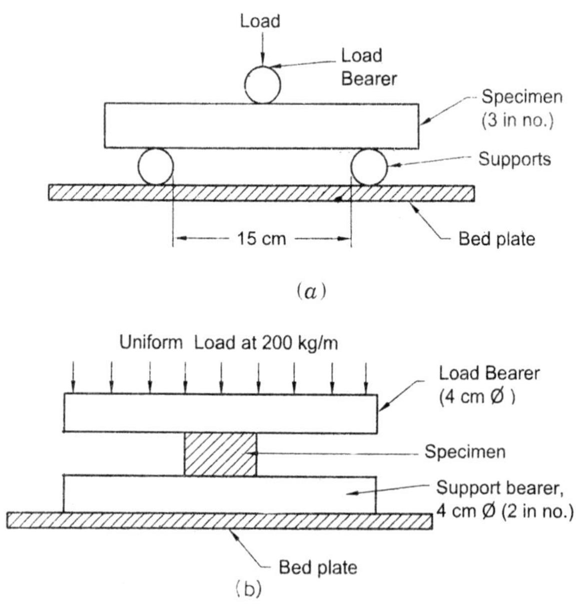

Fig. 6·1.

$$\text{Comp. strength} = \frac{\text{Max. load in } N \text{ at failure}}{\text{Area of bearing face of specimen in mm}^2}.$$

(2) **Transverse Strength.** When tension or comp. forces act on a body of symmetrical form in such a way that their resultant coincides with the axis of the body, they are termed Axial forces, and the stress induced is called Axial stresses. When a member like beam is subjected to bending, transverse stresses develop and their capacity to withstand transverse stresses is called as transverse strength.

Test Process. Three test blocks of size 200 × 50 × 50 mm should be made from a large block of stone to be tested. Test pieces should be taken one from centre and two from edges of the sample. Mark directions of rift and immerse the test pieces in water at 20-30°C for 72 hours and tested in saturated condition.

For dry test, it should be dried at 105 ± 5°C for 24 hours in oven and cool to room temperature at 20 to 30°C in a desicator.

Procedure. Put the specimen on two uniformly supported bearers of 4 cm in dia. Apply load at a uniform rate of 200 kg/m through a 3rd bearer of 4 cm in dia and placed midway and parallel to supports. The length of bearer should be max. width of the specimen to be tested.

$$\text{Transverse strength } (R) \text{ in N/mm}^2 = \frac{WL}{20\,bd^2}$$

where W = central breaking load in N.

L = length of span in mm, b and d are average width and depth of mid sec. of test piece.

Average of the wet and dry tests should be taken.

(3) **Tensile Strength.** The ultimate stress in tension is called the tensile strength of the material. Ultimate stress is the greatest stress which can be produced in a body before rupture occurs. Ultimate stress is the stress on an unit area.

Test Pieces. Three test pieces should be drilled from the rock in form of cylinders. The dia. of the test piece should not be less than 50 mm and dia. : height ratio should be 1 : 2. Prepare test pieces as in case of comp. tests.

Procedure. Put test pieces between steel plates (25 mm width, 10 m thick and length equal to the length of test piece. The movable portion of spherical seated compression plate should be held on spherical seat. Load is applied continuously at a uniform rate. Record max. load when specimen splits. Take average of saturated and dry specimen as in previous cases.

$$\text{Tensile strength} = \frac{0{\cdot}2 \times \text{applied load in N}}{\text{perimeter} \times \text{length of specimen}} = \frac{W}{\pi dl} = S$$

where d is dia, l = length of specimen and S = tensile strength.

(4) **Shear Strength.** Shear is the stress which tends to keep two adjoined plans of a body from sliding one on the other under the influence of two equal and parallel forces acting in opposite directions and forces causing shear are known as shear forces.

Test pieces. Prepare test pieces with the help of saws from the sample collected. Chiesel should not be used, grinding, polishing wheels and abrasive powder is to be used in making the surface smooth. Centre section test piece should be 0·2 mm. Mark load bearing surfaces and direction of rift, dry and a saturated specimen as usual.

For determining shear strength use Dutton Punching shear device.

Beam of testing machine should be kept floating during the test. Take average of three pieces.

Shear strength $(s) = \frac{w_t - w_i}{\pi DT}$ where w_t = total max. load in N indicated by the machine

w_i = Initial load in kg required to bring plunger in contact with the surface of the specimen.

D = dia of plunger

T = Thickness of the test piece in mm.

(5) **Toughness Test.** Toughness is the ability to withstand high stress together with great deformation. Toughness is an index of the ability of material to withstand impact without complete fracture.

Test piece. Test pieces are cut from the rock sample with core drills. It should not be chipped or broken by hammer. Grind test piece by carborundum or emery on a cast iron top with water. The size of cylinders is 25 mm long and 25 mm in dia. The ends of the cylinders should be made plane surfaces, right angle to the axis of cylinders.

Procedure. Cylinder is held without rigid lateral support in the anvil of toughness testing machine. The upper surface of the cylinder should be under the plunger and tangential to the spherical end of the plunger at its lowest point.

A hammer weighing 2 kg should be used with a free fall at 1 cm for the 1st below, 2 cm for 2nd below and an increase of 1 cm fall for each succeeding below until the failure of test occurs.

Three tests should be performed, one perp. other parallel to the plane of structural weakness of the stone, 3rd should be performed on test piece drilled at random.

The toughness will be the height of below at failure. If planes of structural weakness is apparent, average of the three test pieces should be taken.

(6) **Durability Test.** Durability is measured in terms of change of wt. when subjected to repeated change in its environment.

Test pieces. These are three in number, 50 mm cube or 50 mm dia. cylinder with 50 mm height.

Procedure. Take a wt. of w_1 of dried and cooled test piece. Suspend it in super saturated solution of sodium decahydrate at 20 to 30°C for 16 to 18 hours. Dry it in air for 1/2 an hour then in oven at 105 ± 5°C for 4 hours cool it at 20° to 30°C (room temp.). Repeat this cycle 30 times. After completion of 30 cycles, cool test piece to room temp. and wash it. Test piece should be free from sodium sulphate solution. The reaction of the wash water should be tested with $BaCl_2$. Change in weight due to disintegration should be noted by weighing the test piece after every 5 cycles. Cracks development or spelling should be examined during test.

Change in wt. $= \frac{w_1 - w_2}{w_1} \times 100$ percent where

w_1 = original wt. of test piece

w_2 = wt. of test piece after 30 cycles

Durability should be expressed in percentage as change in the wt. Average of three results should be taken as durability value.

If edges show curvilinear structure at the end of test, means stone is weak.

(7) **Specific Gravity Test.** The terms Density and Specific gravity are synonymous in engineering work.

Test Sample. About 0·5 kg of stone from sample is collected, washed and crushed to a max. of 3 mm size particles between hardened steel surfaces. Mix it properly and reduce to 50 gm sample by the method of quartering grind such that it should pass through an I.S. sieve of 150 micron. Remove magnetic material by a magnet if any.

The procedure of finding the true specific gravity of stone is as below:

Take 50 gm sample powder in weight.

Take a dry specific gravity bottle with stopper (properly cleaned) at a temperature of 105 to 110°C and cool it in a desicator to the room temperature 20° to 30°C, weigh it, say it is w_1.

Fill the bottle with the sample powder and again close the stopper and weigh it say it is w_2.

Fill the bottle with distilled water full and close it by the stopper. Now say its weight is w_3. Boil the distilled water at a temperature of 105° to 110°C for 10 minutes and then cool it to room temperature.

Remove the sample powder from bottle and fill 3/4th with distilled water full and close it with the stopper and weight, say it is w_4.

$$\text{True specific gravity} = \frac{w_2 - w_1}{(w_4 - w_2) - (w_3 - w_2)}$$

where w_1 = wt. of empty specific gravity bottle with stopper

w_2 = wt. of bottle with stopper and powder

w_3 = wt. of bottle with stopper, powder and distilled water

w_4 = wt. of bottle with stopper and distilled water.

(8) **Weathering Test.** In the absence of detailed information about the rock it becomes necessary to test its quality before use. For this effect of weather is necessary to be known. Take three test piece of the rock in a cylindrical form of 50 mm dia and 50 mm in height. The edges is rounded to the radius of 3 mm app. and smooth its surface.

Procedure. Take wt. of dried and cooled specimen (w_1), submerge test piece in water at 20°C to 30°C for 24 hours. Totally sink in water and let it be freely suspended. Take wt. in water (w_2). Remove specimen and wipe surface with damp cloth. Take weight (w_3).

Take glass, porcelain or glazed stone ware flat dish of 9 cm in dia. and 1·5 cm in depth. Take 25 ml of water add 2 gm gypsum powder, keep test piece in it and place in open oven for 5 hours. The temperature should be constant at 105° ± 2°C. Remove dish from oven and cool to 25° ± 5°C. This completes the 1st cycle. Add 25 ml water and repeat same process for 30 times.

At the end of 30th cycle, clean test pieces with stiff fibre brush to remove gypsum particles on the surface. Immerse each specimen in water for 24 hours, dry its surface and take wt. (w_4) then in water (w_5) as described earlier. Determine increase or change in absorption by the formula given below :

$$A_1 = \frac{w_3 - w_1}{w_1} \times 100$$

$$V_1 = \frac{w_3 - w_2}{d}$$

$$A_2 = \frac{w_4 - w_1}{w_1} \times 100$$

$$V_2 = \frac{w_4 - w_5}{d}$$

$$\text{So increase in absorption} = \frac{A_2 - A_1}{A_1} \times 100 \text{ percent}$$

Increase in vol. = $\frac{V_2 - V_1}{V_1} \times 100$ percent where

A_1 = original absorption of the test piece in percentage by wt. during 24 hours immersion in water

A_2 = final absorption in percentage by wt. after 30th cycle.

V_1 = vol. of test piece after immersion.

V_2 = final vol. of test piece after 30th cycle.

d = density of water at the temperature of observations

w_1 = wt. of dried test piece before immersion

w_2 = wt. of test piece in water

w_3 = wt. of saturate test piece after immersion

w_4 = final wt. of test piece after immersion (30th cycle)

w_5 = find wt. of test piece in water after 30th cycle.

Defects in Stones

(1) **Vents.** They are small fissures in the stone which makes it liable to decompose.

(2) **Sand and clay holes.** They are holes or cracks in stone which are filled with loose sandy or clayey materials. The loose materials decompose when subjected to weathering action.

(3) **Mottle.** When some chalky substances are present in the stone, it presents spoiled appearance and such stone are unsuitable for use in face work.

(4) **Shakes.** They are very fine cracks in the stone and filled up with calcite which form hard veins of dark colour. This gives unpleasant appearance to the stone surface.

(5) **Shelly bars.** These are small shell or fossils present in stone. When their amount is excessive the stone is liable to decay and hence the use of such stones should be avoided.

Table 6·1. Compressive Strength of Stones

Name of building stone	*Comp. strength in N/mm²*
Igneous origin	
Granite	75 to 135
Synite	90 to 150
Dionite	90 to 150
Basalt	150 to 190
Sedimentary origin	
Sand stone	6·5 to 0
Laterite	1·8 to 3·2
Shale	0·2 to 0·6
Metamorphic origin	
Gneiss	220 to 375
Slate	75 to 216
Lime stone (marble)	60 to 150

Seasoning of Stone. Practically all freshly quarried stone contains a certain amount of moisture known as quarry sap. Hence all works like dressing and moulding of stone etc. is done when the stone is freshly quarried. After dressing or moulding of stone it is stored in a shed without walls, so as to have an open circulation of air. It should be protected from direct rays of sun and rain.

Table 6·2. Stone Beams : Load in kg for 10 cm wide granite

Thickness	*Clear span in metres*								
cm	*0·3*	*0·6*	*0·9*	*1·2*	*1·5*	*1·8*	*2·1*	*2·4*	*3·0*
2·5	18	9	—	—	—	—	—	—	—
5·0	75	36	23	18	—	—	—	—	—
7·5	162	81	54	36	31	—	—	—	—
10·0	288	144	90	72	54	45	36	—	—
12·5	450	223	144	108	90	72	63	—	—
15·0	648	324	216	162	126	108	90	72	5·4
18·0	882	441	288	216	171	144	117	108	81
20·0	1152	576	378	288	225	189	162	135	108
25·0	1800	900	594	450	351	280	252	216	171
30·0	2592	1296	864	648	504	432	360	315	252

Note : (1) Wt. of the beam is 2700 kg/m^3 and factor of safety is 10.

(2) For distributed loads total load will be double.

(3) For slate the loads can be taken as 3 times, for sand stone 1/2 times and for marble the same as above.

6·2(*b*) Bricks. Standard size of brick is $9'' \times 4\frac{3}{8}'' \times 2\frac{3}{4}''$ (23 × 11 × 7 cm) or Indian Standard modular is 19 cm × 9 cm × 7 cm). Its approximate wt. is 8 lbs or 3·6 kg. Classification of bricks is as under :

Class of bricks	*Crushing strength N/mm^2*	*Water absorption %*
1st class	7·00 to 10·5	Not more than 10%
2nd class	5·0 to 7·0	Not more than 20%
3rd class	3·5 to 5·0	Not more than 25%

1st Class Bricks. Well burnt to give an uniform deep red colour having straight and sharp edges (parallel and perp.). It must give a metallic ringing sound when two bricks are struck together. When newly broken it must give an uniform compact structure, free from cracks or flaws.

The surface should not produce any scratch with finger nails. It should not absorb about 1/6th water more than its own wt. when soaked for 10 hours. Its surface should not be too smooth in order to have a proper bond with mortar. It should not break if dropped from a height of 2·1 metre on its end face on ground. Its strength in comp. is 35 kg/cm^2 (min : IS). When it is soaked in cold water a slight efflorescence is caused and its compressive strength reduces by 25%. It is used in all important works, walls of buildings and hydraulic structures. Before use they must be soaked in water for about one hour. When used with lime or cement mortar. For mud mortar they are not soaked with water.

2nd Class Bricks. Hard, well burnt, rough or spotted on surface. It absorbs about 1/4th of water by its own wt. when soaked for about 10 hours. They are used in works of moderate type and in compound walls. Efflorescence ceases when the bricks became saturated in water.

3rd Class Bricks. Yellow in colour, having dull sound when two bricks are struck together, absorbs about 20% of water by wt. when immersed for 10 hours in cold water. They are used in unimportant and temporary works such as huts for labour and false brick work where required.

Over burnt. Over burnt, pinkish in colour, distorted in shape and is sufficient hard. They are used in foundations, rolling and edging of roads and for road ballast.

Clay for bricks. A good earth should be domat or clay mixed with sand. The earth should be free form alkalies (reh) as it provides efflorescence, however a slight percentage is desirable as it gives plasticity to the clay. Excess of alkalies also give white salts in bricks when they are exposed to damp climate. It should be composed of silica 60%, Alumina 20%, Calcium, Iron, manganese, magnesium, sodium, potasium and other substances 20%. Silica helps to check shrinkage, cracking and warping of the bricks but excess of it will make the brick brittle. Clay or alumina makes the earth plastic and hard. Lime about 5% and oxide of iron help as a flux in binding the particles together. Oxide gives the red colour to the brick, but excess of it will turn the brick in bluish colour. Manganese makes the brick yellowish. It must be free from all pebbles of grit. It must weigh about 112 lbs/cft. (1760 kg/m^3). The presence of lime in the earth can be detected by pouring a little of acid on it. Production of efflorescence is an indication of the presence of excess lime. Presence of iron pyrites, salts, pebbles, kankar, modulus and organic matter is harmfull to brick earth.

Field Tests for Brick Clay. If unburnt, dry bricks crack on surface which shows excess of plasticity and mixing a little of sand is required, while if the unburnt bricks are brittle they give an indication of excess of silica and mixing of clay is required, otherwise they will be burnt as jhama. A white tint over the partial dry clay shows the presence of salts and alkalies.

1st class bricks soak about 20%, 2nd class 22% and 3rd class 25% of water by its wt. when soaked for 24 hrs.

Qualities of good bricks

(1) Regularity of form
(2) Uniformity in size, colour and texture
(3) Soundness
(4) Hardness
(5) Strength
(6) Less asbsorption
(7) Resistance to weather
(8) Fine resistance.

Laboratory Tests—(1) Compressive strength (2) Water absorption (3) Efflorescence.

Compressive Strength tests. Take a sharp edge regular brick, soak it in water for 24 hours at room temperature. The brick is taken out from water and any water should be drained. The frog should be filled with mortar 1 : 1 cement and sand of max. 3 mm size. The brick should be packed with damp jute bag which is immersed in water for three days. The bricks are then placed with flat faces horizontal and mortar filled face facing upward between two, three plywood sheets each of 3 mm thickness and centred to the testing machine. Axial load is applied at a uniform rate of 14N/mm^2 per min. till failure occurs. The load at failure is the max. load at which specimen fails.

$$\text{Compressive strength the brick in N/mm}^2 = \frac{\text{Max. load at failure N}}{\text{Average area of the bed face in mm}^2}.$$

Average of 5 bricks should be taken.

Elastic Properties of Bricks. Strain at fracture lies around 10^{-3} Young's modulus ranges $3{\cdot}5 \times 10^4$ kg/cm^2 to $3{\cdot}5 \times 10^4$ kg/cm^2 from low strength to high strength bricks.

The linear expansion of brick should not be more than 0·02%.

The bricks are burnt upto a temperature of 1060 to 1120°C.

Fire bricks. They are moulded from fire or refractory clay burnt to a high temperature in special kilns. They are yellowish white in colour. Fire bricks are used in furnace lining, boilers and chimney flues, where they are subject to intense heat. They do not defuse upto temperature of about 1600°C. Their crushing strength is 125 kg/cm^2 and weighs about 2400 kg/m^3. They absorb water only upto an extent of 5 to 10 percent. Fire clay is nearly pure hydrated silicate of alumina. The greater the percentage of alumina the more refractory the clay will be. The presence of lime or oxide of iron is practically nil subject to max. of 5%. The colour of fire clay is generally grey and a bit greasy to touch.

Fire bricks are laid in mortar of fine clay and not with cement or lime. Their joints are very thin. About 75 kg (0·06 m^3) of fine clay produces 100 nos. of bricks. The bricks are only dipped in the thin paste of the fire clay mortar so as to have a thin joint. Fire clay is found under the seams of coal in coal fields of Raniganj and Raj Mahal (Bihar). It has the following composition.

Silica 56 to 90% ; Alumina 25 to 36% ; Iron Oxide 2 to 5% ; Lime, magnesia, potash and soda 1 to 2%.

Terracota. When stone coverage are difficult and costlier, moulded terracota are prepared in the shape in which they are required by hardware burning agencies. They are soft glazed which gives hard compact and impervious surface. Terracota is prepared from fine clay mixed with crushed pottery and is burnt to a high temperature.

Glazing. Surfaces of earthen ware, stone ware, bricks and tiles etc are glazed to improve their appearance and to make them water proof to protect them from the action of sewage and acidic atmosphere. Salt glazing and enamelling are the two methods of glazing.

Salt Glazing. It is done by throwing common salt in the kiln at the close of burning operation. At the high temperature of about 1300°C the salt vaporises. The vapours act over the expose surface giving a glossy finish and imparts a brownish colour.

Enamelling. This process increases the appearance of the article as well as improves its durability and makes it impervious. Borax, Kaolin, Chalt and colouring agents are mixed together and is fused with all or part of filspar, flint and lead oxide. The resulting molten mass is poured into water to give shattered frit. The frit is then ground with the remaining materials and water to a thick cream known as slip.

Burnt earthen ware known as biscuits are dipped in the slip. It absorbs water being porous and forms a thin layer of glaze. The earthen ware is then dried and again is heated to a lower temperature so as to fuse the glaze.

Glazed Earthenware Tiles. I.S. sizes are 99 × 99 mm and 148·5 × 148·5 mm size. Thickness being 6·5, 8·0 or 9·5 mm.

Porcelain. It is made of Kaoline (China clay) mixed with high proportion of fluxes such as bone ash for bone china and felspar for hard porcelains. It is used in pottery and in electric insulators etc.

Fly ash-Lime bricks. Fly ash is a waste generated from thermal power stations. Good quality, high strength bricks can be produced from fly ash using lime as a binder and sand as inert filler. In some cases chemical is added as an accelerator unlike burnt clay solid bricks fly ash. Sand lime bricks are cured not burnt. The consumption of mortars and plasters have been found to be substantially less than those for burnt clay bricks. The followings are the advantages :

(1) It results in saving of fuel.

(2) Lighter than ordinary burnt clay bricks resulting saving in transport and dead load in design.

Fly ash bricks. There are two type of bricks prepared from fly ash.

(1) Non calcinite bricks—Fly ash is mixed with bonding agent.

(2) Non calcinite bricks—Fly ash clay brick.

(1) **Non Calcinite bricks.** Several combinations are made for example one is 70% fly ash and 20% river sand/bottom ash/pulverised slag as an aggregate with upto 12% sod. silicate (water glass) solution as a binding agent (3% by wt. on a dry basis). The mix is dry pressed and air dried. This can use any type of fly ash and it has been adopted for commercialization.

Calcinite bricks. The process of manufacturer is similar to that of normal clay bricks, except that a certain amount of fly ash is mixed in the clay before moulding the bricks. About 20-29% of sieved fly ash by wt. is mixed with local soil and wetted for 24 hours. The homogeneous plastic material so obtained is used for the moulding of bricks. They are then dried under sun and then burnt in Bull's kiln at a temperature ranging to 950°-1020°C. These bricks have strength 75 kg/cm^2 to 200 kg/cm^2 and water absorption below 16% (IS : 5454-1969). It has also a saving in coal during burning 3 ton to 7 ton for one lack bricks. About 20% lime, 3% gypsum, and suitable foaming agent (aluminium powder) can also be mixed for better results.

Tests for different percentage of fly ash to soils gave (1) comp. strength (2) water absorption (3) efflorescence and (4) volumetric shrinkage in produced bricks. Some results are as below :

Fly ash-lime bricks	Compressive strength	16 to 25 N/mm^2
	Water absorption	5 to 10% by wt.
	Density	1·6 gm/cm^3
Fly ash, lime, sand brick	Density	1·2 to 2·0 gm/cm^3.

Essential requirements as per IS 12894 : 1990

(1) **General Requirements.** Visually the bricks shall be sound compact and uniform in shape. The bricks shall be free from visible cracks. Warpage and organic matter. The bricks shall be solid with or without frog 10 to 20 mm deep on one of its flat side. The bricks shall have smooth rectangular faces with sharp and square corners.

(2) **Dimensions and Tolerances :**

Table 6·3

	L (mm)	W (mm)	H (mm)
Modular size	*a* 190	90	90
	b 190	90	40
Non modular size	*a* 230	110	70
	b 230	110	30

Tolerances length ± 3 mm Breadth, Height ± 2 mm

(3) **Classification.** The fly ash-lime bricks shall be of the following four classes depending upon their average compressive strength.

Class	*Average compressive*	*Strength N/mm^2*
	(Not less than)	*(Less than)*
7·5	7·5	10·0
10	10·0	15·0
15	15·0	20·0
20	20·0	—

(4) **Compressive Strength.** The min. average compressive strength of fly ash-lime bricks shall not be less than the one specified for each class in 6·1 when tested as described in IS 3495 (Part 1) : 1976. The compressive strength of any individual bricks shall not fall below the min. average compressive strength specified for the corresponding class of bricks by more than 20%.

(5) **Drying Shrinkage.** The average drying shrinkage of the bricks when tested by the method described in IS : 41399 : 1989, being the average of three units shall not exceed 0·15%.

(6) **Efflorescence Test.** The bricks when tested according with the procedure laid down in IS : 3495 (Part 3) : 1976 shall have the rating of efflorescence not more than "moderate" upto class 10 and 'slight' for higher classes.

(7) **Water Absorption.** The bricks when tested in accordance with the procedure laid down in IS 3485 (Part 2) : 1076, after immersion in cold water for 24 hours, shall have average water absorption not more than 20% by mass upto class 10 and 15% by mass for higher classes.

Table 6·4. Comparative Features of Flyash-Lime-Bricks and Burnt Clay Bricks

Features/Property	*Fly ash-lime bricks*	*Burnt clay bricks*
1. Comp. Strength	70-175 kg/cm^2	35-125 kg/cm^2
2. Water absorption	13-15%	20% for bricks of compressive strength less than 125 kg/cm^2
3. Limit weight	3-3·2 kg	3·5-4 kg
4. Bulk density	1500-1550 kg/m^3	1600 kg/m^3
5. Durability	Good	Good
6. Efflorescence	Slight	Slight to moderate
7. Coefficient of variation in compressive strength	5-10%	5-15%
8. Fire resistance	Good	Good
9. Shape	Uniform	Non-uniform
10. Fuel consumption (coal)	66 kg % Nos.	200 kg/00 nos.
11. Cement consumption in 1 : 6 cement mortar per m^3 of mass	40-45 kg (for modular size)	62·5 kg
12. Environmental effect	Waste utilisation reduction in pollution of land water and air	Erosion of top soil, atmospheric pollution

Efflorescence in bricks—Causes and Remedial measures :

Main causes in brick efflorescence in buildings :

(1) Existence of salts near buildings

(2) Collection of salt earth in vicinity

(3) Disposal of waste in manure work shops

(4) Use of sea sand in mortar

(5) Presence of stagnant water nearby

(6) Use of salty bricks in construction

(7) Collection of water in structive parts due to wrong design

Remedial measures :

(1) Removal of salts from brick face by wire brushes. This process can be repeated if required. Washing with water is also useful.

(2) Provision of damp-proof courses as dampness is its main cause.

(3) Gypsum plastering over coal tar painting after cleaning the surface by wire brushes including removing of old plaster.

(4) Fixing precasted cement panels over wood frames to have an access to air. These panels are tarcoaled from in side.

(5) Use of over burnt bricks in foundations upto D.P.C. as they are less porous.

(6) Too rich mortar should be avoided as it cracks in sun causing entrance for dampness.

Test for afflorescence bricks. 5 Nos. of bricks are kept in water in a tray upto 1·5 to 3 cm on their short edges in a dry atmosphere. Dry these bricks after soaking water in air. Repeat this process again. Now inspect the salt traces over the surface of bricks.

Bricks containing mag. sulphate more than 0·05% should be rejected as it is a main cause of efflorescence soluble salts of sulphates and chlorides should also be not more than 0·1%.

$$\text{Water absorption in bricks by wt.} = \frac{w_2 - w_1}{w_1} \times 100 \text{ percent}$$

where w_1 is the wt. of dry brick and w_2 is the wt. of saturated brick for 24 hours in water.

Use of peddy waste (husk or bhusi of rice) in brick making

5 to 10% grinded bhusi is mixed in the moulding soil before burning which gives the following results.

(1) 20-25% saving in fuel for burning.

(2) Lesser weight of bricks (15 to 20% lighter than ordinary clay bricks)

(3) Pressure power 70 and 150 kg/cm^2

(4) water absorption 12-18%

(5) Sp. gravity 1·2 to 1·6 gm/cm^2

(6) Calorific value 2800 to 3000 kilo calories/kg which is half to that of coal.

6·3. Lime

Fat lime. Stone lime, white lime, quick lime. It is produced by burning (calcination) of lime stone ($CaCO_3$), the effect of which is to drive off the carbonic acid and moisture it contains. Chemically it is oxide of calcium (CaO). It is in the form of white limps. Fresh quick lime weighs about 1050 kg/m^3. When in a bit combination of mag. oxide and slacks with water, it is known as quick lime.

Slacked lime. (Hydrated lime) When water is poured over quick lime, it absorbs it and cracks to a white powder with a hissing sound, with an evolution of heat and steam. This process is known as slacking.

$$\begin{array}{ccccc} CaO & + & H_2O & = & Ca(OH)_2 \\ \text{quick time} & + & \text{water} & = & \text{slacked lime} \end{array}$$

The volume is increased three to four times. Its weight is about 640 kg/m^3 when fresh. It increases in weight as the time passes on hardening.

Chalk. When quick lime is left for open moist air it absorbs moisture and CO_2 and converts in white inert mass known as chalk, which has no cementing properties. Therefore quick lime is stored in closed stones like cement and should be used as early as possible.

Hydraulic Lime. When kankar or clay mixed lime stone is burnt (calcined) hydraulic lime is produced. It sets in water in 7 to 30 days. It is classified as eminently hydraulic, moderately hydraulic or feebly hydraulic according to its setting time under water.

(*A*) **Eminently Hydraulic Lime.** Used in structures min. compressive strength is 17·5 kg/cm^2 after 14 days.

(*B*) **Moderately Hydraulic or Semi Hydraulic.** Used as mortar for masonry having crushing strength 28·0 kg/cm^2 after 28 days.

(*C*) **Fat Lime.** Used as plastering, white washing in masonry with a certain admixture of surkhi or any other pozzalonic material to produce artificial hydraulic mortar.

Its crushing strength is 12·5 kg/cm^2 after 14 days and 17·5 kg/cm^2 after 28 days.

Class *A* is supplied in hydrated form while *B* and *C* are supplied as quick lime and hydraulic lime.

Hydraulic lime sets under water and hence is used in hydraulic works. It also shrinks less than fat lime. Mixing a small portion of sand improves its quality it is ground to powder and sieved in a mesh of 3·35 mm. Hydraulic lime is slacked before use and not at the time of burning. Excess of water is injurious and hardens it even before use.

Kankar lime should be grinded dry after burning as if it is not grinded it deteriorates rapidly. Lime is grinded in grinding machines.

Table 6·5. Chemical Composition of Building Lime (IS : 712—1964)

Sl. No.	*Constituents*	*Percentage requirements for*				
		Class A	*Class B*		*Class C*	
			quick lime	*hydrated lime*	*quick lime*	*hydrated lime*
1.	Cal. and Mag. oxide (*a*) Min.	60	70	70	85	85
	(*b*) Max.	70	—	—	—	—
2.	Silica Alumina and ferric oxide (min.)	25	15	15	—	—
3.	Insoluble residue in HCl less than silica (max.)	2	3	2	—	—
4.	Insoluble matter in sodium carbonate (max.)	5	5	5	5	5
5.	Loss on ignition (max.)	—	(*a*) 5 for lump lime (*b*) 7 for ground lime		(*a*) 5 for lump lime (*b*) 7 for ground lime	
6.	Carbon dioxide (max.)	5	5	5	5	—

Note : Cementation value $= \dfrac{2{\cdot}8A + 1{\cdot}1B + 0{\cdot}7C}{1{\cdot}0D + 1{\cdot}4\,E}$

A = percentage of silica content by wt.

B = percentage of Alumina oxide by wt.

C = percentage of Ferric oxide by wt.

D = percentage of Calcium oxide by wt.

E = percentage of Magnesium oxide by wt.

Other Materials. (1) Clinker : It is waste from furnaces and resembles burnt coal and is used in light concrete.

(2) **Furnace Slag.** It is blast furnace waste and is used as an aggregate by breaking.

(3) **Coak breaze.** It is obtained from gas works and coke ovens. It is light in weight and porous and is used in light wt. concrete.

(4) **Breaze.** It is general form of furnace ash.

(5) **Lime Punning.** Lime mortar mixed with chopped (cut jute) as 4 kg/m^3 of mortar. •

Test for Strength of a Lime Mortar Joint. Two bricks are laid cross wise with mortar under test (12 mm thick). Bricks should be well soaked in water. After seven days of its joining, the load required to separate them gives its adhesive strength, which should be 1·4 kg/cm^2 for one : two, lime : sand mortar. The ultimate strength in tension of hydraulic should be 7 kg/cm^2 and of fat lime 2·8 kg/cm^2 with 1 : 3 lime sand mortar and its compressive strength should be 4 to 5 times the tensile strength.

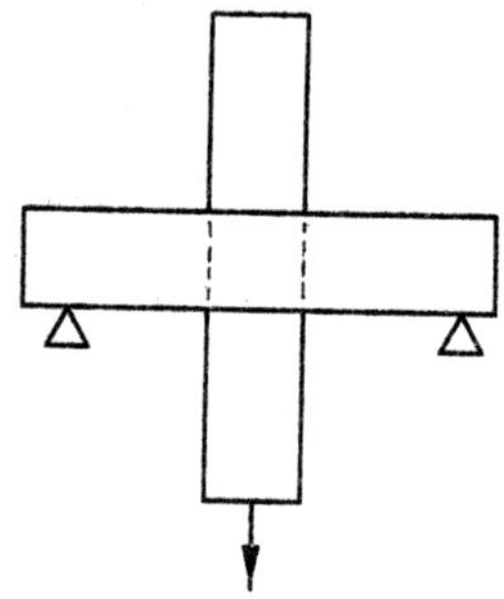

Fig. 6·2.

6·4. Timber

Timber trees—(1) **Babool.** Thorney tree with small leaves. It is not found in big bols. The wood is closed grained and tough and of a pale red colour used for bodies of carts, wheels, ploughs, tent pegs, tool handles, chaukhats and lintels for cheap buildings. Also used in well kerbs.

Bamboo. It is an endogenous tree used for sea holdings, thatched roofs, huts and for scafolding work.

Cheer. Found in hills, light and brown in colour, softer and coarse grained. It seasons well. Do not crook on drying. Used for shutters and other inferior work of houses.

Deodar. Found in hills at higher altitudes. It has tall straight trunk. It gives a smooth surface after painting. It is light coloured with close well marked grains. It takes a fine polish, easy to work, yet strong and durable. It is used for good building shutters and in railway sleepers.

Kail. It looks like chir or deodar, light in weight, soft and look good when painted. It takes a fine polish. Used in door shutters and furniture etc.

Mango. Found throughout in India. The wood is of an inferior quality yet highly used for building works, furniture and door shutters. It is easily taken by white ants.

Sal. A strong wood of sound colour. Highly used in good buildings as beams, chaukhats and lintels etc. It is highly used in railway sleepers. It is hard and closed grained.

Semal. A weak wood tree having big trunks, brown in colour. Mostly used as casing wood and in match factories.

Siris. A hard wood used as a building material, brown to reddish in colour.

Shisham or Sisso. Widely distributed in India. It is dark brown in colour, used in building works in making door shutters, making furniture. It takes a good polish and plainned good. It is hard and strong. Easily taken by white ants if unseasoned or immatured in white colour. It is also used in railway sleepers and canal regulation planks.

Pipal. A weak tree of yellow colour wood. Used as shutter wood in low cost buildings.

Teak. A strong wood, used as a high class building wood in making shutters and chaukhats and in making furniture. It is plainned well and takes a good fine polish. It is less effected by rots.

Toon. A light wood, takes a fine polish and painted well. Weak in strength. It can be compared with Kail in quality. It has a red colour.

Akhrot. A tall tree found in hills, hard. It takes a beautiful polish and plainned well. It is used as furniture wood.

Gular. A weak tree of yellow colour wood. Used as well Kerb and shutters of low cost houses.

Imli (Tammrind). A hard reddish brown wood tree generally becomes yellow upto its maturity. It is used for coal burning and in small works where strength is needed.

Classification of wood on Strength Basis

(1) **Hard wood.** It has no turpentine or resins. Their fibres are more adhesive and is closer grained. It is heavier, stronger and darker in colour. Being hard difficult to work. Resists shearing used in important works where strength is needed. Sal, Shisham, Teak, Babool, Mahogony and oak etc. are their varieties.

(2) **Soft.** It is light coloured and weight having distinct annual layers. Resinous, chir, deodar, kail, walnut spruce pine are their varieties. It is stronger in tension and have well defined fibrous texture. It is used in door shutters and in railway sleepers. It is also known as **Fir wood.**

Time for falling of timber. Newly fell tree in green stage contains thick elaborated sap which is liable to attack by worms or vegitable growth in stagnant air and moisture. It is therefore considered best to fell timber in mid summer when the rising sap consists of nothing more than water and mineral salts in solution, which can be easily disposed off by seasoning. Falling in spring or autumn should be avoided. The tree should be fell on its maturity. When the **heart wood** (wood of inner part of trunk) attains its maximum strength, but if it is allowed to stand too long decay sets in, which is always started from the heart wood. After felling its bark should be removed.

Seasoning of timber. Timber obtained from a newly fell tree in green stage is full of sap and if it is not expelled by proper seasoning is liable to shrink, warp, rot and develop cracks or shakes after it has been placed in position. The following methods of seasoning (drying) timber are in use.

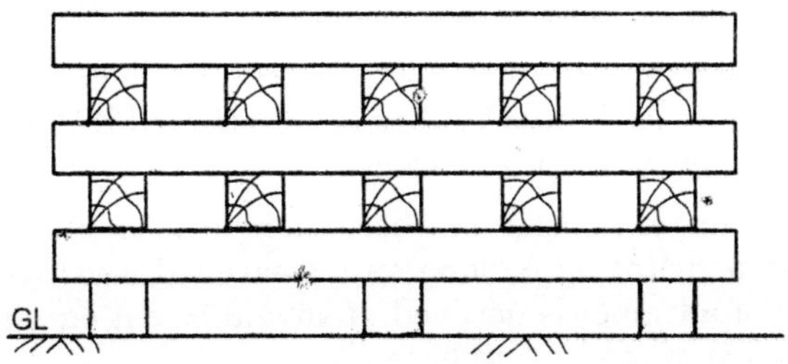

Fig. 6·3

(1) **Natural Seasoning.** After it has been felled, the log roughly squared, should be dried gradually by being stacked on stone or brick supports a little above the ground, with a free space between each log for circulation of air. The drying yard should be well drained, not liable to pass wind and direct rays of sun, perfectly covered. It is best method of seasoning but it takes 2 to 4 years for carpenter or joiners work. While stacked its ends should be protected with some paint or tar.

(2) **Artificial Seasoning**—(*a*) **Water Seasoning.** It consists of immersing the timber in water (preferably running stream) with larger end facing u/s as soon as it is cut. After a fortnight it is taken out and dried in dry air place. The logs should be sink entirely in water, partial immersion being more injurious. This process renders the timber less liable to warp, worm eaten and cracks but it weakens the strength. It is used when the timber is required to use early.

(*b*) **Boiling.** In this process the timber is kept in boiling water or exposed to the action of hot steam for about four hours and is then dried slowly. It impairs the strength and elasticity of timber but reduces its liability to shrinkage.

(*c*) **Desicating or Kiln Seasoning.** The sawn timber is arranged in a chamber of kiln with space for air to circulate. The chamber is artificially heated to about 72°C and air of controlled humidity is blown in for 3 to 12 days to bring down the moisture content to 6%. It is used when seasoning is to be done in large scale.

Table 6·6. Permissible Moisture Content in Timber for Different Uses

Use of Timber	Max. moisture centents percent			
	Zone I	Zone II	Zone III	Zone IV
1. Beams and rafters	12	14	17	20
2. Doors and windows (more than 5 cm thick)	10	12	14	16
3. Doors and windows (less than 5 cm thick)	8	10	12	14
4. Flooring strips for general purpose	8	10	10	12
5. Flooring strips for tea gardens	12	12	14	16
6. Furniture and cabinet work	10	12	14	15
7. Handles	12	12	14	15
8. Pattern making	8	10	12	14

Note : Zone I. Rajasthan, Punjab, M.P., Maharashtra and Gujrat having relative humidity 40 to 50% or less.

Zone II. Kashmir, Himachal, Delhi, U.P., Parts of Gujrat, Maharastra, Andhra and M.P. having relative humidity 40 to 50%.

Zone III. Zones having relative humidity between 50 to 67%.

Zone IV. Zones having relative humidity more than 67%.

$$\text{Percentage moisture} = \left(\frac{w - w_0}{w_0}\right) \times 100$$

where w = wt. of unseasoned wood or original wt. and w_0 = wt. of dry wood.

Decay of Timber. Sources of decay : (*a*) **Fungi.** It is a vegetable growth which develops when the timber has moisture more than 20%. Dry or saturated timber is not effected by fungi. Hair like threads are developed which causes the wood to turn to powder.

(*b*) **Dry rot.** It is caused by confirming the timber in position where there is no circulation of air. It is also produced when charring, taring or painting is done on unseasoned wood. Dry rot convert the wood into powder so when a part of a timber is decayed, it should be cut out and surface protected with paint (when dry) of a solution of copper sulphate.

(*c*) **Wet rot.** It is produced by damp, moisture and the works which are in contact of direct wet weather, even standing tree is effected by wet rot. It is also produced in alternate dry and wet weather conditions. To get rid of wet rot dry timber should be protected by oil paints.

(*d*) **White ants or termite.** It is very injurious to timber and produced in wet or moist air. Some time adjacent to damp parts or in direct contact of rising moisture of earth is effected by it. It turns the timber into white powder.

Preservation of Timber from Decaying. Natural process of preservation consists of seasoning, free circulation of air, protection against moisture, avoiding frequent changes of drying and wetting. However the following protective covers are used. Before using any protective cover the timber should be seasoned perfectly, otherwise the protective coat will close the out side pores, shut up the sap and thereby induce decay. The ends of beams or back face of chaukhats should be preserved with tar coats so that it may not in direct contact of the moisture rising from walls or ground.

(1) **Tarring.** Coal tar (mixed with little of pitch) is applied hot on surfaces which do not need any good appearance.

(2) **Charring.** When some timber is burried in ground charring (smoking) is done to protect against rotting. The timber is quenched with water, when they are charred to a depth of about 1 cm by smoking.

(3) **Creosoting.** The timber is stacked openly in an air tight chamber from which air is evacuated. Creosote oil under a high pressure of about 120 lbs per sq. inch (8 kg/cm^2) at a temperature of 50°C is pumped in as long as timber absorbs it. It protects the timber from rots and white ants. It is used in large works as piles and railway sleepers. Commercial creosote is a dark brown oily liquid obtained from coal tar by distillation at a temperature ranging 350° to 700°F. Coal tar contains about 20 to 30% of creosote in it.

(4) **Painting.** When fine and good surfaces are required oil paints are used as per shade required.

In market ready made timber care chemicals are also available.

(5) **AsCu Treatment.** It is obtained in the form of a powder and consists one part by wt. of $As_2O_5.2H_2O$ (hydrated arsenic pentoxide), three parts $CuSO_4.5H_2O$ (blue vitriol) and 4 parts of $K_2Cr_2O_7$ (pot dichromate).

6 parts of powder by wt. is mixed with 100 parts of water. The solution is applied or sprayed on timber in two coats AsCu treated surfaces can be painted, varnished, polished or waxed as desired. It protects the timber from white ants.

(6) **Orangic Chemicals.** Chemicals like D.D.T. are used as preservatives after desolving it in suitable solvents such as naphtha, kerosene or sprit in cold condition (as they are inflammable). They give clean good surface.

(7) **Fire Resistant Preservatives.** Wood can not be rendered fire proof, but the action of fire can be retarded by use of preservatives. 2 coats of 2% solution of borax or sodium arsenate in a suitable solvent, dilute solution of sodium silicate followed by a cream like paste of slacked lime and finally with a concentrated solution of silicate of soda, solution of amm. diaphosphate, sodium tetraborate or zinc chloride gives a good fire resisting coat.

Note : Contact with hydrated slacked lime with timber is injurious and hence should be avoided.

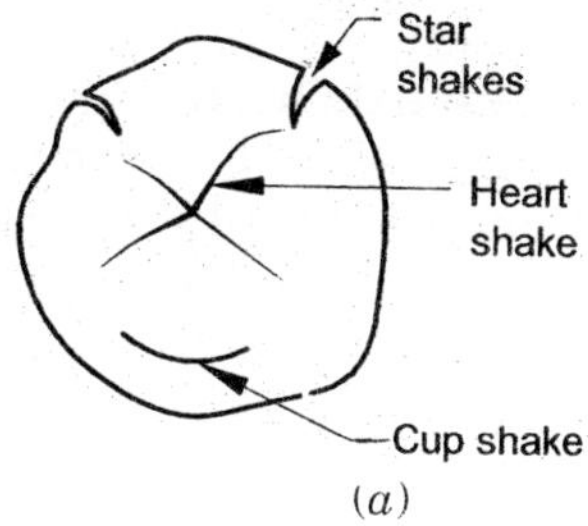

(a)

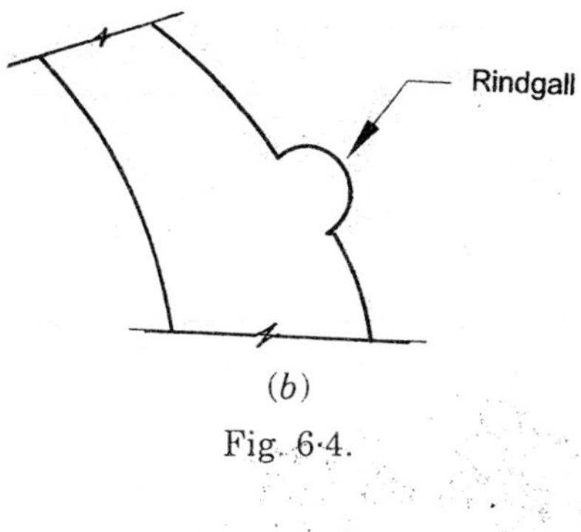

(b)

Fig. 6·4.

Defects in timber. Defects developed during growth of timber :

(1) **Heart shakes.** They are radiated splits from centre through the heart wood.

(2) **Star shakes.** They are radiated and wider towards the outer edge and narrower towards the pitch.

(3) **Cup shakes** or **Ring shake.** They are curved splits and separated from the annual rings.

(4) **Rind galls.** They are healed wounds formed by cutting of branches.

(5) **Upsets.** Defects caused by crushing of wood fibres at places. Twisted fibres are caused by turning of the tree in one direction constantly by wind.

(6) **Knots.** They are old spots of cut branches. By knots continuity of fibres is brocken and the timber is reduced in strength as the knots breaks out or removed even at a small pressure, Large number of knots make a timber unsuitable for work.

(7) **Foxiness.** A yellow or red tinge and dotiness in a specified skin found in some timbers. It is due to over maturity or unsufficient ventilation.

Characteristics of a good timber. It should be obtained from the heart of a sound matured tree from which sap is entirely removed. It must be uniform in colour, close fibred, free from knots, shakes and must have a sweet smell when cut fresh. It must not be wooly nor it should clag the teeth of the saw. A plained surface should have a smooth and bright appearance. Heavy in weight and darker in colour are the qualities of a good strong timber.

General Properties of timber. Its strength is minimum when green, and increases on seasoning to about 20 to 50%. The timber is considered to be seasoned when its weight is reduced by 12%. Timber has a better resistance to load if applied suddenly than applied gradually.

Cut sizes of timber (IS : 1331—1958)

(*a*) **Batten**—A section having max. size 5 cm in either direction.

(*b*) **Plank**—Having max. thickness of 5 cm but width is more than 5 cm.

(*c*) **Scantling**—A section having *x*-sectional dimensions more than 5 cm, but not more than 20 cm in both directions.

(*d*) **Baulks**—Timber having one dimensions more than 5 cm while more than 20 cm in other direction.

Classification of timber :

Class I—Timber having average life of 120 months and over

Class II—Timber having average life of 60 to 120 months

Class III—Timber having average life of 60 months or below.

Grading of Structural Timber (IS : 883—1961)

(1) **Select Grade.** Timbers of this grade should not contain defects. The estimated effect of which tends to reduce the basic strength of timber by more than 12·5%.

(2) **Standard Grade.** Timber of this grade shall not contain defects, the estimated effect of which tends to reduce the basic strength of timber by more than 25%.

(3) **Common Grade.** The timber of this grade shall not contain defects, the estimated effect of which tends to reduce the basic strength of timber by more than 37·5%.

Note : Limited slope of grains in selected grade is 1 in 20 and for common grade 1 in 12 can be allowed. Light timber having a weight less than 75% of the average wt. should not be used for structural purposes.

Table 6·7. Max. Permissible Defects in Standard Grade Timber (IS : 1620—1960)

Width of face mm	*Max. size of knot in mm*		*Max. depth of checks and and shakes of seasoned timber(mm)*	*Max. slope of grain*
	Narrow face 1/4 the width of wide face close to top and bottom edges	*Central half of the width face*		
75	19	14	25	
100	25	25	35	
150	38	38	50	11 in. 15
200	44	50	65	
250	50	57	81	
300	54	75	100	
350	57	81	115	
400	63	87	131	
450	66	93	150	
500	65	100	165	
550	72	103	181	
600	75	106	200	

Note : The defects permissible in select grade can be 50% and in common grade 150% of the above.

Table 6·8. Safe Permissible Stresses for Certain India Timbers

Species	*Average unit wt. at 12% moisture content in kg per cm^2*	*Mod. of Elasticity tonnes/cm^3*	*Permissible stresses in kg/cm^2 for grade I*									*Shear horizontal along grain*		*Durability*
			Bending tension along grain extreme fibre			*Comp. parallel to grain*			*Comp. perp. to grain*					
			I	*O*	W	*I*	*O*	W	*I*	*O*	W			
Khair	1010	134	202	168	134	138	123	100	77	60	49	14	22	High
Shamun	785	148	182	152	124	120	106	88	60	46	38	13	19	Moderate
Red sanders	1105	127	250	209	167	181	161	131	112	91	75	17	24	Moderate
Babool	785	108	182	154	124	112	102	80	65	50	41	15	22	Low
Jamun	850	112	151	126	102	91	84	67	58	45	36	12	17	High
Indian oak	865	125	148	124	98	92	80	66	45	35	29	12	17	Moderate
Sal	865	127	168	140	112	106	94	78	45	35	29	9	13	High
Teak	640	96	140	116	94	88	78	64	40	31	25	10	14	High
Kudal	770	105	130	108	88	88	78	64	36	28	23	9	13	Moderate
Deodar	545	95	102	88	70	78	70	56	26	29	17	7	10	High
Rosewood	755	93	168	140	112	106	92	78	64	50	41	12	17	High
Sissoo	785	89	152	128	102	94	84	66	46	36	29	12	17	Moderate
Mango	690	91	124	102	80	74	66	52	31	24	19	9	14	Moderate
Chir	575	98	84	70	60	64	56	46	22	17	14	6	9	Low
Bunsum	530	86	116	94	78	78	66	56	24	19	15	8	11	Low
Rohini	1155	122	215	179	143	15	134	109	129	101	101	16	23	Moderate

I—Inside location *O*—Outside location *W*—wet location

Factors Effecting Strength of Timber :

(1) **Knots.** Its effect on strength is greater in tension than comp.

(2) **Grain size.** It should be as follows :

(*a*) Common strength ... ... 1 in 10

(*b*) Mod. of elasticity ... ... 1 in 15

(*c*) Mod. of rupture... ... ... 1 in 20

(*d*) Shock resistance ... ... 1 in 25

(3) **Closeness of grains.** Close grained timber is stronger than loose grained, six rings per 2·5 cm may be the minimum in structural timber.

Sap wood. For design purposes no distinction is made between heart and sap wood. While heart wood is more resistant to decay.

Definition of Terms

(1) **Exogeneous Trees.** Trees having annular ring growth as sal, teak, chir etc.

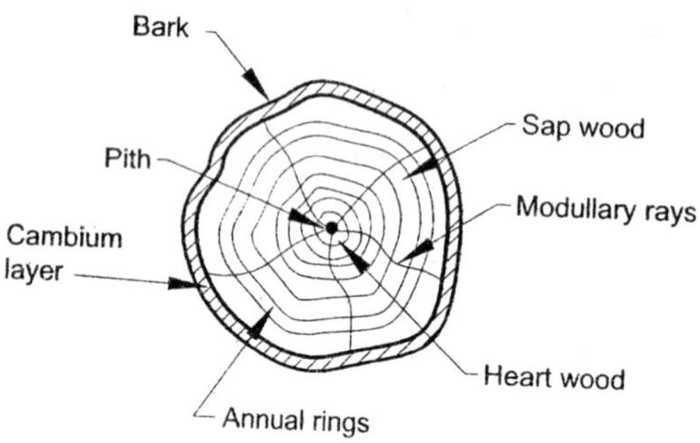

Fig. 6·5.

(2) **Endogeneous.** Having their growth in vertical joints such as bamboo or palm etc.

(3) **Annual rings.** The rings of fibres arranged in concentric circles produced annually in layers.

(4) **Pith.** It is the inner most 1st formed part in a stem of tree.

(5) **Heart wood.** Inner most rings surrounding the pith.

(6) **Sap wood.** Outer rings containing sap and weaker.

(7) **Cambium layer.** Outer most debt ring between the bark and the sap wood.

(8) **Modullary rays.** These are reins radiating from the pith towards bark.

(9) **Bark.** It is outer most protection cover.

(10) **Sap.** A liquidy material.

Vaneering. The layers or slices are cut in continuous thin sheets by revolving the log on lath, with a long sharp knife edge. The log is softened by steaming. They are dried carefully. The vaneers are used when a thin layer of superior wood is glued on an inferior wood. Plywood veneers are glued under pressure in alternate layers of grains (longitudinal and cross wise) to make two ply (2 layers of vaneers). Three ply (three layers of vaneers) and so on in odd numbers. They are available in sizes of 4′ × 8′ or 4′ × 10′.

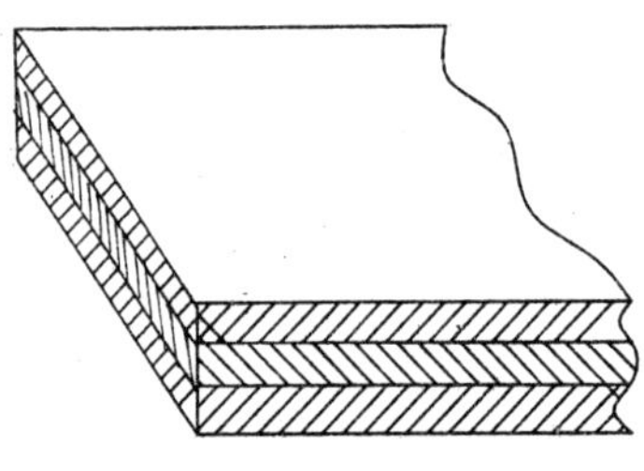

(*a*) Three ply

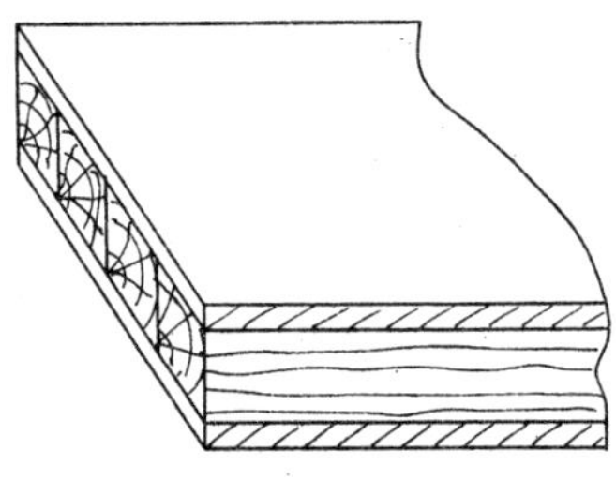

(*b*) laminated board

Fig. 6·6.

Laminated or Batton Board. They are made from vaneers on top and bottom layers with inner core of sawn timber battons of thickness 3/8″ to 2″ glued under pressure.

Fibre Boards. 1/8″ to 1/2″ thick fibre boards are made by pressing hard a heated mass of wood, cane or other vegetable fibres with glue. For light boards straw is used. They have insulating properties and are used in ceilings, dado of walls and partition walls etc.

In market they are sold as hard or straw boards.

Theory of design of timber beams and other sections

1. They are designed to resist B.M. by the formula, $M = fZ$

where M is the B.M. f is the extreme fibre bending stress and Z is the the sec. modulus.

2. The theory is based on the following assumptions :

   (*a*) The sec. plane before bending remain plain after bending.

   (*b*) The stress is within the proportion limit.

   (*c*) Young's modulus is same for tension and compression.

Design of timber sections

Example. Teak wood beam, clear span 5 m, spacing of beams 3 m.

Dead load of span = 3000 N/m^2. Live load = 2000 N/m^2.

Solution.

Dead load on beam = 3000 × 3 = 9000 N/m

Self load (assumed) 500 N/m

Total 9500 N/m (say w_1d)

Live load on beam (say w_2l) = 2000 × 3 = 6000 N/m

Effective span = 5·3 m (bearing assumed as ·30 M

$$\text{Max. B.M. (say } M) = (w_1d + w_2l) \times \frac{l^2}{8}$$

$$= \frac{(9500+6000)(5{\cdot}3)^2\ N\text{-m}}{8} = 54{,}424 \text{ N-m} = 5{,}442{,}400 \text{ N-cm}$$

$$\text{Min width of beam} = \frac{5{\cdot}3 \times 100}{50} = 10{\cdot}6 \text{ cm (being 1/50th of effective span)}$$

Allowable stress for inside location (f) = 13·73 MPa (1 kg/cm^2 = 0·0981 MPa or = 0·1 MPa app.)

$$M = f\frac{bd^2}{6}\ \left(bd^2/6 \text{ being modulus of sec. } z\right);\ M = fz$$

or

$$bd^2 = 6\ M/f = \frac{5{,}442{,}400 \times 6}{13{\cdot}73 \times 100} = 23{,}783 \text{ cm}^3$$

Since depth is not to be more than $3b$.

$$(30)^2 \times b = 23{,}783 \text{ or } b = z^3\sqrt{\frac{23783}{9}} = 13{\cdot}82 \text{ cm (taking } d = 30 \text{ cm)}$$

Use 15 cm wide beam.

$$\text{Depth } d = \sqrt{\frac{23{\cdot}783}{15}} = 39{\cdot}87 \text{ cm, use 40 cm} \times 15 \text{ cm beam.}$$

Dead load per metre : 0·15 × 0·40 × 6278 = 377N.

Hence assumed load w is O.K. (6278 is the density of teak N/cm^2).

Table 6·9. Allowable stresses in wood (1 kg = 9·81 N)

Kind of wood	*Density of 12% moisture*	*Modulus of Elasticity*	*Bending and tension along grain MPa*			*Shear MPa*		*Comp. parallel to grain*			*Comp. perpendicular to grain*		
	N/cm²	*MPa*	*I MPa*	*O MPa*	*w MPa*	*Horizontal in beams*	*Along grain*	*I MPa*	*O MPa*	*w MPa*	*I MPa*	*O MPa*	*w MPa*
Fir	4415	9·22	7·65	6·47	5·49	0·59	0·78	5·89	5·10	4·12	1·57	1·19	0·98
Babool	7701	10·59	17·85	15·11	12·16	1·47	2·16	10·99	10·01	7·85	6·38	4·91	4·02
Deodar	5346	9·32	10·01	8·63	6·87	0·69	0·91	7·65	6·87	5·49	2·55	2·06	1·67
Rose wood	7407	9·12	16·48	13·73	10·99	1·18	1·67	10·40	9·03	7·65	6·28	64·91	4·02
Sissoo	7701	8·73	14·91	12·36	10·01	1·18	1·67	9·22	8·24	6·47	4·51	3·53	2·89
White cedar	7063	10·69	13·15	10·59	8·63	0·98	1·37	7·85	6·87	5·49	2·94	3·34	1·86
Jamun	8339	10·99	14·81	12·36	10·01	1·18	1·67	8·92	8·24	6·57	5·69	4·41	3·53
Walnut	5691	8·43	11·38	9·22	7·65	0·78	1·18	6·47	5·89	4·91	2·26	1·77	1·47
Mango	6769	8·93	12·16	10·01	7·85	0·88	1·37	7·26	6·47	5·10	3·04	2·35	1·86
Kail	5052	9·67	6·47	5·49	4·91	0·59	0·70	5·11	4·51	3·73	1·67	1·28	0·98
Chir	5341	9·61	8·24	6·87	5·89	0·59	0·88	6·28	5·49	9·51	2·16	1·67	1·37
Indian oak	8486	12·26	14·52	12·16	9·61	1·18	1·67	9·03	7·85	6·47	4·41	3·43	2·84
Sal	8486	12·46	16·48	13·73	10·99	0·88	1·28	10·40	9·22	7·65	4·41	3·43	2·84
Rohini	11,331	11·97	21·09	17·56	14·03	1·57	2·26	14·72	13·15	10·69	12·65	9·91	8·04
Teak	6278	9·42	13·73	11·38	9·22	9·83	1·37	8·63	7·65	6·28	3·92	3·04	2·45

Note : *I* = Inside location, *O* = Outside location, *w* = wet location.

Check for Shear

Distribution load w $= 5{\cdot}3\ (w_1d + w_2l) = 5{\cdot}3 \times (9500 + 6000) = 82{,}150\text{N}.$

Max. shear (V) $= \dfrac{w}{l}\left(1-\dfrac{2D}{2}\right) = \dfrac{82{,}150}{2}\left(1-\dfrac{2\times 40}{530}\right) = 34{,}875\ \text{N}$

Shear stress H $= \dfrac{3V}{2bD} = \dfrac{3\times 34{,}875}{2\times 15\times 40} = 87{\cdot}19\ \text{N/cm}^2 < 98$ safe.

Check for deflection

Allowable deflection $= \dfrac{1}{240}\times 530 = 2{\cdot}21$ cm

Total N/m $= 2\,w_1d + \dfrac{3}{4}\,w_2l = 2\times 9500 + \dfrac{3}{4}\times 6000 = 23{,}500$ N/m (say w')

Deflection $= \dfrac{5\,w'\,l^4}{384\,EI} = \dfrac{5\times 23{,}500\times (5{\cdot}3)^4\times (100)^3}{384\times 942\times 1000\times 15\times \dfrac{(40)^3}{12}}$

$= 3{\cdot}2$ Not safe ($2{\cdot}21$ cm is safe)

increase the depth to 45 cm, the deflection $= \dfrac{5\times 2350\times (5{\cdot}3)^4\times (100)^3}{384\times 942\times 1000\times 15\times \dfrac{(45)^3}{12}} = 2{\cdot}1$ cm safe.

Note : At depth 40 cm, the deflection comes to 3·2 cm against safe 2·21 cm, hence the depth is increased to 4·5 cm.

Check for bearing. Max. reaction $= \dfrac{5{\cdot}3}{3}(w_1d + w_2l) = \dfrac{5{\cdot}3}{3}(9500 + 6000) = 41{,}075$ N

Allowable bearing stress = 4 MPa

Bearing length required $= \dfrac{41{,}075}{4\times 150} = 68{\cdot}5$ min. (bearing provided 30/2 = 15 cm is safe)

The final section chosen = 45 cm × 15 cm. **Ans.**

Note : 1 kg = 9·81 Newton N for convenience it is taken 1 kg = 10 N

or 1 N/mm² = 10^6 Pascals = MPa (Mega Pascal)

Example. ***Design of Wood Column.*** *If the teak wood column is 20 cm × 20 cm in size. Determine the safe axial load if the unsupported length is (i) 2 metre (ii) 4 metre (iii) 6 metre.*

Solution. For inside location $f_c||$ = 8·63 MPa

S = unsupported length and d is the least dimension

E = 9420 MPa S/d = Slenderness ratio = K (say)

(*i*) $\dfrac{S}{d} = \dfrac{200}{20} = 10.$ It is a short column

$\because$ allowable load $= A \times f_c|| = 20\times 20\times 8{\cdot}63\times 100 = 345{,}200$ N

(*ii*) $\dfrac{S}{d} = \dfrac{400}{20} = 20 > 11.$ It is not a short column.

$$K = 0{\cdot}702\sqrt{\frac{E}{f_c||}} = 0{\cdot}702\sqrt{\frac{94200}{863}} = 23{\cdot}19$$

The column is intermediate.

Allowable load $= A \times f_c|| \left[1 - \frac{1}{3}\left(\frac{S}{Kd}\right)^4\right] = 20 \times 20 \times 8{\cdot}63 \times 100\left(1 - \frac{1}{3}\left(\frac{20}{23{\cdot}19}\right)^4\right)$

$= 345200 \times 0{\cdot}8156 = 281{,}545$ N

(iii) $\frac{S}{d} = \frac{600}{20} = 30 > 23{\cdot}19$. It is long column.

Allowable load $= A \times \frac{9{\cdot}329\,E}{(S/d)^4} = 20 \times 20 \times 100 = \frac{0{\cdot}329 \times 9420}{(30)^2} = 133{,}741$ N

References : (a) Short column when S/d does not exceed ||

(b) Intermediate column when S/d is between || and K.

(c) Long column when $S/d > K$.

where $K = 0{\cdot}702\sqrt{E/f_c||}$ where E = Young's Modulus.

Permissible load shall be calculated as follows :

(a) For short column $f_c = P/A = f_c||$ where A = sec. area of column and P is total load

(b) For intermediate column $f_c = P/A - f_c|| \left[1 - \frac{1}{3}\left(\frac{S}{Ed}\right)^4\right]$.

(c) For long column $f_c = P/A = \frac{0{\cdot}329\,E}{(S/d)^2}$ where ratio S/d shall not exceed 50.

Note : (1) For circular section it is taken as $d \times d$ square section.

(2) For tapered columns the least dimension is $1^1/_3$ times the small end.

The allowable unit compressive stress at the small end shall not exceed the permissible compressive stress in the direction of grains.

Design of a wood tension member

Net area $A_n = P/f_t$ where A_n is the net area of the wood section; P = tension load and ft is the allowable stress in tension. In case when the load is direct + bending load, the following formula is used $P/(A\,f_t) + M/z \le 1$ where P is the axial tension, A is the X-sec. area, f_t is the allowable tensile stress, M is the bending moment. z is the modulus of section and f_b is allowable stress in bending.

Example. *Design a timber tension member to take a load of 100,000 N. It is connected at the joint by 16 mm bolts. The timber used is fir wood.*

Solution. For inside location $f_t = 7{\cdot}65$ MPa

assuming single piece member $A_n = \frac{100{,}000}{7{\cdot}65} = 13{,}070 \text{ mm}^2$

Gross area app. $= 1{\cdot}25 \times 13{,}070 = 103{\cdot}4 \text{ cm}^2$ (taking area to be 1·25 times)

Diameter of bolt hole $= 16 + 1{\cdot}5 = 17{\cdot}5$ mm

Use 20 cm × 8 cm piece by 2 bolts in a row.

Net area $= 160 - 2 \times \frac{17{\cdot}5}{10} \times 8 = 160 - 28 = 132{\cdot}0 \text{ cm}^2$ (safe)

In above example if nails are used in place of bolts.

Solution. There is no reduction for area when nails are used.

Area required $= \frac{100{,}000}{7{\cdot}65} = 13{,}070 \text{ mm}^2$, use 22 cm × 6 cm piece.

Bolted Joints in Timber

$p = \frac{LD}{P}$ where p = The basic average pressure in timber parallel to the

L = Length of bolt in the central member (equal to the thickness of wood plates)

D = Diameter of the bolt

P = Total load transmitted

$p = K_1 f_c||$ where K_1 is constant given in the table below.

$f_c||$ can be seen in the table 6·9 for the wood used.

L/D is ratio between length and dia. of bolt.

These stresses are for metal plate.

In case timber splice used is of half depth these values of stresses should be multiplied by 0·8.

L/D ratio	1	2	3	4	5	6	7	8	9	10	11	12	13	14
K_1	1·00	1·02	1·00	0·97	0·88	0·76	0·65	0·57	0·51	0·46	0·41	0·38	0·34	0·30

The thickness of metal splice plate is given by the following formula.

$$t = \frac{P}{n\, f_s\left[d - h_n(D + 0{\cdot}15)\right] \times 100} \quad \text{where}$$

t = thickness of plate in cm P = load in N

n = number of plates f_s = Allowable working stress of metal MPa

d = depth of main member in cm h_n = Number of holes at critical section.

D = dia. of bolt in cm.

Example. *Find max. load that a splice can take as given in Fig. The splice plates are 6 cm × 20 cm and the main tension member is 12 cm × 20 cm. The wood used is Fir and number of bolts on each side of the splice is 6 of 20 mm dia.*

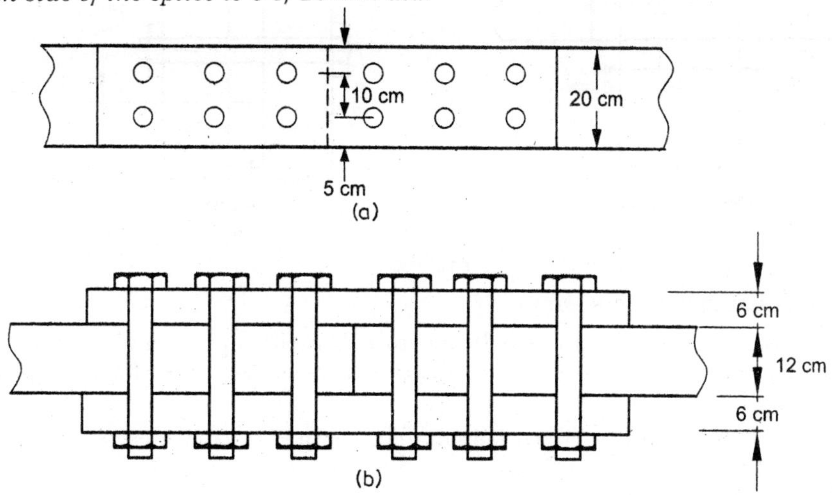

Fig. 6·7.

Solution. From table 6·9 for inside location $f_c|| = 5{\cdot}89$ MPa

$$L/D = \frac{12}{2} = 6. \text{ From Table for } L/D = 6\ K_1 \text{ is } 0{\cdot}76$$

Allowable bearing stress = 0·8 × 0·76 × 5·89 = 3·58 MPa (Being wood splice stress is taken as 0·8).

Allowable load on joint = 6 × 2 × 12 × 3·58 × 100 = 51,552 N

The bolt hole = 20 + 1·5 mm (hole dia. is larger by 1·5 mm than the dia. of bolt)
= 21·5 mm = 2·15 cm.

Net area = (20 – 2 × 2·15) × 12 = 188·4 cm^2 (area of two bolts of the weakest section is to be deducted)

Total bearing area of the bolts = 6 × 2 × 12 = 144 cm^2

0·8 × 144 = 115·2 so net area = 184·4 > 115·2 (safe)

f_t = allowable tensile stress = 7·65 MPa

Tensile force = 7·65 × 100 × 188·4 = 144,126 N

The splice can carry 51,550 N.

Table 6·11. Values of K_2 for values of L/D ratios

L/D ratio	1	2	3	4	5	6	7	8	9	10	11	12	13
K_2	1	1	1	1	1	1	1	0·96	0·86	0·76	0·60	0·61	0·55

Values of K_3 for different dia. of bolts

Dia.	6	10	12	14	16	18	20	22	24	27	30	33	35	39	42	50	75 and over
K_3	2·50	1·75	1·68	1·60	1·52	1·41	1·37	1·33	1·27	1·23	1·19	1·16	1·14	1·12	1·10	1·33	1

Stress to right angle to grain

The distance between the bolts should be

(*a*) c/c spacing 4 times dia. of bolt. In case metal splice plates are used, spacing required should be based on space to tighten the nuts.

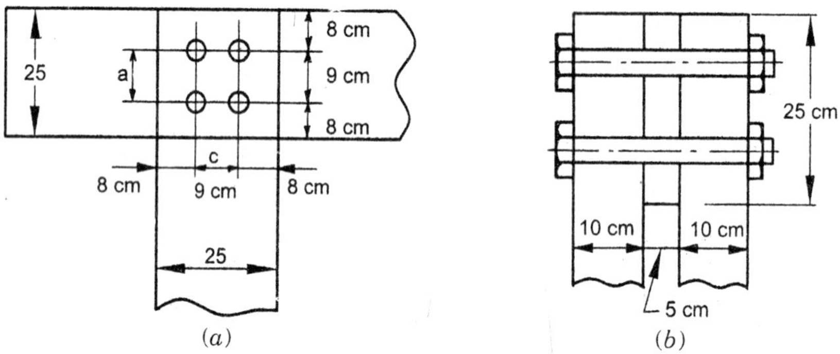

Fig. 6·8.

(*b*) no end distance in this joint.

(*c*) row spacing, min. 2½ times bolt dia. to *L/D* ratios upto 2 and 5 times bolt dia. for *L/D* ratios of 6 or greater. For further ratio of *L/D* intermediate values for row spacing may be used.

(*d*) edge distance, min. 4 times bolt dia. In comp. the edge distance would be at the opposite edge from that as shown in figure.

Note : The allowable bearing stress in the direction perpendicular to the grain is not reduced, if timber cover plates half the thickness of main members are used.

Allowable stress = $K_2 \,.\, K_3 \; f_{c}\perp$

Example. A joint consists of centre member 10 cm in thickness, bolted at right angles by two 5 cm thick pieces. The timber used is fir wood and number of bolts used are 4 and 20 mm dia. The joint is to be used in dry inside location. Find the safe load of joint and depth of timber pieces.

Solution. $f_c\perp = 1{\cdot}57$ MPa (from Table 6·9)

$L/D = 10/2 = 5$; $K_2 = 1$; $K_3 = 1{\cdot}37$

then allowable $q = K_2 \,.\, K_3\, f_c\perp = 1 \times 1{\cdot}37 \times 1{\cdot}57 = 2{\cdot}15$ MPa

Safe load per bolt $= 215 \times 2 \times 10 = 4300$ N

Safe load on joint $= 4 \times 4300 = 17200$ N

Example. A joint consists of centre number 10 cm in thickness bolted at 60° by two 5 cm thick pieces. Timber is fir wood; 4 bolts 20 mm dia. are used, joint is to be used dry inside location. Find safe load of the joint and depth of timber piece.

Solution. $f_c \parallel = 5{\cdot}89$ MPa (from Table 6·9)

$f_c\perp = 1{\cdot}57$ MPa ; $L/D = 10/2 = 5$

$K_1 = 0{\cdot}88$; $K_2 = 1$; $K_3 = 1{\cdot}37$

$P = 0{\cdot}8\, K_1\, f_c \parallel = 0{\cdot}8 \times 0{\cdot}88 \times 5{\cdot}89 = 4{\cdot}15$ MPa

$q = K_2K_3\, f_c\perp = 1 \times 1{\cdot}37 \times 1{\cdot}57 = 2{\cdot}15$ MPa

$$\sin 60° = \frac{\sqrt{3}}{2} \quad \cos 60° = \frac{1}{2}$$

$$f\theta = \frac{pq}{P\sin^2\theta + q\cos^2\theta} = \frac{4{\cdot}15 \times 2{\cdot}15}{4{\cdot}10 \times \frac{3}{4} + 2{\cdot}15 \times \frac{1}{4}} = 2{\cdot}44 \text{ MPa (safe stress)}$$

Safe load per bolt $= 2{\cdot}44 \times 2 \times 10 \times 100 = 4880$ N

Safe load per joint $= 4880 \times 4 = 19{,}520$ N

Inclined members

Safe load per bolt $= 0{\cdot}8\, K_1\, f_c \parallel LD$

$= 0{\cdot}8 \times 0{\cdot}88 \times 5{\cdot}89 \times 100 \times 10 \times 2 = 8293$ N

Safe load per member $= 8293 \times 4 = 33{,}172$ N

$0{\cdot}8 \times$ Bearing area of bolts $= (0{\cdot}8 \times 4 \times 10 \times 2) = 64$ cm²

Net area of member $= (15{\cdot}2 \times 2{\cdot}15) \times 10$

$= 11{\cdot}7 \times 10 = 117$ cm² > 64 (safe)

Use two pieces 15 cm × 5 cm.

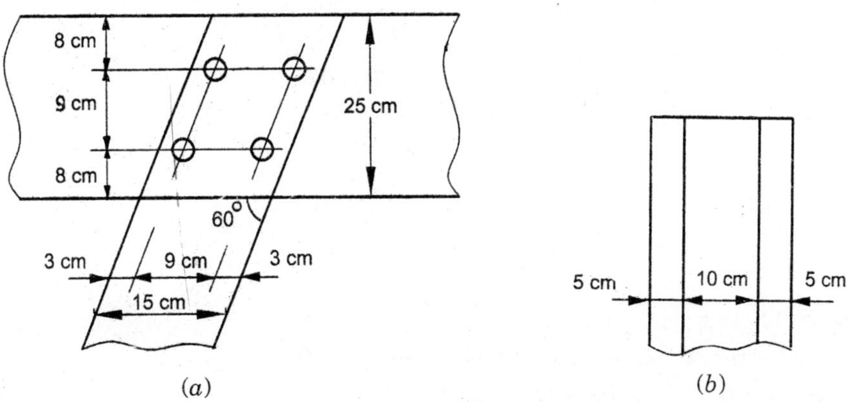

Fig. 6·9.

Nail Joints :

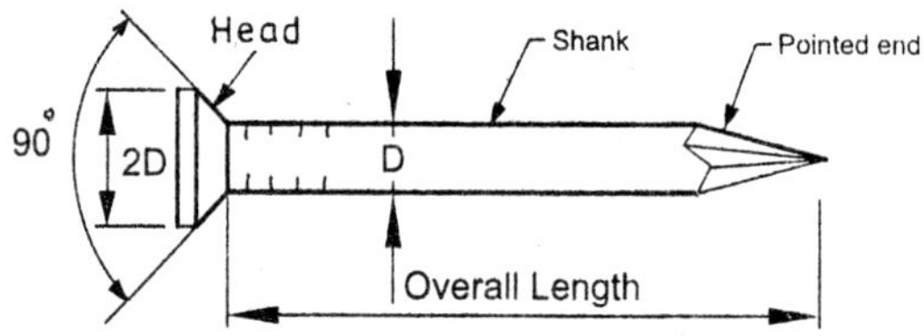

Fig. 6·10.

Table 6·12. Nails

Size of nails in mm	*Dia. of shank mm*	*Dia. of head in mm*	*Length in mm*						*Pre bore hard wood*	*Pre bore soft wood*
(*A*) 10·00, 8·00, 6·30, 5·60,	10·00	20·00						250	—	—
5·00, 4·50 & 4·00	8·00	16·00					225	200	—	—
mm dia. of shank	6·30	12·50					175	150	—	—
(*B*) 3·55, 3·15, 2·80 & 2·50	5·60	1·20					150	125	—	—
mm dia. of shank	5·00	10·00					125	100	4·00	3·55
	4·50	9·00					200	90	3·55	3·15
(*C*) 2·24, 2·00, 1·80, & 1·66	4·00	8·00					90	80	3·15	2·80
mm dia. of shank	3·55	8·00			90	80	70	60	3·80	2·50
	3·15	7·10				70	60	50	2·50	2·24
(*D*) 1·40 and 1·25 mm	2·80	6·20				70	60	50	2·24	2·00
shank dia.	2·50	5·60		70	60	50	45	40	2·00	1·80
Length 2 to 25 cm	2·24	5·60	70	60	50	45	40	35	1·80	1·60
	2·00	5·00	50	45	40	35	30	25	1·60	1·40
Wire nails—wire	1·80	4·50					30	25	—	—
nails are made of	1·60	4·00					25	20	—	—
mild steel	1·40	3·80						20	—	—
	1·24	3·40						20	—	—

Example. A board of teak is 1 metre long and 15 cm wide and 2 cm thick. It is nailed to end supports 6 cm deep, which are made of the same material, if the nails are driven perpendicular to the grain of the supports and if a uniformly distributed load w of 1000 N acts in such a way that it tends to pull the board from the supports. How many 2·24 mm 6 cm long nails should be driven into each end. Check the sec. for bending.

Solution. $$\text{B.M.} = \frac{Wl}{8} = \frac{1000 \times 1000}{8} = 125000 \text{ N-cm}$$

$$Z = \frac{15 \times 2^2}{6} = 10 \text{ cm}^3 = 10{,}000 \text{ mm}^3$$

$$f = \frac{M}{Z} = \frac{125{,}000}{10{,}000} = 12{\cdot}50 \text{ MPa (safe)}$$

Allowable stress for teak inside location is 13·23 MPa

Withdrawal force $= \dfrac{1000}{2} = 500$ N

Sp. gravity of teak = 0·64

Withdrawal strength on one nail = $954 \times (0{\cdot}64)^{2{\cdot}5} \times 0{\cdot}224$

Per cm penetration = 70 N/cm

Length of nail = 6 cm

Penetration in support = 6 – 2 = 4 cm

Withdrawal strength of one nail = 70 × 4 = 280 N

No. of nails required $= \frac{500}{280} = 1{\cdot}79$ or 2 nails required.

6·5. Ferrous metals

Cast Iron. It is an alloy of carbon and iron with or without other elements. Carbon content varies from 1·7 to 4·5%. A line of demarcation is generally drawn between cast iron and steel at 2% of carbon.

The heavy percentage of carbon in cast iron makes it brittle, non malleable and non ductile metal. It can not be forged at any temperature or tempered, rolled, drawn under a hammer or easily welded, but it can be hardened by heating and dipping in cold water. Cast iron cannot be punched or rivetted like steel but it can be easily melted and cast into various shapes and machined. Its melting point is about 1100°C. Have a good resistance to corrosion than other ferrous metals and rusts slowly, but corrodes in sea water. It is classified as under.

(1) **Grey cast iron.** It is strongest variety of cast iron containing free carbon or graphite. It is softer and tougher than white cast iron and can be easily machined. It is used in pipes, cylinders, machine leds and frames etc. It can be distinguished from white cast iron by dropping nitric acid on a clean fractured surface, a black stain is formed on grey cast iron while a brown on white cast iron. It has a dark appearance.

(2) **White cast iron.** It is very hard and brittle and is unsuitable for general castings. Carbon occurs in carbide form. The colour is light.

(3) **Malleable cast iron.** It is anealed white cast iron from which some of the carbon is extracted by heating. It is stronger, less brittle and non malleable and ductile than ordinary cast iron. It is softer and tougher than grey variety and can be bent cold, forged and welded, more resistant to corrosion. It is used in castings such as levers, door fastenings, hinges, pipe fitting, hardware and agricultural implements.

(4) **Chilled cast iron.** It is obtained by melting grey iron and pouring it into cold metallic moulds, causing hard outer surface.

Field test for cast iron. A bar 2·5 cm^2 in section on supports which are 30 cm apart should resist a load of 1 tonne, placed centrally on it, or a load of 200 kg placed centrally on a span of 1·5 m.

Wrought iron. It is purest form of iron containing carbon less than 0·15 percent. It possess important qualities of toughness, ductility and malleability. It can be easily welded at a temperature of 900°C by a hammer but not by fusion as its melting point is about 1500°C. It becomes soft and plastic at red heat and could be easily forged at about 900°C. It can be bent or twisted when either hot or cold. It cannot be casted. It can be hardened by quenching or tempering (sudden cooling). It can be easily threaded in machines. It is used in making spikes, nails, bolts and nuts, wires, chains, horse shoe bars, sheets and plates, ornamental gates, straps for trusses and pipes etc.

Field test. A wrought iron bar should elongate 20% of its length at the time of rupture under a slowly applied tensile breaking stress and fail under a gradually increasing stress of not less than $3t/cm^2$. Rivets and bolt bars should stand bending double when cold without cracking. Bars of over 5 cm dia. should be capable of bending double when cold without cracking to a curve of which the inner radius is twice the thickness of the piece tested the better the iron the more it can bent.

Steel. In steel carbon content is limited to 1·7 percent. A general classification of steel according to carbon content is as follows :

Mild soft steel	Carbon upto 0·23 percent
Med. carbon steel	Carbon upto 0·25 to 0·70 percent
High carbon steel	Carbon upto 0·70 to 1·25 percent
Extra hard or very high carbon steel	Carbon over 1·25 percent.

For rolling thin sheets soft malleable steel is required. For drawing into wires a very soft and ductile steel is required. For making tools a very hard and brittle steel is required. Increase of carbon percentage increases the density and hardness with corresponding decrease in ductility and toughness. The tensile strength, hardness, yield point and elastic limit of plain carbon steels increase with the carbon content upto about 1% of carbon. The higher is the percentage of carbon the lower is the melting point which is between 1535°C for pure iron free from carbon, 1130°C for 18% carbon steel. Steel with carbon less than 0·1% is soft steel. Carbon in structural steel and high tensile steel is not more than 0·30% and in rivet bars not more than 0·25%.

Mild steel. Mild steel contains 0·2 to 0·5% of carbon. It is ductile and elastic. It can be easily forged, cut machined, punched or drilled, welded or rolled. It cannot be hardened or tempered and so cannot be used in making cutting tools. It is highly ductile enables the material to be bent when cold. It elongates to about 25 to 30% of its length before it breaks. It is used in structural steel such as joists, channels, angles, bolts, rivets and sheets etc.

Spring steel. It is high or medium carbon, plain steel or alloyed. Steel is heated upto 760°-780°C, quenched in oil or water. Tempered if required.

Heat treatment of steel. (1) **Hardening.** It is the process of increasing hardness of metal by suitable treatment involving heating and cooling steel is heated upto 950°C to 1000°C according to the thickness of the section and its carbon content and is then quenched.

(2) **Quenching.** It is a process in which the metal is cooled rapidly from a high temperature by soaking in water, brine solution or air. Water and brine solution gives a rapid cooling rate, oil a medium and air is a slow cooling process.

(3) **Tempering.** A hardened steel unless tempered is too hard and brittle for almost all practical purposes. Tempering is softening by reheating of hardened (quenched) steel to a temperature below its critical (light red heat) temperature range (600°C to 650°C) and subsequent cooling in air or quenching in oil or water. Tempering imparts ductility, improves toughness, reduces brittleness and modifies hardness. Slow and uniform heating is essential. Usually reheating is done upto a temperature of 400°C. Tempering in the range of 400°C to 700°C is known as **Drawing.**

Annealing. It is reverse of hardening or can be said as softening or hardness removing. Heating is done slightly above the critical temperature (light red heat) and then allowed to cool slowly. This treatment rids the material of internal stresses set up by uneven cooling or by rolling, forging or by usage which results in the loss of ductility and make the metal brittle. Annealing reduces ultimate strength but increases the ductility and brings back the steel to best physical state to resist fracture under sudden stresses.

Surface hardening. It is effected by heating the surface rapidly with a blow pipe and then quenching it by spraying water and thus rendering the surface hard.

Cold working. Bending and rolling etc. done in cold steel. This improves the physical properties of steel and its strength.

Alloy steel. When metals which have no carbon is mixed with steel.

Definition of Terms

Blow holes—Gas cavities in castings.

Brittleness—Nature of breaking to pieces under impact load.

Creep—Slow stretching or plastic deformation under steady load.

Critical temperature—Melting temperature.

Ductility—It is the property of a metal of being permanently extended or structured by a tensile force, before it fractures.

Hardness—The resistance of a metal to penetration, abrasion or wear. Hardness on Mobs scale : Talk (1), Gypsum (2), Calcite (3), Flour spar (4), Apatitus (5), Feldspar (6) Quartz (7) Topaz (8), Corundum (9), Diamond (10). Diamond being the hardest.

Hard drawn—It is the temper produced in a wire, rod or tube by cold drawing.

High tensile steel—Steel having enhanced mechanical properties and increased resistance to corrosion by the incorporation of some alloying elements.

Ingots—Castings of uniform sizes made of molten steel for subsequent rolling, forging or processing.

Forging—Moulding of a hot piece of metal in different shapes by hammering.

Pickling—Removing scales from steel by immersion in diluted acid bath.

Processing—Another name for annealing.

Rolling—Castings or ingots are passed through rolling machines to shape them into different sections such as bars, *I, L* or *T* sections etc.

Stiffness—It is ability of a material to resist deformation. It it a measure of the modulus of elasticity. The higher the modulus the stiffer the metal.

Tenacity—It is property of a material to resist a tensile force without giving way.

Toughness—It is the resistance of a material to fracture by bending, twisting, fatigue or impact of load opposite to brittleness. The greater the hardness the less will be the toughness. Toughening a material by tempering or annealing decreases tensile strenght and hardness. Toughness enables a material to undergo larger deformation at high stress. Deflection of a test piece under load gives an idea of the toughness of a material.

Field tests for Structural Steel

(1) **Cold bend test for bars.** The specimen is folded double either by pressure or blows by hammer untill two sides became parallel. In the case of bars above 2·5 cm in dia. or thickness, the internal dia. is not greater than 3 times of the dia. or the thickness of the bar. In case of bars 2·5 cm or under in dia. or thickness, the internal dia. of the bend is not greater than twice its dia. or thickness. The specimen should with stand without fracture.

Cold bend test for hard drawn wires. One end of the test piece is firmly gripped in the vice and the free end shall be bent round a radius equal to the dia. of the wire through an angle of 90° and then bent back in the opposite direction round the same radius through an angle of 180°, there after being bent back again through an angle of 90° to come to the original position. The specimen should be withstand without fracture in the above treatment.

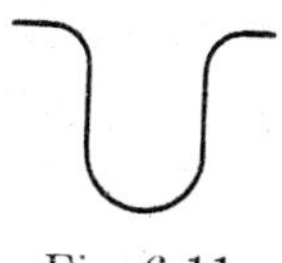

Fig. 6·11.

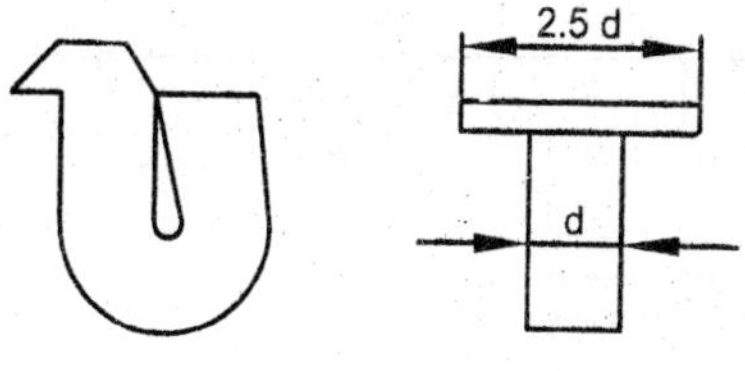

(*a*) (*b*)

Fig. 6·12.

Cold bent test for rivets. The rivet shank shall be capable of being bent cold back on itself and hammered till the two parts of the shank touch without fracture on the outside of the bend. The rivet head shall be capable of being flattened at red heat to a uniform thickness without cracking at the edges until its dia. is 2½ times the dia. of the shank short lengths of rivet bars equal to twice their dia. when cold shall withstand without fracture being compressed to half their length.

Cold bent test for mild steel sheets

Black sheets—Strips of 18 B.G. steel with stand bending through 180° flat on itself without fracture. Whole of the strip of sheet over 16 B.G. shall withstand bending through 180° with an inclined radius equal to 1½ times the thickness of the sheet without fracture.

Galvanised sheets—(1) Sheets of 2·5 cm width shall withstand bending round a rod of dia. 15 times the thickness of the metal without flaking or peeling of zinc coating.

(2) **Doubling test**—as in case of black sheets.

(3) (IS : 227—1951) **Test for galvanised sheets**—(*i*) Test pieces of 230 mm × 75 mm × 100 mm shall be cut both along and across the direction of rolling. Bend test piece shall be selected at the rate of one set of two for every 500 sheets or part thereof.

The specimen of sheets shall withstand bending through 180° around a mandrel having a dia. equal to the thickness of the number of pieces of the same thickness as specified in the table below without pealing or flaking of zinc coating.

Table 6·13.

Zinc coating gm/m²	*Thickness of sheets (mm)*					*Remarks*
	1·6	1·25	1·0	0·8	0·63	
750	10	10	11	12	14	Dia. of mandrel expressed as the number of times the thickness of sheets.
600	8	8	9	10	11	
450	6	6	7	8	8	
375	4	4	5	6	5	

(*ii*) **Temper bend test**—The specimen should be heated in blood red colour and then quenched in water at a temperature not exceeding 80°F. The colour shall be judged in doors in the shade. The test piece shall then withstand without fracture being doubled over either by pressure or by blows from a hammer until the internal dia. is not greater than 3 times the thickness of the test sample and the sides are parallel.

Tensile test—A specially prepared test piece is stretched by a gradually increasing load applied in opposite directions at its ends until the test piece breaks. The tougher the steel the more force will be needed to break it.

Compression test—It is made in a machine which exerts pressure of a compressive nature until the steel gives way and will not recover.

6·14. Properties of cast iron, wrought iron and steel

S. No.	*Property*	*Cast iron*	*Wrought iron*	*Steel*	
				Low or med. mild steel	*High carbon or Hard steel*
1.	Carbon content	2 to 4·5%	0 to 0·25%	0·5 to 0·6%	0·6 to 1·7%
2.	Melting point	1200°C	1500°C	1400°C	1300°C
3.	Sp. gravity	7·25	7·70	7·80	7·90
4.	Ultimate comp. strength t/cm²	7·0	2·0	4·75	12·0 to 25
5.	Ultimate tensile strength t/cm²	1·5	3·75	5·5	8 to 11

Table Contd...

Table Contd...

S. No.	*Property*	*Cast iron*	*Wrought iron*	*Steel*	
				Low or med. mild steel	*High carbon or Hard steel*
6.	Hardness tempering and hardening	very hard, can be hardened by healing and sudden cooling	Tough and more elastic than CI can not be hardened or tempered	Tough and more elastic than WI can be hardened or tempered difficulty	Tougher and more elastic than ms. Can be hardened and tempered easily
7.	Ductility and malleability	Non ductile and malleable (Brittle)	Highly ductile and malleable	Mod. ductile and melleable	Low ductile or malleable
8.	Welding, forging or rolling property	Cannot be welded or rolled into sheets	Can be easily forged, welded and rolled	Can be easily forged, rolled and welded	Can not be easily welded forged or rolled
9.	Stock absorption	Incapable of shock absorption shocks	Can not absorb sudden excessive shocks	Capable of absorption of shocks	Capable of absorption of shocks
10.	Corrosion	Does not rust easily	Rust more rapidly than C.I.	Rusts readily	Rusts readily
11.	Effect of salt water	Becomes soft	Works better than C.I.	Not effected	Not effected
12.	Magnetic property	Can not be magnetised	Can be magnetised temporrily	Can be magnetised permanently	Can be magnetised permanently

Strength of wrought iron—A W.I. bar should elongate 20% of its length at the time of rupture under a slowly applied tensile breaking stress and fail under a gradually increasing stress of not less than 3·5 tonnes per cm^2. Rivet and bolt bars should stand bending double when cold without cracking. Bars over 5 cm in dia. should be capable of bending double when cold without cracking to a curve of which the inner radius is twice the thickness of the piece tested. The better is the iron the more it will bend.

Joining two parts of ferrous or other non-ferrous metals

(1) **Soldering**—Joining of metals by addition of molten filler (solder) metal of different composition at temperature well below the melting point of the metals to be jointed. The melting point of the solder must be lower than that of the metals to be jointed. The temperature is raised by oxy-acetylene flame.

(2) **Brazing**—It is more or less soldering, only the filler material is spatter which is harder and fuses at a high temperature but below the temperature of the metals to be joined.

Flux—In soldering or brazing the function of flux is to desolve the oxides formed during the operation of welding. No single flux is suitable for all metals and alloys. Common fluxes given below.

Iron or steel—Borax, Ammonium chloride.

Stainless steel—Zinc chloride and hydrochloric acid equally.

Galvanised steel—Hydrochloric acid.

Zinc—Zinc chloride, hydrochloric acid, Amm. Phosphate.

Lead—Tallow, Resin.

Copper brass or gun metal—Amm. Chloride, Zinc Chloride, HCl.

Tin—Amm. Phosphate.

Tinned Iron—Resin, Hydrochloric acid.

Lead and Tin pipes—Resin and sweet oil ; Lead and Brass pipes ...Tallow, Resin.

Note : Borax is applied as a paste with brush to the surface for small articles and as a powder to large articles.

Resin is applied by a brush in a solution of resin in methylated sprit.

Table 6·15. Electrodes used in reinforcing bars

Bar size dia in mm	6	10	20	32·40
Electrode size in mm	2	2·5	3	5

Max. dia. of electrodes for welding plates and other sections

Less than 5 mm thick	3·2 mm — 10 SWG
5 mm to 8 mm	4 mm — 8 SWG
8 mm to 10 mm	5 mm — 6 SWG
10 mm to 16 mm	6 mm — 4 SWG
16 mm to 25 mm	9 mm
25 mm or over	9 mm

6·6. Non-Ferrous Metals

Alluminium. Bauxite is the ore from which aluminium is obtained. Alumina is obtained by roasting the coarsely granulated bauxite at a sufficient high temperature by which the water is driven off from the bauxite. After this the dry bauxite is ground finely and heated for several hours under pressure. A little sod. hydrate is also added. The solution is diluted and it is agitated and kept for several hours for precipitation of hydrate. This precipitation is separated, washed and calcined at a temperature of about 1000°C, which produces alumina. It contains one percent impurities such as oxides of sodium, iron and silicon.

Properties of aluminium. Pure aluminium is soft, light in weight and ductile. It is alloyed with other metals like, copper, magnesium, silicon and mangnese etc. which increases its tensile strength and hardness, aluminium is highly resistant to corrosion and conductive to heat and electricity. The specific gravity of aluminium is 2·7. Its tensile strength is low *i.e.* about 100 N/mm^2. It has poor resistance to alkalies and common salt solution. Its resistance against corrosion can be improved by anodizing. Its melting point is 600°C. Thermal conductivity is 0·52 cal/sq. cm/cm/degree c/sec. and coefficient of thermal expansion is about 0·0000125/degree F.

Uses of aluminium. It is used in window frames, wire rods, made of aluminium are most common. Corrugated aluminium sheets for roofing are also used. Aluminium powder is made by powdering aluminium foil into flats of extreme fineness. This powder has a bright silver colour and is used as a pigment in aluminium paints. It is used as a protective cover on steel structures. It is widely used in electric transmission wires in place of copper.

Aluminium alloys. It is alloyed with copper, zinc, silicon and manganese etc. These alloys have better strength and hardness.

Copper. It is obtained from its ore "*copper pyrite*" by crushing and pulverising in ball mills, concentration by forth floatation process. Roasting in excess of air on the hearth of a reverberatory furnace then smelting in blast furnace with little coke and sand. The molten metal is directly run into Bessemer convertor. The blister copper contain about 98% copper. The remaining 2% impurities consisting iron, nickle, zinc, silver and lead etc. is removed by plane electro refining process.

Properties of copper. It is light, tough, strong, durable and malleable metal with good properties of resistance to corrosion in dry air. It can be forged, rolled or can be worked hot or cold and drawn into wire. It has high thermal and electric conductivity. It can be welded, soldered and rivetted easily.

Its physical properties are :

Colour : Flash to pink	: Sp. Gravity : 8-93 ; Melting point : 1083°C to 2310°C
Thermal conductivity	: 0·92 cal/cm^2/cm per degree C/sec.
Coeff. of thermal expansion	: $16·6 \times 10^{-6}$/°C ; Specific heat : 0·092
Electrical resistivity	: 1·7241 micr ohm/m at 20°C
Mech. properties	: Tensile strength (working) 100N/mm^2, ultimate 300N/mm^2
Hardness Brinell	: 60 ; Elongation percent (5 mm dia.) : 30 to 40%
Modulus of elasticity	: 1·24 to 10^6 N/mm^2 ; Poison's ratio : 0·3

Uses of copper. It is widely used in electric wires and cables, Light gauge copper tubes for hot and cold water supply, gas and sanitation services. It is alloyed with zinc to produce brass, as a protective coating for other metals and is used as Dowels in stone masonry.

Lead. Galena (Pb S) is the chief ore of lead and found associated with sulphates of Ag, Zn, Sb and siliceous impurities. Other lead ore are Carrusite $PbCO_3$ and Angle site Pb SO_4.

Extraction. Powdered ore is concentrated by differential floatation process and roasted in air. When the sulphide is oxidised and mixed with coke and smelted in a blast furnace, crude metal is obtained. This crude metal is heated in a reverberatory furnace in an oxidising atmosphere. Lead so obtained contain traces of precious metal like silver and gold which are removed by Parke's process. In melted metal zinc is added. Zinc floats at the top with noble metals and solidifies. The solid metal is removed and zinc is distilled leaving behind the noble metals. The lead metal at lower layer is purified by electrolyte process.

Properties. It has very poor ductility. Due to high malleability it can be rolled into sheets and foils. It can not be drawn into wires. Lead has good casting properties. It has low tensile strength (10 N/mm^2) low melting point (328°C). It can be used on high temperature. On exposure to air a thin layer of oxide is formed on the surface which protect the metal underneath.

Uses. It is used in storage batteries, cable sheathing, alloy for bearings solder and other building materials.

Zinc. The zinc is obtained from the sulphide ore, zinc, blende, ZnS. It also occurs as carbonate (Calamine) and as silicate. The ore is first converted into oxide by roasting, the sulphide ore or by calcining the carbonate, oxide and coal in equal quantity is heated in fire clay retorts. Zinc oxide is reduced to zinc and vapours are condensed above the melting point. The molten zinc is obtained into moulds and is known as 'spelter' and is of commercial use.

Properties and uses. Zinc is weak and brittle metal. Tensile strength in the cast condition is about 50 N/mm^2 which becomes 3 to 4 times on rolling. Due to its brittleness it is rolled at 100°C to 150°C. Melting point is quite low (419°C). Zinc is readily attacked by acids and alkalies. Being more electropositive than iron, zinc coating protect iron and steel structures from corrosion. It is used in making dee-cashing alloys and alloyed with copper to form brass.

Tin. The ore of tin is casset or tin stone SnO_2. It contains 10% tin. The remaining being impurities like silica, wolfram or iron, tungstile and pyrites of copper, iron and arsenic.

Properties. Tin has a low melting point (232°C) and is poor conductor of heat and electricity. Tin exists in two allotropic modifications. Gray tin which is stable below 18°C and white tin which is stable between 18°C and the melting point. If white tin is cooled below 18°C a transformation to powdery grey tin takes place.

Tin is soft, very malleable and ductile, but possess low tensile strength. It does not corrode or tarnish in the atmosphere but reacts with dil. HCl.

Uses. It is used for tin plating and torne plating. Metal is used in the form of piping for alcoholic liquors and distilled water and as foil for wrapping cigarette, in tooth paste tubes, tin amalgam for mirrors etc. It is an important constituent of many alloys like solder, bronze and gun metal.

Alloys

(1) **Brass.** Brass is an alloy of copper and zinc. It's properties vary with the percentage of its constituents. Common brass contains 65 percent copper and 35 percent zinc. Sometimes a small amount of tin is also mixed.

Brass is ductile and malleable at ordinary temperature and can be rolled into sheets, turned into tubes, drawn into wires or cast into moulds. Brass resists corrosion well.

Uses. Brass is used in utensils of kitchen. In buildings as grills, protection sheets and is used in hardwares. Brass surface open to air becomes dull and hence needs polishing.

(2) **Bronze.** It is an alloy of copper, zinc and tin and contains about 80% copper, phosphor, bronze contains about 1% of phosphorous.

Properties of bronze vary with the content of its different constituents. Mangnese bronze is an alloy (which is usually white) of pure copper with 2 to 30 percent manganese.

Uses. It is largely used in building construction for doors, windows, sash frames, grills, balconies, balustrades etc. and in great variety of ornamental purposes.

(3) **Solder.** It is low melting alloy of tin and lead which are used for soldering.

(*i*) **Soft solder**—(Pb-37 to 67%, Sn-31 to 60%, Sb-0·12 to 2%).

They melt at low temperature and used for soldering electrical connections, for sealing tin cans and for joining lead pipes.

(*ii*) **Silver solders**—(Ag-10 to 80%, Cu-15 to 52%, Zn-4 to 48%). It is used for brazing.

(*iii*) **Brazing alloys**—(Sn-32 to 92%, Cu-2·5%) used for soldering steel joints.

(*iv*) **Tinman's solders**—(Sn-66%, Pb-34%) used for joining articles of tin.

Table 6·16. Brass (Copper and zinc alloy)

	Name	*Cu %*	*Zn %*	*Tin %*	*Uses*
1.	Commercial brass	90	10	—	For hardware, forgings, screws column etc.
2.	Dutch metal	80	20	—	Cheap jewellery, drawing and forming flexible bases.
3.	Cartridge brass	70	30	—	For condenser tube, sheets for cold drawings and pressing purposes.
4.	Muntz metal or yellow brass	60	40	—	For casting, hot scambing, screw, springs chain etc.
	Special brass				
	(*a*) Admiralty brass	70	29	1	Propellers and marine works.
	(*b*) Naval brass	62	23	1	Naval work
	(*c*) Aluminium brass	75	23	2	For condensed tubes and marine works
	(*d*) German silver	50	20	3% Ni	For making utensils table ware, bolts, screws, ornaments, plating and small machine parts
5.	Manganese brass	50-60%	36	3	Bush, pinion, pump, rod, very little effected by salt water
6.	Delta metal	60	37	3 iron	Used in place of mild steel (corrosion resisting property is high)
7.	Ordinary brass	·75	25	—	Door handle, lock, bolt, name plate (can be moulded)

6·7. Bituminous Materials

Bitumen is a non-crystalline solid or viscous material derived from petroleum either by natural or refinery process, soluble in carbon-di-sulphide. It is black or brown in colour. They may occur naturally, but are usually made as end products from distillation or as extract from selected petroleum oils. It also occurs in conjuncture with mineral deposite in the form of lake asphalt. Bitumen minerals can be classified as follows :

(1) Asphalt (2) Tar (3) Cut back (4) Emulsion

(1) **Asphalt**—It is a natural or artificial mixture in which bitumen is associated with inert mineral matter. There are two forms of asphalt.

(*a*) **Natural asphalt**—It is a mixture found in nature associated with inert mineral matter.

(*b*) **Residual asphalt**—It is produced when crude petroleum of an ashphaltic base is distilled.

Natural asphalt is further divided in following two categories.

(*i*) **Lake asphalt** is found in the lakes at Trinidad (West Indies) and Bermudaz (Venezuela) at depths varying from 3 metres to 60 metres in which bitumen content is 40 to 70 percent.

(*ii*) **Rock asphalt.** It is naturally occurring as rock formation, usually lime stone or sand stone ultimately associated throughout its mass with bitumen varying 4 to 20 percent by volume.

Asphalt excluding its inside mineral matter consists of :

(*i*) Asphaltness (*ii*) resins and (*iii*) oil.

Hardness in asphalt is due to asphaltness, cementing properties are due to resins and oil provides viscosity.

(2) **Tar**—Tar is produced by the destruction distillation of organic material such as coal, oil, lignite, peat and wood. It is black to dark brown in colour. It is also a by-product of the manufacture of bituminous coke and is soluble in carbon-di-sulphide. The Indian Institute has divided it in 5 grades RT_1 to RT_5 and its viscosity increases as the tar grade increases. Properties of tar depend upon the following factors :

(*i*) raw materials used for manufacture.

(*ii*) Method of distillation

(*iii*) Proportion as the residual matter incorporated.

Asphalt versus tar

(*i*) Asphalt is obtained by fractional distillation of crude petroleum while tar is produced by destructive distillation of organic matter.

(*ii*) Creosote oil, which is used for wood preservation is obtained from tar.

(*iii*) Asphalt is less adhesive than tar.

(*iv*) Tar needs more setting time but hardens much quickly.

(*v*) Tar can be held as a by-product from steel industries and is cheaper than asphalt.

(*vi*) Tar contains higher percentage of carbon and is used for roofing material and joint filler etc. ductility of tar can be increased by mixing it with sufficient quantity of anthracite oil. Mixture of tar and asphalt hardens slowly.

Cut back. Asphalt mixed with liquid solvent is called as cut-back asphalt. The solvent is the distillate of the petroleum or coaltar. Tar distillates are used as solvent in case of tar. Cut-backs are used in repairing cracks in roofs and floors etc.

The object of cut-back is to soften the heavy product and to convert it into a liquid form so that they can be used without heating or may require a light heating. Cut-back contains 20% solvent and remaining 80% either tar or asphalt.

Emulsion. For cold application asphalt is available in the form of emulsion. Asphalt mixed with 50-60% of water together with 1% emulsifying agent, when water evaporates the emulsion breaks and forms a water proofing layer. High viscous emulsion has less covering power and vice-versa.

Asphaltic cement. Asphaltic cement is produced by blowing air at high temperature (225° to 350°C) through asphalt, where it is oxidized and the resulting material is of a plastic nature and is highly resistant to climate variations. It is used for roofing, flooring and in expansion joints in concrete. Excessive high temperature reduce ductility, lower penetration and cause cracking which results in a less homogeneous product. A penetration of 200 to 300 indicate softest grade whereas a penetration of 30 to 40 indicates highest grade.

An asphaltic "flux" is lake asphalt liquified by the addition of asphaltic base petroleum products.

Mastic asphalt. Asphalt or bitumen heated and mixed with mineral fillers sand and or clippings so as to form a coherent, void less, intermeable mass solid or semi solid under normal temperature conditions, but sufficiently fluid, when brought to a suitable temperature to be spreaded by a hand float.

Mastic asphalt provides a water proof membrane which is durable and since it is laid in a mastic state can be moulded easily to confirm to the shape of its base. It is useful in the construction of flat roofs, floors, paving, damp proof courses end in basements 'Asphalt tiles' for flooring are made of asphalt as an alternative to mastic asphalt laid insitu.

Powdered asphalt. Hard solid asphalt with a penetration of 10 or less are called powdered asphalt. It is used for low cast roads with a fluxing medium such a liquid asphalt.

Plastic Bitumen. It consists of bitumen and thinners and a suitable inert filler such as asbestos fibre or powder. The quantity of inert filler used is 40 to 45 percent. It is used for closing leaks and filling cracks to make them waterproof.

Bitumen felt. These are used for checking dampness to go in. They are available in forms of mats impregnated with bitumen or tar. These are sticked to the walls or floors by using bitumen as a binder.

Tests of bituminous material. The solubility of a bituminous material for structural use are : (for detail refer chapter on 'Roads')

(1) Penetration test (2) Softening point test (3) Ductility test.

(4) Flash and fire test (5) Viscosity test (6) Water cement test.

(1) **Penetration test.** This test determines the hardness of these materials by measuring the depth (in tenth of mm) to which a standard needle will penetrate vertically under specified conditions of standard load, time and temperature. The sample is maintined at the standard temperature of 25°C and total load on needle is 100 gm. This test is not used for soft materials like cut-back.

(2) **Ductility** is expressed as the distance in centimetre to which a standard briquette of bitumen can be stretched before the thread breaks. The test is conducted at 27° ± 5°C and at a rate of pull of 50 ± 2·5 mm per minute. Ductility of a bitumen varies from 5 to 100. A value of 50 is specified for bituminous constructions.

(3) The **Softening** points is the temperature at which the substances attains particular degree of softening under specified condition of test. Ring and ball test usually determines softening point bitumen with higher softening point may be preferred in warmer place.

(4) **Viscosity** defines the fluid properly of bituminous material. A low viscosity provides a uniform film thickness for bending action.

(5) The volatiles in bitumen catch fire causing **flash**. This condition is very hazardous. **Flash point** is the temperature at which flash occurs when a small flame is brought in contact with the vapours of a bituminous product gradually heated under standard conditions. Hence precaustions should be taken while heating any bituminous material to avoid fire. **Fire point** is the lowest temperature at which the material gets ignited and burns under specified conditions.

(6) **Water content test.** It is carried out to test the percentage of water present in emulsion. Emulsion may contain 70 percent water.

6·8. Paints

The constituents of a paint are : (*i*) Base (*ii*) Vehicle (*iii*) Colouring pigments (*iv*) Solvent or thinner (*v*) Drier (*vi*) Inert filler.

(*i*) **Base.** White lead, Zinc white, Red lead, Iron oxide and Tatanium white. Base gives body to the paint and are solids. White lead is cheapest, Red lead is used for steel paints while Zinc white is used in paints for decorative purposes.

(*ii*) **Vehicle.** Linseed oil, Nut oil. It helps to spread the bare over the surface.

(*ii*) **Colouring pigments.** The following colouring pigments are used.

Black—Lamp black, vegetable black, graphite.

Blue—Prussian blue, Indigo, Cobalt blue.

Brown—Raw umber, Burnt umber, Vandy ice brown.

Green—Chrome green, Verdigris.

Red—Carmine, Indian red, Red lead, Venetian red, Vermillion.

Yellow—Chrome yellow, Raw siena, Yellow ochre.

Solvent or thinner—Turpentine.

Drier—Litharge and red lead.

Inert filler—Sand, Cal. carbonate, Gypsum, Talk etc. It increases the quantity.

Preparation—Ground the base and mix it by linseed oil to make a paste. It is then thinned by turpentine to a required state and then drier is mixed. It is preferable to mix the drier before use. Add required quantity of colouring pigment according to the shade desired. If required it can be screened in a fine sieve or cloth.

Painting of wood surfaces

(1) **Knotting.** It is done to fill all the knots and crevices in the wood. While lime (Kharia, geru or red lead) pasted with glue, size (rice marh) or lin seed is used for this purpose.

(2) **Stopping.** The fine cracks in wood are filled with fluidy putty (lime mixed with lin seed oil). The surface is then made uniform by rubbing with sand paper.

(3) **Primary coat or priming.** It consists of red lead, white lead in proportion of 1 : 16 with linseed oil and litharge (Chapra) to the required liquidity of the paste.

(4) **Painting.** Painting is done in two or three coats, 1st coat, subsequent coat and the final coat.

Repainting of wood work. If the old surface of the paint is unsound and blustered, the old point is 1st removed as below :

(1) **Removing by blow lamp** by burning. Care should be taken that the part of the wood may not be injured.

(2) **Paint removers.** Though these are ready made paint removers are available in market yet the following method may be used.

(*a*) wet the surface with naphtha (an inflammable oil) till it becomes soft, rub the surface to make clean by a cloth brush.

(*b*) by caustic soda solution having 1 kg of caustic soda to about 5 litres of water. The solution is rubbed on the surface by a cloth brush tied to the end of a long stick. The surface is then washed with clean water.

(*c*) Dissolve about 1/2 kg of local soda (sajji) with two kg of unslacked lime in hot water so as to form a paste. The painted surface is coated with this paste for about three hours and than the paint is removed by a cloth.

(*d*) For smoky painted surfaces or of kitchans a paste containing 1 kg glue with 60 gm of unslacked lime in 4 kg of water is pasted on the surface and after some time the surface should be washed with soap water.

The surface such cleaned is 1st cleaned with soap water. All greasy spots are removed with a solution of a cuastic soda in water. All cracks and holes are filled with putty. The surface is rubbed with sand paper or pumic stone. The paint is then applied in two or three coats as is required.

Painting of plastered surfaces. (1) A solution of creamy lime (kharia) with size (rice water) or POP is done to have a smooth surface, over which linseed oil is coated to have an impervious surface.

(2) A coat of varnish mixed with turpenline is applied two or three coats as desired.

(3) The surfaces of Plaster of Paris (POP) is smoothened by sand paper if it is too rough. A coat of linseed oil is applied to have an impervious surface on which a final coat of plastic paint is done.

(4) On surfaces containing free alkali (reh), the surface is washed with a solution of zinc sulphate.

Now a days ready made wall paints are available in the market known as 'Snowcem' etc. These are known as *cement paints*. The walls is cured for two or three days after their applications.

Cement paints. Cement paints are prepared by 6 kg of cement preferably white, with 5 litres of double boiled linseed oil 10 to 20% of hydrated lime, 4 to 5% sod. or calcium chloride which helps in curing by retaining moisture.

They are used on plastered walls or on cement concrete surfaces. It resist the moisture to eneter into the wall. They are mixed with silica (sand) before use and are painted with brushes of hair. It must be used on the surface after 4 weeks of the final curing of the surface. The surface is 1st cleaned with water (not with soap) and painted in two coats. 2nd coat is done when 1st is dried. About one litre of mixture paint gives about 2 sq. m. of surface and 1·5 sq. m. of rough surface. Two or three coats should be applied as required. The curing must be started after 24 hours and should be continued for three days. 'Birla White' and JK white are sold in market as a trade products.

Aluminium paints. It is silvery and hence is visible in night. It does not oxide and fade. It is done on iron surfaces. One litre of paint covers about 200 to 250 m^2 of surface. It protects iron from corrosion, sea water and acidic atmosphere.

Antique paints. Base of the antique paint is deco paint spray over which antique paint is applied and then cleaned with water. It gives a granular surface on wood work.

Cellulose paints. They are costly and used in 1st class spray painting on motor cars etc. It has great hardness, smoothness and tolerance to heat.

Clear cole. It is a size coating, applied to fill the cores and cracks on wood work and plaster before painting.

Size. A liquidy substances such as rice size (marh).

Mastic. A pasty substance like glues.

Shallac or lac. It is made from exudation of a kind of insect in some varieties of trees. It is soluble in alcohol and in alkaline water solution.

Painting of iron surfaces. (1) Remove all rust by sand paper and wash with lime or caustic soda to remove any grease on the surface. Primary coat is generally oxide of iron (red oxide) subsequent coats and than final coat is applied. Galvanished steel should be washed with solution of copper sulphate before painting.

Varnishes. Varnish contains following constituents :

(1) **Resin.** Copal is common resin, it is hard shinning, brown or yellowish in colour and found embedded in earth. Other resins are mastic amber, gum mastic and lac.

(2) **Solvent.** It is chosen according to the resin used, linseed oil with copal or amber, turpentine oil for common resin or mastic and methylated sprit for lac, wood naphtha is used for cheap varnishes and not used in superior varnishes due to its offensive smell.

(3) **Driers.** Litharge or lead acetate are common driers which must be used in small quantity to avoid any injury to varnish.

Types of varnishes

(1) **Water varnish.** Lac locally known as 'Lal dana' is dissolved in hot water with borax, ammonia, potash or soda just enough to dissolve the lac. It is used in delicate works as painting of wall papers.

(2) **Oil varnish.** They are prepared by dissolving hard resins like copal or amber in oil or in turnpentine. They are slow to dry and are used in superior works.

(3) **Spirit varnishes.** It is prepared by dissolving shellac in methylated spirit (400 gm of shellac, or chapra in one lit. of spirit) without heating. It may be given a little of colouring pigment. A very little amount of plasticizer such as caster oil is some times added. It is also known as french polish.

Varnishing of wood surfaces. Clean the surface. A coat of brown earth, ochre or geru mixed in glue is done on the surface. Clean the surface with sand paper. 2nd coat containing the staining colour with glue is applied and cleaned with sand paper when dry, one or two coats of the desired varnish is then applied.

Wax polish. Mix equal quantity of bees wax and boiled linseed oil and heat slowly, when the mixture is cool add half of the quantity of turpentine oil to that of linseed oil. The mixture is rubbed on the surface with cotton pad. Rubbing is continued till the desired finish is obtained. Vinegar and turpentine is mixed in equal (quantity with Til oil (mitha Tel)) for oiling wood surfaces.

Enamel. When the base of the paint is ground in varnish or in a viscous boiled oil instead of linseed oil, the resultant product has a harder and glosier film and is known as enamel, which makes the paint more acid or alkali proof. Enamels made from synthetic resins are known as synthetic enamel.

Stains. They are used to change or to modify the grains and texture of the wood surface. The main classes are as under :

(1) **Oil stains**—Turnpentine or benzine is added to an oil pigment which are used to colour the stain.

(2) **Water stain**—It is a solution of aniline dyes in water.

(3) **Spirit stains**—They consist of dye stuffs dissolved in acetone or methylated spirit.

(4) **Chemical stains**—These contain no colouring matter. The colour change occurs by action of chemicals like iron salts, pot and sod. trichromates etc.

Glue. Gum of babool or from waste pieces of skins, horns and hoofs of animals by steeping (saturating) them in water and boiling. Straining and casting the product into cakes which is locally known as **saresh.** While using these cakes are boiled in water to make a paste.

Glaziers putty. It is made of whiting (karia powder or geru) with raw linseed oil or glue.

Colouring of wire gauged doors. Lamp black or green powder colour is mixed in turpentine, kerosene or spirit and is then applied on wire gauzes with a pad of cloth.

Angus Smith's solution. Boiled mixture of slacked lime and tar with small quantity of Tallow, resin and lamp black used in C.I. Pipes coating. Tallow is melted and clearified animal fat.

Directions for Enamel Painting

Enamel can easily be applied by brushing or spraying by a spray gun as follows :

First use sand paper to clean the surface thoroughly to make it free from rust, grease and dirt etc. Old loose and flaking paint must be removed by scraping or by other abrasive means. The surface must be perfectly dry.

Use metal primer red oxide for metal, woodorite primer for wood and DCP (ST) for masonry plastered surface by brush or spray gun one or two coats as desired. Second coat must be done when the first is perfectly dry say after 10-12 hours. Sand the surface again after priming use of apcolite KP filler is recommended to fill the dirts and surface imperfections. Apply one more coat of primer if filler is used after sand papering the fillered surface. Use metal sand paper for metal surface and wood sand paper for wooden surface.

Adjust the viscosity of paint or primer by adding 9-10% by volume of thinner T-101 (Turpentine) for application by brush and by adding 27-30% by volume for application by spray for best results. Apply two coats of paint for new surface. However one coat may be sufficient if surface is old painted is not much rough. 2nd coat must be done when the first is perfectly dry say after 10-12 hours. Spray guns operated by compressed air are used for heavy works.

6·9. Miscellaneous Materials

Rigid PVC (Poly Vinyle Chloride). In plastics PVC is a well known material with execellent chemical resistance. However PVC suffers from disadvantages like low impact strength, low stiffness and lack of workability with wood working tools. These disadvantages have been over come with the development of PVC foam.

Phosphorgypsum. It is a by-product produced as a solid waste from phosphoric acid plants. It is the 2nd largest pollutant after fly ash in India. CBRI Roorkee has evolved several methods ranging from washing and thermal to chemical treatments to reduce/motivate the impurities. Wet sieving of phosphogypsum through micron IS sieve helps in removing the major part of impurities through the rejection of coarse particles in phosphogypsum. So extra cost in purification and drying is involved. A small quantity of phosphogypsum is currently used as a cement retarder and larger quantity of it is used as landfill.

It can be used as for making plaster which is the main raw material for making light weight fibrous gypsum plaster boards and blocks, panels for wall partitions, slotted tiles for wall cladding, decorative boards for ceilings and for making super sulphated cement. Recently a durable water resistant gypsum binder has been developed from calcined phosphogypsum and other additives for use in masonry work.

It is used in the following works :

(1) In general masonry as a binder.

(2) Light heat proof block making.

(3) It is reinforced by glass fibres.

(4) In making of mouldings.

(5) Its boards are used in ceilings and partitions.

Prestressed Precast Hollow Cone Slabs. They are generally cast in M-25 conc. The depth of these precast units varies from 150 to 400 mm. The corresponding self weight is 205 kg to 405 kg per m^2. It is usual that a 100 mm thick RCC solid slab can be easily replaced by a prestressed precast hollow cone slab of 150 mm thickness. The main advantage of these hollow cone slabs are :

(1) Speed of erections

(2) Saving in cement conc. fly ash can also be used.

(3) Long spans achievable (4) Structural efficiency.

A hollow conc. slab offers the ideal structural sections by reducing the dead weight in hollow slab whilst at the same time maintaining the full load/span advantages, the reduction of RCC weight in hollow slab versus solid RCC slab could be as high as 30%.

Water Proofing Commercial Compounds : (*i*) **Roll fly seal.** When mixed with water and applied on leaky surfaces, the chemicals in Roll fly seal penetrate deep into water bearing capillaries, react with cement particles and form insoluble crystals which totally and permanently block the passage of water. It remains in the body of the concrete as a catalyst to reactivate the crystallisation process whenever water enters the structure through newly formed capillaries.

After ensuring that all cracks are static and that the substrate is sound, the surface is cleaned of any film of oil, curing compound etc. Any latence from the concrete is removed. Static cracks greater than 1 mm in width are chased out to a '*V*' shaped groove and filled with fly seal mortar.

Application. Mix it in water in ratio 2·5 : 1. Apply creamy slurry on wet surface of conc. within 20 min. of mixing. Apply 2nd coat when 1st becomes green and tacky. Apply plaster or screed of cement sand mortar admixed with plaster master over heated surface when 2nd coat is green and tacky. Cure plaster normally. Plaster coat can be omitted if appearance is unimportant and treated surface can be cured normally.

Coverage depends on porosity of the surface to be treated. For two coat application an average of 8-10 ft^2 per kg of flyseal is achieved.

Roff tile adhesives are formulated exclusively for permanent adhesion of ceramic tiles, mosaic and marble cladding to surfaces that may be subjected to extreme weather conditions. Once Rofftile adhesives are beneath the tiles, there is absolute protection against seepage through the wall or floor. Tiles are not required soaking before use. Curing is also not required. It is non shrinking even at changing temperatures and has a better bond with tiles.

Roff Bond Repair. It is used in mortar and concrete as an admisture to increase water resistance, wear resistance and durability. It is also used as corrosion protection of steel.

Application. Remove oil, grease etc. from surface, wet the surface but keep free of surface water. Prepare slurry with 1·5 to 2 parts of cement to 1 part of Roff Bond repair and mix it to make lumpfree. Apply with a stiff brush leaving no pin holes visible. Do not apply slurry in excess of 2 mm thickness. If 2nd coat is required it should be applied after 20-40 min and at right angle to the 2nd coat. The standard disc is 10 litres of Roff Bond repair per 50 kg of cement. For more demanding critical surface, it can be increased to 15 kg per 50 kg of cement. For details contact Roff Construction Chemicals Pvt. Ltd., 45-A wing, Mittal Tower, Nariman Point, Bombay-400 021.

MC-Fix-ST a quick stopper plug for leakages only water is to be added at the site. The mortar plug developes very high strength in about 5-7 minutes and is stone hard. The application is simple. First chisel the leakage spots or the cracks in dove tail fashion. Brush loose particles dust etc. and moisten the surfaces. Mix MCFix-ST in small quantity with water, kneed it into a paste and then press it in the prepared joint to ensure that no voids are left. Hold it in place until it sets either with hand or trowel. The setting time can be accelerated by using warm water. If still drier surfaces are required a slurry of MC-Fix-ST can be applied. It can be had from MC-Bauchemic (India) Pvt. Ltd., Bombay.

M-seal. It is mixed in cement with water to make a paste and is applied in cracks to check leakage.

Araldite adhesive. Used for joining stone. Feviseal (A Commercial Product)

Fast Setting Epoxy Putty

Feviseal EasiMix is a unique and a novel concept in epoxy putty. It is a 2 in 1 fast setting epoxy putty. Both components are premeasured in a single stick ; ensuring right mixing proportion and strength for every use. Just cut, knead and use. It sets hard within 20 minutes. Final curing strength is achieved in 4 hours. Feviseal Easimix is useful in sealing, gripping, joining and insulating a variety of surfaces like ferrous and non-ferrous metal, procelain, ceramic, marble, granite, ivory, asbestos, glass, wood, leather, rubber, most plastics, etc.

Applications/Usages :

Household. Repairing and sealing overhead/flush tanks, wash basins, pipelines, taps, broken tiles, window panels, wooden furniture, stone sculpture, chipped parts of appliances like knife handles, pressure cooker handles, etc. Fixing screws/nails on the wall. Filling gaps between aluminium sliding window channels and concrete. Useful in art, handicraft, mould and model making, nurals, stained glass paintings, etc.

Industrial. Sealing of blow holes and cracks in castings, metal fabircations, industrial vessels, boats, water supply mains, tanks, concrete sewage pipes, gear boxes, etc. Gives smooth finish to joints and corners in wooden and metal patterns. Useful in dynamic balancing, grouting of machines on floor, repairing internal threads of various types of machines.

Electrical. Sealing and insulating cable joints, terminals, leakages in transformers, and other oil filled electrical switchgears. Covering and insulating underground and overhead twist joints of aluminium conductors.

Automobile. Sealing leakages in radiators, diesel/petrol tanks, water/fuel pumps, engine blocks, gear boxes, differentials, carburettors, silencers, fuel injection pumps, etc. Filling body dents and cracks.

Mastic. Mastic is a thick paste used on floors and runways etc. as the safety material against deterioration of surface either due to chemical action or due to action of water. It is same as Bitumen composition. Some time filler and some pigments are also used to give a desired colour.

It is prepared by heating Bitumen composition to a temperature 170°-205°C which is its softening points. Bitumen having softening point lower than this is not used in mastic preparation. In this liquid bitumen fillers are added to increase its durability some air is blown into it. Cal. Carbonate, silica (sand), Cal. silicates, quartz, earthoxide etc. are used as fillers in mastics. The cooking time when filler material are mixed with bitumen by boiling it is 2 to 3 hours. If aggregates used one of large size, the cooking lime will be less while for smaller size aggregate the cooking time is more. Colouring pigments of desired shade can be mixed in bitumen which it is being cooked. In the acidic climate of factories etc. acids are not to be used as fillers. If alkali content is assumed to be more, the filler used must be resistant to it.

In wooden floors it is not advisable to use mastics. Before applying mastic a layer of bitumen should be applied on surface by Hessian or Jute *i.e.* a solution of bitumen in some solvent cloth. Now a days fibre glass is used to apply bitumen fill. Complete surface must be covered by bitumen felt and no air gap should be left, otherwise adhesion will not be done properly. On this surface mastic is applied by specular in uniform thickness of layer. Mastic is not sprayed as it gives poor surface by spraying. In concrete floors mastic can be applied direct and no bitumen felt is required. The thickness of mastic is generally 5-6 cms. This thickness depends on type of load for which it is subjected. Some times mastic as applied in two layers are over the other I.S. Code specifies 3 cm thickness for floors.

The mastic should be chemical resistant and water proof and resilient. The mastic is applied on the floor where water and acidic possibilities exist. In the floor of industries, grain godowns, food proceedings and dairy etc. mastic is applied. The mastic must be able to beer high temperatures upto 150°C.

Sealant. In expansion and contractive joints provided in concrete pavements, a material which can expand or contract with the conc. so as to keep the joint water tight is used. Such materials are called as **sealant.**

For small works putty which is a mixture of linseed oil and chalk is used when the expansion or contraction possibilities are more a sealant is used. The sealant composed should be water proof and should not crack during temperature variation *i.e.* on contraction and expansion of the conc.

If expansion and contraction is more than 10%, Bitumen based material *i.e.* mastic itself is used as a sealant. Some times in this Butyl, volcanised rubber or neoprene is mixed.

In market bitumen matrix is sold as a sealant which is prepared by reducing proportion of filler in the mastic. If expansion and contraction is more than 10% following special sealants are used.

(*i*) Poly sulphate (*ii*) Silicon rubber (*iii*) Polyurethene and

(*iv*) Acrylic sand, silicate and chalk etc. are the inorganic fillers whilst sand dust, asbestos powder are organic fillers. During change if temperature the filler must adjust itself with the matrix.

Qualities of a good sealant. It must be (*i*) Ignition point must be more than melting point of bitumen.

(*ii*) Bitumen contents should be 80-85%.

(*iii*) Filler contents must be 10 to 15%.

(*iv*) The pour point or the temperature at which can be pourable.

(*v*) Extensability *i.e.* how much it can expand or contact.

(*vi*) Adhesion with the material on which it is used.

For hair cracks or when the crack is smaller than 3 mm, sealant can not be used. For this purpose latex (rubber) is applied in 2 to 3 layers on couple area. Lalac is sold in the market Synthetic rubber sealants are used as they fulfill all the requirements of a good sealant.

Gypsum and Plaster of Paris. It is a white crystalline substance. In composition it is cal. sulphate (79%) with water (209%) of crystallization and is found as a normal in nature in many parts of India. It is colourless but in presence of impurities its colour may be white grey, brown or raddish brown.

Gypsum is soluble in hydrochloric acid or in water. Its specific gravity is 2-3. It rarely found in pure state but it contains varying amount of clay, lime stone, silica and iron compounds etc.

Gypsum plaster and gypsum plaster boards are used very much in buildings. Its boards are used in ceilings and walls of auditorium and hotels etc. when sound insulation is required.

Natural gypsum is 1st crushed and grounded to very fine powder. It is heated in large retorts under constant stirring conditions at a temperature of about 160°-165°C. 14·7% of water goes off as steam and results in the form of hemithydrate of Cal. sulphate (2 Ca SO_4 H_2O). It still contains about 6% of water. This is known as **Plaster of Paris** or gypsum plaster. This is used in paste form also can be poured in moulds to form desired architectural forms for decoration and casting of statues and for repairs of small cracks in wall, giving smooth finish to wall base and also now a days used on roofs for designing borders etc.

If the water is further driven off it results in the formation of an hydrate of Calcium sulphate ($CaSO_4$) and known as 2nd settler plaster. This is used in wall boards and tiles etc. for insulation against heat. Retarded hemi hydrate gypsum plaster if produced by mixing some retarders in Plaster of Paris to delay its setting time.

Gypsum plaster mixed with small proportion of sand and other aggregates for use. It sets with little change in volume and with negligible shrinkage on drying. It is light in weight. It is uneffected by bacteria. The ratio of gypsum plaster and sand is generally 1 : 3 to 1 : 4. It sticks with the fibrous materials.

For manufacture of gypsum plaster (Plaster of Paris or P.O.P.) gypsum is crushed and grinded so as to pass through 100 mesh sieve. After colouring it converts to Plaster of Paris by reducing its water contents. Finally it is grinded and mixed with suitable retarder.

Bags containting gypsum powder (P.O.P.) must be kept in dry and closed place because it picks up moisture from atmosphere. It should not be stored for long periods as it looses strength after three months.

Gypsum plaster boards. These are used now a days in ceilings and walls to have insulation against heat and sound. They are light in weight fire proof nature, neither expand nor contract due to change in temperature. They can be part painted to a desired tint. They can be used without any finish. These boards are made of mixing gypsum plaster with cinder or wood chips and sufficient coats to form other consistency. They are also used in floors.

Mixes for internal plasting by gypsum floors (by volume)

Ball ground	*Under coat*			*Finished coat*		
	Gypsum plaster	*Lime*	*Sand*	*Gypsum plaster*	*Lime*	*Sand*
Brick work or	1/3	1	2·4	1/4-1/2**	1	0-1
building blocks	2#	1-1½	5-6	1	0-1/2	0-1
				1	0-1/2	1
				1/4-1/2*	1	0-1
Precast conc.	2#	1	5	1/4-1/2*	1	0-1
				1	0-1/2	1
Wood or metal lath	2#	1	5	1/4-1/2**	1	0-1
Fibre board or gypsum plaster board	1*	—	1½	1/4-1/2**	1	0-1
				1	0-1/2	1

Anhydrous gypsum plaster * Retarted semi hydrate gypsum plaster
** Either retarted semi hydrate gypsum plaster or suitable anhydrates.

Other gypsum products

(1) **Keens Cement.** It is a type of plaster prepared by calcining pure gypsum above 90°C to semi-hydrate stage, soaking it in solution of potash, alum, rebaking it at temperature about 480°C and grinding. Sometimes it is calcined at about 600°C. It is also very hard and possesses comp. strength about 35 N/mm^2 and sets in 20 minutes to 6 hours time. It is less susceptible to moisture. It has sufficient high resistant against cracking and can be polished. It is used in ornamental plaster works. It can be used either as a base coat by mixing with sand or for finished coat with lime putty to gain early strength.

(2) **Pyrocell.** It is finely grounded gypsum powder containing an admixture which when mixed with water, forms gas which expands the mixture 3 to 4 times in volume. The inflated paste hardens into a light, cellular force resistant mass possessing good accoustical insulating properties.

(3) **Mack Cement.** It is made by burning gypsum at a very high temperature and adding about 0·4 percent of burnt glass bars salt (Na_2SO_4) or pot. sulphate. It is used to form an unusually hard and durable surface colour, can painted well.

If cement is calcined with borax is called as Pasian cement, similarly gypsum calcined with pearl ash is called Pasian gypsum. If gypsum is slacked in petroleum, it forms sirapit. These all are hard burnt plasters. These plasters being very hard are used in corners and angles. They are also used in repair works. They are also used where good appearance is required.

Gypsum laths. These are used as base for plasters. These may be made either solid or perforated. The fibrous covering of laths helps in uniform section and give a fairly strong and durable board with gypsum plaster. These can easily be nailed.

Bake lite. It is used in many electrical and engineering purposes. It is obtained by heating phenol and formal dehydrate in equal amounts in the presence of base. Bakelite *A* has a melting point of 50°C and is soluble in alcohol and acetone. Bakelite *C* is hard insoluble transparent and amber like substance. Bakelite is light in weight has smooth surface, high strength and resistance to shock.

Mica. Mica is found as colourless and in various shades of brown to blue. It is used in electric works. Micanite made from thin pieces of mica into large sheets, using suitable adhesives are cheaper than mica but is inferior in electrical properties.

Lubricants. These are used to minimise the travelled distance between two surfaces while motion. These are generally liquids but there are solid and semi solid lubricants also. Water is the cheapest lubricant but it evaporates as temperature rises, hence it is used as cooling agent instead of lubricant.

Mineral oils, animal oils, vegetable oils are commonly used as liquid lubricants. Their grades vary and depend upon their viscosity, oiliness, stability, specific gravity etc. solid lubricants are graphite, soap stine etc. and are used when surfaces are likely to be subjected for high pressure and motion is at low speed. Grease is semi solid lubricant used commonly. It is prepared by mixing of Palm oil and tallow and boiling it with caustic soda solution and used very much for fans and machines etc.

Gaskets. It is made of leather, rubber, paper and cotton impregnated with grease or oil. It is used as a packing material, in valves and pipe joints to make these leak proof.

Emery cloth and paper. Emery is a mixture of iron oxide and aluminium *i.e.* corundum in crystalline form and used as a grinding material for cutting various surfaces. Emery cloth and emery paper comprise of ground emery of definite degree of fineness attached to calco cloth or paper by glue. Emery cloth or paper is generally used for finishing and polishing metal surfaces. Glass cloth or glass paper consists of ground glass of different fineness attached with glue are used for smoothing surfaces of wood and other surfaces.

Vulcanito polymer sheets. These are made of recycled scrap tyres, thickness varies from 2 mm to 12 mm, having specific gravity approximately 1·4 and are waterproof and acid proof having good resistance property upto 60°C. They are termite proof, anti-corrosive and have good sound proof properties and electrical resistance property. It can be screwed to wooden plants and metal sheets. Hence it is used for cupboards, door frames and partitions etc.

Silica fume. Silica fume is an adhesive of concrete which reduces its porosity and increases its strength and imperviousness. It's trade name is microsilica.

Silica fume is a by product resulting from the reduction of high purity quartz with coal, coat and wood chips in an electric arc furnace during the production of silicon or ferro-silicon alloys. The silica fume, which condenses from the gases escaping from the furnace has very fine spherical particles having diameter of 0·1 micrometer.

Rock dust. It is obtained from stone crushes after screening of different grades of ballast as a dust and is used as fine aggregate in concrete. Though it does not fulfil the requirements of fine aggregate yet it is used as a fine aggregate because it does not adversely effect the requirements of fine aggregate. It increases the workability hence the amount of water to be added is reduced, consequently it improves the strength and compressive strength is also not reduced.

Plastic wood. Plastic wood is synthetic wood widely used as a substitute of wood and plywood. It is non-corrosive and resistant to weather. It has smooth surface. It can be used without smoothing or painting. It can be planed, drilled or sawn just like ordinary wood. It is impervious to insects, termite and chemicals. It absorbs sound and is light in weight. It has good thermal insulating properties.

Rice husk. Rice husk is a waste of rice mills. It is light. It is used as an adderant in cement manufacturing. Used in plaster as a mortar mix. The ash of the husk is also good for many purposes.

Agriculture waste. Husk, sugarcane waste from sugar mills, wheat waste from threshers and coir fibres etc. can be used effectively in manufacture of acoustic boards, thermal insulation boards, light roof ceiling sheets with resin binders. Saw dust of wood is also glued to form an artificial wood which can be moulded in ornamental boards etc.

Fibre. Small pieces called fibre (long and thin) of a certain material are used as reinforcement. They can also be circular or flat. Fibre is described by a parameter called "Aspect ratio". It is the ratio of length to diameter or least lateral diameter in case of flat fibres. It ranges from 30 to 150. Steel fibres are commonly used in concrete in amount of 1%. They are of the following types :

(*i*) **Plastic fibres.** Nylon, polypropylene, polyethylene, rayon, acrylic and polyester are of this type. Nylon and polypropylene have high tensile strength but low elastic modulus. Caricrole is one of the trade name of fibre reinforced concrete with polypropylene.

(*ii*) **Steel fibres.** These have fairly high tensile strength (280-430 N/mm^2) as well as high Young's modulus. (204 × 10^3 N/mm^2). They impart high flexural strength as compound to polypropylene fibres. Steel fibres have high corrosion unless are not treated by surface impregnation or coating. Steel fibres reinforced concrete is known as **wirand conc. Crumbed** or deformed fibres (trade name **duo form**).

(*iii*) **Fibre glass.** E-glass fibres can be used, but these are not alkali resistant hence alkali resistant glass fibre **cemfil** or glass fibre imported with protective coatings are used. The coating may be of polyvinyl acetate. Glass fibres have high tensile strength (1-48 kN/m^3 and high Young's modulus 71·41 × 10^3 N/mm^2).

(*iv*) **Carbon fibres.** Chopped carbon fibres with random array may be used. They are costly.

(*v*) **Asbestos fibres.** These are highly chemical and fire resistant having high tensile strength (560-988 N/mm^2 and high modulus of elasticity (81·68 × 10^3 to 142·8 × 10^3 N/mm^2).

(*vi*) **Cellular fibres.** These have low tensile strength, low E-value and are hygroscopic.

(*vii*) **Coir.** These are cheap compared to others.

(*viii*) **Jute.** They are also very cheap, scrap may be used as fibres.

(*ix*) **Aluminium.** Factory scraps can be used for fibres.

(*x*) **San.** An organic product which is used in ropes etc. having good tensile strength and used for water proofing can also be used as fibres in concrete and improves its ductility only.

Expansion joint filler. These are tar impregnated boards used as joint fillers which are compressible and possess high degree of recovery after compression is released. Joint fillers of wood saw dust impregnated in bitumen are used as joint fillers. Mastic is also used as a road joint filler.

Heat insulations. Materials used for protecting structures from heat are used as heat insulator. Their bulk density is more than 7 kN/m^3 and have low coefficient of heat conductivity. Heat insulating material are bricks, mats, cords, mineral, wood, glass wood etc. They may be organic or inorganic in nature. They must be chemical and fire resistant.

Inorganic insulators. Mineral wood, glass fibres, cellular concrete, foam glass, expanded perlite, and vermiculite, asbestos etc. are used as heat insulators. Cellular concrete is a stone material made up of a solidified binder with uniformally closed pores.

Organic heat insulations. Fibre, fibrolite, reed and peat boards are rigid organic insulations, while felt, corrugated card boards are flexible materials.

Fibre board is sheet material obtained by moulding and subsequent drying of wood fibre with polymers added depending upon their building strength, fibre boards are assigned the gradings such as soft, semi soft, rigid and very rigid. Fibrous boards are manufactured from wood (fine chips of wood) mixed with mineral binder (Portland cement). They are utilised in making partitions and thermal protecting walls.

Reed boards moulded and woven with galvanized wire rectangular in shape are manufactured from reed stems. Peat boards are manufactured from under composed peat by moulding and subsequent drying.

Abrasives. An abrasive is a material which is used for cutting grading surfacing and finishing other materials. They are harder than the material to be cut or grinded. Pure diamond is the hardest and have its hardness as 10 on the Mohr's Scale. The hardness of other is numbered in comparison to it. Other materials are Emery, Garnet, Quartz etc. which are natural abrasives while the artificial abrasives are Boron-Carbide, Silicon, Carbide and Aluminium Oxide etc. These abrasives are used commonly in the preparation of Sand Paper, Sand cloth and grinding wheel cutting bits of stone cutting are also prepared by slicking diamond chips on it. These bits are also used in core diamond drilling of rocks.

Metallic abrasives are made of steel balls whose hardness ranges from 5 to 8·5 and are commonly used for grading clinkers in cement factories. Steel shots are also used for grinding and polishing of stones. Steel balls also used in flour grinding mills. Silicon carbide known as carborundum is used as an abrasive powder for making grinding wheels, polishing cloth and paper. Carborundum bits are used for grinding marble floors. It has high resistance to chemicals and can with stand high temperature specially for grinding iron castings. Boron carbide is also one of the hard abrasives (Hardness 9·5 to 9·7) used for cutting hardened steel and for making nozzles of blasting sand stone. Sand papers are prepared by spreading the particles on the glue coated paper and then drying. The binding paste may be shellac, resin, rubber and ceramic silicate etc.

Adhesives. Adhesion is attraction between unlike surfaces while cohesion is attraction between like surfaces. Due to primary or secondary forces of attraction, adhesives are used to join two or more parts into an unit. Adhesives join the surfaces in three ways (1) Specific adhesion, if surfaces are joined together by intermolecular forces of attraction. (2) Mechanic adhesion if the adhesive fill the voids or porous or rough surfaces and hold the surfaces by interlocking action. (3) Fusion of surfaces which are partially dissolved in the adhesive or its solvent. Adhesives used for bonding the surfaces of wood, metal, plastic and glass are divided as organic adhesives and synthetic adhesive as below :

(*a*) **Animal protein glues.** These glues are obtained from hide trimmings, bones or flashings by boiling in hot water. Animal glues provide strong, tough, easily made joints, but they are effected by damp and moist conditions. It is supplied in the form of flakes, pearls, sheets, cakes, granules, cuber or jelly. Animal glue having three grades depending on the water absorption *i.e.* 18, 15, 10 times the dry weight of glue.

(*b*) **Blood albumin glues.** It is made by drying raw blood and effected by damp and moist.

(*c*) **Casein adhesive.** It is obtained by curdling of skimmed milk by the addition of dilute acid (generally a lemon). Casein is separated, mixed with lime, preserved and sold.

Casein for wet mix glue should pass through. 60 μ sieve and for dry mix glue should pass through 25 μ. Sieve, when shaken for 10 minutes. Casein glue if properly formulated provides highly moisture resistant glue joints but not water proof. It is less resistant to bacterial attack.

(*d*) **Starch adhesives.** It is made from vegetable starch having good dry strength but not resistant to moisture.

Synthetic adhesives. These are mostly resins used in plastic industries and are classed as thermosetting or thermoplastic glues. Thermosetting glues are permanent, once they are set, but the thermoplastic types can be made plastic again by reheating. All of them are strong, water proof and fire proof and the setting time can be regulated by varying the type and amount of the hardener. They are resistant to fungal and possess non-stating qualities. The four main types are phenolic resin, resorcinol resins, urea resin and melamine resins. Nitro-cellulose, ethyl celluloses, vinyl polymers and acrylic resins are of lesser importance for building industry. Phenolic glue and melamine resins require heat and pressure for setting. They are used for plywood and other wood work.

Asbestos. Asbestos is white or yellow colour fibrous mineral composed of silicate of calcium and magnesium with iron oxide and alumina. It is used as an excellent insulator for insulating furnaces, boilers etc. It is used for making fire proof suits of asbestos cloth. Plane and corrugated asbestos sheets are made from asbestos and cement mixed under high pressure. These sheets are fire proof, oxide proof, water proof, insect proof, non conductive, light and are used for building work. They can be nailed, veneered, ground, sawn and pasted. Asbestos fibres are non corrodible and suitable for supply of water, gas and sewage. They are available in white, grey, slaty and light green colours.

Corrugated asbestos sheets are classfied according to size, form and corrugations as under :

Table 6·18.

Type of sheet	*Pitch of corrugation*	*Depth of corrugation*	*Over all width*	*Effective width*	*Nominal thickness*	*Length of sheet*
Corrugated	146 mm	48 mm	1050 mm	1010 mm	6 mm to 7mm	1·5, 1·75, 2, 2·25, 2·5, 2·75, 3·0 metre
Semi-corrugated	338 mm	45 mm	1100 mm	1040 mm	67 mm	1·5, 1·75, 2, 2·25, 2·5, 2·75, 3·0 metre

Cork. Cork is derived from bark of certain trees. It is bad conductor of heat, compressible light *i.e.* 1·5 to 2 kN/m^3 having high elasticity, does not disintegrate, after boiling in water upto three hours and should not expand in any direction. It is used as sound absorbing medium in building as an ingradient of tiles. For reducing vibration in machinery, as insulating material in cold storage industry, in stopper of bottles. Cork lining and in formation of flexible sheet. It is mostly imported from other countries like Portugal, Spain and Morocco. Due to shortage of cork cement-sand mixture is recommended as substitute in cold storage.

Linoleum. It is a mixture of oxydised linseed oil, pulverised cork, sand dust, and colouring pigments, all spreaded in an uniform layer over canvas. The surface may be printed in different patterns. The surface is then made water proof by oil paints. Linoleum having 6·7, 6·0, 4·5, 3·2, 2·0 and 1·6 mm thickness is available in the market. It is used as a floor cover of hospital, offices, drawing room etc. It is made in rolls as well as in tiles. It is not effected by oil but slightly by acid. It can be easily cleaned with soap and is easily wax polished.

Plastics. Various ingredients of plastics are :

(1) **Binder.** These are added to give binding capacity. Cellulose is one most useful available, resins, rayon, waxes and bitumen are also used as binders.

(2) **Filler.** To increase strength of plastics, fillers are mixed. Wood asbestos, mica, glass fibres etc. are used as fillers. Fillers also develop other properties such as less mould shrinkage, increase moldability, electric properties and low moisture absorptions.

(3) **Plasticizer.** To modify plastics, plasticizers are mixed. It also impart strength and toughness. Plasticizers must be of less volatile nature. Glycerine forms glycerol, glycols, naphthalenes, paraffins, cereastyrene is also used as plasticizer.

(4) **Dyes and pigments.** According to the colours desired, different type of pigment are used. The dyes and pigments added must not effect the other properties of plastics. Dyes must

be soluble in water and alcohol etc. While pigments are insoluble. Dyes are of transparent variety. Organic and inorganic chemicals are used as pigments. Earth, metallic salts (organic pigments), zinc chloride, zinc sulphate, calcium (inorganic) etc. are used as ingredients for colouring plastics.

(5) **Catalyst.** In thermosetting plastics to start polymerization of the monomers, catalyst are used. In condensation, stronger inorganic acids such as sulphuric acids and alkalies are used. Whilst in addition oxydising catalyst such as benzyl para oxide is used.

(6) **Lubricants.** Lubricants are mixed to ease the process of making plastics Metallic soaps and shear oils are used as lubricants.

Structure of plastics. Plastics are organic components of carbon. Plastics form when carbon combines with other elements like oxygen, hydrogen and nitrogen.

Types of plastics. Plastics can be divided in two main types :

(1) Thermosetting plastics (2) Thermoplastics

Thermosetting plastics. These are Amino plastics and phenolic resins.

Thermoplastics. These are cellulose derivatives, acrylic resins, polyvinyl and polyethlene.

Miscellaneous plastics. Natural protein, vulcanized fibres and soyabean protein etc. are other types of plastics.

Uses of plastics. The use of plastics in civil engineering technology is unlimited. Doors, furniture, electric fittings. W.C. fittings, drawing boards and decorative articles are wide uses of plastics. PVC pipes are widely used in sanitary and water supply.

In mechanical engineering plastics are used in making gaskets laminated gears and car pulley etc.

In electrical engineering, all fillings, switches and holders etc. are made of plastics. Radio and T.V. cabins are also made of plastics. Polyethylene is widely used in day to day life. It is used as a water sealant in roofs. It is used as a rain protective cover in open placed articles and machines etc.

Rubber. It is naturally produced by the milk (latex) of the rubber plant and as lissa from chir plant. For the preparation, latex is collected in buckets through diagonal slit cut in the bark and coagulated into a solid mass by heat with chemical adulterants like dilute solution of acitic acid at 50°C. This mass after being cured or anticepticized by smoking is the crude rubber. This is the raw material for manufacture of other rubber goods.

This crude rubber is washed and spreaded by knives and mixed with sulphur or other ingredients to form thick slurry "dough" as per requirement and quality of rubber to be produced.

Synthetic rubber. It may be made synthetically by polymerization of the hydrocarbon isoprene. Neoprene is one of the successfull synthetic rubber. Other raw materials in use of synthetically and natural rubbers are petroleum, natural gas, potatos, sugar, coaltar, lime stone, coke, salt, sulphuric acid etc.

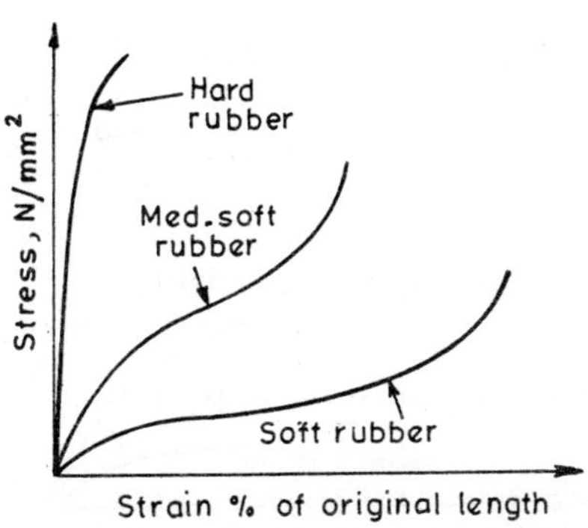

Fig. 6·13.

Properties of rubbers. Soft rubbers can be stretched to 10 times to its original length while the hard rubber is almost as brittle as cast iron. They may be made flexible byheating to moderate temperature. It does not have a constant modulus of elasticity in tension.

Uses. Its uses can be tested as below :

(1) As an ingredient rubber has been used with success with bituminous material as bond in surfacing for roads, yards and school play grounds.

(2) Latex and other forms of unprocessed or semi-processed rubber are used with bitumen for soil stabilization. It increases the surface flexibility to an approachable amount.

(3) Rubber sheets are also used very much in foundation. Rubber floorings are used very much. For all special type of roads rubber is used by mixing in cement or other aggregates.

Table 6·19.

Material	*Elongation at fracture %*	*Modulus of elasticity for small deformation N/mm²*	*Tensile strength at 200°C of tensile strength at room temperature N/mm²*
Natural Rubber			
Soft rubber	800	15·0	
Hard rubber	6	15,000·00	
Sponge rubber		1·5	
Synthetic			
Polychloropene	500		4·0
Thiocol	600		3·2

Glass. Glass is brittle, transparent opaque, semi-transparent and colourless, but can be given desired shades. It is used in door and window panes, toilet and operation rooms. It is also used in decorative purposes and widely used in looking mirrors.

Composition of glass. It is not true solid, but a super cooled liquid with no definite melting point. It is completely non-crystalline. It is a compound silicate of sodium, potassium or calcium, with small quantities of metallic oxides which are melted together at 1200°C to 1500°C and then subjected controlled cooling. It is insoluble in anything except of hydrofluoric acid and strong alkalies.

Varieties of glass. (1) Flat glass used in panes of doors and window. It may be subdivided in two kinds.

(*a*) **Sheet glass.** Glass in sheet form is drawn or rolled. In a continuous process in which sheets of considerable width are drawn up from the furnace of molten glass.

(*b*) **Plate glass.** It is produced as ribbon through rollers. Molten material is poured on the flat heated iron table with a raised rim and rolled to the required thickness with a heavy iron roller. This can be ground smooth and polished.

According to defects, plate glass is divided into silvery and glazing quality. The silvery grade is used in mirrors, while the glazing quality is a little inferior and is used in prestigious buildings. The heavier plate glass is used for shelving, table tops, toilet and partitions etc. glasses produced through rollers can have one surface patterned which obscures direct vision to varying degrees. This type of glass is called figure rolled glass.

(2) **Safety glass.** It can be classified in the following three types :

(*a*) **Laminated safety glass.** It is formed by sandwitch of a plastic material such as cellulose nitrate or acetate or synthetic resins in between two glass sheets. It is generally used in automobiles, metal insulations, sky lights and show cases etc.

(*b*) **Toughened glass.** To produce it, plate glass is heated to the point of softening and suddenly cooled. This produces hardening of surface layers in expanded state. Toughened glass is stronger than ordinary glass. It is used in showcases, furnace doors and countertops etc.

(*c*) **Wired glass.** This is produced by incorporating the wire mesh in the body of the glass during manufacturing in such a way that it takes a midway position between the surfaces of the glass. The main advantage of this type of glass is that the mesh holds the pieces of glass together when cracked. It is also used where some fire resistant is desired.

(3) **Heat insulation of glass.** There are two types of this glass :

(*a*) **Foam glass.** It is obtained by producing glass evolution to occur with in the molten glass at an appropriate stage during manufacturing. Foam glass is an efficient thermal insulating material approaching cork in its performance. It is water proof, termite proof, rigid non-combustible, stable upto a fairly high temperature. Its weight is app. 1-7 kN/m^3 at which its thermal conductivity is 0·067 kcal/m.hr/degree. It is used in buildings, air conditioning and cold storage etc. covering of hot and cold pipes. It is also used for sound proofing.

(*b*) **Glass fibre.** Glass may be softened and drawn mechanically into thread or glass wood which is finer than silk. A glass stand composed of 60 filament. Each filament having a dia. of 0·0036 mm possesses the tensile strength approx. 175 kN/m^2. However glass fibre may have a tensile strength upto 700 kN/m^2. A stand glass fibre may be 1/15th of the dia. of a human hair but have a tensile strength of steel. They may be wooven into fabric or used in loosely packed form. Used as sound or thermal insulators 25 mm of glass is equivalent in terms of thermal conductivity of 42 mm of brick or 62 cm of concrete.

For purpose of heat insulation glass wool is compressed with suitable binder into insulating boards, tiles etc.

Glass fibres is produced in variety of forms (*a*) Lime soda glass containing 10-15% alkali and is known as alkali glass '*A*'. (*b*) above silicate glass having low alkali content and commonly called as '*E*' glass.

Uses of glass fibre. (*i*) **Glass reinforced laminates.** Reinforcement by glass fibres in plastics while they are moulded improve the strength of the material in all directions. It is used in manufacture of corrugated sheeting, mainly for use of roofs and interior decorations.

(*ii*) **Bitumen bonded fibre glass.** For thermal and sound insulation the glass fibres are intermixed with bitumen emulsions and finally compressed in required thickness. The thermal conductivity of these products is about 0·23 kcal/m. hr./deg.

Glass-blocks. Glass blocks are hollow, light transparent texture and are produced by fusing together two pressed semi blocks. Glass blocks may be square, rectangular or angular as desired. They are light diffusing and light transparent varieties and may be colourless. They have sufficient compressive strength but is not used as load bearing member.

Due to the presence of air cell in block this has good thermal insulating effect. Glass blocks have thermal conductivity of the order of 0·36 kcal/m-hr.deg. They are used in bath rooms, stairways and laboratories etc. They are manufactured in 15 cm, 20 cm and 30 cm squares and approximate thickness of 10 cm. The blocks can be set in cement mortar 1 : 1 : 4. They are adequate to carry their own load upto max. height of 6 metres and resist lateral wind pressure.

Other varieties. (1) **Coloured glass** also known as stand glass is made by adding oxides of metals to molten glass.

(*ii*) **Heat absorbing glass.** It is bluish green in colour. This glass has property of absorbing the infrared rays of the sun. Colorex glass is of this type.

(*iii*) **Mirror.** It is a clear sheet of polished plate on the back of which is precipitated a layer of a solution of silver nitrate and ammonia. The back of this layer is protected from dampness with a coat of shellac or varnish and two coats of lead or tar paint.

Opal glass. This type of glass possess opacity in some degree from slight milkness to complete opacity. Acids except hydrofluoric have no effect on glass, while alkalies corrode them.

Blind glass. To make translucent the glass panes of doors and windows a film of paint is applied by a cotton cloth brush, which is made uniform by a cotton cloth padding.

Fly ash and its different uses

Fly ash : A construction material—Fly ash is a biproduct of thermal power stations as a waste. During combustion of coal the products found are classified into two categories, bottom ash and fly ash. The bottom ash is that part of the residue which infused into particles heavy enough to drop out of the furnace. These particles are collected at the bottom of the furnace. Fly ash is that part of the ash which is entrained in the combustion gas leaving the boiler.

The size of ashes consists of fine spherical particles ranging in dia. from 0·5 μ to 100 μ. The pH of fly ash contacted with water may vary from 3 to 12, with the pH for the majority of pulverized coal burned fly ashes contacted with water ranging from 8 to 12.

Coal ash can be classified as (1) bituminous ash and (2) Lignite ash.

Lignite ash having more cal. oxide plus mag. oxide than feric oxide, while bituminous ash has more ferric oxide. The average particle size of lignite fly ashis coarser than bituminous. Free lime is also present in all lignite ashes.

Chemical composition of the ash—Silica (SiO_2), alumina (Al_2O_3) and iron oxide (Fe_2O_3) with smaller amount of cal. oxide (CaO) mag. oxide (MgO) and sulphure (SO_3).

Engineering properties of the ash—Low specific gravity, uniform gradation and lack of plasticity. The specific gravity depends on chemical composition ranging from 2 to 2·6. Bottom ash has higher specific gravity than fly ash. The shear strength depends on compaction.

Fly ash utilization. Fly ash has proven to be a versatile material. The use of fly ash in construction are (1) Manufacture of Portland pozzolana cement and or concrete (2) Brick manufacture (3) As a structural fill and (4) In pavement and subgrade construction. Fly ash is also being used in small quantity in the recovery of minerals and elements such as iron and aluminium oxides, controlling mine fires and subsidence (In mud jacking) remove scaling, grouting and manufacature of light weight aggregates. There has been an increasing use of fly ash as mineral filler in products as rubber, plastics, ceramics, roofing and insulation.

Fly ash mixed cement or concrete. Fly ash is blended either with other ingradients in manufacturing cement or proportioned with other aggregates when mixed. Mixing in concrete serves two purposes (1) In supplements or replaces fine aggregates and (2) it provides effective pozzolanic action.

Fly ash blended cement produce strong and durable concrete and in tributes to increased plasticity (usually with less mixing of water) which improves placing and finishing. It also improves resistance of conc. to sulphate attack and reduces the heat of hydration during massive structures. About 20% replacement of cement by fly ash give optimum benefit. Fly ash is also used in ferrow cement. Percentage of fly ash mixing with cement or concrete is based on the chemical composition of fly ash and the performance required by the structure. Mixing of fly ash 5 to 10% in concrete improves early strength.

Fly ash fills. Fly ash is laid in thin layers and compacted. Structural fills are relatively incompressible and can be used to develop parts, playgrounds and other similar jobs. Mixing lime or cement induces hardening in the fill. It is used in embankments, dyke, tailings, dam construction and (4) Pavement and sub grade construction. Fly ash has a higher optimum moisture content. Fly ash behaves much like a cohesive soil with respect to consolidiation. The coeff. of permeability depends on compaction.

Cement : Fly ash (1 : 7) mix can be used as big stones in the protection works of rivers with 0·5 water fly ash ratio is filled in gunney bags. A proportion of clean Ganga sand can also be mixed.

Table 6·20. Test Results of (Cement + Fly Ash) : Ganga Sand Mix

(C + G.S.) : GS by wt.	Cement fly ash ratio (By vol.)	Water fly ash ratio (By vol.)	Comp. strength kg/cm²			
			Cast and kept in water		Cast out side kept in water for 24 h	
			7 days	28 days	7 days	28 days
1 : 2	1 : 1	0·50	—	—	—	26·47
1 : 2	1 : 3	0·50	—	—	—	13·54
1 : 2	1 : 2	0·50	—	—	—	21·06
1 : 2	1 : 5·67	0·50	—	—	—	10·33
1 : 3	1 : 5·67	0·50	—	—	—	3·00
1 : 3	1 : 2	0·50	—	—	—	15·16
1 : 3	1 : 3	0·50	—	—	—	11·35
1 : 3	1 : 9	0·50	—	—	—	7·74
1 : 3	1 : 1	0·50	—	—	—	19·70
1 : 3	1 : 10	0·57	2·3	3·4	—	—
1 : 3	1 : 7	0·57	4·0	6·0	5·0	6·00
1 : 2	1 : 7	0·57	5·2	5·5	5·4	6·40
1 : 1	1 : 10	0·57	7·0	16·5	8·6	—
1 : 1	1 : 7	0·57	8·4	24·0	12·0	26·00

Test Results of Cement : Fly Ash Mix

Mix ratio by vol.	Water fly ash ratio	Comp. strength kg/cm²					
		Cast and kept in water		Cast out side kept in water at once		Cast outside kept in water after 24 h	
		7 days	28 days	7 days	28 days	7 days	28 days
1 : 7	0·81	5·00	13·30	8·70	14·70	—	22·20
1 : 7	0·57	21·10	33·30	23·00	36·30	28·00	50·00
1 : 10	0·57	3·30	3·20	4·90	4·00	—	3·50
1 : 10	0·40	4·70	5·10	5·50	6·20	6·00	8·50
1 : 7	0·50	—	—	—	—	23·35	60·60
1 : 7	0·45	—	—	—	—	24·70	61·50
1 : 7	0·40	—	—	—	—	17·00	55·76
1 : 10	0·50	—	9·20	—	—	—	7·07
1 : 5	0·50	—	16·51	—	—	—	10·10

Use of Fly Ash and Condensed Silica Fumes in Making Concrete

Fly Ash (FA). Fly ash as already said is a by-product of thermal power plants using coal as the solid fuel. Finely ground coal, passing 75 μm sieve, is injected at high speed along with air into the furnaces at around 1500°C temperature. The carbonaceous content of coal is burnt instantaneously in these furnaces, but other materials like shell and clays consisting of silica, alumina and iron oxide melt in suspension. About 80% of these materials are carried away with the fuel gases out of the furnaces, get rapidly cooled and form fine spherical glassy particles ; the remaining 20% falls to the bottom of the furnaces (furnace bottom ash). These spherical particles in the fuel gases, when removed by electrostatic precipitators before the gases are discharged into the atmosphere, are known as pulverized fuel ash, or simply, fly ash.

Like cement, fly ash also is plant specific and its properties depend on the type of raw coal that is used as the fuel. In trying to identify the factors which influence the properties of concrete made with fly ash, researchers have investigated into its various constituents and properties like chemical composition (particularly SO_3, MgO, the major oxides (SiO_2, AL_2O_3 and Fe_2O_3) contents), the loss on ignition (LOI), the pozzolanic activity index (PAI), fineness, moisture, content and water requirement. The only two properties which may be considered important in this respect are the LOI and the fineness. The fineness, in turn, controls water demand, workability, PAI and the strength of concrete and is, therefore, considered as the most important factor in determining the quality of fly ash for replacing cement upto 20% to 50%.

Condensed Silica Fume (CSF)

Condensed silica fume is by-product of the ferro-silicon alloy and silicon metal industries, where the silicon alloys are produced in submerged-arc type electric furnaces. The chemical reactions taking place in the furnaces at about 2000°C are complex and involve formation of SiO vapour, which subsequently oxidises and condenses in the form of very small spherical particles of non-crystalline silica. The dust, which is carried away with flue gases of the furnaces, and contains these tiny particles, is subsequently removed in bag filters as the hot gasses pass through them, and is known as condensed silica fume or silica dust. After being collected in bag filters, CSF is further processed for controlling the particle size and for removing impurities before being used in concrete.

Silica fume particles have an average diameter of 0·1 micron, (the sizes ranging from 0·01 to 0·3 micron) and are, therefore, 1/50th to 1/100th of the average size of cement and fly ash particles. Surface area of these particles varies from 17000 m^2/kg to 25000 m^2/kg compared to 300-350 m^2/kg for fly ash and 350 to 600 m^2/kg for cement. Bulk density of CSF is generally between 200 and 250 kg/m^3; while specific gravity is 2·2 (compared to 3·1-3·23 for cement and 2·5-2·7 for fly ash).

The chemical composition of CSF depends mostly on the composition of the principal product being made in the furnace, as well as on the design of the furnace itself and is, therefore, plant specific like cement and FA. When the furnace is fitted with a heat recovery system, the exhaust gases exit at about 800°C and most carbon gets burnt. One the other hand, if there is no heat recovery system, the gases leave the furnace at about 200°C and contain some unburnt carbon, CSF produced from such furnaces has a grey colour and higher value of LOI.

Properties of Concrete mix with FA/CSF

Investigations in laboratory as well as actual applications in field indicte that maximum FA content in concrete should generally be limited to around 35% when economy and environmental protection is the primary consideration. When production of high strength concrete is the objective, it is better to limit it to 25%. For CSF, these limits are around 10-15%, most favourable being around 10%. When FA and CSF are used in combination, cementitious material may comprise 75% cement, 20% FA and 5% CSF. Effects of addition of FA and CSF within there ranges on various properties of concrete are described here.

Fresh Concrete

Workability. Presence of FA particles in concrete causes better dispersion of cement flocks, increased particulate packing and a type of ball bearing effect dut to the round shapes of the particles. These effects result in improved workability and reduced water demand. Though the exact extent of these effects are difficult to determine, the consensus amongst the researchers is that FA reduces the water demand of concrete for the same slump. Conversely, if same quantity of water is used, concrete incorporating FA will be comparatively more workable. An approximate norm is that 10% FA replacement is equivalent to increasing the water content by 3%, so far as workability is concerned.

CSF particles, on the other hand, though have a stabilizing effect on the rheology of fresh concrete and reduce the tendency of segregation and blending, make the concrete somewhat sticky. Investigators have reported that the addition of small percentage of CSF (5-10% by weight of cement) does not need the use of any extrawater, or water reducing admixture, to maintain desired slump. For higher percentage of CSF, addition of water reducing agent is necessary. However, in the industry the common practice is to use water reducing agent for all CSF concrete, so that same slump is obtained with less water-to-cementitious materials ratio to achieve higher strength.

Air-Entrainment. Air entrainment in fresh concrete is a desirable property for stability against freeze-thaw attack, a normal phenomenon in cold climate. Fly ash is believed to reduce the air content in fresh concrete, particularly when more than 20% FA (of (C + FA) by weight) is used. The reduction in air content is approximately 2% when FA content is increased from 0 to 50%. For concrete to be used in extreme cold climate, this aspect has to be taken care of.

For use of CSF, experimental data indicate that up to about 10% addition, there is no change in air content of fresh concrete. Beyond 10%, there is progressive reduction. For applications in cold climate where the concrete is likely to be subjected to freeze-thaw cycles, CSF concrete with air entrainment is recommended.

Other effects of FA addition in fresh concrete are reduction in rise in temperature, rate of evaporation, plastic shrinkage cracking and bleeding. Time of setting is marginally increased. Use of CSF, on the other hand, increases the rate of evaporation and plastic shrinkage cracking; and surface of such concrete must be protected immediately after laying in hot climate. In respect of time of setting, CSF content up to 10% has no significant effect ; but beyond that, the setting time progressively increases.

Hardened Concrete

Strength, Rate of Strength Gain and Elastic Modulus. For ultimate compressive strength of concrete made with cement in combination with pozzolanas like FA and CSF, two parameters are most important : the replacement level and, age of concrete.

With FA inclusion, the rate of pozzolanic reaction is comparatively slower. Therefore, when compressive strengths are compared, it is seen that up to about 35% FA, the ultimate compressive strengths at 7-day or 14-day is lower; they are nearly equal to those of reference concrete at 28 days ; and beyond 28 days, the strengths are higher. The reference concrete has same w/c ratio as $W(C + FA)$ ratio of FA concrete, both having similar cementitious material to aggregate ratio.

When CSF is used to replace cement, the early strength at 1-day and 3-day is reduced, especially where water to (cement + CSF) ratio is greater than 0·5. AT 28 days or 90 days, compressive strength of CSF concrete is higher. Concrete technologies are of the opinion that in respect of 28-day strength, effective improving ability of CSF is equivalent to 2 to 5 times that of an equivalent mass of cement, provided water-reducing admixture is also used. This is expressed by the relation[5] :

$$\left(\frac{w}{c}\right)_R = \left(\frac{w}{c + K_S}\right)_S$$

where the subscripts R and S indicate reference and CSF concrete, respectively ; K, is the efficiency factor varying from 2 to 5 ; and w, c, s, are weight of water, cement and CSF, respectively in kg/m^3 of cement.

Module of elasticity of concrete made with pozzolanas in combination with cement, follows similar relationship to its ultimate compressive strength as does that of portland cement concrete to its own strength.

Creep. For the same 28-day design strength, FA concrete exhibits lower creep than portland cement concrete, the difference may be upto 50% depending upon the mix proportions and the age of concrete. The reason for lower creep is higher ultimate strength of the concrete. Though data on creep of CSF concrete are still limited, same trend as in FA concrete may be reasonably assumed.

Permeability. Permeability is a major factor in deterioration of concrete, as more permeable the concrete is, the more will be the ingress of liquids and gases into the body of the concrete. Both FA and CSF, because they cause dense packing and increased hydration of cement and pozzolanic reactions (though delayed in case of FA concrete), reduce the permeability. The presence of FA and CSF leads to greater precipitation of cement gel products than that with portland cement alone, amd more effectively blocks the pores in concrete, thus reducing its permeability. The actual extent of reduction depends on many factors like water-to-cementitious materials ratio, aggregate grading, compaction, efficiency of curing, and the quality and extent of pozzolanas.

Concrete containing pozzolanas have also exhibited better resistance against chemical attacks and alkali-aggregate reactions. In respect of frost attack, FA concrete shows better resistance though air content in fresh concrete somewhat reduces with FA use. Available data for CSF concrete are not conclusive in this respect.

Properties of Concrete using a Combination of FA and CSF as Pozzolanas

From the properties exhibited by concrete using FA or CSF individually to replace cement, it is observed that there may be some marginal adverse effects in their use, particularly for special applications. As an example, it may be seen that with FA addition only, the rate of strength gain is somewhat lower up to 28 days. This affects early removal of forms. CSF concrete, on the other hand, gives increased rate of strength gain from fourth day onwards upto 28 days. Beyond 28 days, the contribution of CSF to strength is negligible, though pozzolanic reaction for FA continues for much longer period. Therefore, these materials, if used in combination, offset the adverse effects and the resulting concrete exhibits all round better performance. With this supposition, extensive researches have been carried out, of late, using cement, FA and CSF together.

It has been reported that a very promising mix of cementitious materials is a combination of 75% cement, 20% FA and 5% CSF. Such a combination not only increases the early-age rate of strength gain, but fully makes up the reduction in 7-day or 14-day strength of FA concrete and at 28 days, the strength is higher than that of FA concrete, especially for low water-to-cementitious materials ratios. In a particular series of experiments with 1 : 5 cementitious materials to aggregate ratio by weight, 0·3 $w/(c + FA + CSF)$ ratio and 3% by weight of $(c + FA + CSF)$ of superplasticizer, an ultimate compressive strength of 70 MPa was achieved at 28-day for such a combination.

Role of FA/CSF in production of High Strength Concrete

Even in early stages of development of high strength concrete (HSC) with cement only, it was observed that HSC required low water-to-cement ratio (less than 0·3) necessitating use of water-reducers, and very high cement content, making it less economically viable. It was also seen that there was a practical limit to cement content at around 500 kg/m^3. Investigations further revealed that the least water-cement ratio have which portland cement can fully hydrate was 0·38, implying that 20%-30% of cement in HSF remained unhydrated and did not contribute to strength development.

Use of pozzolanas like FA or CSF changes the situation very favourably. The pozzolana particles, besides reacting with free lime of cement and contributing to development of strength, bind themselves tightly with cement hydrates in form of flocks, and make more space available for the hydration products of cement grains. Thus, these pozzolana particles make it possible to use increased cement content per unit concrete volume and also improve hydration of cement grains. Therefore, when FA/CSF is used to partly replace cement, not only that the water-to-cementitious materials ratio can be furtehr reduced, but the maximum cement content itself also may be increased, to produce concrete of higher strengths at economically attractive costs.

6·10. Aggregates (Also refer Chapter on R.C.C.)

Aggregates are important ingradients of concrete and mortar. The important conditions for a good aggregate are as follows :

1. It should not be glossy structure. Because proper bond does not develop in glossy structure.

2. The strength of aggregate used should not be less than the strength of cementing material, as it takes the load.

3. The aggregate should not be soft, porous or flaky. It should be angular which can develop proper strength and bond.

4. It should not absorb water more than 5%. It should be free from salt, clay, organic impurities etc. otherwise it will loose strength.

Classification of Aggregates

(*a*) *Fine aggregate* : Size less than 4·75 mm

(*b*) *Coarse aggregate* : Size more than 4·75 mm

Fine aggregate. These are generally known as sand which can be obtained from the following sources.

(*a*) river sand (*b*) pit sand (*c*) sea sand (*d*) fine waste of stone crushing plants.

Sand can also be classified according to the size :

(*a*) Fine sand, fineness modulus 22-26.

(*b*) Medium sand, fineness modulus 26-29.

(*c*) Coarse sand, fineness modulus 29-32.

Bulking of sand. When sand is moistened, film of water form on the particles which tends to hold them apart, causing an increase in volume of sand. This is known as bulking of sand. This bulking goes on increasing with the increase of the percentage of water mixed upto a certain extent after which decrease in bulking goes on with the further increase of water and ultimately it becomes nil when the sand is completely saturated. At its saturation point the volume is found as it was in complete dry condition.

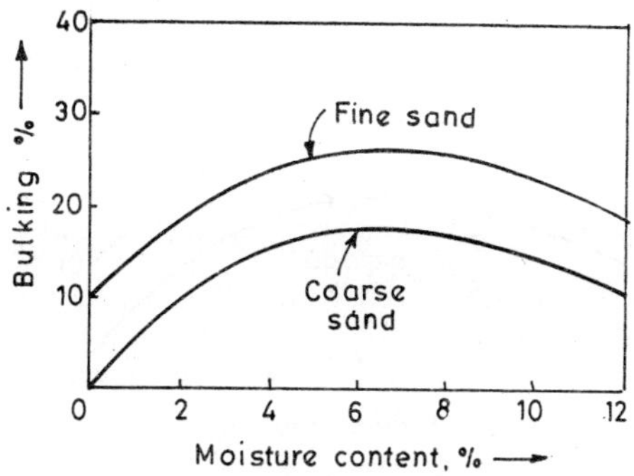

Fig. 6·14. Bulking of sand.

Measurement of Bulking

Dry process. A container of known volume (V) is filled with wet sand. The sand is then dried in an oven at 110 ± 5°C till the surface moisture disappears completely. It is then refilled in the same container (It may be graduated) which gives the unbulked volume say V_1.

Wet process. The unbulked volume can also be determined by filling container having wet sand by more water till it becomes completely saturated and settles down. This volume may again be volume V_1 (unbulked).

$$\text{Percentage bulking of sand} = \frac{V - V_1}{V} \times 100$$

when measuring sand an allowance for this bulking should be made to obtain correct proportion of sand.

Procedure for finding the bulking pattern of a sample of sand

(1) Put the available sand in a container after drying in the oven and measurement of height by a steel scale say it is h

(2) Take out the sand from the container in a tray and mix 2% by weight of sand water and mix it thoroughly by hand. Care should be taken that no particle of sand should go out.

(3) Again fill this 2% wet sand in the container and level it, no tamping is to be done, measure the length again say it is h_1.

(4) Repeat the process by adding 4%, 6% ... of water upto saturation and measure the heights in the container say it is h_2, h_3 and so on.

(5) Calculate the percentage of bulking in each case by the formula $\frac{h_1 - h}{h} \times 100$.

(6) Plot a graph showing the bulking pattern of the sand in trial.

(7) Mark the maximum bulking

Standard sand. Indian standard sand is used for testing cement. It is obtained from Ennore (Tamil Nadu). Equal amount of sand by weight of three variable sizes given below are mixed and used as standard sand.

(1) Passing 2 mm sieve and retained on 1 mm sieve.

(2) Passing 1 mm sieve and retained on 500 μ sieve.

(3) Passing on 500 μ sieve and retained on 90 μ sieve.

This clean, well graded and granular sand is used to te t compressive strength of cement. In case of this sand is not available, clear river sand free of all impurities and of this gradation can be used and results obtained which are 65 to 70 percent correct compared to standard sand.

Note : Previously Leighton-Buzzord sand was imported for this purpose.

Coarse aggregate. These are of two types :

(*a*) Natural gravel (*b*) Crushed aggregate.

(*a*) **Natural aggregate** (Gravel) is found in river beds which is round edged and sieved according to different grades. It is round or oval in shape. It varies from pea gravel, gravel, single to boulders in size 4 mm to 250 mm. It gives a better workability than the crushed sharp edged aggregate.

(*b*) **Crushed aggregate**. Big boulders or stones are crushed in crushers to the desired gauges and screened separately according to the gauges. These aggregates are sharp edged which have a better strength but lesser workability. Dirt or disintegrated parts are removed while screaning. Its specific gravity varies from 2·5 to 2·7 and produces concrete of approximate density 250 kN/m^3.

Other types of aggregates are :

All in aggregate. It is collected from river beds. It is a mixture of all sized gravels therefore it contains a gradation. By further grading manually or mechanically it can be made suitable for a concrete aggregate. The dirt or undesirable materials are removed by screaning. Its strength is about 250 kN/m^3.

Light weight aggregates. This aggregate has a density about 100-120 kN/m^3 and used for producing concrete of light weight. It is not used in heavy structures and can be used in precast blocks or in partition wells etc. it can be produced by crushing pumice rocks or diatermite stone. Volcanic cinder or fly ash can also be used. This provides better insulation and fire resistance. Brick ballast of good 1st class brick is also used where low cost and light weight concrete is required such as in foundations etc.

Heavy weight aggregates. Where it is required to have a high strength concrete heavy weight aggregates are used having density more than 280 kN/m^3. These are magnitite (Fe_3O_4) barytes ($BaSO_4$) and scrap of iron etc. This type of concrete is required to shield against Gamma and X-rays in nuclear reactor and in similar installations for protection works and in counter weights of lifts and bridges.

Properties of Aggregate

(1) **Fineness modulus.** A well graded aggregate is one which is made up of stones or particles of different sizes ranging from large to small. Well graded aggregate contains minimum voids, hence quantity of cement required for max. strength is less.

Fineness modulus of an aggregate is an index number which is roughly proportional to the average size of particles in the aggregate *i.e.* the coarser is the aggregate, the higher the fineness modulus. It is computed by adding the cumulative percentage of material coarser than each of the following I.S. sieves and dividing the sum by 100

$\left(\text{Fineness Modulus} = \dfrac{\text{Cumulative \%age retaining}}{100}\right)$ 80 mm, 40 mm, 20 mm, 10 mm, 4·75 mm, 2·36 mm, 1·18 mm, 600 micron, 300 micron and 150 micron (m). For details refer chapter on R.C.C.

Workability is also a factor for achieving a better strength together with w/c ratio. The better is the gradation lesser will be the voids, lesser the cement required for better strength together with better workability. Possibility of segregation and bleeding will be less.

Fineness Modulus of coarse aggregate is always more than 5. Coarser is the material more the fineness modulus and vice-versa. In concrete fineness modulus of sand should be approximately 2·60 and that of coarse aggregate 6·00.

A known weight of dry aggregate is passed successively through IS sieves in the order given below :

Fine Aggregate. Sieve nos. 4·75, 2·36, 1·18, 600 μ, 300 m, 150 m.

Coarse Aggregate. 80 mm, 40 mm, 20 mm, 16 mm, 10 mm, 4·75 mm, 2·36 mm, 1·18 mm, 600 m, 300 μ and 150 μ.

All in aggregate. 80 mm, 40 mm, 20 mm, 4·75 mm, 600 m, 300 m and 150 m.

The material retained on each sieve is compared with the standard limits and a graph is plotted percentage passing vs. particles size.

Note : (1) Sieving should be started from larger size to smaller gradually.

(2) Shaking should be done backward and forward, left to right, circular and anti-clockwise with frequent jarring. Shaking should be done for 2 minutes on each sieve and weight retained and passed is taken and recorded in a tabular form.

(3) For mechanical sieving by mechanical vibrator, the material is put on the topmost sieve and vibrator is vibrated for a period of 15 to 20 minutes and weight retained on each sieve is noted.

Wt. of sample : *w* = 10 kg **Observation Table**

Sieve No.	*Wt. retained*	*% wt. retained*	*% Passing*	*Cumulative %age retained*
80, 46, 20, 10, 4·76, 2·36, 1·18, 600 m, 300 m and 100 m	Fineness Modulus = $\dfrac{\text{Cumulative \%age retaining}}{100}$			

Flakiness Index. The flakiness index of an aggregate is the percentage by weight of particles in it whose least dimension (thickness) is less than 0·6 of their mean dimension. This test is for the particles greater than 6·3 mm size, higher the flakiness index more flaky, less workability and weaker is the concrete. Impact value and crushing value increases with increase in flakiness index.

Elongation Index. The elongation index of an aggregate is the percentage by weight particles whose greatest dimension, (length) is greater than 1·8 times their mean dimension. The test is not applicable to size smaller than 63 mm. Higher the elongation index more elongated particle it contains. It makes concrete less workable, causes its segregation and produces weak concrete. Crushing value and impact value increases generally with the increase of elongation index.

Angularity number. The angularity number of an aggregate is the amount by which the percentage voids in it after compaction in a prescribed manner exceeds 33. The angularity number ranges from 0 for highly rounded pebbles to 10 and more for crushed stone. In a concrete for a given w/c ratio and aggregate cement ratio. The workability or compaction factor of concrete depends on the angularity of its aggregate.

Thermal Properties

(*i*) Coefficient of thermal expansion

(*ii*) Specific heat

(*iii*) Conductivity.

Mechanical Properties

(*i*) Crushing values

(*ii*) Impact value

(*iii*) Abrasion value : Abrasion is the property of a material by virtue of which it opposes the wearing of the material. Such as the tyres of moving vehicles wears the surfaces of the roads.

It can be ascertained by making scratch on the surface. If a deep scratch is made with a less power on the surface, the stone has less abrasion power.

Blending of aggregates (Proportioning of fine to coarse aggregates)

(2) **By Fineness modulus method :**

$$p = \frac{F_c - F_a}{F_c - F_f}$$

where p is the percentage of fine to be added to coarse. F_c, F_a and F_f are the fineness modulus of coarse, all aggregates (desired mix) and F_f is of fine aggregates respectively, taken separately of each.

If $F_c = 6{\cdot}2$, $F_f = 2{\cdot}0$ and $f_a = 4{\cdot}2$. The $p = \frac{(6{\cdot}2 - 2{\cdot}2) \times 100}{(6{\cdot}2 - 4{\cdot}0)} = 47{\cdot}6\%$ than is to say 47·6 parts of sand is to be added to (100 – 47·6) = 52·4 parts of coarse aggregates.

Trial method. The samples of different ratios are prepared and the heaviest mix of the same volume is taken for use.

Note : Please refer mix design in this case for concrete.

Grading of aggregates. It is particle size distribution of aggregates by sieve analysis. The grading of aggregate coarse to fine has a marked effect on the workability, uniformity and strength of concrete. A well graded and uniformly distributed aggregate produces a dence, hard and compact concrete while the partly graded concrete produces a harsh concrete having max. voids and less density. The gradation of aggregates is given in the table below.

Table 6·21. Grading Limits of Fine Aggregate

I.S. Sieve Designation	*Percentage passing*			
	Zone I	*Zone II*	*Zone III*	*Zone IV*
4·75	90-100	90-100	90-100	100
2·36	60-95	75-100	85-100	95-100
1·18	30-70	55-90	75-100	90-100
600 μ	15-34	35-59	60-79	80-100
300 μ	5-20	8-30	12-40	15-50
150 μ	0-10	0-10	0-10	0-15
app. Fineness modulus	3·5 coarse sand	2·7 medium	2·35 sand	1·18 fine sand

Grading for All in Aggregate

I.S. sieve designation	*Grading limit*	
	40 mm	*20 mm*
80 mm	100	—
40 mm	90-95	100
20 mm	45-75	95-100
4·75 μ	25-45	30-50
600 μ	8-30	10-35
150 μ	0-6	0-6

Grading for Coarse Aggregate

I.S. sieve designation	*%age Passing single size nominal*			*Percentage Passing graded size nominal*		
	40 mm I	*20 mm II*	*12·5 mm III*	*40 mm I*	*20 mm I*	*12·5 mm III*
40 mm	85-100	100	—	95-100	100	—
20 mm	0-20	85-100	—	30-70	95-100	100
16 mm	—	—	100	—	—	—
12·5 mm	—	—	85-100	—	—	95-100
10 mm	0-5	0-20	0-45	10-35	25-55	40-8
4·75	—	0-5	0-10	0-5	0-10	0-10
Fineness mod. app.	8·00	7·00	6·8	7·3	6·6	6·4

Main Factors Effecting Gradings. (1) Surface area of aggregate (2) Workability of mix (3) Relative vol. occupied by aggregate (4) Tendency to segregation (5) Large amount of material less than 300 μ.

Sampling for Tests. (1) If the deposits is an open face of bank or pit, the sample should be taken by channelling the face vertically, bottom to top, so that it will be representative of the material proposed to be used.

(2) Sample of coarse aggregate from stock pits should be taken at or near the top of the pile or near the base or from intermediate points. Further segregation should be avoided.

Samples from top should be taken a bit below the surface where the material is not effected by heat and sun etc. and segregation due to other reasons. From bottom also the sample should be a bit above the ground which may be effected by damp or any other factor.

(3) Sample from wagons, trucks and boats etc. should be taken from 4 or 5 points where segregation etc. is not considered to be effective.

(4) Number and size or quality of samples depend on the type or tests.

Impurity in Aggregates and their tests. The following impurities are found in aggregates :

(*a*) Clay lumps (*b*) Fine silt and fine dust (can be obtained by sedimentation)

(*c*) Soft particles (*d*) Light weight pieces and (*e*) organic impurities.

Organic impurities can be washed by water or by other chemical treatment.

(1) **Field test for impurities.** For measuring silt content in an aggregate or sand sample.

(*a*) In a 200 m litre jar take about 100 ml of sample in a dry condition.

(*b*) Fill the jar with the clear water upto about 150 ml.

(*c*) Keep it about for 24 hours. After 24 hrs. a layer of silt will be seen on the top of the sample. By measuring the thickness of this layer, the percentage amount if impurities with sample can be ascertained.

Let h be the height of the sample in the jar,

h_1 is the height of impurities collected on top of the jar.

then impurities = $\frac{h_1}{h} \times 100$ percent.

Following are the permissible limits for silt content

Natural sand	...	....	4%
Crushed stain sand	....	....	10%
Coarse aggregate	....	....	1%

(2) **Lab Test for Silt content.** Take about 500 gms of sand. Sieve it through 75 micron sieve. Fine material will pass through the sieve. To remove the finer particles further which are still sticked to the sand, wash it by water on the sieve itself till all the finer particles are washed. Put the sand sample on oven and heat upto a temperature of 100-110°C for 24 hours for water to evaporate and weight after 24 hours.

The wt. of the original sample $= w_1$

The wt. of the sample after washing $= w_2$

Percentage of silt $= \frac{w_1 - w_2}{w_1} \times 100$ percent.

The presence of silt clay or dust in excessive quantities is harmful, because owing to their fairness and large surface area, silt and dust increase the amount of water necessary to wet all the particles in the mix. Clay makes a surface coating which interfere with the bond with cement and aggregate and this interfere the strength of the concrete.

Aggregate Impact Test. Toughness is the property of material to resist impact. The aggregate impact value gives relative measure of the resistance of an aggregate to sudden shock or impact which in some aggregate differs from its resistance to a slow compressive load. The test given below is standardized by the Indian Institutes.

The Apparatus Consists of :

(1) A metal base supported firmly over a firm floor. A detachable cylindrical steel cup of internal dia. 102 mm and depth 50 mm is rigidly fastened centrally to the base plate. A mild steel hammer of wt. 135-140 N having the lower end cylindrical in shape, 100 mm in dia. and 50 mm long with 2 mm chamfer at the lower edge capable of sliding freely between vertical guide and fall concentric over the cup. There is an arrangement for raising the hammer and allowing it to fall freely between the vertical guides from a height of 380 mm on the test sample in the cup. The height of fall being adjustable upto 5 mm. A key is provided for supporting the hammer. While fastening or removing the cup (refer Fig. 6·15).

(2) A cylindrical metal measure having internal dia 75 mm and depth 50 mm for measuring aggregate.

(3) A straight metal tamping rod 10 mm dia. and 200 mm long and end is bullet ended.

(4) 1-3 sieves of sizes 12·5 mm, 10 mm and 8·36 mm.

(5) A balance of capacity more than 500 gm. to weight upto an accuracy of 0·1 gm.

(6) A thermostatically controlled drying oven capable of maintaining a temperature of 100-110°C.

Generally aggregates crushing and impact value are similar numerically, but in cases of fine grained highly silicaceous aggregates which are less resistant to impact than to crushing. The impact values are roughly higher by 5 than their crushing values.

The sample under test is kept in a mould is subjected to 15 belows of a metal hammer of weight 14·5 N falling from a height of 380 mm. The quantity of fine material passing through 2·36 mm. IS sieve indicates the toughness of the sample of aggregate. The ratio of weight of material finer than 2·36 mm to the weight of total sample taken is experessed in percentage as the impact value.

Let the original wt. of the oven dry sample is $= w_1$ kg

Wt. of the fraction passing 2·36 mm IS sieve $= w_2$ kg

Aggregate impact value $= \frac{w_2}{w_1} \times 100$ percent.

Preparation of sample for test. The test sample consists of aggregate passing over 12·5 mm. IS sieve and retained on 10 mm. sieve. Dried in an oven for four hours at a temperature of 100-105°C and then cooled. The sample is filled about 1/3rd in the cylindrical measure and temped by 25 bellows with bullet ended rod. Further quantity of aggregate is then added upto 2/3rd full in the cylinder and temped by 25 bellows by the same rod again cylindrical measure now is filled full with the sample and again temped by 25 bellows. The surplus material in the measure is struck of by rod horizontally. The net wt. of the sample in the measure is determined to the nearest gram by the balance. The whole sample is then transferred to the cylindrical cup firmly fixed in the horizontal level base of the machine. The sample in the cup is again temped by 25 bellows.

The hammer in the machine is adjusted at a height of 380 mm from the top of the sample in the steel cup. The hammer is allowed to fall 15 times at an interval of not less than one second.

The sample from the cup is removed and sieved in the IS sieve of 2·36 mm. The fraction passing the sieve is weighed accurately upto 0·1 gm. The fraction retained on the sieve is also weighed and if the wt. of the fraction passing and retained is added together is less than the original wt. of the sample by more than one gm. The test should be discarded and a fresh test is made. Two tests should be made to evaluate the impact vlaue.

Let original wt. of oven dried aggregate be w_1 gm

Wt. of fraction passing in 2·36 mm IS sieve $= w_2$ gm

Aggregate impact factor

$$= \frac{100 \times w_2}{w_1} \text{ percent}$$

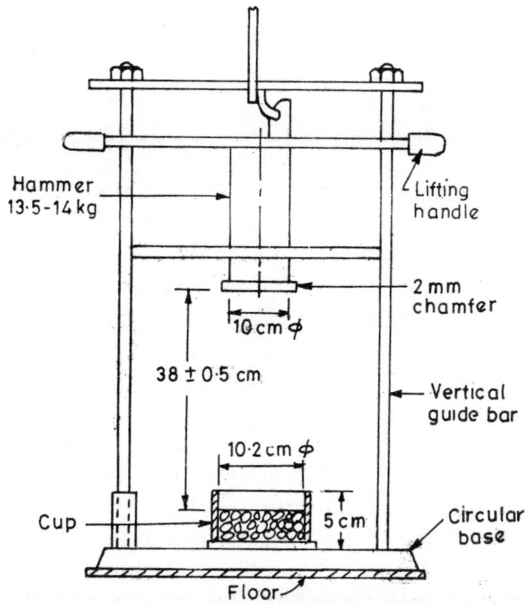

Fig. 6·15. Aggregate impact testing apparatus.

The impact value is used to classify the toughness of the stone, well shaped angular,

cubical stones provide high resistance to impact, whilst flacky and elongated stones provide less resistance.

Impact value below 10—exceptionally strong

10-20—Strong

20-30—Satisfactory, for Road work

above 10—Weak for road surfaces

30— For Bituminous conc., cement conc.

35— For Bituminous bound macadam

45— For base coats of c. conc.

Aggregate Crushing Value Test. The aggregate crushing value gives a relative measure of the resistance of an aggregate crushing under gradually applied compressive load. For a good quality of concrete, aggregate possessing low crushing value is preferred.

The aggregate crushing value should not be more than 45 percent for aggregate used for concrete other than wearing coats, run ways, road sand and airfield pavements.

The apparatus consists of :

(1) A steel cylinder with open ends and internal dia. 152 mm with 225 mm square base, a hole is provided across the stem of the plunger, sot that a rod could be inserted for lifting or placing the plunger in the cylinder. The plunger is provided with a piston of dia. 150 mm.

(2) Cylindrical measure having an internal dia. of 115 mm and height 180 mm.

(3) Steel tamping rod 16 mm dia. and 450-600 mm long with one end bullet ended.

(4) Balance of capacity 30 N with a least count of 1 gm.

(5) Compression testing machine of capacity 40 tonnes or more.

The aggregate crushing value is defined as a ratio of the weight fines passing the specified IS sieve to the total wt. of the sample expressed as a percentage.

Total wt. of Dry sample taken = w_1 N

Wt. of the portion of crushed material passing 2·36 mm IS sieve = w_2 N

Aggregate crushing value = $\frac{w_2}{w_1} \times 100$ percent.

Testing procedure. (1) The sample of aggregate is passed over IS Sieve 12·5 mm and retained on 100 mm sieve is selected for standard test. The aggregate should be in surface dry condition before testing. The aggregate may be dried by heating at temperature 100-110°C for a period of 24 hours and is tested after cooling to room temperature.

(2) The cylindrical measure is filled by the test sample of aggregate in three equal layers. Each layer is tamped by 25 bellows by a bullet ended rod. After the 3rd layer is tamped, the aggregate at the top of the cylindrical measure to levelled by the tamping rod passing horizontally on the sample. About 6·5 kg of aggregate is required for preparing two test samples in a repeat test.

The cylinder of the test apparatus is placed in position on the plate. 1/3rd of the cylinder is filled by the sample and tamped by 25 bellows of the bullet ended rod. Similarly remaining two parts are filled in two operations and tamped by 25 bellows or before in each operation. The level of the surface is levelled by the tamping rod as usual. The total depth of the material in the cylinder after tamping shall be 100 mm and plunger is placed in the position in the testing machine. Load is then applied through the plungers at a uniform rate of 40 kN per minute until the total load to 400 kN. Aggregate including the crushing portion are removed from the cylinder and sieved on 2·36 mm IS Sieve. The material which passes this sieve is collected.

The above crushing test is repeated on 2nd sample of the same weight in accordance with the above test procedure. Thus two tests are made for the same same specimen for taking an average value. Depending on size of aggregate suitable cylinder should be used as given in table below :

Table 6·22. Details for Aggregate Crushing Test Apparatus

Aggregate size passing sieve in mm	*Retained on sieve size in mm*	*Diameter of cylinder to be used in cm*
25-0	20·0	15·0
20-0	12·5	7·5
10-0	6·3	7·5
6·3	4·75	7·5
4·75	3·35	7·5
3·35	2·36	7·5

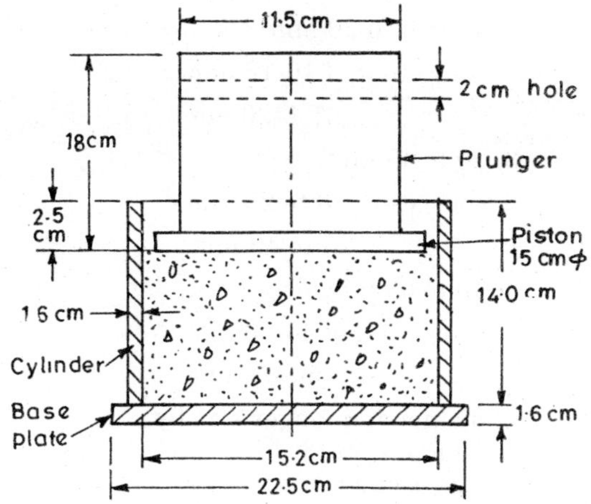

Fig. 6·16. Aggregate crushing test app.

The aggregate crushing value is an indirect measure of crushing strength of the aggregate. Low crushing value indicates strong aggregates as the crushed fraction is low. Thus the test can be used to assess the suitability of aggregates with reference to strength for various types of pavement components.

Note : Aggregate crushing value is also known as A.C.V.

Soundness test of aggregates. Soundness of an aggregate refers to the ability of an aggregate to resist against weather and other atmospheric environment. It may be freezing and thawing, variation of temperature, dampness in atmosphere, presence of CO_2 etc. which directly effect the mineral.

Apparatus consists of :

(1) Container for aggregates made with suitable perforation or with cohesive permit free access and drainage of solution.

(2) IS sieve of size 4·75, 8·10, 12·5, 16, 20, 25, 34, 40, 50, 63 and 80.

(3) Thermostatically controlled over, having capacity to maintain 105 ± 5°C and having an average evaporation rate at least 25 gms per hour.

As a general guide it may be taken that aggregate loss of weight after 10 cycles should not exceed 12% when tested with sod. sulphate and 18% when tested with magnesium sulphate. IRC has specified 12% as the max. permissible loss in soundness test after 5 cycles with sod. sulphate for aggregate to be used in bituminous surface dressing, penetration mecadam and bituminous macadam surfaces.

Procedure of testing. Saturated solution of sod. sulphate (Anhydrous Na_2SO_4 or the crystalline Na_2SO_4, $10H_2O)_4$ is prepared in water at a temperature of 25°-30°C. It should be ensured that the solution is saturated and excess salt is present. The solution is maintained at a temperature of 27° ± 2°C and stirred at frequent intervals until it is used. At the time of using the solution should have a specific gravity of not less than 1·5% and not more than 1·7% and discoloured solution should not be used. It is necessary to use not less than 420 gm of anhydrous salt or 1300 gm of crystalline dehydrate salt per litre of water.

The coarse aggregate specimen may be prepared by sieving it in 4·75 mm IS sieve. The amount of sample should be :

For aggregate

1. 4·75 to 10 mm size ... ... 300 gms
2. 10 mm to 20 mm ... ... 1000 gms
   consisting of 10-12 mm 33%
   12·5-20 mm 67%
3. 20 to 40 mm ... ... 1500 gms
   consisting 20 to 25 mm 33%
   25 to 49 mm 67%
4. 40 to 63 mm size ... ... 3000 gms
   consisting of 40-50 mm 50%
   50-63 mm 50%
5. 80 mm and longer size by ... ... 3000 gms
   20 mm spreaded in sieve size each fraction

The samples should be washed and dried to a constant temperature of 105 ± 5°C and should be taken in quantities and proportion as mentioned above. The samples are then immersed in the prepared solution of sod. sulphate or mag. sulphate for 16 to 18 hours in such a depth of at least 15 mm. The sample contained are covered to avoid the possibility of evaporation of solution and maintained at 27° ± 1°C.

After 16-18 hours the sample is removed and placed in an oven at a temperature of 150 ± 5°C for drying to a constant weight. After this the samples again immersed in solution. This is repeated for 5 to 10 cycles as the case may be. After final cycle the sample is removed, washed to free it from sulphate which can be tested by borium chloride (when there is no white precipitate then borium chlorite is added to wash water. It is presumed that there is no sulphate with wash water). The sample is again dried to a constant weight at 105 ± 5°C temperature. Coarse aggregate fractions are sieved by IS sieve of size mentioned earlier. Each fraction of aggregate is examined visually to see if there is any evidence of extensive splitting, crumbling or disintegration of grains.

The results should be tabulated as below :

(1) Type of solution used for test

(2) Weight of each fraction of sample before test and percentage weight of the fraction.

(3) Weight of each fraction of sample after test.

(4) Percentage loss.

Table 6·23. Results and Observations as Shown in Tabulated Form

Sieve size mm Passing	*Retained*	*Grading of original sample*	*Wt. of lost fraction before test gms*	*% passing from sieve of the test actually % losts*	*Weighed average*
63	40	20	3000	4·8	0·96
40	20	45	1500	9·6	3·6
20	10	23	1000	8·00	2·20
10	4·75	12	300	11·2	1·34
Total		100	5800		8·190

Specific gravity of an aggregate. It is the ratio of the weight of given volume of sample to the weight of equal volume of water. Specific gravity of rocks varies from 2·6 to 2·8.

$$\text{Bulk density of aggregate} = \frac{\text{weight of material in compacted form}}{\text{volume of container}}$$

Void ratio. It is volume of voids to the solid volume occupied by aggregate

$$\text{Void ratio} = \frac{\text{Volume of void}}{\text{Solid volume}}$$

Water absorption of an aggregate. It is the amount of water that an oven dried aggregate can absorb, if put in water for 24 hrs.

Field procedure for determining above ratios is as follows :

(1) Take about 1 kg of sample and weigh it.

(2) Take this sample in any frying Pan and heat gently till the complete surface moisture disappears. As soon as this situation comes sand looses its shining and becomes dull weigh it.

(3) Take a clean dry cylinder of known volume and weigh it accurately say w_1.

(4) Put surface dry sand (from step 2) in this cylinder upto top and weigh it say w_2.

(5) Take out this sand from the cylinder completely and heat it in an oven upto a temperature of 105 ± 5°C till complete moisture is evaporated and sand becomes dry *i.e.* it attains constant weight. Weigh it say w_3.

(6) For getting unit weight of compacted sand, the surface dry sand is filled in cylinder (step-4) in three layers and compacted each layer with 25 bellows of 16 mm diameter, 600 mm long tamping rod. Strike the top and weight it say w_4.

If volume of cylinder = V

$$\text{Water content of sand} = \frac{w_3}{w_2 - w_1} \times 100 \text{ percent}$$

$$\textbf{Bulk density } (\gamma) = \frac{w_2 - w_1}{V} \text{ kg/litre or gm/ml}$$

$$\text{Bulk density of compacted sand} = \frac{w_4 - w_1}{\gamma} \text{ kg/litre}$$

If G_S is the specific gravity of sand

$$\text{Percentage voids} = \frac{G_S - \gamma}{G_S} \times 100$$

Generally the sand is mixed in terms of volume and to convert from weight to volume, weight is always to be divided by the bulk density to get correct volume of sand.

Porosity. The presence of internal pores in the aggregates. Due to the porosity the permeation and absorption effects the bonding properties between aggregate to the cement plaster, resistance of concrete to freezing and thawing as well as chemical solubility and resistance to abrasion are effected. The pores are of various sizes and effects to strength.

Absorption. Water absorption in aggregate is determined by the increase in weight of an oven dried sample when immersed in water for 24 hours. The ratio of increase of weight to the weight of oven dried mass is expressed in percentage, which is termed as absorption.

Moisture content. It is percentage of the weight of saturated to surface dry aggregate and is termed as **moisture content.** The total water content of the moist aggregate is the sum of absorption and moisture in surface. Coarse aggregate holds very much less water than sand and hence contain less moisture contents.

Specific gravity and water absorption test. The appliances required are as follows:

(1) Balance and weights, balance must have a least count of 0·1.

(2) Oven to maintain temperature 100 ± 5°C

(3) Container for water with an arrangement for suspending a basket (wire-basket).

(4) A shallow tray and two pieces of absorbing cloths.

About 2 kg of the aggregate sample is washed thoroughly to remove fines, drained and then placed in the wire basket and then immersed in distilled water at a temperature 22-32°C with a cover of 5 cm of water above the basket. The entrapped air is removed from the sample by lifting the basket of aggregate 25 mm above the base of the tank and allowing it to drop 25 times (at 1 drop per second). The basket and aggregate is kept immersed in water for a period of 24 ± 1/2 hours afterwards.

The basket with the sample is weighted in the water say it is w_1 gm. The basket with sample is taken out of the water and water is allowed to drain for few minute.

The aggregate is collected in an absorbant cloth.

The empty basket is then returned to the tank, jolted for 25 times and weighed in water say it is w_2 gm.

The aggregate placed on absorbant cloth is kept till no more water could be absorbed by the cloth. The aggregate is then transferred to 2nd absorbent cloth and allow to dry for 10 minutes. It is further dried upto 60 minutes on the absorbent cloth. The aggregate should be covered and not let open to atmospheric or sun light. In the 1st 10 minutes a current of unheated air may be used to expedite the drying process. The surface dried aggregate sample is weighed, say it is w_3 gm. The aggregate is placed in a shallow tray and kept on an oven at a temperature of 100 to 110°C for 24 hrs. Then remove it from oven cool in an air tight container and weighed say it is w_4 gm.

Observations are noted as below :

w_1 = wt. of saturated aggregate suspended in water + basket.

w_2 = wt. of basket suspended in water

w_3 = wt. of saturated surface dry agg.

w_4 = wt. of oven dry aggregate.

wt. of saturated aggregate in water $(w_5) = (w_1 - w_2)$ gm

wt. of water equal to the vol. of agg. = $(w_3 - w_5)$ gm

$$\text{True specific gravity} = \frac{w_4}{(w_3 - w_4)}$$

$$\text{Apparent specific gravity} = \frac{w_4}{(w_3 - w_5)}$$

$$\text{Water absorption} = \left(\frac{w_3 - w_4}{w_4}\right) \times 100 \text{ percent}$$

Higher the specific gravity, the higher is the strength of aggregate and harder it is.

Specific gravity : – Gravel = 2·6, Lime stone 2·7 and Granite 2·75

Water absorption. It is a measure of porosity. The absorption is more, the porosity will be more and vice versa. It also effects and reduces workability of concrete.

Moisture contents of aggregate (M.C.)

Let w_1 = wt. of aggregate

$$w_2 = \text{wt. of oven dry aggregate}$$

$$\text{M.C.} = \frac{w_1 - w_2}{w_1} \times 100 \text{ percent}$$

Note : The process in the field can be done on the lines of the above tests.

Testing of absorption and surface moisture

(1) Take a wet sample of about 500 gm, weigh it, say it is w_1.

(2) The sample is heated in a frying pan gently tell all surface moisture disappears and the sample looses its shining and becomes dull, weight it say it is w_2.

(3) The sample is again heated in oven till all of its moisture evporates and the sample becomes dry, weigh it say it is w_3.

$$\text{Then absorption} = \frac{w_2 - w_3}{w_3} \times 100 \text{ percent}$$

$$\text{Surface moisture content} = \frac{w_1 - w_2}{w_3} \times 100 \text{ percent of dry wt.}$$

$$\text{Specific gravity} = \frac{w_2}{w_2 - w_1} \text{ and apparent specific gravity} = \frac{w_3}{w_3 - w_1}.$$

6·11. Concrete

Fibre Reinforced Concrete. Concrete is reinforced with discontinuous discrete fibres. The fibres used are (*i*) Steel fibre, (*ii*) Plastic fibre, (*iii*) Glass fibre, (*iv*) Carbon fibre and (*v*) Asbestos fibres etc. The fibre length may be 6 mm to 7·5 mm. **Aspect ratio** is the ratio of the length of the fibre to the equivalent fibre diameter. This ratio varies from 30 to 150.

Light weight concrete. Porous aggregates are used for light wet concrete. Its density does not exceed 18 kN/m^3. It saves dead load. It has better insulation against heat and sound. Its strength is less.

Aggregates used in light weight concrete

(1) **Cinder or breeze**—Obtained from coal waste, must not have combustible material.

(2) **Pumice stone**

(3) **Foamed slag**—Obtained by rapid quenching of blast furnace slag in water. It should in free form combustible constituents like coke and sulphate.

(4) **Aggregate with no fines**—The properties of rigid weight concrete with porous aggregates are their low density, heat conductivity strength and frost resistance.

(5) Brick bats or ballast

Cellular concrete. It is a type of light wt. concrete, obtained by introducing gas bubbles into plastic cement mix in order to produce a material with cellular structure. Some what similar to sponge rubber. It is also can be said as aerated concrete.

Gas concrete is obtained by chemical reaction generating a gas in the mortar. So that when it sets, it contains a large number of gas bubbles. Finely divided aluminium powder is most commonly used. Its proportion is about 0·2 percent of weight of cement. Powdered zinc and hydrogen per oxide is also used. This generates oxygen, Resin soap which introduces and stabilizes air bubbles during mixing at high speed.

Prepacked concrete. Stones and big size ballast is packed dry and then mortar is blowed by a mortar gun at a pressure which fills the interests of the packed material and thus forms a solid mass.

Guniting. A layer of cement-sand grout is sprayed on the honey combed layers by a cement gun on the existing surfaces to make it compact.

Shot crete concrete. Mortar conveyed through a hose and pneumatically projected to a surface under high pressure. It is a process applied to fill joints and cracks, etc. This contains smaller size of aggregate. There are two methods for the shot creting (1) dry process water is fed before mortar is jetted from nozzle at a high velocity on the surface to be gunited (2) In the wet process water is fed in concrete in the beginning.

Workability of concrete

Factors effecting workability :

(1) Aggregate gradation ; Max size of aggregate

(2) Shape of particles ; angular (crushed), round (Shingle)

(3) Surface texure of aggregates

(4) Mix proportion

(5) Water content

Methods for Assessing workability :

(1) Slump test—(see chapter on concrete and RCC)

(2) Compaction factor apparatus—(see chapter on concrete and RCC)

(3) Flow Table

(4) Vee-Bee test (remoulding test)

(5) Ball penetration test—Kelly penetrometer.

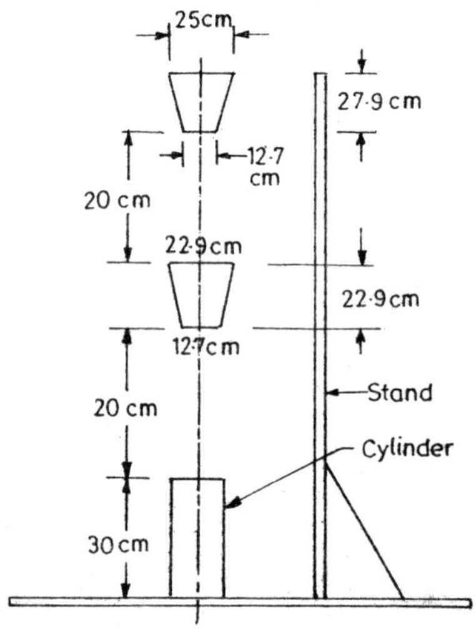

Fig. 6·17. Compacting factor apparatus.

Compaction factor apparatus. Detail operation can be seen in chapter of Concrete & R.C.C.

$$\text{Compaction factor} = \frac{w_1}{w_2} = \frac{\text{wt. of partially compacted concrete}}{\text{wt. of fully compacted concrete}}$$

w_1 = wt. of the concrete left = the cylinder after removing surplus concrete by scrapping.

w_2 = wt. of the concrete in the cylinder filled with fresh concrete in layers and tamped to mix thoroughly to obtain full compaction.

Table 6·24. Compact factor for different workability

Workability of mix	*Compact factor*
Low workability	0·85
Med. workability	0·92
Good workability	0·95
High workability	over 0·95

Flow Table (Workability Test)—apparatus consists of :

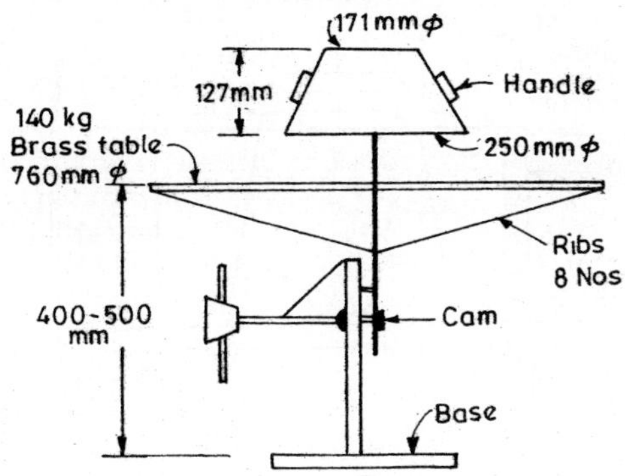

Fig. 6·18. Flow table apparatus or mould.

(1) Flow Table as shown in Fig. 6·18 having a table of 760 mm dia. of brass. With concentric cords marked on it. It is mounted on a concrete box about 400-500 mm in height of wt. not less than 140 kg.

(2) A mould of smooth metal casting in the form of a frustum of a cone with a base of 250 mm in dia. upper surface 171 mm in dia. and 127 mm high. The base and top are open and at right angles to the axis of the cone handles are provided to lift it.

(3) A tamping rod of 16 mm dia. and 600 mm long with one end is rounded.

The flow of the concrete is recorded as the percentage increase in the dia. of the spreaded concrete over the base dia. of the moulded concrete, calculate as below :

$$\text{Flow percent} = \frac{\text{Spread dia.} - \text{original dia.}}{\text{original dia.}}, \text{ original dia. is generally 250 mm}$$

$$\text{Hence flow percent} = \frac{\text{Spread dia. in mm} - 250}{250} \times 100 \text{ percent}$$

The table is cleaned of all dirt. The mould of standard dimension is put on the centre of the table firmly and filled with concrete in two layers, each layer is tamped with 25 bellows by the bullet ended rod (rounded). Overflow if any is removed, cleaned and mould is lifted. Concrete stands on its own weight. The table is then raised by 12·5 mm and dropped. This raising and lowering of table is done for 15 times in 15 seconds. The speed is measured at six places upto 5 mm and average is taken and flow percentage is calculated.

The flow percent can vary from 0 to 150%. A close pattern of spread of concrete gives a good indication of the characteristics of conc. such as tendency for segregation.

VEE-BEE Consistometer

It is an indirect measure of workability in laboratory. Latest I.S. : 456 recommends values of workability of Vee-Bee time in seconds. This method is used for very dry concrete of low workability whose slump value cannot be measured by slump test.

Apparatus consists of :

(1) Vee-Bee consistometer as shown in the figure, 6·19 which contains a slump cone (*B*) placed inside the sheet-metal cylindrical pot (*A*). *A* cone *D* is placed on top of slump cone to pour concrete and which can be moved horizontally. The mounting is fixed on a vibrator.

(2) A tamping rod 16 mm dia. with one end bullet ended (rounded)

(3) Trowel and stop watch etc.

Slump is measured in terms of Vee-Bee seconds. It is the time taken by the concrete to change from conical shape to a cylindrical shape in seconds, which is known as Vee-Bee degree when the cylindrical pot is vibrated.

Procedure of test is as below :

(1) Put the slump (concrete) in cylindrical pot in three layers, each layer is tamped by the

tamping rod by 25 bellows. The concrete is poured by another cone *D*. The slump cone which is placed in the cylindrical container is removed.

(2) The concrete is vibrated by vibrating the cylindrical pot and the stop watch is started. The vibrations are kept continued till the conical shape of concrete is totally converted to the cylindrical shape of the pot. The stop watch is then closed and the reading is taken. Average of six results are taken. The readings are recorded as below. t_1 and t_2 are the readings of stop watch at start and at closing respectively.

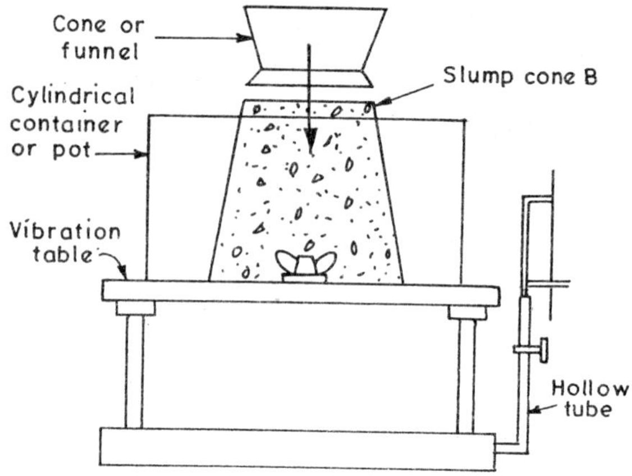

Fig. 6·19. Vee-bee consistometer

S. No.	*Sample No. 1*	*Initial reading of stop watch*	*Final reading of stop watch*	*Vee-Bee degree in seconds* $(t_2 - t_1)$
1				
2				
3	**Note :** 20-10 seconds workability is known as low			
4	5-2 seconds workability is medium			
5				
6				

Table. 6·25. Workability of conc.

Placing condition	*Degree of workability*	*Value of workability*
1. Concrete in shallow section with vibration	Very low	20-10 sec vee-bee time or 0·75 to 0·80 compaction factor
2. Concrete of lightly reinforced section with vibrations	Low	10-5 sec vee-bee time or 0·80 to 0·85 compaction factor
3. Concrete of lightly reinforced sec. without vibrations	Medium	5-3 sec vee-bee time or 0·85 to 0·92 compaction factor or 25-75 mm slump for 20 mm of aggregate
4. Concrete of heavily reinforced section without vibrations	High	Above 0·92 compaction factor or 75-125 mm slump for 20 mm aggregate.

$$\text{Water cement ratio} = \frac{\text{Qty. of water added in litre}}{\text{Qty. of cement in litre}}$$

Less water incompletes the process of hydration and more water improves the workability but forms more voids. Hence conc. does not attain max. strength in both cases.

Poissons ratio of conc. Poissons ratio of concrete is the ratio of lateral strain and the axial strain in a uniaxially stressed body. Its value for conc. varies from 0·1 to 0·3 and generally increases as the modulus of elasticity decreases. Generally a value of 0·15 assumed where ever necessary.

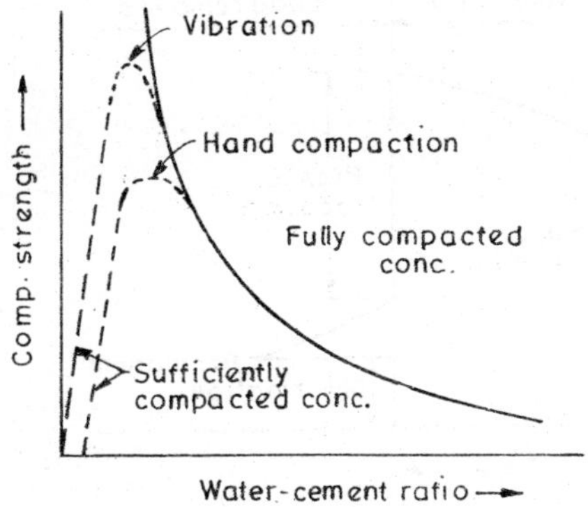

Fig. 6·20. Relation between strength and w/c ratio of conc.

Shrinkage. The volume of concrete elements undergoing air hardening diminish and increases when concrete hardens in water. If evaporation of the mixing water from the hardening cement is not ensured, surface cracks of different sizes appear. The process of cracking is traced to the rapid evaporation of the mixing water from concrete and is referred to as **shrinkage** which is inadmissible in concreting.

The best method of shrinkage control consists in preventing water evaporation from the concrete from the instant when compaction of the mix is terminated. This control is called as **curing** of hardening concrete. This shrinkage due to volume changes in concrete due to loss of moisture at different stages due to different reasons are classified as under :

(1) Plastic shrinkage (2) Drying shrinkage (3) Autogeneous shrinkage and

(4) Carbonating shrinkage.

Plastic shrinkage. Shrinkage of concrete during change of condition of concrete from plastic state to harden state is called plastic shrinkage. It is more in hot climate and under high winds where surfaces are large and exposed to air, the surface of concrete dries very fast, resulting plastic shrinkage even of w/c ratio is high. It is prevented to check rapid loss of water from surface. It can also be checked by closing concrete work in night. Use of aluminium powder is also suggested to offset the effect of plastic shrinkage.

Drying shrinkage. It occurs after the concrete has hardened. Evaporation of water from concrete causes drying shrinkage. This shrinkage is measured by the following formula.

$E_S = 0{\cdot}00125\ (0{\cdot}90 - h)$ where E_S is the shrinkage strain, h = relative humidity in decimals if humidity is 50%, $h = 0{\cdot}5$. The parameters effecting the dry shrinkage are (1) water cement ratio (2) cement content (3) relative humidity (4) type of aggregate 15 size and shape (5) type of cement and (6) admixtures.

Autogeneous shrinkage. When no moisture is allowed to move to and fro from the paste and the temperature is kept constant. It generally occurs in thick masses as in concrete of Dams in order of 100×10^{-5}.

Carbonation shrinkage. It is due to the presence of CO_2 in air. The CO_2 consists calcium hydroxide of hydrated cement to cal. carbonate. This carbonation penetrates beyond the exposed surfaces of conc. only slowly. It results in increase of strength and reduced permeability.

The shrinkage is unrelated to the loads. It can be taken 0·0002 to 0·0003 for computing prestress loss.

Creep. Creep is the property of concrete by which it continues to deform with time under sustained load at unit stress within the elastic range. Factors effecting creep are :

(1) Relative humidity

(2) Creep is inversely proportional to the strength of concrete.

(3) Creep is closely related to w/c ratio.

(4) The age at which load is applied.

(5) Type of cement used—Portland blast furnace cement results in a higher creep.

(6) Fineness of cement effect early development of strength but effects creep.

Effects of creep. (1) It affects strains and deflection.

(2) Creep does not effect strength in plane concrete. But it hastens the approach of the limiting strain at which failure takes place.

(3) The influence of creep on the ultimate strength of simply supported RC beams subjected to sustained load is not significant but the deflection increases considerably.

(4) In RC columns creep results in gradual transfer of load from concrete to steel. So the full strength of the steel and concrete is developed before failure takes place.

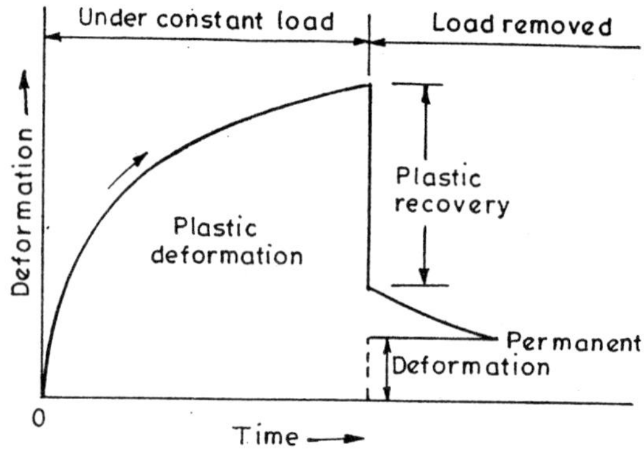

Fig. 6·21. Deformation of conc. under permanent load

(5) Unlike shrinkage the creep is not so harmful and is beneficial in relieving stress concentration and has contributed very considerably to the success of concrete as a structural member.

Bleeding of concrete. A depsoit of white film scum on the surface of concrete due to chemical action. It is due to excessive compaction due to which water comes up. This layer is known as laitance. This layer should be removed by wire brushes for the successive lifts of the conc. Bleeding can be reduced by using less water, adding fine sand or stone crushers waste sand dust. Excess floating (trowelling) is also a cause of it.

Test of concrete

Destructive tests. Concrete once placed, sets and hardens according to time and gains its ultimate strength. Concrete cubes are prepared and tested to ascertain the quality and strength of concrete. The samples of concrete are collected during construction which are loaded till failure to ascertain quality of concrete. The destructive tests have limitations for their use because they involve complete failure of specimen. Therefore these tests can not be applied to check the qualities of material and properties of a structure. These tests are mainly used in routine testing for checking the acceptable specifications and properties created during construction.

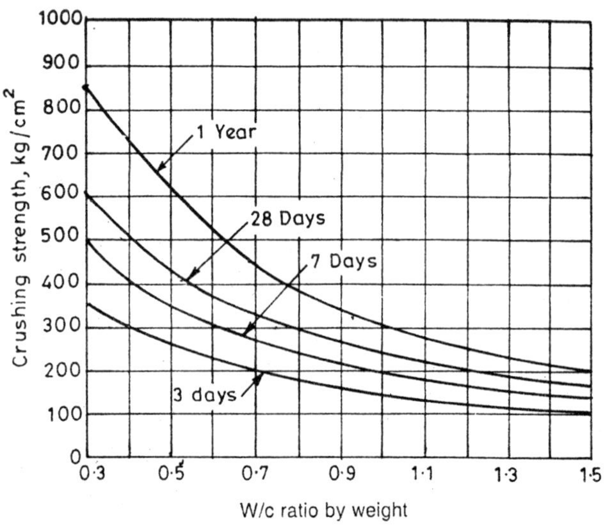

Fig. 6·22.

Undestructive tests. To test quality of concrete of completed structure *i.e.* finished work many types of non-destructive tests are carried out. These tests are the way to have quality control of the work as the structure cannot be loaded to failure, hence only such tests are performed which will not damage the structure. For this purpose some undestructive tests are given below :

(1) **Surface Hardness Test.** This method consists of finding out quality of concrete by testing the hardness of concrete surface, hence it is possible by the following two methods.

(*a*) **Indentation test.** Indentation test is very common for metal, non-metal and alloys but for concrete it is not so popular. William testing pistol and impact hammer are used mainly to find strength of concrete. Indentation marks give idea about the quality compared with a standard specimen.

(*b*) **Rebound hammer test.** Rebound hammer method consists of measuring the elastic rebound of concrete and is used to determine compressive strength of concrete for comparative investigations, Ginbeck pendulum hammer and Frank spring hammers are some of the devices used for measuring hardness of surface. One most common type of rebound hammer used now a days is known as Schmidt hammer, which is detailed as below.

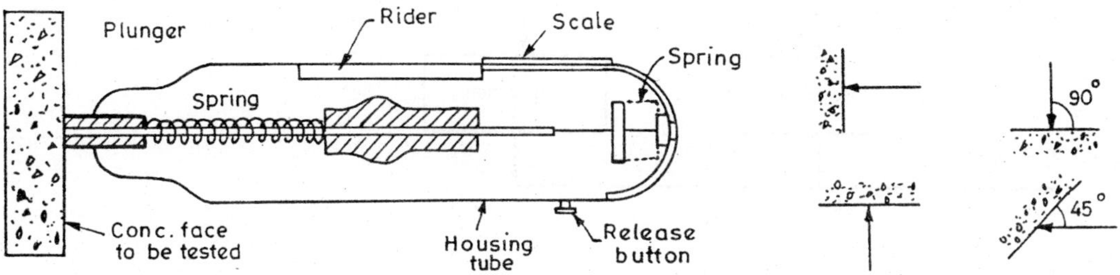

(*a*) Schmidt rebound hammer (*b*)

Fig. 6·23.

Schmidt hammer consists of a spring control hammer that slides on a plunger within a tubular housing when plunger is pressed against the surface of concrete, the mass rebounds from the plunger. It reacts against the force of the spring. The hammer impacts against concrete and the spring control mass rebounds, taking rider with it along the guide scale. Release button which holds the rider in position to take the reading. The distance travelled is measured by graduated scale gives rebound number. Calibrated charts attached on hammer give approximate compressive strength corresponding to rebound number. The calibrated charts show the relation between rebound number, compressive strength of concrete and angle of concrete surface with the rebound hammer. Different possible angles with surfaces are shown in Fig. 6·23 (*b*). Corresponding to these angles, different curves have been developed in comp. strength of concrete versus rebound number.

The procedure consists of cleaning the surface of all dust and cement slurry covering etc. by corburandum stone and then pressing the hammer against the surface to measure rebound number at various places approximately in one metre grid and average should be taken. If average values do not vary by 15% the result may be considered as satisfactory. At individual key points the rebound number may be checked. Even though the results given by this hammer are not so reliable and only give a rough idea of the quality and strength of concrete.

Following points may be considered :

(*a*) Floated or trowelled surfaces give higher results than that of moulded surfaces.

(*b*) Repetition of the rebound on the same point gives lower value.

(*c*) Minimum 5 cm gap be left between the observed point and edge of surface.

(2) **Vibration method.** Also called Dynamic method, consists of generating vibration

in concrete by various methods. The fundamental basis is transmission of sound waves through concrete. This method is further classified as under :

(*i*) Resonant frequency method through sonometer.

(*ii*) Pulse velocity method

(*iii*) Mechanical sonic pulse velocity method and

(*iv*) Ultrasonic pulse velocity method.

(*i*) **Resonant frequency method.** Electrical vibrations are developed at sonic frequencies, whichis the basic principle of transmitting sound through concrete. A mathematical relationship between velocity of sound through material, its resonant frequency and modulus of elasticity of material could be developed. These relations are mainly for homogeneous isotropic and perfectly elastic material, but could be applied to hetrogeneous materials like concrete. Figures given below Fig. (*a*) shows a schematic layout of the apparatus as per ASTM specifications. The

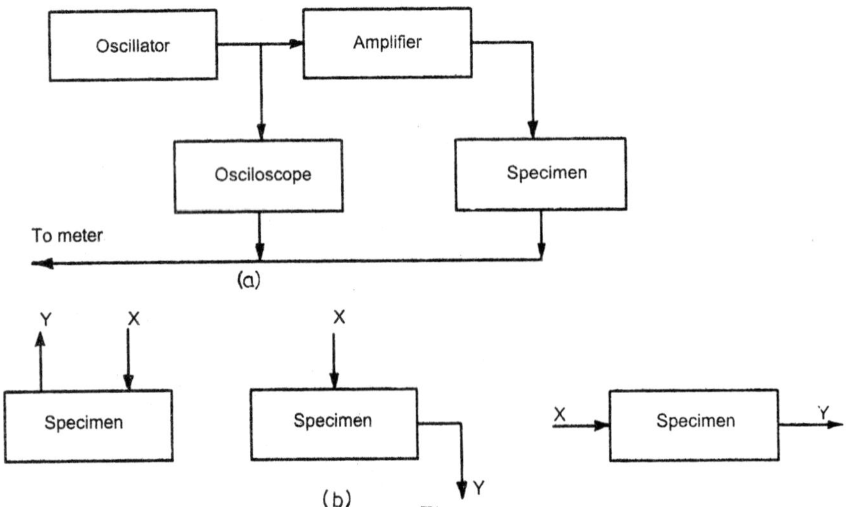

Fig. 6·24.

waves through specimen are transmitted by different ways shown in Fig. 6·24 (*b*). This method is very useful for laboratory testing. As all waves are generated though sonometer. It is also called as "Sonometer method". This method consists of finding dynamic modulus of elasticity and then corelating it with compressive strength of concrete. Various relationships have been established by various agencies like ASTM, BS etc. Various factors like curing, moisture content etc. effects modulus of elasticity. Hence the method can not be relied upon. The variation upto 20 percent was found between test results obtained by cubes and results obtained by this method.

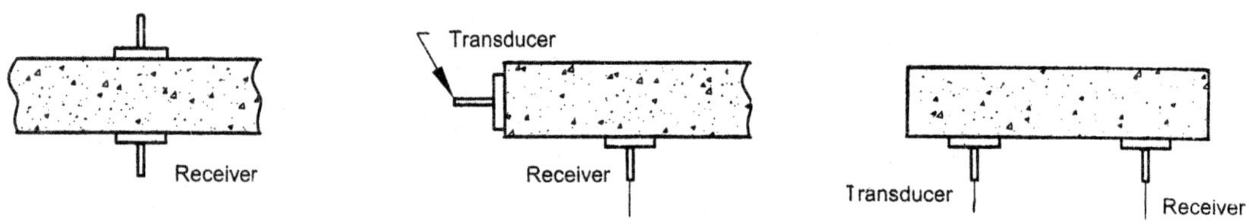

(*a*) Direct transmission (*b*) Semi-direct transmission (*c*) Surface transmission

Fig. 6·25.

(*ii*) **Pulse velocity method.** It involves measurement of time of travel of electronically generating mechanical ultrasonic pulses though the concrete. The system consists of :

(*a*) Electronic circuit generating pulse and

(*b*) Transducers for transferring electric pulses to mechanical energy.

The mechanical energy develops vibration in specimen. The vibrations are of the frequency range 50 to 200 KH_3, determining time to travel for these pulses through a distance of specimen gives pulse velocity of wave generated. Battery operated portable digital ultrasonic tester are becoming popular now a days. As explained in resonant frequency method here also there are three ways of generating pulses or measuring pulse velocity through concrete as shown in figure (*a, b* and *c*). To measure velocity of generation, devices for measuring with an accuracy of 1 micro sec. should be used.

Method of measure of pulse velocity through concrete. Ciganek has used the relationship

$$R = KV^2$$

where R = compressive strength of concrete, V is pulse velocity and K is a factor depending on the composition and preparation of concrete. Following tables give relationship between pulse velocity and codition of concrete.

Table 6·26 (*a*)

Pulse velocity in m/sec.	*General condition of concrete*
4575 and above	Excellent
4575-3660	Good
3660-3000	Satisfactory to poor
3050-2135	Poor
2135 or less	Very poor

Table 6·26 (*b*)

Velocity m/sec.	*Quality*	*Comp. strength in Nw/mm²*
4000 and above	Very good	30 to 35
3500-4000	Good	25 to 30
3000-3500	Medium	20 to 25
3000 and below	Poor	15 to 20

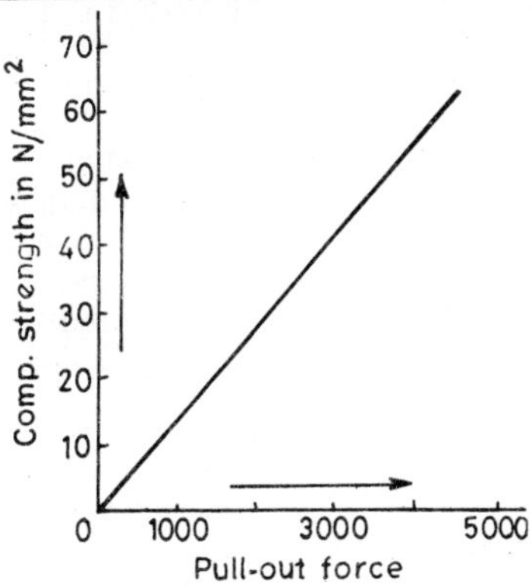

Fig. 6·26.

(3) **Pullout test.** A rod with specially shaped enlarged end is embedded in concrete face during casting of the concrete. The rod is pulled out after setting of the concrete and the force required to pull out of the rod gives an idea of the strength of concrete. A relation is drawn between the pullout force required to the compressive strength of concrete as shown in Fig. 6·26.

(4) **Core test.** Cores from the concrete are drilled from the structure by core drilling machines. These cores are tested as usual for compression and tension etc. The strength obtained must be 75 to 85% from the specified value of the conc. of this specification, based on age conditions.

(5) **Load test.** The load test is generally done in bridges to test the quality of work just after expiry of 28 days from the date of placing concrete. The load applied is equal to the full dead load of the structure plus 1·25 times the imposed load for a period of 24 hrs. and then the

imposed load is removed. The deflection due to imposed load only be recorded. If within 24 hours of removal of the imposed load the structure does not recover at least 75 percent of the deflection under superimposed load, the test may be repeated after a lapse of 72 hrs. If recovery is less than 80 percent the structure be deemed to be unacceptable. If the max. deflection in mm shown during 24 hours under load is less than 40 l^2/D where l is the effective span in metres and the D is over all depth of section in mm. It is not necessary for the recovery to be measured.

(6) **Radioactive method.** The use of X-rays and Gamma rays are used for non-destructive testing of structures now a days. It has been found that X-rays and Gamma rays are absorbed by concrete. The absorption of these rays depends on the density of concrete. When these rays pass through the concrete part of the rays are absorbed and part of the rays are scattered. The scattered rays are shielded and measured and remaining absorbed rays give the density of concrete. Gamma rays are used to measure thickness of concrete of known density.

(7) **Other methods—Nuclear method.** Battery operated magnetic devices that can measure the depth of reinforcement conc. and to detect the position of reinforce bars are now available. Electrical methods are also available to determine the moisture contents of hardened conc. Electric resistivity methods have been used to find out thickness of concrete pavements.

Chiesels are also use to access the strength of concretes.

Conc. Mix Design. The following variables (factors) are considered in a mix design.

(1) Water cement rate (2) Cement Aggregate ratio

(3) Gradation of aggregates (4) Workability of the fresh concrete.

The following methods are developed in the sequence of times.

(1) **Arbitrary method.** Trial mixes are made with different ratio mixes with cement aggregate fine : Aggregate coarse. The maximum strength and workability was judged and the mix is adopted accordingly. It is only a rough estimation.

(2) **Min. void method.** The mix design by this method is based upon the principle of minimum percentage of voids present in the concrete. So as to obtaina dense concrete. It means that the voids created between the coarse aggregate should be filled up by the fine aggregate, similarly the voids between fine aggregate particles should be filled by the cement. Lastly the spaces left between the cement particles should be filled up by water. During this process of setting a chemical reaction takes place between water and cement, which combines all particles of coarse and fine aggregate, forming a solid mass which is known as concrete.

Fig. 6·27.

By this method always a dense and strong mass is not obtained as the particles of the concrete aggregated are not so graded. So that the least amount of water is needed which influences the strength of the concrete.

(3) **Maximum density method.** The minimum void method was further modified by Fuller on the principle that the coarse aggregate is so graded that the mix has the optimum density. He gave an empirical formula for grading of materials as follows :

$$P = 100 \times \sqrt{\frac{d}{D}}$$

where P = the percentage by weight of coarse aggregate material finer than d

D = the max. size of aggregate.

For illustration, to grade a mixture with 16 mm as the maximum size of coarse aggregate and 1 mm as the min. size of fine aggregate the value of P for materials fewer than 1 mm will be given as $P = 100\left[\frac{1}{16}\right]^{1/2} = 25\%$ In this manner, particles of various intermediate sizes should be determined in accordance with Fuller's formula. Experiment has proved the concrete mix designed by this to be of optimum density but it is difficult to have the desired strength due to two reasons.

(*i*) the accuracy if grading is difficult to attain in practice and

(*ii*) no guidelines have been provided to control the amount of water.

(4) **Fineness modulus of aggregates.** To supplement the water cement ratio criteria for concrete proportioning, D.A. Abrams developed in 1918 a method of proportioning of fine to coarse aggregate based on 'fineness modulus' of aggregates as determined by sieve analysis. The water cement ratio and fineness modulus concepts were developed at a about same time and were often confused. For fineness modulus calculation refer chapter of plainand reinforced concrete of this book in coarse aggregates.

For good concrete the value of fineness modulus for coarse aggregate should be between 6 to 8·5 and for fine aggregate between 2 to 3·5. Any increase in the value of fineness modulus of aggregate beyond this given range will result in a harsh mix, while decrease in the value will give an uneconomical mix. But it does not mean that the aggregate should be discarded. It indicates that the mix will require slightly more cement for a given water cement ratio and workability.

The max. size of coarse aggregates selected for a certain work should depend on the size of the least section. The size of the aggregate should not be greater than 1/4 to 1/5 of the min. thicknesss of the section. Larger size of aggregate will provide more economical mix, since it requires less amount of water and cement for a given workability and water cement ratio. Max. size of aggregate is represented by the opening of the sieve next larger to the one on which 15% of the total aggregate is retained. Likewise, the min. of size of aggregate is represented by the sieve, next smaller to the one through which 15% of the aggregate passes. Generally the max. size of the coarse aggregate is 15 cm beyond which it is difficult to handle the mix. uniformly.

A.C.I. Method. The American concrete institute has tabulated various data required for the proportioning of concrete mixes from the normal graded aggregates etc. As per the requirements of a specified design problem, the relevant figures for w/c ratio, quantity of cement and aggregate can be worked out from these tables and the mix can be based in the laboratory. Slight variation as per the test result and requirements of design are made to suit the condition.

Trial Mix Method. The samples of coarse and fine aggregates are mixed together in different known proportions as a trial. These trial mixtures are then felled in moulds and weighed. Weight of each sample per unit volume is calculated. The sample having the maximum weight per uint volume is selected for design.

According to the strength requirement water cement ratio is obtained from charts. Water and cement are mixed together in this proportion and to this the aggregate mixture is added. The aggregate mixture is added in weighted quantity. The slump is tested and the weight of aggregate which gives the required slump is noted.

In this way, the proportion of sand and coarse aggregate will be determined by trial and weight of the cement for a required weight of total aggregate for a given slump. Thus the proportion are designed.

Concrete Mix Design (IS : 10262—1982)

The proportioning of concrete mixes consists of determination of quantities of respective ingradients necessary to produce concrete having adequate but not excessive workability and strength for the particular loading and durability for the exposure to which it will be subjected.

It is emphasized that available ingradients of the concrete most economically be utilised. The basic assumption in this method is that the compressive strength of workable concrete is governed by water cement ratio. The method is also based on using of graded aggregate and is applicable for normal concrete mixes.

The following data are required :

(*a*) Characteristic compressive strength of concrete (fck) after 28 days of laying.

(*b*) Required degree of workability.

(*c*) Type of max. size of aggregate to be used.

(*d*) Standard deviation corresponding to grade of concrete and degree of control.

(*e*) Limitation on w/c ratio (water-cement ratio) and minimum cement requirement as per IS : 456.

The following steps are taken :

Step 1 : *To find characteristic strength and average target strength of concrete mix to be designed.*

Target strength and characteristic strength. Characteristic strength is the min. strength supposed to have by a concrete used in the structure. Samples collected of concrete cubes to find quality of work should not fall below this. So to achieve this target the mix has to be designed for a somewhat higher target of average compression force. This average target is obtained by the following formula.

$$S_{av} = S_{min} + K\phi \text{ where}$$

S_{av} = average design strength at 28 days (Target strength)

S_{min} = characteristic min. strength at 28 days

ϕ = standard deviation

K = a statistic depending on accepted proportion of low results and number of tests. The value of K is given in the table below.

Table 6·27. Tables of *K* Factor

Percentage of results allowed to fall below the Min.	*Factor K*	*Remark*
1 in 5 = 20%	0·84	According to IS : 456—1978 the characteristic strength is defined as that value below which not more than 5% results are expected to fail
1 in 10 = 10%	1·20	
1 in 15 = 6·6%	1·50	
1 in 20 = 5%	1·65	
1 in 40 = 2·5%	1·86	For fall of 1 in 20, K = 1·65
1 in 100 = 1·0%	2·33	so $S_{av} = S_{min} + 1{\cdot}65\ \phi$

$$\text{Standard deviation } \phi = \sqrt{\frac{\sum x - \bar{x}}{n-1}} \text{ (root mean square)}$$

where $\bar{x} = \dfrac{\sum x}{n}$ is the mean strength

$\sum x$ = sum of strength of test cubes and

n = number of cubes

'Variance' is the measure of variability or difference between any simple observed data from the mean strength.

Coefficient of variation :

$$V = \frac{\phi}{\bar{x}} \times 100$$

where V = coefficient of variation expressed in percentage.

The use of coefficient of variation is determining the average design strength

$$S_{av} = \frac{S_{min}}{1 - \frac{KV}{100}}$$

The value of K (Henceworth constant is given in the table below).

Table 6·28

Quality control	*Coefficient of variation*	*Percentage of results to fall below the min.*	*K Henceworth constant*
Attainable in laboratory	5	0·1 (1 in 1000)	3·09
Excellent	10	0·8 (1 in 1067)	2·50
Good	15	1·0 (1 in 100)	2·33
Fair	18	2·5 (1 in 40)	1·96
Poor	18	6·6 (1 in 15)	1·50
		6·00 (1 in 6)	1·00

Note : Generally 1 percent result is allowed to fall below the min. Hence value of K is taken as 2·33.

Grade of cements	*Standard deviation for different degrees of control in N/mm²*		
	very good	*Good*	*Fair*
M-10	2·0	2·3	3·3
M-15	2·5	3·5	4·5
M-20	3·6	4·6	5·6
M-25	4·3	5·3	6·3
M-30	5·0	6·0	7·0
M-35	5·3	6·3	7·3
M-40	5·6	6·6	7·6
M-45	6·0	7·0	8·0
M-50	6·4	7·4	8·4
M-55	6·7	7·7	8·8

Step 2 : Selection of water-cement ratio

The water cement ratio is determined by following two methods :

(*a*) The water-cement ratio by mass is determined by the figure below in which relationship in free water-cement ratio and target compressive strength of concrete is given.

(*b*) The water-cement ratio by mass is also determined from fig. below (*b*) in which relationship between water-cement ratio, 28 days average target compressive strength of concrete and 28 days strength of concrete is given.

The water-cement ratio selected above should be checked against limiting w/c ratio for the requirements of durability and lower of the two values should be taken.

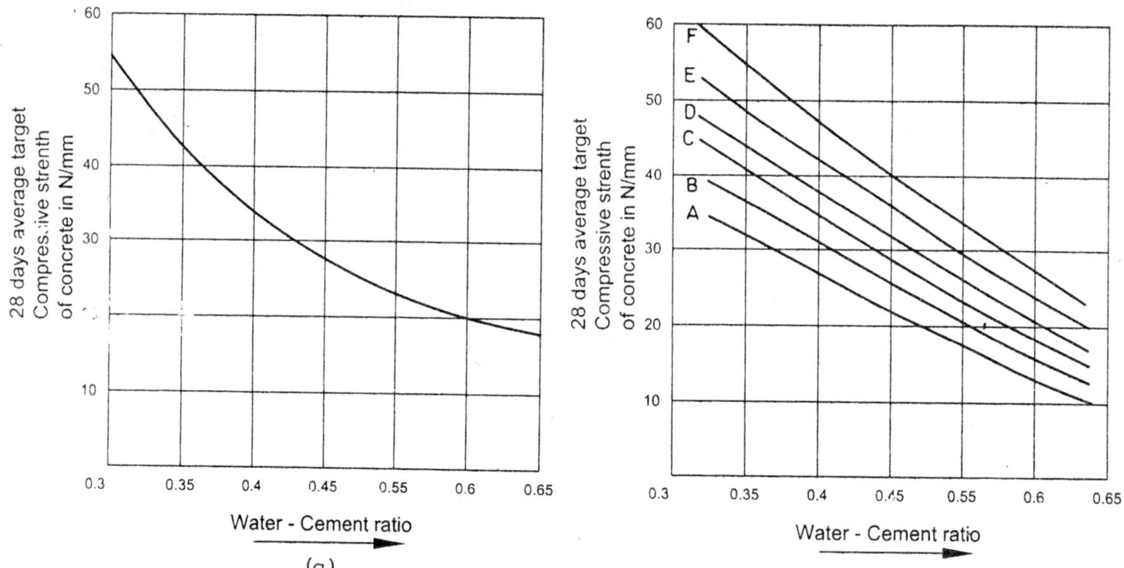

Fig. 6·28.

w/c ratio 28 days—Strength of cement

A = 325-375 kg/cm^2 B = 375-425 kg/cm^2 C = 425-475 kg/cm^2

D = 475-525 kg/cm^2 E = 525-572 kg/cm^2

Step 3 : Next step consists of estimation of approximate amount of entrapped air to expected in normal (non-air entrained) concrete from table below. It depends on the maximum size of aggregate used in concrete.

Table 6·29

Normal maximum size of aggregate	*Entrapped air percentage of volume of concrete*	
10 20 40	3·0 2·0 1·0	Approximate-Air content

Step 4 : For the desired workability, the quantity of mixing water per unit volume of concrete and the ratio of fine aggregate to total aggregate by absolute volume are determined from the table 6·30 depending upon maximum size of aggregate and grade of concrete.

Table 6·30. Approximate sand and water content per cubic metre of concrete

For concrete grade upto M-35 *Maximum size in mm*	*Water content/cu. metre of concrete in litre*	*Sand percent of total aggregate by volume*
10 20 40	208 186 165	40 35 36
For concrete grade above M-35		
10 20	200 186	28 25

These requirements of sand and water content are for angular coarse aggregate and for workability as per compaction factor of 0·80. Further these results are for water-cement ratio of

0·6 and 0·35 for concrete grades upto M-35 and above M-35 respectively. The aggregate used confirms to zone II. For different types of aggregates compaction factor of concrete and water cement ratio. These values of sand and water content are to be adjusted. Generally aggregate confirm to zone II or III for which no adjustment of water content is required to be made. Similarly for change of compaction factor also quantity of sand required does not change. For rounded aggregates the amount of water required is always less. Further the quantity of sand required also decreases. For rounded aggregates quantity of water required is reduced by 15 litres and percentage of sand by 7%.

Step 5 : After knowing the amount of water required and water-cement ratio the quantity of cement is calculated. This quantity of cement in no case shall be less than minimum cement required for durability criteria.

Step 6 : After knowing quantity of water and cement per unit volume of concrete and also of fine to total aggregate. Total aggregate per unit volume of concrete is determined as follows.

$$V = \left[w + \frac{c}{S_c} + \frac{1}{P} \cdot \frac{f_c}{Sf_c} \right] \times 1000 \quad \text{and} \quad V = \left[w + \frac{c}{S_c} + \frac{1}{(1-P)} \cdot \frac{cd}{Sc_a} \right] \times \frac{1}{1000}$$

where V = absolute volume of fresh concrete which is equal to

Gross volume in m^3-volume of entrapped air,

w = mass of water per cu. metre of concrete,

c = mass of cement in kg/cu. metre of concrete,

S_c = specific gravity of cement.

p = ratio of fine aggregate to total aggregate by absolute volume

f_a, cd = total masses of fine aggregate and coarse aggregate in kg/cu.m of concrete respectively.

S_{fa}, S_{ca} = specific gravities of fine aggregate and coarse aggregate.

Step 7 : Batch the mixture to find ratio of various ingradients and to expose w/c ratio.

6·12. Field Engineering Materials and Devices : Shoring, Shuttering, Scaffolding and Underpinning

Shoring. Shoring is employed to prevent a damaged structure due to foundation settlement or other reasons from collapse. It is also used to provide temporary supports to a structure which is being remodelled or where alteration of adjacent foundation are being carried out. Shoring may be provided externally or internally or from both sides of the wall. For light loads or temporary shores generally timber is used. Whereas for supporting heavier loads steel beams or braced sections are employed some times concrete or masonry is also used for shoring. The shores are classified as follows :

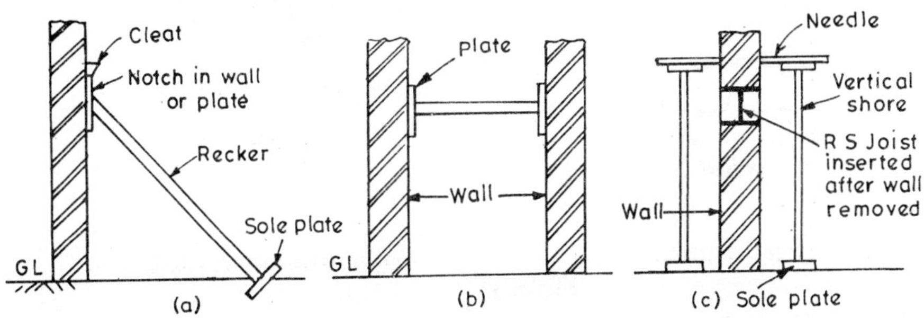

Fig. 6·29.

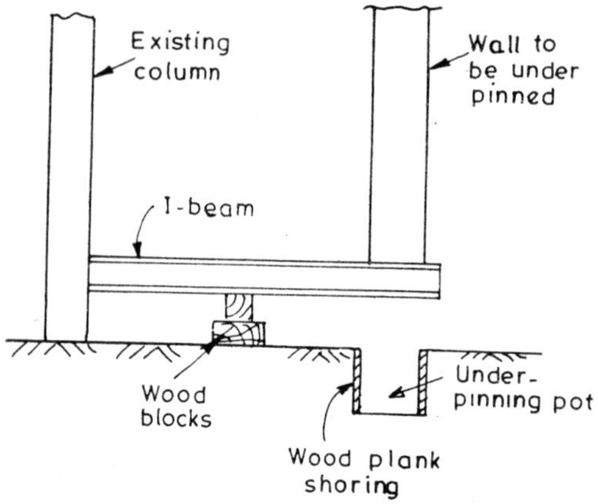

Fig. 6·30. A typical shoring.

(*a*) **Racking shores.** For unimportant and low structures racking shores are used. A trench or notch is made in the wall in which inclined posts are inserted to carry the weight of that part of the wall which is above the shore. The lower edge of the supporting post is fixed by a sole stake and plate. The upper part of the post is also supported by a plate. If in sufficient two or three rackers can be used one above the other as required.

Horizontal or flying shores. When the building has to be entirely demolished, the walls of the adjoining property are supported by horizontal shores.

Vertical or Dead shores. These shores are placed vertically to support walls temporarily, the lower part of which are to be removed for repairs or otherwise the whole load of the roofs etc. is supported by these shores.

Shutterings and form work. Wooden and steel plates used for making forms for laying concrete supported by verticals or rackers (see in detail in the chapter of plane and reinforced concrete.)

Under Pinning. At many times, it is essential to replace or strengthened the foundation of an existing structure. The operation of providing new permanent foundations is known as underpinning. It is generally done due to the settlement of the structure. The methods of underpinning is decided according to the site conditions.

Scaffolding. When the height above floor level becomes more than 1·5 m temporary erection is needed to support a number of plateforms at different levels for the convenience of workers. Scaffold enables the masons to work at various stages of building and to lift the materials for their immediate use at different heights. The following term are used in scaffoldings :

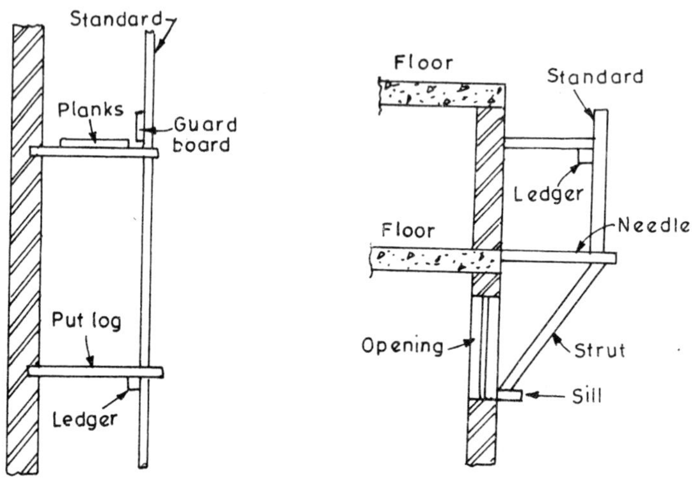

(*a*) Vertical scaffold (*b*) Cantilever scaffold

Fig. 6·31.

(1) **Standard**—Vertical member of a support.

(2) **Ledger**—The horizontal member parallel to the wall.

(3) **Putlog**—It is the transverse piece which is placed on the ledgers and which is supported on the wall at one end. It is at right angles to the wall.

(4) **Transom**—It is putlog supported on ledgers at their both ends.

(5) **Brace**—It is diagonal or cross piece fixed on the standards.

(6) **Guard rail**—It is a rail fixed like a ledger at the working level.

(7) **Briddle**—It is a piece which is used to cover an operating in a wall and it provides support to one end of the putlog at the opening.

(8) **Toe Board**—It is a board fixed parallel to ledgers and supported between the putlogs. It is given as a protective measure on the working plateform.

(9) **Raker**—An oblique support known as Raker.

Types of Scaffolds :

(1) Single or brick layers scaffold
(2) Double or mason's scaffold
(3) Cantilever scaffold
(4) Suspended scaffold
(5) Tensile scaffold
(6) Steel scaffold.

Note : For details see chapter "Plane and Reinforced Concrete".

12. Field Engineering

Fasteners (Refer Fig. 6·32)

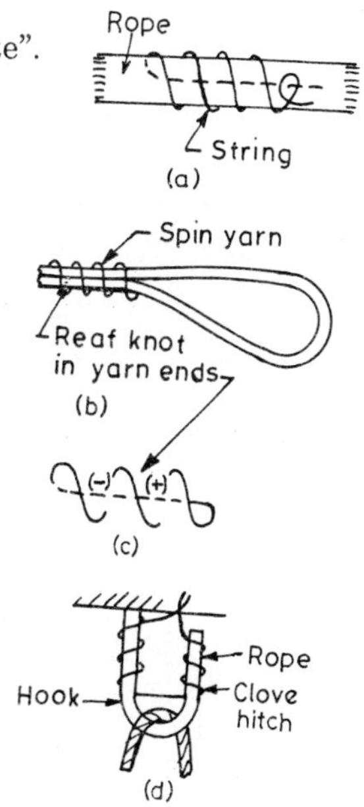

Fig. 6·32.

Whipping. In ropes when the end is wrapped by a string so that the end of the rope may not fray is called as whipping.

Siezing. It is used to prevent two ends of the same rope or different ropes from slipping by a string wrapping.

Mousing. It is done to prevent the rope coming out of the hook. A knot may be used or a string is wrapped.

Bow line. It is used to put a loop in the rope. It is also used to join together the ends of two hossers. (Thick ropes)

Bow line at a height. The height of the rope is used instead of the ends. This knot is made in the same way as the bow line.

Half and two half hitch. They are used for securing a rope to a ladder or for fastening the guys of two derricks or cranes.

Clove hitch. Used for securing scaffolds.

Timber hitch. It is used for the same purpose as the half hitch. It is so form that greater the strain falls on it the lighter it becomes.

Round turn and two half hitches. Used for same purpose as half hitch.

Fishermen's bend. Used when a thick rope is made fast (or fastened) to a ring.

Man harness. It is used for harnessing a man to a thick rope.

Knots. Knots are used for making a stop on a rope to prevent it from fraying or untwisting. They are also used to unit two ropes together. In all the knots we use either simple under hand or over hand loops.

(1) **Thumb knot.** The loose end of the rope is passed through either on over head or an under head loop. It is simplest of all the knots and is firm. The principal use of this knot is in the end of a rope to prevent it from slipping through any thing. It is used at the end of the rope from fraying.

(2) **Reaf knot.** It is generally used for uniting the ends of the two separate pieces of ropes or two separate ends of the same rope. The knot when drawn tight sets flat, when formed of two ropes of equal thickness. It is simplest and best knot for uniting them.

(3) **Single sheet bend.** It is used for joining two ropes of unequal sizes.

(4) **Double bend.** Double bend is given instead of one. It is better than single.

(5) **Hawser bend.** Cordage more than 1″ circumference is known as hawser. It is used to join two hawsers of two thick ropes.

Lashings. They are used for fastening two or more spars (logs) together.

Square lashings. This is used to fix or square a ledger to a standard and is made as follows.

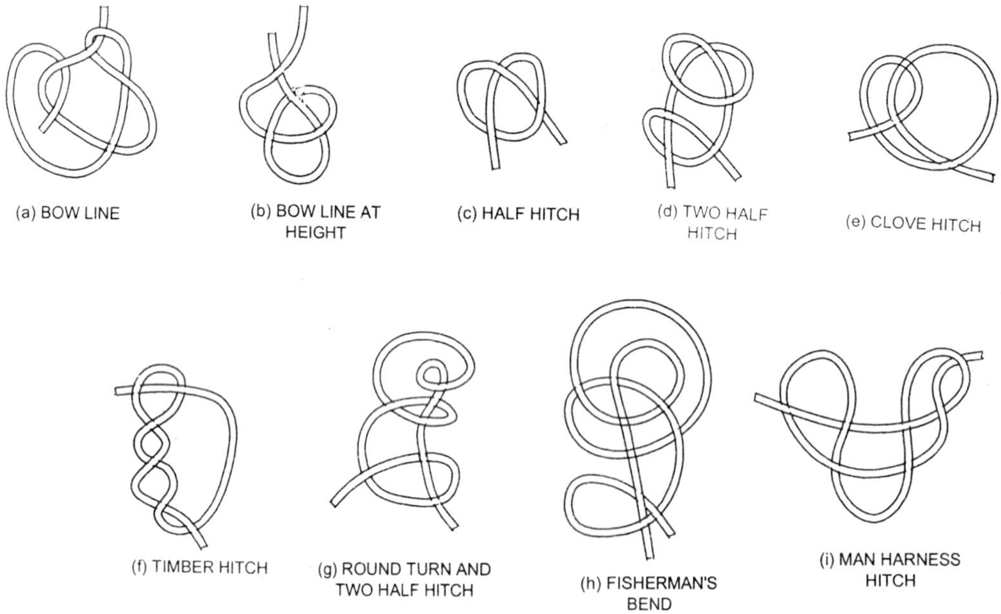

Fig. 6·33.

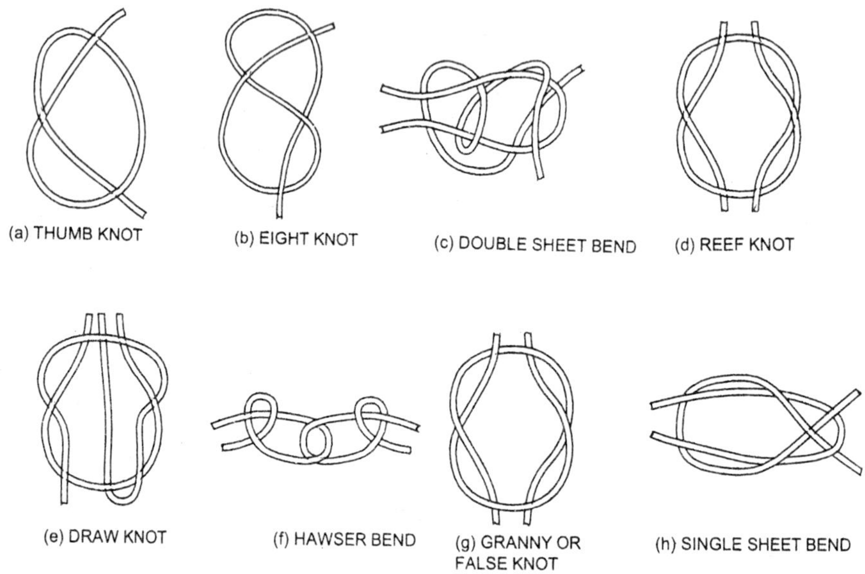

Fig. 6·34.

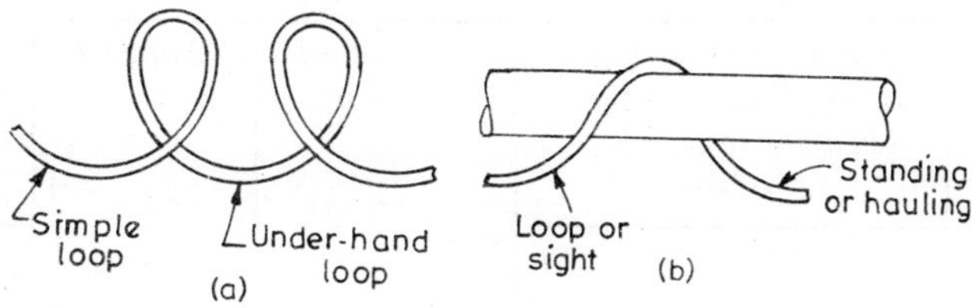

Fig. 6·35

A clove hitch is 1st made round the standard just below the ledger. The short end of the rope is disposed off by twisting it round the long or standing end and the later is then passed up horizontally behind standard down in front of the ledger and again horizontally behind the standard. Three or four turns round the sparks are then taken. Two turns known as trapping turns are next taken in the vertical plane between the two sparks round the four turns just mentioned. These being well between in and trapping turn pulled as tightly as possible. The lashing is completed by making two half hitches on the ledger.

Diagonal lasing. It is made as follows and is used to join diagonal bracings to standards.

The timber or a clove hitch is made round both sparks diagonally across their intersection and then three turns taken round across the diagonal as in the previous case and the lashing is completed by two strapping turns and two half hitches as in the case of square lashings.

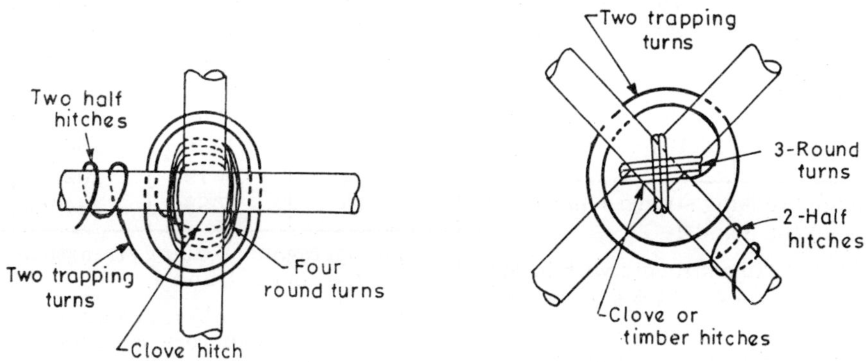

(*a*) Square lashing (*b*) Diagonal lashing

Fig. 6·36.

Ropes

Uncoiling a rope. Layout the coil flat with inside end at the bottom and uncoil by putting the inside end up through the centre of the coil and if possible a long bar should be passed right through the centre of the coil and then supporting the ends of the bar on two pickets (Khunti). The rope can be then unbound the coil which will revolve round the bar by eliminating all kinks and turns.

Care in keeping of cordage. (1) It should be kept against sharp edges by interposing wood packing or rollers.

Table 6·31. Properties of steel wire ropes

Dia. of rope *mm*	*App. wt.* *gm/m*	*Nominal breaking strength in tonnes (Tensile strength of wire)*	
		160-175 kg/m²	*175-190 kg/m²*
1	2	3	4
6 × 190 group of SWR ropes			
8	0·24	3·4	3·7
10	0·44	6·6	7·2
12	0·54	8·6	9·4
14	0·76	10·9	11·9
16	0·94	13·4	14·7
18	1·25	19·3	21·1
20	1·47	22·6	24·6
22	1·84	25·9	28·4
24	2·13	30·0	33·0
25	2·41	34·0	37·6
29	3·05	43·2	47·2
32	3·76	53·3	58·4
35	4·55	64·5	70·6
38	5·43	76·7	84·3
41	6·37	90·4	99·1
44	7·38	104·7	114·8
48	8·48	119·9	132·1
51	9·64	137·2	150·4
54	10·89	154·4	169·7

(1) For aggregate breaking strength add 14·25% to the Figs. in col. 3 and 4

(2) For nominal breaking strength with hard drawn wire main core add 7·5% to the figs. in col. 3 and 4.

(3) For wt. with a wire main core add 11·0% to the wt. given in col. 2.

Constructions : $6 \times \frac{12}{6/1}$; $6 \times \frac{12}{6} + \frac{6F}{1}$

$6 \times \frac{9}{9/1}$ and $6 \times \frac{10}{5} + \frac{5F}{F}$

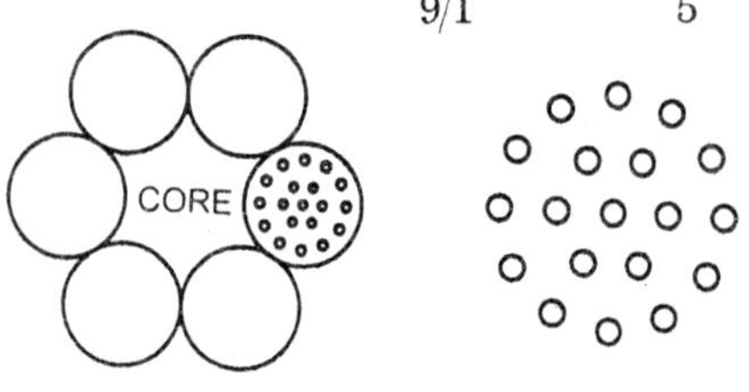

6 × 12/16/1 (*a*) Strand 12/16/1 (*b*)

Fig. 6·37.

Dia. of rope *mm*	*App. wt.* *gm/m*	*Nominal breaking strength in tonnes (Tensile strength of wire)*	
		160-175 kg/m²	*175-190 kg/m²*
1	2	3	4
6 × 37 group of SWR ropes			
10	0·45	6·2	6·8
12	0·60	8·1	8·9
14	0·74	10·3	11·3
16	0·92	12·7	13·9
18	1·32	18·3	20·0
20	1·58	21·4	23·5
22	1·81	24·6	26·9
24	2·10	28·4	31·0
25	2·37	32·5	35·6
29	2·99	40·6	44·7
32	3·69	50·3	55·4
35	4·48	61·0	67·1
38	5·32	72·6	79·8
41	6·25	85·3	93·5
44	7·24	99·1	108·7
48	8·32	113·8	125·0
51	9·46	129·1	142·2
54	10·68	146·3	160·5
57	11·9	163·6	179·8
64	14·79	202·2	221·5
70	17·88	244·9	268·2

(1) For aggregate breaking strength add 21% to the figs. in col. 3 and 4.

(2) For nominal breaking strength with hard drawn wire main core add 7·5% to the fig. in col. 3 and 4.

(3) For wt. with a wire main core add 11% to the wt. given in col. 2.

Construction : $6 \times \frac{14}{7} + \frac{7}{7/1}$;

$6 \times \frac{14}{7} + \frac{7F}{7/1}$;

$6 \times \frac{16}{8} + \frac{8F}{6/1}$;

$6 \times \cfrac{15}{\cfrac{15}{6/1}}$; $\frac{8}{8/1}$;

$6 \times \cfrac{18}{\cfrac{12}{16/1}}$.

Strand 18/12/16/1 (*c*)

Fig. 6·37.

Table Contd...

Dia. of rope	*App. wt.*	*Nominal breaking strength in tonnes (Tensile strength of wire)*	
mm	*gm/m*	*160-175 kg/m²*	*175-190 kg/m²*
1	2	3	4
6 × 24 group of SWR ropes			
8	0·21	3·0	3·3
10	0·39	5·5	6·1
12	0·54	7·6	8·3
14	0·67	9·4	10·4
16	0·80	11·5	12·6
18	1·19	16·8	18·5
20	1·41	20·0	21·9
22	1·64	23·3	25·4
24	1·86	26·4	28·4
25	2·08	29·5	32·0
29	2·68	37·6	41·1
32	3·24	45·7	50·3
35	3·96	55·9	61·5
38	4·76	67·6	73·7
41	5·51	77·7	85·3
44	6·43	90·9	99·6
48	7·44	104·6	114·8
51	8·36	118·9	130·0
54	9·52	134·1	147·3

For aggregate breaking strength add 14·25% in the figs. in col. 3 and 4.

Dia. of rope	*App. wt.*	*Nominal breaking strength in tonnes (Tensile strength of wire)*	
mm	*gm/m*	*160-175 kg/m²*	*175-190 kg/m²*
1	2	3	4
Flattened strand group 11-F			
14	0·85	11·5	12·4
16	1·04	14·6	15·9
18	1·40	21·3	22·9
20	1·66	25·1	26·9
22	2·05	29·0	31·5
24	2·37	33·0	35·6
25	2·68	37·1	40·1
29	3·39	47·2	50·8
32	4·20	58·4	63·5
35	5·06	69·6	75·2
38	6·02	83·3	90·4
41	7·05	98·6	105·7
44	8·26	113·8	124·0
48	9·45	130·1	140·2
51	10·71	148·3	160·5

(1) For aggregate breaking strength add 17·5% in the figs. in col. 3 and 4.

(2) For nominal breaking with a hard wire main core add 7·5% to the figs. in col. 3 and 4.

(3) For wt. with a wire main core add 8% to the fig. in col. 2.

Construction : $6 \times \frac{9}{12/\Delta}$; $6 \times \frac{10}{12/\Delta}$; $6 \times \frac{12}{12/\Delta}$.

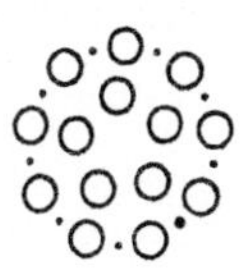

Strand 9/5/1 + 9

(*d*)

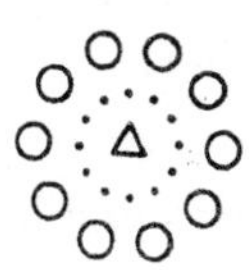

Strand 10/12/Δ

(*e*)

Fig. 6·37

The cores of the strands of flattened strands rope may consist one or more triangular wires or three or more round wires.

Table Contd...

Dia. of rope	*App. wt.*	*Nominal breaking strength in tonnes (Tensile strength of wire)*		*Dia. of rope*	*App. wt.*	*Nominal breaking strength in tonnes (Tensile strength of wires)*	
mm	*gm/m*	*160-175 kg/m²*	*175-190 kg/m²*	*mm*	*gm/m*	*160-175 kg/m²*	*175-190 kg/m²*
1	2	3	4	1	2	3	4
17 × 7 and 18 × 7 group of SWR ropes				34 × 7 group of SWR ropes			
8	0·25		3·6	16	1·04		13·7
10	0·42		7·0	18	1·37		19·7
12	0·57		8·9	20	1·63		23·0
14	0·80		11·6	22	2·02		26·9
16	0·90		14·5	24	2·32		30·5
18	1·32		20·5	25	2·65		35·1
20	1·55		24·2	29	3·35		44·2
22	1·93		27·4	32	4·14		54·9
24	2·23		32·0	35	5·00		66·0
29	2·53		36·6	38	5·93		78·7
29	3·20		45·2	44	8·11		104·6
32	3·96		55·9	51	10·59		136·1
35	4·77		68·6				
38	5·70		81·8				
For aggregate breaking strength add 33·33% to the fig. in col. 4.				For aggregate breaking strength add 43% to the figs. given in col. 4.			

Note : (1) Steel wire ropes for haulage purpose in mines and cranes are constructed 10 to 15% heavier than general engg. purposes. Thinner ropes are kept 10% heavier.

(2) The cordage should be parceled by wrapping it in canvas and bound with spun yard.

(3) Cordage saturated with water should not be applied load more than two-third of its normal working load (A saturated cordage lasts longer than a dry)

(4) Cordage should not be recoiled wet.

(5) Cordage shrinks when wet and hence an allowance for this should be given when used.

Steel wire ropes. Several wires stick together forms a rope. Steel wire ropes are described by the number of their strands and the number of wires in the strand. Several wires makes a strand, several strands make a rope and several ropes (generally three) makes a cable. A wire rope 6 × 19 consists of six strands having 19 wires in each strand. The arrangement of wires in the strand is also classified further.

Terms used in wire ropes :

Strand—It is an assembly of wires laid helically around a centre in one or more layers.

Centre—Material in the centre of strand about which the wires are laid.

Pitch of strand—It is the distance parallel to the axis of the strand in which a wire makes one complete turn about the centre.

Pitch of rope—It is the distance parallel to the axis of the rope to which a strand makes one complete turn about the core.

Core—The material in centre of a wire rope about which the strands are laid. The core may be of fibre or an independent strand.

Helix right hand—A wire helix about the centre similar to the threads of a right hand screw.

Helix left hand—A wire helix about the centre of similar to the threads of a left hand screw.

Diameter of a rope—Diameter of the circumscribed circle enclosing the strands.

Lang's lay ropes—When the direction of the twist (helix) in the strand is the same as that of the strands in the rope.

Ordinary lay ropes—When the direction of the twist in the strand is opposite to that of the strands in the rope.

Galvanized wire type A—When the wires are galvanized either by the hot-dip or electrolytic process and with a thick coating of zinc.

Galvanized wire type Z—When the wires are galvanized either by the hot dip or electrolytic process and with a thinner coating of zinc.

Types of steel wire ropes (IS : 2266—1963)

Main class : (1) Round strand 6 × 19 (2) Round strand 6 × 37 (3) Flattened strand group II F.

Other class : (1) Round strand 6 × 24 (2) Multistrand non-rotating ropes 17 × 7 and 18 × 7.

Specifications of wire ropes. For a wire core wires of tensile strength lower than those of outer wires of rope or strand may be used, but wires of higher tensile strength should not be used.

The rope may be either of ordinary lay or Lang's lay and of right hand unless left hand is specified. The length of the lay of rope should not be greater than eight times the dia. of the rope. The dia. of the rope when measured before tensioning should not be less than the dia. (nominal) by more than 2% and shall not exceed the nominal dia. by more than 5%.

Tensile strength of wire other than core filler should be with in the normal range of 160-175 or 175-190 kg/m^2.

Testing of wire ropes

Sampling. A suitable length from one end should be cut off the rope and unstranded. The wires excluding all core wires should then be well mixed and 36 wires should be taken as follows :

(1) 9 for tensile test, (2) 9 for torsion test, (3) 9 for repeat tensile test in case of failure (4) 9 for repeat torsion test in case of failure.

Galvanizing test can be carried out, out of six wires reserved for repeat tests. When more than one size of wire is used in the rope, the quantities of each size of wire taken for testing should be proportional to their number in the rope.

Storing of steel ropes. (1) Steel ropes should be coiled on reels or drums.

(2) It should be kept under cover and a bit raised from the ground.

(3) It should be avoid sharp bends. The bend should not be more than four times the circumference, to a rough rule the dia. of the pulley should not be less than six times or in extreme cases not more than four times the circumference of the rope.

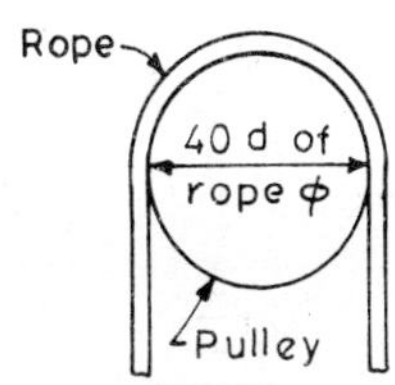

Fig. 6·38

(4) All steel ropes should be lubricated at regular intervals. For this it should be immersed in hot oil for several hours, before being placed in position. Linseed oil is suitable as lubricant.

Joints. Joints in wires should be avoided, but where necessary it should widely apart and staggered. One wire should be joined in 10 m length of strand. For wires over 0·5 mm dia. (24 SWG) the joint should be either brazed or electric welded. If brazed it should be properly scarfed and if welded by electric should be properly annealed. For wires below 0·5 mm thick joint should be used.

Bull dog grips. It is a way of securing the end of a wire rope.

Dia. of rope in mm	*Min no. of grips*
Upto and including 20	3
Over 20 upto and including 32	4
Over 32 upto and including 38	5
For all size ropes	6

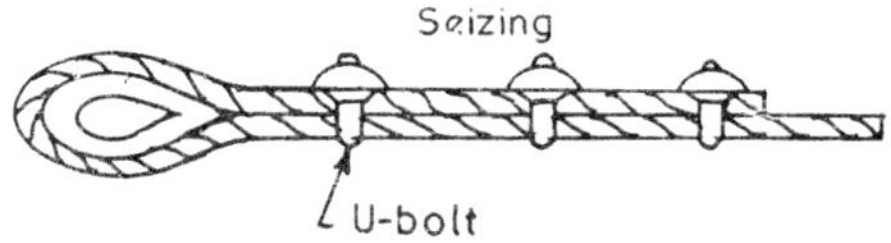

Fig. 6·39.

The end of the rope is spinned with wires. The nut of the V-bolts is kept on the side of the end of rope.

Bull dog grips should be spaced at a distance of approximately six times the rope dia. Bull dog grips are available from 8 mm size to 41 mm size of the rope. The V-bolts of the Bull dog-grips should have a min. tensile strength of 42 kg/mm^2 and max. of 50 kg/mm^2.

Weight Lifting—Blocks and Tackles

Block—A frame consisting of a number of pulleys is known as block.

Pulley—A wheel axial on a pin, fitted with a steeple and hooks.

Tackles—Two blocks connected together by ropes.

Reaving—The operation of passing the ropes round the block.

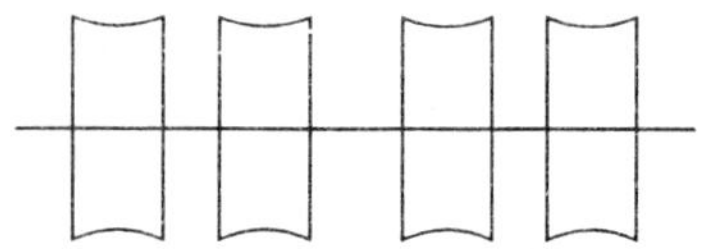

Fig. 6·40.

Overhaul of a tackle—Removing the ropes from the blocks. It is reverse of reaving.

To rack a tackle—Ceiling the two opposite turns of a tackle in order so that the relative position of the block is not changed, even if the running end is left loose.

To round the tackle—To bring the two blocks close together is known as rounding of the tackle.

To choke a block—When the two blocks are as close as they could be, is known as the choking of the block.

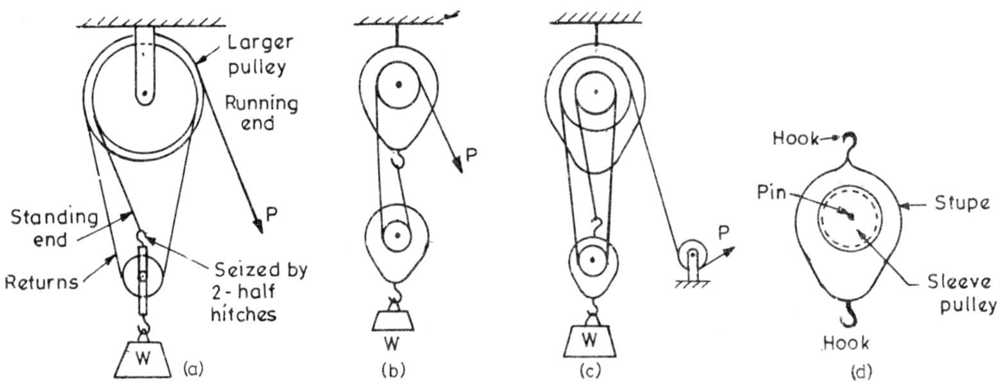

Fig. 6·41.

Care in handling of a blocks

(1) Should be well oiled and free from dirt etc.

(2) All fastenings should be secure.

(3) The ropes should be free from kinks and twist and should run freely over the pulleys.

(4) Tackles must be carried by lifting and must not be dragged along the ground.

(5) The returns should not touch together.

(6) Suspended weight should be placed or lifted easily and not by jerks.

(7) The safe limit of the block should not be exceeded.

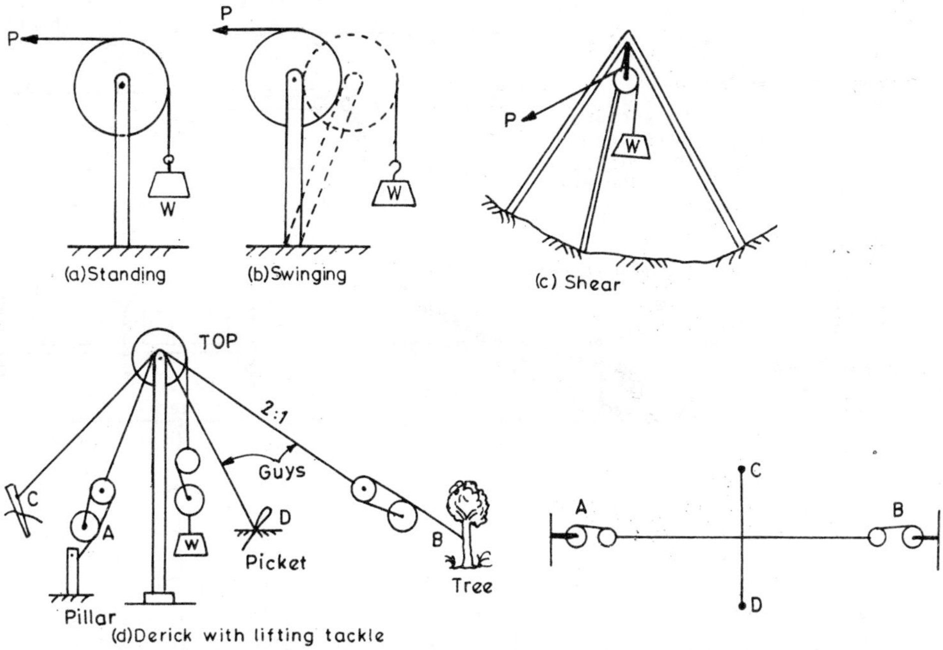

Fig. 6·42. Dericks sheers and guyes.

Anchorages. Anchors are fixed points to which the ropes are fastened. The following are the types of anchorages.

(1) Anchors (2) Existing hold fasts (Natural trees and structural columns etc.)

(2) Pickets (4) Picket and baulk hold fasts (5) Rock hold fasts.

(6) Buried anchors

(1) **Anchors**—These are of iron and about 2 quintals in weight.

(2) **Pickets**—(*a*) Weight of a picket is about 2 quintal or as required.

(*b*) A clove hitch is given just below the eye.

(*c*) Ends are married together.

(3) **Picket and baulk hold fasts**—(*a*) The number of pickets should be same both sides.

(*b*) The pickets should be not less than 200 mm apart.

(*c*) Log (baulk) must base as even as possible against all the pickets in the front rank.

(*d*) Baulk should rest on the ground and should not raised above ground.

(*e*) The rear edge of the logs of square section should be sunk in a narrow trench.

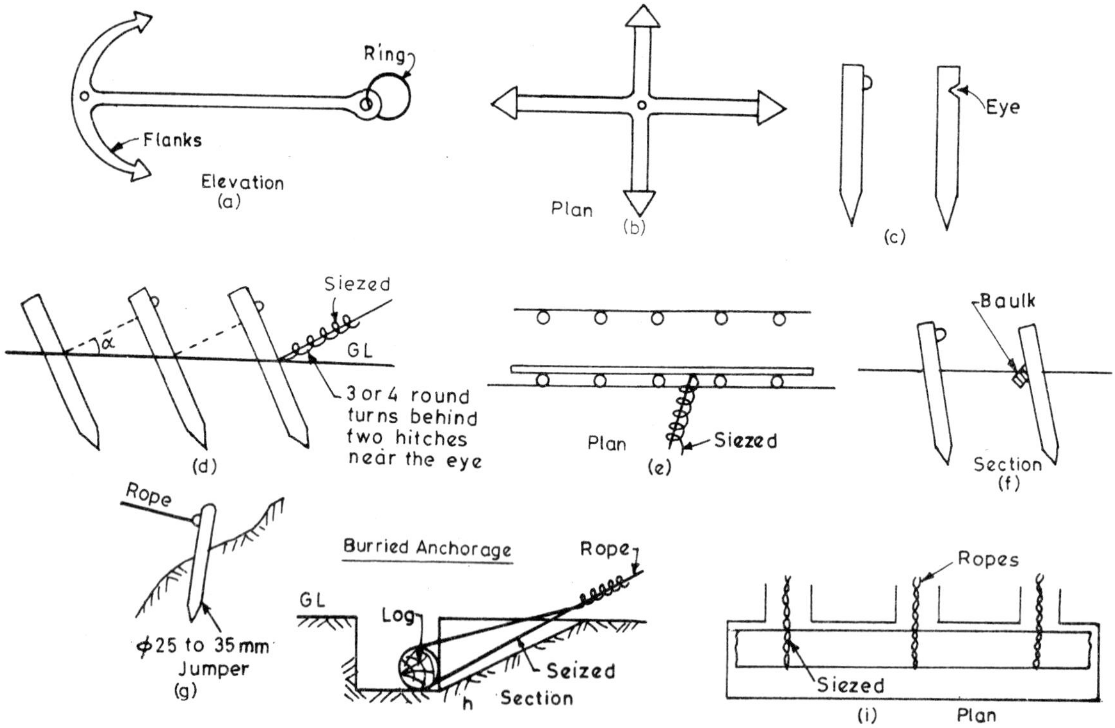

Fig. 6·43.

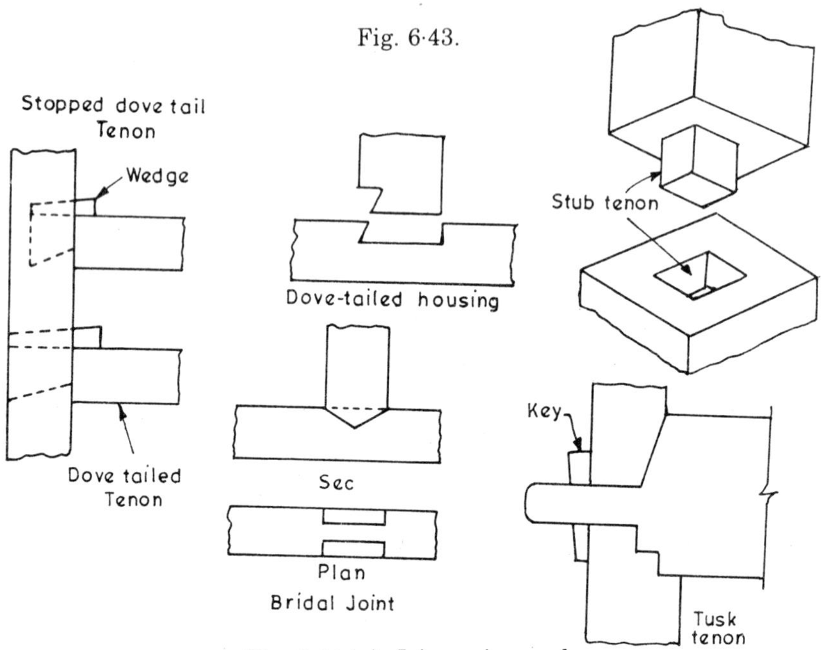

Fig. 6·44 (*a*). Joinery in wood.

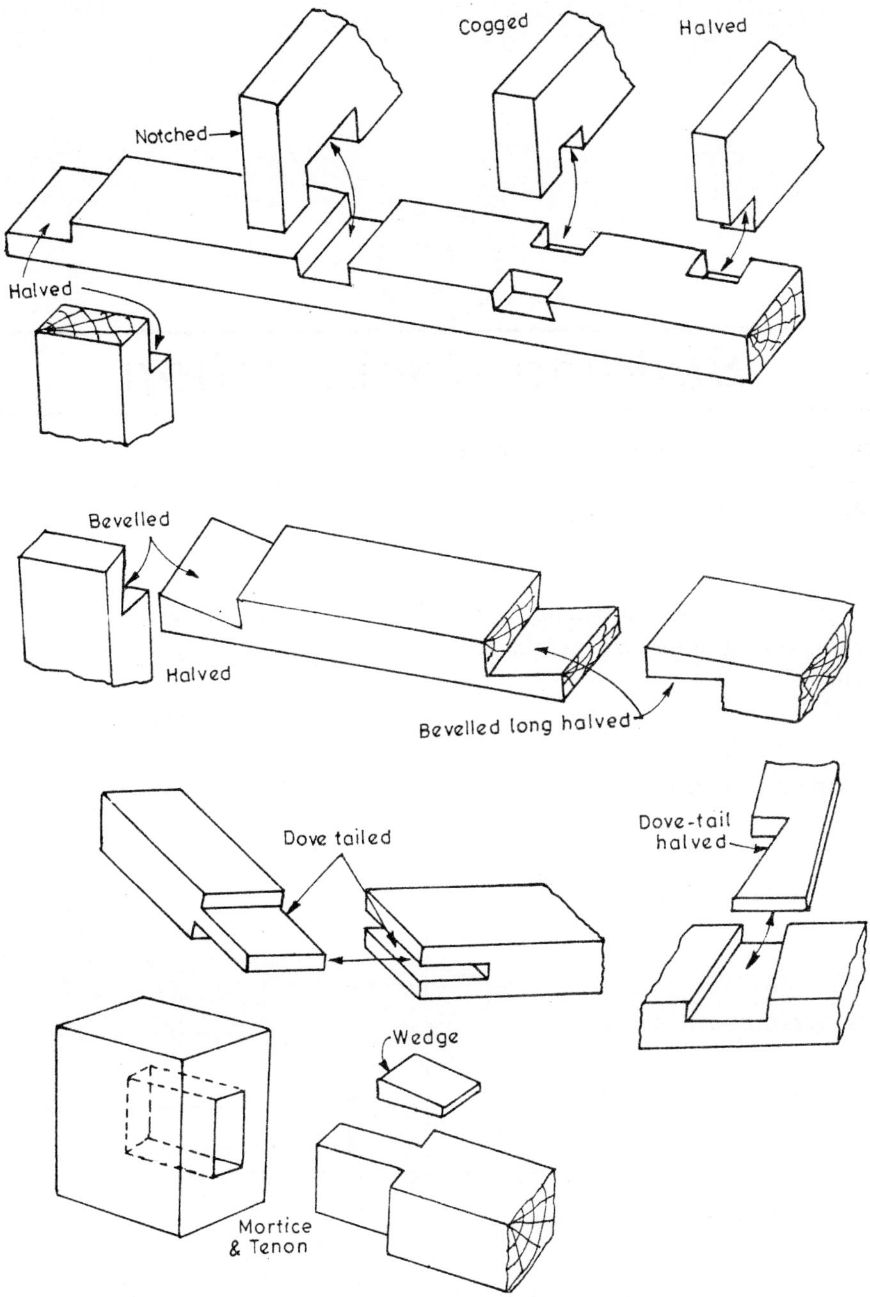

Fig. 6·44 (*b*). Joinery of wood.

Dove tailing—In the joints of the angles such as curbs etc. which areusually of similar sinking dove tailing is used.

Housing—When the entire end or thickness of a piece of member butts and fits into another piece, it is said to be housed.

Mortice and Tenon—For simplicity and efficiency these joints are used.

7

Building Construction

7·1. Denotations or Notations in Drawings

(*a*) Chain dotted centre line

(*b*) Unit of measure is mentioned in the drawing on right side or otherwise mentioned in the dimensions.

(*c*) Long line shown brocken

(*d*) Dimension lines

(*e*) Lines crossing each other.

(*f*) Section lines

(*g*) Long dotted lines indicating position of rear or under unseen construction.

(*h*) Double dotted chain lines indicating forward or over unseen construction

(*i*) Soil drain lines

(*j*) Rain water drain

(*k*) Brick section vermillion or light red

(*l*) Concrete Plain sec. green no. 1; if RC mention.

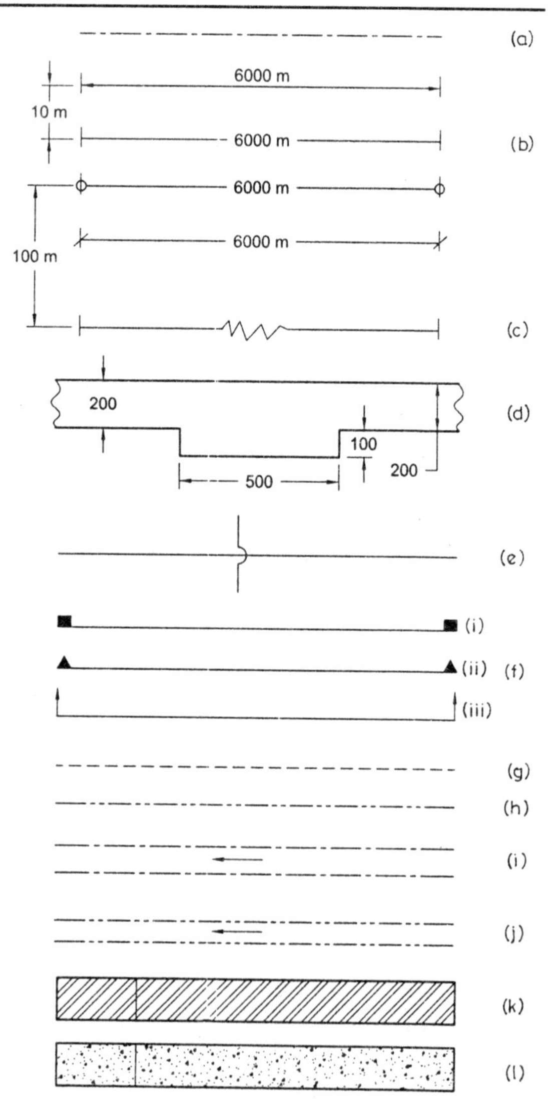

(*m*)	Earth section	Sepia
(*n*)	Rock section	-do-
(*o*)	Stone section	Cobalt blue
(*p*)	Wood unwrot	Raw seinna
(*q*)	Wood wrot if hard wood burnt umber.	Burnt seinna
(*r*)	Plaster	Terreverte
(*s*)	Asphalt or mastic	Discritionary
(*t*)	Marble	Cobalt blue
(*u*)	Opening in roof	
(*v*)	Wood section	

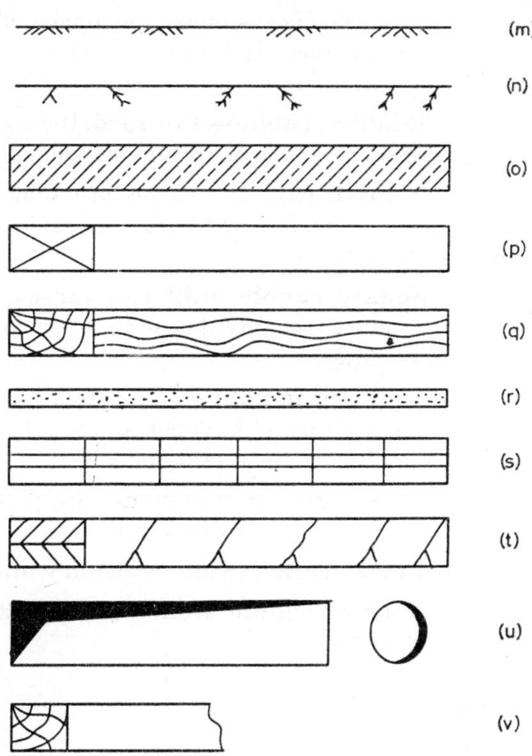

Fig. 7·1 (*a*) to (*v*)

7·2. Stone Walls

(1) **Rubble—**Flint, random rubble Kentish 'rag' (2) Block in course (3) Ashlar

Flint walls. The flints are small and irregular form of stones. The large stones are used on face while smaller are filled inside. The face stones are chipped off to give a good surface.

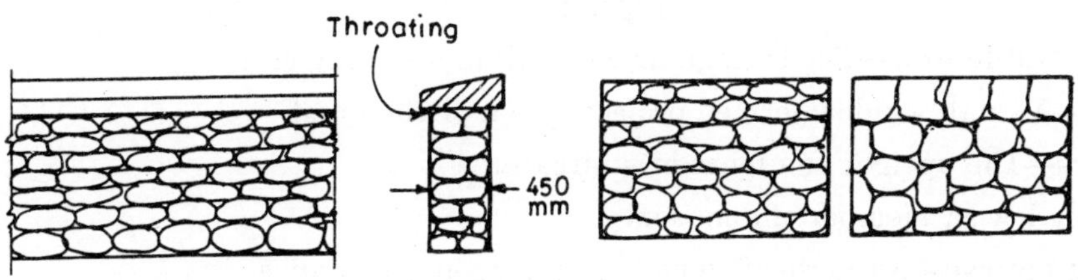

(*a*) Flint (*b*) R.R. coursed

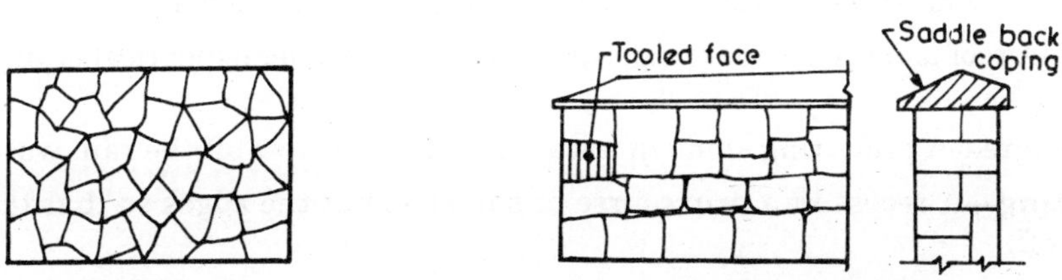

(*c*) Kentish rag (*d*) Square Rubble

Fig. 7·2.

Random rubble—Uncoursed. The stones are of larger size. The face stones are chipped off roughly to give a smooth face. It has no courses in a straight horizontal line.

Random rubble—Coursed. It has courses of unequal thickness of roughly shaped stones.

Kentish rag. The stones are kept in different diagonal shapes on face and back and inside is filled with small packing stones.

Square rubble built to courses. The stones used are square, roughly dressed and set in courses of unequal thickness.

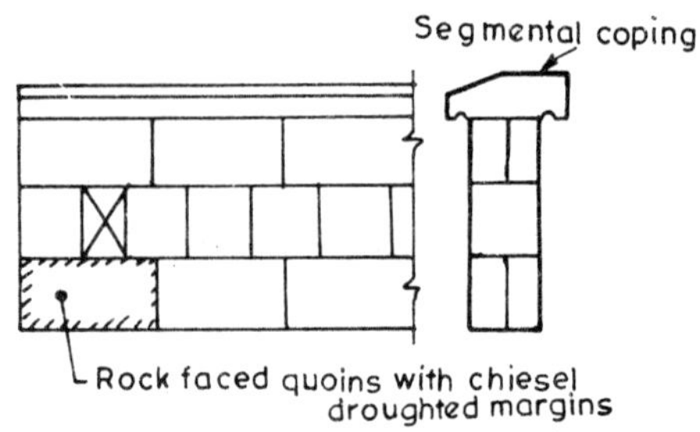

Fig. 7·3. Ashlar

(2) **Block in course.** The stones are squared and are brought to good fair joints. The faces are usually being hammer dressed. Block in course closely resembles to coursed rubble or ashlar according to the quality of work.

(3) **Ashlar.** The face stones are properly squared, plained and bedded in proper bond. The joints are truely horizontal and vertical. The inner fill may be of bricks or random rubble.

7·3. Technical Terms (Stone masonry and walls)

Apex or saddle stone—Highest stone of a gable end, ornamental apex is known as finical or pinnacle.

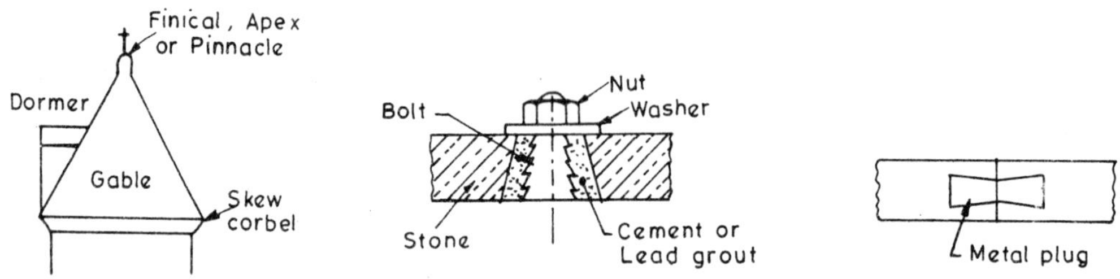

(*a*) (*b*) Rag bolt (*c*) Cramp

Fig. 7·4.

Gable or Gable end—The triangular end wall in a sloping roof.

Dormer—A small window formed projected in a pitched roof.

Balusters—The upright of a fence or staircase.

Base—The lowest member of a masonry.

Blocking course—A course of stones erected upon the cornice.

Bed surface—The surface of a stone perpendicular to the pressure.

Bonders—Long stones placed through from face to back of a wall.

Dome—A roof usually circular or polygonal on plan and hemispherical or any other curve in elevation.

Drip Stone—A projecting stone in a wall in order to throw off the rain water.

Throating—A recess in a drip course or sun shade at the edges so that the rain water may be thrown off.

Dowels—These are the members to resist lateral movement. These may be of hard stone, iron or copper.

Anchor bolt—Long iron bolt employed at the back of cornices that have great projections.

Rag bolts—The ends of the bolts are often fixed by having the end that is let into the stone jagged and run with lead or cement. The mortice being dovetailed shaped to secure it fromany upward pressure.

Cramp—Plate or metal connection.

Coping—The highest and covering course of a masonry forming a water proof top.

Corbel—A piece of stone projecting off a wall to support a projecting feature.

Cornice—The moulded course of a masonry crowning building to throw off the rain water from the wall.

Lacing course—It is a course (generally given in brick work) over the coursed or unbonded walls to give a bond and strength.

Pedestal—A raised base of any type of work over which a machine or a statue is founded.

Arris—When two sloping surfaces meet and produce an external angle.

Template—Pieces of stones placed under the end or bearing of a beam to distribute the weight and save the bearing from crushing.

Flag stone or paving sets—Flat stones used in flooring.

Free stone—A stone obtained by splitting and which is easy to carve.

Bed rock—Any hard rock underlying a soft deposition.

Bedding plane—Junction of two adjacent layers in a sedimentary origin.

Bulls eye—A circular or oval opening in a wall.

Chase—A recess made inside a wall to receive pipes and electric wiring in concealed fittings.

Jambs—Two sides of an opening in a wall. They form a base for chaukhats of openings. Also known as **Reveal.**

Mental—The shelf above a fire place projecting from the wall.

Oriel window—A projecting window on upper floors of a building and does not reach upto the ground.

Pilaster—An attached pier from a wall or a pier to receive load bearing members.

Sleeper walls—Low walls constructed between main walls to provide support to the lowest floor.

Underpinning—Supports provided in existing structure when repairs are done in a lower structure.

Weathering—A slight slope or fall given in the upper surface of cornices, coping, sun shades and window sills etc. to throw off rain water.

Spall—Stone chips or broken bricks.

Bressummer—Steel joists embedded in cone. It is used over varendah posts on which purlins of sloping roof rests. It is also means a beam which carries of wall.

Gargoyle—A stone ware water spout employed in buildings to carry off the rain water from the gutters and projecting sufficiently far to throw the water clear of the building.

Gutters—A channel section placed longitudinally at end of sloping roof to collect rain water.

Secant wall—A wall of cast in situ bored piles.

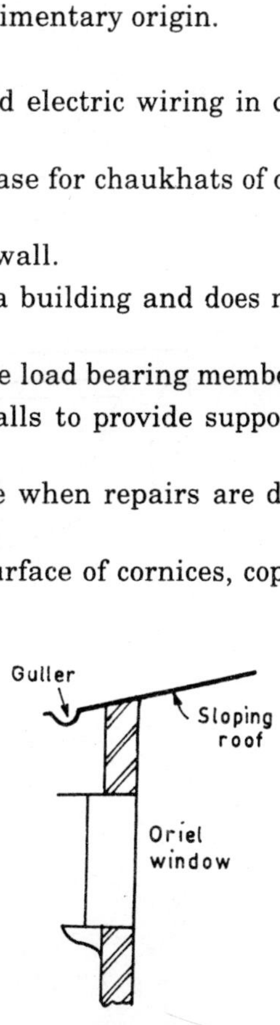

Fig. 7·5.

7·4. Technical terms (Brickwork)

Frog—A depression is formed in the bedding surface of the bricks so as to make a key for the mortar. Manufacturers generally leave their initials in the frog. It is kept upward while laying.

Bed joint—The mortar joints normal to the pressure (6 mm thick)

(*a*) In vertical walls the bed joints are horizontal

(*b*) In batter walls they would be right angle to the batter.

(*c*) In arches right angle to the curve of arch.

Quoins—The external corners of walls. Quoin brick or quoin stone is applied to the corner brick or stone.

Perpends—The vertical joints of the face of walls (10 mm thick)

Stretchers—Bricks laid with their 9″ lengths parallel to the face of the wall.

Headers—Bricks laid with their 4½″ width parallel to the face of wall.

Bats—Pieces of bricks ¼, ½, or ¾ bats is known according to their fractions.

Lap—The horizontal distance between the vertical joints in two successive courses. This should be ¼th the length of brick.

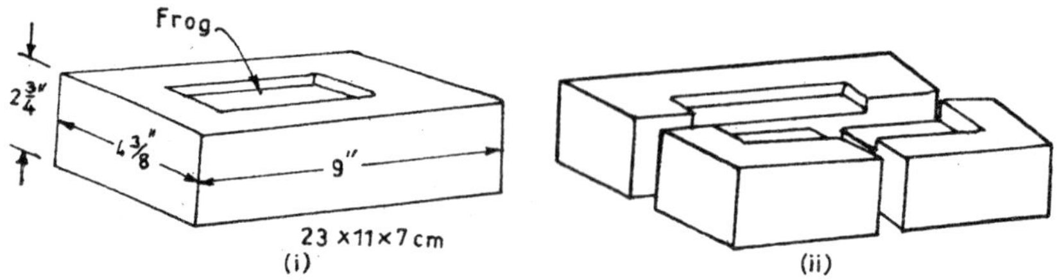

Fig. 7·6. Queen closures

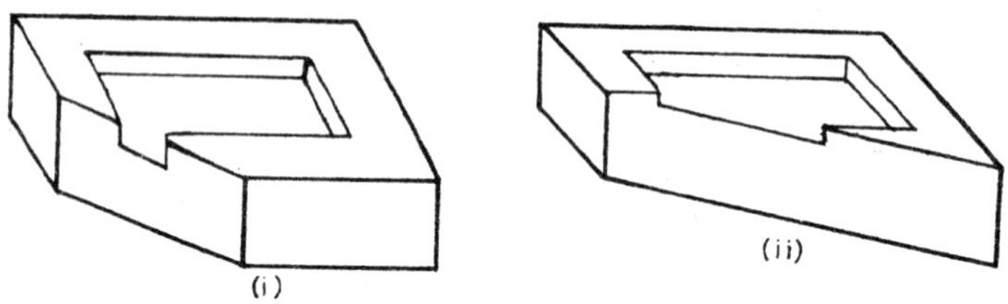

Fig. 7·7. King closures

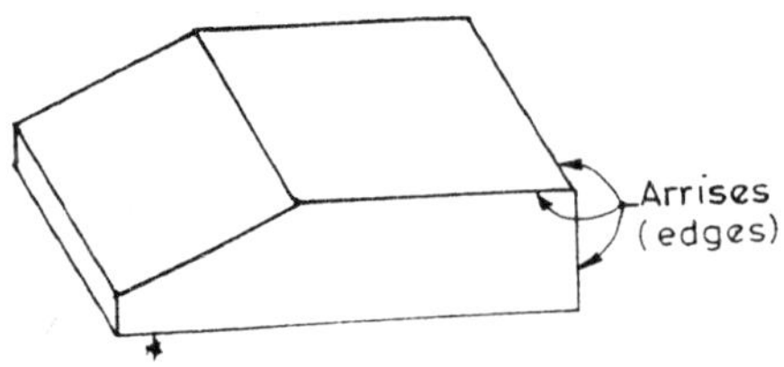

Fig. 7·8. Plinth brick

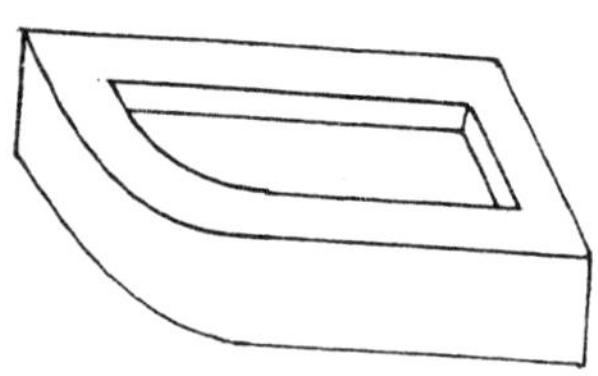

Fig. 7·9. Bull nose

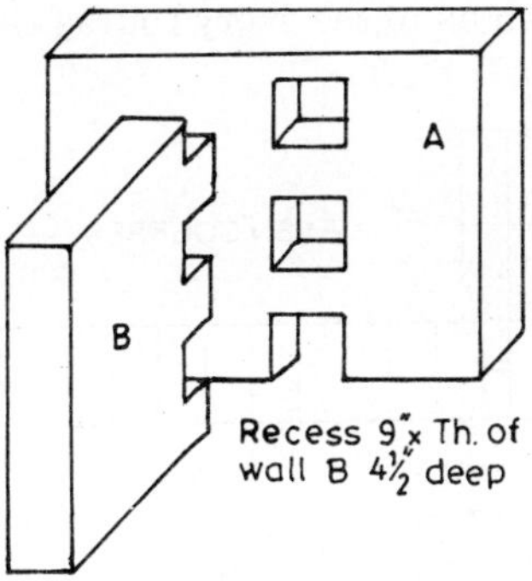

Fig. 7·10. Block bonding of wall *A* to *B*

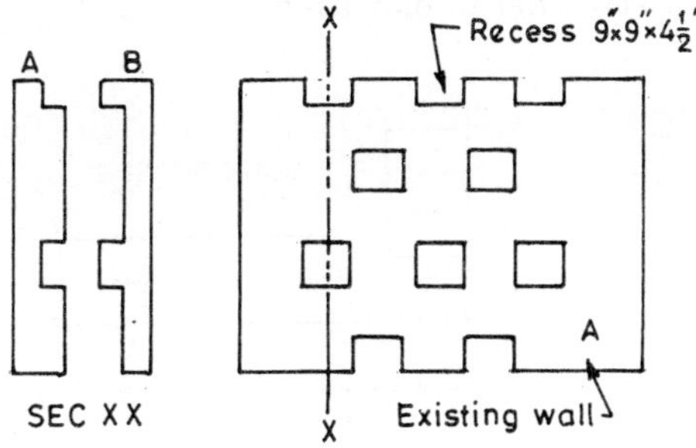

Fig. 7·11. Thickening wall by *B*

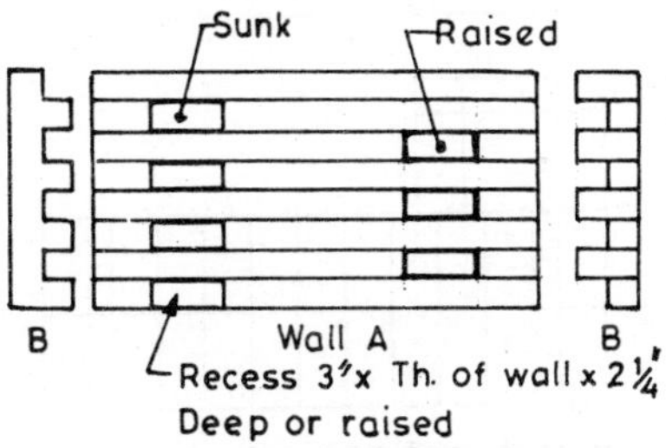

Fig. 7·12. Racking for future lengthening

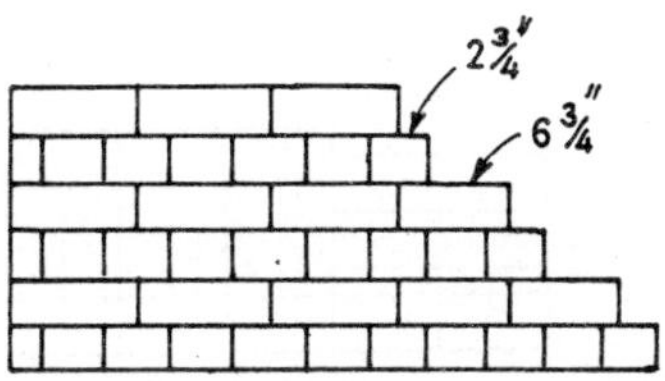

Fig. 7·13. Toothing for future for adding cross walls

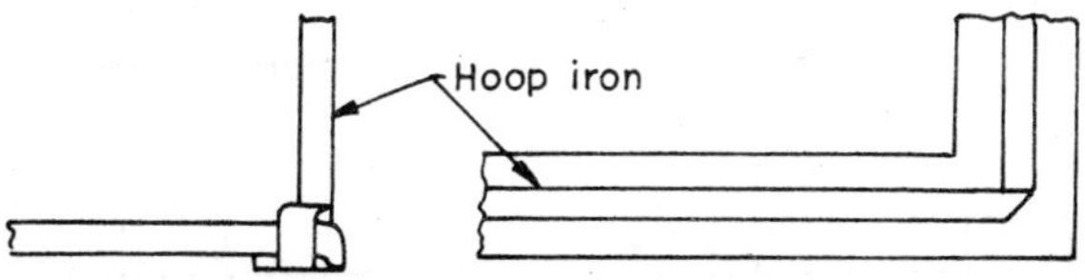

Fig. 7·14. Hoop iron bond.

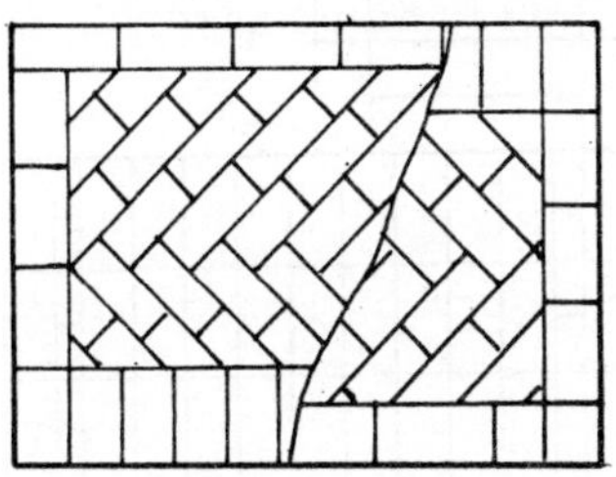

Fig. 7·15. Herring bone bond

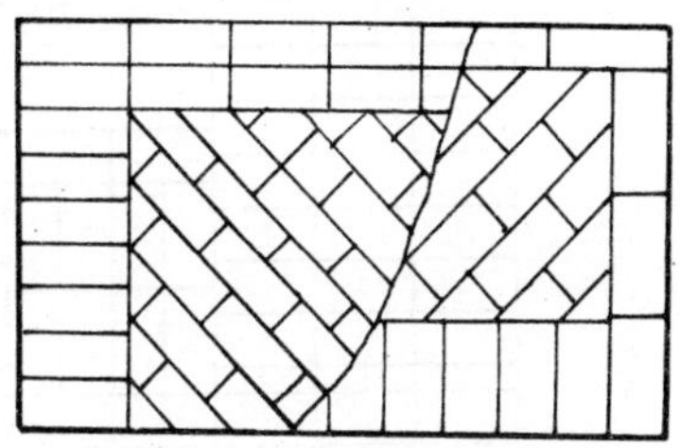

Fig. 7·16. Diagonal bond

Queen closures—Bricks cut half and one quarter along length.

King closures—Bricks cut on corners.

Squint quoins—Bricks cut or moulded on one edge, splayed in order to form projections on walls.

Bull nose—Bricks having one end rounded.

Cow nose—Bricks having both ends rounded or double bull nose.

Racking—Leaving an unfinished end of brick work for future extension of the work.

English bond—Setting of bricks in each layer such as to see every course either a header or a stretcher in elevation.

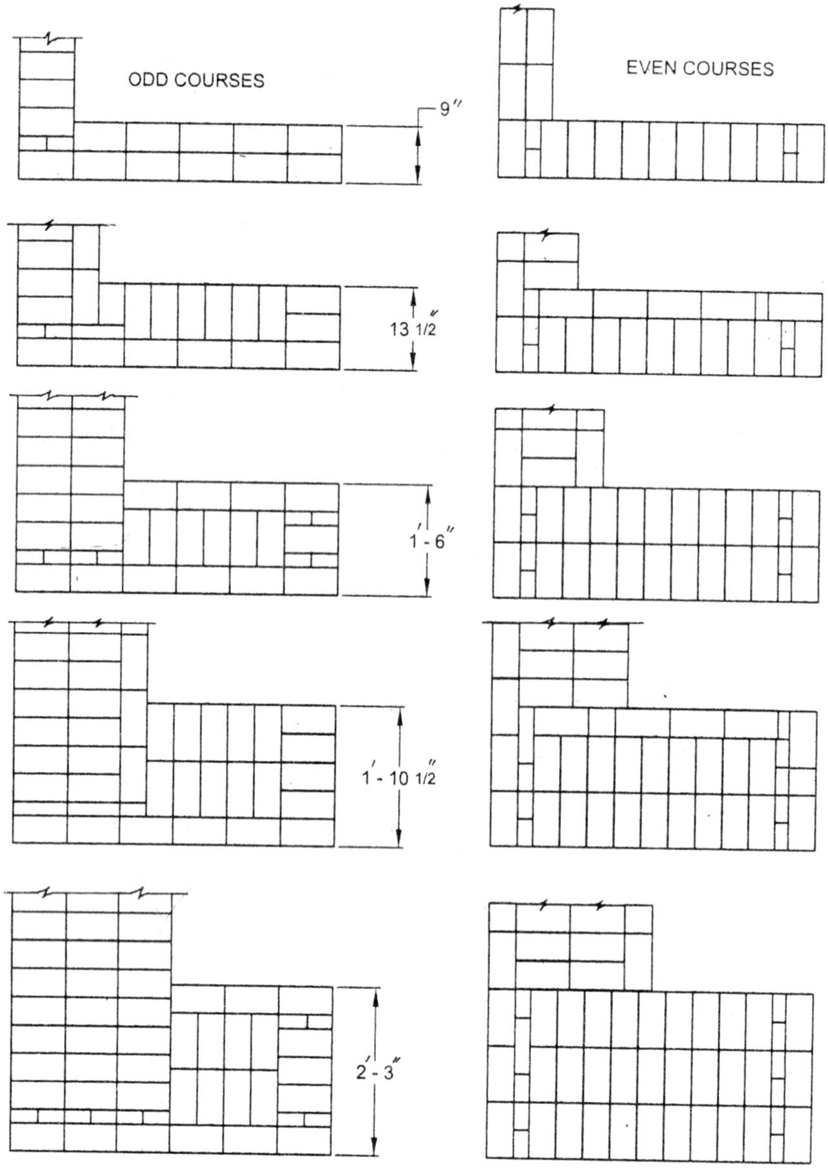

Fig. 7·17. English bond.

Flemish bond—Setting of bricks in each layer such as to see every course alternatively with stretcher and header in elevation.

Herring bone bond—Brick layers laid diagonally starting from the centre of the wall thickness. Generally used in thick walls or floors.

Diagonal bond—Brick courses laid diagonally (laid in thick walls).

String course—A horizontal course projected out in order to divide the height of a building.

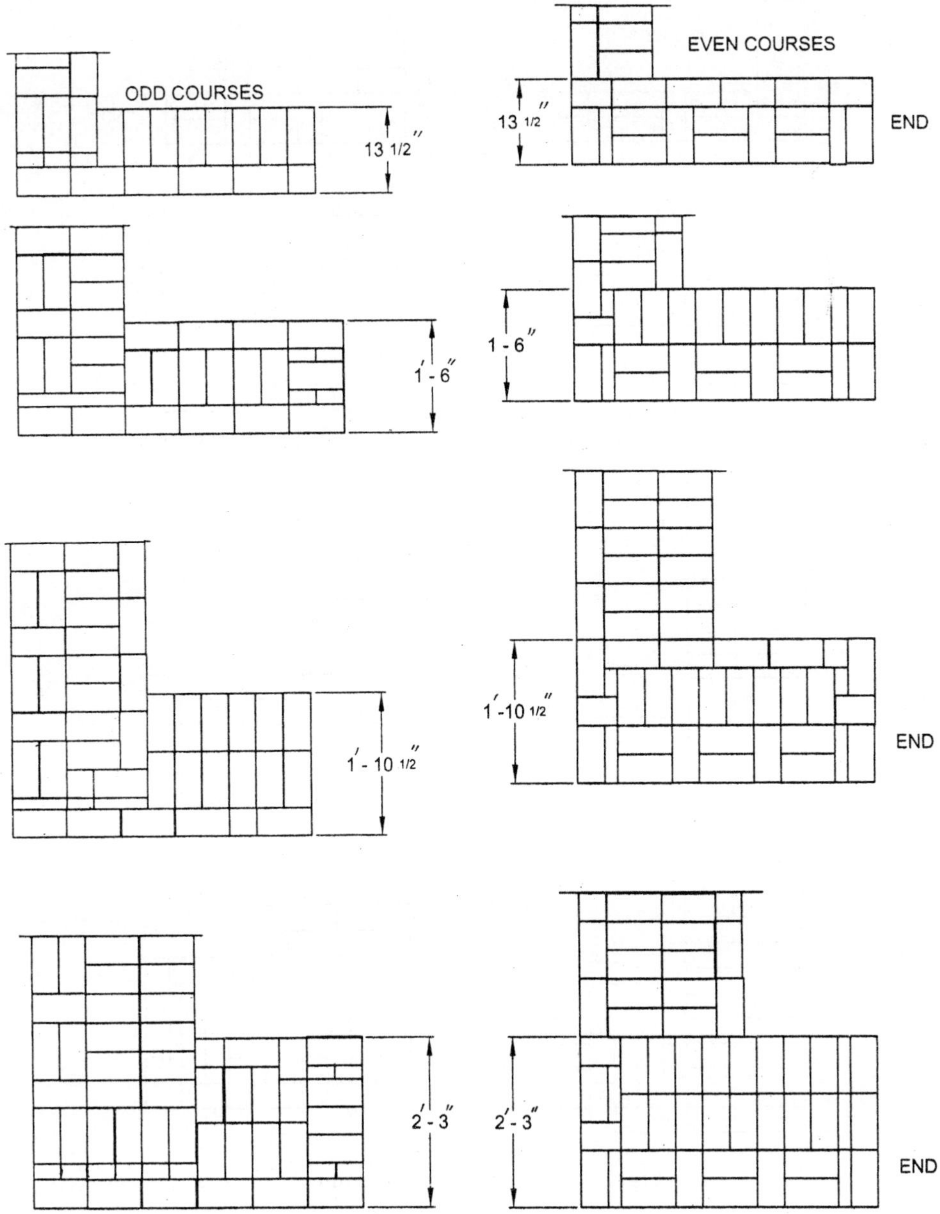

Fig. 7·18. Single flemish bond.

Corbel—A projected course under roofs in side the walls.

Cornice—A projected course on roof out side the walls.

Brick nogging—Brick work filled in between wooden posts, forming a partition wall.

Plinth—Projected area of buildings.

Course—Operation of a brick or stone layer.

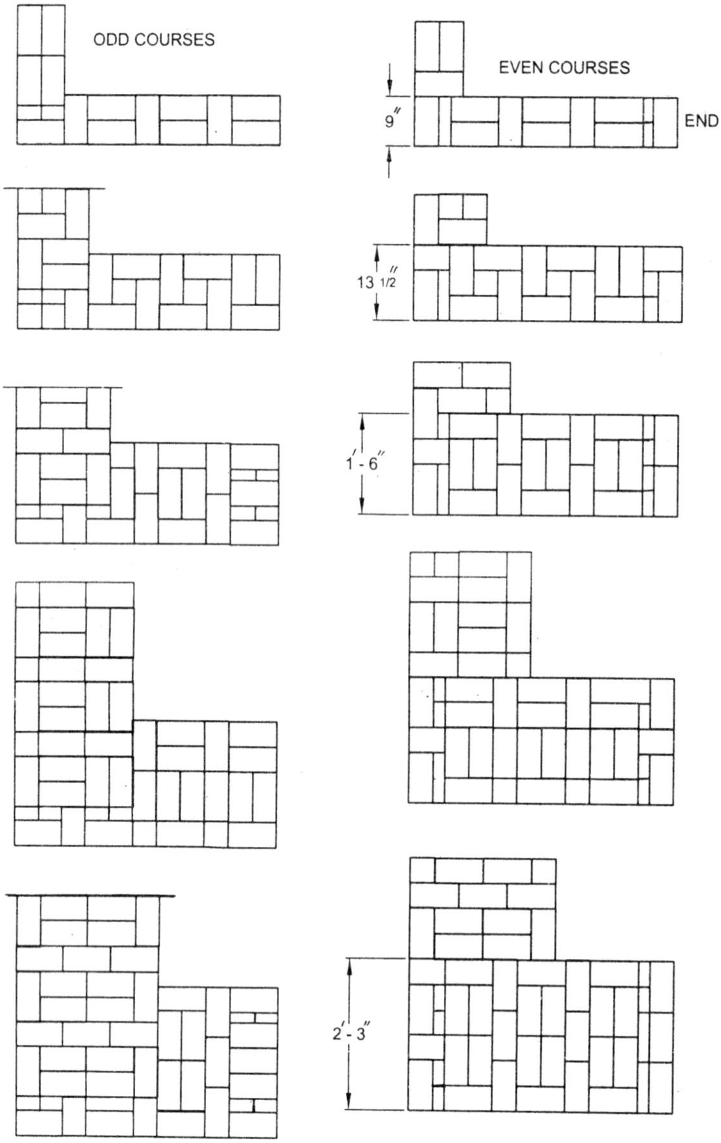

Fig. 7·19. Double Flemish bond.

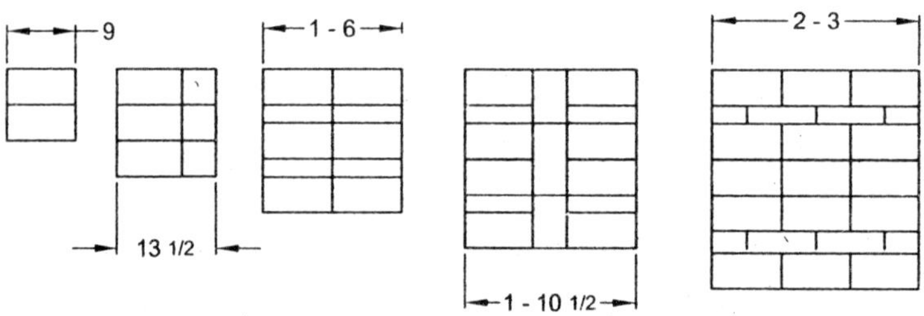

Fig. 7·20. Sq. piers (English bond).

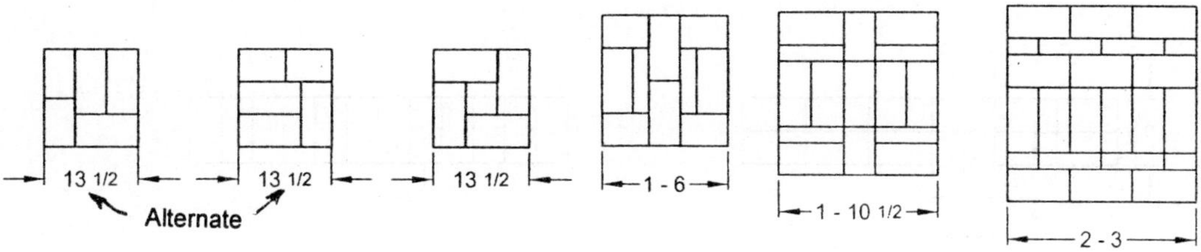

Fig. 7·21. Sq. piers (Flemish bond).

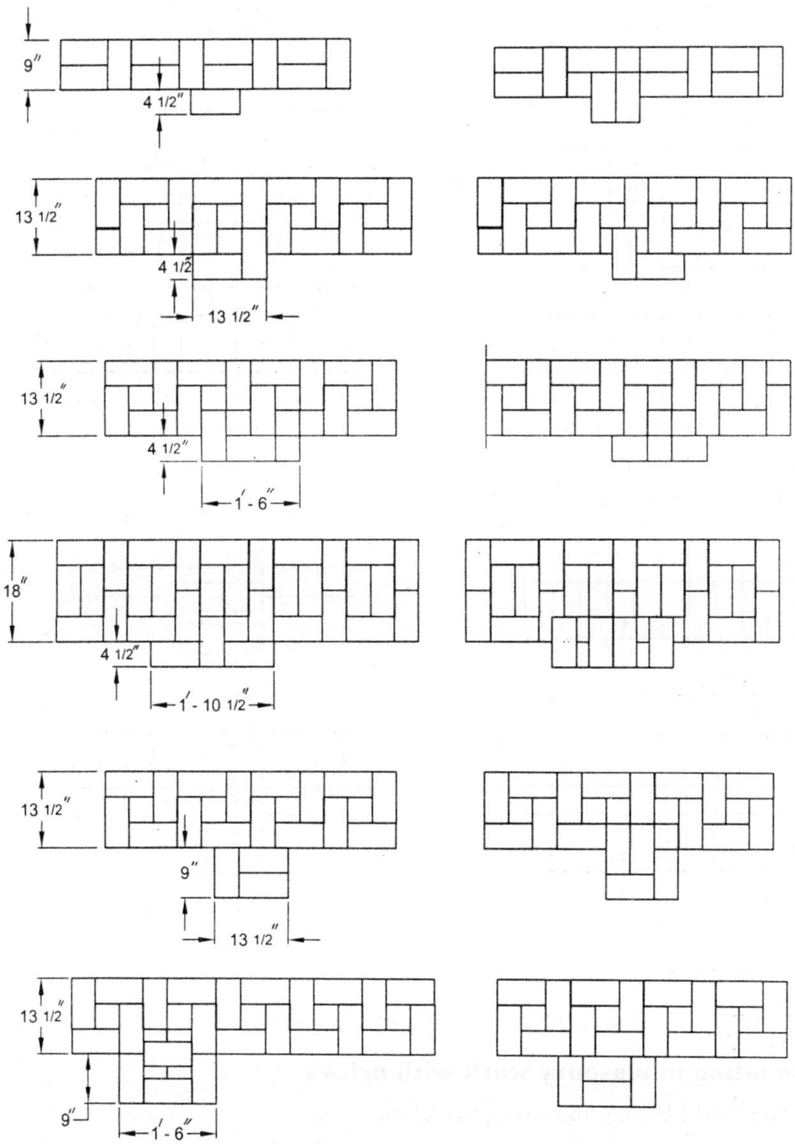

Fig. 7·22. Attached piers flemish bond.

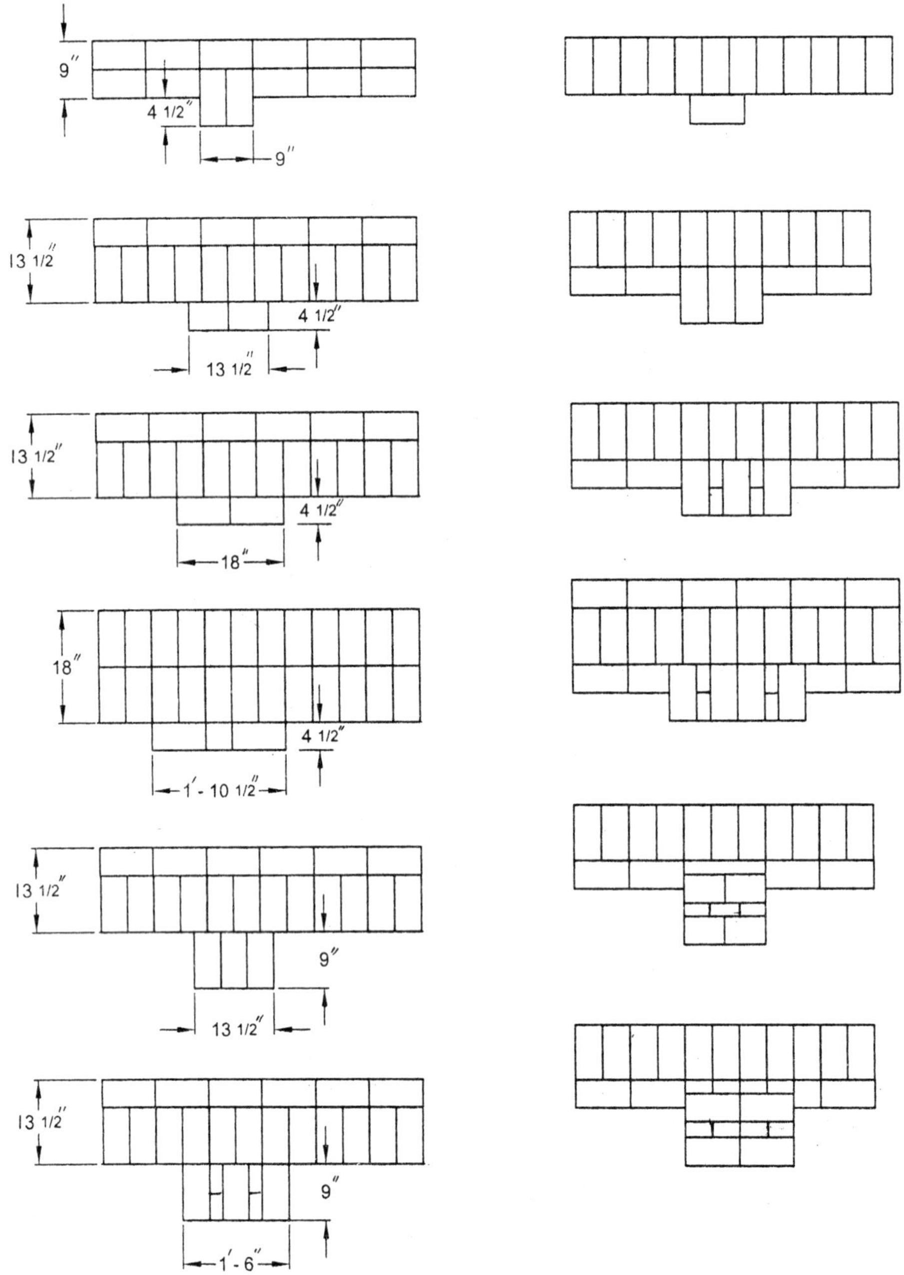

Fig. 7·23. Attached piers English bond.

7·5. Rules for bonding in masonry work with bricks

(1) The top should be one-fourth of the brick.

(2) Brick should be uniform in shape and size. The length of the brick should be equal to twice the width of brick plus thickness of one mortar joint.

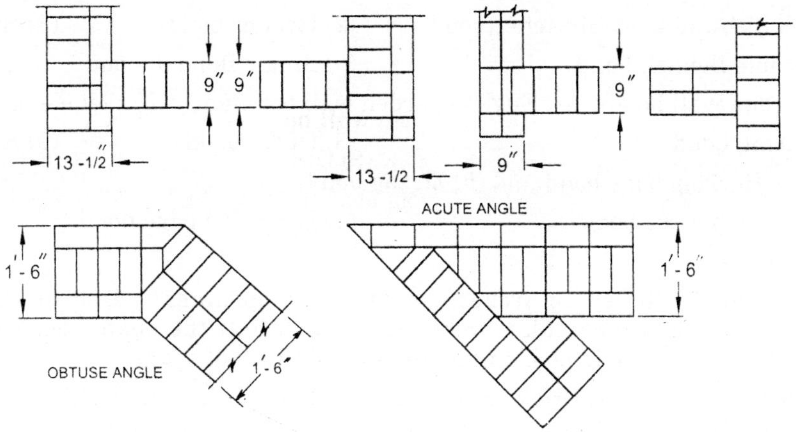

Fig. 7·24. Squin quoins, English bond.

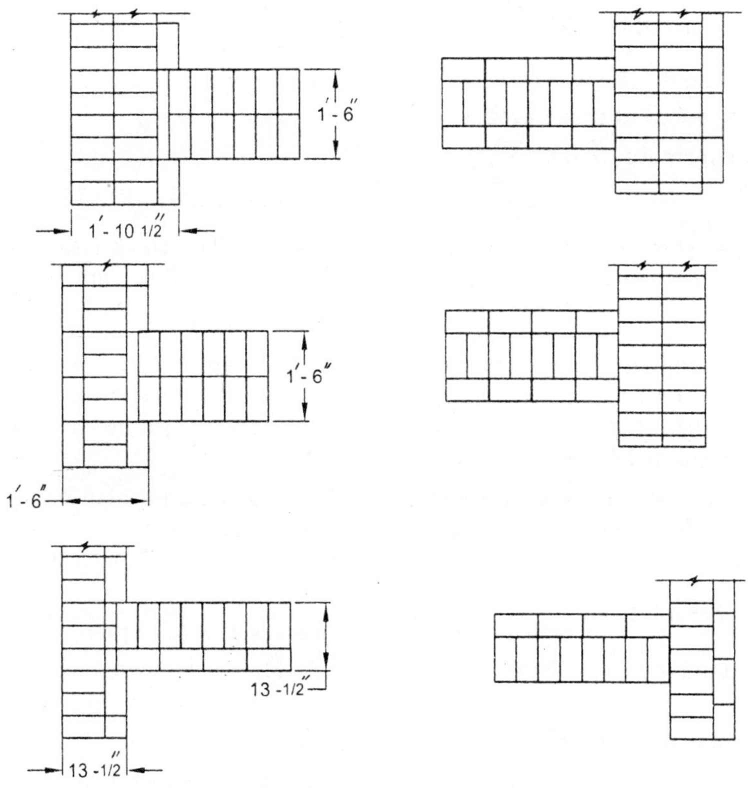

Fig. 7·25. Junctions, English bond.

(3) The vertical joints should be vertically above each other in the alternate courses.

(4) The stretchers should be used only in facing, while hearting should be done in headers only.

(5) The centre line of the header should coincide with the centre line of the stretcher in the course below or above it.

(6) Least number of bats should be used.

Types of bonds. (1) Stretcher bond (2) Header bond (3) English bond (4) Double flemish bond (5) Single flemish bond (6) Garden wall bond : (*a*) English garden wall bond and (*b*) Flemish garden wall bond (7) Facing bond (8) Outer bond (9) Racking bond (10) (*a*) Herring bone bond and (*b*) Zigzag bond (11) English cross bond (12) Brick on edge bond.

7·6. Arched roofs

Rise of arch. Relieving arches over doors or openings = 1/10 to 1/12 of span (for segmental arches). For semicircular arches the rise is half the span, segmental arches are provided in jack arches. Rise in jack arched roofs = 1/6 to 1/8 of span.

Thickness of arches. Brick arches : The thickness is kept in multiple of 4½″ (half brick or brick on edge). Half brick thickness is taken for every 1·5 m span. For heavy loads the min. thickness is kept 9″ (one brick) and it is increased by 4½″ for every 10′ (3 m) increase in span. However following formulae are used for fixing thickness of arches.

$$\text{Transwin formula } t = \frac{\sqrt{R + 0{\cdot}5S}}{4} + 0{\cdot}2 \text{ ft} \; ; \; R = \frac{(0{\cdot}55)^2 + h^2}{2h}$$

where t = thickness of arch, R = rad. of arch, h = rise and S = span.

This formula is for cut stone arches.

$$\text{Rankine formula } t = 0{\cdot}4\sqrt{S}$$

$$t = \sqrt{0{\cdot}2 \times R} \text{ (Single semi-circular arch)} = \sqrt{0{\cdot}2S\,R} \text{ (arches in series).}$$

Jack arches. They are provided for 1 to 1·5 m spans. The thickness is 4½″. These are supported either on the lower flange or an upper flange of an iron T-section. The end spans are provided with a tie rod. The horizontal thrust say P on a tie rod is $P = \frac{12{\cdot}5\,WL}{R}$ where W is the total vertical load in kg/m^2 including dead and live for end span and live load for intermediate spans ; P = Horizontal thrust and L = span in metres. From this horizontal thrust, the section of the tie rod can be calculated for end span which is P/p where p = permissible tensile stress of steel in direct tension (min. 12 mm).

The spacing of the rods is kept about 1 to 1·5 m, but it must also be not less than 20 times of the flange width of the supporting beam.

The tie rods are archored with the anchor plate at their ends with bolts and washers. The area of the anchor plate = $\frac{P}{\text{bearing capacity of the mass of wall or pier}}$. The bearing plate must have a minimum area 75 × 75 mm and 6 mm thick. Mortar is used as 1 : 3 cement or rich lime mortar.

7·7. Technical terms (Arch work)

Voussoirs—The brick or stones which are generally in edge shaped.

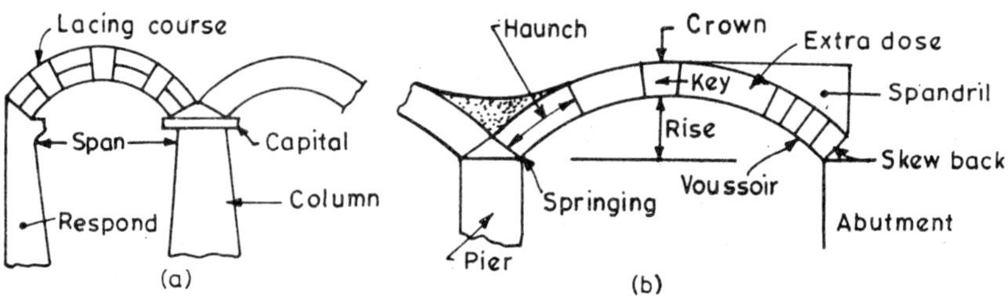

Fig. 7·26. Arcade.

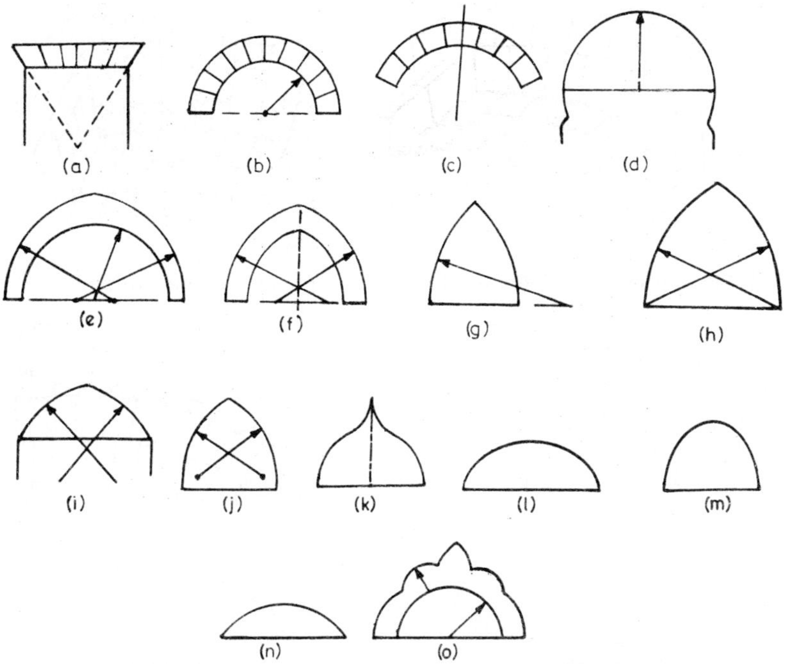

(*a*) Flat;	(*b*) Semi circular;	(*c*) Segmental;	(*d*) Horse shoe;	(*e*) Florentine;
(*f*) Venetian;	(*g*) Lancet;	(*h*) Equilateral;	(*i*) Centred;	(*j*) Moorish;
(*k*) Ogee;	(*l*) Elliptical;	(*m*) Parabolic;	(*n*) Hyperbolic; and (*o*) Lotus;	

Fig. 7·27. Types of Arches.

Springing—The seat of the curved portions of an arch to the abutment. The 1st course over springing is known as **springer.**

Key—The central or upper most layer or course of an arch.

Skew back—The plopping course of an abutment on which the extreme or the lowest voussoir rests.

Intrados or soffit—The under or the concave side of an arch.

Extradose or back—The upper or the convex side of an arch.

Capital—Moulded or carved head of a column.

Respond—The semi column or Corbel forming the end support of an **arcade** (series of arches).

Crown—The highest point of the extradose of an arch.

Haunch—Lower half of the arch from springing to the mid way of the arch.

Spandril—The curved triangular space between the arches *i.e.* vertical from the end of extrados to the tangent of the crown.

Lacing course—The courses which are provided to break the continuity of the ring courses of the arch.

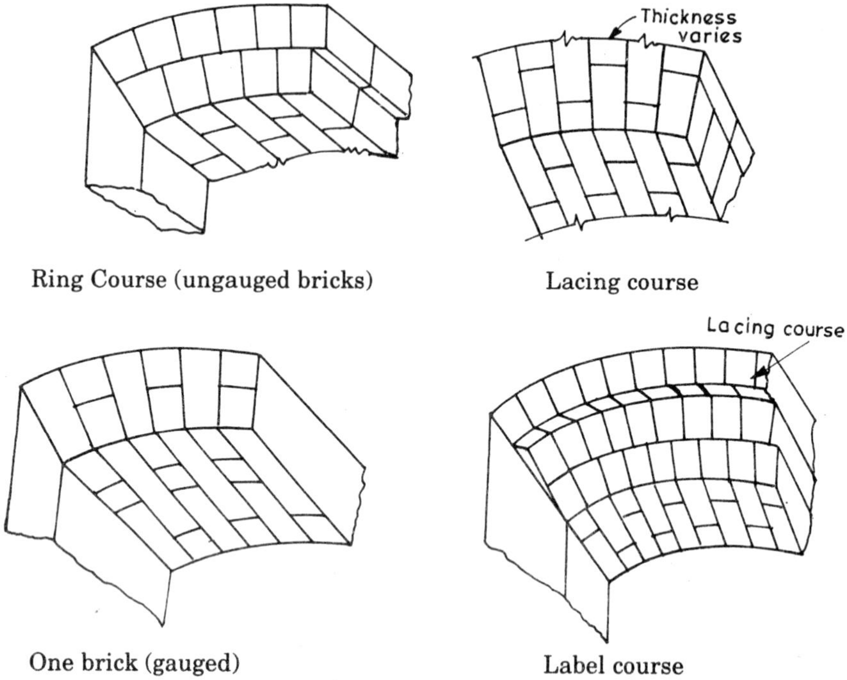

Fig. 7·28. Arch bonds.

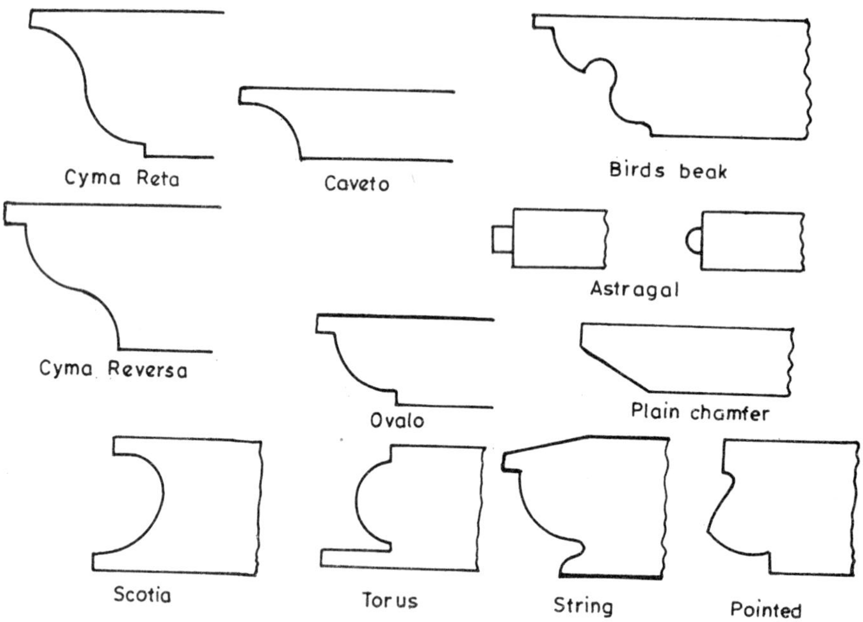

Fig. 7·29. Cornice carvings

Label course—The courses which are provided projected to throw off the rain water as to have a pleasing effect.

Squint arch—An arch having abutment or pier faces parallel, but their ends having angles other than a right angle. Such types of arches are laid when the water or the road way do not cross at right angles to each other.

Inverted arches—These are laid in floors to bear the load on foundations. In such cases the rise is actually a depression.

Vault—An arched structure with series of arches.

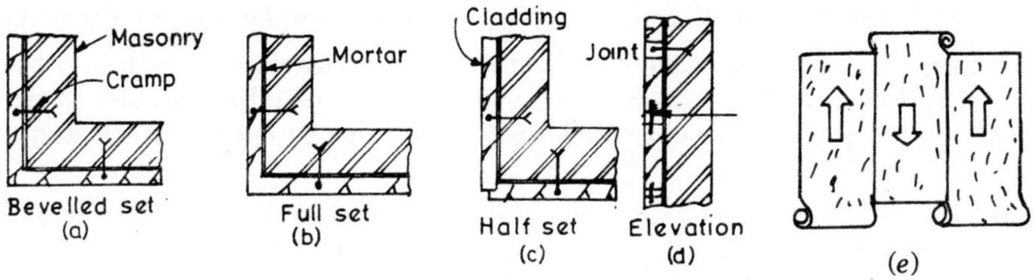

Note : Reverse alternate lengths for perfect match

Corner details (plan) Wall paper

Fig. 7·30. Lining of walls.

Boarder Design Window faces

Fig. 7·31.

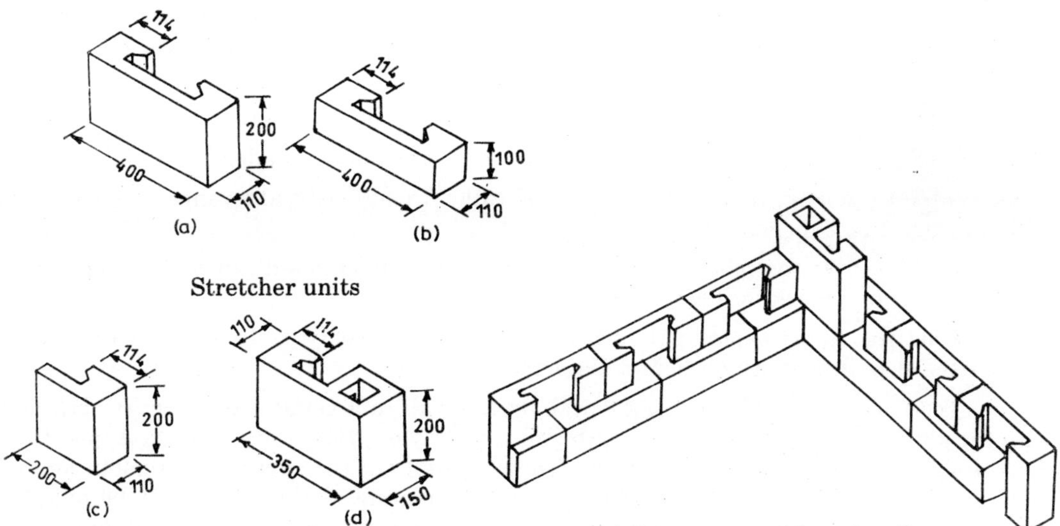

Jamb unit Corner unit (*e*) Corner assemblage detail

Fig. 7·32. Interlocking Block Masonry—Interlocking concrete blocks are prepared and setin mortar.

7·8. Wall lining (Cladding) (Refer Fig. 7·30)

Lining with marble. In order to make exposed surface of walls more pleasing and weather resistant, bricks or stone masonry is lined or cladded with marble sheets (2 to 2·5 cm thick).

In fixing, the slabs are kept 2 cm to 2·5 cm from the face of the wall and are bedded by the rich mortar say 1 : 2 cement and sand in vertical position. The sheets are fixed in position with brass dowels about ¼″ dia. along the lower edges and brass cramps along the top edges of the form as shown in the figure given. Holes are drilled in the top edge of the lower sheet with a brace and bit. Into this the turned down end of the cramp is inserted. The other end of the cramp is usually fish tailed and pinned and fixed into the wall with mortar. Each slab is plumbed and levelled. Arrangements of the joints on covers are also shown in the figure. The edges of the slabs are chipped off bevelled to make a key. An example of this type can be seen in Taj at Agra.

Lining with sand stone. (Dholpur etc.) When the face appearance is required better than the brick or stone and cost is also a guiding factor, sand stone cladding is used on walls. The method is the same as discussed above, cramps and dowels can be used of steel. Example can be seen at Lal Qila at Delhi or Agra.

Lining with glazed tiles. Glazed tiles are available in market in usual size of 6^2 and 4^2 square and in other suitable rectangular forms in different patterns.

The surface of the wall is prepared with rough plaster with coarse sand and cement. On this plastered surface the tiles are stuck with neat cement mortar in desired patterns. Marble chips can be sticked on back face with araldite adhesive to have a better bond.

The brocken pieces of tiles are also used in different patterns on walls. The intersticks are filled with cement mortar prepared by the desired colouring pigment. About one fourth part of mortar is mixed with marble dust, so that hair cracks may not develop. Desired pieces can be cut by glass cutting knife edge.

Paper lining. (Size of Roll : 10 m × 0·62 m. Area 6·2 m^2/Roll).

Surface preparation and pasting directions. The walls should be solid, clean, semi-absorbing and not very smooth. Wherever local flaking paint exists, scrap it and fill interistics with Plaster of Paris prepared from Max-Bond paste and make even the wall wherever walls are good and pre-painted, sand paper them for slight roughness (wall covering will not stick properly on walls very smooth, oily or dusty).

(*a*) Open the rolls and see that all of them are of the same lot.

(*b*) Spread the rolls on ground an d see that the colours, shades are matching.

(*c*) Cut the lengths according to size of wall with sufficient allowance for design matching with an extra 1 or 2 inches.

(*d*) Wherever the label of reverse alternate lengths is found : In that case reverse it and also make a pencil mark for identification.

Pasting. Apply paste at the back of the roll. Also apply paste on the wall, if the wall is lime coated or painted with oil-bound distemper.

Position of the wall covering length on the wall in a vertical position. (Check and align with the plumb line). Take the 2nd length and similarly position it on the wall. Adjust the design matching. In case if the design is free match, overlap it till the edges have smooth and uniform foaming all over (It is important to note that the foaming at the edges may be slightly more than all over. Hence it is important to overlap until uniform foaming is available) Overlap by 6 mm to 10 mm. Please note that the roll is 63 cms and design is 62·5 cms to 63 cms. This compensates extra margin for overlap cutting.

The overlap is then cut with the blades so that the upper and lower wall covering is cut and remove the upper and lower slitted strips, as in the case of overlap cutting in other brands.

Apply on the edges diluted solution of Fevicol (without powder of Max-Bond) and with a pressing putti press it firmly on the wall. Take a wet sponge soaked in clean water. (If water is warm, it will be better as gum dissolves faster in warm water) and mop the design surface so that gum deposits are removed.

Joint sealing patti (J.S.P.). When wall covering is pasted on wall and is in wet condition. In wet condition it expands because of its natural characteristics with in about 7 to 8 Hrs., when it starts drying it starts contracting if the wall surface is weak *i.e.* lime coated/freshly painted/prepared with lambi-patti, the joints open because of the shrinkage along with the plaster. To avoid this a J.S.P. is used.

J.S.P. is pasted on the wall with the wall paper gum, and is centrally positioned on the wall in the joints area. After pasting press the J.S.P. on wall and over this the wall covering edges will be pressed.

Note : JSP is available in three thickness : JSP-50, JSP-25, JSP-17. The JSP-25 is thinner than JSP-50 and thicker than JSP-17. The JSP has to be used accordingly to the body of the wall covering otherwise the JSP under layer will be seen.

Max-Bond Adhesive. (1) It is white so the yellow strains as in other gum is not seen on the surface of wall paper.

(*ii*) It is mixed with anti-fungal agents, which resists fungus formation.

(*iii*) It gives perfect sliding and slow drying for perfect matching to paper.

Mixing of Max-Bond. 1 kg of Max-Bond to be wetted for 12 hrs. Next day add 50% fevicol equivalent and mix it and stir it vigrously. The paste is ready for application. The coverage depends upon the wall but wall painted with plastic paint should give a coverage of 1000 sq. ft. and lime coated 700 to 800 sq. ft.

Max-Bond mixed in plaster of Paris. (*i*) This helps the plaster to be very smooth (*ii*) The drying time is reduced, hence large quantity can be prepared (*iii*) It is stronger.

Note : After applying plaster of Paris on wall allow drying for 2 hrs. min.

Moisture Proof Liner (MPL). This is unique PVC laminate which is pasted on the area (without Max-Bond only fevicol) which is likely to be affected by moisture on temporary basis like that of Monsoon or any other incidental nature. The width of the roll is 2·7 cm and is pasted by overlap. Cutting method (OLC). After the laminate is dry (24 hrs curing time) it is ready to take any other wall covering. Wall covering pasted over MRL should be done with Fevicol only (not to mix Max-bond or equivalent).

7·9. False Ceilings

False ceilings in building is provided to have a pleasing face of the roof and to hide the mechanical and electrical fittings.

(1) **Wood Ceiling.** Wood bottom framing is done a bit below (or as required) the roof on short spans on these frames wooden planks 2 cm thick are pinned having a smooth surface wood battons rests on walls or on long beams of wood.

(2) **Plaster of Paris (POP) Ceiling.** Wood batton framing is done as above. The wood battons are covered with wood chapties (about ½″ thick) for making a covered ceiling. On chapti face pin chicken wire mesh, about a cm lower than the chapti face by means of nails. Plaster the face by about 2 cm in thickness by plaster of Paris, which is reinforced by the chicken mesh. The plaster of Paris hardens on drying. The mortar paste is prepared by mixing water. Smooth the surface by plainer. The edges can be moulded by plywood or plain iron sheet moulds.

(3) Plaster of Paris precasted panels or precasted thermocol slabs—The panels of POP of required size (say 3′ × 3′) are casted in forms by reinforced chicken wire mesh. The bottom face can be given any design desired. The four corners are holed for screws. These panels are screwed on wooden frames laid as above at the distance of the width of panel. The bottom face can be painted by the shade desired in place of POP panels, thermocol slabs can be replaced, which are lighter.

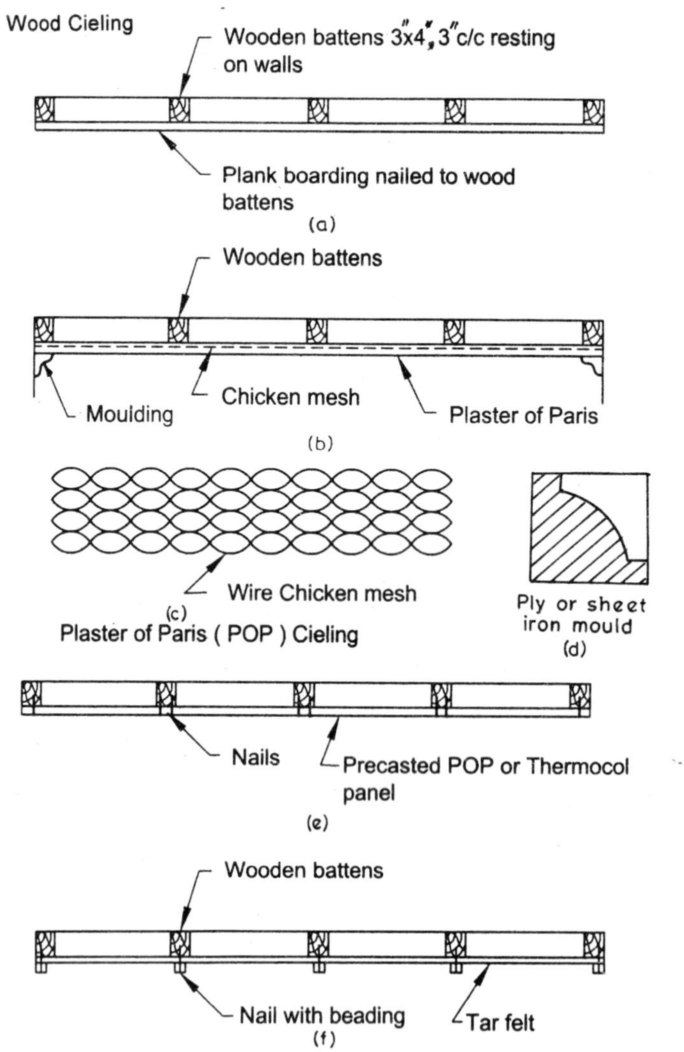

Fig. 7·33.

(4) **Tarfelt Ceiling.** Tarfelt ceilings are provided when low cost is desired. The tarfelt sheets are screwed to the wooden frame with wooden beading in square mesh underneath.

(5) **Bison Panel.** Cement bonded particle boards for false ceilings, partitions and door shutters etc., are also available in market. These are water, fire, weather and termite proof.

7·10. Damp-Proofing in Buildings

Dampness rises in buildings from the following sources :

(1) **Rising dampness.** It rises from the foundations and earth below it.

(2) **Dampness from sides of foundations.** It is due to sub soil water which acts on the sides of the foundations.

(3) Dampness from atmosphere entering from sides of walls.

(4) Dampness entering from top due to atmosphere and rains.

Remedial measures. For rising dampness. A layer of water proofing material is laid at the plinth level in walls and floors above ground level in the following manner :

(*a*) A layer of well burnt brick laid in cement mortar keeping vertical joints unfilled as they are source of rising dampness.

(*b*) A layer of slate set in mortar, vertical joints being kept unfilled or filled with a mortar having water proofing compound.

(*c*) A membrane of lead or copper sheet, mastic asphalt in one or two layers or multi-layer treatment with bitumen felts. Materials like the waxes and fats are unsuitable in the hot areas as they melt at high temperature. Coal tar and bitumen disfigure the original surface and can melt at high temperature.

(*d*) A layer of cement mortar or cement concrete 40 to 50 mm thick consisting of 1 : 2 : 4 stone ballast 4 mm to 10 mm size mix in cement and coarse sand painted over with 2 coats of bitumen. The 1st is applied at the rate of 1·2 kg/cm^2 and the 2nd at 0·7 kg/cm^2 covered with coarse sand at 0·006 m^3/m^2.

(*e*) **Surface treatment.** The pores of the surface are blinded by providing a thin film of water repellent material over the surface. Some of the materials are sod. or potassium silicates, aluminium, mag. or zinc sulphates, barium hydroxide, soap and alum, lime and linseed oil, coal tar resins, shellac, waxes or gums etc.

(*f*) **Integral water proofing.** Some water proofing compounds are mixed in concrete or mortar while mixing. These compounds may be as given in sec '*e*' above or cico, chalk, talc, pudlo or other materials sold in market for this purpose. (See water proofing of concrete in chapter of RCC).

A layer of asphalt or hot coal tar mixed with three parts by weight with dry coarse sand laid in thickness of 10 mm over dry conc. base. In hot places this asphaltic layer is avoided and concrete is used.

I.S. Specification (IS : 1609—1960) of Damp Proofing of Walls

(1) (*i*) To form an effective barrier to moisture under all conditions the damp proofing coarse shall cover the full thickness of the wall excluding rendering and shall not be set back from the wall face for painting. Bed on which the damp proofing coarse is to be laid shall be level, even and free from projections, liable to cause damage to the damp proofing course.

(*ii*) The damp proofing course shall be placed in correct relation to any other damp proofing course *i.e.* for floors so as to provide a complete and continuous barrier to the passage of moisture from below.

(*iii*) Where a vertical damp proofing course is to be laid continuous with a horizontal one a fillet 75 mm in radius shall be provided and the vertical face of the wall or structure shall receive an even bed of mortar, so as to provide a smooth backing for a flexible damp-proofing course.

(2) **Dampness entering from the sides of the foundation walls.**

(*a*) A trench should be cut upto foundation depth or the back fills of the foundations should be filled with graded ballast, gravel and sand then the water should be drained out in a public drain.

(*b*) A layer of tarfelt should be laid with coal tar and then it should be protected by a protection thin wall say half brick thick and back should be filled with graded filter as above. Two or three layers can be laid if the moisture is more.

(3) **Dampness entering from sides of walls.** It is due to moist atmosphere or rain. A best remedy for it is a cavity wall, but it is now out of practice as it is costlier. The joints which are source of water leakage should be pointed with a rich cement mortar. However a water seal layer of cement mortar can be laid on outside of walls, but it makes the moisture inside the

wall (due to rising dampness) trapped and it cannot evaporate even in hot weather, keeping the wall in continuous dampness. So a porous layer of mastic on the wall is better than an impervious one. Throatings are provided in drip courses of windows and sun shades.

Guniting. The surface of masonry is coated by a rich slurry of mortar by spraying it with a gun with pressure, so that all interstices may be filled by mortar and no honey combing is left. It is also used in RCC where heavy reinforcement is provided and in ordinary process concrete can not reach to the interior of reinforcement then guniting process is used.

Shot creting. It is defined as mortar conveyed through hose and projected pneumatically on the surface under pressure at high velocity to fill up concrete in joints and cracks etc. There are two types of shot creting.

(*a*) Wet process—water is added in the conc. in the beginning before shotting.

(*b*) Dry process—water is mixed while shot creting is in progress with the gun together with other ingradients.

Repacking of concrete. The dry stones and big ballast are packed dry with min. voids. The slurry or concrete with smaller aggregate is then injected with cement gun to fill all voids and make the mass solid.

Efflorescence from sides of walls is due to the salts which come out with water coming out in hot weather from the walls leaving a white layer of salt after evaporation. These salts are due to the preparation of bricks with salty earth which should be avoided. This layer of salt is either be removed dry or should be washed with water. A solution of one part of acid (HCl, H_2SO_4 or HNO_3) with five parts of water is good for washing. A solution of zinc chloride with water is also good.

Treatment of floors. Floors laid on soil which contains moisture should be laid with a layer of compacted graded stone or a layer of tar-concrete. Cinder mixed with tar is well compacted over the surface under floor. In wet situations a membrane of water proof paper (Burlap paper) is laid under the floor surface.

Tar concrete. It is mixed concrete with stone grit, coarse sand and tar to give a pasty mass.

Dampness passing from roofs. It is due to the followings :

(1) **Pervious parapets—**It can be get rid if a coping of impervious stone or 1 : 2 : 4 stone grit conc. is laid on top sloping outward. These copings should be corbelled out with a throat.

(2) **Pervious roofs—**Roofs should be made impervious by :

(*a*) Water proofing terraces with a water tight membrane say of polytheline or bitumen under cement conc. 1 : 2 : 4 in stone grit 7 to 10 mm.

(*b*) **Cement cinder concrete roof terracing.** 1 : 4-5 cement and cinder is mixed with required water so as to make a workable paste and a layer of it about 50 mm thick is laid. Cinder (preferably furnace cinder and not the brick cinder) of 12·5 mm nominal size (passing through sieve no. 212 μ and retained 70 to 90 percent on IS sieve no 100 μ) is used. The cinder should be well soaked with water before use. The surface should be plained at a min slope of 1 in 48.

(*c*) **Painting tops of roof slabs or tiles** with neat cement coat, hot bitumen mixed with clean dry sand in two coats. The quantity of bitumen for 1st coat is 120 kg and 70 kg for the 2nd. 0·6 m^3 sand per hundred m^2 surface. This coat should be continued upto top of parapets. Bitumen can be only used if not objected.

(*d*) **Lime concrete terracing.** It is generally laid on arched roofs. However it is also laid on slabed roofs. The surface is cleaned with brushes (wire) and a layer of lime mortar 1 : 2 (lime-surkhi) is spreaded over it about 5 mm in thickness. A mix of 1 : 2 : 4, 1 : 1 : 3 or 1 : 1 : 2

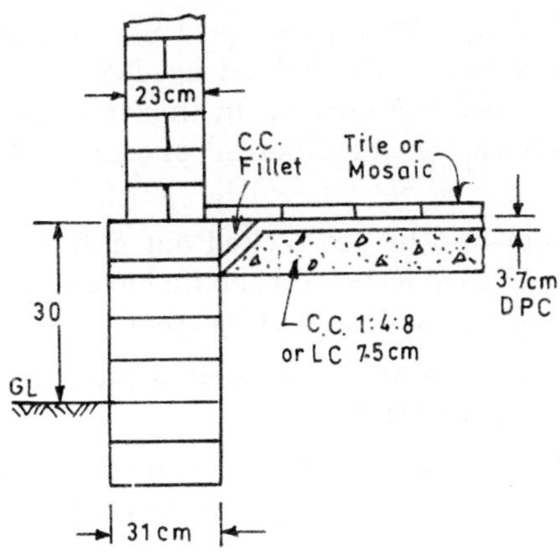

DPC above G.L. wall & floor

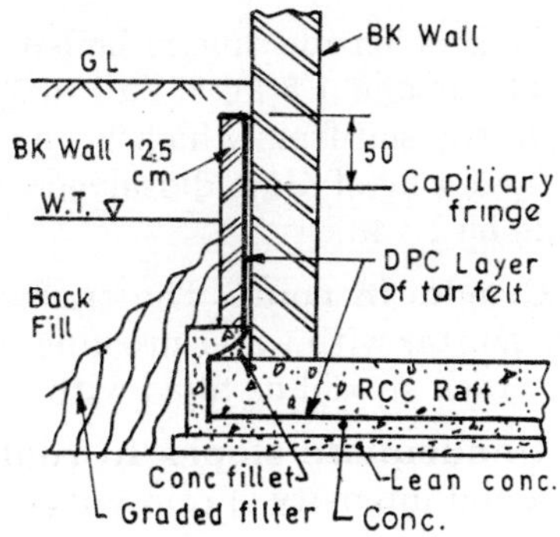

Bal, gravel, sand 15 cm each upto cap. fringe (highest)

DPC below G.L.

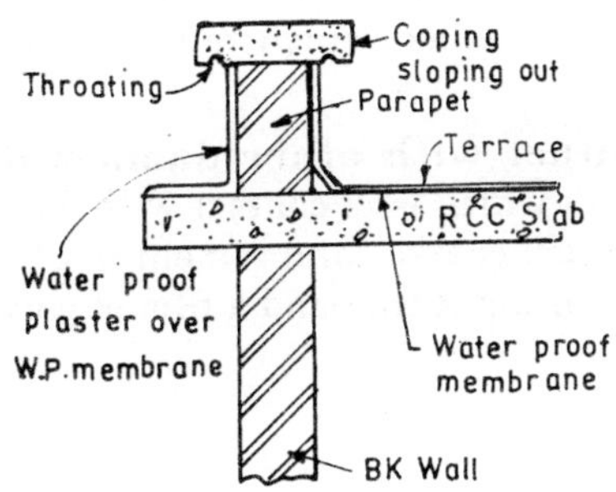

Roof water proofing

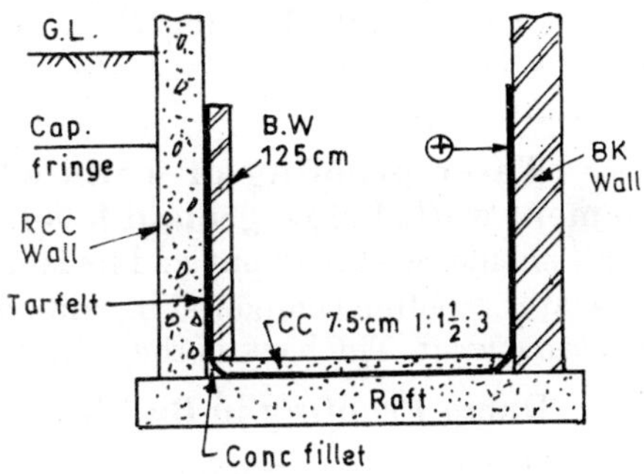

DPC below G.L. (old work)

Parapet moulding

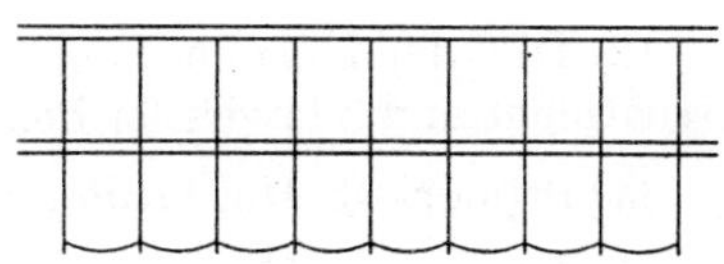

Mouldings in string courses

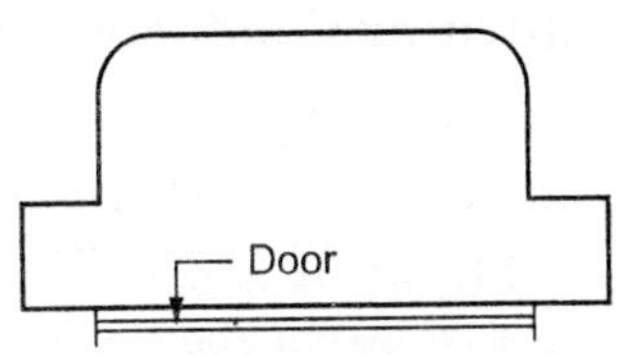

Door projection

Fig. 7·34.

lime-surkhi-brick ballast of 25 mm gauge can also be used. The mortar of lime and surkhi is mixed thoroughly in a pulverising machine and then it should be mixed with ballast and laid on roof with a thickness of 7·5 cm to 12 cm. The surface should be rammed by wooden rammers till the mortar comes on top layer which becomes uniform and porous. The brick ballast should be soaked with water before use. During ramming the surface should be sprinkled with a water solution of jaggery (crude sugar) boiled solution of bail fruit, pulverised San and cereal (Dal) paste. 3 kg of gur and 1·5 kg of bail in 100 litres of water. The ballast used must not have *reh* (salt petre) in the soil from which it has been prepared and burned. In this time in conc. 12 kg of soft soap and 4 kg of alum dissolved in water should be added per m^3 of conc. The final slope of roof should be 1 : 48.

(*e*) **Cracks in roofs.** The cracks in roofs should be 1st racked out and slurry of 1 : 1 cement sand mortar with water proofing compound as used in D.P.Cs should be forced and surface plained, the crack should be filled with tar. See repair of RCC in RCC section.

(3) **Unadequate slopes in roofs.** In heavy rain areas the size of pipes is decided on the roof area and intensity of rain fall (see sec. of Sanitary Engg.)

(4) **Growth of vegetation on roofs.** All vegetation should be cleaned and the crevices in which they are growing should be cleared and grouted with rich mortar having water proofing compound.

(5) **Fixing of water proofing membrane.** Hot bitumen is applied at 1·2 kg/m^2 then polythelene is applied with hand pressure with film face down wards. The paper joints should be overlaped by min. 75 mm. Next layer of bitumen is laid over the membrane, over which terracing is done. The surface of the roof must be clean, washed which must be dry before membrane is applied.

Water proofing of walls which are in contact with other damp walls and basement walls below ground level. The face of the wall which is in contact with damp earth or wall should be racked out and brushed. 1½ cm layer of rich coarse sand cement mortar mixed with water proofing compound in laid on it. This face is then tar coated and a film of polythelene is pasted over it. The back is then filled with sand.

Damp Proofing in Buildings (IS : 1322—1959)

(1) DPC above ground level

(*a*) (*i*) Bitumen applied hot and blown at the rate of 1·5 kg/m^2.

(*ii*) Hessian base self-furnished felt type, grade 2 or 1, type 2 grade 3 or 5.

(2) DPC for basements or structures below ground level apply two layers or below for light treatment and 3 layers for heavy treatment.

(*a*) Primer—(*i*) Hot bitumen applied at the rate of 1·5 kg/m^2

(*ii*) Hessian or fibre base self-finished type 3 grade 2 or type 2 grade 3.

Note : When the load of water is 3 m, layers of felt and bitumen should be added according to pressure developed.

7·11. Lightening Conductors on Buildings

Lightening conductor consists of the following parts :

(*a*) Finial (*b*) Down conductor (*c*) Earth connection

(*a*) **Finial.** It is a 12 mm dia. copper or phosphorous bronze rod painted at the top. It remains at least 30 cm above the pinnacle and about 0·5 metre below. It is also called as terminal. Buildings which are more than 36 m in height and having a top width more than 1·5 m is provided with more than one finial connected by a band. The horizontal distance may be 30 m or they must be provided on all points of importance, such as chimneys, ducts vent pipes and ridges etc.

It must not be laid parallel to any electric conductor or if it is unavoidable, its min. distance must be 21 m. It must be kept separate by non-conductor plates from the inflammable parts of the building. Radio aerials should not be kept upto 1·5 m from the conductor point. Over head lines of high tension electric supply should be also break up and should be carried underground in this region. All metal parts in its vicinity should be earthed.

(*b*) **Down Conductors.** They must run at corners, must not have sharp bends or kinks and must follow the direct possible route. All the bends must have a min. rad. of 30 cm, other wise discharge can take place in building causing damage. No bend should be more acute than 30°. From projections such as sun shades, it must pass through them and should not be passed round. Joints in conductor should be soldered or rivetted. They should be holded by clamps fixed in walls. The clamps must be such that easy expansion or contraction can take place to avoid any kink during expansion. The down conductors are connected to the finial rods.

Copper is better than iron in moist and salt laiden areas of industries. Being cheap aluminium which has double conductivity than copper is now preferable, but it lasts earlier.

(*c*) **Earth Connections.** The ground conductor is laid upto damp soil where it is connected to the electrodes. The conductor inside the ground is protected by charcoal or powdered coke in 15 cm thickness around it (not used in case of copper conductors). If damp soil is not available it must go at least upto 3 metre in ground after which it is connected to the electrodes.

Electrodes. These are generally of copper rods, strips or tubes going upto sub soil water.

(1) **Rods**—12 mm dia. reaching upto sub soil water level and must at least 2·4 m below ground.

(2) **Strips**—Strips should be burried in trenches at least 45 cm deep laid in grids or radial at least 1·8 m apart. Strips are used where rock is encountered less than 2·4 m below ground.

(3) **Pipes**—50 mm gal. iron pipes driven at least 2·4 metre below ground. 1·8 m of the pipe is driven in the sub soil water and is slotted with 3 mm slots. The pipe is filled with fine charcoal powder through which conductor passes upto bottom, where it is soldered with the end of the pipe. Pipes are not used in sub soils having gravel or is filled earth.

(4) **Plates**—90 × 90 × 2·5 mm copper plates (used with copper conductors) should be tinned on both sides. The iron plates are 6 mm thick and is galvanised on both sides and surrounded by charcoal. These plates are burried in the wet soil, if not larger plates are required. They are burried horizontal but preferably vertical. These plates are soldered or riveted with conductors.

Table 7·1. The size of conductors (IS Code)

S. No.	*Material*	*Above ground*	*Below ground*
1.	Round galv. iron wire	No. 0 SWG (8 mm) dia.	No. 4/0 SWG (10 mm) dia.
2.	Galvanized iron strip	20 × 3 mm	32 × 4 mm
3.	Round copper wire or copper clad steel wire	No. 4 SWG (6 mm) dia.	No 0 SWG (8 mm) dia.
4.	Standard copper wire	0·5 sq. cm or 7/3·4 mm dia.	Not allowed
5.	Standard copper strips	30 × 3 mm	20 × 3 mm
6.	Round alum. wire	No. 4/0 SWG (10 mm) dia.	Not allowed
7.	Aluminium	25 × 3 mm	Not allowed

7·12. Anti Termite Treatment—(Protection against white ants)

(1) Pre-construction Treatment—(*a*) **Site preparation**—Remove roots, stumps, dead leaves and waste wood etc. Remove termite mounds by insecticide solution. For this make holes in the mound at several places by crow-bars and insecticide solution is pored in the holes. For a mound having volume of about 1 m^3, 4 litres of emulsion in water is used. Following solutions are used :

Table 7·2.

Chemical	*Concentration by wt.*	*Remarks*
D.D.T.	5%	These chemicals are poisonous hence a proper care should be taken in their use
B.H.C.	0·5%	
Aldrin	0·25%	
Heptachlor	0·25%	
Chlordane	0·5%	

(*b*) **Soil Treatment.** Soil underneath the foundations and around. It is poisoned with insecticides solution as mentioned above by sprayers used in farms and by Maleria Department. The top of foundation concrete is also treated with insecticides solution.

(*c*) **Watering.** Watering is done by hand operation or spraying by compressed air sprayer at 5 litres per sq. m. of surface area. The back fill earth in foundations is treated with insecticide solution at 7·5 litre per m^2 of vertical surface.

(2) **Post Construction Treatment (Existing building)**

Before undertaking any type of treatment a thorough inspection is made of the infestation in the building with a view to determine the extent to which it is spread, and the routes of the entry of termites into the building. A study of structure of the foundation and the ground floor helps in finding out the routes of entry of termites from the soil and also in indicating the mode of treatment required.

The next step is to examine the termites location inside the building. The termites hide outs are located such as ceilings, behind wooden pannels, and electrical fittings etc. Precaution is taken to inject oil or kerosene based solvent into termites channels in wood work and masonry followed by seating openings and spraying the oil/kerosene based solvent. All traces of termite tubes should be removed so that any fresh inspection which may over in future may be detected.

Precaution Measures

(*a*) Extra 3 m width on each side is dug in a depth of 15 cm and flooded with water. Any holes of termites or white ants should be destroyed by hot boiling water. Queen ant should specially be destroyed. A layer of straw on the surface make the ants to come up their holes. This process is only applied in ant prone area. About 500 mm deep trench is dug along the external peripheral wall about 500 mm wide. 12 mm to 18 mm holes at 150 mm centres are made in the trenches, which are filled with Chemical emulsion in water and backfilled. Chemical used should be 15 litres per m^2 of vertical surface of masonry and foundations. The earth fill should be poisoned with emulsion.

(*b*) **Floors.** Holes in floors are drilled and chemical emulsion is filled in them. The holes are then filled with concrete.

(*c*) **Walls.** Holes are drilled in the walls slanting downward and chemical is filled and the holes are then filled with mortar.

(*d*) **Wood Work.** Kerosene mixed with chemical is sprayed or brushed on wood work or on attached area after cleaning all loose effected mass. Holes are dug at 45° and are filled with chemical emulsion by force in the effected portion. Ready made wood care solutions are available in the market.

(*e*) **Masonry Work.** All voids in masonry should be filled by coal tar pitch.

(3) **Construction Treatment**

(*a*) D.P.C. should be provided and take all water proofing cares in it.

(*b*) A solution of half kg of copper sulphate per 20 litres of water should be used in mortar.

This solution is also protective to wood which is soaked for two days for 25 mm thickness of wood.

Yellow arsenic at 6·5 kg/m^3 of masonry and 0·8 kg/m^2 of plaster is mixed in mortar. Being poisonous should not be used on surfaces.

(*c*) Termite sheet of corrosive resistant metal should be provided above the top of masonry of foundation and below wood work. This sheet may be of galvanized iron or copper sheet of min. 0·45 mm thickness.

(*d*) Foundations conc. and masonry surface which is in direct contact with soil should be treated with insecticides solutions.

(*e*) Sub surface of floor should be filled with sand treated with insecticide solution over levelled top of back filling earth.

(*f*) Back filled earth should also be treated with emulsion solution at the rate of 5 litres per m^3 of the filled earth.

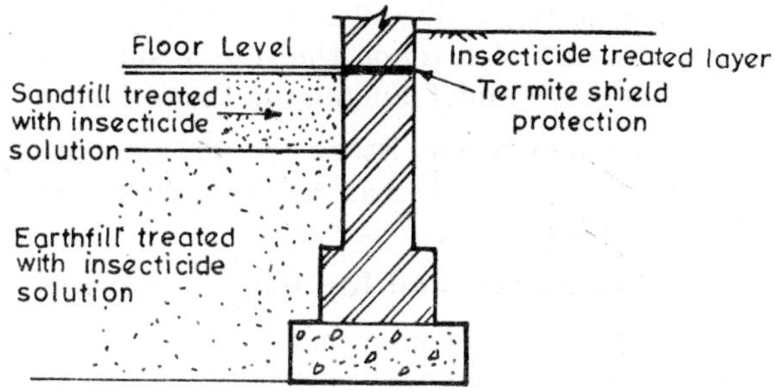

Fig. 7·35.

(*g*) Termites may have an access from any side of the building, so whole of the earth of periphery of the building should also be treated with emulsion solution. An apron should be provided all around in the width of 1 m of conc. 1 : 3 : 6 or bricks on edge as per specification (IS : 277—1962).

7·13. Sound Proofing of Buildings

(1) **Location—**The building should be kept away a noise creating centre.

(2) **Less Openings—**Less openings in walls as sound can pass through openings easily.

(3) **A Reflecting Surface—**Should be provided out side of the wall.

(4) **Air Gap Walls—**Hollow walls.

(5) **Skirting—**A skirting should be provided over floors on the walls.

(6) **Insulating Layer on Walls—**A layer of an insulating material on walls such as fibre boards, hair felt or slag wood is to be provided.

(7) **Floating Floors.** A layer of impervious material (CC 1 : 2 : 4 in stone ballast) 50 mm thick over floor surface or a cinder concrete must be provided.

(8) **Sound Reducing Boards.** These are of strain reed or cork slabs, felt bitumen, slag wood, sponge rubber, asbestos or breeze bricks are also used as sound reducing agents.

Reflection of Sound

Sound waves are reflected in the same manner.as that of light. The angle of incidence from normal is equal to the angle of reflection and vice versa. The concave surface tends to concentrate the reflected waves at certain points. On the other hand a convex surface spreads the reflected sound waves. Sometimes convex surface are employed to spread the sound throughout the room.

Reverberation. The prolongation of the sound after the source ceases is known as reverberation. The time of reverberation according to W.C. Sabine is the time which is required for a sound to decrease to one millionth of its original intensity after stopping the source. The sound decreases as the sound energy is converted to other forms of energy by other surfaces of the building, the furniture, the curtain, the people present and other features like air etc.

Sound Absorption Coefficient. The sound absorption coefficient is an indication of the sound absorpting efficiency of a surface. A surface which could theoretically absorb 100% of impinging sound would have a sound absorption coefficient as 1. Similarly a dense non-porous concrete surface (cast in place) typically absorbs 1 to 2% of incident sound and has a coefficient of 0·015. Another designator term "the noise reduction coefficient (NRC) is calculated by taking a mathematical average of the sound absorption coefficients obtained at frequencies of 250,500, 1000 and 2000 Hertz (CPS).

Sound Transmission Loss. Air borne sound reaching a wall, floor or ceiling produces vibrations in the wall and is radiated with reduced intensity on the other sides. The ratio of sound pressure at level on the source side to the sound pressure level on the radiating side is known as the Sound Transmission Loss (STL). This ratio is expressed as decibels (db).

Impact Noise. Foot steps, dragged chairs, dropped objects, doors and plumbing generate impact noise. Even when air borne sounds are adequately controlled. There can be severe impact noise problems.

Frequency and Intensity of Sounds

Frequency or pitch may be defined as the number of cycles of sound waves per second. The intensity or loudness is defined as the flow of sound energy per unit time through a unit area. Frequency is measuring scale of the quantity of sound and the intensity is the measuring scale of the quantity of sound energy.

Velocity of Sound. The speed at which sound waves propagate in a medium is known as sound velocity. The velocity of sound depends on the followings :

(*a*) Type and density of the medium.

(*b*) The velocity of sound is independent of the frequency of the sound.

(*c*) The velocity of sound depends on the presence of moisture.

(*d*) The velocity of sound depends upon the velocity of the wind.

Table 7·3. The Velocity of Sound in Different Medium

Medium	*Sound velocity at 20°C in m/sec*	
Atmospheric air	343 m/sec	The Frequency of sound varies from 20 to 1500 CPS (cycles per sec). An audible frequency is above 20, below which can not be heard. The audibility depends upon the physical condition of the person.
Pure water	1450	
Granite	6400	
Glass	6000	
Brick	4300	
Concrete	4000	
Iron	5000	
Cork	500	
Rubber	40 to 150	

Table 7·4. Absorption of Sound by different materials

Material	*Absorption coefficient*
Open window	1·00
Ventilators	0·10 to 0·50
40 cm thick wall	0·03

Table Contd...

Table contd...

Material	*Absorption coefficient*
Plaster on wall surface	0·02
Glass agent solid surface	0·03
Marble	0·10
Curtain	0·20
Concrete floor	0·30
Timber floor	0·09 to 9·13
Window glazed	0·18
Metal	0·01

Individual object	*Absorption unit in m^2-Sabins*	
Audience, adult in wood chair	0·45	The unit sound absorption in m^2-Sabin is equal to sound absorption of one sq. meter area of fully open window.
Plain seat	0·02	
Covered seat	0·10 to 0·20	

Quality of good Absorbent Material

(1) A good absorbent must be water proof, strong, good appearence and economical and repairable.

(2) Absorbent must considerably reduce the noise level of the hall. Speaches should be heard clearly and music should be pleasantly enjoyed.

(3) The absorbing capacity depends on the thickness of the absorbing material, porosity density and the frequency of sound.

(4) Acoustic properties of the absorbent depends on their mode of fixing.

(5) Covering destroys the absorbent properties of the material.

(6) Audience of big hall contributes considerably the absorbing factor.

Sound Absorbing Materials. The value of co-efficient of absorption is generally supplied by the manufacturer. The materials are classified as below :

(*a*) Hair felt

(*b*) Acoustic plaster (A plaster which includes granulated insulation material with cement)

(*c*) Compressed cane or wood, fibre board, perforated and imperforated.

(*d*) Wood particle boards.

(*e*) Compressed wood wool.

(*f*) Mineral/glass wool quilts and mats.

(*g*) Mineral/compressed glass wool teles.

(*h*) Composite units of perforated hard boards backed by perforated fibre boards.

(*i*) Composite units of perforated board, hard board, asbestos board, or metal sheet backed by mineral or glass wool quilt or slab.

(*j*) Special absorbed constrained hard boards, teak ply etc. backed by air.

Classification of Sound Absorbants

(*a*) **Porous Absorbants.** On porous absorbants a part of sound is absorbed by the porous surface, while a part is reflected. Such type of absorbents are slag wool, glass wool, wood wool, asbestos fibre spray, foamed plasters and perforated fibre boards.

(*b*) **Resonent Absorbents.** An absorbent material say wood is fixed with an air gap with walls. The sound waves of appropriate frequency cause sympathetic vibrations in the panel, which acts as a diaphragm. The absorption of sound takes place by virtue of the dampening of the sympathetic vibrations in the panel by means of the air space behind the panel. This effect be increased by placing a porous material in the air space.

(*c*) **Cavity Resonators.** It consists of a chamber with a narrow opening in which absorption takes place by resonance of air in the chamber, which gives loss of sound energy.

Defects in Auditorium and their remedies

(1) The pass of the sound should be unobstructed and direct. This makes the sound clear and loud enough for hearing.

(2) It should be checked that non of the subsequent reflection has the same strength as the original sound.

(3) The desired degree of reverberation in the auditorium should be achieved.

General defects in the auditorium

(1) **Reverberation.** The sound once created prolongs for a sufficient period which creats confusion. To rectify it suitable absorbent material should be provided.

(2) **Formation of echoes.** When the reflecting surfaces are located at a distance more than 15 metres and the shape of the hall is undesirable, the echoes are formed. This defect is eliminated by selecting proper shape of the auditorium and making rough and porous surfaces which can disperse echoes.

(3) **Sound foci.** When the interior surfaces of the auditorium are concave the reflected sound waves concentrate at certain spots and produce sound of large intensity. These spots of higher sound intensity are known as sound foci. They can be removed by avoiding concave interiors or by providing absorbent materials on focussing areas.

(4) **Dead spots.** As there is a high concentrations of reflected sound at sound foci. At some spots there is lower sound intensity, the intensity not sufficient for good hearing, then these spots are known as dead spots. Suitable diffusers are used to have properly distributed sound in the hall.

(5) **Loadness.** This is due to insufficient reflecting surfaces, near the source of sound or excessive absorption of sound in the auditorium. To rectify this defect, hard reflecting boards are provided near the source of sound and to adjust the absorption of the hall to obtain an optimum line of a verberation.

(6) **External noise.** This is due to inadequate sound insulation. The external noise enters the hall through loose doors, windows and ventilators. To rectify this defect proper sound insulation is provided to the various components of the auditorium.

Studios acoustics. The rooms where sound is picked up by microphone is known as studio, such as broad cash stations, television stations and sound recording studios. The following precautions are taken in acoustic design of studios.

(1) Noise level in the studio must be in the range of 20 to 30 dB.

(2) There should be no echo formation.

(3) For furnishing the **external** spaces of the building, sound reflecting material should be used.

(4) For finishing the **internal** surface of the studio, sound reflecting material should be used.

(5) The partition walls and the external walls should be rigid enough to resist vibrations and to prevent resonance.

(6) The provision of window should be the minimum.

(7) Air conditioning plant should be isolated and properly insulated such that the vibrations of the plant are not carried inside the studio.

(8) In no case studios are located one above the other. There should be a minimum space of one floor between two consecutive studios in elevation. However a number of studios may be located on the same floor.

(9) Heavy curtains and draperes should be used to control the reverberation time.

(10) Double doors should be provided in the studios.

7·14. Fire Resistance

Characteristics of Fire Resisting Materials

(*a*) Material should be composed of such elements which do not disintegrate under the effect of great heat.

(*b*) The material should have least coefficient of thermal expansion so that excessive expansion of a particular member which may lead to structural instability is prevented.

(*c*) The material should not contract rapidly when it is cooled with water at high temperature.

(*d*) The material should be compact which can not easily catch fire.

Fire Retardants. Fire retardants are chemical compounds designed to give wood flame retardant properties, working properties of these compounds are as follows :

(*a*) Salt melt before wood starts burning and glazes the surface of wood. Hence oxygen for burning cannot go inside.

(*b*) Due to high temperature the salt decompose and gives off such gases which reduce fire.

(*c*) Salt evaporates at least temperature and takes away all heat in evaporation, consequently wood does not catch fire.

Following chemical compounds or salts are used for making timber fire proof :

(*i*) Mono ammonium phosphate (*ii*) Boric acid (*iii*) Borax

(*iv*) Diammonium phosphate and (*v*) Mixture of these salts.

Following materials make effective wood fire proof agent.

Material	Quantity	Method
Sodium silicate	56 gm	Make a solution and apply by means of brush in two coats. 2nd coat must be applied when 1st is dried.
Water	50 gm	
Kastin	75 gm	

Another formula

Material	Quantity	Method
Glass	10 kg	Make a solution and apply on wood surface in two coats at an interval of 6 hours.
Dorcelain	10 kg	
Powdered stone	10 kg	
Calcined lime	5 kg	
Soda silicate	15 kg	

Abel's Process. For making timber fire proofing this method is used. Paint the surface of wood by weak solution of sodium silicate. After that apply slaked pure lime solution whose consistency is that of cream. After that again apply concentrated solution of sodium silicate.

Control of smoke in tall buildings. Due to fire in a part of a tall building the smoke and poisonous gases are produced which flows to the other parts of the building being light, due to which the persons desiring safety feels much difficulty to come out to a safe place. Protection gallery is also provided by which the persons may come out. This protection path should remain uneffected by this smoke for safe passage. The following processes are used to check the entry of smoke to the protection path.

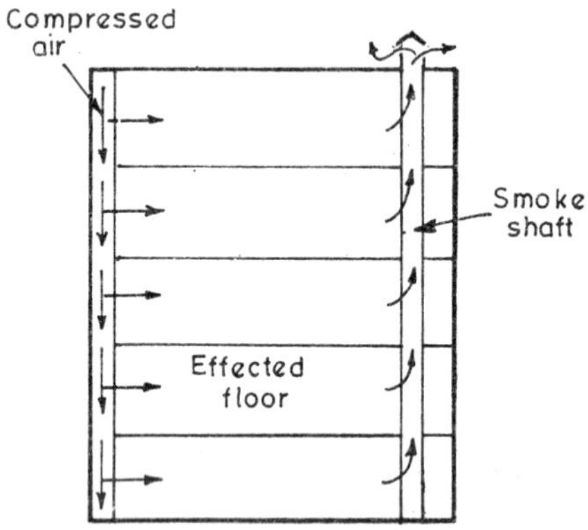

Fig. 7·36. Smoke exit shaft.

(1) **Air Pressure Process.** In this process compressed air is passed in the protection path of the building by compressed air machines. By doing so the hot light smoke from the effected part of the building is checked to come out to the protection path as it is opposed by high pressure air in protection path. Automatic closing doors should be provided which must be opened towards the protection path so that they may be closed due to high pressure of the protection path. These doors should also be automatic opening which should be opened as the pressure is reduced. By closing of the doors the smoke from the effected part is checked to enter in the protection path. So the persons in the building can come out by the safe protection path.

Smoke exit shafts. Smoke exit shafts are provided in the tall building to pass the smoke of the effected part to outside by the exaust fans provided in the shaft roof. Thus the protection path remains uneffected by smoke. The compressed air is passed in the rooms through the smoke protection doors to produce an effected draft.

General Guidelines for Fire Proofing of Buildings

(1) **Alarm System.** This is installed to give an alarm and to call for assistance in case of fire. This system may be automatic or normal. The automatic alarm system is provided in large industrial buildings which can be served in night also. This system sends the alarm to the nearest control point or to the fire brigade station.

(2) **Openings.** Openings are specially provided for fire protection which may be of fire proof materials or wood of min. thickness of 40 mm of hard wood. The openings must have a free and easy approach to outside so that the inhabitants may come out in a short time at the time of any emergency.

(3) **Common Wall.** When two buildings are located side by side. The common wall should have a min. thickness of two bricks and it should be raised above the roof by at least one metre. The fire should not pass to the neighbouring house easily.

(4) **Stairs.** Emergency stairs or ladder should be provided for the use in case of any fire. The ladder should be of fire proof material which may not be effected by fire easily.

(5) **Floors.** Floors should be of RCC of min. thickness of 150 mm sloping out ward so that water may pass when fire fighters are working.

(6) **Fire-Extinguishing Arrangement.** The following equipment must be provided :

(*i*) Manual fire-extinguishing equipment.

(*ii*) Internal hydrants.

(*iii*) Automatic sprinkling installation.

Causes of fires and their prevention

(*a*) Absence of component necessary for combustion.

(*b*) Improper ratio of combustible material to oxygen for the formation of a combustion system.

(*c*) Heat source available is insufficient to ignite a combustion system.

Facing and Plastering. Protecting wooden surfaces by facing materials, plastering is most effective for fire resistance which makes a protective cover for catching fire for wood. The facing materials are :

(*i*) Gypsum plaster, Asbestos cement sheets and brick work etc.

Fire Resisting Treatment of Buildings Materials

(1) **Timber.** The timber is impregnated with fire resisting chemicals as ammonium phosphate and sulphate, sodium arsonate and tetra borate. Borax and boric acid, zinc chloride etc. This treatment retards increase in temperature during fire. Usually 32 to 48 kg of chemical per m^3 of wood are used for moderate protection and 80 to 96 kg/m^3 for high temperature protection.

(2) **Brick work.** Bricks are liable to stand exposed to air for a consideration length of time.

(3) **Stone.** Use of stone is restricted in fire resistance in constructions. Hot stone when cooled produces cracks and leads to failure of structure.

(4) **Steel.** Steel though incombustible has a very low fire resistance, with increase of temperature. The coefficient of elasticity of the metal falls appreciably, rendering the structural members soft and free to expand. When these members are brought in contact of water extinguishing fire, they tend to contract, twist or distort and thus the stability of the entire structure is endangered. Such steel members are enclosed with concrete.

(5) **Glass.** Glass cracks when heated and then suddenly cooled. Reinforced or fibre glass is more fire resistant than ordinary glass.

(6) **Concrete.** The influence of fire on concrete varies with the nature of aggregate and its density. Aggregates found from igneous rocks like granite and trap etc. tends to crack when subjected to fire. Coarse aggregate like foamed slag, cinder and brick are best suited for concrete which has to be fire resistant. The fire disintegrate the RCC for a depth of about 25 mm, hence in a RCC resistant constructions, the thickness of clear cover should be more.

(For detail refer fire resistance in concrete in plane and reinfroced conc. of this volume)

(7) **Asbestos.** Asbestos combined cement products have great fire resistance.

Thermal Insulation and Air Conditioning. The heat is transferred from one place to another by the following three modes :

(1) **Conduction.** One particle of the medium transfers heat to its neighbouring particle and so on. Just as a ball is passed by a man to its adjoining man and so on the ball reaches upto last man.

(2) **Convection.** The heat is passed to the last particle by the 1st particle itself by moving. Such as the ball is passed to the last man standing in a row by the 1st man directly to him.

(3) **Radiation.** The heat is jumped to the last particle from the 1st, just as the 1st man throws a ball to the last man.

The flow of heat is calculated by the following formula

$$H = A\frac{k}{x}(t_1 - t_2)$$

where k = the thermal conductivity of the material

x = thickness of the medium say a wall

t_1 and t_2 the temperature of warmer and colder sides respectively.

H = The total quantity of heat transferred.

Types of Insulating Materials

(1) **Block insulations.** It is made up of cork boards, cellular glass blocks, rubber blocks, mineral work blocks or wood fibres bound together with cement.

(2) **Blanket insulation.** These are made up of flexible fibres materials and are available in rolls. Its thickness varies from 10 to 80 m.

(3) **Bats insulation.** These are soft materials similar to the above type but are smaller in size and greater in thickness.

(4) **Loose fills.** The material like glass wool, wood fibres, wool slag etc. are loosely poured into the studding space and other similar spaces.

(5) **Reflection type insulation.** It is usually metallic foil and depends for its effect not on low conductivity but on its high reflectivity and low emissivity. It is installed in the studding space so as to divide the air space into two or more vertical layers.

Method of Insulations

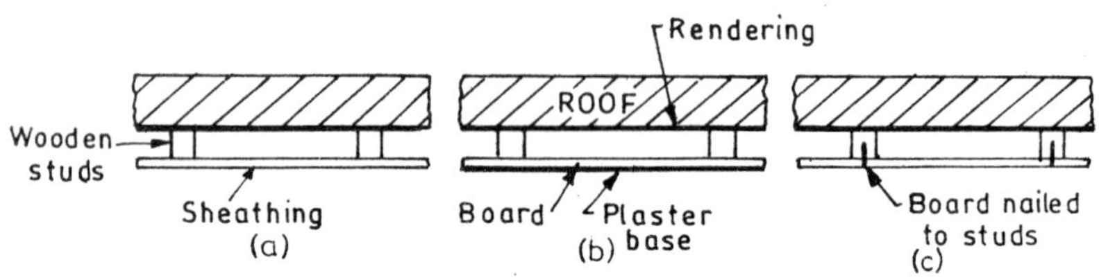

Fig. 7·37.

(*a*) In the rendered roof wooden studs are fixed as joists on which sheathings are fixed by nails.

(*b*) In the rendered roof joists (wooden studs are fixed over which boards are nailed. The base of the boards is plastics).

(*c*) Boards are nailed to the wooden studs.

Vertical insulation on walls. It may be provided by the following devices :

(*a*) Providing wall papers.

(*b*) Plastering by insulating materials like Plaster of Paris.

(*c*) Fixing fibre boards on walls by cleats and nails.

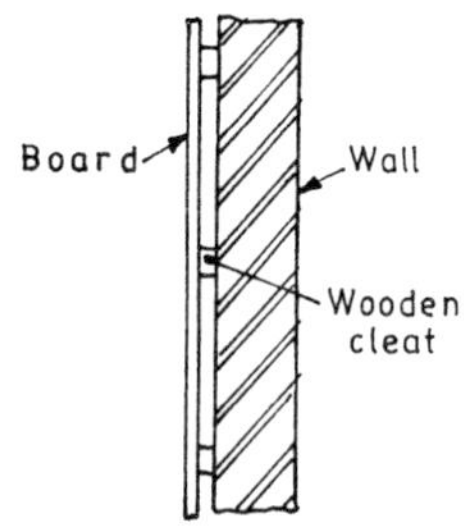

Fig. 7·38.

7·15. Plastering, Pointing and White Washing

(1) **Plastering—Preparation surface for plastering.** Following points are to be followed :

(*a*) The surface of the masonry should be cleaned with wire brushes and all the mortar joints shoiuld be racked out to a depth of 13 to 20 mm by trowel etc. to have a good key to the plaster.

(*b*) All the raised projections more than 13 mm must be chieseld.

(*c*) If the old surface is smooth it should be hacked to make rough.

(*d*) For rendering soffit of the ceilings, a wash of neat cement should be applied.

(*e*) The surface should be plumbed and dot points by plaster mortar is taken at one m^2 grid.

The type of Plaster

(*a*) Lime plaster (*b*) Cement plaster (*c*) Stucco plaster

(*d*) Water proof plaster (*e*) Plaster on lath.

(*a*) **Lime plaster.** Hot lime or hydraulic lime may be used for plastering Hydraulic lime produces a harder and strong plaster, but blistering may occur in it after some times.

Lime mortar containing lime and sand mixture in equal volumes. After mixing it should be grinded in grinding mills. About 1 litre solution of sugar and bel (a fruit) should be added while grinding in about 1 m^3 of mortar.

(*b*) **Cement plaster.** Cement to sand ratios 1 : 3 to 1 : 6 may be used according to the quality and importance of work. The sand should be dry and which should be cleaned with water before proportioning. The bulking of the sand should be taken into account. The thickness of plaster should be 12 mm.

(*c*) **Stucco for exterior walls.** It is prepared by mixing about 1/4th by weight by marble powder in the brown lime mortar. The thickness may be 12 mm. The finished surface should have a thickness of 3 mm with fine mixture of white marble and lime.

(*d*) **Water proof plaster.** In the mixture 1 : 2 of cement to sand, pulverised alum at the rate of 12 kg per m^3 should be added. Some water proofing chemical may also be used in place of alum.

(*e*) **Plaster on lath.** It is the mortar which is plastered over wood or steel and is classified as under :

Metal laths. Various types of metal laths are available in the market such as (*a*) Plain expanded (*b*) Ribbed expanded (*c*) Perforated and (*d*) Dove tailed etc. The sheet should be fixed and stretched lightly with 9 to 12 mm diameter steel rods or steel channels. It contains fire resistant qualities. Two pieces must be overlaped by at least 25 mm and the joint must rest over solid supports.

Plaster is then applied on both sides of the lath (Plaster of Paris may be one of the plasters used). Expanded metal is widely used for this purpose. When lath is fixed over wooden supports, galvanized nails should be used.

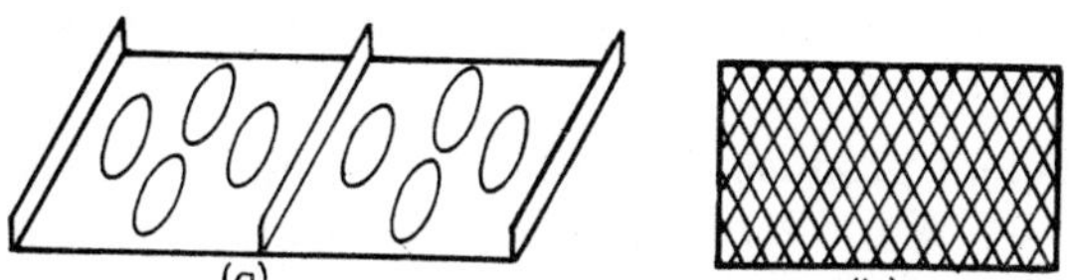

(a) Wooden lath (b) Steel lath

Fig. 7·39.

Wooden laths. It is used to prepare base for plastering timber partition walls and ceilings of timber floors. Wooden laths are attacked by white ants, fungus and other insects and so are strict in use.

Wooden laths consists of 80 to 120 cm in length and 25 mm in width. Thickness of the strips are between 3 to 13 mm. The thicker strips are used for ceiling, where strain is more. The thinner strips are used for walls and partitions where strain is small. They are not fire resistant.

Terms used in Plastering

(*i*) **Background**—Prepared surface on which 1st coat is applied.

(*ii*) **Cracking**—Development of cracks in plaster.

(*iii*) **Crazing**—Hair cracks in plaster on the finished surface.

(*iv*) **Blistering**—Appearance of local swellings in the finished surface.

(*v*) **Dado**—Bottom must part of the plaster of a wall over floor (it may vary from 8 cm to 20 cm) smooth and hard in appearance.

(*vi*) **Dots**—They are small patches of plaster laid on the background for fixing screeds.

(*vii*) **Dubling out.** It is a method of filling in hollow spaces in a solid background befor applying plaster.

(*viii*) **Flaking—**In absence of proper adhesion with the previous coats, some patches of plaster fall down which is known as flaking.

(*ix*) **Gauging—**The process of mixing the various ingradients of plaster is known as gauging.

(*x*) **Hacking—**Clearing out of joints and making the surface rough. It is hammered so that the mortar may stick to the surface.

(*xi*) **Keys—**These are indentation made in the old surface so that a bond may have for the new plaster.

(*xii*) **Peeling—**It is removal of the plaster from the background.

(2) **Pointing—Types of Pointings.** As shown in the figure.

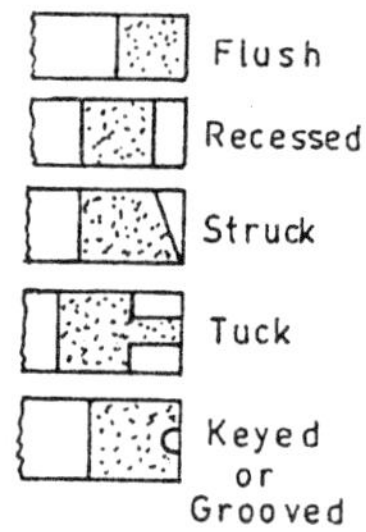

Fig. 7·40. Pointing patterns

Mortar for pointing—Lime mortar with equal part of lime and fine sand.

Cement mortar—In cement or sand in ratio of 1 : 1 to 1·2 as quality required.

Method of Pointing. (1) The surface is brushed with clean water and the joints must be racked out with hard rods having pointed end.

(2) The mortar should be pressed in the racked joint so that the mortar may be fully filled in the grooves.

(3) **White washing.** Fat lime is mixed with water so as to make a good workable liquid mass and is then allowed to rest for 24 hours. 4 gm of gum (gond) or shellac (chapra) or rice marh, 50 gm of common salt, 3 gm of indigo (neel) is mixed with 1 kg of fat lime and the solution is thoroughly mixed and stirred well. This solution should be passed through wire mesh and is then applied by munj or hair brushes on the well cleaned wall. Some soaps and zinc powder as suitable (60% by weight) can also be mixed for good shinning.

White washing with cement. White cement produced by different producers and sold in the market can be used for white washing of walls. White cement is thoroughly mixed in water according to the consistency required and then applied on walls by brushes. The cement wash checks the entry of dampness from out side atmosphere to the walls. The water falled on the walls from different sources is evaporated sortly without entering into them and hence white wash with cement specially for outer walls which are opened to the atmosphere is being replaced widely in place of usual lime washing.

Note : Before white washing old wash should be racked out from old walls and the cracks if any should be filled with lime paste. Birla white and JK white is being sold widely in the market.

(4) **Colour washing and distempering.** Colouring pigments are mixed in white wash liquid to the required extent and shade. The quantity in one operation should be such that it may complete the whole job otherwise patches in shade will occur. Ready made distempers are also available in market either in liquid or in powder form. They are spreaded by hair brush. Some fevicol should be mixed for stickness.

7·16. Flooring. The floors of the buildings are prepared as below :

(1) **Base layer.** As a levelled (in a certain required slope) subgrade of clayey or sandy nature, water is sprinkled, so that it may not suck water from the conc. A layer 75 to 100 mm thick is laid in a lean mix 1 : 6 : 12 in brick or stone ballast, having a gauge of 25 to 40 mm, lime conc. (1 : 2 : 4) slack lime-surkhi-ballast 25 to 40 mm in the same thickness can also be used. Now it should be rammed with 2·5 kg wooden or iron rammers.

(2) **Hard concrete top layer** (Wearing surface). After the lean or thick base concrete has been set or become hard it is wetted with water. A layer of 25 mm to 30 mm thick 1 : 2 : 4 cement conc. with 3 mm to 20 mm graded stone ballast of hard nature say of granite and coarse sand is laid over the wetted base layer after cleaning. The surface is levelled in a proper slope by a big wood or aluminium plainer and rammed by 2·5 kg wooden rammer.

This layer is casted in panels suiting according to the site with a max. of 1 m in grids and laid alternately or in pattern of chequer board, so that no layer is casted immediately after the adjoining is laid. By doing so level is maintained properly and work becomes easier. Its level is kept by leaving the desired share of top surface.

Glass, lead, brass plastic or hard wood strips of 1 mm to 5 mm according to size and thickness of panel and deep according to the depth of conc. are embedded to act as expansion joints. These strips are greased or white washed so that they may not stick to the concrete. If the base conc. sets too hard it must be hacked and cleaned before the wearing surface is laid. The top of strips is kept on the desired floor level.

(3) **Finishing top surfaces.** These are of the following types :

(*a*) **IPS (Indian Pattern Standard).** The top layer is cleaned and wetted. After about two hours a top finishing layer 1 mm in thickness is applied with wet neat cement on the top hard layer with a steel float smoothly and evenly. As soon as it is hardened (Not set initially) it is again plained with iron floats to make a good smooth and even surface. Any excess water on surface should not be dried by dry cement as it cause crazing (hair cracks) but should be waited to let it dry. This layer should be laid before the final set of the top layer.

(*b*) **Flag stone blocks.** Marble, Kota, Dholpur stones and ceramic tiles square pattern pavements are prepared as follows :

A layer of 1 : 2 cement and coarse sand mortar is laid on the base layer in thickness of 10 to 15 mm and the square or rectangular pieces of above stones are pressed on the mortar. The cement used in joints may be of colour matching to the paving blocks. The sharp edges of the slabs should be chipped off from under side to have a good key for joint. Cross joints in the rectangular blocks may be staggered.

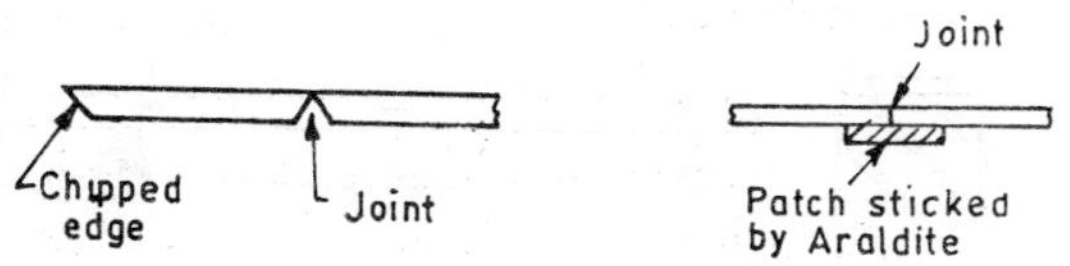

Fig. 7·41. Stone blocks preparation.

In case of translucent white marble slabs neat white cement is spreaded in 1/8″ thickness over natural grey cement mortar to avoid dark shade.

Note : Marble pieces can be joined by Aradite adhesive with a piece under the joint to have a support.

(*c*) **Coloured floors.** On the top layer a mix of 1 : 3 to 1 : 12 according to the darkness of the shade is mixed with cement (preferably white) to colouring pigment as one part. Mixtures of pigment reduces the strength. It is better to use coloured cement in place of colouring pigments (For colouring pigments see RCC). A wet mortar is applied in thickness of about 2 mm and the surface is plained and smoothed. Iron plainer should not be used for smoothening as it crazes the surface (Hair cracks). Trowelling on surface should be repeated as soon as the surface hardens and all trowelling and plaining should be finished before the initial set. Colouring pigments are mixed in white cement. Diamond pattern can be given by using two different colours in alternate panels. This layer should be laid before the final set of the top layer.

Grinding. 1st grinding is done after 3 or 4 days of laying floors with a coarse carborundum No. 40. Stone with coarse sand and water so as to remove all laitence and patches. All crevices in the floor should be closed by the neat cement. 2nd grinding is done after 5 days to 1st with a finer caborundum No. 80 stone, patches if any should be repaired with cement. 3rd grinding should be done after 2 days of the 2nd with carborundum No. 120 and final grinding is done after 3 days to 3rd with hot water and soap by carborundum No. zero. The above grinding schedule is for machine grinding. The vertical grinding on wall skirting and edges of floors is done by hand and should be done only on 3rd day of laying. 2nd and 3rd grinding can be done on subsequent days after repair with neat cement if required so just after grinding of 1st and 2nd operation. In vertical faces where hand grinding is done. Smaller size of chips must be used. Grinder machines for vertical walls are also available.

In case of IPS, granolithic, ironite and coloured floors only one grinding with fine carborundum is done. Mosaic with finer chips need three with finer while thick chips require four grindings with coarser carborundum.

Granolithic finish. A mixure in the proportion of 1 : 2 (cement and hard stone grit 10 mm down to 150 micron) is laid in 12 mm thickness over the concrete top layer. The surface is beaten with a wood float till a slurry part comes up. The top is levelled with a long wood plainer and finished finally. If the top layer is set to sufficiently hardness, it should be hacked cleaned and washed. This type of floors are used where a top strong surface is needed.

PVC floors. On IPS floors PVC tiles 1500 mm × 1500 mm or so are pasted with a solution specially prepared for this purpose and is available in the market. By this a good chequered pattern floors are obtained with two different coloured tiles. **Ceramic tiles** can also be used.

Ironite floors. In granolithic finished surfaces when further hard surface, where heavy machinery works is required, iron grains are mixed with cement in the proportion of 1 : 4 or 1 : 5 by wt. according to the strength required and this iron mixed cement is proportioned with stone grit aggregate (150 μ to 10 mm) in the ratio of 1 : 2 with coarse sand and then the surface is prepared as in the case of granolithic surface finish floors.

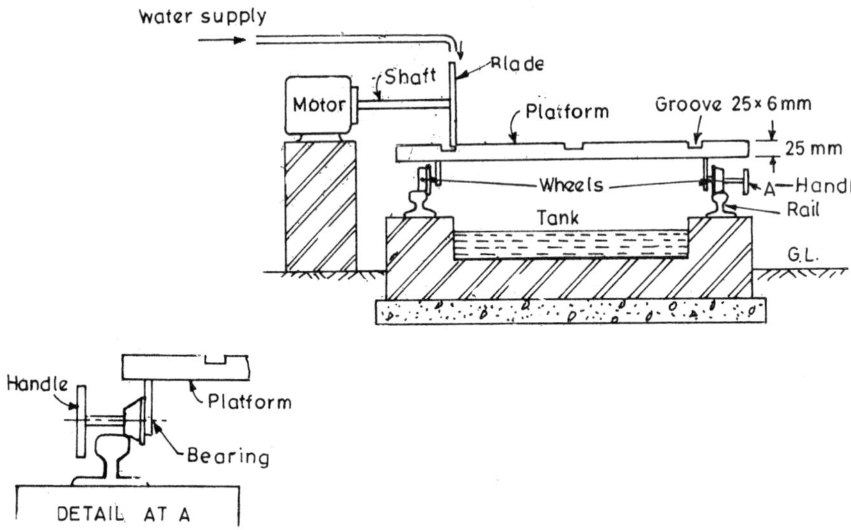

Fig. 7·42. Stone cutter.

Mosaic Marble Floors. (*i*) On the hard top layer a mixture of 1 : 2 (cement to marble chips 3 mm size) in thickness of 6 mm is laid and plained with wood floats to make a top even surface marble powder is mixed with cement in the ratio of 1 : 4 as powder to cement to avoid hair cracks.

(*ii*) When a larger sized marble chips are used to have a wider chipped pattern, the chips are mixed in the ratio of 1 : 2 as above but it is laid in the thickness of 15 mm to 20 mm. The size of chips can be upto 10 mm. The colour of cement is as per shade desired. Grinding and polishing is dealt in separate paragraphs. The chips may be in different coloured shades as desired.

(*iii*) **Terrazzo marble.** A layer of 1 : 2 cement and coarse sand mortar is laid over the top layer in thickness of 10 mm to 15 mm. The marble pieces of different shapes and pattern are pressed on the mortar. The joints can be filled with desired colours of cement or if wider with 1 : 2 cement marble chips mix and the surface is then plained. The marble pieces are locally known as **Kereji.**

Acid resisting floors. The floors over which acid appliances used are made acid resistant by mixing acid resisting chemicals (See chemicals used in RCC sec.) in cement sand mortar in the above conc. floors.

Pressed Concrete Paving Blocks. Conc. Block products are made by applying pressure on wet conc. with 1 : 1 cement mortar.

(4) **Polishing.** After the final grinding oxalic acid is sprinkled over the surface with water and grinded with hard rubber or cotton pads in grinding machine in place of carborundum stone. It is rubbed till a glossy surface is achieved. Next day the surface is wiped with moist cloth and then dried by cotton cloth. A dil. solution of turpentine and bees wax (4 : 1) or with mansion polish (available in market) is applied and rubbed again as above 4 to 5 hrs. to have a polished surface. Saw dust is sprinkled for few days to save the surface from dirt and temperature. About 0·1 litre of polish is needed per m^2 surface.

NB : (1) Oil or cement paints are also used in floor finishes but they require frequent paintings as it wears in use.

(2) The labour cost in grinding and laying etc. is roughly equal to the cost of materials.

(3) Grinding system is usual in flooring. Any individual panel can be repaired or replaced without effecting other panels adjoining to it.

7·17. Ventilation—(1) An opening area not less than 1/12th of the floor area of the room should be provided. The topof this opening area should be not more than 45 cm below the ceiling.

(2) The ratio of fresh air to circulated area should not be less than 1 : 4 special care is needed to ensure the purity and cleanliness of the circulated air. Recirculations should not be adopted where toxic, inflammable dirt or fumes are present.

(3) Duct grills or air inlets may be located in various parts of a room. The most suitable location is in walls at a height of 2 to 3·5 m above the floor. It is desirable that the top of the grill should be 60 cm below the ceiling or twice the height of the grille whichever is greater.

(4) When the air leaving a grille is cooler than the air in a room it tends to fall, conversely warm air tends to rise.

Table 7·5. Thickness of duct metal

Dia. of duct (cm)	*Thickness of sheet in mm*	
	G.I. Sheet	*Aluminium sheet*
15-50	0·63	0·80
51-75	0·80	0·80
76-100	0·80	1·00
101-125	1·00	1·50
Above 125	1·25	1·80

Dampers. All ducts require dampers to control the rate of flow. Such dampers maybe provided in branch ducts in the main fresh air in take and in bye passes round heaters and washers etc.

13. Buildings Air

Table 7·6. Fresh Air to be supplied in buildings

	Type of building	*Min. rate of fresh air to be supplied*
1.	Assembly halls	28·5 m³/hr/head
2.	Canteens	28·5 m³/hr/head
3.	Factories and work shops	
	work rooms	22·5 m³/hr/head
	Lavatories and WCs	2 air changes/hr
4.	Houses and flats	
	Bath rooms and WCs	2 air changes/hr
	Halls and passages	1 air changes/hr
	Kitchens	7 m³/hr
	Living and bed rooms, 8·4 m³/head	20·5 m³/hr/head
	Living and bed rooms, 4·2 m³/head	17·0 m³/hr/head
	Pantries or larders	2 air changes/hr
5.	Shops	28·5 m³/hr/head
6.	Schools	
	Occupational rooms such as class rooms, laboratories etc.	
	2·8 m³/head	42·5 m²/head/hr
	5·6 m³/head	28·5 m²/head/hr
	8·4 m³/head	20·5 m²/head/hr
	11·2 m³/head	17·0 m²/head/hr
	Cloak rooms	3 air changes/hr
	Corridors, lavatories and WCs	2 air changes/hr
7.	Govt. offices	
	56 m³ per head	28·5 m³/hr/head
	8·4 m³ per head	20·5 m³/hr/head
	11·2 m³ per head	17·0 m³/hr/head
	Lavatories and WCs	2 air changes/hr
	Places of entertainment and restaurants	28·5 m³/hr/head

Min. air requirements for ventilation (IS : 650—1955)

Type of enclosure	*Amount of air to be introduced*		*Air space in m³/head*
	Non smokers m³/min/head	*Smokers m³/min/head*	
1. Comfort air conditioning in theatres and other crowded enclosures			
(*a*) where occupants max. duration of stay is 3 hrs/day	0·20	0·57	
(*b*) where stay is longer than 3 hrs. at a time	0·28	0·85	

Table contd...

Table contd...

Type of enclosure	*Amount of air to be introduced*		*Air space in m^3/head*
	Non smokers m^3/min/head	*Smokers m^3/min/head*	
2. Industrial air conditioning			
(*a*) where duration of stay is less than 3 hrs. at a time	0·28 0·20 0·11	0·85 0·57 0·34	5·6 and less 5·6 -11·2 11·2 and more
(*b*) where duration of stay is 3 hrs. or larger at a time	0·34 0·28 0·20	1·02 0·85 0·57	5·6 and less 5·6-11·2 11·2 and above

7·18. Door and Window Opening

Size of doors—

Main gate doors	1·2 × 2·1 m (4′ × 7′)
Outer doors of rooms	1·05 × 1·45 m (3·5′ × 7′)
Inner doors	0·9 × 1·8 m (3′ × 6′)
Bath rooms	0·75 × 1·8 m (2·5′ × 6′)

Sizes of Chaukhats (frames)

Main gate	single shutter	100 × 125 mm (4″ × 5″)
	Double shutter	127 × 150 mm (5″ × 6″)
Main rooms	Single shutter	75 × 115 mm (3″ × 4″)
	Double shutter	127 × 137 mm (5″ × 5½″)
Interior rooms	Single shutter	75 × 115 mm (3″ × 4″)
Windows	Single shutter	75 × 90 mm (3″ × 3½″)
Bathrooms	Single shutter	75 × 75 mm (3″ × 3″)

Double shutters—main shutter is panelled or glazed and otherwise gauzed in the size 1st size figure denotes size perp. to the wall face.

Table 7·7. Thickness of Shutters

Shutter type	*Thickness*	*Width of style*	*Width of rail*
Glazed panelled	45 mm	90 mm (lock and trot upto 150)	115 mm
Panelled	45 mm	90 mm (lock and trot upto 137·5)	115 mm
Bathoned (Bat thickness)	30 mm	Thickness of ledges and braces	25 to 32 mm
Glazed	30 mm	90 mm (No rock rail)	90 mm
Iron barred	30 mm	—	—

Rails are horizontal and style are vertical members

The lock rail centre is kept 0·76 m above the ground

Ledges are horizontal members while braces are inclined stiffners.

Glazed Panelled doors. The lock rail must have two tenons. The thickness of each tenon is 1/3 of the thickness of the shutter and width is kept 5 times of its thickness. For other intermediate rails the thickness of tenon is 1/4 of the thickness of shutter and width 5 times the thickness of the tenon.

The top and bottom rails are tenoned in the style to its full width with a thickness of tenon equal to 1/3 of the thickness of shutter. Sash bars (bars between glazed panels) should be 32 mm wide with a rebate of 10 mm on either side and 20 mm deep. The glass panes should be fastened to the panels by wooden beadings of teak wood (1 × 1·5 cm) nailed to the sash bars or should be fixed by lime putty in a triangular section (Putty is a paste made by mixing chalk, Kharia or geru with linseed oil or adhesives).

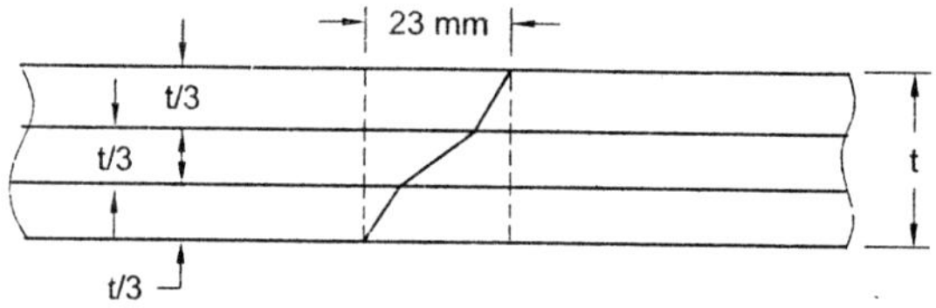

Fig. 7·43. Stone blocks preparation.

In double shutters the meeting junction of the vertical style should be rebated by 1/3 thickness but not less than 2 cm and width not less than 25 mm joints are given and pinned by bamboo pins 10 to 15 mm dia and the joint is then pressed in a clamping vice.

Gauzed doors. Galvanized wire gauze 85 G or 140 G with a wire dia. of 0·56 or 0·71 mm is used. In place of lock rails spring operated bolt is provided. They are generally used in double set of shutters to get rid of mosquitos. The wire gauze can be made black or green by dry lamp black or green powder colour with kerosene or spirit by a pad of cloth. The panes of the glazed doors can be made blind by painting it by white enamel which is made uniform by padding with a cotton cloth pad when the paint is fresh.

Ledged, braced or battoned doors. The horizontal members called the ledges, the sloping members called the braces and the face main shutter vertical pieces nailed together are called battons. The width of ledges and braces is 75 mm to 100 mm while the width of battons is 100 mm (This width is generally kept in the available size of plank and the vertical notches are made to show battons). The braces are sloped down towards the hinged edge.

Louvred (venetianed shutter)—The louvres may be of wood, glass, plastic or asbestos sheets 10 to 12 mm thick 90 mm wide. They are fixed to the end vertical styles at an angle of 45° and covers about half of its width. They are fixed by making a groove in the style 125 mm deep. The loures (venetian) may be fixed or removable.

Door fittings. Brass, iron or stainless steel are provided as below hinges 75 mm to 150 mm, single and double acting spring hinge, sliding, lower or flush bolts and handles etc.

Table 7·8. Wood Shutters (IS 1003—1966)

Type	*Door in mm*		*Window in mm*		*Vent. in mm*	
	Width	*Thickness*	*Width*	*Thickness*	*Width*	*Thickness*
Vertical style top and freeze rail	100 ± 3	40 ± 1	80 ± 3	40 ± 1	80 ± 3	40 ± 1
Lock rail	160 ± 3	40 ± 1	—	—	—	—
Bottom rail	250 ± 3	40 ± 1	80 ± 3	40 ± 1	80 ± 3	40 ± 1
Muriting	100 ± 3	40 ± 1	60 ± 3	40 ± 1	—	—
Glaze base	40 ± 1	40 ± 1	40 ± 1	40 ± 1	40 ± 1	40 ± 1

Figures right of ± indicates tolerance of variation.

Specifications of wooden shutters (IS : 1003—1966)

Type	*Width mm*	*Height mm*	*Type*	*Width mm*	*Height mm*
Doors			**(Window contd.)**		
8 DS 20	700	1905	8 WT 10	340	860

Table contd...

Table contd...

Type	*Width mm*	*Height mm*	*Type*	*Width mm*	*Height mm*
8 DS 21	700	2005	9 WT 10	390	860
9 DS 21	800	2005	10 WT 10	440	860
10 DS 21	900	2005	11 WT 10	490	860
12 DS 21	1060	2005	8 WT 11	340	960
Window			9 WT 11	390	960
5 WS 10	360	860	10 WT 11	440	960
6 WS 10	460	860	11 WT 11	490	960
7 WS 10	560	860	8 WT 12	340	1060
5 WS 11	360	960	9 WT 12	390	1060
6 WS 11	460	960	10 WT 12	440	1060
7 WS 11	560	960	11 WT 12	490	1060
			Ventilators		
5 WS 12	360	1060	6 V 6	500	500
6 WS 12	460	1060	10 V 6	900	500
7 WS 12	560	1060	12 V 6	1100	500

D—denotes door, *W*—window and *V* for ventilator.

S—denotes single shutter while *T*—double shutter

N—number denotes modules, left number denotes width and right height module.

8 WT 10 means a window of double shutter having 8 modules width and 10 modules height. 1 module = 9·94 cm.

Steel Doors, Windows and Ventilator Specifications

The dimensions shown are over all dimensions to the outside frames of steel doors etc. This size is allowed after allowing 3 mm clearance on all four sides for the purpose of fitting the doors, windows or ventilators. The tolerance of variation is ± 1·5 mm width and heights are shown as number of modules as in case of wooden doors. Types are indicated as follows :

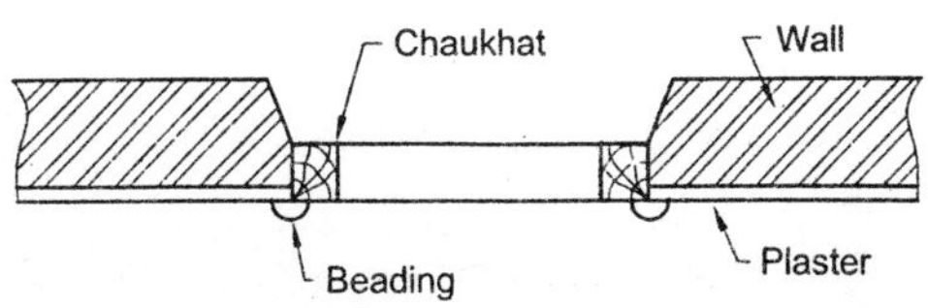

Fig. 7·44.

C = Centre hung shutter

H = With horizontal glazing bars

N = Without horizontal glazing bars

F = Fixed glass panes

S = Side hung shutters

T = Top hung shutters.

7·19. Roofs

Technical terms in roofs

Cleat—A piece of wood or angle fixed in principal rafter to support purlins.

Eaves—The lowest edge of inclined roof.

Hip—A Valley type depression at the junctions of two sloping roofs.

Pitch—The angle of roof from horizontal varies 18°-26″ to 33°-41′.

Sag tie—A vertical member from ridge to the centre of tie to avoid sagging.

Bressumer—Joint spanning over columns to wall in a slope on which purlins to receive rafter rest.

Wind ties—These are flat iron 40 × 6 mm section bolted to the pitched AC or GCI sheet roofs at lowest edge and at interior joints for safety against wind so that sheets may not flew off.

Sheathing—Boards to support coverings, supported on purlins.

Purlins—These are structural members subjected to transverse loads and rest on the principal rafter horizontally. Purlins have a support for sheathing. These are generally fixed on node points. If not possible due to size of roofing sheets etc., then the rafters over which these purlins rest are designed as beams.

Sub purlins—It is secondary system to support tiles etc.

Principal rafter—Inclined top memebrs of truss.

Common rafters—Inclined secondary members resting on purlins to support roof.

Panel—Distance between two adjacent joints in a roof.

Bay—Distance between two adjacent trusses.

Spacing of trusses—It is decided as per site conditions even though an economical formula is used.

$t = 2P + r$ where t = cost of truss, r = cost of covering material and P = cost of purlins.

The economical spacing is generally kept 3 to 5 m for spans upto 15 m and 4·5 to 7·5 m for spans 15 to 30 m.

Camber—Vertical distance between the springing point of truss to the lowest horizontal member. It is generally kept 1/30th to 1/40th of span. A camber equal to 1/480 of span is kept to avoid appearance of any sagging.

Bearings—Ends of trusses over walls or piers. These are properly anchored down with bolts of lengths varying from 90 cm to 140 cm and dia 16 mm upto about 8 m span both the ends may be fixed, but beyond this span either one of the ends is free or both may be free according to span and temperature changes.

General considerations in trussed roofs

(1) Principal rafters must not be longer than 3 m between struts.

(2) Purlins must be fixed at node points which may be also guided by the roofing sheaths size.

(3) M.S. bedding plates of size 30 × 30 × 1·5 cm are fixed over stone or concrete templates.

(4) On the free end lead sheets 3·2 mm thick are provided with a slotted hole 5 cm long and of width 1½ mm bigger than the dia. of anchor bolt passed through it. At the fixed end hole for anchor bolt is round and the lead sheet may also be omitted.

(5) **Minimum size of members in a truss**—flats 50 × 6 mm (thickness, rods 16 mm dia, gusset plates 6 mm thickness, angles 50 × 50 × 5 mm or an equivalent section. Size of rivet or bolt 16 mm.

Max. slenderness ratio in compression members = 100 and tension members = 350. Wind ties on sloped GCI sheet roofs 40 × 6 mm (thick) bolted to roof sheets.

(6) **Gusset plates**—General thickness is 6 mm. At junction of ridge and shoe must be 10 mm, while for spans more than 20 m. It must be upto 14 mm.

(7) **Laps of coverings**—For normal inclination of 18° the end laps in sheets shall not be less than 150 mm. For inclination less than 18° the lap may be increased. The side laps must be such that it may be sheltered from the wind direction, but minimum one corrugation.

The free over hang on eaves from edge to the centre of bolt hole must not be more than 300 mm for 6 mm thick sheets and 400 mm for 7 mm thick sheets. Wherever four corners of sheets over lap, two of them shall be mitred in order to secure perfect fit.

Table 7·9. Internal dia. in tubular members of roof truss at various spans normal loading side slopes 1 : 3 (in mm)

Members	*Truss spacing*		
	3 m c/c	*4 m c/c*	*5 m c/c*
	Span 5 to 6 m (Fig. *A*)		
Principal rafter *ad*	32-L	32-L	40-L
Tie beam *ae*	32-L	32-L	40-L
bc, dc, de	15-L	15-L	15-L
	Span 7·5 m (Fig. *B*)		
Principal rafter *ad*	40-L	40-M	50-L
Tie beam *ae*	32-L	32-M	40-L
ce, cf, bf	20-L	20-L	25-L
de	15-L	15-L	15-L
	Span 10 m (Fig. *C*)		
Principal rafter *ag*			
tie beam *aj*	40-M	50-M	50-M
	40-L	50-L	50-L
	20-L	25-L	25-L
	32-L	40-L	40-L
	15-L	20-L	20-L
	Span 12 m (Fig. *C*)		
Principal rafter *ab*	50-M	65-M	65-M
Tie beam *af*	40-M	50-M	50-M
de	20-M	25-M	25-M
eg	32-M	40-M	20-M
bc, cd, dh, hf	15-M	20-M	20-M
	Span 15 m (Fig. *D*)		
Principal rafter *ai*	65-M	65-M	65-M
Tie beam *ah*	65-M	80-L	80-M
bc, cd, dh, hf	25-L	25-L	25-L
fi	25-L	32-L	40-M
ef	65-M	65-M	65-M
	40-M	40-M	40-M

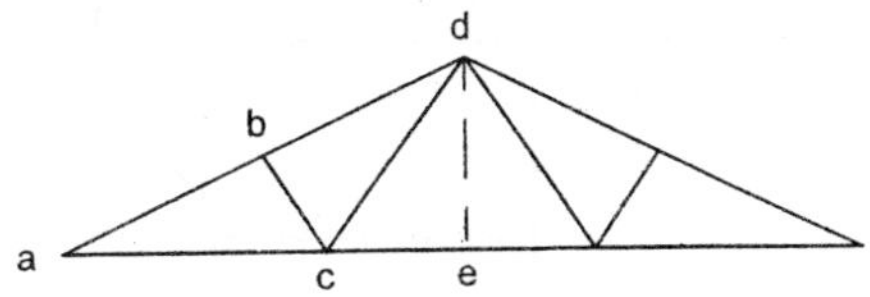

(*A*)

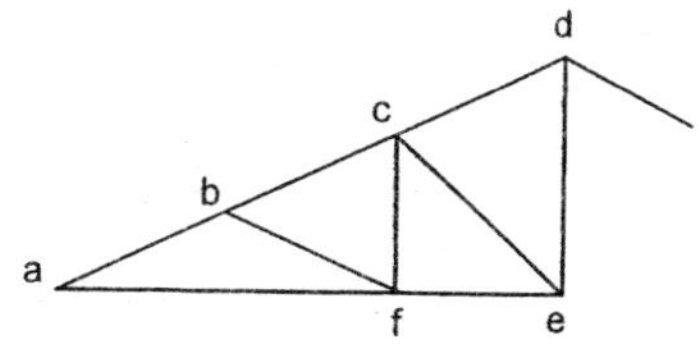

(*B*)

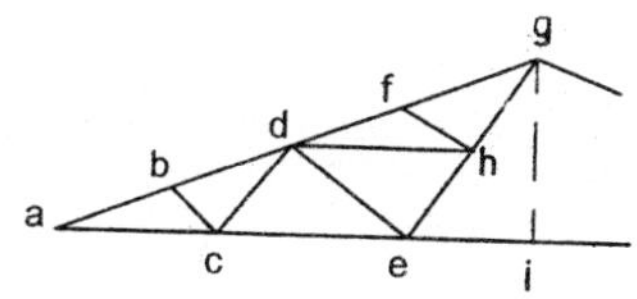

(*C*)

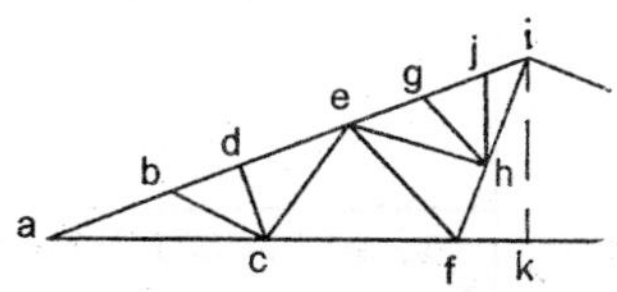

(*D*)

L = Light
M = Medium
H = Heavy
with GCI and AC sheets

Note : See tables of properties of steel tubes. Joints are welded. Table 7·10 *A* and *B*.

Table 7·10 (*A*). Permissible stress in axial compression in steel tubes (IS : 1161—1979)

l/r	*kg/cm*²	*l/r*	*kg/cm*²	*l/r*	*kg/cm*²	*l/r*	*kg/cm*²
0	1250	60	1002	120	674	180	339
10	1217	70	970	130	603	190	304
20	1175	80	929	140	540	200	271
30	1131	90	876	150	490	210	243
40	1080	100	814	160	432	220	219
50	1046	110	745	170	381	230	198
240	180	250	162	300	106	350	71

Table 7·10 (B). Sizes and Properties of Steel Tubes for Structural Purposes

Nominal Bore *mm*	*Outside dia.* *mm*	*Class*	*Thickness* *mm*	*Weight* *kg/m*	*Area of cross sec.* cm^2	*Moment of Inertia* cm^4	*Modulus of section* cm^3	*Radius of gyration* *cm*
(1)	(2)	(3)	(4)	(5)	(6)	(7)	(8)	(9)
15	21·3	L	2·00	0·962	1·21	0·57	0·54	0·69
		M	2·65	1·22	1·55	0·69	0·65	0·67
		H	3·25	1·45	1·84	0·77	0·73	0·65
20	26·9	L	2·35	1·42	1·81	1·38	1·02	0·87
		M	2·65	1·58	2·02	1·50	1·12	0·86
		H	3·25	1·90	2·41	1·72	1·28	0·84
25	33·7	L	2·65	2·04	2·58	3·14	1·86	1·10
		M	3·25	2·46	3·11	3·65	2·16	1·08
		H	4·05	2·99	3·77	4·22	2·51	1·06
32	42·4	L	2·65	2·61	3·31	6·57	3·10	1·41
		M	3·25	3·15	4·00	7·71	3·64	1·39
		H	4·05	3·86	4·88	9·07	4·28	1·36
40	48·3	L	2·9	3·27	4·14	10·70	4·43	1·61
		M	3·25	3·61	4·60	11·73	4·86	1·60
		H	4·05	4·43	5·33	13·90	5·75	1·57
50	60·3	L_1	2·9	4·14	5·23	21·59	7·16	2·03
		L_2	3·25	4·57	5·82	27·33	7·89	2·02
		M	3·65	5·10	6·50	26·17	8·68	2·01
		H	4·5	6·17	7·89	30·90	10·2	1·98
65	76·1	L	3·25	5·84	7·44	44·44	13·0	2·58
		M	3·65	6·53	8·31	54·65	14·4	2·56
		H	4·5	7·92	10·1	65·12	17·1	2·54
80	88·9	L	3·25	6·86	8·74	80·31	18·1	3·03
		M	4·05	8·48	10·8	97·38	21·9	3·00
		H	4·84	10·1	12·8	113·46	28·5	2·40
90	101·6	L	3·65	8·82	11·2	134·9	28·6	3·47
		M	4·05	9·75	12·4	147·9	29·1	3·45
		H	4·85	11·6	14·7	172·9	34·0	3·42
100	114·3	L	3·65	9·97	12·7	194·4	34·0	3·91
		M	4·5	12·1	15·5	234·3	41·0	3·89
		H	5·4	14·5	18·5	274·5	48·0	3·85
110	127·0	L	4·5	13·6	17·3	325·3	51·2	4·33
		M	4·85	14·6	18·6	347·7	54·8	4·32
		H	5·4	16·2	20·6	382·0	60·2	4·30
125	139·7	L	4·5	14·9	19·1	437·2	62·6	4·78
		M	4·85	16·2	20·5	467·6	66·7	4·37
		H	5·4	17·9	22·8	514·5	73·7	4·75
135	152·4	L	4·5	16·4	20·9	572·2	75·1	5·23
		M	4·85	17·7	22·5	612·5	80·4	5·22
		H	5·4	19·5	24·9	674·5	88·5	5·20

Nominal Bore mm	Outside dia. mm	Class	Thickness mm	Weight kg/m	Area of cross sec. cm^2	Moment of Inertia cm^4	Modulus of section cm^3	Radius of gyration cm
(1)	(2)	(3)	(4)	(5)	(6)	(7)	(8)	(9)
150	165·1	L	4·5	17·8	22·7	732·6	88·7	5·68
		M	4·85	19·2	24·4	784·5	95·0	5·67
		H	5·4	21·2	27·1	864·7	105·0	5·65
175	193·7	L	4·85	22·6	28·7	1284	133	6·68
		M	5·4	25·0	31·9	1417	146	6·66
		H	5·9	27·3	34·8	1536	159	6·64
200	219·1	L	4·85	25·7	32·6	1874	171	7·58
		M	5·6	29·4	37·6	2042	195	7·55
		H	5·9	31·0	39·5	2247	205	7·54
225	244·5	H	5·9	34·2	44·2	3149	258	8·44
250	273·0	—	5·9	38·8	49·5	4412	323	9·45
300	323·9	—	6·3	49·5	63·4	7992	493	11·2
350	355·6	—	8·0	68·3	86·5	13111	737	12·3

Note : Steel tubes are designated by their nominal bore and are classified as 'Light'-L ; 'Medium'-M and 'Heavy'-H according to the wall thickness.

Design of Steel Members of Roof Trusses of Various Spans

In design of steel truss members following assumptions are made :

Light Load Roofs. Covered with corrugated iron sheets or asbestos cement sheeting and steel purlins. Total load for design is taken at 100 kg/sq. metre including of wind load at 150 kg/ sq. metre, normal for roof coverings, vertical for truss members (total weights divided by 1·33).

Medium Load Roofs. Covered with single tiles or slates and steel purlins with ceiling. Total load for design is taken at 150 kg/sq. metre (inclusive of wind load, all as for light loading)

Roof slopes 1 in 2 camber of = span/28

Panels equal and equally loaded, spans c/c of bearings will be about 30 cm more.

The following variations will require no alterations in truss sections :

(*a*) Variations of ± 10 percent in the span and spacings of the truss.

(*b*) The omission or inclusion of a boarded ceiling.

(*c*) Inclusion of ventilator at the ridge.

(*d*) If the truss is not cambered or is given a slight camber of say *S*/360 the truss spacings can be increased upto 15 percent.

(*e*) If the panels are reduced from 6 to 4 or from 8 to 6, these will not be appreciable difference, but the principal rafter lengths of panels will be increased necessitating a little heavier angle since it acts as a strut.

Trusses should be lifted at the nodes. Trusses above 12 members should not be slinged at the apex. They should be lifted by slinging at two mid points of the rafters.

Table 7·10 (C). Size of Members for Steel Roof Trusses of Various Spans

Size of *L* members in mm ; Roof Slope 1 in 2

Truss spacing	*3-m centres*	*4-m centres*	*5-m centres*
	5-metres span-Light Loading-4 pannels at 1·4 metres		
Member—P.R., ad	2Ls—50 × 30 × 6	2Ls—50 × 30 × 6	2Ls—50 × 30 × 6
Member dc, bc, ce, ac	1L—50 × 30 × 6	1L—50 × 30 × 6	1L—50 × 30 × 6
	5-metres Span-Medium Loading-4 panels at 1·4 metres		
Member—P.R., ad	2Ls—50 × 30 × 6	2Ls—50 × 30 × 6	
Tie—ac	1L—50 × 30 × 6	1L—65 × 45 × 6	
Member—dc, bc, ce	1L—50 × 30 × 6	1L—50 × 30 × 6	

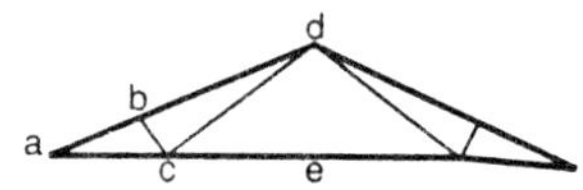

Dia. of Rivets—16 mm ; Thickness of Gussets—10 mm and 6 mm.

Truss spacing	*3-m centres*	*4-m centres*	*5-m centres*
	6-metres Span-Lighting Loading-4 panels at 1·8 metres		
Member—P.R., ad	2Ls—50 × 30 × 6	2Ls—50 × 30 × 6	2Ls—50 × 30 × 6
Tie—ac	1L—50 × 30 × 6	1L—50 × 30 × 6	1L—50 × 50 × 6
Member—dc, bc, ce	1L—50 × 30 × 6	1L—50 × 30 × 6	1L—50 × 30 × 6
	6-metres Span-Medium Loading-4panels at 1·8 metres		
Member—F.R., ad	2Ls—50 × 30 × 6	2Ls—50 × 30 × 6	
Tie—ac	1L—50 × 50 × 6	1L—65 × 45 × 6	
dc, bc, ce	1L—50 × 30 × 6	1L—50 × 30 × 6	

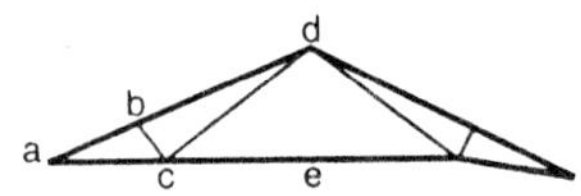

Dia. of Rivets—16 mm ; Thickness of Gussets—10 mm and 6 mm

Truss spacing	*3-m centres*	*4-m centres*	*5-m centres*
	7·5-metres Span-Light Loading-6 panels at 1·4 metres		
Member—P.R., ae	2Ls—50 × 30 × 6	2Ls—50 × 30 × 6	2Ls—50 × 30 × 6
Tie—(end), ac	1L—50 × 30 × 6	1L—65 × 45 × 6	1L—75 × 50 × 6
Tie—(central), cf	1L—50 × 30 × 6	1L—50 × 30 × 6	1L--50 × 30 × 6
Member—bc	1L—50 × 50 × 6	1L—50 × 50 × 6	1L—50 × 50 × 6
Member—ec, dc	1L—50 × 30 × 6	1L—50 × 30 × 6	1L—50 × 30 × 6
	7·5-metres Span Medium Loading-6 panels at 1·4 metres		
Member—P.R., ae	2Ls—50 × 30 × 6	2Ls—50 × 30 × 6	
Tie—(end), ac	2Ls—50 × 30 × 6	2Ls—50 × 30 × 6	
Tie—(central), cf	1L—50 × 30 × 6	1L—50 × 30 × 6	
Member, bc	1L—50 × 50 × 6	1L—50 × 50 × 6	
Member, ec, dc	1L—50 × 30 × 6	1L—50 × 30 × 6	

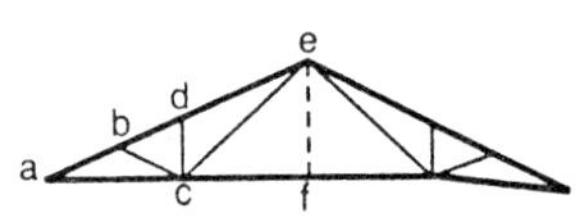

Dia. of Rivets—16 mm ; Thickness of Gussets—10 mm and 6 mm

Truss spacing	*3-m centres*	*4-m centres*	*5-m centres*
	9-metres Span-Light Loading-6 pannels at 1·68 metres		
Member—P.R., ae	2Ls—50 × 30 × 6	2Ls—50 × 50 × 6	2Ls—65 × 45 × 6
Tie (end), ac	1Ls—65 × 45 × 6	1L—75 × 50 × 6	2Ls—50 × 30 × 6
Tie (central), cf	1L—50 × 30 × 6	1L—50 × 30 × 6	1L—50 × 30 × 6
Member, bc	1L—50 × 50 × 6	1L—50 × 50 × 6	1L—50 × 50 × 6
Member, ec, dc	1L—50 × 30 × 6	1L—50 × 30 × 6	1L—50 × 30 × 6

9-metres Span-Medium Loading-6 pannels at 1·68 metres

Member—P.R., ef	2Ls—65 × 45 × 6	2Ls—65 × 45 × 6
Tie (end), ac	2Ls—50 × 30 × 6	2Ls—50 × 30 × 6
Tie (central), cf	1L—50 × 30 × 6	IL—65 × 45 × 6
Member, bc	1L—65 × 45 × 6	IL—65 × 45 × 6
Member, ec,, dc	1L—50 × 30 × 6	IL—65 × 45 × 6

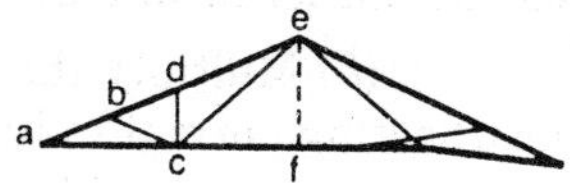

Dia. of Rivets—16 mm ; Thickness of Gussets 10 mm and 6 mm

12-metres Span Light Loading-8 panels at 1·68 metres

Truss spacing	3-m centres	4-m centres	5-m centres
Member—P.R., ah	2Ls—50 × 30 × 6	2Ls—65 × 45 × 6	2Ls—75 × 50 × 6
Tie (end), ae	2Ls—50 × 30 × 6	2Ls—50 × 30 × 6	2Ls—50 × 30 × 6
Tie (central), ej	1L—50 × 30 × 6	1L—50 × 50 × 6	1L—65 × 45 × 6
Member fg, he	1L—50 × 30 × 6	1L—50 × 50 × 6	1L—65 × 45 × 6
Member, de	2Ls—50 × 30 × 6	2Ls—50 × 30 × 6	2Ls—50 × 30 × 6
Member, dc, dg, bc	1L—50 × 30 × 6	1L—50 × 50 × 6	1L—65 × 45 × 6

12-metres Span Medium Loading-8 panels at 1·68 metres

Member—P.R., ah	2Ls—75 × 50 × 6	2Ls—75 × 50 × 6
Tie (end), ae	2Ls—50 × 30 × 6	2Ls—50 × 50 × 6
Tie (central), ej	1L—65 × 45 × 6	1L—65 × 45 × 6
Member, fg, he	1L—75 × 50 × 6	1L—90 × 60 × 6
Member, de	2Ls—50 × 30 × 6	2Ls—50 × 30 × 6
Member, dc, dg, bc	1L—50 × 30 × 6	1L—50 × 30 × 6

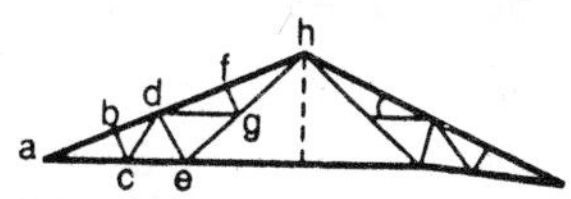

Dia. or Rivets—16 mm ; Thickness of Gussets—10 mm and 6 mm

15-metres Span Light Loading—12 panels at 1·5 metres

Truss spacing	3-m centres	4-m centres	5-m centres
Member—P.R., ak	2Ls—65 × 45 × 6	2Ls—75 × 50 × 6	2Ls—90 × 60 × 6
Tie (end), af	2Ls—50 × 30 × 6	2Ls—50 × 30 × 6	2Ls—50 × 50 × 6
Tie (central), fi	1L—75 × 50 × 6	1L—75 × 50 × 6	1L—90 × 60 × 6
Members, fk	1L—75 × 50 × 6	1L—75 × 50 × 6	1L—90 × 60 × 6
Members, bc, dc, gh, jh	1L—50 × 30 × 6	1L—50 × 30 × 6	1L—50 × 50 × 6
Members, ef, ce, eh	2Ls—50 × 30 × 6	2Ls—50 × 30 × 6	2Ls—50 × 50 × 6

Dia. of Rivets : 16 mm ; Thickness of Gussets—10 mm and 6 mm

15-metres Span Medium Loading—12 panels at 1·5 metres

Member—P.R., ak	2Ls—75 × 50 × 6	2Ls—90 × 60 × 6
Tie (end), af	2Ls—65 × 45 × 6	2Ls—75 × 50 × 6
Tie (central), fc	2Ls—50 × 30 × 6	2Ls—50 × 30 × 6
Members, fk	2Ls—50 × 30 × 6	2Ls—50 × 30 × 6
Members, bc, dc, gh, jh	1L—50 × 30 × 6	1L—50 × 30 × 6
Members, ef, ce, eh	2Ls—50 × 30 × 6	2Ls—50 × 30 × 6

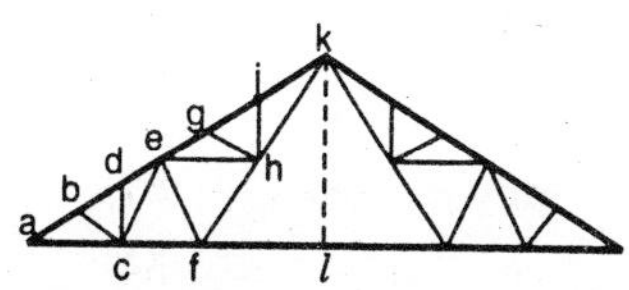

Diametre of rivet = 16 mm ; Thickness of Gussets—12 mm and 8 mm

P.R. is principal rafter.

Design of Steel Roof Trusses by Stress Coefficient Table

To find stress in any number :

(*a*) Multiploy the total dead load carried by the truss including its own weight by the coefficient for dead load.

(*b*) Multiply the total wind load pressure (or the live load to be taken in lieu of the wind load) acting normal to its surface on one side of the roof by the coefficient for wind pressure.

Table 7·10 (D)

S = *Span*, *R* = *Rise*, *C* = *Camber*

Member of truss	*Kind of stress*	*Stress coefficient*			
		$R = S/4$	$C = S/30$	$R = S/3$	$C = S/24$
		Vertical dead load	*Wind load normal to roof surface*	*Vertical dead load*	*Wind load normal to roof surface*
ab	+	·63	·70	·52	·58
bc	–	·08	·07	·07	·05
ac	–	·58	·49	·43	·27
ab	+	·97	1·05	·77	·70
bc	+	·64	·70	·51	·58
bd	+	·31	·69	·24	·58
ad	–	·87	1·13	·65	·80
dc	–	·33	·34	·32	·35
ab	+	1·08	1·24	·86	·86
bc	+	·94	1·10	·74	·80
cd	+	·65	·70	·51	·58
bf	+	·17	·37	·14	·30
ce	+	·25	·55	·21	·51
fc	–	·18	·30	·72	·30
dc	–	·41	·44	·40	·45
fc	–	·77	·92	·52	·63
af	–	·96	1·35	·72	·98
ab	+	·07	1·05	·77	·70
bd	+	·85	1·05	·63	·70
bc	+	·22	·50	·21	·50
ac	–	·87	1·18	·65	·80
ce	–	·54	·45	·41	·28
cd	–	·34	·69	·26	·54

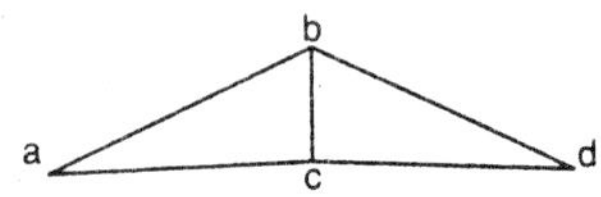

A. Without Camber

B.

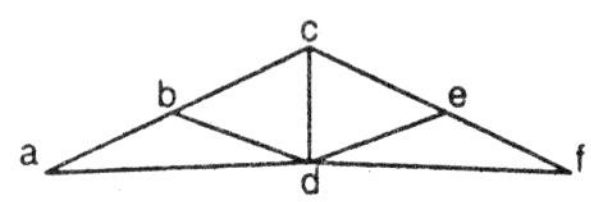

C.

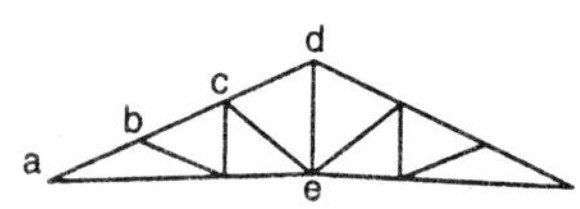

S = Span, R = Rise, C = Camber

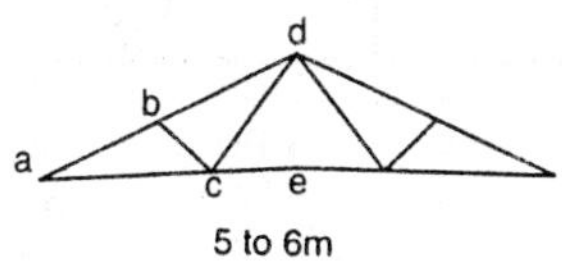

D. Without camber

Member of truss	Kind of stress	$R = S/3$	$\frac{S}{R} = 30°$	$R = S/4$	$C = S/5$
ab	+	·70	·75	·84	1·01
bd	+	·54	·63	·73	·92
bc	+	·21	·22	·22	·23
ac	–	·56	·65	·75	·94
ce	–	·40	·43	·50	·61
cd	–	·19	·22	·25	·31

Same as above with camber=R/6

Member of truss	Kind of stress	$R = S/3$	$\frac{S}{R} = 30°$	$R = S/4$	$C = S/5$
ab	+	·91	1·03	1·20	1·45
bd	+	·77	·91	1·06	1·35
bc	+	·21	·22	·13	·23
ac	–	·77	·91	1·06	1·40
ce	–	·45	·52	·60	·75
cd	–	·36	·42	·49	·63

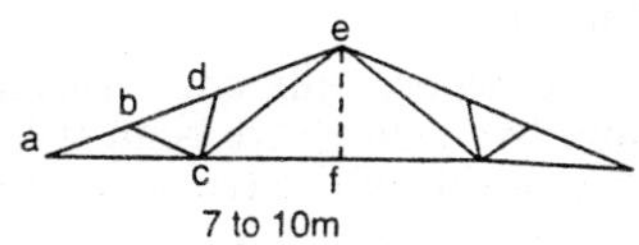

E. Without camber

Member of truss	Kind of stress	$R = S/3$	$\frac{S}{R} = 30°$	$R = S/4$	$C = S/5$
ab	+	·75	·83	·93	1·12
bd	+	·59	·67	·76	·93
de	+	·57	·63	·78	1·00
bc	+	·16	·17	·18	·20
dc	+	·16	·17	·18	·20
ac	–	·63	·72	·83	1·04
cf	–	·36	·43	·50	·63
ce	–	·25	·39	·33	·41

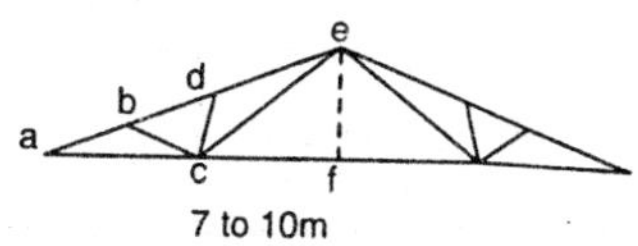

With camber = R/6

Member of truss	Kind of stress	$R = S/3$	$\frac{S}{R} = 30°$	$R = S/4$	$C = S/5$
ab	+	1·02	1·15	1·31	1·61
bd	+	·82	·94	1·08	1·35
de	+	·83	·98	1·16	1·48
bc	+	·17	·19	·21	·27
dc	+	·17	·19	·21	·27
ac	–	·85	1·01	1·18	1·50
cf	–	·45	·52	·60	·75
ce	–	·44	·52	·61	·78

S = Span, R = Rise, C = Camber

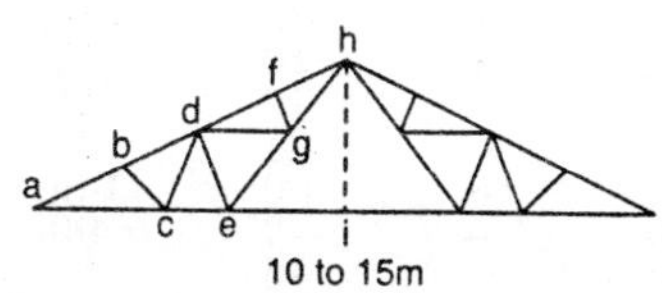

F.

Member of truss	Kind of stress	$R = S/4$ Vertical dead load	$C = S/30$ Wind load normal to roof surface	$R = S/3$ Vertical dead load	$C = S/24$ Wind load normal to roof surface
ab	+	1·13	1·34	·90	·93
bd	+	1·07	1·34	·83	·93
df	+	1·02	1·34	·76	·93
fh	+	·96	1·34	·69	·93
bc	+	·11	·25	·10	·25
fg	+	·11	·25	·10	·25
de	+	·22	·50	·21	·50
ac	–	1·01	1·46	·75	1·06
ce	–	·87	1·13	·64	·81
ej	–	·54	·45	·41	·28
cd	–	·15	·32	·11	·26
dg	–	·15	·32	·11	·26
gh	–	·49	1·01	·36	·80
eg	–	·34	·69	·26	·55

S = Span, R = Rise, C = Camber

Member of truss	Kind of stress	Stress coefficient			
		$R = S/4$	$C = S/30$	$R = S/3$	$C = S/24$
		Vertical dead load	Wind load normal to roof surface	Vertical dead load	Wind load normal to roof surface
ab	+	1·08	1·24	·86	·86
bd	+	1·00	1·24	·81	·94
df	+	·75	·85	·60	·68
bc	+	·15	·33	·14	·34
de	+	·22	·50	·22	·52
dc	–	·59	·43	·18	·42
fe	–	·27	·55	·26	·57
ac	–	·96	1·35	·72	·98
ce	–	·77	·92	·58	·63
eg	–	·56	·47	·42	·28

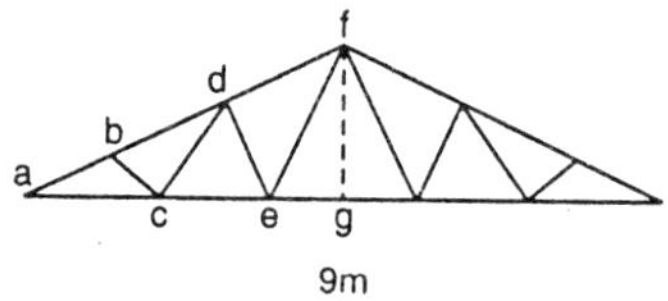

G.

Add (*a*) and (*b*) : This will give the total stress for which a member has to be designed either as a strut or as a tie. This total stress may be divided by 1·33 where wind and dead loads have been taken together.

(*c*) where only one stress co-efficient is given in the table it can be used for a case where both dead and live loads have been resolved to act as one single vertical load. (Wind load is considered to act only on one side of the truss at a time).

(The different tables might give slightly varying results but it will not make any appreciable difference in the final choice of a suitable section).

S = Span, R = Rise, C = Camber

Member of truss	Kind of stress	Stress coefficient				
		$R = S/3$	$\frac{S}{R} = 30°$	$R = S/4$	$C = S/5$	$R = S/6$
ab	+	·80	·90	·98	1·20	1·38
bd	+	·72	·81	·92	1·13	1·34
df	+	·65	·75	·87	1·09	1·30
fh	+	·58	·70	·81	·04	1·27
bc	+	·10	·11	·11	·12	·12
fg	+	·10	·11	·11	·12	·12
de	+	·21	·22	·22	·23	·24
ac	–	·66	·76	·88	1·09	1·30
ce	–	·56	·65	·75	·94	1·13
ej	–	·40	·43	·50	·63	·75
cd	–	·09	·11	·13	·16	·19
dg	–	·09	·11	·13	·16	·19
gh	–	·28	·33	·38	·47	·56
eg	–	·20	·22	·25	·31	·38
ab	+	1·06	1·20	1·37	1·56	1·74
bd	+	·99	1·14	1·31	1·38	1·59
df	+	·92	1·08	1·26	1·60	1·81
fh	+	·85	1·02	1·20	1·55	1·78
bc	+	·10	·11	·11	·12	·12
fg	+	·10	·11	·11	·12	·12
de	+	·21	·22	·22	·23	·24
ac	–	·90	1·06	1·24	1·58	1·79
ce	–	·77	·90	1·06	1·35	1·54
ej	–	·45	·52	·60	·75	·87
cd	–	·13	·15	·18	·23	·26
dg	–	·13	·15	·18	·23	·26
gh	–	·49	·57	·67	·86	·95
cg	–	·36	·42	·49	·63	·70

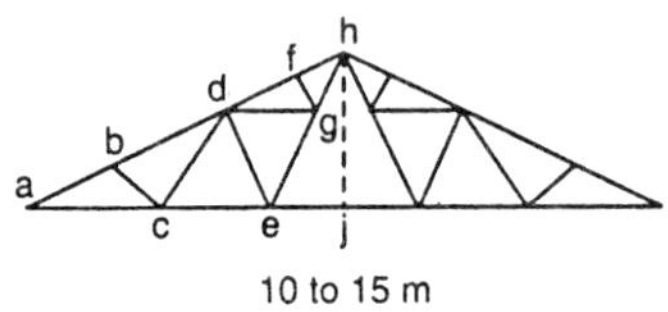

H. Without camber

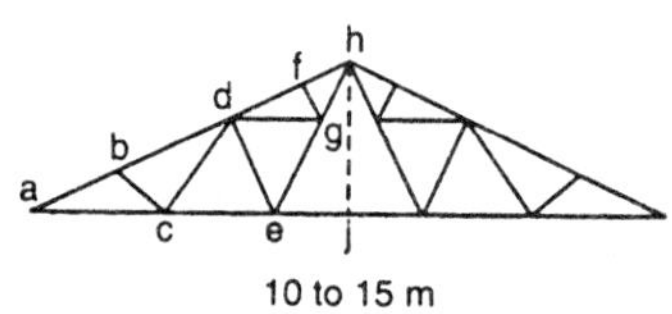

With camber = Rise/6

Member of truss	Kind of stress	Stress coefficient		Length co-efficient
		Dead load (vertical)	Wind load (normal) to roof surface)	
ab	+	1·03	1·21	·093
bd	+	·94	1·10	·093
de	+	·95	1·21	·093
eg	+	·91	1·21	·093
gj	+	·83	1·10	·093
jk	+	·84	1·21	·093
bc	+	·09	·20	·084
dc	+	·09	·20	·084
gh	+	·09	·20	·084
jh	+	·09	·20	·084
ef	+	·22	·50	·140
ac	–	·92	1·49	·156
cf	–	·75	1·12	·156
fl	–	·50	·56	·188
ce	–	·17	·37	·156
eh	–	·17	·37	·156
hk	–	·42	·93	·156
fh	–	·25	·56	·156

S = Span, R = Rise, C = Camber

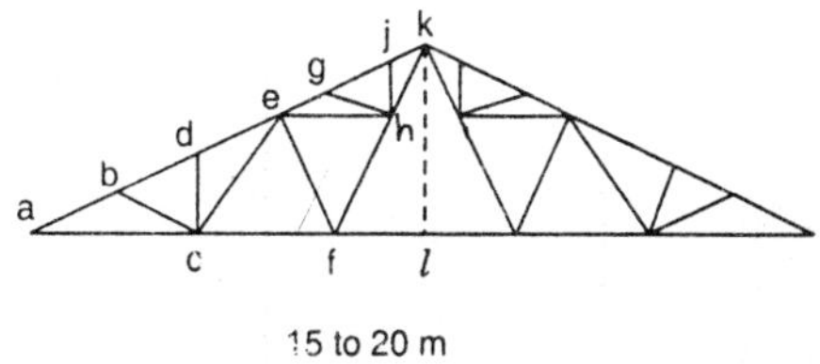

I.

Note :- The above co-efficient are for trusses without camber. If camber is given of say about span/28, loadings may be based on a span of about 20% more to give increased strusses. The rise is : span/4.

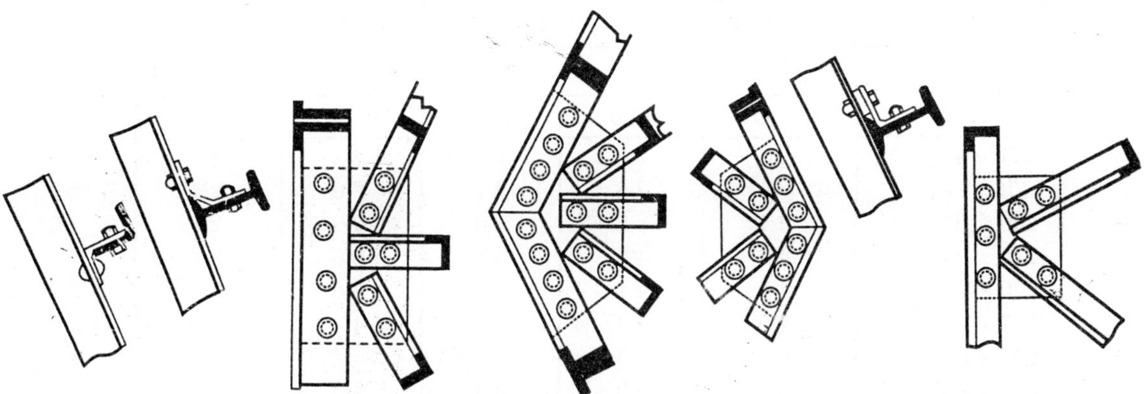

(b) (c)

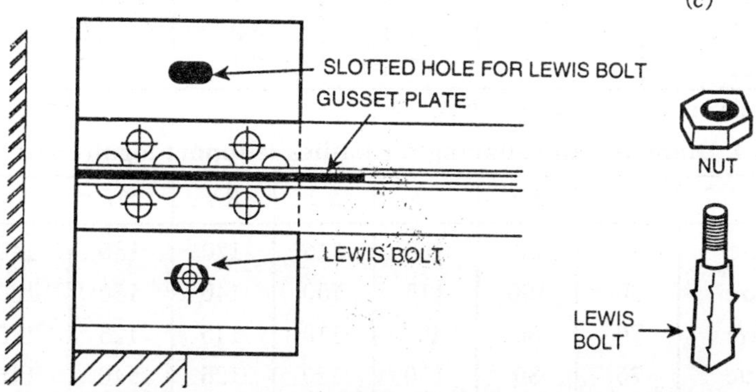

(d)

Fig. 7·45 (*G*) *a* to *d*. Node joints in steel trusses.

Table 7·11. Details of RCC beams on roofs having a load of 500 kg/m² at 300 cm c/c.

Clear span in m	1·5	1·8	2·1	2·4	2·7	3·0
Section in mm	50 × 125	60 × 140	65 × 150	70 × 165	75 × 190	90 × 200
Tensile bar dia. one no. in mm	10	10	10	12	12	14

Details of safe load on kail wood planking in kg/m²

Span in m ↓	*Thickness in mm*				
	25	*40*	*50*	*65*	*75*
0·45	2000	—	—	—	—
0·60	900	3000	—	—	—
0·75	450	1500	3500	—	—
0·90	250	900	2000	4000	—
1·05	—	550	1500	2500	4500
1·20		350	900	1750	**3000**
1·35		250	650	1150	2000
1·50			450	900	1500
1·65			350	650	1150
1·80			250	500	900

For sal multiply by 1·8, for chir 1·4, and for deodar 1·35.

Table 7·13. Spacing of Indian Standard R.S. Joists for different spans in jack arched roofs in metres

Sec. of joist (mm) ↓	*Max. clear span M*					
	0·90	*1·20*	*1·35*	*1·50*	*1·65*	*1·80*
150 × 80	2·8	2·6	2·4	2·2	2·1	2·0
175 × 90	3·0	2·8	2·7	2·6	2·4	2·1
200 × 100	3·4	3·2	3·0	2·9	2·7	2·6
225 × 100	4·2	4·0	3·8	3·6	3·3	3·2
200 × 100	4·4	4·2	4·0	3·8	3·6	3·4
225 × 110	4·9	4·7	4·5	4·3	4·0	3·8
275 × 140	5·6	5·3	5·0	4·7	4·4	4·2
325 × 165	6·3	6·0	5·8	5·5	5·2	5·0
350 × 165	6·7	6·4	6·1	5·9	5·7	5·5
350 × 140	7·7	7·3	6·9	6·6	6·2	5·9
400 × 165	7·8	7·3	7·1	6·8	6·5	6·2

The loads are dead + live = 750 kg/cm².

Table 7·14. Diameter and spacing for ballies (support logs)(Load 500 kg/m²) in mm

Span in m	*1·2*	*1·5*	*1·8*	*2·1*	*2·4*	*2·7*	*3·0*	*3·3*	*3·7*
Deodar 30 cm c/c	75	90	100	115	120	135	140	160	165
45 cm c/c	90	100	115	130	140	150	165	170	185
Sal 30 cm c/c	70	80	95	110	115	125	135	150	160
45 cm c/c	75	80	100	120	125	140	145	165	180

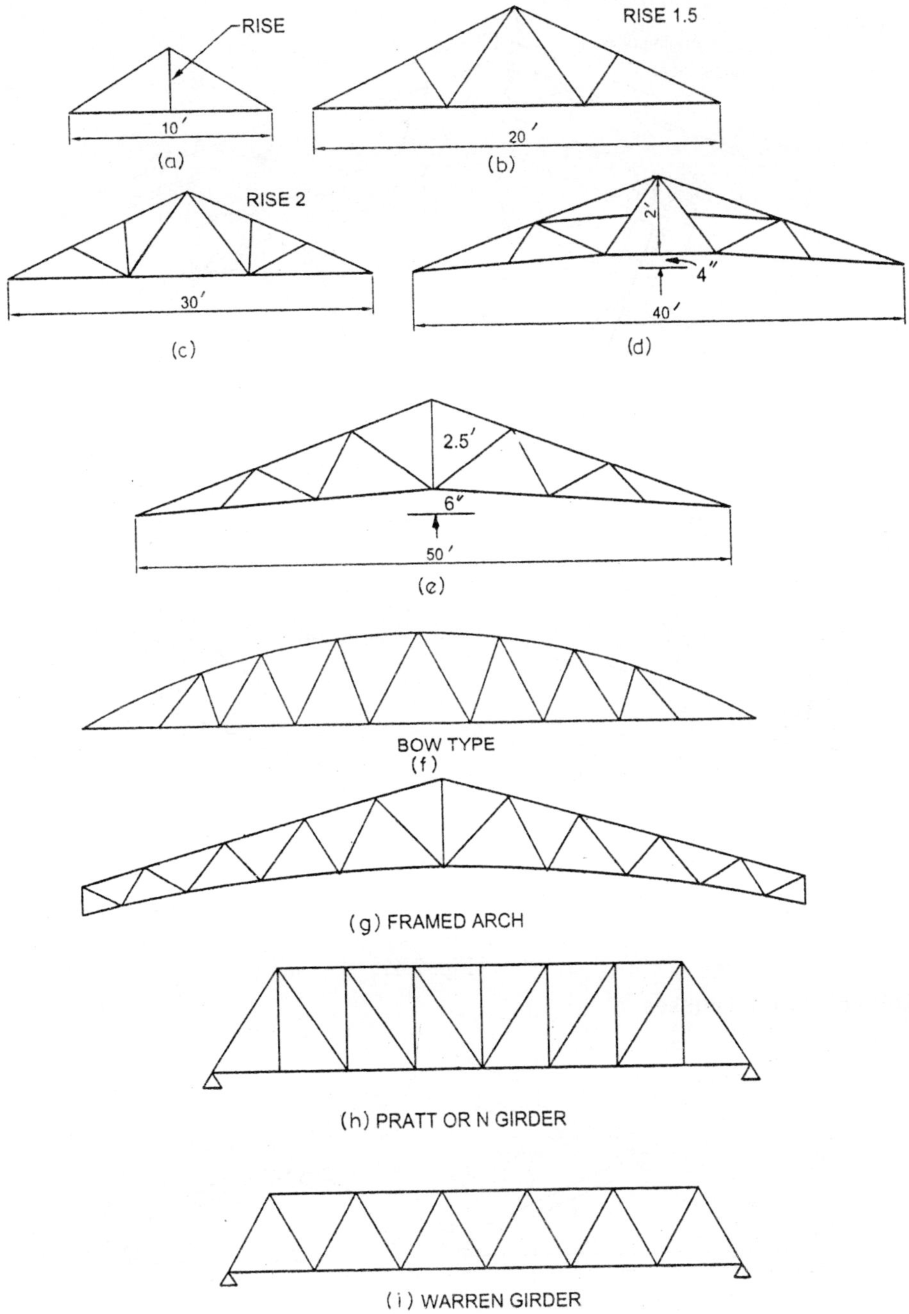

Fig. 7·46. Steel Roofs

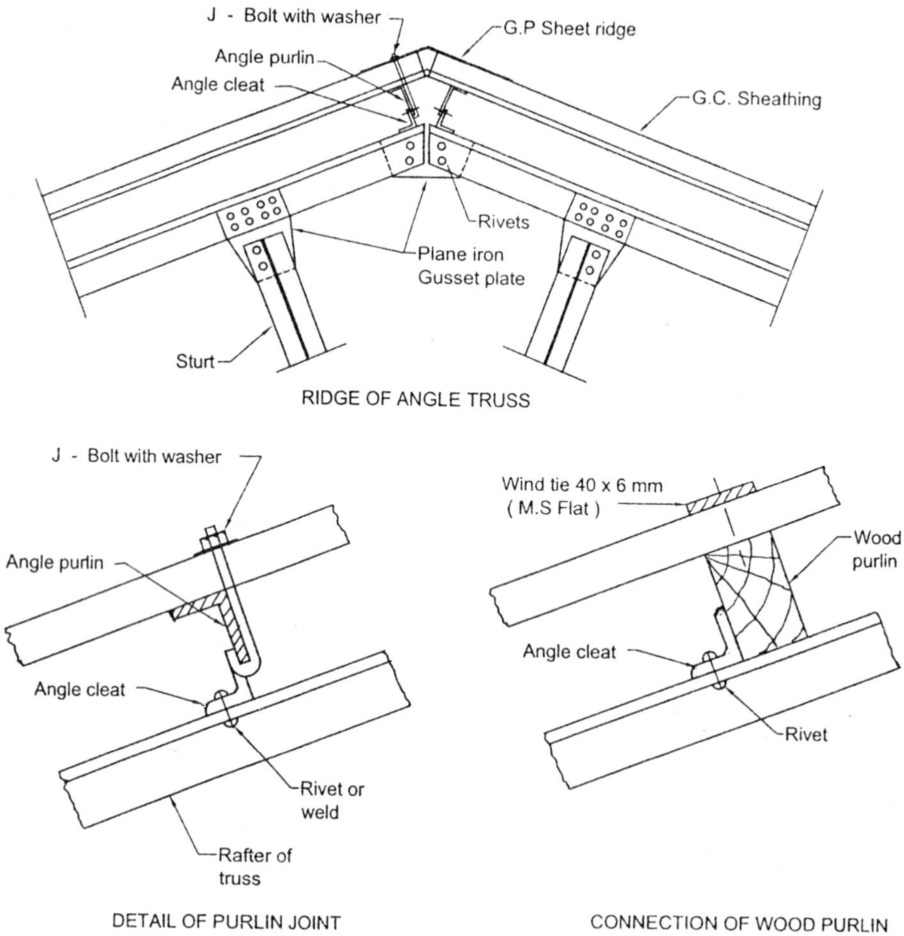

Fig. 7·47.

(1) Details of Wood Trusses

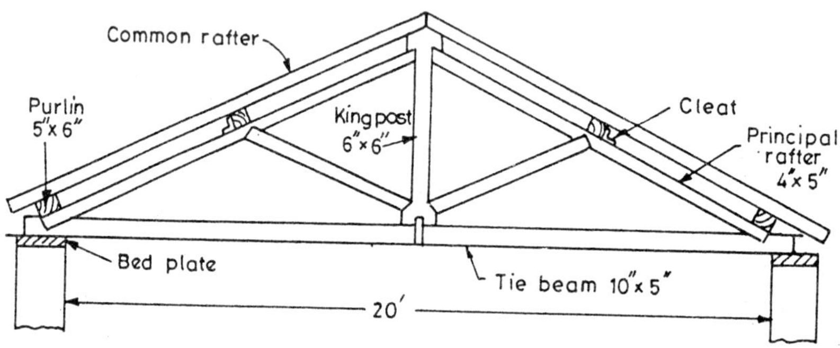

Fig. 7·48 (*a*). King post truss

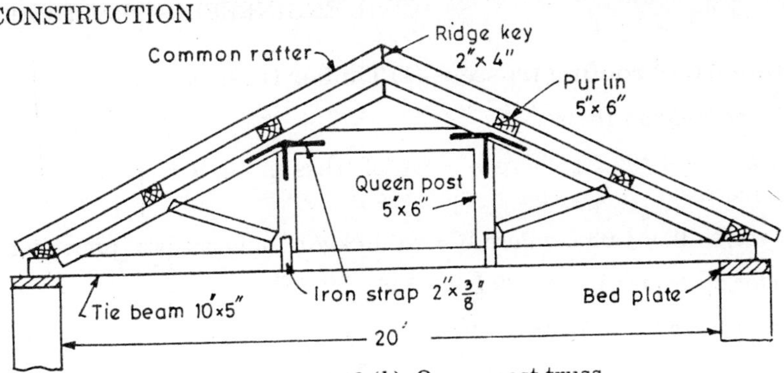

Fig. 7·48 (*b*). Queen post truss

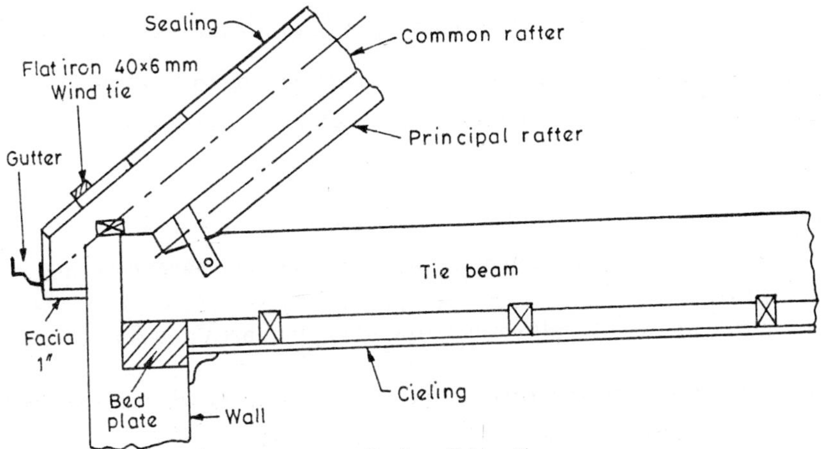

Fig. 7·49. Detail of wall junction

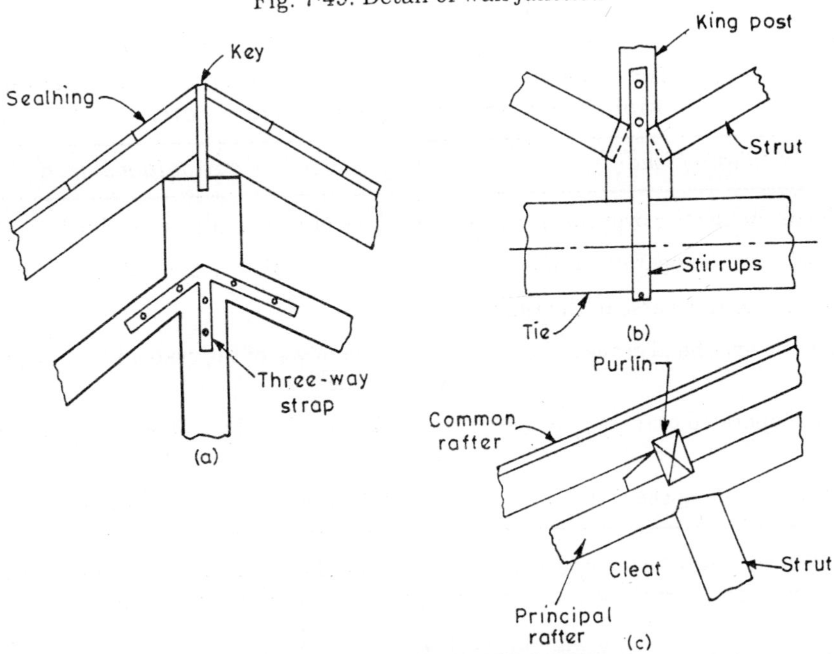

Wood beams of medium type.

SCC in mm : 50 × 95 ; 60 × 110 ; 65 × 120, 75 × 135, 80 × 145, 85 × 160.

Fig. 7·50. Details of king post joint.

Dead loads—Wt. of roofing trusses—(1) **Timber trusses :**

(*a*) *English and Belgian truss* :

$W = 2{\cdot}44\ a\ L(1 + 0{\cdot}492\ L)$ where W = wt. of truss in kg, a = spacing of truss in metres, L = span of truss in metres.

(*b*) *Pitched roofs* : $W = 1{\cdot}03\ L$ where W = wt. in kg/m^2 of horizontal projection of roof.

(*c*) *Flat top for all truss* : $W = 0{\cdot}689\ L + 8{\cdot}545$

(*d*) *Bow string truss* : $W = 0{\cdot}608\ L + 2{\cdot}93$

2. Steel Trusses

(*a*) *Fink type roof truss* : $W = 0{\cdot}0222\ P.A.L.\ (1 + 0{\cdot}3622 \frac{L}{\sqrt{A}}$, W = wt. of truss in kg, P = capacity of truss in kg/m^2 of horizontal projection of roof (150 to 400 kg/m^2)

A = c/c spacing of truss in metres and L = span of truss in metres

(*b*) *Steel truss general* : $W = 0{\cdot}40\left(4{\cdot}42\sqrt{L} + L\right)$

w_2 = wt. of steel truss in kg/sq. m of horizontal area covered.

(*c*) For small spans upto 4 m and pitch 1 : 4 with G.C. sheet covering

$W = \frac{L}{3} + 5$ where W = salt wt. of truss/m^2 of plain area and L = span in metres.

Dead wt. due to partitions. Actual wt. or 100 kg/m^2 whichever is less.

Erection loads. All loads which are probable on the structure during erection period is taken into account.

Live Loads

7·15. Allowance in live loads for gentry crane girders due to vibrations shock, kinetic action and impact of wheels etc.

Type of load	*Additional load*
(*a*) Vertical loads for electric over head cranes	25% of max. static wheel load
(*b*) Vertical load for hand operated cranes	10% of max. wheel loads
(*c*) Horizontal forces transverse to the rails	
(1) For electric over head cranes	10% of wt. of the crab and the wt. lifted by the crane
(2) For hand operated cranes	5% of wt. of the crab and the wt. lifted by the crane
(*d*) Horizontal forces along the rails	5% of the static wheel loads.

(1) The horizontal forces specified in (*c*) and (*d*) should be considered as acting at rail level and being approximately transmitted to the supporting system for both electric and hand operated cranes.

(2) Gantry girders and their vertical supports should be designed on the assumption that either of the horizontal loads (*c*) and (*d*) may act at the same time as the vertical load.

Table 7·16. Increase of live loads due to impact or vibrations

Structure	Impact factor
(*a*) For frames supporting lifts and hoists	100%
(*b*) For foundations, footings and pier supporting lifts and hoisting apparatus	40%
(*c*) For light machinery, shaft or motor units	20% min
(*d*) For reciprocating machinery or power units	50% min

Table 7·17. Live loads on floors (IS)

Loading class No.	*Type of floors*	*Min. live load kg/m² of floor area*	*Alternative min. live load*
1	2	3	4
200	Residential floors, including dwelling houses, floors of tenements, hospitals wards, bed rooms in hotels and dormetories.	200	Subjected to min. of 2·5 times the value in col. (3) for any given slab panel and six times the value in col. (3) for any given beam.
250	Office floors, other than enterance halls, floor of light work rooms. **Note :** The lower value of 250 kg/m² should be taken when separate storage facilities are provided and the higher value of 400 kg/m² should be taken when such provisions are lacking.	250-400	The total load shall be assumed to be uniformly distributed on the entire area of the slab panel or the entire length of the beam.
300	Floors of banking halls, office enterance halls and reaching rooms.	300	
400	Shop floors used for the display and sale of mercandise, floors of work rooms generally, floors of class rooms in schools, floors of places of assembly with fixed seating, churches restaurants, circulation space in machinery halls, power stations etc. occupied by no plants or equipments.	400	Subjected to a min. total load of 2·5 tonnes the value in col. (3) for any given panel and six times the value in col. (3) for any given beam.
500	Floors of ware houses, workshops, factories and other buildings or part of building of similar category for light wt. loads, office floors for storage and filling purposes, floors of places of assembly without fixed seating, public rooms in hotels, dance halls, waiting halls etc.	500	The total load shall be assumed to be uniformly distributed on the entire area of the slab panel or the entire length of the beam.
750	Floors or warehouses, workshop, factories and other buildings or part of buildings of similar category for med. wt. loads.	750	

Table contd...

Table contd...

Loading class No.	*Type of floors*	*Min. live load kg/m² of floor area*	*Alternative min. live load*
1	2	3	4
1000	Floors of warehouses, workshops, factories and other buildings or part of buildings of similar category for heavy wt. loads. Floors of book stores and libraries and roof and pavement, light over basement projecting under the public footpath.	1000	
Stairs	Stairs, landing and corridors for class 200 loading but not liable to over crowding. Stairs, landings and corridors for class 200 loading but liable to over crowding and for all other classes.	300	Subjected to a min. of 130 kg concentrated load at the unsupported end of each step for stairs constructed out of structurally independent cantilever step.
Balconies	Balconies not liable to over crowding (*a*) for class 200 loading (*b*) for all other classes (*c*) Balconies liable to over crowding	 300 500 500	
Garage (light)	Floors for garages for vehicles not exceeding 2·5 tonnes gross wt. (*a*) slab (*b*) Beam	400 400 250	Or combination of actual wheel load whichever is greater subjected to min. of 1½ times the max. wheel load, but not less than 900 kg over 75 cm. sq.
Garage (heavy)	Floors for garages for vehicles not exceeding 4 tonnes gross wt.	750	

Note : (1) Reference to a floor includes a reference to any part of that floor and a reference to slabs includes boarding and beams or ribs spaced not further apart than one metre between centres and a reference to beams means all other beams and ribs.

(2) Fixed seating implies that the removal of the seating and the use of the space for other purposes is improvable. The max. likely load in this case is therefore closely controlled.

(3) The load classification for stairs, corridors, balconies and landings provide for the fact that these often save several occupancies and are used for transporting the furniture and goods.

(4) The loading in workshops, warehouses and factories varies considerably and so there loading, under the terms light, med. and heavy are introduced in order to allow for more economical designs, but the terms have no special meaning in themselves other than the live load for which the relevant floor is designed. It is however important particularly in the case of heavy wt. loads, to assess the actual loads to ensure that they are not in excess of 1000 kg/m² in cases where they are in excess, the design shall be based on the actual loading.

Table 7·18. Live loads on roofs

S. No.	*Type of roof*	*Live load measured on plan*	*Min. line load measured on plan*
1	2	3	4
1.	Flat, sloping or curved roof with slopes upto and including 10°.		

Table contd...

Table contd...

S. No.	*Type of roof*	*Live load measured on plan*	*Min. line load measured on plan*
1	2	3	4
	(*a*) Access provided (*b*) Access not provided for maintenance	150 kg/m^2 75 kg/m^2	(*a*) 375 kg uniformly distributed load over any span of 1 m width of the roof slab and 900 kg uniformly distributed over the span in case of all beams. (*b*) 190 kg uniformly distributed over any span of one m width of the roof slab and 450 kg uniformly distributed over the span in case of beams.
2.	Sloping roofs with slope greater than 10°.	75 kg/m^2 (–) 1 kg/m^2 for every degree increase in slope over 10° upto and including 20° and 2 kg/m^2 for every degree increase in slope over 20°.	Subjected to a min. of 40 kg/m^2.
3.	Curved roofs with slope at springing greater than 10°.	(75 – 345 λ^2) kg/m^2 where $\lambda = h/l$, h = height of the highest points of the structure measured from its springing l = chord width of the roof if singly curved and shorter of the two sides if doubly curved.	Subjected to a min. of 450 kg/m^2.

Note : For special type of roofs with highly permeable and absorbant materials, the contigency of roof material increasing in wt. due to absorption of moisture shall be provided.

The following values of live loads are useful for design.

(*a*) Elevator machine room 1000 kg/m^2

(*b*) Ice skating sink 1250 kg/m^2

(*c*) Telephone exchange room 1000 kg/m^2

(*d*) Transformer room 1000 kg/m^2

The lower values of 250 kg/m^2 should be taken where separate storage facilities are provided and the higher value of 450 kg/m^2 should be taken where such provisions are lacking.

Concentrated live loads with impact and vibrations. This load is due to the installed machinery. The impact factor should not be less than 20% for light machinery. Provisions should also be made while the equipment is being installed or moved for servicing and repairs.

Table 7·19 A. Horizontal load on parapets and balustrades

	Description	*H or load in kg/m run*
(*a*)	Stairways, landings and balconies (Private and domestic)	
	Internal	35
	External	75
(*b*)	All other stairways, parapets and hand rail to roofs	75
(*c*)	Parapets and balustrades in places of assemly likely to be overcrowded	225

Snow Loads. In may be assumed to be 2·5 kg/m^2 per cm depth of snow. In cases where the roof slope is greater than 50°, snow load considerations may be neglected, however if there is any possibility of snow accumulation it must be taken into account.

Loads due to rain. If there is any possibility of accumulation of rain water. The loads must be live loads on roofs load due to this accumulated rain water.

Reduction in floor live loads. In designing columns, walls, piers, their support and foundations, following reduction should be made.

Table 7·19 B.

No. of floors carried by the member	*Percentage reduction on all floors above the member considered*
1	0
2	10
3	20
4	30
5 or more	40

Note : No reduction is made for warehouses, garages, stores and factories and workshops designed for 500 kg/m^2. However factories and workshops designed for live load more than 500 kg/m^2 - the above reduction may be provided that the loading assumed for any column etc. is not less than it would have been if all floors had been designed for 500 kg/m^2 with no reduction.

(1) **Wind loads : Duchemins Formula—**

$$P_n = P\frac{2 \sin \alpha}{1+\sin^2 \alpha} \; ; \; P_H = P\frac{2 \sin^2 \alpha}{1+\sin^2 \alpha} \; ; \; P_V = \frac{2 \sin \alpha \cos \alpha}{1+\sin^2 \alpha}$$ where P = wind pressure on surface normal to the direction of the wind.

P_n = component of wind pressure normal to the inclined roof surface, α = angle which the inclined roof surface makes with the horizontal direction of wind. P_H = horizontal component and P_V is the vertical component.

Table 7·20. The pressures on the roofs based on Duchemen's formula

Slope of roof	*Values of X*				
	3 α = *33° -41′*	$2\sqrt{3}$ α = 30°	*4* α = 26° - 34′	5 α = *21° - 48′*	6 α = *18° - 26′*
$P_n = P_X$	0·848	0·800	0·745	0·653	0·575
$P_V = P_X$	0·706	0·693	0·667	0·606	0·545
$P_H = P_X$	0·471	0·400	0·333	0·242	0·182

In exposed positions 150 kg/m^2 wind pressure on surfaces normal to the direction of wind is sufficient and for protected wind pressure the value of 100 to 125 kg/m^2 can be taken.

(2) **Wind pressure**, $P = ½ K\rho V^2$ where ρ = density of air, V = vel. of wind, K is a constant

depending on the shape and size of obstruction and direction of wind. The density of wind may be taken as 0·006, hence

$$P = 0{\cdot}003\, KV^2$$

Wind pressure on independent lean to roofs

$w = \pm p \sin \alpha$ where w = wind pressure on roofs in kg/m^2.

p = basic wind pressure, α = inclination of roof with the horizontal.

The inclination α and inclined length s of the independently standing lean to roofs are known. For values of α, the value of l/s can be seen from the curve. Knowing s, the value of l can be found out. Knowing the value of l the position of the line of action of R can be found out for l refer figure.

Basic wind pressure *p*. It is an equivalent static pressure in the direction of flow of wind. It is decided by the appropriate authority having regard to local meteorological data.

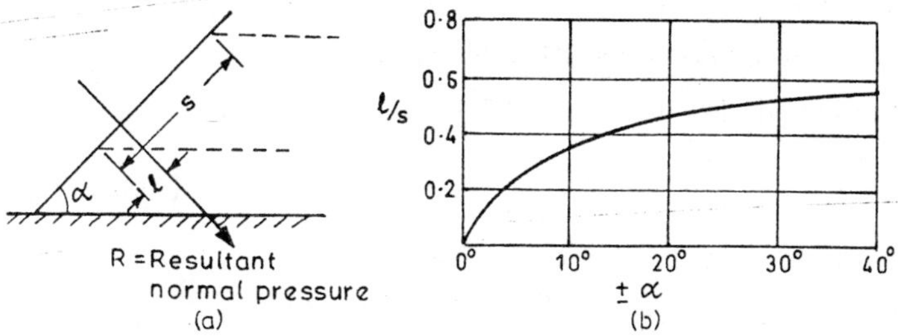

Fig. 7·51.

7·20. Forms of Carpentry Joints

Table 7·21.

Material	*Safe pressure in lbs/in²*			*Remarks*
	Tension	*Comp.*	*Shear*	
Pine	1100	1100		Stress in timber varies widely hence take I.S. values or obtain in laboratory
Oak	1800	1500		
Teak	1800	1500		
Steel	18000	18000	14000	

Example for lap joint

Area of timber sec. = 6 × 6 = 36 sq. in.

Area of strap = 8(1½ × 3/8) = 4·5 sq. in. (for 8 straps of 1½″ × 3/8″)

Area of bolts in single shear = 4·5 sq. in. + (equal to the strap area)

Use 7/8″ dia. bolts, 8 Nos. (area of one bolt = 6 sq. in.)

Check : Load taken by wood section = 36 × 1100 = 39,600 lbs (Pine wood)

Load taken by strap iron + bolts = 4·5 × 18000 = 81,000 lbs

For single shear 81000/2 = 40,500 (safe)

Example for fish joint

Bolts are staggered hence one hole area is deducted from wood sec.

Net area of wood sec. = 6(6 – 7/8) = 30·75 sq. in

Resistance taken by wood sec. $= \dfrac{1100 \times 30{\cdot}75}{2240} = 15{\cdot}3$ tons

Area required for bolt in double shear = $\frac{30 \cdot 75 \times 1100}{18000} = 1 \cdot 9$ sq. in

Mod. ratio $= \frac{1100}{18000} = \frac{1}{16}$

No. of bolts = $\frac{1 \cdot 9}{\cdot 60} = 3 \cdot 2$ or 3 bolts can be used each side of joint ; Sec. area required for steel plate = sec. area required for bolts = 1·92 sq. in. Use 3/8″ plate, 3″ wide.

Area of two nos. steel plates = 2 × 3/8 × 3 = 2·25 sq. in (safe) (against required 1·92 sq. in)

Note : If other side is used by wood plate, the steel plate is used one. If a fished plate is notched in timber by 3/4″ its resistance in shear is increased, hence fish plates notched in timber are stronger than wood plates.

Now effective sec. of wood 6(6 – 2 × 3/4) = 27 sq. in

Area of bolts required in double shear = 27 × 1/16 = 1·7 sq. in

No. of bolts $= 1 \cdot 7 \times \frac{1}{0 \cdot 60} = 2 \cdot 8$ (say 3 on each side of joint)

Area of plate in single shear = 1/8 × 27 = 3·37 sq. in

Thickness of plates = 3·36 ÷ 2 × 6 = 0·28 = 3/8″

Example for Scarf joint

Net area of wood sec. = 8(6 – 3/4) = 42 sq. in

Resistance borne by wood sec $= \frac{42 \times 1120}{2240} = 21$ tons

Area required per bolt in single shear = 21/8 = 2·63 sq. in

No. of 3/4″ bolt $= \frac{2 \cdot 63}{0 \cdot 44} = 6$ Bolts.

Thickness of plate required $= \frac{21}{2 \times 5 \cdot 25 \times 8} = 0 \cdot 25$ in

(5·25 ton per sq. inch being the strength of steel plate of *w.i* in tension)

Let length of the timber be l inch

then $\frac{l \times \frac{2}{3} \times 8 \times 2 \times 150}{2240} = 21$ (assume 2/3 of depth is available for shear along two lines of bolts and 150 strength in shear of wood)

or $l = 29 \cdot 4$ in.

So length of scarf = 30″ and the spacing of bolts = 17″ leaving 6″ on either side.

Forms of joints

Notching—Members resting on other members are notched to have a firm bearing and for adjusting heights.

Cogging—Where one member crosses the other, cogging is used for firm bearing.

Halving—Members crossing each other and are required to flush on one or two faces and have a similar sinking in both to fit each other halved together.

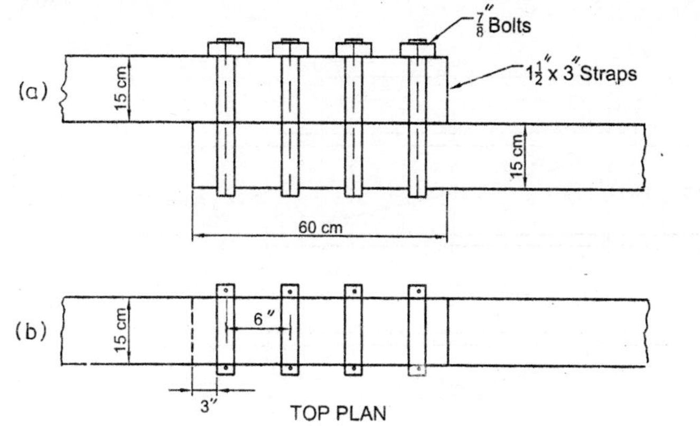

LAP JOINTS

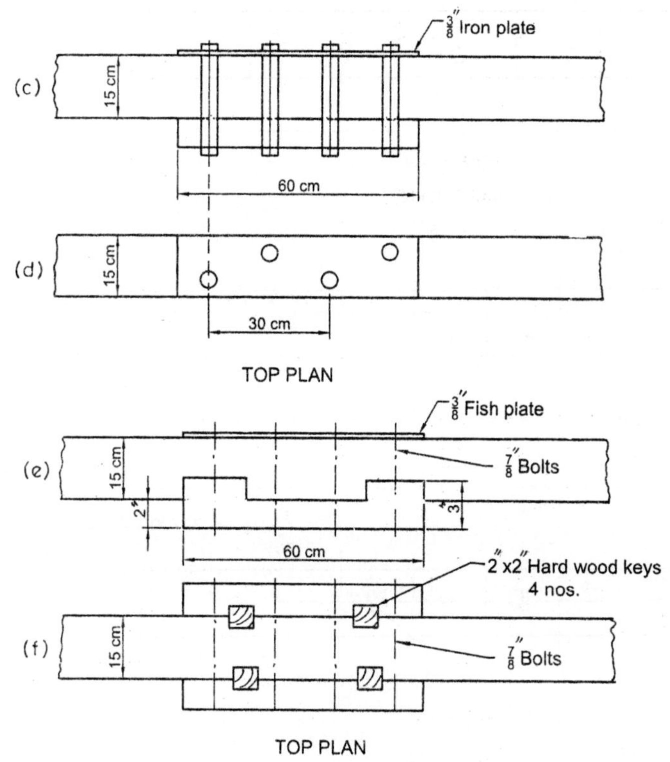

A–FISHED JOINTS

Lap joint— Efficiency is 100%, shrinkage in timber would allow sliding between members. Hence used for temporary purposes.

Fished joint— Satisfactory for tension as well as comp. if iron fish plates are used. If wood plates are used they would require longer than shown for obtaining necessary shearing area.

Fig. 7·52 (*a*) to (*f*).

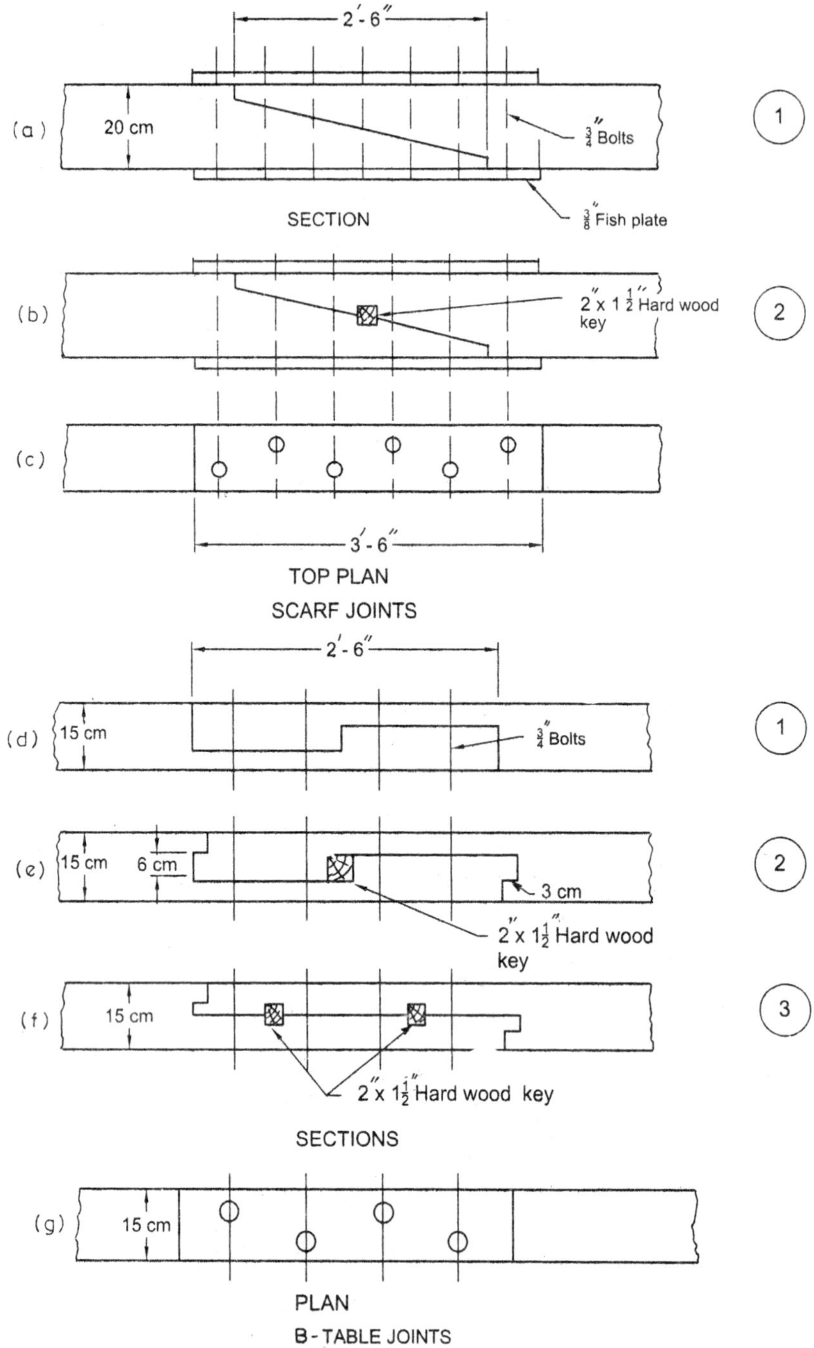

Scarf joint— It's efficiency is 90%. It is used in important structures.

Table joint— Its efficiency is low, as a large amount of section is cut away. These are suitable for lengthening members.

Fig. 7·53 (*a*) to (*g*).

7·21. Building Bye Laws

General terms—Lobby— A central sitting place in a building.

Balcony. A projection including a hand rail or balustrade to serve as passage or sitting out place on floors, locally called "Barja".

Basement or celler— A lower storey of a building below or partly below ground level locally known as "Tehkhana".

Ledge—A shelf like projection supported in any manner what so ever except by means of vertical supports with in a room not having a projection more than a metre locally known as "Tand".

Loft—An intermediate floor between two floors or a residential space in a pitched roof above normal floor level with a max. height of 1·5 m which is constructed or adopted for storage use. Locally known as "duchhatti or Barsati".

Mezzanine floor—An intermediate floor between two floors above ground level. Its head room is more than a loft and used as living.

Corridor—Covered passage in a building.

Exit—Way to go out.

Alleys—Space at the dead end of a road, so as to make a space to turn the vehicle.

Skirting or dado—A strip of flooring raised on the side of walls.

Duarf walls—A wall under verendah or door opening below sill.

Attached pier—A pier which is attached or abutted with a wall.

Porch or porticos—An external construction forming a covered approach to a building.

Chimney—An upright shaft containing one or more flues provided for the conveyance to the outer air of any product of combustion, resulting from the operation of any heat producing appliance.

Detached building—A building whose walls and roofs are independent of any other building with open spaces on all sides as specified.

Semidetached building—A building whose walls and roofs are not independent of other building on all sides except one or two sides.

Mercantile building—Buildings used as shops, stores or market for sale of merchandise purposes.

Hazardous building. Buildings used for manufacturing or processing explosives material or products.

Parapet. A low wall or railing build along the edge of a roof or a floor.

Parking. A area enclosed or unenclosed sufficient in size to park vehicles together with a drive way connected the parking space.

Plinth. The position of a structure between the level of surrounding ground and level of the floor immediately above ground.

Row housing. A row of houses with only front rear and interior open spaces.

Set back line. A line usually parallel to the flat boundaries and laid in each case by the local authority, beyond which nothing can be constructed towards the site boundaries.

Site Interior or Tandor. A site access to which by a passage from a street together with such passage forms part of site.

Storey. The position of a building included between the surface of any floor and the surface of the floor next above it or if there is no floor above it, then the space between any floor and the roof above it.

Street level or grade. The level of the centre line of the street.

Site Plan. Plan showing location of a building at site showing location on all the four directions and streets

Key Plan. A plan showing location of building in the city locating routes and streets to access its location in the city.

Service Plan. A plan showing position of service lines of water supply and drainages etc.

Floor area ratio. (FAR) = $\dfrac{\text{Total covered area of all floors}}{\text{Plot area}}$

Tot-lot – Children's Park

Note : For area definition see "estimating and costing".

Site coverage. The max. covered area for different classes of buildings should be as follows.

(*a*) **Buisness and Commercial Premises.** Should be extended upto 75% of the total area of plot provided that there is sufficient arrangements for off streets facilities for parking loading and unloading of vehicles on the same plot of building.

(*b*) **Industrial Premises.** The covered area may be extended upto 60% of total area of plot provided that the remaining area is sufficient for parking, loading and unloading facilities.

(*c*) **Educational Buildings.** The total built up area on any floor should not be more than 30% of the plot area. The remaining area provided for play grounds and recreational spaces etc.

(*d*) **Residential Buildings— It is as follows :**

Table 7·22

S. No.	*Area of plot*	*Max. permissible covered area*
1.	Upto 200 m^2	66% of plot area on ground floor
		66% of plot area on 1st floor
		On 2nd floor nil except a barsati having 25% of the ground floor
2.	Above 200 to 500 m^2	50% of the plot area or 133 m^2 whichever is more
3.	Above 500 to 1000 m^2	40% of the plot area or 250 m^2 whichever is more
4.	Above 1000 m^2	$33^1/_3$% of the plot area or 400 m^2 whichever is more.

Open Spaces

Table 7·23. Industrial Buildings—The open spaces should be as follows :

S. No.	*Plot size*	*Front* *m*	*Rear* *m*	*Left side* *m*	*Right side* *m*
1.	Upto 150 m^2	3·0	1·5	—	1·5
2.	150 to 200 m^2	3·0	2·0	—	2·0
3.	200 to 250 m^2	3·5	2·0	—	2·5
4.	250 to 300 m^2	3·5	2·5	1·5	2·5
5.	300 to 350 m^2	4·0	2·5	2·0	2·5
6.	350 to 400 m^2	5·0	3·0	2·5	2·5
7.	400 to 450 m^2	5·0	3·0	2·5	3·0
8.	450 to 500 m^2	5·0	3·0	2·5	3·0
9.	500 to 550 m^2	5·5	3·0	2·5	3·0
10.	550 to 1000 m^2	6·0	4·5	4·5	4·5
11.	1000 to 5000 m^2	9·0	4·5	4·5	4·5
12.	5000 to 30,000 m^2	9·0	9·0	4·5	4·5
13.	Above 30,000 m^2	15·0	15·0	15·0	15·0

In case of commercial areas for shopping centre 3·0 m min. open space should be in front and rear. No side space is necessary if they are developed in new scheme.

Rear space is not necessary for back to back shopping centres and for private developed shopping schemes.

Building for business, assembly, mercantile, educational and institutional should have a min. front up in space of 9 m. Side and rear open spaces should be 6 m unless or otherwise specified in relevant cases for special occupancies.

Residential Buildings

Every room intended for habitation should abut on an interior or exterior open space or a verendah.

Exterior Open Spaces. (*a*) Front open space—The min. width is 3 m. In case of two or more sides fronting a street an average width of 3 m, but in no case less than 1·8 m. The above rule is for buildings facing a road upto 12 m in width. In cases of existing built up areas facing the streets less than 7 m, the open space from the centre line of the street to the face of the building should not be less than 4·5.

For plots facing roads upto 18 m in width, the min. front open space should be 4·5 m. The roads more than 18 m in width, the min. front open space is 6 m.

(*b*) **Rear Open Space.** Every building should have a rear yard opening, which forms an integral part of it of an average width of 3 m.

(*c*) **Side Open Space.** Every semi classified and detached building should have side open space forming an integral part of the site not less than 3 m in width.

In case of corner plots the open space should be left on the side having narrower street and if the roads are of the equal width, the space should be left along the longer side of the plot.

(*a*) For heights of buildings above 10 m and upto 25 m there should be increased in the open space at the rate of 1 m for every 3 m or part thereof in height. For heights of buildings above 25 m there should be an increase at the rate of 1 m for every 5 metre upto 30 m. Above 30 m there should be a max. width of 16 m.

Interior Open Spaces. Interior open space such as courtyards etc. should be provided if the habitatble rooms do not abut to any exterior open space not less than 3 m in width.

Exceptions for Open Spaces. (1) A cornice, sun shade or a chhajja not exceeding the width of 0·75 m.

(2) A cantilever portico 2·4 m wide and 4·5 m long in the side set back over the enterance with no access to the top of the portico for use as a sit out place (The height of portico should be at least 2·1 m from the plinth level).

(3) A garage at the rear end of the side open space which will be accountable in the total built up area.

Note : No balcony should be provided within the min. open spaces required.

In case of proposals for erection (alteration of building in existing built up areas on street less than 4 m in width the new plot line shall be set back at 2 m from the centre line of the street and the front open space shall be as per existing provision subject to a min. of 1·5 m.

In case of buildings which are more than 25 years old in existing built up area, the proposed construction on the old structural wall shall be permitted. Subject to permissible coverage of 50% on 1st floor only.

In existing built up areas the coverage shall be governed by the rules given in the table for "covered areas for residential buildings". (Table 7·22)

Basements or semi basements may be provided subject to the condition that the coverage shall be 40% and the height of basement or semi basement shall be max. of 0·9 m from the existing road-level. If there is any violation of this construction shall be counted in calculation of FAR.

Table 7·24. Colouring of Plans

S.No.	*Items*	*Site Plan*			*Building Plan*		
		White Plan	*Blue Print*	*Amm. Print*	*White Plan*	*Blue Print*	*Amm. Print*
1.	Plot lines	Thick Black	Thick Black	Thick Black	Thick Black	Thick Black	Thick Black
2.	Existing street	Green	Green	Green	—	—	—
3.	Future street if any	Green dotted	Green dotted	Green dotted	—	—	—
4.	Permissible build line	Thick Black dotted	Thick black dotted	Thick black dotted	—	—	—
5.	Open spaces	No colour	No colour	No colour	No colour	No colour	No colour
6.	Existing work	Black (out line)	White	Blue	Black	White	Blue
7.	Work proposed for demolition	Yellow hatched	Yellow hatched	Yellow hatched	Yellow hatched	Yellow hatched	Yellow hatched
8.	Proposed work	Red (filled)	Red	Red	Red	Red	Red
9.	Drainage and sewerage work	Red dotted	Red dotted	Red dotted	Red dotted	Red dotted	Red dotted
10.	Water supply work	Black dotted thin	Black dotted thin	Black dotted thin	Black dotted thin	Black dotted thin	Black dotted thin

Table 7·25. Distances of buildings from electric lines (Indian electric rules)

Particular of line	*Vert. distance (m)*	*Hor. distance (m)*
(*a*) Low and med. voltage lines & service lines	2·5	1·2
(*b*) High voltage lines upto and including 33000 volts	3·7	2·0
(*c*) Extra high voltage lines beyond 33000 volts	3·7	2·0
	Plus 0·3 m for every additional 33000 volts or thereof.	Plus 0·3 m for every additional 33000 volts or part thereof.

Requirements of Plots

Interior sites. Means of access of min. width of 3·6 m to reach the site from the street is provided.

Area of Plots. Min. area of 125 sq. m, min. width 6 m and average depth 12 m. In caseof reconstruction in thickly populated area, it can be reduced to 55 sq. m for housing schemes for weaker sections upto 40 sq. m and width 3·6 m.

For industrial area, the min. size of the plot should be 550 sq. m. For service and light industries it can be reduced to 150 sq. m with a min. width of 9 m.

Min. plot area for shops should be 15 sq. m with a min. width of 2·4 m.

In case of plots for assembly occupancies like cinema the min. width of plot should be 30 m and it should front a street not less than 8 m. In case of newly developed areas out side the existing built up area the width of plot for assembly occupancies should not be less than 45 m and should front a street of width not less than 30 m.

Table 7·26 (*a*). App. requirement of floor area and cubic space in buildings (Code of building bye-laws)

Type of Building	*Floor area per head sq. m.*	*Cubic space per head, cu. m.*	*Verendah area %*	*Area taken by walls*
Residential	2·5-3·0	9	10-20	15-20
School	1·0-2·0	4·2	10-20	15-20
Hostel	7·0-10·0	3·0	25-35	15-20
Hospital	8·0-10·0	3·0	25-35	15-20
Factory	2·5-3·0	9-12	25-35	10
Office	2·5-3·0	12-15	25-35	10

Tabl 7·26 (*b*). Size of rooms etc. in Residential buildings (Code of Building Bye-laws)

Room	*Standard in m*	*Ordinary in m*
1. Drawing room	4·2 × 4·8	5·2 × 4·8
2. Dinning room	4·2 × 4·8	Drawing cum dinning
3. Bed room	4·2 × 4·8	3·0 × 4·2
4. Office	3·0 × 3·6	—
5. Guest-room	3·0 × 3·6	—

Table contd...

Table contd...

Room	Standard in m	Ordinary in m
6. Kitchen	3·0 × 3·6	2·5 × 3·0
7. Stone	3·0 × 3·6	2·5 × 3·0
8. Pantry	2·5 × 3·0	2·5 × 3·0
9. W.C. bath combined	1·8 × 2·5	1·8 × 1·8
10. Latrine	1·8 × 2·5	1·2 × 1·2
11. Bath	1·8 × 2·5	1·2 × 1·2
12. Box room	1·8 × 1·8	—
13. Verendah	2·5 to 3·0 wide	1·8 to 2·5 wide
14. Garage	3·0 × 6·0	—
15. Servant room	3·0 × 3·0	3·6
16. Height of main rooms	3·5 × 4·8	2·7 to 3·0
17. Height of other rooms	3·0	2·7 to 3·0

Requirements of Parts of Buildings

Size and area requirements :

1. (*a*) **Habitable rooms :** Min. floor area = 9·5 sq. m and min width = 2·4 m

(*b*) **Rooms of educational Hostels :** Min. size = 7·5 sq. m for single person.

(*c*) **For Double Bedding :** One should not be less than 9·5 sq. m and the other not less than 7·5 sq. m.

(*d*) **For weaker sections :** Single room tenement, one room with min. 9·5 sq m area and min width of 2·4 m and a multipurpose space of area not less than 4·0 sq. m with min. width of 1·5 m.

(*e*) **For double room tenements**, there shall be a living room not less than 9·5 sq. m in area and another room not less than 7·5 sq. m in area.

Kitchen. The area of the kitchen shall not be less than 5·0 sq. m. with the min. width of 1·8 m, where there is a separate store, the size of kitchen may be reduced to 4·5 sq. m. A kitchen which is integrated for eating purposes also, it must have a min. floor area of not less than 9·5 sq. m with a min width of 2·4 m.

In case of a single room tenement a kitchen is not necessary, while for double room tenement kitchen shall not be less than 3 sq. m in area with min. width of 1·2 m.

Bathrooms and water closets. The size of a bath room shall not be less than 1·5 sq. m with the min. width of 1·2 m. A combined bath and water closet must have a floor area not less than 2·8 sq. m with a min width of 1·2 m. The min. floor area for water closet shall be 1·1 sq. m with a min. width of 0·9 m.

Mazzanine floors. If it is used as a living room, the min. floor area shall be 9·5 sq. m. The aggregate area of such mazzanine floor shall be not more than 33·3% of the plinth area of the building.

Loft. Where lofts are provided in kitchen and in other areas, the max. coverage shall be limited to 25% of the room size. Lofts in residential buildings shall be permitted above the corridor space.

Garage. The size of the garage shall be min. of 2·75 × 5·3 m.

Height

Habitable rooms. 2·75 m measured from top of floor to the lowest point of the ceiling, slab or arch. In case of air conditioned rooms a height not less than 2 m from top of floor to bottom of false ceiling. The min. head room under beams shall be 2·4 m.

Kitchen—Not less than 2·75 m.

Bathrooms and water closets—Not less than 2·75 m.

Loft—Head room not less than 1·5 m.

Mazzanine floor—Min. height 2·2 m.

Staircase—The min. head room in a passage under the landing must be 2·2 m.

Industrial buildings—The ceiling height shall not be less than 3·6 m.

Corridor—The min. head room under corridor shall be 2·4 m.

Garages—The min. head room under the garage shall be 2·4 m.

Other Requirements—(1) Bathroom or water closet shall :

(*a*) At least one of its walls shall open to external air.

(*b*) not be directly under or over any room except another laterine, washing place, bath or terrace which is perfectly water tight.

(*c*) Provided with an impervious floor covering, sloping towards the drain and not in any veranda room.

(2) No room containing water closets shall be used for any purpose except as a lavatory and no such room shall open directly to any kitchen or cooking space by a door, window or other opening. Every room containing water closet shall have a door completely closing the entrance to it.

(3) **Mezzanine floor.** A mazzanine floor may be permitted over a room or a compartment provided that

(*a*) It is confirmed to the standards of living rooms as regards lighting and ventilation.

(*b*) It is so constructed as not to interference under any circumstances with the ventilation of the space over and under it.

(*c*) Such mezzanine floor is not sub-divided in to smaller compartments.

(*d*) Such mezzanine floor or any part of it shall not be used as a kitchen.

(*e*) In no case a mazzanine floor shall be sub-divided so as to make it liable to be converted into inventilated compartments.

(4) **Plinth.** The plinth of any part of a building shall be so located with respect to the surrounding ground level or crest of the road level provided adequate drainage. It shall be not less than 0·45 m except in case of public housing where it shall be not less than 0·3 m. The indulating and sloping land shall 1·2 m above the drainage or country water level.

(5) Every interior courtyard or garrage shall be raised at least 0·15 m above the level of the surroundings.

(6) **Roof.** It should be such that it may permit effectional drainage of rain water by means of a sufficient rain water pipe. So that rain water may not cause dampness to any part of the building.

The rain water pipe should be connected to the public drainage system. The rain water pipes should also be affixed to the outer walls or in recess or chases cut or formed in the wall.

Boundary Walls. The height of the boundry walls shall be 1·5 m measured from the centre line of the road. The rear or the side walls can be from 2 m to 3 m in height. The height also changes for different type of buildings such as jails, schools, hospitals etc.

Lighting and Ventilation Requirements. Room shall have one or more aperture in the shape of a window, fan light or ventilator, which are directly open in external air or in a verendah not more than 3 m in width. The openings which are directly connected to the open air should be provided with a sun shade at least 30 cm wide, which can be increased to 60 cm according to the opening. These openings should also cover at least 7·5 cm on either side of the opening. If there is no possibility of natural light or air artificial lightening and ventilation provisions should be made by electric light points and air ducts as provided in air conditioned rooms. The area of the ventilation should not be less than 1/10th of the floor area of the room or dwelling excluding door openings.

Table 7·27. Size of the ventilation shafts for high buildings

S. No.	*No. of storey*	*Size in sq. m*	*Min. width*
1	1, 2	1·2	0·9
2	1, 2, 3, 4	2·8	1·2
3	1 to 6	4·0	1·5
4	1 to 8	5·4	1·8
5	1 to 10	8·0	2·4

Exit requirements. (1) Exits should be clearly visible and the routes to reach the exit should be clearly marked and sign posted to guide the population of floor concerned.

(2) Fire fighting equipments should be suitably located and clearly marked.

(3) Alarm devices should be installed to ensure prompt evacuation of population concerned.

(4) Exits should be so arranged that they may be reached without passing through another occupied unit.

(5) Exits should be well ventilated and lighted. There should be no hinderance in the passage.

(6) Their travel distance should not 22·5 m for residential, educational, institutional and hazardous occupancies and 30 m for assembly, business, mercantile, storage and industrial occupancies.

(7) There should not be less than two exits for buildings over 3 storeys in height servicing every floor area and at least one of them should be internal enclosed stairway.

(8) The location, width and number of exits should be in accordance with travel distance.

(9) Capacity of exit—50 cm width is considered to be one unit width of exit. 25 cm will be counted as half. The occupants per unit exit width.

Table 7·28.

Group of occupancies ↓	*No. of Occupants*	
	Stair way	*Doors*
1. Residential	25	75
2. Educational	25	75
3. Institutional	25	75
4. Assembly	60	90
5. Business	50	75
6. Mercantile	50	75
7. Industrial	50	75
8. Storage	50	75
9. Hazardous	25	40

Other requirements of exits

Door ways. (*a*) Every exit door way shall open into an enclosed stairway, a horizontal exit, on a corridor or passage way providing continuous and protected means of Aggress.

(*b*) No exit door way shall be less than 100 cm in width and shall not be less than 200 cm in height.

(*c*) Exit door way shall open out wards, that is away from the room, but shall not obstruct the travel along any exit. This shall not apply to residential buildings upto 3 storey in height. No door when opened shall reduce the required width of stair way or landing to less than 90 cm, over head or sliding should not be installed.

(*d*) Exit door should not open immediately upon a flight or stairs, a landing equal to atleast the width or the door, should be provided in the stairway at each door way, level of the landing should be the same as that of the floor which it serves.

(*e*) Revolving doors should not be used in exits except in residential, business and mercantile occupancies, but should not constitute more than half the total required width. When revolving doors are considered as required the following assumptions should be made.

(*i*) each revolving door shall be erected one half a unit exit width.

(*ii*) Revolving doors should not be located at the foot of a stair way. Any stair way served by a revolving door should discharge through a lobby or foyer.

Stair way requirements. (*a*) Interior stairs shall be constructed of non combustible material except residential buildings upto three storey in height.

(*b*) Interior stair case should be constructed with at least one side adjacent to an exterior wall and shall be completely enclosed except in residential building upto 3 storey in height.

(*c*) A stair case should not be arranged round a lift shaft unless the later is entirely enclosed by a material or fire resistance rating as required for that type of construction itself.

(*d*) Hollow combustible construction should not be constructed.

(*e*) The min. width of internal stair case should be 100 cm except in case of residential dwellings, the min. width should be 75 cm. In public stair ways it should be 1·37 m.

(*f*) The min. width of treads without noising should be 25 cm for an internal stair case for residential buildings. In the case of other public buildings the min. tread should be 30 cm. The treads should be constructed and maintained in a manner to prevent slipping.

(*g*) The max. height of riser shall be 19 cm. in the case of residential buildings and 15 cm in the case of other buildings.

(*h*) Hand rails should be provided with a min. height of 90 cm from the centre of the tread.

(*i*) Head room from the stair to soffet of roof should not be less than 2·14 m (7′).

(*j*) The max. no. of stairs in a flight should be 12 and min 3. After each flight a landing equal to width of stair should be provided.

Pitch stair slope of stair must be 25° to 40°.

Type of stair cases—(1) Straight—It contains continuous flight in one direction floor to floor. A landing may however be given but the direction will not change.

(2) **Dog legged**—It has two straight flights opposite in direction linked by a half landing.

(3) **Open Newel stair**—It consists two or more flights arranged in such a manner that a clear space called a well occurs between the forward and backward flight.

(4) **Geometrical stair**—When the well in the newel stair is curved.

(5) **Circular stair**—When the space is limited the stair case is made circular with winder steps.

Note : For further detail see, wooden and RCC stairs.

OPEN NEWEL TYPE STAIRCASE

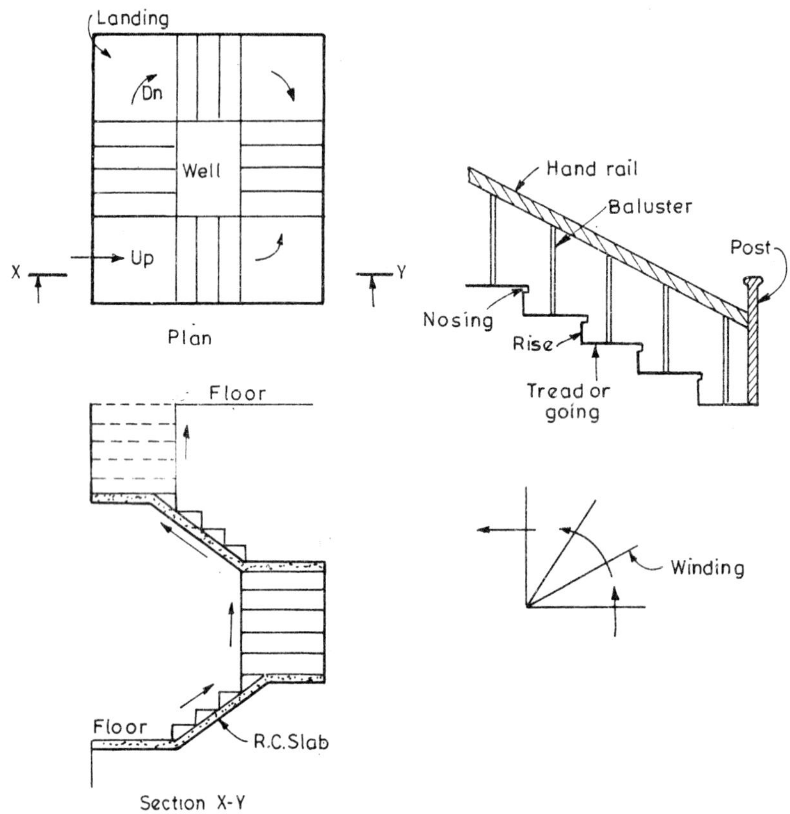

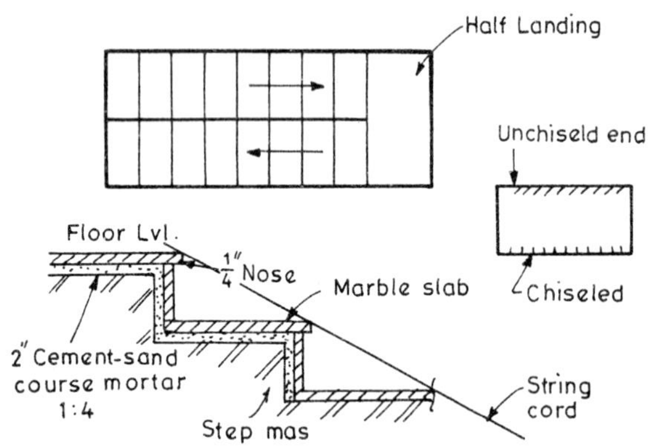

Note :
1. Paving started from ground level going up.
2. False stone is fixed on upper floor level at its proper level and position and a string cord is tied to lower floor level in its proper position and then work is advanced up.
3. Edges of slabs chiselled.

Fig. 7·54. Stone paving of stair case.

Terms used in stairs

(1) **Baluster**—It is the vertical member placed between stringer and hand rail to provide support to the hand rail.

(2) **Balustrade**—The combined frame work of hand rail and balisters and a guide for the climber.

(3) **Flight**—A series of continuous steps without an intermediate landing.

(4) **Landing**—A horizontal platform between two flights of stairs is called landing. A landing gives brief rest during the use of stairs and facilitate in changing of directions. When the landing extends to full width of staircase, it is termed as half spaced landing. It is known as quarter spaced landing when it extends only for half of the staircase width.

(5) **Tread**—The horizontal part of a step which is used to rest the foot while ascending or descending the stairs.

(6) **Riser**—The vertical distance between two consecutive treads.

(7) **Rise**—It is the vertical distance between the surfaces of two consecutive steps.

(8) **Step**—A part of stairs consisting of a tread and a riser which is used to ascend or descend from one floor to the other.

(9) **Nosing**—The outer projection of a tread which is about 1/2 cm and is rounded.

(10) **Line of nosing**—A slanting line (imaginary) joining nose points of the steps. The slope is equal to the slope of the stairs.

(11) **Going**—It is the horizontal distance between the faces of two consecutive risers.

(12) **Head room**—It is the vertical space between the tread of a step and the bottom of the flight or landing immediately above also known as head way.

(13) **Hand rail**—Wooden or metallic rail provided on the side of the stairs at about waist height at an inclination or at level on a landing.

(14) **String**—It is a sloping member which supports the ends of steps in a staircase.

(15) **Walking line**—It is an approximate line of travel of people on a stair and is situated roughly at a distance of about 450 mm from the centre of hand rail.

(16) **Newel post**—It is the vertical member placed at the ends of flights to join the ends of strings and hand rails.

(17) **Pitch**—It is the angle of inclination of the flight to the stairs with the floor.

(18) **Winders**—They are angular or radiating steps and are provided to change the direction in the stairs.

(19) **Curtail step**—The lowest step of a flight employed in geometrical stairs.

(20) **Spendril**—It is a triangular framing under the out side string of an open string stair.

Fire Escapes or External Stairs—(*a*) Fire escapes should not be taken into account in calculating the evacuation times of a building.

(*b*) Entrance of fire escapes should be separate and remote from the internal stair cases.

(*c*) All the fire escapes should be directly connected to the ground.

(*d*) The route of fire escape should be free from all times except a door way leading to the fire escape which shall have the required fire resistance.

(*e*) It must be of non combustible material.

(*f*) Fire escape stairs shall have straight flight not less than 75 cm wide with 23 cm tread and risers not more than 19 cm. The no. of risers should be limited to 16 per flight and min. 3.

(*g*) Hand rails should not be a height less than 100 cm.

Spiral Stair Escapes—The use of spiral stair fire escapes is limited to low occupant load and a building of height of 9 m unless they are connected to plate forms such as balconies and terraces to allow escapes to pause. It should not be less than 150 cm in dia. and should be designed to give an adequate head room.

Ramps. Ramps used in place of stairs should have a min. slope of 1 : 10 and should comply requirements as by a stair way as to enclosure capacity, and limiting dimensions. For special cases slope can be reduced to 1 in 8. The ramp should be provided with a non slipery material on surface.

Lifts—Lifts are provided in buildings more than 15 metre in height.

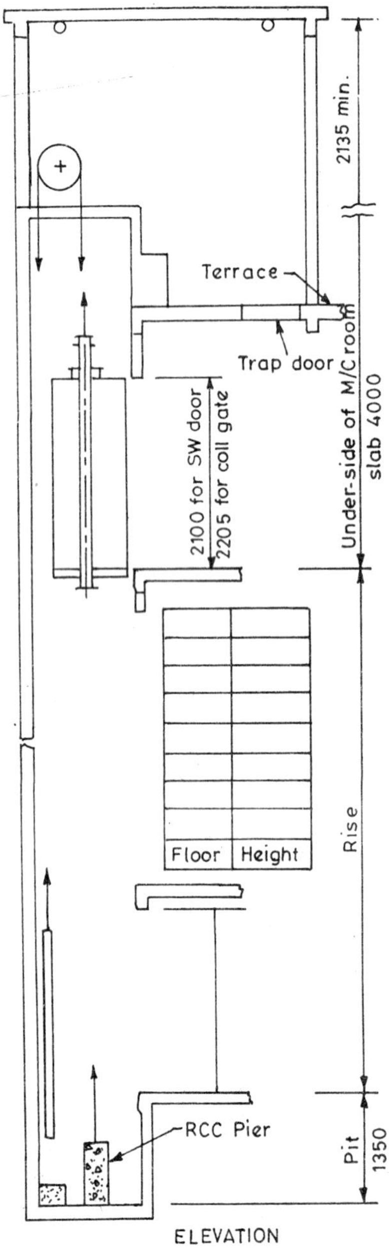

Fig. 7·55.

Owner's Work

1. All civil work holes, grouting etc. and cutouts in machine room floor.
2. Front entrance walls at ground floor must be left unerected until 'OTIS' preassembled carframe etc. installed.
3. Power supply : 400 volts, 3 phase 50 cycles and 230 volts, 1 phase.
4. Reinforced concrete machine room structural floor slab (150 mm thick for 5 & 6 pass/200 mm thick for 8 pass) designed to sustain a min. 1000 kg/sq. m U.D.L.
5. Rolled steel sections for machine beams bearing plates etc. for 6 pass elevator only.

Dimn.	5 pass (340 kg)	6 pass (400 kg)	8 pass (544 kg)
A	1600	1600	1800
B	1200	1400	1500
C	1170	1100	1300
D	820	1000	1100
E	3350	3550	4000

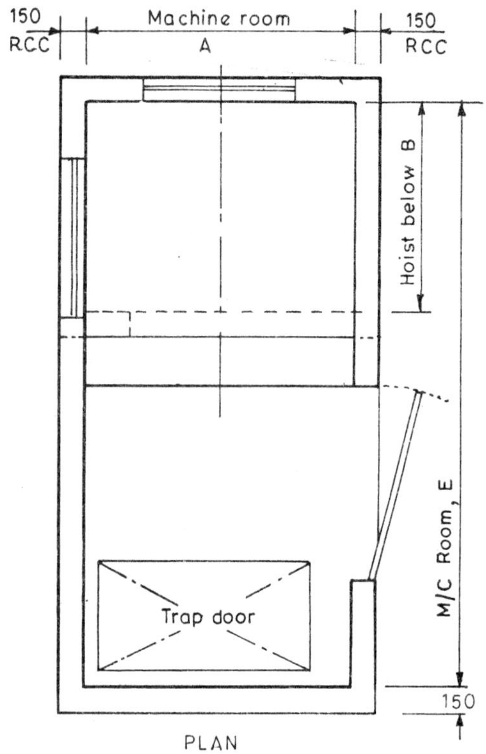

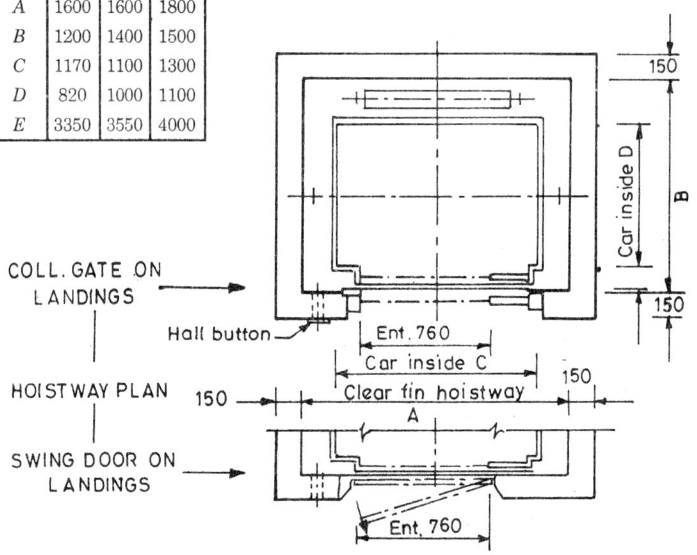

Fig. 7·56.

To be provided in buildings more than 15 m in height.
Specifications. For a particular lift as per OTIS Elevator Co. (India) Ltd.
Speed—0·70 metres per second.
Power supply—230 volts, 50 cycles single phase.
Control—OTIS Thyristor Control System (OTCS-1).
Operation—Single Automatic Push Button.
Machine—General Traction machine placed directly over the insist way.
Car entrance—Protected by steel collapsible gate, black painted finish.
Clear opening—760 mm wide × 2000 mm high.
Hoist way entrances—Wooden swing doors (polished or steel collapsible).
Signals— 1. Up/down direction arrows incorporated in hall button face plates at each landing.
2. Battery operated alarm bell and emergency light.

Table 7·29. Off street parking for motor vehicles

S. No.	*Occupancy*	*One parking space for every*
1.	Residential	
	(*i*) Multifamily residential	Tenement exceeding 200 m^2 carpet area
	(*ii*) Lodging establishments tourist houses and hotels with lodging accommodation	6 guest rooms
2.	Educational*	100 m^2 carpet area or fraction thereof of the administrative office area and public service areas
3.	Institutional (medical)	20 beds
4.	Assembly	30 beds
5.	Government or semi-public business	100 m^2 carpet area or fraction thereof
6.	Mercantile**	100 m^2 carpet area or fraction thereof
7.	Industrial	200 m^2
8.	Storage	100 m^2 upto 500 m^2 area and every 200 m^2 there after.

Note : 1. *In the case of auditoria for educational buildings, parking space shall be provided as per sl. no. 4.

2. **For plots upto 100 m^2 as in the case of shops, parking spaces need not be insisted.

3. Off street parking space for motor vehicles should not be less than 3·0 m^2 and 1·4 m^2 respectively.

4. Other types of vehicles for non-residential and non-assembly occupanices, in addition to the parking area as given in table above, 100% additional area is provided for parking other types of vehicles of this, 60% shall be set apart exclusively for cycles.

5. Off street parking spaces should be provided with adequate vehicular access to a street and the area of the drives aisles and such other provisions required for adequate manoeuvring of vehicles should be exclusive of the parking space stipulated in these rules.

6. In addition to parking space provided for buildings of mercantile (commercial) Industrial and storage, the rate of one such space for loading and unloading activities for each 1000 m^2 of floor area or fraction thereof exceeding the 1st 200 m^2 of floor area should be provided.

7. The parking spaces in cinemas, threatres and places of public assembly should be provided as under.

Table 7·31.

Type of vehicle	*No. of vehicles for which parking*
1. Cars	33 % of the scating capacity *
2. Scooters	10 % of the scating capacity
3. Cycles	25 % of the scating capacity

* See serial no. 4 in the table No. 7·29.

8. The spaces left for parking shall lie in addition to the open spaces left out for lighting and ventilation purposes.

9. Parking lock up garages should be induced in calculation for floor space for FAR Calculations unless they are provided in the basement of a building or under a building constructed on stilts with no external wall.

Projections. No projection of any sort what so ever extending more than 23 cm below a height of 4·3 m, such as projection on the level of chabutra, chhajja, cornice, water spouts, drain, pipes, advertisement boards and the like shall project over the the land of the road or over any drain or over any portions out side the boundaries of the site, provided that projections arising out of the vertical part of the rain water spouts projecting at the road level or the water pipe may be permitted in accordance with the drainage plan.

(1) Sun shades over windows and ventilators shall be projected when permitted by the authority shall fulfill following conditions :

(*a*) No projection of any sort shall be permitted over the land and the road or over any drain or over any portion outside the boundaries of the site below a height of 2·8 m from road level.

(*b*) Sun shades provided above a height of 2·8 m from the ground level shall be permitted to project upto a max. width of 60 cm if the road over which the project exceeds 9 m in width.

(*c*) No projection of any sort what so ever shall be permitted on roads less than 9 m in width or on roads having no foot paths.

(2) **Portico in existing developed areas**—Portico may be allowed on such roads as can leave a min. clear space of 18 m between kerbs or if a stipulation has been made for such construction in the lease deed or in such cases where its construction would completely fill in a gap in the existing arcade provided that these shall be constructed as follows :

(*a*) It shall be not less than 3 m wide and is either cantilevered or supported on thin steel or RCC pillars.

(*b*) Nothing shall be allowed to be constructed on the portico which shall be used as an open terrace.

(*c*) Nothing shall be allowed to project beyond the line of arcades.

(*d*) The space under the portico shall be paved and channelled according to the directions of the authority.

Table 7·31. FAR for different use groups

S. No.	*Use groups*	*FAR*	*Density of the area*	
			Person/Acre	*Person/Ha*
1.	Residential	0·50	50	120
		0·70	75	185
		1·00	100	250
		1·33	150	375
		1·80	200	500
		2·00	250	625
		2·50	300	750
2.	Business/Commercial	1·00	Area neighbourhood shopping centre,	
		1·25	sub-district shopping centre area	
		1·50	District shopping centre area	
		3·00	Central business district area and office area	

Table contd...

Table contd...

S. No.	Use groups	FAR	Density of the area	
			Person/Acre	Person/Ha
3.	Educational	1·00		
4.	Institutional	1·50		
5.	Assembly	1·50		
6.	Assembly	1·50		
7.	Industrial	0·60	Upto 250 m^2	
		0·55	250-300	
		0·50	300-upto 0·5 acre/0·2 Ha	
		0·45	0·5-3 Acre/0·2-1·2 Ha	
		0·40	3-7 Acre/1·2-2·8 Ha	
		0·30	Above 7 Acre/above 2-8 Ha	

Note : FAR values indicated above are for plotted development and in the case integrated development scheme, like integrated housing schemes, shopping centres etc. and service industries. The FAR for occupancies should be decided by the planning authorities.

Table 7·32. FAR and coverage for group housing

S. No.	Gross residential density		Max. coverage	FAR
	Person/Acre	Person/Ha	in %	
1.	50	125	25	0·75
2.	100	250	30	1·25
3.	150	425	$33^1/_3$	1·50
4.	200	500	35	1·75
5.	250	625	35	1·75

Note : (1) Floor area is calculated as area on all floors unless specifically excluded.

(2) The coverage shall be calculated on the basis of the whole area reserved for group housing after deducting.

(*a*) The area of any highway and road upto 25 m and major residential 18 m wide road around and width in the group housing area, residential street, loop streets, cal-de-sec, service lanes and foot paths shall not be deducted.

(*b*) The area of the school (excluding sites for nursery schools) and other community facilities with in the group housing area).

(*c*) The open spaces except play grounds and tot lots of local nature.

Height limitations. The height of the building shall governed by the limitations of FAR open spaces and the width of the streets front of the plots as per details given below.

(*a*) The absolute height of a building shall not exceed 1·5 times the width of the road abutting plus the front open spaces.

(*b*) If a building abuts on two or more streets of different widths, the buildings shall be deemed to face upon the street that has the greater width and the height of the building shall be regulated by the width of that street and may be continued to the height to a depth of 24 m along the narrower street.

(*c*) For building in the vicinity of aerodromes the max. height of such buildings shall be given in a separate table.

Height Exceptions. The following appurtenant structures shall not be included in the height of buildings, roof, tanks, and their supports ventilating air conditioning, lift room and similar service equipment, roof structures, chimneys other than penthouses, parapet walls and architectural fixures not exceeding 1 m unless the aggregate area of such structures including pent houses exceeds one-third of the roof of the building upon which they are erected.

Table 7·33. Height restrictions near aerodromes

S. No.	*Limits of distances from the aerodromes Reference point measured horizontally of buildings, structures or installations*	*Difference between the elevation of the top of the buildings, structures or installations and the elevation of the aerodrome. (Aerodrome reference point)*
1	2	3
(*a*)	**International civil airports and their alternates**	
	(*i*) Between 8534 m and 22,224 m	Less than 152 m
	(*ii*) Between 7315 m and 8334 m	Less than 122 m
	(*iii*) Between 6096 m and 7315 m	Less than 91 m
	(*iv*) Between 4877 m and 6069 m	Less than 61 m
	(*v*) Between 4267 m and 4877 m	Less than 49 m
	(*vi*) Between 3658 m and 4267 m	Less than 37 m
	(*vii*) Between 3048 m and 3658 m	Less than 24 m
	(*viii*) Between 2438 m and 3048 m	Less than 12 m
	(*ix*) Between 2438 m and less	Nil except with the prior conccurrence of the local aerodrome authorities.
(*b*)	**Other civil airports and civil aerodromes**	
	(*i*) Between 7925 m and 22,224 m	Less than 152 m
	(*ii*) Between 6706 m and 7925 m	Less than 122 m
	(*iii*) Between 5486 m and 6706 m	Less than 91 m
	(*iv*) Between 4267 m and 5386 m	Less than 61 m
	(*v*) Between 3658 m and 4267 m	Less than 49 m
	(*vi*) Between 3048 m and 3658 m	Less than 37 m
	(*vii*) Between 2438 m and 3048 m	Less than 24 m
	(*viii*) Between 1829 m and 2438 m	Less than 12 m
	(*ix*) Between 1829 m and less	Nil, except with the prior concurrence of the local aerodrome authorities.

Note : (1) For No. (*vii*), (*viii*) and (*ix*) no trees should be planted with in the limits of the distance indicated thereto.

(2) Irrespective of their distance from the aerodrome (that is beyond 22,224 m of the aerodrome/aerodrome reference point) no radio masts or such similar type of installations exceeding 152 m in height should be erected without prior permission of the concerned aviation authority.

(3) No building, structure, or installation exceeding the heights indicated in (*a*) and (*b*) should be permitted without prior consultation with the local aerodrome authority.

(4) The location of slaughter houses/butcher houses and other areas for activities like depositing of garbage in garbage dumps which would generate the collection of high flying birds like eagles, hawks etc. shall not be permitted with in a radius of 10 km from aerodrome reference point.

7·22. Colony Planning

(1) Residential Colonies

Roads. The residential streets are divided in three categories based on their use and proposed traffic requirements (*i*) service road, (*ii*) collector road, (*iii*) other roads. (For details refer chapter on Roads)

(i) **Service roads.** (a) The min. width of a service road should be 9 m. But a road adjoining a part of any open public space with building only on one side may however, have a min. width of 7·5 m. The 9 m service road can serve upto a length of 300 m. This will be measured from one wider street to another wider street. In case of 5 m wide road it can serve upto 400 m. If the 9 m road ends as a dead road it must have a turn around at the end. The width and depth of the turn around should be of 15 m or an equivalent area in another form permitting turn around. No turn around is required if the number of plots served by such road is less than three.

(b) A road which is longer than 300 m or serves upto 100 plots/houses or is extendable to new areas should be 12 m wide. Such roads can be 400 m in length.

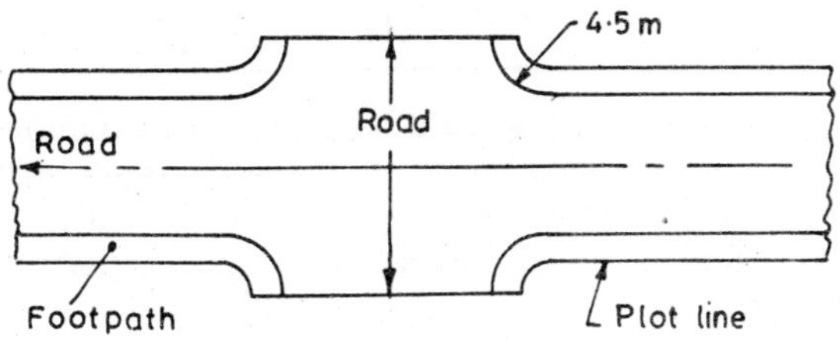

Fig. 7·57.

(c) All junctions of service roads shall have sufficient weaving angle. In no case it shall be less than the space arrived at by drawing quadrant of a circle of 4·5 m radius. At the edge of the actual road lines leaving the width of pedestrian walks (foot path) and the plot boundaries shall be rounded off by drawing a quadrant of the circle of 2·7 m radius at the edge of plot boundaries (see fig.7·57). It can also be provided by cut offs and lots in place of rounded corners.

(d) **Loop street.** The min. width of a loop street should be 9 m and it should cater for a length upto 500 m.

(2) **Collector roads.** These roads are intended for short trip and are also used for direct access to abutting properly as well as access to service roads and dead end roads.

A collector road should serve an area of 200 plots and having an area of not more than 4 Ha exclusively deriving access through it or its service roads. It shall be either of 18 m or 24 m in width.

(3) **Other roads.** (a) **Service lanes**—In row type of housing and in such areas where sewerage system does not exist a 3·5 m service lane should be provided. The length of such service lane should be not more than 300 m.

Conditions of Planning

Service roads should be so laid out, that their use for thorough traffic is automatically discouraged.

Where a sub division abuts on certain major existing or proposed road, the service road along side the major road may be required or provide road with no access to adjacent properties or such other treatment as may be necessary for adequate protection of residential property and to effect separation of through land local traffic.

Path ways and access ways to site and service schemes. In the case of site and service scheme housing colonies for economically weaker sections of society undertaken by public agencies, the min. width of pathways and access ways to dwelling with dwelling are one side of the pathways and open park on the other side should be 3 m and no dwelling should be more than 50 m from any service road of 9 m width. In case of dwellings on both sides, the width of path ways should be 4·5 m and no dwelling facing this pathway should be farther than 80 m from a service road of 9 m width. For lengths longer than the above, the width of the path way with dwelling on both sides should be increased to 6 m subjected to a max. of 150 m distance for any dwelling facing as the pathway from a service road of 9 m.

Commercial, Business and Industrial colonies. The max. length permissible for different classification of roads in areas other than residential should be as indicated below. No road in these areas should be less than 12 m in width.

Table 7·34.

Class of road	*Width*	*Max. length permissible*
1	12 m	200 m
2	18 m	600 m
3	24 m	above 600 m

Alleys. Alleys should be provided in commecial area and industrial except when assured provision is made for service access such as off street loading/unloading and parking consistant with and adequate for the use provided. The width of the alleys where provided should not be less than 6 m and no dead end alley should be permitted unless provided with an adequate turn around facilities.

Junctions. The layout should be provided at the junction of roads in such a way that as far as possible all roads do meet at right angle. Roads meeting at less than 30° should not be permitted unless adequate arrangements for the circulation of traffic with desirable wearing length is available.

Open space—Residential area. The open space in residential area should be in proportion to the density of that area. To work out an over all open space exclusively for active recreation and breathing place the requirements should be worked out on proposed population of the area. The requirements of open place should be provided according to the purpose *i.e.* lot lots parks, play grounds etc. The following criteria may be adopted for arriving at open spaces depending upon density.

Table 7·35.

S. No.	*Density/Acre*	*Density/Ha*	*Open space %*	*Area*	
				Acre/1000	*Ha/1000*
1.	100	250	6	0·6	0·24
2.	150	325	9	0·6	0·24
3.	200	500	12	0·6	0·24
4.	250	625	16	0·65	0·26
5.	300	750	21	0·70	0·28
6.	400	1000	28	0·70	0·28
7.	500	1250	37·5	0·75	0·30

Note : For densities above 500/Acre (1250/Ha) a min. open space of 0·75 acre/1000 (0·30 Ha/1000) should be set apart for this purpose.

Industrial area. In case of layouts in industrial area, the spaces to be left open for parks and green buffers for ecological balance should be as per following scale.

Table 7·36.

Sl. No.	*Industrial plot size in layout*	*Open space %*
1.	upto 500 m^2	5%
2.	550 m^2 - 0·2 Ha	4%
3.	0·2 Ha - 0·8 Ha	3%
4.	0·8 Ha and above	2%

Note : The space is exclusive of space provided for community facilities and amenities given in table.

Layout of plots. The plots in residential areas should be laid out based on the following criteria.

Table 7·37

Plot size	*Development scheme*
Upto 250 m^2	Raw housing
250 m^2 - 500 m^2	Semi detached buildings
above 500 m^2	Detached buildings

Note : Plots which are 6 m to 9 m in width should be developed as row housing scheme.

7·22. Air Conditioning

Ventilation. It involves supplying or removing air by natural or by mechanical means.

(*a*) **Natural means.** These are obtained by cross-ventilation by doors, windows or by ventilators.

(*b*) **Mechanical means.** Exhaust fans are used to extract contaminated air and fans are also used to force the fresh air inside the room. Mechanical system of ventilation may be of the following three types :

(1) **Extract system.** Exhaust fan is used to suck off the contaminated air. This causes decrease in the internal pressure and fresh air finds its way inside the room through leaky doors, windows or the openings provided for the purpose. This system is useful for kitchens and lavatories etc.

(2) **Plenum system.** It is reverse of the extract system. In it air is forced into the room by means of fans but no exhaust fans are provided to remove the contaminated air. The pressure inside the room is higher than that of outside. The contaminated air leaks out automatically through the leakages and opening provided for the purpose. In this case control on air movement is uncertain. This system is mainly utilised in factories. The incoming air can be cleaned, cooled or heated where required.

(3) **Balanced system.** In it exhaust fans are used to extract contaminated air and fans are used to drive the fresh air in. In most buildings it is desirable to extract only about 75% of the quantity of air supplied. In this way circulation of air is possible.

Note : (1) In the case when occupants are more than 50 and the space provided is less than 3 m^2 per person, the mechanical ventilation is must.

(2) An opening area equal to not less than 1/12th of the floor area of the room should be provided. The top of the opening should not be more than 45 cm below the ceiling.

Table 7·38 Fresh air requirement on the bases of body odour concentration

Air space per person $m^3/hour$	*Fresh air supply per person $m^3/hour$*
2·8	42·5
5·6	28·5
8·4	20·5
11·2 and above	17·0

Air conditioning may be classified as under :

(1) **Winter air conditioning**—In this case outside temperature is below the inside. It involves heating, humidification, air distribution and air cleaning.

(2) **Summer air conditioning**—It includes, cooling humidifying and also dehumidifying and air cleaning. The outside temperature is higher than the temperature in side.

(3) **Complete air conditioning—**It includes both heating and cooling, both humidifying and dehumidifying, together with air distribution and air cleaning.

Table 7·39. Requirement of fresh air in different type of buildings

Type of building			*Recommended min. rate of fresh air supply in buildings*
1.	Assembly halls		28·5 m^3/hr/head
2.	Canteens		28·5 m^3/hr/head
3.	Factories and workshops	(*a*) work rooms	22·5 m^3/head
		(*b*) lavatories and W.Cs	2 air changes per hour
4.	House and flats		
	Bath rooms and W.Cs		2 air changes/hour
	Halls and passages		1 air change/hour
	Kitchens		57 m^3/hour
	Living and bed rooms		20·5 m^3/head
			17·0 m^3/head
	Pantries or larders		2 air changes per hour
5.	Shops		28·5 m^3/hour/head
6.	Schools—class rooms, laboratories etc.		42·5 m^3/head/hour
			28·5 m^3/head/hour
7.	Government offices	Office rooms	28·5 m^3/hour/head
		Lavatories and W.Cs	2 air changes per hour
		Places of entertainments	28·5 per hour per head

Air changes per hour for different type of buildings (minimum)

Type of building	*Air changes/hour*
Schools—Class rooms	6
Assembly halls, cloak room, dinning rooms, dormitories	3
Gymnasea, sanotoria, sick room common rooms, lavatories, staff room	2
Laboratories	4
Hospitals—Wards, Dormitories, Day rooms, Dinning rooms, recovery rooms, entrances, internal lavatories	3
Bed rooms, corridors, X-ray rooms, stair cases, lavatories and bath rooms	2
Kitchens	20-40
Laundries	10-20
Boiler houses and smoking rooms	10-15

Air conditioning. The air in the open atmosphere contains many poluted materials such as dust, smoke, fumes, germs and bacteria etc. Moreover the outside temperature is more in summer which it is low in the winter which does not suit the people in both the seasons. Therefore in such environments, natural ventilation or even mechanical ventilation does not serve the purpose for getting rid of the above impurities to go inside the building. In such conditions it is necessary to control the temperature and quality of the outside air which enters inside the building and also to remove the heavy vitiated air at the optimum rates. This problem is solved by airconditioning the buildings in which all the doors, windows and ventilators are kept closed.

The air conditioning process consists of controlling of temperature as well as keep the air free of dirt, bacteria and toxic matter. It is also required that in air conditioning the temperature must vary according to season *i.e.* in summer it must be cooler and in winter it must be hotter than outside temperature. Now it will be discussed that how the summer and winter air conditioning is controlled.

(1) **Winter air Conditioner.** In winter season the external atmospheric temperature is low and this cold air has to be heated before it can be supplied in the room desired to be conditioned. During this process of preheating, the humidity of the air reduces because at higher temperature with the same amount of moisture, this relative humidity decreases. Hence after heating it becomes necessary to increase the humidity of this air by carrying it through a humidifier, where air may be mixed with the water vapour by throwing water over the air with the help of spray nozzles. This humidified air is then passed through **eliminator** plates so as to remove the water droplets if any in the humidified air. This clean hot and optimally air is finally forced out into the space to be conditioned.

Recirculating of air is done as is done in the case of summer air conditioning, because air is to be heated upto lesser extent than the outside air, which causes economy. The flow diagram for winter Air conditioning is shown in Fig. 7B·1(*a*). Preheating may be done by heating or by passing the air over the coils heated by hot water.

(2) **Summer air conditioning.** The process proceeds in the following steps :

(*i*) **Filtration.** Fresh outside air as well as the vitiated recirculated air is first of all passed through a filler, so as to remove the dust particles etc. from it. There are two types of filters (*a*) dry filters (*b*) viscous filters, made of close grained felt or cloth (may be of jute) in a common practice. Now a days a more advanced technology as **"electric precipitation"** is used in high class buildings.

(*ii*) **Dehumidification or cooling and drying.** It is done by cooling of the filtered air by refrigeration below the dew point. By this the extra amount of moisture is condensed, however the humidity of this air increases, because at lower temperature, with the same amount of moisture, the relative humidity increases. Hence after cooling, it becomes necessary to reduce the humidity of air by drying it through a **dehumidifier.** A dehumidifier is in the form of a hygroscopic substance like ammonia, calcium chloride etc. or the air is cooled and dried through the process of condensation. By condensing out necessary amount of moisture and then reheating the same upto the desired temperature. Cooling of the air is done in several ways (*i*) cooling by mechanical refrigeration and (*ii*) by water spray method.

Mechanical refrigeration cools the air like a household refrigerator, and is more suitable to places when temperature is to be lowered substantially. In this method the air is cooled without wetting the same with the help of compressure and metal coils (tubes).

This type of plants are called as Refrigeration plants.

The other type of plants are water spray plants. The water is 1st cooled by refrigerant or by ice. This cooled water is then sprayed on the hot air coming out of the filters. The air, thus gets cooled by evaporation. This method increases the humidity of the air and is generally not found suitable for humid climates.

In both the cooling methods the air is cooled upto dew point, so as to extract some desired moisture from it, and the balance air is reheated upto the desired temperature for final distribution through fans and ducts in the rooms to be conditioned.

In summer the desirable temperature is 21·7°C in which winter it is near 18·9°C. Refrigerating plants are generally rating on ton bases. 1 M-ton being equivalent to heat removal at the rate of 100 CHU (*i.e.* 180 BTh U) per minute. As a rough rule the power required to drive refrigerating plants is 1 BHP per M Ton.

Individual air conditioning machines called room air conditioners are fitted on the windows of rooms ; whereas for large building central air conditioning is adopted. In central air conditioning the conditioned air is produced by keeping the plant in one separate room and distribution ducts are carried to individual rooms and at various points in a big hall. For distributing the conditioned air, through fans and blowers as shown in Fig.

Recirculating air. During summer season, the temperature of room is lower than the temperature of the outside air. It is economical if the used air heated air is used again. This process is called as recirculation of air as is shown in the Fig.

There the air conditioners are designed so as to use the room air again and again and the use of outside air is avoided as can be possible.

Water coolers. In a water cooler an exhaust fan is provided at the front face which blows the air to the space which is to be cooled. The cooling is done by a spray operated by a Tullu Pump (A patent name). Water is filled in the bottom (a type of grass root) of the box which is lifted by the Tullu Pump. On three sides of this box pads of straw or of *khas* are provided for screening of the incoming air.

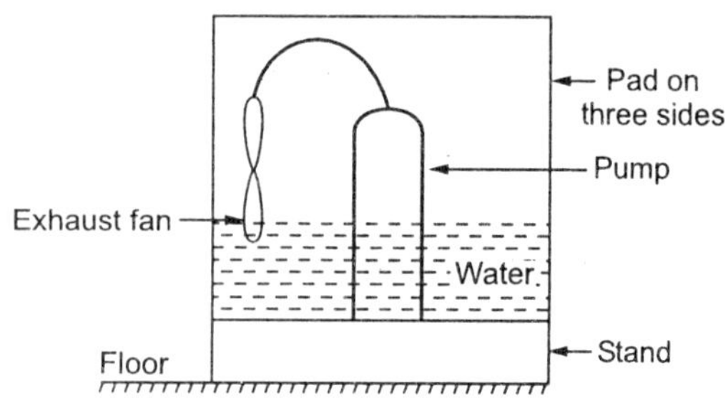

Fig. 7·58. Cooler.

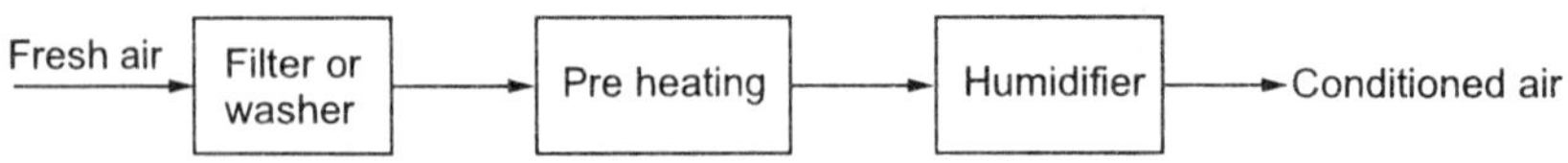

(*a*) Winter AC flow line diagram.

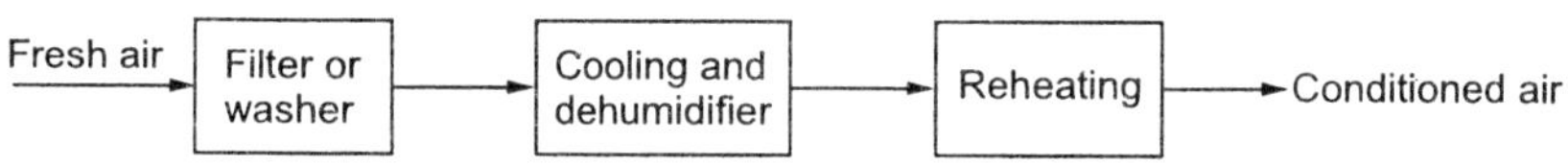

(*b*) Summer AC flow line diagram

Fig. 7·59.

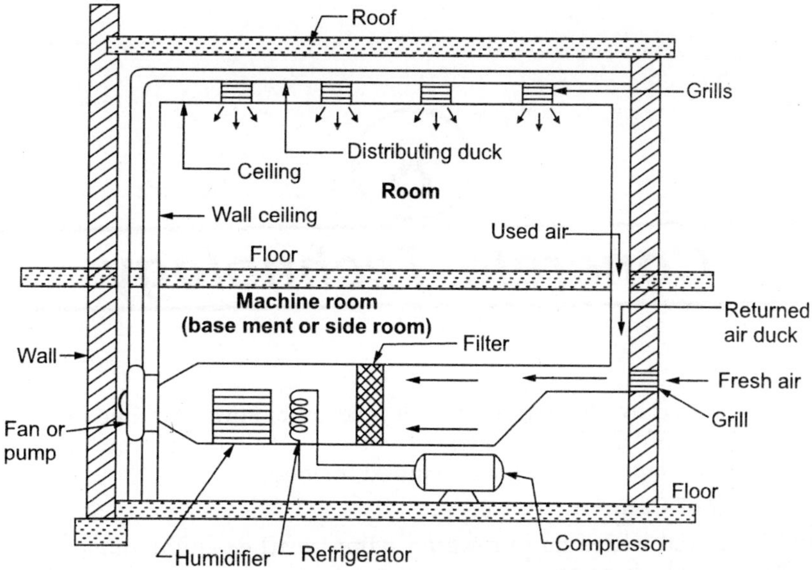

Fig. 7·60. Central system of air conditioning.

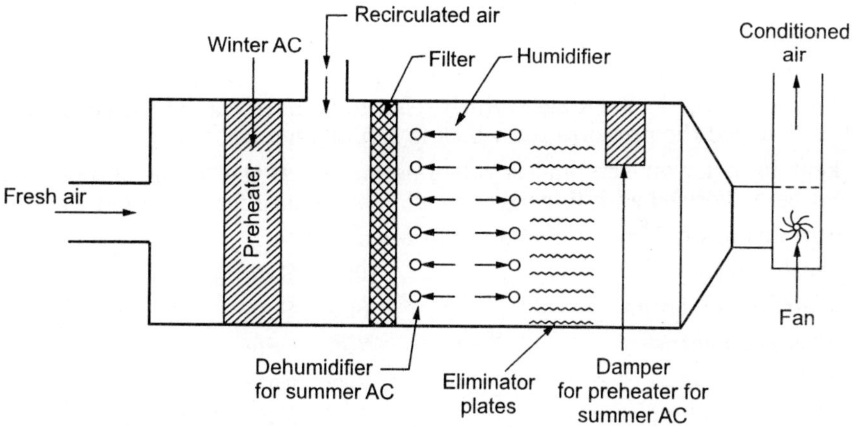

Fig. 7·61. Flow of two way air conditioner.

8

Concrete Technology

8·1. Cement

Cement is produced by burning together a mixture of slica and lime in Partial fusion at a temperature of 1400-1450°C. This heating results in the formation of clinker which is subsequently cooled and grounded to get the required fineness.

8·1·1. Storing of Cement

It should be placed where no rain-water, damp weather and dampness through walls or floors can reach. It should be kept about 200 mm away from walls in the stack of not more than 10 bags in nos.

It should be kept on wooden sleepers 100 or 75 mm thick, kept 200 mm above the floor on wooden supports so that it may be away from capillary moisture.

The stacks should be covered by the terpoline or polythene (Polyethylene) covers to get rid of atmospheric moisture.

It is also some times stored in steel drums which are kept away from moisture to save against rusting, manufacturers store cement in Silos.

Note : The lower bags in the stacks which seem to be hard can be loosened by leaving it through a height. It is called the pressure set, which is actually not set.

Cement kept in moist air sets and is called as air set. If the lumps of any cement is so hard that it can not be pulverised with fingers, it should not be used for important works.

8·1·2. Detoriation of Cement stored is effected as below :

(1) Fresh cement	100%	Safe
(2) After three months	80%	Safe
(3) After six months	75%	Safe
(4) After one year	70%	Safe
(5) After one and quarter year	65%	Safe
(6) After one and half year	60%	Safe
(7) After one and 3/4th year	55%	Safe
(8) After two years	50%	Safe

8·1·3. Contamination of Cement

(1) A sample of cement is burnt in a steel plate. An adultrated sample will change in colour while unadultrated will not.

(2) Make test pats of 5 × 5 × 2 cm in size. If the cement is unadultrated, the pat will have hardened sufficiently in 24 hours to resist any impression of the finger nail. After 24 hours it will not easy to break with pressure of finger.

8·1·4. Tests for Cement

(1) **Samples for Test.** From a quantity of 250 tonnes at least one sample should be tested. Above 250 tonnes one sample for each 250 tonnes should be tested. Each sample must have a mixture of different points, if the cement is stored in heaps and from 12 bags if stored in bags. A final sample should be 10 lbs (4·54 kg) in weight and should be taken as a fair average sample. This test is according to B.S. 112—1947.

(*a*) **Fineness of Cement.** 100 gm or 4 oz of cement shall be sieved on IS sieve no. 90 micron or B.S. no. 170 for 15 minutes. The residue should be weighed and shall not exceed 10% for ordinary. Blast furnace, and pozzuolana cement and 0·05% for rapid hardening cement. Pressure set lumps shall be broken by the fingers and not be rubbed on the sieve mesh.

(*b*) **Soundness Test.** By the Le Chatelier app.—Fig. 8·3. About 100 grams of cement paste be needed. The mould of the apparatus is filled with a cement paste of 0·78 times weight of water to its own weight on a glass plate. The mould is then covered with 2nd glass plate and the whole assembly is then submerged for 24 hours in water at 80°F to 90°F (27 to 32°C). The distance between the pointers of the indicator is measured and noted. Again keep it in the same water and the whole assembly is heated and kept at boiling point for one hour. The mould is then removed from water and allowed to cool. The distance between the indicator points should be measured and noted. The difference between the two readings is expansion of the cement which according to IS specifications should not be more than 10 mm for each type of cement, if kept in air tight place and 5 mm, if cement aerated for 7 days in 75 mm deep layer at humidity 80% before test.

(*c*) **Chemical Composition of Cement.** I.S. specification. It is governed by the following formula :

$$\frac{CaO - 0{\cdot}7SO_3}{2{\cdot}8\ SiO_2 + 1{\cdot}2\ Al_2O_3 + 0{\cdot}65\ FeO_3}$$

$0{\cdot}7SO_3$ is the proportion of lime which is necessary to combine with the sulphuric anhydride.

(1) Ratio of percentage of lime to percentage of Silica, Alumina and iron oxide which is calculated by the above formula not greater than 1·02 and not less than 0·66. The excess of free lime in cement causes unsoundness. Above formula is for ordinary and rapid hardening cement.

Molecular weight of lime	$CaO = 56$
Molecular weight of Silica	$SiO_2 = 60$
Molecular weight of Alumina	$Al_2O_3 = 102$
Molecular weight of Iron oxide	$Ca_2O_3 = 160$
Molecular weight of Sulphuric Anhydride	$SO_3 = 80$

If 2% of sulphuric anhydride is present, the lime which will require to combine with it = $\frac{2 \times 56}{80}$ = 1·4%, *i.e.* 0·7 part of the sulphuric anhydride.

$$\text{Percentage of lime} = \frac{\begin{pmatrix}\text{Percentage of lime after deduction of requirement}\\ \text{for combining with sulphuric anhydride}\end{pmatrix}}{56(\text{Molecular weight of lime})} = a_1(\text{say})$$

$$\text{Percentage of silica} = \frac{\text{Percentage of silica present}}{60(\text{Molecular weight of silica})} = a_2(\text{say})$$

$$\text{Percentage of alumina} = \frac{\text{Percentage of alumina present}}{102(\text{Molecular weight of alumina})} = a_3(\text{say})$$

$$\text{Percentage of iron oxide} = \frac{\text{Percentage of iron oxide}}{1600(\text{Mol. wt. of iron oxide})} = a_4(\text{say})$$

Then $\dfrac{a_1}{2{\cdot}8\,a_2 + 1{\cdot}2\,a_3 + 0{\cdot}65\,a_4}$ should not be more than 1·02 and less than 0·66.

Note : (1) Percentage of different chemicals present in cement is given by the manufacturer or should be chemically determined. A table is also given below.

(2) Rate of percentage of alumina to that of iron oxide not less than 0·66.

(3) The quantity of magnesia should not be more than 6% by weight as its excess causes unsoundness.

Percentage of different chemicals present in cement :

Weight of magnesia	Not more than 5%
Weight of soluble residue	Not more than 1·5 to 2%
Ratio of percentage of alumina to iron oxide	Not less than 0·66%
Total sulphur calculated as silica	Not more than 2·75%
Total loss on ignition	Not more than 4%
In case of blast furnace cement (IS 455—1962)	
Magnesium oxide	8·0%
Sulphur trioxide	3·0%
Sulphide sulphur	1·5%
Manganic oxide	1·5%
Insoluble residue	4·0%
Loss on ignition	1·5%

(4) In soluble residue percentage not more than 2% by weight as detailed below.

(*a*) Mix thoroughly one gram of cement with 4·0 cc of water and 10 cc of concentrated HCl (Specific gravity 1·16), boil the mixture for 10 minutes. Keeping the volume constant by adding water and any lump produced should be broken. Filter the solution and rinse the container five times and wash filter with hot water 10 times.

(*b*) Wash the residue in a beaker with 10 cc of distilled water and boil it for 10 minutes with 30 cc of sodium carbonate solution of twice the normal strength. Filter the solution in the same filter, wash five times with water and then by HCl solution of twice the normal strength and finally with water till it is free from chlorides.

(*c*) The filter paper should be dried and ignited and weighed to give the insoluble residue, which should not be more than 2%.

(5) On heating the sample of cement the moisture and CO_2 which is present in the sample is evaporated. The loss in weight can be obtained by heating the sample before and after heating. The loss should not be more than 5%. The presence of moisture causes hydration of cement.

(6) The total presence of sulphur in the form of sulphuric anhydride (SO_3) produced due to presence of gypsum should not be more than 2·75% when the tricalcium aluminate percentage by weight is 7 or less and 3·0% when it is more than 7. This compound also cause unsoundness. It's process is also so slow that it cannot be perceived by Le Chatelier app. and hence should be chemically measured.

(7) The percentage of lime in low heat cement (after deducting the amount necessary to combine with sulphuric anhydride present) not more than 2·4 (SiO_2) + 1·2 (Al_2O_3) + 0·65 (Fe_2O_3) nor less than 1·9(SiO_2) + 1·2(Al_2O_3) + 0·65(Fe_2O_3). Otherwise the composition comply with conditions mentioned above in serial 2 to 6.

Note : (1) Each symbol in bracket refer to the percentage (By mass of total cement) of the oxide excluding any content of insoluble residue as mentioned in serial 4.

(2) Tri Calcium aluminate (Ca_3Al) is calculated by the formula $Ca_3Al = 2{\cdot}65 (Al_2O_3 - 1{\cdot}69 (FeO_3)$. Where each symbol in bracket refer to the percentage (By mass of total cement) of the oxide excluding of insoluble residue as mentioned in serial 4 above.

(3) Alkali contained (Na_2O) should be upto 0·6%. If such cements are not available use portland pozzuolana cement or cement pozzuolana admixtures.

(*d*) **Test for Normal consistency.** Test several pasts with different water cement ratios. The penetration of 1 cm dia rod (**Vicat's apparatus** 8·3) should be 33 to 35 mm or as desired for a particular job.

(*e*) **Test for setting time.** (*a*) Initial test (*b*) Final test

(*a*) **Initial test.** (The Vicat apparatus refer 8·3) The time from mixing of the cement paste to the penetration of 1 mm needle when it ceases in the paste is known as the initial setting time. It is the time during which a crack developed in concrete can reunit.

(*b*) **Final set.** It is the time taken from the instant of mixing the paste to the instant when the annular attachment "*F*" fails to leave a mark on the paste which the needle makes the same when released. It is the time during which the concrete attains sufficient strength.

	Ordinary cement	*Rapid hardening*	*Low heat cement*	*Blast furnace*	*Pozzuolana cement*
(*a*) Initial setting time	30 min.	30 min.	60 min.	30 min.	30 min
(*b*) Final setting time	10 Hrs.	10 Hrs.	10 Hrs.	10 Hrs.	10 Hrs.

(*f*) **Tensile strength of cement.** Six nos. briquettes of 1 : 3 cement and standard sand mortar of the water cement ratio determined by the formula $P = 0{\cdot}195\ P_n + 2{\cdot}5$. Where P is the percentage of water by weight to that of cement and P_n is the percentage of water to that of cement by weight required for normal consistency are prepared. The mortar is mixed thoroughly till it makes an uniform paste. Fill the mould with paste and tap it by the stapula of the standard size. Make the surface smooth by a trowel. The temperature of the room shall be 58 to 64°F (25 to 30°C) and humidity 90%. These briquettes are kept under water of above temperature till taken out for test. The tensile strength should be as follows :

Table 8·1

1 : 3 (cement : sand)	*Ordinary cement*	*Rapid hardening*	*Blast furnace*	*Pozzuolana cement*
(*a*) 1 day not less than	—	20 kg/cm^2	—	—
(*b*) 3 days not less than	20 kg/cm^2	30 kg/cm^2	20 kg/cm^2	—
(*c*) 7 days not less than	25 kg/cm^2	—	25 kg/cm^2	—
(20 kg/cm^2 = 300 lbs/m^2)				

No tensile test is required for low heat cement.

The tensile strength is tested by the machine shown below Fig. 8·1. The briquette is clamped tight by the screw *A*. The lead shots are allowed to fall from the vessel *V* to vessel *D* which increases the pull on the briquette. On breaking load the supply from vessel *V* to *D* is cutoff automatically by lever arrangement and level of lead shots in the vessel *D* can also be weighed by the lever arm *L*, giving the breaking load.

(g) **Compression strength.** A paste of 1 : 3 cement and standard sand is prepared with 0·4 w/c ratio and mixed well. Time in making shall not less than 3 min. and more than 4 minutes. Mortar for each cube should be made separately. The size of side of the cubes should be 2·78 in. (7·06 cm) at 58 to 64°F (25 to 30°C) ; 50 cm^2 face area and 90% humidity.

The moulds should be made in two blocked steel frames. It shall be oiled from inner surface while joints should be greased. Its base plate should also be greased so that water may not leak. The mould is connected to a vibration machine which runs at 1200 ± 400 r.p.m. The machine runs for two minutes after filling the mould. The moulds are kept in water till the time of test.

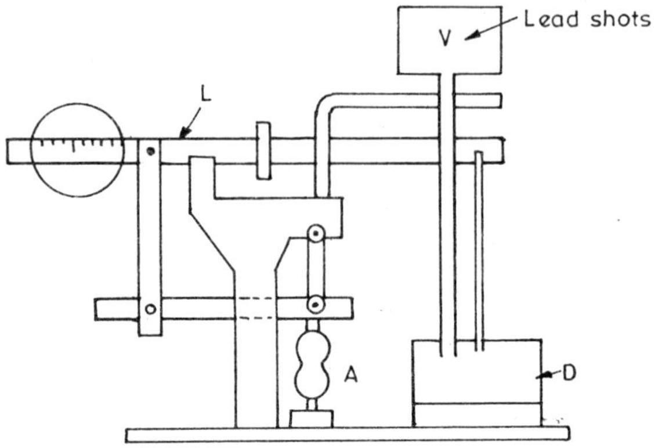

Fig. 8·1.

Determination of Compressive Strength of Cement.

Sl. No.	*Parameter*	*Requirement as per IS : 4031*	*Remarks*
1.	Sampling		As per IS : 3535
2.	Cement for each cube	200 g	
3.	Standard sand for each cube	600 g	As per IS : 650
4.	Water	Potable/Distilled	
5.	Gauging trowel		As per IS : 10086
6.	Vibrating machine, poking rod cube mould		As per IS : 10080
7.	Mixing plate	Non-porous	
8.	Temperature of moulding room, dry materials and water Relative humidity of laboratory	27 ± 2°C 65 ± 5%	
9.	Temperature of moist room Relative humidity	27 ± 2°C 65 ± 5%	
10.	Dry mixing time for cement and standard sand	One minute	
11.	Mixing time for cement standard sand and water	3 minutes min. 4 minutes min.	
12.	Period of vibrations	Two minutes	12000 ± 400 vibrations/min.
13.	Curing tank temperature	27 ± 2°C	
14.	Rate of loading for testing of cube	Starting zero at a rate of 35 N/ sq. mm per min.	Load shall be steady and uniformly applied

Table 8·2. Compressive Strength

(115 gm/cm² = 1600 lbs/in²) *1 : 3 (cement : sand)*	*Ordinary cement*	*Rapid hardening*	*Blast furnace*	*Pozzuolana cement*	*Low heat*
(*a*) 1 day not less than	—	115 gm/cm²	—	—	—
(*b*) 3 days not less than	115 gm/cm²	210 gm/cm²	115 gm/cm²	—	70 gm/cm²
(*c*) 7 days not less than	175 gm/cm²	—	175 gm/cm²	140 gm/cm²	115 gm/cm²
(*d*) 28 days not less than	—	—	—	—	265 gm/cm²

(*h*) **Density of cement.** Density is determined by specific gravity bottle :

(*i*) The weight of bottle empty in air say w_1 gm

(*ii*) The weight of bottle filled with water say its weight = w_2 gm

(*iii*) It is emptied and rinsed with alcohol and dried.

(*iv*) About 20 gms of cement (sieved with B.S. sieve no. 170) is filled in bottle and it is again weighed say its weight is w_3 gm.

(*v*) The bottle is now filled with kerosine or benzene about half of its capacity. Shake it thoroughly so that air from cement may expell till no bubbles come out. The bottle is completely filled with liquid and weighed, let it be w_4 gm.

(*vi*) The bottle is again emptied, cleaned and dried. It is then filled with liquid alone, say now it weighs w_5 gram.

$$\text{Density of cement} = \frac{(w_3 - w_1)d_4}{(w_5 - w_1) - (w_4 - w_3)} \text{ gm/cc}$$

where $d_4 = \dfrac{w_5 - w_1}{w_2 - w_1}$. The normal specific gravity of cement is 3·10. (3·15 ± 0·01)

(*i*) **Field tests of cement.** (1) The colour of the cement should be uniform grey.

(2) Any pressure set lump should be pulverised by finger and thumb.

(3) It should be smoothy in touch, it is gritty if sand is mixed.

(4) The strength can be judged by making a block 3″ × 1″ × 1/2″ with a mortar of 1 : 6 cement and sand. Grip its one end by hand while the other end should be loaded (keeping it horizontal) by steadily increased load. It should not be friable or easily brocken after 3 days immersion in water.

(5) Small pats of 5 × 5 × 2 cm size should be moulded. After 24 hours setting it will resist any impression of the thumb nail. In 48 hours it should not be easily brocken by pressure of finger.

(6) If a sample is heated for about 20 minutes. There should be no change in colour.

(7) Presence of sand in cement can be seen by dissolving the cement in HCl acid. Sand remains undissolved.

(*j*) **Percentage of voids in cement.** Fill a container of 15 cm diameter and 30 cm high with cement upto top, weigh say it is w_1. Fill it with water slowly till it over flows, weigh it again say it is w_2. Now weight of water absorbed by cement : $w_2 - w_1$.

$$\text{Volume of water absorbed by cement} = \frac{w_2 - w_1}{\text{density of water}} = V_2 \text{ (say)}$$

Now the percentage of voids = $\dfrac{V_2}{V_1} \times 100$ where V_1 is the capacity of the container which is already known.

(*k*) **Strength of mortar joint in brick work.** Two bricks are jointed by mortar as shown in Fig. 8·2. Load is applied on the vertical brick gradually. The load at which the joint cracks is noted.

Then strength $= \dfrac{P}{4\frac{1}{2} \times 4\frac{1}{2}}$ units per inch^2, where P is the noted load on cracks $\left(\left(\dfrac{P}{12 \times 12}\right) \text{ units/cm}^2\right)$

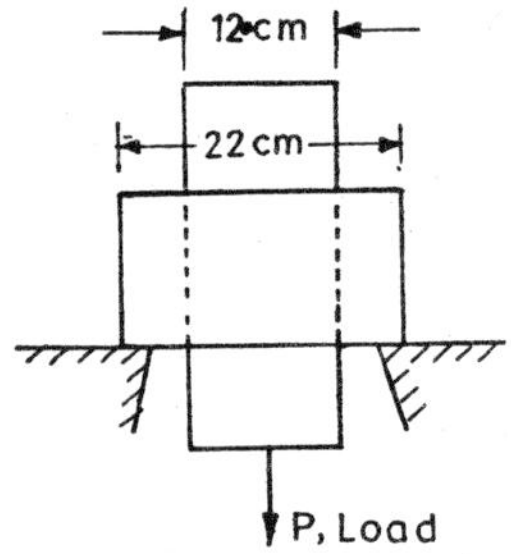

Fig. 8·2.

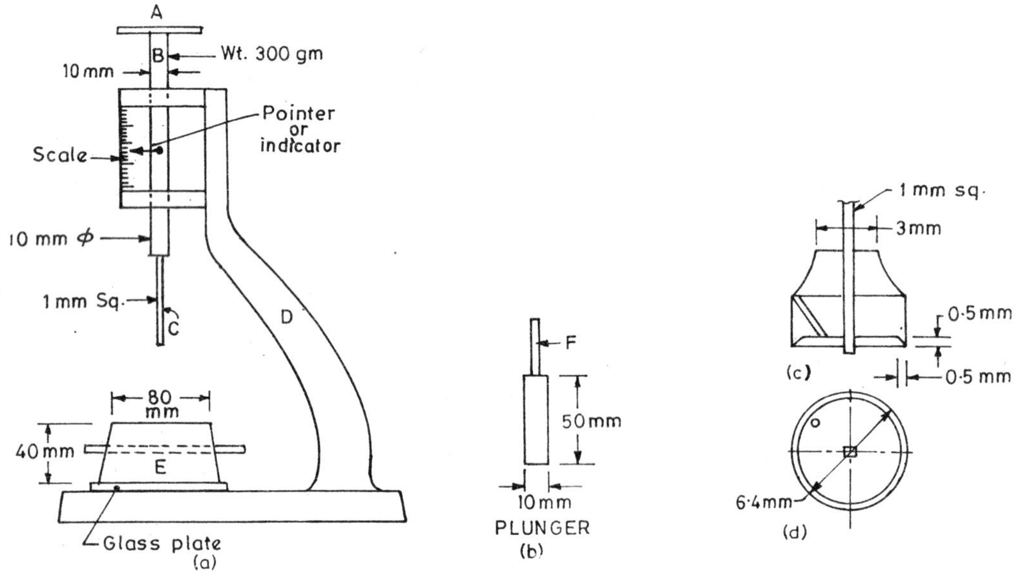

Vicat needle apparatus.

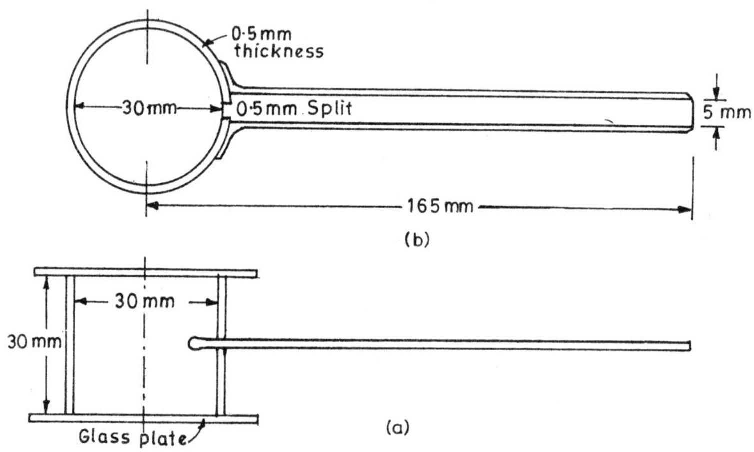

Le Chatelier apparatus.

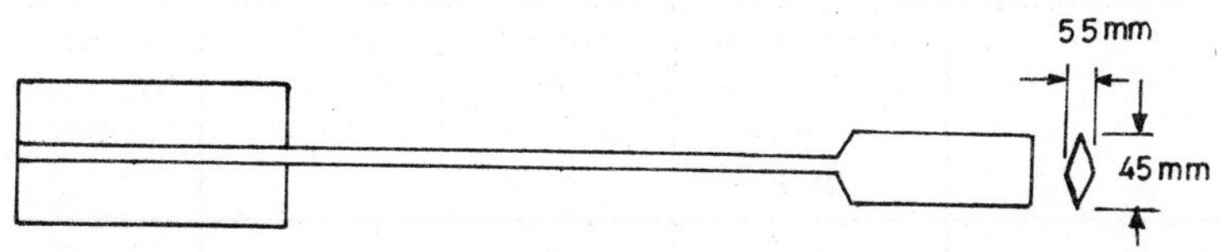

Spatula for tempering paste on mould (all dimensions are in mm)

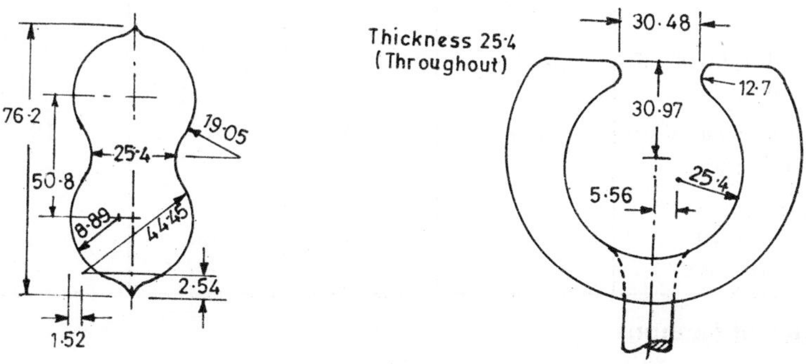

(*a*) Briquate (*b*) Jaws OP apparatus

Apparatus for tensile test of cement.

Fig. 8·3.

Vicat Needle Apparatus. The apparatus consists of a frame D and a movable rod B (10 mm diameter) with a cap A at one end and the removable needle (C) at the other end of 1 mm sq. flat tipped. The rod B carries an indicator which moves on a graduated scale attached to frame D. The cap, rod and needle with all attachments shall together weigh 300 grams. The cement mould consists of a split ring E 80 mm dia and 40 mm high resting on a glass plate (non porous plate). It is used for following tests :

(1) To test the normal consistency of the paste—Needle B is used.

(2) To test the initial setting time—Needle F is used. (Needle F with annular attachment as shown is replaced by the needle C).

For details refer tests for cement. In all operations the needle is released on the paste gently and quickly. The paste of required consistency is filled in the mould and surfaces are plained and cleaned.

Le Chatelier Apparatus. It consists of a split cylinder of brass or any other suitable metal of 0·5 mm thickness and 30 mm internal diameter. It is 30 mm high. Two indicators are attached on either side of split with pointed ends. The distance between the points is 5 mm and the length from centre of split to end = 165 mm. The distance between jaws of the split should be 0·5 mm. Percentage of water for mortar mix is $1\frac{1}{4}\ P = 2{\cdot}5$ where P is the percentage of water.

Paste should be plained by a trowel of spatula of 212·62 gram and not to be tappered by rammers.

Table 8·3. Physical requirements of cement (I.S.).

S. No.	*Property*	*Ordinary portland cement (IS : 269—1958)*	*Rapid Hardening (IS : 269—1956)*	*Low heat (IS : 269—1958)*	*Blast fur. (IS : 455—1962)*	*Pozzuolana (IS : 1489—1962)*
1.	(*i*) Fineness—Maximum residue by weight on IS sieve no. 90 (Present).	10	5	—	10	10
	(*ii*) Minimum Sp. surface by air permeability method in gm/cm^2	2250	3250	3200	2250	3000
2.	Soundness					
	(*i*) Maximum expansion of aerated sample mm.	5	5	5	5	5
	(*ii*) Maximum expansion of unaerated sample mm.	10	10	10	10	10
3.	Max. heat of hydration in cal/gm.					
	7 days	—	—	65	—	—
	10 days	—	—	65	—	—

8·1·5. Types of Cement

Quick Setting, Rapid hardening or high early strength cement

(IS : 8041—1978 and IS : 8102—1978) (1) It contains large proportion of lime and tri calcium silicate.

(2) It is grinded finer.

(3) Calcium chloride about 2% which acts as an accelerator is added when quick setting is needed.

(4) It contains high alumina properties, a mixture of bauxite ($Al_2 O_3 \cdot 2H_2O$) and lime is grinded to the clinker formed.

(5) It contains less gypsum, the setting time is controlled by the percentage of gypsum.

(6) It produces more heat and it shrinks and cracks more after setting.

(7) Having larger surface area due to fineness it needs more water for the same workability. It is more cohesive and reduces separation of water at top called bleeding.

(8) The increasing of the temperature reduces the setting time.

This is used where concrete is laid in water. In closing of water leakages, when load is to be applied earlier, when forms are to be released earlier and for repair work.

Cico and calcium chloride is used as an accelerator. It takes strength earlier, but the ultimate strength is the same. It costs more. In market many other products are also available.

Low setting or low heat cement. (IS : 269—1976). It is used in mass concrete where heat production is to be reduced. In low heat cement the percentage of tricalcium silicate is reduced by say 5%. It is also used where time taken in transite of concrete is more. Its strength is low at early stages, yet its final strength is unaltered. Calcium ligno sulphate is used for this purpose which is to be used in very small quantity only after due experience.

Water proofing of cement. The following water proofers are used.

British products—Pudlo and Impermo.

Indian products—Cico, water seal and Feronite. Many other products are also sold in market which are dealt in later chapters on water proofing.

Cico is supplied as cico no. 1, 2, 3... so on according to the extent of water proofing required. Khana soda, Caustic soda and quick lime are also used as water proofers. These water proofers are sold in market in powder or in liquid form. During manufacture some water proofers are also mixed.

Expanding cements. It expends during setting. It is used for repair work so that it may fill the crevices tight by expansion.

Acid resisting cement. These are silicate base cements. One brand of this cement is Nelson's cement manufactured by Nelson manufacturing company, Bombay. Other brand is made by Pegasur Indian Textilates (Bombay) as "olite". These are used in laboratories and factories of acetic atmosphere.

White cement. In manufacturing of this cement white chalk is used. Calcium and the presence of iron oxide is eliminated (which is the chief cause of the greyish colour of cement) to produce white cement. Oil fuel is used instead of coal fuel. It costs 4 to 5 times more than ordinary cement. It is also known as "snowcrete". There are several brands of white cement available in market. In which 'Birla White' and 'J.K. White' are the main.

Coloured cements. Red and brown colour can be obtained from the grey cement. For other colours white cement is used. Colouring pigments are mixed 5 to 10 percent during grinding, or can be readily mixed in white cement at the time of laying. Any film deposited on surface should be washed by dil HCl (1 : 10) and then with clean water. HCl should be applied on wet water surface.

Table 8·4. Production of coloured cement finishes (IS : 269—1968).

S. No.	*Colour*	*Pigment*	*App. quantity of pigment per 50 kg of white cement in kg*	
			Light shade	*Medium shade*
1.	Grey, blue, black	Germen town carbon or lamp black	0·27	0·55
		Black oxide of M_n. or Mineral black	0·55	1·10
2.	Blue	Ultramarine blue	2·70	4·85
3.	Brownish red or dull brick, red	Red oxide of iron	2·70	4·85
4.	Bright red or verm.	Mineral Turkey	2·70	4·85
5.	Red sand stone to purplish red	Indian red	2·70	4·85
6.	Brown to reddish brown	Mat. brown (oxide)	2·70	4·85
7.	Buff, colonial tint and yellow	Yellow ochre or yellow oxide	2·70	5·50
8.	Green	Chromium oxide or greenish ultramarine blue	3·25	—

Sand and Masonry cements. Ordinary cement when used in brick work, water is soaked, reducing the quantity of water in the mortar, hence some siliceous material is added during grinding. It gives more workability.

Pozzuolana cement. (IS : 1489—1976). A mixture of 40% portland cement and 40% pozzuolana is grinded together. By this a more chemical resistant cement is produced. It has a low heat evolution, strength is highly increased with temperature.

Air entraining cement. It is an ordinary cement mixed with air entraining materials during grinding. The air in the form of minute air bubbles form 0·003 to 0·05 in dia is distributed throughout the mass. This causes more workability, reduce segregation and bleeding. The strength of this concrete is reduced more than 160 p.s.i. The air entraining materials are Resin, Vinsol, Rosan, Darex, oils and fats, sulphuric acid, alkali salts of sulphated organic compounds etc. The amount of sand can be reduced by an amount equal to the volume of bubbles. Air should not be more than 5%. Aluminium powder is also one of the substitutes mixed 0·005 to 0·02% by weight causing formation of hydrogen gas which works as above.

Blast furnace cement. It has low heat evolution and is more durable. At lower temperature its rate of hardening is low.

High alumina cement. It is manufactured by fusing a mixture of aluminous and calcarious materials in suitable proportions during grinding. It develops strength rapidly. More heat evolution and high durability against chemical agents, such as sulphates and sea water. It is black in colour. The raw materials are lime stone and bauxite ($AlO_3 . 2H_2O$) burnt with coal. After cooling it is grinded and all particles of iron are separated by magnetic separators. It contains 40% of lime, 40% aluminium, silica less than 6%. It develops strength even earlier with rapid hardening cement. It's ultimate strength is higher than that of ordinary cement, compressive strength over 6000 lbs/in^2. Due to evolution of heat it is used in cold climates, hence is generally used in cold and frosty weather. It's initial setting time is 3·5 hours and final 4 to 5 hours. The presence of calcium chloride reduces it's strength hence sea water is harmful for this cement. It is kept separate with ordinary cement, nor it is mixed with it. For reducing setting time 1 to 2% hydrated lime is mixed. Cement "Fouder" is one of its brands. It is used in chemical plants and where the concrete is to be used soon as in wars. It connot be used in mass construction work.

Super sulphate cement. Granulated slag, calcium sulphate and Portland cement are mixed together. The cement so produced has low heat evolution and chemical resistance.

Sulphate resistant cements. It is used where structures are constructed under alkalinic water. In this cement silicate percentage is more, while aluminates are less. It develops high ultimate strength and heat generation is not more than low heat cement.

Natural cement. Hydraulic lime and surkhi mixed with cement gives more strength and workability. It decreases bleeding, segregation and heat of hydration. The shrinkage may increase. Period of curing is also higher.

Calcium chloride cement. It contains 2% calcium chloride. It is rapid hardening. Attains strength very early. Forms can be released even after six hours and work can be used only after 16 hours.

Hydrophobic cement. This cement has a property of not being effected in air or dampness. It is prepared from Portland cement clinker in which water repellent chemicals are added during the operation of grinding.

Refractory cement. This cement can with stand high temperatures in the range of 1500°C. It is used in coating of high alumina bricks used in repair of furnace walls.

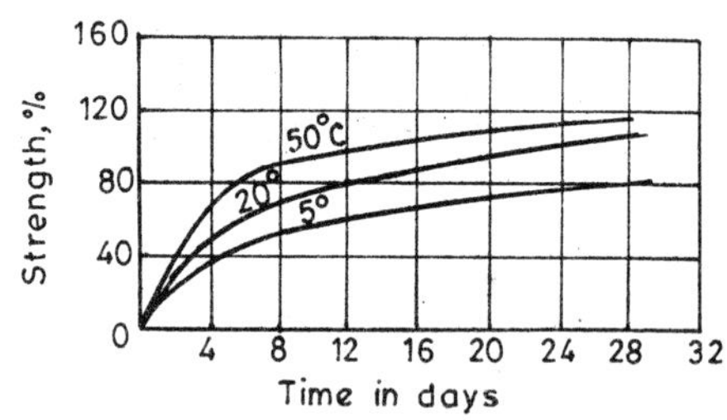

(Ratio 1 : 2 : 4 in stone blast, w/c ratio 0·2)
Fig. 8·4.

Oil well cement. It is used in drilling of oil wells so as to fill the space between the steel lining tube and wall of the well. It sets slowly and hence it has sufficient time to reach large depths before setting. When setting starts it takes strength rapidly.

Red oxide mixed cement. Red oxide is mixed in cement to have a protection of steel against rusting. Some manufacturers are producing such cements.

8·1·6. Strength of Portland cement with age (From date of pouring)

3 days	40%	3 months	110%
7 days	65%	6 months	120%
28 days	100% (Taken as unit)	12 months	130%

Rapid hardening cement		*High alumina cement (1 : 2 : 4)*	
1 day	140 kg/cm^2	7 Hrs.	260 kg/cm^2
2 day	200 kg/cm^2	12 Hrs.	490 kg/cm^2
3 day	260 kg/cm^2	24 Hrs.	520 kg/cm^2
7 day	370 kg/cm^2	3 days	530 kg/cm^2
28 days	480 kg/cm^2		
12 months	530 kg/cm^2		

8·1·7. Different types of cement as classified by the Bureau of Indian Standards

(1) 33 grade ordinary Portland cement (IS 269 : 1989) Low setting. (33 MPa)

(2) 43 grade ordinary Portland cement (IS 8112 : 1989) Medium setting. (43 MPa)

(3) 53 grade ordinary Portland cement (IS 12269 : 1987) High setting. (53 MPa)

(4) Rapid Hardening Portland cement (IS 8041 : 1990)

(5) Portland slag cement (IS 455 : 1989)

(6) Portland Pozzoulana cement (IS 11489 Part-1 : 1991)

(7) Portland Pozzoulana cement (IS 11489 Part-2 : 1991)

(8) Hydrophobic cement (IS 8043 : 1991)

(9) Low Heat Portland cement (IS : 12600 : 1989)

(10) Sulphate resisting Portland cement (IS 12330 : 1988)

(11) High Alumina cement (IS 6452 : 1989)

(12) Super Sulphated cement (IS 6909 : 1990).

Note : (1) Grades 33, 43 and 53 depends on admixture of Pozzoulana, Alumina and Calcium Chloride according to the time based strength required.

(2) Unit weight of Ordinary Portland Cement (O.P.C.) = 1300 ± 50 kg/m^3.

Physical characteristics of various types of cements

Sl. No.	*Type of cement*	*IS : No.*	*Fineness m²/kg (min.)*	*Setting time (min.)*		*Comp. strength MPa*		
				Initial Min.	*Final Max.*	*3 days*	*7 days*	*28 days*
1.	OPC 33 grade	269 : 1989	225	30	600	16	22	33
2.	OPC 43 grade	8112 : 1989	225	30	600	23	33	43
3.	OPC 53 grade	12269 : 1987	225	30	600	22	37	53
4.	OPC (Fly ash base)	1489 Part-2 1991	300	30	600	16	22	33
5.	PSC (Slag cement)	455 : 1989	220	30	600	16	22	33
6.	SDC (Sulphate resisting cement)	12330 : 1988	225	30	600	10	16	33
7.	Rapid hardening cement	8041 : 1990	325	30	600	27	—	—
8.	Railway sleeper class cement	43-5/53-5	370	60	600	—	37·5	—

Table contd...

Table contd...

Sl. No.	Type of cement	IS : No.	Fineness m^2/kg	Setting time (min.)		Comp. strength MPa		
			(min.)	Initial Min.	Final Max.	3 days	7 days	28 days
9.	Low heat portland cement	12600 : 1989	320	60	600	10	16	35
10.	Masonry cement	3466 : 1989	*	96	1440	NS	2·5	5
11.	High aluminium cement	6452 : 1989	225	30	600	35	NS	NS
12.	Super sulphated cement	6909 : 1990	400	30	600	15	22	30
13.	White cement	8042 : 1989	225	30	600	14·4	19·8	29·7

* Residue on 45 m is sieve max. percent (by wet sieving) is 15.

NS Not specified.

8·1·8. Admixtures

Admixtures are materials used in concrete to modify its properties. These are added to the concrete to modify specific properties of the concrete generally calcium chloride, starches, cellulose products, sugars and hydroxylated carboxylic acids are used as admixtures. Admixture should comply with IS : 9103.

Mineral Admixtures

Pozzolana. Pozzolana materials confirming to Indian Standards may be used to provide uniform blending with cement is ensured.

Silica fume. Silica fume confirming to a standard may be used as part replacement of cement provided uniform blending with cement is ensured. It is a by-product of manufacture of silicon.

Fly ash. (Pulverised fuel ash) Confirming to Grade 1 of IS 3812 may be used as part replacement of ordinary Portland cement provided uniform blending with cement is ensured.

Rice husk. Rice husk ash is produced by burning of rice husk, contains large properties of silica. It can range from being as deleterious as silt when incorporated in concrete. Water demand and drying shrinkage should be studied before using rice husk.

Matakaolini. Matakaolini having fineness between 700 to 900 m^2/kg may be used as pozzolana material in concrete. Matakaolini is obtained by calcination of pure or refined Kaolintic clay at a temperature between 650°C and 850°C, followed by grinding to achieve a fineness of 700 to 900 m^2/kg. The resulting material has high pozzoulana city.

Ground Granulated Blast Furnace Slag. Ground granulated blast furnace slag is obtained by grinding granulated blast furnace slag confirming to IS 12089 may be used as part replacement of ordinary Portland cement provided blending with cement is ensured.

The addition of Fe-Cr slag upto 40% along with OPC in slag cement has given good results. Although the Fe-Cr slag cement contains Cr_2O_3 and low glassy structure, the physical results obtained are above the limits of Indian Standards (IS : 455) and comparable with Tisco slag cement manufactured using B.F. slag.

Compressive strength of cement can be further improved by proper granulated of FeCr slag *i.e.*, by rapid cooling of molten slag by high pressure water jets. This will improve glass cement of slag and consequently improve reactively of slag in cement slag blends and hence strength of cement paste. It is possible to use upto 12% L.D. slag as replacement of lime stone in the cement clinker resulting in the additional production to the extent of 10% without addition of extra energy to the kiln.

Studies of NCB revealed that small percentage of steel slag (15 to 20%) alongwith Blast Furnace slag can be used as admixture in making blended cement.

Studies with South African steel slag has indicated that by subjecting the slag to a reduction process the oxides are reduced to iron which is removed with magnetics and returned to the steel plant. The removing slag is used in the production of Portland cement which resulted in a significant reduction in the CO_2 emission in the cement plant. A positive contribution towards waste reduction could thus be made.

8·2. Aggregates

8·2·1. Aggregates are inert materials like broken stones, bricks, river-bed shingle and sand etc., used in concrete. The aggregates, generally larger than 3/16″ (4·75 mm) is called a coarse aggregate while smaller are known as fine. The following are the characteristics of a good aggregate. According to Bureau of Indian Standards (B-IS) or IS 383 : 1970.

(1) Its strength should not be less than the strength of the building material.

(2) It should not be soft, porous, or flaky, free from friable, elongated and laminated particles which are weak in shear porous aggregates give chance for the rusting of the reinforcement due to passage of water through it.

(3) Broken aggregates are better than the round in the sense that it contains better bonding than the round, while the round pebbles are better in the sense that no loose and soft material is left in the pebbles during rolling with river water and it gives good workability and strength for the same quantity of cement used. It has also less voids than the brocken aggregates.

(4) It must not absorve water more than 10% by weight after 24 hours immersion in water (IS specification).

(5) It must be lighter, hard and non abrasive and must have fine resisting properties.

(6) It must be resistant to weather, water and temperature.

(7) It should be clear with impurities like clay, silt, alkalies and organic matter which retards the setting considerably and reduce bondage to cement. The strength of the concrete is also effected by the presence of these substances.

(8) It should be free from mica, because of its soft laminated and absorptive character.

(9) The surface texture is classified as glossy, smooth, granular, rough or pilled, crystalline and honey combed porous. The selection is done according to the purpose.

(10) It should not contain more than 1% of sulphates.

8·2·2. Coarse aggregates

As specified above the aggregates larger than 3/16″ (4·75 mm) and passes from 80 mm sieve are known as coarse aggregates. It can be obtained from the following sources.

(1) Round aggregates can be obtained from the beds of the rivers after screening to different sizes. It is hard more workable and is known as shingle. The bigger size more than 4″ (100 mm) is known as boulder, while pebbles smaller than the size of Pea is known as Pea-gravel and larger than Pea as Bajree.

(2) Crushed aggregates can be obtained by crushing the stones in crushing plants where it is screened in different sizes as ballast.

The source of stones for crushing are—

(*a*) Granite, Basalt and trap which gives a hard ballast generally used in important R.C.C. works.

(*b*) **Sand stones** which gives softer ballast and hence generally used in mass concreting in foundations where is available in vicinant locality. It is porous and give poor concrete which is liable to shrink and cracks and is therefore used in less important works.

(*c*) **Lime stone** is quite good provided if it is hard, crystalline and entirely free from dust. It should not be used in works subjected to intense heat and water due to its porosity. It is effected by acidic climate.

(*d*) **Quartzite.** Used in mass concrete in foundations and roads. It is also used in RCC work.

(*e*) **Blast furnace slag.** Its density should not be more than 78 lbs/cft or 1200 kg/m^3 and should not absorve water more than 10% by weight. It should have low percentage of sulphuric and iron.

(*f*) **Pumice stone.** Furnace clinker, coke, breeze, saw dust and expanded vermiculate etc. are used where light weight concrete is required just as in curtain walls and fillets etc. These are not used in structural members.

(*g*) **Brick bats.** Brocken 1st class or over burnt bricks are used as ballast. It is porous and light. It is used in less important works in foundations and where light weight is needed. It is also sound proof and fire resistant over burnt and Jhama ballast is used in road solling. Earth containing lime and sulphur should be avoided for bricks.

Note : (1) Bricks which are absorvent in nature should be soaked in water before use.

(2) The aggregates should be washed with clear water before use to escape any dust etc.

Concrete with tile waste as coarse aggregate. It is reported that around 30% of the tiles produced in the factories are defective due to various reasons. These waste tiles can be used as coarse aggregate in concrete after crushing. Results of study showed that concrete with mix proportions 1 : 3 : 6 and 1 : 4 : 8 with brocken tile waste as coarse aggregate shows a compressive strength of 4·9 N/mm^2 and 4·1 N/m^2 respectively and water absorption of 3% and 3·4% respectively. The compressive strength of concrete with brocken tile pieces as coarse aggregate is about 50% to 60% of that conventional concrete.

Note : (1) Aggregates should not contain more than 0·5% or sulphates as SO_2 and should not absorb more than 10% of their own mass of water.

(2) Size of aggregate—maximum size of coarse aggregate should be as large as possible with in the limits specified but not greater than one-fourth of the minimum thickness of the member. The reinforcement should be thoroughly surrounded by mortar, which should fill all the corners of the form. In concrete elements with the sections, closely spaced reinforcement or small cover, consideration should be given to the use of 10 mm nominal maximum size.

(3) **Plums.** (big boulders) above 160 mm and upto any reasonable size upto a maximum limit of 20% by volume of concrete may be used. Plumps should be evenly distributed and shall not be closer han 150 mm from the surface.

(4) For heavily reinforced members as in case of ribs of main beams the nominal maximum size of the aggregate is restricted to 5 mm less than the minimum clear distance between the main bars or 5 mm less than the minimum cover to the reinforcement which ever is smaller.

8·2·2A. Storing of aggregates.

The aggregates should be stored in pyramidal shaped heaps. Care should be taken that while pouring aggregates to the heap from the vehicle, fine and bigger ingradiants may not separate or the heavier parts tend to roll on outer edge, while the finer remains in the centre. It should not be stored in a large heap, but should be stored in smaller stacks having about a truck capacity.

8·2·2B. Sampling for test

A sample of about half m^3 should be taken and spreaded on a clean surface. It should be quartered by a trowel. Two opposite quarters should be remixed to make a sample. It should be taken from different heaps and a sample from each heap should be tested.

8·2·2C. Test for durability

It depends on the resistance to wear due to weathering. A sample is immersed in saturated solution of sodium or magnesium sulphate for 18 hours at a temperature of 20°C. The sample is then placed in an oven at a temperature of 110°C and dried to constant weight. This process of wetting and drying should be repeated several times. The aggregate should not show any signs of crumbling. The quantity of sample should be taken according to the requirement.

8·2·2D. Specific gravity of aggregates

The method depends on the size of aggregates. For an aggregate coarser than 10 mm a sample is 1st cleaned with water and is then immersed in distilled water for 24 hours and weighed, say it is w_1. Wipe the surface with damp cloth and weigh say it is w_2. Dry the sample in an oven, cool and weigh again say it is w_3. From the above notes calculate the specific gravity as follows.

$$\text{Density of the sample} = \frac{w_3}{\text{vol. of sample}}$$

$$\text{Specific gravity} = \text{density of sample/density of water}$$

$$\text{Absorption} = \frac{w_2 - w_3}{w_3} \times 100 \text{ by percentage}$$

Note : For aggregate finer than 10 mm a pyconometer is used.

Bulk density. A container of known capacity is filled by aggregate in three equal layers, each layer is tamped with 25 strokes by a tamping rod. The weight of the material in the container divided by its volume gives the bulk density of the aggregate.

8·2·2E. Voids in aggregates

Fill up a quantity of aggregate upto top in a container of volume say V_1 in three layers as above and tamp it by 25 strokes by a tamping rod.

Fill up the container with clean water upto top till it just overflows. Remove the ballast from the container and again measure the volume of the remaining water, say it is V_2. The percentage of voids in ballast $= \frac{V_2}{V_1} \times 100$.

Note : In order to measure the quantity of water remained with ballast in absorbed condition and on surface. Weigh the dry ballast before filling the water in the container and again when it becomes wet. The difference gives the volume of water left with ballast and dividing it with density of water, volume of the water remained with ballast is calculated and this volume should be added to V_2.

Crushing value. A weighed quantity of aggregate is placed in a metal cylinder fitted with a plunger which is subjected to a specific compressive load. The aggregate is then sieved to separate the crushed portion. The weight of the crushed to the total aggregate expressed as percentage as the aggregate crushing value.

Sieve test. A known weight of dry aggregate is passed successively through the following IS sieves in order.

Fine aggregate	475 mm,	2·36 mm,	1·18 mm		
	600 μ,	300 μ,	150 μ		
Coarse aggregate	80 mm	40 mm	20 mm	10 mm	4·75 mm
All in aggregates	75 mm	40 mm	20 mm	10 mm	4·75 mm
Coarse and fine mixed	2·36 mm	1·18 mm	600 μ	300 μ	150 μ

Table 8·5. Aperture size of standard sieves

Width of aperture			Indian standard sieves standard	British standard sieves mesh no.	U.S. Standard sieves standard	Tyler sieves mesh no.
	mm	Inches				
ISO	5·60	0·224	5·60 mm		5·06	3·5
	4·75	0·190	4·75 mm		4·76	4
ISO	4·00	0·160	4·00 mm		4·00	5
	3·35	0·132	3·35 mm	5	3·36	6
ISO	2·80	0·1107	2·80 mm	6	2·83	7
	2·36	0·0949	2·36 mm	7	2·38	8
ISO	2·00	0·0810	2·00 mm	8	2·00	9
	1·70	0·066	1·70 mm	10	1·68	10
ISO	1·40	0·0553	1·40 mm	12	1·41	12
	1·18	0·0474	1·18 mm	14	1·19	14
ISO	1·00	0·0395	1·00 mm	16	1·00	16
	0·850	0·0336	850 micron	18	841 μ	20
ISO	0·710	0·0275	710 micron	22	707 μ	24
	0·600	0·0236	600 micron	25	595 μ	28
ISO	0·500	0·0197	500 micron	30	500 μ	32
	0·425	0·0166	425 micron	36	420 μ	35
ISO	0·355	0·0139	355 micron	44	354 μ	42
	0·300	0·0116	300 micron	52	297 μ	48
ISO	0·250	0·0099	250 micron	60	250 μ	60
	0·212	0·0083	212 micron	72	210 μ	65
ISO	0·180	0·007	180 micron	85	177 μ	80
	0·150	0·006	150 micron	100	149 μ	100
ISO	0·125	0·0049	125 micron	120	125 μ	115
	0·106	0·0041	106 micron	150	105 μ	150
ISO	0·090	0·0035	90 micron	170	88 μ	170
	0·075	0·0030	75 micron	200	74 μ	200
ISO	0·063	0·0026	63 micron	240	63 μ	250
	0·053	0·0021	53 micron	300	53 μ	270
ISO	0·045	0·0018	45 micron	350	44 μ	325

Note : (1) The sieves which have been marked ISO are **international standard of sieves**.

(2) B.S. sieve no. 100 means 100 × 100 apertures (squares) in one inch square area of sieve (B.S. 410 : 1962)

(3) Indian Standard gives the size of arc aperture in mm or in microns.

(4) Size less than 150 μ is known as ultra fine.

The percentage material retained on each sieve is compared with the limits given in the table below.

Table 8·6. Grading limits for fine aggregates (IS : 2386—1965)

I.S. sieve no.	*Percentage passing*			
	Grade-1	*Grade-2*	*Grade-3*	*Grade-4*
100 mm	100	100	100	100
4·75 mm	90-100	90-100	90-100	95-100
2·36 mm	60-95	75-100	85-100	95-100
1·18 mm	30-70	55-90	75-100	90-100
600 μ	15-34	35-59	60-79	80-100
300 μ	5-20	8-30	12-40	15-50
150 μ	0-10	0-10	0-10	0-15

For crushed stone sand is increased by 20%

Table 8·7. Grading limit for coarse aggregate (IS : 3837)

I.S. sieve ↓ *size (mm)*	*Table No.-1* Percentage passing for graded aggregate of nominal size (mm)				*Table No.-2* Percentage passing for single sized aggregate of nominal size (mm)					
	40	20	16	12·5	63	40	20	16	12·5	10
80	100	—	—	—	100	—	—	—	—	—
63	—	—	—	—	85-100	100	—	—	—	—
40	95-100	100	—	—	0-30	85-100	100	—	—	—
20	30-70	95-100	100	100	0-5	0-20	85-100	100	—	—
16	—	—	95-100	—	—	—	—	85-100	100	—
12·5	—	—	—	90-100	—	—	—	—	85-100	100
10	10-35	25-35	30-70	40-85	0-5	0-5	0-20	0-30	0-45	85-100
4·75	0-5	0-10	0-10	0-10	—	—	0-5	0-5	0-10	0-20
2·36	—	—	—	—	—	—	—	—	—	0-5

When the coarse aggregate available at site is ungradial single size coarse aggregate as given in table no. 1 is used and other ingradients as in table no. 2.

Table 8·8. Coarse aggregate by volume for different mixes

Ratio of mix	*Nominal size of aggregate (mm)*	*Part of aggregate of sizes*				
		63 mm	*40 mm*	*20 mm*	*12·5 mm*	*10 mm*
1 : 6 : 12	63	9	—	3	—	—
1 : 6 : 12	40	—	9	3	—	—
1 : 5 : 10	63	7·5	—	2·5	—	—
1 : 5 : 10	40	—	7·5	2·5	—	—
1 : 4 : 8	63	6	—	2	—	—
1 : 4 : 8	40	—	6	2	—	—
1 : 3 : 6	63	4·5	—	1·5	—	—
1 : 3 : 6	40	—	4·5	1·5	—	—
1 : 3 : 6	20	—	—	4·5	—	1·5
1 : 2 : 4	40	—	2·5	1	—	0·5
1 : 2 : 4	20	—	—	3	—	1
1 : 2 : 4	12·5	—	—	—	3	1
1 : 1½ : 3	20	—	—	2	—	1

Table 8·9. Maximum size of aggregate for various uses

Min. dimension of section in cm	*Max. size of aggregate in cm*			
	Reinforced walls beams and columns	*Unreinforced walls*	*Heavy reinforced slabs*	*Light or unreinforced slabs*
6-13	1·2-2·0	2·0	2·0-2·5	2·0-3·8
15-28	2·0-3·8	3·8	3·8	3·8-7·5
30-74	3·8-7·5	7·5	3·8-7·5	7·5
75 or more	3·8-7·5	15·0	3·8-7·5	7·5-15·0

Table 8·10. Properties of Light Weight aggregates

Aggregate	*Unit weight kg/m³*	*Bulk specific gravity*	*Water absorption*	
			weight %	*kg/m³*
Vermiculite	160	1 : 35	128	300
Diatomite	500	1 : 44	75	385
Perlite	144	0·86	153	225
Slag	480-960	1·13-2·26	5-23	48-160
Ash	670-930	1·74-2·10	8-15	24-96
Pumice	700-790	1·46-1·66	29-43	240-270
Shale	960-1220	1·74-2·09	7	—
Slate	625-1170	1·29-2·20	8-15	96-110
Clay	850-1060	1·69-1·98	16-21	176

8·2·3. Fine aggregate (Sand). It is generally known as sand.

Influence of grain size distribution as dilatancy of sand

(1) The simple direct shear test may be utilized to assess the relative dilation values of sand of different grades from various sources. When there are several sources of sand in different grades at disposal, using this simple technique one may choose the best source of sand to be used.

(2) In general coarse the sand higher will be the dilatancy.

(3) Uniformly graded sand exhibits less rate of delatancy than will graded sand nearly at same average grain diameter.

(4) As the normal load increases the dilatancy decreases for each grade and type of load.

Dilatancy means volumetric change accompanying deformation. This is a special property of cohesionless soil. The term dilatancy also can connote thickening or thinning of a joint with granular particles undergoing shear deformation at constant normal stress.

As already classified fine aggregate is a material which passes through 3/16 (4·75 mm) IS sieve and retained on 75 micron sieve sand consists of small grains of silica (SiO_2) and is formed by decomposition of sand silica by action of weather or water. The grains may be round or angular according to source. It may be classified as under :

(1) **Pit sand.** Sand obtained in old abandoned river beds as quarry such as Badarpur quarries, near Delhi. It has sharp angular grains.

(2) **River or lake sand.** Founded in beds of rivers such as in North Indian Rivers Ganga, Chambal, Betwa, Sarda and Satlaj etc. The sand obtained from such sources is mixed with clay silt or mica. Sand is also available in large lakes.

(3) **Sea sand.** Found at coast of sea. It contains round grains and has presence of salt

which effects on concrete and reinforcement and retard setting time. It can be removed by washing. Presence of salts can be tested by taste.

(4) **Crushed stone.** Bye product of ballast crushing plants, left as finish remains. It may contain dust and clay, tends to be flaky which gives a harsh mix.

(5) Fine sand	—	Fineness modulus	2·20 to 2·60
Medium sand	—	Fineness modulus	2·60 to 2·90
Coarse sand	—	Fineness modulus	2·90 to 3·20

Characteristics of a good sand

(1) It should be clean, sharp, angular, hard and durable. Grains chemically inert, free from salt, clay, organic matter and salts. Round grains do not interlock sufficiently.

(2) Grains should pass through a sieve of 400 meshes per m^2. (0·78 mm mesh) and be retained on a sieve of 900 meshes per m^2 (0·5 mm) and should be graded.

(3) The angular grains give best results for tensile strength while the round grains give a better result in compression.

(4) Colour of sand depends on the source of sand. Deep brown colour is due to the presence of the iron traces. Colour of sand matters little if the above qualities are obtained.

(5) Presence of salt, clay and mica, which are the sources of weakness. Mica can be easily detected due to its shining surface, however 6% of silt and 2 to 3 percent of mica can be usually allowed.

Indian Standard of Sand (IS : 650—1955)

(1) Shall be obtained from Ennore (Tamil Nadu)

(2) Shall consist grey or whitish angular (app. spherical) grains of brocken quartz, containing very small amount of elongated or flattened grains.

(3) Shall pass through IS : 842 microns (1 micron = 10^{-3} mm) and not more than 10% by weight shall pass through IS sieve no. 592 microns.

(4) Shall be free from silt and organic impurities.

8·2·3 A. Bulking of sand

When moist sand increases in volume due to the grains of sand getting covered with a thin film of water which prevents them from coming in close contact with one another due to surface tension. Saturated with water, sand is equal in volume to that of perfectly dry sand. When used moist an allowance for this increase should be given in measuring sand. Sand measures should be increased in depth to give an account for this bulking due to presence of moisture. If it is is not done the sand used will be less than required producing honey-combing. The presence of this water is also accounted for calculating water cement ratio, otherwise the water used will be more than required causing increased water cement ratio.

To avoid this the sand is measured by weight in batching plants as the weight of the sand is very little effected by dampness with it, which can be neglected. It may be about 5%.

Table 8·11. Bulking of sand for various moisture contents

Moisture % volume	*Fine sand % volume*	*Medium sand % volume*	*Coarse sand % volume*
1	16	8	6
2	26	16	12
3	32	22	15

Table 8·11 contd.

Table 8·11 contd.

Moisture % volume	*Fine sand % volume*	*Medium sand % volume*	*Coarse sand % volume*
4	36	27	17
5	38	29	18
6	37	28	18
8	35	26	16
10	32	22	12
12	28	19	8
15	22	12	2
17	10	7	0
20	9	6	0
27	0	0	0

Tests for Sand—Field tests (IS : 1542—1960)

(1) **Presence of salts.** It can be checked by taste.

(2) **Presence of silt and clay.** (*a*) Rub a little of sand between the fingers, strain left on figners will indicate the presence of clayee impurities or will leave clayee dust on palm when tested on palm.

(*b*) Vigorously stir a sample of sand in a glass tumbler of water and allow it to rest for about one hour. Amount of clay or silt present in it will settle on the sand and the water will be seen muddy if the sand is mixed with clay or silt. If a tea spoonfull salt is added to a pint of water will quicken the process and silt will settle in a layer on top of the sand. The thickness of the silt layer should not exceed 1/7th or 6% that of sand below it. If the thickness is more than it needs washing. It is known as "decantation test". 1 to 2% silt or clay may improve the plasticity of mortar but excess of it will cause reduction in strength. Meterials passing in B.S. sieve no. 200 (75 μ) is considered to be fine clay or silt. The permissible limits for silt and fine clay is given below as B.S.S. 882.

Natural or crushed gravel sands	4%
Crushed stone sand	10%
Coarse aggregate of any type	1%

Clay forms a thin film on sand particles which reduces adhesion of cement to the sand, retards setting and increases cracks and shrinkage. It increases the requirement of water causing reduction in ultimate strength of mortar.

(3) **Presence of organic impurities.** Stir a sample of sand in a 3% solution (100 gm in 4 litres of water) of caustic soda and keep the bottle corked for 24 hours. If the colour of the liquid turns darker than straw (pale yellow) presence of organic matter is indicated.

This impurity can be removed by washing which also helps in salt removal from sand. These impurities are due to decayed vegetation, humous and factory wastes which retards the setting and strength of the mortar.

(4) **Proportion of sand in concrete mix.** Mix a sample of concrete in water and then pass it through 4·75 mm sieve deposits on the sieve are coarse aggregates, while the material passed is sand and cement. Stir the jar containing the sand and cement mix and allow it to settle sand will settle down and cement will come on the top, thickness of which can be measured and it's proportion to sand can be calculated.

(5) **Bulking in sand.** (*a*) Fill up a container of known height say 30 cm and 15 cm diameter with sand sample upto top. The surplus mass may be removed by a rule, say it's height be H_1. Pour water slowly in the container so that the sand in it may not flow out of the container.

The sand sinks and after some time the water from top of container will start overflowing. It is the condition when the sand becomes saturated with water. Now measure the depth of water from top to the sand surface in container, say it is H_2. Now percentage of bulking is $\frac{H_2}{H_1} \times 100$. The finer the sand the more is the bulking in it.

(*b*) Take a measured volume of bulked sand say V_1. Dry it in a pan on oven till it is perfectly dry. Again measure the volume of this dry sand in a measuring jar, say it is V_2. Now the percentage of bulking is $\frac{V_1 - V_2}{V_1} \times 100$.

Percentage of Voids in Sand. In the container test (5) (*a*), the weight of the container + weight of the wet sand upto height H_2 is taken say it is w_1. Empty the container and dry the sand in the oven till it becomes perfectly dry by heating, and weigh it with the container, say it is w_2. Now the weight of the water in the wet sand in container upto height H_2 is $w_1 - w_2$ and its volume $= \frac{w_1 - w_2}{w}$ where w = weight of water per unit volume = V_2 say.

Specific gravity, Bulk density and Voids of aggregates

Specific gravity—Trap 2·9 ; Granite 2·8 ; Gravel 2·66 ; Sand 2·65.

Bulk density—River sand, Fine 1·44 ; Medium 1·52 ; Coarse 1·60 ; Beach or river shingle 1·60 ; Brocken stone 1·6 ; Stone Screening 1·44 ; Brocken granite 1·68.

Voids in percentage—River sand, Fine 43 ; Coarse 35 ; Mixed and moist 38 ; Mixed and dry 30.

Brocken stone graded, maximum 25 mm 46 ; Maximum 50 mm size 45 ; maximum 63 mm 41 ; stone screening 4·8.

Water absorption of aggregates. By weight : Average sand 1% ; Pebbles and crushed lime stone 1% ; Trap rock and crushed granite 0·5% ; Porous sand stone 7·0% ; Very light and porous upto 25%.

Free water on surface in aggregates

Very wet sand	120 to 160 litres % litres
Moderately wet	80 litres % litres
Moist sand	40 litres % litres
Moist gravel or crushed rock	20 to 40 litres % litres

Note : The coarser is the aggregate, the lesser is the free water it carries.

Specific gravity of Sand. (Fine aggregate below 10 mm). A pyconometer with a metal conical screw top is taken. The sample is dried by a warm air current and is weighed say it is w_1. The aggregate is then placed in the pyconometer filled with water and weighed, say it is w_2. The pyconometer is now emptied, filled with water and weighed, say it is w_3. The sample is then dried in an oven, cooled in an air tight container and weighed say it is w_4.

From the above observations the specific gravity of aggregate can be calculated as below :

Weight of the dry sample = w_4 – weight of the container = w_5 say (weight of container can be weighed separately).

Now specific gravity = $\frac{w_2 - w_5}{w_3}$ (w_5 must be equal to w_1 if there is no wastage).

8·2·4. Fineness modulus of aggregates

Fineness modulus is a number which gives an idea of average fineness of aggregates. To find the fineness modulus of any sample of aggregate, the percentage of the sample (By weight) retained on each of the sieves as given below is determined. The total of these percentages divided by 100 gives the fineness modulus of the sample as shown below. The lesser in the fineness modulus, the finer is the aggregate.

Table 8·12.

B.S. sieve No.	*I.S. sieve No.*	*Percentage retained coarse aggregate*		*Percentage retained fine aggregate*	
		B.S. sieve	*I.S. sieve*	*B.S. sieve*	*I.S. sieve*
100	150 μ	100	100	100	100
52	300 μ	100	100	82	82
25	600 μ	100	100	50	50
14	1·18 mm	100	100	28	28
7	2·36 mm	100	100	16	16
3/16″	4·69 mm	94	94	6	6
3/8″	9·37 mm	60	60	—	—
3/4″	18·75 mm	12	12	—	—
1½″	37·50 mm	—	—	—	—
		666		**282**	

Note : μ is micron = 10^{-3}, 150 μ means 0·150 mm.

Fineness modulus of coarse aggregate $= \frac{666}{100} = 6{\cdot}66$

Fineness modulus of fine aggregate $= \frac{282}{100} = 2{\cdot}82$

If F is the derived fineness modulus of mixture of fine and coarse aggregate having fineness moduli F_1 and F_2 respectively and x is the amount of aggregate to mix with one part of coarse aggregate then $x = \frac{F_2 - F_1}{F - F_1}$.

Table 8·13. Percentage of voids in sand and aggregates

S. No.	*Aggregate type*	*Percentage voids*
1.	Sand moist, fine, passing 18 mesh sieve	43
2.	Sand coarse not passing 18 mesh sieve	35
3.	Sand coarse and fine mixed ordinary	38
4.	Sand dry coarse and fine mixed	30
5.	Gravel	27-37
6.	Gravel and sand mixed	22-25
7.	Ballast 19 mm and under 6% coarse sand	33
8.	Brocken ballast 25 mm and under	46
9.	Brocken ballast 50 mm and under (only dust sieved)	41
10.	Brocken ballast 50 mm and under (stone small sieved out)	45
11.	Brocken ballast 63 mm and under (stone small sieved out)	41
12.	Brick ballast	35-40

Table 8·14. Effect of Fineness Modulus of Coarse aggregate on strength of concrete. Details of observations for a particular test with different fineness modulii of coarse aggregate.

S. No.	*Grade of concrete*	*Cement content*	*Fineness modulus*	*Slump (mm)*	*Compressive strength (N/mm²)*			
					7 days	*14 days*	*28 days*	*60 days*
1.	M-15	348·0	6·41	20	14·40	17·48	21·18	23·70
			6·58	24	14·96	17·70	21·33	24·88
			6·75	30	14·40	17·47	21·85	22·67
2.	M-20	399·0	6·41	20	19·84	23·26	26·67	32·96
			6·58	24	18·15	20·52	24·74	30·67
			6·75	30	17·70	20·52	25·33	28·15
3.	M-35	580·6	6·41	7	27·11	29·92	39·76	41·75
			6·58	12	29·78	32·15	37·20	39·16
			6·75	16	28·67	31·70	35·89	37·48
4.	M-40	618·0	6·41	15	36·12	40·97	44·10	50·03
			6·58	24	35·57	37·22	40·97	46·44
			6·75	32	35·26	40·82	42·69	45·38

Conclusions. (1) The difference in compressive strength corresponding to 28 and 60 days of concrete mixes decreases as the fineness modulus of the coarse aggregate increases.

(2) The slump varies for different mixes with change in fineness modulus of the coarse aggreggate even though the compaction factor, water-cement ratio and the aggregate cement ratio are taken constant.

(3) Even though the Indian Standard method of mix design achieves the target strength at 28 days for leaner mixes, it fails to attain the same for richer mixes. However the target, strength for the richer mixes can be achieved using elongated period of curing.

(4) The approximate sand and water content should be based on target strength rather than the characteristic strength as per IS : 10262 (1982) and the same needs further investigation.

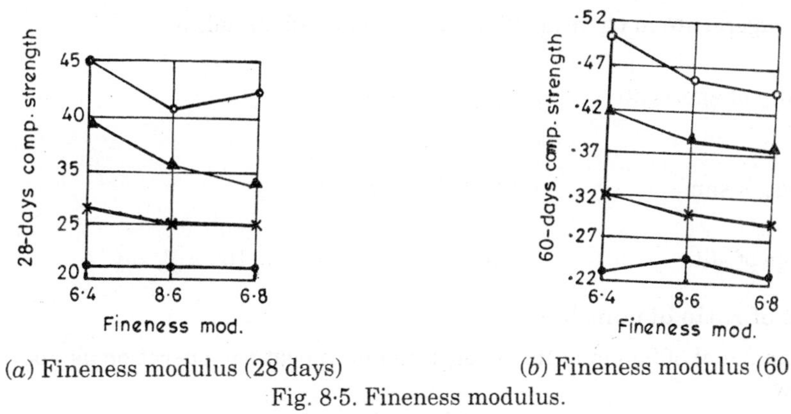

(*a*) Fineness modulus (28 days) (*b*) Fineness modulus (60 days)

Fig. 8·5. Fineness modulus.

Test for density of fine and coarse aggregates and determination of concrete mix ratio of a sample.

(1) **Density and silt content of fine aggregates.** Weigh one kg. of dry sand sample in air in a balance. Put it in the bucket of the Dunagon app. (shown in Fig. 8·6) Add some water and

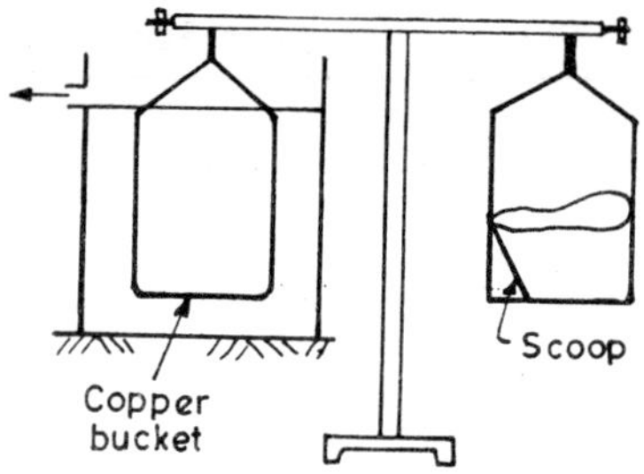

Fig. 8·6. Dunagon buoyancy app.

mix the sample thoroughly. Hang the bucket in the balance and fill water upto brim. Again fill the water in the outer vessel slowly till it flows out. Weight should be taken when all the material settles down and note the weight in the immersed state. Pour out the contents of the bucket on B.S. sieve no. 100 (IS : 150 μ) and wash with clean water. The silt will wash away. Now again weigh the residue on sieve in immersed position on app. and compute the density of sand and its silt content as follows :

Weight of sand in air = 100 gms

Weight of sand in water = w_1 gm (say) as per app. reading.

Weight of (sand-silt) = w_2 gm (say) in water

Density of sand $= \dfrac{100}{1000 - w_1}$ gm/cc

Silt percentage $= \dfrac{w_1 + w_2}{w_1} \times 100 = P_1$ (say)

(2) **Density and silt content of coarse aggregate.**

Weigh 2000 gm (2 kg) of the coarse aggregate in air.

Proceed as above and take weight on B.S. sieve no. 4 and 100 in immersed state (I.S. sieve no. 4·75 and 150 μ).

Material retained on sieve no. 4 is coarse aggregate

Material retained on sieve no. 100 is fine aggregate

Weight of aggregate in air = 2000 gms

Weight of aggregate in water = w_1 gm (say) as per app. reading

Weight of aggregate in (sieve no. 45) = w_2 gms per app. reading.

Weight of aggregate in (sieve no. 100) = w_3 gms per app. reading.

The density of aggregate $= \dfrac{2000}{2000 - w_1}$ gm/cc

Percentage of sand $= \dfrac{w_3}{w_1} \times 100 = P_2$ say

Percentage of silt $= \{(w_1 - w_2 - w_3) \div w_1\} \times 100 = P_3$ say

Analysis of ratio of concrete

Take a sample of 3000 gm of fresh concrete and repeat the operation as above and results noted are as below :

Weight of concrete in air = 3000 gm

Weight of concrete in water = w_1 gm (say)

Weight of residue on sieve no. 4 = w_2 gm (say)

Weight of residue on sieve no. 100= w_3 gm (say)

Compute as below :

	Parameters	*Weight in water*	*Weight in air*
1.	Sample	w_1	3000 gms (1)
2.	Residue on sieve no. 4	w_2 (Coarse aggregate)	$\frac{d_c}{d_c - 1} \times w_2$ (2)
	where d_c is the specific gravity of coarse aggregate		
3.	Residue on sieve no. 100	w_3 (Fine aggregate)	$\frac{dF}{dF - 1} \times w_3$ (3)
	where dF is the specific gravity of fine aggregate		
4.	Cement	$(w_1 - w_2 - w_3)$	$\frac{d_c}{d_c - 1}(w_1 - w_2 - w_3)$ (4)
	where D_c is the specific gravity of cement		
	Total solids = (2) + (3) + (4)		
	Hence water = 3000 – {(2) + (3) + (4)}		

Knowing the weight of cement, fine and coarse aggregates the ratio of the concrete can be determined.

If some sand is mixed in coarse aggregate and silt is mixed in fine aggregate the result will be effected. Determine the actual weights of ingradients as follows :

The actual weight of coarse aggregate $= \dfrac{(2)}{\dfrac{(1) - P_2 + P_3}{100}}$ ...(5)

The actual weight of fine aggregate $= \left[(3) - \dfrac{P_2 \times (5)}{100}\right] \div \left[(1) - \dfrac{b_1}{100}\right]$ ...(6)

The approximate weight of cement *i.e.*, (4) should be deducted by the silt contents of coarse and fine aggregate.

Actual weight of cement $= \dfrac{(4) - (6) \times P_1}{100} - \dfrac{(5) \times P_3}{100}$ ...(7)

Now the ratio of concrete can be determined by (5), (6) and (7) the content on water will remain uneffected.

P_1, P_2 and P_3 will be determined from the samples of the fine and coarse aggregates.

Grading of all in aggregates. All in aggregate is a combined graded aggregate containing both fine and coarse aggregates in different proportions.

Table 8·15.

I.S. sieve No.	*Percentage passing of nominal size*		*Remarks*
	40 mm	*20 mm*	
80	100	---	
40	95-100	100	Fine aggregate should 1st be sieved out by +75 mm sieve and the necessary proportioning should be done by single size aggregate.
40	45-75	95-100	
4·75	25-45	30-50	
600 μ	8-30	10-35	
150 μ	0-6	0-6	

Grading of fine aggregates. Detailed in sieve test of aggregates. As the grading goes finer the zone I to IV. The ratio of fine to coarse aggregate is reduced accordingly from zone I to IV. (Grade I to IV)

Grading according to British Spcifications

Grade	*Size*	*Part(ratio fine to coarse)*		*For small quantity*
I	63 mm	6	63 mm	3 parts
II	40 mm	4	10 mm	1·5 parts
III	20 mm	2		
IV	6·3 mm	1		
Medium aggregate				
	40 mm	5	10 mm	3 parts
	12·5 mm	2	3·35 mm	1 part
	3·35 mm	1		

Sand of above gradings should pass all in 3·35 mm sieve, not more than 30% in sieve no. 850 μ and not more than 60% in sieve no. 4·5 mm.

All in aggregates

Passing 20 mm size mesh	100%	Coarse aggregate
Passing 10 mm size mesh	55-65%	
Passing 4·75 mm size mesh	35-42%	Fine aggregate
Passing 150 μ (B.S. 100)	3%	

Note : (1) A nominal mix 1 : 2 : 4 does not mean, 1 : 6 mix in all in aggregates mix. It may be 1 : 5. The same property is also hold good for other mixes.

(2) For important works the mix should be designed as per site conditions.

(3) The quantity of a aggregate can be slightly reduced for a wetter mix and can be slightly increased for a drier mix. For more plasticity the quantity of sand can be increased slightly. Vice-versa, the sand can be reduced if the plasticity is more.

8·3. Water for concrete

8·3·1. Cement needs about 30% of water of its weight for hydration. In practice some more water is needed for proper workability. This water should be free from dirt, organic matter, sulphure, acids or chlorides causing efflorescence in concrete. Water which is fit for drinking can be said to be fit for concreting. Sea water containing salts, corrodes the steel and disfigures the face and also retards setting. Water containing sugar, marsh, alkalies salt, acids, organic matter and sulphate etc. is harmful to concrete and lessen the strength of concrete. The quantity of water depends on mix proportions, type and grading of aggregates, method of compacation and climatic conditions. Soft water produces a weaker mix. Use of sea water is prohibitive.

8·3·2. Test

(1) The presence of alkalies can be tested by a litmus paper. A rapid change in colour of litmus paper shows the presence of alkalies and acids.

(2) Prepare two cement pats of 25 mm dia and 12 mm thick. One with standard water suitable for concrete while the other with a water under test. Place the pats on an impervious floor for 48 hours. Their setting and hardening times and strengths gained is observed. If the pat under test has the same quality to that of the standard water used pat, the quality of water under test is suitable otherwise not.

(3) (*a*) To neutralize 200 ml sample of water with phenolphaleine as an indicator, it should not require more than 10 ml of 0·2 normal NaOH.

(*b*) To neutralize 200 ml sample of water, using methyl orange as an indicator, it should not require more than 12·5 ml of 0·02 normal HCl.

(*c*) Permissible limits for solids

Organic	200 mg per litre
Inorganic	3000 mg per litre
Sulphates (SO_4)	400 mg per litre
Chlorides (Cl)	2000 mg/litre for plain concrete and 500 mg/litre for RCC
Suspended matter	2000 mg/litre

(4) With the water under test check the compressive strength of the cubes which must be according to the specifications for 28 days, with the distilled water or limited to 90% of it with three similar cubes of 150 mm and should be in accordance with IS 516.

(5) The pH value of water shall generally be not less than 6.

(6) The initial setting time of last block made with the approved cement and the water proposed to be used shall not be less than 30 minute and shall not differ by ± 3·0 minutes from the initial setting time of controlled test block prepared with the same cement and distilled water.

Note : Water for curing can be used as used in mixing. The water for curing should not produce any objectionable or unsightly deposits on the surface. The presence of toxic acid or iron compounds are objectionable.

3·3. Requirement of water in Concrete

(1) For hand compaction about 35 litres per bag of cement.

Table 8·16.

(2) *Mix*	*Quantity of water in litres (Per bag of 50 kg)*	*Remarks*
1 : 1 : 2	21-27	For vibrated concrete 25% of water can be reduced. For wet sand, the quantity of water will further decrease by 20% if bulking is 25%.
1 : 1½ : 3	26-30	
1 : 2 : 4	29-32	
1 : 3 : 6	34-36	
1 : 4 : 8	45-47	

Water requirement per 50 kg of cement bag	*w/c ratio*	*Crushing strength at 28 days in kg/cm²*	*Remarks*
17·5	0·35	530	
20·0	0·40	470	Mix too dry for hand compaction and then add water as required.
22·5	0·45	420	
25·0	0·50	370	
27·5	0·55	320	
30·0	0·60	280	
32·2	0·65	250	Mix water for hand compaction as required.
35·0	0·70	222	
37·5	0·75	200	
40·0	0·80	180	

8·4. Reinforcement Steel (Re bars)

8·4.1. Reinforcement

It can be any of the followings :

(*a*) Mild steel and medium tensile reinforcement confinement to IS : 432 (Part-1982).

(*b*) High strength deformed steel bars (IS : 1786-1982).

(*c*) Hard drawn steel wire fabric (IS : 1566-1982).

(*d*) Structural steel, confirming to grade A (IS : 2062-1992) common section of steel bars are of two types.

(*a*) Plain bars denoted by ϕ.

(*b*) Deformed bars denoted by Φ.

(*a*) Steel type Fe 250 (ordinary mild steel plain bars having characteristic compression strength = 250 N/mm^2) used in designs based on working stresses, of unimportant works and in stirrups of members.

(*b*) Steel type Fe 415 and Fe 500 (High strength steel deformed bars having characteristic compressive strength = 415 N/mm^2 and 500 N/mm^2 respectively used in important structures.

The modulus of elasticity (E_s) of all types of steels are the same as 2×10^5 N/mm^2 both on torsion and compression.

Yield stress of different steels be assumed as the minimum yield stress 0.2% of proof stress.

As the stress strain diagram for Fe 500 is similar to that for Fe 415 and the difference in the yield stress of this type of steels is small so the steel area of steel Fe 500 in design can be found by using factor $\frac{415}{500} = 0.83$. So the area of steel required for Fe 500 = 0·83 × area of steel required for steel Fe 415.

There are certain other local brands are available in market such as Tata, Tricoss, Barnala etc. The strength of which must be checked before use.

(*a*) Cold twisted (Ribbed) (*b*) Hot twisted (Deformed) (*c*) Welded wire fabric.

Fig. 8·7.

Steel used in reinforcement should be free from loose rust, if any should be removed by rubbing with jute bags or sand paper. A slight rusting is however is preferable. The surface of the steel should be free from oil or grease, patches if any should be removed with operation of removing rust.

Zinc coated galvanised reinforcing bars are used to protect steel from corrosion (supplied by Hindustan Zinc LTD.)

Table 8·17. Chemical composition of steel (IS : 1786-1985)

Chemicals	*Strength*				
	Fe 415	*Fe 500*	*Fe 550*	*Fe 570 Ht(ST-58 HT)*	*Fe 540 W – Ht(ST-55 HTω)*
Carbon C	0·30	0·30	0·30	0·27	0·20
Sulphure S	0·060	0·055	0·055	0·055	0·055
Phosphorous P	0·060	0·055	0·050	0·055	0·055
S + P	0·11	0·105	0·10	—	—

Maximum carbon 0·25%.

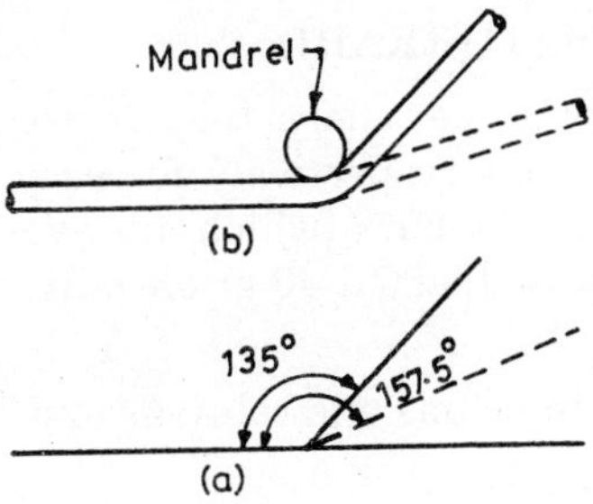

Fig. 8·8.

Tensile strength—Also termed as ultimate tensile stress.

Yield or Proof stress—Stress at which elongation 1st occurs in the test piece without increasing the load during tensile test.

The stress developed during twisting and rise in yield point are a function of pitch of spiral of twist. The most suitable pitch is between 9 and 12 mm dia. single bar. The yield stress will fall if the pitch is outside the range.

Rebend test of steel (Mandrel test). Heat the test piece in boiling water at 100°C for 30 minutes. Cool it and then bend it in mandrel to 135°. Then rebend it to 157·5°. There should be no sign of crack in the test piece.

Nominal size of specimen (ϕ)	*Dia. of mandrel (mm)* (*Fe 415 and 500*)	*Fe 550*
upto and under 10 mm	5ϕ	7ϕ
over 10 mm	7ϕ	8ϕ

Table 8.18. Ribbed tor Steel (IS : 1786 and IS : 456)

1. Substitute of tension reinforcement.

Mild steel (ϕ) mm	8	10	12	16	20	22	25	28	32	36	40	50
Ribbed for steel Φ mm	6	8	10	12	16	18	20	22	25	28	32	38

Note. Original spacing may be reduced by 10%.

Table 8.19.

2. Substitute as compression reinforcement.

Mild steel (ϕ) mm	12	16	20	22	25	28	32	36	40	50
Ribbed for Φ mm	10	14	2 × 12	18	20	2	2 × 18	2 × 20	32	40

Note. For helical bound compression reinforcement the table given for tension reinforcement.

Because of strains in case due to shrinkage and creep and consequent over stressing of compression reinforcement the international code of practice adevices against steel with a yield strength of less than 3000 kg/cm^2 as compression reinforcement (Grade I m.s.) confirming to IS : 226 has yield strength varying from 2600 to 2400 kg/cm^2 and are therefore unsuitable as compression reinforcement.

Table 8.20. Mechanical properties of plain bars.

S. N.	*Property*	*Dia. of bars mm*	*Mild steel*	*Med. Tensile steel*	*Hard Drawn steel*
1.	Ultimate tensile stress kg/mm^2 (Min.)	all sizes	42	58	55
2.	Ultimate elongation in % (Min.)	under 10 mm	16	14	
		10-25 mm	20	18	75
		over 25 mm	24	22	
3.	Proof stress (0.2%) kg/mm^2	upto 25 mm	—	36	—
	Yield stress (kg)/mm^2	25-38 mm	—	34.5	—
		38-50 mm	—	33	—

8·4.2. Grades of steel–TOR-50 ; TOR-55 and TOR-60 (TORKARI)

Rolled 50, 55 and 60 mark followed by Rolled TOR mark as per characteristic design is in-corporated in every bar of TOR-50, TOR-55 and TOR-60 grades respectively for easy field identification both ends of each TOR-50, TOR-55 and TOR-60 grade bars (which are available in 36 Ft. long bars) are painted green, blue and yellow respectively. In TOR-40 grade only rolled TOR mark is incorporated and the bar ends are not painted.

It is recommended that TOR-40 or TOR-50 steel be used in beams and columns and TOR-55 in slabs.

Table 8.21. Chemical Composition (Torkari Steel).

(Percent maximum)	*Tor-40*	*Tor-50*	*Tor-55*	*Tor-60*
Carbon	0·25	0·25	0·30	0·30
Sulphure	0·055	0·055	0·053	0·055
Phosphorus	0·055	0·055	0·055	0·055
Micro Alloys	Optional	0·30	0·30	0·30

Note. For guaranteed weldability carbon equivalent (CE) not to exceed 0.42%. In Tokari the carbon content is restricted to 0.15% though I.S. allows upto 0.3%.

Mechanical Properties (Torkari Steel)

Properties	*Tor-40*	*Tor-50*	*Tor-55*	*Tor-60*
0.2% proof stress/yield stress Min. N/mm^2	415	500	550	600
Elongation, on a gauge length of 5 times the nominal dia. of bar Min. %	14·5	12·0	8·0	6·0
Tensile straight Min. N/mm^2	485	545	585	635

Bend test. No transverse crack should be formed after bending through 180° around a mandrel dia. specified below : (d is dia. of mandrel)

Bars upto and including 20 mm dia.	2d		4d	5d
Bars over 20 mm dia. (d)	3d	4d	5d	6d

Rebend test. No transverse crack should be formed after bending the bar through 45° and reverse bending the same through 22.5° around the following mandrel dia.

Bars upto and including 10 mm dia.	4d	4d	6d	7d
Bars over 10 mm dia.	6d	6d	7d	8d

Characteristic strength for design (limit state) method

	Tor-40	*Tor-50*	*Tor-55*	*Tor-60*
Tension : main bars (N/mm^2)	415	500	550	600
Shear reinforcement (N/mm^2)	415	415	415	415
Compression (N/mm^2)	415	500	550	600

Bend. 60% more than for plain ms bars of same dia.

Table 8·22. Comparison of quantities of various grades of steel in RCC one way continuous slabs.

Size of slab (m)	Depth of slab mm	*Quantity of steel*					
		Tor-40		*Tor-55*			
		Main bars c/c	*Distribution*	*Main bars c/c*	*Saving %*	*Distribution*	*Saving %*
3.05 × 6·10	112·5	8 T @ 200 mm (250/251·31)	6 T @ 225 mm (135/223·4)	5 T @ 100 mm (85/196·4)	27·85	5 T @ 137·5 135/142·8	36·08
3·66 × 7·62	137·5	8 T @ 150 mm (320/335·1)	8 T @ 225 mm (165/223·4)	7 T @ 150 mm (240/256·6)	23·43	5 T @ 112·5 (165/174·5)	21·89

Numbers in brackets show the required/provided area of steel in mm^2.

Table 8·23. Properties of m.s. and Ribbed tor steel rounds (IS : 1786-1985).

Size in mm	*Sec. area in cm^2*	*Wt. / metre kg*	*Perimeter cm*	*Length MT metre*	*Min. bend radius (d = dia.)*	*Remarks*	*Sq. Bars Side in mm*	*Sq. Bars wt / m length kg*
4	0·126	0·099	1·26	10,101		**Nominal dia.**	5	0·20
5	0·146	0·154	1·57	7,014		The dia. of plain	6	0·28
6	0·283	0·222	1·89	4,510		rod (round) having the same	8	0·50
7	0·385	0·302	2·20	3,311		mass/length as	10	0·78
8	0·503	0·395	2·51	2,532		the deformed bar.	12	1·13
10	0·786	0·617	3·14	1,621	4*d*	**Nominal perimeter of the**	14	1·54
12	1·131	0·888	3·77	1,125		**deformed bar.**	16	2·01
14	1·539	1·208	4·40	829		3·14 times the	18	2·54
16	2·012	1·580	5·03	633		nominal dia.	20	3·14
18	2·546	2·000	5·65	500		**Nominal mass.**	22	3·08
20	3·143	2·466	6·28	405		The mass of bar, wire of nominal	25	4·91
22	3·803	2·980	6·91	336		dia. and density	28	6·15
25	4·911	3·854	7·85	260		0·00785 kg/cm^3.	32	8·04
28	6·160	4·830	8·80	207		The wt. of steel is	36	10·17
32	8·046	6·313	10·05	159		taken as 7·85 gms/cu c.m or	40	12·56
36	10·183	7·990	11·31	125	6*d*	0·785 kg/sq. cm	45	15·90
40	12·512	9·864	12·57	101		per m length	50	19·62
45	15·911	12·500	14·14	81		For details refer	56	24·62
50	19·643	15·410	15·71	65		Table 8·99.	63	31·16

4.3. Thermo Mechanical Treatment (TMT)

The reinforcing bar, after coming out of the last stand of the finishing stand of a merchant mill, is made to pass through a specially designed water cooling system. In the cooling bed, the outer surface in contact with high pressure water gets severely quenched and becomes mertensite where as the core remains comparatively hot and austenetic. The quenching treatment is stopped when a determined thickness of mertensite has been formed under the skin. At this stage, when the bar leaves the drastic cooling system, a temperature gradient is established due to heat flow from the core to the outer surface which results in self tempering of the mertensite and increase in field strength of reinforcing bar. The salient properties of TMT bars are :

(*a*) Better weldability and no loss of strength during welding as carbon is restricted 0·2%.

(*b*) Excellent formability due to higher percentage of uniform elongation (22, 20 and 18% for TMT 415,500 and 550 grades respectively). Bend at 1D and rebent at 4D possible against corresponding value of 4D and 7D for CTD bars.

(*c*) Better corrosion resistance.

(*d*) Resistance to fire hazards. No loss of strength upto a temperature of 500°C.

(*e*) Higher fatigue strength and ductility. Therefore most suited for structures and foundations subjected to dynamic and/or seismic loads.

(*f*) Easy working at site. pre welded meshes can be used to eliminate binding at site. Thus saves construction time and space.

(*g*) Satisfies bond requirements of IS : 456-1978).

(*h*) Reduced transportation costs and overall economy.

Table 8.34. Recommended Design Stress (in N/mm²)

Type of stress	*Limit state method of design*					
	415		*500*		*550*	
	TMT	*CTD*	*TMT*	*CTD*	*TMT*	*CTD*
Tension	415	415	500	500	550	550
Axial compress	400	352	400	400	400	400
Bond	60% more than plain bar.					

Notes. 1. Partial safety factor against material of 1·15 to be applied.

2. To account for minimum 0·050 eccentricity in axially load compression members, a factor of 1·1 to be applied.

Additional cost saving by using TMT bars with welded lap joints.

For a dia. = 20 mm ; fy = 415 N/mm² and fck = 15 N/mm² grade of concrete.

Type of lap	*Lap length required*	*Material required*	*Cost*	*Percentage cost saving per joint of a single bar*
Conventional based on Concrete-steel Bonding	Av. 50 dia. = 1000 mm 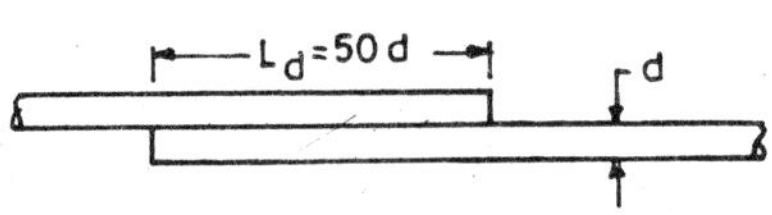	2·47 kg of bar @ Rs. 9800/MT.	Rs. 24	
For welded lap joints 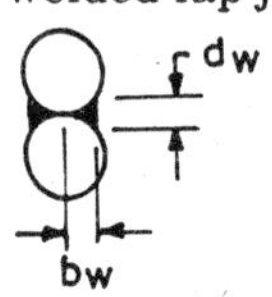	6.3 dia. = 126 mm 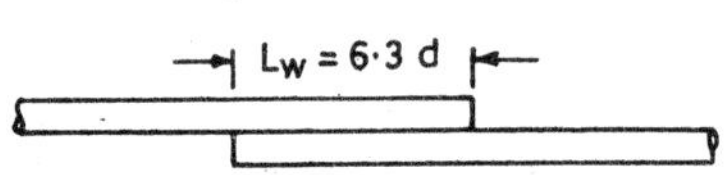	0·31 kg of bar @ Rs. 9800/MT 2·5 electrodes of Δmm dia. and 450 mm long. Includes cost of electrodes 0·2 DA and others.	Rs. 3 Rs. 8	54%

Recommended welding length

For TMT 415 L_w = 6.3 dia. ; TMT 500 L_w = 7·0 dia. ; TMT 550 L_w = 7·5 dia. L_w is length of weld.

8·4.4. Bending, Binding and Placing of Re-bars (It should be done according to IS : 2502)

Bending-Bending die. It has a long lever arm which works as a handle. At one of its ends it has a grip, in which the bar end can be gripped tight and can be bended by the handle. The bar is hold in position by a guide nail fixed on the binding plateform. It is a conventional patent used by the benders and need not to describe in detail. For thin bars a smaller and lighter die can be used while for thicker bars a longer and heavier die is required which has a wider grip end. Bars upto 32 mm can be bended cold, but the thicker bars are cutted by oxy- acetylene flame and bended by a machine operated by power or bended hot (in unavoidable cases).

Binding. At least two fold wire should be used for binding thin rods. For thicker bars 3 to 5 folds of wire must be used. The wire may be black or galvanised of 1·25 mm of soft iron. About 0·5 kg wire is used per quintal of steel. (Black wires are preferred).

A binding hook locally known as "Kundi" is used for binding the bars together tightly. About 200 mm long, 8 mm dia. (according to dia. of steel used) ms bar with a pointed bend tip is used for this purpose. Other end of the hook has a handle made by the bar itself bended in the form of a rectangle. Cross jointing of the bars should not tack welder but should be binded with wires.

Placing—Bottom reinforcement. To give proper cover to the bottom reinforcement, cover blocks of concrete 1 : 2 (cement : coarse sand) or of a richer mix than the mix used in the structure equal to the thickness of the cover required are made. The other sides of the blocks may be 5 cm × 5 cm. A binding wire is embedded in the block to bind it to the reinforcement, so that it may not shift in position. The length of the wire must be sufficient so that it may be binded to the bars. Plastic cover blocks can also be used.

Cover in vertical reinforcement. U bars are provided to give side cover in vertical reinforcement.

Top reinforcement. In order to keep top reinforcement in position chairs locally known as 'Ghories' of suitable sizes and height (suiting the top reinforcement for its load and height) are used at suitable distance apart. The foot of the legs of the chairs are bended in opposite directions to have a better seat.

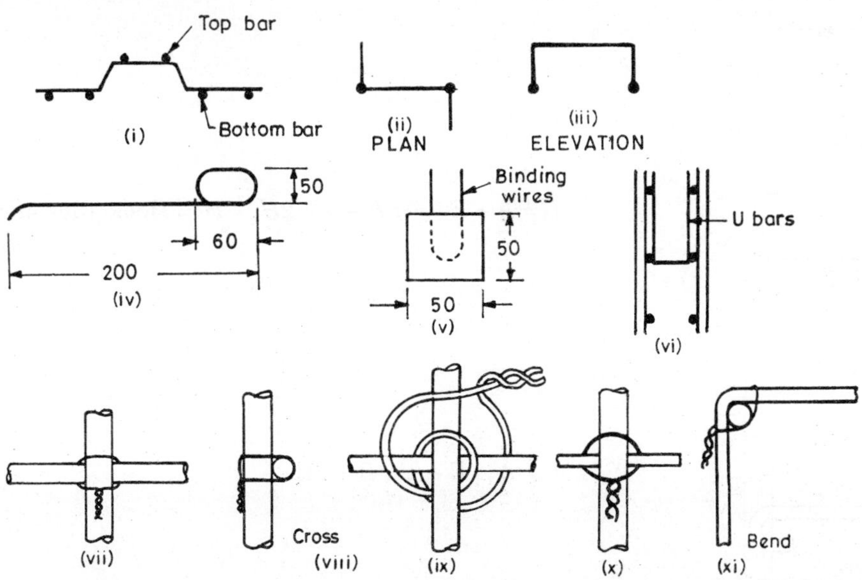

Fig. 8·9.

Precaution in bending, binding and placing of rebars (Reinforcing bars)

1. Tolerances on placing of reinforcement

(*a*) for effective depth 200 mm or less ± 10 mm

(*b*) for effective depth more than 200 ± 15 mm

Cover tolerance. Unless or otherwise not stated the deviation from the required nominal cover by ± 10 mm.

2. Handling. Rough handling or shock loading (prior to embedment and dropping of re-bars from height should be avoided).

3. All welding work. Binding of bars should be done according to IS : 751 and IS 9417.

4. Where reinforcement bars upto 12 mm for high strength deformed steel bars and upto 16 mm for mild steel bars are bent aside at construction joints and afterwards bent back into their original positions. Care should be taken when bending back bars to ensure that the concrete around the bar is not damaged beyond the bend and no kink is left after rebend.

Plate 8-B

Bends in Re Bars

Cut length measured along centre line (Say L)

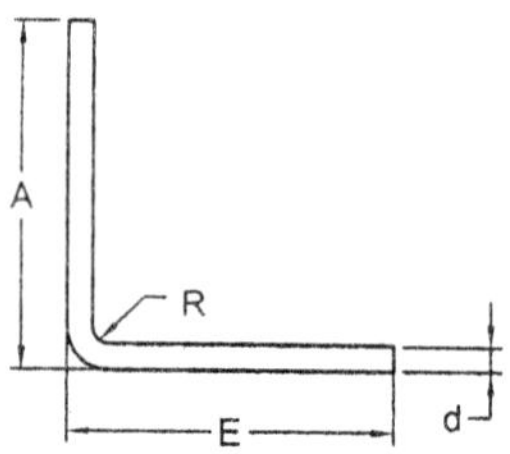

$L = A + E - ½R - d$ $\quad R = 2d$ upto 16 mm

$= 4d$ upto 25 mm

$= 6d$ above 25 mm

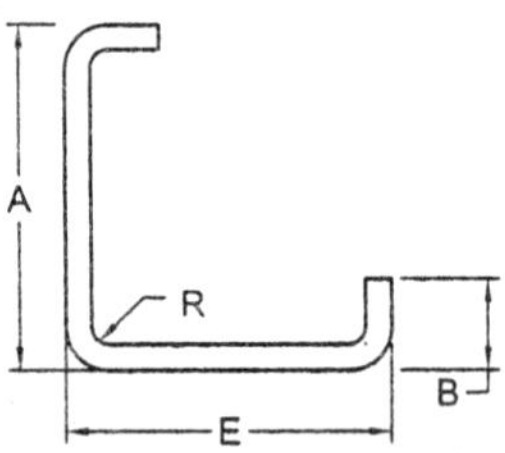

$L = A + E - ½R - d + 2B$ $\quad B$ = Bend allowance

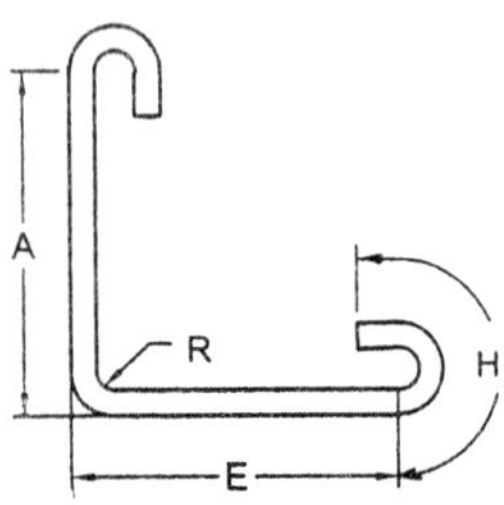

$L = A + E - ½R - d - 2H$ $\quad H$ = Hook allowance

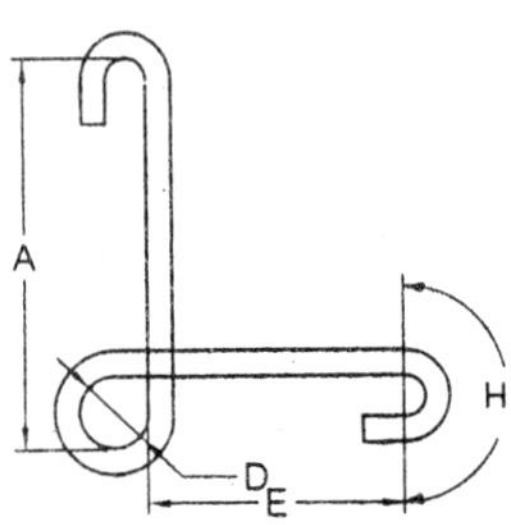

$L = A + E + 1½D + 2H$

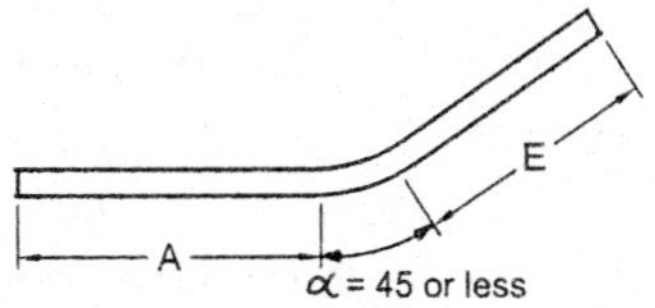

$L = A + E$

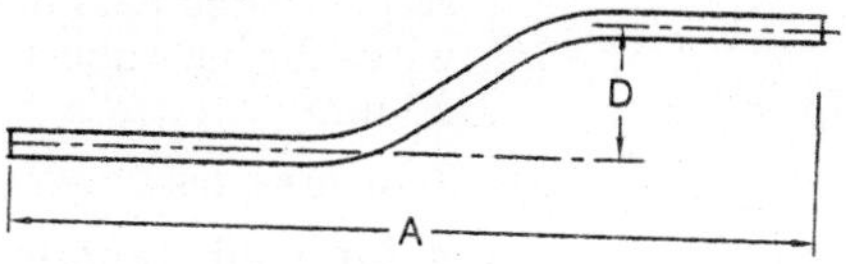

$L = l + 1{\cdot}5D$ when crank angle = 45°

$L = l + 2D$ when crank angle = 30°

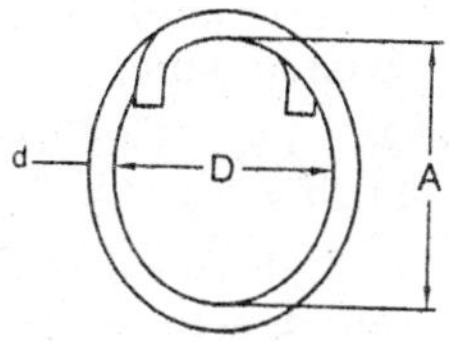

$L = 2A + 2D + 22d$

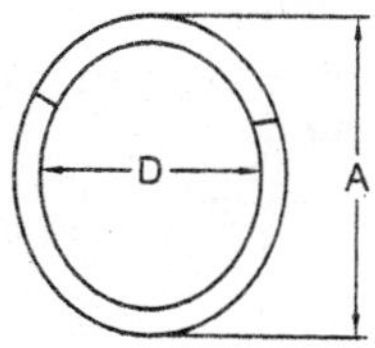

$L = 2A + 2D + 22d$

$L = 2A + 2D + 22d$

D = Inner Dia.

N = No. of turns or part.

P = Pitch of Helix max. $D/3$

$L = N\pi(D + d) = 8d$

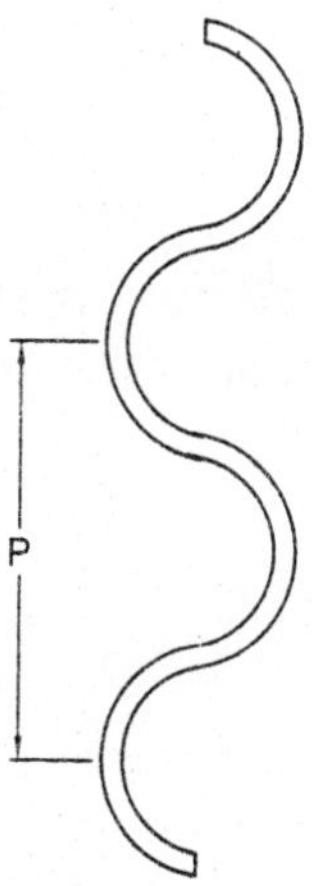

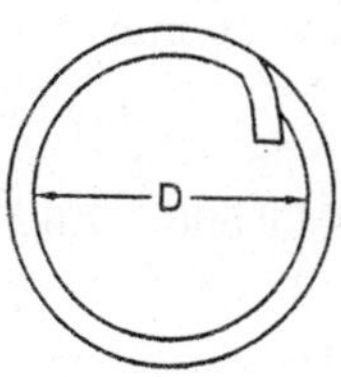

Note. 1. Bars larger than 25 mm Dia. may be bended hot.

2. Bars more than 36 mm dia. needs pressure operated benders.

3. Bars upto 50 mm can be cut by shear and bended by bending machines driven by electric motor at 10 bar/min or 2.5 T/Hr.

The blades of shear machine are made of special alloy with a total life of 40,000 cuts after which no conditioning is needed. The bending machine bend hooks, loops and stirrups. For details contact.

Orient Engineers, Orient Houses, No. 7. Ground Floor, J. Tata Road Mumbai-400020.

END BENDS IN RE BARS

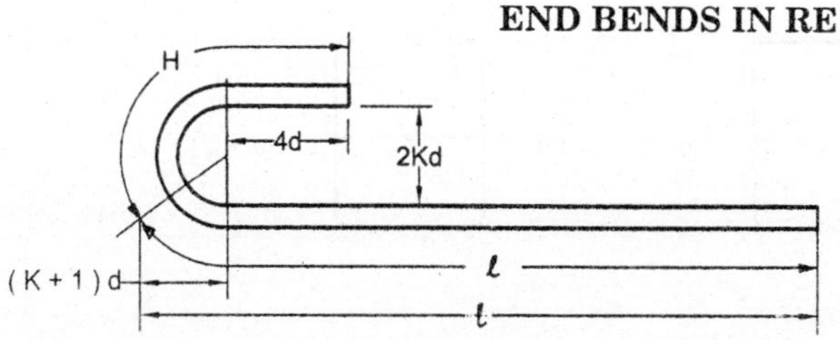

l = Effective length of bar

d = Dia. of bar

H = Hook allowance

B = Bend allowance

K = 2 for ms bars or wires

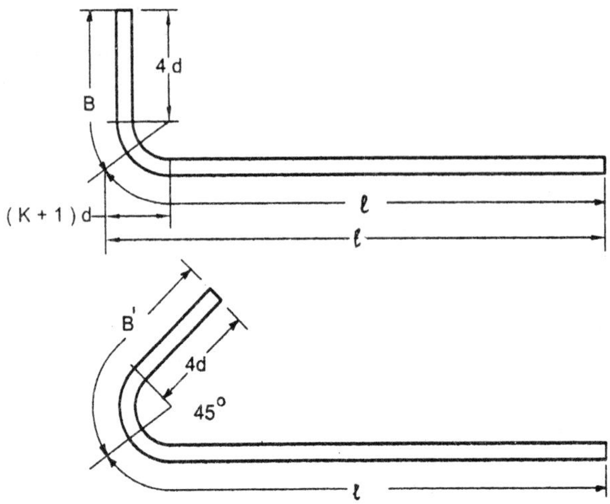

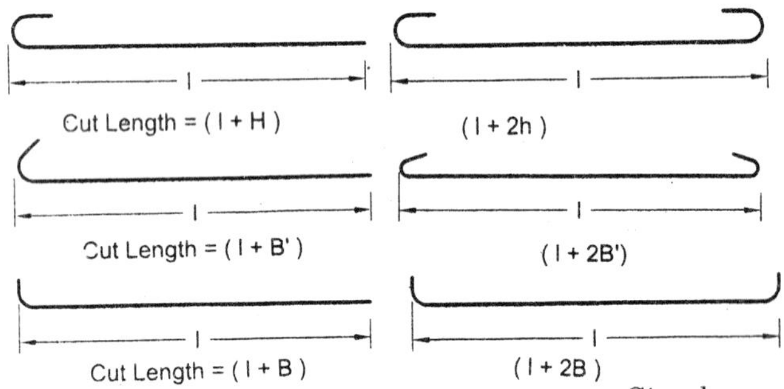

= 3 for med. tensile steel twisted bars or wires for bars above 25 mm

K = 3 for ms bars

= 4 for med. tensile steel twisted

= 6 for cold work twisted bars

H = $9d$, $11d$, $13d$ and $17d$ for

K = 2, 3, 4 and 6 resp. rounded to nearest 5 mm but minimum 75 mm

B' = $6d$, $6.5d$, $7d$ and $7{\cdot}5d$.

Laps in Re Bars

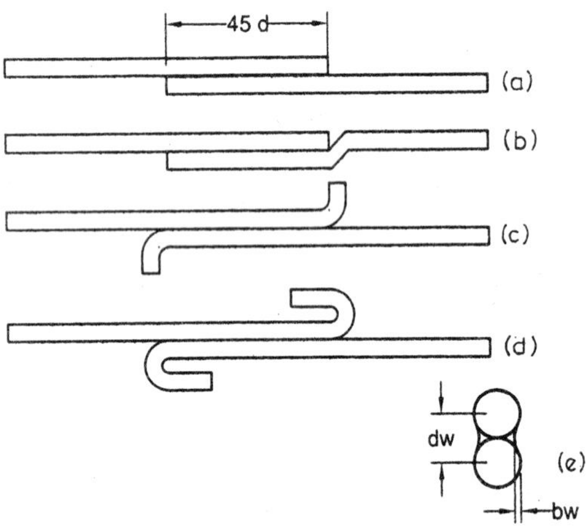

Simple

Joggled

Joggled with bend

Hooked joggled (For m.s.)

Welded – $bw = 0.2d$ or 4 mm

$dw = 0.7d$ or 10 mm

Lw (Length of lap)

TMT 415 = $6{\cdot}3d$; TMT 500 = $7.0d$

TMT 550 = $7{\cdot}5d$.

Stirrups

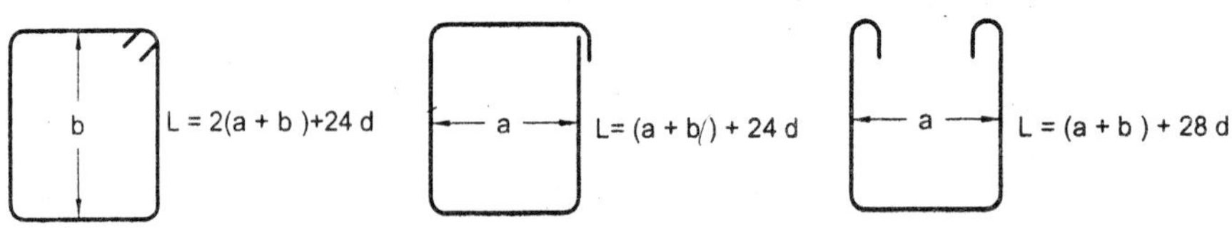

Note : a and b are inner dimensions

Table 8·25. Values of H and B in mm (min. and as recommended).

Size of bar mm	H						B					
	ms		*Med. Tensile*		*Cold twisted*		*ms*		*Med. Tensile*		*Cold twisted*	
	Min.	*Rec.*	*Min.*	*Rec.*	*Min.*	*Rec.*	*Min*	*Rec.*	*Min.*	*Rec.*	*Min.*	*Rec.*
5	75	—	75	—	75	—	75	—	75	—	75	—
6	75	—	75	—	75	—	75	—	75	—	75	—
8	75	—	90	—	105	—	75	—	75	—	75	—
10	90	—	110	—	130	—	75	—	75	—	75	—
12	110	—	130	—	155	—	75	—	75	—	75	—
16	145	—	175	—	210	—	80	—	80	—	95	—
20	180	—	220	—	260	—	100	—	110	—	120	—
22	200	—	240	—	285	—	110	—	120	—	130	—
25	225	—	275	—	325	—	125	—	140	—	150	—
28	250	310	310	365	665	475	145	155	155	170	170	195
32	290	350	350	415	415	445	160	175	175	190	190	225
36	325	395	395	470	470	610	180	200	200	215	215	250
40	360	440	440	520	520	680	200	220	220	240	240	280
45	405	495	495	585	585	765	225	250	250	270	270	315
50	450	550	550	650	650	850	250	275	275	300	300	350

8·4·5. Gas pressure welding for jointing re-bars

Gas pressure welding is a new and convenient method of jointing cold twisted reinforcing bars upto 51 mm dia. Reinforcing bars are usually spliced by laps in which the effectiveness of the splice is accomplished through bond strength with cement concrete. Conventional lap splicing has two distinct disadvantages, namely (*i*) Extra quantity of steel used in laps and (*ii*) Congestion of reinforcement which prevents effective placing and compaction of concrete and which may seriously impair the performance of the structure. It is also difficult to achieve required ductility of RC members where lap splicing is done which is being considerably emphasised now a days in earth quake resistant design of structure.

A relatively new and convenient method of joining reinforcing bars is by the "Gas pressure welding". This is basically a hot forging process, which involves, heating of the bar ends to be joined by oxyacetylene flame and applying hydraulic pressure to effect a solid phase welded joint. Though for these bars Electric Arc Welding is permitted as per IS : 9417, yet there are practical limitations for making butt welded joints as under.

(*a*) Preparation of bar ends to *V* profile.

(*b*) Proper sequencing of welding.

(*c*) Use of different size of electrodes for roof runs and other beads and

(*d*) Cooling of bars after alternate weld to prevent spread of heat effected zone. Electric arc welded lap joints are also not so much effective.

For butt-welded joints, IS : 9417, prescribes that the selected pieces when subjected to a tensile test shall have a strength not less than 90% of the actual tensile strength of the bar, but in no case less than the tensile strength of the bar specified in IS : 1786 (specifications for high strength deformed steel bars and wires for concrete reinforcement). The fracture shall take place away from the weld. It is also necessary that the butt welded joint satisfies the requirements of cold bend-ability as laid down in IS : 9417. The process of gas pressure welding has been in corporated as one of the process in the draft revision of IS : 9417 "Recommendations for welding cold worked steel bars for RCC work".

Equipments required

1. Heating mechanism, consisting of acetylene and oxygen cylinders and multi nozzle burner with regulating valves complete assembly.

2. Clamping mechanism for gripping the bars having a pair of fixed jaws and a pair of movable jaws.

3. Pressing machine with a hydraulic pump operated mechanically or manually.

The following points must be observed.

(*a*) Equipment must be portable and capable of welding in horizontal as well as in vertical positions.

(*b*) The clamping mechanism should ensure perfect alignment of the bars to avoid eccentricity of joints.

(*c*) For different ranges of bars sizes, the nozzles should be spaced so as to ensure uniform heating and to prevent back firing.

(*d*) It should be possible to adjust the flame so as to have carburising flame in the beginning followed by neutral flame.

Process of gas Pressure Welding. The various steps taken are :

1. **Preparation of the bar ends to be jointed.** The ends are not perpendicular to the bar axis. Care should be taken to remove the untwisted ends of the bars. Any impurity just as rust, grease or paint etc. should be removed. For this before welding the end surfaces should be grinded by a grinder such as sand paper or file etc.

2. **Clamping of the bar.** Axis of the bars should be in a straight line to avoid eccentric joint, clamping should be tight to prevent any slippage during compression and gap of 2 to 3 mm must be kept between the bar ends.

3. **Heating-initial.** The bar ends are heated by a multinozzle burner of suitable size. To prevent oxidation of the end faces, the heating in this stage may be done with carburising (reduction) flame. In this stage the burner movement is limited to the end faces to ensure uniform heating throughout the cross-section.

4. **Pressure application-initial.** On sufficient heating of the end faces, pressure is applied by the operation of the hydraulic pump, just sufficient to close up the gap.

5. **Heating final.** As soon as the gap is closed, the flame is changed to neutral flame, and heating of the weld zone is done by gradually increasing the lateral movement of the burner on either side of the joint. Total heating time depends on the size of the bar which ranges 40 sec. to 120 sec. for bars from 16 mm to 28 mm. dia. Care should be taken that the melting of the metal does not take place.

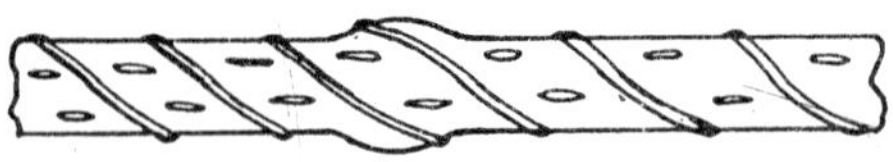

Fig. 8·10. Welded joints.

6. **Pressure application final.** On sufficient heating of the weld zone, final pressure of the order of 30 N/mm^2 to 50 N/mm^2 is applied so that contractions takes place and a smoothly shaped bulge of about 1·4 times the bar dia. is achieved. At this stage the flame is switched off but pressure application is continued for some more time say 3.5 secs.

7. Cooling. The weld portion is allowed to cool gradually in normal atmospheric condition or by pouring water over the joint soon after the flame is switched off.

(*a*) **Air cooling.** The ratio of the ultimate tensile strength of welded bar and that of the parent bar is more than 0·9 (the limit prescribed in IS : 9417) standard deviation ratio of the bars remains quite small indicating consistency of the test results of the process.

Though there is no failure at the joint location, failure takes place in the heating effected zone closed to the joint on heating the cold twisted bars beyond 600°C to 65°C annealing takes place leading to recovery, recrystallisation and grain growth of the metallic structure. This results in progressive lowering of the yield/ultimate tensile strength. The reduction in strength due to effect of heat on cold working takes places, but the same is largely compensated by the increase of cross-section due to formation of bulb.

(*b*) **Water cooling.** Just after the welding is over the cooling with water for four secs. is done. In water cooling failure takes place in the parent bar, meaning thereby that joint performance exceeded in the parent bar on quenching the surface of the hot joint, the heat from core is utilised to temper the mertensitic structure formed on the outer reinforcement, which improves strength as well as ductility on the whole water cooling provides a higher efficiency.

8·4·6. Protection of reinforcement against corrosion

1. **Epoxy Coating** of steel provides good protection in Chloride Carbonated concrete. The fusion bonded process is similar to the one used for coating steel pipes and consists of abrasive blast cleaning of Re-bars, pre-heating them to about 230°C, applying charged epoxy powder on them with electrostatic spray guns and cooling the coated bars in a water quench pool. An effective method to prevent rebars corrosion may be to use a zinc rich epoxy resin for coating rebars before completing the repair. The zinc coating allows electrical contact between the bar and active zinc. Zinc then acts as sacrificial aid protecting the steel. As a precautionary measure all new structures built with epoxy coated bars should induce electrical inter connection of all rebars so that cathodic protection and other electro chemical procedures as well as corrosion testing can be implemented when necessary. In adverse environments additional protective systems like cathodic protection, latest modified or silica fume concrete, calcium nitrite, sealers and other should be considered.

2. **Zinc rich paints** known as cathodic protection to iron are used.

3. **Galvanization** is another protecting treatment for rebars. Galvanizing is also useful for prestressing wires, Galvanizing results in reduction to bond but results of research indicate that bond of galvanized bars is as good as ordinary steel.

4. **Cathodic protection.** By connecting the steel reinforcement as cathode to a small DC current and introducing nodes on or within the concrete surface, oxidation of steel is stopped. The steel cage being forced to be have as a cathode, no longer corrodes.

(*a*) **Red oxide cement.** Some manufacturers mix **red oxide** in the cement while it is in process, which prevents reinforcement from rustings.

8·4·7. Bar bending schedules are prepared before bending the bars, details of which are given below in figure.

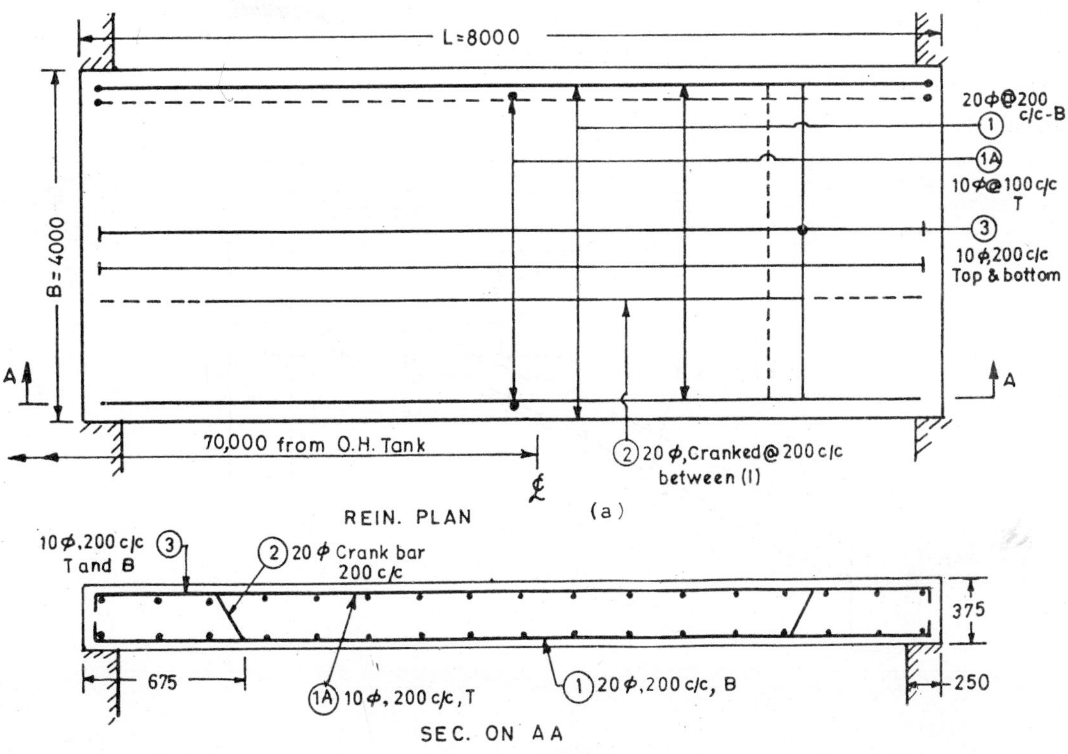

Fig. 8·10.

Note. 1. All dimensions are in mm until and otherwise stated.

2. Firm lines indicate Bottom bars (B)
Dotted lines indicate Top bars (T)
Firm dotted shows crank bars

Table 8·26. Bar Bending Schedule

S. N.	*Location*	*Bar marked*	*Dia. mm*	*No. each*	*Total No*	*Cut length mm*	*Shape*	*Total length m.*
1	Main B	1	20	21	21	8300	7950, 300	174·3
2	Main T	1-A	10	21	21	8300		174·3
3	Main crank	2	20	20	20	8600	5500, 200	170·2
4	Temp.	3	10	2 × 41	82	3950	3950	323·9

The following details should be mentioned in the foot of drawings.

1. Class of IRC loadings and type of supports.
2. Design stress and grade of conc.
3. Modular ratio and clear cover.
4. Details of laps etc.
5. Signatures of authorities.

Openings in slabs

Openings are provided in industrial buildings in roofs for moving of chain tackles etc. These openings are provided with angle curbs at their periphery and are shown in plans as given in Fig. (*a*) and (*b*).

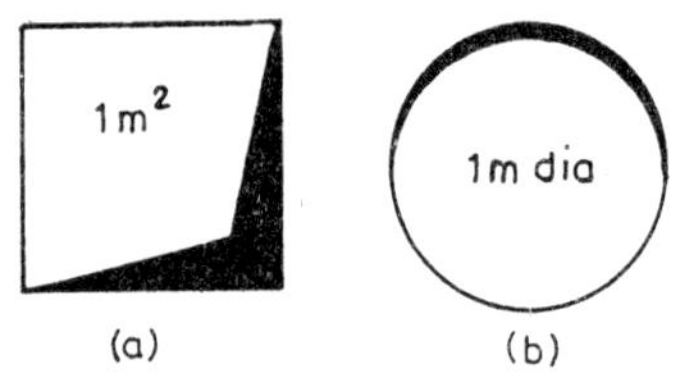

Fig. 8·11.

Typical Section of a Staircase

All dimensions are in mm until and otherwise stated.

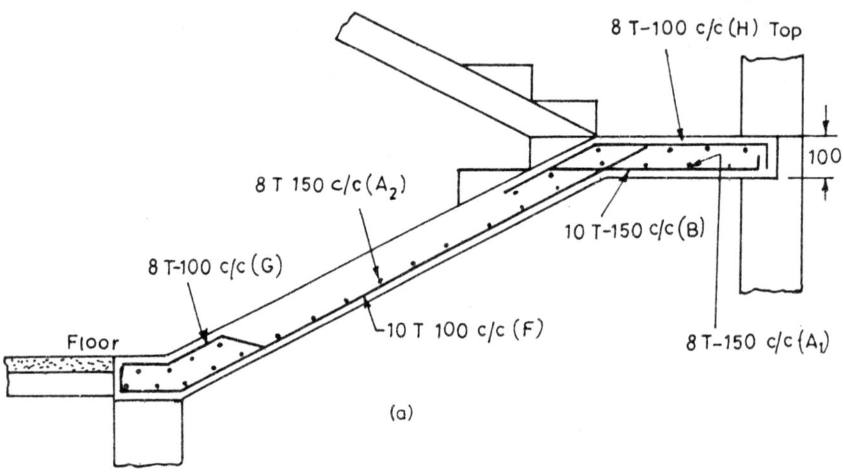

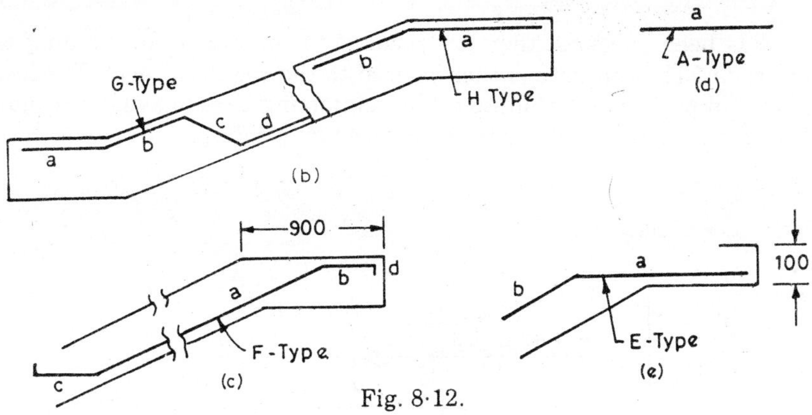

Fig. 8·12.

Table 8·27. Bar Bending Schedule of a Staircase

S. No.	*Type*	*Dia.*	*ϕ or T*	*Spacing c/c*	*Total Nos.*	*Dimensions*						*Remarks*
						a	*b*	*c*	*d*	*e*	*Cut length*	
1	A_1	8	T	150	10	1800					1800	
2	A_2	8	T	150	15	900					900	
3	F	10	T	100	9	2500	700	150	50		3400	
4	E	10	T	150	6	800	500	50			1350	
5	G	8	T	100	9	100	150	100	100		450	
6	H	8	T	100	9	700	500				1200	

Notations of bars in drawings must be such that they may not be complicated and congested to read. The type of different shaped bars are nominated as type *A*, *B*, *C* etc. In one type or shape if the dimensions are different, they are subdivided as A_1 A_2 A_3 or B_1 B_2 B_3 etc. These types and their shapes must also be drawn on the bar bending schedule (BBS). The bars which are placed on top should be marked *T* and for bottom *B*. Bars cranked from bottom to top should be marked *BT* and so on.

8·4.8. Fixers

Jigs. Jigs are used to place the insert plates (discussed in following paragraphs) in horizontal position at its correct location with reference to their centre lines in concrete. Four vertical rods are welded to the reinforcing bars these vertical rods are again welded by four horizontal rods to make a frame. On the horizontal rods the centre lines of the insert plates are marked on both axes by a fine pen or scratch. A fine thread or a horse hair is tied to the centre lines in both directions in opposite rods and the position is taken on the insert plate by a plumb line. The insert plate is welded in position with the reinforcing bars with small pieces of steel rods. The centre line is again checked for accuracy.

Bolt fixing. Jig as shown above is 1st made. Two channels or angles are welded a bit above the surface of the concrete to be laid and below the top of the bolt nut to the horizontal bars of the jig which are already welded accordingly. The angle or the channels are positioned in the centre line of the jig by shifting it on the jig rods as shown in the Fig. 8·13. The bolts are positioned in between the angles (channels) according to the centre line plumbed from jig. The bolt nuts rest on the flange of the angle (channel). After the posi-

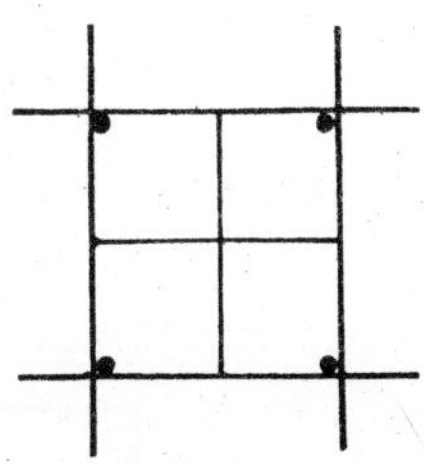

Fig. 8·13.

tion of the bolts has been checked, they are secured to the angles by welding small pieces of iron rods around them. The concrete is then poured to the required level. The lower part of the bolts can be secured in position by welding to the reinforcing bars to avoid any movement during pouring. For this small separate iron rods can be used by welding.

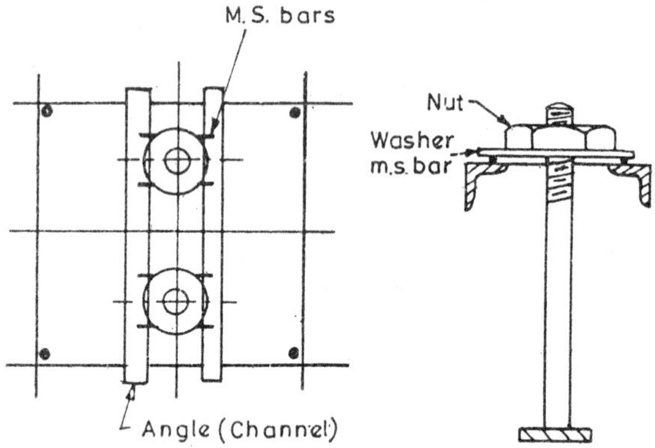

(*a*) Top plan (*b*) Section

Fig. 8·14.

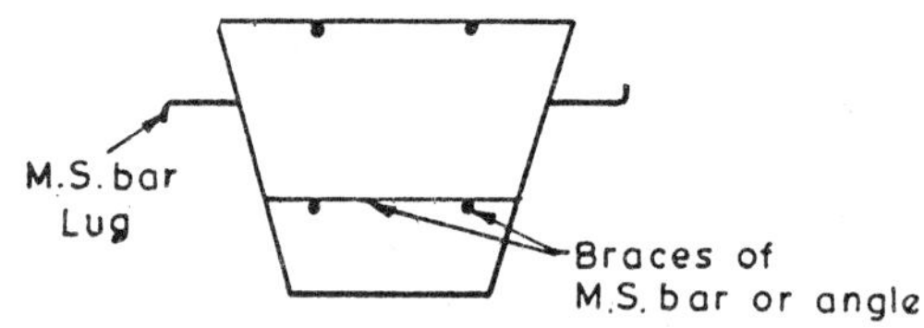

Fig. 8·15. Pockets

Pockets. For grouting hand rails and bolts etc. in future, pockets are left in concrete. These pockets may be shuttered either by solid wood or if bigger by wooden plank boxes. Care should be taken that these pockets are removed as soon as the initial set had occurred or the concrete has come in the position that it can retain its position after removal of the pocket and may not fill the gap again. At least they must be shaked to make loose. If they are left tight it will be difficult to remove them when the concrete has secured its strength. When these pockets are bigger in size, plane iron sheet pockets are made which are left in the concrete. Such pockets must be braced from inside so that they may not twist or bend inside while concrete is being poured. After setting of the concrete these braces may be cut by arc flame if required so.

Inserts. Plates of required size and thickness with lugs of ms round or angles are fixed in concrete for fixing sanitary or electric fillings in future. The lugs may be single, two, four or six in numbers as required according to the size of the plate. Different sizes of plates are shown in the Fig. 8·16 below. These are shown as S_1 S_2 S_3 etc. in the drawings.

Sleeve. Round hollow pipe pieces are left in concrete of walls and roofs for electric cables and sanitary fillings. In drawings these sleeves are shown as Sl_1 Sl_2 Sl_3 etc. according to sizes.

Conduit pipes. Conduit pipes where required for any desired purpose are embedded in the concrete while pouring. They are denoted in the drawings as D_1 D_2 D_3 etc. according to the sizes.

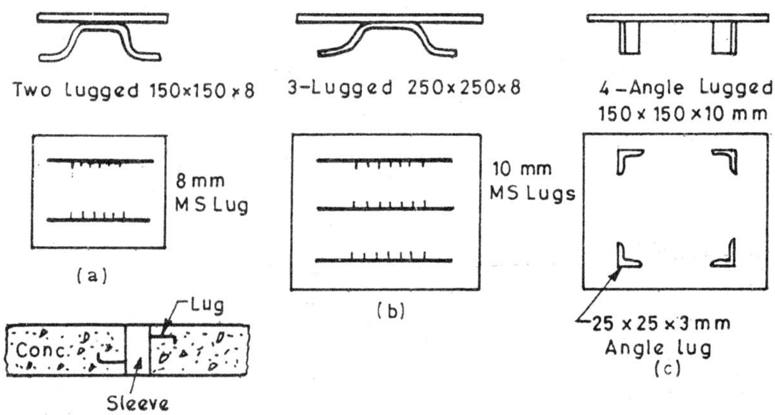

Fig. 8·16. Inserts.

8·5. Centering and Shuttering (Form Work)

8·5·1. Form work and scaffolding systems

(1) **Timber ballies.** Ballies may be of sal, eucalyptus or Jhaoo 75 to 150 mm diameter (diameter of balli is measured about 0·5 m above the lower end). These ballies must be straight 50 mm diameter. Ballies can be used for bracings. Bamboos about 75 mm diameter can also be used. Ballies are tied with coconut cordage to each other.

(2) **M.S. pipes.** These pipes are 50 mm diameter (external) and the thickness of the rim is about 3 mm. The length of the pipes varies from 1 m to 6 m. The length can be increased by th e joint pieces. These are painted with red oxide.

(3) **All purpose pipes.** These are m.s. pipes which can be used in different shapes of frames, having threads and sockets at ends in different directions. These are generally used in high staging.

(4) **Adjustable m.s. pipes.** Acrews, or telescope steel props.—Two m.s. pipes in which upper slides inside the lower one. Lower pipe has a base plate which rests on the ground and disburses the load on the larger area. Upper end of the lower pipe is threaded on which a movable block. Can slide up and down by using threads. Lower pipe has two vertical slits also in which an iron pin can be inserted. The pin bears the end of the upper pipe on it and can be adjusted up or down by lowering or raising the block, which can be operated by a handie to a suitable position. Upper end of the upper pipe is provided with a disc support or a Jack hook with a U-shape hold on which the shuttering members can rest. If there is any looseness in the support it can be tightened by the jack. These supports are available in different heights.

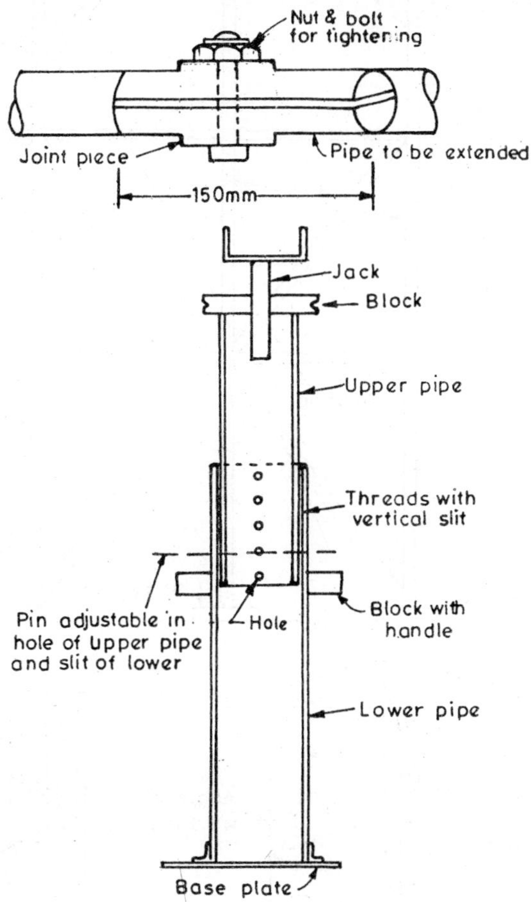

Fig. 8·17. Adjustable prop.

(5) **Wooden vertical supports.** They are ballies (diameter according to the load) upto 6″ diameter. The lower end is supported on a wooden plate. The upper horizontal support is supported by two cross bracings.

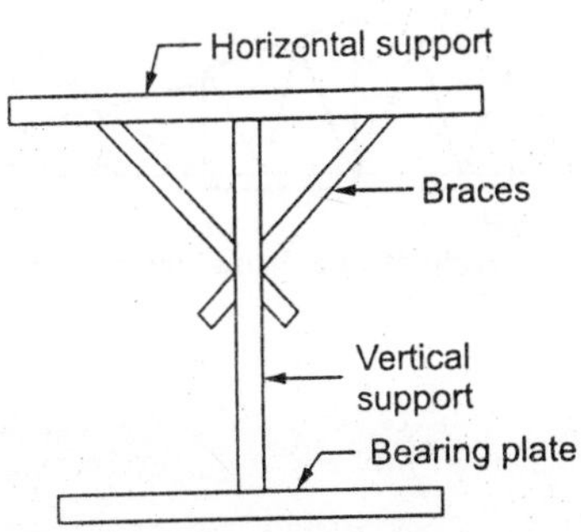

Fig. 8·18. Shuttering of a floor.

(6) **Shoulders.** These are m.s. channel sections provided with holes in the side plates and on the web, so that it may be bolted with shuttering as required. These shoulders are provided on the back of the vertical shuttering. They are provided in vertical as well as in horizontal position on shuttering to take pressure caused by pouring the green concrete. Heavy duty shoulders provided with double channel braces are used where heavy loads are to be handled.

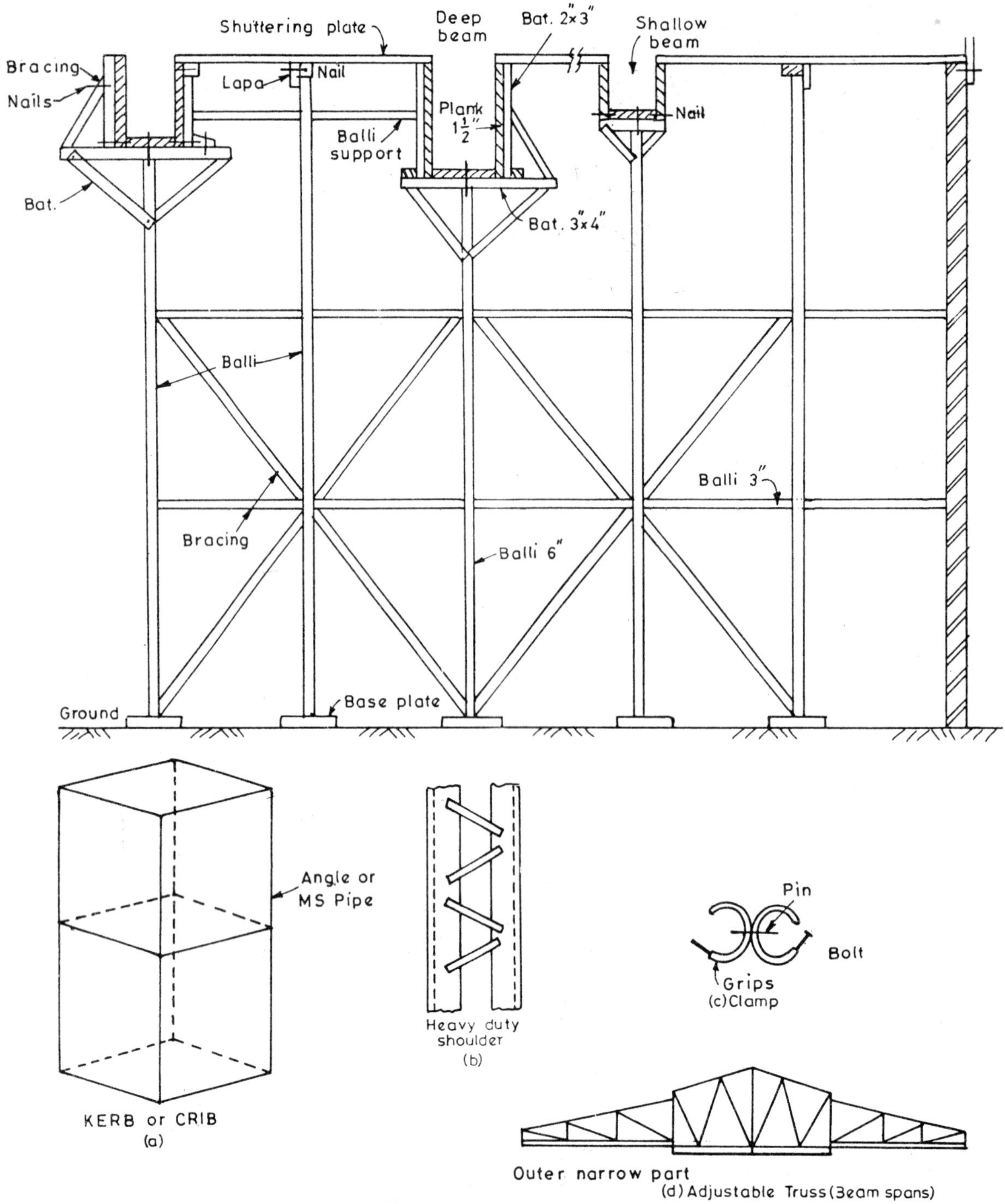

Fig. 8·19. Shuttering of a floor.

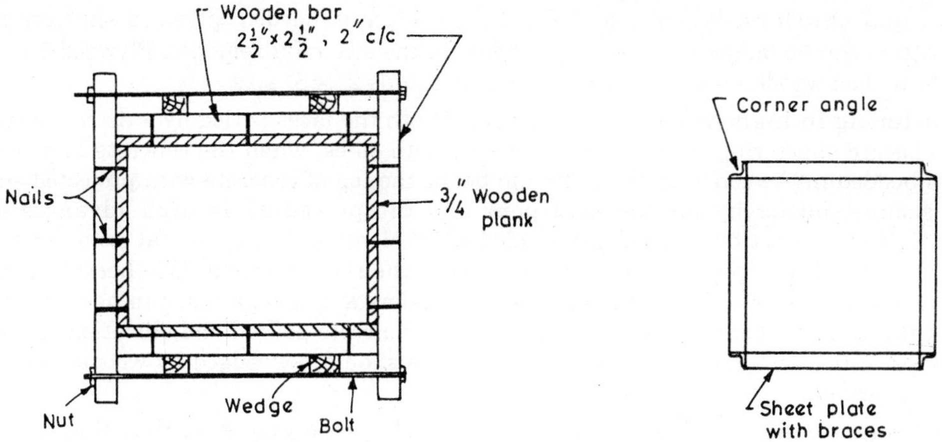

(*a*) Shuttering of col. 12″ × 9″ (wooden) (*b*) Shuttering of col. 9″ × 9″ (steel)

Fig. 8·20.

(7) **Kerbs or Cribs.** Angle iron or m.s. pipe framed blocks are used for staging purposes. These kerbs are prepared in different heights and sections according to the requirements cross bracings are also provided in them in order to ensure a better strength and safty against bulking.

(8) **Adjustable trusses or Beam spans.** To have horizontal support in roof shuttering, the adjustable trusses are used in the long spans. The length of the truss can be reduced or increased by sliding of the end portions inside the middle wider part. The outer portions should slide equally while adjusting length of span.

(9) **Clamps or swirl coupler.** (*a*) ***Movable*** : The m.s. pipes are tied with steel clamps. The two grips of a clamp is connected by a pin on which the grips can take any angular position. The grips have bolts at ends, one end of which is pinned with the grip, while the other can be nutted to the grip at other side.

(*b*) ***Right angle clamp or coupler*** : The two grips are fixed back to back. It is stronger than movable as in the former total load is taken by the pin, but it can only be used as a right angle fastener.

(10) **Shuttering plates at Rt. angle to form a Rt. angle.** (*a*) ***Steel shutters*** **:** They are plane sheet shutters with angle iron at its four edges (or edges pressed) and in intermediate portions. They are painted with red oxide. Holes are drilled in the sides of angles so that one shutter can be bolted to the other or to the shoulder. These shutters are available in sizes of 1 m, 50 cm, 30 cm or 25 cm with a length of 125 m. The thickness of the sheet is 3 mm and angle of bracings are 35 × 35 × 3 mm or 50 × 50 × 5 mm. Steel shutters are used at height where welding can be done easily.

(*b*) ***Wood shutters*** **:** When cheap shutters are needed, they are made by local wood planks 3/4″ thick with local wood braces. The wood should be of impervious nature.

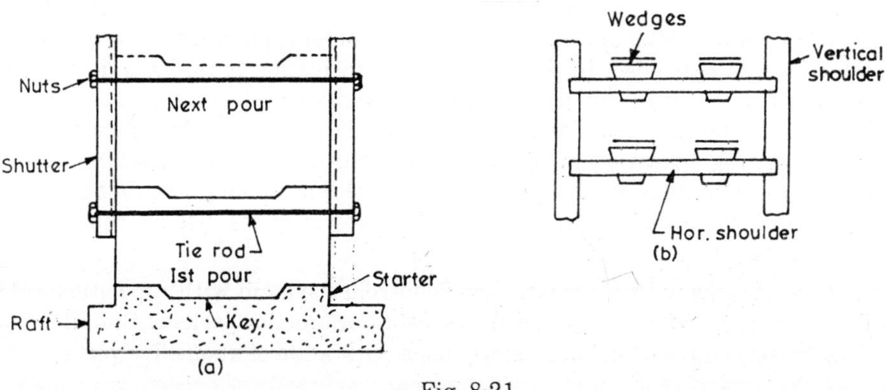

Fig. 8·21.

(*c*) **Plywood shutters.** When a good finishing surface is needed, plywood shutters are used. These shutters can be made in the sizes according to the site requirements. Plywood 10 mm to 12 mm is mounted on wooden frames made of wooden battons 2″ × 3″ size.

(*d*) **Shuttering in high walls.** The shuttering of both the faces is tied by a tie rod bushed at both ends to secure shuttering in position by nuts on both sides, when the concrete is poured, the tie rod is embedded in the concrete about 10 mm below the top of concrete with projected ends both sides to secure shuttering for the neat pour and the procedure is thus advances up. Sometimes the tie rods are not bushed but are welded with a long horizontal bar at its outer face. The inner face is secured by a piece of small bar welded to the reinforcement. The horizontal bar provided outside also works as a horizontal shoulder. Shoulders are also provided in horizontal as well as in vertical position to bear pressure caused by fresh concrete poured and vibrations caused by vibrators, Gaps in the shoulders to the shuttering plates should be wedged by wooden wedges to tighten the shuttering.

(*e*) **Roof shuttering.** (1) Sides of the beams should be so placed so that they can be removed earlier than shuttering of bottom of beam and slabs.

(2) All form work should be greased by mobil oil or diesel mixed with grease so as to give a non-sticky surface. Waste mobil oil of machines can also be used, but it should not grease the steel.

(3) Polythene sheet must be laid over shuttering to ensure lightness of the joints. Asian—MRA form releasing agent is also supplied in market.

(4) While concrete is in progress, the scaffolding and shuttering should be watched regularly and any damage if so, should be repaired immediately.

Normal size of timbers used in form work

(1) Plywood for plates 10 mm to 12 mm (2) Local wood planks 25 to 40 mm

(3) Battons for frames and cross joints 50 to 75 mm and upto 100 mm

(4) Joists for posts and verticals : 100 × 150 mm (5) Ballies for verticals : 100 to 150 mm

(6) Ballies for bracings : 75 to 100 mm.

8·5·2. Modern Shuttering materials and devices

Slipform equiment for silos, tapering chimneys, buildings and steel tank erection—The slipform division of Punjilloyd Ltd. has developed a new three tier slipform shuttering equipment. The first series of jacks are for 6*T* lifting and slipforming function. The 2nd hydraulic system is mounted on the star beams. This is called the inclination control hydraulic system. The 3rd tier is the hydraulically operated spindles and turn buckles which regulate the collapse of shuttering plates reducing the diameter. All jacks, power packs, turn buckles, shutter sliding jacks etc. are available with spare parts. This new system has provision for reducing wall thickness, lifting and change of inclination all hydraulically controlled from a single power pack. The method thus reduces the chances of mannual error and helps in checking diameter, wall thickness and slope of chimneys.

The use of hydraulic jacks and trestles system in steel tank erection works out to be more economical, both time and cost wise. In this system the fabrication of tanks is done in the reverse order *i.e.*, in 1st operation, the topmost vertical sheet is welded, kept in position. Roofing is computed at the ground level itself. Then the structure is lifted and 2nd sheet from the top is added. Like this the lifting operation is done by jacks hydraulically operated from single central power pack. The main advantage in this is that since welding is done at ground level itself, the quality improves, speed of welding increases, scaffolding cost reduces, use of crane is also avoided. These jacks have also been used for lifting Bridge trusses.

Various type of jacks with automatic level controller system with capacities of 1T, 3T, 5T, 6T and 12T have been manufactured and used in steel tank erection jacks with built in safety lock system and lifting trestles have been successfully used with a life of about five years.

8·5·3. Moving scaffolds for high rise buildings

During construction work in high rise buildings as well as during exterior work for maintenance of sky-scrappers, one requires movement of man and material to various locations along the building. The scaffolds are provided with self acting brakes and stand by wire ropes in case of human error. A four suspension system offers stability for changing positions of heavy loads inside the scaffolds have inbuilt system for prevention of excessive tilting. Provision of safety belts, safety net below the scaffold, electromagnetic brakes and hydraulic buffers are some of the special features of the scaffolds.

One of the products for scaffolding worked as "Flag Ship Product" for SGB India is CUPLOK. Its unique "node point" connections where four horizontals can be fastened at one time, along with carefully chosen raw materials and components (such as higher grade YST-2 no. tubes, malleable cast iron top cups forged ledger blades and deep drawn steel bottom cups) makes it the safest fastest and most economical and versatile staging and scaffolding system.

8·5·4. Custom built steel shuttering, centering and scaffolding

Systems manufactured by STB Consultants and Engineers, Mumbai are designed and developed especially to withstand severe climatic conditions and are offered as a package. It has a built in ladder for climbing. A mason can have plateform levels every 900 mm/600 mm, this giving maximum efficiency by working at chest level. A labourer with head load can pass through the gap without bending STB, P-form panels are made of pressed bent section, specially designed to protect ply edges. Panels are light and can be used for slab, walls and columns.

Form work and false work for large waffle slabs. THAKOOR supplied special form work system in corporating dismantable waffle moulds in steel each with the size 1·8 m × 1·85 m with 1·15 mm height. These waffle moulds were placed on special beam bottoms with a drop head arrangement on standards for early striking. The false work system was designed for heavy loads which would enable fast and easy erection and dismantling of the scaffolding. For beams 2·5 m deep × 1·8 m wide at the top with decorative splay construction with a wedge lock system of scaffolding. The standards were designed which would take upto 9 tonnes of leg load. For detail contact :

Fibre glass Coffer moulds and shuttering systems. When using fibre glass moulds, the entire operation of plastering is dispensed with. Glass reinforced plastic shuttering materials and precast moulds have extremely high impact strength, can with stand rough handling and will lost for 100 to 200 repetitions in comparison of plywood, wooden coated moulds which have only the capacity of 5-10 repetitions and have no dimensional stability as well as releasing properly.

Waffle moulds are used in the construction of two way spanning waffle floors, with a mould of 900 mm. In situ concrete waffle slabs allow for major savings to be achieved in concrete and reinforcement.

Emerging trends in form work and scaffolding

New materials such as aluminium, polypropelene and fibre reinforced plastics have entered the market.

One such alternative to traditional shuttering is a form work manufactured in Germany which uses a combination of welded steel mesh and polyethylene shuttering, particularly for foundation application. It has been successfully used on a variety of fast track construction projects in a number of countries. Its outstanding feature is its speed. It reduces concreted pour time from three days to one. Further the ease involved in installation has made it a big hit with construction contractors.

Among the newest products in the form work field is Controlled Permeability Formwork (CPF). This is essentially the incorporation of a layer of material on top of the form which allows air and excess pore water to escape during and after compaction of the concrete while leaving the solid materials in place. Among the benefits recorded for CPF are the improved surface finish with very few flow holes, good surface bond and improved initial surface strength allowing form work to be stick earlier. But the most important result is the reduced water/cement ratio and higher paste volumes in the cover zone provide much better protection against carbonation, chloride penetration and freeze/thaw effects. Modular panel systems are extremely popular today because they provide a high degree of flexibility and reduce the need of special sections.

A fairly versatile system is the unit frame type. This consists of two vertical and one horizontal member with specially designed end fillings and when the three members are assembled together it forms *H* frame. The end fillings on the horizontal also incorporate a fixing device for the longitudinal ledger. The unit frames can be erected one above the other and are spaced at suitable intervals. The advantage of this type of frame is that the units can be spaced at any required intervals and the plateforms can be had at any desired levels.

8·5·5. Wedge lock type of scaffolds

Consist of verticals, ledger, transoms and diagonals. The uprights have housing welded on them at regular intervals. The transoms, ledgers and diagonals have specially designed wedge lock assembles fitted at ends which engage in the housing on the uprights.

This type of scaffolding can be created very fast and does not require any special tool except a small hammer to drive the wedges in. This is extremely used for building scaffold, lowers, inside chimneys, silos and in ship building.

Lock pins are provided on vertical legs to interlock iron braces.

Spigots are provided at the top or bottom of the legs to keep in connecting the frames vertically.

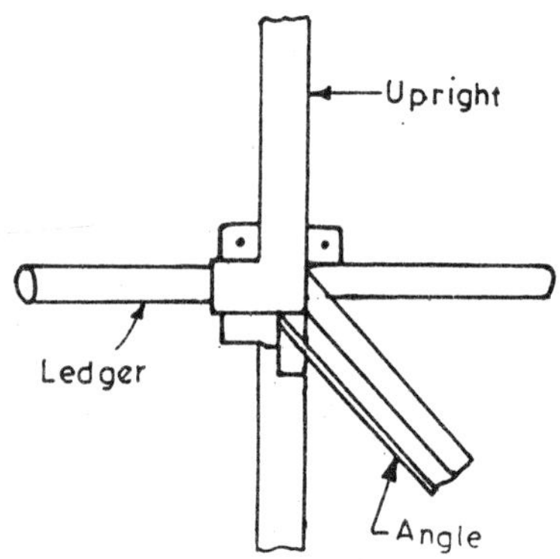

Fig. 8·22.

Inside and external corner angles along with form work fittings such as **locking wedges** etc. are used in shuttering work for different purposes.

5·6. Stay-in-place concrete form work for deck slabs of girder bridges

The form work for the casting of the concrete deck slabs of girder bridges is usually made with plywood panels which are removed after the concrete has set. Relatively thin precast concrete panels are increasingly comming to the force as the stay-in-place alternative to the removable wooden form work. The gross thickness of the deck slab comprises the thickness of the precast panel and that of the concrete cast in place. For a 225 mm thick deck slab, the thickness of the precast panel typically varies between 75 mm to 100 mm. Because of the ease of constructive that it offers. The precast stay-in-place form work has become highly cost effective.

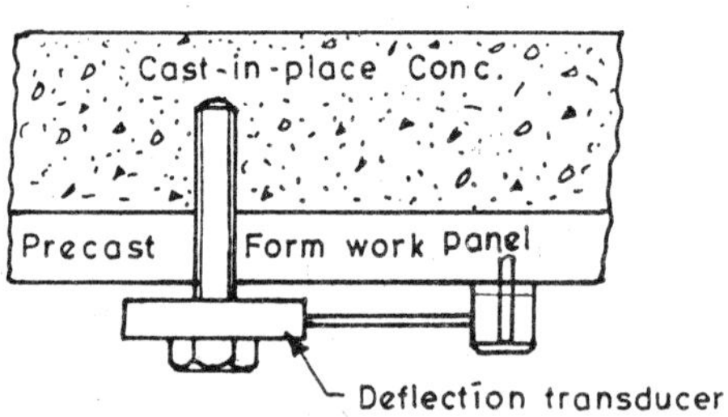

Fig. 8·23. Scheme for measuring the relative horizontal slip between the form work panel and cast in place concrete.

These panels which are between 1·22 m and 2·44 m long in the direction of the girder span are usually cast several at a time in long casting beds. In some cases, several panels are cast as a single unit which is eventually saw-cut into required lengths. The ends of such form work panels are clearly. Smooth and without the producing tendons. In other cases adjacent panels on the casting load have gaps between them, and the strands in these gaps are flame cut so that they produce by upto 150 mm. Part cross-sections of deck slabs with the two types of form work panels are shown in the Fig. 8·24 (*a*) and (*b*) respectively.

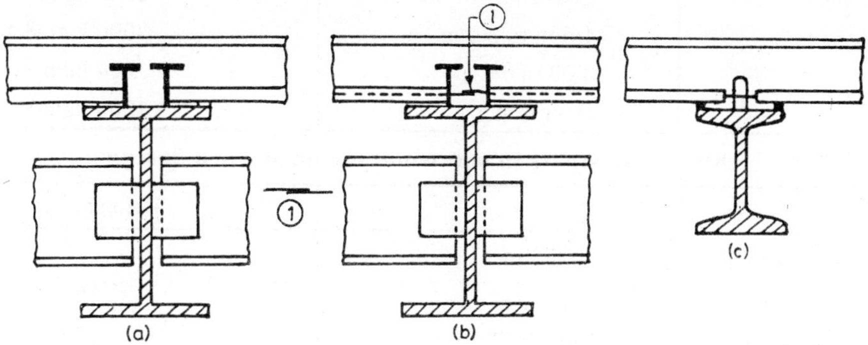

Fig. 8·24. Cross-sections of deck slabs with precast form work panels
(*a*) panels with smooth ends (*b*) panels with producing tendons.

8·5·7. Stripping time for form work (IS : 456—1964 for ordinary Portland cement)

(1) Vertical sides of slabs, walls and columns — 2 days

(2) Bottom of slabs upto 4·5 m span — 7 days

(3) Bottom of slabs above 4·5 m span
Bottom of beams upto 6 m span
Arch rib bottom upto 6 m span — 14 days

(4) Above 6 m span — 21 days

(5) Above 9 m span — 28 days

Note : (1) The supports should not be released suddenly but should be removed gradually so that structure may not have the load suddenly over it.

(2) For rapid hardening 3/7th time of the above (not less than 24 hours).

(3) No load should be allowed over the structure before 28 days.

(4) A rough guide for the strength of the structure is that by blowing with a hammer it must give a hard metallic sound.

(1) The cost of forms is about 1/3 to 1/4 of the cost of RCC tad.

(2) A camber should be given in the mid span of beams and slabs to have a safe guard against bulging.

Table 8·28. Live loads on form work

Members	*Live load in bending in kg/m²*	*Deflection live load in kg/m²*
Sheeting	400	400
Joists	400	200
Ledges	200	200

Horizontal pressure on forms

Structure	*Height of wall or lift*	*Pressure will be equivalent to that of liquid weighing*
Columns	Any height	2000 kg/m^2
Wall, beam sides	Less than 1·5 m	2300 kg/m^2
Walls	1·5 m to 3·0 m	2000 kg/m^2
Walls	3·00 to 6·0 m	1600 kg/m^2
Walls	Over 6 m	1200 kg/m^2

Allowable stress in soft wood for form work design

Stress	*Value in kg/cm^2*
Extreme fibre stress in bending	80
Compression parallel to grain	60
Compression perpendicular to grain	20
Compression shear to grain	8

Value of E may be taken as 1×10^5 kg/cm^2 for calculating deflection.

8·6. Cement Concrete

8·6·1. Batching of Concrete

The operation of batching is considered with proportioning of cement concrete at field. In small works the ingradients ballast and sand is measured by wooden or sheet iron measuring boxes, fitted with two handles to handle the box by two beldars. These boxes are so adjusted in capacity so as to have a quantity equal to one bag of cement *i.e.*, 1·25 cft or 0·0337 cm. Their sizes are generally 1·25′ × 1′ × 1′ or 375 mm × 300 mm × 300 mm. If a part capacity than one bag of cement is required, it is adjusted by reducing the height accordingly. For important works batching of concrete is done by weight in batching plants, weighed by lever balances.

8·6·2. Mixing of Concrete

Concrete is mixed either by mechanical means or by hand in pyramidal stacks of ingradients sand and ballast cement and sand is 1st mixed thoroughly thrice to have a regular colour. This mixed cement sand is then stacked over the ballast of required quantity uniformly. It is then cut by spade or showels thrice or four times till a uniform mass is obtained. Water is added during this mixing according to the requirements.

8·6·3. Mechanical Mixing. There are two main types of mixtures, one tilting in which the drum is tilted to pour the contents while in the other material is discharged by a hopper and drum does not tilt. The mixtures are available in market in capacity ranging from 5 cft to 200 cft. A mixture marked 5/3·5 means that it can lift 5cft dry material and will prepare 3·5 cft of prepared mass. Similarly a mixture marked 100 litres means that it's capacity is for producing 100 litres of prepared mass in one trip. The selection of type is according to availability and quantum of work.

In some mixures ingradients are collected in a hopper which pours it in the revolving drum by a lifting lever. While in some smaller capacaity mixures the ingradients are feeded in the drum by buckets of measured capacity direct.

The engine of some mixures is water cool, having a bucket of water placed at higher platform while some engines are air cooled type.

The following are the normal size of mixures.

Concrete mixtures

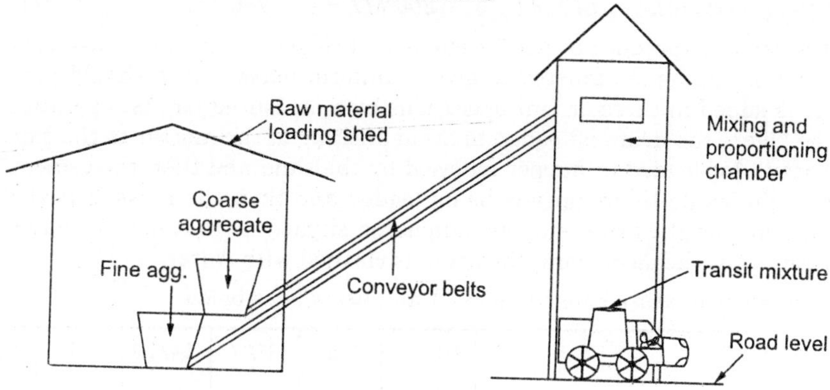

Concrete batching plant

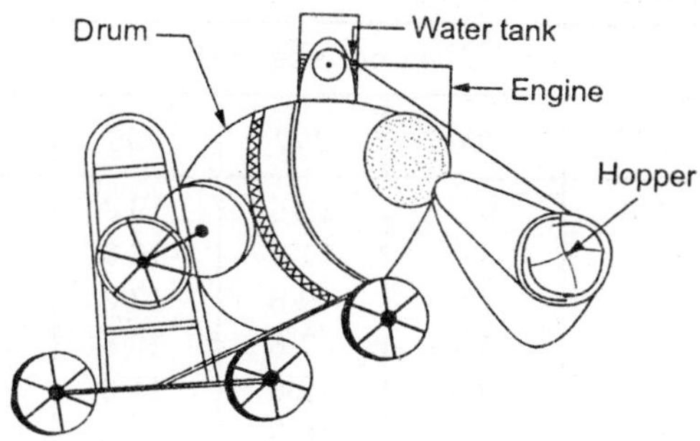

Concrete mixture tilting type with hopper

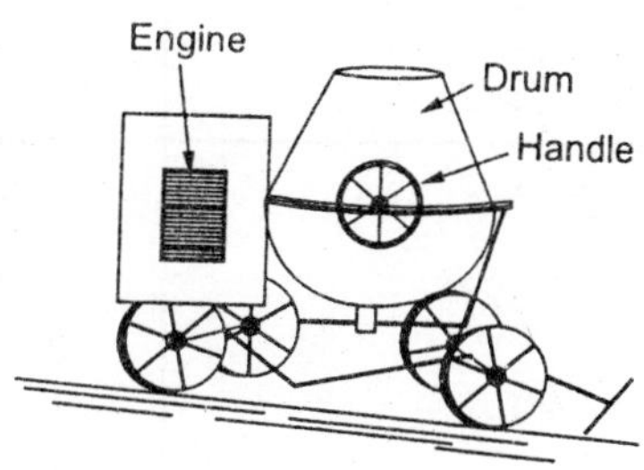

Tilting type concrete mixture without hopper

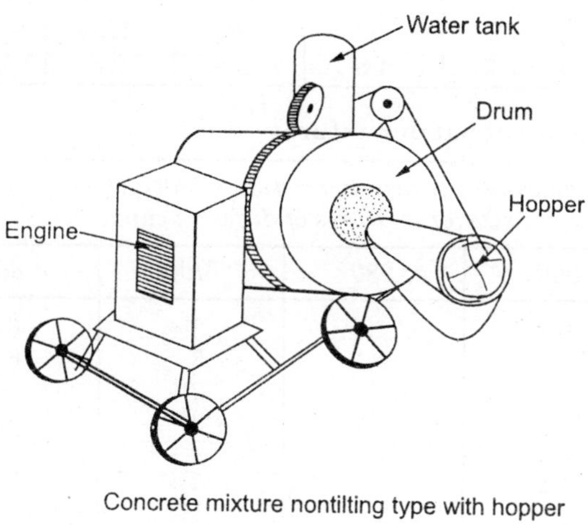

Concrete mixture nontilting type with hopper

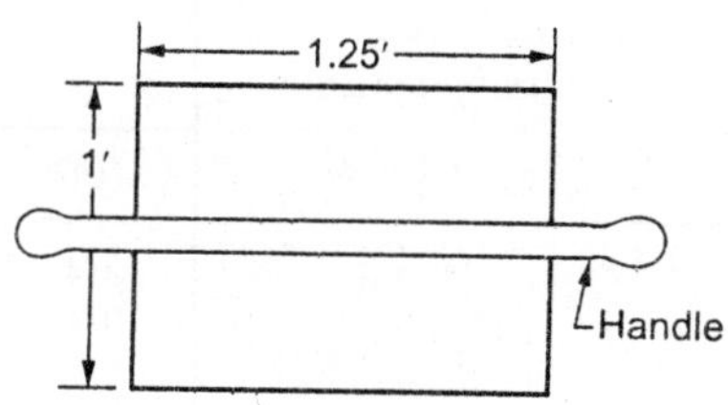

1′ × 1.25′ × 1′ or
Wooden measure of
one cement bag capacity

Fig. 8·25.

Tilting mixtures	*100 T*	*140 T*	*200 T*		
Non tilting mixtures	*140 MT*	*200 MT*	*280 MT*	*400 MT*	*800 MT*

Effort is made to produce a mix for one bag of cement in a trip for avoiding measuring of the cement. Time of mixing is adjusted to give a uniform mass, but it should not be less than 2 minutes. Water is added in three or four operations by a measured jar. 1st operation of addition of water should be before the drum is loaded to avoid sticking of the mortar to the sides of the drum. Coarse aggregate is 1st loaded in hopper followed by the sand and then the cement is added. The drum keeps rotating while the hopper is being loaded and then the mass is feeded to the drum. While mixing is going on the drum may be hammered slightly so that mortar may not stick to the sides of the drum. After the days work, the drum is cleaned with water.

The equivalent mixture capacities in cft and litres is as below :

Capacity in cft	5/3·5	7/5	10/7	14/10	18/12	22/24	45/28
Prepared mass capacity (in litres)	100	140	200	280	340	400	800

Table 8·29. Output of MT mixtures in m³/Hr

Total charging and discharging time in seconds	*Mixing time (min.)*	*Nominal size of mixtures*				
		140	*200*	*280*	*400*	*800*
15	1·0	6·8	9·6	13·6	19·0	38·0
	1·25	5·8	8·0	11·4	16·0	32·0
	1·5	4·8	7·0	9·8	13·6	27·2
	2·0	3·8	5·4	7·6	10·8	21·6
20	1·0	6·4	9·0	12·6	18·0	36·0
	1·25	5·4	7·6	10·8	15·2	30·4
	1·50	4·6	6·4	9·2	13·2	26·0
	2·0	3·6	5·2	7·2	10·4	20·8
30	1·0	5·8	8·0	11·2	16·0	32·0
	1·25	4·8	7·0	9·8	13·8	27·6
	1·5	4·2	6·0	8·4	12·0	24·6
	2·0	3·4	4·8	6·8	9·8	19·2

Table 8·30. Capacity of batch mixtures

Nominal proportion of mix by volume	*No. of 50 kg bags of cement to produce a batch of concrete of suitable size for mixtures of different capacities*				
	100	*200*	*280*	*400*	*800*
1 : 1½ : 3	3/4	1½	2½	3½	6½
1 : 2 : 3	3/4	1½	2	3	6
1 : 2 : 4	1/2	1	1½	2½	5½
1 : 2½ : 5	1/2	1	1½	2	4½
1 : 3 : 5	1/2	1	1½	2	4
1 : 3 : 6	1/2	3/4	1	1½	3
1 : 4 : 8	—	1/2	3/4	1½	3

8·6·4. Transporting of concrete

(1) **By steel pans**. The concrete is filled by showel in the steel pans and is transported on head generally by women labour. Care should be taken that it should be laid in initial setting time. The pan should be placed upside down on the concreting surface.

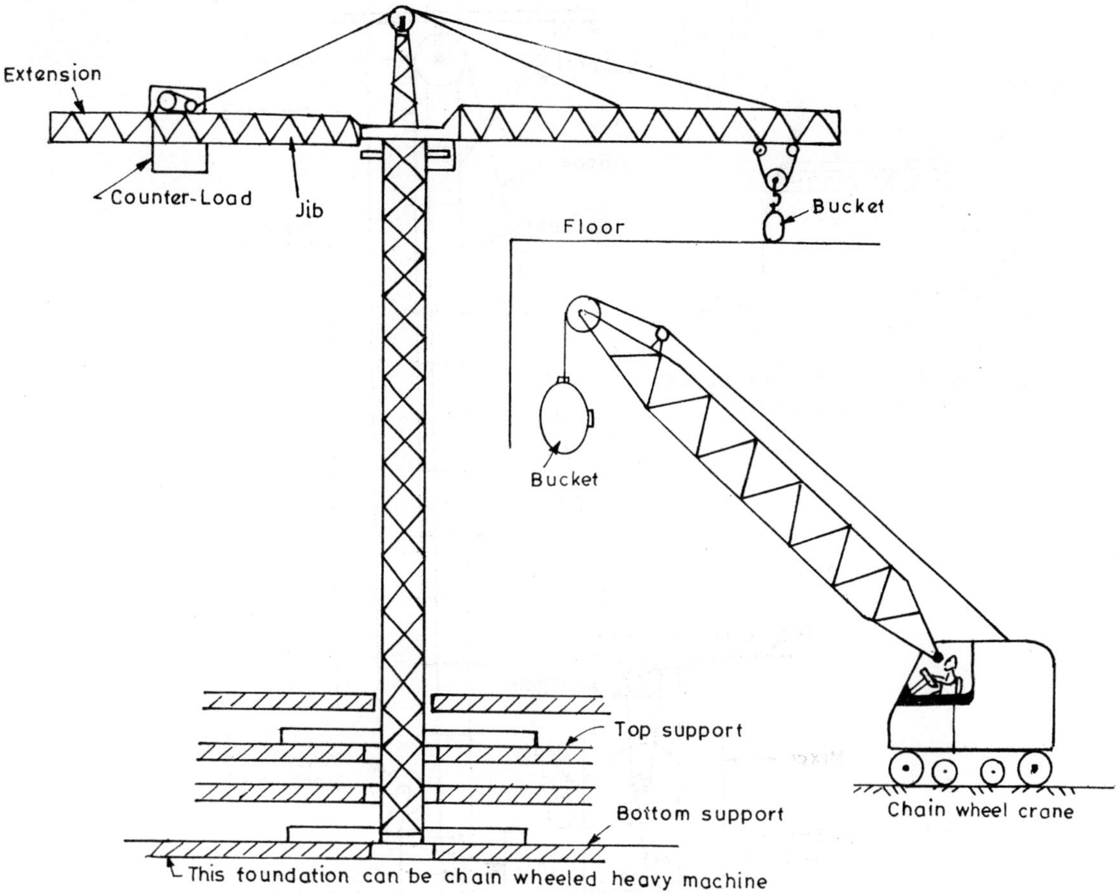

Fig. 8·26. Jib crane lift (Hoist).

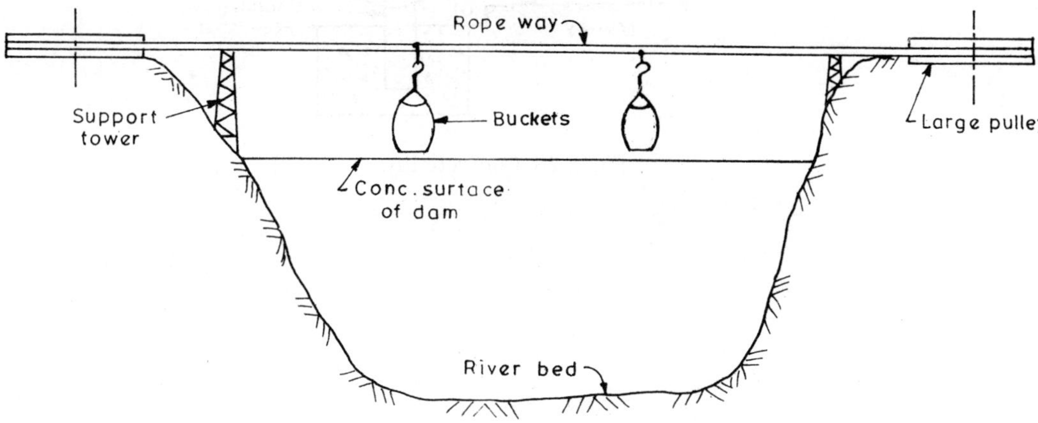

Fig. 8·27. Ropeway hoist.

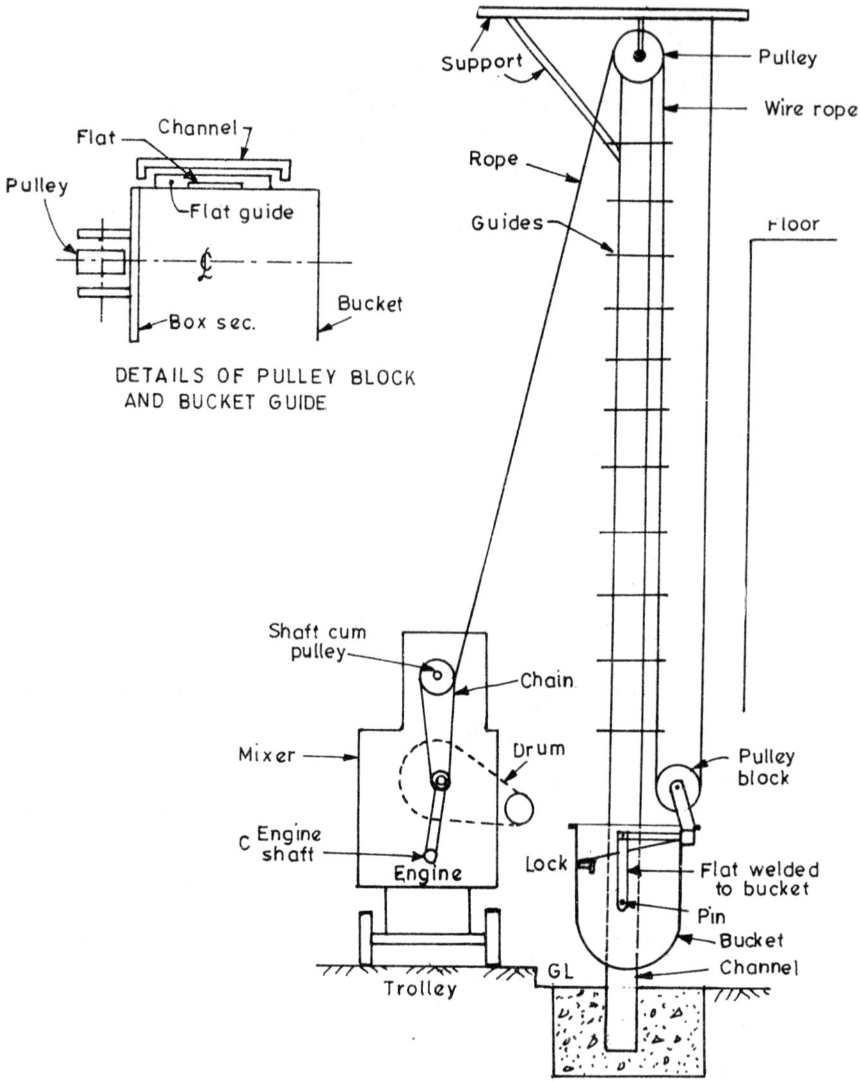

Fig. 8·28. Concrete lift.

(2) **By Transite mixtures.** When the concrete is mixed in batching plants, it is transported in transit mixtures. This method is better because the concrete remains in mixing stage while under transport operation. This method is used for longer leads.

(3) **Buckets moving on wire ropes.** It is used when concrete in mass scale (as in Dams) is done and a vehicle or a man cannot reach to the spot of concreting. The bucket used can be opened on the concrete spot by opening a value fitted in the bottom of bucket.

(4) **By dampers.** The bucket of concrete placed in a dumper is filled under the batching plant and is conveyed to the site by the later where a crane lifts it from the dumpers or truck and pours on the site to be concreted.

(5) **By force pumps.** Concrete pumps are available in capacities ranging from 7·5 to 2·5 m^3/lit. even upto 50 m^3 per hour. Distances upto 300 m horizontal and 30 m vertical can be covered. The concrete can be laid in a slope of 1·8 (8 horizontal to 1 vertical). For larger loads the pumps can be installed in series.

(6) **Lifting of concrete.** (*a*) By cranes the buckets of concrete are lifted by cranes and the concrete is placed on the spot on higher floors.

(*b*) **By lifts**—Buckets of concrete are lifted by lifts having ropes running over pulley operated electrically or mechanically not pattern of a lift is shown in the Fig. 8·26 to 8·28.

8·6·5. Laying of Concrete

In plain mass concrete it is laid in layers of 300 mm in each lift and 150 to 250 mm in case of RCC. The end faces should be shuttered and not to be loose concreted. Before laying the 2nd lift the surface of the 1st lift should be cleaned and wire brushed to remove any loose part (by a small pointed hammer or hacked) or laitance.

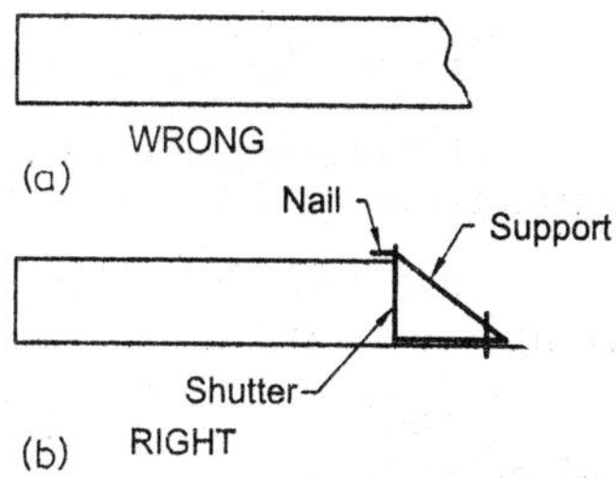

Fig. 8·29.

The vertical edges should be stepped and should not be laid in one vertical joint. The vertical face should be wire brushed or hacked. A slurry of the neat cement mortar (IS specifications) is applied on the previous face about 10 to 15 mm in thickness.

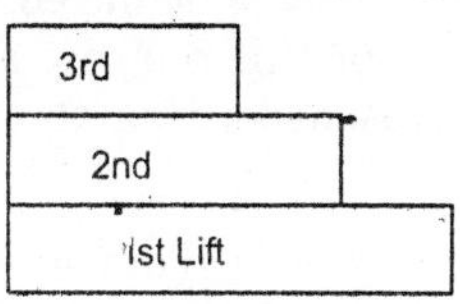

Fig. 8·30.

The concrete in the pan should not be poured from a height but the pan itself with concrete mass should be dropped up side down on the surface to be concreted and then the pan should be lifted by the help of a hook. The next lift should be laid as early as possible before any final setting is taken in the previous one. On old horizontal surface slurry of the mortar 10 to 15 mm thick composed of cement and sand in the same ratio as the mix of the concrete (I.S. specifications) is laid on the surface

(2) **The RCC slabs.** The RCC slabs should be laid in one continuous operation to avoid and cold joint. For large slabs the sides of previous layer should be widened as far as possible with in the initial setting time, however a neat cement slurry should be used if the initial setting time has elapsed. The widening should be advanced in a regular operation as shown in the Fig. The concrete once started should not be stopped till competition. The shutters should be strong so as to bear the load of concrete and vibrations. Horizontal dowels should be left by a suitable bar with embedded length of 40 diameter of bar on each side. A slurry of mortar of 1 : 2 is spreaded in 1 mm thickness over the shuttering to

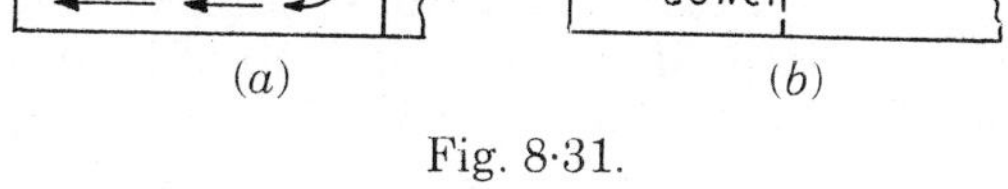

Fig. 8·31.

give a smooth surface and a burlap paper may also be laid over shuttering or on a porous subgrade so that water from the concrete may not be absorbed by the surface.

(3) **RCC in walls and columns.** In walls a lift of about one meter should be taken. While vibrating, water or mortar should not be passed through joints of shutters otherwise honey combing will take place on the joints. The joints should be coked with some water tight material such as putty or jute soaked with tar. In high vertical lifts a key and a vertical dowel should be left for proper bonding of each lift. The embedment of the dowel should be 40 diameter of the bar on each side.

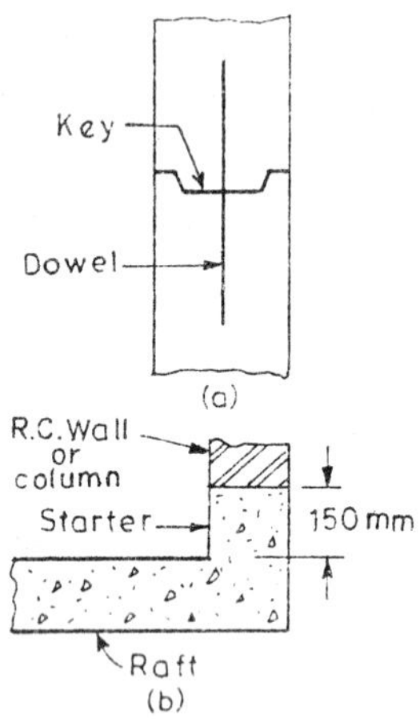

Fig. 8·32.

In columns a thin needle vibrator is used for compaction or a wooden thick rod is used if the stirrups hinder the vibrator. A 15 cm layer should be left to cast with top slab or beam. A 15 cm high starter should be laid with the raft to join with wall.

Beams should be laid as far as possible with the slab. If there is a time lagging the rib of the beam should be laid 15 cm lower so that the slab may not have a contiuous horizontal joint with beam. However the gap of time between the beam and slab should not be more than 2 days. The construction joint on slabs and beams should be given at mid of span.

8·6·6. Compaction of Concrete

Hand compaction for thick plan concrete in foundations is done by ramming with wooden or iron rammers. Care should be taken that while ramming segregation may not take place.

For sharp edges pinning or rodding is done. This operation is done by an iron bar or strong wooden rod.

The surface is rammed by wooden temping with a long template of wood with handles on both sides. In place of wood a flat web bed channel iron can also be used. Shuttering from outside is also hammered to achieve proper compaction inside.

Mechanical compaction. Where a mass concrete is done a good efficiency is achieved by mechanical vibration system in time, quality and economy. The vibrators used for this purpose are electric, diesel or compressed air driven. They are classified in four groups according to the purpose and mode of vibrations.

(*a*) **Internal or immersion type.** These are used in massive concrete works. They are of flexible or rigid types. The rigid type is used in concentrated massive concrete work while the flexible type is used for concrete spreaded in layers, because they consists of long flexible shaft. The needle for thick sections is thicker while for thin sections such as for columns a thin needle is used. These should be immersed in concrete slowly and also should be removed slowly for avoiding cavity formation. Immersion vibrators are also used in concrete underwater such as plugging concrete in well foundations.

(*b*) **External vibrators.** These are damped with shutters which transmitts the vibrations to the concrete. More power is wasted in such type in vibrating the shutters. Shutters are also liable to be loose while vibrating. They give a good side surface to concrete.

(*c*) **Table vibrators.** They are used for precast units.

(*d*) **Surface vibrators.** These vibrators are fixed in a wooden or steel template which can be lifted by handles and transmitts the vibrations to the surface. They are used in road and floors.

Less compaction results in honey combing while excessive gives a hetrogenous mass as heavy ingradients go down leaving the slurry on top.

Capacity of vibrators vary from 4 to 30 m^3 concrete handling per hour. The minimum frequency is 3500 vibrations per minute. The higher is the frequency, the better is the time saving vibrations should be stopped when scum appears on top. Needle of vibrator should reach upto bottom of concrete layer and should not penetrate in the bottom layer laid before. The layers of concrete such as slabs should be vibrated by the needle laid flat.

8·6·7. Curing of Concrete

(1) **Necessity of curing.** For chemical action (called hydration of cement) in setting water is needed for hardening of cement. Water present in the mix dries due to evaporation, heat, wind or due to porous nature of forms. In order to fulfil the requirement of water during hydration a continuous supply of water (curing) is provided to the concrete. This hydration and hardening of concrete is continuous upto one year, but after about a fortnight this process goes very slow and the requirement of water is fulfilled by natural conditions of the atmosphere and hence the curing process is necessary for about a fortnight depending on the type of cement as given below :

Normal portland cement	— 7 to 12 days (Minimum 14 days practically)
Rapid hardening cement	— 24 Hours (Minimum 7 days practically)
High alumina cement	— 24 Hours (Minimum 5 days practically)

The strength of concrete is only 50% if not damp cured to that if damp cured. Its strength will increase about 25% if the curing is continuous for four months.

Due to lack of water proper hydration does not take place and full strength is not achieved. The concrete sets very rapidly in initial stags and if it is not kept damp the shrinkage effect will take place and resulting in loss of strength. The climate conditions also effects the strength of concrete and hence curing.

Concrete gets strength slowly in low temperatures in comparison to high temperatures, hence higher temperatures are more favourable for curing to attain early strength. Due to wind and high temperature water dries earlier and hence continuous curing is needed. The curing should be started as soon as the concrete hardens *i.e.*, about one or two hours after laying.

(2) **Methods of curing.** (*a*) Prevention of loss of concrete moisture (*b*) supplying extra moisture to concrete.

(*a*) **Preventive method.** Forms are removed after water requirement to concrete ceases. Impervious type of forms, painting inside of form work, water proof membrane (polythene paper) using under concrete surface, spraying water on forms, so that they may not dry and liable to absrob water from concrete, subgrades are well wetted before laying concrete are preventive methods.

Concrete is protected by curtains from direct effect of sun and wind. Spraying of propriatory membrane composed for curing such as bitumen emulsions in two coats on surface concrete. They prevent evaporation.

(*b*) **Supplying moisture.** (1) Wet gunny bags are laid on the surface or tied to the vertical columns and are kept wet by spraying or sprinkling water coir matting. Bundles of straw, 5 to 10 cm thick layer of sand dust or sand can also be used. This operation will start after 2 hours of laying of concrete to 24 hours. After which a 25 mm deep layer of water is kept over surface. This water should be filled in 1 m^2 grids may be of lean sand mortar. This operation is called ponding. A surface is ready for ponding if a boy can walk on the surface without leaving foot prints. The ponds should be filled with water periodically as soon as they are likely to dry.

In vertical members like walls curtain of gunny are hunged and are kept wet by spraying water jets. Perforated bottom pots can also be kept on the top edge surface. In columns gunny bags are wrapped and kept wet by water jets.

Under face and side of beams and slabs are cured continuously by force jets. Curing time can be reduced by use of calcium chloride as it absorbs moisture from air.

Steam or hot water can also be used for curing within 24 hours.

The water which is fit for concreting is fit for curing.

Liquid membrane curing compound : Emcoril a liquid membrane curing compound manufactured by M.C. Bauchemic (India Pvt. Ltd. Mumbai). Emcoril is to be brushed or sprayed on the part poured concrete at a very limited stage. It forms a seamless film on the surface of freshly cast concrete and mortars which arrests the evaporation of water from the capillaries and presents quick drying of concrete avoiding cracks and enabling the concrete to hydrate efficiently. Emcoril disintegrates after about one month by virtue of its built film breaking system. It minimizes the shrinkage cracks. Impermeable membranes such as polyethlene sheeting covering closely the concrete surface may also be used to provide effective barrier against evaporation.

8·6·8. Concrete under special situations

(1) **Concrete under water.** Plugging of well and other type of foundations where concrete is laid under water, the following procedure is adopted :

(*i*) **Termic pipe.** It consists of a steel pipe 13 to 15 cm in diameter and length as per site situations. The bottom rests on concrete surface (about 5 cm below concrete) and top surface about 30 cm above the water surface. The top end is provided with a conical hopper in which the concrete mass is poured. The termic should not be emptied to avoid entry of water in it. The pipe is lifted up as the concrete advances. It is shifted at different positions for pouring concrete which can be judged by the depth. A drier mass (slump 100 to 180 mm IS : 456) having less water is used. The cement used must be 10% extra than that required if used in dry condition (IS : 456—1978). Ratio of fine to coarse aggregate must be 1 : 2.

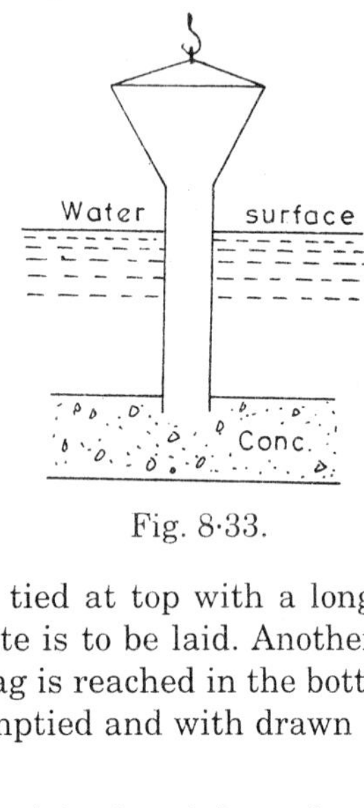

Fig. 8·33.

(*ii*) **Gunny bags** filled with stiff concrete mass and loosely tied at top with a long rope reaching upto full depth is lowered in the bed of water where concrete is to be laid. Another rope hooked in the bottom of bag is also lowered with the bag. When the bag is reached in the bottom, it is turned up side down by pulling hooked rope and thus the bag is emptied and with drawn up for next trip.

(*iii*) **Buckets (skips)** which opens from base by a valve and is closed from the top is lowered a bit higher on the bed where concrete is to be laid in water. The valve in the base is opened by a rope and the mass in the bucked is poured. The bucket is lifted and the operation is repeated till completion.

(*iv*) **Grouting.** A cage of 6 mm m.s. bars with a squared mesh of 50 mm is placed extending to full height of concrete to be laid in water. Stone aggregate 50 to 200 mm is deposited in the cage upto full height and grount of 1 : 2 cement sand slurry with a w/c ratio of 0·6 to 0·8 is sent down with pressure (about 0·2 N/mm^2) through 38 to 50 mm diameter pipes terminating into steel cages placed in lifts of 600 mm. The quantity of grout should be sufficient to fill the voids in the aggregate say about 55%.

Gangway with high lifts. Gangway is made if the concrete is to be laid by manpower on heights. A landing after every 15 m height should be given or it may also be given at bends

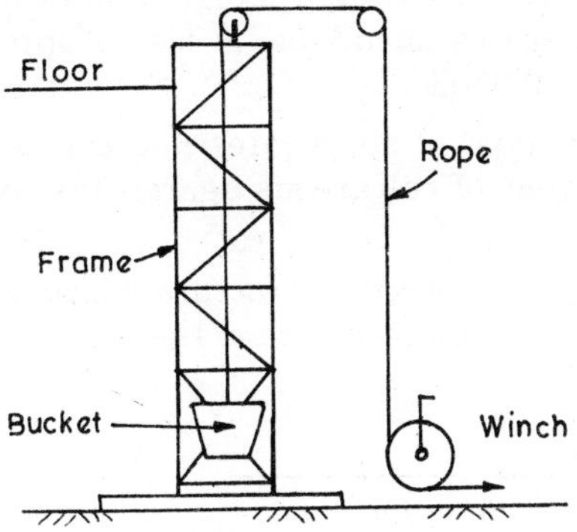

Fig. 8·34.

in gang way. The slope of gang way should be so gentle that a man can climb on it easily. It may be about 1·5 m wide so that a man who is returning down may have a passage by the side of the up going man, side hand rails should also be provided. These gang ways are made with m.s. pipe and clamps or may be of wood ballies winch driven buckets (Hoists)—on tall buildings bucket of concrete is lifted by ropes driven by winch. The bucket moves in side a vertical framed steel tower and is picked up on a plate form on top. The height of the steel frame can be increased as the concrete advances up. The bucket has guide rolls with frame angle so that it may lift smoothly.

Laying concrete down with chutes. Chutes are used when concrete is laid on a lower level than the road. A plain sheet channel folded in suitable size is placed on a suitable slope (generally varies 1 : 3 to 1 : 2) on angle supports. The slope is so adjusted that concrete may step without segregation and leaving the chute clean. The troughs of the chute is washed before and after use. The top and lower end of chute should be placed on easily approached situations.

Elephant chute. It is made by joining G.I sheet made vessels as shown in the Fig. 8·35.

8·6·9. Shortcomings in Concrete

Segregation. To avoid segregation of mix (separation of the ingradients of the mix.). The following points should be attended :

(1) The mix should be properly designed and finer sand be avoided.

(2) Proper handling and transportation of concrete is required. For long leads transit mixtures should be used. Mixture should not be thrown from a height but should be poured ger pan upside down.

(3) Too much vibrations should be avoided.

(4) In chutes mix should not pass with a fast velocity.

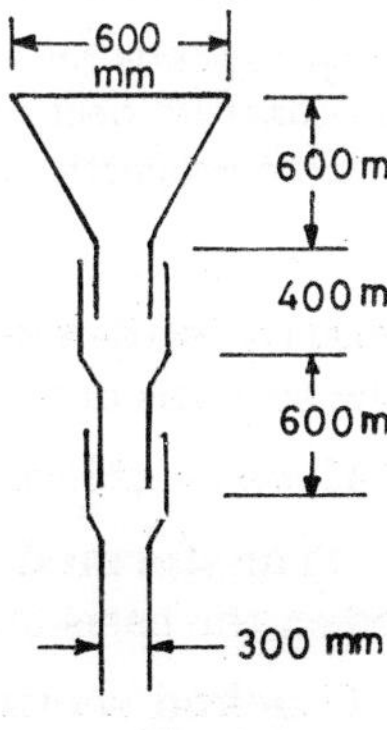

Fig. 8·35.

Bleeding. Appearance of water scum on the surface of concrete (also called laitance) after compaction. It shows that either the water is mixed more than required or the grading is not proper. Excess vibrations also cause bleeding. This scum should be removed as it makes weak bondage with subsequent lifts. Bleeding can be reduced either by decreasing water or using lesser sand. The addition of finely ground inert substance like stone dust also decreases bleeding. In wet aggregates a due allowance for the presence of the water already in aggregates is given. Angular aggregate, fine sand, and ungraded mix needs more water.

Hydration of Cement. For hydration (chemical action) cement needs water and calcium hydroxide and hydrated lime is liberated. Due to heat production in this process temperature goes up and shrinkage occurs on subsequent cooling which results cracks (as water present in concrete evaporates by heat and the mass cools). Hence for further hydration more water is needed which is about 25% of the mass of the cement. When w/c ratio is less than 0·5 complete hydration will not take place, hence water for further hydration is required as curing. Roughly the w/c ratios are kept as follows :

cc 1 : 2 : 4 = 0·6 ; cc 1 : 1½ : 3 = 0·5 ; cc 1 : 1 : 2 = 0·45.

Shrinkage. During hydration concrete shrinks. The drying shrinkage is due to excess cement, water and aluminous cements. In big size aggregates shrinkage is less. Approximate value of total shrinkage strain for designs may be taken on 0·0003.

Expansion of Concrete. It largely depends on type of aggregates and cement used. Aggregates with siliceous contents expands more than that of calcareous aggregates like lime stone. Rich mixes expand more than lean.

Creep of Concrete. It is the permanent strain in a concrete structure which does not disappear on the removal of the external load. Due to this changed strain there is a gradual redistribution of stress between the steel and the concrete.

Table 8·31.

Age of loading	*Creep coefficient*
7 days	2·2
28 days	1·6
1 year	1·1

Note : (1) The ultimate creep strain, estimated as described above does not include the elastic strains.

(2) Ultimate creep strain may be calculated from the creep coefficients (*i.e.*, ultimate creep strain/elastic strain at the age of loading). For long span structure, it is advisable to determine actual creep strain likely to take place.

Creep depends on stress in the concrete, age at loading and deviation of loading. As long as the stress in concrete does not exceed one-third of its characteristic compressive strength, creep may be assumed to be proportional to the stress. Other factors as mentioned above also influence creep.

Stiffness

Relative stiffness. The relative stiffness of the member may be based on the moment of inertia of the sections determined on the basis of the following definitions :

(*a*) **Gross section.** The cross-section of the member ignoring reinforcement.

(*b*) **Transformed section.** The concrete cross section plus the area of reinforcement transformed on the basis of modular ratio.

(*c*) **Cracked section.** The area of concrete in compression plus the area of reinforcement transformed on the basis of modular ratio.

The assumptions made shall be consistent for all the members of the structure throughout.

For deflection calculations, appropriate values of moment of Inertia should be used.

Limit State Serviceability

Deflection. The deflection of a structure or a part thereof shall not adversely effect the appearance or efficiency of structure or finishes. The deflection is limited as below :

(1) The final deflection due to all loads including effects of temperature creep and shrinkage and measured from as cast level of the supports of floors, roofs and all other horizontal members should not normally exceed span/250.

(2) The deflection including the effects of temperature, creep and shrinkage occurring after erection of partitions and the application of finishes should not normally exceed span/35 or 20 mm whichever is less. The span to depth ratios are not greater than the values as below :

(*i*) Span to effective depth ratios for span upto 10 m.

Cantilevers —7 ; simply supported—20 ; continuous — 26.

(*ii*) Spans above 10 m, the values in (*i*) may be multiplied by 10/span in meters, except for cantilever in which case deflection calculation should be made.

Cracking. Cracking in concrete should not effect the appearance or durability of the structure. The acceptible limit of cracking would vary with the type of structure and the environment.

Crack width (W_{cr})

$$W_{cr} = \frac{3Q_{cr}\,\varepsilon_m}{q + \dfrac{2(Q_{cr} - C_{min})}{h - x}}$$

where a_{cr}—distance from the point considered to the surface of the nearest longitudinal bar.

C_{min} = Minimum cover to the longitudinal bar.

ε_m = Average steel strain at the level coned.

h = Overall depth of member.

x = Depth of neutral axis.

The value of ε_m may be calculated as under :

$$\varepsilon_m = S_1 \frac{b(h-x)(a-x)}{3E_s\,A_s(d-x)}$$

where A_s = area of tension steel ; b = width of the section at the centroid of the tension steel.

ε = strain at the level covered, calculated ignoring the stiffening of the concrete in the tension zone.

a = distance from the comp. face to the point at which the crack width is being calculated

d = effective depth of section.

f_s = tensile stress in steel.

f_a = compressive stress in concrete.

E_s = elastic modulus of steel

E_c = elastic modulus of concrete.

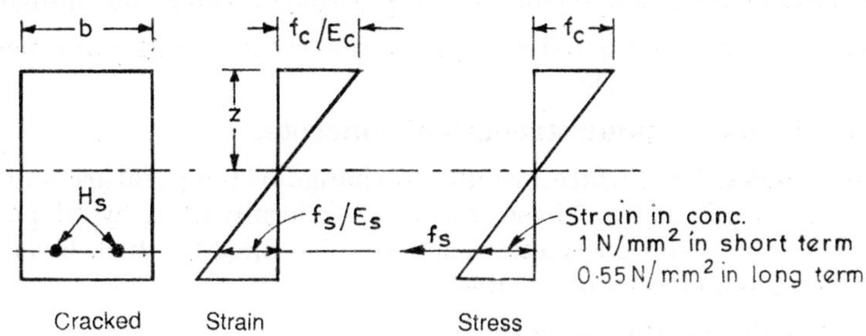

Fig. 8·36.

The average of steel strain can be calculated by the formula given above. Concrete and steel are assumed to be fully elastic.

Elastic modulus of steel (E_s) = 200 kN/mm^2 (For all type of steels)

Elastic modulus of concrete = $5000\sqrt{f_{ck}}$ N/mm^2 in short term in tension air comp. both

(f_{ck} being the characteristic compressive strength of concrete in bending).

Approximately it will normally be calculated equal to the tensile force by a triangular distribution having a value of zero at the neutral axis and a value at the centroid of the tension steel of 1 N/mm^2 instantaneously reducing to 0·55 N/mm^2 in the long term over the tension zone divided by the steel area for a rectangular tension zone.

The surface width of the cracks should not in general exceed 0·3 mm in members where cracking is not harmful.

In members where cracking in the tensile zone is harmful when they are in contact with weather or in harmful water and soil etc. the limit of crack is restricted to 0·2 mm.

For aggressive environments such as 'severe' category the assessed surface width should not be more than 0·1 mm.

8·6·10. Concrete Deterioration

The reasons for deterioration of concrete is due to the following reasons:

(*a*) Excessive fine sand as it needs high water cement ratio. Coarse sand gaps are filled by cement giving a higher binding and strength. While in fine particles gaps are filled with water. However fine sand to a certain percentage gives a better workability.

(*b*) **Frost.** Continuous action of frost and alternate drying and cooling has a detoreous action on concrete.

(*c*) **Rusting of reinforcement.** It is due to porous concrete. Even 0·25 mm gap is sufficient for the passage of moisture which causes rusting of steel. Rust has a more volume than steel and hence it throws up the cover material leaving the bars bare to atmosphere, causing further rusting. The leakage should be grouted and in R.B. work the steel should not touch the bricks. It must have at least 20 mm mortar around.

(*d*) **Honey combing.** It is due to less compaction, segregation, more w/c ratio as excess water evaporates leaving voids in the concrete. Ungraded mix which gives a harsh mix leaving gaps in between.

(*e*) **Cracks in concrete.** It is due to the followings :

(*i*) Expansion during hydration and cooling after that in air causing contraction and ultimately cracks.

(*ii*) Smaller sections attached monolithic with larger causing unequal expansion and contraction. Restrained end members crack more than freely supported one.

(*iii*) Alternate heating and drying in winds, action of water and change of seasons.

(*iv*) **Forms.** Absorptive type and weaker forms creates cracks in concrete. Weaker support to form work is also source of cracks.

(*v*) **Heavy loads** and **pour strength of concrete.**

(*vi*) **Hair cracks.** On surface are due to change of temperature sudden wetting, unsufficient curing and richer mix at top. These cracks are generally filled by "slopping" (filling cracks by thick paste of white paint and putty etc.) They are also filled by thick layer of surface treatment layer, while larger should be cement grouted.

8·6·11. Durability of Concrete

A durable concrete is one that perform satisfactorily in the working environment during it anticipated lift.

Factors influencing durability are :

(*i*) The environment

(*ii*) Cover to reinforcing steel

(*iii*) Type and quality of ingradients

(*iv*) Cement content and water cement ratio

(*v*) Workmanship including compaction and curing, water content during mixing.

(*vi*) Shape and size of the member.

Environmental Conditions. (1) Surface protected from weather, dampness and contact of alkaline soils and water.

(2) Safety from frost, rain water and alkaline solids etc.

(3) Alternate wetting and drying, heat or cold, contact with sea water.

(4) Contact of aggressive chemicals.

Specifications of Concrete

(*i*) Type and grade of mix

(*ii*) Type of cement, sizes of fine and coarse aggregate.

(*iii*) Ratio of ingradients like cement and aggregates.

(*iv*) Water cement ratio and workability slump required.

(*v*) Exposure condition

(*vi*) Maximum temperature at the time of placing.

(*vii*) Method of transportations of concrete and method of placing with type of compaction.

(*viii*) Curing requirement

(*ix*) Degree of supervision etc.

8·6·12. Joints in concrete structures

There are two types of joints in concreting

(1) Construction joints (2) Contraction and expansion joints

(1) **Construction joints** are given during laying of concrete due to stoppage of work due to one or the other reason. Construction joints in plain concrete have been discussed with pouring of concrete and construction joints in RCC are given below.

Beams. These joints are given at the point of minimum shear *i.e.*, at the centre of span. If a beam is crossed by another smaller beam, the joint in the big beam should be given at a distance of about twice the depth of beam or in the middle third portion. Joints on the centre of support wall or column can also be given leaving the other half bearing for the next beam. The joints must not be given at the support of the beam either in case of a wall or column or under the concentrated loads having maximum shear. Construction joints in the smaller beam can be given at a distance of about depth of big or supporting beam. In *T* and *L* beams where the slabs are monolithic with beams effect should be made that rib and slab may be casted in one operation and if in unavoidable conditions when it becomes necessary to stop the work, the joint in the rib about 75 or 100 mm below the slab may be given. The slab should be casted not later than two days in such cases.

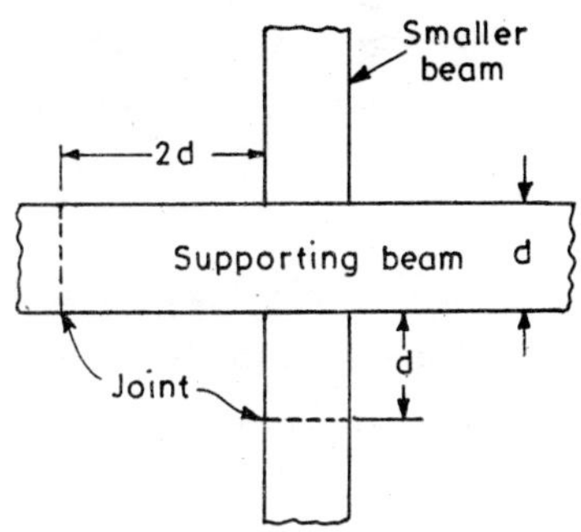

Fig. 8·37.

The end of joints should be supported by shutters leaving an access for the projecting bars. Construction joints should be planned before laying of concrete. So that at the slopage of work it may not be left in any undesirable position.

Slabs. In case of two or four way supported slabs the construction joint must be given in centre or in the middle 3rd portion. In case of continuous slabs over beams joint can be given in the centre of the wall or column.

(*i*) **Contraction and expansion joints.** Due to change of temperature either during construction or after construction the concrete contracts on reduction and expands on increase of temperature causes cracks. On contraction, the cracks widen while on expansion they are shortened. Hence the reduction of temperature is more dangerous than rise. The concrete is weaker in tension than in compression. The contraction cracks are wider or closer due to tension than expansion. Cracks create compression in concrete and hence the contraction joints are provided nearer than expansion joints. The magnitude of contraction is about two to three times to that of expansion. The amount of shrinkage also depends on the quantity of cement and water-cement ratio. Greater the amount of cement and w/c ratio the larger is the shrinkage. Shrinkage is also created due to loss of excess water by evaporation. Shrinkage for 10 m long M-15 concrete is as follows in accordance with w/c ratio.

Table 8·32.

w/c ratio	*Contraction*	
0·3	1·5 mm	Contraction in neat cement is aboutthree times to that of a mortar of 1 : 3 or M-15 concrete.
0·5	4·2 mm	Concrete structures shrinks remarkably in the 1st
0·7	8·0 mm	year of construction than the later years.

The combined effect of shrinkage and temperature changes causes cracks in concrete. The coefficient of expansion of steel and concrete is roughly the same.

Steel	0·0000120	per unit length per degree C
	0·0000067	per unit length per degree F
Plain concrete	0·0000110	per unit length per degree C
	0·0000060	per unit length per degree F
RCC	0·0000117	per unit length per degree C
	0·0000065	per unit length per degree F

The stress produced = coefficient of expansion × Change of temperature × Modulus of elasticity of the RCC.

The spacing and the thickness of the expansion joints are determined.

(*a*) By variation of temperature all over the year's season and

(*b*) The season in which the concrete is laid. Concrete laid in summer may be provided with long spaced joints than laid in winter. As per IS code the structures wider than 45 metres should have one or more joint. In general three must be provided in structures which are larger than 10 metre. The minimum joint width is 6 mm while the maximum width is 25 mm. It is advisable to provide larger no. of joints instead of wider joints. Effort should be made to provide joints on change of sections or as per architectural effects

Spacing for different type of work's joints are given below :

Reinforced concrete walls, distance of vertical joints	10 to 25 m
Unreinforced concrete walls, distance of vertical joints	4·5 m exposed to weather
Unreinforced concrete walls, distance of vertical joints	9·0 unexposed to weather
R.C. roofs protected by layers of mud or other insulator	20 to 30 m
R.C. roofs not protected by layers of mud or other insulator	15 m

Materials used in joints filler are Bitumen, soft wood free from knots. Impregnated fibre board (solistax or nomotax boards) or synthetic rubber packing.

Sawn joints. Joints are cut by saw in road passing for improved riding quality. Continuous laying of concrete and hence saving of time is achieved. The joints are later cut by a saw at desired interval of space and filled with insulating material when the concrete sets.

Concrete saw with diamond cutting wheels is supplied by Build Aids, 19 Centaph road Teynampet Chennai 600018.

8·6·13. Fire Resistance

A structure or structural element required to have fire resistance should be designed to process appropriate degree of resistance to flame penetration, heat transmission and failure. The fire resistance of a structural element is expressed in terms of time in hours. Fire resistance of concrete elements depends upon details of member size, cover of steel reinforcement detailing and type of aggregate (normal weight or light weight) used in concrete.

Minimum requirements of concrete cover and member dimensions for normal weight aggregate concrete numbers so as to have the required fire resistance is shown in the Table 8·33.

The reinforcement detailing should reflect the changing pattern of the structural section and ensure that both individual elements and the structure as a whole contain adequate support, ties, bonds and anchorages for the required fire resistance.

Additional measures such as application of fire resistant finishes, provisions fire resistant false ceilings and superficial steel in tensile zone should be adopted in case the nominal cover required exceeds 40 mm for beams and 35 mm for slabs to give protection against spalling.

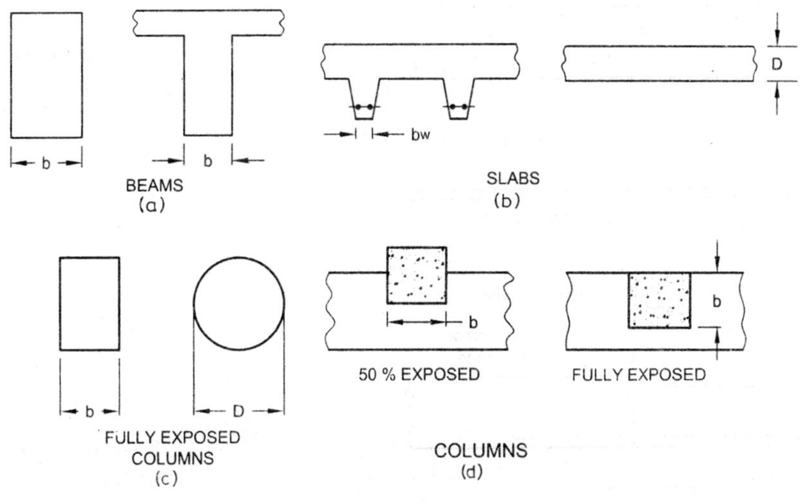

Fig. 8·38. Columns.

Table 8·33. Minimum dimensions of reinforced concrete membes for fire resistance

Fire resistance in Hrs h	*Min. beam width b mm*	*Rib width of slab, b_w mm*	*Min. thickness floors D mm*	*Column dimensions (b or D)* Fully expand mm			*Min wall thickness* $P < 0·4\%$ mm		
				Fully expand mm	*50% expand mm*	*One per expand mm*	*$P < 0·4\%$ mm*	*$0·4\% \le P \le 1\%$ mm*	*$P > 1\%$*
0·5	200	125	75	150	125	100	150	100	100
1	200	125	95	200	160	120	150	120	100
1·5	200	125	110	250	200	140	175	140	100
2	200	125	125	300	200	160	—	160	100
3	240	150	150	400	300	200	—	200	150
4	280	175	170	450	350	240	—	240	180

Table 8·34. Nominal cover to meet specified period of fire resistance

Fire Resistance Hrs	*Nominal cover*						
	Beams		*Slabs*		*Ribs*		*Columns*
h	*Supply supported mm*	*Continuous mm*	*Supply supplied mm*	*Continuous mm*	*Supply supplied mm*	*Continuous mm*	*mm*
0·5	20	20	20	20	20	20	40
1	20	20	20	20	20	20	40
1·5	20	20	25	20	35	20	40
2	40	30	35	25	45	35	40
3	60	40	45	35	55	45	40
4	70	50	55	45	65	55	40

JOINTS

Temperature Joints

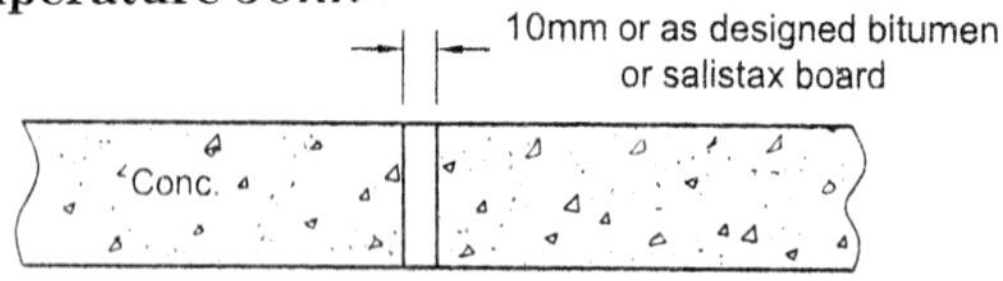

Used in roads

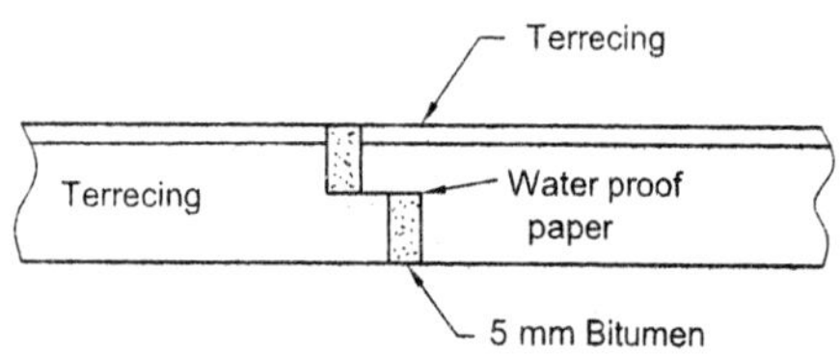

Used in roofs

In terrecing use asphalt layer with expended metal 6 mm or cc M-25 20 mm thick

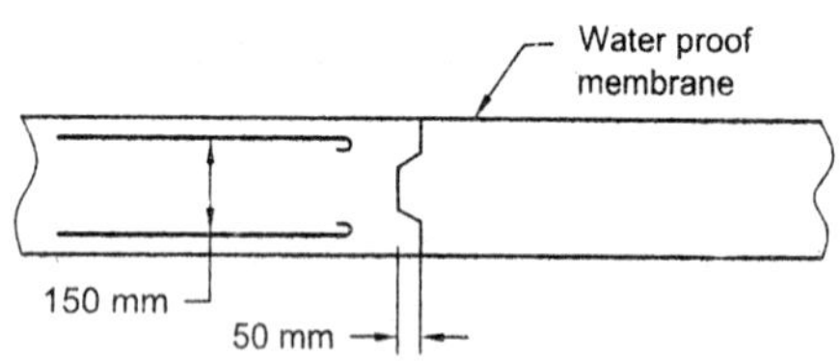

Used in verticals walls for retaining water

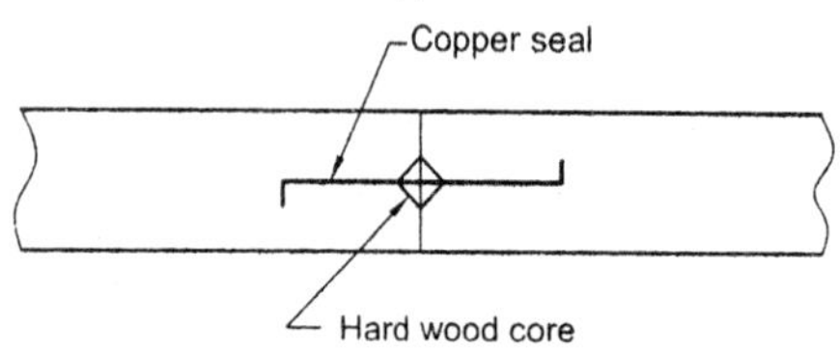

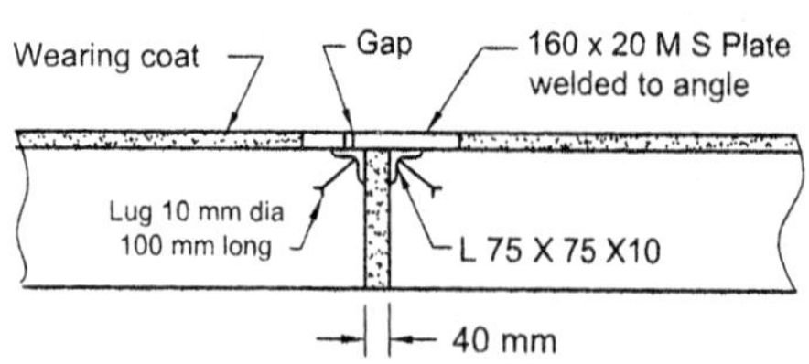

Joint over bridge slab

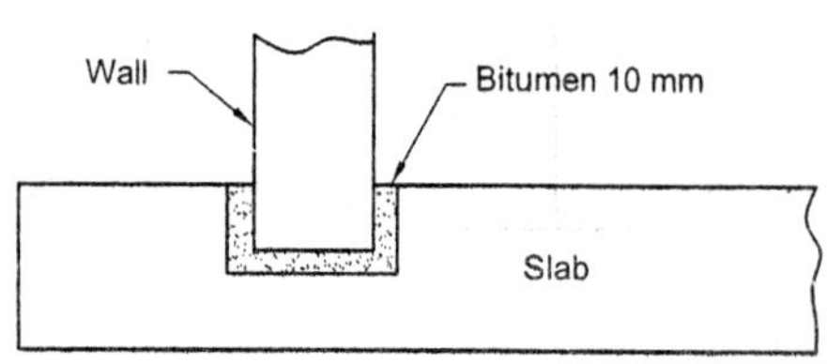

Vertical joint in a water tank wall & slab

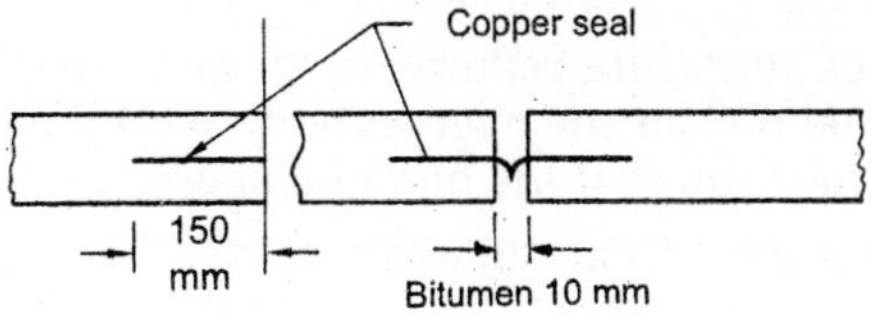

Fig. 8·39. Water proof rubber seal joint (water stop) and copper seal joints.

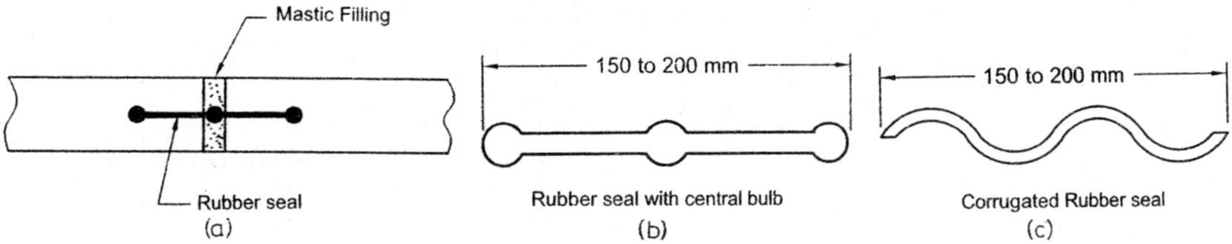

CONSTRUCTION JOINTS

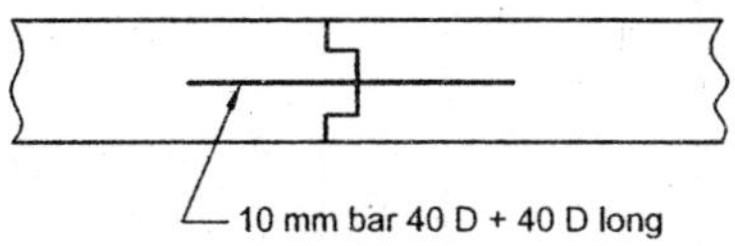

KEYED JOINT

Joint in wall & slabs :
Horizontal and Vertical

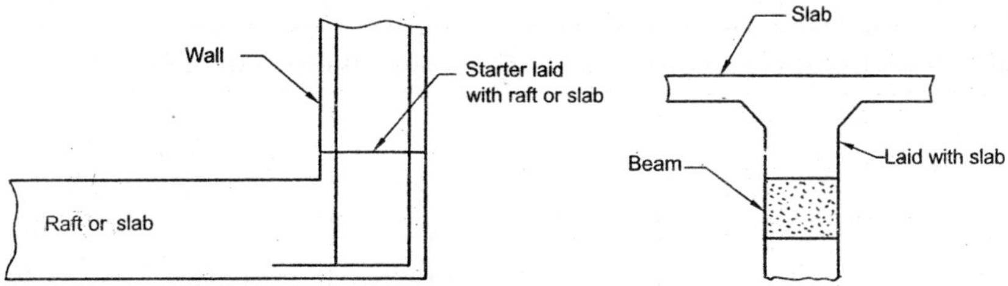

Fig. 8·40.

8·6·14. Tests for Concrete (Also refer chapter of Building Materials)

The compressive strength. It is assessed by cubes crushed to destruction by a machine in the lab 6″ cubes (150 mm) are prepared in a steel mould of two pieces. The frame pieces are bolted together and to the base plate. A sample of concrete is filled in layers in the mould and vibrated by a small vibrator outside the frame wall or by a tamping rod by hand. The rod is 16 mm in diameter and 60 cm long with a bullet end. The strokes penetrate to the full depth of the layer to the following minimum numbers.

Cube 15 cm size	35
Cube 10 cm size	25
Cylinders	30
Beams 15 cm size	175
Beams 10 cm size	100 (The size of tamping bar is 25 mm sq. 40 cm long)

The sides of the frame are oiled with mobil oil and the joints of base and sides are greased so that no water may leak during vibrations. The concrete is filled at 58 to 64°F (25 to 30°C) at 90% humidity. The top is levelled with trowel. The blocks are kept under water till the time of test and then they are tested in a pressure operated machine. The load is applied gradually.

Cylinderical blocks of 150 mm diameter and 300 mm height are also tested. Cylinderical tests give 80% strength to that of cube tests. The crack in the cylinderical blocks occur at 60° while in cube blocks at 45°.

When the nominal size of aggregate reduces to 20 mm, 100 mm size cubes are prepared for test 150 mm size cubes are taken from the aggregate upto 40 mm. For aggregate over 40 mm. the size of block increases to the four times of the nominal aggregate size.

Some times direct pieces are cut from the work for test. These are known as cores.

Effect of shape of test specimen on compressive strength of concrete

The test study conducted on 36 concrete specimens of various shapes constructed with three different grades of concrete yielded the following conclusions and results.

Table 8·35. Details of test specimens

S. No.	*Shape*	*X-sections area (sq. mm)*	*Height mm*	*Grade of conc.*	*No.*	*Remarks*
1.	Cubical (all sides = 150 mm)	22,500	150	M-15 M-20 M-25	3 3 3	**Properties of cement** 1. Normal consistancy 29% 2. Initial setting time 40 minutes
2.	Cylinderical (150 mm dia.)	17,662·5	300	M-15 M-20 M-25	3 3 3	3. Final setting time 160 minutes 4. Fine ness 0·8%
3.	Hexagonal all sides 82·5 mm	17,662·5	300	M-15 M-20 M-25	3 3 3	5. Soundness 1 mm 6. 3 days compressive strength 17·31 N/ mm^2
4.	Triangular (all sides 202 mm)	17,662·5	300	M-15 M-20 M-25	3 3 3	7 days 22·70 N/mm^2 28 days 34·10 N/mm^2

Table 8·36. Compressive strength of test specimens (curing period 28 days)

S. No.	*Mix*		*W/c Ratio*	*Cubical N/mm^2*	*Cylinderical N/mm^2*	*Hexagonal N/mm^2*	*Triangular N/mm^2*
	Grade	*Proportion*					
1.	M-15	1 : 2 : 4	0·5	17·30	12·67	11·60	10·18
				14·87	13·54	12·12	9·91
				15·02	13·28	12·38	10·02
2.	M-20	1 : 1·5 : 3	0·5	23·10	17·28	17·18	14·20
				22·28	18·95	17·02	13·98
				23·00	19·60	17·11	14·32
3.	M-25	1 : 1 : 2	0·5	24·00	21·21	19·42	16·20
				25·21	22·07	19·37	16·42
				26·93	22·00	20·01	16·98

Strength Ratio. The average compressive strength of different shape specimens are non-dimensionalized by dividing average strength obtained from the tests by average strength of cubical specimens and known as strength ratio.

Table 8·37. Non-dimensionalized strength ratios

S. No.	*Average strength N/mm^2*					*Non-dimensionalized strength ratios*			
	Grade of conc.	*Cubical*	*Cylinderi-cal*	*Hexa-gonal*	*Triangu-lar*	*Cubical*	*Cylinder-ical*	*Hexa-gonal*	*Triangu-lar*
1.	M-15	18·4	14·5	13·2	11·4	1·0	0·78	0·72	0·62
2.	M-20	24·6	20·5	18·8	15·7	1·0	0·84	0·77	0·64
3.	M-25	28·3	23·7	21·5	18·2	1·0	0·84	0·76	0·65

Conclusions : (1) The shape of specimen has significant influence on compressive strength of concrete.

(2) The strength obtained from triangular specimen is the lowest and for cubical specimen is the highest.

(3) The strength reduction in the case of triangular specimens is maximum.

Recommendation. In design of sections other than rectangular shape correction factors should be applied to the characteristic strength of concrete specified in section 5·1·1 of IS : 456—1978. However there is a need of further experimentation considering other shapes and l/r ratios.

Concrete strength vs grade of concrete

Strength ratio vs Grade of concrete

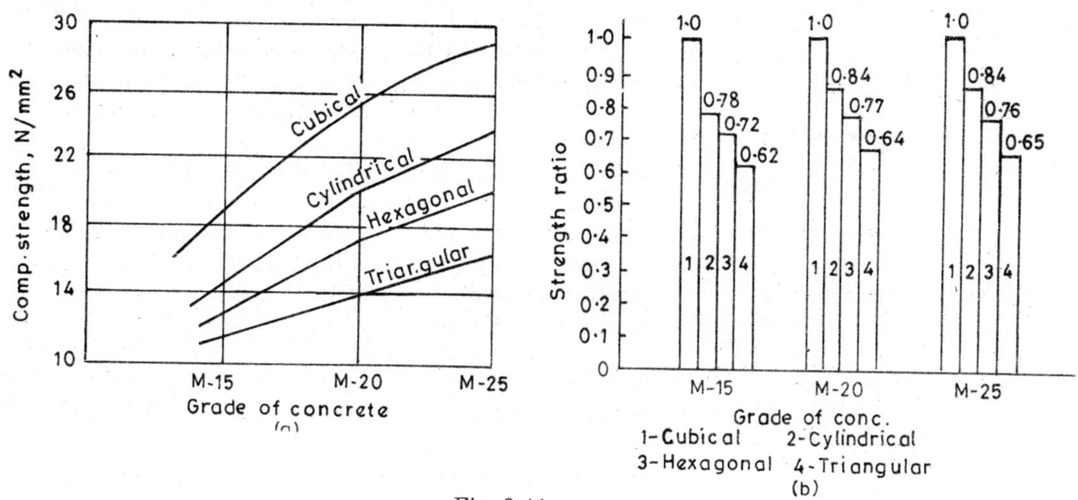

Fig. 8·41.

Direct compressive stress is 0·8 times of the flexural or compressive stress under bending. A working compressive stress is taken to be a factor of safety of 2·4 and 3·0 for cylinderical block strength. For rapid hardening cement minimum cube strength in "work test" is taken at 7 days strength. The rate of loading per minute for both cubes and cylinders should be approximately 140 kg/cm^2. The compressive strength is calculated by dividing the load at failure by the cross-sectional area of the specimen.

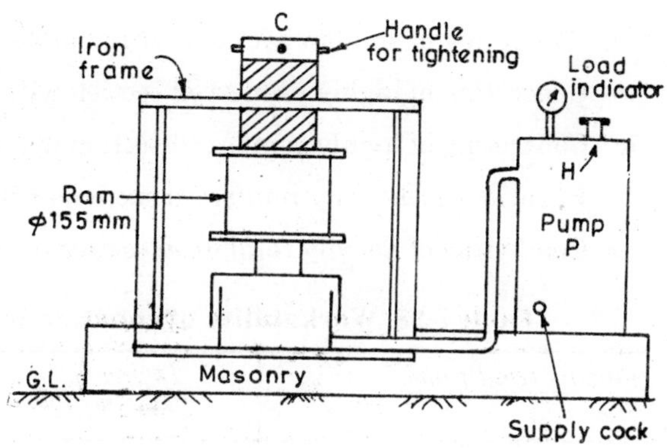

Fig. 8·42. Compressive test machine.

Allowable Standard. Three test specimen are taken for each test as per IS : 456—1957, the average strength of the three specimens should be equivalent to the standard given, with the difference to maximum and minimum of three cubes limited to 15% to the average. If the difference exceeds 15% to the average the specimen must not be accepted.

Compressive testing machine. It has the following working :

(1) Test block is clamped by clamp C.

(2) Pressure is released by pump P.

(3) Pump is operated by handle H.

(4) Pumping is continued till the breakage of test block indicated by red pointer fixed with the load indicator. The red indicator ceases to advance on breakage of the block.

Test for tension—Beam test. A concrete beam of the sample is casted in 100 × 100 mm in section and 400 mm long. The beam rests on roller bearings at 300 mm apart and is loaded by a machine in the centre by a cylinderical load, which gives the extreme fibre stress in bending as rupture of beam in tension side. It is generally 1·5 to 1·8 times to that of a direct load test, which is tested in a direct tension machine as used for test of cement in direct tension. The tensile strength in bending is also known as a modulus of rupture. Tensile strength in flexure (bending) with construction joint is taken 0·8 of the tensile strength in bending without construction joint.

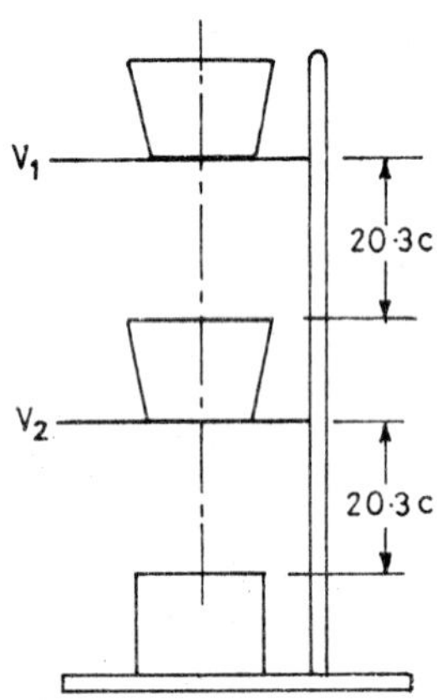

Fig. 8·43.

Workability test. (1) **Compaction test.** By this test a degree of compaction of concrete and the workability is tested. There are two vessels V_1 and V_2 with a valved opening at bottom. A container of 15 cm diameter and 30 cm high is placed at bottom. The distance of the vessels and that of the container is a certain distance which is provided in the apparatus. Fill the sample of container in vessel V_1 and release it by the bottom valve causing it to fall in vessel V_2. Again the bottom valve of V_2 is opened causing the concrete to fall in the container. The extra quantity of concrete is removed by a float moving on the container. The container is removed and weighed say it is w_1. Calculate the theoretical weight of the concrete which is contained in the container taking no voids or air say it is w_2. Now the ratio of w_1 to w_2 is the compaction ratio w_1/w_2. 0·92 is a medium workability. 0·95 is a good and 0·85 is a poor workability.

The compaction factor required for various placing conditions are as below :

(*a*) Concreting of shallow sections with vibrations 0·75 to 0·80

(*b*) Concreting of highly reinforced section with vibrations 0·80 to 0·90

(*c*) Concreting of highly reinforced section without vibrations or heavily reinforced sections with vibrations 0·85 to 0·90

(*d*) Concreting of heavily reinforced section without vibratios 0·85 to 0·92

Table 8·38. Workability of concrete in accordance with IS : 1199

Placing conditions	*Degree of workability*	*Slump*
Blinding concrete Shallow sections Pavements using pavers	Very low	In the very low category of workability where stuck control is necessary, for example pavement quality control concrete measurement of workability by determination of compacting factor will be more appropriate than slump and a value of compacting factor of 0·75 to 0·85 is suggested.

Table contd.

Table contd.

Placing conditions	*Degree of workability*	*Slump*
Mass concrete Lightly reinforced sections in slabs, beams, walls, columns, floors Hand placed pavements, canal lining, strip footing	Low	25-75
Heavily reinforced sections in slabs, beams, walls and columns	Medium	50-100
Slip form works Pumped concrete	Medium	75-100
Trench fill In-situ piling	High	100-150
Tremic concrete	Very high	In the very high category of workability measurement of workability by determination of flow will be appropriate.

Note : For most of the placing conditions, internal vibrators (needle vibrators) are suitable. The diameter of the needle shall be determined based on the density and spacing of reinforcement bars and thickness of sections. For premix concrete vibrators are not required to be used.

Table 8·39. Dimensions of apparatus (compaction test)

Item	*Internal diameter in cm*		*Internal height in cm*
	Top	*Bottom*	
Upper hopper	25·4	12·7	27·9
Lower hopper	22·9	12·7	22·9
Cylinder	15·2	15·2	30·5

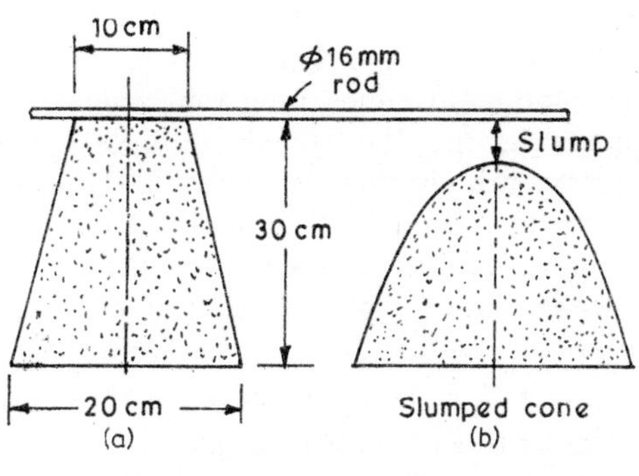

Fig. 8·44. Mould for slump.

Slump test for Consistency

A metal mould in the shape of a frustum of a concrete without top and bottom having 4″ (10 cm) diameter top diameter 8″ (20 cm) bottom and 12″ (30 cm) high is used for the test. The sample of the concrete is filled in the mould in layers of 3″ (7·5 cm) each and each layer is tapped by 25 strokes by 5/8″ (16 mm) diameter bullet ended rod 2′ (60 cm) in length. The rod is so applied that it just reaches to the bottom of layer without disturbing the lower one. The mould is then removed. The vertical settlement is then measured putting the rod on the mould by scale. This vertical settlement of the concrete is known as "slump". The slump for different works as commonly used is as follows (IS : 456—1964).

(1) Road work	25 to 50 mm
(2) Mass concrete	25 to 50 mm
(3) Ordinary beam and slabs (RCC)	50 to 100 mm
(4) RCC of columns, retaining walls etc.	100 to 175 mm
(5) Vibrated concrete	12 to 25 mm
(6) Concrete for walls, thin verticals	75 to 125 mm

Table 8·40. Water contents/m^3 concrete for 75 mm slump

Max. size of coarse aggregate in mm		13	20	25	40	50	75
Water in kg	*Poured aggregate*	200	184	178	166	158	148
	Crushed aggregate	212	200	193	180	172	164

For each 25 mm change in slump, 30% change in w/c ratio is done.

Sampling. A sample about 0·2 m^3 in volume is needed. The sample should be taken when one quarter, one half and three quarters of the contents of the drum of mixure have been discharged. When collected from the site of work it must be collecated from five different positions.

KM-slump Tester of Concrete. A new and simple apparatus called the K.M. slump tester has been newly introduced. It can be used to measure. The consistency, slump and workability of fresh concrete in one minute. Over 450 tests were performed on 28 different mixes of concrete using either normal or light weight aggregates with or without air entraining agent and superplasticizer. The results show that there is a high correlation between the KM slump measured with the app. and the slump measured with standard cone. The apparatus is made up of the following six principal parts :

1. Three chrome-plated steel tubes with external and internal dia. of 1·9 and 1·6 cm centred and placed equidistant at the apexes of an equilateral triangle of sides 7·62 cm and connected to a disc floater. Each tube is 16 cm long from the tip of the solid concrete at the bottom to the soffit of the floater disc. The solid cones facilitate the insertion of the apparatus into the fresh concrete. Two types of openings are provided in each tube. Rectangular slots 5·1 cm long and 0·8 cm wide and 22 round holes 0·64 cm in dia. all distributed uniformly. In fact the tubes are similar to the bottom part of the KM slump tester.

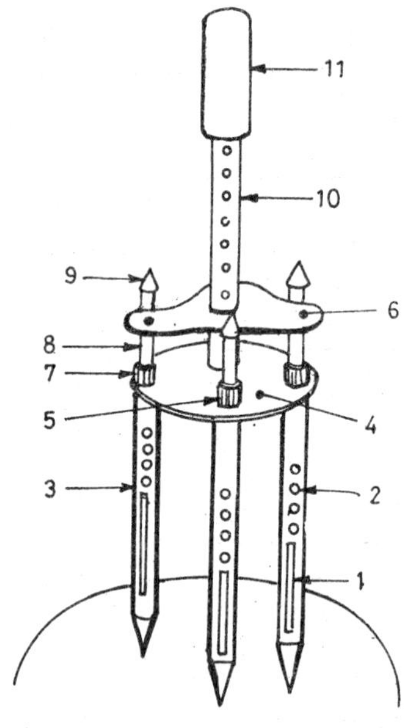

Fig. 8·45. The KM-slump tester.

2. An equilateral triangle aluminium disc floater of thickness 0·4 cm and 18 cm sides rounded at the corners. The disc floater has three equidistant circular holes of dia. 1·9 cm which receive the above tubes. The disc serves to maintain a constant level of insertion of the steel tubes into the concrete by preventing the tester from sinking beyond the pre selected level.

3. Freely movable light hollow plastic rods, one in each of the three tubes 0·95 cm in dia. and 14·5 cm long which may contain graduated scale in cm. The rods are plugged at each end with a plastic cap to prevent cone or any other material from seeping in side. Each of these rods can be used to measure the height of mortar that flows into a corresponding tube. The use

of the KM tester can be had as per instructions given by the manufacturer which is supplied along with the apparatus.

(*a*) Into a pail filled and levelled with fresh concrete.

(*b*) Using the apparatus in a laboratory pan mixer.

Fig. 8·46. The KM-slump tester is inserted into fresh concrete moulds up to the level of disc floater.

4. A graduated aluminium rod of dia. 1·9 cm and length of 30·5 cm fitted at the centre of the disc floater by means of a screw and marked with engraved rings as a scale from 0 to 14 cm. A cylindrical rubber jacket of dia. 3·8 cm and 10 cm long is glued to the top of the rod so as to serve as handle.

5. Three hollow cylindrical aluminium guides of internal and external dia. of 1·3 and 1·9 cm respectively and a length of 2·3 cm filling coaxially with the tubes. They are provided with a horizontal slit at mid depth to receive a wire spring that serves to hold the plastic rods.

6. A top aluminium plate of thickness 0.3 cm with a central circular hole of dia. 2·54 cm acting as a height indicator.

The plate can be slide freely through the central vertical rod and rests on the wire springs when it is not used for measuring purposes. It can be raised and rotated to rest on the caps of the plastic tubes so as to indicate their average height on the vertical scale. The reading corresponds to the average consistency or KM slump of the fresh concrete.

The total weight of the apparatus is 1270 g. The tester is a modified and improved version of the KM-slump tester. The main improvement is the incorporation of three KM slump testers in one apparatus that gives directly the average value of three KM-slump test results as a single reading. Similarly an average of three workability index values can be obtained in a single operation in one minute. The use of the K.M. tester can be had as per instructions given by the manufacturer which is supplied along with the apparatus.

Non destructive tests for concrete (also refer chapter on Building Materials)

Rebound hammer test. Since concrete of block tests is not taken directly from structures, hence there are chances of its being replaced. This probability is finished in rebound hammer test as it is taken direct on structure.

In this test the concrete is directly hitted on surface by a spring loaded hammer and the extent of rebound numbers suggests the strength of conc. Makers supply a calibration cure showing rebound numbers vs. strength values.

Ultrasonic test method. Ultrasonic concrete tester is often used for qualitative assessment of compressive strength of concrete. Neville has classified the quality of concrete from excellent to very poor depending on the pulse velocity through the concrete sample. The qualitative classification as given by Neville has been quantified in the expert system by assigning 25 N/mm^2, 20 N/mm^2, 16·5 N/mm^2, 13·5 N/mm^2 and 11 N/mm^2 to *fck* values for excellent, good fair, poor and very poor quality of concrete respectively. It gives the quality of concrete at each location of each member of a structure.

Residual compressive strength of concrete needs to be determined for evaluating the safety by Rebound Hammer test and ultrasonic test methods suggested in IS : 456-1978 combining the *fck* values obtained from Rebound Hammer and ultrasonic tests, the residual strength of concrete at each location of a particular member is obtained.

Ultrasonic Pulse velocity test. Consists of measuring the time of travel of ultrasonic pulse passing through the material to be tested. The circuit is an electronic circuit for generating pulses and transducers for transforming these electronic pulses into mechanical energy, having vibration frequencies in the range of 15 KHz to 50 KHz. The time of travel between initial onset and the reception of path pulse at the other end is measured electronically. The path length between transducers decided by the time of travel gives us the average velocity of wave propagation : The higher the velocity, the stronger is the concrete.

Non destructive testing systems :

1. Micro cover meter
2. Multi cell surveyor
3. Ultrasonic scope
4. Ultrasonic tester
5. Schmidt hammer
6. H. R. Rebar locator
7. PPR meter
8. Resistivity logger
9. Windsor probe.

Supplied by Aimil Sales and Agencies Pvt. LTD. Mathura Road New Delhi.

Chemical analysis of concrete samples (Chloride penetration test)

Samples of concrete from some selected critical locations should be collected and tested chemically in the laboratory for pH and soluble chloride content. Risk of corrosion for each sample is determined by following the soluble chloride content, the hydorxyle molar activity ratio and the pH value. If the pH is found to be less than 11·5 and the soluble chloride content is more than 750 ppm a weightage factor of 3 is assigned for corrosion risk. However if chloride content is negligible, the weightage factor is assigned is 2. In case the pH values between 11·5 and 12·5 the criterion of chloride hydroxyle molar activity ratio given by Erlin and verback is used. If the chloride content obtained experimentally is greater than that obtained from the criterion a weightage factor of 2 is to be assigned. However if the experimental chloride content is less than the chloride contents obtained from criterion or the pH is more than 12·5, the weightage factor assigned for risk of corrosion is 1.

Visual inspection for corrosion. Selected members of the structure are visually checked for yellow-brown stains, cracking, bulging and spalling of concrete. Comparing the symptoms of corrosion distress with the relevant knowledge base, suitable weightage factors are assigned to them.

Drilled conc. testing. A cylinderical conc. may be drilled from the structure (if allowed) for testing. The cavity so formed must be refilled by a richer mix after welling with water and slurry.

8·6.15. Factors influencing workability

1. **Water.** Addition of water increases workability, while it reduces strength and density of concrete.

2. **Size of aggregate.** Larger size of aggregate for the same mix and w/c ratio increases workability as lower amount of water will require to wet the surface of particles and this saved water makes the mortar more workable.

3. **Coarse and fine aggregate ratio.** If the quantity of the coarse aggregate is increased and fine aggregate is decreased to have the same cement, aggregate and w/c ratio, the workability is increased as in the bigger aggregate less water is used for wetting the surface of the aggregate. This saved water is used for a more flowey mortar.

4. **Particle interlock.** For round shaped gravels workability is more than broken ballast.

5. **Particle interference.** When the mixture is ungraded, the smaller particles can not pass in gaps of bigger particles, hence void formation in which water fills, causing less water for mortar and hence workability is reduced.

6. **Type of admixtures.** The following admixtures influence the workability in the manner shown below.

(*a*) **Air gas entraining agents.** Adding of air entraining materials such as Darex, Vinsol resin and aluminium etc. which causes the gas bubbles formation. The presence of the flexible bubbles increase the workability of concrete. They also checks bleeding.

(*b*) **Addition of Pozzuolana.** Improves the workability.

(*c*) **Presence of chemicals.** Some materials like Linsa Pole liquid at the rate of 10*z* per bag improves workability.

(*d*) **Hydraulic lime or quick lime or powdered Surkhi** gives a better workability and also decreases bleeding, segregation and heat of hydration, however shrinkage will increase.

7. **Types of means used for compaction.** Mechanical vibrations give a better workability than pinning or ramming. For mechanical vibrated concrete about 20% less water and 15% less cement is needed.

8. **Type of reinforcement used.** If reinforcement used is closer then a more fluidy mix is needed than in case of plain conc. or when the reinforcement is used at greater intervals.

9. **Type of form work.** For rough and narrow formwork a more fluidy mixture is needed.

10. Climatic conditions. A less water or lower fluidity is needed for wet, frosted and cold weather surfaces in contact with water need drier mixes.

11. Type of cement used. Rapid hardening cement needs at 4·5 litres more water per 50 kg of cement than ordinary cement. The higher the percentage of cement the higher is the workability.

8·6·16. Factors in fluencing strength of concrete

1. Mixing Time. The strength of concrete increases with time of mixing which ranges 1½ minutes to 3 minutes till the material make a homogenous plastic mass. Excess mixing causes segregation and resulting in reduction of strength.

Mixing times of conc. by mixtures

500 litres or less 1½ min.

700 litres or less 2 min

1000 litres or less 2½ min.

1250 litres or less 2¾ min.

1500 litres or less 3 min.

2. Fineness of Sand. More fine is the sand more will it have the surface area needing more *w/c* ratio water on the surface of the sand particles causes a surface tension which repels each other, causing bulking in sand, resulting less percentage of sand used than required, which gives a lesser strength, hence coarser particles of sand is always better.

3. w/c Ratio. Water used more than that what is required for chemical combination of concrete evaporated leaving pores in the concrete, which decreases the strength. Hence larger *w/c* ratio always reduces the strength. With change of *w/c* ratio tensile strength is less effected than compressive strength. An excess of 10% water reduces strength upto 15% and 30% excess water reduces the strength upto 50%.

4. Compaction. Less compaction causes a heavy compact concrete resulting in a weaker formation of concrete. The extent of compaction is judged by the weight required to the actual weight of concrete poured.

5. Curing. If curing is not to the mark, the hydration process will be slow in lack of moisture causing a weaker concrete.

6. Fatigue and impact. The strength of cement is decreased by vibrations and sudden change of loads and impacts.

7. Effect of temperature. Cold weather retards setting, while hot weather accelerates and ultimate strength however remaining the same. Expansion and contraction of concrete is affected with change of temperature.

Abrasion. The concrete surface is effected by the abrasion of moving vehicles and machines with metal tyres.

8·6·16. General Tables regarding cement concrete

Table 8·41. Increase of compression strength with age

Min. age of member when full design load is expected in months	*Age factor*
1	1·0
3	1·11
6	1·15
12	1·20

Table 8·41. Minimum cement content, Maximum water-cement ratio and Minimum grade of conc. for different exposures with normal weight Aggregates of 20 mm nominal maximum size

Sl. No.	*Exposure*	*Min. cement content kg/m³*	*Plain conc.*		*Reinforced conc.*		*Minimum grade of conc.*
			Max. free water cement ratio	*Min. grading conc.*	*Min cement content kg/m³*	*Max. Free water cement ratio*	
1.	Mild	220	0·60	–	300	0·55	M-20
2.	Moderate	240	0·60	M-15	300	0·50	M-25
3.	Severe	250	0·50	M-20	320	0·45	M-36
4.	Very severe	260	0·45	M-20	340	0·45	M-35
5.	Extreme	280	0·40	M-25	360	0·40	M-40

Notes. 1. Cement contents prescribed in this table is irrespective of the grade of cement. The addition such as fly ash or ground gravitable blast furnace bulge may be taken into account in the conc. composition with respect to the cement content and *w/c* ratio if the suitability is established and as long as the maximum amounts taken into account do not exceed the limit of pozzolana and slag.

2. Minimum grade for plain concrete under mild exposure condition is not specified.

Table 8·43. Total air content by volume of the fresh concrete at the time of delivery to the constructions

Nominal max. size Aggregate mm	*Entrand air percentage*
20	5 ± 1
40	4 ± 1

Table 8·44. Limits of chloride contents of concrete

Type of use of conc.	*Max. total acid soluble chloride content expressed as kg/m³ g conc.*
Conc. containing metal and steam cured at elevated temp. and pre-stressed conc.	0·4
Reinforced conc. or plain conc. containing embedded metal	0·6
Conc. not containing embedded metal or any material requiring protection from chloride	3·6

8·6·18. Concrete mix Design (Also refer chapter on Building Materials)

Properties of ingredients which should be known before designing a mix. either as desired or by field tests (designed or nominal).

1. Slump of the concrete as desired.
2. Crushing strength of concrete as desired (Grade designation).
3. Max. size of fine aggregate available subject to max. 4·75 mm (3/16").
4. Max. size of coarse aggregate available subject to max. 150 mm (6"), 1/4 to 1/5 of the min. Thickness of concrete sec. or 3/4 of the min. cover.
5. Fineness modulus of fine aggregate.
6. Fineness modulus of coarse aggregate.
7. Percentage of voids in fine aggregate.
8. Percentage of voids in coarse aggregate.
9. Percentage of voids in cement.
10. Bulking in fine aggregate.
11. Weight per cu. unit of fine, coarse aggregate and cement.
12. Admixture to be used.
13. Grade of cement.
14. *w/c* ratio.
15. Minimum cement content (for design mix.)
16. Mixture proportion (for nominal mix.)
17. Exposure conditions temperature at time of placing.
18. Method of placing.
19. Maximum cement content.

Steps carried out in designing a concrete mixture

Step 1. To determine the water cement ratio (*w/c*) for the strength desired.

(*a*) **Abram's water cement ratio law.** $P = \frac{A}{B^x}$ where P = crushing strength in lb/in^2, A = constant which is 1400 for very good and round aggregates, 984 for properly graded, thoroughly mixed and fully compacted concrete without voids for improved quality of cements. The value of B depends on quality of cement and conditions of curing. Its value ranges from 4 to maximum up to 13, x is the water cement ratio by volume.

In the formula $P = \frac{A}{B^x} \times \cdot 07$, P = crushing strength in kg/cm^2 of concrete desired.

(*b*) **Boleman formula.** $P = k(c/w - \cdot 05)$ where P = crushing strength of cement in *lbs* per in^2, c/w = cement water ratio by weight, K = constant which is generally 3200.

In the formula $P = 0{\cdot}07\ \text{K}(c/w - 0{\cdot}05)$, P = crushing strength of concrete as desired in kg/cm^2.

(*c*) Table given by different agencies for finding *w/c* ratio for different crushing strength of concrete.

Table 8·45

Strength of conc.		*w/c ratio by vol.*		
lbs/in²	*kg/cm²*	*USBR conc. method*	*Boleman K = 3200*	*S.K. Jain A = 13500 B = 8 (Abram's law)*
4500	315	0·48	0·525	0·53
3750	262	0·56	0·60	0·615
3600	252	0·58	0·615	0·635
2700	189	0·78	0·745	0·76

(*d*) *w/c* ratio for different climatic conditions by volume.

Table 8·46

Climate extreme	*w/c ratio for* Light structures	*w/c ratio for* Hydraulic structures	*w/c ratio for* Heavy structures piers, dams, found etc.
1. Exposed to alternate wetting and drying, freezing and thawing for long periods, sea and sulphate water	0·73	0·73	0·8
2. Exposed to rain and snow, freezing and thawing but not continuously	0·8	0·8	0·9
Moderate			
1. Exposed to ordinary weather, but not continuously in contact of water	0·9	0·8	1·0
2. Protected against rain and frost below ground level not effected with sub soil water or freezing etc.	1·0	0·8	1·1

(*e*) Indian standards from the following Fig. 8·47 which has been plotted from a number of field tests for different crushing strengths designed for 28 days. Setting period for different water cement ratios.

Step 2nd. Proportioning of fine to coarse aggregates and their gradation.

1. Fineness modulus method

(*a*) Grading of fine aggregate by sieve analysis

Table 8·47

B.S. Sieve No./(IS)	4 (4·0 mm)	7 (2·36 mm)	14 (1·18 mm)	25 (600 μ)	52 (300 μ)	100 (150 μ)
Percentage passing by wt.	95-100	80-100	50-85	25-60	10-30	2-10

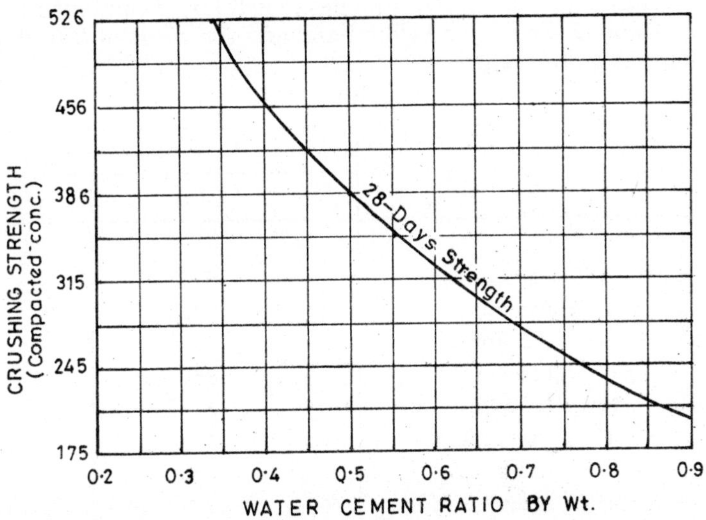

Fig. 8·47.

(b) Grading of coarse aggregate by sieve analysis.

Table 8·48

Max. size of aggregate	*Percentage of coarse aggregate fraction*					
	6″-3″ (150-75) mm	*3″-1½″ (75-38) mm*	*1½″-3/4″ (38-79) mm*	*3/4″-3/8″ (20-9·5) mm*	*3/8″-3/16 69·5-4·75)*	*3/4″-3/16″ (1·9-4·75) mm*
6″ (150 mm)	20-35	20-32	20-30	12-20	8-15	20-35
3″ (75 mm)	0	20-40	20-40	15-25	10-15	25-40
1½″ (38 mm)	0	0	40-55	30-35	15-25	45-60
3/4″ (19 mm)	0	0	0	55-73	27-45	100

Note. In practice available aggregate may not comply the above conditions hence if so not suitable.

(c) Grading of mix (fine and coarse) aggregate.

Table 8·49

Max. size of aggregate	*Percentage passing in the sieve*										
	6″ 150 mm	*3″* 75	*1½″* 38	*3/4″* 19	*3/8″* 9·5	*3/16″* 4·75	*B.S.-7* 2·36	*B.S.-14* 1·18	*B.S.-25* 600 μ	*B.S.-52* 300 μ	*B.S.-100* 150 μ
6″ (150 mm)	100	70	50	36	25	18	12·5	9	6·25	4·5	3
3″ (75 mm)	–	100	70	50	36	25	18	12·5	9	6·25	4·5
1½″ (38 mm)	–	–	100	70	50	36	25	18	12·5	9	6·25
3/4″ (19 mm)	–	–	–	100	70	50	36	25	25	12·5	9

(*d*) Grading of the mix by the formula $P = \frac{A - B}{A - C} \times 100$

where, P = Percentage of fine to combined aggregate by weight.

A = Fineness modulus of coarse, B = Fineness modulus of combined and C = Fineness mod. of fine aggregate. A and C are known before hand and the value of B from the table below. A and C can also be found from the table.

Table 8·50

Max. size of aggregate			*Fineness modulus*	
			Min.	*Max.*
Fine aggregate			2	3·5
Coarse aggregate	3/4″	(19 mm)	6	6·9
	1½″	(38 mm)	6·9	7·5
	3″	(75 mm)	7·5	8·0
	6″	(150 mm)	8·0	8·5
Mixed aggregate	3/4″	(19 mm)	4·7	5·1
	1″	(25·4 mm)	5·0	5·5
	1¼″	(32 mm)	5·2	5·7
	1½″	(38 mm)	5·4	5·9
	3″	(75 mm)	5·8	6·3
	6″	(150 mm)	6·5	7·0

Locate mix aggregate proportion from the size of coarse aggregate, from maximum and minimum, take according to the fineness mod. of fine aggregate to which it corresponds, whether maximum, minimum or average etc. Put all the three values in the above formula and obtain P (P is the percentage of fine, while $100 - P$ is of coarse) by weight.

2. Proportioning by trial. Mixure trial mixes with different proportions of fine to coarse aggregate and weigh (of the same volume). The mix which gives the maximum weight for the same volume is the best.

3. By optimum percentage of sand. Mix several trial mixes with different proportions. It will be found that, that there is only one ratio of fine to coarse for which the cement required is the least for certain water cement ratio for a desired workability or slump. To achieve it a certain mix is tried with different quantities of cement with water in the desired *w/c* ratio, and the quantity of cement for the desired slump is located for the mix. In the same way other mixes are also tried and their cement requirement for a desired slump is located. Now from the test the mix which require the minimum cement is taken as accepted. The percentage of sand in the mix to the combined aggregate is known as optimum percentage of sand.

Step 3. Proportioning of cement and water requirements.

(*a*) **By trial.** In the selected fine to coarse aggregate mix, mix different quantities of cement and water in the different water cement ratio and select the mix which gives the desired slump.

(*b*) According to the maximum size of coarse aggregate from following Table.

Table 8.51

Max. size of aggregate	*3/4"(19 mm)*	*1(25.4)*	*11/2"(38)*	*3"(75)*	*6(150 mm)*
Quality of water in lbs % cft conc./kg/m^3	$\frac{1250}{199}$	$\frac{1200}{191}$	$\frac{1125}{179}$	$\frac{1025}{163}$	$\frac{900}{143}$

From the quality of water so obtained the quantity of cement is calculated for the desired *w/c* ratio.

(*c*) **Fineness modulus method.** Water content by volume for 100 cft concrete is given by the formula $W = \dfrac{29 + Q}{(1{\cdot}15)^F}$ where W = water content in 100 cft concrete in cft ; Q = slump required in inches and F = combined fineness mod. of aggregate.

Other method of Proportioning

Method based on Min voids. Voids in ballast and sand are determined before hand. The cement is mixed in sand a bit more (say 10%) than the voids in sand and then this cement mixed sand is mixed in ballast a bit more (say 15%) than the voids in ballast. The mass is thoroughly saked and water is added to make a plastic mass (workable).

The mix is compacted theoretically yet practically due to the bulking of sand and separation of ballast pieces due to pressure caused by sand, the compactness is not reliable. Excess water also effects the strength.

Method based on Maximum density. Fuller gave a formula for proportioning of concrete in gradations to have maximum density of the mixture.

$P = 100\,(d/D)^{1/2}$ where P is the percentage of fine aggregate by weight including of cement, d is the maximum size of fine aggregate and D is the maximum size of coarse aggregate. If a mix 1 : 6 (cement sand) by wt. is to be mixed and if the value of P obtained from the formula is

50% than in the mix of 100 kg, the cement will be 16.6 kg (100/6). Sand will be 50 – 16.6 = 33.4 kg and ballast will be 50 kg or 16.6 : 34.4 : 50 or 1 : 2 : 3 by weight will be the mix.

The quantity of water has not been regulated in this method hence the strength attained is not reliable.

Table 8·52. Physical properties of material used in conc. design.

Material	*Sp. gravity*	*Wt. per unit vol.*	*Wt per unit vol. of solid material*
Water	1.00	62.4 lb/cft (1 kg/lit.)	62.4 lb/cft (1 kg/lit.)
Cement	3.150	90 lb/cft (1430 kg/m^3)	196.6 lbs/cft (3126 kg/m^3)
Sand	2.637	120 lb/cft (1908 kg/m^3)	164.5 lbs/cft (2616 kg/m^3)
Gravel	2.702	105 lb/cft (1670 kg/m^3)	166.6 lbs/cft (2647 kg/m^3)

Note. 1. In the method mentioned above if the conc. mix so obtained does not give the required slump, the quantity of water may be changed and then change the proportion accordingly.

2. The calculations are for the dry sand. If there is any bulking in the sand an account for the same may be taken in mixing *i.e.*, the bulked quantity of sand should be mixed to the same percentage of bulking extra.

3. The moisture content in the ballast and sand should be determined before hand and its water content should be deducted from the quantity of water required. If some water is absorved by the aggregate, it should be calculated extra than water requirements.

4. As general 15% more sand and 10% more cement are often used than the percentage voids in course and fine aggregate.

5. Percentage of water by volume + percentage of cement by volume + percentage of sand by volume + percentage of ballast by volume (all in compacted stage) = 100.

6. If in place of water, cement quantity is fixed, the requirements of water may be calculated by the quantity of space of voids left for it. Calculate solid volumes of cement, sand and ballast and deduct it from 100. The quantity so obtained is the volume of water needed.

Example. *Design a mix with the following data.*

Grade of concrete M – 250

Crushing strength = *250 kg/cm²*

Slump = *50 mm*

Fineness modulus of coarse aggregate = *6.0*

Fineness modulus of fine aggregate = *2.0*

Maximum size of coarse aggregate = *20 mm*

Wt. of coarse aggregate = *1500 kg/m³*

Wt. of fine aggregate = *1700 kg/m³*

Wt. of cement = *1430 kg/m³*

Voids in cement, fine and coarse aggregate = *50,40 and 50% respectively*

The crushing strength of M – 250 = *250 kg/cm²*

Step 1st. From the table for 250 kg/cm^2, *w/c* ratio by wt. = 0.67

(If climatic conditions are predominated then use table for calculating *w/c* ratio).

Step 2nd. The fineness modulus of combined aggregate (Aggregate size from the tables varies 4·7 to 5·1). As the fineness modulus of fine aggregate is 200 (The minimum provided in the table 2.0 to 3.5) so take 4.7 as the fineness mod of combined aggregate. Now the proportion of fine to combine aggregate

$$P = 100\frac{6-4{\cdot}7}{6-2{\cdot}0} = \frac{1{\cdot}3}{4{\cdot}0} \times 100 = 32{\cdot}5\% \text{ by wt.}$$

So the percentage of coarse aggregate by wt. $= 100 - 32{\cdot}5 = 67.5\%$

Volume 32.5 kg of fine aggregate $= 32.5 \times 1700 = 55250$ kg

Volume of 67.5 kg of coarse aggregate $= 67.5 \times 1500 = 1{,}01{,}250$

So ratio of fine to coarse by volume $= \dfrac{55250}{101750} = 1 : 1{\cdot}9$

Step 3rd. From the table for 20 mm (3/4″ maximum size of coarse aggregate) water required is 200 kg/m^3 of conc.

So the cement required will be 200/0.67 = 300 kg

Volume of 200 kg (200 lit.) of water = 0.20 cm^3.

Volume of 300 kg cement = 300/1430 = 0.210 m^3

Solid volume of 0.2 m^3 of water = 0.2 m^3

Solid volume of 0.21 m^3 of cement $= \dfrac{0{\cdot}21}{2} = {\cdot}1$ (having 50% voids)

So solid volume of water + cement $= 0{\cdot}2 + 0{\cdot}1 = 0{\cdot}3$ m^3

The solid volume of combined aggregate in 1 m^3 conc. remains $(1 - 3) = 0{\cdot}7$ m^3

1 m^3 of fine aggregate contains $(1 - 0.4) = 0.6$ m^3 solid material (having 40% voids)

1 m^3 of coarse aggregate contains $(1 - 0{\cdot}5) = 0{\cdot}5$ m^3 solid material (having 50% voids)

So $0{\cdot}60 + 0{\cdot}5 = 1{\cdot}1$ m^3 of solid combined aggregate contains 2 m^3 of normal material.

So $0{\cdot}7$ m^3 of solid material will have $\dfrac{2}{1{\cdot}1} \times {\cdot}7 = 1{\cdot}28$ m^3 of material having a ratio of 1 : 1·9, the volume of fine to coarse aggregate in 1 m^3 of conc. will be 0·44 m^3 and 0·84 m^3 respectively (Divide 1·28 in ratio of 1 : 1·9)

So	*Water*	*Cement*	*Fine aggregate*	*Coarse aggregate*	
	200 lit.	0·2 m^3	0·44 m^3	0·84 m^3	By vol.
	200 kg	300 kg	248 kg	1260 kg	By wt.

Note. 1 Note 1 to 6 as given above and do accordingly.

2. If the slump of the conc. is not according to the requirement then increase the water and calculate proportions accordingly.

3. If there is bulking in sand, increase the quantity of bulked sand accordingly and take its water into account.

4. Moisture content in ballast should also be accounted.

5. Take 10% more cement and 15% more sand.

6. The coarse aggregate may absorb water, if it requires so and it should not be taken into account for proportioning the mix.

Analysis of ingradients of fresh concrete and then prediction of 28 days strength in compression

Step 1. Take about 200 grms of sand which is being used in conc. and weigh it, say it is w gm. Sieve it through 150 micron IS sieve and weigh the sand retained on 150 micron IS sieve say it is w_1 gm. Then fine sand passing 150 micron IS sieve is $\frac{w - w_1}{w} \times 100 = r_1$ (say) ... (A)

Step 2. Take two representative samples of about one kg each of fresh concrete, care should be taken that no loss of water due to evaporation etc. may occur. These two samples are weighed accurately.

Dry sample no. 1 on heater and determine the percentage of water

wt. of sample no. 1 $= m_1$ gm (say) ...(1)

wt. of sample no. 1 after drying $= m_2$ gm (say) ...(2)

Then the water content $= m_1 - m_2 = m$ (say) which is $\frac{m}{m_1} \times 100 = r_2$ say ... (B)

Step 3. Sample no. 2 should be thoroughly washed by water on sieve no 150 micron. The retained material then dried on heater, cooled and sieved on 475 mm sieve. Then material retained on 4·75 mm sieve shall be coarse aggregate, where as passing material on it is sand silt. The cement contained may be obtained by difference in weights. Knowing absorption of aggregate, water and cement content may be determined as follows.

Wt. of concrete in sample no. 2 $= m_3$ gm (say) ...(3)

Wt. of sample no. 2 after wet sieving on sieve no. 150 micron and drying $= m_4$ (say) ...(4)

Wt. of aggregate retained on 4·75 mm sieve after sieving aggregate of (4) $= m_5$ (say) ...(5)

The aggregate obtained at (5) may be analysed to check the actual grades of coarse aggregate.

Sand $= (4) - (5) = m_4 - m_5 = m_6$ (say) ...(6)

Correction in sand for materials passing on sieve no. 150 micron

$$= \frac{A \times (6)}{100} = \frac{r_1 \times m_6}{100} = m_7 \text{ (say)} \qquad \text{...(7)}$$

Total sand in sample no. 2 $= (6) + (7) = m_6 + m_7 = m_8$ (say) ...(8)

Total water in sample no. 2 $= \frac{(3) \times (B)}{100} = \frac{m_3 \times r_2}{100} = m_9$ say ...(9)

Cement in sample no. 2 $= (3) - (5) - (8) - (9) = m_{10}$ say ...(10)

Cement : Aggregate $= (10)/(5) = m_{10} : m_5 = r_3$ (say)

Total water : cement $= (9) : (10) = m_9 : m_{10} = r_4$ (say)

Free water in sample no. 2 $= m_9 -$ absorption of water in aggregate (say 1%)

$= m_9 - (m_4 + m_7) = m_{11}$ (say) ...(11)

Free water : Cement ratio $= m_{11} : m_{10} = r_5$ (say)

Cement : Sand : Aggregate $= m_{10} : m_8 : m_5$ by weight

Water cement ratio $= m_{11} : m_{10} = r_5$

Note. To obtain mix ratio hy volume, mix ratios obtained by weight are to be divided by the bulk densities of aggregates. The bulk density of cement may be taken as 1·44 kg/lit.

Prediction of 28 days compressive strength of cement may be done for respective water-cement ratio from the curves given.

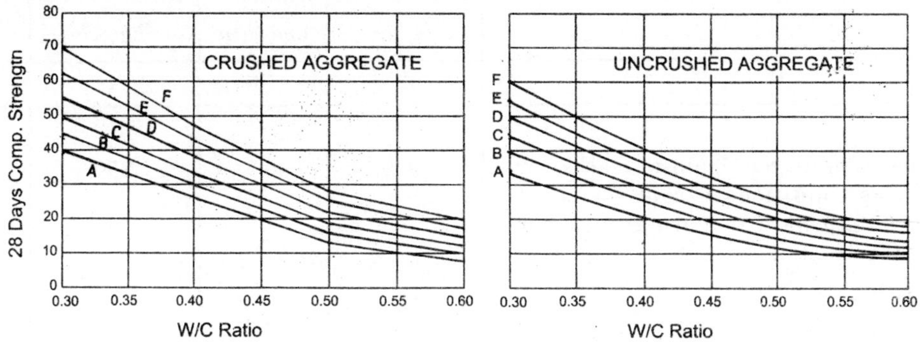

(*a*) (*b*)

Fig. 8.48.

7 days strength of cement according to IS 4031—1968

A = 21·6 –25·0 N/mm^2 B = 25·0 – 29·8 N/mm^2 C = 29·8 – 35·0 N/mm^2

D = 35·0 – 41·5 N/mm^2 E = 41·5 – 48·0 N/mm^2 F = 48·0 – 53·4 N/mm^2

Table 8·53. Proportion of nominal mix of concrete (IS)

Grade of conc.	*Total Qty. of dry aggr. by mass per bag of cement to be taken as the sum of the ingradients mass of fine and coarse aggregates (max. kg)*	*Proportion of fine to coarse aggregates by mass*	*Qty. of water per 50 kg of cement*
M-5	800	Generally 1 : 2 but subjected to an upper limit of 1 : 1½ and a lower limit of 1 : 2½	60
M-7·5	625		45
M-10	480		34
M-15	350		32
M-20	250		30

Note. 1. The proportion of the fine to coarse aggregate should be adjusted from the upper limit progressively as the grading of the fine aggregate becomes finer and the max. size of coarse aggregate becomes larger. Graded coarse aggregate shall be used.

2. The cement content of the mix specified in the above table for any nominal mix shall be proportionally increased if the quantity of water in a mix has to be increased to overcome the difficulty of placement and compaction. So that the water content ratio as specified is not exceeded.

For an average grading of fine aggregate the proportions shall be 1 : 1·5, 1·20 and 2·50 for maximum size of aggregate 10, 20 and 40 mm respectively.

3. In case of vibrated concrete, the limit specified may be suitably reduced to avoid segregation.

4. The quantity of water for RCC should be sufficient but not more than sufficient to produce dense conc. of adequate workability for its purpose.

Table 8·54. Minimum cement content required in cement concrete to ensure durability under specified conditions of exposure

Exposure	*PCC*		*RCC*	
	Min. cement kg/m³	*Max. w/c ratio*	*Min. cement kg/m³*	*Max. w/c Ratio*
(1)	(2)	(3)	(4)	(5)
Miled				
Completely protected against weather or aggressive conditions except for short period of exposure to normal weather during construction	220	0·7	250	0·65
Moderate				
Sheltered from heavy and wind driven rain and against freezing whilst saturated with water, burried conc. in soil and concreted continuously under water	250	0·6	290	0·55
Severe				
Exposed to see water, alternate wetting and drying to freezing whilst wet subject to heavy condensation or corrosive fumes	310	0·3	360	0·45

Note. 1. When the max. *w/c* ratio can be strictly controlled, the cement content in the above table can be reduced by 10%.

2. The min. cement content is based on 20 mm aggregate for 40 mm aggregate, it should be reduced by about 10% for 12.5 mm aggregate, it should be increased by about 10%.

Table 8·55. Nominal conc. mix ratios, grade and water requirement (in M.K.S. units)

Min. ratio	*Grade*	*Mod. ratio*	*Type of work*	*Water per bag of cement*
1 : 6 : 12	M-50		Mass conc. in foundation etc.	70 litres
1 : 5 : 10	M-50		Mass conc. in foundation etc.	60 litres
1 : 6 : 8	M-100		Mass conc. in foundation etc.	45 litres
1 : 3 : 6	M-100	31	Mass conc. super structure *i.e.*, in pier and abutments etc.	34 litres
1 : 2 : 4	M-150	18.7	Normal RCC of roots, slabs, beams and walls	32 litres
1 : 1½ : 3	M-200	13.3	RCC in hydraulic structure, olumns and pipes	30 litres
1 : 1 : 2	M-250	10.0	Heavily located columns, long span beams and arches	27 litres

Note. 1 Grades above 1 : 3 : 6 are not used in RCC work.

2. M-150 in M.K.S. units is equivalent to M15 in S.I. System.

Design of concrete mix according to limit state loading (I.S.)

The mix shall be designed to produce the grade of concrete having the required workability and a characteristic strength not less than appropriate values given in the table below (grades of concrete). The target mean strength of concrete mix should be equal to the characteristic strength plus 1.65 times the standard deviation given in the table below.

Mix design done earlier not prior to one year may be considered adequate for later work provided there is no change in source and the quality of the materials.

Standard deviation for each grade of concrete shall be calculated separately.

Standard deviation based on test strength of sample

(*a*) **Number of test results of samples.** The total number of test strength of samples required to constitute an acceptable record for calculation of standard deviation shall not be less than 30. Attempts should be made to obtain the 30 samples as early as possible, when a mix is used for the 1st time.

(*b*) In case of significant changes in concrete. When significant changes are made in the production of concrete batches (for example changes in the materials used and mix design equipment or technical control), the standard deviation value shall be separately calculated for such batches of concrete.

(*c*) Standard deviation to be brought up to date. The calculation of the standard deviation shall be brought up to date after every change of mix design.

Assumed standard deviation

Where sufficient test results for a particular grade of concrete are not available the value of standard deviation given in table below may be assumed for design of mix in the 1st instance. As soon as the results of samples are available, actual calculated standard deviation shall be used and the mix designed properly. However when adequate past records for a similar grade exist and justify to the designer a value of standard deviation different from that shown—Table below, it is permissible to use that value.

Nominal mix concrete. Nominal mix concrete may be used for M-20 or lower. The proportion of materials for nominal mix concrete shall be in accordance with table 8·53.

A nominal mix is the mix which is designed for specified materials *i.e.* cement and aggregate etc. while a *designed mix* is the mixed design by the materials available for the desired strength.

Table 8·56. Grades of Concrete

Group	*Grade designation*	*Specified characteristic compressive strength of 150 mm cube at 28 days N/mm² f_{ck}*	*Assumed standard deviation*
Ordinary concrete	M-10	10	3·5
	M-15	15	3·5
	M-20	20	4·0
Standard concrete	M-25	25	4·0
	M-30	30	5·0
	M-35	35	5·0
	M-40	40	5·6
	M-45	45	5·0
	M-55	55	5·0
High strength concrete	M-60	60	
	M-65	65	
	M-70	70	
	M-75	75	
	M-80	80	

Notes : (1) In the designation of the concrete mix references to the mix and the number to the specified compressive strength of 150 mm size cube at 28 days N/mm^2.

(2) For concrete of compressive strength greater than 55, design parameters given in the standard may be applicable and the values may be obtained from the specified literature and experimental results.

(3) Concrete of grades lower than these given in the table may be used for plain concrete constructions, lean concrete, simple foundations, foundation for masonry walls and other simple or temporary reinforced concrete works.

(4) These values are corresponding to the site control having proper storage of cement, weigh batching of all materials, controlled ratio of water, regular checking of materials, aggregate gradings and moisture content. Periodical checking of workability and strength, where there is deviation from the above, the values given in the above table shall be increased by 1 N/mm^2.

The tensile strength if concrete can be obtained from the compressive strength using flexural strength (f_{cr}) = $0{\cdot}7\sqrt{(f_{ck})}$ N/mm^2

Similarly the elastic modulus of structural concrete may be assumed as follows :

E_c = $5000\sqrt{(f_{ck})}$ where f_{ck} is the characteristic compressive strength of concrete in bending, tensile and compressive both in N/mm^2 (Short term basis or E_c is the modulus of elasticity of concrete.

E_s = 200 kN/mm^2 (E_s is the modulus of elasticity of all type of steel)

Characteristic strength of materials. Characteristic strength means that value of strength of materials below which not more than 5% of the test results are expected to fall. The characteristic value shall be assumed as the minimun yield stress/0·2% proof stress specified in the relevant I.S. specifications.

Characteristic loads. Characteristic loads means that value of load which has a 95% probability of not being exceeded during the life of the structure.

The I.S. specification regarding loads are as below :

I.S. 875 (Part-1) dead loads, I.S. 875 (Part-2) imposed loads

I.S. 875 (Part-3) wind loads, I.S. 875 (Part-4) snow loads

I.S. 1893 Seismic loads.

8·6·19. Repair of Reinforced Cement Concrete

Repair procedure. Small cracks often become sealed naturally, either with calcium carbonate formed when calcium hydroxide is leached into the crack from the concrete matrix or by small particles of debris, very fine cracks are generally removed by white washing, snowcem or distemper coating. When small cracks remain open, they can be sealed by liquid pressure injection repair systems, using low viscosity epoxy resins. Static cracks could be racked along the exposed surface to a groove with a width of 15-20 mm and depth of 12-20 mm. These should be cleaned with water to remove dirt and filled up with slightly stiff paste of 1 : 2 : 9 (cement : lime : sand) by volume along with some water proofing compound. Active cracks should be racked in the similar manner and cleaned dry by air blasting. A suitable mastic asphalt should then fill the groove after priming it with liquid primer for better contact with the surface. Mastics are generally bitumen based. Larger cracks can be an indications of areas of loose concrete cover which must be removed before repair concrete forming the integral sides of crack or spalls may be friable and the surface atleast will be carbonated, it is necessary therefore to cut back to form a sound and ideally alkaline surface on which to bond the repair.

The part of the concrete that has damaged or spalled off should be removed by chiselling or by hacking and then be cleaned with wire brushes, water or by sand and air blasting.

Repair techniques for concrete. The surface obtained after removal of damaged concrete and cleaning is coated with a cement based material within the period not exceeding the initial setting time. If epoxy based coatings are used, these should be used within the period not exceeding the pot life.

Cement grout injection. For cement grout injection holes are chilled at required intervals. These can be of 25 mm to 50 mm diameter and 6 to 12 mm depth depending on crack size. Aluminium sockets or respective diameter are then fixed in the holes. Special cementation slurry heaving properties of higher compressive and tensile strength and non-shrinkage properties after setting and having expanding properties when green are then injected through sockets till refusal and the voids are completely filled. This is generally done by pressure grouting with a pressure of 8 kg/cm^2.

Epoxy grout crack injection. The spacing of injection points will depend on depth and width of cracks and should help in maximum resin penetration and easy filling of cracks with low operating pressure not exceeding 10 kg/cm^2. Generally the pressure is around 5 to 6 kg/cm^2. When the cracks are inclined, it is usual to commence the injection at the lowest injection point and work upwards as the resin comes out at the next higher injection point. For horizontal cracks the injection can start from one end and proceed along the crack.

Polymer concrete composite injection. Repair of cracks can be easily done by injecting polymer-concrete composite into the cracks.

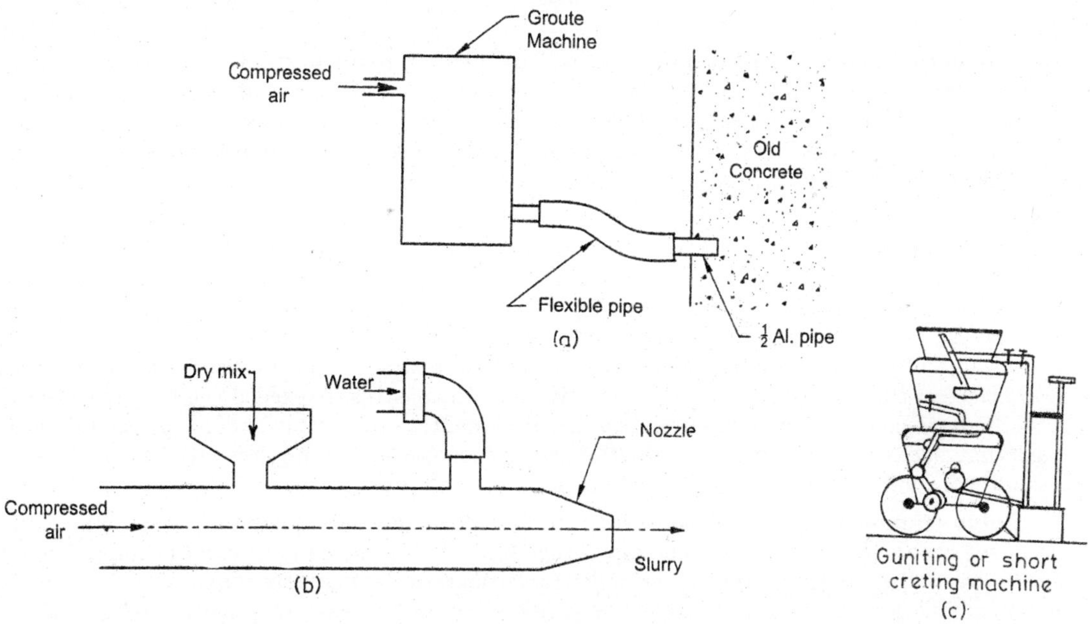

Fig. 8·49.

Guniting or shortcrete is basically a mortar or concrete conveyed through a pressure hose and applied pneumatically at high velocity on a prepared surface. The force of the jet impacting on the surface compacts the material so that it can support itself without sagging even in a vertical face. There are two guniting processes in general use. The wet mix and the dry mix process. The later process is more extensively used for structural repairs. Cracks wider than 0·5 mm should be cut out and filled hand applied mortar with trowel.

Jacketing. It is a process of fastening a durable material over concrete and filling the caving with a grout that provides needed performance characteristics. The materials used for jacekts are metals, rubber, plastic and concrete. Jacketing materials may also be secured by means of bolts, screws, nails or adehsives by bond with existing concrete or by gravity jacketing improves the look of surface and also strengths in against weather.

For rehabilitation of damaged elevated service reservoirs many a times it becomes necessary to enlarge the section of a column. This procedure is called jacketing of column. Jacketing has the following operations :

(1) Removal of damaged concrete from surface.

(2) Injection to seal inner cracks in concrete.

(3) Placing plywood form work and additional reinforcement in width of jacket (with ranges from 100 to 110 mm)

(4) Concreting with at least M-25 mix.

(5) Protecting the new surface with resin based coating.

Note : (1) In vertical faces a wire mesh or expended metal should be tied to reinforcement or to extra bar anchors embedded in the concrete if the thickness of the repair patch is more than 10 cm. So that the repair grout mass may be held in position.

(2) Before dealing with any crack a tail of cement plaster patch should be plastered over the crack with date of patching and should be watched that weather the cracks develop on the tall tail. If the cracks develop with time, indicate any structural weakness which should be studied before repair.

Materials for repair. (1) **Cement based.** Ordinary Portland cement sulphate resisting cement or high alumina cement. It may be applied by hand trowel on big cracks or by spraying dry or wet.

(2) **Resin based.** (*a*) **Polymer resins.** Oil derived resin systems usually applied in adhesive or mortar form. Polyester resins have good general adhesion and rapid curing on dry concrete, but perform poorly in damp and wet conditions. They are not normally applied in thick layers because of the possibility of strucking during curing. The curing time is faster than epoxy resin systems particularly at low temperatures.

Epoxy Resins. Epoxy resins are modern well formulated systems that provide excellent adhesion chemical resistence and performance in dry and damp conditions. Although the nature of cure is exothermic, thermal shrinkage can be reduced to low levels. Their use leads to fast curing even at low temperatures. Epoxy resins can cover a whole range of materials from low viscosity grouts (very useful for the cracks). Epoxy resins have considerable higher coefficient of expansion and lower value of youngs modulus than concrete. These disparities can induce high shear stress at the interface of the repair and base concrete. If these shear stresses exceed the tensile resisting stress of the base concrete, then the repair will subsequently disbond. It should not therefore be assumed that because of the greatly superior compressive and tensile strength of epoxy resin mortars a repair will give monolithic performance.

Polymer modified cement based materials. The addition of polymer latex to portland cement based repair material gives some advantage like much reduced permeability improvement of bond between the repair material and substrate concrete particularly when a slurry coat of polymer modified portland cement is used to prime surfaces increase in tensile strength of the repair, improved workability through minor plasticising of the mix while allowing reduction of water/cement ratio, general improvement in chemical resistance of the repair material and improvements in curing. The different type of polymer notified latex used include Polyvinyle Acetate (PVA) Styrene Butadiene (SBP) Polyvinylidene Chloride (PVDC) acrylic and styrene acrylic lattices. Polyvinyle acetate are not suitable for external use in damp conditions.

Cement Pozzuolanic Modified Materials. Portland cement blended with microsilica, fly ash, calcium nitrate etc. can dramatically reduce the permeability and hence the chloride ion diffusion of concrete.

A good repair material combination has the following properties :

(*a*) Mechanical properties as close to the base material as possible such as, Youngs modulus, coefficient of expansion, compressive and tensile strengths etc.

(*b*) Good adhesion in dry or wet conditions.

(*c*) Low shrinkage during curing and long term.

8·6·20. Protection to Reinforcement

Reinforcement corrosion is the cause of cracking or spalling, it is important to cut the concrete back behind the steel to a depth of at least 12 mm (provided this does not endanger structural stability. The steel should be cleaned to remove all corrosion products. This is best achieved by grit blasting. The steel if sufficiently corroded require replacement. This is achieved by cutting out the corroded length and replacing with a new length of the same type and cross-section, welded to the existing bar at each end, rust or salts on reinforcement should be removed by brushing or by gunny bags. Derusting jelly and phosphating jelly developed by central Electrochemical Research Institute Karaikudi may be used for heavily rusted rods. *Protmax* anti-corrosive for rebars prepared by Cerci Protek, Madras can be used.

Polymer Chemical Grouts. In India new chemical grouts based on polymerisation process and having notoxic effects have been developed and used in several projects. These chemical grouts are epoxy resin based, poly use-thane based and acrylic based. In water soluble polymer grouts when an aqueous catalyst is added, the resultant mixed grout has about the same viscosity as water. The grout will penetrate any soil or rock formation through when water flows and about the same rate. In a predetermine period of time which may be closely controlled from a few seconds to several hours by changing the quantity of catalyst, the grout solution solidifies into a stiff gel. In this manner all voids containing grout solution are sealed with a flexible, continuous gel that prevents the passage of water through the formation. In the case of a soil mass it also binds the soil particles together to provide a moderate increase in shear strength. No natural ground deposits has yet been encountered in which a gel cannot be made to form. The characteristics of chemical reaction are such that the viscosity of the polymer grout solution remains the same until the gel forms. In large works other materials are used to fill the voids in the coarses strata or fissures and the final seal is made by grouting with polymer based chemical grout. Aquagel-9 manufactured by Asian Laboratories, New Delhi is satisfactory on all these counts.

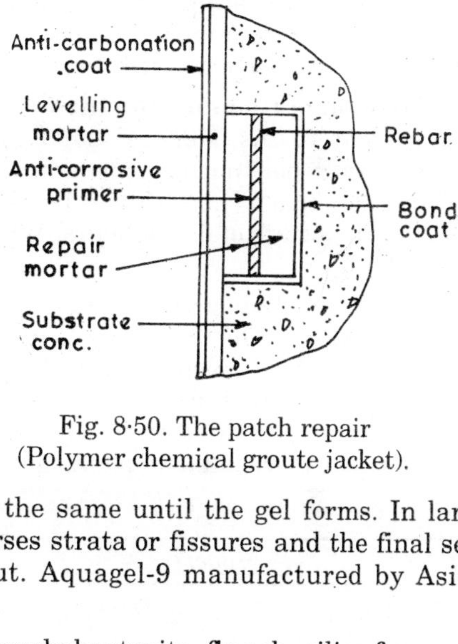

Fig. 8·50. The patch repair (Polymer chemical groute jacket).

Grouts can be divided into two broad categories, namely bentonite, fly ash, silica fume and solution grouts or chemical grouts. Physically the ability of a suspended solids grout to penetrate a formation is limited by the size of the suspended particles and the size of the voids or fissures that are to be grouted. In order to penetrate a formation at desirable pressure and rates without binding the foundation the size of the suspended particle cannot be greater than about one 3rd of the size of the voids.

In a polymer solution in which one is monomer and the other is accelerator (catalyst) a very stiff gel is formed. The 1st reaction starts almost immediately after the 2nd component (catalyst) is added. The rate of reaction is controlled by proper selection of the catalyst system and the environment allows a predetermined amount of time to elapse before polymerization of chemical grout occurs. This is known as the **Induction period** or **Gel time** during which viscosity of the solution remains almost constant. At the end of the induction period heat is evolved.

In dry soils gravitational and capillery forces act quickly to disperse the injected solution. The extent of dispersion may be sufficient to render the gel ineffective. Dispersion can be avoided if the soil is saturated prior to injection of chemical grout and by use of very short gel time. Due to low viscosity polymer chemical grouts can pass any soil from which water can flow.

When the gel is started under conditions of low humidity water evaporates slowly and the gel shrunks. When the same gel is placed under conditions of saturated humidity it reabsorbs the water previously lost and expand to its original volume. The gel is impermeable to water and is rubbery elastic material.

The dye test—is an indication test to trace the path of flow of water and the time required for the grout to trowel enabling the grouting personal to fix minimum gel time in the field.

Equipment—There are three types of equipments which have been used to apply polymer based chemical grout solutions.

(*i*) **Proportioning system.** This system allows one man to control all the factors by mechanical means. The pumping unit has a volume of one lit to 45 litres rang/minimum and pressure range of 0 to 300 psi and weighs approximate 150 kg.

Two solution system. It has been used for same types of applications but it permits working conveniently with only predetermined gel time.

(3) **Batch system.** The grout and the catalyst is mixed in one tank and the batch is then pumped into the ground using almost any type of pump. This system has major limitations hence it is generally abandoned a field work.

Polymer Cement Mortar—is available in many brand names. Some of these are based on no solvent resins, some as solvent based resins and some as polymer emulsions. White emulsion based polymer cement mortar can be advantageously used in moist conditions, resin based polymer cement mortar can be used on dry surfaces only. Emulsion based polymer cement mortar has a pot life of 5 to 6 hours. Where as resin based polymer cement mortar has one to two hours of pot life.

Om Agro Industrial Plastics Pvt. Ltd. Bombay have developed a polymer cement mortar which is marked under the brand name of **Omaicrete** which is a polymer emulsion modified cement mortar. It is formulated for heavy industrial floorings, Hospital floors, restoration of old floors, rehabilitation of distressed RCC structures, repairs to cracked concrete and plaster, water proofing basements, water reservoirs, Aqueducts and RCC terraces etc. A comparison of properties of polymer cement concrete to plain concrete is tested below.

Table 8·57.

Property	*Polymer cement concrete*	*Plain concrete*
Compressive strength kg/cm^2	1200	300
Tensile strength kg/cm^2	150	30
Flexural strength kg/cm^2	350	80
Water absorption	0·5	5·5
Percentage of loss of weight on abrasion test	—	9·5

Polymer cement mortar is generally air cured. It dries in about 8 to 10 Hrs. Hardened mortar has sufficient flexibility. Thus avoiding stresses in floors. It is available in two pack system comprising of a powder and a polymer emulsion.

Repair Techniques. (*a*) For floorings—Clean the surface by grinding, sand blasting or by other means. Unsound concrete should be chiselled and washed. Apply one primer coat on damp surface. Spread polymer cement mortar uniformly in required thickness (3 to 5 mm and 10 mm for industrial floors) and finish smooth by steel trowel. It will dry in 6 to 8 hours. Light water spray curing can be done after 12 hours. For thick (10 mm) floors add coarse aggregate to the powder. These floor can be used after 2 days for light traffic to 7 days for heavy.

Wherever in RCC structures concrete has been damaged beyond a depth of 40 mm a chicken mesh should be provided.

New repair commercial products

(1) **Conbond.** It is a liquid adhesive and strengthener or for CC. It will bond new concrete or cement topping to structurally sound surfaces cement concrete, brick, concrete blocks or ceramic tiles without the usual time considering practice of chipping, roughening, acid washing, scarifying or notching the old surface necessary as a preliminary measure to anchor a new wet concrete or rendering. Inspite of providing mechanical key there has been no definite assurance of a dependable 100% monolithic bond between the old and new surface. Conbond becomes an integral part of the interface between the new concrete and the old surface. Conbond-A a special grade additive allow thin over lays of 25 mm thickness to be laid on existing work out floor surface having high impact and abrasion resistance and have water and chemical resistance properties. It will also eliminate surface curing.

Conbond is a paint like fluid which dries to a thin, flexible film. It eliminates shrinkage cracks that usually appear around the repaired patch. Joints between two different materials like wood concrete or masonry can be achieved by it.

Conbond may be used in concrete repair as follows :

Prepare Poth hole in a square shape with vertical edges. Roughen the surface. Dilute two parts of conbond with one part of water by volume and apply this solution by brush on the entire surface including vertical edges. Mix dry 1 : 3 cement and coarse sand and prepare mortar by adding solution as made above (1 : 2, conbond : water). Fill up the hole with mortar, level the surface by trowel. Cure the surface for a day by covering it with chet burlap. For details contact :

Conteck Chemicals A/3 Panch Tirth Apats. Sarkhej Road, Ahmedabad-380007.

Tapecrete P151 is an acrylic based polymer modified liquid in conjunction with requisite amount of cement improves the properties of cement. It can also be used as a slurry coating and as well as brush coating. It can be used in water retaining structures. For details contact :

FRC Composites India Ltd., 406, Deepali 92, Nehru Place New Delhi-110019.

Aqua Super Set-VW-9. Suitable for under water repairs. The effective water proofing, non-shrinking, stiff and self expanding gel ensuring total water proof repair in water tanks and reservoir etc. For details contact :

Asian Laboratories, 88 New Okhala, Industrial Complex, Phase II, New Delhi-110020.

Crack fill is a unique formulation helps crackfill to expand when it dries hence forcing itself inside the cracks contact :

Jayant Colour and Chemical Industries, Tulsi Ram Gupta Mills Estate, Darukhana, Ready Road, Mumbai-400010.

Expoxy Repair System. Sika Qualcrete. Moisture unsensitive epoxies which can be even used under water for repairs Sika Qualcrete Pvt. Ltd. 24-B, Park Street, Kolkata-700016.

For concrete repair materials contact :

Coromandal Proelorite, 24, Thattan Kulam Road, Madhavaram, Madras-600060.

Corocretin ZnP	—	Primer for Re-bars
Corocretin FSS	—	For facade protection
Corocretin of IHL	—	Injection grade resin
Corocretin SK-4	—	Special adhesive
Corocretin UBL	—	For water storage tanks
Corocretin UBS	—	For chemical resistance.

Acid resisting cement. For chemical plants, available in powder as well as in liquid form. About 2·5 kg powder for 1 litre solution is used. For detail contact (address of "crack fill" given above).

Jayant Colour and Chemicals Industries, Bombay.

Leaking of Concrete Roofs : Causes and Remedies

Causes— • Inadequate drainage provision of the rain water from the roof.

• Use of highly absorbent poor quality brick aggregate.

• Inadequate design detailing giving due consideration to adverse weather conditions to which the roof is subjected to as well as to crack control measures.

• Absence of maintenance of the drainage provisions.

Applying ferro cement layer could be a more effective remedy. The technique could prevent corrosion of the embedded reinforcement if applied immediately after the leak is detected when the damage observed is minimal. The application of the ferro cement to the slab involved :

(*i*) The surface is dried in the sun for 20 days, 10 days on each face.

(*ii*) Preparation of the surface by roughening with chisel and removal of loose materials by blowing air.

(*iii*) Laying of wire mesh 8 × 8 mm spacing and fixing it to the surface by nailing at suitable locations.

(*iv*) Application of the cement mortar on the surface 13 mm or 50 in thickness with 1 : 3 cement and sand.

After 24 hours of applying the cement mortar water was stored on the slab to both serve the purpose of curing as well as to monitor the effectiveness of ferro cement in arresting the seepage of water. The monitoring continued at suitable time interval upto one month.

Precautionary measures to prevent corrosion of re-bars.

(1) use of richer mix *e.g.* 1 : 1·5 : 3

(2) use of deformed bars for better bond

(3) use of dense aggregate *e.g.*, stone chips

(4) proper slope and drainage provisions

(5) easy access to roof and provision for regular maintainable.

Deterioration in concrete roof in majority of cases manifests itself in the cracking of concrete usually caused by corrosion of the re-bars which is associated with a change in volume. This expansive tensile pressures causes the concrete cover to spall off. Preventing the ingress of water and oxygen would greatly minimize the risk of corrosion in the embedded rebars especially in the roof slab, the building part most vulnerable to weathering forces.

8·6·21. Strengthening of RCC beams in bridges

(1) Epoxy bonded flats are fixed to take extra loads/ metal plates are bonded by epoxy resins to the concrete surface

(2) Prestressed cables fixed for taking extra loads.

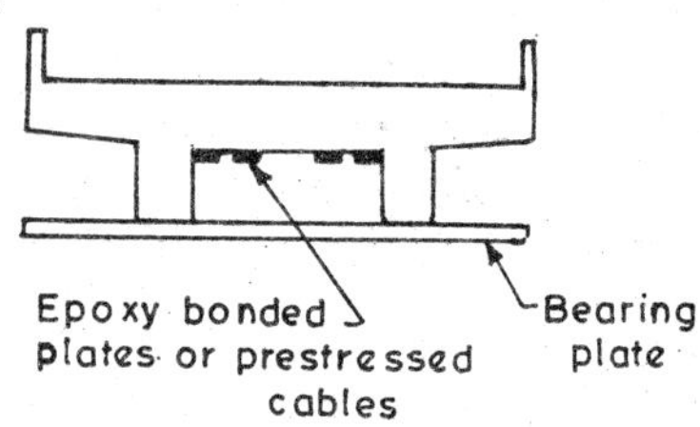

Fig. 8·51.

8·6·22. Special Preparation of Concrete

(1) **Prestressed concrete.** The compressive stresses are produced in a concrete beam in lower tension side by stretching several cold wires of high tensile strength. The concrete is laid when the wires are in tension. After setting of concrete when the wires are released they produce

compression in the tension side of beam which is 1st neutralised on loading and then tension starts functioning. Thus the load carrying capacity of the beam is increased. Such beams are called prestressed beams. Their other details are given in the section of reinforced concrete.

(2) **Prepacked Concrete.** Stones of different grades are packed together so that the smaller stones may insert in the voids of larger ones and so on, and thus a mass is prepared with complete dry stones. A slurry or mortar of the required ratio of cement and sand is pumped with force in iteristies of the packed stone mass and thus a solid cemented mass is prepared. The inner portions are grouted by inserting pipes in the packed stone mass, which are either removed after grouting or are grouted with mortar. These pipes must be of steel. Bigger sized stones can be used in this operation. It is done generally in pavements. It has advantage of compaction time saving and of simplicity. But the quality achieved is not good. A dispersing agent such as cheecol is mixed for making the grout to flow more freely around the stones and voids are filled completely.

(3) **Light weight concrete.** (Sound and heat proofing). Curtain and partition walls are needed with these qualities which can be achieved in the following ways :

(*a*) **By used of light aggregates**, which are given below :

(*i*) **Breeze of coak** obtained from coals.

(*ii*) **Pumice stones** found in nature.

(*iii*) **Foamed slag** obtained by quenching the furnace slag.

(*iv*) **Saw dust mixed in cement** and boiled in water for 10 minutes.

(*v*) **Expanded vermiculite slates**. It is obtained by heating a vermiculite (a mica product) to a suitable temperature, which expends on heating and a light weight material for using as ballast is obtained.

(*vi*) **Cinder Concrete.** 1 part cement to 10 parts cinder gives a good light porous and insulating properties, used on roofs, laid about 6 cm thick in slope of 1 : 50. A water proofing layer is laid over it as cinder concrete is not water proofing.

(*b*) **Concrete with no sand.** In this type of concrete sand is not used, only the coarse aggregate of size 10 mm to 20 mm of the light weight types mentioned above are used in ratios of 1 : 6 to 1 : 10 (cement : aggregate) according to the weight of the aggregate (using 1 : 6 for light) water mixed should be just sufficient to bind the aggregate particles together. More water will cause the flow of aggregate, while less will leave loose particles inside. Due to the absence of sand the space between the aggregate particles remain hollow. The surface can be reduced smooth, with cement, lime or plaster of Paris. Compaction in such concretes should be avoided.

(*c*) **Aeration of Concrete.** Aluminium of zinc (0·005 to 0·02% mixed with cement which causes formation of bubbles of hydrogen in the concrete. These bubbles take place of the mortar in the concrete and then being light in weight makes the concrete light. Sometimes resins and soaps are used which produce bubbles causing the light weight as is done by the hydrogen bubbles. They are mixed in the ratio of 1 : 1000 by weight and is thoroughly mixed in cement in dry state. Water is then mixed, which causes evolution of bubbles. The mould is filled one third in height with the paste so formed after bubbling this mould is filled full. The surplus mass should be removed and the surface should be levelled (collection of water on surface of concrete causes hollow pores after evaporation). These bubbles also force the concrete mortar in sharp edges resulting a tight fit concrete mass. Bond to the rebars is also good.

Light weight concrete is used where sound and heat proofing is primary, while the strength is secondary.

(4) **Early strength cement concrete.** When the structure is to be used earlier or when the forms are to be removed earlier so as to be used on other surface, early strength is needed. In

hydraulic structures early strength is also needed. In cold weather and for repairing cracks etc. the concrete should get strength earlier. The following accelerating agents are used.

(*i*) Addition of 2% of **calcium chloride** by weight with cement retards time of setting upto one 3rd and the normal strength achieved is 170% more in one day, 30% more in seven days and 10% in 28 days which is called the ultimate strength. It also increase workability and hence reduction in w/c ratio for the same strength. A high temperature (70-80°C) is also achieved when the quantity of calcium chloride is reduced, its temperature can be reduced to 40°C to 50°C, but the time to achieve strength is doubled.

(*ii*) Addition of 0·05% of **sugar** by weight of cement reduces the setting time by about 2 hours at 44°C atmospheric temperature. By addition of sugar a leaner mix can also be used and thus cement is saved too much addition of sugar is harmful. It should be mixed in water.

(*iii*) NaOH (Sodium hydroxide or caustic soda) if mixed in 2% quantity by weight of cement, the time of setting is reduced by five minutes. Baking soda (khana soda) also reduces time of setting.

(*iv*) Cico-cico mixed with concrete reduces the time of setting. It is available in market as cico no. 1, 2, 3 etc. according to the grade of setting time. The direction for uses are written on the packages by the maker.

(*v*) **Quick slacked time.** Also retards setting time of mixed with cement.

(*vi*) Early strength cement productions are also sold in the market.

(5) **Slow strength concrete.** When the time of transite and laying of concrete is expected to be more due to distant and hard approach from the batching to the site, and to avoid cracks due to high temperature production during hydration of cement, the slow setting in cement is needed.

(*i*) Calcium lignous sulphate is used. It should be used in very low quantity after due verification of its effect on concrete.

(*ii*) Low heat cement productions can be used if available.

(6) **Heat treatment of concrete.** In mass concrete as in dams and in heavy roofs, high heat is evolved which on cooling causes strain in concrete due to which shrinkage in concrete takes place, which is followed by cracks. Inner surface cool later than the open surfaces. They also create unequal stresses in concrete, resulting shrinkage which creates cracks. The following remedies are used for this.

(*a*) Use of low heat cement.

(*b*) water used should be cold by adding ice etc. while mixing.

(*c*) steel conduit pipes are embedded in the concrete and cold water is circulated in the pipes which do not allow the temperature to rise due to heat evolution. After work these pipes can be closed by pressure grouting.

(*d*) Proper time of laying of concrete is given so that previous layer cools before the 2nd is laid. A formula for regulating the time for laying of concrete is given as, $t = KweH$

where t = rise in temperature in °F, K is a coefficient = 0·0011 (for laying 1′ to 2·5′ lift per day) w is the weight of concrete in lbs/yd^3 of concrete and H is the heat evolved by cement upto 7 days in cal/gm. Hence the temperature t, heat generated H and the height of lift can be adjusted as desired.

(*e*) Aggregates should be cooled with cold water.

(*f*) All ingradients and mixing plants should be kept under covered sheds of straw etc. The mixing plant should be painted white so that they may not absorve more heat from air.

(*g*) Steel shutters should be avoided.

(*h*) Above 38°C work should be abandoned.

(7) **Concrete in cold weather.** The rate of hydration of cement retards in cold weather below 21°C (70°F). When the freezing water below 4°C expands it causes distintegration in concrete. When the temperature falls below 45°C, the concreting work should be abandoned. The following remedial measures are taken :

(*a*) The mixing water is heated to 66°C (150°F). Hot water should not be mixed with cement direct. The aggregates should also be heated to 21°C (70°F). Mixing plant should also be kept warm. Steel shutters should be avoided and timber shutters should be used. These shutters are removed later than their normal time.

(*b*) Temperature of the fresh concrete should not be allowed more than 21°C (70°F) as it require higher quantity of water, on cooling the concrete may crack. So a temperature of 21°C is maintained during laying. An average water cement ratio should be 6·60.

(*c*) Provide layers of straw or other insulating material on the layers of fresh laid concrete (such as polythene paper).

(*d*) A rapid hardening cement containing calcium chloride must be used as it evolves heat during hydration and keep the concrete mass on average temperature. Calcium chloride is mixed in mixing water and is not directly mixed dry with other ingradients. It should also not be mixed with alumina cement which itself has a heat evolving property. It is also not used in RCC work.

(*e*) Sodium chloride (common salts) lowers the freezing point of water. 1 kg per 170° litres of water can be desolved. A bit more quantity can be used for lower temperatures. Excess of salt decreases the strength. More than 5% salt by weight of cement in injurious for strength and also rusts the reinforcement.

(8) **Fire resistance of concrete.** If the concrete is subjected to high temperature, percentage of quartz (sand) is reduced and use of brick ballast is preferable.

(9) Plastic-fibre-reinforced concrete (Polycrete) is used in sanitary ware like manhole covers (Polycrete Enterprises, Meerut, UP).

Table 8·58. Thermal expansion of concrete.

Type of Aggregate	*Coefficient of thermal expansion for concrete/1°C*
Quartzite	$1{\cdot}2$ to $1{\cdot}3 \times 10^{-5}$
Sand stone	$0{\cdot}9$ to $1{\cdot}2 \times 10^{-5}$
Granite	$0{\cdot}7$ to $0{\cdot}75 \times 10^{-5}$
Basalt	$0{\cdot}8$ to $0{\cdot}95 \times 10^{-5}$
Levive stone	$0{\cdot}6$ to $0{\cdot}9 \times 10^{-5}$

Shrinkage. Concrete after pouring in forms is liable to shrink which depends on size of member and environmental conditions mostly influenced by total amount of water resent in concrete at the time of mixing and to a lesser extent by cement contents. Shrinkage in conc. influences stress in the structure.

(10) **Concrete in sea water.** Sea water effects either continuously as in docks and harbers or alternately wetting and drying as in tides. This has a corrosive effect on the reinforcement as well as on concrete. As a remedial measure the following steps are taken :

(*a*) Use large size of reinforcement 65 mm 475 mm with more covering concrete.

(*b*) Use a rich and well graded mix not less than 1 : 1½ : 3 or M-20 with hard stone ballast. Slag, brick ballast, lime stone soft sand stone or other porous aggregates should not be used.

(*c*) Precast structures are prepared as they are well cured and hard, without sharp corners, trowel smooth and surfaces free from cracks etc.

(*d*) Plastering or rendering is avoided.

(*e*) The faces which are effected by scour or ice, the protection is given by wood seething or by big stone crates or concrete formed big precast blocks.

(*f*) When abrasion is anticipated, bitumen coating can be used.

(*g*) Use of sulphate resisting cement high alumina cement and blast furnace cement is considered better than ordinary portland cement, use of finely powdered pozzolana upto 25% increases resistance to adverse attack.

(*h*) Construction joints should not be given below or above the levels of wave action by 60 cm.

(*i*) All steel and materials should be protected from the direct action of salty atmosphere.

(*ii*) **Concrete on alkaline soil.** Ground water with alkalies (soluble phosphate) are injurious to concrete. The presence of sulphaltes in soil can be estimated by the presence of colour less crystals or formation of white scum or efflorscence on the surface (reh deposite in local language) excavated on drying. However if such scum is not present, it does not mean that phosphates are not there. Further a laboratory test should be taken in doubtful cases. The Remedial measures for overcoming the above are as follows :

(*a*) A concrete mix (1 : 1½ : 3) M-20 having a low water cement ratio should be used with use of low sulphate cements like high alumina cement.

(*b*) Kerocine 10% by weight of cement should be added to the mix mortar.

(*c*) Cover for reinforcement should be increased to 50 mm and for foundation rafts upto 100 mm.

(*d*) Construction joints should be minimised.

(*e*) A protective cover of alkali resistant stones or a cover of Plaster of Paris with jute impregnated with lac is applied.

(12) **Fly ash cement.** Fly ash can be replaced by cement to achieve the same strength 20% of cement can be replaced by 27·5% of fly ash for the same strength. This requires reproportioning of aggregate and water cement ratio. Fine aggregate is reduced by 7·5% weight of cement and coarse aggregate is increased by the same amount.

(13) **Vacuum dewatering.** (Collection of water on surface of concrete). Bleeding on surface develops hollow pores when water is evaporated. Therefore this extra water is removed during laying of concrete in a manner shown in figure, with cloth, wire gauge expanded metal and wood sheeting laid in above sequence and water is then pumped off. It reduces water cement ratio.

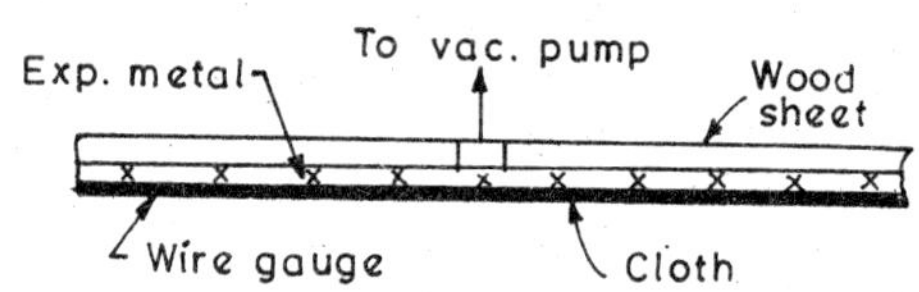

Fig. 8·52.

Concrete encasing R.S. section. R.S. section should not be painted if they are to be encased with concrete. The surface should be cleaned and brushed to remove any rust etc. ungalvanised wire mesh or expended metal, the meshes of which are large enough so as to pass the max. size of aggregate through them, must be wrap round the section. The edges and surface of the section should have a minimum of 50 mm cover and the wraping should pass through the centre of the covering.

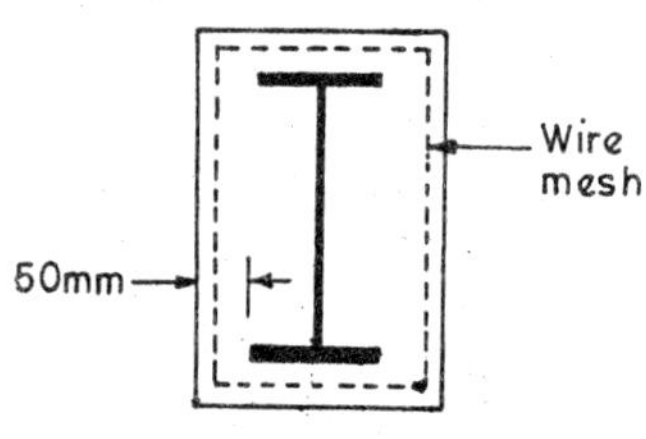

Fig. 8·53.

8·6·23. Sound proofing in concrete. Good acoustical design utilizes both absorptive and reflective surfaces.

Sound Absorption. The amount of sound absorbed by concrete depends upon its porosity. Sound waves reaching a porous surface cause air to flow into and from the surface. The fraction of the air flowing through the pores converts portion of sound energy to heat.

The sound absorption coefficient is an indication of the sound absorbing efficiency of a surface. A surface which could theoretically absorb 100% of impinging sound would have a sound absorption coefficient of 1 similarly a dense, non porous concrete surface (cast in place) typically absorbs 1 to 2% of incident sound and have a coefficient of 0·015.

Noise reduction coefficient (N.R.C.) is calculated by taking a mathematical average of the sound absorption coefficient obtained at frequency of 250, 500, 1000 and 2000 Hertz (CPS). It is expressed to the nearest integral multiple of 0·05. Cast in place concrete would have a NRC of 0·02, while precast units of light weight concrete may have an NRC of as high as 0·60. Where additional sound absorption is desired, cast in place concrete can be coated with spray applied acoustical materials, acoustical tiles can be applied with adhesive or acoustical ceiling can be hung below :

Sound reflection. Many surfaces must be acoustically reflective, not absorptive *i.e.* a panel shell. Hard reflective surfaces on walls and ceilings near the stage in an auditorium, serve as megaphones to direct sound to the audience. Concrete is an excellent material for this.

Air borne sound reaching a wall, floor or ceiling provides vibrations in the wall and is reached with reduced intensity on the other side. The ratio of sound pressure level on the source side to the sound pressure level on the radiating side is known as sound transmission loss (STL). The ratio is expressed in decibels (db).

Carpets and acoustical ceilings can further reduce sound travel by absorbing sound in source and receiving room.

The performance of a building section with an otherwise adequate STL can be seriously reduced by a relatively small hole or any other path which allows sound to bypass the wall. Common flanking paths are openings around doors, pipes, electric boxes and air ducts, suspended ceilings in rooms where walls do not extend from the ceiling to roof or floor above allow sound travel to adjacent rooms. Usually a cm fibre board will provide the desired isolation, when a single concrete wall is used as a sound barrier. It is sometimes desirable to provide a resilient connection between the wall and the building frame to reduce the sound transmission to adjacent wall.

Laterite concrete. Since lateritic soil is abundantly available in India and in other tropical regions of the world, use of these materials for various construction activities could be attempted. From the results it is observed that sand can partially be replaced in concrete without sacrificing its strength. Amount of sand replaced by laterite depends upon the mix proportions—the richer the mix, higher the percentage of sand that can be replaced, 20 percent to 100 percent laterite can be replaced in place of sand, cubes were prepared using three different mix ratios and cured for different curing periods (From 7 to 28 days). Results of the study showed that sand can be replaced by laterite upto 40% in the case of 1 : 15 : 3 mix and upto 20% in the case of 1 : 2 : 4 mix, without affecting any of the properties of the conventional concrete. However the water absorption characteristics of laterite concrete was found to be higher than that of ordinary concrete. The water requirement increases enormously for the same workability of concrete with laterite fines. Further increase in the laterite content decreases the strength and for fully laterized cement concrete the strength in 50% of that of ordinary concrete. The strength of 1 : 3 : 6 mix ratio is decreased by partial or full replacement of sand by laterite soil.

As the grain size of the lateritic soil decreases the compressive strength increases. This was attributed to the increase in cohesive force bending the soil particles. Out of the various curing techniques tried, water curing was found to give highest strength values, while air cured specimen gave the lowest strength values. It is reported that the anchorage bond stress between plain reinforcing bars and laterite concrete. Compares vary well with that of ordinary concrete, but higher than those of light weight concrete.

Impact Noise. Foot steps, dragged chairs, dropped objects, glammed doors and plumbing generate impact noises. Even when air borne sounds are adequately controlled. These can be severe sound impact noise problems.

Electrically conductive floors. Concrete floors in hospital operating rooms and other places, where sparking would be a hazard, may be made electrically conductive with an integral acetylene carbon black admixture, or with specially prepared metallic aggregates or powders which are worked into the fresh concrete surface. For terrazzo work 2% acetylene carbon black by weight of cement has been used satisfactorily in a marble chip topping over a sand bedding course which also contains 3% acetylene carbon black by weight of cement.

8·6·24. Concrete surface finishing

(1) To obtain an even surface after removal of forms hack out (a pointed hammer) all the surface projectors or chip by chiesel. Fill all the crevices by a rich mortar (richer than the original concrete) and let it set for 24 hours. Smooth the surface by a carborandum stone no. 20 and fill any crevices if there by neat cement mortar. Wash the surface after the cement becomes set with soap solution (sunlight soap) wash the surface with equal proportioned cement and quick lime wash snowcem can be applied as a final coat. Quick lime in wash should not be added if the surface is to be snowcemed. 1 kg of common salt mixed with water gives a better result in cement wash.

(2) If the surface is more rough, it should be rendered after giving a coat of 1 : 3 : 10 cement, while lime and sand in 12 mm thickness. This can be done if the surface has not been finally set. If the surface has been set finally, then it should 1st be hacked and then a neat cement slurry should be applied before the rendering is done.

(3) The following protective coats can be applied in all cases. The surface should 1st be cleaned with soap water and wire brushed to remove all loose particles and if any crevices are there, they should be filled with cement sand mortar 1 : 2.

(*a*) **Magnesium or zinc fluosilicate.** The primer coat is prepared with one lb of compound per gallon of water and the subsequent coats are prepared with 2 lbs of chemical with one gallon of water.

(*b*) **Sodium Silicate** (Water glass). It is viscous liquid and is diluted with water three times of its volume. Each coat is allowed to dry for 24 hours before the 2nd is applied. For subsequent coats stronger solutions may be taken. Number of coats should be applied as per site conditions.

For structures under water stronger solution may be taken. 25 litres of liquid is sufficient for furnishing 100 m^2 surface.

(*c*) **Linceed oil.** It is applied hot on dry surface. 2 or 3 coats may be applied. 1st coat should be dry before the 2nd is laid.

(*d*) **Bitumen.** Hot bitumen can be applied in two or three coats.

(*e*) A coat of one kg of calcium chloride with 30 litres of mixing water. Calcium chloride absorbs water from air and hence helps in curing.

(*f*) **Oil paints.** These should be applied when the surface is finally set and there is no need of curing. The surface should be cleaned with zinc sulphate (2 kg to 30 litres of water) and should be free form oil or greases etc. 1st coat should be thin while the subsequent coats may be thicker. Varnishes can also be used for this job.

(*g*) **Cement paints.** The surface is made wet before applying each coat two or three coats may be applied and the surface should be cured for few days, so that the paint may set.

(*h*) Top finish should be done after one hour of laying of concrete, so that excess water on surface may be reduced. A rich mix of 1·2 cement sand with a water proofing compound is spreaded on the surface and is made smooth with long wood or steel plainers or float.

(*i*) A coat of retarding agents should be applied on the form work so that the surface may not finally set when the forms are removed and the final surface may be finished efficiently to have a better bond with the old.

(*j*) The surfaces which are to be plastered or to be brick worked should be roughened after removal of form work.

Architectural surfaces. (*a*) **Exposed aggregate.** Mortar from the surface is removed after the removal of forms and thus an exposed aggregate surface is obtained. Pound aggregates (10 to 25 mm) should be used for the purpose in the concrete.

(*b*) **Rough cost.** A mix of 1 : 6 : 4 (lime, sand shingle 6 mm to 12 mm) is thrown on the surface with a trowel.

(*c*) **Pebble-dash.** A mix of 1 : 1 : 5 cement, lime and sand is applied on the surface in 10 mm thickness. On this mix 6 mm to 12 mm shingle is thrown on the surface when it is still green.

8·6·25. Water proofing of concrete

Water penetrates the concrete in two ways (*i*) when there is hydrostatic pressure on one side of concrete mass. Water travels through continuous channels which ultimately inter connect the two faces of concrete and (*ii*) water may be absorbed by capillary action and travel through the concrete to a face where it evaporates.

The basic solution to reduce voids, number of tunnels and capillaries in concrete is to control water cement ratio alongwith proper mechanical compaction. During hydration the capillaries can get discontinuous or partly blocked due to the formation of 3 $CaO \cdot 2SiO_2 \cdot 3H_2O$ which is called as **Tobermorite** or **Cement gel**. To get this formation of cement gel water cement ratio has to be less than 0·65 to 0·70 above which this product formation in very insufficient and below which it can be proportionately more. Besides this cement gel itself also has very low hydraulic permeability $K_w = 7 \times 10^{14}$ cm/sec. Following these guidelines to attain such conditions and when aided with adequate compaction, it should not be difficult to make a perfectly unpermeable concrete.

Types of integral water proofers. Water proofing admixures can be grouped as :

(*i*) Permeability reducers

(*ii*) Water repellents or hydrophobic (water hating) agents

(*iii*) Others.

Permeability reducers are pore filling and porosity reducing materials which can be further classified into :

(*a*) Very fine particulate matters.

(*b*) Workability air entraining admixures.

(*c*) Accelerators.

Ground sand, lime stone (powdered, bentonite, whiting, P.F.A. dia. tomacceous earths, slag, pumice, colloidal silica, fluoro silicates etc.) are generally available water proofing admixures in the market which are in the powdered form.

It is also preferable that in addition to being fine particles the material has some pozzuolanic character also. This would classify the cement gel due to formation of fine gel of hydrated calcium silicate instead of coarser calcium hydroxide crystals. As mentioned earlier these water proofers are particularly useful if the concrete mix is low cement contents or deficient in fines.

Plasticizers and workability agents obviously avoid the presence of large voids and higher water requirements as per their advocating use. The plasticizers generally work by giving better dispersion of cement and simultaneously reducing the surface tension of the water/aqueous phase. This results into further willing and proper hydration reaction at lesser water requirements.

Similarly air entraining agents also improve workability. In this class, salts of ligno sulphuric acids, ligno sulphonates, urea/napthlene carbohydrates anionic surfactants etc. are involved. Accelerators class of water proofers are considered functionally doubtful as permeability reducers in the long term effect and hence may not be strictly considered as water proofers.

Thus whenever concrete is to be water proofed for external, water pressure user should use the permeability reducer type of admixures and while specifying the product, it should be ascertained from the manufacturer—

(*i*) Besides pore/void filling acation preferably some pozzuolanic reaction also is incorporated in the products.

(*ii*) Plasticizers or air entraining agents also may be formulated in proper dosages and correct discretion.

(*iii*) Plasticizers are mostly sulphonates of various organic compounds and hence a fear of the harmful presence of sulphate ions can not be ruled out. It is mandatory for any user to get the full details about the presence of such harmful ions from the manufacturers and see to it that such determined presence of ions like SO_2, Cl etc. is in the tolerable limits prescribed in various standards :

(*iv*) It shoiuld also be borne in mind that the water proof are useful only in cases of mixes low in cement or deficient in finer. In richer mixes this addition can increase the water demand leading to a less dense and lower strength concrete. Hence it can be inferred that as far as possible such fine particulate water proofers should be used in the plaster coat or top I.P.S. etc. whenever the rich mixes are concerned. This would protect the core concrete from any unwated loss of strength.

Water repellents are another class of products available in the market viz. water repellant or hydrophobies (water hating agents). These compounds generally impart water repellant properties to concrete surface which is due to certain electroplatic charges, impacted to the walls of the concrete. Generally soaps, Butyl, Slearate emulsion and some petroleum products etc. comprise this class.

Water proofing surface coating. Another important classes of water proofing aids are polymeric elastometric sealants and water proofing polymeric coatings.

ACI committe 515 defines—*Water proofing as a treatment of surface or structure to prevent the passage of water under hydrostatic pressure and membrane water proofing consists of surrounding the entire structure with a continuous barrier.* The purpose is to prevent leakage into a usable space or to prevent loss of water from a retaining structure.

To dry surface applied protection membrane (5 apm) is the most modern techniques for the water proofing of buildings and the market all over the world including India. The popularity of these products is due to the simple application procedure and guaranteed results. Surface preparation is thorough and coating is protected by another course of cement some screed or tile etc.

Most of these products are based on epoxies, polyurethenes, silicons, acrylics. Isochloroprenes, polysulphates either used individually or formulated together, of these one pack systems get cured/dried by solvent evaporates or atmospheric air curing.

Few of these systems are available in two packs *i.e.*, resin and curing agents. These chemically cross linked polymers are indeed very tough and water resistant but they are reported to have a few handicaps as well which certainly demand due attention.

(*i*) After chemical cross linking it is reported that the film contracts upto 3 to 4% ; This may result in lifting up of film on a very large scale.

(*ii*) Since this is a two pack system the chemical cross linking process starts at the zero time when the curing agent is added to resin. Hence when the actual application is going on, the material applied at, say zero time, quarters time, half time and then at the end will be different in efficiencies/characteristics, which is due to their various degrees of curing at that particular time.

(*iii*) For the applicator also in such cases the spoilt undesirable brushes means heavy loss. Besides due negligence, delay on the part of painter leads to semi gelling of the material which is either a total loss to the user or in an attempt to somehow apply this semi gelled material. The requisite designed properties would not be achieved by the surface.

(*iv*) Fully dry and thoroughly clean surface is the prime need if any polymer coating either two pack or single pack with air blowers.

(*v*) Extra efforts and additions should be made in the pigmentation to stabilize these coatings from detrimental effect of U.V. radiation.

The worldwide trend is to modify the products property to one pack system. The definite trend is also seen that the systems are often made water based instead of solvent based. This reduces the cost as well as various hazards like fire and pollution etc. Hence for proper choice these sealants and coatings can offer various advantages like ;

(*i*) Total water proofing when applied from the side of hydrostatic pressure.

(*ii*) Can be given any decorative colour if needed thereby obviating additional cost of external painting.

(*iii*) Unlike other external paints such coatings do not catch fungus etc.

(*iv*) They are generally fire resistant, though in few cases evolution of some abnoxious gases is found to be reported.

(*v*) These coatings are U. V. radiation stabilized.

(*vi*) Longer life.

Water proofing can be improved by :

(1) Proper grading of ingradients

(2) Less water cement ratio (0·54 or less)

(3) Fineness of cement

(4) Non porous aggregates

(5) Well mixing, uniform placing, thorough compaction.

(6) Proper curing

(7) Less use of air entraining agents like aluminium powder, which makes the concrete porous due to bubble formation.

Following admixtures also increase water tightness. Their proportioning should be tested at site or as directed by the maker.

(*a*) Addition of fully slacked white lime (hydrated) in the proportions

1 : 2 : 4 concrete 10% by weight of cement

1 : 2½ : 5 concrete 15% by weight of cement

It also increases the workability.

(*b*) The volumes of fines should be a slight more than requirement.

(*c*) Addition of talk, sodium silicate, calcium chloride or soap solution. They are available either in powder or in liquid form. One kg of washing soda with 30 litres of water gives a water proof mortar

(*d*) Cico and other commercial products dealt in the following paras.

Surface water proofing. Surface of the outer faces of walls, cellers (basements), bed of rafts laid under spring level and roofs of buildings are treated with surface water proofers. They are waxes, fats, pudlo, resins, vegetable oils, coal tar or bitumen.

They are applied either in hot molten state or by mixing some volatile solvent on the surface, which is thoroughly cleaned brushed and washed if necessary. They are suitably pressed on the surface so as to fill the pores in the surface.

Boiled linseed oil, paraffin or varnish can be brushed on the surface when the concrete has been well cured and dried. Any pores in surface should be filled with cement mortar and should be cloth cleaned to remove any loose particle.

Floors should be sprinkled with neat cement and should be plained to give a smooth surface.

A membrane called the tarfelt produced by jute clothes soaked in bitumen is also used on surfaces. These tar felts are sold in market and are used for base of rafts laid under spring level and on sides of concrete structures as detailed below :

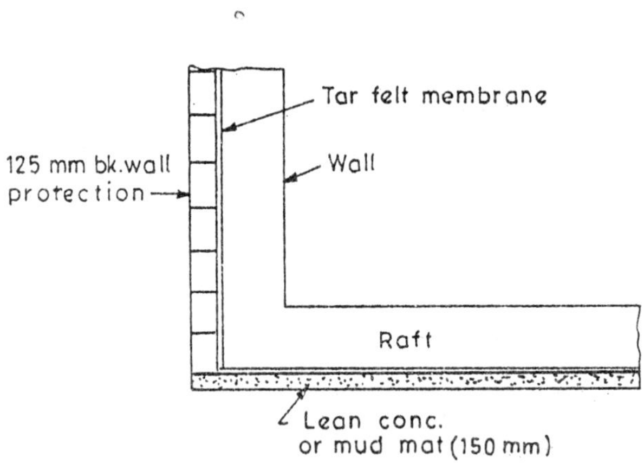

Fig. 8·54.

The surface is cleaned with wire brush. A hot coat of bitumen is laid on the surface over a primary coat. The tarfelt sheet is also coated with bitumen and then it is pasted on the face so produced. More than one layer can be applied to achieve the degree of water lightness required beased on the head of water pressure on the face or the presence of the corrosive salts in the adjoining soil.

The joints horizontal or vertical of the tarfelt should be staggered in each layer and also must have a proper overlap at least 15 cm. There should be no gap or hole in the tarfelt sheet. As even a single hole will make the whole surface ineffective.

Commercial products of water proofing.

Keeping the structural dynamics in mind, water proofing material selected for treatment to leaky structures should have the following characteristics : good adhesion, elasticity greater than that of the member, vapour permeability but impervious to water, resistance to aberration, resistance to chloride and sulphate attack in aggressive environmental conditions and case of application to eliminate applicator error or contractor resistance.

Dichtament DS water proofing system. Comprises mineral based hydraulically set powder, dichtament DS and a liquid polymer component Nafufill BB2. The liquid compound should be mixed with water and then this mixture should be added to the powder until a slurry consistency is obtained. This slurry can be applied to concrete or masonry surfaces by means of paint brushes or rollers. The coated surfaces should be cured. In case of terraces and sanitary areas this coat should be used as sandwich coat before carrying out subsequent treatments like brick bat coba or patent stone tiling etc. For further details contact :

MC-Bauchemic (India) Pvt. Ltd., Sangli Bank Bldg. 296 Perin Nariman Street Fort, Mumbai-400001.

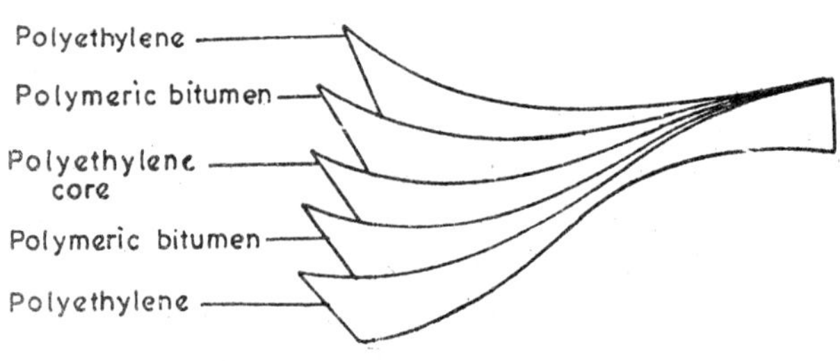

Fig. 8·55. Bituflex polymer filt.

Bituflex polymer felt is an alternative to conventional hession based bitumen felt. It is an elastic polymer membrane made from polymerized bitumen sandwiched between 2 polyethelene layers having a central core of elastomeric polymer. It is laid in conventional way *i.e.* with hot bitumen of 85/25 grade. Thickness is 1 mm-4 mm. It has excellent resistance to ultra violet rays and atmospheric hazards. For details contact :

Greensboro Polychem Pvt. Ltd., 199 Defence Colony Flyover Commercial Complex, New Delhi-110024.

Cico Polygrout is a water reactive chemical grout. Basically it is a low viscosity liquid which reacts with water instantly and forms a foam. The expended foam is microcellular in structure and forms a water barrier. As it expands the foam fills up the cavity where it comes in contact with water and seals it effectively. The rate of reaction and gel time can be controlled by using an accelerator.

Cico polygrout is generally pumped as a single component through low pressure pumps. Due to its low viscosity and expansion during reaction even the smallest cracks, fissures and pores can be impregnated. For details contact :

The Structural Waterproofing Co. Pvt. Ltd. 406 Deepali, 92, Nehru Place, New Delhi-110019.

Cico Aquakem is a two component water based epoxy sealer membrane coating system, specially meant for curing seepage and dampness problem on interior and exterior surfaces.

It gives an excellent finish on the concrete and provides an ideal waterproofing membrane on the concrete floor slabs undercarpets. It retains its flexibility and plasticity and never becomes hard or brittle, which makes it suitable for both interior and exterior application. It has superb adhesion and makes a monolithic bonding on neatly prepared surfaces. It can also be applied on steel and timber.

It is offered in two packs, off white and transparent. Thermal properties can be improved by applying off white Aquakem as it has excellent reflection properties. It is manufactaured by :

The Structural Waterproofing Co. Pvt. Ltd., 406, Deepali, 92, Nehru Place, New Delhi-110019.

Roff Hyguard is a two component polymer modified acrylic cementitious system. It needs on site mixing of the components in the proportion in which they are packed and brush applied to the structure. This does not require curing or further protection. A Hyguard heated surface is suitable for subsequent painting or any decorations and can also be plastered if need be. It has good adhesion properties. For details consult :

Roffe Construction Chemicals Pvt. Ltd., 12C Vikas Centre, S.V. Road, Santacruz (W) Bombay-400054.

Roofix 2000 is a one component product based on modified polymers and free from tar, bitumen and solvents the product supplied in paste like consistency can be applied on cementitious substrates by means of paint brushes or rollers after one coat of primer, Primex 250. The dried coat forms a seamless membrane which is flexible and elastic in nature having a breaking elongation 82%. The coat while still retaining the breathing properties of concrete is resistant to UV rays and does not crack or flake after multiple thermal cycles. It has no pot life considerations. The non toxic production prevents fungus, moss and root growth and therefore very suitable for terrace gardens and underground structures. For details :

M.C. Bauchemic (India) Pvt. Ltd. Mumbai.

Plastofelt is installed by welding a self finished polyster based felt saturated with modified bitumen using a gas flame torch elastomeric system is cold applied, comprising three components *viz.*, a polymer mat sandwiched between two coats of elast-alumin which gives the system a bright aluminium finish. For details STP Ltd, 13th Floor, Shanti Niketan, 8 Camel Street, Kolkata-110017.

Tuffseal. The adhere well with all common building materials, perform well at extreme temperatures and allow 50% joint movement. Totally impervious to water, petro-products, alkalies and mild acids. They remain intact and flexible even after years of exposure. Application of "Tuffseal" includes, expansion joints, construction joints, cracks, window/door fixing, glazing, roofing and floor joints, water tanks etc. For details :

Hindocha Brothers Pvt. Ltd., 25 Rue Francis Martin, P.O. Box No. 85, Pondicherry-605001.

Full Stop is acrylic modified vinyl spray on waterproofing. It is one component water based product with a high coverage area and is applied as a spray to rapidly form a light weight, seamless, impermeable membrane on surfaces of all types such as concrete, brick, wood, metal and asbestos sheeting. It protects walls, ceilings, roofs, storage, tanks, industrial vessels, dams and irrigation channels. It withstands temperature fluctuations and resistant to ultra-violet rays. It resists industrial pollutants and impervious to acidic and alkaline compounds. For details :

Anil Chemicals Ltd., Abinay Theatre Complex, Aurangabad-431001.

Misiwa SH—is cementitiousis water based colourless, hydrophobic property on silicone basis. It is perform solvents, possesses deep penetrating effect and is delivered in ready-to-use consistency. It prevents efflorescence and fungus growth. It can be applied by soft brush or by spraying. It is effective 1-2 hours after application. M.C. Bauchemic (India) Pvt. Ltd. Mumbai.

Liquid Polysulphide Polymers (LP). Used in expansion and construction joints and bindings etc. due to their properties of adhesion, flexibility, chemical resistence, water proofing and protection from ultra-violet rays. For details :

Overseas Water proofing Corporation, A-45, Hauz Khas, New Delhi-110016.

Polysulphide based sealants—are a two part system of cold applied compounds which come in thick pasty form and are chemically cured to form a firm synthetic rubber. The two parts are the base and the accelerator, which are mixed thoroughly, and the system cures chemically after mixing. This sealant becomes tough dry on the surface within 48 hours and takes eight days for a full cure. It comes in two forms, gun grade and pour grade. The gun grade is used for vertical, inclined and overhead applications, while the pour grade is used for horizontal applications. For details :

Overseas Waterproofing Corporation, A-45 Hauz Khas, New Delhi-110016.

Rigid and Flexible Waterproofing

Rigid water proofing renderings. These renderings are coatings of cement sand mortar (1 : 2 or 1 : 3) of 2·5 to 4 cm thickness, consisting of several individual layers of approximately 8-10 mm each to which admixtures are added like **Acro I/Water seal or equivalent**. The admixture helps to fill the pores in the mortar with hydrophobers.

When the cement grains are hydrated, the water repellent admixtures react with the water proof admixtures forming insoluble dry soap which covers the capillery walls. Water soaking to enter the capilleries is repelled and looses so much of pressure that it is prevented from passing. The rendering however breathes, therefore no vapour pressure can build up and rendering does not burst. It should be done after having the surface sufficiently roughed.

Flexible membrane water proofing are very useful on concrete roofs, underground concrete structures, channels and terrace water proofing compounds.

Repellin S101. For a protective finish on the surface which repels water. Water just slides off and the surface remains dry. It is a clear, colourless, silicone based finish. Since it does not block the pores of the surface, water that is already in the surface can escape in the form of water vapours even after repellin is applied. Hair line cracks upto 0·3 mm width are effectively bridged by Repellin S101 coat. It repels water and also dirt which washes away by rain and surface remain clean.

Pidicrete LW. It has good plasticizing properties, makes concrete cohesive and prevents segregation. It saves upto 10% water causing less water cement ratio. It is easily soluble in water and ensures homogeneous mix.

Aquashield SW201. It is a silicone based integral water proofing additive. When its powder is thoroughly mixed, its fine particles get uniformly distributed through the whole depth of plaster and concrete. Only 100 gms of it is required for 30 kg of cement.

Pidifin RGD. It is ready to use single component cement bound surface sealing compound. It can be used against **ground moisture seeping, leakages of the roof** and water reservoirs etc. It forms a rigid film suitable for areas not subjected to cyclic movements. For areas subjected to cyclic movements it is made durable and elastic by adding Pidicrete B, being polymer based, Pidicrete B retains water in mix for a longer period. The bond is through molecular attractions causing a bond between the new and old surface. For details :

Pidilite Industries Ltd., Regent Chambers, 7th floor Jamna Lal Bajaj Marg, Nariman Point, Mumbai-400021.

Unisil Silicone Sealants. It is workable under wider range of temperature (65°C to 200°C) and inert to weather, rain, snow U.V.R. and ozone extremes. These materials do not harden, crack, crumble dryout or become brittle with age. It remain elastic for 20 years. They can with stand chemical attack. For sealing of gaps in roof ridges plumbing, nut bolt sealing, window glazing and showcases etc. these are the ideal products. For details consult :

M/s Universal Silicones and Lubricants Pvt. Ltd., 406, Amit Industrial Estate, 61, Dr. S.S. Rao Road, Parel, Mumbai-400012.

Sikadur 53 is an epoxy which sets under water by displacing moisture.

"Qualitex" acrylic based chemicals along with neat cement slurry in to the structures is injected. These chemicals are soluble in water and hence can penetrate minutest of the cracks and run through entire thickness of the structure. On gelation these chemicals form an impermeable barrier which renders the structure water tight permanently. Even a hydrostatic gravity pressure is sufficient in normal cases however in few cases where (*i*) subsoil water pressure is high (*ii*) thickness of concrete is more we inject the grout with help of mechanised pumps to ensure full penetration in the entire thickness. The injection process is as below :

Step I : Holes about 65 mm dia. and 65·75 mm deep are chiselled about 1 to 1·5 m apart. Nozzles are then fixed in these holes with cement slurry.

Step II : After the nozzles are set for about 24 hours, neat cement slurry mixed with **Qualitex** is injected through these nozzles by gravity pressure or by mechanised pumps as per site requirements so as to reach in the entire thickness.

Step III : The nozzles are either removed or should be grouted by the slurry and the pressure must be remain continued till the slurry sets and attains strength. The surface should now be plastered.

The proportion of the chemicals to ordinary port cement/pozzolana cement shall be 2% by weight. The nozzles may be of G.I. pipe or of aluminium. For details contact :

Foamcrete Insulators, C-4A/53C, Janakpuri, New Delhi-110058.

Grout seal—Cement Water Proofing Chemical for RCC and subsoil.

Water—Water Proofing Consultants, 531 Matia Mahal, Delhi-110006.

Commercial Products for accelerators, Retarders, water proofing, anti-corrosive for rebars and form releasing agents etc. (Directory of Manufacturers) :

(1) **The Ferrosite Company.** 2-Cockbum Lane—Royal Street, Kolkata-16.

Ferrogrout—Non shrinking high strength grout ; Accelerex—Early strength; Retarix—Retarding agent ; Plastex—for workability ; Alastex—Air entraining agent ; Pumpex—Concrete by pumps ; Monolithex—For repair ; Ferroseal—water proofing ; Efflore six—Saltpetre resistive in plaster ; Forrosite—Abrasion resistant and hard surfaces.

(2) **Acro Construction Acids Pvt. Ltd.**—Munshi Niketan, 1/10-B, Asaf Ali Road, New Delhi-110002.

Acro 1—Integral water proofer in liquid (IS : 2645)

Acro 2—Leak plugging in liquid ; Water seal—integral water proofer powder ; Acro seal—Acrylic water proofer ; Acrocrete—Polymer water proofer for cementations surfaces ; Acrofex—water proofing polymer membrane in paste.

Acrocote—Polymer water proofing slurry coating (in 2 packs).

Acroflo—Concrete plasticize and water reducing admixture.

Acroflo AEA—Air entraining agent ; Acrocure—Liquid membrane curing compound ; Acronite—Abrasion resistant and floor hardner ; Acrogrip—Tile adhesive (In two packs).

(3) **Jagat Colour and Chemicals**

Wet seal—water proofer ; Supersonic—Rapid hardner ; Fastonate—Concrete hardness and water proofer ; Jaycor—Acid resistant, super set rapid hardner ; Crack fill—Expansion filler ; Furset—Fire resistant ; Superceme—Decorative water proofing cement coating ; Lion brand—cement colour ; Artcrete—Coloured cement.

(4) **MC-Bauchemic (India Pvt. Ltd.),** Sangli Bank Building, 5th floor, 296, Perin Nariman Street, Fort, Mumbai-400001.

Mould release agents, concrete admixtures, polymer binding agents, curing compounds, water proofers, tile adhesives, surface retarders, floor hardner, dirt proofers, Non shrink high strength grouts and repair products.

(5) **STP Ltd.,** 8 Comel Street, Kolkata-17.

Water proofers, Road surfacing, Floor topping, Pipe coating, corrosion protection, sealants and adhesives.

(6) **Rofte Construction Chemicals Pvt. Ltd.,** 47 Akshaya III, Main, Ist Cross road, Dumlur, II Phase, Banglore.

(7) **Om Agro Industrial Plastics Pvt. Ltd.,** 6-Sarvodaya Industrial Estate, Maha Kali Canes Road, Andheri, East Chakla, Mumbai-93.

Omaxrylic. Polymer water proofing, Omaiplas AB-Polymer cementitious water proofing compound ; Omaicrete—polymer mortar for rehabilitation of structures and constructing seamless flooring, grouting foundation bolts and for wet surfaces.

Lustrecam. Polymer adhesives for cement bases curing not required ; Omai Plus EP 901—Epoxy compound for grouting crack structures under water ; Omai seal-Epoxy Putty for sealing leakages of pipe lines ; Omaiseal 622—Epoxy Putty for sealing cracks under water.

Omai seal 702—Polymer based sealant for filling cracks tile seal for tile joints.

(8) **Greensboro Polychem Pvt. Ltd.,** 199, Defence Colony, Flyover Commercial Complex, New Delhi-110024.

Polydee 10—Prevents leakage ; Siltrex—colourless water repellent treatment ; Polydee Floor Patch—repair poth holes in concrete and RCC requires no water for curing, quick setting ; Grout Fast—quick grout. Polydee Floor Coating—Corrosion resistant ; Polydee 40—Rubberised clay to metric sealant ; Sitrografin—colourless water seal.

(9) **Sika Products**—Concrete admixtures, form releasing agents, curing compounds, surface retarders, water proofers, Bonding and air entraining agents, expanding grouts, synthetic resin products, Abrasives. Sika Qualcrete Ltd., 20-B, Park street, Calcutta-700016.

(10) **The Structural Water Proofing Co. Pvt. Ltd.,** "Cico House" 21/1, Dover Road, Bally Gaunga, Kolkata-700019.

(11) **Asian Laboratories (India)** 88, New Okhla, Industrial Area Complex, New Delhi-110020.

Quickcrete—Fast setting, Non-shrinking.

Shrink Kamp grouts—Expand and grip.

Poly proof—Concrete additive, accelerator, Retarder and water proof.

Poly bond—Bonding new to old concrete in construction joints.

Lik Gunite—Water proofer ; Asian MRA—Form releasing agent.

Poly seal—Epoxy Putty.

(12) **Fosroc Chemicals (India Ltd.),** Shankar House, IV Floor, Mehkri circle, Bangalore-560080

For zinc rich epoxy primer for protection of rebars and other admixtures.

9

(A) Reinforced Concrete Structure (Simple Stress)

9A.1. Principles of design

t = tensile strength of steel (allowable)

c = compressive strength of concrete in bending

m = modular ratio

$$= \frac{\text{mod. elasticity of steel}}{\text{mod. elasticity of conc.}} = \frac{E_s}{E_c}$$

$$= \frac{2800}{3c} = \frac{2800}{3 \times 50} = 18.7 \text{ (I.S.) for concrete mix M-150, having}$$

compressive bending stress 50 kg/cm^2

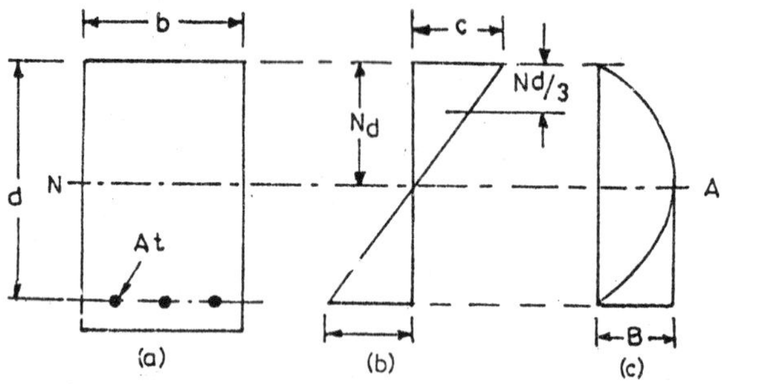

(a) Beam section (b) Bending stress (c) Shear stress

Fig. 9A·1.

where b = width of beam

d = effective depth of beam

N = coefficient of neutral axis $= \frac{1}{1 + t/mc} = \frac{c}{c + t/m}$

J = coefficient of lever arm = 1 – N/3

Q = Resisting moment = ½NCJ

$M = Qbd^2$ Moment of Resistance ...(1)

$A_t = \frac{M}{tjd}$ where A_t = area of steel in tension ...(2)

Shear reinforcement. Intensity of shear stress $S = \frac{F}{bjd}$ ...(3)

where F = S.F. on the section.

If s is within allowable limits then no shear reinforcement is given. If it is more than that allowable stress then shear reinforcement is given as below.

Say, the extra shear force taken by the shear reinforcement is F_s. Then

$$F_s = \frac{A_s \times t \times d}{P}(\sin \phi + \cos \phi) \quad ...(4)$$

where A_s = Area of shear reinforcement in one sec.

t = Tensile stress allowable for steel and which is equal to the allowable shear stress for the steel.

d = effective depth of section.

P = pitch length of the shear reinforcement

ϕ = angle of crank (or crack) due to shear with N.A.

or $P = \frac{A_s.t.d}{F_s}(\sin \phi + \cos \phi)$; $F_s = F - (s.b.jd)$ s being allowable shear stress for 90° angle, the value of $\sin \phi + \cos \phi$ will be 1.

9A.2. Provision of shear reinforcements

(1) Bars which are not required by tension is curtailed a bit away where it is required in the compression zone at an angle 30° in shallow beams to, 45° in deep beams.

The number and spacing of bars available for bending up can be located by the B.M. diagrams. The bars which are bent up can be utilized for –ve B.M. at supports. The bent up part should be deeper than the lever arm *Jd*. Bars which are bent up for shear should not be more than the half of the total tension bars.

Using expression (1) and (2) depth of beam and area of tensile steel can be calculated $x = l/2\ (n_1/n)^{1/2}$; where x = distance from mid span to point of curtailment ; l = effective span, n_1 is no. of bars bent and n = no. of total bars in tension zone.

(2) **By vertical stirrups.** Two legged, four legged or multi-legged. Two and four legged are used in beams and columns while multi legged in slabs. Shear bars in columns are also known as *binders*. Their mode of embedment should be looping around the tension bars. The stirrups can be used with bent-up bars with proper account of shear taken by each. The total area of vertical or slanting sections is considered to take the shear. If there is no bars in top, nominal supporting bars can be provided.

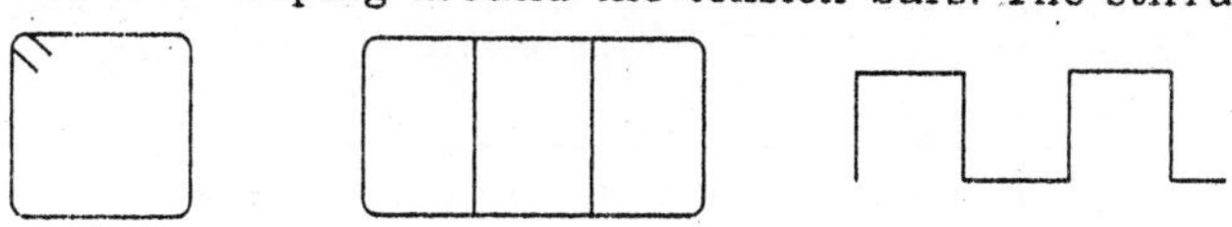

TWO LEGGED FOUR LEGGED MULTI LEGGED

Fig. 9A·2.

9A.3. Bending moment in slabs and beams

Distributed load

(*a*) Simply supported $= \frac{Wl^2}{8}$ at centre (+)

$= \frac{Wl^2}{24}$ at support (–)

(*b*) One end simply supported other fixed or continuous $= \frac{Wl^2}{10}$ at $D/4$ from centre towards free end (+)

$\frac{Wl^2}{24}$ on supports which is free (–)

$\frac{Wl^2}{24}$ on fixed or continuous supports (–)

(*c*) Both ends fixed or continuous = $\frac{Wl^2}{12}$ at centre (+)

$\frac{Wl^2}{12}$ at support (–)

where l is the effective span of the slab (Refer basic rules for designing of beams and slabs)

Impact and vibration allowance (IS : 875 – 1964).

(1) For frames supporting lifts and hoists 100%

(2) For foundations, footing and piers, supporting lifts and hoisting apparatus 40%

(3) For light machines, shaft or motor (Min.) 20%

(4) For reciprocating machines of power units (min.) 50%

9A.4. Basic rules for the design of beams and slabs (IS : 456-1964)

(1) **Effective span**

(*a*) **Freely supported.** Distance between the centres of the supports or the clear distance between the supports plus the effective depth of the beam or slab which ever is smaller.

(*b*) **Continuous.** Where the width of the middle supports is less than 1/12th of the clear span, the rule mentioned above will be followed, when the width of the mid supports is greater than 1/12th of the clear span. The following rules should be followed.

(*i*) In case of fixed at ends, the effective span shall be the clear distance between the supports.

(*ii*) The effective span for the end span of a continuous beam or slab with one end free and the other is continuous, shall be equal to the clear span plus half of the effective depth.

2. **Slab thickness.** The ratio of span to over all depth should not exceed the following rules. However the thickness of floor or roof slab shall not be less than 9 cm.

Sl. No.	*Type of slab*	*Max. value of effective span/over all depth*
1.	Simply supported slab spanning in one direction	30
2.	Continuous slab spanning in one direction	35
3.	Simply supported slab spanning in two directions	35
4.	Continuous slab spanning in two directions	40
5.	Cantilever slabs	12

3. Beam dimensions. The depth of beam for normal loading conditions should be assumed to be 1/20th of the clear span. In the interest of economy the width of a beam should vary for height 3/4th of its depth. For safe in stiffness, the ratio of the span to over all depth should not exceed the following.

Sl. No.	*Type of beam*	*Max. value of effective span/overall depth*
1.	Simply supported beams	20
2.	Continuous beams	25
3.	Cantilever beams	10

(4) **Minimum reinforcement in slabs.** The minimum area of reinforcement (shrinkage and temperature distribution or main reinforcement) to be provided in either direction not be less than :

(*a*) 0.15% of the gross sectional area of concrete where plain bars are used as reinforcement.

(*b*) 0.12% of the gross cross-sectional area of the concrete, where high yield strength deformed bars or welded wire fabric is used as reinforcement.

(5) **Minimum reinforcement in beams.** The minimum area of tensile reinforcement should not be less than :

(*a*) 0.3% of the gross cross-sectional area when plain mild steel bars are used as reinforcement.

(*b*) 0.20% of the gross cross-sectional area when high yield strength deformed bars are used as reinforcement.

(6) **Maximum compressive reinforcement in beams.** The amount of the compressive steel should not exceed 0.4% of the gross cross sectional area.

(7) **Bar sizes.** The dia. of the main reinforcement must not be less than 6 mm nor greater than 50 mm. The dia. of stirrups or distribution, temperature or shrinkage bars not be less than 5 mm, although bars less than 6 mm dia. are seldom used.

(8) **Distance between bars.** (*a*) The minimum distance between two parallel main bars must not be less than the dia. of the bar (in case of the unequal dia. bars, the dia. of larger bar is considered) or 6 mm greater than the maximum size of the coarse aggregate used in concrete, which ever is greater.

(*b*) In case where main bars are provided in two or more layers, the minimum vertical clearance between any two layers shall normally be 15 mm or the maximum size of the coarse aggregate or the maximum size of the bar which ever is greater.

(*c*) The pitch of the main tensile bars in slabs should not exceed three times of the effective depth of the slab or 60 cm which ever is smaller. The pitch of the distribution, temperature or shrinkage bars in the slab shall not exceed five times the effective depth of the slab or 60 cm which ever is smaller.

(9) **Clear cover.** (*a*) In slabs it should not be less than 13 mm or the dia. of the bar which ever is greater.

(*b*) In beams for long bases it should not be less than 25 mm or the dia. of the bar which- ever is greater.

(*c*) The clear cover at each end of bar in beams or slabs should not be less than 25 mm or twice the dia. of the main bar which ever is greater.

(*d*) Where the beam or slab is in contact with earth faces or moisture is subjected to corrosive condition. The cover should be increased between 1.5 mm and 40 mm over and above the values provided in (*a*, *b* and *c*) above.

(10) **Shear in beams.** (*a*) The intensity of shear stress should not exceed 4 times the safe permissible stress for the grade of concrete used.

(*b*) The dia. of the stirrups used shall not be less than 5 mm and their spacing should not exceed the lever arm of the beam. Even if the beam is safe, shear nominal stirrups should be provided throughout the length at a spacing not more than lever arm of the beam (*c.g.* of tension bars to c.g. of compressive bars denoted by jd.)

(*c*) In beams with compressive reinforcement the spacing of the stirrups for the compressive reinforcement should not exceed 16 times the dia. of the anchored bar or 48 times the dia. of the anchoring bar which ever is less. The dia. of the stirrups should not be less than 1/4 times the dia. of the anchored bar.

(*d*) Where steel beam theory has been used for calculating the compressive reinforcement, the spacing of the stirrups should not exceed 8 times the dia. of the compressive bar.

(11) **Bond and anchorage reinforcement.** (*a*) Every bar either in compression or tension should be extended by 12 times the dia. of the bar or 23 cm which ever is more, beyond the point where it is no longer required to resist bending.

(*b*) At the end of every bar an anchorage should be provided which may be in the form of a semi circular standard hook or by introducing 90° bend (L-hook)

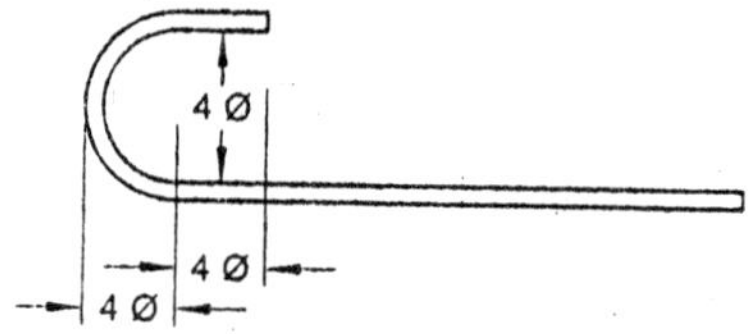

Fig. 9A·3.

The anchorage value of the standard semi circular hook and L hook is taken as 16 and 6 times dia. of the hooked bars respectively.

(12) **Curtailment of bars.** The main bars in beams or slabs may be curtailed or bent up where they are no longer required for bending moment purposes. In a beam at least 25% of the main tensile bars must be extended beyond the support for a distance equal to or greater than minimum bond length. The distance from the centre of beam where a particular rod can be curtailed as calculated by the formula $x = l/2\sqrt{n_1/n}$ where x = distance of the point from mid span where a rod is to be cut or curtailed.

l = effective span of the beam, n_1 = no. of bars to be curtailed and

n = total nos. of bars available at mid span for tension zone.

(13) **Laps in bars.** The laps if any should be provided in a staggered manner.

(1) For bars in tension—the minimum lap should be greater of the followings :

(*a*) 30 dia. of the bar

(*b*) $\dfrac{\text{dia. of the bar} \times \text{actual compressive stress in bar}}{\text{5 times permissible average bond stress}}$

(14) **Weight of R.C.C.** The weight of RCC will be taken as 2400 Kg/m^3

(15) **Modular ratio.** $m = \dfrac{2812}{3C}$, C = maximum permissible compressive stress due to bending in the grade of conc. in Kg/cm^2

(16) **General design requirements** (*a*) Longitudinal reinforcement for direct bending stress.

(*b*) Sectional area of concrete to take direct compressive stress caused by B.M.

(*c*) Provision for anchorage for bonding.

(*d*) Shear reinforcement to be provided to keep the shearing well in permissible stress.

(16) **Causes of failure of R.C. beams.** (*a*) Excessive tension more than the provision of long bars.

(*b*) Excessive compressive stress in concrete than the safe permissible.

(*c*) Excessive shear.

(*d*) Slippage of bars due to lack of anchorage.

(*e*) Bed quality of materials, change of climate conditions and aggressive type of gases or liquids in contact.

9A.5. General data of RC structures

Table 9A.1. Coefficients for rectangular beams

C Kg/cm^2	m	t = 1300 Kg/cm^2			t = 1400 Kg/cm^2			t = 1900 Kg/cm^2		
		Q	N	J	Q	N	J	Q	N	J
50	19	9·07	0·422	0·859	8·74	0·404	0·865	7·41	0·333	0·888
70	13	12·43	0·411	0·862	11·98	0·393	0·868	10·51	0·323	0·892
85	11	15·30	0·418	0·860	14·75	0·400	0·866	12·48	0·329	0·890
100	9	17·67	0·409	0·863	17·01	0·391	0·869	14·35	0·321	0·892
115	8	20·54	0·414	0·861	19·79	0·396	0·867	16·72	0·326	0·891
130	7	23·09	0·411	0·862	22·24	0·393	0·868	18·78	0·323	0·892

9A.2. Permissible shear stress in concrete N/mm². IS : 456-1978

100·As/bd	M-15	M-20	M-25	M-30	M-35	M-40
0·25	0·22	0·22	0·23	0·23	0·23	0·23
0·50	0·29	0·30	0·31	0·31	0·31	0·32
0·75	0·34	0·35	0·36	0·37	0·37	0·38
1·00	0·37	0·39	0·40	0·41	0·42	0·42
1·25	0·40	0·42	0·44	0·45	0·45	0·46
1·50	0·42	0·45	0·46	0·48	0·49	0·49
1·75	0·44	0·47	0·49	0·50	0·52	0·52
2·00	0·44	0·49	0·51	0·53	0·54	0·55
2·25	0·44	0·51	0·53	0·55	0·56	0·57
2·50	0·44	0·51	0·55	0·57	0·58	0·60
2·75	0·44	0·51	0·56	0·58	0·60	0·62
3·00 and above	0·44	0·51	0·57	0·60	0·62	0·63

As is the area of tension steel, b = width and d = effective depth.

Max shear stress in N/mm²

	1·6	1·8	1·9	2·2	2·3	2·5

Table 9A.3. Design Shear stress in concrete N/mm²

0·25	0·35	0·36	0·36	0·37	0·37	0·38
0·50	0·46	0·48	0·49	0·50	0·50	0·51
0·75	0·54	0·56	0·57	0·59	0·59	0·60
1·00	0·60	0·62	0·64	0·66	0·67	0·68
1·25	0·64	0·67	0·70	0·71	0·73	0·74
1·50	0·68	0·72	0·74	0·76	0·78	0·79
1·75	0·71	0·75	0·78	0·80	0·82	0·84
2·00	0·71	0·79	0·82	0·84	0·86	0·88

Table contd.

Table contd.

2·25	0·71	0·81	0·85	0·88	0·90	0·92
2·50	0·71	0·82	0·88	0·91	0·93	0·95
2·75	0·71	0·82	0·89	0·94	0·96	0·98
3·00	0·71	0·82	0·92	0·96	0·99	1·01

Maximum shear stress is N/mm^2

	2·5	2·8	3·1	3·5	3·7	4·0

For solid slabs the design shear strength for concrete shall be K_s where K is a coefficient given below and s is given in table above.

Overall depth of slab (mm)	300 or more	275	250	225	200	175	150 or less
value of K	1·00	1·05	1·10	1·15	1·20	1·25	1·30

Permissible stress in direct tension (when tension is taken by reinforcement alone)

Grade of conc.	*M-10*	*M-15*	*M-20*	*M-25*	*M-30*	*M-35*	*M-40*
Tensile stress μ/mm^2	1·2	2·0	2·8	3·2	3·6	4·0	4·4

Table 9A·4· Coefficients for slab and beams.

C	*t*	*m*	*N*	*J*	*P*	*Q*
50 Kg/cm^2	1400	18·7	0·400	0·810	0·00712	8·7
60 Kg/cm^2	1400	15·55	0·375	0·875	0·00803	9·8
70 Kg/cm^2	1400	13·33	0·400	0·867	0·0010	12·1
80 Kg/cm^2	1400	11·70	0·400	0·867	0·0114	13·9

Table 9A.5. Nominal conc. mix ratios, their grade and water requirement.

Mix. ratio	*Grade*	*Modular ratio*	*Type of work*	*Water required per bag cement*
1 : 6 : 12	M-50		Mass conc. in foundation etc.	70 litres
1 : 5 : 10	M-50		Mass conc. in foundation etc.	60 litres
1 : 4 : 8	M-100		Mass conc. in foundation etc.	45 litres
1 : 3 : 6	M-100	31	Mass conc. in super structure *i.e.* in piers and abutments etc.	34 litres
1 : 2 : 4	M-150	18·7	Normal RCC work of roofs, slabs, beams and walls	32 litres
1 : 1½ : 3	M-200	13·3	RCC in hydraulic structures, columns and pipes	30 litres
1 : 1 : 2	M-250	11·0	Heavily loaded columns, long span beams and arches	27 litres

Note. Grades above 1 : 3 : 6 are not used in RCC work.

Table 9A.6. Permissible stress of conc. in compressive and bond (IS : 456-1964)

Grade of conc.	*Comp. (Kg/cm²)*		*Shear stress Kg/cm²*	*Bond*	
	Bending stress	*Direct stress*		*Average stress*	*Local stress*
M-100	30	25	3·0	4·0	7·0
M-150	50	40	5·0	6·0	10·0
M-200	70	50	7·0	8·0	13·0
M-250	85	60	8·0	9·0	15·0
M-300	100	80	9·0	10·0	17·0
M-350	115	90	10·0	11·0	18·0
M-400	130	100	11·0	12·0	19·0

In design, average bond stress is taken. It is increased by 25% for bars in compression.

Table 9A.7. Permissible stress in tension in various grades of concrete (IS : 456-1964)

Grade of concrete	*Permissible stress in tension in*		*Modular ratio m*	*Shear stress Kg/cm²*
	Direct Kg/cm²	*Bending Kg/cm²*		
M-150	11	15	18	15
M-200	12	17	13	17
M-250	13	18	11	19
M-300	15	20	9	22

Table 9A.8. Strength required for concrete (IS : 456-1964)

Grade of concrete	*Compressive strength in Kg/cm² of 15 cm cubes in crushing*			*Modulus of rupture in tension*	
	Preliminary test	*Work test*			
		7 days (after mix)	*28 days*	*3 days*	*7 days*
M-100	135	70	100	12	17
M-150	200	100	150	15	21
M-200	260	135	200	17	24
M-250	320	170	250	19	27
M-300	380	200	300	21	30
M-350	440	235	350	23	32
M-400	500	270	400	25	34

Table 9A.9. Permissible stress in steel reinforcement (IS : 456-1964)

Type of tress in reinforcement	*Permissible stress in Kg/cm²*			
	m.s. confirming to grade I IS : 432-1960 or IS : 1939-1959	*Med. Tensile steel confirming to IS : 432-1960 IS : 1939-1959*	*Cold twisted steel confirming to IS :1786-1961*	*High yield strength deformed bars and RIbbed Tor steel*
1. Tensile other than in (*a*) helical reinforcement in columns and (*b*) shear reinforcement upto and including 40 mm over 40 mm	1400 1300	Half the guaranteed stress subject to max 1900	1900 1900	2300 2300
upto and including 200 mm over 200 mm			2300 2100	
2. Tension in helical reinforcement in compressive members	1000	1300	1600	
3. Tension in shear reinforcement	1400	1400	1750	
4. Compression in column bars	1300	1300	1750	1900
5. Compression in bars in a beam or slab when the compressive resistance of the conc. is not taken into account	The calculated compressive stress in the surrounding concrete multiplied by the modular ratio or working stress in compressive whichever is less.			
6. Compression in bars in a beam or slab when the compressive resistance of the concrete is not taken into account upto and including 40 mm over 40 mm	1400 1300	Half the guaranteed yield stress subjected to max. of 1900	1900 1900	1900 1900

Note. 1. When mild steel confirming to grade II of IS : 432-1960 is used the permissible stresses shall be reduced by 10% or if the design details have already been worked out on the basis of mild steel confirming to grade I IS : 432-1960 the area of reinforcement shall be increased by 10% of that required of grade I steel.

2. Yield stress of steel for which there is a clearly defined yield point should be taken to 0.2% of proof stress.

3. A factor of safety of 2 is taken which is yield stress/permissible stress.

4. Permissible stress in bending may be exceeded by 33% to that given in Table 9A·9.

5. When the load due to earthquake, temperature or impact is taken into account, the permissible stress should not increase 2600 Kg/cm^2.

6. For welded wire fabrics the permissible stress is 2300 Kg/cm^2.

7. According to IS : 432-1966 mild steel grade I and II has an ultimate tensile strength 4200 Kg/cm^2 and 3800 Kg/cm^2. Medium and high tensile strength steel has an ultimate tensile strength of 5500 kg/cm^2 and 10,000 Kg/cm^2 respectively.

Table 9A.10. Areas of bars in slabs in sq.cm/metre.

Spacing in cms.	*Bar dia. in millimetres*										
	5	*6*	*8*	*10*	*12*	*14*	*16*	*18*	*20*	*22*	*25*
5	3·93	5·65	10·05	15·71	22·62	30·79	40·21	50·89	62·83	76·03	98·17
6	3·27	4·71	8·38	13·09	18·85	25·66	33·51	42·41	52·36	63·38	81·81
7	2·80	4·04	7·18	11·22	16·16	21·99	28·72	36·35	44·88	54·30	70·12
8	2·45	3·53	6·28	9·82	14·14	19·24	25·13	31·81	39·27	47·52	61·36
9	2·18	3·14	5·58	8·73	12·57	17·10	22·34	28·27	34·91	42·24	54·54
10	1·96	2·83	5·03	7·85	11·31	15·39	20·11	25·45	31·42	38·01	49·09
11	1·78	2·57	4·57	7·14	10·28	13·99	18·28	23·13	28·56	34·56	44·62
12	1·64	2·36	4·19	6·54	9·42	12·83	16·75	21·21	26·18	31·68	40·91
13	1·51	2·17	3·87	6·04	8·70	11·84	15·47	19·57	24·17	28·24	37·76
14	1·40	2·02	3·59	5·61	8·08	11·00	14·36	18·18	22·44	27·15	33·06
15	1·31	1·88	3·35	5·24	7·54	10·26	13·40	16·96	20·91	25·34	32·72
16	1·23	1·77	3·14	4·91	7·07	9·62	12·57	15·90	19·63	23·76	30·68
17	1·15	1·66	2·96	4·62	6·65	9·05	11·83	14·97	18·48	22·36	28·87
18	1·09	1·57	2·79	4·36	6·28	8·55	11·17	14·14	17·45	21·12	27·27
19	1·03	1·49	2·63	4·14	5·95	8·10	10·58	13·39	16·53	20·01	25·84
20	0·98	1·41	2·51	3·93	5·65	7·70	10·05	12·72	15·71	19·01	24·54
21	0·93	1·35	2·39	3·74	5·39	7·33	9·57	12·12	14·96	18·10	23·37
22	0·89	1·28	2·28	3·57	5·14	7·00	9·14	11·57	14·28	17·28	22·31
23	0·85	1·23	2·18	3·41	4·92	6·69	8·74	11·06	13·66	16·53	21·34
24	0·82	1·18	2·09	3·27	4·71	6·41	8·38	10·60	13·07	15·84	20·45
25	0·78	1·13	2·01	3·14	4·52	6·16	8·04	10·18	12·57	15·20	19·63
26	0·75	1·09	1·93	3·02	4·32	5·92	7·33	9·79	12·08	14·62	18·88
27	0·73	1·05	1·86	2·91	4·19	5·70	7·45	9·42	11·64	14·08	18·18
28	0·70	1·01	1·79	2·80	4·04	5·50	7·18	9·09	11·22	13·58	17·53
29	0·68	0·97	1·73	2·71	3·90	5·31	6·93	8·77	10·83	13·11	16·93
30	0·65	0·94	1·68	2·62	3·77	5·13	6·70	8·48	10·47	12·67	16·36
32	0·61	0·88	1·57	2·45	3·53	4·81	6·28	7·95	9·82	11·88	15·34
34	0·58	0·83	1·48	2·31	3·33	4·53	5·91	7·48	9·24	11·18	14·44
36	0·54	0·78	1·40	2·18	3·14	4·28	5·58	7·07	8·73	10·56	13·63
38	0·52	0·74	1·32	2·07	2·98	4·05	5·29	6·70	8·27	10·00	12·92
40	0·49	0·71	1·26	1·96	2·83	3·85	5·03	6·36	7·85	9·50	12·27

Preliminary test is the test in laboratory under ideal material conditions while work test is taken in the site lab. with materials available. A factor of safety upto 3·0 is taken in the cube crushing strength.

$$\text{Factor of safety} = \frac{\text{Crushing or characteristic compressive strength in lab.}}{\text{Working strength allowable at site}}$$

Note. 1. S.I. units have been used in IS code 456-1978. In SI units stress is expressed in N/mm^2. 1 kg/cm^2 is taken as 0.1 N/mm^2 or 0.1 kg/mm^2 is taken as 1N/mm^2. N is for Newton $N = 100$ gm.

2. M-100 mix is a mix having a compressive cube crushing strength after 28 days as 100 kg/cm^2 while the same grade represented by M-10 in SI units in compressive crushing strength after 28 days as 10 N/mm^2.

3. For plane concrete permissible tensile strength in bending is taken-as equal to the shear stress without reinforcement.

4. Flexural strength in tension in bending = $0.7\sqrt{fsi}$ where fsi is the crushing compressive strength of concrete in N/mm^2.

5. The tensile strength in bending is about 1.3 to 1.8 to that in direct tension.

6. **Increase in strength with age.** The characteristic compressive strength may be increased by multiplying the following factors.

Full design load/stress is expected	*Age factor*
1 Month	1·0
3 Months	1·10
6 Months	1·15
12 Months	1·20

Note. (1) No increase in respect of age at loading should be allowed when high alumina cement is used.

(2) Where members are subjected to lower direct loading during construction. They should be checked for stresses resulting from combination of direct load and bending during construction.

(3) The permissible stresses or design strengths shall be based on the increased value of compressive strength.

7. $E_C = 5700\sqrt{fsi}$ E_C in the short term modulus of elasticity in N/mm^2.

8. **Thermal expansion in concrete.** Thermal expansion depends on type and quantity of cement, the aggregate, the relative humidity and the size of sections. The value of coefficient of thermal expansion for concrete with different aggregates may be taken as below:

Table 9A·11

Type of aggregate	*Coefficient of thermal expansion for conc. (at 0°C)*
Quartzite	$1{\cdot}2$ to $1{\cdot}30 \times 10^{-5}$
Sand stone	$0{\cdot}9$ to $1{\cdot}20 \times 10^{-5}$
Granite	$0{\cdot}7$ to $0{\cdot}95 \times 10^{-5}$
Basalt	$0{\cdot}8$ to $0{\cdot}95 \times 10^{-5}$
Lime stone	$0{\cdot}6$ to $0{\cdot}90 \times 10^{-5}$

Wind load factors (IS : 875 – 1964). For structures of various plan shapes other than rectangular plan shape, the external pressure acting on the projected area in the plane perpendicular to the wind shall be the product of basic pressure and the factors given in the table below –

Plane shape of the structure	*Ratio length to base width*		
	(0·4)	*(4·8)*	*8·0 or over*
Circular	0·7	0·7	0·7
Octagonal	0·8	0·9	1·0
Square (wind perpendicular to diagonal)	0·8	0·9	1·0
Square (wind perpendicular to face)	1·0	1·15	1·3
Coefficient of friction between conc. and other faces/ type of surface			Coeff. of friction
1. Dry clay, gravel or sand	—	—	0·2 to 0·40
2. Moist clay or sand	—	—	0·3 to 0·35
3. Wet clay	—	—	0·1 to 0·30
4. Rock	—	—	0.5 to 0.60

Table 9A.12.

Shear Resistance of bent up bar in kg/each bar.

Bar dia. (mm)	*t* = 1400 kg/cm² bending		
	$\phi = 30°$ H/V = 1.73 Hor. rest.	45° 1.0	60° 0.58
10	550	778	952
12	791	1120	1371
16	1407	1990	2438
18	1780	2519	3086
20	2198	3110	3809
	t = 1300 kg/cm² (bending)		
22	2474	3494	4280
25	3196	4512	5526
28	4010	5660	6932
32	5234	7393	9054
36	6627	9357	11460

Shear resistance for slabs = KS
(S = permissible stress in shear)

dia.	*value of K*
300 or above	1·00
275	1·05
250	1·10
225	1·15
200	1·20
175	1·25
190 or above	1·30

Shear Resistance value of vertical stirrups Two legged for t = 1400 kg/cm²

Stirrup spacing (mm)	*Fs/d* in kg/cm² (dia. in mm)				
	5	6	8	10	12
5	109	158	281	440	633
7	78	113	201	314	452
8	68	99	176	275	396
10	55	79	141	220	317
12	46	66	117	183	264
14	39	56	100	157	226
16	34	49	88	137	198
18	31	44	78	122	176
20	27	40	70	110	158
25	22	32	56	88	127
30	18	26	47	73	106
35	16	23	40	63	90
40	14	20	35	55	79
45	12	18	31	49	70
50	10	16	28	44	63
55	9	14	25	40	57

Note. (1) Shear value of bar bent at 45° is $0.707\, A_t . t$.

t for steel = 1400 kg/cm². A_t = area of bars.

(2) The value is for one bar, for n bars it will be n times.

9A.6. Check for Bond

(1) Bond stress say $S_b = \dfrac{F}{Sd\ OT}$ (local) ...(5)

Allowable bond stress (S_b) is given in table 9A.4 for different mixes. OT is perimeter of all tension bars. If S_b is more than allowable value, use thinner bars having larger OT. If S_b is still more than allowable bond stress, then ends are hooked to circular, right angle or 45° bend.

(2) $L = \dfrac{t \times d}{4 S_b}$, where L = Anchor length (for tension bars) and t = tensile stress in tension bars.

$L = \dfrac{t_c \times d}{5 S_b}$ where t_c = compressive stress in steel bars in compressive zone and d = dia. of bar.

If the anchor length is more than the length of bar in the section (beam or slab), it must be hooked at ends.

Table 9A·13. Anchor value of hooks in tension bars (circular)

Bar dia. (mm)	6	8	10	12	16	18	20	22	25	28	32	36
Anchor value of hook K in cm	9·6	12·8	16·0	19·2	25·6	28·8	32·0	35·2	40·0	44·8	51·2	57·6

Note. 1. Anchor value of 90° bend is half the circular hook.

2. In slabs or beams where tension bars continue to the end, the straight portion should extend upto centre of bearing before hooks or bends begin.

3. In continuous bars these bars must extend for 20*d* beyond the centre of support before hook begins.

4. There should be a cover of 2*d* or 25 mm (min.) for sides and 3*d* or 40 mm (min.) at top. Hooks should be completely covered with concrete around of it.

5. For bond stress bars are checked for the point of maximum shear force and where the number of bars is min.

6. In case of high yield deformed bars the permissible bond stress is increased by 40% for bars in compressive and 25% for bars in tension.

7. The bond length is measured from the point of max. B.M. to the end of bar (Mid. span in the case of beams) for the bars extend in full span and where the bars are bent up the bond length is measured from the point where the bar cuts the neutral axis to the end of bar in compression zone.

Local bond stress = $S/JdOT$ (S is shear stress)

The local bond stress may exceed 1.75 times permissible direct bond stress.(given in Table 9A·6)

Laps in bars. 1. Lap length say $L = \dfrac{t \times d}{4 \times 5b}$ or 30*d* (d = dia. of bar) whichever is greater.

2. Lap for bars under direct tension = $2L$ or 30*d* which ever is greater.

3. Lap for bars in compression. $L = \dfrac{t_c \times d}{5\,S_b}$ or 24*d* whichever is greater.

Note. 1. The outer lap length can be reduced by giving hooks at ends for restricted conditions as in case of bond. But the minimum straight length of lap should not be less than 15*d* or 20 cm.

2. The overlap should be arranged at point of minimum tensile stress and should be staggered.

3. Length of splice in column bars should be 24*d*, water works 30*d*, vertical bars 30*d* and for hooked circular rings 40*d*.

4. For steel fabrics end should be over lapped by 30 cm and tied together by wires.

5. For bars thicker than 36 mm welding should be done. The strength of weld should be tested. *V* welded joints are used upto bars of 30 mm and double *V* for larger dia. bars.

6. In practice 40 to 50 dia. lap is given, and 6.3 to 7.5 dia. for welded lap joints.

9A.7. Temperature or distribution reinforcement

(*a*) 0.15% of the gross sectional area of the concrete with plain bars and 0.12% for high yield deformed bars.

(*b*) It should be provided uniformly at bottom. It can also be provided in top and bottom both, using top bars as supporting bars.

9A.8. Two way reinforced or Doubly reinforced beams

$$M = (m-1)\,.\,A_C\,C\,\frac{(N-a)}{N}(d-ad) + Qbd^2 \qquad \ldots(6)$$

where A_c = area of steel bars in compressive zone. ad = distance of top of beam to the centre of compressive reinforcement which can be obtained by adding the top cover to the half of the dia. of bar (for compressive)

$$A_t = \frac{Q\,bd^2}{tsd} + (m-1)\,A_c C \frac{\frac{(N-a)}{N}(d-ad)}{t\,(d-ad)} \qquad \text{...(6A)}$$

Equation (6) will give the compressive reinforcement and equation (6A) will give tension reinforcement in two way reinforced beams.

Test in bond and shear. For tension bars is the same as is done in usual beams.

For compressive bars. Find the ratio of the moment M taken by the compressive steel (Formula – 6) to the total moment say it is R, then shear stress in compressive

$$\text{Steel} = \frac{R \times F}{b(d-ad)} \times \frac{(m-1)}{m}$$

It is more than allowable stress, provide stirrups as above.

(Taking allowable shear stress in compression)

Bond stress in compressive steel = $\dfrac{R \times F}{(d-ad)\,O_c}$ where O_c is perimeter compression bars.

The total moment taken = $M + Qbd^2$ where Qbd^2 is the moment taken by the tension bars.

9A.9(A). Design of four way supported slabs (IS : 456-1978)

(1) When the corners of a slab are prevented from lifting the slab is designed as follows :

(*a*) The max BM per unit width in a slab is given by the equation $M_L = \alpha_L\, wB^2$; $M_B = wB^2\, \alpha_b$ where M_L and M_B are moments on strips per unit width on long and short spans respectively. L and B are the long and short spans respectively and W is the total design load per unit area. α_L and α_B are the coefficients for different condition of supports given in the table 7.14.

(*b*) Slabs are considered as divided in middle strips and edge strips as shown in the Fig. 9A.4 below.

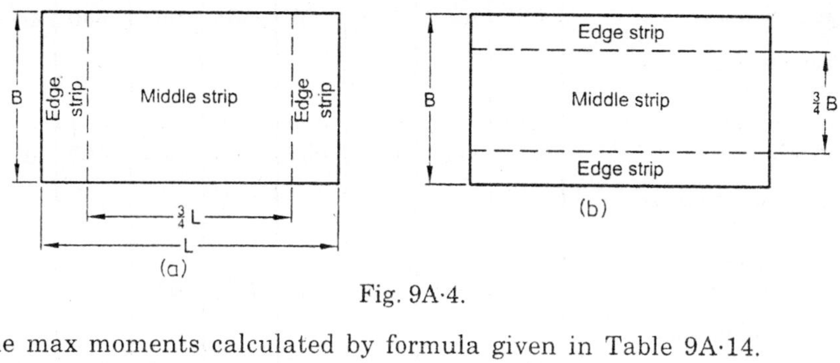

Fig. 9A·4.

(*c*) The max moments calculated by formula given in Table 9A·14.

(*i*) The above apply only to the middle strips and no redistribution should be made.

(*d*) Tension reinforcement provided at mid span in the middle strip shall extend in the lower part of the slab to within 0.256 of a continuous edge or 0.15 L of a discontinuous edge.

(*e*) Over the continuous edges of middle strip, the tension reinforcement shall extend in the upper part of the slab at a distance of 0.15 L from the support and at least 50% shall extend a distance of 0.3 l.

(*f*) At a discontinuous edge, –ve moments may arise according to the fixity at the edges, but a general tension reinforcement equal to 50% of that provided at mid span extending 0.1 L into the span will be sufficient.

(*g*) Reinforcement in edge strip parallel to that edge shall comply with the given in section above and the requirements for tension given below.

Table 9A.14. B.M. coefficients for rectangular pannels supported on four sides with provision of torsion at corners.

Sl. No.	*Type of pannel and moments*	*Short Span coefficients αβ values of L/B*								*Long coefficent αl span all values of L/B*
		1.0	1.1	1.2	1.3	1.4	1.5	1.75	2.0	
1.	*Interior Pannels*									
	–ve Mt at concrete edge	.032	·037	·043	·047	·051	·053	·060	·065	·032
	+ve Mt at mid span	·024	·028	·032	·036	·039	·041	·045	·049	·024
2.	*One short edge discontinuous*									
	–ve Mt at cont. edge	·037	·043	·048	·051	·053	·057	·064	·068	·037
	+ve Mt at mid span	·028	·032	·036	·039	·041	·044	·048	·052	·028
3.	*One long edge discontinuous*									
	–ve Mt at cont. edge	·037	·044	·052	·057	·063	·067	·077	·085	·037
	+ve Mt at mid span	·028	·033	·039	·044	·047	·051	·059	·065	·028
4.	*Two adjacent edges discontinuous*									
	–ve Mt at cont. edge	·047	·053	·060	·065	·071	·075	·0014	·091	·047
	+ve Mt at mid span	·035	·040	·045	·049	·053	·056	·063	·069	·035
5.	*Two short edges discontinuous*									
	–ve Mt at cont. edge	·045	·040	·052	·056	·059	·060	·065	·069	—
	+ve Mt at mid span	·035	·037	·047	·043	·044	·045	·049	·052	·035
6.	*Two long edges discontinuous*									
	–ve Mt at cont. edge	—	—	—	—	—	—	—	—	·045
	+ve Mt at mid span	·035	·043	·051	·057	·063	·068	·080	·088	·035
7.	*Three edges discontinuous one long edge cont.*									
	–ve Mt at cont. edge	·057	·062	·031	·076	·080	·084	·091	·047	—
	+ve Mt at mid span	·043	·048	·053	·057	·060	·064	·069	·073	·043
8.	*Three edges discontinuous one short edge cont.*									
	–ve Mt at cont. edge	—	—	—	—	—	—	—	—	·057
	+ve Mt at mid span	·043	·051	·059	·065	·071	·076	·087	·096	·043
9.	*Four edges discontinuous*									
	+ve Mt at mid span	·056	·064	·072	·079	·083	·089	·100	·107	·056

(*h*) Torsion reinforcement shall be provided at any corner where the slab is simply supported on both edges meeting at the corner with both top and bottom bars placed parallel to the sides of the slab and extending from the edges a minimum distance of 1/5th of the span (shorter). The area of the reinforcement in each of there four layers shall to 3/4th of the area required for the maximum mid span moment.

(*i*) Torsion reinforcement equal to half as provided in section (*h*) shall be provided at a corner contained by edges over only one of which the slab is continuous.

(*j*) Tension reinforcement is not required at any corner contained by the edges over both of which the slab is continuous.

(*k*) Where *L*/*B* is greater than 2. slab is designed as one way slab.

(2) Simply supported slab, no provision to resist torsion at corners and to prevent from lifting.

(*a*) B.M. coefficients for slabs simply supporting as four sides.

Value of *L*/*B*	1·0	1·1	1·2	1·3	1·4	1·5	1·75	2·0	2·5	3·0
α_B	·062	·0074	·084	·093	·099	·104	·113	·118	·122	·124
α_L	·062	·061	·059	·055	·051	·046	·037	·029	·020	·014

(*b*) At least 50% of tension reinforcement provided at mid span should extend to the supports. The remaining 50% should extend to within 0·1 B or 0·1 L the supports as appropriate.

9A.9(B). Circular and Elliptical slabs

Without going in deep detail, the circular slabs are more or less designed as four way supported slabs. Long span may be taken as the major axis and short span as the minor axis of the ellipse. While dia. of the circle can be taken both as long as well as short span.

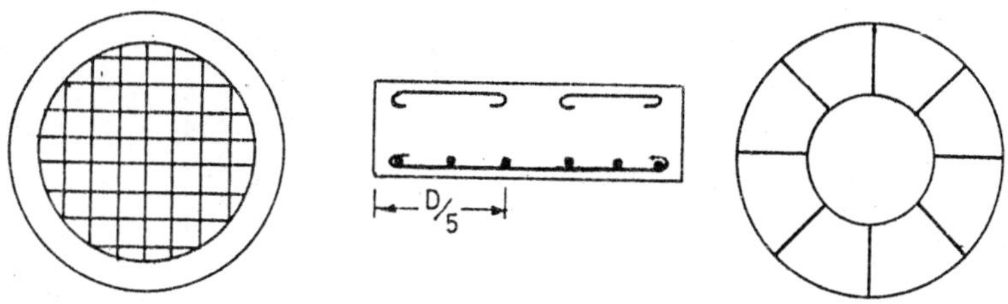

(*a*) Bottom reinforced bars (*b*) (*c*) Top reinforced bars

Fig. 9A·5.

Table 9A.15. RCC Slab (simply supported) in buildings.

Effective span = clear span + bearing ; Min bearing 15 cm or depth of slab

Effective span (m)	*B.M. $\omega l^2/8$ (cm) gm*	*Depth of slab*		*Main rein.*			*Distribution rein.*		
		effective (cm)	*Total (cm)*	*area (cm²)*	*dia. (mm)*	*spacing c/c (cm)*	*area (cm²)*	*dia. (mm)*	*spacing c/c (cm)*
3·70	99,595	10·70	12	7·73	10	10	15·5	6	18
3·30	80,405	9·68	11	6·23	10	12·7	1·245	6	22
3·00	60,075	8·31	10	5·74	10	13·5	1·147	6	24
2·70	46,474	7·30	9	5·30	10	15·5	1·03	6	27
2·40	34,992	6·34	8	4·34	10	18·0	0·87	6	32
2·10	25,468	5·41	7	3·71	8	13·5	0·742	6	37
1·80	18,711	4·64	7	2·72	8	18·0	0·544	6	50
1·50	12,994	3·87	7	1·90	8	76·0	0·38	6	73
1·20	8,316	3·09	7	1·21	8	41·0	0·242	6	115

Note. (1) Main bars should be bent upto 1/5th span from support alternately.

(2) Live load = 147 kg/m^2 (30 lb/ft^2) and

(3) Dead load of Terracing is also 147 kg/m^2 + Dead load of slab calculated separately.

(4) Floor load for multistorey buildings

Live load = 195 kg/m^2 (40 lb/ft^2)

Dead load = wt. of slab itself + 2.5 to 4.0 cm c.c. terracing.

(5) As total loads on roofs and slabs are approximately the same hence the design will hold good.

Table 9A.16. Live loads in buildings

Sl. No.	*Details of works*	*Slabs*				*Beams*			
		Normal load		*Min. Total load*		*Normal load*		*Min. Total load*	
		lb/ft^2	*kg/m^2*	*T*	*MT.*	*lb/ft^2*	*kg/m^2*	*T*	*MT.*
1.	Floors, Residential Hotels, Hospitals	50	250	·25	·25	40	200	1·0	1·0
	Hotels, Hospitals	50	250	·25	·25	40	200	1·0	1·0
	Public Place	100	500	·4	·4	100	500	2·0	2·0
2.	Office, Shops, Schools, Church, Reading rooms	80	400	·4	·4	80	400	2·0	2·0
3.	Assembly and Cinema Halls, Restaurants	100	500	·4	·4	100	500	2·0	2·0
4.	Ware houses, Work shops and factory	150	750	·4	·4	150	750	2·0	2·0
5.	Stores	200	1000	·4	·4	180	900	2·0	2·0
6.	Garriage, Light Vehicle Heavy vehicle	80 150	400 750	·4 ·4	·4 ·4	80 120	400 600	2·0 2·0	2·0 2·0
7.	Stairs, Corridors, Landings stairs (inside)	100	500	·4	·4	100	500	2·0	2·0
	Private residences	50	250	·4	·4	40	200	2·0	2·0
8.	Roofs flat	40	200	·4	·4	30	150	2·0	2·0
	Inclined	15	75	·25	·25	30	150	2·0	2·0

Reinforced Concrete Roof with Filler Slab

Notations : The following notations are adopted :

A_{st} = area of tensile reinforcement in the section ; B = width of flange of T or L-beam

d = effective depth to tension reinforcement ; f_y = characteristic yield strength of steel

l = effective span ; M = bending moment

M_u = ultimate moment ; P_t = percentage of tensile

w = uniformly distributed live load and dead load per running meter

In the fundamental concept of reinforced concrete solid slab, the concrete below the neutral axis is being used as a binder, that is, only the steel reinforcements take the tension. Reinforcements of the slab may be designed in such a way that the balance of binder concrete below the neutral axis may be eliminated considerably. The removal of such concrete by providing centering arrangements will involve a huge cost. To minimize the cost of shuttering, removable fillers, such as sand bags, may be introduced for making patterns, but it costs much for dressing and finishing. If an integrating filler is used, it will not add any extra cost other than the cost of conventional centering and ceiling finishing. For the integrating filler, bricks may be used as they are cheap, can be procured easily and have compressive strength to certain extent.

Example. *In a RC slab of 10 cm thickness, the main reinforcement of 10 mm rods at 20 cm c/c and the distributors of 8 mm rods at 30 cm c/c, brick fillers of size 23 cm × 11 cm × 5 cm may be arranged. These fillers may be placed over centring before/or at the time of concreting conveniently. In this example, savings of 20% of concrete will be affected.*

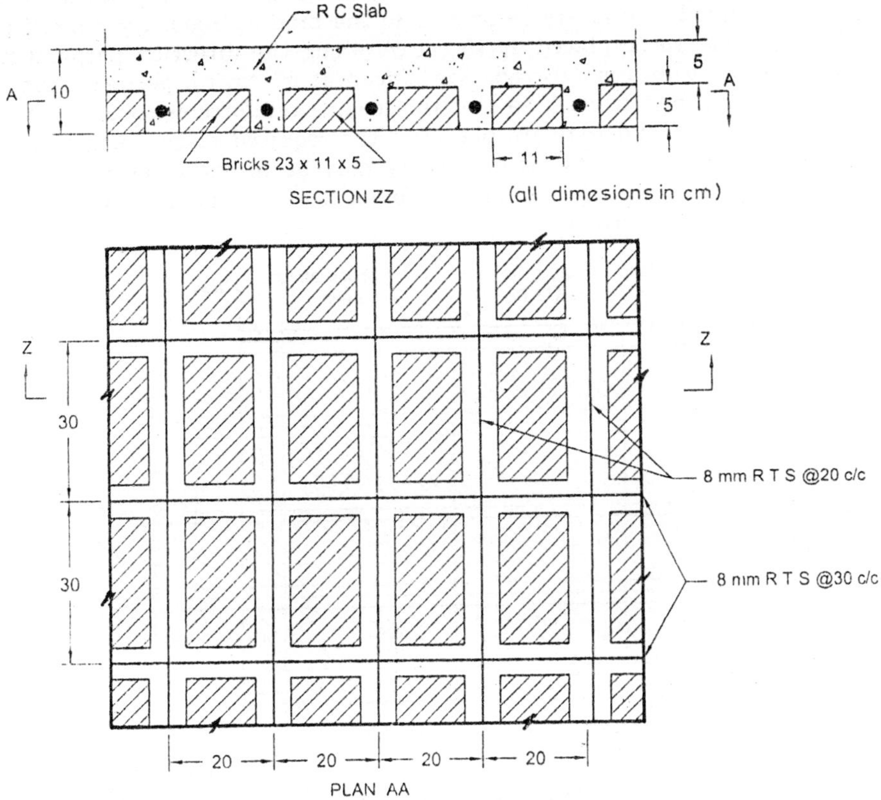

Fig. 9A·6. Arrangement of brick fillers in RC slab.

Hollow clay block slab method (Filler slab)

Hollow clay block slab requires less concrete. Such a floor or roof consists of a thin top slab 3 cm to 9 cm overlying concrete ribs. These ribs may be at 15 cm c/c to 90 cm c/c and may be from 6 cm to 12 cm wide. Spaces between the ribs may be left open, but in order to simplifying the shuttering they are frequently filled (with hollow clay blocks or fillers). The combined depth of rib and slab is determined in the same manner as the depth of a solid slab, and thickness of the top slab is made sufficient to provide adequate compressive area. The thickness of top slab should not be less than one-twelfth of the distance between ribs with a minimum of 3 cm. The ribs are placed together to form a series of tiny T-beams in the middle and *L*-beams at ends. The beams have to be checked for shear and other requirements.

In this method, if the hollow clay blocks are substituted with integrating fillers, there will be savings of about 50% in the concrete. The total cost is reduced and is about 1/5 th.

Procedure for filler slab concrete construction

Centring is done as per the conventional practice. Minor slope may be introduced, if necessary, according to design. Some nominal binder rods, say 3 to 4 of 6 mm MS rods per span, are placed along the direction perpendicular to the proposed tiny T-beams. Tiny T-beam positions are located. From the edge, first one tiny L-beam position will be left, then course of soaked bricks of size 23 cm × 11 cm × 6 cm are placed as stretchers of 23 cm with a thickness of 6 cm over centring between tiny beams, the place is left for tiny T-beam and the process will be completed by engaging some labour. The bricks are to be joined by means of cement mortar in the ratio of 1 : 4 or so. The breaking of joints or bricks will not matter as the same will be finished at the time of finishing ceiling.

Fig. 9A·8 shows that one 8 mm RTS reinforcement for each tiny beams will be placed in the beam gaps provided. These are to be tied to the binding rods. Over brick paving, one set of 6 mm MS rods are to be placed at 45 cm c/c along the direction perpendicular to the tiny beams. Another set of 6 mm MS rods are placed at 30 cm c/c perpendicular to the top rods placed just before to form a mesh so that tiny beams reinforcements are just under them and the mesh is tied. Additional rods are placed at the required places such as over supports and fan hooks. Other service ducts for electricity may be provided by removing bricks at necessary places. The bar bending is simple. Copious water is poured over bricks to avoid absorption of water from concrete.

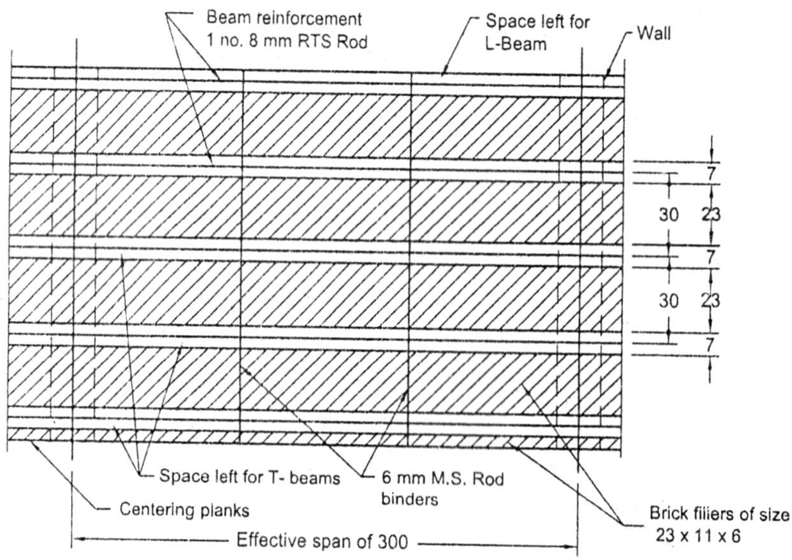

Fig. 9A·7. Plan showing the arrangement of brick fillers over centring.

Concrete of mixture 1 : 2 : 4 using 20 mm granite metal is done, starting from one edge first beam gaps and top simultaneously as usual and completed by ordinary means of ramming and consolidation. The concrete will be cured for 10 days and then centring may be removed. The exposed brick surface is to be watered sufficiently not to absorb water from mortar to be used for ceiling. The ceiling may be finished with cement mortar.

Advantages : The advantages of RC roof are as detailed below :

(1) In this type of RC roof with brick filler slab construction for an area of 55 m^2, there will be savings of 46% of concrete and 54% of steel than the conventional method.

(2) The roof is considered to be flat when the slope of roof does not exceed 10° Hence, for the roof a slope of less than 10° is provided on one side and the weathering course and pressed tiles over the roof are eliminated to have further economy, as adopted for ridge roof for low cost housing.

(3) Thermal comfort is being felt for such type of RC roof with brick filler construction. It is little cooler under this roof than solid slab roof during summer, and a little warmer than the solid slab roof during winter.

(4) As the bricks have a tendency to absorb much moisture, minute quantum of oozing of moisture in the roof, if any, will be absorbed by brick fillers.

5. This type of roof construction does not require any machinery or sophisticated instruments.

Such type of RC roof with brick filler slab construction executed during April 1982 for an area of 55 m^2, having a slope of 15 cm on one side without any weathering course and pressed tiles in a suburban locality is functioning well. Assuming only horizontal expansion in suburban areas, a minimum live load of 75 kg/m^2 is taken into account for the roof without access, resulting in light roof, foundation, etc. to achieve overall economy. For floors of flats for middle income group, this type of roof may be designed accordingly to suit the environment.

Design of top flange slab

In solid reinforced cement concrete slabs, the value of P_t in either direction shall not be less than 0·15 where plain rods are used. Considering 1 m × 1 m slab of thickness of 4 cm, using plain rods on either side,

Area of steel $= \dfrac{100 \times 4 \times 0.15}{100} = 0.6 \text{ cm}^2$

Using 6 mm MS rods,

spacing in either direction $= \dfrac{100 \times 0.283}{0.6} = 47$ cm c/c

To suit the pattern, 6 mm MS rods are placed 30 cm c/c and 45 cm c/c on either side, respectively to form a mesh accordingly.

Design of Tiny T-Beams :

Load per T-beam p.r.m.

Solid RC portion = 0·0162 m^3

Filler portion = 0·0138 m^3

Furnishes 2 × 0·3 × 0.01 = 0·006 m^2

Dead load for RC portion 0·0162 × 2400 = 39 kg

Dead load BK filler portion 0·0138 × 1920 = 26 kg

Dead furnishes portion 0·006 × 1920 = 12 kg

Live load assuming inaccessible roof 75 × ·3 = 23 kg

Total = 100 kg

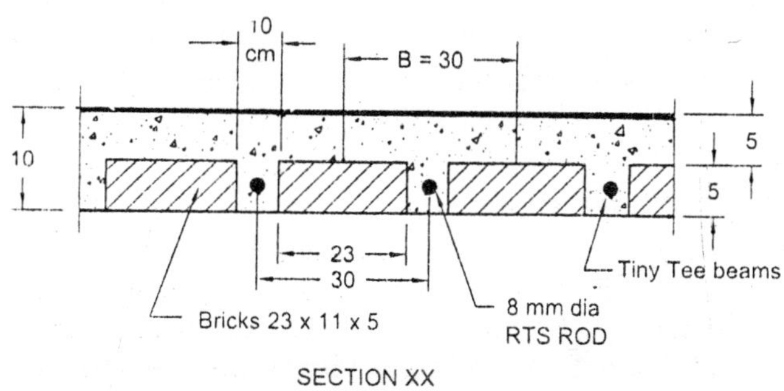

Fig. 9A·8. Section of tiny tee beam

S.F. $= 100 \times 3/2 = 150$ kg

Shear stress $= \dfrac{150}{0.8 \times 7 \times 8.5} = 3{\cdot}15 \text{ kg/cm}^2 < 5 \text{ kg/cm}^2$

Bond stress $= \dfrac{150}{0.8 \times 8.5 \times 2.51} = 8{\cdot}79 \text{ kg per cm}^2 < 14 \text{ kg/cm}^2$

$$Pt = \frac{0.5 \times 100}{7 \times 10} = 0.7$$

For T beams, using 1 : 2 : 4 concrete, the value of Pt is limited to 1·5 hence not required to check since its condition is satisfied.

Conc. mix 1 : 2 : 4

$B = 30$ cm

$d = 10$ cm

$$M = \frac{\omega l^2}{8} = \frac{100 \times 3 \times 3}{8} = 112{\cdot}5 \text{ kg m.}$$

$$Mu = 1{\cdot}5 \times 112{\cdot}5 = 168{\cdot}73 \text{ kg m or } 1{\cdot}655 \text{ k pl-m}$$

$$\frac{Mu}{Bdl} \frac{1{\cdot}655 \times 1000}{30 \times 10 \times 10} = 0{\cdot}55/\text{mm}^2$$

From table $Pt = 0{\cdot}159, As$

$$As = \frac{0{\cdot}159}{100} \times 30 \times 10 \times 0{\cdot}48 \text{ cm}^2$$

Provide 8 mm ϕ 1 No.

It is more than 0·20% as required for RCC beams for top bars.

Design for top flange slab

In solid R.C.C. slabs, the value of *Pt* in either direction shall not be less than 0.15 where plain rods are used. Considering 1 × 1 m slab of thickness 4 cm, using plain rods on either side.

Area of steel $\frac{100 \times 4 \times 0.15}{100} = 0.6 \text{ cm}^2$ using 6 mm^2 M.S. rods

Spacing in either direction = $\frac{100 \times 0{\cdot}283}{0{\cdot}6}$ = 47 cm c/c. Suiting the pattern use 6 mm m.s. bars 30 cm c/c and 45 c/c on either side.

Main reinforcement is provided in the bottom of Tiny T-beam while the distribution is provided in a most suiting the hollow box size in either direction over the main bars. It saves 50% steel.

9A·10. Water Pipes

Water pipes are casted with a rich mortar (say M-20) 1 : 11/2 : 3 with a coarse aggressive not exceeding 4·5 mm. size. These pipes are consolidated by centrifugal vibrations created by revolving the concrete in the forms. The main steel is provided as hoop steel by the following formula.

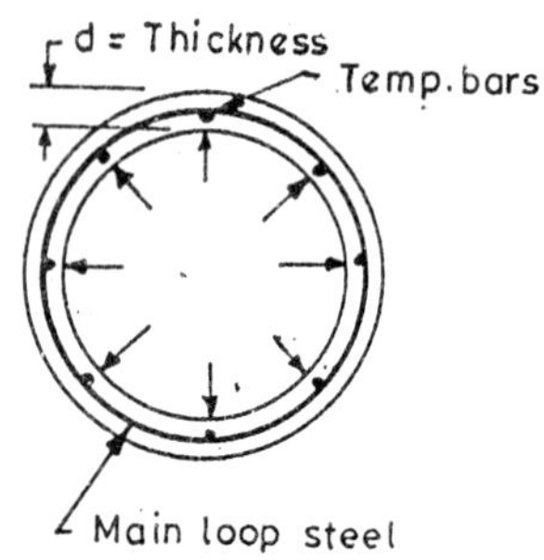

Fig. 9A·9.

Hoop tension = $\frac{pD}{2} = \frac{\omega HD}{2}$ where H = head of water, D = inner dia of pipe, ω =density of water, P = pressure of water in side pipe (in head of water it is ωH) or $As = \frac{\omega HD}{2f_s}$ where A_s = area of steel per unit length of pipe and f_s = permissible stress in steel to check any crack in tension, which may be 1000 kg/cm^2. Density of water = 0·001 kg/cm^3.

The temperature reinforcement is taken to be 0·3%. In case the pipes are subjected to water hammer due to sudden closing, values 3 to 4 times of steel is provided.

Thickness of pipe. It is given by the formula or relation $T = \frac{\omega HD}{2} - A_c + A_s\,(m - 1)$; m being modular ratio which is 13·3 in case of concrete mix 1 : 1 1/2 : 3, A_c = area of concrete.

Taking 1 metre wide strip $A_c = 100 \times d$ where d = thickness of pipe in cm. Knowing other factors d can be calculated in $\frac{\omega HO}{2} = 100d + A_s(m - 1)$. As calculated As area of steel as above.

Permissible stress in conc. relating to resistance to crack.

Position of steel	*ms bars kg/cm²*	*Deformed bars kg/cm²*	*High yield deformed bars kg/cm²*
Steel at 255 mm from water face	1000	1125	1500
Steel away 255 mm from water face	1250	1400	1900

(*a*) As main bars are taken per unit length of pipe.

(*b*) Distribution bars are distributed uniformly on circumference.

9A.11. Design of columns

Short column = $\frac{\text{effective length}}{\text{least lateral dimension}} < 15$ or $\frac{\text{effective span}}{\text{least lateral rad of gyration}} < 50$

Long column = $\frac{\text{effective length}}{\text{least lateral dimension}} > 15$ or $\frac{\text{effective length}}{\text{least lateral rad of gyration}} > 50$

Load taken by short column (with lateral ties) $= P' = C_A + t_c \cdot A_s$ ...(*A*)

Load taken by long column (with helical ties) $= P' = C_{Ak} + t_c \cdot A_s + 2th \times Ah$ ...(*B*)

where P' = load, C = compressive stress in direct compressive = 48 kg/cm² (for *M* 150 concrete)

A = Total area of concrete sec. ; (excluding long steel) ; A_s = Area of long. steel.

t_c = permissible stress in steel in compression = 1300 kg/cm²

A_k = Sectional area of concrete, excluding long. steel (area between helical)

t_h = permissible tensile stress in helical reinforcement = 1000 kg/cm²

A_h = equivalent area of helical bars

$$= \frac{\text{Circumference of the column} \times \text{sectional area of helical bars}}{\text{One pitch height}}$$

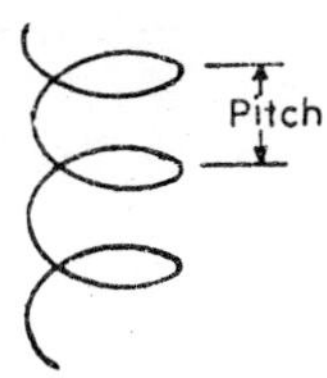

Fig. 9A·10.

Design of short columns

Divide the load by the reduction factor

$P/r = P'$ where P = load given, r = reduction factor

P' = load adopted for design

reduction factor $r = 1{\cdot}5l/30 \times$ least lateral dimension (l being the effective length)

or $$r = 1{\cdot}5\frac{l}{100 \times \text{least lateral rad. of gyration}}.$$

Table 9A·17

L/D	12	15	18	21	24	27	30	33	36	39	42	45
r	1·0	·94	·88	·81	·75	·69	·63	·56	·50	·44	·38	·31

L = least lateral dimension, D = diameter of core for helical bars.

Design the column for load P' as short column.

Plate 9A·1. Types of reinforcement in Columns.

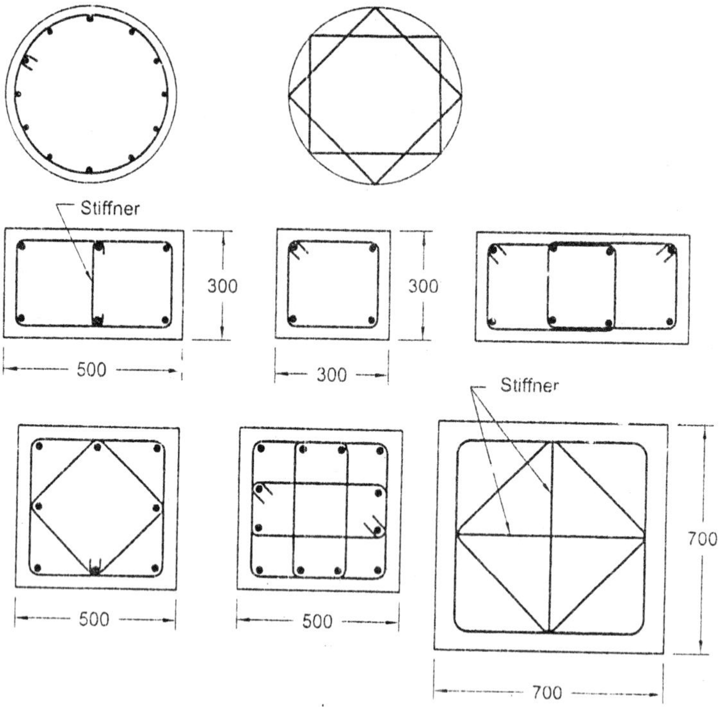

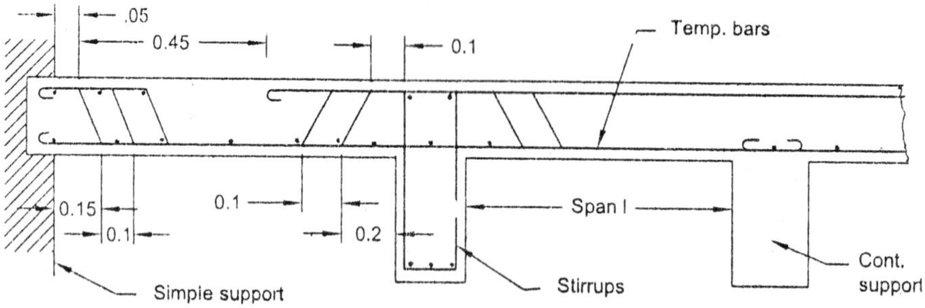

(e)

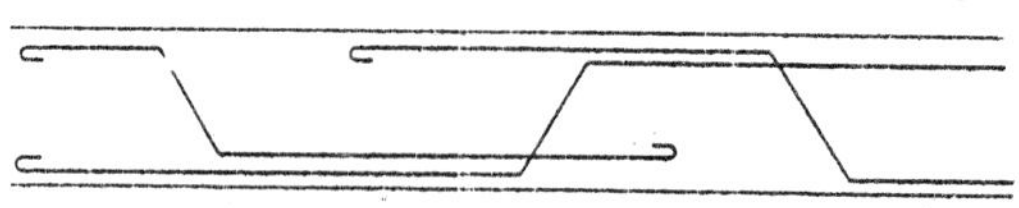

DETAILS OF BENT BARS
(f)

Longitudinal reinforcement

(1) Sectional area of steel must be taken between 0·8 to 8 percent.

(2) Dia. of bar should be between 12 mm and 50 mm.

(3) Spacing between the bars should be more than dia. of bar, 6 mm or max. size of the aggregate whichever is greater.

(4) Number of bars should be more than 6 for spiral reinforcement and one bar should be provided at the centre.

Transverse reinforcement

(1) Volume of bars should not be less than 0·4% of the total volume of the concrete.

(2) Dia. of the bar should not be less than the 5 mm and not more than 25 mm. for spiral reinforcement or lateral reinforcement.

(3) Distance of lateral ties should not be more than :

(*a*) Least lateral dimension of the column.

(*b*) 12 × dia. of long. bar.

(*c*) 30 cm.

It must not be less than 15 cm.

(4) Pitch of the helical should not be more than 7·5 cm or 1/6 of dia. of conc. whichever is less. It should also not be less than 2·5 cm or 3 dia. of the bar whichever is greater.

Column loaded eccentrically

Assume a section of $b \times d$ (d being the higher side). The eccentric loadings are due to brackets in columns, eccentric spacing of columns and the beams or due to any other unsymmetrical load compressive stress on the column $= \frac{\omega}{A} \pm \frac{M}{z}$ ...(1)

A = equivalent concrete area

$= bd + (1{\cdot}5\text{ m} - 1)\,As$;

ω = load on column, M = Moment $= \omega e$

where e is the eccentricity of the load

z = section modulus of the section

$= \frac{I}{d/2}$ (I = moment of inertia of the section)

$$I = \frac{bd^3}{12} + [(1{\cdot}5\text{ m} - 1)As \times (d/2 - a)^2]$$

A_s = Total area of steel (long.). In 1st attempt assume it as per requirement of longitudinal steel

a = cover of steel + $d/2$ of the bar.

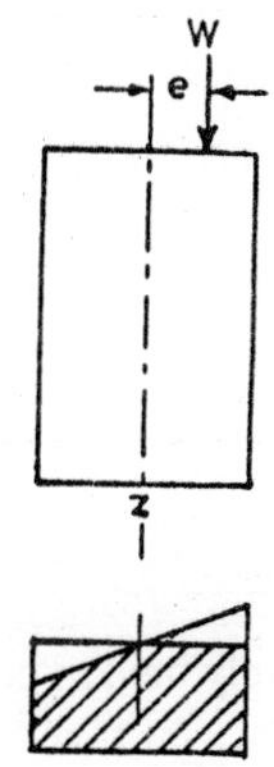

Fig. 9A·11.

Placing all the values in the equation (1) the compressive stress in bending for (+) sign and in direct compressive with (–) sign is obtained. If it is more than permissible, increase the section sides. If less than decrease and check till it is perfect. If the section of the column is restricted then try with different sections of longitudinal steel.

The above formula for finding out the stresses in a RC section for combined bending and direct loads is applicable only so long as the concrete does not crack under the effect of tensile stresses. If it does crack, a part of the section becomes ineffective and unless the position of the neutral axis is known, the value of A, I and Od cannot be found. It is considered that if the tensile stress in concrete does not exceed 1/6th of the safe compressive stress, the whole section may be taken as effective and the above formula is applicable. In cases where the compressive stress on the section varies from a maximum at the extreme fibre to zero at the neutral axis, the safe compressive stress is taken the same as for bending stresses alone.

Cases of combined bending and direct stress in which the eccentricity is not more than 1/4th the depth of the section can be analysed with the help of the above method. The eccentricity should be measured from the c.g. of the equivalent section.

Combined footings

When a column is situated near the edge of a property line and it is not possible to extend the footing on one side of the column, the load on the isolated footing will be eccentric. It is therefore better to design this column in combination with the adjacent internal column, in such a manner that the *c.g.* of the combined footing coincides with the *c.g.* of the loads on the two columns. Such footing may be rectangular or trapezoidal in shape, a combination of the footings is also necessary in case of foundations on poor soils where the footing of one over laps the other.

Foundation with strap beams

If the area of the footing is so arranged that the footing has large areas under the columns and these areas are connected by a narrow beam, the upward reaction will be very near the column loads resetting in a reduction of the maximum bending moment. The connecting beam is called the *strap beam*. This arrangement is specially useful in the case of footings for a wall column. Where it is difficult to make the footing concentric with the column, the two areas under the columns are so arranged that the total area is equal to the bearing area required for the combined load of those columns and the *c.g.* of the areas coincides with the *c.g.* of the columns loads. The actual dimensions of the foundation can only be obtained by trial. The reinforcement of the strap beam will be as an inverted beam.

Values of effective length in columns (IS : 456-1978)

Sl. No.	*Way of end restraint*	*Effective length*
1.	Effectively held in position and restrained against rotation at both ends	0·65 L 
2.	Effectively held in position at both ends, restrained against rotation at one end	0·80 L 
3.	Effectively held in position at both ends but not restrained against rotation	1·00 L 
4.	Effectively held in position and restrained against rotation at one end and at the other restrained against rotation but not held in position	1·30 L 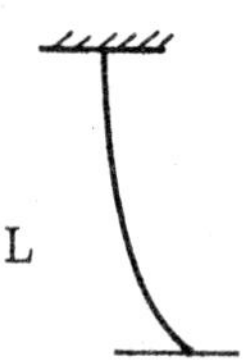

Table contd.

Table contd.

Sl. No.	*Way of end restraint*	*Effective length*	
5.	Effectively held in position and restrained against rotation at one end and at the other partially restrained against rotation but not held in position	1·50 L	
6.	Effectively held in position at one end but not restrained against rotation, and at the other end restrained against rotation but not held in position	2·0 L	
7.	Effectively held in position and restrained against rotation at one end but not held in position nor restrained against rotation at the other end (L being the unsupported length of column)	2·0 L	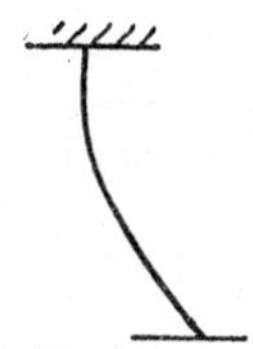

Fig. 9A·12.

Column footings

The footings of columns may be square, rectangular or circular according to the type of column. The footings may be cantilever, stepped or sloped. Total load on columns + weight of column and footing = Safe bearing pressure taken by soil = W (say).

The footing size and depth is designed on the following three factors.

(*b*) **Punching shear.** The footing block must have a sufficient resistance to the column to penetrate or punch a hole in it.

The total shear on the periphery of column base taken by the thickness of the footings = perimeter of the column × thickness of the footing × Punching shear strength of the concrete (for concrete mix 1 : 2 : 4 = 10 kg/cm^2 which is twice the normal shear of the concrete). This total shear is resisted by the soil pressure on the area of the footing projected beyond the column. For a column of square section of side a and footing of b punching shear strength s (permissible $w/b^2\ (b^2a^2) = 4ads$ where d is the thickness of the footing and w = total weight on column including dead weight of column + footing. Knowing other factors s can be calculated. If it is more than permissible then increase the thickness, otherwise by putting the permissible value of shear in punching the thickness of footing can be calculated (In the 1st trial a, b and d are assumed.)

2. **Diagonal shear.** Normal shear acts at 45° from the base of the column to the bottom of footings.

Total shear remained on the footing = $w/b^2\ \{b^2 - (a - 2d)^2\}$

It acts on area $4(a + 2d)\ Jd$

Total shear is also equals to $4(a + 2d)Jd.S.d.$ where S is the permissible shear stress in compression.

Equating the two $w/b^2\ \{b^2 - (a + 2d)^2\} = 4(a + 2d)Jd.Sd$

or $$d = w/b^2\ \{b^2 - (a + 2d)^2\} \div \{4(a + 2d)Jd.S\}$$

$S = 5$ kg/cm^2 for concrete mix 1 : 2 : 4 in compression

3. **Due to BM on the projection.** An unit width is considered in the middle of the footing having a projection of $\frac{b-a}{2}$ from the edge of the column.

BM on this cantilever $= w/8b\ (b - a)^2$ ...(1)

In RCC section M is also equal to Qbd^2 (here b = unity) ...(2)

Equating (1) and (2) we can find d.

Adopt maximum depth obtained in above three cases. Reinforcement can also be calculated as in cantilevers.

General rules for footing design

(1) Load on footing should not exceed the safe bearing capacity of the soil.

(2) In sloped or stepped footings the effective cross section in compression shall be limited by the area above the neutral plain and the angle of the slope or depth and location of steps shall be such that the design requirements are satisfied at every section.

(3) Thickness at the edge of footing in RCC or PCC concrete footings shall be not less than 150 mm for footings on soil nor less than 300 mm above the top of piles for pile footings In case of PCC pedestals the angle α between the plane passing through the bottom edge of the pedestal and the corresponding junction edge of the column with pedestals and the horizontal plain shall be governed by the expression $\tan\alpha \nless 0.9\sqrt{\frac{100\,qc}{fk} + 1.0}$ (IS : 456-1978)

where qc = Calculated max. bearing pressure at the base of pedestal in N/mm^2

fk = Characteristic strength of concrete in 28 days in N/mm^2.

In cases of circular or octagonal columns the face of the column is taken as a side of an inscribed square within the perimeter of circular or octagonal column.

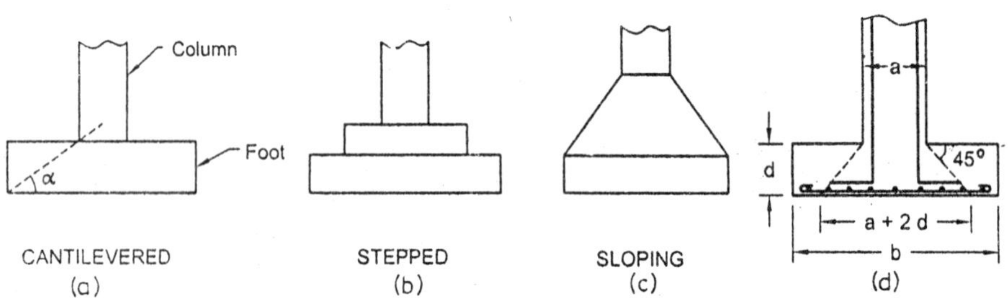

Fig. 9A·13.

Table 9A·18.

Outer dia	*Vertical bars*		*Helical or spiral reinforcement*		*Load carried by column*		
	1300 kg/cm^2 pitch		*bar dia*	*M-15*	*M-20 40 kg/cm^2 (bend)*	*M-25 50 kg/cm^2 (bend)*	*60 kg/cm^2 (bend)*
cm	*Nos.*	*dia. mm*	*mm*	*mm*	*Tonnes*	*Tonnes*	*Tonnes*
15	8	10	32	6	17	18	18
	8	12	28	6	21	22	23
	8	16	26	6	31	31	32

Table contd.

Table contd.

Outer dia cm	Vertical bars 1300 kg/cm² pitch		Helical or spiral reinforcement		Load carried by column		
	Nos.	dia. mm	bar dia mm	M-15 mm	M-20 40 kg/cm² (bend) Tonnes	M-25 50 kg/cm² (bend) Tonnes	60 kg/cm² (bend) Tonnes
20	8	12	32	6	27	29	30
	8	16	28	6	37	39	40
	8	22	26	6	56	57	59
25	8	12	32	8	54	57	60
	8	16	28	8	85	88	91
	8	25	26	8	57	62	69
30	8	12	30	8	57	62	69
	8	22	28	8	86	90	95
	12	25	38	10	122	125	129
35	8	12	30	8	69	76	82
	8	22	40	10	102	108	115
	12	28	36	10	61	167	174
40	8	16	30	8	114	128	142
	8	28	38	10	189	201	214
	12	32	44	12	211	219	227
45	8	16	32	8	114	128	142
	8	32	38	10	189	201	214
	12	36	42	12	276	286	297
50	8	20	34	8	143	160	177
	8	36	38	10	233	249	265
	12	40	42	12	324	337	350
55	8	20	34	8	165	186	207
	8	36	36	10	259	279	299
	12	40	70	16	352	369	386
60	8	22	34	8	195	221	246
	8	40	45	12	321	346	370
	12	46	70	16	391	412	432

Table 9A·19. Design Data for RC Square Short Columns

Size cm	Dia.-No. mm	Area cm²	Load on bars in tonnes (t = 1400 kg per cm²)	Binder Stirrups pitch dia.	Safe load on columns in tonnes		
					c = 60 (M-25) kg/cm²	c = 50 (M-20) kg/cm²	c = 40 (M-15) kg/cm²
15 × 15	12-4	4·52	6·33	16-5	19·56	17·35	15·19
16 × 16	12-4	4·52	6·33	16-5	21·42	18·90	16·39
17 × 17	12-4	4·52	6·33	16-5	23·40	20·55	17·71
18 × 18	12-4	4·52	6·33	16-5	25·50	22·30	19·11
19 × 19	12-4	4·52	6·33	16-5	27·72	24·15	20·59
20 × 20	12-4	4·52	6·33	16-5	30·06	26·10	22·15
21 × 21	12-4	4·52	6·33	16-5	32·59	28·15	23·79
22 × 22	12-4	4·52	6·33	16-5	35·10	30·30	25·51
22 × 22	20-4	12·57	17·60	20-5	45·88	41·17	36·46
23 × 23	12-4	4·52	6·33	16-5	37·80	32·55	27·31

Table contd.

Table contd.

Size	*Dia.-No.*	*Area*	*Load on bars in tonnes (t = 1400 kg per cm²)*	*Binder Stirrups pitch dia.*	*Safe load on columns in tonnes*		
					c = 60 (M-25) kg/cm²	*c = 50 (M-20) kg/cm²*	*c = 40 (M-15) kg/cm²*
cm	*mm*	*cm²*					
23 × 23	24-4	18·10	25·34	20-6	55·99	50·88	45·78
23 × 23	24-8	36·10	50·67	25-8	80·24	75·31	70·38
24 × 24	24-4	18·10	25·34	25-8	28·81	53·24	47·66
24 × 24	12-4	4·52	6·33	16-5	40·60	34·90	29·19
24 × 24	24-8	36·19	50·67	25-8	83·06	77·66	72·26
25 × 25	16-4	8·04	11·26	20-5	48·28	42·11	35·95
25 × 25	28-4	24·63	34·48	20-6	70·50	64·50	58·49
25 × 25	28-4	49·26	68·96	25-8	103·50	97.75	91·99
26 × 26	18-4	10·18	14·25	20-5	54·20	47·54	40·83
26 × 26	30-4	28·27	39·58	20-6	78·44	71·97	65·49
26 × 26	30-8	56·55	79·17	25-8	116·34	110·14	103·9
27 × 27	18-4	10·18	14·25	20-5	57·38	50·19	43·00
27 × 27	30-4	28·27	39·58	20-6	81·59	74·39	67·59
27 × 27	30-8	56·55	79·17	25-8	119·52	112·79	106.07
28 × 28	18-4	10·18	14·25	20-5	60·68	52·94	45·20
28 × 28	30-4	28·27	39·58	20-6	84·92	77·37	69·81
28 × 28	30-8	56·55	74·17	25-8	112·82	115·52	108·27
29 × 29	20-4	12·57	17·60	20-5	67·31	39·08	50·74
29 × 29	30-4	28·27	39·58	20-6	84·92	77·37	69·81
29 × 29	30-8	56·55	79·17	25-8	126·24	118·39	110·55
30 × 30	30-4	12·57	17·60	20-5	70·85	61·97	53·10
30 × 30	30-4	40·72	57·01	25-8	100·57	99·97	91·38
30 × 30	36-8	81·43	114·00	30-8	164·11	154·93	146·74
30 × 30	20-4	12·57	17·60	20-5	78·28	68·17	58·06
32 × 32	36-4	40·72	57·01	25-8	116·01	106·17	96·54
32 × 32	36-8	81·43	114·00	30-8	170·55	161·13	151·70
34 × 34	22-4	15·21	21·24	20-6	89·74	78·33	66·92
34 × 34	30-8	56·55	79·70	25-8	145·14	134·14	123·15
34 × 34	40-8	100·53	140·47	30-8	202·47	192·18	181·89
36 × 36	22-4	15·21	21·29	20-5	118·14	85·33	72·52
36 × 36	32-8	64·34	90·38	30-8	164·20	151·96	139·65
36 × 36	40-8	100·53	140·74	30-8	212·74	200·51	188·53
38 × 38	22-4	15·21	21·24	20-5	107·02	92·73	78·44
38 × 38	34-8	22·63	101·68	20-6	103·76	170·75	156·53
38 × 38	45-8	127·23	198·12	30-8	257·13	243·96	230·79
40 × 40	45-8	127·63	178·12	30-8	266·49	251·76	237·03
45 × 45	24-4	18·10	25·34	20-5	145·35	125·69	105·62
45 × 45	36-8	81·43	114·00	25-8	230.09	211·18	191·74
45 × 45	45-8	127·23	178·12	30-8	291·99	273·01	254·03
50 × 50	20-8	25·14	35·20	20-6	183·69	158·94	134·19
50 × 50	34-12	168·95	152·54	30-8	295·99	272·48	248·17
50 × 50	45-12	190·85	267·19	30-8	405·74	382·65	759·50
55 × 55	22-8	30·48	42·57	20-6	232·75	192·30	152·89
55 × 55	34-12	108·95	152·53	30-8	327·49	298·33	296·17
55 × 55	45-12	190·85	267·19	30-8	427·24	408·89	380·56
60 × 60	24-8	36·19	50·67	25-8	264·50	228·86	193·22
60 × 60	36-12	122·15	171·01	30-8	379·68	344·90	310·12
60 × 60	45-12	190·85	267·19	30-8	471·74	437·65	403·56
65 × 65	24-8	36·19	50·67	20-6	302·00	260·11	218·22
65 × 65	36-12	122·75	171·01	30-8	417·18	776·15	335·12

Table 9A.20. Design data for square footings under RCC columns.

Outer column size (a)	Load on column	Depth of footing (D)	Size of footing and reinforcement at different bearing pressure of soil																		Remarks
			5 tonnes/m^2			10 tonnes/m^2			15 tonnes/m^2			20 tonnes/m^2			25 tonnes/m^2			30 tonnes/m^2			
			Side of foot b	no.	dia.	Side of foot b	no.	dia.	Side of foot b	no.	dia.	Side of foot b	no.	dia.	Side of foot b	no.	dia.	Side of foot b	no.	dia.	
cm	ton.	cm			mm			mm			mm			mm			mm			mm	
15 × 15	14	36	180	10	12	125	8	12	100	8	12	90	8	12	80	8	12	75	8	12	1. Table based on "R.C. Designs Manual" concrete association of India.
20 × 20	21	38	220	18	12	155	12	12	125	12	12	110	12	12	100	12	12	90	12	12	
20 × 20	26	48	240	18	12	170	12	12	140	10	12	120	10	12	105	10	12	100	10	12	
25 × 25	30	42	265	16	16	190	12	16	155	12	16	135	12	16	120	12	16	110	12	16	
25 × 25	35	48	275	16	16	195	10	16	160	10	16	140	10	16	125	10	16	115	10	16	
25 × 25	40	60	300	14	16	210	10	16	175	10	16	150	10	16	135	10	16	125	10	16	
25 × 25	44	70	310	14	16	220	10	16	180	8	16	155	8	16	140	8	16	130	8	16	
25 × 25	49	75	330	16	16	235	10	16	190	8	16	165	8	16	150	8	16	135	8	16	2. Stress-crush-ing (bending) = 50 kg/cm^2; Punching shear in concrete (comp.) = 10 kg/cm^2; Tensile strength of steel 1400 kg/cm^2.
30 × 30	46	50	320	22	16	225	14	16	185	12	16	160	12	16	145	12	16	130	12	16	
30 × 30	51	60	335	20	16	240	14	16	195	12	16	170	12	16	150	12	16	140	12	16	
30 × 30	55	70	350	20	16	245	14	16	200	10	16	175	10	16	155	10	16	145	10	16	
30 × 30	60	75	370	20	16	260	14	16	210	12	16	185	10	16	165	10	16	160	10	16	
30 × 30	74	75	445	18	20	285	20	16	235	14	16	200	14	16	180	14	16	165	14	16	
35 × 35	64	60	380	18	20	265	12	20	220	12	20	190	12	20	170	12	20	155	12	20	
35 × 35	68	70	390	18	20	275	12	20	225	10	20	195	10	20	175	10	20	160	10	20	
35 × 35	73	75	400	18	20	285	12	20	235	10	20	200	10	20	180	10	20	165	10	20	
40 × 40	83	70	425	22	20	300	16	20	250	12	20	215	12	20	190	12	20	175	12	20	3. Nos. of bars are for both directions (long. and cross) provided at bottom spaced equally.
40 × 40	88	75	440	22	20	310	16	20	255	12	20	220	12	20	200	12	20	180	12	20	
40 × 40	95	85	455	22	20	325	16	20	255	12	20	230	12	20	205	12	20	190	12	20	
40 × 40	113	90	500	22	20	355	16	22	290	12	22	250	12	22	225	12	22	205	12	20	
45 × 45	105	75				340	20	20	280	18	20	240	14	20	215	14	20	200	14	20	
45 × 45	112	85				350	20	20	290	16	20	250	14	20	215	14	20	205	14	20	
50 × 50	131	85				380	24	20	310	20	20	270	16	20	240	16	20	220	16	20	
50 × 50	149	90				405	22	22	330	18	22	290	16	22	255	16	22	235	16	22	
50 × 50	162	95				420	28	22	345	20	22	900	16	22	265	16	22	245	16	22	
55 × 55	152	85				410	24	22	335	18	22	290	18	22	260	18	22	235	18	22	4. Dead wt. of column and footing is 10% of the live load on column.
55 × 55	170	95				435	26	22	355	20	22	305	16	22	275	16	22	250	16	22	
55 × 55	183	100				450	28	22	365	20	22	315	16	22	285	16	22	260	16	22	
60 × 60	193	95				460	32	22	375	24	22	325	18	22	295	18	22	265	18	22	
60 × 60	206	100				475	32	22	390	26	22	335	20	22	300	20	22	275	20	22	
60 × 60	225	110				500	36	22	405	26	22	350	18	22	315	18	22	290	18	22	

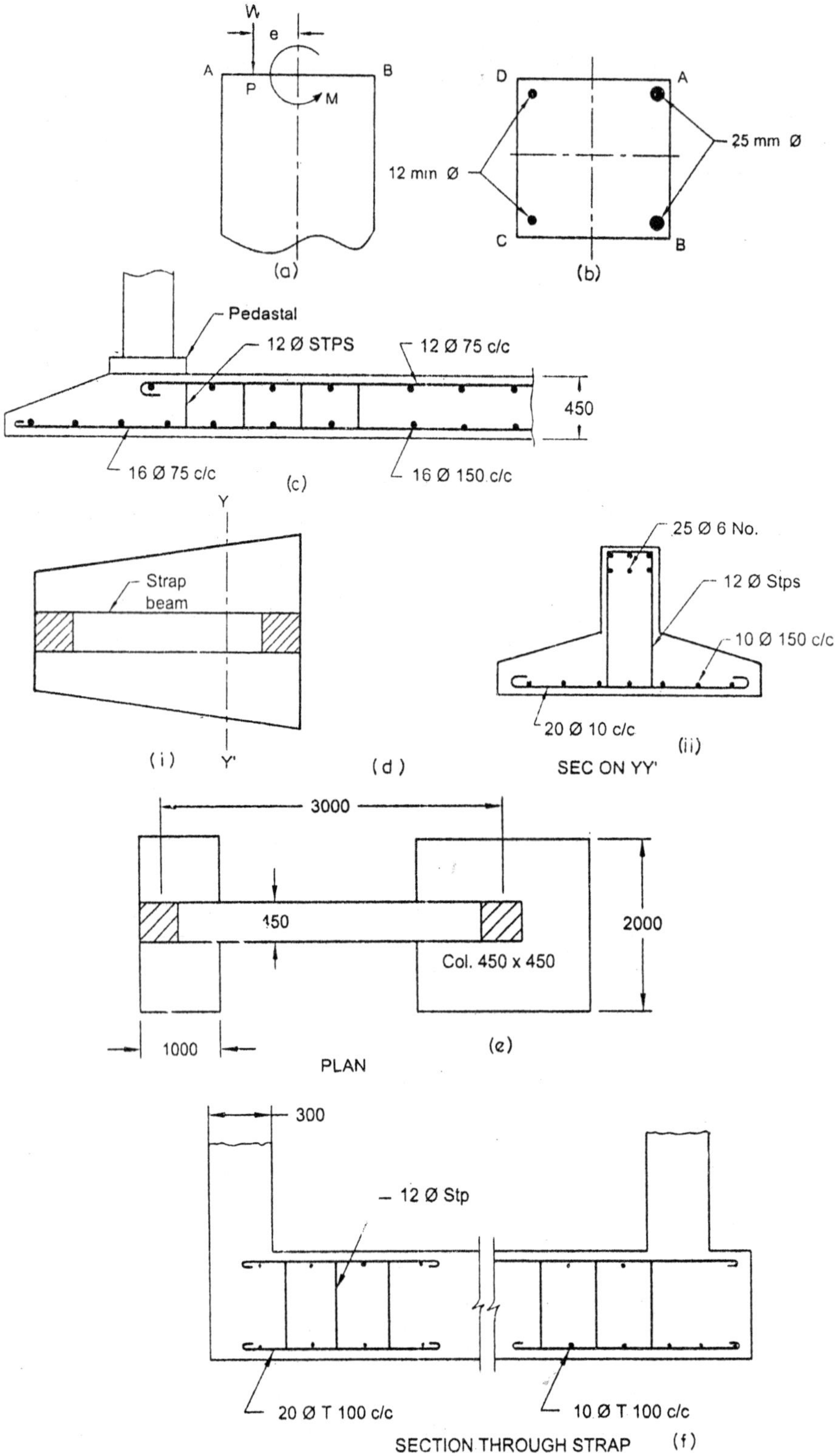
W
e
A
B
P
M
(a)
D
A
C
B
25 mm Ø
12 min Ø
(b)
Pedastal
12 Ø STPS
12 Ø 75 c/c
450
16 Ø 75 c/c
16 Ø 150 c/c
(c)
Y
Strap beam
Y'
(i)
(d)
25 Ø 6 No.
12 Ø Stps
10 Ø 150 c/c
20 Ø 10 c/c
(ii)
SEC ON YY'
3000
450
2000
Col. 450 x 450
1000
PLAN
(e)
300
12 Ø Stp
20 Ø T 100 c/c
10 Ø T 100 c/c
SECTION THROUGH STRAP
(f)

Fig. 9A·14.

9A·12. Design of T-Beam

Design of slab. The end effective span = clear span + 1/2 depth of slab. For intermediate spans, effective span = clear span.

Design the slab as usual. Provide –ve B.M. and extend it to the middle of each span. Bars cranked from bottom can be used as –ve bars. Hence, –ve reinforcement will be provided upto half the span towards beam in end span and in full length in middle spans. 0.2% temperature reinforcement is provided in the bottom of slabs and on the support at the top. Test the bond and shear stress is as usual.

Design of beam

$$M = b_s . d_s . c \frac{2Nd - d_s}{2Nd} jd \qquad ...(A)$$

(Case I when $N.A.$ lies below slab) the above equation will give M, knowing other factors.

(1) b_s = 1/3 of the span of beam

(2) 12 × Depth of slab or width of web.

or (3) centre to centre of beam, whichever is less.

d_s = depth of slab. ; $M = tjd$ will give the reinforcement in the beam.

Case II : (when the $N.A.$ lies in the slab itself when the slab is thick)

For slab use formula $M = Q\ b_s d^2$ ...(B)

and $M = tjd$ ...(C)

Design of the beam can be done with the formula (A)

Design of the beam by economical formula $d = \sqrt{\frac{Mr}{tjd}}$

where r is the ratio of the cost of steel to cost of concrete or $r = \frac{\text{cost of concrete}}{\text{cost of steel}}$

Test in bond and shear is as usual.

Design of T-Beams

There are two **Cases-(1)** when the $N.A.$ lies outside the flange and the compression in the web is negligible. If C_s is the intensity of compressive stress at the bottom of flange then $C_s = C.\frac{Nd - d_s}{Nd}$ where d_s is the thickness of flange.

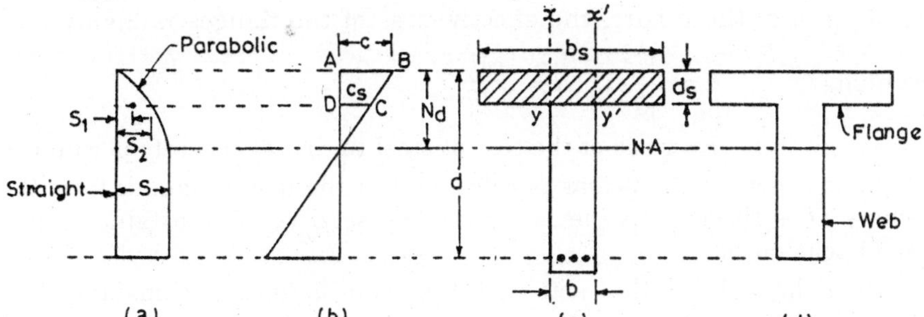

Shear stress Bending stress Sec. of T-beam

Fig. 9A·15.

Total compression in the flange $= b_s d_s \dfrac{(C + Cs)}{2}$

$$= b_s d_s \, C/2\left(1 + \frac{Nd - d_s}{Nd}\right)$$

$$= b_s d_s \, C/2 \frac{(2Nd - d_s)}{Nd}$$ from the flange is negligible,

If the distance of the *c.g.* the compressive forces and that of steel is equal to *jd i.e.* lowering then the moment of resistance of the beam with respect to compressive stress is given by

$$M = b_s d_s \, C \frac{2Nd - d_s}{2Nd} \, jd \qquad \text{... (1)}$$

and $$M = A_t . t . \, jd \qquad \text{...(2)}$$

As usual with respect to tensile stress. The value of '*J*' generally lies between 0.88 and 0.95 increasing with the decrease of d_s/d. It is usual to assume J equal to 0.9 in the preliminary design.

Case (2). If the flange is so thick that the neutral axis lies inside the flange, the bottom portion of flange is in tension and so total compressive stress is equal to $bs \; Nd \; . \; C/2$ as in ordinary section beam.

$$\therefore \quad M = b_s \, Nd \, . \, C/2 \, jd$$

$$= (1/2 \, NCj) b_s \, d^2 = Q b_s d^2$$

This is the same formula as for rectangular beams except that the breadth of the beam in this case is equal to the width of the flange that acts with the beam.

With the help of the equations (1) and (2) the T-beam can be designed for a given moment to the depth and amount of steel can be calculated.

Test for shear

$$V = \frac{F}{d_s jd} \cdot \frac{b_s - b}{b_s} \cdot \frac{Nd}{2Nd - d_s}$$

where F = Total S.F. and is the allowable shear stress

V = Shear max. stress at top fibre of the slab at section XY which must be allowable stress S.

The beam is some times strengthened by means of fillets between the flange and web and the shear stress and also transverse steel bars are placed near the top of the slab. Then bars not only strengthen the connection between the flanges and the stress but also resist any –ve moment that develops due to load on the slab. If the slab cracks due to this moment in the absence of these bars, the effectiveness of the flanges is highly reduced.

For economy $$b = \frac{Mr}{t_j d^2}, \quad d = \sqrt{\frac{Mr}{tjb}}$$

where r = ratio of the cost of steel to cost of concrete per unit in volume.

Note 1. Bond stress in the beams is calculated in the usual manner from the formula $Sa = F/jd\Sigma 0$ where *jd* is the effective lever arm of the section. Sa = attainable bond stress. $\Sigma 0$ = perimeter of tension bars.

2. Breadth of the slab '*bs*' that acts with the beam in such circumstances is the least of the following.

(*a*) 1/3rd of the span of beam.

(*b*) 12 × depth of slab + width of web.

(*c*) Distance between middle point of the adjacent spans of the slab.

Plate 9A·2. RCC Design of a particular building.

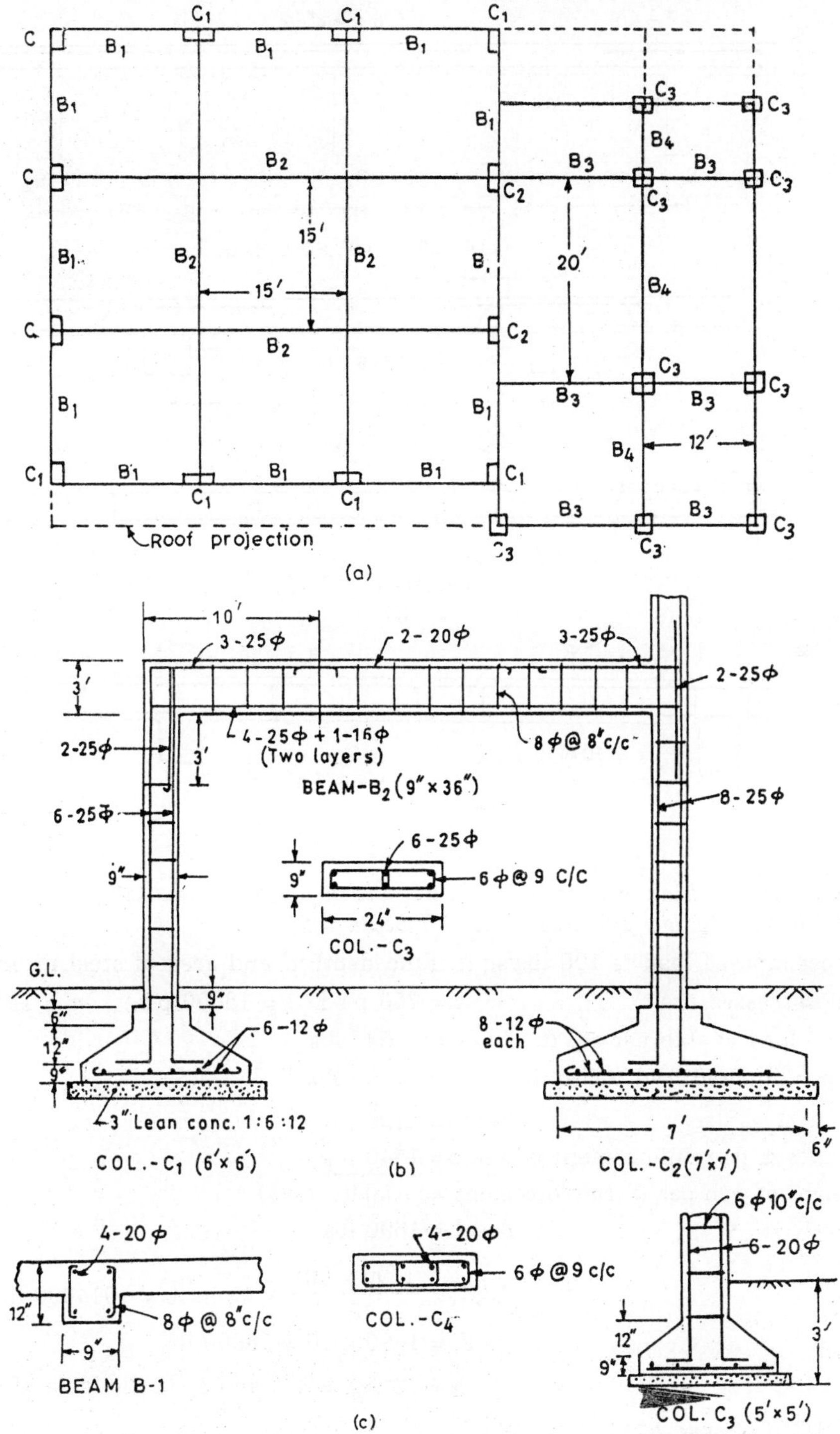

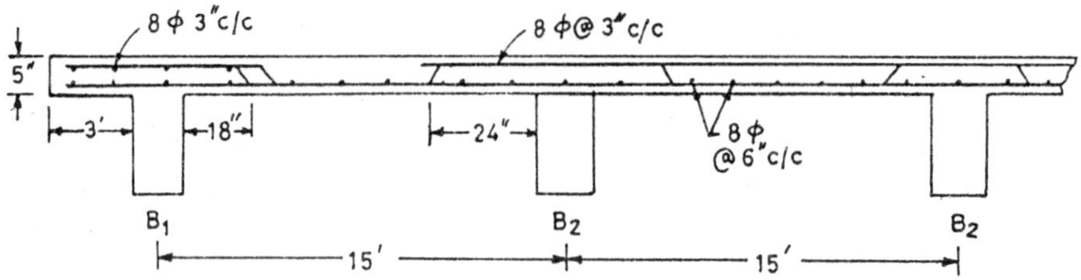

(d) ROOF SLAB FOR HALL

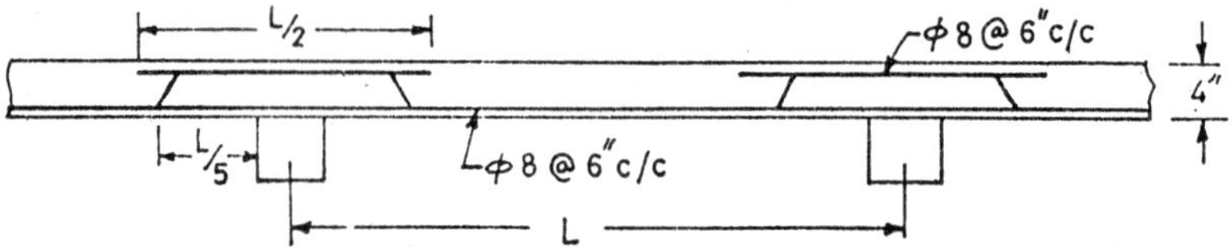

(e)

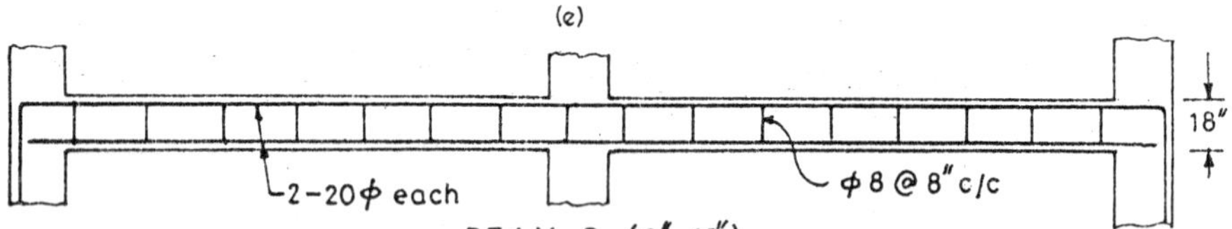

BEAM–B_3 (9"×18")

(f)

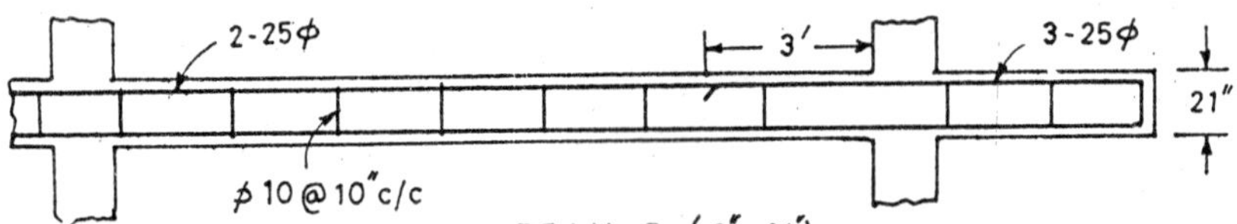

BEAM–B_4 (9"×21")

(g)

Example. *Thickness of roof = 4½", width of the beam 12" monolithic with slab spacing of T-beams 10' c/c. effective span of T-beam = 20'.*

Superimposed load is 100 lbs/sq.ft. Find depth d and area of steel in one beam.

Safe stresses are c = 750 p.s.i t = 18000 p.s.i. m = 18

Dead load of slab per sq. ft. = 54 lbs

Super imposed load per sq. ft. = 100 lbs

Total = 154 lbs

Load per ft. reinforcement of beam = 1540 lbs

Weight of web per ft. reinforcement = 150 lbs (say)

Total = 1690 lbs

$$\therefore \quad \text{B.M.} = \frac{1690 \times 20^2}{8} \times 12 \text{ in lb} = 1014000 \text{ in lb}$$

$$\text{S.F.} = 1690 \times 10 = 16900 \text{ lbs}$$

Here b = 12", d_s = 45" and b_s is the least of the following

(a) 1/3rd of span of beam = 20/3 ft.

(b) 12 × d_s + b = 66 inches

(c) c/c of beams = 10 ft.

Hence bs = 66 inches. Equation (1) gives the depth of the beam based on max. allowable compressive stress. Since it is proposed to use max. allowable. Then in steel also, N = 3/7 and j may be assumed to be 0.9 to start with. It can be lateron checked after the depth and area of steel have been found.

$$\therefore \quad 1014000 = 66 \times 4.5 \times 750 \left(\frac{2 \times 3/7d - 4.5}{2 \times 3/7d}\right) 0.9d \text{ or } d = 10.7 \text{ inches}$$

Economical depth formula, $d = \sqrt{\dfrac{Mr}{tjb}}$ where r = 60

$$= \sqrt{\frac{1014000 \times 60}{18000 \times 0{\cdot}9 \times 12}} = 17{\cdot}3 \text{ inches}$$

Adopt effective depth = 17.3 inches

$$A_t = \frac{1014000}{18000 \times 0.9 \times 17.3} = 3.6 \text{ sq.ms.}$$

After having adopted depth and area of steel, it is now possible to find out the actual lever arm and the stresses may be rechecked.

9A.13. Stairs

Design loads

1. Stairs and landings of residential and office buildings 300 kg/m^2
2. Stairs public places and warehouses 500 kg/m^2
3. Stairs unimportant approaches 150 kg/m^2

Effective span

For stairs without stringers shall be taken as follows – (horizontal distances)

(*a*) When supported on top and bottom risers by beams spanning parallel to the risers, the distance c/c of beams.

(*b*) Where spanning on the edge of a landing slab, which spans parallel with the risers, a distance equal to the going of the stairs plus at each end either half the width of landing or one metre which ever is smaller (Ref. Fig. 9A·16).

(*c*) When the landing slab spans in the same direction as the stairs they shall be considered as acting together to form a single slab and the span determines on the distance c/c of the supporting beams or walls. The going being measured horizontally.

(*d*) **Depth of section.** Minimum thickness perpendicular to the soffit of the stair case.

Waist slab reinforcement details for office residential or for moderate loads spanning over walls or edge beams.

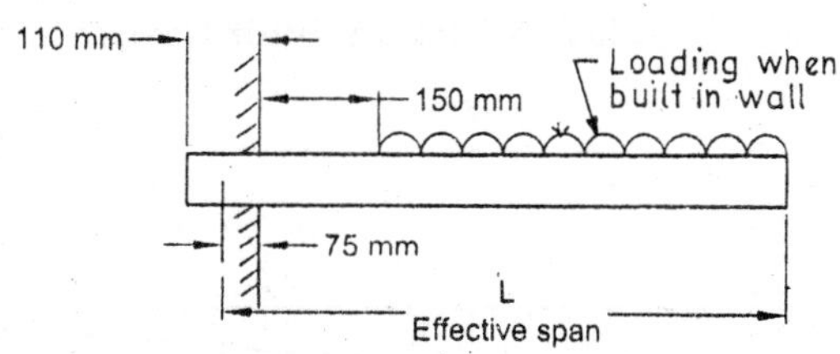

(*a*)

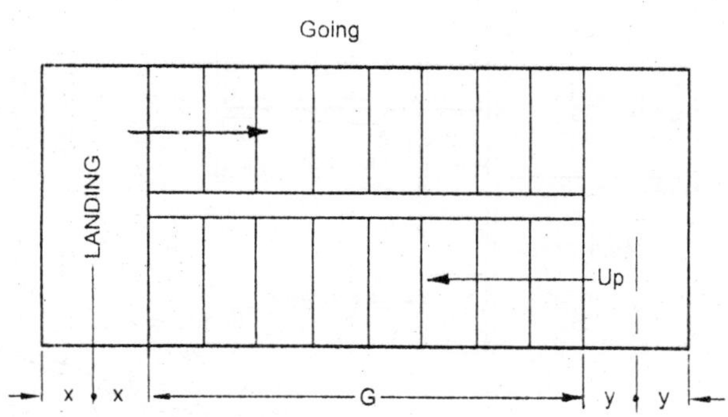

(*b*)

Fig. 9A·16

Table 9A.21

Span in	*Thick-ness of waist slab*	*Main bars*		*Distribution bars*		*Span in*	*Thick-ness of waist slab*	*Main bars*		*Distribution bars*	
		dia.	*spacing c/c*	*dia.*	*spacing c/c*			*dia.*	*spacing c/c*	*dia.*	*spacing c/c*
(m)	*(mm)*	*(mm)*	*(cm)*	*(mm)*	*(cm)*	*(m)*	*(mm)*	*(mm)*	*(cm)*	*(mm)*	*(cm)*
1·5	100	10	15	6	30	4·0	170	16	14	10	25
2·0	100	10	13	6	25	4·5	200	16	12	10	17
2·5	115	10	10	6	22	5·0	225	16	10	10	12
3·0	130	12	14	6	15	5·5	255	16	9	10	12
3·5	150	12	12	10	30	6·0	270	16	7	10	12

(1) Pre-cast slabs anchored in side walls. Tread slabs anchored in side wall at one side, projecting 1.2 m outside of wall with 200 mm anchorage width in wall.

Width = 350 mm

and Thickness = 100 mm

Main bars 2 Nos, 10 mm at top side

Transverse bars 6 cm c/c

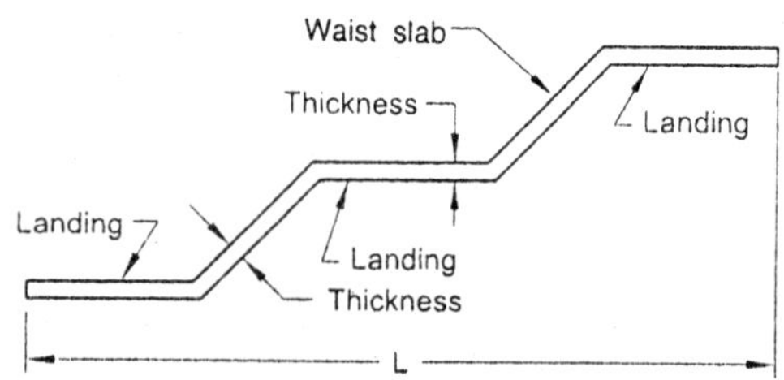

Fig. 9A·16 (*c*)

Plate No. 9A·3A. Stair Cases

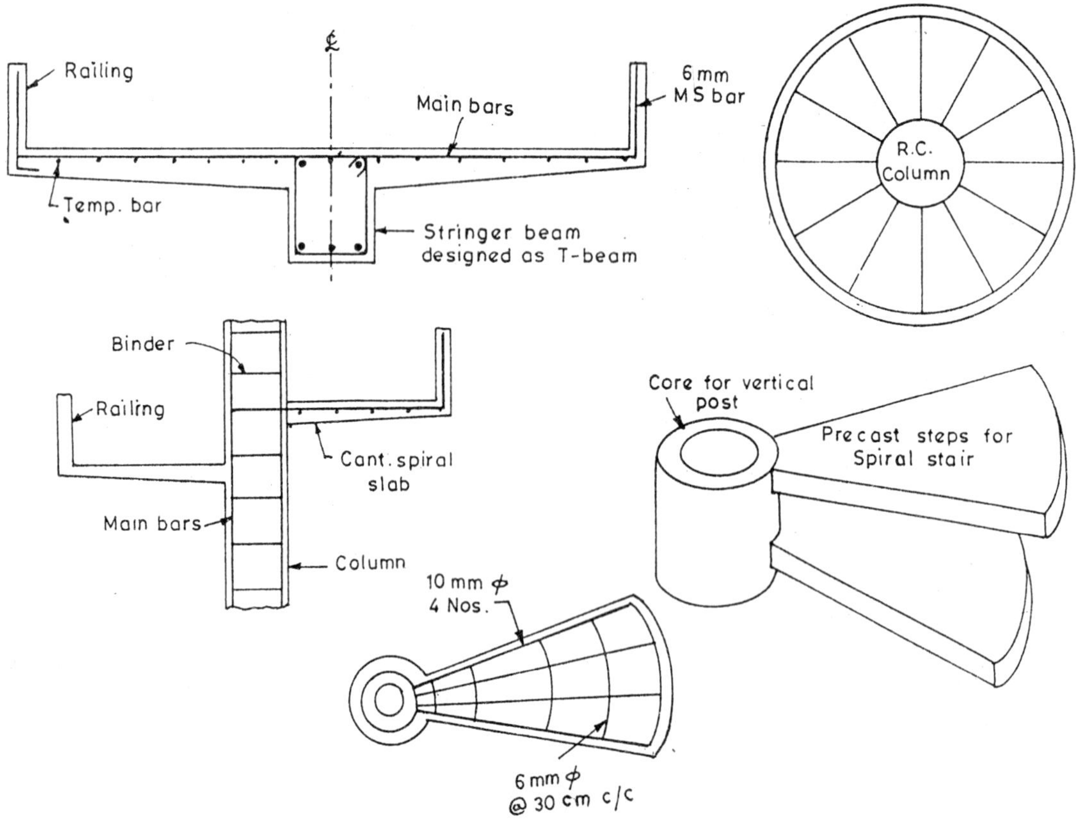

Plate No. 9A·3B

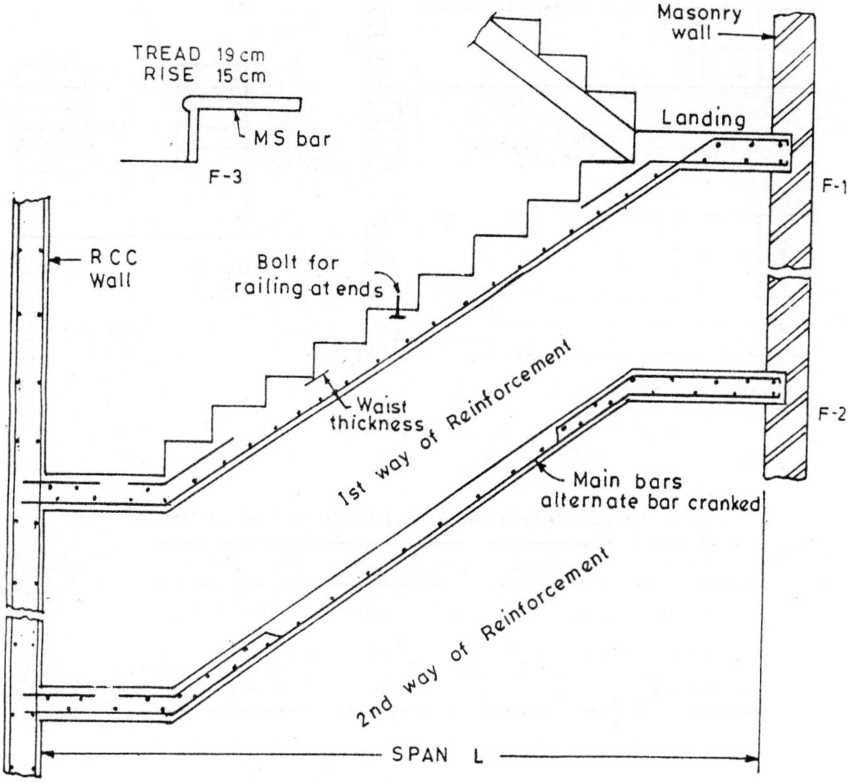

Plate No. 9A·3C

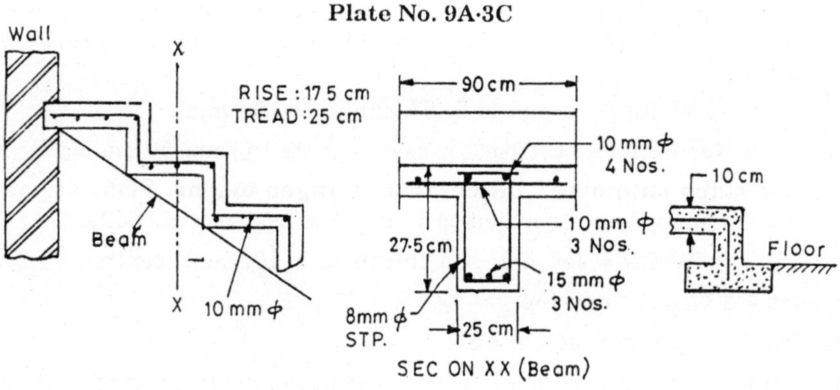

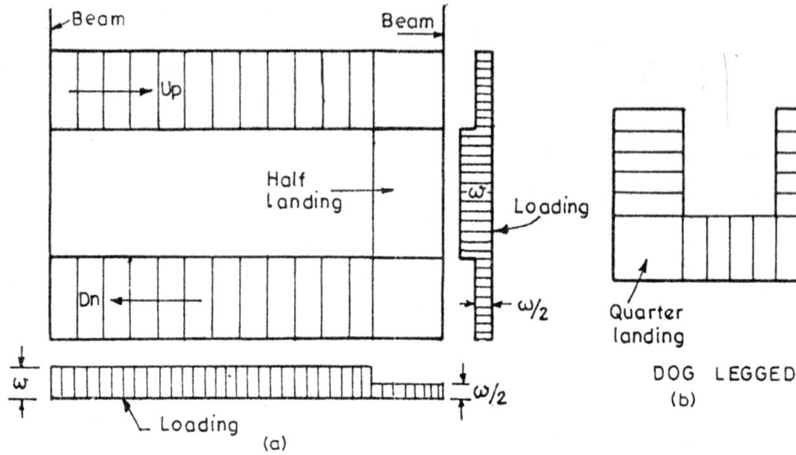

Fig. 9A·17.

Table 9A·22. Optimum dimensions for stair (mm)

Usage	*Tread*	*Rise*	*Min. width*
Public	300	150	1000
Semi Public	275	165	1000
Private	250	175	80

Note. General optimum dimensions 2 × rise + tread = 600 mm

'Tread' can also be said as 'going'.

2. Precast slabs supported on stringer beams on both ends. Slabs are anchored with bolts in the stringer beams which are notched to bear slabs and provided with bolts, casted in the notches.

Width = 30 mm and Thickness = 100 mm

Main bars 3 Nos 6 mm at bottom, transverse bars : 6 mm 30 cm c/c

3. Precast slabs supported on central stringer beams. Slabs are anchored with bolts in the central stringer beam notched to bear slabs casted with bolts.

Width = 350 mm and thickness = 100 mm (centre), 75 mm at ends.

Main bars – 3 Nos. 10 mm top

Transverse bars – 6 mm 30 cm c/c.

Note 1. Holes in slabs are made when casting for bolts of hand rails and stringer beams.

2. Each upper slab projects about 4 cm over the edge of lower.

9A.14. Walls

R.C.C. walls are designed as tied columns for a strip of unit width. The thickness of the wall is kept at least 1/25th of the supported height or length whichever is greater 1/30th of the supporting distance. Load bearing walls must have minimum width of 10 cm, partition walls 7.5 cm and cellar (basement) walls 20 cm. However, the strength of the wall may be increased by the values given below –

Ratio of storey height to length of wall	1.5 or more	1.0	0.5 or less
% increase in length	0	10	20

Note 1. The length of the wall is the overall length or where opening occurs, the length between adjacent opening or between the walls.

2. When the effective height of the wall exceeds 12 times the wall thickness, the slenderness effects should be considered as in columns.

Reinforcement—IS : 456-1978.

Vertical bars

(*a*) 0.0012 of the gross concrete area with deformed bars not larger than 16 mm in dia. and a characteristic strength of 415 N/mm^2 or greater.

(*b*) 0.0015 of the gross area for other type of bars.

(*c*) 0.0012 for welded wire fabric not larger than 16 mm in dia.

(*d*) The spacing of bars must not be farther apart than three times the wall thickness or 450 mm.

Horizontal bars

(*a*) 0.002 of the gross concrete area for deformed bars not larger than 16 mm in diameter and with a characteristic strength of 415 N/mm^2 or greater.

(*b*) 0.0025 for other type of walls.

(*c*) 0.0020 for welded wire fabric not larger than 16 mm in diameter.

(*d*) Should not be spaced farther apart than three times the wall thickness or 450 mm.

Note 1. The minimum reinforcement may not always be sufficient to provide adequate resistance to the effects of shrinkage and temperature.

2. Footings of the walls should be designed on the load bearing capacity of the soil. However, a width twice the thickness of wall and depth half the thickness of the wall are generally provided.

9A.15. Load on lintels

(1) If wall is higher than the vertex of the equilateral triangle. Full triangular load is taken (for B.M.) B.M. = $WL/6$.

(2) (*a*) If wall ends below the vertex, the load of a rectangle from top of lintel to bottom of roof is taken with the base equal to span.

(*b*) For mud mortar take isosceles triangle with base L.

(*c*) For R.R. masonry take rectangle with a height of 1.5 L.

(3) An opening in the triangle, take load on lower opening triangle + load on higher opening triangle – triangle of lower opening at base of above opening.

(4) Uniformly distributed load falling within the triangle is considered by taking into account only that length of the floor lying inside the triangle + lower part of the triangle below floor.

Concentrated loads

(5) If concentrated load is falling inside the triangle then total moment = Moment due to triangle + Moment due to concentrated load . Total moment = $\frac{wL}{6} + \frac{w_1 L}{4}$, w being the load of the triangle and w_1 be the concentrated load.

Plate 9A·4. Lintels

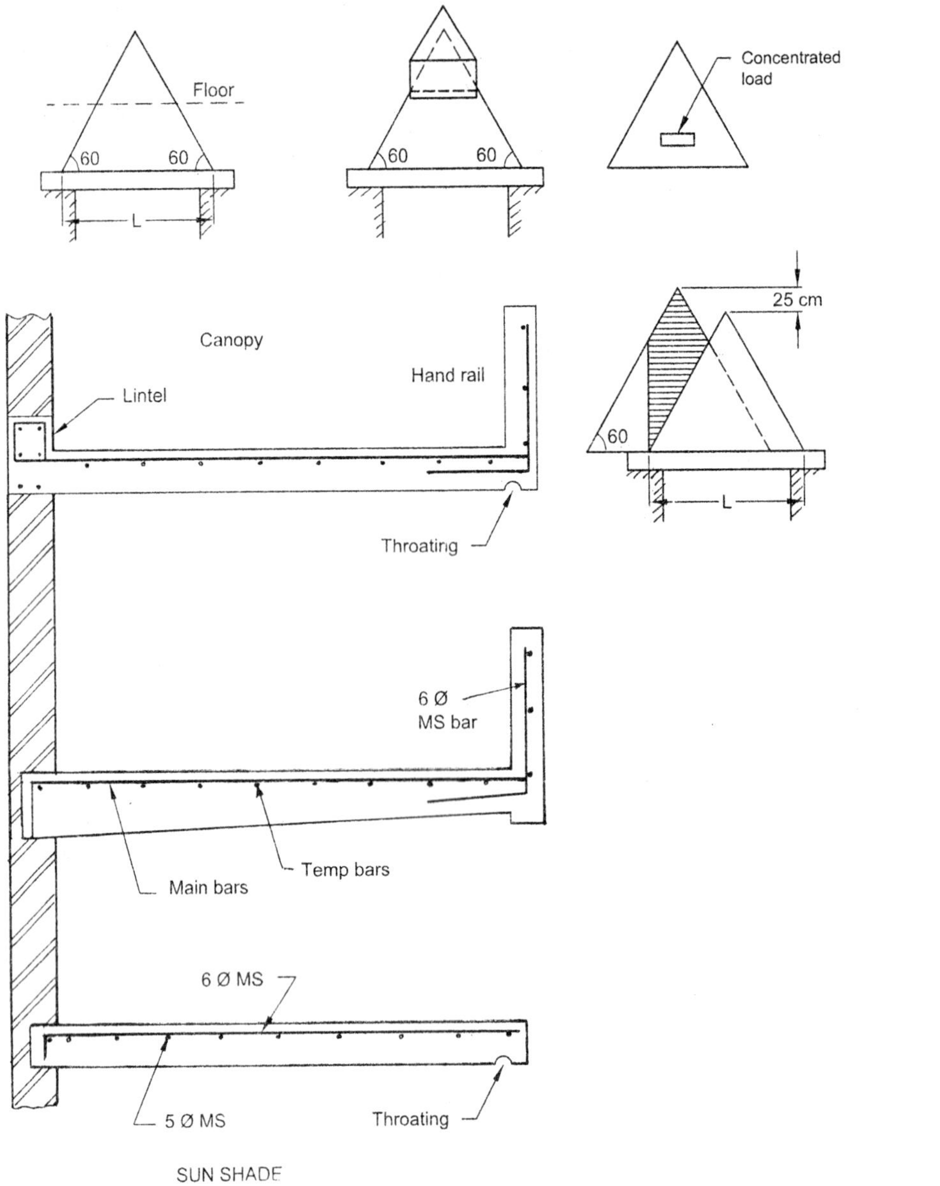

BM due to self distributed load $= \dfrac{wL^2}{8}$ (w = distributed load of lintel itself.)

So total BM $= \dfrac{wL}{6} + \dfrac{w_1L}{4} + \dfrac{wL^2}{8}.$

(6) Point loads outside the triangle should be considered only if they fall within the span of the lintel and below a horizontal line 25 cm above the apex of the triangle. The weight of the masonry is shown hatched must be deducted for such concentrated load.

(7) Concentrated loads above vertex more than span L in height above vertex is neglected and below is added together with load of triangle as discussed in (6) above.

Deflection and thickness in lintels

Deflection must not exceed $\frac{1}{480}$ of the span and depth should not be less than $\frac{1}{20}$th of the span. For stone lintels thickness may be taken approximately 10 cm for a span upto 1 m and 20 cm upto a span of 2 m.

Table 9A.23. Design data for RCC cantilevers, canopies and sun shades.

Projection in (m)	*Overall depth at support (cm)*	*Reinforcing bars*			
		Main tensile dia. (mm)	*Bar at top spacing (cm)*	*Distribution bar*	
				dia. (mm)	*spacing (cm)*
0·5	7	6	30	5	4 Nos·
1·0	12	6	20	5	5 Nos·
1·5	18	10	30	6	30
2·0	25	12	30	6	30
2·5	30	12	25	6	25
3·0	35	12	20	6	25

Note. Make top sloping, thus reducing the thickness at the free end from about 1/2 to 3/4th of the thickness or depth at the supports (walls). Thickness of a cantilever slab at the support should be not less than 1/10 $\left(\text{preferably } \frac{1}{7.5}\right)$ of the projection. Sufficient anchorage to counter balance the weight of the projection is essential. In cantilever slabs of larger dimension thicker bars should be used, which may not be less than 12 mm in diameter. In adequate and lesser stiff bars are likely to bend while concreting.

In built-up RC sun-shades No. 10 wire is provided at 10 cm c/c at right angles to the main bars. Minimum head room from top of pavement is 2.3 m.

Table 9A.24. Reinforcement in lintels (equilateral triangle wall load.

Clear span M/(Ft.)		*Min. bearing cm/(in)*		*Overall depth cm/(in)*		*Thickness of slab cm/(in)*		*Straight bars No.*	*dia. T (mm)*	*Bent up bars No.*	*dia. T (mm)*
1 m	(3'-4")	15 cm	(6")	10 cm	(4")	11	(4.5)	2	(6)	—	—
						22	(9)	2	(6)	1	(6)
						33	(13.5)	2	(8)	1	(8)
1.25	(4′-2″)	15	(6″)	10	(4″)	11	(4.5)	2	(6)	—	—
						22	(9)	2	(8)	1	(8)
						33	(13.5)	2	(8)	1	(8)
1.5	(5′-0″)	15	(6″)	15	(6″)	11	(4.5)	2	(6)	—	—
						22	(9)	2	(8)	1	(8)
						33	(13.5)	2	(8)	2	(8)
1.75	(5′-10″)	15	(6″)	15	(6″)	11	(4.5)	2	(8)	—	—
						22	(9)	2	(8)	2	(8)
						33	(13.5)	2	(10)	2	(10)
2.0	(6′-8″)	20	(8″)	20	(8.5″)	11	(45)	2	(8)	—	—
						22	(9)	2	(8)	2	(8)
						33	(13.5)	2	(10)	2	(10)

Table contd.

Table contd...

Clear span M/(Ft.)		Min. bearing cm/(in)		Overall depth cm/(in)		Thickness of slab cm/(in)		Straight bars		Bent up bars	
								No.	dia. T (mm)	No.	dia. T (mm)
2.25	(7′-6″)	20	(8″)	20	(8.5″)	11	(4.5)	2	(10)	—	—
						22	(9)	2	(10)	2	(10)
						33	(13.5)	2	(12)	2	(12)
2.50	(8′-2″)	25	(10″)	25	(10)	11	(4.5)	2	(10)	—	—
						22	(9)	2	(10)	2	(10)
						33	(13.5)	2	(12)	2	(12)
2.75	(9′-1″)	25	(10″)	25	(10)	11	(4.5)	2	(12)	—	—
						22	(9)	2	(12)	2	12
						33	(13.5)	2	(14)	2	14
3.00	(10′)	30	(12″)	30	(12)	11	(4.5)	2	(12)	—	—
						22	(9.0)	2	(12)	2	12
						33	(13.5)	2	(14)	2	14

Note 1. Bent up bars should be bent at 45° at 1/7th of span from support.

2. Nominal stirrups of 6 mm diameter at 15 cm c/c.

3. For small spans thickness of slab can be reduced to 7.5 cm reinforcement same as for 1 m span.

9A.16. Design of RC water tanks

General rules for design of water tanks.

(1) Economical proportions of circular tanks in diameter = Height (covered)

diameter = 2 Height (open)

Economical proportions of rectangular tanks is cube for covered base square and height half of side (open).

(2) Mixture of concrete is 1 : 1½ : 3 (M-20) with impervious stone ballast and water proofing compound to avoid any sweating (seeping of water on outer face).

(3) Minimum thickness of floor and wall is 25 mm + 1/40 of water depth. (Minimum 10 cm)

(4) Minimum steel in walls and floors is 0.3% in each direction. It can be 0.2 percent for high yield deformed bars. The thinner possible bars should be used. Distribution bars should be placed outside the main bars.

(5) The lift of one layer should be maximum 200 cm.

(6) The tank must be insulated outside for guide against temperature with earth, bitumen, fibre board, or any other material having low thermal conductivity.

(7) Thick shuttering must be avoided as it prevents to escape the heat produced during hydration.

(8) No beams under floor's slab are provided. The supporting columns are provided with drop pannels and capitals.

Design of circular tanks

Wall.(not monolithic with base slab.)

Reinforcement for hoop or circumferential tension. Assuming one metre strip of wall.

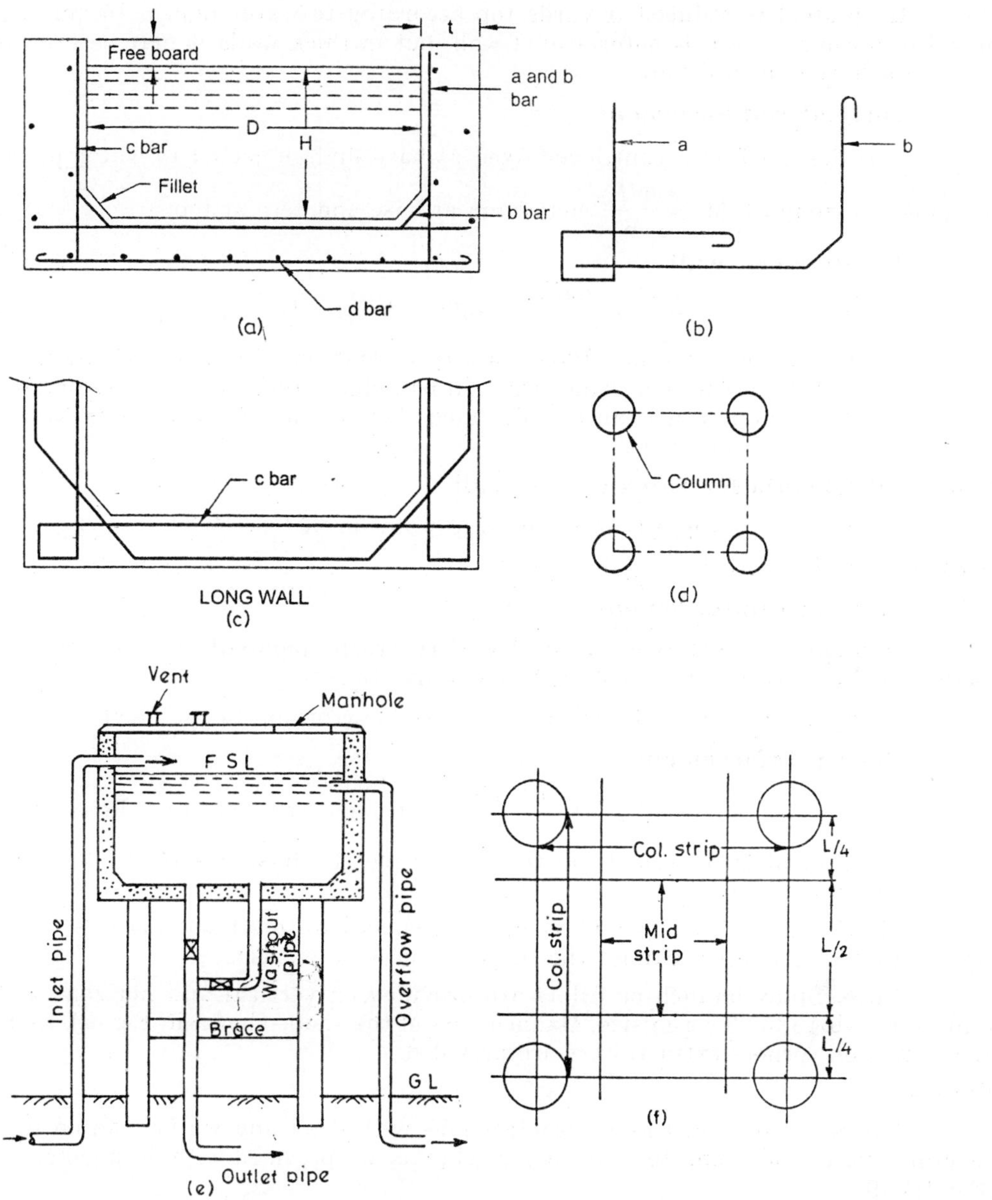

Fig. 9A·18.

$T = \frac{wHD}{2}$ where T = hoop tension, H = head of water in tank

D = inner diameter of tank and w = the weight of water per unit.

$A_s = \frac{T}{f_s}\ ;\ \frac{wHD}{2} = \frac{HD}{2}\ ;$

A_s = area of steel per m height of wall and f_s is the permissible stress in steel against cracking which is 1000 kg/cm^2 for M-20 grade concrete, 1000 being weight of water in kg/m^3.

Hoop steel is reduced towards top according to water depth. In small tanks it is provided in centre (towards outerface) of wall, but in thick walls it may be provided on both faces outside the vertical bars.

Vertical reinforcement

It is designed as a cantilever fixed at base and subjected to water pressure inside the tank. Maximum B.M. = $\frac{wH^3}{6}$ maximum at base and zero at top.

Thickness of wall

$$t = \{A_c + A_s (m - 1)\} \text{ or } \frac{wHD}{2} = \{1000 + A_s (m - 1)\}$$

t = thickness of wall ; 1000 t is area of conc. in 1000 mm high wall, m = 13.3 for M-20 grade conc. Thickness can be reduced towards top according to the height of water which can be calculated. The minimum thickness is 15 cm at bottom and 10 cm at top.

Empirical formula for thickness of wall

t = 3H + 5; where H is the head of water in metre.

Walls (monolithic with floor slab)

Vertical reinforcement

Moment in cantilever at the base (restraint moment) = $a \times wH^3$ ("a" being a coefficient. Refer Reissner's constants for circular tanks)

Every alternate or 3rd bar can be curtailed according to the height.

Hoop reinforcement

$T = b \times \frac{w \times HD}{2}$ "b" being a constant. (refer Reissoner's constants)

Position of maximum hoop tension above the base = CH "C" being a constant (Reissoner's constant).

The distance of hoop reinforcement is reduced to this point towards bottom and top both, with a minimum of 3 times the thickness of wall at base.

Note. Splay haunch or fillets are provided on vertical and horizontal junctions of walls and slab 15 to 23 cm in size. Haunch bars of the shape shown in Fig. 9A·18 are provided at junction on corners extra L bars are provided.

Floors

Floors are designed as horizontal slabs with dead and water load on it. Beams are generally not provided and the supporting columns are provided with drop panel and capitals. (Fig. 9A·19)

Table 9A.25. Reissner's constants for circular tanks.

Constant		*H/D*	*0·2*	*0·3*	*0·4*	*0·5*	*1·0*	*2·0*	*3·0*
		10	·045	·030	·024	·020	·012	·006	·005
a	*(H/t)*	20	·028	·018	·014	·012	·006	·005	·003
		30	·023	·012	·010	·008	·005	·003	·002
		10	·30	·30	·43	·47	·62	·73	·77
b	*(H/t)*	20	·38	·51	·57	·61	·72	·81	·84
		30	·50	·60	·64	·68	·77	·85	·87
		10	—	·55	·50	·45	·38	·30	·27
c	*(H/t)*	20	0·5	·44	·40	·37	·28	·22	·21
		30	0·44	·38	·34	·31	·24	·19	·18

Rectangular tanks with walls monolithic with base slab long walls

Long walls are designed as cantilevers supported at base, with a water pressure from side of the tank with a maximum B.M. = $wH^3/6$. The vertical reinforcement is provided towards the water face, on the water face. However, a nominal reinforcement (0.2%) is also provided. The reinforcement can be curtailed towards top in alternate or 3rd bar according to the depth of water where B.M. is reduced according to the water depth.

Horizontal reinforcement is provided to bear tension due to water pressure. T = 3/4th × $w/2$ where T is the horizontal tension and t = thickness of wall. Knowing T, the reinforcement the thickness of wall can be determined as in circular tanks. (Maximum calculated by cantilever or by horizontal tension load is adopted) 0.2 to 0.3% transverse reinforcement or horizontal reinforcement whichever greater is provided horizontally.

Short walls.

Short walls are designed as slabs spanning the short span in unit wide strips. The maximum B.M. = $\dfrac{wL^2}{16}$ and –ve B.M. = $\dfrac{wL^2}{12}$. Bars for +ve B.M. are provided to the outer face and inner towards the waterside face.

In large tanks counter fort walls are provided with vertical walls at suitable distance apart.

Table 9A.26. Design data for small RCC circular tanks.

Capacity (litres)	*Inside dia. D (m)*	*Depth h includ. free board (mm)*	*Thickness of wall and floor t (mm)*	*Reinforcement*					
				Wall				*Floor*	
				Hor. steel at bot. half		*Vert. steel bars a and b*		*Bars each way bar d*	
				depth bar c dia. (mm)	*spacing (cm)*	*dia. (mm)*	*spacing (cm)*	*dia. (mm)*	*spacing (cm)*
(1)	(2)	(3)	(4)	(5)	(6)	(7)	(8)	(9)	(10)
2,000	1·75	1·00	10	10	20	10	20	10	20
3,500	2·00	1·40	10	10	20	10	20	10	20
5,000	2·75	1·45	10	10	20	10	20	10	20
7,000	2·50	1·55	10	10	20	10	20	10	20
9,000	2·75	1·70	13	10	20	10	20	10	20
14,000	3·00	2·10	13	10	20	10	20	10	20
23,000	3·75	2·25	15	10	17	10	20	10	20
34,000	4·25	2·55	15	10	17	10	20	10	20
45,000	4·75	2·65	18	12	20	12	30	12	30
90,000	6·00	3·25	18	12	12	12	20	12	30

Note 1. Horizontal reinforcement can be reduced towards the top to about 2/3rd of the bottom reinforcement. Thickness of the wall can also be diminished at top.

2. Nominal reinforcement at top of slab of the floor should be provided.

3. Bars provided in vertical reinforcement, alternate bar is bent to form fillet. Horizontal bars ast outer edge is bent to form fillet.

4. Small tanks upto nine thousand litres can be built on peripheral beam, for larger tanks square pannel is formed with beams. Each beam takes 1/4th of total load of triangular shape. The B.M. at centre of each beam will be $wL/6$. The floor slab is designed as two way reinforced.

Table 9A.27. Design data for small RCC square tanks.

Capacity (litres)	Inside dia. D (m)	Depth h includ. free board (mm)	Thickness of wall and floor t (mm)	Reinforcement					
				Wall				Floor	
				depth bar c dia. (mm)	spacing (cm)	dia. (mm)	spacing (cm)	dia. (mm)	spacing (cm)
(1)	(2)	(3)	(4)	(5)	(6)	(7)	(8)	(9)	(10)
2,000	1·5 sq.	1·00	10	6	15	6	15	6	20
3,500	1·8 sq.	1·25	10	6	15	6	15	6	20
5,000	2·0 sq.	1·40	10	6	15	6	15	6	20
7,000	2·3 sq.	1·50	11·5	10	22	10	22	6	20
9,000	2·5 sq.	1·60	11·5	10	20	10	15	6	20
14,000	2·8 sq.	2·00	13	10	18	12	18	6	14
23,000	3·5 sq.	2·10	15	10	16	16	20	6	12
34,000	4·0 sq.	2·30	16	10	·15	16	18	6	10
45,000	4·2 sq.	2·70	18	12	20	16	15	6	10

Note. See above notes for circular tanks.

Table 9A.28. Design data for RC water tanks (large)

L = Position of maximum hoop tension above bottom of tank.

Capacity 1000 litres	Inside dia. (m)	Depth of water (m)	Thickness of wall (cm)	Reinforcement				
				Hori. hoop steel			Vertical steel	
				dia. (mm)	spacing (cm)	Height L (m)	dia. mm	spacing cm
450	11·30	4·50	25·00	16·0	14·5	1·89	12·0	14·0
360	10·10	4·50	22·50	16·0	15·0	1·68	12·0	15·5
225	8·00	4·50	20·00	16·0	17·5	1·58	12·0	17·5
135	6·20	4·50	17·50	12·0	11·5	1·35	12·0	18·5
450	12·65	3·50	20·00	12·0	12·0	1·82	12·0	15·0
360	11·30	3·50	22·50	12·0	12·5	1·61	12·0	16·5
225	8·95	3·50	17·50	12·0	13·0	1·40	10·0	15·5
135	6·95	3·50	17·50	12·0	15·0	1·26	10·0	16·0
450	13·80	3·00	20·00	12·0	14·5	1·80	12·0	16·0
360	12·30	3·00	17·50	12·0	15·5	1·50	12·0	18·0
225	9·75	3·00	15·00	12·0	15·5	1·29	10·0	15·5
135	7·55	3·00	15·00	12·0	17·0	1·17	10·0	18·0
450	15·20	2·50	17·50	10·0	13·5	2·00	10·0	13·5
360	13·55	2·50	17·50	10·0	14·5	1·75	10·0	15·0
225	10·72	2·50	15·00	10·0	15·5	1·40	10·0	16·5
135	8·30	2·50	15·00	10·0	16·5	1·20	10·0	18·0

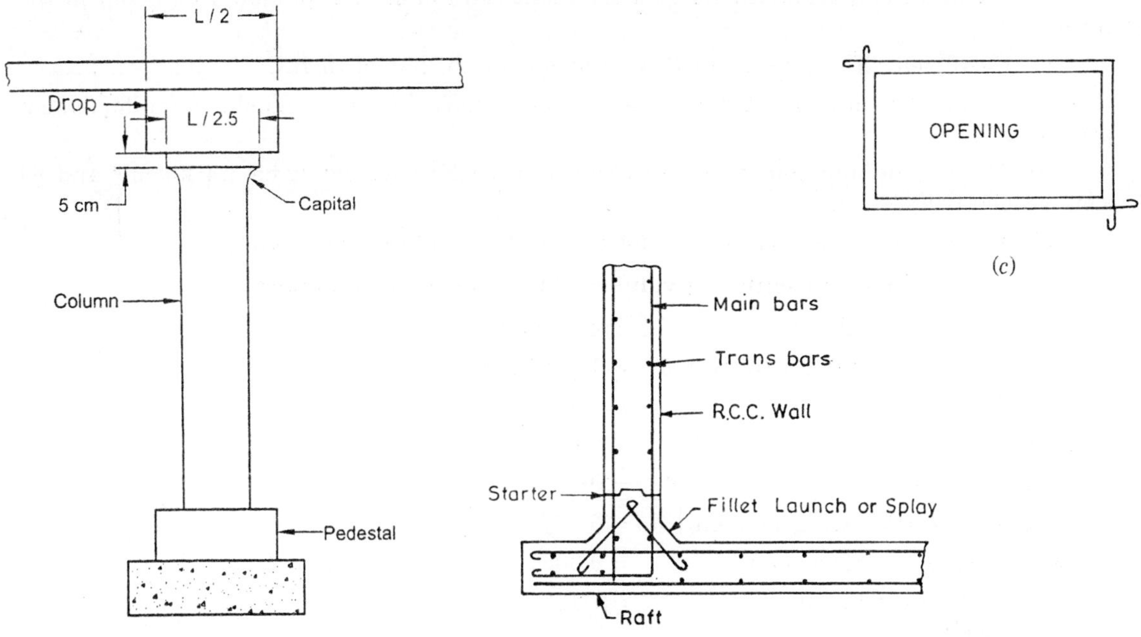

(c)

(a) (b)

Fig. 9A·19.

9A.17. Reinforced brick work

The design procedure for reinforced brick work is almost the same as for RCC work. The following design constants are adopted.

(1) Design bending stress in tension in reinforced bars	1400 kg/cm^2
(2) Design bending stress in compression in B.W. 1 : 3	25 kg/cm^2
(3) Direct compression in B.W. 1 : 3 mortar	14 kg/cm^2
(4) Direct compression in (with hoop binders)	20 kg/cm^2
(5) Direct shear stress (diagonal tension)	1·0 kg/cm^2
(6) Direct Bond stress (Sb)	6·0 kg/cm^2
(7) Modular ratio m	40
(8) Lever arm (j)	0·86
(9) Neutral axis arm (N)	0·42
(10) Moment of resistance Q	4·5

General requirements

(1) The concrete used in joints and in top layer should have a ballast of size 4·75 mm and the thickness of the concrete used on top should be at least 1/3 of the effective depth of slab.

(2) Reinforced bars should not be more than 12 mm.

(3) Over lapping is avoided preferably and if required it should be 45 dia. with ends hooked.

(4) The main thickness of vertical joint should be 40 mm or three times the dia. of bar whichever is greater.

(5) Brick bats should be avoided and should only be given if they are required for proper bonding.

(6) –ve B.M. and temperature reinforcement (Minimum 0.2%) should be given in top concrete.

(7) Coefficient of expansion in R.B. is about 5% to that of in R.C.

(8) Shear stain R.B. must not be more than 3 kg/cm^2 even if the shear reinforcement is provided.

(9) The tensile and compressive strength of bricks used must be 1.4 kg/cm^2 and 84 kg/cm^2 respectively.

(10) Thickness of the slab should not be less than 1/30 of the span.

Design coefficient value of R.C. work in brick ballast

Comp. stress (1 : 2 : 4) = 40 kg/cm^2;
Tensile stress in steel (untested) = 1200 kg/cm^2
Shear stress = 3 kg/cm^2 ;
Modular ratio (m) = 20
Neutral axis (Nd) = 0·40 (d = depth) ;
Lever arm (Resisting moment) Jd = 0.867 d
Percentage reinforcement = 0·0067 bd ;
Q the Moment factor = 7·136
(b is width)

Plate 8·5. Cross section of pre concrete poles

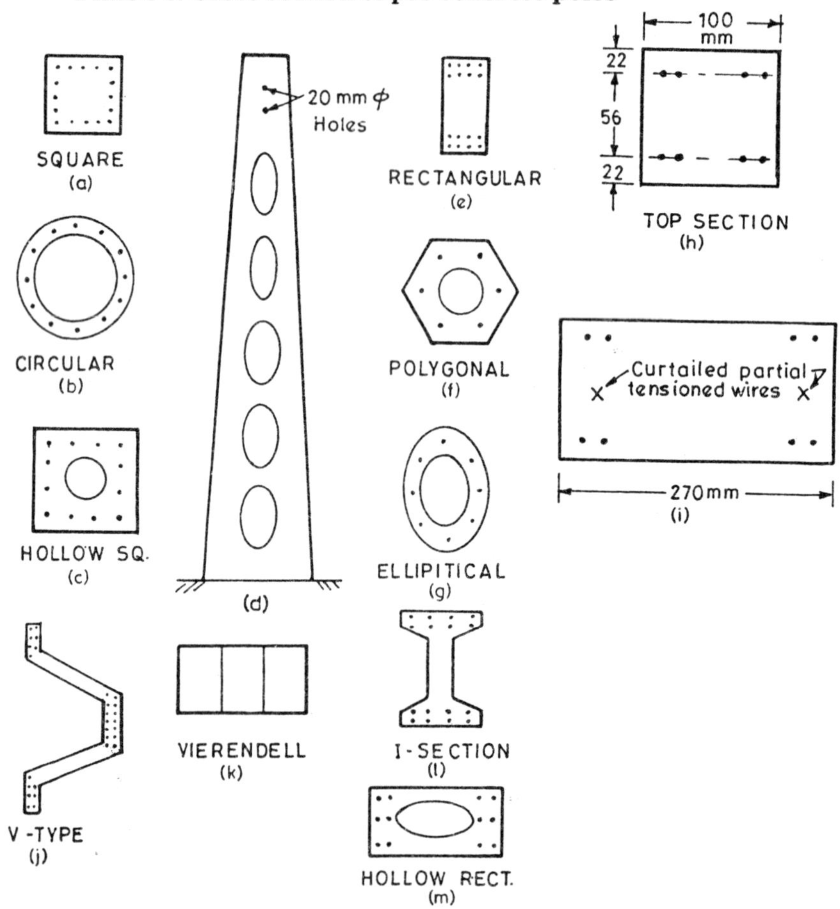

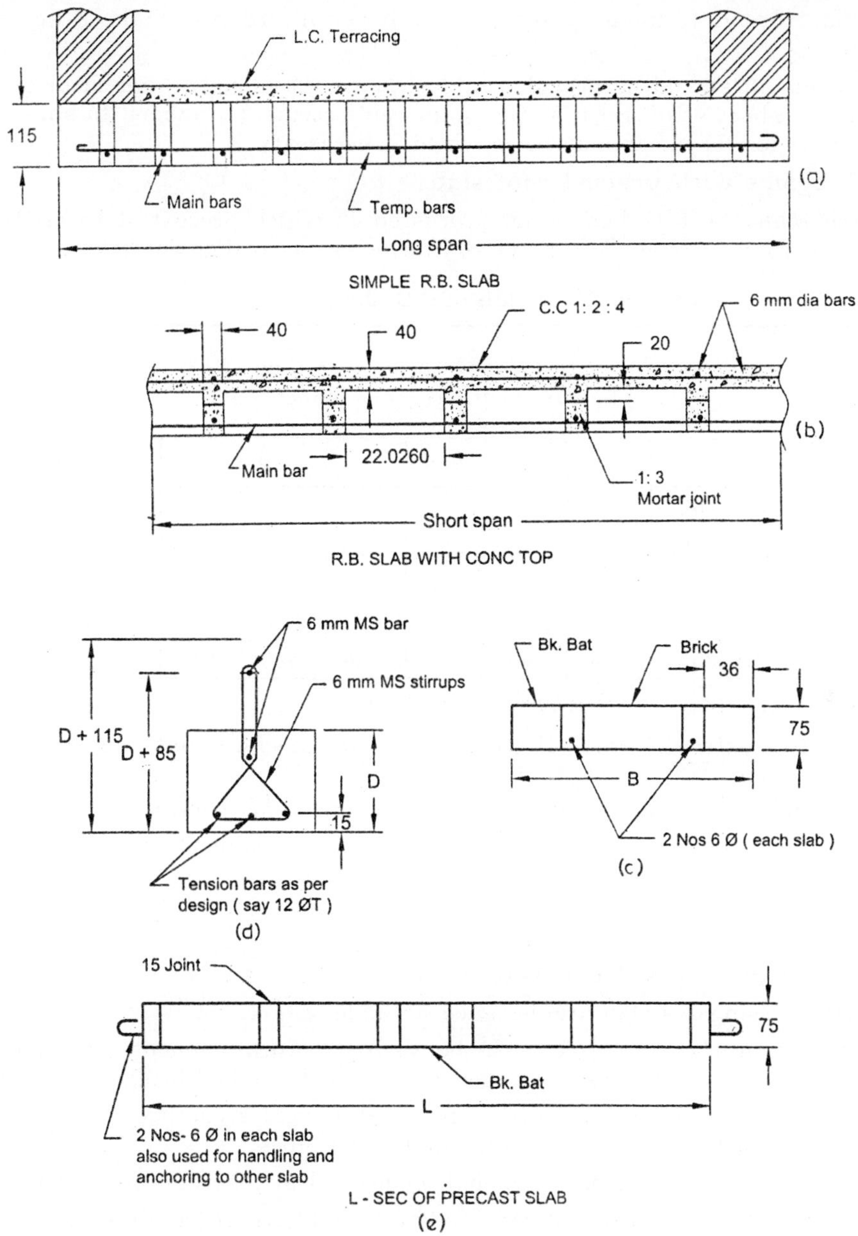

Fig. 19A·20 (*a* to *e*).

Reinforced brick work mixed with R.C.

Such slabs work as a T-beam and hence they are designed as T-beam and slabs. Vertical mortar joint works as a web while the top concrete works as a flange. The top concrete also forms a part of terraced concrete on roofs and floors finish..

Main and temperature bars are provided in vertical joints, where nominal 6 mm to 8 mm bar meshing is provided on top in a grid of 250 to 300 mm. According to 9" brick joints, to avoid any hair or temperature cracks in top layer.

Bars should be well surrounded by mortar and they must not be in touch of bricks.

The vertical mortar joints must be left 20 mm lower in order to make a key to the top concrete layer.

Reinforcement should be provided in each joint. The long 9″ side of brick should be placed parallel to short span. So that the main reinforcement provided to short span may be narrower. Stirrups for shear may be provided if necessary.

Precast R.C. beams with precast roof slabs

In such roofs the R.C. beams are precasted on which precast slabs of R.B, R.C. or stone are placed. In such roofs the cost of shuttering is saved. For detail refer drawing.

Table 9A.29. Details of R.B. slabs (mortar 1 : 3)

Total depth of slab in (inches)	*Safe distributed loads in kg/m² excluding dead loads in various spans in (m)*										*Steel sec. per ft (20 cm) width sq. mm²*	*Depth below centre of steel mm*
	1·22	*1·52*	*1·83*	*2·13*	*2·44*	*2·74*	*3·0*	*3·66*	*4·77*	*4·88*		
3"	600	350	200	100	50						70	20
4·5"	1875	1125	725	475	475	325	175	125			120	20
6"	3450	2100	1350	950	800	450	300	150			160	25
7·5"	5975	3675	1225	1675	1225	875	625	325	125		200	25
9"	8550	5300	3550	2500	1800	1350	1000	550	100		250	32

(1) Compressive stress for B.W. is 25 kg/cm^2.

(2) Add 10% extra for grade II steel and for tor steel use data for replacing m.s. to tor in "Rebars section."

(3) The table is for simply supported slabs having B.M. = $wL/8$.

(4) For other conditions of support the span should be multiplied by factors as detailed below :

having the same load $\frac{wL}{12}$ by 1.12 ; $\frac{wL}{12}$ by 1.25 and $\frac{wL}{12}$ by 1.41.

9A.18. Design of prestressed concrete beams

The prestressing systems are designed as under :

(1) Generation of compressive forces between structural elements and the abutments by flat jacks. This type of prestressing is generally used in arched bridges and pavements.

(2) Development of hoop compression in cylindrical structures by circumferential wire winding. It is used generally in circular tanks and pipes etc.

(3) Use of longitudinal steel (torsional) embedded in concrete or housed in ducts.

(4) Use of distortion of a statically indeterminate structure either by displacement or by rotation of one part relative to the remaining.

(5) Using deflected steel sections by embedding in concrete till final setting and hardening.

(6) Developing limited tension in steel and compression in concrete by using expanding cement.

(7) Prestressing can also be developed by chemical prestressing.

(8) *Thermoelectric prestressing*. The tendons are heated upto 300 to 400°C by passing electric current with in 3 to 4 cm nuts by which they are lengthened 0·4 to 0·5 percent. The bars after cooling try to shorten and is prevented by the fixed anchorage at the two ends. The cooling period is recovered within 12 to 15 minutes. By this process it is possible to induce initial stresses of 500 to 600 N/mm^2 in the tendons. The concrete is placed in the

moulds only after the temperature of the wires fall below 90°C. This method is found to be more economical.

Materials required

Concrete–High strength concrete, 28 days cube strength should at least be 300 kg/cm^2 even concrete upto 500 kg/cm^2 is used.

(*i*) Permissible flexural compressive stress in conc. is 1/3 of cube strength.

(*ii*) Permissible compressive stress at transfer is 1/2 of cube strength.

(*iii*) Tensile strength is 1/10 of the maximum permissible compressive stress or 14 kg/cm^2 in the pretensioned and 10 kg/cm^2 in Post tensioned systems whichever is lower.

(*iv*) Modulus of elasticity of conc. $E_c = 18000\sqrt{F_c}$ where F_c is the cube strength of conc. at 28 days.

Steel—It may be in the form of high tensile, wires cables and bars.

Wires—Hard drawn high tensile steel wires of 2 to 8 mm dia. ultimate tensile strength = 16000 kg/cm^2.

Bars—High tensile alloy steel bars of 9 to 32 mm dia. ultimate tensile strength = 9500 kg/cm^2.

The proof stress of bars and wires should not be less than 80% of the minimum ultimate tensile strength.

The modulus of elasticity *Es* of the wire is $2{\cdot}1 \times 10^6$ kg/cm^2 and of bars is $2{\cdot}0 \times 10^6$ kg/cm^2.

Accounting for all losses, the maximum tensile stress at the point of maximum B.M. should not exceed (*a*) 60% of the ultimate tensile strength of the wires or bars for steel without a definite yield point and (*b*) 80% of the yield stress for steel with a guaranteed yield point.

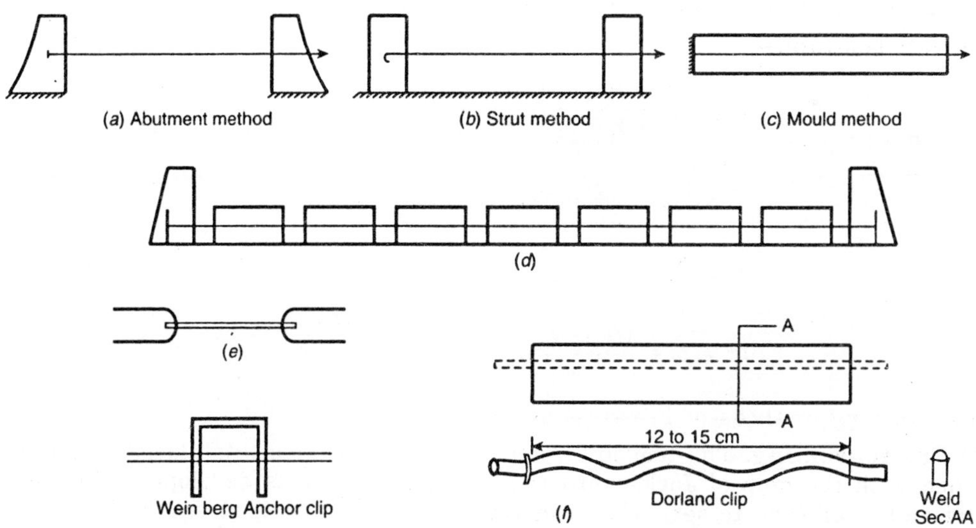

Fig. 9A·21. The helical form of twisted wires in the strand substantially improves the band strength.

Design of beam (Plane tandon)

A = area of cross-section of beam

Y_b = distance of bottom fibre from NA

P = prestressing force

e = eccentricity of prestressing force

p_t = stress due to prestress fibre at top

p_b = stress due to prestress at bottom force

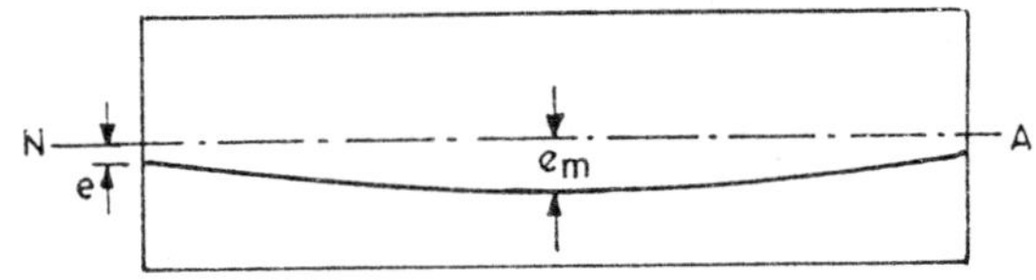

Fig. 9A·22.

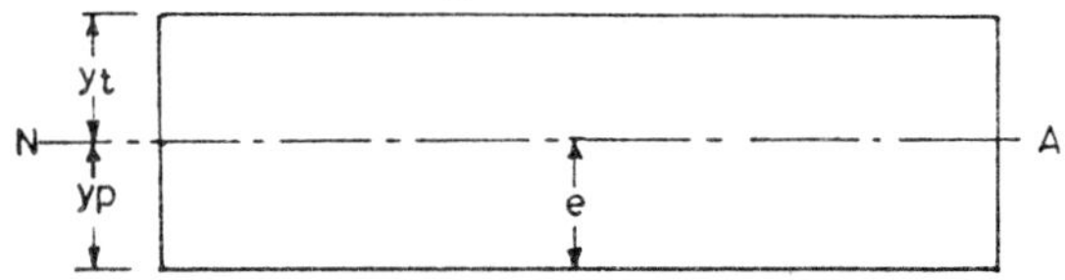

Fig. 9A·23.

Then $$p_t = -\frac{P}{A} + \frac{Pey_t}{I} \quad ...(1)$$

$$p_c = -\frac{P}{A} + \frac{Pey_b}{I} \quad ...(2)$$

Taking p_t as allowable tensile stress in concrete (+ve)

p_c as allowable compressive stress in concrete (–ve)

Solving equation (1) and (2)

$$P = \left\{p_t - \frac{y_t}{y_t + y_b}(p_t - p_c)\right\} A \quad ...(3)$$

$$e = \frac{(p_t - p_c) I}{(y_t + y_b) P} \quad ...(4)$$

Final stress $$P' = P_t - \frac{Y_b}{I}(Md + Ms) = p_t \quad ...(5) \text{ at top}$$

Final stress $$P'' = P_b + \frac{Y_c}{I}(Md + Ms) = p_t \quad ...(6) \text{ at Bottom}$$

Md and Ms being B.M. due to dead load and superimposed loads.

Curved tendons—

$$e_m = \left(\frac{P_t - P_c}{Y_t + Y_b}\right)\frac{I}{P} + \frac{Md}{P} \quad ...(7)$$

$$P = \left\{p_t - \frac{y_t}{y_t + y_c}(p_t - p_c)\right\} A \quad ...(8)$$

$$P' = p_t - \frac{Ms.y_t}{I} = p_c \quad ...(9)$$

$$P'' = p_c + \frac{Ms.y_c}{I} = p_t \quad ...(10)$$

The following methods of Prestressing are used :

(1) Pre tensioning. The tendon (pretensioned reinforcement) is placed in the mould and stretched with the help of Jacks until the required tension is developed. The concrete is then laid and is allowed to set. When concrete attains sufficient strength the Jacks are released. The steel tries to return to its original position and hence causes compression in concrete. This method is generally used in mass product factories.

(2) Post tensioning. The tendons arc provided when the concrete mass sets finally. Some times tendons are placed in the mould and are protected by thin rubber sheaths to come in the direct touch of the concrete. After the concrete attains its full strength the tendons are pulled at one end by jacks while the other end is anchored to the extension required. Finally the gap between the tendon and the concrete is filled by cement grout used in large bridges, dams and nuclear reactors etc. in important projects.

The main advantage of post tensioning is that it allows curved and sloped off cables to vary stress distribution section to section.

In another method ducts are left while concreting and the tendons are inserted and pulled when the concrete sets finally. The spacing of the tendons is controlled by a helical spring in side the tendons. (Fig. 8·23).

Cover for tendons. In order to protect steel tendons from the effect of atmosphere carbonation and humidity these are covered with the concrete. The IS Standard Code (IS : 1343) provides for a minimum clear cover of 20 mm, for protected prestensioned members, 30 mm or the size of the cable whichever is bigger. If the prestressed members are exposed to the atmosphere, the cover requirement are increased by 10 mm.

Table 9A·30 . British cover code requirements for tendons and reinforcement in prestressed concrete.

Condition of exposure	*Min. cement content kg/m^3*	*Max. free w/c ratio* ++	*Nominal grade 30*	*Cover for grade 40*	*Cover of Grade 50*	*Grade more than 50*
Mild	300	0·65	15	15	15	
Moderate	319	0·55	30	25	20	
Severe	370	0·45	40	30	25	
Very severe	—	—	—	60	50	
Extreme severe	310	0·55	50+	40+	25	

+ For max. size of aggregate of 10 mm.

++ When water cement ratio can be strictly controlled.

* For concrete with entrained air only.

Permissible Stress in Steel. The tensile stress in steel at time of tensioning behind the anchorage and after allowing for all possible losses are generally expressed as a fraction of the ultimate tensile strength or proof stress. The recommendations of the various national codes vary marginally with regard to the allowable stress in prestressed members at different stages. The permissible values specified in Indian and British codes are compared in table below.

Table 9A·31

	IS : 1343	*ASI 318-71*	*CP 110-72*
At the time of initial tensioning	80% of the ultimate tensile strength	80% of the ultimate tensile strength but not more than the max. value recommended by the manufacturers	70% of the characteristic strength but not more than the max. 80% provided that additional consideration is given to the stress characteristic of tendons and frictional stress
Immediately after transfer	—	70% of the ultimate tensile strength	—
After allowing for all losses	Not less than 5% of the ultimate tensile strength.	—	—

The Indian Standards prescribe a minimum limit of 2% for the elongation at rupture, when tested over a gauge length of 200 mm.

Advantages of Prestressed Concrete

(1) It can take higher loads in compression to concrete steel structure.

(2) The cross-section of the structure is more efficiently utilized which is cracked under working loads.

(3) Within certain limits a permanent dead load may be counter acted by increasing the eccentricity of the prestressing force in a prestressed element.

(4) Prestressed members possess improved resistance shearing forces due to the effect of compressive prestress, which reduces the principal tensile stress. The use of the curved cables particularly in long span members helps to reduce the shear forces developed at the support sections.

(5) A prestressed flexural member is stiffer under working loads than a R.C. member of the same depth.

(6) The use of the high strength concrete and steel in prestressed members results in stronger members than could be possible by using R.C. The two structural features of prestressed concrete *viz.,* higher strength concrete and freedom from cracks contribution to the improved durability of the structure under aggressive environ conditions.

(7) Prestressing of concrete improves the ability of the material for energy absorption under impact loads. The ability to resist repeated working loads have been proved to be as good as in reinforced concrete.

(8) The prestressed concrete is economical for long spans, standardized precast bridge beams between 10 to 30 m long and precast prestressed piles have proved to be economical in prestressed as in reinforced concrete.

(9) Prestressed concrete has considerable resistance due to its capacity for completely recovering from substantial effect of over loading without undergoing any serious damage.

(10) The prestressed concrete elements crack which temporarily develope under occasional overloading will close up completely when loads are removed since the fatigue strength of prestressed concrete is comparatively better than that of the other materials chiefly due to the small stress variations in prestressing. Steel is recommended for dynamically loaded structures such as railway bridges and machine foundations.

(11) Due to the utilization of concrete in tensile zone a saving of 15 to 30 percent in concrete is possible in compression with reinforced concrete. The saving in steel is higher 60-80 percent mainly due to high permissible stress allowable in the high tensile wires. Although there is a considerable saving in the quantity of the materials used in prestressed concrete members in compression with reinforced concrete members. The economy in cost is not of that significance due to the additional costs increased for the high strength concrete, high tensile steel, machines anchorage and other hard work required for the production of prestress members.

(12) There is an overall economy in using prestressed concrete as the decrease in dead weight reduces the design loads and cost of foundations particularly in major works.

Losses in prestressing. While a pretensioning force is applied on high tensile steel it is lost due to the followings :

Table 9A.32

Type of loss	*Pretensioning*		*Post tensioning*		*Remarks*
Creep*		7%		9%	
Relaxation of steel		3%		3%	
Shrinkage of concrete	3×10^{-4}	7%	$2{\cdot}0 \times 10^{-4}$	4%	I.S. Code
Shortening of concrete		3%		1%	
Friction		–		2%	
Slip		–		2%	
Stress corrosion		–		–	(Cause cracks & heat tructed wires, protected by coatings ducts after prestressing)
		20		21	

* Creep coeff. = 2·2, 1·6 and 1·1 for 7 days, 28 days and 1 year loading respectively (IS : 1343–80)

Creep coeff. = ultimate strain/elastic strain.

Innovative mixture design for prestressed cement concrete poles

Prestressed cement concrete poles have been gradually replacing the traditional poles made of wood, steel and RCC and are widely used for railway, power and signal lines, lighting poles, telephone poles, low and high voltage upto 11 kV electric transmission and sub station towers. Tensioning is done manually by using jacks and pulleys. Elongation required for the designed prestress is predetermined for the required length of line.

Rural electrification (REC) specified the following norms for PCC poles (prestressed cement concrete) for 11 kV and LT line.

The cement concrete mix was designed to the requirement laid down for the controlled concrete in IS : 1343 (1960) 'code of practice for prestressed conc.' and IS : 456 code of practice for plain and reinforced concrete subject to the following special conditions :

(*a*) Maximum works cube strength at 28 days should be at least 420 kg/cm^2 (42 N/mm^2).

(*b*) The concrete handling stress should at least be 210 kg/cm^2 *i.e.* strength at transfer. The prestressed tendons are cut three days after casting and poles lifted from casting beds to curing ponds. Hence, the concrete should have a handling stress of 210 kg/cm^2.

(*c*) The mix should at least contain 380 kg of cement per m^3 concrete.

(*d*) The mix should contain as low a water content as is consistent with adequate workability required at site. If it becomes necessary to add water to increase the workability, the cement content also should be raised in such a way that the original value of water cement ratio is maintained.

(*e*) While conforming to IS : code 383/1970 the nominal maximum size of aggregate shall in no case exceed 12 mm.

The section of 8 m long pole was 270 mm × 100 mm at bottom tapering to 100 mm × 100 mm at top. The clear gap between the wires at broad face was 166 mm at bottom reducing to 20 mm at top. It was conceived that the PCC poles breakage may be due to the smaller size aggregate used.

Table 9A·33. Fatigue Behaviour of steel Fibre Reinforced Concrete Beams

Details of Fibres	*Fibre type*	*Length*	*Diameter*	*Aspect ratio*	*Ultimate strength*
	Crimped	40 mm	0·5 mm	80	1000 MPa
	Trough-shaped	40 mm	0.5 mm	80	1170 MPa
	Straight	40 mm	0·5 mm	80	975 MPa

Steel Fibre Reinforced Concrete Beams

(1) The addition of fibres to the concrete matrix of R.C. beams improved their performances under fatigue loadings as :

(*a*) The fatigue life of all beams, as reflected in the number of cycles to failure, improved considerably with the addition of fibrous. The SFRC (steel fibre reinforced concrete) beams also should have higher rigidity and hence lesser defiective during the entire loading cycle require for all the load ranges tested.

(*b*) The performance of the SFRC beams under fatigue loading improved with an increase in the percentage of volume fraction of the fibres. The behaviour of beams containing trough shaped fibres was superior to those beams containing the other two types of fibres, namely, straight and crimped fibres at 1% and 1.5% volume fraction. Even though the crimped fibres showed higher stiffness, they failed at a much lower number of cycles. For all the SFRC beams the number of cycles to failure considerably reduced as the load range was increased.

(2) Based on the experimental investigations, an empirical equation has been derived to evaluate the deflection of SFRC beams subjected to fatigue loading with the minimum load being kept constant at about 20% of its ultimate load capacity. The value of deflection during the 1st cycle and the number of loading cycles are the two main parameters that are required to compute the deflection at the desired member of loading cycles using the empirical equation.

(3) Rate of change of deflection (or slope) with number of cycles determine the failure under fatigue loading. The slope at failure depends on the type of fibre, range of loading and the volume fraction of fibres. An equation has been derived to obtain the failure slope based on these parameters.

(4) Using the equations for predicting the deflection and on failure slope an empirical relationship has been derived to obtain the number of cycles to failure in SFRC beams. The effects of all the major variables or parameters that influence the behaviour of beams under fatigue loading have been included in the empirical relationship.

Table 9A.34. A test results (Beam designation and strength details).

Dimensions : B = 100 mm D = 150 mm Defection = 130 mm Effective span = 1350 mm

Beam ID	*Type of fibre*	*Volume fraction of fibre*	*Average cube strength of beam concrete MPa*	*Average modulus of rupture MPa*	*Average ultimate flexural load of RC/SF RC beams kN*
Com	–	–	32·62	5·64	44·20
TA	Trough shaped	1·0	36·95	6.78	50·00
TB	Trough shaped	1·5	42·88	10·08	54·50
TC	Trough shaped	2·0	43·68	11·88	53·50
SA	straight	1·0	34·81	6·37	48·00
SB	straight	1·5	35·70	8·77	48·00
CA	Crimped	1·0	39·73	6·41	52·00
CB	Crimped	1·5	43·04	8·83	52·00

Note. Typically TAB represents as SFRC beam with trough shaped fibre with a volume fraction of 1·0% and the figure '8' represents its beam number.

(5) The equation derived were used to predict the fatigue behaviour 9 SFRC beams (*i.e.* number of cycles to failure) which were tested in this programme as well as those reported in the literature and the agreement between the predicted values and experimentally obtained values are within acceptable limits. Design loading under varying system parameters can be derived based on methodology/equating suggested. Finally the improved performance of RC beams with addition of fibres to concrete matrix clearly indicate the suitability of application of fibres in RC structural elements where fatigue loadings are predominant. Concrete is mixed in a conventional tilt up type mixing machine. Fibres are added manually at uniform rate as the concrete is getting mixed in the mixing machine (Fibres at a volume fraction of 2% to improve workability). The volume traction of fibres can be varied 1·0% to 2%.

9A·19. Technical terms used in RCC

(1) **Accelerator.** An admixture which increases the rate of setting of concrete.

(2) **Retarder.** An admixture which retards the rate of setting of conc.

(3) **Flash set.** A sudden set of concrete while in progress.

(4) **Harsh or stiff mix.** A mix which causes a difficulty to work and make concrete. smooth while laying.

(5) **Knocking.** Breaking up and remixing concrete that has not set.

(6) **Effective grain size.** The size of grains which occupy 90% by weight of the whole grains.

(7) **Floating.** Smoothening a surface by a plainer.

(8) **Plum.** Hard big stones used in mass concrete. A plum must not be greater than 1/3rd of the thickness of the concrete in size.

(9) **Pozzalane materials.** Materials like Surkhi or fly ash etc. which increase the workability and reduce evolution of heat in hydration.

(10) **Retemping.** Remixing of mortar, when it has partially set (It can be used in unimportant works).

(11) **Screeding.** A top concrete layer to give final level to the floor. It can be replaced when weared.

(12) **Splicing.** Mass plain concrete below structures to achieve the required level for foundation raft. It is gap between bottom of foundation to a hard good bearing soil strata. It is used to avoid deep foundations.

(13) **Mud mat or lean conc.** A base for laying raft foundation in a lean conc. mix to avoid direct touch of the soil to designed raft.

(14) **Striking.** Removal of forms (cribbing).

(15) **Drop pannel.** Above a column a thickened pedastal is provided under the flat slabs.

(16) **Pan mixture.** A concrete mixture with horizontal pan or drum which is operated by electric paddles.

(17) **Sweeting.** Seeping of water on outer face.

(18) **Peripheral speed.** Circumferencial volume of concrete mixing drum.

(19) **Punning.** Same as ramming or tamping.

(20) **Slicing.** Spading or rodding or punning.

(21) **Uninformity coefficient** $= \dfrac{\text{Size of sieve that will pass 60\% by weight}}{\text{Size of sieve that will pass 10\% by weight}}$.

Super plasticizers. Plastic products used as additives in cement concrete for making it water tight and rapid hardener, etc.

Drift. The maximum horizontal relative displacement (Sway/due to earth quake forces between two successive floors is called a drift. It shall not exceed 0.004 times the difference in levels between these floors.

Pot life. In epoxy resins the period upto which the resin does not initially set.

Epoxy resins. For grouting fine cracks in concrete epoxy resins are injected in the cracks. (It is a liquidy resin which reaches in the cracks by injection and then set in the crack.

Breathing of concrete. Concrete disintegration.

Abrasion. Abrasion of concrete due to wheels of vehicles and by other impacting sources.

Technical Terms in Prestressing

Anchorage. A device used to enable the tendon to impart and maintain prestress in the concrete.

Bonded Prestressed Concrete. Concrete in which prestress is imparted to concrete through a bond between the tendons and surrounding concrete. Pretensioned members belong to this group.

Non-bonded prestressed concrete. A method of construction in which the tendons are not bonded to the surrounding concrete. The tendons may be placed in ducts for most in concrete members or they may be placed outside the concrete section.

Fill prestressing. Prestressed concrete in which tensile stress in the concrete is entirely obviated at working load by having sufficiently high prestress in the members.

Limited or partial prestressing. The degree of prestress applied to concrete in which tensile stress to a limited degree is permitted in concrete under working loads. In this case in addition to tensioned steel considerable proportion of untensioned reinforcement is generally used to limit the width of cracks developed under service loads.

Moderate prestressing. In this type of members no limit is imposed upon the magnitude of the tensile stress at working loads. This form of construction is not really prestressed concrete but is to be regarded as reinforced concrete with reduced cracking and the sections should be analysed according to the rules of reinforced concrete as a case of bonding combined with axial load.

Axial prestressing. Members in which the entire cross section of concrete has a uniform compressive prestress. In this type of prestressing the centroid of the tendons coincides with that of the concrete section.

Eccentric prestressing. A section at which the tendons are eccentric to the centroid resulting in a triangular or trapezoidal compression stress distribution.

Concordant prestressing. Prestressing of members in which the cables follow a concordant profile. In the case of statistically indeterminate structures concordant prestressing does not cause any change in the support reactions.

Non-distortant prestressing. In this type the combined effect of the degree of prestress and the dead weight stress are such that the deflection of the axis of the member is prevented. In such cases the moments due to prestress and dead weight exactly balance the resulting weight in the axial force in the member.

Circular prestressing. Prestressing in round members such as tanks and pipes.

Uniaxial biaxial and triaxial prestressing. It refers to the cases where concrete is prestressed in only one direction, in two directions which are mutually perpendicular to each other and prestressed in three directions which are mutually perpendiculars.

Transfer. The stage corresponding to the transfer of prestress to concrete. For pretensional members transfer takes places at the release of heat from the bulk heads, for postensioned members, it takes place after the completion of the tensing process.

Transmission length. The length of the bond anchorage of the prestressing wire from the end of a pretensioned member to the point of the full steel stress.

Supplementary or untensional reinforcement. Reinforcement in prestressed members which are not tensioned with respect to the surrounding concrete before the application of loads. These are generally used in partially prestressed members.

Cracking load. The loads on the structural element corresponding to an visible crack.

Cap cable. A short curved tendon arranged at the interior supports of a continuous beam. The anchors are in compression zone, while the curved portion is in the tensile zone.

Degree of prestressing. A measure of the magnitude of the prestressing force related to the resultant stress occurrence in the structural member at working load.

Debonding. Prevention of bond between the steel work and surrounding concrete.

Relaxation in steel. Decrease of stress in steel at constant strain.

Relaxation of stress in steel. When a high tensile steel wire is stretched and maintained at constant strain, the initial force in the wire does not remain constant but decreases with time. The decrease of stress in steel at constant strain is known as relaxation.

Tendon splices. In cases where the long tendons are required and the available tendons (prestressing wires) are of short length, the tendons are spliced together in order to increase the length of the tendon.

Hydrogen Embrittlement. Atomic hydrogen is liberated due to the action of acids on high tensile steel which is very injurious to the structure and make it brittle, use of high alumina cement and blast furnace slag in cement which are rich in sulphides and are likely to give rise to production of hydrogen which deteriorates the structure concrete. In order to prevent hydrogen embrittlement, the steel is properly protected from the action of acids. Protection coverages like bituminous crape cover during transport reduces the chances of contamination. The wires should be protected from rain and excessive humidity by keeping them in dry places.

Fig. 9A·35. Design Data for RCC Slabs

Moment of Resistence per metre width kg.m.	*Thickness of slab cm*	*Effective depth cm*	*t. for steel–1400 kg/cm² (Safe bending stress for steel)* *c. Safe crushing stress of conc. in bending = 50 kg/cm²* *m = 18·7* *Length of spans and safe distributed super imposed load excluding wt. of slab*										*Area at per metre width in cm²*	*Main*		*Transverse*		*Quantity of steel % sq.m. of slab area Tonnes*	*Remarks*
			1·5	*2·0*	*2·5*	*3·0*	*3·5*	*4·0*	*4·5*	*5·0*	*5·5*	*6·0*		*Bar dia. mm*	*Spac-ing mm*	*Bar dia. mm*	*Spac-ing mm*		
200	7	5	542	242									3·57	8	14·0	5	20	0·391	
300	8	6	873	408	192								4·28	8	11·5	5	20	0·469	
425	9	7	1296	634	329	164							5·00	8	10·0	6	20	0·543	
560	10	8	1754	880	480	280	125						5·72	10	13·5	6	19	0·633	
700	11	9	2236	1146	636	366	196						6·45	10	12·0	6	17	0·710	
870	12	10		1452	822	485	282	147					7·15	10	10·0	6	15·5	0·776	
1050	13	11		1788	1028	621	373	213	103				7·75	10	10·0	6	14·5	0·845	
1250	14	12		2164	1264	774	484	289	159				8·58	12	13·0	8	24·0	0·932	
1470	15	13			1520	950	600	375	220	110			9·30	12	12·0	8	22·0	1·02	
1700	16	14			1796	1116	726	466	286	160			10·00	12	11·0	8	21·0	1·095	
1960	17	15			2·092	1332	872	572	372	222			10·70	12	10·5	8	14·5	1·153	
2225	18	16				1548	1028	668	458	300			11·45	12	9·5	8	18·5	1·283	
2500	19	17				1766	1148	794	544	344	180		12·15	12	9·0	8	17·5	1·333	
3100	22	19				2232	1492	1022	692	467	292	162	13·57	16	14·5	8	14·5	1·486	
3800	24	21					1904	1324	924	634	424	269	15·00	16	13·0	8	12·5	1·635	
5000	28	24						1828	1298	928	648	428	17·14	16	11·5	10	10·5	1·876	
6200	31	27							1706	1236	896	636	19·28	16	10·3	10	13·5	2·111	

Note :(1) For calculating moment of resistence a dead wt. of slab 24 kg/cm thickness per m² of area is added to the superimposed load.
(2) For tor steel the bars may be replaced as per conversion table m.s. to Tor.
(3) For grade II steel add 14% extra steel.
(4) For continuous and semi-continuous beams safe loads are increased by 50 and 25% respectively. For cantilevers it is reduced to 25% or 1/4th.

Fig. 9A·36. R.C.C. T-Beam Design Details for Different Spans and Loadings

Mix : 1 : 2 : 4 (M-15) $m = 18{\cdot}7$

$c = 50$ kg/cm^2 ; $t = 1400$ kg/cm^2

Superimposed load kg/m	Effective span in metres																Remarks
	2·5		3·0		3·5		4·0		4·5		5·0		5·5		6·0		
	$d \times b$ cm	A_s cm^2	$d \times b$ cm	A_s cm^2	$d \times b$ cm	A_s cm^2	$d \times b$ cm	A_s cm^2	$d \times b$ cm	A_s cm^2	$d \times b$ cm	A_s cm^2	$d \times b$ cm	A_s cm^2	$d \times b$ cm	A_s cm^2	
1300	30×20	3·20	30×20	4·85	30×22	7·15	30×22	9·35	30×22	11·80	35×25	12·00	35×25	15·00	35×25	17·80	
1600	30×20	2·84	30×20	5·85	30×22	8·60	30×22	11·22	30×22	14·20	35×25	14·40	35×25	18·00	35×25	21·40	
1900	30×20	4·48	30×20	7·20	30×22	10·00	30×22	13·10	30×22	16·50	35×25	16·80	35×25	21·00	35×25	25·90	
2200	30×20	5·12	30×20	8·25	30×22	11·44	30×22	15·00	30×22	18·90	35×25	19·20	35×25	24·70	35×25	29·45	
2500	30×20	6·20	30×22	9·50	30×22	12·77	30×22	16·80	35×22	17·50	35×25	21·60	35×25	27·10	45×25	23·70	(1) Based on R.C.C. design manual. The concrete association of India.
2800	30×20	6·90	30×22	10·50	30×22	14·30	30×22	18·70	35×25	19·50	35×25	24·74	45×25	22·00	45×25	26·00	
3100	30×20	7·65	30×22	10·60	35×25	13·00	35×25	16·80	35×25	21·40	45×25	20·00	45×25	25·00	45×25	28·80	
3400	30×20	8·55	30×22	12·65	35×25	14·20	35×25	18·30	35×25	23·90	45×25	21·80	45×25	27·10	50×30	27·50	(2) When untested (commercial quality) steel is used provide 10 extra reinforcement.
3700	30×20	9·25	35×25	11·25	35×25	15·40	35×25	21·22	35×25	25·70	45×25	23·90	50×30	25·30	50×30	30·70	
4000	30×22	10·00	35×25	12·10	35×25	16·60	35×25	21·40	45×25	21·20	50×30	22·40	50×30	27·10	50×30	32·30	
4300	30×22	10·70	35×25	13·00	35×25	17·80	35×25	22·80	45×25	21·90	50×30	24·00	50×30	29·20	50×30	34·30	
4600	35×25	9·40	35×25	13·85	45×25	13·80	45×25	18·00	45×25	23·65	50×30	25·68	50×30	31·60	50×30	36·60	
4900	35×25	10·00	35×25	14·70	45×25	14·70	45×25	19·20	50×30	21·70	50×30	27·70	50×30	33·20	50×30	40·20	
5200	35×25	10·60	35×25	15·50	45×25	15·60	45×25	20·30	50×30	23·65	50×30	28·80	50×30	35·20	50×30	41·75	

Note : (1) d is effective depth, b is width of rib (web) in cm and A_s is the area of steel section in beam under tension in sq. cm.

(2) Load is uniformly distributed on simple supports.

(3) Check the beam in shear.

(4) Total wt. = supported load + wt. of slab (24 kg/cm thickness × width supported by beam) + wt. of rib (web).

(5) Reinforcement should be provided in two rows (one can be taken for small beam). Main reinforcement may be cranked upto 1/5th, take –ve B.M. 1/3rd to 1/2 to its magnitude at 1/4th of the span on either side at 45° and ends hooked.

(6) For supporting stiruups at top provide 2 Nos. hanger bars of 8 mm dia. for small and upto 16 mm for large if no top reinforcement is provided.

(7) Provide nominal stirrups of 6 mm dia. at 12 cm c/c at supports and increase the spacing gradually at centre of span to a distance of effective depth of beam where they are not required to take any shear.

(8) The top slab may be designed as a slab of semifixed ends with –ve B.M. provided at the top of web in the slab.

(B) Limit State Design in RCC

In the method of design based on limit state concept, the structure shall be designed to withstand safety from all the loads liable to act on it throughout its life. It shall also satisfy the serviceability requirements such as iimitations on deflection and cracking. The acceptible limit for the safety and serviceability requirements before failure occurs called a "limit state". The aim of design is to achieve acceptible probabilities that the structure will not become unfit for the use for which it is intended *i.e.* that it will not to reach a limit state. In general the structure shall be designed on the basis of the most critical limit state and shall be checked for other limit states.

For ensuring the above objective, the design should be based on characteristic values for material strengths and applied loads, which take into account the variations in the material strengths and in the loads to be supported. The characteristic values should be based on statistical data if available ; where such data are not available should be based on experience. The design values are derived from the characteristic values through the use of partial safety factors, one for the material strengths and the other for loads. In the absence of special considerations these factors should be the values given below :

Partial safety factors (y_F)

$UL = 1{\cdot}5\ (DL + LL)$ ...(1)

$UL = 1{\cdot}2\ (DL + LL + WL \text{ or } EL)$ ...(2)

y_m for concrete $= 1{\cdot}5$

y_m for steel $= 1{\cdot}15$

UL = Ultimate load
DL = Dead load
LL = Live load
WL = Wind load
EL = Earthquake load

Design strength of material say $f_d = \dfrac{f}{y_m}$ where f is the characteristic strength of material and y_m = partial safety factor appropriate to the material as per limit state considerations.

Designed load $F_d = F.y_f$ where F is the characteristic load and y_f is partial safety factor appropriate to the material of loading according to limit state considerations.

The code gives principles for design of R.C. sections under the following limit states :

(*a*) Flexure (*b*) Compression (*c*) Axial load and uniaxial loading
(*d*) Axial load and biaxial bending (*e*) Shear (*f*) Torsion
(*g*) Deflection (*h*) Cracking.

Limit states (*a*) to (*f*) refer to ultimate limit states or limit states of collapse, which the last two limit states refers to serviceability requirements.

Limit state due to impact, vibrations, fatigue, durability, fire resistance, lightening etc. are satisfied by good quality control, adequate size of members, adequate cover to reinforcement, provision of min. steel area and other special details. Limit state of cracking is satisfied by providing min. steel area and spacing of bars.

Notations

(*a*) **Singly reinforced sections**

x = depth from the comp. face to the neutral axes (general)

x_u = depth of neutral axis (ultimate load) from top of sec.

$x_{u\ max}$ = depth of neutral axis (Maximum) from top of sec.

f = characteristic strength of materials

f_c = comp. stresses in conc.

f_{ck} = characteristic compressive strength of concrete.

f_d = design strength of material

f_s = tensile strength of steel.

f_y = characteristic tensile strength of steel.

E_s = Elastic modulus of steel = 200 kN/mm^2 for all type of steels both in comp. and tension.

E_c = Elastic modulus of conc. = $5000\sqrt{f_{ck}}$ N/mm^2 for comp. and tension both (in short term basis)

m = Modular ratio of steel and concrete = $\frac{E_s}{E_c}$.

Moment of resistances

M_u lim = Maximum moment of resistance.

P_t lim = Limiting percentage of steel corresponding to limiting moment of resistance as M_u lim.

A_{st} = Area of tensile reinforcement.

y_m = Partial safety factor ; for steel = 1·15 ; for concrete = 1·5.

h = Over all depth of section

d = Effective depth of section

b = Width of section.

Q_u = Limiting moment of resistance factor = $Q_u = Q_l \times f_{ck}$

Q_l = Limiting moment of resistance constant.

F = Characteristic load

F_d = designed load ; $F_d = y_m F$

UL = Ultimate load ; DL = Dead load ; LL = Live load

W = Wind load EL = Seismic load.

(1) Elastic modulus of steel, E_s = 200 kN/mm^2 for all type of steels both compression and tension.

(2) Elastic modulus of concrete, $E_c = 5000\sqrt{f_{ck}}$ N/mm^2 both for compressive and tension for short form.

Actual measured values may differ by ± 20% from the values obtained from the above expression.

Note : The modulus of elasticity of concrete is influenced by elastic properties of aggregate, and to a lesser extent by curing and age of concrete mix proportions and type of cement. The modulus of elasticity is related to the compressive strength of concrete.

Tensile strength of concrete. The flexural and stiffening tensile strength of concrete may be obtained by the formula given below from the compression strength of concrete (IS : 576 and IS : 5816 respectively).

Flexural strength of concrete. $f_{cr} = 0{\cdot}7\sqrt{f_{ck}}$ N/mm^2 (in flexural tension with bending)

or Modulus of rigidity $f_{ct} = 0{\cdot}5\sqrt{f_{ck}}$ N/mm (in direct tension)

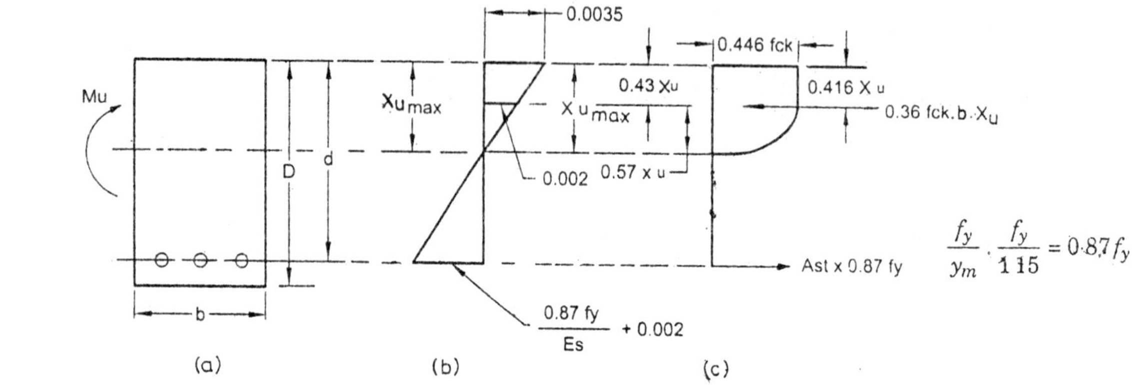

(*a*) Singly reinforced (*b*) Strain diagram (*c*) Stress diagram

Fig. 9B·1.

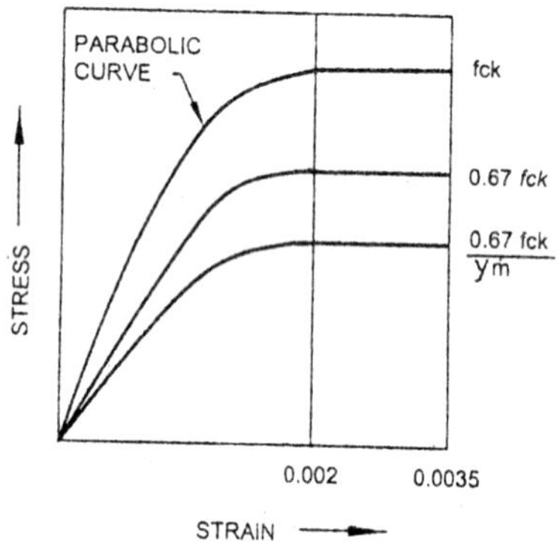

(*a*)

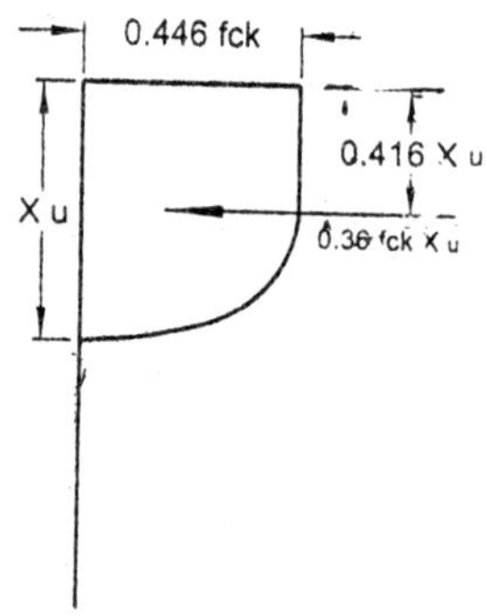

(*b*) Stress

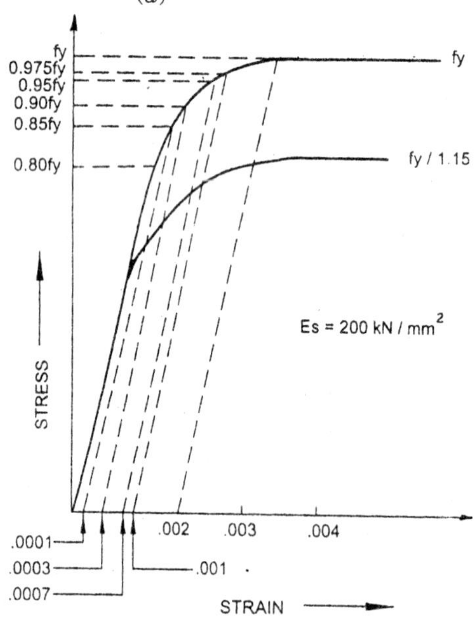

(*c*) Deformed bar

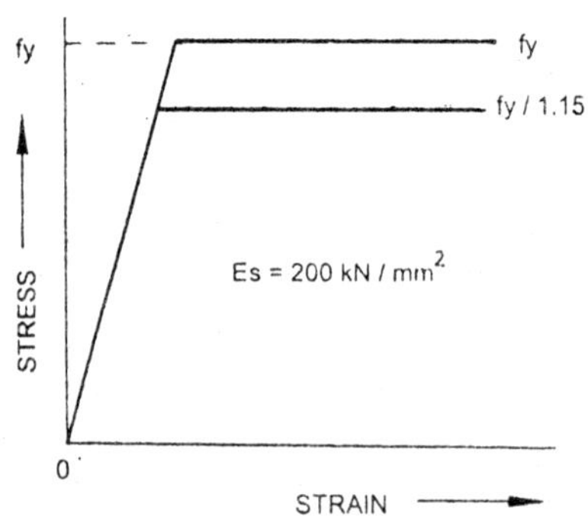

(*d*) Steel bar

Fig. 9B·2.

Shrinkage. The approximate value of total shrinkage strain for design may be taken as 0·0003.

Steel bars Fe 250 (ordinary mild steel plain bars) used in working strain designs of less important works and stirrups for shear.

Steel bars Fe 415 and Fe 500 (High strength steel deformed bars).

The stresses for Fe 500 are almost similar to Fe 415, even then stresses in Fe 500 for design may be taken as $\frac{415}{500} = 0{\cdot}83$ to the steel required for Fe 415.

Behaviour of R.C. members at failure

(*a*) **Tension failure.** Conc. crushed or not crushed, but tension steel will in yield when steel provided is less it yields before the max. crushing strain of concrete (0·0035) is reached. The neutral axis shifts upwards.

(*b*) **Compressive failure.** Concrete crushed and tension steel not in yield. When the amount of tension steel is large *i.e.* the section is over reinforced. The concrete reaches its ultimate crushing strain. (Max. strain 0·0035) before the tension steel start, yielding.

(*c*) **Balanced failure.** Balanced failure is just a transition between the tension and the compression failures. Both the concrete and the steel reaches at their yield stresses simultaneously.

Assumption in the Design of flexural members on limit state

(*a*) Plane sections normal to the axis remain plane after bending.

(*b*) The maximum strain in concrete at the outermost comp. fibre is taken as 0·0035 in bending.

(*c*) The relationship between the compressive stress distribution in concrete and the strain in concrete may be assumed to be rectangle, trapezoid, parabola or any other shape which results in prediction of strength in substantial agreement with the results of tests. An acceptible stress strain curve given in Fig. 9B·2 (*a*). For design purposes, the compressive strength of concrete in the structure shall be assumed to be 0·67 times the characteristic strength f_{ck}. The partial safety factor $y_m = 1{\cdot}5$ shall be applied in addition to this. For the stress strain curve Fig. 9B·2 (*b*) the design stress parameters are as follows :

Area of stress block = $0{\cdot}36\, f_{ck} . x_4$

Depth of centre of compressive force from top fibre in comp. = $0{\cdot}416\, x_4$

(*d*) The tensile strength of concrete is ignored.

(*e*) The stresses in the reinforcement are derived from the representative stress strain curve for the type of steel used. For design purposes the partial safety factor $y_m = 1{\cdot}15$ shall be used.

(*f*) The max. strain in the tension reinforcement in the section at failure shall not be less than

$$\frac{f_y}{1{\cdot}5\, E_s} + 0{\cdot}002 \quad \text{or} \quad \left[\frac{0{\cdot}87\, f_y}{E_s} + 0{\cdot}002\right] \qquad ...(9B{\cdot}1)$$

The assumption (*f*) is made to ensure that the failure of the section is ductile *i.e.* steel undergoes a certain *in-elastic* deformation before concrete fails in comp. Max depth of neutral axis.

In Fig. 9B·1(*b*) consider similar triangles

$$\frac{x_{y.max}}{d} = \frac{0.0035}{0.87\ f_y/E_s + 0.002} \quad \text{...(9B·2)}$$

Table 9B·1. Values of ($x_{u.max}/d$) for different steels

Yield strength of steel, N/mm²	250	415	500
$x_{u.max}/d$	0·531	0·479	0·456

9B·1. Design of singly reinforced sections. (Steel in tension side only)

Refer Fig. 9B·1 and 9B·2 the centroid of the compressive force in the rectangular sec lies at 0·416 $x_{u.max}$ from the extreme comp. fibre.

The total comp. force = Area of sec. × stress = 0·36 $f_{ck}.b.x_{u.max}$.

Lever arm = Distance between the centroid of comp. force and centroid of the tensile force
= (d – 0·416 $x_{u.max}$) refer Fig. 9B·2(b).

The maximum moment of resistance of the section

Mu lim = Force × lever arm = 0·36 $f_{ck}.b.x_{u.max}$ × (d – 0·416 $x_{u.max}$)

or $$Mu \text{ lim} = 0.36 f_{ck}\, bd^2 \frac{x_{u.max}}{d}.\left[1 - 0.416\frac{x_{u.max}}{d}\right] \quad \text{...(9B·3)}$$

Substituting for $\frac{x_{u.max}}{d}$ (refer equation 9·2)

$$Mu \text{ lim} = 0.36 f_{ck}\, bd^2 \frac{0.0035}{0.87\ f_y/E_S + 0.002}\left[1 - \frac{0.0015}{0.002 + 0.87\ f_y/E_S}\right] \quad \text{...(9B·4)}$$

$$\frac{Mu \text{ lim}}{f_{ck}\ bd^2} = \frac{0.0013}{0.002 + 0.87\ f_y/E_S}\left[1 - \frac{0.0015}{0.002 + 0.87\ f_y/E_S}\right] = Ql \quad \text{...(9B·5)}$$

where Ql is defined as limiting moment of resistance constant which depends on characteristic strength f_y and modulus of steel E_s.

This can be written as Mu lim = $Ql\ f_{ck}\ bd^2$ ...(9B·6)

The percentage of steel is obtained by equating total comp. and tensile forces.

Total comp. force = 0·36 f_{ck} b. $x_{u.max}$.

Total tensile force = Area of steel × stress in steel = P_t lim bd(0·07 fy)

where Pt lim is the limiting percentage of steel corresponding to limiting moment of resistance.

Equating two forces

$$P_t \text{ lim } bd\frac{(0.87\ f_y)}{100} = 0.36\ f_{ck}.b.x_{u.max}$$

or $$\frac{P_t \text{ lim } f_y}{f_{ck}} = 41.379\frac{x_{u.max}}{d}$$; substituting for $\frac{x_{u.max}}{d}$ equation (9B·2).

$$P_t \text{ lim}\frac{f_y}{f_{ck}} = \frac{41.379 \times 0.0033}{0.002 + 0.87\ f_y/E_s} = \frac{0.1448}{0.02 + 0.87\ f_y/E_s} = C_P \quad \text{...(9B·7)}$$

where C_P is limiting steel constant, the value of which depenas on f_y, E_s.

The value of E_s = 200 kN per mm^2.

Table 9B·2. Limiting moment of resistance and percentage steel constants for single reinforced rectangular beams

f_y N/mm^2	250	415	500
$Ql = \dfrac{Mu \lim}{f_{ck} K\ bd^2}$	0·149	0·138	0·133
$C_P = \dfrac{P_t \lim f_y}{f_{ck}}$	21·97	19·82	19·87

For particular grade of concrete the limiting moment of resistance can be written as

$$Mu \lim = Q_u\ bd^2 \text{ (refer eqn. 9B·6)}$$

where $\qquad Q_u = Ql \times f_{ck}$

Table 9B·3. Limiting moment of resistance factor Q_u for singly reinforced rectangular beams

f_{ck} N/mm^2	*f_y N/mm^2*			The values of Q_u are obtained by multiplying Ql by appropriate strength of concrete $Q_u = Ql \times fu$ which is given as $\dfrac{Mu \lim}{bd^2}$ N/mm^2
	250	*415*	*500*	
15	2·24	2·07	2·00	
20	2·98	2·76	2·66	
25	3·73	3·45	3·33	
30	4·47	4·14	3·90	

Table 9B·4. Percentage of tensile steel P_t lim for singly reinforced rectangular beams

f_{ck} N/mm^2	*f_y N/mm^2*			$P_t \lim = C_P \times \dfrac{f_{ck}}{f_y}$ C_P can be taken from Table and then multiplying by $\dfrac{f_{ck}}{f_y}$ to obtain P_t lim
	250	*415*	*500*	
15	1·32	0·72	0·57	
20	1·76	0·96	0·76	
25	2·20	1·19	0·94	
30	2·64	1·43	1·13	

Example. *Data : Singly reinforced beam 30 × 60 cm, concrete mix M-15, characteristic strength of steel = 250 N/mm^2. Determine limiting moment of resistance and bending percentage of steel.*

Solution. Assume 25 mm dia. bars and 25 mm clear cover

So effective depth $\qquad = 60 - 25 - 2·5/2 = 56·25$ cm.

From table 9B·4 for f_y $\qquad = 250$ N/mm^2 and $f_{ck} = 15$ N/mm^2

Limiting moment constant $Q_u = \left(\dfrac{M}{bd^2}\right) = 2·24$ N/mm^2

or $$Q_u = \frac{2·24}{1000} \times (1000)^2 \text{ kN/m}^2 = 2·24 \times 10^3 \text{ kN/m}^2$$

Since Mu lim $= Q_u\, bd^2 = 2{\cdot}24 \times 10^3 \times 30/100 \times \left(\frac{56{\cdot}25}{100}\right)^2 = 212{\cdot}6$ kN-m

From Table 9B·4, limiting percentage of steel for f_y 250 N/mm^2 and f_{ck} = 15 N/mm^2 is 1 : 32. **Ans.**

9B·2. Design of Doubly Reinforced Beams (Limit State Design)

Some times it becomes necessary to restrict the dimensions of a beam from structural, architectural or head room requirements. Such beams have to resist more Bending Moment on a single reinforced section. In such cases additional moment is provided by designing the section as a Doubly reinforced section *i.e.* by providing steel both on tension as well as on compression side. Such beams are called as Doubly Reinforced beams.

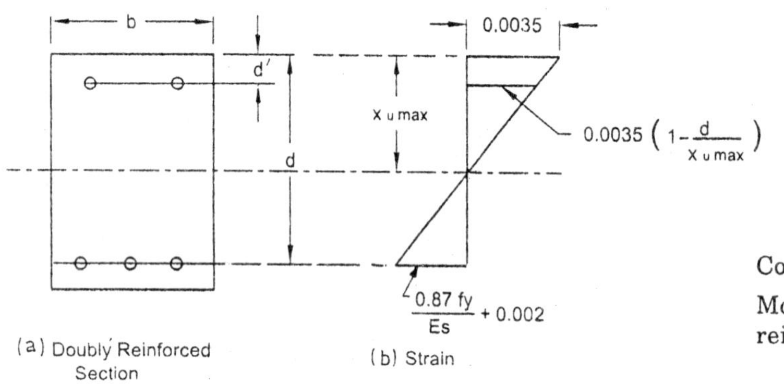

Cover of centre of comp. steel = d^1

Moment of resistance of singly reinforced section

$$Mu \lim = Q_u bd^2$$

Fig. 9B·3.

Q_u (limiting resistance factor) for different concrete grades and type of steel is given in the Table 9B·3. The limiting percentage of the tensile steel A_{st1} corresponding to the limiting moment is given in equation 9·7 $\left(P_t \lim \frac{f_y}{f_{ck}} = C_P\right)$. The values of limiting percentage of steel are given in Tables 9B·2 and 9B·4.

The additional moment of resistance $Mu_2 = Mu - Mu$ lim which is taken by steel on comp. side and additional steel on tension side.

The lever arm for the additional moment is equal to the deistance between the centroids of tension and comp. steel and is equal to $d - d'$.

Additional moment $Mu_2 = A_{st2}\,(0{\cdot}87\, f_y)\,(d - d')$ ...(9B·8)

where A_{st2} = the area of additional tensile steel which can also be obtained from

$$Mu_2 = A_{Sc}\,(f_{Sc} - f_{cc})\,(d - d') \quad ...(9B{\cdot}9)$$

where A_{sc} = area of compression steel

f_{sc} = stress in comp. steel

f_{ce} = comp. stress in conc. at the level of centroid of comp. steel.

A_{sc} the area of comp. steel can also be obtained from the consideration that additional tensile force = additional comp. force.

$$A_{Sc}(f_{Sc} - f_{cc}) = A_{st2}\,(0{\cdot}87\, f_y) \quad ...(9B{\cdot}10)$$

Area of total tensile steel $= A_{st_1} + A_{st_2} = P_t \lim \frac{bd}{100} + A_{st_2}$ ...(9B·11)

A_{sc} can also be obtained from the equations 9B·9 and 9B·10 provided that the values of f_{sc} and f_{cc} are known. For design purposes the depth of neutral axis is taken as x_4 max (as for singly reinforced section). The strain at the level of comp. reinforcement will be equal to

$0{\cdot}0035\left[1 - \dfrac{d'}{x_4\, max}\right]$ as shown, for values of d'/d equal to 0·2 f_{cc} is equal to 0·446 f_{ck} (Fig. 9B·2 (*b*)) and the design steel for mild steel will be $0{\cdot}87f_y$. For cold worked bars the design stress in compression will be less than $0{\cdot}87f_y$ and will depend on the cover to the comp. steel. The allowable stress in comp. reinforcement for cold work bars is given in Table below (9B·5) for various values of cover to the reinforcement (values of d'/d).

Table 9B·5. Allowable stress in comp. steel f_{cc} N/mm² in doubly reinforced beams with cold worked bars

f_y N/mm^2	d'/d			
	0·05	0·10	0·15	0·20
415	355	353	342	329
500	424	412	395	30

Example 9B·1. *Design a R.C. section to resist a factored moment of 600 kN-m inclusive of self weight. The dimensions of the beam are to be restricted to 40 cm × 80 cm. Concrete used in M-15 and characteristic strength of steel is 250 N/mm²*

Solution. Assume 25 mm dia. bars with 25 mm clear cover.

Effective depth $= 80 - 2{\cdot}5 - \dfrac{2{\cdot}5}{2} = 76{\cdot}25$ cm $= 762{\cdot}5$ mm

From Table 9B·3 for f_{ck} 15 N/mm² and $f_y = 250$ N/mm². The limiting moment of resistance constant is 2·24.

Limiting moment of resistance Mu lim $= Q_u\, bd^2$

$$= \frac{2{\cdot}24 \times 400 \times 762{\cdot}5 \times 762{\cdot}5}{1000 \times 1000} \text{ kNm} = 520{\cdot}94 \text{ kNm}$$

Moment of resistance M_{u2} to be supplied by the comp. steel = 600 – 520·94 = 79·06 kN-m

Area of tensile steel A_{st1}, corresponding to limiting moment of resistance from Table 9B·4 is 1·32%.

$$A_{st1} = \frac{1{\cdot}32}{100} \times 400 \times 762{\cdot}5 \text{ mm}^2 = 4026 \text{ mm}^2 = 40{\cdot}26 \text{ cm}^2$$

Cover to centre of comp. steel $= 2{\cdot}5 + \dfrac{2{\cdot}5}{2} = 3{\cdot}75$ cm $= 37{\cdot}5$ mm

Lever arm for moment of resistance due to comp. steel $= d - d' = 762{\cdot}5 - 37{\cdot}5 = 725$ mm

Additional moment $M_{u2} = A_{st2}\,(0{\cdot}87 + y)\,(d - d')$

$$79{\cdot}06 = A_{st2}\left(\frac{0{\cdot}87 \times 250}{1000}\right) \times \frac{725}{1000} \text{ kN-m}$$

$$A_{st2} = 501{\cdot}33 \text{ mm}^2 = 5{\cdot}0133 \text{ cm}^2$$

Total area of tensile steel $= 45{\cdot}2733$ cm²

$$\frac{d'}{d} = \frac{37{\cdot}5}{762{\cdot}5} = 0{\cdot}0492 < 0{\cdot}2$$

Hence comp. stress in steel will be $0{\cdot}87\, f_y$ and $f_{cc} = 0{\cdot}446\, f_{ck}$

$$M_{u2} = A_{sc}(f_{sc} - f_{cc})\,(d - d')$$

$$79 \cdot 06 = A_{sc} = \left(\frac{0 \cdot 87 \times 250 - 0 \cdot 446 \times 15}{1000}\right) \times \frac{725}{1000} \text{ kN-m}$$

$$A_{sc} = \frac{79 \cdot 06 \times 10^6}{725 \times (217 \cdot 5 - 6 \cdot 69)} = 500 \text{ mm}^2 = 5 \text{ cm}^2$$

Area of tensile steel = $45 \cdot 273$ cm^2

Area of comp. steel = 5 cm^2

9B·3. Design of T-Sections

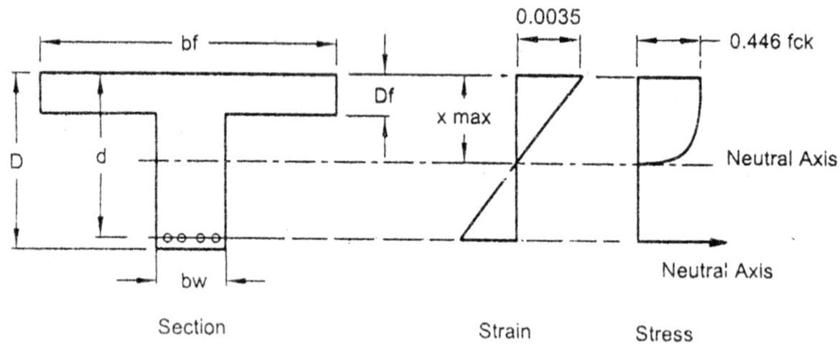

D_f = thickness of flange
d = effective depth of beam
b_w = thickness of web
b_f = effective width of flange

Fig. 9B·4.

Floor slabs and beams are cast together to form a monolithic section. In such a section a portion of slab acts with beam and the section acts as a *T*-beam.

The width of the web is b_w and the effective width of the flange is b_f, which may be taken as the following but not greater than width of the web + ½ sum of the clear distance to the adjacent beams on either side.

(*i*) For *T*-beams, $b_f = \frac{l_0}{6} + b_w + 6\,D_f$; For L – beams, $b_f = \frac{\rho_0}{12} + b_w + 3D_f$

(*ii*) For isolate *T*-beams $b_f = \frac{l_0}{\left(\frac{l_0}{b} + 4\right)} + b_w$. For *L*-beams, $b_f = \frac{0 \cdot 5\, l_0}{\left(\frac{l_0}{b} + 4\right)} + b_w$

where, l_0 = distance between points of few moments.

D_f = thickness of flange and d = effective depth of beam.

b = actual width of flange.

The moment of resistance of *T*-beam is the sum of the moments in concrete in the web of width bw and due to the flange of width b_f. There are two cases in this :

(*a*) **When flange thickness is less than 0·2 *d***

The centroid of compressive force in flange will be $D_f/2$ from the top compressive fibre.

Mu lim *T*-sec. = Mu lim web + Mu lim flange

Mu lim flange = Force × lever arm

$$= 0 \cdot 446\, f_{ck}\,(b_f - b_w)\; D_f \times \left[d - \frac{D_f}{2}\right]$$

Mu lim web is obtained as for singly reinforced section (Equation 9B·3)

So Mu lim web = $0 \cdot 36\, f_{ck} b\, x_{u.max}\,(d - 0 \cdot 416\, x_{u.max})$ it can also be obtained from

Mu lim web = $Q_u\, bd^2$ (values of Q_u are given in Table 9B·3)

The area of the tensile steel is the sum of the areas required for balancing compressive force in web and comp. force in flange.

Percentage of tensile steel for balancing comp. force in web $P_s t_w$ is given by the limiting percentage of steel (Equation 9B·7).

$$P_s t_w = P_t \text{ lim} = \frac{f_{ck}}{f_y} \frac{0.1448}{0.0055 \times 0.87 f_y / E_s} \text{(refer Table 9·4)} \quad \text{(Equation 9B·8)}$$

$$\text{Area of steel } = P_s t_w \times \frac{bw.d}{100} = \frac{bwd}{100} . \frac{f_{ck}}{f_y} \frac{0.1448}{0.0055 \times 0.87 f_y / E_S}$$

where P_{stw} = percentage of tensile steel is web.

The area of tensile steel for balancing comp. force in flange. A_{stf} is obtained by equating total comp. in flange to total tensile force in steel required to balance.

Therefore, Total comp. force = stress × area = $0.446 f_{ck} (b_f - b_w) D_f$

Therefore, $0.446 f_{ck} (b_f - b_w) D_f = 0.87 f_y A_s t_f$ where $A_s t_f$ = tensile steel in flange

or
$$A_{st_f} = \frac{0.446 f_{ck}}{0.87 f_y} (b_f - b_w) D_f$$

Total area of tensile steel in T-sec. = $A_{st_w} + A_{st_f}$ where A_{stw} is the area of steel in web

$$= \frac{b_w . d}{100} . \frac{f_{ck}}{f_y} . \frac{0.1448}{0.0055 + 0.87 f_y / E_c} + \frac{0.446 f_{ck} (b_f - b_w) D_f}{0.87 f_y}$$

(*b*) When flange thickness is larger than 0·2 d :

In such cases the stress in flange is not $0.446 f_{ck}$ throughout the thickness and the stress in flange will be $0.446 f_{ck}$ in some portion of the thickness and less than $0.446 f_{ck}$ in the remaining portion. An approximate expression is given as below to make allowances for such variation. In this expression D_f is replaced by d'_f for moment of resistance due to flange.

$$Mu \text{ lim flange} = 0.446 f_{ck} (b_f - b_w) d'_f \left(d - \frac{d'_f}{2} \right)$$

where
$$d'_f = (0.15 x_{u.max} + 0.65 D_f) \text{ but not greater than } D_f$$

Total moment of resistance = Mu lim web + Mu lim flange

$$= 0.36 f_{ck} b.x_{u.max} (d - 416 x_{u.max}) + 0.446 f_{ck} (b_f - b_w) d'_f \left(\frac{d - d'_f}{2} \right)$$

Area of tensile steel = Area for balancing comp. force in web + Area for balancing comp. force in flange.

Area for balancing force in web in Pt lim web and is given by equation 9B·7 and Table 9B·4. The area of steel for balancing comp. force is obtained by equating total tensile and compressive forces

$$0.446 f_{ck} (b_f - b_w) d'_f = A_{stf} 0.87 f_y$$

or
$$A_{st_f} = \frac{0.446 f_{ck} (b_f - b_w) d'_f}{0.87 f_y}$$

Example 9B·2. *Determine the limiting moment of resistance of a T-Beam shown below. Mixed used M15 and characteristic strength of steel 250 N/mm^2. Also determine area of tensile steel.*

Solution. $0.2\, d = 0.2 \times 60 = 12$ cm

As thickness of slab is less than 0·2, the flange will develop full comp. strength of $0.446 f_{ck}$.

The total moment of resistance = Mu lim web + Mu lim flange

where Mu lim web = $Q_u\, bd^2$

For f_{ck} = 15 N/mm² and f_y = 250 N/mm², the value of limiting moment of resistance Q_u

= 2·24 N/mm² (Table 9B·3)

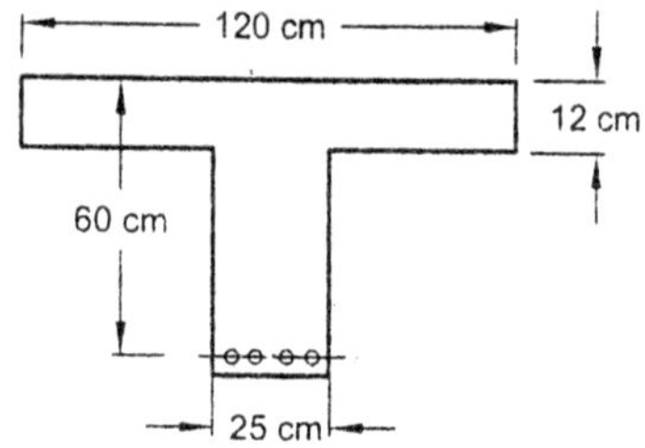

Fig. 9B·5.

$$Mu \text{ lim web} = Q_u\, bd^2 = 2{\cdot}24 \times 250 \times 600 \times 600 \text{ N/mm}^2$$

$$= \frac{2{\cdot}24 \times 250 \times 600 \times 600}{1000 \times 1000} = 201{\cdot}6 \text{ KN-m}$$

Area of steel for this moment of resistance = $P_t \text{ lim} \times \dfrac{bd}{100} = \dfrac{1{\cdot}32 \times 25 \times 60}{100} \text{ cm}^2 = 19{\cdot}8 \text{ cm}^2$

Moment of resistance of the flange $= 0{\cdot}446\, f_{ck}\, (b_f - bw)\, D_f \times \left(d - \dfrac{D_f}{2}\right)$

$$= 0{\cdot}446 \times 15\, (1200 - 250) \times 120 \times \left(600 - \frac{120}{2}\right) \text{ N-m}$$

$$= 0{\cdot}446 \times 15 \times \frac{950}{1000} \times \frac{120 \times 540}{1000} \text{ kN} = 411{\cdot}83 \text{ kN}$$

Total moment of resistance = 201·6 + 411·83 = 613·43 kN-m

Area of steel for this moment of resistance...refer (Equation 9B·8)

$$A_{stf} = \frac{0{\cdot}446\, f_{ck}}{0{\cdot}87\, f_y}(b_f - b_w)D_f = \frac{0{\cdot}446 \times 15}{0{\cdot}87 \times 250}(1200 - 250) \times 120 \text{ mm}^2$$

$$= \frac{0{\cdot}446 \times 15}{0{\cdot}87 \times 250} \times \frac{950 \times 120}{100} \text{ cm}^2 = 35{\cdot}06 \text{ cm}^2$$

Total area of tensile steel = $A_{stw} + A_{stf}$ = 19·8 + 35·06 = 54·86 cm² **Ans.**

9B·4. Shear in Beams

Diagonal cracks are formed in case when shear stress generated exceed shear strength of concrete at 45° to axes of the member. On the experimental basis three different mods of failure which can occur as a result of combinations of shear and bending moment in the section as follows :

(1) **Diagonal tension.** This occurs when shear force is larger as compared to bending moment at 45° to the axis.

(2) **Flexural shear.** This occurs when bending moment is larger as compared to shear force. Such cracks are formed at 90° to the axis.

(3) **Diagonal compression.** This occurs in beams not reinforced against shear and shear force in large. This is characterised by the crushing of the concrete.

Design of beam for shear force (S.F.) is as under :

(1) Find out nominal shear stress S_c by the formula given below :

Beams of uniform depth— $S_c = \dfrac{S_u}{bd}$

Beams of varying depth— $S_c = \dfrac{S_u \pm (Mu \tan \beta)/d}{bd}$

where S_c = Nominal shear stress

S_u = Ultimate S.F. due to design loads

b = Width of member which for flanged section shall be taken as width of the web bw and

d = Effective depth

M_u = Ultimate Bending Moment (BM) at the section

B = Angle between the top and the bottom edges of the beam.

When the B.M. increases numerically in the same direction as the effective depth increases, the –ve sign holds good for the formula of the beams with varying depth, otherwise the +ve sign holds good.

(2) Find out the design shear strength of concrete depending upon the longitudinal tensile steel (refer Table 9B·6 below).

Table 9B·6. Design shear strength of conc. S_d N/mm²

$100\frac{A_s}{bd}$	*Conc. grade*					
	M 15	*M 20*	*M 25*	*M 30*	*M 35*	*M 40 and above*
≤ 0·15	0·28	0·28	0·29	0·29	0·29	0·30
0·25	0·35	0·36	0·36	0·37	0·37	0·38
0·50	0·46	0·48	0·49	0·50	0·50	0·51
0·75	0·54	0·56	0·57	0·59	0·59	0·60
1·00	0·60	0·62	0·64	0·66	0·67	0·68
1·25	0·64	0·67	0·70	0·71	0·73	0·74
1·50	0·68	0·72	0·74	0·76	0·78	0·79
1·75	0·71	0·75	0·78	0·80	0·82	0·84
2·00	0·71	0·79	0·82	0·84	0·86	0·88
2·25	0·71	0·81	0·85	0·88	0·90	0·92
2·50	0·71	0·82	0·88	0·91	0·93	0·95
2·75	0·71	0·82	0·90	0·94	0·96	0·98
3·00 and above	0·71	0·82	0·92	0·96	0·96	1·01

Note : The term A_s is the area of longitudinal tension steel which continues at least one effective depth beyond the section being considered except at support where the full area of tension steel may be used.

(3) Find out the max. shear stress depending upon the grade (refer table below).

Table 9B·7. Max. shear stress $S_{c.max}$ *.N/mm²*.

Conc. Grade	M 15	M 20	M 25	M 30	M35	M 40 and above
$S_{c.max}$ *N/mm²*	2·5	2·8	3·1	3·5	3·7	4·0

(4) If nominal shear stress is greater than max. stress change the sec. increasing either b or d and repeat 1 to 3 steps above.

(5) Now there may be two cases :

(*a*) Nominal stress S_c is less than design shear strength of concrete (S_d). For this case provide min. steel as below :

(*b*) Nominal shear stress exceeds the design shear strength of concrete For this case shear steel can be provided in three different forms.

(*i*) Vertical stirrups

(*ii*) Bent up bars along with stirrups

(*iii*) Inclined stirrups

When bent up bars are used, their contribution towards shear resistance shall not be more than half of the total shear reinforcement.

Shear reinforcement shall be provided to carry a shear equal to $S—S_d \cdot bd$. The strength of shear reinforcement S_s shall be calculated as below :

(a) $S_s = \dfrac{0{\cdot}87 f_y A_{sv} d}{d_v}$ For vertical stirrups

(b) $S_s = \dfrac{0{\cdot}87 f_y A_{sv} d}{d_v}(\sin\alpha + \cos\alpha)$ For inclined stirrup or a series of bars bent up at different x-sections.

(c) $S_s = 0{\cdot}87 f_y A_{sv} \sin\alpha$ For single bar or single group of parallel bars, all bent up at the same x-section

where A_{sv} = Total x-sectional area of stirrup legs or bent up bars with a distance of sv

d_v = Spacing of the stirrups or bent up bars along the length of the member

S_c = Nominal shear stress

S_d = Design shear stress

b = Breadth of the member which for the flanged beams can be taken as breadth of the web

f_y = Characteristic strength of stirrups or bent up bars which shall not be taken greater than 415 N/mm^2.

Angle α is angle of crank of bars.

Note : Solid slabs, the design shear strength for conc. shall be S_{dk} where 'k' has the values.

Table 9B·8. Values

Overall depth of slab	300 or more	275	250	225	200	175	150 or less
K	1·00	1·05	1·10	1·15	1·20	1·25	1·30

9B·5. Columns

Limit State of collapse in compression. In addition to the assumptions made in limit state of collapse design of flexural members (art 9B·1). The following assumptions shall be made.

(a) The max. compression strain in concrete in axial compression is taken as 0·0002.

(b) The max. compressive strain on the extreme fibre with high compression subjected to axial compression in concrete and bending and where is no tension on the section shall be 0·0035 – 0·75 times the strain at the least compressed extreme fibre.

All the members shall be designed for the min. eccentricity equal to the unsupported length of column 1500 + lateral dimension/30 subject to a minimum of 20 mm. Where calculated eccentricity is larger. The min. eccentricity shall be ignored.

Short Axially loaded members in comp. members with lateral ties

The design shall be made on the above assumptions including requirement of min. eccentricity when min. eccentricity does not exceed 0·05 times the lateral dimension. The design is done as below :

$$P_u = 0{\cdot}4 f_{ck} A_c + 0{\cdot}67 f_y A_{sc} \quad \text{...(9B·10)}$$

f_{ck} = characteristic comp. strength of concrete

A_c = Area of concrete

f_y = Characteristic strength of comp. steel and

A_{sc} = Area of longitudinal steel for column.

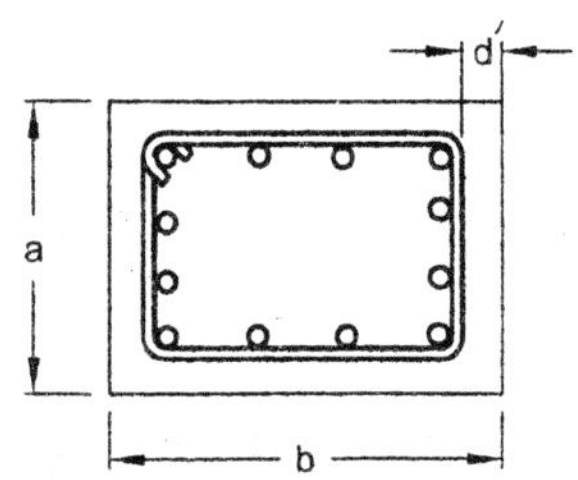

Fig. 9B·6

Members with Helical Reinforcement

The strength of comp. members with helical reinforcement satisfying the requirements given below is taken 1·05 times the strength of similar member with lateral ties.

The ratio of the volume of helical reinforcement to the volume of the core shall not be less than $0{\cdot}36\left(\frac{A_g}{A_c}-1\right)\frac{f_{ck}}{f_y}$.

where A_g = Gross area of the section.

A_c = Area of core of the helically reinforced column measured to an outside diameter of the helix.

f_{ck} = Characteristic comp. strength of concrete and

f_y = Characteristic strength of the helical reinforcement but not exceeding 415 N/mm^2

Example 9B·3. *Determine ultimate load carrying capacity of a 456 mm × 600 mm R.C. column. The column is reinforced with 6 bars of 25 mm dia. Concrete mix used in M 20 and characteristic strength of steel is 415 N/mm². Take column length as 3·2 m.*

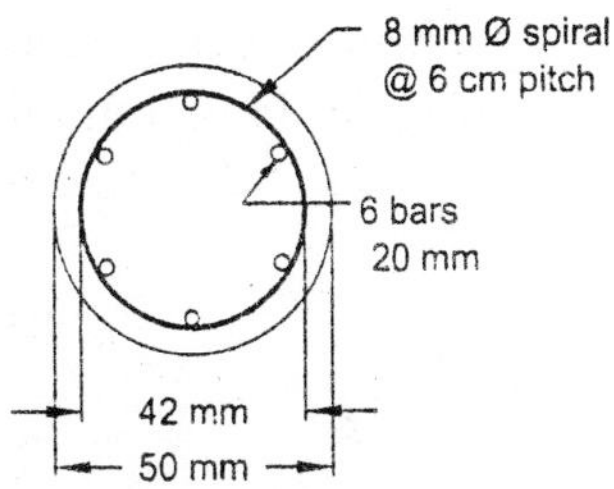

Fig. 9B·7.

Solution. Min. eccentricity in longer dimension is e_{min}

$$= \frac{1}{500} + \frac{D}{30}$$

$$= \frac{312 \times 1000}{500} + \frac{600}{30} = 6{\cdot}4 + 20 = 26{\cdot}4 \text{ mm}$$

$$\frac{e_{min}}{D} = \frac{2{\cdot}64}{60} = 0{\cdot}44 < 0{\cdot}05 \text{ where } D = \text{longer dimension}$$

The min. eccentricity ratio is < 0·05 in both directions. Hence the load carrying capacity is

Ultimate load $P_u = 0{\cdot}4\, f_{ck}\, A_c + 0{\cdot}67\, f_y\, A_{sc}$

where f_{ck} is 20 N/mm^2 ; f_y = 415 N/mm^2.

A_{sc} = Area of 6 bars of dia. 25 mm = 29·45 cm^2 = 2945 mm^2

A_c = Area of concrete = 450 × 600 = 2945 mm^2 = 267055 mm^2

$P_u = 0{\cdot}4 \times 20 \times 267055 + 0{\cdot}67 \times 415 \times 2945$ N

or $$P_u = \frac{0{\cdot}4 \times 20 \times 267055 + 0{\cdot}67 \times 415 \times 2945}{1000} \text{ kN} = 2136 + 818{\cdot}82 = 2955{\cdot}2 \text{ kN}$$ **Ans.**

Example 9B·4. *Find ultimate load carrying capacity of a 50 cm dia. circular R.C. column with 6 bars of 20 mm dia. The column have 8 mm ϕ spiral reinfrocement at 6 cm pitch as shown in Fig. 9B·7. Mix of concrete is M15* and f_y of steel is 250 *N/mm². Effective length of column is 3·0 m.*

Solution. Min. eccentricity $= \frac{l}{500} + \frac{D}{30} = \frac{3000}{500} + \frac{500}{30} = 6{\cdot}0 \pm 13{\cdot}3 = 19{\cdot}3$ mm

$$e_{min} = \frac{20}{500} = 0{\cdot}04 < 0{\cdot}08 \text{ (acceptible) say } 20{\cdot}0 \text{ m}^2$$

Length of each spiral $= \sqrt{\pi D^2 + p^2} = \sqrt{\pi(420+8)^2 + 60^2} = 1321$ mm.

Volume of spiral per mm height $= \dfrac{\frac{\pi}{4} \times 8^2 \times 1321}{60} = 1100$ mm^2

Volume of core per mm height $= \frac{\pi}{4}(420 + 2 \times 8) \times 1 = \frac{\pi}{4} \times (436)^2 = 149301$ mm^2

Ratio of Vol. of spiral to Vol. of core $= \frac{1100}{149301} = 0{\cdot}0074$

The ratio should not be less than $0{\cdot}36 \times A_g\ (A_c - 1)\ f_{ck}/f_y$ for increased capacity.

A_g = gross area of section $= \frac{\pi}{4} \times 500^2 = 196350$ mm^2

$$A_c = \frac{\pi}{4}(420 + 2 \times 8)^2 = 149{,}301 \text{ mm}^2$$

$$\text{Now } 0{\cdot}36\left\{\frac{A_g}{A_c} - 1\right\}\frac{f_{ck}}{f_y} = 0{\cdot}36\left\{\frac{196350}{149301} - 1\right\}\frac{15}{200} = 0{\cdot}0068$$

Actual ratio is $0{\cdot}0074 > 0{\cdot}0068$

The load carrying capacity given in equation 9B·10 will be increased by 1·05.

Area of longitudinal reinforcement = 1885 mm^2

$$P_u = 1{\cdot}05\ (0{\cdot}4\ f_{ck}\ A_c + 0{\cdot}67\ f_y\ A_{sc})$$

or $$P_u = 1{\cdot}05\left[0{\cdot}4 \times 15\left\{\frac{\pi}{4} \times (500)^2 - 1850\right\} + 0{\cdot}67 \times 250 \times 1885\right] \text{kN}$$

or $$P_u = \frac{1{\cdot}05}{1000}(6 \times 194465 + 315737)\text{kN} = 1556 \text{ kN}$$

Ultimate load carrying capacity = 1556 kN **Ans.**

9B·6. Design of Beams

Example 9B·5. *Design a beam for the following data :*

Moment at support = *191·07 kNm*

Moment at span = *81·56 kNm*

Shear force at support = *149·12 kN*

Shear force at span = *32·98 kN*

Solution : Design moment 191·07 kNm (At support)

Size of the beam = 400 × 600

$\therefore$ Effective depth required $= \sqrt{\frac{191{\cdot}07 \times 10^6}{0{\cdot}138 \times 20 \times 400}} = 416{\cdot}02$ mm

Effective depth provided $= 600 - 25 - \frac{20}{2} = 565$ mm

$$\therefore \quad \frac{Mu}{bd^2} = \frac{191{\cdot}07 \times 10^6}{400 \times 565^2} = 1{\cdot}5$$

From tables P_t required = 0·46%

$$\therefore \quad A_{st} \text{ required} = \frac{0{\cdot}46}{100} \times 400 \times 565 = 1039{\cdot}6 \text{ mm}^2$$

Provide 4 – 20 ϕ bars

$$\therefore \quad A_{st} \text{ provided} = 4 \times 314 = 1256 \text{ mm}^2$$

$$P_t \text{ provided} = \frac{1256 \times 100}{400 \times 565} = 0{\cdot}556\%$$

$$\text{Shear stress developed} = \frac{149 \cdot 12 \times 10^3}{400 \times 565} = 0 \cdot 66 \ \text{N/mm}^2$$

Design of shear stress of concrete corresponding to p_t = 0·556% is 0·498 N/mm^2

∴ We have to provide shear reinforcement for a shear force

$$= 149 \cdot 12 - 0 \cdot 498 \times 400 \times 565 \times 10^{-3} = 36 \cdot 57 \text{ kN.}$$

Providing 2L – 10 ϕ stirrups spacing required is

$$S_v = \frac{0 \cdot 87 f_y A_{sv} d}{V_{us}} = \frac{0 \cdot 87 \times 415 \times 2\left(\frac{\pi}{4} \times 10^2\right) \times 565}{36 \cdot 57 \times 10^3} = 875 \cdot 77 \text{ mm}$$

Provide 2L – 10 ϕ stirrups @ 300 c/c

At span

$$\frac{Mu}{bd^2} = \frac{81 \cdot 56 \times 10^6}{400 \times 567^2} = 0 \cdot 63$$

From tables, we get p_t required = – 0·181

$$\therefore \quad A_{st} \text{ required} = \frac{0 \cdot 181}{100} \times 400 \times 567 = 410 \cdot 51 \text{ mm}^2$$

Provide 3 – 16 ϕ bars

$$\therefore \quad A_{st} \text{ provided} = 3 \times 201 = 603 \text{ mm}^2$$

$$\therefore \quad P_t \text{ provided} = \frac{603 \times 100}{400 \times 567} = 0 \cdot 26\%$$

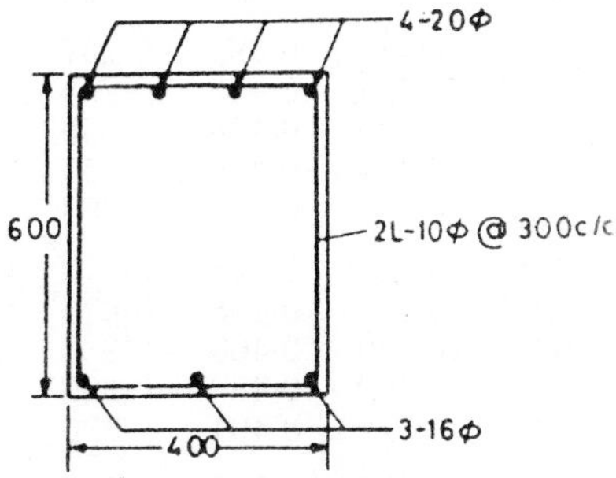

Fig. 9B·8.

$$\text{Shear stress developed} = \frac{32 \cdot 98 \times 10^3}{400 \times 567} = 0 \cdot 145 \ \text{N/mm}^2$$

Design shear stress of concrete corresponding to p_t = 0·26% is 0·366 N/mm^2. So provide only nominal reinforcement. Provide 2L – 10 ϕ stirrups @ 300 c/c

Table 9B·9. Flexure–Reinforcement Percentage, P_t For Singly Reinforced Sections (Concrete mix M15, f_{ck} = 15 N/mm²)

M_u/bd^2, N/mm^2	f_y, N/mm^2 240	250	415	480	500
0·30	0·147	0·141	0·085	0·074	0·071
0·35	0·172	0·166	0·100	0·086	0·083
0·40	0·198	0·190	0·114	0·099	0·095
0·45	0·224	0·215	0·129	0·112	0·107
0·50	0·250	0·240	0·144	0·125	0·120
0·55	0·276	0·265	0·159	0·138	0·132
0·60	0·302	0·290	0·175	0·151	0·145
0·65	0·329	0·316	0·190	0·164	0·158
0·70	0·356	0·342	0·206	0·178	0·171
0·75	0·383	0·368	0·221	0·191	0·184
0·80	0·410	0·394	0·237	0·205	0·197
0·82	0·421	0·405	0·244	0·211	0·202
0·84	0·433	0·415	0·250	0·216	0·208
0·86	0·444	0·426	0·257	0·222	0·213
0·88	0·455	0·437	0·263	0·227	0·218
0·90	0·466	0·448	0·270	0·233	0·224
0·92	0·477	0·458	0·276	0·239	0·229
0·94	0·489	0·469	0·283	0·244	0·235
0·96	0·500	0·480	0·289	0·250	0·240
0·98	0·512	0·491	0·296	0·256	0·246
1·00	0·523	0·502	0·303	0·262	0·251
1·02	0·535	0·513	0·309	0·267	0·257
1·04	0·546	0·524	0·316	0·273	0·262
1·06	0·558	0·536	0·323	0·279	0·268
1·08	0·570	0·547	0·329	0·285	0·273
1·10	0·581	0·558	0·336	0·291	0·279
1·12	0·593	0·570	0·343	0·297	0·285
1·14	0·605	0·581	0·350	0·303	0·290
1·16	0·617	0·592	0·357	0·309	0·296
1·18	0·629	0·604	0·364	0·315	0·302
1·20	0·641	0·615	0·371	0·321	0·308
1·22	0·653	0·627	0·378	0·327	0·314
1·24	0·665	0·639	0·385	0·333	0·319
1·26	0·678	0·650	0·392	0·339	0·325
1·28	0·690	0·662	0·399	0·345	0·331
1·30	0·702	0·674	0·406	0·351	0·337
1·32	0·715	0·686	0·413	0·357	0·343
1·34	0·727	0·698	0·420	0·364	0·349
1·36	0·740	0·710	0·428	0·370	0·355
1·38	0·752	0·722	0·435	0·376	0·361
1·40	0·765	0·734	0·442	0·382	0·367
1·42	0·778	0·747	0·450	0·389	0·373
1·44	0·790	0·759	0·457	0·395	0·379
1·46	0·803	0·771	0·465	0·402	0·386
1·48	0·816	0·784	0·472	0·408	0·392
1·50	0·829	0·796	0·480	0·415	0·398
1·52	0·842	0·809	0·487	0·421	0·404
1·54	0·856	0·821	0·495	0·428	0·411
1·56	0·869	0·834	0·503	0·434	0·417
1·58	0·882	0·847	0·510	0·441	0·423
1·60	0·896	0·860	0·518	0·448	0·430
1·62	0·909	0·873	0·526	0·455	0·436
1·64	0·923	0·886	0·534	0·461	0·443
1·66	0·936	0·899	0·542	0·468	0·449
1·68	0·950	0·912	0·550	0·475	0·456
1·70	0·964	0·925	0·558	0·482	0·463
1·72	0·978	0·939	0·566	0·489	0·469
1·74	0·992	0·952	0·574	0·496	0·476
1·76	1·006	0·966	0·582	0·503	0·483
1·78	1·020	0·980	0·590	0·510	0·490
1·80	1·035	0·993	0·598	0·517	0·497
1·82	1·049	1·007	0·607	0·525	0·504
1·84	1·064	1·021	0·615	0·532	0·511
1·86	1·078	1·035	0·624	0·539	0·518
1·88	1·093	1·049	0·632	0·546	0·525
1·90	1·108	1·063	0·641	0·554	0·532
1·92	1·123	1·078	0·649	0·561	0·539
1·94	1·138	1·092	0·658	0·569	0·546
1·96	1·153	1·107	0·667	0·576	0·553
1·98	1·168	1·121	0·676	0·584	0·561
2·00	1·184	1·136	0·685	0·592	
2·02	1·199	1·151	0·693		
2·04	1·215	1·166	0·703		
2·06	1·231	1·181	0·712		
2·08	1·247	1·197			
2·10	1·263	1·212			
2·12	1·279	1·228			
2·14	1·295	1·243			
2·16	1·312	1·259			
2·18	1·328	1·275			
2·20	1·345	1·291			
2·22	1·362	1·308			
2·24	1·379				

Note—Blanks indicate inadmissible reinforcement percentage $\left(Mu/bd^2 \text{ exceeds } \frac{Mu, \lim}{bd^2} \text{ given in Table 9·3.}\right)$.

Table 9B·10. Flexure–Reinforcement Percentage, P_t For Singly Reinforced Sections (Concrete mix M20, f_{ck} = 20 N/mm²)

M_u/bd^2, N/mm^2	f_y, N/mm^2 240	250	415	480	500
0·30	0·146	0·140	0·085	0·073	0·070
0·35	0·171	0·164	0·099	0·086	0·082
0·40	0·196	0·188	0·114	0·098	0·094
0·45	0·222	0·213	0·128	0·111	0·106
0·50	0·247	0·237	0·143	0·123	0·119
0·55	0·272	0·262	0·158	0·136	0·131
0·60	0·298	0·286	0·172	0·149	0·143
0·65	0·324	0·311	0·187	0·162	0·156
0·70	0·350	0·336	0·203	0·175	0·168
0·75	0·376	0·361	0·218	0·188	0·181
0·80	0·403	0·387	0·233	0·201	0·193
0·85	0·430	0·412	0·248	0·215	0·206
0·90	0·456	0·438	0·264	0·228	0·219
0·95	0·483	0·464	0·280	0·242	0·232
1·00	0·511	0·490	0·295	0·255	0·245
1·05	0·538	0·517	0·311	0·269	0·258
1·10	0·566	0·543	0·327	0·283	0·272
1·15	0·594	0·570	0·343	0·297	0·285
1·20	0·622	0·597	0·359	0·311	0·298
1·25	0·650	0·624	0·376	0·325	0·312
1·30	0·678	0·651	0·392	0·339	0·326
1·35	0·707	0·679	0·409	0·354	0·339
1·40	0·736	0·707	0·426	0·368	0·353
1·45	0·765	0·735	0·443	0·383	0·367
1·50	0·795	0·763	0·460	0·397	0·382
1·55	0·825	0·792	0·477	0·412	0·396
1·60	0·855	0·821	0·494	0·427	0·410
1·65	0·885	0·850	0·512	0·443	0·425
1·70	0·916	0·879	0·530	0·458	0·440
1·75	0·947	0·909	0·547	0·473	0·454
1·80	0·978	0·939	0·565	0·489	0·469
1·85	1·009	0·969	0·584	0·505	0·484
1·90	1·041	1·000	0·602	0·521	0·500
1·95	1·073	1·030	0·621	0·537	0·515
2·00	1·106	1·062	0·640	0·553	0·531
2·02	1·119	1·074	0·647	0·559	0·537
2·04	1·132	1·087	0·655	0·566	0·543
2·06	1·145	1·099	0·662	0·573	0·550
2·08	1·159	1·112	0·670	0·579	0·556
2·10	1·172	1·125	0·678	0·586	0·562
2·12	1·185	1·138	0·685	0·593	0·569
2·14	1·199	1·151	0·693	0·599	0·575
2·16	1·212	1·164	0·701	0·606	0·582
2·18	1·226	1·177	0·709	0·613	0·588
2·20	1·239	1·190	0·717	0·620	0·595
2·22	1·253	1·203	0·725	0·627	0·602
2·24	1·267	1·216	0·733	0·633	0·608
2·26	1·281	1·230	0·741	0·640	0·615
2·28	1·295	1·243	0·749	0·647	0·621
2·30	1·309	1·256	0·757	0·654	0·628
2·32	1·323	1·270	0·765	0·661	0·635
2·34	1·337	1·283	0·773	0·668	0·642
2·36	1·351	1·297	0·781	0·675	0·648
2·38	1·365	1·311	0·790	0·683	0·655
2·40	1·380	1·324	0·798	0·690	0·662
2·42	1·394	1·338	0·806	0·697	0·669
2·44	1·408	1·352	0·814	0·704	0·676
2·46	1·423	1·366	0·823	0·711	0·683
2·48	1·438	1·380	0·831	0·719	0·690
2·50	1·452	1·394	0·840	0·726	0·697
2·52	1·467	1·408	0·848	0·734	0·704
2·54	1·482	1·423	0·857	0·741	0·711
2·56	1·497	1·437	0·866	0·748	0·719
2·58	1·512	1·451	0·874	0·756	0·726
2·60	1·527	1·466	0·883	0·764	0·733
2·62	1·542	1·481	0·892	0·771	0·740
2·64	1·558	1·495	0·901	0·779	0·748
2·66	1·573	1·510	0·910	0·786	0·755
2·68	1·588	1·525	0·919	0·794	
2·70	1·604	1·540	0·928		
2·72	1·620	1·555	0·937		
2·74	1·636	1·570	0·946		
2·76	1·651	1·585	0·955		
2·78	1·667	1·601			
2·80	1·683	1·616			
2·82	1·700	1·632			
2·84	1·716	1·647			
2·86	1·732	1·663			
2·88	1·749	1·679			
2·90	1·766	1·695			
2·92	1·782	1·711			
2·94	1·799	1·727			
2·96	1·816	1·743			
2·98	1·833	1·760			

Note—Blanks indicate inadmissible reinforcement percentage (Percentage of steel exceeds limiting percentage given in Table 9·4)

Table 9B·11. Flexure–Reinforcement Percentage, P_t For Singly Reinforced Sections (Concrete Mix M25, f_{ck} = 25 N/mm²)

M_u/bd^2, N/mm^2	f_y, N/mm^2				
	240	250	415	480	500
0·30	0·146	0·140	0·084	0·073	0·070
0·35	0·171	0·164	0·099	0·085	0·082
0·40	0·195	0·188	0·113	0·098	0·094
0·45	0·220	0·211	0·127	0·110	0·106
0·50	0·245	0·236	0·142	0·123	0·118
0·55	0·271	0·260	0·156	0·135	0·130
0·60	0·296	0·284	0·171	0·148	0·142
0·65	0·321	0·309	0·186	0·161	0·154
0·70	0·347	0·333	0·201	0·174	0·167
0·75	0·373	0·358	0·216	0·186	0·179
0·80	0·399	0·383	0·231	0·199	0·191
0·85	0·425	0·408	0·246	0·212	0·204
0·90	0·451	0·433	0·261	0·225	0·216
0·95	0·477	0·458	0·276	0·239	0·229
1·00	0·504	0·483	0·291	0·252	0·242
1·05	0·530	0·509	0·307	0·265	0·255
1·10	0·557	0·535	0·322	0·279	0·267
1·15	0·584	0·561	0·338	0·292	0·280
1·20	0·611	0·587	0·353	0·306	0·293
1·25	0·638	0·613	0·369	0·319	0·306
1·30	0·666	0·639	0·385	0·333	0·320
1·35	0·693	0·666	0·401	0·347	0·333
1·40	0·721	0·692	0·417	0·360	0·346
1·45	0·749	0·719	0·433	0·374	0·359
1·50	0·777	0·746	0·449	0·388	0·373
1·55	0·805	0·773	0·466	0·403	0·387
1·60	0·834	0·800	0·482	0·417	0·400
1·65	0·862	0·828	0·499	0·431	0·414
1·70	0·891	0·856	0·515	0·446	0·428
1·75	0·920	0·883	0·532	0·460	0·442
1·80	0·949	0·911	0·549	0·475	0·456
1·85	0·979	0·940	0·566	0·489	0·470
1·90	1·009	0·968	0·583	0·504	0·484
1·95	1·038	0·997	0·601	0·519	0·498
2·00	1·068	1·026	0·618	0·534	0·513
2·05	1·099	1·055	0·635	0·549	0·527
2·10	1·129	1·084	0·653	0·565	0·542
2·15	1·160	1·114	0·671	0·580	0·557
2·20	1·191	1·143	0·689	0·596	0·572
2·25	1·222	1·173	0·707	0·611	0·587
2·30	1·254	1·204	0·725	0·627	0·602
2·35	1·285	1·234	0·743	0·643	0·617
2·40	1·317	1·265	0·762	0·659	0·632
2·45	1·350	1·296	0·781	0·675	0·648
2·50	1·382	1·327	0·799	0·691	0·663

M_u/bd^2, N/mm^2	f_y, N/mm^2				
	240	250	415	480	500
2·55	1·415	1·358	0·818	0·708	0·679
2·60	1·448	1·390	0·837	0·724	0·695
2·65	1·482	1·422	0·857	0·741	0·711
2·70	1·515	1·455	0·876	0·758	0·727
2·75	1·549	1·487	0·896	0·775	0·744
2·80	1·584	1·520	0·916	0·792	0·760
2·85	1·618	1·554	0·936	0·809	0·777
2·90	1·653	1·587	0·956	0·827	0·794
2·95	1·689	1·621	0·977	0·844	0·811
3·00	1·724	1·655	0·997	0·862	0·828
3·05	1·760	1·690	1·018	0·880	0·845
3·10	1·797	1·725	1·039	0·898	0·863
3·15	1·834	1·760	1·061	0·917	0·880
3·20	1·871	1·796	1·082	0·936	0·898
3·25	1·909	1·832	1·104	0·954	0·916
3·30	1·947	1·869	1·12[illegible]	0·973	0·935
3·32	1·962	1·884	1·13[illegible]	0·981	0·942
3·34	1·978	1·899	1·144	[illegible]	
3·36	1·993	1·914	1·1[illegible]		
3·38	2·009	1·929	1·162		
3·40	2·025	1·944	1·171		
3·42	2·040	1·959	1·180		
3·44	2·056	1·974	1·189		
3·46	2·072	1·989			
3·48	2·088	2·005			
3·50	2·104	2·020			
3·52	2·120	2·036			
3·54	2·137	2·051			
3·56	2·153	2·067			
3·58	2·170	2·083			
3·60	2·186	2·099			
3·62	2·203	2·115			
3·64	2·219	2·131			
3·66	2·236	2·147			
3·68	2·253	2·163			
3·70	2·270	2·179			
3·72	2·287	2·196			
3·74	2·304				

Note—Blanks indicate inadmissible reinforcement percentage of steel exceeds the limiting percentage given in Table 9·4.

Table 9B·12. Flexure—Reinforcement Percentage, P_t For Singly Reinforced Sections (Concrete Mix M30 f_{ck} = 30 N/mm²)

M_u/bd^2, N/mm²	f_y, N/mm² 240	250	415	480	500
0·30	0·145	0·140	0·084	0·073	0·070
0·35	0·170	0·163	0·098	0·085	0·082
0·40	0·195	0·187	0·113	0·097	0·093
0·45	0·219	0·211	0·127	0·110	0·105
0·50	0·244	0·235	0·141	0·122	0·117
0·55	0·269	0·259	0·156	0·135	0·129
0·60	0·294	0·283	0·170	0·147	0·141
0·65	0·320	0·307	0·185	0·160	0·153
0·70	0·345	0·331	0·200	0·172	0·166
0·75	0·370	0·356	0·214	0·185	0·178
0·80	0·396	0·380	0·229	0·198	0·190
0·85	0·422	0·405	0·244	0·211	0·202
0·90	0·447	0·429	0·259	0·224	0·215
0·95	0·473	0·454	0·274	0·237	0·227
1·00	0·499	0·479	0·289	0·250	0·240
1·05	0·525	0·504	0·304	0·263	0·252
1·10	0·552	0·529	0·319	0·276	0·265
1·15	0·578	0·555	0·334	0·289	0·277
1·20	0·604	0·580	0·350	0·302	0·290
1·25	0·631	0·606	0·365	0·315	0·303
1·30	0·658	0·631	0·380	0·329	0·316
1·35	0·685	0·657	0·396	0·342	0·329
1·40	0·712	0·683	0·411	0·356	0·342
1·45	0·739	0·709	0·427	0·369	0·355
1·50	0·766	0·735	0·443	0·383	0·368
1·55	0·793	0·762	0·459	0·397	0·381
1·60	0·821	0·788	0·475	0·410	0·394
1·65	0·849	0·815	0·491	0·424	0·407
1·70	0·876	0·841	0·507	0·438	0·421
1·75	0·904	0·868	0·523	0·452	0·434
1·80	0·932	0·895	0·539	0·466	0·448
1·85	0·961	0·922	0·556	0·480	0·461
1·90	0·989	0·950	0·572	0·495	0·475
1·95	1·018	0·977	0·589	0·509	0·488
2·00	1·046	1·005	0·605	0·523	0·502
2·05	1·075	1·032	0·622	0·538	0·516
2·10	1·104	1·060	0·639	0·552	0·530
2·15	1·134	1·088	0·656	0·567	0·544
2·20	1·163	1·116	0·673	0·581	0·558
2·25	1·192	1·145	0·690	0·596	0·572
2·30	1·222	1·173	0·707	0·611	0·587
2·35	1·252	1·202	0·724	0·626	0·601
2·40	1·282	1·231	0·742	0·641	0·615
2·45	1·312	1·260	0·759	0·656	0·630
2·50	1·343	1·289	0·777	0·671	0·645
2·55	1·374	1·319	0·794	0·687	0·659
2·60	1·404	1·348	0·812	0·702	0·674
2·65	1·435	1·378	0·830	0·718	0·689
2·70	1·467	1·408	0·848	0·733	0·704
2·75	1·498	1·438	0·866	0·749	0·719
2·80	1·530	1·469	0·885	0·765	0·734
2·85	1·562	1·499	0·903	0·781	0·750
2·90	1·594	1·530	0·922	0·797	0·765
2·95	1·626	1·561	0·940	0·813	0·781
3·00	1·659	1·592	0·959	0·829	0·796
3·05	1·691	1·624	0·978	0·846	0·812
3·10	1·725	1·656	0·997	0·862	0·828
3·15	1·758	1·687	1·017	0·879	0·844
3·20	1·791	1·720	1·036	0·896	0·860
3·25	1·825	1·752	1·055	0·913	0·876
3·30	1·859	1·785	1·075	0·930	0·892
3·35	1·893	1·818	1·095	0·947	0·909
3·40	1·928	1·851	1·115	0·964	0·925
3·45	1·963	1·884	1·135	0·981	0·942
3·50	1·998	1·918	1·156	0·999	0·959
3·55	2·034	1·952	1·176	1·017	0·976
3·60	2·069	1·986	1·197	1·035	0·993
3·65	2·105	2·021	1·218	1·053	1·011
3·70	2·142	2·056	1·239	1·071	1·028
3·75	2·178	2·091	1·260	1·089	1·046
3·80	2·215	2·127	1·281	1·108	1·063
3·85	2·253	2·163	1·303	1·126	1·081
3·90	2·291	2·199	1·325	1·145	1·099
3·95	2·329	2·236	1·347	1·164	1·118
4·00	2·367	2·273	1·369	1·184	
4·05	2·406	2·310	1·391		
4·10	2·445	2·348	1·414		
4·15	2·485	2·386			
4·20	2·525	2·424			
4·25	2·566	2·463			
4·30	2·607	2·502			
4·35	2·648	2·542			
4·40	2·690	2·583			
4·45	2·733	2·623			

Note—Blanks indicate inadmissible reinforcement percentage of steel exceeds the limiting percentage given in Table 9·4.

Table 9B·13. Flexure—Reinforcement Percentanges for Doubly Reinforced Sections (Concrete mix M15)

$f_{ck} = 15\ N/mm^2$
$f_y = 250\ N/mm^2$

Mu/bd^2, N/mm^2	$d'/d = 0.05$		$d'/d = 0.10$		$d'/d = 0.15$		$d'/d = 0.20$	
	P_t	P_c	P_t	P_c	P_t	P_c	P_t	P_c
2·24	1·322	0·002	1·322	0·003	1·323	0·003	1·323	0·003
2·25	1·327	0·007	1·328	0·008	1·328	0·008	1·328	0·009
2·30	1·351	0·032	1·353	0·034	1·355	0·036	1·357	0·039
2·35	1·376	0·057	1·379	0·061	1·382	0·064	1·386	0·068
2·40	1·400	0·082	1·404	0·087	1·409	0·092	1·415	0·098
2·45	1·424	0·107	1·430	0·113	1·436	0·120	1·443	0·128
2·50	1·448	0·132	1·455	0·140	1·463	0·148	1·472	0·157
2·55	1·472	0·157	1·481	0·166	1·490	0·176	1·501	0·187
2·60	1·497	0·182	1·506	0·192	1·517	0·204	1·530	0·217
2·65	1·521	0·207	1·532	0·219	1·544	0·232	1·558	0·246
2·70	1·545	0·232	1·558	0·245	1·751	0·260	1·587	0·276
2·75	1·569	0·257	1·583	0·272	1·599	0·288	1·616	0·305
2·80	1·593	0·282	1·609	0·298	1·626	0·315	1·645	0·335
2·85	1·612	0·307	1·634	0·324	1·653	0·343	1·673	0·365
2·90	1·642	0·332	1·660	0·351	1·680	0·371	1·702	0·394
2·95	1·666	0·357	1·685	0·377	1·707	0·399	1·731	0·424
3·00	1·690	0·382	1·711	0·430	1·734	0·427	1·760	0·454
3·05	1·714	0·407	1·736	0·430	1·761	0·455	1·788	0·483
3·10	1·739	0·432	1·762	0·456	1·788	0·483	1·817	0·513
3·15	1·763	0·457	1·788	0·482	1·815	0·511	1·846	0·543
3·20	1·787	0·482	1·813	0·509	1·842	0·539	1·875	0·572
3·25	1·811	0·507	1·839	0·535	1·869	0·567	1·903	0·602
3·30	1·836	0·532	1·864	0·562	1·896	0·595	1·932	0·632
3·35	1·860	0·557	1·890	0·588	1·923	0·623	1·961	0·661
3·40	1·884	0·582	1·915	0·614	1·950	0·650	1·990	0·691
3·45	1·908	0·607	1·941	0·641	1·977	0·678	2·018	0·721
3·50	1·932	0·632	1·966	0·667	2·004	0·706	2·047	0·750
3·55	1·957	0·657	1·992	0·693	2·031	0·734	2·076	0·780
3·60	1·981	0·682	2·018	0·720	2·059	0·762	2·175	0·810
3·65	2·005	0·707	2·043	0·746	2·086	0·790	2·133	0·839
3·70	2·029	0·732	2·069	0·773	2·113	0·818	2·162	0·869
3·75	2·053	0·757	2·094	0·799	2·140	0·846	2·191	0·899
3·80	2·078	0·782	2·120	0·825	2·167	0·874	2·220	0·928
3·85	2·102	0·807	2·145	0·852	2·194	0·902	2·248	0·958
3·90	2·126	0·832	2·171	0·878	2·221	0·930	2·277	0·988
3·95	2·150	0·857	2·196	0·904	2·248	0·958	2·306	1·017
4·00	2·174	0·882	2·222	0·931	2·275	0·985	2·335	1·047
4·05	2·199	0·907	2·248	0·957	2·302	1·013	2·363	1·077
4·10	2·223	0·932	2·273	0·983	2·329	1·041	2·392	1·106
4·15	2·247	0·957	2·299	1·010	2·356	1·069	2·421	1·136
4·20	2·271	0·982	2·324	1·036	2·383	1·097	2·450	1·166
4·25	2·296	1·007	2·350	1·063	2·410	1·125	2·478	1·195
4·30	2·320	1·032	2·375	1·089	2·437	1·153	2·507	1·225
4·35	2·344	1·057	2·401	1·115	2·464	1·181	2·536	1·255
4·40	2·368	1·082	2·426	1·142	2·491	1·209	2·565	1·284

Table 9B·14. Flexure—Reinforcement Percentages for Doubly Reinforced Sections (Concrete mix M20)

$f_{ck} = 20\ \text{N/mm}^2$
$f_y = 250\ \text{N/mm}^2$

M_u/bd^2, N/mm²	$d'/d = 0{\cdot}05$		$d'/d = 0{\cdot}10$		$d'/d = 0{\cdot}15$		$d'/d = 0{\cdot}20$	
	P_t	P_c	P_t	P_c	P_t	P_c	P_t	P_c
2·99	1·765	0·005	1·765	0·005	1·765	0·006	1·766	0·006
3·00	1·769	0·010	1·770	0·011	1·771	0·011	1·771	0·012
3·05	1·794	0·035	1·796	0·037	1·798	0·039	1·800	0·042
3·10	1·818	0·061	1·821	0·064	1·825	0·068	1·829	0·072
3·15	1·842	0·086	1·847	0·091	1·852	0·096	1·858	0·102
3·20	1·866	0·111	1·872	0·117	1·879	0·124	1·886	0·132
3·25	1·891	0·136	1·898	0·144	1·906	0·152	1·915	0·162
3·30	1·915	0·162	1·923	0·171	1·933	0·181	1·944	0·192
3·35	1·939	0·187	1·949	0·197	1·960	0·209	1·973	0·222
3·40	1·963	0·212	1·974	0·224	1·987	0·237	2·001	0·252
3·45	1·987	0·237	2·000	0·250	2·014	0·265	2·030	0·282
3·50	2·012	0·263	2·026	0·277	2·041	0·293	2·059	0·312
3·55	2·036	0·288	2·051	0·304	2·068	0·322	2·088	0·342
3·60	2·060	0·313	2·077	0·330	2·095	0·350	2·116	0·372
3·65	2·084	0·338	2·102	0·357	2·122	0·378	2·145	0·402
3·70	2·108	0·364	2·128	0·384	2·149	0·406	2·174	0·432
3·75	2·133	0·389	2·153	0·410	2·177	0·434	2·203	0·462
3·80	2·157	0·414	2·179	0·437	2·204	0·463	2·231	0·492
3·85	2·181	0·439	2·204	0·464	2·231	0·491	2·260	0·522
3·90	2·205	0·464	2·230	0·490	2·258	0·519	2·289	0·552
3·95	2·229	0·490	2·256	0·517	2·285	0·547	2·318	0·582
4·00	2·254	0·515	2·281	0·544	2·312	0·576	2·346	0·612
4·05	2·278	0·540	2·307	0·570	2·339	0·604	2·375	0·642
4·10	2·302	0·565	2·332	0·597	2·366	0·632	2·404	0·672
4·15	2·326	0·591	2·358	0·624	2·393	0·660	2·433	0·701
4·20	2·351	0·616	2·383	0·650	2·420	0·688	2·461	0·731
4·25	2·375	0·641	2·409	0·677	2·447	0·717	2·490	0·761
4·30	2·399	0·666	2·434	0·703	2·474	0·745	2·519	0·791
4·35	2·423	0·692	2·460	0·730	2·501	0·773	2·548	0·821
4·40	2·447	0·717	2·486	0·757	2·528	0·801	2·576	0·851
4·45	2·472	0·742	2·511	0·783	2·555	0·830	2·605	0·881
4·50	2·496	0·767	2·537	0·810	2·582	0·858	2·634	0·911
4·55	2·520	0·793	2·562	0·837	2·609	0·886	2·663	0·941
4·60	2·544	0·818	2·588	0·863	2·637	0·914	2·691	0·971
4·65	2·568	0·843	2·613	0·890	2·664	0·942	2·720	1·001
4·70	2·593	0·868	2·639	0·917	2·691	0·971	2·749	1·031
4·75	2·617	0·894	2·664	0·943	2·718	0·999	2·778	1·061
4·80	2·641	0·919	2·690	0·970	2·745	1·027	2·806	1·091
4·85	2·665	0·944	2·716	0·997	2·772	1·055	2·835	1·121
4·90	2·689	0·969	2·741	1·023	2·779	1·083	2·864	1·151
4·95	2·714	0·995	2·767	1·050	2·826	1·112	2·893	1·181
5·00	2·738	1·020	2·792	1·077	2·853	1·140	2·921	1·211
5·05	2·762	1·045	2·818	1·103	2·880	1·168	2·950	1·241
5·10	2·786	1·070	2·843	1·130	2·907	1·196	2·979	1·271
5·15	2·811	1·096	2·869	1·157	2·934	1·225	3·008	1·301

Table 9B·15. Flexure—Reinforcement Percentages for Doubly Reinforced Sections (Concrete mix M25)

$f_{ck} = 25\ N/mm^2$
$f_y = 250\ N/mm^2$

M_u/bd^3, N/mm^2	$d'/d = 0{\cdot}05$		$d'/d = 0{\cdot}10$		$d'/d = 0{\cdot}15$		$d'/d = 0{\cdot}20$	
	P_t	P_c	P_t	P_c	P_t	P_c	P_t	P_c
3·73	2·202	0·002	2·202	0·003	2·202	0·003	2·203	0·003
3·75	2·212	0·013	2·213	0·013	2·213	0·014	2·214	0·015
3·80	2·236	0·038	2·238	0·040	2·240	0·043	2·243	0·045
3·85	2·260	0·064	2·264	0·067	2·267	0·071	2·272	0·076
3·90	2·284	0·089	2·289	0·094	2·294	0·100	2·300	0·106
3·95	2·309	0·115	2·315	0·121	2·322	0·128	2·329	0·136
4·00	2·333	0·140	2·340	0·148	2·349	0·157	2·358	0·167
4·05	2·357	0·166	2·366	0·175	2·376	0·185	2·387	0·197
4·10	2·381	0·191	2·391	0·202	2·403	0·214	2·415	0·227
4·15	2·406	0·217	2·417	0·229	2·430	0·242	2·444	0·258
4·20	2·430	0·242	2·443	0·256	2·457	0·271	2·473	0·288
4·25	2·454	0·268	2·468	0·283	2·484	0·299	2·502	0·318
4·30	2·478	0·293	2·494	0·310	2·511	0·328	2·530	0·348
4·35	2·502	0·319	2·519	0·337	2·538	0·356	2·559	0·379
4·40	2·527	0·344	2·545	0·364	2·565	0·385	2·588	0·409
4·45	2·551	0·370	2·570	0·391	2·592	0·414	2·617	0·439
4·50	2·575	0·395	2·596	0·417	2·619	0·442	2·645	0·470
4·55	2·599	0·421	2·621	0·444	2·646	0·471	2·674	0·500
4·60	2·623	0·447	2·647	0·471	2·673	0·499	2·703	0·530
4·65	2·648	0·472	2·673	0·498	2·700	0·528	2·732	0·561
4·70	2·672	0·498	2·698	0·525	2·727	0·556	2·760	0·591
4·75	2·696	0·523	2·724	0·552	2·754	0·585	2·789	0·621
4·80	2·720	0·549	2·749	0·579	2·782	0·613	2·818	0·651
4·85	2·744	0·574	2·775	0·606	2·809	0·642	2·847	0·682
4·90	2·769	0·600	2·800	0·633	2·836	0·670	2·875	0·712
4·95	2·793	0·625	2·826	0·660	2·863	0·699	2·904	0·742
5·00	2·817	0·651	2·851	0·687	2·890	0·727	2·933	0·773
5·05	2·841	0·676	2·877	0·714	2·917	0·756	2·962	0·803
5·10	2·866	0·702	2·903	0·741	2·944	0·784	2·990	0·833
5·15	2·890	0·727	2·928	0·768	2·971	0·813	3·019	0·864
5·20	2·914	0·753	2·954	0·795	2·998	0·841	3·048	0·894
5·25	2·938	0·778	2·979	0·822	3·025	0·870	3·077	0·924
5·30	2·962	0·804	3·005	0·848	3·052	0·898	3·105	0·955
5·35	2·987	0·829	3·030	0·875	3·079	0·927	3·134	0·985
5·40	3·011	0·855	3·056	0·902	3·106	0·955	3·163	1·015
5·45	3·035	0·880	3·081	0·929	3·133	0·984	3·192	1·045
5·50	3·059	0·906	3·107	0·956	3·160	1·012	3·220	1·076
5·55	3·083	0·931	3·133	0·983	3·187	1·041	3·249	1·106
5·60	3·108	0·957	3·158	1·010	3·214	1·070	3·278	1·136
5·65	3·132	0·982	3·184	1·037	3·242	1·098	3·307	1·167
5·70	3·156	1·008	3·209	1·064	3·269	1·127	3·335	1·197
5·75	3·180	1·033	3·235	1·091	3·296	1·155	3·364	1·227
5·80	3·204	1·059	3·260	1·118	3·323	1·184	3·393	1·258
5·85	3·229	1·085	3·286	1·145	3·350	1·212	3·422	1·288
5·90	3·253	1·110	3·311	1·172	3·377	1·241	3·450	1·318

Table 9B·16. Flexure—Reinforcement Percentages for Doubly Reinforced Sections (Concrete mix M30)

$f_{ck} = 30\ \text{N/mm}^2$
$f_y = 250\ \text{N/mm}^2$

M_u/cd^2, N/mm^2	$d'/d = 0{\cdot}05$		$d'/d = 0{\cdot}10$		$d'/d = 0{\cdot}15$		$d'/d = 0{\cdot}20$	
	P_t	P_c	P_t	P_c	P_t	P_c	P_t	P_c
4·48	2·645	0·005	2·645	0·005	2·645	0·006	2·645	0·006
4·50	2·654	0·015	2·655	0·016	2·656	0·017	2·657	0·018
4·55	2·678	0·041	2·681	0·043	2·683	0·046	2·686	0·049
4·60	2·703	0·067	2·706	0·071	2·710	0·075	2·714	0·080
4·65	2·727	0·093	2·732	0·098	2·737	0·104	2·743	0·110
4·70	2·751	0·119	2·757	0·125	2·764	0·133	2·772	0·141
4·75	2·775	0·144	2·783	0·152	2·791	0·161	2·801	0·171
4·80	2·799	0·170	2·808	0·180	2·818	0·190	2·829	0·202
4·85	2·824	0·196	2·834	0·207	2·845	0·216	2·858	0·233
4·90	2·848	0·222	2·859	0·234	2·872	0·248	2·887	0·263
4·95	2·872	0·248	2·885	0·261	2·899	0·277	2·916	0·294
5·00	2·896	0·273	2·911	0·289	2·927	0·306	2·944	0·325
5·05	2·921	0·299	2·936	0·316	2·954	0·334	2·973	0·355
5·10	2·945	0·325	2·962	0·343	2·981	0·363	3·002	0·386
5·15	2·969	0·351	2·987	0·370	3·008	0·392	3·031	0·417
5·20	2·993	0·377	3·013	0·398	3·035	0·421	3·059	0·447
5·25	3·017	0·402	3·038	0·425	3·062	0·450	3·088	0·478
5·30	3·042	0·428	3·064	0·452	3·089	0·479	3·117	0·508
5·35	3·066	0·454	3·089	0·479	3·116	0·507	3·146	0·539
5·40	3·090	0·480	3·115	0·506	3·143	0·536	3·174	0·570
5·45	3·114	0·506	3·141	0·534	3·170	0·565	3·203	0·600
5·50	3·138	0·531	3·166	0·561	3·197	0·594	3·232	0·631
5·55	3·163	0·557	3·192	0·588	3·224	0·623	3·261	0·662
5·60	3·187	0·583	3·217	0·615	3·251	0·652	3·289	0·692
5·65	3·211	0·609	3·243	0·643	3·278	0·680	3·318	0·723
5·70	3·235	0·635	3·268	0·670	3·305	0·709	3·347	0·754
5·75	3·259	0·660	3·294	0·697	3·332	0·738	3·376	0·784
5·80	3·284	0·686	3·319	0·724	3·359	0·767	3·404	0·815
5·85	3·308	0·712	3·345	0·752	3·387	0·796	3·433	0·845
5·90	3·332	0·738	3·371	0·779	3·414	0·825	3·462	0·876
5·95	3·356	0·764	3·396	0·806	3·441	0·853	3·491	0·907
6·00	3·381	0·789	3·422	0·833	3·468	0·882	3·519	0·937
6·05	3·405	0·815	3·447	0·860	3·495	0·911	3·548	0·968
6·10	3·429	0·841	3·473	0·888	3·522	0·940	3·577	0·999
6·15	3·453	0·867	3·498	0·915	3·549	0·969	3·606	1·029
6·20	3·477	0·893	3·524	0·942	3·576	0·998	3·634	1·060
6·25	3·502	0·918	3·549	0·969	3·603	1·026	3·663	1·091
6·30	3·526	0·944	3·575	0·997	3·630	1·055	3·692	1·121
6·35	3·550	0·970	3·601	1·024	3·657	1·084	3·721	1·152
6·40	3·574	0·996	3·626	1·051	3·684	1·113	3·749	1·182
6·45	3·598	1·022	3·652	1·078	3·711	1·142	3·778	1·213
6·50	3·623	1·047	3·677	1·106	3·738	1·171	3·807	1·244
6·55	3·647	1·073	3·703	1·133	3·765	1·199	3·836	1·274
6·60	3·671	1·099	3·728	1·160	3·792	1·228	3·864	1·305
6·65	3·695	1·125	3·754	1·187	3·819	1·257	3·893	1·336

Table 9B·17. Flexure—Reinforcement Percentages for Doubly Reinforced Sections (Concrete mix M15)

$f_{ck} = 15\ \text{N/mm}^2$
$f_y = 415\ \text{N/mm}^2$

M_u/bd^2, N/mm^2	$d'/d = 0{\cdot}05$		$d'/d = 0{\cdot}10$		$d'/d = 0{\cdot}15$		$d'/d = 0{\cdot}20$	
	P_t	P_c	P_t	P_c	P_t	P_c	P_t	P_c
2·08	0·719	0·003	0·720	0·003	0·720	0·003	0·720	0·003
2·10	0·725	0·009	0·726	0·009	0·726	0·010	0·727	0·011
2·20	0·754	0·039	0·757	0·041	0·759	0·045	0·761	0·050
2·30	0·784	0·069	0·787	0·073	0·791	0·080	0·796	0·089
2·40	0·813	0·099	0·818	0·106	0·824	0·115	0·831	0·127
2·50	0·842	0·129	0·849	0·138	0·857	0·150	0·865	0·166
2·60	0·871	0·160	0·880	0·170	0·889	0·185	0·900	0·205
2·70	0·900	0·190	0·910	0·202	0·922	0·220	0·935	0·244
2·80	0·929	0·220	0·941	0·234	0·954	0·255	0·969	0·282
2·90	0·959	0·250	0·972	0·267	0·987	0·290	1·004	0·321
3·00	0·988	0·280	1·003	0·299	1·020	0·325	1·039	0·360
3·10	1·017	0·311	1·034	0·331	1·052	0·360	1·073	0·399
3·20	1·046	0·341	1·064	0·363	1·085	0·395	1·108	0·438
3·30	1·075	0·371	1·095	0·395	1·117	0·430	1·142	0·476
3·40	1·104	0·401	1·126	0·427	1·150	0·465	1·177	0·515
3·50	1·134	0·432	1·157	0·460	1·183	0·500	1·212	0·554
3·60	1·163	0·462	1·188	0·492	1·215	0·535	1·246	0·593
3·70	1·192	0·492	1·218	0·524	1·248	0·571	1·281	0·631
3·80	1·221	0·522	1·249	0·556	1·280	0·606	1·316	0·670
3·90	1·250	0·552	1·280	0·588	1·313	0·641	1·350	0·709
4·00	1·279	0·583	1·311	0·621	1·346	0·676	1·385	0·748
4·10	1·309	0·613	1·342	0·653	1·378	0·711	1·420	0·787
4·20	1·338	0·643	1·372	0·685	1·411	0·746	1·454	0·825
4·30	1·367	0·673	1·403	0·717	1·443	0·781	1·489	0·864
4·40	1·396	0·703	1·434	0·749	1·476	0·816	1·524	0·903
4·50	1·425	0·734	1·465	0·781	1·509	0·851	1·558	0·942
4·60	1·455	0·764	1·495	0·814	1·541	0·886	1·593	0·980
4·70	1·484	0·794	1·526	0·846	1·574	0·921	1·627	1·019
4·80	1·513	0·824	1·557	0·878	1·606	0·956	1·662	1·058
4·90	1·542	0·855	1·588	0·910	1·639	0·991	1·697	1·097
5·00	1·571	0·885	1·619	0·942	1·672	1·026	1·731	1·136
5·10	1·600	0·915	1·649	0·975	1·704	1·061	1·766	1·174
5·20	1·630	0·945	1·680	1·007	1·737	1·096	1·801	1·213
5·30	1·659	0·975	1·711	1·039	1·769	1·131	1·835	1·252
5·40	1·688	1·006	1·742	1·071	1·802	1·166	1·870	1·291
5·50	1·717	1·036	1·773	1·103	1·835	1·201	1·905	1·329
5·60	1·746	1·066	1·803	1·136	1·867	1·236	1·939	1·368
5·70	1·775	1·096	1·834	1·168	1·900	1·271	1·974	1·407
5·80	1·805	1·126	1·865	1·200	1·932	1·306	2·008	1·446
5·90	1·834	1·157	1·896	1·232	1·965	1·341	2·043	1·485
6·00	1·863	1·187	1·927	1·264	1·998	1·376	2·078	1·523
6·10	1·892	1·217	1·957	1·296	2·030	1·411	2·112	1·562
6·20	1·921	1·247	1·988	1·329	2·063	1·446	2·147	1·601
6·30	1·950	1·278	2·019	1·361	2·095	1·481	2·182	1·640
6·40	1·980	1·308	2·050	1·393	2·128	1·517	2·216	1·678

Table 9B·18. Flexure—Reinforcement Percentages for Doubly Reinforced Sections (Concrete mix M20)

$f_{ck} = 20\ \text{N/mm}^2$
$f_y = 415\ \text{N/mm}^2$

M_u/bd^2, N/mm²	$d'/d = 0.05$ P_t	P_c	$d'/d = 0.10$ P_t	P_c	$d'/d = 0.15$ P_t	P_c	$d'/d = 0.20$ P_t	P_c
2·77	0·958	0·002	0·958	0·002	0·959	0·003	0·959	0·003
2·80	0·967	0·011	0·968	0·012	0·968	0·013	0·969	0·015
2·90	0·996	0·042	0·998	0·045	1·001	0·049	1·004	0·054
3·00	1·025	0·072	1·029	0·077	1·034	0·084	1·038	0·093
3·10	1·055	0·103	1·060	0·109	1·066	0·119	1·073	0·132
3·20	1·084	0·133	1·091	0·142	1·099	0·154	1·108	0·171
3·30	1·113	0·164	1·122	0·174	1·131	0·190	1·142	0·210
3·40	1·142	0·194	1·152	0·207	1·164	0·225	1·177	0·249
3·50	1·171	0·224	1·183	0·239	1·197	0·260	1·212	0·288
3·60	1·200	0·255	1·214	0·271	1·229	0·295	1·246	0·327
3·70	1·230	0·285	1·245	0·304	1·262	0·331	1·281	0·366
3·80	1·259	0·316	1·276	0·336	1·294	0·366	1·315	0·405
3·90	1·288	0·346	1·306	0·369	1·327	0·401	1·350	0·444
4·00	1·317	0·376	1·337	0·401	1·360	0·437	1·385	0·483
4·10	1·346	0·407	1·368	0·433	1·392	0·472	1·419	0·522
4·20	1·375	0·437	1·399	0·466	1·425	0·507	1·454	0·561
4·30	1·405	0·468	1·429	0·498	1·457	0·542	1·489	0·600
4·40	1·434	0·498	1·460	0·530	1·490	0·578	1·523	0·640
4·50	1·463	0·528	1·491	0·563	1·523	0·613	1·558	0·679
4·60	1·492	0·559	1·522	0·595	1·555	0·648	1·593	0·718
4·70	1·521	0·589	1·553	0·628	1·588	0·683	1·627	0·757
4·80	1·550	0·620	1·583	0·660	1·620	0·719	1·662	0·796
4·90	1·580	0·650	1·614	0·692	1·653	0·754	1·696	0·835
5·00	1·609	0·680	1·645	0·725	1·686	0·789	1·731	0·874
5·10	1·638	0·711	1·676	0·757	1·718	0·825	1·766	0·913
5·20	1·667	0·741	1·707	0·790	1·751	0·860	1·800	0·952
5·30	1·696	0·772	1·737	0·822	1·783	0·895	1·835	0·991
5·40	1·725	0·802	1·768	0·854	1·816	0·930	1·870	1·030
5·50	1·755	0·832	1·799	0·887	1·849	0·966	1·904	1·069
5·60	1·784	0·863	1·830	0·919	1·881	1·001	1·939	1·108
5·70	1·813	0·893	1·861	0·952	1·914	1·036	1·974	1·147
5·80	1·842	0·924	1·891	0·984	1·946	1·071	2·008	1·186
5·90	1·871	0·954	1·922	1·016	1·979	1·107	2·043	1·225
6·00	1·900	0·985	1·953	1·049	2·012	1·142	2·078	1·264
6·10	1·930	1·015	1·984	1·081	2·044	1·177	2·112	1·303
6·20	1·959	1·045	2·014	1·114	2·077	1·213	2·147	1·342
6·30	1·988	1·076	2·045	1·146	2·109	1·248	2·181	1·381
6·40	2·017	1·106	2·076	1·178	2·142	1·283	2·216	1·421
6·50	2·046	1·137	2·107	1·211	2·175	1·318	2·251	1·460
6·60	2·075	1·167	2·138	1·243	2·207	1·354	2·285	1·499
6·70	2·105	1·197	2·168	1·276	2·240	1·389	2·320	1·538
6·80	2·134	1·228	2·199	1·308	2·272	1·424	2·355	1·577
6·90	2·163	1·258	2·230	1·340	2·305	1·459	2·389	1·616
7·00	2·192	1·289	2·261	1·373	2·338	1·495	2·424	1·655
7·10	2·221	1·319	2·292	1·405	2·370	1·530	2·459	1·694

Table 9B·19. Flexure—Reinforcement percentages for Doubly Reinforced Sections (Concrete mix M25)

$f_{ck} = 25\ N/mm^2$
$f_y = 415\ N/mm^2$

M_u/bd^2, N/mm^2	$d'/d = 0.05$ P_t	P_c	$d'/d = 0.10$ P_t	P_c	$d'/d = 0.15$ P_t	P_c	$d'/d = 0.20$ P_t	P_c
3·46	1·197	0·002	1·197	0·002	1·197	0·003	1·197	0·003
3·50	1·209	0·014	1·210	0·015	1·210	0·017	1·211	0·019
3·60	1·238	0·045	1·240	0·048	1·243	0·052	1·246	0·058
3·70	1·267	0·076	1·271	0·081	1·276	0·088	1·281	0·097
3·80	1·296	0·106	1·302	0·113	1·308	0·123	1·315	0·137
3·90	1·325	0·137	1·333	0·146	1·341	0·159	1·350	0·176
4·00	1·355	0·167	1·363	0·178	1·373	0·194	1·385	0·215
4·10	1·384	0·198	1·394	0·211	1·406	0·230	1·419	0·254
4·20	1·413	0·229	1·425	0·244	1·439	0·265	1·454	0·294
4·30	1·442	0·259	1·456	0·276	1·471	0·301	1·488	0·333
4·40	1·471	0·290	1·487	0·309	1·504	0·336	1·523	0·372
4·50	1·500	0·320	1·517	0·341	1·536	0·372	1·558	0·412
4·60	1·530	0·351	1·548	0·374	1·569	0·407	1·592	0·451
4·70	1·559	0·382	1·579	0·407	1·602	0·443	1·627	0·490
4·80	1·588	0·412	1·610	0·439	1·634	0·478	1·662	0·530
4·90	1·617	0·443	1·641	0·472	1·667	0·514	1·696	0·569
5·00	1·646	0·474	1·671	0·504	1·699	0·549	1·731	0·608
5·10	1·675	0·504	1·702	0·537	1·732	0·585	1·766	0·648
5·20	1·705	0·535	1·733	0·570	1·765	0·620	1·800	0·687
5·30	1·734	0·565	1·764	0·602	1·797	0·656	1·835	0·726
5·40	1·763	0·596	1·795	0·635	1·830	0·691	1·869	0·766
5·50	1·792	0·627	1·825	0·667	1·862	0·727	1·904	0·805
5·60	1·821	0·657	1·856	0·700	1·895	0·762	1·939	0·844
5·70	1·851	0·688	1·887	0·733	1·928	0·798	1·973	0·884
5·80	1·880	0·718	1·918	0·765	1·960	0·833	2·008	0·923
5·90	1·909	0·749	1·948	0·798	1·993	0·869	2·043	0·962
6·00	1·938	0·780	1·979	0·830	2·025	0·904	2·077	1·002
6·10	1·967	0·810	2·010	0·863	2·058	0·940	2·112	1·041
6·20	1·996	0·841	2·041	0·896	2·091	0·975	2·147	1·080
6·30	2·026	0·871	2·072	0·928	2·123	1·011	2·181	1·120
6·40	2·055	0·902	2·102	0·961	2·156	1·046	2·216	1·159
6·50	2·084	0·933	2·133	0·993	2·188	1·082	2·251	1·198
6·60	2·113	0·963	2·164	1·026	2·221	1·118	2·285	1·238
6·70	2·142	0·994	2·195	1·059	2·254	1·153	2·320	1·277
6·80	2·171	1·024	2·226	1·091	2·286	1·189	2·354	1·316
6·90	2·201	1·055	2·256	1·124	2·319	1·224	2·389	1·356
7·00	2·230	1·086	2·287	1·157	2·351	1·260	2·424	1·395
7·10	2·259	1·116	2·318	1·189	2·384	1·295	2·458	1·434
7·20	2·288	1·147	2·349	1·222	2·417	1·331	2·493	1·474
7·30	2·317	1·177	2·380	1·254	2·449	1·366	2·528	1·513
7·40	2·346	1·208	2·410	1·287	2·482	1·402	2·562	1·552
7·50	2·376	1·239	2·441	1·320	2·514	1·437	2·597	1·591
7·60	2·405	1·269	2·472	1·352	2·547	1·473	2·632	1·631
7·70	2·434	1·300	2·503	1·385	2·580	1·508	2·666	1·670
7·80	2·463	1·330	2·534	1·417	2·612	1·544	2·701	1·709

Table 9B·20. Flexure—Reinforcement Percentages for Doubly Reinforced Sections (Concrete mix M30)

$f_{ck} = 30$ N/mm^2
$f_y = 415$ N/mm^2

M_u/bd^2, N/mm^2	$d'/d = 0{\cdot}05$		$d'/d = 0{\cdot}10$		$d'/d = 0{\cdot}15$		$d'/d = 0{\cdot}20$	
	P_t	P_c	P_t	P_c	P_t	P_c	P_t	P_c
4·15	1·436	0·002	1·436	0·002	1·436	0·002	1·436	0·003
4·20	1·451	0·017	1·451	0·019	1·452	0·020	1·454	0·022
4·30	1·480	0·048	1·482	0·051	1·485	0·056	1·488	0·062
4·40	1·509	0·079	1·513	0·084	1·518	0·092	1·523	0·102
4·50	1·538	0·110	1·544	0·117	1·550	0·127	1·558	0·141
4·60	1·567	0·141	1·575	0·150	1·583	0·163	1·592	0·181
4·70	1·596	0·171	1·605	0·183	1·615	0·199	1·627	0·220
4·80	1·626	0·202	1·636	0·215	1·648	0·235	1·661	0·260
4·90	1·655	0·233	1·667	0·248	1·681	0·270	1·696	0·300
5·00	1·684	0·264	1·698	0·281	1·713	0·306	1·731	0·339
5·10	1·713	0·295	1·729	0·314	1·746	0·342	1·765	0·379
5·20	1·742	0·325	1·759	0·347	1·778	0·378	1·800	0·418
5·30	1·771	0·356	1·790	0·380	1·811	0·413	1·835	0·458
5·40	1·801	0·387	1·821	0·412	1·844	0·449	1·869	0·498
5·50	1·830	0·418	1·852	0·445	1·876	0·485	1·904	0·537
5·60	1·859	0·449	1·883	0·478	1·909	0·521	1·939	0·577
5·70	1·888	0·479	1·913	0·511	1·941	0·556	1·973	0·616
5·80	1·917	0·510	1·944	0·544	1·974	0·592	2·008	0·656
5·90	1·946	0·541	1·975	0·576	2·007	0·628	2·042	0·696
6·00	1·976	0·572	2·006	0·609	2·039	0·664	2·077	0·735
6·10	2·005	0·603	2·036	0·642	2·072	0·699	2·112	0·775
6·20	2·034	0·634	2·067	0·675	2·104	0·735	2·146	0·814
6·30	2·063	0·664	2·098	0·708	2·137	0·771	2·181	0·854
6·40	2·092	0·695	2·129	0·741	2·170	0·807	2·216	0·894
6·50	2·121	0·726	2·160	0·773	2·202	0·842	2·250	0·933
6·60	2·151	0·757	2·190	0·806	2·235	0·878	2·285	0·973
6·70	2·180	0·788	2·221	0·839	2·267	0·914	2·320	1·012
6·80	2·209	0·818	2·252	0·872	2·300	0·950	2·354	1·052
6·90	2·238	0·849	2·283	0·905	2·333	0·985	2·389	1·092
7·00	2·267	0·880	2·314	0·937	2·365	1·021	2·424	1·131
7·10	2·296	0·911	2·344	0·970	2·398	1·057	2·458	1·171
7·20	2·326	0·942	2·375	1·003	2·431	1·093	2·493	1·210
7·30	2·355	0·972	2·406	1·036	2·463	1·128	2·527	1·250
7·40	2·384	1·003	2·437	1·069	2·496	1·164	2·562	1·290
7·50	2·413	1·034	2·468	1·102	2·528	1·200	2·597	1·329
7·60	2·442	1·065	2·498	1·134	2·561	1·236	2·631	1·369
7·70	2·471	1·096	2·529	1·167	2·594	1·271	2·666	1·408
7·80	2·501	1·126	2·560	1·200	2·626	1·307	2·701	1·448
7·90	2·530	1·157	2·591	1·233	2·659	1·343	2·735	1·488
8·00	2·559	1·188	2·621	1·266	2·691	1·379	2·770	1·527
8·10	2·588	1·219	2·652	1·299	2·724	1·414	2·805	1·567
8·20	2·617	1·250	2·683	1·331	2·757	1·450	2·839	1·606
8·30	2·646	1·280	2·714	1·364	2·789	1·486	2·874	1·646
8·40	2·676	1·311	2·745	1·397	2·822	1·522	2·908	1·686
8·50	2·705	1·342	2·775	1·430	2·854	1·557	2·943	1·725

Table 9B·21. Flexure—Reinforcement Percentages for Doubly Reinforced Sections (Concrete mix M15)

$f_{ck} = 15\ N/mm^2$
$f_y = 500\ N/mm^2$

M_u/bd^2, N/mm^2	$d'/d = 0{\cdot}05$		$d'/d = 0{\cdot}10$		$d'/d = 0{\cdot}15$		$d'/d = 0{\cdot}20$	
	P_t	P_c	P_t	P_c	P_t	P_c	P_t	P_c
2·00	0·568	0·001	0·568	0·001	0·568	0·001	0·568	0·002
2·10	0·592	0·026	0·593	0·029	0·595	0·032	0·596	0·036
2·20	0·616	0·052	0·619	0·056	0·622	0·062	0·625	0·070
2·30	0·640	0·077	0·644	0·084	0·649	0·092	0·654	0·105
2·40	0·664	0·102	0·670	0·111	0·676	0·122	0·683	0·139
2·50	0·689	0·127	0·695	0·138	0·703	0·153	0·711	0·173
2·60	0·713	0·153	0·721	0·166	0·730	0·183	0·740	0·208
2·70	0·737	0·178	0·746	0·193	0·757	0·213	0·769	0·242
2·80	0·761	0·203	0·772	0·221	0·784	0·244	0·798	0·276
2·90	0·785	0·228	0·798	0·248	0·811	0·274	0·826	0·310
3·00	0·810	0·253	0·823	0·276	0·838	0·304	0·855	0·345
3·10	0·834	0·279	0·849	0·303	0·865	0·334	0·884	0·379
3·20	0·858	0·304	0·874	0·330	0·892	0·365	0·913	0·413
3·30	0·882	0·329	0·900	0·358	0·919	0·395	0·941	0·448
3·40	0·906	0·354	0·925	0·385	0·946	0·425	0·970	0·482
3·50	0·931	0·380	0·951	0·413	0·974	0·455	0·999	0·516
3·60	0·955	0·405	0·976	0·440	1·001	0·486	1·028	0·551
3·70	0·979	0·430	1·002	0·468	1·028	0·516	1·056	0·585
3·80	1·003	0·455	1·028	0·495	1·055	0·546	1·085	0·619
3·90	1·028	0·481	1·053	0·523	1·082	0·577	1·114	0·654
4·00	1·052	0·506	1·079	0·550	1·109	0·607	1·143	0·688
4·10	1·076	0·531	1·104	0·577	1·136	0·637	1·171	0·722
4·20	1·100	0·556	1·130	0·605	1·163	0·667	1·200	0·757
4·30	1·124	0·582	1·155	0·632	1·190	0·698	1·229	0·791
4·40	1·149	0·607	1·181	0·660	1·217	0·728	1·258	0·825
4·50	1·173	0·632	1·206	0·687	1·244	0·758	1·286	0·860
4·60	1·197	0·657	1·232	0·715	1·271	0·789	1·315	0·894
4·70	1·221	0·682	1·258	0·742	1·298	0·819	1·344	0·928
4·80	1·245	0·708	1·283	0·769	1·325	0·849	1·373	0·963
4·90	1·270	0·733	1·309	0·797	1·352	0·879	1·401	0·997
5·00	1·294	0·758	1·334	0·824	1·379	0·910	1·430	1·031
5·10	1·318	0·783	1·360	0·852	1·406	0·940	1·459	1·066
5·20	1·342	0·809	1·385	0·879	1·424	0·970	1·488	1·100
5·30	1·366	0·834	1·411	0·907	1·461	1·000	1·516	1·134
5·40	1·391	0·859	1·436	0·934	1·488	1·031	1·545	1·169
5·50	1·415	0·884	1·462	0·962	1·515	1·061	1·574	1·203
5·60	1·439	0·910	1·488	0·989	1·542	1·091	1·603	1·237
5·70	1·463	0·935	1·513	1·016	1·569	1·122	1·631	1·272
5·80	1·488	0·960	1·539	1·044	1·596	1·152	1·660	1·306
5·90	1·512	0·985	1·564	1·071	1·623	1·182	1·689	1·340
6·00	1·536	1·011	1·590	1·099	1·650	1·212	1·718	1·375
6·10	1·560	1·036	1·615	1·126	1·677	1·243	1·746	1·409
6·20	1·584	1·061	1·641	1·154	1·704	1·273	1·775	1·443
6·30	1·609	1·086	1·666	1·181	1·731	1·303	1·804	1·478
6·40	1·633	1·111	1·692	1·208	1·758	1·334	1·833	1·512

Table 9B·22. Flexure—Reinforcement Percentages for Doubly Reinforced Sections (Concrete mix M20)

$f_{ck} = 20\ \text{N/mm}^2$
$f_y = 500\ \text{N/mm}^2$

M_u/bd^2, N/mm^2	$d'/d = 0{\cdot}05$		$d'/d = 0{\cdot}10$		$d'/d = 0{\cdot}15$		$d'/d = 0{\cdot}20$	
	P_t	P_c	P_t	P_c	P_t	P_c	P_t	P_c
2·67	0·758	0·002	0·758	0·003	0·758	0·003	0·758	0·003
2·70	0·765	0·010	0·765	0·011	0·766	0·012	0·767	0·014
2·80	0·789	0·035	0·791	0·038	0·793	0·042	0·795	0·048
2·90	0·813	0·061	0·816	0·066	0·820	0·073	0·824	0·083
3·00	0·837	0·086	0·842	0·094	0·847	0·103	0·853	0·117
3·10	0·862	0·111	0·868	0·121	0·874	0·134	0·882	0·152
3·20	0·886	0·137	0·893	0·149	0·901	0·164	0·910	0·186
3·30	0·910	0·162	0·919	0·176	0·928	0·195	0·939	0·221
3·40	0·934	0·188	0·944	0·204	0·955	0·225	0·968	0·255
3·50	0·958	0·213	0·970	0·232	0·982	0·256	0·997	0·290
3·60	0·983	0·238	0·995	0·259	1·009	0·286	1·025	0·324
3·70	1·007	0·264	1·021	0·287	1·036	0·316	1·054	0·359
3·80	1·031	0·289	1·046	0·314	1·064	0·347	1·083	0·394
3·90	1·055	0·314	1·072	0·342	1·091	0·377	1·112	0·428
4·00	1·080	0·340	1·098	0·369	1·118	0·408	1·140	0·463
4·10	1·104	0·365	1·123	0·397	1·145	0·438	1·169	0·497
4·20	1·128	0·391	1·149	0·425	1·172	0·469	1·198	0·532
4·30	1·152	0·416	1·174	0·452	1·199	0·499	1·227	0·566
4·40	1·176	0·441	1·200	0·480	1·226	0·530	1·255	0·601
4·50	1·201	0·467	1·225	0·507	1·253	0·560	1·284	0·635
4·60	1·225	0·492	1·251	0·535	1·280	0·591	1·313	0·670
4·70	1·249	0·517	1·276	0·563	1·307	0·621	1·342	0·704
4·80	1·273	0·543	1·302	0·590	1·334	0·651	1·370	0·739
4·90	1·297	0·568	1·328	0·618	1·361	0·682	1·399	0·773
5·00	1·322	0·593	1·353	0·645	1·388	0·712	1·428	0·808
5·10	1·346	0·619	1·379	0·673	1·415	0·743	1·457	0·843
5·20	1·370	0·644	1·404	0·701	1·442	0·773	1·485	0·877
5·30	1·394	0·670	1·430	0·728	1·469	0·804	1·514	0·912
5·40	1·418	0·695	1·455	0·756	1·496	0·834	1·543	0·946
5·50	1·443	0·720	1·481	0·783	1·524	0·865	1·572	0·981
5·60	1·467	0·746	1·506	0·811	1·551	0·895	1·600	1·015
5·70	1·491	0·771	1·532	0·839	1·578	0·925	1·629	1·050
5·80	1·515	0·796	1·558	0·866	1·605	0·956	1·658	1·084
5·90	1·540	0·822	1·583	0·894	1·632	0·986	1·687	1·119
6·00	1·564	0·847	1·609	0·921	1·659	1·017	1·715	1·153
6·10	1·588	0·873	1·634	0·949	1·686	1·047	1·744	1·188
6·20	1·612	0·898	1·660	0·976	1·713	1·078	1·773	1·223
6·30	1·636	0·923	1·685	1·004	1·740	1·108	1·802	1·257
6·40	1·661	0·949	1·711	1·032	1·767	1·139	1·830	1·292
6·50	1·685	0·974	1·736	1·059	1·794	1·169	1·859	1·326
6·60	1·709	0·999	1·762	1·087	1·821	1·200	1·888	1·361
6·70	1·733	1·025	1·788	1·114	1·848	1·230	1·917	1·395
6·80	1·757	1·050	1·813	1·142	1·875	1·260	1·945	1·430
6·90	1·782	1·076	1·839	1·170	1·902	1·291	1·974	1·464
7·00	1·806	1·101	1·864	1·197	1·929	1·321	2·003	1·499

Table 9B·23. Flexure—Reinforcement Percentages for Doubly Reinforced Sections (Concrete mix M25)

$f_{ck} = 25\ \text{N/mm}^2$
$f_y = 500\ \text{N/mm}^2$

M_u/bd^2, N/mm^2	$d'/d = 0{\cdot}05$		$d'/d = 0{\cdot}10$		$d'/d = 0{\cdot}15$		$d'/d = 0{\cdot}20$	
	P_t	P_c	P_t	P_c	P_t	P_c	P_t	P_c
3·33	0·945	0·001	0·945	0·001	0·945	0·001	0·945	0·001
3·40	0·962	0·019	0·963	0·021	0·964	0·023	0·965	0·026
3·50	0·986	0·044	0·989	0·048	0·991	0·053	0·994	0·060
3·60	1·010	0·070	1·014	0·076	1·018	0·084	1·023	0·095
3·70	1·035	0·095	1·040	0·104	1·045	0·115	1·052	0·130
3·80	1·059	0·121	1·065	0·132	1·072	0·145	1·080	0·165
3·90	1·083	0·146	1·091	0·159	1·099	0·176	1·109	0·200
4·00	1·107	0·172	1·116	0·187	1·126	0·206	1·138	0·234
4·10	1·131	0·197	1·142	0·215	1·154	0·237	1·167	0·269
4·20	1·156	0·223	1·167	0·242	1·181	0·268	1·195	0·304
4·30	1·180	0·248	1·193	0·270	1·208	0·298	1·224	0·339
4·40	1·204	0·274	1·219	0·298	1·235	0·329	1·253	0·373
4·50	1·228	0·299	1·244	0·326	1·262	0·360	1·282	0·408
4·60	1·253	0·325	1·270	0·353	1·289	0·390	1·310	0·443
4·70	1·277	0·350	1·295	0·381	1·316	0·421	1·339	0·478
4·80	1·301	0·376	1·321	0·409	1·343	0·451	1·368	0·512
4·90	1·325	0·402	1·346	0·437	1·370	0·482	1·397	0·547
5·00	1·349	0·427	1·372	0·464	1·397	0·513	1·425	0·582
5·10	1·374	0·453	1·397	0·492	1·424	0·543	1·454	0·617
5·20	1·398	0·478	1·423	0·520	1·451	0·574	1·483	0·651
5·30	1·422	0·504	1·449	0·548	1·478	0·605	1·512	0·686
5·40	1·446	0·529	1·474	0·575	1·505	0·635	1·540	0·721
5·50	1·470	0·555	1·500	0·603	1·532	0·666	1·569	0·756
5·60	1·495	0·580	1·525	0·631	1·559	0·697	1·598	0·790
5·70	1·519	0·606	1·551	0·659	1·586	0·727	1·627	0·825
5·80	1·543	0·631	1·576	0·686	1·614	0·758	1·655	0·860
5·90	1·567	0·657	1·602	0·714	1·641	0·788	1·684	0·895
6·00	1·592	0·682	1·627	0·742	1·668	0·819	1·713	0·929
6·10	1·616	0·708	1·653	0·770	1·695	0·850	1·742	0·964
6·20	1·640	0·733	1·679	0·797	1·722	0·880	1·770	0·999
6·30	1·664	0·759	1·704	0·825	1·749	0·911	1·799	1·034
6·40	1·688	0·784	1·730	0·853	1·776	0·942	1·828	1·068
6·50	1·713	0·810	1·755	0·881	1·803	0·972	1·857	1·103
6·60	1·737	0·835	1·781	0·908	1·830	1·003	1·885	1·138
6·70	1·761	0·861	1·806	0·936	1·857	1·033	1·914	1·173
6·80	1·785	0·886	1·832	0·964	1·884	1·064	1·943	1·207
6·90	1·809	0·912	1·857	0·992	1·911	1·095	1·972	1·242
7·00	1·834	0·937	1·883	1·019	1·938	1·125	2·000	1·277
7·10	1·858	0·963	1·909	1·047	1·965	1·156	2·029	1·312
7·20	1·882	0·988	1·934	1·075	1·992	1·187	2·058	1·346
7·30	1·906	1·014	1·960	1·103	2·019	1·217	2·087	1·381
7·40	1·930	1·039	1·985	1·130	2·046	1·248	2·115	1·416
7·50	1·955	1·065	2·011	1·158	2·074	1·278	2·144	1·451
7·60	1·979	1·090	2·036	1·186	2·101	1·309	2·173	1·486
7·70	2·003	1·116	2·062	1·213	2·128	1·340	2·202	1·520

Table 9B·24. Flexure—Reinforcement Percentages for Doubly Reinforced Sections (Concrete mix M30)

$f_{ck} = 30$ N/mm^2
$f_y = 500$ N/mm^2

M_u/bd^2, N/mm^2	$d'/d = 0{\cdot}05$ P_t	P_c	$d'/d = 0{\cdot}10$ P_t	P_c	$d'/d = 0{\cdot}15$ P_t	P_c	$d'/d = 0{\cdot}20$ P_t	P_c
4·00	1·135	0·002	1·135	0·002	1·135	0·003	1·135	0·003
4·10	1·159	0·028	1·161	0·030	1·162	0·034	1·164	0·038
4·20	1·183	0·054	1·186	0·058	1·189	0·064	1·193	0·073
4·30	1·208	0·079	1·212	0·086	1·216	0·095	1·222	0·108
4·40	1·232	0·105	1·237	0·114	1·244	0·126	1·250	0·143
4·50	1·256	0·130	1·263	0·142	1·271	0·157	1·279	0·178
4·60	1·280	0·156	1·289	0·170	1·298	0·188	1·308	0·213
4·70	1·305	0·182	1·314	0·198	1·325	0·218	1·337	0·248
4·80	1·329	0·207	1·340	0·226	1·352	0·249	1·365	0·283
4·90	1·353	0·233	1·365	0·254	1·379	0·280	1·394	0·318
5·00	1·377	0·259	1·391	0·281	1·406	0·311	1·423	0·353
5·10	1·401	0·284	1·416	0·309	1·433	0·342	1·452	0·388
5·20	1·426	0·310	1·442	0·337	1·460	0·372	1·480	0·423
5·30	1·450	0·336	1·467	0·365	1·487	0·403	1·509	0·458
5·40	1·474	0·361	1·493	0·393	1·514	0·434	1·538	0·493
5·50	1·498	0·387	1·519	0·421	1·541	0·465	1·567	0·528
5·60	1·522	0·413	1·544	0·449	1·568	0·496	1·595	0·563
5·70	1·547	0·438	1·570	0·477	1·595	0·526	1·624	0·598
5·80	1·571	0·464	1·595	0·505	1·622	0·557	1·653	0·633
5·90	1·595	0·490	1·621	0·533	1·649	0·588	1·682	0·668
6·00	1·619	0·515	1·646	0·560	1·676	0·619	1·710	0·703
6·10	1·643	0·541	1·672	0·588	1·704	0·650	1·739	0·738
6·20	1·668	0·566	1·697	0·616	1·731	0·680	1·768	0·773
6·30	1·692	0·592	1·723	0·644	1·758	0·711	1·797	0·807
6·40	1·716	0·618	1·749	0·672	1·785	0·742	1·825	0·842
6·50	1·740	0·643	1·774	0·700	1·812	0·773	1·854	0·877
6·60	1·765	0·669	1·800	0·728	1·839	0·804	1·883	0·912
6·70	1·789	0·695	1·825	0·756	1·866	0·835	1·912	0·947
6·80	1·813	0·720	1·851	0·784	1·893	0·865	1·940	0·982
6·90	1·837	0·746	1·876	0·812	1·920	0·896	1·969	1·017
7·00	1·861	0·772	1·902	0·839	1·947	0·927	1·998	1·052
7·10	1·886	0·797	1·927	0·867	1·974	0·958	2·027	1·087
7·20	1·910	0·823	1·953	0·895	2·001	0·989	2·055	1·122
7·30	1·934	0·849	1·979	0·923	2·028	1·019	2·084	1·157
7·40	1·958	0·874	2·004	0·951	2·055	1·050	2·113	1·192
7·50	1·982	0·900	2·030	0·979	2·082	1·081	2·142	1·227
7·60	2·007	0·926	2·055	1·007	2·109	1·112	2·170	1·262
7·70	2·031	0·951	2·081	1·035	2·136	1·143	2·199	1·297
7·80	2·055	0·977	2·106	1·063	2·164	1·173	2·228	1·332
7·90	2·079	1·002	2·132	1·091	2·191	1·204	2·257	1·367
8·00	2·103	1·028	2·157	1·118	2·218	1·235	2·285	1·402
8·10	2·128	1·054	2·183	1·146	2·245	1·266	2·314	1·437
8·20	2·152	1·079	2·209	1·174	2·272	1·297	2·343	1·472
8·30	2·176	1·105	2·234	1·202	2·299	1·327	2·372	1·507

Table 9B·25. Flexure—Limiting Moment of Resistance Factor, $M_{u,\,lim}/b_w d^2 f_{ck}$, for Singly Reinforced T-Beams, N/mm²

f_y = 250 N/mm²

D_f/d	b_f/b_w									
	1·0	2·0	3·0	4·0	5·0	6·0	7·0	8·0	9·0	10·0
0·06	0·149	0·175	0·201	0·227	0·253	0·279	0·305	0·331	0·357	0·383
0·07	0·149	0·179	0·209	0·239	0·270	0·300	0·330	0·360	0·390	0·420
0·08	0·149	0·183	0·218	0·252	0·286	0·320	0·355	0·389	0·423	0·457
0·09	0·149	0·187	0·226	0·264	0·302	0·341	0·379	0·417	0·456	0·494
0·10	0·149	0·191	0·234	0·276	0·318	0·361	0·403	0·446	0·488	0·530
0·11	0·149	0·195	0·242	0·288	0·334	0·381	0·427	0·474	0·520	0·566
0·12	0·149	0·199	0·250	0·300	0·350	0·401	0·451	0·501	0·551	0·602
0·13	0·149	0·203	0·257	0·312	0·366	0·420	0·474	0·528	0·583	0·637
0·14	0·149	0·207	0·265	0·323	0·381	0·439	0·497	0·555	0·614	0·672
0·15	0·149	0·211	0·273	0·335	0·397	0·458	0·520	0·582	0·644	0·706
0·16	0·149	0·215	0·280	0·346	0·412	0·477	0·543	0·609	0·674	0·740
0·17	0·169	0·218	0·288	0·357	0·427	0·496	0·565	0·635	0·704	0·773
0·18	0·149	0·222	0·295	0·368	0·441	0·514	0·581	0·660	0·733	0·806
0·19	0·149	0·226	0·302	0·379	0·456	0·532	0·609	0·686	0·763	0·839
0·20	0·149	0·229	0·310	0·390	0·470	0·550	0·631	0·711	0·791	0·872
0·21	0·149	0·233	0·317	0·400	0·484	0·568	0·652	0·736	0·820	0·903
0·22	0·149	0·236	0·324	0·411	0·498	0·586	0·673	0·760	0·848	0·928
0·23	0·149	0·240	0·330	0·421	0·511	0·602	0·692	0·783	0·873	0·953
0·24	0·149	0·242	0·334	0·427	0·520	0·613	0·705	0·798	0·891	0·978
0·26	0·149	0·246	0·343	0·440	0·538	0·635	0·732	0·829	0·926	1·023
0·27	0·149	0·248	0·348	0·447	0·546	0·645	0·745	0·844	0·943	1·043
0·28	0·149	0·250	0·352	0·453	0·555	0·656	0·758	0·859	0·961	1·062
0·29	0·149	0·252	0·356	0·460	0·563	0·667	0·770	0·874	0·978	1·081
0·30	0·149	0·255	0·360	0·466	0·572	0·677	0·783	0·889	0·995	1·100
0·31	0·149	0·257	0·365	0·472	0·580	0·688	0·796	0·903	1·011	1·119
0·32	0·149	0·259	0·369	0·479	0·588	0·698	0·808	0·918	1·028	1·138
0·33	0·149	0·261	0·373	0·485	0·597	0·709	0·820	0·932	1·044	1·156
0·34	0·149	0·263	0·377	0·491	0·605	0·719	0·833	0·947	1·061	1·175
0·35	0·149	0·265	0·381	0·497	0·613	0·729	0·845	0·961	1·077	1·193
0·36	0·149	0·267	0·385	0·503	0·621	0·739	0·857	0·975	1·093	1·211
0·37	0·149	0·269	0·389	0·509	0·629	0·749	0·869	0·989	1·109	1·229
0·38	0·149	0·271	0·393	0·515	0·637	0·759	0·880	1·002	1·124	1·246
0·39	0·149	0·273	0·397	0·521	0·644	0·768	0·892	1·016	1·140	1·264
0·40	0·149	0·275	0·401	0·526	0·652	0·778	0·904	1·029	1·155	1·281
0·41	0·149	0·277	0·404	0·532	0·660	0·789	0·915	1·043	1·170	1·298
0·42	0·149	0·279	0·408	0·538	0·667	0·797	0·926	1·056	1·186	1·315
0·43	0·149	0·280	0·412	0·543	0·675	0·807	0·938	1·069	1·200	1·332
0·44	0·149	0·282	0·416	0·549	0·682	0·815	0·949	1·082	1·215	1·349
0·45	0·149	0·284	0·419	0·554	0·689	0·825	0·960	1·095	1·230	1·365

Table 9B·26. Flexure—Limiting Moment of Resistance Factor, $M_{x,lim}/b_w d^2 f_{ck}$, for Singly Reinforced T-Beams, N/mm²

f_y = 415 N/mm²

D_f/d	b_f/b_w 1·0	2·0	3·0	4·0	5·0	6·0	7·0	8·0	9·0	10·0
0·06	0·138	0·164	0·190	0·216	0·242	0·268	0·294	0·320	0·346	0·372
0·07	0·138	0·168	0·198	0·228	0·259	0·289	0·319	0·349	0·379	0·409
0·08	0·138	0·172	0·207	0·241	0·275	0·309	0·344	0·378	0·412	0·446
0·09	0·138	0·176	0·215	0·253	0·291	0·330	0·368	0·406	0·445	0·483
0·10	0·138	0·180	0·223	0·265	0·308	0·350	0·392	0·435	0·477	0·519
0·11	0·138	0·184	0·231	0·277	0·324	0·370	0·416	0·463	0·509	0·555
0·12	0·138	0·188	0·239	0·289	0·339	0·390	0·440	0·490	0·541	0·591
0·13	0·138	0·192	0·247	0·301	0·355	0·409	0·463	0·518	0·572	0·626
0·14	0·138	0·196	0·254	0·312	0·370	0·428	0·487	0·545	0·903	0·661
0·15	0·138	0·200	0·262	0·324	0·386	0·448	0·509	0·571	0·633	0·695
0·16	0·138	0·204	0·269	0·335	0·401	0·466	0·532	0·598	0·663	0·729
0·17	0·138	0·207	0·277	0·346	0·416	0·485	0·554	0·624	0·693	0·762
0·18	0·138	0·211	0·284	0·357	0·430	0·503	0·576	0·649	0·723	0·796
0·19	0·138	0·215	0·291	0·368	0·445	0·522	0·598	0·675	0·752	0·828
0·20	0·138	0·218	0·299	0·379	0·459	0·540	0·620	0·700	0·780	0·861
0·21	0·138	0·221	0·305	0·388	0·471	0·554	0·638	0·721	0·804	0·887
0·22	0·138	0·224	0·309	0·395	0·480	0·566	0·651	0·737	0·822	0·908
0·23	0·138	0·226	0·314	0·402	0·489	0·577	0·665	0·753	0·841	0·928
0·24	0·138	0·228	0·318	0·408	0·498	0·588	0·678	0·768	0·859	0·949
0·25	0·138	0·230	0·323	0·415	0·507	0·600	0·692	0·784	0·876	0·969
0·26	0·138	0·233	0·327	0·422	0·516	0·611	0·705	0·800	0·894	0·989
0·27	0·138	0·235	0·331	0·428	0·525	0·622	0·718	0·815	0·912	1·008
0·28	0·138	0·237	0·336	0·435	0·534	0·632	0·731	0·830	0·929	1·028
0·29	0·138	0·239	0·340	0·441	0·542	0·643	0·744	0·845	0·946	1·047
0·30	0·138	0·241	0·344	0·448	0·551	0·654	0·757	0·860	0·963	1·066
0·31	0·138	0·243	0·349	0·454	0·559	0·664	0·770	0·875	0·980	1·085
0·32	0·138	0·245	0·353	0·460	0·568	0·675	0·782	0·890	0·997	1·104
0·33	0·138	0·248	0·357	0·466	0·576	0·685	0·795	0·904	1·014	1·123
0·34	0·138	0·250	0·361	0·473	0·584	0·696	0·807	0·919	1·030	1·142
0·35	0·138	0·252	0·365	0·479	0·592	0·706	0·819	0·933	1·046	1·160
0·36	0·138	0·254	0·369	0·485	0·600	0·716	0·831	0·947	1·063	1·178
0·37	0·138	0·256	0·373	0·491	0·608	0·726	0·843	0·960	1·079	1·196
0·38	0·138	0·258	0·377	0·497	0·616	0·736	0·855	0·975	1·094	1·214
0·39	0·138	0·260	0·381	0·503	0·624	0·746	0·867	0·989	1·110	1·232
0·40	0·138	0·262	0·385	0·508	0·632	0·755	0·879	1·002	1·126	1·249
0·41	0·138	0·263	0·389	0·514	0·640	0·765	0·890	1·016	1·141	1·267
0·42	0·138	0·265	0·393	0·520	0·647	0·775	0·902	1·029	1·156	1·284
0·43	0·138	0·267	0·396	0·526	0·655	0·784	0·913	1·042	1·172	1·301
0·44	0·138	0·269	0·400	0·531	0·662	0·793	0·924	1·055	1·187	1·318
0·45	0·138	0·271	0·404	0·537	0·670	0·803	0·936	1·068	1·201	1·334

Table 9B·27. Flexure—Limiting Moment of Resistance Factor $M_{u,lim}/b_w d^2 f_{ck}$, for Singly Reinforced T-beams, N/mm²

f_y = 500 N/mm²

D_f/d	b_f/b_w									
	1·0	2·0	3·0	4·0	5·0	6·0	7·0	8·0	9·0	10·0
0·06	0·133	0·159	0·185	0·211	0·237	0·263	0·289	0·315	0·341	0·367
0·07	0·133	0·163	0·193	0·223	0·254	0·284	0·314	0·344	0·374	0·404
0·08	0·133	0·167	0·202	0·236	0·270	0·304	0·339	0·373	0·407	0·440
0·09	0·133	0·171	0·210	0·248	0·286	0·325	0·363	0·401	0·440	0·478
0·10	0·133	0·175	0·218	0·260	0·303	0·345	0·387	0·430	0·472	0·514
0·11	0·133	0·179	0·226	0·272	0·318	0·365	0·411	0·458	0·504	0·550
0·12	0·133	0·183	0·234	0·284	0·334	0·385	0·435	0·485	0·536	0·586
0·13	0·133	0·187	0·241	0·296	0·350	0·404	0·458	0·513	0·567	0·621
0·14	0·133	0·191	0·249	0·307	0·365	0·423	0·481	0·540	0·598	0·656
0·15	0·133	0·195	0·257	0·319	0·381	0·442	0·504	0·566	0·628	0·690
0·16	0·133	0·199	0·264	0·330	0·396	0·461	0·527	0·593	0·658	0·724
0·17	0·133	0·202	0·272	0·341	0·411	0·480	0·549	0·619	0·688	0·757
0·18	0·133	0·206	0·279	0·352	0·425	0·498	0·571	0·646	0·717	0·791
0·19	0·133	0·210	0·286	0·363	0·440	0·516	0·593	0·670	0·747	0·823
0·20	0·133	0·213	0·292	0·372	0·452	0·532	0·611	0·691	0·771	0·850
0·21	0·133	0·215	0·297	0·379	0·461	0·543	0·625	0·707	0·789	0·871
0·22	0·133	0·217	0·302	0·386	0·470	0·555	0·639	0·723	0·808	0·892
0·23	0·133	0·220	0·306	0·393	0·479	0·566	0·653	0·739	0·826	0·912
0·24	0·133	0·222	0·311	0·400	0·488	0·577	0·666	0·755	0·844	0·933
0·25	0·133	0·224	0·315	0·406	0·497	0·589	0·680	0·771	0·862	0·953
0·26	0·133	0·226	0·320	0·413	0·506	0·600	0·693	0·786	0·880	0·973
0·27	0·133	0·229	0·324	0·420	0·515	0·611	0·706	0·802	0·897	0·993
0·28	0·133	0·231	0·328	0·426	0·524	0·622	0·719	0·817	0·915	1·012
0·29	0·133	0·233	0·333	0·433	0·532	0·632	0·732	0·832	0·932	1·032
0·30	0·133	0·235	0·337	0·439	0·541	0·643	0·745	0·847	0·949	1·051
0·31	0·133	0·237	0·341	0·445	0·550	0·654	0·758	0·862	0·966	1·070
0·32	0·133	0·239	0·346	0·452	0·558	0·664	0·770	0·877	0·983	1·089
0·33	0·133	0·241	0·350	0·458	0·566	0·675	0·783	0·891	1·000	1·108
0·34	0·133	0·243	0·354	0·464	0·575	0·685	0·795	0·906	1·016	1·127
0·35	0·133	0·245	0·358	0·470	0·583	0·695	0·808	0·920	1·033	1·145
0·36	0·133	0·248	0·362	0·476	0·591	0·705	0·820	0·934	1·049	1·163
0·37	0·133	0·250	0·366	0·483	0·599	0·716	0·832	0·949	1·065	1·181
0·38	0·133	0·252	0·370	0·489	0·607	0·725	0·844	0·962	1·081	1·199
0·39	0·133	0·254	0·374	0·494	0·615	0·735	0·856	0·976	1·097	1·217
0·40	0·133	0·255	0·378	0·500	0·623	0·745	0·868	0·990	1·112	1·235
0·41	0·133	0·257	0·382	0·506	0·630	0·755	0·879	1·004	1·128	1·252
0·42	0·133	0·259	0·386	0·512	0·638	0·764	0·891	1·017	1·143	1·270
0·43	0·133	0·261	0·389	0·518	0·646	0·774	0·900	1·030	1·158	1·287
0·44	0·133	0·263	0·393	0·523	0·653	0·783	0·913	1·043	1·174	1·304
0·45	0·133	0·265	0·397	0·529	0·661	0·793	0·925	1·056	1·188	1·320

Table 9·27 contd...

Beams can also be designed using tables such as given below

Singly Reinforced Beams f_y = 415 M20 concrete HYSD steel.

Beam No.		B (mm)	D (mm)	d (mm)	M (Nmm) × 10^7	Mu =1·5 M (Nmm) × 10^7	$\frac{M_{u,lim}}{bd^2}$ Tab. 9·3	Mu, lim (Nmm) × 10^7 > Mu →Singly Reinf.	$\frac{Mu}{bd^2}$	(pt) = 100 $\frac{A_s}{bd}$ Tab. 8·10	A_s (mm^2)	No. of 25 φ Bars	Remarks
201	L	600 mm	800 mm	750 mm	41·58	62·37	2·76	93·15 → All beams are singly reinforced except 201 R, 203 R	1·85	·584	2628	5·35 say 6	Top
	M				18·22	27·33			·81	·237	1066·5	2·17 say 3	Bottom
	R				64·83	97·25	DR		2·88	—	—	—	DR (Doubly Rein.)
202	L				18·91	28·37			0·84	·245	1102·5	2·25 say 3	T
	M				7·71	11·57			0·34	·095	427·5	·87 say 2	B
	R				49·59	74·39			2·20	·717	3226·50	6·57 say 7	T
203	L				34·51	51·77			1·53	·470	2115·00	4·31 say 5	T
	M				18·28	27·42			0·81	·237	1066·50	2·17 say 2	B
	R				69·70	104·55	DR		3·10	—	—	—	DR (Doubly Reinf.)
204	L				59·88	89·82			2·66	·910	4095	8·34 say 9	T
	M				12·85	19·28			·57	·165	742·5	1·51 say 2	B
	R				30·89	46·34			1·37	·415	1867·50	3·80 say 4	T
205	L				56·73	85·10			2·52	·848	3816	7·77 say 8	T
	M				12·74	19·11			·57	·165	742·5	1·51 say 2	B
	R				36·66	54·99			1·63	·505	2272·50	4·63 say 5	T
206	L				60·70	91·05			2·70	·928	4176	8·51 say 9	T
	M				12·84	19·26			·57	·165	742·5	1·51 say 2	B
	R				30·57	45·86			1·36	·410	1845	3·76 say 4	T
207	L				57·50	86·25			2·56	·866	3897	7·94 say 8	T
	M				12·75	19·13			·57	·165	742·5	1·51	B
	R				36·35	54·35			1·62	·500	2250	4·58 say 5	T

L – Left Support *M* – Mid Span *R* – Right Support

Beam No.		B (mm)	D (mm)	d (mm)	M (Nmm) × 18	Mu =1·5 M (Nmm) × 10^7	$\frac{M_{u,lim}}{bd^2}$ Tab. 9·3	Mu, lim (Nmm) × 10^7 > Mu →Singly Reinf.	$\frac{Mu}{bd^2}$	(pt) = 100 $\frac{A_s}{bd}$ Tab. 8·10	A_s (mm^2)	No. of 25 φ Bars	Remarks
301	L	800 mm	800 mm	750 mm	51·58	77·37	2·76	124·2 → All beams one singly reinforced	1·72	·535	3210	6·54 say 7	T
	M				24·83	37·25			·83	·240	1440	2·93 say 3	B
	R				73·48	110·22			2·45	·820	4920	10·02 say 11	T
302	L				22·61	33·92			0·75	·218	1308	2·66 say 3	T
	M				8·38	12·57			0·28	·085	510	1·04 say 2	B
	R				51·48	77·22			1·72	·535	3210	6·54 say 7	T
303	L				46·02	69·03			1·53	·465	2790	5·68 say 6	T
	M				24·95	37·43			·83	·240	1440	2·93 say 3	B
	R				80·89	121·34			2·70	·928	5568	11·34 say 12	T
304	L				65·05	97·58			2·17	·705	4230	8·62 say 9	T
	M				17·64	26·46			·59	·169	1014	2·07 say 3	B
	R				36·15	54·23			1·21	·365	2190	4·46 say 5	T
305	L				63·12	94·68			2·10	·678	4068	8·29 say 9	T
	M				17·56	26·34			·59	·169	1014	2·07 say 3	B
	R				38·87	58·31			1·30	·392	2352	4·79 say 5	T
306	L				65·87	98·81			2·20	·717	4302	8·70 say 9	T
	M				17·62	26·43			·59	·169	1014	2·07 say 3	B
	R				35·84	53·76			1·19	·357	2142	4·36 say 5	T
307	L				63·86	95·79			2·13	·690	4140	8·43 say 9	T
	M				17·58	26·37			·59	·169	1014	2·07 say 3	B
	R				38·57	57·86			1·29	·390	2340	4·77 say 5	T

T–Reinforcement at Top *B*–Reinforcement at Bottom

Singly Reinforced Beams — *fy*= 415 N/mm² M20 concrete HYSD Steel

Beam No.		B (mm)	D (mm)	d (mm)	M (Nmm) × 18	Mu =1·5 M (Nmm) × 10⁷	$\frac{M_{u,lim}}{bd^2}$ Tab. 9·3	Mu, lim (Nmm) × 10⁷ > Mu →Singly R	$\frac{Mu}{bd^2}$	(pt) = 100 $\frac{A_s}{bd}$ Tab. 8·10	A_s (mm²)	No. of 20 φ Bars	Remarks
401	L				25·07	37·61			1·11	·330	1485	4·73 say 5	Top
	M	600	800	750	14·74	22·11			·66	·190	855	1·74 say 2	B
	R				41·62	62·43			1·85	·584	2628	8·37 say 9	T
402	L				12·77	19·16			0·57	·165	742·5	2·36 say 3	T
	M	600	800	750	5·54	8·31			·25	·085	382·5	·78 say 2	B
	R				29·17	43·76			1·30	·392	1764	5·61 say 6	T
403	L	600	800	750	28·33	42·50			1·26	·380	1710	5·44 say 6	T
	M				14·71	22·07			·65	·187	841·50	1·71 say 2	B
	R				37·54	56·31			1·67	·520	2340	7·45 say 8	T
404	L				34·48	51·72			1·53	·470	2115	6·73 say 7	T
	M	600	800	750	10·59	15·89	2·76	93·15 → All beams singly reinforced	·47	·135	607·50	1·24 say 2	B
	R				19·70	29·55			·88	·255	1147·50	3·65 say 4	T
405	L				34·57	51·86			1·54	·470	2115	6·73 say 7	T
	M	600	800	750	10·57	15·86			·47	·135	607·50	1·24 say 2	B
	R				20·39	30·59			0·91	·265	1192·50	3·80 say 4	T
406	L				34·91	52·37			1·55	·477	2146·50	6·83 say 7	T
	M	600	800	750	10·59	15·89			·47	·135	607·50	1·24 say 2	B
	R				19·44	29·16			0·86	·250	1125	3·58 say 4	T
407	L				34·94	52·41			1·55	·477	2146·50	6·83 say 7	T
	M	600	800	750	10·50	15·87			·47	·135	607·50	1·24 say 2	B
	R				20·24	30·36			0·90	·264	1188	3·78 say 4	T

Doubly Reinforced Beams — *fy*= 415 N/mm² M20, concrete HYSD steel

Beam No.		B (mm)	D (mm)	d (mm)	M × 10⁷ (Nmm)	1·5 M Mu × 10⁷ (Nmm)	Mu, lim × 10⁷ (Nmm)	$\frac{Mu}{bd^2}$	d'/d	Pt = 100 $\frac{A_{st}}{bd}$ (Tab. 8·10)	p_c = 100 $\frac{A_{sc}}{bd}$	A_{st} (mm²)	A_{sc} (mm²)	No. of 32 φ bars for A_{sv}	No. of 32 φ bars for A_{sc}
101	L				157·55	236·33		4·36		1·425	·480	8122·50	2736	10·10	3·40
	M				92·66	138·99	SR	—		—	—	—	—	—	—
	R				144·93	217·40		4·01		1·320	·380	7524	2166	9·36	2·69
103	L				141·84	212·76		3·93		1·300	·355	7410	2023·5	9·21	2·52
	M				92·94	139·41	SR	—		—	—	—	—	—	—
	R				163·52	245·28		4·53		1·475	·540	8407·5	3078	10·45	3·83
104	L				185·42	278·13		5·14		1·650	·725	9405	4132·50	11·69	5·14
	M				127·20	190·80		3·52		1·176	·229	6703·20	1305·30	8·33	1·62
	R				178·31	267·47		4·94		1·590	0·660	9063	3762	11·27	4·68
105	L				128·69	193·04		3·56		1·185	·245	6754·50	1396·50	8·40	1·74
	M				48·28	72·42	SR	—		—	—	—	—	—	—
	R	600	1000	950	129·01	193·52	149·45	3·57	0·05 (Use 0·05)	1·189	·248	6777·30	1413·60	8·43	1·76
106	L				177·42	266·13		4·91		1·585	·655	9034·5	3733·50	11·23	4·64
	M				126·85	190·28		3·51		1·175	·228	6697·5	1299·60	8·33	1·62
	R				186·99	280·49		5·18		1·660	·735	9462	4189·50	11·77	5·21
109	L				— SR										
	M				67·03	100·55	SR								
	R				107·45	161·18		2·98		1·015	·065	5785·5	370·50	7·19	·46
110	L				135·98	203·97		3·77		1·250	·310	7125	1767	8·86	2·20
	M				84·02	126·03	SR								
	R				153·53	230·30		4·25		1·390	·450	7923	2565	9·85	3·19
111	L				152·53	228·80		4·23		1·385	·445	7894·50	2536·50	9·82	3·15
	M				83·93	125·90	SR								
	R				129·17	193·76		3·58		1·190	·250	6783	1425	8·43	1·77

Singly Reinforced Beams fy= 415 N/mm² M20 concrete HYSD Steel SR

Beam No.	B (mm)	D (mm)	d (mm)	M (Nmm) × 18	Mu =1·5 M (Nmm) × 10^7	$\frac{Mu, lim}{bd^2}$ Tab.8·3	Mu, lim (Nmm) × 10^7 > Mu →Singly R	$\frac{Mu}{bd^2}$	(p_t) = 100 $\frac{A_s}{bd}$ Tab. 8·10	A_s (mm^2)	No. of 20 ϕ Bars	Remarks
501 M	250	450	410	4·66	6·99	2·76	11·60 → All these beams are S.R.	1·66	·520	533	1·70	Top
502 L				3·52	5·28			1·26	·380	389·50	1·24	T
M				1·75	2·63			0·63	·182	186·55	·59	T
R				3·76	5·64			1·34	·405	415·13	1·32	T
503 M				4·66	6·99			1·66	·517	529·93	1·69	T
504 M				4·34	6·51			1·55	·477	488·93	1·56	T
505 M				4·34	6·51			1·55	·477	488·93	1·56	T
506 M				4·34	6·51			1·55	·477	488·93	1·56	T
507 M				4·34	6·51			1·55	·477	488·93	1·56	T

DR - Doubly Reinforced
SR - Singly Reinforced

Singly Reinforced Beams fy= 415 N/mm² M20 concrete HYSD Steel

Beam No.	B (mm)	D (mm)	d (mm)	M (Nmm) × 10^7	Mu =1·5 M (Nmm) × 10^7	$\frac{Mu, lim}{bd^2}$ Tab.8·3	Mu, lim (Nmm) × 10^7 > Mu →Singly R	$\frac{Mu}{bd^2}$	(p_t) = 100 $\frac{A_s}{bd}$ Tab. 8·10	A_s (mm^2)	No. of 32 ϕ Bars	Remarks
105 L	600	1000	950	128·69	DR	2·76	149·45					DR
M				48·28	72·42			1·34	·405	2308·5	2·87 say 3	B
R				129·01	DR							DR
106 L				177·42	DR							DR
M				126·85	DR							DR
R				186·99	DR							DR
107 L				87·65	131·48			2·43	·810	4617	5·74 say 6	Top
M				68·71	103·07			1·90	·602	3431·40	4·27 say 5	B
R				98·20	147·30			2·72	·937	5340·90	6·64 say 7	T
108 L				68·01	102·02			1·88	·595	3391·50	4·22 say 5	T
M				24·31	36·47			·67	·194	1105·90	1·37 say 2	B
R				70·24	105·36			1·95	·621	3539·70	4·40 say 5	T

Singly Reinforced Beams — f_y= 415 N/mm^2 M20 concrete HYSD Steel

Beam No.		B (mm)	D (mm)	d (mm)	M (Nmm) × 10^7	Mu =1·5 M (Nmm) × 10^7	$\frac{Mu, lim}{bd^2}$ Tab.8·3	Mu, lim (Nmm) × 10^7 > Mu → Singly R	$\frac{Mu}{bd^2}$	(p_t) = $100 \frac{A_s}{bd}$ Tab. 8·10	A_s (mm^2)	No. of 32 φ Bars	Remarks
109	L	600	1000	950	93·35	140·03	2·76	149·45	2·59	·880	5016	6·24	Top
	M				67·03	100·55			1·86	·590	3363	4·18	B
	R				107·45	DR							
110	L				135·98	DR							
	M				84·02	126·03			2·33	·769	4383·30	5·45	B
	R				153·53	DR							
111	L				152·53	DR							
	M				83·93	125·90			2·32	·765	4360·50	5·42	B
	R				129·17	DR							
112	L				130·12	DR							
	M				113·49	DR							
	R				195·85	DR							

Singly Reinforced Beams — f_y= 415 N/mm^2 M20 concrete HYSD Steel

Beam No.		B (mm)	D (mm)	d (mm)	M (Nmm) × 10^7	Mu =1·5 M (Nmm) × 10^7	$\frac{Mu, lim}{bd^2}$ Tab.8·3	Mu, lim (Nmm) × 10^7 > Mu → Singly R	$\frac{Mu}{bd^2}$	(p_t) = $100 \frac{A_s}{bd}$ Tab. 8·10	A_s (mm^2)	No. of 32 φ Bars	Remarks
113	L	600 mm	1000 mm	950 mm	199·09	298·64	2·76	149·45	5·51				
	M				118·79	DR							
	R				113·74	170·61			3·15				
114	L				129·03	193·55			3·57				
	M				113·55	DR							
	R				195·96	293·94			5·43				
115	L				199·03	298·55			5·51				
	M				118·78	DR							
	R				113·82	170·73			3·15				
116	L				137·10	205·65			3·80				
	M				83·96	125·90			2·32	·765	4360·50	5·42	B
	R				152·13	228·20			4·21				
117	L				144·42	216·63			4·00				
	M				83·98	125·90			2·32	·765	4360·50	5·42	B
	R				127·70	191·55			3·54				

T-Top Reinforcement, *B*-Bottom Reinforcement

Shear Calculation using tables (Ref. Table 8·6)

f_y = 415 N/mm², f_{ck} = 30 N/mm²

b *mm*	*d* *mm*	p_t	V_u (× 10^6) *N*	τ_c *N/mm²*	V_{uc} (× 10^6) *N*	V_{us} (× 10^6) *N*	*Bar Dia* *mm*	*Spacing Bet. legs* *mm*	A_{sv} *mm²*	S_v *mm*	*Spacing provided* *mm*
1000	1130	0·28	0·0004	0·39	0·44	—	—	—	—	—	No shear reinf-orcement
1000	2314	0·11	2·064	0·29	0·671	1·208	16	200	1005	447	400
1000	2274	0·83	2·064	0·61	1·39	0·674	16	200	1005	1224	400
1000	2274	0·22	1·364	0·34	0·773	0·523	—	—	—	—	No shear reinf-orcement
1000	1890	0·26	1·119	0·37	0·70	0·419	—	—	—	—	No shear reinf-orcement

9B·8. Design Tables for Slabs

Table 9B·28. Moment of Resistance of Slabs, kN-m per metre width

f_{ck} = 15 N/mm^2
f_y = 250 N/mm^2
Thickness = 10·0 cm

Bar Spacing, cm	Bar Diameter, mm 6	8	10	12	Bar Spacing, cm	Bar Diameter, mm 6	8	10	12
5	8·92	14·02	–	–	20	0·00	4·20	6·27	8·55
6	7·59	12·20	–	–	21	0·00	4·01	6·00	8·19
7	6·61	10·77	–	–	22	0·00	3·83	5·74	7·87
8	5·85	9·63	13·56	–	23	0·00	3·67	5·51	7·56
9	5·24	8·70	12·40	–	24	0·00	3·53	5·30	7·28
10	4·75	7·93	11·41	–	25	0·00	3·39	5·10	7·02
11	4·34	7·29	10·56	13·81	26	0·00	3·27	4·92	6·78
12	4·00	6·74	9·82	12·95	27	0·00	3·15	4·75	6·56
13	3·70	6·26	9·18	12·19	28	0·00	3·04	4·59	6·34
14	3·75	5·85	8·61	11·50	29	0·00	2·94	4·44	6·16
15	3·23	5·49	8·11	10·88	30	0·00	2·85	4·30	5·96
16	3·04	5·17	7·66	10·32	35	0·00	0·00	3·72	5·17
17	2·86	4·89	7·26	9·81	40	0·00	0·00	3·27	4·56
18	2·71	4·63	6·90	9·35					
19	0·00	4·40	6·57	8·93					

Note 1. Blanks indicate percentage of reinforcement exceeding limiting value.
Note 2. Zeros indicate inadmissible reinforcement percentage (less than minimum permissible).
Note 3. Bar spacings below the dividing line exceed $3d$.

Table 9B·29. Moment of Resistance of Slabs, kN-m per metre width

f_{ck} = 15 N/mm^2
f_y = 250 N/mm^2
Thickness = 11·0 cm

Bar Spacing, cm	Bar Diameter, mm 6	8	10	12	Bar Spacing, cm	Bar Diameter, mm 6	8	10	12
5	10·15	16·21	–	–	20	0·00	4·74	7·12	9·78
6	8·62	14·02	–	–	21	0·00	4·53	6·81	9·36
7	7·48	12·33	17·37	–	22	0·00	4·33	6·52	8·98
8	6·61	10·99	15·70	–	23	0·00	4·15	6·26	8·63
9	5·92	9·91	14·30	–	24	0·00	3·98	6·01	8·31
10	5·36	9·02	13·12	17·23	25	0·00	3·83	5·79	8·01
11	4·90	8·28	12·11	16·04	26	0·00	3·69	5·58	7·73
12	4·51	7·65	11·25	15·00	27	0·00	3·56	5·38	7·47
13	4·18	7·10	10·49	14·08	28	0·00	3·43	5·20	7·22
14	3·89	6·63	9·83	13·25	29	0·00	3·32	5·03	6·99
15	3·64	6·22	9·25	12·52	30	0·00	3·21	4·87	6·78
16	3·42	5·86	8·73	11·86	35	0·00	0·00	4·21	5·87
17	3·23	5·53	8·26	11·26	40	0·00	0·00	3·70	5·18
18	0·00	5·24	7·84	10·72	45	0·00	0·00	3·30	4·63
19	0·00	4·98	7·47	10·23					

Note 1. Blanks indicate percentage of reinforcement exceeding limiting value.
Note 2. Zeros indicate inadmissible reinforcement percentage (less than minimum permissible).
Note 3. Bar spacings below the dividing line exceed $3d$.

Table 9B·30. Moment of Resistance of Slabs, kN-m per metre width

f_{ck} = 15 N/mm²
f_y = 250 N/mm²
Thickness = 12·0 cm

Bar Spacing, cm	Bar Diameter, mm 6	8	10	12	Bar Spacing, cm	Bar Diameter, mm 6	8	10	12
5	11·37	18·39	–	–	20	0·00	5·29	7·98	11·01
6	9·64	15·84	22·22	–	21	0·00	5·05	7·62	10·53
7	8·37	13·89	19·81	–	22	0·00	4·83	7·30	10·10
8	7·38	12·36	17·83	–	23	0·00	4·62	7·00	9·70
9	6·61	11·13	16·20	21·30	24	0·00	4·44	6·72	9·33
10	5·98	10·12	14·83	19·38	25	0·00	4·27	6·47	8·99
11	5·46	9·27	13·67	18·28	26	0·00	4·11	6·23	8·67
12	5·02	8·56	12·67	17·05	27	0·00	3·96	6·02	8·38
13	4·65	7·95	11·80	15·97	28	0·00	0·00	5·81	8·10
14	4·33	7·41	11·05	15·01	29	0·00	0·00	5·62	7·84
15	0·45	6·95	11·38	14·16	30	0·00	0·00	5·44	7·60
16	0·00	6·54	9·79	13·39	35	0·00	0·00	4·69	6·57
17	0·00	6·17	9·08	12·71	40	0·00	0·00	4·13	5·79
18	0·00	5·85	8·79	12·09	45	0·00	0·00	0·00	5·18
19	0·00	5·55	8·36	11·52					

Note 1. Blanks indicate percentage of reinforcement exceeding limiting value.
Note 2. Zeros indicate inadmissible reinforcement percentage (less than minimum permissible).
Note 3. Bar spacings below the dividing line exceed $3d$.

Table 9B·31. Moment of Resistance of Slabs, kN-m per metre width

f_{ck} = 15 N/mm²
f_y = 250 N/mm²
Thickness = 13·0 cm

Bar Spacing, cm	Bar Diameter, mm 6	8	10	12	16	Bar Spacing, cm	Bar Diameter, mm 6	8	10	12	16
5	12·60	20·58	–	–	–	20	0·00	5·83	8·83	12·24	19·49
6	10·67	17·66	25·06	–	–	21	0·00	5·57	8·43	11·71	18·73
7	9·24	15·45	22·25	–	–	22	0·00	5·32	8·07	11·22	18·02
8	8·15	13·72	19·97	26·22	–	23	0·00	5·10	7·74	10·77	17·36
9	7·29	12·34	18·10	24·03	–	24	0·00	4·89	7·44	10·36	16·75
10	6·59	11·21	16·54	22·14	–	25	0·00	4·70	7·15	9·97	16·18
11	6·02	10·27	15·22	20·51	–	26	0·00	0·00	6·89	9·62	15·64
12	5·53	9·47	14·09	19·10	–	27	0·00	0·00	6·65	9·29	15·14
13	5·12	8·79	13·12	17·86	–	28	0·00	0·00	6·42	8·98	14·67
14	4·77	8·19	12·27	16·77	–	29	0·00	0·00	6·21	8·69	14·23
15	0·00	7·68	11·52	15·80	24·35	30	0·00	0·00	6·01	8·42	13·81
16	0·00	7·22	10·86	14·93	23·21	35	0·00	0·00	5·18	7·28	12·04
17	0·00	6·82	10·27	14·15	22·16	40	0·00	0·00	4·55	6·41	10·66
18	0·00	6·45	9·74	13·45	21·20	45	0·00	0·00	0·00	5·73	9·57
19	0·00	6·13	9·26	12·81	20·31						

Note 1. Blanks indicate percentage of reinforcement exceeding limiting value·
Note 2. Zeros indicate inadmissible reinforcement percentage (less than minimum permissible)·
Note 3. Bar spacings below the dividing line exceed $3d$·

Table 9B·32(*a*). Moment of Resistance of Slabs, kN-m per metre width

f_{ck} = 15 N/mm^2
f_y = 250 N/mm^2
Thickness = 14·0 cm

Bar Spacing,	Bar Diameter, mm					Bar Spacing,	Bar Diameter, mm				
cm	6	8	10	12	16	cm	6	8	10	12	16
5	13·83	22·76	31·99	–	–	20	0·00	6·38	9·68	13·46	21·67
6	11·69	19·48	27·91	–	–	21	0·00	6·09	9·25	12·88	20·81
7	10·12	17·01	24·69	–	–	22	0·00	5·82	8·85	12·34	20·01
8	8·92	15·09	22·10	29·38	–	23	0·00	5·57	8·48	11·84	19·26
9	7·97	13·56	19·99	26·76	–	24	0·00	0·00	8·15	11·38	18·57
10	7·21	12·30	18·24	24·60	–	25	0·00	0·00	7·84	10·96	17·93
11	6·58	11·26	16·77	22·75	–	26	0·00	0·00	7·55	10·56	17·32
12	6·05	10·38	15·51	21·15	–	27	0·00	0·00	7·28	10·20	16·76
13	5·60	9·63	14·43	14·43	–	28	0·00	0·00	7·03	9·86	16·23
14	0·00	8·97	13·49	18·52	28·81	29	0·00	0·00	6·80	9·54	15·73
15	0·00	8·41	12·66	17·44	27·26	30	0·00	0·00	6·58	9·24	15·27
16	0·00	7·90	11·93	16·47	25·94	35	0·00	0·00	5·67	7·98	13·29
17	0·00	7·46	11·28	15·60	24·73	40	0·00	0·00	0·00	7·02	11·76
18	0·00	7·06	10·69	14·82	23·63	45	0·00	0·00	0·00	6·27	10·54
19	0·00	6·70	10·16	14·11	22·61						

Note 1. Blanks indicate percentage of reinforcement exceeding limiting value.
Note 2. Zeros indicate inadmissible reinforcement percentage (less than minimum permissible).
Note 3. Bar spacings below the dividing line exceed 3*d*.

Table 9B·32(*b*). Moment of Resistance of Slabs, kN-m per meter width

f_{ck} = 15 N/mm^2, f_y = 250 N/mm^2, Thickness = 15·0 cm

Bar Spacing,	Bar Diameter, mm						Bar Spacing,	Bar Diameter, mm					
cm	6	8	10	12	16	18	cm	6	8	10	12	16	18
5	15·06	24·95	35·41	–	–	–	20	0·00	6·93	10·54	14·69	23·89	28·13
6	12·71	21·30	30·76	–	–	–	21	0·00	6·61	10·06	14·05	22·89	27·06
7	11·00	18·57	27·13	35·81	–	–	22	0·00	6·32	9·63	13·45	21·99	26·06
8	9·69	16·46	24·24	32·37	–	–	23	0·00	0·00	9·23	12·91	21·16	25·13
9	8·66	14·77	21·89	29·49	–	–	24	0·00	0·00	8·86	12·41	20·39	24·26
10	7·82	13·39	19·95	27·06	–	–	25	0·00	0·00	8·52	11·94	19·67	23·45
11	7·14	12·25	18·32	24·98	–	–	26	0·00	0·00	8·20	11·51	19·00	22·68
12	6·56	11·29	16·94	23·20	–	–	27	0·00	0·00	7·91	11·11	18·38	21·97
13	0·00	10·47	15·75	21·64	33·36	–	28	0·00	0·00	7·64	10·73	17·79	21·29
14	0·00	9·46	14·71	20·28	31·83	–	29	0·00	0·00	7·39	10·38	17·24	20·66
15	0·00	9·13	13·80	19·07	30·17	–	30	0·00	0·00	7·15	10·05	16·72	20·06
16	0·00	8·59	13·00	18·00	28·67	33·32	35	0·00	0·00	0·00	8·68	14·53	17·52
17	0·00	8·10	12·28	17·25	27·30	31·87	40	0·00	0·00	0·00	7·64	12·85	15·54
18	0·00	7·67	11·64	16·18	26·05	30·53	45	0·00	0·00	0·00	6·82	11·51	13·96
19	0·00	7·28	11·06	15·40	24·91	29·28							

Note 1. Blanks indicate percentage of reinforcement exceeding limiting value.
Note 2. Zeros indicate inadmissible reinforcement percentage (less than minimum permissible).
Note 3. Bar spacing below the dividing line exceed 3*d*.

Table 9B·33. Moment of Resistance of Slabs, kN-m per meter width

f_{ck} = 15 N/mm², f_y = 250 N/mm², Thickness = 17·5 cm·

Bar Spacing, cm	Bar Diameter, mm 6	8	10	12	16	18	20	Bar Spacing, cm	Bar Diameter, mm 6	8	10	12	16	18	20
5	18·14	30·41	43·95	–	–	–	–	20	0·00	0·00	12·67	17·77	29·32	35·04	40·53
6	15·28	25·86	37·87	50·17	–	–	–	21	0·00	0·00	12·09	16·97	28·09	33·64	39·01
7	13·19	22·48	33·22	44·59	–	–	–	22	0·00	0·00	11·57	16·25	26·96	32·34	37·59
8	11·61	19·87	29·57	40·05	–	–	–	23	0·00	0·00	11·08	15·58	25·91	31·14	36·26
9	10·36	17·81	26·63	36·32	–	–	–	24	0·00	0·00	10·64	14·97	24·95	30·02	35·02
10	9·36	16·13	24·22	33·21	–	–	–	25	0·00	0·00	10·23	14·40	24·05	28·98	33·86
11	0·00	14·74	22·20	30·57	47·84	–	–	26	0·00	0·00	9·85	13·87	23·21	28·00	32·77
12	0·00	13·57	20·49	28·32	44·78	–	–	27	0·00	0·00	9·49	13·38	22·43	27·09	31·75
13	0·00	12·57	19·03	26·37	42·06	–	–	28	0·00	0·00	9·17	12·93	21·69	26·23	30·78
14	0·00	11·71	17·76	24·67	39·63	46·45	–	29	0·00	0·00	8·86	12·50	21·01	25·43	29·88
15	0·00	10·96	16·64	23·17	37·46	44·10	–	30	0·00	0·00	0·00	12·10	20·36	24·67	29·02
16	0·00	10·29	15·66	21·85	35·50	41·96	–	35	0·00	0·00	0·00	10·44	17·66	21·47	25·36
17	0·00	9·71	14·79	20·66	33·73	40·00	45·82	40	0·00	0·00	0·00	9·17	15·58	18·99	22·51
18	0·00	9·19	14·01	19·60	32·12	38·21	43·93	45	0·00	0·00	0·00	0·00	13·94	17·03	20·23
19	0·00	8·72	13·31	18·64	30·66	36·56	42·17								

Note 1. Blanks indicate percentage of reinforcement exceeding limiting value.
Note 2. Zeros indicate inadmissible reinforcement percentage (less than minimum permissible).

Table 9·34. Moment of Resistance of Slabs, kN-m per metre width

f_{ck} = 15 N/mm² f_y = 250 N/mm² Thickness = 20·0 cm.

Bar Spacing, cm	Bar Diameter, mm 6	8	10	12	16	18	20	22	25
5	21·21	35·88	52·48	69·39	–	–	–	–	–
6	17·84	30·41	44·98	60·41	–	–	–	–	–
7	15·39	26·38	39·32	53·37	–	–	–	–	–
8	15·53	23·39	34·91	47·74	–	–	–	–	–
9	12·07	20·84	31·38	43·15	67·31	–	–	–	–
10	0·00	18·86	28·49	39·35	62·21	–	–	–	–
11	0·00	17·22	26·08	36·16	57·77	–	–	–	–
12	0·00	15·84	24·05	33·44	53·89	63·38	–	–	–
13	0·00	14·67	22·31	31·10	50·47	59·67	–	–	–
14	0·00	13·66	20·81	29·06	47·44	56·33	–	–	–
15	0·00	12·78	19·49	27·27	44·74	53·32	61·43	–	–
16	0·00	12·00	18·33	25·69	42·33	50·61	58·53	–	–
17	0·00	0·00	17·30	24·28	40·16	48·14	55·86	–	–
18	0·00	0·00	16·38	23·01	38·20	45·89	53·41	60·43	–
19	0·00	0·00	15·55	21·87	36·41	43·84	51·15	58·06	–
20	0·00	0·00	14·81	20·84	34·78	41·96	49·07	55·85	–
21	0·00	0·00	14·13	19·90	33·30	40·23	47·14	53·79	–
22	0·00	0·00	13·51	19·04	31·93	38·63	45·35	51·96	–
23	0·00	0·00	12·94	18·25	30·66	37·15	43·69	50·05	58·81
24	0·00	0·00	12·42	17·53	29·50	35·78	42·14	48·37	57·02
25	0·00	0·00	11·93	16·86	28·42	34·51	40·69	40·78	55·33
26	0·00	0·00	11·49	16·24	27·41	33·32	39·34	45·30	53·72
27	0·00	0·00	0·00	15·66	26·47	32·21	38·07	43·90	52·19
28	0·00	0·00	0·00	15·12	25·60	31·17	36·88	42·58	50·74
29	0·00	0·00	0·00	14·62	24·78	30·20	35·76	41·33	49·36
30	0·00	0·00	0·00	14·15	24·01	29·28	34·71	40·16	48·06
35	0·00	0·00	0·00	12·19	20·78	25·42	30·24	35·14	42·38
40	0·00	0·00	0·00	0·00	18·31	22·45	26·78	31·21	37·87
45	0·00	0·00	0·00	0·00	16·37	20·10	24·03	28·07	34·20

Note 1. Blanks indicate percentage of reinforcement exceeding limiting value·
Note 2. Zeros indicate inadmissible reinforcement percentage (less than minimum permissible)·

Table 9B·35. Moment of Resistance of Slabs, kN-m per metre width

f_{ck} = 15 N/mm^2,
f_y = 250 N/mm^2,
Thickness = 22·5 cm

Bar Spacing, cm	Bar Diameter, mm								
	6	8	10	12	16	18	20	22	25
5	24·28	41·34	61·02	81·69	–	–	–	–	–
6	20·40	34·96	52·10	70·66	–	–	–	–	–
7	17·58	30·28	45·42	62·15	–	–	–	–	–
8	15·45	26·70	40·24	55·42	86·82	–	–	–	–
9	0·00	23·88	36·12	49·98	79·45	–	–	–	–
10	0·00	21·59	32·76	45·50	73·14	85·96	–	–	–
11	0·00	19·70	29·96	41·75	67·71	80·09	–	–	–
12	0·00	18·12	27·61	38·56	62·99	74·91	–	–	–
13	0·00	16·77	25·60	35·83	58·87	70·31	81·18	–	–
14	0·00	15·61	23·86	33·45	55·24	66·21	76·79	–	–
15	0·00	0·00	22·34	31·37	52·03	62·54	72·81	–	–
16	0·00	0·00	21·00	29·53	49·16	59·25	69·20	78·62	–
17	0·00	0·00	19·81	27·89	46·59	56·27	65·91	75·13	–
18	0·00	0·00	18·75	26·43	44·27	53·58	62·90	71·91	–
19	0·00	0·00	17·80	25·11	42·16	51·12	60·14	68·93	–
20	0·00	0·00	16·94	23·91	40·25	48·87	57·61	66·18	78·11
21	0·00	0·00	16·16	22·83	38·50	46·81	55·27	63·63	75·39
22	0·00	0·00	15·45	21·84	36·89	44·92	53·11	61·25	72·82
23	0·00	0·00	14·79	20·93	35·42	43·17	51·11	59·04	70·41
24	0·00	0·00	0·00	20·09	34·05	41·55	49·25	56·98	68·14
25	0·00	0·00	0·00	19·32	32·79	40·04	47·52	55·05	66·00
26	0·00	0·00	0·00	18·60	31·61	38·64	45·91	53·24	63·98
27	0·00	0·00	0·00	17·94	30·52	37·33	44·40	51·55	62·07
28	0·00	0·00	0·00	17·32	29·50	36·11	42·98	49·96	60·27
29	0·00	0·00	0·00	16·74	28·54	34·97	41·65	48·96	58·56
30	0·00	0·00	0·00	16·20	27·65	33·89	40·40	47·04	56·95
35	0·00	0·00	0·00	0·00	23·90	29·37	35·12	41·04	50·01
40	0·00	0·00	0·00	0·00	21·04	25·91	31·05	36·38	44·54
45	0·00	0·00	0·00	0·00	18·80	23·18	27·82	32·66	40·13

Note 1. Blanks indicate percentage of reinforcement exceeding limiting value.

Note 2. Zeros indicate inadmissible reinforcement percentage (less than minimum permissible).

Table 9B·36. Moment of Resistant of Slabs, kN-m per metre width

f_{ck} = 15 N/mm^2,
f_y = 250 N/mm^2,
Thickness = 25·0 cm

Bar Spacing, cm	Bar Diameter, mm								
	6	8	10	12	16	18	20	22	25
5	27·36	46·80	69·56	93·98	–	–	–	–	–
6	22·96	39·51	59·21	80·90	–	–	–	–	–
7	19·48	34·18	51·52	70·93	111·08	–	–	–	–
8	0·00	30·12	45·58	63·10	100·48	–	–	–	–
9	0·00	26·91	40·86	56·81	91·59	107·96	–	–	–
10	0·00	24·32	37·02	51·65	84·07	99·79	–	–	–
11	0·00	22·19	33·84	47·34	77·64	92·66	109·90	–	–
12	0·00	20·40	31·17	43·69	72·10	86·43	100·26	–	–
13	0·00	18·87	28·88	40·55	67·28	80·94	94·32	–	–
14	0·00	0·00	26·90	37·84	63·05	76·09	88·99	101·25	–
15	0·00	0·00	25·18	35·47	59·31	71·76	84·20	96·17	–
16	0·00	0·00	23·67	33·37	55·99	67·89	79·87	91·53	–
17	0·00	0·00	22·32	31·51	53·01	64·41	75·95	87·28	–
18	0·00	0·00	21·12	29·84	50·34	61·26	72·38	83·39	98·90
19	0·00	0·00	20·05	28·34	47·91	58·40	69·13	79·81	95·05
20	0·00	0·00	19·07	26·99	45·71	55·79	66·14	76·51	91·45
21	0·00	0·00	0·00	25·75	43·70	53·40	63·40	73·46	88·09
22	0·00	0·00	0·00	24·63	41·86	51·20	60·87	70·64	84·95
23	0·00	0·00	0·00	23·60	40·17	49·18	58·53	68·02	82·01
24	0·00	0·00	0·00	22·65	38·60	47·31	56·37	65·58	79·25
25	0·00	0·00	0·00	21·78	37·16	45·57	54·35	63·31	76·67
26	0·00	0·00	0·00	20·97	35·82	43·96	52·47	61·19	74·24
27	0·00	0·00	0·00	20·21	34·57	42·46	50·72	59·20	71·95
28	0·00	0·00	0·00	19·51	33·40	41·05	49·08	57·33	69·80
29	0·00	0·00	0·00	18·86	32·31	39·74	47·54	55·58	67·76
30	0·00	0·00	0·00	18·25	31·29	38·50	46·09	53·93	65·84
35	0·00	0·00	0·00	0·00	27·02	33·32	40·00	46·94	57·63
40	0·00	0·00	0·00	0·00	23·78	29·37	35·32	41·54	51·21
45	0·00	0·00	0·00	0·00	21·22	26·25	31·61	37·25	46·06

Note 1. Blanks indicate percentage of reinforcement exceeding limiting value.

Note 2. Zeros indicate inadmissible reinforcement percentage (less than minimum permissible).

Table 9B·37. Flexure–Moment of Resistance of Slabs, kN-m Per Meter width

f_{ck} = 15 N/mm² f_y = 415 N/mm² Thickness = 10·0 cm

Bar Spacing, cm	Bar Diameter, mm 6	8	10	12	Bar Spacing, cm	Bar Diameter, mm 6	8	10	12
5	13·53	–	–	–	20	3·98	6·71	9·79	12·91
6	11·72	–	–	–	21	3·80	6·42	9·39	12·44
7	10·32	–	–	–	22	3·64	6·15	9·03	12·00
8	9·21	–	–	–	23	3·49	5·91	8·69	11·59
9	8·31	13·20	–	–	24	0·00	5·68	8·38	11·21
10	7·56	12·16	–	–	25	0·00	5·47	8·08	10·84
11	6·94	11·26	–	–	26	0·00	5·28	7·81	10·50
12	6·42	10·48	–	–	27	0·00	5·09	7·55	10·18
13	5·96	9·80	–	–	28	0·00	4·92	7·31	9·88
14	5·57	9·20	13·04	–	29	0·00	4·77	7·08	9·59
15	5·22	8·67	12·37	–	30	0·00	4·62	6·87	9·32
16	4·92	8·19	11·75	–	35	0·00	3·99	5·97	8·16
17	4·64	7·77	11·20	–	40	0·00	3·51	5·28	7·26
18	4·40	7·38	10·69	–					
19	4·18	7·03	10·22	–					

Note 1. Blanks indicate percentage of reinforcement exceeding limiting value.
Note 2. Zeros indicate inadmissible reinforcement percentage (less than minimum permissible).
Note 3. Bar spacing below the dividing line exceed $3d$.

Table 9B·38. Flexure—Moment of Resistance of Slabs, kN-m Per Metre Width

f_{ck} = 15 N/mm² f_y = 415 N/mm² Thickness = 11·0 cm

Bar Spacing, cm	Bar Diameter, mm 6	8	10	12	Bar Spacing, cm	Bar Diameter, mm 6	8	10	12
5	15·57	–	–	–	20	4·49	7·62	11·21	14·95
6	13·42	–	–	–	21	4·29	7·29	10·74	14·39
7	11·77	–	–	–	22	0·00	6·98	10·32	13·86
8	10·48	16·67	–	–	23	0·00	6·70	9·92	13·37
9	9·44	15·21	–	–	24	0·00	6·44	9·55	12·91
10	8·59	13·97	–	–	25	0·00	6·20	9·21	12·48
11	7·87	12·91	–	–	26	0·00	5·97	8·90	12·07
12	7·27	12·00	–	–	27	0·00	5·77	8·60	11·69
13	6·75	11·20	15·96	–	28	0·00	5·57	8·32	11·34
14	6·30	10·50	15·06	–	29	0·00	5·39	8·06	11·00
15	5·90	9·88	14·26	–	30	0·00	5·22	7·82	10·68
16	5·55	9·33	13·53	–	35	0·00	4·51	6·78	9·33
17	5·24	8·83	12·86	–	40	0·00	0·00	5·99	8·28
18	4·97	8·39	12·26	16·22	45	0·00	0·00	5·36	7·44
19	4·72	7·99	11·71	15·56					

Note 1. Blanks indicate percentage of reinforcement exceeding limiting value.
Note 2. Zeros indicate inadmissible reinforcement percentage (less than minimum permissible).
Note 3. Bar spacings below the dividing line exceed $3d$.

Table 9B·39. Flexure—Moment of Resistance of Slabs, kN-m Per Metre Width

f_{ck} = 15 N/mm^2 f_y =415 N/mm^2 Thickness = 12·0 cm

Bar Spacing, cm	Bar Diameter, mm 6	8	10	12	Bar Spacing, cm	Bar Diameter, mm 6	8	10	12
5	17·61	–	–	–	20	0·00	8·53	12·62	16·99
6	15·12	–	–	–	21	0·00	8·15	12·09	16·33
7	13·23	21·00	–	–	22	0·00	7·80	11·60	15·71
8	11·76	18·94	–	–	23	0·00	7·49	11·15	15·14
9	10·57	17·23	–	–	24	0·00	7·19	10·74	14·61
10	9·61	15·79	–	–	25	0·00	6·92	10·35	14·11
11	8·80	14·56	20·65	–	26	0·00	6·67	9·99	13·64
12	8·12	13·51	19·32	–	27	0·00	6·44	9·65	13·20
13	7·53	12·59	18·14	–	28	0·00	6·22	9·33	12·79
14	7·02	11·79	17·09	–	29	0·00	6·02	9·04	12·41
15	6·58	11·09	16·14	–	30	0·00	5·83	8·76	12·04
16	6·19	10·46	15·30	20·24	35	0·00	0·00	7·59	10·50
17	5·84	9·90	14·53	19·33	40	0·00	0·00	6·70	9·30
18	5·53	9·40	13·84	18·49	45	0·00	0·00	5·99	8·35
19	5·26	8·94	13·20	17·71					

Note 1. Blanks indicate percentage of reinforcement exceeding limiting value.
Note 2. Zeros indicate inadmissible reinforcement percentage (less than minimum permissible).
Note 3. Bar spacings below the dividing line exceed 3*d*.

Table 9B·40. Flexure—Moment Resistance of Slabs, kN-m Per Meter Width

f_{ck} =15 N/mm^2 f_y = 415 N/mm^2 Thickness = 13·0 cm

Bar Spacing, cm	Bar Diameter, mm 6	8	10	12	16	Bar Spacing, cm	Bar Diameter, mm 6	8	10	12	16
5	19·65	–	–	–	–	20	0·00	9·43	14·04	19·04	–
6	16·82	–	–	–	–	21	0·00	9·01	13·44	18·27	–
7	14·69	23·59	–	–	–	22	0·00	8·63	12·89	17·57	–
8	13·03	21·21	–	–	–	23	0·00	8·28	12·39	16·92	–
9	11·71	19·24	–	–	–	24	0·00	7·95	11·92	16·31	–
10	10·63	17·60	24·99	–	–	25	0·00	7·65	11·48	15·74	–
11	9·73	16·21	23·23	–	–	26	0·00	7·37	11·08	15·21	–
12	8·97	15·02	21·68	–	–	27	0·00	7·11	10·70	14·72	22·92
13	8·32	13·99	20·32	–	–	28	0·00	6·87	10·35	14·25	22·30
14	7·75	13·09	19·11	–	–	29	0·00	6·64	10·01	13·81	21·70
15	7·26	12·30	18·03	23·95	–	30	0·00	6·43	9·70	13·40	21·13
16	6·83	11·59	17·07	22·79	–	35	0·00	0·00	8·40	11·66	18·66
17	6·44	10·97	16·20	21·73	–	40	0·00	0·00	7·41	10·32	16·69
18	6·10	10·40	15·41	20·75	–	45	0·00	0·00	6·62	9·25	15·09
19	0·00	9·90	14·69	19·86	–						

Note 1. Blanks indicate percentage of reinforcement exceeding limiting value·
Note 2. Zeros indicate inadmissible reinforcement percentage (less than minimum permissible)·
Note 3. Bar spacings below the dividing line exceed 3*d*·

Table 9B·41. Flexure Moment of Resistance of Slabs, kN-m Per Metre Width

f_{ck} = 15 N/mm^2 f_y = 415 N/mm^2 Thickness = 14·0 cm

Bar Spacing, cm	Bar Diameter, mm 6	8	10	12	16	Bar Spacing, cm	Bar Diameter, mm 6	8	10	12	16
5	21·69	–	–	–	–	20	0·00	10·34	15·46	21·08	–
6	18·52	29·54	–	–	–	21	0·00	9·88	14·79	20·22	–
7	16·15	26·18	–	–	–	22	0·00	9·45	14·18	19·43	–
8	14·31	23·48	–	–	–	23	0·00	9·06	13·62	18·69	–
9	12·84	21·26	–	–	–	24	0·00	8·71	13·10	18·01	–
10	11·65	19·41	27·82	–	–	25	0·00	8·37	12·61	17·37	27·18
11	10·65	17·86	25·80	–	–	26	0·00	8·07	12·17	16·78	26·37
12	9·82	16·53	24·05	–	–	27	0·00	7·78	11·75	16·23	25·61
13	9·10	15·38	22·50	–	–	28	0·00	7·52	11·36	15·71	24·89
14	8·48	14·38	21·14	28·14	–	29	0·00	7·27	10·99	15·22	24·20
15	7·94	13·51	19·92	26·68	–	30	0·00	0·00	10·65	14·76	23·55
16	7·47	12·73	18·84	25·34	–	35	0·00	0·00	9·21	12·83	20·74
17	0·00	12·03	17·87	24·13	–	40	0·00	0·00	8·12	11·34	18·51
18	0·00	11·41	16·99	23·02	–	45	0·00	0·00	7·25	10·16	16·70
19	0·00	10·85	16·19	22·01	–						

Note 1. Blanks indicator percentage of reinforcement exceeding limiting value.
Note 2. Zeros indicate inadmissible reinforcement percentage (less than minimum permissible).
Note 3. Bar spacings below the dividing line exceed *3d*.

Table 9B·42. Flexure—Moment of Resistance of Slabs, kN-m per metre width

f_{ck} = 15 N/mm^2, f_y = 415 N/mm^2 Thickness = 15·0 cm

Bar Spacing, cm	Bar Diameter, mm 6	8	10	12	16	18	Bar Spacing, cm	Bar Diameter, mm 6	8	10	12	16	18
5	23·73	–	–	–	–	–	20	0·00	11·25	16·88	23·12	–	–
6	20·22	32·56	–	–	–	–	21	0·00	10·74	16·14	22·16	–	–
7	17·60	28·77	–	–	–	–	22	0·00	10·28	15·47	21·28	–	–
8	15·58	25·74	–	–	–	–	23	0·00	9·85	14·85	20·47	32·08	–
9	13·97	23·27	33·30	–	–	–	24	0·00	9·46	14·28	19·71	31·05	–
10	12·67	21·23	30·66	–	–	–	25	0·00	9·10	13·75	19·01	30·08	–
11	11·58	19·51	28·38	–	–	–	26	0·00	8·76	13·26	18·35	29·16	–
12	10·67	18·04	26·48	–	–	–	27	0·00	8·45	12·80	17·74	28·30	–
13	9·89	16·78	24·68	32·91	–	–	28	0·00	0·00	12·37	17·17	27·48	–
14	9·21	15·68	23·16	31·06	–	–	29	0·00	0·00	11·97	16·63	26·70	31·22
15	8·62	14·72	21·81	29·40	–	–	30	0·00	0·00	11·59	16·12	25·97	30·43
16	0·00	13·86	20·61	27·89	–	–	35	0·00	0·00	10·02	14·00	22·81	26·97
17	0·00	13·10	19·53	25·53	–	–	40	0·00	0·00	8·82	12·36	20·32	24·18
18	0·00	12·42	18·56	25·29	–	–	45	0·00	0·00	0·00	11·07	18·31	21·89
19	0·00	11·80	17·68	24·16	–	–							

Note 1. Blanks indicate percentage of reinforcement exceeding limiting value.
Note 2. Zeros indicate inadmissible reinforcement percentage (less than minimum permissible).

Table 9B·43. Flexure—Moment of Resistance of Slabs, kN-m Per Metre Width

f_{ck} = 15 N/mm^2,
f_y = 415 N/mm^2,
Thickness = 17·5 cm

Bar Spacing, cm	Bar Diameter, mm 6	8	10	12	16	18	20
5	28·83	46·46	–	–	–	–	–
6	24·47	40·12	–	–	–	–	–
7	21·25	35·25	–	–	–	–	–
8	18·77	31·41	45·24	–	–	–	–
9	16·81	28·31	41·17	–	–	–	–
10	15·22	25·76	37·74	–	–	–	–
11	13·90	23·63	34·82	46·53	–	–	–
12	12·79	21·82	32·31	43·47	–	–	–
13	11·85	20·27	30·13	40·76	–	–	–
14	0·00	18·92	28·22	38·35	–	–	–
15	0·00	17·44	26·55	36·20	–	–	–
16	0·00	16·70	25·04	34·27	–	–	–
17	0·00	15·77	23·70	32·53	–	–	–
18	0·00	14·94	22·50	30·96	–	–	–
19	0·00	14·19	21·41	29·53	46·43	–	–
20	0·00	13·51	20·42	28·22	44·64	–	–
21	0·00	12·90	19·52	27·02	42·98	–	–
22	0·00	12·34	18·69	25·92	41·42	–	–
23	0·00	11·82	17·93	24·90	39·97	–	–
24	0·00	0·00	17·23	23·96	38·61	45·35	–
25	0·00	0·00	16·58	23·09	37·34	43·97	–
26	0·00	0·00	15·98	22·28	36·14	42·66	–
27	0·00	0·00	15·42	21·52	35·02	41·43	–
28	0·00	0·00	14·90	20·81	33·96	40·25	–
29	0·00	0·00	14·41	20·15	32·96	39·14	–
30	0·00	0·00	13·96	19·53	32·01	38·08	–
35	0·00	0·00	12·05	16·91	27·99	33·53	38·89
40	0·00	0·00	0·00	14·91	24·86	29·92	34·91
45	0·00	0·00	0·00	13·33	22·34	26·99	31·64

Note 1. Blanks indicate percentage of reinforcement exceeding limiting value.
Note 2. Zeros indicate inadmissible reinforcement percentage (less than minimum permissible).

Table 9B·44. Flexure—Moment of Resistance of Slabs, kN-m per metre width

f_{ck} = 15 N/mm², f_y = 415 N/mm², Thickness = 20 cm

Bar Spacing, cm	Bar Diameter, mm								
	6	8	10	12	16	18	20	22	25
5	33·93	55·53	–	–	–	–	–	–	–
6	28·72	47·68	–	–	–	–	–	–	–
7	24·89	41·73	60·25	–	–	–	–	–	–
8	21·96	37·08	54·10	–	–	–	–	–	–
9	19·64	33·35	49·05	65·33	–	–	–	–	–
10	17·77	30·30	44·83	60·22	–	–	–	–	–
11	16·22	27·75	41·26	55·81	–	–	–	–	–
12	0·00	25·60	38·22	51·97	–	–	–	–	–
13	0·00	23·76	35·58	48·60	–	–	–	–	–
14	0·00	22·16	33·28	45·64	–	–	–	–	–
15	0·00	20·76	31·26	43·00	–	–	–	–	–
16	0·00	19·53	29·47	40·65	63·97	–	–	–	–
17	0·00	18·44	27·87	38·53	61·08	–	–	–	–
18	0·00	17·46	26·43	36·63	58·43	–	–	–	–
19	0·00	16·58	25·14	34·90	55·98	–	–	–	–
20	0·00	15·78	23·96	33·32	53·71	–	–	–	–
21	0·00	0·00	22·89	31·88	51·61	60·92	–	–	–
22	0·00	0·00	21·91	30·56	49·67	58·89	–	–	–
23	0·00	0·00	21·01	29·34	47·86	56·79	–	–	–
24	0·00	0·00	20·18	28·21	46·17	54·92	–	–	–
25	0·00	0·00	19·42	27·17	44·59	53·15	–	–	–
26	0·00	0·00	18·71	26·20	43·12	51·49	59·48	–	–
27	0·00	0·00	18·05	25·30	41·73	49·93	57·80	–	–
28	0·00	0·00	17·43	24·45	40·43	48·45	56·20	–	–
29	0·00	0·00	16·86	23·67	39·21	47·06	54·69	–	–
30	0·00	0·00	16·32	22·93	38·06	45·74	53·24	–	–
35	0·00	0·00	0·00	19·83	33·18	40·09	46·98	53·62	–
40	0·00	0·00	0·00	17·46	29·39	35·66	41·99	48·21	–
45	0·00	0·00	0·00	15·60	26·38	32·10	37·94	43·75	52·03

Note 1. Blanks indicate percentage of reinforcement exceeding limiting value·

Note 2. Zeros indicate inadmissible reinforcement percentage (less than minimum permissible)·

Table 9B·45. Flexure—Moment of Resistance of Slabs, kN-m Per Metre Width

f_{ck} = 15 N/mm^2,
f_y = 415 N/mm^2,
Thickness = 22·5 cm

Bar Spacing, cm	Bar Diameter, mm								
	6	8	10	12	16	18	20	22	25
5	39·03	64·59	–	–	–	–	–	–	–
6	32·97	55·24	79·65	–	–	–	–	–	–
7	28·54	48·21	70·37	–	–	–	–	–	–
8	25·15	42·75	62·96	84·02	–	–	–	–	–
9	22·48	38·39	56·92	76·67	–	–	–	–	–
10	20·32	34·83	51·91	70·43	–	–	–	–	–
11	0·00	31·88	47·71	65·09	–	–	–	–	–
12	0·00	29·38	44·12	60·47	–	–	–	–	–
13	0·00	27·24	41·03	56·45	–	–	–	–	–
14	0·00	25·40	38·34	52·92	83·48	–	–	–	–
15	0·00	23·78	35·98	49·80	79·20	–	–	–	–
16	0·00	22·36	33·90	47·02	75·31	–	–	–	–
17	0·00	21·10	32·04	44·54	71·75	–	–	–	–
18	0·00	19·98	30·37	42·29	68·50	80·96	–	–	–
19	0·00	0·00	28·87	40·27	65·52	77·70	–	–	–
20	0·00	0·00	27·50	38·42	62·78	74·67	–	–	–
21	0·00	0·00	26·26	36·74	60·25	71·85	–	–	–
22	0·00	0·00	25·13	35·19	57·91	69·23	–	–	–
23	0·00	0·00	24·09	33·77	55·74	66·77	77·40	–	–
24	0·00	0·00	23·14	32·46	53·73	64·48	74·92	–	–
25	0·00	0·00	22·25	31·25	51·85	62·34	72·59	–	–
26	0·00	0·00	21·43	30·12	50·09	60·32	70·38	–	–
27	0·00	0·00	20·67	29·08	48·45	58·43	68·30	–	–
28	0·00	0·00	19·96	28·10	46·91	56·65	66·33	75·57	–
29	0·00	0·00	19·30	27·18	45·47	54·97	64·46	73·58	–
30	0·00	0·00	0·00	26·33	44·11	53·39	62·69	71·69	–
35	0·00	0·00	0·00	22·74	38·36	46·65	55·08	63·42	–
40	0·00	0·00	0·00	20·01	33·93	41·40	49·48	56·79	67·93
45	0·00	0·00	0·00	0·00	30·41	37·20	44·24	51·37	61·87

Note 1. Blanks indicate percentage of reinforcement exceeding limiting value.
Note 2. Zeros indicate inadmissible reinforcement percentage (less than minimum permissible).

Table 9B·46. Flexure—Moment of Resistance of Slabs, kN-m. Per Metre Width

f_{ck} = 15 N/mm²,
f_y = 415 N/mm²,
Thickness = 25·0 cm

Bar Spacing,	Bar Diameter, mm								
cm	6	8	10	12	16	18	20	22	25
5	44·14	73·66	105·62	–	–	–	–	–	–
6	37·23	62·80	91·46	–	–	–	–	–	–
7	32·18	54·69	80·50	107·33	–	–	–	–	–
8	28·34	48·42	71·82	96·78	–	–	–	–	–
9	25·31	43·43	64·79	88·01	–	–	–	–	–
10	0·00	39·37	59·00	80·63	–	–	–	–	–
11	0·00	36·00	54·15	74·36	–	–	–	–	–
12	0·00	33·16	50·03	68·97	–	–	–	–	–
13	0·00	30·73	46·48	64·30	102·14	–	–	–	–
14	0·00	28·64	43·41	60·21	96·44	–	–	–	–
15	0·00	26·81	40·71	56·61	91·29	–	–	–	–
16	0·00	25·20	38·33	53·40	86·64	102·61	–	–	–
17	0·00	0·00	36·20	50·54	82·43	97·98	–	–	–
18	0·00	0·00	34·31	47·96	78·58	93·72	–	–	–
19	0·00	0·00	32·60	45·64	75·07	89·78	–	–	–
20	0·00	0·00	31·05	43·52	71·85	86·15	99·95	–	–
21	0·00	0·00	29·64	41·60	68·89	82·78	96·32	–	–
22	0·00	0·00	28·35	39·83	66·16	79·66	92·91	–	–
23	0·00	0·00	27·17	38·21	63·63	76·76	89·72	–	–
24	0·00	0·00	26·09	36·72	61·28	74·05	86·73	–	–
25	0·00	0·00	25·09	35·33	59·10	71·52	83·92	95·88	–
26	0·00	0·00	24·16	34·05	57·07	69·15	81·28	93·05	–
27	0·00	0·00	0·00	32·86	55·17	66·93	78·79	90·37	–
28	0·00	0·00	0·00	31·74	53·39	64·85	76·45	87·82	–
29	0·00	0·00	0·00	30·70	51·72	62·89	74·23	85·41	–
30	0·00	0·00	0·00	29·73	50·15	61·04	72·14	83·12	–
35	0·00	0·00	0·00	25·66	43·54	53·21	63·18	73·22	87·82
40	0·00	0·00	0·00	0·00	38·46	47·14	56·17	65·36	79·00
45	0·00	0·00	0·00	0·00	34·44	42·30	50·54	58·99	71·71

Note 1. Blanks indicate percentage of reinforcement exceeding limiting value.
Note 2. Zeros indicate inadmissible reinforcement percentage,(less than minimum permissible).

Table 9B·47. Flexure - Moment Of Resistance Of Slabs, kN-m Per Metre Width

f_{ck} = 20 N/mm^2,

f_y = 250 N/mm^2,

Thickness = 10·0 cm

Bar Spacing cm	Bar Diameter, mm			
	6	8	10	12
5	9·21	14·94	0·00	0·00
6	7·79	12·84	18·09	0·00
7	6·75	11·24	16·08	0·00
8	5·96	9·99	14·44	0·00
9	5·33	8·98	13·10	17·27
10	4·82	8·16	11·97	15·93
11	4·40	7·48	11·03	14·77
12	4·05	6·90	10·21	13·76
13	3·75	6·40	9·51	12·87
14	3·49	5·97	8·90	12·09
15	3·26	5·59	8·36	11·40
16	3·06	5·26	7·88	10·78
17	2·89	4·97	7·45	10·22
18	2·73	4·70	7·07	9·71
19	0·00	4·47	6·72	9·26
20	0·00	4·25	6·41	8·84
21	0·00	4·06	6·12	8·46
22	0·00	3·88	5·86	8·11
23	0·00	3·72	5·62	7·78
24	0·00	3·57	5·40	7·49
25	0·00	3·43	5·19	7·21
26	0·00	3·30	5·00	6·95
27	0·00	3·18	4·83	6·71
28	0·00	3·07	4·66	6·49
29	0·00	2·97	4·51	6·28
30	0·00	2·87	4·37	6·09
35	0·00	0·00	3·77	5·26
40	0·00	0·00	3·31	4·64

Note 1. Zeros indicate inadmissible reinforcement percentage.

Note 2. Bar spacings below the dividing line exceed $3d$.

Table 9B·48. Flexure - Moment Of Resistance Of Slabs, kN-m Per Metre Width

f_{ck} = 20 N/mm^2,

f_y = 250 N/mm^2,

Thickness = 11·0 cm

Bar Spacing cm	Bar Diameter, mm			
	6	8	10	12
5	10·44	17·13	24·00	0·00
6	8·82	14·66	20·93	0·00
7	7·63	12·80	18·51	0·00
8	6·73	11·35	16·58	21·90
9	6·01	10·20	14·99	20·00
10	5·44	9·25	13·68	18·39
11	4·96	8·47	12·58	17·01
12	4·56	7·81	11·64	15·81
13	4·22	7·24	10·82	14·77
14	3·93	6·75	10·12	13·85
15	3·67	6·32	9·50	13·04
16	3·45	5·95	8·95	12·31
17	3·25	5·61	8·46	11·66
18	0·00	5·31	8·02	11·08
19	0·00	5·04	7·62	10·55
20	0·00	4·80	7·26	10·07
21	0·00	4·58	6·94	9·63
22	0·00	4·38	6·64	9·22
23	0·00	4·19	6·36	8·85
24	0·00	4·02	6·11	8·51
25	0·00	3·87	5·88	8·19
26	0·00	3·72	5·66	7·90
27	0·00	3·59	5·46	7·63
28	0·00	3·46	5·27	7·37
29	0·00	3·35	5·10	7·13
30	0·00	3·24	4·94	6·91
35	0·00	0·00	4·25	5·97
40	0·00	0·00	3·74	5·25
45	0·00	0·00	3·33	4·69

Note 1. Zeros indicate inadmissible reinforcement percentage.

Note 2. Bar spacings below the dividing line exceed $3d$.

Table 9B·49. Flexure - Moment Of Resistance Of Slabs, kN-m Per Metre Width

f_{ck} = 20 N/mm^2,

f_y = 250 N/mm^2,

Thickness = 12·0 cm

Bar Spacing cm	Bar Diameter, mm			
	6	8	10	12
5	11·67	19·31	27·41	0·00
6	9·84	16·48	23·78	0·00
7	8·51	14·36	20·95	27·64
8	7·50	12·72	18·71	24·97
9	6·70	11·41	16·89	22·73
10	6·05	10·35	15·39	20·85
11	5·52	9·46	14·13	19·24
12	5·07	8·72	13·06	17·86
13	4·69	8·08	12·14	16·66
14	4·37	7·53	11·34	15·60
15	4·08	7·05	10·63	14·67
16	0·00	6·63	10·01	13·85
17	0·00	6·25	9·46	13·11
18	0·00	5·92	8·97	12·44
19	0·00	5·62	8·52	11·84
20	0·00	5·35	8·12	11·30
21	0·00	5·10	7·75	10·80
22	0·00	4·87	7·41	10·34
23	0·00	4·67	7·11	9·92
24	0·00	4·48	6·82	9·54
25	0·00	4·30	6·56	9·18
26	0·00	4·14	6·32	8·85
27	0·00	3·99	6·09	8·54
28	0·00	0·00	5·88	8·25
29	0·00	0·00	5·69	7·98
30	0·00	0·00	5·50	7·73
35	0·00	0·00	4·74	6·67
40	0·00	0·00	4·16	5·87
45	0·00	0·00	0·00	5·24

Note 1. Zeros indicate inadmissible reinforcement percentage·

Note 2. Bar spacings below the dividing line exceed 3*d*.

Table 9B·50. Flexure - Moment Of Resistance Of Slabs, kN-m Per Metre Width

f_{ck} = 20 N/mm^2,

f_y = 250 N/mm^2,

Thickness = 13·0 cm

Bar Spacing cm	Bar Diameter, mm				
	6	8	10	12	16
5	12·90	21·50	30·83	0·00	0·00
6	10·87	18·30	26·62	34·96	0·00
7	9·39	15·92	23·39	31·16	0·00
8	8·26	14·08	20·84	28·04	0·00
9	7·38	12·63	18·79	25·47	0·00
10	6·67	11·44	17·10	23·31	0·00
11	6·08	10·46	15·68	21·48	33·00
12	5·57	9·63	14·48	19·91	30·94
13	5·17	8·92	13·45	18·55	29·11
14	4·81	8·31	12·56	17·36	27·46
15	0·00	7·78	11·77	16·31	25·98
16	0·00	7·31	11·08	15·39	24·65
17	0·00	6·90	10·47	14·56	23·43
18	0·00	6·53	9·91	13·81	22·33
19	0·00	6·19	9·42	13·14	21·33
20	0·00	5·89	8·97	12·53	20·41
21	0·00	5·62	8·56	11·97	19·56
22	0·00	5·37	8·19	11·46	18·78
23	0·00	5·14	7·85	10·99	18·06
24	0·00	4·93	7·53	10·56	17·39
25	0·00	4·74	7·24	10·16	16·77
26	0·00	0·00	6·97	9·79	16·19
27	0·00	0·00	6·72	9·45	15·65
28	0·00	0·00	6·49	9·13	15·14
29	0·00	0·00	6·28	8·83	14·66
30	0·00	0·00	6·07	8·55	14·22
35	0·00	0·00	5·23	7·37	12·34
40	0·00	0·00	4·59	6·48	10·89
45	0·00	0·00	0·00	5·78	9·75

Note 1. Zeros indicate inadmissible reinforcement percentage·

Note 2. Bar spacings below the dividing line exceed 3*d*.

Table 9B·51. Flexure - Moment Of Resistance Of Slabs, kN.m Per Metre Width

f_{ck} = 20 N/mm^2,

f_y = 250 N/mm^2,

Thickness = 14·0 cm

Bar Spacing cm	Bar Diameter, mm				
	6	8	10	12	16
5	14·12	23·68	34·24	0·00	0·00
6	11·89	20·12	29·47	39·06	0·00
7	10·27	17·48	25·83	34·67	0·00
8	9·03	15·45	22·98	31·12	0·00
9	8·06	13·84	20·69	28·20	0·00
10	7·28	12·53	18·80	25·77	39·66
11	6·64	11·45	17·23	23·71	36·97
12	6·10	10·54	15·90	21·96	34·59
13	5·64	9·76	14·76	20·44	32·47
14	0·00	9·09	13·78	19·12	30·58
15	0·00	8·51	12·91	17·95	28·90
16	0·00	7·99	12·15	16·92	27·38
17	0·00	7·54	11·47	16·00	26·01
18	0·00	7·13	10·86	15·18	24·76
19	0·00	6·77	10·32	14·43	23·63
20	0·00	6·44	9·82	13·76	22·59
21	0·00	6·14	9·37	13·14	21·64
22	0·00	5·87	8·97	12·58	20·77
23	0·00	5·62	8·59	12·06	19·96
24	0·00	0·00	8·24	11·58	19·21
25	0·00	0·00	7·93	11·14	18·51
26	0·00	0·00	7·63	10·74	17·87
27	0·00	0·00	7·36	10·36	17·26
28	0·00	0·00	7·10	10·00	16·70
29	0·00	0·00	6·86	9·67	16·17
30	0·00	0·00	6·64	9·36	15·67
35	0·00	0·00	5·72	8·07	13·59
40	0·00	0·00	0·00	7·10	11·99
45	0·00	0·00	0·00	6·33	10·72

Note 1. Zeros indicate inadmissible reinforcement percentage.

Note 2. Bar spacings below the dividing line exceed $3d$.

Table 9B·52. Flexure - Moment Of Resistance Of Slabs, kN.m Per Metre Width

f_{ck} = 20 N/mm^2,
f_y = 250 N/mm^2,
Thickness = 15·0 cm

Bar Spacing cm	Bar Diameter, mm					
	6	8	10	12	16	18
5	15·35	25·87	37·65	49·46	0·00	0·00
6	12·92	21·94	32·31	43·16	0·00	0·00
7	11·15	19·04	28·27	38·18	0·00	0·00
8	9·80	16·82	25·11	34·19	0·00	0·00
9	8·75	15·05	22·58	30·93	0·00	0·00
10	7·90	13·62	20·51	28·22	44·04	0·00
11	7·20	12·44	18·79	25·95	40·94	0·00
12	6·61	11·45	17·33	24·00	38·23	44·42
13	0·00	10·60	16·08	22·33	35·83	41·88
14	0·00	9·87	14·99	20·87	33·71	39·58
15	0·00	9·24	14·05	19·59	31·81	37·50
16	0·00	8·68	13·21	18·46	30·11	35·62
17	0·00	8·18	12·47	17·45	28·58	33·91
18	0·00	7·74	11·81	16·54	27·19	32·34
19	0·00	7·34	11·22	15·73	25·93	30·91
20	0·00	6·98	10·68	14·99	24·78	29·60
21	0·00	6·66	10·19	14·31	23·72	28·39
22	0·00	6·36	9·74	13·69	22·75	27·28
23	0·00	0·00	9·33	13·13	21·86	26·24
24	0·00	0·00	8·96	12·61	21·03	25·28
25	0·00	0·00	8·61	12·13	20·26	24·39
26	0·00	0·00	8·29	11·68	19·55	23·55
27	0·00	0·00	7·99	11·27	18·88	22·78
28	0·00	0·00	7·71	10·88	18·26	22·05
29	0·00	0·00	7·45	10·52	17·68	21·36
30	0·00	0·00	7·21	10·18	17·13	20·72
35	0·00	0·00	0·00	8·78	14·83	18·00
40	0·00	0·00	0·00	7·71	13·08	15·91
45	0·00	0·00	0·00	6·88	11·69	14·25

Note 1. Zeros indicate inadmissible reinforcement percentage.

Note 2. Bar spacings below the dividing line exceed $3d$.

Table 9B·53. Flexure - Moment Of Resistance Of Slabs, kN.m Per Metre Width

f_{ck} = 20 N/mm^2,

f_y = 250 N/mm^2,

Thickness = 17·5 cm

Bar Spacing cm	Bar Diameter, mm						
	6	8	10	12	16	18	20
5	18·43	31·33	46·19	61·76	0·00	0·00	0·00
6	15·48	26·49	39·43	53·40	0·00	0·00	0·00
7	13·34	22·94	34·37	46·96	0·00	0·00	0·00
8	11·72	20·23	30·45	41·87	65·25	0·00	0·00
9	10·45	18·09	27·33	37·76	59·71	0·00	0·00
10	9·43	16·36	24·78	34·37	54·96	64·19	0·00
11	0·00	14·93	22·67	31·53	50·88	59·82	0·00
12	0·00	13·73	20·88	29·13	47·34	55·95	0·00
13	0·00	12·70	19·36	27·06	44·24	52·52	60·23
14	0·00	11·82	18·04	25·26	41·51	49·46	56·99
15	0·00	11·06	16·89	23·69	39·09	46·72	54·04
16	0·00	10·38	15·88	22·30	36·94	44·26	51·57
17	0·00	9·79	14·98	21·06	35·00	42·04	48·93
18	0·00	9·26	14·18	19·96	33·26	40·03	46·70
19	0·00	8·78	13·46	18·96	31·68	38·19	44·66
20	0·00	0·00	12·81	18·06	30·24	36·52	42·78
21	0·00	0·00	12·22	17·24	28·93	34·98	41·05
22	0·00	0·00	11·68	16·49	27·72	33·56	39·45
23	0·00	0·00	11·19	15·80	26·61	32·25	37·96
24	0·00	0·00	10·73	15·17	25·58	31·04	36·58
25	0·00	0·00	10·32	14·59	24·63	29·92	35·30
26	0·00	0·00	9·93	14·05	23·75	28·87	34·10
27	0·00	0·00	9·57	13·54	22·93	27·90	32·98
28	0·00	0·00	9·24	13·08	22·16	26·99	31·93
29	0·00	0·00	8·93	12·64	21·45	26·13	30·94
30	0·00	0·00	0·00	12·23	20·77	25·33	30·02
35	0·00	0·00	0·00	10·53	17·96	21·95	26·09
40	0·00	0·00	0·00	9·25	15·81	19·36	23·07
45	0·00	0·00	0·00	0·00	14·12	17·32	20·68

Note. Zeros indicate inadmissible reinforcement percentage.

Table 9B·54. Flexure - Moment Of Resistance Of Slabs, kN.m Per Metre Width

f_{ck} = 20 N/mm^2,
f_y = 250 N/mm^2,
Thickness = 20·0 cm

Bar Spacing cm	Bar Diameter, mm								
	6	8	10	12	16	18	20	22	25
5	21·50	36·80	54·73	74·05	0·00	0·00	0·00	0·00	0·00
6	18·04	31·05	46·54	63·65	0·00	0·00	0·00	0·00	0·00
7	15·54	26·85	40·47	55·74	87·37	0·00	0·00	0·00	0·00
8	13·64	23·65	35·78	49·55	78·91	0·00	0·00	0·00	0·00
9	12·16	21·12	32·07	44·59	71·85	84·51	0·00	0·00	0·00
10	0·00	19·09	29·05	40·52	65·89	78·02	0·00	0·00	0·00
11	0·00	17·41	26·55	37·12	60·81	72·39	83·28	0·00	0·00
12	0·00	16·00	24·44	34·25	56·44	67·47	78·04	0·00	0·00
13	0·00	14·81	22·64	31·79	52·64	63·16	73·36	82·81	0·00
14	0·00	13·78	21·09	29·65	49·32	59·34	69·18	78·44	0·00
15	0·00	12·88	19·74	27·79	46·38	55·94	65·42	74·47	0·00
16	0·00	12·09	18·55	26·14	43·77	52·91	62·04	70·84	0·00
17	0·00	0·00	17·50	24·68	41·43	50·18	58·97	67·53	0·00
18	0·00	0·00	16·55	23·37	39·33	47·71	56·18	64·49	76·03
19	0·00	0·00	15·71	22·20	37·43	45·47	53·64	61·70	73·04
20	0·00	0·00	14·95	21·13	35·70	43·43	51·31	59·14	70·25
21	0·00	0·00	14·25	20·17	34·13	41·56	49·18	56·77	67·66
22	0·00	0·00	13·62	19·28	32·69	39·85	47·21	54·58	65·23
23	0·00	0·00	13·04	18·47	31·36	38·27	45·39	52·54	62·96
24	0·00	0·00	12·51	17·73	30·14	36·81	43·70	50·65	60·83
25	0·00	0·00	12·02	17·05	29·01	35·45	42·13	48·89	58·84
26	0·00	0·00	11·57	16·41	27·95	34·19	40·67	47·24	56·96
27	0·00	0·00	0·00	15·82	26·98	33·02	39·30	45·70	55·20
28	0·00	0·00	0·00	15·27	26·07	31·92	38·03	44·25	53·54
29	0·00	0·00	0·00	14·76	25·21	30·90	36·83	42·90	51·97
30	0·00	0·00	0·00	14·28	24·42	29·94	35·71	41·62	50·49
35	0·00	0·00	0·00	12·29	21·08	25·90	30·97	36·21	44·17
40	0·00	0·00	0·00	0·00	18·54	22·82	27·34	32·04	39·24
45	0·00	0·00	0·00	0·00	16·55	20·39	24·47	28·72	35·29

Note. Zeros indicate inadmissible reinforcement percentage.

Table 9B·55. Flexure - Moment Of Resistance Of Slabs, kN.m Per Metre Width

f_{ck} = 20 N/mm^2,

f_y = 250 N/mm^2,

Thickness = 22·5 cm

Bar Spacing cm	Bar Diameter, mm								
	6	8	10	12	16	18	20	22	25
5	24·57	42·26	63·27	86·34	0·00	0·00	0·00	0·00	0·00
6	20·60	35·60	53·66	73·89	115·76	0·00	0·00	0·00	0·00
7	17·73	30·75	46·56	64·52	102·98	0·00	0·00	0·00	0·00
8	15·56	27·06	41·12	57·24	92·57	109·29	0·00	0·00	0·00
9	0·00	24·16	36·81	51·42	83·99	99·87	0·00	0·00	0·00
10	0·00	21·82	33·32	46·66	76·82	91·85	106·23	0·00	0·00
11	0·00	19·89	30·43	42·71	70·75	84·96	98·80	0·00	0·00
12	0·00	18·28	28·00	39·37	65·55	79·00	92·27	104·82	0·00
13	0·00	16·91	25·93	36·52	61·05	73·79	86·50	98·70	0·00
14	0·00	15·73	24·14	34·04	57·12	69·22	81·38	93·20	0·00
15	0·00	0·00	22·59	31·89	53·66	65·16	76·81	88·24	104·15
16	0·00	0·00	21·22	29·98	50·60	61·55	72·71	83·75	99·35
17	0·00	0·00	20·01	28·30	47·86	58·31	69·01	79·68	94·93
18	0·00	0·00	18·93	26·79	45·40	55·39	65·67	75·97	90·85
19	0·00	0·00	17·96	25·43	43·18	52·75	62·63	72·58	87·08
20	0·00	0·00	17·08	24·21	41·17	50·35	59·85	69·47	83·59
21	0·00	0·00	16·29	23·09	39·33	48·15	57·31	66·61	80·36
22	0·00	0·00	15·56	22·08	37·65	46·13	54·97	63·97	77·35
23	0·00	0·00	14·90	21·15	36·11	44·28	52·81	61·53	74·56
24	0·00	0·00	0·00	20·29	34·69	42·57	50·81	59·26	71·95
25	0·00	0·00	0·00	19·50	33·38	40·98	48·96	57·15	69·51
26	0·00	0·00	0·00	18·77	32·16	39·51	47·24	55·19	67·22
27	0·00	0·00	0·00	18·10	31·02	38·14	45·63	53·35	65·08
28	0·00	0·00	0·00	17·47	29·97	36·86	44·13	51·63	63·07
29	0·00	0·00	0·00	16·88	28·98	35·67	42·72	50·02	61·17
30	0·00	0·00	0·00	16·33	28·06	34·55	41·40	48·50	59·38
35	0·00	0·00	0·00	0·00	24·20	29·85	35·85	42·11	51·80
40	0·00	0·00	0·00	0·00	21·27	26·28	31·61	37·20	45·91
45	0·00	0·00	0·00	0·00	18·98	23·47	28·26	33·31	41·21

Note. Zeros indicate inadmissible reinforcement percentage.

Table 9B·56. Flexure - Moment Of Resistance Of Slabs, kN.m Per Metre Width

f_{ck} = 20 N/mm^2,
f_y = 250 N/mm^2,
Thickness = 25·0 cm

Bar Spacing cm	Bar Diameter, mm								
	6	8	10	12	16	18	20	22	25
5	27·65	47·72	71·80	98·64	0·00	0·00	0·00	0·00	0·00
6	23·16	40·15	60·77	84·14	133·98	0·00	0·00	0·00	0·00
7	19·93	34·65	52·66	73·30	118·59	140·15	0·00	0·00	0·00
8	0·00	30·47	46·46	64·92	106·23	126·58	0·00	0·00	0·00
9	0·00	27·20	41·55	58·25	96·13	115·24	133·67	0·00	0·00
10	0·00	24·55	37·59	52·81	87·74	105·68	123·40	139·87	0·00
11	0·00	22·38	34·31	48·30	80·68	97·53	114·32	130·41	0·00
12	0·00	20·56	31·56	44·49	74·65	90·52	106·49	122·04	0·00
13	0·00	19·01	29·21	41·24	69·46	84·43	99·63	114·59	0·00
14	0·00	0·00	27·19	38·43	64·93	79·09	93·57	107·96	128·41
15	0·00	0·00	25·43	35·98	60·95	74·38	88·19	102·01	121·93
16	0·00	0·00	23·89	33·83	57·43	70·19	83·38	96·66	116·03
17	0·00	0·00	22·52	31·91	54·29	66·45	79·06	91·83	110·62
18	0·00	0·00	21·30	30·20	51·47	63·08	75·15	87·45	105·67
19	0·00	0·00	20·20	28·67	48·93	60·03	71·61	83·45	101·12
20	0·00	0·00	19·21	27·28	46·63	57·26	68·39	79·80	96·93
21	0·00	0·00	0·00	26·02	44·54	54·73	65·44	76·45	93·06
22	0·00	0·00	0·00	24·87	42·62	52·42	62·73	73·36	89·48
23	0·00	0·00	0·00	23·82	40·86	50·29	60·23	70·51	86·16
24	0·00	0·00	0·00	22·85	39·24	48·33	57·93	67·87	83·06
25	0·00	0·00	0·00	21·96	37·75	46·52	55·79	65·42	80·18
26	0·00	0·00	0·00	21·14	36·36	44·83	53·80	63·13	77·48
27	0·00	0·00	0·00	20·37	35·07	43·26	51·95	61·00	74·96
28	0·00	0·00	0·00	19·66	33·87	41·80	50·22	59·01	72·59
29	0·00	0·00	0·00	19·00	32·75	40·44	48·61	57·14	70·37
30	0·00	0·00	0·00	18·38	31·70	39·16	47·09	55·39	68·28
35	0·00	0·00	0·00	0·00	27·32	33·80	40·73	48·01	59·42
40	0·00	0·00	0·00	0·00	24·01	29·74	35·88	42·36	52·58
45	0·00	0·00	0·00	0·00	21·41	26·54	32·06	37·90	47·14

Note. Zeros indicate inadmissible reinforcement percentage.

Table 9B·57. Flexure - Moment Of Resistance Of Slabs, kN.m Per Metre Width

f_{ck} = 20 N/mm^2,

f_y = 415 N/mm^2,

Thickness = 10·0 cm

Bar Spacing cm	Bar Diameter, mm			
	6	8	10	12
5	14·33	0·00	0·00	0·00
6	12·27	0·00	0·00	0·00
7	10·72	17·11	0·00	0·00
8	9·52	15·40	0·00	0·00
9	8·55	13·98	0·00	0·00
10	7·77	12·79	0·00	0·00
11	7·11	11·79	16·78	0·00
12	6·55	10·92	15·67	0·00
13	6·08	10·18	14·70	0·00
14	5·67	9·52	13·83	0·00
15	5·31	8·95	13·05	17·22
16	4·99	8·44	12·36	16·39
17	4·71	7·99	11·73	15·64
18	4·46	7·58	11·16	14·94
19	4·24	7·21	10·65	14·30
20	4·03	6·87	10·18	13·72
21	3·85	6·57	9·74	13·17
22	3·68	6·29	9·35	12·67
23	3·52	6·03	8·98	12·20
24	0·00	5·79	8·64	11·76
25	0·00	5·57	8·33	11·36
26	0·00	5·37	8·03	10·98
27	0·00	5·18	7·76	10·62
28	0·00	5·00	7·51	10·29
29	0·00	4·84	7·27	9·97
30	0·00	4·69	7·04	9·68
35	0·00	4·04	6·10	8·43
40	0·00	3·55	5·38	7·46

Note 1. Zeros indicate inadmissible reinforcement percentage.

Note 2. Bar spacings below the dividing line exceed 3*d*.

Table 9B·58. Flexure - Moment Of Resistance Of Slabs, kN.m Per Metre Width

f_{ck} = 20 N/mm^2,

f_y = 415 N/mm^2,

Thickness = 11·0 cm

Bar Spacing cm	Bar Diameter, mm			
	6	8	10	12
5	16·37	0·00	0·00	0·00
6	13·97	22·23	0·00	0·00
7	12·18	19·70	0·00	0·00
8	10·79	17·66	0·00	0·00
9	9·69	15·99	0·00	0·00
10	8·79	14·61	20·87	0·00
11	8·04	13·44	19·35	0·00
12	7·40	12·44	18·03	0·00
13	6·86	11·57	16·88	0·00
14	6·40	10·82	15·85	21·04
15	5·99	10·16	14·94	19·94
16	5·63	9·57	14·13	18·94
17	5·31	9·05	13·40	18·04
18	5·03	8·58	12·74	17·21
19	4·77	8·16	12·14	16·45
20	4·54	7·78	11·59	15·76
21	4·33	7·43	11·09	15·11
22	0·00	7·11	10·64	14·52
23	0·00	6·82	10·21	13·97
24	0·00	6·55	9·82	13·46
25	0·00	6·30	9·46	12·99
26	0·00	6·07	9·12	12·55
27	0·00	5·85	8·81	12·13
28	0·00	5·65	8·52	11·75
29	0·00	5·47	8·24	11·38
30	0·00	5·29	7·99	11·04
35	0·00	4·56	6·91	9·59
40	0·00	0·00	6·09	8·48
45	0·00	0·00	5·44	7·60

Note 1. Zeros indicate inadmissible reinforcement percentage.

Note 2. Bar spacings below the dividing line exceed 3*d*.

Table 9B·59. Flexure - Moment Of Resistance Of Slabs, kN.m Per Metre Width

f_{ck} = 20 N/mm^2,
f_y = 415 N/mm^2,
Thickness = 12·0 cm

Bar Spacing cm	Bar Diameter, mm			
	6	8	10	12
5	18·41	0·00	0·00	0·00
6	15·67	25·25	0·00	0·00
7	13·64	22·29	0·00	0·00
8	12·07	19·93	0·00	0·00
9	10·32	18·01	25·76	0·00
10	9·81	16·42	23·70	0·00
11	8·96	15·08	21·93	0·00
12	8·26	13·95	20·40	26·99
13	7·65	12·97	19·06	25·39
14	7·13	12·12	17·88	23·95
15	6·67	11·37	16·83	22·66
16	6·27	10·71	15·90	21·49
17	5·91	10·12	15·07	20·44
18	5·60	9·59	14·31	19·48
19	5·31	9·12	13·63	18·60
20	0·00	8·69	13·01	17·80
21	0·00	8·29	12·44	17·06
22	0·00	7·93	11·92	16·38
23	0·00	7·61	11·45	15·75
24	0·00	7·30	11·00	15·16
25	0·00	7·02	10·59	14·62
26	0·00	6·77	10·21	14·12
27	0·00	6·52	9·86	13·64
28	0·00	6·30	9·53	13·20
29	0·00	6·09	9·22	12·79
30	0·00	5·90	8·93	12·40
35	0·00	0·00	7·72	10·76
40	0·00	0·00	6·80	9·50
45	0·00	0·00	6·07	8·50

Note 1. Zeros indicate inadmissible reinforcement percentage·

Note 2. Bar spacings below the dividing line exceed $3d$·

Table 9B·60. Flexure-Moment Of Resistance Of Slabs, kN.m Per metre Width

f_{ck} = 20 N/mm^2,
f_y = 415 N/mm^2,
Thickness = 13·0 cm

Bar Spacing cm	Bar Diameter, mm				
	6	8	10	12	16
5	20·45	32·66	0·00	0·00	0·00
6	17·38	28·28	0·00	0·00	0·00
7	15·10	24·88	0·00	0·00	0·00
8	13·34	22·20	31·72	0·00	0·00
9	11·95	20·02	28·91	0·00	0·00
10	10·83	18·23	26·54	0·00	0·00
11	9·89	16·73	24·51	32·49	0·00
12	9·11	15·46	22·76	30·39	0·00
13	8·43	14·36	21·24	28·53	0·00
14	7·86	13·41	19·90	26·87	0·00
15	7·35	12·58	18·72	25·38	0·00
16	6·91	11·84	17·67	24·04	0·00
17	6·51	11·19	16·73	22·84	0·00
18	6·16	10·60	15·89	21·74	0·00
19	0·00	10·07	15·12	20·75	0·00
20	0·00	9·59	14·43	19·84	30·85
21	0·00	9·16	13·79	19·00	29·73
22	0·00	8·76	13·21	18·23	28·67
23	0·00	8·39	12·68	17·52	27·69
24	0·00	8·06	12·18	16·87	26·77
25	0·00	7·75	11·73	16·25	25·90
26	0·00	7·46	11·30	15·69	25·08
27	0·00	7·20	10·91	15·16	24·31
28	0·00	6·95	10·54	14·66	23·59
29	0·00	6·72	10·20	14·20	22·90
30	0·00	6·50	9·88	13·76	22·26
35	0·00	0·00	8·53	11·92	19·49
40	0·00	0·00	7·50	10·52	17·33
45	0·00	0·00	6·70	9·41	15·59

Note 1. Zeros indicate inadmissible reinforcement percentage·

Note 2. Bar spacings below the dividing line exceed $3d$·

Table 9B·61. Flexure-Moment Of Resistance Of Slabs, kN.m Per Metre Width

f_{ck} = 20 N/mm^2,
f_y = 415 N/mm^2,
Thickness = 14·0 cm

Bar Spacing cm	Bar Diameter, mm				
	6	8	10	12	16
5	22·49	36·29	0·00	0·00	0·00
6	19·08	31·30	0·00	0·00	0·00
7	16·56	27·48	39·12	0·00	0·00
8	14·62	24·47	35·26	0·00	0·00
9	13·09	22·04	32·06	0·00	0·00
10	11·85	20·05	29·37	38·94	0·00
11	10·82	18·38	27·08	36·20	0·00
12	9·96	16·97	25·12	33·79	0·00
13	9·22	15·76	23·42	31·67	0·00
14	8·58	14·71	21·93	29·78	0·00
15	8·03	13·79	20·61	28·10	0·00
16	7·55	12·98	19·44	26·60	0·00
17	0·00	12·25	18·40	25·24	0·00
18	0·00	11·61	17·46	24·01	0·00
19	0·00	11·03	16·61	22·90	35·87
20	0·00	10·50	15·85	21·88	34·48
21	0·00	10·02	15·14	20·95	33·18
22	0·00	9·58	14·50	20·09	31·97
23	0·00	9·18	13·91	19·30	30·84
24	0·00	8·82	13·37	18·57	29·79
25	0·00	8·48	12·86	17·89	28·80
26	0·00	8·16	12·39	17·26	27·87
27	0·00	7·87	11·96	16·67	27·00
28	0·00	7·60	11·55	16·12	26·18
29	0·00	7·34	11·18	15·60	25·41
30	0·00	0·00	10·82	15·12	24·68
35	0·00	0·00	9·34	13·09	21·56
40	0·00	0·00	8·21	11·54	19·14
45	0·00	0·00	7·33	10·32	17·20

Note 1. Zeros indicate inadmissible reinforcement percentage.
Note 2. Bar spacings below the dividing line exceed $3d$.

Table 9B·62. Flexure-Moment Of Resistance Of Slabs, kN.m Per Metre Width

f_{ck} = 20 N/mm^2,
f_y = 415 N/mm^2,
Thickness = 15·0 cm

Bar Spacing cm	Bar Diameter, mm					
	6	8	10	12	16	18
5	24·53	39·92	0·00	0·00	0·00	0·00
6	20·78	34·32	0·00	0·00	0·00	0·00
7	18·01	30·07	43·16	0·00	0·00	0·00
8	15·90	26·73	38·80	0·00	0·00	0·00
9	14·22	24·06	35·21	0·00	0·00	0·00
10	12·87	21·86	32·20	43·03	0·00	0·00
11	11·75	20·03	29·66	39·91	0·00	0·00
12	10·81	18·48	27·48	37·19	0·00	0·00
13	10·00	17·15	25·60	34·80	0·00	0·00
14	9·31	16·00	23·95	32·70	0·00	0·00
15	8·71	15·00	22·50	30·82	0·00	0·00
16	0·00	14·11	21·22	29·15	0·00	0·00
17	0·00	13·32	20·07	27·64	43·25	0·00
18	0·00	12·61	19·04	26·28	41·40	0·00
19	0·00	11·98	18·11	25·04	39·69	0·00
20	0·00	11·41	17·26	23·92	38·11	0·00
21	0·00	10·88	16·49	22·89	36·64	0·00
22	0·00	10·41	15·79	21·94	35·27	41·27
23	0·00	9·97	15·14	21·07	34·00	39·90
24	0·00	9·57	14·55	20·27	32·81	38·60
25	0·00	9·20	14·00	19·52	31·70	37·38
26	0·00	8·86	13·48	18·83	30·66	36·24
27	0·00	8·54	13·01	18·18	29·69	35·15
28	0·00	0·00	12·57	17·58	28·77	34·13
29	0·00	0·00	12·15	17·01	27·91	33·16
30	0·00	0·00	11·77	16·48	27·09	32·24
35	0·00	0·00	10·15	14·26	23·64	28·29
40	0·00	0·00	8·92	12·56	20·95	25·19
45	0·00	0·00	0·00	11·22	18·81	22·69

Note 1. Zeros indicate inadmissible reinforcement percentage.
Note 2. Bar spacings below the dividing line exceed $3d$.

Table 9B·63. Flexure - Moment Of Resistance Of Slabs, kN.m Per Metre Width

f_{ck} = 20 N/mm^2,
f_y = 415 N/mm^2,
Thickness = 17·5 cm

Bar Spacing cm	Bar Diameter, mm						
	6	8	10	12	16	18	20
5	29·63	48·99	0·00	0·00	0·00	0·00	0·00
6	25·03	41·88	60·33	0·00	0·00	0·00	0·00
7	21·66	36·55	53·29	0·00	0·00	0·00	0·00
8	19·08	32·40	47·66	63·53	0·00	0·00	0·00
9	17·06	29·09	43·08	57·95	0·00	0·00	0·00
10	15·42	26·40	39·29	53·23	0·00	0·00	0·00
11	14·07	24·15	36·10	49·18	0·00	0·00	0·00
12	12·93	22·26	33·39	45·69	0·00	0·00	0·00
13	11·97	20·64	31·05	42·65	0·00	0·00	0·00
14	0·00	19·24	29·01	39·98	62·74	0·00	0·00
15	0·00	18·02	27·22	37·62	59·52	0·00	0·00
16	0·00	16·94	25·64	35·52	56·59	0·00	0·00
17	0·00	15·99	24·24	33·64	53·92	0·00	0·00
18	0·00	15·13	22·97	31·95	51·48	60·74	0·00
19	0·00	14·37	21·84	30·41	49·24	58·03	0·00
20	0·00	13·67	20·81	29·02	47·18	55·77	0·00
21	0·00	13·04	19·87	27·75	45·27	53·67	0·00
22	0·00	12·47	19·01	26·58	43·52	51·71	0·00
23	0·00	11·94	18·22	25·51	41·89	49·88	57·43
24	0·00	0·00	17·50	24·52	40·37	48·17	55·60
25	0·00	0·00	16·83	23·60	38·96	46·57	53·87
26	0·00	0·00	16·21	22·75	37·64	45·07	52·24
27	0·00	0·00	15·63	21·96	36·41	43·65	50·70
28	0·00	0·00	15·10	21·22	35·25	42·32	49·24
29	0·00	0·00	14·60	20·53	34·16	41·07	47·86
30	0·00	0·00	14·13	19·88	33·14	39·89	46·54
35	0·00	0·00	12·17	17·17	28·82	34·85	40·91
40	0·00	0·00	0·00	15·11	25·49	30·93	36·46
45	0·00	0·00	0·00	13·49	22·84	27·80	32·86

Note. Zeros indicate inadmissible reinforcement percentage.

Table 9B·64. Flexure-Moment Of Resistance Of Slabs, kN.m Per Metre Width

f_{ck} = 20 N/mm^2,
f_y = 415 N/mm^2,
Thickness = 20·0 cm

Bar Spacing cm	Bar Diameter, mm								
	6	8	10	12	16	18	20	22	25
5	34·73	58·06	83·47	0·00	0·00	0·00	0·00	0·00	0·00
6	29·28	49·44	72·14	0·00	0·00	0·00	0·00	0·00	0·00
7	25·30	43·02	63·41	84·72	0·00	0·00	0·00	0·00	0·00
8	22·27	38·07	56·52	76·28	0·00	0·00	0·00	0·00	0·00
9	19·89	34·13	50·96	69·29	0·00	0·00	0·00	0·00	0·00
10	17·97	30·93	46·38	63·43	0·00	0·00	0·00	0·00	0·00
11	16·38	28·28	42·54	58·46	0·00	0·00	0·00	0·00	0·00
12	0·00	26·04	39·29	54·20	85·29	0·00	0·00	0·00	0·00
13	0·00	24·13	36·50	50·50	80·23	0·00	0·00	0·00	0·00
14	0·00	22·48	34·07	47·27	75·70	0·00	0·00	0·00	0·00
15	0·00	21·04	31·95	44·43	71·62	0·00	0·00	0·00	0·00
16	0·00	19·78	30·07	41·90	67·93	80·26	0·00	0·00	0·00
17	0·00	18·66	28·40	39·64	64·59	76·59	0·00	0·00	0·00
18	0·00	17·65	26·91	37·62	61·56	73·22	0·00	0·00	0·00
19	0·00	16·75	25·57	35·78	58·79	70·12	0·00	0·00	0·00
20	0·00	15·94	24·35	34·12	56·25	67·25	77·80	0·00	0·00
21	0·00	0·00	23·24	32·61	53·91	64·60	74·94	0·00	0·00
22	0·00	0·00	22·23	31·22	51·76	62·15	72·26	0·00	0·00
23	0·00	0·00	21·30	29·94	49·77	59·86	69·76	0·00	0·00
24	0·00	0·00	20·45	28·77	47·93	57·74	67·41	76·58	0·00
25	0·00	0·00	19·66	27·68	46·21	55·75	65·21	74·24	0·00
26	0·00	0·00	18·94	26·67	44·62	53·89	63·14	72·03	0·00
27	0·00	0·00	18·26	25·74	43·12	52·16	61·19	69·93	0·00
28	0·00	0·00	17·63	24·86	41·73	50·52	59·36	67·95	0·00
29	0·00	0·00	17·04	24·05	40·42	48·99	57·63	66·07	0·00
30	0·00	0·00	16·49	23·28	39·19	47·54	55·99	64·28	0·00
35	0·00	0·00	0·00	20·09	34·00	41·41	49·00	56·58	67·44
40	0·00	0·00	0·00	17·66	30·02	36·67	43·54	50·48	60·63
45	0·00	0·00	0·00	15·76	26·88	32·90	39·16	45·54	55·01

Note. Zeros indicate inadmissible reinforcement percentage.

Table 9B·65. Flexure-Moment Of Resistance Of Slabs, kN.m Per Metre Width

f_{ck} = 20 N/mm^2,
f_y = 415 N/mm^2,
Thickness = 22·5 cm

Bar Spacing cm	Bar Diameter, mm								
	6	8	10	12	16	18	20	22	25
5	39·84	67·13	97·64	0·00	0·00	0·00	0·00	0·00	0·00
6	33·53	57·00	83·94	112·03	0·00	0·00	0·00	0·00	0·00
7	28·95	49·50	73·53	99·30	0·00	0·00	0·00	0·00	0·00
8	25·46	43·74	65·38	89·04	0·00	0·00	0·00	0·00	0·00
9	22·73	39·17	58·83	80·63	0·00	0·00	0·00	0·00	0·00
10	20·52	35·47	53·46	73·64	0·00	0·00	0·00	0·00	0·00
11	0·00	32·40	48·98	67·74	107·44	0·00	0·00	0·00	0·00
12	0·00	29·82	45·20	62·70	100·41	0·00	0·00	0·00	0·00
13	0·00	27·62	41·95	58·35	94·19	0·00	0·00	0·00	0·00
14	0·00	25·72	39·13	54·56	88·65	105·02	0·00	0·00	0·00
15	0·00	24·07	36·67	51·23	83·71	99·56	0·00	0·00	0·00
16	0·00	22·61	34·50	48·28	79·27	94·61	0·00	0·00	0·00
17	0·00	21·32	32·57	45·65	75·26	90·10	104·35	0·00	0·00
18	0·00	20·17	30·85	43·28	71·63	85·98	99·90	0·00	0·00
19	0·00	0·00	29·29	41·15	68·33	82·20	95·78	0·00	0·00
20	0·00	0·00	27·89	39·22	65·32	78·73	91·97	0·00	0·00
21	0·00	0·00	26·62	37·46	62·55	75·53	88·43	100·77	0·00
22	0·00	0·00	25·45	35·86	60·01	72·58	85·14	97·26	0·00
23	0·00	0·00	24·38	34·38	57·66	69·84	82·08	93·96	0·00
24	0·00	0·00	23·40	33·02	55·49	67·30	79·22	90·87	0·00
25	0·00	0·00	22·50	31·76	53·47	64·93	76·55	87·96	0·00
26	0·00	0·00	21·66	30·60	51·59	62·72	74·04	85·22	0·00
27	0·00	0·00	20·88	29·52	49·84	60·66	71·69	82·63	0·00
28	0·00	0·00	20·16	28·51	48·21	58·72	69·48	80·20	95·50
29	0·00	0·00	19·48	27·57	46·67	56·90	67·40	77·89	92·97
30	0·00	0·00	0·00	26·68	45·23	55·19	65·44	75·71	90·57
35	0·00	0·00	0·00	23·00	39·19	47·97	57·10	66·38	80·10
40	0·00	0·00	0·00	20·21	34·56	42·41	50·63	59·05	71·70
45	0·00	0·00	0·00	0·00	30·91	38·00	45·46	53·16	64·86

Note. Zeros indicate inadmissible reinforcement percentage.

Table 9B·66. Flexure-Moment Of Resistance Of Slabs, kN.m Per Metre Width

f_{ck} = 20 N/mm^2,
f_y = 415 N/mm^2,
Thickness = 25·0 cm

Bar Spacing cm	Bar Diameter, mm								
	6	8	10	12	16	18	20	22	25
5	44·94	76·20	111·81	0·00	0·00	0·00	0·00	0·00	0·00
6	37·78	64·56	95·75	129·04	0·00	0·00	0·00	0·00	0·00
7	32·59	55·98	83·65	113·88	0·00	0·00	0·00	0·00	0·00
8	28·65	49·41	74·23	101·79	0·00	0·00	0·00	0·00	0·00
9	25·56	44·21	66·70	91·97	0·00	0·00	0·00	0·00	0·00
10	0·00	40·00	60·55	83·84	133·56	0·00	0·00	0·00	0·00
11	0·00	36·52	55·43	77·01	123·93	0·00	0·00	0·00	0·00
12	0·00	33·60	51·10	71·20	115·53	136·82	0·00	0·00	0·00
13	0·00	31·11	47·40	66·20	108·14	128·69	0·00	0·00	0·00
14	0·00	28·96	44·19	61·85	101·61	121·41	0·00	0·00	0·00
15	0·00	27·09	41·40	58·03	95·80	114·87	133·27	0·00	0·00
16	0·00	25·45	38·93	54·65	90·61	108·96	126·88	0·00	0·00
17	0·00	0·00	36·74	51·65	85·93	103·60	121·02	0·00	0·00
18	0·00	0·00	34·78	48·95	81·71	98·73	115·64	0·00	0·00
19	0·00	0·00	33·02	46·52	77·88	94·28	110·70	126·55	0·00
20	0·00	0·00	31·43	44·33	74·39	90·21	106·14	121·66	0·00
21	0·00	0·00	29·99	42·32	71·19	86·47	101·93	117·10	0·00
22	0·00	0·00	28·67	40·49	68·25	83·02	98·03	112·84	0·00
23	0·00	0·00	27·47	38·82	65·55	79·83	94·40	108·87	0·00
24	0·00	0·00	26·36	37·27	63·04	76·87	91·03	105·16	0·00
25	0·00	0·00	25·33	35·85	60·73	74·12	87·88	101·67	121·56
26	0·00	0·00	24·39	34·52	58·57	71·55	84·94	98·41	117·96
27	0·00	0·00	0·00	33·30	56·56	69·16	82·19	95·34	114·55
28	0·00	0·00	0·00	32·15	54·68	66·92	79·60	92·45	111·31
29	0·00	0·00	0·00	31·08	52·93	64·82	77·18	89·72	108·24
30	0·00	0·00	0·00	30·08	51·28	62·85	74·89	87·15	105·33
35	0·00	0·00	0·00	25·92	44·37	54·53	65·20	76·18	92·75
40	0·00	0·00	0·00	0·00	39·09	48·15	57·71	67·62	82·78
45	0·00	0·00	0·00	0·00	34·94	43·10	51·76	60·78	74·70

Note. Zeros indicate inadmissible reinforcement percentage.

9B·9. Design Tables for Columns

Table 9B·67. Eccentrically loaded columns

f_{ck} = 15 MPa, f_y = 250 MPa, a = 1/6

Percentage steel on each side		k=0·3	k=0·4	k=0·5	k=0·6	k=0·7	k=0·8	k=0·9	k=1·0	k=1·1	k=1·2
p = 0·5	Pu/BD	1·587	2·127	2·667	3·207	4·168	5·229	6·166	7·036	7·594	7·971
	e/D	0·842	0·685	0·572	0·483	0·332	0·219	0·146	0·091	0·053	0·035
p = 1·0	Pu/BD	1·553	2·093	2·633	3·173	4·555	6·137	7·471	8·657	9·421	9·952
	e/D	1·323	1·048	0·859	0·720	0·435	0·255	0·159	0·095	0·055	0·035
p = 1·5	Pu/BD	1·520	2·060	2·600	3·140	4·943	7·046	8·777	10·634	11·248	11·932
	e/D	1·821	1·422	1·153	0·962	0·521	0·282	0·169	0·098	0·056	0·034
p = 2·0	Pu/BD	1·486	2·026	2·566	3·106	5·330	7·954	10·082	12·257	13·075	13·913
	e/D	2·337	1·809	1·455	1·209	0·595	0·303	0·175	0·100	0·057	0·034
p = 2·5	Pu/BD	1·453	1·993	2·533	3·073	5·718	8·863	11·388	13·88	14·902	15·894
	e/D	2·870	2·209	1·765	1·462	0·659	0·320	0·181	0·102	0·058	0·034
p = 3·0	Pu/BD	1·419	1·959	2·499	3·039	6·105	9·771	12·693	15·502	16·729	17·874
	e/D	3·420	2·622	2·083	1·720	0·715	0·333	0·185	0·103	0·059	0·034
p = 3·5	Pu/BD	1·336	1·926	2·466	3·006	6·493	10·680	13·999	17·124	18·556	19·855
	e/D	3·994	3·050	2·410	1·984	0·764	0·344	0·188	0·104	0·059	0·034
p = 4·0	Pu/BD	1·352	1·892	2·432	2·972	6·880	11·588	15·304	18·747	20·383	21·835
	e/D	4·587	3·493	2·745	2·254	0·807	0·354	0·191	0·105	0·060	0.034

Table 9B·68. Eccentrically loaded columns

f_{ck} = 15 MPa, f_y = 250 MPa, a = 1/8

Percentage steel on each side		k=0·3	k=0·4	k=0·5	k=0·6	k=0·7	k=0·8	k=0·9	k=1·0	k=1·1
p = 0·5	Pu/BD	1·587	2·127	2·667	3·207	3·959	5·046	6·008	6·829	7·472
	e/D	0·905	0·727	0·6063	0·511	0·388	0·234	0·166	0·104	0·068
p = 1·0	Pu/BD	1·553	2·093	2·663	3·173	4·138	5·772	7·156	8·357	9·178
	e/D	1·458	1·136	0·929	0·785	0·552	0·313	0·193	0·117	0·074
p = 1·5	Pu/BD	1·520	2·060	2·600	3·140	4·317	6·498	8·304	9·836	10·883
	e/D	2·035	1·556	1·259	1·050	0·703	0·362	0·213	0·126	0·079
p = 2·0	Pu/BD	1·486	2·026	2·566	3·106	4·496	7·224	9·452	11·314	12·589
	e/D	2·638	1·991	1·598	1·328	0·841	0·401	0·228	0·132	0·082
p = 2·5	Pu/BD	1·453	1·993	2·533	3·073	4·675	7·950	10·600	12·793	14·299
	e/D	3·269	2·440	1·946	1·612	0·969	0·433	0·239	0·138	0·085
p = 3·0	Pu/BD	1·419	1·959	2·499	3·039	4·854	8·676	11·747	14·271	15·999
	e/D	3·930	2·904	2·304	1·902	1·088	0·459	0·249	0·142	0·087
p = 3·5	Pu/BD	1·386	1·926	2·466	3·006	5·033	9·402	12·895	15·750	17·705
	e/D	4·622	3·385	2·671	2·199	1·198	0·481	0·256	0·145	0·088
p = 4·0	Pu/BD	1·352	1·892	2·432	2·972	5·212	10·128	14·043	17·228	19·410
	e/D	5·349	3·883	3·048	2·502	1·300	0·501	0·263	0·148	0·090

Table 9B·69. Eccentrically Loaded Columns

f_{ck} = 15 MPa, f_y = 250 MPa, a = 1/10

Percentage steel on each side		k=0·3	k=0·4	k=0·5	k=0·6	k=0·7	k=0·8	k=0·9	k=1·0	k=1·1
p = 0·5	Pu/BD	1·587	2·127	2·667	3·207	3·834	4·973	5·914	6·793	7·399
	e/D	0·940	0·754	0·627	0·528	0·427	0·273	0·179	0·113	0·074
p = 1·0	Pu/BD	1·553	2·093	2·633	3·1373	3·888	5·553	6·968	8·187	9·033
	e/D	1·529	1·188	0·970	0·812	0·639	0·355	0·216	0·132	0·085
p = 1·5	Pu/BD	1·520	2·060	2·600	3·140	3·942	6·170	8·022	9·580	10·666
	e/D	2·144	1·636	1·323	1·102	0·846	0·420	0·244	0·145	0·092
p = 2·0	Pu/BD	1·486	2·026	2·566	3·106	3·996	6·786	9·076	10·973	12·298
	e/D	2·786	2·099	1·684	1·399	1·047	0·474	0·265	0·155	0·097
p = 2·5	Pu/BD	1·453	1·993	2·533	3·073	4·050	7·403	10·130	12·367	13·931
	e/D	3·459	2·578	2·055	1·701	1·242	0·519	0·282	0·163	0·102
p = 3·0	Pu/BD	1·419	1·959	2·499	3·039	4·104	8·019	11·184	13·760	15·564
	e/D	4·162	3·073	2·436	2·011	1·432	0·556	0·295	0·169	0·105
p = 3·5	Pu/BD	1·386	1·926	2·466	3·006	4·158	8·636	12·238	15·153	17·197
	e/D	4·900	3·585	2·828	2·327	1·618	0·589	0·306	0·174	0·107
p = 4·0	Pu/BD	1·352	1·892	2·432	2·972	4·212	9·252	13·292	16·547	18·870
	e/D	5·675	4·115	3·230	2·650	1·798	0·617	0·316	0·179	0·110

Table 9B·70. Eccentrically loaded columns

f_{ck} = 20 MPa, f_y = 250 MPa, a = 1/6

Percentage steel on each side		k=0·3	k=0·4	k=0·5	k=0·6	k=0·7	k=0·8	k=0·9	k=1·0
p = 0·5	Pu/BD	2·118	2·835	3·555	4·275	5·416	6·657	7·771	8·804
	e/D	0·737	0·600	0·504	0·426	0·305	0·209	0·143	0·090
p = 1·0	Pu/BD	2·075	2·791	3·511	4·231	5·793	7·554	9·063	10·408
	e/D	1·103	0·875	0·721	0·605	0·389	0·240	0·155	0·095
p = 1·5	Pu/BD	2·033	2·746	3·466	4·186	6·169	8·451	10·354	12·012
	e/D	1·489	1·158	0·944	0·789	0·462	0·265	0·164	0·098
p = 2·0	Pu/BD	1·990	2·702	3·422	4·142	6·545	9·348	11·645	13·616
	e/D	1·892	1·451	1·172	0·976	0·527	0·285	0·171	0·100
p = 2·5	Pu/BD	1·948	2·657	3·377	4·097	6·924	10·245	12·937	15·220
	e/D	2·312	1·754	1·407	1·167	0·585	0·302	0·177	0·102
p = 3·0	Pu/BD	1·906	2·612	3·332	4·052	7·298	11·142	14·228	16·824
	e/D	2·751	2·067	1·648	1·363	0·637	0·316	0·081	0·104
p = 3·5	Pu/BD	1·863	2·568	3·288	4·008	7·674	12·039	15·519	18·428
	e/D	3·210	2·391	1·895	1·562	0·684	0·328	0·185	0·105
p = 4·0	Pu/BD	1·821	2·523	3·243	3·963	8·050	12·936	16·811	20·032
	e/D	3·690	2·727	2·149	1·767	0·727	0·338	0·189	0·106

Table 9B·71. Eccentrically loaded Columns

f_{ck} = 20 MPa, f_y = 20 MPa, a = 1/8

Percentage steel on each side		*k*=0·3	*k*=0·4	*k*=0·5	*k*=0·6	*k*=0·7	*k*=0·8	*k*=0·9	*k*=1·0
p = 0·5	*Pu/BD*	2·115	2·835	3·555	4·275	5·208	6·475	7·616	8·663
	e/D	0·777	0·632	0·530	0·448	0·347	0·233	0·158	0·101
p = 1·0	*Pu/BD*	2·071	2·791	3·511	4·231	5·376	7·190	8·752	10·126
	e/D	1·195	0·941	0·774	0·649	0·476	0·286	0·182	0·112
p = 1·5	*Pu/BD*	2·026	2·746	3·466	4·186	5·544	7·904	9·888	11·589
	e/D	1·633	1·259	1·024	0·885	0·597	0·330	0·201	0·121
p = 2·0	*Pu/BD*	1·982	2·702	3·422	4·142	5·712	8·619	11·023	13·052
	e/D	2·089	1·588	1·281	1·065	0·711	0·366	0·215	0·128
p = 2·5	*Pu/BD*	1·937	2·657	3·377	4·097	5·880	9·334	12·159	14·515
	e/D	2·567	1·928	1·544	1·280	0·819	0·397	0·227	0·134
p = 3·0	*Pu/BD*	1·892	2·612	3·332	4·052	6·047	10·049	13·295	15·978
	e/D	3·068	2·280	1·814	1·500	0·921	0·423	0·237	0·138
p = 3·5	*Pu/BD*	1·848	2·568	3·288	4·008	6·215	10·763	14·431	17·441
	e/D	3·597	2·644	2·092	1·724	1·017	0·416	0·245	0·142
p = 4·0	*Pu/BD*	1·801	2·523	3·243	3·963	6·383	11·478	15·567	18·904
	e/D	4·143	3·021	2·378	1·954	1·108	0·466	0·253	0·145

Table 9B·72. Eccentrically Loaded Columns

f_{ck} = 20 MPa, f_y = 250 MPa a = 1/10

Percentage steel on each side		*k*=0·3	*k*=0·4	*k*=0·5	*k*=0·6	*k*=0·7	*k*=0·8	*k*=0·9	*k*=1·0
p = 0·5	*Pu/BD*	2·115	2·835	3·555	4·275	5·083	6·365	7·523	8·579
	e/D	0·803	0·652	0·545	0·461	0·375	0·250	0·168	0·108
p = 1·0	*Pu/BD*	2·071	2·791	3·511	4·231	5·126	6·971	8·566	9·957
	e/D	1·248	0·981	0·805	0·675	0·538	0·318	0·201	0·125
p = 1·5	*Pu/BD*	2·026	2·746	3·466	4·186	5·169	7·576	9·609	11·336
	e/D	1·714	1·320	1·072	0·895	0·699	0·376	0·226	0·138
p = 2·0	*Pu/BD*	1·982	2·702	3·422	4·142	5·212	8·182	10·662	12·715
	e/D	2·200	1·670	1·345	1·119	0·857	0·425	0·247	0·148
p = 2·5	*Pu/BD*	1·937	2·657	3·377	4·097	5·255	8·787	11·695	14·093
	e/D	2·708	2·033	1·626	1·848	1·012	0·467	0·263	0·156
p = 3·0	*Pu/BD*	1·892	2·612	3·332	4·052	5·297	9·392	12·737	15·472
	e/D	3·240	2·407	1·914	1·582	1·165	0·504	0·277	0·163
p = 3·5	*Pu/BD*	1·848	2·568	3·288	4·008	5·340	9·998	13·780	16·851
	e/D	3·797	2·795	2·210	1·821	1·315	0·536	0·289	0·168
p = 4·0	*Pu/BD*	1·803	2·523	3·243	3·963	5·383	10·603	14·823	18·229
	e/D	4·382	3·197	2·515	2·065	1·463	0·565	0·299	0·173

Table 9B·73. Eccentrically Loaded Column

f_{ck} = 25 MPa, f_y = 250 MPa, a = 1/6

Percentage steel on each side		k=0·3	k=0·4	k=0·5	k=0·6	k=0·7	k=0·8	k=0·9	k=1·0
p = 0·5	Pu/BD	2·647	3·544	4·444	5·345	6·665	8·086	9·378	10·587
	e/D	0·663	0·548	0·463	0·392	0·288	0·202	0·140	0·090
p = 1·0	Pu/BD	2·594	3·489	4·389	5·289	7·030	8·972	10·655	12·175
	e/D	0·963	0·770	0·638	0·537	0·358	0·230	0·151	0·094
p = 1·5	Pu/BD	2·541	3·433	4·333	5·233	7·395	9·858	11·933	13·762
	e/D	1·275	0·999	0·818	0·684	0·422	0·253	0·160	0·097
p = 2·0	Pu/BD	2·488	3·377	4·277	5·177	7·760	10·744	13·210	15·349
	e/D	1·601	1·236	1·002	0·835	0·480	0·272	0·167	0·100
p = 2·5	Pu/BD	2·435	3·321	4·221	5·121	8·126	11·630	14·488	16·937
	e/D	1·941	1·481	1·192	0·990	0·533	0·288	0·173	0·102
p = 3·0	Pu/BD	2·382	3·266	4·166	5·066	8·491	12·515	15·765	18·524
	e/D	2·296	1·734	1·386	1·147	0·581	0·302	0·178	0·104
p = 3·5	Pu/BD	2·329	3·210	4·110	5·010	8·856	13·401	17·043	20·111
	e/D	2·667	1·996	1·586	1·309	0·625	0·314	0·182	0·106
p = 4·0	Pu/BD	2·276	3·154	4·054	4·954	9·221	14·287	18·320	21·698
	e/D	3·056	2·267	1·791	1·473	0·666	0·325	0·186	0·107

Table 9B·74. Eccentrically Loaded Columns

f_{ck} = 25 MPa, f_y = 250 MPa, a = 1/8

Percentage steel on each side		k=0·3	k=0·4	k=0·5	k=0·6	k=0·7	k=0·8	k=0·9	k=1·0
p = 0·5	Pu/BD	2·644	3·544	4·444	5·344	6·457	7·904	9·224	10·448
	e/D	0·700	0·579	0·484	0·410	0·321	0·222	0·153	0·098
p = 1·0	Pu/BD	2·589	3·489	4·389	5·289	6·614	8·607	10·347	11·895
	e/D	1·038	0·834	0·681	0·572	0·428	0·268	0·175	0·109
p = 1·5	Pu/BD	2·33	3·433	4·333	5·233	6·770	9·311	11·471	13·343
	e/D	1·391	1·100	0·883	0·738	0·530	0·307	0·192	0·118
p = 2·0	Pu/BD	2·477	3·377	4·277	5·177	6·927	10·014	12·595	14·790
	e/D	1·760	1·378	1·090	0·908	0·627	0·341	0·206	0·125
p = 2·5	Pu/BD	2·421	3·321	4·221	5·121	7·084	10·718	13·718	16·238
	e/D	2·146	1·668	1·303	1·081	0·720	0·370	0·218	0·131
p = 3·0	Pu/BD	2·366	3·266	4·166	5·066	7·241	11·422	14·842	17·685
	e/D	2·551	1·970	1·521	1·258	0·809	0·395	0·228	0·135
p = 3·5	Pu/BD	2·310	3·210	4·110	5·010	7·397	12·125	15·966	19·133
	e/D	2·974	2·287	1·745	1·439	0·894	0·418	0·237	0·139
p = 4·0	Pu/BD	2·254	3·154	4·054	4·954	7·554	12·829	17·089	20·580
	e/D	3·419	2·619	1·976	1·624	0·976	0·438	0·244	0·143

Table 9B·75. Eccentrically Loaded Column

f_{ck} = 25 MPa, f_y = 250 MPa, a = 1/10

Percentage steel on each side		k=0·3	k=0·4	k=0·5	k=0·6	k=0·7	k=0·8	k=0·9	k=1·0
p = 0·5	Pu/BD	2·644	3·544	4·444	5·345	6·332	7·794	9·132	10·364
	e/D	0·720	0·591	0·496	0·420	0·343	0·236	0·161	0·104
p = 1·0	Pu/BD	2·589	3·489	4·389	5·289	6·364	8·389	10·164	11·728
	e/D	1·081	0·856	0·706	0·593	0·476	0·294	0·190	0·120
p = 1·5	Pu/BD	2·533	3·433	4·333	5·233	6·395	8·983	11·195	13·092
	e/D	1·457	1·130	0·921	0·770	0·608	0·345	0·213	0·132
p = 2·0	Pu/BD	2·477	3·377	4·277	5·177	6·427	9·577	12·227	14·456
	e/D	1·850	1·413	1·142	0·951	0·738	0·390	0·233	0·142
p = 2·5	Pu/BD	2·421	3·321	4·221	5·121	6·459	10·171	13·259	15·820
	e/D	2·261	1·705	1·368	1·135	0·867	0·429	0·249	0·150
p = 3·0	Pu/BD	2·366	3·266	4·166	5·066	6·491	10·766	14·291	17·184
	e/D	2·691	2·007	1·601	1·324	0·995	0·464	0·263	0·157
p = 3·5	Pu/BD	2·310	3·210	4·110	5·010	6·522	11·360	15·322	18·548
	e/D	3·142	2·320	1·839	1·517	1·121	0·495	0·275	0·163
p = 4·0	Pu/BD	2·254	3·154	4·054	4·954	6·554	11·954	16·354	19·912
	e/D	3·616	2·644	2·085	1·714	1·247	0·524	0·286	0·168

Table 9B·76. Eccentrically Loaded Columns

f_{ck} = 15 MPa, f_y = 415 MPa, a = 1/6

Percentage steel on each side		k=0·3	k=0·4	k=0·5	k=0·6	k=0·7	k=0·8	k=0·9	k=1·0
p = 0·5	Pu/BD	1·588	2·127	2·667	3·207	4·167	5·228	6·165	7·021
	e/D	1·147	0·910	0·750	0·632	0·447	0·310	0·224	0·159
p = 1·0	Pu/BD	1·556	2·093	2·633	3·173	4·555	6·136	7·471	8·642
	e/D	1·951	1·505	1·221	1·021	0·645	0·411	0·287	0·206
p = 1·5	Pu/BD	1·525	2·060	2·600	3·140	4·942	7·045	8·776	10·263
	e/D	2·788	2·119	1·703	1·419	0·812	0·486	0·332	0·238
p = 2·0	Pu/BD	1·493	2·026	2·566	3·106	5·330	7·953	10·081	11·883
	e/D	3·661	2·754	2·198	1·825	0·954	0·544	0·365	0·261
p = 2·5	Pu/BD	1·461	1·993	2·533	3·073	5·717	8·861	11·387	13·504
	e/D	4·571	3·409	2·705	2·240	1·078	0·590	0·391	0·279
p = 3·0	Pu/BD	1·429	1·959	2·499	3·039	6·104	9·769	12·692	15·125
	e/D	5·523	4·088	3·227	2·665	1·185	0·627	0·411	0·293
p = 3·5	Pu/BD	1·397	1·926	2·466	3·006	6·492	10·677	13·997	16·746
	e/D	6·517	4·789	3·762	3·098	1·280	0·658	0·428	0·304
p = 4·0	Pu/BD	1·366	1·892	2·432	2·972	6·879	11·586	15·303	18·367
	e/D	7·559	5·516	4·313	3·542	1·364	0·684	0·442	0·314

Table 9B·77. Eccentrically Loaded Columns

f_{ck} = 15 MPa, f_y = 415 MPa, a = 1/8

Percentage steel on each side		k=0·3	k=0·4	k=0·5	k=0·6	k=0·7	k=0·8	k=0·9	k=1·0
p = 0·5	Pu/BD	1·587	2·127	2·667	3·207	3·959	5·046	6·008	6·879
	e/D	1·244	0·981	0·808	0·679	0·524	0·358	0·255	0·182
p = 1·0	Pu/BD	1·553	2·093	2·633	3·173	4·138	5·772	7·156	8·357
	e/D	2·151	1·650	1·337	1·117	0·813	0·500	0·343	0·246
p = 1·5	Pu/BD	1·520	2·060	2·600	3·140	4·317	6·498	8·304	9·836
	e/D	3·097	2·340	1·880	1·564	1·077	0·611	0·407	0·290
p = 2·0	Pu/BD	1·486	2·026	2·566	3·106	4·946	7·224	9·452	11·314
	e/D	4·086	3·053	2·437	2·021	1·320	0·699	0·455	0·323
p = 2·5	Pu/BD	1·453	1·993	2·533	3·073	4·675	7·950	10·601	12·793
	e/D	5·121	3·790	3·009	2·487	1·545	0·771	0·493	0·348
p = 3·0	Pu/BD	1·419	1·959	2·499	3·039	4·854	8·676	11·749	14·271
	e/D	6·204	4·552	3·596	2·964	1·753	0·831	0·523	0·368
p = 3·5	Pu/BD	1·386	1·926	2·466	3·006	5·033	9·402	12·897	15·750
	e/D	7·340	5·341	4·200	3·452	1·946	0·882	0·548	0·384
p = 4·0	Pu/BD	1·352	1·892	2·432	2·972	5·212	10·128	14·045	17·228
	e/D	8·532	6·158	4·818	3·950	2·126	0·926	0·569	0·398

Table 9B·78. Eccentrically Loaded Columns

f_{ck}= 15 MPa, f_y = 415 MPa, a = 1/10

Percentage steel on each side		k=0·3	k=0·4	k=0·5	k=0·6	k=0·7	k=0·8	k=0·9	k=1·0
p = 0·5	Pu/BD	1·587	2·127	2·667	3·207	3·834	4·937	5·914	6·793
	e/D	1·302	1·024	0·824	0·708	0·577	0·389	0·276	0·197
p = 1·0	Pu/BD	1·553	2·093	2·633	3·173	3·888	5·553	6·968	8·187
	e/D	2·268	1·737	1·407	1·174	0·935	0·561	0·381	0·272
p = 1·5	Pu/BD	1·520	2·060	2·600	3·140	3·942	6·170	8·022	9·580
	e/D	3·278	2·473	1·985	1·651	1·283	0·699	0·458	0·325
p = 2·0	Pu/BD	1·486	2·026	2·566	3·106	3·996	6·786	9·076	10·973
	e/D	4·332	3·233	2·579	2·138	1·621	0·812	0·518	0·365
p = 2·5	Pu/BD	1·453	1·993	2·533	3·073	4·050	7·403	10·130	12·367
	e/D	5·435	4·019	3·189	2·636	1·951	0·907	0·565	0·395
p = 3·0	Pu/BD	1·419	1·959	2·499	3·039	4·104	8·019	11·184	13·760
	e/D	6·590	4·832	3·815	3·144	2·272	0·986	0·603	0·420
p = 3·5	Pu/BD	1·386	1·926	2·466	3·006	4·158	8·636	12·238	15·153
	e/D	7·801	5·673	4·458	3·664	2·584	1·054	0·635	0·440
p = 4·0	Pu/BD	1·352	1·892	2·432	2·972	4·212	9·252	13·292	16·547
	e/D	9·072	6·544	5·119	4·196	2·889	1·114	0·661	0·456

Table 9B·79. Eccentrically Loaded Columns

f_{ck} = 20 MPa, f_y = 415 MPa, a = 1/6

Percentage steel on each side		k=0·3	k=0·4	k=0·5	k=0·6	k=0·7	k=0·8	k=0·9	k=1·0
p = 0·5	Pu/BD	2·116	2·835	3·555	4·275	5·416	6·657	7·772	8·804
	e/D	0·959	0·769	0·638	0·538	0·393	0·281	0·204	0·145
p = 1·0	Pu/BD	2·071	2·791	3·511	4·231	5·793	7·554	9·063	10·408
	e/D	1·568	1·217	0·994	0·832	0·554	0·367	0·260	0·187
p = 1·5	Pu/BD	2·027	2·746	3·466	4·186	6·169	8·452	10·355	12·012
	e/D	2·203	1·681	1·358	1·132	0·895	0·435	0·303	0·212
p = 2·0	Pu/BD	1·983	2·702	3·422	4·142	6·545	9·349	11·646	13·616
	e/D	2·867	2·160	1·732	1·438	0·820	0·490	0·335	0·241
p = 2·5	Pu/BD	1·938	2·657	3·377	4·097	6·921	10·246	12·938	15·221
	e/D	3·561	2·605	2·115	1·751	0·931	0·535	0·362	0·259
p = 3·0	Pu/BD	1·894	2·612	3·332	4·052	7·298	11·143	14·229	16·825
	e/D	4·288	3·166	2·509	2·071	1·031	0·573	0·383	0·274
p = 3·5	Pu/BD	1·850	2·568	3·288	4·008	7·674	12·040	15·521	18·429
	e/D	5·050	3·696	2·914	2·398	1·121	0·606	0·401	0·287
p = 4·0	Pu/BD	1·805	2·523	3·243	3·963	8·050	12·938	16·812	20·033
	e/D	5·849	4·244	3·330	2·732	1·202	0·634	0·416	0·297

Table 9B·80. Eccentrically loaded columns

f_{ck} = 20 MPa, f_y = 415 MPa, a = 1/8

Percentage steel on each side		k=0·3	k=0·4	k=0·5	k=0·6	k=0·7	k=0·8	k=0·9	k=1·0
p = 0·5	Pu/BD	2·115	2·835	3·555	4·275	5·208	6·475	7·616	8·671
	e/D	1·031	0·822	0·681	0·574	0·450	0·316	0·229	0·162
p = 1·0	Pu/BD	2·071	2·791	3·511	4·231	5·376	7·190	8·752	10·141
	e/D	1·715	1·327	1·080	0·904	0·676	0·436	0·305	0·218
p = 1·5	Pu/BD	2·006	2·746	3·466	4·186	5·544	7·904	9·888	11·612
	e/D	2·429	1·847	1·490	1·241	0·888	0·534	0·364	0·259
p = 2·0	Pu/BD	1·982	2·702	3·422	4·142	5·712	8·619	11·023	13·083
	e/D	3·176	2·385	1·910	1·586	1·088	0·616	0·411	0·292
p = 2·5	Pu/BD	1·937	2·657	3·377	4·097	5·880	9·334	12·159	14·553
	e/D	3·957	2·941	2·341	1·937	1·277	0·685	0·449	0·317
p = 3·0	Pu/BD	1·892	2·612	3·332	4·052	6·047	10·049	13·295	16·024
	e/D	4·774	3·516	2·784	2·297	1·455	0·744	0·480	0·338
p = 3·5	Pu/BD	1·848	2·568	3·288	4·008	6·215	10·764	14·431	17·495
	e/D	5·631	4·111	3·238	2·664	1·623	0·796	0·507	0·356
p = 4·0	Pu/BD	1·803	2·523	3·243	3·963	6·383	11·478	15·567	18·965
	e/D	6·531	4·728	3·706	3·040	1·783	0·841	0·529	0·370

Table 9B·81. Eccentrically loaded columns

f_{ck} = 20 MPa, f_y = 415 MPa, a = 1/10

Percentage steel on each side		k=0·3	k=0·4	k=0·5	k=0·6	k=0·7	k=0·8	k=0·9	k=1·0
p = 0·5	Pu/BD	2·115	2·835	3·555	4·275	5·083	6·365	7·523	8·579
	e/D	1·074	0·855	0·707	0·595	0·488	0·340	0·245	0·175
p = 1·0	Pu/BD	2·071	2·791	3·511	4·231	5·126	6·971	8·566	9·957
	e/D	1·803	1·392	1·132	0·947	0·762	0·483	0·335	0·240
p = 1·5	Pu/BD	2·006	2·746	3·466	4·186	5·169	7·576	9·609	11·336
	e/D	2·565	1·947	1·569	1·306	1·032	0·603	0·405	0·290
p = 2·0	Pu/BD	1·982	2·702	3·422	4·142	5·212	8·182	10·652	12·715
	e/D	3·360	2·521	2·017	1·673	1·297	0·705	0·462	0·328
p = 2·5	Pu/BD	1·937	2·657	3·377	4·097	5·255	8·787	11·695	14·093
	e/D	4·193	3·113	2·476	2·049	1·558	0·794	0·509	0·360
p = 3·0	Pu/BD	1·892	2·612	3·332	4·052	5·297	9·392	12·737	15·472
	e/D	5·064	3·726	2·948	2·432	1·815	0·871	0·548	0·385
p = 3·5	Pu/BD	1·848	2·568	3·288	4·008	5·340	9·998	13·780	16·851
	e/D	5·978	4·361	3·433	2·824	2·068	0·938	0·581	0·407
p = 4·0	Pu/BD	1·803	2·523	3·243	3·963	5·383	10·603	14·823	18·220
	e/D	6·936	5·017	3·931	3·225	2·316	0·998	0·609	0·425

Table 9B·82. Eccentrically loaded columns

f_{ck} = 25 MPa, f_y = 415 MPa, a = 1/6

Percentage steel on each side		k=0·3	k=0·4	k=0·5	k=0·6	k=0·7	k=0·8	k=0·9	k=1·0
p = 0·5	Pu/BD	2·647	3·544	4·444	5·344	6·665	8·086	9·378	10·582
	e/D	0·844	0·684	0·571	0·482	0·360	0·261	0·191	0·135
p = 1·0	Pu/BD	2·594	3·489	4·389	5·289	7·030	8·972	10·655	12·165
	e/D	1·332	1·045	0·856	0·718	0·495	0·337	0·241	0·173
p = 1·5	Pu/BD	2·541	3·433	4·333	5·233	7·395	9·858	11·933	13·747
	e/D	1·840	1·418	1·177	0·959	0·617	0·399	0·281	2·303
p = 2·0	Pu/BD	2·488	3·377	4·249	5·177	7·760	10·744	13·210	15·329
	e/D	2·370	1·803	1·450	1·205	0·727	0·450	0·312	0·226
p = 1·5	Pu/BD	2·435	3·321	4·221	5·121	8·126	11·630	14·488	16·912
	e/D	2·923	2·201	1·759	1·457	0·827	0·494	0·339	0·245
p = 3·0	Pu/BD	2·382	3·266	4·166	5·066	8·491	12·515	15·765	18·494
	e/D	3·501	2·613	2·076	1·714	0·919	0·532	0·352	0·260
p = 3·5	Pu/BD	2·329	3·210	4·110	5·010	8·856	13·401	17·043	20·076
	e/D	4·105	3·039	2·401	1·977	1·004	0·564	0·370	0·273
p = 4·0	Pu/BD	2·276	3·154	4·054	4·954	9·221	14·287	18·320	21·658
	e/D	4·738	3·481	2·736	2·246	1·081	0·593	0·386	0·285

Table 9B·83. Eccentrically loaded columns

f_{ck} = 25 MPa, f_y = 415 MPa, a = 1/8

Percentage steel on each side		k=0·3	k=0·4	k=0·5	k=0·6	k=0·7	k=0·8	k=0·9	k=1·0
p = 0·5	Pu/BD	2·644	3·544	4·444	5·344	6·457	7·904	9·224	10·448
	e/D	0·903	0·727	0·605	0·510	0·404	0·290	0·211	0·150
p = 1·0	Pu/BD	2·589	3·489	4·389	5·289	6·614	8·607	10·347	11·895
	e/D	1·454	1·133	0·926	0·776	0·591	0·393	0·279	0·200
p = 1·5	Pu/BD	2·533	3·433	4·333	5·233	6·770	9·311	11·471	13·343
	e/D	2·029	1·552	1·255	1·047	0·768	0·481	0·333	0·239
p = 2·0	Pu/BD	2·477	3·377	4·277	5·177	6·927	10·014	12·595	14·790
	e/D	2·629	1·984	1·593	1·324	0·938	0·556	0·377	0·270
p = 2·5	Pu/BD	2·421	3·321	4·221	5·121	7·084	10·718	13·718	16·238
	e/D	3·258	2·432	1·940	1·606	1·100	0·621	0·414	0·296
p = 3·0	Pu/BD	2·366	3·266	4·166	5·066	7·241	11·422	14·842	17·685
	e/D	3·916	2·895	2·296	1·896	1·255	0·678	0·446	0·318
p = 3·5	Pu/BD	2·310	3·210	4·410	5·010	7·397	12·125	15·966	19·133
	e/D	4·606	3·373	2·662	2·191	1·403	0·729	0·473	0·336
p = 4·0	Pu/BD	2·254	3·154	4·054	4·954	7·554	12·829	17·089	20·580
	e/D	5·330	3·869	3·038	2·493	1·546	0·774	0·496	0·352

Table 9B·84. Eccentrically loaded columns

f_{ck} = 25 MPa, f_y = 451 MPa, a = 1/10

Percentage steel on each side		k=0·3	k=0·4	k=0·5	k=0·6	k=0·7	k=0·8	k=0·9	k=1·0
p = 0·5	Pu/BD	2·644	3·544	4·444	5·344	6·332	7·794	9·132	10·364
	e/D	0·938	0·753	0·626	0·527	0·434	0·309	0·224	0·160
p = 1·0	Pu/BD	2·589	3·489	4·389	5·289	6·364	8·389	10·164	11·728
	e/D	1·524	1·185	0·968	0·810	0·657	0·431	0·303	0·218
p = 1·5	Pu/BD	2·633	3·433	4·333	5·233	6·395	8·983	11·195	13·092
	e/D	2·137	1·632	1·319	1·099	0·877	0·537	0·367	0·264
p = 2·0	Pu/BD	2·477	3·377	4·277	5·177	6·427	9·577	12·227	14·456
	e/D	2·777	2·093	1·679	1·394	1·095	0·629	0·421	0·301
p = 2·5	Pu/BD	2·421	3·321	4·221	5·121	6·459	10·171	13·259	15·820
	e/D	3·447	2·569	2·048	1·696	1·312	0·711	0·466	0·332
p = 3·0	Pu/BD	3·366	3·766	4·166	5·066	6·491	10·766	14·291	17·184
	e/D	4·148	3·063	2·428	2·004	1·526	0·784	0·504	0·358
p = 3·5	Pu/BD	2·310	3·210	4·110	5·010	6·522	11·360	15·322	18·548
	e/D	4·883	3·573	2·818	2·319	1·738	0·849	0·538	0·380
p = 4·0	Pu/BD	2·254	3·154	4·054	4·954	6·554	11·954	16·354	19·912
	e/D	5·654	4·101	3·218	2·641	1·948	0·908	0·567	0·399

Table 9B·85. Eccentrically Loaded Columns

f_{ck} = 15 MPa, f_y = 250 MPa,

	$a = \frac{1}{6}$			$a = \frac{1}{8}$			$a = \frac{1}{10}$		
$\frac{P_u}{BD}$	$\frac{M_u B}{(P_u)^2}$	f_s = stress in steel	$P = \frac{A_t \times 100}{BD}$	$\frac{M_u B}{(P_u)^2}$	f_s	$P = \frac{A_t \times 100}{BD}$	$\frac{M_u B}{(P_u)^2}$	f_s	$P = \frac{A_t \times 100}{BD}$
1	2	3	4	5	6	7	8	9	10
0·1	155·56	217·5	1·10	171·5	217·5	1·15	181·40	217·5	1·19
0·2	38·89	217·5	1·10	42·88	217·5	1·15	45·35	217·5	1·19
0·3	17·28	217·5	1·10	19·06	217·5	1·15	20·16	217·5	1·19
0·4	9·72	217·5	1·10	10·72	217·5	1·15	11·34	217·5	1·19
0·5	6·22	217·5	1·10	6·86	217·5	1·15	7·26	217·5	1·19
0·6	4·32	217·5	1·10	4·76	217·5	1·15	5·04	217·5	1·19
0·7	3·17	217·5	1·10	3·50	217·5	1·15	3·70	217·5	1·19
0·8	2·43	217·5	1·10	2·68	217·5	1·15	2·83	217·5	1·19
0·9	1·92	217·5	1·10	2·12	217·5	1·15	2·24	217·5	1·19
1·0	1·56	217·5	1·10	1·72	217·5	1·15	1·81	217·5	1·19
1·1	1·29	207·7	1·18	1·42	216·5	1·16	1·20	217·5	1·19
1·2	1·08	177·6	1·35	1·19	191·8	1·31	1·26	199·8	1·29
1·3	0·92	153·8	1·55	1·01	168·4	1·49	1·07	176·7	1·46
1·4	0·79	131·2	1·82	0·88	146·2	1·72	0·93	154·6	1·67
1·5	0·69	109·9	2·17	0·76	125·1	2·01	0·81	133·7	1·93
1·6	0·61	8·96	2·67	0·67	105·0	2·39	0·71	113·7	2·27
1·7	0·54	89·6	3·40	0·59	85·8	2·92	0·63	94·7	2·73
1·8	0·48	51·9	4·60	0·53	67·6	3·71	0·56	76·6	3·37

Table 9B·86. Eccentrically loaded column

f_{ck} = 20 MPa, f_y = 250 MPa,

	$a = \frac{1}{6}$			$a = \frac{1}{8}$			$a = \frac{1}{10}$		
$\frac{P_u}{BD}$	$\frac{M_u B}{(P_u)^2}$	f_s = stress in steel	$P = \frac{A_t \times 100}{BD}$	$\frac{M_u B}{(P_u)^2}$	f_s	$P = \frac{A_t \times 100}{BD}$	$\frac{M_u B}{(P_u)^2}$	f_s	$P = \frac{A_t \times 100}{BD}$
1	2	3	4	5	6	7	8	9	10
0·1	206·90	217·5	1·46	228·20	217·5	1·54	241·40	217·5	1·58
0·2	51·73	217·5	1·46	57·05	217·5	1·54	60·35	217·5	1·58
0·3	22·99	217·5	1·46	25·36	217·5	1·54	26·82	217·5	1·58
0·4	12·93	217·5	1·46	14·26	217·5	1·54	15·09	217·5	1·58
0·5	8·28	217·5	1·46	9·13	217·5	1·54	9·66	217·5	1·58
0·6	5·75	217·5	1·46	6·34	217·5	1·54	6·71	217·5	1·58
0·7	4·22	217·5	1·46	4·66	217·5	1·54	4·93	217·5	1·58
0·8	3·23	217·5	1·46	3·57	217·5	1·54	3·77	217·5	1·58
0·9	2·55	217·5	1·46	2·82	217·5	1·54	2·98	217·5	1·58
1·0	2·07	217·5	1·46	2·28	217·5	1·54	2·41	217·5	1·58
1·1	1·71	217·5	1·46	1·89	217·5	1·54	2·00	217·5	1·58
1·2	1·44	217·5	1·46	1·58	217·5	1·54	1·68	217·5	1·58
1·3	1·22	217·5	1·46	1·35	217·5	1·54	1·43	217·5	1·58
1·4	1·06	215·8	1·48	1·16	217·5	1·54	1·23	217·5	1·58
1·5	0·92	196·3	1·62	1·01	210·2	1·59	1·07	217·5	1·58
1·6	0·81	177·6	1·79	0·89	191·8	1·74	0·94	199·8	1·72
1·7	0·72	159·6	2·00	0·79	174·1	1·92	0·84	182·3	1·89
1·8	0·64	142·4	2·24	0·70	157·1	2·13	0·75	165·5	2·08

Table 9B·87. Eccentrically loaded Columns, Steel on one side

f_{ck} = 25 MPa, f_y = 250 MPa

$\frac{P_u}{BD}$	$a = \frac{1}{6}$			$a = \frac{1}{8}$			$a = \frac{1}{10}$		
	$\frac{M_u B}{(P_u)^2}$	f_s = stress in steel	$p = \frac{A_t \times 100}{BD}$	$\frac{M_u B}{(P_u)^2}$	f_s = stress in steel	$p = \frac{A_t \times 100}{BD}$	$\frac{M_u B}{(P_u)^2}$	f_s = stress in steel	$p = \frac{A_t \times 100}{BD}$
1	2	3	4	5	6	7	8	9	10
0·1	259·00	217·5	1·83	285·60	217·5	1·92	302·10	217·5	1·98
0·2	64·75	217·5	1·83	71·40	217·5	1·92	75·53	217·5	1·98
0·3	28·78	217·5	1·83	31·73	217·5	1·92	33·57	217·5	1·98
0·4	16·19	217·5	1·83	17·85	217·5	1·92	18·88	217·5	1·98
0·5	10·36	217·5	1·83	11·42	217·5	1·92	12·08	217·5	1·98
0·6	7·19	217·5	1·83	7·93	217·5	1·92	8·39	217·5	1·98
0·7	5·29	217·5	1·83	5·83	217·5	1·92	6·17	217·5	1·98
0·8	4·05	217·5	1··83	4·46	217·5	1·92	4·72	217·5	1·98
0·9	3·20	217·5	1·83	3·53	217·5	1·92	3·73	217·5	1·98
1·0	2·59	217·5	1·83	2·86	217·5	1·92	3·02	217·5	1·98
1·1	2·14	217·5	1·83	2·36	217·5	1·92	2·50	217·5	1·98
1·2	1·80	217·5	1·83	1·98	217·5	1·92	2·10	217·5	1·98
1·3	1·53	217·5	1·83	1·69	217·5	1·92	1·79	217·5	1·98
1·4	1·32	217·5	1·83	1·46	217·5	1·92	1·54	217·5	1·98
1·5	1·15	217·5	1·83	1·27	217·5	1·92	1·34	217·5	1·98
1·6	1·01	217·5	1·83	1·12	217·5	1·92	1·18	217·5	1·98
1·7	0·90	217·5	1·83	0·99	217·5	1·92	1·05	217·5	1·98
1·8	0·80	207·9	1·92	0·88	217·5	1·92	0·93	217·5	1·98

Table 9B·88. Eccentrically Loaded Columns Steel in one side

f_{ck} = 15 MPa, f_y = 415 MPa

$\frac{P_u}{BD}$	$a = \frac{1}{6}$			$a = \frac{1}{8}$			$a = \frac{1}{10}$		
	$\frac{M_u B}{(P_u)^2}$	f_s = stress in steel	$p = \frac{A_t \times 100}{BD}$	$\frac{M_u B}{(P_u)^2}$	f_s = stress in steel	$p = \frac{A_t \times 100}{BD}$	$\frac{M_u B}{(P_u)^2}$	f_s = stress in steel	$p = \frac{A_t \times 100}{BD}$
1	2	3	4	5	6	7	8	9	10
0·1	143·80	361·05	0·60	158·05	361·05	0·63	167·70	361·05	0·64
0·2	35·95	361·05	0·60	39·63	361·05	0·63	41·93	361·05	0·64
0·3	15·98	361·05	0·60	17·61	361·05	0·63	18·63	361·03	0·64
0·4	8·99	361·05	0·60	9·91	361·05	0·63	10·48	361·05	0·64
0·5	5·75	361·05	0·60	6·34	361·05	0·63	6·71	361·05	0·64
0·6	3·99	361·05	0·60	4·40	361·05	0·63	4·66	361·05	0·64
0·7	2·93	361·05	0·60	3·23	361·05	0·63	3·42	361·05	0·64
0·8	2·25	361·05	0·60	2·48	361·05	0·63	2·62	361·05	0·64
0·9	1·78	330·86	0·65	1·96	345·64	0·65	2·07	353·92	0·66
1·0	1·44	298·20	0·72	1·59	313·59	0·72	1·68	322·25	0·72
1·1	1·19	267·54	0·81	1·31	283·46	0·80	1·39	292·43	0·80
1·2	1·00	238·71	0·90	1·10	255·06	0·89	1·16	264·30	0·88
1·3	0·85	211·55	1·01	0·94	228·25	0·99	0·99	237·72	0·98
1·4	0·73	185·91	1·16	0·81	202·91	1·12	0·86	212·57	1·06
1·5	0·64	161·67	1·33	0·70	178·92	1·26	0·75	188·73	1·23
1·6	0·56	138·73	1·55	0·62	156·17	1·45	0·66	166·10	1·40
1·7	0·50	116·98	1·84	0·55	134·57	1·68	0·58	144·60	1·61
1·8	0·44	96·32	2·24	0·49	114·03	1·98	0·52	124·14	1·88

Table 9B·89. Eccentrically loaded columns, steel on one side

f_{ck} = 20 MPa, f_y = 415 MPa

$\frac{P_u}{BD}$	$a = \frac{1}{6}$			$a = \frac{1}{8}$			$a = \frac{1}{10}$		
	$\frac{M_u B}{(P_u)^2}$	f_s = stress in steel	$p = \frac{A_t \times 100}{BD}$	$\frac{M_u B}{(P_u)^2}$	f_s = stress in steel	$p = \frac{A_t \times 100}{BD}$	$\frac{M_u B}{(P_u)^2}$	f_s = stress in steel	$p = \frac{A_t \times 100}{BD}$
1	2	3	4	5	6	7	8	9	10
0·1	191·70	361·05	0·80	211·30	361·05	0·84	223·60	361·05	0·86
0·2	47·93	361·05	0·80	52·83	361·05	0·84	55·9	361·05	0·86
0·3	21·30	361·05	0·80	23·48	361·05	0·84	24·84	361·05	0·86
0·4	11·98	361·05	0·80	13·21	361·05	0·84	13·98	361·05	0·86
0·5	7·67	361·05	0·80	8·45	361·05	0·84	8·94	361·05	0·86
0·6	5·36	361·05	0·80	5·87	361·05	0·84	6·21	361·05	0·86
0·7	3·91	361·05	0·80	4·31	361·05	0·84	4·56	361·05	0·86
0·8	3·00	361·05	0·80	3·30	361·05	0·84	3·49	361·05	0·86
0·9	2·37	361·05	0·80	2·61	361·05	0·84	2·76	361·05	0·86
1·0	1·92	361·05	0·80	2·11	361·05	0·84	2·24	361·05	0·86
1·1	1·58	356·81	0·80	1·75	361·05	0·84	1·85	361·05	0·86
1·2	1·33	330·87	0·87	1·47	345·64	0·87	1·55	353·92	0·88
1·3	1·13	306·17	0·94	1·25	321·42	0·94	1·32	329·99	0·94
1·4	0·98	282·63	1·02	1·08	298·30	1·01	1·14	307·12	1·01
1·5	0·85	260·17	1·10	0·94	276·20	1·09	0·99	285·25	1·09
1·6	0·75	238·71	1·20	0·83	255·06	1·18	0·87	264·30	1·17
1·7	0·66	218·19	1·32	0·73	234·81	1·29	0·77	244·23	1·27
1·8	0·59	198·54	1·45	0·65	215·41	1·40	0·69	224·97	1·38

Table 9B·90. Eccentrically loaded columns, steel on one side

f_{ck} = 25 MPa, f_y = 415 MPa

$\frac{P_u}{BD}$	$a = \frac{1}{6}$			$a = \frac{1}{8}$			$a = \frac{1}{10}$		
	$\frac{M_u B}{(P_u)^2}$	f_s = stress in steel	$p = \frac{A_t \times 100}{BD}$	$\frac{M_u B}{(P_u)^2}$	f_s = stress in steel	$p = \frac{A_t \times 100}{BD}$	$\frac{M_u B}{(P_u)^2}$	f_s = stress in steel	$p = \frac{A_t \times 100}{BD}$
1	2	3	4	5	6	7	8	9	10
0·1	239·60	361·05	1·00	264·01	361·05	1·04	279·50	361·05	1·07
0·2	59·90	361·05	1·00	66·03	361·05	1·04	69·88	361·05	1·07
0·3	26·62	361·05	1·00	29·34	361·05	1·04	31·06	361·05	1·07
0·4	14·98	361·05	1·00	16·51	361·05	1·04	17·47	361·05	1·07
0·5	9·58	361·05	1·00	10·56	361·05	1·04	11·18	361·05	1·07
0·6	6·66	361·05	1·00	7·34	361·05	1·04	7·76	361·05	1·07
0·7	4·89	361·05	1·00	5·39	361·05	1·04	5·78	361·05	1·07
0·8	3·74	361·05	1·00	4·13	361·05	1·04	4·37	361·05	1·07
0·9	2·96	361·05	1·00	3·26	361·05	1·04	3·45	361·05	1·07
1·0	2·40	361·05	1·00	2·64	361·05	1·04	2·80	361·05	1·07
1·1	1·98	361·05	1·00	2·18	361·05	1·04	2·31	361·05	1·07
1·2	1·66	361·05	1·00	1·83	361·05	1·04	1·94	361·05	1·07
1·3	1·42	361·05	1·00	1·56	361·05	1·04	1·60	361·05	1·07
1·4	1·22	351·51	1·02	1·35	361·05	1·04	1·40	361·05	1·07
1·5	1·06	330·87	1·09	1·17	345·64	1·09	1·20	353·92	1·10
1·6	0·94	311·02	1·16	1·03	326·17	1·16	1·09	334·69	1·16
1·7	0·83	291·91	1·23	0·91	307·42	1·23	0·97	316·15	1·23
1·8	0·74	273·52	1·31	0·82	289·34	1·30	0·86	298·26	1·30

Table 9B·91. Columns with Compression and Uniaxial Bending can also be designed by using following tables : f_{ck} 20 N/mm^2

Member No.	*b* *mm*	*D* *mm*	*d* *mm*	*Mu* (× 10^9) *Nmm*	*Pu* (× 10^6) *N*	$\frac{Mu}{f_{ck}\, bD^2}$	$\frac{Pu}{f_{ck}\, bD}$	$\frac{P}{f_{ck}}$	*As required* *mm*^{2}	*Bar Dia* ϕ *mm*	*Spacing* *mm*	$A_{S(**)}$ *provided* *mm*^{2}
1	1000	9400	9330	14·73	–5·73	0·009	0·025	0	*3396	ϕ32	200	8040
2	1000	9400	9330	53·91	–7·50	0·020	0·027	0·0025	7050	ϕ32	200	8040
3	1000	9400	9330	53·91	–7·50	0·020	0·027	0·0025	7050	ϕ32	200	8040
4	1000	1200	1130	0·113	–9·92	0·003	0·276	0	*5879	ϕ32	200	8040
5	1000	2384	2314	5·478	–6·14	0·032	0·085	0	*3638	ϕ32	200	8040
6	1000	2384	2274	3·720	+8·76	0·022	0·122	0·05	35760	2 Rows (ϕ40 +ϕ32) +2 × ϕ32	200	36700
7	1000	2384	2274	4·520	+8·76	0·027	0·122	0·05	35760	2 Rows (ϕ40 +ϕ32) +2 × ϕ32	200	36700
8	1000	10000	9930	14·787	–8·25	0·005	0·03	0	*4889	ϕ32 +ϕ25	200	12950
9	1000	10000	9930	35·32	–8·25	0·011	0·03	0	*4889	ϕ32 +ϕ25	200	12950
10	1000	10000	9930	43·30	–20·25	0·014	0·068	0	*12000	ϕ32 +ϕ25	200	12950
11	1000	10000	9930	39·10	–15·67	0·013	0·05	0	*9286	ϕ32 +ϕ25	200	12950
12	1000	10000	9930	35·31	–8·26	0·011	0·05	0	*4895	ϕ32 +ϕ25	200	12950
13	1000	10000	9930	14·79	–8·26	0·005	0·05	0	*4895	ϕ32 +ϕ25	200	12950
14	1000	2384	2274	2·74	–11·97	0·016	0·167	0	*7093	2 Rows ϕ25 +ϕ20	200	8050
15	1000	2000	1890	4·82	–11·51	0·04	0·19	0	*6821	2 Rows ϕ25 +ϕ20	200	8050

* Steel is provided for minimum reinforcement of 0·8% of area required to resist direct stress.

9B·10. Crack width calculations

Beam No.	Properties of the section				Reinforcement				M_u (×10⁹)(N-mm)	Tensile Force (T × 10⁶) (N)	x (mm)	z (mm)	Stress in tension steer			Prop. of crack width			Strain at that point ($\varepsilon_1 \times 10^{-3}$)	avg. strain ($\varepsilon_m \times 10^{-3}$)	Design surface crack width (mm)
	b_t (mm)	h (mm)	d (mm)	d' (mm)	A_S (mm^2)	ρ ($\times 10^{-3}$)	A_{sc} (mm^2)	ρ' ($\times 10^{-3}$)					f_{s_1}	f_{s_2}	$f_s = f_{s_1} + f_{s_2}$	a_{cr} (mm)	C_{min} (mm)	a' (mm)			
1	1000	1200	1130	70	3140	2·78	3140	2·78	0·075	—	209	1080	22	—	22	50	50	1200	0·118	–0·99	un-cracked
2	1000	2384	2274	110	18835	8·28	18835	8·28	2·48	5·84	639	2091	63	155	218	50	50	2384	1·20	0·80	0·12
3	1000	2384	2274	110	18835	8·28	18835	8·28	3·01	5·84	639	2091	80	155	235	50	50	2384	1·29	0·89	0·13
4	1000	2000	1890	110	4910	2·60	4910	2·60	3·21	—	340	1775	368	—	368	50	50	2000	1·98	1·10	0·18

Following pile spacings should be used to keep the cost of the pile cap minimum:

Table 9B·93.

Type of pile	*Minimum spacing centre-to-centre of piles*
Bearing piles in hard stratum.	2 to $2\frac{1}{2}$ times diameter of pile or minimum 0.8 m
Bearing piles in hard bed rock.	2 times diameter or minimum 0.6 m
Friction piles.	3 to 5 times diameter or minimum 1.0 m.

9B·11. Design Data for Reference

App. 9B·1A. Areas of Bars at Given Spacings Values in cm² per Meter Width

Spacing cm	Bar Diameter, mm 5	6	8	10	12	14	16	18	20	22	25	28	32
5	3·93	5·65	10·05	15·71	22·62	30·79	40·21	50·89	62·83	76·03	98·17	123·15	160·85
6	3·27	4·71	8·38	13·09	18·85	25·66	33·51	42·41	52·36	63·36	81·81	102·68	134·04
7	2·80	4·04	7·18	11·22	16·16	21·99	28·72	36·35	44·88	54·30	70·12	87·96	114·89
8	2·45	3·53	6·28	9·82	14·14	19·24	25·13	31·81	39·27	47·52	61·36	76·90	100·53
9	2·18	3·14	5·58	8·73	12·57	17·10	22·34	28·27	34·91	42·24	54·54	68·42	89·36
10	1·96	2·83	5·03	7·85	11·31	15·39	20·11	25·45	31·42	38·01	49·09	61·57	80·42
11	1·78	2·57	4·57	7·14	10·28	13·99	18·28	23·13	28·56	34·56	44·62	55·98	73·11
12	1·64	2·36	4·19	6·54	9·42	12·83	16·75	21·21	26·18	31·68	40·91	51·31	67·02
13	1·51	2·17	3·87	6·04	8·70	11·84	15·47	19·57	24·17	29·24	37·76	47·37	61·86
14	1·40	2·02	3·59	5·61	8·08	11·00	14·36	18·18	22·44	27·15	35·06	43·98	57·45
15	1·31	1·88	3·35	5·24	7·54	10·26	13·40	16·96	20·94	25·34	32·72	41·05	53·62
16	1·23	1·77	3·14	4·91	7·07	9·62	12·57	15·90	19·63	23·76	30·68	38·48	50·27
17	1·15	1·66	2·96	4·62	6·65	9·05	11·83	14·97	18·48	22·36	28·87	36·22	47·31
18	1·09	1·57	2·79	4·36	6·28	8·55	11·17	14·44	17·45	21·12	27·27	34·21	44·68
19	1·03	1·49	2·65	4·13	5·95	8·10	10·58	13·39	16·53	20·01	25·84	32·41	42·33
20	0·98	1·41	2·51	3·93	5·65	7·70	10·05	12·72	15·71	19·01	24·54	30·79	40·21
21	0·93	1·35	2·39	3·74	5·39	7·33	9·57	12·12	14·96	18·10	23·37	29·32	38·30
22	0·89	1·28	2·28	3·57	5·14	7·00	9·14	11·57	4·28	17·28	22·31	27·99	36·56
23	0·85	1·23	2·18	3·41	4·92	6·69	8·74	11·06	13·66	16·53	21·34	26·77	34·97
24	0·82	1·18	2·09	3·27	4·71	6·41	8·38	10·60	13·09	15·84	20·54	25·66	33·51
25	0·78	1·13	2·01	3·14	4·52	6·16	8·04	10·18	12·57	15·20	19·63	24·63	32·17
26	0·75	1·09	1·93	3·02	4·35	5·92	7·73	9·79	12·08	14·62	18·88	23·68	30·93
27	0·73	1·05	1·86	2·91	4·19	5·70	7·45	9·42	11·64	14·08	18·18	22·81	29·79
28	0·70	1·01	1·79	2·80	4·04	5·50	7·18	9·09	11·22	13·58	17·53	21·99	28·76
29	0·68	0·97	1·73	2·71	3·90	5·31	6·93	8·77	10·83	13·11	16·93	21·23	27·73
30	0·65	0·94	1·68	2·62	3·77	5·13	6·70	8·48	10·47	12·67	16·36	20·52	26·81
32	0·61	0·88	1·57	2·45	3·53	4·81	6·28	7·95	9·82	11·88	15·34	19·24	25·13
34	0·58	0·83	1·48	2·31	3·33	4·53	5·91	7·48	9·24	11·18	14·44	18·11	23·65
36	0·54	0·78	1·40	2·18	3·14	4·28	5·58	7·07	8·73	10·56	13·63	17·10	22·34
38	0·52	0·74	1·32	2·07	2·98	4·05	5·29	6·70	8·27	10·00	12·92	16·20	21·16
40	0·49	0·71	1·26	1·96	2·83	3·85	5·03	6·36	7·85	9·50	12·27	15·39	20·11

App. 9B·2A. Areas of Given Numbers of Bars in cm²

Number of Bars	Bar Diameter, mm 6	8	10	12	14	16	18	20	22	25	28	32	36
1	0·28	0·50	0·79	1·13	1·54	2·01	2·54	3·14	3·80	4·91	6·16	8·04	10·18
2	0·56	1·00	1·57	2·26	3·07	4·02	5·08	6·28	7·60	9·81	12·31	16·08	20·35
3	0·84	1·50	2·35	3·39	4·61	6·03	7·63	9·42	11·40	14·72	18·47	24·12	30·53
4	1·13	2·01	3·14	4·52	6·15	8·04	10·17	12·56	15·20	19·63	24·63	32·17	40·17
5	1·41	2·51	3·92	5·65	7·69	10·05	12·72	15·70	19·00	24·54	30·78	40·21	50·89
6	1·69	3·01	4·71	6·78	9·23	12·06	15·26	18·85	22·80	29·45	36·94	48·25	61·07
7	1·97	3·51	5·49	7·91	10·77	14·07	17·81	21·99	26·60	34·36	43·10	56·29	71·25
8	2·26	4·02	6·28	9·04	12·31	16·08	20·35	25·13	30·41	39·27	49·26	64·34	81·43
9	2·54	4·52	7·06	10·17	13·85	18·09	22·90	28·27	34·21	44·17	55·41	72·38	91·60
10	2·82	5·02	7·85	11·31	15·39	20·10	25·44	31·41	38·01	49·08	61·57	80·42	101·78
11	3·11	5·52	8·63	12·44	16·93	22·11	27·99	34·55	41·81	53·99	67·73	88·46	111·96
12	3·39	6·03	9·42	13·57	18·47	24·12	30·53	37·69	45·61	58·90	73·89	96·51	122·14
13	3·67	6·53	10·21	14·70	20·01	26·13	33·08	40·84	49·41	63·81	80·04	104·55	132·32
14	3·95	7·03	10·99	15·83	21·55	28·14	35·62	43·98	53·21	68·72	86·20	112·59	142·50
15	4·24	7·54	11·78	16·96	23·09	30·15	38·17	47·12	57·02	73·63	92·36	120·63	152·68
16	4·52	8·04	12·56	18·09	24·63	32·17	40·71	50·26	60·82	78·54	98·52	128·68	162·86
17	4·80	8·54	13·35	19·22	26·17	34·18	43·26	53·40	64·62	83·44	104·67	136·72	173·03
18	5·08	9·04	14·13	20·35	27·70	36·19	45·80	56·54	68·42	88·35	110·83	144·76	183·21
19	5·37	9·55	14·92	21·48	29·24	38·20	48·34	59·69	72·22	93·26	116·99	152·80	193·39
20	5·65	10·05	15·70	22·62	30·78	40·21	50·89	62·83	76·02	98·17	123·15	160·85	203·57
Circumference of Given Numbers of Bars in c.m.													
1	1·88	2·51	3·14	3·71	4·40	5·03	5·65	6·28	6·91	7·85	8·80	10·05	11·31
2	3·76	5·02	6·28	7·42	8·86	10·06	11·30	12·56	13·82	15·70	17·60	30·10	22·62
3	5·64	7·53	9·42	11·13	13·20	15·09	16·45	18·84	20·73	23·55	26·40	30·10	33·93
4	7·52	10·04	12·56	14·84	17·60	20·12	22·60	15·12	27·64	21·40	25·20	40·20	45·24
5	9·40	12·55	15·70	18·55	22·00	25·15	28·25	31·40	34·55	29·25	44·00	50·25	56·55
6	11·28	15·06	18·84	27·26	26·40	30·78	33·90	37·68	41·46	47·10	52·80	60·30	67·86
7	13·46	17·57	21·98	25·97	30·28	35·21	39·55	43·96	48·37	54·95	61·60	70·35	79·17
8	15·04	20·08	25·12	29·68	35·20	40·24	45·20	50·24	55·28	62·86	70·40	80·40	90·48
9	16·92	22·59	28·26	33·39	39·60	45·27	50·85	56·52	62·19	70·65	79·20	90·45	101·79
10	18·80	25·10	31·40	37·10	44·00	50·30	56·50	62·90	69·10	78·50	88·00	100·50	113·10

App. 9B·3A. Deflection Formulae for Prismatic Beams and Cantilevers

(Also refer chapter 4)

Load type		*Deflection*	
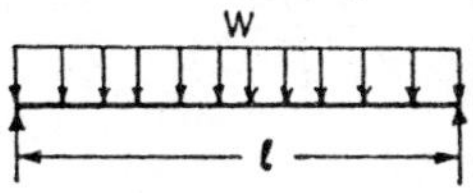	$\frac{5}{384} \times \frac{Wl^3}{EI}$	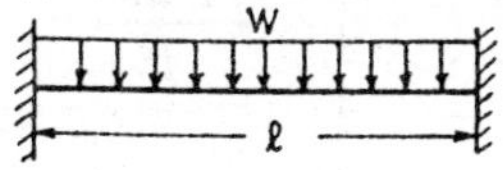	$\frac{Wl^3}{384\ EI}$
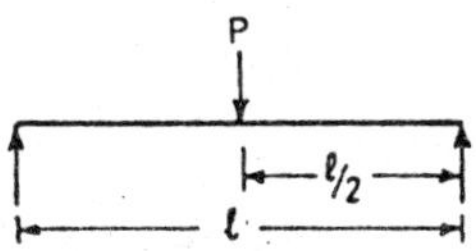	$\frac{Pl^3}{48\ EI}$	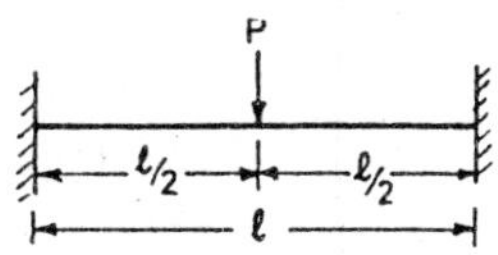	$\frac{Pl^3}{192\ EI}$
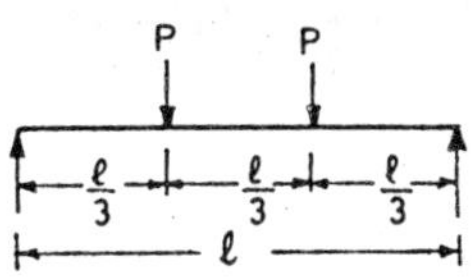	$\frac{23\ Pl^3}{648\ EI}$	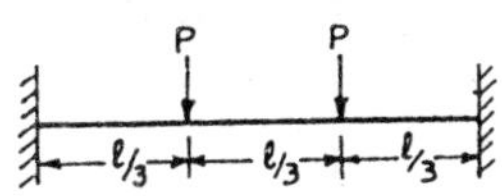	$\frac{5\ Pl^3}{648\ EI}$
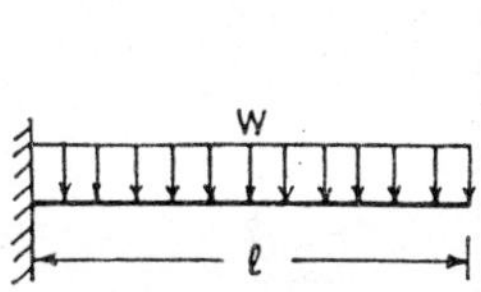	$\frac{Wl^3}{8\ EI}$	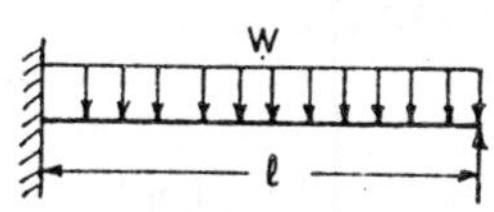	$\frac{Wl^3}{185\ EI}$
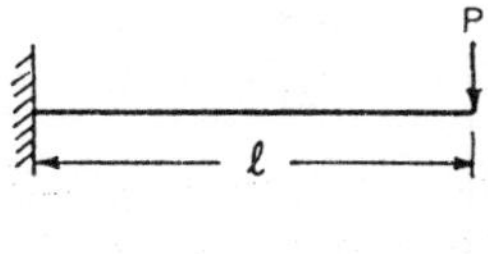	$\frac{Pl^3}{3\ EI}$	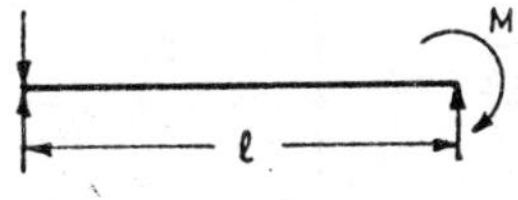	$\frac{1}{16} \times \frac{Ml^2}{EI}$ $\frac{Pl^3}{48\sqrt{5}\ EI}$

Note : W is total distributed load

App. 9B·4A. Fixed End Moments for Prismatic Beams. (Also refer chapter 4)

Load Type	M_{FA}	M_{FB}
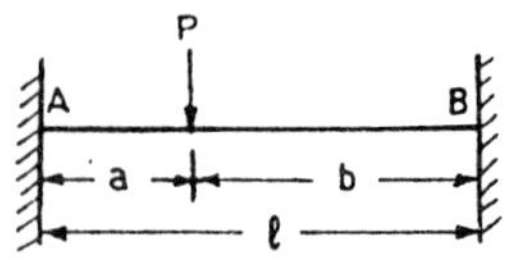	$+\frac{P\,ab^2}{l^2}$	$-\frac{P\,a^2b}{l^2}$
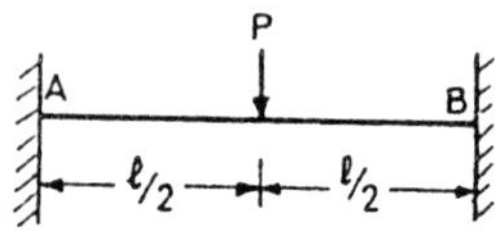	$+\frac{Pl}{8}$	$-\frac{Pl}{8}$
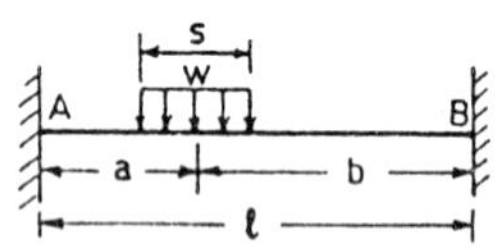	$+\frac{ws}{12\,l^2}\left[12\,ab^2+s^2(l-3b)\right]$	$-\frac{ws}{12\,l^2}\left[12\,a^2b+s^2(l-3a)\right]$
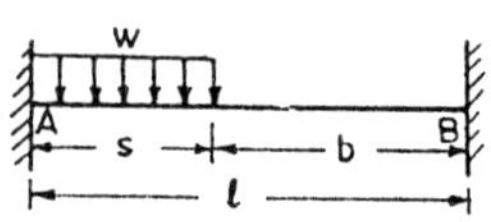	$+\frac{ws^2}{12\,l^2}\left[2l(3l-4s)+3s^2\right]$	$-\frac{ws^2}{12\,l^2}(4l-3s)$
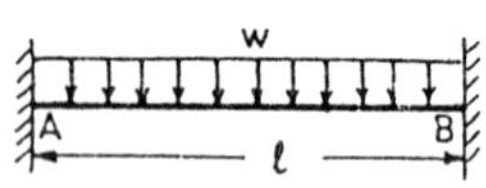	$+\frac{wl^2}{12}$	$-\frac{wl^2}{12}$
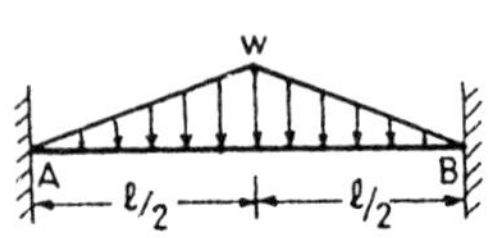	$+\frac{5\,wl^2}{96}$	$-\frac{5\,wl^2}{96}$
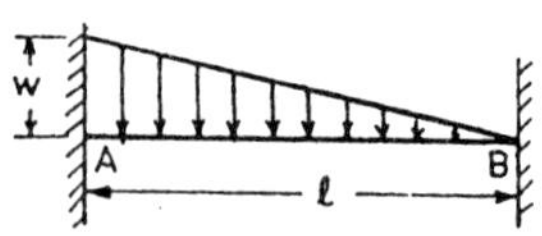	$+\frac{wl^2}{20}$	$-\frac{wl^2}{30}$
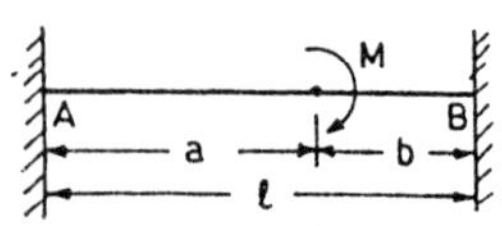	$-M\frac{b}{l}\left(2-\frac{3b}{l}\right)$	$-M\frac{a}{l}\left(2-\frac{3a}{l}\right)$

Note : w is the load per unit length

App. 9B·5A. Moments in Walls Spanning Horizontally

Form of Container	*Support moment formulae*	*Bending moments $M = ql^2_1/k$ Bending-moment coefficients k*							*Reaction formulae (i.e. shearing force)*
		Ratio of l_2/l_1							
		1/2	*3/4*	*1*	*5/4*	*3/2*	*7/4*	*2*	
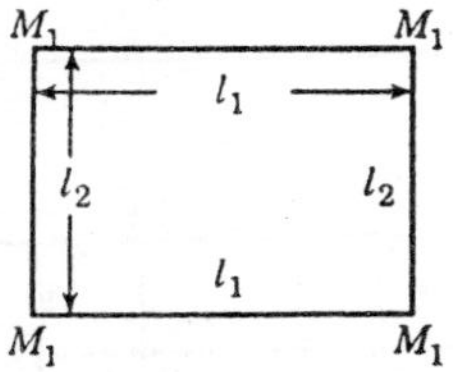	$M_1 = \frac{q(l_1^3 + l_2^3)}{12(l_1 + l_2)}$	16·00	14·77	12	9·14	6·86	5·19	4·00	$R_{l1} = \frac{1}{2} q l_1$ $R_{l2} = \frac{1}{2} q l_2$
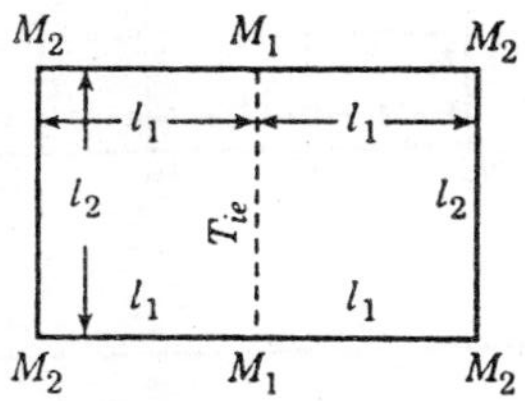	$M_1 = \frac{q(l_1^3 + 3l_1^2 l_2 - l_2^3)}{12(l_1 + 2l_2)}$	10·11	10·61	12	15·02	22·59	60·63	—	$R_{l1} = \frac{1}{2} q l_1 + \frac{M_2 - M_1}{l_1}$
	$M_2 = \frac{q(l_1^3 + 2l_2^3)}{12(l_1 + 2l_2)}$	19·20	16·27	12	8·56	6·19	4·61	3·53	$R_{l2} = \frac{1}{2} q l_2$
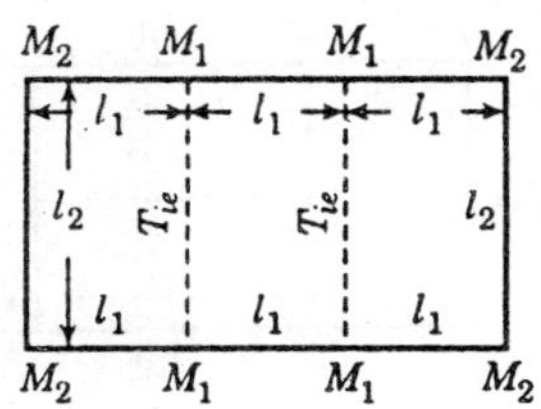	$M_1 = \frac{q(3l_1^3 + 6l_1^2 l_2 - l_2^3)}{12(3l_1 + 5l_2)}$	11·23	11·44	12	12·99	14·61	17·32	22·29	R_{l1} (end span) $= \frac{1}{2} q l_1 + \frac{M_2 - M_1}{l_1}$
	$M_2 = \frac{q(3l_1^3 + 5l_2^3)}{12(3l_1 + 5l_2)}$	18·21	15·85	12	8·70	6·34	4·73	3·63	R_{l1} (central span) $= \frac{1}{2} q l_1$ $R_{l2} = \frac{1}{2} q l_2$
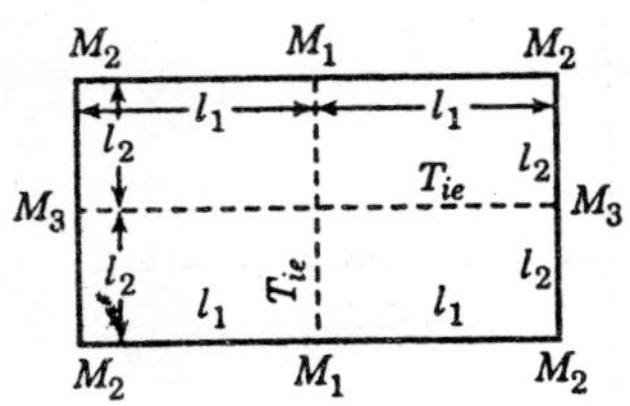	$M_1 = \frac{q(l_1 + l_2)(2l_1 - l_2)}{24}$	10·67	10·97	12	14·22	19·20	34·91	—	$R_{l1} = \frac{1}{2} q l_1 + \frac{M_2 - M_1}{l_1}$
	$M_2 = \frac{q(l_1^3 + l_2^3)}{12(l_1 + l_2)}$	16·00	14·77	12	9·14	6·86	5·19	4·00	$R_{l2} = \frac{1}{2} q l_2 + \frac{M_2 - M_3}{l_2}$
	$M_3 = \frac{q(l_1 + l_2)(2l_2 - l_1)}{24}$	—	27·43	12	7·11	4·80	3·49	2·67	

(Table contd...)

Form of Container	Support moment formulae	Bending moments $M = ql_1/k$		Bending-moment coefficients k					Reaction formulae (i.e. shearing force)
		Ratio of l_2/l_1							
		1/2	3/4	1	5/4	3/2	7/4	2	
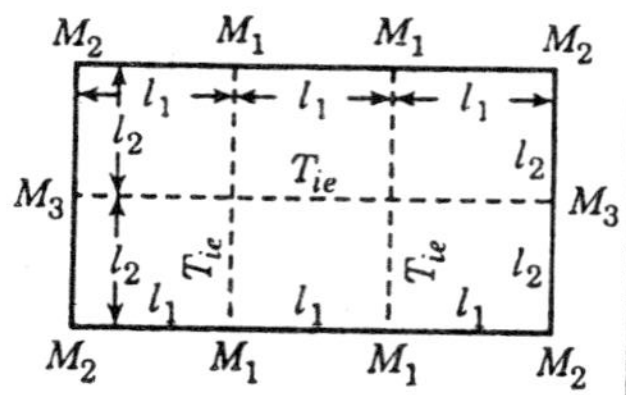	$M_1 = \frac{q(6l_1^3 + 6l_1^2 l_2 - l_2^3)}{12(6l_1 + 5l_2)}$	11·49	11·61	12	12·73	13·94	15·89	19·20	R_{l1} (end span) $= \frac{1}{2}ql_1 + \frac{M_2 - M_1}{l_1}$
	$M_2 = \frac{q(6l_1^3 + 5l_2^3)}{12(6l_1 + 5l_2)}$	15·40	14·43	12	9·32	7·08	5·40	4·17	R_{l1} (central span) $= \frac{1}{2}ql_1$
	$M_3 = \frac{q(5l_2^3 + 9l_1 l_2^2 - 3l_1^3)}{12(6l_1 + 5l_2)}$	—	28·04	12	7·06	4·75	3·45	2·63	$R_{l2} = \frac{1}{2}ql_2 + \frac{M_2 - M_3}{l_2}$
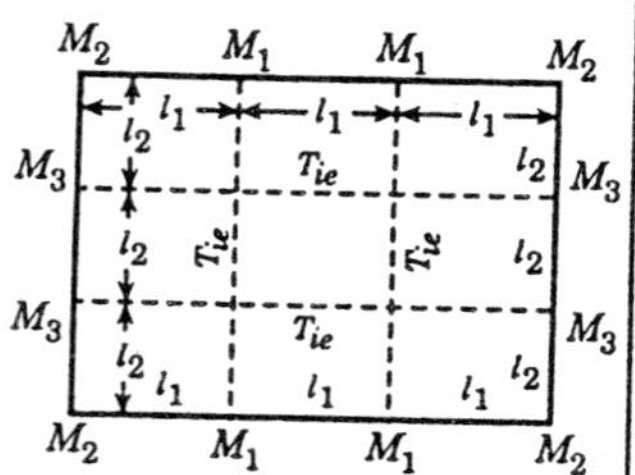	$M_1 = \frac{q(5l_1^3 + 6l_1^2 l_2 - l_2^3)}{60(l_1 + l_2)}$	11·43	11·57	12	12·80	14·12	16·27	20·00	R_{l1} (end span) $= \frac{1}{2}ql_1 + \frac{M_2 - M_1}{l_1}$
	$M_2 = \frac{q(l_1^3 + l_2^3)}{12(l_1 + l_2)}$	16·00	14·77	12	9·14	6·86	5·19	4·00	R_{l1} (central span) $\frac{1}{2}ql_1$
	$M_3 = \frac{q(5l_2^3 + 6l_1 l_2^3 - l_1^3)}{60(l_1 + l_2)}$	80·00	23·41	12	7·44	5·11	3·74	2·86	R_{l2} (end span) $= \frac{1}{2}ql_2 + \frac{M_2 - M_3}{l_2}$
									R_{l2} (central span) $= \frac{1}{2}ql_2$

App. 9B·6A. Geometric Properties of Uniform Sections

Section	Area, A	Section modulus, J_c	Second moment of area, I	Radiation of gyration, i
Rectangle 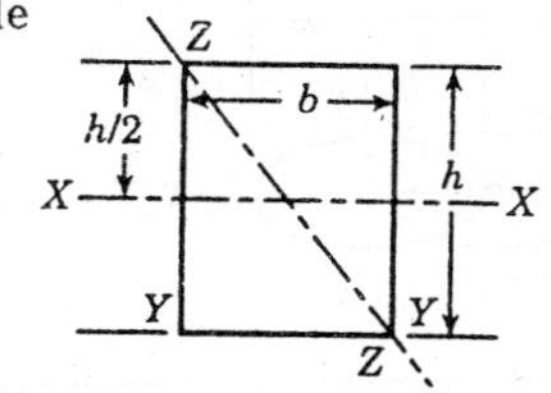	bh	About XX : $\frac{1}{6}bh^2$ About ZZ : $\frac{1}{6}\frac{b^2h^2}{\sqrt{(b^2+h^2)}}$	About XX : $\frac{1}{12}bh^3$ About YY : $\frac{1}{3}bh^3$ About ZZ : $\frac{1}{6}\frac{b^3h^3}{(b^2+h^2)}$	About XX : $h/\sqrt{12} = 0{\cdot}2887h$
Trapezium 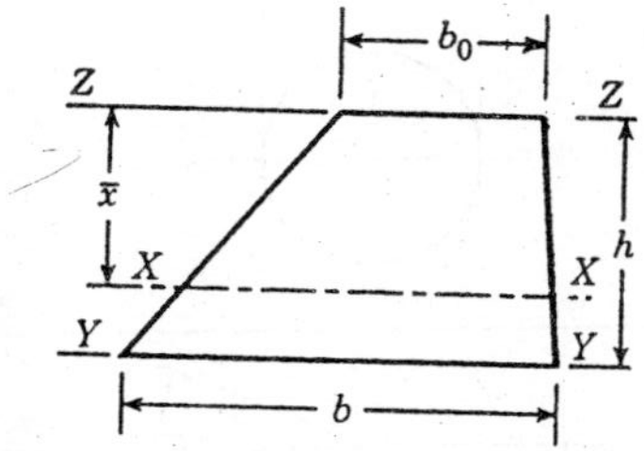	$\frac{1}{2}h(b_0+b)$	About XX to b_0 : $\frac{(b^2+4bb_0+b_0^2)h^2}{12(b+2b_0)}$ To b : $I_{xx}/(h-\bar{x})$ where $\bar{x} = \frac{1}{3}h\left(\frac{2b+b_0}{b+b_0}\right)$	About XX : $\frac{(b^2+4bb_0+b_0^2)h^3}{36(b+b_0)}$ About YY : $I_{xx} + A(h-\bar{x})^2$ About ZZ : $I_{xx} + A(\bar{x})^2$	About XX : $\sqrt{\frac{I_{xx}}{A}}$
Triangle 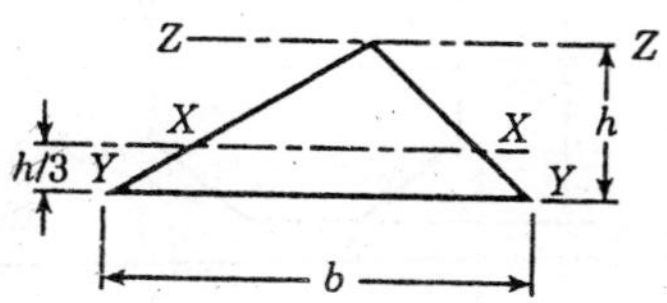	$\frac{1}{2}bh$	About XX to apex : $\frac{1}{24}bh^2$ About XX to base : $\frac{1}{12}bh^2$	About XX : $\frac{1}{36}bh^3$ About YY : $\frac{1}{12}bh^3$ About ZZ : $\frac{1}{4}bh^3$	About XX : $h/\sqrt{18} = 0{\cdot}2357h$
Flanged section 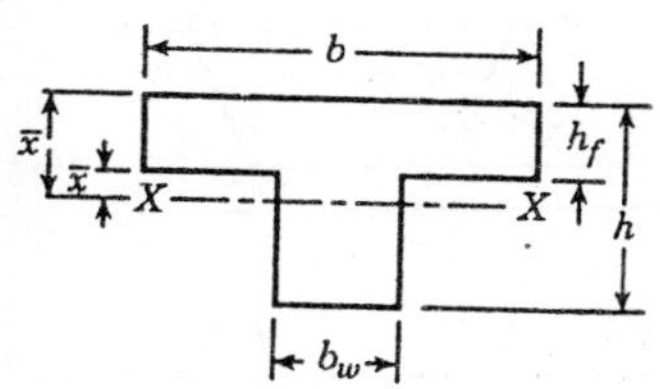	$bh_f + b_w(h-h_f)$	About XX : $\frac{I_{xx}}{\bar{x}}$ or $\frac{I_{xx}}{h-\bar{x}}$ $\bar{x} = \frac{h_f^2(b-b_w)+h^2b_w}{2[h_f(b-b_w)+hb_w]}$	About XX : $\frac{1}{3}\left[b\bar{x}^3 + b_w(h-\bar{x})^3 - (\bar{x}')^3 - (b-b_w)\right]$ where $\bar{x}' = \bar{x} - h_f$	About XX : $\sqrt{\frac{I_{xx}}{A}}$

(*Table contd...*)

Section	*Area, A*	*Section modulus, J_c*	*Second moment of area, I*	*Radiation of gyration, i*
Hexagon 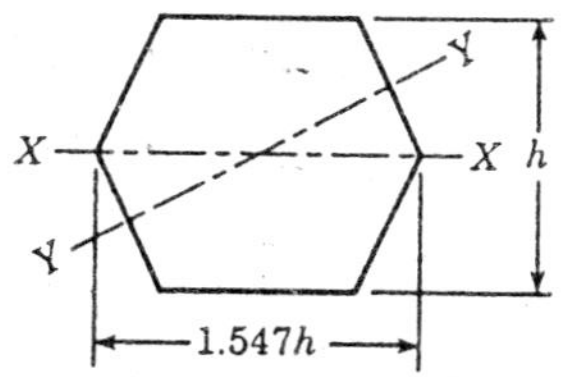	$0{\cdot}8660h^2$ (side = $0{\cdot}5774h$)	About XX : $0{\cdot}1203h^3$ About YY : $0{\cdot}1042h^3$	About XX or YY : $0{\cdot}0601h^4$	About XX or YY : $0{\cdot}2635h$
Octagon 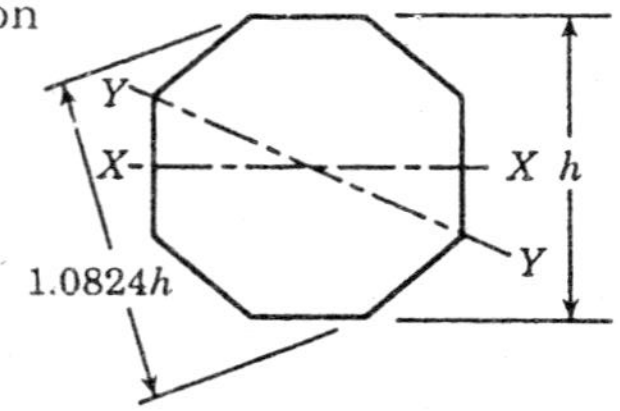	$0{\cdot}8284h^2$ (side=$0{\cdot}4142h$)	About XX : $0{\cdot}1095h^3$ About YY : $0{\cdot}1011h^3$	About XX or YY : $0{\cdot}0547h^4$	About XX or YY : $0{\cdot}2570h$
Circle 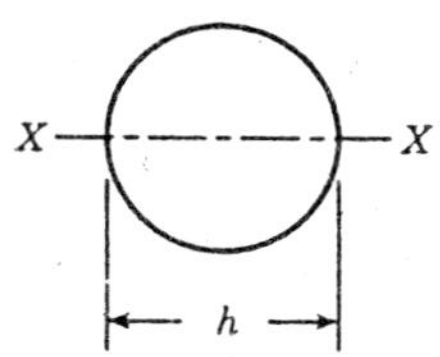	$0{\cdot}7854\,h^2 = \frac{\pi}{4}h^2$	About XX : $\frac{1}{32}\pi h^3 = 0{\cdot}0982\,h^3$	About XX : $\frac{1}{64}\pi h^4 = 0{\cdot}0491\,h^4$	About XX : $0{\cdot}2500h$
Ellipse 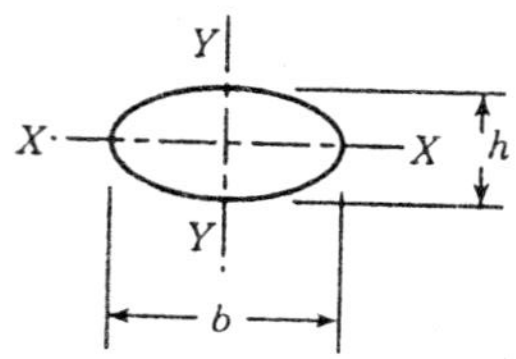	$\frac{1}{4}\pi bh$ $= 0{\cdot}7854bh$	About XX : $\frac{1}{32}\pi bh^2 = 0{\cdot}0982bh^2$	About XX : $\frac{1}{64}\pi bh^3 = 0{\cdot}0491bh^3$	About XX : $0{\cdot}2500h$

(Table contd...)

Section		Area, A	Section modulus, J_c	Second moment of area, I	Radiation of gyration, i
Sector of cylinder	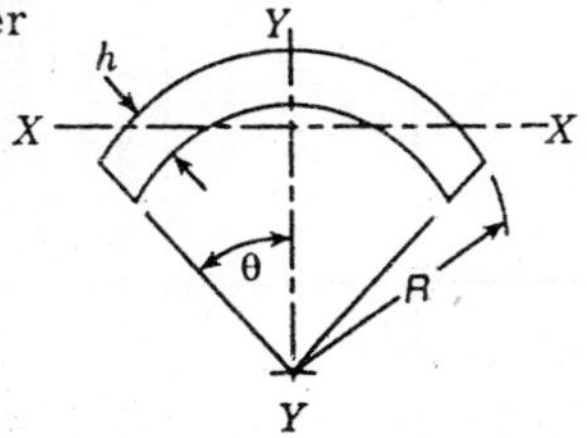	$\theta h(2R - h)$	About XX to top : I_{xx}/y_t^* About XX to bottom : I_{xx}/y_b^*	About XX : I_{xx}^* About YY : I_{yy}^*	About XX : $\sqrt{\dfrac{I_{xx}}{A}}$

$$y_t^* = R\left\{1 - \frac{2 \sin\theta}{3\theta}\left(1 - \frac{h}{R} + \frac{1}{2-(h/R)}\right)\right\} \qquad y_b^* = R\left[\frac{2\sin\theta}{3\theta(2-(h/R))} + \left(1 - \frac{h}{R}\right)\frac{2\sin\theta - 3\theta\cos\theta}{3\theta}\right]$$

$$\text{About XX : } I_{xx}^* = R^3 h\left\{\left[1 - \frac{3h}{2R} + \left(\frac{h}{R}\right)^2 - \frac{1}{4}\left(\frac{h}{R}\right)^3\right]\left[\theta + \sin\theta\cos\theta - \frac{2\sin^2\theta}{\theta}\right] + \frac{h^2\sin^2\theta}{3R^2\,\theta(2-(h/R))}\left[1 - \frac{h}{R} + \frac{1}{6}\left(\frac{h}{R}\right)^2\right]\right\}$$

$$\text{About YY : } I_{yy}^* = R^3 h\left\{\left[1 - \frac{3h}{2R} + \left(\frac{h}{R}\right)^2 - \frac{1}{4}\left(\frac{h}{R}\right)^3\right][\theta - \sin\theta\cos\theta]\right\}$$

App. 9B·7A. Reinforcement. (Bending Schedule)

Shape No.	Method of measuring bending dimensions	Total length of bar	Sketch to be given in schedule
1.		A	Straight
2.		A + h	
3.		A + 2h	
4.		A + n	
5.		A + 2n	
6.		If r is non-standard use shape code 14 A + B – (½r + d)	
7.	or	A + B + C – 2(½r + d) A + B + C – 2(½r + d)	or
8.	Non-standard radius	A + 0.57B + C – ½πd	
9.	D shall be at least 2d or	If angle with horizontal is 45° or less A + B + C	or
10.		If angle with horizontal is 45° or less A + B + C + n	
11.		If angle with horizontal is 45° or less A + 2B + C + E	
12.		A + B + C – (½ r + d)	
13.		A + B + C	
14.	(Non-standard)	If r is standard use shape code 6 A + B – (½r + d)	
15.	or	A + B + C + D – 3(½r + d)	or
16.		A + B + C + D + E – 4(½r + d)	
17.		A + B + C + D + E – 2(½r + d)	
18.	or	A + B + C + D + E – 4(½r + d)	or
19.		2(A + B) + 20d	
20.		If angle with horizontal is 45° or less A + C	
21.	r (Non-standard)	A	

Shape No.	Method of measuring bending dimensions	Total length of bar	Sketch to be given in schedule
22.	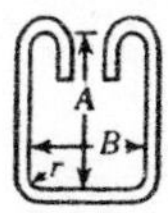 See also note 1	2A + B + 25d	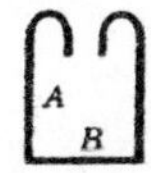
23.	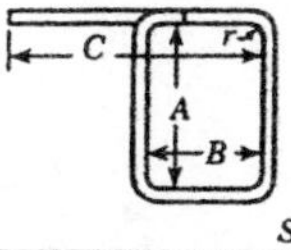 See also notes 1 & 2	2A + B + C + 10d	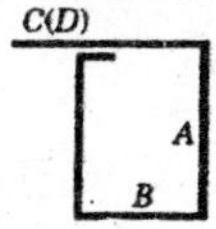
24.	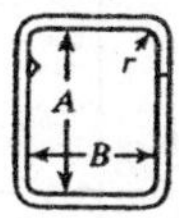 See also note 1	2A + 3B + 20d	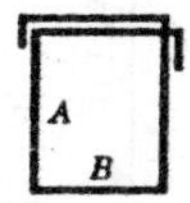
25.	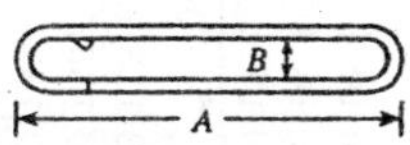	2A + 3B + 22d	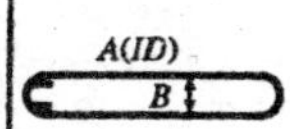
26.	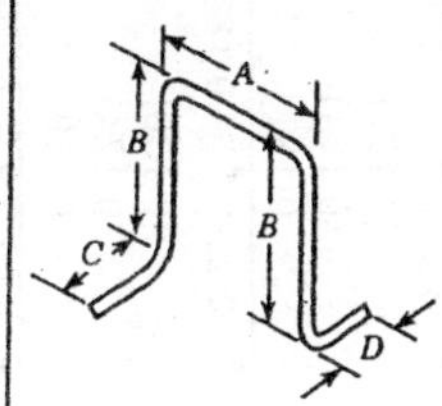	A + 2B + C + D − 4(½ r+d)	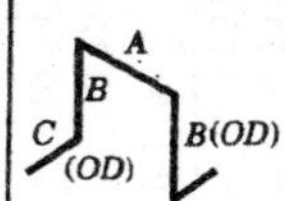 Isometric view
27.	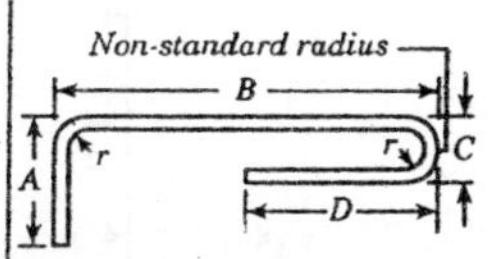	A + B + 0.57C + D ½ r−2.57ϕ	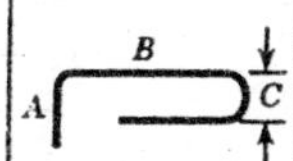
28.	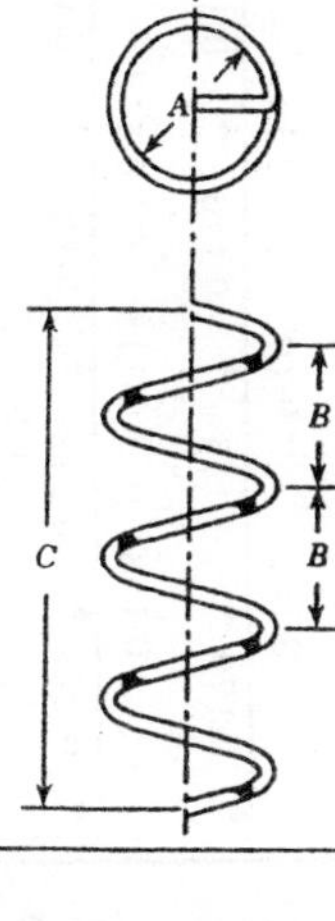	where B is not greater than A/5 $\frac{C}{B}$ π (A + d) + 8d Where d is size of bar	Helix A internal dia. B pitch of helix C overall height of helix Dimensions (mm)
29.	All other shapes		A dimensioned sketch of the shape must be given on the schedule

Notes

1. The position of the dimensions in the figure indicates whether a dimension is internal or external. If the shape is such that there may be doubt as to which is the inside of the bar, arrows should be shown in the bending schedule or the dimension must be marked with the suffix OD (outside dimension) or ID (inside dimension).
2. ϕ diameter of bar
   r radius of bend (standard unless otherwise stated)
   h hook allowance
   n bend allowance
   Hook and bend allowances, standard radii of bends, and values of (r/2) + ϕ with standard radii are as follows :

Bar diameter (mm)	(r/2) + ϕ Mild steel (mm)	(r/2) + ϕ High-yield steel (mm)	Critical min. radius (shape no. 21) (mm)
6	12	18	2·40
8	16	24	2·75
10	20	30	3·50
12	24	36	4·25
16	32	48	7·50
20	40	60	14·00
25	50	100	30·00
32	64	128	43·00
40	80	160	58·00
50	100	200	—

3. For critical radii of bars of this shape, see above table.

Dimensions of binders, links etc. are inside dimensions. Radii at corners to be half diameter of bar enclosed by binder etc. (to be stated if non-standard)

Allowances for links

Dia.	10ϕ	20ϕ	22ϕ	25ϕ
mm	mm	mm	mm	mm
6	60	120	140	150
8	80	160	180	200
10	100	200	220	250
12	120	240	270	300

App. 9B·8A. Continuous Beams—Moments from Equal Loads on Equal Spans.

Load	All spans loaded (e.g. dead load)	Imposed load (sequence of loaded spans to give max. bending moment)
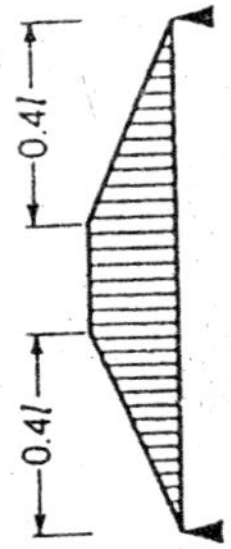	0·155 0·094 ▲ 0·094	0·155 0·127 ▲ 0·127
	0·124 0·124 0·107 ▲ 0·040 ▲ 0·107	0·145 0·145 0·134 ▲ 0·102 ▲ 0·134
	0·133 0·089 0·133 0·103 ▲ 0·054 ▲ 0·054 ▲ 0·103	[0·133] [0·089] [0·133] (0·144) (0·133) (0·144) 0·149 0·133 0·149 0·132 ▲ 0·109 ▲ 0·109 ▲ 0·132
	0·131 0·098 0·098 0·131 0·104 ▲ 0·050 ▲ 0·066 ▲ 0·050 ▲ 0·104	[0·131] [0·098] [0·098] [0·131] (0·144) (0·132) (0·132) (0·144) 0·149 0·138 0·138 0·149 0·133 ▲ 0·107 ▲ 0·115 ▲ 0·107 ▲ 0·133
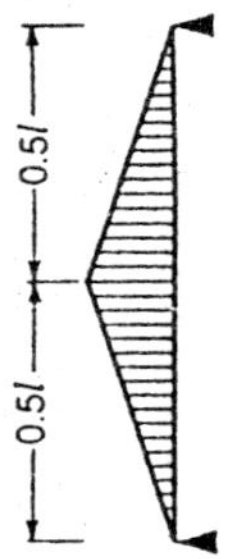	0·156 0·095 ▲ 0·095	0·156 0·129 ▲ 0·129
	0·125 0·125 0·108 ▲ 0·042 ▲ 0·108	0·146 0·146 0·136 ▲ 0·104 ▲ 0·136
	0·134 0·089 0·134 0·104 ▲ 0·056 ▲ 0·056 ▲ 0·104	[0·134] [0·089] [0·134] (0·145) (0·134) (0·145) 0·151 0·134 0·151 0·134 ▲ 0·111 ▲ 0·111 ▲ 0·134
	0·132 0·099 0·099 0·132 0·105 ▲ 0·051 ▲ 0·068 ▲ 0·051 ▲ 0·105	[0·132] [0·099] [0·099] [0·132] (0·145) (0·133) (0·133) (0·145) 0·150 0·139 0·139 0·150 0·135 ▲ 0·109 ▲ 0·117 ▲ 0·109 ▲ 0·135
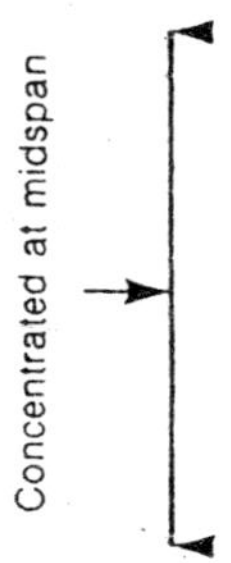	0·188 0·156 ▲ 0·156	0·188 0·203 ▲ 0·203
	0·150 0·150 0·175 ▲ 0·100 ▲ 0·175	0·175 0·175 0·213 ▲ 0·175 ▲ 0·213
	0·161 0·107 0·161 0·170 ▲ 0·116 ▲ 0·116 ▲ 0·170	[0·161] [0·107] [0·161] (0·174) (0·161) (0·174) 0·181 0·161 0·181 0·210 ▲ 0·183 ▲ 0·183 ▲ 0·210
	0·158 0·118 0·118 0·158 0·171 ▲ 0·112 ▲ 0·132 ▲ 0·112 ▲ 0·171	[0·158] [0·118] [0·118] [0·158] (0·174) (0·160) (0·160) (0·174) 0·179 0·167 0·167 0·179 0·211 ▲ 0·181 ▲ 0·191 ▲ 0·181 ▲ 0·211

Table contd...

Load	All spans loaded (e.g. dead load)	Imposed load (sequence of loaded spans to give max. bending moment)
Concentrated at third points 	0·167 ▲ 0·111 ▲ 0·111 ▲	0·167 ▲ 0·139 ▲ 0·139 ▲
	0·133 0·133 ▲ 0·122 ▲ 0·033 ▲ 0·122 ▲	0·156 0·156 ▲ 0·144 ▲ 0·100 ▲ 0·144 ▲
	0·143 0·095 0·143 ▲ 0·119 ▲ 0·056 ▲ 0·056 ▲ 0·119 ▲	[0·143] [0·095] [0·143] (0·155) (0·143) (0·155) 0·160 0·144 0·160 ▲ 0·143 ▲ 0·111 ▲ 0·111 ▲ 0·143 ▲
	0·140 0·105 0·105 0·140 ▲ 0·120 ▲ 0·050 ▲ 0·061 ▲ 0·050 ▲ 0·120 ▲	[0·140] [0·105] [0·105] [0·140] (0·155) (0·142) (0·142) (0·155) 0·159 0·148 0·148 0·159 ▲ 0·144 ▲ 0·108 ▲ 0·115 ▲ 0·108 ▲ 0·144 ▲
Uniformly distributed 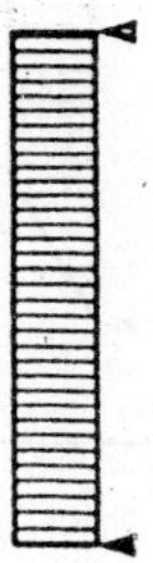	0·125 ▲ 0·070 ▲ 0·070 ▲	0·125 ▲ 0·096 ▲ 0·096 ▲
	0·100 0·100 ▲ 0·080 ▲ 0·025 ▲ 0·080 ▲	0·117 0·117 ▲ 0·101 ▲ 0·075 ▲ 0·101 ▲
	0·107 0·071 0·107 ▲ 0·077 ▲ 0·036 ▲ 0·036 ▲ 0·077 ▲	[0·107] [0·071] [0·107] (0·116) (0·107) (0·116) 0·121 0·107 0·121 ▲ 0·099 ▲ 0·081 ▲ 0·081 ▲ 0·099 ▲
	0·105 0·079 0·079 0·105 ▲ 0·078 ▲ 0·033 ▲ 0·046 ▲ 0·033 ▲ 0·078 ▲	[0·105] [0·079] [0·079] [0·105] (0·116) (0·106) (0·106) (0·116) 0·120 0·111 0·111 0·120 ▲ 0·100 ▲ 0·079 ▲ 0·086 ▲ 0·079 ▲ 0·100 ▲
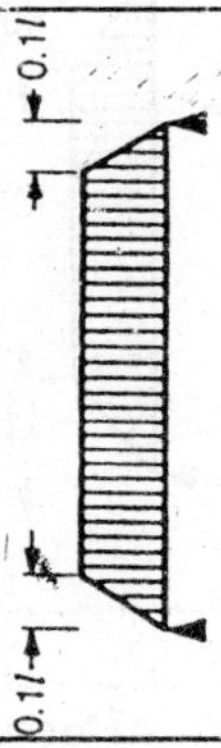	0·136 ▲ 0·077 ▲ 0·077 ▲	0·136 ▲ 0·105 ▲ 0·105 ▲
	0·109 0·109 ▲ 0·088 ▲ 0·028 ▲ 0·088 ▲	0·127 0·127 ▲ 0·111 ▲ 0·083 ▲ 0·111 ▲
	0·117 0·078 0·117 ▲ 0·085 ▲ 0·040 ▲ 0·040 ▲ 0·085 ▲	[0·117] [0·078] [0·117] (0·127) (0·117) (0·127) 0·131 0·117 0·131 ▲ 0·109 ▲ 0·089 ▲ 0·089 ▲ 0·109 ▲
	0·115 0·086 0·086 0·115 ▲ 0·086 ▲ 0·037 ▲ 0·051 ▲ 0·037 ▲ 0·086 ▲	[0·115] [0·086] [0·086] [0·115] (0·126) (0·116) (0·116) (0·126) 0·131 0·121 0·121 0·131 ▲ 0·110 ▲ 0·087 ▲ 0·094 ▲ 0·087 ▲ 0·110 ▲

Table contd...

Table contd...

Load	All spans loaded (e.g. dead load)	Imposed load (sequence of loaded spans to give max. bending moment)
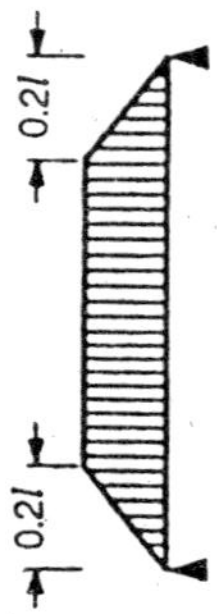	0·145 0·084 ▲ 0·084 0·116 0·116 0·095 ▲ 0·032 ▲ 0·095 0·124 0·083 0·124 0·092 ▲ 0·045 ▲ 0·045 ▲ 0·092 0·122 0·092 0·092 0·122 0·093 ▲ 0·041 ▲ 0·056 ▲ 0·041 ▲ 0·093	0·145 0·114 ▲ 0·114 0·135 0·135 0·120 ▲ 0·090 ▲ 0·120 [0·124] [0·083] [0·124] (0·135) (0·124) (0·135) 0·140 0·124 0·140 0·118 ▲ 0·096 ▲ 0·096 ▲ 0·118 [0·122] [0·092] [0·092] [0·122] (0·135) (0·123) (0·123) (0·135) 0·139 0·129 0·129 0·139 0·119 ▲ 0·095 ▲ 0·102 ▲ 0·095 ▲ 0·119
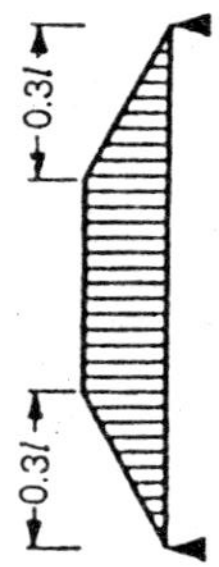	0·151 0·090 ▲ 0·090 0·121 0·121 0·102 ▲ 0·036 ▲ 0·102 0·130 0·086 0·130 0·098 ▲ 0·050 ▲ 0·050 ▲ 0·098 0·127 0·096 0·096 0·127 0·099 ▲ 0·046 ▲ 0·062 ▲ 0·046 ▲ 0·099	0·151 0·121 ▲ 0·121 0·141 0·141 0·128 ▲ 0·097 ▲ 0·128 [0·130] [0·086] [0·130] (0·140) (0·130) (0·140) 0·146 0·130 0·146 0·126 ▲ 0·103 ▲ 0·103 ▲ 0·126 [0·127] [0·096] [0·096] [0·127] (0·140) (0·129) (0·129) (0·140) 0·145 0·135 0·135 0·145 0·127 ▲ 0·102 ▲ 0·109 ▲ 0·102 ▲ 0·127

Bending moment = (coefficient) × (total load on one span) × (span)
Bending moment coefficient :

above line apply to negative bending moment at supports

below line apply to positive bending moment in span

Coefficients apply when all spans are equal (or shortest ⊁ 15% less than longest). Loads on each loaded span are equal. Moment of inertia same throughout all spans.

Bending moments is square brackets (imposed load) apply if all spans are loaded.

Bending moments coefficients in curved brackets (imposed load) apply if two spans only are loaded.

App. 9B·9A.

Table (A)Freely Supported R.C. slabs for Road Bridges and Culverts

(Clear span 3 ft. to 25 ft.)

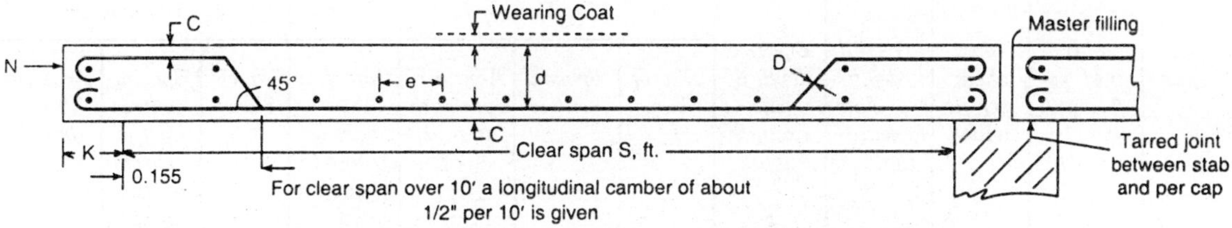

For clear span over 10′ a longitudinal camber of about ½″ per 10′ is given.

C = Clear cover min. 1″

D = Diameter of main reinforcement bar

e = Spacing of distribution bars

h = Effective span $S + d$

T = Thickness of bearing slab a pier cap $= 0{\cdot}25 + 0{\cdot}025\ S'$

d = Effective depth to the centre of main bars

N = End cover 1½ of $2D$ which ever is more

K = Length of bearing = 0·5 to 0·045 which ever is less

K = Length of bearing = $0{\cdot}5 + 0{\cdot}04\ S'$ or 1·4′ whichever is less

H = Over all depth = $d + C + D/2$

Table (A) For wearing coat upto 3″ thick (Details of Reinforcement)

Clear span	*Max. B.M. per ft. width H*	*Max. S.F. per H-width*	*Overall depth of slab exclud-ing w.c.*	*Effective depth of slab exclud-ing w.c.*	*Main bars*				*Distribution bar*		
					Dia. of bars	*Spacing centres*	*Area per foot width at mid span*	*No. of main bars cranked at each end*	*Dia. of bars*	*Spacing centres in the central portion of the span*	*Area per foot width*
1	*2*	*3*	*4*	*5*	*6*	*7*	*8*	*9*	*10*	*11*	*12*
FT.	*IN.LBS*	*LBS*	*IN.*	*IN.*	*IN.*	*IN.*	*SQ.IN.*	*NOS.*	*IN.*	*IN.*	*SQ.IN.*
S	*M*	*V*	*H*	*d*	*D*	—	A_s	—	—	e^e	—
3	34,000	3,970	7·00	5·75	3/8	3½	0·408	nil	3/8	7	0·189
4	46,000	4,440	7·00	5·75	1/2	4¼	0·554	nil	1/2	9¾	0·241
5	56,000	4,520	8·00	6·75	1/2	4	0·586	1 in every 4	1/2	9½	0·250
6	93,000	5,670	9·25	8·00	1/2	3	0·785	1 in every 4	1/2	8¼	0·285
7	1,13,000	6,050	10·00	8·69	5/8	4¼	0·868	1 in every 4	1/2	7¾	0·304
8	1,38,000	6,250	11·00	9·69	5/8	4	0·920	1 in every 4	1/2	7½	0·314
9	1,59,000	6,590	11·75	10·37	3/4	5¼	1·010	1 in every 4	1/2	7½	0·314
10	1,90,000	6,660	12·75	11·37	3/4	4¾	1·120	1 in every 4	5/8	11	0·335
12	2,50,000	7,210	14·25	12·87	3/4	4¼	1·248	1 in every 2	5/8	10½	0·351
14	3,20,000	7,630	16·00	14·50	3/4	3¾	1·413	1 in every 2	5/8	10	0·368
15	3,57,000	7,860	17·00	15·50	1	6¼	1·510	1 in every 2	5/8	10	0·368
16	3,94,000	8,150	17·75	16·25	1	6	1·571	1 in every 2	5/8	9¾	0·378
18	4,74,000	8,630	19·25	17·75	1	5½	1·714	1 in every 2	5/8	9½	0·388
20	5,67,000	9,260	21·00	19·50	1	5	1·885	1 in every 2	5/8	9	0·409
22	6,62,000	9,760	22·50	21·00	1	4½	2·090	1 in every 2	5/8	8¾	0·421
24	7,55,000	10,380	24·00	22·50	1	4¼	2·216	1 in every 2	3/4	12	0·442
25	8,30,000	10,750	25·00	23·50	1	4	2·356	1 in every 2	3/4	12	0·442

Table contd...

Table (B) For wearing coat upto 3" and upto 9" thick

Clear span	Max. B.M. per ft. width	Max. shear per ft. width	Overall depth of slab exclud-ing w.c.	Effective depth of slab exclud-ing w.c.	Main bars				Distribution bar		
					Dia. of bars	Spacing centres	Area per foot width at mid span	No. of main bars cranked at each end	Dia. of bars	Spacing centres in the central portion of the span	Area per foot width
1	2	3	4	5	6	7	8	9	10	11	12
FT.	IN.LBS	LBS	IN.	IN.	IN.	IN.	SQ.IN.	NOS.	IN.	IN.	SQ.IN.
S	M	V	H	d	D	—	A_s	—	—	e^e	—
3	34,000	3,970	7·00	5·75	3/8	3½	0·408	nil	3/8	7	0·189
4	46,000	4,440	7·00	5·75	1/6	4¼	0·334	nil	1/2	9¾	0·241
5	56,000	4,520	8·00	6·75	1/2	4	0·386	1 in every 4	1/2	9½	0·250
6	1,02,000	5,670	9·50	8·19	5/8	4½	0·818	1 in every 4	1/2	7½	0·314
7	1,21,000	6,050	10·25	9·10	5/8	4¼	0·808	1 in every 4	1/2	7½	0·314
8	1,47,000	6,250	11·25	9·44	5/8	3¾	0·982	1 in every 4	1/2	7½	0·314
9	1,70,000	6,590	12·00	10·62	3/4	5	1·060	1 in every 4	1/2	7½	0·325
10	2,04,000	6,660	13·00	11·62	3/4	4¾	1·120	1 in every 4	1/2	7¼	0·325
12	2,73,000	7,210	15·00	13·62	3/4	4	1·325	1 in every 2	5/8	10½	0·351
14	3,51,000	7,660	16·75	15·37	3/4	3½	1·510	1 in every 2	5/8	9¾	0·378
15	3,91,000	7,980	17·75	16·25	1	6	1·570	1 in every 2	5/8	9½	0·388
16	4,37,000	8,310	18·50	17·00	1	3¾	1·640	1 in every 2	5/8	9¼	0·398
18	5,26,000	8.930	20·25	18·75	1	3¼	1·795	1 in every 2	5/8	9	0·409
20	6,28,000	9,550	22·00	20·50	1	4¾	1·983	1 in every 2	5/8	8¾	0·421
22	7,42,000	10,330	23·73	22·25	1	4¼	2·216	1 in every 2	5/8	8½	0·433
24	8,66,000	11,170	25·30	24·00	1	4	2·356	1 in every 2	3/4	11½	0·462
25	9,35,000	11,310	26·50	25·00	1	3¾	2·510	1 in every 2	3/4	11½	0·462

Note : (1) The design tables apply to slabs of bridges and culverts with a clear road width of not less than 2 traffic lanes.

(2) Main reinforcement governed by bond and shear considerations upto span of 4 ft.

(3) In table B the values of B.M. for spans upto 5 ft. and values of shear for spans upto 12 ft. have been kept for convenience. The same as Table (A), although for a 9 in wearing coat (w.c.) actual requirements would be some what less owing to dispersion effect.

(4) The no. of main bars to be bent up towoards the support should not exceed that indicated in the tables. The no. has been so fixed as to keep bond and tensile stresses on the residual bottom bars within the permissible limits.

(5) The area of distribution reinforcement should be not less than $1/\sqrt{L}$ times the area of the main re-inforcement. Distribution bars should be securely welded or wired to the main bars as every alternate joint.

(6) If full length bars are not available and the joints have to be provided, lap joints of length 40D are permissible provided no joint comes at mid span and all joints are well staggered.

Design Loading—IRC standard class 'A' (Revised 1947) wheel load train.

Design Stresses—Concrete (f_c) = 750 lbs per sq. in. ; steel (f_s) = 18,000 lbs/sq. in.

Modular Ratio Fixed—15

App. 9B·10A. Conversion table for change of one type of steel into another, valid for tension steel bars of slabs, beams and footings only (for columns—no direct conversion permitted)

Type of steel	Diameter of bars in mm														
F_s 250	6	8	10	12	14	16	18	20	22	24	25	26	28	30	32
F_s 415	–	6	8	10	12	14	14	16	18	20	20	22	22	24	25
F_e 500	–	6	8	10	10	12	14	16	16	18	18	20	20	22	24

Notes : 1. This conversion table is based on the principle that steel area is directly proportional to yield stress.

2. This conversion table is conservative and may be used only in emergency when necessary design aids are not available.

App. 9B·11A. Area and Centre of Gravity for different Cross-sections. (Refer Chapter 2)

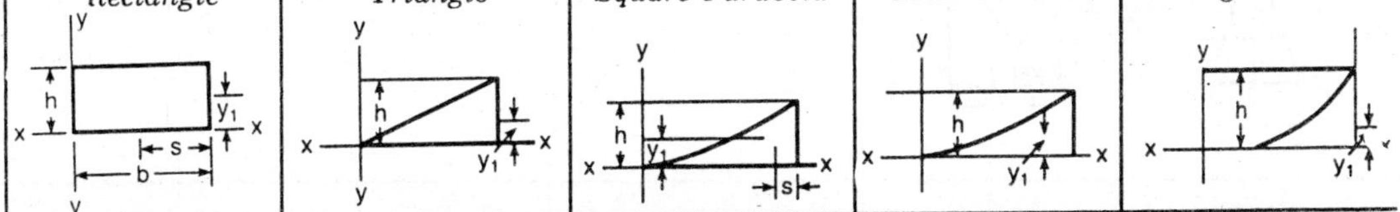

	Rectangle	Triangle	Square Parabola	Cubic Parabola	4th deg. Parabola
A	1.b.h.	1/2.b.h.	1/3.b.h.	1/4.b.h	1/5.b.h.
s	1/2 b	1/3 b	1/4 b	1/5 b	1/6 b
y_1	1/2 h	2/6 h	3/10 h	4/14 h	5/18 h
Eqn.	$y = h$	$y = \frac{h}{b}.x$	$y = \frac{h}{b^2}.x^2$	$y = \frac{h}{b^3}.x^3$	$y = \frac{h}{b^4}.x^4$

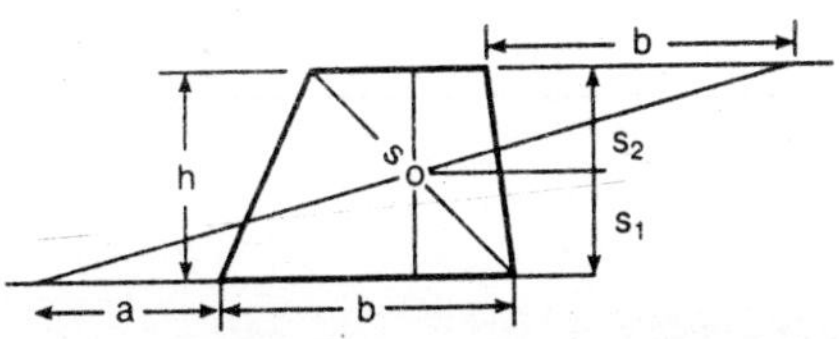

Trapezium $A = \frac{a+b}{2}.h$

$$s_1 = \frac{h(2a+b)}{3(a+b)},\ s_2 = \frac{h}{3}\frac{(2b+a)}{(a+b)}$$

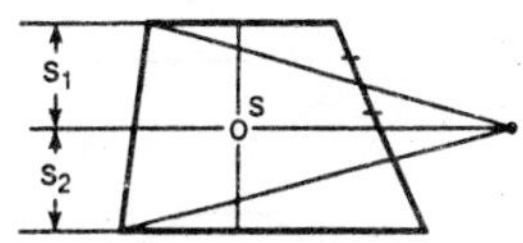

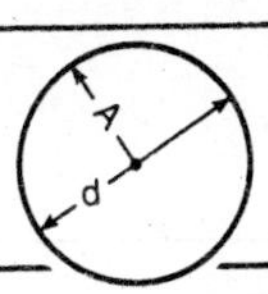

$A = \pi r^2 = \pi d^2/4$

Circum. $= 2\pi r$
$= \pi d$

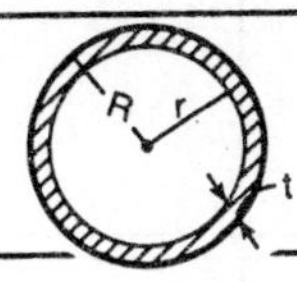

$A = \pi(R^2 - r^2)$
$= (D^2 - d^2)/4$
$= \pi(R + r)t$ or $2\pi(R - t/2).t$

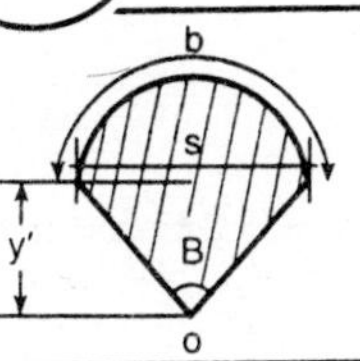

$A = br/2$
$= \pi r^2 \beta/180$
$b = \pi r \beta/180$
$y_1 = \frac{2}{3}.\frac{r.s}{b}$

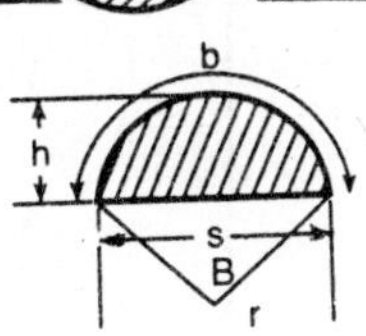

$A = \frac{br}{2} - \frac{s.(r-h)}{2}$

$s = 2\sqrt{h(2r-h)} \doteq 2r . \sin\frac{\beta}{2}$

$A = \frac{2}{3}s . h$(for small β)

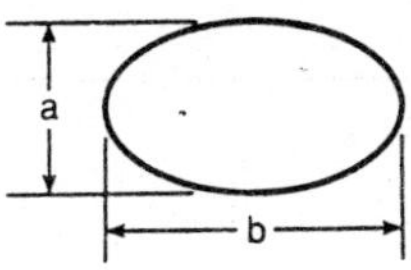

Square parab.
$A = 2/3\ b . h$
$s_1 = 3/8\ b.$
$s_2 = \frac{2}{5}h$

Ellipse :
$A = \pi a b/4$

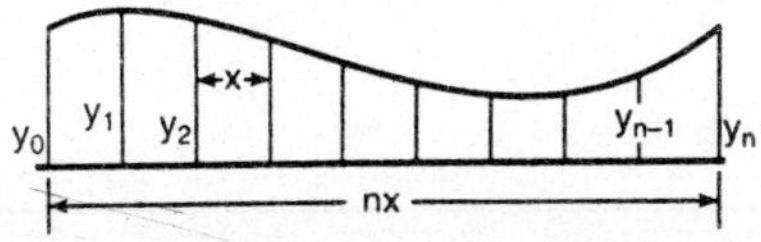

1. Simpson's Rule : (n-even)

$$A = \frac{x}{3}[y_o + 2(y_2 + y_4 + ...) + 4(y_1 + y_3 + ...) + y_n]$$

2. Approximate Rule : (Trapezium)

$$A = \frac{x}{2}[y_o + 2(y_1 + y_2 + y_3 + ...) + y_n]$$

App. 9B·12A. Volume and Surface Area of Different Bodies (Refer Chapter 2)

Body	*V = volume, S = Surface area of body*
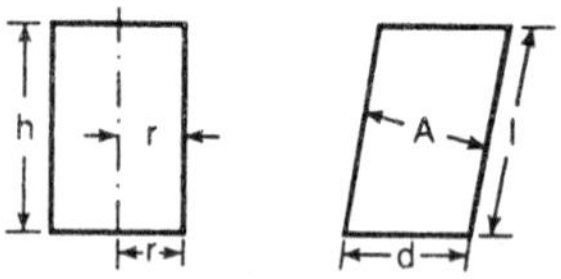	**Cylinder :** 1. $V = \pi r^2 h,\ S = 2\pi r h$ 2. $V = A.l = \pi r^2 . \frac{h}{l} . l = \pi r^2 h$ S = length of circumference at A × length l.
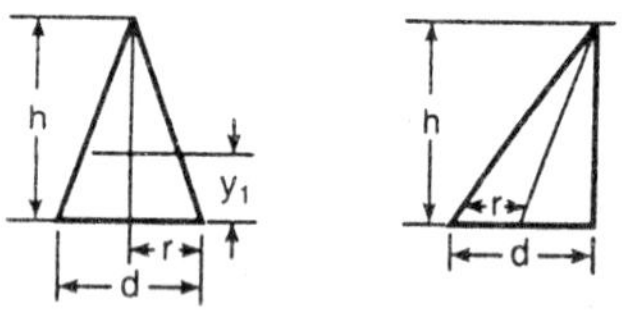	**Cone :** $V = \frac{1}{3} A.h. = \pi r^2\ h/3,\ S = \pi r.l = \pi r\sqrt{r^2 + h^2},\ y_1 = h/4$
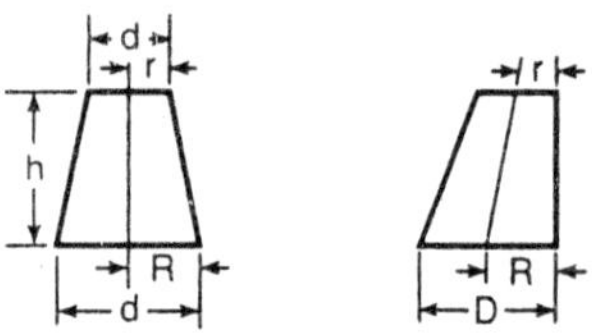	**Part of cone :** $V = \frac{\pi h}{3}(R^2 + r^2 + R.r)\ S = \pi .l.(R + r)$ $= \pi(R + r)\sqrt{(R - r)^2 + h^2}$
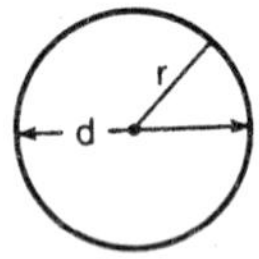	**Sphere :** $V = \frac{4}{3}\pi r^3 = \pi d^3/6,\ S = \pi d^2 = 4\pi . r^2$
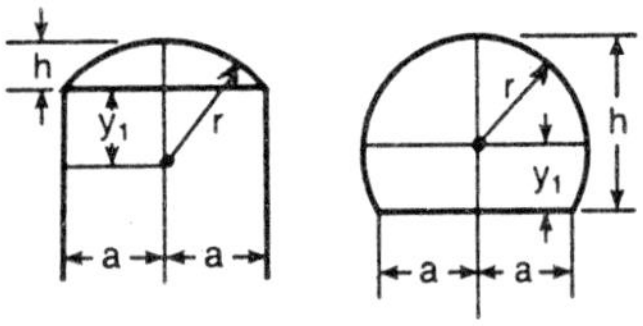	**Part of Sphere :** $V = \pi h^2\left(r - \frac{h}{3}\right) = \frac{\pi h}{6}(3a^2 + h^2),\ S = 2\pi r\ h = \pi(a^2 + h^2)$ $y_1 = 3/4\frac{(2r - h)^2}{3r - h},\ a = \sqrt{h(2r - h)}$
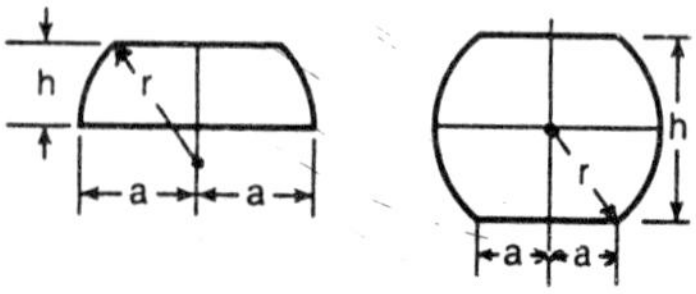	**Part of Sphere :** $V = \frac{\pi h}{6}(3a^2 + 3b^2 + h^2),\ S = 2\pi r . h$

App. 9B·13A. Centre of Gravity, Section Modulus & Moment of Inertia for Different Sections (Refer Chater 2)

Section	*C.G.* (y)	I	$Z = I/y$
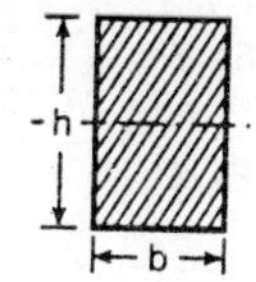 (1) 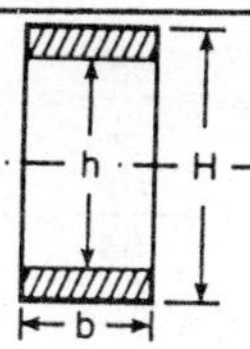 (2)	1. $\frac{h}{2}$ 2. $\frac{H}{2}$	1. $\frac{bh^3}{12}$ 2. $\frac{b}{12}(H^3 - h^3)$	1. $\frac{bh^2}{6}$ 2. $\frac{b}{6H}(H^3 - h^3)$
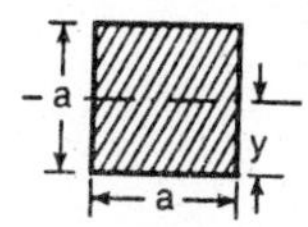 (3) 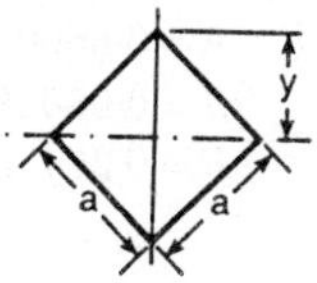 (4)	3. $\frac{a}{2}$ 4. $\frac{a}{2}\sqrt{2}$	3. $\frac{a^4}{12}$ 4. $\frac{a^4}{12}$	3. $\frac{a^3}{6}$ 4. $0{\cdot}1179\ a^3$
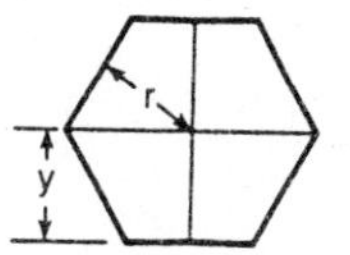 (5) 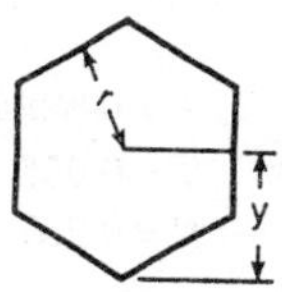 (6)	5. $0{\cdot}866\ r$ 6. r	5. $0{\cdot}5413\ r^4$ 6. $0{\cdot}5413\ r^4$	5. $\frac{5}{8}r^3 = 0{\cdot}625\ r^3$ 6. $0{\cdot}5413\ r^3$
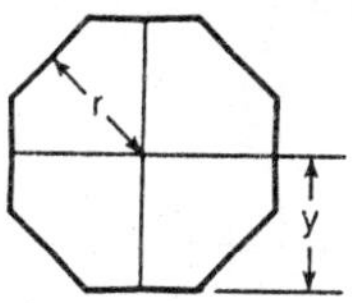 (7)	7. $0{\cdot}924\ r$	7. $0{\cdot}6381\ r^4$	7. $0{\cdot}6906\ r^3$
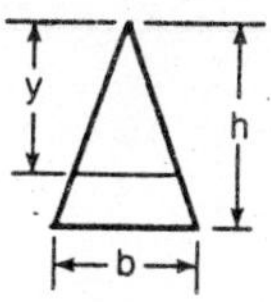 (8) 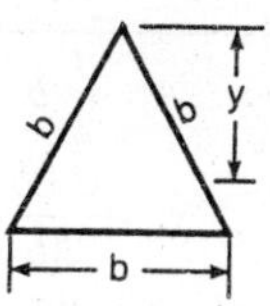 (9)	8. $\frac{2}{3}h$ 9. $0{\cdot}5778\ b$	8. $I_x = \frac{bh^3}{36}\ I_y = \frac{hb^3}{48}$ 9. $= 0{\cdot}018\ b^4$	8. $Z_x = \frac{bh^2}{24}\ Z_y = \frac{hb^2}{24}$ 9. $= 0{\cdot}0313\ b^3$
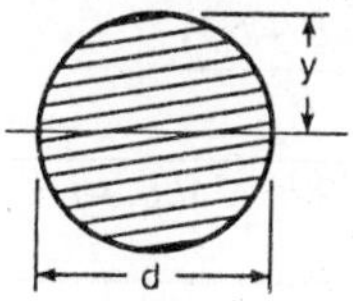 (10) 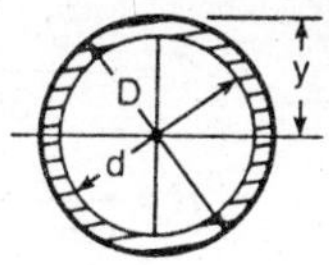 (11)	10. $\frac{d}{2}$ 11. $\frac{D}{2}$	10. $\frac{\pi d^4}{64} = 0{\cdot}049\ d^4$ 11. $\frac{\pi}{64}.(D^4 - d^4)$	10. $\frac{\pi d^3}{32} = 0{\cdot}1\ d^3$ 11. $\frac{\pi}{32}.\frac{D^4 - d^4}{D}$
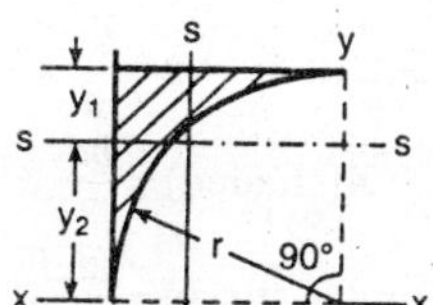	12. $y_1 = 0{\cdot}2234\ r$ $y_2 = 0{\cdot}7766\ r$	12. $I_s = 0{\cdot}0075\ r^4$ $I_x = I_y = 0{\cdot}137\ r^4$ $I_{xy} = \frac{r^4}{8}$ $I_{ss} = 0{\cdot}0044\ r^4$	12. $Z_{s_2} = \frac{0{\cdot}0075\ r^4}{y_2}$ $= 0{\cdot}00966\ r^3$ $= 0{\cdot}01\ r^3$

App. 9B·14A. Properties of Sections

Dash-and-dot lines are drawn through centers of gravity

A = area of section I = moment of inertia R = radius of gyration

Section	Properties	Section	Properties
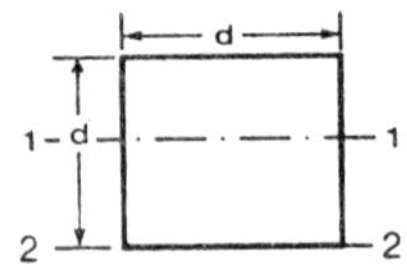	$A = d^2$ $I_1 = \dfrac{d^4}{12}$ $I_2 = \dfrac{d^4}{3}$ $R_1 = 0{\cdot}2887\ d$ $R_2 = 0{\cdot}5774\ d$	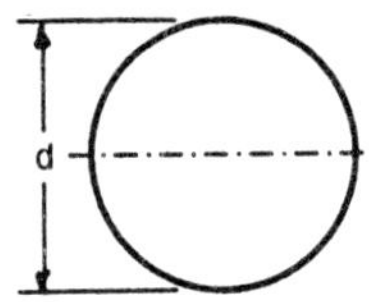	$A = \dfrac{\pi d^2}{4} = 0{\cdot}7854\ d^2$ $I = \dfrac{\pi d^4}{64} = 0{\cdot}0491\ d^4$ $R = \dfrac{d}{4}$
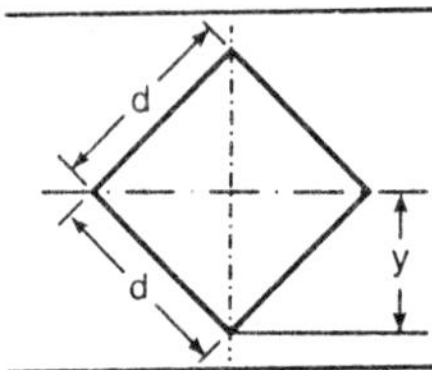	$A = d^2$ $y = 0{\cdot}7071\ d$ $I = \dfrac{d^4}{12}$ $R = 0{\cdot}2887\ d$	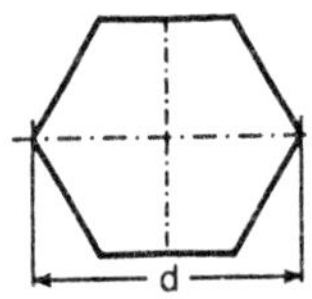	$A = 0{\cdot}8660\ d^2$ $I = 0{\cdot}060\ d^4$ $R = 0{\cdot}264\ d$
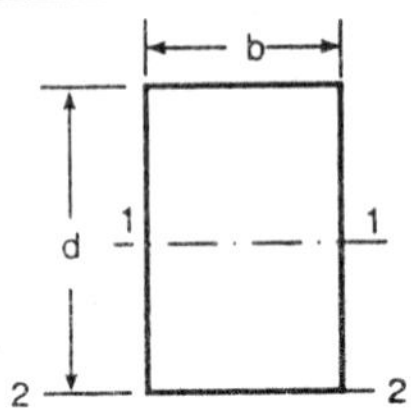	$A = bd$ $I_1 = \dfrac{bd^3}{12}$ $I_2 = \dfrac{bd^3}{3}$ $R_1 = 0{\cdot}2887\ d$ $R_1 = 0{\cdot}5774\ d$	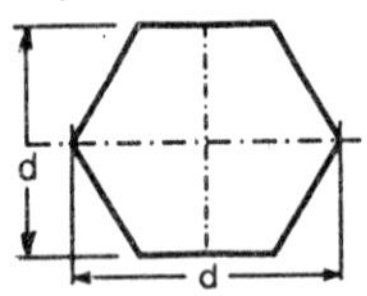	$A = 0{\cdot}8284\ d^2$ $I = 0{\cdot}055\ d^4$ $R = 0{\cdot}257\ d$
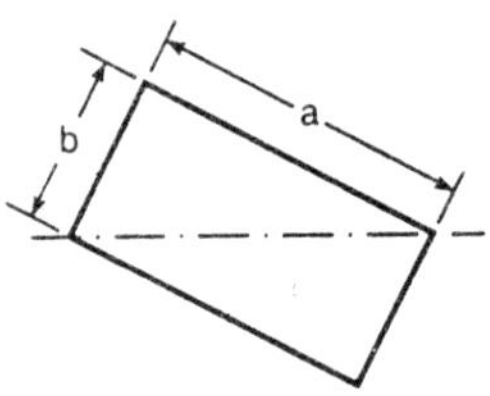	$A = bd$ $y = \dfrac{bd}{\sqrt{b^2 + d^2}}$ $I = \dfrac{b^3 d^2}{6(b^2 + d^2)}$ $R = \dfrac{bd}{\sqrt{6(b^2 - d^2)}}$	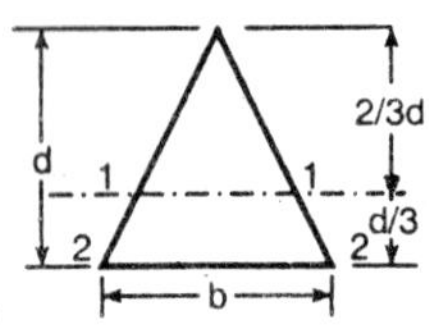	$A = \dfrac{bd}{2}$ $I_1 = \dfrac{bd^3}{36}$ $I_2 = \dfrac{bd^3}{12}$ $R_1 = 0{\cdot}236\ d$ $R_2 = 0{\cdot}408\ d$
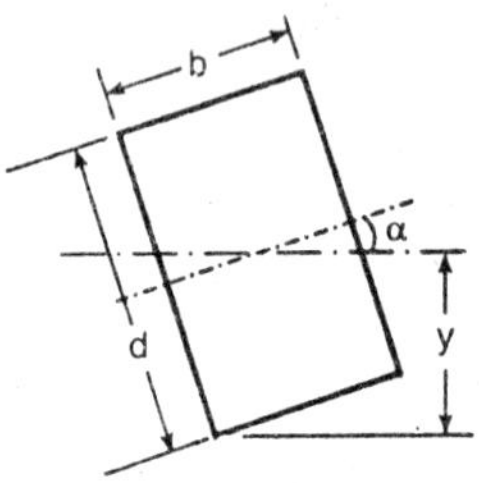	$A = bd$ $y = \dfrac{b \sin \alpha + d \cos \alpha}{2}$ $I = \dfrac{bd(b^2 \sin^2 \alpha + \alpha^2 \cos^2 \alpha)}{12}$ $R = \sqrt{\dfrac{b^2 \sin^2 \alpha + d^2 \cos^2 \alpha}{12}}$	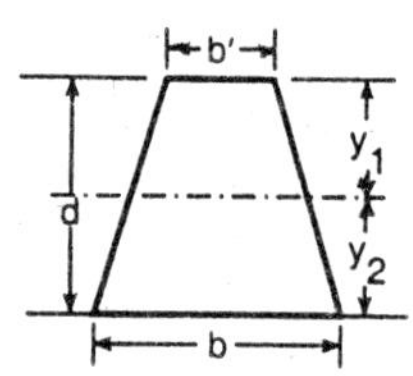	$A = \dfrac{d}{2}(b + b')$ $y_1 = \dfrac{d(2b + b')}{3(b + b')}$ $y = \dfrac{d(b + 2b')}{3(b + b')}$ $I = \dfrac{d^2(b^2 + 4bb' + b'^2)}{36(b + b')}$ $R = \dfrac{d}{6(b + b')}\sqrt{2(b^2 + 4bb' + b'^2)}$
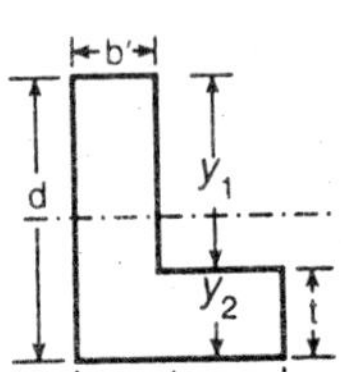	$A = bt + b'c$ $y = \dfrac{d^2 b' + t^2(b - b')}{2(bt + b'c)}$ $y_1 = d - y$ $I = \dfrac{b' y_1^3 + by^3 - (b - b')(y - t)^3}{3}$	Section of Parabola 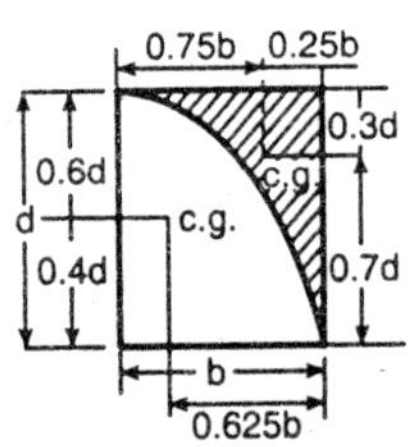	Equation : $y^2 = \dfrac{b^2}{d}x$ $A(\text{shaded}) = \dfrac{bd}{3}$ $A(\text{under curve}) = \dfrac{2bd}{3}$

Table contd...

Table contd...

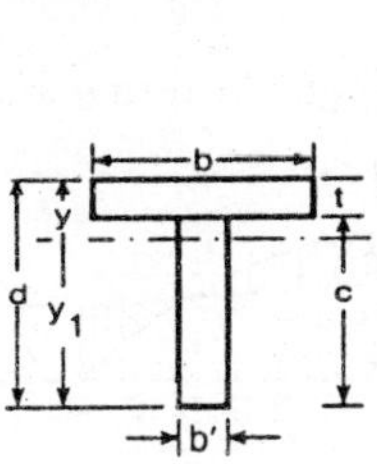

$$A = bt + b'c$$

$$y = \frac{d^2b' + t^2(b - b')}{2(bt + b'c)}$$

$$y_1 = d - y$$

$$I = \frac{b'y_1^3 + by^3 - (b - b')(y - t)^2}{3}$$

$$R = \sqrt{\frac{I}{A}}$$

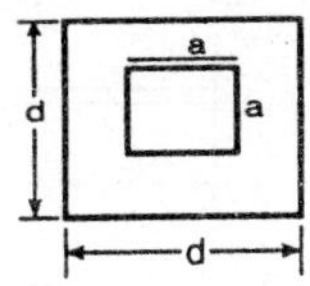

$$A = d^2 - a^2$$

$$I = \frac{d^4 - a^4}{12}$$

$$R = \sqrt{\frac{d^2 + a^2}{12}}$$

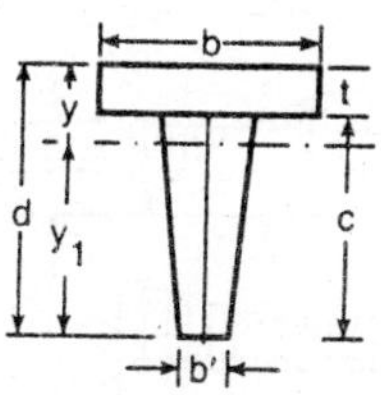

$$A = bt + \frac{c(a + b')}{2}$$

$$y = \frac{3bt^2 + 3b'c(d + t) + c(a - b')(c + 3t)}{3[2bt + c(a + b')]}$$

$$y_1 = d - y$$

$$I = \frac{4bt^3 + c^3(3b' + a)}{12} - A(y - t)^2$$

$$R = \sqrt{\frac{I}{A}}$$

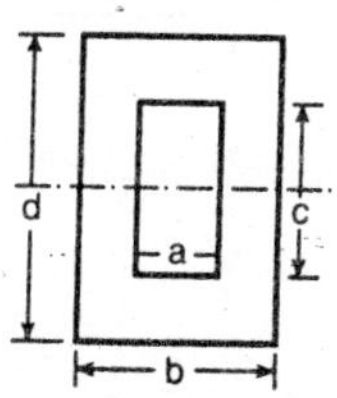

$$A = bd - ac$$

$$I = \frac{bd^2 - ac^2}{12}$$

$$R = \sqrt{\frac{bd^3 - ac^3}{12(bd - ac)}}$$

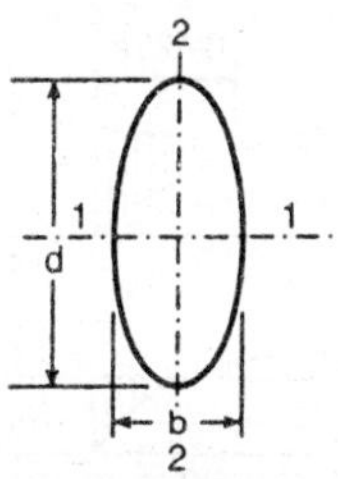

Ellipse

$$A = 0{\cdot}7854\, bd$$

$$I_1 = \frac{\pi bd^3}{64} = 0{\cdot}0491\, bd^3$$

$$I_2 = \frac{\pi b^3 d}{64} = 0{\cdot}0491\, b^3 d$$

$$R_1 = \frac{d}{4},\; R_2 = \frac{b}{4}$$

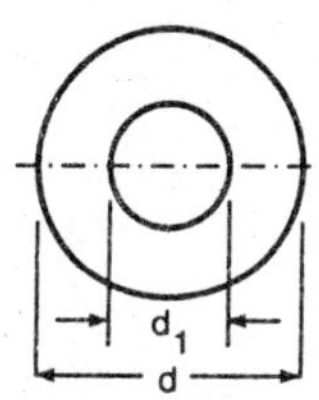

$$A = \frac{\pi(d^2 - d_1^2)}{4}$$

$$= 0{\cdot}7854(d^2 - d_1^2)$$

$$I = \frac{\pi(d^4 - d_1^4)}{64}$$

$$= 0{\cdot}0491(d^4 - d_1^4)$$

$$R = 1/4\sqrt{d^2 - d_1^2}$$

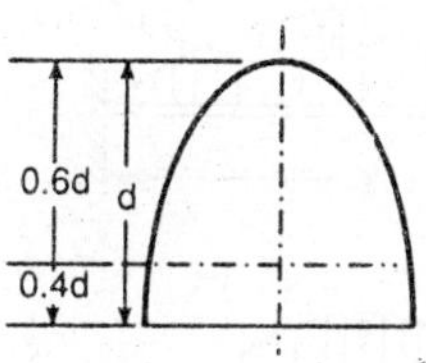

Parabola Equation :

$$y^2 = \frac{b^2}{4d}.x$$

$$A = \frac{2bd}{3}$$

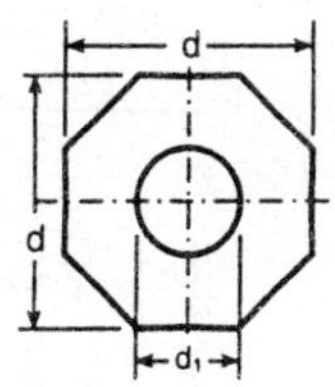

$$A = 0{\cdot}8284\, d^2 - 0{\cdot}7854\, d_1^2$$

$$= 0{\cdot}7854(1{\cdot}055\, d^2 - d_1^2)$$

$$I = 0{\cdot}0547\, d^4 - 0{\cdot}0491\, d_1^4$$

$$= 0{\cdot}0491(1{\cdot}115\, d^4 - d_1^4)$$

$$= 0{\cdot}0491[(1{\cdot}056)^2 d^4 - d_1^4]$$

$$R = \frac{1}{4}\sqrt{1{\cdot}056\, d^2 + d_1^2}$$

App. 9B·15A. Coefficients for Moments in Beams with Fixed Ends
Moments in Beams of Constant Section and with Fixed Ends

$$M = m \cdot w \cdot L$$

m = coefficient taken from diagram, W = total load on beam, L = length of beam, a = length in terms of L.

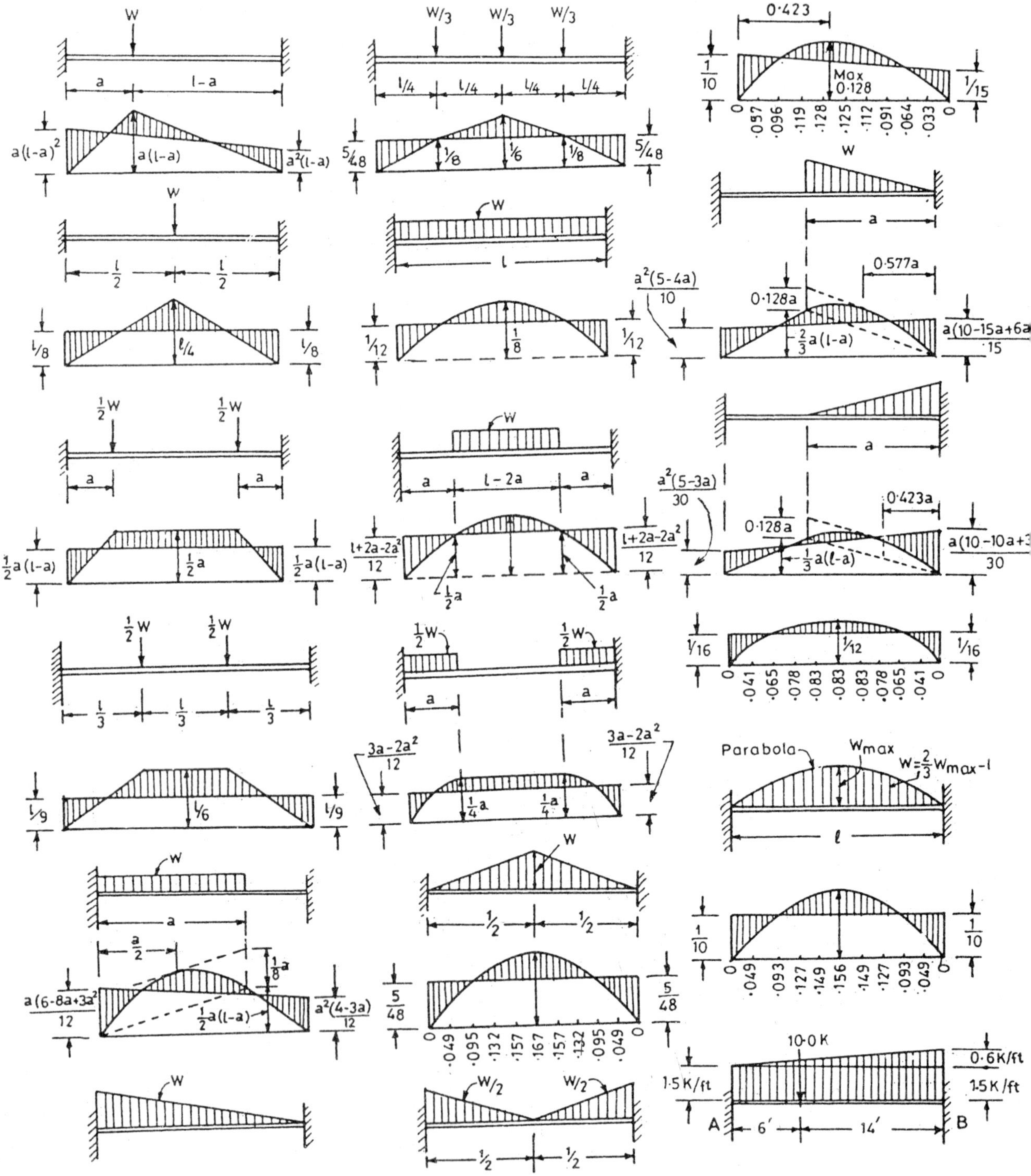

App. 9B·16A. Reactions, Bending Moments and Deflections of Free Cantilevers and Simply Supported Beams (Also (Also refer Chapter 4)

Load	Reaction	Bending Moment	Deflection
1. 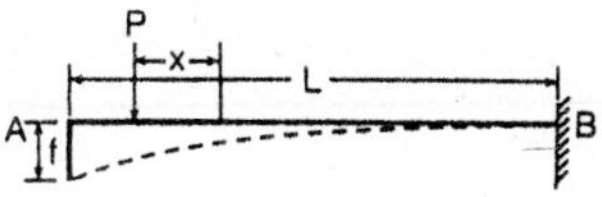	$B = P$	$M_x = -P_x$ $MaxM = -PL$	$f = \frac{1}{3}\frac{PL^3}{EI}$
2. 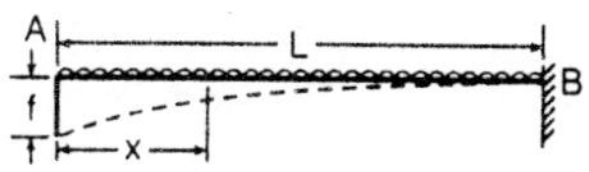	$B = qL$	$M_x = -\frac{qx^2}{2}$ $MaxM = \frac{qL^2}{2}$	$f = \frac{qL^4}{8EI}$
3. 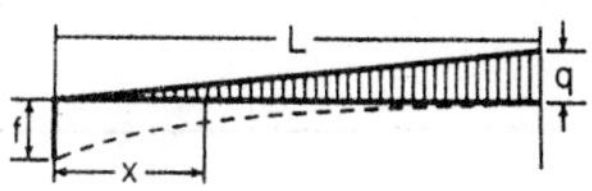	$B = \frac{qL}{2}$	$M_x = \frac{qx^3}{6L}$ $Max\ M = \frac{qL^2}{6}$	$f = \frac{1}{30}\frac{qL^4}{EI}$
4. 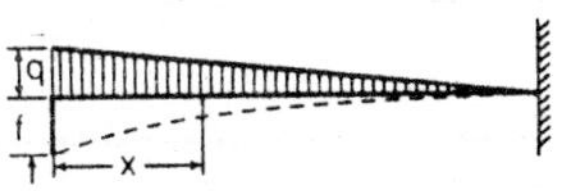	$B = \frac{qL}{2}$	$M_x = \frac{qL^2}{6}\left(\frac{3x^2}{L^2} - x^3/L^3\right)$ $Max\ M = -qL^2/3$	$f = \frac{11}{120}\cdot\frac{qL^4}{EI}$
5 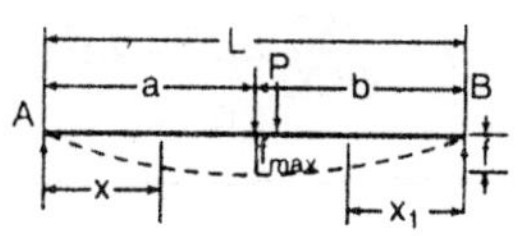	$A = \frac{Pb}{L},\ B = \frac{Pa}{L}$	$M_x = \frac{Pb}{L}x$ $Max\ M = \frac{P_{ab}}{L}$	$f = \frac{1}{3}\frac{P}{EI}\frac{a^2b^2}{L}$, max f, at, $x = a\sqrt{\frac{1}{3} + \frac{2b}{3a}}$ for $a > b$ $x_1 = b\sqrt{\frac{1}{3} + \frac{2}{3}\frac{a}{b}}$, for $a < b$
6. Same as 5, with $a = b = L/2$	$A = B = \frac{P}{2}$	$M_x = \frac{P}{2}x,\ Max\ M = \frac{PL}{4}$	$f = \frac{1}{48}\frac{PL^3}{EI}$
7. 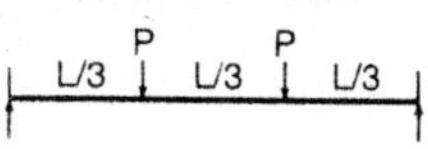	$A = B = P$	$MaxM = PL/3$	$f = \frac{23}{648}\frac{PL^3}{EI}$
8. 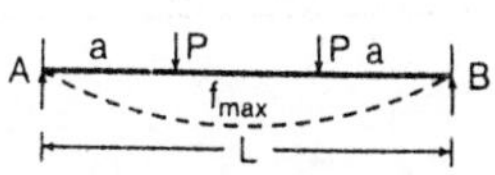	$A = B = P$	$MaxM = Pa$	$Maxf = \frac{Pa}{24\ EI}(3L^2 - 4a^2)$
9. 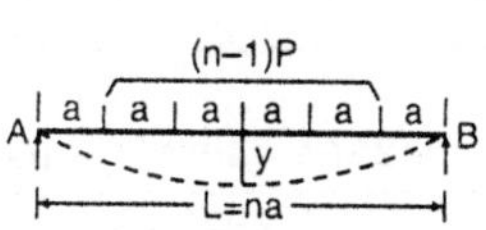	$A = B = \frac{n-1}{2}P$ P P L/3 | L/3 | L/3 $n = 3$	$Max\ M = k_M\ PL$ P P P L/4 | L/4 | L/4 $n = 4$	$f = k_f\frac{PL^3}{EI}$ P P P P L/5 | L/5 | L/5 | L/5 | L/5
		KM 1/3 kf 23/648	1/2 3/5 19/384 63/1000
10. 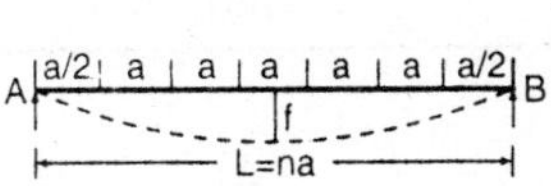	L/4 | L/2 | L/4 $n = 2$ $A = B = \frac{n}{2}P$	L/6 | L/3 | L/7 | L/8 $n = 3$ $Max\ M = k_M\ PL$	L/5 | L/4 | L/4 | L/9 | L/8 $f = k_f\frac{PL^3}{EI}$
		KM 1/4 Kf 11/384	5/12 1/2 53/1296 41/768

Table contd...

Table contd...

No.	Case	Reactions	Moments	Deflection
11.	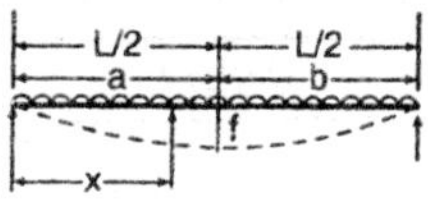	$A = B = \frac{qL}{2}$	$M_x = \frac{qx}{2}(L - x)$ $Max\ M = \frac{qL^2}{8}$	$f = \frac{5}{384} \cdot \frac{qL^4}{EI}$
12.	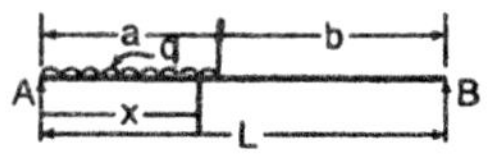	$A = \frac{qc}{2L}(2L - c)$ $B = \frac{qc^2}{2L}$	$M_x = A_x - \frac{qx^2}{2}$ $Max\ M = \frac{qc^2}{8L^2}(2L - c)^2$ $at: x = \frac{A}{q}$	
13.	Same as 12 with $c = \frac{L}{2}$	$A = \frac{3}{8}qL\ B = \frac{1}{8}qL$	$Max\ M = \frac{9}{128}qL^2$	
14.	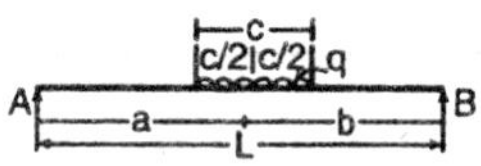	$A = \frac{qbc}{L}$ $B = \frac{qac}{L}$	$Max\ M = \frac{qabc}{2L^2}(2L - c)$ $at: x = \frac{A}{q} + d$	
15.	Same as 14 with $a = b = \frac{L}{2}$	$A = B = \frac{qc}{2}$	$Max\ M = \frac{qc}{8}(2L - c)$	
16.	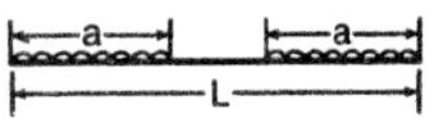	$A = B = qa$	$M_x = \frac{q}{2}(2a - x)x$ $Max\ M = qa^2/2$	$f = \frac{qa^2}{48EI}(3L^2 - 2a^2)$
17.	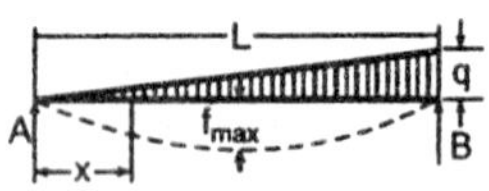	$A = \frac{1}{6}aL$ $B = \frac{1}{3}qL$	$M_x = \frac{qL_x}{6}\left(1 - \frac{x^2}{L^2}\right)$ $Max\ M = \frac{1}{9\sqrt{3}}qL^2$ $= 0.064\ qL^2$ At $x = L/2,\ M = \frac{qL^2}{16}$ At $x = L/2,\ M = \frac{qL^2}{16}$	$Max\ f = 0.00652\frac{qL^4}{EI}$
18.	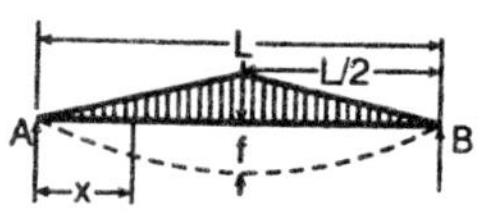	$A = B = \frac{qL}{4}$	$M_x = \frac{qLx}{2}\left(1/2 - \frac{2}{3}\frac{x^2}{L^2}\right)$ $Max\ M = \frac{qL^2}{12}$	$f = \frac{1}{120}\ \frac{qL^4}{EI}$
19.	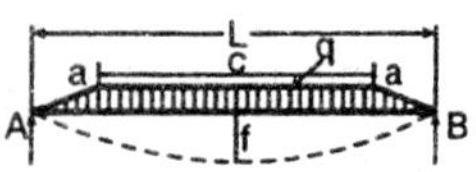	$A = B = \frac{q(L - a)}{2}$	$Max\ M = \frac{q}{24}(3L^2 - 4a^2)$	$f = \frac{q(25L^4 - 40a^2L^2 + 16a^4)}{1920\ EI}$
20.	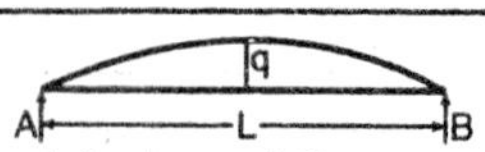 2nd parabola	$A = B = \frac{qL}{3}$	$Max\ M = \frac{5}{48}qL^2 = qL^2/9.6$	$f = \frac{61}{5760}qL^4$
21.	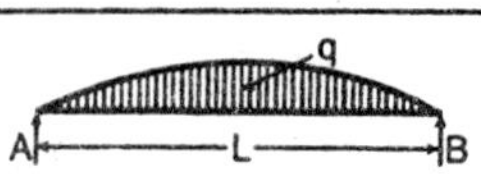 sin-curve	$A = B = \frac{qL}{\pi}$	$Max\ M = qL^2/\pi^2$	

Table contd...

Table contd...

Case	Reactions / Shear	Moments	Deflections
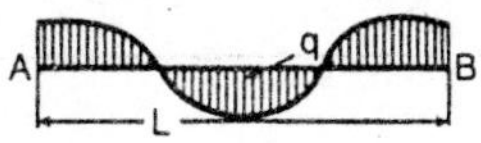 22. cos-curve	$A = B = 0$ $Q_{max} = \frac{qL}{2\pi}$	$Max\ M = qL^2/2\pi^2$	
23. 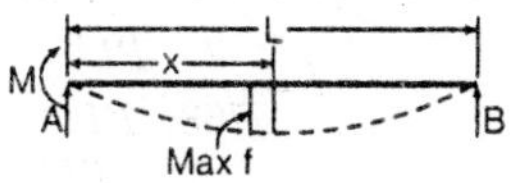	$A = -B = \frac{M}{L}$	$M_x = M\frac{L-x}{L}$	$Max\ f = \frac{1}{15{\cdot}59}.\frac{ML^2}{EI}$ at $x = 0{\cdot}423\ L$ at $x = 0{\cdot}5L$ $f = \frac{ML^2}{16\ EI}$
24. 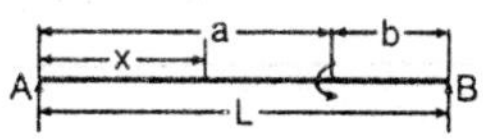	$A = -B = \frac{M}{L}$	$M_x = M\frac{x}{L}$ for $x \le a$ $M_x = -M\frac{L-x}{L}$ for $x \ge a$	
25. 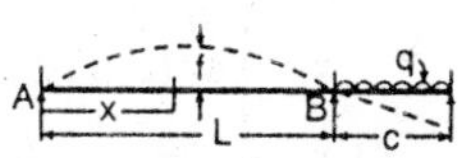	$A = -\frac{qc^2}{2L}$ $B = q\left(c + \frac{c^2}{2L}\right)$	$M_x = \frac{qc^2}{2}.\frac{x}{L}$ $M_B = -qc^2/2$	$f = \frac{qc^2\ L^2}{18\sqrt{3}\ EI}$ $f_1 = \frac{qc^3}{24\ EI}(4L + 3c)$
26. 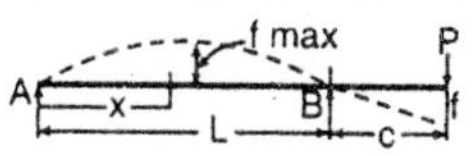	$A = \frac{P_c}{L}$ $B = \frac{P(L+c)}{L}$	$M_x = Ax = -\frac{Pcx}{L}$ $M_B = -Pc$	$Max\ f = \frac{c}{9\sqrt{3}}.\frac{PL^2}{EI}$ at $x = 0{\cdot}577L$, $f_1 = \frac{L+c}{3}.\frac{Pc^2}{EI}$
27. 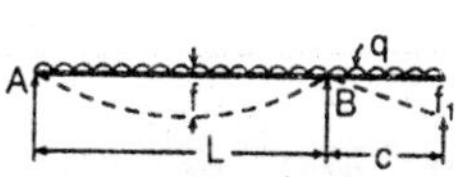	$A = \frac{q}{2L}(L^2 - c^2)$ $B = \frac{q}{2L}(L+c)^2$	$Max\ M_f = \frac{q}{8L^2}(L+c)^4$ $M_B = -\frac{qc^2}{2}$	$f = \frac{qL^2}{384\ EI}(5L^2 - 12c^2)$ at $x = \frac{L}{2}$, $f_1 = -\frac{qc}{24\ EI}\left[c^2(4L+3c) - L^3\right]$
28. 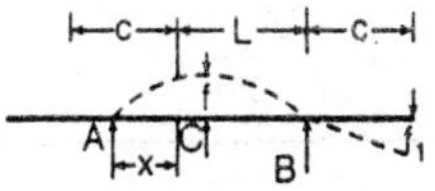	$A = B = P$	$M_A = M_B = -P_c$	$f = \frac{PL^2c}{8\ EI}$, $f_1 = \frac{Pc^2}{3\ EI}\left(c + \frac{3L}{2}\right)$
29. 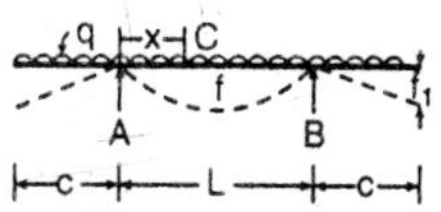	$A = B = \frac{q}{2}(L + 2c)$	$M_x = Ax\left(1 - \frac{c}{x} - \frac{x}{L+2c}\right)$ for $x \le c : M_x = -\frac{qx^2}{2}$ $M_A = M_B = -\frac{qc^2}{2}$ $M_c = \frac{qL^2}{2}\left(\frac{1}{4} - \frac{c^2}{L^2}\right)$ for $c = 0{\cdot}3536\ L$, $M_C = +\frac{qL^2}{16}$	$f = \frac{1}{16}.\frac{qL^4}{EI}\left(\frac{5}{24} - \frac{c^2}{L^2}\right)$ $f_1 = \frac{1}{24}.\frac{qL^4}{EI}\left(3\frac{c^4}{L^4} + 6\frac{c^3}{L^3} - \frac{c}{L}\right)$

Table contd...

App. 9B·17A. Reactions, Bending Moments and Deflections of Beams with one or Two Supports Fixed.

1.	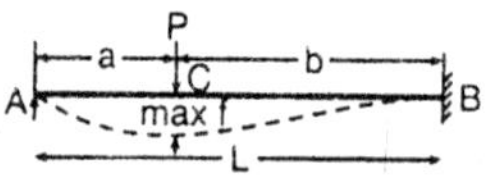	$A = \frac{Pb^2}{2L^3}(2L + a)$ $B = \frac{Pa}{2L^3}(3L^2 - a^2)$	$M_B = -\frac{Pab}{2L^2}(L + a)$ $M_C = \frac{Pa}{2}\left(2 - 3\frac{a}{L} + \frac{a^3}{L^3}\right)$	$f_c = \frac{Pa^2 b^3}{12\, EIL^3}(4L - b)$
2.	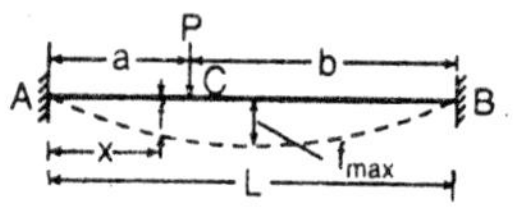	$A = \frac{5}{16}P,\ B = \frac{11}{16}P$	$Max\ M = M_B = -\frac{3}{16}PL$ $M_C = \frac{5}{32}PL$	$f = \frac{7}{768}.\frac{PL^3}{EI}$ $Max\ f = \frac{1}{48\sqrt{5}}.\frac{PL^3}{EI}$ $x = 0{\cdot}4471$
3.	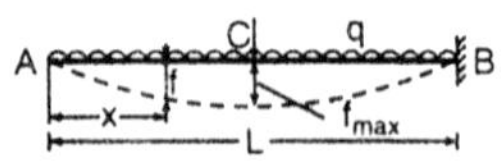	$A = \frac{3}{8}qL,$ $B = \frac{5}{8}qL$	$M_x = \frac{qLx}{2}\left(3/4 - \frac{x}{L}\right)$ $Max\ M = M_B = -\frac{qL^2}{8}$ $M_C = \frac{9}{128}$ at : $x = \frac{3}{8}L$ $= 0{\cdot}07\ qL^2$ at : $x = \frac{3}{8}L$	$Max\ f = \frac{1}{185}.\frac{qL^4}{EI}$ $x = 0{\cdot}4215\ L$ At At $x = \frac{L}{2}\ f = \frac{1}{192}\ \frac{ql^4}{EI}$
4.	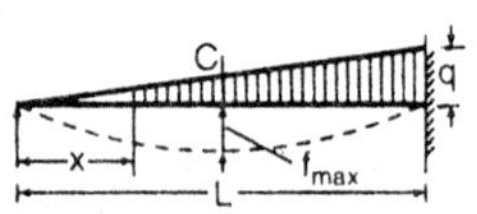	$A = \frac{1}{10}qL$ $B = \frac{2}{5}qL$	$M_x = \frac{qLx}{2}\left(\frac{1}{5} - \frac{x^2}{3L^2}\right)$ $Max\ M = M_B = -\frac{qL^2}{15}$ $M_C = 0{\cdot}0298\ qL^2\ x = 0{\cdot}4471\ L$	$Max\ f = \frac{1}{420}.\frac{qL^4}{EI}$ $x = 0{\cdot}447L$
5.	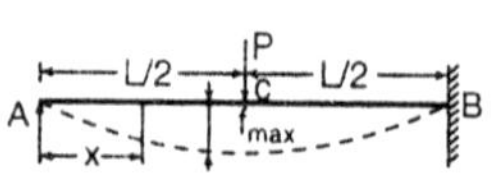	$A = \frac{Pb^2}{L^3}(L + 2a)$ $B = \frac{Pa^2}{L^3}(L + 2b)$	$M_A = -P\frac{ab^2}{L^2}\ M_B = -P\frac{a^2b}{L^2}$ $Max M = M_c = 2P\frac{a^2b^2}{L^3}$	$f_C = \frac{1}{3L^3}.\frac{Pa^3 b^3}{EI}$ $Max f = \frac{2}{3(3L - 2a)^2}\ \frac{Pa^2 b^3}{EI}$ $x = \frac{L^2}{3L - 2a}$
6.	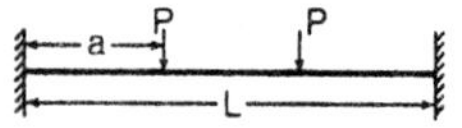	$A = B = P$	$M_A = M_B = -\frac{Pa}{L}(L - a)$ $\max M = \frac{Pa^2}{L}$	
7.	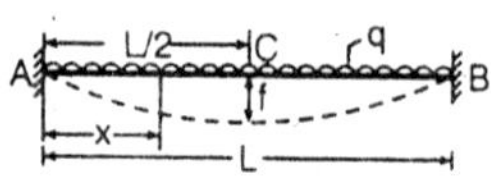	$A = B = \frac{qL}{2}$	$M_x = -\frac{qL^2}{2}\left(\frac{1}{6} - \frac{x}{L} + \frac{x^2}{L^2}\right)$ $Max\ M = M_A = M_B = -\frac{qL^2}{12}$ $M_C = \frac{qL^2}{24}$	$f = \frac{1}{384}.\frac{qL^4}{EI}$

Table contd...

Table contd...

8. 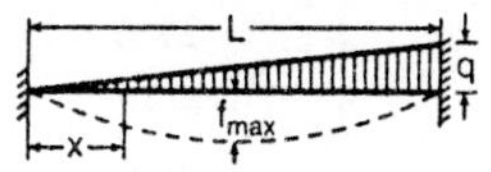

$$M_X = \frac{qL^2}{60}\left(2 - 9\frac{x}{L} + 10\frac{x^3}{L^3}\right)$$

$$M_A = \frac{qL^2}{30}$$

$$A = \frac{3}{20}qL,\ B = \frac{7}{20}qL \quad Max\ M = M_B = -\frac{qL^2}{20}$$

$$M_C = \frac{qL^2}{46{\cdot}6},\ x = 0{\cdot}548\ L$$

$$Max\ f = \frac{1}{784}.\frac{qL^4}{EI}$$

$$x = 0{\cdot}525\ L$$

---

9. 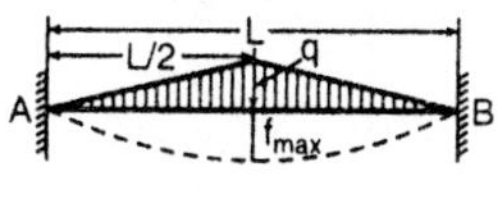

$$A = B = \frac{qL}{4}$$

$$Max\ M = M_A = M_B = -\frac{5}{96}qL^2$$

$$M_C = \frac{qL^2}{32}$$

$$f = \frac{1}{549}.\frac{qL^4}{EI}$$

---

10 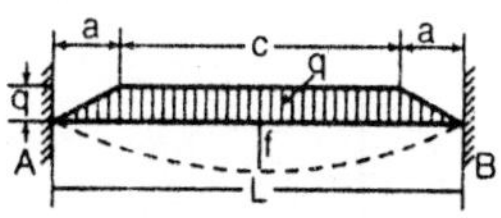

$$A = B = \frac{q(L - a)}{2}$$

$$Max\ M = M_A = M_B$$

$$= -\frac{q}{12}\left(L^2 - 2a^2 + \frac{a^3}{L}\right)$$

$$M_C = \frac{q}{24}\left(L^2 - \frac{2a^3}{L}\right)$$

$$f = \frac{q(L^4 - 2a^3\ L)}{209\ EI}$$

---

11. 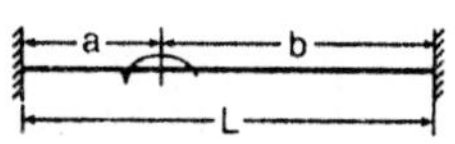

$$A = -B = 6M\frac{ab}{L^3}$$

$$M_A = -M\frac{b}{L^2}(3a - L)$$

$$M_B = M\frac{a}{L^2}(3b - L)$$

---

12. 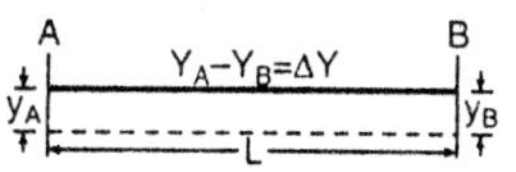

$$A = -B = -\frac{12\ EI}{L^3}\Delta Y\ YM_A = -M_B = \frac{6\ EI}{L^2}\Delta Y$$

Sinking of supports

---

13. 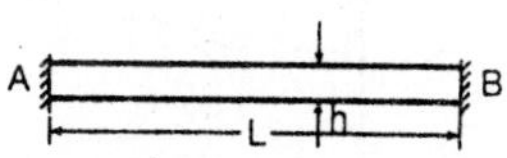

$$A = B = 0 \qquad M_A = M_B = -\frac{EI}{h}\Delta t\ \alpha_t$$

Temperature change

App. 9B·18A. Data of G.I. Sheeting

Gauge	*Thickness cm*	*Weight (kg/m²)*	*Moment of inertia I per m width (cm⁴)*	*Section Modulus Z per m width (cm³)*	*Allowable bending stress (kg/cm²)*
16	0·159	17·6	8·75	9·15	1100
18	0·126	14·2	6·97	7·26	1060
20	0·0995	11·27	5·46	5·75	1020
22	0·0795	9·30	4·37	4·57	985
24	0·063	7·34	3·42	3·66	945

App. 9B·19A. Unit Weight (range) of Materials (Also refer Chapter 3)

S.No.	*Material*	*Unit weight (kN/m^3)*	*S.No.*	*Material*	*Unit weight (kN/m^3)*
1.	Bitumen	0·1		sand stone	22-24
2.	Brick			slate	27·5
	common, refractory	16-19	9.	Timber	6-11
	heavy duty	24-25		Casuarina	8·4
	aggregate	10-14		Cypress	5·1
	dust (*surkhi*)	10-11		oak, sal	8·5
	masonry	19-22		mahogany	6·6
3.	Cement			mango	6·8
	ordinary	14·1		rose	8·2
	rapid hardening	12·5		sandal	9
	mortar	20		teak	6·3
4.	Cement concrete		10.	Grains	
	foam	8-10		(stored/stacked)	6·5-8
	light weight aggregate	10-14	11.	Fruits	3·5
	lean	22-23	12.	Sugar, Flour	7-7·5
	plain	23-24	13.	Vegetables	5-7
	RCC	23-26	14.	Coal	8·5-11
	PSC	24·26	15.	Fertilisers	11.5
5.	Glass	24-25	16.	Plastics	11-14
6.	Lime		17.	Oils	7-8·5
	powder	6-11	18.	Paints	9·5
	plaster	17	19.	Diesel oil	9·4
	mortar	15·18	20.	Petrol	6·8
	concrete	18·19	21.	Metals	
7.	Soils			aluminium	25-27
	undisturbed earth	13-19		copper	87·6
	Clay : compact dry	14		iron (pig)	70·6
	compact wet	20		(wrought)	75·5
	gravel : loose	16		lead	111
	compact	19·21		gold	189
	sand : dry	15-16		platinum	210
	wet	17-20		silver	103
	compact	18		brass	80-84
	silt (dry-wet)	16-19		steel	76·8
8.	Stone		22.	Miscellaneous	
	aggregate	16-19		ashes	6-7·5
	gravel (loose)	16		clinker	7·8
	(rammed)	19		rubber	12-14
	basalt	28-29		slag	15
	granite	23-26		furs	9
	lime	20-23		cotton	11-13
	marble	26·5		(compressed)	

App. 9B·20A. Weight per Unit Surface Area (Also refer Chapter 3)

S. No.	*Product*	*Thickness*	*Weight/(kN/100 m^2)*
1.	Asbestos cement sheets		
	plain	5 mm	9
	corrugated	6 mm	12-13
2.	Boards		
	cork compressed	10 mm	4
	fibre hard boards	medium 10 mm	4·5-7·5
	fire insulation	9 mm	3-4
	wood particle		4-11
3.	Expanded mesh		2·5-8
4.	Bitumen sheets		
	fibre base		2-3
	hessian base		2·1-3·6
5.	Linoleum sheets		
		1·6 mm	2·1
		4·4 mm	5·7
6.	Mastic pad	10 mm	21
7.	Plaster		
	acoustic	10 mm	7·8
	fibrous	10 mm	8·8
	gypsum	10 mm	18·5
8.	Galvanised iron sheets		
		1·0 mm	8·4
		1·6 mm	13·1
9.	Plywood	1 mm	0·7
10.	Plaster	25 mm	44
11.	Roof Tiles		110-170

App. 9B·21A. Design Live Loads on Roofs (Also refer Chapter 4)

S. No.	*Type of roof*	*UDL (kN/m^2)*	*Minimum*
1.	Flat, sloping, or curved with slopes		
	(*a*) access not provided	0·75	1·9 kN/m or 4·5 kN per span
	(*b*) access provided (*i.e.* staircase provided)	1·50	3·75 kN/m or 9 kN per span
2.	Sloping roof with slope (θ) greater than 10°	0·75-0·20 (θ – 10°)	0·4 kN/m^2
3.	Curved roofs with slope $\gamma = h/L$	$(0{\cdot}75 - 0{\cdot}52\ \gamma^2)$	0·4 kN/m^2

App. 9B·22A. Design Live Load on Floors

S. No.	Type of floor	UDL (kN/m^2)	Concentrated load (kN)
1.	*Dwelling Houses*		
	(*a*) all rooms except corridors, balconies, stairs, store	2	1·8
	(*b*) corridors, balconies, store, stairs	3	4·5
2.	*Hostels, Hotels, Lodges*		
	(*a*) living, bed, and bath rooms	2	1·4
	(*b*) kitchens, laundries, corridors, stairs, lobbies	3	4·5
	(*c*) restaurants, balconies	4	2·7
	(*d*) stores	5	4·5
	(*e*) plants and boiler rooms	5	6·7
	(*f*) garages for vehicles of weight		
	2·5 *t*	2·5	9
	4·0 *t*	5	9
3.	*Institutional and Educational Buildings*		
	(*a*) bed rooms, toilets	2	1·8
	(*b*) class rooms, dining, restaurants	3	2·7
	(*c*) kitchens, X-ray, operating, reading rooms with separate storage	3	4·5
	(*d*) corridors, stairs	4	4·5
	(*e*) balconies	4	1·5 kN/m at end
	(*f*) plant rooms	4-5	4·5
4.	*Office buildings*		
	(*a*) rooms with separate storage	2·5	2·7
	(*b*) rooms without separate storage	4	4·5
	(*c*) banking and dining halls	3	2·7
	(*d*) corridors	4	4·5
	(*e*) record, vaults, strong rooms	5	4·5
	(*f*) stationary stores	4/m height	9
5.	*Commercial buildings*		
	(*a*) office	2·5	2·7
	(*b*) kitchen/dining	3	4·5/2·7
	(*c*) retail shops	4	3·6
	(*d*) corridors, stairs	4	4·5
	(*e*) plant, boiler	5	6·7
	(*f*) balconies	4	1·5 kN/m at edge
6.	*Industrial buildings*		
	(*a*) work areas without machinery	2·5	4·5
	(*b*) work areas with machinery		
	light duty	5	4·5
	medium duty	7	4·5
	heavy duty	10	4·5
	(*c*) dining rooms	3	2·7
	(*d*) kitchens	3	4·5
	(*e*) corridors, stairs not subjected to machinery	4	4·5
	(*f*) corridors, stairs subject to machinery/ wheeled vehicles	5	4·5
7.	*Storage buildings* (actual loads can be computed)		
	(*a*) storage & work houses	2·4/m height	7
	minimum	7·5	

Table contd...

Table contd...

	(*b*) cold storage	5·0/m height	9
	minimum	15	9
	(*c*) corridors, stairs	4	4·5
	(*d*) corridors, stairs, with machinery movement	5	4·5
	(*e*) plant room	7·5	4·5
8.	*Assembly halls*		
	(*a*) fixed seat area	4	
	(*b*) without fixed seating	5	3·6
	(*c*) restaurants, corridors, stairs	4	4·5
	(*d*) stages	5	4·5
	(*e*) balconies	4	1·5 kN/m at outer edge
9.	Loads on Parapets and Balustrades : The following loads will be assumed to act at handrail or coping level.		
	Description	*Horizontal load*	
	Stair ways, landings and balconies		
	(Private and domestic : Internal force	25 lb/ft.	37 kg/m
	External force	50 lb/ft.	72 kg/m
	All other stair ways, parapet	50 lb/ft.	74 kg/m
	Parapets and balustrades in place of assembly Design should be checked against wind and seismic loads	150 lb/ft.	223 kg/m

10\. **Reduction in imposed floor loads on columns etc.**

Excepting for factories, workshops, ware houses, garages and storage buildings, reduction in the assumed live loads on floors may be made in designing columns, walls, peirs, their supports and foundations as follows :

Storey below the top most storey	1st	2nd	3rd	4th	others
Reduction, % of the live load	10	20	30	40	50

Where a single span of a beam or girder supports not less than 500 ft.^{2} of floor at one general level, the live load may be reduced in the design of the beam or girder by 5% for each 500 ft.^{2} supported subject to a max. reduction of 23%. This reduction or that given above whichever is greater may be considered in the design of columns etc.

10

Steel Structures

As per BIS Code : IS 800 : 2007 (Indian Standards)

10·1. General

10·1·1. Technical Terms

(1) **Accidental Loads.** Loads due to explosion, impact of vehicles, or other rare loads for which the structure is considered to be vulnerable as per the user.

(2) **Accompanying Load.** Live (imposed) load acting along with leading imposed load but causing lower actions and/or deflections.

(3) **Action Effect or Load Effect.** The internal force, axial, shear, bending or twisting moment, due to external actions and temperature loads.

(4) **Action.** The primary cause for stress or deformations in a structure such as dead, live, wind, seismic or temperature loads.

(5) **Actual Length.** The length between centre-to-centre of intersection points, with supporting members or the cantilever length in the case of a free standing member.

(6) **Beam.** A member subjected predominantly to bending.

(7) **Bearing Type Connection.** A connection made using bolts in 'snug-tight' condition, or rivets where the load is transferred by bearing of bolts or rivets against plate inside the bolt hole.

(8) **Braced Member.** A member in which the relative transverse displacement is effectively prevented by bracing.

(9) **Brittle Cladding.** Claddings, such as asbestos cement sheets which get damaged before undergoing considerable deformation.

(10) **Buckling Load.** The load at which an element, a member or a structure as a whole, either collapses in service or buckles in a load test and develops excessive lateral (out of plane) deformation or instability.

(11) **Buckling Strength or Resistance.** Force or moment, which a member can withstand without buckling.

(12) **Built-up Section.** A member fabricated by interconnecting more than one element to form a compound section acting as a single member.

(13) **Camber.** Intentionally introduced pre-curving (usually upwards) in a system, member or any portion of a member with respect to its chord. Frequently, camber is introduced to compensate for deflections at a specific level of loads.

(14) **Characteristic Load (Action).** The value of specified load (action), above which not more than a specified percentage (usually 5 percent) of samples of corresponding load are expected to be encountered.

(15) **Characteristic Yield/Ultimate Stress.** The minimum value of stress, below which not more than a specified percentage (usually 5 percent) of corresponding stresses of samples tested are expected to occur.

(16) **Column.** A member in upright (vertical) position which supports a roof or floor system and predominantly subjected to compression.

(17) **Compact Section.** A cross-section, which can develop plastic moment, but has inadequate plastic rotation capacity needed for formation of a plastic collapse mechanism of the member or structure.

(18) **Constant Stress Range.** The amplitude between which the stress ranges under cyclic loading is constant during the life of the structure or a structural element.

(19) **Corrosion.** An electrochemical process over the surface of steel, leading to oxidation of the metal.

(20) **Crane Load.** Horizontal and vertical loads from cranes.

(21) **Cumulative Fatigue.** Total damage due to fatigue loading of varying stress ranges.

(22) **Cut-off Limit.** The stress range, corresponding to the particular detail, below which cyclic loading need not be considered in cumulative fatigue damage evaluation (corresponds to 10^8 numbers of cycles in most cases).

(23) **Dead Loads.** The self-weights of all permanent constructions and installations including the self-weight of all walls, partitions, floors, roofs, and other permanent fixtures acting on a member.

(24) **Deflection.** It is the deviation from the standard position of a member or structure.

(25) **Design Life.** Time period for which a structure or a structural element is required to perform its function without damage.

(26) **Design Load/Factored Load.** A load value obtained by multiplying the characteristic load with a load factor.

(27) **Design Spectrum.** Frequency distribution of the stress ranges from all the nominal loading events during the design life (stress spectrum).

(28) **Detail Category.** Designation given to a particular detail to indicate the *S-N* curve to be used in fatigue assessment.

(29) **Discontinuity.** A sudden change in cross-section of a loaded member, causing a stress concentration at the location.

(30) **Ductility.** It is the property of the material or a structure indicating the extent to which it can deform beyond the limit of yield deformation before failure or fracture. The ratio of ultimate to yield deformation is usually termed as ductility.

(31) **Durability.** It is the ability of a material to resist deterioration over long periods of time.

(32) **Earthquake Loads.** The inertia forces produced in a structure due to the ground movement during an earthquake.

(33) **Edge Distance.** Distance from the centre of a fastener hole to the nearest edge of an element measured perpendicular to the direction of load transfer.

(34) **Effective Lateral Restraint.** Restraint, that produces sufficient resistance to prevent deformation in the lateral direction.

(35) **Effective Length.** Actual length of a member between points of effective

restraint or effective restraint and free end, multiplied by a factor to take account of the end conditions in buckling strength calculations.

(36) **Elastic Cladding.** Claddings, such as metal sheets, that can undergo considerable deformation without damage.

(37) **Elastic Critical Moment.** The elastic moment, which initiates lateral-torsional buckling of a laterally unsupported beam.

(38) **Elastic Design.** Design, which assumes elastic behaviour of materials throughout the service load range.

(39) **Elastic Limit.** It is the stress below which the material regains its original size and shape when the load is removed. In steel design, it is taken as the yield stress.

(40) **End Distance.** Distance from the centre of a fastener hole to the edge of an element measured parallel to the direction of load transfer.

(41) **Erection Loads.** The actions (loads and deformations) experienced by the structure exclusively during erection.

(42) **Erection Tolerance.** Amount of deviation related to the plumbness, alignment, and level of the element as a whole in the erected position. The deviations are determined by considering the locations of the ends of the element.

(43) **Exposed Surface Area to Mass Ratio.** The ratio of the surface area exposed to the fire (in mm^2) to the mass of steel (in kg).

Note : In the case of members with fire protection material applied, the exposed surface area is to be taken as the internal surface area of the fire protection material.

(44) **Fabrication Tolerance.** Amount of deviation allowed in the nominal dimensions and geometry in fabrication activities, such as cutting to length, finishing of ends, cutting of bevel angles, etc.

(45) **Factor of Safety.** The factor by which the yield stress of the material of a member is divided to arrive at the permissible stress in the material.

(46) **Fatigue.** Damage caused by repeated fluctuations of stress, leading to progressive cracking of a structural element.

(47) **Fatigue Loading.** Set of nominal loading events, cyclic in nature, described by the distribution of the loads, their magnitudes and the number of applications in each nominal loading event.

(48) **Fatigue Strength.** The stress range for a category of detail, depending upon the number of cycles it is required to withstand during design life.

(49) **Fire Exposure Condition**

(*a*) *Three-sided fire exposure condition.* Steel member incorporated in or in contact with a concrete or masonry floor or wall (at least against one surface).

Notes : (1) Three-sided fire exposure condition is to be considered separately unless otherwise specified.

(2) Members with more than one face in contact with a concrete or masonry floor or wall may be treated as three-sided fire exposure.

(*b*) *Four-sided fire exposure condition.* Steel member, which may be exposed to fire on all sides.

(50) **Fire Protection System.** The fire protection material and its method of attachment to the steel member.

(51) **Fire Resistance.** The ability of an element, component or structure, to fulfil for a stated period of time, the required stability, integrity, thermal insulation and/or other expected performance specified in a standard fire test.

(52) **Fire Resistance Level.** The fire resistance grading period for a structural element or system, in minutes, which is required to be attained in the standard fire test.

(53) **Flexural Stiffness.** Stiffness of a member against rotation as evaluated by the value of bending deformation moment required to cause a unit rotation while all other degrees of freedom of the joints of the member except the rotated one are assumed to be restrained.

(54) **Friction Type Connection.** Connection effected by using pre-tensioned high strength bolts where shear force transfer is due to mobilisation of friction betweeen the connected plates due to clamping force developed at the interface of connected plates by the bolt pre-tension.

(55) **Gauge.** The spacing between adjacent parallel lines of fasteners, transverse to the direction of load/stress.

(56) **Gravity Load.** Loads arising due to gravitational effects.

(57) **Gusset Plate.** The plate to which the members intersecting at a joint are connected.

(58) **High Shear.** High shear condition is caused when the actual shear due to factored load is greater than a certain fraction of design shear resistance.(See 9·2·2)

(59) **Imposed (Live) Load.** The load assumed to be produced by the intended use or occupancy including distributed, concentrated, impact, vibration and snow loads but excluding, wind, earthquake and temperature loads.

(60) **Instability.** The phenomenon which disables an element, member or a structure to carry further load due to excessive deflection lateral to the direction of loading and vanishing stiffness.

(61) **Lateral Restraint for a Beam.** (*see* 134)

(62) **Leading Imposed Load.** Imposed load causing higher action and/or deflection.

(63) **Limit State.** Any limiting condition beyond which the structure ceases to fulfil its intended function (*see also 186*).

(64) **Live Load** (*see 159*).

(65) **Load.** An externally applied force or action (*see also* 134).

(66) **Main Member.** A structural member, which is primarily responsible for carrying and distributing the applied load or action.

(67) **Mill Tolerance.** Amount of variation allowed from the nominal dimensions and geometry, with respect to cross-sectional area, non-parallelism of flanges, and out of straightness such as sweep or camber, in a product, as manufactured in a steel mill.

(68) **Normal Stress.** Stress component acting normal to the face, plane or section.

(69) **Partial Safety Factor.** The factor normally greater than unity by which either the loads (actions) are multiplied or the resistances are divided to obtain the design values.

(70) **Period of Structural Adequacy under Fire.** The time (t), in minutes, for the member to reach the limit state of structural inadequacy in a standard fire test.

(71) **Permissible Stress.** When a structure is being designed by the working stress method, the maximum stress that is permitted to be experienced in elements, members or structures under the nominal/service load (action).

(72) **Pitch.** The centre-to-centre distance between individual fasteners in a line, in the direction of load/stress.

(73) **Plastic Collapse.** The failure stage at which sufficient number of plastic hinges have formed due to the loads (actions) in a structure leading to a failure mechanism.

(74) **Plastic Design.** Design against the limit state of plastic collapse.

(75) **Plastic Hinge.** A yielding zone with significant inelastic rotation, which forms in a member, when the plastic moment is reached at a section.

(76) **Plastic Moment.** Moment capacity of a cross-section when the entire cross-section has yielded due to bending moment.

(77) **Plastic Section.** Cross-section, which can develop a plastic hinge and sustain plastic movement over sufficient plastic rotation required for formation of plastic failure mechanism of the member or structure.

(78) **Poisson's Ratio.** It is the absolute value of the ratio of lateral strain to longitudinal strain under uni-axial loading.

(79) **Proof Stress.** The stress to which high strength friction grip (HSFG) bolts are pre-tensioned.

(80) **Proof Testing.** The application of test loads to a structure, sub-structure, member or connection to ascertain the structural characteristics of only that specific unit.

(81) **Prototype Testing.** Testing of structure, sub-structure, members or connections to ascertain the structural characteristics of that class of structures, sub-structures, members or connections that are nominally identical (full scale) to the units tested.

(82) **Prying Force.** Additional tensile force developed in a bolt as a result of the flexing of a connection component such as a beam end plate or leg of an angle.

(83) **Rotation.** The change in angle at a joint between the original orientation of two linear member and their final position under loading.

(84) **Secondary Member.** Member which is provided for overall stability and or for restraining the main members from buckling or similar modes of failure.

(85) **Semi-compact Section.** Cross-section, which can attain the yield moment, but not the plastic moment before failure by plate buckling.

(86) **Serviceability Limit State.** A limit state of acceptable service condition exceedence of which causes serviceability failure.

(87) **Shear Force.** The inplane force at any transverse cross-section of a straight member of a column or beam.

(88) **Shear Lag.** The in plane shear deformation effect by which concentrated forces tangential to the surface of a plate gets distributed over the entire section perpendicular to the load over a finite length of the plate along the direction of the load.

(89) **Shear Stress.** The stress component acting parallel to a face, plane or cross-section.

(90) **Slender Section.** Cross-section in which the elements buckle locally before reaching yield moment.

(91) **Slenderness Ratio.** The ratio of the effective length of a member to the radius of gyration of the cross-section about the axis under consideration.

(92) **Slip Resistance.** Limit shear that can be applied in a friction grip connection before slip occurs.

(93) **S-N Curve.** The curve defining the relationship between the number of stress cycles to failure (N_{sc}) at a constant stress range (S_c), during fatigue loading of a structure.

(94) **Snow Load.** Load on a structure due to the accumulation of snow and ice on surfaces such as roof.

(95) **Snug Tight.** The tightness of a bolt achieved by a few impacts of an impact wrench or by the full effort of a person using a standard spanner.

(96) **Stability Limit State.** A limit state corresponding to the loss of static equilibrium of a structure by excessive deflection transverse to the direction of predominant loads.

(97) **Stickability.** The ability of the fire protection system to remain in place as the member deflects under load during a fire test.

(98) **Stiffener.** An element used to retain or prevent the out-of-plane deformations of plates.

(99) **Strain.** Deformation per unit length or unit angle.

(100) **Strain Hardening.** The phenomenon of increase in stress with increase in strain beyond yielding.

(101) **Strength.** Resistance to failure by yielding or buckling.

(102) **Strength Limit State.** A limit state of collapse or loss of structural integrity.

(103) **Stress.** The internal force per unit area of the original cross-section.

(104) **Stress Analysis.** The analysis of the internal force and stress condition in an element, member or structure.

(105) **Stress Cycle Counting.** Sum of individual stress cycles from stress history arrived at using any rational method.

(106) **Stress Range.** Algebraic difference between two extremes of stresses in a cycle of loading.

(107) **Stress Spectrum.** Histogram of stress cycles produced by a nominal loading event design spectrum, during design life.

(108) **Structural Adequacy for Fire.** The ability of the member to carry the test load exposed to the standard fire test.

(109) **Structural Analysis.** The analysis of stress, strain, and deflection characteristics of a structure.

(110) **Strut.** A compression member, which may be oriented in any direction.

(111) **Sway.** The lateral deflection of a frame.

(112) **Sway Member.** A member in which the transverse displacement of one end, relative to the other is not effectively prevented.

(113) **Tensile Stress.** The characteristic stress corresponding to rupture in tension, specified for the grade of steel in the appropriate Indian Standard, as listed in Table 1.

(114) **Test Load.** The factored load, equivalent to a specified load combination appropriate for the type of test being performed.

(115) **Transverse.** Direction along the stronger axes of the cross-section of the member.

(116) **Ultimate Limit State.** The state which, if exceeded can cause collapse of a part or the whole of the structure.

(117) **Ultimate Stress** (*see* 1·113).

(118) **Wind Loads.** Load experienced by member or structure due to wind pressure acting on the surfaces.

(119) **Yield Stress.** The characteristic stress of the material in tension before the elastic limit of the material is exceeded, as specified in the appropriate Indian Standard, as listed in Table 1.

(120) **Zone.** Portion.

10·1·2. Units

For the purpose of design calculations the following units are recommended.

(*a*) Forces and loads, in kN, kN/m, kN/m^2;

(*b*) Unit mass, in kg/m^3;

(*c*) Unit weight, in kN/m^3;

(*d*) Stresses and strengths, in N/mm^2 (MN/m^2 or MPa); and

(*e*) Moments (bending, etc.), in kNm.

For conversion of one system of units to another system, IS 786 (Supplement) may be referred.

10·1·3. Convention for Member Axes

Unless otherwise specified convention used for member axes is as follows (Fig. 10·1) :

(*a*) *x-x* along the member.

(*b*) *y-y* an axis of the cross-section.

(*i*) perpendicular to the flanges, and

(*ii*) perpendicular to the smaller leg in an angle section.

(*c*) *z-z* an axis of the cross-section

(*i*) axis parallel to flanges, and

(*ii*) axis parallel to smaller leg in angle section.

(*d*) *u-u* major axis (when it does not coincide with *z-z* axis).

(*e*) *v-v* minor axis (when it does not coincide with *y-y* axis).

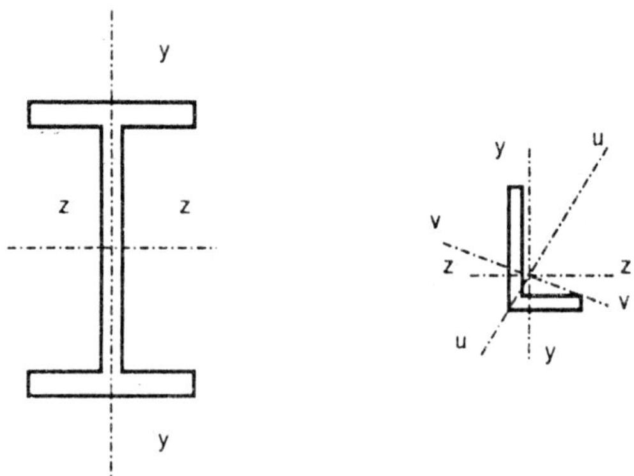

Fig. 10·1. Axes of members.

10·2. Materials

The material properties given in this section are nominal values, to be accepted as characteristic values in design calculations.

10·2·1. Structural Steel

The provisions in this section are applicable to the steels commonly used in steel construction, namely, structural mild steel and high tensile structural steel.

All the structural steel used in general construction, coming under the purview of this standard shall before fabrication conform to IS 2062.

Structural steel other than those specified above may also be used provided that the permissible stresses and other design provisions are suitably modified and the steel is also suitable for the type of fabrication adopted.

Steel that is not supported by mill test result may be used only in unimportant members and details, where their properties such as ductility and weldability would not affect the performance requirements of the members and the structure as a whole.

However, such steels may be used in structural system after confirming their quality by carrying out appropriate tests in accordance with the method specified in IS 1608.

10·2·2. Properties

Physical properties of structural steel irrespective of its grade may be taken as:

(*a*) Unit mass of steel, ρ = 7850 kg/m^3.

(*b*) Modulus of elasticity, $E = 2{\cdot}0 \times 10^5$ N/mm^2 (MPa)

(*c*) Poisson ratio, $\mu = 0{\cdot}3$

(*d*) Modulus of rigidity, $G = 0{\cdot}769 \times 10^5$ N/mm^2 (MPa)

(*e*) Co-efficient of thermal expansion $\alpha_t = 12 \times 10^{-6}$/°C.

Mechanical Properties of Structural Steel. The principal mechanical properties of the structural steel important in design are the yield stress, f_y; the tensile or ultimate stress, f_u ; the maximum percent elongation on a standard gauge length and notch toughness. Except for notch toughness, the other properties are determined by conducting tensile tests on samples cut from the plates, sections, etc. in accordance with IS 1608. Commonly used properties for the common steel products of different specifications are summarized in Table 10·1.

10·2·3. Connections

Rivets shall be manufactured from steel conforming to IS 7557. They may also be manufactured from steel conforming to IS 2062 provided that the steel meets the requirements given in IS 1148.

Rivets shall conform to IS 1929 and IS 2155 as appropriate.

High tensile steel rivets, shall be manufactured from steel conforming to IS 1149.

Bolts, Nuts and Washers. Bolts, nuts and washers shall conform as appropriate to IS 1363 (Parts 1 to 3), IS 1364 (Parts 1 to 5), IS 1367 (Parts 1 to 20), IS 3640, IS 3757, IS 4000, IS 5369, IS 5370, IS 5372, IS 5374, IS 5624, IS 6610, IS 6623, IS 6639, and IS 6649. The recommendations in IS 4000 shall be followed.

Steel Casting. Steel casting shall conform to IS 1030 or IS 2708.

Welding Consumable. Covered electrodes shall conform to IS 814 or IS 1395, as appropriate.

Filler rods and wires for gas welding shall conform to IS 1278.

The supply of solid filler wires for submerged arc welding of structural steels shall conform to IS 1387.

The bare wire electrodes for submerged arc welding shall conform to IS 7280. The combination of wire and flux shall satisfy the requirements of IS 3613.

Filler rods and bare electrodes for gas shielded metal arc welding shall conform to IS 6419 and IS 6560, as appropriate.

Table 10·1. Tensile Properties of Structural Steel Products

Sl. No.	Indian Standard	Grade / Classification	Properties: Yield Stress MPa, Min	Properties: Ultimate Tensile Stress MPa, Min.	Properties: Elongation, Percent, Min.
(1)	(2)	(3)	(4)	(5)	(6)
(*i*)	IS 513	O	—	—	—
		D	280	270-410	28
		DD	250	270-370	32
		EDD	220	270-350	35
(*ii*)	IS 814	Ex40xx	330	410-540	16
		Ex41xx	330	410-540	20
		Ex42xx	330	410-540	22
		Ex43xx	330	410-540	24
		Ex44xx	330	410-540	24
		Ex50xx	360	510-610	16
		Ex51xx	360	510-610	18
		Ex52xx	360	510-610	18
		Ex53xx	360	510-610	20
		Ex54xx	360	510-610	20
		Ex55xx	360	510-610	20
		Ex56xx	360	510-610	20
(*iii*)	IS 1079	O	—	—	—
		D	—	240-400	25
		DD	—	260-390	28
		EDD	—	260-380	32
(*iv*)	IS 1367 (Part 3)	3·6	—	330	25
		4·6	—	400	22
		4·8	—	420	—
		5·6	—	500	20
		5·8	—	520	—
		6·8	—	600	—
		8·8 ($d \leq 16$ mm)	640 1)	800	12
		8·8 ($d > 16$ mm)	660 1)	830	12
		9·8	720 1)	900	10
		10·9	940 1)	1040	9
		12·9	1100 1)	1220	8
(*v*)	IS 1875	1	200	370	26
		1A	220	410	25
		2	230	430	24
		2A	250	460	22
		3	270	490	21
		3A	280	540	20
		4	320	620	15
		5	350	710	13
		6	370	740	10

Sl. No.	Indian Standard	Grade / Classification	Yield Stress, *d* or *t* ≤20	Yield Stress, *d* or *t* > 20	Ultimate Tensile Stress	Elongation
(*vi*)	IS 1990	S_t 37	220	200	360-440	26
		S_t 42	250	240	410-500	23

Sl. No.	Indian Standard	Grade / Classification	Yield Stress, *t* ≤16	Yield Stress, *t* >16 and ≤40	Yield Stress, *t* >40 and ≤60	Yield Stress, *t* >60 and ≤100	Yield Stress, *t* >100 and ≤350	UTS, *t* ≤60	UTS, *t* >60 and ≤100	UTS, *t* >100 and ≤350	Elongation, *t* ≤60	Elongation, *t* >60 and ≤350
(*vii*)	IS 2002	1	235	225	215	200	185	360-480	360-480	350-480	24	23
		2	265	255	245	215	200	410-530	410-530	400-530	22	21
		3	290	285	280	255	230	460-580	450-570	440-570	21	20

Table (Contd.)

Sl. No.	*Indian Standard*	*Grade / Classification*	*Properties*				
			Yield Stress MPa, Min			*Ultimate Tensile Stress MPa, Min.*	*Elongation, Percent, Min.*
(1)	(2)	(3)	(4)			(5)	(6)
			d or *t*				
			<20	20-40	>40		
(*viii*)	IS 2062	E 165 (Fe 290)	165	165	165	290	23
		E 250 (Fe 410 W) A	250	240	230	410	23
		E 250 (Fe 410 W) B	250	240	230	410	23
		E 250 (Fe 410 W) C	250	240	230	410	23
		E 300 (Fe 440)	300	290	280	440	22
		E 350 (Fe 490)	350	330	320	490	22
		E 410 (Fe 540)	410	390	380	540	20
		E 450 (Fe 570) D	450	430	420	570	20
		E 450 (Fe 590) E	450	430	420	590	20
			d or *t*				
(*ix*)	IS 3039	I	≤25	> 25 and ≤ 50			
		II	230	220		400-490	22
		III	235	235		400-490	22
			235	235		400-490	22
(*x*)	IS 6240	Grade 1	240			350-450	25
		Grade 2	245			360-450	34
(*xi*)	IS 7557	Annealed Condition	160			330-410	30
		As-Drawn Condition	190			410-490	20
(*xii*)	IS 9295	HFC 210/CDS 210/ERW210	210			330	20
		HFC 240/CDS 240/ERW240	240			410	18
		HFC 310/CDS 310/ERW310	310			450	15
(*xiii*)	IS 10748	1	170			290	30
		2	210			330	28
		3	240			410	25
		4	275			430	20
		5	310			490	15

Notes : 1. Percent of elongation shall be taken over the gauge length $5{\cdot}65\sqrt{S_o}$, where S_o = Original cross-sectional area of the test specimen.

2. Abbreviation : O = Ordinary, D = Drawing, DD = Deep Drawing, EDD = Extra Deep Drawing.

1) Stress at 0·2 percent non-proportional elongation, *Min*.

10·3. General Design Requirements

10·3·1. Methods of Design

Structure and its elements shall normally, be designed by the *limit state method*. Account should be taken of accepted theories, experimental information and experience and the need to design for durability. Calculations alone may not produce safe, serviceable and durable structures. Suitable materials, quality control, adequate detailing and good supervision are equally important.

Where the limit states method cannot be conveniently adopted; the working stress design may be used.

10·3·2. Loads and Forces

For the purpose of designing any element, member or a structure, the following loads (actions) and their effects shall be taken into account, where applicable, with partial safety factors and combinations.

(*a*) Dead loads;

(*b*) Imposed loads (live load, crane load, snow load, dust load, wave load, earth pressures, etc.);

(*c*) Wind loads;

(*d*) Earthquake loads;

(*e*) Erection loads;

(*f*) Accidental loads such as those due to blast, impact of vehicles, etc; and

(*g*) Secondary effects due to contraction or expansion resulting from temperature changes, differential settlements of the structure as a whole or of its components, eccentric connections, rigidity of joints differing from design assumptions.

Dead loads should be assumed in design as specified in IS 875 (Part 1).

Imposed loads for different types of occupancy and function of structures shall be taken as recommended in IS 875 (Part 2). Imposed loads arising from equipment, such as cranes and machines should be assumed in design as per manufacturers/suppliers data. Snow load shall be taken as per IS 875 (part 4).

Wind loads on structures shall be taken as per the recommendations of IS 875 (Part 3).

Earthquake loads shall be assumed as per the recommendations of IS 1893 (Part 1).

The erection loads and temperature effects shall be considered as specified in 3·3 and 3·4 respectively.

10·3·3. Erection Loads

All loads required to be carried by the structure or any part of it due to storage or positioning of construction material and erection equipment, including all loads due to operation of such equipment shall be considered as erection loads. Proper provision shall be made, including temporary bracings, to take care of all stresses developed during erection. Dead load, wind load and also such parts of the live load as would be imposed on the structure during the period of erection shall be taken as acting together with the erection loads. The structure as a whole and all parts of the structure in conjunction with the temporary bracings shall be capable of sustaining these loads during erection.

10·3·4. Temperature Effects

Expansion and contraction due to changes in temperature of the members and elements of a structure shall be considered and adequate provision made for such effect.

10·3·5. Load Combinations

Load combinations for design purposes shall be those that produce maximum forces and effects and consequently maximum stresses and deformations. The following combination of loads with appropriate partial safety factors (*see* Table 10·4) may be considered.

(*a*) Dead load + imposed load,

(*b*) Dead load + imposed load + wind or earthquake load,

(*c*) Dead load + wind or earthquake load, and

(*d*) Dead load + erection load.

Note : In the case of structures supporting cranes, imposed loads shall include the crane effects as given below in crane loads.

Wind load and earthquake loads shall not be assumed to act simultaneously. The effect of each shall be considered separately.

The effect of cranes to be considered under imposed loads shall include the vertical loads, eccentricity effects induced by the vertical loads, impact factors, lateral (surge) and longitudinal (horizontal) thrusts, not acting simultaneously, across and along the crane rail, respectively.

The crane loads and their combinations to be considered shall be as indicated by the customer. In the absence of any specific indications, the load combinations shall be as given below :

(*a*) Vertical loads with full impact from one loaded crane or two cranes in case of tandem operation, together with vertical loads without impact from as many loaded cranes as may be positioned for maximum effect, along with maximum horizontal thrust from one crane only or two in case of tandem operation;

(*b*) Loads as specified above, subject to cranes in maximum of any two bays of the building cross-section shall be considered for multi-bay multi-crane gantries;

(*c*) The longitudinal thrust on a crane track rail shall be considered for a maximum of two loaded cranes on the track; and

(*d*) Lateral thrust (surge) and longitudinal thrust acting across and along the crane rail respectively, shall be assumed not to act simultaneously. The effect of each force, shall however be investigated separately.

While investigating the effect of earthquake forces, the resulting effect from dead loads of all cranes parked in each bay, positioned to cause maximum effect shall be considered.

The crane runway girders supporting bumpers shall be checked for bumper impact loads also, as specified by the manufacturers.

Stresses developed due to secondary effects such as handling; erection, temperature and settlement of foundations, if any, shall be appropriately added to the stresses calculated from the combination of loads with appropriate partial safety factors.

10·3·6. Geometrical Properties

The geometrical properties of the gross and the effective cross-sections of a member or part thereof, shall be calculated on the following basis :

(*a*) The properties of the gross cross-section shall be calculated from the specified size of the member or part thereof or read from appropriate table.

(*b*) The properties of the effective cross-section shall be calculated by deducting from the area of the gross cross-section, the following :

(1) The sectional area in excess of effective plate width, in case of slender sections.

(2) The sectional areas of all holes in the section except for parts in compression. In case of punched holes, hole size 2 mm in excess of the actual diameter may be deducted.

Table 10·2. Limiting Width to Thickness Ratio

Compression Element			*Ratio*	*Class of section*		
				Class 1 Plastic	*Class 2 Compact*	*Class 3 Semi-compact*
(1)			(2)	(3)	(4)	(5)
Outstanding element of compression flange	Rolled section		b/t_f	9·4ε	10·5ε	15·7ε
	Welded section		b/t_f	8·4ε	9·4ε	13·6ε
Internal element of compression flange	Compression due to bending		b/t_f	29·3ε	33·5ε	42ε
	Axial compression		b/t_f	Not applicable		
Web of an I, H or box section	Neutral axis at mid-depth		d/t_w	84ε	105ε	126ε
	Generally	If r_1 is negative :	d/t_w	$\frac{84\varepsilon}{1+r_1}$ but ≤ 42ε	$\frac{105 \cdot 0\varepsilon}{1+r_1}$	$\frac{126 \cdot 0\varepsilon}{1+2r_2}$ but ≤ 42ε
		If r_1 is positive :	d/t_w		$\frac{105 \cdot 0\varepsilon}{1+1 \cdot 5r_1}$ but ≤ 42ε	
	Axial compression		d/t_w	Not applicable		42ε
Web of a channel			d/t_w	42ε	42ε	42ε
Angle, compression due to bending (Both criteria should be satisfied)			b/t d/t	9·4ε 9·4ε	10·5ε 10·5ε	15·7ε 15·7ε
Single angle, or double angles with the components separated, axial compression (All three criteria should be satisfied)			b/t d/t $(b + d)/t$	Not applicable		15·7ε 15·7ε 25ε
Outstanding leg of an angle in contact back-to-back in a double angle member			d/t	9·4ε	10·5ε	15·7ε
Outstanding leg of an angle with its back in continuous contact with another component			d/t	9·4ε	10·5ε	15·7ε
Stem of a T-section, rolled or cut from a rolled I- or H-section			D/t_f	8·4ε	9·4ε	18·9ε
Circular hollow tube, including welded tube subjected to : (*a*) moment			D/t	$42\varepsilon^2$	$52\varepsilon^2$	$146\varepsilon^2$
(*b*) axial compression			D/t	Not applicable		$88\varepsilon^2$

Notes :

(1) Elements which exceed semi-compact limits are to be taken as of slender cross-section.

(2) $\varepsilon = (250/f_y)^{1/2}$

(3) Webs shall be checked for shear buckling when $d/t > 67\varepsilon$, where, b is the width of the element (may be taken as clear distance between lateral supports or between lateral support and free edge, as appropriate), t is the thickness of element, d is the depth of the web, D is the outer diameter of the element (*see* Fig. 10·2)..

(4) Different elements of a cross-section can be in different classes. In such cases the section is classified based on the least favourable classification.

(5) The stress ratio r_1 and r_2 are defined as:

$$r_1 = \frac{\text{Actual average axial stress (negative if tensile)}}{\text{Design compressive stress of web alone}}$$

$$r_2 = \frac{\text{Actual average axial stress (negative if tensile)}}{\text{Design compressive stress of overall section}}$$

10·3·7. Types of Elements

(*a*) **Internal elements.** These are elements attached along both longitudinal edges to other elements or to longitudinal stiffeners connected at suitable intervals to transverse stiffeners, for example, web of I-section and flanges and web of box section.

(*b*) **Outside elements or Outstands.** These are elements attached along only one of the longitudinal edges to an adjacent element, the other edge being free to displace out of plane, for example, flange overhang of an I-section, stem of T-section and legs of an angle section.

(*c*) **Tapered elements.** These may be treated as flat elements having average thickness.

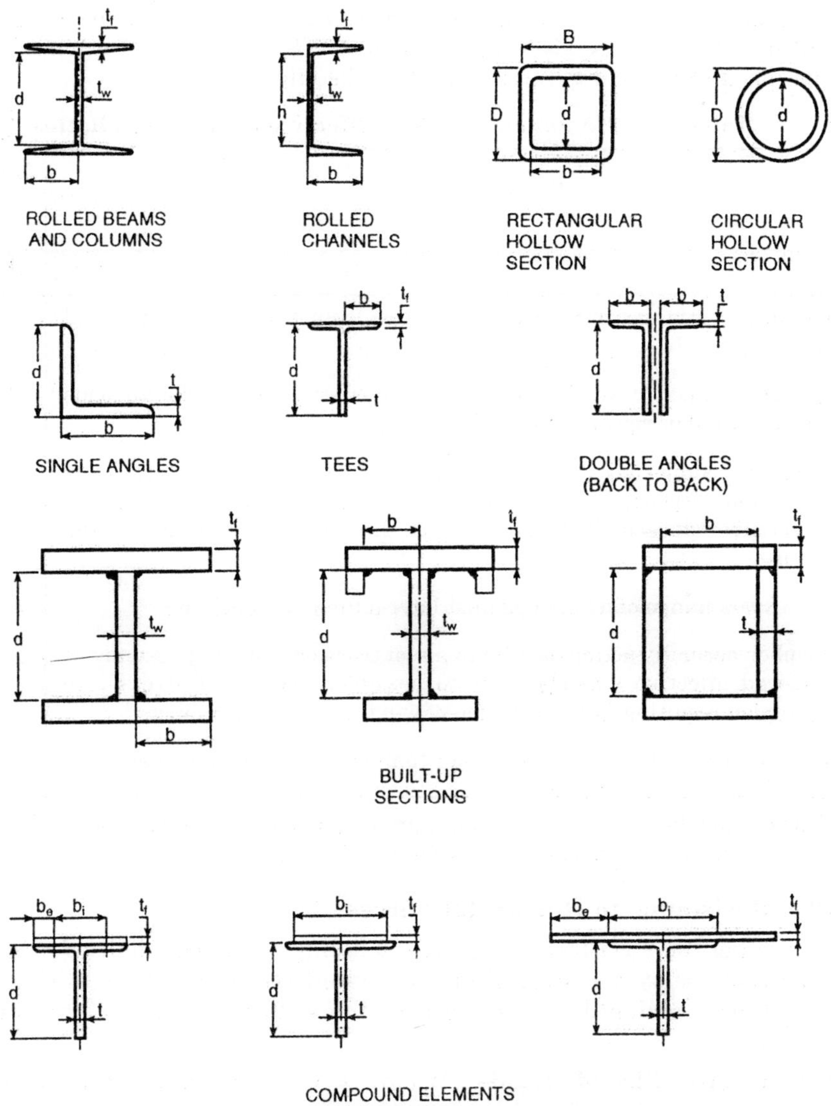

b_i—Internal Element Width

b_e—External Element Width

Fig. 10·2. Dimensions of sections.

10·3·7·1. Compound Elements in Built-up Section (*see* Fig. 10·2)

In case of compound elements consisting of two or more elements bolted or welded together, the limiting width to thickness ratios as given in Table 10·2 should be considered on basis of the following:

(*a*) Outstanding width of compound element (b_e) to its own thickness.

(*b*) The internal width of each added plate between the lines of welds or fasteners connecting it to the original section to its own thickness.

(*c*) Any outstand of the added plates beyond the line of welds or fasteners connecting it to original section to its own thickness.

10·3·8. Maximum Effective Slenderness Ratio

The maximum effective slenderness ratio, *KL/r*, values of a beam, strut or tension member shall not exceed those given in Table 10·3. '*KL*' is the effective length of the member and '*r*' is appropriate radius of gyration based on the effective section.

Table 10·3. Maximum Values of Effective Slenderness Ratios

Sl. No.	*Member*	*Maximum Effective Slenderness Ratio (KL/r)*
(1)	(2)	(3)
(*i*)	A member carrying compressive loads resulting from dead loads and imposed loads	180
(*ii*)	A tension member in which a reversal of direct stress occurs due to loads other than wind or seismic forces.	180
(*iii*)	A member subjected to compression forces resulting only from combination with wind/earthquake actions, provided the deformation of such member does not adversely affect the stress in any part of the structure.	250
(*iv*)	Compression flange of a beam against lateral torsional buckling.	300
(*v*)	A member normally acting as a tie in a roof truss or a bracing system not considered effective when subject to possible reversal of stress into compression resulting from the action of wind or earthquake forces[1].	350
(*vi*)	Members always under tension[1] (other than pre-tensioned members)	400

[1] Tension members, such as bracing's, pre-tensioned to avoid sag, need not satisfy the maximum slenderness ratio limits.

10·3·9. Resistance to Horizontal Forces

In designing the steel frame work of a building, provision shall be made (by adequate moment connections or by a system of bracing) to effectively transmit to the foundations all the horizontal forces, giving due allowance for the stiffening effect of the walls and floors, where applicable.

Eccentrically Placed Loads. Where a wall, or other gravity load, is placed eccentrically upon the flange of a supporting steel beam, the beam and its connections shall be designed for torsion, unless the beam is restrained laterally in such a way as to prevent the twisting of the beam.

10·3·10. Expansion Joints

In view of the large number of factors involved in deciding the location, spacing and nature of expansion joints, the decision regarding provision of expansion joints shall be left to the discretion of the designer.

Structures in which marked changes in plan dimensions take place abruptly, shall be provided with expansion joints at the section where such changes occur. Expansion joints shall be so provided that the necessary movement occurs with minimum resistance at the joint. The gap at the expansion joint should be such that;

(*a*) It accommodates the expected expansion/contraction due to seasonal and durinal variation of temperature, and

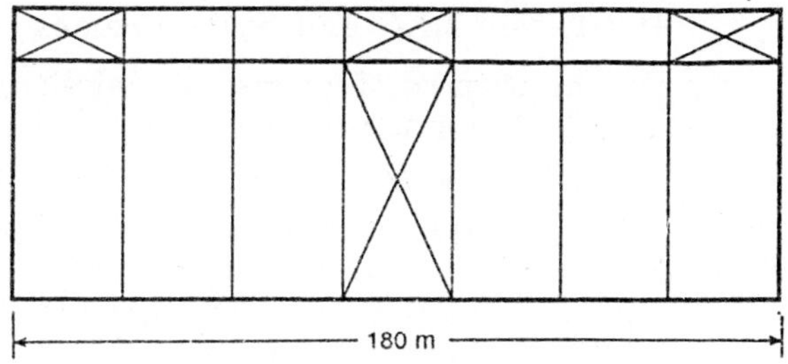

End of Covered Building/Section

Fig. 10·3. Maximum Length of Building with one bay of bracing

(*b*) It avoids pounding of adjacent units under earthquake. The structure adjacent to the joint should preferably be supported on separate columns but not necessarily on separate foundations.

The details as to the length of a structure where expansion joints have to be provided may be determined after taking into consideration various factors such as temperature, exposure to weather and structural design.

If one bay of longitudinal bracing is provided at the centre of the building or building section, the length of the building section may be restricted to 180 m in case of covered buildings and 120 m in case of open gantries (*see* Fig. 10·3).

If more than one bay of longitudinal bracing is provided near the centre of the building/section, the maximum centre line distance between the two lines of bracing may be restricted to 50 m for covered buildings (and 30 m for open gantries) and the maximum distance between the centre of the bracing to the nearest expansion joint/end of building or section may be restricted to 90 m (60 m in case of open gantries). The maximum length of the building section thus may be restricted to 230 m for covered buildings (150 m for open gantries). Beyond this, suitable expansion joints shall be provided (*see* Fig. 10·4).

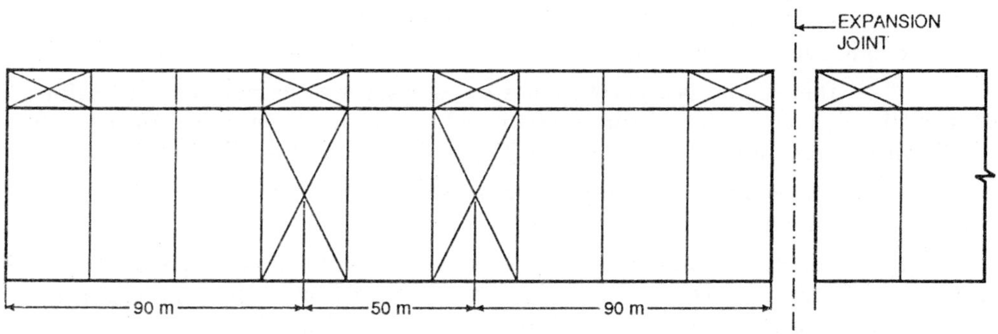

Fig. 10·4. Maximum length of building/section with two bays of bracings.

The maximum width of the covered building section should preferably be restricted to 150 m beyond which suitable provisions for the expansion joint may be made.

Note : When the provisions of these sections are met for a building or open structure, the stress analysis due to temperature is not required.

10·4. Structural Analysis

10·4·1. Non-sway and Sway Frames

For the purpose of analysis and design, the structural frames are classified as non-sway and sway frames as given below:

(*a*) **Non-sway frame.** One in which the transverse displacement of one end of the member relative to the other end is effectively prevented. This applies to triangulated frames and trusses or to frames where in-plane stiffness is provided by bracings, or by shear walls, or by floor slabs and roof decks secured horizontally to walls or to bracing systems parallel to the plane of loading and bending of the frame.

(*b*) **Sway frame.** One in which the transverse displacement of one end of the member relative to the other end is not effectively prevented. Such members and frames occur in structures which depend on flexural action of members to resist lateral loads and sway, as in moment resisting frames.

(*c*) A rigid jointed multi-storey frame may be considered as a non-sway frame if in every individual storey, the deflection δ, over a storey height h_s, due to the notional horizontal loading.

10·4·2. Rigid Construction. In rigid construction, the connections between members (beam and column) at their junction shall be assumed to have sufficient rigidity to hold the original angles between the members connected at a joint unchanged under loading.

10·4·3 Semi-rigid Construction. In semi-rigid construction, the connections between members (beam and column) at their junction may not have sufficient rigidity to hold the original angles between the members at a joint unchanged, but shall be assumed to have the capacity to furnish a dependable and known degree of flexural restraint. The relationship between the degree of flexural restraint and the level of the load effects shall be established by any rational method or based on test results (*see* Annex F).

10·4·4. Simple Construction. In simple construction, the connections between members (beam and column) at their junction will not resist any appreciable moment and shall be assumed to be hinged.

10·4·5. Base Stiffness

In the analysis of all structures the appropriate base stiffness about the axis under consideration shall be used. In the absence of the knowledge of the pedestal and foundation stiffness, the following may be assumed:

(*a*) When the column is rigidly connected to a suitable foundation, the stiffness of the pedestal shall be taken as the stiffness of the column above base plate. However in case of very stiff pedestals and foundations the column may be assumed as fixed at base.

(*b*) When the column is nominally connected to the foundation, a pedestal stiffness of 10 percent of the column stiffness may be assumed.

(*c*) When an actual pin or rocker is provided in the connection between the steel column and pedestal, the column is assumed as hinged at base and the pedestal and foundation may be appropriately designed for the reactions from the column.

(*d*) In case of (*a*) and (*b*), the bottom of the pedestal shall be assumed to have the following boundary condition in the absence of any detailed procedure based on theory or tests :

(1) When the foundation consist of a group of piles with a pile cap, raft foundation or

an isolated footing resting on rock or very hard soil, the pedestal shall be assumed to be fixed at the level of the bottom of footing or at the top of pile cap.

(2) When the foundation consist of an isolated footing resting on other soils, pedestal shall be assumed to be hinged at the level of the bottom of footing.

(3) When the pedestal is supported by a single pile, which is laterally surrounded by soil providing passive resistance, the pile shall be assumed to be fixed at a depth of 5 times the diameter of the pile below the ground level in case of compact ground or the top level of compact soil in case of poor soil overlying compact soil.

(4) When the column is founded into rock, it may be assumed to be fixed at the interface of the column and rock.

10·4·5·1. Simple Construction. Bending members may be assumed to have their ends connected for shear only and to be free to rotate. In triangulated structures, axial forces may be determined by assuming that all members are pin connected.

10·4·6. Notional Horizontal Loads. To analyze a frame subjected to gravity loads, considering the sway stability of the frame, notional horizontal forces should be applied. These notional horizontal forces account for practical imperfections and should be taken at each level as being equal to 0·5 percent of factored dead load plus vertical imposed loads applied at that level. The notional load should not be applied along with other lateral loads such as wind and earthquake loads in the analysis.

The notional forces should be applied on the whole structure, in both orthogonal directions, in one direction at a time, at roof and all floor levels or their equivalent. They should be taken as acting simultaneously with factored gravity loads.

The notional force should not be,

(*a*) applied when considering overturning or overall instability,

(*b*) combined with other horizontal (lateral) loads;

(*c*) combined with temperature effects; and

(*d*) taken to contribute to the net shear on the foundation.

The sway effect using notional load under gantry load case need not be considered if the ratio of height to lateral width of the building is less than unity.

10·4·7. Elastic Analysis

Assumptions

Individual members shall be assumed to remain elastic under the action of the factored design loads for all limit states.

The effect of haunching or any variation of the cross-section along the axis of a member shall be considered, and where significant, shall be taken into account in the determination of the member stiffness.

10·4·8. Plastic Analysis

Application. The effects of design action throughout or on part of a structure may be determined by a plastic analysis. The distribution of design action effects shall satisfy equilibrium and the boundary conditions.

Requirements. When a plastic method of analysis is used, all of the following conditions shall be satisfied, unless adequate ductility of the structure and plastic rotation capacity of its members and connections are established for the design loading conditions by other means of evaluation:

(*a*) The yield stress of the grade of the steel used shall not exceed 450 MPa.

(*b*) The stress-strain characteristics of the steel shall not be significantly different from those obtained for steels complying with IS 2062 or equivalent and shall be such as to ensure complete plastic moment redistribution. The stress-strain diagram shall have a plateau at the yield stress, extending for at least six times the yield strain. The ratio of the tensile strength to the yield stress specified for the grade of the steel shall not be less than 1·2. The elongation on a gauge length complying with IS 2062 shall not be than 15 percent, and the steel shall exhibit stain-hardening capability. Steels conforming to IS 2062 shall be deemed to satisfy the above requirements.

(*c*) The members used shall be hot-rolled or fabricated using hot-rolled piates and sections.

(*d*) The cross-section of members not containing plastic hinges should be at least that of compact section, unless the members meet the strength requirements from elastic analysis.

(*e*) Where plastic hinges occur in a member, the proportions of its cross-section should not exceed the limiting values for plastic section.

(*f*) The cross-section should be symmetrical about its axis perpendicular to the axis of the plastic hinge rotation.

(*g*) The members shall not be subject to impact loading, requiring assessment or fluctuating loading, requiring a fatigue assessment.

10·4·9. Restraints

If practicable, torsional restraint (against lateral buckling) should be provided at all plastic hinge locations. Where not feasible, the restraint should be provided within a distance of *D*/2 of the plastic hinge location, where *D* is the total depth of section.

The torsional restraint requirement at a section as above, need not be met at the last plastic hinge to form, provided it can be clearly identified.

10·4·10. Stiffeners at Plastic Hinge Locations

Web stiffeners should be provided where a concentrated load, which exceeds 10 percent of the shear capacity of the member, is applied within *D*/2 of a plastic hinge location. The stiffener should be provided within a distance of half the depth of the member on either side of the hinge location and be designed to carry the applied load. If the stiffeners are flat plates, the outstand width to the thickness ratio, *b*/*t*, should not exceed the values given in the plastic section (Table 10·2). Where other sections are used the ratio $\left(\frac{I_{so}}{I_t}\right)^{t/2}$ should not exceed the values given for plastic section (Table 10·2).

where I_{so} = second moment of area of the stiffener about the face of the element perpendicular to the web; and

I_t = St. Venant's torsion constant of the stiffener.

The frame shall be adequately supported against sway and out-of-plane buckling by bracings, moment resisting frame or an independent system such as shear wall.

10·5. Limit State Design

10·5·1. In the limit state design method, the structure shall be designed to withstand safely all loads likely to act on it throughout its life. It shall not suffer total collapse under accidental loads such as from explosions or impact or due to consequences of human error to an extent beyond the local damages. The objective of the design is to achieve a structure that will remain fit for use during its life with acceptable target reliability. In other words, the probability of a limit state being reached during its lifetime should be very low. The acceptable limit for the safety and serviceability requirements before failure occurs is called a limit state. In general, the structure shall be designed on the basis of the most critical limit state and shall be checked for other limit states.

10·5·2. For achieving the design objectives, the design shall be based on characteristic values for material strengths and applied loads (actions), which take into account the probability of variations in the material strengths and in the loads to be supported. The characteristic values shall be based on statistical data, if available. Where such data is not available, these shall be based on experience. The design values are derived from the characteristic values through the use of partial safety factors, both for material strengths and for loads. In the absence of special considerations, these factors shall have the values given in this section according to the material, the type of load and the limit state being considered. The reliability of design is ensured by satisfying the requirement:

Design action or load ≤ Design strength

Limit states are the states beyond which the structure no longer satisfies the performance requirements specified. The limit states are classified as:

(*a*) Limit state of strength ; and (*b*) Limit state of serviceability.

The limit states of strength are those associated with failures (or imminent failure), under the action of probable and most unfavourable combination of loads on the structure using the appropriate partial safety factors, which may endanger the safety of life and property. The limit state of strength includes:

(*a*) Loss of equilibrium of the structure as a whole or any of its parts or components.

(*b*) Loss of stability of the structure (including the effect of sway where appropriate and overturning) or any of its parts including supports and foundations.

(*c*) Failure by excessive deformation, rupture of the structure or any of its parts or components.

(*d*) Fracture due to fatigue.

(*e*) Brittle fracture.

The limit state of serviceability include :

(*a*) Deformation and deflections, which may adversely affect the appearance or effective use of the structure or may cause improper functioning of equipment or services or may cause damages to finishes and non-structural members.

(*b*) Vibrations in the structure or any of its components causing discomfort to people, damages to the structure, its contents or which may limit its functional effectiveness. Special consideration shall be given to systems susceptible to vibration, such as large open floor areas free of partitions to ensure that such vibrations are acceptable for the intended use and occupancy.

(*c*) Repairable damage or crack due to fatigue.

(*d*) Corrosion, durability.

(*e*) Fire.

10·5·3. Actions. The actions (loads) to be considered in design include direct actions (loads) experienced by the structure due to self weight, external actions etc., and imposed deformations such as that due to temperature and settlement.

Classification of Actions. Actions are classified by their variation with time as given below :

(*a*) *Permanent actions* (Q_p) : Actions due to self-weight of structural and non-structural components, fittings, ancillaries, and fixed equipment, etc.

(*b*) *Variable actions* (Q_v) : Actions due to construction and service stage loads such as imposed (live) loads (crane loads, snow loads, etc.), wind loads, and earthquake loads, etc.

(*c*) *Accidental actions* (Q_a) : Actions expected due to explosions, and impact of vehicles, etc.

Characteristic Actions (Loads). The Characteristic Actions, Q_c, are the values of the different actions that are not expected to be exceeded with more than 5 percent probability, during the life of the structure and they are taken as:

(*a*) the self-weight, in most cases calculated on the basis of nominal dimensions and unit weights.

(*b*) the variable loads, values of which are specified in relevant standard.

(*c*) the upper limit with a specified probability (usually 5 percent) not exceeding during some reference period (design life).

(*d*) specified by client, or by designer in consultation with client, provided they satisfy the minimum provisions of the relevant loading standard.

10·5·4. Design Actions (l). The design actions, Q_d is expressed as $Q_d = \sum_k \gamma_{fk} Q_{ck}$

where γ_{fk} = partial safety factor for different loads k, given in Table 10·4 to account for:

(*a*) Possibility of unfavourable deviation of the load from the characteristic value,

(*b*) Possibility of inaccurate assessment of the load,

(*c*) Uncertainty in the assessment of effects of the load, and

(*d*) Uncertainty in the assessment of the limit states being considered.

The loads or load effects shall be multiplied by the relevant γ_f factors, given in Table 10·4, to get the design loads or design load effects.

Table 10·4. Partial Safety Factors for Loads, γ_f for Limit State

Combination	*Limit State of strength*					*Limit State of Serviceability*			
	DL	*LL*[1]		*WL/EL*	*AL*	*DL*	*LL*[1]		*WL/DL*
		Leading	*Accompanying*				*Leading*	*Accompanying*	
(1)	(2)	(3)	(4)	(5)	(6)	(7)	(8)	(9)	(10)
DL + LL + CL	1·5	1·5	1·05	—	—	1·0	1·0	1·0	—
DL + LL + CL+	1·2	1·2	1·05	0·6	—	1·0	0·8	0·8	0·8
WL/EL	1·2	1·2	0·53	1·2					
DL + WL/EL	1·5(0·9)[2]	—	—	1·5	—	1·0	—	—	1·0
DL + ER	1·2(0·9)[2]	1·2	—	—	—	—	—	—	—
DL + LL + AL	1·0	0·35	0·35	—	1·0	—	—	—	—

1) When action of different live loads is simultaneously considered, the leading live load shall be considered to be the one causing the higher load effects in the member/section.

2) This value is to be considered when the dead load contributes to stability against overturning is critical or the dead load causes reduction in stress due to other loads.

Abbreviations :

DL = Dead Load, LL = Imposed load (Live loads), WL = Wind load, CL = Crane load (vertical/Horizontal), AL = Accidental load, ER = Erection load, EL = Earthquake load.

Note : The effects of actions (loads) in terms of stresses or stress resultants may be obtained from an appropriate method of analysis.

10·5·4·1. Design Strength. The Design Strength, S_d is obtained as given below from ultimate strength, S_u and partial safety factors for materials, γ_m given in Table 10·5.

$$S_d = S_u/\gamma_m$$

where partial safety factor for materials, γ_m account for :

(*a*) Possibility of unfavourable deviation of material strength from the characteristic value,

(*b*) Possibility of unfavourable variation of member sizes,

(*c*) Possibility of unfavourable reduction in member strength due to fabrication and tolerances, and

(*d*) Uncertainty in the calculation of strength of the members.

10·5·5. Factors Governing the Ultimate Strength

10·5·5·1. Stability. Stability shall be ensured for the structure as a whole and for each of its elements. This should include, overall frame stability against overturning and sway.

10·5·5·1·1. Stability against overturning. The structure as a whole or any part of it shall be designed to prevent instability due to overturning, uplift or sliding under factored load as given below :

(*a*) The Actions shall be divided into components aiding instability and components resisting instability.

(*b*) The permanent and variable actions and their effects causing instability shall be combined using appropriate load factors as per the Limit State requirements, to obtain maximum destabilizing effect.

(*c*) The permanent actions (loads) and effects contributing to resistance shall be multiplied with a partial safety factor 0·9 and added together with design resistance (after multiplying with appropriate partial safety factor). Variable actions and their effects contributing to resistance shall be disregarded.

(*d*) The resistance effect shall be greater than or equal to the destabilizing effect. Combination of imposed and dead loads should be such as to cause most severe effect on overall stability.

Sway Stability. The whole structure, including portions between expansion joints, shall be adequately stiff against sway. To ensure this, in addition to designing for applied horizontal loads, a separate check should be carried out for notional horizontal loads to evaluate the sway under gravity loads.

Fatigue. Generally fatigue need not be considered unless a structure or element is subjected to numerous significant fluctuations of stress. Stress changes due to fluctuations in wind loading normally need not be considered. When designing for fatigue, the partial safety factor for load, γ_f equal to unity shall be used for the load causing stress fluctuation and stress range.

Plastic Collapse. Plastic analysis and design may be used, if the requirement specified under the plastic method of analysis are satisfied.

10·5·6. Limit State of Serviceability

Serviceability limit state is related to the criteria governing normal use. Serviceability limit state is limit state beyond which the service criteria specified below, are no longer met :

(*a*) Deflection limit, (*b*) Vibration limit,

(*c*) Durability consideration, and (*d*) Fire resistance.

Unless specified otherwise, partial safety factor for loads, γ_f of value equal to unity shall be used for all loads leading to serviceability limit states to check the adequacy of the structure under serviceability limit states.

Table 10·5. Partial Safety Factor for Material, γ_m

Sl. No.	*Definition*	*Partial Safety Factor*	
(*i*)	Resistance, governed by yielding, γ_{m0}	1·10	
(*ii*)	Resistance of member to buckling, γ_{m0}	1·10	
(*iii*)	Resistance, governed by ultimate stress, γ_{mf}	1·25	
(*iv*)	Resistance of connection	*Shop Fabrications*	*Field Fabrications*
	(*a*) Bolts-Friction Type, γ_{mf}	1·25	1·25
	(*b*) Bolts-Bearing Type, γ_{mb}	1·25	1·25
	(*c*) Rivets, γ_{mr}	1·25	1·25
	(*d*) Welds, γ_{mw}	1·25	1·50

Deflection. The deflection under serviceability loads of a building or a building component should not impair the strength of the structure or components or cause damage to finishings. Deflections are to be checked for the most adverse but realistic combination of service loads and their arrangement, by elastic analysis, using a load factor of 1·0. Table 10·6 gives recommended limits of deflections for certain structural members and systems. Circumstances may arise where greater or lesser values would be more appropriate depending upon the nature of material in element to be supported (vulnerable to cracking or not) and intended use of the structure, as required by client.

Table 10·6. Deflection Limits

Type of Building (1)	*Deflection* (2)	*Design Load* (3)	*Member* (4)	*Supporting* (5)	*Maximum Deflection* (6)
Industrial Buildings	Vertical	Live load/Wind load	Purlins and Girts	Elastic cladding	Span/150
				Brittle cladding	Span/180
		Live load	Simple span	Elastic cladding	Span/240
				Brittle cladding	Span/300
		Live load	Cantilever span	Elastic cladding	Span/120
				Brittle cladding	Span/150
		Live load/Wind load	Rafter supporting	Profiled Metal Sheeting	Span/180
				Plastered Sheeting	Span/240
		Crane load (Manual operation)	Gantry	Crane	Span/500
		Crane load (Electric operation up to 50 t)	Gantry	Crane	Span/750
		Crane load (Electric operation over 50 t)	Gantry	Crane	Span/1000
	Lateral	No cranes	Column	Elastic cladding	Height/150
				Masonry/Brittle cladding	Height/240
		Crane + wind	Gantry (lateral)	Crane (absolute)	Span/400
				Relative displacement between rails supporting crane	10 mm
		Crane + wind	Column/frame	Gantry (Elastic cladding ; pendent operated)	Height/200
				Gantry (Brittle cladding ; cab operated)	Height/400

Table (Contd.)

Table (Contd.)

Type of Building (1)	*Deflection* (2)	*Design Load* (3)	*Member* (4)	*Supporting* (5)	*Maximum Deflection* (6)
Other Buildings	Vertical	Live load	Floor and Roof	Elements not susceptible to cracking	Span/360
				Elements susceptible to cracking	Span/360
		Live load	Cantilever	Elements not susceptible to cracking	Span/150
				Elements susceptible to cracking	Span/180
	Lateral	Wind	Building	Elastic cladding	Height/300
				Brittle cladding	Height/500
		Wind	Inter storey drift	—	Storey height/300

10·6. Design of Tension Members

10·6·1. Tension Members

Tension members are linear members in which axial forces act to cause elongation (stretch). Such members can sustain loads upto the ultimate load, at which stage they may fail by rupture at a critical section. However, if the gross area of the member yields over a major portion of its length before the rupture load is reached, the member may become non-functional due to excessive elongation. Plates and other rolled sections in tension may also fail by block shear of end bolted regions.

The factored design tension T, in the members shall satisfy the following requirement :

$$T < T_d$$

where T_d = design strength of the member.

The design strength of a member under axial tension, T_d is the lowest of the design strength due to yielding of gross section, T_{dg}; rupture strength of critical section, T_{dn} ; and block shear T_{db}.

10·6·2. Design Strength Due to Yielding of Gross Section

The design strength of members under axial tension, T_{dg} as governed by yielding of gross section, is given by

$$T_{dg} = A_g f_y / \gamma_{m0}$$

where f_y = yield stress of the material,

A_g = gross area of cross-section, and

γ_{m0} = partial safety factor for failure in tension by yielding (*see* Table 10·5).

10·6·3. Design Strength Due to Rupture of Critical Section

Plates. The design strength in tension of a plate, T_{dn} as governed by rupture of net cross-sectional area, A_n at the holes is given by

$$T_{dn} = 0{\cdot}9\, A_n f_u/\gamma_{m1}$$

where γ_{m1} = partial safety factor for failure at ultimate stress (*see* Table 10·5).

f_u = ultimate stress of the material, and

A_n = net effective area of the member given by,

$$A_n = \left[b - nd_h + \sum_i \frac{p_{si}^2}{4\,g_i} \right] t$$

where b, t = width and thickness of the plate, respectively,

d_h = diameter of the bolt hole (2 mm in addition to the diameter of the hole, in case the directly punched holes),

g = gauge length between the bolt holes, as shown in Fig. 10·5,

p_s = staggered pitch length between line of bolt holes, as shown in Fig. 10·5,

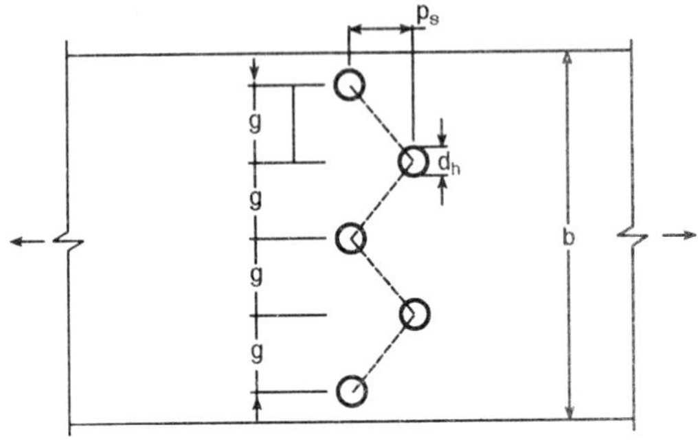

Fig. 10·5. Plates with bolts holes in Tension.

n = number of bolt holes in the critical section, and

i = subscript for summation of all the inclined legs.

Threaded Rods. The design strength of threaded rods in tension, T_{dn}, as governed by rupture is given by

$$T_{dn} = 0{\cdot}9\, A_n f_u / \gamma_{m1}$$

where A_n = net root area at the threaded section.

Single Angles. The rupture strength of an angle connected through one leg is affected by shear lag. The design strength, T_{dn} as governed by rupture at net section is given by:

$$T_{dn} = 0{\cdot}9\, A_{nc}\, f_u/\gamma_{m1} + \beta\, A_{g0}\, f_y/\gamma_{m0} \qquad ...(i)$$

where

$$\beta = 1{\cdot}4 - 0{\cdot}076\, (w/t)\, (f_y/f_u)\, (b_s/L_c) \le (f_u \gamma_{m0} / f_y \gamma_{m1}) \ge 0{\cdot}7 \qquad ...(ii)$$

where w = outstand leg width,

b_s = shear lag width, as shown in Fig. 10·6, and

L_c = length of the end connection, that is the distance between the outermost bolts in the end joint measured along the load direction or length of the weld along the load direction.

For preliminary sizing, the rupture strength of net section may be approximately taken as:

$$T_{dn} = \alpha\, A_n\, f_u/\gamma_{m1}$$

where α = 0·6 for one or two bolts, 0·7 for three bolts and 0·8 for four or more bolts along the length in the end connection or equivalent weld length :

A_n = net area of the total cross-section;

A_{nc} = net area of the connected leg;

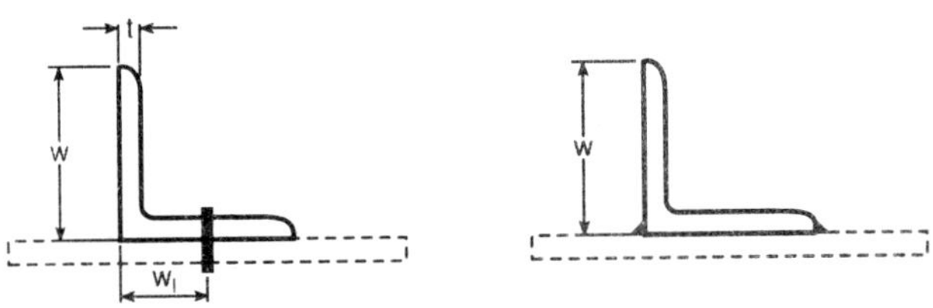

$b_s = w + w_l - t$ $\qquad$ $b_s = w$

Fig. 10·6. Angles with single leg connections

A_{g0} = gross area of the outstanding leg; and

t = thickness of the leg.

Other Section. The rupture strength, T_{dn} of the double angles, channels, I-sections and other rolled steel sections, connected by one or more elements to an end gusset is also governed by shear lag effects. The design tensile strength of such sections as governed by tearing of net section may also be calculated using equation (*i*), where β is calculated based on the shear lag distance, b_s taken from the farthest edge of the outstanding leg to the nearest bolt/weld line in the connected leg of the cross-section.

10·6·4. Design Strength Due to Block Shear

The strength as governed by block shear at an end connection of plates and angles is calculated as given below.

Bolted Connections. The block shear strength, T_{db} of connection shall be taken as the smaller of,

$$T_{db} = \left[A_{vg} f_y / \left(\sqrt{3}\, \gamma_{m0}\right) + 0{\cdot}9 A_{tn} f_u / \gamma_{m1}\right]$$

or

$$T_{db} = \left[0{\cdot}9 A_{vn} f_u / \left(\sqrt{3}\, \gamma_{m1}\right) + A_{tg} f_y / \gamma_{m0}\right]$$

where A_{vg}, A_{vn} = minimum gross and net area in shear along bolt line parallel to external force, respectively,

A_{tg}, A_{tn} = minimum gross and net area in tension from the bolt hole to the toe of the angle, end bolt line, perpendicular to the line of force,

f_u, f_y = ultimate and yield stress of the material, respectively.

Welded Connection. The block shear strength, T_{db} shall be checked for welded end connections by taking an appropriate section in the member around the end weld, which can shear off as a block.

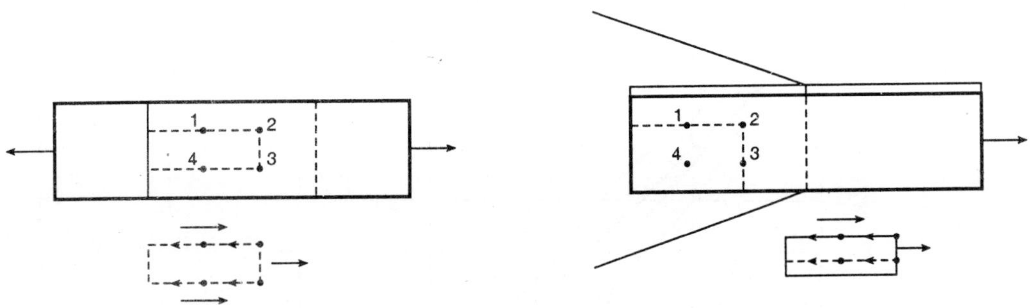

(*a*) Plate (*b*) Angle

Fig. 10·7. Block shear failure.

10·7. Design of Compression Members

10·7·1. Design Strength

Common hot rolled and built-up steel members used for carrying axial compression, usually fail by flexural buckling. The buckling strength of these members is affected by residual stresses, initial bow and accidental eccentricities of load. To account for all these factors, the strength of members subjected to axial compression is defined by buckling class *a*, *b*, *c* or *d* as given in Table 10·7.

The design compressive strength P_d, of a member is given by :

$$P < P_d$$

where $P_d = A_e f_{cd}$

where A_e = effective sectional area.

f_{cd} = design compressive stress, obtained.

The design compressive stress, f_{cd} of axially loaded compression members shall be calculated using the following equation :

$$f_{cd} = \frac{f_y/\gamma_{m0}}{\phi + \left[\phi^2 - \lambda^2\right]^{0.5}} = \chi f_y/\gamma_{m0} \le f_y/\gamma_{m0}$$

where $\phi = 0.5[1 + \alpha(\lambda - 0.2) + \lambda^2]$

λ = non-dimensional effective slenderness ratio

$$= \sqrt{f_y/f_{cc}} = \sqrt{f_y\,(KL/r)^2/\pi^2 E}$$

$$f_{cc} = \text{Euler buckling stress} = \frac{\pi^2 E}{(KL/r)^2}$$

where KL/r = effective slenderness ratio or ratio of effective length, KL to appropriate radius of gyration, r;

α = imperfection factor given in Table 10·7;

χ = stress reduction factor (*see* Table 10·8) for different buckling class, slenderness ratio and yield stress

$$= \frac{1}{\left[\phi + \left(\phi^2 - \lambda^2\right)^{0.5}\right]}$$

λ_{m0} = partial safety factor for material strength.

Note : Calculated values of design compressive stress, f_{cd} for different buckling classes are given in Table 10·9.

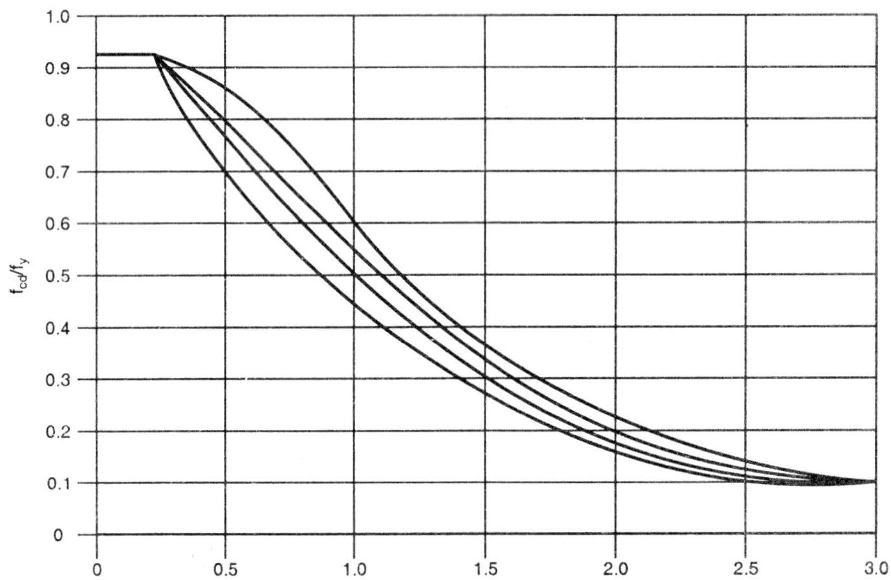

Fig. 10·8. Column buckling curves.

Table 10·7. Imperfection Factor, α

Buckling Class	*a*	*b*	*c*	*d*
α	0·21	0·34	0·49	0·76

Table 10·8(a) Stress Reduction Factor, χ for Column Buckling Class a.

KL/r ↓	Yield Stress, f_y (MPa)																		
	200	210	220	230	240	250	260	280	300	320	340	360	380	400	420	450	480	510	540
10	1·000	1·000	1·000	1·000	1·000	1·000	1·000	1·000	1·000	1·000	1·000	1·000	1·000	1·000	1·000	1·000	1·000	1·000	1·000
20	1·000	0·999	0·998	0·997	0·995	0·994	0·993	0·993	0·990	0·988	0·986	0·984	0·983	0·981	0·979	0·977	0·975	0·972	0·970
30	0·977	0·975	0·974	0·972	0·970	0·969	0·967	0·965	0·961	0·957	0·954	0·951	0·948	0·946	0·943	0·938	0·934	0·930	0·925
40	0·952	0·949	0·947	0·944	0·942	0·939	0·937	0·934	0·926	0·921	0·916	0·911	0·906	0·901	0·896	0·888	0·881	0·873	0·865
50	0·923	0·919	0·915	0·911	0·908	0·904	0·900	0·896	0·884	0·876	0·867	0·859	0·851	0·842	0·834	0·820	0·807	0·794	0·780
60	0·888	0·883	0·877	0·871	0·865	0·859	0·853	0·847	0·828	0·816	0·803	0·790	0·777	0·763	0·750	0·730	0·710	0·690	0·671
70	0·846	0·837	0·829	0·820	0·811	0·803	0·794	0·785	0·758	0·740	0·722	0·703	0·686	0·668	0·651	0·626	0·602	0·579	0·557
80	0·793	0·781	0·769	0·757	0·746	0·734	0·722	0·710	0·675	0·653	0·631	0·610	0·589	0·570	0·551	0·525	0·501	0·478	0·458
90	0·730	0·715	0·700	0·685	0·671	0·657	0·643	0·628	0·590	0·565	0·542	0·520	0·500	0·481	0·463	0·439	0·416	0·396	0·377
100	0·661	0·644	0·627	0·610	0·594	0·579	0·564	0·549	0·510	0·486	0·463	0·443	0·424	0·407	0·390	0·368	0·348	0·331	0·314
110	0·591	0·573	0·555	0·538	0·522	0·507	0·492	0·478	0·440	0·418	0·397	0·379	0·362	0·346	0·332	0·312	0·295	0·279	0·265
120	0·525	0·507	0·489	0·473	0·458	0·443	0·429	0·416	0·381	0·361	0·343	0·326	0·311	0·297	0·284	0·267	0·252	0·238	0·226
130	0·466	0·448	0·432	0·416	0·402	0·388	0·376	0·364	0·332	0·314	0·298	0·283	0·269	0·257	0·246	0·231	0·217	0·206	0·195
140	0·413	0·397	0·382	0·368	0·355	0·342	0·331	0·320	0·291	0·275	0·260	0·247	0·235	0·224	0·214	0·201	0·189	0·179	0·170
150	0·368	0·353	0·339	0·326	0·314	0·303	0·293	0·283	0·257	0·243	0·229	0·218	0·207	0·197	0·189	0·177	0·166	0·157	0·149
160	0·329	0·316	0·303	0·291	0·280	0·270	0·261	0·252	0·229	0·215	0·204	0·193	0·184	0·175	0·167	0·157	0·147	0·139	0·132
170	0·296	0·283	0·272	0·261	0·251	0·242	0·233	0·225	0·204	0·192	0·182	0·172	0·164	0·156	0·149	0·140	0·131	0·124	0·117
180	0·267	0·255	0·245	0·235	0·226	0·218	0·210	0·203	0·184	0·173	0·163	0·155	0·147	0·140	0·134	0·125	0·118	0·111	0·105
190	0·242	0·231	0·222	0·213	0·205	0·197	0·190	0·183	0·166	0·156	0·147	0·140	0·133	0·126	0·121	0·113	0·106	0·100	0·095
200	0·220	0·210	0·202	0·193	0·186	0·179	0·172	0·166	0·151	0·142	0·134	0·127	0·120	0·115	0·109	0·102	0·096	0·091	0·086
210	0·201	0·192	0·184	0·177	0·170	0·163	0·157	0·152	0·137	0·129	0·122	0·115	0·110	0·104	0·099	0·093	0·087	0·083	0·078
220	0·184	0·176	0·169	0·162	0·155	0·149	0·144	0·139	0·126	0·118	0·111	0·106	0·100	0·095	0·091	0·085	0·080	0·075	0·071
230	0·170	0·162	0·155	0·149	0·143	0·137	0·132	0·128	0·115	0·108	0·102	0·097	0·092	0·088	0·083	0·078	0·073	0·069	0·065
240	0·157	0·149	0·143	0·137	0·132	0·127	0·122	0·118	0·106	0·100	0·094	0·089	0·085	0·081	0·077	0·072	0·068	0·064	0·060
250	0·145	0·138	0·132	0·127	0·122	0·117	0·113	0·109	0·098	0·092	0·087	0·082	0·078	0·074	0·071	0·066	0·062	0·059	0·056

Table 10·8(*b*) Stress Reduction Factor, χ for Column Buckling Class *b*.

KL/r ↓	*Yield Stress, f_y* (MPa)																		
	200	*210*	*220*	*230*	*240*	*250*	*260*	*280*	*300*	*320*	*340*	*360*	*380*	*400*	*420*	*450*	*480*	*510*	*540*
10	1·000	1·000	1·000	1·000	1·000	1·000	1·000	1·000	1·000	1·000	1·000	1·000	1·000	1·000	1·000	1·000	1·000	1·000	1·000
20	1·000	0·998	0·996	0·994	0·993	0·991	0·990	0·986	0·983	0·981	0·978	0·975	0·972	0·970	0·967	0·963	0·960	0·956	0·953
30	0·963	0·961	0·958	0·955	0·953	0·950	0·948	0·943	0·938	0·933	0·929	0·924	0·920	0·915	0·911	0·904	0·898	0·892	0·886
40	0·925	0·921	0·917	0·913	0·909	0·906	0·902	0·895	0·887	0·880	0·873	0·866	0·859	0·852	0·845	0·835	0·825	0·815	0·805
50	0·883	0·877	0·872	0·866	0·861	0·855	0·850	0·839	0·829	0·818	0·808	0·798	0·787	0·777	0·767	0·752	0·737	0·722	0·708
60	0·835	0·827	0·820	0·812	0·805	0·798	0·790	0·775	0·761	0·746	0·732	0·718	0·704	0·691	0·677	0·657	0·638	0·620	0·602
70	0·781	0·771	0·761	0·751	0·742	0·732	0·722	0·703	0·685	0·667	0·649	0·632	0·615	0·599	0·584	0·561	0·540	0·520	0·502
80	0·721	0·709	0·697	0·685	0·673	0·661	0·650	0·627	0·606	0·585	0·566	0·547	0·529	0·512	0·496	0·474	0·453	0·434	0·416
90	0·657	0·643	0·629	0·615	0·602	0·589	0·576	0·552	0·530	0·508	0·488	0·470	0·452	0·436	0·421	0·400	0·380	0·363	0·346
100	0·593	0·577	0·562	0·548	0·534	0·520	0·507	0·483	0·461	0·440	0·421	0·403	0·387	0·372	0·358	0·339	0·321	0·306	0·291
110	0·531	0·515	0·500	0·485	0·471	0·458	0·445	0·422	0·401	0·381	0·364	0·348	0·333	0·319	0·306	0·289	0·274	0·260	0·247
120	0·474	0·458	0·443	0·429	0·416	0·403	0·391	0·370	0·350	0·332	0·316	0·301	0·288	0·276	0·265	0·249	0·236	0·223	0·212
130	0·423	0·408	0·394	0·380	0·368	0·356	0·345	0·325	0·307	0·291	0·276	0·263	0·251	0·240	0·230	0·217	0·204	0·194	0·184
140	0·378	0·364	0·350	0·338	0·327	0·316	0·306	0·287	0·271	0·256	0·243	0·231	0·221	0·211	0·202	0·190	0·179	0·169	0·161
150	0·339	0·325	0·313	0·302	0·291	0·281	0·272	0·255	0·241	0·227	0·215	0·205	0·195	0·186	0·178	0·167	0·158	0·149	0·142
160	0·305	0·292	0·281	0·271	0·261	0·252	0·243	0·228	0·215	0·203	0·192	0·182	0·174	0·166	0·158	0·149	0·140	0·133	0·126
170	0·275	0·264	0·253	0·244	0·235	0·227	0·219	0·205	0·193	0·182	0·172	0·163	0·155	0·148	0·142	0·133	0·125	0·118	0·112
180	0·249	0·239	0·229	0·220	0·212	0·205	0·198	0·185	0·174	0·164	0·155	0·147	0·140	0·133	0·128	0·120	0·113	0·106	0·101
190	0·227	0·217	0·208	0·200	0·193	0·186	0·179	0·168	0·157	0·148	0·140	0·133	0·127	0·121	0·115	0·108	0·102	0·096	0·091
200	0·207	0·198	0·190	0·183	0·176	0·169	0·163	0·153	0·143	0·135	0·128	0·121	0·115	0·110	0·105	0·098	0·092	0·087	0·083
210	0·190	0·182	0·174	0·167	0·161	0·155	0·149	0·140	0·131	0·123	0·117	0·110	0·105	0·100	0·096	0·090	0·084	0·080	0·075
220	0·174	0·167	0·160	0·154	0·148	0·142	0·137	0·128	0·120	0·113	0·107	0·101	0·096	0·092	0·088	0·082	0·077	0·073	0·069
230	0·161	0·154	0·147	0·141	0·136	0·131	0·126	0·118	0·111	0·104	0·098	0·093	0·088	0·084	0·080	0·075	0·071	0·067	0·063
240	0·149	0·142	0·136	0·131	0·126	0·121	0·117	0·109	0·102	0·096	0·091	0·086	0·082	0·078	0·074	0·070	0·065	0·062	0·058
250	0·138	0·132	0·126	0·121	0·117	0·112	0·108	0·101	0·095	0·089	0·084	0·080	0·076	0·072	0·069	0·064	0·060	0·057	0·054

Table 10·8(c) Stress Reduction Factor, χ for Column Buckling Class c.

KL/r ↓	Yield Stress, f_y (MPa)																		
	200	210	220	230	240	250	260	280	300	320	340	360	380	400	420	450	480	510	540
10	1·000	1·000	1·000	1·000	1·000	1·000	1·000	1·000	1·000	1·000	1·000	1·000	1·000	1·000	1·000	1·000	1·000	1·000	1·000
20	0·999	0·997	0·994	0·992	0·990	0·987	0·985	0·981	0·976	0·972	0·968	0·964	0·961	0·957	0·953	0·948	0·943	0·938	0·933
30	0·948	0·944	0·941	0·937	0·933	0·930	0·926	0·920	0·913	0·907	0·901	0·895	0·889	0·883	0·877	0·869	0·861	0·853	0·845
40	0·896	0·891	0·885	0·880	0·875	0·870	0·866	0·856	0·847	0·838	0·829	0·820	0·812	0·803	0·795	0·783	0·771	0·760	0·748
50	0·841	0·834	0·827	0·821	0·814	0·807	0·801	0·788	0·776	0·763	0·752	0·740	0·729	0·717	0·706	0·690	0·675	0·660	0·645
60	0·783	0·774	0·765	0·757	0·748	0·740	0·732	0·716	0·700	0·685	0·670	0·656	0·642	0·628	0·615	0·596	0·578	0·561	0·544
70	0·722	0·711	0·700	0·690	0·680	0·670	0·660	0·641	0·623	0·605	0·588	0·572	0·557	0·542	0·528	0·508	0·489	0·471	0·454
80	0·659	0·646	0·634	0·622	0·611	0·600	0·589	0·568	0·548	0·529	0·512	0·495	0·479	0·464	0·450	0·430	0·412	0·395	0·379
90	0·596	0·583	0·569	0·557	0·544	0·533	0·521	0·499	0·479	0·460	0·443	0·426	0·411	0·397	0·383	0·365	0·348	0·332	0·318
100	0·536	0·522	0·508	0·495	0·483	0·471	0·459	0·438	0·418	0·400	0·384	0·368	0·354	0·341	0·328	0·311	0·296	0·282	0·269
110	0·480	0·466	0·453	0·440	0·428	0·416	0·405	0·385	0·366	0·349	0·333	0·319	0·306	0·294	0·283	0·268	0·254	0·242	0·230
120	0·430	0·416	0·403	0·391	0·379	0·368	0·358	0·339	0·321	0·306	0·291	0·278	0·267	0·256	0·246	0·232	0·220	0·209	0·199
130	0·385	0·372	0·360	0·348	0·337	0·327	0·317	0·299	0·283	0·269	0·256	0·244	0·234	0·224	0·215	0·203	0·192	0·182	0·173
140	0·346	0·333	0·322	0·311	0·301	0·291	0·282	0·266	0·251	0·238	0·227	0·216	0·206	0·197	0·183	0·178	0·168	0·160	0·152
150	0·311	0·300	0·289	0·279	0·269	0·261	0·252	0·237	0·224	0·212	0·202	0·192	0·183	0·175	0·168	0·158	0·149	0·141	0·134
160	0·281	0·270	0·260	0·251	0·242	0·234	0·227	0·213	0·201	0·190	0·180	0·172	0·164	0·156	0·150	0·141	0·133	0·126	0·120
170	0·255	0·245	0·236	0·227	0·219	0·212	0·205	0·192	0·181	0·171	0·162	0·154	0·147	0·140	0·134	0·126	0·119	0·113	0·107
180	0·232	0·223	0·214	0·206	0·199	0·192	0·186	0·174	0·164	0·155	0·147	0·139	0·133	0·127	0·121	0·114	0·107	0·102	0·096
190	0·212	0·203	0·195	0·188	0·181	0·175	0·169	0·158	0·149	0·140	0·133	0·126	0·120	0·115	0·110	0·103	0·097	0·092	0·087
200	0·194	0·186	0·179	0·172	0·166	0·160	0·154	0·144	0·136	0·128	0·121	0·115	0·110	0·105	0·100	0·094	0·089	0·084	0·079
210	0·178	0·171	0·164	0·158	0·152	0·146	0·141	0·132	0·124	0·117	0·111	0·105	0·100	0·096	0·092	0·086	0·081	0·076	0·072
220	0·164	0·157	0·151	0·145	0·140	0·135	0·130	0·122	0·114	0·108	0·102	0·097	0·092	0·088	0·084	0·079	0·074	0·070	0·066
230	0·152	0·145	0·140	0·134	0·129	0·124	0·120	0·112	0·105	0·099	0·094	0·089	0·085	0·081	0·077	0·073	0·068	0·065	0·061
240	0·141	0·1[illegible]	0·0129	0·124	0·120	0·115	0·111	0·104	0·098	0·092	0·087	0·082	0·078	0·075	0·071	0·067	0·063	0·060	0·056
250	0·131	0·125	0·120	0·115	0·111	0·107	0·103	0·096	0·090	0·085	0·081	0·076	0·073	0·069	0·066	0·062	0·058	0·055	0·052

Table 10·8(*d*) Stress Reduction Factor, χ for Column Buckling Class *d*.

KL/r ↓	*Yield Stress, f_y* (MPa)																		
	200	*210*	*220*	*230*	*240*	*250*	*260*	*280*	*300*	*320*	*340*	*360*	*380*	*400*	*420*	*450*	*480*	*510*	*540*
10	1·000	1·000	1·000	1·000	1·000	1·000	1·000	1·000	1·000	1·000	1·000	1·000	1·000	1·000	1·000	1·000	1·000	1·000	1·000
20	0·999	0·995	0·991	0·988	0·984	0·980	0·977	0·970	0·964	0·958	0·952	0·946	0·940	0·935	0·930	0·922	0·915	0·908	0·901
30	0·922	0·916	0·911	0·906	0·901	0·896	0·891	0·881	0·872	0·863	0·855	0·847	0·839	0·831	0·823	0·813	0·802	0·792	0·782
40	0·848	0·841	0·834	0·828	0·821	0·815	0·808	0·796	0·784	0·773	0·762	0·751	0·741	0·731	0·721	0·707	0·694	0·681	0·668
50	0·777	0·768	0·760	0·752	0·744	0·736	0·728	0·713	0·699	0·685	0·672	0·659	0·647	0·635	0·624	0·608	0·592	0·577	0·563
60	0·707	0·697	0·687	0·678	0·668	0·659	0·651	0·634	0·617	0·602	0·587	0·573	0·560	0·547	0·535	0·517	0·501	0·486	0·471
70	0·640	0·629	0·618	0·607	0·597	0·587	0·578	0·559	0·542	0·526	0·510	0·496	0·482	0·469	0·456	0·439	0·423	0·408	0·394
80	0·576	0·564	0·553	0·542	0·531	0·521	0·511	0·492	0·474	0·458	0·442	0·428	0·414	0·402	0·390	0·373	0·358	0·344	0·330
90	0·517	0·505	0·493	0·482	0·471	0·461	0·451	0·432	0·415	0·399	0·384	0·370	0·357	0·345	0·334	0·319	0·304	0·292	0·280
100	0·464	0·451	0·440	0·428	0·418	0·408	0·398	0·380	0·363	0·348	0·334	0·321	0·309	0·298	0·288	0·274	0·261	0·249	0·239
110	0·416	0·404	0·392	0·381	0·371	0·361	0·352	0·335	0·319	0·305	0·292	0·281	0·270	0·259	0·250	0·237	0·226	0·215	0·206
120	0·373	0·361	0·350	0·340	0·330	0·321	0·313	0·297	0·282	0·269	0·257	0·246	0·236	0·227	0·219	0·207	0·197	0·187	0·179
130	0·336	0·325	0·314	0·305	0·295	0·287	0·279	0·264	0·251	0·239	0·228	0·218	0·209	0·200	0·193	0·182	0·173	0·164	0·157
140	0·303	0·292	0·283	0·274	0·265	0·257	0·250	0·236	0·224	0·213	0·203	0·194	0·185	0·178	0·171	0·161	0·153	0·145	0·138
150	0·274	0·264	0·255	0·247	0·239	0·231	0·224	0·212	0·201	0·190	0·181	0·173	0·165	0·159	0·152	0·144	0·136	0·129	0·123
160	0·249	0·240	0·231	0·223	0·216	0·209	0·203	0·191	0·181	0·171	0·163	0·155	0·149	0·142	0·137	0·129	0·122	0·116	0·110
170	0·227	0·218	0·210	0·203	0·196	0·190	0·184	0·173	0·164	0·155	0·147	0·140	0·134	0·128	0·123	0·116	0·110	0·104	0·099
180	0·207	0·199	0·192	0·185	0·179	0·173	0·167	0·157	0·149	0·141	0·134	0·127	0·122	0·116	0·111	0·105	0·099	0·094	0·089
190	0·190	0·183	0·176	0·169	0·164	0·158	0·153	0·144	0·136	0·128	0·122	0·116	0·111	0·106	0·101	0·095	0·090	0·085	0·081
200	0·175	0·168	0·162	0·156	0·150	0·145	0·140	0·132	0·124	0·118	0·112	0·106	0·101	0·097	0·093	0·087	0·082	0·078	0·074
210	0·161	0·155	0·149	0·143	0·138	0·134	0·129	0·121	0·114	0·108	0·102	0·097	0·093	0·089	0·085	0·080	0·075	0·071	0·068
220	0·149	0·143	0·138	0·133	0·128	0·123	0·119	0·112	0·105	0·100	0·094	0·090	0·086	0·082	0·078	0·074	0·069	0·066	0·062
230	0·138	0·133	0·128	0·123	0·118	0·114	0·110	0·104	0·097	0·092	0·087	0·083	0·079	0·075	0·072	0·068	0·064	0·061	0·058
240	0·129	0·123	0·119	0·114	0·110	0·106	0·103	0·096	0·090	0·085	0·081	0·077	0·073	0·070	0·067	0·063	0·059	0·056	0·053
250	0·120	0·115	0·110	0·106	0·102	0·099	0·095	0·089	0·084	0·079	0·075	0·071	0·068	0·065	0·062	0·058	0·055	0·052	0·049

Table 10·9(*a*) Design Compressive Stress, f_{cd} (MPa) for Column Buckling Class *a*.

KL/r ↓	Yield Stress, f_y (MPa)																		
	200	210	220	230	240	250	260	280	300	320	340	360	380	400	420	450	480	510	540
10	182	191	200	213	218	227	236	255	273	291	309	327	345	364	382	409	436	464	491
20	182	191	200	208	217	226	235	252	270	287	305	322	339	357	374	400	425	451	476
30	178	186	195	203	212	220	229	245	262	279	295	311	328	344	360	384	408	431	454
40	173	181	189	197	205	213	221	237	253	268	283	298	313	328	342	363	384	405	425
50	168	176	183	191	198	205	213	227	241	255	268	281	294	306	318	336	352	368	383
60	162	169	175	182	189	195	202	214	226	237	248	258	268	278	286	299	310	320	329
70	154	160	166	171	177	182	188	197	207	215	223	230	237	243	249	256	263	268	274
80	144	149	154	158	163	167	171	178	184	190	195	199	204	207	210	215	219	222	225
90	133	137	140	143	146	149	152	157	161	164	168	170	173	175	177	179	182	184	185
100	120	123	125	128	130	132	133	136	139	141	143	145	146	148	149	151	152	153	154
110	107	109	111	112	114	115	116	118	120	121	123	124	125	126	127	128	129	129	130
120	95·5	96·7	97·9	98·9	100	101	101	103	104	105	106	107	107	108	109	109	110	110	111
130	84·6	85·5	86·3	87	87·7	88·3	88·8	89·8	90·6	91·3	92·0	92·5	93·0	93·5	93·9	94·4	94·9	95·3	95·7
140	75·2	75·8	76·4	76·9	77·4	77·8	78·2	78·9	79·5	80·0	80·5	80·9	81·3	81·6	81·9	82·3	82·6	83·0	83·2
150	67·0	67·4	67·9	68·2	68·6	68·9	69·2	69·7	70·2	70·6	70·9	71·2	71·5	71·8	72·0	72·3	72·6	72·9	73·1
160	59·9	60·3	60·6	60·9	61·1	61·4	61·6	62·0	62·4	62·7	62·9	63·2	63·4	63·6	63·8	64·0	64·3	64·5	64·6
170	53·8	54·1	54·3	54·6	54·8	55·0	55·1	55·5	55·7	56·0	56·2	56·4	56·6	56·7	56·9	57·1	57·3	57·4	57·6
180	48·6	48·8	49·0	49·2	49·3	49·5	49·6	49·9	50·1	50·3	50·5	50·6	50·8	50·9	51·0	51·2	51·3	51·5	51·6
190	44·0	44·2	44·3	44·5	44·6	44·7	44·9	45·1	45·3	45·4	45·6	45·7	45·8	45·9	46·0	46·2	46·3	46·4	46·5
200	40·0	40·2	40·3	40·4	40·5	40·7	40·7	40·9	41·1	41·2	41·3	41·4	41·5	41·6	41·7	41·8	41·9	42·0	42·1
210	36·6	36·7	36·8	36·9	37·0	37·1	37·2	37·3	37·4	37·6	37·7	37·8	37·8	37·9	38·0	38·1	38·2	38·3	38·3
220	33·5	33·6	33·7	33·8	33·9	34·0	34·0	34·2	34·3	34·4	34·5	34·5	34·6	34·7	34·7	34·8	34·9	35·0	35·0
230	30·8	30·9	31·0	31·1	31·2	31·2	31·3	31·4	31·5	31·6	31·6	31·7	31·8	31·8	31·9	31·9	32·0	32·1	32·1
240	28·5	28·5	28·6	28·7	28·7	28·8	28·8	28·9	29·0	29·1	29·1	29·2	29·3	29·3	29·4	29·4	29·5	29·5	29·6
250	26·3	26·4	26·5	26·5	26·6	26·6	26·7	26·7	26·8	26·9	26·9	27·0	27·0	27·1	27·1	27·2	27·2	27·3	27·3

Table 10·9(*b*) Design Compressive Stress, f_{cd} (MPa) for Column Buckling Class *b*.

KL/r ↓	*Yield Stress, f_y (MPa)*																		
	200	*210*	*220*	*230*	*240*	*250*	*260*	*280*	*300*	*320*	*340*	*360*	*380*	*400*	*420*	*450*	*480*	*510*	*540*
10	182	191	200	209	218	227	236	255	273	291	309	327	345	364	382	409	436	464	491
20	182	190	199	208	217	225	234	251	268	285	302	319	336	353	369	394	419	443	468
30	175	183	192	200	208	216	224	240	256	271	287	302	318	333	348	370	392	414	435
40	168	176	183	191	198	206	213	228	242	256	270	283	297	310	323	342	360	378	395
50	161	167	174	181	188	194	201	214	226	238	250	261	272	283	293	308	322	335	347
60	152	158	164	170	176	181	187	197	207	217	226	235	243	251	259	269	279	287	295
70	142	147	152	157	162	166	171	179	187	194	201	207	213	218	223	230	236	241	246
80	131	135	139	143	147	150	154	160	165	170	175	179	183	186	190	194	198	201	204
90	120	123	126	129	131	134	136	141	144	148	151	154	156	159	161	163	166	168	170
100	108	110	112	114	116	118	120	123	126	128	130	132	134	135	137	139	140	142	143
110	96·5	98·3	100	101	103	104	105	107	109	111	112	114	115	116	117	118	119	121	121
120	86·2	87·5	88·6	89·7	90·7	91·7	92·5	94·1	95·4	96·6	97·7	98·6	100	100	101	102	103	104	104
130	76·9	77·8	78·7	79·5	80·3	81·0	81·6	82·7	83·7	84·6	85·4	86·1	86·8	87·3	87·9	88·6	89·2	89·8	90·3
140	68·7	69·4	70·1	70·7	71·3	71·8	72·3	73·1	73·9	74·6	75·2	75·7	76·2	76·6	77·1	77·6	78·1	78·5	78·9
150	61·6	62·1	62·6	63·1	63·6	64·0	64·3	65·0	65·6	66·1	66·6	67·0	67·4	67·7	68·1	68·5	68·9	69·2	69·5
160	55·4	55·8	56·2	56·6	56·9	57·3	57·5	58·1	58·5	59·0	59·3	59·7	60·0	60·3	60·5	60·9	61·2	61·5	61·7
170	50·0	50·3	50·7	51·0	51·2	51·5	51·7	52·2	52·5	52·9	53·2	53·5	53·7	53·9	54·1	54·4	54·7	54·9	55·1
180	45·3	45·6	45·9	46·1	46·3	46·5	46·7	47·1	47·4	47·7	47·9	48·1	48·3	48·5	48·7	48·9	49·2	49·3	49·5
190	41·2	41·5	41·7	41·9	42·1	42·2	42·4	42·7	42·9	43·2	43·4	43·6	43·7	43·9	44·0	44·2	44·4	44·6	44·7
200	37·6	37·8	38·0	38·2	38·3	38·5	38·6	38·9	39·1	39·3	39·5	39·6	39·8	39·9	40·0	40·2	40·3	40·5	40·6
210	34·5	34·7	34·8	35·0	35·1	35·2	35·3	35·5	35·7	35·9	36·0	36·2	36·3	36·4	36·5	36·6	36·8	36·9	37·0
220	31·7	31·9	32·0	32·1	32·2	32·3	32·4	32·6	32·8	32·9	33·0	33·1	33·2	33·3	33·4	33·6	33·7	33·8	33·9
230	29·2	29·4	29·5	29·6	29·7	29·8	29·9	30·0	30·1	30·3	30·4	30·5	30·6	30·7	30·7	30·8	30·9	31·0	31·1
240	27·1	27·2	27·3	27·3	27·4	27·5	27·6	27·7	27·8	27·9	28·0	28·1	28·2	28·3	28·3	28·4	28·5	28·6	28·7
250	25·1	25·2	25·3	25·3	25·4	25·5	25·6	25·7	25·8	25·9	26·0	26·0	26·1	26·2	26·2	26·3	26·4	26·5	26·5

Table 10·9(*c*) Design Compressive Stress, f_{cd} (MPa) for Column Buckling Class *c*.

KL/r ↓	Yield Stress, f_y (MPa)																		
	200	210	220	230	240	250	260	280	300	320	340	360	380	400	420	450	480	510	540
10	182	191	200	209	218	227	236	255	273	291	309	327	345	364	382	409	436	464	491
20	182	190	199	207	216	224	233	250	266	283	299	316	332	348	364	388	412	435	458
30	172	180	188	196	204	211	219	234	249	264	278	293	307	321	335	355	376	395	415
40	163	170	177	184	191	198	205	218	231	244	256	268	280	292	304	320	337	352	367
50	153	159	165	172	178	183	189	201	212	222	232	242	252	261	270	282	295	306	317
60	142	148	153	158	163	168	173	182	191	199	207	215	222	228	235	244	252	260	267
70	131	136	140	144	148	152	156	163	170	176	182	187	192	197	202	208	213	218	223
80	120	123	127	130	133	136	139	145	149	154	158	162	165	169	172	176	180	183	186
90	108	111	114	116	119	121	123	127	131	134	137	140	142	144	146	149	152	154	156
100	97·5	100	102	104	105	107	109	112	114	116	119	120	122	124	125	127	129	131	132
110	87·3	89·0	90·5	92·0	93·3	94·6	95·7	97·9	100	102	103	104	106	107	108	110	111	112	113
120	78·2	79·4	80·6	81·7	82·7	83·7	84·6	86·2	87·6	88·9	90·1	91·1	92·1	93·0	93·8	94·9	95·9	96·8	97·6
130	70·0	71·0	71·9	72·8	73·5	74·3	75·0	76·2	77·3	78·3	79·2	80·0	80·7	81·4	82·0	82·9	83·6	84·3	84·9
140	62·9	63·6	64·4	65·0	65·6	66·2	66·7	67·7	68·6	69·3	70·0	70·7	71·2	71·8	72·3	72·9	73·5	74·1	74·6
150	56·6	57·2	57·8	58·3	58·8	59·2	59·7	60·4	61·1	61·7	62·3	62·8	63·3	63·7	64·1	64·6	65·1	65·5	65·9
160	51·1	51·6	52·1	52·5	52·9	53·3	53·6	54·2	54·8	55·3	55·7	56·1	56·5	56·9	57·2	57·6	58·0	58·4	58·7
170	46·4	46·8	47·1	47·5	47·8	48·1	48·4	48·9	49·3	49·8	50·1	50·5	50·8	51·1	51·3	51·7	52·0	52·3	52·6
180	42·2	42·5	42·8	43·1	43·4	43·6	43·9	44·3	44·7	45·0	45·3	45·6	45·8	46·1	46·3	46·6	46·9	47·1	47·3
190	38·5	38·8	39·0	39·3	39·5	39·7	39·9	40·3	40·6	40·9	41·1	41·4	41·6	41·8	42·0	42·2	42·5	42·7	42·9
200	35·3	35·5	35·7	35·9	36·1	36·3	36·5	36·8	37·0	37·3	37·5	37·7	37·9	38·1	38·2	38·4	38·6	38·8	39·0
210	32·4	32·6	32·8	33·0	33·1	33·3	33·4	33·7	33·9	34·1	34·3	34·5	34·7	34·8	34·9	35·1	35·3	35·4	35·6
220	29·9	30·1	30·2	30·4	30·5	30·6	30·8	31·0	31·2	31·4	31·5	31·7	31·8	31·9	32·1	32·2	32·4	32·5	32·6
230	27·6	27·8	27·9	28·0	28·2	28·3	28·4	28·6	28·8	28·9	29·1	29·2	29·3	29·4	29·5	29·7	29·8	29·9	30·0
240	25·6	25·7	25·9	26·0	26·1	26·2	26·3	26·4	26·6	26·7	26·9	27·0	27·1	27·2	27·3	27·4	27·5	27·6	27·7
250	23·8	23·9	24·0	24·1	24·2	24·3	24·4	24·5	24·7	24·8	24·9	25·0	25·1	25·2	25·3	25·4	25·5	25·6	25·7

Table 10·9(d) Design Compressive Stress, f_{cd} (MPa) for Column Buckling Class d.

KL/r ↓	*Yield Stress, f_y* (MPa)																		
	200	*210*	*220*	*230*	*240*	*250*	*260*	*280*	*300*	*320*	*340*	*360*	*380*	*400*	*420*	*450*	*480*	*510*	*540*
10	182	191	200	209	218	227	236	255	273	291	309	327	345	364	382	409	436	464	491
20	182	190	198	206	215	223	231	247	263	279	294	310	325	340	355	377	399	421	442
30	168	175	182	189	197	204	211	224	238	251	264	277	290	302	314	332	350	367	384
40	154	161	167	173	179	185	191	203	214	225	235	246	256	266	275	289	303	316	328
50	141	147	152	157	162	167	172	182	191	199	208	216	224	231	238	249	258	268	277
60	129	133	137	142	146	150	154	161	168	175	182	188	193	199	204	212	219	225	231
70	116	120	124	127	130	133	137	142	148	153	158	162	167	171	174	180	184	189	193
80	105	108	111	113	116	118	121	125	129	133	137	140	143	146	149	153	156	159	162
90	94·1	96·4	98·6	101	103	105	107	110	113	116	119	121	123	126	128	130	133	135	137
100	84·3	86·2	87·9	89·6	91·1	92·6	94·0	96·7	99·1	101	103	105	107	108	110	112	114	116	117
110	75·6	77·0	78·4	79·7	81·0	82·1	83·2	85·3	87·1	88·8	90·4	91·8	93·1	94·4	95·5	97·1	98·5	100	101
120	67·8	69·0	70·1	71·1	72·1	73·0	73·9	75·5	77·0	78·3	79·5	80·6	81·7	82·6	83·5	84·7	85·8	86·9	87·8
130	61·0	62·0	62·8	63·7	64·5	65·2	65·9	67·2	68·3	69·4	70·4	71·2	72·1	72·8	73·5	74·5	75·4	76·2	76·9
140	55·0	55·8	56·5	57·2	57·8	58·4	59·0	60·0	61·0	61·8	62·6	63·3	64·0	64·6	65·2	66·0	66·7	67·3	67·9
150	49·8	50·4	51·0	51·6	52·1	52·6	53·1	53·9	54·7	55·4	56·0	56·6	57·2	57·7	58·1	58·8	59·3	59·9	60·4
160	45·2	45·7	46·2	46·7	47·1	47·5	47·9	48·6	49·3	49·9	50·4	50·9	51·3	51·7	52·1	52·7	53·1	53·6	54·0
170	41·2	41·6	42·1	42·4	42·8	43·1	43·5	44·1	44·6	45·1	45·5	45·9	46·3	46·7	47·0	47·4	47·8	48·2	48·6
180	37·7	38·0	38·4	38·7	39·0	39·3	39·6	40·1	40·5	41·0	41·3	41·7	42·0	42·3	42·6	43·0	43·3	43·6	43·9
190	34·5	34·9	35·2	35·4	35·7	35·9	36·2	36·6	37·0	37·4	37·7	38·0	38·2	38·5	38·7	39·1	39·4	39·6	39·9
200	31·8	32·0	32·3	32·5	32·8	33·0	33·2	33·6	33·9	34·2	34·5	34·7	35·0	35·2	35·4	35·7	35·9	36·2	36·4
210	29·3	29·6	29·8	30·0	30·2	30·4	30·5	30·9	31·2	31·4	31·7	31·9	32·1	32·3	32·5	32·7	32·9	33·1	33·3
220	27·1	27·3	27·5	27·7	27·9	28·0	28·2	28·5	28·7	29·0	29·2	29·4	29·6	29·7	29·9	30·1	30·3	30·5	30·6
230	25·2	25·3	25·5	25·7	25·8	26·0	26·1	26·4	26·6	26·8	27·0	27·1	27·3	27·5	27·6	27·8	27·9	28·1	28·2
240	23·4	23·6	23·7	23·9	24·0	24·1	24·2	24·5	24·7	24·8	25·0	25·2	25·3	25·4	25·5	25·7	25·9	26·0	26·1
250	21·8	22·0	22·1	22·2	22·3	22·5	22·6	22·8	22·9	23·1	23·2	23·4	23·5	23·6	23·7	23·9	24·0	24·1	24·2

The classification of different sections under different buckling class *a, b, c* or *d*, is given in Table 10·10. The stress reduction factor χ, and the design compressive stress f_{cd}, for different buckling class, yield stress, and effective slenderness ratio is given in Table 10·8 for convenience. The curves corresponding to different buckling class are presented in non-dimensional form, in Fig. 10·8.

10·7·2. Effective Length. Where the boundary conditions in the plane of buckling can be assessed, the effective length, *KL* can be calculated on the basis of Table 10·11. Where frame analysis does not consider the equilibrium of a framed structure in the deformed shape (second-order analysis or advanced analysis), compression members in such cases can be calculated using the procedure given in Annexure A-1. The effective length of stepped column in single storey buildings can be calculated using the procedure given in Annexure A-2.

10·7·3. Eccentric Beam Connection. In cases where the beam connections are eccentric in plan with respect to the axes of the column, the same conditions of restraint as in concentric connection shall be deemed to apply, provided the connections are carried across the flange or web of the columns as the case may be, and the web of the beam lies within, or in direct contact with the column section. Where practical difficulties prevent this, the effective length shall be taken as equal to the distance between points of restraint, in non-sway frames.

10·7·4. Compression Members in Trusses. In the case of bolted, riveted or welded trusses and braced frames, the effective length, *KL*, of the compression members shall be taken as 0·7 to 1·0 times the distance between centres of connections, depending on the degree of end restraint provided. In the case of members of trusses, buckling in the plane perpendicular to the plane of the truss, the effective length, *KL* shall be taken as the distance between the centres of intersection.

10·7·5. Angle Struts

Single Angle Struts. The compression in single angles may be transferred either concentrically to its centroid through end gusset or eccentrically by connecting one of its legs to a gusset or adjacent member.

Loaded through one leg. The flexural torsional buckling strength of single angle loaded in compression through one of its legs may be evaluated using the equivalent slenderness ratio, λ_e as given below:

$$\lambda_e = \sqrt{k_1 + k_2\,\lambda_{vv}^2 + k_3\,\lambda_\varphi^2}$$

where k_1, k_2, k_3 = constants depending upon the end condition, as given in Table 10·12.

$$\lambda_{vv} = \frac{\left(\dfrac{l}{r_{vv}}\right)}{\varepsilon\sqrt{\dfrac{\pi^2\varepsilon}{250}}} \quad \text{and} \quad \lambda_\varphi = \frac{(b_1 + b_2)/2t}{\varepsilon\sqrt{\dfrac{\pi^2\varepsilon}{250}}}$$

where l = centre-to-centre length of the supporting member,

r_{vv} = radius of gyration about the minor axis,

b_1, b_2 = width of the two legs of the angle,

t = thickness of the leg, and

ε = yield stress ratio $(250/f_y)^{0\cdot5}$.

Table 10·10. Buckling Class of Cross-Sections

Cross-Section	*Limits*	*Buckling About Axis*	*Buckling Class*
(1)	(2)	(3)	(4)
Rolled I-Sections 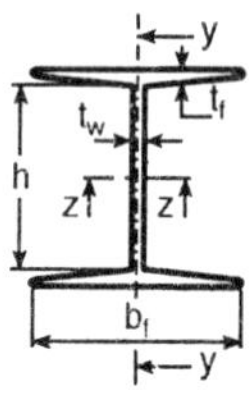	$h/b_f > 1{\cdot}2$: $t_f \le 40$ mm	z-z y-y	a b
	$40 \le$ mm $< t_f \le 100$ mm	z-z y-y	b c
	$h/b_f \le 1{\cdot}2$: $t_f \le 100$ mm	z-z y-y	b c
	$t_f > 100$ mm	z-z y-y	d d
Welded I-Section 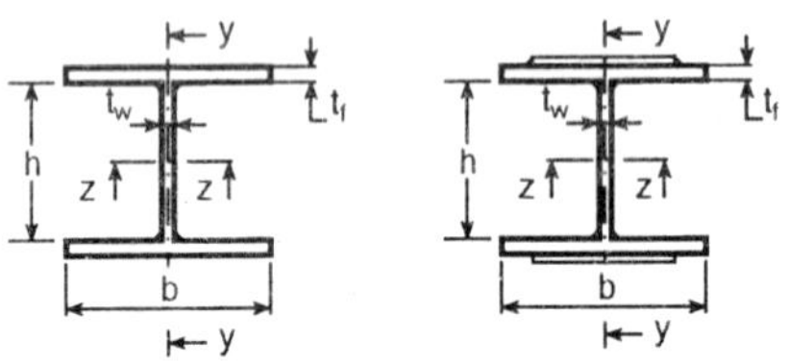	$t_f \le 40$ mm	z-z y-y	b c
	$t_f > 40$ mm	z-z y-y	c d
Hollow Section 	Hot rolled	Any	a
	Cold formed	Any	b
Welded Box Section 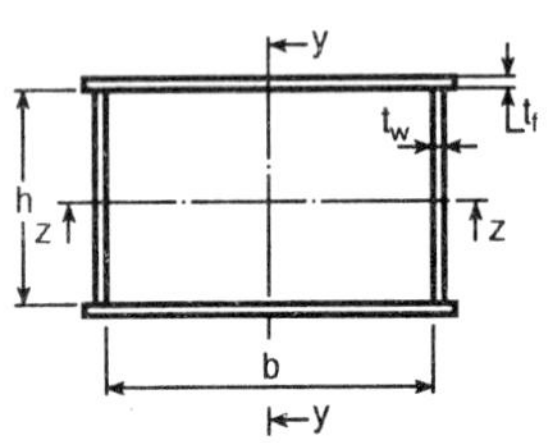	Generally (except as below)	Any	b
	Thick welds and $h/t_f < 30$ $h/t_w < 30$	z-z	c y-y c
Channel, Angle, T and Solid Sections 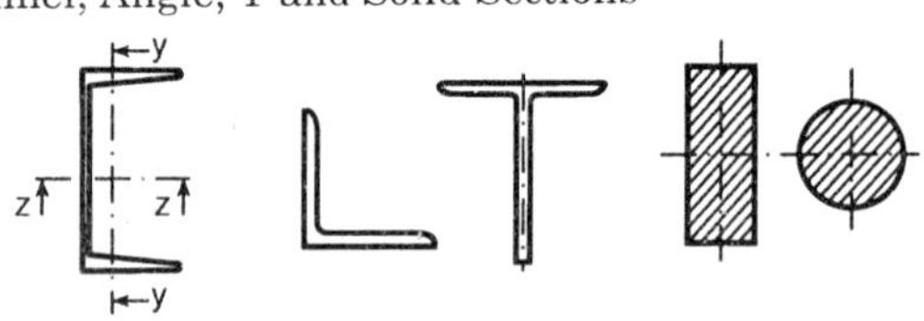		Any	c
Built-up Member 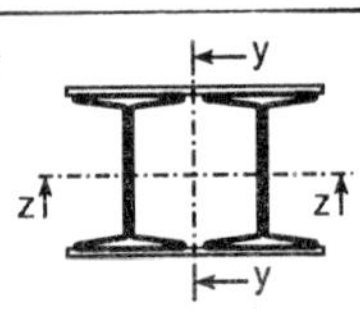		Any	c

Table 10·11. Effective Length of Prismatic Compression Members

Boundary Conditions				*Schematic Representation*	*Effective Length*
At one end		*At the other end*			
Translation	*Rotation*	*Translation*	*Rotation*		
(1)	(2)	(3)	(4)	(5)	(6)
Restrained	Restrained	Free	Free	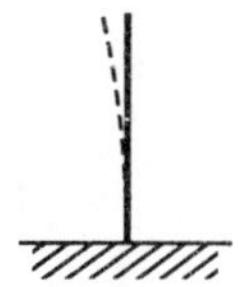	2·0 L
Free	Restrained	Free	Restrained		
Restrained	Free	Restrained	Free	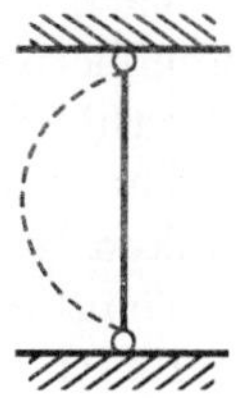	1·0 L
Restrained	Restrained	Free	Restrained		1·2 L
Restrained	Restrained	Restrained	Free	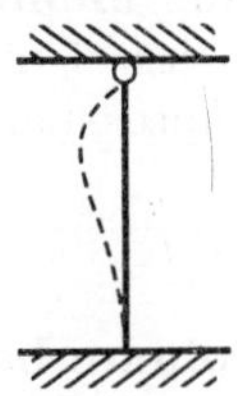	0·8 L
Restrained	Restrained	Restrained	Restrained	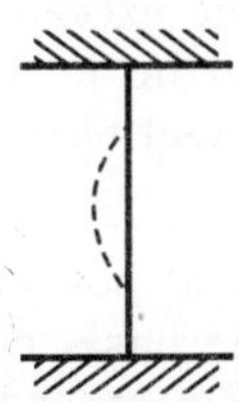	0·65 L

Note : L is the unsupported length of the compression member.

Table 10·12. Constants k_1, k_2 and k_3

Sl. No.	*No. of Bolts at each End Connection*	*Gusset / Connecting Member Fixity* [1]	k_1	k_2	k_3
(1)	(2)	(3)	(4)	(5)	(6)
(*i*)	≥ 2	Fixed	0·20	0·35	20
		Hinged	0·70	0·60	5
(*ii*)	1	Fixed	0·75	0·35	20
		Hinged	1·25	0·50	60

[1] Stiffness of in-plane rotational restraint provided by the gusset/connecting member.

For partial restraint, the λ_e can be interpolated between the λ_e results for fixed and hinged cases.

Double Angle Struts. For double angle discontinuous struts, connected back to back, on opposite sides of the gusset or a section, by not less than two bolts or rivets in line along the angles at each end, or by the equivalent in welding, the load may be regarded as applied axially. The effective length, *KL*, in the plane of end gusset shall be taken as between 0·7 and 0·85 times the distance between intersections, depending on the degree of the restraint provided. The effective length, *KL*, in the plane perpendicular to that of the end gusset, shall be taken as equal to the distance between centres of intersections. The calculated average compressive stress (design stress f_{cd}) shall not exceed the values as specified in Article 10·7·1. The angles shall be connected together over their lengths so as to satisfy the requirements that the ratio of most unfavourable slenderness ratio of each member between the intermediate connections is not greater than 40 or 0·6 times the most unfavourable ratio of slenderness of the strut as a whole whichever is less.

Double angle discontinuous struts connected back-to-back, to one side of a gusset or section by one or more bolts or rivets in each angle, or by the equivalent in welding, shall be designed as single angle strut and the angles shall be connected together over their lengths so as to satisfy the requirements.

Continuous Members. Double angle continuous struts such as those forming the flanges, chords or ties of trusses or trussed girders, or the legs of towers shall be designed as axially loaded compression members, and the effective length shall be taken in accordance with section 10·7·3.

10·8. Columns

10·8·1. Column bases. Column bases should have sufficient stiffness and strength to transmit axial force, bending moments and shear forces at the base of the columns to their foundation without exceeding the load carrying capacity of the supports. Anchor bolts and shear keys should be provided wherever necessary. Shear resistance at the proper contact surface between steel base and concrete/grout may be calculated using a friction coefficient of 0·45.

The nominal bearing pressure between the base plate and the support below may be determined on the basis of linearly varying distribution of pressure. The maximum bearing pressure should not exceed the bearing strength equal to 0·6 f_{ck}, where f_{ck} is the smaller of characteristic cube strength of concrete or bedding material.

If the size of the base plate is larger than that required to limit the bearing pressure on the base support, an equal projection c of the base plate beyond the face of the column and gusset may be taken as effective in transferring the column load as given in Fig. 10·9, such that bearing pressure on the effective area does not exceed bearing capacity of concrete base.

10·8·2. Gusseted Bases. For stanchion with gusseted bases, the gusset plates, angle cleats, stiffeners, fastenings, etc, in combination with the bearing area of the shaft, shall be sufficient to take the loads, bending moments and reactions to the base plate without exceeding specified strength. All the bearing surfaces shall be machined to ensure perfect contact.

Where the ends of the column shaft and the gusset plates are not faced for complete bearing, the weldings, fastenings connecting them to the base plate shall be sufficient to transmit all the forces to which the base is subjected.

Column and base plate connections. Where the end of the column is connected directly to the base plate by means of full penetration butt welds, the connection shall be deemed to transmit to the base all the forces and moments to which the column is subjected.

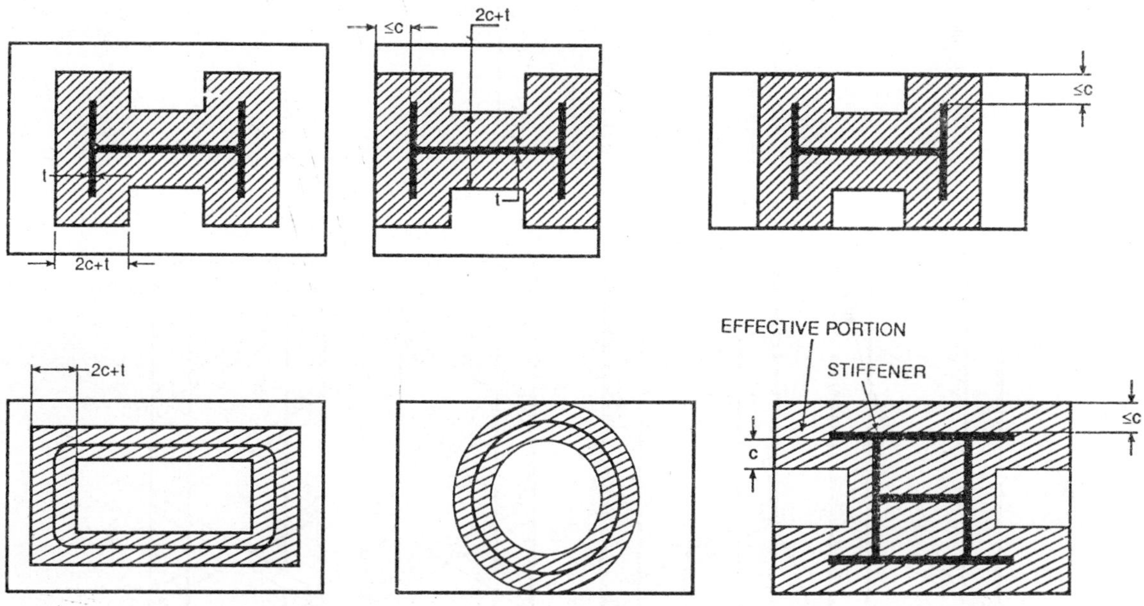

Fig. 10·9. Effective Area of a Base Plate.

10·8·3. Slab Bases. Columns with slab bases need not be provided with gussets, but sufficient fastenings shall be provided to retain the parts securely in place and to resist all moments and forces, other than direct compression, including those arising during transit, unloading and erection.

The minimum thickness, t_s of rectangular slab bases, supporting columns under axial compression shall be

$$t_s = \sqrt{2{\cdot}5w\left(a^2 - 0{\cdot}3b^2\right)\gamma_{m0}/f_y} > t_f$$

where w = uniform pressure from below on the slab base under the factored load axial compression;

a, b = larger and smaller projection, respectively of the slab base beyond the rectangle circumscribing the column; and

t_f = flange thickness of compression member.

10·8·4. Laced Columns

(1) Members comprising two main components laced and tied, should where practicable, have a radius of gyration about the axis perpendicular to the plane of lacing not less than the radius of gyration about the axis parallel to the plane of lacing (*see* Fig. 10·10A and 10·10B).

(2) Except for tie plates as specified in 10·7·7, double laced system (*see* Fig. 10·10B) and single laced systems (*see* Fig. 10·10A) on opposite sides of the main components shall not be combined with cross members (ties) perpendicular to the longitudinal axis of the strut (*see* Fig. 10·10C), unless all forces resulting from deformation of the strut members are calculated and provided for in the design of lacing and its fastenings.

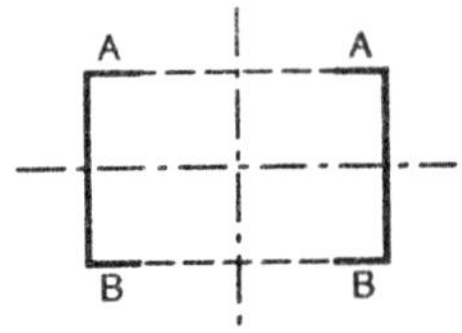

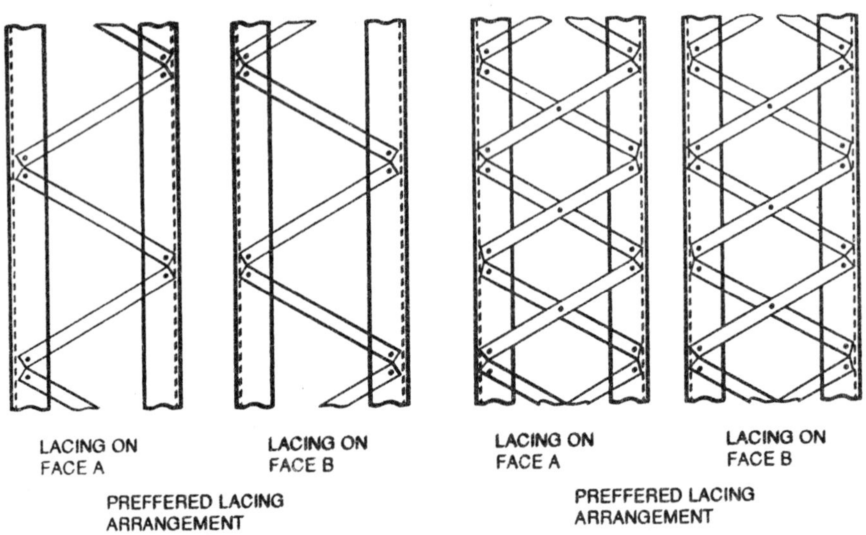

(A) Single Laced System (B) Double Laced System

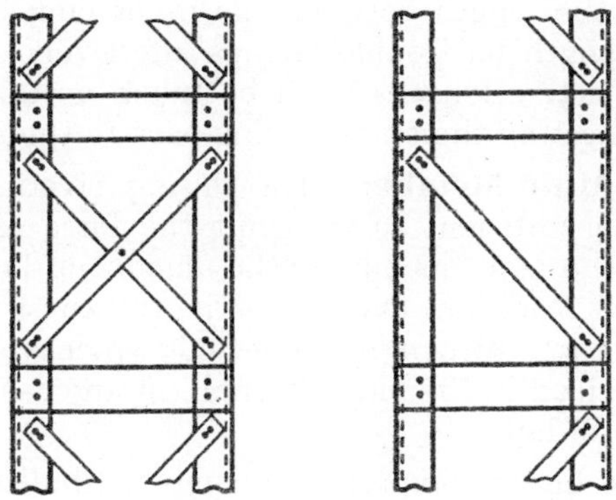

(C) Double laced and single laced system combined with cross numbers.

Fig. 10·10. Laced columns.

(3) Single laced systems, on opposite faces of the components being laced together shall preferably be in the same direction so that one is the shadow of the other, instead of being mutually opposed in direction.

(4) The effective slenderness ratio, $(KL/r)_e$, of laced columns shall be taken as 1·05 times the $(KL/r)_0$, the actual maximum slenderness ratio, in order to account for shear deformation effects.

(5) **Width of Lacing Bars.** In bolted/riveted construction, the minimum width of lacing bars shall be three times the nominal diameter of the end bolt/rivet.

(6) **Thickness of Lacing Bars.** The thickness of flat lacing bars shall not be less than one-fortieth of its effective length for single lacings and one-sixtieth of the effective length for double lacings.

Rolled sections or tubes of equivalent strength may be permitted instead of flats, for lacings.

(7) **Angle of Inclination.** Lacing bars, whether in double or single systems, shall be inclined at an angle not less than 40° nor more than 70° to the axis of the built-up member.

(8) **Spacing.** The maximum spacing of lacing bars, whether connected by bolting, riveting or welding, shall also be such that the maximum slenderness ratio of the components of the main member (a_1/r_1), between consecutive lacing connections is not greater than 50 or 0·7 times the most unfavourable slenderness ratio of the member as a whole, whichever is less, where a_1 is the unsupported length of the individual member between lacing points, and r_1 is the minimum radius of gyration of the individual member being laced together.

(9) Where lacing bars are not lapped to form the connection to the components of the members, they shall be so connected that there is no appreciable interruption in the triangulation of the system.

10·8·5. Design of Lacings

(1) The lacing shall be proportioned to resist a total transverse shear, V_t at any point in the member, equal to at least 2·5 percent of the axial force in the member and shall be divided equally among all transverse-lacing system in parallel planes.

(2) For members carrying calculated bending stress due to eccentricity of loading, applied end moments and/or lateral loading, the lacing shall be proportioned to resist the actual shear due to bending.

(3) The slenderness ratio, KL/r, of the lacing bars shall not exceed 145. In bolted/riveted construction, the effective length of lacing bars for the determination of the design

strength shall be taken as the length between the inner end fastener of the bars for single lacing, and as 0·7 of this length for double lacings effectively connected at intersections. In welded construction, the effective lengths shall be taken as 0·7 times the distance between the inner ends of welds connecting the single lacing bars to the members.

(4) **Attachment to Main Members.** The bolting, riveting or welding of lacing bars to the main members shall be sufficient to transmit the force calculated in the bars. Where welded lacing bars overlap the main members, the amount of lap measured along either edge of the lacing bar shall be not less than four times the thickness of the bar or the thickness of the element of the members to which it is connected, whichever is less. The welding should be sufficient to transmit the load in the bar and shall, in any case, be provided along each side of the bar for the full length of lap.

(5) **End Tie Plates.** Laced compression members shall be provided with tie plates at the ends of lacing systems and at intersection with other members/stays and at points where the lacing systems are interrupted.

10·8·6. Battened Columns

(1) Compression members composed of two main components battened should preferably have the individual members of the same cross-section and symmetrically disposed about their major axis. Where practicable, the compression members should have a radius of gyration about the axis perpendicular to the plane of the batten not less than the radius of gyration about the axis parallel to the plane of the batten (*see* Fig. 10·11).

(2) Battened compression members, not complying with the requirements specified in this section or those subjected to eccentricity of loading, applied moments or lateral forces in the plane of the battens (*see* Fig. 10·11), shall be designed according to the exact theory of elastic stability or empirically, based on verification by tests.

Note : If the column section is subjected to eccentricity or other moments about an axis perpendicular to battens, the battens and the column section should be specially designed for such moments and shears.

(3) The battens shall be placed opposite to each other at each end of the member and at points where the member is stayed in its length and as far as practicable, be spaced and proportioned uniformly throughout. The number of battens shall be such that the member is divided into not less than three bays within its actual length from centre-to-centre of end connections.

(4) The effective slenderness ratio $(KL/r)_e$ of battened columns, shall be taken as 1·1 times the $(KL/r)_0$, the maximum actual slenderness ratio of the column, to account for shear deformation effects.

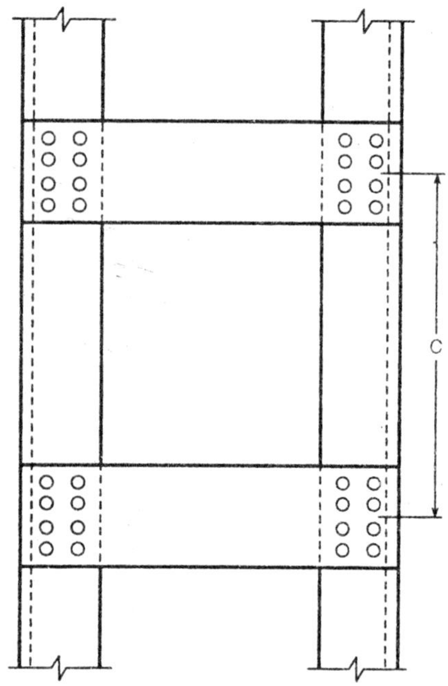

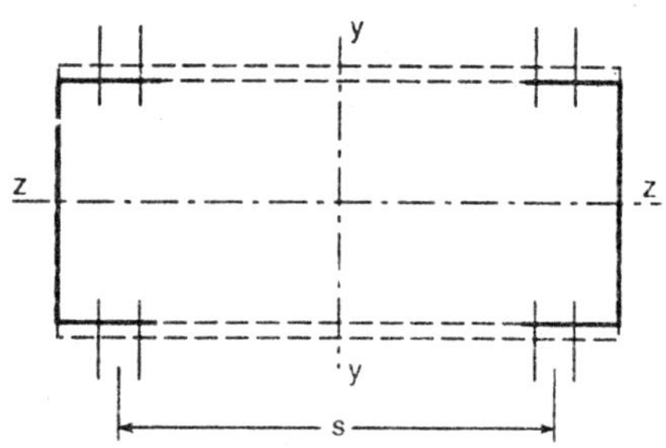

Fig. 10·11. Batten column section.

Table 10·13(a) Design Bending Compressive Stress Corresponding to Lateral Buckling, f_{bd}, $\alpha_{LT} = 0{\cdot}21$.

$f_{cr,b}$ ↓	f_y 200	210	220	230	240	250	260	280	300	320	340	360	380	400	420	450	480	510	540
10000	181·8	190·9	200	209·1	218·2	227·3	236·4	254·5	272·7	290·9	309·1	327·3	345·5	363·6	381·8	409·1	436·4	463·6	490·9
8000	181·8	190·9	200	209·1	218·2	227·3	236·4	254·5	272·7	290·9	309·1	327·3	345·5	363·6	381·8	409·1	436·4	463·6	490·9
6000	181·8	190·9	200	209·1	218·2	227·3	236·4	254·5	272·7	290·9	309·1	327·3	345·5	363·6	381·8	409·1	436·4	463·6	490·9
4000	181·8	190·9	200	209·1	218·2	227·3	236·4	254·5	272·7	290·9	309·1	327·3	345·5	363·6	381·8	409·1	436·4	463·6	490·9
2000	181·8	190·9	200	209·1	218·2	227·3	236·4	254·5	272·7	290·9	309·1	327·3	345·5	363·6	381·8	409·1	436·4	463·6	490·9
1000	169·1	179·5	186	196·5	202·9	209·1	219·8	229·1	245·5	261·8	275·1	291·3	300·5	323·6	332·2	355·9	370·9	384·8	412·4
900	169·1	179·5	186	194·5	200·7	204·5	215·1	231·6	242·7	258·9	272	291·3	300·5	316·4	328·4	339·5	366·5	380·2	392·7
800	167·3	177·5	184	190·3	196·4	206·8	212·7	224	240	258·9	268·9	284·7	293·6	301·8	324·5	335·5	349·1	370·9	387·8
700	163·6	171·8	182	188·2	192	202·3	208	226·5	237·3	250·2	259·6	278·2	286·7	294·5	305·5	327·3	340·4	352·4	363·3
600	161·8	168	176	181·9	194·2	197·7	203·3	218·9	226·4	244·4	253·5	261·8	276·4	287·3	294	306·8	322·9	333·8	343·6
500	161·8	166·1	172	179·8	185·5	188·6	200·9	208·7	218·2	232·7	244·2	248·7	259·1	269·1	274·9	286·4	296·7	301·4	314·2
450	158·2	164·2	168	173·5	183·3	186·4	191·5	206·2	215·5	224	231·8	242·2	248·7	258·2	263·5	274·1	279·3	292·1	294·5
400	150·9	162·3	166	169·4	174·5	184·1	186·7	196	204·5	215·3	222·5	229·1	238·4	243·6	248·2	257·7	261·8	264·3	274·9
350	147·3	152·7	162	165·2	170·2	172·7	179·6	188·4	193·6	200·7	210·2	212·7	221·1	225·5	229·1	233·2	240	241·1	245·5
300	143·6	147	152	154·7	161·5	163·6	167·8	175·6	182·7	186·2	194·7	196·4	196·9	203·6	206·2	212·7	213·8	217·9	220·9
250	134·5	137·5	142	144·3	148·4	152·3	153·6	160·4	163·6	165·8	170	173·5	179·6	178·2	179·5	184·1	183·3	185·5	191·5
200	121·8	124·1	126	129·6	130·9	134·1	134·7	137·5	141·8	142·5	145·3	147·3	148·5	149·1	152·7	151·4	152·7	153	157·1
150	101·8	103·1	104	104·5	16·9	106·8	108·7	109·5	111·8	113·5	114·4	114·5	117·5	116·4	118·4	118·6	117·8	120·5	122·7
100	74·5	76·4	76	77·4	76·4	77·3	78	78·9	79·1	78·5	80·4	81·8	79·5	80	80·2	81·8	82·9	83·5	83·5
90	67·3	68·7	70	69	69·8	70·5	70·9	71·3	70·9	72·7	74·2	72	72·5	72·7	72·5	73·6	74·2	74·2	73·6
80	61·8	63	62	62·7	63·3	63·6	63·8	63·6	65·5	64	64·9	65·5	65·6	65·5	64·9	65·5	65·5	64·9	68·7
70	54·5	55·4	56	56·5	56·7	56·8	56·7	56	57·3	58·2	58·7	58·9	58·7	58·2	57·3	57·3	56·7	60·3	58·9
60	47·3	47·7	48	48·1	48	50	49·6	48·4	49·1	49·5	49·5	49·1	48·4	50·9	49·6	49·1	52·4	51	49·1
50	40	40·1	40	41·8	41·5	40·9	40·2	40·7	40·9	40·7	43·3	42·5	41·5	43·6	42	40·9	43·6	41·7	44·2
40	32·7	32·5	32	33·5	32·7	34·1	33·1	33·1	32·7	34·9	34	32·7	34·5	32·7	34·4	32·7	34·9	32·5	34·4
30	25·5	24·8	26	25·1	26·2	25	26	25·5	24·5	26·2	24·7	26·2	24·2	25·5	26·7	24·5	26·2	27·8	24·5
20	16·4	17·2	18	16·7	17·5	18·2	16·5	17·8	16·4	17·5	18·5	16·4	17·3	18·2	19·1	16·4	17·5	18·5	19·6
10	9·1	9·5	8	8·4	8·7	9·1	9·5	7·6	8·2	8·7	9·3	9·8	10·4	7·3	7·6	8·2	8·7	9·3	9·8

Table 10·13(*b*) Design Bending Compressive Stress Corresponding to Lateral Buckling, f_{bd}, $\alpha_{I/T}$ = 0·49.

$f_{cr,b}$ ↓	f_y																		
	200	210	220	230	240	250	260	280	300	320	340	360	380	400	420	450	480	510	540
10000	181·8	190·9	200·0	209·1	218·2	227·3	236·4	254·5	272·7	290·9	309·1	327·3	345·5	363·6	381·8	409·1	436·4	463·6	490·9
8000	181·8	190·9	200·0	209·1	218·2	227·3	236·4	254·5	272·7	290·9	309·1	327·3	345·5	363·6	381·8	409·1	436·4	463·6	490·9
6000	181·8	190·9	200·0	209·1	218·2	227·3	236·4	254·5	272·7	290·9	309·1	327·3	345·5	363·6	381·8	409·1	436·4	463·6	490·9
4000	181·8	190·9	200·0	209·1	218·2	227·3	236·4	254·5	272·7	290·9	309·1	327·3	345·5	363·6	381·8	409·1	436·4	463·6	490·9
2000	181·8	190·9	200·0	209·1	218·2	227·3	236·4	254·5	272·7	290·9	309·1	327·3	345·5	363·6	381·8	409·1	436·4	463·6	490·9
1000	160·0	164·2	170·0	179·8	185·5	190·9	196·2	211·3	220·9	235·6	247·3	255·3	266·0	280	290·2	302·7	318·5	329·2	343·6
900	154·5	164·2	170·0	173·5	183·3	188·6	193·8	203·6	218·2	226·9	238·0	252·0	262·5	269·1	282·5	290·5	305·5	319·9	333·8
800	152·7	158·5	168·0	171·5	176·7	181·8	191·5	201·1	210·0	224·0	234·9	242·2	252·2	258·2	271·1	282·3	296·7	306	319·1
700	150·9	154·6	160·0	169·4	172·4	177·3	182·0	196	207·3	215·3	222·5	232·4	238·4	247·3	259·6	270	279·3	292·1	304·4
600	145·5	150·8	154·0	161·0	168·0	172·7	177·3	188·4	193·6	203·6	213·3	222·5	228	236·4	244·4	253·6	261·8	273·5	274·9
500	140·0	145·1	150·0	154·7	159·3	161·4	167·8	175·6	185·5	192	200·9	206·2	214·2	218·2	225·3	229·1	240	245·7	250·4
450	134·5	141·3	144·0	148·5	152·7	156·8	160·7	168	177·3	186·2	191·6	196·4	203·8	210·9	213·8	220·9	231·3	236·5	235·6
400	129·1	135·5	138·0	142·2	148·4	150	153·6	162·9	169·1	174·5	182·4	183·3	193·5	196·4	202·4	208·6	209·5	217·9	220·9
350	123·6	129·8	132·0	135·9	139·6	143·2	148·9	152·7	158·2	162·9	170	173·5	176·2	181·8	183·3	192·3	196·4	199·4	206·2
300	118·2	122·2	126·0	129·6	130·9	134·1	137·1	142·5	147·3	154·2	157·6	157·1	162·4	167·3	168	175·9	178·9	180·8	181·6
250	109·1	112·6	116·0	117·1	120·0	122·7	125·3	129·8	130·9	136·7	139·1	140·7	145·1	149·1	148·9	151·4	152·7	157·6	157·1
200	98·2	101·2	102·0	104·5	104·7	109·1	108·7	112	117·3	119·3	120·5	121·1	124·4	127·3	126	130·9	130·9	129·8	132·5
150	83·6	84·0	86·0	87·8	89·5	88·6	89·8	91·6	95·5	96·0	95·8	98·2	100·2	101·8	103·1	102·3	104·7	106·6	103·1
100	63·6	63·0	64·0	64·8	65·5	65·9	66·2	68·7	68·2	69·8	71·1	68·7	69·1	72·7	72·5	73·6	74·2	74·2	73·6
90	58·2	57·3	60·0	58·5	61·1	61·4	61·5	61·1	62·7	64·0	64·9	65·5	65·6	65·5	64·9	65·5	65·5	64·9	68·7
80	52·7	53·5	54·0	54·4	54·5	54·5	54·4	56	57·3	58·2	58·7	58·9	58·7	58·2	61·1	61·4	61·1	60·3	58·9
70	47·3	47·7	48·0	48·1	48·0	50·0	49·6	50·9	49·1	49·5	52·5	52·4	51·8	50·9	53·5	53·2	52·4	55·6	54·0
60	41·8	42·0	42·0	41·8	43·6	43·2	42·5	43·3	43·6	43·6	43·3	45·8	44·9	47·3	45·8	45·0	48·0	46·4	49·1
50	36·4	36·3	36·0	35·5	37·1	36·4	37·8	38·2	38·2	37·8	37·1	39·3	38·0	40·0	38·2	40·9	39·3	37·1	39·3
40	29·1	30·5	30·0	29·3	30·5	29·5	30·7	30·5	30·0	32·0	30·9	32·7	31·1	32·7	30·5	32·7	30·5	32·5	34·4
30	23·6	22·9	22·0	23·0	24·0	22·7	23·6	22·9	24·5	23·3	24·7	22·9	24·2	25·5	22·9	24·5	26·2	23·2	24·5
20	16·4	15·3	16·0	16·7	15·3	15·9	16·5	15·3	16·4	17·5	15·5	16·4	17·3	18·2	15·3	16·4	17·5	18·5	14·7
10	9·1	7·6	8·0	8·4	8·7	9·1	9·5	7·6	8·2	8·7	9·3	9·8	6·9	7·3	7·6	8·2	8·7	9·3	9·8

Table 10·14. Critical Stress, $f_{cr,b}$.

KL/r ↓	h/t_f 8	10	12	14	16	18	20	25	30	35	40	50	60	80	100
10	22551·2	22255·1	22092·6	21994·1	21929·8	21885·7	21854·0	21805·4	21779·0	21763·1	21752·7	21740·5	21733·8	21727·2	21724·2
20	6220·5	5947·9	5794·5	5700·0	5637·8	5594·7	5563·8	5515·8	5489·7	5473·8	5463·5	5451·4	5444·8	5438·2	5435·1
30	3149·3	2905·9	2764·6	2676·0	2616·7	2575·3	2545·3	2498·5	2472·8	2457·1	2447·0	2434·9	2428·3	2421·7	2418·6
40	2036·1	1821·2	1693·0	1610·8	1555·1	1515·8	1487·0	1441·7	1416·5	1401·1	1391·0	1379·0	1372·5	1365·9	1362·8
50	1492·9	1303·2	1187·3	1111·8	1059·9	1022·7	995·3	951·7	927·1	912·0	902·0	890·2	883·7	877·1	874·2
60	1178·0	1009·5	905·0	835·6	787·4	752·4	726·4	684·6	660·9	646·1	636·4	624·7	618·2	611·7	608·7
70	973·9	823·2	728·5	664·8	620·1	587·4	562·9	522·9	500·0	485·5	476·0	464·4	458·0	451·7	448·7
80	831·3	695·4	609·2	550·7	509·1	478·4	455·3	417·2	395·1	381·2	371·8	360·5	354·1	347·7	344·7
90	725·9	602·6	523·6	469·5	430·9	402·2	380·4	344·2	322·9	309·3	300·2	289·1	282·8	276·5	273·5
100	644·7	532·0	459·3	409·3	373·2	346·4	325·8	291·4	270·9	257·7	248·8	237·9	231·8	225·5	222·5
110	580·4	476·6	409·3	362·9	329·2	303·9	284·5	251·8	232·1	219·3	210·8	200·1	194·0	187·8	184·8
120	527·9	431·9	369·5	326·0	294·5	270·7	252·3	221·2	202·4	190·1	181·6	171·2	165·2	159·1	156·2
130	484·3	395·0	336·8	296·1	266·5	244·1	226·7	197·1	179·0	167·1	158·8	148·6	142·8	136·7	133·9
140	447·6	364·2	309·5	271·5	243·4	222·3	205·8	177·5	160·2	148·7	140·7	130·8	125·0	119·0	116·2
150	416·0	337·8	286·6	250·6	224·2	204·2	188·4	161·5	144·8	133·7	126·0	116·3	110·6	104·7	101·9
160	388·7	315·2	266·8	232·8	207·8	188·8	173·9	148·2	132·0	121·3	113·9	104·3	98·8	93·0	90·1
170	364·9	295·4	249·6	217·5	193·7	175·6	161·4	136·7	121·3	111·0	103·6	94·4	89·0	83·2	80·4
180	343·9	278·0	234·6	204·1	181·5	164·2	150·6	127·1	112·2	102·2	95·2	86·0	80·7	75·0	72·3
190	325·2	262·6	221·3	192·3	170·7	154·2	141·2	118·6	104·3	94·6	87·8	79·0	73·7	68·1	65·3
200	308·3	248·8	209·6	181·7	161·2	145·4	133·0	111·3	97·5	88·1	81·4	72·8	67·8	62·2	59·5
210	293·3	236·5	198·9	172·4	152·7	137·6	125·7	104·8	91·5	82·4	75·9	67·5	62·6	57·1	54·5
220	279·5	225·3	189·3	163·9	145·1	130·6	119·1	99·0	86·2	77·4	71·2	62·9	58·1	52·7	50·1
230	267·1	215·2	180·7	156·3	138·2	124·3	113·3	93·9	81·5	72·9	66·9	58·9	54·1	48·8	46·2
240	255·8	205·8	172·8	149·4	132·0	118·6	108·0	89·3	77·2	69·0	63·1	55·3	50·6	45·4	42·8
250	245·3	197·3	165·6	143·0	126·3	113·4	103·2	85·1	73·5	65·5	59·7	52·1	47·5	42·4	39·8
260	235·7	189·5	159·0	137·3	121·1	108·7	98·8	81·3	70·1	62·3	56·7	49·3	44·8	39·7	37·2
270	226·8	182·3	152·8	131·9	116·3	104·3	94·7	77·9	67·0	59·4	53·9	46·8	42·2	37·3	34·8
280	218·6	175·7	147·2	126·9	111·9	100·2	91·1	74·7	64·1	56·8	51·5	44·4	40·0	35·2	32·7
290	210·9	169·4	141·9	122·3	107·8	96·6	87·7	71·8	61·5	54·3	49·2	42·2	38·1	33·2	30·8
300	203·8	163·7	137·1	118·1	104·1	93·2	84·5	69·1	59·1	52·1	47·1	40·4	36·2	31·5	29·0

10·8·7. Design of Battens

(1) **Battens.** Battens shall be designed to carry the bending moments and shear forces arising from transverse shear force V_t equal to 2·5 percent of the total axial force on the whole compression member, at any point in the length of the member, divided equally between parallel planes of battens. Battened member carrying calculated bending moment due to eccentricity of axial loading, calculated end moments or lateral loads parallel to the plane of battens, shall be designed to carry actual shear in addition to the above shear. The main members shall also be checked for the same shear force and bending moments as for the battens.

Battens shall be of plates, angles, channels, or I-sections and at their ends shall be riveted, bolted or welded to the main components so as to resist simultaneously a shear $V_b = V_tC/NS$ along the column axis and a moment $M = V_tC/2N$ at each connection,

where V_t = transverse shear force as defined above;

C = distance between centre-to-centre of battens, longitudinally;

N = number of parallel planes of battens; and

S = minimum transverse distance between the centroid of the rivet/bolt group/ welding connecting the batten to the main member.

(2) **Tie Plates.** Tie plates are members provided at the ends of battened and laced members, and shall be designed by the same method as battens. In no case shall a tie plate and its fastenings be incapable of carrying the forces for which the lacing or batten has been designed.

(3) **Size.** When plates are used for battens, the end battens and those at points where the member is stayed in its length shall have an effective depth, longitudinally, not less than the perpendicular distance between the centroids of the main members. The intermediate battens shall have an effective depth of not less than three quarters of this distance, but in no case shall the effective depth of any batten be less than twice the width of one member, in the plane of the battens. The effective depth of a batten shall be taken as the longitudinal distance between outermost bolts, rivets or welds at the ends. The thickness of batten or the tie plates shall be not less than one-fiftieth of the distance between the innermost connecting lines of rivets, bolts or welds, perpendicular to the main member.

(4) The requirement of bolt size and thickness of batten specified above does not apply when angles, channels or I-sections are used for battens with their legs or flanges perpendicular to the main member. However, it should be ensured that the ends of the compression members are tied to achieve adequate rigidity.

(5) **Spacing of Battens.** In battened compression members where the individual members are not specifically checked for shear stress and bending moments, the spacing of battens, centre-to-centre of its end fastenings, shall be such that the slenderness ratio (KL/r) of any component over that distance shall be neither greater than 50 nor greater than 0·7 times the slenderness ratio of the member as a whole about its z-z (axis parallel to the battens).

10·9. Members Subjected to Bending

Members subjected to predominant bending shall have adequate design strength to resist bending moment, shear force, and concentrated forces imposed upon and their combinations. Further, the members shall satisfy the deflection limitation presented in Section 5, as serviceability criteria. Member subjected to other forces in addition to bending or biaxial bending shall be designed in accordance with combined forces.

10·9·1. Effective Span of Beams. The effective span of a beam shall be taken as the distance between the centre of the supports, except where the point of application of the reaction is taken as eccentric at the support, when it shall be permissible to take the effective span as the length between the assumed lines of the reactions.

10·9·2. The factored design moment, M at any section, in a beam due to external actions, shall satisfy

$$M \le M_d$$

where M_d = design bending strength of the section.

When the design shear force (factored), V exceeds $0{\cdot}6\ V_d$, where V_d is the design shear strength of the cross-section the design bending strength, M_d shall be taken.

$$M_d = M_{dv}$$

where M_{dv} = design bending strength under high shear.

10·9·3. Holes in the Tension Zone

(*a*) The effect of holes in the tension flange, on the design bending strength need not be considered if

$$\left(A_{nf}/A_{gf}\right) \ge \left(f_y/f_u\right)\left(\gamma_{m1}/\gamma_{m0}\right)/0{\cdot}9$$

where A_{nf}/A_{gf} = ratio of net to gross area of the flange in tension,

f_y/f_u = ratio of yield and ultimate stress of the material, and

γ_{m1}/γ_{m0} = ratio of partial safety factors against ultimate to yield stress (*see* 5·4·1).

When the A_{nf}/A_{gf} does not satisfy the above requirement, the reduced effective flange area, A_{ef} satisfying the above equation may be taken as the effective flange area in tension, instead of A_{gf}.

(*b*) The effect of holes in the tension region of the web on the design flexural strength need not be considered, if the limit given in (*a*) above is satisfied for the complete tension zone of the cross-section, comprising the tension flange and tension region of the web.

(*c*) Fastener holes in the compression zone of the cross-section need not be considered in design bending strength calculation, except for oversize and slotted holes or holes without any fastener.

Table 10·15. Effective Length for Simply Supported Beams, L_{LT}

Sl. No.	*Conditions of Restraint at Supports*		*Loading Condition*	
	Torsional Restraint	*Warping Restraint*	*Normal*	*Destabilizing*
(1)	(2)	(3)	(4)	(5)
(*i*)	Fully restrained	Both flanges fully restrained	0·70 L	0·85 L
(*ii*)	Fully restrained	Compression flange fully restrained	0·75 L	0·90 L
(*iii*)	Fully restrained	Both flanges fully restrained	0·80 L	0·95 L
(*iv*)	Fully restrained	Compression flange partially restrained	0·85 L	1·00 L
(*v*)	Fully restrained	Warping not restrained in both flanges	1·00 L	1·20 L
(*vi*)	Partially restrained by bottom flange support connection	Warping not restrained in both flanges	1·0 L + 2 D	1·2 L + 2 D
(*vii*)	Partially restrained by bottom flange bearing support	Warping not restrained in both flanges	1·2 L + 2 D	1·4 L + 2 D

Notes : 1. Torsional restraint prevents rotation about the longitudinal axis.

2. Warping restraint prevents rotation of the flange in its plane.

3. D is the overall depth of the beam.

Table 10·16. Effective Length, L_{LT} for Cantilever of Length, L

Restraint Condition		*Loading Condition*	
At Support	*At Top*	*Normal*	*Destabilizing*
(1)	(2)	(3)	(4)
(*a*) Continuous, with lateral restraint to top flange 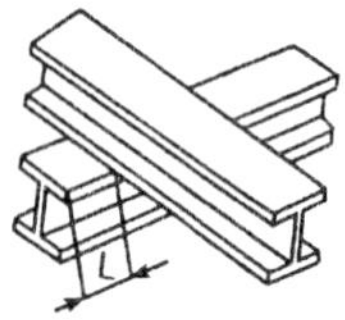	(*i*) Free (*ii*) Lateral restraint to top flange (*iii*) Torsional restraint (*iv*) Lateral and torsional restraint	3·0 *L* 2·7 *L* 2·4 *L* 2·1 *L*	7·5 *L* 7·5 *L* 4·5 *L* 3·6 *L*
(*b*) Continuous, with partial torsional restraint 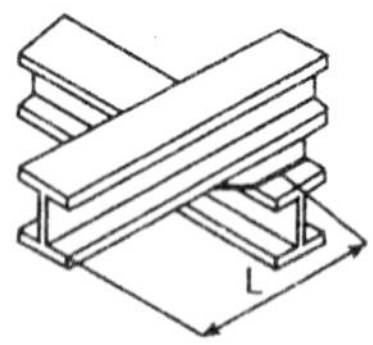	(*i*) Free (*ii*) Lateral restraint to top flange (*iii*) Torsional restraint (*iv*) Lateral and torsional restraint	2·0 *L* 1·8 *L* 1·6 *L* 1·4 *L*	5·0 *L* 5·0 *L* 3·0 *L* 2·4 *L*
(*c*) Continuous, with lateral and torsional restraint 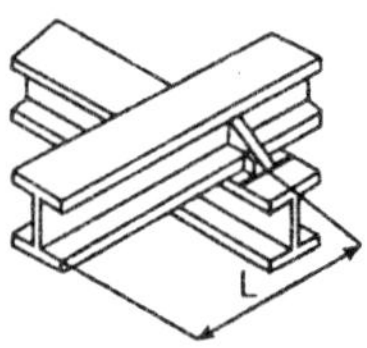	(*i*) Free (*ii*) Lateral restraint to top flange (*iii*) Torsional restraint (*iv*) Lateral and torsional restraint	1·0 *L* 0·9 *L* 0·8 *L* 0·7 *L*	2·5 *L* 2·5 *L* 1·5 *L* 1·2 *L*
(*d*) Restrained laterally, torsionally and against rotation on plan 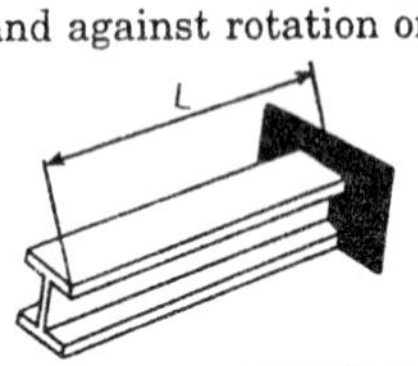	(*i*) Free (*ii*) Lateral restraint to top flange (*iii*) Torsional restraint (*iv*) Lateral and torsional restraint	0·8 *L* 0·7 *L* 0·6 *L* 0·5 *L*	1·4 *L* 1·4 *L* 0·6 *L* 0·5 *L*

Top restraint conditions

(*i*) Free	(*ii*) Lateral restraint to top flange	(*iii*) Torsional restraint	(*iv*) Lateral and torsional restraint
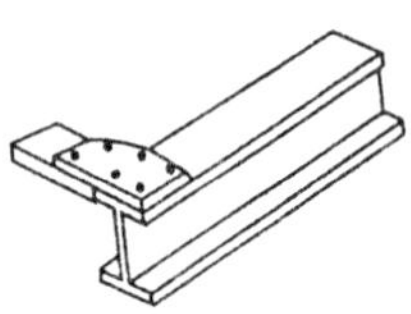	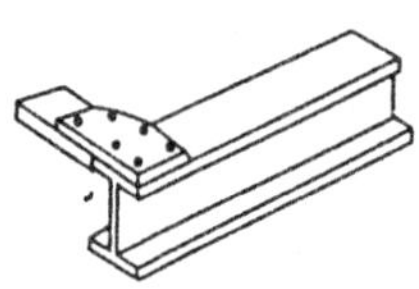	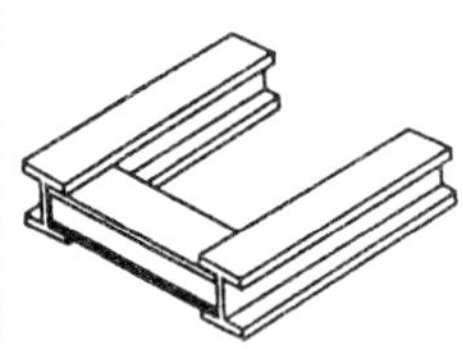	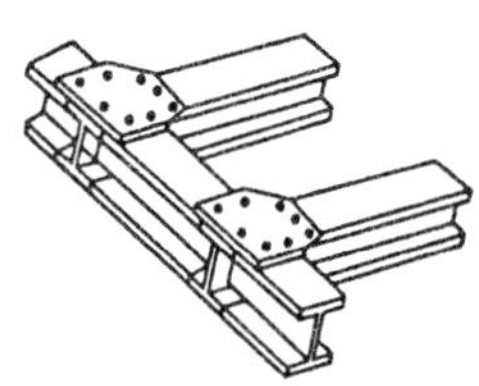

10·9·4. Shear. The factored design shear force, V, in a beam due to external actions shall satisfy

$$V \le V_d$$

where V_d = design strength

$= V_n/\gamma_{m0}$

where γ_{m0} = partial safety factor against shear failure (*see* 5·4·1).

The nominal plastic shear resistance under pure shear is given by :

$$V_n = V_p$$

where $$V_p = \frac{A_v\, f_{yw}}{\sqrt{3}}$$

A_y = shear area, and

f_{yw} = yield strength of the web.

The shear area may be calculated as given below:

I and channel sections :

Major Axis Bending :

Hot-Rolled — $h\, t_w$

Welded — $d\, t_w$

Minor Axis Bending :

Hot-Rolled or Welded — $2b\, t_f$

Rectangular hollow sections of uniform thickness :

Loaded parallel to depth (h) — $A\, h/(b + h)$

Loaded parallel to width (b) — $A\, b/(b + h)$

Circular hollow tubes of uniform thickness — $2A/\pi$

Plates and solid bars — A

where A = cross-section area,

b = overall breadth of tubular section, breadth of I-section flanges,

d = clear depth of the web between flanges,

h = overall depth of the section,

t_f = thickness of the flange, and

t_w = thickness of the web.

Note : Fastener holes need not be accounted for in plastic design shear strength calculation provided that :

$$A_{vn} \ge \left(f_y/f_u\right)\left(\gamma_{m1}/\gamma_{m0}\right) A_v/0{\cdot}9$$

10·9·5. Stiffened Web Panels

(1) **End Panels Design (*see* Fig. 10·12).** The design of end panels in girders in which the interior panel (panel A) is designed using tension field action shall be carried in accordance with the provisions given in Fig. (refer Figs. 10·12, 10·13 and 10·14)

10·9·6. Design of Beams and Plate Girders with Solid Webs

10·9·6·1. Minimum Web Thickness. The thickness of the web in a section shall satisfy the following requirements :

(1) **Serviceability requirement**

(a) When transverse stiffeners are not provided, $\dfrac{d}{t_w} \le 200\varepsilon$ (web connected to flanges along both longitudinal edges).

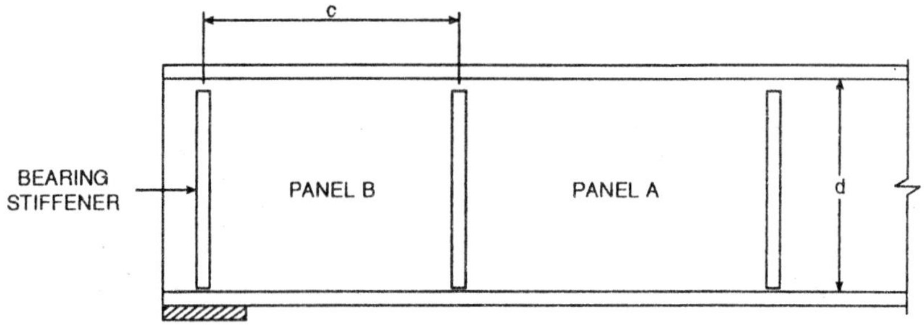

Notes : 1. Panel A is designed utilizing tension field action.

2. Panel B is designed without utilizing tension field action.

3. Bearing stiffener is designed for the compressive force due to bearing plus compressive force due to the moment M_d.

Fig. 10·12. End panel designed not using tension field action.

(2) **End Panels Designed Using Tension Field Action** (*see* Fig. 10·13 and Fig. 10·14)

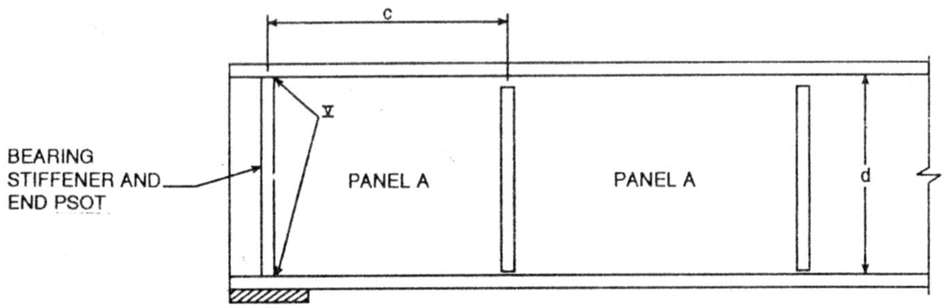

Notes : 1. Panel A is designed utilizing tension field action.

2. Panel B is designed utilizing tension field action.

3. Bearing stiffener and end post is designed for combination of compressive loads due to bearing and a moment equal to 2/3 M_n.

Fig. 10·13. End panel designed using tension field action (single stiffener)

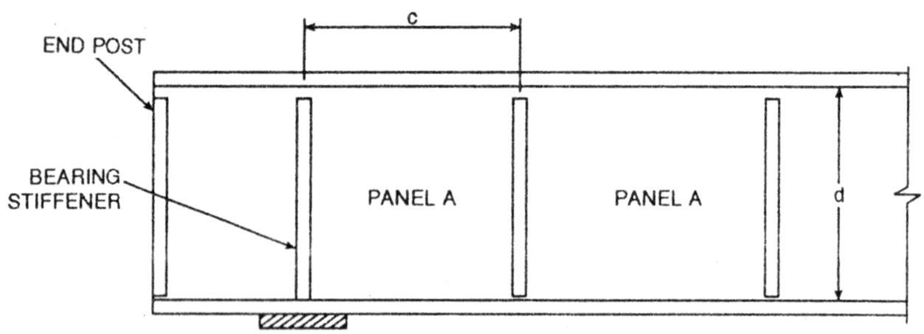

Notes : 1. Panel A is designed utilizing tension field action.

2. Bearing stiffener is designed for compressive force due to bearing.

3. End post is designed for horizontal shear R_u and moment M_u.

Fig. 10·14. End panel designed using tension field action (Double stiffener).

$$\frac{d}{t_w} \le 90\varepsilon \text{ (web connected to flanges along one longitudinal edge only),}$$

(*b*) When only transverse stiffeners are provided (in webs connected to flanges along both longitudinal edges),

(*i*) when $3d \ge c \ge d$

$$\frac{d}{t_w} \le 200\varepsilon$$

(*ii*) when $0{\cdot}74\, d \le c < d$

$$\frac{c}{t_w} \le 200\varepsilon_w$$

(*iii*) when $c < d$

$$\frac{d}{t_w} \le 270\varepsilon_w$$

(*iv*) when $c > 3d$, the web shall be considered as unstiffened.

(*c*) When transverse stiffeners and longitudinal stiffeners at one level only are provided ($0{\cdot}2\, d$ from compression flange).

(*i*) when $2{\cdot}4d \ge c \ge d$

$$\frac{d}{t_w} \le 250\varepsilon_w$$

(*ii*) when $0{\cdot}74\, d \le c \le d$

$$\frac{c}{t_w} \le 250\varepsilon_w$$

(*iii*) when $c < 0{\cdot}74\, d$

$$\frac{d}{t_w} \le 340\varepsilon_w$$

(*d*) When a second longitudinal stiffener (located at neutral axis is provided).

$$\frac{d}{t_w} \le 400\varepsilon_w$$

where d = depth of the web,

t_w = thickness of the web,

c = spacing of transverse stiffener (*see* Fig. 10·12 and Fig. 10·13),

ε_w = yield stress ratio of web = $\sqrt{\dfrac{250}{f_{yw}}}$, and

f_{yw} = yield stress of the web.

10·9·6·2. Compression Flange Buckling Requirement. In order to avoid buckling of the compression flange into the web, the web thickness shall satisfy the following:

(*a*) When transverse stiffeners are not provided

$$\frac{d}{t_w} \le 345\varepsilon_f^2$$

(*b*) When transverse stiffeners are provided and

(*i*) when $c \geq 1{\cdot}5\ d$

$$\frac{d}{t_w} \leq 345\varepsilon_f^2$$

(*ii*) when $c < 1{\cdot}5\ d$

$$\frac{d}{t_w} \leq 345\varepsilon_f$$

where d = depth of the web,

t_w = thickness of the web,

c = spacing of transverse stiffener (*see* Fig. 10·12 and Fig. 10·13),

ε_f = yield stress ratio of web = $\sqrt{\dfrac{250}{f_{yf}}}$ and

f_{yf} = yield stress of compression flange.

10·9·7. Sectional Properties. The effective sectional area of compression flanges shall be the gross area with deductions for excessive width of plates as specified for compression members (*see* Section 7) and for open holes occurring in a plane perpendicular to the direction of stress at the second being considered.

The effective sectional area of tension flanges shall be the gross sectional area with deductions for holes.

The effective sectional area for parts in shear shall be given.

10·9·8. Flanges. In riveted or bolted construction, flange angles shall form as large a part of the area of the flange as practicable (preferably not less than one-third) and the number of flange plates shall be kept to a minimum.

In exposed situations, where flange angles are used, at least one plate of the top flange shall extend over the full length of the girder, unless the top edge of the web is machined flush with the flange angles. Where two or more flange plates are used, tacking rivets shall be provided, if necessary to comply with the requirements of Section 10 (connections).

Each flange plate shall extend beyond its theoretical cut-off point, and the extension shall contain sufficient rivets, bolts or welds to develop in the plate, the load calculated for the bending moment on the girder section (taken to include the curtailed plate) at the theoretical cut-off point.

The outstand of flange plates, that is the projection beyond the outer line of connections to flange angles, channel or joist flanges or in the case of welded constructions their projection beyond the face of the web or tongue plate, shall not exceed the values given in 3·7 (*see* Table 2).

In the case of box girders, the thickness of any plate, or the aggregate thickness of two or more plates, when these plates are tacked together to form the flange, shall satisfy the requirements given in 3·7 (*see* Table 2).

10·9·9. Flange Splices. Flange splices should preferably, not be located at points of maximum stress. Where splice plates are used, their area shall be not less than 5 percent in excess of the area of the flange element spliced; their centre of gravity shall coincide, as nearly as possible, with that of the element spliced. There shall be enough bolts, rivets or welds on each side of the splice to develop the load in the element spliced plus 5 percent but in no case should the strength developed be less than 50 percent of the effective strength of the material spliced. In welded construction, flange plates shall be joined by complete penetration butt welds, wherever possible. These butt welds shall develop the full strength of the plates.

10·9·10. Connection of Flanges to Web. The flanges of plate girders shall be connected to the web by sufficient rivets, bolts or welds to transmit the maximum horizontal shear force resulting from the bending moment gradient in the girder, combined with any vertical loads which are directly applied to the flange. If the web is designed using tension field method, the weld should be able to transfer the tension field stress, f_{yw} acting on the web.

10·9·11. Bolted/Riveted Construction. For girders in exposed situations and which do not have flange plates for their entire length, the top edge of the web plate shall be flush with or above the angles, and the bottom edge of the web plate shall be flush with or set back from the angles.

10·9·12. Welded Construction. The gap between the web plates and flange plates shall be kept to a minimum and for fillet welds shall not exceed 1 mm at any point before welding.

10·9·13. Webs

Effective sectional area of web of plate girder. The effective cross-sectional area shall be taken as the full depth of the web plate multiplied by the thickness.

Note : Where webs are varied in thickness in the depth of the section by the use of tongue plates or the like, or where the proportion of the web included in the flange area is 25 percent or more of the overall depth, the above approximation is not permissible and the maximum shear stress shall be computed on theory.

10·9·13·1. Splices in Webs

(1) Splices and cutouts for service ducts in the webs should preferably not be located at points of maximum shear force and heavy concentrated loads.

Splices in the webs of the plate girders and rolled sections shall be designed to resist the shears and moments at the spliced section (*see* Annex. F).

In riveted or bolted construction, splice plates shall be provided on each side of the web. In welded construction, web splices shall preferably be made with complete penetration butt welds.

(2) Where additional plates are required to augment the strength of the web, they shall be placed on each side of the web and shall be equal in thickness. The proportion of shear force assumed to be resisted by these plates shall be limited by the amount of horizontal shear which they can transmit to the flanges through their fastenings, and such reinforcing plates and their fastenings shall be carried up to the points at which the flange without the additional plates is adequate.

10·9·14. Stiffener Design

(1) When the web of a member acting alone (that is without stiffeners) proves inadequate, stiffeners for meeting the following requirements should be provided:

(*a*) *Intermediate transverse web stiffener*—To improve the buckling strength of a slender web due to shear.

(*b*) *Load carrying stiffener*—To prevent local buckling of the web due to concentrated loading.

(*c*) *Bearing stiffener*—To prevent local crushing of the web due to concentrated loading.

(*d*) *Torsion stiffener*—To provide torsional restraint to beams and girders at supports.

(*e*) *Diagonal stiffener*—To provide local reinforcement to a web under shear and bearing.

(*f*) *Tension stiffener*—To transmit tensile forces applied to a web through a flange.

The same stiffeners may perform more than one function and their design should comply with the requirements of all the functions for which designed.

10·10. Connections

10·10·1. Location Details of Fasteners

Clearances for Holes for Fasteners (Table 10·17). Bolts may be located in standard size, over size, short slotted or long slotted hole.

Table 10·17. Clearances for Fastener Holes

Sl. No.	*Nominal Size of Fastener, d mm*	*Size of the Hole = Nominal Diameter of the Fastener + Clearances mm*			
		Standard Clearance in Diameter and Width of Slot	*Over size Clearance in Diameter*	*Clearance in the Length of the Slot*	
				Short Slot	*Long Slot*
(1)	(2)	(3)	(4)	(5)	(6)
(*i*)	12 – 14	1·0	3·0	4·0	2·5 *d*
(*ii*)	16 – 22	2·0	4·0	6·0	2·5 *d*
(*iii*)	24	2·0	6·0	8·0	2·5 *d*
(*iv*)	Larger than 24	3·0	8·0	10·0	2·5 *d*

10·10·2. Minimum Spacing. The distance between centre of fasteners shall not be less than 2·5 times the nominal diameter of the fastener.

10·10·3. Maximum Spacing

(1) The distance between the centres of any two adjacent fasteners shall not exceed $32t$ or 300 mm, whichever is less, where t is the thickness of the thinner plate.

(2) The distance between the centres of two adjacent fasteners (pitch) in a line lying in the direction of stress, shall not exceed $16t$ or 200 mm, whichever is less, in tension members and $12t$ or 200 mm, whichever is less, in compression members : where t is the thickness of the thinner plate. In the case of compression members wherein forces are transferred through butting faces, this distance shall not exceed 4·5 times the diameter of the fasteners for a distance equal to 1·5 times the width of the member from the butting faces.

(3) The distance between the centres of any two consecutive fasteners in a line adjacent and parallel to an edge of an outside plate shall not exceed 100 mm plus $4t$ or 200 mm, whichever is less, in compression and tension members; where t is the thickness of the thinner outside plate.

(4) When fasteners are staggered at equal intervals and the gauge does not exceed 75 mm, the spacing specified in 10·10·2 and 10·10·3 between centres of fasteners may be increased by 50 percent, subject to the maximum spacing specified in 10·10·3·1.

10·10·4. Edge and End Distances

(1) The edge distance is the distance at right angles to the direction of stress from the centre of a hole to the adjacent edge. The end distance is the distance in the direction of stress from the centre of a hole to the end of the element.

In slotted holes, the edge and end distances should be measured from the edge or end of the material to the centre of its end radius or the centre line of the slot, whichever is smaller. In oversize holes, the edge and end distances should be taken as the distance from the relevant edge/end plus half the diameter of the standard clearance hole corresponding to the fastener, less the nominal diameter of the oversize hole.

(2) The minimum edge and end distances from the centre of any hole to the nearest edge of a plate shall not be less than 1·7 times the hole diameter in case of sheared or hand-flame cut edges; and 1·5 times the hole diameter in case of rolled, machine-flame cut, sawn and planed edges.

(3) The maximum edge distance to the nearest line of fasteners from an edge of any un-stiffened part should not exceed 12 $t\varepsilon$, where $\varepsilon = (250/f_y)^{1/2}$ and t is the thickness of the thinner outer plate. This would not apply to fasteners interconnecting the components of back to back tension members. Where the members are exposed to corrosive influences, the maximum edge distance shall not exceed 40 mm plus $4t$, where t is the thickness of thinner connected plate.

10·10·5. Tacking Fasteners

(1) In case of members when the maximum distance between centres of two adjacent fasteners as specified in 10·10·4·3 tacking fasteners not subjected to calculated stress shall be used.

(2) Tacking fasteners shall have spacing in a line not exceeding 32 times the thickness of the thinner outside plate or 300 mm, whichever is less. Where the plates are exposed to the weather, the spacing in line shall not exceed 16 times the thickness of the thinner outside plate or 200 mm, whichever is less. In both cases, the distance between the lines of fasteners shall not be greater than the respective pitches.

(3) All the requirements specified in 10·10·52 shall generally apply to compression members, subject to the stipulations in Section 10·7 affecting the design and construction of compression members.

(4) In tension members (*see* Section 6) composed of two flats, angles, channels or tees in contact back to back or separated back to back by a distance not exceeding the aggregate thickness of the connected parts, tacking fasteners with solid distance pieces shall be provided at a spacing in line not exceeding 1000 mm.

(5) For compression members covered in Section 10·7, tacking fasteners in a line shall be spaced at a distance not exceeding 600 mm.

10·10·6. Countersunk Heads. For countersunk heads, one-half of the depth of the countersinking shall be neglected in calculating the length of the fastener in bearing. For fasteners in tension having countersunk heads, the tensile strength shall be reduced by 33·3 percent. No reduction is required to be made in shear strength calculations.

10·10·7. Bearing Type Bolts

10·10·7·1. Effective Areas of Bolts

(1) Since threads can occur in the shear plane, the area A_e for resisting shear should normally be taken as the net tensile stress area, A_n of the bolts. For bolts where the net tensile stress area is not defined, A_n shall be taken as the area at the root of the threads.

(2) Where it can be shown that the threads do not occur in the shear plane, A_e may be taken as the cross section area, A_s at the shank.

In the calculation of thread length, allowance should be made for tolerance and thread run off.

10·10·8. Shear Capacity of Bolt. The design strength of the bolt, V_{dsb} as governed shear strength is given by:

$$V_{dsb} = V_{nsb}/\gamma_{mb}$$

where V_{nsb} = nominal shear capacity of a bolt, calculated as follows:

$$V_{nsb} = \frac{f_u}{\sqrt{3}}(n_n A_{nb} + n_s A_{sb})$$

where f_u = ultimate tensile strength of a bolt,

n_n = number of shear planes with threads intercepting the shear plane;

n_s = number of shear planes without threads intercepting the shear plane;

A_{sb} = nominal plain shank area of the bolt; and

A_{nb} = net shear area of the bolt at threads, may be taken as the area corresponding to root diameter at the thread.

10·10·9. Bearing Capacity of the Bolt. The design bearing strength of a bolt on any plate, V_{dpb} as governed by bearing is given by:

$$V_{dpb} = V_{npb}/\gamma_{mb}.$$

where V_{npb} = nominal bearing strength of a bolt

$= 2{\cdot}5\ k_b\ d\ t\ f_u$

where k_b is smaller of $\frac{e}{3d_0}, \frac{p}{3d_0} - 0{\cdot}25, \frac{f_{ub}}{f_u}, 1{\cdot}0$;

e, p = end and pitch distances of the fastener along bearing direction;

d_0 = diameter of the hole;

f_{ub}, f_u = ultimate tensile stress of the bolt and the ultimate tensile stress of the plate, respectively,

d = nominal diameter of the bolt; and

t = summation of the thicknesses of the connected plates experiencing bearing stress in the same direction, or if the bolts are countersunk, the thickness of the plate minus one half of the depth of countersinking.

The bearing resistance (in the direction normal to the slots in slotted holes) of bolts in holes other than standard clearance holes may be reduced by multiplying the bearing resistance obtained as above, V_{npb}, by the factors given below:

(*a*) Over size and short slotted holes — 0·7, and

(*b*) Long slotted holes — 0·5.

Note : The block shear of the edge distance due to bearing force may be checked as given in 10·6·4.

10·10·10. Tension Capacity. A bolt subjected to a factored tensile force, T_b shall satisfy:

$$T_b \leq T_{db}$$

where $T_{db} = T_{nb}/\gamma_{mb}$

T_{nb} = nominal tensile capacity of the bolt, calculated as:

$$0{\cdot}90\ f_{ub}\ A_n < f_{yb}\ A_{sb}\ (\gamma_{mb}/\gamma_{m0})$$

where f_{ub} = ultimate tensile stress of the bolt,

f_{yb} = yield stress of the bolt,

A_n = net tensile stress area as specified in the appropriate Indian Standard (for bolts where the tensile stress area is not defined, A_n shall be taken as the area at the bottom of the threads), and

A_{sb} = shank area of the bolt.

Table 10·18. Typical Average Values for Coefficient of Friction (μ_f)

Sl. No.	*Treatment of Surface*	*Coefficient of Friction,* μ_f
(1)	(2)	(3)
(*i*)	Surfaces not treated	0·20
(*ii*)	Surfaces blasted with short or grit with any loose rust removed, no pitting	0·50
(*iii*)	Surfaces blasted with shot or grit and hot-dip galvanized	0·10
(*iv*)	Surfaces blasted with shot or grit and spray-metallized with zinc (thickness 50-70 μm)	0·25
(*v*)	Surfaces blasted with shot or grit and painted with ethylzinc silicate coat (thickness 30-60 μm)	0·30
(*vi*)	Sand blasted surface, after light rusting	0·52
(*vii*)	Surfaces blasted with shot or grit and painted with ethylzinc silicate coat (thickness 60-80 μm)	0·30
(*viii*)	Surfaces blasted with shot or grit and painted with alcalizinc silicate coat (thickness 60-80 μm)	0·30
(*ix*)	Surface blasted with shot or grit and spray metallized with aluminium (thickness > 50 μm)	0·50
(*x*)	Clean mill scale	0·33
(*xi*)	Sand blasted surface	0·40
(*xii*)	Red lead painted surface	0.1

10·10·11. Welds and Welding. Requirements of welds and welding shall conform to IS 816 and IS 9595, as appropriate.

(1) **End Returns.** Fillet welds terminating at the ends or sides of parts should be returned continuously around the corners for a distance of not less than twice the size of the weld, unless it is impractical to do so. This is particularly important on the tension end of parts carrying bending loads.

(2) **Lap Joint.** In the case of lap joints, the minimum lap should not be less than four times the thickness of the thinner part joined or 40 mm, whichever is more. Single end fillet should be used only when lapped parts are restrained from openings. When end of an element is connected only by parallel longitudinal fillet welds, the length of the weld along either edge should not be less than the transverse spacing between longitudinal welds.

(3) A single fillet weld should not be subjected to moment about the longitudinal axis of the weld.

10·10·12. Size of Weld

(1) The size of normal fillets shall be taken as the minimum weld leg size. For deep penetration welds, where the depth of penetration beyond the root run is a minimum of 2·4 mm, the size of the fillet should be taken as the minimum leg size plus 2·4 mm.

(2) For fillet welds made by semi-automatic or automatic processes, where the depth of penetration is considerably in excess of 2·4 mm, the size shall be taken considering actual depth of penetration subject to agreement between the purchaser and the contractor.

(3) The size of fillet welds shall not be less than 3 mm. The minimum size of the first run or of a single run fillet weld shall be as given in Table 10·19, to avoid the risk of cracking in the absence of preheating.

(4) The size of butt weld shall be specified by the effective throat thickness.

10·10·13. Effective Throat Thickness

(1) The effective throat thickness of a fillet weld shall not be less than 3 mm and shall generally not exceed $0{\cdot}7t$, or $1{\cdot}0t$ under special circumstances, where t is the thickness of the thinner plate of elements being welded.

Table 10·19. Minimum Size of First Run or of a Single Run Fillet Weld

Sl. No.	*Thickness of Thicker Part mm*		*Minimum Size mm*
	Over	*Up to and including*	
(1)	(2)	(3)	(4)
(*i*)	—	10	3
(*ii*)	10	20	5
(*iii*)	20	32	6
(*iv*)	32	50	8 of first run 10 for minimum size of weld

Notes : 1. When the minimum size of the fillet weld given in the table is greater than the thickness of the thinner part, the minimum size of the weld should be equal to the thickness of the thinner part. The thicker part shall be adequately preheated to prevent cracking of the weld.

2. Where the thicker part is more than 50 mm thick, special precautions like pre-heating should be taken.

(2) For the purpose of stress calculation in fillet welds joining faces inclined to each other, the effective throat thickness shall be taken as K times the fillet size, where K is a constant, depending upon the angle between fusion faces, as given in Table 10·20.

(3) The effective throat thickness of a complete penetration butt weld shall be taken as the thickness of the thinner part joined, and that of an incomplete penetration butt weld shall be taken as the minimum thickness of the weld metal common to the parts joined, excluding reinforcement.

10·10·14. Effective Length or Area of Weld

(1) The effective length of fillet weld shall be taken as only that length which is of the specified size and required throat thickness. In practice the actual length of weld is made of the effective length shown in drawing plus two times the weld size, but not less than four times the size of the weld.

(2) The effective length of butt weld shall be taken as the length of the continuous full size weld, but not less than four times the size of the weld.

Table 10·20. Values of K for Different Angles Between Fusion Faces

Angle Between Fusion Faces	60°–90°	91°–100°	101°–106°	107°–113°	114°–120°
Constant, K	0·70	0·65	0·60	0·55	0·50

(3) The effective area of a plug weld shall be considered as the nominal area of the hole in the plane of the faying surface. These welds shall not be designed to carry stresses.

(4) If the maximum length l_j of the side welds transferring shear along its length exceeds 150 times the throat size of the weld, t_t, the reduction in weld strength as per the long joint should be considered. For flange to web connection, where the welds are loaded for the full length, the above limitation would not apply.

10·15. Intermittent Welds

(1) Unless otherwise specified, the intermittent fillet welding shall have an effective length of not less than four times the weld size, with a minimum of 40 mm.

(2) The clear spacing between the effective lengths of intermittent fillet weld shall not exceed 12 and 16 times the thickness of thinner plate joined, for compression and tension joint respectively, and in no case be more than 200 mm.

(3) Unless otherwise specified, the intermittent butt weld shall have an effective length of not less than four times the weld size and the longitudinal space between the effective length of welds shall not be more than 16 times the thickness of the thinner part joined. The intermittent welds shall not be used in positions subject to dynamic, repetitive and alternating stresses.

10·10·16. Weld Types and Quality. For the purpose of this code, weld shall be fillet, butt, slot or plug or compound welds. Welding electrodes shall conform to IS 814.

(1) **Fillet welds.** Design strength of a fillet weld, f_{wd} shall be based on its throat area and shall be given by:

$$f_{wd} = f_{wn}/\gamma_{mw}$$

where $f_{wn} = f_u/\sqrt{3}$

f_u = smaller of the ultimate stress of the weld or of the parent metal, and

γ_{mw} = partial safety factor (*see* Table 10·5)

10·10·17. Butt Welds. Butt welds shall be treated as parent metal with a thickness equal to the throat thickness, and the stresses shall not exceed those permitted in the parent metal.

10·10·18. Stresses Due to Individual Forces. When subjected to either compressive or tensile or shear force alone, the stress in the weld is given by:

$$f_a \text{ or } q = \frac{P}{t_t\, l_w}$$

where f_a = calculated normal stress due to axial force, in N/mm^2;

q = shear stress, in N/mm^2;

P = force transmitted (axial force N or the shear force Q);

t_t = effective throat thickness of weld, in mm; and

l_w = effective length of weld, in mm.

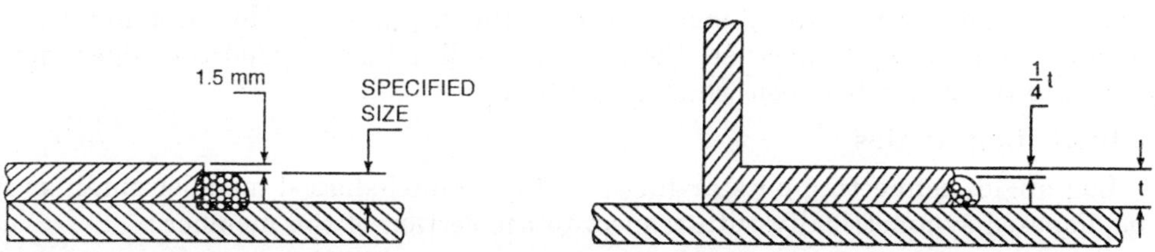

Fig. 10·15. Fillet welds on square edge of plate or round toe of rolled section.

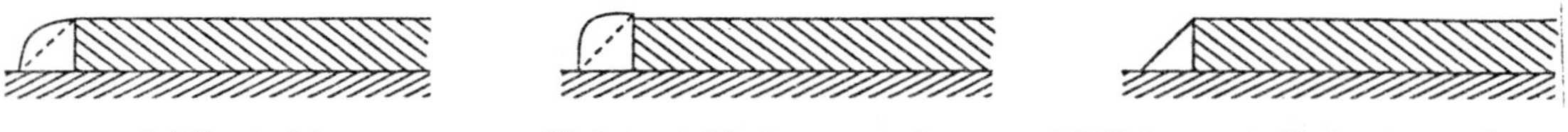

(*a*) Desirable (*b*) Acceptable because of full throat thickness (*c*) Not acceptable because of reduced throat thickness

Fig. 10·16. Full size fillet weld applied to the edge of a plate or section.

10·10·19. Combined bearing, bending and shear. Where bearing stress, f_{br} is combined with bending (tensile or compressive), f_b and shear stresses, q under the most unfavourable conditions of loading in butt welds, the equivalent stress, f_e as obtained from the following formula, shall not exceed the values allowed for the parent metal:

$$f_e = \sqrt{f_b^2 + f_{bf}^2 + f_b\, f_{br} + 3q^2}$$

where f_e = equivalent stress;

f_b = calculated stress due to bending, in N/mm²;

f_{br} = calculated stress due to bearing, in N/mm²; and

q = shear stress, in N/mm².

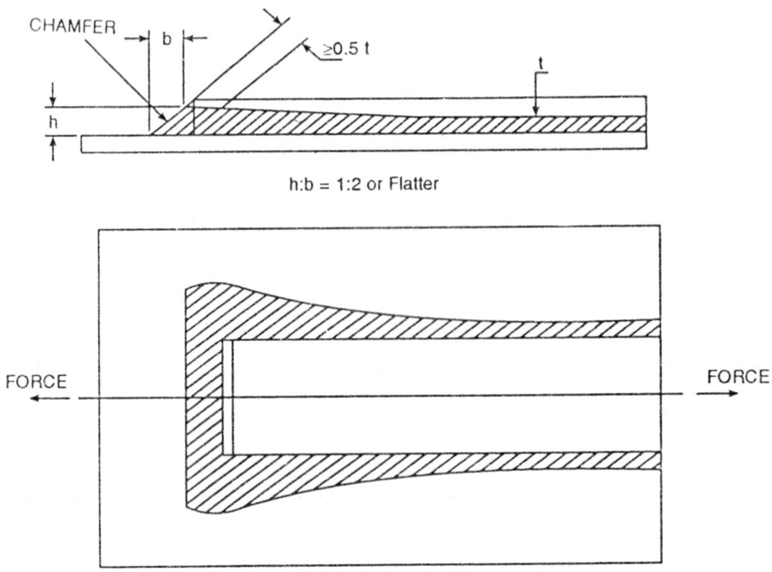

Fig. 10·17. End fillet weld normal to direction or force.

10·10·20. Where a packing is welded between two members and is less than 6 mm thick, or is too thin to allow provision of adequate welds or to prevent buckling, the packing shall be trimmed flush with the edges of the element subject to the design action and the size of the welds along the edges shall be increased over the required size by an amount equal to the thickness of the packing. Otherwise, the packing shall extend beyond the edges and shall be fillet welded to the pieces between which it is fitted.

10·10·21. Lug Angles

(1) Lug angles connecting outstanding leg of a channel-shaped member shall, as far as possible, be disposed symmetrically with respect to the section of the member.

(2) In the case of angle members, the lug angles and their connections to the gusset or other supporting member shall be capable of developing a strength not less than 20 percent

in excess of the force in the outstanding leg of the member, and the attachment of the lug angle to the main angle shall be capable of developing a strength not less than 40 percent in excess of the force in the outstanding leg of the angle.

10·11. Working Stress Design

10·11·1. General design requirements of Section 10·3 shall apply in this section.

The working stress shall be calculated applying respective partial load factor for service load/working load.

In load combinations involving wind or seismic loads, the permissible stresses in steel structural members may be increased by 33 percent. For anchor bolts and construction loads this increase shall be limited to 25 percent. Such an increase in allowable stresses should not be considered if the wind or seismic load is the major load in the load combination (such as acting along with the dead load alone).

10·11·2. Tension Members

Actual Tensile Stress. The actual tensile stress, f_t on the gross area of cross-section, A_g of plates, angles and other tension members shall be less than or equal to the smaller value of permissible tensile stresses, f_{at}, as given below:

Actual tensile stress, $f_t = T_s / A_g$

The permissible stress, f_{at} is smallest of the values as obtained below:

(*a*) As governed by yielding of gross section

$$f_{at} = 0{\cdot}6\ f_y$$

(*b*) As governed by rupture of net section

(1) *Plates under tension* : $f_{at} = 0{\cdot}69\ T_{dn}/A_g$

(2) *Angles under tension* : $f_{at} = 0{\cdot}69\ T_{dn}/A_g$

(*c*) As governed by block shear

$$f_{at} = 0{\cdot}69\ T_{db}/A_g$$

where T_s = actual tension under working (service) load,

A_g = gross area,

T_{dn} = design strength in tension of respective plate/angle calculated.

T_{db} = design block shear strength in tension of respective plate/angle calculated.

10·11·3. Compression Members. The actual compressive stress, f_c at working (service) load, P_s of a compression member shall be less than or equal to the permissible compressive stress, f_{ac} as given below:

Actual compressive stress, $f_c = P_s/A_c$

The permissible compressive stress, $f_{ac} = 0{\cdot}60\ f_{cd}$

where A_e = effective sectional area (gross area – hole area if not rounded or bolted).

f_{cd} = design compressive stress.

Column Bases. The thickness of a simple column base, t_s shall be calculated as:

$$t_s = \sqrt{3w\left(a^2 - 0{\cdot}3b^2\right)/f_{bs}}$$

where w = uniform pressure from below on the slab base due to axial compression;

a, b = larger and smaller projection of the slab base beyond the rectangle circumscribing the column, respectively; and

f_{bs} = permissible bending stress in column base equal to $0{\cdot}75\ f_y$.

10·12. Design and Detailing for Earthquake Loads

10·12·1. Steel frames shall be so designed and detailed as to give them adequate strength, stability and ductility to resist severe earthquakes in all zones classified in IS 1893 (Part I) without collapse.

10·12·2. Load and Load Combinations

Earthquake loads shall be calculated as per IS 1893 (Part I), except that the reduction factors recommended in 10·12·3 may be used.

In the limit state design of frames resisting earthquake loads, the load combinations shall conform to Table 10·4.

In addition the following load combination shall be considered as required as below:

(*a*) 1·2 Dead Load (DL) + 0·5 Live Load (LL) ± 2·5 Earthquake Load (EL); and

(*b*) 0·9 Dead Load (DL) ± 2·5 Earthquake Load (EL).

10·12·3. Response Reduction Factor. For structures designed and detailed as per the provision of this section, the response reduction factors specified in Table 10·21 may be used in conjunction with the provision in IS 1893 for calculating the design earthquake forces.

Table 10·21. Response Reduction Factor (*R*) for Building System

Sl. No.	*Lateral Load Resisting System*	*R*
(1)	(2)	(3)
(*i*)	*Braced Frame Systems* :	
	(*a*) Ordinary Concentrically Braced Frames (OCBF)	4
	(*b*) Special Concentrically Braced Frame (SCBF)	4·5
	(*c*) Eccentrically Braced Frame (EBF)	5
(*ii*)	*Moment Frame System*:	
	(*a*) Ordinary Moment Frame (*OMF*)	4
	(*b*) Special Moment Frame (SMF)	5

10·12·4. Connections, Joints and Fasteners

10·12·4·1. All bolts used in frames designed to resist earthquake loads shall be fully tensioned high strength friction grip (HSFG) bolts or turned and fitted bolts.

10·12·4·1. All welds used in frames designed to resist earthquake loads shall be complete penetration butt welds, except in column splices, which shall conform to 10·12·5·2.

10·12·4·1. Bolted joints shall be designed not to share load in combination with welds on the same faying surface.

10·12·5. Columns

10·12·5·1. Column Strength. When P_r/P_d is greater than 0·4, the requirements in 10·12·5·1·1 and 10·12·5·1·2 shall be met.

where P_r = required compressive strength of the member, and

P_d = design stress in axial compression as obtained from 10·7·1·2.

10·12·5·1·1. The required axial compressive and axial tensile strength in the absence of applied moment, shall be determined from the load combination in 10·12·2·3.

10·12·5·1·2. The required strength determined in 10·12·5·1·1 need not exceed either of the maximum load transferred to the column considering 1·2 times the nominal strength of the connecting beam or brace element, or the resistance of the foundation to uplift.

10·12·5·2. Column Splice

10·12·5·2·1. A partial-joint penetration groove weld may be provided in column splice, such that the design strength of the joints shall be at least equal to 200 percent of the required strength.

10·12·5·2·2. The minimum required strength for each flange splice shall be 1·2 times $f_y A_f$, where A_f is the area of each flange in the smaller connected column.

Continuity plates (tension stiffener) (*see* Fig. 10·18) shall be provided in all strong axis welded connections except in end plate connection.

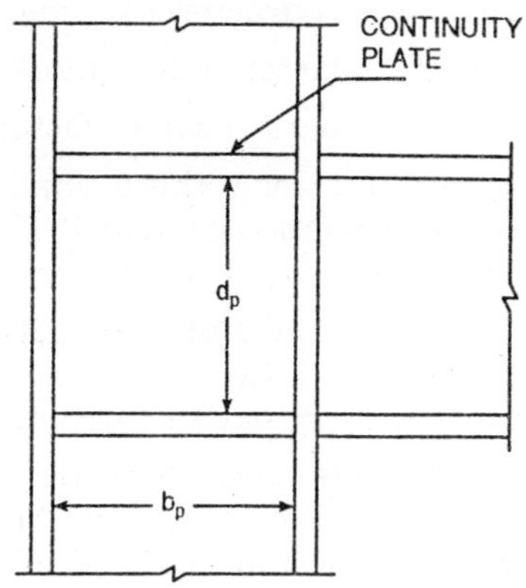

Fig. 10·18. Continuity plates.

10·13. Testing

10·13·1. Types of Test

Acceptance Test

(1) This is intended as a non-destructive test for confirming structural performance. It should be recognized that the loading applied to certain structures might cause permanent distortions. Such effects do not necessarily indicate structural failure in acceptance test. However, the possibility of their occurrence should be agreed to before testing.

The load for acceptance test, $F_{test,\,a}$ shall be determined from:

$F_{test,\,a}$ = (1·0 × self weight) + (1·15 × remainder of the permanent load) + (1·25 × variable load).

The assembly shall satisfy the following criteria:

(*a*) It shall demonstrate substantially linear behaviour under test loading, and

(*b*) On removal of the test load, the residual deflection shall not exceed 20 percent of the maximum-recorded deflection.

If the above criteria are not satisfied the test may be repeated one more time only, when the assembly shall satisfy the following criteria:

(*a*) It shall demonstrate substantially linear behaviour on the second application of test loading, and

(*b*) Corresponding recorded residual deflection in the second test shall not exceed 10 percent of the maximum deflection during the test.

(2) **Strength Test.** Strength test is used to confirm the calculated resistance of a structure or component. Where a number of items are to be constructed to a common design, and one or more prototypes are tested to confirm their strength, the others may be accepted without any additional test, provided they are similar in all relevant respects to the prototype.

Before carrying out the strength test, the specimen should first be subjected to and satisfy the acceptance test. Since the resistance of the assembly under test depends on the material properties, the actual yield strength of all the steel materials in the assembly shall be determined from coupon (test piece as defined in IS 1608) tests. The mean value of the yield strength, f_{ym} taken from such tests shall be determined with due regard to the importance of each element in the assembly. The strength test load $F_{test,\,s}$ (including self weight) shall be determined from:

$$F_{test,\, s} = \gamma_{mi}\, F_d \left(f_{ym} / f_y \right)$$

where f_y = characteristic yield stress of the material as assumed in the design

F_d = factored design load for the ultimate limit state, and

γ_{mi} = partial safety factor for the type of failure, as prescribed in this standard.

At this load there shall be no failure by buckling or rupture of any part of the structure or component tested. On removal of the test load, the deflection should decrease by at least 20 percent of the maximum deflection at $F_{test,\, s}$.

(3) **Test to Failure (Ultimate Strength Test).** The objective of a test to failure is to determine the design resistance from the ultimate resistance. In this situation it is still desirable to carry out the acceptance and strength tests, before test to failure.

Not less than three tests shall be carried out on nominally identical specimens. An estimate should be made of the anticipated ultimate resistance as a basis for such tests. During a test to failure, the loading shall first be applied in increments up to the strength test load. Subsequent load increments shall then be determined from consideration of the principal load deflection plot. The test load resistance, $F_{test.R}$ shall be determined as that load at which the specimen is unable to sustain any further increase in load. At this load, gross permanent distortion is likely to have occurred and in some cases such large gross deformation may define the test limit. If the deviation of any individual test result exceeds 10 percent of the mean value obtained for all the three tests, at least three more tests shall be carried out. When the deviation from the mean does not exceed 10 percent of the mean, the design resistance may be evaluated as given below:

(*a*) When the failure is ductile, the design resistance, F_d may be determined from:

$$F_d = 0{\cdot}9\, F_{test,\, Min.} \left(f_y / f_{ym} \right) / \gamma_{m0}$$

where $F_{test,\, Min.}$ = minimum test result from the test to failure

f_{ym} = average yield strength as obtained from the material tests, and

f_y = characteristic yield stress of the grade of steel.

(*b*) In the case of a sudden (brittle) rupture type failure, the design resistance may be determined from:

$$F_d = 0{\cdot}9\, F_{test,\, Min.} \left(f_u / f_{um} \right) / \gamma_{m1}$$

where f_u = characteristic ultimate stress of the grade of steel used, and

f_{um} = average ultimate tensile strength of the material obtained from tests.

(*c*) In the case of a sudden (brittle) buckling type failure, the design resistance shall be determined from:

$$F_d = 0{\cdot}75\, F_{test,\, Min.} \left(f_y / f_{ym} \right) / \gamma_{m0}$$

(*d*) In ductile buckling type failure in which the relevant slenderness λ can be reliably assessed, the design resistance may be determined from:

$$F_d = 0{\cdot}9\, F_{test,\, Min.} \left(\chi f_y / \chi_m f_{ym} \right) / \gamma_{m0}$$

where χ = reduction factor for the relevant buckling curve, and

χ_m = value of χ when the yield strength is f_{ym}.

(4) **Check Tests.** Where a component or assembly is designed on the basis of strength tests or tests to failure and a production run is carried out of such items, an appropriate number of samples (not less than two) shall be selected from each production batch at random for check tests.

The samples shall be carefully examined to ensure that they are similar in all respects to the prototype tested, particular attention being given to the following:

(*a*) Dimensions of components and connections;

(*b*) Tolerance and workmanship; and

(*c*) Quality of steel used, checked with reference to mill test certificates.

Where it is not possible to determine either the variations or the effect of variations from the prototype; an acceptance test shall be carried out as a check test.

In this check test, the deflections shall be measured at the same positions as in the acceptance test of the prototype. The maximum measured deflection shall not exceed 120 percent of the deflection recorded during the acceptance test on the prototype and the residual deflection should not be more than 105 percent of that recorded for the prototpye.

(5) **Test Conditions**

(*a*) Loading and measuring devices shall be calibrated in advance.

(*b*) The design of the test rig shall be such that:

(*i*) Loading system adequately simulates the magnitude and distribution of loading;

(*ii*) It allows the specimen to perform in a manner representative of service conditions;

(*iii*) Lateral and torsional restraint, if any, should be representative of those in service;

(*iv*) Specimen should be free to deflect under load according to service condition;

(*v*) Loading system shall be able to follow the movements of the specimen without interruption or abnormal restraints; and

(*vi*) Inadvertent eccentricities at the point of application of the test loads and at the supports are avoided.

(*c*) Test load shall be applied to the unit at a rate as uniform as practicable.

(*d*) Deflections should be measured at sufficient points of high movements to ensure that the maximum value is determined.

(*e*) If the magnitude of stresses in a specimen is to be determined, the strain at the desired location may be measured and the corresponding stress calculated.

(*f*) Prior to any test, preliminary loading (not exceeding the characteristic values of the relevant loads) may be applied and then removed, in order to set the test specimen on to the test rig.

(6) **Test Loading.** Where the self-weight of the specimen is not representative of the actual permanent load in service, allowance for the difference shall be made in the calculation of test loads to be applied.

On the attainment of maximum load for either acceptance or strength tests, this load shall be maintained for at least 1*h*. Reading of load and deflection shall be taken at intervals of 15 min and the loading shall be maintained constant until there is no significant increase in deflection during a 15 min period or until at least 1*h* has elapsed.

The test load shall be equal to the design load for the relevant limit state in proof testing.

(7) **Acceptance for Strength.** The test structure, sub-structure, member or connection shall be deemed to comply with the requirements for strength if it is able to sustain the strength test load for at least 15 min.

`It shall then be inspected to determine the nature and extent of any damage incurred during the test. The effects of the damage shall be considered and if necessary appropriate repairs to the damaged parts carried out.

Acceptance for Serviceability. The maximum deformation of the structure or member under the serviceability limit state test load shall be within the serviceability limit values appropriate to the structure.

10·14. Durability

General. A durable steel structure is one that performs satisfactorily the desired function in the working environment under the anticipated exposure condition during its service life, without deterioration of the cross-sectional area and loss of strength due to corrosion. The material used, the detailing, fabrication, erection and surface protection measures should all address the corrosion protection and durability requirements.

10·14·1. Requirements for Durability

(1) **Shape, Size, Orientation of Members, Connections and Details.** The design, fabrication and erection details of exposed structures should be such that good drainage of water is ensured. Standing pool of water, moisture accumulation and rundown of water for extended duration shall be avoided.

The details of connections should ensure that:

(*a*) All exposed surfaces are easily accessible for inspection and maintenance; and

(*b*) All surfaces, not so easily accessible are completely sealed against ingress of moisture.

10·14·2. Exposure Condition

General environment. The general environment, to which a steel structure is exposed during its working life is classified into five levels of severity, as given in Table 10·22.

Table 10·22. Environmental Exposure Conditions

Sl. No.	*Environmental Classification*	*Exposure Conditions*
(1)	(2)	(3)
(*i*)	Mild	Surfaces normally protected against exposure to weather or aggressive condition as in interior of buildings, except when located in coastal areas
(*ii*)	Moderate	Structural steel surfaces: (*a*) exposed to condensation and rain (*b*) continuously under water (*c*) exposed to non-aggressive soil/ground water (*d*) sheltered from saturated salt air in coastal areas
(*iii*)	Severe	Structural steel surfaces: (*a*) exposed to severe frequent rain (*b*) exposed to alternate wetting and drying (*c*) severe condensation (*d*) completely immersed in sea water (*e*) exposed to saturated salt air in coastal area
(*iv*)	Very severe	Structural steel surface exposed to: (*a*) sea water spray (*b*) corrosive fumes (*c*) aggressive sub soil or ground water
(*v*)	Extreme	Structural steel surfaces exposed to: (*a*) tidal zones and splash zones in the sea (*b*) aggressive liquid or solid chemicals

10·14·3. Abrasion. Specialist literature may be referred for durability of surfaces exposed to abrasive action as in machinery, conveyor belt support system, storage bins for grains or aggregates.

10·14·4. Exposure to sulphate attack. Appropriate coatings may be used when surfaces of structural steel are exposed to concentration of sulphates (SO_3) in soil, ground water, etc.

When exposed to very high sulphate concentrations of more than 2 percent in soil and 5 percent in water, some form of lining such as polyethylene, polychloroprene sheet or surface coating based on asphalt, chlorinated rubber, epoxy or polymethane material should be used to completely avoid access of the solution to the steel surface.

10·14·5. Corrosion Protection Methods. The methods of corrosion protection are governed by actual environmental conditions as specified in IS 9077 and IS 9172. The main corrosion protection methods are given below:

(*a*) Controlling the electrode potential,

(*b*) Inhibitors, and

(*c*) Inorganic/metal coatings or organic/paint systems.

10·14·6. Surface Protection. In the case of mild exposure, a coat of primer after removal of any loose mill scale may be adequate. As the exposure condition becomes more critical, more elaborate surface preparations and coatings become necessary. In case of extreme environmental classification, protection shall be as per specialist literature. Table 10·23 gives guidance to protection of steelwork for different desired lives.

Table 10·23(*a*) Protection Guide for Steel Work Application—Desired Life of Coating System in Different Environments

Sl. No.	*Atmospheric Condition / Environmental Classification*	*Coating System*					
		1	*2*	*3*	*4*	*5*	*6*
(1)	(2)	(3)	(4)	(5)	(6)	(7)	(8)
(*i*)	Normal inland (rural and urban areas), mild	12 years	18 years	20 years	About 20 years	About 20 years	Above 20 years
(*ii*)	Polluted inland (high airborne sulphur dioxide), moderate	10 years	15 years	12 years	About 18 years	15-20 years	Above 20 years
(*iii*)	Normal coastal (as normal inland plus high airborne salt levels), severe	10 years	12 years	20 years	About 20 years	About 20 years	Above 20 years
(*iv*)	Polluted coastal (as polluted inland plus high airborne salt levels), very severe or extreme	8 years	10 years	10 years	About 15 years	15-20 years	Above 20 years

Table 10·23 (*b*) Protection Guide for Steel Work Application—Specification for Different Coating System (Shop Applied Treatments

Sl. No.	*Protection*	*Coating System*					
		1	2	3	4	5	6
(1)	(2)	(3)	(4)	(5)	(6)	(7)	(8)
(*i*)	Surface preparation	Blast clean	Blast clean	Blast clean	Blast clean	Girt blast	Blast clean

Table (contd.)

Table (contd.)

Sl. No.	*Protection*	*Coating System*					
		1	2	3	4	5	6
(1)	(2)	(3)	(4)	(5)	(6)	(7)	(8)
(*ii*)	Pre-fabrication primer	Zinc phosphate epoxy, 20 μm	2 pack zinc-rich epoxy, 20 μm	—	2 pack zinc-rich epoxy, 20 μm	—	Ethyl zinc silicate, 20 μm
(*iii*)	Post-fabrication primer	High-build zinc phosphate modified alkyd, 60 μm	2 pack zinc-rich epoxy, 20 μm	Hot dip galvanized 85 μm	2 pack zinc rich epoxy, 25 μm	Sprayed zinc or aluminium	Ethyl zinc silicate, 60 μm
(*iv*)	Intermediate coat	—	High-build zinc phosphate, 25 μm	—	2 pack epoxy micaceous iron oxide	Sealer	Chlorinated rubbed alkyd, 35 μm
(*v*)	Top coat	—	—	—	2 pack epoxy micaceous iron oxide, 85 μm	Sealer	—

Table 10·23(*c*) Protection Guide for Steel Work Application—Specification for Different Coating System (Site Applied Treatments)

Sl. No.	*Protection*	*Coating System*					
		1	*2*	*3*	*4*	*5*	*6*
(1)	(2)	(3)	(4)	(5)	(6)	(7)	(8)
(*i*)	Surface preparation	As necessary	As necessary	No site treatment	As necessary	No site treatment	As necessary
(*ii*)	Primer	Touch in	Touch in	—	—	—	Touch in
(*iii*)	Intermediate coat	—	Modified Alkyd Micaceous iron oxide, 50 μm	—	Touch in	—	High-build Micaceous iron oxide Chlorinated rubber Micaceous, 75 μm
(*iv*)	Top coat	High-build Alkyd finish, 60 μm	Modified Alkyd Micaceous iron oxide, 50 μm	—	High-build Chlorinated rubber	—	High-build oxide chlorinated rubber, 75 μm

10·15. Fire Resistance

The requirements shall apply to steel building elements designed to exhibit a required fire-resistance level (FRL) as per the relevant specifications.

(1) For protected steel members and connections, the thickness of protection material (h_i) shall be greater than or equal to that required to give a period of structural adequacy (PSA) greater than or equal to the required FRL.

(2) For unprotected steel members and connections, the exposed surface area to mass

ratio (k_{sm}) snall be less than or equal to that required to give a PSA equal to the required FRL.

Fire Resistance Level. The required FRL shall be as prescribed in IS 1641, IS 1642 and IS 1643, as appropriate or in building speçifications or as required by the user or the city ordinance. The FRL specified in terms of the duratinn (in minutes) of standard fire load without collapse depends upon:

(*a*) the purpose for which structure is used, and

(*b*) the time taken to evacuate in case of fire.

Period of Structural Adequacy (PSA). The calculation of PSA involves:

(*a*) Calculation of the strength of the element as a function of temperature of the element and the determination of limiting temperature;

(*b*) Calculation of the thermal response of the element, that is calculation of the variation of the temperature of the element or the parts of the element with time, when exposed to fire; and

(*c*) Determination of PSA at which the temperature of the element or parts of the element reaches the limiting temperature.

Determination of Period of Structural Adequacy. The period of structural adequacy (PSA) shall be determined using one of the following methods:

(*a*) *By calculation*:

(1) determining the limiting temperature of the steel (T_1) in accordance with 10·15·5; and

(2) determining the PSA as the time (in min) from the start of the test to the time at which the limiting steel temperature (t) is attained, in accordance with 10·15·6 for protected members and 10·15·7 for unprotected members.

(*b*) By direct application of a single test in accordance with 10·15·8; or

(*c*) By calculation of the temperature of the steel member by using a rational method of analysis confirmed by test data or by methods available in specialist literature.

Variation of Mechanical Properties of Steel with Temperature

Variation of Yield Stress with Temperature. The influence of temperature on the yield stress of steel shall be taken as follows for structures of mild steels and high strength low alloy steels:

$$\frac{f_y(T)}{f_y(20)} = \frac{905 - T}{905} \leq 1{\cdot}0$$

where $f_y(T)$ = yield stress of steel at T°C,

$f_y(20)$ = yield stress of steel at 20°C (room temperature) and

T = temperature of the steel in °C.

This relationship is shown by Curve 1 in Fig. 10·18.

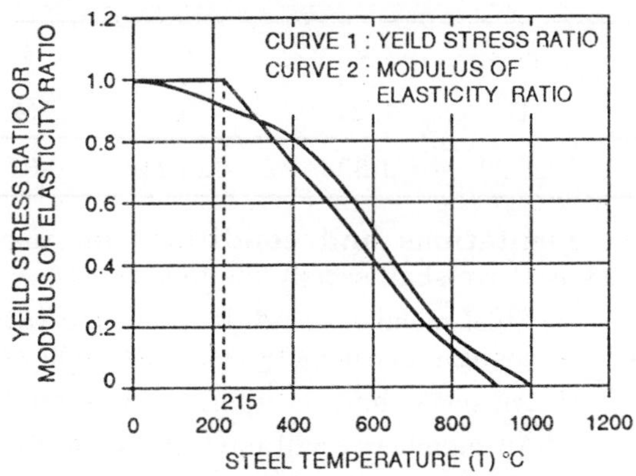

Fig. 10·19. Variation of Mechanical Properties of Steel with Temperature.

For temperature less than 215°C no reduction in the yield stress need to be considered.

Variation of Modulus of Elasticity with Temperature. The influence of temperature on the modulus of elasticity shall be taken as follows for structures of mild steels and high strength low alloy steels:

$$\frac{E(T)}{E(20)} = 1{\cdot}0 + \left[\frac{T}{2000\left[\ln\left(\frac{T}{1100}\right)\right]}\right]$$

when $0°C < T \le 600°C$

$$= \frac{690\left(1 - \frac{T}{1000}\right)}{T - 53{\cdot}5}$$

when $600°C < T \le 1000°C$

$E(T)$ = modulus of elasticity of steel at T °C, and

$E(20)$ = modulus of elasticity of steel at 20°C (room temperature).

This relationship is shown by curve 2 in Fig. 10·19.

Regression Analysis. The relationship between temperature (T) and time (t) for a series of tests on a group shall be calculated by least-square regression as follows:

$$t = k_0 + k_1 h_i + k_2 \frac{h_i}{k_{sm}} + k_3 T + k_4 h_i T + k_5 \frac{h_i T}{k_{sm}} + k_6 \frac{T}{k_{sm}}$$

where t = time from the start of the test, in min;

k_0 to k_6 = regression coefficients from test data;

h_i = thickness of fire protection material, in mm;

T = steel temperature, in degrees celsius obtained from test as given, $T > 250°C$; and

k_{sm} = exposed surface area to mass ratio, in 10^3 mm²/kg.

In lieu of test results, the values for coefficients in Table 10·24 may be used in the equation above when the test satisfies the conditions below:

Table 10·24. Regression Coefficients, *k*

k_0	k_1	k_2	k_3	k_4	k_5	k_6
(1)	(2)	(3)	(4)	(5)	(6)	(7)
– 25·90	1·698	– 13·71	0·0300	0·0005	0·5144	6·633

Limitations and conditions on use of regression analysis. Test data to be utilized as above shall satisfy the following:

(*a*) Steel members shall be protected with board, sprayed blanket or similar insulation materials having a dry density less than 1000 kg/m³;

(*b*) All tests shall incorporate the same fire protection system;

(*c*) All members shall have the same fire exposure condition;

(*d*) Test series shall include at least nine tests;

(*e*) Test series may include prototypes which have not been loaded provided that stickability has been demonstrated; and

(*f*) All members subject to a three-sided fire exposure condition shall be within a group in accordance with 10·15·9.

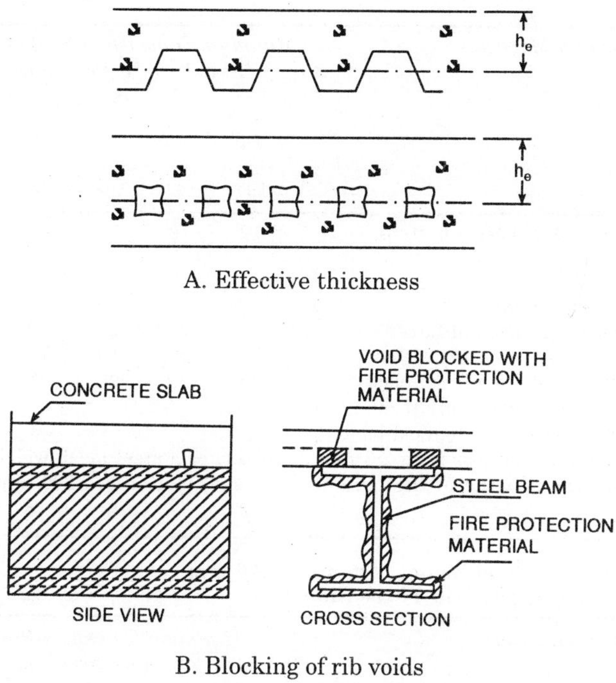

Fig. 10·20. Three sided fire exposure condition Requirements.

A regression equation obtained using prototypes with a four-sided fire exposure condition may be applied to a member with a three-sided fire exposure condition provided that stickability has been demonstrated for the three-sided case.

Fire Resistance Rating. The fire resistance rating of various building components such as walls, columns, beams, and floors are given in Fig. 10·20. Fire damage assessment of various structural elements of the building and adequacy of the structural repairs can be done by the fire resistance rating for encased steel column and beam (Table 10·25A and B).

Table 10·25A. Encased Steel Columns, 203 mm × 203 mm (Protection Applied on Four Sides)

Sl. No.	*Nature of Construction and Materials*	*Minimum Dimensions Excluding Any Finish, for a Resistance of mm*				
		1h	*1½ h*	*2h*	*3h*	*4h*
(1)	(2)	(3)	(4)	(5)	(6)	(7)
(*i*)	Hollow protection (without an air cavity over the flanges)					
	(*a*) Metal lathing with trowelled lightweight aggregate gypsum plaster[1)]	13	15	20	32	—
	(*b*) Plasterboard with 1·6 mm wire binding at 100 mm pitch, finished with lightweight aggregate gypsum plaster less than the thickness specified					
	(1) 9·5 mm plaster board	10	15	—	—	—
	(2) 19 mm plaster board	10	13	20	—	—
	(*c*) Asbestos insulating boards, thickness of board:					
	(1) Single thickness of board, with 6 mm cover fillets at transverse joints	—	19	25	—	—
	(2) Two layers, of total thickness	—	—	—	38	50
	(*d*) Solid bricks of clay, composition or sand lime, reinforced in every horizontal joint, unplastered	50	50	50	75	100
	(*e*) Aerated concrete blocks	60	60	60	—	—
	(*f*) Solid blocks of lightweight concrete hollow protection (with an air cavity over the flanges)	50	50	50	60	75

Table (contd.)

Table (contd.)

Sl. No.	Nature of Construction and Materials	Minimum Dimensions Excluding Any Finish, for a Resistance of mm				
		1h	1½ h	2h	3h	4h
(1)	(2)	(3)	(4)	(5)	(6)	(7)
(ii)	Asbestos insulating board screwed to 25 mm asbestos battens	12	19	—	—	—
(iii)	Solid protections					
	(a) Concrete, not leaner than 1 : 2 : 4 mix (unplastered):					
	(1) Concrete not assumed to be load bearing, reinforced[2)]	25	25	25	50	75
	(2) Concrete assumed to be load bearing	50	50	50	75	75
	(b) Lightweight concrete, not leaner than 1 : 2 : 4 mix (unplastered) concrete not assumed to be load bearing, reinforced[2)]	25	25	25	25	25

1) So fixed or designed, as to allow full penetration for mechanical bond.

2) Reinforcement shall consist of steel binding wire not less than 2·3 mm diameter, or a steel mesh weighing not less than 0·5 kg/m². In concrete protection, the spacing of the reinforcement shall not exceed 200 mm in any direction.

Table 10·25B. Encased Steel Beams, 406 mm × 176 mm (Protection Applied on Three Sides)

Sl. No.	Nature of Construction and Materials	Minimum Thickness Protection for a Fire Resistance of mm					
		½h	1h	1½h	2h	3h	4h
(1)	(2)	(3)	(4)	(5)	(6)	(7)	(8)
(i)	Hollow protection (without an air cavity beneath the lower flanges):						
	(a) Metal lathing with trowelled lightweight aggregate gypsum plaster[1)]	13	13	15	20	25	—
	(b) Plasterboard with 1·6 mm wire binding at 100 mm pitch, finished with lightweight aggregate gypsum plaster less than the thickness specified[2)]						
	(1) 9·5 mm plaster board	10	10	15	—	—	—
	(2) 19 mm plaster board	10	10	13	20	—	—
	(c) Asbestos insulating boards, thickness of board:						
	(1) Single thickness of board, with 6 mm cover fillets at transverse joints	—	—	19	25	—	—
	(2) Two layers, of total thickness	—	—	—	—	38	50
(ii)	Hollow protection (with an air cavity below the lower flange)						
	(a) Asbestos insulating board screwed to 25 mm asbestos battens	9	12	—	—	—	—
(iii)	Solid protections						
	(a) Concrete, not leaner than 1 : 2 : 4 mix (unplastered):						
	(1) Concrete not assumed to be load bearing, reinforced[3)]	25	25	25	25	50	75
	(2) Concrete assumed to be load bearing	50	50	50	50	75	75
	(b) Lightweight concrete, not leaner than 1 : 2 : 4 mix (unplastered)[4)]	25	25	25	25	40	60

1) So fixed or designed, as to allow full penetration for mechanical bond.

2) Where wire binding cannot be used, expert advice should be sought regarding alternative methods of support to enable the lower edges of the plasterboard to be fixed together and to the lower flange, and for the top edge of the plasterboard to be held in position.

3) Reinforcement shall consist of steel binding wire not less than 2·3 mm in diameter, or a steel mesh weighing not less than 0·5 kg/m². In concrete protection, the spacing of the reinforcement shall not exceed 200 mm in any direction.

4) Concrete not assumed to be load bearing, reinforced.

Table 10·26. Straightness Tolerances Incorporated in Design Rules

Sl. No.	*Criterion*	*Permitted Deviation*
(1)	(2)	(3)
(*i*)	Straightness of a column (or other compression member) between points which will be laterally restrained on completion of erection	0·001*L* generally, and 0·002*L* for members with hollow cross-sections; where, *L* is the length between points which will be laterally restrained.
(*ii*)	Straightness of a compression flange of a beam, relative to the weak axis, between points, which will be laterally restrained on completion of erection	0·001*L* generally, and 0·002*L* for members with hollow cross-sections; where, *L* is the length between points which will be laterally restrained

ANNEXURE-A
Determination of Effective Length of Columns

A-1. Method for Determining Effective Length of Columns in Frames

In the absence of a more exact analysis, the effective length of columns in framed structures may be obtained by multiplying the actual length of the column between the centres of laterally supporting members (beams) given in Fig. 10·21 and 10·22 with the effective length factor *K*, calculated by using the equations given below, provided the connection between beam and column is rigid type:

(*a*) **Non-sway Frames (Braced Frame).** A frame is designated as non-sway frame if the relative displacement between the two adjacent floors is restrained by bracings or shear walls. The effective length factor, *K*, of column in non-sway frames is given by (*see* Fig. 10·20)

$$K = \frac{[1 + 0{\cdot}145(\beta_1 + \beta_2) - 0{\cdot}265\,\beta_1\beta_2]}{[2 - 0{\cdot}364(\beta_1 + \beta_2) - 0{\cdot}247\,\beta_1\beta_2]}$$

(*b*) **Sway Frames (Moment Resisting Frames).** The effective length factor *K*, of column in sway frames is given by (*see* Fig. 10·21):

$$K = \left[\frac{1 - 0{\cdot}2(\beta_1 + \beta_2) - 0{\cdot}12\,\beta_1\beta_2}{1 - 0{\cdot}8(\beta_1 + \beta_2) + 0{\cdot}6\,\beta_1\beta_2}\right]^{0{\cdot}5}$$

where β_1, β_2 are given, $\beta = \dfrac{\sum K}{\sum K_C + \sum K_b}$

K_c, K_b = effective flexural stiffness of the columns and beams meeting at the joint at the ends of the columns and rigidly connected at the joints, and these are calculated by:

$$K = C\,(I/L)$$

I = moment of inertia of the member about an axis perpendicular to the plan of the frame.

L = Length of the member equal to centre-to-centre distance of the intersecting member.

C = Correction factor as shown in Table 10·27.

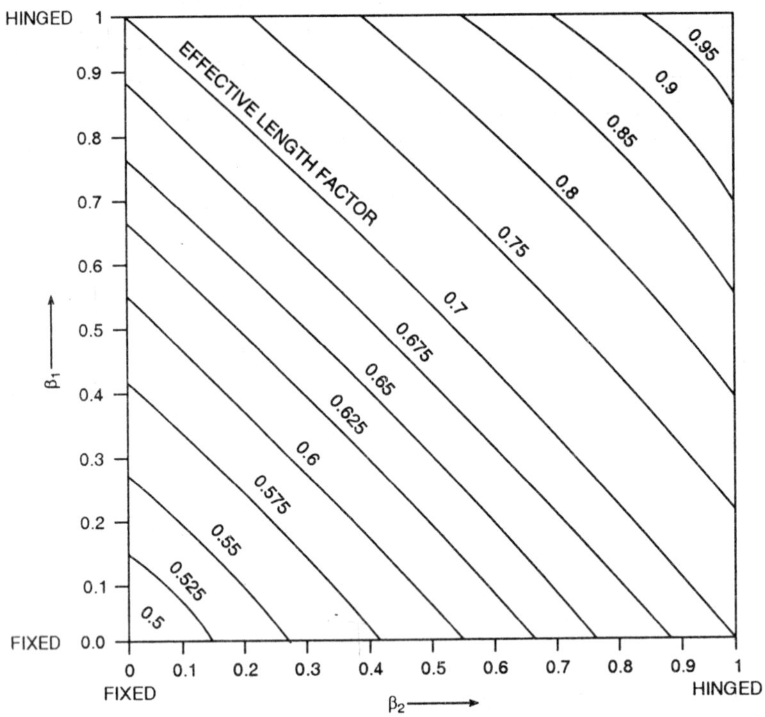

Fig. 10·21. Column effective length factor—non-sway frame.

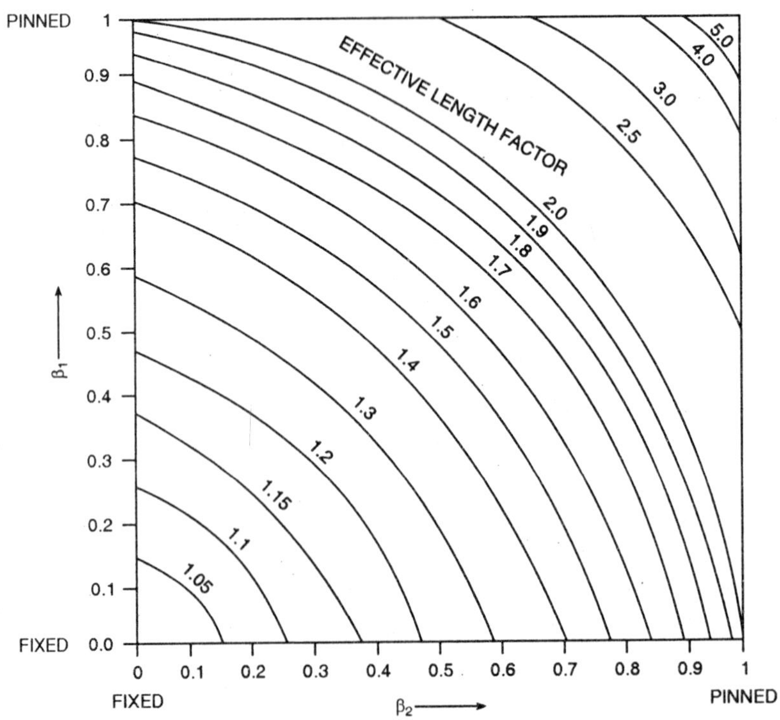

Fig. 10·22. Column effective length factor—sway frame.

Table 10·27. Correction Factors for Effective Length

Sl. No.	*Far End Condition*	*Correction Factor, C*	
		Braced Frame	*Unbraced Frame*
(1)	(2)	(3)	(4)
(*i*)	Pinned	$1{\cdot}5(1-\bar{n})$	$1{\cdot}5(1-\bar{n})$
(*ii*)	Rigidly connected to column	$1{\cdot}0(1-\bar{n})$	$1{\cdot}0(1-0{\cdot}2\,\bar{n})$
(*iii*)	Fixed	$2{\cdot}0(1-0{\cdot}4\,\bar{n})$	$0{\cdot}67(1-0{\cdot}4\,\bar{n})$

Note : $\bar{n} = \dfrac{P}{P_e}$

where P_e = elastic buckling load, and P = applied load.

A-2. Method for Determining Effective Length for Stepped Columns (*see* 10·7·2·2)

Single Stepped Columns. Effective length in the plane of stepping (bending about axis *z-z*) for bottom, and top parts for single stepped column shall be taken as follows (*see also* Fig. 10·23).

Note : The provisions of given here are applicable to intermediate columns as well with stepping on either side, provided appropriate values of l_1 and l_2 are taken.

A-3. Effective Length for Double Stepped Columns

Effective lengths in the plane of steppings (bending about axis *z-z*) for bottom, middle and top parts for a double stepped column shall be taken as follows (*see* also Fig. 10·23).

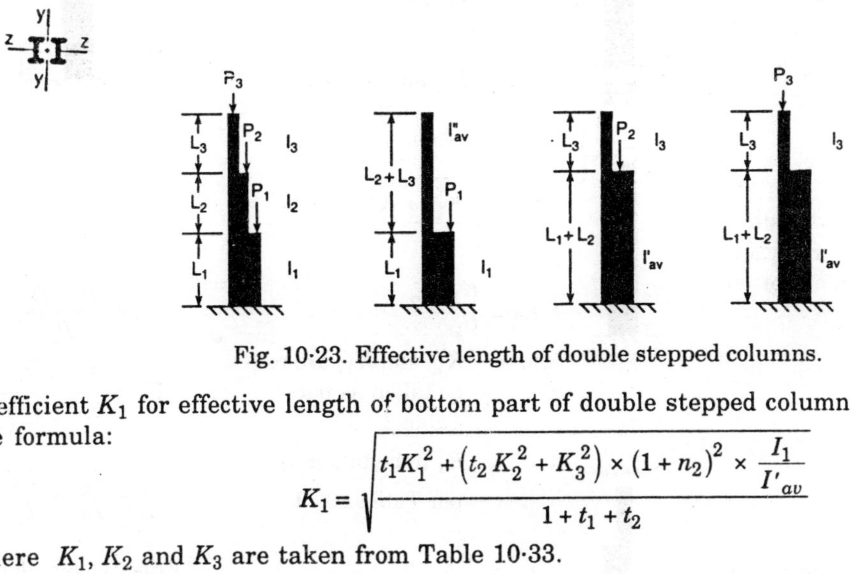

Fig. 10·23. Effective length of double stepped columns.

Coefficient K_1 for effective length of bottom part of double stepped column shall be taken from the formula:

$$K_1 = \sqrt{\frac{t_1 K_1^2 + \left(t_2 K_2^2 + K_3^2\right) \times (1 + n_2)^2 \times \dfrac{I_1}{I'_{av}}}{1 + t_1 + t_2}}$$

where K_1, K_2 and K_3 are taken from Table 10·33.

$$t_1 = \frac{P_1}{P_3},\quad t_2 = \frac{P_2}{P_3},\quad n_2 = \frac{L_2}{L_1}$$

I'_{av} = average value of moment of inertia for the lower and middle parts

$$= \frac{I_1 L_1 + I_2 L_2}{L_1 + L_2}$$

I''_{av} = average value of moment of inertia for the middle and top parts

$$= \frac{I_2 L_2 + I_3 L_3}{L_2 + L_3}$$

Value of coefficient K_2 for middle part of column is given by formula:

$$K_2 = \frac{K_1}{C_2}, \text{ and}$$

coefficient K_3 for the top part of the column is given by:

$$K_3 = \frac{K_1}{C_3} \le 3$$

where $$C_2 = \frac{L_2}{L_1}\sqrt{\frac{I_1(P_2+P_3)}{I_2(P_1+P_2+P_3)}}, \quad C_2 = \frac{L_3}{L_1}\sqrt{\frac{I_1P_3}{I_3(P_1+P_2+P_3)}}$$

Note : The provisions of D-3 are applicable to intermediate columns as well with steppings on either side, provided appropriate values of I_1, I_2 and I_3 are taken.

Table 10·28. Effective Length of Single Stepped Columns

Sl. No. (1)	*Degree of End Restraint* (2)	*Sketch* (3)	*Effective Length Coefficients* (4)	*Column Parameters for All Cases* (5)
(*i*)	Effectively held in position and restrained against rotation at both ends		$K_1 = \sqrt{\frac{K_{12}^2 + K_{11}^2(\alpha-1)}{\alpha}}$ $K_2 = \frac{K_1}{C_1} \le 3$ where K_{12} and K_{11} are to be taken as per Table 10·29.	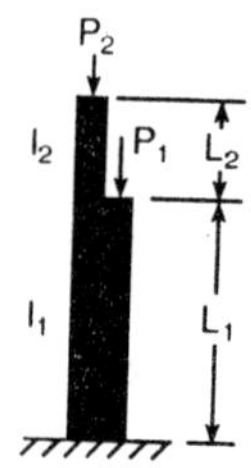
(*ii*)	Effectively held in position at both ends and restrained against rotation at bottom end only		$K_1 = \sqrt{\frac{K_{12}^2 + K_{11}^2(\alpha-1)}{\alpha}}$ $K_2 = \frac{K_1}{C_1} \le 3$ where K_{12} and K_{11} are to be taken as per Table 10·30	$a = \frac{P_1+P_2}{P_2}$ $C_1 = \frac{L_2}{L_1}\sqrt{\frac{I_1}{I_2\alpha}}$ $\frac{i_2}{i_1} = \frac{I_2}{L_2} \times \frac{L_3}{I_1}$
(*iii*)	Effectively held in position and restrained against rotation at bottom end, and top end held against rotation but not held in position		K_1 to be taken as per Table 10·31 $K_2 = \frac{K_1}{C_1} \le 3$	Effective length of bottom of column in plane of stepping $= K_1L_1$
(*iv*)	Effectively held in position and restrained against rotation at bottom end, and top end neither held against rotation nor held in position		K_1 to be taken as per Table 10·32 $K_2 = \frac{K_1}{C_1} \le 3$	Effective length of top part of column in plane of stepping $= K_2L_2$

Table 10·29. Coefficients of Effective Lengths K_{12} and K_{11} for Columns with Both Ends Effectively Held in Position and Restrained Against Rotation

I_2/I_1	Coefficients K_{12} and K_{11} for L_2/L_1 Equal to 0·1	0·2	0·3	0·4	0·5	0·6	0·7	0·8	0·9	1·0	1·2	1·4	1·6	1·8	2·0
	Coefficient K_{12} ($P_1 = 0$)														
0·05	0·74	0·94	1·38	1·60	1·87	2·07	2·23	2·39	2·52	2·67	3·03	3·44	3·85	4·34	4·77
0·1	0·67	0·76	1·00	1·20	1·42	1·61	1·78	1·92	2·04	2·20	2·40	2·60	2·86	3·18	3·41
0·2	0·64	0·70	0·79	0·93	1·07	1·23	1·41	1·50	1·60	1·72	1·92	2·11	2·28	2·45	2·64
0·3	0·62	0·68	0·74	0·85	0·95	1·06	1·18	1·28	1·39	1·48	1·67	1·82	1·96	2·12	2·20
0·4	0·60	0·66	0·71	0·77	0·82	0·93	0·99	1·08	1·17	1·23	1·39	1·53	1·66	1·79	1·92
0·5	0·59	0·65	0·70	0·77	0·82	0·93	0·99	1·08	1·17	1·23	1·39	1·53	1·66	1·79	1·92
1·0	0·55	0·60	0·65	0·70	0·75	0·80	0·85	0·90	0·95	1·00	1·10	1·20	1·30	1·40	1·50
	Coefficient K_{11} ($P_2 = 0$)														
0·05	0·65	0·67	0·71	0·85	1·01	1·17	1·31	1·41	1·50	1·57	1·67	1·74	1·78	1·82	1·86
0·1	0·64	0·65	0·65	0·65	0·78	0·92	1·05	1·15	1·25	1·33	1·45	1·55	1·62	1·68	1·71
0·2	0·62	0·64	0·65	0·65	0·66	0·73	0·83	0·92	1·01	1·09	1·23	1·33	1·41	1·48	1·54
0·3	0·60	0·63	0·64	0·65	0·66	0·67	0·73	0·81	0·89	0·94	1·09	1·20	1·28	1·35	1·41
0·4	0·58	0·63	0·63	0·64	0·64	0·66	0·68	0·75	0·82	0·88	1·01	1·10	1·19	1·26	1·32
0·5	0·57	0·61	0·63	0·64	0·64	0·65	0·68	0·72	0·77	0·83	0·94	1·04	1·12	1·19	1·25
1·0	0·55	0·58	0·60	0·61	0·62	0·63	0·65	0·67	0·70	0·73	0·80	0·88	0·93	1·01	1·05

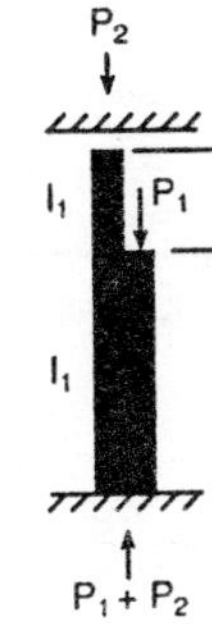

Note : Intermediate value may be obtained by interpolation.

Table 10·30. Coefficients of Effective Lengths K_{12} and K_{11} for Columns with Both Ends Effectively Held in Position and Restrained Against Rotation at Bottom End Only.

I_2/I_1	Coefficients K_{12} and K_{11} for L_2/L_1 Equal to 0·1	0·2	0·3	0·4	0·5	0·6	0·7	0·8	0·9	1·0	1·2	1·4	1·6	1·8	2·0
	Coefficient K_{12} ($P_1 = 0$)														
0·05	0·97	1·66	2·10	2·43	2·72	2·92	3·08	3·24	3·48	3·73	4·22	4·85	5·36	6·00	6·58
0·1	0·83	1·21	1·57	1·95	2·14	2·33	2·46	2·60	2·76	2·91	3·28	3·61	4·03	4·43	4·85
0·3	0·78	0·90	1·09	1·27	1·44	1·60	1·74	1·86	1·98	2·11	2·35	2·51	2·76	2·99	3·25
0·5	0·78	0·86	0·99	1·10	1·22	1·35	1·47	1·57	1·67	1·76	1·96	2·15	2·34	2·50	2·76
1·0	0·78	0·85	0·92	0·99	1·06	1·13	1·20	1·27	1·34	1·41	1·54	1·68	1·82	1·97	2·10
	Coefficient K_{11}/($P_2 = 0$)														
0·05	0·67	0·67	0·82	1·16	1·35	1·48	1·58	1·65	1·69	1·74	1·81	1·84	1·86	1·88	1·90
0·1	0·67	0·67	0·73	0·93	1·11	1·25	1·36	1·45	1·52	1·57	1·66	1·72	1·77	1·80	1·82
0·3	0·67	0·67	0·67	0·71	0·80	0·90	0·99	1·08	1·15	1·22	1·33	1·41	1·48	1·54	1·59
0·5	0·67	0·67	0·67	0·69	0·73	0·81	0·87	0·94	1·01	1·07	1·17	1·26	1·33	1·39	1·44
1·0	0·67	0·67	0·67	0·68	0·71	0·74	0·78	0·82	0·87	0·91	0·99	1·07	1·13	1·19	1·24

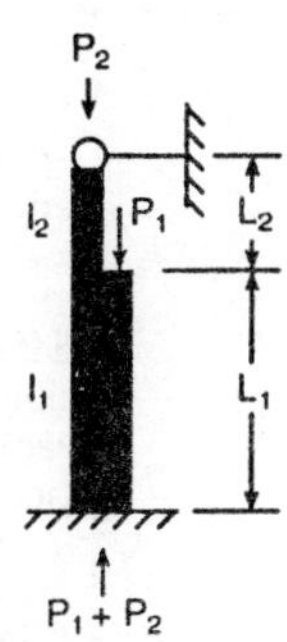

Note : Intermediate value may be obtained by interpolation.

Table 10·31. Coefficients of Effective Lengths K_1 for Columns Effectively Held in Position and Restrained Against Rotation at Bottom End and Top End Held Against Rotation but not Held in Position

	Coefficients K_1 for I_2/I_1 Equal to														
C_1	0·1	0·2	0·3	0·4	0·5	0·6	0·7	0·8	0·9	1·0	1·2	1·4	1·6	1·8	2·0
0	2·0	1·8	1·7	1·67	1·6	1·55	1·50	1·4	1·43	1·4	1·37	1·3	1·1	1·10	1·0
0·5	2·0	1·9	1·8	1·74	1·6	1·65	1·61	1·5	1·55	1·5	—	—	—	—	—
1·0	2·0	2·0	2·0	2·00	2·0	2·00	—	—	—	—	—	—	—	—	—
1·5	2·0	2·2	2·3	2·48	—	—	—	—	—	—	—	—	—	—	—
2·0	2·0	2·6	2·9	—	—	—	—	—	—	—	—	—	—	—	—
2·5	2·5	3·1	3·5	—	—	—	—	—	—	—	—	—	—	—	—
3·0	3·0	3·7	4·1	—	—	—	—	—	—	—	—	—	—	—	—

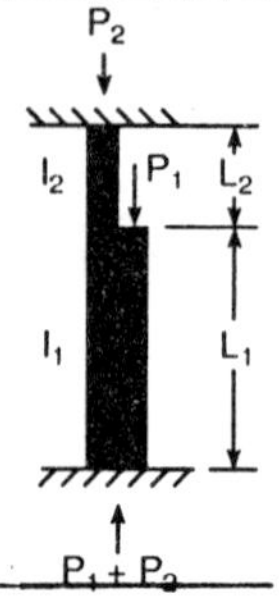

Note : Intermediate values may be obtained by interpolation.

Table 10·32. Coefficients of Effective Lengths K_1 for Columns with Top Ends Free and Bottom End Effectively Held in Position and Restrained Against Rotation

	Coefficients K_1 for I_2/I_1 Equal to														
C_1	0·1	0·2	0·4	0·6	0·8	1·0	1·2	1·4	1·6	1·8	2·0	2·5	5·0	10	20
0	2·0	2·0	2·0	2·0	2·0	2·0	2·0	2·0	2·0	2·0	2·0	2·0	2·0	2·0	2·0
0·5	2·0	2·14	2·24	2·36	2·47	2·57	2·67	2·76	2·85	2·94	3·02	—	—	—	—
1·0	2·0	2·73	3·13	3·44	3·74	4·00	—	—	—	—	—	—	—	—	—
1·5	3·0	3·77	4·35	4·86	—	—	—	—	—	—	—	—	—	—	—
2·0	4·0	4·90	5·67	—	—	—	—	—	—	—	—	—	—	—	—
2·5	5·0	6·08	7·00	—	—	—	—	—	—	—	—	—	—	—	—
3·0	6·0	7·25	—	—	—	—	—	—	—	—	—	—	—	—	—

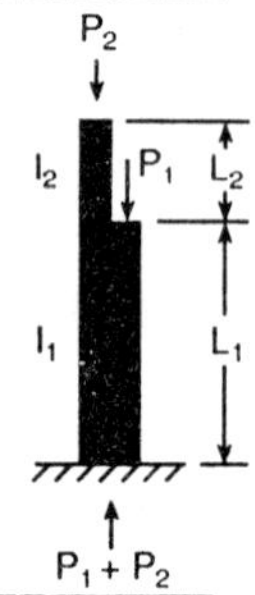

Note : Intermediate values may be obtained by interpolation.

Table 10·33. Values of K_1, K_2 and K_3

Sl. No.	*Degree of End Restraint*	*Sketch*	K_1	K_2	K_3	*Column Parameters for All Cases*
(1)	(2)	(3)	(4)	(5)	(6)	(7)
(*i*)	Effectively held in position and restrained against rotation at both ends		$K_1 = K_{11}$ where K_{11} is taken from Table 10·29	$K_2 = K_{11}$ where K_{11} is taken from Table 10·29	$K_3 = K_{12}$ where K_{12} is taken from Table 10·29	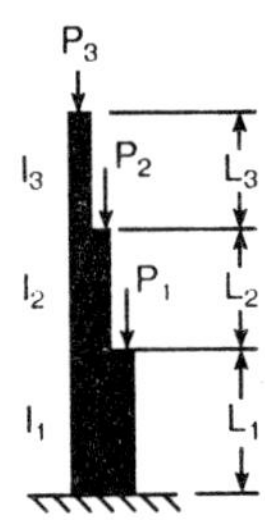
(*ii*)	Effectively held in position at both ends and restrained against rotation at bottom end only	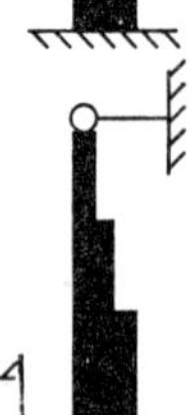	$K_1 = K_{11}$ where K_{11} is taken from Table 10·30	$K_2 = K_{11}$ where K_{11} is taken from Table 10·30	$K_3 = K_{12}$ where K_{12} is taken from Table10·30	
(*iii*)	Effectively held in position and restrained against rotation at bottom end, and top end held against rotation but not held in position		$K_1 = K_1$ where K_1 is taken from Table 10·31 with $C_1 = 0$	$K_2 = K_1$ where K_1 is taken from Table 10·31 with $C_1 = 0$	$K_3 = K_1$ where K_1 is taken from Table 10·31 with $C_1 = \frac{L_3}{L_1 + L_2}\sqrt{\frac{I_{av}}{I_3}}$	

Table (contd.)

Table (contd.)

Sl. No.	*Degree of End Restraint*	*Sketch*	K_1	K_2	K_3	*Column Parameters for All Cases*
(1)	(2)	(3)	(4)	(5)	(6)	(7)
(*iv*)	Effectively held in position and restrained against rotation at bottom end, and top end neither held against rotation nor against translation		$K_1 = 2$	$K_2 = 2$	$K_3 = K_1$ where K_1 is taken with $C_1 = \dfrac{L_3}{L_1 + L_2}\sqrt{\dfrac{I_{av}}{I_{31}}}$	

ANNEXURE-B
Connections (Splices)

B·1. General

The requirement for the design of splice and beam to column connection as well as recommendation for their design shall be as given below.

B·2. Beam Splices

For rolled section beam splices located away from the point of maximum moment, it may be assumed that the flange splice carries all the moment and the web splice carries the shear (*see* Fig. 10·24). However in the case of a deep girder, the total moment may be divided between the flange and the web in accordance with the stress distribution. The web connection should then be designed to resist its share of moment and shear. Even web splice is designed to carry only shear force, the moment about the centroid of the bolt group on either side of the splice should be designed for moment due to eccentricity.

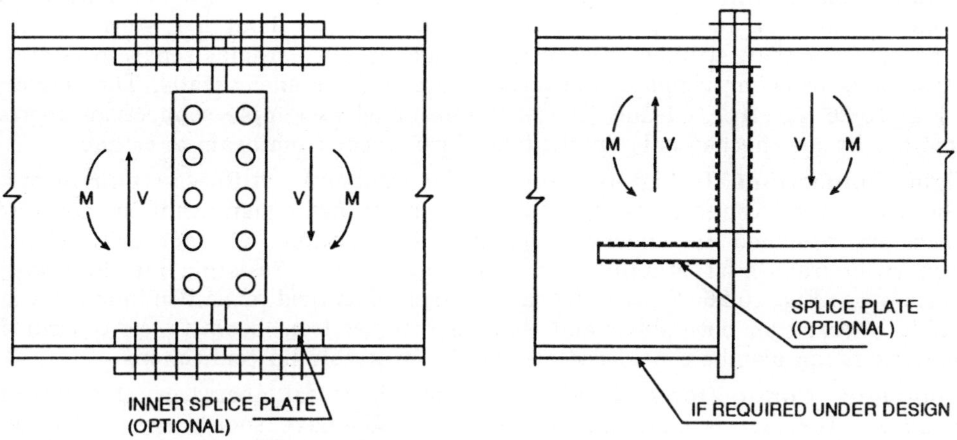

Conventional Splice (Typical) End Plate Splice

Fig. 10·24. Beam splices.

Flange joints should preferably not be located at points of maximum stress. Where splice plates are used (*see* Fig. 10·24), their area shall not be less than 5 percent in excess of the area of the flange element spliced; and their centre of gravity shall coincide, as nearly as possible with that of the element spliced. There shall be enough fasteners on each side of the splice to develop the load in the element spliced plus 5 percent but in no case should the strength developed be less than 50 percent of the effective strength of the material spliced. Wherever possible in welded construction, flange plates shall be joined by complete penetration butt welds. These butt welds shall develop the full strength of the plates. Whenever the flange width or thickness changes at the splice location, gradual transition shall be made in the width/thickness of the larger flange.

When beam splice is located at the point of inflection of a continuous beam, the flange splicing requirement given above may be relaxed appropriately.

B·3. Column Splice

Where the ends of compression members are faced for bearing over the whole area, they shall be spliced to hold the connected parts aligned. The ends of compression members faced for bearing shall invariably be machined to ensure perfect contact of surfaces in bearing (*see* Fig. 10·25).

Where such members are not faced for complete bearing the splices shall be designed to transmit all the forces to which the member is subjected at the splice location.

Wherever possible, splices shall be proportioned and arranged so that centroidal axis of the splice coincides as nearly as possible with the centroidal axes of the members joined, in order to avoid eccentricity; but where eccentricity is present in the joint, the resulting stress considering eccentricity shall be provided for.

If a column flange is subjected to significant tension or if the faces are not prepared for bearing, or if full continuity is required without slip, only HSFG bolts shall be used.

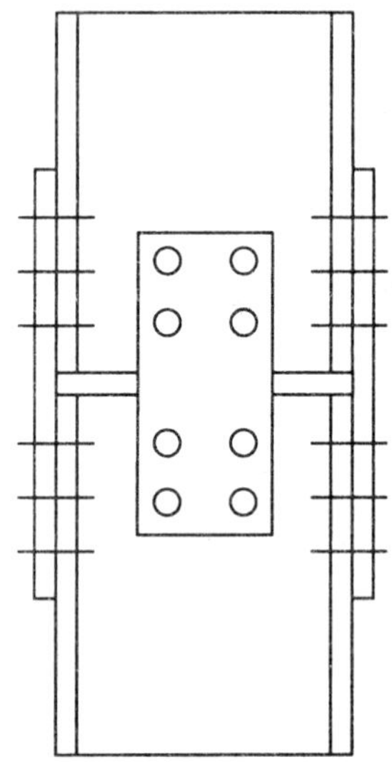

Fig. 10·25. Column splices (Typical)

B·4. Beam-to-Column Connections

Simple Connections. Simple connections are assumed to transfer only shear at some nominal eccentricity and typically used in frames up to about five stories in height, where strength rather than stiffness govern the design. In such frames separate lateral load resisting system is to be provided in the form of bracings or shear walls. The connections shown in Fig. 10·26 (A), (B), (C) and (D) can be assumed as simple connections in framed analysis and need to be checked only for the transfer of shear from beam to column.

Rigid Connections. In high-rise and slender structures, stiffness requirements may warrant the use of rigid connections. Rigid connections transfer significant moments to the columns and are assumed to undergo negligible deformations at the joint. These are necessary in sway frames for stability and also contribute in resisting lateral loads. The connections shown in Fig. 10·26 (E), (F), (G) can be assumed as rigid connection in frame analysis and need to be checked for both shear and moment transfer from beam to the column. Fully welded connections can also be considered as rigid beam to column connections.

Semi-rigid Connections. Semi-rigid connections fall between the two types mentioned above. The fact is that simple connections do have some degree of rotational rigidity as in the semi-rigid connections. Similarly rigid connections do experience some degree of joint deformation and this can be utilised to reduce the joint design moments.

The moment-rotation relationship of the connections have to be determined based on experiments conducted for the specific design or based on the relationship derived from tests, presented in specialist literature. The simplest method of analysis will be to idealize the connection as an equivalent rotational spring with either a bilinear or non-linear moment rotation characteristics. The classification proposed by Bjorhovde combined with the Frey-Morris model can be used with convenience to model semi-rigid connections, as given in the next section.

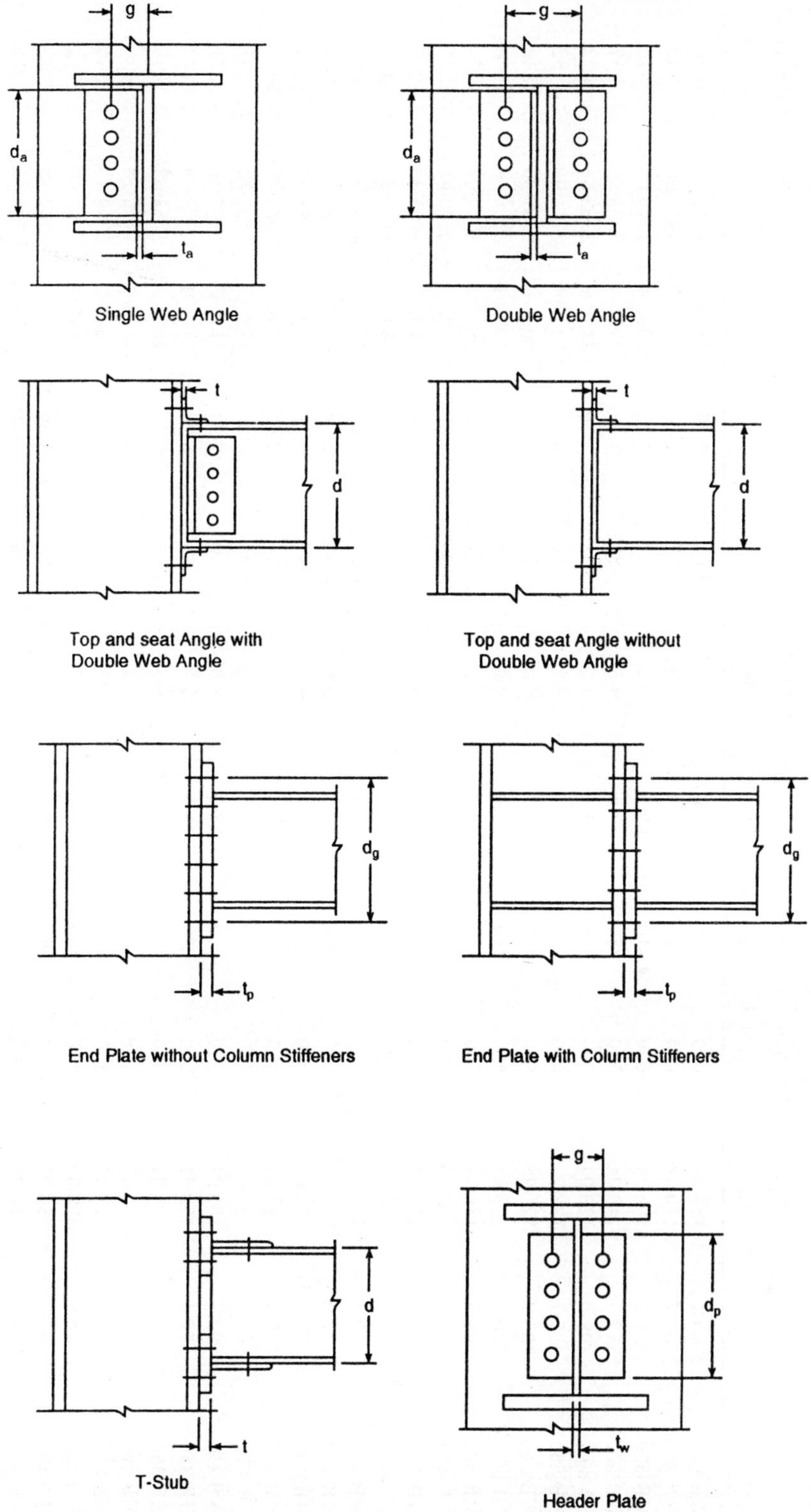

Fig. 10·26. Size parameter for various types of connections

Table 10·34. Plastic Properties of Beams

Designation	*Weight per Metre*	*Sectional Area*	*Depth of Section*	*Width of Flange*	*Thickness of Flange*	*Thickness of Web*	*Radii of Gyration*		*Section Modulus*	*Plastic Modulus*	*Shape Factor*
	kg/m	cm^2	(D) *mm*	(b_f) *mm*	(t_f) *mm*	(t_w) *mm*	(r_z) *cm*	(r_y) *cm*	(Z_{ez}) cm^3	(Z_{pz}) cm^3	(Z_{pz}/Z_{ez})
(1)	(2)	(3)	(4)	(5)	(6)	(7)	(8)	(9)	(10)	(11)	(12)
ISWB 600	*145·1	184·86	600	250	23·6	11·8	25·01	5·35	3854·2	4341·63	1·1265
ISWB 600	*133·7	170·38	600	250	21·3	11·2	24·97	5·25	3540·0	3986·66	1·1262
ISMB 600	*122·6	156·21	600	210	20·8	12	24·24	4·12	3060·4	3510·63	1·1471
ISWB 550	*112·5	143·34	550	250	17·6	10·5	22·86	5·11	2723·9	3066·29	1·1257
ISLB 600	*99·5	126·07	600	210	15·5	10·5	23·98	3·79	2428·9	2798·56	1·1522
ISMB 550	103·7	132·11	550	190	19·3	11·2	22·16	3·73	2359·8	2711·98	1·1492
ISWB 500	*95·2	121·22	500	250	14·7	9·9	20·77	4·96	2091·6	2351·35	1·1242
ISLB 550	*86·3	109·97	550	190	15·0	9·9	21·99	3·48	1933·2	2228·16	1·1526
ISMB 500	86·9	110·74	500	180	17·2	10·2	20·21	3·52	1808·7	2074·67	1·1471
ISHB 450	92·5	117·89	450	250	13·7	11·3	18·50	5·08	1793·3	2030·95	1·1325
ISHB 450	87·2	111·14	450	250	13·7	9·8	18·78	5·18	1742·7	1955·03	1·1218
ISLB 500	*75·0	95·50	500	180	14·1	9·2	20·10	3·34	1543·2	1773·67	1·1493
ISWB 450	79·4	101·15	450	200	15·4	9·2	18·63	4·11	1558·1	1760·59	1·1300
ISHB 400	82·2	104·66	400	250	12·7	10·6	16·61	5·16	1444·2	1626·36	1·1261
ISHB 400	77·4	98·66	400	250	12·7	9·1	16·87	5·26	1404·2	1556·33	1·1155
ISMB 450	*72·4	92·27	450	150	17·4	9·4	18·15	3·01	1350·7	1533·36	1·1500
ISLB 450	*65·3	83·14	450	170	13·4	8·6	18·20	3·20	1223·8	1401·35	1·1451
ISWB 400	66·7	85·01	400	200	13·0	8·6	16·60	4·04	1171·3	1290·19	1·1271
ISHB 350	72·4	92·21	350	250	11·6	10·1	14·65	5·22	1131·6	1268·69	1·1212
ISHB 350	67·4	85·91	350	250	11·6	8·3	14·93	5·34	1094·8	1213·53	1·1085
ISMB 400	*61·5	78·40	400	140	16·0	8·9	16·05	2·84	1020·0	1176·18	1·1498
ISLB 400	*56·9	72·43	400	165	12·5	8	16·33	3·15	965·3	1099·45	1·1390
ISWB 350	56·9	72·50	350	200	11·4	8·0	14·63	4·03	887·0	995·49	1·1223
ISHB 300	63·0	80·25	300	250	10·6	9·4	12·70	5·29	863·3	962·18	1·1145
ISHB 300	58·8	74·85	300	250	10·6	7·6	12·95	5·41	836·3	921·68	1·1021
ISMC 400	*49·5	62·93	400	100	15·3	8·6	15·48	2·83	754·1	891·03	1·1816
ISMB 350	52·4	66·70	350	140	14·2	8·1	14·32	2·84	779·0	889·57	1·1421
ISLB 350	49·5	63·01	350	165	11·4	7·4	14·45	3·17	751·9	851·11	1·1320
ISLC 400	*45·7	58·25	400	100	14·0	8·0	15·50	2·81	699·5	825·02	1·1794
ISWB 300	48·1	61·33	300	200	10·0	7·4	12·66	4·02	654·8	731·21	1·1167
ISHB 250	54·7	69·71	250	250	9·7	8·8	10·70	5·37	638·7	708·43	1·1092
ISLB 325	*43·1	54·90	325	165	9·8	7·0	13·41	3·05	607·7	687·76	1·1317

Table 10·34. (Continued)

Designation	Weight per Metre	Sectional Area	Depth of Section	Width of Flange	Thickness of Flange	Thickness of Web	Radii of Gyration		Section Modulus	Plastic Modulus	Shape Factor
	kg/m	cm^2	(D) mm	(b_f) mm	(t_f) mm	(t_w) mm	(r_z) cm	(r_y) cm	(Z_{ez}) cm^3	(Z_{pz}) cm^3	(Z_{pz}/Z_{ez})
(1)	(2)	(3)	(4)	(5)	(6)	(7)	(8)	(9)	(10)	(11)	(12)
ISHB 250	51·0	64·96	250	250	9·7	6·9	10·91	5·49	618·9	678·73	1·0967
ISMC 350	*42·1	53·66	350	100	13·5	8·1	13·66	2·83	571·9	672·19	1·1754
ISMB 300	*44·2	56·26	300	140	12·4	7·5	12·37	2·84	573·6	651·74	1·1362
ISLC 350	*38·8	49·47	350	100	12·5	7·4	13·72	2·82	532·1	622·95	1·1707
ISLB 300	*37·7	48·08	300	150	9·4	6·7	12·35	2·80	488·9	554·32	1·1338
ISHB 225	46·8	59·66	225	225	9·1	8·6	9·58	4·84	487·0	542·22	1·1134
ISWB 250	40·9	52·05	250	200	9·0	6·7	10·69	4·06	475·4	527·57	1·1097
ISHB 225	43·1	54·94	225	225	9·1	6·5	9·80	4·96	469·3	515·82	1·0987
ISMC 300	*35·8	45·64	300	190	13·6	7·6	11·81	2·61	424·2	496·77	1·1711
ISMB 250	37·3	47·55	250	125	12·5	6·9	10·39	2·65	410·5	465·71	1·1345
ISLC 300	*33·1	42·11	300	100	11·6	6·7	11·98	2·87	403·2	466·73	1·1576
ISLB 275	*33·0	42·02	275	140	8·8	6·4	11·31	2·61	392·4	443·09	1·1305
ISHB 200	40·0	50·94	200	200	9·0	7·8	8·55	4·42	372·2	414·23	1·1129
ISHB 200	37·3	47·54	200	200	9·0	6·1	8·71	4·51	360·8	397·23	1·1010
ISWB 225	33·9	43·24	225	150	9·9	6·4	9·52	3·22	348·5	389·93	1·1189
ISMC 250	*30·4	38·67	250	80	14·1	7·1	9·94	2·38	305·3	356·72	1·1684
ISMB 225	31·2	39·72	225	110	11·8	6·5	9·31	2·34	305·9	348·27	1·1385
ISLB 250	*27·9	35·53	250	125	8·2	6·1	10·23	2·33	297·4	338·69	1·1388
ISLC 250	28·0	35·65	250	100	10·7	6·1	10·17	2·89	295·0	338·11	1·1462
ISWB 200	28·8	36·71	200	140	9·0	6·1	8·46	2·99	262·5	293·99	1·1200
ISMC 225	*25·9	33·01	225	80	12·4	6·4	9·03	2·38	239·5	277·93	1·1605
ISLC 225	*24·0	30·53	225	90	10·2	5·8	9·14	2·62	226·5	260·13	1·1485
ISLB 225	*23·5	29·92	225	100	8·6	5·8	9·15	1·94	222·4	254·72	1·1453
ISMB 200	25·4	32·33	200	100	10·8	5·7	8·32	2·15	223·5	253·86	1·1358
ISHB 150	34·6	44·08	150	150	9·0	11·8	6·09	3·35	218·1	251·64	1·1538
ISHB 150	30·6	38·98	150	150	9·0	8·4	6·29	3·44	205·3	232·52	1·1326
ISHB 150	27·1	34·48	150	150	9·0	5·4	6·50	3·54	194·1	215·64	1·1110
ISMC 200	*22·1	28·21	200	75	11·4	6·1	8·03	2·23	181·9	211·25	1·1614
ISLC 200	*20·6	26·22	200	75	10·8	5·5	8·11	2·37	172·6	198·77	1·1516
ISWB 175	22·1	28·11	175	125	7·4	5·8	7·33	2·59	172·5	194·20	1·1258
ISLB 200	*19·8	25·27	200	100	7·3	5·4	8·19	2·13	169·7	184·34	1·1370
ISMB 175	*19·3	24·62	175	90	8·6	5·5	7·19	1·86	145·4	166·08	1·1422
ISMC 175	*19·1	24·38	175	75	10·2	5·7	7·08	2·23	139·8	161·65	1·1563

Table 10·34. (*Continued*)

Designation	*Weight per Metre*	*Sectional Area*	*Depth of Section*	*Width of Flange*	*Thickness of Flange*	*Thickness of Web*	*Radii of Gyration*		*Section Modulus*	*Plastic Modulus*	*Shape Factor*
	kg/m	cm^2	(*D*) *mm*	(b_f) *mm*	(t_f) *mm*	(t_w) *mm*	(r_z) *cm*	(r_y) *cm*	(Z_{ez}) cm^3	(Z_{pz}) cm^3	(Z_{pz}/Z_{ez})
(1)	(2)	(3)	(4)	(5)	(6)	(7)	(8)	(9)	(10)	(11)	(12)
ISLC 175	*17·6	22·40	175	75	9·5	5·1	7·16	2·38	131·3	150·36	1·1452
ISLB 175	*16·7	21·30	175	90	6·9	5·1	7·17	1·93	125·3	143·30	1·1437
ISJB 225	*12·8	16·28	225	80	5·0	3·7	8·97	1·58	116·3	134·15	1·1535
ISJC 200	13·9	17·08	200	70	7·1	4·1	8·08	2·18	116·1	133·12	1·1465
ISWB 150	17·0	21·67	150	100	7·0	5·4	6·22	2·09	111·9	126·86	1·1337
ISMC 150	16·4	20·88	150	75	9·0	5·4	6·11	2·21	103·9	119·82	1·1533
ISMB 150	14·9	19·00	150	80	7·6	4·8	6·18	1·66	96·9	110·48	1·1401
ISLC 150	14·4	18·36	150	75	7·8	4·8	6·16	2·37	93·0	106·17	1·1416
ISLB 150	14·2	18·08	150	80	6·8	4·8	6·17	1·75	91·8	104·50	1·1384
ISJC 175	*11·2	14·24	175	60	6·9	3·6	7·11	1·88	82·3	94·22	1·1449
ISJB 200	*9·9	12·64	200	60	5·0	3·4	7·86	1·17	78·1	90·89	1·1639
ISMB 125	13·0	16·60	125	75	7·6	4·4	5·20	1·62	71·8	81·85	1·1399
ISMC 125	12·7	16·19	125	65	8·1	5·0	5·07	1·92	66·6	77·15	1·1585
ISLB·125	11·9	15·12	125	75	6·5	4·4	5·19	1·69	65·1	73·93	1·1356
ISJC 150	9·9	12·65	150	55	6·9	3·6	6·9	1·73	62·8	72·04	1·1472
ISLC 125	10·7	13·67	125	65	6·6	4·4	5·11	2·05	57·1	65·45	1·1462
ISJB 175	*8·1	10·28	175	50	4·6	3·0	6·83	0·97	54·8	64·22	1·1799
ISMB 100	8·9	11·4	100	50	7·0	4·2	4·00	1·05	36·6	41·68	1·1389
ISJB 150	*7·1	9·01	150	50	4·6	3·0	5·98	1·01	42·9	49·57	1·1556
ISJC 125	7·9	10·07	125	50	6·6	3·0	5·18	1·60	43·2	49·08	1·1362
ISMC 100	9·2	11·70	100	50	7·5	4·7	4·00	1·49	37·3	43·83	1·1750
ISLB 100	8·0	10·21	100	50	6·4	4·0	4·06	1·12	33·6	38·89	1·1573
ISLC 100	7·9	10·02	100	50	6·4	4·0	4·06	1·57	32·9	38·09	1·1576
ISJC 100	*5·8	7·41	100	45	5·1	3·0	4·09	1·42	24·8	28·38	1·1442
ISMC 75	6·8	8·67	75	40	7·3	4·4	2·96	1·21	20·8	24·17	1·1904
ISLB 75	6·1	7·71	75	50	5·0	3·7	3·07	1·14	19·4	22·35	1·1522
ISLC 75	*5·7	7·26	75	40	6·0	3·7	3·02	1·26	17·6	20·61	1·1710

Note : Sections having 'weight per meter' marked with an asterik (*) may be chosen as the section is lighter having high Z_p as compared to sections below it.

Appendix : Steel Tables

Properties of Structural Steel Sections

Table 10A·1. Indian Standard Rolled Steel Beams

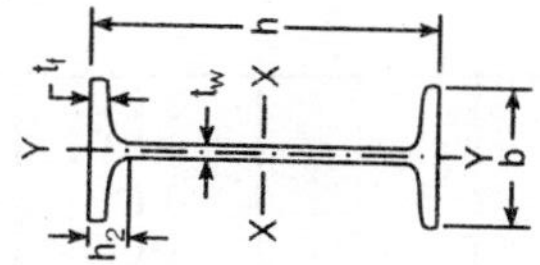

Designation (including Depth h in mm)	Weight per meter w kg	Sectional area A cm^2	Width of flange b mm	Thickness of flange t_f mm	Thickness of web t_w mm	Moment of Inertia I_{xx} cm^4	Moment of Inertia I_{yy} cm^4	Radius of Gyration r_{xx} cm	Radius of Gyration r_{yy} cm	Modulus of section Z_{xx} cm^3	Extreme Fibre to Root fillet h_2 mm	Torsional constant J cm^4	Plastic Modulus Z_p cm^3
ISWB 600	145·1	184·86	250	23·6	11·8	115626·6	5298·3	25·01	5·35	3854·2	46·05	249·3	4341·6
ISWB 600	133·7	170·38	250	21·3	11·2	106198·5	4702·5	24·97	5·25	3540·0	42·90	187·2	3986·7
ISMB 600	122·6	156·21	210	20·8	12·0	91813·0	2651·0	24·24	4·12	3060·4	45·15	158·1	3510·7
ISWB 550	112·5	143·34	250	17·6	10·5	74906·1	3740·6	22·86	5·11	2723·9	38·30	110·7	3066·3
ISLB 600	99·5	126·69	210	15·5	10·5	72867·6	1821·9	23·98	3·79	2428·9	39·90	74·1	2798·6
ISMB 550	103·7	132·11	190	19·3	11·2	64893·6	1833·8	22·16	3·73	2359·8	41·25	115·0	2712·0
ISWB 500	95·2	121·22	250	14·7	9·9	52290·9	2987·8	20·77	4·96	2091·6	34·50	68·2	2351·4
ISLB 550	86·3	109·97	190	15·0	9·9	53161·6	1335·1	21·99	3·48	1933·2	36·95	59·6	2228·2
ISMB 500	86·9	110·74	180	17·2	10·2	45218·3	1369·8	20·21	3·52	1808·7	37·95	77·5	2074·7
ISWB 450	79·4	101·15	200	15·4	9·2	35057·6	1706·7	1863	4·11	1558·4	33·00	59·6	1760·6
ISLB 500	75·0	95·50	180	14·1	9·2	38579·0	1063·9	20·10	3·34	1543·2	34·90	45·9	1773·7
ISMB 450	72·4	92·27	150	17·4	9·4	30390·8	834·0	18·15	3·01	1350·7	35·40	64·2	1553·4
ISLB 450	65·3	83·14	170	13·4	8·6	27536·1	853·0	18·20	3·20	1223·8	33·00	36·2	1401·4
ISWB 400	66·7	85·01	200	13·0	8·6	23426·7	1388·0	16·60	4·04	1171·3	29·75	37·2	1290·2
ISMB 400	61·6	78·46	140	16·0	8·9	20458·4	422·1	16·15	2·82	1022·9	32·80	46·9	1176·2
ISLB 400	56·9	72·43	165	12·5	8·0	19306·3	716·4	16·33	3·15	965·3	31·90	27·9	1099·5
ISWB 350	56·9	72·50	200	11·4	8·0	15521·7	1175·9	14·63	4·03	887·0	27·25	25·3	995·5
ISMB 350	52·4	66·71	140	14·2	8·1	13630·3	537·7	14·29	2·84	778·9	31·00	32·4	889·6
ISLB 350	49·5	63·01	165	11·4	7·4	13158·3	631·9	14·45	3·17	751·9	30·85	20·7	851·1
ISWB 300	48·1	61·33	200	10·0	7·4	9821·6	990·1	12·66	4·02	654·8	24·95	17·1	731·2
ISLB 325	43·1	54·90	165	9·8	7·0	9874·6	510·8	13·41	3·05	607·7	29·25	13·8	687·8
ISMB 300	44·2	56·26	140	12·4	7·5	8603·6	453·9	12·37	2·84	573·6	29·25	21·7	651·7
ISLB 300	37·7	48·08	150	9·4	6·7	7332·9	376·2	12·35	2·80	488·9	27·45	11·1	554·3
ISWB 250	40·9	52·05	200	9·0	6·7	5943·1	857·5	10·69	4·06	475·4	23·10	12·0	527·6
ISMB 250	37·3	47·15	125	12·5	6·9	5131·6	334·5	10·39	2·65	410·5	27·95	18·7	465·7
ISLB 275	33·0	42·02	140	8·8	6·4	5375·3	287·0	11·31	2·61	392·4	25·65	8·6	443·6
ISWB 225	33·9	43·24	150	9·9	6·4	3920·5	448·6	9·52	3·22	348·5	21·80	11·5	389·9
ISMB 225	31·2	39·72	110	11·8	6·5	3441·8	218·3	9·31	2·34	305·9	25·85	13·9	348·3
ISLB 250	27·9	35·53	125	8·2	6·1	3717·8	193·4	10·23	2·33	297·4	23·70	6·4	338·7
ISWB 200	28·8	36·71	140	9·0	6·1	2624·5	328·8	8·46	2·99	262·5	20·60	8·2	293·8

Table contd...

Table contd...

Designation (including Depth h in mm)	Weight per meter w kg	Sectional area A cm^2	Width of flange b mm	Thickness of flange t_f mm	Thickness of web t_w mm	Moment of Inertia I_{xx} cm^4	Moment of Inertia I_{yy} cm^4	Radius of Gyration r_{xx} cm	Radius of Gyration r_{yy} cm	Modulus of section Z_{xx} cm^3	Extreme Fibre to Root fillet h_2 mm	Torsional constant J cm^4	Plastic Modulus Z_p cm^3
ISMB 200	25·4	32·33	100	10·8	5·7	2235·4	150·0	8·32	2·15	223·5	23·65	9·5	253·9
ISLB 225	23·5	29·92	100	8·6	5·8	2501·9	112·7	9·15	1·94	222·4	22·35	5·6	254·7
ISWB 175	22·1	28·11	125	7·4	5·8	1509·4	188·6	7·33	2·59	172·5	17·75	4·4	194·2
ISLB 200	19·8	25·27	100	7·3	5·4	1696·6	115·4	8·19	2·13	169·7	17·15	3·6	184·3
ISMB 175	19·3	24·62	90	8·6	5·5	1272·0	85·0	7·19	1·86	145·4	20·25	4·7	166·1
ISLB 175	16·7	21·30	90	6·9	5·1	1096·2	79·6	7·17	1·93	125·3	16·70	2·7	143·3
ISJB 225	12·8	16·28	80	5·0	3·7	1308·5	40·5	8·97	1·58	116·3	11·95	1·0	134·2
ISWB 150	17·0	21·67	100	7·0	5·4	839·1	94·8	6·22	2·09	111·9	16·70	3·0	126·9
ISMB 150	14·9	19·00	80	7·6	4·8	726·4	52·6	6·18	1·66	96·9	18·05	2·8	110·5
ISLB 150	14·2	18·08	80	6·8	4·8	688·2	55·2	6·17	1·75	91·8	16·55	2·2	101·5
ISJB 200	9·9	12·64	60	5·0	3·4	780·7	17·3	7·86	1·17	78·1	10·25	0·7	90·9
ISMB 125	13·0	16·60	75	7·6	4·4	449·0	43·7	5·20	1·62	71·8	17·90	2·5	81·8
ISLB 125	11·9	15·12	75	6·5	4·4	406·8	43·4	5·19	1·69	65·1	14·80	1·7	73·9
ISJB 175	8·1	10·28	50	4·8	3·2	479·3	9·7	6·83	0·97	54·8	10·00	0·5	64·2
ISMB 100	11·5	14·60	75	7·2	4·0	257·5	40·8	4·20	1·67	51·5	17·50	2·0	58·7
ISJB 150	7·1	9·01	50	4·6	3·0	322·1	9·2	5·98	1·01	42·9	9·80	0·5	49·6
ISLB 100	8·0	10·21	50	6·4	4·0	168·0	12·7	4·06	1·12	33·6	13·50	1·1	38·9
ISLB 75	6·1	17·21	50	5·0	3·7	72·7	10·0	3·07	1·14	19·4	11·65	0·5	22·4
ISHB 450	87·2	111·14	250	13·7	9·8	39210·8	2985·2	18·78	5·18	1742·7	31·9		1955·2
ISHB 450	92·5	117·89	250	13·7	11·3	40349·9	3045·0	18·50	5·08	1793·3	31·9		2030·9
ISHB 400	77·4	98·66	250	12·7	9·1	28083·5	2728·3	16·87	5·26	1404·2	29·9		1566·4
ISHB 400	82·2	104·66	250	12·7	10·6	28823·5	2783·0	16·61	5·16	1444·2	29·9		1626·4
ISHB 350	67·4	85·91	250	11·6	8·3	19159·7	2451·4	14·93	5·34	1094·8	27·0		1213·5
ISHB 350	72·4	92·21	250	11·6	10·1	19802·8	2510·5	14·65	5·22	1131·6	27·0		1268·7
ISHB 300	58·8	74·85	250	10·6	7·6	12545·2	2193·6	12·95	5·41	836·3	25·1		921·7
ISHB 300	63·0	80·25	250	10·6	9·4	12950·2	2246·7	12·70	5·29	863·3	25·1		962·2
ISHB 250	51·0	64·96	250	9·7	6·9	7736·5	1961·3	10·91	5·49	618·9	23·2		678·7
ISHB 250	54·7	69·71	250	9·7	8·8	7983·9	2011·7	10·70	5·37	638·7	23·2		708·4
ISHB 225	43·1	54·94	225	9·1	6·5	5279·5	1353·8	9·80	4·96	469·3	22·2		515·6
ISHB 225	46·8	59·66	225	9·1	8·6	5478·8	1396·6	9·58	4·84	487·0	22·2		542·2
ISHB 200	37·3	47·54	200	9·0	6·1	3608·4	967·1	8·71	4·51	360·8	20·8		397·2
ISHB 200	40·0	50·94	200	9·0	7·8	3721·8	994·6	8·55	4·42	372·2	20·8		414·2
ISHB 150	27·1	34·48	150	9·0	5·4	1455·6	431·7	6·50	3·54	194·1	19·0		215·6
ISHB 150	30·6	38·98	150	9·0	8·4	1540·6	460·3	6·29	3·44	205·3	19·0		232·5
ISHB 150	34·6	44·88	150	9·0	11·8	1635·6	494·9	6·09	3·35	218·1	19·0		251·6

Table 10A·2. Indian Standard Rolled Steel Beams

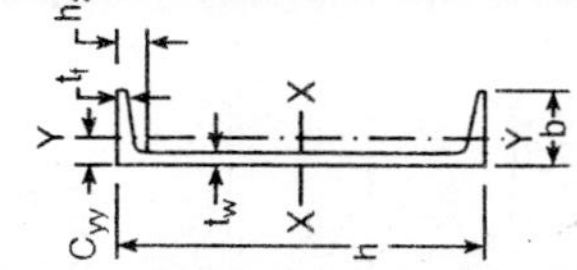

Designation	Weight per meter w kg	Sectional area A cm^2	Width of flange b mm	Thickness of flange t_f mm	Thickness of web t_w mm	Centre of Gravity C_{yy} cm	Moment of Inertia I_{xx} cm^4	Moment of Inertia I_{yy} cm^4	Radius of Gyration r_{xx} cm	Radius of Gyration r_{yy} cm	Section Modulus Z_{xx} cm^2	Extreme Fibre to Root fillet h_2 mm	Torsional constant J cm^4	Plastic Sections Modulus Z_p cm^3
ISMC 400	49·4	62·93	100	15·3	8·6	2·42	15082·8	504·8	15·48	2·83	754·1	33·6	31·7	891·0
ISLC 400	45·7	58·25	100	14·0	8·0	2·36	13989·5	460·4	15·50	2·81	699·5	31·4	24·6	825·0
ISMC 350	42·1	53·66	100	13·5	8·1	2·44	10008·0	430·6	13·66	2·83	571·9	30·9	22·1	672·2
ISLC 350	38·8	49·47	100	12·5	7·4	2·41	9312·6	394·6	13·72	2·82	532·1	29·1	17·4	623·0
ISMC 300	35·8	45·64	90	13·6	7·6	2·36	6362·6	310·8	11·81	2·61	424·2	29·6	19·1	496·8
ISLC 300	33·1	42·11	100	11·6	6·7	2·55	6047·9	346·0	11·98	2·87	403·2	27·3	13·2	466·7
ISMC 250	30·4	38·67	80	·14·1	7·1	2·30	3816·8	219·1	9·94	2·38	305·3	28·7	17·6	356·7
ISLC 250	28·0	35·65	100	10·7	6·1	2·70	3687·9	298·4	10·17	2·89	295·0	25·5	9·9	338·1
ISMC 225	25·9	33·01	80	12·4	6·4	2·30	2694·6	187·2	9·03	2·38	239·5	27·1	11·9	277·9
ISLC 225	24·0	30·53	90	10·2	5·8	2·46	2547·9	209·5	9·14	2·62	226·5	24·5	7·7	260·1
ISMC 200	22·1	28·21	75	11·4	6·1	2·17	1819·3	140·4	8·03	2·23	181·9	24·9	8·7	211·3
ISLC 200	20·6	26·22	75	10·8	5·5	2·35	1725·5	146·9	8·11	2·37	172·6	20·0	7·3	198·8
ISMC 175	19·1	24·38	75	10·2	5·7	2·20	1223·3	121·0	7·08	2·23	139·8	23·3	6·3	161·6
ISLC 175	17·6	22·40	75	9·5	5·1	2·40	1148·4	126·5	7·16	2·38	131·2	18·2	5·0	150·4
ISJC 175	13·9	17·77	70	7·1	4·1	1·97	1161·2	84·2	8·08	2·18	116·1	15·8	2·1	133·1
ISMC 150	16·4	20·88	75	9·0	5·4	2·22	779·4	102·3	6·11	2·21	103·9	21·7	4·3	119·8
ISLC 150	14·4	18·36	75	7·8	4·8	2·38	697·2	103·2	6·16	2·37	93·0	16·5	2·9	106·2
ISJC 175	11·2	14·24	60	6·9	3·6	1·75	719·9	50·5	7·11	1·88	82·3	14·5	1·6	94·2
ISMC 125	12·7	16·19	65	8·1	5·0	1·94	416·4	59·9	5·07	1·92	66·6	19·8	2·8	77·2
ISJC 150	9·9	12·65	55	6·9	3·6	1·66	471·1	37·9	6·10	1·73	62·8	14·4	1·4	72·0
ISLC 125	10·7	13·67	65	6·6	4·4	2·04	356·8	57·2	5:11	2·05	57·1	14·2	1·6	65·4
ISJC 125	7·9	10·07	50	6·6	3·0	1·64	270·0	25·7	5·18	1·60	43·2	13·1	1·1	49·1
ISMC 100	9·2	11·70	50	7·5	4·7	1·53	186·7	25·9	4·00	1·49	37·3	18·0	1·7	43·8
ISLC 100	7·9	10·02	50	6·4	4·0	1·62	164·7	24·8	4·06	1·57	32·9	12·8	1·1	38·1
ISJC 100	5·8	7·41	45	5·1	3·0	1·40	123·8	14·9	4·09	1·42	24·8	11·5	0·5	28·4
ISMC 75	6·8	8·67	40	7·3	4·4	1·31	76·0	12·6	2·96	1·21	20·3	16·8	1·2	24·2
ISLC 75	5·7	7·26	40	6·0	3·7	1·35	66·1	11·5	3·02	1·26	17·6	12·3	0·7	20·6

PROPERTIES OF STEEL SECTIONS

Table 10A·3. Indian Standard Rolled Steel Sections (equal angles)

Designation $A \times B$	Thickness d mm	Sectional area a cm^2	Weight per metre w kg	Centre of gravity $C_{xx} = C_{yy}$ cm	Moment of further $I_{xx} = I_{yy}$ cm^4	Radii of Gyration $r_{xx} = r_{yy}$ cm	Radii of Gyration r_{vv}
ISA 5050	5·0	4·79	3·8	1·41	11·0	1·52	0·97
	6·0	5·60	4·5	1·45	12·9	1·51	0·96
ISA 5555	5·0	5·27	4·1	1·53	14·7	1·67	1·06
	6·0	6·26	4·9	1·57	17·3	1·66	1·06
	8·0	8·18	6·4	1·65	22·0	1·64	1·06
	10·0	10·02	7·0	1·72	26·3	1·62	1·06
ISA 6060	5·0	5·75	4·5	1·65	19·2	1·82	1·16
	6·0	6·84	5·4	1·69	22·6	1·82	1·15
	8·0	8·96	7·0	1·71	29·0	1·80	1·15
	10·0	11·0	8·6	1·85	14·8	1·73	1·15
ISA 6565	5·0	6·25	4·9	1·77	24·7	1·99	1·26
	6·0	7·44	5·8	1·81	29·1	1·98	1·26
	8·0	9·76	7·7	1·89	37·4	1·96	1·25
	10·0	12·00	9·4	1·97	45·0	1·94	1·25
ISA 7070	5·0	6·77	5·3	1·89	31·1	2·15	1·36
	6·0	8·06	6·3	1·94	36·8	2·14	1·36
	8·0	10·58	8·3	2·02	47·4	2·12	1·35
	10·0	13·02	10·2	2·10	57·2	2·10	1·35
ISA 7575	5·0	7·27	5·7	2·02	38·7	2·31	1·46
	6·0	8·66	6·8	2·06	45·7	2·30	1·46
	8·0	11·38	8·9	2·14	59·0	2·28	1·45
	10·0	14·02	11·0	2·22	71·4	2·26	1·45
ISA 8080	6·0	9·29	7·3	2·18	56·0	2·46	1·56
	8·0	12·21	9·6	2·27	72·5	2·44	1·55
	10·0	15·05	11·8	2·34	87·7	2·41	1·55
	12·0	17·81	14·0	2·42	101·9	2·39	1·54
ISA 9090	6·0	10·47	8·2	2·42	80·1	2·77	1·75
	8·0	13·79	10·8	2·51	104·2	2·75	1·75
	10·0	17·03	13·4	2·59	126·7	2·73	1·74
	12·0	20·19	15·8	2·66	147·9	2·71	1·74
ISA 100100	6·0	11·67	9·2	2·67	111·3	3·09	1·95
	8·0	15·39	12·1	2·76	145·1	3·07	1·95
	10·0	19·03	14·9	2·84	177·0	3·05	1·94
	12·0	22·59	17·7	2·92	207·0	3·03	1·94
ISA 110110	8·0	17·02	13·4	3·00	195·0	3·38	2·14
	10·0	21·06	16·5	3·08	238·4	3·36	2·14
	12·0	25·02	19·6	3·16	279·6	3·34	2·13
	15·0	30·81	24·2	3·27	337·4	3·31	2·13
ISA 130130	8·0	20·22	15·9	3·50	328·3	4·03	2·55
	10·0	25·06	19·7	3·58	402·7	4·01	2·54
	12·0	29·82	23·4	3·66	473·8	3·99	2·54
	15·0	36·81	28·9	3·78	574·6	3·95	2·53
ISA 150150	10·0	29·03	22·8	4·06	622·4	4·63	2·93
	12·0	34·59	27·2	4·14	735·4	4·61	2·93
	15·0	42·78	33·6	4·26	896·8	4·58	2·92
	18·0	50·79	39·9	4·38	1048·9	4·54	2·91
ISA 200200	12·0	46·61	36·6	5·36	1788·9	6·20	3·92
	15·0	57·80	45·4	5·49	2197·7	6·17	3·91
	18·0	68·81	54·0	5·61	2588·7	6·13	3·90
	25·0	93·80	73·6	5·88	3436·3	6·05	3·88

Table 10A·4. Indian Standard Rolled Steel Unequal Angles

Designation	Thickness t	Sectional area a	Weight per Metre w	Center of Gravity		Moments of inertia		Radii of Gyration			tan α
	mm	cm^2	kg	c_{xx} cm	c_{yy} cm	I_{xx} cm^4	I_{yy} cm^5	r_{xx} cm	r_{yy} cm	r_{vv} cm	
ISA 5030	5·0	3·78	3·0	1·72	0·74	9·3	2·5	1·57	0·81	0·63	0·35
	6·0	4·47	3·5	1·76	0·78	10·9	2·9	1·56	0·80	0·63	0·35
ISA 6040	5·0	4·76	3·7	1·95	0·96	16·9	6·0	1·89	1·12	0·85	0·44
	6·0	5·65	4·4	1·99	1·00	19·9	7·0	1·88	1·11	0·85	0·43
	8·0	7·37	5·8	2·07	1·08	25·4	8·0	1·86	1·10	0·84	0·42
ISA 6545	5·0	5·26	4·1	2·07	1·08	22·1	8·6	2·05	1·28	0·96	0·47
	6·0	6·25	4·9	2·11	1·12	26·0	10·1	2·04	1·27	0·95	0·47
	8·0	8·17	6·4	2·19	1·20	32·3	12·8	2·02	1·25	0·95	0·46
ISA 7045	5·0	5·52	4·3	2·27	1·04	27·2	8·8	2·22	1·26	0·96	0·41
	6·0	6·56	5·2	2·32	1·09	32·0	10·3	2·21	1·25	0·96	0·41
	8·0	8·58	6·7	2·40	1·16	41·0	13·1	2·19	1·24	0·95	0·40
	10·0	10·52	3·3	2·48	1·24	49·3	15·6	2·16	1·22	0·95	0·39
ISA 7550	5·0	6·02	4·7	2·39	1·16	34·1	12·2	2·38	1·42	1·07	0·44
	6·0	7·16	5·6	2·44	1·20	40·3	14·3	2·37	1·41	1·07	0·44
	8·0	9·38	7·4	2·52	1·28	51·8	18·3	2·35	1·40	1·06	0·43
	10·0	11·52	9·0	2·60	1·36	62·3	21·8	2·33	1·38	1·06	0·42
ISA 8050	5·0	6·27	4·9	2·60	1·12	40·6	12·3	2·55	1·40	1·07	0·39
	6·0	7·46	5·9	2·64	1·16	48·0	14·4	2·54	1·39	1·07	0·36
	8·0	9·78	7·7	2·73	1·24	61·9	18·5	2·52	1·37	1·06	0·38
	10·0	12·02	9·4	2·81	1·32	74·7	22·1	2·49	1·36	1·06	0·38
ISA 9060	6·0	8·65	6·8	2·87	1·39	70·6	25·2	2·86	1·71	1·28	0·44
	8·0	11·37	8·9	2·96	1·48	91·5	32·4	2·84	1·69	1·28	0·44
	10·0	14·01	11·0	3·04	1·55	110·9	39·1	2·81	1·67	1·27	0·43
	12·0	16·57	13·0	3·12	1·63	129·1	45·2	2·79	1·65	1·27	0·42
ISA 10065	6·0	9·55	7·5	3·19	1·47	96·7	32·4	3·18	1·84	1·39	0·42
	8·0	12·57	9·9	3·28	1·55	125·9	41·9	3·16	1·83	1·39	0·42
	10·0	15·51	12·2	3·37	1·63	153·2	50·7	3·14	1·81	1·38	0·41
ISA 10075	6·0	10·41	8·0	3·01	1·78	100·9	48·7	3·15	2·19	1·59	0·55
	8·0	13·36	10·5	3·10	1·87	131·6	63·3	3·14	2·18	1·59	0·55
	10·0	16·50	13·0	3·19	1·95	160·4	76·9	3·12	2·16	1·58	0·55
	12·0	19·56	15·4	3·27	2·03	187·5	89·5	3·10	2·14	1·58	0·54
ISA 12575	6·0	11·66	9·2	4·05	1·59	187·8	51·6	4·01	2·10	1·62	0·37
	8·0	15·38	12·1	4·15	1·68	245·5	67·2	4·00	2·09	1·61	0·36
	10·0	19·62	14·9	4·24	1·76	300·3	81·6	3·97	2·07	1·61	0·36
ISA 12595	6·0	12·86	10·1	3·70	2·22	203·2	102·1	3·97	2·82	2·03	0·57
	8·0	16·98	13·3	3·80	2·31	266·0	133·3	3·96	2·80	2·02	0·57
	10·0	21·02	16·5	3·88	2·39	325·8	162·7	3·94	2·78	2·02	0·57
	12·0	24·98	19·6	3·96	2·47	382·6	190·4	3·91	2·76	2·01	0·56
ISA 15075	8·0	17·42	13·7	5·23	1·58	407·2	70·2	4·83	2·01	1·60	0·27
	10·0	21·56	16·9	5·32	1·61	499·1	85·3	4·81	1·99	1·59	0·26
	12·0	25·62	20·1	5·41	1·69	587·0	99·5	4·74	1·97	1·58	0·26
ISA 150115	8·0	20·58	16·2	4·46	2·73	465·7	238·9	4·76	3·41	2·45	0·58
	10·0	25·52	20·0	4·55	2·82	573·3	293·4	4·74	3·39	2·44	0·58
	12·0	30·38	23·8	4·64	2·90	676·5	345·3	4·72	3·37	2·44	0·58
	15·0	37·52	29·5	4·76	3·02	823·5	418·6	4·69	3·34	2·43	0·57
ISA 200100	10·0	29·03	22·8	6·96	2·01	1210·0	209·2	6·46	2·68	2·14	0·27
	12·0	34·59	27·2	7·05	2·10	1431·7	246·2	6·43	2·67	2·13	0·26
	15·0	42·78	33·6	7·18	2·22	1750·5	298·1	6·40	2·64	2·12	0·26
ISA 200150	10·0	34·00	26·7	5·99	3·51	1377·9	669·6	6·37	4·44	3·21	0·56
	12·0	40·56	31·8	6·08	3·60	1634·9	793·2	6·35	4·42	3·21	0·56
	15·0	50·25	39·4	6·20	3·72	2005·8	969·9	6·32	4·39	3·20	0·55
	18·0	59·76	46·9	6·33	3·84	2359·9	1136·9	6·28	4·36	3·19	

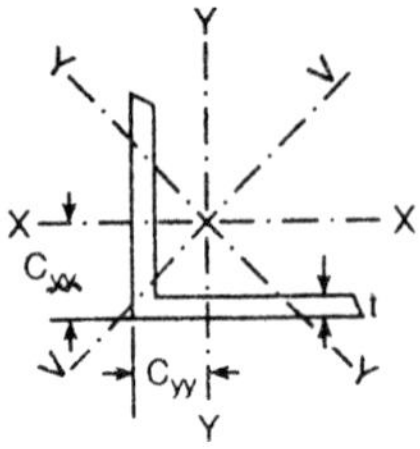

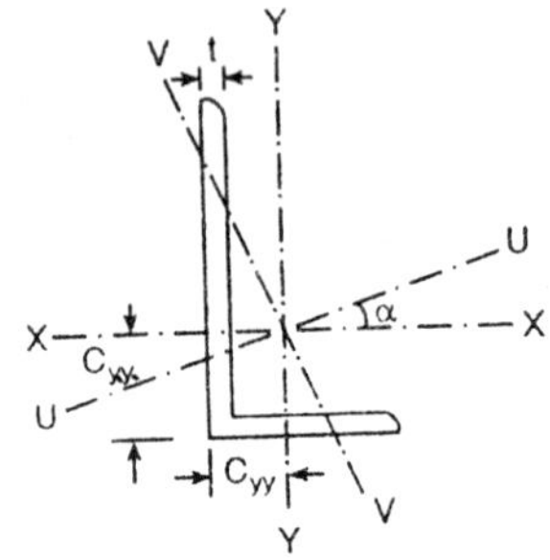

Table 10A·5. Indian Standard Rolled Steel Tee Bars

Designation		Weight per Metre *w* kg	Sectional area *a* cm²	Width of Flange *b* mm	Thickness of Flange t_f mm	Thickness of Web t_w mm	Centre of Gravity C_{xx} cm	Moments of Inertia I_{xx} cm⁴	I_{yy} cm⁴	Radii of Gyration r_{yy} cm
ISNT	20	0·9	1·13	20	3·0	3·0	0·60	0·4	0·2	0·39
ISNT	30	1·4	1·75	30	3·0	3·0	0·83	1·4	0·6	0·57
ISNT	40	3·5	4·48	40	6·0	6·0	1·20	6·3	3·0	0·82
ISNT	50	4·5	5·70	50	6·0	6·0	1·44	12·7	5·9	1·02
ISNT	60	5·4	6·90	60	6·0	6·0	1·67	22·5	10·1	1·21
ISNT	80	9·6	12·25	80	8·0	8·0	2·23	71·2	32·3	1·62
ISNT	100	15·0	19·10	100	10·0	10·0	2·79	173·8	79·9	2·05
ISNT	150	22·8	29·08	150	10·0	10·0	3·95	603·8	267·5	3·03
ISHT	75	15·3	19·49	150	9·0	8·4	1·62	96·2	230·2	3·44
ISHT	100	20·0	25·47	200	9·0	7·8	1·91	193·8	497·3	4·42
ISHT	125	27·4	34·85	250	9·7	8·8	2·37	415·4	1005·8	5·37
ISHT	150	29·4	37·42	250	10·6	7·6	2·66	573·7	1096·8	5·41
ISST	100	8·1	10·37	50	10·0	5·8	3·03	99·0	9·6	0·96
ISST	150	15·7	19·96	75	11·6	8·0	4·75	450·2	37·0	1·36
ISST	200	28·4	36·22	165	12·5	8·0	4·78	1267·8	358·2	3·15
ISST	250	37·5	47·75	180	14·1	9·2	6·40	2774·4	532·0	3·34
ISLT	50	4·0	5·11	50	6·4	4·0	1·19	9·9	6·4	1·12
ISLT	75	7·1	9·04	80	6·8	4·8	1·72	41·9	27·6	1·75
ISLT	100	12·7	16·16	100	10·8	5·7	2·13	116·6	75·0	2·15
ISJT	75	3·5	4·50	50	4·6	3·0	2·00	24·8	4·6	1·01
ISJT	87·5	4·0	5·14	50	4·8	3·2	2·50	39·0	4·8	0·97
ISJT	100	5·0	6·32	60	5·0	3·4	2·81	63·5	8·6	1·17
ISJT	112·5	6·4	8·14	80	5·0	3·7	3·01	101·6	20·2	1·58

Note : For the followings, please refer the chapter "Estimating and Costing" or "Building Materials".

1. Size and weight of expanded metal (X-PM) sheets.
2. Weights and sizes of standard steel (Block Sheets).
3. Comparison of weights of sheets of different metals.
4. Weights of standard sizes of steel strips.
5. Weights and sizes of standard steel plates.
6. Weights of standard corrugated galvanised steel sheets.
7. Wire and sheet metal gauges.

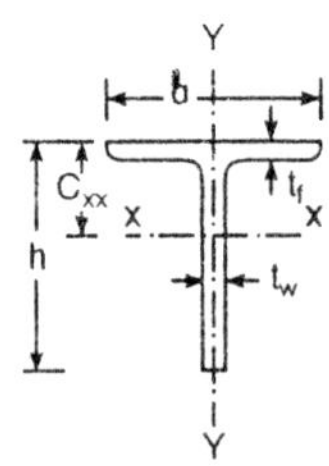

Table 10A·6(*i*). Properties of Steel Tubes for Structural Purposes (Metre units)

Nominal Bore (mm)	*Outside diameter (mm)*	*Class*	*Thickness (mm)*	*Weight (kg/m)*	*Area* (cm^2)	*Movement Inertia* (cm^4)	*Sections Modulus* (cm^3)	*Radius of gyration (cm)*
15	21·3	Light	2·00	0·952	1·21	0·57	0·54	0·69
		Medium	2·65	1·22	1·55	0·69	0·65	0·69
		Heavy	3·25	1·45	1·84	0·78	0·73	0·65
20	26·9	Light	2·35	1·41	1·81	1·38	1·02	0·87
		Medium	2·65	1·58	2·02	1·51	1·12	0·86
		Heavy	3·25	1·90	2·41	1·72	1·28	0·84
25	33·7	Light	2·65	2·01	2·58	3·14	1·86	1·10
		Medium	3·25	2·44	3·11	3·65	2·16	1·08
		Heavy	4·05	2·97	3·77	4·22	2·15	1·05
32	42·4	Light	2·65	2·58	3·31	6·57	3·60	1·41
		Medium	3·25	3·14	4·00	7·71	3·64	1·39
		Heavy	4·05	3·84	4·88	9·07	4·28	1·36
40	48·3	Light	2·90	3·25	4·14	10·70	4·43	1·61
		Medium	3·25	3·61	4·60	11·73	4·86	1·60
		Heavy	4·05	4·43	5·63	13·90	5·76	1·57
50	60·3	Light	2·90	4·11	5·23	21·60	7·16	2·03
		Medium	3·65	5·10	6·50	26·17	8·68	2·01
		Heavy	4·50	6·17	7·89	30·91	10·8	1·98
65	76·1	Light	3·25	5·80	7·44	49·45	13·0	2·58
		Medium	3·65	6·51	8·31	54·66	14·4	2·57
		Heavy	4·50	7·90	10·1	65·14	17·1	2·54
80	88·9	Light	3·25	6·81	8·74	80·33	18·1	3·03
		Medium	4·05	8·47	10·8	97·40	21·9	3·00
		Heavy	4·85	10·1	12·8	113·5	25·5	2·98
90	101·6	Light	3·65	8·74	11·2	134·9	26·6	3·47
		Medium	4·05	9·72	12·4	147·9	29·1	3·45
		Heavy	4·85	11·6	14·7	173·0	34·0	3·43
100	114·3	Light	3·65	9·89	12·7	194·4	34·0	3·91
		Medium	4·50	12·1	15·5	234·4	41·0	3·89
		Heavy	5·40	14·4	18·5	274·6	48·1	3·86
125	139·7	Medium	4·85	16·2	20·5	467·8	60·0	4·77
		Heavy	5·4	17·8	22·8	514·6	73·7	4·75
150	165·1	Medium	4·85	19·2	24·4	784·7	95·1	5·69
		Heavy	5·4	21·2	27·1	804·9	104·8	5·65

Table 10A·6(*ii*). Properties of Steel Tubes for Structural Purposes (Inch units)

Nominal Bore (inch)	*Outside diameter (inch)*	*Class*	*S.W.G.*	*Thick-ness (inch)*	*Weight (lb/th)*	*Area Inertia (in^2)*	*Movement Modulus (in^4)*	*Sections gyration (cm^3)*	*Radius of gyration (in)*
1/2	17/32	Light	14	0·080	0·640	0·192	0·014	0·034	0·279
		Medium	12	0·104	0·822	0·242	0·017	0·040	0·264
		Heavy	10	0·128	0·977	0·288	0·019	0·045	0·257
3/4	$1\frac{1}{16}$	Light	13	0·092	0·944	0·281	0·033	0·063	0·345
		Medium	12	0·104	1·06	0·313	0·036	0·068	0·341
		Heavy	10	0·128	1·27	0·376	0·042	0·079	0·333
1	$1\frac{11}{32}$	Light	12	0·104	1·35	0·405	0·078	0·117	0·441
		Medium	10	0·128	1·64	0·489	0·091	0·136	0·432
		Heavy	8	0·160	2·00	0·593	0·166	0·158	0·422
$1\frac{1}{4}$	$1\frac{11}{16}$	Light	12	0·104	1·73	0·517	0·163	0·193	0·561
		Medium	10	0·128	2·11	0·627	0·192	0·227	0·553
		Heavy	8	0·160	2·58	0·768	0·226	0·268	0·543
$1\frac{1}{2}$	$1\frac{29}{32}$	Light	11	0·116	2·19	0·652	0·262	0·275	0·634
		Medium	10	0·128	2·43	0·715	0·284	0·298	0·630
		Heavy	8	0·160	2·98	0·878	0·337	0·354	0·620
2	$2\frac{3}{8}$	Light	11	0·116	2·76	0·823	0·527	0·443	0·800
		Medium	9	0·144	3·42	1·01	0·631	0·531	0·790
		Heavy	7	0·176	4·14	1·22	0·740	0·623	0·780
$2\frac{1}{2}$	3	Light	10	0·128	3·90	1·15	1·19	0·795	1·02
		Medium	9	0·144	4·38	1·29	1·32	0·880	1·01
		Heavy	7	0·176	5·31	1·56	1·56	1·04	1·00
3	$3\frac{1}{2}$	Light	10	0·128	4·58	1·36	1·93	1·10	1·19
		Medium	8	0·160	5·69	1·68	2·53	1·34	1·18
		Heavy	6	0·192	6·76	2·00	2·74	1·56	1·17
4	$4\frac{1}{2}$	Light	9	0·144	6·64	1·97	4·68	2·08	1·54
		Medium	7	0·176	8·44	2·39	5·60	2·49	1·53
		Heavy	5	0·212	9·71	2·86	6·58	2·92	1·52
5	$5\frac{1}{2}$	Medium	6	0·192	10·9	3·20	11·3	4·11	1·88
		Heavy	5	0·212	12·0	3·52	12·3	4·48	1·87
6	$6\frac{1}{2}$	Medium	6	0·192	12·9	3·80	18·9	5·83	2·23
		Heavy	5	0·212	14·3	4·19	20·7	6·38	2·22

Table 10A·7. Weights of m.s. round and square bars (British Units)

Dia. or Size	*Round bars*			*Square bars*		
	Area (sq. inches)	*Perimeter*	*Wt/Ft. (lbs)*	*Area (sq. inches)*	*Perimeter (inch)*	*Wt/Ft. (lbs)*
1/4	0·049	0·78	0·17	0·062	1·00	0·21
5/16	0·077	0·98	0·26	0·098	1·25	0·33
3/8	0·110	1·28	0·38	0·141	1·50	0·48
7/16	0·150	1·37	0·51	0·191	1·75	0·65
1/2	0·196	1·57	0·67	0·250	2·00	0·85
9/16	0·248	1·77	0·84	0·316	2·25	1·08
5/8	0·307	1·96	1·04	0·391	2·50	1·33
11/16	0·371	2·16	1·26	0·473	2·75	1·61
3/4	0·442	2·36	1·50	0·563	3·00	1·91
13/16	0·518	2·55	1·76	0·660	3·25	2·24
7/8	0·601	2·75	2·04	0·766	3·50	2·60
15/16	0·690	2·98	2·35	0·879	3·75	2·99
1	0·785	3·19	2·67	1·007	4·00	3·40
$1\frac{1}{8}$	0·994	3·53	3·38	1·266	4·25	4·30
$1\frac{1}{4}$	1·227	3·93	4·17	1·563	4·50	5·31
$1\frac{1}{2}$	1·770	4·71	6·00	2·25	6·00	7·65

Metric Units

Size (mm)	*sq. cms.*	*cms.*	*kg/m*	*mm*	*sq. cms.*	*kg/m*
3	0·20	1·57	0·15	0·25	2·0	0·20
5·5	0·24	1·73	0·19	0·30	2·2	0·24
6	0·28	1·88	0·22	0·36	2·4	0·28
7·8	0·38	2·20	0·30	0·49	2·8	0·38
8	0·50	2·51	0·39	0·64	3·2	0·50
9	0·64	2·83	0·50	0·81	3·6	0·64
10	0·79	2·14	0·62	1·00	4·0	0·78
11	0·95	3·46	0·75	1·21	4·4	0·95
12	1·13	3·77	0·89	1·44	4·8	1·13
14	1·54	4·40	1·21	1·96	5·6	1·54
16	2·01	5·03	1·58	2·56	6·4	2·01
18	2·54	5·65	2·00	3·24	7·2	2·54
20	3·14	6·28	2·47	4·00	8·0	3·14
22	3·50	6·91	2·98	4·84	8·8	3·80
25	4·91	7·85	3·85	6·25	10·0	4·91
28	6·16	8·80	4·83	7·54	11·20	6·15
32	8·04	10·05	6·31	10·24	12·8	8·04
36	10·18	11·31	7·39	12·96	14·4	10·17
40	12·57	12·57	9·86	16·00	16·0	12·56
45	15·90	14·14	12·49	20·25	18·0	15·90
50	19·64	15·76	15·41	25·00	20·0	19·62
56	24·63	17·59	19·34	35·36	22·4	24·62
63	31·71	19·79	24·47	39·69	25·20	31·16
71	39·59	22·31	31·08	50·49	28·40	39·57
80	50·27	25·13	39·46	64·00	32·00	50·24
90	63·62	28·27	49·94	81·00	36·00	63·58
100	78·54	31·42	61·66	100·00	40·00	78·50

Table 10B·1. Safe Loads for Indian Standard Angles used as Ties

Size of Angle Leg × Leg × Thickness	*Weight per Metre Length Single Angle*	*Single Angle Ties*			*Double Angle Ties*		
		Equal Angles	*Unequal Angles*		*Equal Angles*	*Unequal Angles*	
		Connected by one leg	*Shorter leg connected*	*Longer leg connected*	*Connected by one leg*	*Shorter leg connected*	*Longer leg connected*
mm	*kg*	*Safe Loads (Tensile) in Metric Tonnes*					
(1)	(2)	(3)	(4)	(5)	(6)	(7)	(8)
50 × 30 × 3	1·8	—	2·5	2·3	—	6·6	5·2
50 × 30 × 3	2·3	2·7	—	—	6·9	—	—
50 × 30 × 4	2·4	—	3·3	3·0	—	8·7	6·7
50 × 30 × 5	3·0	—	4·1	3·6	—	11	8·3
50 × 50 × 4	3·0	3·5	—	—	9·0	—	—
50 × 30 × 6	3·5	—	4·8	4·3	—	13	9·7
60 × 40 × 5	3·7	—	5·3	4·5	—	13	10
50 × 50 × 5	3·8	4·4	—	—	11	—	—
55 × 55 × 5	4·1	4·6	—	—	12	—	—
65 × 45 × 5	4·1	—	6·0	5·1	—	15	12
70 × 45 × 5	4·3	—	6·1	5·6	—	16	13
60 × 40 × 6	4·4	—	6·3	5·3	—	16	12
60 × 50 × 6	4·5	5·1	—	—	13	—	—
60 × 60 × 5	4·5	5·2	—	—	13	—	—
75 × 50 × 5	4·7	—	6·8	6·2	—	17	14
55 × 55 × 6	4·9	5·4	—	—	14	—	—
65 × 45 × 6	4·9	—	7·1	6·1	—	18	14
80 × 50 × 5	4·9	—	6·9	6·6	—	18	15
65 × 65 × 5	4·9	5·8	—	—	15	—	—
70 × 45 × 6	5·2	—	7·3	6·6	—	19	15
70 × 70 × 5	5·3	6·5	—	—	16	—	—
60 × 60 × 6	5·4	6·1	—	—	16	—	—
75 × 50 × 6	5·6	—	5·8	7·3	—	20	17
75 × 75 × 5	5·7	7·1	—	—	18	—	—
60 × 40 × 8	5·8	—	8·2	6·9	—	21	16
65 × 65 × 6	5·8	6·9	—	—	17	—	—
80 × 50 × 6	5·9	—	6·0	7·8	—	18	17
70 × 70 × 6	6·3	7·7	—	—	19	—	—
55 × 55 × 8	6·4	7·0	—	—	18	—	—
65 × 45 × 8	6·4	—	9·2	7·9	—	23	18
70 × 45 × 8	6·7	—	8·7	6·6	—	24	19
75 × 75 × 6	6·8	8·4	—	—	21	—	—
90 × 60 × 6	6·8	—	7·0	9·3	—	25	21
60 × 60 × 8	7·0	8·4	—	—	21	—	—
80 × 80 × 6	7·3	9·2	—	—	23	—	—
75 × 50 × 8	7·4	—	7·6	9·6	—	23	22
100 × 65 × 6	7·5	—	8·0	10	—	23	22

Table contd...

Table contd...

Size of Angle	*Weight*	*Single Angle Ties*			*Double Angle Ties*		
	per Metre Length Single Angle	*Equal Angles*	*Unequal Angles*		*Equal Angles*	*Unequal Angles*	
Leg × Leg × Thickness		*Connected by one leg*	*Shorter leg connected*	*Longer leg connected*	*Connected by one leg*	*Shorter leg connected*	*Longer leg connected*
mm	*kg*	*Safe Loads (Tensile) in Metric Tonnes*					
(1)	(2)	(3)	(4)	(5)	(6)	(7)	(8)
65 × 65 × 8	7·7	9·0	—	—	23	—	—
80 × 50 × 8	7·7	—	7·7	10	—	24	23
55 × 55 × 10	7·9	8·5	—	—	22	—	—
100 × 75 × 6	8·0	—	9·2	10	—	29	24
90 × 90 × 6	8·2	11	—	—	26	—	—
70 × 70 × 8	8·3	10	—	—	25	—	—
70 × 45 × 10	8·3	—	12	10	—	30	24
60 × 60 × 10	8·0	10	—	—	25	—	—
75 × 75 × 8	8·9	11	—	—	27	—	—
90 × 60 × 8	8·9	—	9·2	12	—	27	27
75 × 50 × 10	9·0	10	9·2	12	—	28	27
65 × 65 × 10	9·4	11	—	—	28	—	—
80 × 50 × 10	9·4	—	9·4	13	—	29	28
80 × 80 × 8	9·6	12	—	—	30	—	—
100 × 65 × 8	9·9	—	10	13	—	31	30
70 × 70 × 10	10·2	12	—	—	31	—	—
100 × 75 × 8	10·5	—	12	14	—	33	32
90 × 90 × 8	10·8	14	—	—	34	—	—
75 × 75 × 10	11·0	13	—	—	34	—	—
90 × 60 × 10	11·0	—	11	15	—	34	34
80 × 80 × 10	11·8	15	—	—	37	—	—
100 × 100 × 8	12·1	15	—	—	38	—	—
100 × 65 × 10	12·2	—	13	16	—	38	36
90 × 60 × 12	13·0	—	13	18	—	40	40
100 × 75 × 10	13·0	—	15	17	—	41	39
90 × 90 × 10	13·4	17	—	—	42	—	—
80 × 80 × 12	14·0	17	—	—	43	—	—
100 × 100 × 10	14·9	9	—	—	46	—	—
100 × 75 × 12	15·4	—	—	20	—	48	46
90 × 90 × 12	15·8	20	—	—	50	—	—
100 × 100 × 12	17·7	22	—	—	55	—	—

Note : (*i*) Safe allowable loads have been rounded off to the nearest tonne for practical application

(*ii*) All angles are connected by one leg : longer leg connected of unequal angles.

(*iii*) Double angles are fixed on both sides of the gusset. Where fixed on one side, the allowable loads shall be only 90% of the tabulated loads.

(*iv*) Rivet hole/holes have been deducted from the gross areas to arrive at the allowable loads.

Table 10B·2. Safe Loads for Indian Standard Angles used as Struts

Size of Angle Leg × Leg × Thickness mm	*Weight per Metre Length Single Angle kg*	*Double Angle ⅂⎾ Struts (Back to Back) — Effective Lengths in Metres*												
		1·0	*1·5*	*2·0*	*2·5*	*3·0*	*3·5*	*4·0*	*4·5*	*5·0*	*5·5*	*6·0*	*"EL"*	*Axis*
		Safe Loads in Metric Tonnes											*m*	
50 × 50 × 4	3·0	0·7	7·0	4·8	3·3	2·2	1·6	—	—	—	—	—	2·5	*x—x*
50 × 50 × 5	3·8	11	8·6	5·9	4·0	2·7	1·9	—	—	—	—	—	2·5	*x—x*
55 × 55 × 5	4·1	12	10	7·5	5·3	3·6	2·6	1·9	—	—	—	—	3·0	*x—x*
65 × 45 × 5	4·1	12	11	8·7	6·4	4·6	3·3	2·5	1·9	—	—	—	3·0	*y—y*
70 × 45 × 5	4·3	12	11	8·9	6·5	4·7	3·4	2·5	1·9	—	—	—	3·0	*y—y*
50 × 50 × 6	4·5	13	10	7·0	4·6	3·2	2·2	—	—	—	—	—	2·5	*x—x*
60 × 60 × 5	4·5	13	12	9·1	6·6	4·7	3·4	2·5	—	—	—	—	3·0	*x—x*
75 × 50 × 5	4·7	14	13	11	8·3	6·2	4·6	3·4	2·6	—	—	—	3·5	*y—y*
55 × 55 × 6	4·9	14	12	8·8	6·2	4·2	3·0	2·2	—	—	—	—	2·5	*x—x*
65 × 45 × 6	4·9	15	13	10	7·8	5·7	4·1	3·1	2·4	—	—	—	3·0	*y—y*
80 × 50 × 5	4·9	15	13	11	8·3	6·2	4·5	3·4	2·6	—	—	—	3·5	*y—y*
65 × 65 × 5	4·9	15	13	11	8·3	6·2	4·5	3·4	—	—	—	—	3·5	*x—x*
70 × 45 × 6	5·2	15	14	11	7·9	5·7	4·1	3·1	2·4	—	—	—	3·0	*y—y*
70 × 70 × 5	5·3	—	—	13	10	7·6	5·7	4·3	3·3	2·6	—	—	3·5	*x—x*
60 × 60 × 6	5·4	16	14	11	7·9	5·6	4·1	3·0	—	—	—	—	3·0	*x—x*
75 × 50 × 6	5·6	17	15	13	10	7·5	5·5	4·2	3·2	—	—	—	3·5	*y—y*
75 × 75 × 5	5·7	—	—	14	12	9·2	7·1	5·4	4·2	3·3	2·7	—	4·0	*x—x*
65 × 65 × 6	5·8	17	16	13	9·4	7·3	5·3	4·0	—	—	—	—	3·5	*x—x*
80 × 50 × 6	5·9	18	16	13	10	7·6	5·5	4·2	3·2	—	—	—	3·5	*y—y*
70 × 70 × 6	6·3	—	—	15	12	9·0	6·8	5·1	3·9	3·1	—	—	3·5	*x—x*
55 × 55 × 8	6·4	19	16	11	7·9	5·4	3·9	2·9	—	—	—	—	2·5	*x—x*
65 × 45 × 8	6·4	19	17	14	10	7·8	5·6	4·2	3·2	—	—	—	3·5	*y—y*
70 × 45 × 8	6·7	20	18	14	11	7·8	5·6	4·2	3·2	—	—	—	3·0	*y—y*
75 × 75 × 6	6·8	—	—	17	14	11	8·4	6·4	5·0	3·9	3·1	—	4·0	*x—x*
90 × 60 × 6	6·8	—	—	18	15	12	9·1	7	5·4	4·3	3·5	2·8	4·0	*y—y*
60 × 60 × 8	7·0	21	18	14	10	7·2	5·2	3·9	—	—	—	—	3·0	*x—x*
80 × 80 × 6	7·3	—	—	19	16	13	10	7·9	6·1	4·9	4·0	3·2	4·0	*x—x*
75 × 50 × 8	7·4	22	20	17	13	10	7·6	5·8	4·4	—	—	—	3·5	*y—y*
100 × 65 × 6	7·5	—	—	20	17	14	11	8·7	6·8	5·5	4·4	3·6	4·5	*y—y*
65 × 65 × 8	7·7	23	21	17	13	9·4	6·8	5·1	—	—	—	—	3·5	*x—x*
80 × 50 × 8	7·7	23	21	18	14	10	7·6	5·7	4·4	—	—	—	3·5	*y—y*
55 × 55 × 10	7·9	23	19	14	9·5	6·5	4·6	3·4	—	—	—	—	2·5	*x—x*
100 × 75 × 6	8·0	—	—	23	21	18	15	12	10	8·3	6·7	5·6	5·0	*y—y*
90 × 90 × 6	8·2	—	—	23	20	17	14	11	8·9	7·1	5·8	4·8	4·5	*x—x*
70 × 70 × 8	8·3	—	—	20	15	12	8·7	6·6	5·0	4·0	—	—	3·5	*x—x*
70 × 45 × 10	8·3	25	22	18	14	10	7·3	5·5	4·2	—	—	—	3·5	*y—y*
60 × 60 × 10	8·6	25	22	17	12	8·7	6·3	4·6	—	—	—	—	3·0	*x—x*
75 × 75 × 8	8·9	—	—	22	18	14	11	8·2	6·4	5·0	4·1	—	4·0	*x—x*

Table contd...

Table contd...

Size of Angle *Leg × Leg × Thickness* *mm*	*Weight per Metre Length Single Angle* *kg*	*Double Angle ⅂⎾ Struts (Back to Back)*												
		Effective Lengths in Metres												
		1·0	*1·5*	*2·0*	*2·5*	*3·0*	*3·5*	*4·0*	*4·5*	*5·0*	*5·5*	*6·0*	*"EL"*	*Axis*
		Safe Loads in Metric Tonnes											*m*	
90 × 60 × 8	8·9	—	—	23	20	16	12	9·6	7·4	6·0	4·8	3·9	4·0	*y—y*
75 × 50 × 10	9·0	27	25	22	17	13	9·8	7·4	5·7	—	—	—	3·5	*y—y*
65 × 65 × 10	9·4	28	25	21	15	11	8·1	6·1	—	—	—	—	3·5	*x—x*
80 × 50 × 10	9·4	28	26	22	17	13	9·8	7·4	5·7	—	—	—	3·5	*y—y*
80 × 80 × 8	9·6	—	—	25	21	17	13	10	7·9	6·3	5·1	4·2	4·0	*x—x*
100 × 65 × 8	9·9	—	—	27	23	19	15	12	9·4	7·5	6·0	5·0	4·5	*y—y*
70 × 70 × 10	10·2	—	—	24	19	14	10	7·9	6·1	4·8	—	—	3·5	*x—x*
100 × 75 × 8	10·5	—	—	30	27	24	20	17	14	11	9·2	7·7	5·5	*y—y*
90 × 90 × 8	10·8	—	—	30	26	22	18	14	12	9·2	7·6	6·2	4·5	*x—x*
75 × 75 × 10	11·0	—	—	27	22	17	13	9·9	7·8	6·1	4·9	—	4·0	*x—x*
90 × 60 × 10	11·0	—	—	29	25	30	16	12	9·5	7·6	6·1	5·0	4·0	*y—y*
80 × 80 × 10	11·8	—	—	31	26	20	16	12	9·5	7·6	6·1	5·1	4·0	*x—x*
100 × 100 × 8	12·1	—	—	34	32	28	23	19	16	1·3	11	8·4	3·5	*x—x*
100 × 65 × 10	12·2	—	—	33	29	24	19	15	12	9·6	7·7	6·4	4·5	*y—y*
90 × 60 × 12	13·0	—	—	35	30	24	19	15	12	9·4	7·6	6·2	4·5	*y—y*
100 × 75 × 10	13·0	—	—	37	34	30	26	21	18	14	12	9·8	5·5	*y—y*
90 × 90 × 10	13·4	—	—	37	32	27	22	18	14	11	9·2	7·5	4·5	*x—x*
80 × 80 × 12	14·0	—	—	36	30	24	18	14	11	8·0	7·1	5·1	4·0	*x—x*
100 × 100 × 10	14·9	—	—	42	39	34	29	24	20	16	13	11	5·0	*x—x*
100 × 75 × 12	15·4	—	—	44	41	36	31	26	21	18	14	12	5·5	*y—y*
90 × 90 × 12	15·8	—	—	43	38	32	26	21	16	13	11	8·8	4·5	*x—x*
100 × 100 × 12	17·7	—	—	50	46	40	34	28	23	19	15	13	5·0	*x—x*

Notes for struts :

(1) Safe load figures have been rounded off to the nearest tonne beyond 10 tonnes for ease of practical application.

(2) Tabulated loads are for ratio of slenderness upto but not exceeding 250.

(3) "EL" is the effective span beyond which ratio of slenderness exceeds 180.

(4) Safe loads are on the basis of full unit stress since the sections are more often used as bracings and as secondary members than as main members.

(5) Single angle struts are double riveted or double bolted or with welded end connections where struts are single bolted or are with single riveted end connections (in case of small sections) only 80% of the tabulated loads shall be allowed.

(6) For double angle struts back to back connected to both sides of a gusset or a member by a single rivet or bolt, only 80% of the tabulated loads shall be allowed.

(7) In double equal angles longer legs are connected back to back. (Shorter legs connected take lesser loads).

(8) Space between back to back of double angle struts has been taken as 6 mm.

(9) Effective length of a strut is taken as centre to centre of fastening at each end.

(10) Radius of gyration on x-x axis of two angles back to back is the same as for single angle as x-x axis.

(11) When two angles are placed heel to heel (starred) the least radius of gyration for both angles is the same as for single angle on x-x axis.

(12) The least allowable safe loads have been taken whether as the x-x or y-y axis.

Table 10B·3. Safe Loads for Indian Standard Single Angles used as Struts

Size of Angle Leg × Leg × Thickness mm	*Weight per Metre Length Single Angle kg*	*Single Angle L Struts — Effective Lengths in Metres*						*"EL" m*
		1·0	*1·5*	*2·0*	*2·5*	*3·0*	*3·5*	
		Safe Loads in Metric Tonnes						
50 × 50 × 4	3·0	3·3	1·8	1·0	—	—	—	1·5
60 × 40 × 5	3·7	3·5	1·7	0·9	—	—	—	1·5
50 × 50 × 5	3·8	4·1	2·2	1·2	—	—	—	1·5
55 × 55 × 5	4·1	4·9	2·9	1·6	10	—	—	
65 × 45 × 5	4·1	4·4	2·4	1·3	—	—	—	1·5
70 × 45 × 5	4·3	4·7	2·5	1·4	—	—	—	1·5
60 × 40 × 6	4·4	4·1	2·0	1·1	—	—	—	1·5
50 × 50 × 6	4·5	4·8	2·6	1·4	—	—	—	1·5
60 × 60 × 5	4·5	5·7	3·6	2·2	1·3	—	—	2·0
55 × 55 × 6	4·9	5·8	3·4	1·9	1·2	—	—	1·5
65 × 45 × 6	4·9	5·2	2·8	1·5	—	—	—	1·5
65 × 65 × 5	4·9	6·5	4·5	2·8	1·7	1·1	—	2·0
70 × 45 × 6	5·2	5·6	3·0	1·6	—	—	—	1·5
70 × 70 × 5	5·3	7·3	5·4	3·5	2·2	1·5	—	2·0
60 × 60 × 6	5·4	6·8	4·3	2·5	1·5	—	—	2·0
75 × 50 × 6	5·6	6·7	4·0	2·3	1·4	—	—	1·5
60 × 40 × 8	5·8	5·3	2·6	1·4	—	—	—	1·5
65 × 65 × 6	5·8	7·8	5·3	3·3	2·1	1·4	—	2·0
80 × 50 × 6	5·9	7·0	4·2	2·4	1·4	—	—	1·5
70 × 70 × 6	6·3	8·7	6·4	4·2	2·6	1·8	—	2·0
55 × 55 × 8	6·4	7·6	4·5	2·5	1·5	—	—	1·5
65 × 45 × 8	6·4	6·8	3·7	2·0	—	—	—	1·5
70 × 45 × 8	6·7	7·2	3·9	2·1	—	—	—	1·5
75 × 75 × 6	6·8	9·6	7·4	5·0	3·3	2·2	1·6	2·5
60 × 60 × 8	7·0	8·9	5·6	3·3	2·0	—	—	2·0
80 × 80 × 6	7·3	10	8·5	6·0	4·1	2·8	2·0	2·5
75 × 50 × 8	7·4	8·7	5·2	2·9	1·8	—	—	1·5
65 × 65 × 8	7·7	10	6·9	4·3	2·7	1·8	—	2·0
80 × 50 × 8	7·7	9·1	5·4	3·0	1·8	—	—	1·5
55 × 55 × 10	7·9	9·3	5·5	3·1	1·9	—	—	1·5
70 × 70 × 8	8·3	11	8·3	5·4	3·4	2·3	—	2·0
70 × 45 × 10	8·3	8·8	4·7	2·5	—	—	—	1·5
60 × 60 × 10	8·6	11	6·9	4·0	2·5	—	—	2·0
75 × 75 × 8	8·9	12	9·7	6·5	4·3	2·9	2·0	2·5
90 × 60 × 8	8·9	12	8·3	5·2	3·3	2·2	—	2·0
75 × 50 × 10	9·0	11	6·3	3·6	2·2	—	—	1·5
65 × 65 × 10	9·4	12	8·5	5·3	3·3	2·2	—	2·0

Table 10B·4. Safe Loads for Indian Standard Single Angles used as Struts

Size of Angle *Leg × Leg × Thickness* *mm*	*Weight per Metre Length Single Angle* *kg*	*Single Angle L Struts* *Effective Lengths in Metres* *1·0*	 *1·5*	 *2·0*	 *2·5*	 *3·0*	 *3·5*	 *4·0*	 *4·5*	*"EL"* *m*
		Safe Loads in Metric Tonnes								
80 × 50 × 10	9·4	11	6·6	3·7	2·3	—	—	—	—	1·5
80 × 80 × 8	9·6	14	11	7·8	5·3	3·6	2·5	—	—	2·5
100 × 65 × 8	9·9	14	10	6·7	4·3	2·9	—	—	—	2·5
70 × 70 × 10	10·2	14	10	6·6	4·2	2·8	—	—	—	2·0
100 × 75 × 5	10·5	15	12	8·9	6·1	4·1	2·9	—	—	2·5
90 × 90 × 8	10·8	—	14	10	7·5	5·2	3·8	—	—	3·0
75 × 75 × 10	11·0	15	12	8·0	5·3	3·5	2·5	—	—	2·5
90 × 60 × 10	11·0	15	10	6·3	4·0	2·6	—	—	—	2·0
80 × 80 × 10	11·8	17	14	9·6	6·5	4·4	3·1	—	—	2·5
100 × 100 × 8	12·1	—	16	13	9·9	7·3	5·3	4·0	3·0	3·5
100 × 65 × 10	12·2	17	12	8·2	5·2	3·5	—	—	—	2·5
90 × 60 × 12	13·0	17	12	7·5	4·7	3·1	—	—	—	2·0
100 × 75 × 10	13·0	19	15	11	7·4	5·1	3·6	—	—	2·5
90 × 90 × 10	13·4	—	17	13	9·1	6·4	4·6	3·4	—	3·0
80 × 80 × 12	14·0	20	16	11	7·6	5·2	3·7	—	—	2·5
100 × 100 × 10	14·9	—	20	16	12	9·0	6·4	4·9	3·7	3·0
100 × 75 × 12	15·4	22	18	13	8·8	6·0	4·2	—	—	2·5
90 × 90 × 12	15·8	—	20	15	11	7·6	5·5	4·0	—	3·0
100 × 100 × 12	17·7	—	24	19	14	11	7·6	5·8	4·4	3·0

Table 10B-5. Corrugated Galvanized Iron Sheets

The following table gives the span the sheets will carry for a load of 100 kg/sq. metre

Gauge No.	*16*	*18*	*20*	*22*	*24*	*26*	
Length in metres (without laps)	2·2	2·1	1·8	1·6	1·4	1·2	Cantilevers will be only 1/4 of these lengths
With end lap of 23 cm and riveted	2·7	2·4	2·0	1·8	1·6	1·4	

Table 10B-6. Safe Loads for Single Indian Standard Channels used as Columns

Size of Channel *Depth × Width Web thickness* *mm*	*Weight per Metre Length* *kg*	*"Effective Height" in Metres* *4·0*	 *5·0*	 *6·0*	 *7·0*	 *8·0*	 *9·0*	 *10·0*	 *11·0*	 *12·0*	*"EH"* *metres*
		Safe Loads in Metric Tonnes Based on X-X Axis									
75 × 40 × 3·7	5·7	4·4	3·0	2·0	1·4	—	—	—	—	—	5·0
75 × 40 × 4·4	6·8	5·1	3·4	2·3	1·6	—	—	—	—	—	5·0
100 × 50 × 4·0	7·9	8·9	6·7	5·1	3·8	2·8	2·2	1·7	—	—	7·0
100 × 50 × 4·7	9·2	10	7·8	5·8	4·3	3·2	2·5	1·9	—	—	7·0
125 × 65 × 4·4	10·7	14	12	10	7·9	6·3	4·9	3·9	3·2	2·6	9·0
125 × 65 × 5·0	12·7	17	14	12	9·3	7·3	5·7	4·6	3·7	3·0	9·0
150 × 75 × 4·8	14·4	20	19	17	14	12	9·6	7·8	6·4	5·3	11·0
150 × 75 × 5·4	16·4	23	21	19	16	13	11	8·8	7·1	6·0	10·0

Table contd...

Table contd...

Size of Channel *Depth × Width Web thickness mm*	*Weight per Metre Length kg*	*"Effective Height" in Metres*									*"EH"*
		4·0	*5·0*	*6·0*	*7·0*	*8·0*	*9·0*	*10·0*	*11·0*	*12·0*	
		Safe Loads in Metric Tonnes Based on X-X Axis									*metres*
175 × 75 × 5·1	17·6	26	25	23	20	17	15	13	11	8·9	—
175 × 75 × 5·7	19·1	28	27	24	22	19	16	13	11	9·5	—
200 × 75 × 5·5	20·6	31	30	28	26	23	21	18	15	13	—
200 × 75 × 6·1	22·1	33	32	30	28	25	22	19	16	14	—
225 × 90 × 5·8	24·0	36	35	34	32	30	27	24	22	19	—
225 × 80 × 6·4	25·9	39	38	37	35	32	29	26	30	27	—
250 × 100 × 6·1	28·0	43	42	41	39	37	35	32	29	26	—
250 × 80 × 7·1	30·4	46	45	44	42	40	37	34	30	27	—
300 × 100 × 6·7	33·1	51	50	50	48	47	45	43	40	37	—
300 × 90 × 7·6	35·8	55	54	53	52	50	48	46	43	40	—
350 × 100 × 7·4	38·8	60	60	59	58	57	55	53	51	49	—
350 × 100 × 8·1	42·1	65	65	64	63	61	60	58	55	53	—
400 × 100 × 8·0	45·7	71	71	70	69	68	67	65	64	61	—
400 × 100 × 8·6	49·4	77	76	76	75	74	72	70	69	66	—

(*i*) Safe load figures have been 'rounded off' to the nearest tonne beyond 10 tonnes for practical application.

(*ii*) The safe loads tabulated are for ratio of slenderness up to but not exceeding 250.

(*iii*) "*EH*" is the "effective height" beyond which the safe loads indicated are for ratio of slenderness exceeding 180.

Table 10B-7. Safe Loads for Single Indian Standard Channels used as Columns

Size of Channel *Depth × Width Web thickness mm*	*Weight per Metre Length kg*	*"Effective Height" in Metres*									*"EH"*
		2·0	*2·5*	*3·0*	*3·5*	*4·0*	*4·5*	*5·0*	*5·5*	*6·0*	
		Safe Loads in Metric Tonnes Based on Y-Y Axis									*metres*
75 × 40 × 3·7	5·7	3·2	2·0	1·3	—	—	—	—	—	—	2·0
75 × 40 × 4·4	6·8	3·6	2·2	1·5	—	—	—	—	—	—	2·0
100 × 50 × 4·0	7·9	6·5	4·4	3·0	2·1	—	—	—	—	—	2·5
100 × 50 × 4·7	9·2	7·0	4·7	3·2	2·2	—	—	—	—	—	2·5
125 × 65 × 4·4	10·7	12	9·5	7·1	5·2	4·0	3·0	2·4	—	—	3·5
125 × 65 × 5·0	12·7	14	10	7·5	5·4	4·0	3·1	—	—	—	3·0
150 × 75 × 4·8	14·4	18	15	12	9·4	7·2	5·6	4·4	3·6	—	4·0
150 × 75 × 5·4	16·4	20	16	12	9·3	7·0	5·5	4·3	3·5	—	3·5
175 × 75 × 5·1	17·6	23	19	15	12	8·9	6·9	5·5	4·4	—	4·0
175 × 75 × 5·7	19·1	24	19	15	11	8·4	6·5	5·2	4·1	—	4·0
200 × 75 × 5·5	20·6	26	22	17	13	10	8·0	6·3	5·1	—	4·0
200 × 75 × 6·1	22·1	27	22	17	13	9·7	7·6	6·0	4·8	—	4·0
225 × 90 × 5·8	24·0	32	28	23	18	15	12	9·3	7·4	6·2	4·5
225 × 80 × 6·4	25·9	33	28	22	17	13	10	8·0	6·5	—	4·0
250 × 100 × 6·1	28·0	39	35	30	25	20	16	13	11	9·0	5·0
250 × 80 × 7·1	30·4	39	32	26	20	15	12	9·4	7·6	—	4·0
300 × 100 × 6·7	33·1	46	42	35	29	24	19	15	13	10	5·0
300 × 90 × 7·6	35·8	48	42	34	27	22	17	14	11	9·1	4·5
350 × 100 × 7·4	38·8	54	48	41	33	27	22	17	14	12	5·0
350 × 100 × 8·1	42·1	59	52	45	36	30	24	19	16	13	5·0
400 × 100 × 8·0	45·7	64	57	48	39	32	25	20	17	14	5·0
400 × 100 × 8·6	49·4	69	62	52	43	35	28	22	18	15	5·0

(*i*) Safe load figures have been 'rounded off' to the nearest tonne beyond 10 tonnes for practical application.

(*ii*) The safe loads tabulated are for ratio of slenderness up to but not exceeding 250.

(*iii*) "*EH*" is the "effective height" beyond which the safe loads indicated are for ratio of slenderness exceeding 180.

Table 10B-8. Safe Concentric Loads for Indian Standard H Beams used as Column (No. 2)

Size of H Beam *Depth × Width × Web thickness* *mm*	*Weight per Metre Length* *kg*	*Radius of Gyration on x-x Axis* *cm*	*"Effective Height" in Metres*								
			4	*5*	*6*	*7*	*8*	*9*	*10*	*11*	*12*
			Safe Loads on Metric Tonnes Based on x-x Axis								
150 × 150 × 5·4	27·1	6·50	39	36	33	28	24	20	16	13	11
150 × 150 × 8·4	30·6	6·29	44	41	36	31	25	21	17	14	12
150 × 150 × 11·8	34·6	6·09	49	45	39	33	27	23	18	15	12
200 × 200 × 6·1	37·3	8·71	56	55	52	49	45	41	36	31	27
200 × 200 × 7·8	40·0	8·55	60	58	56	52	48	43	37	33	28
225 × 225 × 6·5	43·1	9·80	66	64	62	60	56	52	48	43	38
225 × 225 × 8·6	46·8	9·58	71	70	67	64	60	56	50	45	40
250 × 250 × 6·9	51·0	10·91	78	77	75	73	70	66	62	57	52
250 × 250 × 8·8	54·7	10·70	84	82	80	78	75	70	65	60	54
300 × 250 × 7·6	58·8	12·95	91	90	89	87	86	82	79	75	71
300 × 250 × 9·4	63·0	12·70	97	96	95	93	90	88	84	80	75
350 × 250 × 8·3	67·4	14·93	105	104	103	102	100	98	95	92	89
350 × 250 × 10·1	72·4	14·65	112	111	110	109	107	105	102	98	94
400 × 250 × 9·1	77·4	16·87	120	120	119	118	117	115	114	110	108
400 × 250 × 10·6	82·2	16·61	128	127	126	125	123	121	119	117	113
450 × 250 × 9·8	87·2	18·78	136	135	135	134	132	131	129	127	125
450 × 250 × 11·3	92·5	18·50	144	144	143	142	140	139	137	135	132

Notes for Columns Tables No. 1 and 2.

(*i*) For "Effective Height" see under "Design of Columns".

(*ii*) The safe loads tabulated are for ratio of slenderness up to but not exceeding 250.

(*iii*) "*EH*" is the "Effective Height" in Table No. 1 beyond which the safe loads indicated are for ratio of slenderness exceeding 180.

(*iv*) When two beams are placed side by side (which are laced or battened), the radius of gyration on the *Y-Y* axis will increase depending upon the spacings between the beams and which would be greater than the radius of gyration on the *X-X* axis even if the beams are abutting together. In that case the radius of gyration given for single beams on *X-X* axis may be taken for calculating concentrated loads on simple columns.

(*v*) Safe load figures have been 'rounded off' to the nearest tonne beyond 10 tonnes for practical application.

Table 10B-9. Data for Double Channels Used as Columns

For Single Channels				*Radius of Gyration on Y-Y Axis*		*Distance S between two channels when $R_{XX} = R_{YY}$ (approx.)*
Size of Channel Depth × Width × Web thickness	*Weight per Metre Length*	*Sectional area*	*Radius of Gyration on x-x Axis*	*When abutting back to (S o)] [*	*With flanges butting [ ]*	
mm	*kg*	*cm²*	*cm*	*cm*	*cm*	*mm*
75 × 40 × 3·7	5·7	7·26	3·02	1·85	2·93	28
100 × 45 × 3·0	5·8	7·41	4·09	1·99	3·41	48
75 × 40 × 4·4	6·8	8·67	2·96	1·78	2·95	27
125 × 50 × 3·0	7·9	10·07	5·18	2·29	3·72	65
100 × 50 × 4·0	7·9	10·02	4·06	2·26	3·73	42
100 × 50 × 4·7	9·2	11·70	4·00	2·13	3·78	45
150 × 55 × 3·6	9·9	12·65	6·10	2·40	4·21	85
125 × 65 × 4·4	10·7	13·67	5·11	2·89	4·91	58
175 × 60 × 3·6	11·2	14·24	7·11	2·57	4·65	105
125 × 65 × 5·0	12·7	16·19	5·07	2·73	4·95	55
200 × 70 × 4·1	13·9	17·77	8·08	2·94	5·48	115
150 × 75 × 4·8	14·4	18·36	6·16	3·36	5·64	68
150 × 75 × 5·4	16·4	20·88	6·11	3·13	5·73	70
175 × 75 × 5·1	17·6	22·40	7·16	3·38	5·63	88
175 × 75 × 5·7	19·1	24·38	7·08	3·13	5·75	90
200 × 75 × 5·5	20·6	26·22	8·11	3·34	5·67	118
200 × 75 × 6·1	22·1	28·21	8·03	3·11	5·78	110
225 × 90 × 5·8	24·0	30·53	9·14	3·59	7·05	155
225 × 80 × 6·4	25·9	33·01	9·03	3·31	6·18	130
250 × 100 × 6·1	28·0	35·65	10·17	3·96	7·85	142
250 × 80 × 7·1	30·4	38·67	9·94	3·31	6·18	150
300 × 100 × 6·7	33·1	42·11	11·98	3·84	7·98	182
300 × 90 × 7·6	35·8	45·64	11·81	3·52	7·13	185
350 × 100 × 7·4	38·8	49·47	13·72	3·71	8·10	222
350 × 100 × 8·1	42·1	53·66	13·66	3·74	8·07	215
400 × 100 × 8·0	45·7	58·25	15·50	3·67	8·14	258
400 × 100 × 8·6	49·4	62·93	15·48	3·73	8·09	255

Table 10B-10. Safe Concentric Loads for Indian Standard Steel H Beams used as Columns (No. 1)

No	Size of H Beam Depth × Width × Web thickness mm	Weight per Metre Length kg	Radius of Gyration on Y-Y Axis cm	"Effective Height" in Metres — Safe Loads in Metric Tonnes Based on Y-Y Axis (Least Radius of Gyration): 2·0	2·5	3·0	3·5	4·0	4·5	5·0	5·5	6·0	6·5	7·0	7·5	8·0	8·5	9·0	9·5	10·0	11·0	12·0	"EH"	No.
1	150 × 150 × 5·4	27·1	3·54	40	38	35	31	26	22	19	16	13	11	10	8	7	6						6·0	
2	150 × 150 × 8·4	30·6	3·44	45	42	38	34	29	24	20	17	14	12	10	9	8	7						6·0	
3	150 × 150 × 11·8	34·6	3·35	50	47	43	37	31	26	22	18	15	13	11	9	9							6·0	
4	200 × 200 × 6·1	37·3	4·51	56	55	53	50	46	42	37	33	29	25	23	19	17	15						8·0	
5	200 × 200 × 7·8	40·0	4·42	60	59	56	53	49	44	39	34	30	26	23	20	17	15	13	12	11	8·5		7·5	
6	225 × 225 × 6·5	43·1	4·96	66	64	62	60	57	53	48	43	38	34	30	27	24	21	18	16	15	12	10	8·5	
7	225 × 225 × 8·6	46·8	4·84	71	70	67	65	61	56	51	46	40	36	32	28	24	21	19	17	15	12	10	8·5	
8	250 × 250 × 6·9	51·0	5·49	78	77	75	73	70	67	62	57	52	47	42	38	34	30	27	24	22	18	14	9·5	
9	250 × 250 × 8·8	54·7	5·37	84	82	80	78	75	70	66	60	54	49	44	39	35	31	28	25	22	18	15	9·5	
10	300 × 250 × 7·6	58·8	5·41	90	89	87	84	80	76	71	65	59	53	48	43	38	34	30	27	24	20	16	9·5	
11	300 × 300 × 9·4	63·0	5·29	96	95	92	89	85	80	75	68	61	55	49	44	39	35	31	27	25	20	17	9·5	
12	350 × 250 × 8·3	67·4	5·34	103	102	99	96	92	87	80	74	67	60	53	47	43	38	34	30	27	22	18	9·5	
13	350 × 250 × 10·1	72·4	5·22	111	109	106	102	98	92	85	77	69	62	55	49	44	39	35	31	28	22	18	9·0	
14	400 × 250 × 9·1	77·4	5·26	118	117	113	110	105	99	91	83	75	67	60	54	48	42	38	33	30	24	20	9·0	
15	400 × 250 × 10·6	82·2	5·16	126	123	120	116	110	103	95	86	78	69	62	55	49	43	38	34	31	25	20	9·0	
16	450 × 250 × 9·8	87·2	5·18	133	131	127	123	117	110	101	92	83	74	68	59	52	46	41	36	33	26	22	9·0	
17	450 × 250 × 11·3	92·5	5·08	141	139	135	130	123	115	106	95	85	76	68	60	53	47	42	37	33	27	22	9·0	

Table 10B-11. Safe Concentric Loads for Indian Standard Steel H Beams used as Columns (No. 1)

No.	Size of Channel Depth × Width × Web thickness mm	Weight per Metre Length kg	Section Modulus cm³	2 × shear carrying capacity Tonnes	"L" m	Span in Metres 1·0	1·5	2·0	2·5	3·0	3·5	4·0	5·0	6·0	7·0	8·0	9·0	No.
						Safe Loads in Metric Tonnes												
1	75 × 40 × 3·7	5·7	17·6	5·2	1·5	2·1	1·4	1·0	—	—	—	—	—	—	—	—	—	
2	100 × 45 × 3·0	5·8	24·8	5·6	1·0	3·0	2·0	1·5	1·1	0·8	—	—	—	—	—	—	—	
3	75 × 40 × 4·4*	6·8	20·3	6·2	2·0	2·4	1·6	1·2	—	—	—	—	—	—	—	—	—	
4	125 × 50 × 3·0	7·9	43·2	7·0	1·5	5·2	3·5	2·6	2·1	1·5	—	—	—	—	—	—	—	
5	100 × 50 × 4·0*	7·9	32·9	7·6	1·5	3·9	2·6	2·0	1·4	1·1	—	—	—	—	—	—	—	
6	100 × 50 × 4·7*	9·2	37·3	8·8	2·0	4·5	3·0	2·2	1·6	1·3	—	—	—	—	—	—	—	
7	150 × 55 × 3·6*	9·9	62·8	10·2	1·5	7·5	5·0	3·8	3·0	2·5	2·0	1·6	—	—	—	—	—	
8	125 × 65 × 4·4*	10·7	57·1	10·4	2·0	6·9	4·6	3·4	2·7	2·1	—	—	—	—	—	—	—	
9	175 × 60 × 3·6	11·2	82·3	12·0	1·5	9·9	6·6	4·9	4·0	3·3	2·8	2·3	—	—	—	—	—	
10	125 × 65 × 5·0*	12·7	66·6	11·8	2·0	8·0	5·3	4·0	3·2	2·5	—	—	—	—	—	—	—	
11	200 × 70 × 4·1*	13·9	116·1	15·4	1·5	14	9·3	7·0	5·6	4·6	4·0	3·5	2·6	—	—	—	—	
12	150 × 75 × 4·8*	14·4	93·0	13·6	2·0	11	7·4	5·6	4·5	3·7	3·0	2·5	—	—	—	—	—	
13	150 × 75 × 5·4*	16·4	103·9	15·4	2·5	12	8·3	6·2	5·0	4·2	3·4	2·8	—	—	—	—	—	
14	175 × 75 × 5·1	17·6	131·3	16·8	2·0	16	10	7·9	6·3	5·3	4·5	3·7	—	—	—	—	—	
15	175 × 75 × 5·7	19·1	139·8	18·8	2·5	17	11	8·4	6·7	5·6	4·8	4·0	—	—	—	—	—	
16	200 × 75 × 5·5	20·6	172·6	20·8	2·0	21	14	13	8·3	6·9	5·9	5·2	3·7	—	—	—	—	
17	200 × 75 × 6·1	22·1	181·9	23·0	2·5	22	15	11	8·7	7·3	6·2	5·5	4·1	—	—	—	—	
18	225 × 90 × 5·8	24·0	226·5	24·6	2·5	27	18	14	11	9·1	7·8	6·8	5·2	—	—	—	—	
19	225 × 80 × 6·4	25·9	239·5	27·2	2·5	29	19	14	11	9·6	8·2	7·2	5·5	—	—	—	—	
20	250 × 100 × 6·1	28·0	295·0	28·8	2·5	—	24	18	14	12	10	8·8	7·1	5·4	—	—	—	
21	250 × 80 × 7·1	30·4	305·3	33·6	2·5	—	24	18	15	12	10	9·2	7·3	5·6	—	—	—	
22	300 × 100 × 6·7	33·1	403·2	38·0	2·5	—	32	24	19	16	14	12	9·7	8·1	6·2	—	—	
23	300 × 90 × 7·6	35·8	424·2	43·0	2·5	—	34	25	20	17	14	13	10	8·5	6·6	—	—	
24	350 × 100 × 7·4	38·8	532·1	49·0	2·5	—	43	32	25	21	18	16	13	11	9·1	7·4	6·0	
25	350 × 100 × 8·1	42·1	571·9	53·6	2·5	—	46	34	27	23	20	17	14	11	9·8	8·0	6·5	
26	400 × 100 × 8·0	45·7	699·5	60·4	2·5	—	56	42	34	28	24	21	17	14	12	10	8·5	
27	400 × 100 × 8·6	49·4	754·1	65·0	2·5	—	60	45	36	30	26	23	18	15	13	11	9·4	

Table 10B-12. Safe Distributed Loads for Indian Standard Steel Beams (contd.)

No.	Size of H Beam Depth × Width × Web thickness mm	Weight per Metre Length kg	Section Modulus cm^3	2 × shear carrying capacity Tonnes	"L" m	Span in Metres 1·0	1·5	2·0	2·5	3·0	3·5	4·0	4·5	5·0	5·5	6·0	No.
						Safe Loads in Metric Tonnes											
25	250 × 125 × 6·9*	37·3	410·5	32·6	3·5	52	34	26	21	17	15	13	11	10	8·4	7·0	
26	225 × 150 × 6·4*	33·9	348·5	27·2	4·0	44	29	22	18	15	12	11	9·5	7·8	—	—	
27	275 × 140 × 6·4	33·0	392·4	33·2	3·0	49	33	25	20	16	14	12	11	9·9	8·8	7·4	
28	225 × 110 × 6·5	31·2	305·9	27·6	3·0	38	26	19	15	13	11	9·6	8·3	6·8	—	—	
29	200 × 140 × 6·1*	28·8	262·5	23·0	3·5	33	22	16	13	11	9·4	8·2	6·5	5·2	—	—	
30	250 × 125 × 6·1	27·9	297·4	28·8	3·0	37	25	19	15	12	11	9·4	8·3	7·4	6·8	5·1	
31	200 × 100 × 5·7*	25·4	223·5	21·6	3·0	28	19	14	11	9·4	8·0	6·9	5·5	4·4	—	—	
32	225 × 100 × 5·8	23·5	222·4	24·6	2·5	28	19	14	11	9·4	8·0	7·0	6·0	5·0	—	—	
33	175 × 125 × 5·8	22·1	181·9	19·2	3·0	22	14	11	8·7	7·2	6·1	4·6	—	—	—	—	
34	200 × 100 × 5·4	19·8	169·7	20·4	2·5	21	14	11	8·6	7·2	6·1	5·3	4·2	3·4	—	—	
35	175 × 90 × 5·5	19·3	145·4	18·2	2·5	18	12	9·2	7·3	6·1	5·1	4·0	—	—	—	—	
36	150 × 100 × 5·4*	17·0	111·9	15·4	2·5	14	9·4	7·0	5·6	4·6	3·4	2·6	—	—	—	—	
37	175 × 190 × 5·1	16·7	125·3	16·8	2·0	16	10	7·9	6·3	5·2	4·4	3·4	—	—	—	—	
38	150 × 80 × 4·8*	14·9	96·9	13·6	2·0	12	8·1	6·1	4·9	3·9	2·9	2·2	—	—	—	—	
39	150 × 80 × 4·8*	14·2	91·8	13·6	2·0	12	7·7	5·8	4·6	3·7	2·8	2·1	—	—	—	—	
40	125 × 75 × 4·4*	13·0	71·8	10·4	2·5	9·0	6·0	4·5	3·5	2·5	—	—	—	—	—	—	
41	225 × 80 × 3·7	12·8	116·3	15·8	1·5	15	9·8	7·4	5·9	4·9	4·2	3·7	3·2	1·6	—	—	
42	125 × 75 × 4·4*	11·9	65·1	10·4	2·0	8·2	5·5	4·1	3·2	2·3	—	—	—	—	—	—	
43	100 × 75 × 4·0*	11·5	61·5	7·6	2·5	6·5	4·3	3·3	2·6	1·4	—	—	—	—	—	—	
44	200 × 60 × 3·4*	9·9	78·1	12·8	1·0	9·8	6·6	4·9	3·9	3·3	2·8	2·4	1·9	1·6	—	—	
45	175 × 50 × 3·2	8·1	54·8	10·6	1·0	6·9	4·6	3·4	2·8	2·3	1·8	1·5	—	—	—	—	
46	100 × 50 × 4·0*	8·0	33·6	7·6	1·5	4·2	2·8	2·1	1·6	0·9	—	—	—	—	—	—	
47	150 × 50 × 3·0	7·1	42·9	8·6	1·0	5·4	3·6	2·7	2·2	1·8	1·3	1·0	—	—	—	—	
48	75 × 50 × 3·7*	6·1	19·4	5·2	1·5	2·4	1·6	1·1	—	—	—	—	—	—	—	—	

Table 10B-13. Safe Distributed Loads for Indian Standard Steel Beams (R.S. Joints)

No.	Size of H Beam Depth × Width × Web thickness	Weight per Metre Length	Section Modulus	2 × shear carrying capacity	"L"	Span in Metres																					No.
						3·0	3·5	4·0	4·5	5·0	5·5	6·0	7·0	8·0	9·0	10·0	10·5	11·0	11·5	12·0	12·5	13·0	13·5	14·0	14·5	15·0	
						Safe Loads in Metric Tonnes																					
	mm	kg	cm^3	Tonnes	m																						
1	600 × 250 × 11·8	145·1	3854·2	133·8	6·5	162	139	121	108	97	88	81	69	61	54	49	46	44	42	40	37	34	31	29	27	25	1
2	600 × 250 × 11·2	133·7	3540·0	127·0	6·0	149	127	111	99	89	81	74	64	56	50	45	42	41	39	37	34	31	29	27	25	23	2
3	600 × 210 × 12·0	122·6	3060·4	136·0	5·0	129	110	96	86	77	70	64	55	48	43	39	37	35	33	32	29	27	25	23	22	20	3
4	550 × 250 × 10·5	112·5	2723·9	109·2	6·0	114	98	85	76	69	62	57	49	43	38	34	33	31	28	26	24	22	—	—	—	—	4
5	550 × 190 × 11·2*	103·7	2359·8	116·4	4·5	99	85	74	66	59	54	50	42	37	33	30	28	26	24	22	21	19	—	—	—	—	5
6	600 × 210 × 10·5	99·5	2428·9	119·0	4·5	102	87	76	68	61	56	51	44	38	34	31	22	28	27	25	23	21	20	18	17	16	6
7	500 × 250 × 9·9	95·2	2091·6	93·6	5·5	88	75	66	59	53	48	44	38	33	29	26	25	21	23	18	—	—	—	—	—	—	7
8	500 × 180 × 10·2*	86·9	1808·7	96·4	4·0	76	65	57	51	46	41	38	33	28	25	22	22	18	20	16	—	—	—	—	—	—	8
9	550 × 190 × 9·9	86·3	1933·2	103·0	4·0	81	70	61	54	49	44	41	35	30	27	24	23	22	20	18	17	16	—	—	—	—	9
10	450 × 200 × 9·2	79·4	1558·1	78·2	4·5	65	56	49	44	39	36	33	28	25	21	17	16	14	—	—	—	—	—	—	—	—	10
11	500 × 180 × 9·2	75·0	1543·2	87·0	4·0	65	56	49	43	39	35	32	28	24	22	19	17	16	14	13	—	—	—	—	—	—	11
12	450 × 150 × 9·4	72·4	1350·7	80·0	3·5	57	49	43	38	34	31	28	24	21	19	15	13	12	—	—	—	—	—	—	—	—	12
13	400 × 200 × 8·6*	66·7	1171·3	65·0	4·5	49	42	37	33	21	27	25	21	18	14	12	—	—	—	—	—	—	—	—	—	—	13
14	450 × 170 × 8·6	65·3	1223·8	73·2	4·0	51	44	39	34	39	28	26	22	19	17	14	—	—	—	—	—	—	—	—	—	—	14
15	400 × 140 × 8·9	31·6	1022·9	67·2	3·5	43	37	32	29	26	23	21	18	16	12	10	—	—	—	—	—	—	—	—	—	—	15
16	350 × 200 × 8·0*	56·9	887·0	53·0	4·5	37	32	28	25	22	20	19	16	12	9·5	—	—	—	—	—	—	—	—	—	—	—	16
17	400 × 165 × 8·0	56·9	965·3	60·4	3·5	41	35	30	27	24	22	20	17	15	12	9·5	—	—	—	—	—	—	—	—	—	—	17
18	350 × 140 × 8·1	52·4	778·9	53·6	3·5	33	28	24	22	20	18	16	14	10	8·3	—	—	—	—	—	—	—	—	—	—	—	18
19	350 × 165 × 7·4*	49·5	751·9	49·0	3·5	32	27	24	21	19	17	16	13	10	8·1	—	—	—	—	—	—	—	—	—	—	—	19
20	300 × 200 × 7·4	48·1	654·8	42·0	4·5	27	24	21	18	16	15	13	10	—	—	—	—	—	—	—	—	—	—	—	—	—	20
21	300 × 140 × 7·5	44·2	573·6	42·6	3·5	24	21	18	16	14	13	12	8·7	—	—	—	—	—	—	—	—	—	—	—	—	—	21
22	325 × 165 × 7·0	43·1	607·7	43·0	3·5	25	22	19	17	15	14	13	10	—	—	—	—	—	—	—	—	—	—	—	—	22	—
23	250 × 200 × 6·7*	40·9	475·4	31·6	5·0	20	17	15	13	12	9·8	8·2	—	—	—	—	—	—	—	—	—	—	—	—	—	23	—
24	300 × 150 × 6·7	37·7	488·9	38·0	3·5	21	18	15	14	12	11	10	7·4	—	—	—	—	—	—	—	—	—	—	—	—	—	24

Note : (*a*) The tabulated loads are calculated uniformly distributed loads on a simply beam and include the weight of the

(*b*) Allowable loads are in direct to the length of the span except where exceeds the limit of 1/325 of the the loads have been reduced in value (in right hand end columns) so as to keep the deflections with in limits.

(*c*) Length of bearings to take full shear at the ends should not be less than half of the depth of the beam.

(*d*) Column "*L*" gives the lengths of spans upto which tabulated loads are safe even without supports.

(*e*) Beams marked with an asterisk (*) are not economical except when depth is limited. Channels can be used, their economy should be checked.

(*f*) Make proper provision in cases eccentric loads or any other special condition of loadings.

(*g*) Check the sections for its shearing carrying capacity. Where the total load is the excess of the tabulated "shear carrying capacity" of the beam its web should be strengthened with web stiffners.

(*h*) Safe load figures have been rounded off to the nearest tonne beyond 10 tonnes for ease of practical application.

(*i*) The allowable loads have been calculated on the assumptions that the beams have adequate lateral supports to the compression flange at distances apart not exceeding 20 times the width of the flanges. Where a beam is not provided with adequate lateral supports with floors or cross beams etc., the tabulated loads have to be reduced in value.

11

Soil Mechanics

11·1. Types of soils

Soil. Soil is an aggregate material of mineral grains, loose or moderately cohesive, in-organic or organic in nature, the grains of which may be separated by simple mechanical means *i.e.*, by agitation in water.

Rock. Hard and compact aggregate of mineral grains cemented together to form a solid, compact and hard mass.

11·1·1. Classification of soil according to their mode of deposition:

Alluvial. Soils transported by water of rivers etc. such as river deposits, sand, gravel silt and clay.

Acolian soil—Soil transported by wind such as sand dunes etc.

Loustrum soil—Soil deposited in the bottom of lakes.

Marine—Solid deposits in sea water.

Glacial—Soils which are deposited by glacial activity.

11·1·2. Classification of soil according to engineering purposes:

Sand and gravel—They are cohesion less soils may be angular or rounded mineral grains. Sand and gravel is distinguished according to their grain size. Particles more than 2 mm size are known as gravel.

Silt. It is fine grained soil with little or no plasticity. If a sample of silt is taken on palm, the surface of the silt appears glossy (shining and smooth).

Organic silt. It is fine grained, more or less plastic soil which is finely divided organic matter mixed with it. The colour of silt is grey. They are less permeable than sand.

Clay. It is composed of fine to very fine particles of weathered rock. Clays are plastic in nature and hard. On shaking on palm they leave no dirt. Some times organic particles are mixed in the clay which are called organic clays.

Black cotton soil. In organic in nature, occurs mostly in central India. They are worst foundation soil and cracks on temperature effects on surface.

Peat—It is compound of vegetable matter, compressible and unsuitable for foundations.

Hard pan. A very dense accumulated mass of soil (clay, sand and gravel) cemented together to form a rock like mass that does not soften by water and excavated by pick axes.

Domat. It is mixed with clay and sand. It is a good soil for agriculture and engineering foundations.

Humous. It is dark black soil formed by decomposition of vegetable matter. It is unfit as foundation soil.

Permeable soils. The soils through which water can pass. Which opposes the passage of water are called **impervious**.

Force of cohesion. It is the force of attraction between the particles of the same substance.

Force of adhesion. It is the force of attraction between the particles of different substances.

Confined strata. It is impermeable strata while **unconfined** is a permeable strata.

Colloids. Gluey matter (sticky) found in clays consisting of very fine particles (0.002 mm) which absorbs moisture. These are fine particles which remain suspended in water and do not settle by gravity. They slow the motion of water in soil.

Shale—A compressible laminated clay. It is plastic when wet but becomes hard on drying.

Loam. A soft deposit consisting mixture of different grades of sands, silt and clay. It is slightly sticky and smooth. Squeezed when dry. The loams which contains a part of organic matter is good for cultivation.

Grit—A coarse sand or sharp fine gravel having angular grains.

Drift—A superficial deposits on the earth crust.

Diluvium—A glacial deposit.

Incoherent alluvium—It is soil composition of loose granular graded material.

Non alluvial. Soils formed by disintegration of rocks. There are no silt problems for channels passing through this soil. It has hard beds.

Laterite soil—They are usually porous and well drained but lack in common nutrients.

Red soil. This is crystalline and formed by disintegration of sand stone deposits. It is not uniform in structure. At some places it is a good cultivated and at some places not. It is also not much suitable for an irrigation scheme. It is found in North India, Bihar and South.

Grain size classification

(*a*) U·S· Bureau of soil classification

Type of Soil	*Grain Size*
Fine gravel	2·0-1·0 mm
Coarse sand	1·0-0·5 mm
Sand	0·5-0·25 mm
Fine sand	0·25-0·1 mm
Very fine sand	0·1-0·05 mm
Silt	0·05-0·005 mm
Clay	less than 0·005 mm.

(*b*) **MIT classification**

Coarse sand	2·0-0·6 mm
Med. sand	0·6-0·2 mm
Fine sand	0·2-0·06 mm
Coarse silt	0·06-0·02 mm
Med. silt	0·02-0·006 mm
Fine silt	0·006-0·002 mm
Clay	less than 0·002 mm

(c) **Boulders**	greater than 200 mm
Cobbles	200-80 mm
Pebbles	80-2·36 mm
Gravels	60-2·00 mm.

11·2. Soil properties

Weight-volume relationship. The soil mass consists of solids and voids. The voids may be partially or wholly filled with water or air

$V = V_a + V_w + V_s$ and also $V_v = V_a + V_w$

where V = total volume of the soil, V_a = volume of air in the voids

V_w = volume of water in the voids, V_s = volume of solid particles

V_v = Total volume of voids.

1. Porosity. Porosity η is the ratio of the total volume of voids to the total volume of the soil *i.e.* $\eta = \dfrac{V_v}{V} = \dfrac{V_a + V_w}{V_a + V_m + V_s}$

2. Voids ratio. Void ratio e is the ratio of the total volume of voids to the volume of the solids *i.e.* $e = \dfrac{V_v}{V_s} = \dfrac{V_a + V_w}{V_s}$. It is more finer soil than coarse.

3. Degree of saturation. Degree of saturation S is the ratio of volume of water to the total volume of voids in a soil mass *i.e.* $S = \dfrac{V_w}{V_v} = \dfrac{V_w}{V_a + V_w}$ expressed in percentage as

$$S = \frac{V_w}{V_v} \times 100.$$

Type of sand	*Degree of saturation in percentage*
Dry sand	0
Humid sand	1-25
Damp sand	25-30
Moist sand	75-99
Saturated sand	100

The total weight of the soil mass W, consists of the following :

$W = W_w + W_s$ where W_w = weight of water, W_s = weight of solid.

The weight of air is negligible and so taken as zero.

4. Moisture content. Moisture content W of a soil is the ratio of weight of water to the weight of solids *i.e.* $W = \dfrac{W_v}{W_s}$. The weight used in the expression is of that water which is lost when the soil is heated to a temperature of 105°C to 110°C till its weight becomes constant.

5. Density, bulk density or unit weight of soil. It is weight of soil per unit mass or d (density) $= \dfrac{W}{V} = \dfrac{W_s + W_w}{V_s + V_v} = G \times dw \left(\dfrac{HW}{1+e}\right)$ where G = specific gravity of solid and dw = unit weight of water (gm/cc). The bulk density depends on type of soil, compaction and its moisture content. The weight of solid matter per unit volume of the soil is known as the dry density of the soil.

6. Specific gravity of soil (G). It is ratio of the density of soil to that of water. Its value varies between 2·65 to 2·75. (G = weight per unit volume of soil/weight per unit volume of water.) It can be determined by specific gravity bottles or a pycnometer.

Table 11·1. Specific gravities of important soils

Soil type	*Specific gravity*	*Soil type*	*Specific gravity*
Clay	2·44-2·92	Kaolin	2·47-2·58
Chalk	2·63-2·81	Silt with organic matter	2·40-2·50
Loam	2·65-2·75	Bentonite clay	2·34
Silt	2·68-2·72	Peat	1·26-1·80
Lime	2·70	Humus	1·37
Quartz and Sand	2·64-2·65	Peat	0·50-0·80
Quartzite	2·65	Sphagnuna 25% decomposed	

7. Optimum moisture content (OMC). It is percentage by weight of the dry soil at which a specified amount of compaction will produce maximum density in a soil.

For sand and gravel OMC varies 8 to 10%, 15% for silts and 15 to 20% for clays. The change in moisture content changes the value of angle of repose, amount of compaction required and cohesive strength of a soil. The density of the solids alone is some times known as absolute density.

Note. The bearing capacity of any soil usually increases with increasing dry density and decreasing moisture content. It is, therefore, necessary to compact soils to the maximum possible density. High density assures greater shear strength and imperviousness, moisture content effects more in the fine grained soils than coarse grained.

Index Properties. These are classified as soil grain properties and soil aggregate properties.

1. Soil grain properties. They are classified as grain size and grain shape properties.

(*a*) **Grain size property.** It is determined by passing the soil through a set of sieves having square opening. Sieving is not possible for grains smaller than 0·073 mm. Hence finish fraction obtained from a sieve analysis (BS sieve no. 200 or IS sieve no. 75 μ) has to be further analysed by a process of measurement of rate of settlement of soil particles in suspension by means of a hydrometer.

A known weight of dry soil is placed on a set of sieves arranged according to their sizes and shaken for about 10 minute in a sieve shaker. The soil retained on each sieve is weighed.

(*b*) **Grain shape**

(*i*) **Bulky grains.** Such soil grains are formed by mechanical break down of rock masses. When the soil formation takes place initially these grains have sharp edges and are termed angular and after an interval of time they worn out at edges.

(*ii*) **Flaky or shale like grains.** They are laminated and are then compared to their length and breadth. Clay minerals are usually of this type.

(*iii*) **Needle like grains.** A needle like grain shape is exhibited by a special group of clay minerals **'Kaolinetes'**.

2. Soil aggregate properties.

(*a*) **Elasticity of soils.** If the soil changes in shape and volume on the application of external load, but if it regains its original shape and volume on the removal of this load is known as an elastic soil, and the extreme limit to which a soil can repeatedly strained without causing fracture of the original shape is the resilience of the soil.

$$H_c = \frac{4\,T\cos\alpha}{d.\gamma w} \qquad \text{where } H_c = \text{capillary rise}$$

where T = force of surface tension, d = inner dia. of the tube

α = angle of contact, H_c is the rise in the water in the tube

The value of T decreases slightly with temperature. Its maximum value at 4°C = $75{\cdot}6 \times 10^{-6}$ kN/m i.e. 75·6 dynes or $\frac{75{\cdot}6}{981} = 0{\cdot}077$ gm wt/cm. The value at 20°C = $72{\cdot}8 \times 10^{-6}$ kN/m and at 30°C = $70.2\ 10^{-6}$ kN/m approximately. For practical purposes it can be taken as 75×10^{-6} kN/m. (between glass-water).

The height H_c is measured from the lower tangent of the meniscus which is concave.

For clear glass and water the mansacus is semi spherical and hence the angle α = 0. So that $H_c = \frac{4\,T}{d.\gamma w}$ since cos α = 1 or $H_c = \frac{0{\cdot}306 \times 10^{-4}}{d}$ m since γ_w for water is 1 and $4T$ is taken = $0{\cdot}306 \times 10^{-4}$ app.

Capillary rise for 1 mm dia $= \frac{0{\cdot}306 \times 10^{-4}}{1 \times 10^{-3}}$ m = 0·306 m = 30·6 cm

Capillary rise for 1 mm dia $= \frac{0{\cdot}306 \times 10^{-4}}{1 \times 10^{-3}}$ m = $3{\cdot}06 \times 10^{-2}$ m = 3·06 cm

Capillary rise for 1 cm dia. $= \frac{0{\cdot}306 \times 10^{-4}}{1 \times 10^{-2}}$ m = $0{\cdot}306 \times 10^{-2}$ m = 0·306 cm

It can then be seen that the capillary rise is highest in the smallest dia. tube

Table 11·2. Capillary rise and capillary pressures in different soils

Soil type	*Size of particle (mm)*	*Range of capillary rise H_c in cm or capillary pressure in gm wt/cm²*	*Capillary pressure in kN/m²* $= col(3) \times \frac{10^4}{10^3} \times \frac{9{\cdot}81}{10^3}$ $= \text{col}(3) \times 10$
1	2	3	4
Fine gravel	2-1	2-10	0.2-1
Coarse sand	1-0.5	10-15	1-1.5
Med. sand	0.5-0.25	15-30	1.5-3
Fine sand	0.25-0.05	30-100	3-10
Silt	0.05-0.005	100-1000	10-100
Clay	0.005-0.0005	1000-3000	100-300
Colloids	< 0.0005	> 3000	> 300

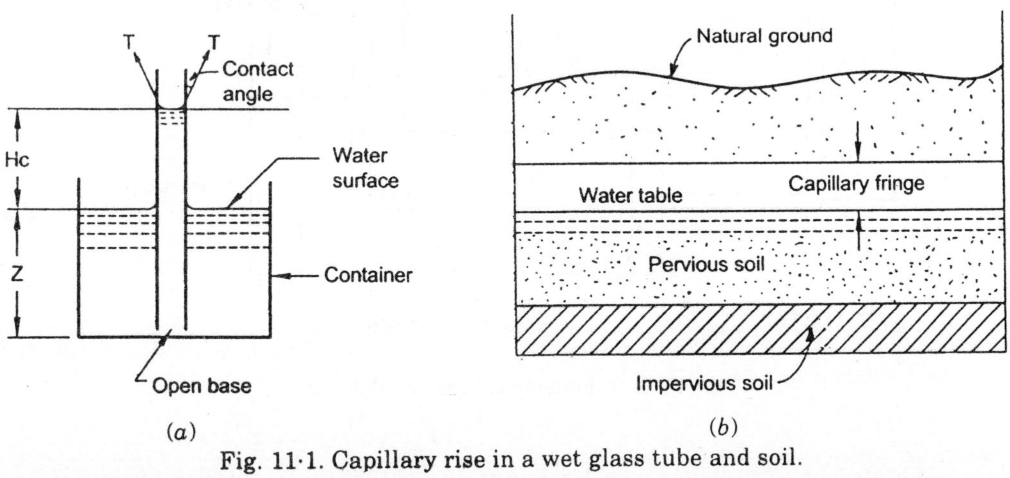

Fig. 11·1. Capillary rise in a wet glass tube and soil.

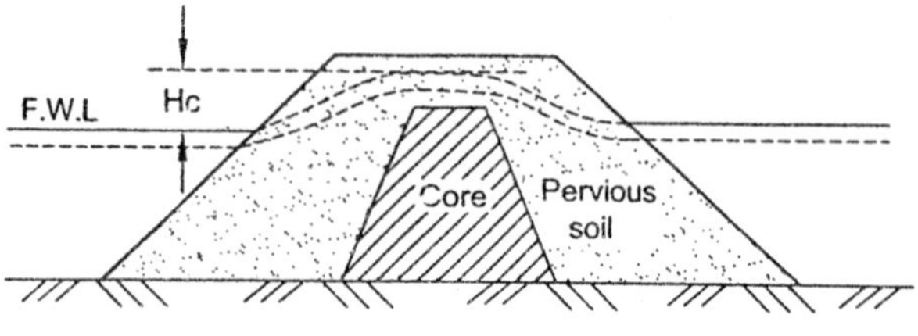

(c) Capillary syphoning in earthen dams.

Fig. 11·1. Capillary rise in a wet glass tube and soil

(b) **Compressibility.** It is the decrease in volume per unit increase of load. Its measure of rate at which consolidation proceeds is given by coefficient of consolidation. If a moist mass of gravel sand or silt is subjected to compression they suffer no significant volume change. But if a moist mass of clay is subjected to compression, moisture and air may be expelled resulting reduction in the volume of clay, which is not immediately recovered when the load is withdrawn.

Compressibility of sand and silt varies with density and compressibility varies directly with water content and inversely with cohesive strength. Clays and other compressible soils are known to swell when external load is removed.

(c) **Permeability.** The property of soil by virtue of which fluids are permitted to percolate through it is known as permeability. The passage of water through inter spaces or pores of the soil is called percolation. The soils which allow the passage of water through them are called permeable or pervious while those who do not allow are called impermeable or impervious. The flow through permeable soils is governed by the **Darcy's law** as follows.

The rate of flow is proportional to the gradient or $Q = KIA$ where Q = rate of flow, I = the gradient in flow lines, A = area of flow and K is a constant depending on the type of soil known as Darcy's coefficient of permeability. Permeability of cohesive soils is very small while of non cohesive soils is large. Therefore the permeability of a particular soil is a constant and is a property of the soil mass and not of individual particles.

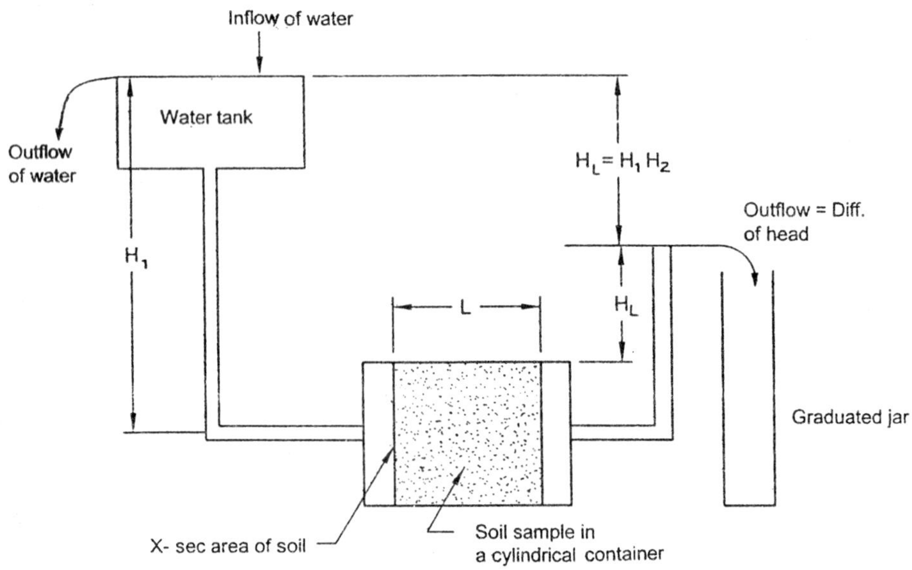

Fig. 11·2. Dimensional laminar flow app.

$$\text{Darcy's law} = Q = K\frac{H_L}{L}\cdot A \;(H_L/L = \text{slope I})$$

Table 11·3. Typical values of permeability (K)

S. No.	*Soil Type*	*K in cm / sec.*	
1.	Gravel	10^1 to 10°	
2.	Coarse sand	10° to 10^{-1}	$K = \frac{Q, L}{H_L \cdot A}$
3.	Med. sand	10^{-1} to 10^{-2}	
4.	Fine sand	10^{-2} to 10^{-3}	Q is known from
5.	Silty sand	10^{-3} to 10^{-4}	the graduated jar.
6.	Delhi silt	7×10^{-5}	
7.	Boston Blue clay	6×10^{-7}	
8.	London Clay	1.5×10^{-9}	

Permeability of stratified soil deposits.

Case I. When flow is parallel to bedding planes.

Flow along x-axis.

$$K_x = \left[\frac{K_1 d_1 + K_2 d_2 + K_3 d_3 \ldots\ldots}{d_1 + d_2 + d_3 \ldots\ldots}\right]$$

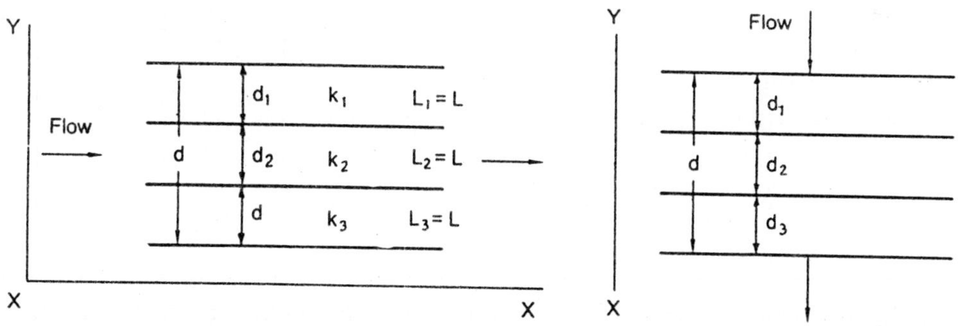

(a) (b)

Fig. 11·3.

Case II. When flow is perpendicular to bedding planes.

Flow along y-axis

$$K_y = \left[\frac{d_1 + d_2 + d_3 + \ldots\ldots}{\frac{d_1}{K_1} + \frac{d_2}{K_2} + \frac{d_3}{K_3} + \ldots\ldots}\right]$$

(*d*) **Capillarity.** Due to the capillary action the water rises up in the pores of the soil (due to surface tension) even against gravity. The rate is more in fine particles than in coarse particles. The capillary rise in a wet soil may be 4 to 5 times the rise in the same soil when dry. Gravel has practically no capillary rise, sands and silts have 20 cm to 120 cm and clays have a rise upto 120 cm or more (details see in hydraulics chapter)

(*e*) **Cohesion.** It is the internal molecular attraction which resists the shear of the soil. Cohesion of a soil decreases as the moisture content increases. Cohesion is more in clays than in sands and is independent of the external load.

(*f*) **Internal friction.** It is due to the resistance of grains to sliding over each other and is the characteristic of the coarse material of particle size more than about 0.002 mm. The magnitude of the internal friction of granular mass depends on the grading moisture content and load to which it is subjected. It is high with angular grains, rough surface, increased load and is reduced in the presence of lubricant such as water. For coarse material it is usually assumed that the particle size distribution giving the greatest dry density has the greatest internal friction. The strength of a non cohesive soil depends entirely on internal friction. The resistance in sliding of grain particles of soil mass depends on the angle of internal friction. The true **angle of internal friction** of clay is seldom zero and may be as much as 26°. For silts the angle is about 20° and for dry sand as much as 34°.

(*g*) **Plasticity.** It is the property of a soil to undergo large deformations when stressed without cracking or crumbling. Plasticity is a major characteristic of all cohesive soils and is due to the lubricating effect of the water films between adjacent particles. Cohesionless soils are non plastic.

(*h*) **Atterberg limits**

Table 11·4. Atterberg's limits for some common soils

S. No.	*Soil type*	*Clay size particles* %	*Silt size particles* %	*Sand size particles* %	*L.L.* (w_1)	*P. L.* (*WP*)	*P. L.* or I_p (*WL* – *WP*)
1.	Moutmosillonite-Na	100	0	0	710	54	656
2.	Illite-Na	100	0	0	120	53	67
3.	Kaolinite-Na	100	0	0	33	32	21
4.	Delhi Silt	15	70	15	32	22	10
5.	Ghaggar clay	33	58	4	51	25	26
6.	Dhan ausi clay	35	64	1	51	30	21
7.	Bean shale	30	68	2	35	19	16
8.	Mombay marine clay	66	32	2	90	40	50
9.	London clay	50	–	–	74	25	49

(*i*) **Liquid limit (LL).** It is the minimum water content at which a Pat of soil, cut by a groove of standard dimension, expressed as percentage of the dry weight of the soil will flow for a distance of 1.25 cm (1/2 in) like a liquid when jarred (tapped) slightly by 25 blows in a standard liquid approximately. At this limit the cohesion is practically zero.

Most of the clay soils have LL about 50 to 90 percent. Fat clays which are highly plastic, having a high content of colloidal particles have high LL while lean clays have low LL. Presence of organic matter in clay increases LL and lowers the P.L. If sand or silt is added to clay its LL is lowered. A LL between 20 and 40 indicates a mixture of sand or silt predominating. Peats have a very high LL of several hundred percent but a small PL.

(*ii*) **Plastic limit PL.** The plastic limit indicates the percentage of moisture at which the soil changes with decreasing wetness from a plastic to a semi plastic state or with increasing wetness from the semi solid to the plastic state. It is the lower limit of plastic state and is the moisture content at which a thread of soil can be rolled without breaking until it is only 3 mm in dia. When it just begins to crumble under pressure exerted by the hand. A small increase in moisture above the PL will destroy cohesion and shear strength of the soil.

Sand gravel and peat do not posses plasticity and have no plastic limit and can not be rolled into threads at any moisture content. Clays and colloids posses a high degree of plasticity and silts have only occasionally a PL. Clays have an average PL 45, colloids 46 and silts 20. A soil having high clay contain usually high LL and PL and less cohesive soils have lower figures.

The LL and PL signifies at limit at which a solid passes from solid to liquid or plastic stage.

(*iii*) **Plasticity index (PI).** It is a numerical difference between the liquid and plastic limit of a soil and indicates the magnitude of the range of moisture content over which the soil is in plastic condition. It indicates the fineness of the soil and its characteristics as regards plasticity and cohesiveness *i.e.* its power to change shape without altering its volume. A high value of PI indicates excess of clay or colloids, when the PL is equal or greater than the LL, the PI is zero.

	LL	*PL*	*PI*
Sand	20	0	0
Silt	27	20	7
Clay	100	46	45
Colloids	399	45	0

(*iv*) **Shrinkage limit (SL).** It is the limiting moisture content in percentage of the dry weight of the soil at which a further reduction in the moisture by evaporation will not cause any further decrease in the volume of the soil mass but at which an increase in the moisture content will cause an increase in the volume of the soil mass. Evaporation in water causes shrinkage in a soil upto a certain degree, beyond which decrease in volume does not occur ; at this stage the soil has reached its shrinkage limit. The SL indicates the moisture content at the point at which the soil passes from the semi-solid to the solid state and is a means of describing the pore space present in a soil after it has been allowed to compact itself to the maximum density obtainable by shrinkage.

The lower the SL of the soil the greater is the possible volume change corresponding to a given variation in the moisture content of the soil. For friable soils SL may be any where between the LL and 50 percent of LL and for feebly plastic 25 to 30%, for med. plastic 20 to 25%, for highly plastic 15 to 20%. There is no definite relation between PL and SL.

(*v*) **Consistency or liquid index (LI).** It is defined as the natural moisture content of the soil in excess of PL expressed as a percentage of PL.

$$\frac{\text{Natural moisture content} - \text{PL}}{\text{Liquid limit} - \text{Plastic limit}} \times 100 \text{ percent}$$

It is a measure of the consistency of a soil. Soft clays have LI approximate 100 percent while stiff clays have a LI which approximates to zero and may be even –ve.

(*vi*) **Field moisture equivalent (FME).** It is the percentage moisture of a soil at which the demands for absorbed water are fully satisfied and at which a drop of water placed on the smooth surface of the soil will not be absorbed immediately but will spread out over the surface.

11·3. Field test for soil identification

1. Visual inspection of dry soil. The physical state in regard of soil size, plasticity and angular conditions.

2. Identification of wet soil. Take a small quantity of wet soil on the palm, touch it with finger. If the soil is clayey a soapy touch is felt, for sandy soil a roughness will be experienced and for silty clay if squeezed between fingers, moisture will come out. Clay sticks with fingers and dries slowly but silt dries quickly and dusted off when dry leaving stain on palm.

3. Thread test. Take a sample of about 1 cm^3. Wet it if necessary and roll it to a thread on palm or on a smooth surface to a dia of about 3 mm. If crumbling does not occur (breaking to pieces), fold to thread and re-role as before and go on repeating the process until the moisture content of the soil has been reduced by drying during repetition to the plastic limit where crumbling occurs. The soil can be identified by the help of the plastic limit from the following table.

Table 11·5.

Division and subdivision	*Soil group description*	*Sign*
1. Gravity soils of which more than half of the coarse grains are larger than IS sieve 480	1. Well graded gravels or gravel sand mixtures with clay binder.	GB
	2. Well graded gravels or gravel sand mixtures, little or not fines.	GW
	3. Clayey gravels poorly graded or gravel sand clay mixtures.	GC
	4. Silty gravel or poorly graded gravel sand silt mixtures.	GM
	5. Poorly graded or gravels sand mixtures, little or no fines.	GP
2. Sandy soils (more than half of the coarse grains are smaller than IS sieve 480)	1. Well graded sands or gravelly sands with clay binder.	SB
	2. Well graded sands or gravelly sands little or no fines.	SW
	3. Clayey sands poorly graded or sand clay mixtures.	SC
	4. Silty sands or poorly graded sand silt mixtures.	SM
	5. Poorly graded sand or gravelly sands little or no fines.	SP
3. Fine grained in organic soils (more than 1/2 of the total material is smaller than IS sieve no. 8.)	1. Silt and very fine sand rock flour, silty to clayey fine sands with low plasticity.	ML
(*a*) In organic silts and clays with low than the med. compressibility.	2. Gravelly clays, sandy clays, silty clays, lean clay with low plasticity.	CL
	3. Clay of med. plasticity.	CI
(*b*) In organic silt and clays with low to med. compressibility.	4. Very compressible micaceous or dia atomaceous fine silty soils.	HM
	5. Clay of high plasticity.	
4. Silt and clay with high compressibility.	1. Silt and silt clays of low plasticity.	OL
	2. Clays of med. to high plasticity very compressible.	OH
5. Peat	1. Peat and other highly organic swamp soils.	PT

4. Dilatancy test. Prepare a pat of particles retained in IS sieve no. 425 μ of the soil sample in the size of 2 cm^3. Add water as required to make the paste non sticky and scft. Take the sample on palm and shake it vigorously in horizontal direction striking the hand with the other hand several times till the surface becomes glossy. When the sample is squeezed between the fingers the water and gloss disappears from the surface, the pat stiffens and finally crumbles. The appearance of water on the sample during shaking and disappearance during squeezing identifies the character of the fines in a soil. Very fine clean sands give the quickest and more distinct reaction while plastic clay has no reaction. In organic silts such as typical rock floor shows a moderate quick reaction.

5. Core cutter method for dry density of natural or compacted soil. It consists of a steel cutter 10 cm internal dia and 13 cm high. It has also 2.5 cm high dolly and a rammer with other equipments. If not known measure the inside dimensions of the cutter and calculate its capacity say *V*, weigh the cutter without dolly say it is *W*. Place the dolly on the cutter and insert it in the soil by ramming slightly till about 1 cm of the dolly goes in side the soil. Dig out the cutter from the ground remove the dolly and trim the soil above the cutter by a trowel. Care should be taken while the cutter is lifted from the soil that no soil may remain out of which is of the share of the cutter. For this the trowel for lifting must be used. Weigh the cutter with soil and without dolly say it is W_1. If water content is known the dry weight of the soil can be calculated and hence its dry density per cc. If not known, the soil inside the cutter may be heated on an oven at 105°C till a constant wt. remains or say it is W-2 with the container. Then water content is $W_1 - W_2$.

6. Sand replacement method for calculating dry density in situ. Dig a hole of known capacity and collect its soil and weigh say it is W_1. Again fill this hole with dry sand of known bulk density and weigh it. Then capacity of the hole $= \dfrac{\text{weight of sand}}{\text{density of sand}}$. The moisture content of the soil scooped can be determined as above. Knowing the volume of the soil scooped and its moisture content dry density can be calculated.

7. Collection of undisturbed samples. A steel, brass or aluminium tube having out side dia. 40, 45, 55, 65, 75, 125 mm with wall thickness in mm 1.25, 1.25, 1.25 ; 1.7, 1.7, 3.15 respectively are used. The height of the tube is 5 to 10 times of the dia. for sand penetration and 10 to 15 times of the dia. for day penetration subject to maximum of 60 cm. The lower edge is hevelled as a cutting shoe.

For easy working a wider pit at sample site is dug in the middle of which a **matam** of original is soil left of the bigger size than the sample is required. Over this matam the sampler is penetrated with the hammer upto the required depth, and then the sampler is lifted with the help of a trowel or spatula from the bottom. The extra soil of matam is removed.

Chunk samples. It is an open ends cylindrical container and is put over the undressed soil. The top is fitted by a flat bottomed rammer till full depth of the sampler penetrates in the soil. The sampler is removed by a spatula from bottom. The sides and top loose cover is coated with paraffin so that soil may not stick to the sampler walls. The height of the sampler can be reduced accordingly to the height of the sample required.

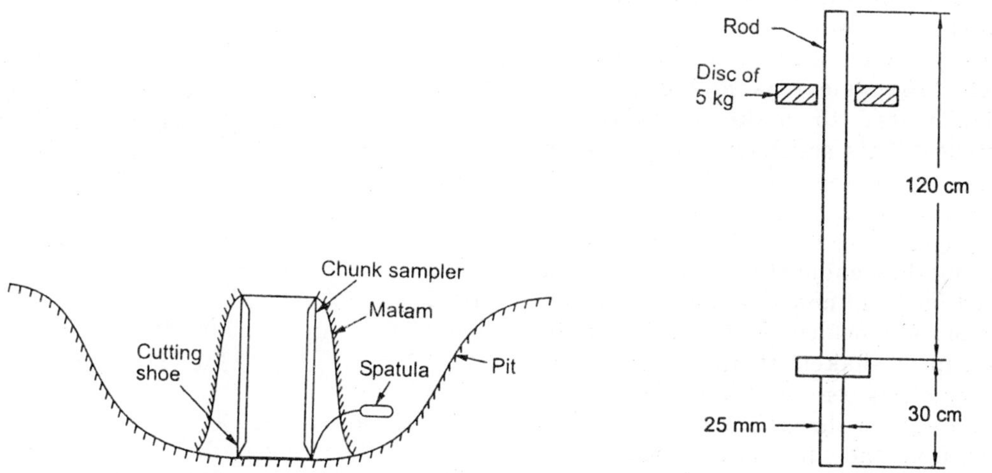

(*a*) Chunk sampler (*b*) Consolidation field test.

Fig. 11·4

8. Field test for consolidation of sand. A rod of steel (or plunger) 25 mm dia. and 1.5 metre long with both ends flat is taken. A disc having a weight of 5 kg moves up and down in the rod at stops at the base which is 30 cm from the lower end. For testing a sand foundation for its compactness, the disc is allowed to drop from the top of the rod to the base repeatedly till the lower 30 cm penetrates full. The no. of blows are recorded for full penetration and should be compared with the blows of a standard compacted sand foundation.

Soil Tests (in lab. and field)

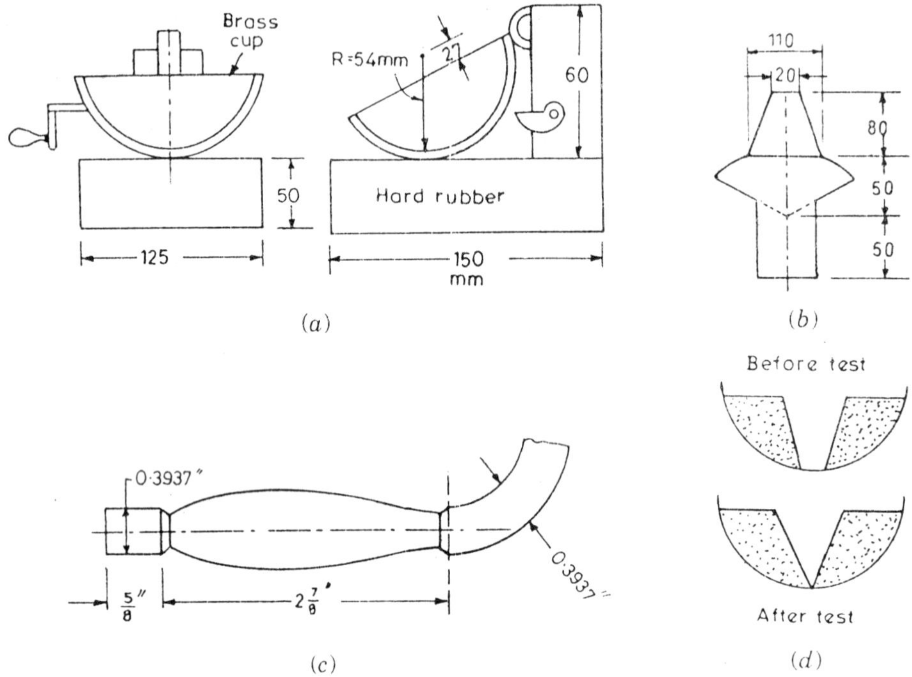

Fig. 11·5. Liquid limit apparatus.

Determination of liquid limit (LL). It is measured in a "liquid limit app." shown in the Fig. (11·5 *a* to *e*). About 120 gm of the specimen passing through 425 μ sieve is mixed thoroughly with distilled water to make a paste of uniform consistency. This soil paste is then placed in the brass cup of the app. and is levelled with a spatula. A groove is cut with either the cassagrande type grooving load (*b*) or the ASTM type grooving load (*c*). By turning the handle of the apparatus once the cup is raised by 1 cm and falls back again on the hard rubber block provided. In the test the grooved pat in the cup is shaken at an uniform and constant rate of two blows per sec. The no. of blows required to close the groove through a distance of 1.25 cm (1/2") are noted. The soil is immediately removed from the cup and kneeded. The blow count is then repeated. The difference in two successive blows should normally be with in ± 2. The water content of the paste is determined at every set of test and is repeated for different moisture contents. A graph is drawn of the number of blows plotted on the scale (abscissa) and ordinate as the water content on the natural or arithmetic scale. The test should always proceed from the drier to the wetter condition of the soil. The plotted curve is a straight line as near as possible. The liquid limit is read corresponding to 25 blows on the abscissa. The no. of blows used for the above plot be between 10 to 40.

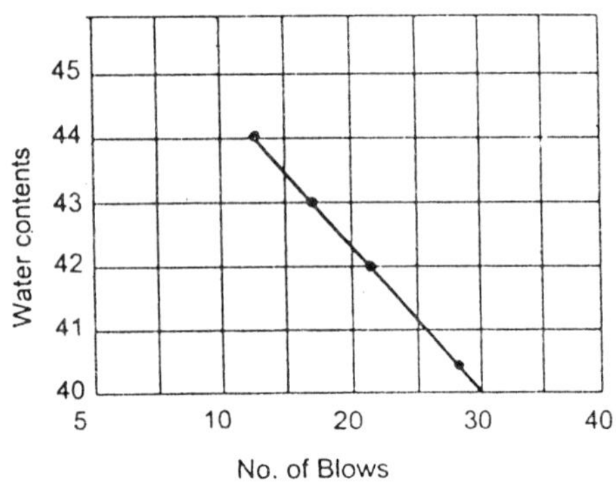

Fig. 11·5 (*e*). Flow curve.

Plastic limit test. Mix well about 30 gm of soil passing a 425 μ sieve with distilled water in a dish or on glass plate till it is plastic enough so as to make a ball. Take about 10 gm of the mass from the ball and roll into a thread on the ground glass plate with fingers till it is reached to a dia. of 3 mm, remould the soil thread to a ball again. Repeat this threading and remoulding process till the thread just starts crumbling at a dia. of 3 mm. Determine the water content of the crumbled thread. Repeat the process thrice with the test sample and take the average of the result of these water contents which is the required plastic limit.

Test for moisture content. There are a no. of methods for this test namely (*a*) oven dry method (*b*) Sand-bath method (*c*) Pycnometer test and (*d*) density method. oven dry method is a practical and easy method which is as follows—

Place a sample of soil about 50 gm if fine grained and 250 to 300 gm if coarse grained in a container with lid and weight say it is W_1. Place the container without lid in the oven and dry for 16 to 24 hrs. at a controlled temperature of 105°C to 110°C till constant weight is achieved. After drying remove the container from the oven allow to cool after replacing the lid on the container in a desiccator and weight say it is W_2. Cool and clean the container and weigh it with the lid say it is W_3. Then the water content = $\frac{W_1 - W_2}{W_2 - W_3} \times 100$ per cent.

Shrinkage limit test. Mix about 50 gm of soil passing a 425 μ sieve with distilled water in amount sufficient to fill the voids completely and make the soil pasty with out inclusion of air bubble.

In an empty "shrinkage container" the inside of which is coated with vaseline or any other grease. Fill the container completely with wet sample. Strike off top surface with a straight edge and the container is cleaned from out side and weigh it say it is W_1. Dry the soil container in an oven till the volume just becomes constant at a temperature of 105°C to 110°C cool and weigh say it is W_2 clean and dry the shrinkage container and weigh say it is W.

Take a mercury container larger than the capacity of the shrinkage container and fill it with mercury upto top till overflows. Keep this container in a wider vessel and fill the dry mass of the soil of shrinkage container in the mercury container, due to which mercury equal to the volume of the dry soil mass will overflow in the wider vessel. The weight of the spilled mass of the mercury can be obtained by the difference of weight of filled vessel-empty vessel. The volume of the splitted mass = volume of the dry soil mass in the shrinkage container = mass of the splitted mercury divided by the SP. gravity of mercury which is 13.6 gm/cc = V_2 (Say).

$$\text{Now shrinkage limit} = \frac{\text{Weight of water in saturated soil at shrinkage limit}}{\text{Weight of dry soil in the container}}$$

$= (W_1 - W_2) - W(V_1 - V_2)$ where V_1 = volume of the saturated mass which is equal to the capacity of the shrinkage container

W = SP. gravity of water = 1 gm/cc

Consolidation test. It is performed by Jodhpur consolidometer. An undisturbed sample of the soil is collected in a metal ring or cylinder. Two porous stones are kept on either face of the cylinder to facilitate drainage of the sample during test. The test load is applied on the upper stone vertically, gradually and the shrinkage in volume is noted at every set of load till the shrinkage ceases. When the equilibrium of load is reached *i.e.* no further settlement occurs even at the increase of load, the limiting load is noted. The data so obtained is plotted in the form of a dial reading shrinkage verses time curve for each load. Time required for consolidation is proportional to the square of the thickness of a soil stratum. Since the time rate of consolidation is a function of permeability of a soil, it determines the coefficient of permeability indirectly.

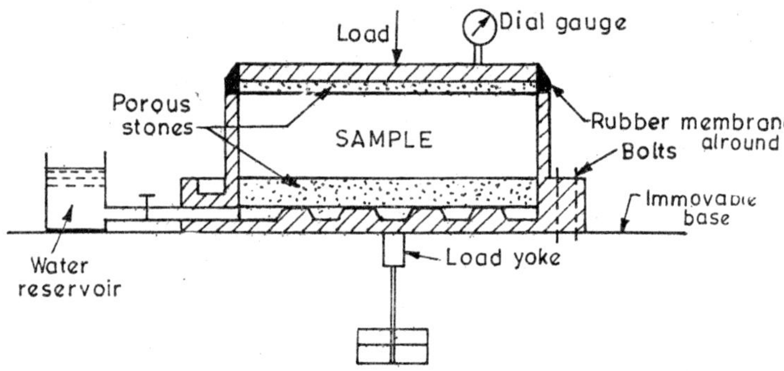

IS : 2720—1965 : Size of sample Dia. 60 mm. Thickness = 20 mm (Min.)
Note : Dia. to thickness ratio min. 3. Thickness not less than 10 × Max. Dia.

Fig. 11·6. Consolidometer.

Permeability measurements. (1) **Field method.** The average permeability of a soil stratum below the water table if a tube well exists or is constructed. So as to penetrate the stratum fully. Two observation wells or holes are needed at known distance apart away from the well. The well is continuously pumped at a steady discharge rate, till the water level inside the well becomes constant.

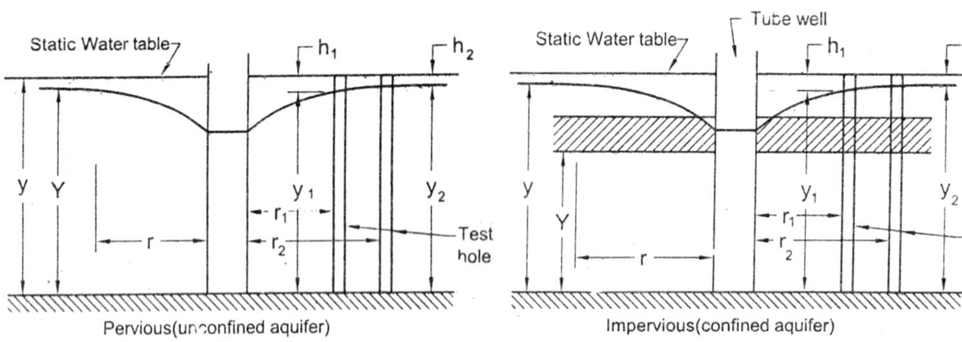

CASE I CASE II

Fig. 11·7. Measurement of Field permeability.

Case I. When in unconfined aquifer the pre water surface or the water table is inside the stratum itself. Discharge of well $Q = K\dfrac{dy}{dr}.2\pi ry$ or $K = Q\ \log_e \dfrac{r_2}{r_1}\Big/\pi\,(y_2^2 - y_1^2)$.

Case II. When in confined aquifer, the stratum is overlain by an impervious stratum, and the water table lies above the test stratum, inside the impervious stratum or in another structure still higher.

Discharge of well Q $=K\ dy/dr\ .\ 2\pi ry$ or $K = Q\ \log_e r_1/r_2/2r_1Y(y_2 - y_1)$ where K is constant of permeability.

r_1 =horizontal distance from the tube well to the neared test hole and r_2 to the farther test hole.

y_1 =Vertical head of the neared test hole from the impervious stratum to the water surface and y_2 = the farthest test hole.

Y =the vertical head between impervious layer to the pre water surface in 1st case and head between two impervious layers in the 2nd case.

2. Laboratory method (a) Constant head permeameter. Two porous screens are placed in a vertical cylinder. The inside area of the soil cylinders gives the area of x-section of the Sample A. The length L is measured between two porous plates. The soil sample is 1st saturated by connecting the source of supply to the bottom, the water rises up through the Sample and expels the air in the pores upwards. The constant level water supply is then connected to the top of the Sample. So that ready flow conditions develop under a constant head. A constant level is maintained in the source of supply by always having a small over flow taking place at its top. The soil Sample is placed in a constant head chamber which is filled to the brim at the start of the experiment so that any further water entering into it must overflow. The difference between the water levels in the supply and the constant head chamber gives the constant head H.

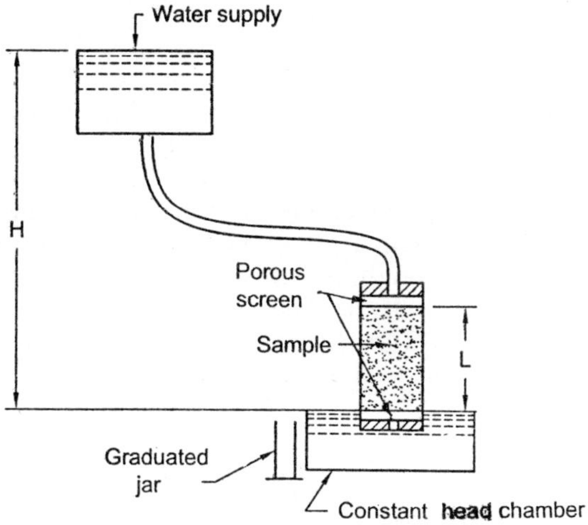

Fig. 11·8 (a) Constant head permeameter.

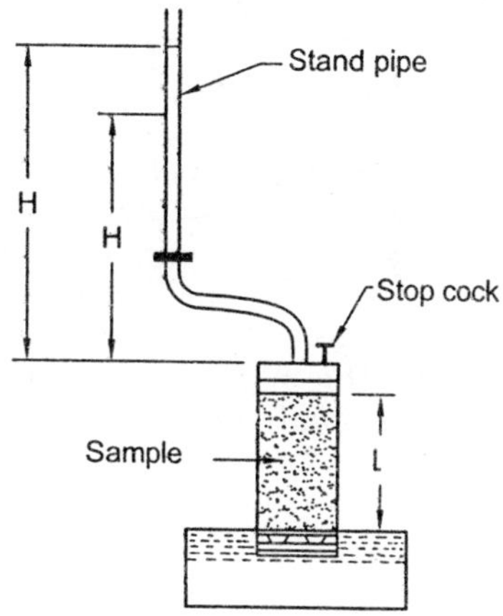

Fig. 11·8 (b) Variable head permeameater.

The quantity of water overflowing, the constant head chamber is collected in a graduated jar for a known time. Then by 'Darcy's law' $Q = K/A$ or $K = QL/HA$.

In impervious soils, the quantity of seepage is very small hence this constant head permeameter is suitable for pervious soils only.

(b) **Variable head permeameter.** It is widely used in all type of permeable or non permeable soils. It consists of two porous plates at the ends of a cylindrical mould, the length and area of which is determined as above. For accurate measurements the mould should be placed in a constant head chamber as above which should be full to the brim at the start of experiment. After all the air has been exhausted from the sample and the mould has been filled upto the top, its cover is filled and tightened. A graduated stand pipe or burette of inside area a is connected to the inlets provided in the top cover by a flexible tubing. A stop cock also provided in the top cover, is then opened for a short time to allow any air bubble entrapped with in to escape. The stop cock is then closed. Seepage now takes place from the burette, through the saturated sample and into the constant head chamber from which it overflows and spills out. The head causing flow through the sample at any instant is the difference between the water level in the stand pipe and that in the constant head chamber, while the later remains constant, the formal falls as the water percolates through the sample. The time it required for the water level in the burette to fall from a mark at height H_1 to another mark H_2 above the same water level in the chamber is noted by Darcy's law.

$$= a \frac{dh}{dt} = K\,(H/L)\,A \quad \text{or} \quad K = \frac{2.3\,aL}{At} \log_{10} H_1/H_2$$

The rate of fall of water level can be adjusted to convenient and accurate measurements by adjusting the area of the stand pipe, larger area being needed for more pervious soils.

Table. Coefficient of permeability of some soils

Type of soil	*Coefficient permeability in cm / sec.*
Clay	0·000001 or less
Silt	0·0005 – 0·0001
Silty sand	0·002 – 0·0001
Fine sand	0·05 – 0·001
Sand mixture	0·01 – 0·005
Coarse sand clean	0·1 – 0·01
Clean gravel	1·0 or more

Direct shear test. The test is performed in a shear box which contains of two parts, the upper fixed frame and the lower moveable frame. The two halves of the box are screwed together and the test sample is placed in the box, one half being in each frame. Depending on the type of test porous plates or brass gratings are placed on the top and bottom of the sample. The screws joining the two halves of the box are removed before subjecting the sample to shear. The spacing screws which pass through the upper part of the box, are turned so that there is a small space between the two halves. The spacing of the two halves is governed by the maximum size of the soil particles. This space is also increased for loose soils. The upper half should not ride on a soil grain between the edges.

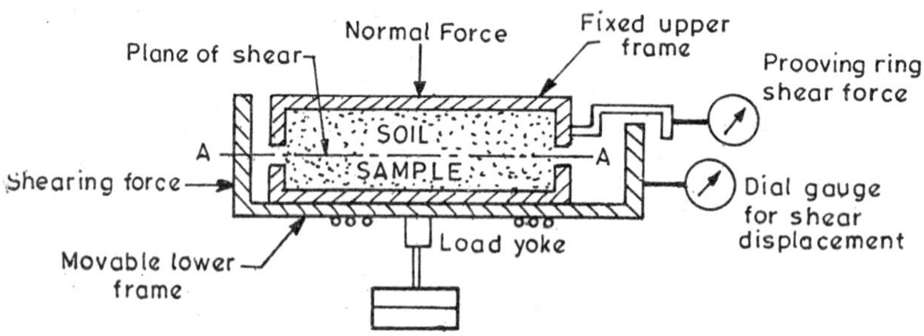

Fig. 11·9 (*a*) Direct shear apparatus.

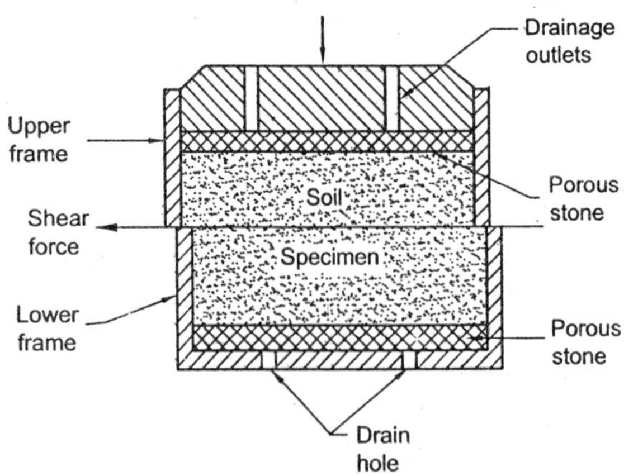

Fig. 11·9 (*b*). Shear box text apparatus.

A vertical load w per unit area is applied to the upper frame by placing loads on the loading yoke. The sample is subjected to shearing stress at the plane of separation *AA*. Shear is caused by application of shearing force to the lower frame while the upper frame is held fixed in position. The shearing force is increased either gradually or in steps and is measured by means of a proving ring. The relative motion between the upper and lower frames is called the shearing displacement and is measured on the dial gauge.

California bearing ratio test. The test is done for pavements design. The apparatus consists of a mould having an internal dia. of 150 mm and a total height of 175 mm, out of which 50 mm high removable. Caller is attached at its top. The base plate is perforated. A circular plunger of 50 mm dia. (according to Indian standard) is placed in the centre of the top of the soil sample. A hydraulic jack pushes the speci-men upwards while the plunger is held in position, causing the plunger to penetrate into the specimens. The force is indicated by a gauge on the hydraulic jack, while the penetration is measured by a dial gauge attached to the plunger and abutting against the top of the coller Annular weights of 2.5 kg each with the central hole, slightly larger than the plunger dia. can be placed on the soil specimen to simulate the weight of the pavement. The test may be done on undisturbed or remoulded sample. The for-mer in case when the subgrade is not to be disturbed while the later in case when the subgrade is to be compacted.

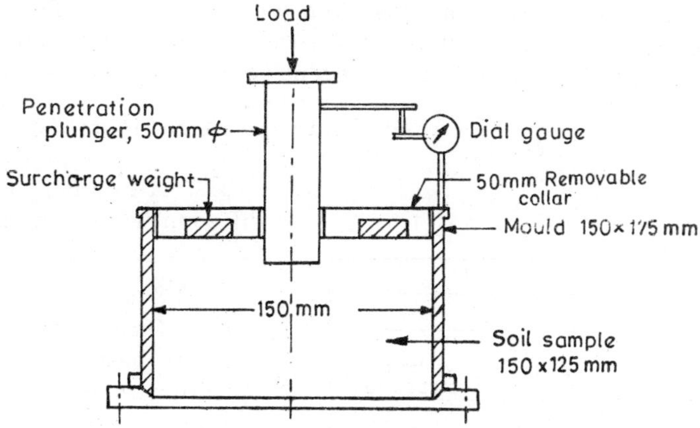

Fig. 11·10. California bearing ratio apparatus.

California Bearing Ratio (CBR) is a measure of load carrying capacity of a standard soil as 100. A standard crushed rock specimen has been taken as a standard having 100% value. The standard 100 CBR is one in which a load of 1360 kg penetrates a flat plunger with base of area 14·3 cm^2 to a distance of 0·25 mm at a rate of 0·125 mm per min.

The load is a applied to the plunger to obtain a constant rate of penetration of 1·25 mm (0·05 inch) min. In the usual type of apparatus the rate of penetration is controlled by a stop watch. Reading of the load should be taken at the following penetrations—0·025, 0·05, 0·075, 0·10, 0·15, 0·20, 0·30, 0·40 and 0·50 inches.

The penetrations is plotted against the load and a smooth curve drawn, through the plotted points the values of the loads at penetration of 0·1 inch (0·25 mm) and 0·2 inch (0·50 mm) are read from this curve and expressed as percentages of the standard loads of 3000 lbs (1360 kg) and 4500 lbs (2040 kg) respectively. The standard loads were obtained from tests on a sample of crushed stone which was defined as having a CBR of 100%. The larger of the two percentages gives the CBR of the given material.

Test for optimum moisture content (IS). The apparatus consists of a mould 100 mm internal dia. and 127.3 mm high having a capacity of 1000 cc and of known weight say W. It has a detachable coller at the top and the mould is bolted to the base plate.

The soil to be tested is mixed with a measured quantity of water thoroughly. The mould is filled with this wet earth in three equal layers. Each layer is compacted with a rammer having a weight of 2.6 kg and a drop of 310 mm. Each of the three layers is given 25 blows evenly to all sides. For heavy compaction 4.89 kg weight rammer with a 450 mm drop is used. The soil is filled a little higher than the mould in the collar. The collar should be removed and the level of the soil in the mould should be levelled by a trowel, removing extra soil above the mould. The mould is

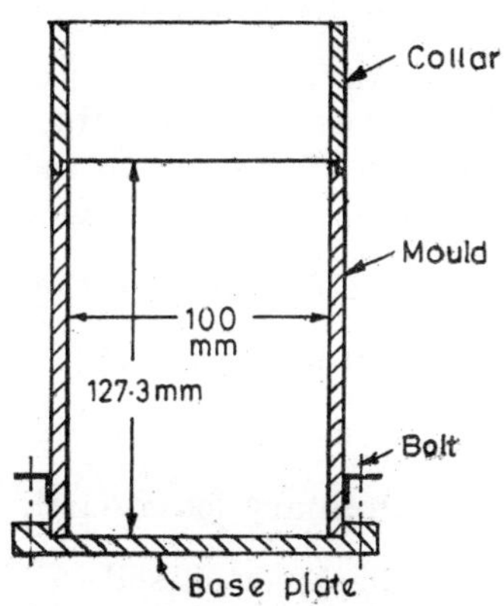

Fig. 11·11 (*a*).

then removed from the base and weighed say W_1. Then the weight of the wet soil in the mould is $W_1 - w$; w is the moisture content in the compacted soil in the mould, determined by drying the sample in the oven. (weight wet soil – weight dry soil) weight of the moist soil per cc $= \frac{W_1 - w}{1000}$ Say Dw hence the weight of dry soil per cc $= \frac{Dw}{1+w}$, Say Dd.

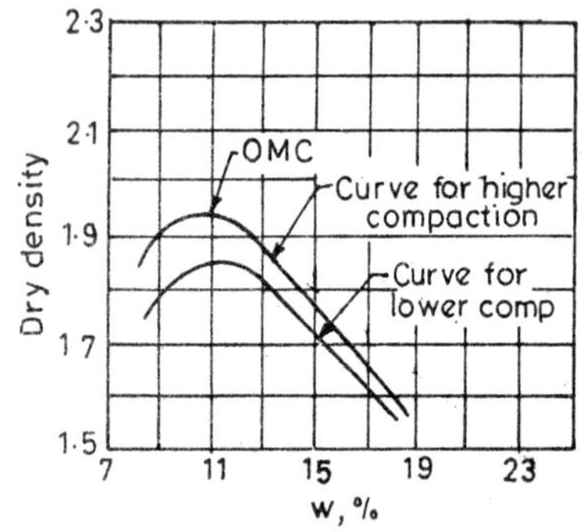

Fig. 11·11 (*b*). Shear box text apparatus.

A number of such observations are taken with different water contents in the soil and a curve is plotted for that compaction, with $w\%$ as x-axis and Dry density as y-axis.

Other series of curves for different compactions can also be drawn. It is seen from the curve that the optimum moisture for a certain compaction which is higher is less than the optimum moisture for lower compaction.

Note. As a guide the PL of a soil may be considered approximately to represent optimum moisture content.

At a given moisture content the maximum possible compaction would be obtained when all the air is expelled, but in practice a certain air will remain in water in minute bubbles.

Moisture content in the soil plays a main part in the compaction of soils. By mixing of the water, the particles of the soil are surrounded by a water film making them more lubricant. The more water is mixed the more lubricacy is achieved by which particles slip easily in the voids of the soil expelling the air out. But a stage comes when whole of the intersticks of the soil is filled by the water and on compacting this water opposes, the entry of soil particles, hence it can be said that there is a certain limit only to which the addition of water can help in compaction. This stage is called as optimum moisture content (OMC). This OMC is also effected by the quantum of the compaction applied. The higher the compaction load the lesser is the water content is needed for optimum condition.

11·4. Compaction of Earthen Embankments

Sand. Sand is compacted better by vibrations created by vibro rammers or vibro-rollers. OMC has no effect on sand.

Sandy clay—Can be consolidated by penumatic tyres and sheep foot rollers etc.

Clay. As the clay containing clods, mixing of water at site while ramming is in progress does not effect the soil efficiently. Hence it is better to wet the borrow area before excavation of the soil to the extent of optimum moisture content. The clods if any should be broken by hand rammers before compaction.

The following settlement allowance is given per metre height of loose material.

Soft or loose rock, laterite or gravel	8 cm
Firm compacted earth	12 cm
Ordinary loose earth	16 cm
Black cotton soil	24 cm

Table 11·6. Thickens of layers in different type of soils in one operation of consolidation

Type of plant	*Silt and heavy clay*	*Sandy soil*	*Gravel shingle or loose sand*	*Fragmented rock with 10 mm maximum size*
8 mm steep foot roller	15-20 cm	—	Loose sand should be damped	—
5 ton smoother Roller	—	20-30 cm	—	—
Tractor	—	—	30 cm	—
Heavy smooth rollers	—	—	—	30-60 cm

As a thumb rule total vertical settlement of a well consolidated embankment is about 1/20 of its height. One metre height in small channels is given with the following settlement allowance.

All works rolled and watered	8 cm
Rolled but not watered	16 cm
Niether rolled nor watered	24 cm

Note : 1. After one rainy season the embankment is considered to be 50% settled, after 2 monsoons 75% and after 3 monsoons 87.5% is considered to be settled.

2. The outer slopes are kept 150 cm extra, which is cut after consolidation to the proper section to ensure complete consolidation on outer slopes. **Slope compactors** are also used on slopes.

Compaction equipments

Smooth drum Rollers. These machines are self propelled or the towed type with small steel roll surfaces. In self propelled type it can be three roll (Tricycle configuration) or tandem two rolled types. The contact area between the drum of the machine and the surface of the soil is a narrow strip and as a result the stress in the soil fall off rapidly as depth in the layer increases. The drum has negligible penetration in the soil.

Pneumatic tyre rollers. This type of machine relies on dead weight acting upon pneumatic-tyred wheels to produce the compaction effort. There are single axle machines and double axle machines. Single axle machines are towed by tractor with a single axle set of wheels usually three or four. Double axle machines are self propelled or towed by tractor. They have two axle sets, the rear axle set arranged so that its wheels track is in the gaps in the wheel tracks of the front axle set. The tyres have significant penetration into the soil.

Impact rollers. It consists of a square conc. block with steel conversing having rounded corners. The impact roller is claimed to produce compaction to a considerable depth with certain soils and to be applicable to a wide range of soil types.

Sheep foot rollers. These machines can be towed or self propelled and the drums consists of a cylinderical shell with producing "feet". These foots can be tapered or can be of "club" type. The soil is supposed to be consolidated when the impression by the feet is not more than 12 mm achieved by 16 to 20 trips. The density of top layer should be about 1.48.

Tamping foot/Pad foot rollers. It is modified sheep foot roller. The producing face area is much larger than in sheep foot.

Grid rollers. These machines are designed to be towed by a tractor and have a compacting roll comprising of heavy steel mesh of square pattern. They are appropriate for the compaction of shallow layers of soft rock due to their ability to crush particles with high peak stresses under the points of contact of the steel mesh. Where heterogeneous soils occur, especially mixtures of wet and dry plastic goods, the grid tends to.become blocked with soil and the benefits of the potential high peak stresses can be test.

Vibratory rollers. These rollers consists of a cylinderical steel drum with one rotating eccentric weight mounted at the centre of the drum. The rotating eccentric weight produces vibrations which causes the roller to bounce against the soil. These rollers are very effective in compacting cohesionless soils in thick layers.

Oscillating rollers. These rollers are characterised by two rotating eccentric weights in side a cylinderical steel drum which are phased to produce horizontal vibrations. In these rollers the drum mover lifts off the ground and produces horizontal dynamic stresses. These rollers offer greater driver comfort and produce less damaging influence on adjacent structures.

Vibratory plate compactors. These machines have a flat plate in contact with the soil on which either one or two eccentrically weighted shafts are mounted. Because of their much smaller size these vibrators have lower out put and are used for compaction of cohesionless soils in confined areas and spaces. These are electric driven and is operated by dragging by hand such as plane vibrators in RCC work.

Vibrotampers. These are engine drive reciprocating machines which acts on a spring system through which vertical oscillations with an amplitude of about 10-80 mm are set up in a base plate. It has a mass of about 50-150 kg. It is used for the compaction of most type of soils in confined areas and spaces.

11·5. Use of geogrids for ground improvements. The development of use of geosynthetic in ground improvement is only an exclusive of the earlier techniques like bamboo facines etc. The options that are available are through mechanical, hydraulic and chemical treatment.

The destruction between a geogrid and a geotextile is that the former is also a filter where as the later is a non filter. A geogrid functions by restraintment and reinforcement by using a geogrid in ground improvement technique we look forward to improving the bearing capacity as well as to restricting the settlement within permissible limit and if possible to avoiding differential settlement totally.

A geogrid is distinguished by its reinforcement characteristics from other geosynthetic materials which is primarily due to its ability with the aggregates. This has led to the stage that wherever a geogrid is used to improve bearing capacity it is called as a reinforced soil.

Soil Stabilization using additives. When a poor quality soil is encountered at construction site, the structure can be designed accordingly or the unsatisfactory soil can be replaced with a suitable soil borrowed from near by area. Another option is to modify the properties of the existing soil so that it meets the design requirements. The soil stabilization can be achieved in a variety of ways :

(*a*) By using mechanical means *i.e.* compaction (*b*) By drainage including electrical osmosis (*c*) By using thermal energy *i.e.* calcination (*d*) Improving the gradation of the soil by adding other soil, aggregate or gravel etc. (*e*) By adding of chemical stabilization agents such as lime, cement or fly ash etc. Local soils can also be mixed with industrial/agro wastes like fly ash, slag, rice husk ash etc. So as to improve their properties and make them suitable for high way construction. This also helps the problem of disposal of this waste materials.

These additives are both organic and inorganic. The chemicals which are considered as chemically active are lime, cement, pozzolana, since they react with soils forming cementing compounds.

Additives like bitumen, resin etc. are inactive additives because soil is stabilized by water proofing and/or adhesion between soil particles.

Lime Stabilization. It has been observed that clayey soils respond better to lime stabilization. When lime is added to highly plastic soil it undergoes chemical reaction with clay particles produce the binding material. Three types of reactions occur when lime is mixed with moist soil. First calcium ions cause reduction in plasticity of cohesive soils by ion exchange and soil becomes more friable and workable. Hence preliminary addition of one to two per cent of lime to fine grained soils tends their plasticity and improves mixing with other stabilizers like cement or bitumen if necessary. The 2nd reaction is the carbonation of lime by atmospheric carbon dioxide, forming calcium carbonate, a weak cementing material. The 3rd reaction namely pozzolana reaction is slow and results in the formation of long term cementation of compacted mixture of lime and soil. This involves interactions between hydrated lime and ciliceous and aluminous minerals in the soil to form cementation compounds. Indian Roads Congress (IRC) has recommended that the calcium oxide/Calcium hydroxide content in the lime to be used for stabilization, should be at least 70% since the quantity of lime varies widely.

The quantity of lime required depends mainly on plasticity index. As little as half per cent has been used for soils of low P.I. However normal requirement is 4% to 6% by dry weight. The lime can be applied to the soil in two ways, dry or as a slurry. Better penetration is obtained when it is used as slurry. After 1st mixing the material is lightly compacted at or some what above the optimum moisture content and is then allowed to cure for three or four days. The lime is spreaded on soil surface, and then mixed by rotillor used for road construction.

Stabilization by cement. All types of soils except highly organic are unimproved by cement Stabilization. For Stabilization to be economically feasible it is considered that the percentage passing B.S. sieve no 200 should generally be less than 35% and should in no case exceed 50%. The liquid limit should be less than 40% and the plastic index less than 18%. The usual range of percentage of cement by weight is 5 to 15%. The lower limit being appreciable for sandy soils while the higher to clayey soils.

Adequate compaction is essential for obtaining satisfactory strength in soil cement. As compaction attained depends on moisture content, it is therefore necessary to maintain the optimum moisture content during compaction of soil cement. The steps required are pulverisation of soil, dry mixing, wet mixing after necessary quantity of water has been added, spreading and compaction and finally curing for 7 days by covering with wet straw or sand. Some chemicals like gypsum improves the soil cement properties.

Lime pozzolana Stabilization. Presence of clay size particles is necessary for improvement of soils using lime and silty, sandy soils generally have low or negligible content and are therefore not amenable to lime stabilization. Pozzolana which are essentially siliceous materials having cementing properties of their own react with lime at ordinary temperature and in the presence of moisture resulting in the formation of cementaneous compounds pozzolana can be a naturally occurring materials such as volcanic dust or artificial materials like fly ash, rice husk ash, pulverized blast furnace slag, ground bricks (surkhi) etc. of these materials fly ash has the greatest potential and lime fly ash mixes have been used to stabilise soils for improving the sub grade or for constructing the sub base and the base course layers of the pavement. The ratio of the time to pozzolana and ratio of the lime pozzolana to soil are the important determinants of the properties of stabilised soil mixture. Usually the ratio between the lime and pozzolana varies from 1 : 1 to 1 : 9. Increasing the lime pozzolana percentage beyond a certain limit does not bring in common strength gain of the soil. The behaviour of lime soil and lime pozzolana soil are identical in many respects. Both reduce the plasticity, increase the strength and reduce the volume change in soil and enhance the durability.

Bitumen Stabilization. Bituminous materials such as asphaltic bitumen, tars or emulsions have been successfully employed for soil Stabilization. It works as a binder as well as water proofing agent. In dry climates bituminous material as a binder is sprayed on the soil surface. If soil has a moderate cohesion the surface can carry light traffic in dry weather but because slippery after rains.

Bitumen mixed with solvent called a cut back. Solvent may be a petroleum product. Cut back or Bitumen emulsions which contain about 5% water can also be used with dry sandy soils. The mixing is carried out at moisture contents above the plastic limit. As water dries out to the optimum percentage for compaction, compaction may be carried out. Cut back bitumen can be added to pulverised soils as in soil contents. For water proofing bitumens containing a high percentage of wax are most effective.

Resin-Stabilization. Resinous materials like vinsol-resin and Resin which are products of distillation of pine trees have been employed to a limited extent for water proofing of soils. The addition of about 1% of resin to the soil reduces its water absorption to almost 1/10th of the untreated soil. Resins do not have appreciable influence on the cohesion or angle of internal friction of soils are almost solely used for water proofing.

Molasses Stabilization. Addition of molasses lead to increased moisture retention and cementation. It is subjected to fungal action and improvement of strength is not significant.

Other chemical additives used for Stabilization

(*a*) **Sodium chloride.** It is used as dust palliative for roads. It reduces permeability and to some extent improves strength. Being high soluble in water it washes away and hence is used as a short term stabiliser.

(*b*) **Sodium silicate.** It alone or with combination with other chemicals stabilize the sandy soils. This chemical has the ability to react with soluble calcium salts in water to form cementing agents.

(*c*) **Calcium chloride and calcium sulphate.** Hygroscopic property of calcium chloride is made use to reduce evaporation loss. It is usual as dust palliative on roads or the controlling placement moisture. This is also used for soil grouting. In combination with sodium silicate, calcium sulphate has been used as additive to accelerate setting.

(*d*) **Sodium hydroxide.** Used to stabilise lateritic soils. Its caustic in nature makes its handling difficult and it absorbs carbon dioxide quickly and losses its effectiveness.

(*e*) **Aluminium salts.** These salts have useful effect on soil stability or resistance to action of water.

(*f*) **Organic compounds.** In Di-hydrogenated tallow dimethyle ammonium chloride the clay particles tend to fluctuate when this salt is added and this results in lowering the plasticity of soil. This reduces the moisture intake by soil, thereby improving the soil.

Other mixes. Soil can be improved by adding locally available materials like sand, gravel, kanker and brick bats etc. Depending on the type of soil and gravel, the mix proportions are determined. The size of aggregate must preferably be less than 25 mm size and the ratio of soil and aggregate should be 2 : 1 by volume. Sand clay mixes have been used (or a non plastic material like fly ash and silt) according to IRC, their plastic index range must be 9-11 when used in wearing course and six when used as sub base course.

Dynamic compaction of soils. It involves the repeated dropping a large conc., cast iron or steel hammers from predetermined heights. Typically hammer's range from 5 to 30 tonnes in weight and drop heights from 10 to 25 metres. The repeated application of high energy impacts causes deep densification of the deposits being treated densification to depth of 5-15 metres are to line and upto 30 metres have been reported. This process increase the bearing capacity, reduction in total and differential settlement and decrease in liquifaction potential.

11·6. Soil Nailing. The term soil nailing refers to relatively small dia. bars inserted into the ground directly or by drilling and grouting and angled into the soil in such a manner they develop tensile axial force. Soil nailing has two main applications, namely for slope Stabilization and retaining structures. Soil nailing technique involves three basic processes. Excavation, nail installation and face stabilization. The order of last two steps is often reversed depending on

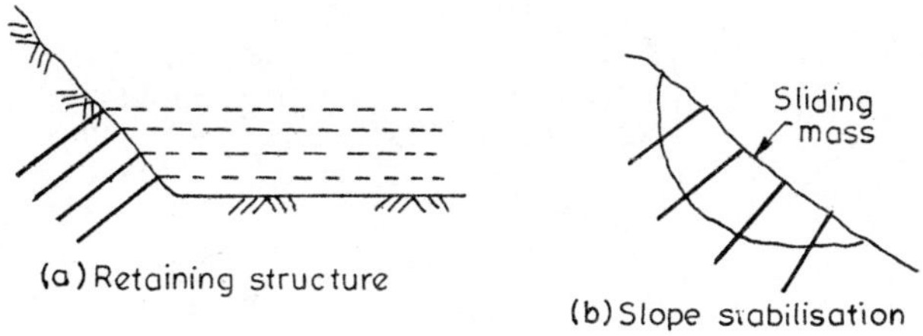

Fig. 11·12. Soil nailing.

the ground conditions. The procedure depends on weather the soil nails are being used to create a new structure or stabilise an existing one. It also depends on the soil properties and the inclination of the slope or excavation.

Excavation. The table below provides an indication of typical excavation depths of necessary vertical cuts in different type of soils excavation depths of nearly vertical cuts (Gassler, 1990)

Table 11·7.

Type of soil	*Cut depth*
(1)	(2)
Sandy gravel	
1. Having capillary cohesion	0·5 m
2. Cemented	1·5 m
Sand	
1. Medium dense with capillary cohesion	1·2 m
2. Cemented	2·0 m
3. Dense with capillary cohesion	1·5 m
Silt	
	1.2 to 2·0 m (depending on structure stability of the grain skeleton and water cement)
Clay	
1· Normally consolidated	1·5 m
2· Over consolidated	2·5 m

Installation of nails. The nails in general consists of steel bars with dia. of 20 mm to 28 mm (Maximum 50 mm) and length 5-10 m. The spacing of nails is usually one per 1 m to 2 m of cut face, resulting in a nailing density of 0.5 to 1 nail m^2.

Installation of nails is done by either drilling and grouting or by deriving. The most common method of installing nails is by predrilling, then inserting the steel bar centrally into the bore hole of dia. 70 mm to 120 mm and grouting. The function of the grout is to provide an increased bond with the soil. However it also provides the advantage of increased corrosion protection, double corrosion protection for permanent structures can also be provided by a corrugated PVC sheath as used in anchor technology.

In cohesive soils, the bore holes should always be kept dry to attain a good grout to ground bond. If the bore holes does not remain stable one should use casings but not supporting suspension such as bentonite.

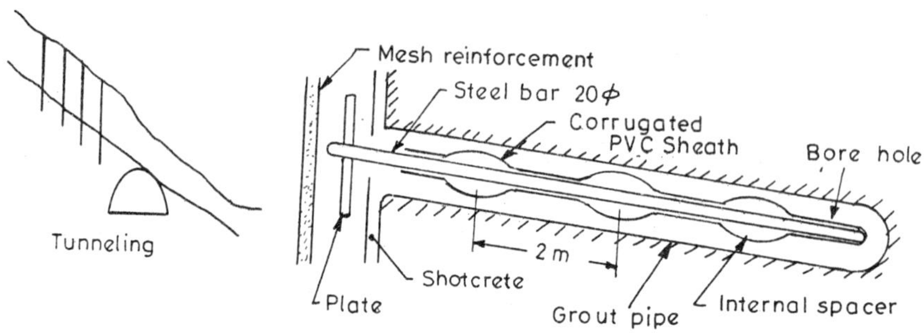

Fig. 11·13. Permanent nail of German standard.

Driven nails are typically solid circular or tubular bars. The major advantage with driven nails is that they can be installed rapidly especially in soils where drilling requires casing of the bore hole. The disadvantage with this type of nail are the much lower bond between the nail and the soil and a lower degree of corrosion protection. Driven nails are often limited in length and a higher density is required as per German codes of practice. Soil nails can be classified based on corrosion requirements as:

1. Temporary nails for service period of less than two years.

2. Permanent nails (For service period of more than two years). Now a days nearly all the nails are grouted for two seasons.

(*a*) The bond between the steel and the soil is essentially increased by grouting.

(*b*) A good corrosion problem is provided by the grout for temporary service periods, particularly in unfavourable environments.

A good temporary nail of German standard is shown in Fig. 11·15. The thickness of the cement or mortar coating has to be 15 mm at least so that the minimum dia. of a (predrilled) bore hole is determined by the dia. of the steel bar and the minimum thickness of the grout coating. The concentricity of the steel bar with the bore hole imparted for an uniform grout cover is provided by centralizers which should be placed at regular intervals of about 1.5 m to 2.0 m along the nail.

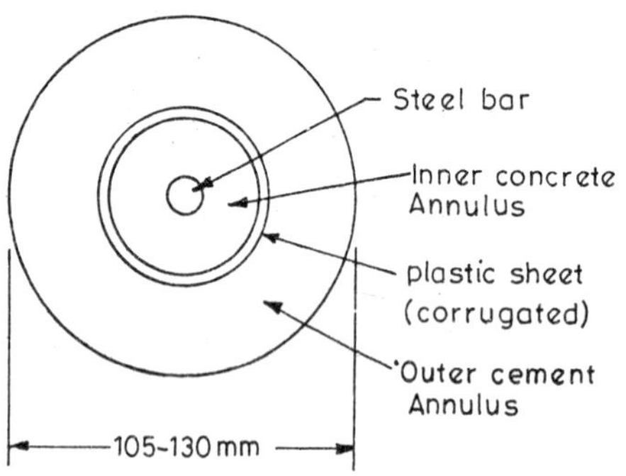

Fig. 11·14. Cross-section of permanent nail of German standard

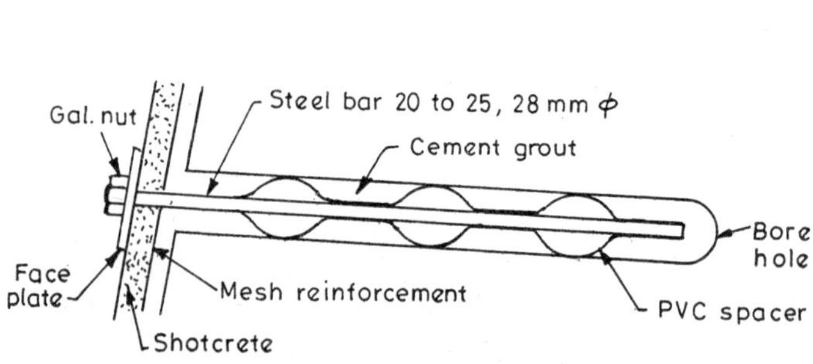

Fig. 11·15. Temporary nail of German standard.

An example of a grouted permanent of German standard is shown in the Fig. 11·15 in which the steel bar is protected by an outer sheath of plastic material. This sheath of corrugated shape enclosed in an inner cement annulus of at least 5 mm thick around the steel bar. Fig. 11·14 shows a cross-section of a permanent nail.

11·7. Facing. The object of facing is to prevent local soil failure and hence excessive displaccments of the structure. The most common form of the face Stabilization is a layer of shotcrete reinforced by a single layer steel mesh. For deep excavations or permanent works a double layer of shotcrete may be applied. The thickness of the shotcrete generally lies between 80 mm and 200 mm. The facing has to be sprayed using a dry mixture (1000 kg and 0.4 mm, 400 kg gravel 4.8 mm and 450 kg cement) to which the water will be given through a jet. Admixture can be incorporated to accelerate setting and to minimise rebound. In permanent nailing two nail head consisting of plate nail end and nut can be protected against corrosion by attaching a small wire mesh around the head and spraying another layer of shotcrete of about 5 cm thickness.

Several facilities have contributed to the growing popularity some of which are given below.

1. It is flexible readily accommodating variations in soil conditions and work programmes as excavation progresses.

2. Construction of soil nailing is done by staged excavation from top down exploiting natural ground.

3. It is an ideal method for soils like alluvial soil, fine sand, cemented sand weathered rock laterite etc.

Design considerations. Just as in the design of gravity retaining walls the stability of a nailed structure must be checked against both external and internal faces as depicted in Fig. 11·15 regarding external faces.

1. The reinforced zone must not overturn.

2. The reinforced zone must be able to resist the outward thrust from the unreinforced interior without sliding.

3. The combined loading from the reinforced zone self weight and the lateral soil thrust, it is resisting must not cause a foundation bearing failure.

4. The stability of remaining structure must be checked against the deep seated over all failure mechanism.

Regarding internal stability, the reinforcing elements must be installed in a pattern dense enough to ensure an effective interaction with the soil in the reinforced zone. The reinforcement elements must also have sufficient length and capacity to ensure a stable reinforced zone in particular.

(*a*) Each individual reinforcement should be capable of holding the soil immediately surrounding it in equilibrium. This local stability aspect dictates the spacing of the reinforcement only.

(*b*) Over all slip failure in the reinforced zone must also be considered to ensure against failure by insufficient bond or breaking of the reinforcement. These criteria govern the required length of reinforcement.

In slope stabilization inclusions are generally placed more or less perpendicular to the failure surface and shear stress and bending moments are mainly developed in the bars. The behaviour of natural soil in slope stabilization in largely dependent on the stiffness of the reinforcement. Soil nailing has an actual effectiveness to slow the sliding rate, but may be in a adequate for permanent stabilization, particularly in slopes already subjected to large displacements leading to residual shear strength in soil.

A great attention has to be given to water conditions so as not to obstruct natural flow by grouting and creates pore pressures which would decrease the available shear strength along the failure plane surface.

In retaining structures inclusions are placed approximately horizontal and are subjected mainly to tensile forces in a way similar to reinforced earth.

Stabilization of soil by Baryte Powder. It is barain sulphate ($BaSO_4$) and is a waste as a top layer in mines and occurs as white gray or buff coloured crystals or in massive form. It has high sp. gr. as 4·65. CaO and BaO is present in baryte powder as 0·43% and 65·7% respectively.

It's mixture in Black Cotton Soil decreases the possibility of expansion and contraction of soil and thereby making it more suitable for foundation of works.

Table 11·8. External and internal forces on nailed structures

	External	*Min. Fs*
Overturning	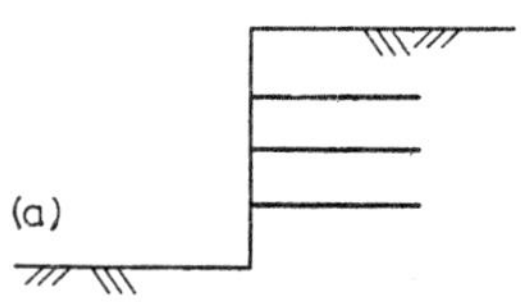	2·0
Sliding	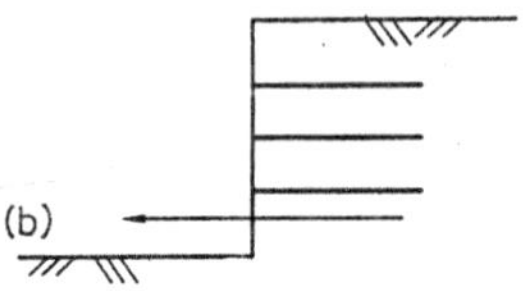	1·5
Bearing capacity	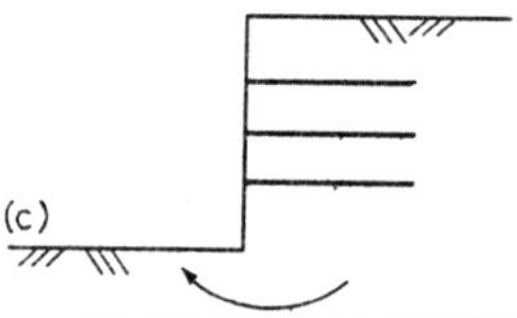	3·0
Overall slope	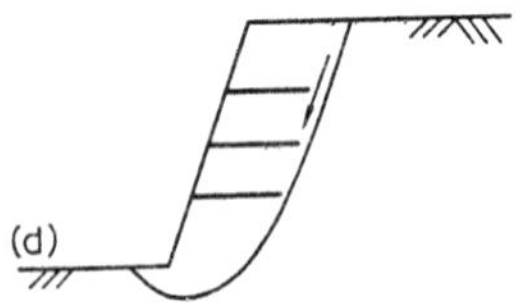	1·4 (1·2)
Pull out	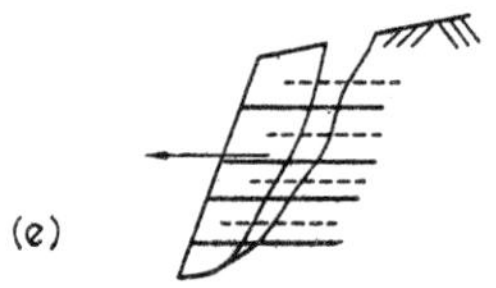	2 soil/ grout 2 steel/ grout
Tensile		$F_{max.} \le 0{\cdot}55ty$
Head and Facing	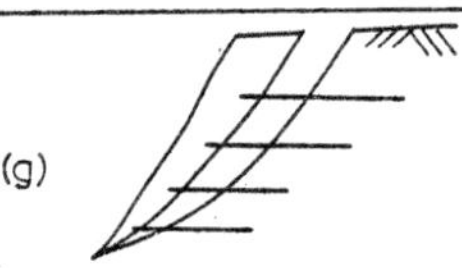	30 m bearing capacity

Fig. 11·16. Vibroflot.

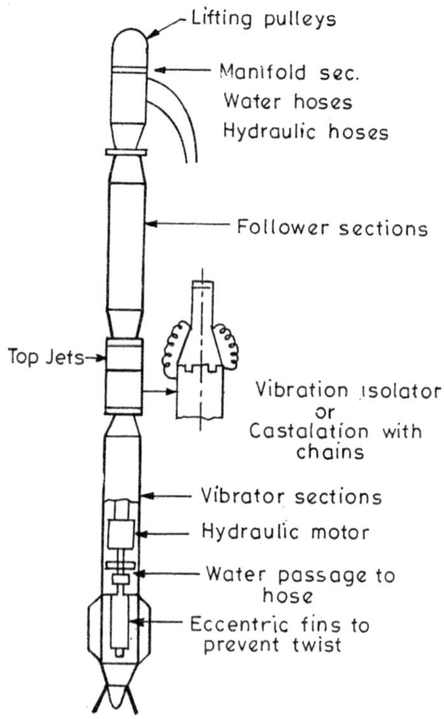

Fig. 11·17 (*a*). Vibroflot.

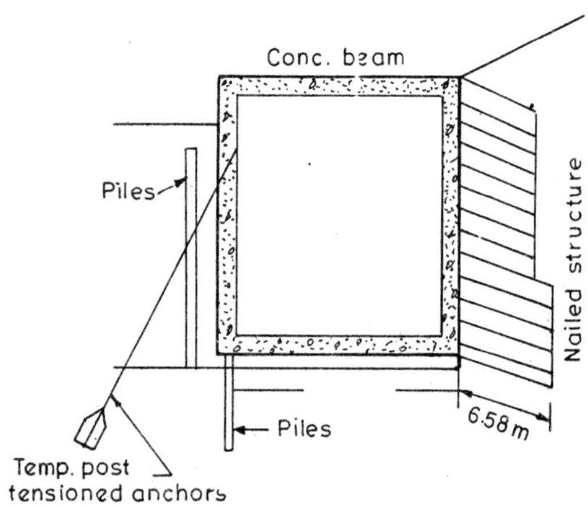

Fig. 11·17 (*b*). Marcy bed rock.

11·8. Drainage. Drainage is essential in excavation using soil nailing. It should be provided as in other retaining structures. It may be omitted if water pressure is very unlikely for temporary nail walls but not for permanent walls. Depending on circumstances various type of drainage methods such as short tubes in the facing among the nails, back facing drains consisting of either vertical strips of filtering geotextiles or perforated tubes or long chain pipes slotted can be used for draining the outer within and behind the nailed structure.

Strengthening by vibro flotation. At some installations stone columns adopted for RCC building, cooling towers and grade slabs. Field load test on columns have suggested that the col. is tend to bulge under the load and the surrounding soil tries to counteract the same by passive resistance. As the settlement of the col. and the surrounding soil is to be same and because of the much higher modulus of the stone col. to stone col. is stressed to many times higher than the soil. Thus the stress on the soil is relieved. Together with the high proportion of the replacement of the soil by the relatively in compressible stone metal. This results a reduction of the settlement.

In most of the cases, stone columns were laid in a triangular pattern, the spacing varying from 1 to 2.2 m with some concentration under the shell and periphery beyond the shell. It has been widely reported that at about 1/2 to 1/3 radius from periphery, settlement may be comparable magnitude as that at the centre and in recent past some concentration in that area has been made in the layout to cater for the extra, settlement *i.e.*, by aiming at a higher reduction.

Procedure. Vibro flot (vibro needle attached with suitable follow on tubes about 400 mm in dia. is sunk through the soft soil with bottom water jets and vibration. The vibration is created by an eccentric weight rotated about a vertical axis giving a lateral oscillating load of about 10 tonnes. The rotation of the eccentric is by a hydraulic motor, vibration is isolated at castellation junction so that vibration does not propagate to the follow on tubes. Surging is done for a couple of times to push out the accumulator effluent.

After the final depth is reached the vibro assembly is raised by 500 to 600 mm about the final depth and the top water jets are opened at bottom water jets reduced.

Use of compressed air also in vogue. However soil conditions need to be stiff and position of water table plays an important part in selecting compressed air as a jetting flout. So far no site has been encountered in India where compressed air can be utilised. 100 mm/75 mm down stone metal is poured around the vibro flot and allowed to sink against up flowing water. After dumping about 0.4 m^3 of metal the vibro flot is lowered and is allowed to penetrate in side the stone metal to compact the stone metal. Compression is indicated with sharp rise in pressure gauge during this operation. The above process is repeated to form a vibro stone column. In case of loose sand compaction sand is poured through the annular space.

11·9. Soil improvement by stone columns, chemical grouting and geotextiles. Stone columns are compacted columns of gravel or crushed rock installed in soft soils. They provide vertical support for overlying structures or embankments and also functions as drains for the soft soil. They can be used also to resist shear in horizontal and inclined directions. Stone column systems are somewhat like pile foundations except that pile caps. Structural connections and deep penetration into under lying form strata are not required. Stone columns are more compressible.

A cylinderical vertical hole is made by a vibrating probe penetrating by setting and under its own weight. Gravel back fill is dumped into the hole in increments of 0.4 to 0.8 m and compacted by the probe which simultaneously displaces the material readily into the soft soil. The dia. of the column ranges from 0.6 to 1.0 m, column lengths may be upto 20 m. Square or triangular grid patterns are used with centre to centre col. spacings of 1.5 to

3.5 m. When used in foundations, the supporting capacity and settlement are of primary concern. When used for stability purposes under embankments or in slopes the shear strength of columns is of primary interest. Both analytical and experience indicate that the allowable vertical stress (pv) on a single col. can be expressed as $pv = \frac{25S}{F_s}$ where S is the undrained shear strength of the soft ground soil and F_s is the factor of safety which is generally taken as 3. As actual analytical design is based on many factors such as cross-sec. of the column, their spacing and relative stiffness etc. of materials is complicated, so the actual design is based on field test and experience.

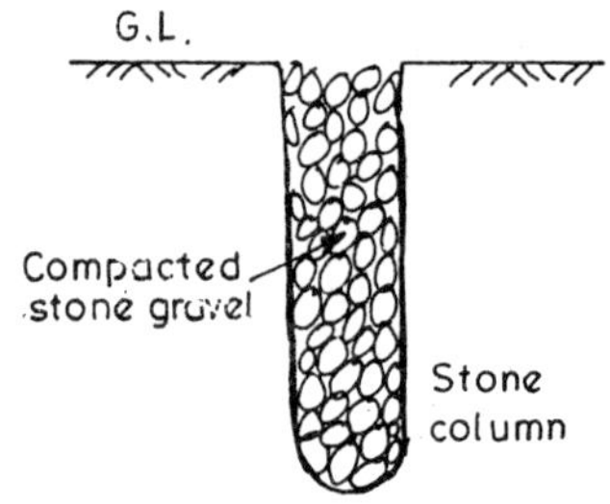

Fig. 11·18.

Chemical grouting. Grouting is a process where by fluid-like materials, either in suspension or solution form are injected into sub surface soil or rock for one or more of the purposes. (*a*) To decrease permeability (*b*) To increase shear strength (*c*) To decrease compressibility.

There are three types of grouting :

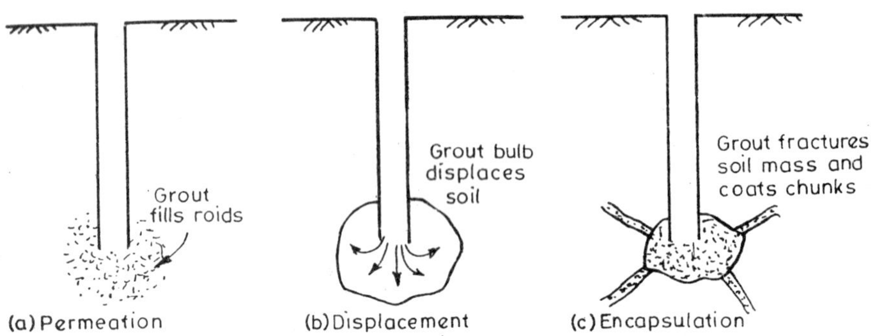

Fig. 11·19.

1. Permeation grouting. Here the grout fills the soil pores. There is essentially no change in the volume or structure of the original ground.

2. Displacement grouting. In this mode, a stiff mixture fills voids and remains more or less intact and exerts pressure on soil and thereby density the medium.

3. Encapsulation or uncontrolled displacement grouting. Here the grout is injected under high fluid pressure due to which the ground is fractured hydraulically and the grout rapidly penetrates into the fractured zone. The grout coats but does not permeate the individual chunks of soil.

Grout types. Permeation grouts are of two types. Particulate or suspension grouts are made up of cement, soil or clay or mixture of these chemical grouts are composed of various materials in solution. Displacement or compaction grouts are stiff, slow slump mixtures of cement, soil and or clay with water. Lime sluries are the most commonly used encapsulation-type grouts. Chemical grouts in some detail :

Chemical grouts have certain advantages over particulate grouts. Chemical grouts can penetrate smaller pores, have lower viscosity and there is a better control of set time but its technology is complex and costs are high. The most common grouts are silicates, lignins, resins, acrylamides and urethanes. Grouts containing 25-30% silicates are typical water proofing. Sodium silicate (Na_2SiO_4 watergas) is also commercial available material.

Grouting methods. Boring of holes can be read in piling system. There are several types of grout injection methods, three of which are as follows.

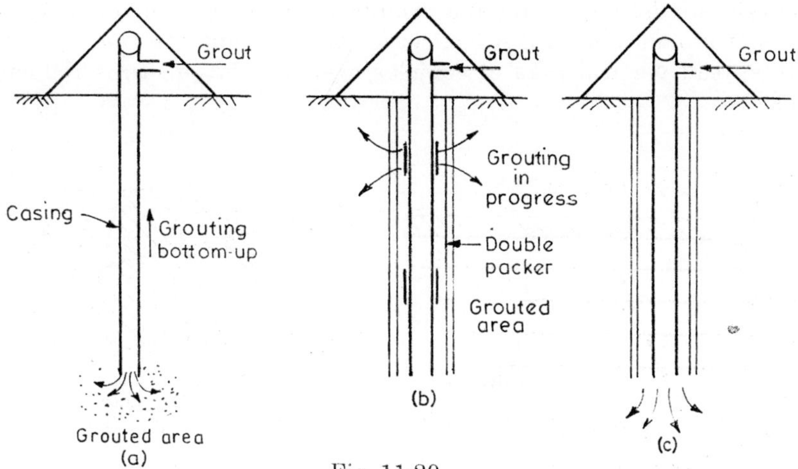

Fig. 11·20.

Bottom up driving. Drives the casing to full depth, with draw it to a specified elevation and then inject the grout. The process continues upward to the surface.

Sealed in Sleeve pipe injection—allows for several injections at the same elevation. Injection is done by a double packer which is inserted in the sleeve pipe to the desired location.

Simultaneous drilling and grouting. Allows for injection during rotary drilling. At predetermined distance, the drill rod is withdrawn and grout is injected into the soil through a separate drill rod. The process continues from the top downward. It is only suitable for pervious granular soils.

Note. The effect of the injected grout should be watched on the underground water table so that it may not harm the people who use this water for drinking etc.

11·10. Geotextiles. Geotextiles are fabrics made of fibrous materials mainly synthetic like polypropolene, polyester, polythelone, nylon etc. A new system of reinforcement called the Websol system was introduced which in corporated non metallic reinforcement like synthetic fibres. The use of synthetic fibres open up new possibilities for use of the fabrics embedded in soil for a variety of other purposes. It was discovered that the new composite material made of synthetic fabric and soil has not only improved mechanical properties but also excellent and useful hydraulic properties.

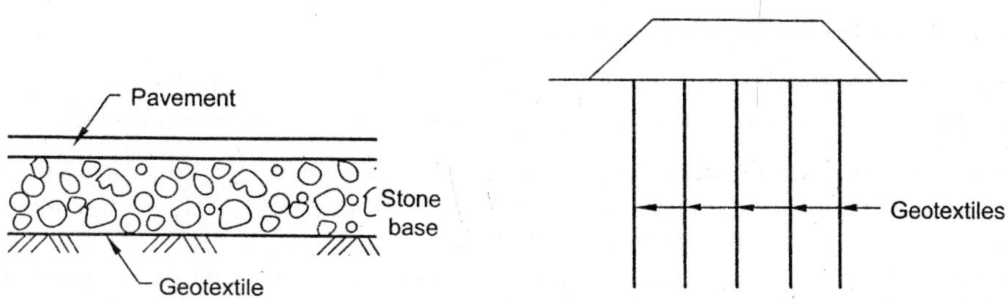

(*a*) Dissipating water pressure and drainage.

(*b*) Vertical and horizontal drainage of soft sub soil.

Fig. 11·21.

The present day "geotextiles" which is also called as geo-synthetics geo-membranes, geogrid etc. serve several functions such as separation, reinforcement, drainage, erosion control and imperbeable membranes. Geotextiles is also useful in construction of temporary roads over marshy lands, peat soils and compressible clays. A layer of fabric between the surface of the soft ground and gravel box serves both to separate the materials and prevent mixing and to spread vertical load of vehicles over foundation, thus reducing the induced shear stresses.

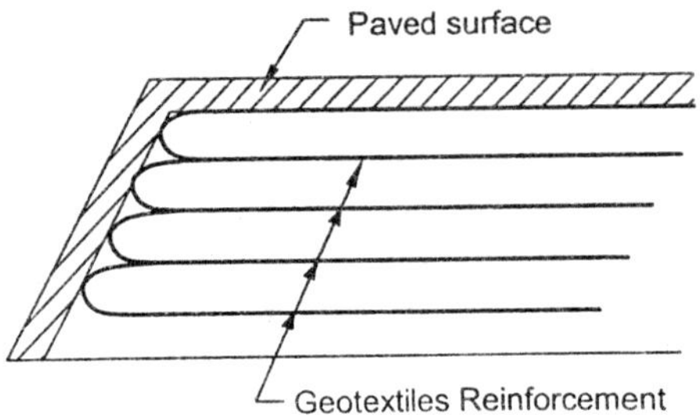

(*c*) Geotextile reinforcement in embankments.

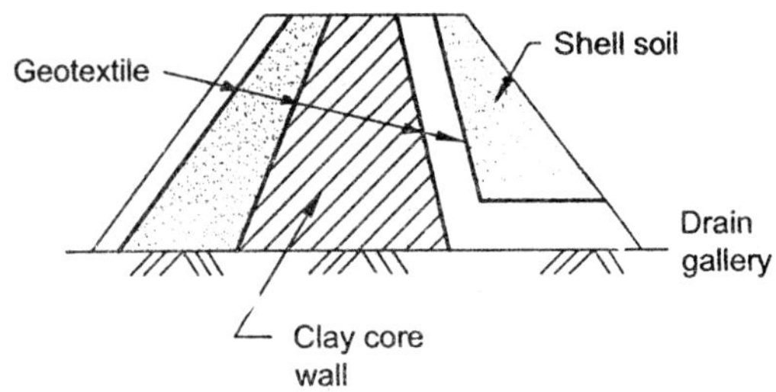

(*d*)

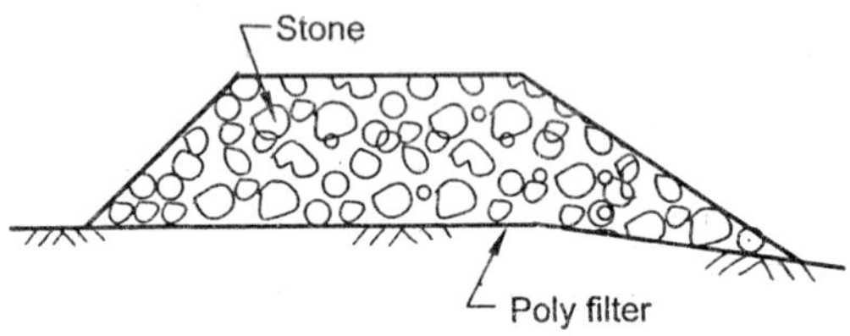

(*e*)

Fig. 11·21.

11·11. Tunnelling

11·11·1. Geotechnical classification of tunnelling projects

(*a*) Where worst ground conditions were met with, like squeezing ground, Dwelling and upheaving ground a flowing ground etc. and where gassy conditions are met with (category I)

(*b*) Where acute geotechnical problems were encountered like Fault zones, Shear zones, Thrust zones and excessive roof fall etc. (category II).

(*c*) Where no classified geotechnical problems were encountered (Category III).

11·11·2. Construction methodology

(*a*) **Manual method.** Excavation is done with pickaxes, hand shovels, pneumatic breakers. Mucking is done with small trolleys pushed manually or mechanically.

(*b*) **Conventional method.** Drilling and blasting is used. Drilling is done with jack hammers operated by compressed air, Pusher legs or autofeeds with or without drilling jumbo plateforms. The tunnel is supported with heavy steel supports and back filled with concrete. The drill holes are drilled at line of least resistance and are filled with explosives (Gelatine or Gelamax.), on the top of which a detonator is fixed which in turn is carried by a fuse coil, which is ignited from a safe distance apart. In important works electric detonators are used. A mixture of diesel and ammonium sulphate is also filled and compacted over the explosive which works as a catalytic agent. The quantity of explosive depends on the type of rock, position of least resistance etc., even as a fare estimate about 5 kg gelatine is required to explode 1 cu m. of the rock. Gases from the tunnels are evacuated by exhaust fans followed by plane galvanized sheet conduits leading to open atmosphere. Cavitation and chimney formation is controlled by timber of steel sections.

(*c*) **Modern method.** Modern equipment like Miner TBM, Electro hydraulic drill jumbo, Rock bolting Jumbo, Robot arm for shotcreting etc., and modern methods like NATM (New Austrian Tunnelling Method) and shotcreting and rock bolting are extensively adopted.

11·11·3. Classification according to progress achieved

(*a*) **Construction method A.** Using conventional method and equipment.

(*b*) **Construction method B.** Using modern technology as well as use of latest state of art equipment.

Box-jacking. Box Pushing is a method of Jacking precast RCC boxes to form a horizontal opening below ground or through embankments. In this process a RCC thrust bed of suitable size is casted near the tower of the embankment. The top level of this bed coincides with the bottom level of the proposed box. Rectangular RCC segments are cost in suitable lengths as rails embedded in the thrust bed. The 1st piece of rectangular RCC box is cast with a built in mild steel cutting edge around the front of the shield.

This section of box is cast along the alignment of the push. The other box sections may be cast either along the same alignment or away from the site of the 1st box depending on the availability of space. In the later case the concrete box has to be pushed laterally to bring it into alignment before pushing. The jacking rigs rest on the thrush bed designed to take the horizontal force required for pushing.

As jacking progresses, the lead unit with the shield penetrates into the embankment and excavation from the face of the shield is carried out mechanically or manually. The muck is removed either by a trolley running on temporary rails installed inside the concrete box or by head loads. After the 1st unit advances to the end of the thrust bed, the 2nd unit is telescoped into it through an intermediate jacking station (I.J.S.). This unit has facilities for housing additional jacks to cater for the load required to jack the 1st unit, with the rear box and the jacking rigs locked in position. The jacking rigs transferred to the rear end of the 2nd unit and the I.S.J. are utilised alternately to push the rear and the 1st box. The length of push after such an operation is restricted by the range of the hydraulic ram, which is 250 mm.

The jacking rig is a rectangular steel frame 3.7 m × 0.9 m in outside dimensions, constructed to hold hydraulic jacks. This rig is placed on the thrushtbed to cover the pin pocket in such a way that the ram of the hydraulic jack rests against the vertical steel pin in the pin pocket. The hydraulic rams pin the box units by pushing the frame against the jacking pin through a series of packing pieces placed in scale the frame between the hydraulic ram and the mild steel pin. The packing pieces are increased until there is no room for more packing pieces in the frame. Depending upon the total jacking load, two or more such frames are used for pushing.

An intermediate jacking station is made by wrapping 20 mm m.s. plate round the concrete box. The dimensions of the opening allows free pretelescopic movement of the subsequent cast iron box units. It has also arrangements to hold the required number of hydraulic jacks butting against two concrete box faces. An example for it is the widening of "Delhi Road under bridge" in which M-43 mix is adopted.

Table 11·9. Instrumentation for tunnels

Parameters	*Instruments*
1. Lateral movement	(*a*) Digital in clinometer (Borehole) (*b*) Digital netmeters.
2. Pore water pressure	Piezometers
3. Soil and rock deformations, settlement and heave	Single and multiple Bonehole Extensometer, sondex settlement system
4. Convergence	Tape extensometer
5. Stress in steel	Vibrating wire strain gauge
6. Load	Centre hole load cells
7. Stress in conc. lining	Total pressure cells
8. Rock man insitu properties in Bore holes	(*a*) Godown jack (*b*) USBM Bone hole deformation gauge (*c*) CSIRO (Australia) Hollow inclusion cell (*d*) Minipac (Hydrotractive) system
9. Crack monitoring in ground	Three dimensional crack meter
10. Ground vibration	Peak vibration monitors
11. Automation in Instrumentation.	Intelligent data acquisition system

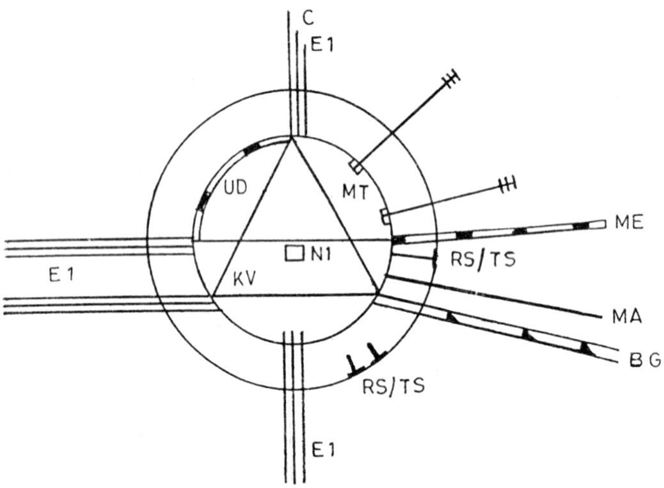

EI – Extensometer
NI – Invert Bolt
MA – Measuring Anchor
MT – Anchor load cells
ME – Multiple Extensometer
RS – Pressure cells for radial stress
TS – Pressure cells for tangential stress
BG – Rock pressure cells in Bore holes
KV – Convergence Measuring Section. Inner Convergence
UD – Perimeter Deformation Measure-ment with Segment and radial deformation

Fig. 11·22. Typical section of an Instrumented Tunnel.

12

Hydraulics

12·1. (1) **Atmospheric Pressure.** Pressure exerted by atmosphere. (The column of air above a place)

At sea level = 14·7 lbs/in² = 1·033 kg/cm²

= 34′ head of water = 30″ or 76 cm of mercury.

It reduces as the altitude of a place is increased from mean sea level according to the following data :

Table 12·1.

Altitude in metres → *Atmospheric pressure* ↓	*0*	*500*	*1000*	*1500*	*2000*	*3000*	*5000*
(*a*) *mercury in cm*	76	72	67·7	63·7	59·6	53·0	41·3
(*b*) *water in m*	10·3	9·8	9·2	8·6	8·1	7·2	5·6

The atmospheric pressure is measured as a head of mercury or water which can stand in a basometric tube against atmospheric pressure. The specific gravity of mercury is 13·5.

For standard 1 metre atmosphere = 1 kg/cm² (14·22 lbs/in²)

= 73·5 cm of mercury head (29″)

= 10 m of water head (32·8 ft)

Absolute pressure = Atmospheric Pressure + Gauge Pressure

Gauge pressure is the reading which is measured on a gauge taking atmospheric pressure as a datum of zero. For sub atmospheric pressure the gauge pressure is a –ve figure, so in this case

Absolute pressure = Atmospheric Pressure – Vacuum Pressure

where vacuum pressure is a pressure above vacuum.

Pascal's law. Pressure applied on a surface of liquid is transferred equally in all directions and acts normal to the surface of vessel.

(2) **Statics.**

(*i*) $p = wH$

where p = intensity of pressure

w = weight of water per unit

H = head of water

(*ii*) $P = wA\bar{x}$ (vert. surface)

P = total pressure

A = area of surface

$\bar{x}$ = distance of centre of area from surface

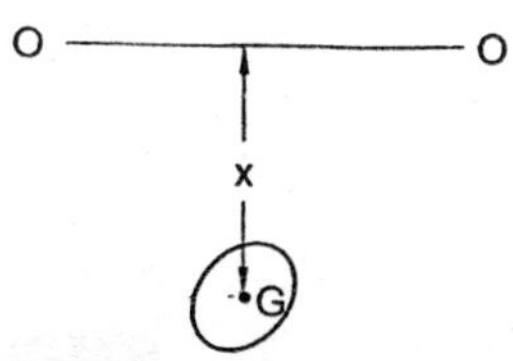

Fig. 12·1.

$\bar{h} = \dfrac{I_0}{A\bar{x}}$ G is the centre of gravity

C is centre of pressure

I_0 = moment of inertia of the Fig. about OO

$\bar{x}$ = depth of centre of area from OO

$\bar{h}$ = depth of centre of pressure from OO

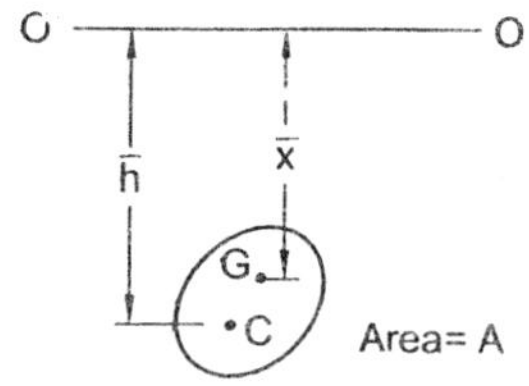

Fig. 12·2.

(iii) $P = wA\bar{x}$ (Inclined surface at an angle θ from horizontal)

$$\bar{h} = \frac{I_B \sin^2 \theta}{A\bar{x}}$$

$$I_B = \frac{I_g + A\bar{x}^2}{\sin^2 \theta}$$

I_B = moment of inertia of the surface about B

I_g = moment of inertia of the surface about G

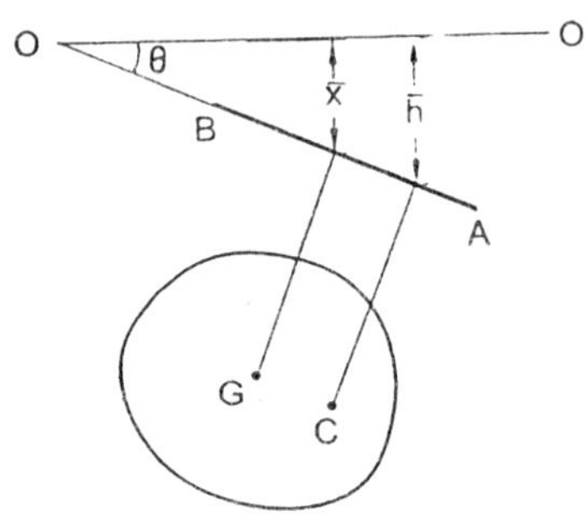

Fig. 12·3.

(iv) $P = \dfrac{1{\cdot}86 \times wV^2}{2g}$

where P = Pressure due to running water having a velocity V normal to the plane

$$P_1 = \frac{P \times 2 \sin^2 \alpha}{1 + \sin^2 \alpha}$$

where P_1 = Pressure due to running water on a plane inclined at an angle α from horizontal.

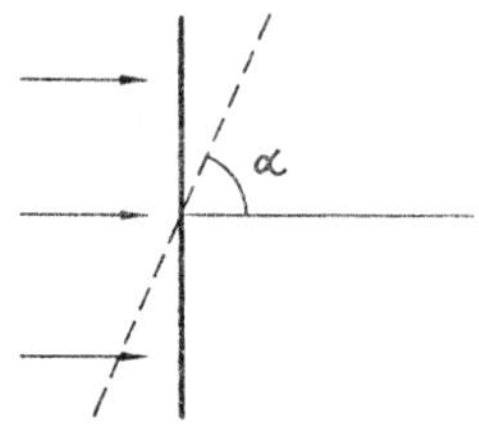

Fig. 12·4.

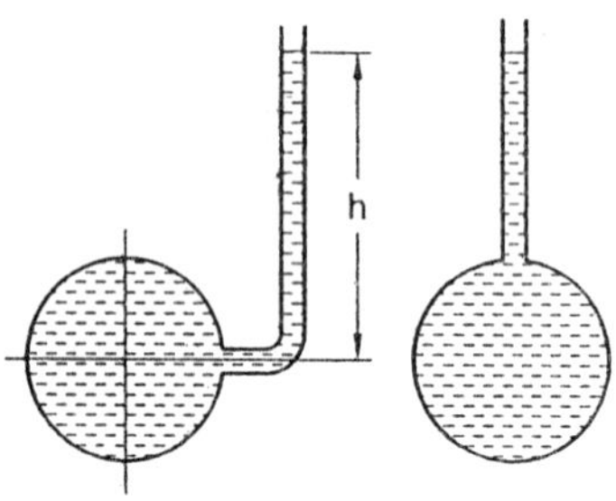

$P = wh$ kg/m^2

w = Sp. wt. of liquid in pipe

w = Sp. wt. of water

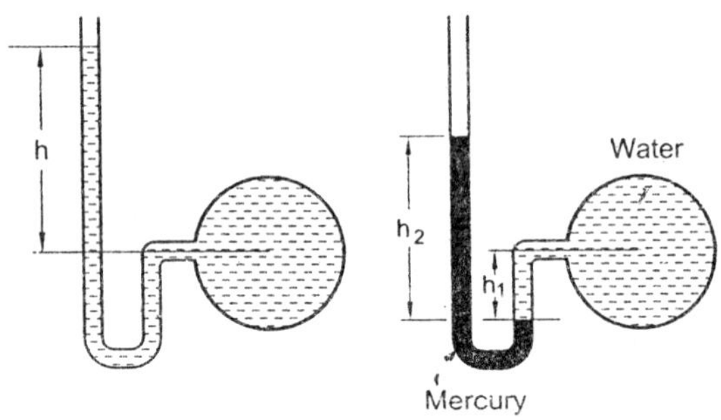

$P = w_m h_2 - wh_1$

w_m = Sp. wt. of mercury

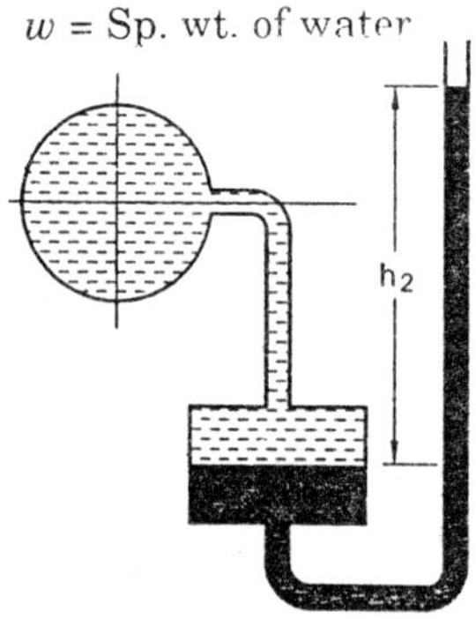

$P = w_m \times h_2$

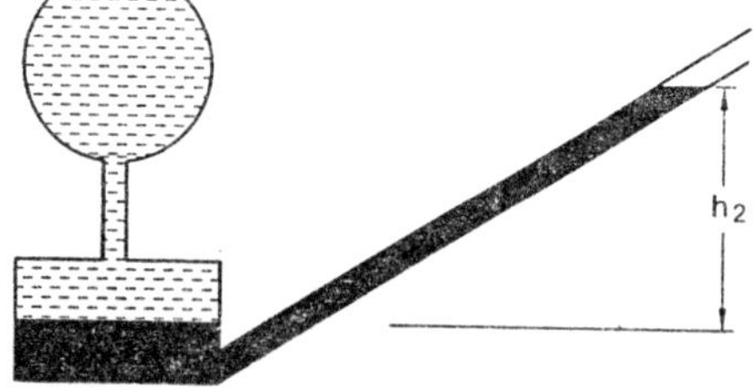

$P = w_m h_2$

s(d) Inclined tube sensitive manometer.

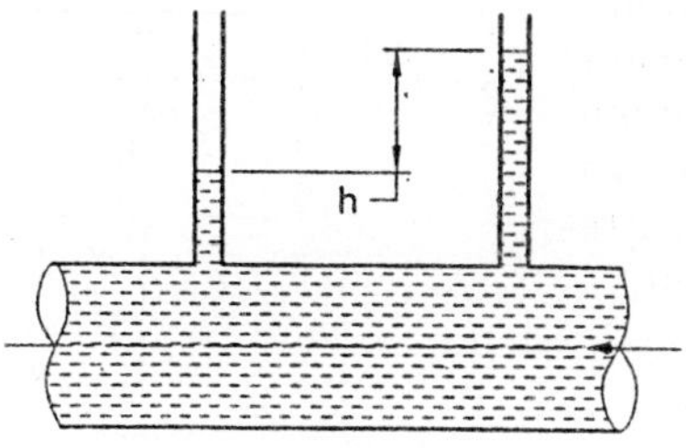

wh = Pressure difference is the same pipe
(e) Differential manometers

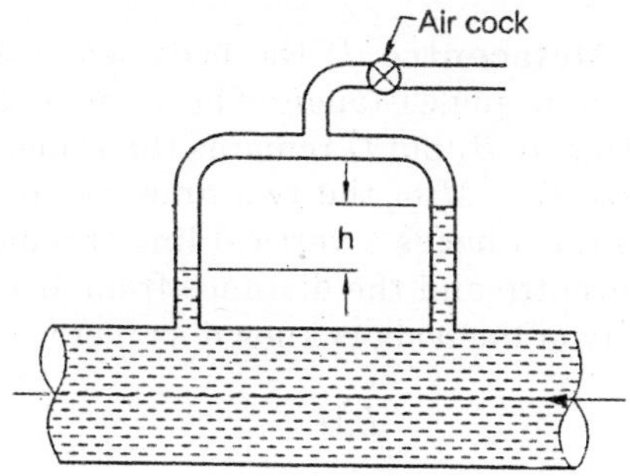

Pressure difference = wh
(f)

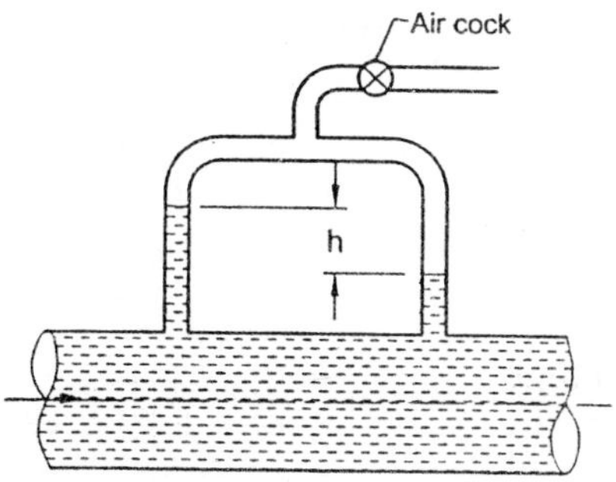

Pressure difference = $w_m h$
(g)

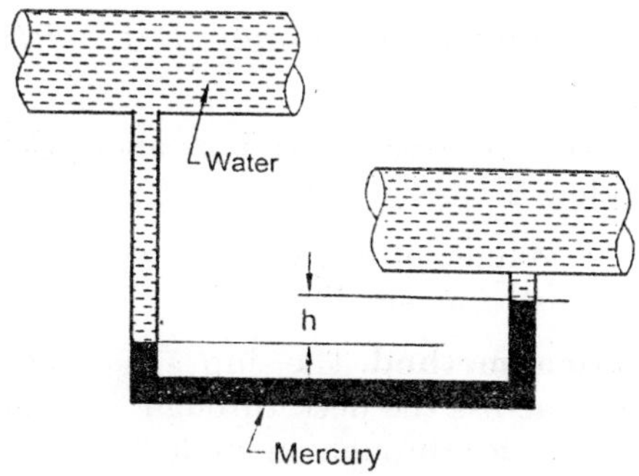

Pipes are at different levels
(h)

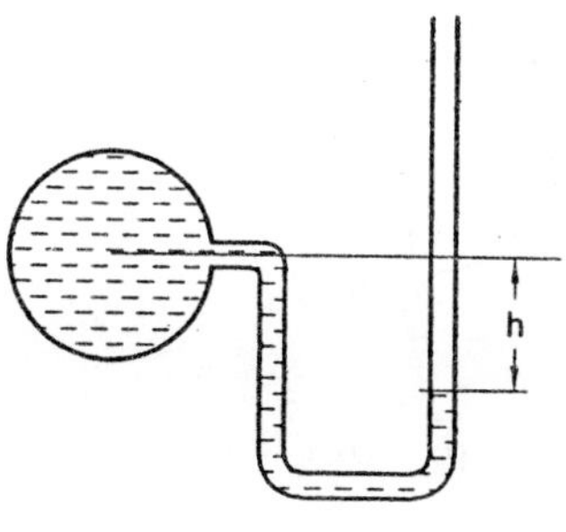

–ve pressure = wh

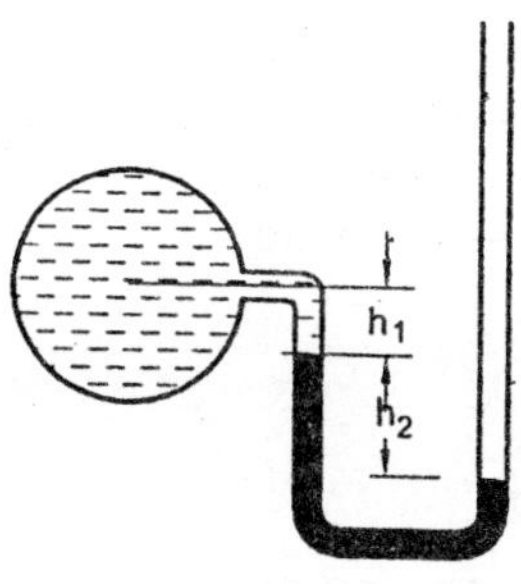

$p = h_2 w_m - wh_1$(–ve)

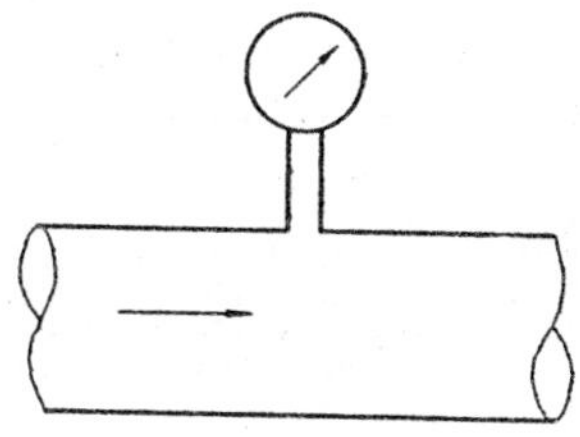

Pressure Gauge

(i) Pressure in pipes (kg/mm^2).

Fig. 12·5

(3) **Buoyancy of liquid**

Archimedes Principle. When a body is totally or partially immersed in a fluid, it is buoyed up (lifted up) by a force which is equal to the weight of the fluid displaced by the body.

The force by which the body is lifted up is known as the force of buoyancy say P and acts upward vertically from the centre of gravity of the displaced liquid which is known as the centre of buoyancy (say B). The weight of the body W acts downward vertically and passes from its centre of gravity say G. If the body is in equilibrium or rest the points B and G lies in a vertical line and the weight of water displaced is equal to the weight of the body and the body will float

$$P = W \text{ (body upright)}$$

Metacentre. If the body which floats is tilted slightly at an angle θ (angle of heel) the centre of buoyancy will change to B_1 but G remains the same, then the point of intersection M of the two lines are passing through BG and the other is a vertical line through B, is known as metacentre and the distance from M to G the centre of gravity of the body is known as metacentric height

$$BM = \frac{I}{V}$$

where I = moment of inertia of a horizontal section (top plan) of vessel at water line along a longitudinal axis yy.

Hence metacentric height $GM = BM \pm BG = I/V + BG$

The –ve sign used where G is above B and +ve where G is below B.

V = volume of liquid displaced angle of heel is being small upto 10°.

Practical method. The ship is moved by rolling a weight say m across the deck through a distance l by which the ship moves through an angle θ.

Then metacentric height $GM = \dfrac{ml}{w \tan\theta}$

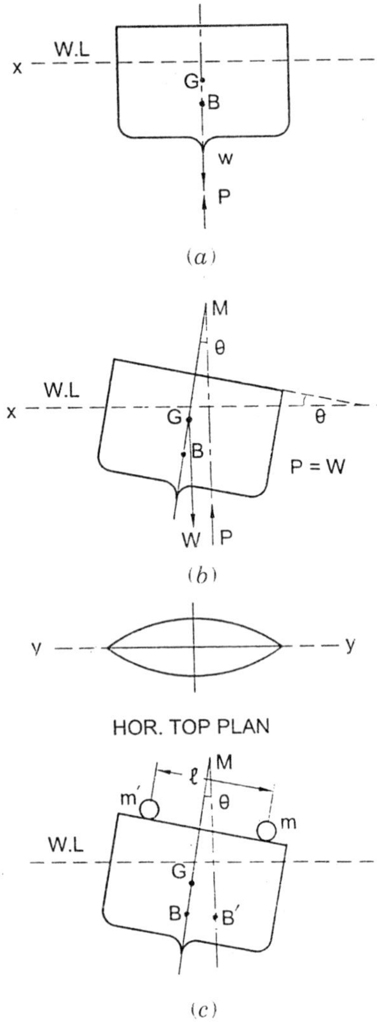

Fig. 12·6.

(4) **Bernauli's Theorem.** For any mass of flowing water in which there is a continuous connection between all particles, the total head of water on each particle (datum head + velocity head + pressure head) is the same.

$$z + \frac{P}{w} + \frac{V^2}{2g} = z_1 + \frac{b_1}{w} + \frac{V_1^2}{2g}$$

Consider a section of a reservoir (see Fig. 12·7)

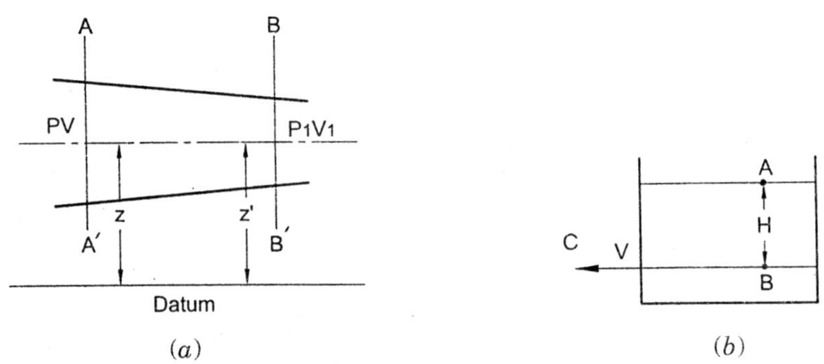

Fig. 12·7.

Total energy at $A = H + O + O$, at $B = O + H + O$, at $C = O + O + \frac{V^2}{2g}$. Taking the line through centre of origin as datum, then

$$H = \frac{V^2}{2g} \text{ or } V = \sqrt{2gH}$$

(5) **Venturimeter.** The discharge through venturimeter

$$= q = K\,C\sqrt{H}$$

where H is the difference of head read by the height of water in piezometers m_1 and m_2.

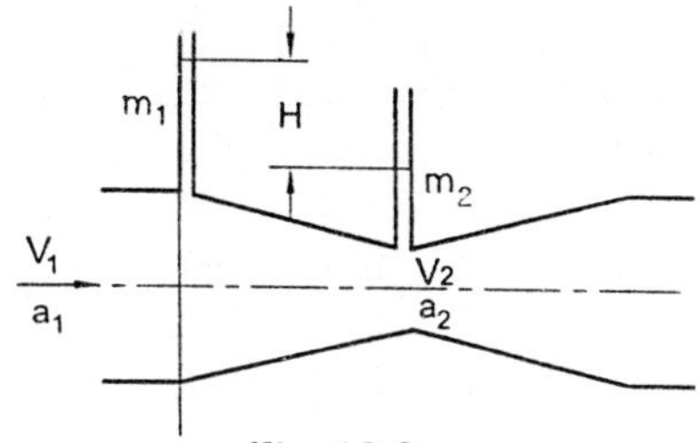

Fig, 12·8.

$$C = \frac{a_1\,a_2}{\sqrt{a_1^2 - a_2^2}}\sqrt{2g}$$

which is constant for a venturimeter. K = loss of head due to friction etc. and is constant for a venturimeter.

Manometer. It is a tube usually bent in the form of U, containing a liquid of known specific gravity. The surface of the liquid changes according to the pressure change. When one limb of the menometer or a piezometer is opened to the atmosphere it is known as open menometer while when both the limbs are connected to two pressures, it gives the difference of the two pressures and is known as differential menometer.

(6) **Centrifugal head on a revolving liquid** $= \frac{V_2^2}{2g} - \frac{V_1^2}{2} = \frac{p}{w}$

Centrifugal force $= \frac{w}{g} w^2 r$

V_1 = tangential velocity at rad. R_1

V_2 = tangential velocity at rad. R_2

$r_1 = wR_1$ and $r_2 = wR_2$

where w is the angular velocity of revolution of arm about an axis xx_1. The water in the arm is filled from radius R_1 to radius R_2.

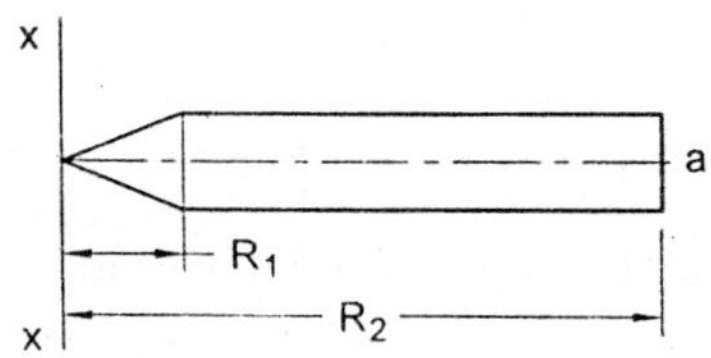

Fig. 12·9. Nozzles.

(7) **Kinetic energy of a jet** $= \frac{waV^2}{2g}$

where w = weight of water/unit, V = velocity of water through nozzle.

Metric H.P. of jet of water through a nozzle

$$= \frac{\text{weight of water in kg/sec.} \times \text{available head in m}}{75}$$

$$\frac{A}{a} = \sqrt{\frac{\delta + l}{D}}$$

where A = area of pipe, D = dia. of pipe, l = length of pipe, a = area of nozzle, f = coefficient of friction.

Table 12·1. Discharge through nozzles at different heads

ft.	*m*	*lb per in²*	*kg per cm²*	*Dia. of nozzles in mm*									
				10		*12*		*15*		*20*		*25*	
				Ht m	*Q lit/m*	*Ht m*	*Q lit/m*	*Ht m*	*Q lit/m*	*Ht m*	*Q lit/m*	*H m*	*Q lit/m*
10	3·05	4·3	·30	2·7	14	3·0	55	3·0	86	3·0	125	3·0	220
20	6·10	8·6	·60	5·2	19	5·8	78	5·8	122	5·8	175	5·8	311
30	9·14	13·0	·91	7·3	24	8·2	95	8·5	149	8·5	215	8·8	381
40	12·2	17·3	1·22	9·1	28	10·7	111	11·0	172	11·3	248	11·5	440
50	15·2	21·6	1·52	10·4	31	12·8	123	13·4	192	13·7	277	14·0	494
60	18·3	26·0	1·83	11·3	34	14·9	135	15·5	210	15·8	303	16·5	540
70	21·3	30·3	2·13	11·9	36	16·8	145	17·7	227	18·3	328	18·9	585
80	24·4	34·6	2·44	12·2	39	18·3	156	19·5	234	20·4	350	21·3	621
90	27·4	39·0	2·74	11·9	41	19·8	165	21·3	258	22·2	372	23·5	658
100	30·5	43·3	3·15	11·3	43	21·0	174	22·9	272	24·1	392	25·6	694
120	36·6	52·0	3·66	—	—	22·9	190	25·6	298	27·4	429	29·6	762
140	42·7	60·6	4·27	—	—	24·1	206	27·7	322	30·2	463	33·2	821
160	48·8	69·3	4·88	—	—	24·4	220	29·3	343	32·3	496	36·6	880
180	54·9	78·0	5·49	—	—	24·1	233	30·2	365	34·1	526	39·3	934
200	61·0	86·6	6·10	—	—	22·9	246	30·5	385	35·3	553	41·7	984
220	67·1	95·1	6·71					30·2	403	36·3	581	44·2	1033
240	73·1	110·40	7·31					29·3	421	36·6	607	45·7	1079
260	79·2	126·6	7·92					28·0	438	36·3	632	47·2	1123
280	85·3	121·2	8·53					25·6	455	35·7	655	48·2	1165
300	91·4	130·0	9·14					22·9	472	34·1	676	48·8	1207

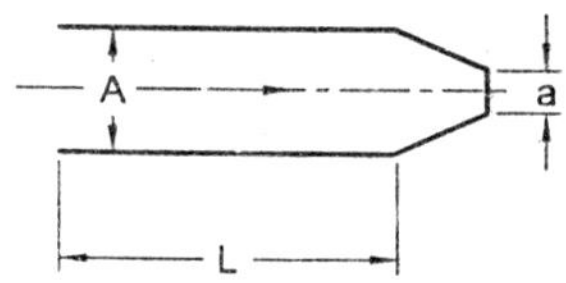

(8) **Pitot tube.** The rise of water in the Pitot tube above external water level due to the running water say $h = K \frac{V^2}{2g}$; $V = \sqrt{2gH}$ where V = velocity of water, H = head of water and K is a constant for loss of head due to friction etc.

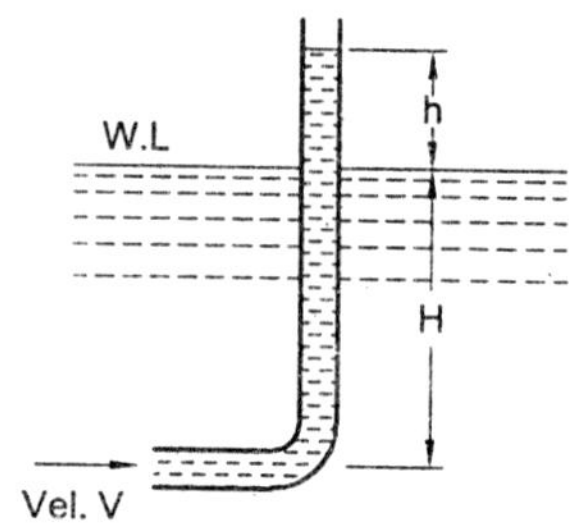

Fig. 12·11. Pitot tube.

(9) **Hammer blow in pipes.** If valves in pipes of flowing water are closed suddenly successive pulsating pressure waves are set due to the kinetic energy loss of water, with a noise known as **knocking**. The sudden rise of pressure in a pipe due to closure of valve is known as Hammer blow.

$$\text{Intensity of pressure} = \frac{wlV}{gt} \text{ (valve closed gradually)}$$

$$w = \text{specific weight of water} = V \times \sqrt{\frac{Kw}{g}} \text{ (valve closed suddenly)}$$

l = length of pipe

V = Velocity of flow, t = closing time of valve in second and

K = Bulk modulus of elasticity of water.

(10) **Surface tension** = T kg/mm of periphery

α = angle of contact

d = diameter of tube
w = specific weight of liquid
h = height of liquid column in tube.

Then $$h = \frac{\Delta T \sin \alpha}{wd}$$

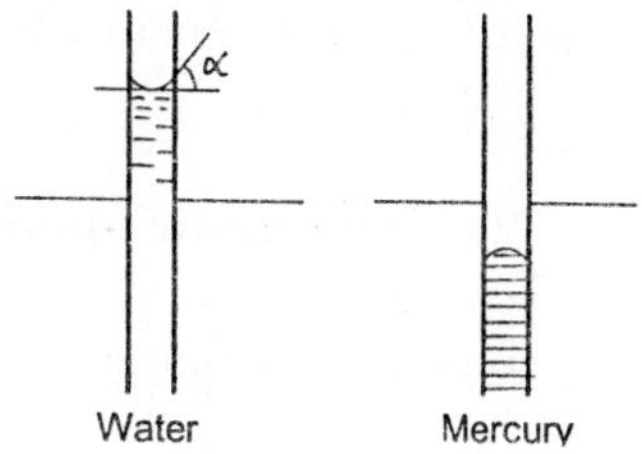

Fig. 12·12. Surface tension

12·2. Orifices

(*a*) **Sharp edged orifice.** Coefficient of contraction say C_C

$$= \frac{\text{area of jet at vena contracta } a}{\text{area of orifice } A} = \frac{a}{A}$$

Coefficient of velocity $= C_V = \dfrac{\text{Actual velocity}}{\text{Theoretical velocity}} = \dfrac{V}{\sqrt{2gH}}$

Coefficient of discharge $= C_d = \dfrac{\text{Actual discharge}}{\text{Theoretical discharge}} = \dfrac{C_V\sqrt{2gH} \times C_C A}{A\sqrt{2gH}} = C_V \times C_C$

$$C_V = \sqrt{\frac{x^2}{4yH}}$$ x and y are the coefficients of a point in the jet

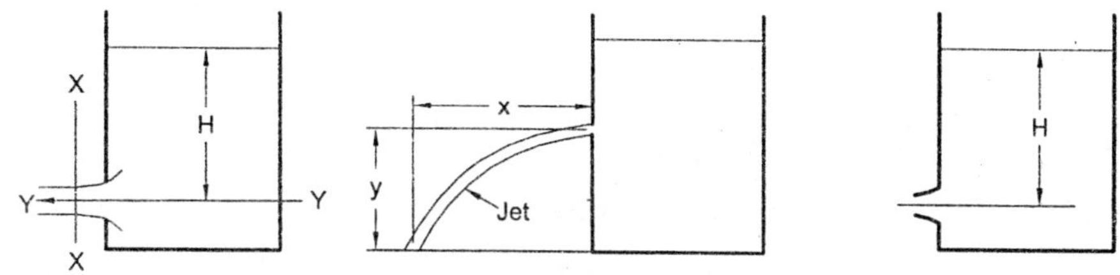

(*a*) Simple orifice. (*b*) Sharp edged. (*c*) Bell mouthed
Fig. 12·3.

(*i*) Discharge through small sharp edged orifice

$= C_d \cdot A\sqrt{2gH}$, for bell mouthed $C_d = 0{\cdot}97$
for shallow water $C_d = 0{\cdot}62$

(*ii*) Discharge through large vertical orifices

$$= \frac{2}{3} C_d \times B\sqrt{2g}\left(H_2^{3/2} - H_1^{3/2}\right),\ B = \text{width of orifice}$$

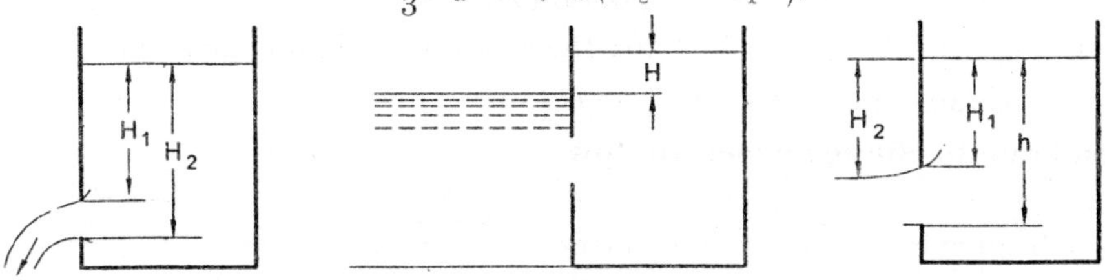

(*d*) Large vertical. (*e*) Submerged. (*f*) Part submerged
Fig. 12·13.

(*iii*) Discharge through drowned orifice (submerged)

$= C_d . A\sqrt{2gH}$, H = difference of head of either sides

(*iv*) Discharge through partial submerged orifice (Partial drowned)

= Sum of the discharges of lower drowned + discharge of the upper free part.

$$= \frac{2}{3} C_d \times B\sqrt{2g}\left(H_2^{3/2} - H_1^{3/2}\right) + C_d\, B(h - H_2)\sqrt{2gH}$$

(*v*) Circular openings – Discharge = $C_d \pi R \sqrt{2g\,H}\left(1 - \frac{1}{32}\frac{r^2}{H^2}\right)$

r = rad. at vena contracta, R = rad. of opening, C = 0·6 nearby

(*vi*) **Triangular openings**

Base up discharge $= \frac{2}{3} C_d\, B\sqrt{2g}\left(\frac{2}{3}\,\frac{H^{5/2} - H_1^{5/2}}{H - H_1} - H_1^{3/2}\right)$

Base down discharge $= \frac{2}{3} C_d\, B\sqrt{2g}\left(H^{3/2} - \frac{2}{5}\,\frac{H^{5/2} - H_1^{5/2}}{H - H_1}\right)$

where H is the head from lower point and H_1 of the upper.

(*vii*) Time of emptying vessel through orifice in base

$$T = \frac{2A\sqrt{H_1 - H_2}}{C_d \cdot a\sqrt{2g}}$$

where T = time of emptying from H_1 to H_2

A = sectional area of tank

a = area of orifice

if H = 0 (*i.e.* emptying full) then $T = \dfrac{2A\sqrt{H_1}}{C_d \cdot a\sqrt{2g}}$

(*viii*) Time of flow from one vessel to another

$$T = \frac{T\,2A_1\left(H_1^{1/2} - H_2^{1/2}\right)}{C_d - a\sqrt{2g}\left(1 + \frac{A_1}{A}\right)}$$

where T = Time of flow, A_1 and A_2 are the areas of two vessels and H_1 and H_2 are the difference of head at beginning and end of flow.

(*ix*) Discharge from a vessel with inflow

$$T = \frac{2A}{K^2}\left[Q \times \log_e\left(\frac{Q - K\sqrt{H_2}}{Q - K\sqrt{H_1}}\right) + K\left(\sqrt{H_2} + \sqrt{H_1}\right)\right]; \; K = C_d \cdot a\sqrt{2g}$$

Q = Discharge of inflow, H_1 and H_2 are the heads at beginning and end

T = time to change the head from H_1 to H_2.

12·3. Loss of head due to change of sec. of flow

(*i*) Loss of head due to sudden enlargement $= \left(\frac{V_1 - V_2}{2g}\right)^2$

(*ii*) Loss of head due to sudden contraction and entrance at pipes $= \dfrac{0.5\,V^2}{2g}$

(*iii*) Loss of head due to obstruction $= \left\{\frac{A}{C_C(A - a)} - 1\right\}\frac{V^2}{2g}$

(*iv*) Loss of head due to change in direction $= \dfrac{K\,V^2}{2g}$

K depends on the angle and rad. of bend for 90° elbows it is unity. It is ultimately lost in friction of the eddies formed.

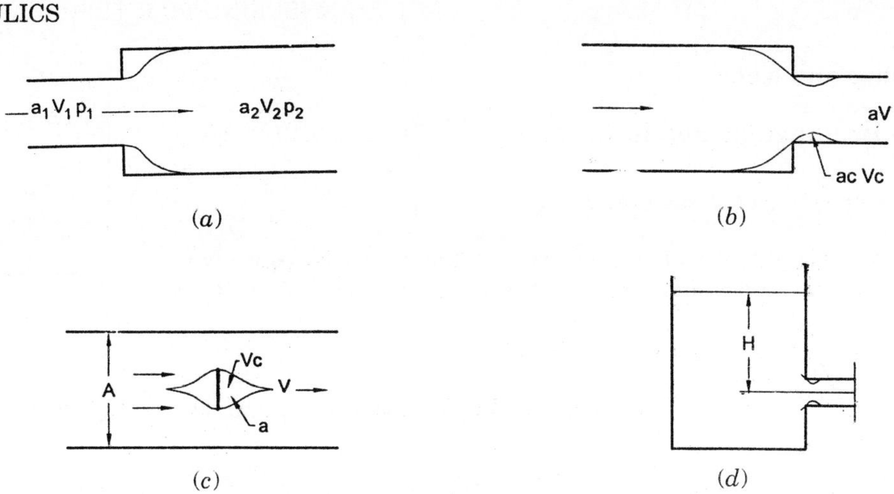

Fig. 12·14.

12·4. Mouth pieces

(*i*) **External mouth piece.** Loss of head $= 0{\cdot}375\,\dfrac{V^2}{2g}$

$$C_V = \frac{1}{\sqrt{1{\cdot}375}} = 0{\cdot}855 \qquad C_C \text{ at vena contracta} = 0{\cdot}62$$

(*ii*) **When mouth piece is running full** C_C at free end = 1

So $C_d = C_C \times C_V = 1 \times {\cdot}855 = 0{\cdot}855$. Hence by fitting a mouth piece the discharge is increased.

$H_c = H_a - 0{\cdot}89\,H$, where H_c is the pressure at vena contracta.

H_a = atmospheric pressure. If H_c becomes less than 34′ (10·2 m) of water or practically 26′ (7·8 m) of water separation takes place.

(*iii*) **Convergent mouth piece.** It is an external mouth piece in which loss of head due to sudden contraction and enlargement is eliminated, so its coefficient of discharge is unity, but due to frictional losses it is practically 0·975.

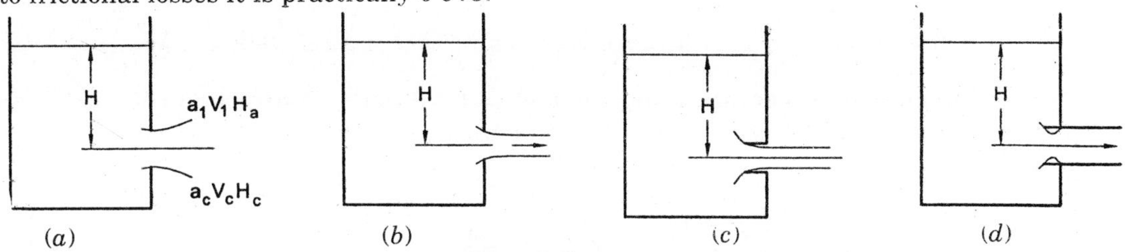

Fig. 12·15.

(*iv*) **Divergent mouth piece.** For a steady flow $\dfrac{a}{a_c} = \sqrt{1 + \dfrac{H_a - H_c}{H}}$ for maximum vacuum pressure of 26′ (7·8 m) $\dfrac{a}{a_c} = \sqrt{1 + \dfrac{7{\cdot}8}{H}}$.

(*v*) **Internal mouth piece.**

H = Height of water ; a = area of mouth piece

a_c = contracted jet area, V = velocity through mouth piece

Running free : $ac = \dfrac{a}{2}$, Discharge $= 0{\cdot}5\,a\sqrt{2gH}$; $C_d = 0{\cdot}5$

Running full : $ac = \dfrac{a}{2}$, Discharge $= a\sqrt{gH}$; $C_d = \dfrac{1}{\sqrt{2}} = 0{\cdot}707$

12·5. Notches and weirs

(a) **Rectangular notch.** Discharge $Q = \frac{2}{3} C_d \sqrt{2g}\ L\ H^{3/2}$ for a particular weir $\frac{2}{3} C_d \sqrt{2g}\ L$ = const. K, $C_d = 0.62$.

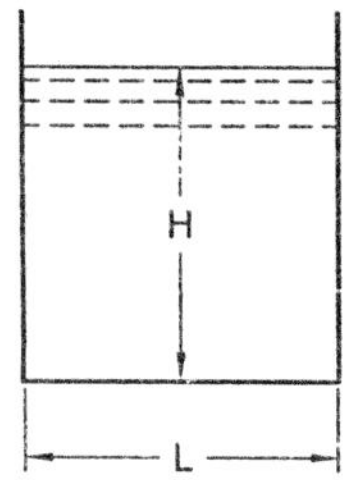

Fig. 12·16 (a).

Note : Height of water over crest is known as **Nappe.** This formula is for no end contractions. For n contractions L will be reduced to

$$L_1 = (L - 0.1\, nH)$$

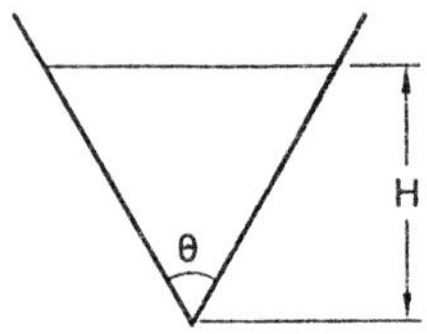

Fig. 12·16 (b).

(b) **Triangular V-notch.** Discharge $Q = \frac{8}{15} C_d \sqrt{2g} \tan \frac{\theta}{2} H^{5/2}$

assuming $C_d = 0.6$; $Q = 2.56 \tan \frac{\theta}{2} H^{5/2}$ (FPS units)

$$= 1.417 \tan \frac{\theta}{2} H^{5/2} \text{ (MKS units)}$$

(c) **Francis formula for sharp edged rectangular weirs with n contractions** (For one span $n = 2$)

$$Q = 3.33\ (L - 0.1\, nH)\ H^{3/2} \text{ in FPS units}$$

$$= 1.84\ (L - 0.1\, nH)\ H^{3/2} \text{ in MKS units}$$

If the channel has the same width at ends as water end contractions will be zero.

(d) **Sharp-edged weir with no end contractions**

$$Q = \frac{2}{3} \sqrt{2g} L\ H^{3/2} \left(0.605 + \frac{1}{1.05\ H - 3} + \frac{0.08\ H}{P} \right) \text{ Rehbock's formula}$$

P is the height of weir crest from bottom of channel of approach in m.

(e) **Bazin's formula for rectangular weirs.**

$$Q = m \sqrt{2g}\ L\ H^{3/2} \left(m = \frac{2}{3} C_d \right) m \text{ also } = 0.405 + \frac{0.00384}{H}$$

(f) **Discharge of rectangular weirs with a velocity of approach V_a.** If the area of the channel is greater than the area of the weir water section or water is approaching with a velocity V_a then discharge

$$Q = \frac{2}{3} C_d \sqrt{2g}\ L \left[\left(H + \frac{V_a^2}{2g} \right)^{3/2} - \left(\frac{V_a^2}{2g} \right)^{3/2} \right]$$

Francis formula with n contractions

$$Q = 3.33\ (L - 0.1\, nH) \left\{ H_1^{3/2} - \left(\frac{V_a^2}{2g} \right)^{3/2} \right\} ;\ H_1 = H + \frac{V_a^2}{2g}$$

(g) **Syphon spillway**

$$Q = C_d\ A \cdot \sqrt{2g\ H}\ ;\ C_d \text{ ranges } 0.6 \text{ to } 0.75$$

A_1 = area of cross-section of spillway pipe.

The syphon spillway takes more discharge and it utilises the whole difference of head of reservoir and over flow channel.

Table 12·3. Flow through Syphon (lit/sec)

Conduit dia.	Head in cm			
	5	10	15	20
10	0·05	0·07	0·08	0·09
20	0·19	0·26	0·37	0·73
30	0·42	0·59	0·73	0·84
40	0·75	1·06	1·79	1·49
50	1·17	1·63	2·02	2·33

(*h*) **Discharge through broad crested weir.**

$$Q = C_d \cdot b \cdot h\sqrt{2g(H-h)} \times L$$

for maximum distance $h = \frac{2}{3}H$

In broad crests discharge is reduced by 25%.

$$Q_{max} = 1{\cdot}7\, C_d\, LH^{3/2} \text{ for } h = \frac{2}{3}H$$

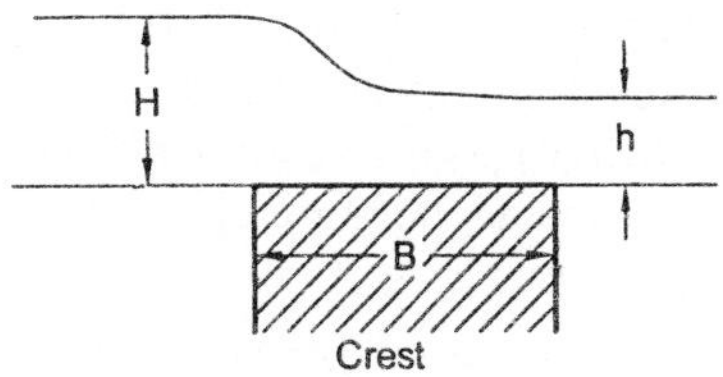

Fig. 12·16 (*c*).

Note : For end contraction reduce L by $0{\cdot}1\, nH$.

(*i*) **Round crested weirs.** $Q = C_d\, L\, H^{3/2}$, C_d = 2 to 4·5 depending on shape of crest.

(*j*) **Cippalletti weir or trapezoidal weir.** (Side slopes 1 : 4)

$Q = 1{\cdot}86\, LH^{3/2}$ (L = width of crest at bottom. Q in cum/sec with velocity of approach Q = $1{\cdot}86\, L\, (H + 1{\cdot}5\, h)^{3/2}$, h = head due to velocity of app. $= \frac{V_a^2}{2g}$, where V_a is velocity of approach.

(*k*) **Ogee shaped weir.** $Q = 2{\cdot}21\, LH^{3/2}$

Its discharge is about 1·5 times to that of a broad crested weir.

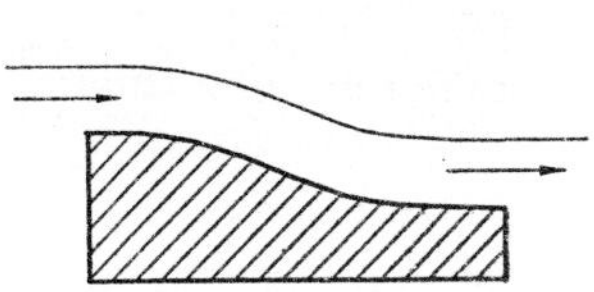

(*d*)

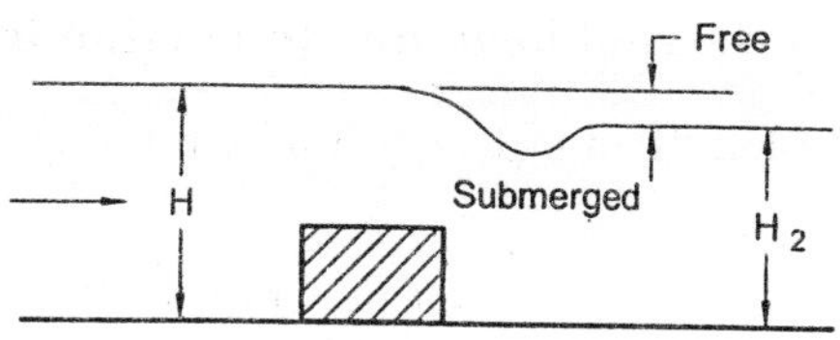

(*e*)

Fig. 12·16.

(*l*) **Flow over a submerged weir.**

Q = Discharge through submerged part + discharge through free part

$$= \frac{2}{3} C_d \sqrt{2g} \cdot L(H_1 - H_2)^{3/2} + C_d\, LH_2\{2g(H_1 - H_2)\}^{1/2}$$

The drowned portion is called as tail water.

(*m*) **Trapezoidal weir.** It may be taken as a combination of rectangular and triangular weir :

$$Q = \frac{2}{3} C_{d1} \sqrt{2g} \cdot L\, H^{3/2} + \frac{8}{15} C_{d2} \sqrt{2g} \tan\frac{\theta}{2} H^{5/2}$$

(*n*) **Flumes** (*a*) Standing wave flume

$$Q = 1{\cdot}705\, KBD^{3/2}; \text{ where, } Q = \text{discharge in cumecs,}$$

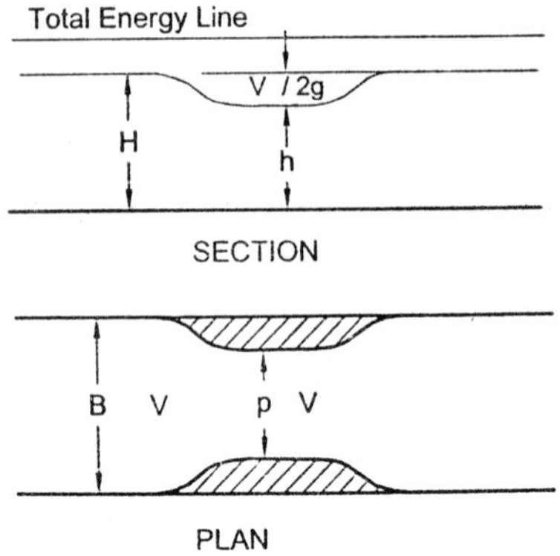

Fig. 12·17.

K is a constant depending on the relative proportions of the flume dimensions to be determined experimentally, B = throat width in m and $D = D_1 + h_0$ where D_1 is the length of water over sill of throat in m, h_0 is the head of water due to velocity of approach.

(*h*) **Venturi flume :** $Q = \dfrac{B \cdot H \times bh\sqrt{2g}\,\sqrt{H-h}}{\left(B^2H^2 - b^2h^2\right)^{1/2}}$

for maximum discharge $Q = 3{\cdot}09\ bH^{3/2}$

Note : A deposite of silt u/s of weir reduces its discharge coefficient. The inclined faces of the weir increases the discharge coefficient. Battering the u/s face of the crest increases the discharge by 10% over the weir when the batter is 1 : 1. Battering the d/s face does not effect the discharge. However the stability point of view d/s batter can be given. Rounding of the u/s edges of the crest increases the discharge by about 10%.

Time of emptying a reservoir by a rectangular weir.

$$T = \frac{2A}{\frac{2}{3}C_d\sqrt{2g}L}\left(\frac{1}{H_2^{1/2}} - \frac{1}{H_2^{1/2}}\right)$$

where H_1 and H_2 are the heads of water before and after the emptying process.

Table 12·4. Values of C in the formula $Q = CH^{5/2}$ for triangular notches

Head in m	0·10	0·15	0·2	0·3	0·4	*Angle notch*	60°	45°	30°	11¼°
Value for 90° notch	1·39	1·384	1·328	1·371	1·369	*Value of C*	2·40	1·38	0·815	0·275

12·6. Flow through pipes

(*a*) **Loss of head due to friction in pipes** $= \dfrac{uflV^2}{d{\cdot}2g}$

where l = length of pipe, d = dia. of pipe, f is a constant depending on the frictional resistence of the pipe.

$$f \text{ for new pipes} = 0{\cdot}005\left(1 + \frac{1}{12d}\right)$$

$$f \text{ for old pipes} = 0{\cdot}01\left(1 + \frac{1}{12d}\right)$$

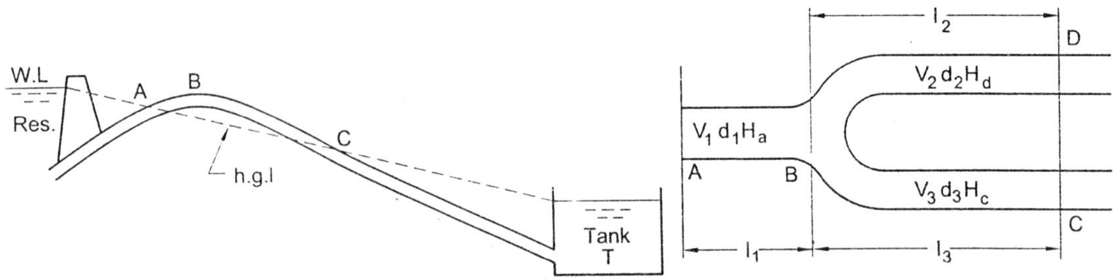

(*a*) (*b*)

Fig. 12·18

(*b*) If a pipe line *ABC* discharges water from reservoir *R* to tank *T*. The hydraulic gradient line (*h.g.l.*) due to friction falls from *R* to *T* and at the points *A* to *C* pressure is atmospheric and at B below atmospheric. If it reaches below 8′ absolute or 26′ of water vacuum separation will take place.

(c) **Parallel flow through pipes :**

$$\text{Route } ABD = H_a - H_d - \frac{4fl_1V_1^2}{d_1 2g} - \frac{4fl_2V_2^2}{d_2 \cdot 2g} = \frac{V_2^2}{2g} \quad ...(1)$$

$$\text{Route } ABC = H_a - H_c - \frac{4fl_1V_1^2}{d_1 2g} - \frac{4fl_3V_3^2}{d_3 \cdot 2g} = \frac{V_3^2}{2g} \quad ...(2)$$

$$V_1 d_1^2 = V_2 d_2^2 + V_3 d_3^2 \quad ...(3)$$

From equation (1), (2) and (3) V_1, V_2 and V_3 can be obtained.

(d) **Time of emptying a tank by a pipe :**

$$T = \frac{8A\sqrt{\dfrac{H\,4fl}{d}}}{\pi\, d^2 \sqrt{2g}} \times \left(H_1^{1/2} - H_2^{1/2}\right)$$

where, A = area of tank

l = length of pipe

H_1 = head of water above outlet pipe at beginning of operation

H_2 = head of water above outlet pipe at end of operation

(e) **Power from pipes carrying water :**

$$\text{Metric H.P. } (C_V) = \left(H \times V - \frac{4flV^2}{2g\,d}\right)\frac{wa}{75}$$

where, f = frictional resistance coefficient

H = head of water

V = velocity of water

d = dia. of pipe, l = length of pipe

w = density of water

$$\text{Efficiency of transmission} = \frac{H - h_f}{H}$$

where, h_f = loss of head due to friction

(f) **Thickness of pen stock conduits** $= t = \dfrac{pd}{2ft\,n}$

t = thickness of steel pipe, d = internal dia. of pipe, p = internal pressure in pipe to which it is subjected, ft. = permissible tensile stress of pipe material, η = efficiency of longitudinal joint.

(η = 1 for seamless pipes, 0·9 for welded joints, 0·75 for double riveted and 0·63 for single riveted joint). The values are taken for taking water hammer and rusting in consideration. The minimum thickness of steel pipes = 5 mm.)

Minimum thickness of C.I. pipes $= t = \dfrac{d}{50} + 0{\cdot}9$ cm if casted horizontally

$= \dfrac{d}{60} + 0{\cdot}9$ cm if casted vertically

Economical velocity of water in penstocks $= \dfrac{1}{8}\sqrt{2gH}$ m/sec (*g*) **Chezy's formula for velocity in pipes.** $V = c\sqrt{mi}$

for pipes $i = \frac{h_f}{l}$ where h_f is loss of head due to friction and l = length of pipe, m = hyd. mean radius = $\frac{r}{2}$ where r = inner radius of pipe.

Table 12·5.

Pipe dia. in cm	1·25	2·5	7·5	15	30	60	90
Chezy's const. C	36	44	54	58	60	61	61·5

(*h*) Critical velocity in pipes = velocity at which flow changes from laminar to turbulent due to friction in pipes.

12·7. Flow through open channels (also refer design of channels in irrigation sec.)

Chezey's formula : $V = C\sqrt{mi}$ m = hyd. mean depth = $\frac{\text{area}}{\text{wetted perimeter}}$

Bazin's formula : $C = \frac{157{\cdot}5}{1 + \frac{K}{m^{1/2}}}$ i = slope in fraction

Values of *K* in Bazin's *C*

Smooth *C* plaster or planned wood	0·109
Clear smooth sides of wood, brick or stone etc.	0·29
Dirty sides	0·5
Smooth randum rubble	0·833
Good earth	1·54
Sides of natural earth	2·35
Earth with weed sides	3·17

Manning's formula : $\frac{1{\cdot}486}{N} m^{2/3} i^{1/2}$ ft./sec. ; $\frac{1}{N} m^{2/3} i^{1/2}$ m/sec.

For values of *N* and (for other details refer "Irrigation sec.")

For maximum discharge in trapezoidal section $m = \frac{d}{2}$ (d = depth of water)

For maximum velocity in circular section $i = 1{\cdot}62\, r$ (r = radius)

For maximum discharge in circular section $d = 1{\cdot}9^r$

Critical depth $= \frac{r^2}{g}$

Table 12·6. Approximate discharge over a rectangular weir, one ft. wide without end contractions in m³/min. $Q = 3{\cdot}33\, LH^{3/2}$

H in m	*Q in m³/min*	*H in m*	*Q in m³/min*
0·305	5·59	0·610	15·81
0·335	6·45	0·686	18·73
0·366	7·34	0·762	22·11
0·400	8·27	0·838	25·51

Table contd...

Table contd...

H in m	*Q in m^3/min*	*H in m*	*Q in m^3/min*
0·427	9·24	0·914	29·06
0·457	10·25	1·067	36·62
0·490	11·27	1·219	44·76
0·518	12·38	1·371	53·41
0·549	13·49	1·524	62·55
0·579	14·62	1·676	72·16

Table 12·6 A. Channel capacities in litres/sec. for various channel slopes and sections. Channels are trapezoidal with side slopes 1½′-1′ (hor. : vert.) and roughness coeff. 0·035.

Channel Slope		*Bed width B and water depth H in metres*								Channels with weeds and bushes n = 0·025, 0·035
		B 0·10	0·15	0·20	0·25	0·30	0·40	0·50	0·60	
		H 0·15	0·25	0·30	0·40	0·50	0·65	0·85	1·00	
1/10,000	0·01%	2·5	9·3	16	33	59	121	243	375	
1/5,000	0·02%	3·6	13	23	47	84	172	345	518	
1/2,000	0·05%	5·6	21	36	74	133	271	545	845	
1/1,000	0·1%	7·8	30	51	107	190	390	770	1200	
1/500	0·2%	11·0	42	71	148	266	540	1090	1690	
1/333	0·3%	13·5	51	87	183	330	670	1330	2065	
1/250	0·4%	15·5	59	100	212	380	765	1540	2305*	
1/200	0·5%	17·0	66	113	237	422	855	1720*	2670*	
1/100	1·0%	24·0	94	160	330	593*	1210*	2430*	3775*	

* Velocities greater than 1 m/sec.

Table 12·6B. Discharge through standard cipalleti trapezoidal weirs in ltrs/sec.

H	*Width of crest of weir (B in cms)*							
cm	*25*	*50*	*75*	*100*	*125*	*150*	*175*	*200*
1	0·5	0·9	1·4	1·8	2·3	2·7	3·2	3·7
2	1·3	2·6	3·9	5·2	6·5	7·8	9·2	11
3	2·4	4·8	7·2	9·6	12	14	17	19
4	3·7	7·4	11	15	19	22	26	30
5	5·2	10	16	21	26	31	36	42
6	6·8	14	21	27	34	41	48	55
8	10·5	21	32	42	53	63	74	84
10	15·0	29	44	59	73	88	103	118
12	19·0	39	58	70	93	116	135	155
14	24	49	73	97	122	146	170	195

Table contd...

Table contd...

H	Width of crest of weir (B in cms)							
cm	*25*	*50*	*75*	*100*	*125*	*150*	*175*	*200*
16		60	89	119	149	178	208	238
18		71	106	142	177	212	248	284
20		83	125	166	208	249	291	333
25			174	232	290	349	407	465
30			229	305	382	458	535	611
35				391	481	577	674	770
41				477	588	705	823	941
45				571	701	842	982	1122
50					822	986	1150	1314

The conditions for measurement for a rectangular weir also apply to a cipalleti weir. The standard side slopes are 1 hor. to 4 vert. Discharge $Q = 1{\cdot}86$ in cu.m./sec.

Values of coefficient of discharge for various type of works having notches

1.	Small opening with shallow water	0·57
2.	Shear edge thin plates	0·62
3.	Short round tubes	0·63
4.	Ordinary lock sluices	0·62
5.	Conical divergent mouth piece	0·50
6.	Orifice in thin walls 2 to 3 times to the dia. of orifice	0·82
7.	When thickness is short	0·61
8*a*.	Re-entrant tube projected 2½ times of dia. (in side)	0·73
b.	When length of re-entrant mouth piece is equal to inside dia.	0·52
9.	Bell mouth orifice, vena contracta will rounded	0·97
10.	Sharp edged orifice with covering mouth piece	0·98
11.	Opening having bottom at the level of reservoir with pointed piers	0·86
12.	Sluices in lock gates	0·83
13.	Narrow bridges openings	0·90
14.	Sluices without side walls	0·66
15.	Canal lock gates	0·70

Weirs

1.	Broad crested flat top	0·577
2.	Narrow crests less than 90 cm	0·623
3.	Weir overfalls in full width of channel end contraction suppressed	0·666

12·8. Measurements of flow in open channels (Discharge)

Open channel. The term open channel applies for any passage through which water is flowing, when the free surface of water is in contact of atmosphere. The channel may be covered at top or open. If covered it must not run full, otherwise the pressure might rise above or fall below the atmospheric. A pipe which is not running full may be classed as an open channel. An open channel may be of uniform sections such as canals, sewer and aquaduct or it may be an irregular cross-section as rivers and streams.

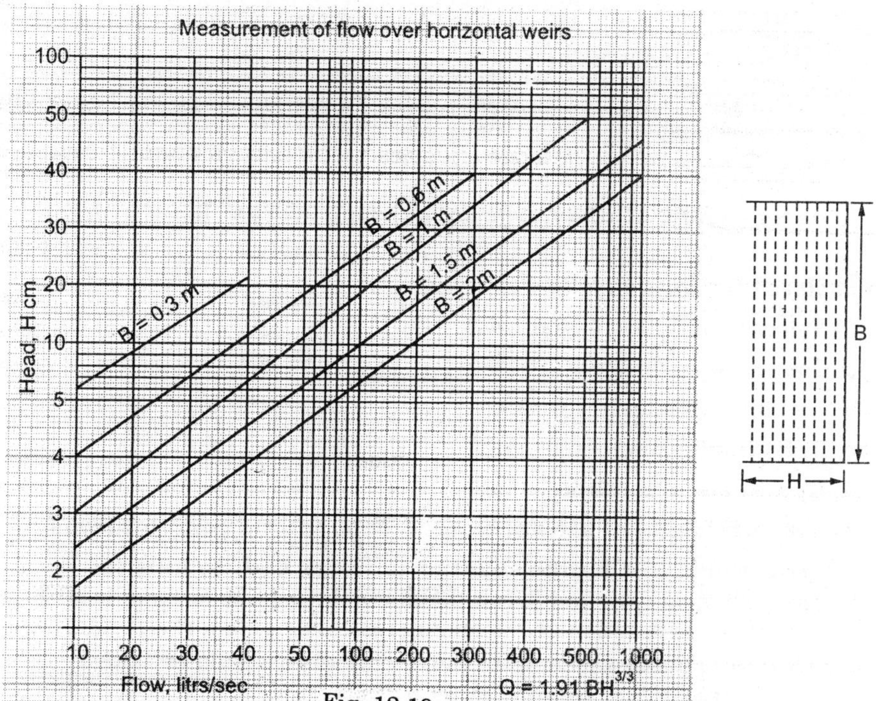

Fig. 12·19.

Water running through an open channel is subjected to a frictional resistance at the wetted surface of the channel due to which the velocity of flow is not uniform throughout the section, being smaller towards the sides. As the pressure through out is not atmospheric the head causing flow is entirely due to slope of the channel which is overcome by the friction of the sides. For calculating discharge through the channel mean velocity of whole section is taken into account.

Discharge. Discharge is a product of area o water swept and velocity.

(1) **Measurement of area of water swept.** (*a*) **Site work.** The work on site has different conditions on different sites.

(*i*) Channel having uniform bed, such as irrigation channel and rock bed in hills.

(*ii*) Channels having flexible beds such as rivers in plains.

(*iii*) Channels which can be measured across by a rope as in small irrigation channels.

(*iv*) Channels which cannot be measured across by a rope such as in big canals and rivers.

(*v*) Can be measured, when channel is dry and when channel is not running.

(*b*) **Office computations by recorded data.** Generally following methods are used according to the accuracy required, availability of time, means and records available.

(*i*) Graphical method

(*ii*) Simpson's rule

(*iii*) Trapezoidal rule

(*iv*) Dividing channel into compartments.

(2) **Velocity of water.** The velocity is generally taken by the following means, according to the accuracy required, means available and site conditions.

(*i*) Surface floats

(*ii*) Double or submerged floats

(*iii*) Velocity rods

(*iv*) Current meters

(*v*) Pitot tube

(3) **Assessment of discharge by existing works** (Refer hydraulics irrigation and bridges)

(*a*) Head over crest on falls and weirs.

(*b*) Velocity in flumes of channels

(*c*) Channel dimensions

(*d*) By afflux on masonry works

(*e*) By hydraulic jump.

(4) **By Chemical method**

(5) **Measurements of area of water swept and its computations.**

(A) Site work. (*i*) **Channel having uniform bed.** In hills the bed and sides of the channel is generally firm rock and it can taken stable at least for one flood. It will be better in such cases that the cross section of the channel is taken before the flood. However the section can be taken after the floods also and the mean of the two should be taken.

(*ii*) **Channels having flexible beds.** In plains where channel runs in ordinary soil, the cross-section must be taken when the channel is running at the same time when its velocity is taken. If for some reason it is not possible to observe cross-section when channel is running, it should be taken when the channel is dry before and after the flood or running and mean of the two should be taken. (Not desirable for highly flexible beds).

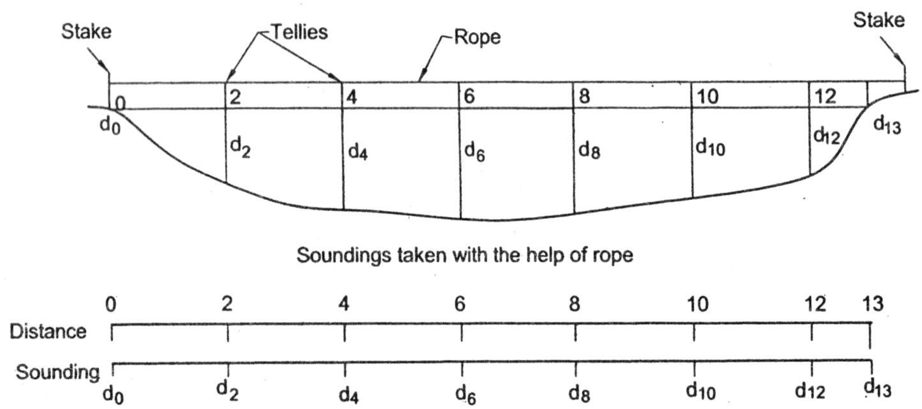

Fig. 12·20.

(*iii*) **Channels which can be measured across by a rope.** Cross-sections in small channels such as distributries etc. should be taken by a rope passing across the channel, having tellies at equal intervals on which the soundings should be taken. When rope sags due to large width of the channel, a metallic wire with tellies should be taken. In canals a stout manila rope should run with wire rope for the support of the sounding.

(*iv*) **Channels which cannot be measured across by a rope.** Channels which cannot be measured across by a rope, the cross section is taken before the flood or in running if the bed is flexible. Soundings are taken as directed in the following articles.

(*v*) **Cross-sectioning when the channel is dry.** In such cases fix a B.M. on one bank and take a cross-section at equal intervals by a levelling instrument. Distances should be measured by a tape or by stadia of the instrument. The cross section should be starded above the H.F.L. or F.S.L. and also be finished above F.S.L. or H.F.L.

(*vi*) **Cross-section when the channel is running.** The level of the water is taken by a gauge or from a B.M. by a levelling instrument. Soundings are taken by a rope or by a theodolite as detailed below. It needs two operations.

(*a*) Horizontal control (*b*) Vertical control.

(*a*) **Horizontal control.** Method of locating soundings.

(*i*) **Location by transite and stadia.** In this method a transit theodolite is set up at a point on one bank and stadia reading are taken on a stadia rod held on the bottom of a boat at the instant the soundings are taken. The transit station should be near the water level or zero of the horizontal distance.

(*ii*) **Location by range and time interval.** In this method the sounding boat is rowed with a uniform speed along the range and soundings are taken at a regular interval of time. The method is practical in low speed and shallow water.

(*iii*) **Location by range and one angle from the bank.** (Refer Fig. 12·21 (*a*) In this method the boat is kept on the range and one angle between the base line and the boat is observed

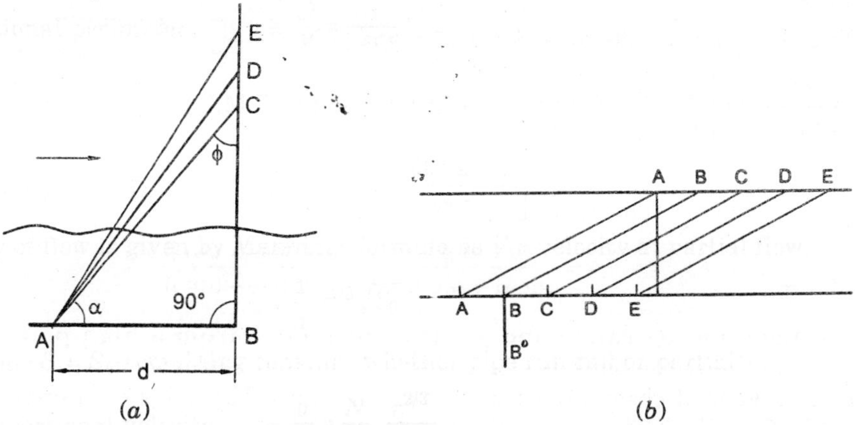

(*a*) (*b*)

Fig. 12·21.

with a theodolite, set up near the one end of the base line, at the instant the soundings are made, when a signal is given from the boat. Thus as in the figure a theodolite is set up at *A*, on the base line *AB* at right angles to the range and with both plates clamped at zero. The station *B* is bisected loosening the upper plate the telescope is directed to the boat man and angle α is recorded. The distance *BC* of the position of the soundings = $d \tan \alpha$ where *d* is the perpendicular distance of *A* from the range line and α is the angle observed.

(*iv*) **Locating by intersecting ranges.** (Refer Fig. 12·21 (*b*) In this method signals *ABCDE* and *A'B'C'D'E'* ... are fixed on both banks and soundings in a boat are taken by ranging *A* to *A'*, *B* to *B'* *C* to *C'* etc. The sounding interval can be measured by increasing *B'B°* at site on one bank.

(*v*) **Location by range and one angle from the boat.** By an angular measurement of

ϕ taken from the boat with a sexant at the time of sounding to same point *A* already located on the map. Here $y = d \cot \phi$. y = distance of boat from the point *B* at bank and d = distance of *B* from the point *A*. "refer Fig. for serial (*iii*)", locating sounding from one angle from the bank). The point *A* might be conveniently marked with a ranging rod. The direction of the line *BCD* ... may be determined by ranging from the bank.

(*vi*) **Location by range and two angles from bank.** A much more expeditious method of locating soundings is by means of simultaneous angular measurements taken from two instrument stations on bank. It require two instrument men on bank and one sounding party on boat. Thus if *A* and *B* are the two stations (see Fig. 12·22) the position of which on the map are known, a theodolite is set up at each (Plane tables would be practicable in some cases).

Each operator selects some definite referring object already plotted on the map (possibility the station at which the other instrument is fixed) and with the vernier of the horizontal scale clamped at zero direct the cross hair of the telescope to this. The lower plate is then clamped and the telescope is then directed to some definite mark on the boat and reading is taken as a signal is given by the sounding party. The position of each sounding is observed in this way.

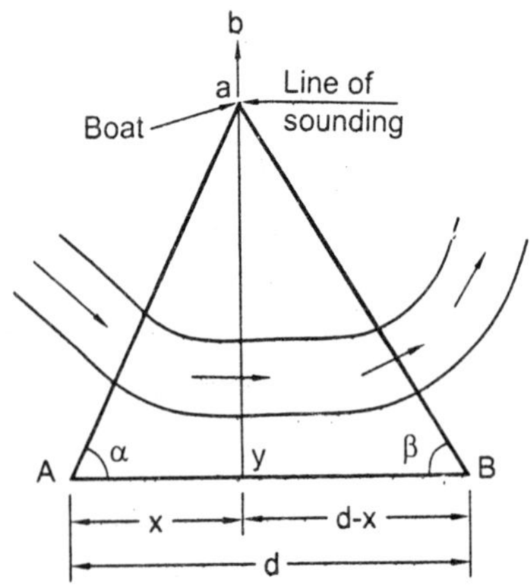

Fig. 12·22.

Almost invariably the points would be plotted by means of a protector, but if desired the co-ordinates of each position could be calculated and plotted with a linear scale.

Thus let *d* be the distance *AB* and α and β be the observed angles at *A* and *B* each measured from the other station as a referring object and let the co-ordinates of the position of the boat be *x* and *y* from *A*.

Then $$y = x \tan \alpha = (d - x) \tan \beta$$

$$\therefore \quad x(\tan \alpha + \tan \beta) = d \tan \beta$$

$$x = \frac{d \tan \beta}{\tan \alpha + \tan \beta}, \quad y = \frac{d \tan \alpha \tan \beta}{\tan \alpha + \tan \beta}$$

(*vii*) **Location by range and polar co-ordinates from a high point on the bank.** When the ground near the bank is of a moderately high altitude, the position of sounding may be located by means of observations from one theodolite. The polar co-ordinates of the points being there by furnished. The observations would include :

(*a*) A horizontal angle or bearing α from some referring object shown on the map.

(*b*) A vertical angle of depression.

Then knowing the reduced level of the instrument axis and the water level at the time of observations the horizontal distance may be calculated *e.g.* if the height of the instrument axis above the water surface be *h* and the angle of depression be θ, the horizontal distance *r* from the instrument station to the sounding point is

$$r = h \cot \theta$$

and if this is measured along a line upon the plan having a bearing α from the referring object the required point is located.

If preferred, the rectangular co-ordinates with reference to the instrument station as origin may be computed

$$x = r \cos \alpha = h \cot \theta \cos \alpha ; \quad y = r \sin \alpha = h \cot \theta \sin \alpha$$

(*viii*) **Location by range and two angles from boat.** The position of the soundings may be located by means of two simultaneous angular observations to three well defined points already marked upon the map. If no permanent natural objects are available poles may be errected and their positions may be plotted on the map by ordinary survey methods. In this method only one instrument and observer is required in the boat. The location of points by this method gives rise to "three point problem". Let the angle observed be θ_1 and θ_2.

Mechanical method. An instrument known as station pointer having three legs, middle fixed and other two adjustable having a point fulcrum or common centre of their fiducial edges. It is set with the measured angles θ_1 and θ_2 between its fiducial edges of the arms. Move the instrument on the paper so as the three edges pass from the station observed simultaneously.

Graphical method. In this method in place of the instrument the angles θ_1 and θ_2 are drawn from a point O on a tracing paper and these three radiating lines sketch is moved on the plan so as the three stations coincide the lines simultaneously.

(*b*) **Vertical control.** (*i*) **Sounding rod.** Sounding rods are convenient in shallow water up to depth of about 5 cm. They are made of sound and straight wood and are fitted at the bottom

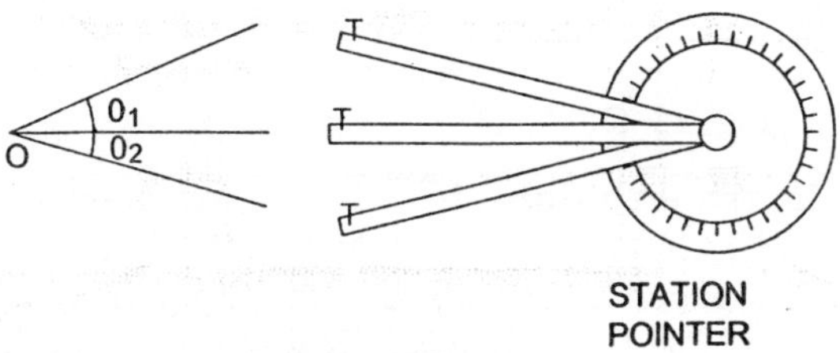

Fig. 12·23.

with a flat iron or lead shoe of sufficient weight to hold it up right in water and of sufficient bottom area to prevent it from sinking into the ground. If the samples of the bed are required the shoe is provided with a cup shaped cavity. The rods are graduated for reading the depth of water. Their section is closed brackets to cut the water and avoiding heading of water on it.

(*ii*) **Lead lines.** These are used for depths beyond 5 m. The lead lines consists of a hemp, cotton or brass chain having at its end a weight called lead. The rope is marked with tellies. It is thrown in water so as to reach the bottom vertically down of the sounding boat.

(*iii*) **Sounding machine.** It consists of a machine which makes a click on the boat. The click after rebounding from the bed is again heard at the boat. The time interval multiplied by the velocity of sound in water gives twice the depth of water.

Velocity of sound in water $= \left(\dfrac{K_g}{w}\right)^{1/2}$ where K = bulk modulus of elasticity. It varies with density and hence to a small extent with temperature and pressure. Also with salinity being about 9% greater on average for sea water than fresh water. At 50°F for fresh water K = 3,00,000 lb/in^2 *i.e.* 43·2 × 10^6 lbs/ft^2. For sea water K = 1·09 × 43·2 × 10^6 lbs/ft^2, g = 32·2 but varies with locality. w = 62·4 for fresh water and 64·3 lbs/ft^3 for sea water. For above formula the velocity of sound is fresh water = 4720′/sec. and in sea water 4850′/sec. An average of 4800′/sec.

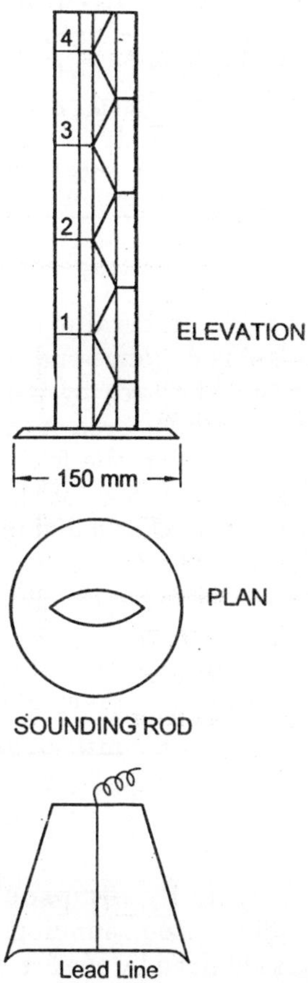

Fig. 12·24.

(B) Computation of area of cross section.

(*i*) **By graphical method.** By dividing the section in squares—The whole section of the channel, taking water surface as datum is plotted on a graph sheet to a scale. The no. of squares are counted and area of x-section is computed. If the horizontal and vertical scales are different, the area of a square is computed by the respective scales and the whole area is computed by counting the squares. Squares less than half is omitted and more than half or half is taken full in counting.

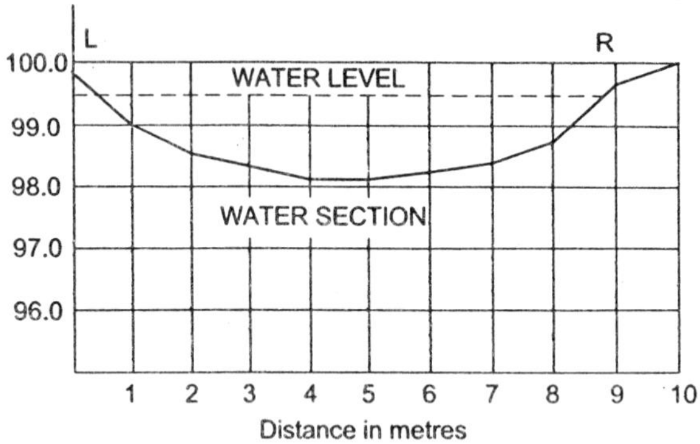

Area of 1 cm² = 1 m² (in graph)

10 × 10 = 100 columns = 1 m² (in graph)

Nos. of columns 850 = 8·5 m² (in graph)

Fig. 12·25.

(*ii*) **By dividing the section in trapezoidals.** In this method a series of parallel equidistant lines are ruled on a tracing. The constant distance between them representing some round number of feet or metres. The tracing paper is then placed over the plan so that the area is exectly enclosed between the parallel lines. The figure is thus divided into a number of strips. The curved ends of which are replaced by perpendicular. The sum of the lengths of these rectangles thus obtained multiplied by common breadths, gives the required area. The length of each strip is scaled by the oridnary plotting scales or the computing rule.

(*iii*) **By trapezoidal method.** Area (say A) = $\left\{\text{sum of all soundings} - \dfrac{\text{sum of 1st and last}}{2}\right\} \times d$

where d = interval of distance. If the last sounding is not a regular distance and is a part of distance interval, then 1st find the area by ignoring the last sounding and add afterwards the area of the last triangle or trapezium. If in an observation the following six soundings d_1 to d_6 were obtained as a regular interval l and last sounding d_7 has been obtained at a distance l_1 then

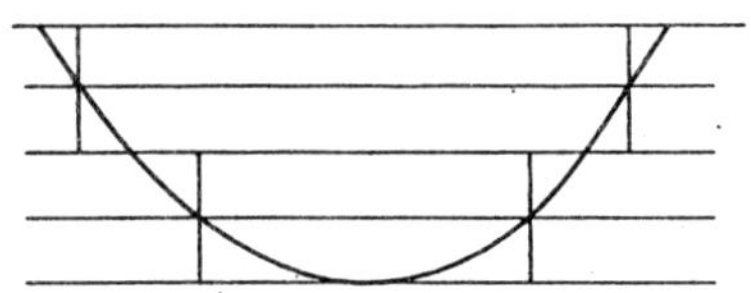

Fig. 12·26.

$$A = \left(d_1 + d_2 + d_3 + d_4 + d_5 + d_6 - \frac{d_1 + d_6}{2}\right) l + \frac{d_6 + d_7}{2} \times l_1$$

In this method it is presumed that the surface between soundings are of straight lines. 1st sounding is taken at the zero of the chainage.

(*iv*) **By mid ordinate rule.** In this rule soundings are taken at the middle of section. Let the soundings are d_1, d_2, d_3, d_4 and d_5 at a distance l apart and let the last sounding is d_6 at a distance of l_1 then $A = (d_1 + d_2 + d_3 + d_4 + d_5)\, l + d_6 l_1$. 1st sounding is taken at the middle of 1st section.

(*v*) **By Simpson's rule.** To the sum of 1st and last soundings add twice the sum of remaining odd soundings and four times the sum of all even soundings. Multiply the total sum thus obtained by one 3rd of the common distance between the soundings and the result so obtained gives the area. Let the soundings are d_1, d_2, d_3, d_4 ... d_n and common distance be l then

$$A = \frac{l}{3}[(d_1 + d_n) + 2(d_3 + d_5 + d_7 + \ldots) + 4(d_2 + d_4 + d_6 + \ldots)]$$

In this rule it is presumed that the surface between the soundings is parabola hence this rule is also known as parabolic rule. 1st sounding is taken at the zero of the chainage.

(*vi*) **By dividing into compartments.** When the channel is big, the whole width of the channel is divided in equal compartments. The width is divided in odd no. of compartments so that there is always a central compartment.

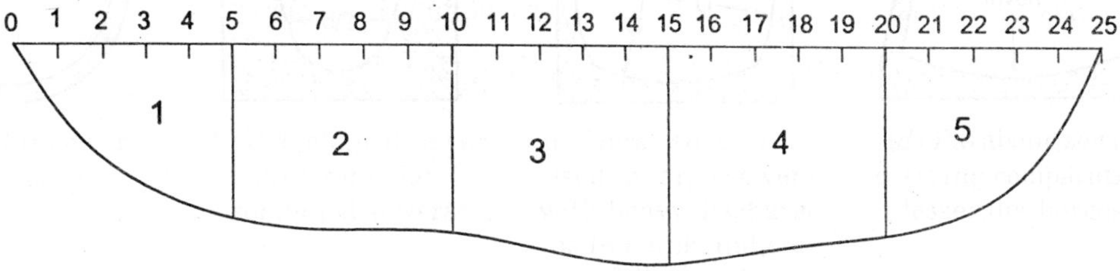

Fig. 12·27.

The process is decided at site and velocity is observed in the middle of each compartment. The area and velocity for each compartment is calculated separately and then adding together will give the whole discharge. Suppose in an observation $d_0, d_1, d_2, d_3 \ldots d_{25}$ soundings are taken. The compartments are 1st—d_0 to d_5, 2nd—d_5 to d_{10}, 3rd—d_{10} to d_{15}, 4th—d_{15} to d_{20} and 5th—d_{20} to d_{25}. The velocity observed be V_1, V_2, V_3, V_4 and V_5 in the middle of each compartment by velocity rods. The common distance be l.

$$\begin{aligned}
\text{Then} \quad Q &= \left(d_0 + d_1 + d_2 + d_3 + d_4 + d_5 - \frac{d_0 + d_5}{2}\right) l \times V_1 \\
&+ \left(d_5 + d_6 + d_7 + d_8 + d_9 + d_{10} - \frac{d_5 + d_{10}}{2}\right) l \times V_2 \\
&+ \left(d_{10} + d_{11} + d_{12} + d_{13} + d_{14} + d_{15} - \frac{d_{10} + d_{15}}{2}\right) l \times V_3 \\
&+ \left(d_{15} + d_{16} + d_{17} + d_{18} + d_{19} + d_{20} - \frac{d_{15} + d_{20}}{2}\right) l \times V_4 \\
&+ \left(d_{20} + d_{21} + d_{22} + d_{23} + d_{24} + d_{25} - \frac{d_{20} + d_{25}}{2}\right) l \times V_5
\end{aligned}$$

(*vii*) **When soundings are at irregular distances.** When the soundings are taken at irregular intervals due to some controlled or sharp edged points, the following two methods are used for computing the area.

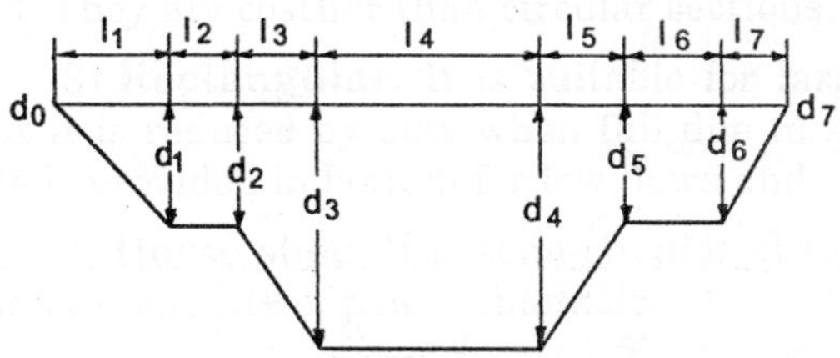

Fig. 12·28.

1st method. In this method the area of each trapezoid is computed separately by multiplying the base by the mean of the soundings on its sides. By adding, these the area is obtained from the Fig. 12·28

$$A = \frac{d_0 + d_1}{2} \times l_1 + \frac{d_1 + d_2}{2} \times l_2 + \frac{d_2 + d_3}{2} \times l_3 + \frac{d_3 + d_4}{2} \times l_4 + \frac{d_4 + d_5}{2} \times l_5 + \frac{d_5 + d_6}{2} \times l_6 + \frac{d_6 + d_7}{2} \times l_7$$

2nd method—By co-ordinates. In this method the co-ordinates of various controlling points are taken with reference to an origin *O*, and they are tabulated in the form below :

Points	*Co-ordinates*		*Points*	*Co-ordinates*		*Points*	*Co-ordinates*	
	x	y		x	y		x	y
A	x_1	y_1	*D*	x_4	y_4	*F*	x_6	y_6
B	y_2	y_2	*E*	x_5	y_5	*G*	x_7	y_7
C	x_3	y_3						

The co-ordinates are arranged in the form of determinants

$$\begin{matrix} y_1 & & y_2 & & y_3 & & y_4 & & y_5 & & y_6 & & y_7 & & y_1 \\ & \times & & \times & & \times & & \times & & \times & & \times & & \times & \\ x_1 & & x_2 & & x_3 & & x_4 & & x_5 & & x_6 & & x_7 & & x_1 \end{matrix}$$

Then $\quad \Sigma P = (y_1 x_2 + y_2 x_3 + \ldots y_7 x_1)$

$\quad \Sigma Q = (x_1 y_2 + x_2 y_3 + \ldots y_7 x_1)$

Then $\quad \text{area} = \frac{1}{2}(\Sigma P - \Sigma Q)$

(*viii*) **Instrumental method.** This method consists of determining the area of a given Fig. by the use of a planimeter (refer survey section). Makers also give a note for its use.

Examples for calculating area of *x*-section.

Example 1. *In a distributory the following field notes are taken. Calculate the area of x-sec. of the sec. of water.*

Distance from L to R (m)	*Soundings in m*	*Distance from L to R (m)*	*Soundings in m*
0	0·20	2·5	1·20
0·5	0·85	3·0	1·11
1·0	1·20	3·5	1·15
1·5	1·21	4·0	1·10
2·0	1·23	4·5	0·70
		5·0	0·00
			Sum 9·95

Mean of 1st and last $= \frac{0{\cdot}20 + 0}{2} = 0{\cdot}10$

Common distance $= 0{\cdot}5$ m

So area $= \left(\text{Sum of soundings} - \frac{\text{1st} + \text{last}}{2}\right) l$

where $(l = \text{common distance} = 0{\cdot}5)$

$= (9{\cdot}95 - 0{\cdot}10) \times 0{\cdot}5 = 4{\cdot}93 \text{ m}^2.$

Example 2. *In a channel field notes are as below. Calculate x-sec. of water.*

Distance	*0*	*1*	*2*	*3*	*4*	*5*	*6*	*7*	*8*	*9*	*10*	*10·5*
Soundings	*0·5*	*1·01*	*1·95*	*2·00*	*2·00*	*2·00*	*2·00*	*2·02*	*2·00*	*2·00*	*0·75*	*0·18*

Note : Here the last sounding is not at a regular distance of 1 m. It is at 0·5 m. So 1st calculate the area of cross-section by ignoring the last sounding *i.e.* calculate for sounding 0 to 10 m and then add of last trapezoid.

Sum of the soundings from 0·0 to 10·0 m = 18·23

Mean of 1st and last at 10 m $= \dfrac{0{\cdot}50 + 0{\cdot}75}{2} = 0{\cdot}63$

Area from 0·0 to 10 m $= (18{\cdot}23 - 0{\cdot}63) \times 1 = 17{\cdot}60 \text{ m}^2$

Area of the last trapezoid from 10·0 m to 10·5 $= \dfrac{0{\cdot}75 + 0{\cdot}18}{2} \times 0{\cdot}5 = 0{\cdot}23 \text{ m}^2$

Total area $= 17{\cdot}60 + 0{\cdot}23 = 17{\cdot}83 \text{ m}^2$

Example 3. *The following sounds are taken in a river at 25′ regular interval. Calculate area of x-sec. of water by Simpson's rule*

$A = \dfrac{\text{Distance interval}}{3}$ (1st + last sound + 2 times of sum of remaining odd sounds + 4 times of remaining even sounds).

Soundings 9·8, 12·9, 17·6, 15·9, 19·8, 12·9, 24·5, 22·2 and 18·9

$$A = \frac{25}{3}\{9{\cdot}8 + 18{\cdot}9 + 2(17{\cdot}6 + 19{\cdot}8 + 24{\cdot}5) + 4(12{\cdot}9 + 15{\cdot}9 + 21{\cdot}9 + 22{\cdot}2)\}$$
$$= 3700{\cdot}83 \text{ sq. ft.}$$

Example 4. *The cross-section of a channel when dry was taken by a levelling instrument. The field notes are given below. Calculate the area of cross-section of water at a water-level of 99·0. Regular distance was 50′ and last level was taken at a distance of 30′.*

Distance in ft	*Reading*			*H.I.*	*R.L.S.*	*Remarks*
	Back	*Inter*	*Fore*			
0	5·02			105·02	100·00	B.M. at Rt. bank
50	4·25		7·91	101·36	97·11	Bed
100	5·19		6·11	100·44	95·25	Bed
150	4·82		8·27	106·99	92·17	Bed
200	4·91		4·76	107·14	92·23	Bed
250	5·00		4·96	97·18	92·18	Bed
300	5·03		4·46	97·75	92·72	Bed
350	4·98		4·87	97·86	92·88	Bed
400	4·99		2·86	99·99	95·00	Bed
450	5·11		2·86	102·24	97·13	Bed
480			2·01		100·23	Left bank
	49·30		49·07 = 0·23	Arith. check 100·23 – 100 = 0·23		

Let at right bank water starts with sounding 0·0 at x' from B.M.

Then $\dfrac{x}{50 - x} = \dfrac{1}{1{\cdot}89}$ or $x = 17$

Difference in water level and B.M. at 0 $= 100 - 99 = 1{\cdot}00$

Difference in 50′ station point and W.L. $= 99{\cdot}0 - 97{\cdot}11 = 1{\cdot}89$

Let left bank water ends at y from last station.

Then $\dfrac{y}{3 - y} = \dfrac{1{\cdot}23}{1{\cdot}87}$ or $y = 12$

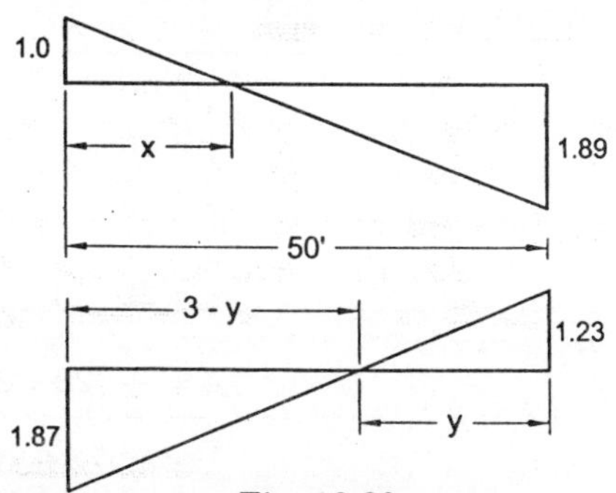

Fig. 12·29.

(Difference in last B.M. – W.L. = 1·23 (90 ~ 100·23))

(Difference in 450 point and W.L. = 90 – 97·13 = 1·87)

Soundings	*R.L. of bed*	*Water level*	*Difference in sounding*
0	100·00	99·0	(–) 1·00
50	97·11	99·0	1·09
100	95·25	99·0	3·75
150	92·17	99·0	6·83
200	92·23	99·0	7·77
250	92·18	99·0	7·72
300	92·72	99·0	6·28
350	92·88	99·0	6·12
400	95·00	99·0	4·00
450	97·13	99·0	1·87
480	100·23	99·0	1·23

The soundings can be arranged in the following table :

Distance	17	50	100	150	200	250	300	350	400	450	480
Soundings	0	1·89	3·75	6·82	7·77	7·72	6·28	6·12	4·00	1·87	0·00

Here the 1st and last soundings are not at equal interval, so 1st ignore it. Now the sum for 50′ to 450′

$$= 1{\cdot}89 + 3{\cdot}75 + 6{\cdot}82 + 7{\cdot}77 + 7{\cdot}72 + 6{\cdot}28 + 6{\cdot}12 + 4{\cdot}00 + 1{\cdot}87 = 46{\cdot}22$$

Mean of 50′ and 450′ soundings $= \dfrac{1{\cdot}89 + 1{\cdot}87}{2} = 1{\cdot}88$

So area from 50′ to 450′ = (46·22 – 1·88) 50 = 2217·0 ft^2

Area of 1st triangle $= \dfrac{1{\cdot}89}{2} \times 33 = 31{\cdot}10$

Area of last triangle $= \dfrac{1{\cdot}87}{2} \times 18 = 16{\cdot}83$

Total = 2217·0 + 31·1 + 16·83 = 2264·93 ft^2

Example 5. *Following sounds are taken at a discharge site. Calculate the area of cross-section*

Distance	0	20	50	90	135	ft
Soundings	20	25	15	18	28	ft

$y_1 = 20$ $\quad d_1 = 20 - 0 = 20$

$y_2 = 25$ $\quad d_2 = 50 - 20 = 30$

$y_3 = 15$ $\quad d_3 = 90 - 50 = 40$

$y_4 = 18$ $\quad d_4 = 135 - 90 = 45$

$y_5 = 28$

$$A = \frac{20}{2}(20 + 25) + \frac{30}{2}(25 + 15) + \frac{40}{2}(15 - 18) + \frac{45}{2}(18 + 28)$$

$$= 450 + 600 + 660 + 1035 = 2745 \text{ ft}^2$$

Example 6. *Taking the data as in Example 5. Find the area by co-ordinates.*

	Co-ordinates	
	x	*y*
a	0	20
b	20	25
c	50	15
d	90	18
e	135	28
f	135	0

Arranging in determinant form $\frac{20}{0} \times \frac{25}{20} \times \frac{15}{50} \times \frac{18}{90} \times \frac{28}{135} \times \frac{20}{20}$

$$\Sigma P = (20 \times 20 + 25 \times 50 + 15 \times 90 + 18 \times 135 + 28 \times 0) = 9210$$

$$\Sigma Q = (0 \times 25 + 20 \times 15 + 50 \times 18 + 90 \times 28 + 135 \times 20) = 3720$$

$$A = \frac{1}{2}(\Sigma P - \Sigma Q) = \frac{1}{2}(9210 - 3720) = 2745 \text{ ft}^2$$

(6) **Measurements of velocity and its computations**—Distribution of velocity of water. The velocity distribution in an open channel is illustrated in the Fig. 12·30. The mean velocity is obtained in the centre of the channel just below the surface from where it drops towards the sides as well as towards the bottom.

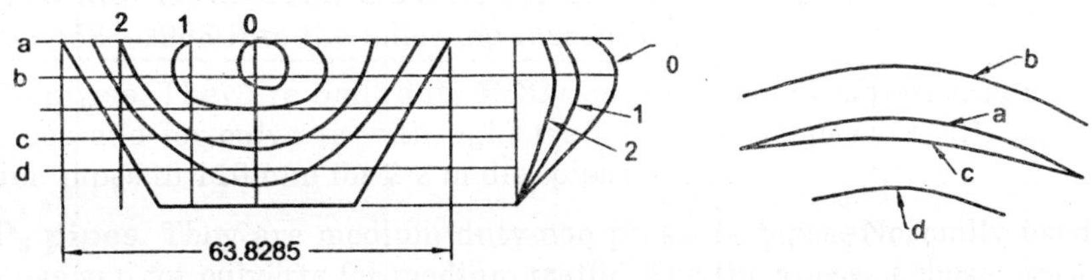

Fig. 12·30.

The main problem in obtaining the channel discharge is to measure the mean velocity. For measurements of mean velocity a straight and smooth reach of the channel far away from any disturbing influence and having a fairly constant cross-sectional area should be selected.

The following methods are adopted for measuring mean velocity :

(*i*) Surface floats or single float (*ii*) Sub surface or double floats

(*iii*) Velocity rods (*iv*) Current metres

(*v*) Pitot tube (refer hydraulics)

In all cases the cross-section of the stream is divided into a number of compartments except for small channels and the mean velocity is measured separately for each compartment. A rope is marked with tags of different colours to show the compartments and their central lines. This rope is stretched across the stream perpendicular to the direction of flow. Add the discharge of all these compartments to get the total discharge of the channel.

(*i*) **Surface Float Method.** The length of run over which the velocity is observed should be selected according to the size of the channel and accuracy required. By taking large runs a better accuracy is obtained, but there are also many contingencies due to wind and obstruction in flow which effects the accuracy in long runs adversely. For float any hollow piece of metal, a piece of wood or cork which is lighter than water and whose centre of gravity lies on the surface is selected, usually cow dungs are used for this purpose. It should not be so light that it may be effected by wind. The marked rope should be stretched a few ft. up the water level and the two other ropes should be stretched perpendicular to the direction of flow at the beginning and end of the run. In cases of large rivers four flags on either bank, 2 u/s of the site of cross section and 2 d/s should be fixed in direction perpendicular to the flow at the ends of the run. The time should be taken by stop watch as (the float is released a bit u/s of the run) float just passes the ropes or the range of the flags. To get better results the time should be recorded as the float crosses the plan of rope and its image in the water.

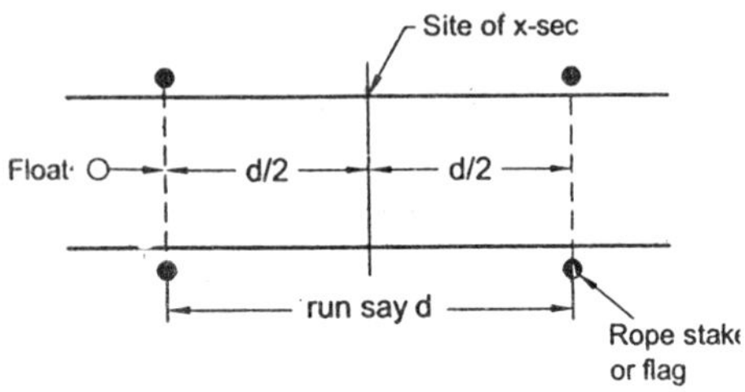

Fig. 12·31.

Let the time taken by the float be t and the run be d so velocity = d/t

A no. of such observations should be taken, the average of which is taken for computations of velocity.

In cases of single floats it is average mid surface velocity. The mean velocity is obtained by multiplying it by a coefficient C, determined experimentally with known discharges. This coefficient is found to be dependent on the hydraulic mean depth R and the Rougocity coefficient N of the channel. The values used in U.P. Irrigation department are shown in the table below :

Table 12·7.

Value of R		*Value of C (Earth channels)*		
m	*ft*	*N = 0·020*	*N = 0·0225*	*N = 0·0250*
·15	·5	·095	·670	·646
·23	·75	·719	·694	·671
·3	1·0	·734	·710	·688
·78	1·25	·744	·721	·699
·48	1·50	·752	·729	·708
·52	1·75	·758	·736	·715
·6	2·0	·764	·742	·721
·75	2·50	·771	·750	·730
·9	3·00	·777	·756	·736
1·05	3·5	·782	·761	·742
1·2	4·0	·786	·766	·746
1·35	4·5	·789	·769	·750
1·5	5·0	·792	·772	·753
1·8	6·0	·796	·777	·758
2·1	7·0	·799	·780	·762
2·4	8·0	·803	·784	·765
2·7	9·0	·805	·786	·768
3·0	10·0	·807	·788	·770

Hydraulic mean depth *R*. The method for finding out the hydraulic mean depth which is area/wetted perimeter will be clear by the following example.

In col. (1) common distances are recorded. Col. (2) shows depth of soundings.

Distance L to R (1)	*Sounding (2)*	*Difference (3)*	*Hypotenuse (4)*
0	0·5	—	—
1	1·9	1·4	1·72
2	2·8	0·9	1·34
3	3·1	0·3	1·04
4	3·2	0·1	1·00
5	3·2	0	1·00
6	3·2	0	1·00
7	3·2	0	1·00
8	3·3	0·1	1·00
9	3·3	0	1·00
10	3·2	0·1	1·00
11	3·1	0·1	1·00
12	3·0	0·1	1·00
13	2·7	0·3	1·04
14	1·3	1·4	1·72
	41·0		15·86

Col. (3) differences of two consecutive soundings, while col. (4) gives hypotenuse of the differences obtained direct from a table given separately. The difference of two consecutive soundings gives the perpendicular height of the proceeding points.

(–) *mean of 1st and last sound*

$$= \frac{0{\cdot}5 + 1{\cdot}3}{2} = 0{\cdot}9$$

$41{\cdot}0 + 0{\cdot}9 = 40{\cdot}1$

$A = 40{\cdot}1 \times 1 = 40{\cdot}1$

$$R = \frac{40{\cdot}1}{17{\cdot}60} = 2{\cdot}27$$

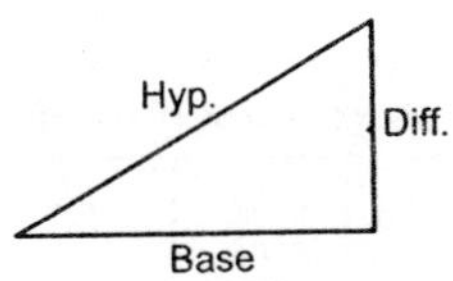

Fig. 12·32.

(+) *1st and last sound*

0·5

1·3

Total W.P. = 17·66

From table $R = 2{\cdot}27$ and $N = {\cdot}0225$ for earth channels, $C = 0{\cdot}746$

The hypotenuse of the base and difference of soundings gives the wetted length. Adding these hypotenuse with the 1st and last soundings will give the W.P. Area = (sum of all the soundings – mean of 1st and last) × common distance. If the last distance is not a common distance and is less of it. Its area should be added separately as already discussed in computing areas.

If the last sounding is at a distance say 0·5 m, the hypotenuse should be calculated at distance 0·5 m, instead of 1 m and rest operation is the same.

Some emperical formulae for finding out mean velocity from surface velocity are given below :

(1) **Bezin's formula.** $V = K\,V_s$; where, K is a coefficient, V_s is surface velocity and V = mean velocity.

In the following table : *a* for earthen channels, *b* for smooth plastered surface, *c* for cut stones, brick work etc, *d* for Rubble masonry. (See after Table 12·8 and 12·9).

Table 12·8. Hypotenuse Tables

Depth	Hypotenuse				
	Base 5	*1·0*	*2·0*	*5·0*	*10·0*
·1	·51	1·00	2·00	5·00	10·00
·2	·54	1·02	2·02	5·00	10·00
·3	·58	1·04	2·02	5·01	10·00
·4	·64	1·08	2·04	5·02	10·01
·5	·71	1·12	2·06	5·02	10·01
·6	·78	1·17	2·09	5·04	10·02
·7	·86	1·22	2·11	5·05	10·02
·8	·94	1·28	2·15	5·06	10·03
·9	1·03	1·34	2·19	5·08	10·04
1·0	1·12	1·41	2·24	5·10	10·05
1·1	1·21	1·49	2·28	5·12	10·06
1·2	1·30	1·56	2·33	5·14	10·07
1·3	1·79	1·64	2·38	5·17	10·08
1·4	1·49	1·72	2·44	5·19	10·10
1·5	1·58	1·80	2·50	5·22	10·11
1·6	1·63	1·89	2·56	5·25	10·13
1·7	1·77	1·97	2·62	5·28	10·14
1·8	1·87	2·06	2·69	5·31	10·17
1·9	1·96	2·15	2·76	5·35	10·18
2·0	2·06	2·24	2·83	5·38	10·20
2·1	2·16	2·33	2·90	5·42	10·20
2·2	2·26	2·42	2·97	5·46	10·24
2·3	2·35	2·51	3·05	5·50	10·26
2·4	2·45	2·60	3·12	5·55	10·28
2·5	2·55	2·69	3·20	5·59	10·31
2·6	2·65	2·79	3·28	5·64	10·33
2·7	2·75	2·88	3·36	5·68	10·36
2·8	2·84	2·97	3·44	5·72	10·38
2·9	2·94	3·01	3·52	5·78	10·41
3·0	3·04	3·16	3·61	5·83	10·44

Table 12·9. Velocities in m/sec over a 100 m run

Time secs.	*Vel.*	*Diff.*	*Time secs.*	*Vel.*	*Diff.*	*Time secs.*	*Vel.*	*Diff.*	*Time secs.*	*Vel.*	*Diff.*
2·0	5·00	·214	4·0	2·50	·06	6·0	1·07	·03	8·0	1·25	·02
2·1	4·76	·22	4·1	2·44	·06	6·1	1·64	·03	8·1	1·23	·01
2·2	4·54	·19	4·2	2·38	·06	6·2	1·61	·03	8·2	1·22	·02
2·3	4·35	·18	4·3	2·33	·06	6·3	1·59	·03	8·3	1·20	·01
2·4	4·17	·17	4·4	2·27	·05	6·4	1·56	·02	8·4	1·19	·01
2·5	4·00	·15	4·5	2·22	·05	6·5	1·54	·03	8·5	1·18	·02
2·6	3·85	·15	4·6	2·17	·05	6·6	1·51	·02	8·6	1·16	·01
2·7	3·70	·13	4·7	2·12	·04	6·7	1·49	·02	8·7	1·15	·01
2·8	3·57	·12	4·8	2·08	·04	6·8	1·47	·02	8·8	1·14	·02
2·9	3·45	·12	4·9	2·04	·04	6·9	1·45	·02	8·9	1·12	·01
3·0	3·33	·11	5·0	2·00	·04	7·0	1·43	·02	9·0	1·11	·01
3·1	3·22	·10	5·1	1·96	·04	7·1	1·41	·02	9·1	1·10	·01
3·2	3·12	·09	5.2	1·92	·04	7·2	1·39	·02	9·2	1·09	·02
3·3	3·03	·09	5·3	1·98	·04	7·3	1·37	·02	9·3	1·07	·01
3·4	2·94	·08	5·4	1·85	·03	7·4	1·35	·02	9·4	1·06	·01
3·5	2·86	·08	5·5	1·82	·03	7·5	1·33	·02	9·5	1·05	·01
3·6	2·78	·08	5·6	1·79	·03	7·6	1·31	·02	9·6	1·04	·01
3·7	2·70	·07	5·7	1·75	·03	7·7	1·30	·02	9·7	1·03	·01
3·8	2·63	·07	5·8	1·72	·03	7·8	1·28	·02	9·8	1·02	·01
3·9	2·56	·08	5·9	1·69	·02	7·9	1·27	·01	9·9	1·01	·01

Table 12·10. Values of K for different surfaces

R	0·5	1·0	2·0	3·0	4·0	5·0	6·0	7·0	8·0	9·0	10·0	15·0	20·0	50·0
a	·58	·65	·71	·72	·75	·76	·77	·78	·78	·78	·78	·79	·80	·81
b	·84	·85	·85	·85	·85	·85	·85	·85	·85	·85	·85	·85	·85	·86
c	·81	·82	·83	·83	·83	·83	·84	·84	·84	·84	·84	·84	·85	·85
d	·74	·77	·79	·80	·81	·81	·81	·81	·81	·82	·82	·82	·82	·83

(2) **Mosin Formula.** $V = 0{\cdot}705\ V_S + {\cdot}003\ V_S^2$, V_S is the surface velocity and V = mean velocity.

(3) The following coefficients for working out mean velocity from surface velocity are given by Trans Am Society of L.E. Vol. 66 as worked out by Grumeky $V = C \times V_S$.

Table 12·11.

Width of stream / Average depth	5	10	15	20	30	40	50	100
C	1·01	0·97	0·94	0·92	0·89	0·87	0·85	0·82

The above coefficients are for sandy beds, for rough sandy beds the coefficients are reduced by 90 to 95%.

(4) The mean velocity on a vertical (not near the sides of a channel) relative to the surface velocity is shown in table below.

Table 12·12.

Depth of a vertical		*Values of Na*			
ft.	*m*	*0·016*	*0·020*	*0·025*	*0·030*
0·5	·15	·87	·84	·82	·78
1·0	·30	·87	·84	·82	·78
5·0	1·5	·90	·90	·89	·85
10·0	3·0	·91	·91	·90	·86
20·0	6·0	·91	·91	·90	·88

Na is the Lacey's coefficient of Rougocity

(5) Bezin also given a formula : $V = V_S - \frac{K}{3}(Di)^{1/2}$

where, V = mean velocity, V_S = surface velocity, K = Coefficient = 36·2 (app.)
D = depth and i = slope of bed.

(2) **Double float or sub surface floats.** Double floats consists of a surface float to which a hollow metal sphere heavier than water is attached by a cord. The velocity is observed by time required by the float to travel the known length of the run. This velocity will be mean velocity of the surface velocity and the velocity at the depth at which the lower float is carried. In this method effect of the wind is minimised, even though due to some effect of wind and resistence of cords etc. following coefficient due to Cunningham is used to obtain the velocity at a mean depth or mean velocity $V = \frac{1}{4}\left(V_S + 3 \times V_{3/5}\right)$.

V_S = Surface velocity and $V_{3/5}$ in the velocity at depth $\frac{3}{5}$ D.

If the velocity is determined at half the depth.

The mean velocity = $V = 0{\cdot}98\ V_{1/2}$ where $V_{1/2}$ is velocity at $\frac{1}{2}$ depth.

In the above two readings the float at surface is a small float to minimise the wind action. Generally the floats are taken of equal size and the mean velocity is taken by adjusting the lower float at a depth of $0{\cdot}8D$.

(3) **Velocity by rods :** (*a*) Wooden (*b*) Telescopic.

(*a*) **Wooden rods.** These are straight wood rods of about 25 mm (1") dia, weight at bottom to float it vertical. It is wholly immersed except for a small portion at the top. They are made of various lengths to suit different depths. It gives the mean velocity along the vertical section of that compartment, hence there is no necessity of multiplying it by a coefficient. However an allowance by a coefficient dealt in next para according to site may be given for the portion by which the rod is kept above the bed of the channel to avoid obstruction.

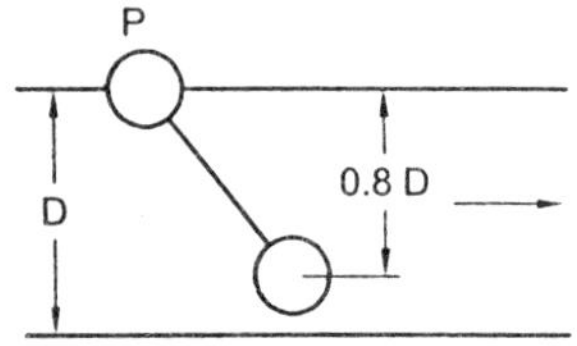

Fig. 12·33.

(*b*) **Telescopic rods.** The telescopic rods used for measuring velocity are in common use. (Telescopic means tube which slides on the other to adjust its length, telescopic name is only due to the fact that such tubes were primarily used in telescopes.

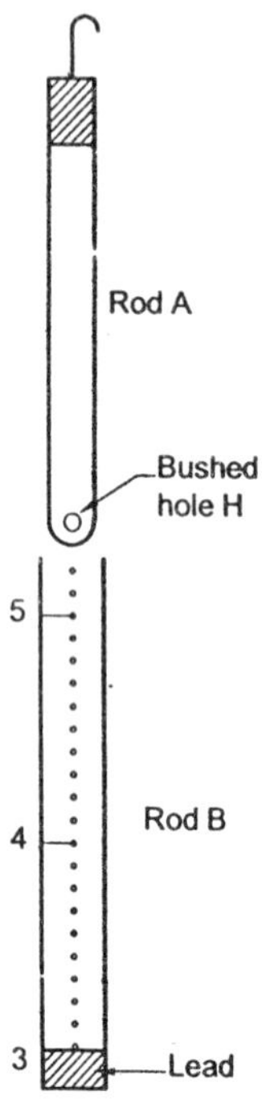

Fig. 12·34.

The telescopic velocity rod consists of a galvanised iron hollow water tight tube *A* of about 1¼" (31 mm) dia which slides in another hollow tube *B*. Tube *A* which is hollow and water light consists at its top a three legged hook for lifting and dropping it in the current by a thin string holded by two persons on either bank of the channel. The top 3" to 1½" (75 mm to 37 mm) portion of the rod is painted black and remains outside the surface of the water when floating. The quantity of water displaced by this rod below the black portion is equal to the weight of the whole assembly of rod *A* and *B* so as to make it floating according to the law of floatation. Rod *B* which slides over rod *A* is loaded with lead at its bottom so as to make the rod float vertical and the quantity of lead also adjusts the weight of the whole assembly equal to the water displaced by it. Holes of about 1/4" (6 mm) dia at interval of 1" (25 mm) are punched in the rod *B* in a vertical line by which the length of the rod is adjusted by fixing with a screw to the bushed hole *H* of rod *A*. The length of rod is measured from the bottom of rod *B* to the black mark of rod *A* which can be read directly by the marks provided by the sides of the holes of rod *B* against bush hole *H*. For different ranges of lengths rods are manufactured by the makers. The sounding chart of the channel is taken at equal intervals and different compartments are formed from this sounding chart. Velocity in the middle of a certain compartment gives the average velocity of that compartment, by which discharge of that compartment is computed. Sum of all these compartments discharge gives the discharge of the whole channel. In order to adjust the length of the rod for a certain compartment, the middle sounding of that compartment is located from the sounding chart and the rod is adjusted for 3" (75 mm) less or 0·6 *D* (depth) of this sounding so that it may flow free at depth 0·94 *D*. No coefficient is practically taken, however the following relation gives the coefficient used for the uncovered depth of rods.

Table 12·13.

l/D	·75	·80	·85	·90	·93	·95	·96	·97	·98	·99
$\frac{V_{mean}}{V_{observed}}$	·954	·961	·968	·975	·981	·986	·989	·992	·996	1·00

A relation deduced by Francis for shorter rods is as below

$$V = V_V\left[1\cdot012 - 0\cdot116\left(\frac{d_1}{d}\right)^{1/2}\right]$$

where V = mean velocity of the vertical section on which the rod moves.

V_V = observed velocity, d = depth of water and

d_1 distance from bottom of rod to bed.

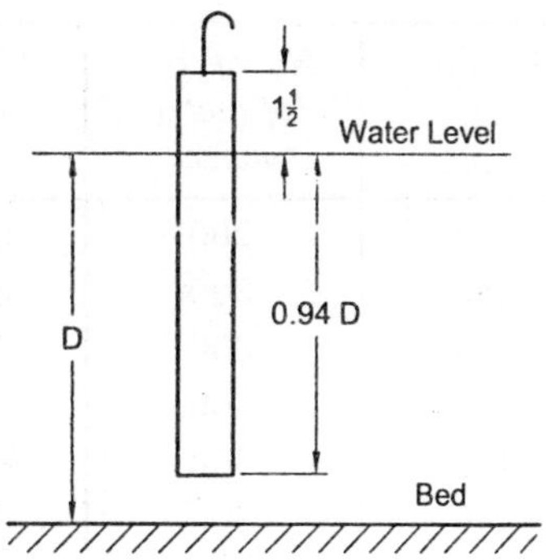

Fig. 12·35.

Lacey's Formula : $V_{mean} = 2V_{0\cdot 8D} + V_{0\cdot 4D}$

where $V_{0\cdot 8D}$ and $V_{0\cdot 4D}$ are the velocities observed with the velocity rods of length equal to $0\cdot 8D$ and $0\cdot 4D$ respectively. D being the average depth of water in the rod course.

(4) **Current meters.** Floats and rods are suitable for only small channels such as canals and drains. But for large rivers current meters are used. Current meters are mechanical devices usually containing a small wheel or propeller blades rotated by the force of flowing water. A tail of fins to keep the instrument aligned in the direction of flow. The speed of rotation depends on the velocity of flowing water. The instrument is provided with an automatic counter which indicates a fixed no. of revolutions by momentarily closing an electric current which cause an electric bell to ring or a bulb is lighted or a head phone to buzz.

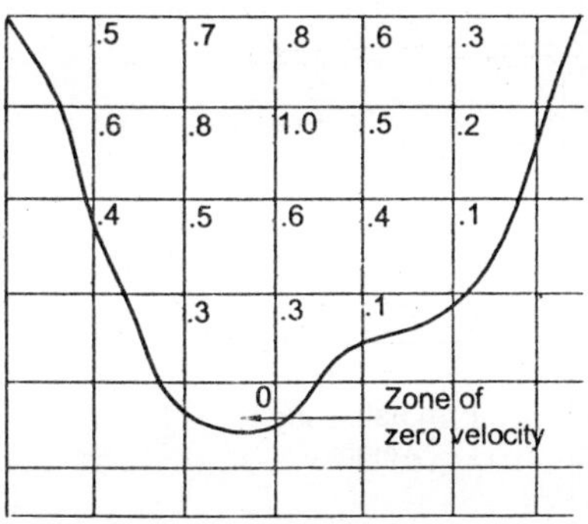

Fig. 12·36.

Precaution. (1) While calculating area of cross section it should be ascertained that there is no zone of still water due to some local pit at the site of x-sec. If there is any such zone it should be deducted from the area of x-sections. It can be located by the zero velocity zones at vertical sections.

(2) The wind should be normal. An account for favourable or unfavourable wind should be made, which can be estimated by taking same discharge in different wind conditions.

(3) The site should be straight and clear of all weed growth, debris or eddies etc.

Calibration of meter. The meter is suspended from a projection fitting out in front of the boat and immersed at least 0·6 m to eliminate any surface effects.

The boat is then towed or sculled over a known distance in still water at a constant speed as possible. The no. of revolutions recorded by the meter and the time taken being also noted. The boat being in rear of the meter so that it may not disturb the water until the meter has passed through it and consequently does not effect the reading.

From this data calculated the relative velocities of the meter and the water and also the number of revolutions per second or the time taken to complete such 50 revolutions, and from a series of such experiments a law may be discovered connecting their quantities. The equation, table or curve so ascertained will be applicable to observations made in a flowing stream from a stationary boat or from a bridge it is the velocity relation to the meter which is measured in each case.

Example. The following example shows some of the results obtained by towing a meter through still water in the manner described above.

Table 12·14.

Distance ft	*No. of rev. of meter wheel*	*Time sec.*	*t = time for 50 rev.*	*n = rev. per sec.*	*v = vel. ft/sec.*	*log v*	*log t*
162	200	57	14·25	3·51	2·84	·453	1·154
240	300	67	11·17	4·48	3·59	·555	1·048
273	350	70	10	5	3·9	·591	1
245	300	60	10	5	4·08	·611	1
181	350	62	8·86	5·75	4·53	·656	·947
240	300	46	7·67	6·53	5·22	·718	·885
240	300	41	6·81	7·32	5·85	·767	·834

The instrument is "mono" if the clicks are recorded after every revolution or "penta" if it is clicked after 5 revolutions of the blades. The velocity of flow of water can be computed from the calibrations chart or as information supplied with the instrument. A fish shaped heavy weight is attached to the bottom to keep the instrument vertical. The meter is suspended from a boat or from some other convenient position such as bridge by means of a chain or rope which is heavily weighted at the lower end to prevent any appreciable deflection as already discussed. Since such deflection renders uncertain, the position of the point at which the velocity is measured. Some times instead of a chain or cord an iron rod is used and this is probably better for swift currents. Since the rod can rest on the bed of the river (rod has a flat bottom such as is provided in sounding rods) and may be more easily held in position after it has been adjusted vertically by the aid if necessary, of a wire or cord attached to its lower extremity. Such rods are generally used in shallow water.

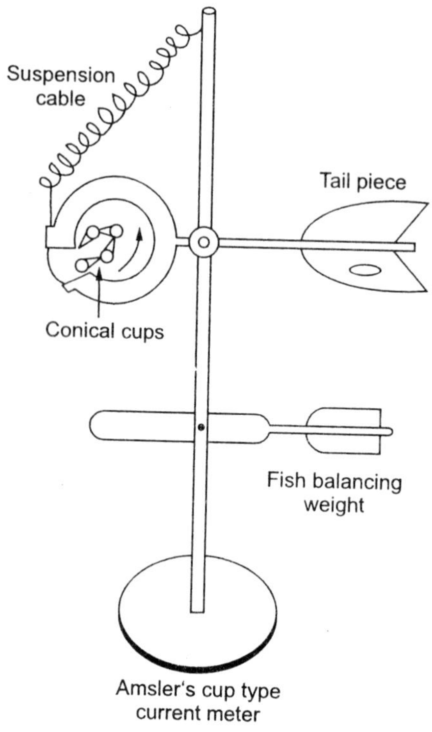

Fig. 12·37. Current meter.

The meter rests upon a coller clamped to the rod at any required height above the bottom, in such a manner that it is perfectly free to rotate in a horizontal plane, and thus by the action of the rudder shown in the figure it adjusts to meet the current.

If suspension by means of a chain or cord there is a certain freedom of motion in a vertical as well as in horizontal plane, but the former motion is prevented if the suspension is by mean of a rod. There are a number of type of instruments. Curve (1) shows the relationship between v and n, as this is a straight line, the equation is of the form

$$v = cn + b \qquad ...(1)$$

where c and b are constants.

Substituting values taken from the diagram such as $v = 3$, $n = 3{\cdot}77$ and $v = 6$, $n = 7{\cdot}54$, we get

$$3 = 3{\cdot}77\,c + b \qquad ...(2)$$

$$6 = 7{\cdot}54\,c + b \qquad ...(3)$$

Multiplying (2) by 2 and substracting from (3) and therefore

from (2) $\quad c = \dfrac{3}{3{\cdot}77} = 0{\cdot}796$

i.e. the equation is $v = 0{\cdot}796\,n$ ...(4)

Curve (2) shows the relationship between v and t and curve (3) that between $\log v$ and $\log t$.

Assuming the euqation to curve (2) is of the form $v = \dfrac{k}{t^P}$ where k and P are constants, the curve (3) which is a straight line has the equation

$$\log v = \log k - P \log t \qquad ...(5)$$

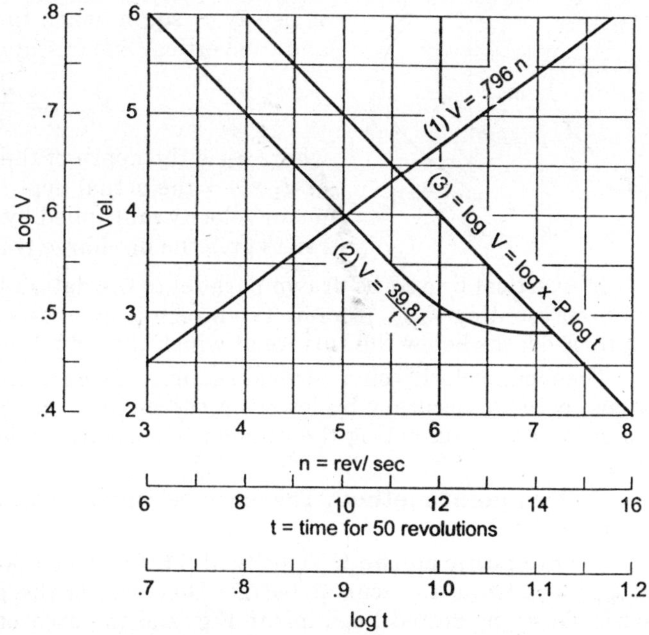

Fig. 12·38.

...(5)

but when $\log t = 0$, $\log v = \log k$ and also $P = \dfrac{\log k - \log v}{\log t} = \tan \theta$, where θ is the slope of the line (3) when the scales are equal.

The two logarithmic scales being equal and θ being 45°. $P = \tan 45 = 1$ and curve (2) is a rectangular hyperbola. As the origin of the coordinates is not shown on the diagram k may be found by the substitution of say $\log v = u$ and $\log t = 1{\cdot}2$ in equation (5). These equations being obtained from curve (3) *i.e.* $4 = \log k - 1{\cdot}2$ or $\log k = 1{\cdot}6$, $k = 39{\cdot}81$.

The equation of the meter over the range of velocity covered by the experiments are therefore

$$v = {\cdot}796\,n \qquad ...(6)$$

$$v = \frac{39{\cdot}81}{t} \qquad ...(7)$$

Determination of mean velocity on a vertical section

(*a*) **Vertical velocity curve distribution or six point method.** A no. of observations generally six $0{\cdot}1D$, $0{\cdot}2D$, $0{\cdot}4D$, $0{\cdot}6D$, $0{\cdot}8D$ and $0{\cdot}9D$ of velocity may be taken from surface to the bottom and the curve of distribution is plotted. The product of area of any particular vertical strip and the average velocity on its centre line gives the discharge through that section and the summation of these partial discharges over the whole width of the river gives the total discharge of the stream.

Much of this work may be done graphically at the same time a considerable amount of information may be obtained regarding the distribution of velocities in the section.

To determine the value of mean velocity on any specified vertical section a curve may be plotted showing the velocities at different depths.

$$V_{mean} = \frac{\text{area of enclosed curve}}{\text{mean depth of section}}$$

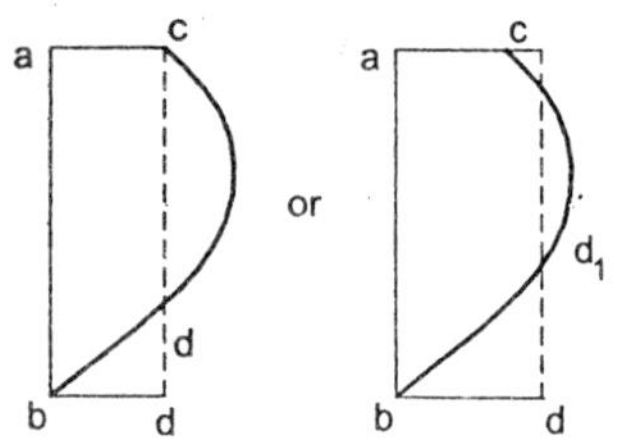

Fig. 12·39.

If the area is determined by a planimeter or otherwise to be say a_1 sq. in. when the velocity scale is V ft/sec to an inch and the vertical linear scale is q ft to an inch. Then

$$V_{mean} = \frac{a_1\, Vq}{d_1\, q} = \frac{a_1 V}{d_1}$$

where d_1 is the depth of the cross-section on the plain in inches or $d_1 \times q$ = the actual depth of the river at that point in ft. This mean velocity multiplied by the area of vertical strip to which it refers give the discharge through the strip.

If a vertical line cd be drawn parallel to the datum line ab of the velocity curve and at a distance representing V_{mean} from it. The intersection of this line with the curve of velocity shows the depth or depths below the surface at which the actual velocity is equal to the mean.

The mean velocity on a vertical section may be as alternative be obtained, though not to the same degree of accuracy by lowering the meter at a constant rate from the surface to the bottom of the river and noting the number of revolutions recorded with the corresponding time interval.

(*b*) **Two point method.** The mean velocity at 0·2D and 0·8D of the total depth from the surface may be taken.

(*c*) **One point method.** Velocity at 0·6D may be taken as the mean velocity. In a certain case V_{mean} was found to occur at 0·67D. The locus of the point for various parts of the cross-section is shown by dotted lines in the Fig. and the area enclosed by this by the area of cross-section.

$$= \frac{10{\cdot}44 \text{ in}^2 \text{ on the plane for } V_{mean}}{15{\cdot}55 \text{ in}^2 \text{ on the plane for section}} = 0{\cdot}67$$

(*d*) **Area velocity integration method.** It is based on the velocity distribution curves of verticals. A velocity distribution diagram for the section (see Fig. 12·40) is prepared showing curves of equal velocity.

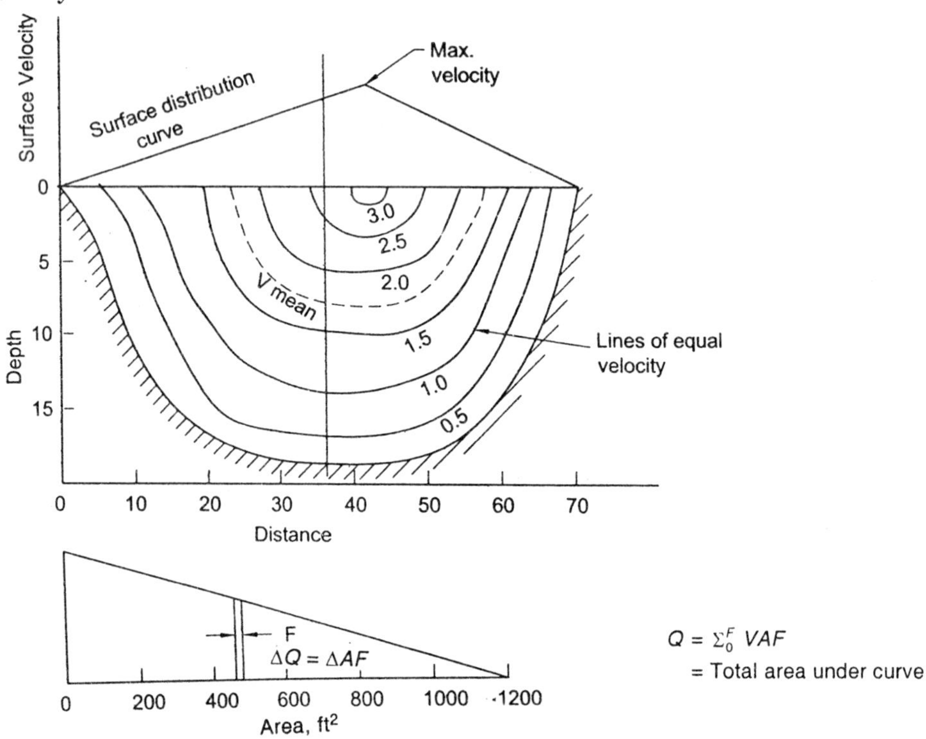

Fig. 12·40.

Starting from the curves of maximum velocity. The area enclosed by the equal velocity curves and the water surface are marked with the ordinates indicating the velocity and the abscissa indicating the covering area. Area enclosed by the velocity area curve represents the discharge of the x-section concerned.

(e) Other method for calculating discharge from the curves is contour interval velocity method. In this method the area between two contours is computed either by a graph or by a planometer and then it should be multiplied by the mean of the volume of these two contours. Adding all these results so obtained will give the discharge through the section. Suppose a_1, a_2, a_3, a_4, a_5 and a_6 are the areas between the velocities ·5, 1·0, 1·5, 2·0, 2·5, 3·0, 2·7 (surface).

$$\text{Then total discharge} = a_1 \times \frac{\cdot 5 + 1\cdot 0}{2} + a_2 \frac{1\cdot 0 + 1\cdot 5}{2} + a_3 \frac{1\cdot 5 + 2\cdot 0}{2} + a_4 \frac{2\cdot 0 + 2\cdot 5}{2} + a_5 \frac{2\cdot 5 + 3\cdot 0}{2} + a_6 \frac{3\cdot 0 + 2\cdot 7}{2}$$

By this method the discharge is calculated for the whole section and not only for a particular section.

(f) **Prismoidal formula.** V_0, V_1, V_2, V_3, V_4, V_5 ... V_b are the velocities at top and subsequent points upto V_b the bed.

Then $$V_m = \frac{1}{18}\{(V_0 + V_b) + 4(V_1 + V_3 + V_5 + \ldots\ldots) + 2(V_2 + V_4 + \ldots \text{ upto } V_b)\}$$

(g) **Method for turbulent flow.** The velocity curve at different depths is extrapolated from the last measured point from the bed.

By calculating $V_x = V_a \left(\frac{x}{a}\right)^{1/n}$ where V_x = velocity in the extrapolated zone at any point at a distance x from the bed.

V_a = velocity in the last measured point at a distance a from the bed. The average of 7 may be used for n in most cases.

The computations may be simplified by integration and the mean velocity $(V_x)_m$ in this zone is given by the following relation.

$$(V_x)_m = \frac{n}{n+1} V_a \text{ } (V_x \text{ being velocity at any point } x \text{ from bed})$$

(h) **Empirical formulae**

(i) $$V = \frac{V_S + 2V_d + V_b}{4}$$

V = mean velocity, V_b = velocity at bed, V_S = surface velocity, V_d = velocity at middle depth.

(ii) Prof. Von Wagner's formula

$$V = 0\cdot 705\ V_S + 0\cdot 003 V_S^2$$

(iii) Morin's formula

$V = V_b + 10\cdot 87\sqrt{RS}$; $V_b = V_S + 10\cdot 87\sqrt{RS}$, R and S are hyd. mean depth and slope respectively.

(iv) The relation between mean, surface and bottom velocities are sometimes given by $V = \cdot 85\ V_S = 1\cdot 34\ V_b$.

(v) The following coefficients are recommended by Buckly for measured depth from surface.

Table 12·15.

Depth	*Coeff.*	*Depth*	*Coeff.*	*Depth*	*Coeff.*	*Remarks*
·1 ·2 ·3	·85 ·89 ·91	·4 ·5 ·6	·95 ·98 1·002	·7 ·8 ·9	1·046 1·102 1·174	Observed velocity at certain depth multiplied by the coefficient gives the mean velocity.
				bed	1·339	

Example 1. *The following observations were made while taking discharge of a branch canal. Calculate its discharge. The run for velocity rods was 100′. The velocity was observed in 5 compartments 0′-15′, 15′-30′, 30′-45′, 45′-60′, 60′-77′.*

Distance	*Soundings*		*Timings*
0	·5	I compartment	30 secs.
5	4·0		31 secs. or $\frac{93}{3} = 31$ secs.
10	7·0		32 secs. $V_m = 3{\cdot}32'$/sec.
15	7·5		93 $V_m = (100/\text{mean time})31$ secs.
20	7·6	II compartment	28 secs.
25	7·6		27 secs. or $= \frac{84}{3} = 28$ secs.
30	7·7		29 secs. $V_m = 3{\cdot}57'$/sec. 84
35	7·7	III compartment	25 secs. or $= \frac{74}{3} = 24{\cdot}7$ secs.
40	7·5		26 secs.
45	7·4		24 secs. $V_m = 4{\cdot}05'$/sec. 74
50	7·4	IV compartment	27 secs. or $= \frac{80}{3} = 26{\cdot}7$ secs.
55	7·5		26 secs. $V_m = 3{\cdot}75'$/sec.
60	7·3		27 secs. 80
65	7·3	V compartment	
70	6·3		35 secs. or $= \frac{105}{3} = 35{\cdot}3$ secs.
75	4·0		36 secs. $V_m = 2{\cdot}83'$/sec. 35 secs.
77	1·0		105

Note : A coefficient for the rod may be applied as given in previous paras.

1st compartment : Soundings 0·5 Discharge = area × velocity

4·0 = 75 × 3·22 = 241·5 cusecs

7·0

7·5

19·0

$$(-)\ \frac{7{\cdot}5 + {\cdot}5}{2} = 15{\cdot}0,\ A = 15{\cdot}0 \times 5 = 75 \text{ sft.}$$

2nd Compartment : Soundings 7·5, 7·6, 7·6, 7·7 — total 30·4

Discharge = area × velocity
= 114 × 3·57 = 407 cusecs

$$(-)\ \frac{7 \cdot 7 + 7 \cdot 5}{2} = 22 \cdot 8,\ A = 22 \cdot 8 \times 5 = 114 \cdot 0$$

3rd Compartment : Soundings 7·7, 7·5, 7·4, 7·4 — total 30·0

Discharge = area × velocity
= 113·0 × 4·05 = 457·7 cusecs

$$(-)\ \frac{7 \cdot 7 + 7 \cdot 4}{2} = 22 \cdot 4,\ A = 22 \cdot 4 \times 5 = 112 \cdot 0$$

4th Compartment : Soundings 7·4, 7·4, 7·5, 7·3 — total 29·6

Discharge = area × velocity
= 111 × 3·75 = 416·3 cusecs

$$(-)\ \frac{7 \cdot 4 + 7 \cdot 3}{2} = 22 \cdot 2,\ A = 22 \cdot 2 \times 5 = 111 \cdot 0$$

5th Compartment : Soundings 7·3, 7·3, 6·3, 4·0 — total 24·9

Here as last sounding is not at regular interval so 1st ignore it and then add its area separately.

Discharge = area × velocity
= 102·5 × 2·83
= 290 cusecs

$$(-)\ \frac{7 \cdot 3 + 4 \cdot 0}{2} = 19 \cdot 5,\ A = 19 \cdot 5 \times 5 = 97 \cdot 5$$

Area of last trapezoid $= \frac{4 \cdot 0 + 1 \cdot 0}{2} \times 2 \cdot 0 = 5 \cdot 0$

Total area of compartment = 97·5 + 5·0 = 102·5

Total discharge of the channel = 241·5 + 407·0 + 457·7 + 416·3 + 290·0 = 1812·5 cusecs

Example 2. *While taking discharge of a minor, the following observations were taken. Velocity taken by a float. Calculate its mean velocity, Run = 30′, wind normal.*

Distance	*Soundings*	*diff.*	*hyp.*	*Timings*
0	0	—	—	
1	·6	0·6	1·17	95 secs.
2	1·5	0·9	1·34	93 secs.
3	1·9	0·4	1·08	94 secs.
4	1·9	—	1·00	28·2 or average 94 secs.
5	1·9	—	1·00	
6	1·9	—	1·00	Velocity = $\frac{30}{94}$ = 0·32′/sec.
7	1·4	0·5	1·12	(from table at R = 1·3, N = 0·0225
8	1·0	0·4	1·08	Coefficient = 0·772
8·5	0·6	0·4	0·64	So V_{mean} = 0·32 × 0·722 = 0·23′/sec.)
		Total	9·43	

$$A = 12\cdot1 - \left(\frac{0 + 1\cdot0}{2}\right) + \frac{1\cdot0 + 0\cdot6}{2} \times 0\cdot5 = 13\cdot0$$

$$\text{W.P.} = 9\cdot43 + \text{1st} + \text{last soundings} = 9\cdot43 + 0 + 0\cdot6 = 10\cdot03$$

$$\text{Hyd. mean depth} = \frac{13\cdot0}{10\cdot03} = 1\cdot3$$

Chemical Method: The chemical method is a direct method for estimation of discharge without observing the mean velocity and x-sectional area. The procedure consists of introducing a solution of a known strength of some chemical usually common salt uniformly over a cross-section at a known rate and determining the average concentration of the chemical by taking out samples at some distance d/s, when the solution may be considered to have mixed properly with the stream. Let q be the rate of introducing solution in volume/unit of time (cft/sec).

w = The concentration of salt solution wt./unit volume (lbs/cft)

Q = The discharge of the stream = volume/unit time (cusecs)

W = The concentration of salt in stream (wt./unit volume (lb/cft))

Since total weight of salt at the two sections must be the same

$qw = QW$ or $Q = q.w/W$

A no. of samples should be taken from all over the section and the average taken out. It should also be seen that the salt is thoroughly mixed at the d/s section. This method is suitable where x-section and velocity can not be taken practically, such as in hills where due to boulders and rapids x-sectioning is not possible. The salt is mixed thoroughly due to rapids in hills.

Measurement of discharge in small rocky and irregular streams as in hills. In hill gaderas (streams) having small discharges and irregular boulder bed with rapids a certain length is channelised with proper section by masonry and then dischare is taken as in other channels.

When the discharge is too small, a bucket of known capacity is filled and the time of filling it is noted by a stop watch, by which the discharge can be calculated.

7. Instructions given by Central Board of Irrigation and Power for observing discharges.

(1) **Selection of site.** The following points should be kept in view while selecting a discharge site.

(*a*) Discharge and gauge sites should be in a straight reach of as large a length as possible. The length of the straight reach should be at least four times the width of the channel but not less than 150 metres in any case. The reach to be chosen should be stable-neither silting nor scouring.

(*b*) The x-section within the reach should be reasonably uniform at all times of the year.

(*c*) The site should be reasonably away from bridges, falls, regulators and offtakes to avoid their effect on water flow.

(*d*) The flow in the reach should be uniform in the cross section of channel.

(*e*) The site should be easily accessible and as far as possible should be near a village.

(*f*) A normal section should be located in the middle of the selected reach. Subsidiary sections for fixing slope, gauges should be at the u/s and d/s ends of the straight reach.

(*g*) As far as possible the site where there are not many trees, obstructing the view should be selected.

(*h*) The whole flow should be divergent as possible from the prevailing wind direction.

(2) **Location of gauges.** The following considerations should be taken for location of gauges. Ordinarily ends discharge site has a gauge site as well.

(*a*) To find out the general slope in a particular reach of the channel, a number of gauges should be fixed in the reach. The minimum length between the extreme gauges should be such that their minimum drop in the water level of 0·2 ft. (·06 m). If other u/s and d/s gauges are available for the same channel section and discharge, these may also be obtained.

(*b*) For recording different water levels at either bank gauges should be fixed on both banks. The mean of the two gauges should be taken as the gauge reading at the site.

(*c*) Gauges should be easily accessible at all times of the day and during all seasons to ensure collection of accurate and reliable data.

(3) **Installation of gauges.** Gauges should be fixed permanently. The following points of installing gauges may be taken as a guide.

(*a*) Gauge wells should be preferably be constructed for the purpose. If not provided some stilling expedients such as tin sheets etc. should be used.

(*b*) Masonry pillers either existing or specially constructed for the purpose can be used.

(*c*) Iron rails, posts or girders may be fixed permanently into the ground on concrete foundations.

(*d*) Wooden poles may be driven firmly into the ground to serve as temporary gauge but these are not liable to be tempered with.

(*e*) The gauges at each site should be sufficiently longer to enable recording of water levels at various discharge stages during different periods. It can either be fixed in one length or in parts.

(*f*) When fixed in parts, the gauges should ordinarily be in lengths of 2 metre each.

(*g*) Sloping gauges are preferable to vertical gauges as greater accuracy is obtained with the former. For installing such gauges the bank should be dressed to one unifrm slope, and provided with a concrete floor.

(*h*) Pneumatic gauges may be used where available. Efforts should be made towards automation.

(*i*) The gauges should be graduated in metres, decimals and centimetres.

(*j*) The gauges should be enamel painted iron gauges.

(*k*) Each gauge should have its zero R.L. fixed below the lowest recorded water level at the site. It should be connected with the G.T.S. benchmarks for determining R.L. of its zero.

(*l*) The B.M. should be fixed near each gauge site for easy check.

(*m*) Maps should be prepared to show discharge sites, position of the gauges, Bench marks, and channel reach and should be kept with gauge register at site and a copy sent to office for record.

(4) **Frequency record gauges.** (*a*) Through the data required for designing channels, mainly full supply records of gauges for various discharges are also desirable to determine gauge discharge relationship. It is well known that this relationship depends largely on the sedimentation carried by the channel and the gauges may be entirely different depending upon whether the river from which the canal draws is rising or falling.

(*b*) Gauges should be recorded twice daily in the morning and evening at fixed hours. In addition to routine gauge recording gauge should be read before and after each field measurements of discharge and silt charge and mean of the two accepted as the gauge for the observation.

Table 12·16. Discharge observations

Segmentation channel capacity	*Approximate surface width*	*No. of verticals for depth & velocity*
(*a*) Above 3000 cusecs (85 cumecs)	About 120′ (35 m)	11
(*b*) Between 500-3000 cusecs (15-85 cumecs)	Between 50′-120′ (15-35 m)	9
(*c*) Between 50-500 cusecs (15-15 cumecs)	Between 15′-50′ (4·5 m-15 m)	5
(*d*) Below 50 cusecs (15 cumecs)	Below 15′ (4·5)	3

Occasionally an engineer incharge may increase the number of verticals to check the adequacy of the number of verticals indicated above.

Velocity observations

(*a*) The mean velocity at any vertical should be measured with a current meter in channels with depth more than 4′ (1·2 m) by taking the average of velocities observed at 0·2*D* and 0·8*D* (*D* being the depth at the vertical in question from the surface).

It is desirable to check this periodically by measuring velocities at close intervals (say 0·10 *D*) to arise at the velocity distribution and derive the mean velocity therefrom.

(*b*) In channels of capacity 500 cusecs (15 cumecs) or below and with water depth less than 4′ (1·2 m) velocity rods are accurate means of observing velocities. The mean velocity at any vertical should be measured with help of Lacey's telescopic velocity rods. By Lacey's method according to which $V_{mean} = 2\ V_0\ 0{\cdot}8D + V_0\ 0{\cdot}4D$ where $V_0\ 0{\cdot}8D$ and $V_0\ 0{\cdot}4D$ are the velocities observed with the velocity rods of lengths equal to 0·8*D* and 0·4*D* respectively (*D* being the average depth of water in the rod coursets). These velocity rods can be got manufactured in Rourkee by various firms.

(*c*) For average small channels discharge can conveniently be measured with a measuring device if available in the reach, such as standing wave, flume, cippoletti weir or *V*-notch.

(*d*) Temperature of channel water just below surface should be measured with 0·50°C thermometer.

(*e*) The meter can be suspended in the following manner :

(*i*) Upto depth 2-3 metre. The metre should be suspended by means of a rigid rod with swivel.

(*ii*) For depth more than 4 m and low velocities *i.e.* 1 m/sec or less, the meter should be suspended with a cable suspension with 8 to 14 kgm fish weight.

(*iii*) When depths are more than 3 m but less than 6 m and velocities do not exceed 2 m/sec and boat can be controlled by wire rope, meter can be suspended by rack and pinion arrangement where rack and pinion arrangement is not available, it should be necessary to permit using cable suspension with heavier weight and allowing for air and wet line correction (Refer "Stream gauging" by M.G. Hiranandani and S.V. Chitale, Govt. of India Publication).

Mechanics of Fluids

Fluid—Definition and Classification

Fluid. Fluid is a substance which is capable of flowing. It can not preserve its shape and size for any length of time unless it is restricted into a particular form depending upon the shape of its surroundings. Thus it would flow in a layer of small thickness over a large area, if the surroundings are removed. A small amount of shear stress as a result of shear force exerted on the fluid will distort it and the change of shape will be continuous as long as the force continues to be applied. Thus in equilibrium a fluid will not be able to sustain shear stress.

Ideal fluid. When the displacement of any particle of fluid no resistance if encountered, it will be known as an ideal fluid. An ideal fluid can not be compressed and is not viscous.

Practical fluid. Conditions pertaining to an ideal fluid are mostly not obtainable in practice and some resistance is always experienced by the fluid when it is displaced. Some shear stress will also exist and some frictional work will be done, such a fluid will be known as a practical fluid.

Classification of fluids. Fluids are classified into liquids and gases including vapour.

Liquids. Fluids which are not able to be compressed, occupy definite volumes and are not affected by the change in temperature. They assume the shape of the vessel containing these.

Gases. Fluids capable of being compressed and expanded are known as gases and they confirm to the shape and volume of the vessel they are contained in. Any change in the temperature of a gas will affect its volume and pressure.

Fluid mechanics. It is a branch of science which deals with the behaviour at rest and in motion of fluids. Theoretically all liquids and gases do not come in the scope of fluid mechanics, but it is confined to the study of all liquids and those gases which are mostly in compressible. Highly compressed gases are governed by thermodynamics.

Hydromechanics. It is a branch of mechanics confined to the study of liquids only. It is sub-divided into the flowing breaks :

(*i*) **Hydrostatics.** It deals with the study of liquids under rest without any motion.

(*ii*) **Hydrodynamics or hydrokinematics.** It deals with the study of ideal and practical liquids in motion, but is concerned with the relations between velocities and acceleration of liquids and the forces causing the same.

Hydraulics. It deals with the application of hydromechanics to engineering problems. It is derived from the Greek word meaning water and pipe.

Fluid properties. These are discussed as below :

(*a*) **Specific weight.** It is generally denoted by (w) and is defined as the weight (force) per unit volume of the fluid. It is also known as weight density. It is a function of temperature and pressure

as $w = W/V$ where W = the weight of the fluid and V = Volume of fluid.

The **specific weight** is w is expressed in gm per cubic cm in (G.C.S. system) or kg per cu.metre (in MKS system).

Specific Density. It is the weight of water in 1000 kg m^3 or 0·001 kg/cm^3 or 1 gm/cm^3 at normal temperature and pressure of 4°C and 760 mm mercury respectively at mean sea level.

(*b*) **Mass density or Density.** (also known as specific mass) of fluid is defined as its mass per unit volume. It is generally denoted by (ρ).

$$\text{Weight} = \text{Mass} \times \text{acceleration due to gravity}$$

$$\therefore \quad \text{Mass density} = \frac{\text{weight density}}{g} \text{ or } \rho = \frac{w}{g} = \frac{\text{kg.sec}^2}{\text{m}^4}$$

$$\text{The mass density of water} = \frac{w}{g} = \frac{1{,}000}{9{\cdot}81} = \frac{102 \text{ kg sec}^2}{\text{m}^4}$$

The density of fluids varies with the change of temperature as well as with the change of pressure. The table below give the value of specific mass (ρ) or mass density against temperature.

Table 12·17.

T in °C	0	10	20	40	60	80	100
w in kg/m³	1,000	1,000	998	992	983	972	958
$\rho = \frac{kg\ sec^2}{m^4}$	101·9	101·9	101·7	101·1	100·2	99·1	97·8

(*c*) **Specific gravity** (Sp. gr.) of a fluid is the ratio of its density to that of a standard substance at a standard temperature. For liquid pure water is taken as a standard substance at 4°C. Specific gravity of water is 1 and that of mercury is 13·5 to 13·6.

$$\text{Specific gravity of liquids} = \frac{\text{Specific weight of liquid}}{\text{Specific weight of water}}$$

(*d*) **Viscosity.** Viscosity is derived from the word "viscous" which means sticky, adhesive, tenacious. Therefore it is a properly by virtue of which it offers resistance to shear.

Consider a fluid consist of a number of parallel layers as shown in Fig. 12·41. The upper layer will have a tendency to slide over the lower one, but depending upon the type of fluid (its adhesive capacity), the two layers will show a resistance and shear. Thus the rate of flow of tar or thick syrup would be slower than that of water as the adhesive property of tar or thick syrup will offer more resistance to sliding or shear.

Fig. 12·41.

Newton's law of viscosity states that for a given rate of angular deformation of fluid the shear stress is directly proportional to the viscosity.

The shear stress to a moving fluid is proportional to the velocity gradient in a direction normal to the area under consideration in the same way as a stress is proportional to the strain in a solid or stress. It can be said that V is a function of μ, the distance measured normal to the solid wall.

or $$f_s \;\alpha\; \frac{d_v}{d_y} \quad \text{or} \quad f_s = \mu \frac{d_v}{d_y}$$

where μ is the coefficient of viscosity, absolute viscosity, dynamic viscosity or simply viscosity.

Units of μ can be easily found

$$\mu = \frac{f_s}{f_y} = \frac{\text{kg m}^{-2}}{\text{m sec}^{-1}\ \text{m}^{-1}} = \text{kg}\ \frac{\text{sec}}{\text{m}^2}$$

in c.g.s. units, the unit of viscosity is poise or

$$1 \text{ poise} = 1\ \frac{\text{dyne.sec}}{\text{cm}^2}\ ; \quad 1 \text{ kg(force)} = 981 \times 10^3 \text{ dyne}$$

$$\therefore \quad 1 \text{ poise} = \frac{1}{98{\cdot}1}\ \frac{\text{kg.sec}}{\text{m}^2} \quad \text{and } 1 \text{ m}^2 = 10^4 \text{ cm}^2$$

Helmholze suggested the value of μ for water as below

$$\mu = \frac{0{\cdot}01776}{1 + 0{\cdot}03368\,T + 0{\cdot}000221T^2} \text{ poise.}$$

where T is the temperature in degree C.

Viscosity of a liquid decreases with the rise of temperature on the other hand viscosity of a gas increases with rise of temperature. The changes of pressure has a little effect on the absolute viscosity.

(*e*) **Kinematic viscosity.** It is the ratio of absolute viscosity to mass density.

or $$V = \frac{\mu}{\rho} = \frac{\mu}{w/g} = \frac{\text{kg sec}}{\text{m}^2} \cdot \frac{\text{m}^4}{\text{kg sec}^2} = \frac{\text{m}^2}{\text{sec}}$$

In c.g.s. units, the unit of kinematic viscosity is stoke

and $$1 \text{ stoke} = 1 \text{ cm}^2/\text{sec}.$$

Table 12·18. Values of kinematic viscosity V for water

Temp.	°C	*0*	*5*	*10*	*20*	*30*	*40*	*60*	*80*	*100*
μ	10^6 kg sec m^{-2}	183·2	154·7	133·2	102·3	81·8	66·5	47·9	36·3	28·8
	poise	0·0178	0·01518	0·0131	0·01009	0·00804	0·00654	0·00478	0·00366	0·00295
V	10^6 m^2.sec^{-1}	1·78	1·518	1·310	1·009	0·804	0·654	0·478	0·366	0·295
μ	Stoke	0·0178	0·01518	0·01310	1·01009	0·00804	0·00654	0·00478	0·00366	0·00245

Determination of viscosity and kinematic viscosity. It can be determined by the following methods.

(*a*) **Capillary tube.** Poiseville showed that the volume V of a liquid or gas flowing per sec. through a horizontal capillary tube (Fig. 12·41) of given radius r and length l under a constant difference in pressure ΔP between two end is inversely proportioned to the viscosity of the liquid. The volume of the fluid through the tube in t secs given by

$$V = \frac{\pi r^4 . \Delta P . t}{8 \rho \mu} \quad \text{or} \quad Q = \frac{V}{t} = \frac{\pi d^4}{128} . \frac{\Delta P}{l} . \frac{1}{\mu}$$

The lesser is the volume of fluid flowing through the tube per unit time, the larger the viscosity.

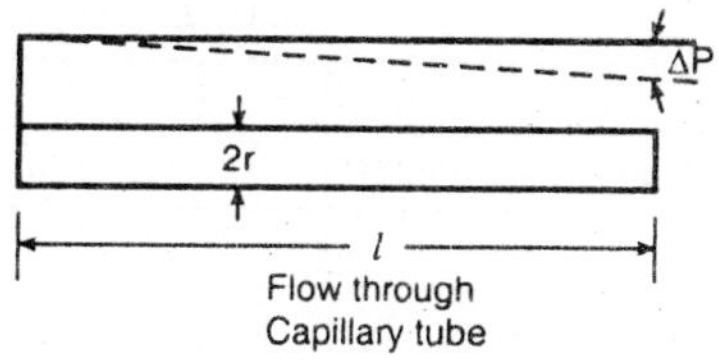

Fig. 12·42.

(*b*) **By viscometer.** It is an instrument to measure viscosity. It measures some quantity which is a function of viscosity. The quantity measured is usually the time taken to pass in certain volume of liquid through an orifice filled in the bottom of viscometer. The temperature of liquid while it is being passed through the orifice should be maintained constant.

A say bolt universal viscometer consists of a vertical tube 12·35 ± 0·1 mm long and 1·765 ± 0·015 mm dia. The time in seconds to pass 60 cc of any liquid for the determination of viscosity in "second say bolt". The following empirical relations are used to determine kinematic viscosity in stokes

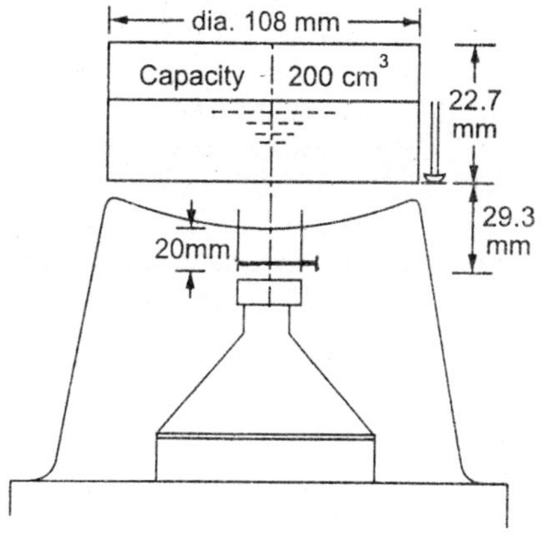

Fig. 12·43.

(*a*) Say bolt universal viscometer, $\upsilon = 0{\cdot}0022\,t - \dfrac{1{\cdot}8}{t}$

(*b*) Red wood viscometer $\quad \upsilon = 0{\cdot}0026\,t - \dfrac{1{\cdot}175}{t}$

(*c*) Engle viscometer $\quad \upsilon = 0{\cdot}00147\,t - \dfrac{3{\cdot}74}{t}$

where t = time in seconds required for various viscometers.

Compressibility. The compressibility of various substances including fluids are inversely proportioning to their volume modulus of elasticity. The variation of volume of fluids by means of resistance is known as compressibility. It decreases with the increase in temperature of fluid as the volume module increases with the increase of temperature, water looses 0·007 of its original volume for each tonne of pressure applied over a unit area. Mercury losses 1/6th of that of water.

Water is generally assumed as in compressible for most of the hydraulic problems. But in case of water flowing through pipes its compressibility can not be ignored.

Expressing compressibility of fluid by its bulk modulus of elasticity, consider a force when applied on any fluid, its volume V decreases by an amount dV. This decrease is proportioned to the force per unit area (*i.e.* p) of the fluid

or $$p \propto \frac{dV}{V} \text{ or } p = -K\frac{dV}{V} \text{ or } K = -\frac{p}{dV/V}$$

where K is a constant and is called as coefficient of compressibility of the fluid or as bulk modulus of elasticity, which remains nearly the same for all temperatures for liquids. For water K = 20,000 kg/cm^2 at ordinary temperature and pressure.

Vapour pressure. Liquids which are open to atmosphere have a tendency to evaporate because of the molecules escaping from its surface. When the liquid is confined in an enclosed vessel, it evaporates into the space between the surface of liquid and that of the vessel and thus exerts partial pressure known as vapour pressure.

If the pressure above the liquid surface is lowered by some means, the evaporation starts again, until the pressure of vapour is such that no further evaporation can occur. Thus when the pressure above the liquid surface is equal to the vapour pressure of the liquid the "boiling" starts. Therefore water may boil even at room temperature if the pressure above the water is reduced considerably. At high altitudes water boils at a temperature lower than 100°C. Vapour pressure increases with the rise of temperature.

Table 12·19. Vapour pressure versus temperature

Temp. °C	*0*	*5*	*10*	*15*	*20*	*40*	*60*	*80*	*100*
Vapour pressure kg/cm^2	0·00623	0·00889	0·0125	0·01737	0·238	0·775	2·033	4·75	10·35
m of water	0·0623	0·0889	0·125	0·1737	0·238	0·775	2·033	4·75	10·35

Cohesion. It is a property of fluid by which molecules of the same kind of fluid are attracted. This property enable the liquid to resist tensile stress.

Adhesion. It is property of fluid by which molecules of different kinds of liquid are attracted to each other or molecules of a liquid are attracted to another body. This enables the two different kinds of liquids to adhere to each other.

Note : When water is flowing through hydraulic machines such as turbines or pumps etc. and if it reaches to low pressure region, where the evaporation commences, the bubbles are formed. These bubbles travel along the flow till they may reach a high pressure region where they will suddenly collapse giving rise to high pressure. The pressure is so high that if the bubbles collapse on metallic surface of machine, the cavities are formed on them. This phenomenon is known as **cavitation**.

Pressure gauge connection in pipes. The following points are observed :

(*a*) Drilling should be perpendicular to the pipe wall.

(*b*) Dia. of hole *d* should be between 3 to 5 mm. Smaller holes are liable to be choked while larger holes may cause error in measurement by change in pressure at pressure point. Dia. should be 15 to 20 mm.

(*c*) For connecting the gauge piping outside, 10 mm bore pipe with gas threads will suffice.

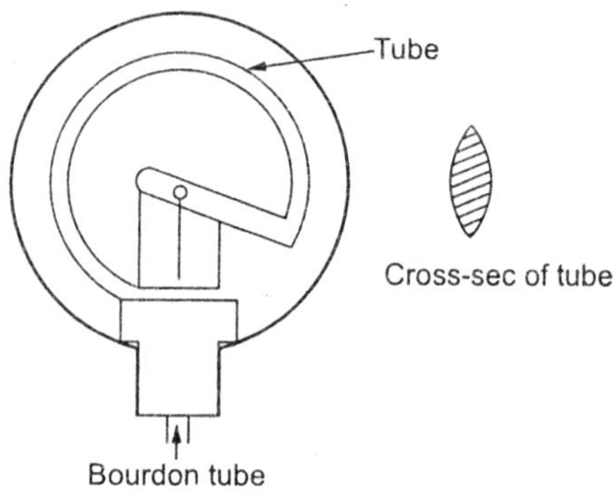

Fig. 12·44. Pressure gauge.

(*d*) Connecting pipes should be full of liquid. No air pockets should present.

Diaphragm pressure gauge (pressure gauge without liquid). A corrugated diaphragm is used. Elastic deformation of the diaphragm under pressure is transmitted by a similar arrangement to a point needle. This type of gauge is used to measure relatively low pressures. The instrument must be calibrated before use. The Aneroid barometer operates as a similar principle.

13

Irrigation Engineering

13·1. Irrigation terms

(1) **Irrigible area.** Area which can be irrigated in the command of the land, if the supply is unlimited and marked on the sajra sheet with water sheds. It is also known as **Gross Commanded Area** (G.C.A.).

(2) **Culturable commanded area (CCA).** From the area which can be irrigated, the culturable area is sorted out, which is known as the Culturable Commanded area.

(3) **Intensity of irrigation.** As the water available in the canal (or river) is limited, a percentage of the culturable commanded area is taken to be proposed for irrigation (proposed area) according to the supplies available. This is known as the intensity of irrigation. Intensity of irrigation is also proposed to avoid adverse effects on canal introducing, such as water logging etc.

(4) **Assessment of water requirements.** Once the intensity has been fixed out, the area to be irrigated is calculated, water requirements are calculated as below.

(5) **Duty of canal water.** It is number of hectares irrigated by a discharge averaging one cumec at head for a specified period known as **Base period.** It includes all the losses in the channel below the head. Hence the duty at the head of a canal is less than the head of a distributary and at the head of a distributary is less than the head of a minor due to increased losses.

(6) **Outlet factor.** Duty calculated neglecting all losses is known as outlet factor or outlet discharge factor.

(7) **Depth of water.** It is the depth of water which will require to mature a crop if whole of the water supplied is considered to remain standing without any loss due to percolation or evaporation. For design purposes this depth of water is considered for the peak period of demand. It is denoted by Δ.

8. Base period. It is the period in which the demand of water remains at peak and the channels are designed on the requirement of this period, which obviously will fulfil the requirement, when the demand is not keen. A channel designed for requirement of Rabi is known as **Rabi channel** and the period of keen demand is known as **Kor period.** In Rabi or winter period, the supply in the river is also limited. A channel designed for fulfilling the requirements of Kharif is known as a **Kharif channel.** A study of the table of area statistics will make the things clear itself.

9. Relation between water depth (Δ), duty (d) and Base Period (B). Δ is in metres, duty in hectares and base period in no. of days.

$$\Delta = \frac{8{\cdot}64\, B}{d} \qquad \ldots(1)$$

one cumec day = 8·64 hectare meter. One cumec day means, one cumec running for a day of 24 hours = 86,400 m^3.

Hectare meter means one metre depth of water in a hectare = 10,000 m^3.

Discharge Q = Area to be irrigated/duty.

In F.P.S. : $\Delta = \frac{2B}{d}$; 1 Acre ft. = 43560 cu. ft. and 1 cusec day = 1.98 say 2 Acre ft.

10. Overlap allowance. When period of one phase overlaps the other to start with, an allowance for this extra water requirement is made in the design.

11. Paleo. It is the 1st watering before sowing the crop.

12. Kore watering. 1st watering for a crop, the depth of water for this period is known as **Kor depth** and the period of this watering is known as **Kor period.** It is period of keen demand of water as every field in this period is demanding water. The channels are designed for the water depth of this period. This period is also taken as **base period** for design.

13. The source of water for irrigation may be (*a*) hygroscopic in the form of dew or mist etc. (*b*) capillary water of the soil and (*c*) gravitational or surface water.

13·2. Canal Irrigation

Main crops of India

Kharif—1 April to 30th Sept.

Rabi—10 Oct. to 31 March

Zaid—1 April to 30 Jun. (Moong, Urd or Melons etc.)

Table 13·1. Information for different crops.

Crop	*Sowing time*	*Harvesting time*	*Seed requirement per Hectare (kg)*	*Average yield per hectare (tonnes)*	*Total water depth Δ (cm)*	*Remarks regarding irrigation requirements*
Kharif						
1. Maize (Macca)	Jun.	Sep.-Oct.	13·50	1·1 to1·3	45	Usually nil except paleo
2. Early paddy (Dhan)	July	Oct.	90	0·9 to 1.1	90	When rain has a long gap
3. Transplanted paddy (Jarhan)	July	Oct.	90	1·3 to 1·6	125	When rain has a long gap and in Oct.
4. New varieties of paddy	July	Oct.	90	3·0 to 4·0	125	Continuous submergence
5. Spiked millet (Bajra)	July-Aug.	Oct	1·5 to 2·0	0·6 to 0·7	30	Seldom irrigated
6. Great Millets (Juar)	July	Oct.	5·0	0·7	30	After cutting of Rabi, usually used as fodder
7. Arhar	July-Aug.	April	15·0	0·7	30	Not irrigated
8. Urd-Moong	Aug.	Dec.	15·0	0·55	30	Not irrigated
9. Ground nut (Moong phali)	May	Nov.-Dec.	25 to 30	1·80	45	Paleo is required
10. Cotton (Kapas)	May-June	Dec.	10 to 15	0·35 to 0·45	45	Paleo is required
11. Til	July-Aug.	Dec.	10 to 15	0·35	-	Seldom irrigated
12. Sugarcane	Feb.	Dec.-Mar.	2750	25 to 30	90	Regular irrigation
Rabi						
1. Wheat (Desi)	Oct.	Mar.-Ap.	90 to 130	1·5 to 2·0	40	
2. Wheat (New variety)	Nov.-Dec.	April	90 to 130	4 to 6	80	Generally four watering

Table contd...

Table contd...

3. Barley (Jau)	Oct.	Mar.-Ap	90-130	1·35	45	One watering
4. Gram (Chana)	Sep.	Mar.	40-50	1·10	30	Seldom irrigated
5. Peas (Matar)	Oct.-Nov.	Mar.	40-50	1·20	55	2 watering
6. Potato (Aloo)	Oct.	Feb.	185	13-35	60-90	Irrigated every week
7. Mustard (Sarsaun)	Oct.	Feb.-Mar.	10-15	0·70	45	
8. Tobacco (Tambakoo)	Oct.-Feb.	Feb.-Mar.	50	1·0	60	To be irrigated frequently

Duty of certain crops in India (approximate and average in hectares/Cu. m. of water)

Sugar cane	730	Rice	775
Other Kharif	1500	Rabi	1800
Perennials	1100	Hot fodder	7500

13·3. Losses in canals. The losses are due to seepage and evaporation and are due to the following reasons :

1. Permeability of the strata.

2. Sub soil water level.

3. Age of canal. In old canals losses are less due to deposite of silt layer than in new.

4. Type of sections. The more is the wetted perimeter, the more are the losses.

5. Silt charge and silt grade. The purer is the water more are the losses.

6. In larger velocities, losses are more.

Losses due to Seepage and evaporation in North India

(*a*) Main canal and branches upto head of distribution system 15-20 percent.

(*b*) In distribution channels upto head of distribution system 6-7 percent.

(*c*) Water courses upto head of distribution system 17-21 percent.

(*d*) In fields upto head of distribution system 8·25 percent.

U.P. standard. Losses to seepage and evaporation per km length of channel = $\frac{1}{200}(B + D)^{2/3}$ where B = bed wealth and D = water depth in metres.

In general losses in ordinary clayey loam = 0·8 cumecs per million sq.m. of wetted perimeter.

In sandy loam = 9·6 cumecs per million sq.m. of W.P. (wetted perimeter)

In Tamil Nadu the loss allowance/million sq.m. of wetted perimeter or surface is as follows :

1. Rocks = 0·90 cumecs
2. Black cotton soil = 1·51 cumecs
3. Alluvial soil = 2·42 cumecs and
4. Decayed rock or gravel = 3·0 cumecs.

Transpiration losses in channels unaffected by fluctuation in water table (according to Khuslani in cumecs per million sq. m. of wetted perimeter.)

Table 13·2. Transpiration losses.

Type of soil	New channels	Old channels
1. Impervious clay loam	1·2	0·9
2. Medium clay loam with a layer of hard pan at 60 to 90 cm depth	1·51	1·20
3. Medium clay loam		2·10 1·51
4. Ordinary clay loam		2·5 1·80

Table contd...

Table contd...

Type of soil	*New channels*	*Old channels*
5. Silty clay loam	2·85	2·42
6. Silt loam	3·16	3·70
7. Loam	3·30	3·00
8. Sandy clay loam, gravelly clay loam	3·46	3·16
9. Sandy loam	5·12	3·62
10. Loose sand	5·73	5·12
11. Gritty soil	6·93	5·73
12. Gravelly sand	8·74	6·93
13. Gravelly soil porous	10·6	8·74
14. Gravel	21·1	10·6

13·4. Suitability of canal water for irrigation

1. It must be free from alkalies. The land which contains alkalies as "reh" is not fit for canal alignment.

2. Salts of calcium and magnesium are not harmful upto 0·03%. Sodium salts are injurious even 0·003% can be tolerated with calcium salts which retards the harmful effect of sodium.

3. The presence of Pot. nitrate is good for agricultural use.

4. Water containing Sodium carbonate or Sodium bicarbonate hardens the soil and there is likely hood of water logging.

5. Some factory waste water produces weed growth in the channels hence should be avoided. Running the channels with less discharge is also a cause of weed growth.

Table 13·3. Standards of irrigation water

Class of water	*Sod. Carbonate in percentage*	*Total Salt content*	*Boron ppm (Parts per million)*
I	60	0·700	00-0·5
II	60·75	700-2000	0·5-2·0
III	75	over 2000	over 2·0

Class I is suitable for plants and class III is harmful while class II is considered to be partly good.

Antiwater logging measures

1. By providing seepage drains in area

2. By boring tube wells in the area by which the water table is lowered and the water pumped can be used for other suitable use.

3. By lining of the canals and channels.

13·5. Silt in canals

1. Distribution of silt at different depth of a channel. It is about 60 to 70 percent by weight at surface and above 130% near the bed. At a depth of about 0·6 D (D is the depth of water from surface) where the velocity is mean, the silt carried by the water is a fare average.

2. At bends the silt deposits are greater at inside and is less at outer curve and hence the depth of water is less inside and more outside. The location of heads is avoided at bends due to either excess or less silt charge.

3. A certain amount of silt grade and charge is necessary in canal water as it helps in forming a water tight layer on the channel section, which reduces seepage losses, forms berms and acts as a fertilizer for the crops. Hence the channels are so designed that they may have the required silt grade and charge with them. Silt grade is size and charge is quality.

4. Weight of silt is about 1280 to 1300 kg/m^3 and the voids ranging from 45 to 55 percent.

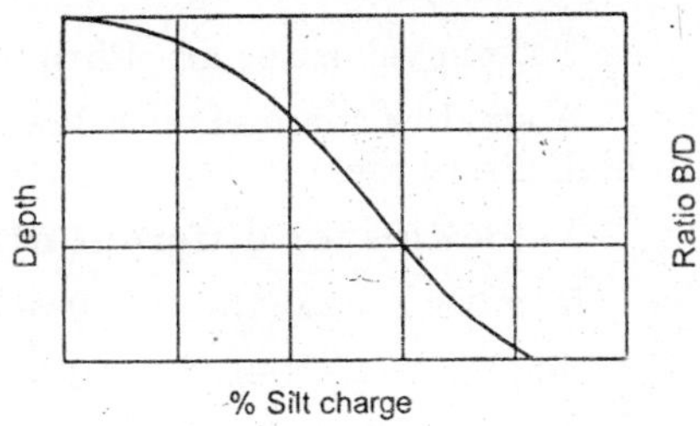

Fig. 13·1.

13·6. Velocity in channels

Critical velocity. It is the velocity which is neither silting nor scouring. Its ratio with the actual velocity is known as critical velocity ratio = V/V_0 (C.V.R.) where V = actual velocity and V_0 = critical velocity. Finer silts having less critical velocity (less than 1·0) and coarser sand has critical velocity more than 1·0.

The usual velocity in different channels (Earthen)

Main canals	1·1	m/sec.
Branch canals	0·9	m/sec.
Big Distributaries.	0·75	m/sec.
Small Distributaries	0·60	m/sec.
Minors	0·45	m/sec.
Water courses	0·30	m/sec.

1. Canals are generally not made deeper than 2·7 m as on this depth the velocity increases than 1·1 m/sec.

Mean non scouring velocities in different soils

Soft earth or very fine clay	8-9	cm/sec
Soft or fine clay	15-30	cm/sec
Very fine pure sand	23-30	cm/sec
Very light loose sand or silt	30-45	cm/sec
Course sand or light sandy soil	45-60	cm/sec
Average sandy soil and good loam	60-75	cm/sec
Sandy loam	75-85	cm/sec
Light ordinary earth or Sandy bed	75-90	cm/sec
Average loam or alluvial soil	85-90	cm/sec
Firm loam, clay loam	90-115	cm/sec
Firm gravel or clay	110	cm/sec
Stiff soil, clay, ord. gravel soil or clay and gravel	115-120	cm/sec
Broken stone and clay	150	cm/sec
Grass	90-150	cm/sec
Coase gravel, cobbles, shingle, shale	150-180	cm/sec
Conglomerates, cemented gravel, soft slate, tough hard Pan, soft sedimentary rock	180-245	cm/sec
Soft rock	135-245	cm/sec
Hard rock	305-460	cm/sec
Very hard rock or concrete	480-760	cm/sec
Boulder lining	150	cm/sec
Burnt clay tile lining	180	cm/sec

Cement conc. lining 200 cm/sec

Bottom velocities are 4/5th to 3/4th of the above.

A smaller channel with low discharges can take higher velocities than a large channel with high discharge.

Velocities for different dia. stones to move in a river

V. m/sec.	0·15	0·3	0·6	0·91	1·22	1·52	2·13
dia. mm.	0·9	3·6	16	32	57	89	1.78

Chailly's Formula-$V = 5{\cdot}67\sqrt{Gd}$; $d = \dfrac{V^2}{85}$

where d = dia. of stone in foot and G = specific gravity of stone (2·65).

Regime channel. A channel which is neither silting nor scouring or a channel having critical velocity.

13·7. Design of Channels on Kennedy's Silt Theory for Alluvial Soils

The equations to be used are

1. Q = A.V. where Q = Discharge, V = actual velocity, A = area of channel section.
2. V = $\text{KmD}^{0.64}$ (Kennedy's equation)

where m = critical velocity ratio (C.V.R.), D = depth of water and
K = a coefficient depending on the type of soil

3. $V = C\sqrt{RS}$, where C is Chezy's coefficient, R = hyd. mean depth and S = slope in fraction.

Values of *m* (C.V.R.)

Type of soil	*Value of m*
1. Silt of *R* Indus in Pakistan	0·70
2. Coarse silt or debris of hard soil	1·30
3. Sandy loam silt	1·20
4. Coarser light sandy silt	1·10
5. Light sandy silt as in rivers of N. India	1·00

Generally higher values of m are assumed in head reaches and lower values towards tail.

Values of Kennedy's coefficient K

Very fine silt (Sarda Canal)	0·41
Light Sandy Silt	0·53
Fine Sand Silt (Punjab Canals)	0·55
Coarser light sandy silt	0·57
Fine sand silt (Burma rivers)	0·59
Sandy loam (Madras Rivers)	0·65
Coarse silt and coarse sand	0·70
Sand and small Bajree	0·70 to 0·97
Bajree and gravel	1·62 to 1·95
Gravel and Boulder	1·95 to 2·27
For Godavary Basin	$V_0 = 0{\cdot}39\ D^{0{\cdot}55}$
For Krishna Basin	$V_0 = 0{\cdot}53\ D^{0{\cdot}59}$

Velocity V is the mean velocity of a channel known as actual velocity

In Chezy's formula $C = \frac{S^{1/16}}{N}$ in metric units.

In Kutter's formula $C = \dfrac{23 + \frac{1}{N} + \frac{0.00155}{S}}{1 + \left(23 + \frac{0.00155}{S}\right)\frac{N}{\sqrt{R}}}$ Metric units $\qquad C = \dfrac{41.66 + \frac{1.811}{N} + \frac{0.00281}{S}}{1 + \left(41.66 + \frac{0.0028}{S}\right)\frac{N}{\sqrt{R}}}$ F.P.S. units

where N = Rugocity constant

Value of N for North India	*Channels*
1. Poor lined sections	0·015
2. Good lined sections	0·02
3. Very good earthen sections	0·0225
4. Good earthern sections	0·025
5. In different earthen sections	0·0275
6. Poor earthen sections	0·030
7. Cement surface	0·01
8. Masonry new	0·015

Pipes	
Glazed and steel pipes	0·01
C.I. rough sewers	0·015
Existing sewers in bad condition	0·01

Table 13·4. Values of C in formula $V = C\sqrt{RS}$ (where S is slope in fraction)

R in Ft.	*Values of C*		
	N = ·020	*N = ·0225*	*N = ·0250*
0·5	58	53	47
0·75	65	58	52
1·0	70	62	56
1·25	74	66	59
1.50	77	·69	62
1·75	80	71	64
2·0	82	73	66
2·50	86	76	69
3·0	89	79	71
3·5	92	81	73
4·0	94	83	75
4·5	95	85	78
5·0	'97	86	78
6·0	100	89	80
7·0	102	91	82
8·0	104	92	83
9·0	105	93	84
10·0	107	95	85

Known details for design of a channel

1. Slope of bed—From L-section say 1′ per mile = 1/5280.
2. Rugocity coefficient N-from above tables.
3. Discharge Q-Designed separately from area statistics.
4. Side slopes—According to channel sections say 1/2 : 1

Proceed as below

1. Assume a trial value of D, the depth of water (say 2m)
2. Work out actual velocity V from the formula $V = \text{Km } D^{0.64} = K\frac{V}{V_0}D^{0.64}$ or $V_0 = KD^{0.64}$

since $m = 1$ (for regime) $V_0 = KD^{\cdot 64}$ | Regime channel is neither silting nor scouring

3. Calculate A by the formula $A = Q/V$

The values of K is taken from the tables which is 0·55 for N. India.

4. Assume a bed width as B, then the area $A = BD + D^2/2$ (side slopes 1/2 : 1) knowing A and D, B can be calculated.

5. Calculate Chezy's C from Kutter's equation or from tables assuming a suitable value for N.

6. The actual velocity $V = C\sqrt{RS}$ knowing R and S, V the actual velocity can be calculated.

Then the critical vel. ratio $= \dfrac{\text{Value of } V \text{ calculated in Sl. 6}}{\text{Critical vel. obtained in Sl. 2}}$

The critical velocity ratio (C.V.R.) must be within 1·0 to 1·1 for regime. If not try, with another water depth D.

Note. Kennedy's channel is a trapezoidal section.

13·8. Design of Channels on Lacey's Theory

1. Calculate V (actual vel.) by the equation

$$V = \left(\frac{Qf^2}{140}\right)^{1/6} \text{ in metric units} \qquad V = \left(\frac{Qf^2}{4}\right)^{1/6} \text{ in F.P.S. Units} \quad ...(1)$$

where Q = Discharge, $f = 1{\cdot}76\sqrt{dm}$ where f is silt factor and dm = max. size of particle in mm.

2. Calculate hyd. mean depth $R = 2{\cdot}5\dfrac{V^2}{f}$ (metric units)

$$R = 3/4\frac{V^2}{f} \quad \text{(F.P.S. units)} \quad ...(2)$$

3. Area $A = Q/V$ ...(3)

4. Wetted Perimeter $P = 4{\cdot}75\sqrt{Q}$ (metric units)

$$P = 8/3\sqrt{Q} \quad \text{(F.P.S. units)} \quad ...(4)$$

Knowing A, P and R, side slopes as per soil and site conditions, say 1/2 : 1 ;

$$A = BD + D^2/2 \quad ...(5)$$

$$P = B + \sqrt{5}\,D \quad ...(6)$$

From equations (5) and (6), B and D can be calculated.

Note. Lacey's regime channel is a semi elliptical channel not having sharp edges.

5. Slope of bed $S = \dfrac{f^{5/3}}{3340\,Q^{1/6}}$ (metric units)

$$S = \frac{f^{5/3}}{1844\,Q^{1/6}} \quad \text{(F.P.S. units)} \quad ...(7)$$

Note. 1. By Lacey's method the slope of bed is calculated according to the channel conditions and not on the basis of L-section or topography as in case of Kennedy.

2. Lacey's theory does not apply on southern basins as silt there is non coherent and soil is non alluvial.

Table 13·5. Value of (f) given by Lacey for silts

1.	Very fine silt	0·40	6.	N. Indian canals near Roorkee	0·70
2.	Fine silt as Madras	0·50	7.	Fine silt in Krishna	0·80
3.	Fine silt as Jammu	0·60	8.	Fine silt in Punjab canals	0·85
4.	Fine silt as Sardar Valley	0·70	9.	Fine silt in Ganga canal dys.	0·85
5.	North Indian Canals U.P.	0·62	10.	Fine silt in Ganga at Soron	0·90

Take 0·90 for head reaches and 0·80 for tail reaches

Lacey's Regime Definitions

Regime Channel. A channel is said to be in regime if it flows in coherent unlimited alluvium of the same character as that transported and the silt grade and charge are constant.

Initial Regime. It is the state of channel that has formed its section only and yet not secured the longitudinal slope.

Final Regime. A channel which has attained its section and longitudinal slope is said to be a channel in final regime.

Permanent Regime. A channel section protected by linning is said to be in permanent regime. There is no chance of change in section and longitudinal slope. Regime theory is not applicable to such channels.

13·9A. Design of Channel Dimensions by Garrett's Diagrams

Garrett's diagrams are based on Kennedy theory. Proceed as below :

(1) Find the point of intersection say x, of the discharge curves marked on top and bottom axes to the horizontal line of the slope marked on the left ordinate of the diagrame for the designed value of N (say 0·0225).

(2) From this point of intersection x, imagine a vertical line intersecting the various bed widths curves. Each such intersecting point say y, with bed width has a certain water depth marked on Rt ordinate and the critical velocity V_0 on a horizontal line from this point y.

(3) Tabulate several points of bed width and corresponding water depth and their critical velocities V_0 read directly or interpolated as below.

(4) On the left hand portion of the diagrams, there is a set of bed widths velocity curves. In conjunction with these bed width-velocity curves the abscissa indicates velocity and not discharges. In order to find out the velocities for a particular pair of bed-widths and depth, 1st find out the point of intersection of depth line with the corresponding bed width velocity curves. From the intersections say z, draw a vertical to the slope line for the channel and from the point on the slope line come along the velocity curve to the abscissa which gives the value of velocity.

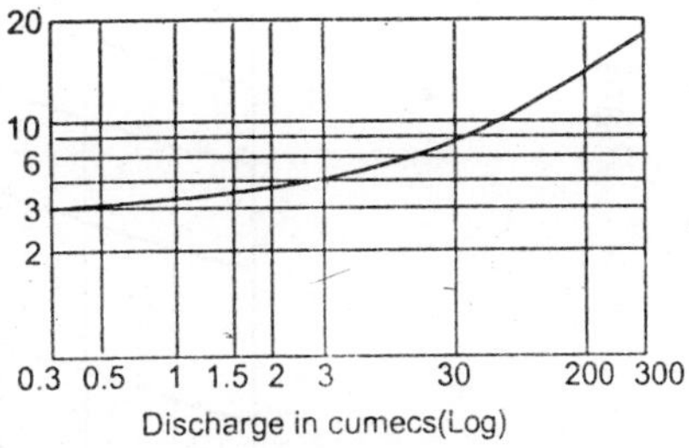

Fig. 13·2. Bed width to depth ratio (for unlined channels).

(5) As the velocities from the diagrams are given on 1/2 : 1 side slopes so in practice, the actual velocity is calculated by dividing the discharge by the area of cross-section so obtained.

(6) Calculate the value of V/V_0 for different sets and choose the required one having the approximate value of V/V_0 desired.

(7) Same diagrams can be used for other values of N. For this in the top nomograms a vertical arrow makes the value for which the curve has been plotted and other values are shown on left and right of the scale. If the diagrams are to be used for a different value of N, measure the distance between that value and the arrow on nomograms and shift the position of point x_1, obtained before to the same extent and in the same direction horizontally. The vertical AB is then to be erected on this shifted point and the rest of the procedure for obtaining B and D is the same. The velocity V in such cases are best obtained by calculation of discharge divided by area.

Note. The bed slope has already been decided on the basis of topography of the land or otherwise.

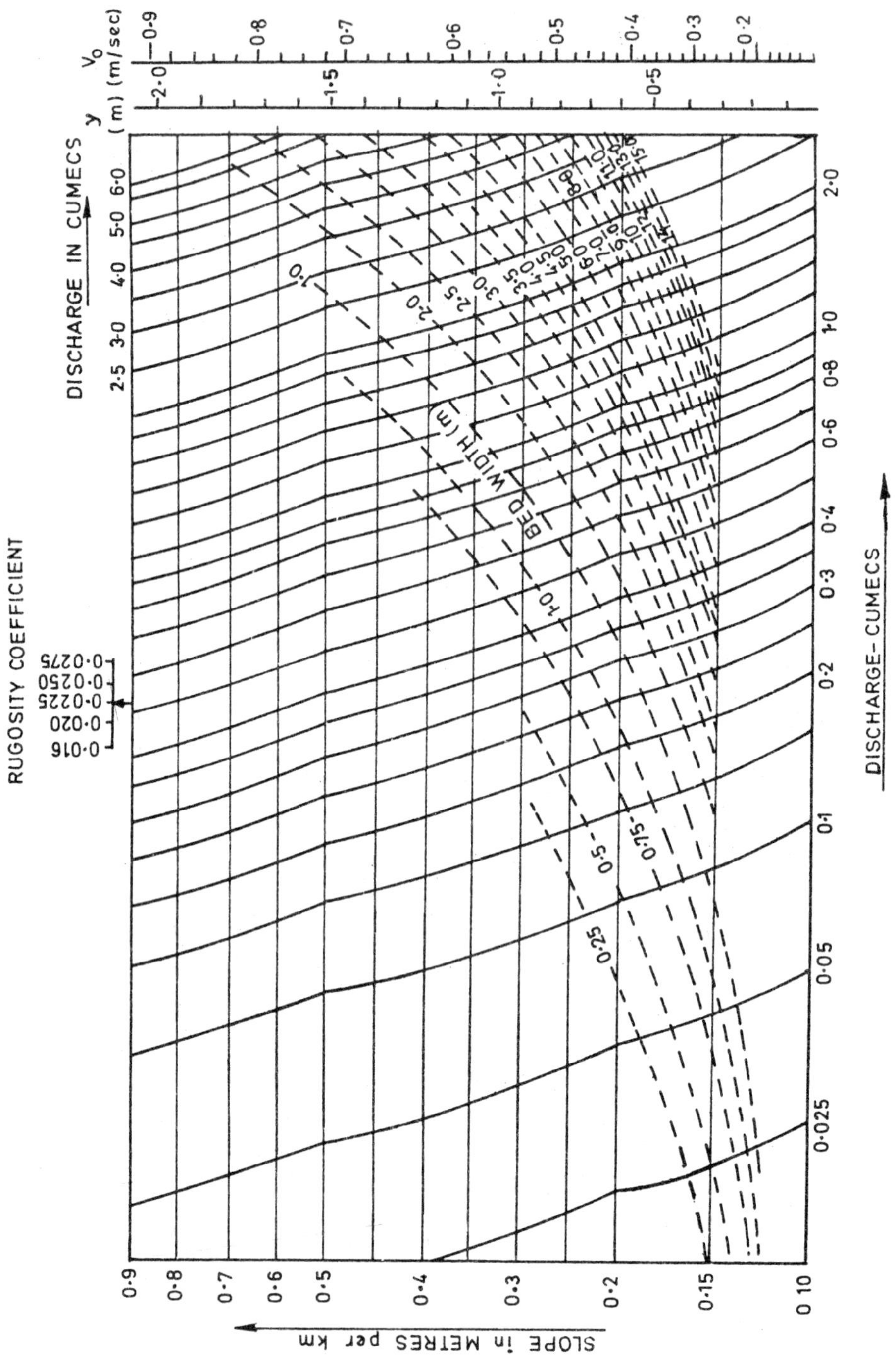

Plate. 13.1. Garret's Diagram No. 1

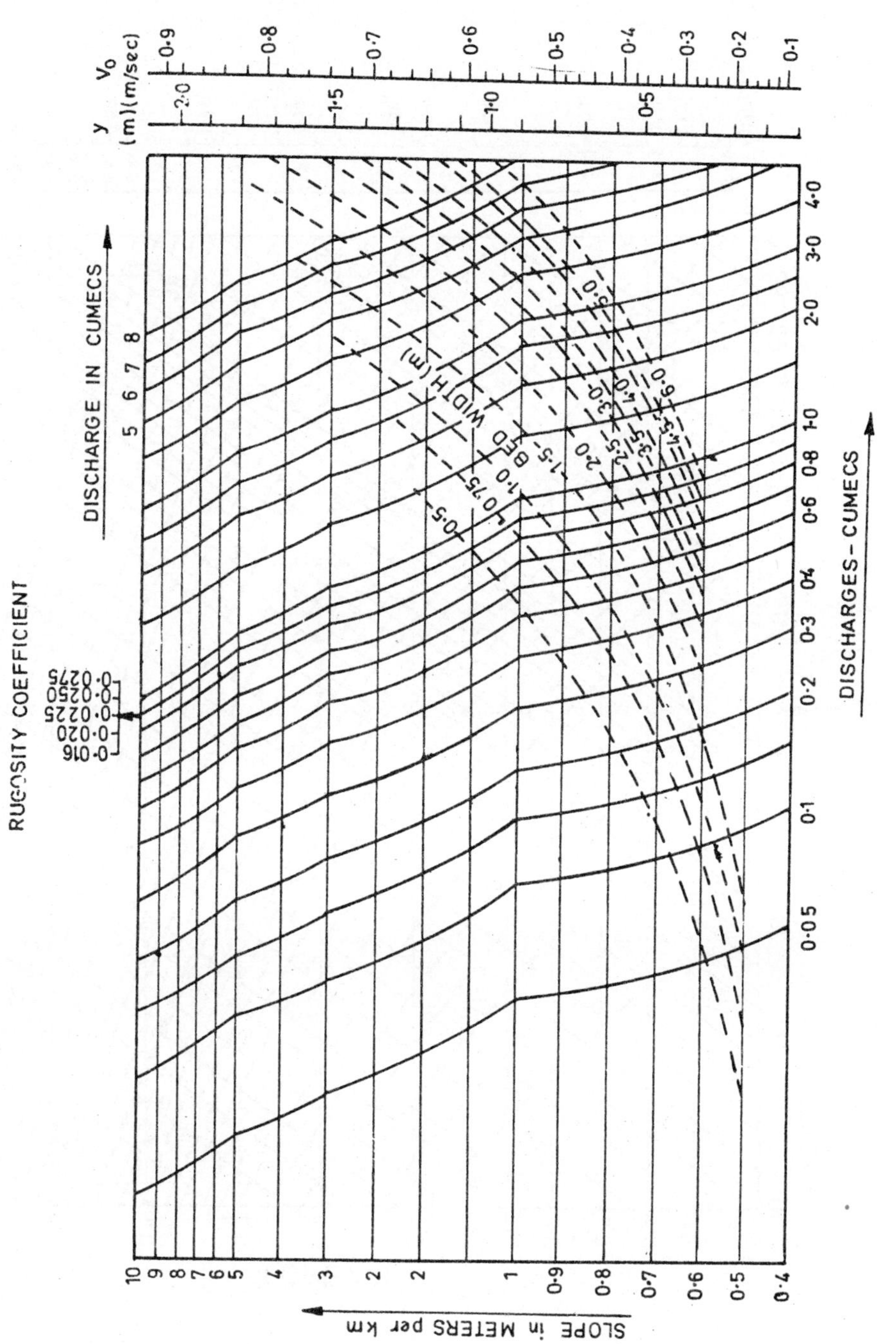

Plate. 13.2. Garret's Diagram No. 2

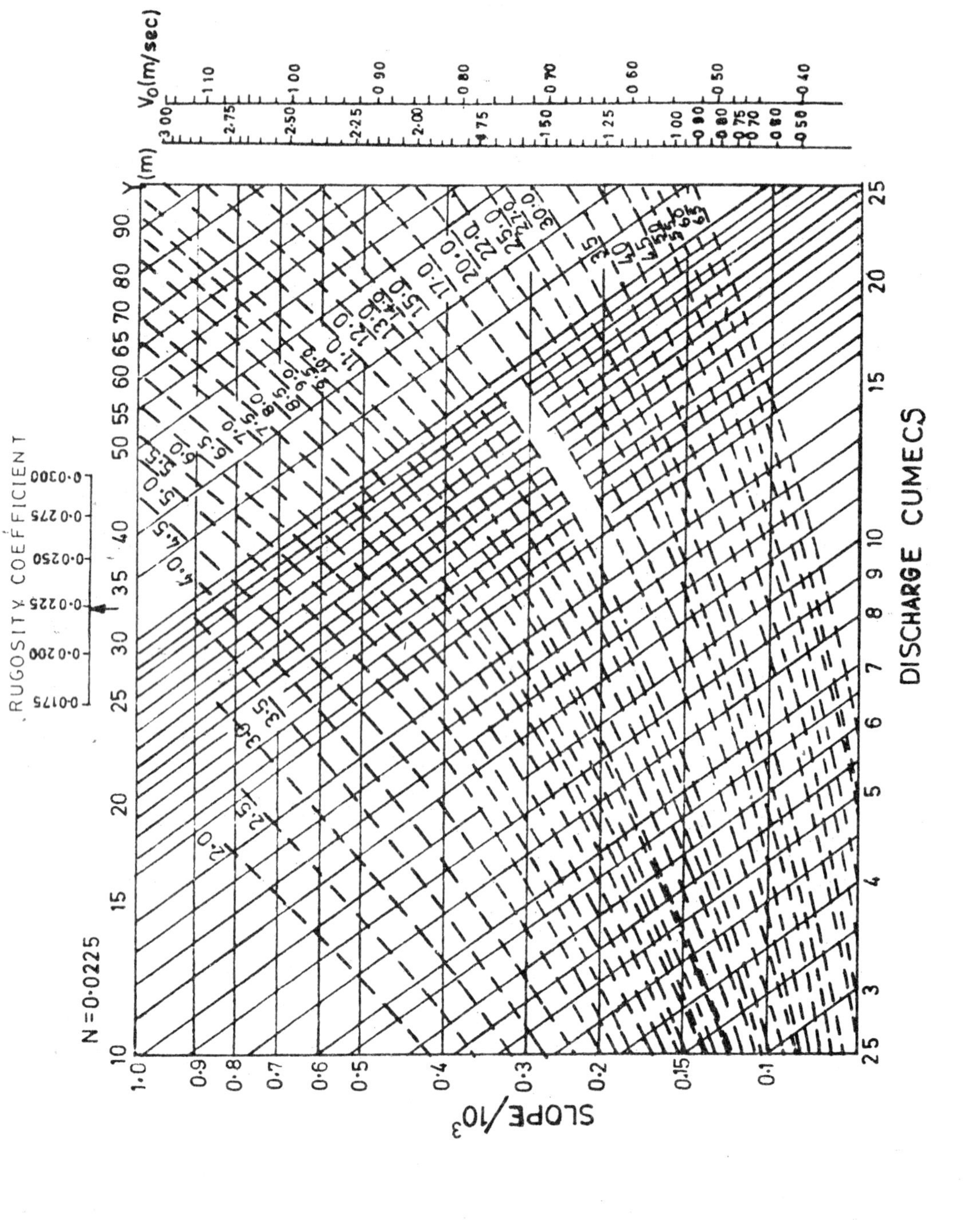

Plate. 13.3 Garret's Diagram No. 3

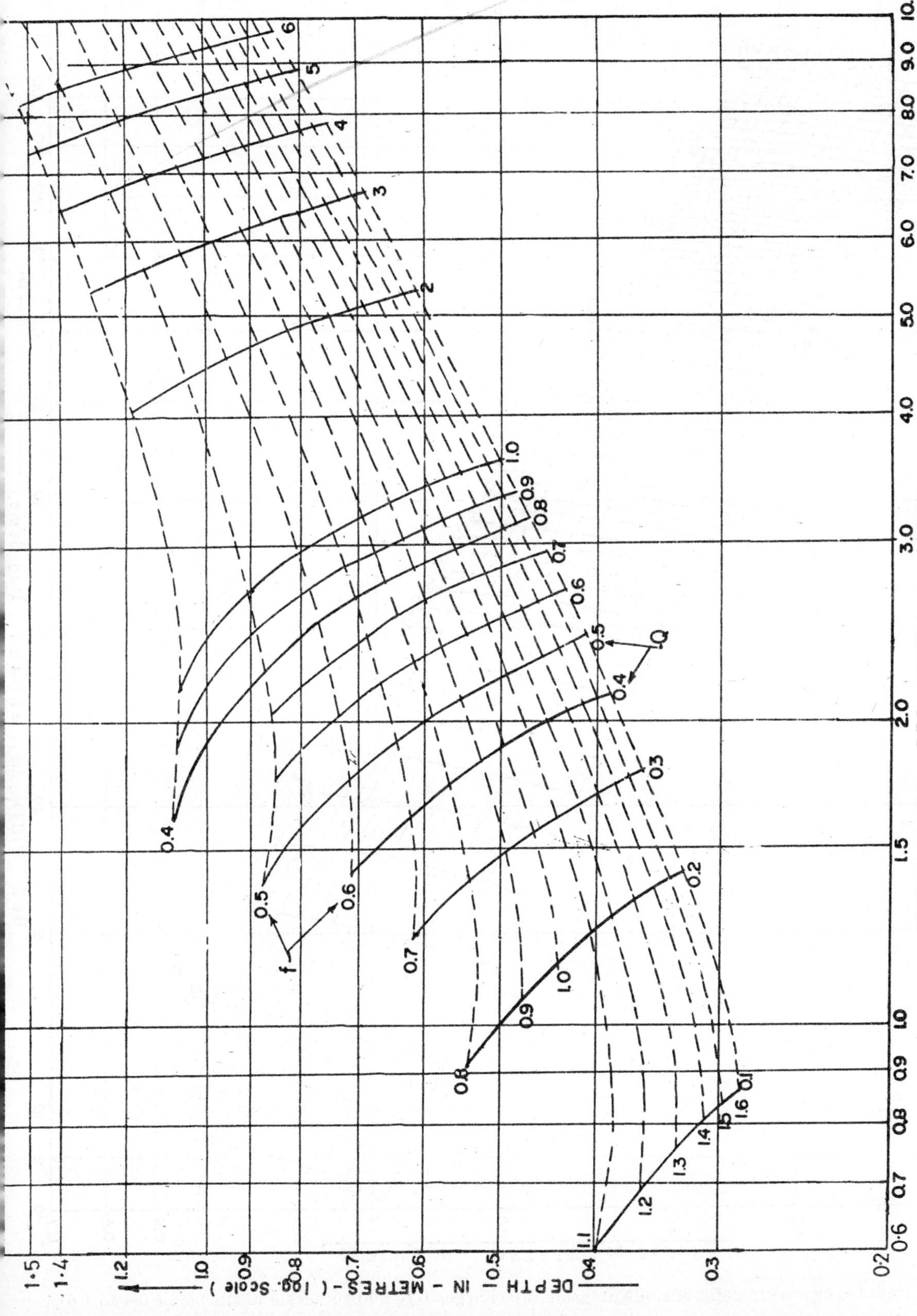

Plate 13·4. Lacey's regime dimensions diagram (Discharges 0·1 to 6·0 cumecs and silt factor 0·4 to 1·6).

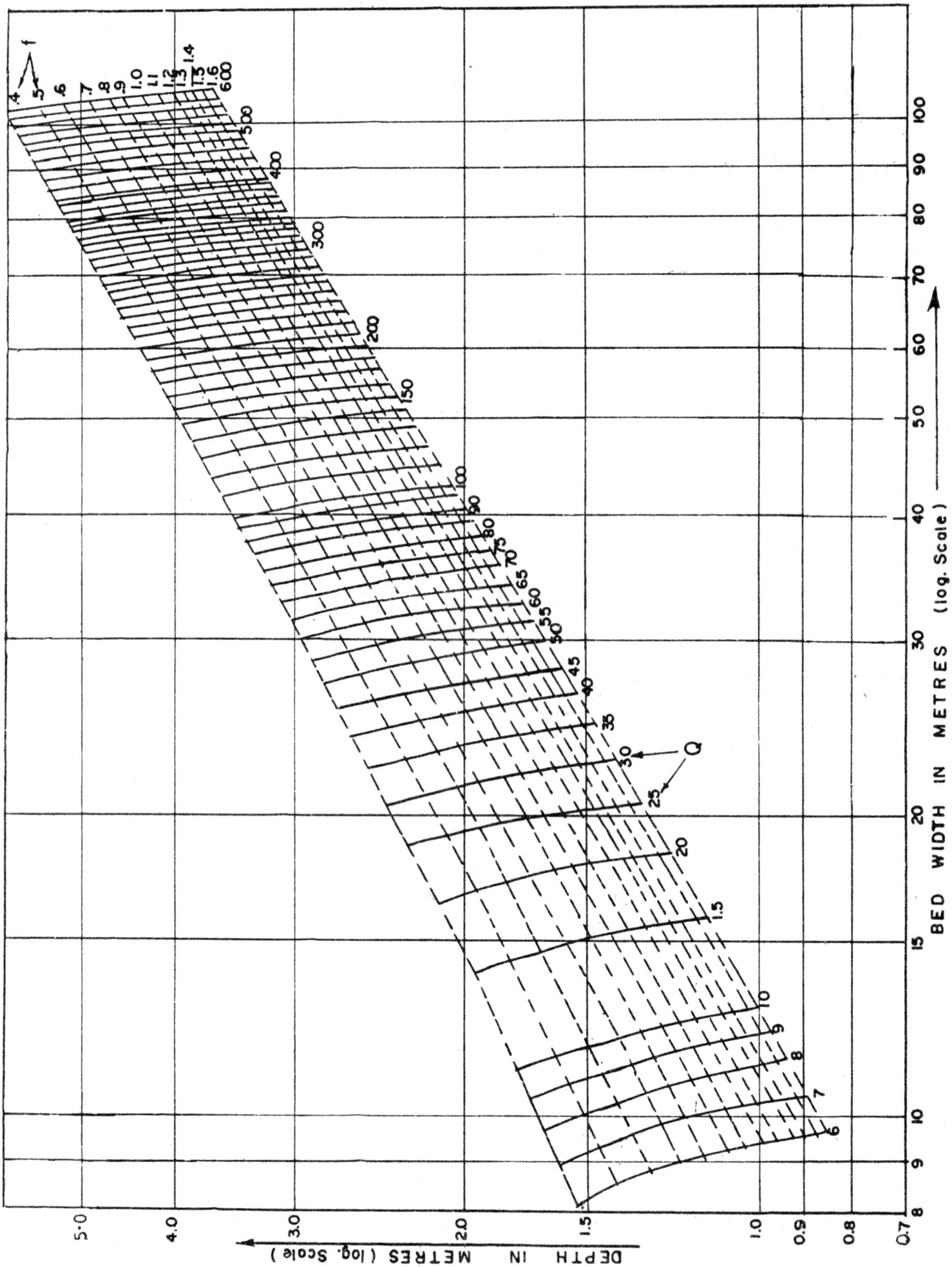

Plate 13·5. Lacey's regime dimensions diagram (discharges 6 to 600 cumecs and silt factor 0·4 to 1·6)

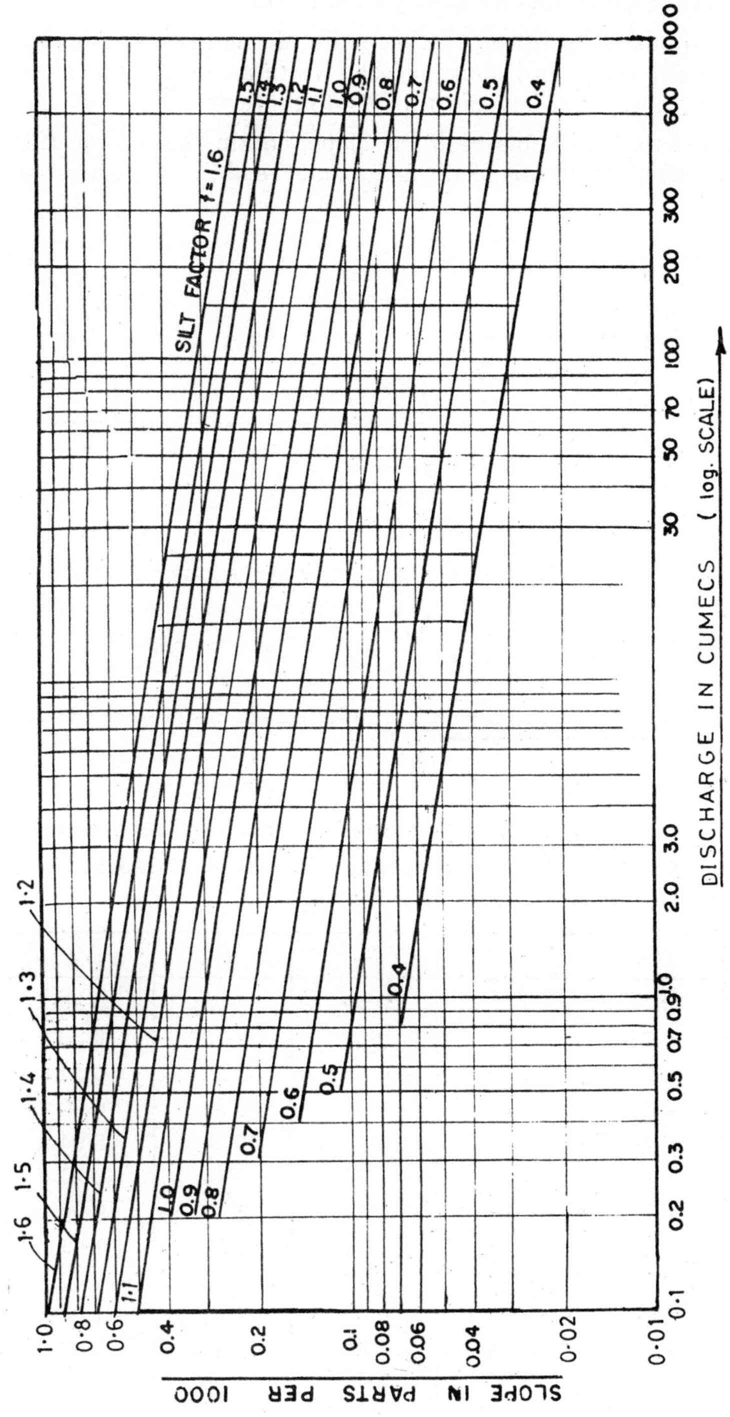

Plate 13·6. Lacey's regime slope diagram.

13·9B. Design of Channels by Lacey's Diagrams

1. Find out the point of intersection of discharge and silt factor curves for a designed discharge and silt factor and then read bed-width as abscissa and water depth on ordinate by the vertical and horizontal lines for this point of intersection.

2. From the 2nd table read the slope, obtain the intersection of the given discharge ordinate with the slanting line of silt factors and read the slope against the point of intersection on the y-axis.

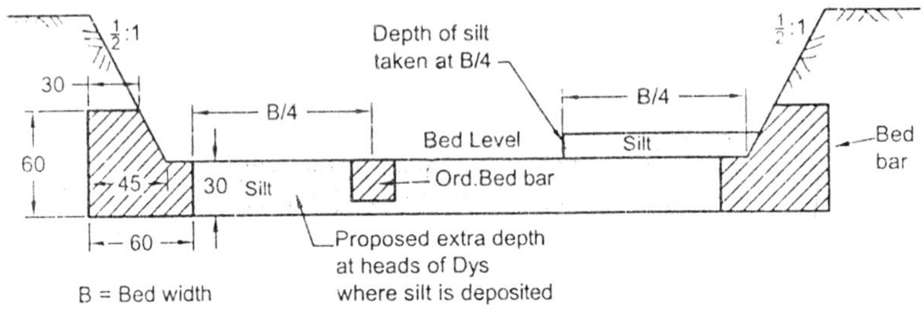

Note : All dimensions are in cm until and other wise mentioned.

Fig. 13·3. Sketch of Shavaksha type bed bar.

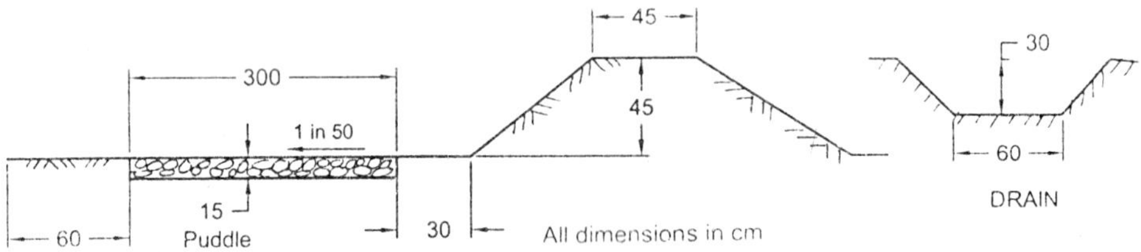

Fig. 13·4. Puddling section of canal service road.

Table 13·6. Values of V_0 in Kennedy's formula for different depths ; V in m/sec. and D in metres.

Side slopes 1/2 : 1 and K = 0·55

D	V_0	D	V_0	D	V_0	D	V_0
0·15	0·16	1·13	0·59	2·04	0·86	2·96	1·10
0·30	0·26	1·22	0·62	2·13	0·89	3·05	1·12
0·40	0·30	1·31	0·65	2·22	0·91	3·14	1·14
0·46	0·33	1·37	0·67	2·29	0·93	3·20	1·15
0·52	0·36	1·43	0·70	2·35	0·94	3·26	1·17
0·61	0·42	1·52	0·72	2·44	0·97	3·35	1·19
0·70	0·43	1·61	0·74	2·53	0·99	3·44	1·25
0·76	0·46	1·68	0·76	2·59	1·01	3·50	1·22
0·82	0·48	1·74	0·78	2·65	1·02	3·57	1·24
0·91	0·52	1·83	0·80	2·74	1·04	3·66	1·25
1·00	0·55	1·92	0·83	2·83	1·07	4·57	1·45
1·07	0·57	1·98	0·85	2·89	1·08	6·10	1·74

For Sind Canals multiply the value by 0·75. The ratio of bed width to depth should be between 1 and 5.

Bed width to water depth	3·5	4	4·5	5	6	9
Discharge in cumecs	0·28	0·71	2·83	5·66	14·16	28·31

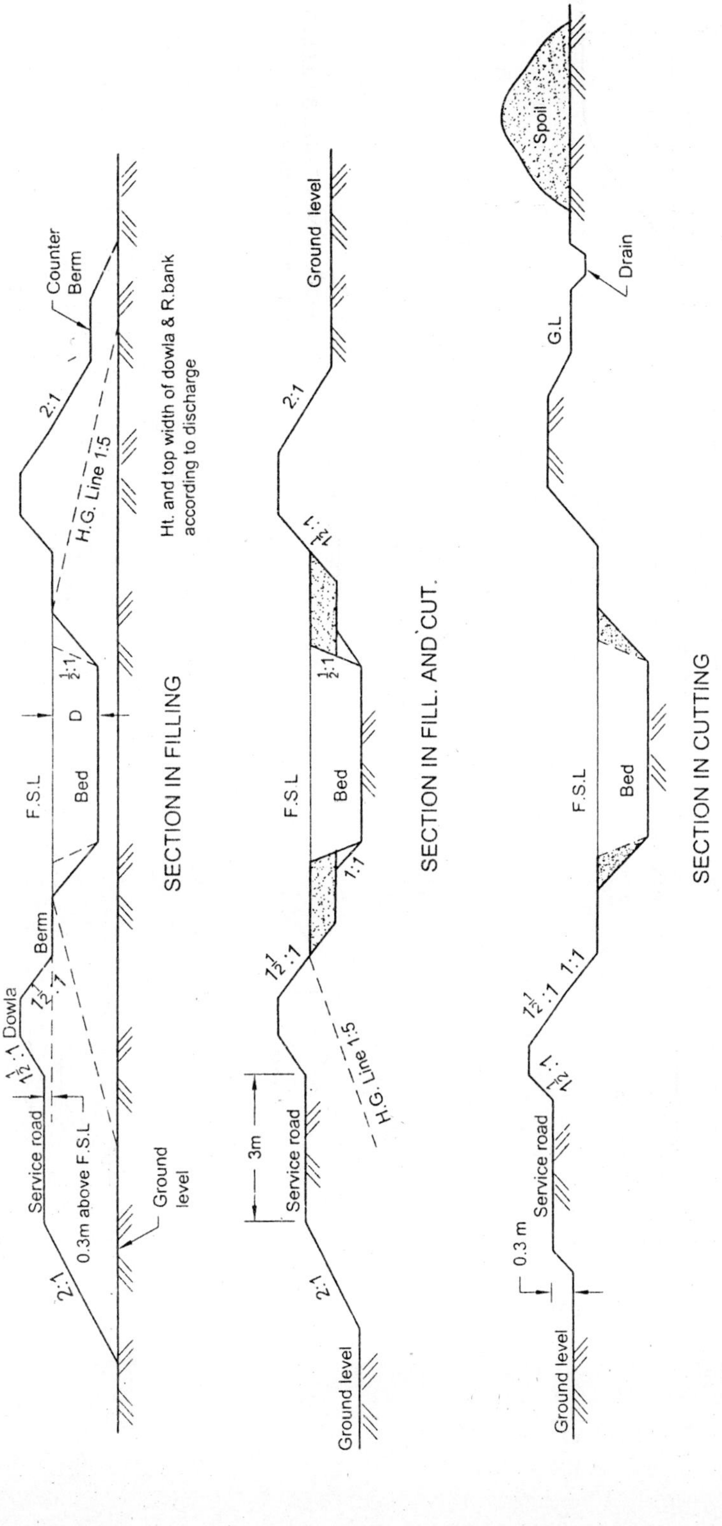

(c) Section in cutting.

Note : For dimensions see Tables.

Fig. 13·5.

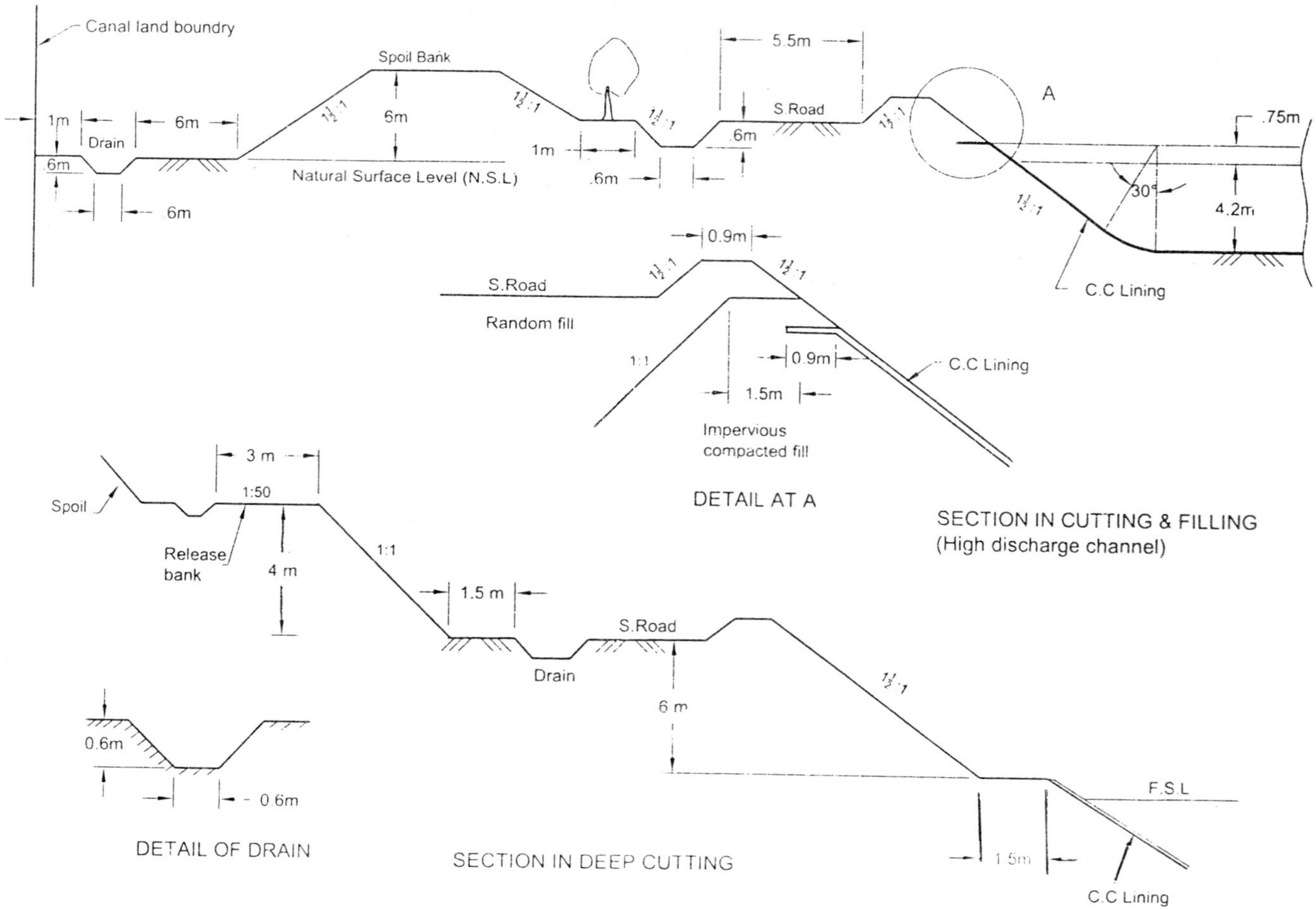

Note : (1) For dimensions see Tables; (2) Dimensions are in metre until and otherwise stated.

Fig. 13·5.

Table 13·7. Design data for Earthen channels based on Kennedy's Theory.

N = ·0225 Side slopes 1/2 : 1

Discharge		B.W.	W.D.	Bed slope	V/V_0	Mean Vel.
cusecs	cumecs	m	m	1 in		m/sec.
1	2	3	4	5	6	7
2	·06	0·61	0·30	2500	1·00	0·24
4	0·11	0·82	0·37	2500	1·03	0·30
6	0·17	1·07	0·43	2860	1·00	0·31
8	0·23	1·22	0·46	2860	1·03	0·33
10	0·28	1·45	0·49	3330	0·92	0·34
12	0·34	1·60	0·53	3330	1·00	0·36
16	0·45	1·83	0·58	3640	1·00	0·38
20	0·57	2·01	0·61	3640	1·00	0·40
30	0·85	2·44	0·68	3640	1·02	0·44
40	1·13	2·82	0·78	4000	0·98	0·46
50	1·42	3·13	0·84	4000	1·00	0·47
60	1·70	3·35	0·88	4000	1·00	0·51
70	1·98	3·36	0·91	4000	1·01	0·53
80	2·26	3·96	0·97	4000	0·97	0·54
90	2·55	4·11	1·02	4000	0·98	0·54
100	2·83	4·42	1·04	4440	1.00	0·55
125	3·54	4·88	1·11	4440	1·00	0·58
150	4·25	5·18	1·12	4440	1·00	0·61
175	4·95	5·64	1·23	4440	1·01	0·63
200	5·66	5·94	1·31	4440	1·01	0·66
250	7·08	6·70	1·43	4440	1·01	0·71
300	8·56	7·31	1·46	4440	1·03	0·71
350	9·91	8·08	1·57	5000	0·97	0·71
400	11·3	8·69	1·61	5000	1·06	0·74
450	12·7	9·30	1·68	5000	1·00	0·76
500	14·2	9·75	1·72	5000	1·00	0·77
600	17·0	10·7	1·83	5000	1·00	0·79
700	19·8	11·9	1·86	5000	1·01	0·82
800	22·6	12·8	1·92	5000	1·01	0·86
900	25·5	14·0	1·95	5000	1·02	0·87
1000	28·3	15·3	1·98	5000	1·03	0·91
2000	56·6	25·4	2·26	5700	1·03	0·94
5000	142	56·5	2·50	6670	0·98	0·97
10,000	283	105	2·59	6670	1·02	1·03
20,000	566·3	212	2·72	8000	0·94	0·975

13·10. Best sections of max. discharge in small channels having no silt.

1. **Closed channels** ... circular

2. **Open channels** (*a*) Semicircle (*b*) Rectangular with bed width twice the water depth or hyd. mean depth is half the depth (*c*) Trapezoidal semi hexagonal when a semi circle inscribed touches all the three sides with rounded corners.

A trapezoidal section having side slopes n : 1 must have the relation

$$B = 2{\cdot}0\, D\left(\sqrt{n^2+1} - n\right) ; \qquad D = \left\{A \div \left(2\sqrt{n^2+1} - n\right)\right\}^{1/2}$$

Triangular. Right angled triangle having both sides equal.

Circular. Depth of water = 0·810 dia.; Hyd. mean depth = 0·304 dia.

Wetted perimeter = 2·245 dia ; For maximum discharge – Depth of water = 0·95 dia.

Hyd. mean depth = 0·286 dia ; Wetted perimeter = 2·60 dia. ; Depth of water = 2·83.

Table 13·8. SIDE SLOPES—Cutting

Nature of bank	*upto 2·5 m depth*	*2·5-4·5 m depth*
1. Firm rock	1/8 : 1	1/8-1/4 : 1
2. Soft rock	1/4 : 1	1/4-1/2 : 1
3. Alluvial soil firm gravel, compacted earth, hard mooram	1/2 : 1	1/2 -3/4 : 1
4. Stiff earth or clay	1 : 1	1½ : 1
5. Ordinary gravel	1¼ : 1	1½ : 1
6. Ord. earth, soft clay, dry sand, sandy or gravelly loam	1½ : 1	2 : 1
7. Loose earth or loose sandy loam	2 : 1	3 : 1
8. Wet sand	2½ : 1	4 : 1
9. Light sand wet clay	3 : 1	3-4 : 1

Alluvial soils. In practice a cutting of 1 : 1 slope is done which is silted to 1/2 : 1 during running and forms a berm at F.S.L. In non alluvial soils cutting according to above rule is done which does not silt up as in case of alluvial soils. For estimate purposes calculations are done for a slope of 1 : 1 while in design 1/2 : 1 slope is considered.

Filling. 1½ : 1 to 2 : 1 slopes are given according to the soils. In good domat soil a slope of 1½ : 1 can be given while in loose soils a slope of 2 : 1, in sandy soils a slope of 3 : 1 and in very loose sand upto 4 : 1 is given. The outer slopes are flatter than the inside slopes. In spoils a slope of 1½ : 1 or a stable slope which may not slip as in service road is given. In big lined canals slope of 1 : 1 and in small channels (distributary and minors) a slope of 1/2 : 1 is given with lining.(Refer Table 13·12).

13·11. Allowable Curves in Channels—Unlined canals

Table 13·9.

Dis. in cumecs	Below 0·3	·3 to 3·0	3 to 15	15 to 30	30 to 85	above 85
Minimum rad. of curve in (m)	100	150	300	600	900	1500

Curves on lined Canals

Discharge in cumecs	42-70	70-140	140-210	210-280	280 and above
Minimum rad. of curve in m	300	450	600	760	900

Note. (1) The super elevation should be given in side the curve and the outer side having more velocity must be pitched by boulders or with crates.

Table 13·10. Schedule of Area statistics and channel Dimensions for ....canal.

Below K.M.	*Cross commanded area (hectares)*	*Culturable commanded area (hectares)*	*Controlling area to be irrigated (hectares) 15%*	*Outlet Discharge factor*	*Losses in reach (cumecs)*	*Total losses (cumecs)*	*Design Discharge cumecs*	*Bed slope, cm/km*	*Bed width (m)*	*Water depth (m)*	*Free board in (m)*	*Ht. of bank above G.L.*	*Width of bank*	*Vel. in m/sec.*	V/V_0	*Remarks*
0	30,000	22,500	3,775	756	0·017	0·488	5·44	20	7·2	1·2	0·6	1·00	2·25	0·58	0·944	
1	25,000	18,750	2812·5	756	0·010	0·471	4·61	20	6·0	1·2	0·5	1·00	2·0	0·582	0·947	
2	20,000	15,000	2,250	756	0·014	0·454	3·79	22·5	6·0	1·05	0·5	0·90	2·0	0·55	0·95	
3	15,000	11,250	1,687·5	756	—	0·440	2·94	22·5	4·2	1·05	0·5	0·925	2·0	0·56	0·96	
					so on											

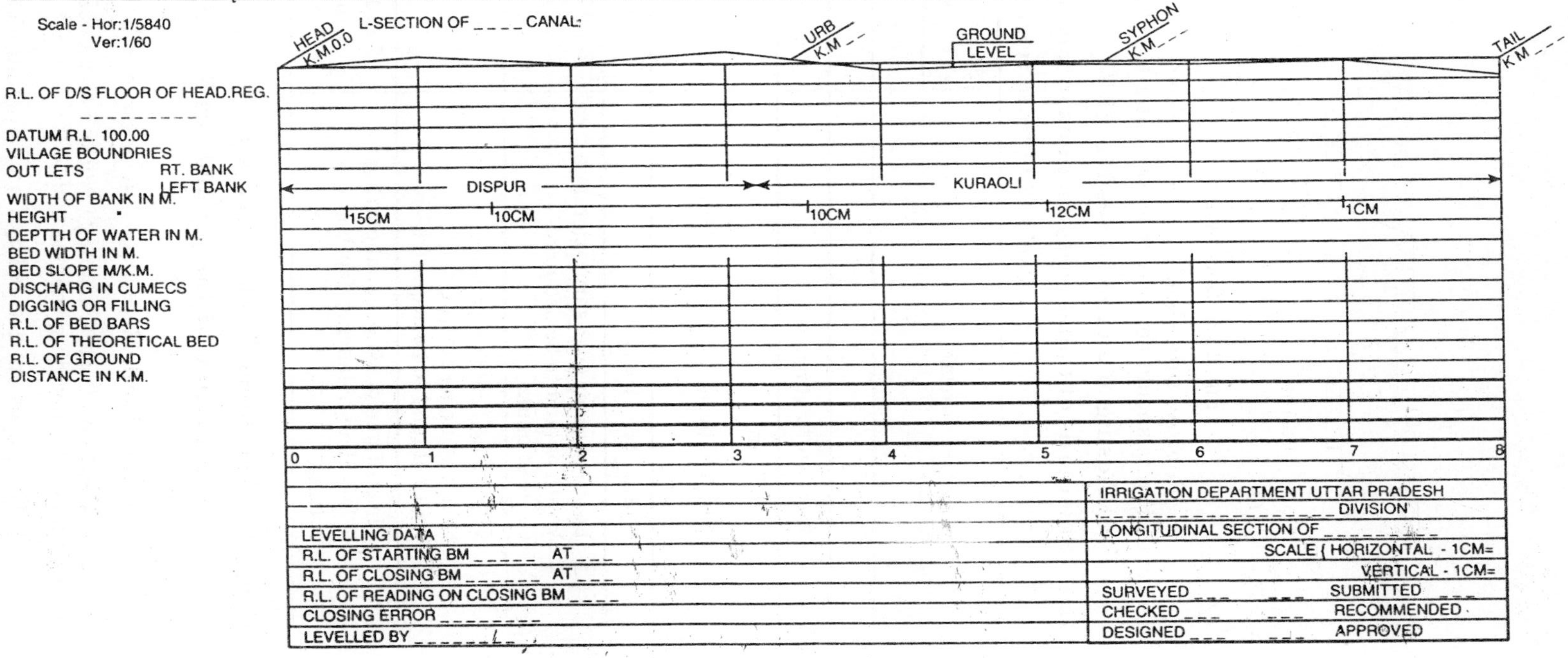

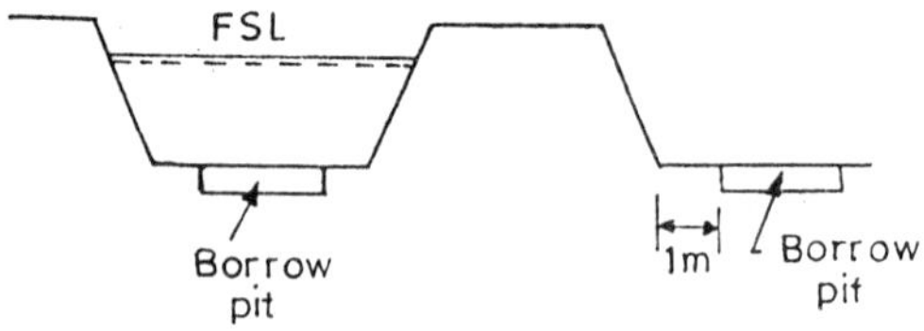

Fig. 13·6. Borrow pits.

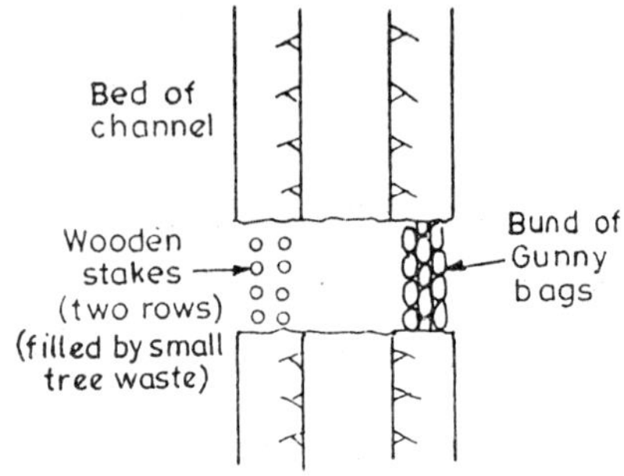

Fig. 13·7. Closing of a breach in channel

(2) **Borrow pits** should be taken either from the bed of the channel or from outside. The outside pits should be away from the outer toe of the bank. (Min. 1 metre)

(3) **Closing of a breach. See Fig. 13·7.**

13·12. Standards of Canal cross-sections in metres

Table 13·11 (Also refer Table 13·12)

Items	*Main and Branch canals*		*Distributaries*		*Minors*	
	150-30	*30-10*	*10-5*	*5-1*	*1-0·3*	*Below 0·3*
		(*in cumecs*)				
Max. width of bank	3·0	2·5	2·25	2·0	1·5	1·0
Free board	0·9	0·75	0·6	0·5	0·4	0·3
Width of berms Min. Max.	0·6 + 1/4 of the full supply depth 0·6 + 1/2 of the full supply depth					
Width of road way	6·0	5·0	5·0	3·5	3·5	NIL
Depth of cover over saturation line Width of land to be acquired Clear of banks	1·0	0·8	0·5	0·5	0·5	0·5
When canal cutting is deeper than balancing cutting width of land to be acquired.	5·0 metre		Half the height of bank above ground subject to min. 1 m			
Clear of banks when canal cutting is less than balancing depth of cutting	Full height of bank + 5·0		Full height of bank above G.L. + 1·5			

13·13. (*a*) Bed-slopes. The bed slope is decided on the following :

1. **Topography of the ground.** (*a*) Economical depth of cutting (*b*) Flow irrigation considerations.

2. **Type of soil.** More slope can be given in hard soils than in poor soils.

3. Position of cross drainage works ; some obligatory points such as H.F.L. etc., which makes a factor for deciding the bed slope.

4. The slopes are decided by Lacey's regime slope equations if designed on Lacey's theory.

Usual slopes which are given in North Indian canals.

Main canal and branches 1 in 10,000 to 1 in 7000

Distributaries and Minors 1 in 6000 to 1 in 3000

In F.P.S. system – 0·48, 0·56, 0·64, 0·72, 0·80, 0·96, 1·00, 1·2, 1·4, 1·6 and 2·0 per mile (slopes in foot are usually given).

(*b*) Stage Discharge Curves. This is a curve between discharge and depth of water in a channel. Stage or depth is plotted as ordinate (y-axis) and discharge as abscissa (x-axis). These curves must be checked periodically as the regime conditions of a channel are always changing.

(*c*) Berms. According to Indian standard. (Refer Table 13·12).

In cutting. 1½ : D1 at F.S.L., both banks where D is depth of water. It becomes 2D on silting.

Half cutting and half filling. 1¾ D at ground level both banks.

It becomes 2.5D on silting on F.S.L.

Filling. 2D at F.S.L. both banks which becomes 3D on silting.

Note. In practice width of berm is kept over D subject to min. of 0·6 metre. The slopes take 1/2 : 1 slope in silting. According to discharge—(U.P. standard)

Upto 4·25 cumecs = 0·6 + 1/2D both banks at F.S.L.

4·25 to 28 cumecs = 1·25 + 1/2 D both banks at F.S.L.

28 cumecs and above $= 1{\cdot}25 + 1/2\ \text{D} + \dfrac{\text{Full supply discharge}}{28}$

Punjab standard

Cutting. 1·5D on service road side and 2D on riding banks side at F.S.L.

Half cutting and half filling. 2D on either side at ground level which silts and forms berm at F.S.L.

Filling. 3D on either side.

Top of banks. Details are given in tables.

Service roads. Details are given in figures for filling section. For normal cutting service road (Inspection road) is provided 0·3 m above general ground level giving a slope of 1 : 30 to 1 : 40 when the ground level changes. In deep cutting service roads are provided at such a level (see x-sec. in deep cutting) that the inspection of the channel may be easy. It should be joined to the general ground level (when met with) with a gradient of 1 : 30 to 1 : 40, when deep cutting finishes. Indeep cutting side drains are provided to drain off the rain water. (refer Table 13·12)

(*d*) Dowla Section. Details are given in the figures 13·5 and Table 13·12.

Free board. The height of the top of bank from F.S.L. according to Indian Standard –

upto 14·0 cumec discharge = 0·5 m

above 14·0 cumec dis. = 0·75 m

According to Punjab Canals –

Lined main canal and branches0·75 m

Unlined branches 0·75 m

Unlined distributaries 0·45 m

(see tables for further details)

Table 13·12. Details of Channel Sections for Different Discharges

Discharge in cumecs		*Min. Total width of banks in m.*	*Free board in bank above F.S.L.*	*Width of service road*	*Height of S.R. from F.S.L.*	*Width of berm*	*Side slopes*		*Dowla*		
From	*To*						*Cutting*	*Filling*	*Top width*	*Side slope*	*Height*
1	2	3	4	5	6	7	8	9	10	11	12
0·05	0·3	1·20	0·45	-	0·15	0·6	1·1	1½ : 1	0·45	1½ : 1	0·3
0·3	0·6	1·20	0·45	3·0	0·15	0·9	1·1	1½ : 1	0·45	1½ : 1	0·3
0·6	3·0	1·5	0·45	3·6	0·15	0·9	1·1	1½ : 1	0·45	1½ : 1	0·3
3·0	6·0	1·8	0·60	3·6	0·30	0·9	1·1	1½ : 1	0·45	1½ : 1	0·4
6·0	15·0	2·1	0·60	3·6	0·30	1·2	1·1	1½ : 1	0·50	1½ : 1	0·4
15·0	30·0	2·7	0·60	3·6	0·45	1·5	1·1	1½ : 1	0·50	1½ : 1	0·4
30·0	60·0	3·0	0·75	4·5	0·45	1·8	1·1	1½ : 1	0·50	1½ : 1	0·5
60·0	70·0	3·0	0·75	4·5	0·60	1·8	1·1	1½ : 1	0·50	1½ : 1	0·5
70·0	100·0	3·6	0·9	5·4	0·60	2·4	1·1	1½ : 1	0·50	1½ : 1	0·5
above	100·0	4·8	0·9	6·0	0·75	2·4	1·1	1½ : 1	0·50	1½ : 1	0·5

1. Saturation or hydraulic gradient

Ordinary loam	1 : 4
Sandy loam	1 : 5
Fine silt and sand	1 : 6

The earth cover to H.G.L. should be at least 0·45 to 0·60 and it should be within outer toe of the bank.

If it crosses the bank, it should either be flattened or a counter berm should be provided.

2. For sandy soils the side slopes should be 1½ : 1 and 2 : 1 in cutting and filling respectively.

3. The height of SR in cutting can be reduced.

4. Berm can be provided as half the full supply depth or if provided on G.L. half of the depth of digging subjected to min. of 0·6 m.

5. Section of side and cross drains should be 0·5 m B.W. and 0·30 m depth with side slopes 1½ : 1.

Note. 1. Road way as well as banks must have an outward cross slope of 1 : 30 to 1 : 40.

2. Min. height of S.R. from G.L. should be 0·30 m.

3. Slope of ramps on village road, should be 1 : 30 to 1 : 40.

4. Slope of ramps of S.R. should be 1 : 40.

5. In Bhoor reaches the canal S.R. must be puddled or metalled for high traffic in width of 3·0 m and depth 0·15 in centre of S.R.

6. In reaches of spoils, side drains and cross drains must be provided, side drain must be at the edge of straight and cross drain at an interval of 50 m or as considered better as per site conditions.

Table 13·13. showing area in Hectares to be irrigated by different size outlets

Ventage inches/ c.m.	Discharge in cusecs				8 Kor week				6 Kor week				4 Kor week				3 Kor week			
	Flow	*0-20% lift*	*20-50% lift*	*Above 50% lift*	*Flow*	*0-20% lift*	*20-50% lift*	*Above 50% lift*	*Flow*	*9-20% lift*	*20-50% lift*	*Above 50% lift*	*Flow*	*0-20% lift*	*20-50% lift*	*Above 50% lift*	*Flow*	*0-20% lift*	*20-50% lift*	*Above 50% lift*
3/7·5	0·2	0·15	-	-	20	15	-	-	16	12	-	-	10	8	-	-	8	6	-	-
4/10	0·4	0·3	0·25	0·2	41	31	26	20	31	23	19	13	20	15	13	10	15	12	10	8
5/12·5	0·68	0·5	0·38	0·3	70	51	31	52	52	39	29	23	35	26	20	15	26	19	15	12
6/15	0·9	0·66	0·55	0·4	92	60	41	79	69	51	42	31	46	34	28	20	34	26	21	15
6 + 3/15 + 7·5	1·1	0·8	0·69	0·5	113	82	51	84	84	62	53	39	56	41	35	26	42	30	26	19
6 + 4/15 + 10	1·3	0·95	0·8	0·6	133	97	62	100	100	73	62	46	67	49	41	31	50	36	31	23
6 + 5/15 + 12½	1·6	1·15	0·93	0·7	164	118	72	123	123	88	72	54	82	59	48	36	62	44	34	27
6 + 6/2 + 15	1·8	1·3	1·1	0·8	186	133	82	139	139	100	84	62	92	67	56	41	69	50	42	31

Outlet factor for Rabi = 460 Hectares/m^3, Sugarcane = 370 Hectare/m^3 and Rice = 318 Hectare/m^3.

Table 13·14. Discharge through Irrigation outlets in cumecs

Ventage (dia. of pipe in cm.)	Free over fall	Outlet with submerged out fall		
		0-20% lift area	*21-50 lift area*	*over 50% lift area*
15	0·025	0·0185	0·0154	0·011
12·5	0·019	0·0140	-	-
10	0·011	0·0080	0·0074	0·006
7	0·006	0·0040	-	-

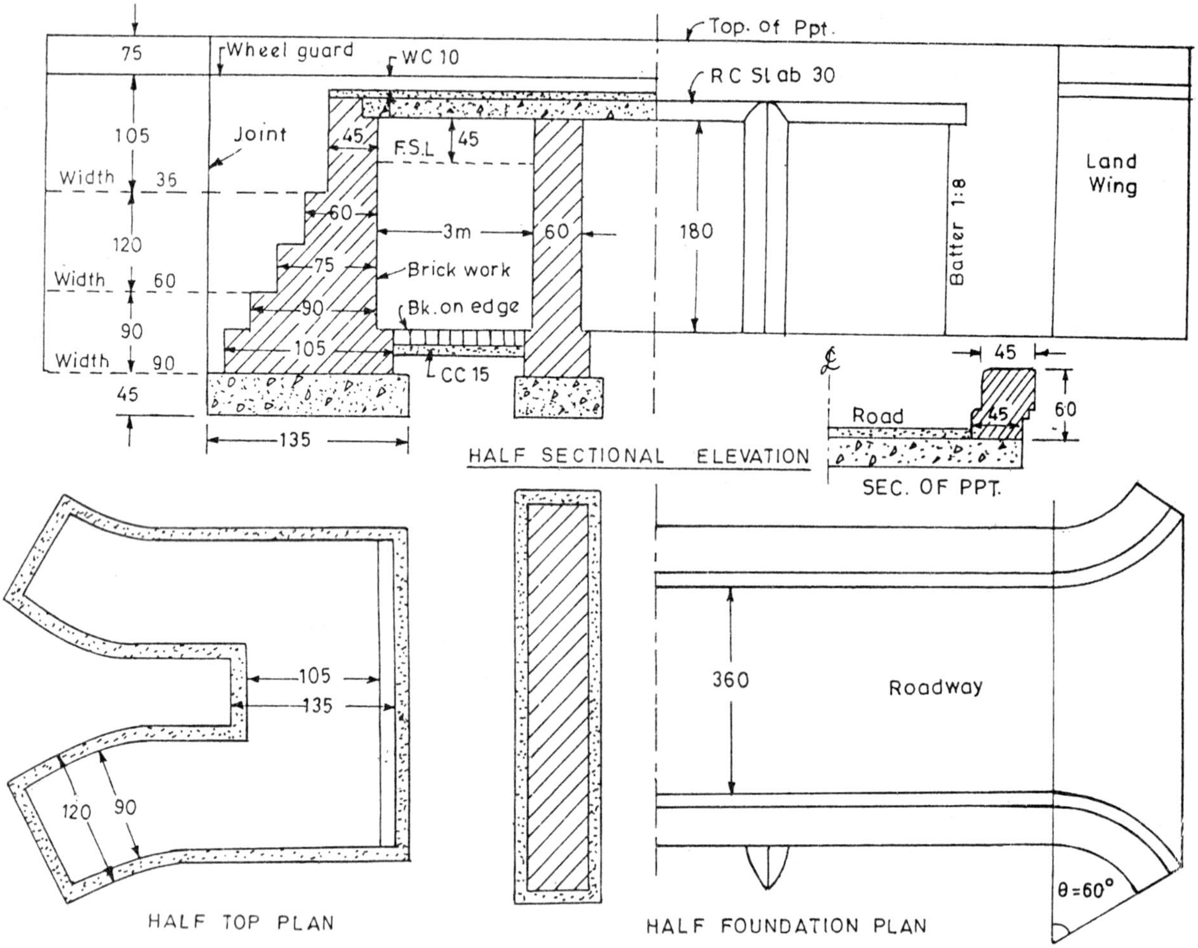

(Dimensions are in mm)

Fig. 13·9. Village road bridge (V.R.B.) canal pattern.

1·14. Design Criteria of Channels and Masonary Works (bridges) IDUP

(1) (*a*) No direct outlets are provided on main canals and branches having discharges over 14·0 cumecs or 500 cusecs.

(*b*) No minor is economical having a discharge less than 0·06 cumecs or 2 cusecs.

(2) **Service Road.** Generally a service road must be provided on channel having length more than 3 kms. (refer Table 13·12).

Service road must be at least 0·3 m above F.S.L. and general ground level. According to Indian Standards the width of S.R. should be as follows.

3·5 m upto 0·56 cumecs

4·0 m from 0·56 to 14 cumecs

5·0 m from 14 cumecs and above

(3) **Berm.** According to Indian Standards the width of berm should be as below :

In cutting 2 × D at F.S.L. on both banks, where D = depth of water.

In filling 3 × D at F.S.L. on both banks, where D = depth of water.

Note. In practice generally width of berm is kept 1D subject to min. 0·6 m.

(After silting it takes a slope of ½ : 1)

(4) **Dowla.** On main canal and branches.

Top width = 0·6 m, Height 0·6 m from S.R., side slopes 1·5 : 1.

Top width = 0·5 m, Height = 0·5 m from S.R., Side slopes 1·5 : 1 Dys. and Mrs.

(5) Non riding bank – Top width 1·5 m upto 0·56 cumecs

2·0 m from 0·56 to 2·83 cumecs

2·5 m from 2·83 to 14·0 cumecs

35 m above 14·0 cumecs

(6) **Free board.** According to Indian Standards

Unlined channels : Lined main canal and branches 0·75 m

0·5 m upto 14·0 cumecs (Dy. and Mrs)

0·75 m above 14·0 cumecs (Main canal and branches)

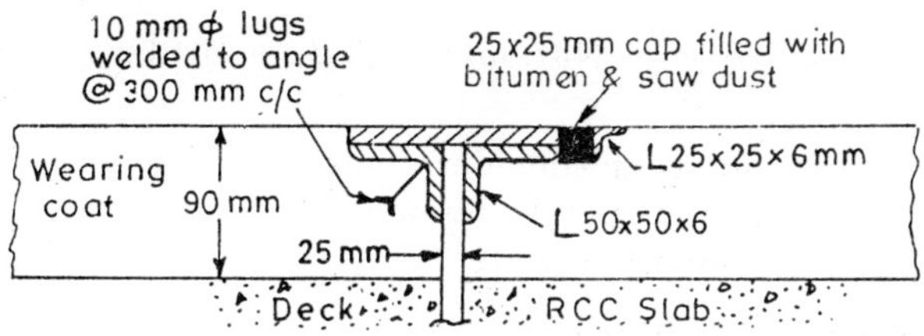

Note : In V.R.B's 25 mm thick joint may be filled with bitumen and saw dust.

Fig. 13·10.

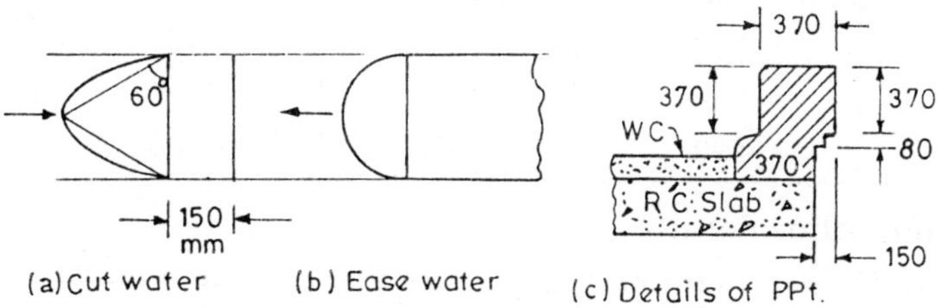

Fig. 13·11.

Bridges on Canals (for details refer Chapter in Bridges)

V.R.B. (Village road bridge). Road way 4·25 m IRC class A loading.

D.R.B./P.R.B. (District and Provincial road bridges). Road way 7·5 M class *AA* loading.

Spacing of bridges. The spacing of two adjacent bridges should not be less than 1 km.

Water way. Water way between inner faces of abutments shall be as below :

$B + D$ for discharge Q upto 5·6 cumecs B is bed width, D is depth of water

$B + D/2$ for discharge Q more than 5·6 cumecs and Q is the discharge.

Note. The clear water way excluding width of piers should not be kept less than B.

Free Board. Free board between F.S.L. of the channel and the bottom of the deck slab or bottom of beams and bearings should be as below :

Free board in metres	Discharge Q in cumecs
0·45 m	For Q less than 5·6 cumecs
0·60 m	For Q more than 5·6 cumecs

Note. In heavy cutting arched bridges of masonry or RCC are preferred.

Spans. Spans should be equal and odd in numbers. Simply supported slabs for spans upto 6 m shall be provided. For spans more than 6 m span *T*-beams are economical.

Depth of foundations. (*a*) For *VRB/DRB* and discharge below 14 cumecs the depth of foundations for abutments and peirs should be as below :

Dis. in cumecs	*Depth below bed or ground whichever is less in m*	*Thickness of found. concrete in m*	*Offset of concrete in m*
upto 1	1·00	0·30	0·15
1 to 3	1·20	0·30	0·15
3 to 14	1·50	0·45	0·20

(*b*) Above 14 cumecs P.R.B. and National highways Bridges of foundation should be designed on design criteria.

(*c*) Depth of foundations on scour considerations should not be less than 1·2 m below the max. anticipated scour (1·5 R) from H.F.L. So depth of foundation below bed = $(1·5R - D) + 1·2$ m (R is hyd. mean depth) D is depth of water.

Width of Abutments wings and peirs.

(*a*) Top width at slab level in m.

Span in m	*Abutment*	*Peir*	*Water &land wings*	*Thickness of concrete*
upto 3	0·58	-	0·38	0·30
3 to 6	0·69	0·69	0·38	0·30
above 6	0·92	0·79	0·38	0·30

Bottom width and other details

(*a*) **Wings.** The top width of 0·38 m should be kept upto top of the banks and width of land wings at G.L. should be 0·5 H. The water face of the wing should be kept vertical above bed. Providing 150 mm offsets upto the level of the concrete H is the height of the wing above bed or G.L. as the case may be. (G.L. for land wing and bed for water wing.)

(*b*) **Abutments**

Upto 3 m span	width at bed level 0·6 H	H is the height of abutment above bed.
3 M to 6 m	width at bed level 0·7 H	
More than 6·0 m	width at bed level 0·8 H	

Water face of the abutment should be kept vert. For span more than 6·0 m it may be battered in 1 : 10. Below bed it can be sloped at 1/2 : 1 (H : V) upto cone. The earth face should be kept vertical below bed level width of the abutment should be equal to the width of decking slab, *u/s* and *d/s* faces of the abutment should be kept vertical upto the concrete level.

(*c*) **Peirs.** For spans upto 6·0 m faces of peirs shall be vertical, for above spans it can be battered to 1 : 12 one step of 60 mm be kept at bed level upto a depth of 30 m, thereafter a batter of ·3 : 4 (H : V) be provided on both faces. The ratio of height of the peir to its width should not exceed 6. The length of straight portion in u/s and d/s shall be 150 mm extra to the width of decking slab, thereafter equilateral 60° nose shall be provided.

(*d*) **Land wings.** Land wings should be segmented with a radius of double the distance from back end of abutment to the end of daula, subtending on angle of 30° at centre. Its foundation should be kept 0·60 m below G.L. and the triangular portion between abutment concrete and land wings conc. be filled with lean concrete 1 : 6 : 12.

(*e*) **Wearing coat.** It should have an average thickness of 75 mm in cc 1 : 1½ : 3.

(*f*) **Road level.** It must as per site conditions and should be at least 0·30 m above G.L.

(*g*) **Approach slab.** In case of VRB it should be brick on edge in full width of road way. In P.R.Bs and National Highways, reinforcement of 10 mm tor bars at 150 mm mesh at top and bottom of slab should be provided. It should be provided in full road width and length not exceeding 3·5 m or the edge of land wings. One side of it should be rested on abutment while the other side should rest on a toe wall resting on ground or on firm soil.

(*h*) Drainage pipes of 75 mm of steel should be provided on both edges of kerbs at every span or max. distance 3·0 m. (divide as per site conditions) projecting 75 mm below slab and flush with wearing coat on top.

(*i*) Construction joint must be provided at the junctions of land wing and abutments from ppt. to conc. of 12 mm thickness.

1·15. Salts in soils. All salts of Sodium and calcium chloride are harmful. Harmful salts are also called alkali salts. Sodium carbonate is the most harmful and also called as "Black alkali". If the percentage of total harmful salts does not exceed 0·18%, the yield from the soil is not generally effected, but if the salts exceed 0·25%, the soil becomes in fertile. The injurious Sodium salts should not be more than 0·10%. Sodium carbonate 0·25% of sodium chloride and 0·50% of sodium sulphide.

Potassium salts are good for crop. Carbonates and sulphates of calcium are not sufficiently soluble in water and are thus not harmful for crops.

Land Reclamation from salts

(*i*) **Leaching Process.** The land is continuously kept flooded with water which percolates downwards carrying salts with it. Open or covered drains are provided to carry away this percolated water. The surface drains also take away salts with it while drained. The soil must not allowed to dry as on drying the salts come up due to capillary action.

(*ii*) **Scraping Top Surface.** The top layers containing salts are scrapped in a thickness of 2 cm or more. It is not a permanent cure as salts again come up by capillary action.

(*iii*) **By Using Chemicals.** The harmful salt sodium carbonate is neutralized by addition of Calcium Sulphate *i.e.* gypsum in the soil.

(*iv*) **By Cultivation of Some Crops.** Berseem, guar, dhancha, Bajra and San etc. are some crops which absorb a bulk of alkaline salts and improve the yield of the field.

Soil conservation. Protection of soil from erosion by rain water.

1. By growing vegetation in the area including plantation.

2. By providing bunds across the flow of water.

13·2. DAMS

2·1. Earthen Dams

Foundation of earth dams. The foundation should be got cleared by all debris etc. up to a depth where a natural soil is reached. The roots of trees should be removed and pit so formed must be filled with good earth and compacted. The surface should be benched in *V* shapes or in the shape of saw teeths up to a depth which may give a good key to the dam section. The foundation may lie on the following types of soils.

1. **Rock.** The bed should be cleaned by water and air jets. The faults and fractures are grouted with a cement sand slurry. The benching in bed is also done in shape of jaw teeths.

2. **Sand and gravel.** "The foundation in the sand can be laid as detailed ahead. The only sand formation which are unsuitable are fine loose sand having a void ratio larger than the critical which may loose their shear strength and will liquidify and flow in saturated condition. The sands having more than critical void ratio must be compacted by pile driving or by penuematric rolling vibrators.

Critical void ratio. When the water in the non-cohesive saturated soil is drained out and it is subjected to shear it will either increase or reduce in volume. The dense soils increase while the loose soils decrease in volume. There is a stage of compaction at which there is neither decrease nor increase in volume. The voids in this stage are called 'in critical void condition'. The percentage of voids above the critical is known as super critical while less as subcritical.

Soil consolidation. In saturated pervious soils when water is drained out, soil particles take the space of water and the soil is thus reduced in volume. This process is called consolidation.

The samples of the soil in the foundation area are collected by auger brings at a regular distance apart or on controlling points. The water table is also located on boring strata charts.

3. **Clay.** Detailed ahead with effects of shear.

Materials for earthen dams. Auger boring samples are taken from the borrow area in a grid of regular interval apart. The dam section composed of only one type of soil are called **homogeneous sec.** The following criteria of a good soil for a dam is taken.

Sand and gravel. It is a good resistant of friction and shear but are no adhesive and too much permeable and therefore not good for dams, if used alone, therefore it is mixed with clay in certain proportions given below.

Clay. Non permeable, swells and cracks on drying and therefore not used alone in dam sections except in core walls.

Gravel and sand with 25 to 30 percent of clay or moorum is a good soil combinations for a dam section even without core walls.

The following proportions gives a good dam material :

Sand 0·02 to 2 mm size	60 to 80 percent
Silt 0·002 to 0·02 mm size	12 to 25 percent
Clay below 0·002 mm size	8 to 15 percent

The plasticity index may be taken as 8·5 to 12·0

Composition with aggregate

Sand retained 45 to 60 percent on 250 μ sieve)	50%
Clay (should be taken more if dry and less if wet)	17%
Aggregate (graded upto 12 mm)	33%

Earth from the area containing alkalies like **reh** or **peat** and **humous soil** must not be taken for a dam.

The top layer containing grain or any other undesirable material should be removed. The soil for a clayee core wall should be sufficient stiff. A wet ball of about 10 cm in dia. must not fall to pieces when emersed in water. In short a clay which is good for tile making is good for a core wall.

Testing porocity of the foundation. Dig one metre deep pits. Line their sides with impermeable clay. Fill the pit with water and keep full for 24 hours, and observe the rate of loss of water.

Design Procedure for an Earthen Dam

(1) **Safety against over-topping free board.** A conservative free board is given over the spill way crest. It must be as follows :

(*i*) Head over crest of spillway in max. flood + 1·5 times the wave height + A safety factor ranging 1 to 3.

(*ii*) For 4·5 m high dams = 1·5 m
4·5 m to 7·5 m = 1·8 m
Above 7·5 m = 2·1 m
} above full reservoir level (F.R.L.)

(*iii*) By stevension formula

$$h = 1{\cdot}5\sqrt{F} + 2{\cdot}5 - F^{1/4} \text{ for } F \text{ less than } 10$$

$$h = 1{\cdot}5\sqrt{F} \quad \text{for } F \text{ more than } 10$$

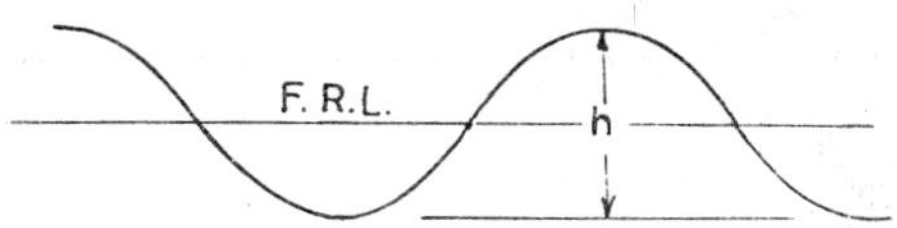

Fig. 13·12.

where h is the height of wave from crest to trough, F = fetch or longest straight reach of water behind the dam in nautical miles of 6076 ft. The height of the wave from still water F.R.L. (Full reservoir level) may be taken as 2/3 h, so the net. free board above the still water is taken as 3/4 $h + \dfrac{V^2}{2g}$ where V is velocity of wave propagation and is given by $V = 5 + 2h$ in ft/sec.

(*iv*) D.A. Molitor formula

$$h = 0{\cdot}032\sqrt{V.F} + 0{\cdot}763 - 0{\cdot}271\sqrt{F} \text{ when } F \text{ is less than 32 km.}$$

$$h = 0{\cdot}032\sqrt{V.F} + 0{\cdot}763 - 0{\cdot}271\sqrt{F} \text{ when } F \text{ is greater than 32 km.}$$

where V is wind velocity in km per hour and F is fetch length in km.

(*v*) As per USBR recommendations

Table 13·15.

Nature of spill way	*Height of Dam*	*Free board*
Free	Any	Min. 2 m and max. 3 over max. flood level
Controlled	Less than 60 m	2·5 m above top of gates
Controlled	Above 60 m	3·0 m above top of gates

Breaching Section. An earthen breaching section is provided which leads to a natural drain by a channel. In any emergency the breaching section which is lower and have less width can be cut and the water may pass to the drain without damaging the structure or area below the dam.

Top width. It is decided by the following emperical formula :

$B = H/5 + 3$ ...(1) $B = 0{\cdot}55H^{1/2} + 0{\cdot}2H$ ...(2)

$B = 1{\cdot}65 \times (H + 1{\cdot}5)^{1/2}$ ...(3) where B = Top width and H = height of dam.

The top width is also given by strange (given in the following articles).

Dimensions for minor bunds

Depth of water in m	*Breadth of water spread in m*	*Top width in m*	*Free board in m*
1·5 to 3	under 100	1·2	1·0
3 to 5	100-300	1·5	1·2
5 to 7	300-500	2·0	1·5
over 7	500 and above	2·8	2·0

A wide top has an advantage for future raising of bund.

(2) **Safety of the slopes.** The slopes are generally kept flatter than the natural angle of repose of the soil and still more flatter when the material is wet. The u/s faces are flatter than the d/s. The following rules can however be taken to decide the slopes of the dams.

Table 13·16. Strange Table

Height of dam above foundation	*Height of dam above high flood*	*Top width (m)*	*u/s slope*	*d/s slope*
upto 4·5 m	1·2-1·5 m	1·8	2 : 1	1½ : 1
upto 4·7 m	1·5-1·8 m	1·8	2½ : 1	1¾ : 1
upto 7·7 m	1·8 m	2·4	3 : 1	2 : 1
upto 15·2 m	2·1 m	3·0	3 : 1	2 : 1

Terzagi Table

Type of material	*u/s slope*	*d/s slope*
Homogeneous well graded material	2½ : 1	2 : 1
Homogeneous coarse silt	3 : 1	2½ : 1
Homogeneous silty clay (height less than 15 m)	2½ : 1	2 : 1
Homogeneous (height more than 15 m)	3 : 1	2½ : 1
Sand + gravel with clay core	3 : 1	2½ : 1
Sand + gravel with R.C. core wall	2½ : 1	2 : 1
Sandy soils	4 : 1	3 : 1

(3) **Safety against seepage.** The seepage line also known as (Phreatic line, saturation line, percolation line) shows the position of static water head in different sections of the dam which is equal to the atmospheric pressure. A capillery fringe over the seepage line has minor negative pressure and so can be neglected in design or a small margin is taken for it.

The seepage line must not fall out side the outer surface of the dam section, there must be a min. cover of 60 cm above it.

(*a*) **Seepage lines** form a shape of a parabola called the base parabola and can be represented by the formula $\sqrt{x^2 + y^2} = x + S$, where S is the focal distance. The saturation lines are shown firm in the Fig. 13·13.

The nature of the parabola is determined for the soil of which the dam is to be constructed. The position of the point of focus is fixed according to the type of the soil at the point of discharge of the slope gradient given ahead for different type of soils.

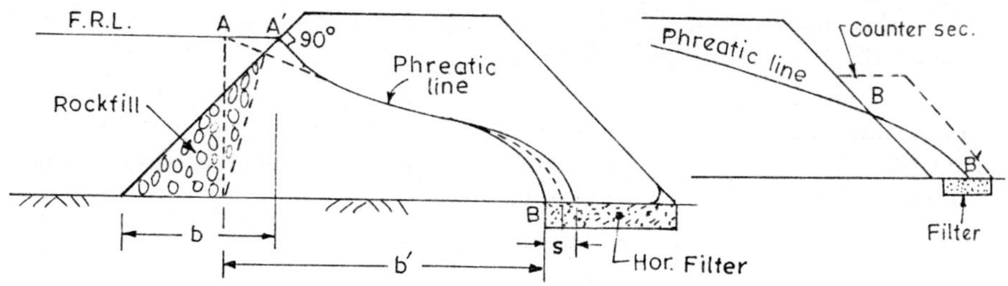

Fig. 13·13.

(*b*) **Equipotential lines** are the lines of parabolas having the same focus (shown dotted in the Fig. 13·14 (*c*)) which represents the line of equal static head and hence they cross the seepage line at an equal horizontal distance from base.

(*c*) In filter toe or rock fill toe the seepage lines drops vertically.

(*d*) The seepage line enters the dam section a bit u/s (at point *A*) of the point which the F.R.L. cuts the inner *B* slope at *A*′ equal to 0·3 times the distance from the top edge of the dam to the point *A*′. This point is known as the entrance point and is denoted by *A* in the Fig. 13·13.

(*e*) The seepage line from the point *A*′ enters normal to the slope and joins phreatic line in a smooth curve.

(*f*) The point at which the parabola emerges out the outer face of the slope is known as point of discharge and is marked by B in the figure. This point is also emerges a bit inside equal to the focal distance or to say at focus of the parabola.

(*g*) In order to bring the discharge point inside the dam section (If it falls out), a filter toe or a rock fill toe is provided. If the discharge point is too higher either the outer slope is flattened, or a puddle core wall is provided in which the seepage line slopes in a steeper slope and emerges at the toe of the core wall. The slope of the saturation line becomes vertical in the rock fill toe or filter toe and it travels horizontally in the horizontal filter. The width of the core wall at base is determined by the saturation gradient in core material.

(*h*) In all cases a horizontal filter is provided from the point at which the seepage line joins the base or to have a horizontal flow.

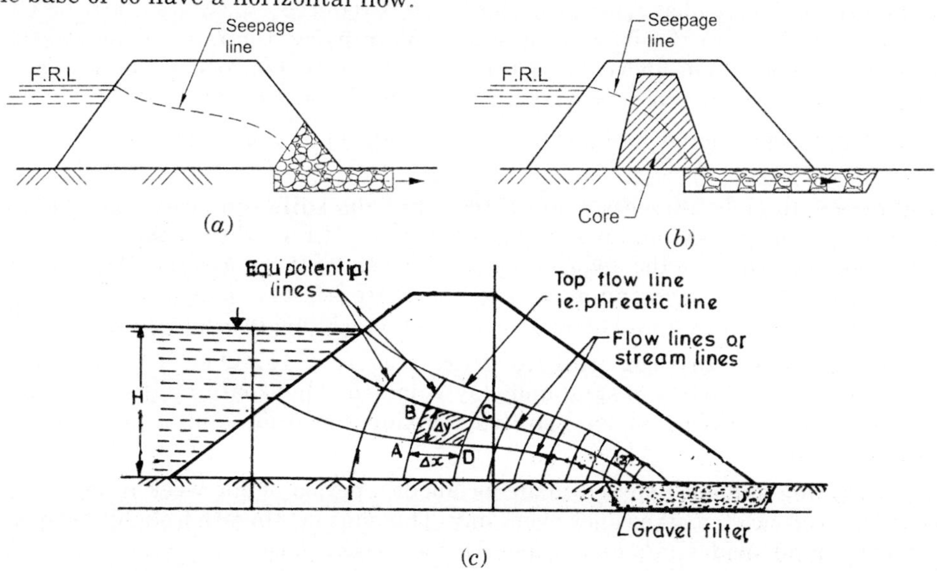

Fig. 13·14.

(*i*) When the foundation is laid on a pervious layer, though it does not effect the seepage line, yet a core wall as shown in the Fig. 13·15 (*a*) is provided at site from the top of the impervious layer to the point where it covers the seepage line.

Impervious clay blankets are also provided when the bottom impervious layer is too blow the foundation surface and thus the provision of such a deep core is not possible. These blankets are provided at the u/s toe in a length of about 10 × depth of water in a thickness of 1 m at dam section to a thickness of 0·5 m at the other end. (Fig. 13·15(*c*))

(*j*) In practice saturation line is taken as gradients as below with u/s and d/s corrections as discussed above.

Good clay	1 : 3	The focus of the parabola may be taken as the point of discharge of this saturation line to the base. The position of focus in core walls is also decided by the saturation gradient in core clay say 1 : 2 to 1 : 3.
Compacted soil	1 : 4	
Average soil sandy loam	1 : 5	
Bad soils	1 : 6	
Fine silt	1 : 6	
Fine sand	1 : 8	
Coarse sand	1 : 10	

In U.P. and Punjab following data is also adopted for hydraulic gradients

where	F.S.L. is 1·2 m above natural surface	1 : 4
	F.S.L. is 1·2 m to 1·50 m natural surface	1 : 5
	F.S.L. is more than 1·5 m natural surface	1 : 6

Note. The hydraulic gradient line must be covered by soil at least by 1·5 m in dams and 0·5 m in canal banks where it can be covered by providing counter berms.

Core walls. The core walls may be provided in the middle of the section or in the sides. The side core walls near the water face prevents percolation but it is open to cracking due to alternate wetting and drying due to fluctuation in the level of water.

The Puddle cores are 1·2 m to 2·5 m wide at top and sides are sloped in a slope of 1 : 12 or 1 : 10 to the ground level below which the thickness is reduced quickly to about 60 cm wider than top and carried down in the foundation upto 0·30 m below the impervious stratum. The top of core walls is kept 30 cm above the F.R.L. and 60 cm to 1 m below top of bank, where height of dam is more than 20 m a masonary core wall should be provided.

A water tight obstruction is known as **core wall** when above ground and as **cut off** when made below ground level.

Sand cores. In embankments made of **freacherous soils** sand cores may be provided. It is keyed 1 m below the ground and is kept upto F.R.L. or H.F.L. with a top width of 1 m to 2 m with side slopes according to the angle of repose of the sand. It reduces the danger of breaches due to cavities formed by burrowing animals or temperature cracks in clay as any hole developed is filled by the slip of sand into it and sand also does not crack due to temperature change.

Composition of clay for puddle. Pure clay is never used as it cracks due to temperature changes. 1 : 2 parts of sand and clay is mixed. Clay containing sodium carbonate is considered to be good. In place of sand shifted (screaned) moorum and in place of clay black cotton soil can be used.

The clay is dug and left exposed to air for about a period of one week in layers of 30 cm and should be watered two to three times every day. This mass is then thoroughly pugged either in a pugmill or by hand spades in a homogenous plastic mass. A core clay may be considered to have the same properties as a brick clay.

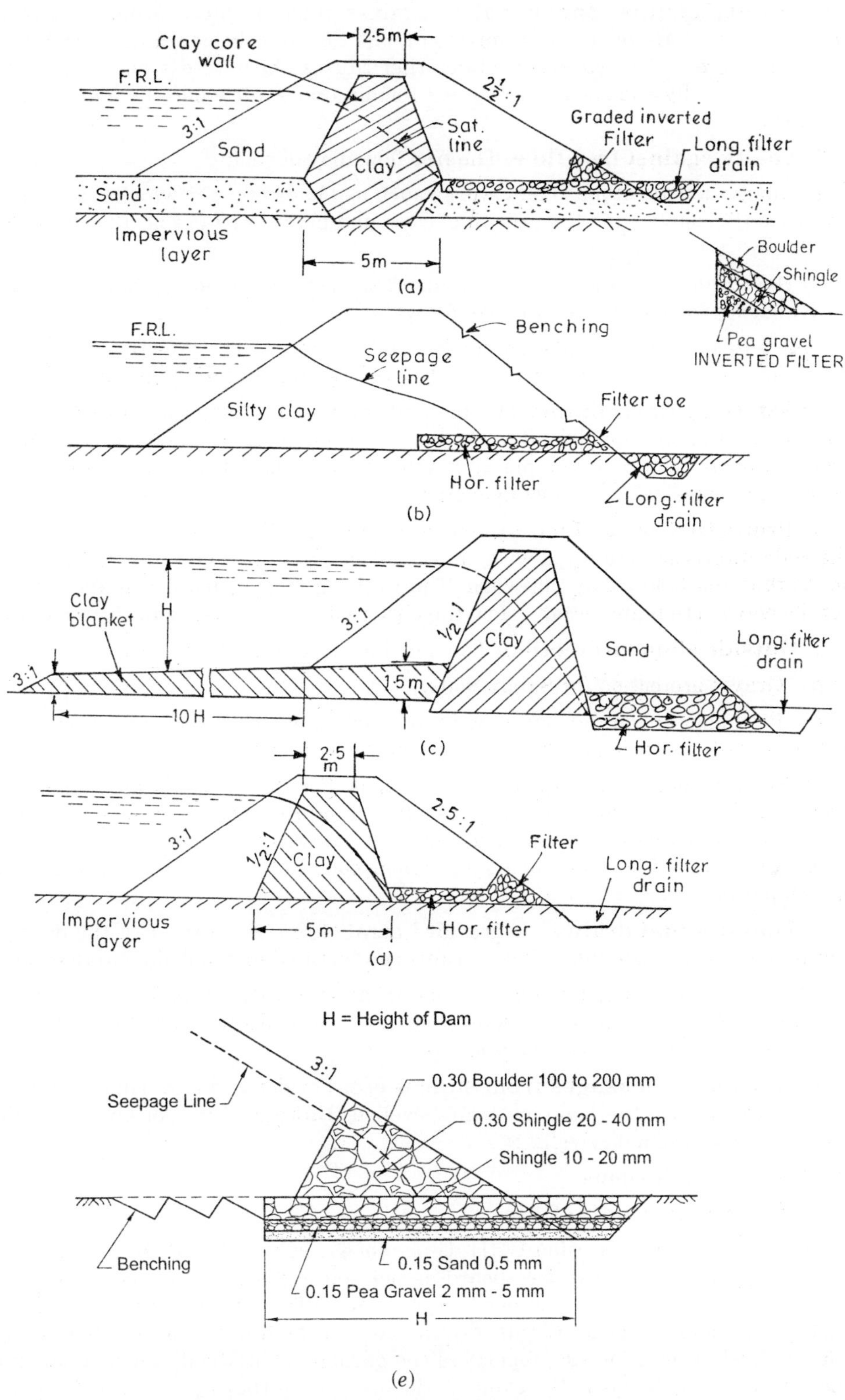

Fig. 13·15. Typical dam sections.

(4) **Safety against shear.** Safety against shear is more prominent in clayee soil foundations. Clayee soils have two components one due to cohesion and other due to friction. The former is more or less constant while other causes shear stress which must be checked, must increase gradually and shear stress must remain under allowable shear stress with a proper factor of safety.

(5) **Safety against free flow.** The free flow may develop :

(*a*) Along the side of masonary works such as heads etc., for which a proper bond to the masonry and sides is given and the growth of weed and plant must not be allowed at the masonry works.

(*b*) Due to decayed roots of the plants. The roots must not be burried in the bank as after decaying they form a source of travel for water.

(*c*) Due to animals like rats, porcupine and crocodiles. The growth of such animals must not be allowed in reservoirs. Owl posts must be provided for the safety against rats.

(6) **Safety against piping.** The toe and the toe of a horizontal filter is covered by an inverted filter so that any bubbling if takes place, the soil particles may not come out with them. If the percolation is seen at other places it must be covered by an inverted filter so that soil particles may not come out with flowing water.

(7) **Protection of u/s face by errosion action.** Side pitching is provided on the u/s face. The wide interistics are filled with small stones while the small interistics are filled with moorum, so that soil below may not wash. The pitching is provided 0·6 m above the maximum height of the wave action and 0·6 m below the outlet sill of the head or to the toe of the slope.

(8) **Outside slope protection.** The out side slope is provided with

(*a*) Gravel protection for Sandy Soils.

(*b*) Provision of counter berms with side drains which discharge either in the natural ground if meets with or through pipes to drain off the rain water.

(*c*) Providing doob grass turfing on the slopes. For this the soil upto a depth of 75 mm is loosened and if it is not suitable for dub grass growth a proper earth is imported and spreading over the slope in a thickness of 50 mm. The surface is watered to be moist and the grass is planted over it. This work should be done during early monsoons so that the grass may be rooted during the monsoon period.

(9) **Longitudinal drains** are provided parallel to the outer toe of the dam to drain off the water into a natural drainage. These drains can be filled to avoid sloughing of the toe.

(10) **Protection against water erosion at the outer toe.** The plantation of willow (Majnoo), Kikar, Kans (Sarkanda) is done about in 30 m width beyond the toe to safe the dam from any water errosion from out side torrents.

(11) **Closing of leakages from sluices etc.** Powdered dung, leaves are thrown u/s of the leakages which close the leaks on being swelled. **Bakola** (fibres of dhak) are filled in the leakages which close them on swelling.

Phreatic line in Earth Dams

Case I with horizontal filter

Take a homogenous section GHH′ G′ as shown in the Fig. 13·16 (*b*) with a horizontal filter FG′, taking side slopes and free board as per soil and site conditions. Take a point A on the F.R.L. such as $AB = 0{\cdot}3\ HB$ (As per Cassa grande). The phreatic line is considered to be a parabola having the base GG' and focus F (inner edge of the filter). The equation of the parabola can be determined from the basic property of the parabola, viz. the distance of any point $P(x, y)$ on the parabola from its focus is the same as the distance of that point $P(x, y)$ from a line called directrix. Taking the point F(Focus) as the origin the equation of the parabola can be written as

AB 0.3 HB

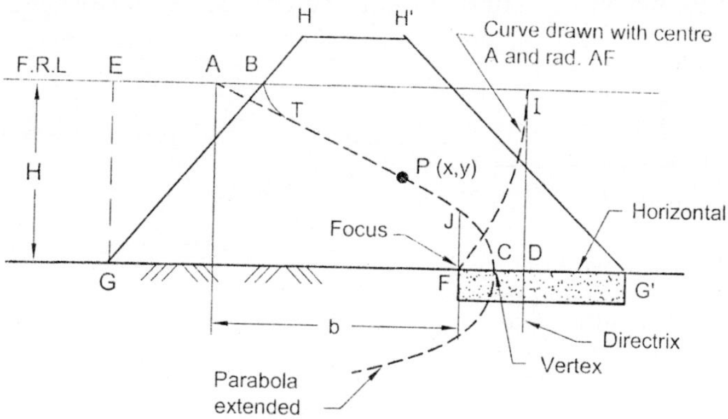

Fig. 13·16. Phreatic line, dam with horizontal filter & homogeneous

$$\sqrt{x^2 + y^2} = x + FD$$

where FD is known as the focal distance and the vertical line through D is the directrix.

Let the distance from the point A to F (horizontal distance) be b, and the focal distance FD be S then the expression becomes

$$\sqrt{x^2 + y^2} = x + S \quad \text{or} \quad \sqrt{b^2 + H^2} = b + S \quad \text{or} \quad S = \sqrt{(b^2 + H^2)} - b$$

from which S can be calculated.

The focal distance S can also be measured by drawing the FI with centre A and radius AF so as to intersect the horizontal water surface produced at I. The centre point (C) of FD will be the vertex of the parabola. The rest of the parabola can be drawn by the equation $\sqrt{x^2 + y^2} = x + S$. Knowing S mark the curve BT, by joining BT such that BI is roughly perpendicular to slope line GB. Now the phreatic line is the curve $BTJC$.

The discharge can also be calculated by drawing the flownet as below by the formula

$$q = KS$$

where q = discharger, S = focal distance and K = coefficient of permeability.

Case II. Phreatic line with no filter. Toe and section Homogeneous. The procedure is the same as in 1st case, only the focus is taken on the outer toe of the section. In this case the phreatic line will go outside of the Dam Section causing sloughing and remains saturated. The base parabola $BIJC$ will cut the d/s slope at J, extend beyond the dam toe upto the point C *i.e.* the vertex to the parabola. The seepage line will however emerge at K, meeting the d/s face tangent-

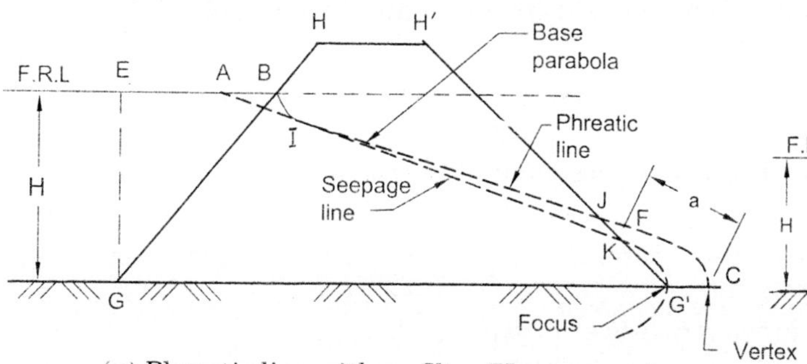

(*a*) Phreatic line with no filter (Homogenous).

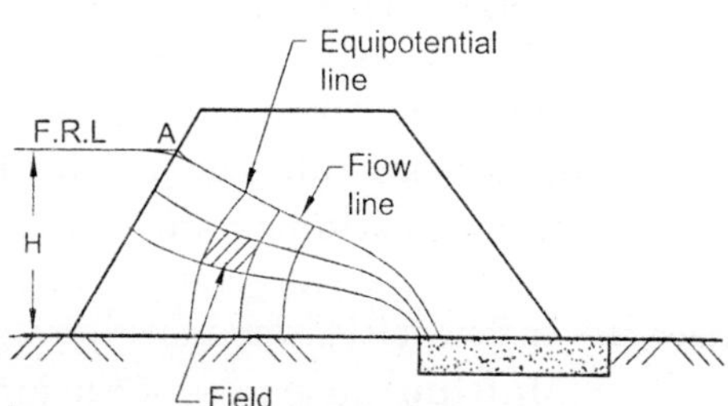

(*b*) Flownet in earthen dam.

Fig. 13·17.

ially there. The portion *KF* is known as the discharge face and always remains saturated. The correction *JK* say (Δa) by which the parabola is to be shifted downward can be determined as follows –

$$\Delta a = (a + \Delta a)\left[\frac{180° - \alpha°}{400°}\right]$$

α *in degrees*	$\dfrac{\Delta a}{a + \Delta a}$	*Remarks*
30	0·36	Intermediate values can be interpolated as read out from the graph plotted between α and $\dfrac{\Delta a}{a + \Delta a}$ with the values given here
60	0·32	
90	0·26	
120	0·18	
130	0·16	
150	0·10	
180	0·0	

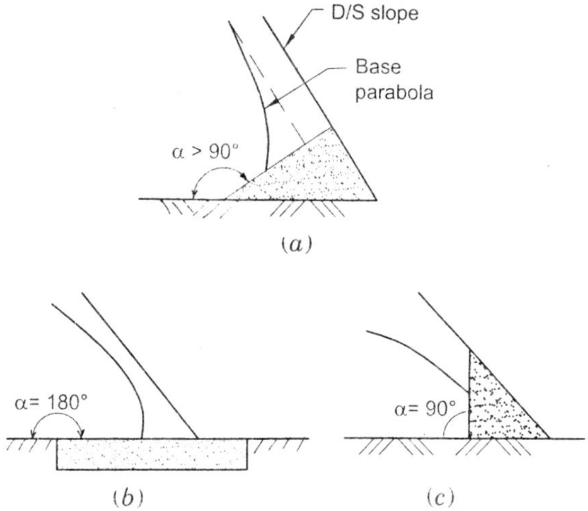

Fig. 13·18. Various type of discharge faces.

Analytical methods for determining the position of point *K*.

Case (*a*) when α<30°

$$a = \frac{b'}{\cos\alpha} - \sqrt{\frac{b'^2}{\cos^2\alpha} - \frac{H^2}{\sin^2\alpha}}$$

Values of *a*, *b*′, α and *H*, we defined in the Fig. 13·19 (*a*).

Case (*b*) when α is between 30° – 60°

$$a = \sqrt{b^2 + H^2} - \sqrt{b^2 - H^2 \cot\alpha}$$

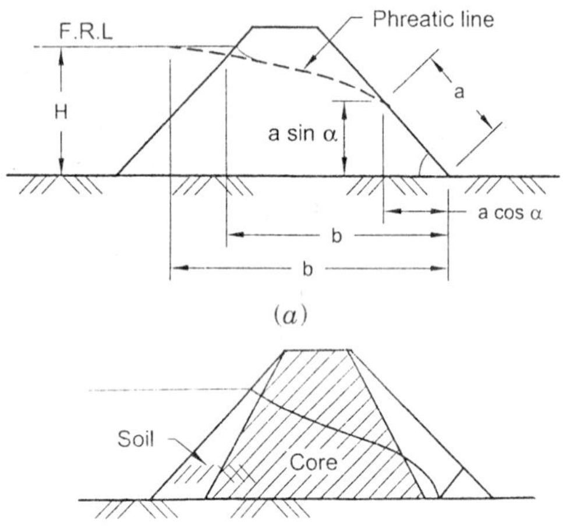

Fig. 13·19.

Case III. Phreatic line for a Zoned Section

In this case a zoned section having a central impervious core, such as shown in the Fig. 13·19 (*b*), the effect of the outer zone can be neglected altogether.

The focus of the base parabola will therefore be located at the d/s toe of the core. The phreatic line can then be drawn as usual freehand, correctness required at suitable places.

2·2. Storage reservoirs

Dams are constructed to create lakes or reservoirs behind themselves, according to the purpose, these reservoirs are classified in the following categories.

They are also called as impounding or river reservoirs.

1. **Conservation or storage**

2. **Flood control.** Storage reservoirs or detension basins ; Retarding basins or retarding reservoirs or flow mitigation reservoirs.

3. **Multipurpose** in which hydroelectric power is generated.

1. **Conservation reservoirs.** Conservation storage is meant to conserve or to save the surplus water brought down by a river during the period when the supply exceeds the current

demand, for utilisation later on during periods when demand outstrips natural flow of the river. Conservation of water may be required for any one or more of the purposes like irrigation hydroelectric power, navigation, water supply to towns or industries and recreation etc.

2. **Flood control.** The aim of the flood control storage is to hold over some of the flood waters of a river when the discharge rate reaches a storage likely to cause damage in the valley down stream and to release them gradually at a safe rate when the flood recedes. Such storage dams are also called as pick up retarding basins or detension basins.

3. **Multipurpose or Hydropower dams.** By such reservoirs which are stored to a high elevation, the potential so achieved is used for generation of hydro-power together with the above purposes of irrigation and flood protection.

Selection of a site for a dam. Storage can obviously be obtained by constructing a barrier across a depression receiving run off from a considerable catchment or across a well defined stream. For economic feasibility of a storage project it is necessary that the length of the barrier or dam should be as small as possible and for a given height, it should store the max. volume of water. It therefore follows that the primary consideration for locating a dam is that the river valley at the site should be relatively narrow, but should open out u/s to provide a large basin for a reservoir. The configuration of contours required for such a site will follow a general pattern similar to that shown in the fig. Other requirements for a good dam site is as below.

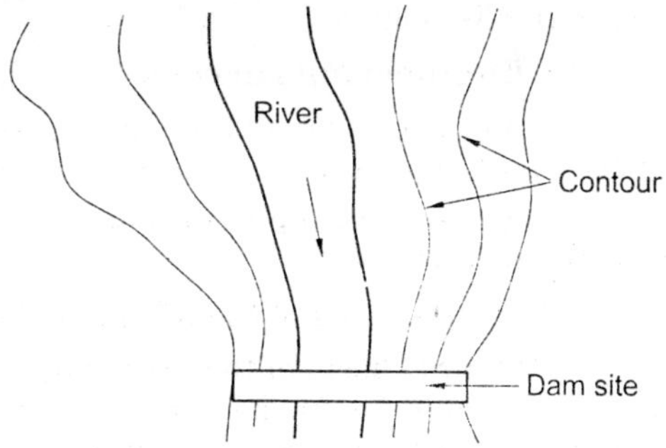

Fig. 13·20.

(1) **Suitable foundations.** For a concrete or masonry dam, solid rock at the surface or within a reasonable depth below it is essential. On other formations the height such dams is limited to about 15 metres.

Rockfill and earthen dams would have more flexible foundation requirements. The cost of dam in such cases is materially effected.

(2) A major portion of the dam should be on the higher contours than the river valley, so as to save its cost and to have a proper drainage.

(3) **A suitable site for a spillway** should be available. Spillway is a structure which is provided to pass the surplus water to the river or to any other drainage after filling the maximum capacity of the reservoir. The best site is that at which the 'gorge' (a narrow valley with steep high banks) portion is separated from the flow by a hillock with its surface above the top of the dam (see Fig. 13·21). If such confirmation is available, the spill way section can be built independently of the dam. At such a site either the flank may be used to provide a separate spill way and the main valley spanned by an earthen similar dam, or the spillway may be provided together with a concrete dam in the main gorge, while the flanks are built in earth at low cost.

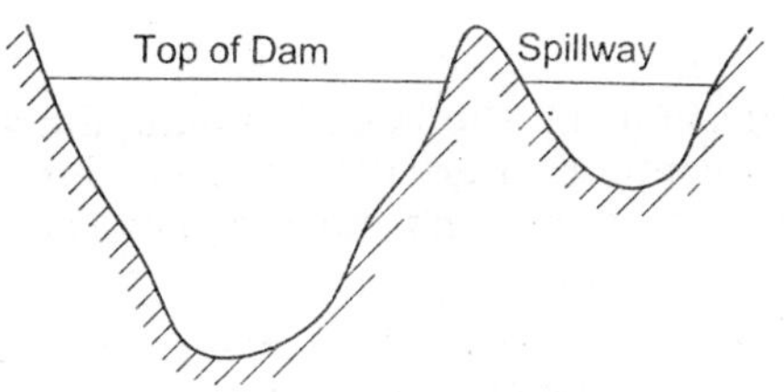

Fig. 13·21.

(4) **Materials.** The construction materials such as, aggregate, stones and sand etc. should be available in the vicinity of the work. However the cement may be collected from some neighbouring cement factory. If the lime stone is available nearby either the lime can be used in construction or a mini cement factory can be installed nearby the lime stone rocks.

In case of earthen dams the problem of construction material is limited.

(5) **The rim of the reservoir basin should be watertight** so that the collected water

may not pass away from the pervious basin. For this purpose some times a treatment of waterproofing materials is done to make the surface watertight.

(6) **The property and land submerged must not be valuable** in comparison to the benefits achieved by the dam.

(7) **There must be a rail or road** construction in the vicinity of the construction sites.

(8) **There must be a suitable site for the dwellings** of the workers and must have a site for a proper storage of the construction materials.

Investigation and planning of the dam projects. For this purpose following type of invesitgation is required :

(1) **Engineering surveys.** The following surveys are done for this purpose.

(*a*) A contour plan of the entire reservoir area together with its catchments are prepared. As a reconnaissance survey of India maps may be consulted.

(*b*) A map showing locations of railway and road lines also showing location of factories etc. should be prepared.

(*c*) Cross-section of the u/s sides should also be taken.

(*d*) Shajra sheets of the area should be procured from the revenue records. The spot levels of *x*-section should be marked on these sheets. By the help of these levels on the sajra sheets, the catchment area and the area submerged can be marked by different coloured wool threads.

2. **Geological investigations.** The exploration work for any important dam project has an important geological aspect. The geological investigation is required for determining (*a*) The suitability of foundation (*b*) The watertightness of the rock or soil concerned. (*c*) Location of quaries for construction materials. A program of sub surface exploration is made with an engineering geologist for the exploration work in which soil samples, of borings in case of soils and drill cores in case of rocks are collected, by which the suitability of foundation and building materials are find out on the basis of which the designs are prepared. For this purpose diamond core drilling and side drifts are explored in rocky portions.

3. **Hydrological survey.** In the hydrological survey following investigations are done :

(*a*) The discharge of the river is measured regularly during the whole year, and the past records are collected from the concerning departments such as State Irrigation Deptt. or Central Water and Power Commission.

(*b*) The rain fall record is collected from the concerning departments such as state irrigation and metrological department by which the probable run off can be estimated.

Estimation of capacity and area submerged

Calculation of capacity

(*a*) **By contours.** The contour interval required depends on the height of dam and side slopes in the basin. For the map of the reservoir area a contour interval of 3 m for dams of moderate height would normally be sufficient while for high dams and steep slopes contour interval of 5 m to 6 m would be acceptable.

From the contoured map of the reservoir area, the water spread of the reservoir at any elevation is directly determined by measuring the area at that contour by a planimeter (refer Estimating chapter). The water spread at various elevation may then be plotted as an area submerged curve for reference (Fig. 13·22). The capacity curve may be determined by taking contour areas at equal intervals and summing up by trapezoidal or Simpson's rule. According to the former the volume V, between two contour at an interval H and having areas A_1 and A_2 is given by

$V = H/3\,(A_1 + A_2 + \sqrt{A_1 A_2}\,)$. According to the latter, the volume between any odd number of contour is given by

$V = H/6$ (Twice the area of odd contour + four times the area of the even contour–area of the 1st and last contour.

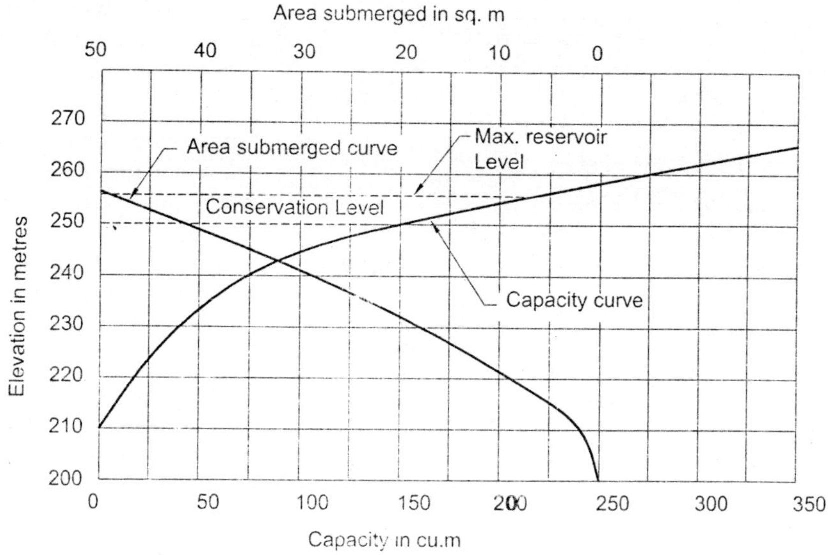

Fig. 13·22. Elevation v/s capacity and area submerged curve.

The area can be computed either by planimeter or by plotting on graph sheets and then counting the squares of the graph. The area can also be computed by Simpson or the trapezoidal rule as described earlier.

The volume upto various elevations having been determined as above, they are plotted in the form of a 'Capacity curve' showing the capacitv of the reservoir below different elevations. The capacity is measured in million cu. metres. The capacity in million cubic metre directly indicate the irrigation potentiality of the stored water.

The map of the reservoir area also indicates the land and property to be submerged under the reservoir and enables estimation of compensation to be paid to the owners. The time schedule according to which they must be moved as water is gradually headed up behind the dam.

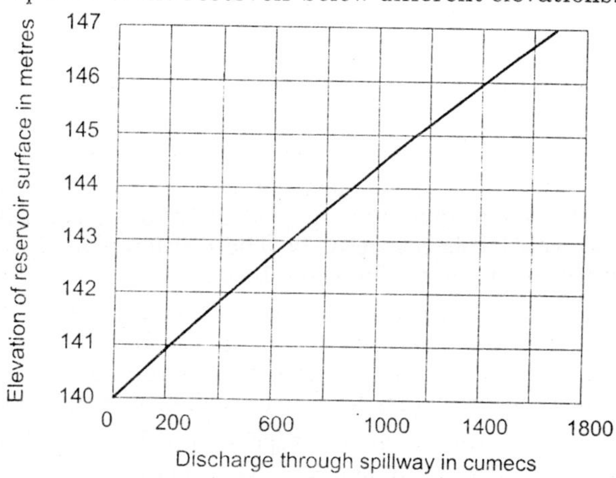

Fig. 13·23. Elevation-outflow curve

Flood routing. The following three curves should be available for carrying out the computations on trial and error method of reservoir routing.

(*a*) The inflow flood hydrograph (Fig. No. 13·24)

(*b*) The capacity and the area curve u/s elevation. (Fig. 13·22)

(*c*) Elevation outflow curve. (Fig. 13·23)

Steps involved in computation

(*i*) Divide the inflow flood hydrograph into a number of small intervals. The time interval should be so chosen, as not to miss the peak values.

(*ii*) Fix the normal pool level at which the spill way crest is provided and the level at which the flood enters the reservoir ; the two are generally taken to be the same, as it is assumed that at this worst design flood enters the reservoir only after the reservoir is full up to the normal pool level.

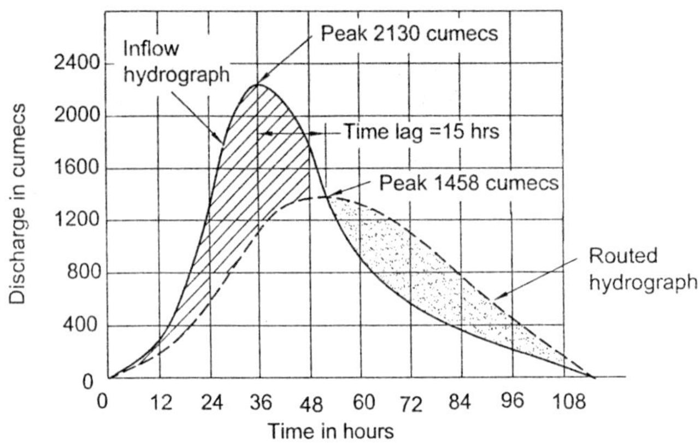

Fig. 13·24. Hydrograph showing flood and routed flood

(*iii*) Work out the spill way and the outlet discharge rating curves (Fig. 13·24).

(*iv*) Work out the elevation capacity curve for the reservoir from the elevation area curve, if the former is not given, using cone formula

i.e. $V = \Sigma \frac{h}{3}(A_1 + A_2 + \sqrt{A_1 A_2})$

where h is the contour interval.

(*v*) Start with the Ist interval and compute the total inflow during the interval by multiplying the average inflow rate at the beginning and the end of the interval, with the period of the interval.

$$I_v = \frac{I_1 + I_2}{2} \times t$$

where I_1, I_2, I_v = rate of inflow at the start of the interval, I_2 is the rate inflow at the end of the interval and I_v is the rate of average inflow volume during the interval respectively

t = Duration of interval.

(*vi*) Compute the total outflow during the interval

$$O_v = \frac{O_1 + O_2}{2} \times t$$

where O_1, O_2 and O_v are the outflow rates at the start of interval, end of interval and average outflow volume during the interval and t = Duration of interval.

(*vii*) The reservoir level at the start of the flood (start of the 1st interval) is known. Assume a trial value for the reservoir level at the end of interval.

(*viii*) Using the elevation storage curve for the reservoir, determine the storage S_1 and S_2 at the beginning and the end of the interval, corresponding to the known and the assumed reservoir levels respectively. Their differences $S_2 - S_1 = \Delta S$ represent the amount of flood stored in the reservoir during the interval.

(*ix*) Add the volume of outflow O_v obtained in step (*vii*) to the values of ΔS obtained in step (*viii*) and compare it with inflow volume I_v calculated in step (*v*). The two values must be equal ($I_v = O_v + \Delta S$). If this is so the assumed reservoir level is correct, otherwise change it and repeat the procedure let this coincidence is obtained.

(*x*) All the above steps should be repeated for other time intervals, till the entire flood is routed or still further, till the reservoir level returns to pre flood pool level.

(*xi*) Outflow ordinates are plotted so as to obtain the outflow hydrograph. The point at which it crosses the inflow hydrograph gives the peak out flow rate. From this time, the rate of flow begins to fall due to decrease in the flow rate.

(*xii*) The time lag between the two peaks is evaluated to give the time lag. The whole of the operation is tabulated in Table no. 13·17.

This flood approaches a reservoir with an uncontrolled spill way the rest of which is kept at R.L. 140·0 m.

The outflow hydrograph is plotted from col. (7) of the above Table no. 13·17 and as shown in Fig. 13·24 by the dotted curve. The point at which it intersects the inflow hydrograph, represents the peak of the routed flood. The peak of outflow flood works out to be 1458 cumecs while the peak of the inflow flood was 2130 cumecs. The time lag is found to be 15 hours (Fig. 13·24) the max. reservoir level is found as 1441·8.

Table 13·17.

Time from start, Hrs.	*Time interval (t), Hrs.*	*Reservoir elevation at the beginning of interval*	*Inflow at start of interval (I.L.)*	*Inflow at the end of interval (I_2)*	*Val. of inflow during the interval* $I_V = (I_i + I_2)/2$	*Outflow at the start of interval (O_1)*	*Trial reservoir elevation at the end of interval*	*Outflow at the end of interval (O_2)*	*Mean outflow vol. (O_V) =*	*Storage capacity at start of interval (S_1)*	*Storage capacity at end of interval (S_2)*	*Change in storage during the interval* $\Delta S = (S_2 - S_1)$	*Outflow volume and change in storage ; ($O_V + \Delta S$)*	*Compare $O_V + \Delta S$ with I_V i.e. col. (14) with col. (6) and Remarks*
1	2	3	4	5	6	7	8	9	10	11	12	13	14	15
Hours	Hours	m	I_1 m³/s	I_2 M. m³	I M.m³	O_1 m³/s	m	O_2 m³/sec.	O_v M/m³	S_1 reck-ned. over spillway crest M. m³	S_2 M. m³	$(S_2 - S_1)$ *i.e.* (ΔS) M.m³	$O_v + \Delta S$ M.m³	whether $(O_v + \Delta S)$ is large or small as compared to (I_v)
For example :														
0-6	6	140	0·0	50	0·54	0·0	140·1 140·03	5·67 0·88	0·06 0·01	0·0	1·2 0·525	1·2 0·525	1·26 0·535	Large and hence change the trial value OK

Same examples are given below for the observation :

Time for start, Hrs	0	6	12	18	24	30	36	42	48	51	60	66	78	90	102	114
Discharge in cumecs	0	50	280	610	1290	1900	2130	1900	1600	144	1060	781	500	370	220	130

From the Fig. 13·24 it follows that the reservoir should be able to hold in storage the volume of water represented by hatched area between the two curves which represents the excess of inflow over outflow during the rising stage, which would then be gradually released during the falling stage. If the reservoir comes back to its orginal level, the total volume under the natural and the moderated hydrographs would be the same and the hatched area representing excess supply held in storage will be equal to the dotted area representing the volume released from storage.

Designing of the Reservoir Capacity

Catchment Yield. Long range run off from a catchment is called as *catchment yield.* The total yearly run-off expressed as the volume of water entering or passing the outlet point of the catchment is thus known as the catchment yield and is expressed in Mm^3 or Mha.m.

The annual yield of the catchment upto the site of a reservoir, located at the given point along a river will thus indicate the quantum of water that will annually enter the reservoir and will thus help in designing the capacity of the reservoir. This will also help to fix outflows from the reservoir, since the outflows are dependent upon the inflows and the reservoir losses.

Reservoir yield. The amount of water that can be drawn from a reservoir in any specified time interval is called the reservoir yield, which naturally depend upon the inflow into the reservoir and the reservoir losses.

The annual inflow to the reservoir *i.e.* the catchment yield is represented by the mass curve of inflow, where as the inflow from the reservoir called the *reservoir yield* is represented by the mass demand line or the mass curve outflow. Both these curves decide the reservoir yield ignoring reservoir losses which can be accounted separately. The past rainfall data available in the catchment say of last 35 years is used to work out the maximum yield of the catchment. For example the worst rainfall year has a 100 m.ha.m. of yield which the maximum yield in the best rainfall year say 200 M.ha.m. There we can get the 100 ha.m. yield throughout the period while we can get only for one year the yield of 200 M.ha.m. Therefore dependability is only $\frac{1}{35} \times 100 = 3\%$ while for 100 M.ha.m. we can have 100% dependability.

Firm yield. The yield corresponding to the worst (most dry) or the most critical year record is called firm yield or the safe yield.

Secondary yield. Water available in excess of the firm yield during years of higher inflow is designated as secondary yield.

Dependable yield. In order to obtain an agreement, average media is generally adopted and an intermediate dependability percentage value (p) such as 50% or 75% may be used to compute the **dependable yield or the design yield.**

Computing the Dependable Catchment Yield. The dependable yield corresponding to a given dependability percentage p is given by the formula.

$m = N\frac{p}{100}$ for which the following procedure is adopted, in the expression N is the number of years for which the rainfall data is available while m is the order number.

Table 13·18.

Year	*Rainfall in cm*	*Year*	*Rainfall in cm*	*Year*	*Rainfall in cm*
1956	98	1968	76	1980	104
1957	100	1969	118	1981	120
1958	101	1970	86	1982	108
1959	99	1971	92	1983	102
1960	85	1972	96	1984	80
1961	112	1973	93	1985	109
1962	116	1974	88	1986	122
1963	78	1975	94	1987	115
1964	160	1976	107	1988	140
1965	66	1977	110	1989	138
1966	184	1978	208	1990	60
1967	90	1979	114		

The above data is arranged in the descending order mentioning several number.

Order No.	*Rainfall in descending order in cm*	*Order No.*	*Rainfall in descending order in cm*	*Order No.*	*Rainfall in descending order in cm*	*Order No.*	*Rainfall in descending order in cm*
1	208	10	115	19	101	28	88
2	184	11	114	20	100	29	86
3	160	12	112	21	99	30	85
4	140	13	110	22	98	31	80
5	138	14	109	23	96	32	78
6	122	15	108	24	94	33	76
7	120	16	107	25	93	34	66
8	118	17	104	26	92	35	60
9	116	18	102	27	90		

For example in the equation $m = P/100$ we compute m for 60/0 dependability

$$m = N\frac{p}{100} = 35 \times \frac{60}{100} = 21.$$

Now in the above table at Sl. no. 21 we get the rainfall as 99. So the value of $m = 99$

Similarly for the dependability of 75 we get $m = 35 \times \frac{75}{100} = 26.5$ therefore we get the rainfall between Sl. 26 and 27 in the ratio of $5/10 = 1/2 = \frac{92 + 90}{2} = 91$ cm.

Converting the dependable rainfall value into the dependable yield value

Some Emperical Relation and formulae are given by different workers, which are as below :

(1) Binnies percentages (2) Strange's tables (3) Barlow's Tables

(4) Lacey's Formula (5) Inglis Formula and (6) Khosla's formula.

Table 13·19. Binnies Monsoon Yield Percentages.

Monsoon rainfall p in cm	*Monsoon yield percentage*	*Monsoon rainfall p in cm*	*Monsoon yield percentage*	*Monsoon rainfall p in cm*	*Monsoon yield percentage*
25	7·0	85	31·0	122·5	43·7
30	9·0	90	33·0	125·0	44·4
35	11·0	95	35·0	127·5	45·0
40	13·0	100	37·0	130·0	45·6
45	15·0	102·5	37·9	132·5	46·2
50	17·0	105·0	38·7	135·0	46·8
55	19·0	107·5	39·5	137·5	47·3
60	21·0	110	40·3	140·0	47·9
65	23·0	112·5	41·0	142·5	48·4
70	25·0	115·0	41·7	145·0	49·0
75	27·0	117·5	42·4	147·5	49·5
80	29·0	120·0	43·1	150·0	50·0

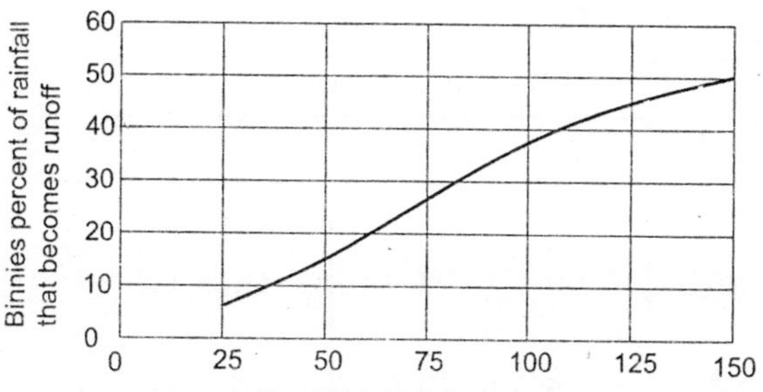

Fig. 13·25. Binnies monsoon rainfall runoff curve

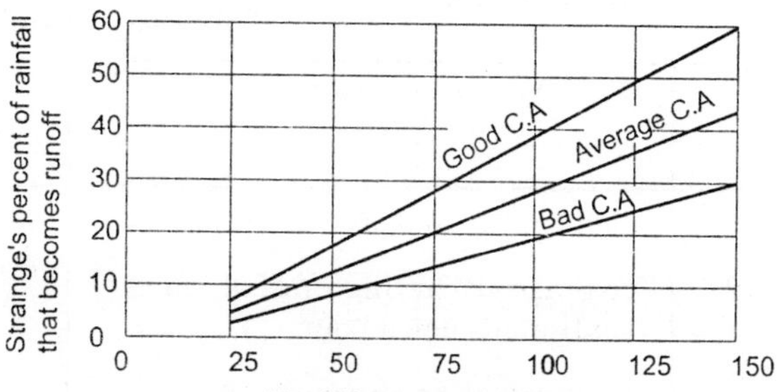

Fig. 13·26. Strange's monsoon rainfall runoff curve

Table 13·20. Stranges percentage Table. Good catchments are more and min. ; Average-intermediate type ; Bad-which give low yields.

Monsoon rain-fall in cm	*Runoff % age for catchments designated for*			*Monsoon Rainfal in cm*	*Runoff % age for catchment designated for*		
	Good	*Average*	*Bad*		*Good*	*Average*	*Bad*
25·0	4·3	3·2	2·1	107·5	40·9	30·6	20·4
30·0	6·2	4·6	3·1	110·0	42·0	31·5	21·0
35·0	8·3	6·2	4·1	112·5	43·1	32·3	21·5
40·0	10·5	7·8	5·2	115·0	44·3	33·2	22·1
45·0	12·8	9·6	6·4	117·5	45·4	34·0	23·2
50·0	15·0	11·3	7·5	120·0	46·5	34·8	23·8
55·0	17·3	12·9	8·6	122·5	47·6	35·7	23·8
60·0	18·5	14·6	9·7	125·0	48·8	36·6	24·4
65·0	21·8	16·3	10·9	127·5	49·9	37·4	24·9
70·0	24·0	18·0	12·0	130·0	51·0	38·2	25·5
75·0	26·3	19·7	13·1	132·5	52·0	39·0	26·0
80·0	28·5	21·3	14·2	135·0	53·3	39·9	26·6
85·0	30·0	23·1	15·4	137·5	54·4	40·8	27·2
90·0	33·0	24·7	16·5	140·0	55·5	41·6	27.7
95·0	35·3	26·4	17·6	142·5	56·6	42·4	28·3
100·0	37·5	28·1	18·7	145·0	57·8	43·3	28·9
102·5	38·5	28·9	19·3	147·5	58·9	44·1	29·4
105·0	39·5	29·8	19·9	150·0	60·0	45·0	30·0

Table 13·21. Barlow's Run off percentages.

S.No.	*Class of catchment*	*Description of the cathment*	*Run off percentage (K)*
1.	*A*	Flat cultivated absorbent soils	10
2.	*B*	Flat partly cultivated stiff soils	15
3.	*C*	Average catchment	20
4.	*D*	Hills and plains with little cultivation	25
5.	*E*	Very hilly and steep catchment with little or no cultivation	33

The above values of run off percentages are for the average type of monsoons and are to be modified by the application of the following coefficients according to the nature of season.

Values of Barlow's coefficient to be multiplied with *K* in the above Table to obtain true run off.

S. No.	*Nature of season*	*Class of catchment*				
		A	*B*	*C*	*D*	*E*
1.	Light rain, no heavy down pour	0·7	0·8	0·8	0·8	0·8
2.	Average or varying rainfall, no continuous down pour	1·0	1·0	1·0	1·0	1·0
3.	Continuous down pour	1·5	1·5	1·6	1·7	1·8

(4) **Lacey's Formula :** Yield $Q = \left[\dfrac{P}{\dfrac{1 + 304.8\ \text{m}}{Pn}}\right]$

where m = a constant called monsoon duration factor which is given in the table below.

n = a constant called catchment factor, the values of which are given for different classes of catchment (as defined by Barlow) Table below.

Table 13·22. Values of m (monsoon duration factor)

S. No.	*Duration of monsoon*	*factor m*
1.	Bed year	0·5
2.	Normal year	1·2
3.	Good year	1·5

Values of *n* (catchment factor)

S. No.	*Class and description of catchment*	*Value of n*
1.	*A.* Flat cutter value absorbent soils	0·25
2.	*B.* Flat partly cultivated stiff soils	0·60
3.	*C.* Average catchment	1·00
4.	*D.* Hills and plains with little cultivation	1·70
5.	*E.* Very hilly and steep catchments with little or no cultivation	3·45

(5) **Inglis Formula**

(*a*) For ghat areas with rainfall equalling or exceeding 200 cm

Yield = $(0{\cdot}85\,P - 30{\cdot}48)$ cm where P is rainfall in cm.

(*b*) For non-ghat areas with rainfall P less than 200 cm.

$$\text{Yield} = P\,\frac{(P - 17.78)}{2 - 54}\ \text{cm where } P \text{ is rainfall in cm}$$

(6) **Khosla's Formula :**

$$\text{Yield } Q = P - 0{\cdot}48\,T_m$$

where Q = yield in cm;
P = rainfall in cm;
T_m = mean annual temperature of the area

Based on recent researches. It can be applied in whole of the country, without bothering for the region.

Table 13·23. Dependable discharge values obtained from the river.

S. No.	*Daily mean discharge m³/s range*	*Year 1981 No. of days the flow belongs in the given range (class interval)*	*Year 1982 No. of days the flow equalled the class range of col. (2)*	*Year 1983 of days the flow alled the range of use in col. (2)*
1	2	3	4	5
1.	100-90·1	0	6	10
2.	90-80·1	16	19	16

Table contd...

Table contd...

S. No.	*Daily mean discharge m³/s range*	*Year 1981 No. of days the flow belongs in the given range (class interval)*	*Year 1982 No. of days the flow equalled the class range of col.(2)*	*Year 1983 No. of days the flow equalled the range use in col. (2)*
3.	80-70·1	27	25	38
4.	70-60·1	21	60	67
5.	60-50·1	43	51	58
6.	50-40·1	59	38	38
7.	40-30·1	64	29	70
8.	30-20·1	22	48	29
9.	20-10·1	59	63	26
10.	10-0 (negligible)	54	26	13

Note : The daily flows in a river for three consecutive years are given in the table by class interval along with the number of days the flow belongs to this class, are 50% and 75% dependable flows (annual and daily) for the river.

With the given daily flows, we will calculate the annual yields for the 3 given years as compared in the table below. Since daily discharge figures are given in range (interval), mid value of range (interval) can be assumed to be the flow discharge, which when multiplied by no. of days, will give yield during these days, summation of yield values over 365 days will give annual yield as shown in table below, which is self explanatory.

Table 13·24.

			Year 1981		*Year 1982*		*Year 1983*	
S. No.	*Daily mean discharge range (m³/s) in descending order*	*Mean value of daily discharge range*	*No. of days for which the flow equalled to that given in col. (3)*	*Yield (mm³) = [(3) × (4) × 86400/10⁶ (3) × (4) × 0·0864]*	*No. of days for which flow equalled to that of col. (3)*	*Yield (mm³) = ·00864 × col. (3) × col. (6)*	*No. of days for which flow equalled to that of col. (3)*	*Yield (mm³) = 0·0864 × col. (3) × col. (8)*
(1)	(2)	(3)	(4)	(5)	(6)	(7)	(8)	(9)
1.	100-90·1	95·05	0	0	6	49·55	10	82·08
2.	90-80·1	85·05	16	117·50	19	139·54	16	117·50
3.	80-70·1	75·05	27	174·96	25	162·0	38	246·24
4.	70-60·1	65·05	21	117·94	60	336·96	67	376·27
5.	60-50·1	55·05	43	204·34	51	242·35	58	275·62
6.	50-40·1	45·05	59	229·39	38	147·77	38	147·74
7.	40-30·1	35·05	64	193·54	29	87·70	70	211·60
8.	30-20·1	25·05	22	47·52	48	103·68	29	62·64
9.	20-10·1	15·05	59	74·34	63	81·65	26	33·70
10.	10-Negligible	5·05	54	23·33	26	11·23	13	5·62
	Σ = Total		365	1182·86	365	1361·98	365	1539·09

The river yield for 3 years is calculated by summing of Col. (5), (7) and (9). Let these yields are arranged in descending order.

Year	*Annual yield* (mm^3)	*Order No. m*
1983	1559·09	1
1982	1361·98	2
1981	1182·86	3
		$N = 3$

Order no. m for $p\%$ dependability $= \dfrac{P}{100} \times N$.

(*i*) Order no. for 75% dependability $= \dfrac{75}{100} \times 3 = 2{\cdot}25$

since order no. 2·25 is not an integer, the mean value of yield corresponding to Sl. No. 2 and 3 will be taken as yield for 75% dependability given as

$$= \left(\frac{1361.9 + 1182.86}{2}\right) = 1272{\cdot}42 \text{ M.m}^3$$

Hence annual flow with 75% dependability = 1272·43 M.m^3

Daily flood discharge with 75% dependability

$$= \frac{1272{\cdot}48 \times 10^6}{365 \times 864{\cdot}00} \text{ M}^3\text{/sec.} = (40{\cdot}34)^3 \text{ m}^3\text{/sec.}$$

(*ii*) Order No. for 50% dependability $= \dfrac{P}{100} \times N = \dfrac{50}{100} \times 3 = 1{\cdot}5$

since No. 1·5 is not integer. The mean value of yield corresponding to order no. 1 and 2 shall be taken as the yield of 50% dependability given as

$$= \frac{1559{\cdot}09 + 1361{\cdot}98}{2} = 1460{\cdot}54 \text{ M.m}^3$$

Hence annual flow for 50% dependability $= \dfrac{1460{\cdot}54 \times 10^6}{365 \times 86400} \text{ m}^3\text{/sec.} = 46{\cdot}31 \text{ m}^3\text{/sec.}$

Fixing the Reservoir Capacity for the Computed Value of the Dependable Yield of the Reservoir Catchment

After deciding the dependable yield for proposed reservoir the reservoir capacity is decided as follows :

The annual water demand is computed by estimating the crop water requirement including transit losses and any other water demand required to meet the water supply needs or the d/s requirement of water release if any, the reservoir losses at about 15% of the water demand is then added to obtain the live or the net storage required to meet the given demand. Dead storage is now added to this live storage to obtain the gross storage required to meet the demand. The reservoir capacity however cannot exceed the catchment yield (inflow into a reservoir) and hence the reservoir capacity is fixed at a value which is lesser of the value of the assessed gross storage required to meet the demand and the assessed dependable yield for the reservoir site. The full tank level (F.T.L) or the full reservoir level (F.R.L.) is finally computed for the elevation capacity curves.

The dead storage level or the dead storage required in the above computation is usually fixed at higher of the following values.

(*a*) Dead storage = rate of silting × life of the reservoir.

(*b*) Dead storage = 10% of gross storage or net water demand.

(*c*) Dead storage level being equal to the full supply level of the soil offtaking canal at the reservoir site.

The reservoir capacity, the reservoir inflow and the outflow from the reservoir are governed by the storage equation as below.

Inflow – outflow – losses = Increase in storage.

If the inflow data is not available for the past years, a nearby catchment the data of which is available can be taken as a guide and the new rain gauge station and the discharge site u/s of the proposed dam is established and the information now obtained can be compared from the past records. So that any difference can be located.

Estimation of required storage capacity. A flow hydrograph for the stream at the dam site having been obtained and plotted for a large number of previous years (roughly 25 to 30 yrs.), it is possible to determine the storage requirement for a given outflow pattern to be maintained during all these years. The best method of doing so is with the help of 'Mass curves'. Mass curves are plots of accmulated flow against time.

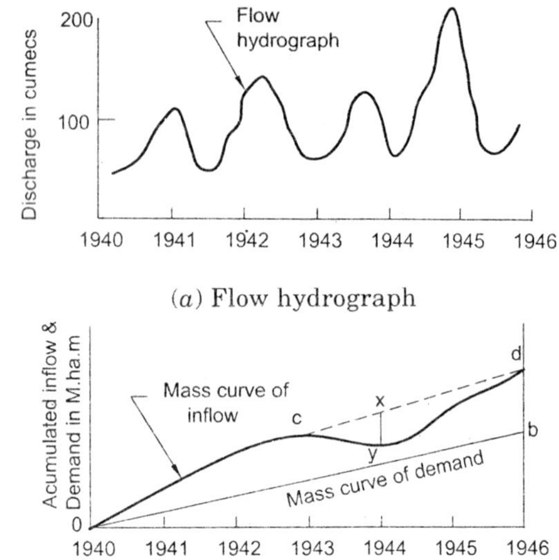

Fig. 13·27. Mass curve of inflow.

Fig. 13·27 (*a*) flow hydrograph and Fig. 13·27 (*b*) mass curve of inflow shows the discharge over time and the mass curve of inflow respectively.

The area under the 1st curve upto a given time is equal to the ordinate of the 2nd curve at the same time, necessary adjustment being made for the units and the scales of the two curves. Obviously, a mass curve must continuously rise as it shows accumulated inflow, if there were no inflow at all during some period it would be horizontal during that period, if there is a high rate of inflow, the curve rises steeply. Thus relatively dry periods are indicated as hollows on the mass curve. Similarly a mass curve of demand may be plotted by accumulating the required outflow. If a constant rate of discharge is required from the reservoir, the mass curve of demand would be a straight line rising from the origin. In Fig. (*b*) *od* represents the mass curve of inflow, while *ob* represents the mass curve of demand resulting from a constant rate of discharge. From an inspection of the mass curve of inflow, *cd* appears to be the driest period on record. From the beginning of this period at *c*, a line parallel to *ob*, the mass curve of demand is drawn to intersect the mass curve of inflow again at *d*. Then the largest vertical ordinate between this line and the mass inflow curve as indicated by *xy* on the figure represents the volume which must be held in storage to tide over this dry period. This is so because, assuming the reservoir to be full at c - there is a total inflow represented by the vertical distance between y and c and there is a total withdrawal represented by the vertical distance between x and c leaving a gap of volume represented by xy which must be met from storage. If there are other dry period indicate on the mass curve, the same procedure should be followed for each and the largest requirement of storage determined accordingly. The requirement of storage so obtained would be the net storage which must be available for utilisation and must be increased by the quantity lost by evaporation or seepage.

It is not necessary that the mass curve of demand should be a straight line. In fact, it would be seldom be so, as water would be withdrawn from the reservoir in such a way as to obtain maximum benefit from it, and this would practically always involve varying rates of withdrawal according to seasons, or according to available head which is determined by reservoir level at that time, or some other factors. If the demand is not constant, the mass curve of demand has to be computed from the hydrograph of demand in the same way as mass curve of inflow is computed from the inflow hydrograph. The accumulated volumes of outflow according to the pattern of demand upto a given time are plotted as ordinate against that time to obtain the mass curve of demand. The required storage capacity can again be obtained in the same way. From the beginning of a dry cycle, the mass curve of demand is superimposed as the *mass* curve of inflow till the two meet again and the largest vertical ordinate between the two gives the requirement of storage. (Fig. 13·28) shown to a larger scale the same dry cycle as represent by cd in Fig. (13·27 (b) while the mass curve of demand is now irregular. The requirement of net storage from this cycle is given by the largest vertical ordinate $x'y'$.

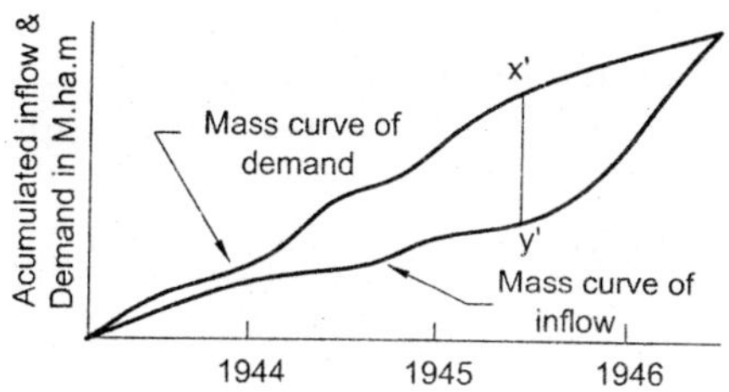

Fig. 13·28.

Reservoir losses. There is always some loss in a reservoir from absorption, percolation and evaporation, which are discussed as below :

Absorption losses will depend on the type of soil forming the reservoir basin. They may be quite large in the beginning but will gradually fall off as the pores get saturated and will not be a significant factor in planning.

Percolation or seepage losses are small in most cases, but they may be significant in some, where there may be outlets under the hills or under the base of the dam provided by continuous seams of porous strata or fractured rock, the reservoir basin should be carefully checked for water lightness by experts in geology and soil mechanics. If appreciable leakage is likely to take place the problem should be analysed as accurately as possible and allowed for an economic studies of the project.

Evaporation losses. The evaporation losses from a reservoir depends upon several factors such as water surface area, water depth, humidity, wind velocity, temperature, atmospheric pressure and quality of water. The evaporation loss from a reservoir under the given atmospheric conditions can be easily estimated by measuring the **standard pan evaporation** and multiplying the same by the pan coefficient.

The evaporation losses become very significant in a hot and humid country like India and realistic estimation of these losses is quite important. In northern and south-central India average losses are taken as below on mean exposed water surface area. (Table 13·25)

Table 13·25.

Month	*Losses in cm*	
	North India	*South and Central India*
January	7	10
February	9	10
March	13	18
April	16	23
May	27	25
June	24	18
July	18	15
August	14	15
September	14	15
October	13	13
November	9	10
December	8	10

The following controlling methods are also used :

1. Wind breakers
2. Covering of the water surface
3. Reduction in exposed surface area
4. Use of underground storage
5. Integrated operation of reservoirs
6. Uses of chemicals for retarding the evaporation

Reservoir Sedimentation. The sediment in the reservoirs are due to the erosion in the catchment as well as in the river itself.

1. **Sheet erosion.** It includes the erosion in the catchment due to rains, the water of which brings the eroded mass to the river by drains.

2. **Channel erosion.** It includes river bank erosion and transportation of this eroded material in the river itself.

Factors Affecting the Erodability of a Soil

(*i*) **Particle size of soil.** Larger the particle size lesser will be the erosion.

(*ii*) **Slope of land.** Greater the slope of land larger will be the erosion.

(*iii*) **Vegetation.** The thick will be the vegetation, lesser will be the erosion.

(*iv*) **Presence of salt and collodials in the soil.** The binding materials like Kaolinite, montmorillonite and biotite etc. do help on increasing the force of cohesion between the soil particles, thereby reducing the erobility of the soil.

(*v*) **Moisture content of the soil.** The greater the moisture content of the soil, the lesser is the erosion.

(*vi*) **Soil compaction.** The higher is the soil compaction the lesser is the erosion.

(*vii*) **Soil properties.** The characteristics of the soil, such as soil erosion texture, structure, stratification, permeability and imposition etc., do affects the soil binding, which in turn will neutralise to force of weathering agents.

(*viii*) **Human activities.** The mining, Agricultural ploughing and project etc. do increase the erosion.

(*ix*) **Rain fall.** Characteristics, the intensity and quatity of rainfall affects the erosion.

$$\text{Trap Efficiency } (\eta) = \frac{\text{Total sediment deposited in the reservoir}}{\text{Total sediment flowing in the river}}$$

Capacity inflow ratio (*f*) or $f = \eta\left(\frac{\text{Inflow\#}}{\text{Capacity}}\right)$

Silting control in reservoir. There are pre-construction and post-construction.

Preconstruction control. These control measures are adopted before or in duration of construction, they are as below.

(*i*) **Selection of dam site.** The silting depends upon the erosion caused in the catchment area and in the river itself. So the dam site should be selected by keeping this factor in mind.

(*ii*) **Reservoir design.** If the reservoir capacity is less than its average annual run off, thus leading to a considerable escape from the reservoir, the rate of silting is less than if the reservoir is capable of holding the entire annual runoff or more. Thus it would prolong the life of the reservoir if the dam is built lower in the 1st instance with allowance in its structural design for its being raised in stages as its capacity is encroached up to the silting, rather than providing the final capacity in the 1st instance.

The outlets in the dam should be adequate and distributed over different elevations.

(*iii*) **Construction of check dams.** Small dams must be constructed u/s of the new proposed dam which may trap a large amount of sediment in them before reaching the proposed dam.

(*iv*) **Vegetation screens.** Vegetation screen may be developed in the catchment area as well as in the u/s reaches of the river. It will check the flow of the sediment to the dam and also will help in the check of erosion in the catchment.

(*v*) **Under Sluices** must be constructed so that heavier silt may pass through them and a clearer water may be stored in the live storage. The sluices may be utilised in flushing out the silt deposits in the reservoirs.

Post construction control. (*i*) It must be tried that the surplus flood water must pass during floods as it is loaded with a major part of silt.

(*ii*) Mechanical stirring of the sediment so that it may remain in motion and could not be settle in bed and pass will flow of water.

(*iii*) Soil conservation program is made in the catchment and it should be planted to avoid soil erosion. In the soil conservation program cross bunds are made to check erosion and grass is planted and grazing of grass is controlled.

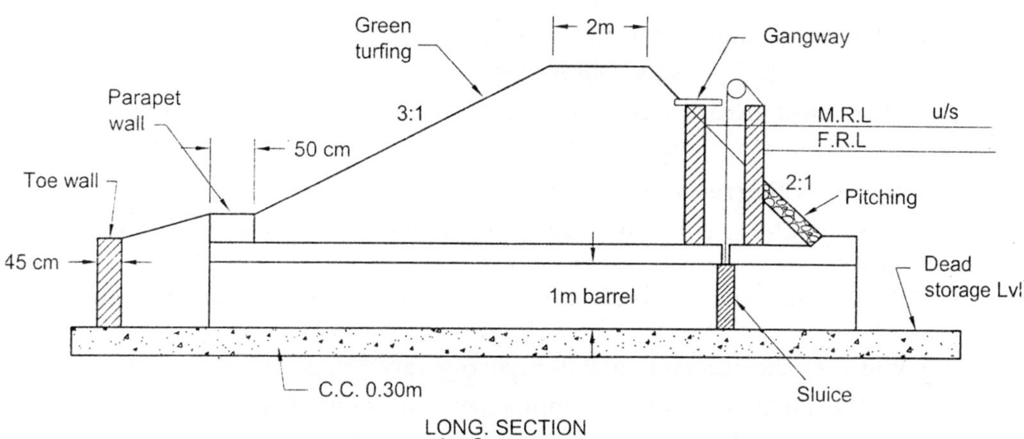

(*a*) **Long-section**

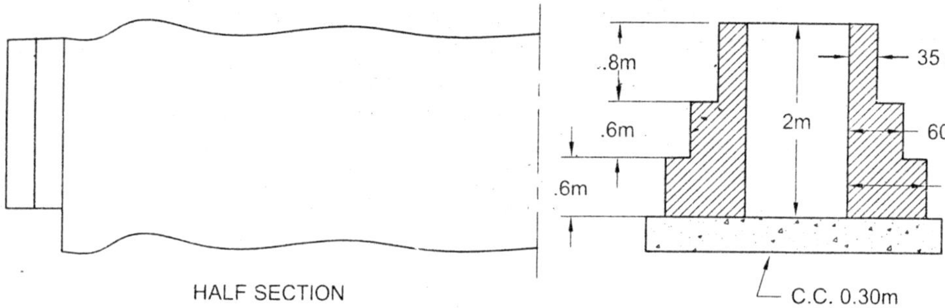

(*b*) Half plan (*c*) Cross-section

Fig. 13·29. Head of channel off taking from reservoir.

Emperical equations for yield of total sediment

(1) **By Jogelkar's Equation :** $Q_s = 0.59\,(A)^{-0\cdot24}$

where Q_s annual silting rate in M.m^3 per 100 sq. km in catchment area.

For example $Q = 0\cdot59(A)^{-0\cdot24}$

where A = catchment area in sq. km.

$= 0\cdot59\,(1830)^{-0.24} = 0\cdot10$ M.m^3/100 sq. km

being $A = 1830$ sq. km

(2) **By Khosla's Equation :**

$Q_s = 0.323\,(A)^{-0\cdot28}$

where Q_s = Annual silting rate in M.m^3/100 sq. km. per year

A = catchment area in sq. km.

(This equation gives always lower estimate of sediment yield at a site.)

(3) **Varshney's equations :** Varshney and Raichin have proposed following equations.

(*i*) Upto 130 sq. km. catchment for hilly rivers.

$Q_s = 0.395\,(A)^{-0\cdot311}$ where Q_s and A represents as above

(*ii*) For rivers draining in plains

$Q_s = 0\cdot392\,(A)^{-0\cdot302}$

(*iii*) For area greater than 130 sq. km for North India catchments.

$Q_s = 1\cdot534(A)^{-0\cdot264}$

(*iv*) For South India River upto 130 sq. km.

$Q_s = 0\cdot46(A)^{-0\cdot468}$

(*v*) For areas greater than 130 sq. km for South India catchments

$Q_s = 0\cdot277\,(A)^{-0\cdot194}$

(4) **By Swami's Regression equation :** $V_s = C.B.(V_{ci})^{0\cdot94}\,(S_0)^{0\cdot84}$

where V_s = cumulative volume of sediment deposited in the reservoir in M.m^3 (Million metre^3)

C = Regression constant with safe value of the order of 1·16. However a value less than 1·16 may be adopted depending on the reservoir.

B = Width of the reservoir at full reservoir level in m.

V_{ci} = Commulative volume of inflow per unit width B of the reservoir.

S_0 = Bed slope of the river.

Example : $V_s = C.B.\ (V_u)^{0.94}\ (S_0)^{0.84}$

where $C = 1.6$; $B = 500$; $S_0 = 0.006$

or $V_s = 1.16\ (500) \times (0.006)^{0.84} \times (V_u)^{0.94}$

$= 8.837\ (V_{ci})^{0.084} = 212.48$

(Value of V_{ci} given in the table for the river)

Here V_s = Commulative volume of sediment deposits in M.m^3

(If the commutative value of V_s is for say 9 years)

Q_s = Sedimentation rate % sq. km. catchment per year

Then
$$Q_s = \frac{V_s}{9} \times \frac{100 \text{ sq. km.}}{\text{Catchment area of } 1830 \text{ km}^2}$$

$$= \frac{212.8}{9} \times \frac{100}{1830}$$

$= 1.29$ million m^3/100 sq. km.

From Similar Catchments. Sediment yield of an unmeasured water shed (Q_{S_2}) can be computed from sedidment yield of a measured catchment Q_{S_1} of similar topography, land cover and land use on area proportion bars as

$$(Q_{S_2}) = Q_{S_1}\left(\frac{A_2}{A_1}\right)$$

where A_1 and A_2 = area of catchment of unknown and known catchments respectively in sq. km.

The annual siltation of similar catchments in mm^3/100 sq. km/year is observed and the same is utilised for the catchments of a new scheme.

Measuring suspended sediment load. Sediment samples are collected from the river site in bottles of standard design at a depth of 0·6 D below the surface (D being the depth of water) or at two depths at 0·2 D and 0·8 D. These bottles are called as sampler. The collected sample of sediment is then analysed in the laboratory either by a **gravimeter** or by hydrometric method to determine the quantum of coarse sediment (particle size higher than 0·2 mm), medium size sediment (particle of size between 0·075 mm to 0·2 mm) and of fine sediment (particle size less than 0·075 mm) separately. Their sum will indicate the total sediment load present in the given volume of water sample. Sediment load present in the water sample is then expressed as ppm (parts per million) as

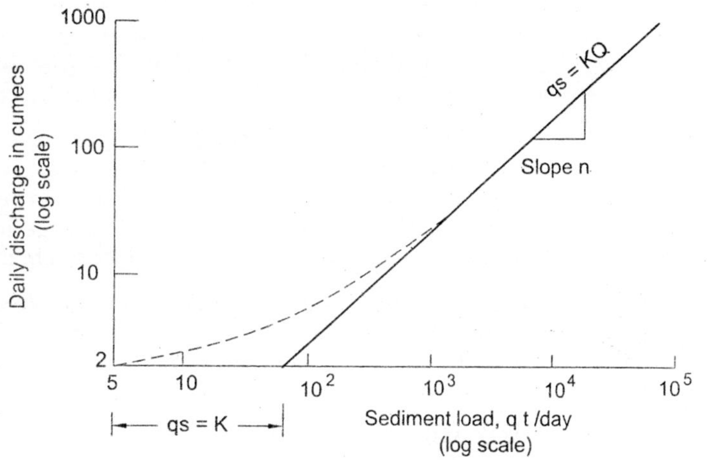

Fig. 13·30. A sediment rating curve.

$$\text{Sediment load in ppm} = \frac{\text{Dry mass of sediment}}{\text{Total mass of original sample including the mass of sediment and water}} \times 10^6$$

This value can be converted into *t*/day by multiplying the average unit weight of sediment (say 1·2 t/m^3) with the total volume of daily inflow in m^3. (t = ton)

From a number of such samp-les a curve can be drawn with sedi-ment load, $q_s = f$ per day on log scale *vs* discharge in m^3/sec.

The bed load can be calculated by using the available emperical equations or on adhoc basis of 2·5625% of the suspended load as to calculate the load total sediment load (sum of suspended load + bed load).

Yield from a reservoir. It is the quantity of water which can be supplied from the reservoir in a specified interval of time. The maximum amount of water that can be guaranteed during a critical dry period is known as the safe or firm yield. The amount of water available in excess of safe yield during high floods is called secondary yield.

Storage zones of a reservoir. These zones are divided as under—

(1) **Normal pool level or Maximum conservation level.** It is the maximum elevation to which the reservoir water surface will rise during normal operating conditions (see Fig. 13·31). It is equivalent to the elevation of the spillway crest or the top of spillway gates for most cases.

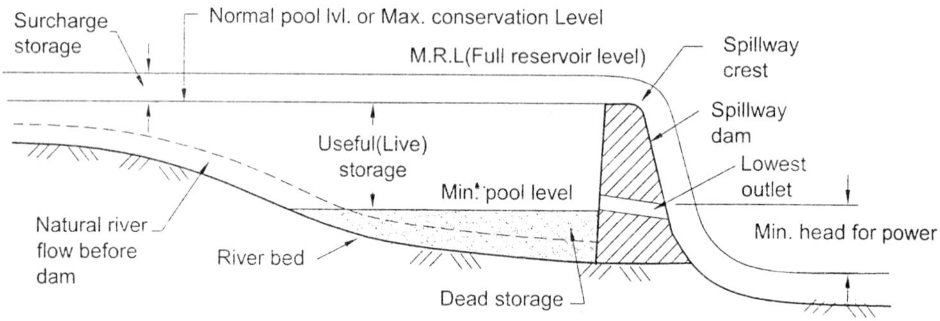

Fig. 13·31.

(2) **Minimum pond (pool) level.** The lower water surface elevation, which has to be kept under normal operating conditions in a reservoir, is called the minimum pool level. This level may be fixed by the elevation of the lowest outlet in the dam or may be guided by the minimum head requires for effective functioning of turbines.

(3) **Useful (live) and dead storage.** The volume of water stored in a reservoir between the minimum and normal pool levels is called the useful or live storage, while water stored in the reservoir below the minimum pool level is known as the Dead storage, and it is not of much use in the operation of the reservoir. The useful storage may be subdivided into conservation storage and flood-mitigation storage in multi-purpose schemes.

(4) **Maximum pool level or full reservoir level during high floods.** Water is discharged over the spillway, but will cause the water level to rise in the reservoir above the normal pool level. The maximum level to which the water rises during the worst design flood is known as the maximum pool level.

Surcharge storage. The volume of water stored between the normal pool level and the max. pool level is called surcharge storage. Surcharge storage is an uncontrolled storage, in the sense that it exerts only till the flood is in progress and cannot be retained for later use.

Bank Storage. When the reservoir is tilted up, certain amount of water seeps into the permeable reservoir banks. This water comes out as soon as the reservoir gets depleted. This volume of water is known as bank storage, and may amount to several percent of the reservoir volume depending as the geological formation.

Valley storage. Even pre-reservoir construction the stream has its own water unit which is called as valley storage. After the construction of the reservoir the net increased storage = capacity of the reservoir – valley storage.

Effective storage in flood mitigation = Useful storage + Surcharge storage – Valley storage corresponding to the rate of inflow in the reservoir.

Flood control reservoirs are of the two types :

(*a*) **Retarding reservoir.** In the retarding reservoirs the outlets and the spillway are not controlled by gates or valves. The discharge capacity of the outlets is such that the total outflow through them or over the spillway would not exceed the safe capacity of the river down stream in the event of highest flood. The retarding reservoirs have the advantage of lower initial cost and elimination of possibility of human error or negligence in their operation.

(*b*) **Detention Basin.** A flood control reservoir provided with outlets controlled by gates is called a **detention basin.** A detention basin is more costly initially due to the additional cost of gates and lifting machines and also in subsequent maintenance as a regular staff has to be maintained to operate the gates. The detention basins also involve the possibility of human error or negligence in their operation. On the other hand, they provide greater flexibility and also permit release of a larger discharge, subject to the safe maximum capacity of the channel below in the earlier stages of flood as the discharging capacity can be restricted by gates if it tends to rise above the maximum permissible value with increasing heads on the outlets.

Multi purposes reservoir. Multi purpose reservoirs have the following uses :

1. Conservation of water for irrigation and water supply.

2. Flood protection and soil conservation.

3. Conservation of Hydroelectric power.

Regulation of the reservoirs. Guiding curves and tables are prepared for the efficient regulation and to avoid any mistake in the operation of the gates over spillways. A table of such type is given below for the regulation during whole year of a particular reservoir.

Date of the year	*Permissible reservoir level demand storage R.L. 600 ft.*
Upto 11 August	600
31st August	605
1st Sept.	617
11th Sept.	623
21st Sept.	627
1st Oct. and onward	630 (F.R.L. = Full reservoir level)

2·3. Spillways

Location. A spillway can be constructed either in the body of the dam itself or at one end of it. The spillway in the body itself or one end of it can only be constructed on masonry dams. In earthen or rockfill dams it is not feasible.

If the dam is earthen or rock fill the spillway must be constructed entirely away from it independently in a saddle. If a deep narrow gorge with steep banks, separated from a flank by a hillock with its level above the top of the dam such as shown in the figure is available. The spillway can be best built independently off the dam. Such saddle dams can even be constructed in the case of masonry dams.

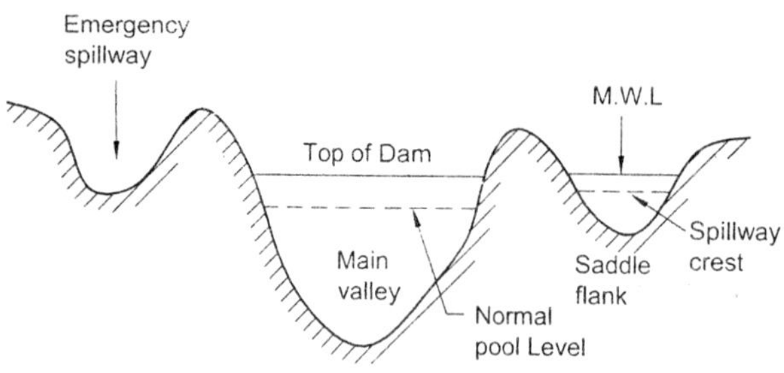

Fig. 13·32.

Emergency spillway. Emergency considered purely as an additional factor of safety, or keeping in mind that the maximum flood hydrograph has a probability of occurrence of once in many years. The main spillway may be designed for a some what smaller discharge and the emergency spillway depends to come into action if that discharge is exceeded during the useful life time of the reservoir. In the case of earthen dams the former view prevails while in the case of concrete dams later view can be taken in order to reduce the cost of the main dam. In such cases an emergency spillway may be provided as shown in the Fig. 13·32.

Types of spillway. The spillways can be divided in the following five types according to the type of construction.

1. Straight drop 2. Overflow or Ogee 3. Trough or Chute 4. Side channel
5. Shaft and 6. Syphon.

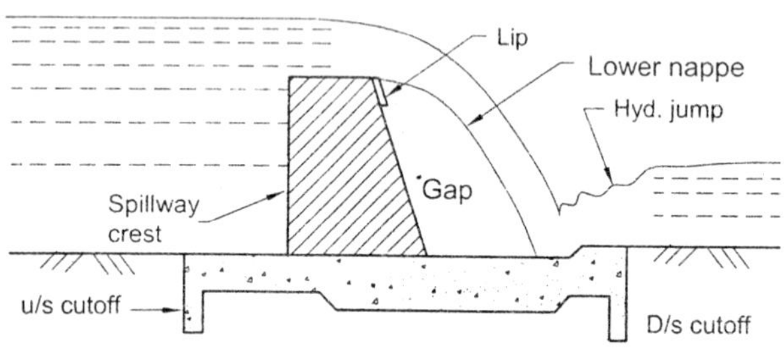

Fig. 13·33. Under side of nappe to be ventilated.

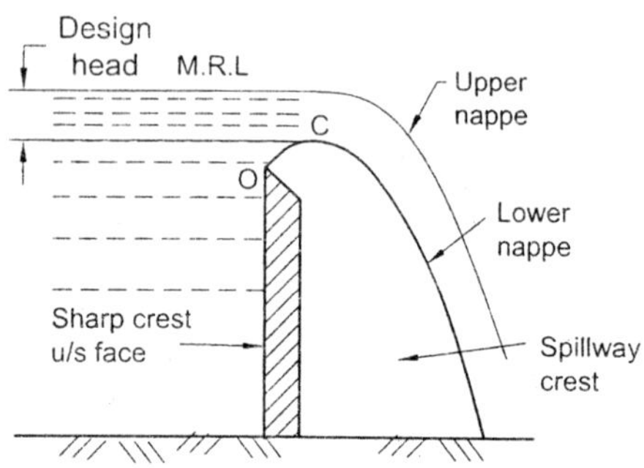

Fig. 13·34. Ogee spillway with ventilation u/s face.

(1) **The straight or overfall type of spillway.** It is used in low reservoirs and is just a weir. A lip is given in the upper d/s edge so that water may fall away from the face of the weir. A gap between the lower nappe and the weir wall is formed which creates a vacuum in it (pressure lower than the atmosphere) which creates cavitation and formation of bubbles which disturbs the easy flow of the water jet. It is therefore a proper ventilation is required to avoid pulsating and fluctuating effects of the jet. The design of such type of dams is just like a well. The d/s face may however be battered for a better stability.

Ogee spillway. It is a type of an outflow spill way. In this type the u/s face of the dam crest is kept vertical, but however it may be splayed in some cases to have a better stability. The d/s face of the dam is kept in the shape of a parabola. The shape of the lower nappe can be determined by the principle of projectile. It generally rises slightly to point C as it originates from the crest O (The tip of the sharp edge and then falls to make a parabolic curve flow if the space between sharp edged weir and the lower nappe is filled with concrete. The weir so formed will have a profile similar to an ogee curve, and hence it is called an ogee weir. The lower nappe will then become the crest of the spillway since the lower nappe of the freefalling jet will be different for differed heads over the crest of the sharp crested weir, the profile of the ogee weir is generally confined to the lower nappe that would be obtained for maximum head over the spill way *i.e.* upto the maximum reservoir level (MRL).

In ogee weirs the falling water slids over the curved profile of the spillway, there is no space between water and crest of the spillway under normal design conditions.

Cavitation. Since the profile of the crest is designed for a particular head which is called as **designed head** (H_d). But in practice the actual load of water as the spillway crest called the operating head may be less or more than the designed head. If the operating head on the spill way is more than the designed head the lower nappe of the falling jet may leave the ogee profile, thereby generating negative pressure at point of separation. The generation of by vacuum or –ve pressure *i.e.* pressure below atmospheric pressure, may lead to formation of bubbles or cavities in the water. These cavities or bubbles filled with air, vapour and other gases are formed in a liquid, where as the absolute pressure *i.e.* atmospheric pressure, vacuum pressure of the liquid is close to its vapour pressure, so as to commence evaporation. Such a condition may arise when the head of water is more than the designed head (since the project is designed for the designed head) and consequently high velocity jet causes reduced pressure or –ve pressure in the lower region of the river jet.

Such cavities on moving d/s may enter a region where the absolute pressure is much higher. This causes the vapour in the cavity to condense and return to liquid with a resulting explosion or collapse of the cavity when the cavity collapse extremely by high pressure are generated. The continuous bombardment of these explosions will thus take place near the surface of the weir causing fatigue failure of the materials. The small particles of concrete or masonry are thus broken away. Causing formation of pits on its surface a spongy appearances. This damaging section of cavitation is called splitting. The cavitation plus the vibration from the alternate making and breaking of contact between the water and face of the spill way, may thus result in said structural damage to the spillway crest on the other hand if the head of the water or the operating head is less than the designed head the falling jet would adhere to the crest of the ogee spillway causing positive hydraulic pressure and thereby reducing the discharge coefficient of the weir.

Table 13·26. Design procedure of the crest of spillway. Taking *O* as origin and *x* and *y* as co-ordinates the profile can be obtained by the tabulation given below—

x/H_d	y/H_d		x/H_d	y/H_d	
	Lower nappe	*Upper Nappe*		*Lower nappe*	*Upper Nappe*
0	– 0·125	0·831	1·5	– 0.738	– 0.088
0·10	– 0·033	0·807	2·0	– 1·393	– 0·743
0·25	– 0·000	0·763	3·0	– 3·303	– 2·653
0·50	– 0·034	0·668	4·0	– 6·013	– 5·363
0·75	– 0.128	0·539	5·0	– 9·523	– 8·873
1·0	– 0·283	0·373			

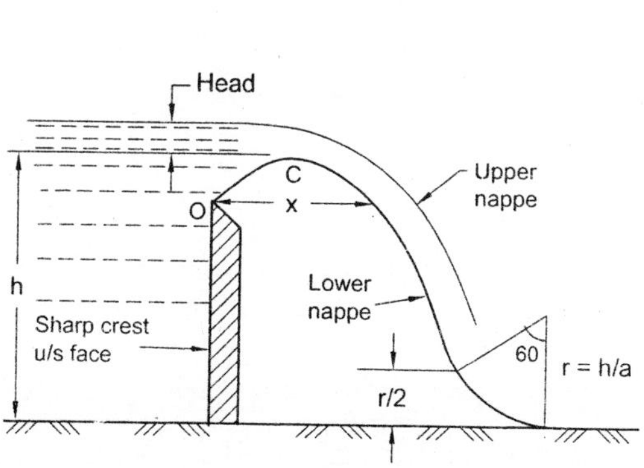

Fig. 13·35. Crest spillway

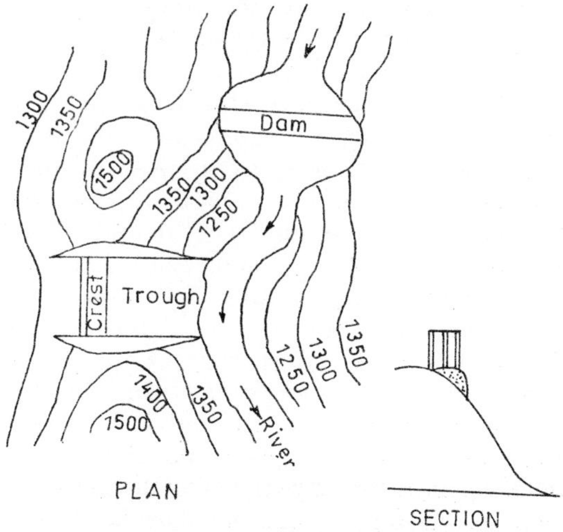

Fig. 13·36. Trough (chute) spillway

(2) **Trough or Chute Spillway.** It is not possible to provide the overfall spillway for earthen and rock fill dams. For concrete dams also, the narrowness of the valley, the erodible nature of river bed or some other reason may make it undesirable to provide the overfall spill way. In such cases some sort of spillway must be provided separately from the main dam. Out of such the trough or the Chute spillway is the simplest.

The trough type spillway is provided in a saddle from which a channel leads the water to the river below the dam. The crest of the spill way is of low height or even flat depending on the natural level of the saddle. If the saddle has a lower level than the full reservoir level then a weir has to be built upto that level and ogee shape may be given to it in order to obtain a high discharge coefficient. On the other hand if the saddle has a higher level than the full reservoir level, it has to be excavated to the later level and in that case the weir crest would normally be left flat as it would seldom be economical to excavate rock in order to build an ogee shaped weir.

The slope of the 'Chute' or trough *i.e.* the channel below the weir for conveying the spilled water is usually kept just sufficient to meet the requirement of flow for as long a distance from the crest as possible without bringing the trough bed into filling. After that the slope is made as steep as possible without endangering the stability or getting into heavy excavation. This arrangement keeps excavation at the minimum and keeps high velocities and possibility of scour away from the spillway. The trough bed should be kept entirely in digging through out its length and its side slopes designed to be stable with an adequate factor of safety, as any slide blocking the trough at flood time may lead to over topping of the main dam with disastrous results. Except in case of solid rock with no horizontal joints, concrete paving of the trough is necessary in all cases. The thickness to the lining should be kept 0·30 to 0·45 cm. Contraction joints should be provided at an interval of 10 to 15 m in either direction. Light reinforcement about 0·25% of concrete area is usually provided in the lining. This reinforcement should not cross the joints.

Bends should be avoided in the trough so far as possible as they may lead to hydraulic jump at hypercritical velocities. If a bend is absolutely unavoidable, it should be made as gentle as possible and adequate allowance should be made in the paving of in the side slopes for super elevation of water on the outside of the curve. The spillway provided in **Tehri Dam** is a trough spillway.

(3) **Side Channel Spillway.** In the trough spillway the water flows in the trough at right angles to the dam axis of the main dam, while in the side channel spill way it flows parallel to the water of the main dam.

This type of spillway is suited to narrow canyons where the overflow type is ruled out, for some reasons and where is no saddle of sufficient width is available to accomodate a trough type spillway. A typical layout of a side channel is illustrated in the fig. (13·37). It will be seen that if the same crest length were to be provided normal to the conveyance channel or trough below the farther end of the crest would be in prohibitively heavy excavation. The flow conditions in the side channel are unique as the water entering the channel has no momentum in the direction it has to take. The slope in the side channel must be sufficient not only to overcome friction losses but to provide acceleration in the direction of flow.

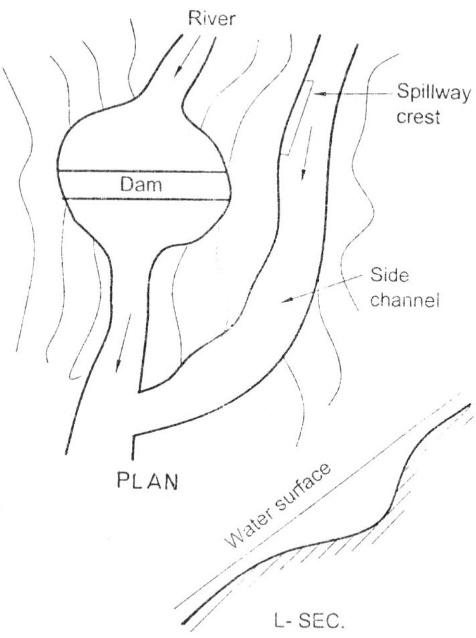

Fig. 13·37. Side channel spillway.

(4) **Shaft spillway.** The shaft spillway consists of a vertical funnel, the lower end of which is turned at right angles and connected to a horizontal tunnel. The water flows over a circular crest and enters the vertical shaft from which it is delivered by a horizontal tunnel to the river channel below the dam. The shaft spillway is divided into two types. (1) The standard spillway and (2) the broad crested spillway. The two types are illustrated in Fig. 13·38 (*a*) and (*b*) respectively. In the former case, the crest is shaped to the curve of the falling nappe of water over a circular sharp crested weir of the same dia. under the design head. The coefficient of discharge is relatively high for this crest and the required crest length and hence the diameter of the crest relatively smaller. On the other hand the

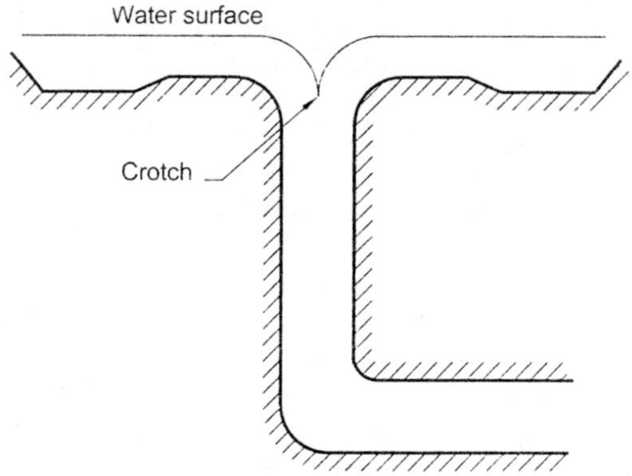

(*a*) Shaft spillway

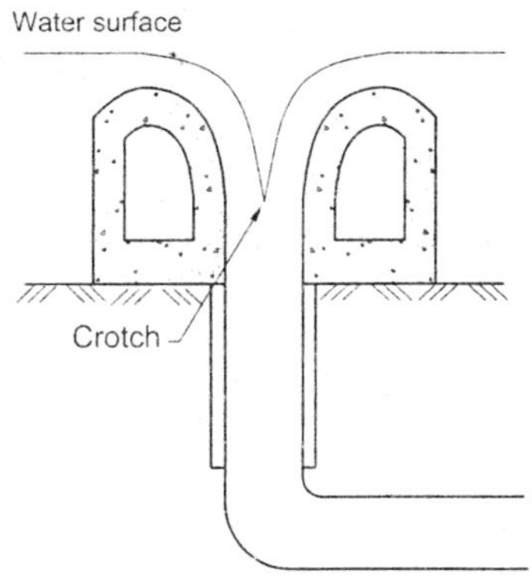

(*b*)

Fig. 13·38.

'crotch' section where the upper nappe from all around the circumference meets is lower in this case than in the 2nd case requiring a comparatively larger funnel diameter upto the crotch section. The broad crested shaft spillway requires a larger outer dia. of the crest because of a lower value of the discharge coefficient but the crotch section is higher and the required funnel dia. smaller upto the crotch than in the former case. For this reason, the standard section is preferable in locations where the spillway has to be constructed in concrete in its top portion as the quantity of concrete required would be smaller, and the broad crested spillway is preferable when the entire spillway has to be provided in excavation as due to smaller funnel diameter the rock excavation required would be less.

Siphon spillway. The siphon spillways are based on the principle of siphonic action in an inverted bent pipe (see Fig. 13·39). If such a pipe is once filled with water it will continue to flow so long as the liquid surface is higher than the lower leg of the pipe. Unless of course the upper leg gets exposed earlier. The velocity through the pipe would be obtained by equating the total head H. to the velocity head at the exit end of the pipe pluss the losses in the pipe.

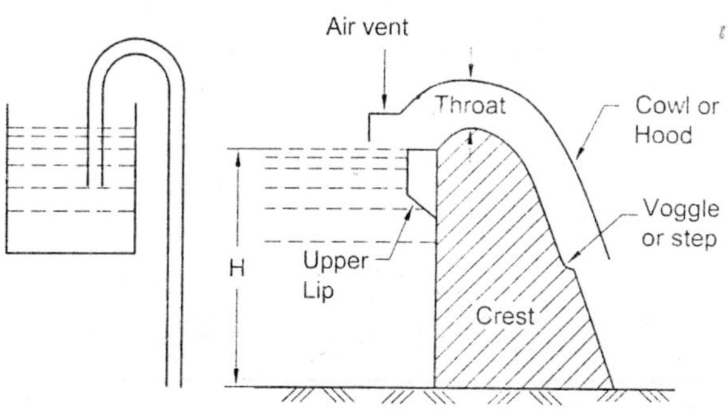

Fig. 13·39.

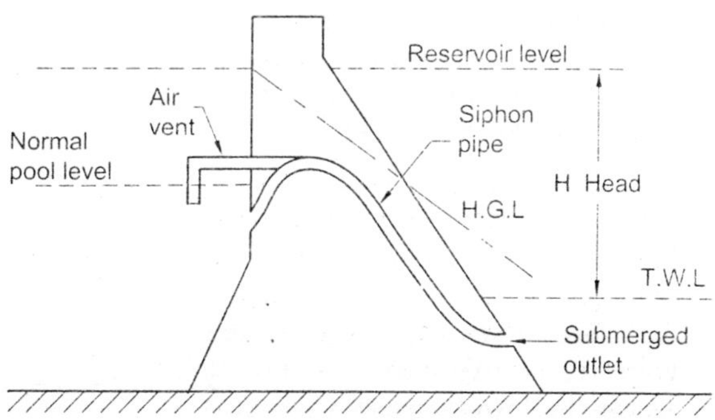

Fig. 13·40. Tilted outlet type siphon spillway.

A Siphon Spillway consists of a siphon pipe, one end of which is kept on the u/s side and is in contact with the reservoir, while the other end discharges water on the D/s scale.

Tilted outlet type of a Siphon Spillway. When the valley is very narrow and no space is available for constructing a separate spill way, the siphon pipe can be installed within the dam body as shown in the Fig. (13·40). An air vent pipe may be connected with the siphon pipe. The level of the air ventilation pipe may be kept at normal pool level, while the entry pipe of the siphon pipe may be kept still lower so as to prevent the entry of debris etc. in the siphon. The outlet of the siphon may be submerged so as to prevent the entry of the air in the siphon.

When the water in the reservoir is upto or below the normal pool level, air enters the siphon through the vent and siphonic action cannot take place when once the water level in the reservoir goes above the normal pool level and if once the siphon is filled with water (primed) the water will start flowing through the siphon by siphonic action. The outflow will continue till the water level in the reservoir falls back to normal pool level. As soon as it happens, the air will enter the siphon through new exposed air vent and the flow will stop.

The discharge equation shows that the discharge through a siphon spillway is sufficiently independent of the water surface elevation of the reservoir. If the water surface in the reservoir rises the discharge through the spillway is affected to a less extent, because change in H is small as compared to corresponding change in head over an ogee type spillway. Hence the discharge through the siphon is nearly always at capacity, when once the water level has risen above the normal pool level. This makes the siphon spillway particularly advantageous in purposing of sudden surges of water, such as may occur in canals and fore bays when the outlet gates are closed rapidly. As the rise of water above the crest level is smaller due to higher discharging capacity even at the start of inflow flood above normal pool level, the height of the non-overflow section of the dam can be kept smaller for the same height of overflow section.

Some times it may not be possible to keep the outlet submerged in tail water because of limitations of –ve pressure at the crossing in such cases the outlet can be left open above the water level but air entry through the outlet have to be controlled by priming devices. The effective head H in such a case will be difference of reservoir water level and outlet level of siphon.

Priming devices. When the outlet cannot be sealed by the tail water some other devices called the 'Priming' are used which lead to an automatic priming if the siphon at a certain rise of water level above the crest. The maximum rise of water level is called priming depth. In Fig. 13·41 (a) the priming is accomplished by means of a slap called joggle which reflects the sheet of water to strike against the lever end of the cover or head, thus sealing the lever end from the atmosphere. Some times, an additional baby siphon may be installed as a priming device as shown in the Fig. 13·41 (b).

When the water level reaches slightly above the crest, the baby siphon which is an additional siphon starts running full. The sheet of water issues from it, is arranged to shoot across the lower end of the main siphon, so as to seal it from the atmosphere.

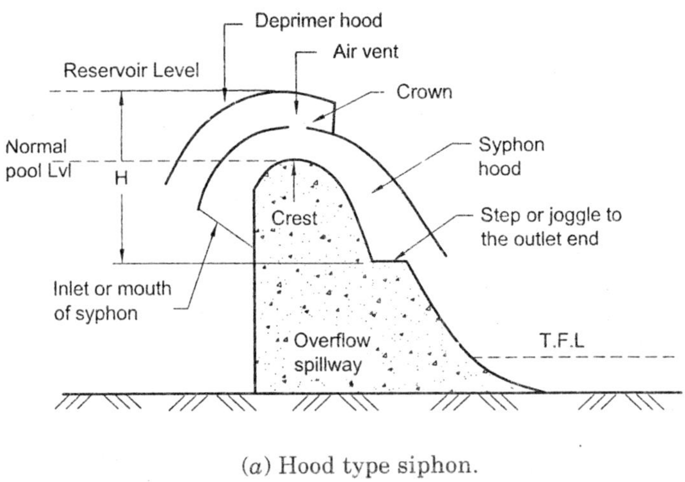

(a) Hood type siphon.

Hooded type of siphon spillway. In this case a reinforced concrete hood is constructed over the ordinary overflow section of a gravity dam. The inlet of this hood is kept submerged so as to prevent the entry of debris, ice etc. A small depriming hood is kept above the main hood and both these hoods are connected by an air vent and the deprimer hood is kept at normal pool level. The principle of functioning of both types of installations is essentially the same except for the initial filling up of the siphon or 'priming. At normal pool level (F.R.L.), the water stand up in the crest of the spill way. If now a flood enters the reservoir, the water level would start rising and a sheet of water would start flowing over the spill way crest. Since the water level is above the deprime hood, the air entry at the inlet is sealed. The air entry at the outlet is also sealed by the tail water etc. Hence the water spilling over the crest, strikes all the remaining air from the hood within minutes. Siphon action gets established after the air in the bend over the crest have been completely exhausted.

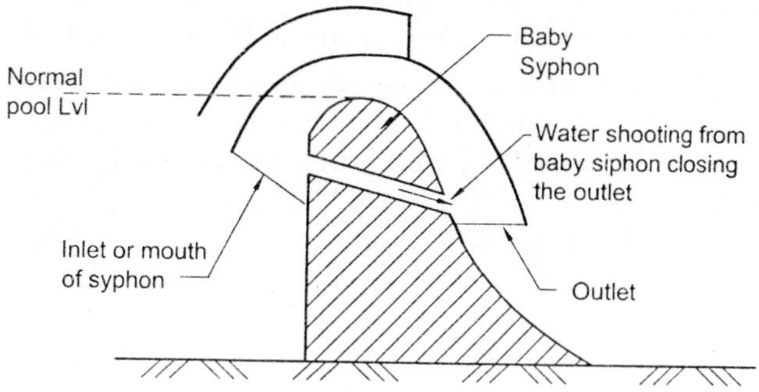

(*b*) Baby siphon.

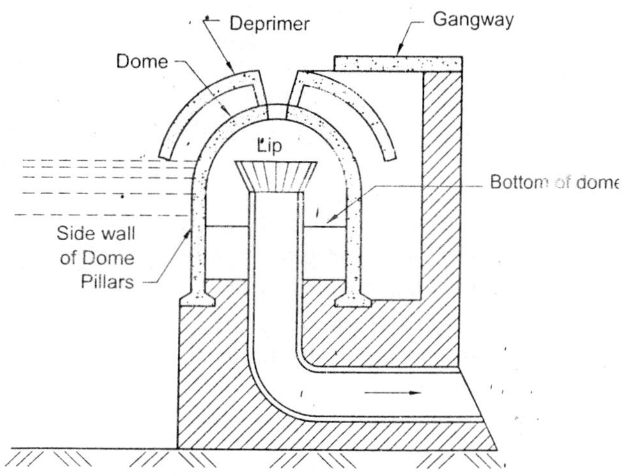

(*c*) Volute siphon spill way.
Fig. 13·41.

Discharge. The velocity head $= \dfrac{V^2}{2g} = H$ or $V = \sqrt{2gH}$

Discharge $(Q) = C_d . A \sqrt{2gH}$ where C_d = coeff. of discharge which is usually about 0.9, A = sec. area and H = Head of water

H = the difference of water level in the reservoir and the tail water level for submerged outlet.

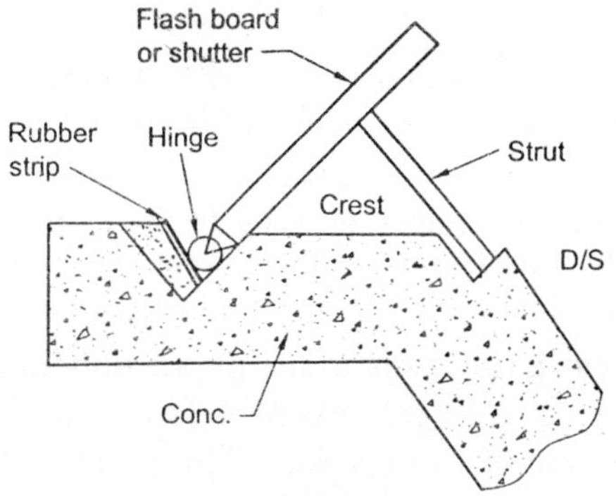

Fig. 13·42. Dropping shutters.

Spillway crest gates. In order to control the supply of water above the crest, shutters are provided over the spillway crest. The following type of shutters are used according to the requirement and situation.

(1) **Dropping shutters or permanent flash boards.** Flash board consist of wooden panels usually 1·0 m to 1·25 m high. They are hinged at the bottom and are supported against the

water pressure by struts. The shutters fall flat on the crest when the d/s supporting struts are tripped, hence they are not suitable for curved crests.

These shutters can be raised or lowered from a overhead cable way or a gangway. Various types of automatic hoisting or dropping shutters are used these days. Automatic shutters do not function well when interfered by floating debris or ice etc. These are used for minor works.

(2) **Stop logs.** Stop logs are sal or any other hard wood planks or sleepers in which two nails on either side is hooked for lifting them. The hooks are beatened to make them flat in the middle to have a grip with wood plank. On either side of the plank steel hoops are nailed to protect the edges of the planks. These planks are placed one over the other and are lifted by a long bamboo hook supporting the nails of the planks. The stop logs are used in very unimportant works. However the regulators are provided with grooves in their piers for use in any emergency if hoisting system fails.

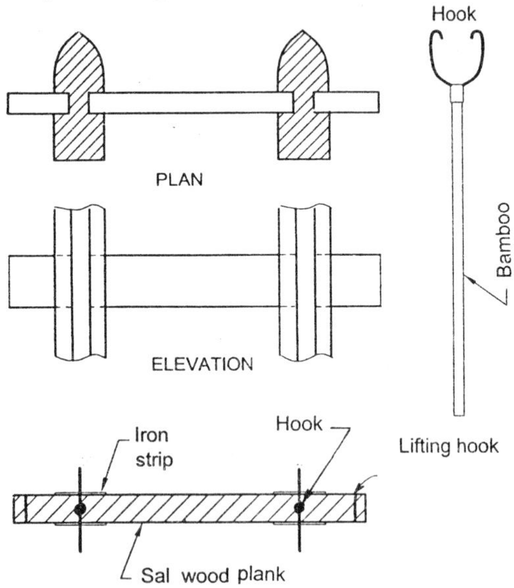

Fig. 13·43. Stop logs.

(3) **Vertical lift gates.** Vertical lift gates spanning horizontally between pier grooves. The grooves are generally provided with steel channels of suitable size so as to provide a smooth bearing surface leaving sufficient bearing strength and are known as groove guides, the gates move vertically in groove guides and hoisted up and down by hoist machines. These gates are generally of steel but in some unimportant works they may be of wood.

In the bearing of slide gates there is a huge amount of friction which is minimised by placing cylindrical rollers between the bearing surfaces, of the gate and the guide grooves. A train of rollers or wheels is therefore generally placed between the gate and the d/s guide, so that the sliding friction is much smaller. These rollers may be placed independent of the gate and the guide for thus eliminating axle friction. When the rollers are neither attached in the gate nor to the guide grooves but rolls vertically between the two when the gate is moved, is known as **stony gate** or **free roller gate.** When the rollers are attached to the gate and ride in tracks on the d/s side of the groove guide is known as **fixed wheel gate** or **fixed roller type gate.** Rubber seals are used to seal the openings between the u/s lead plate and the sides of the pier grooves.

The gate is counter balanced by counter weight beam which is loaded to take about half weight of the gate. Hence the hositing force is required to overcome the frictional force only.

To reduce the height of the operating plateform, high gates may be broken up into two horizontal sections so that the upper portion may be lifted and removed from the guides before the lower portion is moved. This also reduces the loads on the hositing machine.

The discharge through a partially raised vertical gate takes place by an undershot orifice flow and the discharge formula is given by $Q = C_d . A \sqrt{2gH}$ where A is the area of the opening and H is the water head above the centre line of the opening. The normal size of gates is 15 m × 15 m.

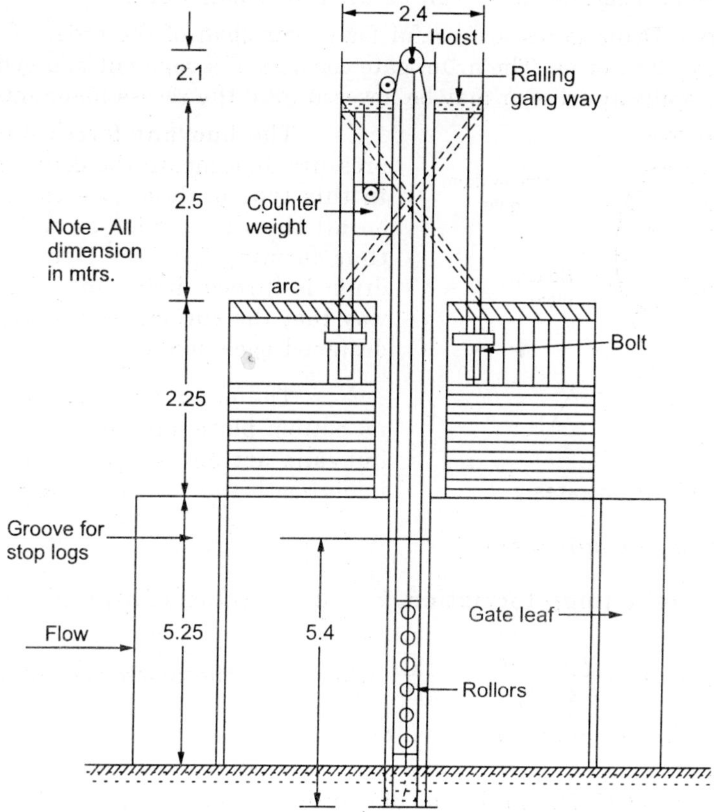

Fig. 13·44. Vertical lift gates.

Radial or the Tainter Gates. A radial gate has a curved water supporting face made of steel. The curved water face which is in the shape of a sector of a circle is properly braced by steel frame work which is pivoted on horizontal shafts called trunnion or pins (Fig. 13·45).The pins are anchored in the d/s portion of the spillway peirs. The gate can thus rotate about the fixed horizontal axis. Hoisting cables are attached to the gate and lead to winches on the hoisting plate form. The winches are usually motor driven or operated manually in emergencies.

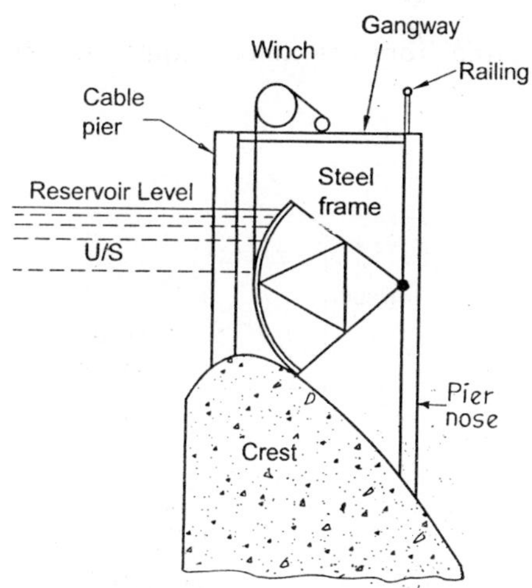

Fig. 13·45. Radial gates.

The water face segment is made concentric in the supporting pins so that the entire water thrust passes through the pins, thus creating no moment against the lifting of the gate. Hence the lifting force is required only against the weight of the gates. The friction between the seats and the piers and the frictional resistance of the pins counter weights in order to counter balance the self weight, may also be used, which further reduce the lifting force. More over the hoisting load is nearly constant for all gate openings. Hence radial gates can be used with smaller lifting for all heads and hand operated hoist can be used for small work.

Drum gates. Drum gates are useful for longer span of the order of 40 m or 50 and medium heights say 10 m or so. The drum gate consists of a segment of a cylinder which may be raised above the spillway crest or may be lowered into the recess made into top of spillway.

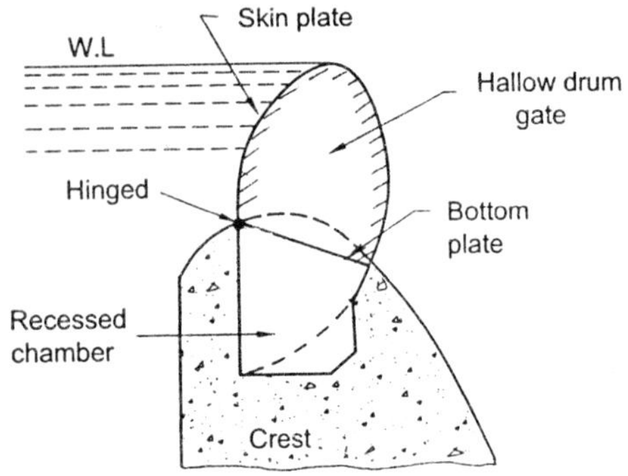

Fig. 13·46. Drum gates.

The buoyant forces due to head water pressure underneath the drum, aids in its lifting. In this type of dam gate the drum is enclosed on all the three sides as well as on the ends, thus forming a water light vessel. When the drum is turned, it fits into the recess in such a way that the surface become coincident with the designed ogee shape of the crest.

The other type of drum gates may have no bottom plate and shall be raised only by the buoyant action of water entering the recess underneath the skin plate of the drum.

Energy dissipation on spillways

(1) **By hydraulic jump formation.** For the formation of hydraulic jump the following relation must follow $D_2 = \frac{D_1}{2} + \sqrt{\frac{D_1^2}{4} + \frac{2q^2}{gD_1}}$. where q is the discharge intensity, D_1 and D_2 are the pre jump and post jump water depths.

For a given head H, D_1 can be calculated by the relation $V_1 = \sqrt{2gH}$. Moving V_1 and discharge intensity q, the water depth will be $= \frac{q}{V_1}$ (H = water Head known). D_1, D_2 can be calculated from the above expression $D_2 = \frac{D_1}{2} + \sqrt{\frac{D_1^2}{4} + \frac{2q^2}{gD_1}}$.

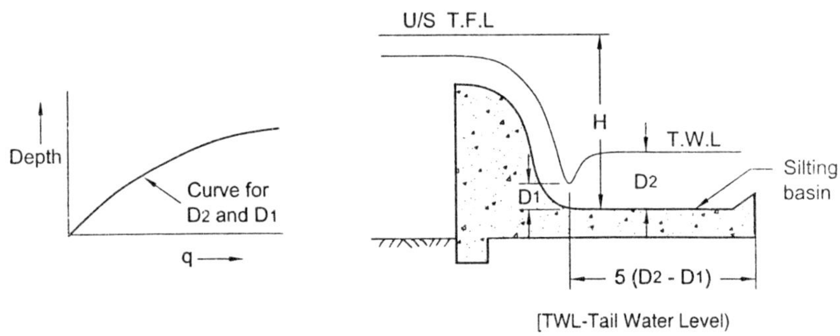

(a) (b)

Fig. 13·47.

Now in the D/S channel of river the depth D_2' can be calculated by the gauge discharge curves. But it is not necessary that this value of D_2' may be in coincidence with the calculated value of D_2 by the above expression. There may be following possibilities which are resolved accordingly.

Case I. When the value of D_2 and D_2' is in concidence then the jump will form on the toe of the glacier which is the ideal condition.

Case II. When the d/s D_2' is higher than D_2.

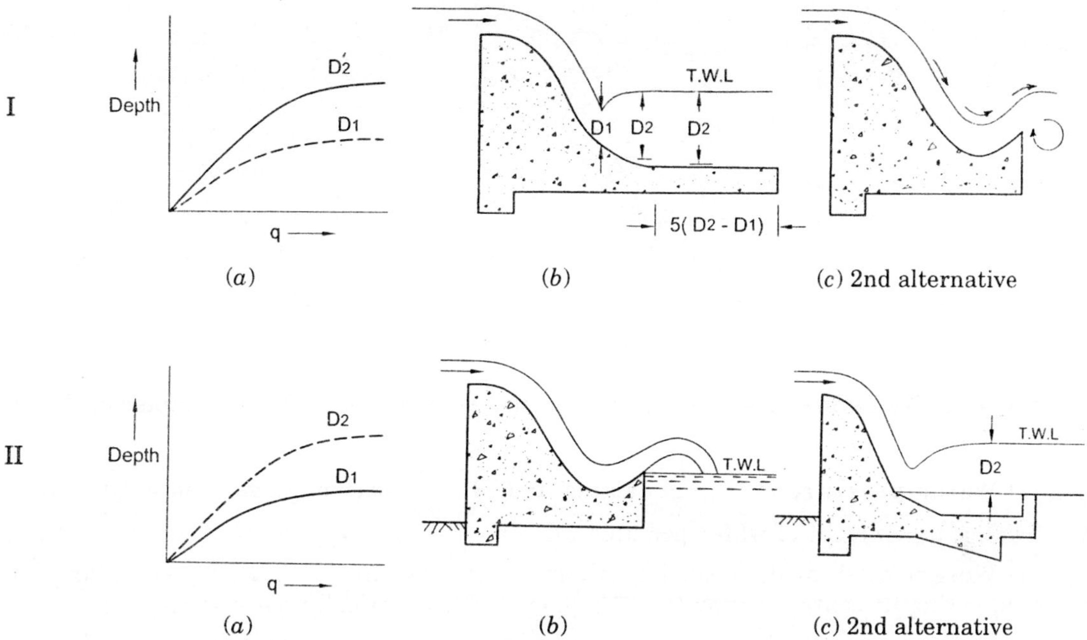

Fig. 13·48.

Case III. When the d/s D_2 is lower then D_2 (Refer figure below) :

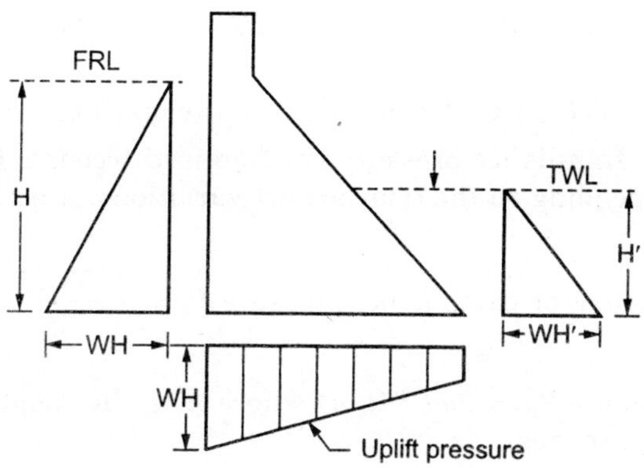

Fig. 13·49. Pressure diagram.

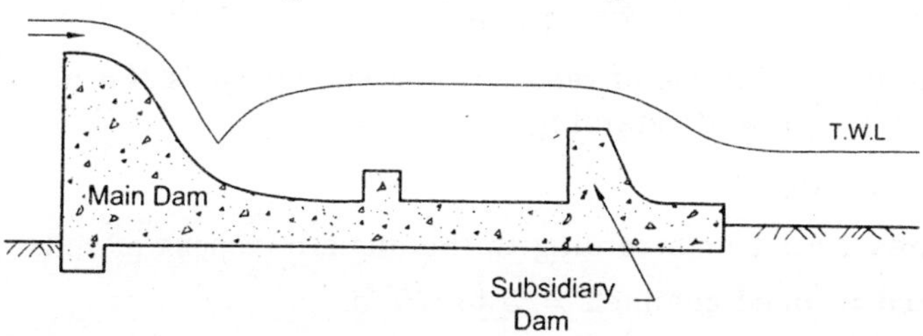

Fig. 13·50. Subsidiary dam.

Stilling Basins

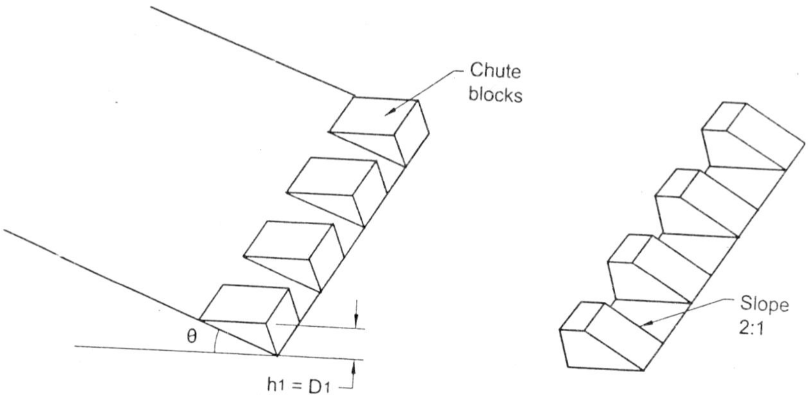

Fig. 13·51.

2·4. Gravity Dams. Loads on gravity dams are as follows : (Refer Chapter 4, Water Pressure on Dams)

(1) **Water pressure.** $P = \frac{wH^2}{2}$ acting at $H/3$ from bottom of dam horizontal. H = depth of water, w = weight of water per unit.

(2) **Weight of dam.** W = section of dam × unit weight of masonry of the dam per unit length, acting at centre of gravity of the dam section vertically downwards.

(3) **Uplift pressure.** It is due to seepage of water under foundations due to falls or due to drainage galleries provided in the body of the dam, uplift pressure at head = wH.

Uplift pressure at toe = wH'

Uplift pressure due to gallery = $[H' + 1/3\,(H - H')]\,w$ where H' is the depth of water towards toe.

The uplift pressure acts at centre of gravity of the uplift diagram.

(4) **Ice pressure.** In hills ice pressure is taken into account. Its magnitude varies from 25 kg/cm^2 to 15 kg/cm^2 depending on the temperature variations. It acts linearly along the length of the dam at lake level.

(5) **Seismic pressure** or earthquake pressure $P_e = \frac{0{\cdot}555\, wH^2 g}{10}$ and acts at $\frac{4H}{3\pi}$ above the base.

(6) **Wave pressure**—$P_w = 2wh^2$ (t/m) where h is the height of waves (discussed in earthen dams) from trough to crest.

(7) **Silt pressure**—$P_s = 1/2\ \phi h \left(\frac{1 - \sin\theta}{1 + \sin\theta}\right)$ where ϕ is the weight of the submerged silt per unit cube and θ is the angle of repose of the silt and h is the height of silt deposits. For further details refer dam and retaining walls.

13·3. Lining of channels

(1) **Side slopes** 1·5 : 1 or according to the angle of repose of soil.

(2) **Free board** in lined channels = ·5 to ·75 m.

(3) **Bank width** for lined channels = 8 m in cutting and filling in main canals ; 6·5

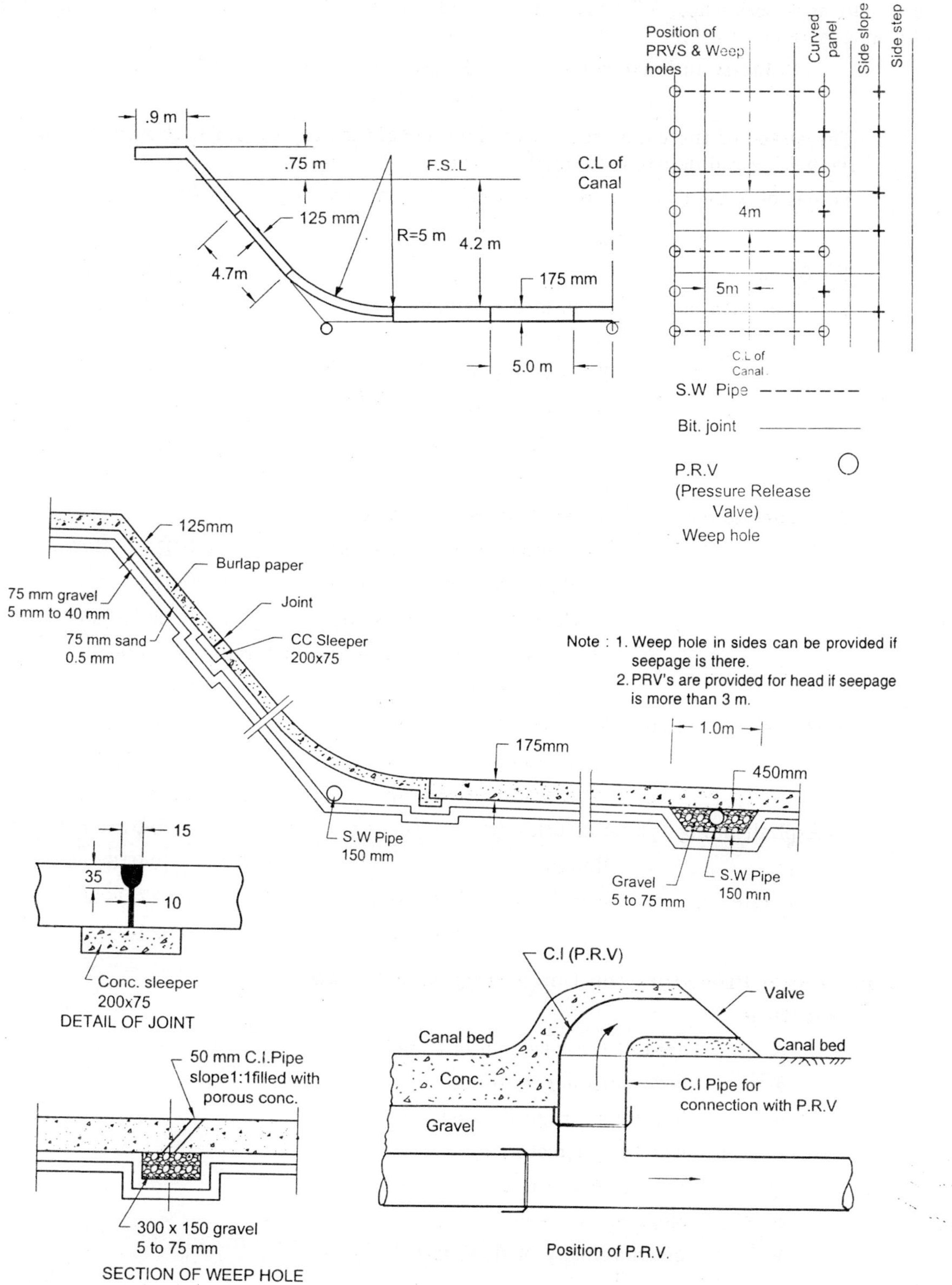

Fig. 13·52. Details of filter toe.

m in cutting in branches, 6·5 m on service road side and 5 m on riding bank side in filling of branch canals.

Velocity in lined canals = 2 m/sec or by the formula

$$V = R^{2/3} S^{1/2}/N$$

The shape of the canal section in lined canals is trapezoidal with corners rounded by a curve having radius equal to depth of water.

Values of N for lined canals with straight alignment (IS : 4745-1968)

	Surface	N
1. Brick		0·014-0·017
2. Cone with surface	(*a*) formed no finish	0·013-0·017
	(*b*) Trowel finish	0·012-0·014
	(*c*) Float finish	0·013-0·015
	(*d*) Float finish with gravel at bottom	0·015-0·017
	(*e*) Gunite good section	0·016-0·019
	(*f*) Gunite wavy section	0·018-0·022
3. Concrete bottom float finished sides as below		
	(*a*) Dressed stone in mortar	0·015-0·017
	(*b*) Random stone in mortar	0·017-0·020
	(*c*) Cement Rubble masonry	0·020-0·025
	(*d*) Cement Rubble masonry plastered	0·016-0·020
	(*e*) Dry rubble rip rap	0·020-0·030
4. Gravel bottom sides	(*a*) Formed from concrete	0·017-0·020
	(*a*) Random stone in mortar	0·020-0·023
	(*b*) Dry Rubble (riprap)	0·023-0·033
5. Asphalt lining	Smooth	0·013
	Rough	0·016
6. Concrete lined excavated rock	(*a*) Good sec.	0·017-0·020
	(*b*) Irregular sec.	0·022-0·027

Simple Design Procedure for Lined Irrigation Canals

Notation

A : area of cross-section of canal, m^2

b : bed width of the canal, m

N : Manning's rugosity coefficient

P : wetted perimeter, m

Q : discharge in the canal, m^3/s

S : slope of the canal

V : mean velocity of flow, m/s

X : $\tan^{-1} \dfrac{1}{Z} = \theta$

y : depth of canal, m $\alpha = b/y$

Z : side slope of canal (horizontal : vertical)

ψ, ϕ : non-dimensional factors

Introduction

There is at present an increased emphasis in conserving water by lining of irrigation canals. Lining also helps in reducing the cross-section of canal and its bed slope. In order to reduce the resistance in canal, sharp corners are avoided in the section. For small discharges, a triangular section is modified to have a circular arc at the bottom. For higher discharges, a trapezoidal section is used with circular arcs at the corners.

In design problems normally the discharge, bed slope, Manning's coefficient (depending on the material used for lining) ; and the side slope (depending on angle of repose of soil) are given. An assumption can be made as regards one of the parameters, namely, (*a*) maximum allowable velocity, V ; (*b*) $\alpha = b/y$ ratio ; and (*c*) the depth of flow y.

In all these cases, even though the procedure is by the simple application of Manning's formula, it involves sometimes tedious trial and error calculations. It is possible to devise graphical aids in the design. They are found to be less accurate and are not quite easy to use. The aim is to suggest some formulae for design which can be easily calculated by aid of a hand calculator and in some cases with simple and short trial and error procedure.

The parameters of triangular section with circular arc are :

If $$X = Z + \tan^{-1} 1/Z \quad ...(1)$$

$$A = XY^2 \quad ...(2)$$

and $$P = 2XY \quad ...(3)$$

In a trapezoidal section with circular corners the parameters are

$$A = y^2 (\alpha + X) \quad ...(4)$$

and $$P = y(\alpha + 2X) \quad ...(5)$$

and $$\alpha = b/y \quad ...(6)$$

It may be noted that when $\alpha = 0$ the parameters for trapezoidal section reduce to that of the triangular section.

Equations of flow

The discharge $$Q = \frac{A}{N}(A/P)^{2/3} S^{1/2}$$

$$= \frac{A^{4/3}}{N}(A/P^2)^{1/3} S^{1/2}$$

$$(P^2/A)^{1/3} = (A^{4/3} S^{1/2})/(QN)$$

or a shape factor $$\psi = P^2/A = (A^4 S^{3/2})/(Q^3 N^3) \quad ...(7)$$

Another useful equation can be derived as :

$$Q = \frac{A}{N}(A/P)^{2/3} S^{1/2} = (A^{5/3} S^{1/2})/(P^{2/3} N)$$

$$(Q N)/S^{1/2} = A^{5/3}/P^{2/3} \quad ...(8)$$

Simplified Equations

(*A*) The shape factor $P^2/A = (A^4 S^{3/2})/(Q^3 N^3)$

$$\psi = P^2/A = \{y(\alpha + 2X)\}^2/\{y^2 (\alpha + X)$$

$$= \alpha + 3x + X^2/(\alpha + X) \quad ...(9)$$

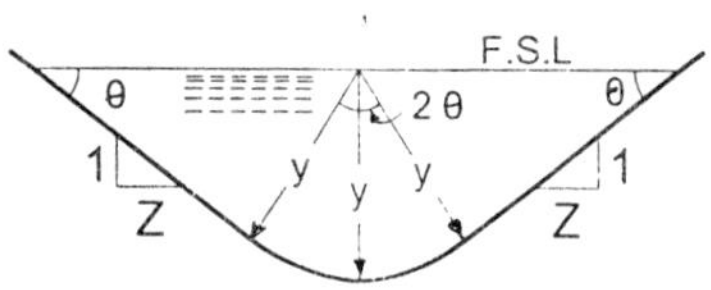

(*a*) Triangular canal with circular bottom

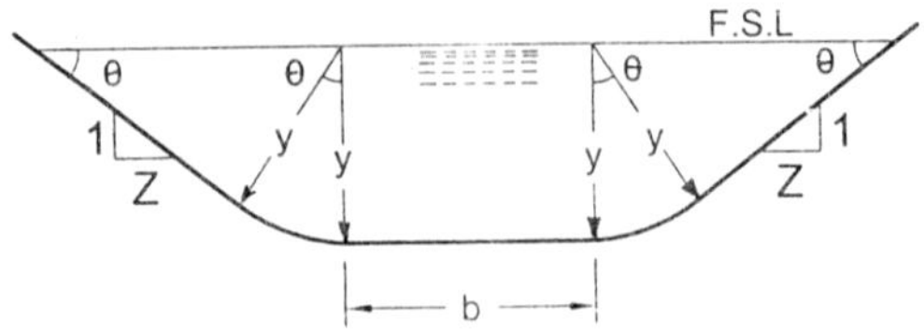

(*b*) Trapezoidal canal with circular arc's

Fig. 13·53.

Hence for a given α, ψ can be easily calculated and substituting in eqution (7), A and later y from equation (4) can be determined.

In case α is to be calculated from given value of ψ it can be done by a simple iteration as :

An over-estimated value of α =

$$\alpha_1 = \psi - 3X \qquad ...(10)$$

$$\alpha_{i+1} = \alpha_1 - X^2 (\alpha_i + X) \qquad ...(11)$$

which will converge very easily.

In case of triangular channels $\alpha = 0$ and hence $\psi = P^2/A = 4X$ and the calculations are simplified.

(*B*) The factor $QN/S^{1/2} = A^{5/3}/P^{2/3}$

$$= \{y^2(\alpha + X)\}^{5/3}/\{y(\alpha + 2X)\}^{2/3}$$

Hence, $\phi = (QN)/(y^{8/3}S^{1/2})$

$$= (\alpha + X)^{5/3}/(\alpha + 2X)^{2/3} \qquad ...(12)$$

This factor is nondimensional and for $1 < Z < 2$ it could be expressed within 1% error by the equations :

$$\phi = 0{\cdot}9\ \alpha + 0{\cdot}174\ Z^{1{\cdot}8} + 0{\cdot}94,\ \alpha < 2 \qquad ...(13)$$

$$\phi = 0{\cdot}97\ \alpha + 0{\cdot}15\ Z^{1{\cdot}8} + 0{\cdot}85,\ 2 \le \alpha < 8 \qquad ...(14)$$

$$\phi = 0{\cdot}99\ \alpha + 0{\cdot}3\ Z + 0{\cdot}55,\ \alpha \ge 8 \qquad ...(15)$$

These derived equations can greatly simplify the design as illustrated by the following examples.

Design Examples

Example 1. *Design a lined canal section for discharge of 50 m³/s at 1 in 10000 bed slope. Assume N = 0.018 and side slope³ 1·25 : 1.*

Solution.

$$Q = 50 \text{ m}^3/\text{s} ;\ S = 1/10000 ;\ N = 0{\cdot}018 ;\ Z = 1{\cdot}25.$$

Hence $X = Z + \tan^{-1} 1/Z = 1{\cdot}925$

Since the discharge is less than 85 m³/s, a triangular channel with circular arc may be used.

i.e. $\alpha = 0 ;\ \psi = P^2/A = 4X = 7{\cdot}7$

$$A = [(7{\cdot}7 \times 50^3 \times 0{\cdot}018)^{3/4}/(1/10000)^{3/2}] = 48{\cdot}625$$

$$A = y^2X \ : \text{Hence } Y = \sqrt{48{\cdot}675/1{\cdot}925} = 5{\cdot}03 \text{ m}$$

$$V = Q/A = 1{\cdot}027 \text{ m/s}$$

Example 2. (*a*) *Design a trapezoidal shaped concrete lined canal to carry a discharge of 100 m³/s at a slope of 25 cm/km. The side slope of canal is 1·5 : 1. The value of N may be* *taken as 0·016. Assume velocity as 1·5 m/s. (b) Design the same canal, if instead of giving the limiting velocity, b/y ratio is given[2] as 8.*

Solution.

(*a*)

$$Q = 100 \text{ m}^3/\text{s} \; ; \; S = 25/100000 \; ; \; N = 0{\cdot}016$$

$$V = 1{\cdot}5 \text{ m/s} \; ; \; Z = 1{\cdot}5 \; ; \; X = Z + \tan^{-1} 1/Z = 2{\cdot}088$$

$$A = Q/V = 100/1{\cdot}5 = 66{\cdot}667 \text{ m}^2$$

$$\psi = P^2/A = (A^4 S^{3/2})/(Q^3 N^3) = 19{\cdot}063$$

$$\alpha_1 = \psi - 3X = 19{\cdot}063 - 3 \times 2{\cdot}088 = 12{\cdot}799$$

$$\alpha_2 = 12{\cdot}799 - (2{\cdot}088)^2/(12{\cdot}799 + 2{\cdot}088) = 12{\cdot}506$$

$$\alpha_{i+1} = 12{\cdot}799 - (2{\cdot}088)^2/(12{\cdot}506 + 2{\cdot}088) = 12{\cdot}500$$

Hence $\alpha = 12{\cdot}5$

$$A = 66{\cdot}667 = y^2(\alpha + X) \; ;$$

Hence $y = (66{\cdot}667/14{\cdot}588)^{1/2} = 2{\cdot}138$ m

$$b = 12{\cdot}5 \times 2{\cdot}138 = 26{\cdot}725 \text{ m}$$

(*b*) $\alpha = 8$; Hence $\psi = \alpha + 3X + X^2/(\alpha + X) = 14{\cdot}696$

$$\psi = 14{\cdot}696 = (A^4 S^{3/2})/(Q^3 N^3)$$

Hence $A = [(14{\cdot}696 \times Q^3 N^3)/S^{3/2}] = 62{\cdot}47 \text{ m}^2$

$$A = 62{\cdot}47 = y^2(\alpha + X) \; ; \; y = [62{\cdot}47/(8 + 2{\cdot}088)]^{1/2} = 2{\cdot}488$$

$$b = 2{\cdot}488 \times 8 = 19{\cdot}91 \text{ m.}$$

Example 3. *Design a concrete lined canal to carry a discharge of 400 m³/s at a slope of 1 in 10000. The side slopes of canal are 1.25 : 1 and Manning's N may be taken as 0·014. The depth[4] is limited to 5 m.*

Solution.

$$Q = 400 \text{ m}^3/\text{s} \; ; \; S = 1/10000 \; ; \; N = 0.014 \; ; \; y = 5 \text{ m} \; ; \; Z = 1{\cdot}25$$

$$X = Z + \tan^{-1} 1/Z = 1{\cdot}925$$

$$\phi = \frac{QN}{y^{8/3} S^{1/2}}$$

$$= (400 \times 0{\cdot}014)/\{5^{8/3} \times (1/10000)^{1/2}\} = 7{\cdot}66$$

From equation (14),

$$7{\cdot}66 = 0{\cdot}97\,\alpha + 0{\cdot}15 Z^{1{\cdot}8} + 0{\cdot}85 \text{ if } 2 < \alpha < 8$$

$$\alpha = (1/0{\cdot}97) \times [7{\cdot}66 - 0{\cdot}15 Z^{1{\cdot}8} - 0{\cdot}85] = 6{\cdot}79$$

which is between 2 and 8.

Hence $b = 6{\cdot}79 \times 5 = 33{\cdot}95$ m

Discussion and Conclusion

The factor $\psi = P^2/A$ is a nondimensional parameter reflecting the slope of the canal. For sections with circular arcs at corners as in Fig. 13·53 (*b*), P^2/A is given by simple expression of the aspect ratio, $\alpha = b/y$ and parameter X reflecting the side slope. The application of Manning's formula gives the expression $P^2/A = (A^4 S^{3/2})/(Q^3 N^3)$ which can be useful in solving problems of canal design. The factor $\phi = (QN)/(y^{8/3} S^{1/2})$ is a functions of α and Z and appropriate equations can be used for design problems where depth of canal is given. The calculations are suitable to be done using a hand calculator and give very accurate results in a short time.

The following types of linings are used :

(1) Permeable lining such as dry bricks on edge stone, or block Kankar.

(2) Impervious lining like

(a) Flag stone (b) Brick tile

(c) Asphaltic (d) Asphalt concrete

(e) Soil cement (f) Concrete lining.

Soil Cement. Cement 2 to 8 percent is mixed in sandy soils.

Asphaltic lining. A thin layer of hot asphalt is sprayed over the prepared sub grade. A cover of 300 mm of good earth is laid over the asphalt in layer and will rammed. Ready made asphaltic membranes are also available which can be laid over subgrade.

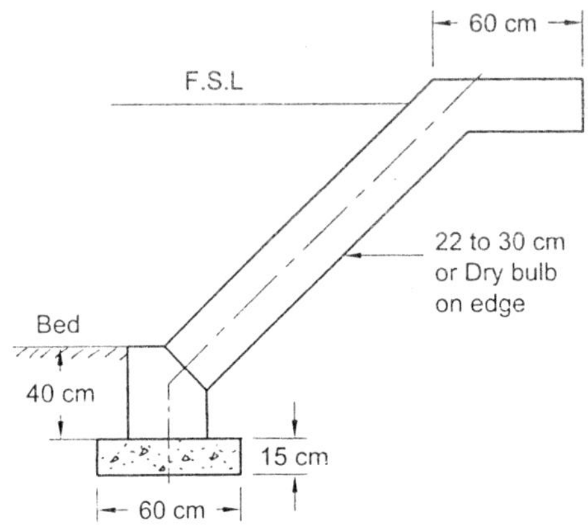

Fig. 13·54.

Asphaltic concrete. A mixture of hot asphalt with sand and stone aggregate in a desired workable ratio and thickness is laid over the subgrade.

Irrigation and Power Research Institute Amritsar in its paper published in 1990 entitled "why sediments deposit in lined channels" upset the previous belief that the cupshape (Mehbub section) has got higher carrying capacity than the conventional trapezoidal section. It was found that the silt transport capacity of rigid boundry channels (lined channels) was found to be proportional to the square of the ratio of hydraulic mean depth to the central depth of flow and in the case of the cup shaped section this parameter had a smaller value than compared to that of a rectangular or trapezoidal section. This indicated that the Mehbub's recommendations was wrong and cup shaped line section had lower silt carrying capacity than unlined trapezoidal section before lining. Hence adoption of cup shaped section should be avoided unless water to be carried is silt free such as tube wells or Bhakra dam water.

13·4. River Training Works

13·4·1. Marginal embankment or bunds. They are provided to protect an area situated behined the bund from the adverse effects of floods. The followings are the effects and their remedies.

(a) **Increase in the velocity.** The erosion effect of the velocity on the bund is minimised by pitching of the water side face of the bund. The velocity can be determined by the Lacey's equation for rivers discussed in design of channels.

(b) **Increase in water surface.** It is overcome by the provision of the adequate height of the bund. The rise inside the basin of the bund can be decided by studing a cross-section of the basin with bunds on the basis of the discharge likely to pass during floods with a velocity as calculated above. $Q = AV$ from which area can be calculated and the rise in height in the x-section is computed on graph.

(c) **The effect due to increased height at u/s of the bund.** The bund should meet the u/s ground gradually and the achievement of the level of the natural ground (having higher level than H.F.L.) keeping a slow upward slope in top of bund, so that the u/s area may not be effected.

(d) **Effect on the d/s of bund.** The bund should be tied to the natural ground by giving a smooth curve. The d/s area should be planted by doob grass so that it may not cause erosion.

(*e*) **Drainage of the area behind the bund.** Sluice gates are provided at drainages which are closed during floods and opened as the flood recedes to pass the water in the drain. Outlets with valves are provided to achieve the above effect automatically. The valve is hinged at top, rests on a sloping face of the pipe which closes during flood due to the water pressure over it, while it opens when flood recedes by the water in the pipe automatically.

13·4·2. Guide banks. They are provided u/s of a hydraulic structure. However they may also be provided at the d/s of the work. The purpose of the guide bank is as follows :

1. To give a straight and smooth entry to the work.
2. To protect the worksides from out flanking.

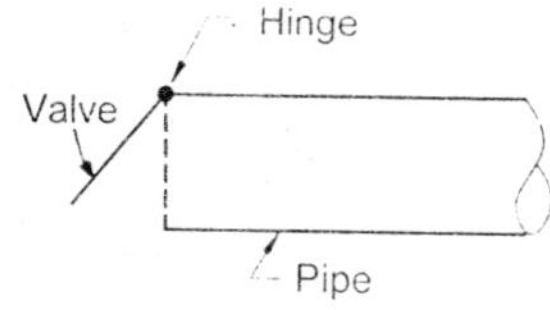

Fig. 13·55.

They are provided at both ends either parallel or in a converging stage towards the work with a bell mouthed entry. The banks are designed as earthen sections discussed in design of earthen dams with a top level at highest flood level keeping a due account for the afflux u/s of the work. The water side of banks are pitched and toe is provided with a launching or subsiding apron having a width of 1·5 times height of bank above scoured depth sloping at a slope of a 2 : 1. Thickness of the launching apron should be 1½ times the thickness of the pitching provided in slopes. If there is any scour it should be filled by dumping boulders. The scoured depth is calculated by Lacey's formula already discussed in bridge foundations. The total length of bund is kept 10 percent extra to the water way of the work, after which it is returned in a circular curve having radius as given in the table. This curved portion is called as impregnable head. The u/s subtended angle is kept as 120° to 145°. The pitching and the launching appron is provided on both sides of the bund. No spurs and groyens are provided on guiding bunds as they produce eddies and swirls.

Table 13·27. Radii and curves provided in the impregnable head in Ft.

Type of soil	*Probable max. scour in Ft.*	*Fall per mile in River in inches*			
		6	*9*	*12*	*18*
Very coarse sand	Below 20	250	300	350	400
Coarse	Above 20	310	375	440	500
Coarse	Below 30	360	425	490	670
	Above 30	430	520	590	700
Medium	Below 40	425	550	625	850
	Above 40	550	650	750	850
Fine	Below 50	590	675	760	850
	Above 50	725	825	925	1020
Very fine	Below 60	700	800	900	1000
	Above 60	900	1000	1100	1200

Radius of d/s ends of Guide bunds.

Half the above with a minimum such that it may maintain a proper curve.

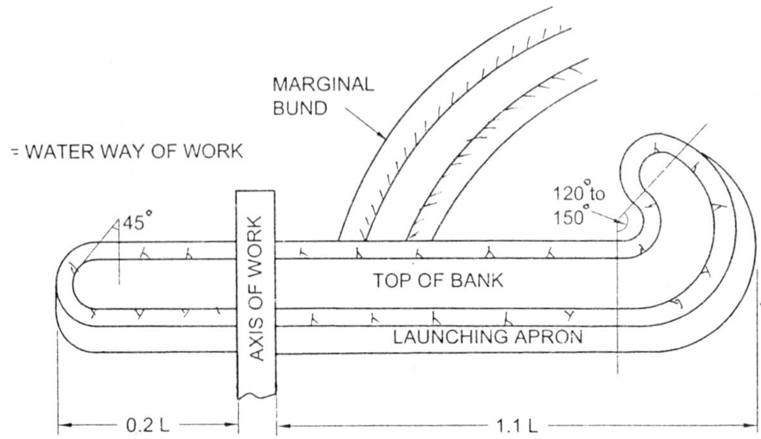

(*a*) Plan

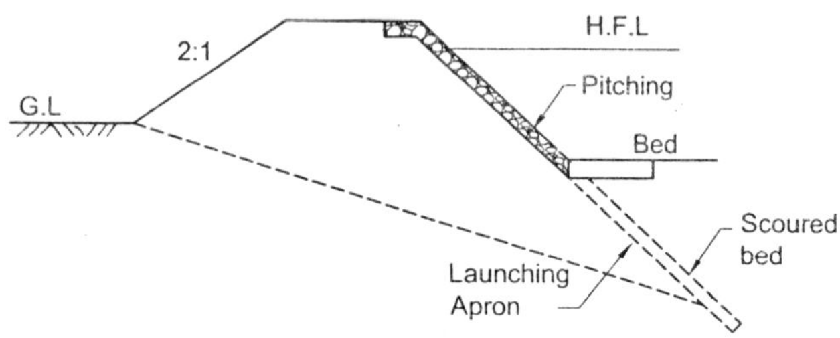

(*b*) Section

Fig. 13·56. Guide bund details.

13·4·3. Spurs. They are provided to protect a work from direct hit of the current to avoid emboyment or damage. By the provision of spurs, the direction of flow of current is diverted away from the work. Spurs provided in series forms a still pond in between causing silting in them. The directing spurs may be as shown in the figure. The spurs pointing d/s are called attractive and diverts the current again. The spurs pointing u/s are called repelling spurs and diverts the current away.

The spurs are divided as solid or impervious according to the material. A masonry or Boulder filled wooden crate is an example of solid type while the impermeable spurs are made by filling bushes in the wooden crates. The impermeable spurs cause silting as there is a still water in between them. They are more flexible and cheap.

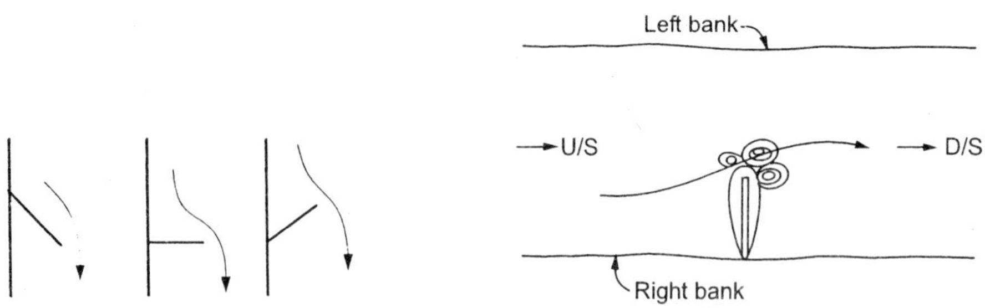

(*a*) Spurs. (*b*)

Fig. 13·57.

13·4·4. Groynes. Groynes are the embankment type structures, constructed transverse to the river flow, extending from the bank into the river. That is why, they may also be called 'Transverse Dykes'. They are constructed, in order to protect the bank from which they are extended, by deflecting the current away from the bank. As the water is unable to take a sharp embayment, the bank gets protected for certain distance upstream and downstream of the groyne. However, the nose of the groyne is subjected to tremendous action of water, and has to be heavily protected by pitching, etc. The action of eddies reduces from the head towards the bank, and, therefore, the thickness of slope pitching and upon can be reduced accordingly.

13·5. Foundations of Hydraulic Works

5·1. Design Principles of Hydraulic Works

The hydraulic works are subjected to the following effects :

(1) Hydraulic pressure (2) Seepage effect (3) Hydraulic jump.

(1) **Hydraulic pressure,** wH where w, weight of water/unit and H = head of water. The floor and the side works such as wings and abutments are subjected to this pressure and can be designed accordingly.

(2) **Seepage effect.** It comprises two factors, 1st piping and 2nd uplift.

Piping effect. The water under the floor of a hydraulic structure travells in stream lines according to the Darcy's law with velocity $K.H/L$ where L = length of creep of water and K is a cœfficient known as the coefficient of permeability of the soil. H is the head of water.

According to Bligh this water creeps along with the lower surface (where it is in touch with the soil) of the structure as shown in the figure. While according to Khosla water creeps along the shortest route available as shown in the next figure and not along the surface and hence the intermediate piles if shorter in depth are ineffective. Now a days works are being designed on Khosla's theory.

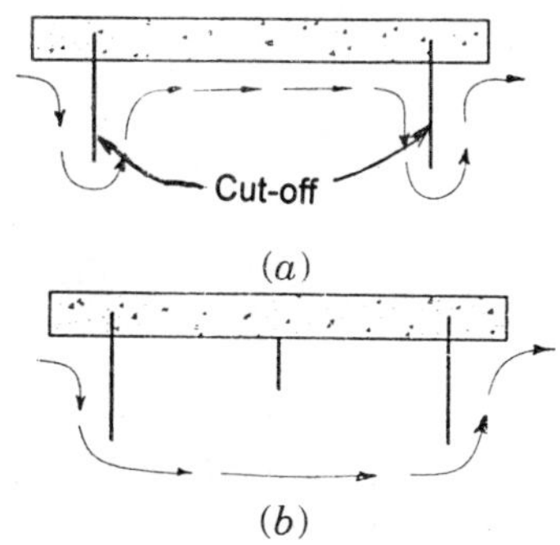

Fig. 13·58.

It is evident from the Darcy's law that as the length of creep increases the velocity goes on decrease. When this water emerges at the d/s end it has some residual velocity with it which is not dissipated during transit. This residual velocity is known as **exit velocity** or the **exit gradient**. The soils particles are brought up with water due to this velocity and lead to increased porosity of the soil and subsidence of the floor. In order to decrease this velocity or exit gradient d/s piles are provided to lengthen the creep. D/s filter is also provided to check the flow of soil particles from emerging water. (The flow of soil particles is also known as **bubling or boiling**)

According to Khosla the exit gradient say $G_E = \dfrac{H}{d}\dfrac{1}{\pi\sqrt{\lambda}}$ where d = depth of d/s pile line from the d/s floor level or the scoured depth if bed is scoured.

$$\lambda = 1 + \frac{\sqrt{1+d^2}}{2}$$

and $\alpha = b/d$, b being the total length of floor.

This value of exit gradient must be such that it may not cause scour and is called as **critical velocity** and is equal to $(1 - n)(w_1 - 1)$ where w_1 is the unit weight of the soil and n = porosity constant which is the ratio of the voids to the total volume. In practice the seepage gradients are taken as given in earthen dam section for different soils.

Uplift effect. The percolating water under floors exerts an upward pressure on the floor till it emerges at the d/s end. This pressure goes on decreasing according to length of the creep and is counter balanced by an equal weight of concrete in the floor. Say t is the thickness of the concrete at a particular sections than $t = \frac{H' - t}{G - 1}$ where H' is the head of water at the point under consideration. G = weight of concrete per unit volume. It is evident from the thickness formula that the thickness of the concrete is dependent of the head of water. Hence u/s of crest, the head is always is less than d/s, so it is always tried that the maximum length of the floor is provided at the u/s end (even a minimum length must to be provided at d/s, by which the remainder u/s is decided, which can be provided in a nominal thickness which can bear erosion).

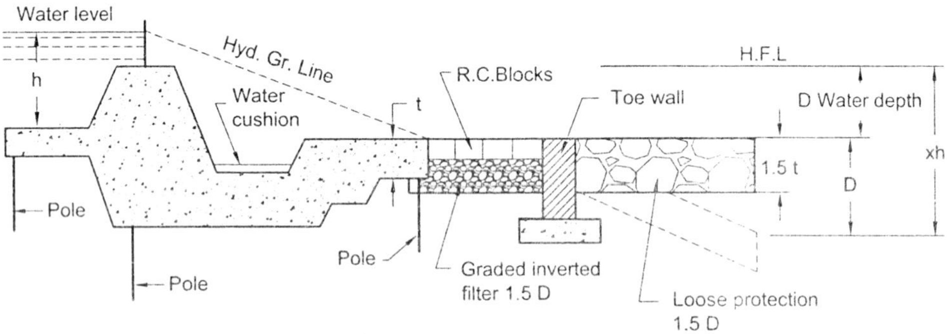

Fig. 13·59. Typical water cushion and D/s filter.

The u/s cut off reduces the head due to a sudden increase of creep length by its provision and effects in whole of the d/s length for floor thickness. So the u/s pile line is most effective.

Marking of the seepage or the hydraulic gradient line. It is started from the u/s end of the floor at its water surface and correction due to piles, thickness of floor and due to slopes in floor at all its controlling points is marked and hydraulic gradient line is decided. The corrections are calculated on the basis of Khosla's curves. The other approach is according to the creep length and seepage gradient of the soil concerned.

(3) **Hydraulic jump.** When a mass of water flowing with a hypercritical velocity over a crest of weir or on glacies meets with a mass of water flowing with a subcritical velocity an abrupt rise in the level of the former takes place with a great turbulance. This phenomenon is called as hydraulic jump and acts as an energy dissipating device. As energy $= \frac{(D_2 - D_1)^3}{4 D_1 D_2} = H_2$ is destroyed during the process. D_1 and D_2 being the depths of water flowing fast and slow. Due to reduction of energy the length of d/s protection works is decreased.

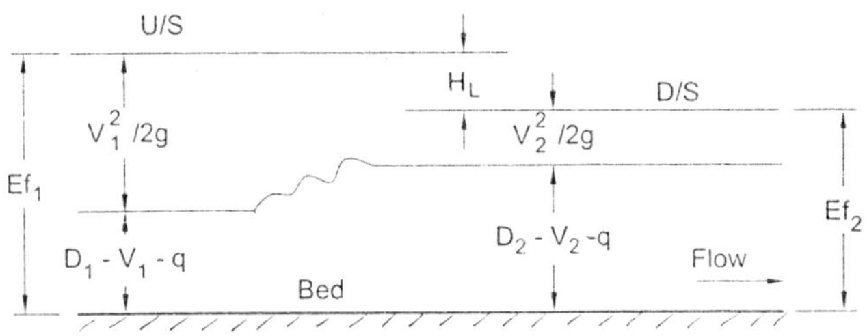

Fig. 13·60. Hydraulic jump.

(4) **Other d/s energy dissipation devices.** Two rows of staggers friction concrete blocks of suitable sizes are provided at the d/s edge of the water cushion trough or on d/s toe of the impervious floor.

Water cushion troughs. A depressed trough is provided at the d/s of the crest of a weir or fall.

(5) **D/s Filter.** A floor of filter D/S of the impervious floor is provided. Heavy cubical blocks of concrete are casted over the filter, having gaps between them to make the water pass.

Rough computation of seepage line, pressures and length by seepage gradient

Take hydraulic gradient as 1:7 for the soil concerned.

(1) The drop at u/s pile = $d/7$ in hydraulic gradient. (d being the depth of u/s pile)

(2) The drop from u/s to d/s pile = $b1/7$. ($b1$ being distance between the u/s and d/s piles)

(3) The drop at d/s pile due to rise of creep = $d1/7$. ($d1$ being the depth of the u/s pile)

Total drop in hydraulic gradient line = $d/7 + b1/7 + d1/7$.

(4) The required length of creep = $7h$, where h is the total drop in hydraulic gradient at site.

The residual head = $7h - (d/7 + b1/7 + d1/7)$

This can be overcomed either by increasing the floor length or by providing deeper piles to increase the creep length. Otherwise proper d/s filter is to be provided so that subgradation in soil may not develop due to the remaining velocity of sub soil water under the floor.

5·2. Bligh's Creep Theory. According to Bligh the percolating water follows the outline of the base of the foundation of the work. The length of path thus traversed by water is called 'the length of creep'. The total length b_1 is lost in the creep length L at a uniform rate. The loss of head per unit length of creep or h_1/L is called the hydraulic gradient. Bligh makes no difference between horizontal and vertical creep. Considering a horizontal floor with three vertical cut offs as shown in Fig. 13·61. The seepage water will then follow the path indicated by arrows and the creep length L will be given by $L = b + 2d_1 + 2d_2 + 2d_3$. The rate of loss of head or the hydraulic gradient is therefore $h_1/L = h_1/(b + 2d_1 + 2d_2 + 2d_3)$ per unit length of creep. There will be losses of head equal to $h_1/(L \times 2d)$, $2h_1/(L \times 2d_2)$ and $h_1/(L \times 2d_3)$ respectively in the planes of the three vertical cutoffs and the hydraulic gradient line will be drawn as shown in the Fig. 13·60. According to Bligh to ensure the safety of the work the following two criteria are required to be followed.

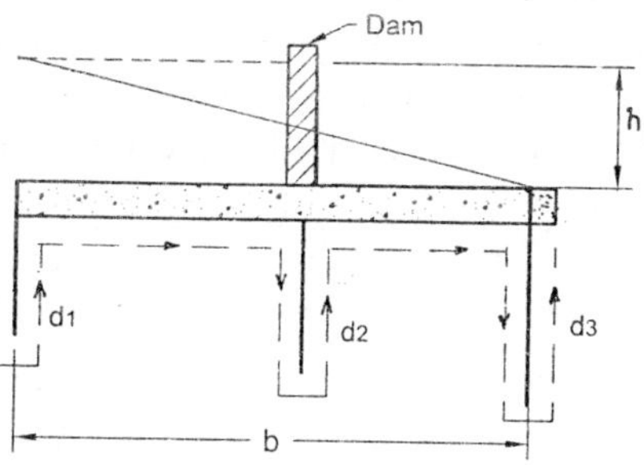

Fig. 13·61. Bligh's creep length.

Safety against piping. The length of creep should be sufficient to provide a safe hydraulic gradient according to the type of soil or $L = Ch$, where C is Bligh's coefficient for the soil. The following values of C were recommended by him.

(*i*) For fine mica coarse sand in North Indian Rivers $C = 15$

(*ii*) For coarse grained sand $C = 12$

(*iii*) For sand mixed with boulder, gravel and loam soda $C = 5$ to 9

The hydraulic gradient is then $1/C$ and hence according to Bligh there is no danger for the foundation if hydraulic gradient $\leq 1/C$. In the above consideration the loss of head is considered as the difference of u/s and d/s water levels, while in worst position the head is equal to the level of crest (water is full upto crest with no water in the d/s of the crest) to the d/s floor level.

Safety against uplift pressure. At any point, the hydraulic gradient line measures the extent to which there is residual head to cause uplift pressures. If a piezometric pipe is bored through the impervious floor upto its bottom, water will rise up in the pipe to the level of the hyd. gradient line. Supposing that the height of the hyd. gradient line above the bottom of the floor at any point is h', the uplift pressure exerted by water at that point is wh' (where w = density of water). If the floor thickness at the point is t and specific gravity of the so material of floor be G, the downward force per unit area due to weight of floor is twG. For equilibrium, the two must balance. Then $wh' = twG$ or $t = \frac{h'}{G}$ or $h' = tG$.

The ordinate h' from the HG line to the bottom of the floor can only be known if the thickness of the floor is determined.

Now $h' = tG$ deduct t from both sides

$$h' - t = t(G - 1)$$

$$t = \frac{h' - t}{G - 1}$$

Here $(h' - t)$ is the ordinate dropped from the H.G. line to the top of the floor, which is known in all cases. Dividing it by $(G - 1)$ or the submerged specific gravity of the floor material the thickness of the floor is directly determined.

The u/s floor can be kept at the minimum practicable thickness while the d/s floor thickness is designed to resist uplift. So as far as practible the maximum length of floor should be provided u/s while the balance should be provided d/s upto certain extent the thickness of the floor can roughly be taken equal to the ordinate from the H.G. line to the top of floor as a safer side as the specific gravity of soil is generally equal to 2·5 and submerged specific gravity = 1·5.

5·3. Reforms of Sh. AN Khosla over Bligh's theory

(*i*) The outerfaces of end sheet piles were much more effective than inner one's and the horizontal length of floor.

(*ii*) The intermediate sheet piles if smaller in length than the outer one's were ineffective except for local redistribution of pressure.

(*iii*) Undermining of floor starts from the tail end. If the hydraulic gradient at exit is more than that the '*critical gradient*' for the particular subsoil, the soil particles move with the flow of water thus causing progressive degradation of the sub soil resulting in cavity formation and ultimate failure. This phenomena is also called as boiling or piping or undermining.

(*iv*) It is absolutely eventual to have a reasonable deep vertical cut off at the d/s end to prevent undermining.

Table 13·28. Values of Lane's safe hydraulic gradient for different soils.

Type of soil	*Value of Lane's coefficient C_1*	*Lane's safe hydraulic gradient should be less than*
1. Very fine sand or silt	8·5	1/8·5
2. Fine sand	7·0	1/7
3. Coarse sand	5·0	1/5
4. Gravel and sand	3·5 to 3·0	1/3·5 to 1/3
5. Boulders, gravel and sand	2·5 to 3·0	1/2·5 to 1/3
6. Clayey soils	3·0 to 1·6	1/3 to 1/1·6

Concept of flownets. The seeping water does not creep along the bottom contour of impervious floor as stated by Bligh, but this water moves along a set of stream lines as shown in Fig. 13·62. This steady seepage in a vertical plane for a homogeneous soil can be expressed by Laplacian equation.

$$\frac{d^2\phi}{dx^2} + \frac{d^2\phi}{dz^2} = 0$$

where ϕ = flow potential = K_h ; where K is the coefficient of permeability of soil as defined by Darcy's law and h is the residual head at any point with in the soil.

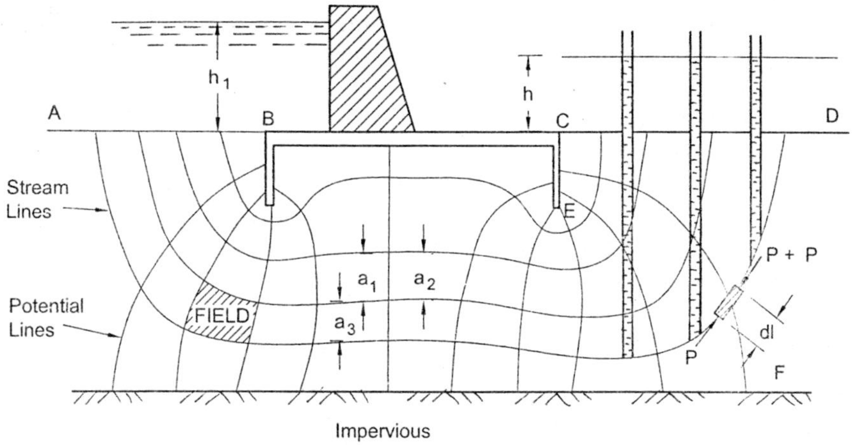

Fig. 13·62. Flownet of stream lines and equipotential lines.

The above equation represents two sets of curves viz. (*a*) Stream lines (*b*) Equipotential lines. The resultant flow diagram showing both the sets of curves is called a **flownet.**

Stream lines. A set of stream lines which indicate the paths adopted by particles of water flowing through the sub soil. Every particle entering the soil at a given point u/s of the work will trace out its own path and will represent a stream line. The first stream line follows the outline of the base of the work and is the same as Bligh's path of creep. Other stream lines follow smooth curves providing a gradual transition from the outline of the foundation to a semi ellipse, if the previous soil medium extends to a very large depth. In case there is an impervious boundary at a certain depth, the last stream line will follow the impervious boundary and the intermediate stream lines will represent a smooth transition from the 1st stream line to the last.

(*a*) **Equipotential lines.** (*a*) Treating the d/s bed as datum and assuming no water on the d/s side, it can be easily stated that every stream line possesses a head equal to h_1 while entering the soil, and when it emerges at the d/s end into the atmosphere, its head is zero. Thus the head h_1, is entirely lost during the seepage of water along the stream line.

At every intermediate point in its path, there is a certain residual head (h) still to be dissipated in the remaining length to be traversed to the d/s and this fact is applicable to every stream line, and hence there will be points on different stream lines having the same value of residual head h. If such points are joined together, the curve obtained is called a equipotential line.

Every particle of water on line AB having a residual head $h = h_1$ and on CD is having a residual head $h = 0$ if there is no water d/s and hence AB and CD are equipotential lines.

Since an equipotential line represents the joining of points of equal residual heads and hence if piezometers were installed on the equipotential lines, the water will rise in all the tubes to the same level.

(*b*) The seepage water exerts a force at each point in the direction of flow and tandential to it as shown in the Fig. 13·63. The force *F* has an upward component from the point where the stream line turns upward. For soil grains to remain stable, the upward component of this force should be counterbalanced by the submerged weight of the soil grain. This force has the maximum disturbing tendency at the exit end, because the direction of this force at the exit point is vertically upward and hence full force acts as its upward component. For the soil grain to remain stable the submerged weight of soil grain should be more than this upward disturbing force. The disturbing force at any point is proportional to the gradient of water pressure at that point. This gradient of pressure of water at the exit end is called the exit gradient. In order that the soil particles at each remains stable, the upward pressure at each should be safe.

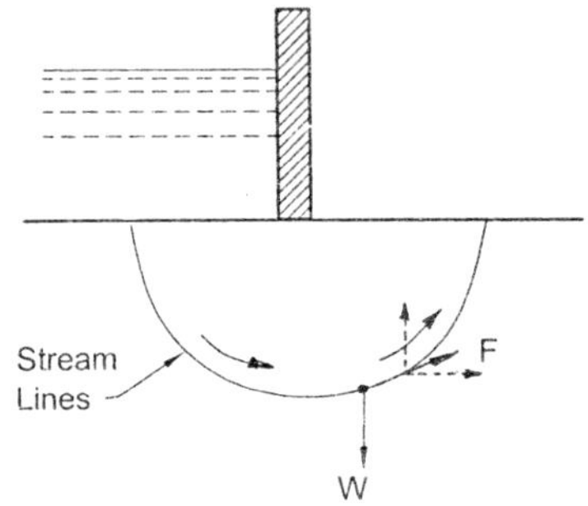

Fig. 13·63.

(*c*) The stream lines and an equipotential lines intersect each other at right angles as the particles of flowing water leads the path of steepest pressure gradient which is normal to the equipotential lines at all points. We can draw innumerable stream lines and equipotential lines. But in order that a flow net may be conveniently drawn and interpolated, a limited number of curves of either type are drawn so that every **field** or the space enclosed between two adjacent equipotential line and flow lines is an **'elementary square'** or a figure having all angles roughly right angles and their average dimensions are equal.

Critical exit gradient or the critical gradient. The exit gradient is called to be critical when the upward disturbing force on the grain is just equal to submerged weight of the grain at the exit when a factor of safety equal to 4 or 5 is used, the exit gradient can be taken as safe against piping.

Table 13·29. Khosla's safe exit gradients

Type of soil	*Safe exit gradient*
Shingle	0·25 to 0·20
Course sand	0·20 to 0·17
Fine soil	0·17 to 0·14

When the exit gradient or the **residual head** at exit is more than the submerged weight of the soil particles, the soil particles come up with water causing sub gradation of soil and ultimate subsidence of the foundation. This action is called as **bubling, undermining** or **piping**.

Under critical conditions exit gradient = $(1 - n)(S - 1)$ where

n= porosity of soil material and S = Specific gravity of the soil.

For soils as river sands S = 2·65 and n = 0·4, then the value of critical exit gradient = $(1 - 0{\cdot}4)(2{\cdot}65 - 1) = 1{\cdot}0$.

Hence exit gradients equate 1/4 to 1/5 of the critical value is safe against piping.

The undermining of the floor at d/s end can be checked by

(*a*) Providing a deep cut off of the d/s end to reduce the exit gradient.

(*b*) Providing a deeper cut off at u/s to reduce the head at the begging so that the lesser thickness may be provided to the floor and ultimately the reduced head to reach at the d/s end.

(*c*) To provide d/s filters to check the bubling so that soil particles may not go up with water which is comping up.

The depth of d/s pile is decided on this basis :

(*a*) **Maximum depth of scour.** The sheet piles must be atleast 3 m below the maximum scour depth.

(*i*) **Safe exit gradient.** It saves the structure against piping.

(*ii*) Uplift pressure due to the hydraulic jump. (details given is hydraulic jump)

Use of flownet in design. Once the flow net for a given problem is obtained, all the effects of seepage can be computed from it. The distribution of uplift pressure on the base is determined by the inter section of the equipotential lines with the base. Wherever an equipotential line meets the base, the position of the hydraulic gradient line can be determined by measuring the residual head h represented by that equipotential line, above the level of the d/s bed. For example, if the total number of potential drops is 11, the residual head where the 7th line meets the base will be 7/11 h, to be measured above the d/s bed level. Once the hydraulic gradient line is plotted, the thickness of the floor can be worked out.

The rate of loss of head or the gradient of exit is determined from the fields at the exit. If Δh is the loss of head between two successive equipotential lines $\left(= \frac{h_1}{N_d}\right)$ (N_d being the no. of line) and a the distance apart at any place between the last equipotential line CD and the last but one equipotential line EF, the exit gradient at that place is $\frac{\Delta h}{a}$ as is obvious from the Fig. 13·63, the two equipotential lines are closest together just at the d/s end of the work and the hydraulic gradient is steepest there. This steepest value of exit gradient should be within safe limits. The configuration of the flownet depends on the geometry of the figure *i.e.* the shape of the foundation, the depth of the impervious boundary and the levels of the u/s and d/s beds. Under the same boundary conditions and applied head, the pressure distribution and the exit gradient will be independent of the type of soil so long as it is homogeneous and follows Darcy's law. The critical gradient depends on the porosity and the specific gravity of the soil.

In small works where the d/s or u/s cut offs are not provided the Bligh's theory can be used. Even though a d/s cut off is still must be provided to ensure safety, though not necessary according to the Bligh's theory.

Methods of drawing flownets. There are a number of method of drawing flownets, some of them are given below :

(*a*) **Graphical sketching.** The stream lines and the equipotential lines are adjusted by trial to confirm the boundary conditions and to divide the flow net into fields which are true elementary squares.

(*b*) **The electrical analogy method** makes use of the fact that the same Laplacian equation is also applies to distribution of electrical potential through a homogeneous conducting medium. The relaxation method is a process of numerical integration to solve the Laplacian equation.

The method that is generally is being used for designing Hydraulic works is the "Method of independent variables" evolved by Dr. Khosla as it is simple to use, quick and accurate.

Khosla's Method of independent variables for pressures and exit gradients for seepage below a weir.

The principle of the method of independent variables evolved by Dr. Khosla consists of breaking up a complex profile into a number of simple profile each of which is independently amenable to mathematical treatment. Mathematical solutions of flownets have been obtained for a number of such simple standard forms, the most useful of which are :

(*a*) A straight horizontal flow of negligible thickness with a sheet pile line at either end Fig. (*i*) and (*ii*).(Fig. 13·64) (*b*) A straight horizontal floor depressed below the bed but with no vertical cut off (Fig. (*iii*)).

(*c*) A straight horizontal floor of negligible thickness with a sheet pile line at some intermediate position (Fig. *iv*)

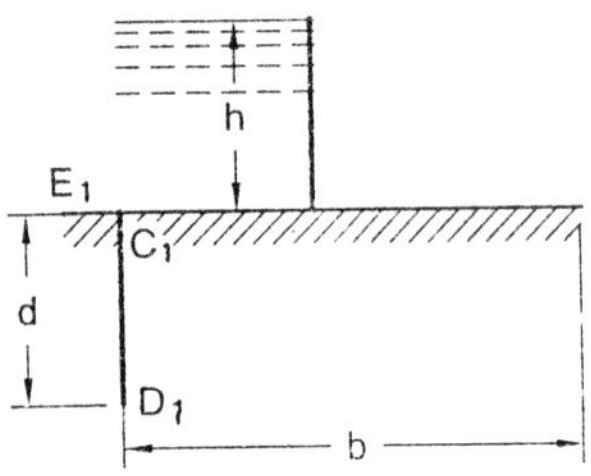

$$\phi_{C_1} = 100 - \phi_E$$

$$\phi_{D_1} = 100 - \phi_D$$

(*i*)

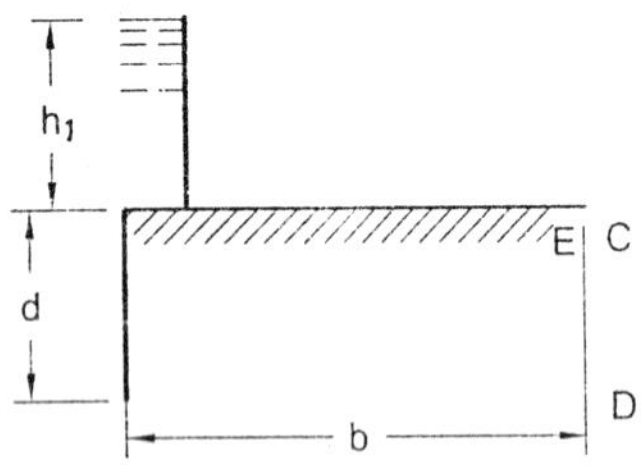

$$\phi_E = \frac{1}{\pi}\cos^{-1}\left(\frac{\lambda - 2}{\lambda}\right) \quad \text{where } \lambda = \frac{1 + \sqrt{1 + \alpha^2}}{2}$$

$$\phi_D = \frac{1}{\pi}\cos^{-1}\left(\frac{\lambda - 1}{\lambda}\right) \quad \alpha = \frac{b}{d} \text{ (respectively)}$$

(*ii*)

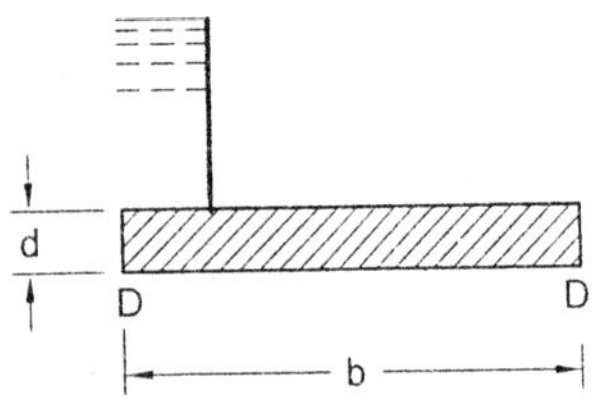

$$\phi_{D'} = \frac{2}{3}(\phi_E - \phi_D) + \frac{3}{\alpha^2}$$

$$\phi_{D'_1} = 100 - \phi_{D'}$$

(*iii*)

$$\phi_E = \frac{1}{\pi}\cos^{-1}\left(\frac{\lambda_1 - 1}{\lambda}\right);\ \phi_D = \frac{1}{\pi}\cos^{-1}\left(\frac{\lambda_1}{\lambda}\right);\ \phi_C = \frac{1}{\pi}\cos^{-1}\left(\frac{\lambda_1 + 1}{\lambda}\right)$$

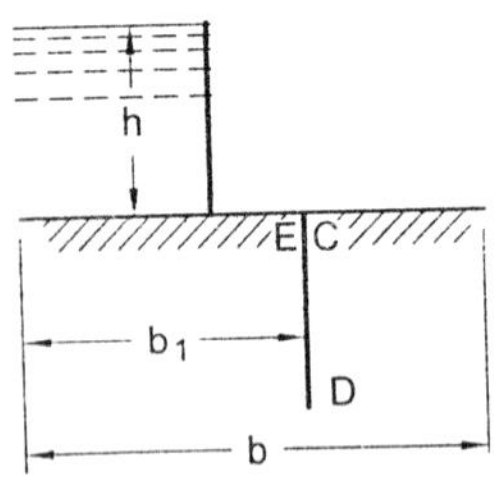

$$\text{where } \lambda = \frac{\sqrt{1 + \alpha_1^2} + \sqrt{1 + \alpha_2^2}}{2};\ \lambda_1 = \frac{\sqrt{1 + \alpha_1^2} - \sqrt{1 + \alpha_2^2}}{2}$$

$$\alpha_1 = \frac{b_1}{d};\ \alpha_2 = \frac{b_2}{d}$$

(*iv*)

Fig. 13·64.

The results of the mathematical solutions of these forms are presented in the form of curves (Khosla's Curve Plate 13·8 (*a*)) from which the percentage pressures or the proportion of the residual head to the total seepage head can be determined at key points or the junction points of sheet piles with flow in the figs. *i, ii* and *iv* and the bottom corners of the floor in Fig. (*iii*). The pressures at intermediate points are assumed to vary along a straight line. This does not introduce any appreciable error. The exit gradient for the form (*ii*) can be determined from curve (*c*). This is the only form important from point of view of exit gradients as it is found that a vertical cut off at d/s end is essential for keeping it at a safe value. The directions for reading the curves are given in the curves themselves and are self explanatory. The principle of reversibility of flow is made use of to reduce the number of curves required. If the direction of flow is reversed, other conditions remaining the same, the flow net pattern remains unaltered. Thus if percentage pressures are known for a sheet pile line at d/s end (Fig. (*ii*) at the key point *E*, *D* and *C*, if the flow is reversed. These points correspond to *C*, *D* and *E* respectively (Fig. (*i*) and the percentage pressures at the later will be 100% pressure of the former.

The percentage pressure observed from the curves for the simple forms into which the profile is broken up, have been demonstrated to hold for the assembled profile as a whole subject to certain correction as given below :

(*i*) **Correction for thickness of floor.** In the standard forms with vertical cut offs, the thickness of the floor is assumed to be negligible. Thus as observed from the curves, the pressure at the junction points *E* and *C* pertain to the level at the top of the floor where as the actual junction is with the bottom of the floor. The pressures at the actual points *E* and *C* are interpolated by assuming straight line variation from this hypothetical point *c* to *D* and also from *D* to *C* (Fig. 13·65 (*a*)).

(*ii*) **Correction for the mutual interference of sheet piles.** Let *C* be the correction to be applied as percentage of head, *b*′, the distance between the two pile lines, *D*, the depth of the pile line, the influence of which has to be determined to the neighbouring pile of depth *d*. *D* to be measured below the level at which interference is desired.

d, depth of pile on which the effect of pile of depth *D* is sought to be determined and

b, the total floor length (Fig. 13·65)

Then $$C = 19\sqrt{\frac{D}{b'}}\left(\frac{d+D}{b}\right)$$

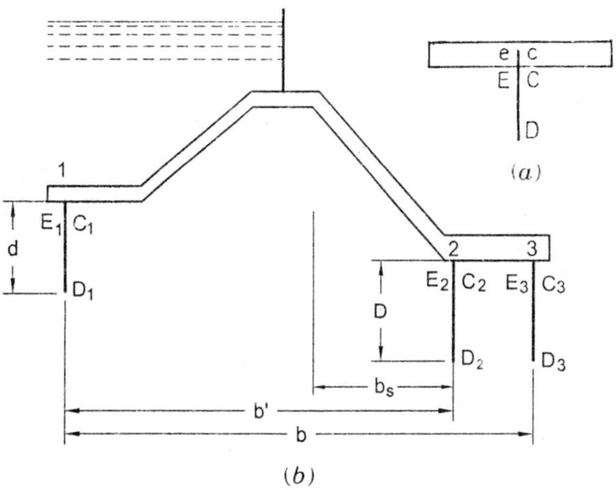

Fig. 13·65.

This correction is + ve for points in the rear or backwater and –ve for points forward in the direction of flow. This equation does not apply to the effect of an outer pile on an intermediate pile if the later is equal to or smaller than the former and is at a distance less than twice the length of the outer pile (in Fig. 13·65(*b*)), the dimensions have been marked as they will apply to point *C* on pile line owing to the influence of pile line 2. The effect of interference of a pile is to be determined only for the face of the adjacent pile towards the interfering *i.e.* pile No. 2 will interfere with the d/s face of pile No. 1 and u/s face of pile No. 3.

(*iii*) **Correction for the slope of the floor.** A correction is applied for a sloping floor and is taken as +ve for the down and – ve for the up slopes following the direction of flow. Values of correction of standard slope such as 1 : 1, 2 : 1, 3 : 1 etc.

Table 13·30. Table for slope correction

Slope, Horizontal : Horizontal	*Correction factor*	*Slope, Horizontal : Vertical*	*Correction factor*
1 : 1	11·2	5 : 1	2·8
2 : 1	6·5	6 : 1	2·5
3 : 1	4·5	7 : 1	2·3
4 : 1	3·3	8 : 1	2·0

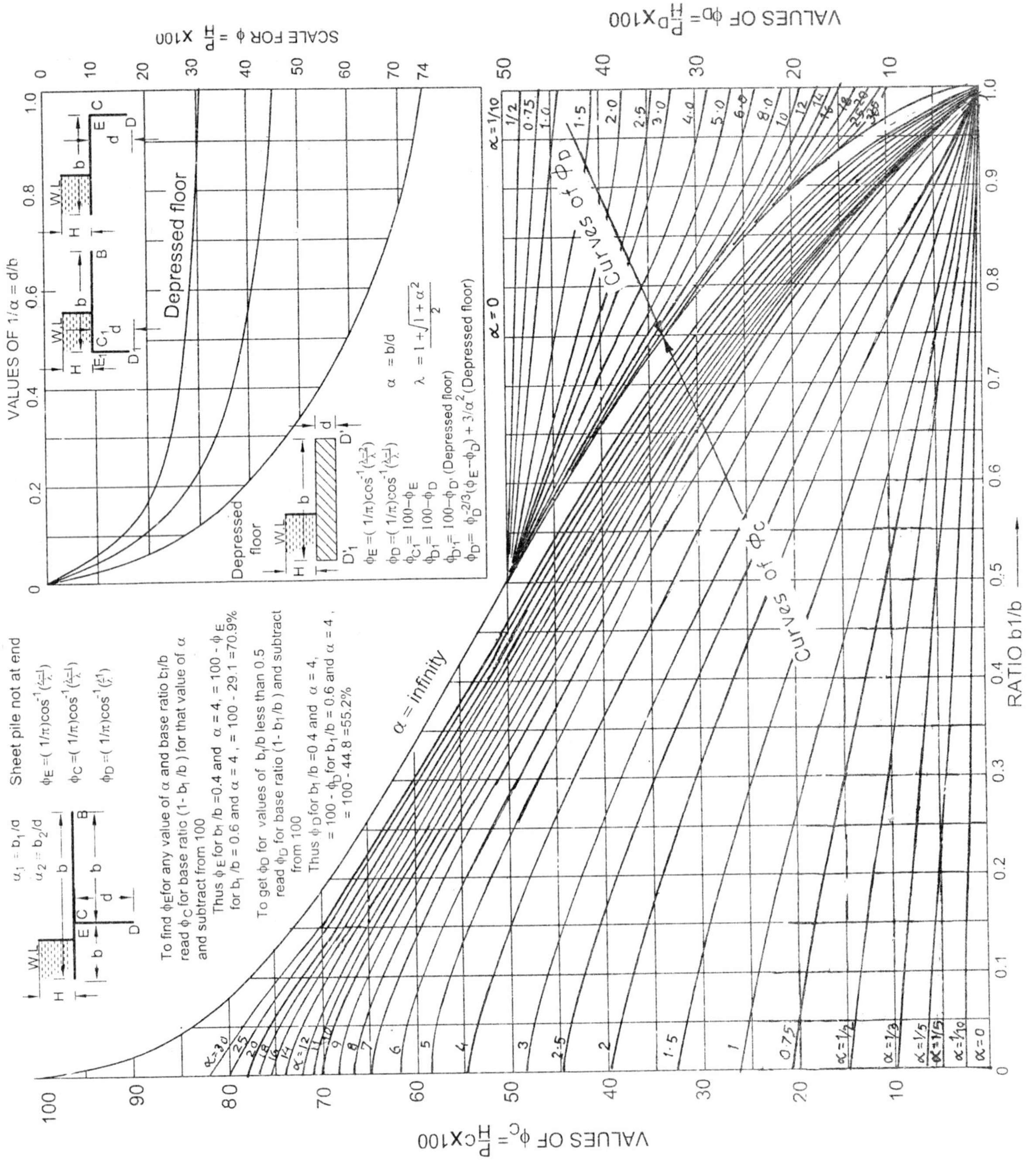

Plate. 13·8 (*a*). Khosla's Pressure Curve

The correction factor given above is to be multiplied by the horizontal length of the slope and divided by the distance between the two pile lines between which the sloping floor is located. This correction is applicable only to the key points of the pile line fixed at the start or the end of the slope.

This correction is applicable to the point E of pile No. 2 in the direction of flow and will be obtained by multiplying the appropriate figure for the above table by $\frac{b_s}{b}$. The correction is –ve for the up and +ve for the down slopes.

Exit gradient. It has been determined that for a standard form consisting of a floor of length b with a vertical cut off of depth d at its d/s end Fig. (13·65) the exit gradient G_E is given by the equation.

$G_E = \frac{h}{d} \cdot \frac{1}{\pi\sqrt{\lambda}}$ where λ is a function of $\alpha = b/d$. From the curves (Khosla's Curves Plate 13·8 (b)) for any value of $\alpha = b/d$, the corresponding value of λ or directly that of the function $\frac{1}{\pi\sqrt{\lambda}}$ can be read off. Knowing the values of h and d, the value of G_E is easily calculated. It is obvious from the equation $G_E = h/d \cdot \frac{1}{\pi\sqrt{\lambda}}$, that if $d = 0$, G_E is infinite. It is therefore essential that a vertical cut off should be provided at the d/s end of the floor. In case scour takes place d/s of the work, the effective depth of the cut off must be measured below scoured bed for use of the above expressions.

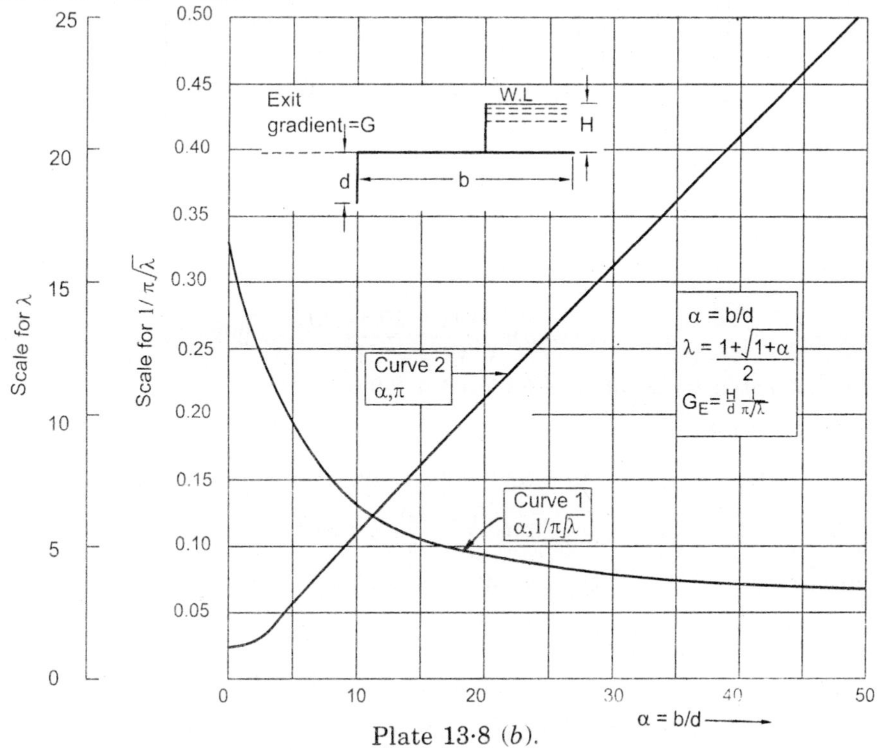

Plate 13·8 (b).

Procedure. To start with assume a width b of the floor equal to = CH, where C = coeff., Bligh's hydraulic gradient (or Lane's safe hydraulic gradient) and H is the head of water. Prepare u/s and d/s pile lines according to the site conditions. The u/s pile line must be taken some what more as it effects the thickness of the d/s floor but it can be done up to a certain extent. The d/s pile line may be taken about 3 m deeper than the scoured depth or as per site conditions. The middle pile line can be taken deeper than the outer pile lines as the shorter pile in the middle is ineffective.

After calculating exit gradient the floor length or the depth of the piles can be readjusted to reach to a safer position of the floor and structure.

Example illustrating the use of Khosla's curves

u/s pile line

$$d = 320 - 298 = 22'$$

$$b = 163,\ 1/\alpha = \frac{22}{163} = 0{\cdot}135$$

From the Khosla's curves

$$\phi_D = 77{\cdot}7\% \ ; \ \phi_c = 68\%$$

ϕ_c correction for thickness of floor $= \dfrac{320 - 317.5}{22}(77{\cdot}7 - 68) = 1{\cdot}1\% \ (+)$

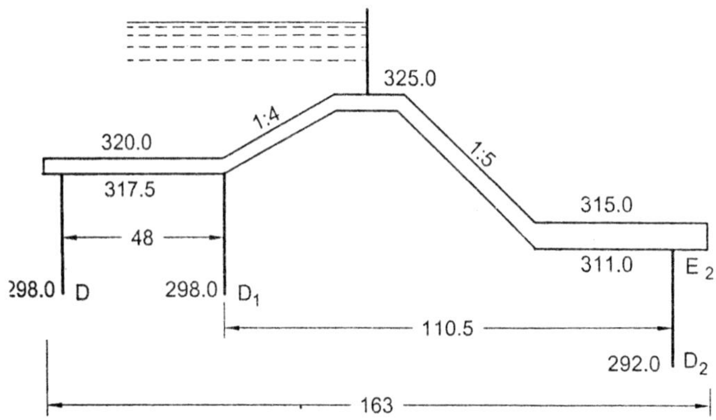

Fig. 13·66.

ϕ_c correction for interference of 2nd pile line

$$= 19\sqrt{\frac{19.5}{48}} \times \frac{19.5 + 19.5}{163} = 2{\cdot}9\% \ (+)$$

Hence corrected value of $\phi_c = 68 + 1{\cdot}1 + 2{\cdot}9 = 72\%$

Intermediate pile line

$$d = 320 - 298 = 22, \quad b/d = \frac{163}{22} = 7{\cdot}4 = \alpha$$

$$b_1 = 50, \ \frac{b_1}{b} = \frac{50}{163} = 0{\cdot}307$$

From curves $\qquad \phi_{E_1} = 71{\cdot}4\%, \ \phi_{D_1} = 61{\cdot}4\%, \ \phi_{C_1} = 53{\cdot}2\%$

ϕ_{E_1} correction for thickness of floor

$$= \frac{320 - 317{\cdot}5}{22} \times (71{\cdot}4 - 61{\cdot}4) = 1{\cdot}1\% \ (-)$$

ϕ_1 correction for interference of 1st pile line $= -\ 2{\cdot}9\%$

The value remaining the same as both pile lines are equal and placed at the same depth.

Corrected $\qquad \phi_{E_1} = 71{\cdot}4 - 1{\cdot}1 - 2{\cdot}9 = 67{\cdot}4\%$

ϕ_{C_1} correction for depth $\qquad = \dfrac{320 - 317{\cdot}5}{22} \times (61{\cdot}4 - 53{\cdot}2) = 0{\cdot}9\% \ (+)$

ϕ_{C_1} correction for interference of 3rd pile line

$$d = 317{\cdot}5 - 298 = 19{\cdot}5$$

$$D = 317.5 - 292 = 25{\cdot}5$$

Hence correction $= 19\sqrt{\dfrac{25{\cdot}5}{110{\cdot}5}} \times \dfrac{25{\cdot}5 + 19{\cdot}5}{163} = 2{\cdot}5\%\ (+)$

ϕ_{C_1} correction for slope—From table of slope corrections

For a slope 1 in 4 = 3·3% (–) as slope is upward in direction of flow

Length of slope = 8′ and the distance between the two pile lines = 110·5′,

hence actual correction to be applied $= 3{\cdot}3 \times \dfrac{8}{110{\cdot}5} = 0{\cdot}24\%\ (-)$.

Hence corrected value of $\phi_{C_1} = 53{\cdot}2 + 0{\cdot}9 + 2{\cdot}5 = 0{\cdot}24 = 56{\cdot}4\%$

d/s pile line— $d = 3/5 - 292 = 23'$, $1/d = d/b = \dfrac{23}{163} = 6{\cdot}143$

$$\phi_{D_2} = 23\%\ ;\ \phi_{E_2} = 33\%$$

ϕ_{E_2} correction for depth $= \dfrac{315 - 311}{23}(33 - 23) = 1.7\%\ (-)$

ϕ_{E_2} correction for interference of intermediate pile line—

$$D = 322 - 298 = 13'$$

$$d = 311 - 292 = 19$$

Correction $= 19\sqrt{\dfrac{13}{110{\cdot}5}} \times \dfrac{13 + 19}{163} = 1{\cdot}3\%\ (-)$

Hence corrected value of $\phi_{E_2} = 33 - 17 - 1{\cdot}3 = 30\%$

Exit gradient

Let the water be headed upto a level of 335·0 on the u/s side with no flow d/s

The seepage head $h_1 = 335 - 315 = 20'$

The depth of cut off $d = 315 - 292 = 23'$

$$\alpha = \frac{b}{d} = \frac{163}{23} = 7{\cdot}1\%$$

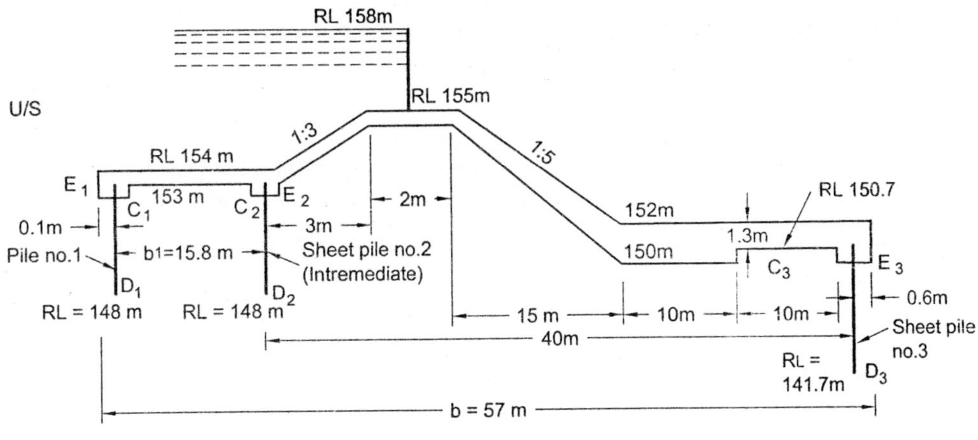

Fig. 13·67.

From Figs., of Khosla's curves, $C = \dfrac{1}{\pi\sqrt{\lambda}} = 0{\cdot}158$ for $\alpha = 71$

Hence $$G_E = \frac{h_1}{d} \cdot \frac{1}{\pi\sqrt{\lambda}} = \frac{20}{23} \times 0{\cdot}158 = 0{\cdot}137$$

The exit gradient with no scour, will therefore be 0·137 or 1 in 7·3 (Safe)

Determination of : (*i*) Percentage pressure at key points

(*ii*) Exit Gradient

(*iii*) Drawing of hydraulic gradient line with pond level at u/s and no water at d/s.

(1) **u/s pile line No. (1)**

Total length of floor $= b = 57{\cdot}0$ m

Depth of us/pile line $= d = 154{\cdot}00 - 148{\cdot}00 = 6{\cdot}0$ m

$$\alpha = \frac{b}{d} = \frac{57{\cdot}0}{6{\cdot}0} = 9{\cdot}5\ ;\ \frac{1}{\alpha} = \frac{1}{9{\cdot}5} = 0{\cdot}105$$

From curve (*a*) $\phi_{C_1} = 100 - 29 = 71\%$

$\phi_{D_1} = 100 - 20 = 80\%$

These values of ϕ_{C_1} and ϕ_{D_1} needs corrections as below

(*a*) **Correction at C_1 for mutual interference of piles, ϕ_{C_1}** is affected by intermediate pile No. 2

$$\text{Correction} = 19\sqrt{\frac{D}{b_1}}\left(\frac{d+D}{b}\right)$$

where D = Depth of Pile No. 2 = 153·00 − 148·00 = 5·0

d = Depth of Pile No. 1 = 153·0 − 148·0 = 5·0 m

b_1 = Distance between two piles = 15·8 m

b = Total floor length = 57·0 m

$$\text{Correction} = 9\sqrt{\frac{5}{15{\cdot}7}}\left(\frac{5+5}{57}\right) = 1{\cdot}88\%$$

Since the point C_1 is in rear in the direction of flow, the correction is (+ ve)

∴ The correction due to pile interference on C_1 = 1·88% (+ ve)

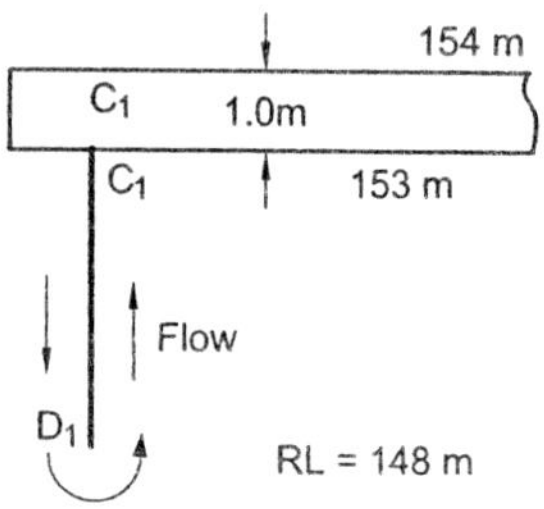

Fig. 13·68 (*a*).

(*b*) **Correction of C_1 due to thickness of floor**

Pressure calculated from curve of C_1', Fig 13·68 (*a*), but we want the pressure at C_1. Pressure at C_1 shall be more than at C_1' as the direction of flow is from C_1 to C_1' as shown and hence the correction will be (+ve)

or $$D = \left[\frac{80\% - 71\%}{154{\cdot}0 - 148{\cdot}0}\right] \times (154{\cdot}00 - 153{\cdot}00) = \frac{9}{6} \times 1 = 1{\cdot}5\%(+\text{ve})$$

(*c*) Correction due to slope at C_1 is nil as this point is neither situated at the start nor at the end of a slope.

∴ Corrected $\phi_{C_1} = 71\% + 1{\cdot}88\% + 1{\cdot}5\% = 74{\cdot}38\%$

and $\phi_{D_1} = 80\%$

(2) For intermediate pile line No. (2)

$d = 154{\cdot}00 - 148{\cdot}00 = 6{\cdot}0$ m

$$b = 57{\cdot}0 \text{ m}\ ;\ \alpha = \frac{b}{a} = \frac{57{\cdot}0}{6{\cdot}0} = 9{\cdot}5$$

Using curves of Plate 13·8 (*b*) we have b_1 in this case = 0·6 + 15·8 = 16·4 m and b = 57·0 m

∴ and $\frac{b_1}{b} = \frac{16.4}{57.0}$ = 0·298 is the base ratio

$$1 - \frac{b_1}{b} = 1 - 0.298 = 0.702$$

ϕ_{E_2} = 100 – 30% = 70% (where 30% is ϕ_C for a base ratio of 0·702 and α = 9·5)

ϕ_{C_2} = 56% (For C base ratio 0·298 and α = 9·5)

ϕ_{D_2} = 100 – 37 = 63% (where 37% is ϕ_D for a base ratio of 0·702 and α = 9·5)

Correction for ϕ_E

(*a*) **Correction at E$_2$ for sheet pile lines.** Pile No. (1) will affect the pressure at E_2 and since E_2 is in forward direction of flow, this correction will be –ve. The amount of this correction is given as—

$$19\sqrt{\frac{D}{b_1}}\left[\frac{d+D}{b}\right]$$

where D = Depth of pile No. 1, the effect of which is considered is
= 153·0 – 148·0 = 5·0 m
d = Depth of pile No. 2 the effect of which is considered
= 153·0 – 148·0 = 5·0 m
b_1 = distance between two pile lines = 15·8 m
b = total length of floor = 57·0 m

Correction $= 19\sqrt{\frac{5}{15.7}}\left(\frac{5+5}{57}\right)$ = 1·88% (– ve)

(*b*) **Correction at E$_2$ due to floor thickness**

$$= \frac{\phi_{E2} - \phi_{D2}}{\text{Distance between } E_2D_2} \times \text{Thickness of floor}$$

$$= \frac{70\% - 63\%}{(154 - 148)} \times 1.0 = 7/6 \times 1.0 = 1.17\%$$

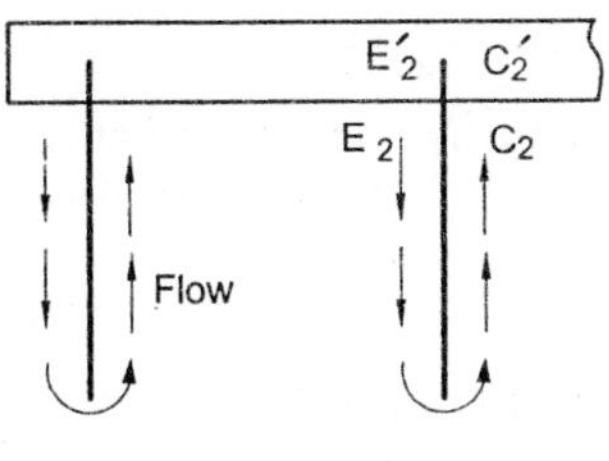

Fig. 13·68 (*b*)

Since the pressure above bed at E_2' and not at E_2 (See Fig. 13·68 (*b*)) and by looking at the direction of flow, it can be stated easily that the pressure at E_2 should be less than that at E_2', hence the correction is –ve.

∴ Correction at E_2 due to floor thickness = 1·17% (– ve)

(*c*) **Correction at E$_2$ due to slope** is nil as the point E_2 is neither situated at the start of the slope nor either end of slope.

Hence the corrected percentage pressure at E_2 = corrected ϕ_{E_2} = 70% – 1·88% – 1·17%
= 66·95%

Correctness for ϕ_{C2}

(*a*) Correction at C_2 due to pile interference at C_2 is affected pile No. (3) and since the point is in the backwater in the direction of flow, this correction is (+ ve). The amount of this correction is as below

$$= 19\sqrt{\frac{D}{b'}} \times \left(\frac{D+d}{b}\right)$$

where D = depth of pile No. 3, the effect of which is considered below the level at which interference is desired.

= 153·0 – 141·7 = 11·3

d = Depth of pile No. 2, the effect on which is considered

= 153·0 – 148·0 = 5·0 m

b' = Distance between the pile No. 2 and pile No. 3 = 40·0 m

b = Total floor length = 57·0 m

$$\text{Correction} = 19\sqrt{\frac{11{\cdot}0}{40{\cdot}0}} \times \left(\frac{11{\cdot}3 + 50}{57{\cdot}0}\right) = 2{\cdot}89\% \text{ (+ ve)}$$

(*b*) Correction at C_2 shall be more than that at C_2', and since the observed pressure is at C_2', this correction shall be (+ ve) and its amount is the same as was calculated for the point E_2 = 1·17%

Hence correction at C_2 due to floor thickness = 1·17% (+ ve)

(*c*) Correction at C_2 due to slope. Since the point C_2 is selected at the start of a slope of 3 : 1 *i.e.* upslope in the direction of flow. The correction is (– ve).

Correction factor for 3 : 1 slope from table = 4·5

Horizontal length of the slope = 3 m

Distance between two pile lines between which the sloping floor is located = 40·0 m

$$\therefore \quad \text{Actual correction} = 4{\cdot}5 \times \frac{3}{40} = 0{\cdot}34\% \text{ (– ve)}$$

Hence correction ϕ_{C1} = 56% + 2·89% + 1·17% – 0·34% = 59·72%

(3) **D/S pile line**

$$d = 152{\cdot}0 - 141{\cdot}7 = 9{\cdot}3 \text{ m}$$

$$b = 57{\cdot}0 \text{ m}$$

$$1/\alpha = \frac{d}{b} = \frac{10{\cdot}3}{57{\cdot}0} = 0{\cdot}181$$

From curves of plate (*a*) we get

$$\phi_{D3} = 32\%$$

$$\phi_{E3} = 38\%$$

Correction for ϕ_{E3}

(*a*) Correction due to piles. The point E_3 is effected by pile No. 2 and since E_3 is in the forward direction of flow from pile No. 3, the correction is (– ve) and its amount is given by—

$$19\sqrt{\frac{D_1}{b}}\left(\frac{d+D}{b}\right).$$

where D = Depth of pile No. 2, the effect of which is considered = 150·7 – 148·0 = 2·7 m

d = Depth of pile No. 3, the effect on which is considered

= 150·7 – 141·7 = 9·0 m

b' = Distance between piles = 40·0 m

b = Total floor length = 57·0 m

$$\text{The correction} = 19\sqrt{\frac{2{\cdot}7}{40}} \times \left(\frac{9 + 2{\cdot}7}{57}\right) = 1{\cdot}02\% \text{ (– ve)}$$

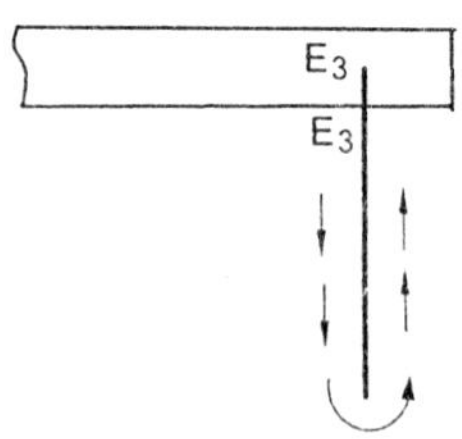

Fig. 13·68 (*c*).

(*b*) **Correction due to floor thickness.**

It can be stated that the pressure at E_3 shall be less than E_3' and since the pressure observed from curves is E_3' ; This correction is –ve and its amount is as below

$$= \frac{38\% - 32\%}{152{\cdot}0 - 141{\cdot}7} \times 1{\cdot}3 = \frac{16}{10{\cdot}3} \times 13 = 0{\cdot}76\% \text{ (– ve)}$$

(*c*) Correction due to slope at E_3 is nil, as the point E_1 is neither situated at the start nor at the end of any slope.

Hence corrected ϕ_{E_3} = 38% – 1·02 – 0·76% = 36·22%

The corrected pressure at various key points are tabulated as below :

u/s pile No. 1	*Intermediate Pile No. 2*	*d/s Pile No. 3*
ϕ_{E1} = 100%	ϕ_{E2} = 66·95%	ϕ_{E3} = 36·22%
ϕ_{D1} = 80·0%	ϕ_{D2} = 63·0%	ϕ_{D3} = 32·0%
ϕ_{C1} = 74·38%	ϕ_{C2} = 59·72%	ϕ_{C3} = 0%

Exit Gradient. Let the water is headed up to RL 158·0 m (pond level) on u/s side while No flow d/s.

The maximum seepage head $= H = 158{\cdot}0 - 152{\cdot}0 = 6{\cdot}0$ m

The depth of d/s cut off OH $= d = 152{\cdot}0 - 141{\cdot}7 = 10{\cdot}3$ m

Total floor length $= b = 57{\cdot}0$ m

$$\alpha = \frac{b}{d} = \frac{57{\cdot}0}{10{\cdot}3} = 5{\cdot}33$$

For value of $\alpha = 5{\cdot}53$, $\frac{1}{\pi\sqrt{\lambda}}$ (from the Khosla's curves is equal to 0·18. Hence G_E = $\frac{H}{d} \cdot \frac{1}{\pi\sqrt{\lambda}} = \frac{6{\cdot}0}{10{\cdot}3} \times 0{\cdot}18 = \frac{1}{9{\cdot}53} = 0{\cdot}105$ *i.e.* 1 in 9·53 (Safe)

Plotting of the Hydraulic gradient line. The percentage pressures calculated above will be used for plotting the H.G.L.

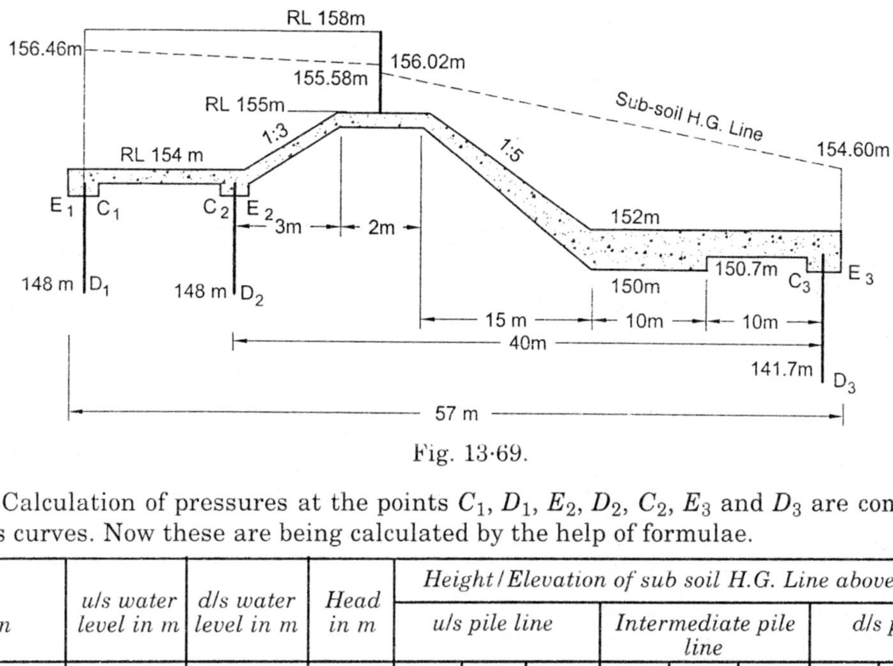

Fig. 13·69.

Calculation of pressures at the points C_1, D_1, E_2, D_2, C_2, E_3 and D_3 are computed with Khosla's curves. Now these are being calculated by the help of formulae.

Flow condition	*u/s water level in m*	*d/s water level in m*	*Head in m*	*Height/Elevation of sub soil H.G. Line above datum*								
				u/s pile line			*Intermediate pile line*			*d/s pile line*		
				ϕ_{E_1} 100 %	ϕ_{D_1} 80 %	ϕ_{C_1} 74·38 %	ϕ_{E_2} 66·95 %	ϕ_{D_2} 63·0 %	ϕ_{C_2} 59·72 %	ϕ_{E_3} 36·22 %	ϕ_{D_3} 32·0 %	ϕ_{C_3} 0 %
Pond level u/s with no water	158·0	152·0	6·0	6·0	4·8	4·46	4·02	3·78	3·58	2·68	1·92	0·0
d/s				158·0	156·8	156·46	156·02	155·78	155·58	154·17	153·92	152·0

(1) **u/s pile line No. 1**

$$b = 57 \text{ m} \quad d = 154{\cdot}00 - 148{\cdot}00 = 6{\cdot}00 \text{ m}$$

$$\alpha = \frac{b}{d} = \frac{57}{6} = 9{\cdot}5$$

ϕ_E for such a case is given by as $\phi_E = \dfrac{1}{\pi}\cos^{-1}\left(\dfrac{y-2}{\lambda}\right)$

where $$\lambda = \frac{1+\sqrt{1+\alpha^2}}{2} \quad \text{or} \quad \lambda = \frac{1+\sqrt{(9{\cdot}5)^2}}{2} = 5{\cdot}28$$

Therefore $$\phi_E = \frac{1}{\pi}\cos^{-1}\left(\frac{5{\cdot}28-2}{5{\cdot}28}\right) = \frac{1}{\pi}\times 51{\cdot}65°\times\frac{\pi}{180°} = 0{\cdot}287\% \textit{ i.e. } 28{\cdot}7\%$$

$$\phi_{C1} = 100 - \phi_E = 100 - 28{\cdot}7 = 71{\cdot}3\% \text{ (against 71\% as before)}$$

Similarly from curve Fig. (*a*)

$$\phi_{E_1} = 100 - \phi_D$$

where $$\phi_D = \frac{1}{\pi}\cos^{-1}\left(\frac{\lambda-1}{\lambda}\right) = \frac{1}{\pi}\cos^{-1}\left(\frac{5{\cdot}28-1}{5{\cdot}28}\right) = 0{\cdot}199 \text{ say } 19{\cdot}9\%$$

$\therefore$ $$\phi_{D_1} = 100 - 19{\cdot}9 = 80{\cdot}1\% \quad \text{(against 80\% as before)}$$

(2) Intermediate pile line No. 2 (as given in Fig. (*d*).

$$\phi_{E_2} = \phi_E = \frac{1}{\pi}\cos^{-1}\left(\frac{\lambda_1-1}{\lambda}\right)$$

$$\phi_{C_2} = \phi_C = \frac{1}{\pi}\cos^{-1}\left(\frac{\lambda_1+1}{\lambda}\right)$$

$$\phi_{D_2} = \phi_D = \frac{1}{\pi}\cos^{-1}\left(\frac{\lambda_1}{\lambda}\right)$$

where $$\lambda = \frac{\sqrt{1+\alpha_1^2}+\sqrt{1+\alpha_2^2}}{2}$$

$$\lambda_1 = \frac{\sqrt{(1+\alpha_1^2)}-\sqrt{(1+\alpha_2^2)}}{2}$$

$$\alpha_1 = \frac{b_1}{d}\ ;\ \alpha_2 = \frac{b_2}{d}$$

From Fig. of the given example

d = depth of intermediate pile = 154·0 – 148·0 = 6·0 m

α_1 = floor length u/s of intermediate pile line = 16·4 m

α_2 = floor length d/s of intermediate pile line = 40·6 m

Therefore $$\alpha_1 = \frac{16{\cdot}4}{6} = 2{\cdot}73$$

$$\alpha_2 = \frac{40{\cdot}6}{6} = 6{\cdot}77.$$

Therefore $$\lambda = \frac{\sqrt{1+(2{\cdot}73)^2}+\sqrt{1+(6{\cdot}77)^2}}{2} = \frac{2{\cdot}907+6{\cdot}843}{2} = 4{\cdot}875$$

$$\lambda_1 = \frac{2{\cdot}907 - 6{\cdot}843}{2} = -\,1{\cdot}968$$

Using $\phi_{E_2} = \frac{1}{\pi}\cos^{-1}\left(\frac{\lambda_1 - 1}{\lambda}\right) = \frac{1}{\pi}\cos^{-1}\left(\frac{-1{\cdot}968 - 1}{4{\cdot}875}\right) = 0{\cdot}708$ *i.e.* 70·8%
(against 70% as before)

Using $\phi_{D_2} = \phi_D = \frac{1}{\pi}\cos^{-1}\left(\frac{\lambda_1}{\lambda}\right) = \frac{1}{\pi}\cos^{-1}\left(\frac{-1{\cdot}968}{4{\cdot}875}\right) = 0{\cdot}632$ *i.e.* 63·2%
(against 63% as before)

Using $\phi_{C_2} = \phi_C = \frac{1}{\pi}\cos^{-1}\left(\frac{\lambda_1 + 1}{\lambda}\right) = \frac{1}{\pi}\cos^{-1}\left(\frac{-1{\cdot}968 + 1}{4{\cdot}875}\right) = 0{\cdot}564$ *i.e.* 56·4%
(against 56% as before)

(3) For d/s pile line No. 3 w.r.t. (Fig. (*b*)) for this example.

$$b = 57{\cdot}0 \text{ m} \qquad \alpha = 152{\cdot}0 - 141{\cdot}7 = 10{\cdot}3 \text{ m}$$

$$\alpha = \frac{b}{a} = \frac{57}{10{\cdot}3} = 5{\cdot}33\ ;\ \lambda = \frac{1 + \sqrt{1+\alpha^2}}{2} = \frac{1 + \sqrt{1 + 5{\cdot}53^2}}{2} = 3{\cdot}31$$

$$\phi_{E_2} = \phi_E = \frac{1}{\pi}\cos^{-1}\left(\frac{\lambda - 2}{\lambda}\right) = \frac{1}{\pi}\cos^{-1}\left(\frac{3{\cdot}31 - 2}{3{\cdot}31}\right) = \frac{1}{\pi}66{\cdot}65^6 \times \frac{\pi}{180} = 0{\cdot}37$$

i.e. 37% (against 38% as before)

$$\phi_{D_2} = \phi_D = \frac{1}{\pi}\cos^{-1}\left(\frac{\lambda - 1}{\lambda}\right) = \frac{1}{\pi}\cos^{-1}\left(\frac{3{\cdot}31 - 1}{3{\cdot}31}\right) = 0{\cdot}254 \text{ i.e. } 25{\cdot}4\%$$

(against 26% as before)

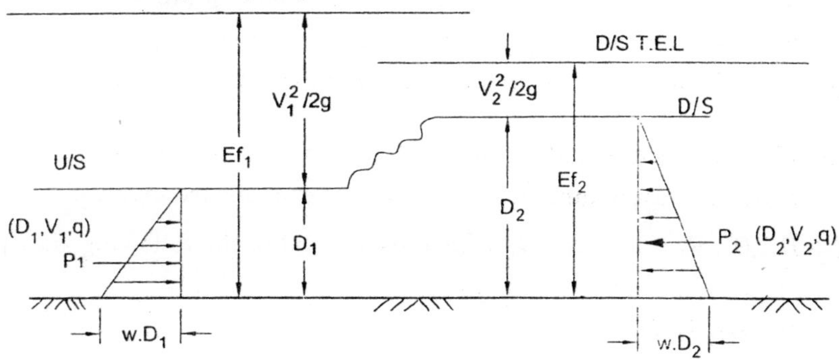

Upstream Hydraulic pressure distribution $= P_1 = ½\, w.D_1^2$ Downstream pressure distribution $= P_2 = ½\, w.D_2^2$

D = depth V = Velocity q = Discharge intensity

Fig. 13·70.

5·4. Hydraulic jump (Standing wave). When a mass of water flowing with a hypercritical velocity and low depth *i.e.* super critical flow meets with a mass of water flowing with a sub-critical velocity and high depth *i.e.* subcritical flow and an abrupt rise in the level of the former takes place with a great turbulance. The phenomena is called as hydraulic jump, and is generally accompanied by dissipating most of the kinetic energy of supercritical flow. Such a phenomenon may occur over a crest of water, on glacis of a spillway or at the place where a steep channel slope suddenly turns flat. Energy lost during the process is

$$H_L = \frac{(D_2 - D_1)^3}{\Delta D_1 D_2}$$

where D_1 and D_2 being the depths of water flowing fast and slow respectively.

When water falls over a spillway, vertical or a glacis fall, it acquires a lot of momentum and velocity, which may cause large scale erosion and scouring at the d/s of the work if not checked or controlled. The high head produced at the point of jump creates heavy uplift on the floor. Moreover this phenomenon of hydraulic jump can be used as a energy dissipating device.

Undular jump. If the jump is low *i.e.* change in depth is small, the water will not rise abruptly but will pass with a number of undulations. In such a case the energy dissipation is low and incomplete.

Direct jump. The change in depth is high *i.e.* the jump is high and abrupt with great turbulence. Such a jump involves large scale energy dissipation and has an important roll in the design of hydraulic structures.

Initial depth. The depth of water before the jump is known as initial depth D_1.

Sequent depth. The post jump depth of water is known as the sequent depth D_2.

Types of jump. The jump on a horizontal floor can be divided as below, depending on the Froude No. F_1. For $F_1 = 1$ the flow is critical and no jump will form.

(*i*) $F_1 = 1$ to 1·7, the water surface shows undulations and the jump is undular jump.

(*ii*) $F_1 = 1·7$ to 2·5, a series of small rollers develop on the surface of jump, but the d/s water surface remains smooth. The velocity through out is fairly uniform and energy lost is low. This type of jump is called a weak jump.

(*iii*) $F_1 = 2·5$ to 4·5. There is an oscillating jet entering the jump bottom to surface and back again with no periodicity. Each oscillation produces a large wave of irregular period which travel for miles with unlimited damage. This jump is called as oscillating jump.

(*iv*) $F_1 = 4·5$ to 9·0. The jump is well balanced and its performance is the best. The energy dissipation ranges from 45 to 70%. The jump is called as steady jump.

(*v*) $F_1 = 9·0$ and more. It is strong jump and energy dissipation is upto 85%.

The ranges of Froude No. given above are not definite and may overlap depending to the local conditions.

Rapids. When the bed is undulating, jumps formed are called as rapids.

Usually in any hydraulic jump following eight variables are involved.

E_{f1}, E_{f2}, D_1, D_2, V_1, V_2, q and H_L which are related to the following six equations :

(*i*) $$D_1.D_2\,(D_1 + D_2) = \frac{2q^2}{g}$$

(*ii*) $$H_L = \frac{\left(D_2 - D_{-1}\right)^3}{4D_1D_2}$$

$$E_{f1} = D_1 + \frac{V_1^2}{2g}$$

$$E_{f2} = D_2 + \frac{V_2^2}{2g}$$

$$V_1 = \frac{q}{D_1}$$

$$V_2 = \frac{q}{D_2}$$

If any two variables are known the remaining six can be worked out by using six equations mathematically. The mathematical calculations being complicate and to avoid large calculations, Blench has given some curve by taking q and H_L as known variables (The discharge intensity q and H_L are known. The value of E_{f2} can be found out from the curves direct.)

If the curves are not available the following mathematical equation can be used to evaluate D_1 and D_2 by known values of q and H_L.

$$D_C = \text{critical depth} = \left[\frac{(q^2)}{g}\right]^{1/3}$$

Now express.
$$\frac{D_1}{D_C} = (X) \text{ say}$$
$$\frac{D_2}{D_C} = (Y) \text{ say}$$
$$\frac{H_L}{D_C} = (Z) \text{ say(where } H_L \text{ and } D_C \text{ is known hence } Z \text{ is known)}$$

Relations between Z and X and Z and Y are worked out as :

$$Z = \frac{-X^6 + 20X^3 + 8 - (X^4 + 8X)^{3/2}}{16\,X^2}$$

$$Z = \frac{-Y^6 - 20Y^3 - 8 - (Y^4 + 8Y)^{3/2}}{16\,Y^2}$$

For different values of X and Y, the values of Z can be tabulated and curves X-Z and Y-Z plotted to read value of X and Y for known values of Z.

To obtain more direct solution, C.P. Swami has obtained an approximate solution to Y-Z curves and related Y with Z by the equation.

$$Y = 1 + 0{\cdot}93556\ Z^{0\cdot368} \text{ for } Z < 1$$

and
$$Y = 1 + 0{\cdot}93566\ Z^{0\cdot240} \text{ for } Z > 1$$

From the known value of Z, value of Y *i.e.* $\frac{D_2}{D_L}$ can be calculated to finally compute the value of D_2.

With known values of Z and X, value of X *i.e.* $\frac{D_1}{D_L}$ can also be computed by using the equation

$$Z = \frac{(Y - X)^3}{4XY}$$

This computed value of X *i.e.* D_1/D_L can be used to compute D_1.

Values of E_{f1} and E_{f2} can also be computed by using the values of X and Y as below :

$$\frac{E_{f1}}{D_C} = \varepsilon = X + \frac{1}{2X^2}$$

$$\frac{E_{f2}}{D_C} = \eta = Y + \frac{1}{2Y^2}$$

Location of jump profile on sloping glacis

Position of the jump. Let the water is passing over the crest of a weir. Then the discharge q (per unit width) = $C_d H^{3/2}$ where H is the head measured from the top of crest to the total energy line (T.E.L.) and C_d is a coefficient of discharge. Knowing the discharge intensity q and H the head over crest to the u/s T.E.L. For the given discharge the depth of water in the d/s is known from the gauge discharge curves of the channel. This fixes the T.E.L. d/s by adding $\frac{V_2^2}{2g}$ in the depth D_2. The difference of level in the T.E.L. of u/s and d/s gives H_L.

Knowing q and H_L, E_{f2} can be obtained from Blench curves. Substracting E_{f2} from d/s total energy line, the level at which the jump will form can be easily obtained and hence the position of the point P is fixed. Knowing E_{f2}, E_{f1} can be calculated by $E_{f1} - E_{f2} = H_L$. The corresponding values of D_1 and D_2 for the known values of E_{f1} and E_{f2} can be directly read from the 'Energy of Flow curves' given by Montague.

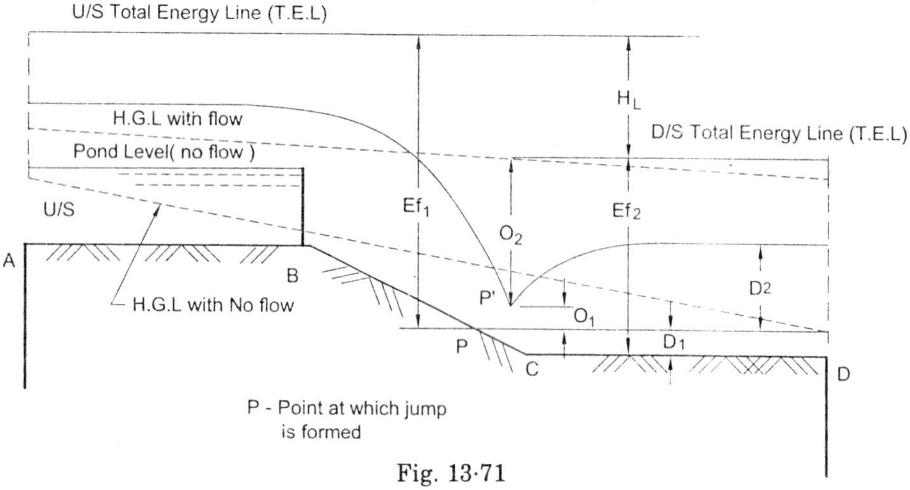

Fig. 13·71

Profile u/s of the jump. The water surface profile u/s of the point P can be drawn by the help of Montague curves. For different values of E_{f1} on the glacis (B to P) the value of E_{f1} will be maximum at the point P. With the values of E_{f1} the values of D_1 will go on decreasing and the point P will go up on the glacis. The values obtained E_{f1} *vs* D_1 can be plotted upto point B from P. The values of E_{f1} will change according to the discharge intensity q, and thus the profile of water surface can be drawn upto top of glacis.

Similarly from the curve E_{f2} *vs* D_2 d/s profile of water surface can be drawn.

Loss of Energy (H_L) in the hydraulic jump (standing wave)—

$$H_L = E_{f1} - E_{f2} \text{ where } E_{f1} = D_1 + \frac{V_1^2}{2g}\ ;\ E_{f2} = D_2 + \frac{V_2^2}{2g}$$

$$H_L = \left[D_1 + \frac{V_1^2}{2g}\right] - \left[D_2 + \frac{V_2^2}{2g}\right]$$

$$= (D_1 - D_2) + \frac{1}{2g}\left(V_1^2 - V_2^2\right) = (D_1 - D_2) + \frac{1}{2g}\left(\frac{q^2}{D_1^2} - \frac{q^2}{D_2^2}\right)$$

or

$$H_L = (D_1 - D_2) + \frac{q^2}{2g}\left[\frac{D_2^2 - D_1^2}{D_1^2 . D_2^2}\right]$$

(From momentum equation $D_1 D_2 (D_2 - D_1) = \frac{2q^2}{g}$ or $\frac{q^2}{2g} = \frac{D_1 D_2}{4}(D_2 + D_1)$

Substituting in the above, we get

$$H_L = (D_1 - D_2) + \frac{D_1 D_2}{4}(D_2 + D_1)\left[\frac{D_2^2 - D_1^2}{D_1^2 D_2^2}\right] = (D_2 - D_1)\left[\frac{(D_2 + D_1)^2}{4 D_1 D_2} - 1\right]$$

$$= (D_2 - D_1)\left[\frac{(D_2 + D_1)^2 - 4 D_1 D_2}{4 D_1 D_2}\right] = (D_2 - D_1)\left[\frac{(D_2 - D_1)^2}{4 D_1 D_2}\right]$$

or $$H_L = \frac{(D_2 - D_1)^{1/3}}{4 D_1 D_2}$$

To make the hydraulic jump as an energy dissipator the following points should be noted :

(*a*) On a level floor with low friction, the position of jump is unstable. For a slight change in depth or velocity, the position of the hydraulic jump varies through a wide range. The position of jump on a horizontal and smooth floor can not be predicted.

(*b*) On the sloping glacis, the position of the jump can be closely predicted. On the sloping glacis, however it is only the horizontal component of the velocity of hypercritical jet, which takes part in the impact, the vertical component remains uneffected.

(*c*) The length of jump is approximately five times the height, while the beginning of the jump is fairly definite, its lower end is indefinite.

(*d*) In sloping glacis the energy dissipation is less. As the position of jump is definite hence a sloping glacis is preferred than level floor.

(*e*) A level floor being indefinite prolongs even to the loose approns and create there a great erosion causing ultimate failure of work.

Uplift pressures in the jump trough. In the 1st case when water is only ponded upto top of the crest while no water is passing d/s, exerts maximum uplift on the floor and measured from the hydraulic gradient line at the point concerned.

In the 2nd case the problem of uplift is considered when the water is flowing down from the crest to the d/s of the work and hydraulic jump is forming, the seepage head is the difference between the water level u/s and d/s, which is usually much smaller than the seepage head h_1 in the former case with no flow. The hydraulic gradient line has been drawn for this case as well. The net ordinate of uplift pressure in this case is to be measured from the hydraulic gradient line to the water surface as the rest of the uplift pressure will be exactly counter balanced by the weight of the water standing on the floor. It is obvious that for most of the floor length, the uplift in this case will be smaller than that in the former. In the trough of the hydraulic jump, however it may not be so. In the Fig. 13·71 the ordinate O_1 measures the net uplift pressure for no flow conditions and the ordinate O_2 when a hydraulic jump is forming at this section. The requirement of the floor thickness should be obtained by taking the larger of the two ordinates and dividing by the submerged density of the floor material, (G-1). It follows that with the jump forming at a particular section, the thickness of the floor at that section and for some distance u/s of it may be governed by later condition. The position of the hydraulic jump will itself vary with varying discharge intensities and with in the range of jump formation, the floor at every section has to be designed for the largest uplift pressure which can occur at that section. For determining the uplift pressures at and u/s of the jump it is necessary to plot the water surface profile of the jump. In the jump trough the turbulance is maximum and uplift pressure is also more and hence a strong mix of cement is used in the trough area.

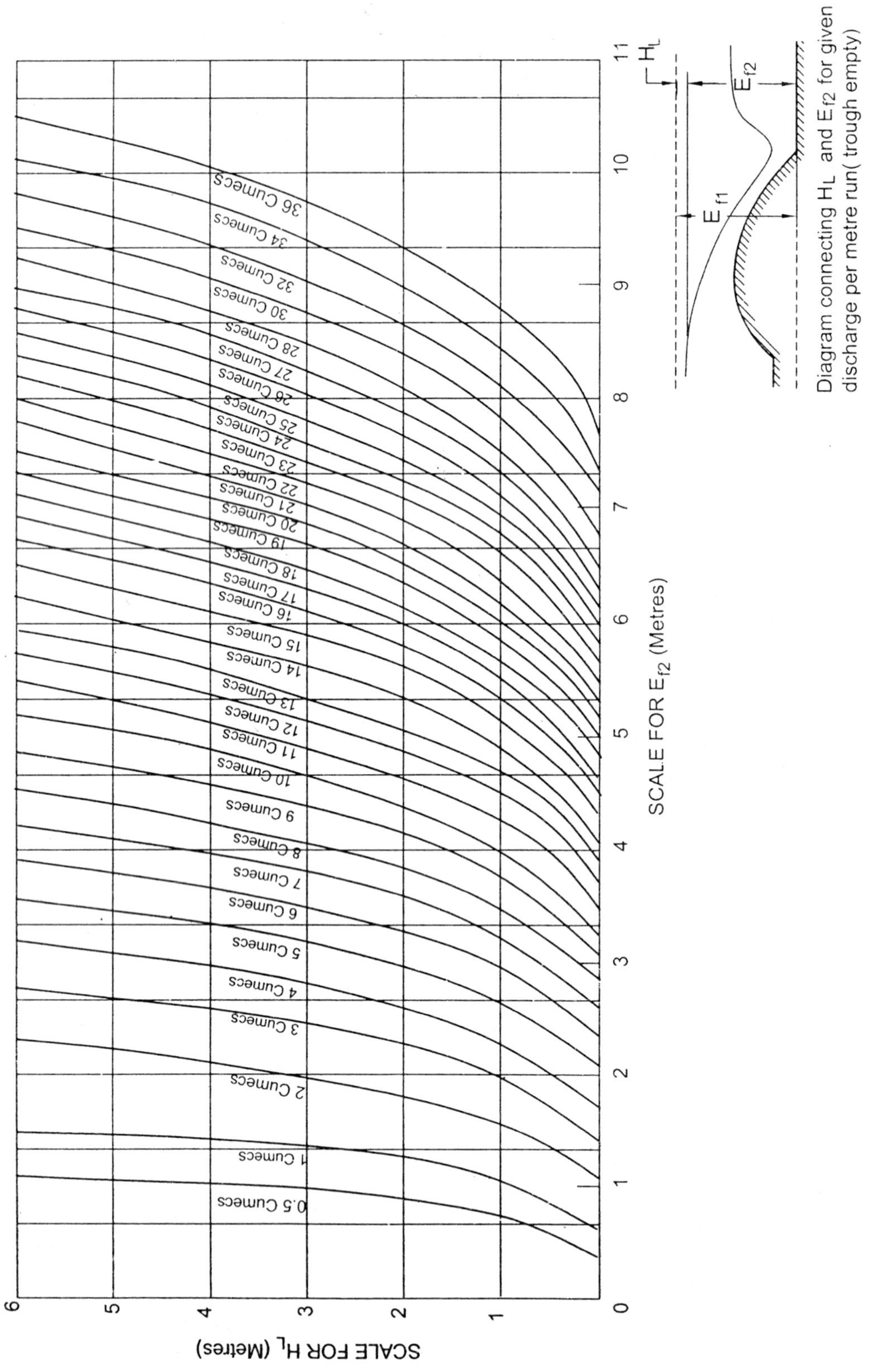

Plate no. 13·9·1. Blench curves.

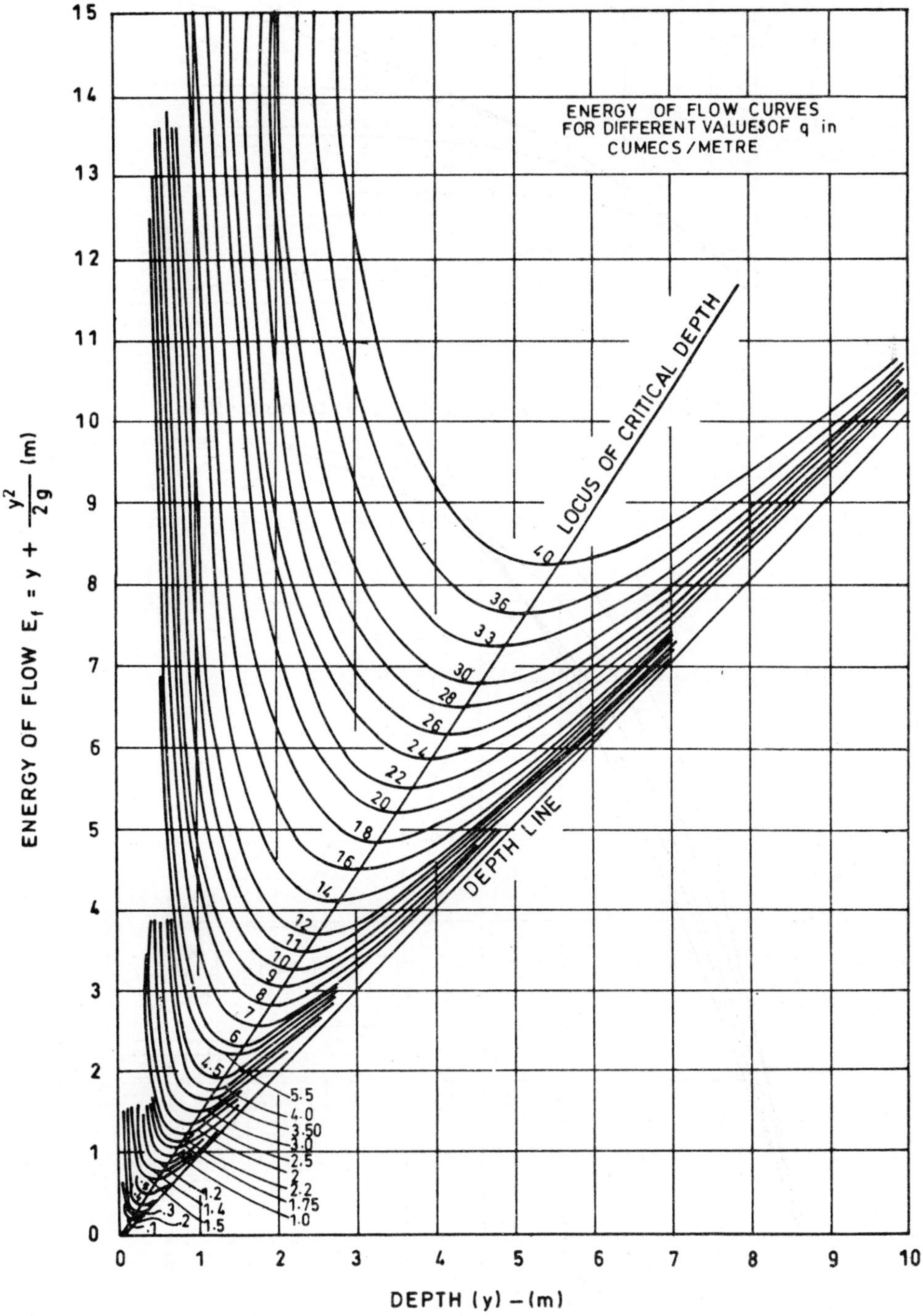

Plate No. 13·9·2. Montague's curves.

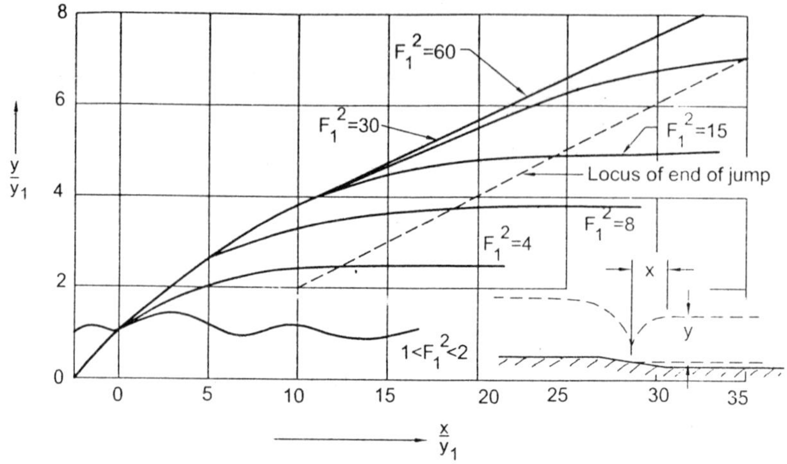

Plate 13·9·3 (*a*). Curve for plotting post pump profile.

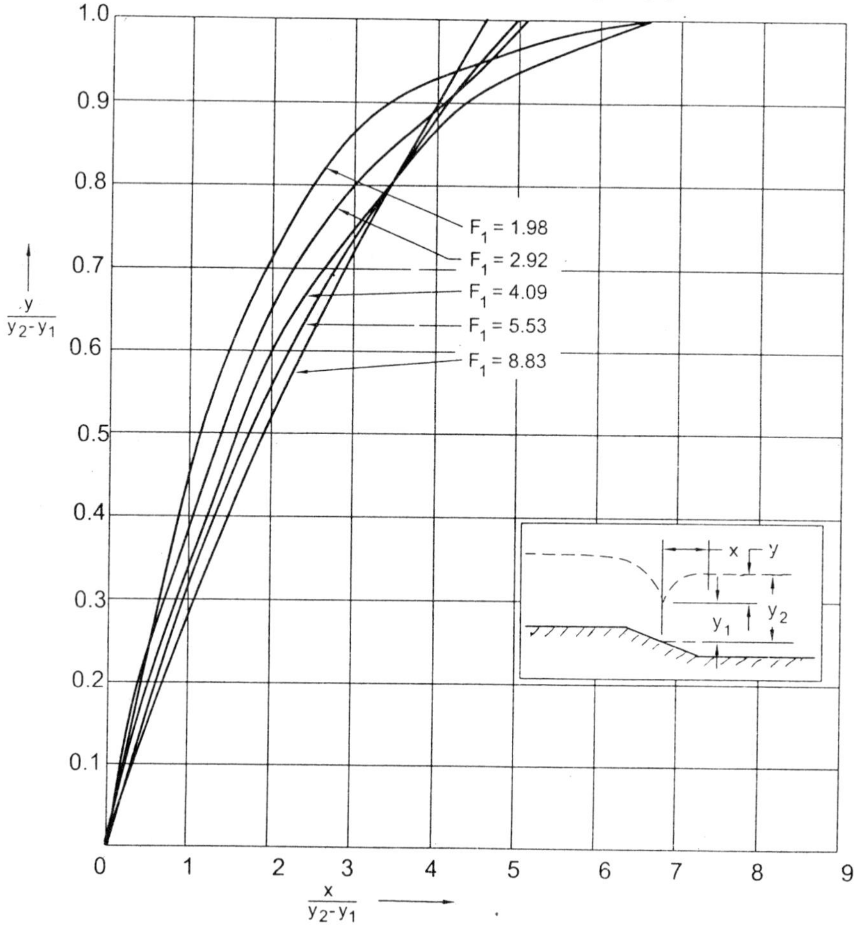

Plate 13·9·3 (*b*). Alternate curve for plotting post jump profile.

13·6. Canal Masonry and Cross Drainage Works

6·1 Canal Head Works

Diversion Head Works. The works which are constructed at the head of the canal in order to divert the river water towards the canal, so as to ensure a regulated continuous supply of silt free water with a certain minimum head into the canal are known as Diversion Head works.

Weir. The purpose of diverting of river water into the canal is accomplished by constructing a barrier across the river so as to raise the water level on the u/s side of the barriers and thus to feed the main canals taking off from the u/s side on one or both of its flanks. The ponding of water can be achieved either by a permanent pucca raised crest across the river or by raised crest with falling counter balanced gates or shutters on the crest. If a part or entire ponding of water is achieved by a raised crest Fig. 13·72 (*a*) or by crest together with shutters (Fig. 13·72 (*b*)), then this barrier is known as a weir. Such weirs cause an afflux above the barrier during floods.

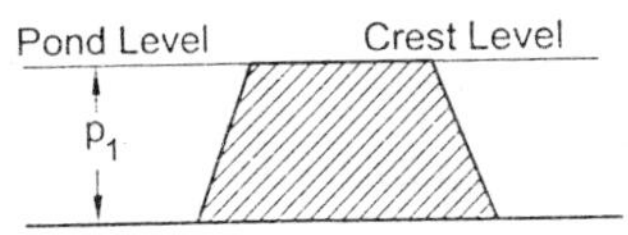

(*a*) Weir without shutters

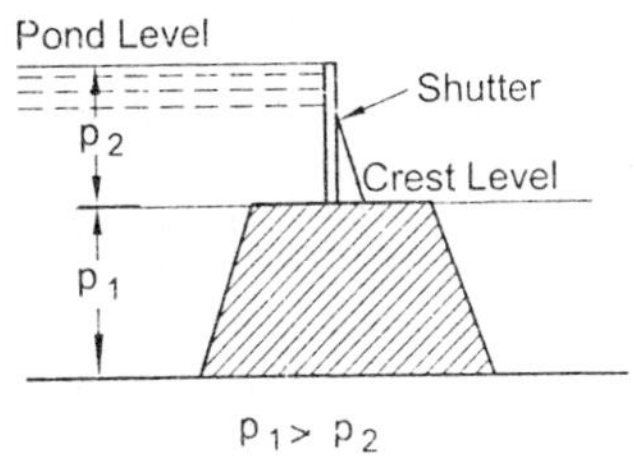

(*b*) Weir with shutter

Fig. 13·72.

Barrage. If most of the ponding is done by gates and a smaller or nil part of it is done by raised crest, then the barrier is known as a barrage. The ponding if done by a barrage then the gates can be opened during floods and the afflux (the rise in H.F.L. of the river) can be minimised even upto nil because the inflow and outflow can be controlled to a much extent by suitably manupulation of gates.

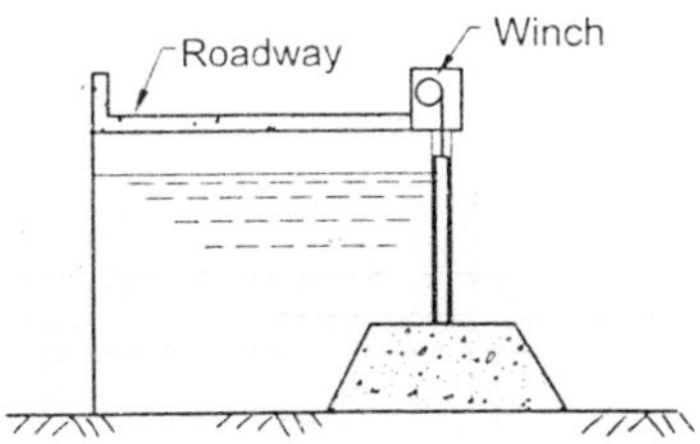

(*c*) Barrage with small crest

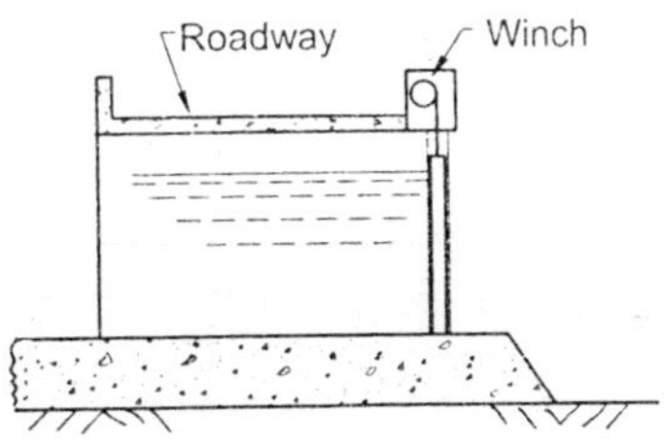

(*d*) Barrage with floor (without crest)

Fig. 13·72.

Gravity and non-gravity weirs. When the weight of the weir together with its floor balances the uplift pressure caused by the head of the water seeping below the weir, it is called a **gravity weir.** On the other hand if the weir floor is designed continuous with the divide piers as reinforced structure, such that the weight of the concrete slab together with the weight of divide piers, keep the structure safe against the uplift, then the structure may be called as a **Non-gravity weir.**

Afflux. The rise in the highest flood level (H.F.L.) u/s of the weir, caused due to the construction of the weir across the river is called **afflux.**

In the initial stages, the water level raised due to afflux upto a distance equal to the length of backwater curve. But with a passage of time, the river bed rises due to silting by the reduction in flow velocity u/s of the weir (Area or depth increases and velocity decreases). The effect therefore, travels u/s till the river bed slope u/s of the weir is the same as was before its construction. It is generally taken as 1 metre in the design of weirs.

Pond level. The water level required in the under sluice pocket u/s of the canal head regulation, so as to feed the canal with its full supply, is known as **Pond level.** The F.S.L. of the canal depends upon the level of the area to be irrigated and the slope of the canal. The pond level is generally computed by keeping it 1·0 to 1·2 m above the canal F.S.L. The pond level under sluice pocket is always maintained so as to ensure a firm supply to the canal. Hence the head available at the canal head regulator is the difference of the level of pond level and F.S.L. of the canal. It is fixed keeping in mind the fluctuation of bed of canal due to silting which can effect the F.S.L. of the canal.

Type of Weirs. (*a*) Masonry weirs with vertical drop.

(*b*) Rock fill weir with sloping aprons

(*c*) Concrete weirs with sloping glacis

(*d*) Barrage with divide piers and regulating gates with a roadway to go across.

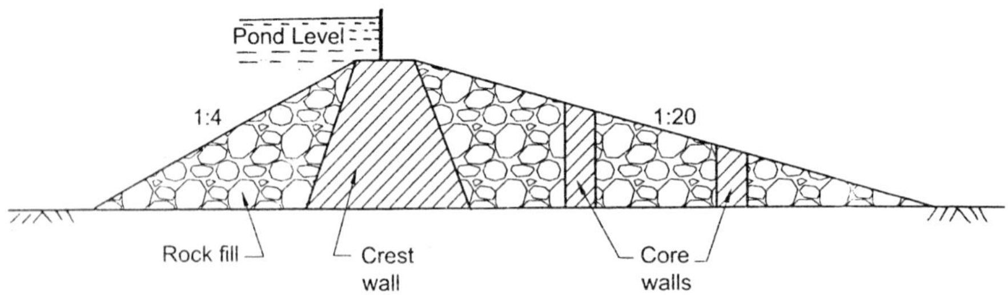

(*a*) Rockfill weir with sloping aprons.

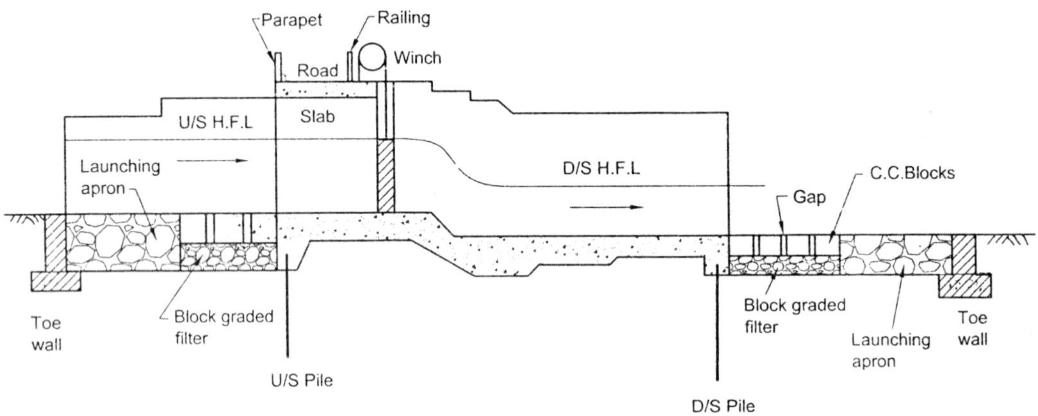

(*b*) Barrage founded on permeable soil.

(1) In a barrage weir is divided in bays with regulation gates.

(2) Each bay has a peir with grooves for gates, founded on wells with floor concrete as capping slab.

(3) It has a road way to go across the river.

(4) Foundation of the barrage may be on RCC raft. The raft with peirs and decking slabs takes the load of uplift.

Fig. 13·73

6·2. Components of the Diversion Head Works. A typical layout of diversion head-works consists of :

(1) Main weir (2) Under sluices (3) Divide wall

(4) River Training works (5) Fish ladder.

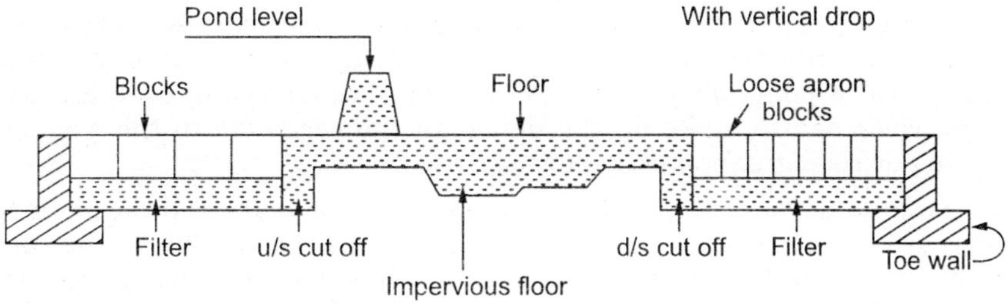

Fig. 13·74.

(1) **Main weir.** In the design of the main weir following points are observed :

(*i*) **Water way and discharge intensity (q) per unit width.** A likely figure to be adopted for the water way of a weir is Lacey's stable perimeter during highest flood discharge. It should be remembered that the regime conditions are disturbed after the construction of a weir and the Lacey's formula is not strictly followed. It was considered that the shoal formation could be checked by limited water way, but it is not so. Most existing weirs have a clear water way from 10% to 50% more than the Lacey's regime perimeter. With a larger discharge intensity, the action on floor will more intensive and the sections will be heavier when the crest length is reduced.

Crest level. The level of the crest of the weir will be determined by the permissible afflux during the maximum flood, the discharge intensity and the pond level.

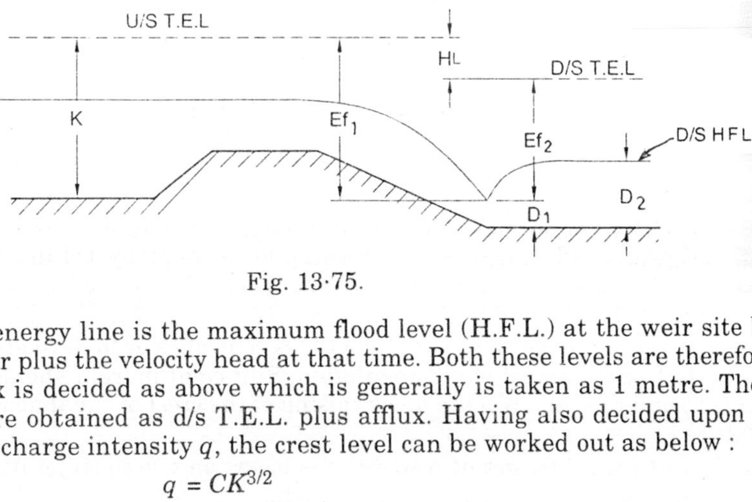

Fig. 13·75.

The d/s total energy line is the maximum flood level (H.F.L.) at the weir site before the construction of the weir plus the velocity head at that time. Both these levels are therefore known. The permissible afflux is decided as above which is generally is taken as 1 metre. The u/s total energy line is therefore obtained as d/s T.E.L. plus afflux. Having also decided upon the water way and hence the discharge intensity q, the crest level can be worked out as below :

$$q = CK^{3/2}$$

where $C = 3{\cdot}09$ and K is the intercept between the u/s energy line and the crest or the static head + velocity head over crest.

The crest level can now be obtained by subtracting K from the level of the u/s energy line. The difference between the crest level so obtained and the pond level is to be made up by shutters or gates. If the height of the shutters is to be reduced, either the permissible afflux has to be increased or the discharge intensity reduced by increasing the water way.

The crest level having been determined, the u/s energy line will remain fixed for a general value of the discharge intensity. The d/s total energy line will have to be some what lowered for purposes of designs to allow for a possible drop in the maximum flood level after the construction of the weir due to retrogression of d/s bed levels. A lowering of 0·30 m will be sufficient in most cases. Thus while the u/s T.E.L. remains unaffected, the d/s T.E.L. will be depressed by 0·30 m to account for retrogression, so that the difference between the two is H_L = Afflux + 0·30 m.

Effect of construction of a weir on the regime of a river. The 1st effect of the construction of a weir is flattening of the water surface slope for some distance behind or u/s of the weir due to ponding up of supplies. This results in reduction of sediment transportation power in that reach so that the river drops a part of its sediment load resulting in the formation of sholes and islands in the pond. The relatively cleaner water passing over the weir picks up sediment from the river bed to make up the deficit in the cargo d/s to the weir and causes a progressive lowering or retrogression of d/s levels.

The above effects develop and continue for a number of years and the shole formation u/s of the weir increases, the resistance to flow of water is increased due to the tortuous route that the water has to take round about the sholes. To overcome this resistance increased head is required and the river starts to regain its original slope thus extending the afflux more and more u/s (refer Fig. 13·76). A stage is gradually reached when the u/s pond absorbs no more silt. As the offtaking canal lakes a comparatively silt free water, the silt burden will go d/s, while the discharge going down will be below normal. This will lead to silt deposite and long range recovery d/s of the weir.

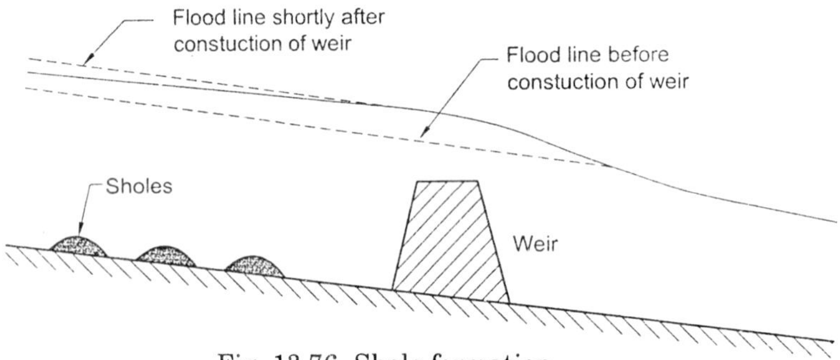

Fig. 13·76. Shole formation.

The main effects on the design are :

(*a*) To account for retrogression, the high flood on the d/s side is drepressed by 0·30 m, while river water surface in lower discharges is depressed still more and the stability of hydraulic jump tested under these conditions. The stability against critical gradient should also be checked after considering the d/s river bed retrogression.

(*b*) Restoration of normal slope u/s of the weir leads to increased flood levels and hence the top of the guide and marginal bunds should be kept by taking this affluxed level in consideration. This stage will reach after several years. The top of marginal bunds should join the contour above H.F.L.

(*c*) Recovery of the d/s bed levels sometimes continues even beyond the original bed levels. This will lead to loss of control of silt regulation. Sufficient margin should be provided between the canal F.S.L. and the pond level to allow raising of the crest of canal head regulator if necessity arises in future.

Design of foundations of a weir. It is based on two considerations

(*a*) Surface flow (*b*) Sub-surface flow

(*a*) **Surface flow.** (*i*) Depth of sheet pile lines in relation to scour.

(*ii*) Length of the d/s floor.

(*iii*) Thickness of floor on the sloping glacis with reference to hydraulic jump.

(*iv*) Length and thickness of u/s and d/s loose aprons.

(*v*) Length, shape and free board of guide and marginal banks.

(*b*) **Sub surface flow.** (*i*) Total length of impervious floor and depth and location of sheet pile lines.

(*ii*) Exit gradient at the end of the impervious floor.

(*iii*) Thickness of the d/s impervious floor for uplift pressures.

(*iv*) Provision of inverted filter.

(*a*) **Design for surface flow.** Depth of d/s pile line is determined by

(*i*) With a suitable length of the d/s impervous floor, it gives a safe exit gradient under maximum head. If the exit gradient is unsafe, either the d/s sheet pile line is deepened or the length of d/s floor is increased.

(*ii*) On the maximum scour depth, the depth of u/s pile line is determined only on the consideration of scour depth, while the d/s pile lines is designed both on the exit gradient as well as on maximum scour depth considerations. The max. scour depth

$$R = 0{\cdot}9\left(\frac{q^2}{f}\right)^{1/3}$$ where R = maximum scour depth below H.F.L.

q = discharge intensity, which is different for weir and under sluices portion and should be designed separately.

f = silt factor is determined by observing the water surface slope of the river at high flood and substituting it in Lacey's slope equation. Lacey's depth of scour R is applicable to regime flow only. Lacey gave following classes of scour.

Class	*Reach*	*Depth of scour*	
A	Straight	1·25 R	Likely to occur any where below loose apron
B	Moderate bend	1·50 R	Likely to occur along the aprons of guide banks in straight reach.
C	Severe bend	1·75 R	Below the noses of guide banks, or below the loose aprons in case heavy swirls
D	Right angled bend	2·0 R	

Design of Launching aprons. It is in depth of 1·5 R u/s of the concrete floor, 2·0 R for d/s concrete floor, 2·25 R at noses of guide banks, 1·5 R for transition from nose to straight portion of guide banks and 1·25 R in straight portions.

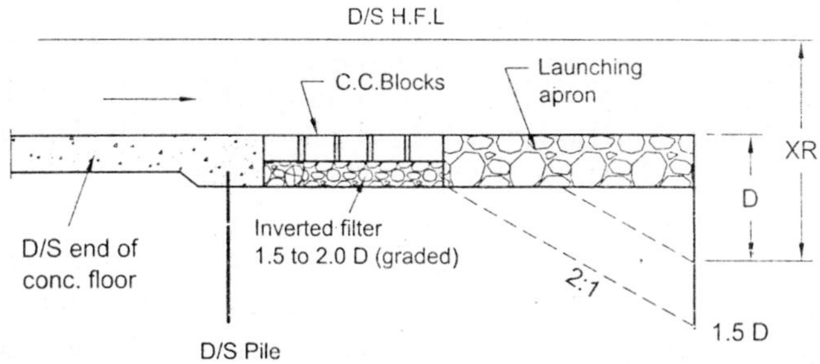

Fig. 13·77. Launching apron.

Loose Protection. d/s of concrete floor end = 1·5 to 2·0 D where D = Top of apron to maximum scour depth R. (R is the depth of maximum scour from the H.F.L. for different conditions).

Loose apron u/s of the floor. Just u/s of the concrete floor a block protection of 0·6 m thick concrete blocks over 0·6 m of packed stone should be provided for a length of D in the same manner as provided in the d/s of the weir concrete floor.

Launching aprons for guide banks and afflux bunds are also provided in the same manner.

Design of d/s floor. According the hydraulic jump conditions, the glacis should be sloped down at a slope of 1 : 3 to 1 : 5 for maximum dissipation of energy.

Level of d/s floor. The level of d/s floor is decided on the consideration that the jump must not form lower than the toe of the glacis. The location is made with different discharge intensities with the help of 'Blench curves'. The check should be made for different discharge intensities. It is usually, be found that the jump shifts lower for smaller discharge intensities particularly when the effect of retrogression is taken into account. It may be noted that while the high flood level is not reduced materially due to retrogression, a reduction of 0·3 m being normally all that may be expected, then water level may go down 1 m to 1·5 m during low supplies due to retrogression. The new intensities for which a check should be made is that corresponding to a head provided by pond level on u/s side of the crest. If a smaller discharge is to be passed, some of the gates can be closed and a miminum head equal to the pond level maintained on the others. The level of the d/s floor is so decided that the jump may occur in the sloping glacis in all conditions.

Length of the d/s floor. It is discussed in case of hydraulic jump that the hydraulic jump disturbances die at a distance of five times the jump height. Therefore the length of d/s floor is so provided that the d/s protection works such as launching aprons etc. may not come in the effect of turbulance created by the hydraulic jump. Therefore length of the d/s horizontal floor below the toe of the glacis should not be less than $5(D_2 - D_1)$ during high floods.

Design of glacis for uplift pressure during floods. The hydraulic jump travels over the glacis for different discharge intensities, it is therefore necessary to determine the maximum uplift pressure on each section for all discharge conditions and design it for the same.

(*b*) **Design for sub-surface flow.** The **length of d/s horizontal floor**, the level and hence the length of glacis are fixed by hydraulic jump conditions.

The **top width of crest** is determined by practical basis and in order of the 2·5 m or so.

The u/s slope of crest is taken as 1 : 2 and d/s slope as 1 : 3 to 1 : 5.

The **u/s floor length** is decided by keeping the d/s length as minimum possible on the basis of design, the exit gradient or hydraulic jump and rest of the total mav be provided u/s but a minimum on practical consideration is to be provided.

Exit gradient and depth of d/s pile line. The exit gradient for a floor with total length equal to b and depth of d/s pile line below scoured bed is given by

$$G_E = \frac{H}{d} \times \frac{1}{\pi\sqrt{\lambda}}$$

where H is the applied static head and λ is a function of α or b/d. The critical gradient for a soil is given by $(1 - n)(G - 1)$ and has a value near to unity (refer sub soil flow) for average soils. The exit gradient should be lower than the critical gradient to provide a margin of safety. The safety factor may be 1 : 4 to 1 : 7. The following factors of safety are recommended

Single	4 to 5	For detail design of floor on soils refer Bligh and
Coarse sand	5 to 6	Khosla's Theory for foundations on permeable soils
Fine sand	6 to 7	for uplift and hydraulic jump etc.

(*c*) **The under sluices.** The under sluices are openings in between divide wall and canal head regulator in the weir wall with a crest at low level on the same side as the canal. These openings are fully controlled by gates in all type of weirs. The crest of the under sluices is often kept at the lowest level in the cold weather cross section of the river at the site of the weir. It is also related to the crest level of the canal head regulator. For scouring of silt deposits in front of the regulator it is necessary that the crest of the under sluices should be lower than the crest of the head regulator by at least 1·2 meter, if no special work to exclude silt from the canal is provided. If a silt excluder, or a work to entry of silt into the canal is to be provided. This difference of level is 1·8 to 2·1 meter. The objects of under sluices are :

(*i*) To maintain a clear and well defined river channel towards the canal head regulator. As the crest of the under sluices is at low levels, a deep channel develops towards them and bring the low winter discharge towards them for easy diversion into the canal. **If two canals off-take on either side of the weir two under sluices will be required, one for each.**

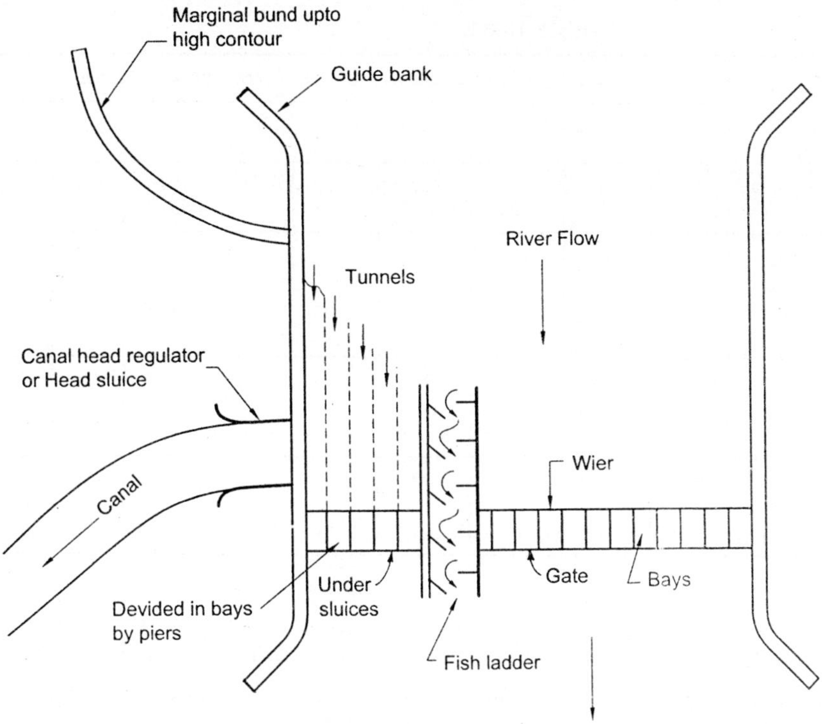

1. Level of crest of under sluices must be lower than that of weir.
2. Bays of under sluices provided with gates.
3. Bays of weir are provided with gates.

Fig. 13·78. Typical layout of a diversion head work.

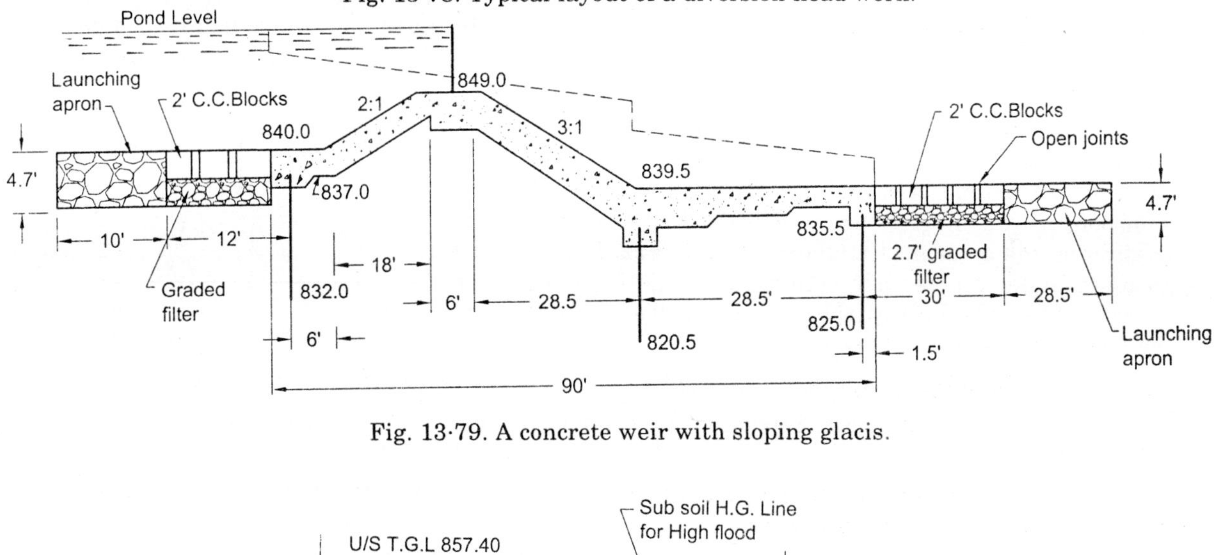

Fig. 13·79. A concrete weir with sloping glacis.

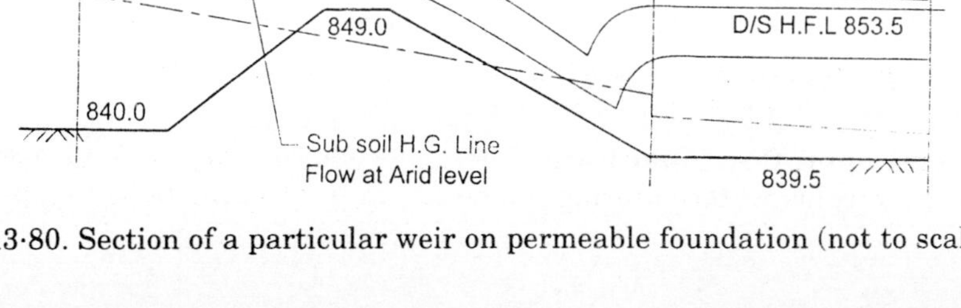

Fig. 13·80. Section of a particular weir on permeable foundation (not to scale).

Table 13·31.

Condition of flow	d/s water level	u/s water level	Head	*Elevation / Ht. of sub soil H.G. line above datum*								
				u/s pile line			*Intermediate pile line*			*d/s pile line*		
				ϕ_E 100%	ϕ_D 81%	ϕ_C 70·02%	ϕ_{E_1} 50·97%	ϕ_{D_1} 41%	ϕ_{C_1} 34·84%	ϕ_{E_2} 33·1%	ϕ_{D_2} 27%	ϕ_{C_2} 0%
No flow	839·50	852·0	Ht. 12·5	12·5	10·13	9·89	6·38	5·12	4·36	4·10	3·38	0
Max. Head			Elevation	852·0	849·63	849·30	845·88	844·62	843·86	843·60	842·88	839·50
High flood			Ht. 3·58	3·58	2·90	2·83	1·84	1·47	1·25	1·19	0·97	0
			Elevation	857·08	856·40	856·33	855·34	854·97	854·75	854·69	854·47	853·50
Low pond level			Ht. 7·0	7·0	5·67	5·53	3·57	2·87	2·44	2·32	1·89	0
			Elevation	852·0	850·67	850·53	848·87	847·87	847·44	847·32	846·89	845·0

(*ii*) To scour the silt deposited on the river bed in the pocket u/s of the canal head regulator. As relatively clearer water is taken into the canal the coarser part of the sediment is deposited in front of the canal head regulator. This is scoured by opening the under sluices.

(*iii*) To pass the winter freshets and low floods without dropping the weir shutters, the raising of which entails a good deal of labour and time, except for barrages which have gates. All weirs are usually provided with dropping shutters. Whenever water is surplus to canal requirements has to be passed across the weir. So long as the surplus water to be escaped does not exceed the under sluices capacity. It is escaped through the under sluices and the weir shutters are kept raised up.

The weir shutters have to be dropped only to pass down the high floods. The weir shutters are dropped only on the 1st floor as expected and raised again at the end of the monsoon. As the shutters are to be raised when water is still passing on the crest it is a laborious and hazardous job. The gates of under sluices are controlled by gates and can be operated by a platform at the top, and are used for passing the low floods whenever they come.

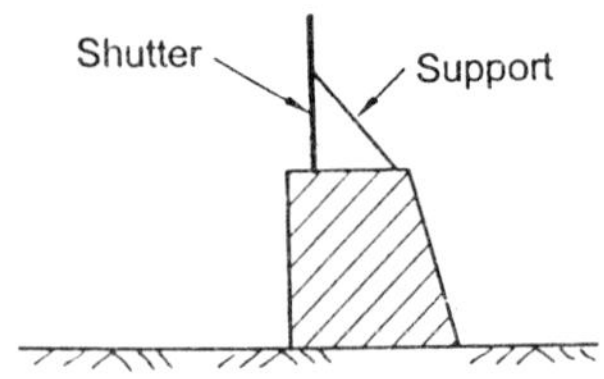

Fig. 13·81. Weir droping shutters.

The discharging capacity of the under sluices is usually determined as below :

(*i*) To ensure scouring capacity. They should be able to take at least double the canal discharge.

(*ii*) They should be able to pass winter freshets and low flood during the dry months without dropping of the weir shutters.

(*iii*) They should pass 10 to 15% of the maximum flood discharge to reduce the length of the rest of the weir.

(*iv*) The design of the sluice floor is the same as weir. The discharge intensity being more in under sluices, more d/s protection works are required.

(*d*) **Silt control on head works.** The following two alternatives are used to control silt entry.

(*a*) **Semi open flow operation.** The under sluices may be kept open to the required extent to escape surplus water entering the pocket in front of the head regulator, the top water passing into the canal. The two streams of water have to divide out in front of the head regulator, one passing into the canal and the other escaping down the under sluices, which maintains a certain velocity in the pocket causing silt to remain in suspension and the turbulance which enables even some of the coarse material to rise up and enter into the canal. The advantage of this system is that there is continuous scouring of silt and the canal does not have to be closed.

(*b*) The second method, called the **method of still pond regulation**, the scouring sluices are kept closed when the canal is running. Only the as much supply enters the pocket as is required for the canal, the surplus being escaped over some other section of the weir. The velocity of water in the pocket is therefore, very much reduced as a smaller discharge enters through the same water way. The silt is thus enabled to settle down and relatively clear water enters the canal. The system is only practicable where the canal head regulator has a high crest above the u/s floor of the under sluices. The silt is allowed to accumulate in the pocket till it reaches within about 0·6 m of the crest. The canal is then closed and the sluices opened till the entire deposit is washed away. The scouring operation takes about 24 hours and for this period the supply to the canal is interrupted. The canal can then be opened and the sluices closed till scouring again becomes necessary. The drawback in this system is that the canal has to be closed each month for 24 hours causing waste of discharge and loss of irrigation.

If the canal off tanks on the both banks, then the sluices are to be constructed on both the banks.

Other devices to control silt entry. These are of two types:

(1) **Silt excluder.** These works are constructed in the river bed in front of the head regulator. Their function is to prevent coarse silt from entry to the canal.

(2) **Silt extractors or silt ejectors.** These are constructed on the canal a little d/s of the head regulator. These serve to remove some of the silt which has already entered the canal from head. The waste silted water is passed to the river a bit d/s of the weir through an escape.

Silt excluders. A silt excluder consists of rectangular tunnels with the top level of the roof covering at the level of the crest of the canal head regulator. The water approaching towards the canal head regulator is nearly separated into two parts by the roof slab of the excluder tunnels. The part of the top enters into the canal and that underneath carrying most of the silt load flows through the tunnels and is escaped from the under sluices.

The discharge taken by the tunnels is about 20% of the canal discharge. A minimum velocity of 2 to 3 m per sec. must be maintained in the tunnels to keep them free from sediment deposit. Hence the required sectional area of the tunnel = discharge/velocity. The height of the tunnel opening is determined by the level. Hence between the pocket bed to the crest level of the head minus thickness of the roof slab of the tunnel. Now the total water way of the tunnels = cross-sectional area/height. The total water way required for the tunnels divided by the number of tunnels will give the span of one tunnel. The thickness of the position of tunnels should be accounted for. The opening of the tunnels in the under sluices can be operated by one gate opening or two or three openings by combining some tunnels in one gate opening of the under sluices. As shown in the Fig. 13·82 three tunnels are combined to be operated by one sluice gate opening.

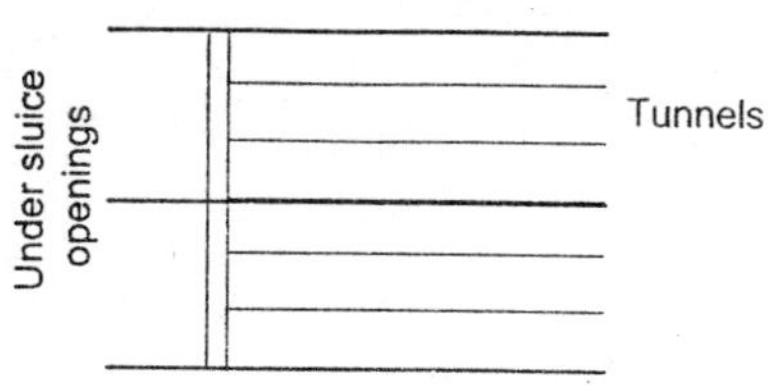

Fig. 13·82.

The slab of the tunnels should be designed for full water head on the slab considering no water is flowing in the tunnels and they have been closed for cleaning purposes.

Normally the crest level of the under sluice pocket is kept equal to the deepest bed level of the river during non monsoon season, whereas the crest level of the weir is kept higher by about 1 to 1·5 m. As the level of under sluice pocket is deeper, a channel is developed which helps the regular supply to the head even in the dry season. The under sluices or the **scouring sluices** also helps in scouring and removing the deposited silt by these tunnels hence they are also called as scouring sluices.

Silt ejector or silt extractor. A silt extractor or ejector essentially consists of a horizontal diaphragm slab a little above the canal bed which separates out the bottom layers. Under the diaphragm there are tunnels to eject the heavy silt laden bottom water into an escape channel. The tunnel entrances have to be so designed that there is no disturbance at entry and then the velocity has to be quickly accelerated to the high value required under the diaphragm to prevent the tunnels from being clogged. The canal bed is slightly depressed under the diaphragm and the height of the tunnel is from 0·5 to 1 m. The acceleration of the velocity is achieved by quickly but steadily reducing the cross sectional area by shear lined vanes. As the lengths of the tunnels are different, the head loss in the three would be different, if all the three were to take the same discharge. As the difference between the water level in the canal and the water level in the escape chamber or the available head is the same for all the tunnels, the shorter

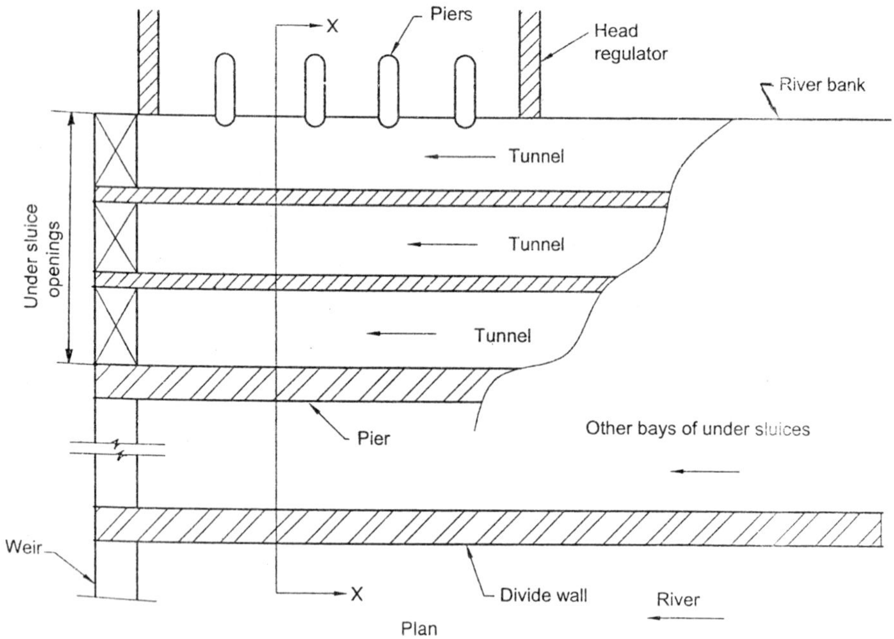

Fig. 13·83 (*a*).

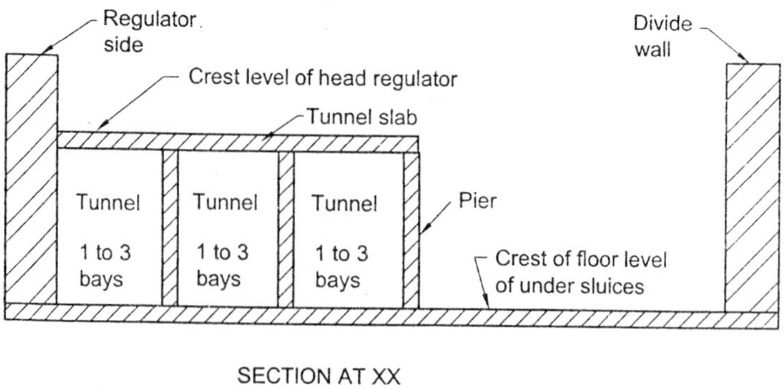

(Note : Scale of Plan and Section is different)

Fig. 13·83 (*b*). Silt excluder.

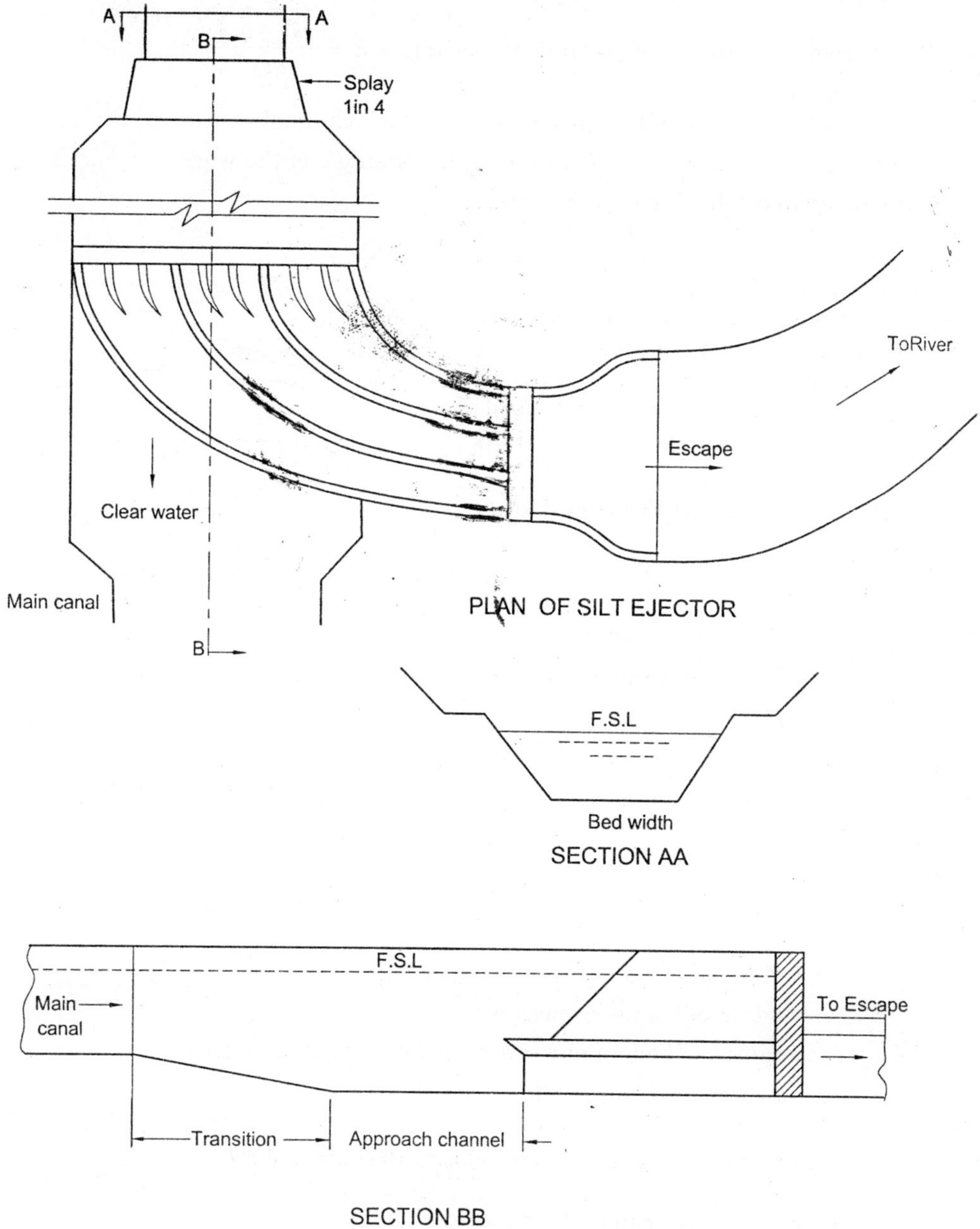

Note : The bed of the escape just d/s of the ejector should be higher than the H.F.L. of the drain in which the ejector escape will fall.

Fig. 13·84.

tunnel would tend to take higher discharge than the longer one.This would mean a higher velocity of entry in the shorter tunnel (nearest to the escape channel) than in the other and would lead to disturbances at entry. To counteract this possibility either the shorter tunnel may serve a larger width of the canal than a longer one or the tunnel cross sections may be altered, each serving an equal width. The tunnel discharge is regulated by means of gates at the outlet end. The escape channel should have sufficient slope to carry the silt laden water without getting silted up and should lead the water by the most economical path back to the river.

The efficiency of silt excluders and silt ejectors = $E = \dfrac{qs_a - qs_c}{qs_a}$

where E = efficiency of the work.

qs_a = the concentration of silt charge in the approach channel

qs_c = the concentration of the silt charge in the canal d/s of the work.

Curved approach. A channel carries less sediment load at the outside of a curve than the average sediment load of the channel as there is concentration of sediment on the inside of the bend. It would thus be desirable to construct a canal head works to obstruct the river water from the outside of a curve. A curved divide wall to provide a curved approach towards the canal head regulator has been successfully experimented.

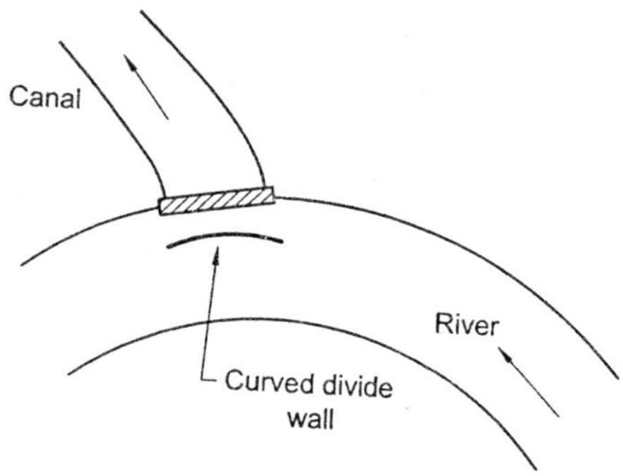

Fig. 13·85.

Losses in tunnels. (*i*) **Frictional loss.**

$$h_f = \frac{n^2.V^2.L}{R^{4/3}} \text{ (Mannings Formula)}$$

where h_f = Head loss in metres

L = Length of tunnel in metres

R = Hydraulic mean depth in metres

n = Mannings Rugosity coefficient

(*ii*) **Loss due to bend.** $h_b = F\left(\dfrac{V^2}{2g}\right)\left(\dfrac{\theta}{180^\circ}\right)$

where $F = 0{\cdot}124 + 3{\cdot}134\left(\dfrac{S}{2r}\right)^{1/2}$

θ = angle of deviation

S = width of tunnel in metres

r = radius of bend along centre line of tunnel in metres

h_b = head loss in metres due to bend.

(*iii*) Transition loss due to change of velocity in contraction $h_c = 0{\cdot}1\left[\dfrac{V^2}{2g} - \dfrac{V_1^2}{2g}\right]$

where V_1 = velocity in canal u/s in m/sec.

V_2 = velocity in tunnel in m/sec.

h_c = head loss in metres in contraction

(*iv*) Transition loss due to change of velocity in expansion $h_c = \left[\dfrac{V_2^2}{2g} - \dfrac{V_3^2}{2g}\right]$

where V_2 = velocity in the tunnel

V_3 = velocity in the d/s of tunnel

Divide wall. The divide wall is a masonry or concrete wall constructed at right angle to the axis of the weir and separates the main weir from the under sluices. The divide wall extends to up side beyond the beginning of the canal regulator and on the d/s side upto the end of the loose protection of the under sluices. The length u/s of the wall is about 0·8 of the length (width) of the under sluices. The top width of the divide wall is 1·5 to 2·5 metres according to the discharge passing over the weir. These walls are founded on wells in its entire length. Wells are founded either on a firm strata to the near scour depth or to meet with the frictional pressure by the load. Its main functions are :

(*a*) It separates the main weir from the under sluices since the bed level, of under sluices are lower than that of the weir.

(*b*) It helps a turbulance free water entry to the head and since the water to the sluice pocket is non turbulant hence the silt free entry of water in the head is possible.

(*c*) It leads a cross currents less water upstream of the weir.

Design considerations. The divide walls can be designed as a cantilever retaining walls subjected to silt pressure and water pressure from the under sluice side. For the worst case the design should be checked for full silt pressure on the under sluice pocket side, with equal water on both sides during low floods and also for maximum differential water head when full discharge is passing through the under sluices and no discharge is passing the weir. The values of different pressure may be taken arbitrarily as 1·0 m for water head and about 2·0 for silt pressure.

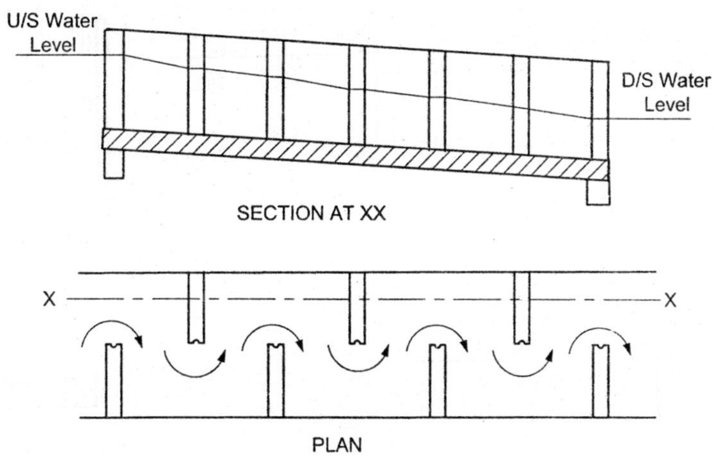

Fig. 13·86. Fish ladder.

Fish ladder. There are some migratory type of fishes in the Indian rivers which move one part of the river to other parts according to the season. These fishes are called as anadromous fish. Such type of fishes are Hilsa, and Salman etc. Some fishes are found to move from u/s (hills) to the d/s (Plains) in the beginning of the winter season in search to warmer water and to their spawning ground u/s, slightly before monsoons in the month of May or June. If no arrangement is made in the weir or the dam to enable to fish to pass u/s or d/s, then such migratory fishes have been found to strike the weir again and again till death, therefore arrangements are made to provide passage to the fishes.

It is seen that some fishes can travel u/s against a velocity of 3 to 3·5 m/sec. There is usually a head difference of 5 to 6 metres from u/s to d/s of the river at the weir. If only some open gap is left, the fishes can not cross the high velocity in the gap. Some arrangements are made to minimise the high velocity by providing some hurdles (baffles) to check the velocity and to dissipate the energy, pool type and step channel types are commonly used as fish ladders in weirs and barrages. In this type of ladder, the space between the weir and the divide wall is provided with oblique walls and holes are also staggered so that the fish can take rest after passing one hole before it move to the other. Some times the fish ladder is provided with in the divide wall itself.

Fish ladders in the high dams (more than 100 m) are not found to be practicable so the fishes are transferred mechanically from u/s to d/s or d/s to u/s by trucks or trolleys etc. Fishes can not pass from the turbines or spillways, if the head is less than 5 m or so they can pass with very less mortality. A wrongly designed fish ladder will work as a fish trap and will be of no use.

River training works. It can be seen in the article of river training works. In addition the spurs should be made in marginal bunds where retrogression is possible.

Canal Head Works. The canal head works provide the following purposes.

(*i*) To regulate supply of water entry to the canal.

(*ii*) To control the entry of silt.

(*iii*) To prevent the river floods to enter into the canal.

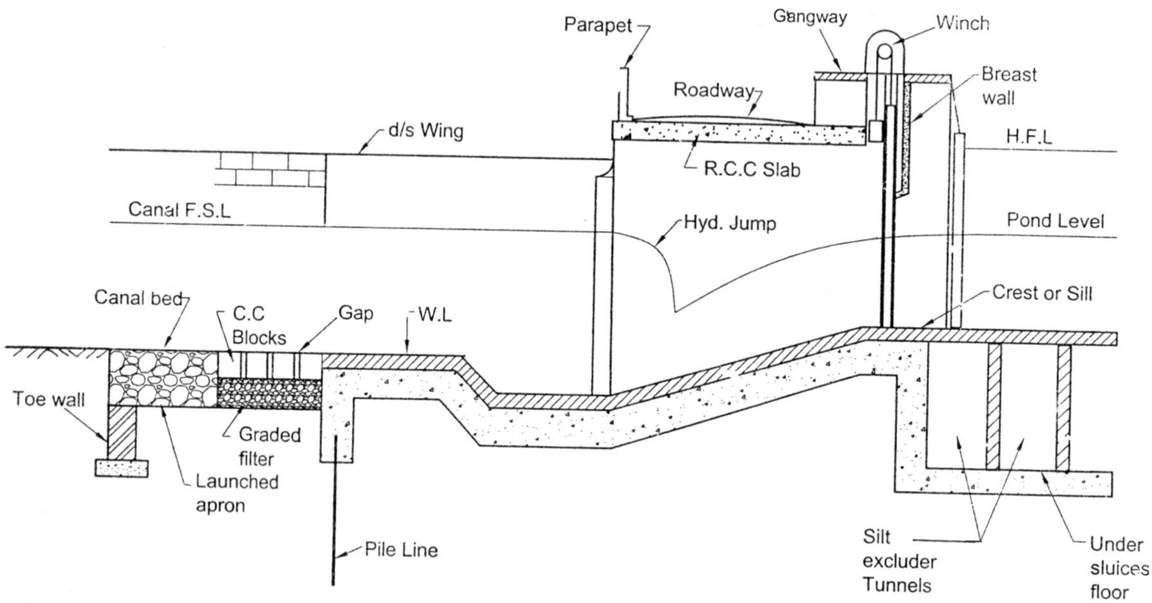

Fig. 13·87. L-section of a canal head regulator.

The heads are constructed generally at right angles to the weir. But in the recent days it may be kept at (90 to 120°) for providing smooth entry of water into canal.

The regulator is divided in spans operated by gates. In old days smaller gates were used but now a days bigger gates are used as the mechanical technology has been developed and thus spaces taken by piers is reduced and hence economical. The maximum height of these gate openings called **head sluices** will be equal to the difference of pond level and crest level of the regulator. The entry of the silt into the canal is controlled by keeping the crest (sill) of the head regulator by about 1·2 to 1·5 metres higher than the crest of the under sluices. If a silt excluder is provided the regulator crest is further raised by 0·6 m to 0·7 m. The silt deposited before the head regulator can be removed by under sluice openings.

The sill (crest) of the regulator is governed by the silt as well as discharge considerations as the full discharge has to be passed from the head openings the height of which is equal to the difference of pond level and sill level. The smaller the height of openings the larger will be the length of the sill or in other words if the sill level is raised too much, the clear water way of the regulator will increase and thereby making it more costly. Since a regulator is provided with a very wide and shallow water way, the drowned weir formula is used to calculate the discharge and is given as below :

$$Q_1 = \frac{2}{3} C_{d1}\sqrt{2g}.B\left[(h + h_v)^{3/2} - h_v^{3/2}\right] \text{(Free weir equation)}$$

$$Q_2 = C_{d2}.B.h_1\sqrt{2g.(h + h_v)} \text{ (drowned weir equation)}$$

Total discharge $= Q_1 + Q_2$

or $$C_d = \frac{2}{3} C_{d1}\sqrt{2g}.B\left[(h + h_v)^{3/2} - h_v^{3/2}\right] + C_{d1}.B.h_1.\sqrt{2g(h + h_v)}$$

The values of C_{d1} and C_{d2} may be taken as 0·577 and 0·80 respectively.

where h = Difference of the u/s and d/s water level *i.e.* (pond level – Maximum anticipated F.S.L. of canal after making due allowance for future silting of canal)

h is called the utilised head or working head or designed head for the regulator and is generally taken as half of the available head, where available head is equal to the difference of pond level and actual FSL of the canal.

h_v = Head due to velocity of approach.

B = Clear width of water way

h_1 = Depth of d/s water level above the crest

i.e. (maximum anticipated FSL of canal minus sill level)

When all other variables are fixed and known, value of clear water way width B can be calculated.

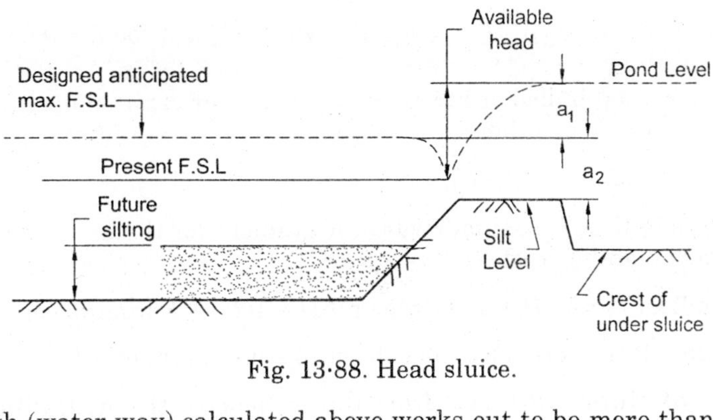

Fig. 13·88. Head sluice.

The width (water way) calculated above works out to be more than the normal width of canal d/s of the head, in such case sill level can be lowered so as to increase the head and to decrease water way to make it equal to the width of canal. If it is not possible due to the silt exclusion conditions then the water way of the head is kept the same and it is joined to the canal width by giving a transition curve by contracting the wings.

To check the entry of flood water into the canal a breast wall of RCC is provided above the pond level. This wall spans in each span and is made above the H.F.L. The breast wall is designed to take up its own weight together with the head or water on the sluice pocket side considering that no flow is going into the canal and water is headed upto H.F.L. on the sluice pocket side.

The length and thickness of horizontal floor, glacis, protection aprons etc. is designed on the same principles as are applicable to weir design. The worst condition for uplift pressure occurs when high flood is passing over the weir and there is no flow in the canal.

6·3. Design of Sarda type fall

(1) Length of crest L = Bed width B (For future development it can be as bed width + water depth = $B + D$)

(2) **Type of crest.** For discharge upto 15 cumec : rectangular with vertical faces. For discharge above 15 cumec trapezoidal with u/s batter 1 : 3 and d/s batter 1 : 8.

(3) Top width of crest b : *Rectangular crest* — $0{\cdot}55\sqrt{d}$ metres; *Trapezoidal crest* — $0{\cdot}55\sqrt{H+d}$ metres

d = height of crest from d/s bed = $D + F - H$, where F is drop in bed.

H = head over crest. To start with assume trial value of H or start with as given in serial 5 below.

(4) **Base width.** $\dfrac{H+d}{G}$ (If more than b give offsets upto u/s bed)

In case of trapezoidal crest determine base width by batter, but not less than d/G. G being the specific gravity of the material or masonry which may be taken as 2.

(5) Value of H : $Q = 1{\cdot}835\, LH^{3/2}\left(\dfrac{H}{b}\right)^{1/6}$ (Rect. crest) ; $Q = 1{\cdot}99\, LH^{3/2}\left(\dfrac{H}{b}\right)^{1/6}$ (Trap. crest)

Calculate H knowing other factors, compare with assumed and try till perfect.

For submerged falls

$$Q = C_d\, L\sqrt{2g}\left(\frac{2}{3}F^{3/2} + h_d\sqrt{F}\right) \text{ where } C_d \text{ is a coeff.} = 0{\cdot}65$$

F = drop in bed or F.S.L.; h_d = head over crest on d/s side. Calculate h_d knowing others.

(6) The height of crest = $(D + F - h_d)$

(7) **Floor.** Length of floor l. Assume hydraulic gradient for the soil say 1 : n then length of floor = nd (d being the height of crest).

(a) d/s length of floor $l_d = 2\,(D + 4)$ + drop or $2(D + 1{\cdot}2^n) + F$ from toe of crest.

(b) The remaining floor is provided u/s subject to a minimum of 5H.

(c) **Thickness of floor.** Ordinate from top of floor to the hydraulic gradient line considering with no flow with water filled upto top of crest in u/s side) divided by the submerged specific gravity of concrete $(G - 1)$. The specific gravity of concrete may be taken as 2·25. The thicknesses t_1, t_2, t_3 ... at distances x_1, x_2, x_3 ... from the toe of the crest will be $\dfrac{y_1}{1{\cdot}25}, \dfrac{y_2}{1{\cdot}25}, \dfrac{y_3}{1{\cdot}25}\cdots$ subject to minimum of 0·30 m for small falls and 0·5 for large falls and should be designed on Khosla's theory. y_1, y_2, y_3 ... are the ordinates from H.G.L. to top of floor with no flow, and water is filled upto top of crest.

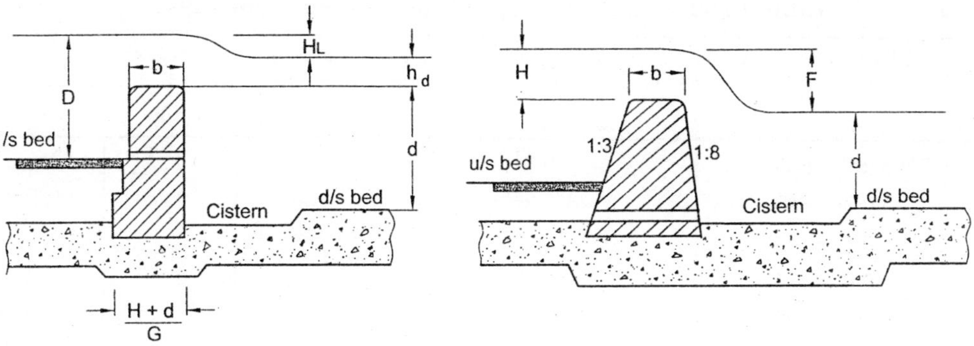

(a) (b)

Fig. 13·89.

Other factors to be provided are :

(1) A nominal thickness at u/s of the floor is kept to be 0·3 m for small falls and 0·5 m for large falls.

(2) A masonry or concrete of 1 m depth (for large falls upto 1·5 m) cut off wall is provided at the d/s end of the floor of about 0·3 m in width.

(3) At top of the concrete floor provide a protective masonry cover of about 10 cm to 15 cm in thickness.

(4) 2 to 4 m length of u/s floor is brick pitched in a slope of 1 : 10. At the u/s floor level weep holes in the crest is provided to drain off the water when the supply in the channel is cut off about 15 cm in dia. at the interval of 1 m apart.

(5) The section of the crest must be checked for actual stability for large falls.

(6) D/s cistern – length $= 5\sqrt{\text{head over crest} \times \text{drop}}$

$$\text{depth} = \frac{1}{6}\sqrt{\text{head over crest} \times \text{drop}}$$

or
$$\frac{1}{4}\,(\text{head over crest} \times \text{drop})^{2/3}$$

U/s Protection

U/s wings. Radius : 5 to 6 H upto end of u/s floor. The end of the wings must enter in the bank straight to about 0·6 m to 1 m.

Foundation of the wing. At u/s top of concrete of floor.

U/s pitching. A nominal length of pitching may be provided at u/s in a slope of 1 : 1.

D/s Protection

D/s wings. The u/s wings are stepped down to form d/s wings after the crest to the required level of d/s. These are kept vertical upto the end of the cistern, after which they are warped to 1 : 1. The end of the wing is also returned in the bank to a length of 1 to 1·5 m. The length is about 3 m beyond the d/s floor. There should also be a free board 0·5 to 1 m in the top of the wing.

Bed protection. A pitching in the bed is also provided upto the end of d/s pitching. Upto 1st curtain wall, c.c. block 1 × 1 × ·5 m size may be provided over a filter material in 30 cm thickness.

Table 13·32. Details of d/s pitching in Sarda type falls

S.No.	*Head over crest in m*	*Total length of pitching d/s side (m)*	*Remarks*	*Curtain walls*	
				number	*depth (m)*
1.	upto 0·30	3		1	0·3
2.	0·30-0·45	3 + 2*F*	Horizontal upto end of masonry wings, after which 1 : 10	1	0·3
3.	0·45-0·60	4·5 + 2*F*		1	0·45
4.	0·60-0·75	6·0 + 2*F*		1	0·6
5.	0·75-0·90	9·0 + 2*F*		1	0·75
6.	0·90-1·0	13·5 + 2*F*		2	0·90
7.	1·0-1·2	18·0 + 2*F*		2	1·0
8.	1·2-1·5	22·5 + 2*F*		3	1·3
9.	1·5-1·75	27 + 2*F*		3	1·5
10.	1·75 – 2·0	33 + 2*F*		4	1·5

Note : All the wing sections are designed as a retaining wall considering channel empty, with earth pressure on the back (saturated). Weep holes may also be given in the wing walls.

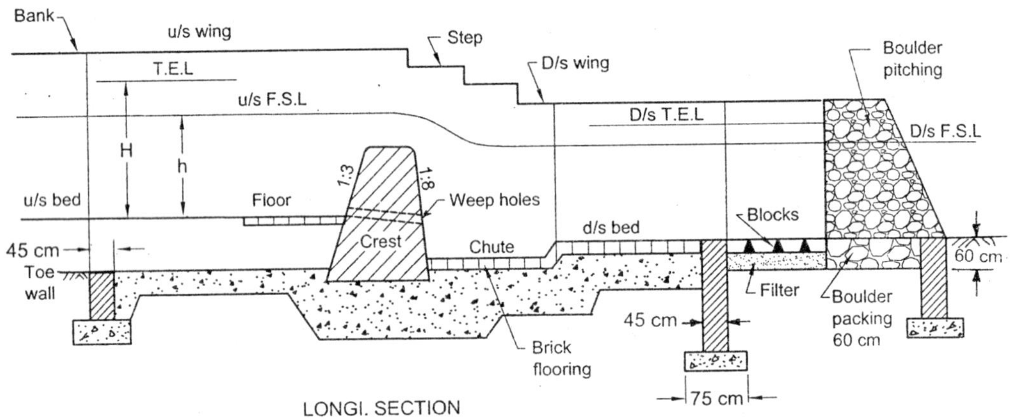

Note : Thickness of floor and depth of toe walls as per design.

(*a*) Longitudinal section Trapezoidal crest Sarda type fall.

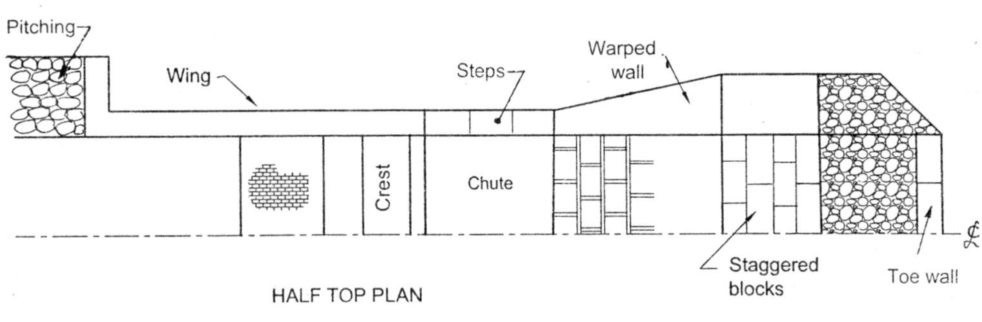

(*b*) Half Top Plan.

Fig. 13·90.

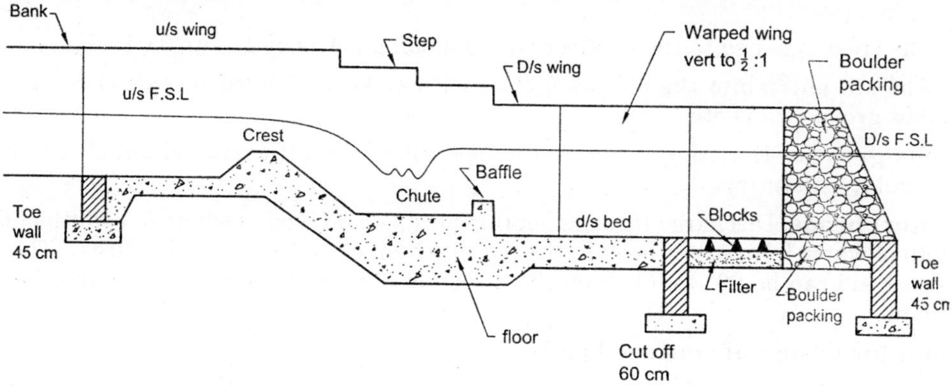

Fig. 13·91. L-section of a sloping glacis baffle fall.

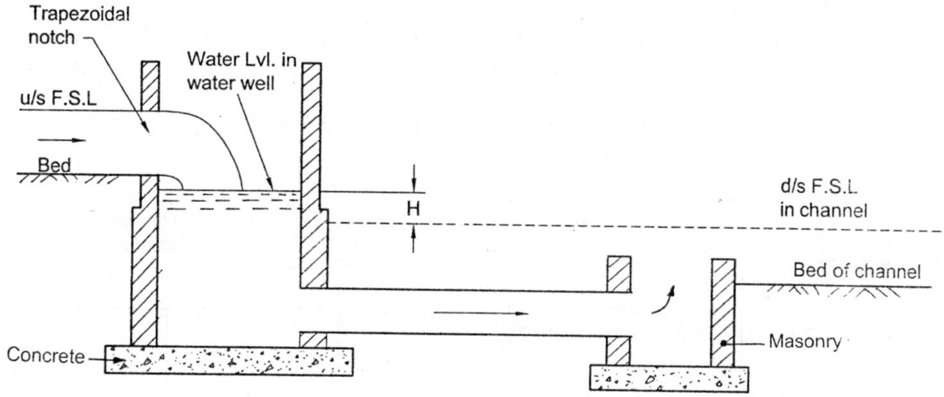

(*a*) Syphon well drop fall

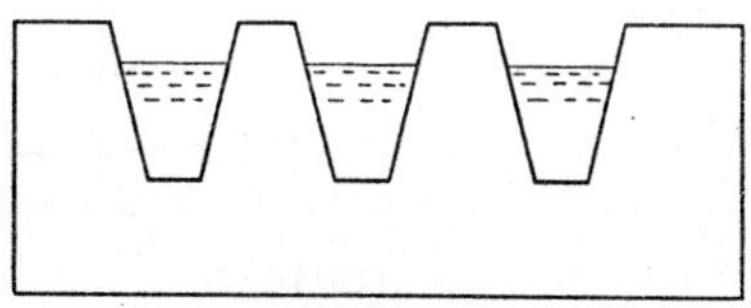

(*b*) Notch fall.

Fig. 13·92.

6·4. Head and cross Regulators of channels

$$Q = \frac{2}{3} C_1 L\sqrt{2g}\left[(h+h_a)^{3/2} - (h_a)^{3/2}\right] + C_2 L \times d\sqrt{h+h_a}$$

where Q = discharge in cumecs

L = waterway length in m

h = diff. in water level u/s and d/s in m for the channel

h_a = head due to velocity of approach

d = depth of d/s water level above crest level

$C_1 = 0{\cdot}577$, $C_2 = 0{\cdot}80$

h_a can be neglected being too small and observe following criteria :

(1) Crest of the cross regulator is kept equal to the u/s bed of the parent channel.

(2) Crest of the distributary head regulator is kept about 0·3 to 1 m above the crest of the cross regulator.

(3) The crest is joined to the d/s floor with a sloping glacis of 2 : 1 to 3 : 1.

(4) The silt entry into the offtaking channel may be controlled by raised crest, King's Vanes or Gibbs groyne walls etc.

Gibbs groyne. It is the perforated wing wall of the off-taking channel into parent channel to regulate silt entry.

Venturi heads. Discharge through venturi head $Q = 3{\cdot}00\ bd^{2/3}$ where b = width of throat and d = depth of water from water level in the parent channel to the silt of the throat. The angle of the venturi head can be 90° to 60° from the direction of flow of the parent channel for a bed width upto 6 m.

Rules for design of venture heads :

(1) **Width of throat.** Must not be less than 1/3 of the bed width of the parent channel or the width determined by the fomrula $b = \dfrac{Q}{2\,bd^{2/3}}$ whichever is greater. Where there is a regulator d/s of the head in the parent channel or where there is a large head available, the throat width may be kept 1/4 of the bed of the parent channel or the width obtained by the formula $b = \dfrac{Q}{2\,d^{2/3}}$ whichever is more subject to minimum of 0·6 m.

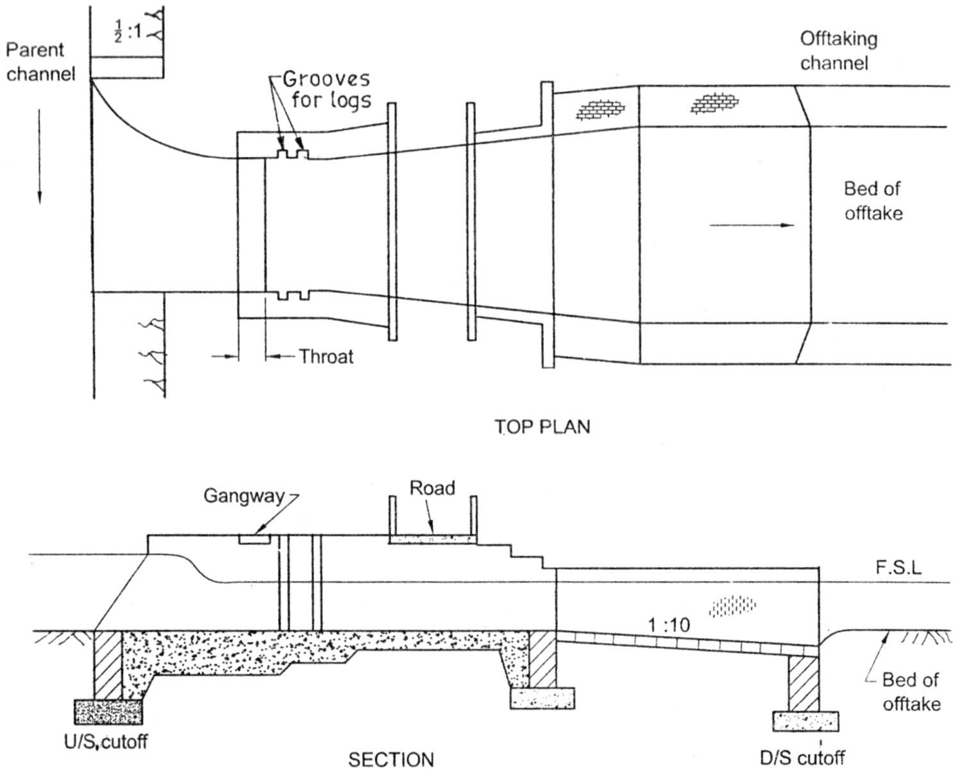

Fig. 13·93. Head of a distributary.

(2) **Drop in the level** of parent channel to the off-taking channels should be at least $d/8$.

(3) The throat should be set back by $1{\cdot}4\ b + 6$ from the F.S.L. line of the parent channel. The side slopes of parent channel are 1 : 2.

(4) **Length of throat.** It should be 2·5 d.

The u/s and d/s connections are self evident from the figure.

Discharge through a venturi flume in channels.

$$Q = \frac{K\, a_1 d_2}{\sqrt{a_1^2 + a_2^2}} . \sqrt{2gh}$$

where Q = discharge, a_1 = area at section (normal), a_2 = area at flumed section (width × depth)

h = difference of head of water surfaces of normal and flumed section.

K = coefficient due to friction which is 0·95 to 0·1.

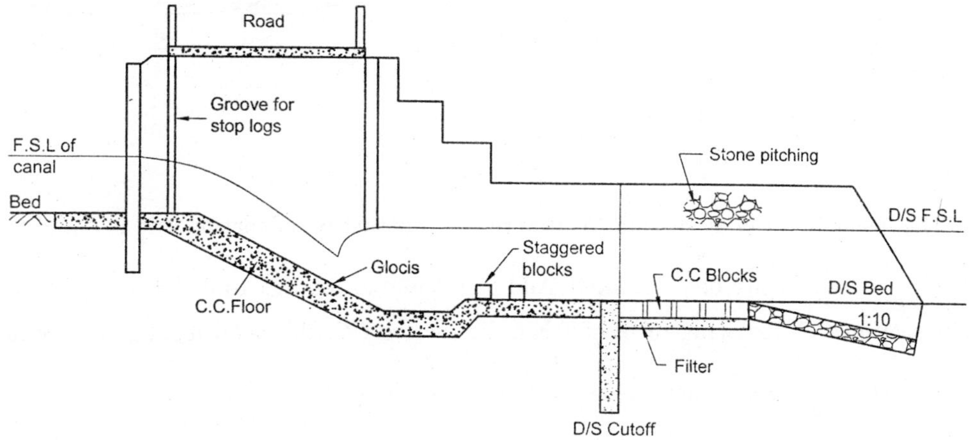

Fig. 13·94. Section through a cross regulator or head regulator of a branch canal.

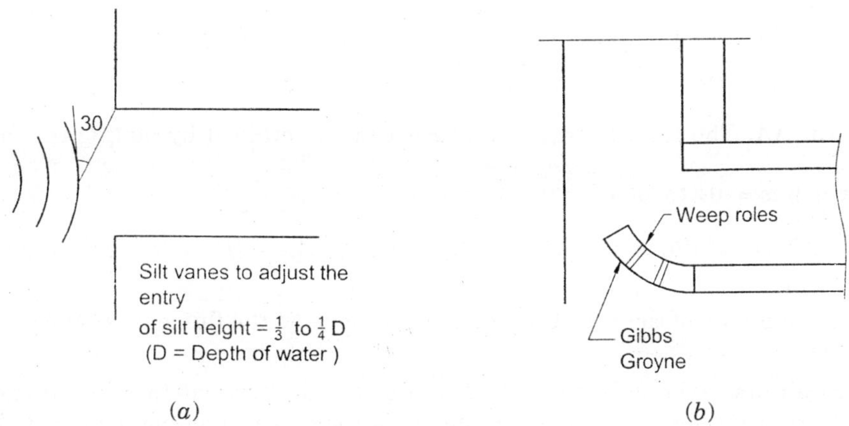

Fig. 13·95.

6·5. Contraction of water way (Flume). The angle of entry must not be steeper than 30° while the angle of departure not steeper than 22½°. Now consider section AA at entry, section BB at u/s contracted section, CC at d/s contracted section and DD at d/s section of departure.

Section DD. Take a datum of level say 100. The depth D_4 and velocity V_4 (known) hence the level of the total energy line

$$= 100 + D_4 + \frac{V_4^2}{2g} \quad \text{(Now known)} \qquad ...(1)$$

Section *CC*. The depth D_3 is known and velocity V_3 is also calculated by Q/A where the width of flume is also known.

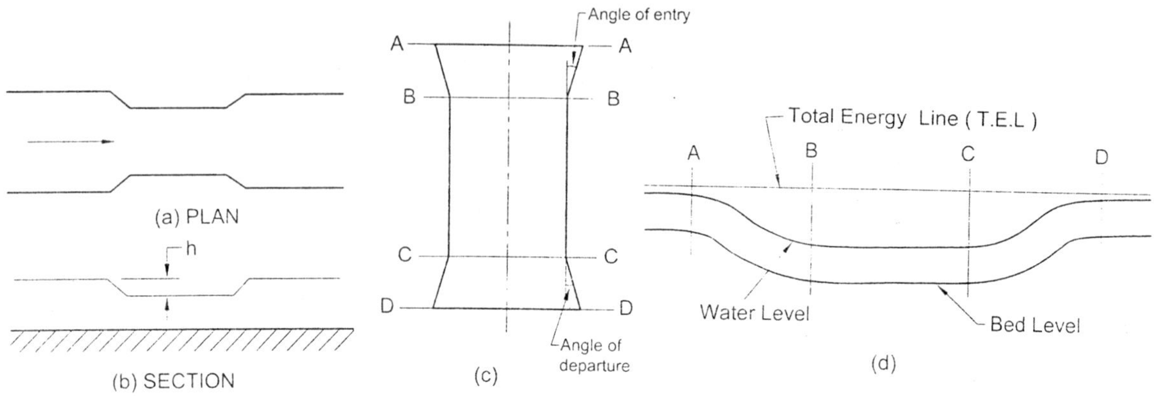

Fig. 13·96.

The loss of energy at section *CC* due to the contraction of section and is equal to 0·10 to 0·30 of $\frac{V_3^2 - V_4^2}{2g}$ which can be calculated. Add it in the total energy line (T.E.L.) of *DD* to obtain T.E.L. at section *CC*. Knowing level of T.E.L. at section *CC*, the head level can be obtained by deduction of $D_3 + \frac{V_3^2}{2g}$ and hence the level of bed at section *CC* is calculated.

Section *BB*. The only loss is due to friction which can be calculated by the Mannings formula. Add it to T.E.L. of section *CC* to obtain T.E.L. at section *BB*. Now the bed level of section

BB = level of T.E.L. at section $BB - \left(D_2 + \frac{V_2^2}{2g}\right)$. D_2 is known and V_2 can be computed knowing the section of flume at *BB*.

Section *AA*. The total energy line at *AA* can be obtained by adding the loss between *AA* and *BB* which is = ·01 to ·03 of $\frac{V_2^2 - V_1^2}{2g}$.

The bed level of flume at *AA* = T.E.L. at section *AA* – (D_1 + loss at section *AA* due to contraction).

Hence the profile of the bed section and water level of the flume is obtained for a desired section of flume.

6·6. Syphons. Average velocity of 2 to 3 m/sec. is assumed to pass through syphons. Higher values are taken for a higher discharge and stronger construction materials is also used in their construction.

Divide the discharge by this assumed velocity which will give the required cross-sectional water way for the syphon. If head way is restricted the linear water way can be obtained by dividing the superficial water way. According to site conditions if the linear water way is restricted the head way can be obtained accordingly. The linear water can be divided into a number of bays.

Afflux u/s of the syphon. $h = (1 + f_1 + f_2 \times L/R)\,\frac{V^2}{2g} - \frac{V_a^2}{2g}$

where h = afflux in ft..; V = velocity in syphon, V_a = velocity of approach *i.e.* velocity in the drain, L = length of barrel, f_1 = coefficient of loss of head at entry = 0·505 for sharp edge and 0·80 for bell mouthed entry. $f_2 = a\,(1 + b/R)$ where R = hydraulic mean depth of barrel in ft. a and b are as follows :

Table 13·33.

Type of Material	a	b
Smooth iron pipe	0·00497	0·084
Encrusted pipe	0·00996	0·084
Smooth cement plaster or plained wood	0·00316	0·10
Ashlar, brick work	0·00401	0·23
R.R. masonry or stone pitching	0·00507	0·83

f_2 is a coefficient such that loss of friction head = $\dfrac{f_2 L}{R} \times \dfrac{V^2}{2g}$

6·7. Outlets. Outlets are divided in the following three classes :

(1) **Non modular outlets.** These are the outlets in which the discharge is effected by the water surface in the supply channel as well as in the gul. Submerged weirs and outlets are the examples of this type. The head can be increased by clearing the guls. These type of outlets are used in lift irrigation areas. In distributaries and minors they are fixed 22·5 cm below the F.S.L. By fluctuation of water supply in channel head over the outlet fluctuates. In main canals and branches outlets are not given directly, however if desired they are provided at a suitable depth from F.S.L. considering the minimum supply. The discharge through such outlets can be determined by the formula $Q = CA\sqrt{2gH}$ where H is head causing flow, A = area of outlet and C is a coefficient which depends on the length and friction in pipes combined.

Value of *C*

(1) Outlet pipes of cement and earthen ware free over fall		= 0·63
	Submerged	= 0·80
(2) Cast iron	Free over all	= 0·63
	Submerged	= 0·74

In practice a value of 0·70 is taken due to obstruction etc. The length of pipe is 3·0 to 4·0 metre. The entry of silt in such outlets is adjusted itself according to head available, even though a better silt entry is improved by lowering the upper end of the pipe which does not effects the head.

The **efficiency** of an outlet is the ratio of the head required to the head supplied.

Minimum modular head is the minimum head required to function the outlet.

Modular limits. The extreme values of any factor at which a module or semi module ceases to act.

(2) **Semi modules.** When the water level in the supply channel effects the discharge due to fluctuations in its water surface and water level in the gul does not have any effect on the discharge of the outlet. Such cases are of free over fall outlets. These type of outlets are used when there is no silt problem in the supply channel, otherwise on high heads more silt can enter in the module.

Open flume semi module with free water surface. It is a weir constructed with throat in which hypercritical velocity is produced. Expansion is provided at outlet end to obtain the recovery of head. The discharge Q through such outlets = $KB\,.\,D_1^{3/2}$ where B is the width of throat and D_1 is the height from bed of throat to the water level in the supply channel. K is a coefficient which is as follows :

B_1 *in Ft/cm*	*value of K*
0·2 to 0·3/6 to 9	2·90/1·60
0·3 to 0·4/9 to 12	2·95/1·64
Over 0·4/12 cm	3·00/1·65

For cm in metric units Q is in cumecs and B_1 and D_1 in metres. The coefficient remain with variation in head and the hydraulic jump keeps the discharge independent of the tail water level. The minimum modular head for this is $0{\cdot}2D$. At lower heads the jump is drawned and the discharge formula does not hold. The depth of crest of the throat is 0·9 times the depth of water in channel. The higher crest will produce higher velocity and lower, lower velocity than proportioned. The efficiency of such outlets are 80 to 90%. To minimise the risk of choking of the throat, the minimum width of the throat is kept to be 0·06 m. In narrower throats the velocity is hypercritical and the share of silt increases, while in the wider throats the velocity is reduced and hence the share of silt is also reduced.

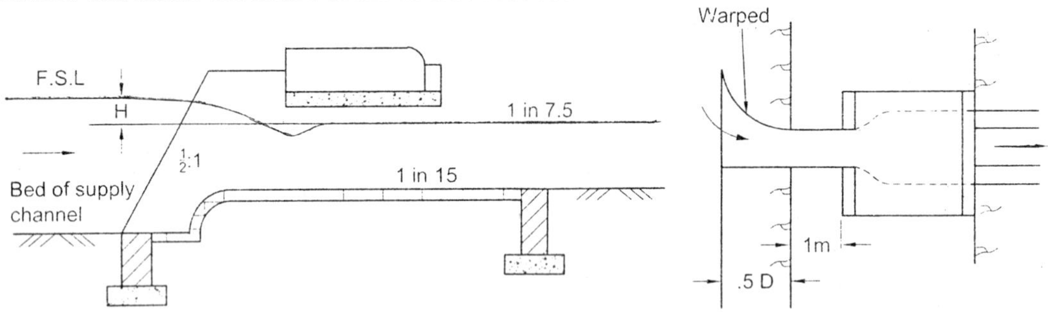

Fig. 13·97. Open flume semi module.

Orifice semi module. It consists of an orifice provided with a gradually divergent flume at d/s side. The flow through the orifice is hypercritical and is independent of tail water level. The u/s curve is warped from vertical to ½ : 1 while the d/s is sloping to a slope of ½ : 1. The length of the throat is 0·6 m. Below the throat (gullet) the side walls diverges in a circular arc of rad. 7·5 m. The slope in the bed is 1 : 15 while the roof block is curve of lemniscate and lifts at a slope of 1 : 7·5. The discharge from such semi module is $7{\cdot}3\, B_1 D_1 \sqrt{H_1}$ where B_1 is the width of orifice. D_1 is the height of the smallest section and H_1 is the head from the water level in supply channel to the lowest point of the roof block. The minimum modular head = $0{\cdot}82\, H_1 - \frac{B_1}{2}$ and if the available head is less than this, the discharge formula will not hold. The value of H_1 is $0{\cdot}3D$ (where D is depth of water in supply channel.) If the value of H_1 is lower the module will be sub-proportional and if more it will be above proportional. The roof level can be adjusted as per requirements.

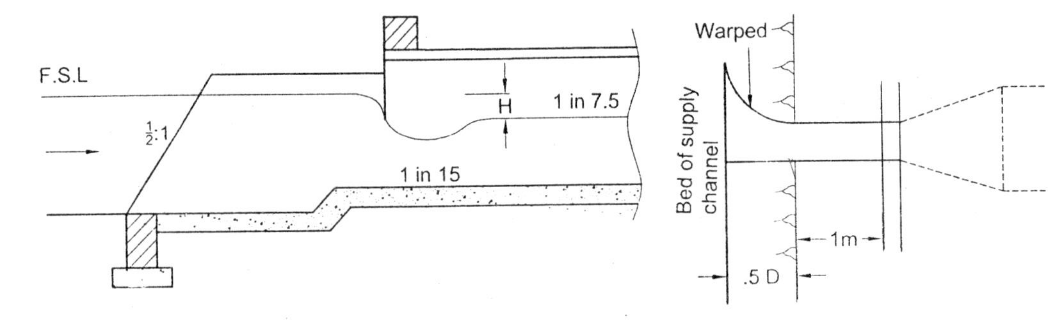

(*a*) (*b*)

Fig. 13·98. Orifice semi module.

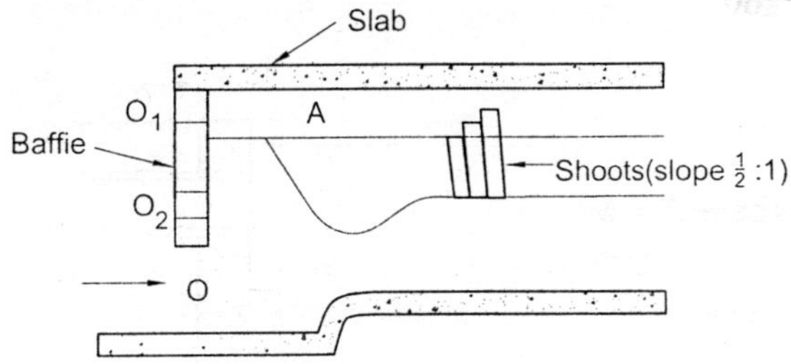

Fig. 13·99. Khanna rigid orifice semi module.

Khanna's Rigid Orifice Semi Module. It is an orifice module as discussed above with additional sloping shoots (slope ½ : 1) of rising heights in steps of 0·15 m provided in roof block and opening in a chamber A to counteract the increase in discharge due to increasing head in the supply channel. The water enters in the orifice through wider opening O (see Fig. 13·99) and shorter O_1 and O_2, during the normal water level in the supply channel. When the water in the supply channel is increased and enters in the chamber A (The differential chamber) it rushes through the lower shoot to the orifice. The back flow through shoots impinges the flow in orifice and dissipates the additional energy. If the level in the supply channel is further increased it enters in the next higher shoot and reduces the additional energy further and the function advances. The number of shoots can be increased according the fluctuation in the supply channel. The module works even if the shoots are choked only the increased energy is not dissipated.

(3) **Rigid Modules.** An outlet which gives a constant fixed discharge irrespective of the water level in the supply channel as well as level in the water course. These are used when the water is supplied on the volumetric basis. In practice these modules are generally not used as they are expansive and different to operate.

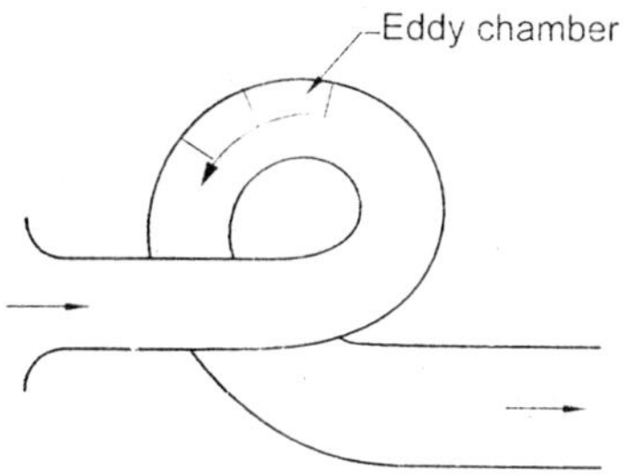

Fig. 13·100. Gibb's module.

Gibbs Module. It consists of a bell mouthed spiral pipe curved upto an eddy chamber in which the baffles are provided against the flow direction from the roof. The diameter of the outlet is more than inlet due to which velocity at outlet is decreased. As the head increases in the supply channel the rate of discharge increases which is blocked at the outlet due to slow velocity and water rushes back towards the eddy chamber and opposes the supply causing it to reduce. The baffle walls hanged from the roof of the eddy chamber which has required opening at the lower end also opposes the increased supply causing a back flow, which reduces the increased supply.

Silting capacity of an outlet. Entry of silt depends on the following :

(1) **Position of the sill.** The lower is the sill of outlet the more is the silt entry.

(2) **The quantum of the contriction of the flume.** The narrower throats give higher velocity and hence greater amount of silt entry.

(3) **Slope of the pipe.** The greater is the slope, the greater is the quantity of silt entry due to increased velocity.

Proportional outlet. The outlet in which the value of flexibility is one. If it is more than one, the outlet is hypercritical and vice-versa.

Flexibility. The ratio of the rate of change of discharge of outlet to the ratio of the change of discharge of supplying channel.

Efficiency. It is the ratio of the head recovered to the head put in. The loss in the working head required the more efficient is outlet to be.

Minimum modular head (M.M.H.). It is the minimum head required to function an outlet.

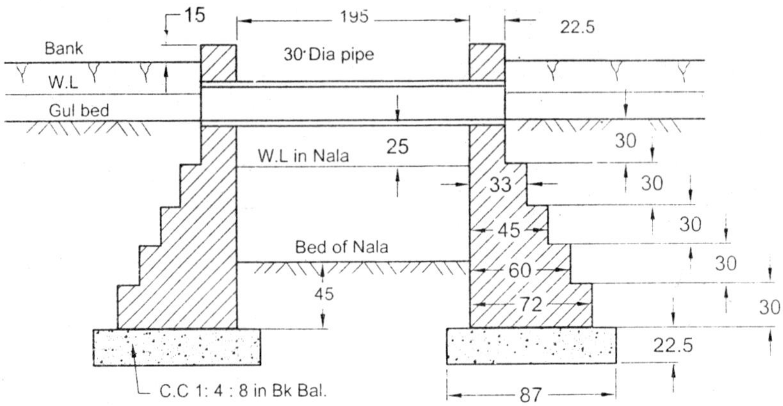

SECTION AT AB

Culvert bed of gul higher than bed of nala crossing.

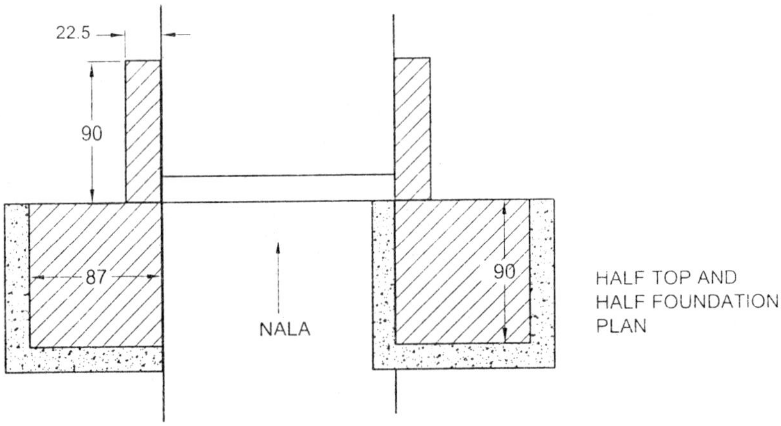

Note : All dimensions are in cm until and otherwise stated.

Fig. 13·101.

6·8. Design procedure for cross drainage works. The stepwise points are as below :

(1) Canal parameter in bed width, water depth, bed level and full supply level with discharge are already given in canal cross-section.

(2) Bed level of drain can be obtained by observing *L*-section of the drain about 10 km u/s and 10/km d/s of the proposed work and slope of the drain can be estimated by this long section by taking an average line.

The high flood level can be ascertained by local enquiries. The enquiry must be done from several old persons of the area or from the flood marks on trees, existing H.F.L. marked on pucca works u/s or d/s of the work.

The water way of the river can be computed by the Lacey's expression

$$P = 4{\cdot}75\sqrt{Q}$$

where P = the wetted perimeter in metres and Q is the discharge of the river

The discharge can be computed as per directions given in the chapter of Hydrology or as discussed in the chapter of measurement of flow in open channels.

Hume Pipe Culvert—Road is above the Gul

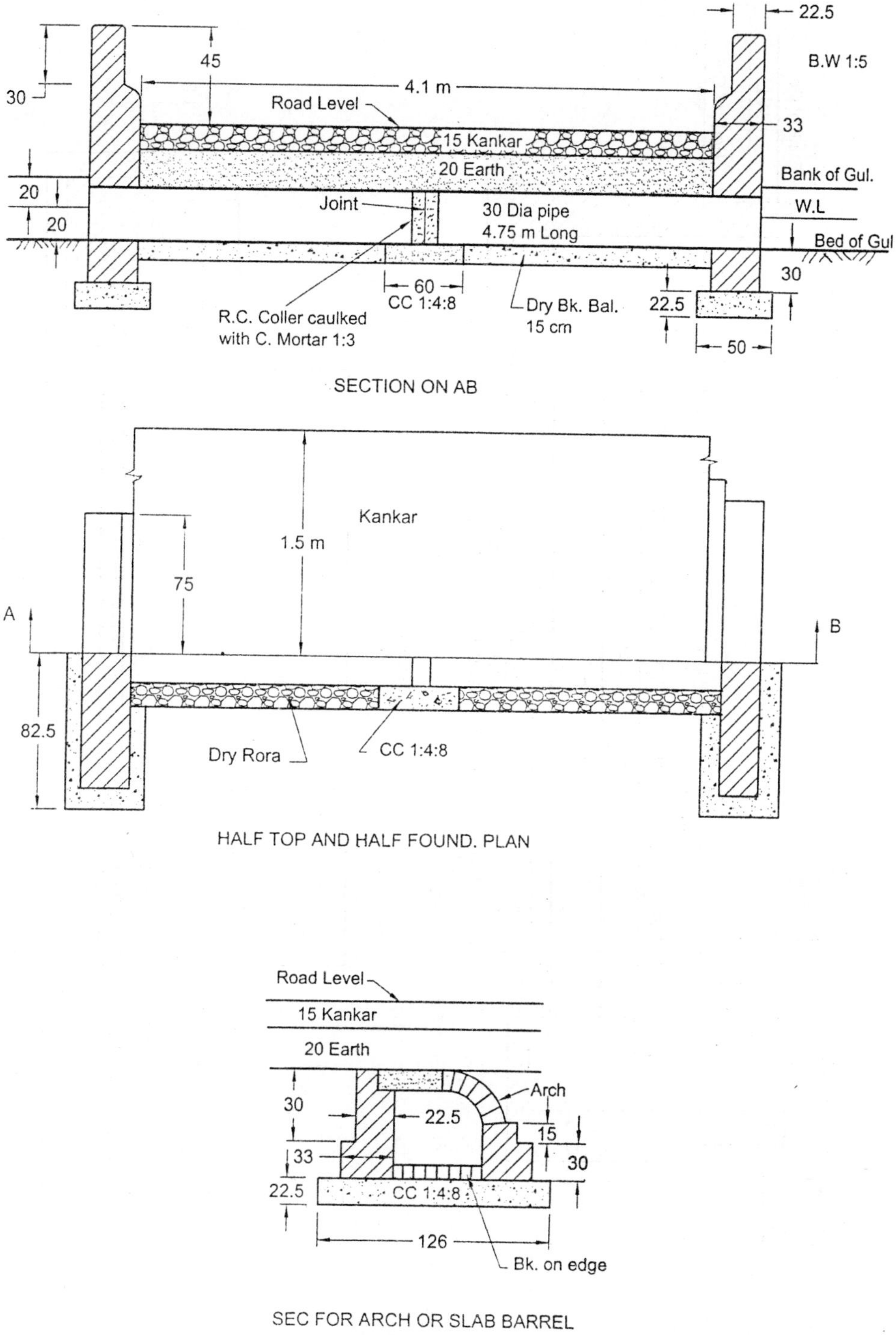

Fig. 13·102. Gul culverts.

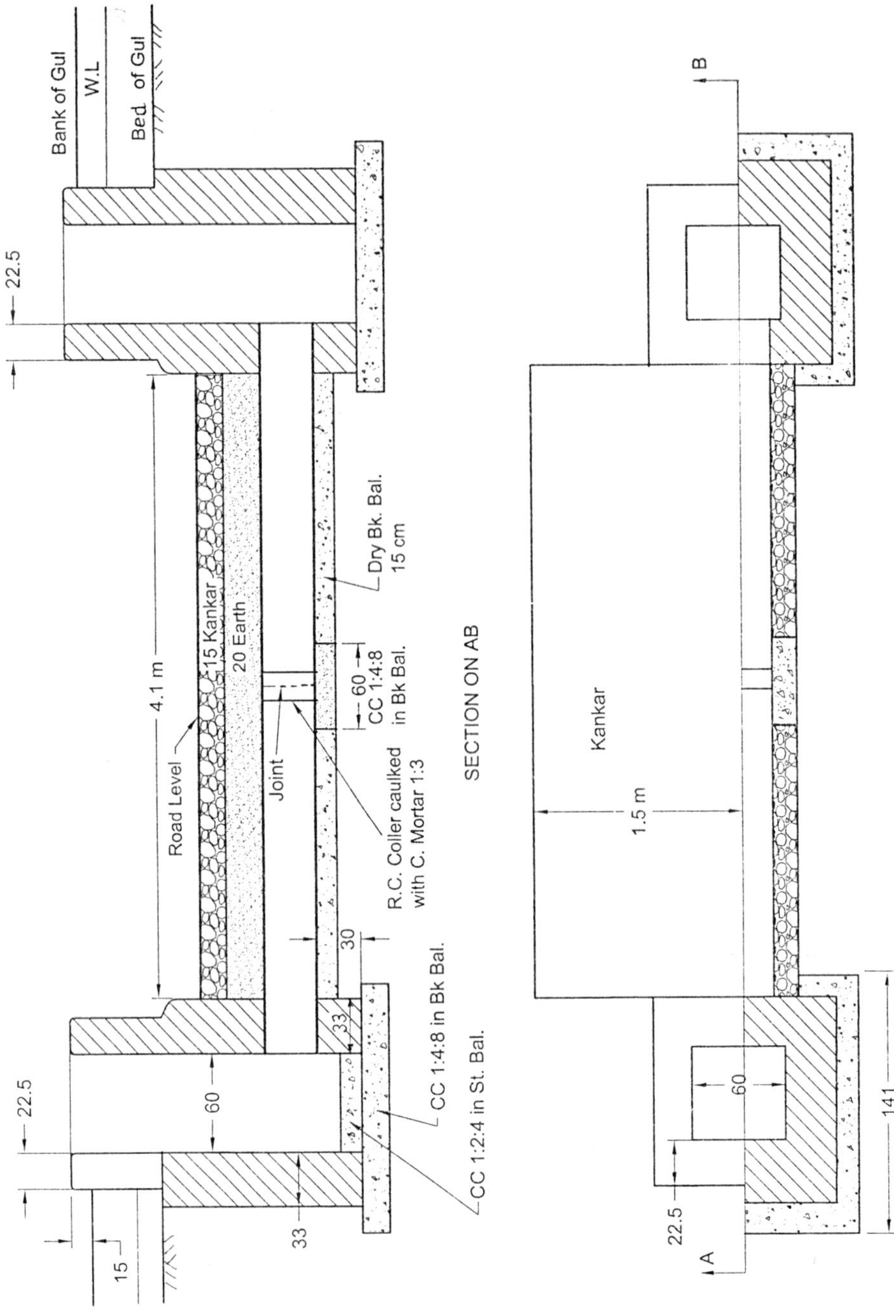

(All dimensions in cm untill and unless mentioned)

Fig. 13·103 Hume pipe siphon when road is lower than gul bed.

Cross-sections u/s and d/s of the work is also taken and the wetted perimeter can be marked on a graph sheet and an average of the two is taken. A value of 0·8 of wetted perimeter as water way may however be taken for big rivers.

For small drains the water way may be taken as bed width + water depth.

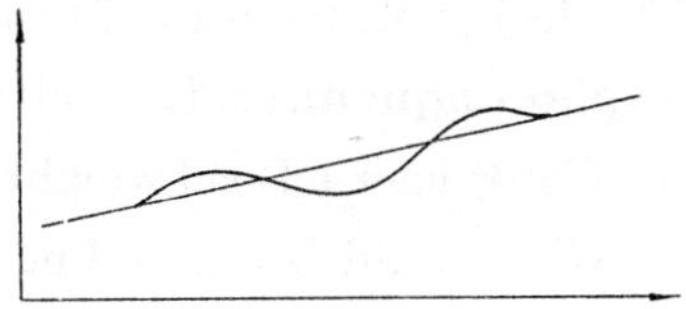

Fig. 13·104.

Size of barrels of Siphon or Syphon aqueducts can be decided by 1st calculating the headway. The waterway or the span is decided by the wetted perimeter and assuming a velocity of 2 to 3 m/sec the head way can be calculated as $Q = AV$ or $A = \frac{Q}{V}$ or $b.h = \frac{Q}{V}$; knowing the span b the head way $h$can be calculated. Knowing h the floor can be depressed according to levels available.

Afflux and head loss in syphon barrels. Due to friction etc. a certain amount of h (head) is lost during passage of water through barrels. Unwin given a formula for loss of head as below :

The total head loss due to the (i) entry loss = $f_1 \frac{V^2}{2g}$ (ii) Friction loss = $\frac{f_2 L V^2}{2gR}$ and exit loss = $\frac{V^2}{2g}$.

$$h = \left[1 + f_1 + f_2 \frac{L}{R}\right] \frac{V^2}{2g} - \frac{V_a^2}{2g}$$

where L = length of barrel

R = hydraulic mean radius of the barrel

V = velocity of flow through the barrel

V_a = velocity of approach and is often neglected

f_1 = coefficient of head loss at entry = 0·505 for unshaped mouth and 0·08 for bell shaped mouth.

f_2 = A coefficient such that the loss of head through the barrel due to surface friction is given by $f_2 \times \frac{L}{R} \cdot \frac{V^2}{2g}$ where $f_2 = a\left(1 + \frac{b}{R}\right)$. and the values of a and b for different materials may be taken as below

Table 13·34.

Material of the surface of barrel	*a*	*b*
Smooth iron pipe	0·00497	0·025
Encrusted pipe	0·00996	0·025
Smooth cement plaster	0·00316	0·030
Ashlar or brick work	0·00401	0·070
Rubble masonry or stone pitching	0·00507	0·250

D/s H.F.L. remain unchanged by the construction of the work so u/s H.F.L. can be obtained by adding the value of afflux h.

Due to rise in H.F.L. due to afflux the top level of guide and marginal bunds u/s of the work are also to be raised. The afflux and the reduced by giving a bell mouth entry and by providing smooth surface of the barrel.

Aqueduct. Design of the roof of the drain or the bottom of the trough. The worst condition is that the channel is running full and drain is dry. In such a condition the only load on the trough is its own load plus the weight of water on it for which it can be designed easily.

The design of side wall of trough is done as a water relating wall.

Syphon aqueduct. It involves three conditions :

(*a*) Water load + Dead weight of trough.

(*b*) When uplift is full and no water load.

The amount of uplift pressure exerted by the drain water on the roof (base) of the trough can be evaluated by drawing the hydraulic gradient line (H.G.L.) as shown in the Fig. 13·109. The uplift pressure at any point of the roof (base) of the trough will be equal to the vertical ordinate between the H.G.L. and the underside of the trough at that point as shown in the figure. From this uplift diagram. it is very evidence that the maximum uplift occurs at the u/s end point near the entry. The uplift pressure on the under side of the trough at the u/s end will be = (u/s water level – entry loss – level of the underside of the trough). The slab thickness should be designed to withstand this maximum uplift. The slab should be designed for larger load (load due to water pressure and load due to uplift. Reinforcement may be provided on both the sides to meet with both the conditions.)

When the uplift pressures are greater, the slab may be anchored to the peirs to take this extra load as shown in the Fig. 13·105.

Design of the floor of drain in the barrel due to the uplift pressure by the spring water. The maximum uplift will occur in the worst condition when no water is flowing in the drain and water table has risen upto the drainage bed.

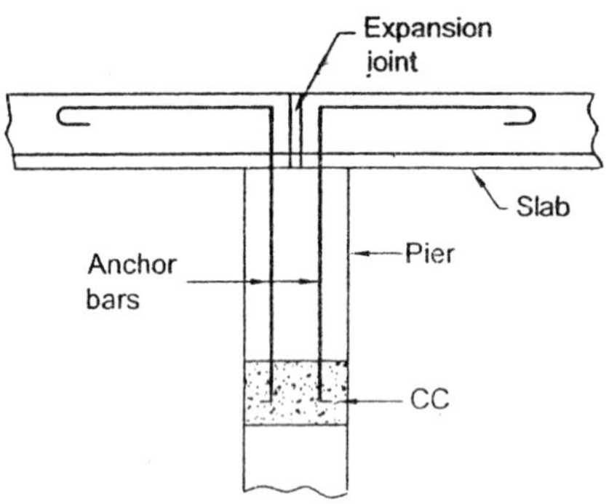

Fig. 13·105.

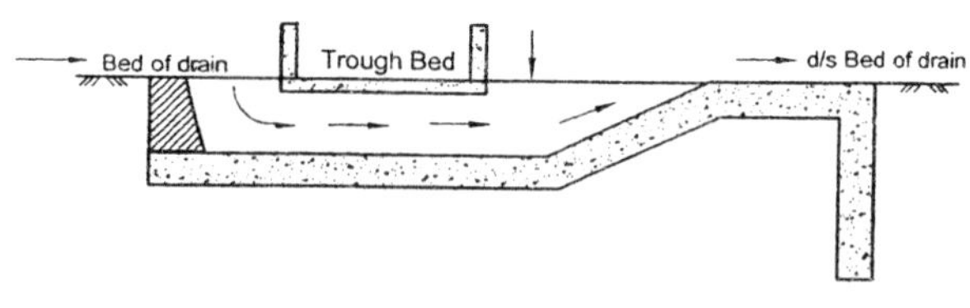

Fig. 13·106.

In such cases uplift is equal to the difference in the bed level of the drain to the amount of depression in the barrel for which bed concrete may be provided accordingly.

Uplift due to the seepage of water from the canal. It is a most important and tedious part of the design of river bed floor due to uplift by the canal water and is considered for the worst position when canal is running full with no water in the drain. In this case as the flow is three dimensional, therefore it is possible to work out uplift on the basis of two dimensional flow, hence Bligh's theory will prevail in this case. For larger works the uplift pressures must be checked by model studies.

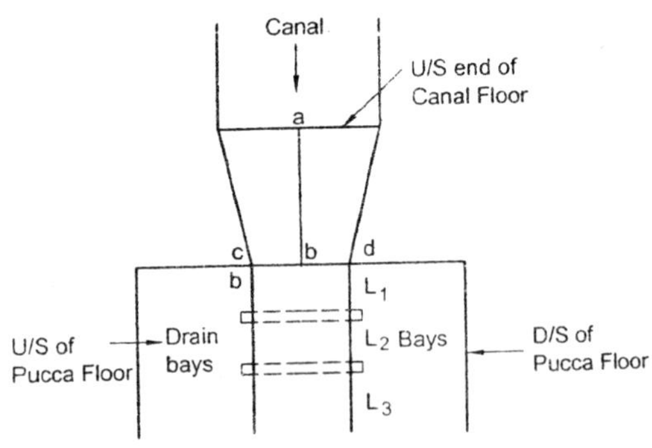

Fig. 13·107.

The seepage flow occurs from the beginning of Pucca floor of canal trough at point (a) and reappears in the drainage bed on either side of the impervious floor along the centre of the floor of the 1st culvert bay say point (c) or (d) as given in the Fig. 13·107. Point b is the point under the centre of the floor of the 1st culvert bay.

Seepage from point a to b and from b to c can be known. The total creep length will then be equal to $ab + bc$. If H is the total seepage head (*i.e.* H = F.S.L. of canal – d/s bed level of drain), the residual head at the point b (*i.e.* H_b) is then given by Bligh's theory as equal to

$$H_b = H - \left(\frac{H}{ab + bc} \times ab\right) \text{ or } H_b = H - \left(\frac{H}{ab + bc} \times bc\right)$$

The floor of the syphon aquaduct must be designed for the total uplift which is equal to the sum of the uplift due to seepage plus uplift due to static head. The total uplift may be partly resisted by the weight of the floor and partly by bending in reinforcement.

Method for reducing the uplift on the floor. The uplift on the bottom floor may be reduced in two ways.

(*i*) By extending the u/s impervious floor of the canal trough on either side of the drain so as to increase the creep length (ab). A puddle apron may be used in place of concrete floor if clay is easily available.

(*ii*) By providing drain holes (weep holes) in the bottom floor. An inverted filter must be provided under the floor to help in preventing the soil particles from getting out from the holes. But these holes and filter may be choked after sometime and thus becomes ineffective.

Wings. There are two types of wings in aqueducts :

(1) **Canal or the land wings.** These wings provide a string connection between the masonry and concrete sides of a canal trough and earthen canal banks. These wings are generally warpe in plan so as to change the canal section from trapezoidal to rectangular. They should be extended upto the end of splay. These wings may be designed as retain walls (bearing earth pressure with no water in canal). The foundation of these wings should not be left on filled earth, they should go deep on firm strata.

Drainage or water wings. These wing walls retain and protect the earthen slopes of the canal, guide the drainage water entering and leaving the work and join to the guide banks and also provide a vertical cut off for the water seeping from the canal into the drainage bed. The foundation of these wings should be taken below the deeper anticipated scour in the river. The sections of these wings should be capable of withstanding the maximum earth pressure likely to come on them.(Refer Fig. 13·108 (a))

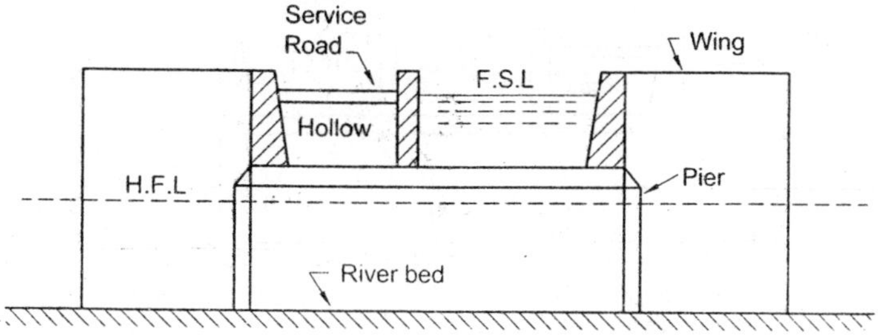

Cross-section

Note : (1) It can be designed just as a bridge. The roof slab is capable to take water load of channel.

(2) The side walls should be capable of taking water pressure of channel and is to be designed as water retaining wall.

Fig. 13·108 (a) Aqueduct.

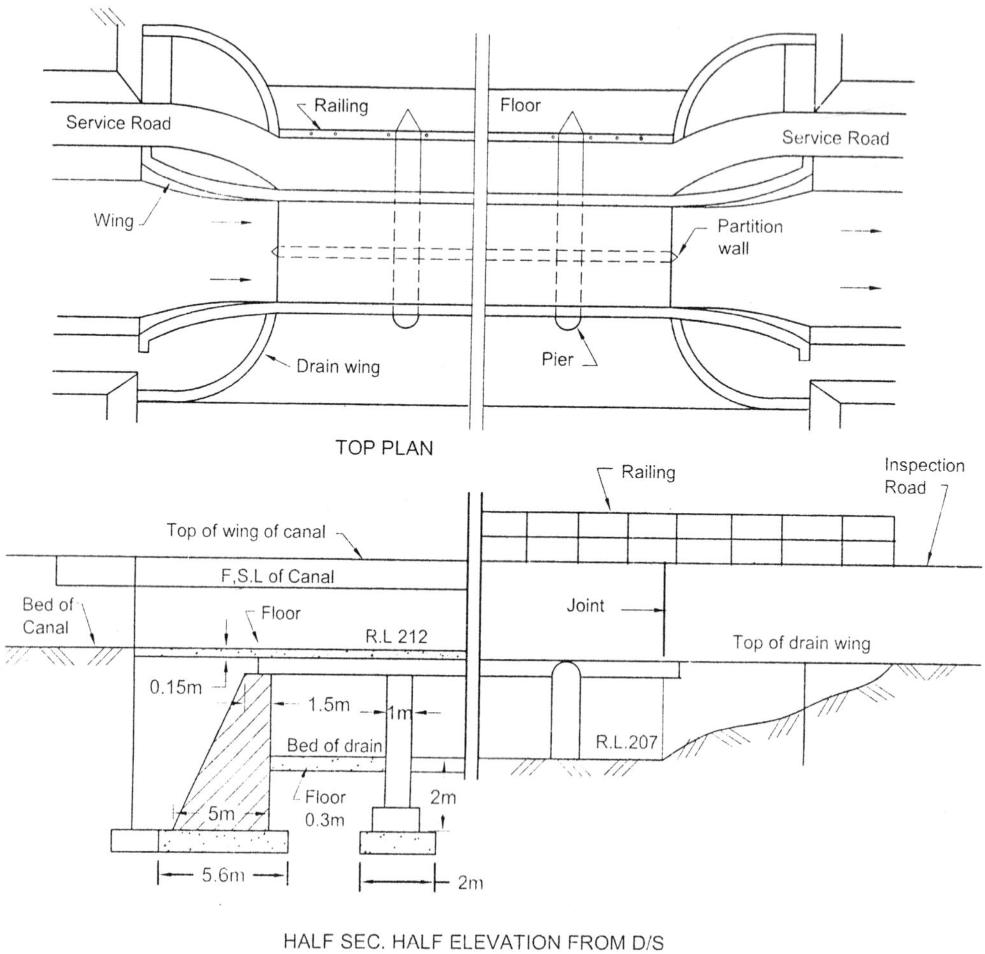

Fig. 13·108.

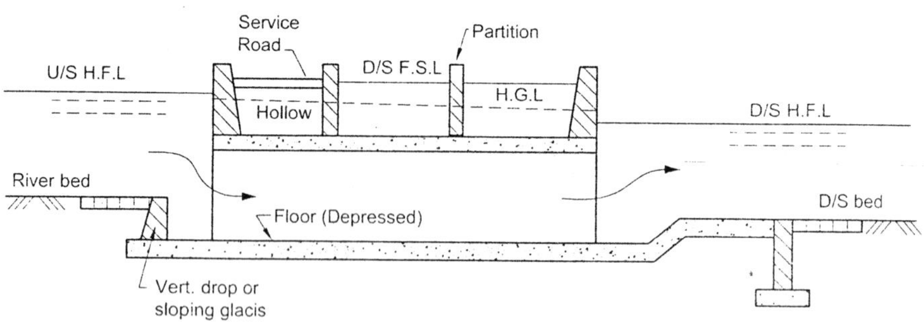

Note : Roof slab is designed for load when drain is full and canal empty for uplift of drain water as well as canal full and drain empty both ways; side wall for water pressure of canal as water retaining wall.

Fig. 13·109. Syphon aqueduct.

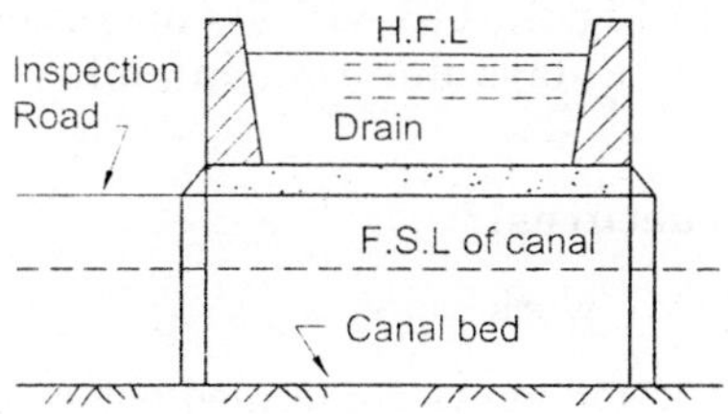

Fig. 13·110. Super passage.

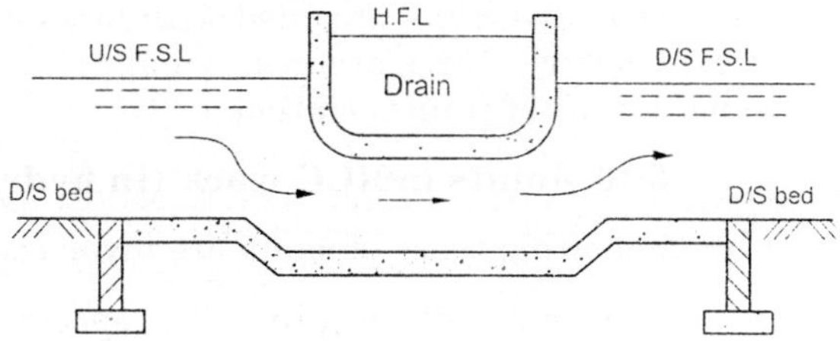

Fig. 13·111. Canal syphon.

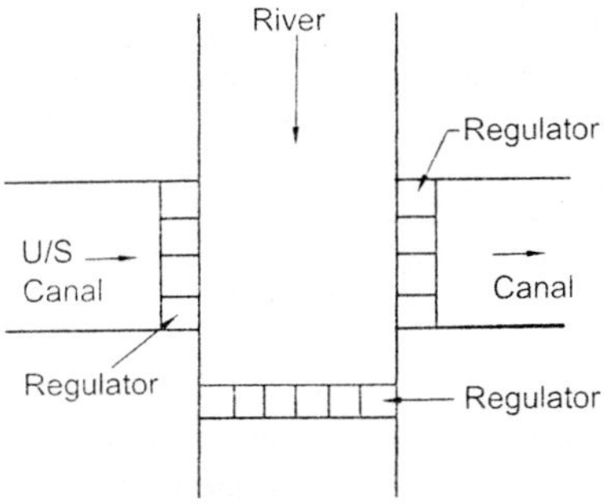

Level crossing

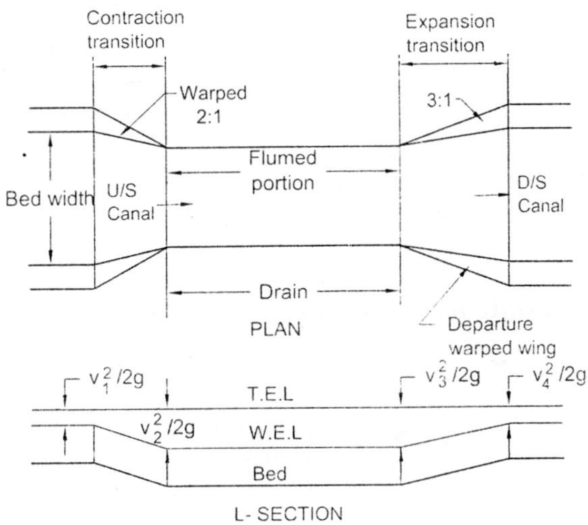

Fig. 13·112. Canal flume.

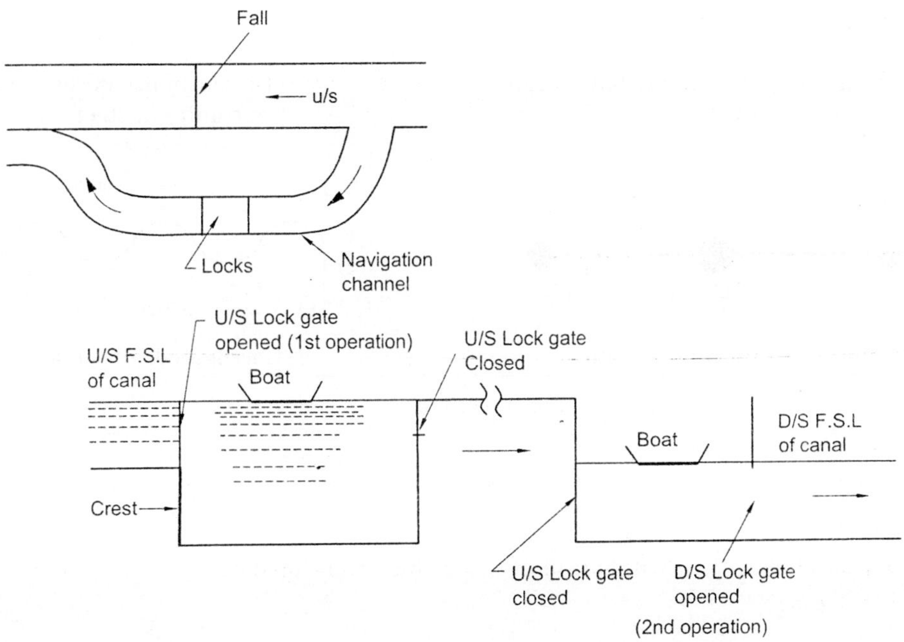

Fig. 13·113. Half section half elevation from d/s.

6·9. Canal navigation (Locks). Where there are falls in canals, a navigation channel is constructed which is provided with locks as shown in Fig. 13·113 with its operation which is self explanatory. Navigation in canals is not done now a days due to availability of modern cheaper means of transportation.

6·10. Joints in RCC work (In hydraulic structures)

Following types of joints are involved in the R.C.C. work :

(1) **Construction joints.** The spacing of construction joints is planned before and should be at regular intervals.

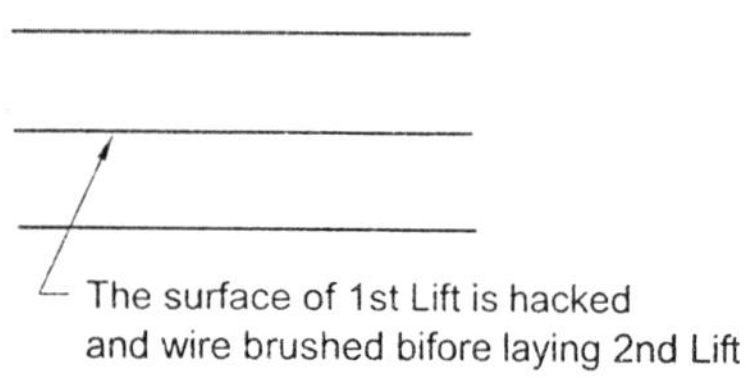

(*a*)

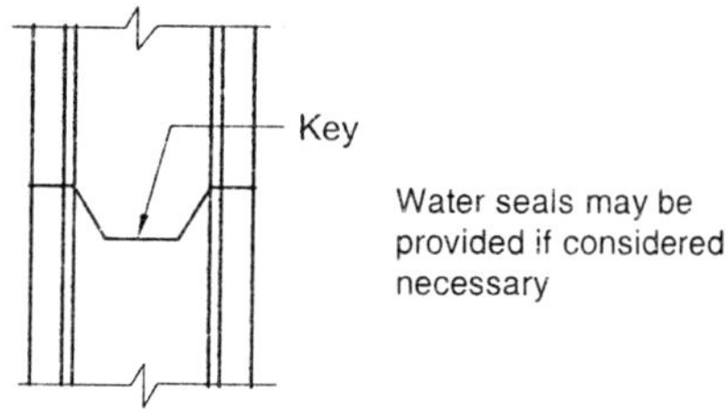

(*b*)

Fig. 13·114.

(2) **Contraction joints**

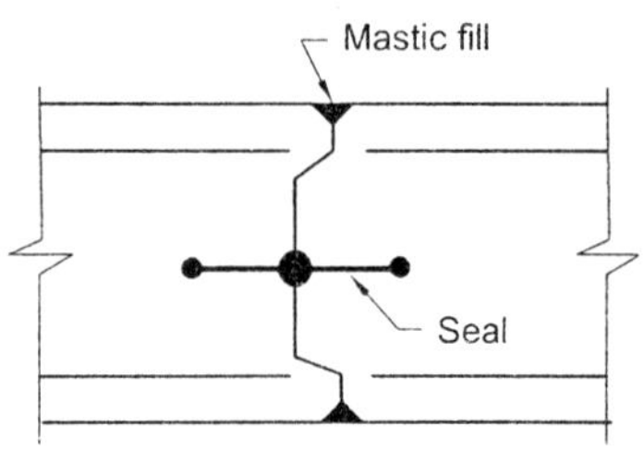

(*a*) Discontinuity in concrete but no gap
Discontinuity in steel.

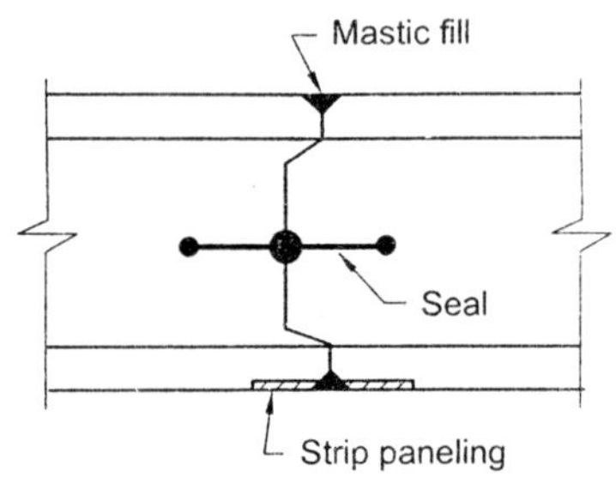

(*b*) Discontinuity in concrete
Continuity in steel.

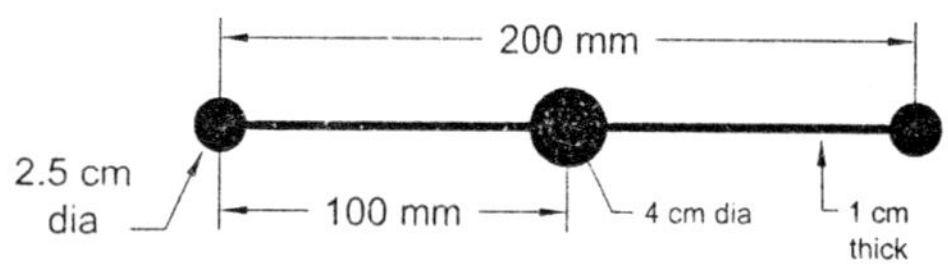

(*c*) Rubber seal with central bulb.

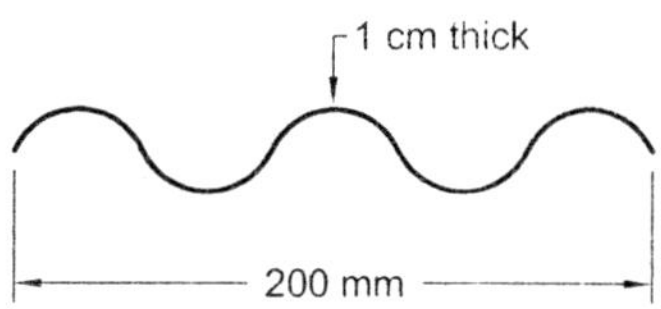

(*d*) Corrugated rubber seal.

Fig. 13·115 (*a*).

Sealing Compounds are :

(1) Asphalt

(2) Bitumen

(3) Coal tar pitch with or without filler such as lime stone or slate.

(4) Bars of PVC.

(3) Expansion joints

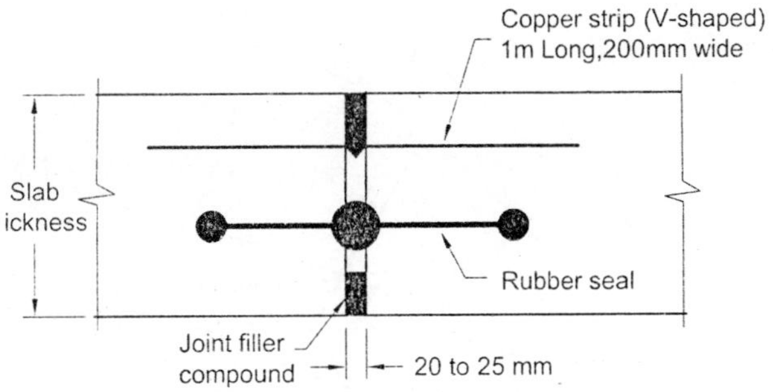

Fig. 13·115 (*b*).

(4) Sliding joints

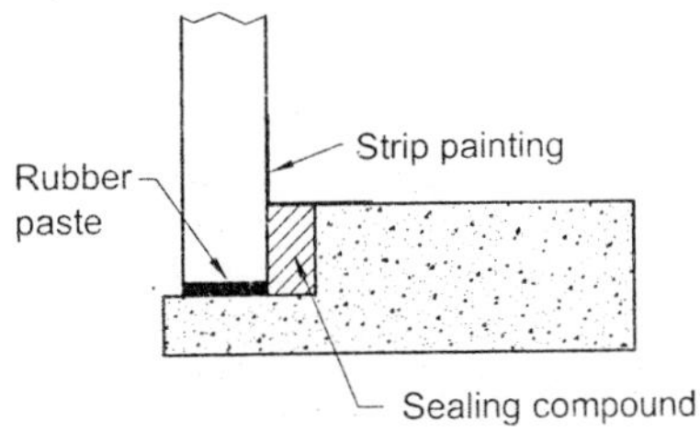

Fig. 13·116.

(5) Other types of joints

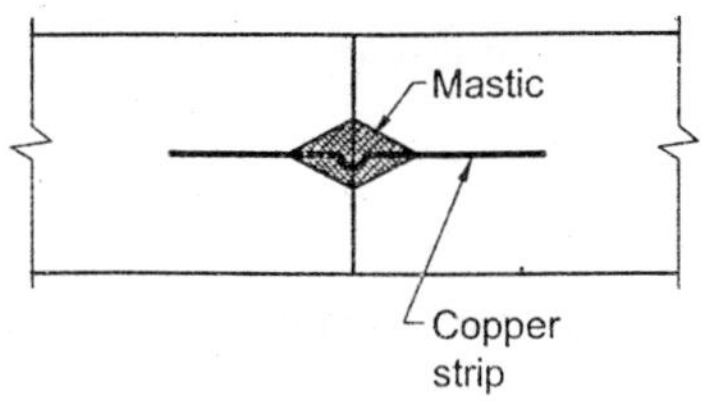

(*a*)

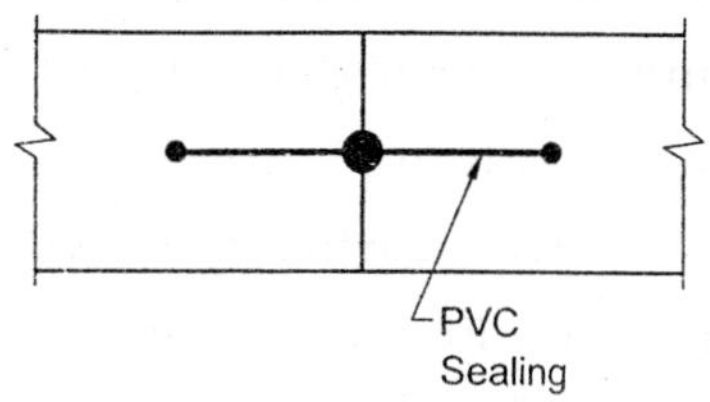

(*b*)

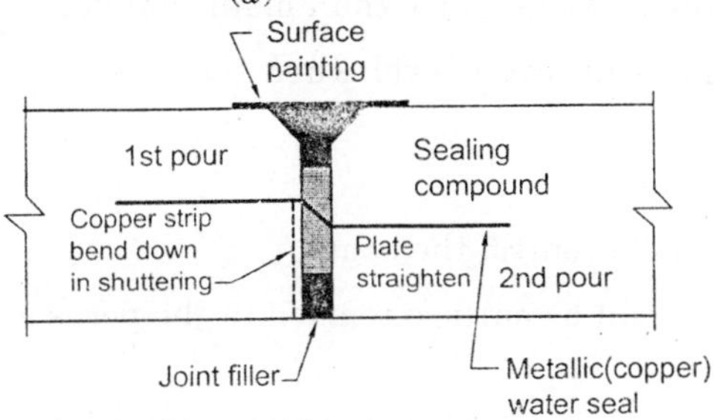

(*c*)

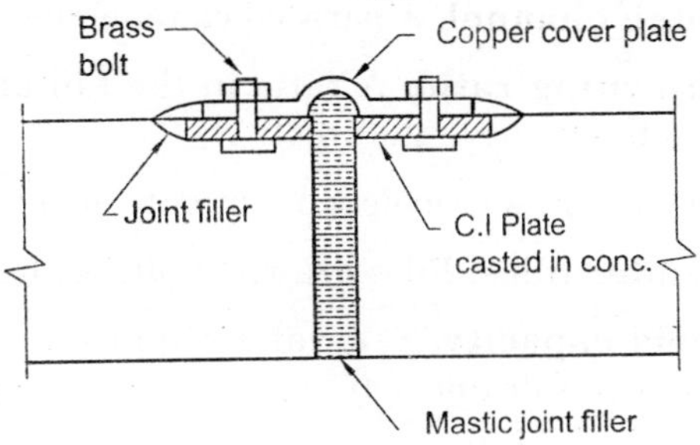

(*d*) copper joint cover plate joint

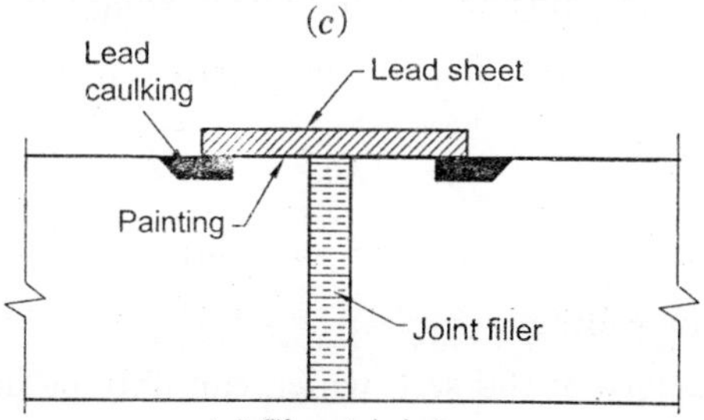

(*e*) Sheet joint

Fig. 13·117.

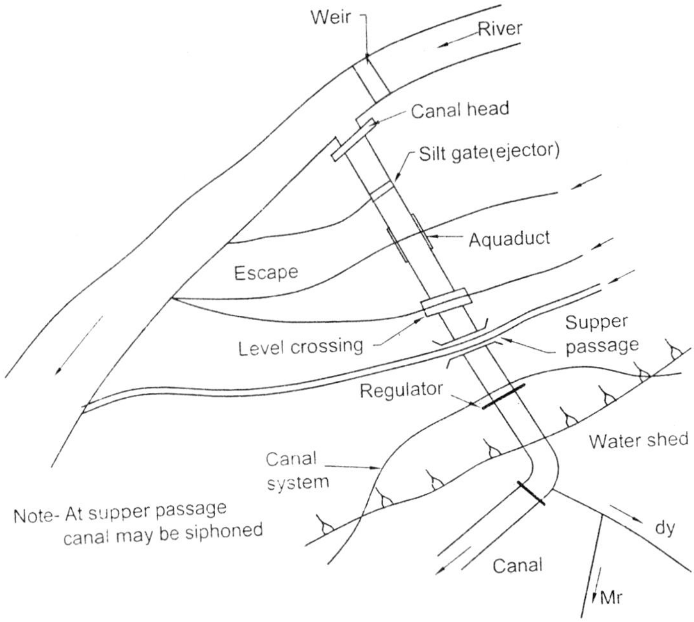

Fig. 13·118. Cross-drainage works on canals.

13·8. Technical Terms in Irrigation Engineering

Caving. Erosion of channel banks by undermining action of water.

Capillarity. Rise of water in soil pores against gravity by force of surface tension.

Conservative works. Works which store water during rains.

Crop ratio. For every crop there is fixed percentage for irrigation according to the availability of supply.

Ditch channel. A parallel channel, having different slope than main channel.

Drowning ratio. A ratio in the tail and head water level when they are in drowned stage *i.e.* both are above the crest.

Dry crop. A crop dependent entirely on rain.

Fender piles. Piles drawn at offtake heads to control the boats.

Field capacity. The water retained in the soil by surface tension in the pores after the surface water has drained off.

Flank wall. Retaining walls u/s and d/s of an abutment. It may be a wing wall.

Flared or warped walls. A retaining or wing wall sloped from vertical at u/s side to a slope say ½ : 1 towards the d/s side.

Groyne. Spurs or transverse dykes.

Hydraulic fill dam. A dam constructed with sand, clay and gavel etc.

Rock fill dam. Earthen dam compacted by rolling.

Hygroscopic water. Moisture on the surface of the soil, which can only be driven off by heat and not by gravity.

In coherent alluvium. Soil composed of loose granular graded material.

Leaching. Washing out of salts from the upper zone of the soil by flowing and draining.

Pen stock. A closed conduit for supplying of water under pressure to the turbines in a hydroelectric plant.

Pick up weir. A weir made across a river to raise the water level so that it may be diverted into a canal few km d/s of a storage reservoir.

Diversion weir. Weirs to divert the flow of river to the canal.

Diversion head works. Head works made on a river from which perinial flow is diverted to the head.

Storage head works. Head works provided in a storage reservoir to direct water into the canal.

Rapids. Inclined falls in bed of canals or rivers.

Inverted filters. A layer of graded material (Pea gravel, shingle to stone at top) provided at outer toe of earthen dams as safety against piping.

After bay—Tail race of a water power plant.

Arid—Dry area

Urban—Populated area

Baffle—A wall provided d/s of a cistern to head up water.

Bell bund—Guide bund for training a work.

Breast wall—A face wall in front of a head regulator to retain the water in the river.

Isoboths—Lines drawn on map from the places having equal level of under ground water.

Rating—A relation between two mutual dependent quantities. Such as no. of revolutions of the fins of a current meter to the discharge and the process of establishing this relation is known as rating of the current meter.

Riprap. A protective graded layer of stones (gravel to stone) on the water surface against erosion.

Suppressed weir. A weir having the same width as channel u/s of it as well as bed level and sides are also coincident with the channel section to avoid and end constriction.

Talus. A d/s protection in the floor of a weir or fall made of concrete blocks founded over a filter bed.

Infiltration. The process of entrance of rain or snow melted water into ground.

Percolation. Motion of rain or surface water after entering in ground.

Aquifers. Layers of soil containing ground water.

Aquifuge. Impervious soil which neither contain water nor allows flow of water through it.

Specific yield. Specific yield of an aquifer is the quantity of water flows out by gravity in percentage of volume of water after being saturated.

Specific retention. The percentage retention of volume of water in an aquifer after being saturated against gravity.

Tail cluster. Tail outlet.

Gullies. Rain cuts.

Sloughing. Flow of saturated soil mass due to seepage.

Piping. Building of fine soil particles with seepage water.

Shoals. Heap of silt deposits u/s of newly constructed weir.

Draw down. Fall of seepage line like dipression head in a well.

Consumptive use of water. This is also called as **Evapo-transporation water.** Loss of water due to transporation, evaporation and in weed growth included in depth of water for irrigation for a crop.

Transporation. It is the process by which plants dissipate water from the surface of their leaves, stacks and trunks in the process of their growth.

Coefficient of transmissibility. Rate of flow of water in m^3/day through a vertical strip of an aquifer of one metre width and extending the full saturation height under a unit hydraulic gradient at 60°F.

Nappe. The head of water over the crest.

Yield. Regular supply of water.

Chute. A depressed trough d/s on hydraulic work to dissipate energy.

13·7. Sub Soil Water Irrigation

13·7·1 Well Irrigation

Mota. Impervious bed of clay, cemented sand, kankar or other hard material which lies a metre or so below the water table. The layer of hard material above water table are not counted as mota.

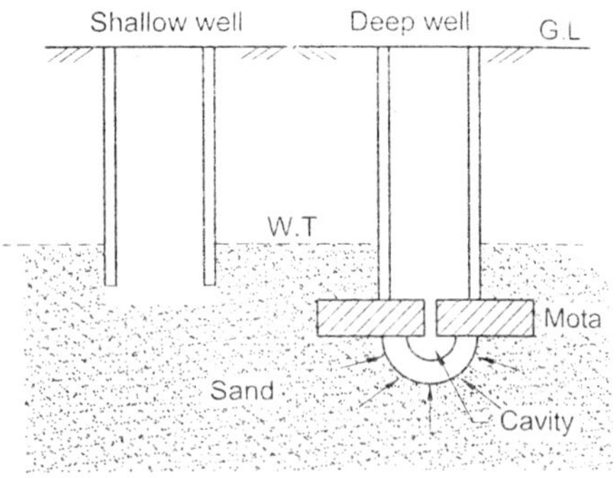

Fig. 13·119.

Shallow wells. Wells founded over pervious stratum and draw their supply from surrounding and bottom soil.

Deep wells. Wells founded over mota. The supply in such wells is taken from another pervious layer below the layer of mota through a hole. A deep well may be higher than a shallow. The name is only technically based and not on the actual depth. Water in such wells is drawn by a cavity formed in the pervious layer below mota after the fines have been drawn up.

Cone of depression or depletion. When water is withdrawn from a well, its level goes down and stabilise on a lower level that than of the water table out side. The depression so created between the original water level of the water table and the water level in the well is called as depression head. As water travels from out side to the well a gradual loss of head occurs in shape of an inverted cone surrounding the well. The shape of water surface so formed is known as the cone of depression, cone of exhaustion or a draw down curve. The radius of the base of this curve is known as the radius of influence and the cone as a cone of influence. But there is a practical limit for this depending on the critical velocity for a particular strata for pumping. Depression head goes on increasing till the rate of withdrawal of water equals to the recuperation. The depression depends upon the nature of the stratum. In sand the gradient is 1 : 20 to 1 : 50, while in chalk it may be 1 : 10. The dpression head goes down by increasing the rate of withdrawal.

13·7·2. Aquifers

The geological material which yields the water to the well is called an *aquifer*. While the geological formation of stratum of impervious material which does not admit ground water is called an **aquiclude.**

(*i*) **Unconfined aquifers.** Unconfined aquifers, also called as non artesian aquifers are the top most water bearing strata having no confined impermeable over-burden lying over them. The ordinary gravity wells 2 to 5 m dia. which are excavated through such top most aquifers are known as unconfined wells. The water level in these wells will stand at the level of the water table as shown in Fig. 13·120. Such wells are therefore also known as water table or gravity wells.

(*ii*) **Confined aquifers.** When an aquifer is covered on its upper and under surfaces by an impervious strata (aquicludes) and is also inclined so as expose the aquifer somewhere to the catchment area at a higher level for the creation of sufficient hydraulic head is called a confined aquifer or an **artesian aquifer.** A well dug through such an aquifer yields water that flows out automatically under the hydraulic head and rushes out upto the height of hydraulic gradient line such wells are called the **artesian** or the flowing wells (well No. 3) in the Fig. 13·121. If the pressure surface, (hydraulic gradient line) which is an imaginary surface and represents the magnitude of hydrostatic pressure available lies above the ground surface, the well will be an artesian well, where as if the pressure surface is below the ground surface, the well be artesian but non flowing and will require a pump to bring the water to the ground surface (in Fig. 13·121 well (1) and well (2).

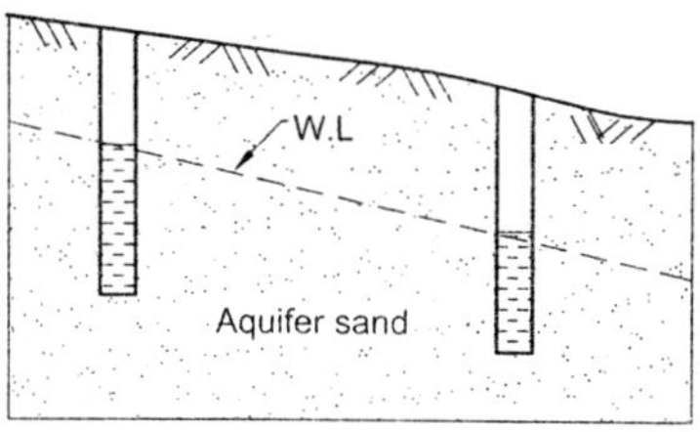

Fig. 13·120. Gravity well.

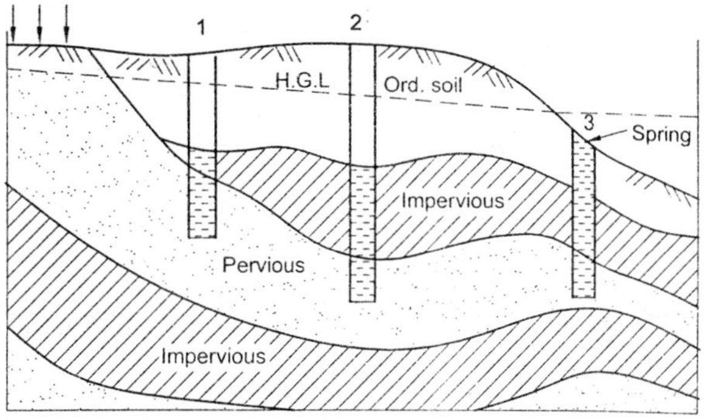

Fig. 13·121.

Thiem's formula for the unconfined aquifer

$$Q = \frac{\pi K\left(h_2^2 - h_1^2\right)}{2{\cdot}3 \log_{10} \dfrac{r_2}{r_1}}$$

or

$$Q = \frac{2\pi T(S_1 - S_2)}{2{\cdot}3 \log_{10} \dfrac{r_2}{r_1}}$$

where T = coefficient of transmissibility ($T = Kd$, taking h_1 and h_2 nearly equal = d)

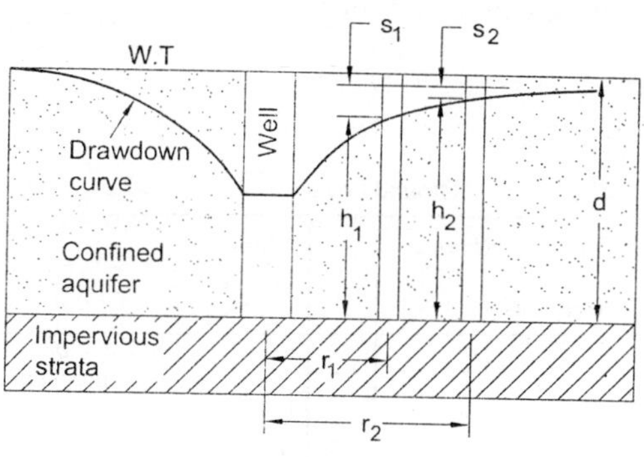

(a)

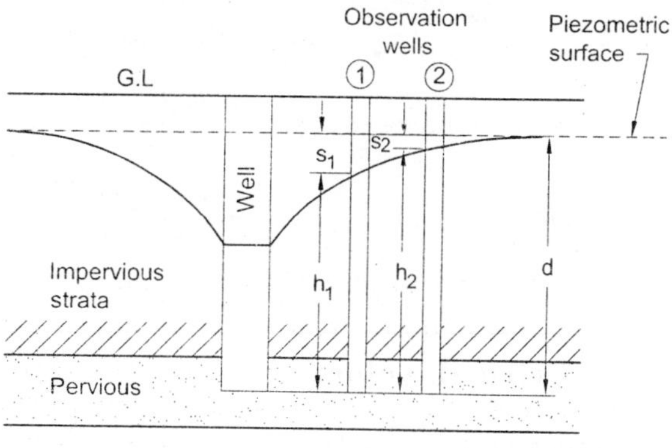

(b)

Fig. 13·122.

Thiem's formula for confined aquifers

$$Q = \frac{2\pi K H(s_1 - s_2)}{2{\cdot}3 \log_{10} \dfrac{r_2}{r_1}}$$

or
$$Q = \frac{2\pi T(s_1 - s_2)}{2{\cdot}3 \log_{10} \frac{r_2}{r_1}}$$

where $T = KH$.

Efficiency of a well. The draw down is α to discharge Q. The discharge per unit of draw down is called specific capacity of the well.

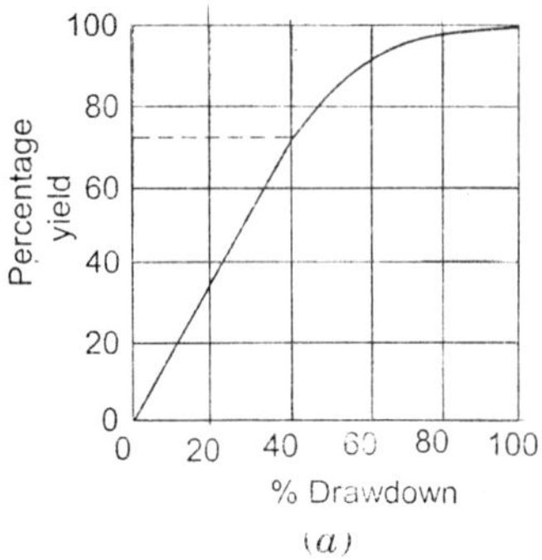

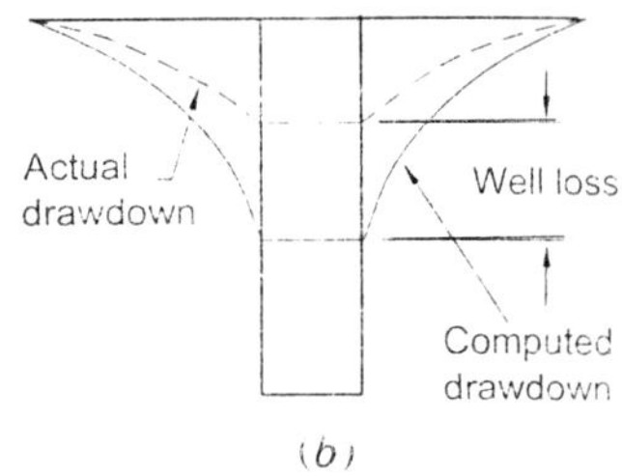

Fig. 13·123.

From the curve it is seen that yield is proportioned to the draw down upto 40% and after that increases abruptly. At 100% draw down it is 100% but in actual it is somewhat lesser. The percentage by which it is reduced is known as the efficiency of the well. It may be of the order of 70%.

Critical Hydraulic Gradient

If the seepage pressure p_s becomes equal to the pressure due to submerged weight of the soil, then evidently the effective pressure is reduced to zero. In such a limiting case, the cohesionless soil looses all its shear strength and the soil particles will have a tendency to move up in the direction of low, with the slightest increase in p_s. This phenomenon of lifting soil particles which starts when p_s and submerged weight of the soil is called the **quick condition**, boiling condition or **quick sand**. The hydraulic gradient corresponding to this situation (just starting) is called the **critical hydraulic gradient** (i_c).

In other words it becomes ic then

$$\gamma_{sub}\, L = L\, i_c.\, \gamma_w \text{ or } i_c = \frac{\gamma_{sub}}{\gamma_w} \text{ (being the length of flow)}$$

Now we have $$\gamma_{sub} = \frac{\gamma_w(G-1)}{1+e} \text{ or } i_c = \frac{\gamma_w(G-1).1}{(1+e)\,\gamma_w} \text{ or } i_c = \frac{G-1}{1+e}$$

Hence $$i_c = \frac{\gamma_{sub}}{\gamma_w} = \frac{G-1}{1+e}$$

where G = specific gravity of soil and

e = void ratio of soil.

Critical velocity. When the rate of withdrawal is increased, a stage will come when the soil particles come with water. This velocity of withdrawal of water is known as critical velocity, the head formed as a critical head and the yield of water as critical yield. It is also known as the capacity of the well.

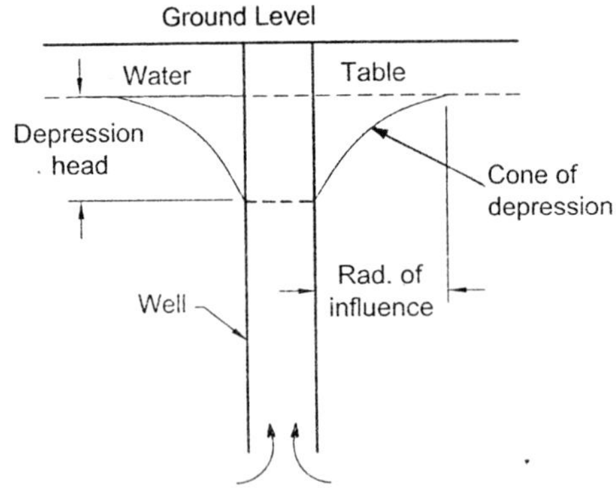

Fig. 13·124.

Due to above reason, the supply in the open well is not taken more than the critical velocity due to danger of subsidence, while in deep wells more supply can be taken by increasing the cavity. Even in deep wells velocity or withdrawal of water is limited as for large velocity the cavity will increase causing a danger for the collapse of mota.

Porosity. Percentage of voids present in a given volume of soil.

$$\text{Porosity} = \frac{\text{Total volume of voids } i.e. \text{ volume of water required say } V_v \text{ to saturate the dry simple of the soil}}{\text{Total volume of soil say } (V)}$$

Table 13·35. Porosity of few rock formations

Sl. No.	*Type of rock formation*	*Porosity*	*Value of K (permeability const.)*
1.	Granite, quartzite	1·5%	$0{\cdot}6 \times 10^{-5}$
2.	Slate, shale	4%	4×10^{-5}
3.	Lime stone	5 to 10%	4×10^{-5}
4.	Sand stone	10 to 15%	0·004
5.	Sand and gravel	20 to 30%	0·4
6.	Only gravel	25%	4·0
7.	Only sand	35%	0·04
8.	Clay and soil	45%	$0{\cdot}04 \times 10^{-5}$

Permeability/Transmissibility

Permeability is defined as the ability of a rock or unconsolidated sediment to transmit or pass water through itself.

Transmissibility. The capacity of the soil of unit width and full depth (*i.e.* width $b = 1$ and depth $= d$ or $A = d$) to transmit water is known transmissibility while in permeability whole of the mass $(b \times d)$ is considered for flow through the soil concerned.

Darcy's Law. Discharge through a soil is directly proportional to the Head loss (H_L) and the area of cross-section A of the soil and inversely proportional to the length of flow (L).

or $$Q = K\frac{H_L}{L}.A$$

where Q = discharge which is flowing, H_L = Head loss,

L = Length of flow and A = Area of cross-section of flow.

K is a constant which is known as the permeability or the coefficient of permeability. This constant changes with the type of soil. So the permeability is different to different soils.

Permeability may be defined as the rate of flow of water through a unit cross-sectional area of the water bearing material under a unit hydraulic gradient at a temperature of 20°C.

$$\text{Specific yield} = \frac{\text{Volume of water obtained by gravity drainage}}{\text{Total volume of material drained}} \times 100$$

$$\text{Specific retention or field capacity} = \frac{\text{Volume of water held against gravity drainage}}{\text{Total volume of material drained}} \times 100$$

13·7·3. Tube wells : (1) Cavity tube wells (2) Strainer tube wells.

(1) **Cavity tube wells.** These are almost the same as cavity wells, the only differentce that instead of well shaft a tube is bored below the mota or to a stratum having a good water. A cavity is formed at the bottom of the tube as in well shafts. In tube wells cavity may be developed even in pervious aquifers.

(2) **Strainer wells.** The procedure of boring is discussed in the boring of piles in bridge foundations. The diameter of the casing or housing pipe is kept generally 150 to 300 mm wider

than the strainer intended to be installed. The casing pipe is not bored below 3 m, if the soil below permits or can retain itself. A strainer is then designed with pores according to the size of sand particles to be excluded from entry in well for different aquifers. The strainer is provided only in water bearing strata and blind pipes are provided in the impervious non water bearing strata according to the strata chart.

At the bottom a bail plug is provided so that the soil below the plug may not enter in the strainer. This bail plug is provided with an eye inside to lift or lower the strainer by a rope. A blind pipe of about 1·2 to 1·5 m is provided above the bail plug to join the strainer and the bottom of the bail plug is kept a bit above the lowest bored point so that it may not give way due to weight of the whole pipe. Some times a conical steel drive point or head is provided in place of bail plug. The strainer is fixed in position and held at the top. Casing pipe is withdrawn if provided in pieces of 1 m together with pea gravel shrouding of graded material 2·5 to 3 times the size of the sand. The bottom 60 cm is filled with pea gravel mixed with coarse sand. If casing pipe is not provided this gravel can be filled from top around the whole strainer. The round gravel which passes through a screen, 4 meshes to one lineal cm (with max. 6 mm) and retained on a 16 mesh to one cm screen is used. It should be free of dirt etc. A compressed air blown from top which is passed out through gravel taking all dirt with it. The reduction of section from casing to strainer pipe is sealed with water tight material.

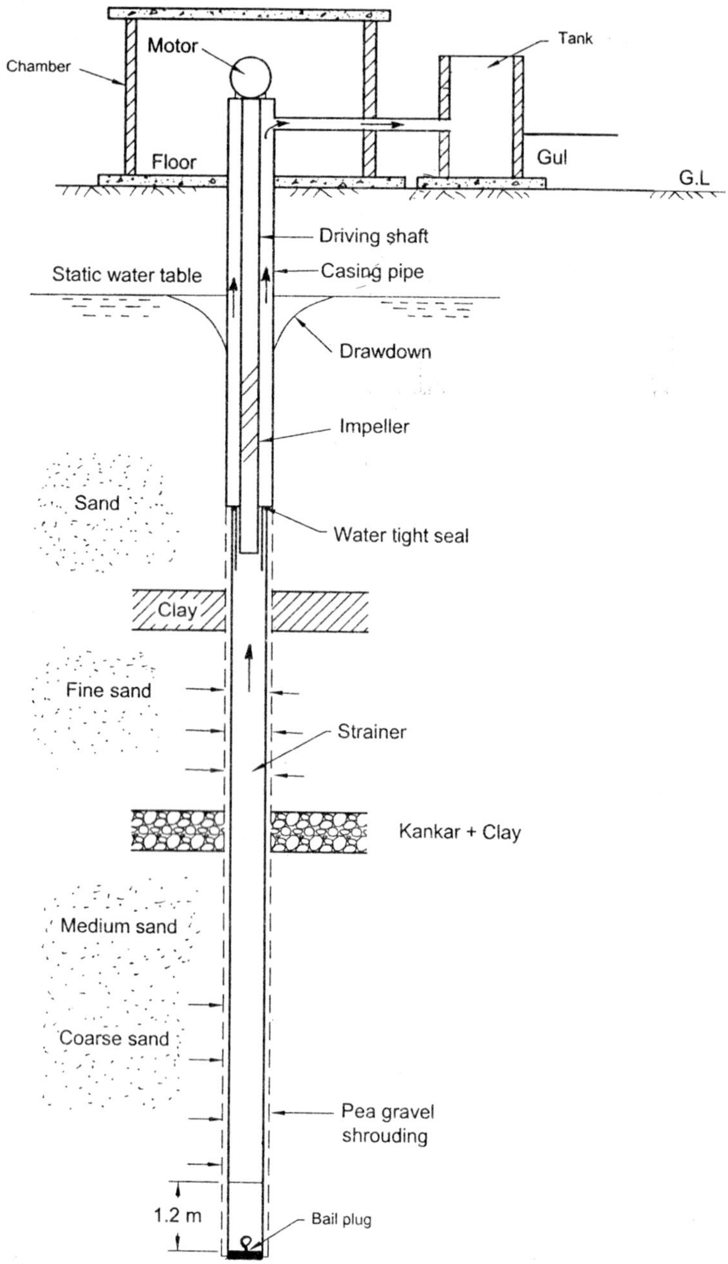

Fig. 13·125. Stramer tube well.

Strainers. Strainers are generally made of wrought iron, brass or other non ferrous metals about 3 mm thick or more according to the diameter of the strainer. The strainer generally consists of a (1) tubular shaft with small pores punched according to the size of the particles to be kept away from entry in the pipe. The maximum size of particles allowed is kept according to the purpose used.

(2) A wire gauze of brass or copper wrapped round a slotted tube (slots are kept staggered) or perforated pipe. A small annular space is left between the screen and the slotted tube according to the maximum dia. of the particle to be passed in, otherwise most of the area of the slots will be covered by the wires of the gauze and the effective area thus be reduced. The cross sectional area of the slots of the pipe is kept equal to the opening of the meshes of the wire gauze, so that no change of velocity occurs. Unperforated area of the tube is kept about twice the perforated area to prevent eddies and back flow. The horizontal motion of the particles is checked by the upward motion of the water and hence the slots are kept sloped up. The following methods are used for the manufacturing of these pipes.

(*i*) To make the operation simpler, the slots are cut in a sheet and then it bent round and brazed both in horizontal and vertical joints.

(*ii*) Wedge shaped wires are wounded at a certain pitch on the slotted tube keeping the wider edge outside and narrow inside, so that the slots are wedge shaped. It checks choking of the strainer.

(*iii*) The strainer should have maximum water area per metre of length, must be uncorrosive and of one metal to avoid danger of electrolytic action.

(*iv*) In temporary borings used for lowering water table in construction of hydraulic works such as dams for laying their foundations below water table, a slotted tube or a frame is wrapped by jute strings or jute cloths, which can be left in after laying of foundation as a strainer.

13·7·4. Types of Pumps used. (Working style classification)

(1) **Horizontal spindle pumps.** Horizontal pumps with horizontal spindle were commonly used till recent. In this case the pump and the motor is kept at the lowest water table in a sump house founded at lowest water table to ensure constant priming with a water tight concrete plug.

(2) **Bore hole Pumps.** The impeller is kept in a vertical position below the lowest position of the depression head which is rotated by a drive shaft. Motor is fitted at the ground level with a vertical axis of rotation attached with the drive shaft. In such cases deep pump house are not required to be built as in case of horizontal spindle pumps.

(3) **Submersible pumps.** In such cases the pump together with motor is kept under water below depression head and is suspended by a vertical shaft or cable fixed at ground level.

Duty of well water. It is an area commanded by a well in dry years for irrigation.

Depth of water in well irrigation. It is about 2/3rd to that in canal irrigation.

Yield from different diameter of strainers and housing pipes in bore hole and submersible pumps.

Table 13·36.

Yield in litre per sec.	*Nominal size of pump bore (cm)*	*Max. size of housing pipe in (cm)*	*Minimum size of housing pipe (cm)*
6	10	15	12·5
5-11	12·5	20	15
10-25	15	25	20
22-40	20	30	25
37-57	25	35	30
53-82	30	40	35
75-112	35	50	40
100-190	40	60	50

Economic diameter of pumping mains

Bore of pipe (mm)	150	225	250	300	350	400	500	600	700
Thousand lit/Hr.	27	54	109	163	215	245	445	590	900

The economic pumping is between 85 to 135 cm/sec. Too small diameter is uneconomical and too large is also wasteful.

Types of Pumps (mechanical classification)

(1) Displacement type. Reciprocating and rotary pumps.

(2) Velocity pumps (3) Centrifugal pumps

(1) **Reciprocating pumps.** A piston or plunger alternately drews water into the cylinder in intake stroke and delivers out on the discharge stroke. These pumps are used for high pressure and small discharges.

(2) **Rotary type.** In these pumps water is drawn by a rotary impeller and forces up into the delivery pipe. It works as a drill of a carpenter.

(3) **Centrifugal type.** It has an impeller with radial vanes which draw water into the centre of pump and discharges out by centrifugal force of the rotating impeller.

Consumption of fuel in different type of prime movers/HP/Hr.

Steam	*Diesel*	*Petrol*	*Electricity*	*Mobile oil*
2 kg coal	1/4 lit.	1/3 lit.	1 unit	1/10 of the oil

The electric motors have 95%, Diesel 75% and steam 65% efficiency.

Fig. 13·126 graph showing power required for different dicharges at different heads (Fig. 13·126).

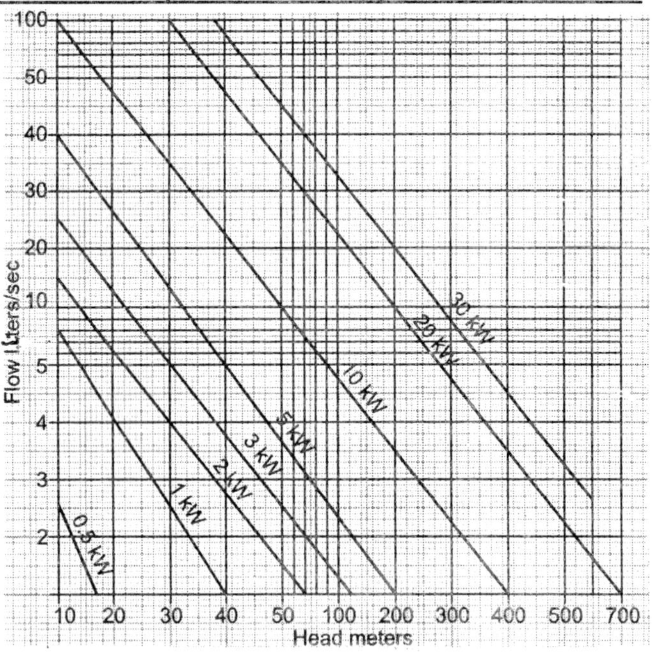

Fig. 13·126. K.W. demand of pumps required to provide various flows at different pumping heads.

Suction and delivery pipes. Water can be lifted upto 34′ (10·36 m) due to the atmospheric pressure. But due to friction losses it can lift only 4·5 to 7·3 metres in practice. The lifting head is taken as 4·88 for centrifugal pumps and 6 metre for reciprocating pumps. At altitudes the suction is reduced by 30 cm for every 300 metre rise in height due to low atmospheric pressure.

Suction pipes are larger in dia. than delivery pipes. The diameter of the suction pipe is 7 mm bigger for 25 mm delivery pipe and about 10 mm for 32-80 mm delivery pipes. For delivery pipes above 100 mm the suction and delivery pipes are of the same dia. The horizontal suction pipes are of maximum 300 m long, having a slope of 1 : 80 rising towards the pump. The foot valve of the suction pipe must have a minimum clearance of 60 cm around it so that no mud etc. may enter into the pipe. Suction and delivery pipes are provided with valves so that water may not vacate the suction pipe or enter in pump from delivery side when not in use or even in running position. For pumps fitted below water level no valve is required in the suction pipe as it is self priming. Pumps which are kept above water level priming is done by filling water before use.

Horse Power of a Pump Motor

$$\text{The power of the motor} = \frac{w.Q.H}{\eta} \quad \text{(N.m/sec. } i.e. \text{ watts)}$$

$$\text{H.P. (metric)} = \frac{\text{watts}}{735} = \frac{w.Q.H}{735\,\eta}$$

where Q = discharge to be delivered in cumecs

H = total lift *i.e.* the head against which the motor has to work in meters.

w = unit weight of water in N/m^3

η = Efficiency of the pumping set and is generally taken as 65% (*i.e.* 0·65) for centrifugal or borehole pumps

The total head H against which the motor has to work consists of :

(*a*) Maximum depth of water level below the ground level

(*b*) Maximum depression head

(*c*) Frictional losses in the tube pipe including the losses of bends and strainer openings

(*d*) Velocity head.

The frictional losses in the pipe (h_f) may be calculated by the formula :

$$h_f = \frac{f' l v^2}{2gd}$$

where f' = coefficient of pipe friction which is generally taken as 0·024

l = length of the pipe line including vertical and horizontal lengths

d = dia. of pipe line.

The losses due to bends and strainer openings are generally taken as 25 to 30% of the frictional losses in pipes.

By the above the H.P. of the motor can be calculating easily.

13·7·5. Discharge from tube wells

Horse Power of a pump – H.P. = $\dfrac{w\,QH}{75 \times \text{efficiency}}$, where w = unit wt. of water in kg/m^3, Q = discharge in cumecs to be delivered and H = head of water to be lifted.

British H.P. = 55 ft. lbs/sec.

Metric H.P. = 75 kg m/sec.

1 metric H.P. = 0·73 kilo watts

Discharge through a right angled V-notch (α = 90°)

$Q = \dfrac{8}{15} c_d \sqrt{2g}\, H^{2\cdot5} \tan\dfrac{\alpha}{2}$, Q is discharge, c_d = co-efficient of discharge usually 0·6, H = head over V-notch.

For right angled V-notch $Q = \dfrac{8}{15} c_d \sqrt{2g}\, H^{2/5}$

$= 2{\cdot}568\, H^{2\cdot5}$ cusecs (H in ft.)

$= 2{\cdot}363\, H^{2\cdot5}$ cumecs (H in m)

$= 577780\, H^{2\cdot5}$ gal/hr (H in ft.)

$= 43778\, H^{2\cdot5}$ lit./hr (H in m)

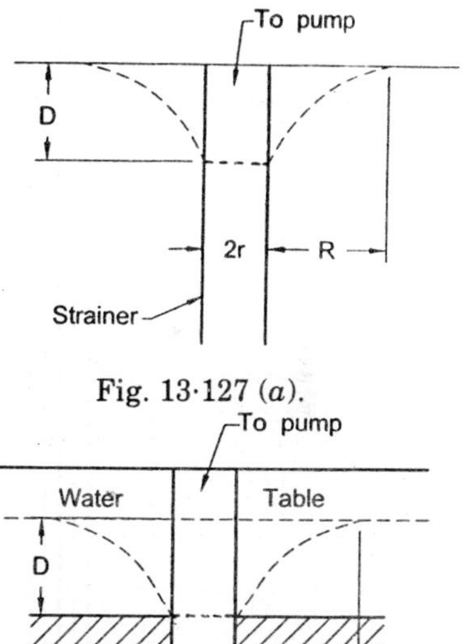

Fig. 13·127 (*a*).

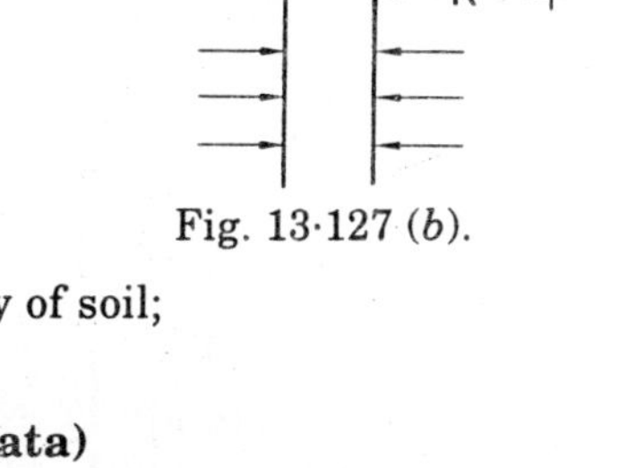

Fig. 13·127 (*b*).

Discharge through a strainer well (unconfined strata)

$$Q = \frac{2\pi KD\left(L + \dfrac{D}{2}\right)}{\log_e \dfrac{R}{r}}$$

where L = Operation lengths of strainer

D = Depression head

R = Rad. of influence; K = Coefficient of permeability of soil;

Q = Discharge

Discharge through a strainer well(confined strata)

$$Q = \frac{2\pi KDL}{\log_e \dfrac{R}{r}}$$

For flow 30 lit./sec., size of strainer = 150 mm; Vel.= 1·5 m/sec.
For flow of 45 lit./sec., size of strainer = 150 mm Vel.= 2·4 m/sec.
For flow of 45 lit./sec., size of strainer = 250 mm Vel.= 0·91 m/sec.
and head of 3·7 m

13·7·6. House hold pump strainer. 1·2 to 2·4 m long, made of iron containing a dia. of 40 to 60 mm.

In tube wells yield = 50 lit./hr per 1000 sq. cm of strainer area per 30 cm head. A tube well upto 30 to 45 m long water bearing strata will give about 2500 lit./mm under a head of 5·4 metre.

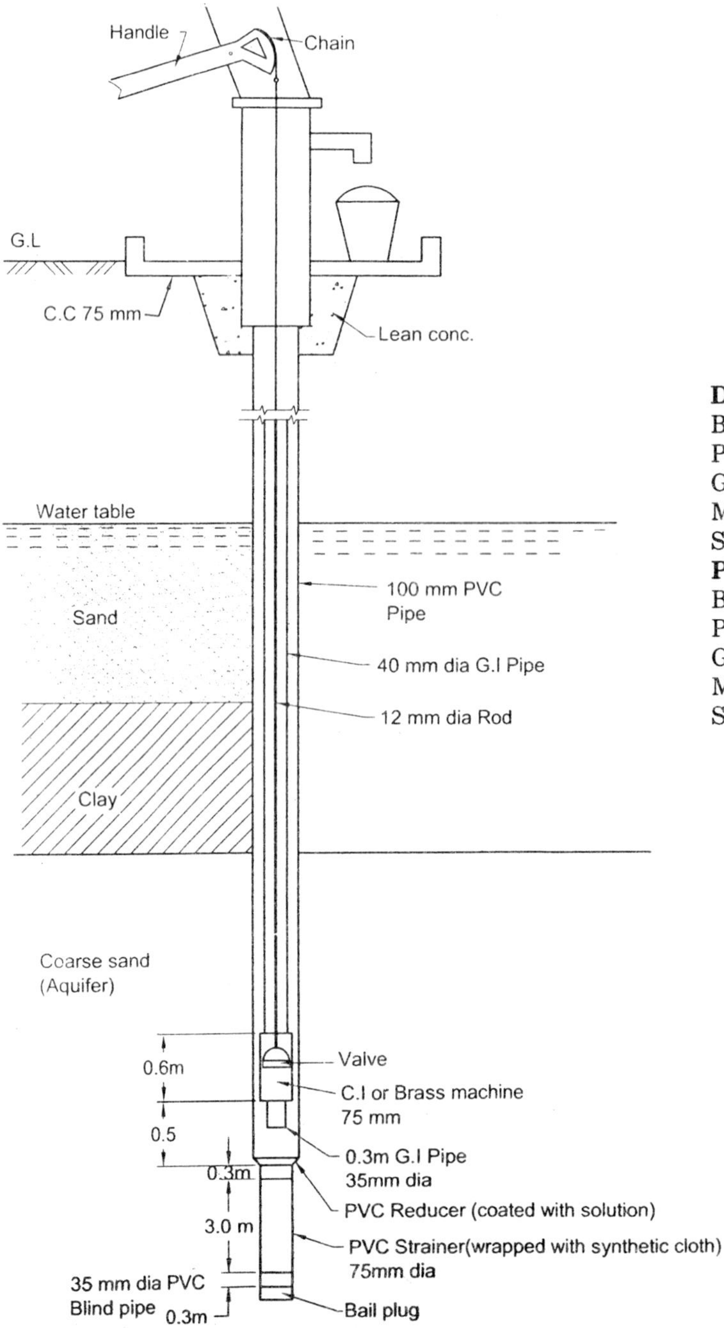

Domestic Pump

Boring	3″ dia.
P.V.C. pipe	2½″ dia.
G.I. pipe	1½″ dia.
Machine	2½″ dia.
Strains	2½″ dia.

Public Pumps

Borings	5 to 6″ dia.
P.V.C. pipe	4″ dia.
G.I. pipe	1¾″ dia.
Machine	3″ dia.
Strainer	3″ dia.

Fig. 13·128. Double hand pump.

Practical determination of velocity of sub soil water

Select two wells at a distance of say L apart.

(1) 1st inject some salt say amm. chloride in u/s well and note it's effect in the d/s well. The time taken from the moment of injection in upper well to the moment effect perceived in the d/s well gives the time to cover a distance L which can give the velocity of flow.

(2) Take the difference of the water level in two wells in vicinity by which the head (difference of water levels) can be determined. The observations must be taken at the same time.

Note : The presence of salt in the d/s well can be detected by increase in electrical conductivity method. Addition of fluorescent or fluorescain solution which turns from reddish to green in ammonium chloride water.

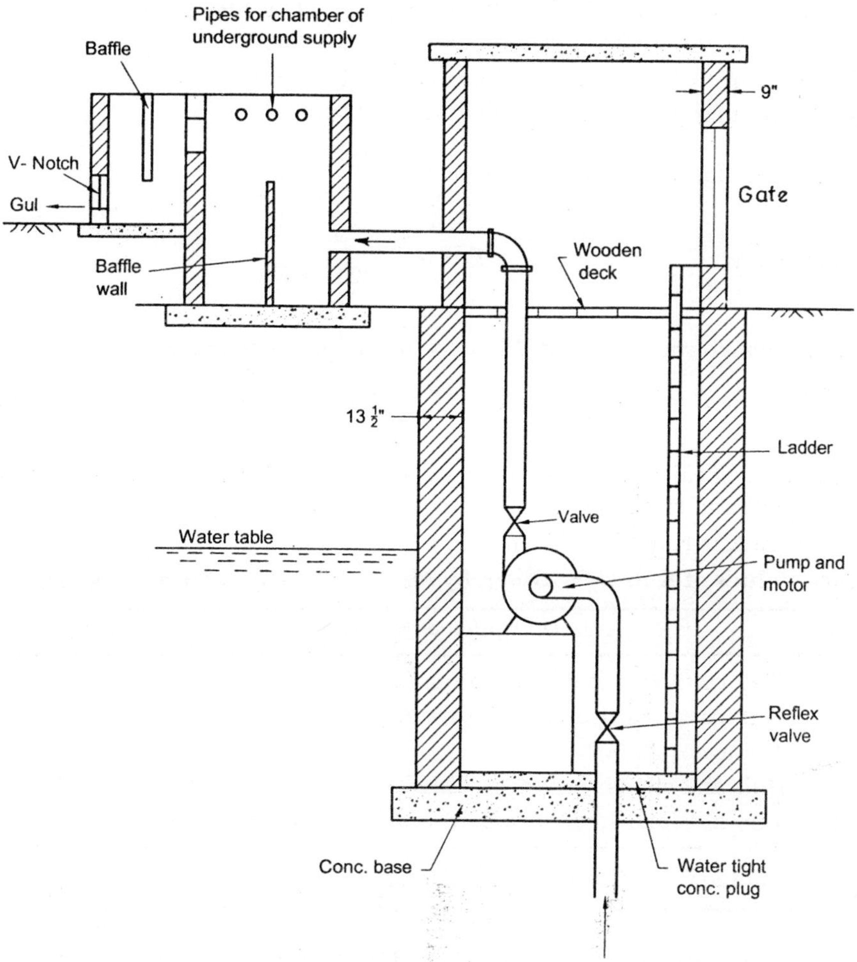

Fig. 13·129. Section of a tubewell with horizontal spindle.

13·8. Technical terms in wells and tube wells

(1) **Slip of pump.** The reduction of discharge due to leakage and friction below the theoretical discharge.

(2) **Static head.** The head to which water is lifted from water level to discharge point.

(3) **Static water level.** It is the level to which water will stand tube while idle while tube well is idle.

(4) **Discharge head.** It is the vertical distance from the centre of the discharge outlet to the centre of the pump.

(5) **Suction head.** It is the vertical distance from the centre of the pump to the level of the water, the draw down should be added to get the working head.

13·9. Hydrology of floods

13·9·1. Catchment area method for normal flows. In certain drains discharge is estimated by multiplying cathment area by an assumed factor, $Q = CA$ where C is a factor, discharge per sq. km of catchment area. This factor is estimated from some neighbouring drains of known discharge and catchment area. The factor so obtained is used as a practice for other drains in the vicinity. In northern India a factor of 0·05 to 0·2 cumecs per km^2 of catchment area is used. (5 to 20 cusecs per mile^2 of catchment). In practice higher values are taken for designing of masonry works for keeping future development in mind.

13·9·2. Estimation of flood run off from rainfall

(*a*) Inglish formula for ghat areas $R = 0{\cdot}85\,P - 30{\cdot}5$

(*b*) Inglish formula for non ghat areas $R = \left(\dfrac{P-128}{254}\right)P$

(*c*) Lacey's formula $R = \dfrac{P}{1+\left(\dfrac{304-8F}{P.S.}\right)}$

where F is total rainfall of storm in cm and S is slope in fraction (one in two $= \frac{1}{2} = 0{\cdot}5$).

(*d*) Khoslas formula $R = P - \dfrac{T-32}{3{\cdot}74}$ where T is time of concentration, R is run off and P is rainfall in centimetre.

Note : The water of rainfall for surface flow after evaporation and absorption is called runoff. The ratio of runoff and rainfall is called "run off coefficient".

(*e*) $R = KP$ where K is runoff coefficient.

Table 13·37. Values of K in U.P. (Given by Mr. T. G. Barlow) for average rain

Catchment class	*Description of catchment*	*Runoff percent*
A	Flat, cultivated and black cotton soil	10
B	Flat, partly cultivated various soils	15
C	Average	20
D	Hills and plains with little cultivation	35
E	Very hilly and steep with hardly any cultivation	45

The above percentage is multiplied by the following coefficients according to nature of season.

Nature of seasons	*Class of catchment*				
	A	*B*	*C*	*D*	*E*
1. Light rains, no heavy down pour	0·70	0·80	0·80	0·80	0·80
2. Average or varying rain, no continuous down pour	1·0	1·0	1·0	1·0	1·0
3. Continuous down pour	1·50	1·50	1·60	1·70	1·80

Daily runoff (By Strange) for South India

Daily rainfall (mm)	*Runoff percentage and yield with original state of ground*					
	Dry		*Damp*		*Wet*	
	Percentage	*Yield mm*	*Percentage*	*Yield mm*	*Percentage*	*Yield mm*
6·25	—	—	—	—	8	0·5
12·5	—	—	6	0·75	12	1·5
18·75	—	—	8	1·50	16	3·0
25	3	0·15	11	2·75	18	4·5
31·25	5	1·50	14	4·37	22	6·88
37·5	6	2·25	16	6·0	25	9·37
43·75	8	3·5	19	8·31	30	13·1
50	10	5·0	22	11·0	34	17·0
62·5	15	9·37	29	18·15	43	26·9
75	20	15·0	37	27·75	55	41·5
100	30	30·0	50	50·0	70	47·0

Strange curve on the above

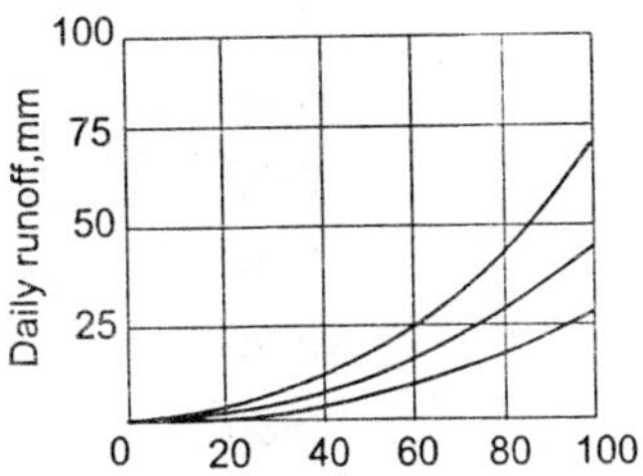

(*a*)

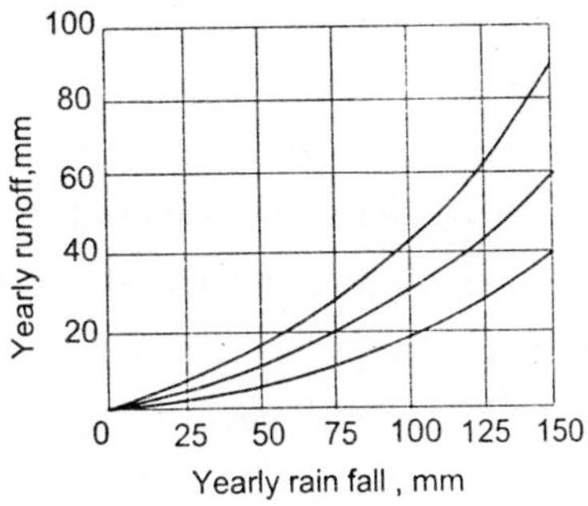

(*b*)

Fig. 13·130.

(*f*) **By infiltration.** Infiltration is the rain water which is absorbed by the soil. The infiltration capacity of a soil may be very considerable in beginning of storm, but is fairly constant likely to be reached later on. If there is interruption of rain fall, the infiltration will again remain higher at beginning but will reach to a fairly constant later on. During early stages of storm there is period for which there is no surface flow and all the water is absorbed by the soil. This loss measured in cm is known as "**initial loss**".

Infiltration index. It is the ratio of the rain water absorbed to the total rainfall of the storm. The following procedure is adopted for calculating the infiltration index.

(*a*) Select a known hydrograph of the past of the basin of the river and calculate from it the runoff available for a flood of period (deducting baseflow) say Q_1.

(*b*) Prepare mass rainfall curves for the rain gauge stations of the area and calculate the runoff available from the thiesien's polygon or isoliyetal line method, say it comes to Q_2.

(*c*) So $Q_2.F = Q_1$ where F is the infiltration index. Knowing Q_1 and Q_2 the value F of the infiltration index can be calculated. This infiltration index can be used for determining run off available for a basin from the mass rainfall curves.

Infiltration index is defined as an average rate of loss, such that the volume of rainfall in excess of that ratio would be equal to volume of surface flow.

Total run off. Infiltration loss = surface flow or excess of rain fall.

13·9·3. Discharge calculation from intensity of rainfall.

Intensity of rain fall. The maximum rain fall during a short period (say once in hour)

$i = \frac{F}{2}\left(1+\frac{1}{t}\right)$ where i = maximum intensity of rain fall mm/hr, F = total rainfall of the storm and t = duration of storm in hours.

For design purposes $I = i\left(\frac{2}{T+1}\right)$ where I is the design or critical intensity and T = Time in which the rainfall is concentrated. The maximum flood discharge in a catchment can be calculated by the formula $Q = \frac{IAK}{36}$ where Q = total runoff in cumecs, I as above, A = area of catchment in hectares and K is a factor of imperviousness which can be taken as follows.

1.	Steep bare rocks	0·90
2.	Steep wooded rocks	0·80
3.	Hills lightly covered, ordinary ground	0·70
4.	Built up areas of cities (dense)	0·70–0·90
5.	Built up areas of cities (not dense)	0·50–0·70
6.	Built up areas of cities (unmettled) roads	0·2-0·5
7.	Clayee soils stiff and bare	0·60
8.	Clayee soils light covered	0·50
9.	Loam lightly cultivated or covered	0·40
10.	Loam largely cultivated	0·30
11.	Suburbs with gardens lawns and macadam roads	0·30
12.	Sandy soil light growth	0·20
13.	Sandy soil covered heavy bushes	0·10
14.	Jungle area	0·1–0·2
15.	Park lawns meedows and cultivated area	0·5 to 0·25

Note : (1) Maximum value should be taken for small districts having steep slopes and minimum for large flatter areas.

(2) Runoff for pan shaped (sector of a circle) is more than fern shaped (elongated) catchments.

(3) Rough surfaces in catchment reduce the runoff while the smoother surface increase.

(4) 65 to 55% runoff of the total precipitation is expected in costal 55-30% in intermediate and 30 to 15% in dry zones.

(5) Rainfall loss in evaporation and absorption 30 to 50%
percolation 15 to 50%
available runoff 25·55%

(6) The heaviest rainfall of a place is taken as 1·51 of the average of last 35 years.

A.N. Khosla's Empirical formula

$R_m = P_m - L_m$ where R_m, P_m and L_m are monthly runoff, precipitation and losses respectively in a basin.

$L_m = \frac{T_m - 32}{95}$, T_m = average monthly temperature when > 40°F.

For T_m less than 40°F, values of L_m are as follows :

T_m	40°	30°	20°	10°	0°
L_m	0·84	0·70	0·60	0·50	0·40 inches

The formula for annual rainfall

$$R_A = P_A - xT_A$$

where R_A, P_A and T_A are annual runoff, precipitation and average temperature in °F. x is coefficient for the catchment which can be obtained from a number of catchments of known runoff and rainfall in the vicinity and is generally taken as 0·50.

13·9·4. Assessment of Discharge of Rivers

(*i*) **By Emperical Formulae :** Lacey's formula $V = 16\ m^{2/3}\ i^{1/3}$ (F.P.S.) for flexible beds (m = hydraulic mean depth and i is slope in fraction).

Manning's formula. $V = \dfrac{1.486}{N}\ m^{2/3}\ i^{1/2}$ (F.P.S.)

$$= \frac{1}{N}\ (m^{2/3}\ i^{1/2})\ \text{(M.K.S.)}$$

For value of N refer hydraulic and irrigation chapters, Lacey's wetted perimeter $L_w = \dfrac{8}{3}\sqrt{Q}$ F.P.S.

For above expressions, the cross-section of the channel may be plotted when it is dry or in normal flow which can give m the hydraulic mean depth. Surface slope of water will give the slope. The velocity so obtained must be multiplied by cross-sectional area upto H.F.L. The wetted perimeter can be measured when the channel is dry from H.F.L. points of one bank to other. H.F.L. points may be obtained from local enquiries from old persons or from old marks on masonry works. For local enquiries several persons should be referred to arrive on correct information.

(*ii*) **Assessment of discharge by past records**

(*a*) If the **hydrograph** (gauge-discharge curve) of a channel at lower gauges is available, it can be extended to the known H.F.L.

(*b*) **By enveloping curves.** For certain streams of different catchments, enveloping curves for catchment area to discharge are plotted. These curves may be used as a guiding area discharge curve for that area.

(*c*) **By coefficient of variation.** For two rivers, the simultaneous variation in discharge is observed from which a coefficient of variation between these rivers is established. If high flood discharge of one is known, the high flood discharge on the other can be estimated by multiplying the H.F.L. discharge of 1st by variation coefficient. Suppose for a discharge of 100 cumecs in stream A the simultaneous discharge in B is 150 cumecs, so the variation coefficient is 1·5. Now for a flood discharge of 1000 cumecs in A as $1.5 \times 1000 = 1500$ cumecs in B.

(*iii*) **By rainfall statistics.** From the rainfall records, the flood discharge of an area can be estimated, which depends on the quantity of rainfall, losses due to transporation and evaporation of the catchment area. The transpiration losses depend on the type of soil, topography of the country and vegetation in the catchment area, while the evaporation losses depends on the relative humidity, temperature, velocity of wind and hours of sunlight. Before estimating the quantity of inflow in a stream due to rain fall the following terms should be defined.

Terms used in rainfall study

Base flow. It is flow in a channel which is already before the flood water reaches in the stream. It is perinial flow. It is due to underground water.

Initial loss. Loss of water in a basin before any flow takes place. The value of initial loss in inches or mm whichever may be the procedure under practice is ascertained from the site investigations before which the flow takes place. It can be assessed on the rain gauge stations by the amount of rainfall measured before any surface flow takes place.

Intensity of rain. It is the rate at which the rain is falling, and is expressed as cm/hr., but this rate at which the rain falls, changes continuously throughout the storm. It may be 4 cm in one hour giving an average rainfall average as 4 cm/hr. However even during this time it may be 5 cm/hr. or even 3 cm/hr. An idealized curve showing the intensity variation with time is shown in the Fig. 13·131(*c*) and is known as **time intensity pattern.**

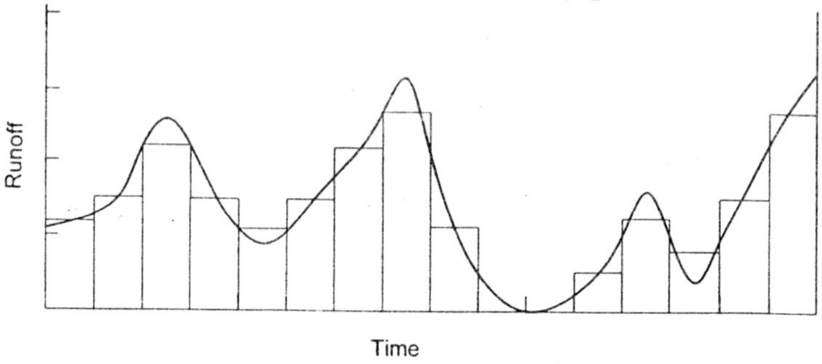

Fig. 13·131(*a*). Inflow Hydrograph.

The above time, intensity curve is generally assume to be made up of straight lines as shown in the Fig. and is called a **rain hyetograph.** A hyetograph is therefore a plot of rainfall intensity against time as a bar chart.

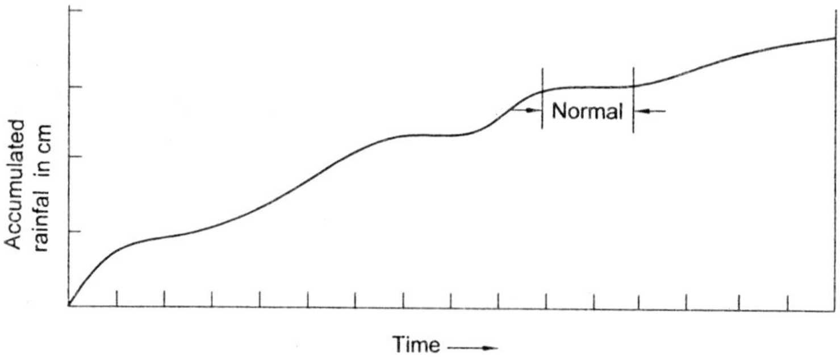

Fig. 13·131(*b*). Mass rainfall curve

The area under a hyetograph represents the total rainfall received in that period. The time interval depends on the purpose. For larger catchment it may be as large as 6 hours.

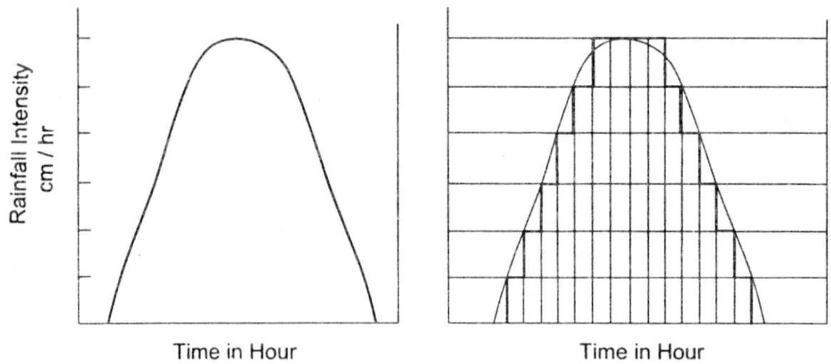

Fig. 13·131 (*c*). Time intensity pattern—Rain Hyetograph.

Mass rainfall curve and inflow hydrograph. Inflow or rain hydrograph is a plot of rainfall against time. It can be represented as a bar chart, while the mass rainfall curve is a plot of accumulated precipitation against time and is called as a mass curve of the storm. The ordinate in the mass curve at a particular time interval represents the total rainfall upto that time in rainfall curve. A straight horizontal line in the mass curve represents a period of no rainfall.

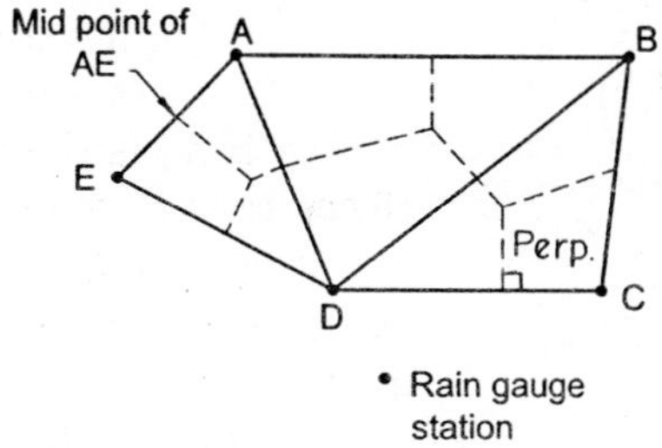

Fig. 13·132. Theissen's polygons.

Assessment of mean rainfall over a drainage basin. The drainage basin is divided in sub areas and rain gauge stations are evenly distributed over the all area, the rainfall at different areas or stations may vary, and an average value of the rainfall is calculated for the entire area. The methods given below are used to compute an average rainfall.

(1) **Arithmetic mean method.** It consists of averaging all the amounts that have been recorded at various rain gauge stations and computed as below.

$$P = \frac{P_1 + P_2 + P_3 \ldots P_n}{n}$$

where P = mean precipitation on the basin

$P_1, P_2, P_3 \ldots P_n$ are respective precipitation at stations

(1), (2), (3), ... (n) are the no. of rain gauge stations

The rain gauges should be located evenly in the basin.

(2) **Theissen's Polygon method.** In this method adjacent stations are joined by straight lines, thus dividing the entire area into series of triangles. Perpendicular bisectors are erected on each of these lines, thus forming a series of polygons each containing only one rain gauge station. It is assuming that the entire area within any polygon is a measure to the rainfall station that is included in the polygon than to any other rainfall station. The rainfall recorded at that station is therefore assigned to that polygon. If P is the mean rainfall on the basin and the area of the basin is A then

$$P = \frac{A_1P_1 + A_2P_2 + A_3P_3 + \ldots A_nP}{A}$$

where $P_1, P_2, P_3 \ldots P_n$ represents rainfalls at the respective stations and surrounding polygons have the areas $A_1, A_2, A_3 \ldots A_n$ respectively. A graphical representation of this method is shown in the Fig. 13·133.

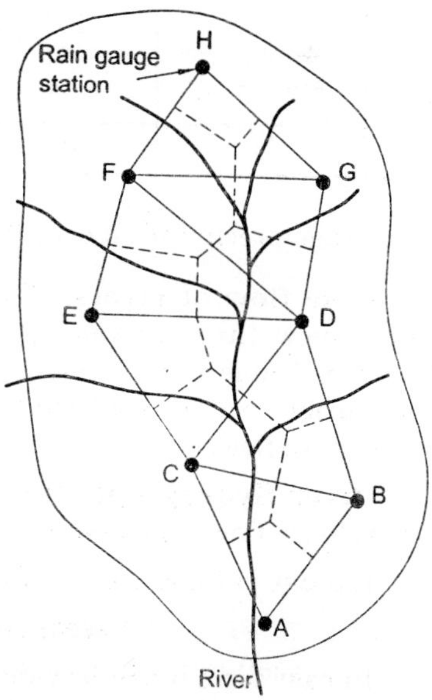

Fig. 13·133.

(3) **Isohyetal method.** Isohyetal lines are the lines drawn on a map joining the stations of the same rainfall. After the rainfall at each station is plotted, the area between the adjacent isohyets is either estimated on graph sheet or measured by a planimeter. Let the areas $A_1, A_2, A_3 \ldots A_n$ be the areas in between contours respecti-

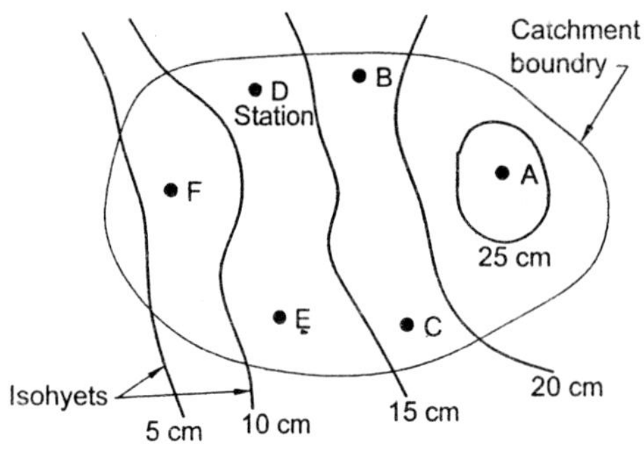

Fig. 13·134. Isohyetal method of computing average rainfall.

vely, then the mean precipitation P in the basin is given by

$$P = \frac{P_1A_1 + P_2A_2 + P_3A_3 + \dots P_nA_n}{A_1 + A_2 + A_3 + \dots A_n}$$

If A_n is the area between contours of 5 and 10 cm, then P_n = 7·5 cm.

Catchment area. It is the area at a point on the river (or work site) in which the rain water from the basin reaches to the river.

Water shed. It is a ridge line in a basin from which the rain water flows on either side of it.

Table 13·38.

Isohyet mm	*Area between each Isohyet and basin boundary in km²*	*Net incremental area between two Isohyet i.e. A_1, A_2, A_3 in km²*	*Average rainfall on the incremental area i.e. average of two Isohyets i.e. P_1, P_2, P_3 in mm*	*Rainfall vol. on incremental areas i.e. P_1A_1, P_2A_2, P_3A_3 ; col. (3) × col. (4) in mm km²*	*Remarks*
(1)	(2)	(3)	(4)	(5)	(6)
21	543	543*	21**	11403	* For the end contour, this is the area between the end Isohyets and the basin boundary.
20	1345	802	20·5	16441	
19	2030	685	19·5	13357	
18	2545	515	18·5	9527	
17	2955	410	17·5	7175	
16	3280	325	16·5	5362	** The average volume being the same as the value of the end Isohyet.
15	3535	255	15·5	3952	
14	3710	175	14·5	2537	
13	3080	170	13·5	2295	
12	3915	35	12·5	437	
	Σ	3915		72486	

$$\text{Average precipitation over the basin} = \frac{\Sigma PA}{\Sigma A} = \frac{72486}{3915} \text{ mm} = 18{\cdot}51 \text{ mm}$$

Base flow of rivers. When there is no surface run off either from the rains or from melting of snow, the river water is derived from the ground water. This results in a study lowering of the water Table and a constantly receiving stream flow (discharge) until a rain occurs to produce surface water as a base flow. This reduced perinial flow of river due to subsoil water is known as base flow.

River Hydrograph. It is a graph plotted discharge against time for the flow of a river minus the base flow. The resulting discharge of the river is called as direct run off (D.R.F.).

Excess rainfall. Also called as effective rainfall and represented as below :

Excess rainfall = Rainfall – Initial basin loss – Infiltration.

In easy form it can be said as surface flow.

Infiltration. When rain starts some of its water is absorbed by the top layer and then it

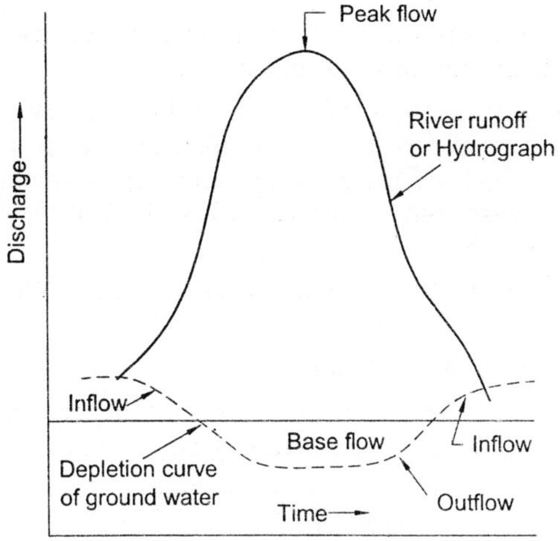

Fig. 13·135.

starts moving down to the soil where it is trapped in the voids of the soil and becomes sub soil water. The process where by the water enters the surface layer and then moves downward towards the water table (or spring level) is called as infiltration.

The infiltration depends upon the amount of voids in the soil which in turn does not depend upon the size of the soil particles, but rather upon the arrangement, sorting, shape and degree of compaction. Therefore different soils which have different above qualities of soil have different capacities of absorbing water. The maximum rate at which a soil in any given condition is capable of absorbing water is called its **infiltration capacity** and is generally denoted by the letter (p).

It is evident that the rain will enter the soil at full capacity rate (f) till the rainfall rate exceeds the infiltration capacity. When the rain intensity is less than the infiltration capacity the prevailing infiltration rate will approximately be equal to the rain fall rate. Hence the actual prevailing infiltration rate may be equal to or less than the infiltration capacity. This is actually prevailing rate at which the water will enter the given soil at any given time and is known as **infiltration rate.** The water below the spring level is known as the ground water and the water above the **spring level** (water table) is known as the **soil moisture.**

If the rain intensity (p) exceeds the infiltration capacity (f), the difference is called the excess rainfall rate (pe). This excess water first of all accumulated on the ground as **surface detension** (D) and then flows over into the streams. Above the water table there is a fringe of water due to surface tension and is known as **capillary fringe**.

Infiltration Capacity Curve. The infiltration capacity curve is a graphical representation of the variation of infiltration capacity with time during and a little after rain.

The infiltration capacity is very high at the beginning of a rain storm that occurs after a long dry spell. During the continuous rain the infiltration capacity is reduced due to several reasons such as **surface detension, soil moisture compaction due to rain and working of fines etc.** After some period say 3 hours or so it tends to become constant. A typical infiltration capacity curve as shown in the Fig. 13·136 (a).

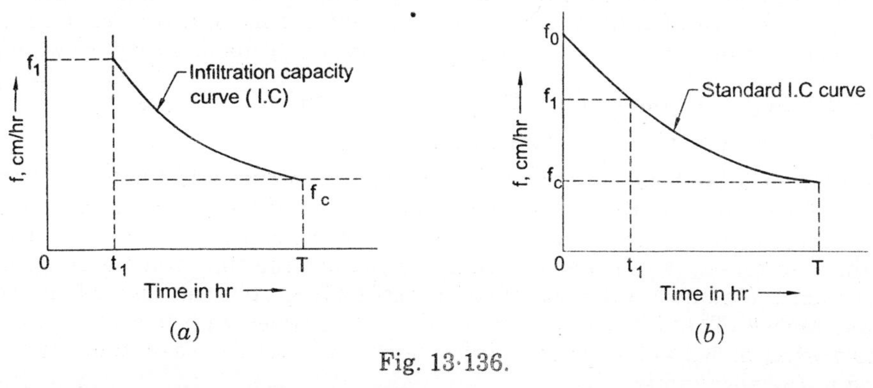

Fig. 13·136.

where (Fig. 13·136) O = Origin, the time is counted fr/om the start of rain

t_1 = Time during which there is no infiltration and the entire rain is used up in interception and depression storage.

Sometimes the value of f to be used for computing the surface runoff due to a given storm from a given drainage basin, in that case, the value of f is 1st of all calculated from another known storm. This value of f is so calculated as to include interception and depression storage in the infiltration itself. The curve will then be represented as shown in Fig. 13·136 (*b*). This is known as standard infiltration capacity curve, in which :

f_0 = value of infiltration capacity at $t = 0$, it may be twice, thrice or any other times of f_c.

f_c = constant value of infiltration reached towards the end.

The values of (f) may be different for soils of different texture and with other conditions since the curve reaches a constant value hence it is an exhaustive type. Horton given an expression as below for the I.C. curve.

$$f = f_c + (f_0 - f_c)\, e^{-Kt}$$

where f_c = The rate of infiltration after it reaches a constant value

f_0 = Infiltration capacity at the start

f = Infiltration capacity at any time t

t = Time from the start of rain and

K = a constant

Field Method for determining Infiltration Capacity by infiltrometer or Rain Simulator. It consists of two shallow **concentric rings of sheet metal.** It is placed on the ground such as its lower end is in ground while the upper end is above the ground. Water is filled in both the compartment upto the same level. The outer ring checks the water of inner ring to spread over a large area, after penetrating below the bottom of the ring. The rate at which the water is required to be added to the inner ring in order to keep constant level will directly give an idea of the infiltration capacity. The curve of infiltration against time may be plotted. The test may be taken at different places of the basin for an average result. In this way the nature and properties of the curve can be found.

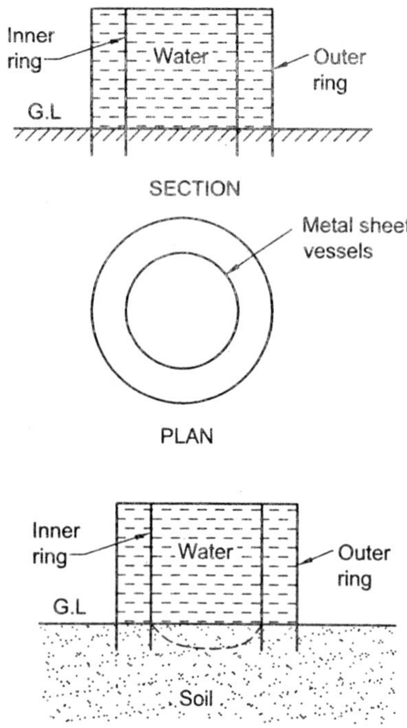

Fig. 13·137. Infiltrometer.

In order to take a better result a **simulator** is used for creating an artificial rain. The difference between the rainfall during a certain interval of time and the resultant run off will give us the amount of infiltration (F) during that interval and the quantity (F) when divided by the duration (t) will give us the value (f) the rate of infiltration $\boldsymbol{F = P - Q}$ or $\boldsymbol{f = \dfrac{P - Q}{t}}$ where P = total rain, Q = total run off and t = time duration.

There exists a lag between the time when rainfall occurs and the time when the water appears as surface runoff at the outlet of the basin. Therefore the infiltration starts at the beginning of excess rainfall and continues not only upto the end of rain but for some more time even after the rain ceases. From the rain intensity pattern the time when excess rain ceases is known. And from the point of inflexion of the runoff hydrograph, the time when overland flow ceases is also known. The difference between these two times will give us this extra period. 1/3rd of which when added to the excess rainfall period, will give us the total time of infiltration (t) to be used in the above relation.

Computing runoff by runoff coefficient. The volume of runoff can directly be computed approximately by the following relation

$$Q = KP$$

where Q = Runoff ;

P = Precipitation and K a constant depending upon the imperviousness of the drainage area.

This relation is generally used for urban areas and not used for rural areas and for big storms.

Table 13·139. The Values of Runoff Coefficient (K)

S. No.	Type of area		Value of K		
			Flat land 0 to 5% slope	*Rolling land 5% to 10% slope*	*Hilly land 10 % to 30% slope*
1. (a)	Urban areas				
	30% area impervious (Paved)		0·40	0·50	—
	50% area impervious (Paved)		0·55	0·65	—
	70% area impervious (Paved)		0·65	0·80	—
(b)	Single family residence in urban areas		0·3		
2.	Cultivated areas -	Open sandy loam	0·30	0·40	0·52
		clay and silt loam	0·50	0·60	0·72
		Tight clay	0·60	0·70	0·82
3.	Pastures	Open sandy loam	0·10	0·16	0·22
		Clay and silt loam	0·30	0·36	0·42
		Tight clay	0·40	0·55	0·60
4.	Wooded land and Forested areas				
		Open sandy loam	0·10	0·25	0·30
		Clay and silt loam	0·30	0·35	0·50
		Tight clay	0·40	0·50	0·60

Computing Runoff by Infiltration Capacity Curve. If infiltration curve (infiltration capacity vs time) is superimposed on the rainfall hydrograph, the resultant amount will represent nothing but the runoff.

Infiltration index. Infiltration index (F) is defined as an average rate of loss such that the volume of rainfall in excess of that rate will be equal to the volume of surface runoff.

$$F = \frac{\text{Total infiltration during period of rainfall excess}}{\text{Period of rainfall excess}}$$

$$= \frac{P-Q}{t}$$

where P = total precipitation

Q = Total runoff and t = time of storm

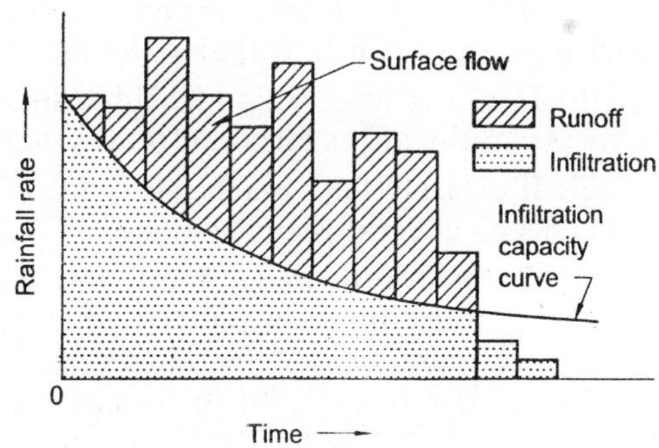

Fig. 13·138. Infiltration—run off curve.

It is the ratio of the rain water absorbed to the total rainfall of the storm.

9·5. Peak Flow. There are three general approaches to the problem of determining peak flow rates.

(1) **Study of Past Records of Floods.** The study of past floods on the stream in question or on neighbouring or similar streams is the first obvious step in forecasting future peaks. For Indian Rivers enveloping curves from observed floods have been plotted by Mr. Kanwar Sain (Fig. 13·139).

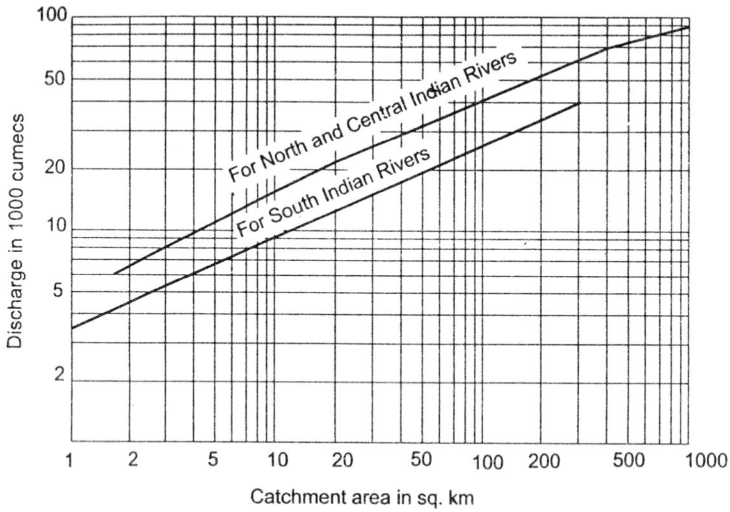

Fig. 13·139. Envelope curves.

If records of past flood peaks are available for the stream in question the future estimate may be based on them. Generally it would be possible to obtain high flood level records more easily than high flood discharge records. If some engineering work is located on the river, the past high flood levels at that site would be marked on it and may be taken as authentic. Where high flood level is established by enquiry from residents on the side of the stream, it is necessary to check from a large number of people, as erroneous information may be given by some. Indications may sometimes be obtained from high water marks like floating debris deposited in branches or trees by receding flood or water marks on banks.

Once the H.F.L. has been established, the following method can be utilised for establishing the high flood discharge.

(*i*) If there is any weir or dam exists near the site, the head on the crest will determine the discharge, since H.F.L. will give the top of the nappe.

(*ii*) If afflux at a flumed bridge has been observed, approximate discharge can be calculated from the afflux formula (refer bridge section of this book).

(*iii*) If a farely long reach (straight) of the river is available, velocity can be calculated with the Lacey's general regime equation $V = 16^{2/3}, 5^{1/3}$, where

R = hydraulic mean depth and S is the slope (in fraction). The cross section can be surveyed and plotted when the river is dry. Even in the time of flood some soundings can be taken to plot the cross-section. From the x-section the area upto H.F.L. and the hydraulic mean depth can be computed. This method is only applicable for the rivers of flexible beds. For streams with rocky beds Manning's expression may be used for determination of velocity (refer measurement of flow in open channels), but it would be subject to the uncertainty involve in value of rugosity coefficient.

(*iv*) If there are actual observations of discharge at lower gauge values are available, the curve for low discharge can be extended to H.F.L.

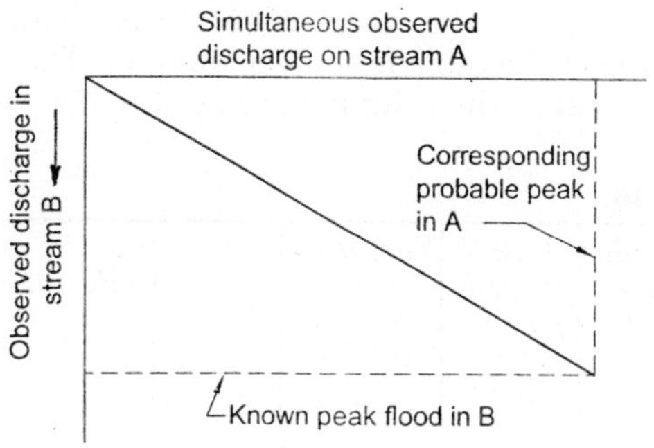

Fig. 13·140.

(*v*) If sufficient records are not available, for the stream in question, but they are available for other streams of that area, a plot similar to that in Fig. 13·139 should be made with enveloping curve fitted to cover the point. From the envelope so plotted the discharge per sq. km of catchment and hence the total flood discharge can be determined. If records on a number of such streams are not available, the enveloping curve Fig. 13·139 can be utilised as a limit. The allowanace for the variation in characteristics of the drainage area and the main feature affecting the flood producing capacity must be accounted for.

(*vi*) A curve on stream *A* of known hydrology vs the stream *B*, the hydrology of which is required is drawn, from which the peak discharge on stream *B* can be computed with reference to the peak of stream *A*.

(2) **Flood frequency method.** The flood frequency studies may however be more usefully employed for the following purposes :

(*i*) Determination of **coefficient of variation** which measures the departure from the mean and is a quantitative measure of the flood characteristics of a stream. If one stream is being used as a basis of comparison for determining the peak on another and if the coefficients of variation of the two are determined for a representative and equal period and compared, that with the larger coefficient of variation has the greater flood producing capacity.

(*ii*) Special studies involving small frequencies, smaller than the period of available records, such as the determination of the maximum discharge likely to occur with in the construction period of a dam on the river for which diversion arrangements must be made, or the percentange of years in which a given discharge will be exceeded in future for assessment of probable flood damage and the resulting economic benefits of flood control measures, the method consists of the following steps :

(1) The plotting of existing flood records in the form of a frequency probability curve.

(2) The extrapolation of this curve if long frequency floods are to be predicted, to intervals of time greater than the length of records.

Two approaches are possible in the application of the theory of probability to a study of floods frequencies.

(*a*) Basic stage method involves a consideration of all floods that exceeded a given basic stage during the period of record.

(*b*) Yearly flood method uses only the maximum flood during each year of record.

The 1st method is considered more accurate, but the results are not materially different. In any case the degree of accuracy expected is not such as to justify the use of elaborate methods and hence the 2nd and simplest method may as well be used.

Let p = The probable percentage of future years in which a flood equal to or greater than a discharge Q will occur.

n = Number of years during the period of record that a flood Q was equalled or exceeded.

y = Total number of years of record.

I = Future flood frequency in years = $\dfrac{100}{p}$

Then according to law of probability $p = \dfrac{100\,n}{y}$

The method is illustrated in table below. The total no. of years of record is 20 and the maximum yearly peak is entered in col. 2. The working of the table is self explanatory. The value of p and I are tabulated in columns 5 and 6, and the rest of the columns are used to determine, the coefficient of variation C_v.

Table 13·40.

Year	Max. yearly peak Q (Cusecs)	Col. 2 arranged in order of magnitude	n, the no. of times the year's peak was equalled or exceeded	p, % age of years, the years peak was equalled or exceeded	I = 100/p future flood frequency years	Col. 3 as proportion of mean flood	Variation from mean V (col 7)-1	V^2	Remarks
1	2	3	4	5	6	7	8	9	10
1937	30,300	28,900	20	100	1	·633	– ·367	·135	
1938	45,000	29,800	19	95	1·05	·653	– ·347	·121	
1939	42,500	30,300	18	90	1·11	·664	– ·334	·112	
1940	60,000	32,700	17	85	1·18	·716	– ·284	·081	
1941	35,600	35,600	16	80	1·25	·78	– ·220	·048	
1942	28,900	36,400	15	75	1·33	·797	– ·203	·041	$p = 100\ n/y$
1943	47,400	37,700	14	70	1·43	·825	– ·175	·031	$y = 20$ years
1944	39,200	39,200	13	65	1·54	·859	– ·141	·020	for this
1945	32,700	41,600	12	60	1·67	·912	– ·088	·008	example
1946	80,500	41,800	11	55	1·82	·916	– ·084	·007	$I = 100/p$
1947	54,100	42,500	10	50	2·00	·936	– ·068	·005	
1948	43,000	43,000	9	45	2·22	·942	– ·058	·003	
1949	37,700	45,000	8	40	2·50	·987	– ·013	·000	$C_V = \sqrt{\frac{\Sigma V^2}{y} - 1}$
1950	48,800	45,100	7	35	2·86	·988	– ·012	·000	
1951	29,800	47,400	6	30	3·33	1·04	·040	·002	
1952	89,900	50,100	5	25	4·00	1·095	·095	·009	
1953	45,100	54,100	4	20	5·00	1·135	·135	·018	
1954	41,600	60,000	3	15	6·61	1·314	·314	·049	
1955	36,400	80,500	2	10	10·00	1·762	·762	·580	
1956	50,100	89,900	1	5	20·00	1·970	·970	·942	
	Total	9,11,600					$\Sigma V^2 = 2{\cdot}262$		
	Mean	45,580					$C_V = 0{\cdot}345$		

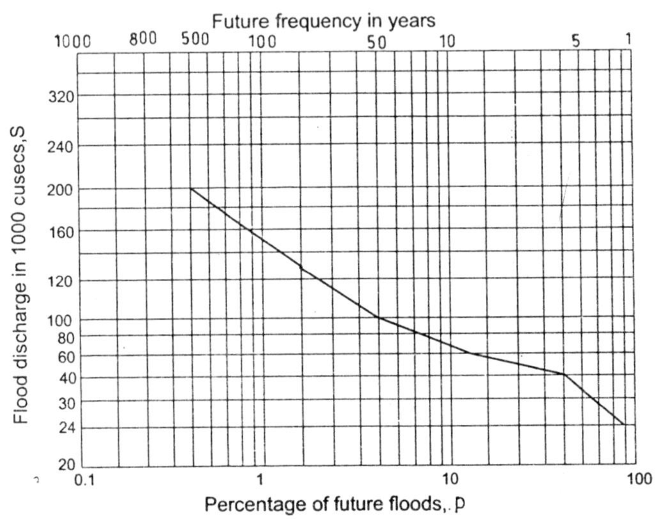

Fig. 13·141.

Values of peak discharges from Column 2 are plotted as ordinates and percentage from Column 5 as abscissas on probability paper as indicated in Fig. 13·141. A curve drawn through the plotted points may be extended to obtain an extrapolated value of the flood discharge Q, which may be expected to be equalled or exceeded, on an average in p percent of future year or occurrence in I years *i.e.* in the example given 100 years frequency flood is 1,80,000 cusecs and the discharge expected to occur once in five years is 58,000 cusecs.

The coefficient of variation comes to 0·345.

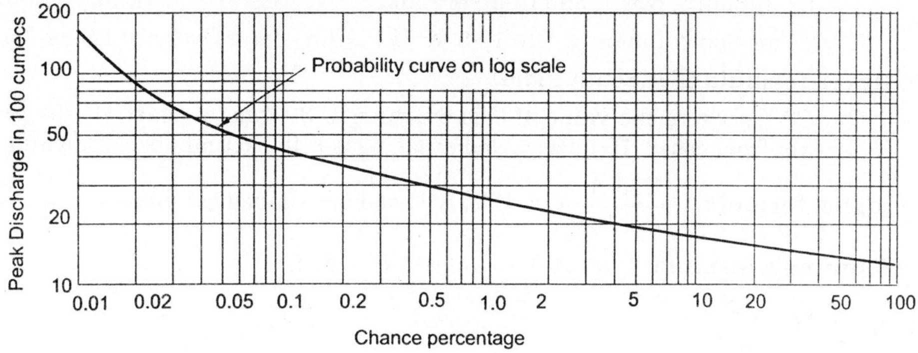

Fig. 13·142.

Probability Plotting on Emperical Relations. In the given table peak flood data is arranged in the descending order and to assign the ranking number (m) to each flood. The severest flood will thus be placed at the top with its ranking as 1. The 2nd severest flood will be placed at number 2 position and its ranking number will also be 2. The lightest flood will be placed at the last place (Nth places and its ranking no. will be N).

The probability is then computed by the emperical **California Formula** as $p = \frac{m}{N}$ and the recurrence interval $(T) = \frac{1}{p} = \frac{N}{m}$.

After values of recurrence interval (T) for different floods are calculated, a graph can be plotted between the frequencies and flood discharges, which can be extended if desired, as to extrapolate the value of flood magnitude corresponding to any high value of frequency. The flood discharge for any other frequency can also be determined from the plotted graph.

However many times a graph is plotted between $\frac{100}{T}$ (called exceedence probability (P) in percent or chance percent) and the flood discharge. A simple graph paper can be used and the curve obtained is as in Fig. 13·143. Some times it is drawn on logarithmic paper. (Fig. 13·143).

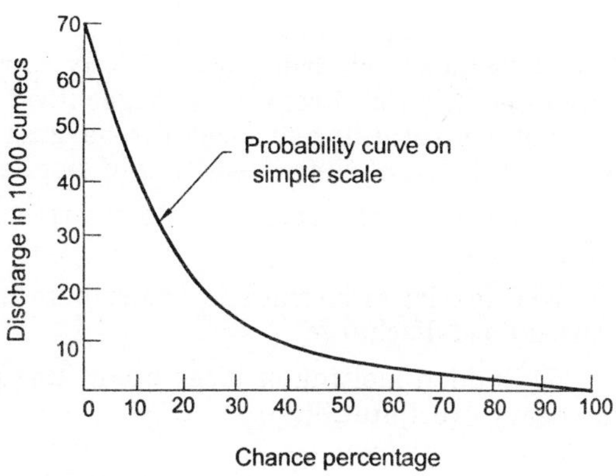

Fig. 13·143.

Other formulae are $p = \frac{m}{N+1}$ (Welbull Formula)

$p = \frac{m - 0.5}{N}$ (Hazen Formula)

$p = \frac{m - 0.3}{N + 0.4}$ (Chegodayev Formula)

$$p = \frac{m - 0.44}{N + 0.12} \quad \text{(Blom Formula)}$$

(3) **Catchment Area Formulae.** For maximum flood discharge

(*a*) Dicken's formula $Q = CA^{3/4}$ (for North and Central India)

where Q = Peak flood in cumecs, A = catchment area in $(\text{km})^2$ and C is a coefficient, which varies from 1·67 to 10·5 on large Indian Rivers but actual observation are upto 22 in South, North and Central India,

C = 22 for South India, 13·5 to 19·5 for U.P., Bihar and Orissa, 11·3 for North India

(*b*) **Ryves formula** (For South India)

$Q = CA^{2/3}$, where the value of C is 6·8 with in 80 k.m. of coast, 8·3 for 80 to 2400 km from coast, 10·0 for curled areas near hills, actual observed value upto 37

(*c*) **Inglis' formula.** $\dfrac{123\,A}{\sqrt{A + 10\,A}}$ or $123\sqrt{A}$ (For Fem shaped catchments)

(*d*) **Fanning's formula.** $Q = CA^{5/6}$ where $C = 254$

(*e*) $Q = CAR^4 \dfrac{\sqrt{S/A}}{455}$

where C is a coefficient = 0·50 for rural areas and 0·75 in average

S = slope in fraction of m/1000

The main factors affecting the flood producing capacity are :

(1) Storm rainfall characteristics, including type of storms and their intensity and duration.

(2) Storage capacity of the catchment or its ability to retain water temporarily above or below ground and to regulate the run off-storage capacity of any form holds the rain water and releases it gradually subsequently, resulting in reduction of peak discharges. Storage may be provided in the form of (*i*) artificial ponds (*ii*) natural lakes and swamps (*iii*) underground storage (*iv*) storage a ground by vegetation.

(3) Slopes of drainage area influencing the period of retention of water on ground and hence its infiltration into the ground.

(4) Shapes of drainage area. In rivers having its tributaries in the shape of a fan (Fig. 13·142(*a*) in which each tributary is likely to reach the main stream at approximately at the same time resulting in a relatively larger flood discharge in the main river. On the other hand if the tributaries of different sizes discharging into the main stream in the shape of fan Fig. (13·142 (*b*) at different times resulting in smaller floods.

(5) The general direction of flow of rivers in relation to general direction of movement of rainfall centres.

(6) Capacity of barriers in the stream to release water suddenly which creates a highly augmented flood discharge.

(7) Sudden melting of large quantities of snow due to rise of temperature at the same time as heavy precipitation.

(*a*) Pan shaped catchment

(*b*) Fern shaped catchment

Fig. 13·144.

Table 13·41. Heavist rainfall in one hour (in mm) for important places (India)

Place	mm	Place	mm	Place	mm
Agartala	66	Dumri	66	Mukhim	57
Ahmedabad	80	Durgapur	90	Nagpur	78
Aligarh	51	Gangtok	81	Nandurbar	73
Allahabad	65	Gannavaram	61	New Delhi	79
Amiridevi	53	Gauhati	61	N. Lakhimpur	65
Amritsar	74	Gaya	70	Okhala	76
Anantapur	38	Gorkha	62	Okhaidunga	52
Asansol	86	Gwalior	63	Palganj	56
Aurangabad	61	Hazaribagh	78	Panumber	37
Bazdora	70	Hirakund	82	Panchat hill	71
Bafra Tawa	63	Hydrabad	102	Pathankot	68
Bangalore	58	Imphal	48	Patna	59
Bangalore central	61	Indore	60	Pokhara	62
Barakachar	51	Jabalpur	77	Pune	47
Barhi	56	Jogdal Pur	73	Port-Blair	61
Baramula	75	Jaipur	55	Punasa	75
Baroda	71	Jamshedpur	62	Pupanki	77
Barrachpore	58	Jamni	60	Purki	49
Bhim Kund	60	Jawai Dam	98	Raipur	49
Bhopal	72	Jharsuguda	77	Ramgarh	56
Bhubneshwar	46	Jodhpur	60	Sagar Island	94
Bhuj	49	Tonkdam	46	Shilong	43
Bishangarh	60	Kathmandu	44	Sindri	50
Bokaro	58	Khalari	63	Sonepur	78
Bombay	129	Khujrawan	66	Sri Nagar	22
(Santa Cruz) Bombay	91	Kodaikonal	83	Shanti Niketan	49
Kalkota	62	Konar	59	Topujang	59
Chambal	84	Luchipur	63	Tehri	41
Chandwa	46	Lucknow	70	Tezpur	63
Cherapunji	127	Madras	62	Thikri	61
Coimbatore	80		73	Tilawa Dam	80
Dadeldhura	36	Mahabaleshwar	51	Tirichnapalli	78
Dhanbad	74	Maithon	54	Trivendrum	96
Dhanwar	20	Manglore	72	Venguria	66
Dholpar	47	Marmagao	60	Verawal	64
Dibrugarh	93	Mawsynram	127	Visakahapatnam	63
Dum Dum	68	Minicoy	70		

The max. rainfall of a place is usually taken to be 1·51 times the average annual rainfall of 35 years.

9·6. Unit Hydrograph. Unit hydrograph is a way for determining the hydrograph of surface run off (rainfall excess). The method involves the preparation of standard unit hydrographs caused by rainfalls of specified durations, such as 4 hours, 6 hours, 12 hours etc. This standard *T*-hour unit duration hydrograph containing one cm of excess rain is used to work out the hydrograph caused by any other rain of the same duration and containing any other amount of excess rain.

A T-hour unit hydrograph is thus defined as the hydrograph of run off produced by an intense excess rain fall of 1 cm, during uniformly over the entire drainage basin and at a uniform rate for the short specified duration of *T*-hour. Since the rainfall excess is nothing but surface runoff, the volume of water contained in the unit hydrograph shall be equal to 1 cm depth over the basin area.

The specified duration of *T* hours was termed as the unit duration and the storm of this duration was called the unit storm.

The application of unit hydrograph of 1 cm excess rain for the computation of the direct run off hydrograph resulting from an excess rain of *D* cm or vice versa is based upon the following assumptions :

(*i*) **Time invariance.** The run off produced from a given drainage basin due to a given effective rainfall, shall always be the same irrespective of the time of its occurrence. In other words, the run off response of a basin to a given effective rain fall is assumed to be time invariant.

(*ii*) **Linear Response.** The runoff response of a drainage basin to the excess rain fall assumed to be linear. Linear response means that if an input $x_1\ (t)$ causes an output $y_1\ (t)$ and an input $x_2\ (t)$ causes an output $y_2\ (t)$ than an input $x_1(t) + x_2(t)$ will raise an output $y_1(t) + y_2(t)$. In other words an input equal to $D.\ x_1\ (t)$ will cause an output equal to $D{\cdot}y_1\ (t)$. It therefore follows that if the excess rain fall of *D* cm occurs in a duration of *T* hour. Then the resulting run off hydrograph will have its ordinates equal to *D* times the ordinates of unit hydrograph. Since the area of the resulting direct run off hydrograph shall increase by the ratio *D*, the base of this hydrograph shall be the same as that of the unit hydrograph. The hydrograph of any other storm of specified duration (*T*-hour) will thus have the same shape as that of the unit hydrograph of the same duration (*T* hours) but with ordinates of flow is proportional to their run off volumes.

Storm of different intensities produce different volumes of excess rain, but of a particular duration, will thus have the same shape of their direct run off hydrographs. Different unit hydrographs for different durations can be prepared, and a particular unit hydrograph when prepared for a paritcular duration can be utilised for evaluating the run off hydrograph of any other storms of the same duration by multiplying the ordinates of unit hydrograph by *D*. The assumption of linear response in an unit hydrograph thus enables the method of super position to be used to derive the direct run off hydrographs. Accordingly if two rainfall excess each of *T* hour duration occur consecutively, then their combined effect can be obtained by superposing the respective run off hydrographs with due care being taken to account for the time lag between the two sequence of events.

For large catchments the unit hydrograph process is not so reliable as the rain fall in whole of the area is not uniform during the same period. The areas exceeding 5000 sq. km are not considered fit for this process of unit hydrograph. The areas below very very small areas amount say 2 sq. km are also not fit for this process as there is other contingencies which effects the rain fall calculation and are greater than the normal.

Preparation of a unit hydrograph. First of all the run off rates in cm/hour resulting from the given storm are plotted against time in hours so as to obtain direct run off hydrograph for the given storm. The total area (D) contained with in this hydrograph as calculated by a planimeter or by the Simpson's rule etc. This will represent nothing but the volume of run off in cm depth of water on the basin.

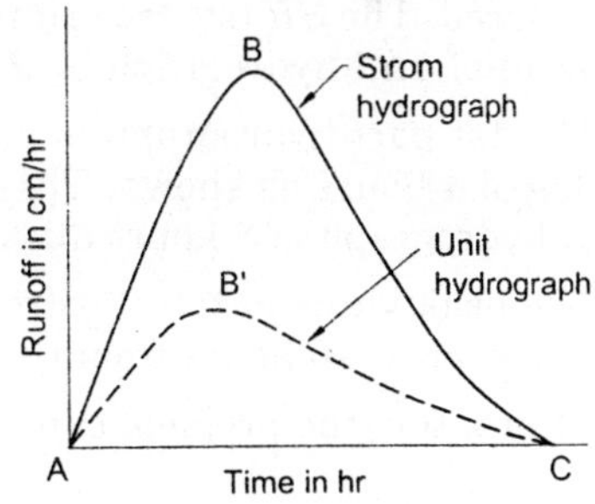

Fig. 13·145 (a).

The ordinates of this hydrograph ABC as in Fig. 13·145 (a) are multiplied by $\frac{1}{D}$ cm so as to obtain the ordinates of a unit hydrograph $AB'C$. For example the area ABC is 3 cm depth of water, then ordinates of unit hydrograph can be obtained by multiplying the ordinates of storm hydrograph by 7/3. To make the process clear the following example is studied.

Example. In a typical 4 hour storm producing 50 mm of excess rain from a basin, the following flows in the stream are recorded.

Time in hours	Flow in cumecs
0	0·0
2	1·22
4	4·05
6	6·75
8	5·67
12	3·375
16	1·75
20	0·0

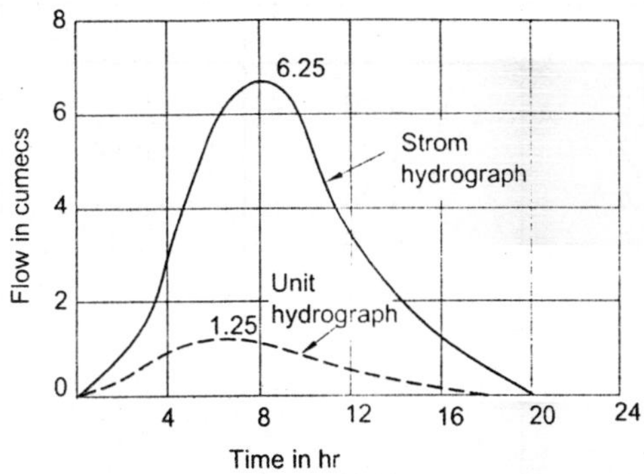

Fig. 13·145 (b)

(a) Plot the unit hydrograph of run off for this storm.

(b) Estimate as accurately as possible the peak flow and the time of its occurrence in a flood created by a 8 hours storm which produces 2·5 cm of effective rain fall during the 1st four hours and 3·75 cm of effective rain fall during the 2nd 4 hours, assuming the base flow to be negligible. 1st the hydrograph of the run off obtained from the given storm of 4 hours duration is plotted, by using the various given values of time and flow. This is shown by the upper curve 1 in the Fig. 13·145 (b).

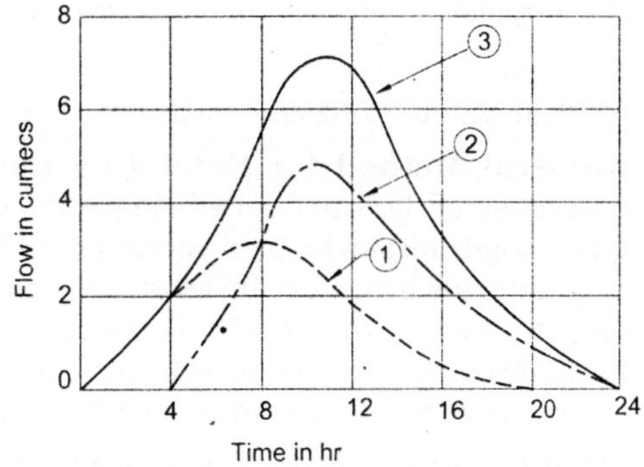

Fig. 13·146. S.R. Hydrograph.

Since the hydrograph contain 5 cm of run off volume, we must multiply its ordinates by 1/5 *i.e.* we must divide its ordinates by 5 in order to obtain unit hydrograph of 4 hours duration. This is shown by the lever curve (2) in Fig. 13·145 (b).

The storm of 8 hours duration has been divided into two parts each of 4 hours duration. During the 1st part 2·5 cm of excess rain is produced and during the 2nd part 3·75 cm of excess rain is produced. The *SR* (surface run-off) hydrograph for the 1st part is obtained by multiplying the ordinates of unit hydrograph by 2·5 and that for 2nd part by multiplying by 3·75.

The 1st part hydrograph is plotted as curve (1) in Fig. 13·146 and 2nd part as curve (2) but at a lag of 4 hours as shown. These two hydrographs are added together, so as to obtain the final total hydrograph of 8 hours duration rain. This is shown by curve (3) in the Fig. 13·146.

The peak value of total hydrograph is found to be 7·32 cumecs and it occurs at a time t = 10 hours *i.e.* after 10 hours from the start of rain.

Alternately the problem can be solved analytically as given in the table below :

Table 13·42.

Time in hour	*Ordinates of storm hydrograph of 5 cm*	*Ordinates of unit hydrograph of 1 cm = col (2) + 5*	*Ordinates of 1st 4 hour hydrograph producing 2·5 cm rain = 2·5 × col (3)*	*Ordinates of 2nd 4 hour hydrography producing 3·75 cm rain at a lag of 4 hour = 3·75 × col. (3)*	*Total 8 hour hydrograph ordinates in cumecs = col (4) + (5)*
1	2	3	4	5	6
0	0·00	0·00	0·00	—	0·00
2	1·22	0·24	0·61	—	0·61
4	4·05	0·81	2·02	0·00	2·02
6	6·75	1·35	3·37	0·90	4·27
8	5·67	1·15	2·83	3·03	5·86
10	—	—	2·26*	5·06	7·32**
12	3·375	0·68	1·69	4·31	6·00
16	1·35	0·27	0·67	2·55	3·23
20	0·00	0·00	0·00	1·01	1·01
24	—	—	—	0·00	0·00

* Interpolated between upper and lower values corresponding to 8 and 12 hours *i.e.* $\frac{2{\cdot}83 + 1{\cdot}69}{2}$ = 2·26.

** Peak value = 7·32 cumecs at t = 10 hr.

General Method for Extending the Discharge Curve. For this purpose we must have the x-section of the site from which we can compute the areas of water sections of the channel at different gauges either by planimeter or by Simpson's rule. A curve is plotted between gauge and area (gauge, u/s area curve). This curve may be plotted on the gauge discharge curve itself. From these two curves, the velocity curve can also be drawn as (mean velocity = Discharge/Area) on the same drawing. The mean velocity curve is generally found to be concave upward while the area curve is generally found to be convex upward as shown in the Fig. 13·147.

After having determined, the mean velocity curve, the problem left is only to extend the same. The velocity given by Manning's formula

$$V = \frac{1}{n} R^{2/3} S^{1/2}.$$

But $\frac{1}{n} S^{1/2}$ is almost constant for higher river stages. We may therefore write

$$V = KR^{2/3}$$

where K is a constant and R = hydraulic mean depth.

From the cross-section we can have the area and the wetted perimeter so the hydraulic mean depth at different stages can be worked out. The value of K can be calculated for various known gauge height which can be applied for higher gauge the velocity at higher gauges can be worked out from the formula $V = KR^{2/3}$.

Now the velocity × Area of cross-section = Discharge at the higher gave in question.

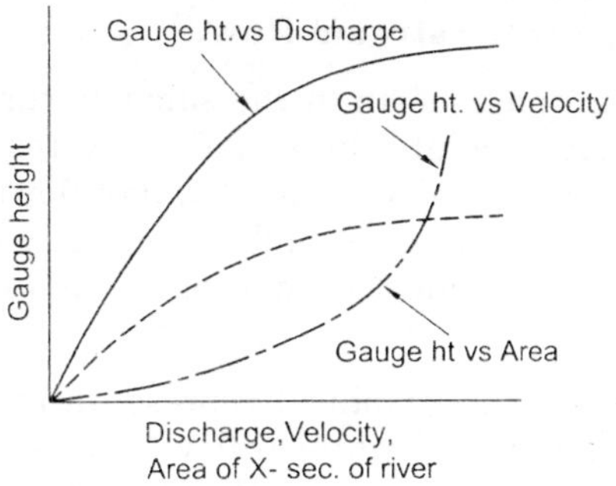

Fig. 13·147.

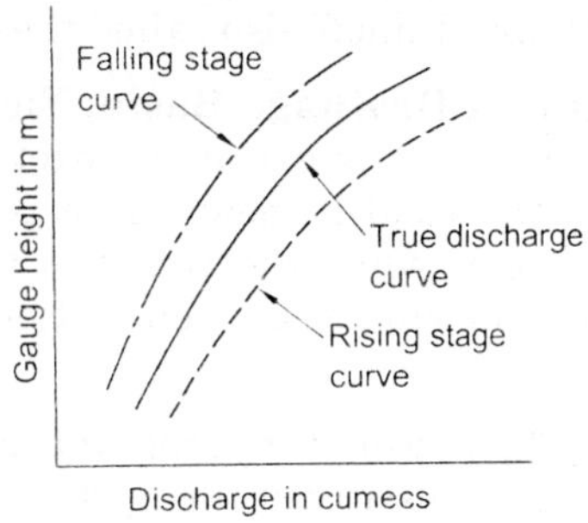

Fig. 13·148.

During a rising stage the measured discharge is more than the true discharge for a given gauge height while in the falling stage it is less than the true discharge hence an average of the two is taken as a true discharge and a curve is plotted for this true discharge.

9·7. General Terms in Flood Hydrology

Rainfall Interception. The quantity of rainfall absorbed by trees, buildings and other objects before reaching on the ground.

Ground Rainfall. The difference between the total rainfall and the rainfall interception is called as ground rainfall.

After the **depression storage** (storage in depressions like ponds etc.) is filled, the rain intensity p continues to create the infiltration capacity of the soil (f), the difference appears as **rainfall excess** which initially accumulates on the ground as **surface detension** (D) and then flows as **overland flow** on the basin surface before entering a stream channel. The water that reaches the stream channel of a basin in this manner is called a surface runoff (S.R.O.) or direct runoff. The surface runoff can therefore occur only from those storms which can contribute to excess rainfall and are simply not dissipated in fulfilling the interception, depression storage and infiltration need of the basin. Excess rainfall = Rainfall – Interception – Depression Storage – Infiltration. Excess rainfall also = Rainfall – Initial Basin loss – Infiltration. So the total of the interception plus depression storage for a basin is called the **initial loss, Basin loss** or the **initial basin recharge.**

Potential infiltration = Sum of total basin loss and infiltration. Therefore excess rainfall = (Rainfall – Infiltration) where infiltration includes initial loss.

The excess water flowing as **overland flow or channel flow** in a water shed, finally, appears as surface runoff at the outlet of the basin but only after filling the capacity of its stream channel. This storage at any instant is known as **channel storage** and is likely to reduce the peak rate of surface runoff at the basin outlet.

Catchment area. The area of which the rain water goes to the outlet of a drain. This area is called as the catchment at the point on the drain.

Water shed. It is a ridge line from which the rain water flows on either sides of it.

Initial and Residual rain. The rain that falls in the beginning of a storm before the depression storage is completely filled is called the initial rain and the rain that falls near the end of the storm at a rate less than the infiltration capacity is called the residual rain.

Depression storage. The storage in the depressed areas such as ponds etc. of the basin in the 1st rain is called the depression storage.

Runoff and surface runoff. Runoff includes all the water flowing in the stream channel at any given section, while the surface runoff includes only the water that reaches the stream channel without 1st percolating down the water table. Surface runoff is also called as the **Direct Runoff** (DRO) and Runoff also called the discharge or the **stream flow.**

Yield of a Drainage Basin. Yield of a drainage basin in the same as runoff, with the only difference that it is expressed over long periods, while the runoff is expressed for short periods. Thus the yield is generally expressed as the total volume of water flowing per year, such as $M.m^3$/year, while the runoff is the instantaneous rate, and is generally expressed as volume of water flowing at a given section of the river in one second or one hour such as in m^3/s or m^3/h.

Base flow. Runoff hydrograph for a river is the graphical representation of the river discharge, which constitutes the surface runoff and ground water inflow (called base flow). In order to obtain the surface runoff graph we must substract the base flow from the runoff graph. It is therefore becomes necessary to understand the movements of ground water flow into the river.

Ground water Depletion curve or Base flow curve. The hydrograph of the river from the time when water table is at maximum height to the time when there is no flow is nothing but the hydrograph of ground water inflow in the river and is known on the ground water depletion curve.

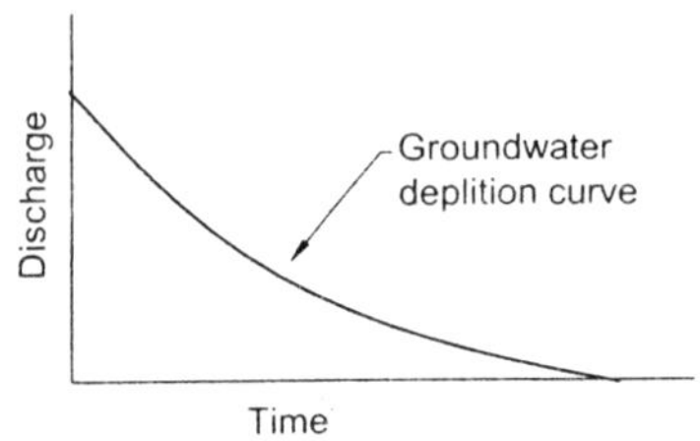

Fig. 13·149. Ground water depletion curve.

Field capacity. Immediately after a rain, when all the gravity water has drained down the water tables, a certain amount of water is retained on the surface of the soil grows by molecular attraction. This is known as **pellicular water** when the water which any soil can retain indefinitely against gravity is expressed in terms of depth of water as if it were spread on the basin is known as field capacity.

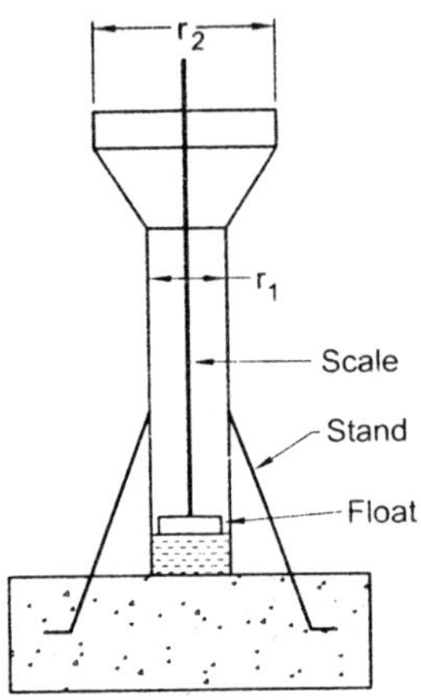

Fig. 13·150 (*a*) Simple rain gauge.

Intensity, of a rain is the rate at which it is falling, the duration is the time for which it is falling with that given intensity, and frequency is the number of times of falls.

Isopluvial lines. Lines of equal rainfall drawn on a map is called as isopluvial line.

Simple rain gauge. It consists of a G.I. plate sheet cylindrical lower limb with closed bottom and have another inverted frustum of a conical top with cylindrical strip edging of larger radius than the lower limb open at the top. The rain water is collected in the lower longer cylindrical limb and is catched by the upper conical limb.

Scale which is graduated in the ratio of $\frac{r_1}{r_2}$ (r_1 is the radius of lower limb and r_2 is the radius of upper limb). Upper conical limb is the actual rain catchment area.

The rain gauge is fitted on the roofs of inspection bungalows, school or other Public buildings and is read by the Patrol of the building. It is secured in triangular stand which is seated in concrete on the roof. There must not be a tree or any other hindrance in the vicinity that may check the free rainfall in the rain gauge. Or the rain must have free access to the rain gauge. Let r_1 and r_2 be the radius of lower and upper limbs and l_1 and l_2 be the length of the two limbs respectively. Then

$$\pi r_1^2 l_1 = \pi r_2^2 l_2 \text{ or } \frac{l_1}{l_2} = \frac{r_2^2}{r_1^2} \text{ (The ratio of the scale)}$$

Symon's non recording rain gauge. It is a rain gauge which is widely being used in Indian meteorological departments and is sketched in the Fig. 13·150 (*b*) and is self explanatory in the figure itself. The non recording type rain gauges do not record the rain but they only collect the rain water. The collected rain is then measured by means of graduated cylinders so as to directly represent the rainfall volume in cm of water depth as below :

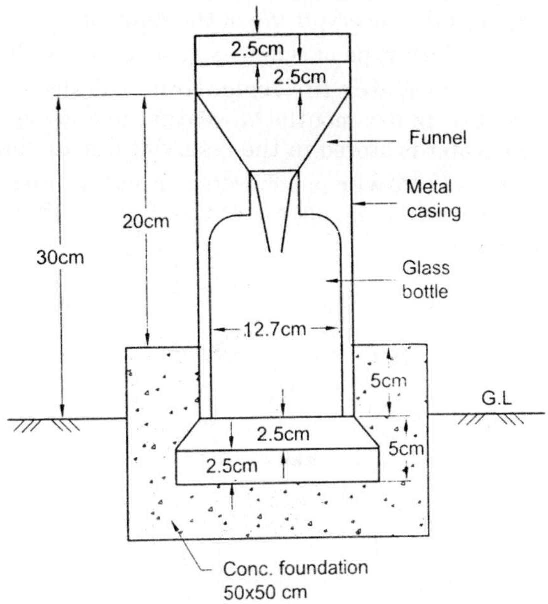

Fig. 13·150 (*b*). Symon's non recording rain gauge.

$$\frac{\text{Volume of water collected in cm}^3}{\text{Area of the aperture of the gauge in cm}^2} = \text{cm. depth of rain fallen.}$$

13·10. Water and Power Resources

10·1. River Valley Projects

(1) **Diversion Power Projects.** A dam is constructed in a narrow valley of a river. A power tunnel is dug on one side of the dam which joins the main river in a loop so as to give a minimum length of approach. On the d/s end of the tunnel when it joins the river a power house is constructed which in turn joins the river by a tail race channel. Water which could be stored u/s of dam is utilised during peak periods of demand.

In hills the river flows with a steep slope while the power tunnel is constructed with gentle slope. Moreover the length of flow of the river is more due to zigzag flow while the length of the tunnel is less due to straight and direct route. Due to above two reasons we recover a sufficient head of water at the junction of river and tunnel, which is utilised for generating power. Maneribhali in the Bhagirathi valley is an example of this type of projects. Power house is constructed above the H.F.L. of the river D/s of the dam.

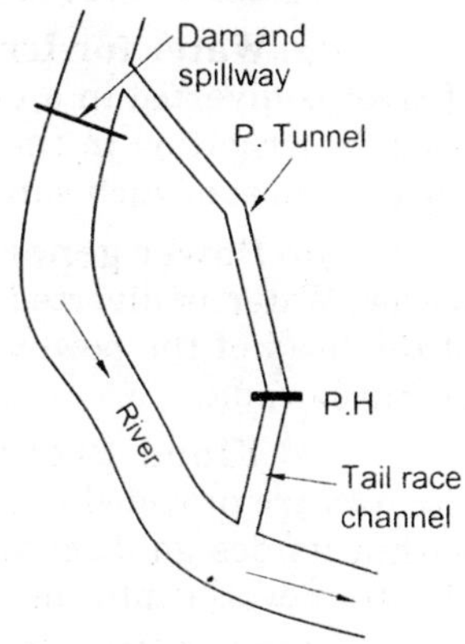

Fig. 13·151. Diversion power project.

(2) **Storage Multi-purpose Projects.** A high dam is constructed in a narrow gorge of a river, which has got a sufficient wide valley u/s of the proposed dam site with a revinous, unpopulated and uncultivable area, in which sufficient high storage can be achieved u/s of the proposed dam.

A power house is constructed at one side of the dam in its d/s side. The flood water is stored in the reservoir u/s of the dam site.

Such type of schemes give three fold benefits:

(*a*) **Water for irrigation.** The flood water which goes waste to the sea is utilised for irrigation in dry months of weather and as well as in rainy season for rice and other such crops. This water is stored in the reservoir during floods u/s of the dam.

(*b*) **Power** is generated from the raised head of water in the u/s of dam. Power house is constructed at the d/s toe of the dam which gives the benefit of the raised level of the water in the river.

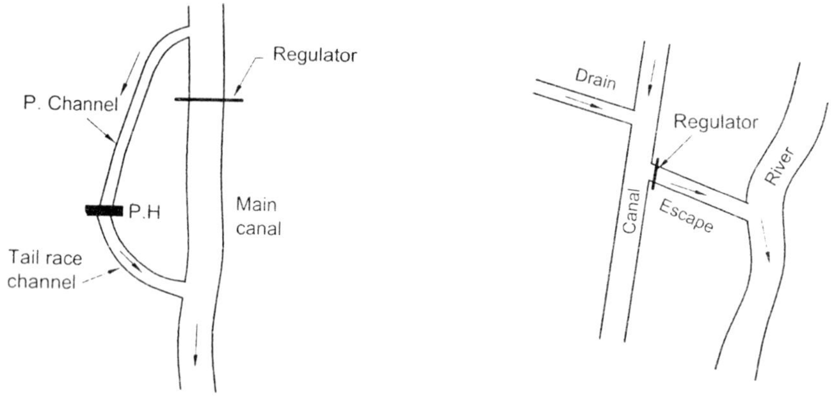

Fig. 13·152. Canal multi purpose works.

(*c*) **Flood Protection.** The flood water which creates destruction in the d/s plane reaches of the river is picked up by the dam so that the extra flood water is checked to go in d/s reaches all of a sudden. Moreover this water is utilised for irrigation in the same reaches in which it creates destruction in the peak demand period of Rabi. Such type of dams are also called as pick up dams. Tehri dam is an example of such projects in Bhagirathi valley. It is known as divided fall development.

Plane Projects of Rivers. Such projects have two fold benefits :

(*a*) **Water for Irrigation.** A barrage or weir is constructed across the river and the water of river is diverted in a canal by a head regulator on one or both sides of the river. The canal is used for irrigation in the d/s reaches of the river at one side of it. Ganga and Sarda canals are the examples of such canals.

(*b*) **Power generation.** The head of water above a fall in the canal is used for generating power. Water is diverted towards the power house through a power channel by a regulator d/s of the head of the power channels. Khatima Power house is an example of such a power house on Sarda canal.

(*c*) **Flood Protection.** Some drains are outleted in the canal during rainy season. Escapes are provided to pass this or any other extra water to the river, so that the canal remains within its design discharge capacities. It should be noted that this activity is avoided to pass the drain water into the canal as far as possible.

Availability of water in different types of Projects.

In **divesion power projects** the minimum available perinial flow can be utilised while an extra water is passed by the spill way.

In diversion canals also the minimum perinial flow can be utilised while the surplus water is passed in the river by sluices.

Storage reservoirs—A regular supply in the dry months of the year is calculated from the available storage between full reservoir level and the dead storage. This regular supply can be given to the irrigation schemes d/s of the dam. The regular supply is also a basis for the supply of water to the power house. As the head of water fluctuates in the dam, a regular supply is stored in a surge tank at the level of dead storage. The head available for the power house is the dead storage and the d/s flood level of the river. The power house can be constructed a little far from the toe of the dam to utilise the head in the bed of river d/s the dam toe.

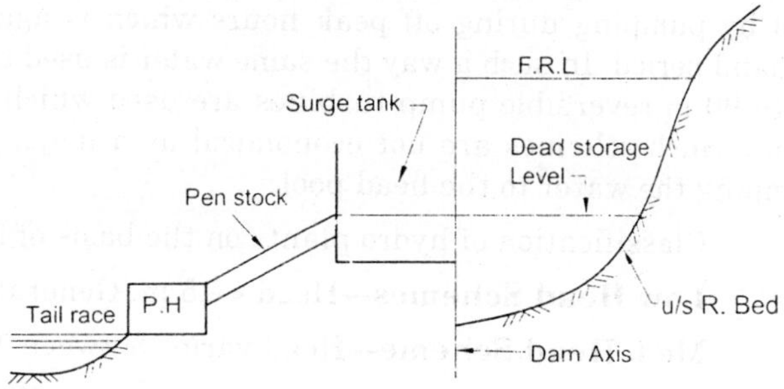

(*a*) Section

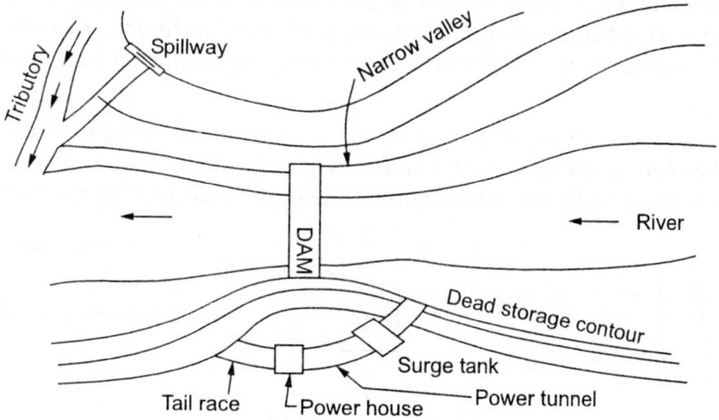

(*b*) Plan

Fig. 13·153.

(3) **Power from tides.** Water of a rising tide enters in the month of the river when rising upto the level of maximum tide, which is stored in a tank operated by sluices. When the tide goes down the valves of the sluices are closed. The head of this stored water is utilised in time of low tide for generating power.

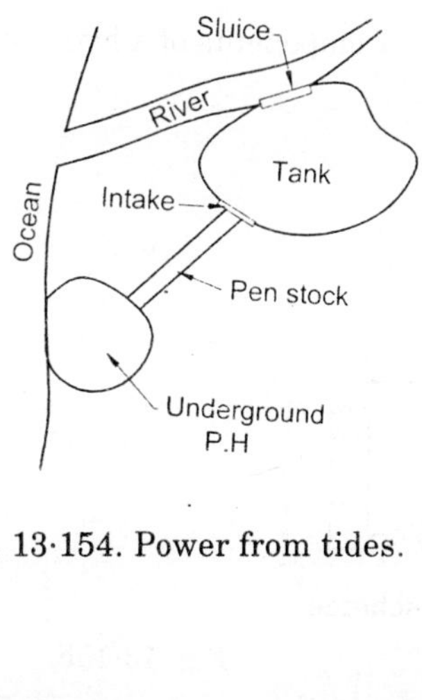

Fig. 13·154. Power from tides.

(4) **Pumped storage.** The tail race pool water of a power project is pumped to the head pool by pumping during off peak hours which is again used for running turbines in the peak demand period. In such a way the same water is used again and again. For heads varying between 15 to 90 m reversible pump turbines are used which can function both as turbine as well as a pump. Such schemes are not economical as a major part of the power generated is wasted in pumping the water to the head pool.

Classification of hydro plants on the basis of head available :

Low Head Schemes—Head < 15 m. Generally diversion schemes.

Med. Head Scheme—Head varies between 15 to 60 m. These are low storage schemes.

High Head Scheme—Head is more than 60 m. These are generally storage dams. Such as Bhakra Dam or Rihand Dam in U.P.

(5) In hill streams or on falls of a canal micro hydel schemes are constructed. In hill streams which have a steeper slope in their bed is utilised by constructing a small off take channel with a smaller slope and the head thus obtained is utilised in hydro power by constructing mini power houses. The water is diverted to the power grid by making a temporary bund of rock fill across the stream.

In the cases of small falls in canals a part of water is diverted in a mill channel u/s of the fall and the head of fall is utilised in the shape of a mini power house or a mini-mill on the mill channel. A series of flour mills are constructed in Ganga canal in U.P. on its falls. (Fig. 13·155).

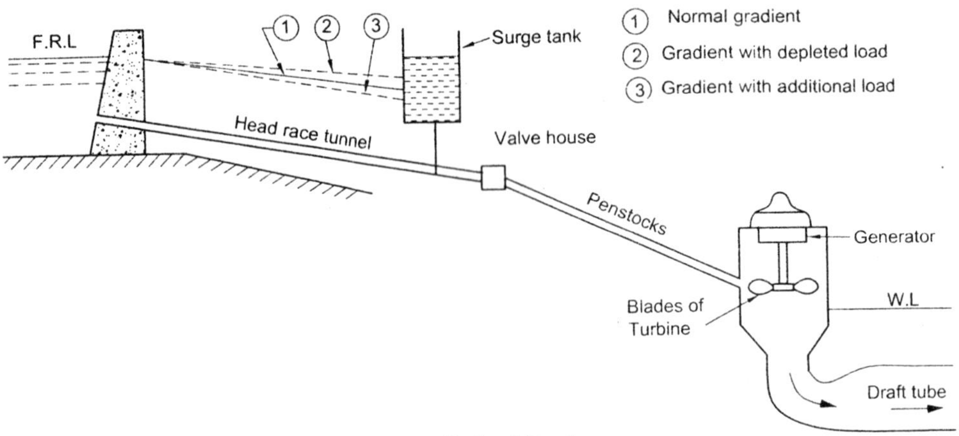

Components of a hydel scheme.

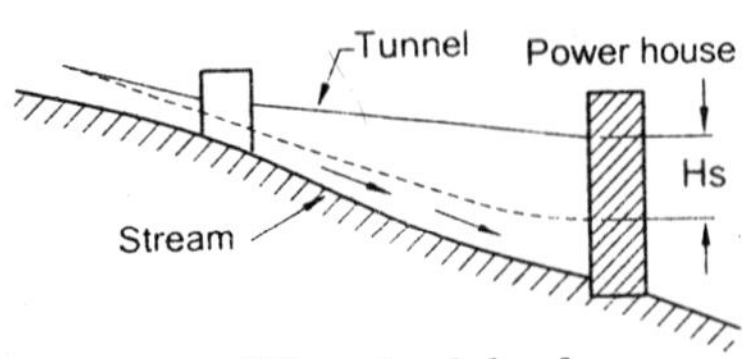

Micro hydel scheme

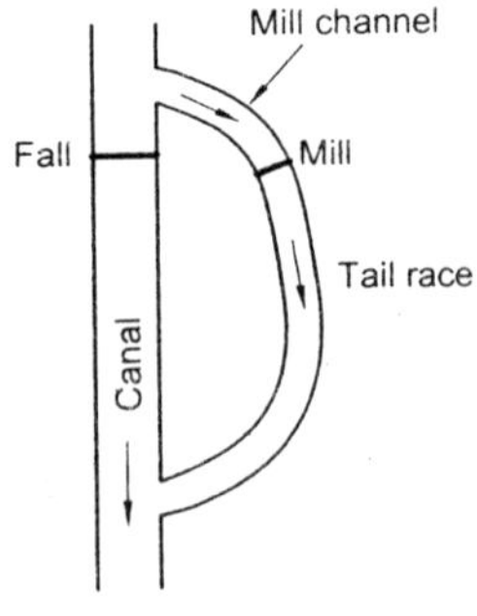

Fig. 13·155.

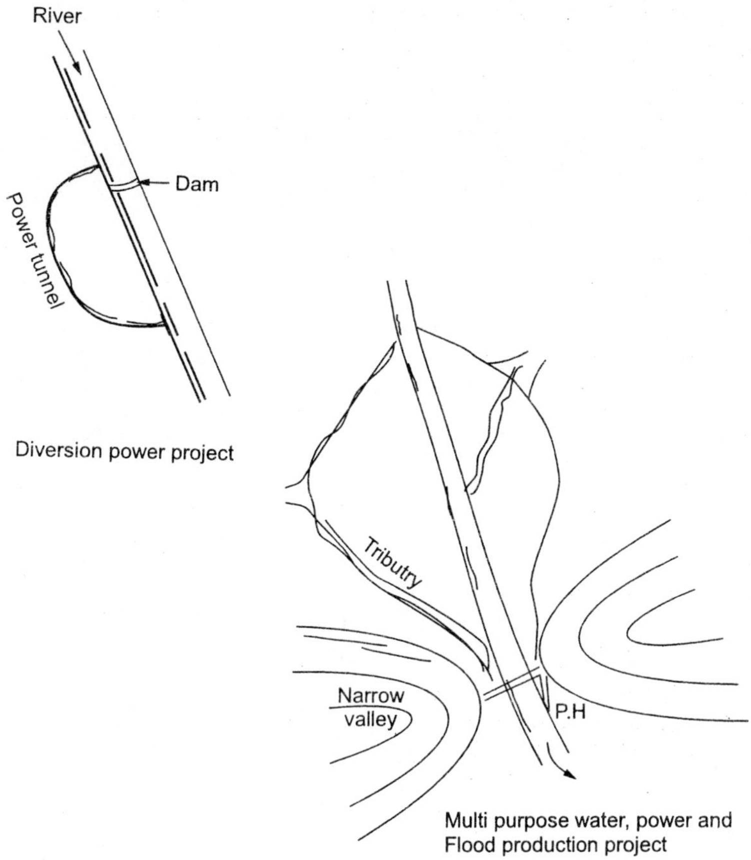

Fig. 13·156.

Power Potential of a Power Generating Unit. Let the discharge available be Q cumecs. H be the head available in (metres), w is the density of water and η be the efficiency of the unit.

The hydro energy available $= w \cdot Q \cdot H$ (wt. of water = 9·81 kN/m^3)

so $= 9{\cdot}81 \times Q \times H$ kN.m/sec (*i.e.* K watts)

Electrical energy or power in K watts is given as

$$P = 9{\cdot}81\ \eta\ QH \text{ (K watts)}$$

Metric H.P. generated $= \dfrac{9{\cdot}81\ \eta Q \times H}{0{\cdot}735} = 13{\cdot}33\ \eta\ QH$

If the efficiency is 80%, electrical energy $= 9{\cdot}81 \times 0{\cdot}8 \times Q{\cdot}H\ H{\cdot}\text{kW}$
$= 7{\cdot}84{\cdot}QH = 8\ QH$ kW

where H = design head in metres, Q = design discharge in cumecs and P = power generated in kW.

10·2. Important terms used in Hydro power :

(1) **Normal Water Level.** (N.W.L.) The hightest level of water in the reservoir that is maintained without any spill way discharge either with a gated or non gated spill way.

(2) **Minimum Water Level.** (M.W.L.) The level of water which produces minimum net head on the power units (*i.e.* 65% of design head H).

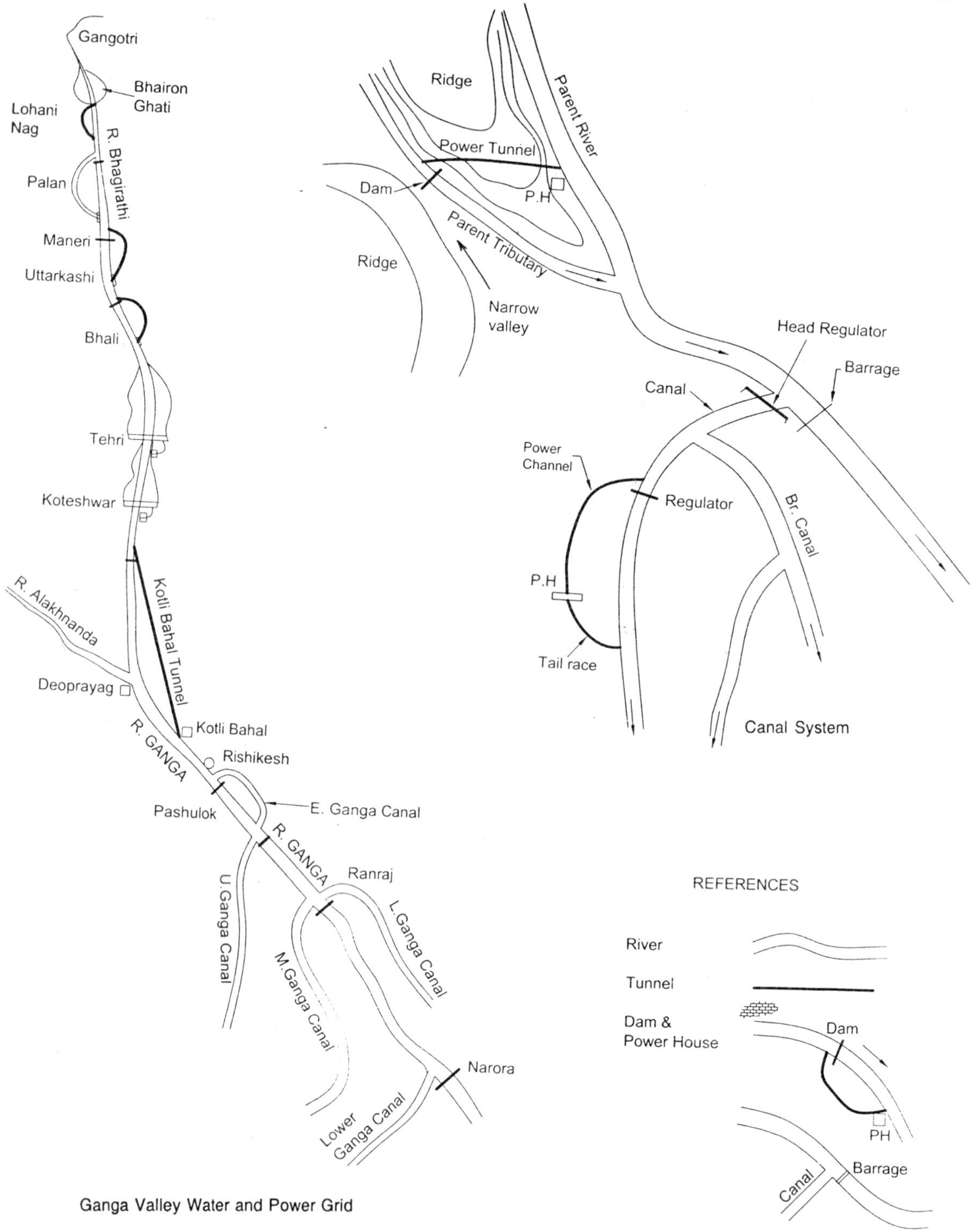

Fig. 13·157. Water and power resources Ganga river valley and its canal projects.

(3) **Weighted Average Level** (W.A.L.) The level above and below which equal amounts of power is developed during an average year *i.e.* 50% units between N.W.L. and W.A.L and 50% units between W.A.L. and M.W.L.

(4) **Design Head.** It is the net head under which the turbine reaches peak efficiency at synchronous speed. Generally the design head = W.A.L. – M.W.L. The difference of N.W.L. and M.W.L. is 125% of design head.

Rated Head. It is head at which the turbine functioning at full gates opening will produce a power output equal to be specified in the name plate of the turbine. This rated head should be equal to the design head of the turbine, so as to ensure maximum overall plant efficiency.

Gross Head. Gross head is the difference in the water level elevations at the point of diversion of water for the hydel scheme and the part of return of water back to the river.

Operating Head. Operating head is the simultaneous difference between the elevations of water surface in the foreway and the tail race, after making due allowance for approach and exit velocity heads.

Operating head = T.E.L. at fore way entrance – T.E.L. at tail race exit.

Net Head or Effective Head. The effective head is the net head applied to the turbine and is given by the difference of head at the point of entry and exit of turbine and include the respective velocity and pressure head at both places.

Installed Capacity at the Power House. The total capacity in kilowatt or million kilowatts of all the turbine-generator unit installed in power house is called its installed capacity.

Dependable Capacity. It is the load carrying capacity of the power house with respect to load characteristics during a specified time interval and is decided by the power factor capability and the load on the power house.

Load Factor. It is defined as the ratio of average load over a certain period of time to the peak load during the same period. Depending upon the period chosen, we may have different load factors, such as daily, monthly or annual load factors.

$$\text{Load factor} = \frac{\text{Average load over a certain period}}{\text{Peak load during that period}}$$

The area under a load curve is plotted (twice in hours as x-axis v/s load in kilowatt y-axis) it would evidently represent the energy consumed in kilowatt hour (kWH). Thus an annual load factor may also be defined as the ratio of the actual energy consumed during that year to the peak demand assumed to continue for one year.

$$\text{Annual load factor} = \frac{\text{Total yearly electrical units (kWH) produced}}{\text{(Max. Power demand in KW)} \times 365 \times 24}$$

The maximum load determines the capacity of the units, while the load factor gives an idea of the degree of utilisation of the capacity. For example an annual load factor of 0·6 would indicate that the machines are produced 60% of their yearly rated capacity (maximum production capacity).

Demand Factor. A consumer is provided the connected load of a certain rating (Kilowatts). He may or may not use the whole load at one time, as he may use a part of it. The ratio of the maximum demand at any particular time to the connected load is known as the demand factor.

Capacity or the Plant Factor. It is the ratio of average output of the plant for a given period of time to plant capacity.

$$\text{Capacity factor} = \frac{\text{Average load (average given period of time)}}{\text{Plant capacity}}$$

In other words the capacity factor is the ratio of the energy actually produced by the plant in any given period to an energy, it would be capable of producing at its full capacity during that period. For example if a plant with a capacity of 10,000 kW were to produce 40,000 kW when operating for 100 hours then,

$$\text{Capacity factor} = \frac{40,000/100}{10,000} = 0{\cdot}4 \text{ or } 40\%$$

$$= \frac{\text{Energy actually produced in a given time}}{\text{Maximum energy that can be produced by the plant during the given time}}$$

The capacity factor and load factor would become identical if the peak load is equal to the plant capacity *i.e.* when plant is allowed to be used upto its maximum capacity or there is no reserve capacity. However load factor would be different, if the plant is not used to full capacity. In the above example if the peak load is 8,000 kW (as against the station capacity of 10,000 KW) then,

$$\text{Load factors} = \frac{40,000/100}{8000} = 50\% \text{ as against the capacity factor of } 40\%.$$

The reserve capacity would then be

$$\text{Peak load} = \text{Plant capacity}/(1 + R)$$

where R = Reservoir capacity expressed in fraction of plant capacity.

$$8000 = \frac{10,000}{1+R} \text{ or } (1 + R) = \frac{10,000}{8000} \text{ or } R = 0{\cdot}25 \text{ i.e. } 25\%$$

i.e. at 25% *RC* ; Peak load × 1·25 = installed capacity.

$$\frac{\text{Utilisation factor or Plant use Factor}}{\text{Utilisation factor (UP)}} = \frac{\text{Water actually utilised for power production}}{\text{Water available at the river}}$$

If the water head is assumed to be constant then the utilisation factor would be

$$\text{UP} = \frac{\text{Maximum power utilised}}{\text{Maximum power available}},$$ the value of utilisation factor usually varies from 0·4 to 0·9 for a hydel plant depending upon the plant capacity, load factor and storage.

Firm Power. The net amount of power which is continuously available from a plant without any break on firm or guaranteed basis is known as firm power. This power should be available under the most adverse hydraulic conditions. The consumers can always be sure of getting this power.

Secondary Power. The excess power available over the firm power during the off peak hours or during mansoon etc. is known as secondary power. There is no guarantee for secondary power and it is supplied to the consumer on 'as and when available' basis.

Power Factor. $$\text{Power Factor} = \frac{\text{Actual power in Kilowatt (kW)}}{\text{Apparent power in Kilowatt-amperes (kVA)}}$$

The power factor can never be greater than unity. Its value depends upon the relationship between the inductance and resistance in the load. A load with very little inductive such as lighting bulbs, will have a power factor close to unity. The usual system load has a power factor varying between 0·8 to 0·9, but if various induction motors are installed in the load, then power factor may be as low as 0·5. Since the electrical machines are generally rated in kVA. The actual power developed depends much upon the power factor. This is the reason, why most of the electric supply undertakings do stress upon the consumers, to reduce their inductance and improve their power factors.

10·3. Major Components of a Hydroelectric Scheme

(1) **Forebay.** In case of diversion schemes, the fluctuation in the demand of water to the power house is balanced by a small reservoir in front of the intake when the demand is less

the water is stored in this reservoir and when the demand increases the maximum water requirement is fulfilled by this stored water. There is always a spillway is provided in the foreway to pass surplus water.

In case of reservoir, the reservoir itself works as a foreway.

In case of canals the canal itself control this fluctuation.

(2) **Intake Structure.** It is an entry of structure through which the water enters into the head race tunnel or head race channel.

(3) **Trash races.** Flat iron grid racks are provided in the entry gates of the intakes so that no debris or ice etc. may pass into the penstocks so that in turbine blades and other parts of the Power House accessories may damage. The racks spacing is kept according to the situation of coming water. The allowable velocity of water entering the trash racks is 0·6 to 1·6 m/sec. A floating boom is often placed in the storage reservoir so as to trap as much ice and floating debris as possible and thus to avoid their entry to the canal.

The forebay must be provided with a spillway or a bypass channel to pass the surplus water.

The following accessories are necessary on trash tracks.

(*a*) A trolley and gang way arrangement is required to clean the trash racks.

(*b*) Penstock closing gates with hoisting machines.

(*c*) Ice removal equipment such as floating booms should be provided.

(*d*) Silting basins are provided in the foreway so that coarse sand may be checked to enter into the intakes.

(4) **Penstocks.** Penstocks are huge diameter pipes which carry water under pressure from the storage reservoir to the turbines. Penstocks may be of RCC or of steel. Each turbine must have a separate penstock but for long penstocks or head race tunnels they can be divided at the lower end.

Penstock closing gates are usually provided at the enterance in the fore bay. The gates can be closed to permit repair of the penstocks. An air vent and vent pipe connecting the top of the penstock with the open air is provided down stream from the gate. Such a vent permits the entry of the air into the penstock as soon as the gates are closed and water is drawn off through the turbine wheels. In the absence of such an arrangement serious negative pressures will be exerted on the penstocks and may cause the penstocks to collapse. The water in the vent pipe should not be frozen, otherwise entry of air will be prevented. Before opening the main head gate, the penstock if empty should be filled through a bypass. So that surge of water may not damage the turbine.

Penstocks must be designed to bear the hammer blow due to sudden closing of the valves to check the entry of water into the turbines. Sharp bends should be avoided in penstocks because they cause loss of head and require special anchorages.

The penstocks may be burried on exposed. The exposed penstocks are supported on cradles and carried across ravines on trestles. The uncovered penstocks are costlier than buried penstocks but their inspection and repair is easy. The penstocks may be tunnels or ducts.

(5) **Surge Tank (Surge Chamber).** A simplest type of a surge tank consists of a cylindrical chamber open to the atmosphere and connected to the penstocks. When the load is rejected by the Power House turbines, the water level in the surge tank rises which decreases the head causing decrease in the flow u/s of it, while when additional load comes, the immediate demand is met by drawing water from the surge tank which increases the flow gradient and thus accelerate the flow from the reservoir. When the load is steady, the water level in the surge chamber remains constant at the level of normal hydraulic gradient line. A surge tank thus reduces the pressure fluctuations in the conduit pipe (penstocks) considerably and thus prevents

additional water hammer pressures from being exerted upon the walls of the conduit. The surge chamber should be high enough to prevent any overflow of water even at full load rejected by the turbines. Different types of surge chambers are used and the selection must be based according to the site conditions.

(6) **Outlet gates.** The outlets of the draft tube should be provided with gates so that the draft tube can be de-watered for repairs. If the span between tail race piers is not too high, limb legs may be used for this purpose. For larger spans steel stop logs or steel gates can be used with hoisting machinery for operation of these gates.

(7) **Tail race.** The channel into which the water is discharged after passing through the turbines is known as tail race. When the power house is close to the river or stream, then outcoming water is directly discharge into the stream while when the stream is far off from the power house the water is discharged by a channel from power house to the stream which is known as the tail race channel. It should be kept in mind that the high flood water should not enter into the draft tube in any case. The channel is so designed that it may not be got silted or scoured by the river water.

(8) **Power House.** The power house is a structure which carries the turbine, dynamo, switch boards, trash racks etc. when the trash racks are provided just above the penstocks. The sub-structure of a turbine may be a concrete structure.

(9) **Draft tube.** The draft tube is a conduit which connects the outlet of a reaction turbine runner to the tail race. Water as it emerges out of the runner, flows through this pipe of gradually increasing diameter and comes to the tail race level. The advantage of having a draft tube instead of letting the water fall into the atmosphere as

(1) Effective pressure head is increased by an amount $= \dfrac{H_2 + V_2^2 - V_3^2}{2g}$ as explained below

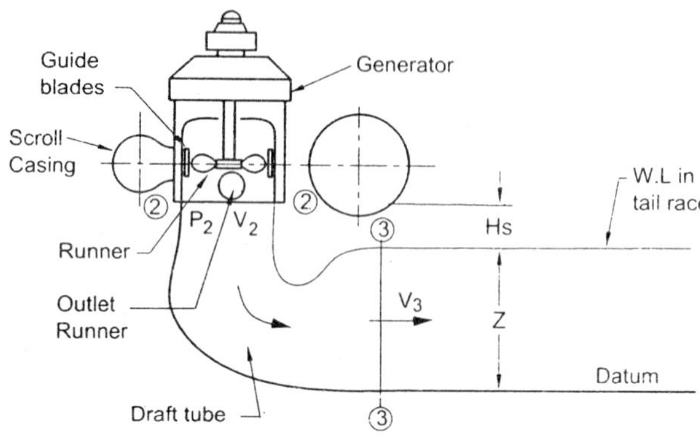

Fig. 13·158. Draft tube.

Considering the Fig. $\dfrac{p}{w} + z + H_3 + \dfrac{V_2^2}{2g} - \dfrac{Pa}{w} + z + \dfrac{V_2^2}{2g}$ or $\dfrac{p_2}{w} = \dfrac{Pa}{w} + \dfrac{V_3^2}{2g} - \dfrac{V_2^2}{2g} - H_3$

$$= \frac{p_2}{w} - \left[H_3 + \frac{V_2^2}{2g} - \frac{V_3^2}{2g}\right]$$

(w = density of water)

Hence the –ve pressure created at the outlet of runner

$$= H_s + \frac{V_2^2 - V_3^2}{2g}\ .$$

This should not exceed the vacuum pressure of water. So if gradually increasing the dia. of this pipe we are able to reduce the velocity $V_2 = 0$, then the net increase in head

$$= H_s + \frac{V_2^2}{2g}$$

(*ii*) The draft tube permits the turbines to be installed at a higher level than the tail water level, which facilitates the maintenance etc. of the turbine.

10·4. Hydraulic Turbines. Turbines are hydraulic machines which convert hydraulic energy into mechanical energy which is converted to **Electrical Energy** by the generators which are directly coupled with the shaft of the turbine and thus generates electrical energy.

In general a turbine consists of a wheel called runner which is provided with specially designed blades or buckets. The water with large hydraulic energy striking the runner and makes it to rotate. This rotation of the runner is passed on to the generator by coupling. This results in rotating the generator armature and thus producing electrical power. The hydraulic turbines are divided in two classes.

(*i*) Impulse or velocity turbine (*ii*) Reaction or pressure turbine.

(*i*) **Impulse or velocity turbine.** In impulse turbine all the energy of the water is converted into velocity before entering the wheel by expanding through a nozzle or guide vanes from the penstocks. The pressure of the water is atmospheric, hence the wheel must not run full, in which case it must be placed at the foot of the fall and above the tail race. The water may be admitted over part of the circumference only or over the wheel circumference. Pelton wheel is an example of such type of turbine.

Let V = velocity of entering water then $H = \frac{V^2}{2g}$.

Energy absorbed by wheel per unit weight of water $= H - \frac{V_1^2}{2g} = \frac{V^2}{2g} - \frac{V_1^2}{2g}$

where H = head of water and V_1 = velocity of escaping water.

The water coming out of the nozzle in the form of free jet is made to strike on a series of buckets mounted on the periphery of a wheel (See Fig. 13·159). This causes the wheel to revolve in open air, and water is in contact with only a part of the wheel at a time.

An impulse turbine is low speed turbine and is used for high heads of about 150 to 1000 m. Since it works at high head comparatively low discharge is required to run it for the same power.

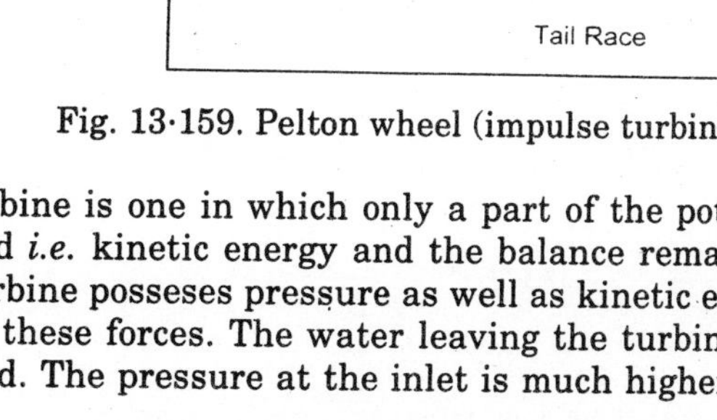

Fig. 13·159. Pelton wheel (impulse turbine)

(*ii*) **Reaction turbine.** A reaction turbine is one in which only a part of the potential energy of water is converted into velocity head *i.e.* kinetic energy and the balance remains as pressure head. Thus the water entering the turbine posseses pressure as well as kinetic energy. The wheel is rotated under the action of both these forces. The water leaving the turbine also contains some pressure as well as velocity head. The pressure at the inlet is much higher than the pressure at the outlet. Since the entire flow takes place under pressure, a closed casing is absolutely necessary, so as to prevent any access of atmospheric air into the turbine. Since the water flows under pressure through such a turbine, the wheels of this turbine are submerged and water enters all around the periphery of the wheel. Francis and Kaplan turbines are examples of such turbines.

Let H be the head of entering water and V_1 be the velocity of leaving water.

Then energy given by the wheel per unit of water weight $= H - \frac{V_1^2}{2g}$.

Difference between Pelton wheel (Impulse type) and Francis (Reaction type) turbine

(*i*) In Pelton wheel total potential head is converted into kinetic head for affecting the motion of the runner. While in Francis turbine only a part of it is converted.

(*ii*) In Pelton wheel, water strikes only a few wheels at a time while in Francies wheel, the water flows like that in a closed conduit. The runner is always full of water and than all the blade are simultaneously striken by water.

(*iii*) In Pelton wheel the water falls freely in the atmosphere, while in Francis wheel the water is taken upto the tail race by means of a closed draft tube, and thus the whole passage of water is totally enclosed.

The Specific Speed of Turbine

$$N_S = \frac{N\left(\sqrt{P_1}\right)}{H^{5/4}}$$

where N = Normal working speed of turbine in R.P.M.

P_1 = Turbine output in horse power

H = Net or effective head in metres.

Table 13·43. Specific Speed of Various Turbines

S. No.	*Type of turbine*	*Density of head in m*	*Specific speed in R.P.M. (revolution per minute)*
1.	Pelton turbine	over 150 (high heads)	10 to 35
2.	Francis turbine	25 to 450 (Med. heads)	100 to 300
3.	Kaplan and propelled turbines	1 to 70 (Low head)	300 to 1000

The selection of a turbine is done on the basis of head and load conditions.

14

Bridges and Foundation

1. BRIDGES

1·1. Waterway

(*a*) (*i*) Irrigation channels = bed width + water depth

For future development = bed width + 2 water depth

(*ii*) Rivers : (*a*) By Lacey's wetted perimeter $P_w = 8/3\ Q^{1/2}$

Q is discharge in cusecs and water way in ft.

or $P_w = CQ^{1/2}$, Q is discharge in cumecs and water way in metre.

$C = 4{\cdot}8$ normally but varies 4·5 to 6·3 according to local conditions.

(*b*) By *x*-section of the site—Three cross-sections of the site are taken, one at the site, other at 100 m u/s and 3rd 100 m d/s of the site. The water way is kept equal to span or width in the cross-section at H.F.L., average of the three sections is taken.

1·2. Depth of Foundation

(*i*) On the maximum scour depth (Say D)

$D = 0{\cdot}4272\ (Q/f)^{1/3} = 0{\cdot}9\ (q^2/f)^{1/2}$ where D is measured from top of H.F.L. in metre. Q = total discharge in cumecs and q is the intensity of discharge per metre. f = silt factor for the soil.

Depth of maximum scour = 1·25 D for straight reach

1·50 D for moderate bend

1·75 D for severe bend

2·00 D for right angled bend, nose of piers

2·75 D for u/s noses of guide banks.

Silt factor depends on the size of the particle, $f = 1{\cdot}76\sqrt{d_m}$ where d_m = mean size of soil particle.

Silt factor can also be determined by Lacey's slope equation

$$S = \frac{f\,5/3}{1844\,Q1/6} \text{ (F.P.S. units, } Q \text{ in cusecs) or } S = \frac{f\,5/3}{3340\,Q1/6} \text{ (m.k.s.) units } Q \text{ in cumecs.}$$

where S = slope of river which can be determined by observing water surface levels of the river in floods taken in one continuous operation, so that discharge conditions may not change.

Table 14·1. Lacey's Silt Factor *f* for different types of soils.

S.No.	*Type of bed soil*	*Particle size mm*	*Value of f*
1.	Very fine silt	0·052	0·400
2.	Godavary, west India silt	0·081	0·500
3.	Fine silt	0·120	0·600
4.	Fine silt, Krishna delta type	0·158	0·700
5.	Medium silt, Ganga canal	0·233	0·850
6.	Standard silt	0·323	1·000
7.	Medium silt	0·505	1·250
8.	Coarse sand	0·725	1·500
9.	Fine bajre and sand	0·988	1·750
10.	Heavy sand	0·290	2·000

Minimum Grip Length. The grip length is taken to be 1/3 of the depth of maximum scour for roads bridges, (as per IRC code) and 1/2 of the depth of maximum scour for Railway bridges (as per practice of Railways). The foundation depth should therefore be kept at least $1^1/_3$ of the maximum scour depth below H.F.L. for road bridges and 1½ of the maximum scour depth for Railway bridges below H.F.L.

It is further recommended that the minimum depth of embedment below the maximum scour depth should not be less than 2 metres for piers and abutments with arches and 1·2 m for piers and abutments supporting other type of structures. The well depth below the maximum scour level is called the **grip length**. This grip length is the real embedded length of the well.

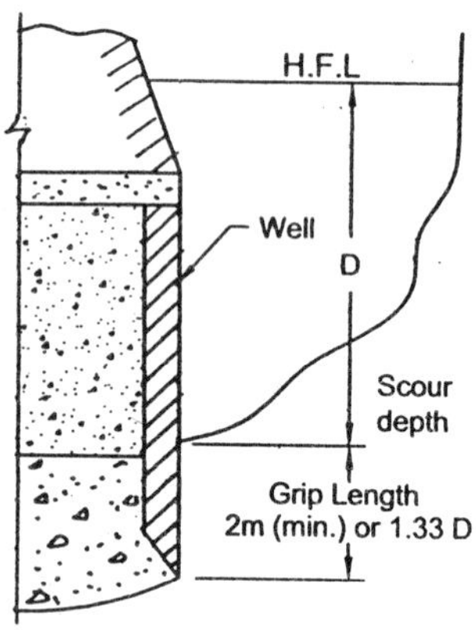

Fig. 14·1.

Maximum Scour depth on existing bridges. Existing water way is less than the regime width of the channel.

$D' = D(W/L)^{2/3}$ where D' = scoured depth when the actual width (L) is less than the regime width (W) of the channel.

D is normal scour depth when $L = W$. The velocity under bridge in such cases is increased by 10% and scoured depth u/s of the bridge by the amount of afflux.

Depth of maximum sounding at bridge site. A sounding chart is prepared at the bridge site and the maximum depth of scour at site is located from it. It may be taken as a normal depth of scour and the scoured depth may be adopted as detailed above for different type of reaches.

Scour depth according to Gale = $1{\cdot}67\ d + r$ where d = deepest observed scour on low water level and r = flood rise.

Foundations of Bridges

(*i*) **Foundations on the rock.** All debris from the foundations is removed and the surface is dented with chisels. For sloping foundations in rocks, the masonry should be anchored to rock by dowels.

(*ii*) **Based on bearing capacity of soils.** The following safe loads are taken in bridge foundations for different soils.

Table 14·2. Safe loads on Bridge foundations for different soils.

Type of soil		Load tonnes/m^2	
		deep found	shallow found
1.	Aluminium and silt	24	15
2.	Confined quick sand	34	20
3.	Fine sand	44	29
4.	Coarse sand	54	39
5.	Mixed sand and clay	34	24
6.	Hard clay	58	44
7.	Hard Pan	88	68
8.	Rock	195	195

(*iii*) **On loose soils by Rankine's Formula.** $h = P/W\left(\frac{1-\sin\phi}{1+\sin\phi}\right)^2$ where h = minimum depth of foundation in m below G.L., P = safe permissible pressure on base in kg/m^2, W = wt. of soil in kg/m^3 and ϕ is the angle of repose of the soil, subject to minimum of 1 min. This formula is used in small culverts where scour is not anticipated G.L. may be taken as the bed level of the channel.

(*iv*) **Well foundations.** Dealt separately.

1·3. Afflux. It is hearing up of water u/s of bridges due to insufficient water way.

(*a*) Meriman formula $$h_a = \frac{V^2}{2g}\left\{\left(\frac{A}{cd}\right)^2 - \frac{A}{A_1}\right\}$$

(*b*) Moles worth formula $$h_a = \left(\frac{V^2}{58{\cdot}6} + 0{\cdot}05\right)\left\{\left(\frac{A}{a}\right)^2 - 1\right\}$$

where $cd = 0{\cdot}75 + 0{\cdot}35\,(a/A) - 0{\cdot}1\,(a/A)^2$ app.

h_a = afflux height in ft. ; V = velocity of approach which is generally is the velocity of the stream, A = Natural water way, A_1 = enlarged area of water u/s of bridge due to afflux (take app. afflux to start) and a = contracted area under bridge.

Note : To convert the result in metre multiply by 0·3048.

(*c*) $$h_a = \frac{V^2}{2g}\left\{\frac{L^2}{C_c^2 - L_1^2} - \frac{D^2}{(D+h)^2}\right\};$$

where D = normal depth of channel ; L = normal width of channel ;
V = normal velocity in channel ; C_c = Coefficient of contraction and
L_1 = contracted water way of channel

Taking coefficient of contraction to be 0·95 and $\frac{D}{D+h_a} = 1$ (roughly)

$$h_a = \frac{V^2}{2g}\left\{\frac{1{\cdot}1L^2}{L_1^2} - 1\right\}$$ neglecting velocity of approach, $h_a = \frac{V_1^2}{2g}$ or $\frac{V_1^2}{2g}\left(\frac{1{\cdot}1L^2}{L_1^2}\right)$

where V_1 = velocity in the contracted section.

Length of back water curve (say l)

$$l = 2\,h_a \cdot \frac{dl}{dh_a} \qquad \text{...(1)}$$

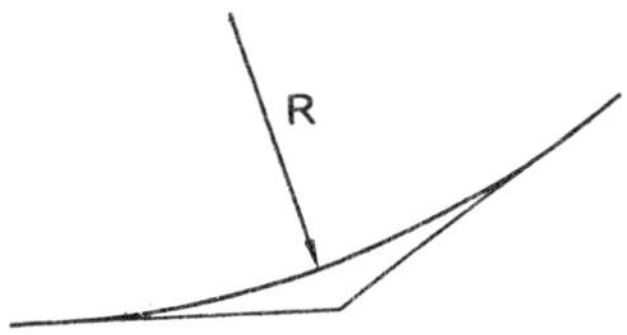

Fig. 14·2

1st method from Mannings formula

$$V = 1/N\, m^{2/3}\, i^{1/2} \qquad ...(A)$$

Calculate V the normal velocity, knowing other factors for a channel (here slope i is in fraction, m is hyd. mean depth) N is manning's coeff. :

Velocity along contracted section

$$= V_1 = \frac{Q}{(D + h_a)L_1} = \frac{A \times V}{(D + h_a)L_1} \qquad ...(B)$$

From equation (B) the value of V_1 can be calculated

$$V_1 = C_1\sqrt{mi} = \frac{1}{N} m_1^{2/3}\, i^{1/2} = \frac{1}{N} m_1^{1/6}\sqrt{m_1 i}$$

or

$$C_1 = \frac{1}{N} m_1^{1/6} \qquad ...(C)$$

from which C_1 can be calculated.

For contracted section $m_1 = \dfrac{A_1}{P_1} = \dfrac{(D + h_a)L_1}{2(D + h_a)}$ ...(D)

will give the value of m_1.

The slope of the free water surface $= \dfrac{dh}{dl} = \left\{L - \dfrac{V_1^2}{C_1^2 \cdot m_1} \div \left(1 - \dfrac{V_1^2}{gh_1}\right)\right\}^1$

So l the length of back water curve $= 2h_a \dfrac{dl}{dh_a}$.

Note : The height of u/s works and foundations of d/s works should be designed after keeping afflux considerations.

1·4. Free board or vertical clearance. It is measured from bottom of slab or bottom of bottom most girder of the deck or centred half of the arch opening to the H.F.L. or F.S.L. of a channel. It is kept on the following considerations. The afflux is taken into account.

(a) Upto 0·3 channels = 0·15 m These clearances are above the afflux level.

3 to 3 channels = 0·45 m

3 to 30 channels = 0·60 m

30 to 300 channels = 0·90 m

300 to 3000 channels = 1·5 m

For navigable rivers = 2·4 to 3·0 m

(b) For arched bridges (with afflux) : Difference from intradose crown to H.F.L. must be $D/10 + R/3$ where D = depth of water and R = rise of arch.

(c) The bottom of bearing must be at least 50 cm above H.F.L. taking afflux into account.

1·5. Clear roadway between kerbs and vertical clearance.

(a) Village road bridges	3·8 m (12·5′)	Single lane
(b) District road bridges	7·5 m (25′)	Double lane
(c) Arterial road bridges	9·75 m (32′)	Double lane
(d) Provincial road bridges and National highways	15 m (50′)	Four lane

The width of central verge where provided shall be minimum 1·2 m

(*e*) The minimum width of foot ways is 1·22 m (IRC) but practically 1·8 m

(*f*) Vertical clearance between the bridges from the formation of the road is 5 m. For foot ways it is 2·25.

1·6. Abutments and Piers

Table 14·3. Top width of abutments and piers for slab, girder or arched bridges

	Cement masonry		*Lime masonry*	
Clear span, m	*Abutment, m*	*Piers, m*	*Abutment, m*	*Piers, m*
3	0·40	0·50	0·50	0·6
6	0·70	1·00	1·20	1·3
12	1·00	1·20	1·30	1·4
24	1·30	1·60	1·70	1·9
40	1·70	1·90	2·0	2·2
60 and above	1·90	2·20	2·4	2·5

Table 14·4. Bottom width of abutments and piers

	Slab		*Arches*	
Type	*Abutment*	*Piers*	*Abutment*	*Piers*
Village road bridge	0·6 H	Vert. face	0·7 H	Vert. face
District road bridge	0·8 H	Vert. face	0·9 H	Batter 1 : 8
Provincial road bridge	1·0 H	Batter 1 : 12 to 1 : 30	1·4 H	Batter 1 : 12 to 1 : 24

H is the height of abutment above concrete to springing. A batter of 1 : 12 to 1 : 24 is given in abutments and in piers, a batter of 1 : 12 is given in larger piers and 1 : 30 in short piers.

For spans upto 3 m the top width of abutment is 75 cm and for above in road slabs is 83 cm.

Short piers may have a vertical side. The width of pier at foundation level shall not be less than 1/3 of the height.

Top width of piers for spans other than arches (IRC Class AA)

Span in m	*Upto 3 m*	*3-5 m*	*5-7 m*	*7-10 m*
Top width	60 cm	70 cm	80 cm	95 cm

Min. top width for simply supported spans should be such as to accommodate to the bridge seats with clearance of 15 cm between the bay. Length of the pier is usually made to exclude 1½ tunes the top width beyond the centre line of the outer girder or truss. The length of cut water (u/s nose) and ease water (d/s nose) are not counted in the length.

Pier caps. It's thickness must be minimum of 225 mm upto a span of 25 m and 300 mm for longer. The reinforcement must be 2% provided in both ways top and bottom.

1·7. Approach slabs. These are provided between road and reinforced decking slabs and are laid so that no live load surcharge is required in the design of abutments. This slab is considered to distribute the live load. When the span of the bridge is less than 1·0 m a road metalling 23 cm thick can do and 25 cm upto a span of 1·5 m.

For embankments more than 3 m in height, approach slabs are unavoidable or otherwise the thickness of the abutment should be increased to take equivalent surcharge due to live load.

The approach slabs on arterial roads should be 3·5 m wide and 30 cm thick with main bars 20 mm diameter placed at 1200 cm c/c and distribution bars of 16 mm placed at 30 cm c/c, every 4th main bar is to be bent up.

In village road bridges, the width of approach road slab should be 1·5 m and thickness 21 cm, main bars 12 mm diameter 20 cm c/c and distribution bars 8 mm @ 25 cm c/c. Main bars are placed parallel to the centre line of road. The sub grade of the slab should be well compacted. One edge of the slab rest on the abutment while the other end should rest on a toe wall.

1·8. Earth Cushion. Height between the top of abutment and road level when earth pressure is considered for design, the pressure due to weight of earth cushion will be taken as level surcharge.

Height of abutment	*Earth Cushion*
1·5 m	1·2 m
3·0 m	1·2 m
5·3 m	1·0 m
6·0 m	0·9 m

1·9. Wings. They are provided to retain the earth slope of embankments. Water wings are used in case of water sides of bridges in rivers and canals.

Canal wings. They are provided in the full height from foundation to the canal bank and is shouldered in the bank for about 1 m. They may be of the following types. The top level is either the springing of decking clab or arch at the top of the free board.

(*a*) **Quadrental.** Generally provided u/s of the canal masonry works.

(*b*) **Right angled** with return walls at right angle—Provided d/s of the canal masonry works.

(*c*) **Warped or flared.** Provided at d/s of canal works. They are warped from vertical at abutment face to cope with side slopes of the canal bank and is then shouldered to it at right angle.

River water wings. The top is kept either at the springing of the decking slab or arch or the top of free board from H.F.L. and then it is sloped downwards at natural angle of repose of the earth of embankment to a height of 60 cm to 1·20 m above the ground level or the normal water level as considered better according to site conditions. Where the height of embankment is less than 2-5 m, it must be equal to the half of the height or minimum 50 cm. It is then returned at right angle to the bank for about 1 m or so (IRC 1970).

Splayed wings. Wings which have an angle (30° or 45°) in plan are known as splayed wings.

The bottom width in sloped and splayed wings is reduced with the reduction of height by keeping it equal to height/3. The embankments are protected by pitching 1 m above H.F.L. keeping due consideration of afflux.

Land wings. Land wings are provided in canals to give a guide to the traffic. The foundation of the land wing is kept 1 m below ground level. Top width = height/12 or 0·45 m whichever is less and bottom width height/3. The road side face is kept vertical below wheel guard upto 1 m while the outer slope is provided in a slope of 1 : 8. The remaining width of foundation is offsetted towards road side.

Vertical joints. Vertical joints between wings and abutments are provided at their junction to allow any mutual displacement.

Sections of the wings. Top width = $H/12$ or 0·45 m whichever is less. Width at ground level = $0{\cdot}4h$ and width at top of concrete is $0{\cdot}5\ H$. Where H = height from bottom of foundation concrete to top of wing and h = height from ground level to top of wing.

Water face. Vertical upto bed of channel and then a slope of 1 : 1 upto foundation (in offsets of 12 cm), warping from vertical to 1/2 : 1 or 1 : 1 upto bed and then vertical upto foundation concrete. However in high abutments and piers, a batter of 1 : 7 to 1 : 8 can be provided.

Back face. Determined by the nature of waterface and bottom width. The backface is sloped in offsets of 12 cm. In warped walls vertical water edge has slope in backside and end edge having desired warped slope has backside vertical.

Note : The above section of wings and abutments are on the basis of thumb rules, must be checked for actual load.

1·10. Parapets and railings

Parapets. The height above the kerb varies from 0·3 m to 0·75 m. Top width is provided with a minimum of 35 cm and maximum 45 cm. These are generally constructed of brick work or of stone.

Railings. The height of railing above kerb = 1·1 m. The bottom rail should be not more than 15 cm above kerb and the adjacent vertical clearance between two horizontal rails should not be more than 0·30 m. Vertical posts must have a minimum distance of 1·5 m. The height of railing for cycle bridge must be 15 cm more.

Hill roads are provided with dry stone guard parapets of 45 cm in thickness and 60 cm in height with 15 cm thick masonry tops. Curves and embankments are also provided with guard parapets. Empty drums of the tar are also used by filling earth and placing upside down painted white.

In causeways guide posts are provided which are either of wood or steel angles, painted black and white.

1·11. Drain holes and drainage of road way. By a proper camber the water can be diverted to the sides. Drain hole pipe sleeves are provided in the sides of decking to pass off the rain water down.

1·12. Approaches. (1) **Vertical control.** A horizontal surface upto 4·5 m to 9·0 m is provided from the face of the abutment after which a gradient of 1:30 to 1:50 is provided ranging from village roads to arterial bridges.

(2) **Horizontal control.** A straight reach varies from 6 to 15 m subject to the visibility of road and type of road. Arterial bridges must be provided with 15 m straight reach. On curves the degree of curve must not be more than 6° with a minimum of 4° with speed limitations.

1·13. Bearings. (1) **Rigid bearings.** These are provided on abutments and piers below the slab or beams. The thickness and width is provided according to loads and type of deckings. The minimum width is 0·30 m and thickness 0·25 m for spans upto 3 m and 38 cm width upto 6 m. A tarred paper is also kept between the slab and the plate.

(2) **Sliding plate bearing.** A metal plate is rigidly fixed with the girder which rests over another plate which is also rigidly fixed on the bed block resting over abutment. The plate which is rigidly fixed in the girder slides over the plate fixed in bed block on expansion or contraction. A clearance is kept between the girder end and back wall over abutment for this temperature movement. The plate is of the anti-corrosive metal like phosphor bronze. These can be used upto spans of 14 m and a maximum pressure of 30 kg/cm^2. For larger spans and in case of girder bridges a sole plate is rigidly fixed underneath the girder ends which rests on another plate rigidly connected to the bed block or the lap in which slotted holes are made for the movement of the bolt connecting to the girder with abutment cap keeping the motion under control.

(3) **Roller bearings.** For large spans more than 20 m roller and rocker bearings are used. Rocker bearings can allow a slight angular movement, while roller bearings can move in longitudinal direction only. The rollers slide on the bearing plate. Rollers are solid and have diameters 8 cm to 25 cm.(Also refer steel structure)

1·14. Loads to be taken in design of bridges.

IRC class A-A : For roads leading to factories and National highways.

IRC class A : For roads leading to factories and Provincial roads.

IRC class B : For village and unimportant roads.

(*a*) **Dead Loads.** It is due to the load of the structure itself.

$$\text{Slabs} = 100 + 9L \text{ in lbs/ft}^2 \text{ of floor}$$

$$\text{T-beams} = 100 + 5L \text{ in lbs/ft}^2 \text{ of floor}$$

L = Clear span. For wearing coat add 40 lb/ft^2 extra.

(*b*) **Live Loads.** Loads due to traffic and vehicles moving over Live loads on foot ways is taken as 400 kg/m^2 for general pedestrians and animals. For foot ways having higher loads the loads can be taken as 500 kg/m^2.

(*c*) **Impact.** It is due to dynamic action of vehicles moving on it. It is generally taken as percentage of live loads. The general rule is IRC class A and B for spans 3 to 4·5 m = $\dfrac{4\cdot5}{6+L}$ for concrete bridges and $\dfrac{9}{13\cdot5+L}$ for steel bridges.

For spans below 30 m it will be 50% for concrete bridges and 54·5% for steel bridges. For spans above 4·5 m it is 8·8% more for concrete bridges and 15·4% more for steel bridges (L = length of span in metres)

For IRC class AA loadings it is taken as 25% extra for spans upto 12 m in concrete bridges and 23 m in steel bridges. After which it is taken according to above relations.

The impact is considerably reduced by the provision of earth cushion over the road slab or arches. The impact is reduced to half when a cushion of 60 cm is provided over the slab or arch crown, and is practically nil for a depth of one metre (cushion). But the dead loads are increased.

(*d*) **Wind loads.** It is horizontal load on bridges and is calculated as below :

(*i*) Deck bridges—area seen in elevation including railing.

(*ii*) Through bridges—one and a half time of above.

(*iii*) Half through bridges—Area as calculated in item (*i*) plus half area of the structure above railing. The intensity of wind load is taken as 20 lb/ft^2 (97·6 kg/m^2) in the areas where the velocity of wind is moderate and 40 lbs/ft^2 (195·22 kg/m^2) for the areas having high wind velocities.

Wind loads on moving vehicles can be taken as 200 lbs/ft^2 (297 kg/m^2) at a point 5′ (1·5 m) above the deck level.

Table 14·5. Wind Pressure and Wind Velocities

H (m)	*V (km/hr)*	*P (kg/m^2)*	*H (m)*	*V (km/hr)*	*P (kg/m^2)*
0	80	40	30	147	141
2	91	52	40	155	157
4	100	63	50	162	171

Table contd...

Table contd...

H (m)	*V (km/hr)*	*P (kg/m²)*	*H (m)*	*V (km/hr)*	*P (kg/m²)*
6	107	73	60	168	183
8	113	82	70	173	193
10	118	91	80	177	202
15	128	107	90	180	210
20	136	119	100	183	217
25	142	130	110	186	224

H = average height in metres of the exposed surface above the mean retarding surface.

V = horizontal velocity of wind in km/hr at height H.

P = horizontal wind pressure in kg/m^2 at height H.

The lateral wind force against any exposed moving live load will be as follows :

(1) Ordinary highway bridges 300 kg/linear m.

(2) Highway carrying train way 450 kg/linear m.

(*e*) **Centrifugal forces.** When the bridges is situated on a curve

$$C = \frac{WV^2}{127\,R}$$

where C is centrifugal force in tonnes acting normally to the traffic at height of 1·2 m above the road level, W = total live load in tonnes per linear m, V = maximum design speed of vehicle using the bridge in km/hr and R is radius of curvature in m.

(*f*) **Buoyancy.** If the bridge is founded on homogeneous impermeable strata no provision for buoyancy is made. For bridges founded on coarse sand a single buoyancy shall be allowed in submerged bridges.

(*g*) **Rolling stocks** (IRC)

Table 14·6.

Descriptions	*Loaded wt. in tonnes*	*Unloaded wt. in tonnes*
1. Single truck single deck	9·6	7·9
2. Single deck Bogie car	15·3	12·7
3. Double deck Bogie car	21·5	16·0

(*h*) **Horizontal forces due to water.** In case of trough bridges it can be calculated by the formula $P = 52\,K \times V$ where P is the pressure in kg/m^2 and velocity V in m/sec. It is rated for 6 m depth or more values of K is as under :

Square face	1·5
Semi-circular ends	0·66
Equilateral triangle	0·50
Triangle having nose angle more than 60°	0·70
Triangle having nose angle more than 90°	0·90
Arcs of circles	0·45

(*i*) **Surcharge due to live load (IRC-6)**

Table 14·7.

Abutment depth below road level (*m*)	*IRC class AA*		*IRC class A*		*IRC class B*	
	Single lane	*Multi lane*	*Single lane*	*Multi lane*	*Single lane*	*Multi lane*
0·2	26	15·4	14·3	17·2	8·3	10·0
1·0	15	9·1	8·5	10·0	5·1	5·8
2·0	8	5·5	5·1	6·1	3·0	3·7
3·0	6·8	4·1	2·8	4·6	3·3	2·7
4·0	5·5	3·3	3·0	3·5	1·8	2·1
6·0	3·8	2·3	2·2	2·6	1·3	1·5
8·0	3·0	1·8	1·7	2·0	1·0	1·2
10·0	2·6	1·5	1·4	1·7	0·9	1·0

(1) Length of abutment = 4·5 m for single lane and 7·6 for multi lane.

(2) Angle of internal friction of soil = 30° and wt. of soil = 100 kg/m^2.

(3) Resultant force acts in horizontal direction.

(*j*) **Velocities under water on bridges**

Sandy beds	0·7-10′/sec	Clayed bed	1·2′/sec
Pebble beds	3-3·5′/sec	Shingle bed	4′/sec
Stratified rock	6′/sec	Hard rock	10′/sec

(*k*) **Tractive forces.** Due to traction effects of moving vehicles caused by the application of breaks etc. It acts longitudinally along the centre line of road, which tend to over turn the abutment and is about 20% of total live load on span.

IRC class AA loading	14 tonnes	
IRC class A loading	5 + 0·4L	where L = clear span
IRC class B loading	60% of class AA	

(*l*) **Earth pressure.** Calculated as per loading on retaining walls, where the outer face of the abutment is scoured, the height of pressure is taken from the scoured bed.

(*m*) **Temperature, seismic and erection loads** are taken as per detailed calculations.

1·15. Types of bridges. (1) **Skew bridges.** The angle of crossing with road should not exceed 60°. The slabs can be designed taking the skew length (span along centre line of road) as span, though the stress conditions in skew bridges are somewhat tedious, yet the above criteria can be used as a fair one. The depth of foundation is kept more due to increased scour depth on skew sites.

Johnarry's Slab (S 145 and S 445). The slab designated as S 145 is a centrally loaded skew slab having simple supports on two opposite edges with 45° skew angle. The dimensions and reinforcement pattern are shown in Fig. 14·3 (*a*) and (*b*). The finite element mesh is shown in other Fig. The other slab designated as S 445 is also a skew slab of identical size, shape and reinforcement as that of S 145, but subjected to a uniformly distributed load.

EI-Hafez's Skew Slab. One of the skew slabs designated as Model no. 3 with 45° skew angle supported on two opposite edges and tested by EI-Hafez is selected for analysis. The over all slab thickness is 100 mm. The concrete cover from bottom surface of the slab to the centre of the main reinforcement is 15 mm. Fig. 14·3 (*c*), (*d*) and (*e*) shows dimensions, element grid system adopted and loading arrangement for the slab. The longitudinal and transverse reinforcements are represented in other figures.

Reinforcement in Skew Slabs (Dimensions in mm)

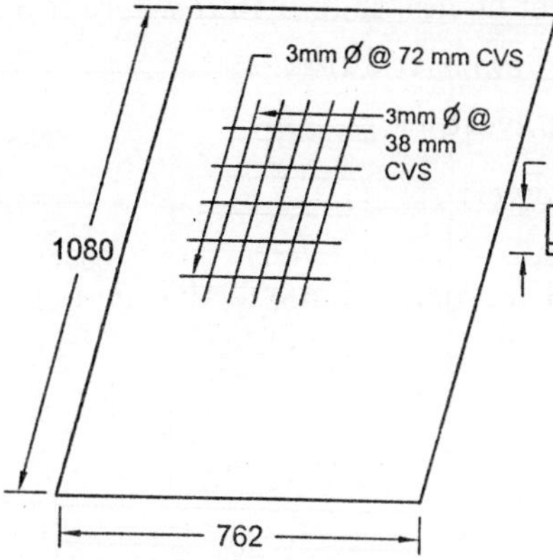

(*a*) Reinforcement for Johnarry's slab 145

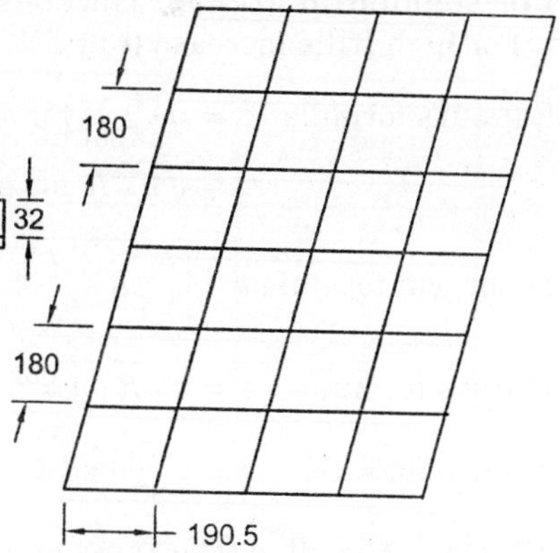

(*b*) Element discretisation for Johnarry's slab 145

Mark	Length	Dia.
1	2940	12
2	2240	12
3	1940	12

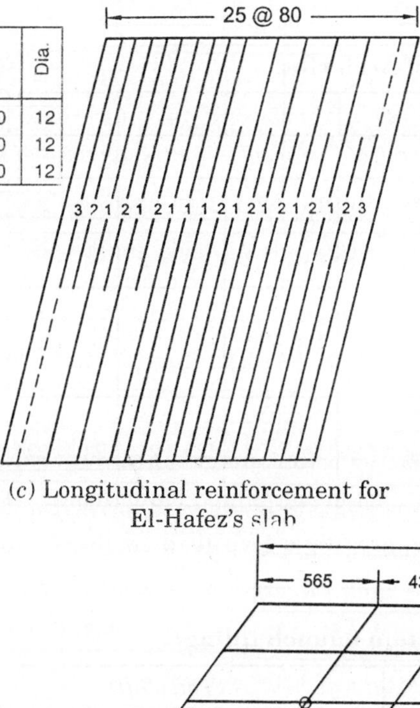

(*c*) Longitudinal reinforcement for El-Hafez's slab

Mark	Length	Dia.
1	1970	10
2	905	12
3	1545	12
4	1673	12
5	1970	12

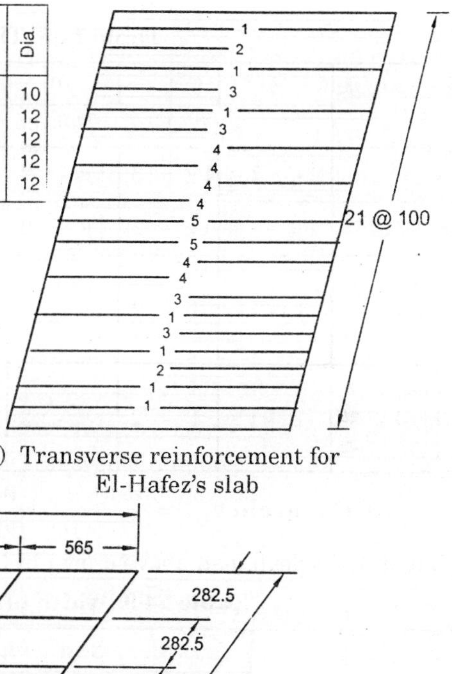

(*d*) Transverse reinforcement for El-Hafez's slab

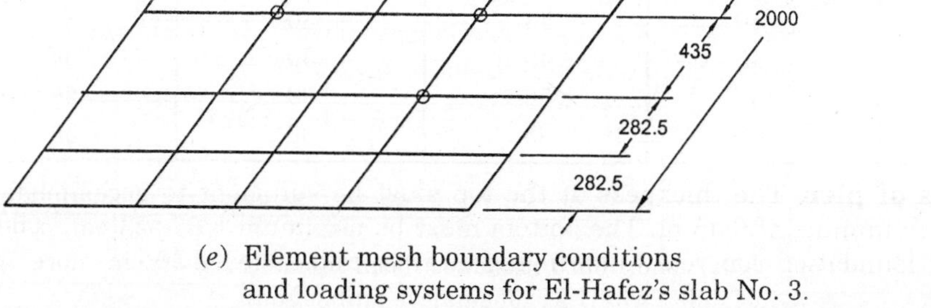

(*e*) Element mesh boundary conditions and loading systems for El-Hafez's slab No. 3.

Fig. 14·3.

(2) **Arched bridges.** Thickness of arch rib (t) in inches for masonry arches.

(a) **For segmental arches.** Thickness t should not be less than 0·45 R where R = radius of soffit in ft. For high frills increase it by 5%.

(b) Rankin's formula $t = \sqrt{1{\cdot}2\ R}$ for single span culvert

$= \sqrt{1{\cdot}7\ R}$ for multi span culvert

(c) Tyant win formula $t = \left[\left(\sqrt{R + \frac{l}{L}}\right)\Big/4\right]^{+0{\cdot}2}$ l = clear span ; L = effective span.

(d) Hurst's formula $t = n\sqrt{R}$, n = no. of spans.

(e) French formula $t = \left(\frac{l}{30}\right) + 1{\cdot}1$

(f) IRC class A loading (thickness of arch)

Seg × rise = ¼ span, effective span = clear span + 0·8 thickness of arch.

depth of haunch filling at pier $= \dfrac{\text{rise + thickness of arch}}{2}$

Table 14·8. Thickness of Arch ribs.

Effective span ft.	4	8	10	15	20	25	30	35	40
	(T – C) T = Thickness of arch at crown, C = no. of 9″ course at crown in ft.								
B. W. 1 : 3	1⅛ - 1½	1⅛ - 2	1⅛ - 2	1½ - 2	1⅞ - 2	1⅞ - 2¼	2¼ - 2½	2¼ - 2½	2⅝ - 2½
B.W. 1 : 2	1⅛ - 1½	1⅛ - 2	1½ - 2	1⅞ - 2	1⅞ - 2	2¼ - 2	2⅝ - 2	3 - 2	3¾ - 3⅛
Stone mas. 1 : 3 or c.c. blocks 1 : 3 : 6	1 - 1½	1 - 2	1½ - 2	1¼ - 2	1½ - 2	1⅓ - 1¾	1¾ - 2½	1⅞ - 2½	2½ - 2½
Stone mas. 1 : 2 or c.c. blocks 1 : 2 : 4	1 - 1½	1 - 2	1¼ - 2	1½ - 2	1¾ - 2	1⅞ - 2	2 - 2½	2¼ - 2½	2½ - 2½

(g) **RCC arches.** $t = \sqrt{l} + \frac{l}{10} + \frac{W_1}{200} + \frac{W_2}{400}$ where W_1 = live load in lb/ft^2 uniformly distributed, W_2 = dead load above crown in lb/ft^2.

Table 14·9. Width of wall to retain haunch filling

Span	*Base width*		*Top width*	
	Stone (cm)	*Brick (cm)*	*Stone (cm)*	*Brick (cm)*
Upto 3 m	50	34	30	34
6 m	45	45	30	34
9 m	53	56	30	34
12 m	60	68	30	34

Thickness of pier. The thickness at the top must be sufficient to accommodate both skew backs with a minimum of 0·45 m. The bottom must be minimum $h/3$ + 23 cm, h being the height from top of foundation concrete to springing of arch, and at least 30 cm more than top width with batter.

Rise. It must be clear span/2 for segmental arches. The masonry arches are not recommended in seismic zones over spans of 6 m.

Depth of haunch at pier and abutment = $\frac{V+t}{2}$; V = rise ; t = thickness of rib.

(3) **Submersible bridges.** Submersible bridges are generally provided on drains, which have a low perinial flow and a high flood flow which reduces in an hour or so. The bridge is designed to take perinial flow keeping all factors in view as in an ordinary bridge. The top of the bridge is not provided with solid parapets but only guide pillars are given which may be of wood or of concrete. So that flood flow may pass over the bridge. These bridges are provided with d/s protection works consisting of pitching and wire crates of boulders in bed. The slab is designed for buoyancy consideration having static water uplift and velocity head due to flowing water besides other loads.

(*a*) **Causeways or Irish bridges.** These are submerged bridges having no openings and are provided on nallas which remain dry during most of the year. In flood period the water flows over the formation level. The level of the foundation at crossing of nallas is lower than the level of the road on either sides. D/S of the causeway may be provided with guide bars. The formation may be of concrcte about 15 cm over boarder solling. u/s and d/s edges are provided with toe walls. Cross slope in causeway is equal to the slope of nalla subject to maximum of 1 : 30. The stream is not constracted at causeway.

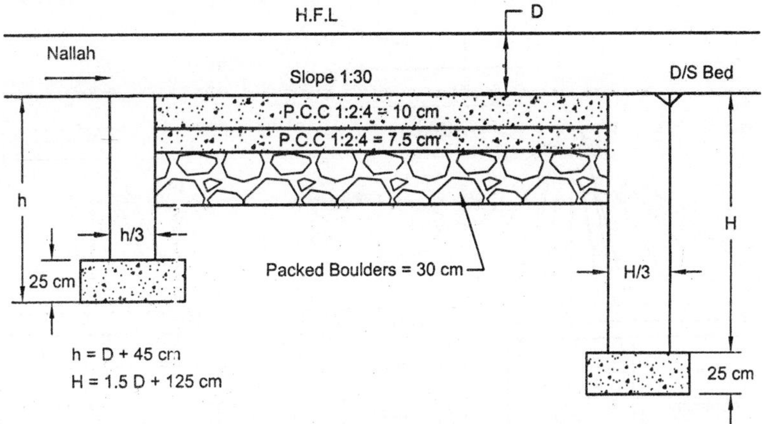

Fig. 14·4. Section of causeway.

(*b*) **Scuppers.** These are provided in hill drains and acts as a submersible. The perinial flow which is limited to about 0·1 cumec passes from an opening of about 0·6 m in span and about 1 m high. The top is covered by successive corbelling of the stones on roof while an earth cushion is given under the formation slab concrete. A catch pit 1 m^3 may be provided u/s of the scupper to hold boulder etc.

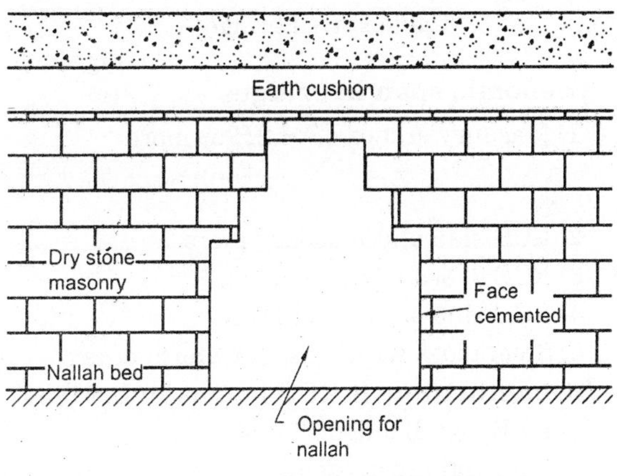

Fig. 14·5. Section of scupper.

(4) **Culverts. Pipe culvert—** Pipe culverts are provided to pass low discharges over nallahs. The joints of pipes are caulked with bitumen and hemp or with cement sand mortar. The joints are also founded on concrete base 0·3 m thick and upto centre half of the pipe in height, covering 25 cm on the sides. The end edges are provided with light abutments and wings as in ordinary culverts. (refer gul culverts in Irrigation section).

Wood crossings. On shallow streams temporary wood crossings are constructed to pass foot traffic. The trestle bends of two cross ballies are framed by tecking in between. These trestles work as a pier over which a wooden decking is made. The bridge is also supported by ropes. These are generally used in hill nallas.

Floating or pontoon bridges. Pontoons or boats are floated in a line (straight) reach at suitable distance apart over which wood decking is provided to pass traffic. Light vehicles can pass over such bridges.

(5) **Suspension bridges.** Two ropes are stretched across the river over two masonry or steel pillars on either side passing over pulleys. The ends of these ropes are anchored in ground. From these ropes suspender rods are suspended by a grip on the rope at upper end and the lower end is bolted to I or channel sections placed longitudinal to the ropes. On these longitudinal sections cross wooden decking is provided.

Cable Stayed Bridge

Prestress in Cable-stayed bridges. Unlike cables of suspension bridges, cables of **cable stayed bridges** are used as means of external prestressing for the deck. By suitable adjustments of cable post tensions, it is possible not only to counteract the dead load girder deflection, or moment, but also to partly counteract the worst live load effects. This may reduce the deflection, moment, curvative and extreme fibre flexural stresses of the girder.

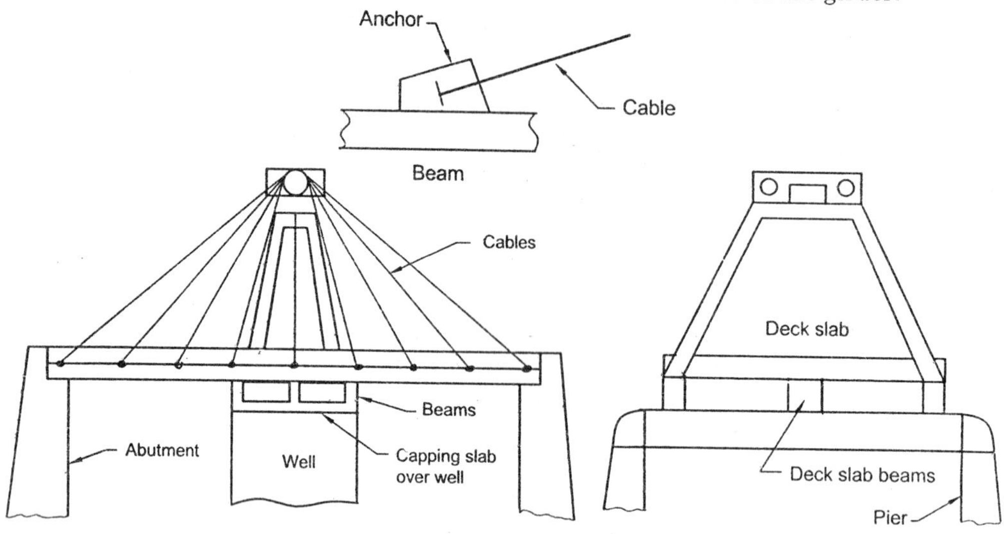

Cable stayed bridge   Cross section

Fig. 14·6.

1·16. Economic span in bridges

(1) Masonry arches : $S = 2H$ or more — L = clear span, H = height from bottom of foundation concrete to bottom of slab or bottom of key stone in arches.

(2) RCC slab and masonry piers : $L = 1\frac{1}{2} H$

(3) RCC T-beams and slabs : $L = 1\frac{3}{4} H$

(4) RCC slab on pile bents : $L = \frac{3}{4} H$

(5) Steel truss with masonry abutments : $L = 3H$

Strengthening of RCC beams in bridges :

(*a*) By Epoxy Bonded Plates

(*b*) External prestressing

(*a*) Additional epoxy bonded plates are fixed to take extra loads.

(*b*) Prestressed cables are fixed for taking extra loads.

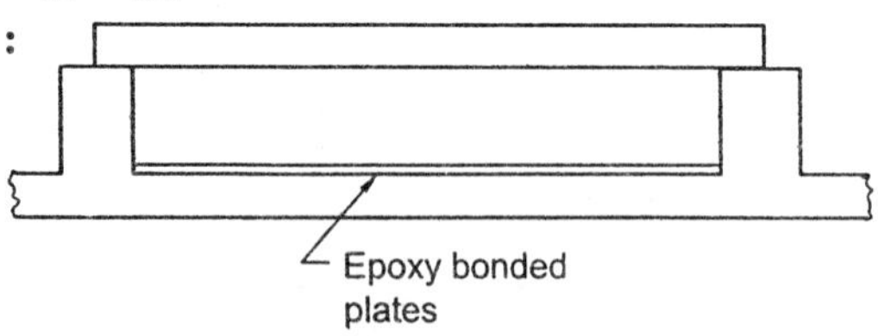

Fig. 14·7.

1·17. Technical Terms

Boil or Blow—Water perculating from ground.

Air lock—In cassion foundations a passage to the inside of shaft which is under pressure due to compound air for working.

Coffer dam—A temporary dam made to check the entry of water inside a work from a stream. It is made when a well foundation is low in river water or when the passage of flow is diverted to a bye pass channel in case of dam foundations.

Dump bell pier—A twin pier consisting of two columns connected by a web.

Gorge—Valley in hills or a narrow passage between hills.

Over bridge—A road bridge over an another crossing road.

Revetment—Material such as concrete blocks, wire crates or big stones used in down stream protection works.

Skin stress or friction. A stress or friction around the top skin of a shaft, well or member.

Under bridge—A road bridge constructed under an other cross obstruction, may be a road or rail line.

Via duct—A long and multi span bridge constructed over a dry valley.

Water cushion—A trough d/s of hydraulic works made by depressing bed to dissipate energy.

Through bridge—A bridge in which the carriage way is supported on the bottom of main supporting members.

Head room—Difference of level between the highest point of the vehicle under a bridge to the lowest point of the bridge decking under side.

1·18. Reference Tables

Equivalent load of vehicles on the backful of an abutment (IRC). In case of bridge abutments, the concentrated loads due to the wheel or truck load of any of IRC standard vehicles placed on the back fill shall be considered to have the same effect as equivalent heights of surcharge of earth as given below :

Table 14·10. Height of Surcharge of Earth in Bridges

Depth of abutment below road level (m)	*Height in m for the concentrated surface loads due to the wheel or truck loads for the following IRC standard loads.*					
	IRC class AA and class 70R loads		*IRC class A loads*		*IRC class B loads*	
	Single lane	*Mutli lane*	*Single lane*	*Multi lane*	*Single lane*	*Multi lane*
1	2	3	4	5	6	7
0·2	26·0	15·4	14·3	17·2	8·0	10·0
1·0	25·0	9·1	8·5	10·0	5·1	5·8
2·0	8·0	5·5	5·1	6·1	3·0	3·7
3·0	6·8	4·1	3·8	4·6	2·3	2·7
4·0	5·5	3·3	3·0	3·5	1·8	2·1
6·0	3·8	2·3	2·2	2·6	1·3	1·5
8·0	3·0	1·8	1·7	2·0	1·0	1·2
10·0	2·6	1·5	1·4	1·7	0·9	1·0

Table 14·11. Details of reinforcement for RCC slab for bridges for class AA loading upto 7·5 M road way (IRC)

Clear span (m)	Overall depth (cm) D	Effective depth (cm) DC	Max. dead load B.M./unit width kg/mm	Max. live load B.M./unit width kg/mm	Max. S.F. at edge/unit width kg/m	Main reinforcement At: Area of steel At sq. mm	Main reinforcement At: Dia. of bar mm	Main reinforcement At: Distance apart mm	–ve BM At_1: Area of steel sq. mm	–ve BM At_1: Dia. of bar mm	–ve BM At_1: Distance apart cm	Temp. rein. At_2: Area of steel sq. mm	Temp. rein. At_2: Dia. of bar mm	Temp. rein. At_2: Distance apart mm
1	2	3	4	5	6	7	8	9	10	11	12	13	14	15
1·0	20·0	16·7	245	2240	5,525	14·362	16	14·0	7·181	16	28·0	4·31	12	26·0
1·5	22·5	19·2	473	2840	6,981	16·755	16	12·0	8·378	16	24·0	5·02	12	22·5
2·0	26·0	22·7	768	3950	8,340	19·200	16	10·5	9·590	16	21·0	5·76	12	19·5
2·5	30·0	26·7	1275	5400	8,685	23·037	16	8·5	11·827	16	17·0	7·12	12	15·5
3·0	33·5	30·2	1907	6660	10,344	26·928	16	7·5	13·464	16	15·0	8·07	16	25·0
3·5	38·0	34·5	2728	8700	10,928	31·416	20	10·0	15·708	20	20·0	9·42	16	21·5
4·0	42·0	38·5	4162	10,060	11,110	34·906	20	9·0	17·453	20	10·0	10·47	16	19·5
4·5	45·0	41·2	4018	11,600	11,320	37·759	25	13·0	18·880	25	26·0	11·32	16	18·0
5·0	48·25	44·7	5882	12,900	11,716	39·332	25	12·5	19·666	25	25·0	11·79	16	17·0
5·5	51·0	47·2	7292	14,020	13,060	42·765	25	11·5	21·380	25	23·0	12·83	16	15·5
6·0	55·5	51·8	9171	16,500	14,000	46·850	25	10·5	23·428	25	21·0	14·05	16	14·0

(a) Compressive stress c.c. 1 : 2 : 4 = 52·7 kg/cm² (750 psi)

(b) Tensile stress of steel = 1285 kg/cm² (18000 psi)

(c) m = 18

(d) Crushing strength of concrete after 28 days = 150 kg/cm²

(e) No bars are to be bent up upto 2 m span = 2150 psi Specified bars are to be provided for –ve B.M. in full space at top for spans more than 2 m, alternate bar are to be bent up at specified distance from support (·17 of span).

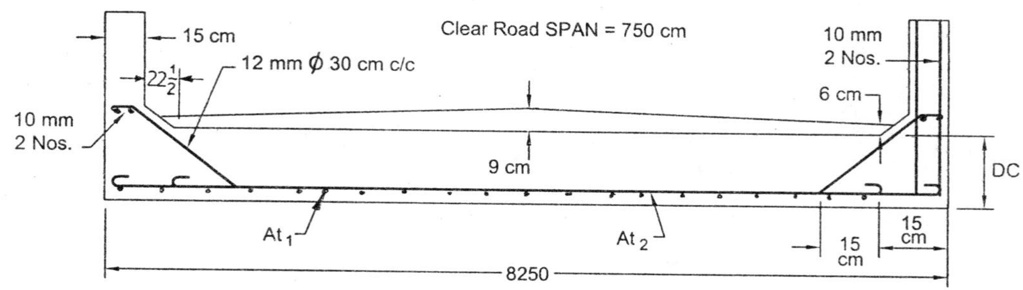

Fig. 14·9

Table 14·12. Masonry arches for culverts (IRC class A loading two lanes)

Clear span	*(m)*	*1·0*	*1·25*	*1·5*	*2·0*	*2·5*	*3·0*	*4·5*	*5·0*	*6·0*	*7·5*	*9·0*	*10·5*	*12·0*
Arch thickness at	cm	25	30	30	35	35	35	40	45	55	60	65	70	80
crown	in	9	13·5	13·5	13·5	13·5	13·5	18	18	22·5	22·5	27	27	31·5
Earth Cushion	cm	45	45	45	50	60	60	60	60	60	70	75	75	75
Haunch filling	cm	25	30	35	45	50	60	70	90	100	120	145	160	190
Abutment Top E_1	cm	65	75	85	90	100	110	120	130	155	175	200	230	245
E_2	cm	70	80	90	95	110	115	140	140	160	190	210	230	250
Pier top P_1	cm	40	50	55	60	70	75	80	85	100	110	130	150	175
P_2	cm	50	60	70	70	80	80	90	90	110	130	140	160	180
Found depth G_1	cm	30	30	40	40	45	45	55	55	60	75	75	75	75
G_2	cm	45	45	55	55	60	60	75	80	85	90	100	40	115

Abutment top E_1 = stone masonry 1 : 3

E_2 = 1st class B.W. 1 : 3

Pier top P_1 = stone masonry 1 : 3

P_2 = 1st class brick work 1 : 3

Found depth G_1 = cement concrete 1 : 3 : 6

G_2 = cement concrete 1 : 4 : 8 or lime concrete.

The masonry of arch must be in 1 : 3 cement mortar or 1 : 3 : 6 concrete blocks.

Table 14·13. Details of reinforcement for bridges class A loading

Clear span (m)	*BM/M width in*	*S.F. per M width kg-cm*	*Total thickness of slab excluding wearing of coat*	*Reinforcement*			
				Main			
				φ in mm	*spacing, c/c*	*φ in mm*	*spacing c/c*
1	2	3	4	5	6	7	8
0·90	1,17,500	5,558	18	10	8		
1·20	1,64,300	6,216	19	12	10		
1·50	2,00,000	6,328	20	12	10	12	
1·80	3,33,000	7,938	23	12	8	12	21
2·10	4,03,500	8,470	25·4	16	11	12	20
2·40	4,43,000	8,750	27·5	16	10	12	18
2·70	5,68,000	9,226	30	18	13	12	18
3·00	6,78,500	9,324	32	18	12	14	28
3·60	8,92,800	9,994	36	18	10	14	26
4·20	11,42,800	10,682	40	18	10	17	25
4·50	12,74,900	11,004	42·5	25	15	14	25
4·80	16,07,000	11,426	44	25	15	14	24
5·40	16,92,750	12,082	48	25	14	14	21
6·00	20,24,870	12,964	53	25	12	14	23
6·60	23,64,150	13,664	56	25	12	14	23
7·20	26,91,300	14,532	60	25	11	18	30
7·50	29,64,100	15,050	62·5	25	10	18	30
8·10	33,32,000	16,128	68	25	10	18	28
9·00	42,49,700	18,032	75	25	9	18	27

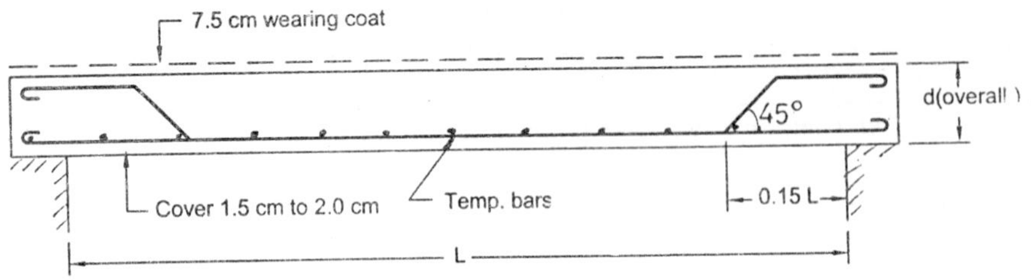

Fig. 14·8 Reinforcement for bridges class A loading.

Note : No bar to be bent upto 2·0 m span. Specified bars are to be provided (12 mm bars 20 mm c/c) for –ve B.M. in full space at top. Alternate bars are to be bent up at specified distances from its supports in spans above 2·0 M (0·17 of span).

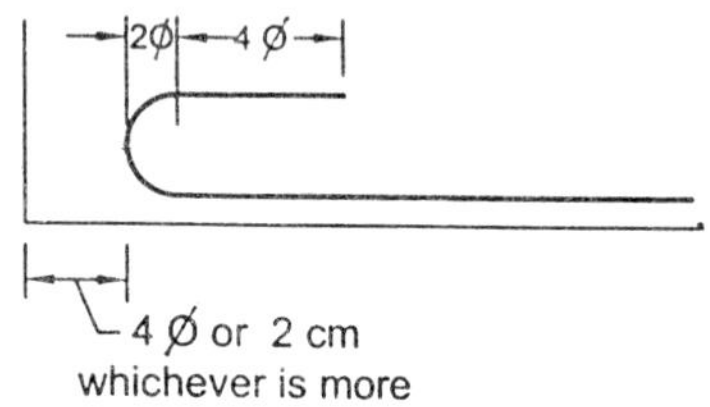

Fig. 14·9 Detail of bend.

2. BEARING CAPACITY OF SOILS

Plate load test. The loading plate which is made of a metal is kept in a pit excavated in ground at a depth equal to the roughly estimated depth of the foundation. The rigid plate is loaded with gradually increasing load and the settlement are noted for each increment of load. The ultimate bearing capacity is then taken as the load at which the plate starts sinking rapidly.

The rigid bearing plate is square in section of minimum 30 cm × 30 cm to maximum of 75 × 75 cm in size. Thickness must not be less than 1 cm to be sufficient to withstand effectively the bending stresses likely to be caused by the maximum anticipated load.

The size of the pit in which the test plate is kept should not be less than five times the size of the plate. A square hole is dug in the pit which is a bit bigger than the size of the plate so as the plate can be placed in it easily. The depth of the hole d is calculated by the formula.

$$d = D_f \cdot \frac{b}{B}$$

where b = width of the plate, B = estimated width of the foundation/footing and D_f = depth of foundation.

The plate is usually loaded by a hydraulic jack. The reaction of the jack is borne by—

(*i*) gravity loaded plateform or (*ii*) By reaction truss method

(*i*) In the gravity loading method (see Fig. 14·10) a platform is constructed over a vertical column resting on the test plate and the loading is done by sand fill gunny bags or big concrete blocks or boulder etc. The actual load on the test plate is applied by the hydraulic jack as a reaction loading only.

(*ii*) In the case of the reaction truss, the reaction of the hydraulic jack is borne by a steel truss, which is usually anchored at both ends into the ground soil through soil anchors, which are firmly driven into the ground by hammers. Guy ropes are tied for lateral stability of the truss. (See Fig. 14·11).

The hydraulic jack is operated by a remote control in which loading rate can be adjusted to the requirement. A dial gauge G known as load dial is provided on the hydraulic jack to read the applied load. The settlement of the plate is measured by a set of two, three or four dial gauges placed on the plate at 180°, 120° or 90° apart. The dial gauges which are sensitive to road upto 0·02 mm are fixed on independent supports so that they may not disturb during the test.

Procedure. Before starting of actual loading, the plate is preloaded with a load of 7 kN/m^2 (70 gm/cm^2) which is removed before the actual loading.

The plate is loaded in steps and the settlement after each loading is recorded. We have to wait till almost full settlement takes place. It is generally one hour for sandy soils and may as

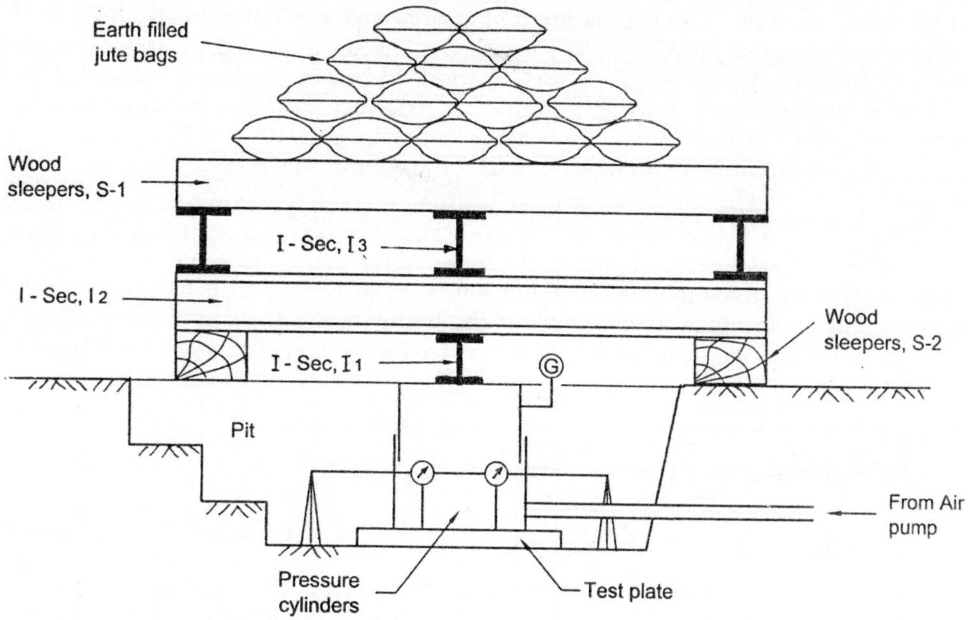

(a)

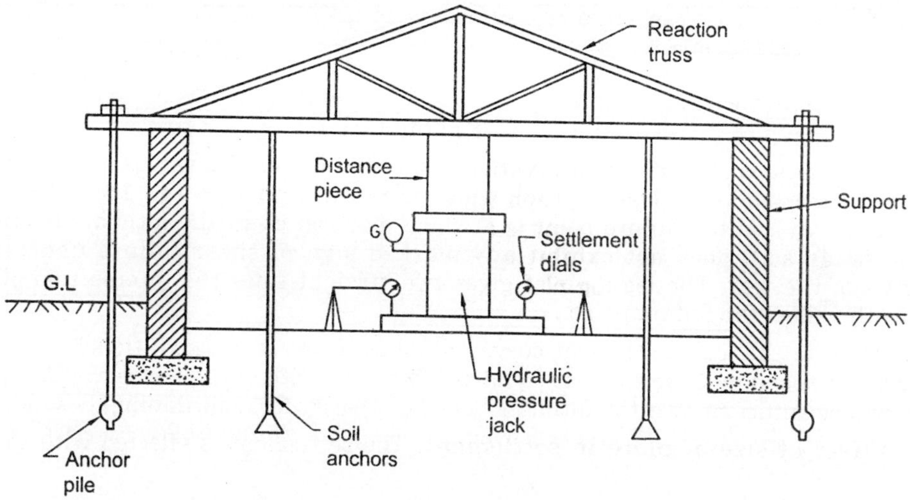

(b)

Fig. 14·10. Bearing capacity of soil.

high as 24 hours for clays. The load is gradually increased and the corresponding settlement is noted after each increasement of load. The load is increased till the failure occurs, *i.e.*, settlement increases rapidly without any extra loading, or the load becomes equal to at least 1·5 times the load to be used in the design. According to the I.S. code each load increasement should be about 1/5th of the roughly estimated load of bearing capacity or 1/10th of the estimated ultimate bearing capacity but in no case exceeding 100 kN (10 *t*) in any one step.

Since water table has a prominent influence on the bearing capacity of sandy and gravelly soils so if the water table exists above the level of footing it should be lowered by pumping and the bearing plate should be kept or seated after the water table is lowered just below the footing level. Even if on water table is located within 1 m below the base of the footing, the load test should be made at the level of the water table itself to ensure exclusion of the capillary zone above the water table, which otherwise likely to affect the load settlement curve on an unsafe side.

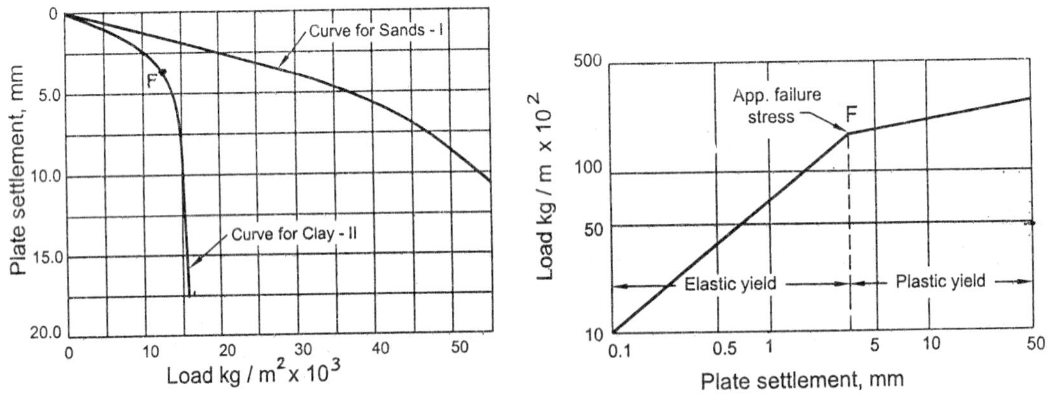

(*a*) Plot of simple graph. (*b*) Plate settlement mm log scale

Fig. 14·11.

The typical curves of the observation of the load intensities versus settlement are drawn on a graph paper and on a log-log graph which is recommended by IS : 1888-1962. In curve, II representing clay soil the failure point is *F* which may represent the ultimate bearing capacity, curve I (sandy soil) does not exhibit any marked sign of shear failure under the loading intensities of the test. The log-log plot gives two straight lines the intersection of which may prominently reflect the failure point.

When in the load settlement curve no failure point is marked, then the failure may be assumed corresponding to settlement equal to 1/5th the width of the test plate. A factor safety of 2 to 2·5 will be sufficient over the ultimate bearing capacity for determining its safe value.

Effect of size of plate in settlement. The settlement is effected with the size of the plate.

Terzaghi and peck formula $S_P = S_F \left[\frac{b(B + 0{\cdot}3)}{B(b + 0{\cdot}3)}\right]^2$ for sandy soils.

where S_p and S_F are the settlement of plate and settlement of footing respectively.

B = width of footing and b = width of plate

For clayey soils, the actual settlement of foundation (*DH*) is compacted on theoretical basis although it can be approximated by the relation $S_F = S_P B/b$ (for clays).

Bond (1961) has suggested the following relation :

$$\frac{S_F}{S_P} = \left(\frac{B}{b}\right)^{n-1} \quad \text{for } C - \phi \text{ soils (clay-sandy soils)}$$

where n is a coefficient depending upon the type of the soil. The value of n in the above relation can be determined by performing the plate load test on different sized plates. In the absence of such test data, the following values of n can be adopted :

Table 14·14.

Type of soil	*Suggested values of n*
Clay	0·03 - 0·05
Sandy clay	0·08 - 0·10
Loose sand	0·20 - 0·25
Medium to dense sand	0·25 - 0·35
Dense sand	0·40 - 0·50

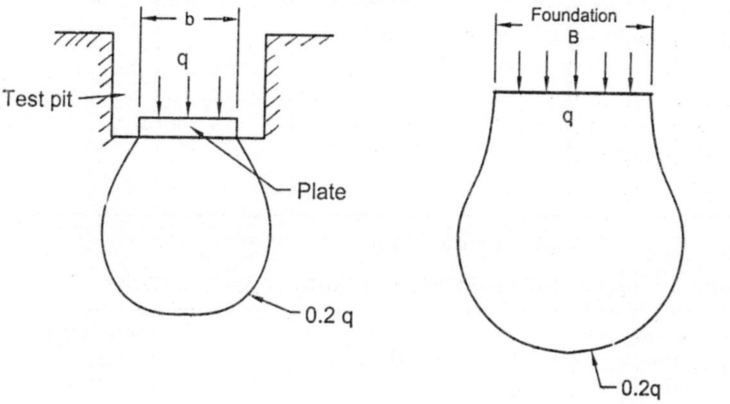

(*a*) Pressure bulb below test plate (*b*) Pressure bulb below footing

Fig. 14·12.

Limitations for Plate load test. (1) The test can be done only on uniform soils over a sufficient depth. As on ununiform beds their settlements are not uniform.

(2) The settlement is not the same for different size of plates, so the test should be taken with different size of plates and at different depths.

Standard Penetration Test (S.P.T.). This test is done usually in sandy soils. The device used for taking out soil samples is called a split barrel sampler. The sampler consists of a barrel having internal dia. 33 mm and outer dia. as 50 mm and 650 mm length connected to the end of boring rods.

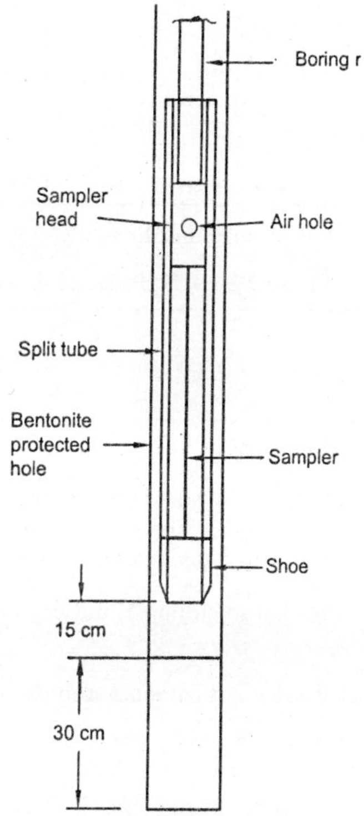

Fig. 14·13. Split barrel sampler

IS : 2131—1981 gives guidelines for performing the test. The test is performed on a clean hole 75 to 150 mm in dia. and supported on sides by a casing or by mud. The sampler is driven into the undisturbed soil below the bottom of the test hole by means of a 65 kg hammer falling freely through a height of 75 cm.

The sampler is 1st driven by 15 cm depth so as to seat the sampler and to bypass any disturbed sand at the bottom of the bore hole. The sampler is further driven into the ground by 30 cm more (total 45 cm) and the number of hammer blows required to drive the subsequent 30 cm of sampler *i.e.*, 15 to 45 cm is noted as Nob. which is called as **sandard penetration resistance (Nob).** During this operation number of blows for each 7·5 cm penetration are noted including initial 15 cm penetration. After this the sampler is driven out and sand extracted.

Table 14·15.

Penetration Resistance (N) Empirical correlation with Soil Properties for Sands					**Penetration Resistance (N) Empirical Correlation with Soil Properties for cohesive soils**			
Penetration resistance i.e., S.P.T. values	*Relative density or consistency**	*%age relative density*	*App. moist density in kN/m².*	*App. φ in degrees***	*Penetration resistance N blows*	*Consistency*	*Saturated density in kN/m³*	*Unconfined comp. strength (q_a) in kN/m²*
—	—	6	—	—	0	very-very soft	—	0
4	Very loose	15%	11·2-11·6	28°	2	Soft	16-19·2	25
10	Loose	35%	14·4-18·4	30°	4	Medium	17·6-20·8	50
20	Moderately dense	50%	16-19·8	32°	8	Stiff		100
30	Medium dense sand	65%	17·6-20·8	36°	16	Very stiff	19·2-22·4	200
50	Dense	85%	17·6-22·4	42°	32	Hard		400
750	Very dense	100%	20·8-24·4	45°				

* Given by Terzeghi and Peak ** Almost a straight line

Table 14·16. Safe Bearing Capacity (q_a) of Different Type of Soils as per I.S. Code

S. No.	*Description*	*Safe bearing capacity kN/m²*	*S. No.*	*Description*	*Safe bearing capacity kN/m²*
	Cohesionless soils			**Cohesive soils**	
1.	Gravel and sand, compact and offering high resistance to penetration when excavated by tools	450	1.	Soft sale hard or stiff clay in in deep bed, dry	450
2.	Coarse sand compact and dry	450	2.	Medium clay readily idented with a thumb nail	250
3.	Medium sand compact and dry	250	3.	Moist clay and sand clay mixture which can be idented with strong thumb pressure	150
4.	Fine sand, silt dry lumps easily pulverised by the fingers	150	4.	Soft clay, idented with moderate thumb pressure	100
5.	Loose gravel or sand gravel mixture ; loose coarse to medium sand dry	250	5.	Very soft clay which can be penetrated several inches with the thumb	50
6.	Fine sand loose and dry	100	6.	Black cotton soil or other shrinkable or expansive clay in dry condiition (50% saturated)	150

Such penetration tests are usually carried out at depth intervals of 0·75 to 1·5 m upto a depth equal to the width B of the footings or preferably 1·5 B. In case of gravely soils the driving shoe is replaced by a solid 60° conc.

When the test is performed below spring level (water table) care must be taken to avoid entry of water through the bottom of the bore hole as this would tend to loosen the sand due to upward seepage pressure. Water on the other hand, should be added in the bore hole as necessary, to maintain the water table level in the bore hole, so as to balance any excess pore water pressure.

Bearing Capacity of Soils—Analytical Method

Shallow Foundations—When $D_f < B$

Deep Foundations—When $D_f > B$

Terzaghi's general equation for bearing capacity of soils

$$q_f = \underset{I}{\underline{C.(N_c)}} \times \underset{II}{\underline{\gamma . D_f .(N_q)}} \times \underset{III}{\underline{1/2\,\gamma\,\beta(N_y)}}$$

where c = shear strength of soil (cohesion)

y = self wt. of soil

D_f = depth of foundation

1st term is the contribution due to constant component of shear strength (c) of the soil.

2nd term is the contribution due to surcharge of soil over the footing.

3rd term is the contribution due to bearing capacity from the self wt. of the soil.

Table 14·17. Terzaghi's Bearing Capacity Factors (Strip values)

Angle of repose	*General shear failure*			*Local shear failure*		
ϕ	H_c	N_q	N_y	N_c	N_q	N_y
0	5·7	1·0	0·0	5·7	1·0	0·0
5	7·3	1·6	0·5	6·7	1·4	0·2
10	9·6	2·7	1·2	8·0	1·9	0·5
15	12·9	4·4	2·5	9·7	2·7	0·9
20	17·7	7·4	5·0	11·8	3·9	1·7
25	25·1	12·7	9·7	14·8	5·6	3·2
30	37·2	22·8	19·7	19·0	8·3	5·7
34	52·6	36·5	35·0	23·7	11·7	9·0
35	57·8	41·4	42·4	25·2	12·6	10·1
40	95·7	81·3	100·4	34·9	20·5	18·8
45	172·3	173·3	297·5	51·2	35·1	37·7
48	258·3	287·9	780·1	66·8	50·5	60·4
50	347·5	415·1	1153·2	81·3	65·6	87·1

Expressions for Terzaghi's Constants given by Prandtl (1921) and Reissner (1924)

$$N_q = \left[\tan^2\left(45° + \frac{\phi}{2}\right)\right] \times \left[e^{\pi \tan \phi}\right]$$

$$N_c = (N_q - 1) \cot \phi$$

$$N_y = 1{\cdot}8\,(N_q - 1) \tan \phi$$

The values of N_q, N_c and N_y as obtained from three equations at different values of ϕ are lesser than those of Terzaghi and one plotted as below.

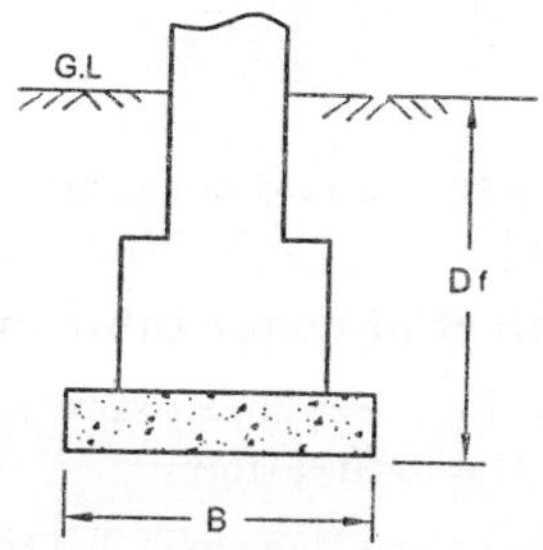

Fig. 14·14.

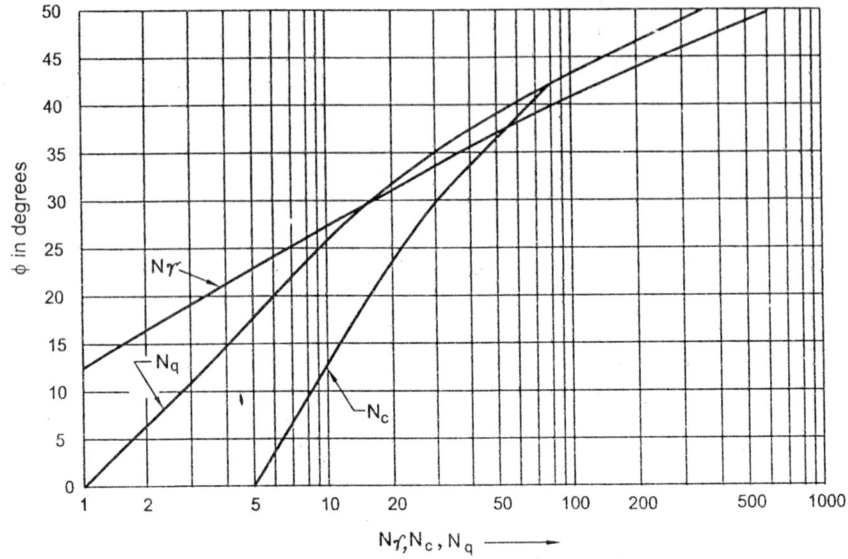

Fig. 14·15.

When $\phi = 0$ such as for saturated soils the value for N_c in the above equation becomes ∞ and hence indeterminate in such case the ultimate bearing capacity is determined by the Prandtl equation given below.

$q_f = 5{\cdot}14$ Cu + $\gamma\ D_f$ in saturated clays under undrained conditions taking value of $N_c = 5{\cdot}14$ and $\phi = 0$. (Cu ultimate shear strength of soil)

Terzaghi gave following shape factors to be multiplied in strip values of q_f, N_y and N_y to obtain the values of the bearing capacity factors as relevant

(*a*) For rectangular footings

$$N_{c(v)} = \left(1 + 0{\cdot}3\frac{B}{L}\right)N_c$$

$$N_{y(v)} = \left(1 - 0{\cdot}2\frac{B}{L}\right)N_y$$

$$N_{q(v)} = N_q$$

For square footings (*i.e.* $B/L = 1$)

$$N_{cs} = 1{\cdot}3\ N_L$$

$$N_{y(s)} = 0{\cdot}8\ N_y$$

$$N_{q(s)} = N_q$$

For circulated footings

$$N_{c(c)} = 1{\cdot}3\ N_c$$

$$N_{y(c)} = 0{\cdot}8\ N_y$$

$$N_{q(c)} = N_q$$

These values of shape factors were given by Terzaghi and are still relevant and are widely used.

Effect of water table on the coefficients N_q and N_y

In the Terzaghi's expression for q_f, it is assumed that the water table is sufficiently below the foot of the foundation.

There are two cases for the position of the water table below foundation.

Case (1) : When water table is below the foundation.

In this case b may be upto zero *i.e.* water table (W.T) upto the base of foundation.

In this case there is no effect on the value of N_q and N_y will be effected.

Case (2) : When water table is above the foot of foundation.

In such cases submerged unit wt. of soil is 1/2 of the bulk unit wt. y of the soil.

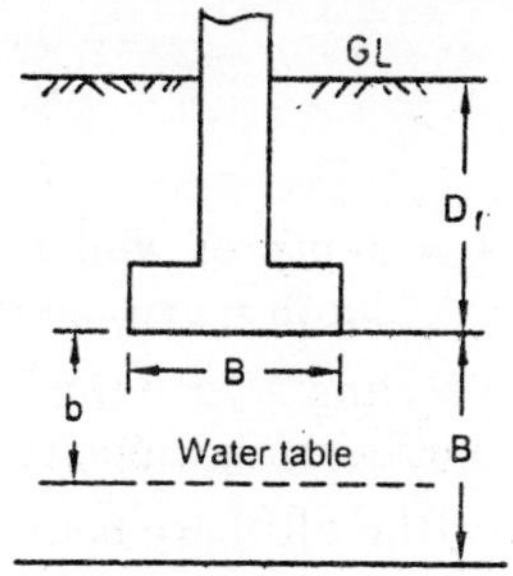

Fig. 14·16.

Teng's Water table correction factors :

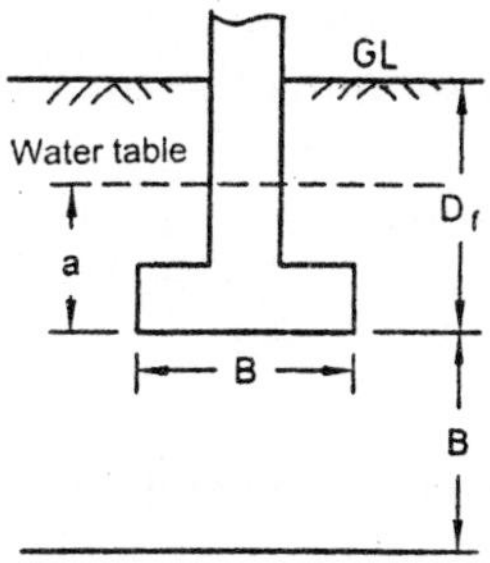

Fig. 14·17.

Reduction factor due to water table (W.T.) for N_y term R

$$w_y = \left(0{\cdot}5 + \frac{0{\cdot}5b}{B}\right) \le 1.$$

where $b = 0$ *i.e.* water table is at base of footing, then $Rw_y = 0{\cdot}5$ (full reduction)

Reduction factor due to W.T. for N_q term

$$Rw_2 = \left(1 - \frac{0{\cdot}5a}{D_f}\right) \le 1.$$

When $a = D_f$ *i.e.* water table is at ground level then $Rw_q = 0{\cdot}5$ (full reduction).

Skemptons Design for Shallow and Deep Footings in Cohesive Soils ($\phi_4 = 0$)

For purely cohesive soils, such as saturated clays existing under undrained conditions, Skempton has related this ultimate bearing capacity to a factor say N'_c which depends upon D_f/B ratio. The equation is given as $q_f = Cu\ N'_c + y.D_f$ for $\phi_u = 0$. This equation used in purely cohesive soils and particularly in deep foundation ($D_f > B$).

The values of N'_c for different values of D_f/B rates are governed by the following equations :

(*i*) For strip footing :

$$N'_c = 5\left[1 + 0{\cdot}2\frac{D_f}{B}\right]$$ with a maximum value of 7·5 and minimum value of 5·14.

(*ii*) For rectangular footings

$$N'_{c(v)} = N'_c \times \left[1 + \frac{0{\cdot}2B}{L}\right]$$ where N'_c is given by the above equation.

(*iii*) For square or circular footing

$N'_{c(s)} = N'_c \times 1{\cdot}2$ where N'_c is again given by the above equation.

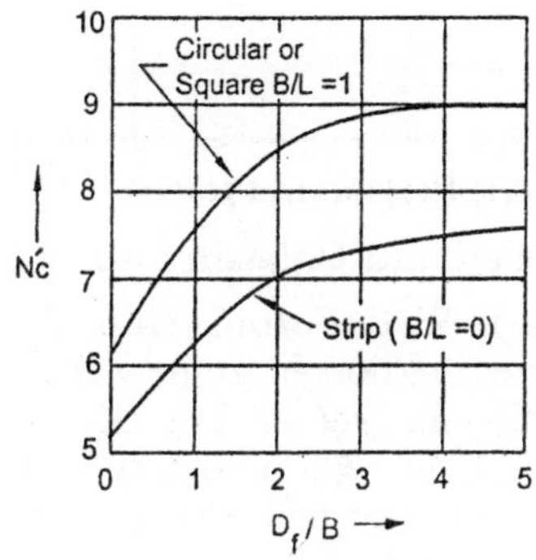

Fig. 14·18.

The values of N'_c for different values of D_f/B are plotted in the Fig. 14·18.

Ultimate Safe bearing Capacity of a Foundation well—

$$Q_f = q_f.A_b + f_s A_s$$

The values of q_f can be computed by using the Basic Terzaghi's equation with correlation for the shape of the footing. For circular well in granular soils, the value of q_f can be written as—

$$q_f = [1{\cdot}3C\,N_c + 7D_f.N_q + 0{\cdot}6\,y\,B.N_y]$$

where B = width of footing or diameter of well.

D_f = depth of well foundation *i.e.* depth of bottom of well from the maximum scour depth = grip length.

N_c, N_q and N_y are the Terzaghi's bearing capacity factors and which can be obtained from the formula of bearing capacity of soils given by Terzaghi

Now the ultimate bearing capacity (Q_f) can be written as below :

$$Q_f = [1{\cdot}3\,C.N_c + yD_f.\,N_q + 0{\cdot}6\,yB.N_y] \times \left(\frac{\pi B^2}{4}\right) + \left[f_s.2\pi.\frac{B}{2}.D_f\right]$$

The values of q_f for cohesion soils may be obtained by skemptons equation given in the chapter of bearing capacity of soils.

The value of skin friction (f_s) averages over the cylinderical length of the well can be computed by load tests. Its approximate value can also be computed by using the equation

$$f_s = K_0\,\bar{q}_0.\tan\delta' \quad \text{or} \quad f_s = K_0\left(\frac{y\,D_f}{2}\right)\tan\delta'$$

where K_0 = coefficient of earth pressure at rest. It is also represented by K_R.

A conservative value of K_0 is taken as 0·45 for wells.

δ' = angle of friction between the well surface and the surrounding sand and is equal to 0·75 ϕ (δ' is the angle of friction)

The value of skin stress (f_s) also gives the resistance which is expected to be encountered during sinking of well through the soil.

Table 14·18. Values of Skin Friction (f_s) for well foundation (Terzaghi and Peck 1948)

S. No.	*Type of soil*	f_s *in kN/m*^{2}
1.	Silt and soft clay	7·25-30
2.	Very stiff clay	48-192
3.	Loose sand	12-33
4.	Dense sand	33-86
5.	Dense gravel	48-96

3. BRIDGE FOUNDATIONS

Well and Caisson Foundations

3·1. Well Foundation. A curb of reinforced concrete or timber (for wells upto 1·8 m diameter with kikar or gular wood) is laid a bit above the water table. The outer dia. of the curb is about 50 mm greater than the outer diameter of the stiening so that the later may not stick to the sides of soil. The masonry in the stiening of well is completed about one metre above the ground level upto a working platform. The due time for setting of concrete of the curb and masonry of steining is given. The hoop iron strips of 75 mm × 6 mm must be provided at suitable interval in the centre of the steining to reinforce it and must be covered with 15 cm thick concrete 1 : 2 : 4. The steining masonry will advance up as sinking goes on.

Sinking of the well is done by scooping or grabbing out soil from the well by iron scoopers (locally known as Jham) or by dredger operated by cranes or winch in large works. The jham can be operated by manual labour. The scooper or the dredger has lever arrangements in its bottom, so that by giving up and down motions to the scooper by a rope, the soil fills in the downward motion and is not allowed to go out by the valve in upward motion. (The valve closes by the load of the soil in the scooper) and thus by giving repeated up and down motions the scooper is filled full and is then lifted up and emptied out side by opening of the valve. The process is repeated till the well reaches upto desired depth. During sinking dewatering by a pump helps in sinking as the water brings soil particles with it leaving a hollow below the curb and the well sinks due to load over it. The top of steining is loaded with earth filled jute bags or **kent ledge** (filling cc blocks in angle iron frames) which help in sinking and also controls the verticality of the well, which is checked by a plumb. When the desired top of the well is achieved a false masonry is done over the steining in a lean cement mortar to facilitate in further operations. A cavity is made below the curb by the scooper which is filled (plugged) by concrete upto about 0·3 m above the curb by a funnel shaped vessel (Details in cement concrete). Sand is then filled upto about one meter below the top of steining over which concrete is again filled upto 0·15 m below the top (to make a key for the capping slab). Before plugging of sand water tightness of the bottom plug is checked by dewatering a bit below the water table. If the level of water in well increases, the plug is not water tight and should further be plugged by a rich mortar.(Refer Fig. 14·19)

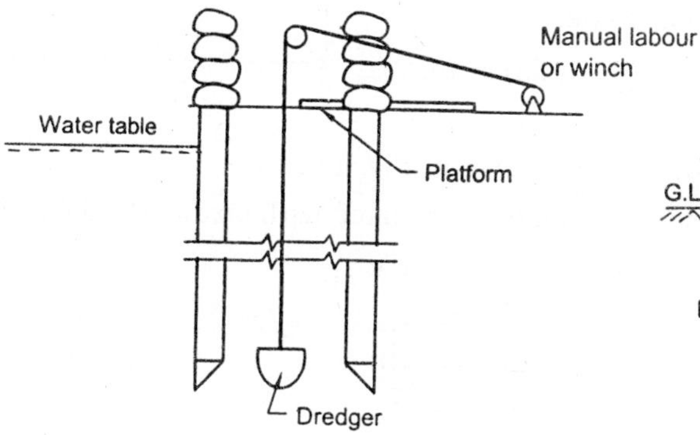

(*a*) Water table

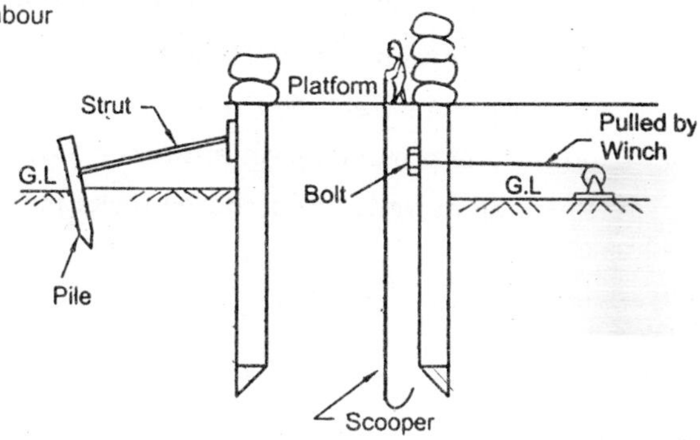

(*b*) Tilt rectification

Fig. 14·19.

The wells are founded on mota (a stiff clay layer) or is sunk so deep so as to retain its position by friction.

Table 14·19. Thickness of steining of wells in cm (Masonry)

Depth of well from G.L. in m	*Dia. of well in m*						*Remarks*
	1·5	*3·0*	*4·5*	*6·0*	*9·0*	*12·0*	
3·0	40	40	40	50	50	50	1. Where high skin friction is expected the thickness may be increased.
6·0	40	50	50	50	60	70	
9·0	50	50	50	60	70	90	
12·0	50	60	60	70	80	100	2. For R.R. masonry the thickness must be increased by 10 to 15 cm.
18·0	60	60	70	80	90	100	
24·0	60	70	80	90	—	—	
30·0	70	80	90	110	—	—	
36·0	70	90	100	—	—	—	

RCC steining should not be less than 45 cm or less than the following for circular wells.

(a) For sandy soil —Thickness = $1 \cdot 0\left(\frac{H}{100}+\frac{D}{10}\right)$

(b) For soft clay —Thickness = $1 \cdot 1\left(\frac{H}{100}+\frac{D}{10}\right)$

(c) For hard strata —Thickness = $1 \cdot 25\left(\frac{H}{100}+\frac{D}{10}\right)$

(d) For boulder, kankar, slate —Thickness = $1 \cdot 25\left(\frac{H}{100}+\frac{D}{8}\right)$

(e) For rectangular or twin D shaped —Thickness = $C\left(\frac{H}{100}+\frac{L}{10}\right)$

C for sandy soil = 1·0, soft clay = 1·1, Hard clay = 1·15 and for boulder, stones/pebbles etc. = 1·2.

D = external dia. of well

H = depth of sinking below bed

L = Longer site of double D end to end.

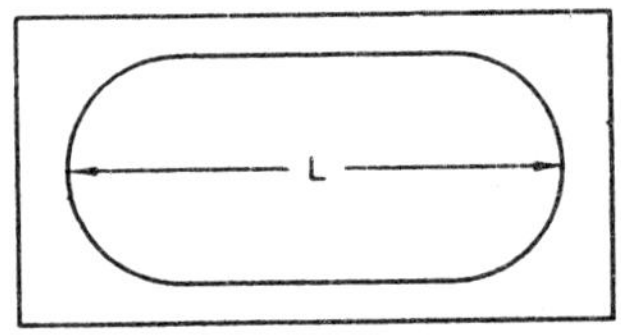

Fig. 14·20.

Reinforcement. (a) Vertical bars 9 kg/m^3 both forces total.

(b) Hoop bars 3·25 kg/m^3 minimum cover is 7·5 cm.

(c) Curb is provided with minimum 72 kg/m^3 as shown in Fig. 14·21(e).

Plugging of wells and fishered rocks may be done by clay mixed with straw (Paddy straw, rice husk)

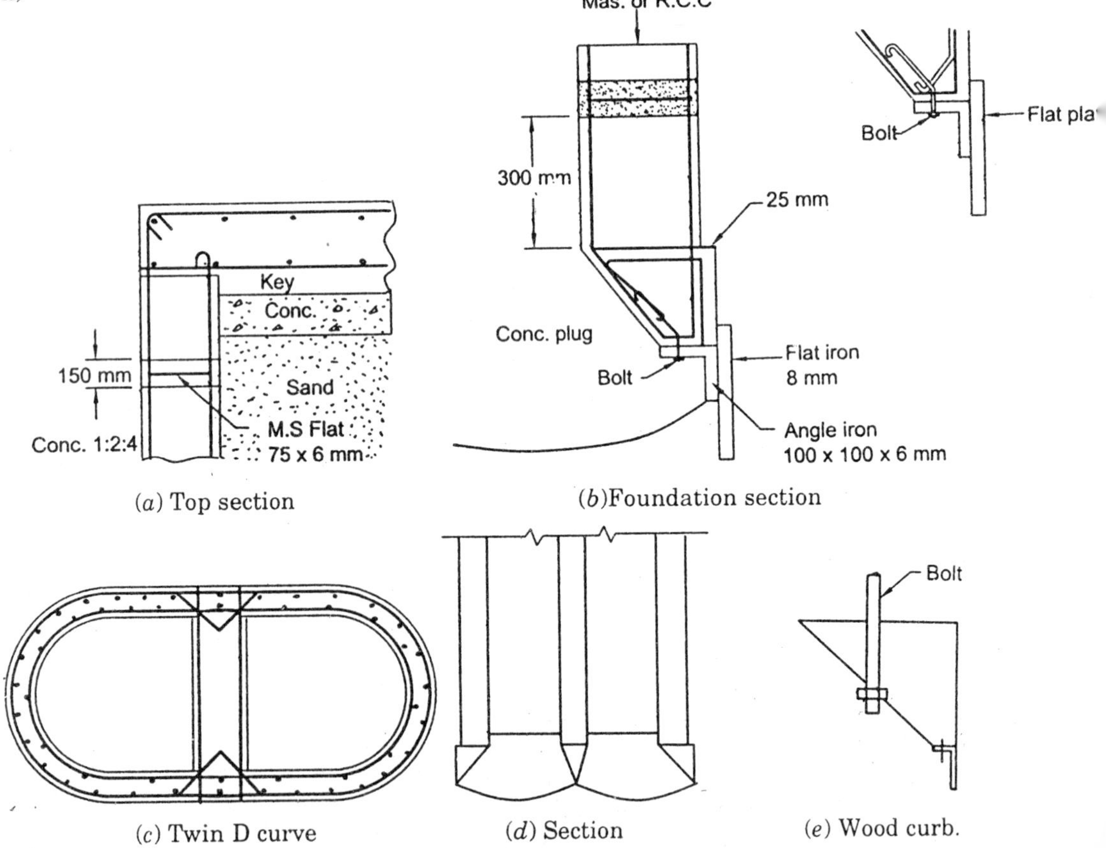

[*The reinforcement may be provided according to loads and size of well*]

Fig. 14·21.

Thickness of steining. The vertical width of a well is called as **steining**.

(*i*) **For brick masonry (circular wells).** $t = \left(\frac{D_f}{40} + \frac{D_0}{8}\right)$ for sandy strata.

The above thickness is increased by 10% for soft clay and 25% for hard clay

where t = thickness of steining

D_0 = outer dia. of well in cm.

D_f = The depth of well below the river bed at the time of sinking in cm.

(*ii*) **For cement concrete (Circular wells)**

$$t = \left(\frac{D_f}{100} + \frac{D_0}{10}\right) \text{ for sandy strata}$$

The above thickness is increased by 10% for soft clay and 25% for hard clay, for laterite, shale or other hard materials like boulder and kankar etc.

$$t = 1{\cdot}25\left(\frac{D_f}{100} + \frac{D_0}{8}\right)$$

(*iii*) For cement concrete (rectangular or oblong wells).

$$t = \left(\frac{D_f}{100} + \frac{L}{10}\right) \text{ for sandy strata}$$

where L = outside longest side of the well in cm.

(The minimum specified thickness of RCC steining = 22·5 cm)

The above thickness is increased by 10% for clay, 15% for hard clay and 28% for laterite, shale or similar hard strata.

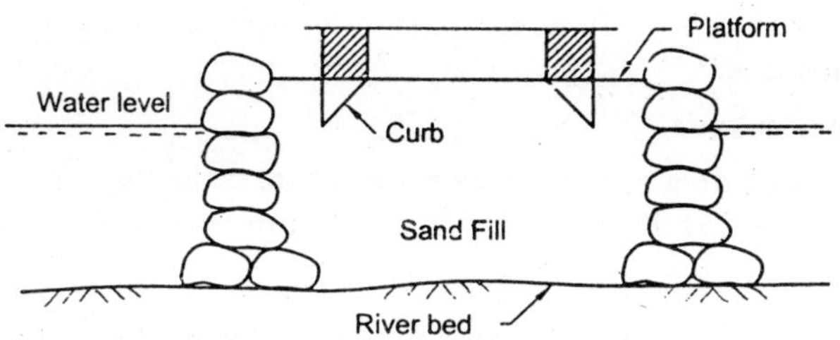

Fig. 14·22.

Laying of well curb

(*a*) **When curb is laid on a dry bed.** The curb is laid by digging trench of the size of the curb on the bed level. The steining is made upto about 1 m height. The earth is scooped out from the curb which is sinked down due to the load on the steining. The operation goes on and below the water table the dredges is used.

(2) **In the bed of the river.** A ring band of sand filled gunny bags is made. The bags should not be filled light. So that there may be no leakage through the bags. If the bags are loosely filled they will set and will form a good bond to avoid any leak.

The ring bund is filled with sand upto about 1 m above the water level and a plateform is made over it, on which the curb is land and the procedure goes on as above.

Cassions. When foundations are to be laid in water, wood or steel boxes called cassions made according to the size of the pier (foundation) and braced from inside to take load from outside are prepared on bank and are floated to the site on exact location and the masonry is started in its bed which is closed. Due to the weight of the masonry or concrete the caisson sinks to the bed and makes a part of the foundation itself. Some times sides are removable and are removed when the masonry sets.

In shallow foundation the box is opened from top and bottom. The soil from the cassion is removed and thus the cassion sinks to the required foundation level in water.

Forces acting on a well foundation. After assessing all relevant forces in magnitude, direction and point of application and their worst possible combinations they can be converted into an equivalent force and two horizontal forces (one acting across the pier and other acting along the pier) as indicated below :

W = resultant of all the vertical forces.

P = resultant of all external forces acting across piers.

P' = resultant of all the external horizontal forces acting along the pier (is usually ignored).

Brief description of all the forces are given below :

(*i*) **Dead loads.** The weight of the well itself including the weight of super structure on it.

(*ii*) **Live loads.** For Railway bridges are taken according to Indian Railway Bridges rules while for the road bridges according to the live loads specified by IRC Code-6—1966 titled "standard specifications and code of Practice for Road Bridges Sec-II loads and stresses".

(*iii*) **Impact loads.** The impact is only considered in the design of pier cap and the bridge seat on abutment.

(*iv*) **Wind loads.** The wind loads on the structure located above the water level are calculated according to the Provisions of IS : Code I.S. : 875. The wind loads act on the exposed area (in elevation) and thus it acts laterally (horizontally) on the bridge.

(*v*) **Water Pressure.** Water pressure due to water current acts on the part of the sub-structure which lies between the water level and the maximum scour level on piers standing parallel to the direction of the water flow, the intensity of water pressure is given by—

$P = CV^2$ where P = intensity of water pressure (kN/m^2)

C = a constant, the value of which depends on the shape of the well. Its value is given to be maximum of 773 for square ended pier to minimum 232 for piers with cut and ease water noses.

V = Velocity of the flowing water (m/s).

It is assumed that the value of P obtained above is the maximum value to be expected at the top surface of water. The pressure is assumed to be zero at the maximum scour level. The variation is then assumed to be linear.

The surface value V is assumed to be equal to $\sqrt{2}$ times the average velocity. Even when the flow is parallel to the pier, a transverse force equal to 20% of that acting parallel to the pier is taken to allow for oblique flow.

If however the water current makes an angle θ with the axis of the pier, the pressure along the axis of the pier and transverse to it are given as :

Water pressure along the axis $= P \cdot \cos^2 (20° \pm \theta)$

Water pressure transverse to axis $= P \cdot \sin^2 (20 \pm \theta)$

(*vi*) **Longitudinal forces.** The longitudinal forces are due to the tractive and breaking forces of the traffic on the bridge deck. These depend on the type of vehicles and the bearings between the deck and the pier. The forces are transmitted through the bearings and the friction in movable bearings. According to IRC code a longitudinal force μW is taken on the free bearings and the balance on fixed bearings, where W is the total reaction and μ is the coefficient of friction.

(*vii*) **Temperature.** Longitudinal forces are induced due to the temperature changes on account of resistance of the bearings against the movement due to variation of temperature.

(*viii*) **Buoyancy forces.** Buoyancy of water around the pier and well reduces the effective weight of the well and that of the soil surrounding the well. For pervious foundation soil like coarse sand and shingle, full buoyancy equal to the weight of the equivalent volume of displaced water should be considered. For semi-pervious foundation soil it is suitably reduced.

(*ix*) **Centrifugal force.** In bridges cured in plain, centrifugal force is transmitted through bearings.

(*x*) **Earth pressure.** The horizontal pressure due to passive and active states of surrounding foundation soil can be computed by the Rankine's or Coulomb's theories. The passive resistance to movement of the well by the external horizontal forces acting on the bridge deck is calculated only for the soil depth existing below the maximum scour level.

(*xi*) **Seismic forces.** The structures constructed in seismic zones, the seismic forces should be considered, as per IS Code (IS : 1893). This force which is acting on all components of the structure is specified as αW where W = the weight of the component and α is the seismic coefficient. The value of α depends upon the seismic zone. Its value generally lies between 0·1 g to 0·3 g. The seismic force acts through the centre of gravity of the component. It may act in any direction, but is assumed to be acting in one direction at any one time. The seismic forces are considered separately along the axis of the pier and transverse to it.

Sub-soil explorations

Ground water table or spring level. The position of ground or sub-soil water level is necessary for proceeding with sub-soil exploration and investigations. The position of spring level in surrounding wells is recorded in various seasons of the year. This information is available in meterological department and in State Irrigation Department. Chemical analysis of the soil is also necessary as it effects the foundation materials of the structure.

Classification of various methods of soil exploration is as below :

(1) (*a*) Open test pits (*b*) Dug wells

(2) Borings (Drilled wells)
(*i*) Tube boring
(*ii*) Auger boring
(*iii*) Wash boring
(*iv*) Percusion boring
(*v*) Demand core drilling

(3) Geophysical methods

(4) Concrete penetrator

Note : Drilled wells yield more water than dug wells, because the former has several water bearing strata for taking out water, while in the later only one water bearing strata is available for yield.

(1) **Open test pits.** Upto sub-soil water table open pits rectangular or square can be dug and can be preserved for test in road projects etc. where deep explorations are not required. From these pits soil samples disturbed or undisturbed can be collected which are preserved in polyethylene bags for testing. A strata chart for the same may be prepared. (Fig. 14·24)

Collection of undisturbed samples (chunk sampling). In this process the soil upto the bottom of the pit is cut in the shape of a standing heap or a tower. A wooden box or any other suitable container (cylinderical) with open ends is placed over this dressed standing soil mass. The empty space between the sides of the soil and the container is filled by moist saw dust or by any other suitable packing material such as molten paraffin wax. The top cover of the container is closed. The bottom of the soilmass is detached by a spatula and the container is reversed upside

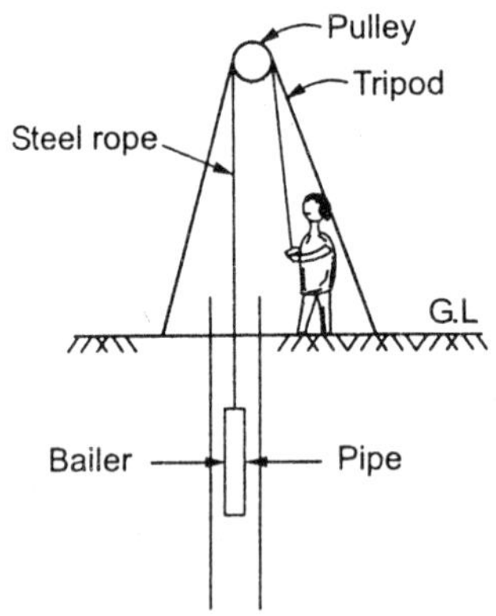

Fig. 14·23. Tube boring.

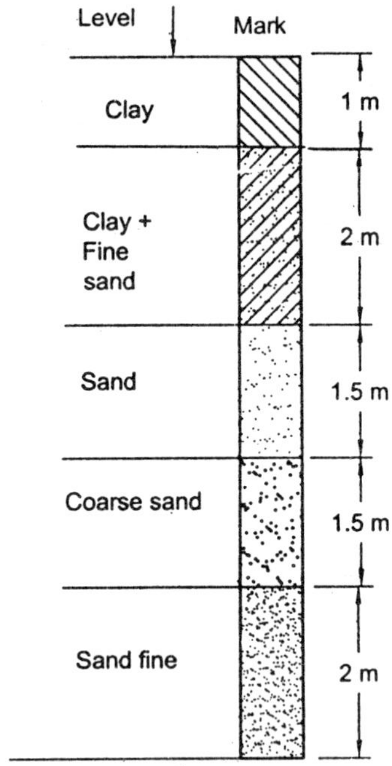

Fig. 14·24. STRATA CHART

down. A portion of a soil is removed, surface smoothened, pored with paraffin wax and lid closed at this end also. The enclosed box contained this undisturbed soil sample can easily be transported to the laboratory for further testing. They are generally required for shear tests of the soil.

(2) **Borings**

(*i*) **Tube boring.** A m.s. pipe of the desired bore dia. is inserted in the ground upto water table in a pit dug manually or by an auger. The soil form the m.s. tube (casing pipe) is removed by the boiler (discussed later). The boiler is moved up and down with the help of a rope tied to the bailer's top end and is passing over a pulley by manual labour. This operation is just the same as is used in boring of domestic hand pumps. The bailer scoops out the soil from the bore hole in its each operation and the pipe is driven down by applying load on it through a wooden clamp. It is an easy and popular way of boring which is widely used.

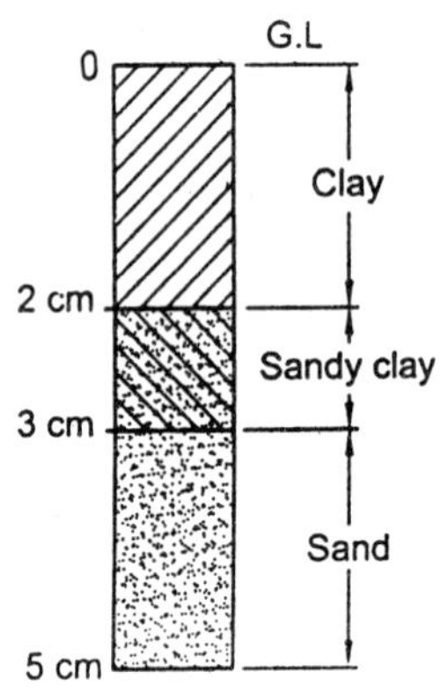

Fig. 14·25. Chunk sampling.

(*ii*) **Auger method.** By auger sampling can be done for shallow depths required generally for road projects upto water table manually. The different type of augers are used for digging holes. In general a scooper is fixed with a handle. A man inserts the auger in the hole with force, the scooper takes out some soil in it, which is removed from it after lifting the auger. The operation is repeated till the required depth is reached. The handle can be extended by adding pieces to it by scokets as the handle itself is a pipe.

(*a*) **Cylindrical type auger.** A cylindrical sharp edged blade is pushed in the ground by force (applied suddenly). By doing so the soil enters inside the blade which is removed out side the hole. By repeated operations the hole advances down. A hole upto spring level can be dug by this auger. The length of the handle can be increased by adding rods (which are tubes) by sockets.

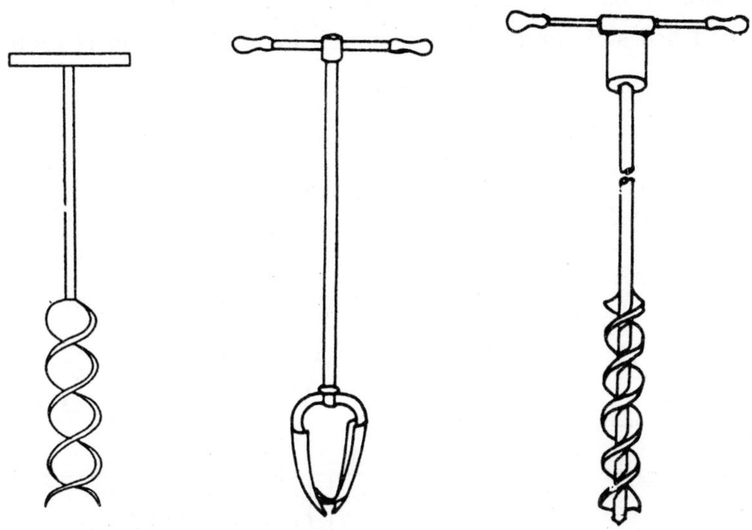

Fig. 14·26. Augers.

(*b*) **Post hole auger.** It contains two blades and is operated by rotating the handle by hand or mechanically.

(*c*) **Helical.** It contains screw type blades and is operated by rotating the handle. It is of the shape of the drill of a carpenter's which is used for making holes in woods etc.

(*iii*) **Wash boring or water jet boring.** Wash boring method is used when a deep boring is to be done in a less time. The unit of boring consists of :

(*a*) A casing pipe of about 3 m in length is inserted in the ground by making a hole by an auger.

(*b*) A **choping bit** is fixed at the lower end of a wash pipe and is inserted in the casing pipe.

(*c*) The choping bit which is perforated and from which water coming through the wash pipe comes out with pressure in the cavity below the casing pipe. The cavity is formed by the water which comes out with force from the choping bit.

(*d*) Water coming out with velocity from the perforations of the bit makes a slurry with the scooped soil which passes up through the anular space between casing and the wash pipe.

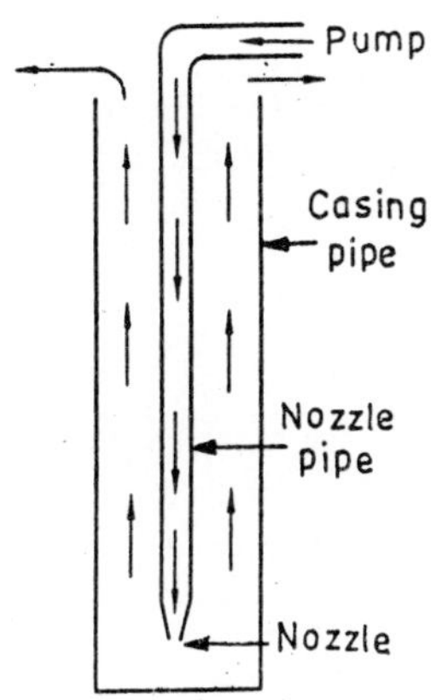

Fig. 14·27. Wash boring.

(*e*) This soil mixed water comes out above ground level through a *T*-connection fixed on the top of the casing pipe.

(*f*) Water is feeded from a pump through a hose pipe to the washing pipe which remains continue during the operation.

(*g*) When the cavity is developed a piece is joined in the casing pipe as well as in wash pipe and the connections are made again. The process goes on till the fixed depth of boring is achieved.

(*h*) The samples of soil are collected by silted soil in a tank which is coming from the waste soil mixed water.

(*i*) If undisturbed soil samples are required a sampler spoon is replaced in place the choking bit.

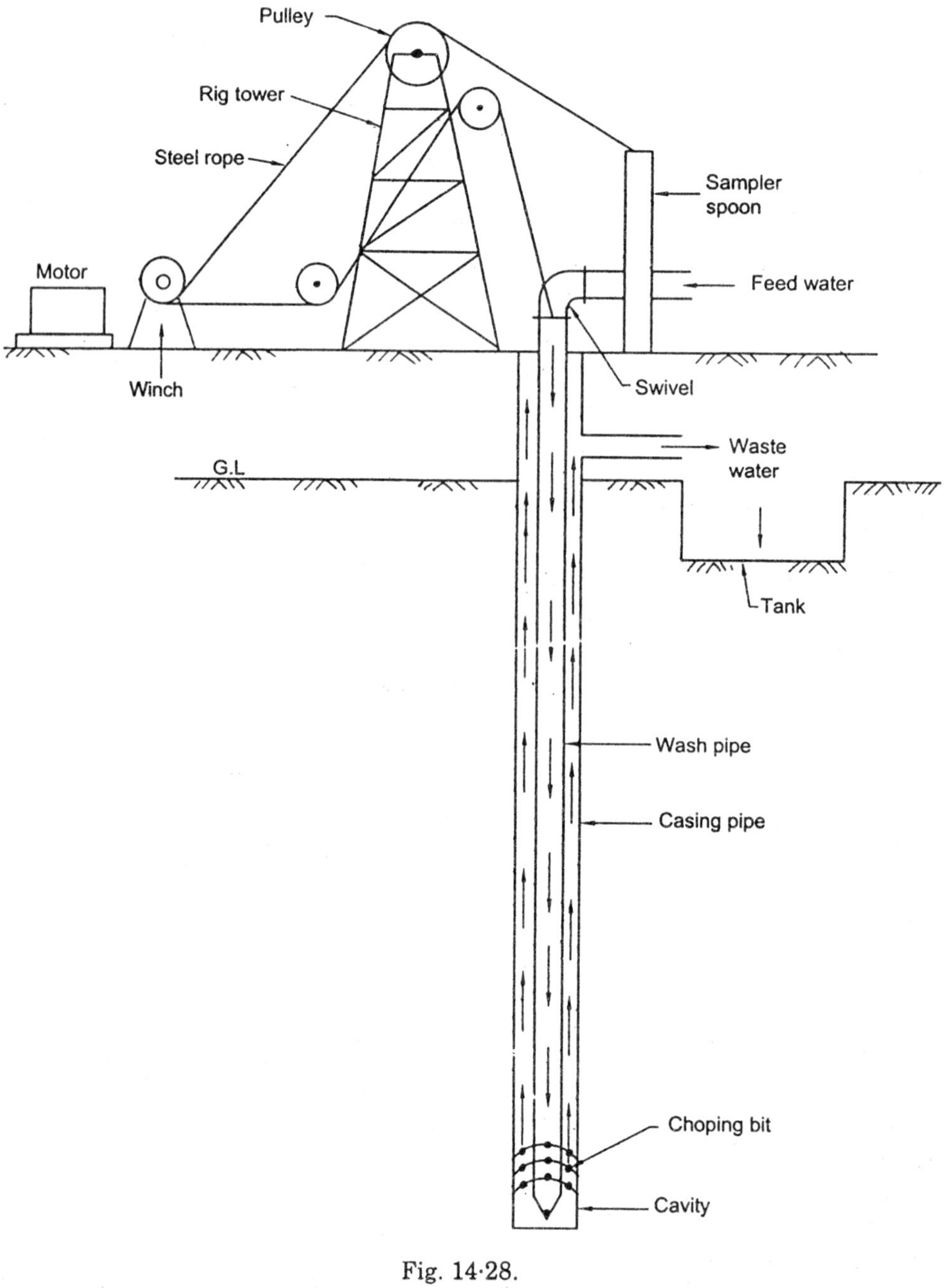

Fig. 14·28.

(*j*) The connection of the water hose pipe to the waste pipe is provided with a swivel joint so that waste pipe and the choping bit can be twisted when they are raised and dropped on the soil at the bottom of the hole. By doing so the cutting of the soil is facilitated.

(*k*) For ordinary boring the casing pipe used commonly of 60 mm in dia. For larger borings, pipes of larger dia. can be used. Similarly the dia. of the waste pipe can be changed.

(*l*) Suitable weight can be placed on the casing pipe by a clamp for easy and fast boring.

(*m*) For routine laboratory tests about 10 kg soil sample is collected and a chart is prepared of soil samples and depths with reference to level point on the ground. The chart is known as **log of borehole.**

(*iv*) **Percussion Drilling.** A percussion drilling rig drills a hole by a heavy chopping bit, attached to a string of solid rod of square or round in section, called a boring rod. This boring rod provides enough weight to the bit which may sometimes however be joined with a heavy element called the sinker bar, before being attached to the boring rod.

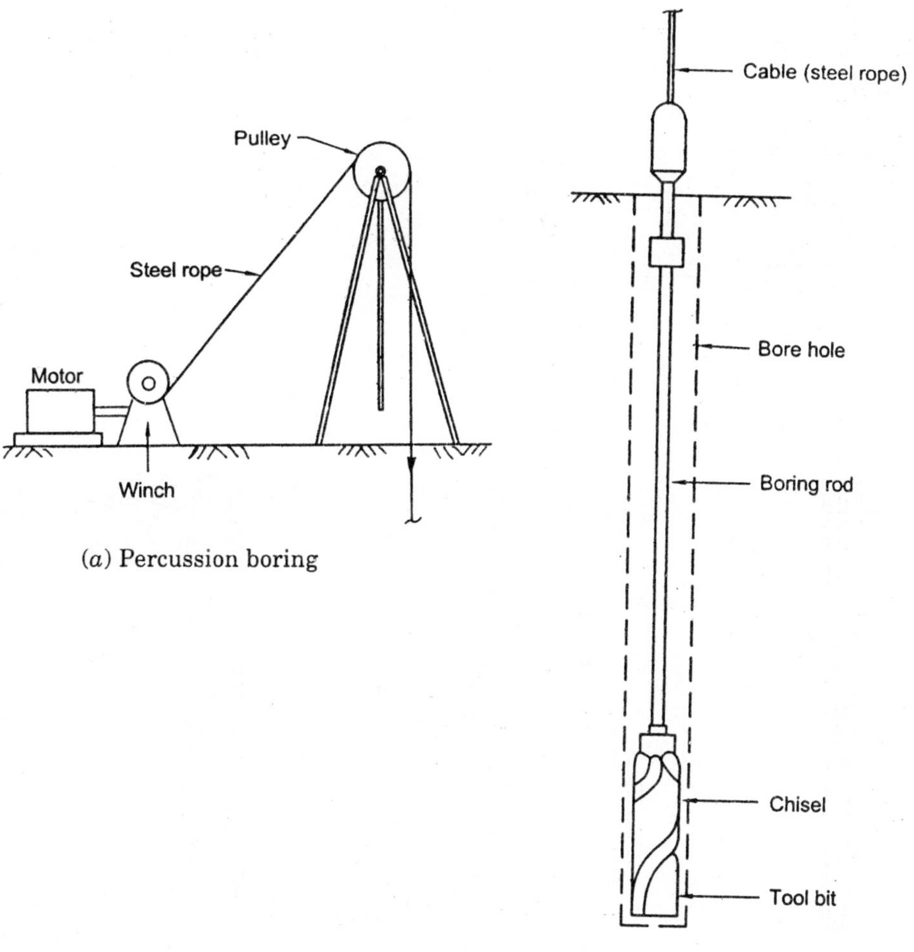

(*a*) Percussion boring

(*b*) Percussion drilling

Fig. 14·29.

The tool bit attached with the boring rod is carried by a steel cable and is alternatively raised and dropped by means of a winch unit so as to break the soil. Water is added to the hole during boring above the water table, so that it forms a slurry with the broken soil, which can be bailed out at intervals through a boiler.

Percussion boring is done in hard soils where ordinary boring or wash boring is unpracticable.

The bailer is replaced in place of the tool bit when slurry from the hole is to be removed. The bailer is generally consists of a barrel of about 2 metre in length with a cutting shoe at the bottom and a valve just above the cutting shoe which opens upward in the downward motion of bailer and allows the slurry or sand etc. to enter in the bailer casing while it checks it to go out in the upward motion of the bailer. In fact the bailer itself works as a cutting unit in case of drilling in soft soils.

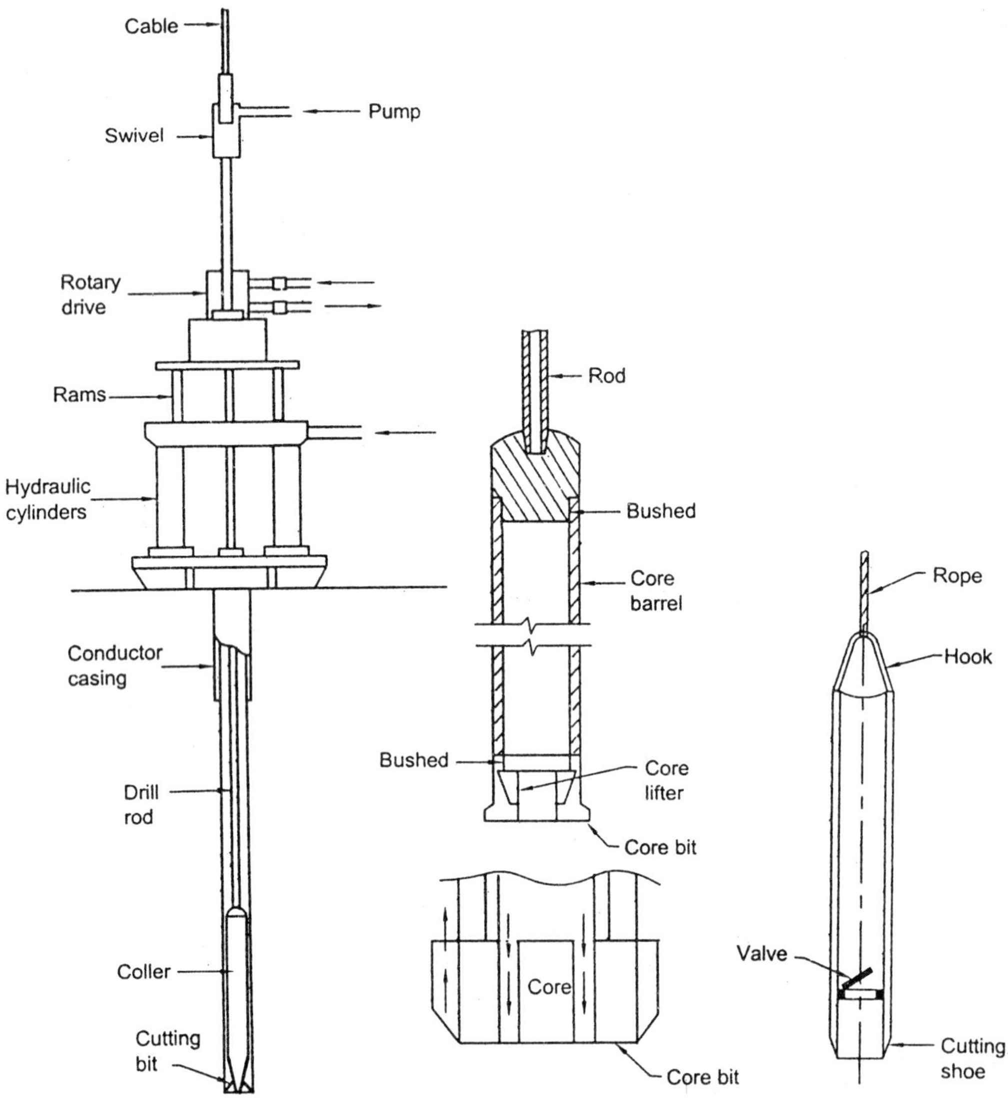

(*a*) Drilling maching (*b*) Details of core barrel (*c*) Bailer

Fig. 14·30.

(*v*) **Rotary diamond core drilling.** The core drilling using a diamond coring bit is adopted for rocks and hard clays and makes it possible to collect intact soil samples, as the bit cuts an annular hole in the stratum, and the intact soil core enters the core barrel, to be collected as a sample. Typical core diameters are 40 mm, 55 mm and 75 mm, but can rank as high as 165 mm.

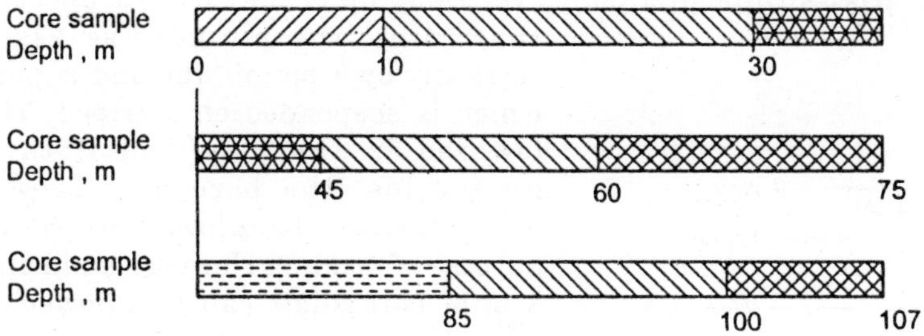

Fig. 14·31. Core sampling case.

This drilling method is quick and fast. It is not however suitable for gravely soils. The samples can be preserved in a wooden cage box in order of serial as occured.

In the case of drilling casing pipes are not used as the sides of the hole can stand being in hard strata. Even in cases for sides are unstable or sand, a slurry of cement or thixotropic volcanic clay in water is circulated to coat and to support the sides of the drill hole in such loose strata. By doing so the permeable strata is also sealed. After passing cement the operation is kept closed for some days so that the cement may set with the sandy sides of the drill hole.

(3) **Geophysical method**

(*i*) **Seismic sound waves method.** This method is based on the principle that sound waves are created by explosives and get reflected from a strong strata below. The time of travel is measured. The sound waves travel faster in solid rocks than fissured or disintegrated rocks. The thickness of the rock is computed as $t = \frac{\text{Vel.} \times \text{time}}{2}$ where t = thickness of the rock, v = vel. of the sound in the rock concerned and t = time taken to travel and in reflection back.

The radiating shock waves are received by the vibrator detector known as geophone or seismic-meter. The time of travel is automatically recorded.

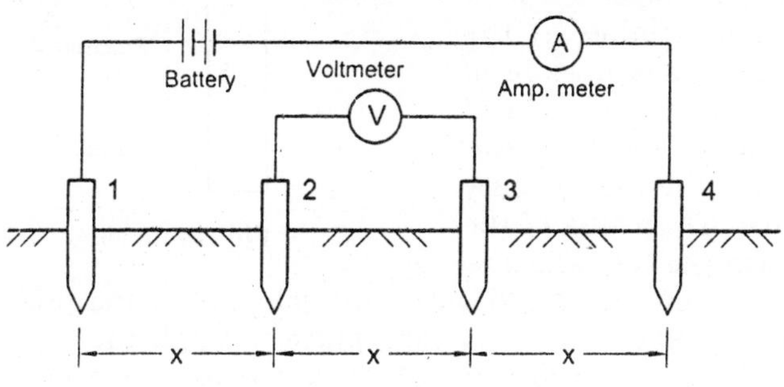

Fig. 14·32. Electric resistance method.

(*ii*) **Electrical Persistively Method.** The thickness of the layer of rock is computed by the electrical resistance offered by the rock. Dense rocks offers more reistance than the the less denser rocks.

(4) **Probing or a Concrete Penetrator.** A steel bar 25 to 40 mm dia. with a pointed end is driven into the ground either by its own weight or blows by hammer till it reaches at a firm strata. The type of soil is examined by the soil sticked to the sides of the rod. By the quantum of the blows over it, a rough idea of the hardness of the soil is made.

3·3. Verticality of the bore holes. The verticality of a bore hole can be checked by a plumb line suspended by the side of the bore hole shaft, but when the shaft is not so high above the ground, this process is not possible. In such cases a plumbing disc is prepared which consists of two (with two or three perforations to pass water) discs a bit less in dia. than the hole of sheet iron about 3 mm thick fitted in an iron rod 25 mm dia. at a distance of about 3 m or according to the depth of the hole by nuts. The upper disc is provided with a hook from which a steel wire is attached, which passes through a pulley vertically up of the hole. At upper end of the bore hole shaft pipe, the plumb disc assembly is adjusted vertically by a plumb line and is passed over the pulley which is suspended on a tripod. The assembly is now lowered in the hole and if the wire shows any inclination, the bore hole is not in plumb. This inclination can be allowed according to the depth and purpose of drilling. However an inclination of 10 mm per 3 m of bore shaft can be allowed where submersible pumps are not installed. The non verticality of the shaft can be rectified as follows.

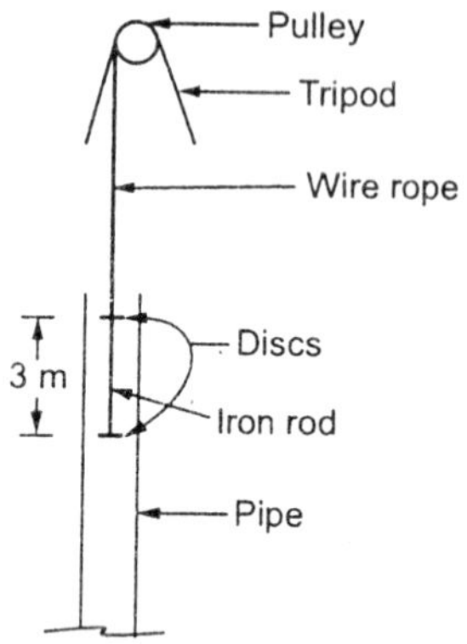

Fig. 14·33 (*a*)

The earth towards the leaning side of the shaft is loosened either by long cross bars or by a side boring in case of deep shafts and removed. A push about a meter deep from ground level is given by a jack till the shaft does not come in plumb. The side of the shaft so becoming hollow is filled with gravel and earth and will compacted so that it may not come back to its previous leaning position, after the removal of the pushing force.

Extraction of bore hole pipes. The strainer pipe can be lifted by a hook tied in a rope passing over a pulley on a tripod. The hook is lowered in the strainer pipe which picks up the eye of the bail plug which is fitted at the lower end of the strainer pipe and then the hook is lifted. When the bore hole pipe sticks to the surrounding earth for low depths it can be lifted by a crow-bar or a wood sleeper lever acted on a clamp which is tightly fixed on the upper end of the shaft. The fulcrum for the lever may be of filled jute bags or wood log. For longer depths jacks must be used.

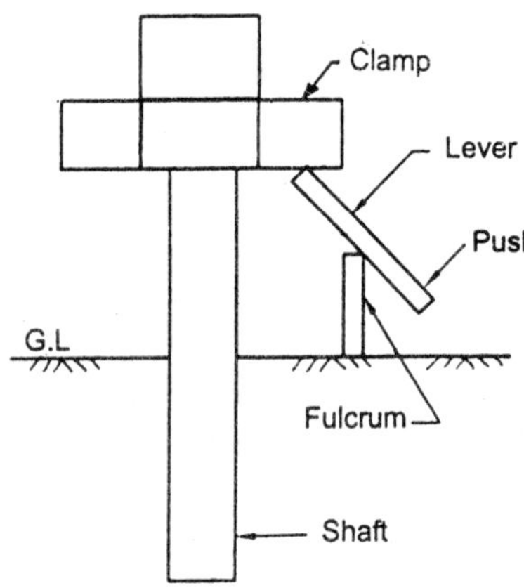

Fig. 14·33 (*b*)

Water Perculation Test. It is an important item in surface exploration for foundation, studies at the various river valley project sites. The examination of cores from the drill holes gives only a general idea of the physical condition of the rock, while the results of the water perculation is useful to determine the permeability of the strata pierced by the drill hole. The value of the coefficient of permeability obtained from the test which is the overall value for rock including loss, into cracks, fissures and joints etc., and provides an approximate estimate of the possible leakage that may take place through the zone in the foundation upon the impoundment of the reservoir, by which the extent of grouting and foundation can be provided for the contemplated work.

Quantity of water to be used in test. The test is of the pumping in type, that is they are based on measuring the amount of water accepted by the ground, through the open bottom of a pipe or through an uncased or ungrouted section of the hole. If water contains silt etc. will plug the test section and will give low permeability result. The pure supply may be assured by filtering or silting. If the climatic conditions demand to raise the water temperature to one degree C higher than ground temperature so as to preclude the creation of air bubble in the ground, which may greatly reduce acceptance of water by test section.

Packers. Washers, pneumatic or hydraulic type. Leather cup packers are used for rock formations where holes drilled, retain their proper size. Mechanical packers used in moderately hard formations, pneumatic packers are used in soft rocks.

Procedure. The test is conducted in uncased and ungrouted sections of the drill holes by a single or double packer. In certain formations it may not be possible to use packer or there is danger of packer being stick in the hole. In such cases, the hole is grouted in the earlier stage and the bore is further extended for carrying out test and the packer is fixed in the grouted zone.

The single packer method is used where the full length of the hole cannot stand uncased/ungrouted in soft rocks such as sand stone, clay shale etc. or where it is considered necessary to have permeability values side by side with drilling as the case of where multiaquifers are present. In this method the hole should be drilled upto a depth desirable for test. Cone barrel should then be removed and hole cleaned with water until clear water returns. The packer should be fixed at the desired level above the bottom of the hole and the test performed.

Double packer method. In this method the hole should be drilled to the final depth desired and cleaned with water until clear water returns. Two packers connected to the ends of a perforated drill rod of a length equivalent to the test section should be fixed in the drill hole. The bottom of the perforated rod should be plugged before the double packer tests are proceeded with. The test may be done from bottom upwards or from top downwards. To start the test from bottom and then work upward is more convenient.

The tests are recommended to be performed in 1·5 or 3 m test sections, so that the entire hole is covered, depending upon the geological conditions. For shear zones or highly jointed zone a lesser length of section is used. However the test length should not less than 5 times the dia. of the bore hole. The test section should be confined by one packer or 2 packers. The water level in the hole section should be determined by electrical device. The water level should be noted at short intervals of time usually 10 to 15 min. till three consecutive readings show constant values, which should be taken as the depth of the water table. This measurement is done for determining the hydraustatic pressure in the test zone and is used for calculating the permeability of the horizon. If the measurements show no ground water the fault should be recorded.

Water should then be pumped into the section under pressure. Each pressure should be maintained until the reading of water intake at interval of 5 min. Show a nearly constant reading of water intake for one particular pressure at the coller. The constant rate of water intake should be noted. The test should be commenced with a low pressure at the coller and increased limited to the availability of suitable rock cover to prevent uplift or to a maximum equivalent to $H + x$ (where H is the hydraulic head to which the strata should be subjected due to contemplated structure and x is the loss due to friction) is achieved. Frictional losses can be determined by means of a chart prepared for this purpose. In order to avoid unheaval of the rock foundations test pressure are generally limited to the followings :

Table 14·20. Limit Test Pressure

Rock type	*Limit of test pressure applied to the test zone in g/cm² per m of rock head*
(*i*) Unconsolidated or poorly consolidated sedimentary foundation	115
(*ii*) Horizontally consolidate bedded sedimentary formation	175
(*iii*) Hard igneous and metamorphic rocks	230

Precautions. (1) Holes should be capped when not in operation.

(2) When intake of water in the test sections is more than that which the pump can deliver it is advisable to reduce the section.

(3) The maximum length of test section is 3 m.

(4) The holes should be thoroughly flushed with clean water before test.

When the core recovery is more than 70%, cores should be per flushed with water under pressure until the wash is clear. When recovery is poor less than 70% the holes are liable to collapse by the disturbance of water. They are cleaned by gentle surging (by moving a rubber block).

(5) Try to use larger dia. rods to reduce the friction.

(6) The gauge should be located between the swivel and the packer and not between water meter and swivel or pump to water meter.

(7) All joints should be water tight and it should be noted that the packers are not leaking as it causes to rise the water level in the hole or even water can overflow from the nipple.

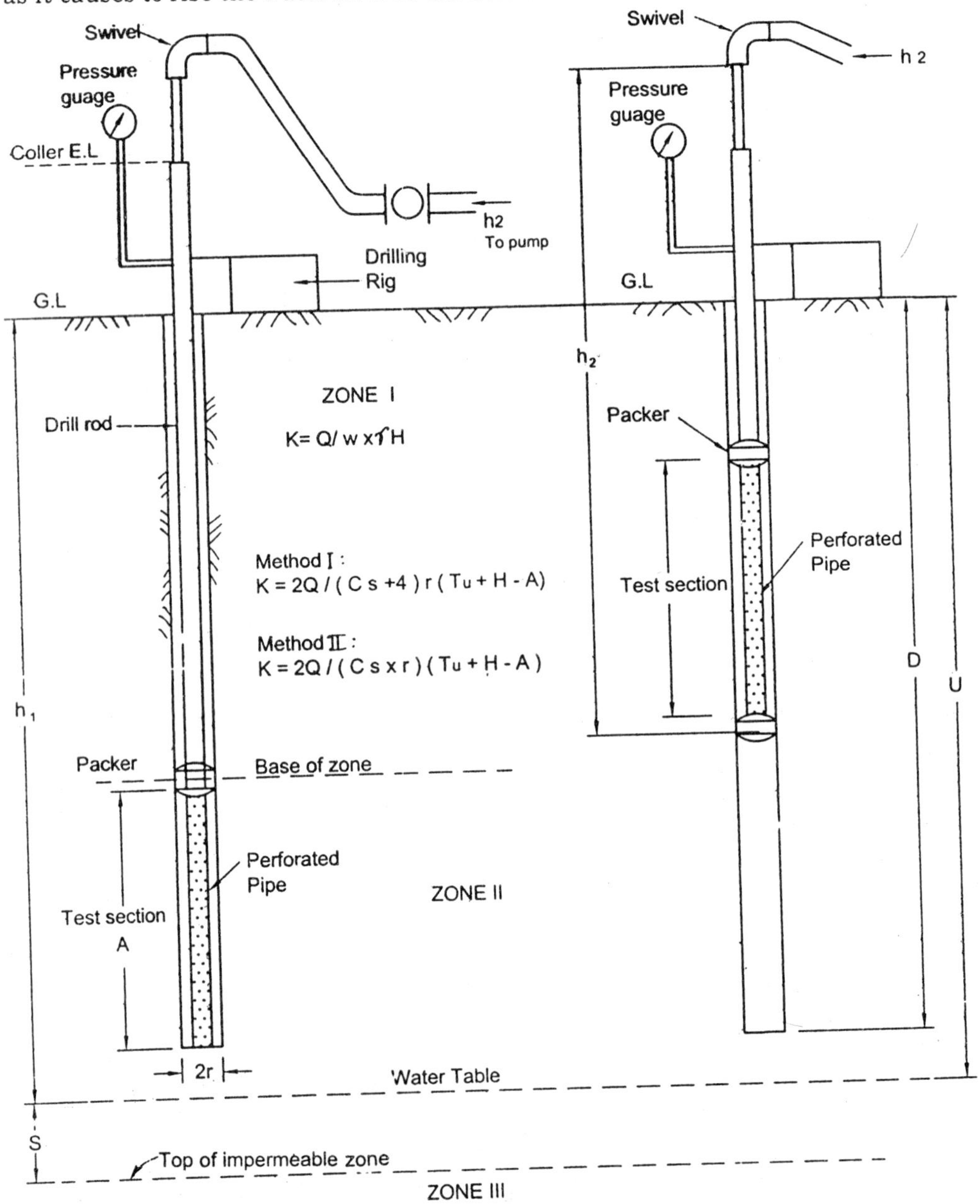

Method I : $K = Q/[C_s + A]\gamma H$ Method II : $K = Q/C_s \times \gamma H$

Fig. 14·34. Layout of single packer and double packer.

Format for presentation of data of In Situ Permeability test in bed rock

Dated :...............

(1) Name of Project	(7) Dia. of drill hole	
(2) Drill hole No.	(8) Total depth of hole	
(3) Feature	(9) Depth tested : From To Total	
(4) Coller elevation	(10) Depth of ground water	
(5) Height of water swivel above coller	(11) Size of drill rod/pipe	
(6) Type of drilling	Note if any	

Table 14·21. Permeability Test Data

Test sec.		*Meter reading of water inlake (lit)*				*Water intake lit/min*					
From	*To*	*Initial reading*	*Reading after 5 min.*	*Reading after 10 min.*	*Reading after 15 min.*	*1st 5 min. (Col. 4 − 3)*	*2nd 5 min. (Col. 5 − 4)*	*3rd 5 min. (Col. 6 − 5)*	*Average of last two readings*	*Water pressure at coller kg/cm²*	*Permeability in cm²*
1	2	3	4	5	6	7	8	9	10	11	12

Limitations. $Q/a \leqq 0{\cdot}10$; $S \geqq 10r$ in method II. Thickness of packer = $10r$.

A = Length of test section in m, a = Surface area of test sec. in m^2

(In method I = area of wall + area of bottom)

C_u = Conductivity coefficient in unsaturated bed (see Fig. 14·34)

C_s = Conductivity coefficient in saturated bed (see Fig. 14·34)

D = Distance of ground surface to bottom of hole in m.

H = Effective head = $h_1 + h_2 - L$ in m

h_1 = In test above water table—distance between swivel and bottom of hole

In test below : water table—distance between swivel and water table in m.

K = Coefficient of permeability in m/s under unit gradient.

(multiply by 100 to get the value in cm/sec.)

L = Head loss in pipe due to friction in m of water (for quantities less than 18·1/min. (in 32 mm pipe it may be ignored).

Q = Steady flow into well in m³/sec., r = rad of test hole in m.

S = Thickness of saturated material in m.

$T_u = U - D + H$

U = Thickness of unsaturated material in m.

X = Per cent of unsaturated stratum $\left(\dfrac{H}{T_u}\right) \times 100$ (see Fig. 14·34).

h_2 = Applied pressure at coller in m of water.

Piles. (1) **Classification of piles according to the material used.**

(*a*) **Wood piles.** Timber piles are used in unimportant foundations such as retaining walls, roads or banks of canals etc. They are cheap, but are undurable especially in alternate wet and dry situations. They are also used for reinforcing the soil. If always kept wet they are quite stable. The timber used in piles are sal, teak, Deodar or Babool etc. Timber piles should be impregnated with solignum, creosote or any other anti rot treatment. Timber piles are round or square in section. Round sections are available from the trunks direct while the square sections are prepared from the heart wood after sawing. The dia. of the round sections obtained from trunks should be measured 0·30 m below the wider edge. The lower edge is fitted with an iron conical shoe nailed to the lower end of the pile, which must be sufficiently thick at bottom. The upper edge is fitted with an iron steel cap or band about 50 to 75 mm wide and 10 to 15 mm thick, so as to bear the blow of the hammer. The general rules for timber piles are as follows :

(1) The load on each timber pile should not exceed 9 tonnes and the compressive stress calculated at sec. of mid length of pile should not exceed 85% of the permissible stress parallel to grain for a ratio of l/d = 11. Depth varies from 1·5 m to 12 m, according to the loads and type of timber. The ratio of width to depth must not be less than 1/20.

(2) Partially exposed piles should be designed as columns in respect of exposed portions.

(3) General size of the timber pile 15 × 15 cm to 36 × 36 cm for square and 20 cm to 36 cm in dia. for round piles. Piles used for compaction of ground should not be less than 10 cm in dia. and the sheet pile should not be less than 5 cm thick and 15 cm wide.

(4) c/c distance between the piles should not be less than 75 cm except in sheet piles where they are driven close together having grooves and tongues at edges.

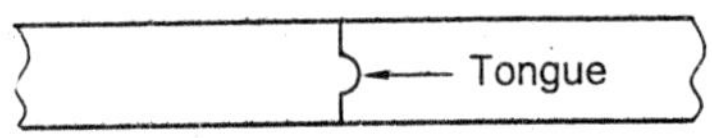

Fig. 14·35.

(5) Weight of the ram and monkey must be minimum 100 kg to maximum upto 1000 kg depending on the size of the pile and nature of soil.

Table 14·22. Safe load in tonnes for Timber piles.

Dia. (mm)	*Length in m*					
	2·0	*3·0*	*6·0*	*9·0*	*12·0*	*15·0*
100	5·3	4·0	—	—	—	—
150	13·8	11·5	7·2	—	—	—
230	33·2	20·3	22·0	16·2	—	—
300	61·5	57·6	45·9	36·2	28·8	27·6
380	47·7	93·2	79·0	64·9	53·8	45·2

(*b*) **R.C.C. Piles.** They may be precast or cast in situ.

Precast piles—Basic rules for the design of precast piles.

(1) **Main reinforcement.** It must not be less than the followings :

(*a*) 1·25 per cent of the gross sectional area of the pile, for piles upto 30 times their least width.

(*b*) 1·5 per cent of the gross sectional area for the pile of length upto 40 times the least width.

(*c*) 2·0 per cent of the gross-sectional area of the pile for piles of length upto 4·0 times their least width.

(2) **Lateral reinforcement.** Like columns it must be provided in the form of links or hoops of m.s. bars 5 mm dia. The volume of the lateral reinforcement must not be less than 0·2% or the gross volume of the pile and the distance apart of links c/c must not be less than the half of

the least width of the pile. Lateral reinforcement at both the ends must not be less than 0·6% of the volume in a distance equal to 3 times the width of the pile and the transition from close to normal reinforcement should be done gradually. If the pile is to be driven in a hard strata in top portion a close helix should be provided.

The longitudinal bars should be held apart by cross m.s. spacers. (forks) 12 mm to 15 mm at least 1·5 m c/c or 6 mm links should be provided.

The clear cover must be minimum of 5 cm and when it is liable to be effected by sea water it must be minimum 6 cm.

Top of longitudinal bars should be kept exposed to have a monolithic joint with the pile capping slab.

(3) The dia. of precast concrete pile varies from 38 cm to 64 cm and their length upto 30 m. Sometimes to improve the bearing capacity of the pile the lower ends are enlarged.

(4) A 30 m long pile can carry loads upto 50 tonnes.

(5) A cutting shoe at the bottom, conical in shape of steel and an iron band cap at top of the pile is also provided.

(6) They are coated with tar before driving.

Cast insitu piles with casing. A thin steel casing is lowered in the bore which prevents soil and ground water from mixing with fresh concrete, it also saves the quantity of concrete which goes waste to fill in the irregularities. But it reduces the bond and friction of pile.

Cast insitu without casing. In this type of piles the steel casing is withdrawn as concrete is poured in. These piles have good bond and friction on sides.

Table 14·23. Safe load in tonnes for precast RCC piles

Section of pile mm	*Max. load tonnes*	*Max. length m*	*Dia. in mm of 8 bars (main)*					
			Length of bar in m					
			6	*9*	*12*	*15*	*18*	*21*
250 × 250	25	9·1	16	20	—	—	—	—
300 × 300	40	12·2	20	22	25	—	—	—
350 × 350	55	16·8	20	22	25	28	—	—
400 × 400	75	19·8	—	22	25	28	32	—
450 × 450	90	22·9	—	—	25	28	32	36

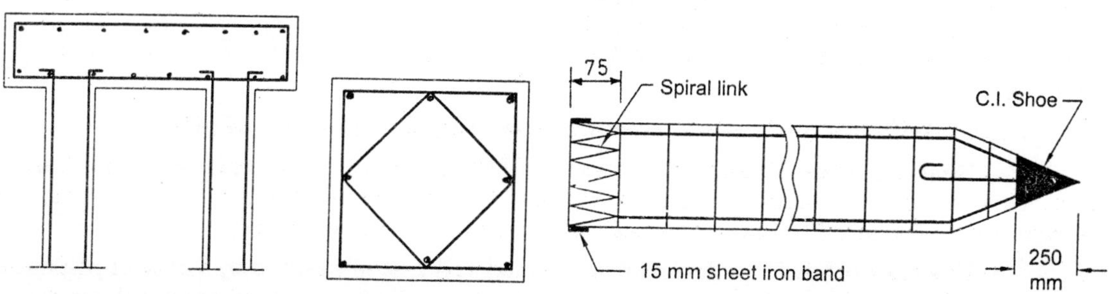

(*a*) Foundations raft over piles (*b*) Section of precast pile (*c*) Long section of precast pile

Fig. 14·36.

(c) **Steel piles.** (i) ***H* Piles**—They cause less disturbance to the soil. They are driven in single pieces upto to 60 m depth. Maximum load ranges 40 to 70 tonnes for friction piles. Exposed top cover is protected by concrete cover.

(ii) **Pipe piles**—The pipes having a dia. of 500 mm and a wall thickness of 12·5 mm have been allowed to carry 120 tonnes when bearing on rocks.

(iii) **Sheet piles**—These are used in canal masonry works to provide an impervious cut off. They are driven edge to edge. The edges are gripped to each other by tongues or clutches. In high piles anchor rods are provided at top which can be anchored in the concrete behind the pile or in soils with an anchor block. While piles are driven care should be taken that grooves must not be out of the tongue or there must be no declutching in order to achieve a perfect water tight cut off. A right angle bends a *T*-sec. is welded to hold the grip of the right angle row of pipes.

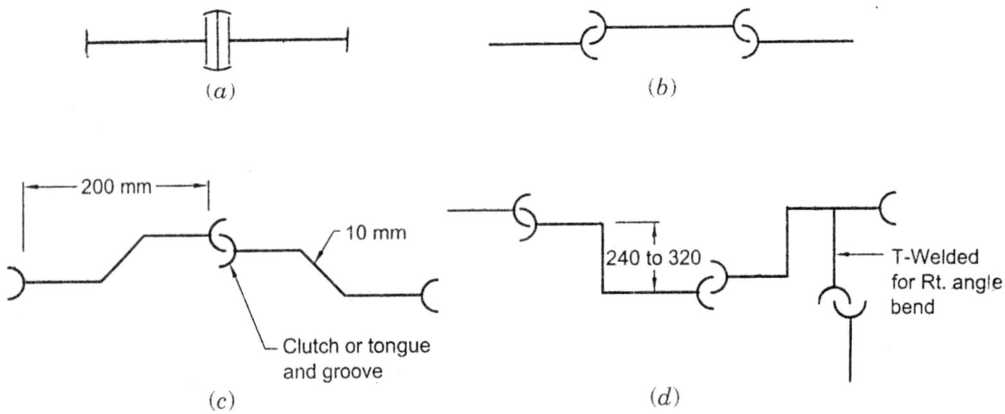

Fig. 14·37. Sheet piles.

Anchor or bulk head. They are generally used in water front constructions where either the water level is high or soil encountered are soft. It is similar to cantilever sheet piles and are supported near its top by means of anchor rods connected to an anchor dead man at suitable intervals. The wall is usually provided on the inner face of the sheet pile.

When the bulk head is built in open water and the fill placed behind it later. It is called a fill bulk head. If the bulk head is constructed in natural ground and the earth is removed in front of its face, it is called dredge bulk head.

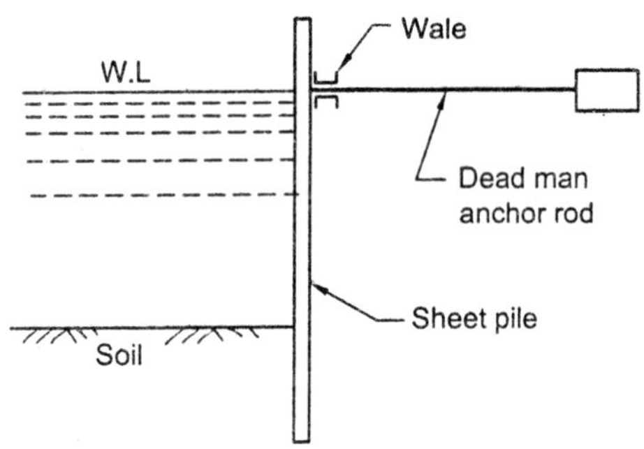

Fig. 14·38.

(2) **Classification of piles according to loading and purpose of pile**

(a) **Bearing piles.** Piles driven in soft soil but resting on hard strata are called bearing piles. This section is designed as a load bearing column. The load which a pile can take in bearing = $\pi r^2 \times P$ where P = bearing capacity of soil and r = radius of the pile.

(b) **Friction piles.** Piles designed on soft soil and rest in position by virtue of resistance provided by friction between the pile and the surrounding soil ($2\pi r \times \mu R$) where r is the radius of pile, l = length of pile, μ the coefficient of friction between the pile material and the soil in contact. R is the reaction due to the pressure of the soil.

$R = \frac{1}{2} C_P w l^2$ where C_P is the coefficient of pressure of soil $= \dfrac{1+\sin\phi}{1-\sin\phi}$. w is the weight of soil per cubic unit and ϕ is the angle of repose of the soil. l the length of the pile can be calculated knowing other variables.

The total load taken by a pile in bearing and friction $= P\pi r^2 + \frac{1}{2}\mu(2\pi rl \times C_P wl^2)$. Such piles are called floating piles. A minimum factor of safety is 3. In above expression P is the bearing capacity and μ is the coefficient of friction of the pile and soil.

(*c*) **Laterally loaded piles.** When the load applied on a pile is normal to the direction of pile it is said to be loaded laterally such as walls and piers.

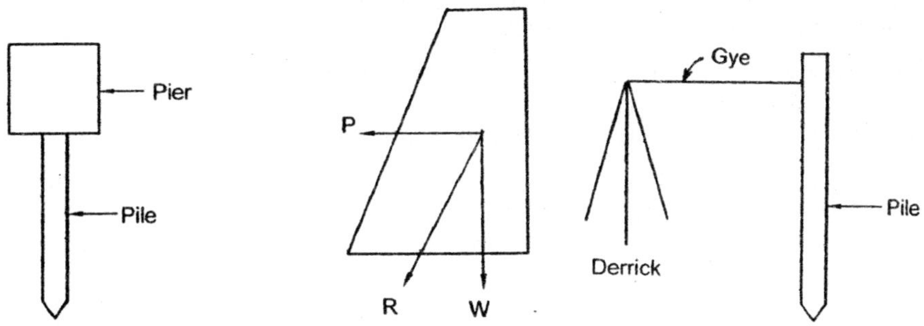

(*a*) (*b*) (*c*)

Fig. 14·39.

(*d*) **Battered piles.** Piles driven at an angle are called battered piles, as in case of retaining walls. They are provided when the load is eccentric and produce a slanting resultant. They are also called as racking piles.

(*e*) **Tensioned piles.** When the load on a pile is applied such that it creates tension in pile. Such as a pile which holds a gye.

(*f*) **Compression piles.** When the soil is compressed by the pile load, such piles are called compression piles.

(*g*) **Scour piles.** When the foundation of piers and abutments are subjected to a scour, they are founded on piles which are driven deeper than the maximum scour depth. Such piles are called scour piles.

(*h*) **Cut off piles.** These piles are driven to check the piping of the sub soil water and are used in hydraulic structures such as barrage or dams etc. at their u/s and d/s faces to increase the length of creep. These piles are of sheet iron and are driven side by side with no gap.

(3) **Classification based on mode of driving.** (*a*) **Pressure driven piles.** These pipes are driven by blows at top of the pile. They are either precast RCC piles, sheet piles or timber piles.

(*a*) **Cast in situ piles.** They are generally of plain or reinforced concrete. The holes are bored in the soil as detailed in boring or exploration section. The concrete is poured by a conical vessel in the shape of a funnel provided with a tube under it. The lower end of the tube of the funnel is kept a bit above the pouring spot in the hole. The concrete is then poured and the end of the tube is raised as the concrete advances up. The concrete in the core of the funnel is controlled by a valve provided at the neck of the funnel. After pouring a lift of the desired height, the concrete is consolidated by lowering a plunger, by having it up and down by a rope on a pulley. The casing pipe is withdrawn gradually as the concrete advances up. Sometimes when the soil in the hole is so stiff that it can maintain its position. The soil in the hole is also made stiffer by passing a slurry of stiff clay or cement paste if the strata is a bit sandy. In such cases when the side soil cannot remain in its position, the thin steel casing is provided in which concrete is filled. The piles which are piled without this thin casing has a good grip in the soil and also have a better load bearing capacity, though the quantity of concrete used is more in order to fill the irregularities. The thin casing is left inside and the casing pipe is used only upto for 2 or 3 m depth.

(*b*) **Driven and cast in situ piles.** Thick casing pipes which can bear heavy blows are driven by giving blows from top. The pipes are jointed by threads on the ends as the piling advances. The lower pipe has a detachable cutting shoe of cast iron which is left in ie, while the casing pipe is withdrawn. On the top a wooden chardwood say tamrind, (Imli) driving cap is fitted on which the blows are applied by a piston operated by steam or compressed air. For light work driving by monkey can be done. In such cases the soil around the pipe is consolidated and thus its capacity of load bearing is increased.

When the operation of driving the pile is finished, concrete with required reinforcement (lowered 1st) is poured in the hole and the casing pipe is lifted up by jacks as the concrete advances up. The casing pipe should be greased before piling.

(*c*) **Under reamed piles.** After boring is carried out to the required depth, the base of the intermediate portions are enlarged in the form of a bulb by a tool known as under reamer. Intermediate bulbs are also reamed to get a good grip and load bearing capacity.

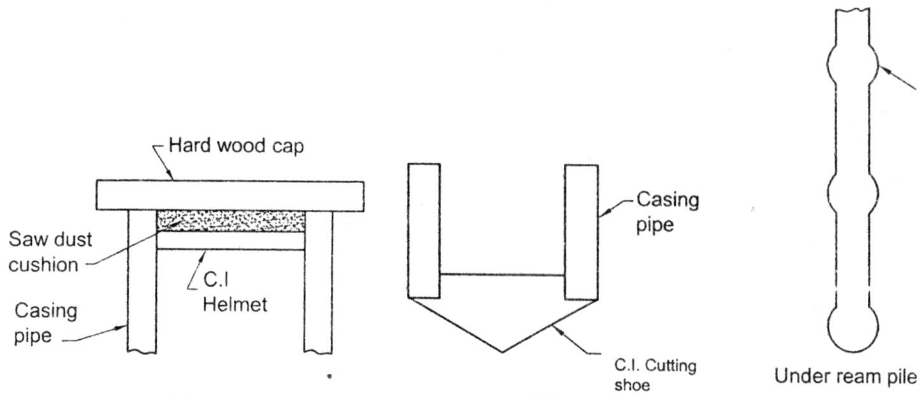

Fig. 14·40.

Pile driving equipment. (1) **Drop hammer.** The weight of the drop hammer ranges between 450 to 2250 kg. The rate of driving piles by this method is slow and pile head is injured by the impact of hammer.

(2) **Single acting hammer.** This hammer is operated by steam or compressed air, that raises the weight which falls by gravity. This hammer can strike 50 to 55 blows per minute. The stroke length or the length of fall should not exceed 1·35 m and the weight of the hammer should be at least half the weight of the pile.

(3) **Double acting hammer.** The steam pressure plays its part both in upward and downward movement of the hammer. No. of blows per minute varies between 100 to 200. Weight of the hammer is 2000 to 4000 kg and the length of drop is 1·5 m.

(4) **Water jet method.** The soil below the pile is shifted by blowing water jets through a pipe under a pressure of 7 to 17·5 kg/cm^2. Sometimes jet pipes are imbedded in the precast piles at their axis for blowing water. The jet pipe is kept 15 to 30 cm below the shoe of the pile through which soil washes up by the nozzle of the pipe and the pile sinks in the space made hollow by the jet. The blowing of the pipe is stopped about a metre above the required depth which is completed

by the hammer so as to avoid any hollow below the pile shoe.

Followers. It is an intermediate member between the head of the pile and the hammer. When it becomes necessary to drive the pile head below the reach of the hammer, these followers are used in between.

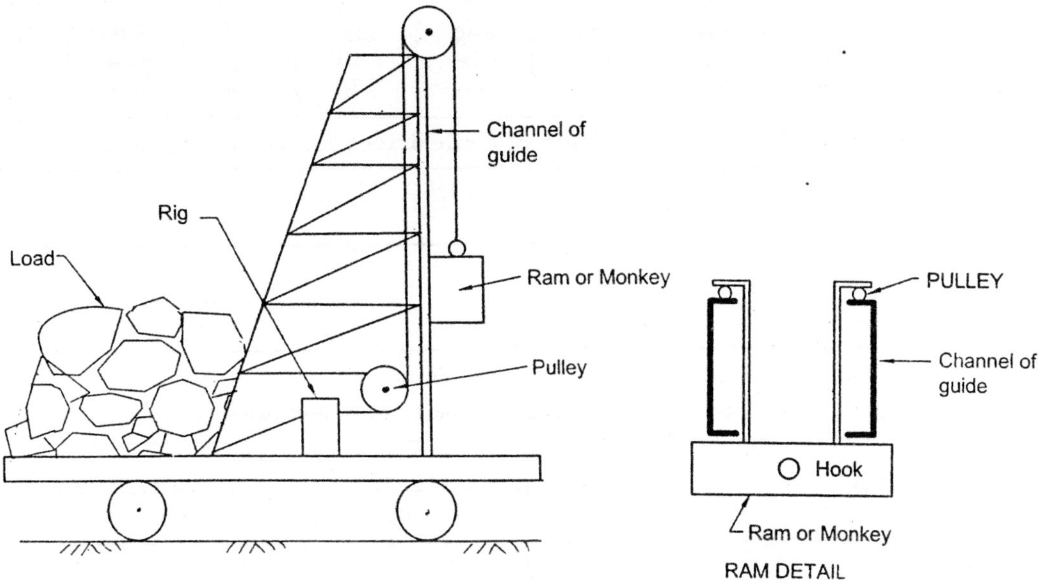

Fig. 14·41. Pile Driving Plant.

Driving heads or cushion blocks. To safeguard the pile heads against splitting while driving, the pile head is protected by a cast iron helmet. The helmet is fitted with a timber stub-dolly at its top and a cushion or packing of saw dust, coirmat coiled hemp rope or asbestos fibre etc. is placed between the timber dolly and the pile head. The hammer blows are given on the timber dolly which may be a hard wood like tamrind (Imli). It must not be more than 25 mm thick.

For easy penetration the precast piles may be tapered at their lower end.

Anvil—It is a part of a power operated hammer which receives the blows of the ram and transfers to the pile.

Safe load on pile

$P = 16{\cdot}7\ WH/(S + 2{\cdot}54)$ free drop hammer

$P = 16{\cdot}7\ H(W + ap)/(S + 0{\cdot}254)$ Double acting steam hammer

P = Safe load on pile in kg, W = weight of monkey in kg

p = mean effective steam presure in kg/cm^2

a = piston area in cm^2

H = height of fall in m

S = Average penetration of a pile in cm per blow measured as the average of the cast 5 to 10 blows under a drop hammer or as the average of the cast 20 blows under steam hammer

$D = 16\ WH/(S + 0{\cdot}25)$ with steam hammer

$p = 16\ WH/(S + 2{\cdot}5)$ with drop hammer, where S is the penetration (taken average of three blows)

Table 14·24. Safe load on piles in tonnes

H in m → / Penetration ↓mm	*150 kg monkey*			*300 kg monkey*			*1000 kg monkey*		
	1·22	*1·83*	*2·44*	*1·22*	*1·83*	*2·44*	*1·22*	*1·83*	*2·44*
6	0·96	1·44	1·92	1·92	2·88	3·84	6·40	9·60	12·80
13	0·80	1·20	1·60	1·60	2·40	3·20	5·33	8·66	10·67
19	0·69	1·03	1·37	1·37	2·06	3·74	4·57	6·86	9·10
25	0·60	0·90	1·28	1·20	1·80	2·40	4·00	6·00	8·00

Table 14·25. Test for a safe depth of a pile driven for taking the load

Penetration of last blow (mm)	*Wt. of monkey (kg)*	*Fall of monkey (m)*
5 mm for 30 blows	400	1·5
6 mm for 10 blows	760	4·6
5 mm for 10 blows	400	9·0

Set—Penetration of the pile per blow in the last blows.

Table 14·26. Load bearing capacity of bored piles

Type of soil	*Dia. of pile (cm) (cm)*	*Length of pile*			
		2m	*2·5m*	*3m*	*4m*
Firm at	25	2	4	5	7
60 cm and	30	3	5	6	7
stiff at 2·5 cm	35	4	6	7	8
stiff at 60 cm	25	2	6	8	—
and hard at	30	3	7	9	—
2·5 m	35	4	9	11	—

General design considerations of pile foundation

(1) No pile shall be less than 30 cm in dia.

(2) Piles should be spaced sufficiently apart to ensure that the zones of soil surrounding them from which the piles derive support do not overlap to such an extent that their bearing values are reduced and the settlement increased. In case of friction piles the c/c spacing must not be less than 100 cm or the circumference of the piles whichever is greater. The spacing for bearing piles should not be less than 75 cm or twice the least width whichever is greater. The maximum spacing c/c must be 4 times the dia. of the pile.

(3) The error of the position in plan to the site must not be more than 7·5 cm and the maximum error in verticality must not be more than 2% of the length of the pile. If it is more, the pile cap must be redesigned or an extra pile must be driven.

(4) The cap of the pile should extent at least 15 cm beyond the edge of the pile and its minimum thickness must be 60 cm.

(5) The reinforcement of the pile should extend in the cap and the top of the pile must be embedded in cap not less than 7·5 cm.

Sand pile foundations. On weaker soils the sand piling system is used. Holes in foundation are made by pegs, augers or sludgers, according to the depth and dia. The holes are spaced diagonally so that each hole is 60 cm apart to the adjacent. These holes are filled with sand. The dia. of the hole varies from 15 cm to 30 cm and depth 60 cm to 3 m according to the load and type of soil. The spacing is kept 0·50 m to 3 m or according to the arrangements of columns of the structure. The filled sand is compacted well and the concrete of the top slab must reach in the hole 15 to 30 cm.

Drag down on piles—Consolidation of upper soil layers after pile installation.

Load test for a pile. The test is done in the following steps :

(1) A pit about 0·2 m below the top of pile is dug in the ground.

(2) The top of the pile is levelled so as to have a good seat for an iron test plate.

(3) Three rows of steel I-sections, which may be adequate to suport the load under test. The lowest section I-1 should be of a heavier section and must be supported in ground on its both sides. The edges of the middle I-2-sections (Three in no. min.) with firm base must be supported on two long strong wooden sleepers *S*-2 placed firmly over ground. I-sec I-3 which are three or more in nos. are placed cross wise over I-sections I-2 to distribute the load evenly. The top of the I-sec. I-3 is provided with a plateform of wooden sleepers *S*-1 on which the earth filled jute bags are stacked in a proper bond, so as to give more load than the required load under test. The lower flange of I-sec I-1 is made to touch the pressure cylinder *S*, the bottom of which rests on a steel sheet over the pile top under test. The situation of I-sec. I is thus adjusted at the time of its placing at a proper position which is checked by placing the pressure cylinder on the pile, so that it may not remain loose or so tight. For a loose position packings can be used and for tight the top of the pile should be chiselled. After the pressure cylinder has been set in position the pressure is increased gradually by an air pump which is read on a gauge *G* having least count of 0·02 mm and recorded in the form of a table. The sinking of the pile is also recorded against each pressure reading. The sinking of the pile is noted on a scale through a pointer which is fixed to the upper edge of the pile by a clamp.

The test load should be 1½ times the proposed safe load value of the pile group. The test load should be applied in equal increments of 10 tonnes at intervals of 12 hours till the proposed working load has been applied. After the safe working load has been applied the increments of 10 tonnes will be made every 24 hours till the full test load has been reached. Full test load shall remain for seven days deviation of settlement will be made every six hours till working load is reached, thereafter 3 hours till full test load is reached and finally every 24 hours.

The test load should be removed in decreaments not exceeding 10 tonnes with intervals of not less than one hour. The rebound shall be recorded after each decreament. The finished rebound should be recorded 24 hours after entire test load has been removed. The test is accepted as satisfactory if—

(*i*) The total set under full test load after a period of 7 days does not exceed 12·5 mm and if the ultimate settlement after removal of test load does not exceed 6 mm.

(*ii*) The general behaviour of pile or the pile group during the test does not disclose any defect.

(*iii*) For a group of end bearing piles the allowable load may be taken as the allowable load for one pile multiplied by the no. of piles in the group.

For a group of friction piles the allowable load shall be allowable load for one pile multiplied by the no. of piles in the group and the efficiency of the pile group. The efficiency of the pile group shall be calculated by the following formula.

$$e = \frac{1 - \theta(n-1)m + (m-1)n}{90\,mn}$$

e = efficiency of pile group. m = no. of rows of piles

n = no. of piles in each row, $\theta = \tan^{-1} d/s$ in degrees.

d = pile dia. in cm, s = pile spacing in cm c/c

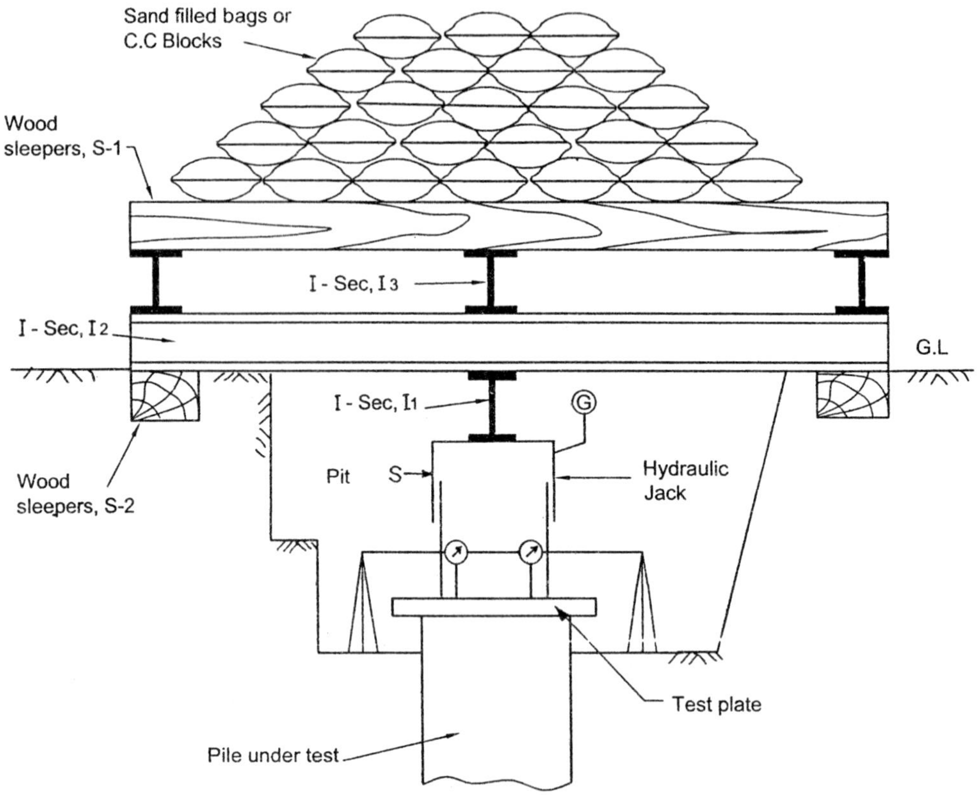

Fig. 14·42. Load test for pile.

Different building codes specify different settlement criteria for determining the ultimate or directly the allowable load such as—

(*i*) The settlement should not exceed 10% of the pile dia. for ultimate load.

(*ii*) The settlement should not exceed 1 cm for allowable load.

(*iii*) The pile should not settle more than 5 cm under twice the design load and not more than 2 cm under the design load.

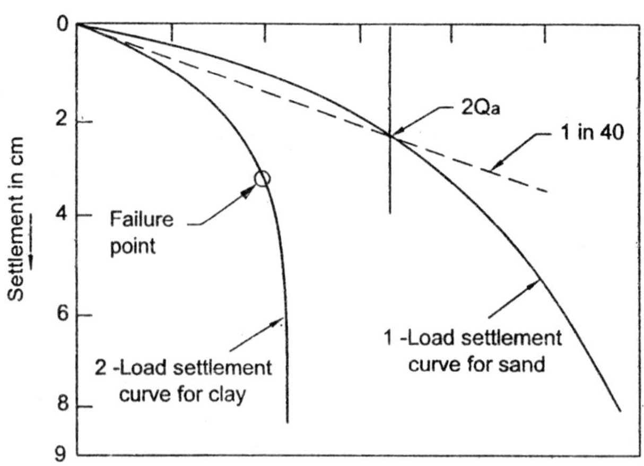

Fig. 14·43. Typical load settlement curves for sand and clay.

In such a double specification, the load corresponding to 2 cm settlement say Q_1 and that corresponding to 5 cm settlement. Say Q_2 would be read out and then the minimum of Q_1 and $Q_1/2$, evidently be taken as the design load.

(*iv*) At twice the design load the settlement per 10 kN should be less than 1/40 cm. For such a specification a line at a slope 1/4 (*i.e.* 2 cm settlement for 800 kN) is drawn and the point where it cuts the load settlement curve will read out twice of the design load *i.e.* $2Q_a$.

These different design criteria will determine different values of the design load, and in fact one of them may be specified depending upon the type of the structure which has to come on the proposed pile system.

Testing of pile capacity by under reamed reaction pile method

The old testing method of piles by direct loading is very inconvenient and cumbersome. Central Building Research Institute, Roorkee has deviced more convenient and cheaper method by using under reamed reacation piles.

In this testing method the test pile is kept in centre of the double under reamed reaction piles which are kept at 30° from normal. In the reaction piles 50 mm dia. reinforcing anchor bars bushed on both ends are embedded. These bars can be taken out after test for further use in other tests. This anchor bar is used for taking uplift resistance by the inclined under reamed piles. In the lower end of the anchor bar a 100 × 100 × 12 mm m.s. reaction plate is inserted and bolted from underneath. This plate is greased so that it can leave the anchor bar when unscrewed from top. The concrete in the pile is filled and the anchor bar is twisted so that it has no bond with the inclined pile concrete and can be easily removed after test. By doing so the m.s. plate with bolt is left inside the pile.

The upper end of the anchor bar is joined to other extra rod (70 mm dia.) which reaches upto the required height by coupler turn buckles and is bolted to the reaction frame by spherical headed bolts over a plate through holes in the later (made from a 25 mm bar).

The pressure on the test piles is taken from the reaction piles by hydraulic jack.

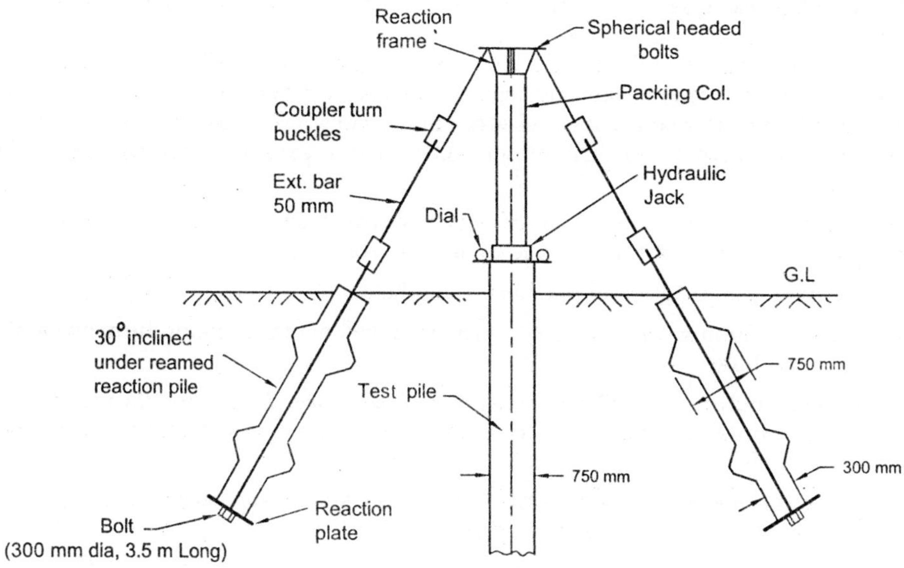

Fig. 14·44.

Reaction frame. It is constructed by 30 cm long and 10 cm dia. steel log on the ends of which 30 cm and 100 cm dia. 25 mm thick iron plates are fixed. For the distribution of load 10 mm thick vertical plates are welded in between the reaction plates. In the 100 cm dia. plate inclined 75 mm dia. rod bolt bushed to 50 mm threads is bolted with spherical headed nuts through inclined holes. The extension rods can be tightened in correct position in the inclined holes of the reaction plate.

Packing column. The space between the test pile and the reaction frame is filled with a strong packing column.

The packing column is constructed by 200 mm dia. pipe inside of which spiral reinforcement is provided and the pipe is then filled with concrete. In order to make this column more strong 25 mm × 25 mm angle iron rings are welded outside of this column. On the both ends of the iron pipe 37·5 cm dia., 25 mm thick plates are welded so that it may rest easily on the test pile and reaction frame.

The no. of reaction piles is decided according to load capacity of the test pile. The design of reaction piles can be done according to the CBRI, Roorkee Publication, 1978 and Indian Standard no. 2911 Vol. III-1980.

About 12 reaction piles are needed for 300 *t* load and 8 nos. for 200 *t* load.

5. Other types of piles

Micropiles for underpinning of structures. Micropiles are small dia. (150 mm) piles constructed by using a small rotary rig to form piles by using repeated injection process. The method of construction of micro piles gives minimum disturbance to the surrounding soils and structures and hence is ideally suited for the piles required for under pinning of structures and also where piles have to be constructed very close to the existing structures or where head room and working space is extremely limited.

The piles can be constructed in almost all types of soils and rocks. The capacity of each pile in compression is about 25*t* and in tension 10*t* to 15*t*. These piles are therefore ideally suited for carrying compressive or tensile forces. Only small amount of bending moments can be taken by the micropiles. However since these piles can be constructed in virtually any direction, it is possible to reduce the bending moment on the piles by using inclined piles.

Method of construction. The equipment for installing micropiles is a small rotary drilling machine. The rig is of such a design that it can be accommodated in a very low head room area of only 3 m high and small working space of only 2 m × 3 m. With this machine there are no problems in drilling through existing brick or reinforced concrete walls as well as old foundations. Even cutting reinforcing bars and steel plates does not present any difficulty. The rigs are normally powered with an electric motor. Where more area is available engine driven equipment can be used.

For grouting the piles a collodial grout mixture and high pressure injection pump is required. The maximum pressure of the pump is to be upto 100 kg/cm^2.

The main steps in construction of piles are given below :

(*a*) A bore hole of 150 mm dia. is drilled to the required depth by using **bentonite slurry** to stablise the sides of the hole.

(*b*) A tube-a-manchett pipe (TAM) is lowered into the hole. This pipe (65 mm dia. heavy class) has slots at design intervals, which are covered by rubber sleeves through which repeated injection of grout is possible.

(*c*) After fixing the pecker just above the lower most sleeve sheath grout is injected into the hole, which displaces the bentonite slurry completely.

(*d*) Through each of the TAM sleeves high pressure injection is carried out to form grout bulbs around the hole.

(*e*) A 32 mm or 36 mm dia. tor steel rod is lowered into the TAM pipe and annular gap between the rod and the pipe is filled with grout.

(*f*) For good bonding between the pile head and the pile cap shear connectors are welded to the exposed TAM pipe.

(*g*) Generally neat cement grout having a water cement ratio of 0·5 is used for grouting and this grout has a compressive strength of about 300 to 400 kg/cm^2 depending upon the exact water cement ratio.

This process is covered by Indian Patent No. 118640 micropiles are done where special repair jobs and strengthening of existing foundations to increase height of buildings are needed. For many bridge structures where loads have to be increased due to increased rail or road traffic, strengthening of old foundations are required. For this purpose micropiles are an ideal solution.

Under Reamed piles. Under reamed piles are bored cast in situ concrete piles having one or more number of bulbs formed by enlarging the pile stem. These piles are best suited in soils where considerable ground movements occur due to seasonal variations, filled up grounds or in soft soil strata. Provision of under reamed bulbs has the advantage of increasing the bearing and uplift capacities. It also provides better anchorage at greater depths. These piles are efficiently used in machine foundations over bridges, electrical transmission lower foundations and water tanks. Indian Standard IS 2911 (Part III) 1980 covers the design and constructions of under reamed piles having one or more bulbs. According to the code the dia. of the under reamed bulbs may vary from 2 to 3 times the stem dia. depending upon the feasibility of construction and design requirements. These piles are of the following two types :

(1) Single bulb called single under reamed (2) Double bulb called double under reamed

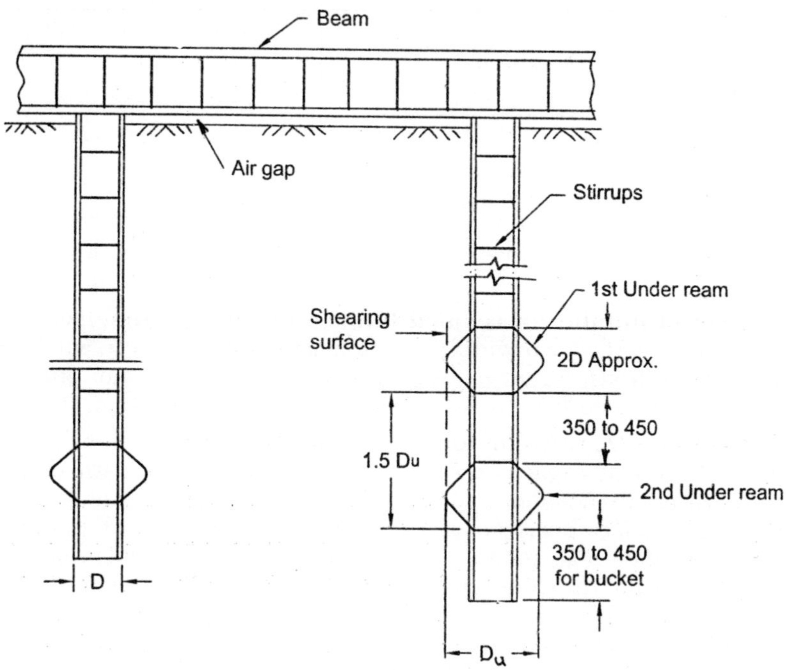

The spacing between any two piles < 1·5 D_u
(All dimensions are in mm)

Fig. 14·45. (Under reamed piles).

The code suggests a spacing of 1·25 to 1·5 times the bulb dia. for the bulbs. An angle of 45° with horizontal is recommended for all under reamed bulbs. This code also gives mathematical expressions for calculating the bearing and uplift capacities. Pile load capacity was found to vary with the number of bulbs and with the spacing ratio S/D_u or S/d adopted (where S = distance between the piles, D_u = dia. of under reamed bulbs and d = dia. of pile.)

Table 14·27. Recommended S/D_u and S/d values for under reamed piles.

Reference	Number of bulbs	Spacing
1. Patnakar (1970)	Pile capacity for one bulb in colasis 25%. For two bulbs 600% and for three bulbs 700% over simple pile	For optimum capacity two bulbs $S/D_u = 6$ or $S/d = 15$, for three bulbs $S/D_u = 5$ or $S/d = 12$
2. Agarwal and Jain (1971)	—	For optimum capacity $S/D_u = 1{\cdot}25$ to 1·5
3. Sona Pal and Thakkar (1977)	—	For optimum capacity $S/D_u = 2{\cdot}5$
4. IS : 2911 (Part III) 1980	More than two bulbs are not advisable	$S/D_u = 1{\cdot}25$ to 1·5.
5. Ray and Raymond 1983	—	Maximum value of $S/D_u = 1{\cdot}25$ to 1·5

(1) Influence of angle of under reamed bulbs on load carrying capacity and settlement.

Table 14·28.

Sl. No.	Description	Ultimate load Q_u (N)	Settlement corresponding to ultimate load S_u mm
1.	Simple pile	650	12·40
2.	Pile under reamed angle 45°	2350	9·90
3.	Pile under reamed angle 0°	2450	7·80

Conclusion. The difference in capacities of the pile with under reamed angle 45° and 0° is only marginal.

(2) **Effect of number of reamed bulbs on bearing capacity.** It can be seen from the figure that the ultimate load carrying capacity increase significantly with the provision of under reamed bulbs. The increase in ultimate load carrying capacity is not effected very much by the increase in the ratio beyond 2·5.

(3) **Effect of S/D_u ratio on load carrying capacity.** It can be seen from the figure that the ultimate load carrying capacity increases steadily upto a S/D_u ratio of 2·5, beyond of which it decreases. This observation is found to be valid irrespective of the number of bulbs. Also it can be seen from the Fig. that position of three or more number of under reamed bulbs are advantageous only when S/D_u is less than two. Generally the number of under reamed bulbs is restricted to two from the construction point of view. The spacing ratio S/D_u of 2·5 is recommended for these piles to give maximum capacity. It can also be noted that the spacing ratio of 1·25 to 1·5 times the dia. of under reamed bulbs suggested in IS : 2911 (1980) is not the optimum. Theoretical expression for pile load capacity suggested by Sona Pal and Thakkar.

$$Q_u = \frac{\pi}{4}\left(D_u - D^2\right)\left\{\frac{1}{2}D(D_u - D)n\,y\,N_y + y N_q \sum_{r=1}^{r=n} dr\right\} + \frac{\pi}{4}D^2\left(\frac{1}{2}D_y\,N_y + y\,D_1\,N_q\right) + \frac{1}{2}ny\tan\delta\left\{K\,D\,D_1^2 + KD\left(D_f^2 - D_n^2\right)\right\}$$

where D_u = dia. of under reamed bulbs
Q_u = ultimate bearing capacity of pile
D = dia. of pile.

$$+\frac{1}{2}\pi\gamma \tan\phi\left\{K\, D_u\left(D_n^2 - D_1^2\right)\right\}$$

$N_y\, H_q$ = Bearing capacity factor

dr = Depth of the centre of the different under reamed bulbs below ground level

D_f = Total depth of pile below G.L.

d = Angle of wall friction

D_1 = depth of the centre of the 1st under reamed bulb

D_n = depth of the centre of the last under reamed bulb

K = Earth pressure constant

K' = Passive earth pressure constant

Casting of under reamed piles. Under reamed bulb piles are developed by CBRI, Roorkee for black cotton soil and for other weaker soils. The piles may be vertical or may be slanted in an angle according to load direction. The work is proceeded in following steps.

(1) Bore a pile hole of the required diameter by a spiral drill to the depth of 1st bulb.

(2) At the bulb position the special mechanical arrangement is opened which can cut the hole in the shape of the bulb when rotated.

(3) The work of drilling bore and bulbs proceeded in the downward direction till the required depth.

Table 14·29. Ultimate load capacities with different methods

S. No.	*S/D$_u$*	*No. of bulbs*	*Observed ultimate load capacity (N)*	*Predicted ultimate load N*		
				Modified Method (N)	*IS method N*	*Sona Pal and Thakkar N*
1	—	—	800	995	1000	995
2	1·5	2	850	1850	1610	1780
3	1·5	3	1050	2580	2150	2480
4	1·5	4	1100	3200	2610	3080
5	1·5	5	1950	3830	3005	3590
6	2·0	2	1300	1900	1600	1890
7	2·0	3	1700	2650	2060	2650
8	2·0	4	2250	3270	2445	3240
9	2·0	5	2900	3740	2740	3700
10	2·5	2	2300	1940	1540	2020
11	2·5	3	3050	2700	1970	2850
12	2·5	4	3150	3250	2280	3460
13	2·5	5	3200	3610	2480	3850
14	3·0	2	2100	1980	1510	2200
15	3·0	3	2950	2720	1885	3100
16	3·0	4	2600	3200	2120	3700
17	3·0	5	3050	3440	2220	3980
18	3·5	2	1900	2020	780	2400
19	3·5	3	2350	2730	770	3380
20	3·5	4	2700	3120	730	3950

Note : (1) Expression suggested in IS method can be used with spacing ratio S/D_u less than 2·5.

(2) For values of S/D_u = 2·5 or more use Sona Pal and Thakkar expression.

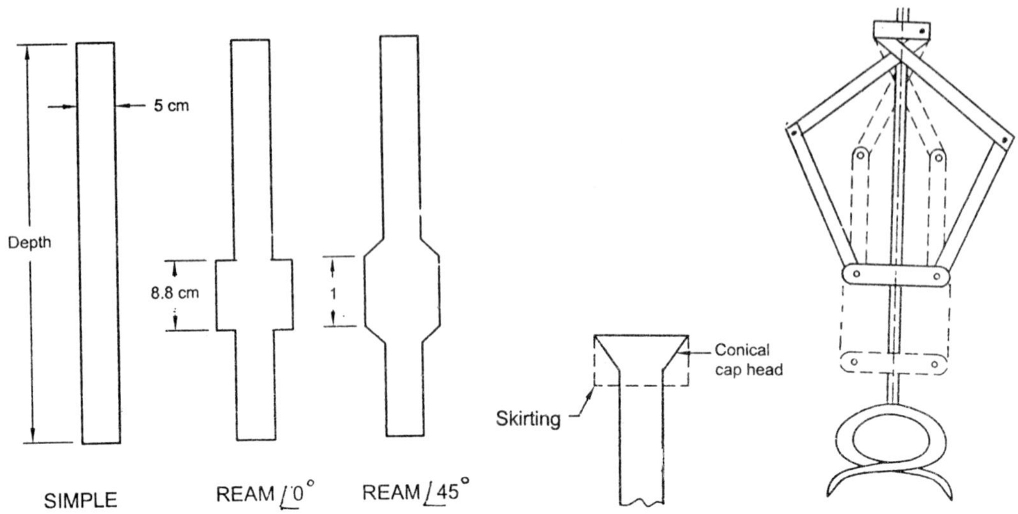

(a) (b) (c) (d) (e) Pile under reamer

Fig. 14·46.

Design of granular pile foundations. In recent years on granular piles research has been carried out to increase bearing capacity by introducing peripheral restrainment on the individual pile upto the critical length (3*d*). In the method suggested the top portion of the pile upto a certain depth is replaced by an inverted cone of granular mass. By adopting this method the critical length of a granular pile can be reduced effectively. It has been found that the increased capacity of this pile is more than that of the pile constructed on peripheral restrain (3*d*), when the depth of the conical shaped granular mass on the top of the pile is equal to half the spacing, keeping the base of the concrete equal to the spacing provided. It is found that the conical shaped granular mass at cap head of pile can eliminate the extra cost of making peripheral restrainment of individual pile.

For making conical shaped cap head at pile top the sub soil of diameter 3 times the pile dia. (*D*) around the pile is scraped out at the angle of 45° such that the vertex of the cone intersect the pile axis at a depth of 1·5 *D*. Tests are performed as per IS : 1888—1982. The load is applied through a hydraulic jack and frame, and the successive loads were increased after achieving 90% settlement during the previous load and this is continued till failure occurred. Pressure-settlement curves for each test is drawn on log-log paper and the ultimate pressure is evaluated from the curves.

Improvement of Bearing Capacity of Conical base Cap head piles. The following table gives an idea of the improvements achieved by providing conical head piles over peripheral restrained and other piles.

Table 14·30. Ultimate bearing pressure for different type of piles

Diameter and length of pile and loading area dia.	*Unrestrained pile with level ground*	*Peripheral restrained pile at pile top with level ground*	*Unrestrained pile with conical shaped cap at pile top*
28/40/120 mm	1·3 MPa	1·78 MPa	1·82 MPa
50/64/150 mm	1·20 MPa	1·76 MPa	1·80 MPa

Effect of Skirting and Padding on improved bearing capacity. From the following table it is found that the improved bearing capacity due to skirting of loaded area, skirted padding in level ground and conical base ground are found as 1·5 times, 3·55 times, 5·44 times over the normal ground. The improved bearing pressure due to skirting and padding on conical base is 3·75 times over simply improved area in level ground.

Table 14·37. Effect of skirting and padding on improved bearing capacity

Granular pile dia./length	*Dia. of loading area and skirted area*	*Ultimate bearing pressure in MPa*		
		Level ground	*Level ground with with sand padding*	*Conical base and sand padding*
38/490 mm	120mm/150 mm	1·35	3·20	4·90

Bearing Capacity of piles (Individual piles)

Q_f = Load taken by base + Load taken by skin friction or

$Q_f = q_f \,.\, A_b + f_s \,.\, A_s$

where,

Q_f = Ultimate load that can be applied at the top of the pile.

q_f = Ultimate bearing capacity of the stratum on which the pile is supported

A_b = Area of the pile section at the base

f_s = Average ultimate friction or shearing resistance of the soil per unit area

A_s = Cylindrical surface area of the pile (*i.e.* perimeter × length of pile)

The weight of the soil removed is roughly equal to the weight of the pile and is hence ignored.

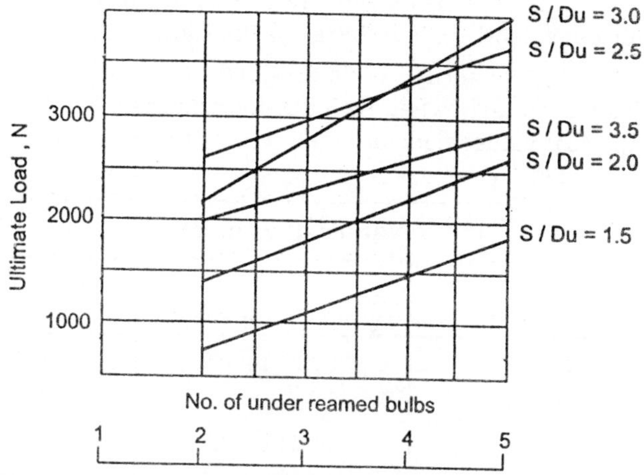

(*a*) Variation of ultimate load with number of bulbs for different S/D_u ratios.
Fig. 14·47.

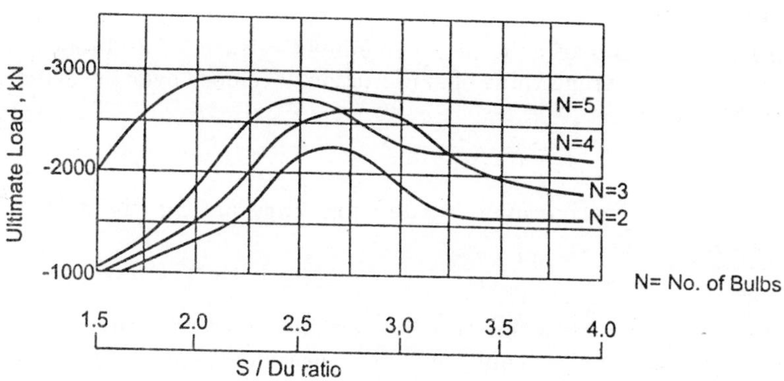

(*b*) Variation of ultimate load with S/D_u ratios having different bulbs.
Fig. 14·47.

In pile foundations where ($D_f > 15B$) is called a **deep foundation or deep piles** and where ($D_f < 15B$) is known as **shallow foundation or shallow piles** ; where D_f = depth of pile and B = lateral dimension of pile.

Computing bearing Capacity (B.C.) of piles in sandy soil

$Q_f = q_f \,.\, A_b + f_s \,.\, A_s$ values of q_f as per Terzaghi equation

$$q_f = c \,.\, N_c + (\gamma\, D_f)\, N_q + ½\, \gamma\, B \,.\, N_1$$
$$= \gamma\, D_f\, (N_q)$$

for piles in sands since c the shear strength of sand = 0 ; Depth of pile D_f is very large compared to B (lateral dimension of pile) and hence the term ½ $\gamma B\, N_y$ is negligible as compared to the term $\gamma\, D_f\, N_q$.

Hence for piles in sands $q_f = \gamma\, D_f \,.\, N_q$ where D_f = depth or length of pile embedded in sand.

$\gamma\, D_f$ represents the effective over burden pressure at the bottom or the base of the pile of embedded depth D_f (surcharge of the soil).

The factor N_q as determined by Terzaghi for a shallow footing cannot be applied to deep piles particularly when $D_f > 5B$. Berezantzev, Khristoppher and Golubkov (1961) developed some emperical values depending on ϕ and D/B ratio for evaluating the factor N_q which is given in the table below.

Values of q_c in kN/m²			**Values of N_q**	
Type of soil	*Values of q_c in kN/m²*	*ϕ(angle of repose) in degrees*	*For D_f/B = 25*	*For D_f/B = 50*
Gravels	800 N-1000N	28	12	9
		30	7	14
Sand	500 N-600 N	32	25	22
		34	40	37
Silty sands	300 N-400 N	36	58	56
		38	89	88
Silts and clayey silts	200 N	40	137	136

where N is the SPT-N values

Note : Intermediate values of D/B can be computed in ratio of difference between 25 and 50. The value of f_s which is the average value of skin friction developed over the cylindrical surface of the pile is given by the equation.

$$f_s = K_s \,.\, \overline{q_0} \tan \delta$$

where $\overline{q_0}$ = The average effective over burden pressure acting along the embedded length

$$= \frac{O + y\, D_f}{2} = \frac{y.D_f}{2}.$$

δ = angle of friction between the pile surface and the surrounding sand and can emperically be taken as equal to 0·75 $\phi°$ for concrete piles and 20° for steel piles.

K_s = average coefficient of lateral earth pressure acting along the embedded length D_f. The value of K_s for piles has been emperically given as 1·0 for loose sands and z = 0 for dense sand. These values should be further reduced by ½ for small displacement piles such as steel piles of H-section.

The values of q_f and f_s stand valid till D_f is less than a certain maximum value roughly equal to $15B$ to $20B$ which is called as **critical depth**. Below this critical depth the values of q_f as well as f_s won't change with D_f, but are found to remain approximately in uniform soil conditions. Hence for depths below critical depth the computation of the bearing capacity of piles is not found to be valid.

Computations of B.C. of piles in sandy soils by SPT-*N* Value. Given by Meyerhof (1976).

$$q_f = 40\,N\,\frac{D_f}{B} \text{ (limited to 400)} \qquad \text{For piles driven in sand in kN/m}^2$$

where N is the SPT-N value in vicinity of pile base

$$f_s = 2\,\overline{N} \text{ for piles driven in sand in kN/m}^2$$

where $\overline{N}$ = SPT-N value average over the embedded depth D_f

The above values of f_s should be multiplied by ½ for small displacement such as steel H-sections.

For bored piles the above values of q_f should be multiplied by $^1/_3$ and value of f_s by $^1/_3$ to obtain their corresponding values.

Then q_f for bored piles = ½ q_f for driven piles.

f_s for bored piles = ½ f_s for driven piles.

Example. *Depth of pile driven = 9 m in sandy soil, size of pile = 40 cm × 40 cm. The standard penetration test results are as below.*

Compute factors of safety if compressive load applied on pile = 1100 kN.

$Q_f = q_f \,.\, A_b \times f_s \times A_s$	*Depth in m*	1·5	3	4·5	6	7·5	4	10·5	12
where $q_f = 40\ N\ D_f/B$ *(limited to 400 N)*	*SPT-N value*	4	5	12	12	20	24	35	39

N for D_f = 9 m is 2·4 (from the table)

B = width of pile = 0·4 m

$$q_f = 40\,N \times \frac{9}{0\cdot4} \text{ kN/m}^2 = 900 \text{ N (limited to 400 N)}$$

$$q_f = 400\,N = 400 \times 24 = 9600 \text{ kN/m}^2$$

A_b = Area of the pile at the base $= 0\cdot4 \times 0\cdot4 = 0\cdot16$ m²

$f_s = 2\,\overline{N}$ kN/m² where $\overline{N}$ = average N over 9 m depth

$$= \frac{4+6+12+12+20+24}{6} = 13$$

$$f_s = 2\,\overline{N} = 2 \times 13 = 26 \text{ kN/m}^2$$

$$A_s = 4B\,(D_f) = 4 \times 0\cdot4 \times 9 = 14\cdot4 \text{ m}^2$$

$$D_f = 9600 \times 0\cdot16 + 26 \times 14\cdot4 = 1910 \text{ kN ; Factor of safety (F.S.)} = \frac{Q_f}{Q} = \frac{1910}{1100} = 1\cdot74$$

Compute factor of safety (F.S.) by using Bearing Capacity equation if ϕ for soil for N = 20 is 32° and N_q for ϕ = 33° and D_f/B of 22·5 is 24. Since $q_f = \gamma\, D_f \,.\, N_q$ where D_f = 9 m ; B = 0·4 m and $D_f/B = \dfrac{9}{0\cdot4} = 22\cdot5$; N_q = 24 (given).

Note : From table given by Terzaghi equation for N = 20 at depth 7·5 m, ϕ = 32° and as given this example is 33°. Further in Table for the values of N_q for ϕ = 32° and D_f/B = 22·5 the value of N_q is approximately $= \left(25 - \dfrac{3}{25} \times 2\cdot5\right) = 24\cdot4$ which in the example is given as 29 hence even if these values are not given we could have calculated them.

Now $q_f = 18 \times 9 \times 24$ (Assume γ = 18 kN/m³) = 3888 kN/m²

Machine Foundations :

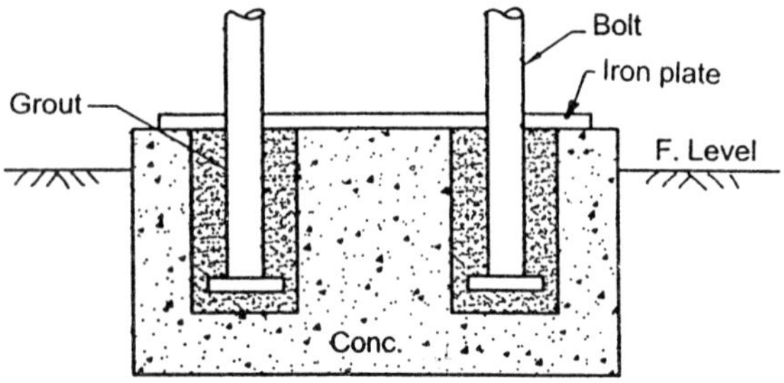

Simple foundation

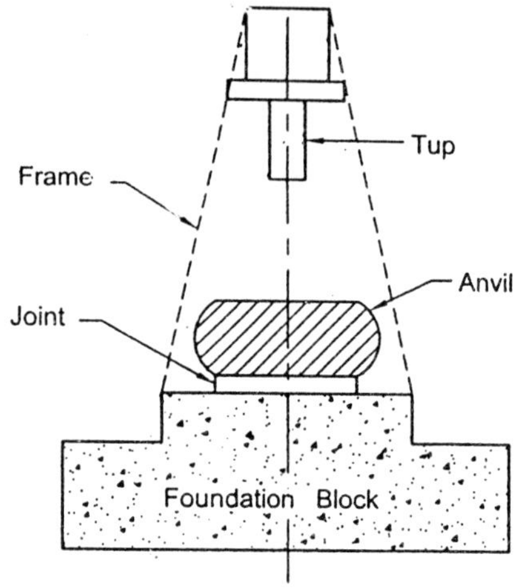

Impact type

Foundations resting on soil

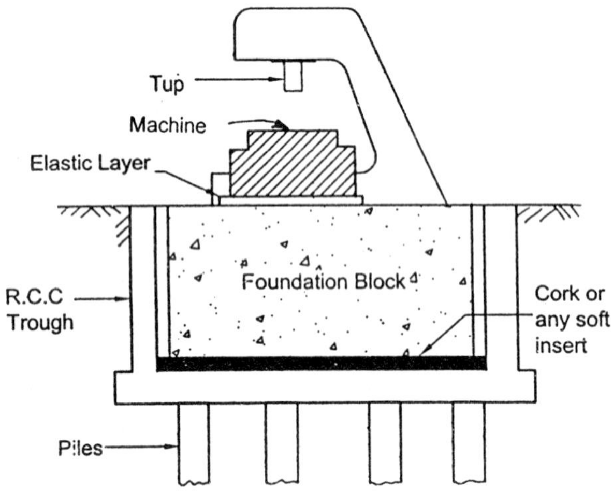

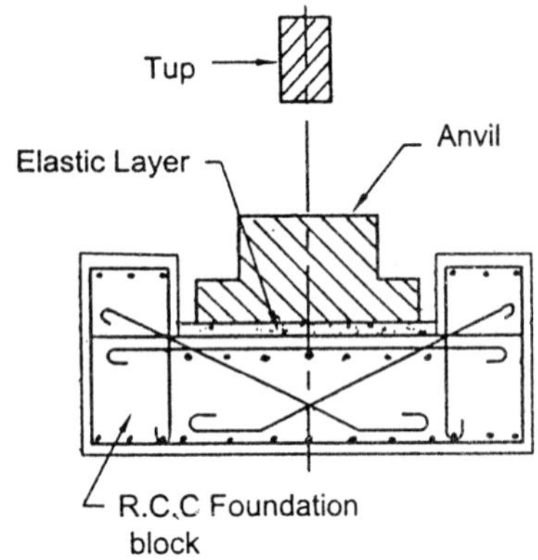

Foundation on piles

Fig. 14·48.

Also $\quad f_s = K_s \times \overline{q_0} \tan \delta$ where $\overline{q_0} = \dfrac{\gamma D_f}{2}$ (as discussed above)

$$= \frac{18 \times 9}{2} = 81 \text{ kN/m}^2$$

$K_s = 1{\cdot}5$ (assume as it is medium sand)

$\delta = 0{\cdot}75\ \phi° = 0{\cdot}75 \times 32° = 24°$

$f_s = 1{\cdot}5 \times 81 \times \tan 24° = 54 \text{ kN/m}^2$

In $\quad Q_f = q_f \times A_b + f_s \times A_s$; $\quad A_b = 0{\cdot}4 \times 0{\cdot}4 = 0{\cdot}16 \text{ m}^2$

$A_s = 4 \times 0{\cdot}4 \times 9 = 14{\cdot}4 \text{ m}^2$

$$Q_f = 3888 \times 0{\cdot}16 + 54 \times 14{\cdot}4 = 1400 \text{ kN}$$

$$F.S. = \frac{Q_f}{Q} = \frac{1400}{1100} = 1{\cdot}27$$

Table 14·33. Spacing of piles.

Type of pile	*Minimum spacing centre to centre of piles*
1. Bearing piles in hard stratum	2 to 2½ times diameter of piles or minimum 0·8 m.
2. Bearing piles in hard bed rock	2 times diameter or minimum 0·6 m.
3. Friction piles	3 to 5 times diameter or minimum 1·0 m.

15

Roads

15·1. Technical Terms

Arterial or trunk roads—A part of national highway which joints important road system of the country.

Blind alley—A road which has a dead end at one of its ends.

Carriage way—Pucca portion of a road designed for vehicular traffic.

Road way—Carriage way plus both the side shoulders or berms.

Right of way—Land required and reserved for a road.

Traffic lane—It is an unit of carriage way supposed to carry single line of vehicular traffic.

Urban roads—Roads built in built up areas of cities.

Subway—An underground passage for pedestrians, vehicles or for any other type of water or sanitry pipes.

Shoulder, haunch or berm—Space left in sides of carriage way which can be utilised in emergency for crossing and overtaking of vehicles.

Asphaltic cement—A mixture of asphalt and bitumen.

Bituminous cement—A general term for bituminous substances which serve as a binder.

Straight run bitumen—It is steam refined bitumen prepared by direct distillation of a crude oil.

Flash point—The lowest temperature at which vapour starts forming.

Matrix—It is a binding base.

Tack coat—It is coat between the new and the old surface of a road to bind them together.

Grabbing—Uprooting and removing the stumps and roots.

Lockspit or Daghbel—A bench line demarcating a layout.

Macadom—A road metal below 75 mm size.

Pot holes—Local depressions in a road due to wearing.

Scarifying—Loosing of the top surface by manual or mechanical means.

Stripping—The operation of cleaning the site of work.

Crazing—Breaking up a surface layer in irregular shaped areas.

Fascines—Grass bundles laid on a sandy track to pass temporary traffic.

Hairpin bends—Zig zag bends in hill roads to cope with gradient in road.

Collie walls—Outer edge protection by rough stone dry walls. (In hill roads)

Water bound macadum—The base layer of a road bounded by metal and soil particles and consolidated by water.

Cement bound macadum—The base layer of a road metal bounded and consolidated with cement.

Skids—Undulations on roads to the projecting stones causing rough surfaces.

15·2. Classification of Non-urban Roads in India

(1) **National Highways.** They connect capitals of states, ports, foreign highways, large towns and industrial centres. They can be deemed to be the primary road network of the country. They traverse through out of India and are of national importance for strategic and administrative purposes.

(2) **State Highways.** These roads are the main centres of traffic within a state serving important cities and are connected to the National Highways and important roads of other states.

(3) **District roads.** These roads take off from the main roads of the state. According to an importance, some of these are known as major district roads while the other are known as other district roads.

(*i*) Major district roads (*ii*) Other district roads.

(4) **Village roads.** These roads connect the major roads to the villages or are connected from villages to villages.

In Road Development Plan (1981-2001), the classification is slightly suggested as under :

(A) **Primary system** (*i*) Express ways, (*ii*) National Highways.

(B) **Secondary system** (*i*) State Highways, (*ii*) Major district roads.

(C) **Tertiary system** (*i*) Other district roads, (*ii*) Village roads.

The classification system adopted for urban highways in this country along with a brief description of each class is given below :

(1) **Express ways.** These are defined as divided highways for motorised traffic with full or partial control access and provided generally with grade separation at intersections. Their main function is to provide for movement of heavy volume of motorised traffic at high speeds. They connect major points of traffic generation and are intended to serve trips of medium and long lengths between residential areas, industrial or commercial concentrations and the central business district. They are generally provided with grade separating at intersections. Parking and unloading of goods and pedestrian traffic are not permitted in their facilities.

(2) **Arterial streets.** Arterial streets is a general term denoting a street primarily meant for through traffic on a continuous route. These alongwith express ways where exists serve as the principal network for through traffic flow. These streets should be coordinated with existing and proposed express way systems to provide for distribution and collector street system. Continuity is the prime essential of arterial streets to ensure efficient movement of through traffic. A properly developed and designed arterial street system would help to identify residential neighbourhoods, industrial cities and commercial areas. These streets are generally spaced at less than 1·5 km in highly developed and central business areas and at 8 km or more in sparsely developed urban fringes. The arterial streets are generally divided highways with fully or partially controlled access. Parking loadings and unloading activities are usually restricted and regulated. Pedestrians are allowed to cross only at intersections/designed pedestrian crossings.

(3) **Sub-arterial streets.** These are streets of somewhat lower level of travel mobility than the arterial streets. The emphasis in access to adjoining areas is more in case of these streets than in the case of arterial streets. Parking loading and unloading are usually restricted and regulated. Pedestrians are allowed to cross only at intersections. Their spacing varies from about 0·5 km in the central business district to 3 to 5 km in the suburban fringe.

(4) **Collector streets.** A collector street is one intended for collecting and distributing the traffic to and from local streets and also for providing access to arterial streets. They may be located in residential neighbourhoods, business areas and industrial areas. Normally fuel access is allowed on these streets from abutting properties. There are few parkings restrictions except during peak hours.

(5) **Local streets.** A local street is one primarily intended for access to residence, business or other abutting property. Such a street normally does not carry large volume of traffic. The traffic carried either originates or terminates along its length. A local street may be residential, commercial or industrial, depending upon the prominent use of the adjoining land. A local street allows unrestricted parkings and pedestrian moment.

(1) **Express ways.** Express ways, motor ways and free ways denotes a superior type of high way facilities, designed for high speeds, high traffic volumes and safety. The term motor way is common in U.K.

The characteristics of express ways :

(1) They have high speeds. A design speed is 120 km/hour (usually).

(2) They have dual carriage way separated by a median, so that each carriage way may be used solely for one direction. However as a 1st stage there are some two lane undivided express ways too.

(3) They have on crossings provided with over bridges or under passes.

(4) They have access control which permits traffic to enter or leave the facility only at designed locations.

(5) Slow moving traffic is not allowed on express ways.

(6) Their construction and maintenance is of superior quality.

15·2·2. Design Standards. The following are the typical values being used in the interim period on some of the projects.

(1)	**Right of way**	90 to 100 m		
(2)	**Design speed**	Plain Terrain	: 120 km/hr	
		Rolling Terrain	: 80-100 km/hr	
		Hilly Terrain	: 60-70 km/hr	
(3)	**Carriage way width**	2 × 2 lane	2 × 7·5 m	
		2 × 3 lane	2 × 11·25 m	
(4)	**Paved shoulder (Berm)**	Left side including 0·5 m edge strip	2·5 to 3·0 m	
		Right side including 0·5 m edge strip	0·7 to 1·0 m	
(5)	**Unpaved shoulder**	Left side	1·0 to 1·5 m	
(6)	**Median width**	2 × 2 lane	12-15 m (So as to accommodate future 6 lane)	
		2 × 3 lane	4-5 m.	
(7)	**Gradient**	Plain Terrain	Ruling	2·0 percent
			Max.	2·5 percent
		Rolling Terrain	Ruling	2·0 percent
			Max.	3·0 percent
		Hilly Terrain	Ruling	4·0 percent
			Max.	5·0 percent
(8)	**Radius of horizontal curves**	Plain Terrain	Desirable	2600 m

		Min.	700 m
	Rolling Terrain	Desirable	450 m
		Min.	300 m
	Hilly Terrain	Desirable	175 m
		Min.	125 m
(9) **Super elevation**	Plain and Rolling Terrain	7 percent	
	Hilly Terrain	8 percent	
(10) **Camber**	Bituminous pavement	2·5 percent	
	Cement conc. (Pavement)	2·0 percent	
	(Shoulder)	1·0 percent (more than that of pavement)	

(11) **Safe stopping sight distances**

Design speed km/hr	*Safe stopping sight distance (m)*
60	80
70	100
80	120
90	150
100	180
110	220
120	250

(12) **Interchanges :** Design speed for interchange elements (km/hr)

Terrain	*Left turning ramps*	*Right turning ramps / loops*
Plain/Rolling	70-90	50
Hilly	40-50	30-40

Gradient : Ramps/Diagonal connections 4 percent

Loops 5 percent

Width of ramps (1) Road way 12 m

(2) Carriage way: 5·5 m for traffic upto 16,000 PCUs/day (Public Carriage Unit)

7·5 m for traffic above 16000 PCU per day and (Public carrier unit upto 32,000 PCUs/day

(3) Paved shoulder 1·5 m on either side

(4) Radius of curvature :

Loop/Ramp design speed km/hr	*Radius (m)*
90	300
70	180
80	130
50	85
40	55

(13) **Speed Change Lanes**

Design speed of turning road way curves (km/hr)		*Stopped condition*	*25*	*30*	*40*	*50*	*60*	*65 and above*
Design speed of High way (km/hr)	*Length of taper (m)*	*Total length of declaration lane including taper (m)*						
65	60	100	90	85	75	60	—	—
80	70	130	120	115	110	110	85	—
100	80	150	150	145	140	130	120	100
110	90	165	165	160	150	145	140	115
120	100	180	180	170	160	150	145	125
Design speed of High way (km/hr)	*Length of taper (m)*	*Length of acceleration lane including taper (m)*						
65	60	—	100	75	70	—	—	—
80	70	—	210	190	180	150	120	—
100	80	—	340	320	300	270	240	180
110	90	—	465	450	420	370	300	250
120	100	—	550	500	450	400	350	300

(14) **Bridges and viaducts.** The width should be the same as that of the approach pavement.

(15) **Culverts.** Culverts should accommodate the full express way including carriage way, median and shoulders.

(16) **Clearance.** The minimum vertical clearance shall be 5·5 m.

(17) **Width of under pass** for accommodating cross roads (refer Fig. 15·1(*a*)).

(18) **Width of structure** with express way at ground level (refer X-sec. Fig. 15·1(*b*)).

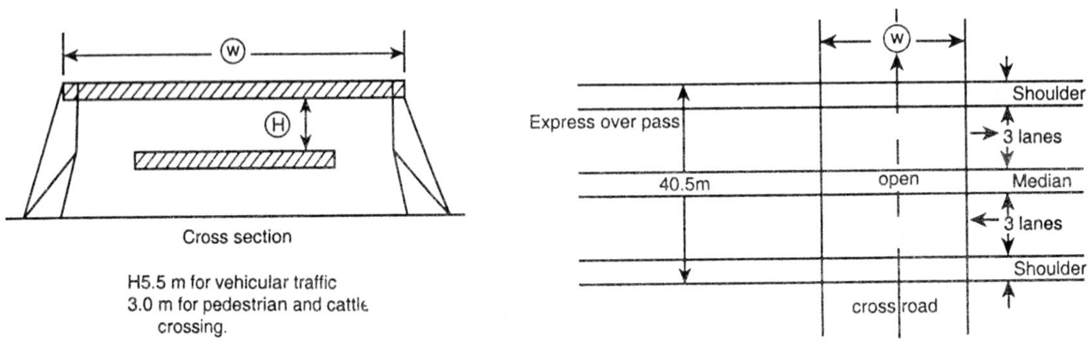

Under pass for cross roads in expressways

Fig. 15·1

15·2·3. Safety Barriers on Expressways—Since express ways have high speed facilities, therefore it is desirable to provide safety barriers. Edge barriers are provided on road embankments by the height and slope of an embankments. The barriers can be steel beam type, concrete of wire type.

Expressway signs and Road markings. The signs and markings should be visible and easily read by the drivers of fast moving vehicles. Since express ways are access controlled and are cut off from the local information sources. There should be adequate information signs to facilitate the traveller. The letters should be of large size, symbols should be large and legend should be short. The signs must be of reflective type and over head type, even if reflectorised, do not get sufficient light from the beam of a car. Hence they should be illuminated. It is convenient to provide over head gantry signs for effective visibility. All edge strips should be marked with reflectorised continuous line and lane markings should be of broken reflected type.

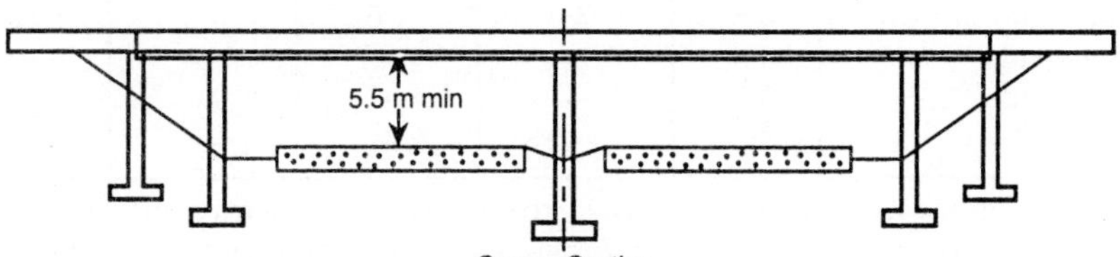

Cross - Section

Fig.15.2(a)

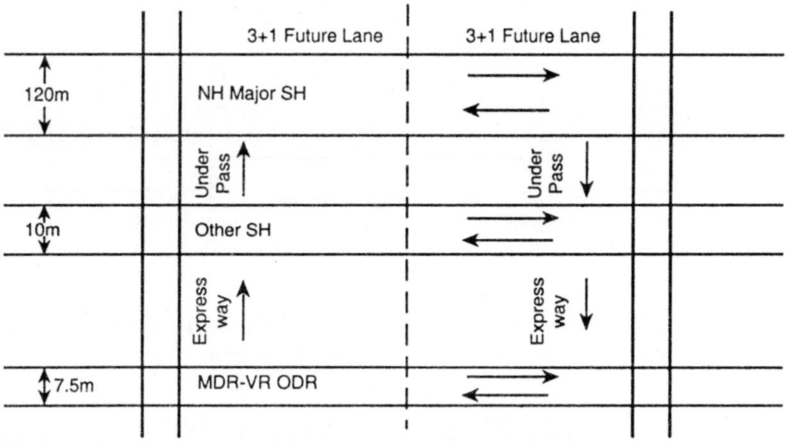

(*b*)

Fig. 15·2. Cross road above expressway.

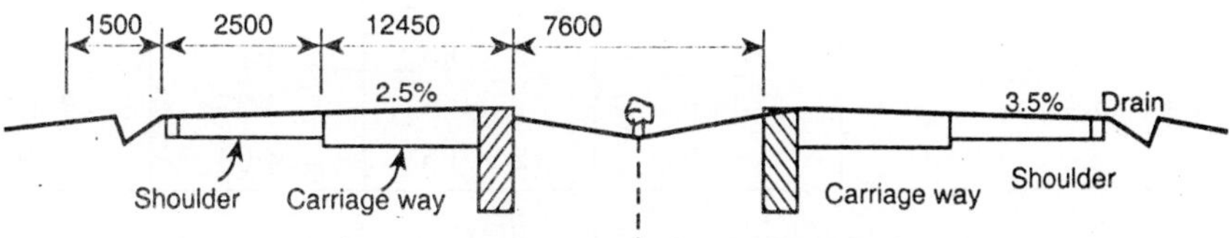

Cross-sec of 2×3 lane express way

(All dimensions are in mm)

Fig. 15·3. Cross-sec. 2 × 3 lane expressway.

15·2·4. Rest Areas. Rest areas are provided all along major highways particularly on express ways. The facilities provided are :

- Parking
- Toilets
- Open area, garden/parks
- Restaurants
- Telephone
- First aid
- Picnic tables
- Fueling shop
- Repair workshops

They can be provided on either side of the roads.

15·2·5. Standard of roads

Table 15·1. Width of carriage way and road way (IRC) and Right of way (Total land) width

Type of road	*Width of carriage way*				*Width of road way*	
	Single lane (m)	*Two lane without raised kerb (m)*	*Two lane with. raised kerb (m)*	*Multilane pavement per lane (m)*	*Single lane (m)*	*Double lane (m)*
1. National and state highway	3·8	7·0	7·5	3·5	12·0	12·0
2. Major district roads	3·8	—	—	—	10·0	—
3. Other district roads	3·8	—	—	—	8·0	—
4. Village roads	3·8	—	—	—	7·5	—

Note : (1) For multilane carriage ways the width of road way will be governed by central verge, foot paths, cycle tracks etc. and width of road way (formation width) is to be designed according to the requirement in each case.

(2) The foot path ways are to be kept 1·5 m wide.

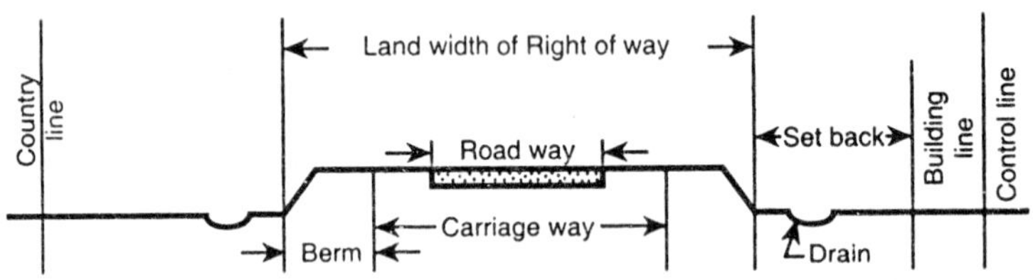

Fig. 15·4

Table 15·2. Width of carriage way, road way and right of way (Hill roads)

Type of road	*Carriage way (m)*	*Shoulder (m)*	*Road way (m)*	*Road land*	
				Built up area	*Open area*
1. National and state high way					
(*a*) Single lane	3·75	2 × 1·25	6·25	20	24
(*b*) Two lane	7·0	2 × 0·9	8·8	20	24
2. Major district road	3·75	2 × 0·5	4·75	15	18
3. Other district road	3·75	2 × 0·5	4·75	12	15
4. Village roads	3·00	2 × 0·5	4·00	9	9

Single lane = 6·71 m wide, Double lane = 7·32 m wide.

Notes : (1) The road way given above is between kerbs without parapet thickness.

(2) In hard rock reaches the width of shoulder may be reduced by 0·4 m either side in double roads and 0·2 m in other cases.

(3) In roads covered by snow, the roadway may be increased by 1·5 m in district and village roads.

(4) On culverts, scuppers and cause way full road width is provided.

(5) The minimum set back building line should be 5 m in normal cases and 3 m in exceptional cases. The width due to deep cutting and filling will be extra.

(6) For design of subway, foot bridges and other facilities, the space required by a pedestrian taken as an ellipse with a major axis of 0·6 m and minor axis as 0·45 m. The space between pedestrians while walking is generally assumed to be 2·5 m which roughly corresponds to a time headway of 2 sec.

Terrain classification

Level	0-10% cross slope of country
Rolling	10-25% cross slope of country
Mountainous	25-60% cross slope of country
Steep	Greater than 60% cross slope of country

Table 15·3. Terrain classification suggested in road user cost study

Terrain classification				*Rise and fall (m/km)*	*Curvature deg/km*
1.	Plain	(*a*)	Low curvature	0-15	0-50
		(*b*)	High curvature	0-15	above 51
2.	Rolling	(*a*)	Low curvature	16-30	0-100
		(*b*)	High curvature	16-30	above 101
3.	Hilly	(*a*)	Low curvature	over 31	0-20
		(*b*)	High curvature	over 31	above 201

Slow moving vehicles	*Bullock cart*	*Horse drive*
Length	5·87 m	4·11 m
Speed	3·78 km/hr	12·24 km/hr
Headway between two vehicles	1·0 m	0·8 m

The following particulars for cycles may be noted :

Length of cycles	1·91 m
Length of cycle rickshaw	2·09 m
Mean speed of cycles	15·63 kPH
Average headway between cycles	2 m
Lateral space occupied by one cycle	0·6 m when in group of 5 and 1·0 m for single cycle

Power driven cycles

Make	*Max. power (B.H.P)*	*Overall length (m)*	*Wheel bore (m)*	*Ground clearance cm*	*Weight kg*
Bajaj	4·5 to 12·5	1·77 to 1·95	1·17 to 1·275	10 to 16	85 to 115
Hero Honda	7·0 to 7·5	1·88 to 1·96	1·20 to 1·24	13·5 to 16·5	92 to 101
Vespa	3·5 to 8·0	1·68 to 1·76	1·17 to 1·23	11 to 16	69 to 107

Pedestrians. Speed of walk of pedestrians is considered in design of traffic signals. The average walking speed of a pedestrian is 0·75 m to 1·8 m per sec. The speed assumed in manual of uniform traffic control devices as 1·2 m/sec. for timing of pedestrian signals. The speed of a pedestrian depends on his age and health conditions.

Table 15·4. Width of carriage way on road bridges (IRC)

Type of bridge	*Clear width of carriage way between the kerbs (m)*	
1. Single lane bridge (VRB)	3·8	Min. straight level
2. Double lane bridge (DRB)	7·5	length should be
3. Bridge on high ways with four lane (dual carriage way on both sides) on either side of central dividing verge (PRB and National highways)		of 30 m on either side

Table 15·5. Minimum land width for roads

Type of road	*Open and agricultural land*				*Urban and Industrial area width of land*		*Mountainous*	
	Width of land		*Build line*	*Control line*			*Upper areas*	*Built up areas*
	Normal (m)	*Range (m)*	*Overall width (m)*	*Overall width (m)*	*Normal (m)*	*Range (m)*	*Normal (m)*	*Normal (m)*
1. National and state roads	30	30-60	60-65	140	25	25-60	24	20
2. Major district roads	20	20-30	50	100	15	15-20	18	15
3. Other district roads	15	15-25	25	40	10	10-15	15	12
4. Village roads	15	15-20	25	30	10	10-15	9	9

Note : (1) The land width also called **right of way** depends on the type of cutting and filling and availability of land.

(2) Set back for building lines from road will be 6 m for National and Provincial roads and 3 m for others.

Table 15·6. Gradient in high ways (IRC)

Type of terrains	*Gradient*		
	Ruling	*Limiting*	*Exceptional*
Plain	1 : 30	1 : 20	1 : 15
Hills	1 : 20	1 : 15	1 : 12

Absolute maximum gradient for short lengths not exceeding 60 m in one K.M.

For deep roads 1 : 15 1 : 12

Gradient at curves 1 : 30

Maximum sustained gradient with safety in operation 1 : 20

Maximum gradient at hair pins bend or other sharp curves wi[illegible]nside curves of 8 to 15 m 1 : 40 and which is never to be exceeded by 1 : 20 and should be flat at least 30 m above the hair pin bend.

For heavy commercial vehicles maximum gradient 1 : 30

Urban roads maximum gradient 1 : 25

Pedestrian ramps maximum gradient 1 : 10

Cycle tracks maximum gradient 1 : 30

Animal traction maximum gradient 1 : 7·5

Table 15·7. Size of vehicles commonly found in India

S. No.	*Type of vehicle*	*Breadth m*	*Length m*	*Height m*	*wheel base m*
1.	Maruti 800 car	1·34	3·30	1·41	2·18
2.	Premier Padmini car	1·46	3·93	1·47	2·34

Table contd...

Table contd...

S. No.	Type of vehicle	Breadth m	Length m	Height m	Wheel base m
3.	Ambassador car	1·68	4·31	1·60	2·50
4.	Jeep	1·75	3·73	1·70	2·31
5.	Truck single unit	2·4 to 2·5	6·97	3·10	4·25
6.	Bus single unit	2·00	7·0 to 9·5	3·22	4·0 to 5·2
7.	Three wheeler auto	1·30	2·49	1·30	2·0

Rolling resistance. When vehicle wheels roll over the road surface, the tyres get deformed due to the irregularities and the roughness of the surface. The road itself may deflect, if the wheel load is high. When the speed, shocks and impact are caused due to motion on an irregular surface. All these factors cause hindrance to motion. The smoother the surface is the less the resistance caused. This resistance is known as the "Rolling resistance".

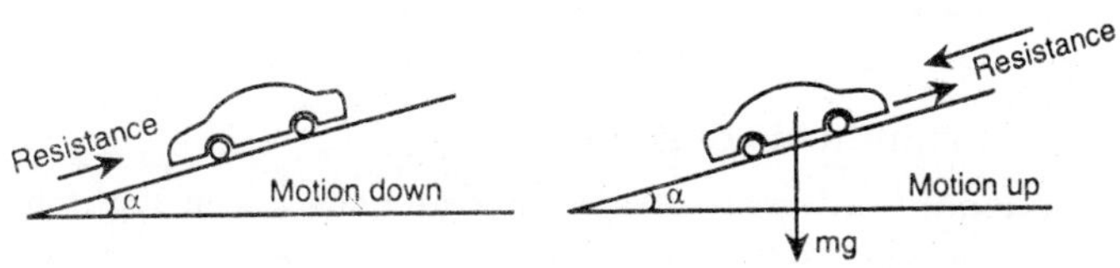

Fig. 15·5.

Table 15·8. Values of coefficient of Rolling Resistance for some typical surfaces

S. No.	Type of Surface	Coefficient of rolling resistance
1.	Road with smooth chippings or gravel surfaces treated with bituminous binders	0·02 to 0·025
2.	Chippings or gravel surfaces not treated with binder having small pot holes	0·03 to 0·04
3.	Cobble stone pavement	0·04 to 0·05
4.	Cement concrete and asphalt surfaces	0·01 to 0·02
5.	Earth road, smooth dry and compact	0·03 to 0·06
6.	Ploughed field saturated and swampy ground, loose sand	0·15 to 0·30 and over

Values of Rolling Resistance coefficient from Indian studies

1. Asphaltic concrete	0·01
2. Premixed carpet in good condition	0·016
3. Premixed carpet in bad condition	0·022
4. Water-bound macadam in good condition	0·025
5. Water-bound macadam in bad condition	0·037
6. Gravel/Earth	0·046

Rolling Resistance of Road way surfacing materials

Surfacing material	*Rolling resistance (kg/1000. kg GVM**	*Equivalent grade %***
1. Portland cement concrete	10	1·0
2. Asphalt concrete	12	1·2
3. Gravel compacted	15	1·5
4. Earth, sandy, loose	37	3·7
5. Crushed aggregate, loose	50	5·0
6. Gravel loose	100	10.0
7. Sand	150	15·0
8. Pea gravel	250	25·0

* G.V.M. ; Gross vehicle mass

** Rolling resistance expressed as equivalent gradient

Rolling resistance = $P_f = mfg$ where m mass of vehicle in kg, f = coefficient of rolling resistance, g = acceleration due to gravity in m/sec^2, P_f = rolling resistance in N.

15·2·6. Cross-sectional standards of roads

The cross-sectional standards of a high way consists of right of way, roadway central median, shoulders, camber, side slopes, horizontal and vertical clearances etc.

(1) **Right of way.** The road land width which is the width of land secured and preserved in public interest for road development. The right of way should be adequate to accommodate all the elements that make up the cross-section of the high way and may reasonably provide for future development.

Table 15·9. Right of way width for different class of roads in India

Class of Road	*Right of way width in metres*					
	Plain and rolling terrain				*Mountainous and steep terrain*	
	Rural areas		*Urban areas*		*Rural areas*	*Urban areas*
	Normal	*Range*	*Normal*	*Range*	*Normal*	*Normal*
1. National and state highways	45	30-60	30	30-60	24	20
2. Major district roads	25	25-30	20	15-25	18	15
3. Other district roads	15	15-25	15	12-20	15	12
4. Village roads	12	12-18	10	10-15	9	9

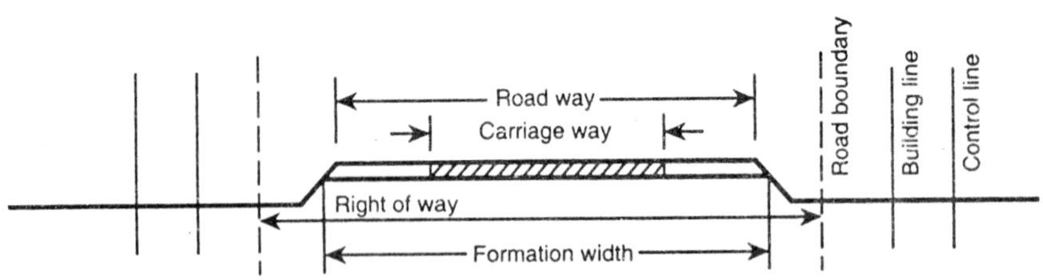

Typical cross sec. of a road boundary

Fig. 15·6.

Table 15·10. Standards for building lines and control lines in India

Class of road	*Plain and rolling terrain*			*Mountainous and steep terrain distance between building line and road boundary (metres)*			
	Rural areas		*Urban and industrial area distance between building line and road boundary (m)*	*Rural area*		*Urban area*	
	Width between building lines m	*Width between control line m*		*Normal*	*Exceptional*	*Normal*	*Exceptional*
1. National and state high ways	80	150	3-6	5	3	5	3
2. Major district roads	50	100	3-5	5	3	5	3
3. Other district roads	25-30*	35	3-5	5	3	5	3
4. Village roads	25	30	3-5	5	3	5	3

* If the land width is equal to the width between building lines indicated in this column, the building lines shall be set 2·5 m from the road land boundary lines.

Control line is a line which represents the nearest limits of the future uncontrolled building activity in relation to a road. This signifies that though building activity is not totally banned between the building line and the control line. The nature of the buildings permitted here is controlled. A "building line" is a line on either side of the road, between which and the road no. building activity is permitted at all.

Table 15·11. Space standards for urban roads

S. No.	*Category of road*	*Minimum space in metres*
1.	Express ways (6 lane divided)	60
2.	Arterial street (4 lane divided) with cycle tracks	50-65
3.	Sub-arterial streets (4 lane)	30-40
4.	Collector street (4 lane)	20-35
5.	Local street such as main residential street, shopping street in residential area, minor residential street and cul-de-sac.	10-70

Table 15·12. Road way width—Standards of road way width (Indian standard)

	High way classification		*Width of road way in metres*	
			Plain and rolling	*Mountainous street*
1.	National and state high ways	(*a*) Single lane	12·0	6·25
		(*b*) Two lane	12·0	8·8
2.	Major district roads	(*a*) Single lane or two lane	9·0	4·75 (single lane)
3.	Other district roads	(*a*) Single lane	7·5	4·75
		(*b*) Double lane	8·0	4·75
4.	Village roads (single lane)		7·5	4·0

Note : For roads with more than two lanes, the road way width has to be worked out to suit the number of lanes, medians (if any) and shoulders.

Carriage way width. Generally a width of 3-4 metres is taken for each traffic lane. Single lane pavements in India are 3·75 metre wide, where as two lane pavements (without raised curbs) are 7·0 m wide when raised curbs are provided two lane pavements are made 7·5 metres in width. An intermediate width of 5·5 metres is commonly used in India. For less important roads with two lanes. For multilane pavements provided with paved shoulders 0·9 metres wide on either side to facilitate crossing and overtaking manoeuvres.

Median (Central reserve). A central reserve or a median is the longitudinal space separating dual carriage-ways. The function of the median are :

(*i*) To separate the opposing streams of the traffic.

(*ii*) To minimise head light glare

(*iii*) To include space for safe operation of crossing and turning vehicles at intersections at grade *i.e.* right turning pockets.

(*iv*) To provide a stopping area in a case of emergency.

Indian practice is to provide a minimum width of 5·0 metre for rural highways which is relaxed to 3·0 metres in restricted conditions. For urban cities a width of 5·0 is considered desirable but a minimum width of 1·2 m is accepted. In American practice minimum value of 1·2 m to maximum of 18·3 or more for rural highways. For urban free ways a minimum of 7·3 metres to 5·0 is taken.

Shoulder or Berms. A shoulder is a portion of the road way contiguous with the travelled way and is intended for accommodation of stopped vehicles, emergency use and lateral support of base and surface courses.

The width of shoulder should be adequate for giving working space around a stopped vehicle. Current Indian practice for two lane roads suggests shoulder width of 2·5 metres for rural highways.

Curbs or kerbs. It is a vertical or a sloping member along the edge of a pavement or shoulder, forming part of gutter, strengthening or providing the edge, and clearly defining the edge to vehicle operators. Curbs are classified as "Barrier" and "mountable". Barrier kerbs are designed to discharge vehicles from leaving the pavement. The face may be vertical or sloping and the height may range from 15 to 25 cm. Mountable curbs are those which can be easily crossed by vehicles if required. They are used at medians and channelizing islands.

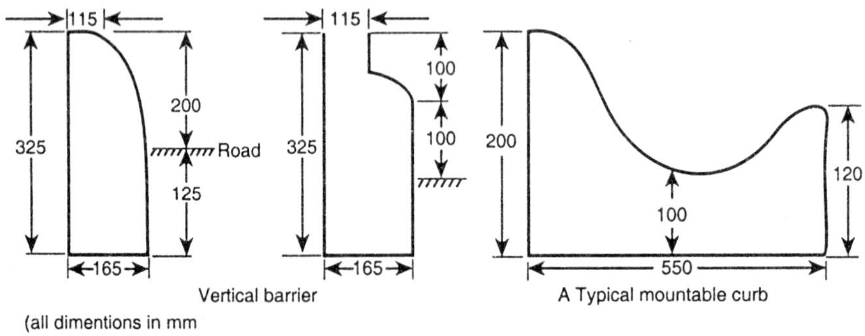

Fig. 15·7.

Side slopes. The side slopes are given according to the soil or embankment and degree of its consolidation. It ranges from ½ : 1 to 3 : 1

Ordinary soil	2 : 1 to 1 : 1
Disintegrated rock	½ : 1
Shaft rock and shale	¼ : 1 to $^1/_8$: 1
Hard rock	almost vertical
High embankments in ordinary soil	upto to 3 : 1

15·2·7. Lateral and vertical clearance. Lateral clearance is the distance between the extreme edge of the carriage way to the face of a structure. Vertical clearance is the height above the highest point of the travelled way to the lowest point of the overhead structure. Current Indian standards are summarized as below :

Type of roads		*Minimum lateral clearances*
A. Rural High ways (1) Single carriage way		
(*i*) National and state high ways	:	Normal 2·5 metres, exceptional 2·0 metres
(*ii*) Major and other district roads	:	Normal 2·0 metres exceptional 1·5 metres
(*iii*) Village roads	:	Normal 1·5 metres exceptional 1·0 metres

In the footpaths are provided the lateral clearance should be the width of the footpath plus one metre.

(2) **Divided carriage ways**

(*i*) Left hand clearance as in 1 above

(*ii*) Right hand side clearance : 2·0 metres desirable 1·5 metres minimum

B. Urban Roads

(1) **Single carriage ways.** For kerbed roads, the carriage way width widens on both sides under structures (underpass etc.) by 0·25 metres in the case of lower category urban roads and by 0·5 metres in the case of higher category urban roads to account for kerb shyness. If a footpath does not form the cross section of the urban road, the minimum lateral clearance in addition to the above values shall be 0·5 metres for lower category roads and 1 metre for higher category roads. When a raised footpath is provided it is not necessary to have additional clearance beyond the width of the footpath.

(2) **Divided carriage ways.** The extra width to account for kerb shyness as kerbed roads is the same as in (1) above. The lateral clearance on the left shall be same as in (1) above. Right hand clearance shall be in addition to the factor to account for kerb shyness, 0·5 metres in the case of lower category roads and 1 metre in the case of higher category roads.

The minimum vertical clearance shall be at least 5 metres. However in urban areas this should be increased to 5·5 metres so that double decker buses could also be accommodated.

Intersections—When two roads cross each other is known as intersection. Some typical intersections are shown as below.

Algrade. When all roads cross at a junction on the same level is known as Algrade.

Access control. Cross streets at very close intervals impede the safe movement of traffic and give rise to ribbon development. Control of access is one of the effective ways of checking ribbon development.

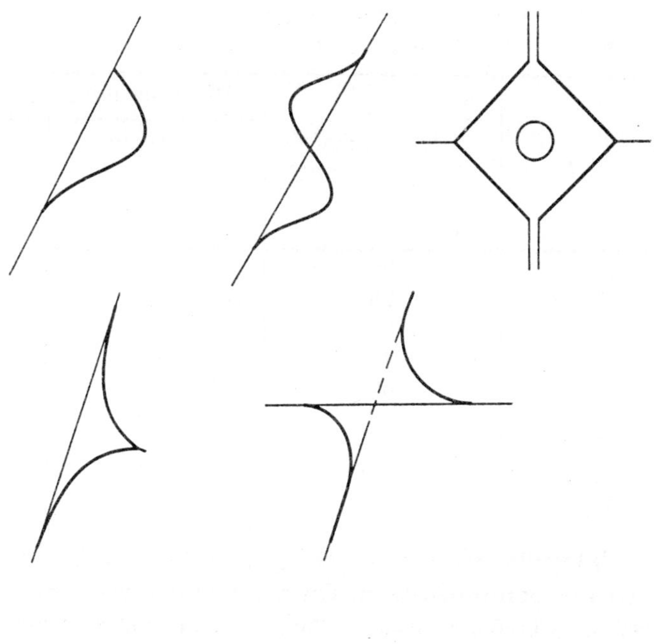

Fig. 15·8.

On rural sections of important trunk routes, it is desirable to exercise limited access control. This is especially necessary in the case of by-passes and high ways in the urban fringe. Indian practice is to limit access to individual private property at a spacing not closer than 300 metres. For intersections of public roads, a spacing not less than 750 metres is normally practised. If parallel service roads are provided connections from these should not be closer than 750 metres.

Bridle path for mules : Maximum 1 : 100 to 150

Handled up gradient : Without increase of power

Junction of roads should be located away from gradients. The gradients should be eased at curves.

Ruling gradient. A gradient which is given as a rule in a normal cases.

Limiting gradient. A grade which should not be exceeded as it is a limit of gradient.

Exceptional gradient. A gradient which is given in exceptional cases, where it becomes obligatory due to surrounding features.

Handled upgrade. A gradient at which a vehicle tends to drag back due to its load without any increase in motive power.

The top or hump of road should be horizontal for about 30 m.

Gradient for road roller max. 1 : 5

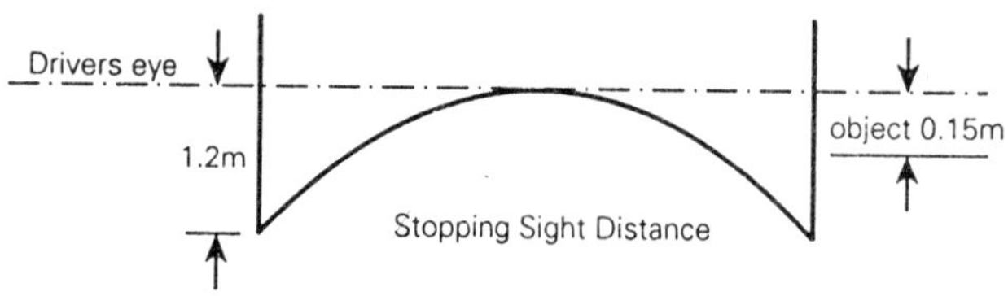

Fig. 15·9.

Table 15·13. The minimum sight distance is the distance along the road in which a driver whose eye is assumed to be 1·2 m above the road surface can see an object 0·10 m high on the road.

Design speed in km/Hr	*Absolute min. stopping distance (m)*	*Min. overtaking sight distance (m)*		
		*Single lane two way traffic**	*Two lane (undivided) two way traffic*	*Min. visible distance, major roads at inter-sections (m)*
20	20	40	—	—
25	25	50	—	—
30	30	60	—	—
40	45	90	165	—
50	60	120	235	110
60	80	160	300	135
65	90	180	340	145
80	120	240	470	180
100	180	300	640	220

* **Opposing vehicles.** The stopping sight distance is double than one way traffic.

Grade compensation. On horizontal curves the vehicle needs extra force which is compensated by giving an easier gradient on the curve. A curve having a curvature more than 6° or radius less than 300 m, should always be compensated when a grade of 3% or over.

$$\text{Compensation in \% grade} = \frac{250}{\text{radius of curvature}}$$

15·2·8. Design Control of Roads

Table 15·14. Suggested Design Speeds for Rural Highways

Classification	*Plain terrain*		*Rolling terrain*		*Mountainous*		*Steep terrain*	
	Ruling	*Min.*	*Ruling*	*Min.*	*Ruling*	*Min.*	*Ruling*	*Min.*
National and state highways	100	80	80	65	50	40	40	30
Major district roads	80	65	65	50	40	30	30	20
Other district roads	65	50	50	40	30	25	25	20
Village roads	50	40	40	35	25	20	25	20

Suggested Design Speeds for Urban Streets

Arterial roads	·80 K.P.H.
Sub-arterial roads	60 K.P.H.
Collector streets	50 K.P.H.
Local streets	30 K.P.H.

A design speed of 120 K.P.H. is being adopted for express ways in India.

Design Hour Volume. The unit for measuring traffic on highway is the annual average daily traffic volume, abbreviated as A.A.D.T. It is equal to the total annual volume of traffic divided by the number of days in the year. A.A.D.T. can be easily estimated where continuous traffic counts are maintained. Where only periodic counts are maintained, it can be established by applying correcting factors. A knowledge of traffic in terms of AADT is not of much use—geometric designs, since it does not represent the variations in traffic during various months of the year, days of the week and hours of the day. A commonly used unit for geometric design is the 30th highest hourly volume abbreviated as 30 HV. It is defined as the hourly volume that is exceeded by 29 hourly volumes during a designated year. For average American conditions, the 30HV is about 15 percent of the AADT in the case of Rural Highways and is about 8 to 12 percent of the AADT in the case of urban streets. It may be noted that a design hour volume of 8 to 10 percent of the AADT has been suggested for use for Indian conditions for capacity determinations.

The results of some Indian surveys on rural sections of National Highways are tabulated as below :

Table 15·15. 30th HV on some Indian Highways

S. No.	*State*	*30th HV as percentage of AADT*
1.	Tamil Nadu (N.H. 45)	8·4
2.	Rajasthan (N.H. 8)	9·9
3.	Orissa (N.H. 5)	9·3
4.	Maharashtra (N.H. 6)	9·8
5	Maharashtra (N.H. 4)	7·3

This shows that a value of 8 to 10 percent AADT may be assumed to be the 30th HV under Indian conditions. The Design Hour Volume (DHV) should be the 30th HV for the future year selected for design.

Directional Distribution of Traffic. For 2 lane highways, the design hour volume in the total traffic in both directions of travel. For highways with more than two lanes, it is desirable to know the directing distribution of traffic. Though this distribution has to be found from traffic surveys, a rough approximation can be assume 67 percent of total traffic to travel in one direction under the design conditions. The design has to be taken into account both the morning and evening peak situations.

Traffic Composition. Traffic composition has a vital effect or capacity and other design considerations. In this country, the traffic is heterogeneous in character, consisting of fast driven cars, trucks, buses and slow animal driven vehicles. It is customary in this country to express the traffic volume in terms of **Passenger Car Units (PCUs).** The values indicated in the Table below have been suggested for rural conditions.

Table 15·16. PCU Equivalent as per Indian Practice

Vehicle Type	*PCU*
1. Passenger car, pickup van or auto rickshaw	1·00
2. Motor cycle, scooter or cycle	0·50
3. Agricultural tractor, light commercial vehicle	1·50
4. Truck or bus	3·00
5. Tractor-trolleys, agricultural tractor	4·50
6. Cycle rickshaw	2·00
7. Hand cart	3·00
8. Horse driven vehicle	4·00
9. Bullock cart (for small cart a value is 6·00 can be taken)	6·00 to 8·00

Future traffic assessment. The design parameters are taken according to the design year, the design passed for flexible pavements varies from 15 to 25 years, the future traffic estimates should be calculated to include the following :

(1) Current traffic (2) Future traffic : (*a*) Traffic growth (*b*) Development of traffic

Table 15·17. Standards of dimensions for design vehicles in metres

Authority/Country	*Maximum length*						
	Max. width	*Max. height*	*Passenger car*	*Single unit truck*	*Semi trailer*	*Truck tractor*	*Single unit bus*
AASHTO (USA)	2·59	4·12	5·8	9·14	16·8	8·91	—
UK	2·5	4·57 (bus)	5·5	11·0	18·0	13·0	—
IRC (1983)	2·5	3·8-4·2 (truck) 4·75 (Double decker bus)	—	11·0	16·0	18·0	12·0

Turning radii of some vehicles are given in table below :

Turning radii of AASHTO (Design Vehicles in metres)

Design vehicle type	*Passenger car (P)*	*Single unit truck (S.U.)*	*Semi trailer cargo (WB-50)*	*Semi trailer full (WB-60)*
Min. turning radius (m)	7·32	12·8	13·72	13·75
Min. inside radius (m)	4·65	8·61	6·00	6·85

Maximum axle loads in different countries (Tonnes)

AASHTO (USA)	Single axle	9·0	Tandem axle	14·5
UK	Single axle	10·0	Tandem axle	—
IRC	Single axle	10·2	Tandem axle	18·0

The maximum weight of vehicles depends upon the number, configuration and spacing of axles.

Selection of design vehicle for the design of a highway is governed by the type of volume of traffic that is expected to use the highway. For example, the design of a superior facility, such as motorway or expressway in residential area can be done by using the passenger car design vehicle.

Capacity. Capacity is the maximum flow that can be accommodated on a highway facility. But the maximum flow occurs when the speed falls down to nearly a half of the speed under low volume conditions. Hence it is not desirable to design the highway facility for maximum capacity conditions. But for a flow much below the capacity

$$C = \frac{1000\,V}{S}$$ where C = Capacity in vehicles/Hr/lane

V = Speed in km per hr.

S = Average spacing between successive moving vehicles

Table 15·18 (*a*). Design capacity of rural motor way

Type of carriage way	*Daily design capacity*	*Peak hourly design capacity per tonne PCU/Hr*
Dual 2 – lane	53,000	1000
Dual 3 – lane	50,000	1000
Dual 4 – lane	66,000	1000

Design capacity of multilane highways in rural areas per AASHTO practice

Type of highway	*Design capacity PCUs per hour per 3·66 m lane*
1. Free ways and express ways with partial control of access and with little interference from cross traffic, rural (average running speed 75-80 KPH)	1000
2. Free way suburban (running speed 65-75 KPH)	1700
3. Major high ways with moderate interference from cross-traffic and road sides (average running speed 75-80 KPH)	700-900
4. Major highways with considerable interference from cross traffic and road sides (average running speed 65-75 KPH)	500-700

Design capacity of dual carriage way other than motor ways in U.K.

Carriage way width	*Design capacity PCUs/day (Passenger car unit)*
Dual 14·6 m	66,000
Dual 11·00 m	50,000
Dual 7·30 m	33,000

Design capacities for arterial streets and urban highways

Type of Highway	Design capacity (Passenger cars per hour per 3·65 lane)
1. Major suburban highway with moderate interference from cross traffic and road sides, level service C	700-900
2. Major suburban highway, considerable unit from cross traffic and road sides, level of service C	500-700
3. Arterial street, traffic signals average 1·6 km or more apart, parking prohibited and refuse provided for stalled vehicles, level of service C	400-600
4. Arterial streets, traffic signals average less than 1·6 km apart, parking prohibited.	as governed by capacity of critical intersections.

Practical capacities of two-way urban roads in U.K.

	2 lane			3 lane		4 lane			6 lane
Effective width of carraige way (m)	6·00	6·75	7·30	9·00	10·00	12·0	13·5	14·6	22
Description	Capacity in PCUs per hour (both directions of flow)				Capacity in PCUs per hour (one direction of flow)				
1. Urban motor ways with grade separation and no frontage access							3000		4500
2. All purpose roads with no frontage access on standing vehicles permitted negligible cross traffic	1200	1350	1500	2200	2000	2000	2400	2200	3600
3. All purpose street with high capacity junctions and "no waiting" restrictions	800	1000	1200	1600	1800	1200	1500	1350	2500
4. All purpose street with capacity restricted by waiting vehicles and junctions	300 to 500	450 to 600	600 to 750	900 to 1100	1100 to 1300	800 to 900	100 to 1200	900 to 1000	1600 to 2000

Possible Design Capacities of two lane rural highway as per AASHTO practice

Possible capacity	Design capacity in vehicles per hour for average running speed of		
2000 vehicles/Hour	60-66 KPH 1500	65-75 KPH 1150	75-80 KPH 900

Table 15·18 (b). Suggested Design surface volume for Indian conditions

Terrain	Curvature (Deg. per km)	Design service volume (DCU/day)
	Two lane roads	
1. Plain	Low (0-50), High (above 51)	1500 12,500
2. Rolling	Low (0-100), High (above 101)	11,000 10,000

Table contd...

Table contd...

Terrain	*Curvature (Deg. per km)*	*Design service volume (PCU/day)*
3. Hilly	Low (0-200), High (above 201)	7,000 5,000
	Intermediate road lane	
1. Plain	Low (0-50), High (above 51)	6,000 5800
2. Rolling	Low (0-100), High (above 101)	5700 5600
3. Hilly	Low (0-200), High (above 201)	5200 4500
	Single lane roads	
1. Plain	Low (0-50), High (above 51)	2000 2000
2. Rolling	Low (0-100), High (above 101)	1800 1800
3. Hilly	Low (0-200), High (above 201)	1800 1400

For four lane high ways, the suggested design service volume is 35000-40,000 as per IRC.

The U.K. standards provide for a design capacity of 9000-PCUs per day for a two lane road, which corresponds to a level of service B, the peak hour volume being 10% of the daily volume.

Pavement Surface Finish. For the fast motor traffic, one of the desirable characteristics is a reasonably smooth surface. The advantages of the smooth surface is as below :

(1) **Higher speeds.** The higher the smooth run of the road surface, the higher the velocity can be achieved by a vehicle.

(2) **Less fuel consumption.** The fuel consumed in a vehicle is proportional to the work required to be done to overcome various resistances (air resistance, frictional resistance and grade resistance). The frictional resistance is a function of the coefficient of friction of tyre-road interference, smoother surfaces thus bring about considerable fuel economy.

(3) **Less wear and tear of tyres.** Rough roads shorten the tyre life.

(4) **Riding comfort.** Smooth roads have higher riding comfort and the rough roads have a jerky motion.

(5) **Safety.** Roads which are full of pot holes, ruts and corrugatory endanger the safety of travel since the possibility of sudden failure of vital parts increases in bad roads. However extremely smooth roads increase the chance of skidding. Thus clear smoothness is to be aimed that has to be a compromise between the conflicting needs of anti-skid properties and economic and comfortable travel.

Types of Pavements. From the structural performance point of view the pavements are classified as below :

(*i*) Flexible (*ii*) Rigid (*iii*) Semi rigid (*iv*) Composite

(*i*) **Flexible.** A flexible pavement is essentially a layered system which has low flexural strength. Thus the external load is largely transmitted to the subgrade by the lateral distribution with increasing depth. Because of the low flexural strength, the pavement deflects momentarily under load but rebounds to its original level on removal of load. The pavement thickness is so designed that the shears on the subgrade soil are kept with in its bearing power and the sub grade is prevented from excessive deformations. This implies that in a flexible pavement the subgrade plays an important role as it carries the vehicle load transmitted to it through a permanent deformation suffered by the subgrade and its resistance to such deformation. If the pavement itself is very strong, but if constructed on loose and poor subgrade it can fail. W.B.M. is an example of flexible pavements.

(*ii*) **Rigid.** A rigid pavement derives its capacity to withstand loads from the flexural strength or beam strength (modulus of elasticity) permitting the slab to bridge over minor irregularities in the subgrade, sub-base or base upon which it rests. This implies that the inherent strength of the slab itself is called upon to play a major role in resisting the wheel load. Minor imperfections or localised weak spots in the material below the slab can be taken care of by the slab itself. This is not to underrate the role of the subgrade soil. In fact a good stable and uniform support is necessary for a rigid pavement as well. But as long as a certain minimum requirement is met within this regard the performance of the rigid pavement is more governed by the strength of the slab itself by the subgrade support. Cement concrete road is an example of this type of road.

A third category of pavement has become popular during recent times, known as semi rigid pavements. It represents an intermediate state between the flexible and the rigid pavement. It has much lower flexural strength compared to concrete slabs, but it can also derive support to the lateral distribution of loads through the pavement depth as in a flexible pavement. Typical examples of a semi rigid pavement are the lean, concrete, base, soil cement and lime puzzalona concrete construction.

(*iii*) **Composite pavement.** Composite pavement is one which comprises of multiple structurally significant layer of different, sometimes heterogeneous composition. A typical example is the brick-sandwiched concrete pavements, which has been tried in India. It consists of top and bottom layers of cement concrete which sandwich a brick layer in the neutral axis zone. The design of composite pavement lies outside the well established fields of flexible or rigid pavements, design and is still in its infancy.

15·2·9. Paved surfaces. The road surfaces which are finished either by bituminous or by concrete surfaces.

Unpaved roads. The roads having their surfaces either finished by earth or, by gravel or by kankar.

Comparison of rigid and flexible pavements

(1) The cement concrete roads (rigid roads) is much more precise structural analysis than a flexible pavement. This is because of the fact that the flexural strength of concrete which is used as the main basis for design is well understood. On the other hand flexible pavement designs are mainly empirical.

(2) **Life.** The life of cement roads is about 40 years. Many of the road constructed in the 4th decade is performing well still now while the flexible roads have their life only 10 to 20 years.

(3) **Maintenance.** The cement concrete paved roads needs less maintenance. The hard surface can withstand the abrasion caused by iron tyred vehicles (bullock carts) in India and studded tyres in the west used under shabby conditions. The surface is unaffected by spillage of oil, lubricants and water. Bituminous surfaces on the other hand need great in puts in maintenance. Sealing cracks making good pot holes, resurfacing and resealing are done very frequently. The surface is affected by spillage of oil, lubricant and water. The surface is also affected by natural agencies like air, water and temperature. The cost of post maintenance of a two lane bituminous road comes to about 30,000 to 1,00,000 per km per year, while the cost of maintenance of cement concrete roads come to Rs. 5000 to 10,000 per km per year.

(4) **Initial cost.** The initial cost of a cement concrete road may be higher than a flexible road but its maintenance and long life goes ultimately to be economic in comparison to the flexible roads.

(5) **Stage construction.** The flexible roads can be enhanced easily in factor by laying extra layers, which is not possible in the cement roads. The cold joints are formed if the cement road is widened or thickened while in the flexible road it is not so.

(6) **Availability of materials.** In the pavement of roads, stone ballast, very small shredded pebbles, sand cement and bituminous substances are in need. Cement is always in

shortage so a major work with cement can not be started before arranging regular cement supply while the bituminous substances can be arranged easily in comparison to cement.

(7) **Surface characteristics.** Surfaces of the cement concrete roads are more smooth than the bituminous roads. Ruts and pot holes are formed easily by moving vehicles, which require more maintenance. But the smoothness of the flexible roads can be achieved by repainting. A cement concrete road has a skidless surface.

(8) **Penetration of water.** The flexible roads are not so water proof as the cement concrete roads. If the joints of cement concrete roads are faulty, water can penetrate the subgrade and will moisen it causing **mud pumping.**

(9) **Utility location.** In the sides of roads particularly in cities utility poles like electric or telephone and their underground lines generally are dug, which is not so easy in case of concrete roads. The pits are dug which is ultimately is filled by bituminous concrete.

(10) **Glare and night visibility.** Cement concrete has a grey colour which can cause glare under sunlight, while the bituminous road are free from this defect. The bituminous roads need more light during night in comparison to cement roads.

(11) **Traffic dislocation during repairs.** Cement take 28 days for setting so the traffic is hindered for such a long time, while the flexible roads can be used immediately.

(12) **Environmental considerations.** During construction heating of bituminous substances produce a hazardous smoke with an unpleasing odour while in cement it is not so.

(13) **Overall economy.** Though the initial cost of a cement road is more yet it is overall economic, considering its life and maintenance than a bituminous road.

15·2·10. Low cost roads. (1) **Brick roads.** Bricks on edge are paved over a 10 cm thick dry brick ballast, subgrade which is rammed by iron rammers and is blinded with earth. The surface of the earth profile is made by giving a proper camber or superelevation where required and compacted. The bricks are laid in diagonal or herring bone bond. The top is blinded by the earth so as to fill up the interistes of the brick bond.

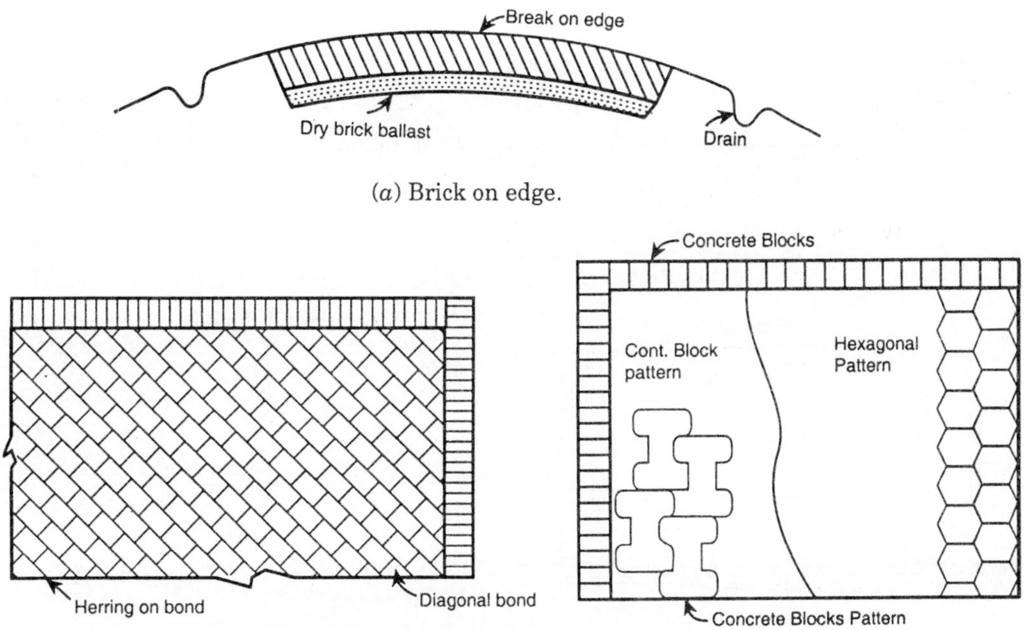

(*a*) Brick on edge.

(*b*) Bricks in herring bone

(*c*)

Fig. 15·10.

(2) **Concrete block paving.** Concrete blocks are laid over the dry brick ballast subgrade as in case of brick on edge paving. Different patterns of concrete blocks are available in the market which can be paved on such pavements. If required in large scale, these can be moulded at the site. The mix of concrete is 1 : 2 : 4 when the size of coarse aggregate is 2 to 3 mm.

(3) **Kankar (Pebble) roads.** In the areas where bichwa kankar (kankar of small size about 4 to 5 cm) is rammed in two layers of 10 cm each over the well prepared earthen subgrade on the flat over burnt bricks. The kankar (pebble) layer is rammed by iron rammers with watering. The kankar roads become muddy in rains with metallic wheeled traffic.

(4) **Earthen roads.** The canal service roads are generally kept earthen. A layer of 10 cm clay puddle is provided over the required width (3 to 4 m).

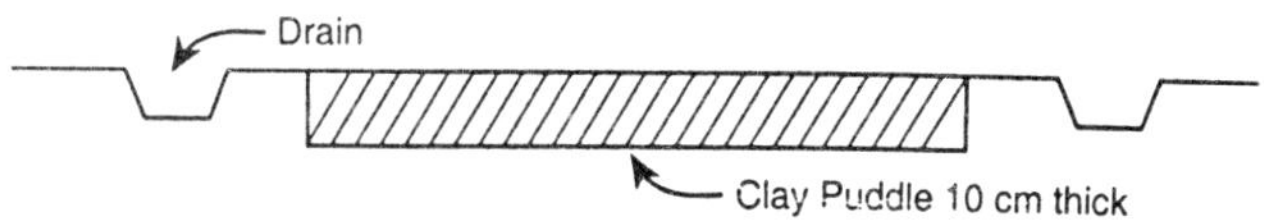

Fig. 15·11.

Drainage of Roads. (1) **Roads in digging.** Drains are constructed at the edge of the road boundary as suitable longitudinally, which end to the level or low grounds. The drains may be *kachcha* or (masonry) lined as required.

(2) **Land Ground Roads.** The longitudinal and the cross drains are constructed. The cross drains are constructed at suitable intervals while the longitudinal drains lead to a low land area.

(3) **Roads in Filling.** Longitudinal masonry drains are constructed on both edges of the road, while the cross masonry drains are constructed on outer slope of the embankment of road which lead to the low lying areas or in a side longitudinal drain at the toe of embankment leading to a low lying area.

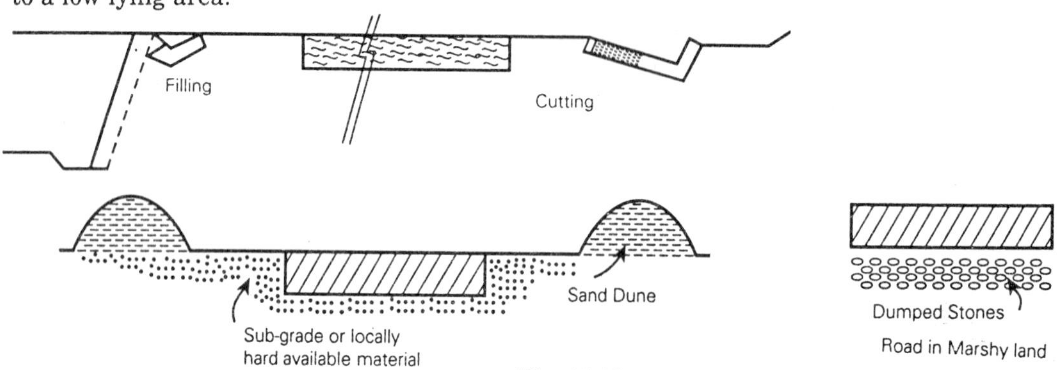

Fig. 15·12.

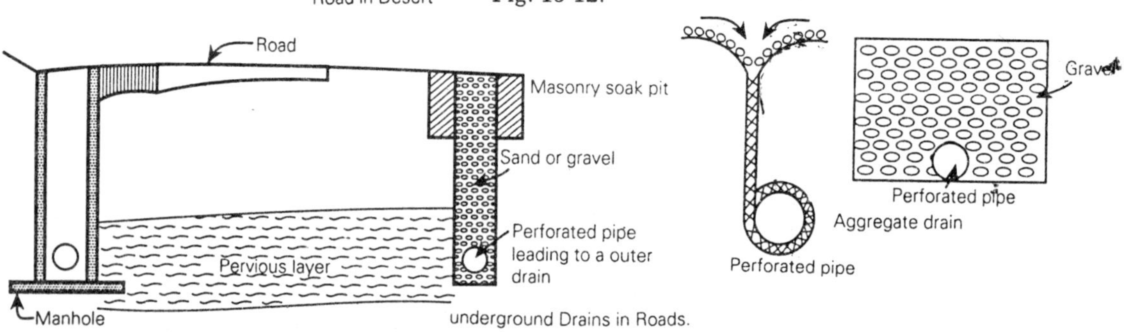

Fig. 15·13 (*a*)

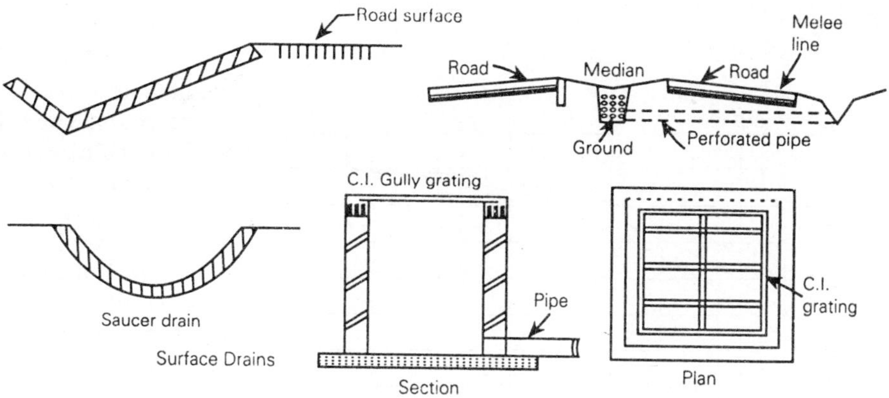

Fig. 15·13 (*b*)

15·2·11. Low volume roads. Low volume roads are a special category roads subjected to a relatively small number of heavy roads. In view of their relatively low usage and the relatively low level of risk involved. AASHTO recommends a low level of reliability (50% for) design. Reliability may be defined as "the probability that any particular type of distress will remain below or within the permissible level during the design life". For low volume roads having gravel surface AASHTO considers 10^5 applications of equivalent single axle load of 80 kN of the maximum traffic level and 10,000 as the minimum level, for design purposes. In terms of the number of commercial vehicles plying per day low volume roads are generally considered to be receiving no more than 50 commercial vehicles per day, as in case of rural roads with gravel surfacing in India. Somewhat lower geometric design standards for low volume roads are generally acceptable in comparison to medium and high traffic intensity high ways.

The following roads may come in this category.

(1) **Rural or village roads.**

(2) **All weather roads.** The total period of interruption of such type of roads should not exceed 10 days due to weather. The pavement should consist of metalling (WBM) or higher type where rain fall is more than 150 cm/year and should at least be of material better than local soil, such as mooram, gravel, kankar or laterite etc. where the rainfall is less than 150 cm/year.

(3) **Fair weather roads.** These roads may be taken in a stage of development to be improved subsequently for conversion into all weather type.

(4) **Low cost water crossings.** Crossways, fords or pave dips may be of such types of roads.

(5) Rural roads of village network.

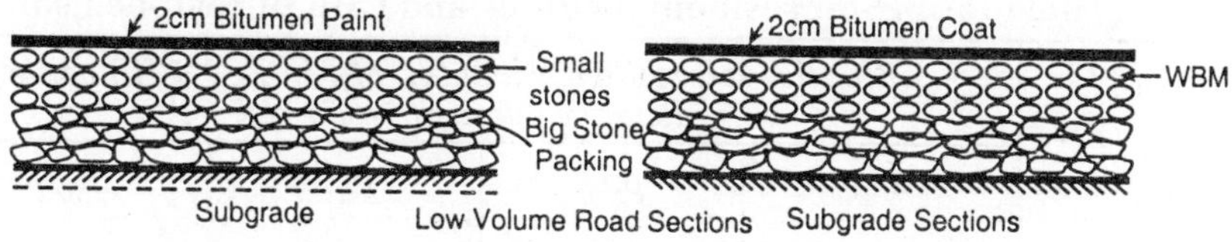

Fig. 15·14.

15·2·12. The CBR method of design. In the flexible pavement design of CBR method, traffic is considered in terms of vehicles (pneumatic tyred) like trucks, buses etc. per day in the design year. However in the rural areas of India, these could be a sizable number of solid. Wheeled carts on the roads especially in the harvesting season, which can cause considerable damage to the pavement. While the choice of CBR *A, B* and *C* would cover the range of commercial vehicles on roads in the rural areas, this design method does not take into account for the solid wheeled concrete traffic.

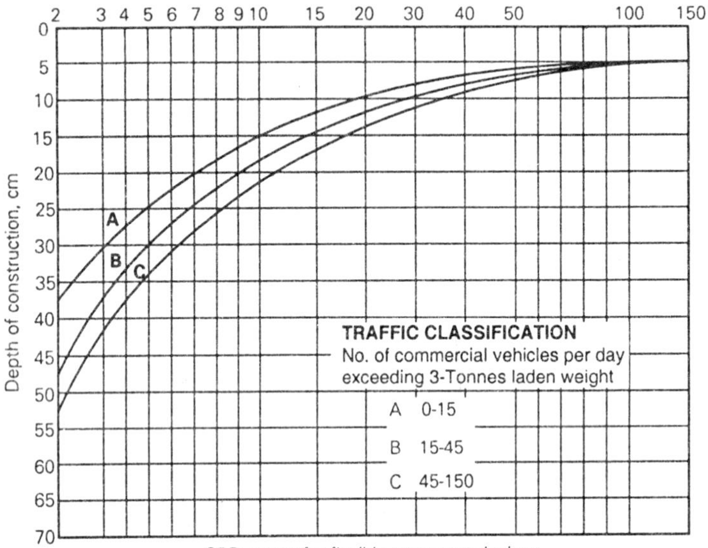

CBR curves for flexible pavement designs.

Fig. 15·15

The subgrade strength is determined in terms of the CBR value. The compacted density and moisture content of specimens very significantly effect the CBR value. For rural roads it is a requirement that upto a depth of at least 300 mm below the formation, the subgrade soil should invariably be compacted at least 95% of the maximum dry density obtained in standard proctor compaction task. For carrying out the CBR terms for subgrade strength, therefore the dry density of specimens should be 95% of maximum Proctor density.

The moisture contents of the specimens at which the CBR test value is to be determined depends on a number of local environmental factors such as depth of water taken and its functions, rainfall, the permeability of soil, drainage conditions and the extent of water proofing by the surfacing. In respect of rural roads, which usually have thin pavements comprising granular materials generally unsealed (and even when sealed only in thin bituminous treatment is provided which by no standards can be considered completely water proof) with unsealed shoulders (berms), box type construction etc. it is reasonable to assume that in most cases, the subgrade will be nearly saturated at least during the rainy season, except for roads in arid regions. The recommended general practice is therefore to cater to the worst condition of saturation by soaking the soil specimens under water for a period of 4 days before testing for the CBR value. (California Bearing Ratio). Lastly it is to be recognized that in the use of CBR design curves, there is an in-built resulting minimum level of serviceability which may be at a higher level than what may be considered as the acceptible minimum for the low volume roads in rural areas.

Table 15·19. Soil resilient modulus and CBR of road-bed soil

Climatic Region	*Effective soil resilient modulus 'M_R' in PSI (CBR value in brackets)* Relative quality of road bed soil*				
	Very poor	*Poor*	*Fair*	*Good*	*Very good*
Wet, no freeze	2800 (CBR = 1·87)	3700 (CBR = 2·40)	5000 (CBR = 3·33)	6800 (CBR = 4·53)	9000 (CBR = 6·33)
Dry, no freeze	3200 (CBR = 2·13)	4100 (CBR = 2·73)	5600 (CBR = 3·73)	7900 (CBR = 5·27)	11,700 (CBR = 7·80)

*Using the relationship M_R (DS_i) = 1500 + CBR.

15·2·13. Super elevation. It is provided on curves to compensate centrifugal forces

$$E = \frac{V^2}{225\,R} \text{ (I.R.C.) where } E = \text{super elevation in metres/m of road way}$$

V = design speed in km/hour and R = radius of curvature in m.

Maximum super elevation : Plains — 1 : 20 in all cases

Hills — 1 : 8 in national highways

1 : 8 in other roads.

Super elevation should not be less than camber.

15·20. Values of super elevation on different radii of curves and speeds

Radius of curve (m)	*Design speed in km / hour*							
	Flat terrain				*Hilly terrain*			
	32	48	64	80	24	32	40	48
30	—	—	—	—	0·067	—	—	—
45	0·067	—	—	—	0·056	0·067	—	—
60	0·067	—	—	—	0·042	0·067	0·067	—
75	0·060	—	—	—	0·034	0·060	0·067	—
90	0·050	0·067	—	—	0·028	0·056	0·067	0·067
120	0·038	0·067	—	—	0·021	0·038	0·038	0·067
150	0·030	0·067	0·067	—	0·017	0·030	0·046	0·067
180	0·025	0·056	0·067	—	0·014	0·025	0·039	0·056
240	0·019	0·042	0·067	0·067	—	—	—	—
300	0·015	0·034	0·060	0·067	—	—	—	—
420	—	0·024	0·043	0·067	—	—	—	—
600	—	—	0·030	0·047	—	—	—	—
900	—	—	0·020	0·031	—	—	—	—

Design speed 100 km/hour. The values of super elevations are :

Radius in m	370-700	800	900	1000	1100	1200	1500	2000
Super elevation	0·067	0·056	0·050	0·045	0·040	0·038	0·030	0·023

Radius in m beyond which no super elevation is needed.

Design speed km/hr.	*Water bound macadam*		*Black top*	*Cement concrete*
	Camber 1 in 36	*Camber 1 in 48*	*Camber 1 in 60*	*Camber 1 in 72*
25	100	130	170	200
30	180	230	300	360
40	270	360	460	560
50	400	530	700	800
60	700	960	1200	1400
80	1100	1500	1900	2300
100	1600	2200	2500	2500

Super Elevation Rates. Super elevation on curves is intended to counteract a part of the centrifugal force, the remaining part being resisted by lateral friction.

Super elevation can be provided either totally counteract the centrifugal force or to counteract a fixed proportion of the centrifugal force. In the former case, the super elevation needed would be more than 1 in 1·5 on sharp curves causing in convenience to slow moving vehicles. Since super elevation has to be limited to 0·07 or 0·10 as per Indian practice, maximum friction would have to be relied upon when the sharpest possible curve is traversed. When a vehicle negotiates a flat curve, friction would not be developed to the maximum. This is not balanced design. It is desirable that the super elevation should be such that a moderate amount of friction is developed while negotiating flat curves and friction not exceeding the maximum allowable value be developed at sharp curves. Therefore designing the super elevation to fully counteract the centrifugal force developed at a friction of the design speed will provide the necessary balance.

The above is achieved as per U.K. practice by providing full super elevation for a speed of 23·2 percent of the design speed such that 40 percent of the centrifugal force is counteracted by super elevation.

$$e = \frac{\left(0.632\,V^2\right)}{127\,R} = \frac{V^2}{314\,R}$$

As per Indian practice super elevation is calculated on the assumption that it should counteract the centrifugal force developed at three fourth the design speed. Thus

$$e = \frac{0.75\,V^2}{127\,R} = \frac{V^2}{225\,R}.$$

The super elevation calculated by this equation is restricted to 0·07 and 0·10.

Table 15·21. Radii beyond which super elevation is not needed for different cambers and speeds

Design speed, K.P.H	*Radius in metres beyond which no super elevation is needed for values of camber of*					
	4%	*3%*	*2·5%*	*2%*	*1·7%*	*Remarks*
20	50	60	70	90	100	When the radius is greater than those given in this table it is however desirable to remove the adverse crown in the outer half of the carriage way and super elevate at the normal crown slope.
25	70	90	110	140	150	
30	100	130	160	200	240	
35	140	180	220	270	320	
40	180	240	280	350	420	
50	280	370	450	550	650	
65	470	620	750	950	1100	
80	700	960	1100	1400	1700	
100	1100	1500	1800	2200	2600	

National and state highway	2286	Normal camber can do and no super elevation is needed.
Major district roads	1981	
Other district roads	1372	
Village roads	610	

The normal cambered section of a highway can itself be continued on a curve where the super elevation calculated is less than the camber from formula $R = \frac{V^2}{225\,R}$. Substituting the value for camber in this formula, the minimum radius beyond which no super elevation is needed is given in the table 15·20.

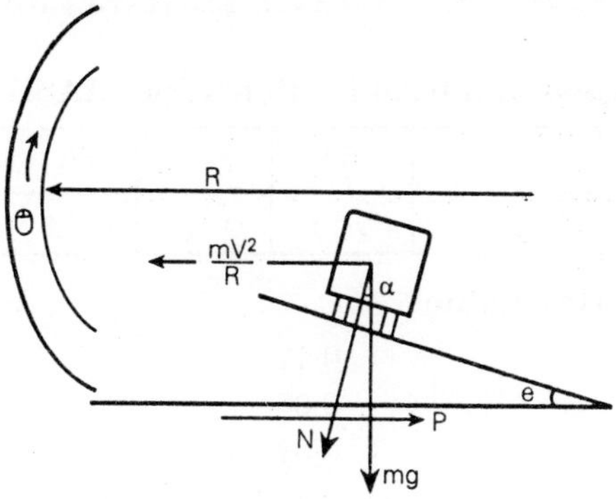

Fig. 15·16.

Notations

m = mass of vehicle
V = speed of vehicle in m/sec
R = radius of curve in metres
g = acceleration due to gravity
P = side friction force resisting the centrifugal force = Nμ
N = normal force
μ = coefficient of lateral friction
α = angle of super elevation
e = rate of super elevation, tan α

The centrifugal force = $\frac{mV^2}{R}$

For equilibrium, resolving forces parallel to the inclined plane

$$\frac{mV^2}{R}\cos\alpha = mg\sin\alpha + P = mg\sin\alpha + N\mu$$

$$= mg\sin\alpha + \mu\left\{mg\cos\alpha + \frac{mg\,V^2}{R}\sin\alpha\right\}$$

obtained by resolving forces at right angles to the inclined plane.

Therefore $\frac{V^2}{gR} = \tan\alpha + \mu + \frac{\mu V^2}{gR}\tan\alpha$

The term $\frac{\mu V^2}{gR}\tan\alpha$ being too small, can be neglected. Thus

$\frac{V^2}{gR} = e + \mu$, expressing speed as $V = K.P.H.$

$$\frac{V^2}{127\,R} = e + \mu$$

If the entire centrifugal force counteracted by superelevation, frictional force will not be called into play. Thus μ = 0, in the equation $\left(\frac{V^2}{127\,R} = e + \mu\right)$.

The super elevation then provided is said to be equilibrium super elevation. In such case the pressure on the inner and outer wheels will be equal.

Coefficient of lateral friction as per AASHTO

Design speed (KPH)	50	65	80	100	120	130
Maximum lateral friction values	0·16	0·15	0·14	0·13	0·12	0·11

Maximum super elevation value

AASHTO	0·12
UK	0·07
IRC for hill roads	0·07 (for snow bound areas)
	0·10 (for non snow bound areas)

Minimum radii of curves. Equation $\frac{V^2}{127\,R} = e + \mu$ can be written as

$$R = \frac{V^2}{127\,(e + \mu)}$$

Adopting values of e = 0·07 or 0·10 and μ = 0·15 as per current Indian practice, the formula becomes :

$R = 0{\cdot}0357\ V^2$ (for plain and rolling terrain)

$R = 0{\cdot}0315\ V^2$ (for hill roads which are not snow bound)

$R = 0{\cdot}0357\ V^2$ (for hill roads which are snow bound)

since the current Indian standards give two values for design speed (*i.e.* Ruling and Minimum) the above formulae yield two values for radius, the ruling radius and the absolute minimum radius.

15·2·14. Curves in highways

Table 15·22. Ruling and absolute minimum radii of curve in metres (IRC)

Design speed km/hr.	*Flat or rolling country*		*Hilly and restricted areas*	
	Ruling min. rad.	*Absolute min. rad.*	*Ruling min. rad.*	*Absolute min. rad.*
25	—	—	50	30
30	100	50	60	50
40	130	60	100	60
50	170	100	130	100
60	250	150	—	—
80	300	250	—	—

Table 15·23. Minimum radii of horizontal curves

Classification of Road	*Plain terrain*		*Rolling terrain*		*Mountainous terrain*				*Steep terrain*			
					No snow affected area		*Snow bound area*		*No snow affected area*		*Snow bound area*	
	Ruling min.	*Absolute min.*	*Ruling min.*	*Absolute min.*	*Ruling min.*	*Absolute min.*	*Ruling min.*	*Absolute min.*	*Ruling min.*	*Absolute min.*	*Ruling min.*	*Absolute min.*
1. National and state Highway	360	230	230	159	80	50	90	60	50	30	60	33
2. Major District roads	230	155	105	90	50	30	60	33	30	14	33	16
3. Other District roads	155	90	98	60	30	20	23	23	20	14	23	15
4. Village roads	90	60	60	45	20	14	23	15	20	14	20	15

Table 15·24. Minimum radii of horizontal curves for hill roads (IRC)

Type of road	*Mountainous terrain*				*Sleep terrain*			
	Area uneffected by snow		*Snow effected area*		*Area uneffected by snow*		*Snow effected area*	
	Ruling min. (m)	*Absolute min. (m)*	*Ruling min. (m)*	*Absolute min. (m)*	*Ruling min. (m)*	*Absolute min. (m)*	*Ruling min. (m)*	*Absolute min. (m)*
1. National and state highways	80	50	90	60	50	30	60	33
2. Major district roads	50	30	60	33	30	14	33	15
3. Other district roads	30	20	33	23	20	14	23	15
4. Village roads				15	20	14	23	15

Note : Ruling and absolute radii are for ruling design speed and minimum design speed respectively.

Table 15·25. Transition curves : Length for various speeds and radii of curve (IRC)

Curve rad.	*Design speed in km per hour*									
	Plain and rolling country					*Hilly tracts*				
(m)	*30*	*50*	*60*	*80*	*100*	*20*	*25*	*30*	*40*	*50*
20	—					20	35			
30	80					15	25	30		
40	65						20	25		
50	50						15	20		
60	45							20		
70	—							15		
80	40								25	55
90	30								25	45
100	25	70							20	45
125	—	—							15	35
150	20	45	65							30
200	15	45	50							20
250	—	30	40	85						18
300		25	35	75						15
400		20	25	55	100					
500		—	20	45	90					
600			—	35	80					
800				30	60					
1000				—	50					

Note : Beyond rad. 1000 m provision of transition curve is not needed

Transition curve. An ease out curve joining a curve to a tangent or another curve of different radius.

Minimum radii and length of vertical curves (IRC)

Speed km/hour	25	30	35	40	50	60	80	100
Minimum radius (m)	60	105	135	165	240	415	650	930
Minimum length (m)	100	12	15	20	30	40	50	60

Extra width of Pavements at Curves (IRC)*

Radius of curve (m)	upto 60 m	60-150	150-300	300-500	above 500
Extra width (m)	1·2	0·9	0·6	0·3	—

Table 15·26. Minimum set back at horizontal curves, two lane carriage way

Radius at road centre (m)	*Set back in metres*					
	D-V *20 20*	*D-V* *45 70*	*D-V* *60 50*	*D-V* *90 65*	*D-V* *120 80*	*D-V* *180 100*
20	5·0	—	—	—	—	—
50	3·2	7·0	—	—	—	—
75	2·8	5·5	13·0	—	—	—
100	2·5	5·0	11·0	—	—	—
125	2·5	3·7	9·0	11·0	—	—
150	2·5	3·6	7·0	9·8	—	—
175	2·5	3·3	6·5	8·0	13·0	—
200	2·5	3·0	6·0	7·6	11·0	—
250	2·5	3·0	5·0	6·5	8·5	—
275	2·5	3·0	5·0	6·0	8·0	12·5
300	2·5	3·0	4·0	6·0	7·5	15·5
350	2·4	2·8	3·5	5·0	7·0	13·0
400	2·4	2·7	3·5	4·5	6·5	12·9
450	2·4	2·6	3·0	4·4	6·0	11·0
500	2·4	2·5	3·0	4·0	5·5	10·2
550	2·4	2·5	3·0	4·0	5·4	9·5
600	2·3	2·5	3·0	4·0	5·0	9·3

Minimum set back at horizontal curves single lane carriage way

	D-V *20 20*	*D-V* *25 25*	*D-V* *30 30*	*D-V* *45 40*	*D-V* *60 50*
14	3·4	—	—	—	—
15	3·2	—	—	—	—
20	2·4	3·8	—	—	—
23	2·1	3·3	—	—	—
30	1·7	2·6	3·7	—	—
33	1·5	2·3	3·4	—	—
50	1·0	1·6	2·2	5·0	—
60	—	1·3	1·4	4·2	—
80	—	—	1·4	3·1	5·6
100	—	—	1·1	2·5	4·5
120	—	—	0·9	2·1	3·7
150	—	—	—	1·7	2·3

Note : *(1) Extra width should be equally distributed on inner and outer sides except in case of sharp curves in hills with radius of curve less than 60 m. Widening should be in the inside only.

(2) The widening will start at the tangent point of the curve and should progressively increased at uniform rate till the maximum designed widening is reached, where the full designed super elevation is achieved.

2·15 Hair pin bends. In hills when a height is achieved in a short length, sharp circular curves are given zigzag going up. The following standards are taken in hair pin bends.

1. Minimum design speed ...20 km/hr
2. Minimum road way at sub unit ...11·5 m for double lane
   (*a*) National and state highways ...9·0 m for single lane
   (*b*) District roads ...7·5 m
   (*c*) Village roads ...6·5 m
3. Minimum length of transition ...15·0 m
4. Minimum radius of inner curve ...14·0 m
5. Gradient ...Maximum 1 : 40
   Minimum 1 : 200
6. Approach gradient not steeper than 1 : 20 for 40 m
7. Super elevation in circular portion curve ... 1 : 10 to 1 : 15
8. Inner and outer rings should be concentric

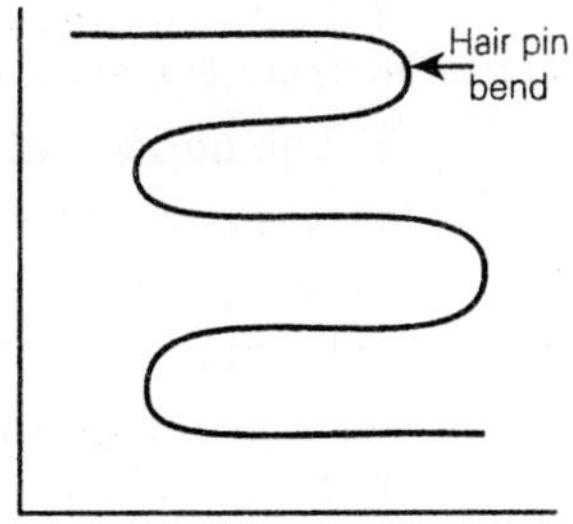

Fig. 15·17.

Camber. It is provided in straight reaches

Minimum value of camber in roads (IRC)

1. For concrete roads ... 1 : 72
2. For Bituminous roads ... 1 : 62
3. For water bound macadum ... 1 : 36 to 1 : 48
4. For mooram and kankar ... 1 : 24 to 1 : 30
5. For earth roads and footpaths ... 1 : 36 to 1 : 25
6. In berms (paved roads) ... 1 : 20 to 1 : 48
7. In berms (kachcha roads) ... 1 : 16 to 1 : 24

Note : (1) Steeper values are taken for high rainfall areas.

(2) The crown surface is covered to a shape of a parabola or ellipse.

Table 15·27. Design speed for different class of roads in km/hr

Type of road	*Plain*	*Rolling*	*Hilly*	*Steep*
1. National and State roads	80-100	65-80	40-50	30-40
2. Major district roads	65-80	60-65	30-40	20-30
3. Other district roads	50-65	40-50	25-30	20-25
4. Village roads	40-50	35-40	20-25	20-25
Urban roads				
1. Arterial	80 km/hr.			
2. Sub-arterial	60 km/hr.			
3. Collector road	50 km/hr.			
4. Local road	30 km/hr.			

Note : The lower or higher values are adopted according to the intensity of traffic and traffic control measures etc. 30 m is the minimum turning radius for a large truck.

Horizontal clearance. A horizontal distance measured at right angle to road alignment between road way or carriage way edge and a pole carrying any over head line or structure as under :

(1) Poles carrying any over head line or structure except in urban areas be erected at least 10·0 m away from the nearest edge of roadway with a minimum of 5 m from nearest line of avenue trees. In case of any future development the clearance shall reckoned from what will be the edge of road way.

(2) In mountainous : The poles should be erected preferably on the valley side as far away as possible from the edge of road.

(3) The horizontal clearance of poles of street lightening.

(*a*) Roads with raised kerb—Minimum 30 cm from edge of raised kerb (60 cm preferred)

(*b*) Roads without raised kerb—At least 15 m from edge of carriage way subject to minimum of 5 m from centre line of carriage way.

Vertical clearance. It is a vertical clear distance between the crown of carriage way to the lowest point of head conductor. The lowest point should be determined after accounting the sag as under :

1. Conductors carrying voltage upto 110 volts — 5·5 m
2. Conductors carrying voltage upto 660 volts — 6·0 m
3. Conductors carrying voltage upto 650 volts — 6·5 r.

It is as per statutory provisions of the Indian electricity rules

4. Urban roads minimum — 5·5 m
5. Railway electric traction (B.G.) — 5·87 m
   Railway non-electric traction (B.G.) — 4·88 m
6. Pedestrian or cycle way — 2·5 m

Traffic equivalent factors. (Taking a passenger car as an unit) The factors for others are fixed to calculate the intensity of traffic m nos.

1. Passenger car, tempo, autorickshaw ... 1·0
2. Cycle, motor cycle or scooter ... 0·5
3. Truck, Bus, Tractor ... 3·0
4. Horse driven vehicle ... 4·0
5. Bullock cart ... 6·8

15·2·16. Lives of roads

1. Water bound macadam with regular repair ... 2 years
   Surface dressing single coat ... 3 years
2. Bituminous grouted macadam ... 8 years
3. Premix bitumix carpet ... 8-15 years
4. Sheet asphaltic surface ... 15 years
5. Concrete roads ... 25-40 years.

Table 15·28. Suitability of road for a particular traffic

Nature of traffic	*Intensity of traffic tonnes/ width pēr day*	*Suitable type of road*
1. Light	Less than 160	Earth, mooram, kankar or gravel
2. Medium	160-330	Water bound macadam or 15 cm thick concrete road
3. Heavy	230-500	Grouted, bituminous macadam (two coats) 15 cm cement concrete
4. Very heavy	500-1400	Bituminous grouted, macadam, asphaltic or 17·5 cm RCC.
	1400-3500	Sheet asphaltic or 20 cm RCC
	3500-5000	22·5 cm RCC.

15·3. Road binding materials

Tar. Obtained from destructive distillation of coal.

Bitumen. A bi-product of petroleum.

Asphalt. A mineral product.

Road tar. It is divided in fine grades according to viscosity. Grade increases with increase of viscosity.

(1) **RT-1.** Penetrating substance, used in surface painting and in cold climates of hill roads. It is applied cold.

(2) **RT-2.** An oily substance, applied by heating at a temperature of 93-104°C on road surface painting in moderate climatic conditions.

(3) **RT-3.** Applied hot by heating to a temperature of 104°C to 116°C used in surface painting and premix light carpets.

(4) **RT-4.** Heated to a temperature of 132°C and used in premix carpets.

(5) **RT-5.** Heated upto a temperature of 138°C and used in grouting.

The above grades are subdivided as A, B, C etc. based on viscosity.

Bitumen. Bitumen obtained direct from distillation of petroleum is known as **straight run bitumen.**

Straight run bitumen is when blown with air to attain a rubbery consistency is known as **Blown bitumen.**

When straight run bitumen is blended with a volatile substance or solvent is known as **cut back.** The substances may be petrol, kerosene, or diesel etc. and is used without heating when straight run bitumen is thinned by water it is known as **bitumen emulsion.** In emulsions bitumen particles remain suspended in water in presence of emulsifying agent while in cut back the particles are dissolved in the solvent.

Straight run bitumen. According to Indian standards it is classified in six grades according to their penetrations below R-25, R-35, R-45, R-65, R-90 and R-200.

Blown bitumen. It is divided in following six grades, 85/25, 85/40, 95/15, 115/15, 135/10 and 135/6. The numerator denotes the softening point and the denominator the penetration point. The figure 85/40 means a softening point of 85°C and a penetration of 40. The blown bitumen has higher melting point and greater resistance to flow.

Cut back. Cut backs are used without heating or with a little heating. Cut backs are classified in the following three classes :

(1) **RC (Rapid Curing or setting).** A light material used as a primer. It becomes sticky to fingers when applied on surface.

(2) **MC (Medium curing or setting).** Used in surface dressing. It gives a kerosene like odour.

(3) **SC (Slow curing or setting).** Heavy type used in premixing. It gives an odour of a lubricating oil when heated.

The above three types are each divided in six grades starting from 0 to 5 as RC-0, RC-1, RC-2 etc. according to their viscosity (fluidity) percentage of bitumen and temperature at which they can be used. No '0' contains about 40% bitumen and No. '5' contains about 80% bitumen and is used at high temperature and is more viscous.

Emulsions. They are chocolate brown in colour. They can be applied cold in damp climates and on damp surfaces, while the cut backs are used on dry surfaces. Emulsions do not fat under traffic. They are of the following three classes.

(1) **RS (Rapid setting).** Used in surface painting and grouting and for seal coats having about 50 percent of bitumen.

(2) **MS (Medium setting).**

(3) **SS (Slow setting).** Used in premixing works and for patch repairs in wet weather. It contains about 60% bitumen. It can be used at normal atmospheric temperature.

The term cutting, curing or breaking can also be used in place of setting. The setting rate is assessed as follows :

Take some clean gravel in a pan and try to mix the emulsion by a spoon. A fast setting emulsion will not mix properly while a slow setting will mix with gravel and will stick to it and spoon.

Sulphur as a road binder in road construction

(1) The hardness of the bitumen can be changed by changing quantity of sulphur.

(2) The quantity of bitumen can be saved 30 to 40% by adding sulphur to it.

(3) The load bearing capacity of road is increased by adding sulphur to bitumen.

(4) The mixture of sand (natural or artificial), bitumen and sulphur is found very useful in road construction.

(5) By adding sulphur to bitumen the working temperature of the binder is reduced results saving in the heat energy.

(6) No change is required in the present construction machinery.

(7) A new binder can be produced chemically by sulphur.

Asphalt. When found naturally it is called natural or rock asphalt, when prepared by distillation in a refinery it is called residual or mastic asphalt. It may be said to be a mixture of bitumen and some inert substances.

Table 15·29

Grade	*Purpose (IRC)*
85/25 and 95/15	Expansion and contraction joints, insulation coats in buildings
85/25 and 105/15	D.P.C., cold storage, insulations, pipe coating
85/25 and 85/40	Sticking of bitumen felts
115/15 and 135/10	Manufacture of bitumen felts.

Quantity of spreading coarse aggregate and bituminous binder (IRC)

Compacted thickness	*Quantity of aggregate / 10 m^2*	*Quantity of binder kg/10 m^2*
50 mm	0·63 m^3	50 straight run bitumen, 60-65 RT-4/RT-5
75 mm	0·90 m^3	68 straight run bitumen, 82-88 RT-4/RT-5

Quantity required for premixing-hot bitumen/cut back

	52-56 kg/m^3 for aggregate	12 mm and above
	56-64 kg/m^3 for aggregate	10 mm size
	115 kg/m^3 for aggregate	stone grit
	128 kg/m^3 for aggregate	coarse sand
Tar :	66-80 kg/m^3 for aggregates	
	118 kg/m^3 for coarse sand	

Note : Different firms such as Burman Shell, Standard Vacuum Oil Co., Shalimar and Coltex Supply Bitumen and Tar products by different trade marks and brands for different purposes of works for different temperatures.

General properties of Bitumen

(*i*) They contain predominantly hydrocarbons, with small quantities of sulphur, oxygen, nitrogen and metals.

(*ii*) They are predominantly soluble in carbon disulphide (CS_2) the portion insoluble in CS_2 being generally less than 0·1%.

(*iii*) Most bitumen are colloidal in nature.

(*iv*) Bitumens are thermoplastic they soften on heating and harden on cooling.

(*v*) They have no specific melting point. Boiling and freezing point, though a form of softening point (Ring and Ball) is used in their characteristics.

(*vi*) Bitumens are insoluble in water.

(*vii*) They are highly impermeable to the passage of water.

(*viii*) They are generally hydrophobic (water repellant), but may be made hydrophilic (water leaking) by the addition of small quantity of surface active agents.

(*ix*) They are chemically inert.

(*x*) They oxidise slowly.

As a good road metal Bitumen should have the following qualities :

(*a*) It should be well hydrated at the time of mixing to coat the aggregates evenly by a thin film. Fluidity is achieved either by heating or by cutting back with a thin flux or by emulsifying the bitumen.

(*b*) It should have low temperature susceptibility or it should exhibit little change in viscosity with change in temperature. At least within the range of temperature prevailing on the road, *i.e.* should show uniform viscosity characteristics. This property becomes very difficult of fulfilment in the case of regions having well temperature range as in Northern India. If the binder have low temperature susceptibility, it will not become soft during the summer nor hard and brittle in cold weather.

(*c*) The bitumen should have a good amount of volatiles wet and it should not loose them excessively when subjected to higher temperature. This will ensure its durability.

(*d*) The bitumen should be ductile and not brittle.

(*e*) The bitumen should be capable of being heated to the temperature at which it can be easily mixed without any fire hazards.

(*f*) The bitumen should have good affinity to the aggregates and should not be shipped off in the continuous presence of water.

Solubility. All bitumens are soluble— CS_2 (carbon disulphide). Insolubles indicate the presence of minerals. IS specifications require 99% solubility.

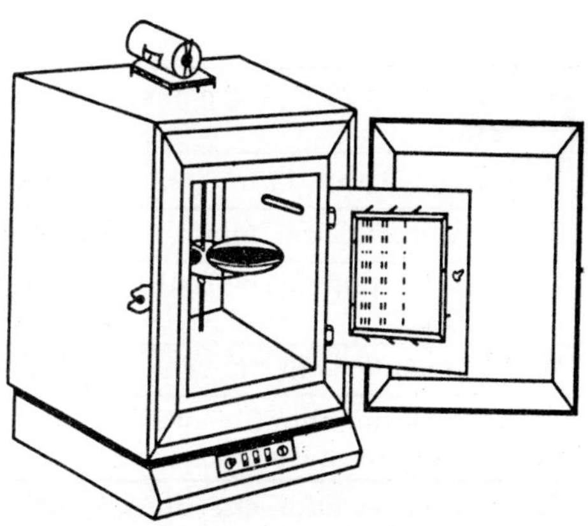

Fig. 15·18. Thin film oven test.

Thin Film Oven Test

In this test, a sample of bitumen is subjected to hardening conditions as would be expected during hot mixing operations. A 50 ml sample of bitumen is placed in a flat bottomed sample pan 140 mm inside diameter and 10 mm deep. The weighed sample and container are placed in a shelf which rotates at 5 to 6 r.p.m. for 5 hours in a ventilated oven (Fig. 15·18). maintained at 163°C. The loss in weight of the sample is expressed as a percentage of the original weight. The hardened bitumen sample is then poured into a container for use in the viscosity or penetration test.

A Rolling Thin Film Oven Test (RTFOT) is a similar test which is considered to simulate the short term ageing or hardening that occurs during the mixing process.

I.S. requirements for paving bitumens

The Indian Standard requirements for paving bitumens are given in Table 15·30.

Cutbacks

All hard penetration grade bitumens require to be heated to a specified temperature during use so as to bring down the viscosity to a value at which the coating of the aggregates with the binder film becomes possible ; the aggregates also have to be heated. To overcome this difficulty, cut-backs are used. A cut-back is a bitumen, the viscosity of which has been reduced by a volatile diluent. Depending upon the diluent used, there are three types of cut-backs :

Rapid-Curing (RC) : Bitumen which has been fluxed or blended with a naphtha type of distillate.

Medium Curing (MC) : Bitumen which has been fluxed or blended with a kerosene type of distillate.

Slow Curing (SC) : A liquid residue produced in the refining process, containing little or no volatile constituents.

Table 15·30. Requirements for Paving Bitumens (Ref. 5)

S. No.	*Characteristics*	*Requirements for Grades*						*Methods of Test, Ref. to*
		S 35	*S 45*	*S 55*	*S 65*	*S 90*	*S 200*	
(1)	(2)	(3)	(4)	(5)	(6)	(7)	(8)	(9)
(*i*)	Specific gravity at 27°C, Min.	0·99	0·99	0·99	0·99	0·99	0·99	IS 1202 : 1978
(*ii*)	Water, percent by mass, Max.	0·2	0·2	0·2	0·2	0·2	0·2	IS 1211 : 1978
(*iii*)	Flash point, Cleveland open cup, °C, Min.	175	175	175	175	175	175	IS 1209 : 1978
(*iv*)	Softening point °C	50 to 65	45 to 60	45 to 60	40 to 55	35 to 50	30 to 45	IS 1205 : 1978
(*v*)	Penetration at 25°C, 100 g, 5 sec., 1/10 mm	30 to 40	40 to 50	50 to 60	60 to 70	80 to 100	175 to 225	IS 1203 : 1978
(*vi*)	Penetration ratio*, Min.	35	35	35	35	35	35	—
(*vii*)	Ductility at 27°C, cm, Min.	50	75	75	75	75	—	IS 1208 : 1978
(*viii*)	Paraffin wax content, percent by mass, Max.	4·5	4·5	4·5	4·5	4·5	4·5	IS 10512 : 1983
(*ix*)	Frass breaking point, °C, Min.	– 4	– 4	– 6	– 6	– 8	– 10	IS 9381 : 1979
(*x*)	Loss on heating, thin film oven test, percent by mass, Max.	1	1	1	1	1	2	IS 1212 : 1978
(*xi*)	Retained penetration after thin film oven test, 25°C, 100 g, 5 sec. 1/10 mm, percent of original, Min.	55	55	52	52	47	42	IS 9382 : 1979

(*Table contd...*)

Table contd...

S. No.	Characteristics	Requirements for Grades						Methods of Test, Ref. to
		S 35	S 45	S 55	S 65	S 90	S 200	
(1)	(2)	(3)	(4)	(5)	(6)	(7)	(8)	(9)
(*xii*)	Matter soluble in trichloroethylene, percent by mass, Min.	99	99	99	99	99	99	IS 1216 : 1978
(*xiii*)	Viscosity at :							
	(*a*) 60°C, Poises	2500 ± 500	2000 ± 400	1500 ± 300	1000 ± 200	500 ± 100	250 ± 50	IS 1206 (Part 2) : 1978
	(*b*) 135°C ; cost, Min.	220	210	180	150	110	20	IS 1206 (Part 3) : 1978

$$* \text{ Penetration ratio} = \frac{\text{Penetration at } 4°\text{C},\ 200\ g,\ 60\ s}{\text{Penetration at } 25°\text{C},\ 100\ g,\ 5\ s} \times 100$$

15·3·1. Filler. The aim of a filler, is to give a workable mix which makes nonporous and smooth surface. Silt is a good filler. Filler should be dry and pulverised with no clods. Lime can be mixed with sand instead of cement. Sand should pass in 4·75 mm mesh. It should be mixed hot and heated to a temperature of 150°-160°C in a hot bin, while binder is heated to a temperature of 150°-160°C and then both are mixed in a pug mill. Sand should be mixed 1st.

15·3·2. Penetration. It is the measure of hardness of a binder and is the distance measured in units of 1/10 mm by penetration of a blunt pointed needle in a sample at 25°C with 100 gm load in 5 seconds. The lower is the penetration the harder is the asphalt. A variation of 10 points may be taken upto 90 points. 80-100 means a variation of 80 to 100 in penetration.

15·3·3. Viscosity. Higher the viscosity of a binder, greater is the strength, hence for heavy traffic binders having high viscosity are good. Too much high viscosity imparts brittleness. Binders having low viscosity can be used in cold weather, while binder having high viscosity are used at high temperatures. High viscosity resists water more than low viscosity.

Viscosity is the property of a fluid that determines the resistance offered by the fluid to a shearing force under laminar flow condition. It is thus opposite of fluidity. Dynamic or absolute viscosity (η) is the internal friction resulting from unit tangential force acting on planes of unit area separated by unit distance of fluid, producing unit tangential velocity. The unit of measurement of dynamic viscosity in SI units is Ns/m^2 (Newton second per sq. metre) and in c.g.s. unit is Poise (dyne per sq. cm); Ns/m^2 = 10 Poise.

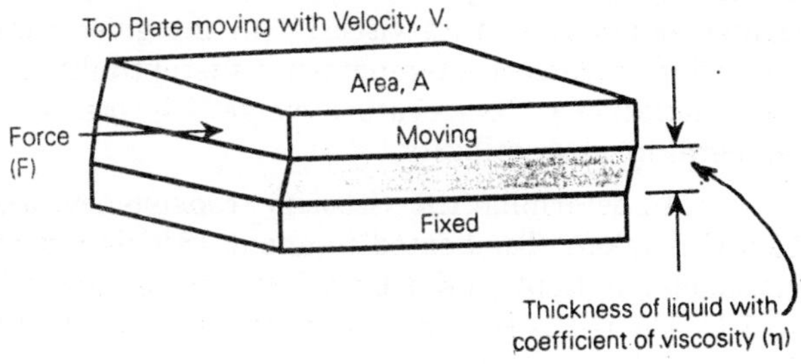

For simple liquids $F = \eta \frac{A_V}{d}$ *i.e.* $\eta = \frac{F_d}{A_V}$

Fig. 15·19. Concept of viscosity.

Kinematic viscosity (η) is the quotient of dynamic viscosity and the density of fluid (ρ). Thus

$$\gamma = \frac{\eta}{\rho}$$

The unit of kinematic viscosity is sq. m/per sec. (m^2/sec) in S.I. units.

and Stoke (cm^2/sec) in c.g.s. units.

One centi stoke = 0·01 stoke, one centi poise = 0·01 poise.

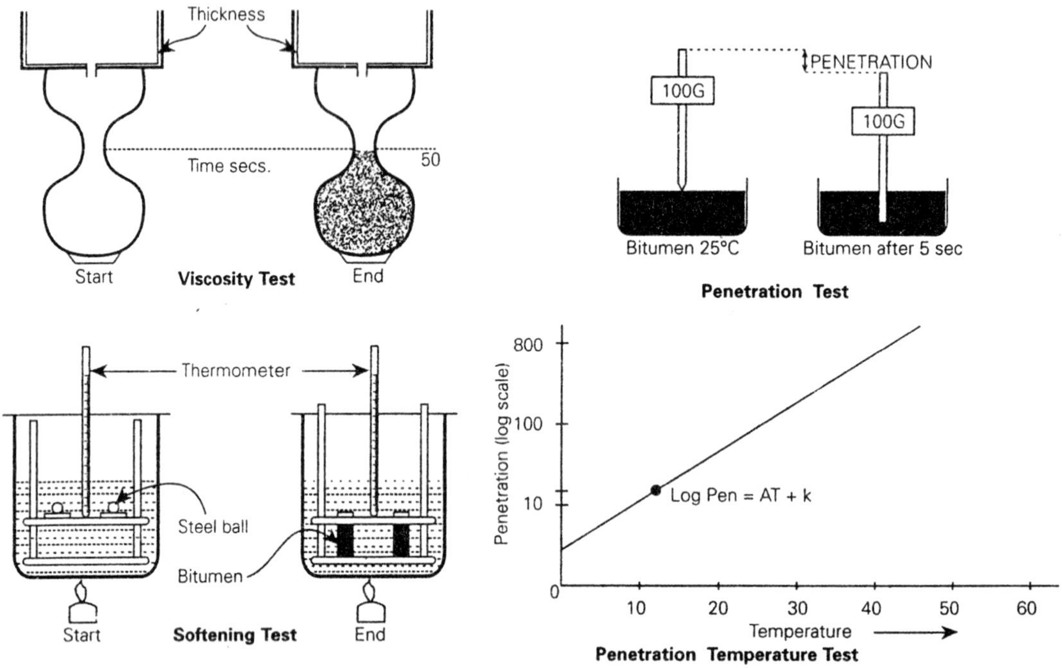

Fig. 15·20.

Temperature susceptibility

The rate of change of viscosity or consistency of a given bitumen determines its temperature susceptibility. This property is used in designing satisfactory bituminous mixes for use in any given range of temperature. The criterion is that the bitumen should exhibit as little change as possible in its viscosity in the given range of temperature change. The most common method to characterise temperature susceptibility is to find the **Penetration index (PI).** Plotting log penetration vs temperature we get log (pen) = $AT + K$. The slope of line A is an indication of temperature susceptibility.

To determine the viscosity (consistency) a standard viscometer surrounded in a bath at 15·5°C is taken. Tar heated to about 18°C is put in the viscometer. The orifice in the bottom of viscometer is kept closed by a ball pointed rod till the tar comes down to the temperature of 15·5°C. The rod is then removed off the orifice and the tar coming out is collected in a graduated flask and the time for taking a collection of 50 cc is noted. This time expressed in seconds is known as the consistency of the tar at 15·5°C.

15·3·4. Softening point. The softening point gives an idea of temperature susceptibility. Higher the softening point the higher will be the temperature susceptibility of tar.

A test tube 1·25 cm^3 of tar is hanged in beaker of water at 25°C. The beaker is surrounded by a water bath. The cube is kept 1·25 cm above the base of beaker. The water in the bath is heated slowly till the cube softens and touches the base of the beaker. As soon as this stage reaches the temperature in the beaker noted which represents the softening temperature of the tar.

15·3·5. Specific gravity. Weigh a measuring flask empty say it weighs w_1. Fill it with distilled water full and weigh say it is w_2. Fill the flask half with tar and weigh say it is w_3, again fill the remaining part by water and weigh say it is w_4. Then specific gravity of tar

$$= \frac{w_3 - w_1}{(w_2 - w_1) - (w_4 - w_3)} = \frac{\text{weight of tar}}{\text{weight of equal volume of water}}$$

The specific gravity of road making tar bitumen varies from 1·02 to 1·04. Tar varies 1·16 to 1·28.

Note : (1) The temperature of water is kept at 15·5°C. The flask which is known as Pyknometer has its capacity of 25 cc.

(2) For a dry mass, its weight is taken say it is M_1. Suspend it in a water bath at 15·5°C and take its weight in water say it is M_2, then the specific gravity = $M_1/(M_2 - M_1)$.

(3) Pure bitumen has its specific gravity varying from 1·00 to 1·02. An asphalt having specific gravity less than unity should not be used and should be softened to the required penetration by adding solvent.

Loss of weight on heating. A piece of 50 gm when heated to 163°C for 5 hours. The loss in weight should be noted which must be less than 3%.

15·3·6. Ductility. A standard briquette of asphalt at 25°C is stretched at the rate of 5 cm/ min. by two tensile forces applied on either ends. The distance stretched without rupture measured in cm is known as the ductility, which should not be less than 50 mm.

15·3·7. Brittleness. Brittleness is the state when fracture occurs without appreciable deformation at low stress. This property is very important in determining the desirable properties of a bituminous mixture. The Fran Break Point test is the most generally adopted procedure for determining brittleness. The test involves a thin film of bitumen (0·5 mm thick) formed on a flexible metal plaque. The film is bent under standardised conditions. The Break Point is that temperature at which cracking occurs.

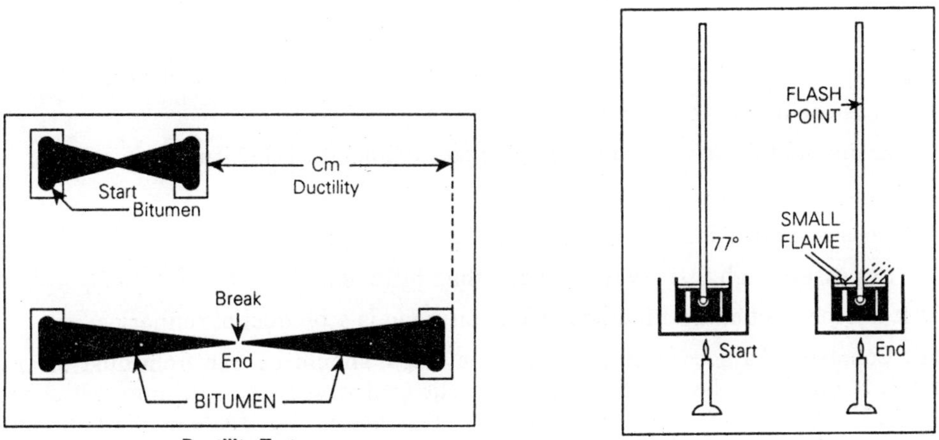

Ductility Test

Flash Point Test

Fig. 15·21.

15·3·8. Heat stability. The bituminous binder liquifies at about 90°C above their softening points. Such changes are reversible. At higher temperature the effects are studied by three tests.

(*i*) Flash point (*ii*) Fire test and spontaneous ignition temperature

(*iii*) Loss on heating.

(*i*) Flash Point of a bitumen is that temperature at which it gives off vapours, which ignite in the presence of a flame, but do not continue to burn. The flash point is an indication of critical position above which precautions are taken against hazard. The ISI list (Pensky-Martin Method) involves a cup into which the bitumen is filled. The bitumen sample is heated at a rate of 5-6°C per minute. The stirring of the material is kept continuous. The test flame is applied at intervals. The flash point is taken as the temperature read on the thermometer when the flame causes a bright flash in the interior of the cup in a closed system and at the surface of the material in an open system.

If heating is kept continue beyond the flash point, the vapour ignite in the presence of a flame and continue to burn indicating the **Fire Point** temperature. There is no standard method to determine the "Spontaneous Ignition Temperature" which can only be broadly indicated.

The effect of head on bituminous binder is the loss of volatile constituents, due to this loss the binder hardens. The loss on heating is achieved by the following method.

A 50 gm sample is maintained at a temperature of 163°C for 5 hours. The loss of weight is expressed as a percentage of the original weight is determined I.S. specifications stipulate a maximum 1% loss for all bituminous except 180/200 pen for which the maximum is 2%. The penetration of bitumen after the test is also determined in percentage of the original penetration which should be a minimum of 60%.

15·3·9. Comparative Properties of tar and bitumen

(1) Tar is a poor resistant than bitumen for weather.

(2) Tar is more sensitive to temperature than bitumen *i.e.* it softens and bleeds more than bitumen, hence it is not so good for road work than bitumen.

(3) Tar becomes brittle in cold weather, while bitumen does not.

(4) Tar is less effected by water than bitumen.

(5) Tar takes more setting time in precoated work than bitumen.

(6) Tar hardens quickly and bitumen slowly.

(7) The specific gravity of tar is more than bitumen.

(8) Tar produces less slippery surface than bitumen.

(9) Requirement of tar is 10% less than bitumen for the same type of work.

(10) Tar is cheaper than bitumen.

(11) Tar does not dissolve in kerosene and petroleum oil while bitumen is soluble.

(12) Tar is more adhesive than bitumen.

(13) It looses volatile matter more rapidly than bitumen.

(14) Tar possess high toxicity (poisonous) than bitumen.

(15) It is biproduct of steel industry while bitumen is a product of refineries.

Grit. Consists of a good, hard, tough stone chips, should be free from dust or any other organic matter. It must also be free from loose, porous or decayed stone. 15 mm grit should pass on a screen of 15 × 15 mm sq. mesh and should be retained on I.S. sieve no. 320 and should be uniformly graded in between these sizes.

15·3·10. Emulsions. Some of the cut backs can be handled when the binder and the aggregates are cold, but still some need to be heated. By emulsification of binders can be liquified even at normal atmospheric temperature about 0°C. An emulsion is a relatively stable dispension of a liquid, minutely subdivided (disperse phase) in another liquid in which it is not soluble (continuous phase). In a bituminous emulsion, bitumen is the disperse phase and water the continuous phase. Stability of the emulsion is achieved by the use of an emulsifying agent contained in the aqueous phase.

Based on the type of emulsifier used, the bitumen particles can be negatively charged or positively charged. Emulsions having negatively charged bitumen particles are called anionic emulsions and those having positively charged particles are called cationic emulsions. The emulsifier used for the anionic emulsions are normally fatty acids derived from mineral, vegetable or wood sources sapnified with the sodium or potassium hydroxide. The emulsifiers in cationic emulsions are generally amine salts made by reacting hydrochloric acid or acetic acid with an organic amine or demine IS : 3117—1965 contains the requirements of anionic emulsions. Cationic emulsions are covered by IS : 8887—1978. Emulsions became popular in the recent period. There are following advantages of emulsions.

(*i*) They are more tolerant than penetration grade bituminous in the presence of dampness, although they should not be used in the presence of free water on the road surface or on aggregates.

(*ii*) Because emulsions are relatively low viscosity at normal temperature they eliminate the need to heat the aggregates and binder and thus conserve energy.

(*iii*) Their use reduces environmental pollution especially because unlike cut back bitumen. They do not release normal smoke in the atmosphere.

(*iv*) They can be used in the cold weather.

(*v*) They can be easily used as patch repair since they do not require heating

(*vi*) They are good sealants because they penetrate in fine cracks.

(*vii*) The emulsions are costlier and since they contain substantial water their transportation is also costlier.

There are three types of emulsions as per I.S. specification 8887 as

(*a*) Rapid setting (RS) ; (*b*) Medium setting (MS) and (*c*) Slow setting (SS).

The emulsions are further classified by numbers and letters related to viscosity of the emulsions and hardness of the base straight run bitumen. The letter "*C*" in front of the emulsion type denotes cationic while the absence of "*C*" denotes anionic. The numbers in the classification relate to the viscosity *i.e.* MS-2 is more viscous than MS-1 ; the "*h*" means harder base bitumen and "*S*" stands for the softer base bitumen. In the anionic grades, the "*HF*" before the grade indicates high float as measured by the float test. High float types have a gel quality that permits a thicker film of bitumen on the aggregate particles.

Anionic	*Cationic*
RS-1	CRS-1
RS-2	CRS-2
MS-1	—
MS-2	CMS-2
MS-2*h*	CMS-2*h*
HFMS-1	—
HFMS-2	—
HFMS-2*h*	—
HFMS-2*s*	—
SS-1	CSS-1
SS-1*h*	CSS-1*h*

A new set of emulsion grades have come up ending in *P*(*s* or *l*) *i.e.* HFRS-2*P* implies a modified bitumen emulsion.

The emulsion breaks down on application to the road. In this process, the particles of the binder in the emulsion separate from the aqueous component and forms a coherent film of binder. The breaking down process changes the brown colour of the emulsion in black. The water contents evaporate leaving behind the bitumen particles which get more closely packed together.

Practically all grades of straight run of bitumen can be emulsified. Tar or tar bitumen blend can also be emulsified.

15·3·11. Guideline for the selection of a bituminous binder (According to Physical Conditions)

(*i*) Whether it is of spraying or mixing specifications.

(*ii*) Climatic conditions—especially temperature range.

(*iii*) Traffic characteristics—whether the traffic is light, medium or heavy.

(*iv*) Plant availability—whether hot mix plant or by any other equipment.

(*v*) Nature of work—whether it is maintenance work or a large scale job.

The Bitumen is available in drums of 166 kg each.

15·3·12. Tar. Coal is carbonised for the production of metallurgical coke needed for the manufacture of steel. Coal is also carbonised for the production of town gas. In this process coal tar is obtained as a byproduct. Road tar is produced by the refining of coal tar. The process is indicated in the chart below :

Coal

Metallurgical coke | Gas | Coal tar distillation

Napthalene | Creosote | Carbolic oil | Anthracene oil | Road tar

Manufacture of Road Tar and its byproducts

Table 15·31. Guide to selection of bituminous binders (According to grade and type of binder)

S. No.	*Type of binder*	*Application*
1.	30/40 Penetration grade	1. Penetration macadam in normal summer temperature and in plains 2. Hot mix asphaltic concrete in normal summer temperature and in plains 3. Bituminous macadam (hot mix) in normal summer temperature and in plains.
2.	60/70 Penetration grade	1. Penetration macadam and in winter and at high altitude. 2. Hot mix asphaltic concrete in normal summer temperature and in plains. 3. Hot mix Bituminous macadam in summer climate and in plains.
3.	80/100 Penetration grade	1. Surface dressing, seal coat and premixed chipping carpet in normal summer temperature and in plains. 2. Penetration macadam in summer temperature and in plains. 3. Hot mix asphaltic concrete and bituminous macadam in summer temperature and in plains. 4. Hot mix asphaltic concrete and bituminous macadam in winter temperature and at high altitudes.
4.	180/200 Penetration grade	1. Surface dressing, seal coat and premixed chipping, carpet at winter temperature and at high altitude. 2. Penetration macadam at winter temperature and at high altitudes. 3. Hot mix asphaltic concrete and macadam at winter temperature and at high altitudes.

Table contd...

Table contd...

S. No.	Type of binder	Application
5.	Cut back RC-3	1. Surface dressing and seal coats at normal summer temperature and in plains. 2. Cold-mix macadam and bituminous carpets at summer and winter temperature, both in plains and high altitudes. 3. Surface dressing and seal coats at winter temperature and at high altitudes.
6.	Emulsions	1. Cold weather work. 2. Remote area work. 3. Wet condition of aggregate. 4. Maintenance and patch repair work. 5. Sealing of fine cracks. 6. Prime coat and lack coat.
7.	Medium-curing and slow curing cut backs.	Priming

The coal belt in India finishes the coking coal (metallurgical coke) needed for the steel mills. A number of coke ovens have been set up to manufacture coking coal-tar which is the residue, is further processed at Jharia and Kolkata. Creosote is used for preservation of wooden sleepers. The residue known as pitch is processed further to get various grades of road tar.

Road tar was used for road construction in India since 1913 when roads in the Govt. place, Calcutta were constructed with tar. The Mall in Lahore was 1st surfaced with tar in 1916. During the period 1920-1950 tar used to be a popular binder tar road construction in India.

The serious shortage of petroleum and bitumen in the past decades has sparked fresh thinking as the possibility of manufacture of road tar on a large scale for road construction.

Table 15·32. Grades of Road Tars for different purposes (IS : 215—1961)

Grade	Uses
RT-1	Surface dressing for very cold weather conditions and at high elevation on hill roads.
RT-2	Surface dressing under normal climatic conditions.
RT-3	A. Surface dressing and renewal coats. B. Precoating chippings ; light chipping carpet.
RT-4	Premix for macadam.
RT-5	Grouting.

Table 15·33. Standard specification for Road Tar (IS : 215—1961)

	Characteristic	RT-1	RT-2	RT-3	RT-4	RT-5
1.	Viscosity					
	(*a*) Temperature °C	35	40	45	55	65
	(*b*) Seconds	30-56	30-55	35-60	40-60	—
2.	E.V.T. °C	32-36	27-41	40-46	53-57	63-68

Table contd...

Table contd...

	Characteristic	*RT-1*	*RT-2*	*RT-3*	*RT-4*	*RT-5*
3.	Softening point of the residue	48	50	52	54	56
4.	Water content %	0·5	0·5	0·5	0·5	0·5
5.	Distillation %					
	(*a*) Below 200	0·5	0·5	0·5	0·5	0·5
	(*b*) 200-270	4-12	2-9	1-6	0-5·4	0-4
	(*c*) 270-300	4-10	4-8	3-6	2-7	1-5
	(*b* and *c*) max.	16	14	12	10	7
6.	Phenol % by volume	2·0	2·0	2·0	2·0	1·0
7.	Naphthalene % weight	4·0	3·5	3·0	2·0	2·0
8.	Matter insoluble into toluene %	22	22	24	24	24
9.	Specific gravity	1·16-1·26	1·16-1·26	1·18-1·28	1·18-1·28	1·18-1·28

Low temperature Tar. The coal tar produced in the manufacture of coking coal results from carbonisation at high temperature (above 1000°C). In recent years the need to increase the availability of binders has given rise to a new technology of tar manufacture. This is known as "low temperature carbonisation" since the carbonisation of coal is carried out in the temperature range of 600-750°C in a smokeless fuel process. The crude tar so produced is now being successfully used for manufacturing road tars.

15·3·13. Modified Binders. Tar and bitumen has their own characteristic but when they are mixed by proper blending, provide a good binder having excellent qualities. Bitumen has greater durability and lower temperature susceptibility than tar. But bitumen has poor adhesion with certain stone aggregates in the presence of water resulting in stripping. Tar has better adhesion with aggregates because of the presence of phenol. Tar when exposed to weather hardens. Tar mixers show better steel resistance properties than bitumen mixers. The bitumen blend exhibits the following betterments :

(*a*) As more and more bitumen is blended with tar, the benzene insoluble, which is normally not a binding material is decreased. The mixer thus has a better binding property.

(*b*) The softening point is increased and the penetration is lowered. Thus the temperature susceptibility of bitumen is lowered. The viscosity temperature relationship is considerably improved.

(*c*) It is now common in other countries also to mix bitumen and tar in proportions approaching 50-50. There are problems such as incompatibility, since bitumen and tar are chemically differ. But with careful control, the materials can be blended.

15·3·14. Rubberised Tar and Bitumen. The addition of a small quantity of rubber in tar and bitumen reduces its viscosity with temperature significantly. The softening point is increased and brittleness is reduced. The elasticity of the binder is increased with the addition of rubber. In places such as bus stands, rotary, intersection and sleep grades where frequent accelerations and deceleration are frequent, the rubber addition checks the flow and the mix is toughened. Rubber increases the resistance to brittle practice at low temperature and improves the adhesion of the binders to the aggregate. Gilsonite and TBM super is used and crumb rubber powder is used for this purpose. The suggested dosage is 12 percent by weight of binder.

Table 15·34. Polymerised bitumen—The following Bitumen modifier are used

Sl. No.	*Type of modifiers*	*Example*	*Indicative close level, % by weight of bitumen*
1.	Plastics : Thermoplastics Thermosets	Polyethylene (PE) Ethylenevinol acetate (EVA) Epoxy resins	 3-6 3-5
2.	Elastomers Natural rubber Synthetic elastomers	Dry rubber contents Butadiene copolymer (SBA) Styrene butadiene styrene black copolymer (SBS)	 2-4 3-5
3.	Reclaimed Rubbers	The crumb rubber powder further improved by additives	10-12

Surface Courses of Bitumen. (1) Prime coats (2) Tack coats.

Prime coats. A prime coat is an initial application of a low viscosity liquid bituminous material to an absorbent surface preparatory to any superimposed bituminous treatment in construction.

Tack coat. It is an application of a bituminous binder to an existing surface (black topper or otherwise) to ensure a bond between the new construction and the old surface.

The aim of the prime coats. Bituminous specification often to be provided directly on the untreated layers of gravel etc. These courses contain considerable voids and have considerable porosity. Due to this the moisture can penetrate into the layer either from the superimposed layer, from the sides or from the underneath due to capillary action. This is overcome by applying a low viscosity liquid bitumen to such surface to penetrate the surface, plug capillary voids and coat and bound dust and loose mineral particles. The process hardens or toughens the surface and promotes adhesion between it and its superimposed layer.

The aims of the tack coat. The difference in a tack and a prime coat is that unlike the latter, the binder does not penetrate into the layer receiving the new application. It remains at the interface between the old surface and the new one and promotes necessary bond between the two.

15·3·15. Field application of bitumen. The bitumen may be applied either manually or by mechanical means on the road surface. In the manual process the bitumen is heated in the half cut (in horizontal direction) bitumen empty drums (spared after the use) and then it is transferred into the cans provided with a fountain at its neck, by spoons made for the purpose. By these cans the bitumen is spreaded manually on road surface. The manual process is generally used for repair work.

In the mechanical process the bitumen is heated in U-shaped boilers generally of a capacity 800-1000 litres. A hand pump at the end of the boiler pumps the binder into a container. The binder is sprayed through a nozzle. The rate of the application of the binder can be raised by adjusting the height of the nozzle over the road. The bitumen pressure distribution consists of a truck mould lane with heating arrangements. The heated binder is sprayed through a series of nozzles spaced along a horizontal pipe.

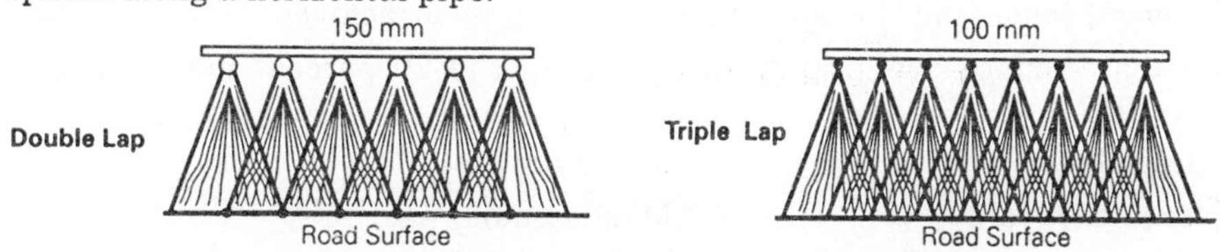

Nozzles for spraying bitumen from Pressure distributor

Fig. 15·22.

The binder is to be sprayed longitudinally along the road length and not transversely to avoid corrugations.

Table 15·35. Heating temperatures for surface dressing

Binder		*Heating temperature*
80/100 penetration grade		163-175°C
Cut back	RC-3	27-66°C
Road tar	RT-2	33-104°C
	RT-3	104-115°C
Emulsions		Heating not required

The cover aggregates are generally spreaded by manual methods. Spreading is done by baskets. The aggregates are then brushed by hard brooms. If emulsions are used then the chippings are applied as soon as the emulsion breaks (turns black). Stone grits are used in mechanical construction.

Rolling should be done immediately with a steel tyred roller 6-10 tonnes capacity as soon as the aggregates are spreaded. This will ensure proper embedment to the aggregates into the soft binder. Pneumatic tyred rollers are known to give better performance since they do not crush the aggregate.

The rolling should proceed from the edges towards the centre. On super elevated portions, the rolling should proceed from the inner to the outer edge. The grade and cross-section should be checked by means of 3 m straight edge and counter boards respectively. The maximum permissible variation is 12 mm in the longitudinal profile and 8 mm in the cross profile.

Traffic should perferably be prevented for 24 hours during which period the binder will harden. Once the binder has set, pneumatic tyred traffic has a beneficial effect on it. It facilitates interlocking of the particles so as to obtain a uniform mosaic covers of aggregates.

Two coats of a surface dressing need a renewal coat after every 3-5 years depending upon the traffic.

15·3·16. Premix carpets. The precoated chipping carpets are open grading premixed materials used as a thin surfacing layer. The thickness as prescribed in India is 20 mm. A seal coat is provided in regions of a high rainfall.

Comparison with two coats surface dressing versus premix carpets

(*i*) Premixing effectively coats the full surface of the aggregates.

(*ii*) There is no loss of aggregates due to traffic as in case of surface dressing.

(*iii*) The quantity of aggregates used in a 20 mm carpet with seal coat is 0·36 m^3 per 10 m^2, as against 0·25 m^3 per 10 m^2 in the case of two coat surface dressing. Thus the former is thicker and better than latter.

The disadvantages are :

(*i*) The premix carpet requires a mixer, whereas two coat surface dressing requires the minimum of equipment consisting of a boiler with a hand spray attachment.

(*ii*) Two coat surface dressing is cheaper than the 20 percent mm carpet material specification as per IRC.

Los Angles value	Maximum 35
Aggregate impact value	Maximum 30
Flakeness index	Maximum 25 percent
Stripping	Maximum 25 percent

Table 15·36. The size and quantity of aggregates for 20 mm carpet

	Material	*Correlation*	*Quantity of 10 m^2*
1.	Aggregates for premixing 12 mm	Passing 20 mm and retained on 10 mm square mesh	0·18 cu. m.
	10 mm	Passing 12 mm and retained on 6·3 mm square mesh	0·09 cu. m.
2.	Sand or fine grit for seal coat in low rainfall areas	Sand having fineness modulus more than 2·5. Fine grit passing IS : 1·70 mm and retained on IS : 180 microns	0·60 cu. m.
3.	Course aggregates to seal coat in high rainfall areas, 6·3 mm.	Passing 10 mm and retained on 2·36 mm sq. mesh	0·09 cu. m.

The binder can be of the following types :

(1) 80/100 penetration grade bitumen

(2) 180/200 penetration grade bitumen

(3) Road tar RT-3

(4) Cut back RC-3.

Table 15·37. Quantity of binder to 20 mm premix carpet

Course	*Binder quantity in kg per 10 m^2*		*Remarks*
	Bitumen	*Tar*	
1. Premixing	14·6	19·7	For 80/100 penetration grade bitumen using cold mix process, it has been found necessary to flux the binder 3-5% kerosene.
2. Premixed seal coat for low rainfall area	6·8	9·8	
3. Premix seal coat for high rainfall area	9·8	—	

Field process. The existing surface is made clean of dust or cracked mud, by brushing and sweeping. Irregularities such as pot holes are made up with precoated chips and rammed. The edges are marked out by ropes. Immediately before laying the carpet, the tack coat is sprayed by hand operated sprayers.

The premixing operation with penetration grade bitumen or road tar can either cold mix or hot mix. In this form, the bitumen is suitably flow but the aggregates are not heated. In the latter, the aggregates are also heated and there is no need for fluxing bitumen. For small works improved drum mixers may be used.

Table 15·38. The heating temperature of the binder for premix carpet

Binder	*Heating temperature*
1. 80/100 penetration grade	150-165°C
2. Road tar RT-3	105-110°C

The mixed material is emptied on the trenchers or wheel burrows and spreaded on the road surface. Spreading and laying a thin carpet of 20 mm can best be done manually by means of forks and rakes. Camber boards are used for checking cross profile. Rolling is done by power roller of 6-10 tonnes, as soon as a sufficient length say 15 metres of carpet has been laid. The rolling is done longitudinally starting at the edges and proceeding towards the crown. On super elevated curves, the rolling is started from the inner side of the curves, proceeding towards the outer edge. The speed of rolling should not exceed 5 km/hour. The successive layers should overlap the previous ones by at least half the width of the rear wheel. The roller wheels can be moistened with water to prevent adhesion of the materials to the wheels. The tolerance in the final surface should be 10 mm in the longitudinal profile when measured with a 3 m straight edge and 6 mm with cross profile.

Seal coat is laid as early as possible. In areas of low rainfall (less than 150 cm per year) premixed seal using sand or fine grit is laid. In areas of heavy rainfall (more than 150 cm per year), liquid seal coat is laid. The liquid seal coat is laid just like a 2nd coat of surface dressing.

Traffic can be allowed preferably after 24 hours of laying seal coats.

The 20 mm precoated chipping carpet has a life of about 6 to 8 years. Every 3-4 years, the seal coat is renewed as a period of normal maintenance.

15·3·17. Built up spray grout (BUSG). Built up spray grout is a method of building up a flexible pavement in which single size stones are laid in layer of thickness equal to the size of the stones and a very small quantity of bituminous binder is grouted. The binder so grouted smears the surface of the stone aggregate and imparts an adhesion amongst the aggregates of one layer as well as between the aggregates of one layer and those of the layers above. This adhesion takes place only at the contact points between aggregate interfaces. The layers are usually built up in thicknesses of 40 mm and the total compacted thickness of the course usually built is not above 75 mm.

15·3·18. The specification as recommended by IRC

(*i*) A tack coat is 1st applied to the water-bound macadam surface, the quantity of binder may be reduced if the existing pavements is black topped.

(*ii*) Course aggregates of the gradation given in the table below are spreaded at the rate of 0·5 cu. m. per 10 m^2 to a uniform depth.

Table 15·39. Gradation of Aggregates for BUSG

% Passing Sieve Size IS :	*Coarse aggregate*	*Key aggregates*
50 mm	100	—
25 mm	35-70	—
20 mm	—	100
12·5 mm	10-15	35-70
4·75 mm	—	0-15
2·36 mm	0-5	0-5

(*iii*) The stone layers then rolled by an 8-10 tonnes power roller.

(*iv*) The first application of binder is then provided at the temperature appropriate for spraying. The specified rate is 12·5 kg-150 kg per 10 m^2.

(*v*) Immediately thereafter the 2nd layer of coarse aggregates at the rate of 0·5 cu. m. per 10 m^2 is spreaded and compacted.

(*vi*) The 2nd application of binder is then applied at the rate of 12·5 kg to 15·0 kg per 10 m^2.

(*vii*) Immediately thereafter, key aggregates at the rate of 0·13 cu. m per 10 m^2 are applied approximately. They are then rolled into position until they are finally embedded in the surface.

(*viii*) Since built up spray grout is an open graded specification, it should be covered with the wearing coarse before opening the traffic. However in exceptional circumstances, the surface may be opened to limited traffic, provided the speed of vehicles is restricted to 16 km per hour.

(*ix*) The wearing course should be at least 20 mm pre mix carpet.

15·4. Water Bound Macadam Roads (W.B.M.)

15·4·1. Sub Grade. A good sub grade has the following qualities :

(*i*) It must contain sand 70 to 80%, silt 10 to 20% and clay 5 to 10% in a consolidated bonded form.

(*ii*) A sub grade having a bearing capacity less than 5½ tonnes per m^2 should be removed upto a depth of 15 cm. A soil containing above grading with an optimum water content must be laid, levelled and rolled in a depth of 15 cm consolidated. For checking the percentage of different constituents the following field tests can be applied.

(*a*) Shake thoroughly a sample mixed in water in a beaker and then allowed to rest. The clay will remain suspended in water, silt and sand will settle in the bottom. The lower layer will be of sand and upper of silt, which can give an idea of the percentage of silt and sand in the sample.

(*b*) For checking the percentage of clay, a known quantity of the sample is taken and the above test is repeated. The quantity of silt and sand is separated, dried and weighed. The whole sample quantity minus the silt and sand is the percentage of clay.

(*c*) To check the percentage of clay, make small balls of the sample and place it in a beaker of water. If it falls to pieces the presence of sand is dominant and if they retain, a percentage of clay is evident.

Sub grade on black cotton soils. Remove 15 cm of the soil, mix it with 4 percent by weight with fat lime. Pulverise thoroughly and lay on the sub-grade. Roll it with a 8 to 10 tonne roller.

Stabilization of poor soils in sub grade by bitumen. Spray hot bitumen on the surface of sub grade at the rate of 450 litres % m^2 and roll with 8 tonnes roller. If there is any sub soil water is present in the sub grade, it should be drained by cutting a side drain which should be dewatered till the soling is completed.

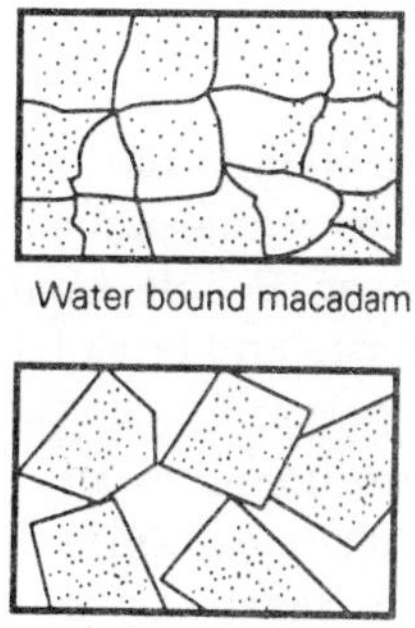

Water bound macadam

Built-up spray grout

Fig. 15·23.

Soling. (Foundation hard core or bottoming). Following materials can be taken for soling.

(1) **Over burnt brick bats**, which do not soak more than 1/4th weight of water to its own weight, when immersed in water for one hour. Over burnt bricks can also be laid dry on edge across the longitudinal axis of road with its long side or laid in herring bone or diagonally. Top blended with mooram or kiln rubbish.

(2) **Stone.** Stones must have the maximum size equal to the thickness of the soling. The broadest face should rest on the sub grade, long side across roadway and should be packed as dense as possible. Fill the interistics by smaller stones and fine gaps by mooram or sand. If the biggest stone has lesser size than the thickness of the soling then fill the interistics by other suitable stones so as to achieve the final thickness. In no case it must be laid in two layers. Camber in the surface of the soling is also given as required. It must then be compacted by a 8 to 10 tonne roller. A layer of sand or mooram 10 cm thick under soling over sub grade gives a good cushion for better distribution of load. The thickness of soling varies from 20 to 30 cm.

Selection of stone. It must be hard tough, dense and weather proof. Hardness can be tested by scratching a line by a pen knife. If the line is deep and distinct, the stone is soft. The toughness can be tested by a blow of a hammer. If it breaks to pieces, it is not tough. Denseness can be tested by its weight per unit volume. If it gives effloresence by a drop of sulphuric acid, the stone is likely to be effected by CO_2 in air. It's texture can be justified by the grains seen in a fresh fractured stone. The fresh brocken stone surface must have a bright granular surface. It must not soak water more than one percent by weight when immersed for one hour in water. It must also not be liable to be abrased. The abrasion can be tested by rolling pieces of stone in a drum. If it crumbles in powder it is not abrasion proof and is not good for road.

Granite, Basalt, Trap and Diorite are used as road metal. Broken stone is always better than round in road work. Sometimes sides of soling are provided thicker at edges for protection which is known as **haunching.**

15·4·2. Base. The thickness of the base varies from 7·5 cm to 16 cm depending on the type of load to be taken by the road. The base top should always be 30 cm higher than the sub soil water level or the level of the water in the side drain. 15% extra depth is laid to give an account for consolidation. The base should be laid in two layers with a minimum of 7·5 cm thickness. Each layer should be consolidated separately and the top layer should be blended and should be opened to traffic for about 6 weeks. The consolidation should be done by 6 to 8 tonne three wheeled roller and should be watered during rolling. Thickness of the metal should be 90 mm to 20 mm.

Table 15·40. Grading of Coarse Aggregate for W.B.M. (IRC)

Grade No.	*Size range*	*Sieve No.*	*Passing percentage by weight*
1.	90 to 40 mm	100 mm	100
	Over burnt brick aggregate	80 mm	65-85
		63 mm	25-60 Sub base
		40 mm	0-15 coarse
		20 mm	0-5
2.	63 to 40 mm soft	80 mm	100
	Stones : Lime stone flint	63 mm	90-100 For lower
	Kankar (Pebble) quartzite	50 mm	35-70 layer
	Laterite and brick ballast	40 mm	0-15
		20 mm	0-5
3.	50 to 20 mm	63 mm	100
	Hard stone granite	50 mm	95-100 For top
	Trap, Basalt, diorite etc.	40 mm	37-70 layer
		20 mm	0-10
		10 mm	0-5

Base Compaction

Material	*Weight of roller*	*Thickness of loose material*	*Moisture content*
1. Hard brick bats or crushed stone	10 tonne or more	20 cm	Not required
2. Ashes clinker	8 tonne	15 cm	12·2%
3. Clayee gravel (stable)	8 tonne	23 cm	6-10%
4. Clayee sand, lean concrete	6-8 tonne	23 cm	10-18% concrete Nil

Sub base. When the sub grade is of poor quality, a layer known as sub base is interposed between the soling and the sub grade of a granular material such as rubble, brick bats, clinker etc. It is generally put under a concrete road.

While laying base the ruts and pot holes formed in soling should be repaired by removing the defective portion. In case of existing roads, the surface should be scarified and should be brought to the required shape after repair. If the thickness of the renewal coat is 6·5 cm or over no scarifying is needed and the old surface should be scored with lines 4 cm deep, 7·5 cm wide and in grids of 2 metres apart in order to provide a key. On sides to protect it and to have a guide for thickness of base bricks on end are fixed or a daula of mud is made.

The metal is considered to be compacted when a piece of stone about 3″ size is crushed by the roller and if it drivens in the base metal it is considered that the compaction is not to the mark. A bullock cart should also not leave a mark on the surface for proper compaction. Over compaction is also harmful and should be avoided.

After the road has been fully consolidated a one cm. thick layer of sand or mooram should be spreaded and the road should be opened for traffic. After four days the road is watered and after 15 days a light rolling and repairing of loosened material is done.

Brick metal absorbs about 10% extra binder and can be used where stone metal is not available or the road is to be used for a light traffic.

15·4·3. Screening and blending. It is pebble stones used to fill up the interstices of the base by screening material like kiln rubbish, mooram, dust or gravel. It is spreaded over the surface dry and filled in the interstices by brushes or hand brooms. Rolling and spreading goes on simultaneously till all the interstices are filled. Any rut or pot hole should be filled by aggregate and screening material and rolled. After the interstices are filled the screening material is spreaded about 1 cm thick watered and rolled to give a smooth surface. After the screening is over the road should be closed for a day for giving a setting time for screening. Too much thickness of screening material should be avoided.

Blending should always be done in the 2nd layer of base and not in the 1st layer.

Table 15·41. Grading of Screenings for W.B.M. (IRC)

Grade No.	*Size range*	*Screen designation*	*Percentage by wt. passing*
A	12·5 mm	12·5 mm	100
		10·0 mm	90-100
		4·75 mm	10-30
		150 μ	18
B	10 mm	10 mm	100
		4·75 mm	85-100
		150 μ	10-30

Note : (*a*) 4·75 and 150 μ used in place of No. 480 (ISI) and No. 15 (ISI).

(*b*) In case of soft aggregates, screening may be eliminated.

(*c*) Type A grade can be used with grade 1 of aggregates
Type B grade can be used with grade 3 of aggregates
Type AB grade can be used with grade 2 of aggregates

Table 15·42. Approximate quantity of coarse aggregate and screenings required for 10 cm compacted base of W.B.M. road for 10 m² area

Coarse aggregate			*Screenings*		
Grade No.	*Size range*	*Loose quantity m³*	*Grade No. (mm)*	*Loose quantity m³*	*Crushed as moorum or gravel-Loose quantity*
I	90-40 mm	1·21-1·43	*A*(12·5)	0·4-0·44	0·44-0·47 m³
	For 7·5 cm compacted thickness				
II	63-40 mm	0·91-1·07	*A*(12·5)	0·18-0·21 (base layer)	0·33-0·35 m³
				0·14-0·17 (surface layer)	
III	50-20 mm	-do-	*B*(9·0)	0·3-0·33 (base layer)	-do-
				0·27-0·30 (base layer)	
				0·24-0·26 (surface)	
				0·22-0·24 (layer)	

Grading of metal in W.B.M.

I	*II*	*III*	*IV*
5 cm-50%	5 cm-60%	5 cm-60%	4 cm-60%
4 cm-25%	2 cm-30%	4 cm-30%	2·5 cm-30%
2 cm-15%	1/2 cm-10%	2 cm-10%	1 cm-10%
1 cm and below 10%			

15·4·4. Grouting and Painting of Water Bound Roads

After the base layer has been consolidated, the grouting and painting is done in the following steps.

(1) **Primary or tack coat.** (*a*) Any pot hole must be closed with the metal in the base layer, levelled and rammed. The surface should be cleaned of all loose dust, sand or mooram. In old surfaces, wire brushed and air blows should be used.

(*b*) Road tar no. 3 heated to a temperature of 200°-225°F (95-105°C) or asphalt 80-100 penetration heated to 350°-375°F (175°-190°C) should be sprayed at the rate of 220 kg% m^2 of road surface (45 litre % sft) or upto such a quantity that the interstices are properly filled by cans or mechanical sprayers, and should be brushed to make even.

(*c*) Hard stone grit or chips (6 mm to 20 mm or ¼″ to ¾″) should be spreaded evenly on surface at the rate of 1·35 m^3% m^2 of road surface. The surface should be rolled by four trips of 8-10 tonne three wheeled roller. The road should be opened for traffic after 24 hours.

(2) **2nd coat.** (*a*) Loose grit of the 1st coat should be removed and if any pot hole is there, should be repainted by tar mixed grit used in 1st coat. Tar no. 3-A heated to 220° to 240°F (105°-115°C) and asphalt 80-100 penetration heated to a temperature of 375°F (190°C) should be spreaded and coated even with cans or sprayers and brushed at the rate of 120 kg% m^2 (25 lb% sft).

(*b*) Dry stone chips or grit (3 mm to 12 mm) or 1/8″ to 3/8″ should be spreaded evenly at the rate of 0·75 m^3%m^2 (2·2 cft% sft). It should then be rolled four times by a 8-10 tonne roller (three wheeled). The road should be opened for traffic after 24 hours.

15·4·5. Salient points on water bound macadam roads (W.B.M.)

(1) W.B.M. name is due to road Engineer Sir John Macadam of England, who introduced this process of road construction. The ballast of size 40 mm is known after his name as Macadam.

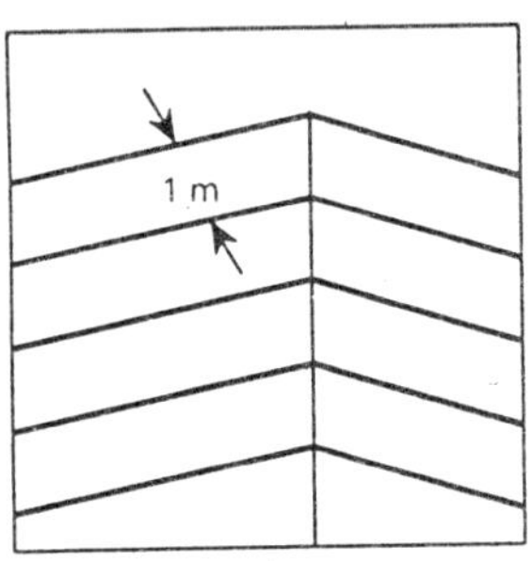

Fig. 15·24.

(2) Road rolling is started from edges of road and advanced towards centre.

(3) Premixed water bound macadam is a developed method for the areas having water scarcity and crowded areas. It costs 25% extra.

(4) 50 mm deep and 50 mm wide cross drains at an interval of 1 m are made to drain off surplus water in W.B.M. at rolling.

(5) 1 m^2 W.B.M. requires an average 50 litre of water.

(6) Broken ballast is better than round.

(7) Sub base 100 mm thick, base 75 mm.

In rammed 75 mm thick W.B.M. material required 0·91 m^3 to 1·07 m^3 coarse ballast and 0·18 m^3 to 0·21 m^3, fine ballast. 0·06 m^3 to 0·09 m^3 binding earth (It may be sandy) for per 10 m^2.

In 100 mm thick W.B.M. coarse ballast 1·21 m^3 to 1·43 m^3, fine ballast 0·40 m^3 to 0·44 m^3 and 0·08 m^3 to 0·1 m^3 binding earth per 10 m^2 coarse ballast—Category (1) 90-40 mm. Category (2) 60-40 mm. Category (3) 50-20 mm (category 1 is used in sub base and category 2 and 3 in base coats).

Fine ballast—10 mm to 12·5 mm screened ballast used to fill interstices. Binding Earth—Plasticity 4 to 6 (Sub base). Binding Earth—Plasticity 6 to 9 (Base Coats).

15·5. Bitumen bound macadam roads. In these types of roads, sub grade and soling is done as in W.B.M. The base metal is bound together by asphalt or tar either by premixing or by grouting.

Bitumen grouted roads. It may be either full grouted or semi-grouted. When the binding material penetrates to the full depth of the base material is said to be full grouted and when it penetrates to a part of its depth it is known as semi-grouted. It may be done also on old W.B.M. surfaces.

Full grouted. (*a*) **Coarse aggregate layer.** The old W.B.M. surface or top surface of soling in new road is brought to proper profile by repair which is known as reconditioning.

A layer of 7 to 9 cm loose metal (5 to 7·5 cm compacted) is layered and rolled by 10-12 tonnes roller to partial consolidation so as to leave voids for binder material to fill in.

Table 15·43. The loose aggregate should confirm the following grading

Percent Passing Sieve no.	*Compacted thickness*	
	5 cm	*7·5 cm*
63 mm	—	100
50 mm	100	—
38 mm	—	35-70
25 mm	35-70	—
19 mm	—	0-15
12 mm	0-15	—
9 mm	—	—
4·75 mm	—	—
2·36 mm	0-5	0-5

The coarse aggregate should be spreaded as follows by manually or by spreader.

50 mm compacted thickness $0{\cdot}63\ m^3$ per $10\ m^2$

15 mm compacted thickness $0{\cdot}90\ m^3$ per $10\ m^2$

(*b*) **Key aggregate layer.** A layer over the hot bitumen on the course aggregate layer is known as key aggregate layer which should confirm the following grading.

Percent Passing Sieve no.	*Compacted thickness*	
	5 cm	*7·5 cm*
38 mm	—	—
25 mm	—	100
19 mm	100	35-70
12 mm	35-70	—
9 mm	—	0-15
4·75 mm	0-15	—
2·32 mm	0-5	0-5

Key aggregate should be spreaded at the rate of $0{\cdot}15\ m^3$ per $10\ m^2$ for compacted surface of 5 cm and $0{\cdot}18\ m^3/10\ m^2$ for compacted surface of 7·5 cm.

(*c*) After the coarse aggregate is laid and compacted the approximate road binder is spreaded at the following rate at an appropriate temperature.

Compacted thickness 5 cm (*i*) Straight run bitumen 50 kg/10 m^2

(*ii*) RT-4/RT-5, 60-65 kg/10 m^2

Compacted thickness 7·5 cm (*i*) Straight run bitumen 68 kg/10 m^2

(*ii*) RT-4/RT-5, 82-88 kg/10 m^2

Asphalt or tar 7·0 to 9·0 kg per m^2 of the surface.

(*d*) For keying the big stones, stone chippings of 2 cm size is spreaded at the rate of 1·8 m^3% m^2 of the surface and should be rolled on and opened to traffic after 24 hours.

(*e*) **Seal coat.** The above surface is rough and hence about 7 days after a seal coat is provided to make the surface smooth and impervious.

1 or 2 cm thick surface layer consisting of bitumen at the rate of 1 to 1·2 kg/m^2 and stone grit (chips) 9 mm size are used at the rate of 1·2 m^3% m^2 of the road surface.

It is then rolled with 8 tonne roller and opened to traffic after 24 hours. When seal coat is used as a surface dressing it is known as liquid seal and when premix layer is used it is known as premix seal coat.

(*f*) **For cold process**

(*i*) emulsion for road surface 8 to 11 lit./m^2 of road surface for 7·5 cm thick layer.

(*ii*) emulsion for seal coat 1·25 lit./m^2 of road surface.

(*iii*) stone metal 2 cm to 5 cm at 0·90 m^2 per 10 m^2 of surface for 7·5 cm thick layer.

(*iv*) key stone 1·2 cm size at 1·8 m^3% m^2 of surface.

(*v*) seal coat, 2·0 cm chips at the rate of 1·2 m^3/m^2 of surface.

Semi grouted. The base surface which is blended by sand or mooram is cleaned with wire brushes upto a depth of 2 to 2·5 cm (W.B.M.). Tar or asphalt at the rate of 2·5 kg/m^2 of surface in hot state is applied. Immediately after this 12 mm size stone chips are spreaded at 1·2 to 1·8 m^2% m^2 of the surface. The surface is then rolled and allowed for traffic after which a seal coat is given about a week later. For cold process, semi grouted method emulsion at the rate of 4 lit./m^2 of surface is used.

15·5·1. Pre coated grit carpetting. In old roads a thickness of 2·5 to 7·5 cm is provided according to the intensity of traffic in one coat, while in new roads it is laid 6 to 12 cm thick in two layers. The edges are wood shuttered coated with binder, brick edged (left in sites after laying of carpet), mud dolla or protected by thick ropes (in case of thin carpets) to the required height.

The mettled road is cleaned of dust and loose material. All pot holes should be filled with metal according to the old layer rammed with binder. Further steps are taken as follows :

(*a*) **Priming or Tack coat.** When the thickness of the carpet is less than 2·5 cm, tack coat is applied so that a bond between the old surface and the carpet is achieved. Bitumen, shelismac, or shelspra (Trade names) heated to a temperature of 158-170°C (320°-340°F) or Tar no. 34 heated to 103-114°C (220°-240°F) is spreaded on the clean surface at the rate of 1 kg per m^2 of surface with sprayer or by cans made uniform by long brushes. In cold weather Priming coat can also be laid before laying 5 or 7·5 cm thick carpets. The carpetting layer is laid immediately after tack coat.

(*b*) **Premix coating up to 7·5 cm thickness.** Road metal and binder both are heated separately to about 18°C and then they are mixed in a bitumen mixture. The hot mass is spreaded by spreader or manually levelled and rolled to the required thickness. The surface is opened for traffic for few days before the sealing coat is laid. For 2·5 cm thick light (4 tonne) rollers are used.

For small scale the mass may be heated in drums and carried to site by borrows, while in the large works where mass is heated in 'hot mixing plants' it is carried to site in dumpers, which turns it to the spreaders operated mechanically which spreads it in a regular uniform layer. The layer is compacted by 8-10 tonne roller (3 wheeled) two times.

Table 15·44. Material required for hot mixed premixed carpets

Thickness of layer		*Size of metal*	*Rate per 10 m^2 of surface*	*Rate per m^2 of metal*
Loose (cm)	*Compacted (cm)*	*(cm)*	*(metal)*	*(binder)*
7·5	6·0	2·5-3·5	0·90-1·10 m^3	Bitumen 55 kg/m^2
5·0	3·75	2·0-2·5	0·60-0·75 m^3	Bitumen 55 kg/m^2
2·5	2·0	1·0 chips	0·33-0·4 m^3	Bitumen 60 kg/m^2

Grading of material for premix carpets

Percent Passing Sieve size (mm)	*Base coarse compacted thickness mm*			
	5 cm		*7·5 cm*	
	I limit	*II limit*	*I limit*	*II limit*
63	—	—	100	100
50	100	100	—	90-100
40	—	90-100	35-70	35-65
25	35-70	50-80	—	20-40
20	—	—	0-15	—
12	0-15	10-30	—	5-20
10	—	—	—	—
4·75	—	—	—	—
2·36	0-5	—	0-5	—
0·075	0-3	0-5	0-3	0-5

Note : (1) For hot mixes bitumen used are 30/40, 60/70 and 80/100 penetration.

(2) For cold mixes RT-4, cut back and emulsions are used 3·0 to 4·5% by weight of mix aggregate which must have low porosity.

(3) If tar is used in place of bitumen both material and tar are heated to a temperature of 120°C separately and then mixed together laid and rolled by 8 ton roller.

(4) When thickness is more than 5 cm, layer is known as thick carpet for less than 5 cm but more than 2·5 cm thin carpet and for less than 2·5 cm it is known as premix carpet or mat.

(5) Full grout surface is costlier than premix but is superior.

(6) For small jobs mixing can be done in iron sheet plates by shovels.

(7) The carpetting work is preferably done in hot weather and should be kept continued in rains or wet weather.

15·5·2. Bituminous Concrete Pavements or Premix Coating 6 to 12 cm thick laid in two layers

1st coat. (*a*) Two parts of chips (angular) 12 mm (½″) passed in 12·5 mm mesh and retained in 10 mm mesh with one part of angular chips 10 mm (3/8″) passing in 12 mm mesh and retained in 6·3 mm mesh should be mixed with 30 to 35% fine aggregate passing in 3 mm mesh and should be mixed in a mixing drum in dry state. When sufficient fine aggregate is not used it requires a water proof seal coat.

(*b*) Tar no. 3*A* heated to 220°F (103-114°C) or 80-100 penetration bitumen heated to 370°F (115°C) is poured in the mixing drum and mixed homogeneous with the chips. This mixed mass is brought to the site in borrows or by dumpers in case when it is mixed in hot mixing plants at large scale. Spreaded by mechanical spreaders and rolled two times by a 8-10 tonnes three wheeled roller in the required thickness of 5 to 8 cm. The quantity of grit and binders are given in a separate table below :

2nd or top wearing coat. It is kept 1·5 to 4 cm thick. The quantities of chips and binder is given below. 30 to 35% of fine aggregate is mixed by weight of the total grit to achieve a smooth and water tight surface. The surface is rolled 3 times by a 8-10 tonne roller.

Sand Flushing. After rolling sand or mooram is spreaded on the surface at 0·3 m^3 % m^2 of the road surface (left % sft) and rolled again till a smooth surface is achieved and the traffic is opened after 24 hours.

Size, quantity of stone chips and binder requirement

1st coat. Aggregate : 12 mm passing through 12-5 mm mesh and retained on 10 mm. sieve at 1·4 to 1·5 m^3 % m^2 of surface.

Binder : 150 to 175 kg % m^2 of road surface for bitumen, 175 to 200 kg % m^2 of road surface for cut backs and road tars over the primary coated surface.

2nd coat. Aggregate : 10 mm passing in 12·5 mm mesh and retained on 6·3 mm mesh at 0·9-1·1 m^3 % m^2 of surface or the coated surface.

Binder : 9·4-108 kg % m^2 of road surface for bitumen.

108-132 kg % m^2 of road surface for cut back and road tars.

Seal coats. For 5·0 and 7·5 cm thick carpets, 1·25 cm thick sealing coat is provided with 6 mm chips 0·17-0·2 m^2 for 10 m^2 of surface binded by bitumen heated to 180°C in a heating bin at 64 kg per m^3 of chips.

For 2·5 cm thick carpets, 1/2 cm thick coat is laid in coarse sand. 170 μ binded by bitumen at 128 kg/m^3 of sand which will be 0·05 m^3 per 10 m^2 of surface. The surface is rolled with 4 tonne roller with cut backs and emulsions heating is not required. The surface is then opened for traffic after 24 hours.

Sheet asphalt pavements. Foundation—15 cm thick cement concrete foundation as rigid is laid in proper camber.

Base. 4 to 6 cm thick compacted asphalt concrete as below.

Binder coarse. 6 mm to 24 mm size graded stone mixed with equal volume of 0·12 mm to 2·4 mm well graded sand with asphalt at the rate of 48 kg/m^3 of stone plus 128 kg/m^3 of sand is mixed and is laid in 4 to 8 cm thickness and rolled over the foundation concrete as base.

Top sheet asphalt or wearing coat. It is 2·5 cm thick and is made as asphalt mortar as below.

It consists of sand and filler (lime stone dust or portland cement) in the ratio of 4 : 1 and asphalt at the rate of 128 kg/m^3 of sand plus 192 kg/m^3 of the filler, mixed together. Sand and asphalt is 1st heated to required temperature and then they are mixed in a mixture. Filler is added in the mixing plant. The asphalt mortar is thus prepared and is laid over the binder coarse in a thickness of 2·5 cm and rolled with a 10 tonne roller. This layer is known as the sheet asphalt layer.

Table 15·45. Grading of aggregates in Bituminous concrete

Sieve size (mm)	*Percentage by weight*	
	Limit I	*Limit II*
20	—	100
12·50	100	80-100
10·0	80-100	75-90
4·75	55-75	50-70

Table contd...

Table contd...

Sieve size (mm)	Percentage by weight	
	Limit I	Limit II
2·36	35-50	35-50
0·60	18-29	18-29
0·30	13-23	13-23
0·15	8-16	8-16
0·075	4-10	4-10

15·6 Cement Concrete Roads

Sub grade. A proper slope, camber and super elevation is given in the sub grade. Sub grade remain 30 cm projected on either side of the road metal. The rest of the preparation is the same as in W.B.M. roads. Kankar subgrades are undesirable as it expands due to its further formation.

Soling. It may be flat brick or brick ballast 3″ consolidated (4″ loose). Joints blended by sand in each case. 3″ stone layer consolidated can also be used.

Base. A layer of water bound macadam 15 cm thick consolidated (18 cm loose). Materials as described in W.B.M. such as kankar, blast furnace slag or over burnt bricks etc. It must be blended by mooram watered and rammed. After becoming dry the surface should be wire brushed and joints must be cleaned 15-20 mm deep so that the concrete may have a key in the base. After being cleaned a sand cement slurry 1 : 3 or 1 : 4 mortar is spreaded over the surface and grouted. Stone chips of 2 mm size is also mixed in the grout and the mortar is made of 1 : 2 : 4 consistency. This process is known as "Cement Bonded Macadam". A fresh layer of consolidated 10 cm thickness (12 cm loose) of 4 to 5 cm size stones may also be laid over the W.B.M. surface and rolled with 8 tonne roller and the slurry of 1 : 2 : 4 consistency as above is grouted. These surfaces are called **Cement grouted macadam.**

15·6·1. Cement Sandwiched macadam. A 5 cm thick consolidated (6·5 cm loose) layer of 4 to 5 cm size stones is rolled over which a thick layer (4 cm) of 1 : 2 cement sand mortar is laid. Another layer of 4 to 5 cm stones 6·5 cm thick (loose) is laid over the mortar layer and rolled with 12 tonne roller. The mortar enters the interstices of the stones and makes a solid mass and about 10 cm thick layer is produced. This operation is done within the initial set time of the cement and the surface must be cured with water.

15·6·2. Collodial concrete roads. Over W.B.M. or on natural sub grade a layer of 15 cm compacted (18 cm loose) is compacted of 4 to 7 cm stones by 10 tonne roller. A cement grout 1 : 2 cement sand with 35 litre water per bag is grouted over the surface so as to fill all the interstices. 4 bags of cement will require for every m^3 of metal. In case of natural sub grade an insulating layer is provided below metal layer.

15·6·3. All concrete roads. Thickness of the slab must be as follows. Grade of concrete M-15 for normal and M-20 for heavy traffic.

Axle load of 8100 kg with constant traffic — 10 cm
Traffic intensity of 15 tonnes — 7·5 cm

Table 15·46. Thickness of concrete roads (IRC)

Type of sub grade	Thickness of base (cm)	Traffic intensity					
		Very heavy	Heavy	Medium	Medium light	Light	Very light
Very stable	Nil	23	20	18	15	13	10
Normal	8	25	23	20	18	15	13
Unstable	8-5	28	25	23	20	18	15
RCC (Rein. kg/m^2)	—	7	5·4	5·4	3·8	3·8	2·7

Thickness based on daily no. of loaded 8 tonne vehicle passing

Upto 200	7·5 cm thickness
200-350	15 cm thickness
350 and over	20 cm thickness

$$t = \left(\frac{3W}{M}\right)^{1/2} \text{ cm}$$

where t = thickness of slab ; W = static load on road at one wheel in kg which varies according to the place.

M = Safe mod. of rupture of concrete in kg/cm^2 say 24·6 kg/cm^2 when concrete has ultimate crushing strength of 246 kg/cm^2 after 28 days.

Note : The thickness is increased at edges and corners, rest remain in equal thickness. A camber of 1 : 72 may be given.

15·6·4. General considerations for a concrete slab for roads

(1) For a better sub base a lean concrete 1 : 4 : 8 or 1 : 5 : 10 in brick ballast 15 cm thick is laid.

(2) When the sub grade consists of an alkalinic soil or capillary water, a water proof paper must be laid if slab concrete is laid direct. The water proof paper (Berlap Paper) acts against the following :

(*a*) Prevents rise of salts and moisture by capillary action.

(*b*) Checks the entry of cement water from concrete slab to the sub grade.

(*c*) Separates the slab from sub grade so that slab may have any lateral movement without any increase of friction.

(*d*) A wearing layer of about 50 mm thickness may be laid over slab in richer mortar say M-20 within the time of initial set.

(3) A sand cushion of 20 mm thickness must be laid on old surfaces when used as a base. So that slab may have a separate movement over the old surface.

15·6·5. Reinforced Cement Concrete Roads

The following points are observed in the reinforced concrete slabs on roads.

(1) A well consolidated and firm sub grade does not need any reinforcement.

(2) Tensile and temperature stresses are produced at top due to direct hit of sun, while weak sub grades having different bearing capacities at different points produce stresses at the bottom. Hence keeping above points in view reinforcement is provided both at top and bottom.

(3) The usual reinforcement of 3 kg/m^2 of surface area for moderate traffic and 5 kg for heavy traffic is provided. The following formula is also used for providing reinforcement both longitudinally as well as transversely.

$A_S = (lfw)/2t$; A_S = area of steel section in cm^2/metre width.

l = length of the panel between joints in m.

f = coefficient of friction between sub grade and slab, usually 1 to 2.

w = weight of the slab concrete/m^2 of surface in kg taking weight of concrete as 2400 kg/m^3.

t = working stress of steel in kg/cm^2 (1400).

Note : (1) The road is opened for traffic after 28 days with proper curing.

(2) Cover is kept 4 to 5 cm.

(3) Welded wire fibres are also provided as reinforcement which are available in market in shape of rolls in different widths. 2·2 kg/m^2 of surface can be provided upto maximum of 3·8 kg/m^2.

Tie bars. Tie bars are provided across longitudinal joints so that the load may be shared and slabs may not settle unequally. These bars can also be provided across transverse joints. The lap width 40 to 50 of the diameter of rod must be embedded on each sides. The area of steel section can be calculated by following formula per metre.

$A_S = (bfw)/t$ where A_S = area of steel section in cm^2, b = width of panel in m, w = weight of concrete per m^2 of surface.

t = Allowable working stress of steel (1400 kg/cm^2) and f = coefficient of friction between slab and subgrade.

Table 15·47. Detail of the bars for two lane longitudinal joint at centre

Slab thickness (cm)	*Diametre (mm)*	*Maximum spacing (cm)*	*Minimum length (cm)*	
			M.S. bars	*Tor bars*
15	8	38	40	30
	10	60	45	35
20	10	45	45	35
	12	64	55	40
25	10	30	45	35
	12	45	55	40
	14	62	65	46

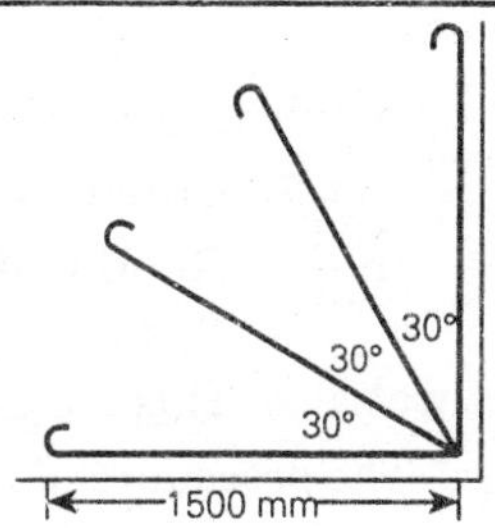

Extra reinforcement at corners

Cover = 50 mm, diameter of bar = 16 mm

15·6·6. Joints in Concrete roads

Table 15·48. Spacing of transverse expansion joints of 25 mm thickness

Period of construction	*Roughness of found*	*Max. spacing in m (Slab thickness in cm)*		
		15	*20*	*25*
Winter (Oct-March)	Smooth	50	50	60
	Rough	140	140	140
Summer (April-Sept.)	Smooth	50	90	120
	Rough	140	140	140

Slab thickness in cm

Type of slab/spacing (m)	*10*	*15*	*20*
Plain concrete slabs	4·5	4·5	4·5
RCC slabs	4·5	13·0	14·0
Welded fabric reinforcement (kg/m^2)	2·2	2·7	3·8

Longitudinal joints. The width of longitudinal joints is according to the width of carriage way subject to a maximum of 4 m. The transverse joints may be staggered at the longitudinal joints to avoid concentration of weakness at one cross point. Transverse joints provided staggered can give a crack along the joint of the adjoining slab.

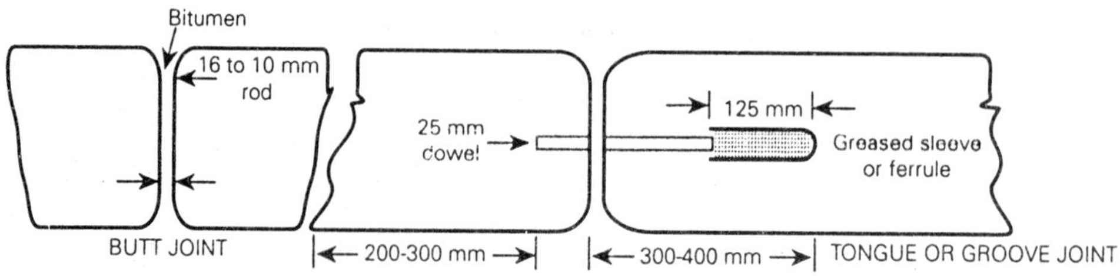

Fig. 15·25.

Sleeve or ferrule is a G.I. pipe greased from inside and which is a bit bigger than the dowel.

Joint filler. Remoulded fillers : Nomotax, salistax boards can be prepared by soaking of cork, fibrous jute and rubber in bitumen equivalent to thickness of joint. These are also available in market.

Cast in situ fillers. Sand asphalt and saw dust in proportion of 6 : 3 : 1 is mixed and poured hot in the joint. In place of saw dust/rice waste can also be used.

15·6·7. Concrete Mix Design

Indian Road Congress (IRC) method—IRC 44 of 1972

The method was basically designed for pavements, but could be applied to other concrete structures also. This method takes into account the compressive strength of cement also.

The procedure of mix design consists of the following steps :

(1) The following data is required for mix design :

(*a*) Decide the 28 days compressive strength of concrete for which the mix is to be designed and to calculate average compressive strength by standard deviation or coefficient of variation.

(*b*) Maximum size of aggregate to be used, its type and grading.

(*c*) Decide degree of workability in terms of slump, depending on the type of work.

(*d*) Find 7 days compressive strength of cement.

(*e*) Specific gravity of cement, sand and coarse aggregate. Find also the fineness modulus of sand and sieve analysis.

(*f*) Find the moisture content of fine aggregate if any and water absorption of aggregate.

(2) The water cement ratio based on 7 days compressive strength of cement and 28 days average compressive crushing strength of mix to be designed is decided.

(3) Knowing the sieve analysis of the coarse aggregate, obtain a combination grading which is very near to the suggested grading given below :

Table 15·49. Suggested Coarse Aggregate Grading

Percentage passing sieve size					*Maximum size of aggregate in mm*
Zone	*40 mm*	*20 mm*	*10 mm*	*4·75 mm*	
A	100	34-40	16-18	6	40

Table contd...

Table contd...

Zone	Percentage passing sieve size 40 mm	20 mm	10 mm	4·75 mm	Maximum size of aggregate in mm
B	100	40-45	18-20	6	
C	100	45-53	20-25	0	
A	100	100	21-32	0	
B	100	100	31-40	6	
C	100	100	40-52	0	20

(4) Using maximum size of aggregate, find out water content in kg/cu.m. of concrete and sand content in percent of total aggregate by absolute volume as shown in table below :

Max. size of aggregate mm	*Water content saturated surface dry basis per cu.m. concrete (kg)*	*Sand is percent of total aggregate by absolute volume*
80	172·0	28·0
40	175·0	33·5
25	177·5	38·0
20	178·0	40·0

The values given in the above table are for specified type of angular aggregate with w/c ratio of 0·5 and slump of 25 mm and for fineness modulus of sand as 2·60. For other conditions the adjustment is required to be made as shown below :

Table 15·50. Adjustment of values in water and sand content for the conditions

Change in conditions stipulated for table	*Adjustments required in* Water content	Sand content
Each 0·5 increase or decrease in w/c ratio	0	+ 1%
Each 0·1 increase or decrease in F.M. of sand	0	+ 0·5%
Each 25 mm increase or decrease in slump	± 4%	0
Rounded aggregate	– 15 adhoc	– 6 to 8%

(5) Knowing the w/c ratio and water content (*w*). The cement content (*c*) is determined.

(6) Using table given below find out the volume of entrapped air corresponding to maximum size of aggregate.

Table 15·51. Water requirement litre/m³ of concrete for different slumps and maximum size of aggregate

Slump in mm	*Water requirement in litre/m³ of concrete for maximum size of aggregate of* 10 mm	12·5 mm	20 mm	25 mm	40 mm	50 mm	80 mm	150 mm
30-50	205 (180)	200 (175)	185 (165)	180 (160)	160 (145)	155 (140)	145 (135)	125 (120)

Table contd...

Table contd...

Slump in mm	Water requirement in litre/m³ of concrete for maximum size of aggregate of							
	10 mm	12·5 mm	20 mm	25 mm	40 mm	50 mm	80 mm	150 mm
80-100	225 (200)	215 (190)	200 (180)	195 (175)	175 (160)	170 (155)	160 (150)	140 (135)
150-180	240 (215)	230 (205)	210 (190)	205 (185)	185 (170)	180 (165)	170 (160)	– –
App. entrapped Air content percent	3 (8)	2·5 (7)	2 (6)	1·5 (5)	1 (4·5)	0·5 (4)	0·3 (3·5)	0·2 (9)

Note : Values given in bracket are for air entrapped concrete.

(1) These are values for well shaped angular coarse aggregate.

(2) The slump values for concrete containing aggregates of size larger than 40 mm are based on slump test.

(7) Calculate the total aggregate content per unit volume of concrete using the following equation :

$$V = \left[W + \frac{C}{S_c} + \frac{P.A.}{S_s} + \frac{(1-P)A}{S_a}\right]\frac{1}{1000}$$

where V= absolute volume of wet mix. = gross volume (1 cubic metre)—the volume of entrapped air.

C = Weight of cement in kg per cubic metre of concrete.

A = Weight of total aggregate in kg per cubic metre of concrete.

P = Proportion of sand in total aggregate determined on the basis of absolute volume.

S_c, S_s and S_a are specific gravities of cement, sand and C,A, respectively.

(8) Knowing the w/c ratio, cement content, total aggregate content and percentage of sand contain the mix proportion can be computed.

This must be adjusted if the coarse aggregate absorbs moisture or sand content moisture if any.

15·7. General

15·7·1. Faults in roads. (1) **Bleeding or Flushing.** The exudation of surplus bitumen or tar on roads. It is also called as faulting.

(2) **Streaking or strictions.** Non uniform applications of binders.

(3) **Scabbing or dislodgement.** Insufficient use of binder.

(4) **Corrugations.** Undulated surface.

(5) **Waving.** Flow of road metal due to excess use of binder in hot weather.

(6) **Ridges.** Ups in a road surface.

15·7·2. Output of 8-10 tonne three wheeled roller per day.

1.	Earth work in embankment 150 mm thick compacted layer	400 m^3
2.	Mooram, gravel, sub base 150 mm thick compacted layer	300 m^3
3.	Mooram, gravel, sub base 100 mm thick compacted layer	250 m^3
4.	Water bound macadam sub base 100 mm thick compacted	35 m^3
5.	Water bound macadam sub base 75 mm thick compacted	30 m^3
6.	Surface dressing single coat	370 m^2
7.	Surface dressing two coats	550 m^2
8.	Premix carpet 25 mm thick	600 m^2

9. Premix carpet 20 mm thick — 740 m^2
10. Liquid seal coat for premix carpet — 1000 m^2
11. Sand seal for premix carpet — 2000 m^2
12. Asphaltic concrete 25-40 mm thick — 370 m^2

15·7·3. Material required for Patch repairs of roads

(*a*) Light traffic	12-15 m^3	Patch repairs annually
Medium traffic	16-25 m^3	per km of road length
Heavy traffic	30-60 m^2	for 3-8 m width

For portion of gradients add 25% extra

(*b*) Painting pot holes with binder	3 lit./m^2
Binder for premixing	48 kg/m^3 of metal

Table 15·52. Minimum size of stone metal for road work (IRC)

Type of stone	*Hand broken* *mm*	*Mechanical crushed* *mm*
1. Heavy soft stone, lime stone, laterite etc.	75	—
2. Hard stone like granite gneiss, quartzite sand stone etc.	50	30
3. Hard tough stone like bsalt and trap	38	25

15·7·4. Gabions or G.I.wire crates. Gabions are large G.I. wire mesh crates filled with boulders. These crates are placed in embay-ments of water coarses to check further erosion.

Gabions (G.I. wire crates) are also used for making retaining walls. The following considerations are taken in making Gabion retaining walls :

(*i*) The resultant force *R*, of the thrust *P* of the backfill and the weight *W* of the wall should pass through the middle 3rd of the base *B* of the wall.

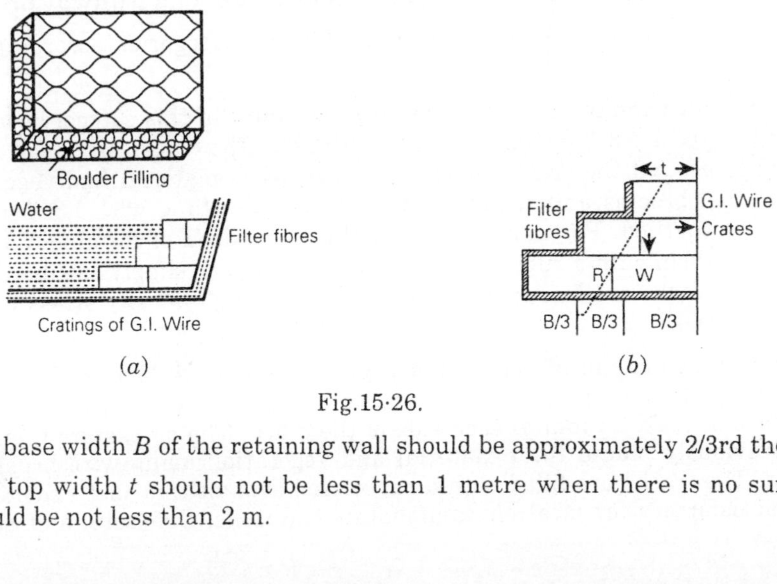

Fig.15·26.

(*ii*) The base width *B* of the retaining wall should be approximately 2/3rd the height *H*.

(*iii*) The top width *t* should not be less than 1 metre when there is no surcharge, with surcharge it should be not less than 2 m.

(iv) If relatively higher size aggregate is used in filling the wire mesh crates, the base width may be suitably increased.

(v) Counterforts may be provided where considered necessary.

(vi) The base can be taken into ground to form a key for increasing the resistance.

(vii) Provide adequate drainage to carry water away the wall.

(viii) A Gabion wall may be built in steps.

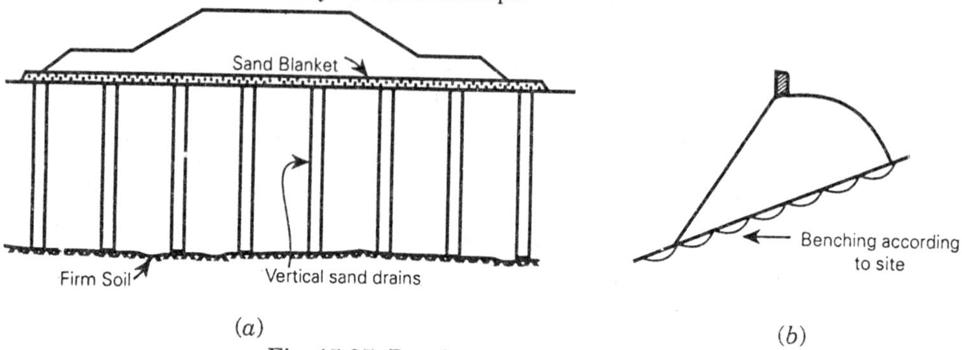

Fig. 15·27. Benching of slopes in embankments.

Table 15·53. Swelling of soils

S. No.	Type of soil	Swell percentage (range)	Average value which can be used for calculation
1.	Clean sand or gravel	5-15	10
2.	Top soil	10-25	20
3.	Loamy soil	10-35	20
4.	Common earth	20-45	25
5.	Clay	30-60	35
6.	Solid rock when blasted	50-80	60
7.	Murram	25-35	30

15·7·5. Crack Repair Methodology for Renovation of a Runway or Road Pavement

The cracks have been divided into the following categories according to the width of cracks.

(1) **Repair of cracks of width less than 6·4 mm.** In this category some cracks may be not wide enough to receive any sealing material with ease. The cracks are repaired by cleaning the pavement surface around the cracks of all dirt, dust, loose material and vegetation using wire brush, stiff bristled brooms and compressed air and then filling with hot asphalt AC-20 by a pressure injection method. For narrow cracks, this comprised of forming V-type 25 mm deep grooves and filling them with a rubberized sealing compound or simply sealing the crack with hot mix asphalt if the cracks are less than 6·4 mm in width. High density stress relief fabric is laid over the repaired cracks.

(2) **Repair of cracks of width between 6·4 mm and 25 mm.** In order to repair the cracks the vertical faces of the cracks are sand blasted to a depth of at least 25 mm and the pavement surface at least 25 mm to each side of the crack. The cracks are then cleaned of loose debris, dirt, previously placed filler material and vegetation using wire brushes, shovels and compressed air. The cracks are filled with a rubberized asphalt that met Federal specification S-SS-1401 and satisfactory for local environmental conditions. Concrete joint sealer of the hot-

poured elastic type (ASTM 1190) which meets the requirements of ASTMD 1191 is also used. Care is taken to ensure that the material is not heated to too high a temperature or too long a time. Direct heating is not used. A tack coat of hot AC-20 is then applied followed by placing a 500 mm wide patented fabric. The width of the asphalt tack coat application is the fabric width (500 mm) plus 50 mm on each side and is applied no further in advance of material placement that could be accomplished without loosing adhesive abilities of the tack. Fabric is sized and cut in such a way that it overlapped the cracks to be repaired with a minimum at each end by 300 mm. The fabric also overlapped a minimum of 63 mm in the direction of paving operation. (See Fig. 15·28)

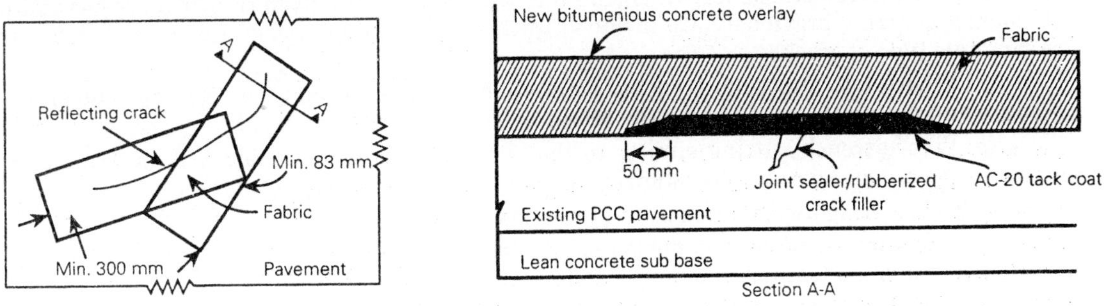

(*a*) (*b*)

Fig. 15·28.

Repair of Cracks of width greater than 25 mm. Three types of cracks of this category are identified :

Type I : Single non interconnected cracks which are relatively straight and where cutting of grooves could be done without causing damage/disturbance in the areas adjoining the cracks. Cracks of this type are repaired using the following procedure.

(*a*) Trenches 300 mm wide and 75 mm deep are formed as shown in figure using concrete cutting wheel/machine.

(*b*) The debris and the milled materials are removed using sweepers with vacuum hose attachment.

(*c*) Using air compressure with hose and nozzle attachment. The remaining dust is blown from the trench.

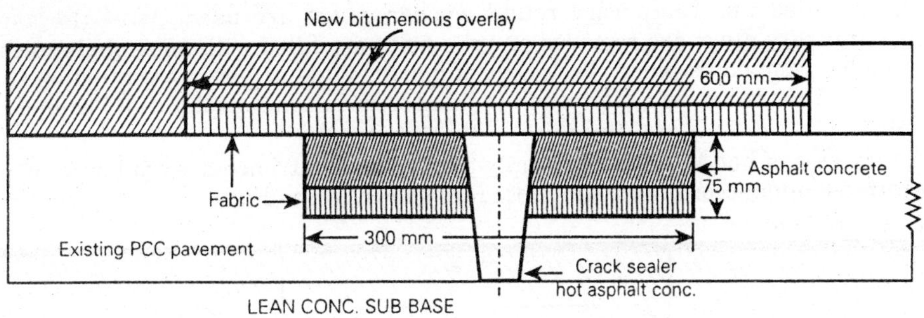

Fig. 15·29.

(*d*) Cracks/cavity at the bottom of the trench, if present is filled up using either a liquid sealer (as in case of 6·4 to 25 mm wide cracks) or a hot mix asphalt similar to that used for the surface course (for large cracks and cavities). A hand tamper is used to compact the hot mix asphalt in the bottom of the trench.

(*e*) A tack coat of hot AC-20 is applied on the bottom surface and the edges of the trench.

(*f*) A high density stress absorbing fabric is placed.

(*g*) Additional tack coat using the same material as in step (*e*) is applied on top of the fabric.

(*h*) The trench is then filled with hot mix asphalt, similar to that specified for surface mix and compacted to 98% laboratory density using a roller. The surface of the compacted asphalt mix is at the same grade as the existing PCC slabs.

(*i*) A tack coat of hot AC-20 is applied on the trench area and another layer of fabric similar to that used at the bottom of the trench, but of width of 600 mm is placed.

(*j*) Hot mix asphalt overlay is placed following the placement at the second layer of fabric. Prior to hot mix overlay, the top of the fabric is tack coated over along with the existing surface at a rate determined by trials.

Type 2 : Large cracks for which 150 mm wide and 75 mm deep trenches are cut and filled with asphalt concrete previously are included in this type. The following procedure is adopted for repairing this type of cracks :

(*a*) Where 300 mm wide trenches could be cut without damaging the adjacent areas, the procedure and materials specified for the repair of Type 1 cracks are used.

(*b*) Where trench cutting similar to that for type 1 is not possible without damaging the concrete in the adjoining area, the following steps are adopted for repair of the cracks.

(*i*) The existing asphalt mix in the trench is flowed out.

(*ii*) The vertical edges and bottom of the trench are cleaned and all foreign materials are removed using a joint cleaning machine and devices including hand tools.

(*iii*) All loose materials and debris is removed from the trench using sweepers with vacuum hose attachment.

(*iv*) If no crack/cavity is found at the bottom of the trench, the trench is filled up with asphalt as shown in the fig. Tack coat of hot AC-20 is uniformly applied on the edge and the bottom of the trench before placement of the hot mix asphalt. The mix is compacted using vibratory rollers. The level of compacted asphalt is the same as the adjacent PCC slab. If on completion of step (*iii*) of this method, a large cavity is found at the bottom of the trench, it is filled up with a surface course of hot mix asphalt and compacted to the level of the bottom of the trench. The mixture is tamped appropriately in place as shown in Fig. Tack coat of hot AC-20 is uniformly applied on the vertical edge and bottom of the trench and trench is filled with hot mix asphalt and compacted to the level of the PCC slab. If however on completion of step (*iii*) of this method, cracks are found at the bottom of the trench, 50 mm diameter holes are drilled along the crack 600 mm c/c upto the bottom of the slab. Using an air compressor with hose and nozzle attachment, the dust from the holes is blown out. An asphalt (AC-40) meeting the requirements of ASTM D3381 is heated to a safe temperature to make it sufficiently fluid suitable for pumping through the holes using a pressure distributor at a pressure of 175 kPa to 415 kPa until the cracks upto the bottom of the trench are filled up. Temporary round wooden plugs are used. After the asphalt had hardened, the temporary plugs are removed and the holes are filled with an asphalt surface course mixture, thoroughly tamped in place. Tack coat of hot AC-20 is uniformly applied on the vertical edge and bottom of the trench and the trench is filled with hot mix asphalt and compacted to the level of PCC slab.

(*v*) A tack coat of hot AC-20 is uniformly applied on the trench area followed by placement of fabric of width 500 mm according to the procedure shown in the Fig.

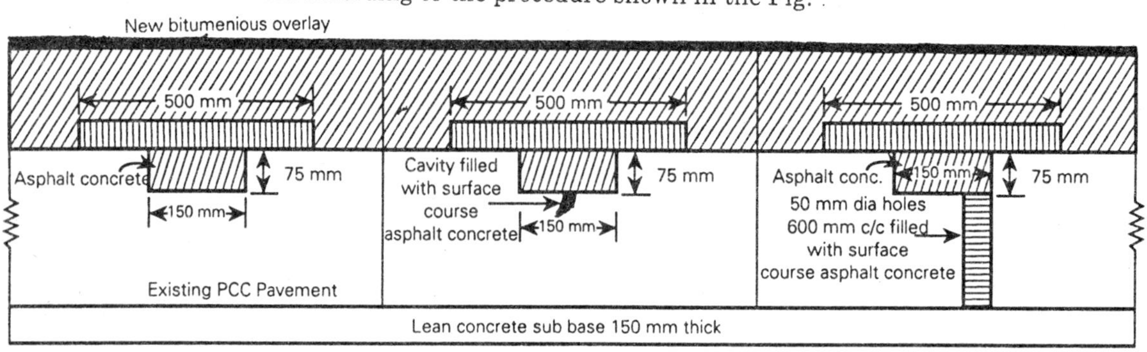

Fig. 15·30.

(*vi*) Hot mix asphalt overlay is then placed after an uniform application of tack coat of hot AC-20 on the fabric and the existing surface as mentioned in step (*i*) for type 1 cracks.

Type 3 : Presence of many random and interconnected wide cracks where trench cutting similar to that for type 1 cracks would not be feasible and any attempt to groove cutting is likely to cause serious damage to the pavement. These cracks are repaired using the following method.

(*a*) 50 mm diameter holes are drilled through the entire slab on 600 mm c/c along the crack.

(*b*) Debris from the holes is removed and using compressed air. The holes are cleaned of dust, any loose and foreign materials.

(*c*) The cracks and holes are filled up using materials as mentioned in step (*iv*) for type 2 cracks.

(*d*) Tack coat of hot AC-20 is then uniformly applied and high density fabric of width 500 mm is placed following standard procedures as shown in the figure.

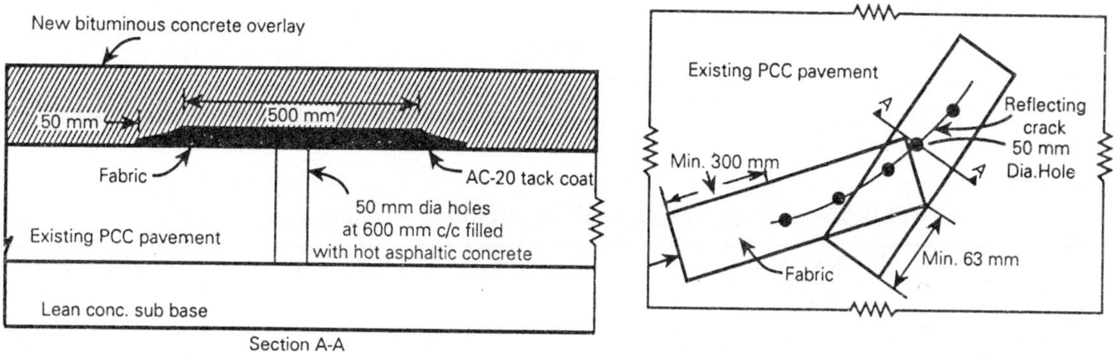

Fig. 15·31.

Plums above 160 mm and above upto any reasonable size may be used in plain concrete work upto a maximum limit of 20 percent by volume of concrete. Plums should be distributed evenly and shall not be closer than 150 mm from the surface.

Prevention of road cracks by rubber-bitumen membrane and its interlayers

Due to the oxidation, the flexibility of bitumen is reduced and it becomes hard causing cracks on roads. If these cracks are covered by bitumen alone or by cement concrete, the cracks develop again and thus the maintenance cost is increased.

By tests it is found that the mixture of bitumen with rubber (which can be economically obtained from waste rubber types) and waste propylene is useful for filling road cracks.

The mixture of rubber with other polymers increases the penetration viscosity and penetration ratio, which reduces the temperature sensitivity and thus brittle no. causing reduction in thermal cracks. Flexibility is recovered and the capacity to bear the tension due to cracks is increased. In this way on new surfaces so prepared possibility of repetition of cracks is reduced. On practical investigation it is found that 0·6 mm to 0·2 mm rubber particles are suitable to be mixed with bitumen.

For the decomposition of rubber primary temperature should be more than 200°C and the ash contents in rubber must be less than 5%.

Preparation of rubber-bitumen mixture. It is prepared in a high speed mixture plant. For 100-120 kg mixture of rubber-bitumen 0·25 HP electric motor is suitable. This quantity is sufficient for 100-120 m^2 of cracked surface. 85 kg of bitumen is heated till it is totally melted in a container upto a temperature of 160°C, then 100 kg waste rubber type powder is mixed and the container is revolved with 500 r.p.m. in a temperature not more than 180°C. Then 5 kg lime-stone slacked powder is mixed for 15 min. and the mass so prepared is known as rubber-bitumen mixture.

Quantity of rubber-bitumen mixture :

For cracks wide upto	3 mm	8-10 kg per 10 m^2
	3-5 mm	10-12 kg per 10 m^2
	5-10 mm	12-15 kg per 10 m^2

It is used either as a layer or as a membrane.

Process of laying rubber-bitumen layers. The surface is cleaned by brushes or compressed air and it must be perfectly dry. 8 to 9 kg mixture is taken in 15 kg containers having 2 mm diameter apertures and is spreaded evenly on the road surface by special brushes used for this purpose.

This layer of rubber-bitumen is covered and rolled with roller with the ballast as follows in a quantity 1^3 to 1·2 m^3 % m^2 of road surface.

6-10 mm ballast for cracks upto 5 mm

6-12 mm ballast for cracks above 5 mm.

Process of spreading rubber-bitumen membrane. If the cracks are more than 3 mm in width, the rubber-bitumen layer is left open for traffic for 5-6 months after which 20-25 mm thick premixed bitumen core is covered on this layer. By doing so the repetition of cracks on the new surface is stopped.

Table 15·54. Physical properties of rubber-bitumen polymers

Type of mixture	*Penetrative viscosity no.*	*Penetrative ratio %*	*Trance brittle no. °C*	*Recovery of flexibility %*
80/100 bitumen	– 1·1	30	– 8	10
10 % rubber + 90% bitumen	+ 1·0	35	– 12	35
5% propylene + 95% bitumen	+ 1·2	46	– 13	30

15·8·1. Road Construction Machinery

Table 15·55. Machines used in road construction

Type of	*Kind of machine*
1. Clearing and grabbing	Tractor dozer, rooter or ripper
2. Excavation of soil	Shovels, scapers, dozers and drag lines
3. Transportation of soil	Scrapers, dumpers and trucks
4. Spreading earth	Grader and dozer
5. Watering	Water tankers, sprinkles, pumps and piping system
6. Compaction	Rollers of different type, sheep foot roller and the above masonry itself helps consolidation while these are working their own jobs.

Tractors. The tractors have the following uses :

(1) To pull or push loads, for mounting many types of accessories like bulldozer blades, rippers, front end shovels, hoes, draglines, clamshells, trenchers, winches, side booms, fronted bucket loaders, pipe layers etc.

(2) For pulling down other obstruction.

(3) As a power driver when other power source is not available.

(4) **Crawler tractors** have a low maximum speed about 10 km per hour and are used where high speed is not primary. They can be used in local roads or even in fields. However pneumatic wheeled tractors are used for moving at high speeds upto 50 km per hour on firm ground.

Cutting buckets can also be towed by the tractors so that it can be used as a scraper, loader or a dozer. The earth can be transported by this bucket or to say it can cut the earth at one place and can fill it at another place.

Dozer. Generally known as Bull dozer. It has a 3 to 3·5 m long blade which is 0·9 to 1·2 m in height mounted in front of it . If the blade can be set at an angle then it is called as an angle dozer. It can do the following works.

(*a*) Clearing and grabbing land of vegetation and tree.

(*b*) Removing top soil from borrow areas.

(*c*) Opening up plot road formations in steep hill sides to such a width that other equipment can move in and complete the work.

(*d*) Spreading earth in layers.

(*e*) Clearing construction sites from debris.

Dozers can be crawler mounted or pneumatic wheel type. Crawler mounted dozers have a speed of about 25 km per hour. It may be 4 to 5 km per hour for wheeled dozers. The dozers are used for moving earth over short lead upto 100 m.

The dozers are available in size ranging from 65 to 200 H.P.

Table 15·56. Output of dozers in earth work

Type / size	*Output in cu.m. per hour in borrow pit measure*				
	Load 15 m	*Load 30 m*	*Load 60 m*	*Load 90 m*	*Load 100 m*
Crawler type					
65 HP	45	30	15	10	8
80 HP	75	50	25	18	15
130 HP	85	55	20	20	18
Wheeled type					
165 HP	90	60	35	25	20

Scrapers. Scrapers dig their own load, as they move forward. They combine the operation of digging, loading, handling and discharging. A cutting blade, which can be raised or lowered upto 20 cm is pulled through the earth causing it to travel up the face of the blade into the bowl of the scraper. Some of the earth falls forward into a carrying apron. When the bowl is full, the apron is lowered to prevent spillage and the cutting edge is raised. After hauling the material is dumped by lowering the cutting edge to the desired height above the fill and opening the front apron. The blade then serves as a strike off beam.

These two types of scrapers (*i*) towed scrapers and (*ii*) motorised scrapers. Towed scrapers are used that hauls, say 150-500 mm at a maximum speed of 10 km per hour and is towed by a tractor. It has a capacity of 8 cu.m. and require 90 B.H.P. tractor for towing. For longer hauls upto 500-1500 m motorised scrapers are used having speed of 30 km per hour or more. Since motorised scrapers can not develop a high tractor effect, a Pusher tractor—dozer is needed to push it. Motorised scrapers have a capacity of 8-10 cu.m. Their efficiency is 50 to 60 percent.

Table 15·57. Output of scrapers in cu.m./hour (In borrow pit measure)

Soil type	*8 cu.m. struck capacity (towed scraper) One way lead of (in metres)*					*12 cu.m. struck capacity (motorised scraper) One way lead of (in metres)*						
	150	*175*	*250*	*300*	*350*	*300*	*450*	*600*	*750*	*900*	*1200*	*1500*
1. Light loam or grumbly soil	45	40	35	30	25	60	55	45	40	35	30	25
2. Sand and gravel	45	40	35	30	25	60	55	45	40	35	30	25
3. Good common earth	45	40	35	30	25	58	50	45	40	35	30	25
4. Clay hard and tough	40	38	33	28	23	55	50	40	38	35	28	23
5. Muram	40	38	33	28	23	55	50	40	28	35	28	23
6. Hard muram												
7. Clay, wet and sticky	40	38	33	28	23	55	50	40	38	35	28	23

Graders. The graders are used for spreading the heaped earth in layers. The graders are either towed or self propelled. The grader has a blade of about 3·5 m and its effective length during working is 2·75 m. The blade can be set at any angle. It has a 100-110 H.P. motor to propell. The speed is about 3 kmph. The spreading is about 1300 sq.m. per hour assuming 65% operating efficiency and 50 min. working hours. The volume of earth spreader is about 200 cu.m./ Hr. in a layer of 15 cm.

Crushers. Crushers break large stones to small pieces of different sizes. These are of the following types :

(1) Jaw crusher (2) Gyratory crusher (3) Concrete crusher

(4) Roll crusher (5) Impact or hammer mill (6) Rod and ball mill

The common sizes of crushers are 400 mm × 350 mm and 400 mm × 225 mm.

Table 15·58. Output of crushers

Size mm	*RPM*	*BHP*	*Output in T per hour without dust and over size for a closed laid setting*	
			16 mm	*30 mm*
300 × 175	365/400	15/20	5	10
400 × 225	365/400	22/25	7	16
750 × 375	300/385	30/35	—	30

Transporting equipment. Trucks having rated load 7½ tonnes, though loading upto 12 tonnes.

Dumpers or Tripers. Dumpers are used to transport the materials. Their speed is 20-30 kmph. The dumpers are provided with a hydraulic lift by which the material can be unloaded by lifting the tiper container. The loading is done by shovels. Their capacity varies for 3 cu.m. to 20 cu.m. struck volume.

Water tankers. Water tankers of 4000 to 5000 litres capacity are used widely. A sprinkling attachment with a bar provides for uniform distribution at any desired space.

Compaction equipments

Three Wheeled 8-10 T Road Roller. It is diesel powered 35 B.H.P. road roller. The diameter of the front roll is about 105 cm, its width being about 100 cm. The diameter of the rear roll is around 145 cm, its width being about 50 cm. The rolling width around 2 metres. The front roll gives a load of around 35 to 40 kg/cm width and the front roll gives a load of 70-80 kg/cm width. The speed of rolling is in the range 15 to 65 km per hour. The output of a three wheeled roller 8-10 T for various jobs.

Table 15·59. Compacting equipments and their application

Sl. No.	Compacting equipment	Application
1.	Road roller, 8-10 T, three wheeler	1. Earth work roller
		2. Soil stabilisation
		3. Rolling granular bases, (*W B M*), murram etc.
		4. Rolling, surface dressing, premix carpet, mix seal bituminous macadam, built up spray grout.
		5. Break down, rolling of asphaltic concrete.
2.	Road roller 6 T or 8 T tandem	1. Surface dressing
		2. Finish rolling of asphaltic concrete.
3.	Sheep foot rollers	1. Rolling cohesive soils
4.	Pneumatic tyred roller	1. Rolling, non-plastic sites and silty soils
		2. Intermediate roller of asphaltic concrete.
5.	Vibratory roller	1. Compacting sand and cohesionless soils.
		2. Compacting all type of soils for obtaining high densities.
		3. Compacting granular bars and sub bases to obtain high densities.
		4. Compacting bituminous bases and surfaces to obtain high degree of compaction.
6.	Frog rammer	1. Compacting sand and cohesionless soils.
		2. Compacting in restricted spaces.

Table 15·60. Output of three wheeled 8-10 T roller

Sl. No.	Job	Passes	Output/day of 8 hours
1.	Earth work, murram, gravel, soil stabilisation	6 passes	425 cu.m.
		9 passes	300 cu.m.
		12 passes	200 cu.m.
2.	Water bound macadam		40 cu.m.
3.	Surface dressing	1st coat	650 sq.m
		2nd coat	930 sq.m
4.	Premix carpet	Carpet	500 sq.m
		Seal coat	900 sq.m
5.	Built up spray grout		300 sq.m
6.	Bituminous macadam		300 sq.m
7.	Mix seal		500 sq.m
8.	Asphaltic concrete, 46 mm	40 mm	300 sq.m

Sheep Foot Rollers. These are hollow circular drums of steel 1·2-1·5 m long and 0·9-1·2 m diameter with legs or tamping feet on the circumferential area at the rate of 12-18 per sq. m of area. They are assembled in units of 1, 2, 3 or 4 drums. The tamping feet on the drums are slaggered into rows. The length of the feet should be at least sufficient to pass through 3/4th of the thickness of the loose layer and is usually 15-20 cm. The rollers can be ballasted with water. The weight of a single drum is in the range 1200-1800 kg when empty and 2000 to 2800 kg when ballasted. A tractor of 45 H.P. can pull a single drum and are of 70-90 H.P. can pull double drum. An average speed is 4 kmph.

Sheep foot rollers are suitable for cohesive soils and the moisture content of the soil should be preferably near their plastic limits. The number of passes of sheep foot rollers depends upon the type of soil, moisture content and density desired. Generally 8-10 passes are needed.

Table 15·61. Output of double drum sheep foot rollers

Depth of loose layer	*Out put per day in cu.m.*				
	8 passes	*10 passes*	*12 passes*	*14 passes*	*16 passes*
20	540	440	360	310	260
22½	600	500	400	360	310
25	690	510	450	400	350

Frog Rammers. Frog rammers are used for compacting cohesionless soils and in an inaccessible and restricted locations where ordinary rollers can not work. They are worked by pneumatic system or by diesel engine. The weight varies from 30 kg to one tonne.

Pneumatic Tyred Rollers. Pneumatic tyred rollers consist of a box mounted over two axles, the rear axle having one more wheel than the front and the wheels of the front axles are so arranged that they are located in plan in between the rear wheels. Generally there are four wheels in the front and five in the rear. The assembly is loaded to get a pressure of around 300 kg per linear meter measured along the axle. Weights in the range 12-48 tonnes are common.

When compacting soils the layer thickness should be 10-20 cms. The roller is suitable for compacting non plastic soils and silty soils. The optimum speed is 4 kmph. They are either self propelled or towed by tractors.

Pneumatic tyred rollers are also used for intermediate rolling of dense asphaltic concrete. Rollers of 12 T-18 T are used. The tyre pressure should be a minimum of 0·5 M.N/m^2. The number of passes required is about 8-12 pneumatic roller is generally required for an output of 25 cu.m/ hour.

Vibratory Rollers. Both cohesive and non-cohesive materials can be compacted by vibratory rollers. The layer thickness can be significantly increased resulting in economy. For example as against a layer thickness of 250 mm for soils compacted by a static roller, thickness of over 1000 mm can be easily compacted by vibratory rollers. Similarly as against a layer thickness of 50 mm for bituminous layers compacted by a static roller layer thickness of 250 mm can be compacted by a vibratory roller.

Vibratory rollers are now being manufactured in India. For compacting soils and granular layers, a frequency of 1500-2500 vibrations per min. and an amplitude of 0·8 to 1·5 mm are recommended. For bituminous courses a frequency in the range of 2000-3000 V.P.M. and an amplitude in the range 0·4-0·8 mm are recommended.

Vibratory Plate Compactors. Being light in weight, very mobile and easy to handle by hand, the vibrating plate compactor is a popular tool for compaction in small works, such as pot holes patching. Commonly the vibrating effect is achieved by installation of a rotating eccentric weight in the system. The plate compactor is normally provided with a long steel handle so that the operator can walk behind it and can control the operation. For working in very tight and inaccessible areas, vibrating plate compactors can be equipped with a run of control arrangements.

Hand Operated Vibratory Rollers. For compaction in small and irregular shaped areas, where ordinary rollers cannot find access, small capacity compactors can be used. A typical design comprises a double drum walk behind roller with two vibrating drums and weight rank of only 0·4 to 1·0 tonnes.

Compound Rollers. Some rollers are in combination of two different type of rollers. One having vibrating drum in front and the rear axle having 3 or 4 pneumatic tyres with a weight range of 4-15 tonnes.

Bituminous Equipments. The bitumen is stored in 155-162 kg drums or in special bulk handling depots. In bulk system of handling hot bitumen is filled in rail tank wagons or tank lorries at the refinery. Bitumen tank lorries have a capacity in the range of 6-12 T. The bitumen tank traveler having capacity of 3-6 T are towed by the tractors.

Bitumen Boilers. The capacity of a boiler may be 100-10,000 litres. The small boilers are heated by coal or fire wood while the large boilers are heated by oil burners.

Bitumen Pressure Distributors. A bitumen pressure distributor is a tank of capacity 5000 to 20,000 litres mounted on a lorry, having oil fired burners and a pump. A spray bar unit with nozzles is fitted at the rear of the tank just above the road surface. Bitumen can be applied at a pressure on to the road surface in connection with specifications like surface dressing. Grout of macadam built up spray grout, seal coat and tack coat etc. The quantity of bitumen can be accurately controlled by a metering device. The speed at which the vehicle operates, controls the rate of spread. The width of spray bar can be set out at any deserved value.

Bituminous Hot Mix Plant. For the production of a hot bituminous paving mixture aggregates are blended, heated and dried and then mixed thoroughly with bitumen. The two types of mixing facilities which are widely used can be classified as under :

(*A*) Batch Mixing Plant (*b*) Drum Mixing Plant.

Both the above types are also be classified as (*i*) stationary *i.e.* permanently situated and not required to be dismantled and renewed or (*ii*) portable *i.e.* capable of being dismantled and moved by road or rail.

Batch Mixing Plant. In a batch mixing plant various sizes of aggregates in storage bins are withdrawn in predetermined quantities to make one batch before mixing with a predetermined quantity of bitumen. It comprises the following :

(*a*) **Cold Aggregate Storage Bins of Different Aggregate Sizes.** These should be at least four in number with discharge gates to control the flow of aggregates of different sizes in the desired amounts. Filler is not included in these bins and is handled differently, since it is to be protected from moisture.

(*b*) **Conveyor and Cold Elevators.** The cold aggregate feeding system discharges into a conveyor in preset quantity to give the required gradings and then into the cold elevator which discharges into the dryer.

(*c*) **Dryer.** The main function of a drier are (*i*) removal of moisture from the aggregates accomplished by the heat of the dryer which vapours the moisture and the vapour is drawn off by the draught and (*ii*) to heat the aggregates so that they are of the right temperature for mixing with bitumen in the pug mill.

(*d*) **Temperature Measuring Device.** It is essential for the control of quantity of the mix.

(*e*) **Dust Collector.** Provided for the prevention of pollution as well as to reduce loss of fines upsetting design gradings.

(*f*) **Hot Elevators.** These consist of a system of buckets elevators housed with in a cover chamber.

(*g*) **Hot Screening Unit.** The hot material carried by the elevators are discharged over a multi deck (usually a deck) vibrating table screen which separates the different aggregate functioning into the different hot bins.

(*h*) **Hot Aggregate Bins.** These are temporary storage for the hot aggregates of different sizes. They have discharge gates opening at the bottom.

(*i*) **Filler Silo.** Because of its fineness, the filler material is stored separately in a filler silo and after weighing the hopper discharges the filler material into the mixture generally after bitumen has been admitted into the mixture.

(*j*) **Bitumen Supply Arrangement.** It consists of (*i*) Bitumen storage (*ii*) Bitumen heating and circulation (*iii*) Bitumen metering. For each boiler bitumen may either be pumped into a special bucket of known weight and weighed on a scale or it may be measured in a volume by meter.

(*k*) **Measuring and Mixing of Aggregates and Bitumen.** The aggregate is drawn from hot bins in predetermined quantity and dropped into a pug mill mixture in batches. The required amount of bitumen is added and mixed with aggregates. The hot aggregates and the hot bitumen are thoroughly mixed in the pug mill mixture.

(*l*) **Discharge into Truck or Hot Storage Silo.** After the mixing operation has been completed the final mixture is discharged from the bottom of the pug mill mixture directly to the hauling truck below or taken to a hot storage silo for temporarily storing the mix, before haulage.

When compound to the batch mixing plant discharged above the **Drum Mixing Plant** is without the hot aggregate bins and the pug mill mixer. It only consists of a cold aggregate feed system, a rotating drum mixture (the drum mixture not only mix the aggregate but also blends the aggregates and bitumen into the designed mix, the heating unit or flame being at the upper end of the drum with cold aggregate entering the drum at the flame end), a bitumen supply system, a dirt collector system and a surge silo. In a continuous plant to leave the Drum Mixing Plant provision of surge or storage bins is an absolute necessity. Various capacities of hot mix plants.

20-30 T/hour ; 30-40 T/hour ; 40-60 T/hour ; 60-90 T/hour ; 80-120 T/hour.

Minimum hot mix plants have a capacity of 3-5 T per hour or 6-10 T per hour.

Cold Mixing Plants. Cold mix asphalt plants are those where there is no arrangement for heating the aggregates. Only the bitumen is heated, when required and added to the mixture. Cold mixing generally clarifies light chipping carpets and slurry seals etc. The plants available in India have a capacity of 0·15 to 0·20 cu.m or 0·30 to 0·35 cu.m. They are mounted on a steel chassis having pneumatic wheels.

Paver Finisher. A paver finisher is indispensable for laying hot mix hot laid bituminous material to any desired specification. The equipment is self propelled and is capable in laying the bituminous material to any desired thickness and partially compact it by means of a vibrating screen. The paver has a hopper into which the rear dump trolly can discharge the mix. The paver may be crater mounted (tracked) or equipped with rubber tyres, which permit a greater degree of freedom for movement. The crawler mounting machines are more stable and can support greater width of screed. The screed width can be adjusted generally in the range 2 to 5 m. The bituminous may discharge from a tipper lorry into the receiving hopper in the front portion of the paver is carried along the conveyor through flow control gates to the augers which describes the material in front of the screed to the full width of the screed. A strike off beam which also helps the mat controls the layer thickness. The paver finisher operates at speed 1·5-10 m/min. A speed of 3-5 m/min. will be found generally acceptible. The width of the mat, can be adjusted in the range of 2-5 m. The cross profile can be controlled by adjusting the screed of the strike off beam. Paver finisher of a capacity 45-75 T/hour are generally used for road work.

8·2. Road Maintenance Machines

Multipurpose Road Maintenance Machine. It is a versatile machine for carrying out a number of road maintenance works. The basic machine is similar to a wheel tractor. It is specially designed and equipped with various attachments to perform the following functions :

(*a*) **Grader.** Hydraulically controlled. It can handle all grading jobs.

(*b*) **Bull-dozer.** Can be operated independently or in combination with the under body blade for spreading and levelling.

(*c*) **Loader.** To load out any excess material.

(*d*) **Scarifier.** To loosen many type of materials including ice.

(*e*) **Snow plough.**

(*f*) **Berm loader.**

(*g*) **Vibrator Plate Compactor.** It can be used for compaction of earth, gravel and asphalt surfaces.

(*h*) **Hydraulic broom.** Its width is about 2 m and is used for cleaning of road surfaces.

Pothole Patching Machine. It is a trailer mounted machine adopting on all in one approach to the repair of potholes. It uses compressed air to blow debris out of the holes and then sprays hot oil at high velocity into it for tack coat. There after smaller chips are coated with an emulsified oil and shot through a nozzle into the hole at a speed of over 100 km/ph. After the oiled chips have filled the hole a thin layer of clear chips is applied. Since the chips are blown in at high speed, they compact themselves uniformly from bottom up. It is fast and takes about 30 seconds to repair a 6 inch round potholes.

Spray Patcher. In the spray patch repair method the aggregate and binder normally bitumen are applied separately. It entails repairing the hole with penetration macadam and sand dressed. The equipment is mounted on a pick up track and consists of an insulator tank for the binder, an LPG burner, a petrol engine driven pump and manual spray bar. There is a space for storing aggregate and sand on the plateform of the truck. A fork lift type crane is also mounted on the truck to facilitate loading unloading of barrels. The spray patch method has been found successful for all minor repairs including potholes, surface cracks, alligator cracking and aggregate stripping defect in surface dressing.

Portable Asphalt Mixture/Recycler. For repair of potholes and other maintenance work. It has the following features :

(*a*) Small capacity ranging from a batch of 200 kg upwards or continuous type.

(*b*) Highly mobile and can be towed at high speed by a truck, van or car.

(*c*) Can be used for repairing new asphalt, recycling reclaimed material or reheating cold mix asphalt.

(*d*) Oil fixed or LPG gas burner for heating.

(*e*) Special burner and arrangement for not impairing the quantity of binder by oxidation.

(*f*) Hydraulic controls.

(*g*) Optional attachments like hand spray nozzle for binder hydraulic or pneumatic jack hammer and tamper.

Heated and Insulated Transport. It is a compact and portable insulated storage box for transporting hot mix asphalt material from the plant to repair sites with reheating arrangements.

Combined Bitumen Sprayer and Aggregate Spreader. The combined spreader is suitable for mounting as a tail gate unit to a tipping truck and is easily detachable. The hydraulic power, compressed air and electricity is supplied by the truck systems. It has following operations and controls :

(*a*) Variable width spreading in steps from 0·3 m to 2·7 m achieved with the help of a aggregate shutters and of spraying nozzles.

(*b*) The aggregate flow is regulated by adjusting the gap shutters and the rotary speed of the speeding roller with variable speed hydraulic transmission.

(*c*) The quantity of binder is proportioned by the size of easily interchangeable spray nozzles and the vehicle speed controlled by hand operated engine accelerator.

(*d*) The bitumen system provides for circulation of bitumen in the spray bar and nozzle valves to prevent clogging of nozzles. Heating is done by a thermostatically controlled LPG burner.

(*e*) On and off control of the spray bar nozzle valves and the aggregate shutters is synchronized so that a satisfactory overlapping between binder and aggregate is obtained.

(*f*) The spreader is operated by the driver himself. A micro process governs all requisite functions.

(*g*) For deciding the correct speeding width, a trance sight is arranged in the visual field of the driver.

Tail board chip spreaders. The unit is made of two sizes *i.e.* 2·25 m and 2·5 m spread and designed for easy fitting to most fitting truck bodies. The spreading width may be varied infinitely between 0·3 m to 2·5 m. Optional quick release scatter plates are available with a full width operator plateform which allows the operator to ride with the machine and operate the controls safely. Feed opening can be adjusted to allow clearance of aggregates varying upto 20 mm Feed gate has adjustable opening and calibration to suit different size of aggregates. To further assist the flow and to break up lumps of coated chippings, an agitator is provided in the throat. Driving the feed roller is via a clutch powered by a fifth wheel which gets power from the ground with the movement of tipper.

15·9·1. Road Signs. *Importance of Road Signs* : (1) To give warning to hazardous situations.

(2) To give important information to the road vehicle drivers regarding control of the vehicles and situations.

(3) To supply information about the road situations etc.

Classes of Signs. (1) **Cautionary or warning signs.** To inform the road drivers or users about the hazardous situations.

(2) **Mandatory or Regulatory signs.** To warn the users of road about certain laws, regulations or restrictions which are to be followed and non-compliance of which is liable to legal action.

(3) **Informatory signs.** These are guidance to the road users in respect of direction and place identifications, facilities like road side rest areas and petrol pumps and parking etc.

Positions of signs on the road side. (1) The road signs are normally placed to the left side of the carriage way but may be repeated as 'overhead signs' of the local conditions if so warrant.

(2) On kerbed roads, no part of the sign should be less than 0·6 m away from the kerb edge. On unkerbed roads it must be ensured that no part of the sign comes in the way of vehicular traffic ; no part of the sign should be less than 2 m from the edge of carriage way.

(3) The bottom edge of the lowest portion of the sign should not be less than 2 m above the kerb on kerbed roads and not less than 1·5 m above the top of the pavement on unkerbed roads.

(4) A sign may be placed on the median of a divided carriage way if placing it on left hand side is not considered effective length for a given set of site conditions.

(5) The signs should be so sited as not to cause any hinderance to the movement of the vehicles on the carriage way and where placed on the shoulder/footpath/refuse island, the obstruction to the pedestrians should be minimised.

(6) Signs may also be fixed on existing utility posts like electric or telephone etc. if conveniently located.

Visibility signs, particularly warning signs and mandatory signs should have respective material like luminous paints or reflective devices or should be lighted for better visibility and legibility at night, except those in lighted street of populated areas.

Cautionary or triangle Warning Signs. The cautionary signs as shown in Plate 15·1 are in the shape of an equilateral triangle with the apex pointing upwards. These signs have red border and black symbols on white background. The side of the triangle is 900 mm for normal sized signs and 600 mm for small sized signs, while the width of the border is 70 mm and 45 mm respectively. Details regarding sizes of symbols etc. are stipulated by IRC. In urban locations, these signs should be about 50 metre away from the points of hazard, which may be adjusted to suit site conditions. In non-urban locations, these signs should be located at the following distances in advance of the hazard.

Table 15·62.

	Plain or rolling terrain	*Hill terrain*
National highways and State highways	120 m	60 m
Major district roads	90 m	50 m
Other district roads	60 m	40 m
Village roads	40 m	30 m

Mandatory Road Signs. There are two most important signs in this category (*i*) stop (*ii*) give way. The "stop" sign is 900 mm × 900 mm is octagonal in shape and is red in colour with a 30 mm white border. A small size version is 600 mm × 600 mm with a 20 mm border. The "give way" sign is an equilateral triangle having each side of 900 mm in shape, white in colour with a 70 mm red border as shown in the Fig. A small sized version has a side of 600 mm with 45 mm border. Other mandatory/regulatory signs as shown in Fig. are circular in shape with 600 mm diameter for normal size 400 mm diameter for small size and are white in colour with red border of 65 mm and 45 mm respectively ; the width of red oblique bar is 60 mm and 40 mm respectively. A smaller size of 300 mm diameter may be used in conjunction with traffic light signals or on bollards on traffic islands. Width of red borders and red oblique bar in such border and red slanting bars, but the back ground is blue instead of white as in other signs of this type. Details on sizes of numbers and symbols in black are stipulated by IRC.

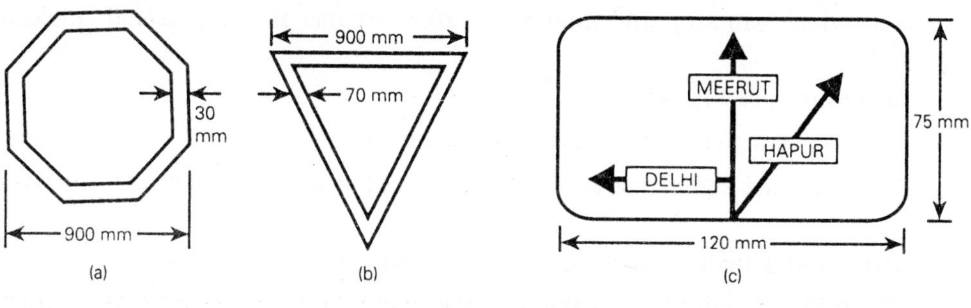

Fig. 15·32.

Information Signs. They are generally (800 mm × 600 mm) rectangular for normal size and (600 mm × 450 mm) for small size. The size of square (as in parking signs) is 400 mm for normal size and 300 mm for small size. Details on sizes of various symbols are stipulated by the IRC. Then signs have white background, black letters and arrows and with black border. Some of the more common informatory signs are shown in the Fig. The size of these signs depends on the massage and size of letters.

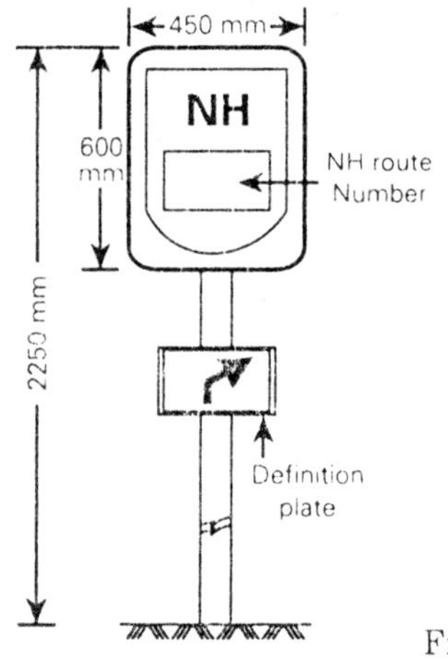

Fig. 15·33.

15·9·2. Traffic Signals. Traffic signals are needed for the control of conflecting streams of vehicular and pedestrian traffic at intersection.

Advantages of Traffic Signals :

(*i*) They can provide information for an orderly movement of traffic.

(*ii*) When proper geometric layouts and control measures are employed, they can increase the traffic holding capacity of the intersection.

(*iii*) They can reduce the frequencies of certain types of accidents, especially the right angle type and pedestrian accidents.

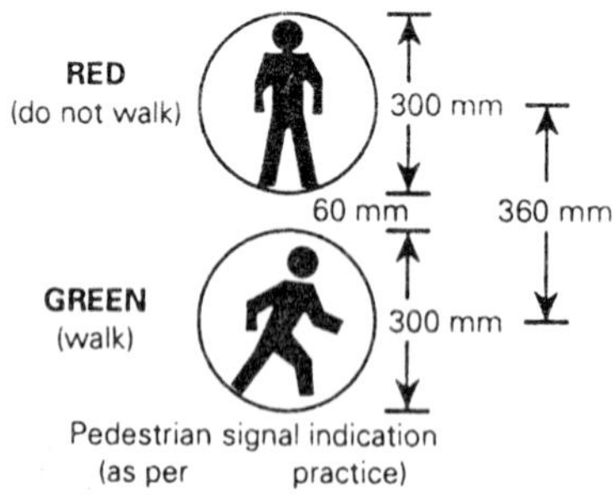

Fig. 15·34.

(*iv*) Under favourable conditions, they can be co-ordinated to provide for continuous or nearly continuous movement of traffic at a definite speed along a given route.

(*v*) They can be used to interrupt heavy traffic at intervals to permit other traffic or pedestrian to cross.

(*vi*) Traffic signals dispense with police control and thus be economical.

(*vii*) If properly designed and set, they can assign right way impartially to traffic unlike manual controls which can stop and interrupt traffic streams at the personal thinking of the traffic controller.

Disadvantages of Signals :

(*i*) Delay in vehicular motion during off peak hours.

(*ii*) Unwarranted signal installation tend to encourage the disobedience of the signal indications.

(*iii*) Drivers may induce less adequate and unsafe routes to avoid delay.

(*iv*) When the installations breakdown, due to any fault or power break, confusions and difficulties are arised.

Indian Practice of Signals. The Indian practice is to have an amber period of 2 seconds as a transition interval between termination of related green movement and exhibition of a red indication or between termination of a red indications and commencement of related green movement.

Pedestrian Signal Indications. The Indian standard on traffic signals for pedestrians as shown in Fig. The red standing man represents the **Don't cross** indication and the green walking man represents the cross indication.

Flashing Amber. A flashing amber signal is a hazard indication, normally used to warn of obstruction and intersections to supplement regulatory signs and to warn of midlock cross walks.

Signal Face. In Indian practice the minimum number of lenses in a signal face is three (red, amber and green). The lenses in a signal face can be arranged in a vertical or a horizontal straight line. The relative position top to bottom or left to right are red, amber and green. A simple signal face with three lenses in a vertical line is indicated in the Fig. A traffic signal has a signal face mounted on a vertical post or provided over head.

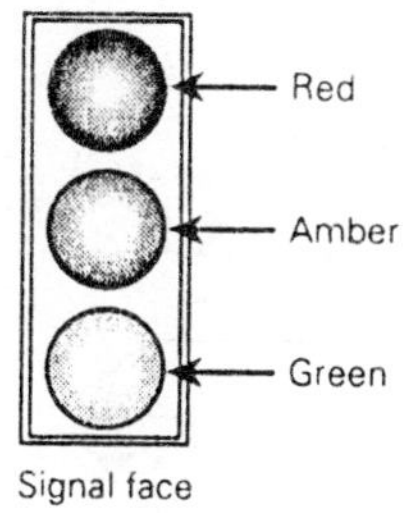

Fig. 15·35.

Illumination of Signals. The American practice requires that the signals should be illuminated as to be visible from a distance of at least 0·4 km under normal atmospheric conditions.

Detailed Indian specifications for the illumination of signals are contained in IS—1974.

Location of Signals. It is desirable to have at least two signal installations (*i*) Primary signal (*ii*) Secondary signal. Primary signals are located near stop line, while the secondary signals are provided diagonally opposite to primary signals. Primary signal is installed at 0·9 m from the stop line while the secondary signal is installed on the back of Primary signal intended for opposing traffic, diagonally opposite the Primary signal.

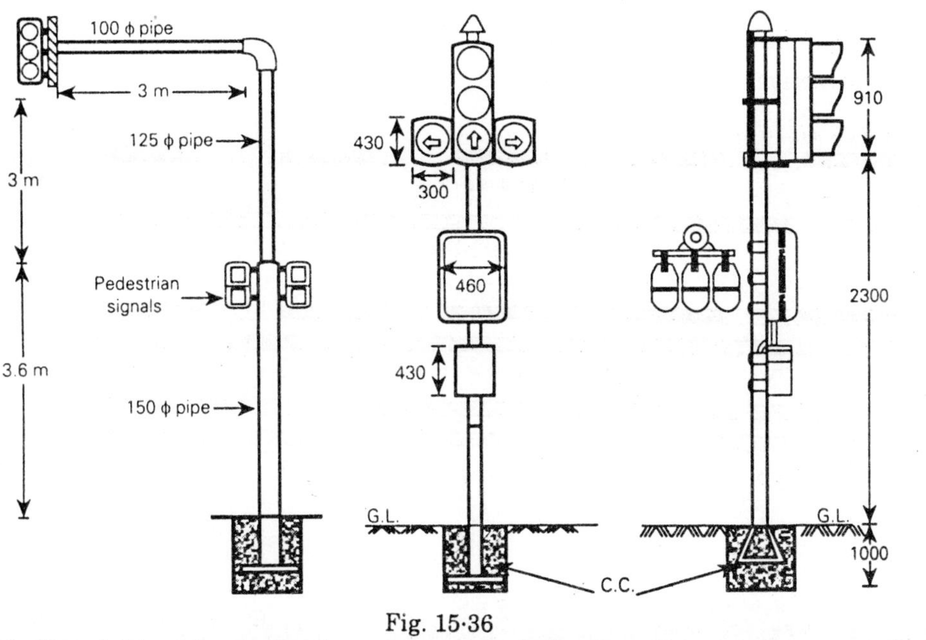

Fig. 15·36

9·3. Road Markings. Road markings are defined as lines patterns, words or other devices, except signs, set into applied or attached to the carriage way or kerbs or to objects within or adjacent to the carriage way, for controlling, working, guiding and informing the road users.

Aim of road markings. (*a*) To guide and control traffic on the roads.

(*b*) To serve as a psychological barrier.

(*c*) To delineate traffic path and its lateral clearance from traffic hazards.

(*d*) To aid pedestrians and cyclists in channelising their movement into safe locations.

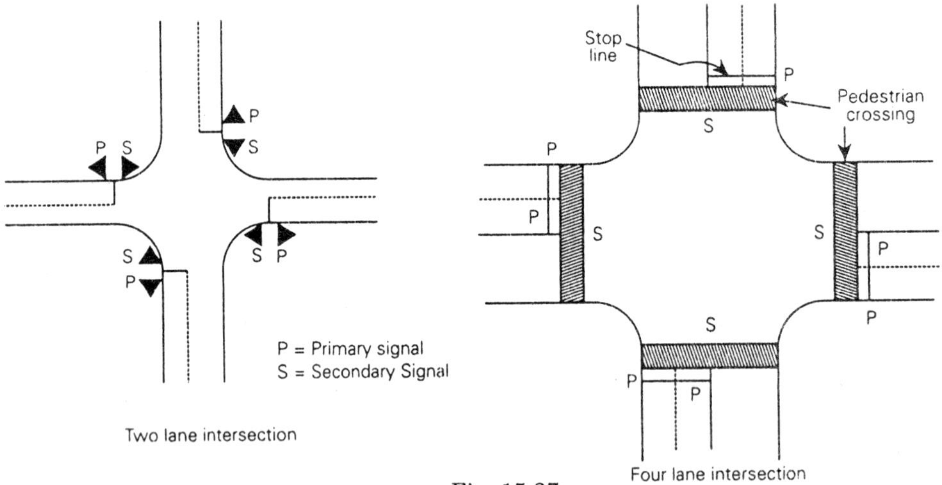

Fig. 15·37.

Classification of road markings. (*A*) **Carriage way markings :**

(*i*) **Longitudinal markings.** These markings are placed along the direction of traffic for the guidance of drivers. These are white in colour except for the following, which are yellow in colour.

(*a*) Lines indicating parking restrictions

(*b*) Obstruction approach markings.

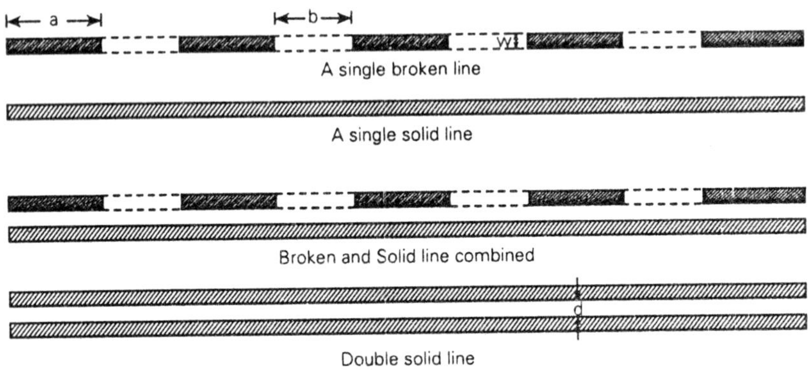

a & *b* will depend on application

c, *d*, *e* = 100

W = 100, for rural areas

W = 150, for urban areas

Fig. 15·38.

(*c*) No overtaking zone markings.

(*d*) Continuous centre line may optionally be yellow.

Broken lines indicate that traffic permitting, these may be crossed.

Solid lines however are restrictive and are not permitted to be crossed except for entry or exit from a premises or a side road or to avoid a stationary obstruction.

Double solid lines indicate maximum restrictives and are not to be crossed except in an emergency.

In a combination of broken and solid lines, a solid line may be crossed with direction, if the broken line of the combination is nearer to the direction of travel. Vehicles from opposite direction are not permitted to cross the solid line.

The various longitudinal markings include the followings :

(*a*) centre lines

(*b*) traffic lines

(*c*) no passing zones

(*d*) working signs

(*e*) boarder edge lines

(*f*) bus lane markings

(*g*) cycle lane markings.

(*ii*) **Marking at intersections.** The type of carriage way for a particular intersection is dependent on a number of variables like speed characteristics and availability of space.

The markings in this category may be further sub-divided into markings in approaches to intersections and markings in the intersection area. The different types of markings under each of these two groups are as under :

(*a*) Markings on approaches to intersections

(*i*) Stop lines

(*ii*) Give way lines

(*iii*) Pedestrian crossings

(*iv*) Cyclist crossings

(*v*) Markings on speed change lane

(*vi*) Direction arrows

(*vi*) Protected right turn lanes

(*b*) Markings in intersection areas, marking at rotaries.

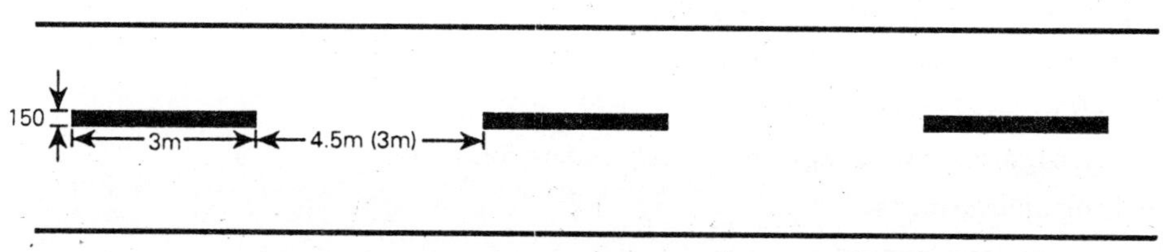

15·39 (*a*) Centre line marking for a two lane road

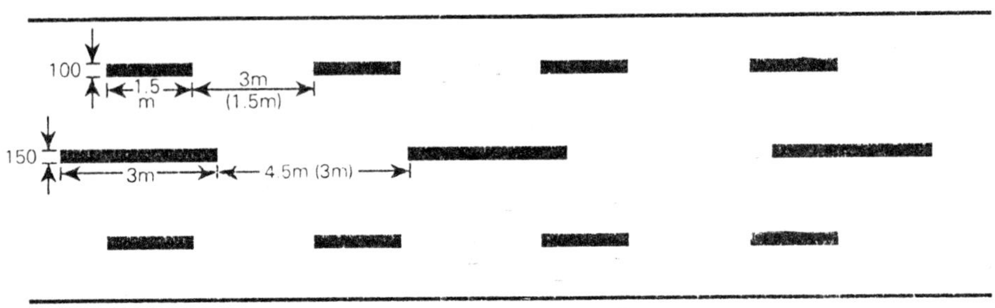

Fig. 15·39 (*b*) Lane line and broken centre line marking for a four lane road

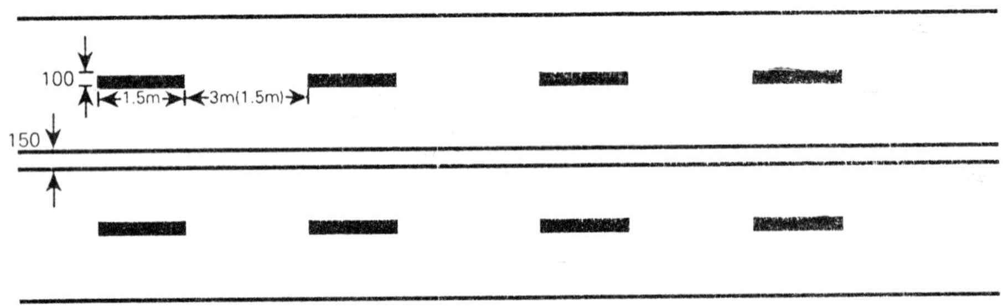

Fig. 15·39 (*c*) Centre barrier line marking for four lane road

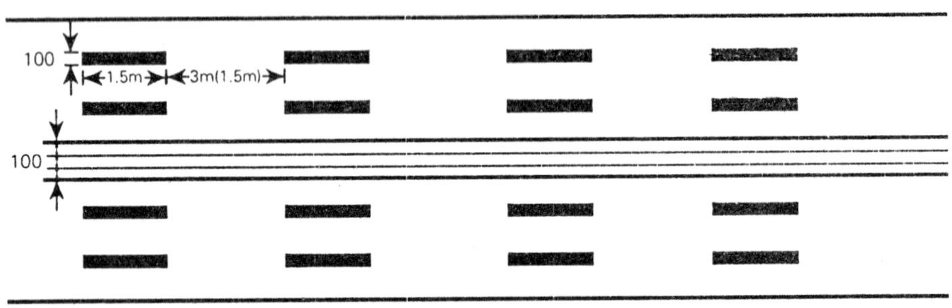

Fig. 15·39 (*d*) Centre barrier line marking for a six lane road

Note : Figures in brackets to be used on curves and approaches to intersections.

(*c*) **Markings on Hazardous Locations.** The more common road markings falling under this category include the following :

—Carriageway width transition markings

—Median width transition markings

—Obstruction approach markings

—Road-Rail level crossings.

(*d*) **Markings for Parking.** These include the following :

—Parking space limits

—Parking restrictions

—Bus stops

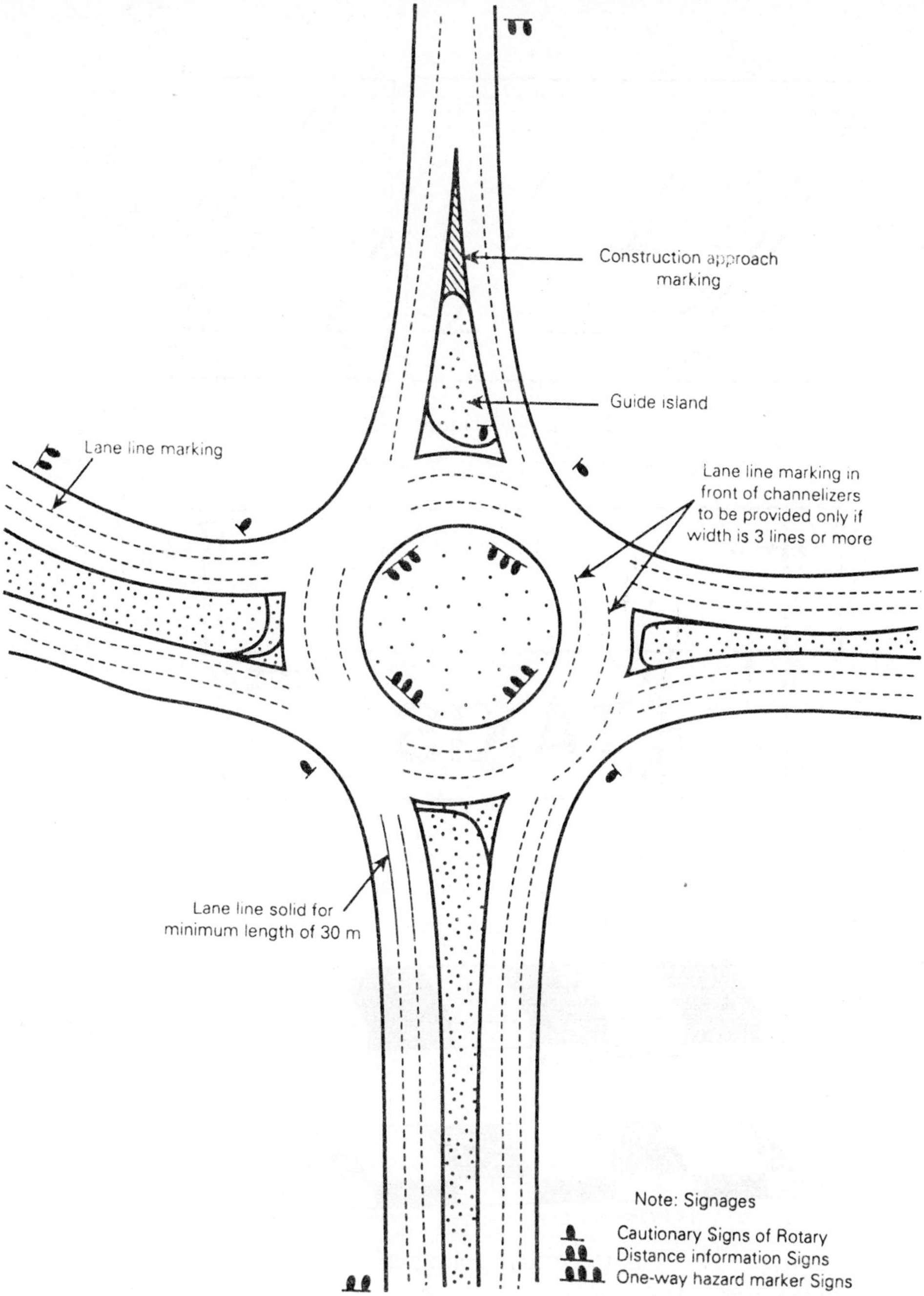

Fig. 15·40. Typical road markings at rotaries.

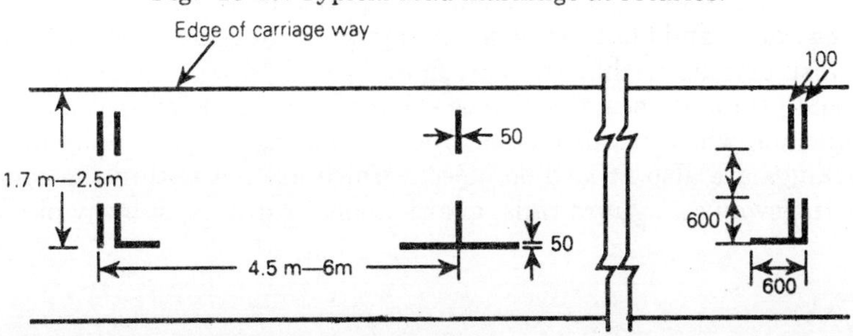

(a) Parallel marking

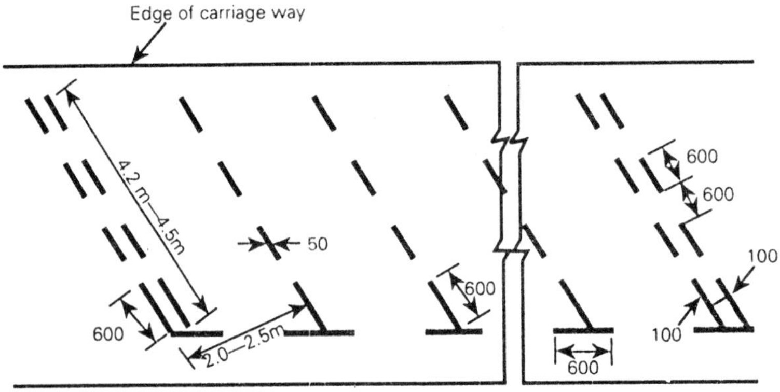

(*b*) Angled parking

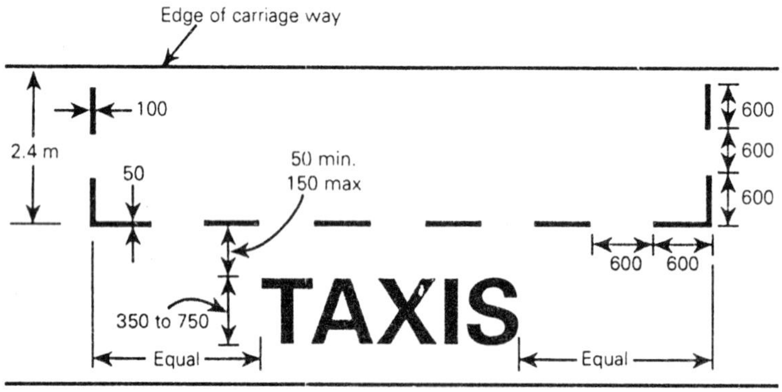

(*c*) Parking for taxis

Note : Width of Bay shall change as per site requirements and type of vehicles.

Fig. 15·41. Typical markings for parking spaces.

Fig. 15·41 shows typical markings for parking spaces.

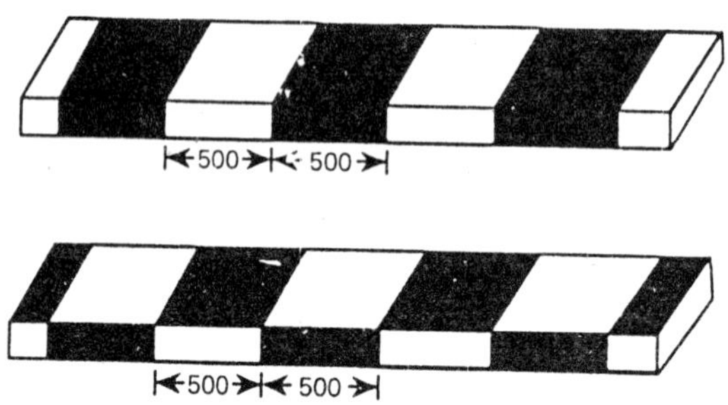

Fig. 15·42. Kerb markings.

(*vi*) **Object Markings.** Markings are also needed on physical obstructions within the carriageway, adjacent to the carriageway and on speed breakers as they may be serious hazards to the moving traffic *e.g.* piers and abutments, monuments, traffic islands, signs and signal supports, poles, trees etc. Obstructions within the carriageway should be marked by not less than five alternating black and yellow stripes, the stripes sloping downwards at an angle of 45° towards the side of the obstruction on which traffic passes. The alternating stripes should not be less than 100 mm in width. Markings are also needed on objects which are not within the carriageway but are adjacent to the carriageway *e.g.*, guard rails, guard stones or drums, subway piers and abutments,

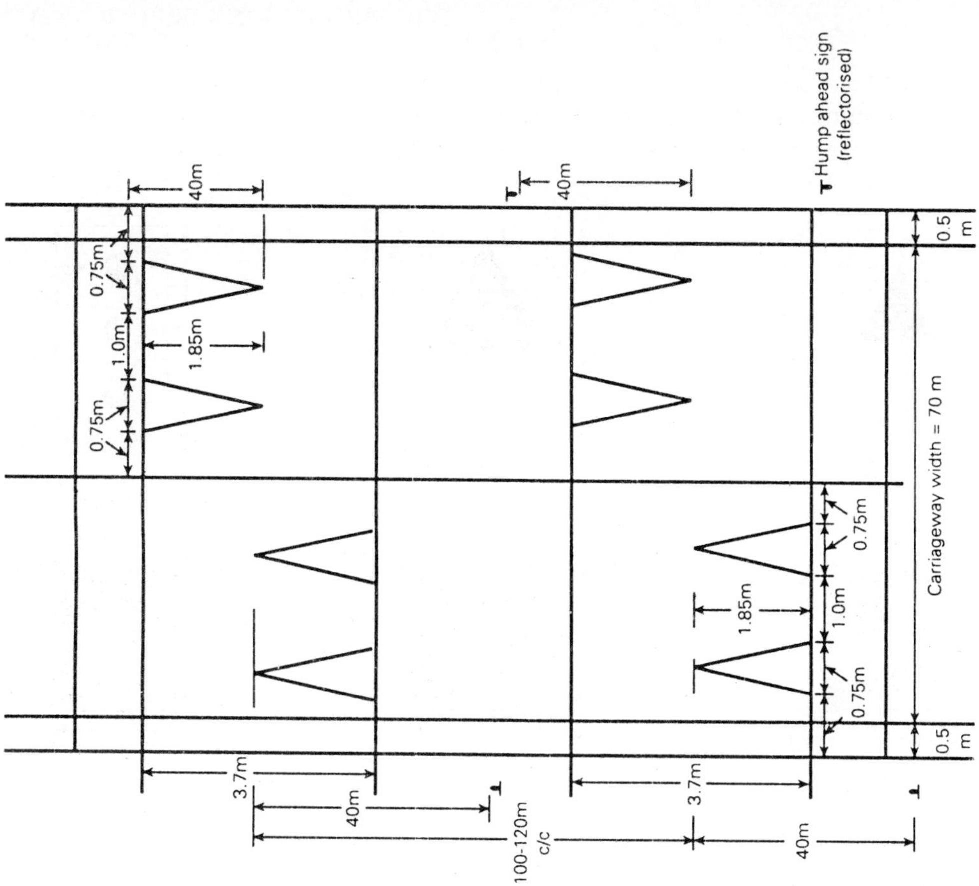

Fig. 15·43. Markings on speed breakers.

culvert head walls, trees etc. In fact, all objects located within 1·5 m beyond the formation width of the road should be painted. Poles close to the carriageway should be marked with alternate black and white horizontal stripes upto a height of 1·25 m above the road level, the stripes being uniform and not less than 100 mm in width. Objects which are not likely to be hit unless a vehicle runs off the carriageway should be painted solid white ; on trees, marking should be upto a height of 1·25 m above the road level with a 300 mm band in black paint in the middle. Speed breakers where warranted should be painted in white to give visual warning to drivers in addition to posting suitable advance warning signs on the roadside located 40 m in advance of the first speed breaker.

15·9·4. Word Messages. Word messages, painted on the pavement, like STOP ; SLOW ; BUS ; BUS LANE ; KEEP CLEAR ; SCHOOL ; RIGHT TURN ONLY ; EXIT ONLY can also be used for providing information to drivers to guide, warn or regulate traffic. While the messages RIGHT TURN ONLY andEXIT ONLY should be used only to supplement the directional arrows, the legends SCHOOL, SLOW and STOP should be used only in support of standard signs. All these legends are painted on the pavement in white and should be reflectorised, except on well-illuminated roads. The letters should be elongated in the direction of traffic ; letter height in the direction of travel should be 1·25 m for speeds upto 50 km per hour and 2·5 m for speeds above 50 km per hour. There should be a minimum 0·3 m clear at either side of the lane/carriageway and in between letters.

15·9·5. Safety during construction. Construction and maintenance activities go on even when traffic operations remain continue. This gives rise to serious hazards. Safety can be ensured through various measures such as :

— Installing proper traffic control devices and signs (preferably reflectorised for right visibility.

—Observing safety rules and by placing traffic marshals to guide the traffic.
—Marking legally mandatory for the contractors to follow safety measures.
—Caution boards placing before the work started.

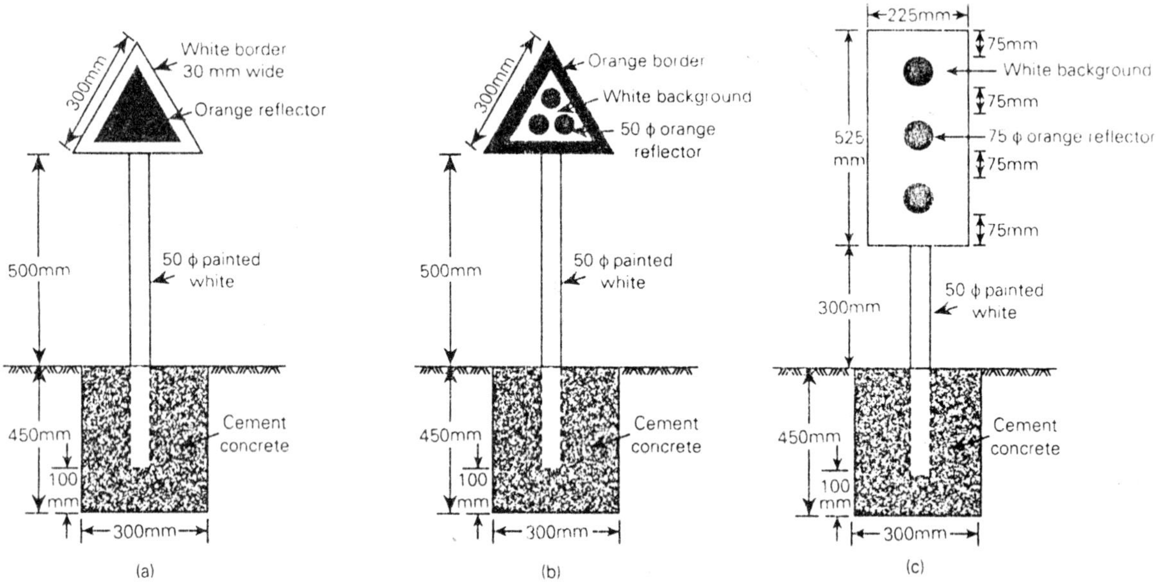

Fig. 15·44. Typical design of object markers.

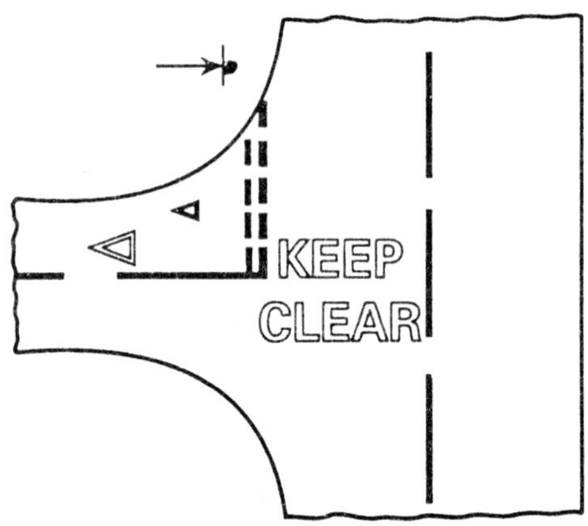

Fig. 15·45. Keep clear word message.

15·9·6. Traffic Impact Attenuators

On modern highways like the Expressways and busy National High ways where vehicles travel at very high speeds, collision of speeding vehicles with fixed objects (like bridge abutments and structural columns etc.) is a common type of road accidents. The exit gore areas in interchanges (*i.e.*, the area downstream from the shoulder intersection point of the main carriageway and an exit road) is a common area where serious accidents are known to take place. Traffic Impact Attenuators or Crash Cushions are protective systems which prevent errant vehicles from impacting hazards by either smoothly decelerating the vehicles to a stop when hit head-on, or by redirecting it away from the hazard for glancing impacts. These barriers are used to shield rigid

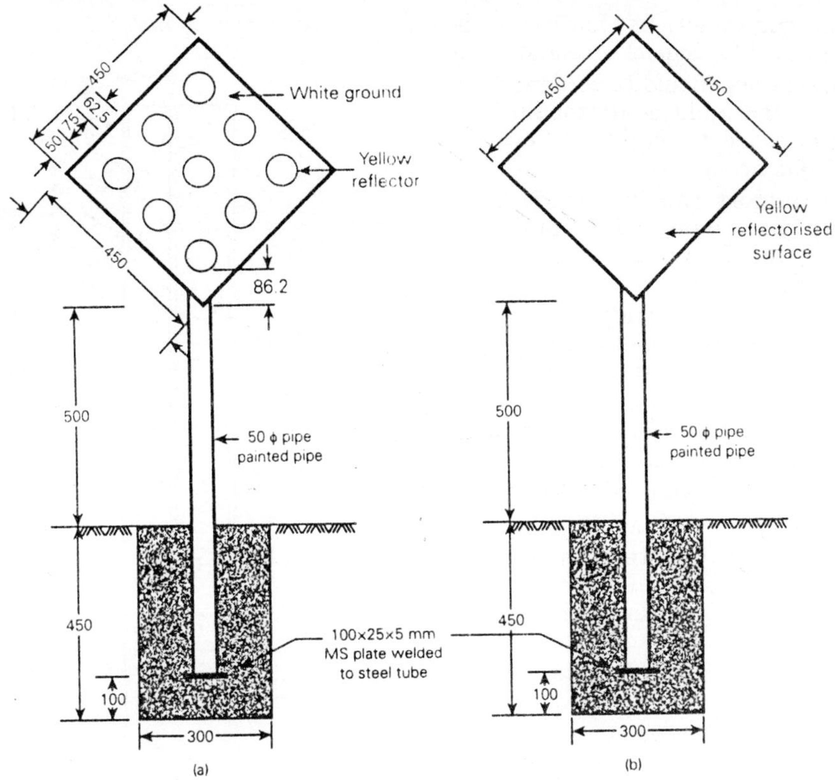

Fig. 15·46. Design of large reflectors.

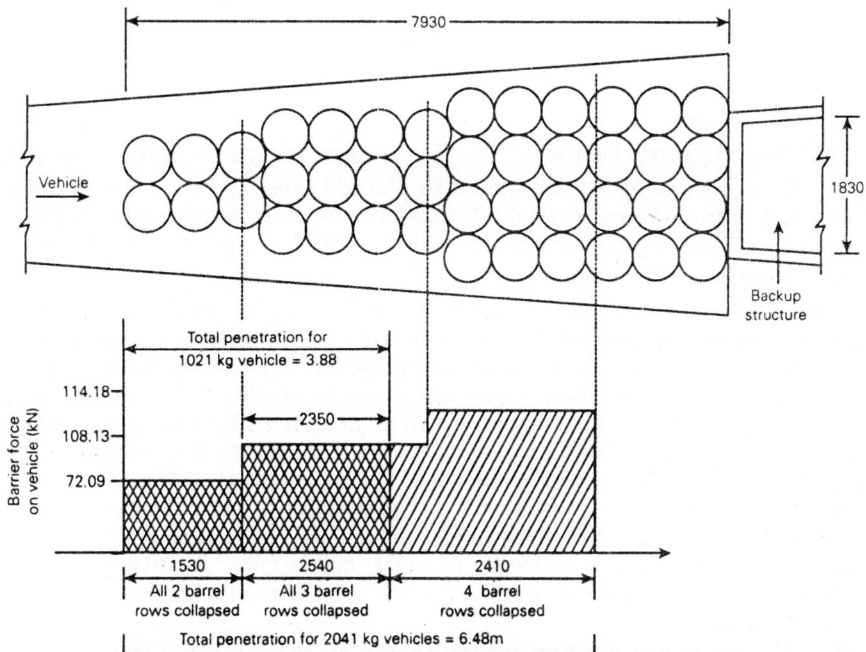

Fig. 15·47. Traffic impact attenuator using empty steel drums.

objects or hazardous conditions that cannot be removed, relocated or made breakway. The main design considerations for impact attenuators are :

— The attenuators should be designed to provide the additional stopping distance needed for crashes above 55 to 65 Km/hr., and

— The attenuators should provide a stopping force near, but slightly less than, the design frontal crush force on the vehicle.

There are many types of traffic impact attenuators in use in developed countries but the ones most relevant to Indian conditions are :

— Empty Steel Drum Assembly

— Hi-Dro Cell cluster and

— Cushions of scrap tyres.

Road Edge Barriers

It is a longitudinal system used to shield vehicles from hazards on the edge of a road and is provided at the following locations :

— Embankment with high fills and steep slopes.

— Near roadside obstacles.

— Bridge rail ends.

— At specific locations for ensuring safety of bystanders, pedestrians and cyclists.

— Dangerous ditches.

— Steep grades.

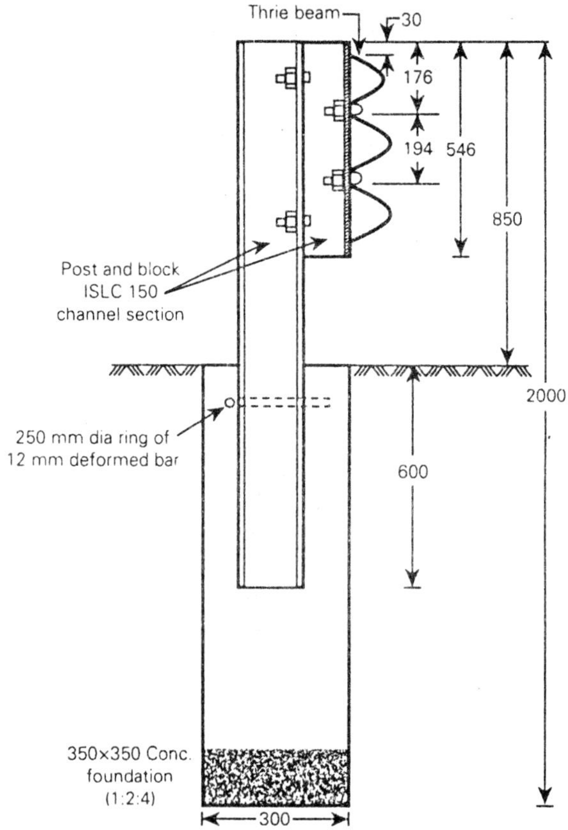

Fig. 15·48. Details of Thrie beam steel barrier.

The types of road edge barriers commonly used abroad are:

(1) "W" beam type steel barrier. (2) Thrie beam type steel barrier. (3) Wire rope barrier.

Ordinarily a road edge barrier should be placed beyond 2·5 m of the travelled way. In case of embankments, a minimum distance of 60 cm should be maintained between the barrier and the start of embankment slope or a hazard to prevent the wheels dropping over the edge.

15·9·7. Roadside Rest Areas

The need. Specially designed studies abroad on high speed highways have shown that watchfulness or vigilance in driving declines after about 30 minutes of continuous driving. If the driver then receives some mental stimulation, his efficiency can be maintained for another 30 minutes. It is, therefore, very necessary from the overall consideration of highway safety that well planned and well designed rest areas adjacent to or near the highway be provided with facilities such as seats, shelter sheds, litter bins, toilets, maps, picnic tables, restaurant/vending stands, adequate parking space etc. Such rest areas should also provide the needed soothing environment, preferably by the side of a lake or waterfall, in a garden with shady areas free from noise and other pollution. After spending some time in a rest area, drivers can resume their journey with the desired level of vigilance and watchfulness. In India, only limited facilities are available adjacent to at the highway in form of roadside dhabas, which are often substandard and do not measure to the required standards.

15·9·8. Highway Safety Appurtenances

With the increasing speeds and higher volumes of traffic plying on highways, provision of safety appurtenances is becoming increasingly necessary. The following safety appurtenances, which are of immediate relevance in the Indian context have been covered as below :

(*i*) Delineators (*ii*) Traffic impact attenuators
(*iii*) Road side rest areas (*iv*) Traffic safety barriers (*v*) Traffic aid posts.

Delineators. Delineators are light retro-reflecting devices mounting by the side of the road way to indicate the road way alignment, espcially for night driving. The three broad types are as below :

(*a*) Road way indicators (*b*) Hazard markers (*c*) Object marking

Road way indicators. These are installed to delineate the edges of the road way (road formation) in order to guide drivers about any abrupt changes *i.e.* sharp curves, abrupt reduction in pavement width *i.e.* from four lane divided to two lanes) and where the alignment may be confusing for some similar reason. These road way indicators should be in form of vertical posts or in form of ballasted drums. However ballasted drums are not favoured mainly because of the damage that they can cause to an out of control vehicle some typical designs of the vertical post type road way indicators are shown in the Fig. 15·49.

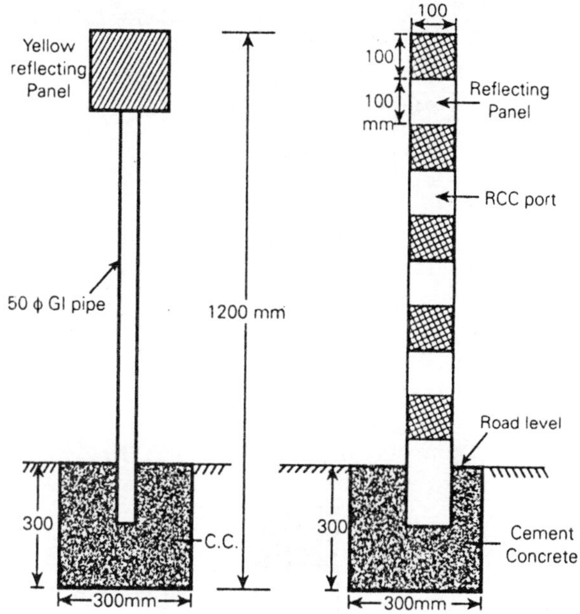

Fig. 15·49. Delineators of different types.
(All dimensions are in mm)

Hazard Markers. These are provided to define obstructions such as guard roads, abutments, pens, barrier rails, etc. In its most common form a hazard marker is a striped board painted alternately black yellow

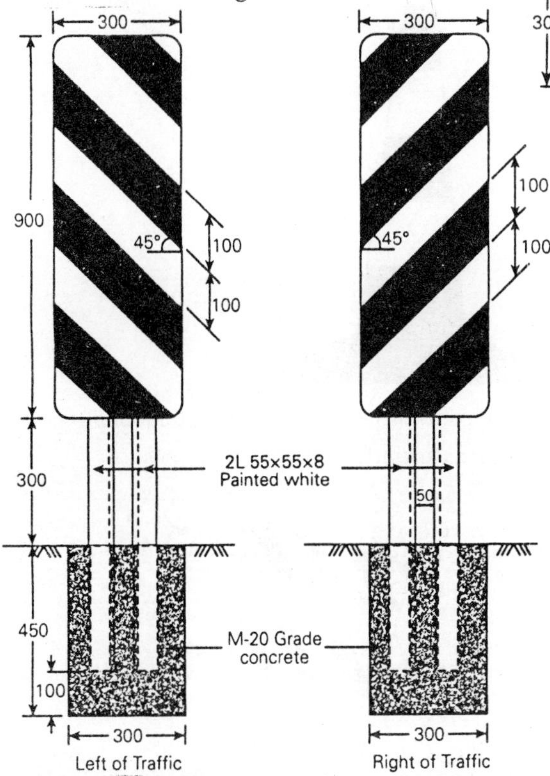

Note : The stripes slope down at 45° towards the side on which traffic is to pass.

Fig. 15·50. Typical design of hazard markers.

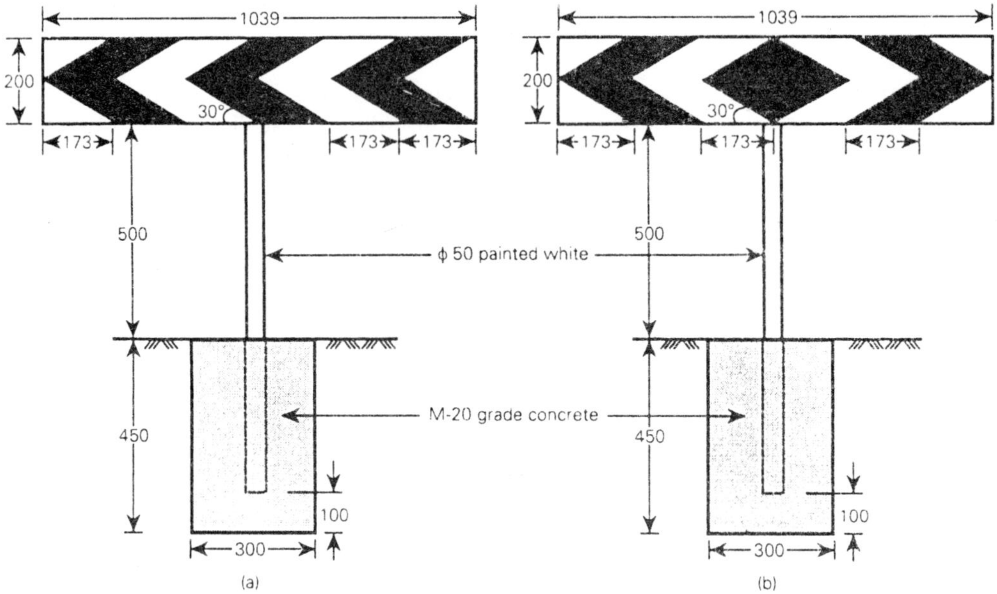

(*a*) One-way hazard marker for Rotary island

(*b*) Two-way hazard marker for T-junction

Fig. 15·51. Hazard marker design.

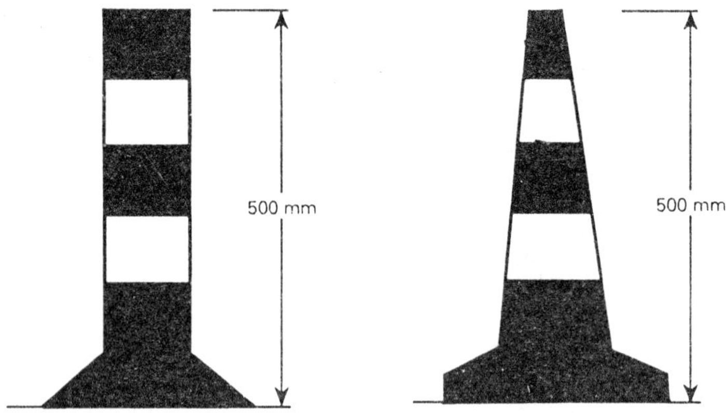

The stripes are 10-15 cm in width and are alternately in reflectorised white and orange colours.

Fig. 15·52. Cones and tubular markers (with alternate white and orange stripes).

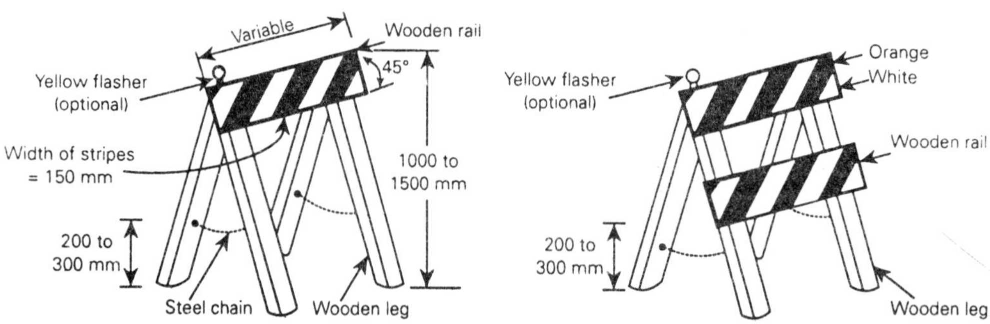

(*a*) Movable type barricade (*b*) Movable type barricade

Fig. 15·53. Movable type barricade.

conventionally ; a colour combination of alternate white orange (reflectorised) is however more suitable. A typical design is shown in the Fig. 15·51(*a*) on rotary island on T-junctions, typical designs for one way and two way hazard is shown in Fig. 15·51(*b*).

(*a*) Delineators without reflectors in black and yellow alternate colours.

(*b*) Delineators with circular reflector.

(*c*) Delineator with square reflector.

(*d*) Amber colour panel delineator.

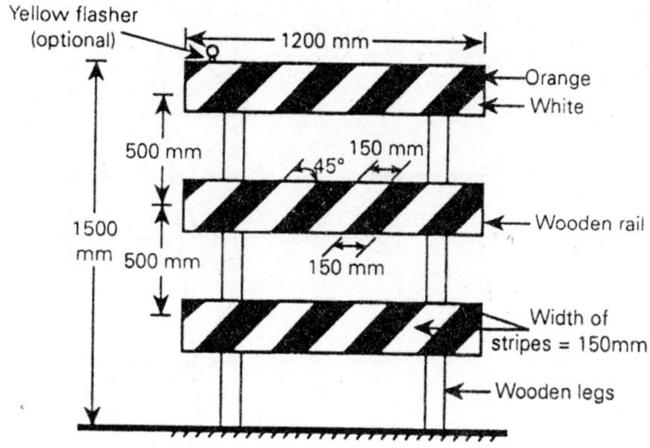

Fig. 15·54. Fixed type barricade.

15·10·1. Planning of a Road Project. (*a*) **Route Surveys.**

(1) Preliminary survey—It consists of a reconnaissance survey which is done (*a*) by touring around and about the area (*b*) by aerial survey (*c*) by survey of India maps of the area.

(2) When the rough route of the road is fixed by reconnaissance the proposed alignment is walked on the side and the final location of road is marked on the land.

(3) On the proposed alignment of the road so marked on the ground longitudinal section of the road is taken at spot levels at about 200 m interval from a standard bench mark of Survey of India and the levelling is closed on the standard bench mark to ascertain any closing error. If the error is beyond the permissible, the levelling operation is repeated. The L-sec. is plotted on a graph sheet. The points of drainage crossings are also marked on it.

(4) Cross-sections of the points of *L*-section at 200 m apart is taken so as to compute the earth work involved in the construction.

(5) The drainage points so marked on the *L*-section is analysed for their hydrology so as to design the cross drainage work on it.

(6) The alignment so proposed is marked on the shajra sheets which are available in the Revenue department, by which the land acquisition papers are prepared. For doing so the alignment is marked on the ground and by which the actual covered plots are marked and their area which has to be acquired is computed plotwise. The width of land (right of way) is calculated from the *x*-sections.

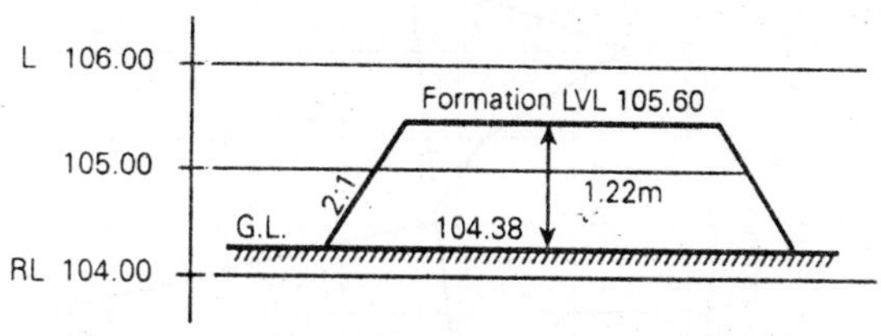

Fig. 15·55. Cross section of road at KM 3·00.

(*b*) **Drainage Studies.** Surface run off of the drains crossing the alignment is determined and the expected discharge which may pass in them is computed from their study of hydrology (for this refer hydrology section in Irrigation Engineering).

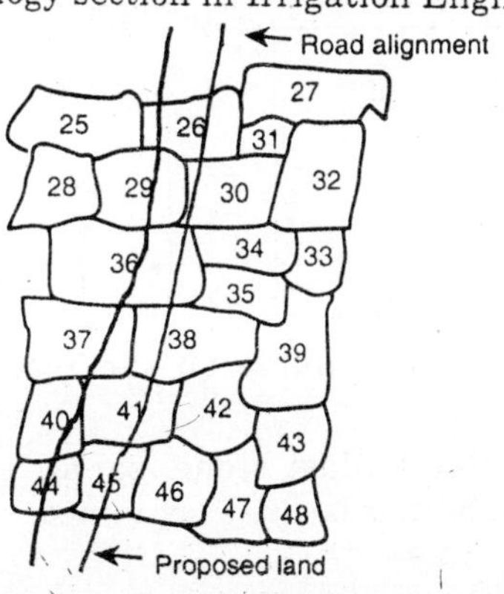

(*c*) **Sub Surface Studies.** For this the spring level of wells in the area is studied by which the position of water table in the area is ascertained, which is utilised when the foundations of the cross drainage works are done.

(*d*) **Soil Surveys.** The soil samples over the alignment is taken by digging pits or by anger borings. On proposed masonry works the percussion boring can be done.

(*e*) **Traffic Survey.** This involves the volume of traffic which is liable on the road, the Accident Studies are also done. The future enhancement of the traffic is also forecasted. The growth rate of the traffic is also ascertained.

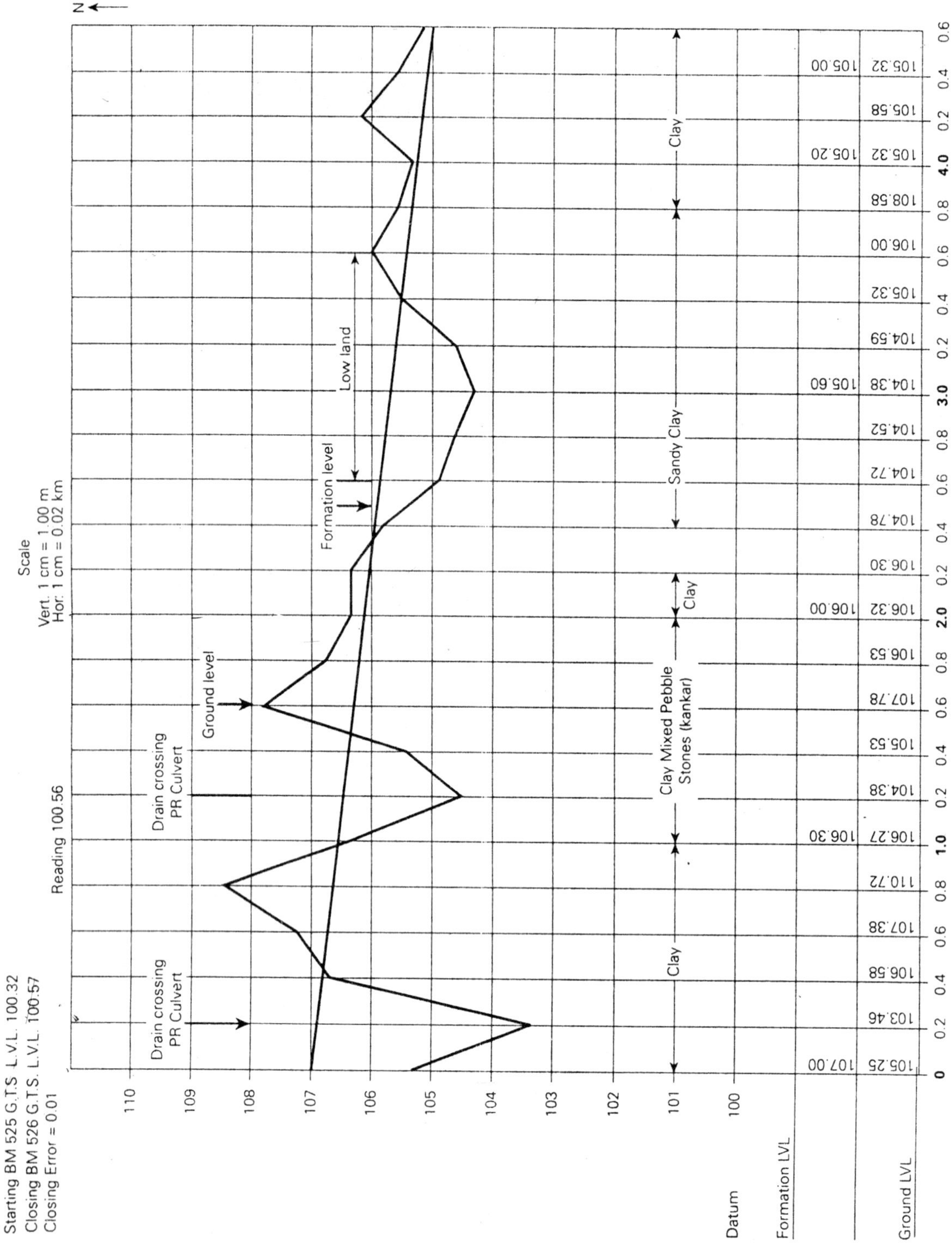

L-section of proposed Khanjar Pur road.

Fig. 15·57.

(*f*) **Exle Load Surveys.** The type of vehicles which are liable on the road after construction and their expected load.

(*g*) **Material Surveys.** The construction material like ballast stone, sand, cement, bitumen etc. which may be used in construction and their availabilities is also ascertained.

(h) Labour position both skilled and unskilled as available in the area.

(i) Rail and road line availability so as to transport the construction materials.

(j) Position of *Abadies* along the site of the road alignment.

15·10·2. Planning of a Hill Road. In continuation of the Planning of Plane road some special features are observed in hill road planning which are as follows :

(1) The levelling of the alignment of hill road is obstructed at vertical rocks or on streams. In such cases the levelling operation is connected by loop survey. In actual footpath 1 metre wide is constructed along the alignment which is hindered at the vertical rocks, so this foot path is connected by loops either at lower level where it cross the cliff or at higher level where it is possible to cross the cliff. The level is done either direct vision across the cliff or along the foot path. The chainage is adjusted according to actual length measured by steel wires.

(2) X-sections are taken by step method due to the steep slope of the hill, which is connected by the level station of the *L*-section.

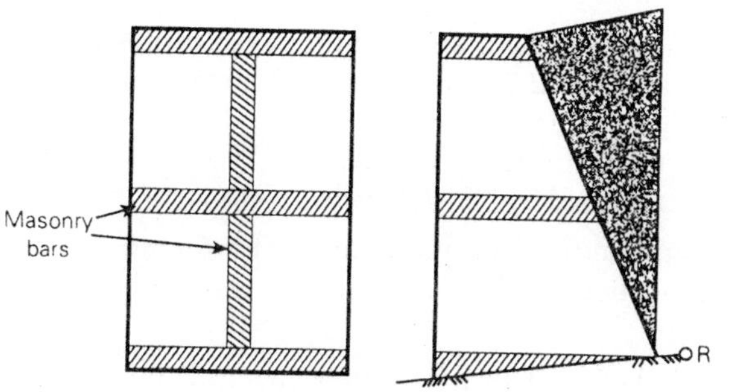

Fig. 15·58.

(3) The Geological survey is done of the alignment rocks, so as to classify the rocks which has to be cut during construction. The geological survey is also necessary to access the stability of slopes and also to have an idea about the siesmology of the terrain.

(4) After levelling is done, the chainage, back cutting and level pillars are constructed so as to have a grid for the contractors before and after tendering during constructions.

(5) In hills the back cutting side is generally cut vertical and the width is maintained by constructing retaining or walls which may be of dry or cement masonry.

(6) In back side where the slope is unstable breast walls are constructed. These may be of dry masonry.

(7) The top and bottom of these walls are made of cement masonry. Some vertical and horizontal bars of masonry are also provided.

15·11. Aboriculture—Road side Plantation

Road side trees must be fairly hardy and robust, these can stand winds and storms. The trees must be shady but not sending out large branches. Too rapid growing trees should be avoided as they are invariably short lived and have very brittle branches. The species selected must be either truely evergreen such as the mango, nearly evergreen such as Margosa, or be leaf during summer. Trees that develop straight and clean trunk upto a height of about 3 to 3·6 m from the ground level and then spread out are suitable. They should be deep rooted as shallow spreading roots injure pavements by absorbing moisture from the subgrades. All species of trees having large and thick leaves should be avoided as they require more moisture than the small leaved varieties. Trees with small sized thin leaves like the tamarind and the margosa stand drought very well as they need much less water than the large and thick leaved varieties.

Trees with valuable fruits or wood and trees like babul, which shed thorns, or those requiring much care and water for growing are not suitable for road side planting. Those trees which shed their leaves during April and May months are not also suitable. The nature of the road has also be taken into consideration in selecting the type of the trees for planting. Where houses are proposed to be built close to the road or on narrow roads, thick growing large trees are not suitable.

Trees dry up the soil in summer and reduce the volume of the sub grade which may be upto 6 percent, and thus drop the road surface and crack it. In heavy clay soils keep fast growing trees at least 15 metres away from the road.

Do not plant trees of incongruous habits together *i.e.* banyan, babul or cork tree. It is preferable to have mixed planting *i.e.* trees of different varieties, so that the plants flower and bear fruits in different seasons and shedding of leaves takes place in different parts of the year. In storms and gales only some of the varieties are uprooted. Tall graving varies with straight stems may be planted (such as eucalyptus) at some selected spots to serve as effective land marks.

Trees should be planted 1·8 to 3 metres away from the outer edge of the side width (berm) or minimum horizontal clearance should be 6·7 metres for single lane roads increasing clearance by 1 metre for each additional lane width. Rows or opposite side of road should be staggered *i.e.* each tree should come not opposite a tree in the road on the other side but midway between two trees on that side.

The trees must not interfere with the traffic on the road and should have stumps free from branches for a height of 2·4 to 3 metres on high ways and 2·7 to 3·3 metres is streets in towns. If the branches grow horizontally it may be necessary to shorten some of these, but the height of 3·3 metres of the Ist branch must not be exceeded. Prune the trees in such a way that the natural shape of the foilage is retained as far as possible it is called as "*Sath Tarashin*" in local language.

Telegraph, telephone or electric poles should be fixed normally at least 1·5 metres outside the existing road edge and if possible at the road boundaries so as not to interfere with tree growth by loopings.

No tree should be planted by the road side before it is 1·5 m high, most of the failures in road side planting are due to use of too small seedlings or of trees which have not had their roots formed by being transplanted in the nursery.

Where trees have to be cut down for road widening purposes, those at the north and east side should be removed, and those on the south and west retained. The later give most shades during the hotest part of the day. The chief influences exerted by the presence of trees upon the road surface is a reduction of daily or annual ranges of temperature of surface. This definitely prevents licking up of tar and the formation of pot holes and ruts and prolong the life of the surface. Rays of the sun have a deleterious effect both upon tar and bitumen, and the presence of trees along the road reduces that effect. The value of shade, therefore apart from comfort is not in considerable in keeping tarred surface in good condition. For earth and water bound macadum roads trees have a great effects in that by reducing the surface temperature. They minimize the loss of moisture content in the soil in hot weather. Trees have the disadvantage as surfaces hold the dust created by motor traffic.

Spacing of Trees. Suitable spacing for road side trees is from 9 to 15 metre according to the species for road side trees, the average being taken about 80 trees in a kilometer.

The distance apart however should not be less than the diameter of the crown of a fully developed tree, and most of the trees will be about 9·15 metre apart. In dry districts the comparatively slow growing trees can be planted at a larger interval of say 15 metres and fast growing and less valuable trees interpolated so that some shade would be available as soon as possible. Then intermediate trees can be cut down as soon as the more permanent trees attain a height of 3 to 3·2 metres. Special care should be taken for planting trees at road curves so that they do not obstruct the vision. While in growth the lower branches must be cut out to have a higher growth of the tree.

No tree should be planted within 6 metres of any masonry work and this distance should be increased to 24 metres minimum preferably 60 where possible, with trees of spreading roots such as pipal, gular, pilkhan and burgad as the roots of these trees grow into the joints of masonry and damage them.

Suitable spacing of different trees :

Banyan	12 m	Bahera	15 m	Indian cork	6 m
Jamun	12-15 m	Karanji	10 m	Khinni	12 m
Mahua	12-15 m	Mango	11-12 m	Neem	10 m
Pipal	12-17 m	Siris	12 m	Imli (Tamarind)	12 m
Teak	12-15 m				

Numbering of Trees. Scraping the bark for numbering should be done so as not to peel it off. Only the dry scales should be scraped for an array 15 cm × 15 cm at 1·2 metre above the ground level and facing the road. Nos. should be written in black paint and the back ground should preferably be white.

Canal side Plantation. On canal service road this plantation is done generally on the same basis as on roads.

In canals the plantation is done in cutting portion beyond the side drain on the spots. No plantation is generally done in the filling reaches as the roots may be a cause of leakage after they are rooted.

In filling reaches generally grass planting is done to save the embankment from rain torrents.

In portions where errosion is possible willow (Majnoo) plantation is done.

Protection of the Plantation. (1) One gardener is sufficient for a length of 4-5 km. according to the availability of water and age of plants.

(2) Spraying of dilute mixture of lime water and blue vitrial (copper sulphate or neela thotha) solution or tobacco solution destroy most of the pests. 50 gm of copper sulphate is dissolved in 1 litre of boiling water. 4 litres of lime water is added afterwards at the time of spraying. Boil 100 gm of dry tobacco leaves in a litre of water for about an hour. Dissolve in the 25 gms hard soap (sun light) add 6 litres of cold water for use.

(3) Parasite plants should be completely removed root and all and destroyed, preferably the branch effected by parasite should be cut off. The cut should be done by a saw and not by axe.

(4) The cuts made by saw or knife during prunning must be preferrred and must be protected from moisture. Putting a ring of white wash around the branch to be cut is a good plan.

(5) The tree which is in growth, newly grown lower branches should be cut off so that the higher branches may grow easily as the lower branches take the nourishment before reaching to the higher branches.

(6) Cavities formed during prunning due to any carelessness should be filled as follows :

(*a*) Clean the dead wood from the cavity by scrapping and fill it with concrete 1 : 2 : 4 after cleaning with potassium permanganate solution.

(7) Stems of the big trees should be coal tarred upto 60 cm height at every alternate year.

(8) The trees should be prunned every year. The best period for prunning is end of February, just before the leaves appear and the sap begins to rise when growth is least active.

(9) **Lopping.** Lopping is done to train the tree to develop a certain shape during its growth ; extra branches are removed. The proper time for lopping is either September or February.

(10) **Weeding.** The excessive growth of grass around young plants should be removed by roots and not merely cut as that is very injurious to the growth of plant.

(11) **Felling of trees.** When the trees matured, it should be cut. A hollow should be dug around the base, and the trunk cut through as low as possible. The hollow then filled up to cover the roots.

Some trees which are planted on road side.

(1) **Mango (Aam).** A fruity and shady tree, with branches. The wood is used as timber in buildings.

(2) **Jamun (Jamboo).** A fruity and shady tree with branches. The wood is used in buildings as timber.

(3) **Neem.** A timber and shady tree having small fruits which can be used in medicines.

(4) **Eucalyptus.** A long trunk tree without or short branches. Used as ballies in scaffolding work.

(5) **Shisham.** A shady tree with branches. Used as a timber in building works.

(6) **Kikar or Babool.** A thorny unshading tree. Used as a fuel wood.

(7) **Tun.** A handsome shady tree. The wood is light and smooth ground, used in furniture work.

(8) **Chir.** A hilly tree. Wood used as a timber.

(9) **Deodar.** A hilly tree, strong wood used as timber.

(10) **Teak, or Sagaun.** A good timber tree. Used in buildings, doors and used in furniture.

(11) **Tamarind (Imli).** A shady tree. Its heart wood is very hard. It is sound fruits.

(12) **Sumbal or saimal.** A high tree with beautiful flowers. Its wood is used in match factories.

(13) **Siris.** A flowery tree with hard timber.

(14) **Pipal.** A good shady tree, with small fruits. It has a rough timber and is used in the an important buildings.

Plantation methods. The following are the plantation methods of trees :

(*a*) By seeds (*b*) Transplantation

(*a*) Some trees are sowed by seeds in the spot just as kikar, mango and jamun etc.

(*b*) A variety of trees are sowed in the nursery and then transplanted to the desired spots. The plant is dug with some earth with its roots and then planted at a desired spot.

(*c*) Some plants are sowed in polyethelene bags and when they are about a foot high is transplanted at the desired spots. The polyethylene bag is removed before planting at a new spot. Eucalyptus is such type of variety.

Note : The trees are protected by animals etc. by providing tree guard made of honey combed bricks or steel strips upto the time till these are matured.

Table 15·63. Sectional area of typical sections of breast walls (Area = 0·06 + $S^2/12$)

Slant height in m	*Area in sq. m.*	*Slant height in m*	*Area in sq. m*	*Slant height in m*	*Area in sq. m*
0·50	0·32	3·0	2·55	5·50	5·82
0·60	0·39	3·10	2·66	5·60	5·97
0·70	0·46	3·20	2·77	5·70	6·13
0·80	0·53	3·30	2·80	5·80	6·28

Table contd...

Table contd...

Slant height in m	*Area in sq. m.*	*Slant height in m*	*Area in sq. m*	*Slant height in m*	*Area in sq. m*
0·90	0·61	3·40	3·00	5·90	6·44
1·00	0·68	3·50	3·12	6·00	6·60
1·10	0·76	3·60	3·24	6·10	6·76
1·20	0·84	3·70	3·36	6·20	6·92
1·30	0·92	3·80	3·48	6·30	7·09
1·40	1·00	3·90	3·61	6·40	7·25
1·50	1·09	4·00	3·73	6·50	7·42
1·60	1·16	4·10	3·86	6·60	7·59
1·70	1·26	4·20	3·99	6·70	7·76
1·80	1·35	4·30	4·12	6·80	7·93
1·90	1·44	4·40	4·25	6·90	8·11
2·00	1·53	4·50	4·39	7·00	8·28
2·10	1·63	4·60	4·52	7·10	8·46
2·20	1·72	4·70	4·66	7·20	8·64
2·30	1·82	4·80	4·80	7·30	8·82
2·40	1·92	4·90	4·94	7·40	9·00
2·50	2·02	5·00	5·08	7·50	9·19
2·60	2·12	5·10	5·23	7·60	9·37
2·70	2·22	5·20	5·37	7·70	9·36
2·80	2·33	5·30	5·52	7·80	9·75
2·90	2·44	5·40	5·67	7·90	9·94
				8·00	10·13

15·11·1. Curves

Extra width of road on curve

Rad. of curve (M)	*Extra width (M)*
14-20	1·50
20-30	1·20
30-60	0·90
60-150	0·60
above 150	Nil

Rad. of 8 m wide roads

Rad. of curve in m	*Convex*	*Concave*
15	20·50	9·50
20	25·50	10·50
25	30·20	19·86
30	35·20	24·80
40	40·90	35·10
50	54·90	45·10
70	74·60	65·40

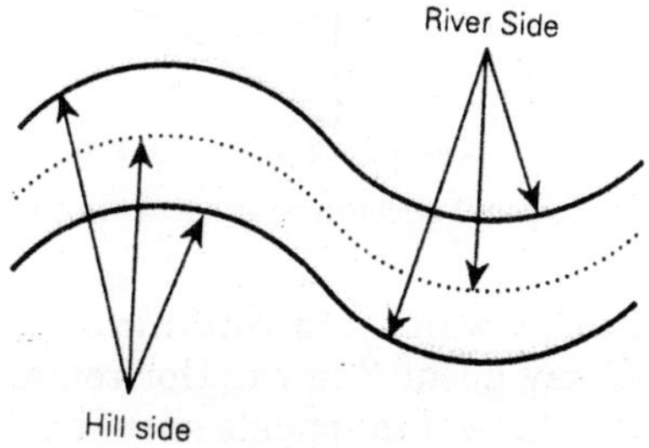

Fig. 15·59.

15·12. Hill Roads

15·12·1. (Also refer article 15·10·2 and table 15·2)

Area of retaining walls for a typical section

Table 15·64. Retaining walls and breast walls.

Top width 0·6 M, front batter 1 : 3 ; Area = 0·6325 S + $\frac{S^2}{6}$ + 0·06, S = Slant height back vertical.

Slant height (m)	*Base width (m)*	*Area in sq. metre*			*Total area in sq. m*
		0·63255	*$S^2/6$*	*0·06*	
0·5	0·8	0·3160	0·041	0·06	0·417
1·0	0·96	0·6325	0·167	0·06	0·859
1·5	1·13	0·949	0·375	0·06	1·384
2·0	1·29	1·265	0·666	0·06	1·491
2·5	1·46	1·581	1·041	0·06	2·682
3·0	1·63	1·898	1·500	0·06	3·458
3·5	1·80	2·214	2·041	0·06	4·315
4·0	1·96	2·530	2·666	0·06	5·259
4·5	2·13	2·846	3·375	0·06	6·281
5·0	2·30	3·162	4·266	0·06	7·388
5·5	2·47	3·479	5·041	0·06	8·580
6·0	2·63	3·795	6·000	0·06	9·859
6·5	2·80	4·111	7·041	0·06	12·654
7·0	2·97	4·428	8·166	0·06	12·654
7·5	3·14	4·744	9·375	0·06	14·179
8·0	3·30	5·060	10·656	0·06	15·386
8·5	3·47	5·376	12·041	0·06	17·477
9·0	3·64	5·693	13·500	0·06	19·253
9·5	3·81	6·009	14·041	0·06	21·110
10·0	3·97	6·325	16·666	0·06	23·051

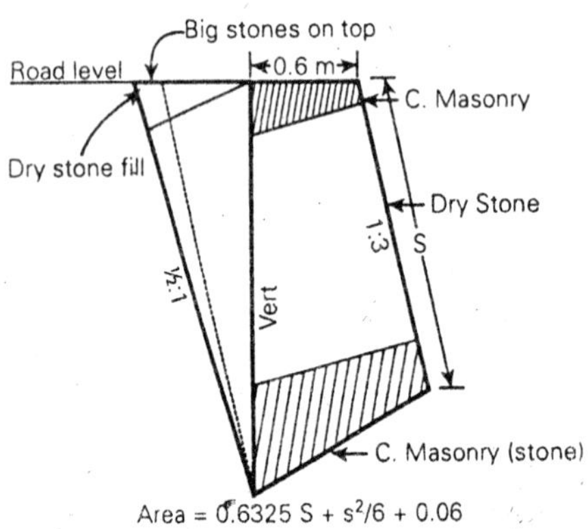

(*a*) Typical section of a retaining wall

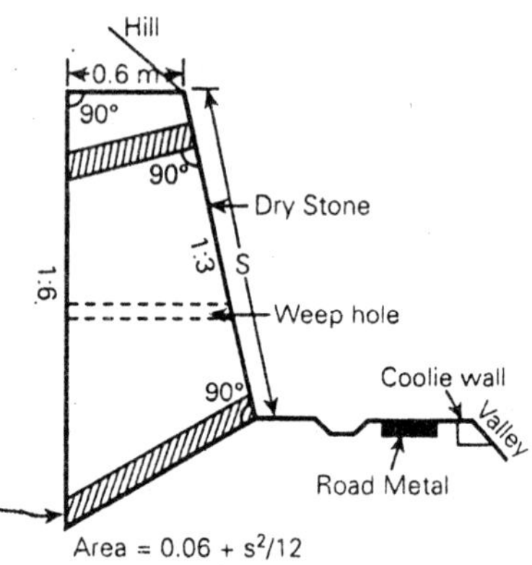

(*b*) Typical section of a breast wall.

Fig. 15·60.

Breast walls and retaining walls are provided with masonry grid panels at regular interval of say about 3 m c/c. Horizontal panel walls is also provided in high walls. The interval between two horizontal panels should not be more than 3 m c/c. The thick width of the panel walls may be 60 m having a sec. equal to that of the wall.

Coolic walls. These are small retaining walls of dry stones at the edge of a hill road.

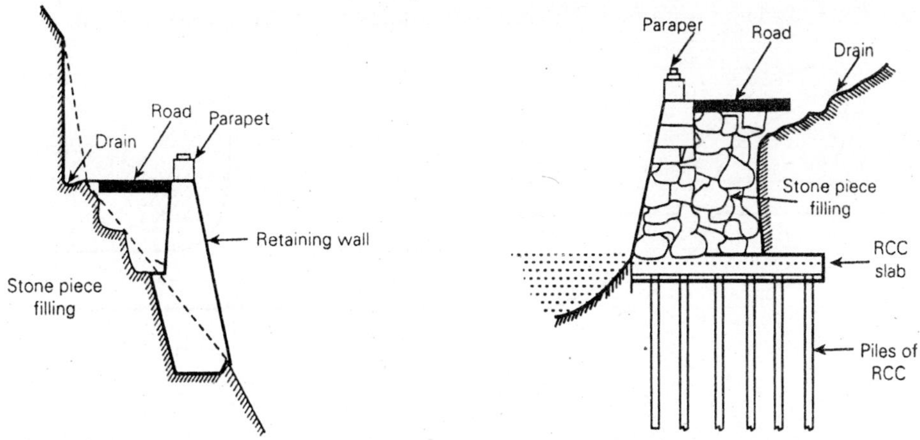

(*a*) Retaining wall on vertical rock (*b*) Retaining wall on piles

Fig. 15·61.

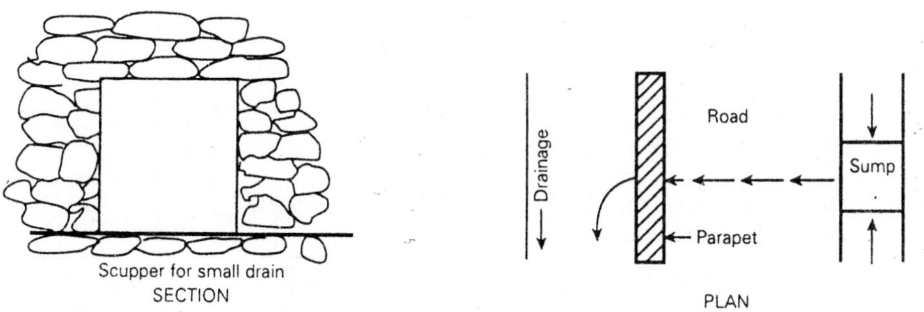

Fig. 15·62.

15·13. Traffic Control

Road crossings. (1) The radius of the kerb line at the junction should be 11 m.

(2) Road crossing at an acute angle are crossed at right angles by giving curves. The minimum angle is 50° and in any obligatory case not less than 30°.

Angle of inter-section	*Rad. for cars upto 6 m length (m)*	*Rad. for bus or truck (m)*
90	10-12	17·2
105	12	20
120	15	23
135	20	30
150	40	50

T-Junctions or Bifurcations

Speed km/hr.	25	32	40	50	56	60	80
Sight distance (m)	20	30	40	50	70	80	120

Rotary. Circular rotaries are provided at right angle or radial crossings, while elliptical are provided at acute angle crossing. According to IRC design speed of vehicles is about 40 km/hr.

Normally for 30 metre diameter central island a speed of 25 km/hr and for 30 m diameter a speed of 40 km per hour can be maintained. The minimum diameter of the island is 20 m.

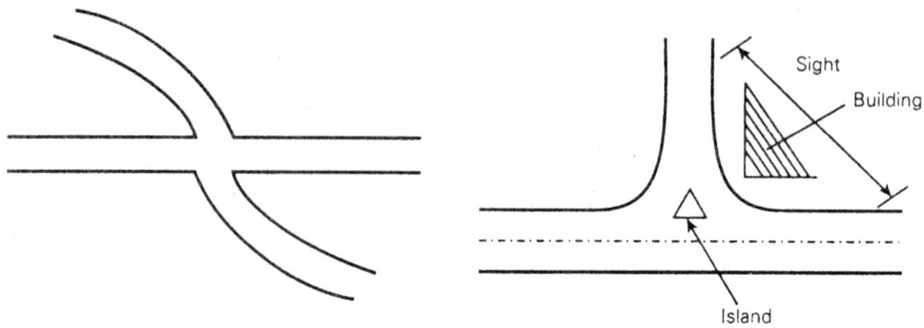

Fig. 15·63. Acute angle crossing

The width of road around the island must be more than 1/4 of the total width of all the radial roads or widest road plus one lane which ever is more. The width of carriage way at rotary exit and entrance should be a bit more than normal of a radial road. The weaving length must be three times the widest limb of the round about subject to minimum of 45 m.

A bit before the entrance to the traffic **guide island** refuge or pedestrian islands are provided where the pedestrians can cross the road. Signal posts are provided on the islands which can be seen by the users for their guidance.

Radius of kerb at entry should be 12 and at exit 23 m. According to IRC radius at entry should be minimum to the radius of the island and at exit 1½ times to that at entry subject to minimum of 33 m for 30 km and 50 for 40 km/hr. speed. The height of the kerb should be 10 cm to 15 cm above road level painted in black and white strips.

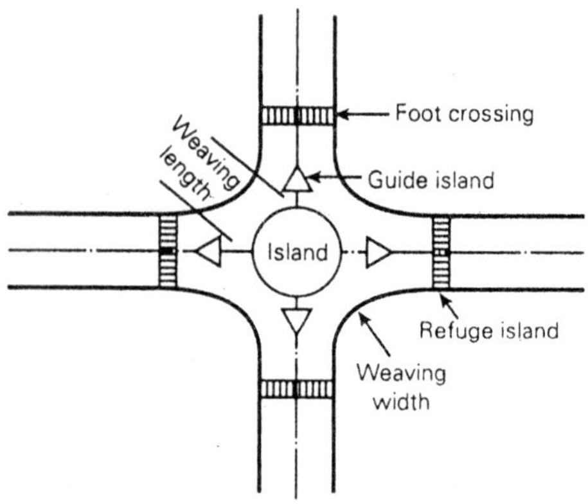

Fig. 15·64. Rotary

15·14. Use of Fly ash and steel plant slag in road work

15·14·1. Use of steel plant slags in road construction and cement. Iron and steel industry gives rise to colossal amounts of byproducts and waste materials such as aircooled slag, granulated slag, fly ash and flue dust. These materials pose serious problems of disposal and cause environmental pollution. One sector where these wastes can be utilised in bulk is road construction. The mixes of blast furnace slag, steel slag and granulated slag not only possess sufficiently high strength but are durable also and hence can be used in base or sub-base course of road pavement.

15·14·2. Physical and Chemical properties of slags. Slag may take on several forms, according to the various means of cooling to which it is subjected after having the blast furnace *e.g.* (*a*) It may be left to cool slowly and in open air, giving a crystallised slag suitable for crushing known as "air cooled slag".

(*b*) It may be subjected to sudden cooling by using water or air, giving a vitrified slag which in the 1st case is known as granulated slag and in the 2nd case as **pelletised slag.**

(*c*) It may be water cooled under certain conditions where the steam produced gives rise to what is known as **"expanded slag"**.

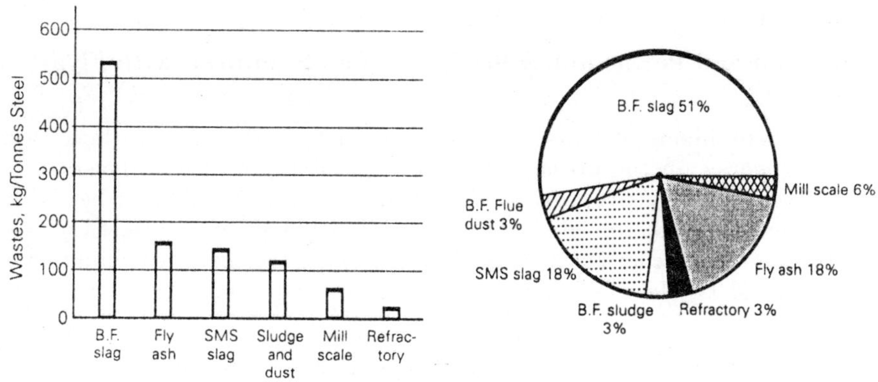

Fig. 15·65.

Air cooled slag. Air cooled blast furnace slag (commonly known as BF Slag) is produced by putting the molten slag into a pit where it is allowed to cool slowly in open air. Crystallisation takes place resulting in material like a fine granulated igneous rock. Because of its similarity to igneous rocks, it has found extensive use as concrete aggregate, road surfacing stone and road base course material. In crystalline blast furnace slag the principle mineralogical phase lies in the series from akermanite ($2CaOMgO_2SiO_2$) to gehlenite ($2CaO.Al_2O_3$-SiO_2). When slags have a high lime content they may contain dicalcium silicate ($2CaOSiO_2$). This inclusion can cause disruption of the slag through volume increase. If sulphur is present in a reactive leachable form mainly as calcium sulphide, problems may also occur.

Granulated slag. Granulated blast furnace slag (GBFS) is produced when the molten slag in the temperature range of 1250°C and 1500°C from the blast furnace is chilled rapidly by a water jet resulting in vesicular, vitreous material of predominantly coarse sand like particles. GBFS has an ability to hydrate in the presence of water to move stable compounds. It therefore seems to have a great potential for use as a binder for stabilisation of road bases and sub bases. For the use in the manufacturing of slag cement, ground granulated slag (GGS) is produced by finely grinding the granulated slag. To produce GGS from slag it is necessary to dry the material and finely grind it to around 370 m^2/kg fineness. This tends to be slightly greater than the fineness of cement. In this form GGS can replace substantial quantities of cement in a concrete mix 25-50% by weight of cement is replaced by Blast furnace slag. The GGS is activated by the alkalies [$Ca(OH_2)$] and sulphates ($CaSO_4$) in cement. However the alkalies and sulphur also contribute to the reaction products, essentially the same as in the hardening process of portland cement. Apart from economic benefit, GGS cement has other desirable properties such as low heat of hydration. Heat generated during hydration of GGS mixed cement concrete is low enough to be considered as a low heat cement.

Steel making slag. Steel making slag (SMS) is produced during the manufacture of steel. To produce steel it is necessary to further refine molten iron to remove carbon and make additions of materials such as manganese, silicon, chrome and tatanium. This refinement stage imparts the properties such as strength, hardness, toughness and flexural strength. The slag produced from steel making is quite different from blast furnace slag. SMS slag has a higher density with more uncombined free lime (upto 4%). This free lime hydrates in the presence of moisture and causes volume instability. It is for this reason that some countries specify weathering of the material. However, the free lime content of steel slag has a potential for activation of granulated slag. In Europe and Australia, SMS slag has been combined with air cooled BF Slag and GBFS to produce commercially a stabilised mixture for use in road base and sub base. Not dissimilar in appearance to an igneous rock, steel slag chemical compositions vary greatly but generally they have a higher CaO/SiO_2 proporption than B.F. Slag.

15·14·3. Compaction and Permeability Study of a Soil Stabilised with Flyash, Lime and Na_2CO_3.

The disposal problems of flyash can be reduced by utilising it in large quantities in various engineering works. In the present study, the possibility of use of flyash to improve the compaction and permeability properties of a locally available soil has been investigated experimentally. Apart from this, the effect of lime as stabilising agent and Na_2CO_3 as an additive, when added to the soil-flyash combination has also been investigated. A combination of 70% soil, 28% flyash, 1% lime and 1% Na_2CO_3 has been found to give best results against the optimum use of flyash in soil.

Introduction. The alarming magnitude of flyash, a by-product of combustion of pulverized coal in boilers of thermal power plants, and its uncontrolled disposal, has attracted wide attention. According to an estimate a 200 MW capacity generation unit produces $2t$ of flyash every minute requiring 50,000 acres of precious land for disposal during the life span of 30 years, making its management is an herculean task. In addition, deteriorating quality of coal as well as scarcity of available disposal sites will further aggravate the situation.

A review of the present status of flyash utilisation indicates that its use in large quantities in civil engineering industry has not been satisfactory, even though many applications have been reported, as compared to developed countries where its utilisation has reached a level of 25% or more. Considering the problems faced by the community, innovative use and safe disposal of the flyash has become the need of the hour so that instead of a waste product, the flyash could considered as a useable by-product.

One way of disposing flyash is to use it for soil stabilisation. With the large availability of flyash at low cost and its stabilisation properties in the presence of lime, it is expected that a combination of flyash, lime and an additive with sodium element, can stabilise and reduce the permeability of local soil. This will be a potential replacement for clay which has already been recommended as permeability reduction material, but at large cost.

15·14·4. Laboratory Investigation

Disturbed samples of locally available soil were collected from Sutlej river near Kandror village, District Bilaspur (HP). The flyash was transported from Guru Nanak Dev Thermal Power Plant, Bhatinda (Punjab). In the first phase, the grain size distribution and Atterberg limits of the soil and flyash were determined as per standard IS code procedure.

In the second phase, Proctor compaction tests were conducted based on IS 2720 (Part VII)—1986 using the standard Proctor tests, on the base material, *i.e.*, soil, as well as on the mixture of soil with different proportion of flyash, lime and Na_2CO_3. For each test on the mixture, care was taken to thoroughly mix the different materials in dry state prior to the addition of water, so as to ensure uniform distribution of the additional material in the matrix of the base material. Alongwith the compaction tests, as compacted saturated samples in the Proctor mould were then taken for permeability tests using variable head permeameters without disturbing the sample. Each sample was subjected to saturation by first keeping overnight in water and the applying back pressure to remove any entrapped air before the start of the experiments. For each series of soil and/or mixture, tests were conducted for at least five moisture contents, and a minimum of three tests were conducted for each moisture content so as to ensure the repeatability of the results.

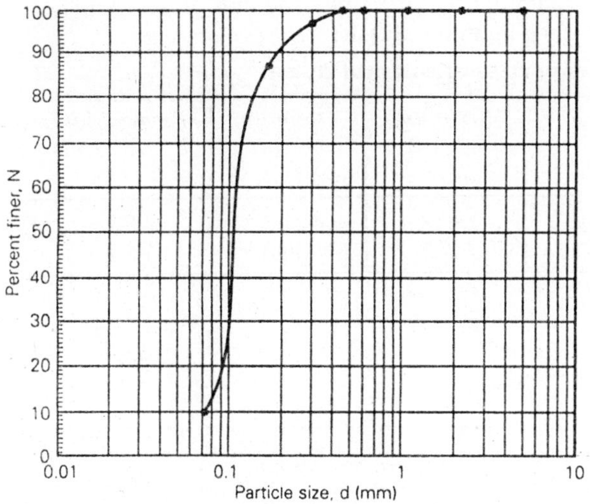

(a) Particle size distribution (Kandror soil).

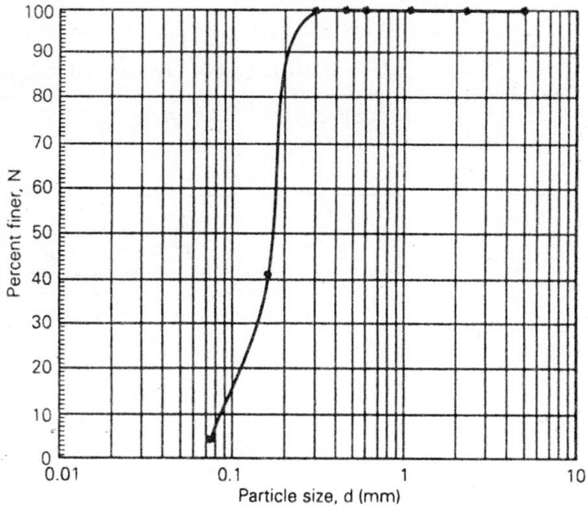

(b) Particle size distribution (Bhatinda flyash).

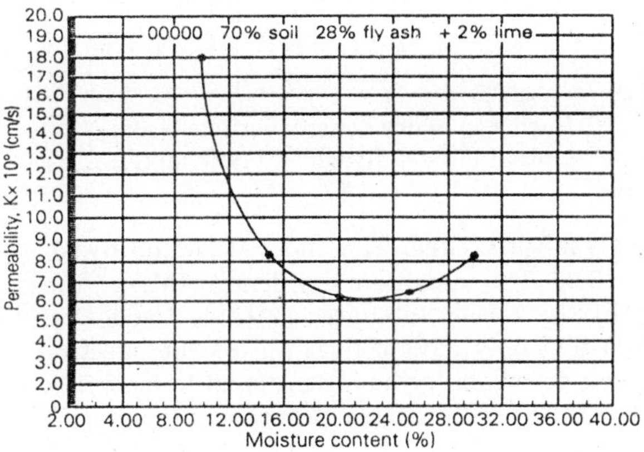

(c) Variation of permeability with moisture content for soil, flyash and lime mixture.

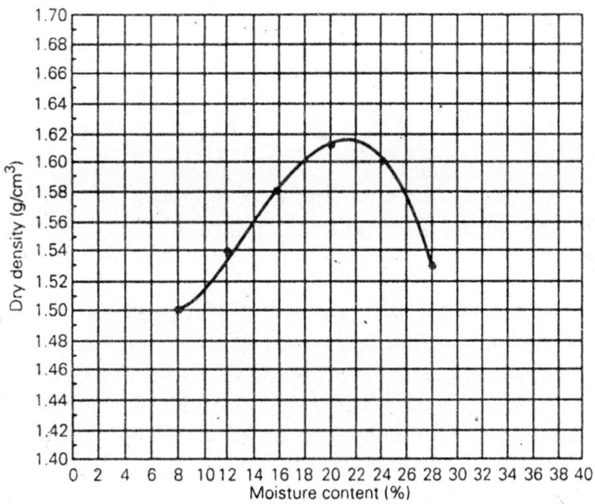

(d) Variation of dry density with moisture content for soil.

Fig. 15·66.

Results and Discussions. The grain size distribution curves of the soil and flyash have been plotted in Fig. 15·66 (*a* & *b*) while the Atterberg's limits alongwith the compaction characteristics and permeability of the same are given in Table 15·65. The permeability of soil, flyash or any other combination was obtained by plotting permeability against moisture content as shown in typical plot (Fig. 15·66 (*c*)) and then noting the permeability against the optimum moisture content, which is obtained from the corresponding plot between dry density and moisture content as shown in a typical plot in Fig. 15·66 (*d*). It can be noted from the Figs. 15·66 (*a* & *b*) and the Table 15·66 that the locally available soil is predominantly very fine sand and plastic while on the other hand flyash is predominantly fine, sand-sized and non-plastic.

Table 15·65. Geotechnical properties of soil and flyash

Material	*Specific gravity*	*Liquid limit, %*	*Plastic limit, %*	*Maximum dry density, g/cm³*	*Optimum moisture content, %*	*Permeability k × 10⁵, cm/s*
Soil	3·00	33·3	30	1·618	21·5	3·2
Flyash	2·14	52·4	non plastic	1·222	36·0	5·4

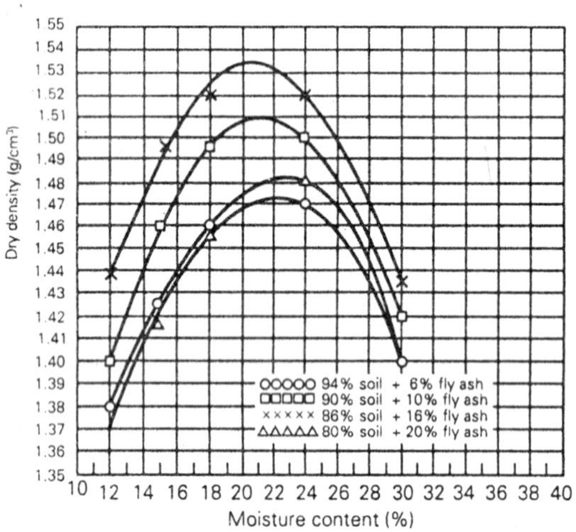

(*e*) Variation of dry density with moisture content for soil and flyash mixture.

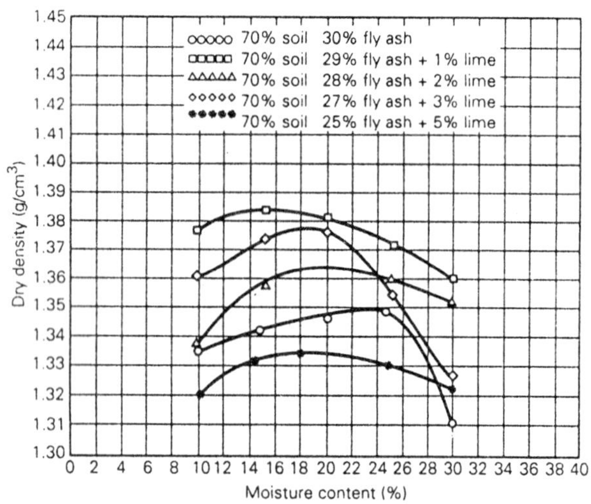

(*f*) Variation of dry density with moisture content for soil, flyash and lime mixture.

Fig. 15·66.

15·14·6. Engineering Properties of Soil-flyash Mixture. The effect of adding flyash on the compaction behaviour of soil is shown in Fig. 15·66. The maximum dry density (MDD), the optimum moisture content (OMC) and the permeability have been tabulated in Table 15·66. One can note from the Table 15·66 and the Fig. 15·66 (*e*) that only 15% of flyash gives the effective results with the combination of soil. The corresponding permeability has been found to be 0·42 × 10^{-5} cm/s as against the permeability of soil (3·2 × 10^{-5}) showing a decrease, though not appreciable, in the permeability of the mixture.

Table 15·66. Compaction and Permeability data of present study

S. No.	*Mix Designation*	*Maximum dry density, g/cm³*	*Optimum moisture, %*	*Permeability k × 10⁵, cm/s*
1.	94% soil + 6% flyash	1·475	22·0	1·600
2.	90% soil + 10% flyash	1·509	21·5	0·780
3.	85% soil + 15% flyash	1·532	20·5	0·420

Table contd...

Table contd...

S. No.	Mix Designation	Maximum dry density, γ_d, g/cm^3	Optimum moisture, %	Permeability $k \times 10^5$, cm/s
4.	80% soil + 20% flyash	1·482	23·1	1·400
5.	70% soil + 30% flyash	1·385	24·5	6·100
6.	70% soil + 29% flyash + 1% lime	1·385	16·0	0·340
7.	70% soil + 28% flyash + 2% lime	1·367	20·0	0·610
8.	70% soil + 27% flyash + 3% lime	1·378	18·0	1·340
9.	70% soil + 25% flyash + 5% lime	1·335	19·5	2·100
10.	70% soil + 29·5% flyash + 0·5% Na_2CO_3	1·395	20·0	1·070
11.	70% soil + 29% flyash + 1% Na_2CO_3	1·442	17·5	0·250
12.	70% soil + 28% flyash + 2% Na_2CO_3	1·405	19·0	0·590
13.	70% soil + 28·5% flyash + 1% lime + 0·5% Na_2CO_3	1·420	19·0	0·915
14.	70% soil + 28% flyash + 1% lime + 1% Na_2CO_3	1·502	17·5	0·218
15.	70% soil + 27% flyash + 1% lime + 2% Na_2CO_3	1·430	18·0	0·512

It has already been established[6, 7] that increase in flyash percentage to fine soils reduces the unit weight, compressive strength and the maximum dry density. Therefore, to increase the use of flyash greater than 15%, it was thought to add certain stabilising agents such as lime and/or adding some additives like Na_2CO_3 to the soil-flyash mixture.

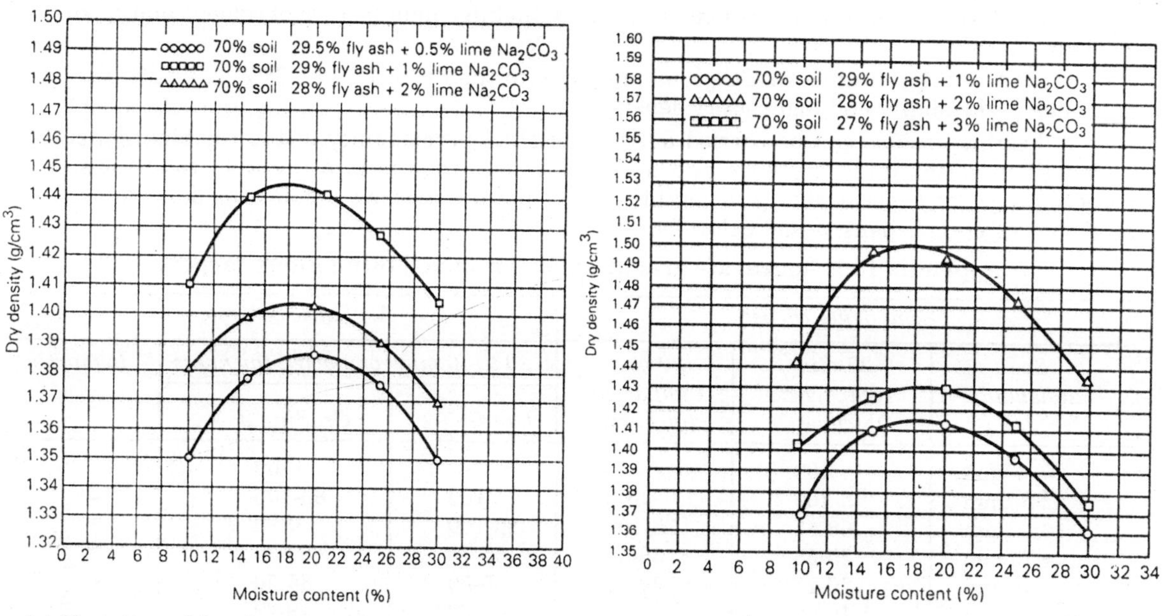

(*g*) Variation of dry density with moisture content for soil, flyash and Na_2CO_3 mixture.

(*h*) Variation of dry density with moisture content for soil, flyash, lime and Na_2CO_3 mixture

Fig. 15·66.

15·14·5. Effect of Addition of Lime on Soil-flyash Mixture. By keeping the percentage of flyash and stabilising agent as 30% the usual tests were conducted on different combinations of soil-flyash-lime and are given in Fig. 15·66 (*f*) and Table 15·66. The stabilising agent used here is locally available hydrated lime. It can be seen that a combination of 70% soil, 29% flyash and 1% lime gives the maximum dry density and the minimum permeability. The permeability of the combination ($3{\cdot}4 \times 10^{-6}$) is nearly half the permeability of 70% soil and 30% flyash mixture.

Effect of Addition of Na_2CO_3 on Soil-flyash Mixture

Literature shows that the addition of stabilising agent alone will not fulfill the strength requirement. As such certain additives like Na_2CO_3 or gypsum may improve the strength and permeability characteristics. Sodium carbonate in anhydrous form was used in the present study. Fig. 15·66 (*g*) and Table 15·66 also shows the results of the usual tests in case of soil, flyash and Na_2CO_3 combination keeping the percentage of flyash and additives as 30%. The results show a further decrease in permeability for the combination of 70% soil, 29% flyash and 1% Na_2CO_3 which is an improvement over the soil-flyash-lime combination.

Effect of Addition of Na_2CO_3 on Soil-flyash-lime Mixture

Table 15·66 also shows the test results for mixture of soil, flyash lime and Na_2CO_3 obtained from Fig. 15·66 (*h*). From this it is noted that a combination of 70% soil, 28% flyash, 1% lime and 1% Na_2CO_3 shows a further reduction in the permeability, though not appreciable, as compared to soil-flyash-Na_2CO_3 combination and an appreciable increase in the maximum dry density.

Conclusions :

(1) It is possible to reduce the permeability of a locally available soil by using flyash and adding certain stabilising agents like lime and additives like Na_2CO_3.

(2) In the soil-flyash mix, flyash content beyond 15% does not reduce the permeability nor improve the dry density.

(3) Addition of lime to the soil-flyash mix allows more reduction in the permeability as it provides the additional strength and stabilising effect to the soil-flyash mixture.

(4) Fly ash is used in roads embankments minefills, manufacture of cement and raising of low lying lands.

(5) A soil-flyash-lime-Na_2CO_3 combination with the ratio of 70% : 28% : 1% : 1% gives the minimum permeability and highest dry density.

Further studies can be carried out to check the permeability of the combination stated under different confining pressure and normal stresses to simulate the field conditions. The reduced range of the permeability so obtained may be useful in some engineering applications like protective layer on expansive soil below foundation.

Appendix 15·1. Aggregate gradation for premixed bituminous carpets.

	Semi dense carpets		*Asphaltic concrete*		
Sieve designation	*25 mm compacted thickness*	*20 mm compacted thickness*	*20 to 40 mm compacted thickness*		*Remarks*
			Grading-1	*Grading-2*	
20 mm	100	—	—	100	*% by wt. passing the sieve*
12·5 mm	75-100	100	100	80-100	
10 mm	60-85	75-100	80-100	70-90	
4·75 mm	35-55	36-55	55-75	50-30	
2·36 mm	20-25	20-15	35-50	35-50	
600 micron	10-22	10-22	18-29	18-29	
300 micron	6-10	6-16	13-23	12-23	
150 micron	4-12	4-12	18-16	8-16	
75 micron	2-8	2-8	4-10	4-10	
Binder content	5·5% wt. of the total mix		7 to 7·5% by wt. of the total mix		

—The binder considered is straight run bitumen of a suitable grade.

—These mixes are suitable as wearing courses.

—Asphaltic conc. as wearing course is of single layer 25 to 50 mm thick. For compacted layer thickness of 25 to 40 mm any of the two gradings could be used, but for layer thickness of 40-50 mm only grading no. 2 may be used.

—Thickness need filter.

Appendix 15·2.

I. Surface painting, surface dressing or surface roads.

Quantity of materials required % m² of road surface

Binder				*Stone chippings*		
Bitumen kg	*Cut back kg*	*Tar kg*	*Emulsion kg*	*Nominal size mm*	*Quality cu.m*	
Single coat work Light density rubber tyre traffic on water bound macadum						
2·25	—	—	—	12	1·65	
170-200	200-220	120-225	225	12	1·42-1·50	
Simultaneous two coats work Medium density ruber tyred traffic on water bound macadam						
170-200	200-200	200-225	—	12	1·40-1·50	Ist coat
—	—	—	200	12	1·35	
100-120	120-150	120-150	100-130	10-6	0·90-1·00	2nd coat
Repairing old painted surfaces-subsequent or renewal coat						
100-120	100-120	120-170	—	10-6	0·90-1·10	
—	—	—	100-125	6-3	0·80-0·90	

Note : (1) Add 2·5% for wastage of binder and 5% wastage of aggregate.

(2) The binders should be fluid enough after spraying on the road to wet thoroughly both the surface and the cover aggregate when the later is spread. Too hard a grade of bitumen will not maintain the necessary fluidity.

(3) Less tar is required for dry climates.

(4) Lesser quantities of binders and smaller sizes of aggregates are for dense and compact surfaces and for lighter traffic.

(5) If the base is to be treated consists of a porous surface, a primer should be employed prior to surface painting.

II. Premixed bituminous close-textured (dense) carpets.

Aggregate required % m² of road surface

Nominal size of aggregate (mm)	*Aggregate in cu. metres for consolidated thickness of carpet in cu.m.*													
	2·5	*6*	*5*	*4*	*2·5*	*4*								
50	4·38						For light intensity traffic such as garden paths and drives. Also for providing a thin wearing course over existing cement concrete roads (also called bituminous streets).							
40	2·29	3·48												
25		2·32	2·88											
20			1·92	4·80	2·28									
—														
12					1·52	3·60	2·10	1·56	1·5	0·99				
10							0·90	1·04	—	0·66	1·80	1·95		
6											0·60		2·25	
Medium coarse sand	3·65	2·90	2·40	2·40	1·90	1·80	0·95	2·50	1·65	0·65	0·60	0·90	0·30	1·95

As far as practicable surface painting shall be carried out only when the atmosphere temperature in shade is 16°C or above.

Appendix 15·3.
Aggregate gradation for 75 mm and 50 mm compacted thickness of Bituminous Macadam(premix)-IRC

Sieve Designation mm	*75 compacted thickness*		*50 mm compacted thickness*		*Remarks*
	percent by wt. passing the sieve				
	Grade A	*Grade B*	*Grade A*	*Grade B*	
63	100				The binder (straight run bitumen) shall be 3·5 and 4·0% by weight of the total mix for aggregate grading no. A and B respectively. The optimum binder content is based on the surface area of the aggregate.
50	90-100		100		
40	35-65	100	90-100		
25	20-40	70-100	50-80	100	
20	—	50-80	—	70-100	
12·5	5·20	—	10-30	—	
10	—	—	—	35-60	
4·75	—	10-30	—	15-35	
2·36	—	5-20	—	5-20	
7·5 μ	0·5	0-4	0-5	0-4	

Aggregate gradation for mix seal surfacing 20 mm thick premix dense carpet

Sieve designation	*Percentage by weight passing the sieve*	
(mm)	*Type-A*	*Type-B*
12·5	—	100
10	100	70-100
4·75	40-85	90-100
2·36	5-20	5-20
75 m	0-4	0-4

Quantity of Aggregate and Binders % m^2

Aggregate	2·7 m^3	2·7 m^3
Binder	220 kg	190 kg

Binder for premixing

(*a*) Using hot bitumen/cut back
50 to 56 kg/m^3 of aggregate 12 mm size and above
56 to 64 kg/m^3 of aggregate 10 mm size
115 kg/m^3 for stone grit
128 kg/m^3 for coarse sand

(*b*) Using tar
66 to 80 kg/m^3 for aggregate
118 kg/m^3 for coarse sand

(*c*) Using cold emulsions
96 kg/m^3 for stone grit

Note : The size of aggregate given are of nominal size according to IRC classification.

The quantities given are only approximate for estimating purpose (which in fact are very variable and depend upon many factors).

5% should be added to the aggregate and 2·5% to the binder for wastage.

Table 15·67. Recommended Values of Camber for Different Types of Road Surfaces.

Sl. No.	*Types of Road Surface*	*Range of Camber in areas of rainfall range*	
		Heavy	*Light*
1.	Cement concrete and high type bituminous surace	1 in 50 (2·0%)	1 in 60 (1·70%)
2.	Thin bituminous surface	1 in 40 (2·50%)	1 in 50 (2·0%)
3.	Water bound macadam and gravel pavement	1 in 33 (3·0%)	1 in 40 (2·5%)
4.	Earth	1 in 25 (4·0%)	1 in 33 (3·0%)

Table 15·68. Width of Carriageway.

S. No.	*Class of Road*	*Width of carriageway*
1.	Single lane	3·75 m
2.	Two lane without raised kerbs	7·00 m
3.	Two lane with raised kerbs	7·50 m
4.	Intermediate carriageway (except on important road)	5·50 m
5.	Multilane-Pavements	3·50 m per lane

Table 15·69. Width of Roadway of Various Classes of Roads

S. No.	*Road classification*	*Roadway width (m) at*	
		Plain and Rolling terrain	*Maintainous and steep terrain*
1.	National and State Highway		
	(*a*) Single lane	12·0	6·25
	(*b*) Two lanes	12·0	8·80
2.	Major District Roads		
	(*a*) Single lane	9·0	4·75
	(*b*) Two lanes	9·0	—
3.	Other District Roads		
	(*a*) Single lane	7·50	4·75
	(*b*) Two lanes	9·0	—
4.	Village roads-single lane	7·50	4·00

Table 15·70. Longitudinal coefficient of Friction.

S. No.	*Speed (kmph)*	*Longitudinal coefficient of Friction, f*
1.	20 to 30	0·40
2.	40	0·38
3.	50	0·37
4.	60	0·36
5.	65	0·36
6.	80	0·35
7.	100	0·35

Table 15·71. Type of Terrain and Cross, Slope of Country

S. No.	*Terrain classification*	*Cross slope of the country (f)*
1.	Plain	0 to 10
2.	Rolling	10 to 25
3.	Mountainous	25 to 60
4.	Steep	greater than 60

Table 15·72. Design speed on Rural Highways

S. No.	*Road Classification*	*Design Speed (kmph) for various terrains*							
		Plain		*Rolling*		*Mountainous*		*Steep*	
		Rolling	*Min.*	*Rolling*	*Min.*	*Rolling*	*Min.*	*Rolling*	*Min.*
1.	National and state Highway	100	80	80	65	50	40	40	30
2.	Major District Roads	80	65	65	50	40	30	30	20
3.	Other District Roads	65	50	50	40	30	25	25	20
4.	Village Roads	50	40	40	35	25	20	25	20

Table 15·73. Design Speed for Different Classes of Urban Roads.

S. No.	*Type of Road*	*Design Speed (kmph)*
1.	Arterial	80
2.	Sub-Arterial	60
3.	Collector Road	50
4.	Local street	30

Table 15·74. Gradients for Roads in Different Terrains

S. No.	*Terrain*	*Rulling*	*Limiting*	*Exceptional*
1.	Plain or polling	3·3%	5%	6·70%
2.	Mountanious terrain, and steep terrain having elevation more than 3000 m above mean sea level	5·0% (1 in 20)	6% (1 in 16·70)	7% (1 in 14·30)
3.	Steep terrain upto 3000 m above mean sea level	6% (1 in 16·70)	7% (1 in 14·30)	8% (1 in 12·70)

Table 15·75. Length of Transition Curve

S. No.	*Criteria for length of transition curve*	*Length of Transition curve (m)*
1.	Based upon actual superelevation *SE* (cm)	7·20 (*SE*)
2.	Based upon cant deficiency (*D*) for max. speed (kmph)	$0{\cdot}073 \times D \times V_{max}$
3.	Based upon *SE* and V_{max}	$0{\cdot}073 \times (SE) \times V_{max}$

Table 15·76. Speed from the Length of Transition Curve

S. No.	*Criteria for Speed*	*Speed (kmph)*
1.	For speed upto 100 kmph	
	(*a*) based upon actual superelevation (*SE*)	134 × *L/SE*
	(*b*) based upon cant deficiency (*D*)	13·4 *L/SE*
2.	For speed above 100 kmph	
	(*a*) based upon *SE*	19·8 × *L/SE*
	(*b*) based upon *D*	19·8 × *L/D*

Table 15·77. Marshall Mix Design Criteria for Bituminous Concrete

S. No.	*Te4st Property*	*Specified value*
1.	Marshall Stability, (kg)	340 (minimum)
2.	Flow value, 0·25 mm units	8 to 16
3.	Air voids in total mix, V_v %	3 to 5
4.	Voids filled with bitumen, *VEB* %	75 to 85

Table 15·78. Mix Design Criteria for Bituminous Concrete by Asphalt Institute

S. No.	*The property*	*Medium and eight traffic*	*Heavy anve very heavy traffic*
1.	Stability, kg	845-910	> 910
2.	Voids, total mix, %	2-5	2-6

Table 15·79. Volume According to Group Index Method of Pavement Design

S. No.	*Number of vehicles per day*	*Traffic volume (commercial vehicles)*
1.	Less than 50	Light
2.	50 to 300	Medium
3.	Over 300	Heavy

Table 15·80. Subgrade Evaluation based upon Group Index Value

S.I.	*Evaluation of Subgrade*	*Group Index Range of Subgrade*
1.	Good	0-1
2.	Fair	2-4
3.	Poor	5-9
4.	Very poor	10-20

Table 15·81. Range of Variables in GI Equation

S. No.	*Variables*	*Range of Variables*	*Remarks*
1.	a	$35 < a < 75$ (0 to 40)	Passing 7 sm
2.	b	$15 < b < 35$ (0 to 40)	Passing 7 sm
3.	c	$40 < c < 60$ (0 to 20)	Liquid limit
4.	d	$10 < d < 30$ (0 to 20)	Plasticity Index

Table 15·82. Physical Requirements of Stone Aggregate for Surface Coat

S. No.	*Test on aggregate*	*Allowable Value*
1.	Los Angles abrasion test	35%
2.	Impact test	30%
3.	Flakiness Index	25%
4.	Water absorption	1%
5.	Stripping test (CRRI Test)	25%

Table 15·83. The Physical Requirement of Stone Aggregate for Penetration Mecadam

S. No.	*Test on Aggregate*	*Allowable Value*
1.	Abrasion test	40%
2.	Impact test	30%
3.	Flakiness Index	25%
4.	Stripping test (CRRI test)	25%
5.	Loss with Sodium Sulphate 5 cycles	12%

16

Railways

16·1. Gauges on Indian Railways

(1) **Broad Gauge (B.G.).** It is kept 1676 mm (5′-6″). It is adopted on main and trunk lines.

(2) **Meter Gauge (M.G).** It is kept 1000 mm (3′-3$^3/_8$″). It is adopted mainly on feeder lines.

(3) **Narrow gauge (N.G.).** It is kept 762 mm or 610 mm (2′-6″ or 2′-0″). It is adopted in difficult terrain. Such as of hills or on the link lines of projects to the railway head for the carriage of construction material.

(1) **Broad gauge** routes are classified based on speed criteria in the following five categories :

Group	*Sanctioned speed*
A	160 kmph
B	130 kmph
C	Suburban sections of Mumbai and Kolkata
D	100 kmph
E	Other sections and Branch lines

(2) **Meter gauge routes.** The meter gauge routes are classified based on their importance, the traffic carried and maximum permissible speed in the following three categories :

(*i*) Trunk routes (*ii*) Main routes (*iii*) Branch lines.

In 1984 three meter gauge routes are classified as under :

(*i*) ***Q*-routes.** The routes on which traffic density is more than 2·5 G.M.T. with maximum permissible speed more than 75 kmph.

(*ii*) ***R*-routes.** The routes on which the traffic density is more than 1·5 G.M.T. with speed potential of 75 kmph.

(*iii*) **S-routes.** The routes on which traffic density is less than 1·5 G.M.T. with a speed potential less than 75 kmph.

(3) **Recommended ruling gradients on railways**

Type of terrain	*Ruling gradient*
Plain country	1 in 125 to 1 in 200
Hilly country	1 in 40 to 1 in 80

Table 16·2. Maximum permissible degree of curves and their compensation

Gauge	*Maximum, degree*	*Compensation*
B.G.	10°	0·04%
M.G.	16°	0·03%
N.G.	40°	0·02%

Rails. The size of rail is designated with its weight of one yard with a letter *R*. 100 *R* rail means a rail of one yard weighing 100 lbs.

The rails are used as follows on different lines :

B.G. main lines 90 *R* (44·6 kg/m)
Branch lines 75 *R* (37·1 kg/m)
M.G. main lines 60 *R* (29·8 kg/m)
Branch lines 50 *R* (24·8 kg/m)

The rails are laid with their top surface laid at 1 in 20 towards centre of track. This helps in embracing the rail top to the concerned tread of the wheel.

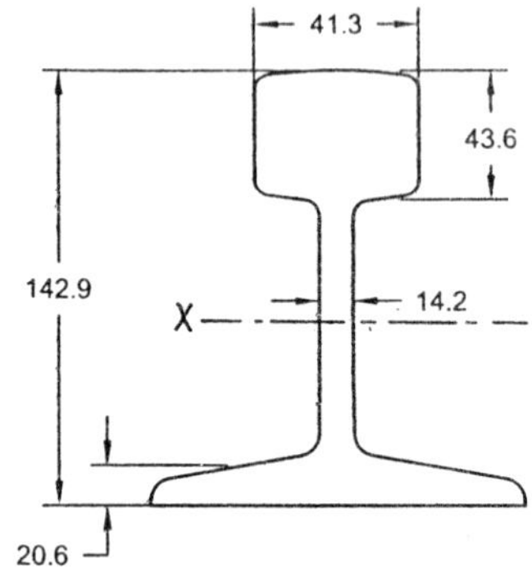

Fig. 16·1. Flat foot rail.

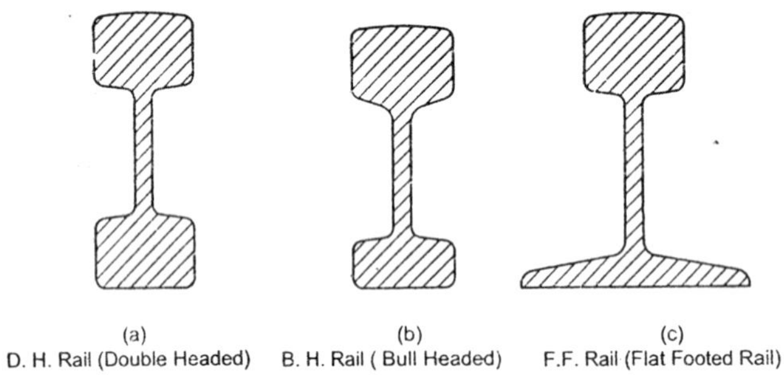

Fig. 16·2.

(*a*) **Double Headed Rail** (or Dumb bull). In such a rail section both the top and bottom sections are kept the same, so that they can be inverted when one is weared. But in actual practice the bottom is also weared out together with the top and hence is not used by inverting.

(*b*) **Bull Headed Rail.** The top section of the rail is heavier than the bottom. Therefore chairs are to be provided on the sleeper to secure the rail, hence these type of rails are expansive.

(*c*) **Flat Footed Rails.** It is also known as vignole on the name of its designer. A flat footed rail is an inverted to shape. Its top head is a slight heavier than that of the double bull head. Now a days these are widely used.

Table 16·3A. Standard Rail Sections

Gauge	*Type of rails*			
	MKS units		*FPS units*	
	Rail sec.	*Wt. (kg/m)*	*Rail sec.*	*Wt. lbs/yd.*
Broad gauge (B.G.)	60 kg	60 kg/m	—	—
	52 kg	52 kg/m	—	—
	90 *R*	44·69 kg/m	90 *R*	90 lbs/yd.
Meter gauge (M.G.)	90 *R*	44·69 kg/m	90 *R*	90 lbs/yd.
	75 *R*	37·24 kg/m	75 *R*	75 lbs/yd.
	60 *R*	29·79 kg/m	60 *R*	60 lbs/yd.
	50 *R*	24·82 kg/m	50 *R*	50 lbs/yd.
Narrow gauge (N.G.)	50 *R*	24·82 kg/m	50 *R*	50 lbs/yd.

Table 16·3B. Properties of Flat Footed Rails used on Indian Railways (Fig. 16·1)

Bottom width *inches*	*Weight of Rail in lbs/yard*	*Distance from top of rail to N.A. inches*	*Section moduli about XX*	*Moment of inertia about XX*	*Radii of gyration about XX*	*Total depth* *inches*
5·000	100 FF	3·03	15·40	46·70	2·18	6·000
5·375	90 R	2·95	13·05	38·45	2·09	5·625
5·375	90 BSS FF	2·80	12·33	34·51	1·98	5·375
5·000	87 FF	2·59	11·50	29·72	1·86	5·150
2·375	84 BH	2·87	9·50	27·27	1·83	5·469
2·500	85 BH	2·94	10·46	30·70	1·91	5·550
2·406	78 DH	2·72	10·00	27·47	1·92	5·437
4·812	75 R	2·61	9·72	25·36	1·86	5·062
4·812	75 BSS FF	2·49	9·23	22·97	1·77	4·812
2·375	75 DH	2·60	8·63	22·45	1·73	5·187
4·000	74 FF	2·52	8·16	20·56	1·67	4·750
4·500	70 FF	2·44	7·46	18·21	1·65	4·562
2·437	68 DH	2·50	7·86	19·66	1·71	5·000
2·125	68 BH	2·91	7·63	22·19	1·81	5·343
2·750	64 DH	2·50	7·32	18·30	1·73	5·000
4·000	62 FF	2·32	6·91	16·03	1·62	4·500
4·312	60 R	2·31	7·04	16·26	1·66	4·500
4·312	60 BSS	2·25	5·77	12·98	1·48	4·312
4·000	60 FF	2·13	6·57	13·99	1·54	4·250
3·875	58½ FF	2·20	3·56	12·22	1·46	4·312
3·937	59 BSS	1·97	5·13	10·10	1·44	3·937
3·500	50 FF	2·00	5·03	10·06	1·43	4·000
3·500	40 BSS	1·75	3·47	6·35	1·29	3·500
3·250	35 BSS	1·62	3·04	4·94	1·20	3·250
3·105	35 FF	1·67	3·06	5·09	1·21	3·307
3·000	30 BSS	1·50	2·39	2·59	1·11	3·000

For old rails the moment of inertia and section modules should be reduced by 12·5%, where proposed to be used as beams.

Min. Radius of gyration at right angle to XX is about $^1/_3$ to $^1/_2$.

The weight of rail is decided on the following factors :

(*i*) Heaviest axle load on the track.

(*ii*) Maximum permissible speed on the track.

(*iii*) Depth of ballast cusion.

(*iv*) Type and density of sleeper.

(*v*) Gauge of track.

Table 16·4. Specification of different Rail Sections

	(90 R) 44·69 kg/m	*52 kg/m*	60 kg/m
(1) Type of gauge	Broad	Broad	Broad
(2) Traffic density	10 G.M.T.	20-25 G.M.T.	35 G.M.T. (million/km/annum)
(3) Speed of trains	100 kmph	upto 130 kmph	upto 160 kmph
(4) Axle load	upto M.L. standard	upto M.L. standard	upto M.L. standard
(5) Life	20 to 25 years	20 to 25 years	20 to 25 years

52 kg/m Rail Section in Indian Railway Design have some improved features

(*a*) Thicker head (67 mm) ... ... For greater wear

(*b*) Greater height (156 mm) ... ... For more stiffens

(*c*) Steeper equal fishing plans ... ... For even wear.

However the foot width is kept almost the same as 90 *R* section.

The ratio of the weight of rail to the weight of locomotive axle as 1/510 *i.e.*

$$\frac{\text{Weight of rail in tonnes}}{\text{Weight of locomotives in tonnes}} = \frac{1}{510}$$

A thumb rule to obtain the maximum axle load with relative to a given section in lbs/yard is as under :

Maximum axle load = 500 × sectional weight of rail in lbs/yard

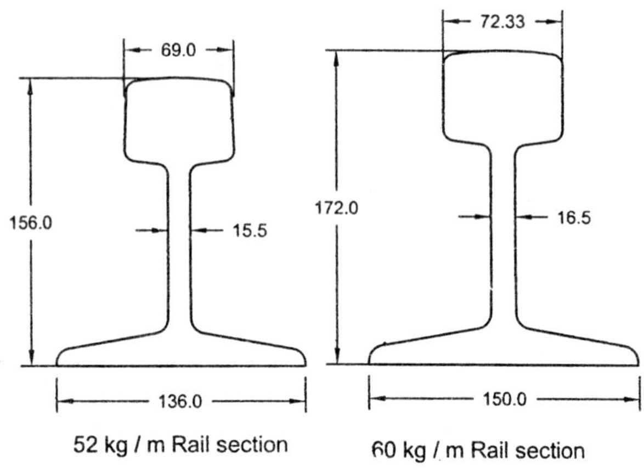

Fig. 16·3.

Advantages of heavy Rails

(*i*) Suitability to Electric and Diesel Engines

(*ii*) These require low sleeper density

(*iii*) These provide more strength

(*iv*) Less deflection between adjacent sleepers.

Table 16·5. Comparison of Flat footed v/s Bull head rails

Flat footed rails	*Bull headed rails*
1. More strong for same cross-section and weight.	1. Less strong for same section and weight.
2. Bearing plates for fixing rails are wooden sleepers	2. Bearing plates for fixing rails wooden sleepers not required.

Table contd...

Table contd...

Flat footed rails	*Bull headed rails*
3. Fastening of rails to sleepers on wooden sleepers is less costly.	3. Fastening on wooden sleepers is more costly.
4. Fitting, laying and relaying is easy.	4. Fitting of these rails is difficult, they are supported on chairs.
5. Arrangement and maintenance of points and crossings is simple and cheaper.	5. Arrangement and maintenance of points is complicated and costlier.
6. The rolling wheels affect the rail fittings and thus disturb the alignment.	6. The rolling wheels do not affect the rail fittings quickly. Thus maintain good alignment.
7. Daily inspection of these rails is not must.	7. Daily inspection of these rails for the wooden keys is required.
8. Initial cost is low.	8. Initial cost is high.
9. These rails provide more rigidity to the vertical loads.	9. These rails provide less rigidity to the vertical loads.
10. Replacement procedure for these rails is easy	10. Replacement procedure for these rails is complicated.
11. The maintenance cost is less.	11. The maintenance cost is more.

Composition of Rail Steel		**Revised Composition of Rail Steel in 1980**	
Carbon	0·55 to 0·68	Carbon	0·45 to 0·60
Manganese	0·65 to 0·90	Manganese	0·95 to 1·40
Silicon	0·05 to 0·03	Silicon	0·05 to 0·30
Sulphur	0·08 or less	Sulphur	0·06 (max.)
Phosphorus	0·05 or less	Phosphorus	0·06 (max.)

Note : (*i*) The combined Carbon and Manganese contents for medium manganese rails should not be less than 1·45% and if the carbon is less than 0·5% the total content of carbon and manganen should not be less than 1·55%.

(*ii*) The maximum content of carbon and manganese should be limited to 1·95%.

Length of Rails :	Broad gauge (B.G.)	13 m (42 ft.)
	Meter gauge (M.G.)	12 m (39 ft.)
	Narrow gauge (N.G.)	12 m (39 ft.)

It is always desirable not to have a rail piece shorter than the longest rigid base of the wagons *i.e.*, the distance between two adjacent axles. In India the wheel base of wagons is 3·66 m (12 ft.). Hence the pieces of rail having length less than 3·66 m (12′) should not be used on through tracks. However in the interest of smoother running, rail closures should be longer 5·5 metre and should neither be located near to each other nor in proximity to junctions of different types of rails sleeper, bridges, level crossings and ash pits etc.

Corrugations in Rails. The rails whose top surface develops alternate ridges and hollows varying in shape and size (0·05 mm to 0·4 mm in depth) 2 to 8 cm apart are called corrugated rails. When vehicle pass over the such corrugation an unpleasant noise is created, probably due to locking of air in the corrugations. Such rails are also called as roaring rails. Empty wagons create more corrugations than the loaded one.

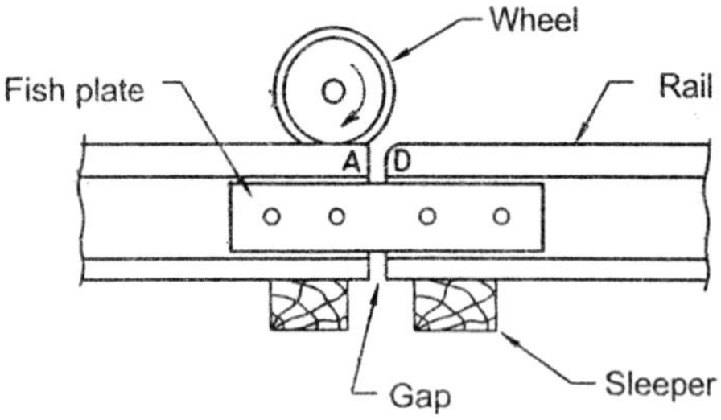

(a) Wear at the end of rail

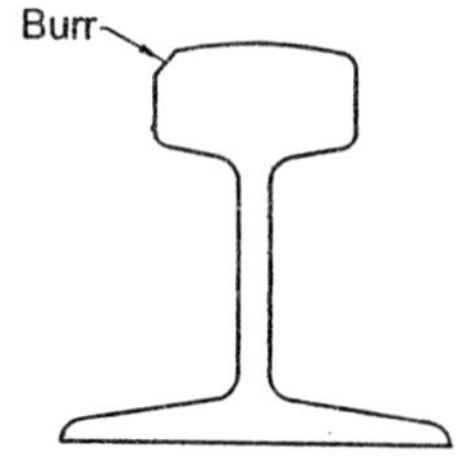

(b) Wear at the top of rail

Fig. 16·4.

(1) **Wear at end of rail.** The wear of rails at the ends is always more than the wear at the top of rails. This wear is caused primarily due to the blows at the ends by the wheels of locomotives during jumping over an expansion gap such as *AB* in the Fig. 16·4.

(2) **Wear at the top of rail.** The wear of the rail table is due to abrasion of the rolling wheel over the rails and due to heavy loads. When a heavy load is concentrated on an extremely small surface on the rail, the stress in the rail exceeds the elastic limit and the metal in the rail flows. The flow of metal occurs on the top of the rail. The projection of metal beyond the original section of the rail on the gauge side are called burrs.

(3) **The wear on sides of rails.** This type of wear primarily occurs on the curves when a vehicle negotiates a curve, it has a tendency to move towards the outside of the curve due to centrifugal force. The tendency of other wheels moving off the rails on curves is countracted by raising the level of outer rail a little above that of the inner rail of the track. The wheel flanges exert a thrust on the inner side of the outer rail and thus the grinding of the rail by the flanges occurs. Rigidity of the wagons also causes the wheel flange to develop a tendency to bite into the side of the outer railhead.

Let *A* and *B* be the front wheels and *C* and *D* be the rear wheels of any rigid wagon (Fig. 16·5). Apparently outer wheels *A* and *C* have to travel a longer distance than the inner wheels *B* and *D*. This is due to the fact that the curve distance *CA* is greater than curve distance *DB*. However due to rigid connection between the wheels, the outer and inner wheels cover the same distance. This causes the inner wheels to slip over the inner rail and thus the inner side of the top of the head of the inner rail gets eroded.

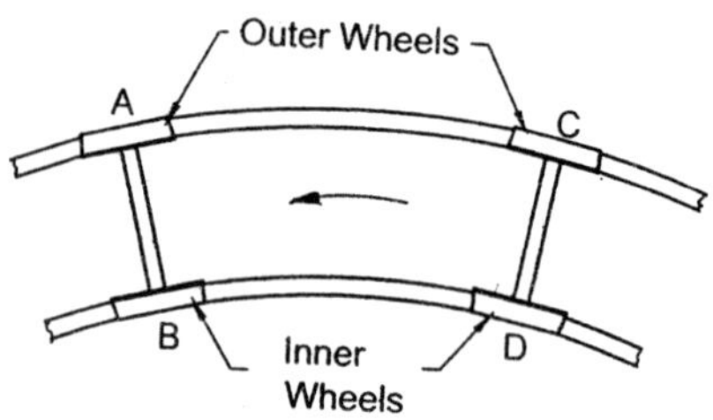

Fig. 16·5.

Movement of wheels of the wagons *AB* on curve as shown in Fig. 16·5.

The main causes of wear of the side of the head of rails may be summarised as under :

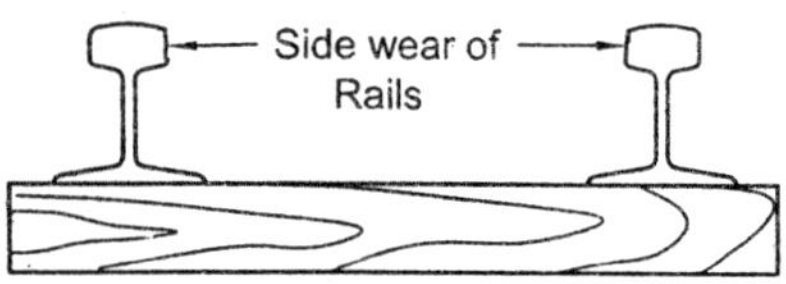

Fig. 16·6

(*i*) Grinding action of the flanges of outer wheels on the inner side of the head of the outer rail due to the thrust exerted by the centrifugal force.

(*ii*) Biting action of the flanges of the outer wheels on the inner side of the head of the outer rails due to rigidity of the vehicle.

(*iii*) Slipping action of the inner wheels in the inner side of the head of the inner rails on curves.

Side wears of rails is shown in the Fig. 16·6.

Measures taken to reduce rail wear

(1) **Provision of special alloy steel rails.** At places of excessive wear special alloy steel rails may be used. Inspite of their high cost use of such rails is justified to reduce the wear of rails.

(2) **Proper track maintenance.** A proper maintenance evidently results in the check of the wear of the rails. The maintenance of correct gauge helps to reduce wear of rails.

(3) **Proper expansion gaps.** The reduction in the gap of rails (upto an allowable limit) results in the reduction of wear of the ends of the rails. As in welded long rails, the expansion gaps are eliminated so the wear of the rails is also reduced.

(4) **Interchanging of rails.** The inner and outer rails on the curve should be interchanged after few years. By doing so the heavily worked out faces are integrated.

(5) **Welding of ends.** Welding or delogging of the battered ends at proper time reduces the wear of rails.

(6) **Providing of check rails.** Check rails holds the back of the flange of the inner wheel and thus prevents the outer wheels to strike and damage the outer rail. The check rail is fastened suitably to the inner rail. The gap between the inner rail and check rail is kept 44 mm for B.G. Check rails are generally provided on curves of 8 degrees and above on B.G. tracks and 14 degrees and above on M.G. tracks.

(7) **Lubrication of rail faces.** Lubrication of the gauges face of the outer rail reduces the wear of the rails common lubricants are :

(*i*) Lime seprified grease on mineral oil base.

(*ii*) Mixture of grease and graphite.

(*iii*) Mixture of plumb-bage and axle oil.

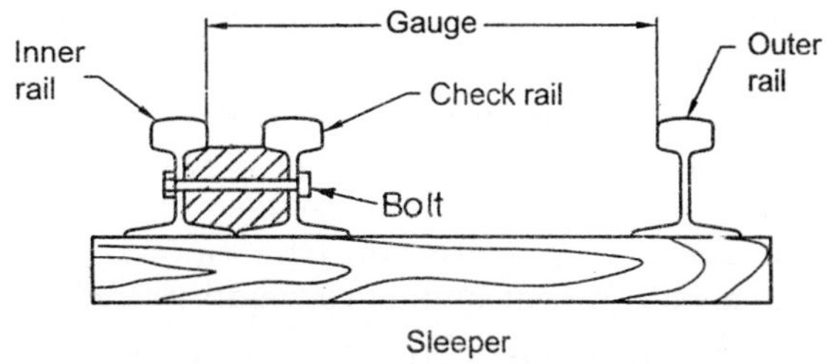

Fig. 16·7. Check rails.

(8) **Providing inward slope to rail table.** Providing inward slope to the rail table by adjusting the wooden sleepers or by inserting candid bearing plates, reduces the wear of the rails.

(9) **Providing proper super elevation.** On curves reduces the wear.

Changing of rails. The worn out rails are replaced on the following situations.

(1) When the wear exceeds 5% of the total weight of the rail section.

(2) When the fish plates are struck or cut by wheel flanges.

(3) When the gauge side gets worn out by 3 mm.

(4) When the gauge side of the head is worn to the shape of the wheel flange. In such a condition the wheels tend to mount the top of rail.

(5) When the top of rail is worn out by 9·5 mm.

(6) When either head or web gets split.

The wearing of thé rails is accessed by the reduction of its standard weight. Secondly the head dimensions are compared with a new one.

The failure of a rail may occur in the following forms :

(*i*) **Crushed Head.** The rail head which get fallened and sagged are called crushed heads. The defect is developed due to slipping of wheels, flat spots on wheels and weak support at the rail ends. The flat spots on the wheel are developed due to skidding of the wheels on the rails. The weak end supports are made by loose fish bolts.

(*ii*) **Split Heads.** The rail heads which develop a crack in the middle or get split up into two parts are called split heads. When the surface of the crack appears smooth and dark, the defective rail is known as piped rail. This defect is primarily due to the manufacturing process (formation of a cavity) or due to shrinkage of the metal.

(*iii*) **Split web.** The web which gets split up in two pieces is called a split web. Such a split is generally, though not necessarily runs through the fish bolt holes.

(*iv*) **Square Break.** When the rail breaks completely in vertical plane, it is called to have a square break.

(*v*) **Angular Break.** When the rail breaks completely in an inclined plane, it is known as inclined break.

(*vi*) **Horizontal fissures.** The fissure which develops in the rail head and goes on increasing gradually, is called co-horizontal fissure. This is probably caused due to worn out fish plates or insufficient ballast packing under the joint sleeper.

(*vii*) **Battered ends.** The hammered down and flattened rail ends due to impact of running wheels is called battered end or **Crippled end**. This defect is primarily caused due to excessive gap and loose fish plates and also not supporting the rails ends firmly. The difference between the level of rail at a point 30 cm away from the rail end and at the rail end is the value of rail end battering. Rail end battering exceeding 3 mm is not desirable.

(*viii*) **Flattering of rail table.** The rail table of the inner rail on curves gets flattened due to a combination of high contact stresses and high lateral forces. Flattering of rails gives a clear indication that the rail is unsuitable for the type of track and track traffic density.

(*ix*) **Corrosion.** This defect is caused due to acid gases developed in the moisture coating of the rail. Rail corrosion is more in industrial and coastal areas near water columns, ash pits, wet tunnels and passenger yards receiving excessive discharges of night soil by the train users. For protecting the rails from corrosive effects, the Indian Railway have recommended a coat of zinc chromate or red oxide primer.

(*x*) **Hogged Rails.** The rails whose ends get deflected downward due to battering action of the moving wheels on their ends are called hogged rails. The hogging of rails ends also increases due to loose packing under the joints and loose fish plates. The defect of rails causes a discomfort to the passengers due to rough riding conditions.

Remedial steps for hogging of rails

(1) **Cropping.** The hogged portion of the rail about one meter in length at the effected end may be cropped and fresh holes drawn for fixing the fish plates. The cutting of rails may be done either on the site or in a nearby workshop. After cutting of the defective ends, the rail is pulled back to a distance equal to the cropped length.

(2) **Replacing.** In this method the defective rail is replaced.

(3) Welding of the rail after removing of the hogged portion.

(4) **Dehogging.** The hogged portion is rectified mechanically by axes etc.

(5) **By passing.** The hogged portion is straighted by crow bars and is then packed.

Measurement of hogging. A straight rule of about one meter is placed over the hogged portion on straight reach of the rails in both sides and then the hogging is measured by a steel tape.

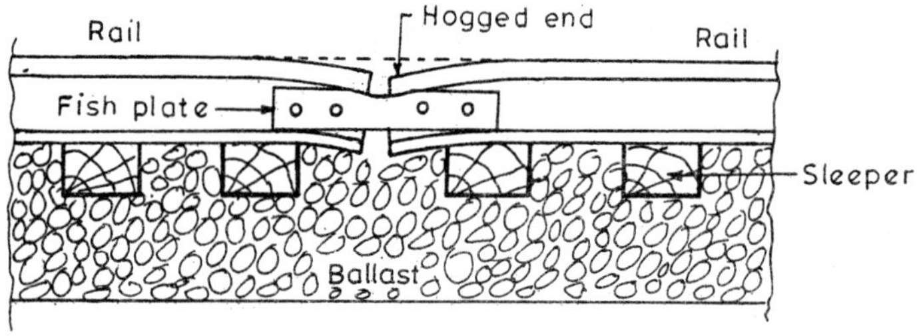

Fig. 16·8. Hogging of rails

Buckling of rails. The rail track which gets distorted due to prevention of free expansion of rails particularly in hot weather, goes out of its position or alignment. This phenomenon is known as buckling of rails.

Causes of buckling of rails. The causes of buckling are as follows :

(*i*) **Insufficient expansion gap.** The force of linear expansion throws the track out of position.

(*ii*) **Too light fish plates.** If the fish plates are too light, the rail ends do not move freely and so it gets buckled.

(*iii*) **Insufficient ballast.** The insufficient ballast fails to provide adequate resistance to the track.

(*iv*) **Inadequate fastening.** If the fastening of rails is insufficient the rail may buckle.

(*v*) **Excessive creap.** If the track develops excessive creep the expansion joints get jammed and the rail get buckled.

(*vi*) **Welded rails.** If the welded plates are not properly held the linear expansion becomes more, the ends gets jammed and thus buckling is caused.

(*vii*) **Non lubrication of the fish plates.** For non lubrication of fish plates, the force of friction increases between the fishing plane, and thus the rails develop bending and buckling.

Life of rails. In India the life of a rail is 60 years as an average.

Marking on the rails. The rails are marked with the details of their weight, maker, year of manufacture etc. The following is a type of marking :

GIP 90R BS TIS CO
52 KG MM HSL V 70→

Here 52 kg means rail weights 52 kg per meter

MM means the rail is made of medium manganese steel.

HSL stands for Hindustan Steel Ltd.

V70 stands for May 1970 the month and year of manufacture.

→ shows the direction of the top of the ingot from which the rail was rolled.

16·3. Rail Joints. The adjoining ends of rails are held together in correct position in both horizontal as well as in vertical planes, by fish plates and four holes in fish plates and in rails by four bolts. The fish plates are so designed that these fit the under side of the rail head and top of the rail foot ensuring that fish plates do not touch the web of the rails.

The rail joint provides a continuous rail path and is a weak point of the rail.

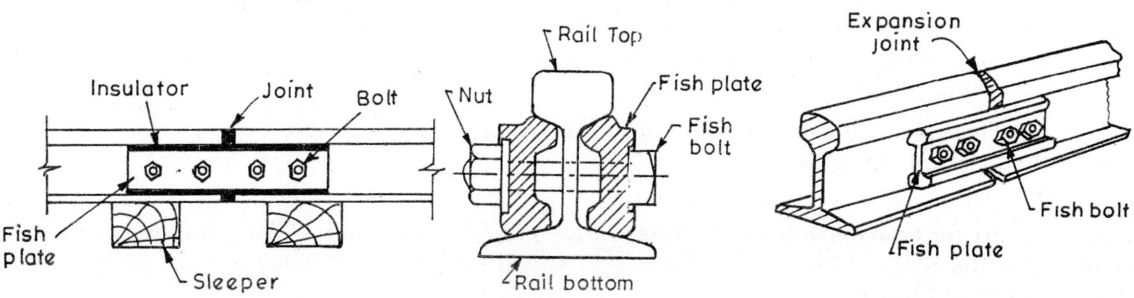

(*a*) Elevation (*b*) Rail bottom section (*c*) Isometric view

Fig. 16·9. Rail joint

A good rail joint must have the following qualities :

(1) It should provide the same strength and stiffness as the other parts of rail have.

(2) It should have sufficient gap to allow a free expansion of the rails due to temperature changes.

(3) It should have the same level and line of the two rails.

(4) It should be so arranged that the connected rails can be lifted easily without disturbing the other rails.

(5) Its initial cost and maintenance should be minimum.

(6) The fish plates should not touch the rail so as to allow a free expansion of the rails.

Type of rail joints. The joints are classified as under :

(1) **Suspended joints.** The rail joint is suspended on the two sleepers. In suspended joints a portion of both the rails acts as a cantilever. Due to the hammering action of the wheels of the moving trains, the packing under the sleepers get loosened [Refer Fig. 16·9 (*a*)]

(2) **Supported joints.** The rail joint is directly supported on a sleeper. Running of trains on supported joints is normally hard. In case the rail joint is packed too hard, to prevent it from setting, it makes the ends of the rails battered while wave motion is carried across the joint. The sleeper which supports the joint gets worn out quickly and hence its maintenance becomes a problem.

In the **Duplex sleeper** plate of size 85 cm × 75 cm is used to support the ends of the two sleepers. These joints are only used in sidings.

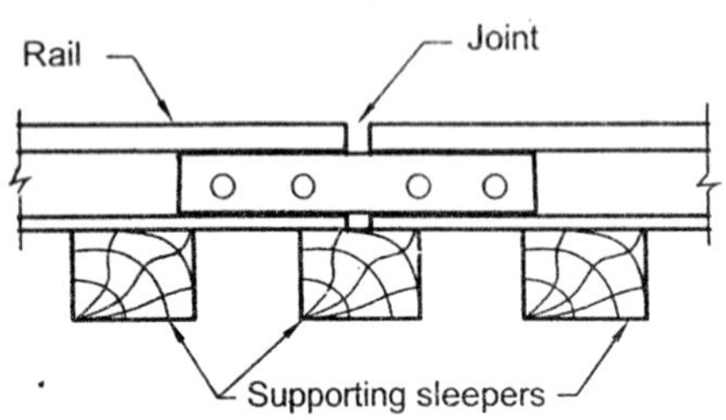

Fig. 16·10. Supporting joint.

(3) **Bridge joints.** The rail joint which is supported over a metal plate serving as a bridge between adjacent sleepers is called a bridge joint. The bridge plate is placed at the bottom of rails on two sleepers. The sleepers on either side of the joints are notched to accommodate the bridge plate. The bridge joints were designed on the theoretical principle that the joint will act as the yielding fixed support. In actual practice it was found quite unsuitable and hence the use of this type of rail joint is not in practice.

(4) **Square joints.** If the rail joints of parallel rails are exactly opposite each other, the joints are called to be the square joints.

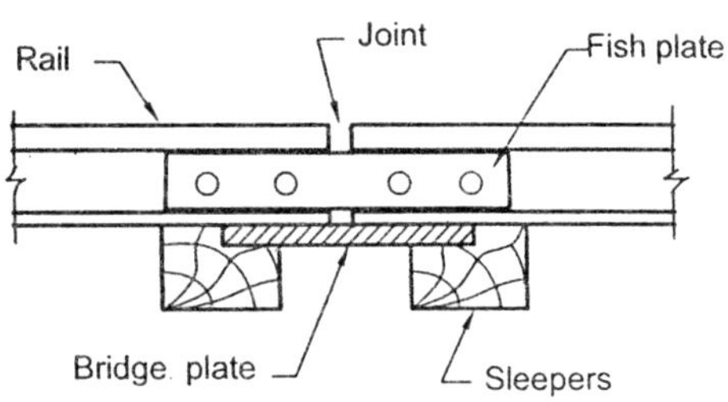

Fig. 16·11. Bridge joint.

(5) **Staggered joints.** When a rail joint is kept facing the centre of this opposite parallel rail, it is known as a staggered joint or mid stagger. Staggered joints are provided on the curves and have the following considerations :

(*i*) They produce smoother running of trains on curves, than that of square joints.

(*ii*) They reduce the tendency of pushing the track out of line by centrifugal force. They also prevent formation of shoulders and kinks at the joints. This happens due to weakness of the track at the joints as the centrifugal force tends to push out the track more at the joint than elsewhere.

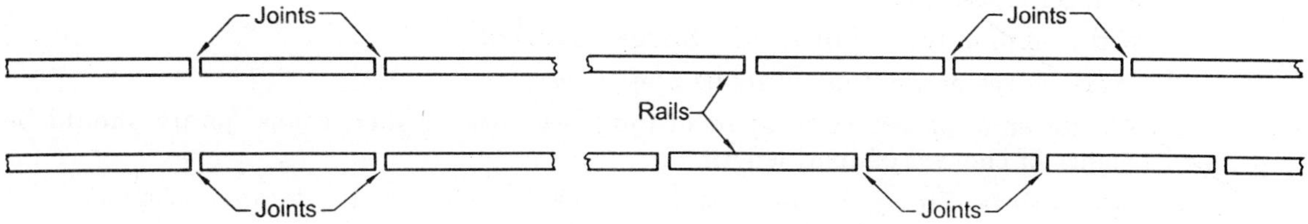

(*a*) Square joint (*b*) Staggered joint

Fig. 16·12.

(*iii*) They ensure uniform vertical continuity of the railway track.

(*iv*) The number of impacts at the joints are doubled but their intensity is halved. However the number of sleepers per rail length increases by one. In India staggered joints are only provided on curves and not on straight portion of tracks as it causes excessive rolling of vehicles.

(6) **Short staggered joints.** The joints which are kept 20 to 30 cm out of square are called staggered joint. The advantages of short staggered joints are :

(*i*) To avoid two weak points directly facing each other.

(*ii*) To reduce impact at joints by half, although the number of impact are doubled.

(*iii*) To provide a uniform vertical continuity of the track. The short staggered joints, however result in bunching of sleepers.

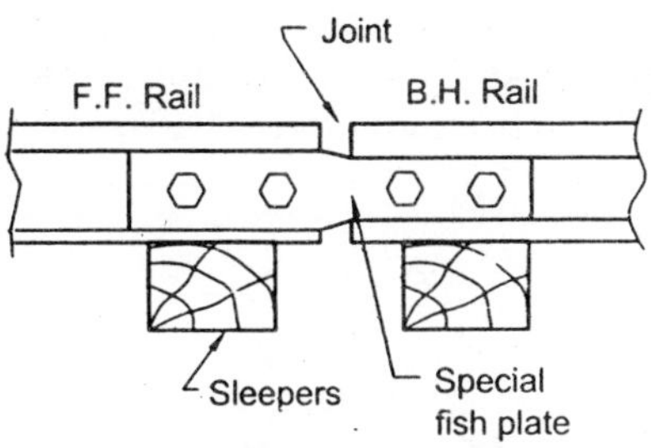

Fig. 16·13. Composite joint

(7) **Compromise joints.** The joint at which two rails of different sections are jointed together by means of special type of fish plates which fit both the rails is known as compromise joint. This type of joint is provided when a flat footing rail is joined with a bull headed rail or a bull headed rail with a flat footed rail.

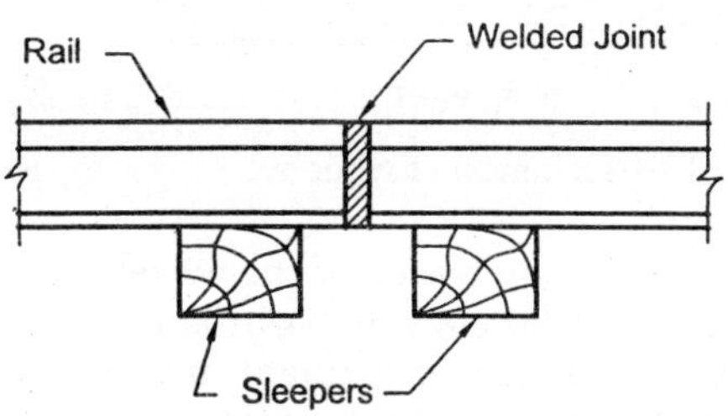

Fig. 16·14. Weld joint

(8) **Welded joints.** When the rail joint is joined by welding, it is called welded joint.

(9) **Insulated rail joint.** The rail joint in which an insulating material is inserted for obstructing the flow of electric current beyond the track circulated portion is called as an insulated joint.

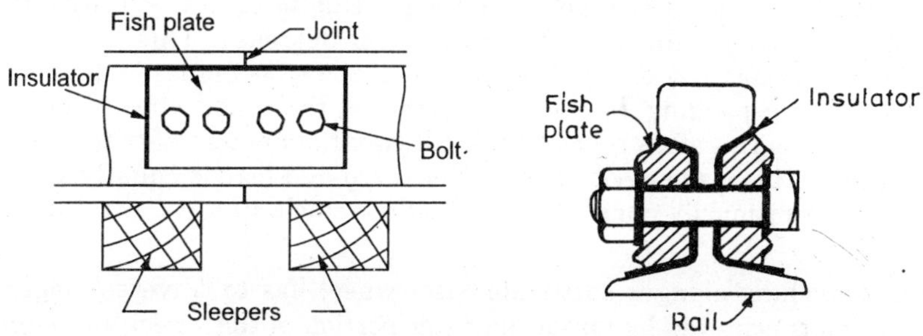

Fig. 16·15. A insulated joint

Avoidance of joints. At the following situations the joints are avoided :

(1) At level crossings.

(2) Within 3 m of the approach of a bridge abutment.

(3) Over bridges of any type of spans 6 m or less.

(4) At the ends of centre of span of long bridges. In such cases, joints should be provided at points of one 3rd of span length.

Gaps at joints. These are provided for the expansion of rails. Its amount depends on the length of rail and the maximum temperature which may occur in the area. Too less gap may cause buckle of rails while too large gaps may damage the ends of rails. The minimum gap of 1 mm is kept even at the largest temperature. It is calculated as follows :

$$e = L \alpha t \times 10^3$$

where e = expansion gap in mm

L = Length of rail in metres (say 13 m)

α = Coefficient of expansion of rail steel, *i.e.*, 0·00001152/degree C.

Lubrication of joints. In order to facilitate expansion of rails and to retard the wear on the fishing plates and rails.

Lubricant. A stiff paste of plum bago (graphite) and kerosene oil in proportion of 3 : 2. For lubricating the fish plates and nuts, black oil reclaimed oil is generally used.

16·4. Coning of wheels. In the beginning the train wheels were provided flat treads and the distance between the running faces of the flanges were kept almost equal to the gauge. It was observed that the sides of the tops of rails get worn out rapidly due to frictional forces between the flange and rails. As such the distance between the running faces of wheels is reduced further so as to provide a clean space between the flanges and the rails. The idea was that the wheels will move freely without coming in contact with rails. But due to slight irregularities in the alignment and gauge the wheels develop a tendency to move laterally to strike the rails. This caused a slight shock which in turn made the journey discomfortable in addition to development of kinks on the head on rails due to impacts.

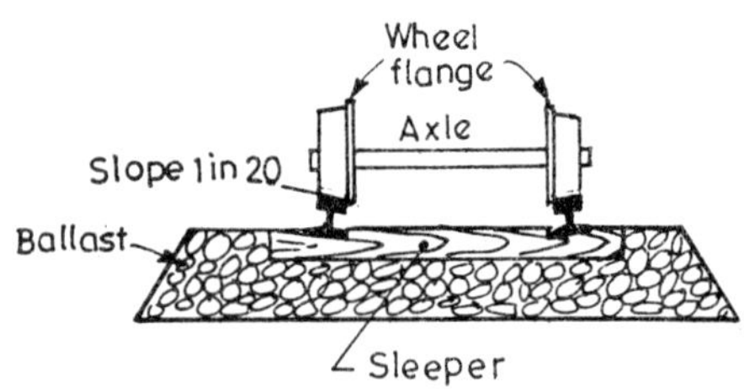

Fig. 16·16. Coning of wheels.

To overcome these defects the modern designer suggested that the treads of the wheels of railway vehicles should not be flat. Instead they recommended a 1 in 20 slope out wards in the form of a frustum of a wire. When the wheels having conincal surface travel on straight and level track. The circumference of the treads of both the wheels attached to the same axle remain equal. Because the wheels are get on axle and there is sufficient space between the flanges and rails. The tendency of lateral moment of the wheels develops. Due to conical surfaces, the circumference of the outer wheel increases and that of inner wheel decrease. This is automatically balanced because of the wheels move laterally. The portion of the wheel of large diameter comes with head of outer rail and corresponding smaller dia portion of the inner wheel comes on the head of the inner rail. The wheels therefore retreat back till equal diameters of both the wheels are over the centres of the rails. This way smooth riding is ensured and load is equally shared by the two rails. Coning of wheels is primarily done to maintain the vehicle in the central portion with respect to the track.

While travelling along a curve the outer wheel has to traverse longer distance than the inner wheel, which is achieved by larger diameter portion of the wheel by coming over the head of outer rail due to coning surface. This continues till a straight track is reached and wheels retreat back till equal diameters of wheels are on the centres of the rails. The vehicle also develop a tendency to move towards the outer rail due to centrifugal force. This makes the circumference of the head of the wheels of the vehicles on the outer rails, greater than that of the inner wheels. This is a favourable condition which helps the outer wheel to travel a greater distance on outer rail than that travelled by the wheel on the inner rail. This condition is very much useful if the axles are not connected to rigid frame of the vehicle.

Due to rigidity of the vehicle frame with axles, the trailing axle develops a tendency to move towards the inner rail. Thus a full advantage of coning of wheels is not utilised on curves.

As soon as the outer wheel moves outwards its circumference increases and hence, the wheel develops a tendency to return back to its normal position without shrinking the rail. The increased circumference also forces the wheel to slide. Sliding and frictional forces stop the further movement of the outer wheel outwards and this saves the flange to come in contact with the side of rail head. Coning of the wheels therefore ensure smoother riding.

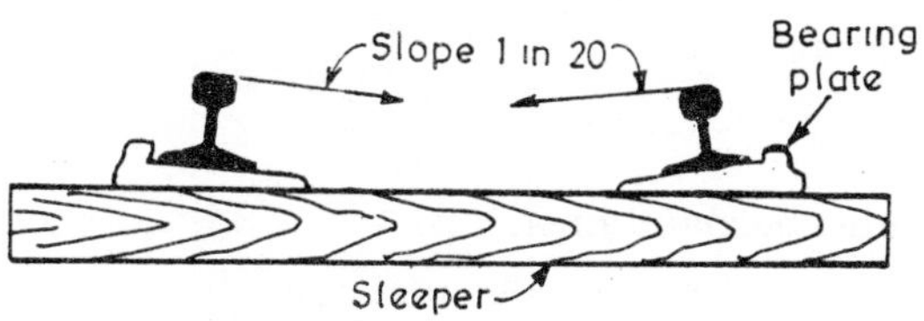

Fig. 16·17. Canted bearing plates.

Tilting of rails. To reduce the wear of the sleepers and lateral bending stresses the rails are not laid flat. The top of the rails is bolted inwards at a slope of 1 in 20 which is also the slope of the conical surface of the wheel. The tilting of rails is done either by adzing the wooden sleepers or by providing control bearing plates.

Tilting of rails has been adopted on the Indian Railways. It may however be noted that rails in switches and crossings and along the length track below them are not tilted.

Slipping of wheels on curves. Due to rigidity of the wheel base, the outer wheel travels a greater distance than the inner wheels on a curve, because the circumference of the tread, increases as soon as the wheel moves towards the rail. In case the lateral movement of this wheel is insufficient to account for the given curvature, the outer wheel starts skidding to cover the extra distance.

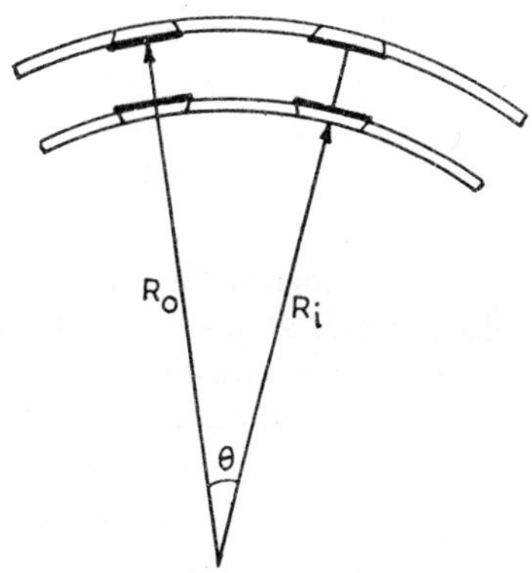

Fig. 16·18. Slipping of wheels

The formula for the amount of skidding is derived as below :

Let R= radius of the curve, R_0 radius of outer rail

R_1 = radius of inner rail

G = gauge of track

θ = angle subtended by wheel base in radians

The distance travelled by outer wheel $= R_0 - \theta$

The distance travelled by inner wheel $= R_i\,\theta$

Slip distance $= R_0\,\theta - R_i\,\theta = \theta\,(R_0 - R_i)$ ...(1)

(But $R_0 = R + G/2$ and $R_i = R - G/2$)

Substituting these values in equation (1) we get

Slip distance $= \theta\,\{R + G/2 - R + G/2\} = \theta\, G$

For B.G. Track, $G = 1{\cdot}676$ m

Slip $= \dfrac{2\pi\theta}{360°} \times 1{\cdot}676$ where θ is in degrees $= 0{\cdot}02925\ \theta°$ *i.e.*, 0·029 m per degree of central angle.

16·5. Creep of rails. The longitudinal movement of rails in the track is called the creep of rails. Due to creeping of rails the following effects are noticed :

(1) The rail joints are widened at two point where creep starts.

(2) Spike heads scratch the rail webs and flanges.

Causes of creep. (1) **Wave formation theory.** The portion under the wheel depressed down while it lifts at the rear and front of the wheel which just forms a wave like formation on the rail.

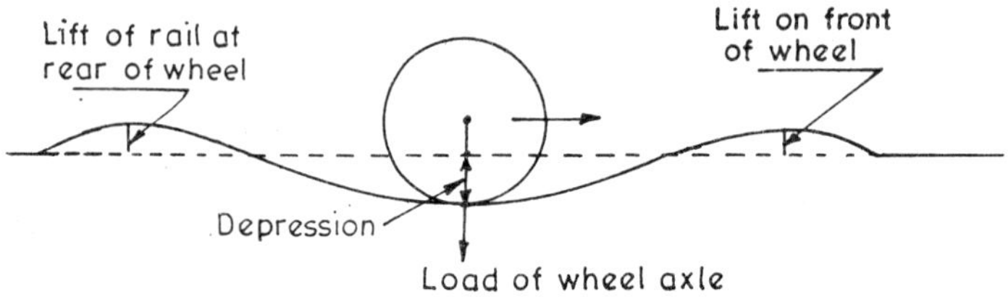

Fig. 16·19.

To reduce the creep two following qualities must be maintained :

(a) Increased stiffeners of the rail (b) Stable soil foundation

(c) Angular ballast for better interlocking.

(2) **Percussion theory.** This theory is based on the assumption that the moving wheels of the train over an expansion gap at the rail joint, depresses the 1st encounter rail end B. Due to this the other end C of the adjacent rail gets elevated, instantaneously. The moving wheel thus strikes the raised end C in quick succession.

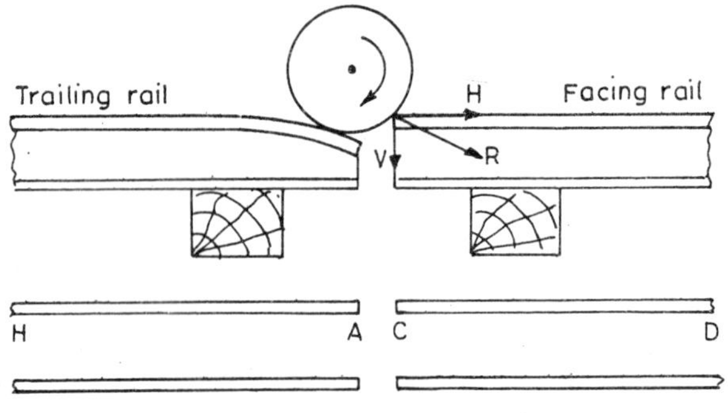

(a) (b)

Fig. 16·20.

The horizontal component H of the Reaction R at the point of contact of the raised end C, pushes, the rail CD in the direction of motion of the train. Due to accumulated effect of a number of wheels of the moving train in quick succession, creep in the rail is developed. Factors responsible for this creep are :

(1) Worn out fish plates (2) Loose fish bolts

(3) Loose packing of ballast at joint (4) Wide expansion gap

(5) Heavy axle load and (6) High speed of vehicles.

(3) **Drag Theory.** This theory is based on the assumption that the backward thrust on the driving wheels of the locomotive of the train pushes the rail of the track backward and other wheels of the locomotive and the vehicle, push the rail in the direction of travel of the train as already explained in the wave theory. As the number of driving wheels of the locomotive are a few as compared to the other wheels, the net amount of creep of rails results in the direction of motion of the train.

(4) **Change of temperature.** The creep in the rails is also due to the expansion and contraction due to change of temperature. It also depends on whether the track remains in sun or in shade.

(5) **Starting and stopping of trains.** When a train starts and gains an acceleration, the backward thrust of the engine wheels tends to push the rails backwards while stopping of a train applies brakes which tends to push the rail forward.

(6) **Unbalanced traffic.** If heavy traffic moves in one direction and the light traffic in the other direction on a single track, unequal creep occurs. The net effect of creep in the direction of movement of heavier traffice is more. In the case of double line tracks, the movement of trains remains unidirectional and as such creep develops in both the tracks in the direction of movement of trains.

Other reasons of creep development

(*a*) Loose fittings | (*b*) Bed quality of sleepers
(*c*) Bad alignment of the curves | (*d*) Too light or too dark gauges
(*e*) Gradients of track | (*f*) Life of rails
(*g*) Uneven placing of sleepers | (*h*) High embankments
(*i*) Weight of rails | (*j*) Type of soil of base.

16·6. Sleepers. Sleepers are the base of the rails which secures the rails in proper position. The following type of sleepers are used.

(1) **Wooden sleepers.** The usual wood of sleepers are (*i*) Sal, (*ii*) Deodar, (*iii*) Chir etc. Now a days as the timber is going costlier other types of the sleepers are in use.

Table 16·6. Dimensions of Wooden Sleepers

Gauge	*Size*						*Bearing area in (sq. m)*	*Bearing area (sq. ft.)*
	cm			*ft.*				
	L	*B*	*H*	*L*	*B*	*H*		
BG	275	25	13	9′	10″	5″	0·465	5·00
MG	180	20	11·5	6′	8″	4½″	0·310	3·33
NG	150	18	11·5	5′	7″	4½″	0·209	2·25

Adzing of wooden sleepers. In wooden sleepers grooves are made to fit the rails in a slope of 1 : 2.

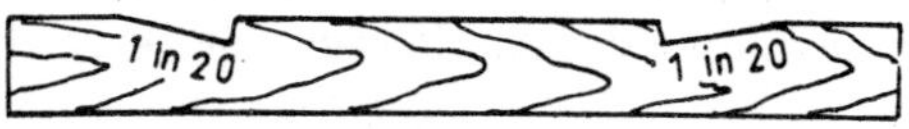

Fig. 16·21.

Precautions in use of wooden sleepers. The following precautions are followed :

(1) The sleepers are of seasoned wood, and free from sap, knots, cracks and shakes etc.

(2) On either side of a joint of rail wood sleepers are used.

(3) Centre line of track should coincide with centre of the sleeper.

(4) The hard wood side is kept at bottom and the sapwood upward.

(5) The central 90 cm length of sleeper should never be packed with ballast to avoid central bound defects *i.e.*, rocking of sleepers, when the ballast below the rail seat gets loosened.

(6) The sleepers on deck bridges should never be adzed. However bearing blasts should be used.

(7) At point of crossings the min. number of sleepers for B.G. track are :

Turn out	*No. of sleepers*
1 in 12	70
1 in 8½	51

Steel sleepers. As timber sleepers have a short life and costlier overall. Hence steel sleepers are being replaced in place of wooden sleepers. Steel sleepers are in the form of inverted channels with folded ends. These sleepers are made out of rolled steel plates of about

12 mm thickness. The end of the rolled section are flattened out in the shape of a spade to hold ballast. The rail seats of a steel sleeper are provided a cant of 1 in 20.

Types of steel sleepers. The various type of steel sleepers used in Indian Railways are :

(1) Lugs or jaws pressed sleepers (2) Sleepers with loose lugs or jaws

(3) Clip bolt type of sleepers (4) Saddle or spring type sleepers.

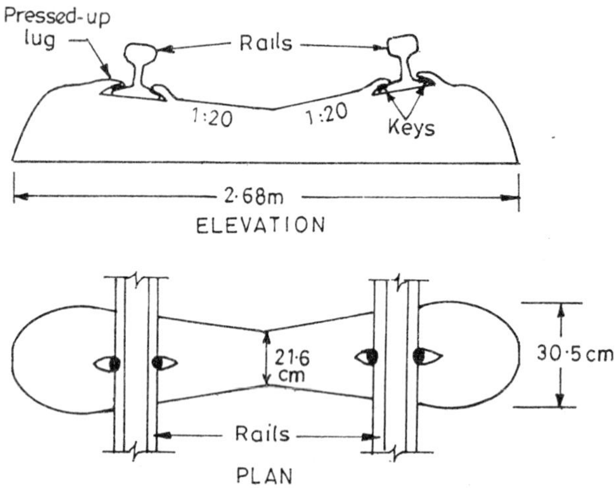

Fig. 16·22. Lugs of jaws pressed sleepers.

(1) **Lugs or jaws pressed sleepers (Fig.16·22).** In this type of steel sleepers, lugs or jaws are pressed out of the plate itself to accommodate the rails and the keys. Such type of sleepers usually get cracks at the corners of the lug holes. They require a lot of maintenance because the lugs give way to the movement of the keys. Variation and impact of the moving loads also loosen the keys. Hence proper gauge gets disturbed.

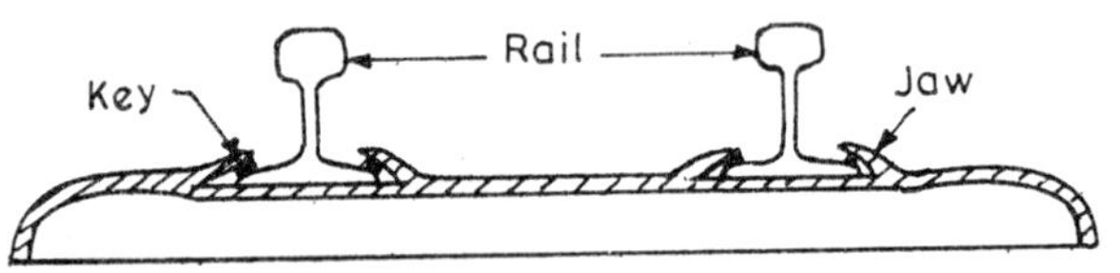

Fig. 16·23. Steel sleeper with loose jaws and lugs.

(2) **Sleepers with loose lugs and jaws (Fig. 16·23).** Instead of lugs pressed out of the sleeper plate, two loose jaws or lugs are provided to hold each rail. This type of sleeper is an improvement on the pressed jaw type. In loose jaw type sleepers, holes are drilled in the sleeper plate at proper position to accommodate the loose jaws. In between the jaws and rails, keys are inserted as in the case of pressed up lugs.

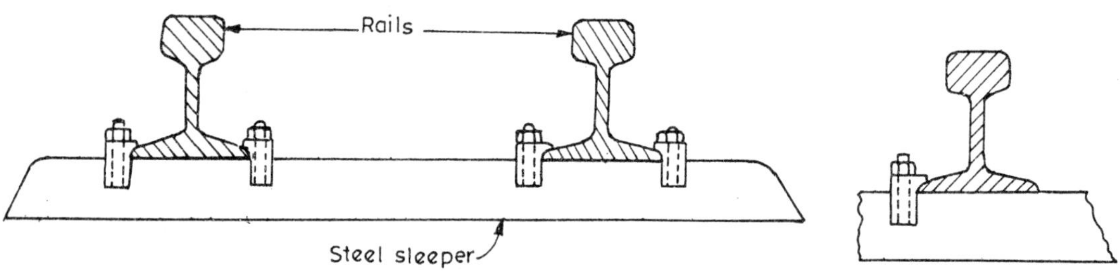

(*a*) Steel sleeper of clip bolt type (*b*) Detail of bolt

Fig. 16·24.

(3) **Clip bolt type steel sleepers (Fig. 16·24).** In this type of sleepers bolts and clips are used for holding the rails. Four clips and four bolts are used for each rail. Because the holes

for inserting bolts are small and circular, the cracks do not develop. These sleepers can be used for rails of various sections by simply using different size of clips and shifting the bolts positions in the bolt holes. The gauge adjustment is also possible by altering the bolt positions. Clip bolts and four key type sleepers also prevent the creep.

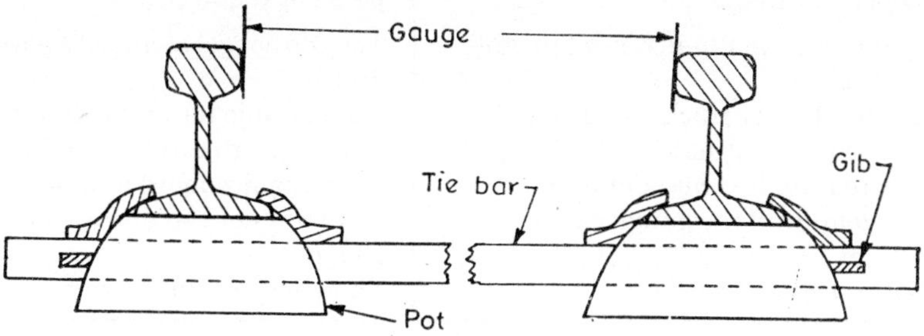

Fig. 16·24(*c*). Cast iron pot sleeper.

(4) **Saddle or spring type sleepers.** In these sleepers, the rail seat is provided with a saddle plate which is fixed to the sleeper with holes. The saddle plate strengthens the rail seat.

To increase the life of steel sleepers these are dipped into hot coal tar so on to protect them from corrosive action.

Cast Iron Sleepers. The cast iron sleepers are of the following types :

(1) Pot or bowl sleepers

(2) Plate sleepers

(3) CST-9 sleepers

(4) Rail free Duplex sleepers.

(1) **Pot or bowl sleepers** (Fig. 16·25) These cast iron sleepers are in the form of two elliptical hollow pots, each placed under each rail and connected together by a tie bar (51 mm × 13 mm) by means of a cotter and gib. Under the rail seat, the metal surface of the bowl is adzed to give the rail the necessary cant.

CST-9 sleepers. The cast iron sleepers now used on Indian Railway is known as the CST-9 sleepers. The design of these sleepers is a combination of a plate sleepers and pot sleeper. CST-9 sleeper was designed by the 9th trail and hence it is called CST-9 (Central Standard Trial-9). It is essentially a composite sleeper. With cast iron plate joined by a flexible steel tie bar with the help of four cotters. The rails are held to the sleeper by a single two way key provided on the gauge side. By changing relative position of four cotters, gauge may be adjusted upto ± 5 mm.

The rail seat of CST-9 sleeper along the rails is only 15 mm wide. Because of narrow bearing the rocking of the sleepers under the wave motion of the rails tend to reduce. This type of sleepers provide firm support and good lateral and longitudinal stability to the rails. The local bearing area of both the plates is equal to that of a standard B.G. woods sleeper *i.e.*, 5 sq. ft. (0·46 m)^2. The useful life of a C.S.T. sleeper is 30 to 50 years.

Plate sleepers. This type of sleeper consists of rectangular plates 864 × 305 mm size. The 305 mm side is laid parallel to the rails. Projecting ribs under the plates are provided for lateral stability. Both the plates are connected across the track by means of a tie bar keys, collars etc. These are also used as in the case of pot sleepers.

Duplex sleepers. This sleeper has been designed to be used at rail joints to prevent the cantilever action between the supports of two CST-9 sleepers, one on either side of the joint. A duplex sleeper is also known as rail free duplex sleeper. These are however not been found satisfactory because the rail ends supported on duplex sleeper. These are get severely flattened. This is why no further detail of Duplex sleepers is required.

Table 16·7. Comparision cast iron v/s steel sleepers

Item	*Steel sleeper*	*Cast iron sleeper*
1. Life	About 25 to 30 yrs. frequent renewal of sleepers not required	About 35 to 50 yrs. frequent renewal of sleepers not required
2. Corrosion	Easily corroded hence not suitable in moist areas	They do not get corroded, hence suitable in most areas
3. Insulation	Not suitable for track circuiting	Not suitable for track circuiting
4. Handling	They require normal handling	They require careful handling
5. Fittings	They require less number of fittings	They require more number of fittings
6. Gauge	They maintain the gauge easily	They are not capable of maintaining correct gauge
7. Scrap value	Their scrap value is less	Their scrap value is more

R.C.C. Sleepers. RCC sleepers are of two types :

(1) A through concrete sleeper (2) Two slabs joints by a tie bar

(1) **Through type.** In through type RCC sleepers cracks generally develop on the tension side when these are stressed due to heavy moving loads. The cracks are very minute in the beginning, but due to repetition of the impacts the loads of the fast moving trains these cracks tend to enlarge. Hence RCC sleepers of this type fail only due to this reason.

Fig. 16·26. Through type RCC sleeper

(2) **Two block RCC sleepers.** The concrete sleepers in the Indian Railways are only due to the shortage of wooden sleepers and costlier steel sleepers. The block of RCC sleepers are exclusively used for B.G. yards.

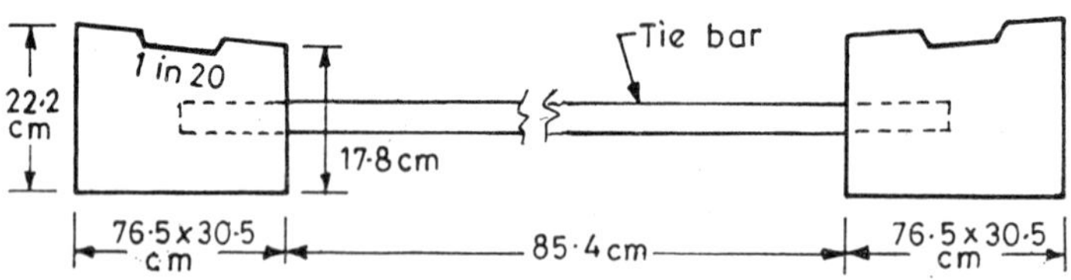

Fig. 16·27.

The main features of the RCC two block sleepers are :

(*i*) The rail seat is designed to carry a 10 tonne load without any lateral thrust.

(*ii*) The size of rail seat — 22 cm × 30 cm × 17 cm

(*iii*) Overall length of sleepers — 247·5 cm

(*iv*) Wt. of the sleeper — 170 kg

(*v*) Main reinforcement in blocks — (*a*) Top — 5 Nos., 8 mm dia. of steel
(*b*) bottom — 2 Nos., 8 mm dia. of steel

(*vi*) Fastenings—Steel clip and spring washer fitted to dowel.

Prestressed sleepers—(*i*) Pre tensioned (*ii*) Post tensioned

For both the types, high tension steel wires 5 mm or less in dia. are used. In case of pre tensioned sleepers, the wires are placed in continuous moulds about 150 m long, anchored at one end to an abutment and stretched by hydraulic mobile jacks applied at the other end when desired tension is attained, the jack end is welded and anchored to another abutment. The freely mixed concrete is then poured into the moulds. On hardening the concrete, the reinforced wires are cut close to the specimen size. The bond strength developed between the concrete and steel wire prevents, the slipping of the wires.

Ballast less track. In metro services lines the rails are directly supporting on concrete floor with the help of specially designed elastic fastenings. This type of track is called as ballast less track.

16·7. Ballast. Its size varies from 19 to 50 mm which is well graded. The ballast may be of trap or round stone (Granite, Basalt, Trap) and may be of the following materials :

(1) Broken stones (2) Gravels (3) Sand
(4) Mooram (5) Cinder (ash) (6) Brick bats
(7) Kankar (8) Ballast earth.

The section of a track is given below :

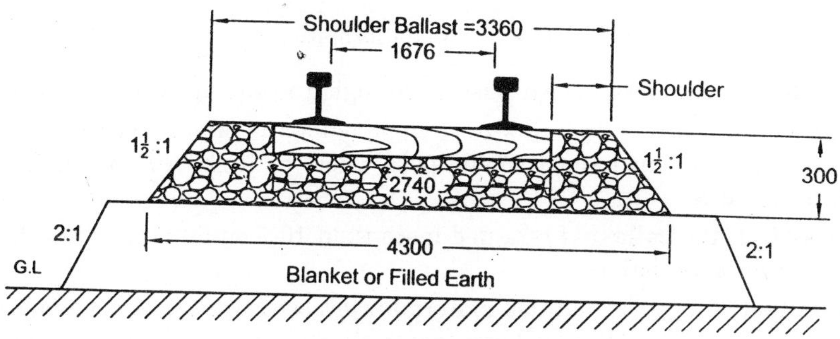

Fig. 16·28. Broad gauge.

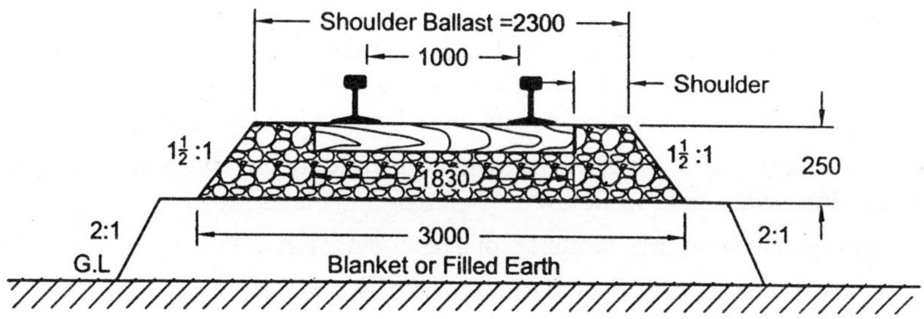

Fig. 16·29. Meter gauge.

Table 16·8. Dimensions of Ballast Section

Gauge	*Width, c*	*Depth, d*	*Size of Ballast*	
B.G.	335 cm	203 mm	1. For wooden sleeper track	50 mm
M.G.	229 cm	152 mm	2. For steel sleeper track	40 mm
N.G.	183 cm	152 mm	3. For points and crossings	25 mm
(Liable to a bit change according to the situation)			4. Concrete sleepers	65 mm
			5. For points and crossings (For trunk routes)	40 mm
			(small size ballast crushes to dust due to heavy loads)	

Main characteristics of Ballast. (1) **Quality.** Stone ballast should consist of hard and durable stone and should not contain more than 10 per cent dust.

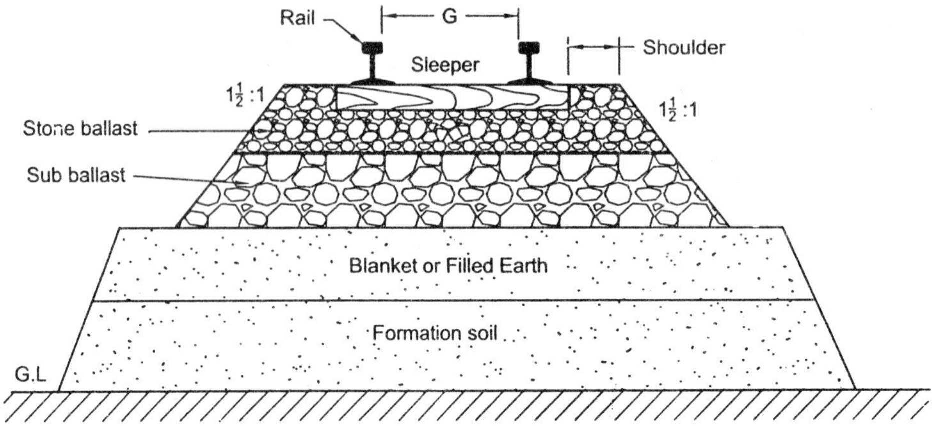

Fig. 16·30. Blanket formation.

The track ballast material which passes through 10 mm sq. mesh is classified as dust.

(2) **Standard size.** The standard size of stone ballast is 50 mm. When sieved through 60 mm sq. mesh sieve. 100 per cent ballast should pass where as it should not retain more than 10 per cent on 50 mm sq. mesh.

(3) **Over size.** If the ballast is retained more than 10% on 50 mm sq. mesh or 25 mm sq. mesh, it is called as over sized ballast.

(4) **Sub-ballast.** A layer of suitable material interposed between the stone ballast and the formation soil is called as sub ballast. Cheap materials such as sand, gravels, mooram etc. are used as sub-ballast. The sub-ballast is provided only to the same width as that of the ballast. Its thickness is 15 cm.

The functions of the sub ballast is to distribute the loads of the rolling stock more evenly over larger area of the formation soil or to say it increases the stability of the track and reduces the amplitude of sleeper vibration and ballast acceleration.

Blanket. The layer of a suitable material provided on the top of a poor formation is called a blanket. Its functions are as below :

(*i*) It improves the bearing capacity of the formation.

(*ii*) It avoids interpenetration of ballast and the soil.

(*iii*) It avoids the formation of ballast pockets.

(*iv*) It prevents the bottom soil to heave up and thus avoids mud pumping situation it is provided on the full width of formation.

The materials for blanket sand, gravel and moorum is of the thickness of 30 cm to 60 cm according to the soil of the formation.

Other techniques related to the ballast

(*a*) **Ballast cushion.** The depth of ballast below the bottom of sleeper, normally measured under the rails, is called as ballast cushion.

(*b*) **Shoulder ballast.** The ballast provided beyond the sleeper edge on either side.

(*c*) **Shoulder width.** The projected length of the ballast top line beyond the sleeper edge is called as shoulder.

(*d*) **Crib ballast.** The ballast confined between the sleepers is called crib ballast.

(*e*) **Ballast section.** The section of the ballast taken in between the sleepers normal to the track alignment is called ballast section.

The ballast provided above the sleeper's top has no use.

The minimum depth of ballast $d = \frac{S - W}{2}$ where S is the shoulder width and W = width of sleeper.

The following points may be noted :

(*i*) Average height of the rail above formation level is about 52 cm *i.e.*, 18 cm the height of rail and bearing plate, 13·8 cm the thickness of the sleeper and 20 cm, the thickness of ballast under B.G. sleeper.

(*ii*) The minimum depth of ballast below sleeper bottom is 15 cm for both B.G. and M.G.

(*iii*) A cross slope of 1 in 40 is provided on the formation sloping on either side for proper drainage of ballast section.

Extra ballast on curves. The extra ballast on the outer shoulder provides better stability to the track in coping with the centrifugal forces generated by the moving vehicles on curves.

On outside of the curves move ballast is needed as under :

Table 16·9.

Rad. of curve	*Gauge*	*Max. Shoulder*
600 m	B.G.	400 mm
600 m	M.G.	400 mm
300 m	N.G.	330 mm

The quantity of ballast. The quantity of ballast required per m tangent length of railway track on curves flatter than 600 m with various depth of ballast cushion are as below :

Table 16·10.

Gauge		*Recommended depth*	*Quantity of ballast*
B.G.	Trunk route (CWR)	300 mm	1·588 m^3
	Trunk route (SWL)	250 mm	1·375 m^3
	Main line	200 mm	1·107 m^3
	Broad line	150 mm	0·965 m^3
M.G.	Trunk route	250 mm	0·965 m^2
	Main line	200 mm	0·817 m^3
	Broad line	150 mm	0·673 m^3

Note : A slight variation in quantity of ballast may be according to the sleeper used. Wooden and concrete through sleepers require slightly less ballast than on pot or trough sleepers.

The ballast should be renewed after a certain period, they make an impervious layer (check the proper drainage) and is crushed under loads of traffic.

16·8. Rail Fixers and Fasteners. Various types of fixures and fasteners are used in order to fix the rails, sleepers etc. in position. These are of the following types :

(1) Fish plates (2) Bolts (3) Spikes

(4) Chairs (5) Keys, cotters and the bars (6) Bearing plates

(7) Check rails (8) Guard rails (9) MCI insert

(10) Rubber pads etc.

(1) **Fish plates.** Dealt in detail in the chapter on joints in rails.

(2) **Composition of steel for fish plates.** Carbon 0·3 to 0·4 % ; Manganese less than 0·8% ; silicon less than 0·15% ; Sulphur and phosphorus less than 0·06%.

Dimensions of standard fish plates.

(*i*) For 90 *R* and heavier rail section 610 mm long.

(*ii*) The dia. of the holes in fish plates is kept 2 mm longer than the bolt dia.

(*iii*) The dia. of hole in the rail is kept 7 mm larger than the dia. of bolt.

(*iv*) Bolts are provided square heads.

For flat footed rails, bone shaped fish plates are used whereas for B.H. rails increased depth fish plates are used.

Compound fish plates. Fish plates for joining two different type of rails are specially designed according to the combination of the rails. See Fig. 16·13. Joints of rails.

Bolts. There are three types of bolts : (1) Fish plate bolts ; (2) Fang bolt ; (3) Hook bolts.

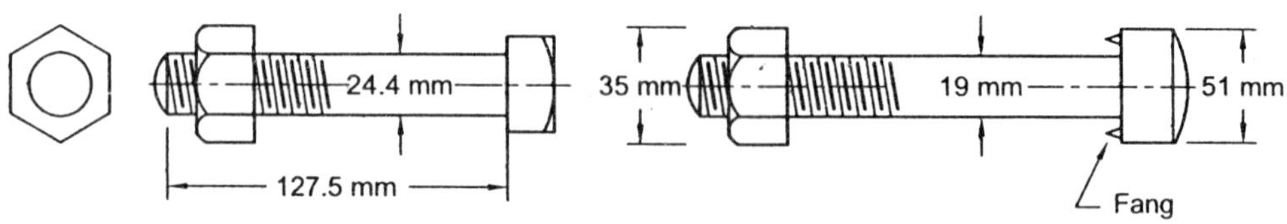

(*a*) Fish bolt for 90 R rail. (*b*) Fang bolt.

Fig. 16·31.

(1) **Fish bolt.** Fish bolts are used in the fixing fish plates to the rails.

(2) **Fang bolt.** Fang bolts are provided with a number of fangs (teeth) on the inner side of their heads. These bolts are used for fixing chairs with sleepers. The square of fang nut is 51 mm square with projections to hold the wooden sleepers from the bottom. The dia. of round fang bolt is kept 19 mm and its length is kept sufficient enough to pass through the sleeper and chair and to have a projected length for tightening the nut. They are specially used in locations when gauge is required to be maintained properly *i.e.*, slide chairs to sleepers under switches.

(3) **Hook bolts.** When sleepers rest on girders over bridges, the rails are fixed to the sleepers with standard dog spikes or skrew spikes. The fastening of sleepers with girders is done with bolts having a special head. These bolts are called as Hook or Dog bolts. The head of the hook bolt grips the flange of the girder and its vertical position is threaded through the holes bored in sleepers. Two hook bolts are sufficient for each sleeper. Bearing plates are invariably used on bridges. On the top end of the bolt an arrow mark is stamped for the maintenance staff to enable them to check the position of hook on the under side of the sleeper.

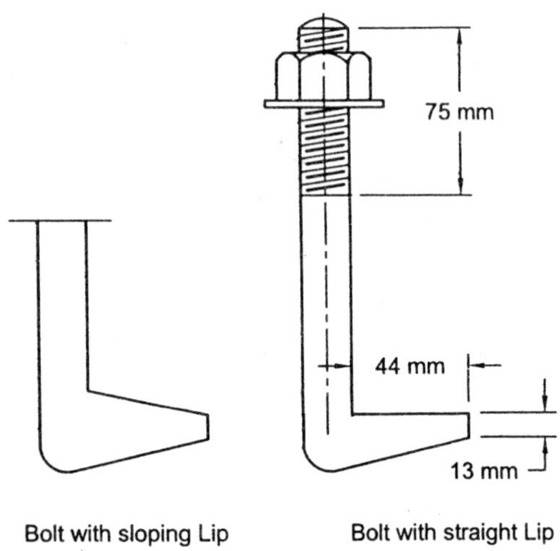

Fig. 16·32

Spikes. Spikes are used for fixing the rails on sleepers with or without bearing plates below the rails. The various types of spikes are given below :

(1) Dog spike (2) Screw spike (3) Round spikes (4) Elastic spikes

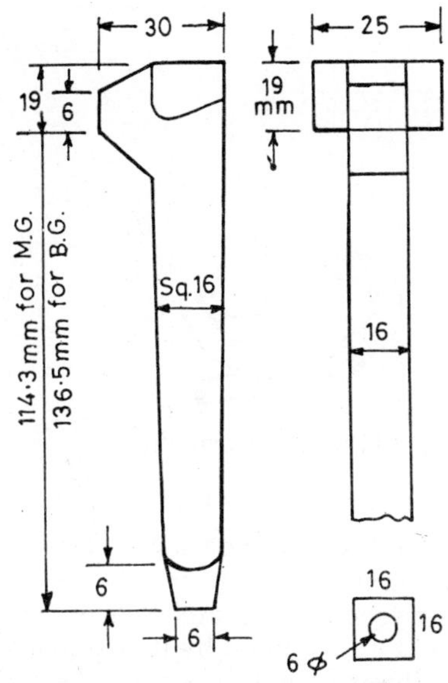

(a) (b)

Fig. 16·33. A dog spike.

Dog spike. The dog spikes are used for fixing F.F. rails to wooden sleepers. The section of the spike is square and the lower end is either blunt pointed or chisel shaped. (See Fig. 16·33)

Fixing of dog spikes. Bore the holes with the augurs right through the sleeper at appropriate positions. For hard wood sleepers 16 mm and for soft wood sleepers 14 mm holes have been standardised.

Insert the spike in the hole vertically till the shank touches the edge of the rail foot. If the head is not pulled up more than 3 to 5 mm, the spike should not be driven back as constant hammering of the spikes, loosens its grip by smoothing the sides of the spike hole.

Screw Spikes. Screw spikes or coach screws are slightly tapered screws provided with special threads. The head is circular (about 50 mm) dia. with a square protection. The length of these spikes varies with gauge. For B.G. its length is 170 mm and the dia. of the bottom end is 9·5 mm. The screw spikes or rail screws do not destroy wooden sleepers by spike killing.

Round spikes. As is the name the section is round having a dia. of 19 mm. These have blunt ends and their length varies according to gauge of the track. Round

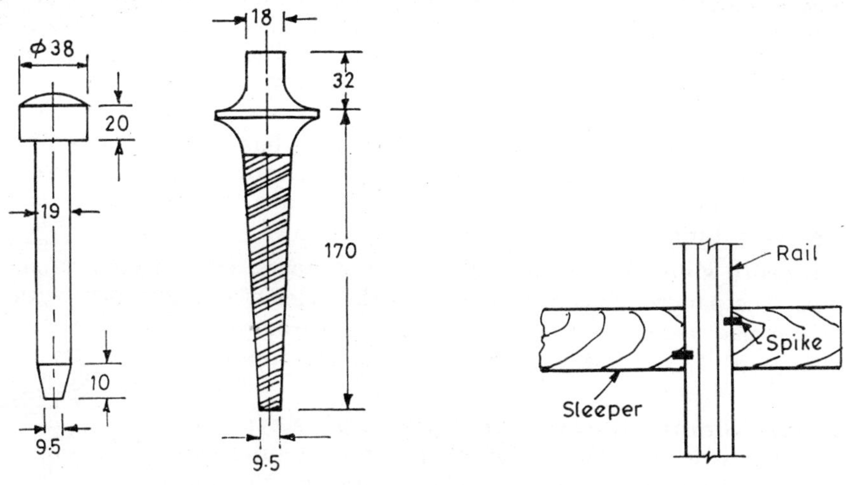

(a) (b)

Fig. 16·34. A screw spike.

spikes are used for fixing the rails on the wooden sleepers using anti creep bearing plates. These are used for fixing chairs and B.H. (Bull headed) rails to wooden sleepers and also for fixing slide chairs on points and crossings. Their use has become practically obsolete these days.

Elastic spikes. The elastic spikes are available in variety of forms, the standard type of elastic spike is shown in Fig. 16·35.

A steel spring and a specially shaped head are provided in this spike. These provide better grip with the foot of a flat footed rail and are not easily driven out due to wave motion of rails carrying heavy moving axle loads. In these spikes the wear and tear of rails is reduced, creates less noise and reduces the creep. To reduce corrosion these are galvanised.

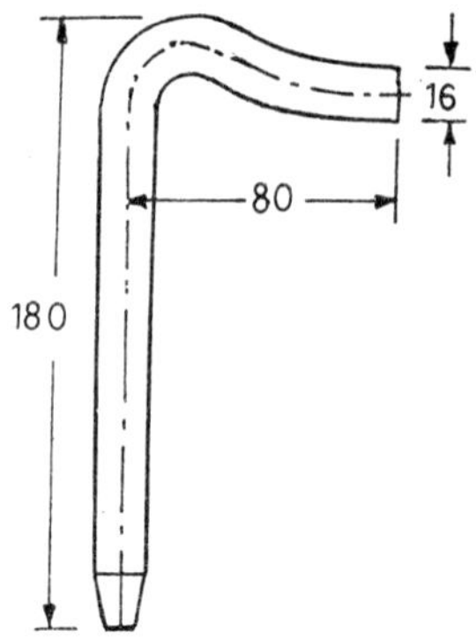

Fig. 16·35. An elastic spike

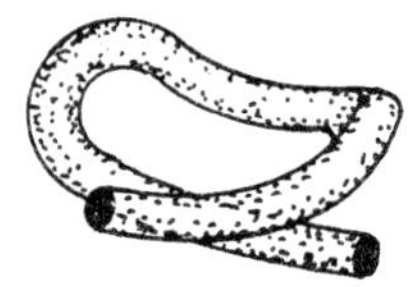

Fig. 16·36. A pandral clip

Modern Elastic Fasteners. The commonly used elastic fastenings are as under :

(*a*) **Pandral clips.** The pandral rail clip or elastic rail clip is a fit and forget type of fastenings. This clip is made of silica Mn. spring steel bar of 21 mm duly heat treated. A toe having 718 kg is quite adequate to restrict the rlative movement between the rail and sleeper. The Pandral clips ability to handle extreme loads in ardous conditions is exemplified by its extensive use on Railways. This clip system is able to withstand the rigrous climatic conditions with the rail temperature ranging from 70°C to below the freezing point. This clip can be suitably fixed on wooden, steel or concrete sleepers with the arrangements as given below.

For wooden sleepers. A base plate of steel or cast iron is fixed on the sleeper with the help of either dog or screw spikes. The base plate is provided with grooves on both sides of the rail for inserting the Pandrol clip with an ordinary hammer. The base plate is given the required slope of 1 : 20 inward and a rubber pad is also inserted between the rail and the base plate to give necessary cushioning effect.

For steel sleepers. In case of steel sleepers a base plate made of steel having grooves on both sides is welded on the sleepers. The pandrol clips are inserted into the grooves with a hammer. For repair work the sleepers are transported to the workshops which creates a great difficulty.

For concrete sleepers. In case of concrete sleepers, cast in pandrol shoulders hold the pandrol clips. The pandrol clips are inserted in the holes of the shoulders with an ordinary hammer. A rubber pad usually 4·5 mm thick is provided between the rail bottom and sleeper for making the assembly doubly elastic.

(*b*) **Double Shank Elastic Rail Spikes.** This type of spikes is made from a rectangular section of spring steel suitably heat treated. It has two 14 mm square shanks to hold the sleeper and has two rectangular bars which press the lower flange of the rail. The spikes exert a toe load of 1500 kg to 1800 kg in LWR tracks. Double shank spikes are more suitable where no anticreep anchors are necessary.

Fig. 16·37. Double shank elastic spike.

Chairs. Chairs are used for holding double headed (D.H.) and Bull headed (B.H.) rails on the sleepers with proper gauge. The chairs are invariably made of cast iron and they distribute the load from the rail on the sleeper through the flat bottoms. A chair has two jaws sufficiently wide apart for the rail to be placed on it. The lower table of B.H. rail rests on the base of the chair. The inner jaw is tightly held against the web of the rail. The rail seal of the chair is tilted inwards 1 in 20. A key is insisted between the outer face of the web of rail and outer jaw. The chairs are fixed with the sleepers by means of three spikes, two on the gauge side and one on the outer side. Some times four bolts may also be used.

The keys which are inserted between the saw and the web of rail to keep the rail in position may be either of wood or metal and they may be either straight or tapered.

The chairs have to be fixed on a level bar on the sleeper so as to avoid the risk of breaking the chair due to loads being concentrated on a small area.

For fixing the double head rails on iron sleeper, the jaws are cast with pot or plate. The shape of the jaw is similar to that of wooden sleepers.

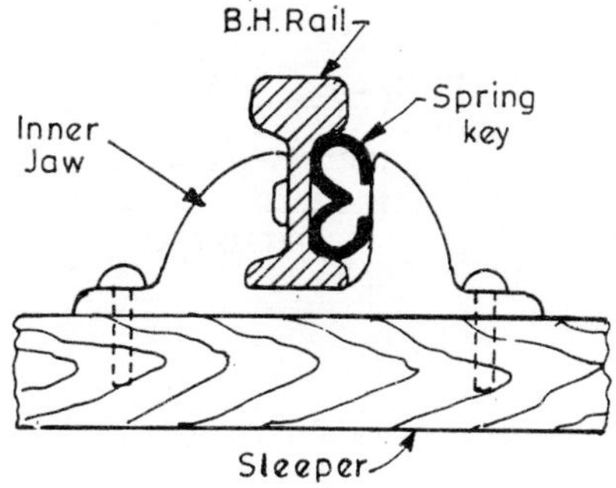

Fig. 16·38. A chair for B.H. rail.

(1) **Keys.** A small tapered piece of wood or metal which is used to fix a rail to the chair is known as key. Keys may be either straight or tapered. Wooden keys are cheep but are liable to be rotten. Therefore steel keys of different designs are used. The common type of metal keys are :

(*a*) Stuart's key (*b*) Morgan key

(*c*) Coiled key

(*a*) **Stuart's key.** Consists of steel plate bent in the form of English letter **E** and a steel plate wedge. The wedge is inserted in the gap between ends of the key to keep it tight against the web of the rail and outer jaw of the chair.

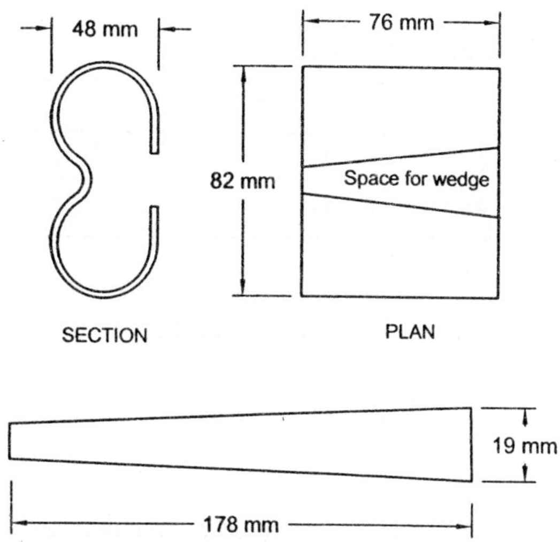

Fig. 16·39. Details of Stuart key.

(*b*) **Morgan's key or two way key.** The length of the two way key is about 176 ± 2 mm for B.G. track with a taper of 1 in 12. These keys are universally employed with cast iron chairs tough sleepers, pot sleepers CBT-9 sleepers. As these keys are manufactured by M/s Morgan Ltd. hence the name.

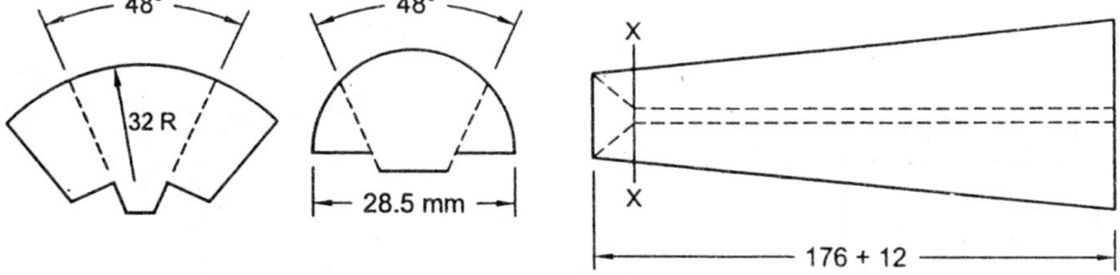

Fig. 16·40. Morgan's key.

(*c*) **Other closed coil key.** An open closed key as is shown in the figure 16·41.

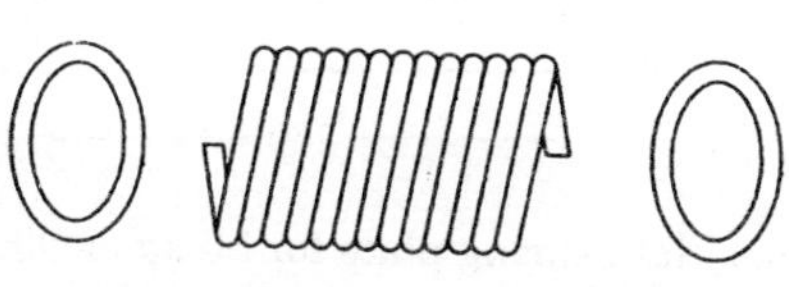
Fig. 16·41. Closed coil key.

(2) **Cotters.** The cotters are used for fixing the tie bars with cast iron sleepers. A cotter is a wedge shaped mild steel plate with a split in either horizontal or vertical plane. Based on the method of splitting, cotters are classified as below in Indian Railways.

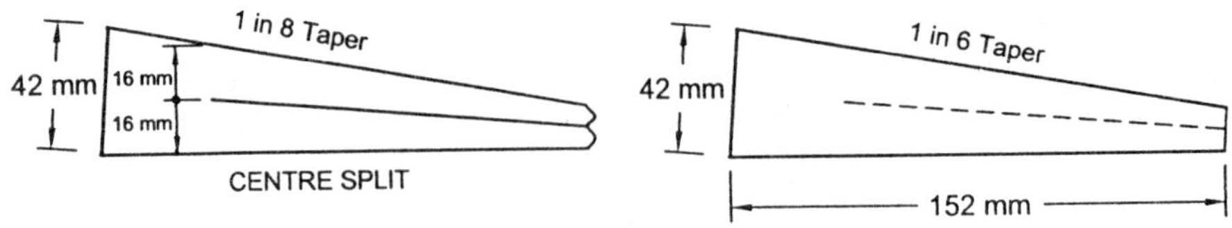

Fig. 16·42. Cotters.

(*a*) Centre split cotter (*b*) Side split cotter.

On account of easy splitting and comparatively longer life split cotter is most commonly used.

(3) **M.S. Tie bars.** Mild steel tie bars are used to connect and hold the pots or bowls together. In case of plate sleepers the tie bars extend to the outer edges of the pots or plates or a little beyond the rail seat. Long tie bars are preferred to counteract the tendency of the pots to tilt inwards under heavy moving loads.

Table 16·11. The dimension of standard tie bars.

Gauge	*Length (mm)*	*Width (mm)*	*Thickness (mm)*
B.G.	2720	50	12
M.G.	1870	45	10

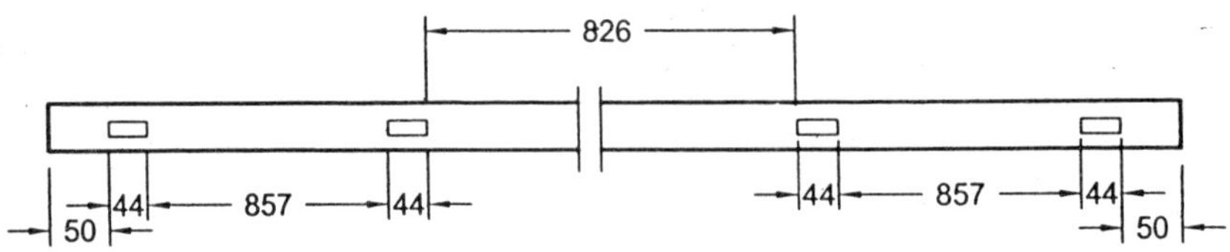

Fig. 16·43. A tee bar for B.G.

Bearing plates. These are rectangular plates of mild steel, cast iron, wrought iron or malleable steel which are interposed between the foot of a flat footed rod and wooden sleepers to distribute the load on large area are called bearing plates.

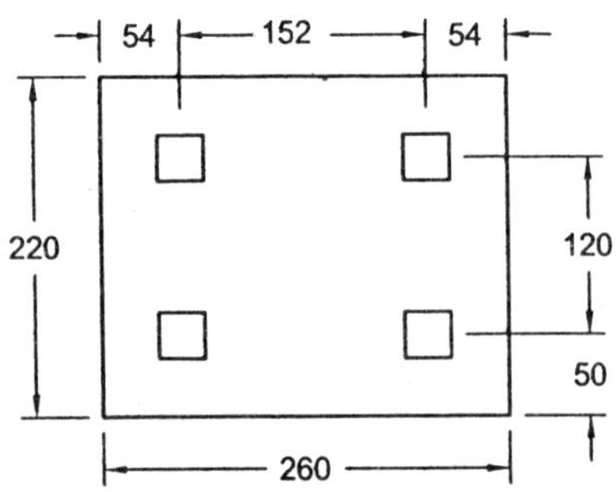

(*a*) Flat bearing plate for 50 kg or 90 rail sec.

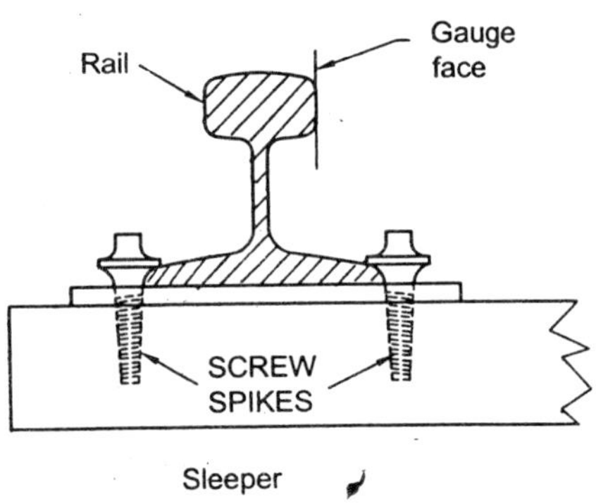

(*b*) M.S. flat bearing plate

Fig. 16·44.

The dimension of steel bearing plates commonly used are :

Gauge	*Length perp. to rail*	*Width parallel to rail*	*Thickness*	*Weight*
B.G.	254 mm	229 mm	18 mm	6·25 kg
M.G.	203 mm	165 mm	18 mm	4·00 kg

Check Rails. The rails which are introduced along a inner track on sharp curves for reducing the wear of rails are called check rails. Check rails are also provided along the straight rails opposite the crossings in turn outs.

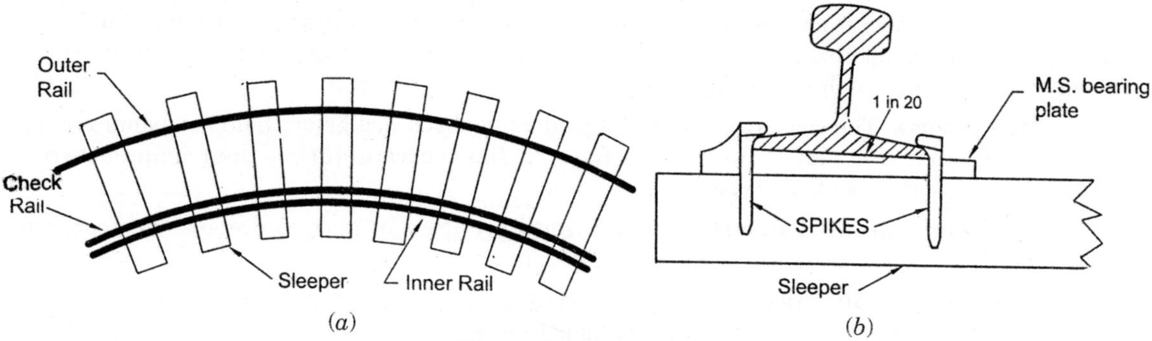

Fig. 16·45. Check rail.

While negotiating a curve, the wagon has a tendency to move upward and the inner face of the wheel rubs against the check rails and thus the flange of the outer wheel is prevented from coming in contact with the side of out rail load. Whereas in case of points and crossings, the check rails serve the purpose of guiding the wheel flange. Through the narrow clearance available at the nose of crossing. The check rails are fixed to the flat footed inner rails with bolts through distance pieces of cast iron known as 'check blocks'. The check rails are provided on curves of 8° and over for B.G. and 14° and over for M.G. tracks. The worn rails which becomes unfit for through tracks are generally used as check rails.

If the gauge is widened on the curve, the distance between the worn rail and check rail is also increased by half the widening of the curve. The heads of the check rails and running rail are kept at same level. The size of check blocks ensure the required clearance. Check rails are also flared at the ends to prevent the wheel flange from sinking them (Fig. 16·45), with B.H. rails double chairs are used for holding the check rails.

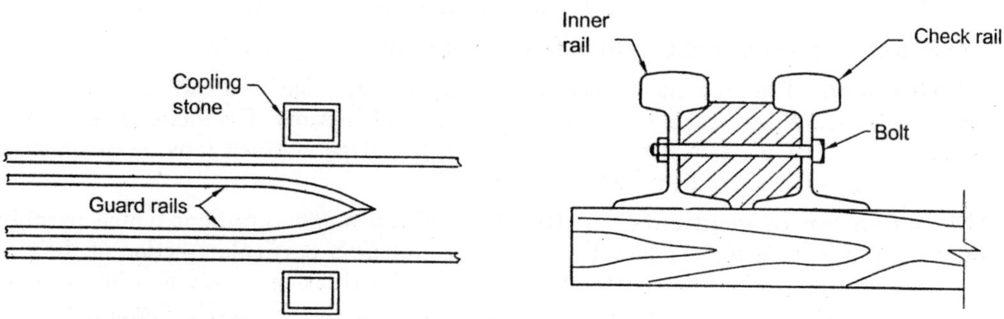

(*a*) Guard rails (*b*) Check block

Fig. 16·46.

Guard rails. The rails which are provided on bridges of long spans with open flow to the running rails in order to prevent derailed wheels from falling off the bridge, are called guard rails. These are fastened to sleepers at a fixed distance apart.

Guard rails are also provided on level crossings to provide a path way cleared to the running wheels.

In case of bridges the guard rails are fixed at 250 mm from end running rail. The top of the guard rails generally kept at the same level as that of the running rail. In no case it should be kept higher than running rail. These may be kept 25 mm lower than the running rail. The guard rail on bridge are joined with the fish plates. The two guard rails cover at point 5·7 m for B.G. track and 4·5 m for M.G. tracks beyond the end of the bridges. The ends of the guard rails are bent down to prevent the hanging points of the running vehicles to strike them.

Sometimes the guard rails also fixed out side the inter rail space and parallel to the running rail. The main function of a guard rails is to maintain the sleepers at correct distances. The outer guard rails are flared at the ends.

MCI inserts. The cast iron pandral shoulders as discussed before hold the pandral clips. The malleable cast iron (MCI) inserts are fixed in the concrete during their manufacturing process. These inserts are of two types.

(*i*) **Stem type MCI inserts.** These inserts are used in normal pretensioned concrete sleepers. The weight of the stem type insert is 1·6 kg per piece.

(*ii*) **Gate type MCI inserts.** These inserts are used in post tenstioned concrete sleepers. The app. weight of gate type MCI insert is 1·7 kg per piece.

Rubber pads. A rubber pad is interposed between the foot of rail and cement sleepers. The main functions of a rubber pad are :

(*i*) It dampens and absorbs the vibration of the rail.

(*ii*) It easily absorbs the shocks.

(*iii*) It resists the lateral movement of the rail.

(*iv*) It prevents abrasion of the rail bottom surface.

(*v*) It provides good electrical insulation for a electrified track.

In Indian railways grooved rubber pads of 4·5 mm thickness made of a special quality rubber are used.

In case track circuiting is not required, the rubber pad may be replaced by steel liner of the same shape and size.

16·9. Railway Track Geometrics. There are following design parameters of railway track :

(1) Gradients (2) Grade compensation (3) Radius and degree of curve

(4) Super elevation or Cant (5) Safe speed of trains

(1) **Gradients.** The amount of slope in longitudinal direction in a railway track is known as gradient or grade. When track rises in the direction of motion of vehicles, the gradient is known as up gradient or position gradient while when the slope of track falls in its longitudinal direction as known as down gradients or (–ve) gradient.

Classification of gradients : (*i*) **Ruling gradients.** The gradient which permits the maximum weight of a train to be pulled by a locomotive along a particular section of the track is known as 'Ruling gradient for that particular section of the track or to say a ruling gradient is maximum gradient which may be permitted on the section of the track. The hauling capacity of a locomotive on a track is inversely proportional to the upgradient of the tracks. On steeper gradients more powerful locomotives are employed. To obtain efficient haulage at the lowest cost, he track section should be provided a gentle slope as far as possible. It is also advantageous to have a rising gradient followed by a falling gradient. The amount of energy used up while climbing up the gradient, may be saved while descending the falling gradient. Moreover if a rising gradient is followed by a falling gradient, the high speed gained by the locomotive at the lowest end of the falling gradient may be suitably utilised to climb the rising gradient. The ruling gradient is decided according to the length of the gradient and locations in addition to the gradient itself.

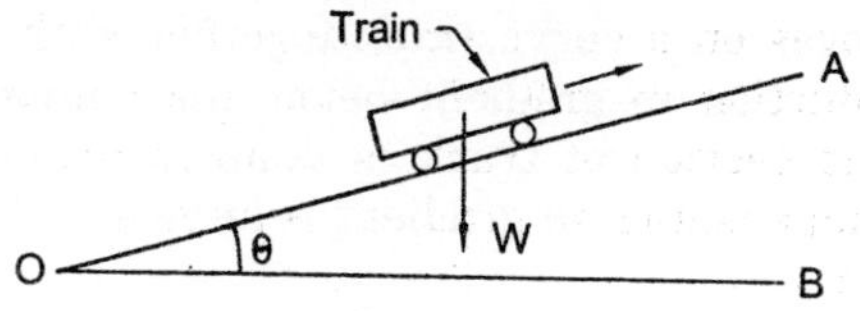

Fig. 16·47.

Grade resistance. Extra amount of energy required by a locomotive on the gradients

$$\text{Grade resistance} = W \times \frac{1}{\text{rate of grad.}}$$

where θ = slope of the track, W = load of the train.

Though there is no fixed ruling gradient is fixed, it varies area to area yet a tentative gradients are adopted as under :

In plain 1 in 150 to 1 in 200

In hills 1 in 100 to 1 in 150

It is a general rule that all the gradients provided after compensation for curvature should be either equal to or flatter than the ruling gradient and in no case the gradient should exceed the specified value of the ruling gradient for the section of the track.

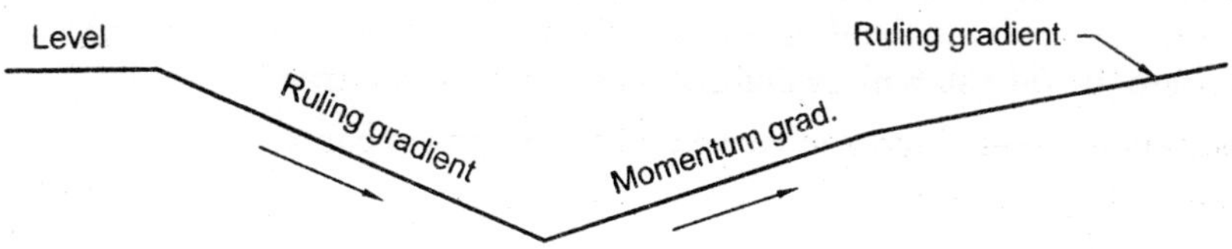

Fig. 16·48.

Momentum gradient. The up gradients which exceeds the ruling gradient along which an increased load of the train may be hauled by the locomotive after gaining momentum during descending a falling gradient is called a momentum gradient. In rolling terrain, a falling gradient is usually followed by a rising gradient. In the falling gradient a vehicle attain a sufficient moment while descending, which is utilised in the up gradient where the vehicle can climb even at sleeper gradient than the ruling gradient due to extra kinetic energy which it has gained during descending. This up gradient which is more than the ruling gradient is known as the momentum gradient. The momentum gradient can only be utilised if the locomotive is not closed while descending so that the momentum which it has gained may not destroyed.

Pusher gradient. In steep gradient more than the ruling gradient an extra locomotive is used at the end of the train to push the train up. This gradient is known as the pusher or the helper gradient. The pusher gradient is generally given in hilly terrian in order to reduce the length of the train. While deciding the pushing of gradient, the hauling capacity of locomotive and the loads are taken in account so that no energy is wasted. The examples of pusher gradient are :

1 in 37 on B.G. track along Western Ghat near Lonavala.

1 in 25 on M.G. track along Siliguri Darjeeling railway track.

Gradient in station yards. The track at the station yards are kept almost lined, but keeping on drainage of the yard in view a gradient of 1 in 1000 upto a maximum limit of 1 in 400 is given.

Gradient stones are provided on the track where the gradient is changed. The indication on the stone indicates as under level track, up gradient in 300 or down gradient as 1 in 250.

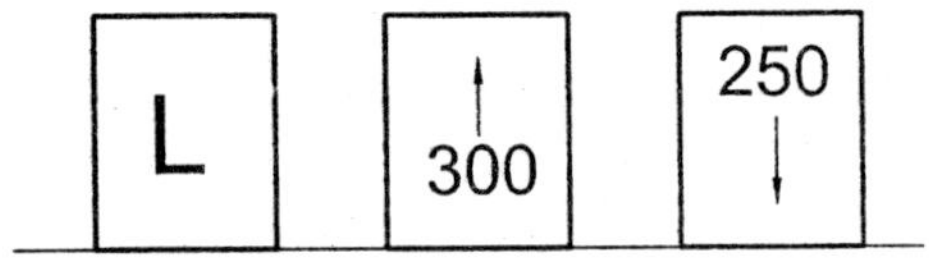

Fig. 16·49.

Grade compensation. When ever a vehicle moves on a curve track together with a gradient, a reduction in gradient below the ruling gradient of this section of track is done in order to compensate the extra tractive force required. This compensation in gradient is known as the "grade compensation". The recommended compensations are :

B.G. track 0·04 % per degree, M.G. track 0·03 % per degree, M.G. track 0·02 % per degree.

Example. *If the ruling gradient is 1 : 30 for a particular section of a track on B.G. line and the curve is 4 degree. What should be the actual gradient ?*

Solution. Grade compensation for 4° curve = 0·04 × 4 = 0·16%

Ruling gradient is 1 in 300, $= \frac{1}{300} \times 100 = 0{\cdot}33\ \%$

Hence the required grad. = Ruling gradient – grade compensation

$= 0{\cdot}33 - 0{\cdot}16 = 0{\cdot}17\%$ or 1 in 58

Curves in railway tracks. The curves in railways are generally kept circular *i.e.*, the radius of the curve remains the same throughout the entire curve.

Degree of railway curve. "The angle subtended at the centre of the curve by an arc of 100 ft. (30·5 m) length is defined as degree of curve" or "the angle subtended at the centre of the curve by a chord of 100′ (30·5 m) is defined as the degree of curve."

Relation between degree of curve and the radius of curve.

(*a*) Based on arc of 30·5 m length

Let R be the radius of curve and θ = degree of curve

Total circumference = $2\pi R$ makes 360° at the centre

$\therefore$ 30·5 m arc makes an angle $= \frac{360}{2\pi R} \times 30{\cdot}5 = \theta°$

$$\therefore \quad \theta = \frac{360 \times 30{\cdot}5}{2\pi R} = \frac{1747{\cdot}52}{R}$$

or $$\theta = \frac{1750}{R} \text{ (rounding 1747·52 to 1750)}$$

i.e. for 1° curve the radius = 1750 metres.

(*b*) Based on chord of 30·5 m length

Let R = radius of curve and θ be the angle of curve

The angle *AOB* is the degree of curve.

Construction. Draw a perpendicular bisector *OC* on the chord *AB*

Now $$\sin\frac{\theta}{2} = \frac{AB}{AO} = \frac{15{\cdot}25}{R} \text{ or } \frac{15{\cdot}25}{R} = \frac{\sin\theta}{2} \text{ where } \theta \text{ is a degrees}$$

$$= \frac{D}{2} \times \frac{\pi}{180} \text{ (}\sin\theta = \theta \text{ if } \theta \text{ is in radians)}$$

or $$\theta = \frac{15{\cdot}25 \times 2 \times 180}{\pi R} = \frac{1747{\cdot}523}{R} \text{ or } \theta = \frac{1750}{R}$$

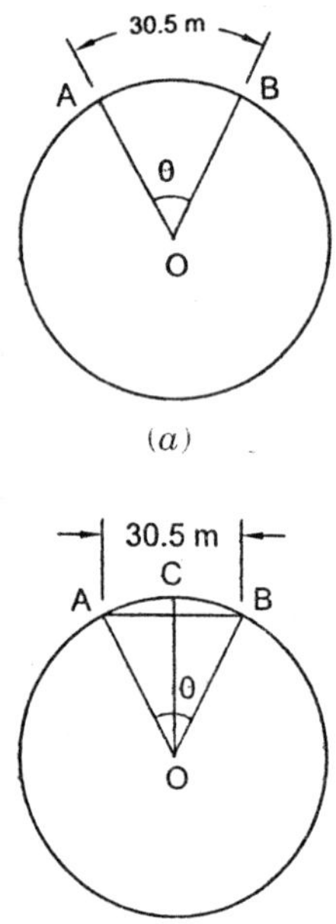

(*a*) (*b*)

Fig. 16·50.

(*i*) Some engineers in railways adopt the degree of curve $\theta = \dfrac{1720}{R}$ which is based on a chord/arc length of 30 m.

(*ii*) The degree of curve based on chord/arc length of 100 is as $\theta = \dfrac{5730}{R}$ where R is a feet

Adverse effects of the curves on the track

(*i*) The length of train is restricted

(*ii*) The maximum permissible speed is restricted on curves

(*iii*) The use of heavy locomotives is to be restricted.

(*iv*) The chances of derailment increases.

(*v*) The running of trains on curves is not smooth.

(*vi*) Extra fittings on track is needed.

(*vii*) Maintenance cost is increased.

The factors kept in mind when deciding a rail curve.

(*i*) **Wheel base of the vehicle.** The distance between two adjacent wheel axles of a bogie is called as "base of vehicle". In case the radius of curve is small the degree of curve is large. The vehicle does not move freely and the chances of derailment increases.

(*ii*) **Sharpness of the curve**. The sharper is the curve the greater is the force required by the locomotives.

(*iii*) **Amount of super elevation.** The super elevation is increased with the degree of curvature.

Permissible Degree of curves on tracks

B.G. = 10° M.G. = 16° M.G. = 40°

Relation between radius and version of a curve

$$V = \frac{12.5\,C^2}{R} \quad \text{when} \quad V = \text{version of the curve}$$

C = length of the long chord

R = radius of the curve

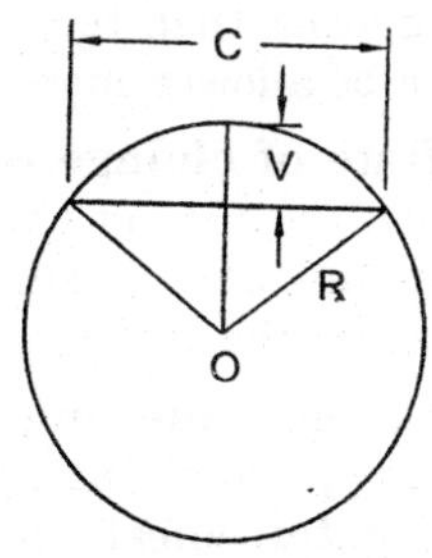

Fig. 16·51.

16·10. Super elevation. Due to the centrifugal forces the outer wheel of a vehicle is raised a slight vertical distance above the rail level. In order to compensate it, the outer rail is raised in level, which is called as super elevation.

Centrifugal force $F = \dfrac{WV^2}{gR}$

Super elevation $e = \dfrac{V^2 G}{gR}$

where V = velocity of vehicle in m/sec.

G = gauge of the track in metres

R = Radius of curve

g = acceleration due to gravity

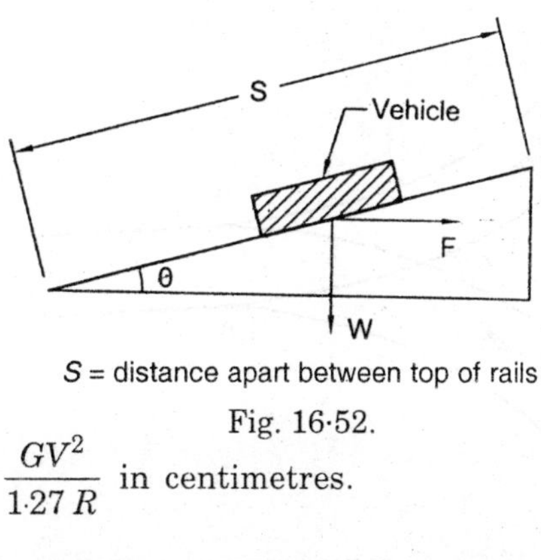

S = distance apart between top of rails

Fig. 16·52.

If the velocity is in k.m. per hour then $e = \dfrac{GV^2}{1.27\,R}$ in centimetres.

Super elevation on different tracks

B.G. track $e = \dfrac{1.676\,V^2}{1.27\,R} = 1.315\,V^2/R$

M.G. track $e = \dfrac{1{\cdot}000\, V^2}{1{\cdot}25\, R} = 0{\cdot}800\, V^2/R$

M.G. track $e = \dfrac{0{\cdot}762\, V^2}{1{\cdot}27\, R} = 0{\cdot}60\, V^2/R$

Maximum permissible super elevation and cant deficiency. It is practically noticed that the super elevation is affected by frictional resistance, coning of wheels, body of the vehicle and the weighted average speed of moving vehicle. The maximum permissible super elevation on Indian Railways is as under :

B.G. Track	Metre Gauge	Narrow Gauge
165 mm	102 mm	76 mm

It is about 1/10 of the gauge.

Cant Deficiency. The equilibrium cant is provided on the basis of the equilibrium speed of different trains running on a track. The equilibrium speed for a fast moving train is always less than the maximum speed of a train. Hence the super elevation required for high speed trains is greater than the equilibrium cant. The shortening of the actual super elevation for high speed trains is called 'cant deficiency'. The cant deficiency may be defined as the difference between the cant necessary for the maximum permissible speed on curve and the actual cant provided. Higher cant deficiency causes more unbalanced centrifugal force and discomforts to the passengers.

Cant excess. The cant excess may be defined as the difference between the equilibrium cant and the theoretical cant required for the given lower speed. When a train moves along a curve at a speed lower than the equilibrium speed, a cant excess occurs. In Indian Railways, cant excess should not be allowed more than 75 mm on B.G. and 65 mm for M.G. for all types of rolling stocks.

Rate of change of cant is the amount by which cant is increased or decreased per sec. is called as the rate of change of cant. An increase or decrease of 38 mm of cant per sec. by a train travelling at a maximum permitted speed is said to have a rate of change of cant of 38 mm per sec. along the transition curve.

Gauge widening on curves. When a train passes on a curve, the outer wheel has to travel more distance than the inner one. This is compensated by (*a*) coning of the wheels due to which on outer wheel the longer diameter of cone is effective while on the inner wheel the smaller dia. is effective (*b*) By widening the gauge as follows :

B.G. exact upto 4°, 6 mm slack, from 4° to 6° and 13 mm slack from 6° to 10° curves.

M.G. exact upto 6°, 6 mm slack from 6° to 10° and 13 mm slack from 10° to 16° curves.

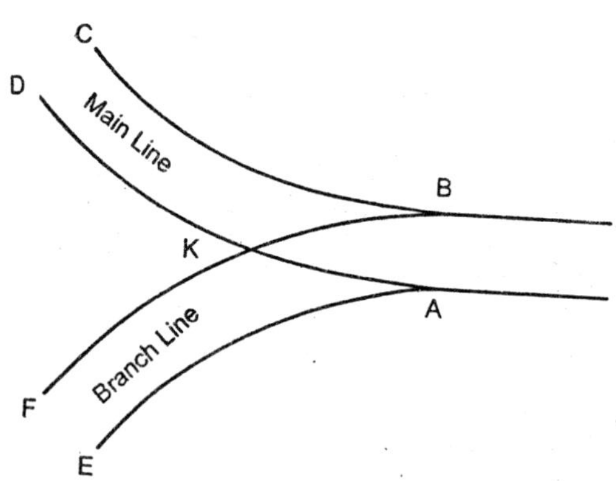

Fig. 16·53. Negative super elevation.

Negative super elevation or –ve cant. When a branch line bifercates from a main line on a curve of contrary flexure, the super elevation necessary for the average speed of trains running over the main line can not be provided. The speed of the trains over the diverging track and main line track has to be reduced considerably. The reason for this reduction is that on the branch line track the inner rail remains at higher level than the outer rail.

Considering the curvature of the tracks, the following condition should satisfied :

(1) On the main line point A should be higher than B, try an amount S_1 (Super elevation of main line). Refer Fig. 16·53.

(2) On the branch line, point B should be on higher level than A by an amount S_2 (super elevation on branch line)

(3) The point K on both tracks should be on the same level.

But the contrary conditions (1) and (2) can not be fulfilled simultaneously with in one layout. In such situation a small amount of cant deficiency is permitted and accordingly speeds on both the tracks are restricted, particularly on the branch line. The amount by which the actual super elevation falls short of the equilibrium super elevation is called cant deficiency or negative super elevation.

Weighted average speed. The super elevation depends on the velocity of the train. In actual position all the trains moving on a track can not be supported to have the same velocity as is designed for calculating super elevation. Moreover the super elevation are provided for a certain speed can not be changed for every speed respective to each train. Hence to overcome as to minimum of average speed is compromised for design and the super elevation is provided on the track according to it. This average speed is known as weighted average speed. The calculation for the average speed is done as under :

$$\text{Weighted average speed} = \frac{V_1 n_1 + V_2 n_2 + V_3 n_3 \ldots V_n n_n}{n_1 + n_2 + n_3 \ldots + n_n}$$

where $V_1, V_2, V_3 \ldots V_n$ are the speeds of the $n_1, n_2, n_3 \ldots n_n$ trains.

Equilibrium speed as per Indian Railways

(*a*) If the maximum allowable speed on B.G. and M.G. sections is 50 kmph or more.

i.e. $V_{max} \geq 50$ kmph

(*i*) Average speed $= \frac{3}{4} \times V_{max}$ subject to minimum of 50 kmph.

(*ii*) Average speed = Safe speed of the curve obtained by "Martin's" formula. The lesser of the two values is accepted for the section.

(*b*) If the maximum allowable speed of the section on B.G. and M.G. tracks is 50 kmph or less *i.e.*

$V_{max} \leq 50$ kmph

(*i*) Average speed = average sanctioned speed for the section

(*ii*) Average speed = safe speed of the curve obtained by Martin's formula

Safe speed on curves. Maximum speed of a train depends on the, gauge, super elevation, presence of transition curves at the ends and the weight of the train and is called the safe speed on the curve. The safe speed is the speed which remains safe from the danger of overtuning or derailment etc. The safe speed is calculated by the following methods :

(*a*) **Martin's formula for safe speed**

For B.G. and M.G. tracks with suitable transitions

$V = 4{\cdot}4\sqrt{R - 70}$ where R is the radius of curve in metres

For B.G. and M.G. tracks without transition curves

$V = \frac{4}{5}$th of the speed with transition curves $= 3{\cdot}52\sqrt{R - 70}$

For N.G. tracks (2′ 6″) with suitable transition curves

$V = 3{\cdot}65\sqrt{A - 6}$ subject to a maximum of 50 kmph

For N.G. tracks (2′ 6″) without transition curves

$$V = 2{\cdot}92\sqrt{R-6} \text{ subject to maximum of 40 km per hr.}$$

(*b*) **Safe speed based on super elevation**

Super elevation $$e = \frac{GV^2}{127\,R} \text{ or } V = \sqrt{\frac{127\,R \times e}{G}}$$

The value of e in the above equation is the sum of actual super elevation and the specified cant deficiency.

(*c*) **Safe velocity based on length of transition curve**

(*i*) For the normal speeds upto 100 kmph $V = \dfrac{134\,L}{e}$ ...(1)

where L = the length of the transition curve based on the rate of change of cant as 38 mm/sec for normal speeds upto 100 kmph and 55 km/sec for speeds exceeding 100 kmph. Super elevation e is in mm.

For normal speed upto 100 kmph, $V = \dfrac{134\,L}{d}$ ...(2)

The cant deficiency d is in mm.

The lesser value of the speeds obtained from equation (1) and (2) is accepted as the safe speed.

(*ii*) For normal speeds exceeding 100 kmph.

$$V = \frac{198\,L}{e} \quad \text{...(1)}$$

$$V = \frac{198\,L}{d} \quad \text{...(2)}$$

The lesser value of speed obtained from equation (1) and (2) is accepted value as the safe speed.

(*d*) **Maximum sanctioned speed for the section.** The speed for the section determined by the factors such as track conditions. Standard of locking, and type of locomotives etc. is known as maximum sanctioned speed of the section.

16·11. Points and Crossings

Turn out. (Points and crossings). The assembly of various components which enables trains to move from one track to other track either parallel or diverging from the 1st track is called as turn out or points and crossings.

(1) Points (2) Crossings

(1) **Points.** The components of points.

(*a*) **Stock rails.** The rails of main line track against which tongue rails singly fit are called stock rails.

(*b*) **Tongue rails.** The tapered rails whose thicker ends known as heel are fixed to the main track and thinner ends known as toe of the switch to obtain a snug fit with the respective stock rails, are called tongue rails, switch rails or point rails. By moving the tongue rails the flanged wheels of the trains are diverted from one track to the other. In India straight tongue rails are used.

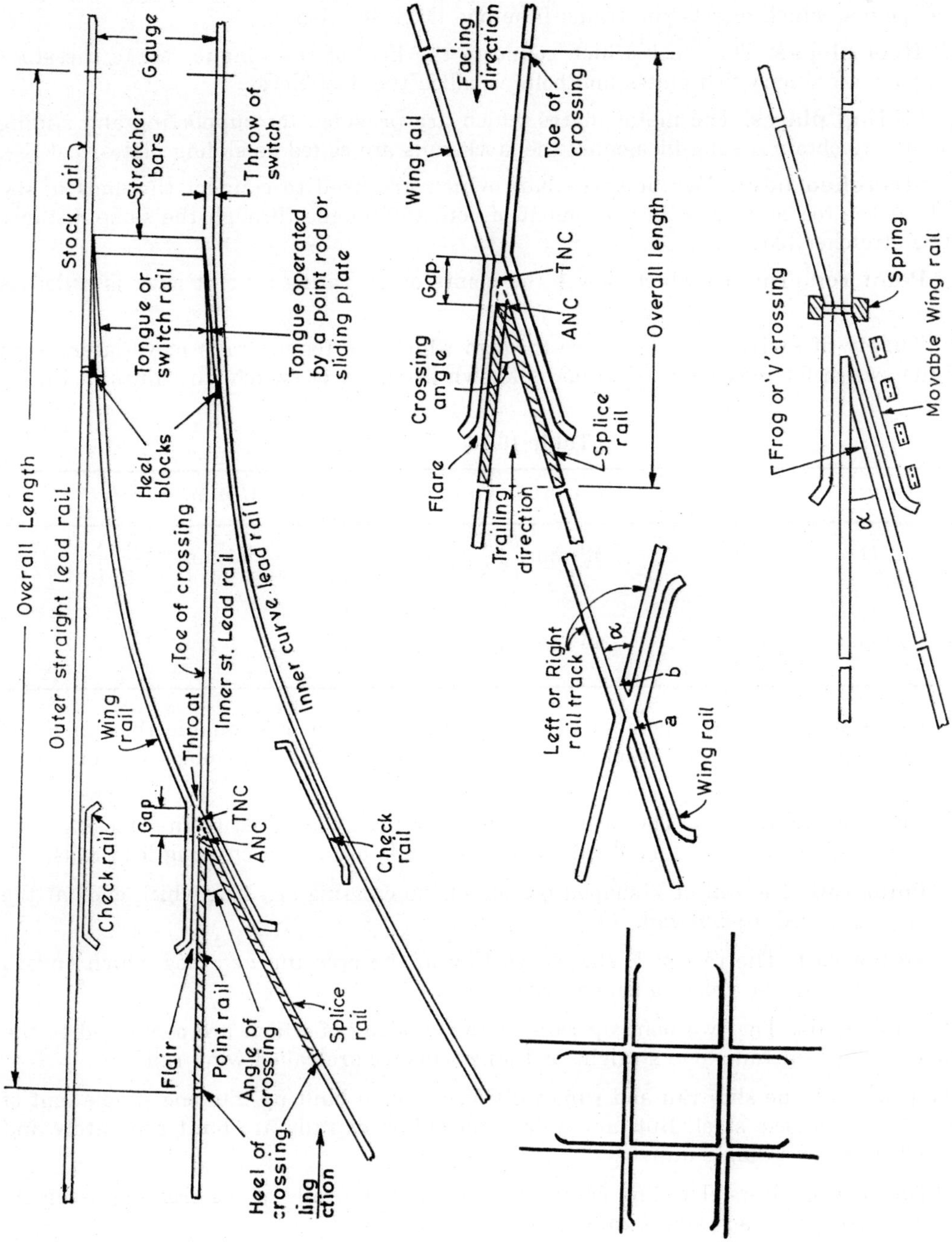
Gauge
Throw of switch
Stretcher bars
Stock rail
Tongue or switch rail
Tongue operated by a point rod or sliding plate
Heel blocks
Overall Length
Outer straight lead rail
Toe of crossing
Inner st. Lead rail
Inner curve lead rail
Wing rail
Throat
Gap
TNC
ANC
Check rail
Flair
Point rail
Angle of crossing
Splice rail
Heel of crossing
Facing direction
Toe of crossing
Wing rail
Overall length
Gap
TNC
ANC
Crossing angle
Splice rail
Flare
Trailing direction
Left or Right rail track
α
b
a
Wing rail
Frog or 'V' crossing
Spring
Movable Wing rail
α

Fig. 16·54.

(*c*) **Switch.** A stock rail and its respective tongue rail form a switch. A set of switches is known as points, which directs the trains from one track to other.

(*d*) **Heel blocks.** The block which connects the heel of the tongue rail to the stock rail, with a pair of ordinary fish plates and bolts is called the heel block.

(*e*) **Sliding plates.** The metal plates which are provided for supporting and sliding the tongue rails to obtain a snug fit against the stock rails are called as sliding plates.

(*f*) **Stretched bars.** Two or three bars which are used to connect the ends of the tongue rails at the toe to ensure the movement of both the tongue through the same distance are called as stretcher bars.

(*g*) **Point rod.** The rod which moves the points by operating a point lever is called as point rod.

(*h*) **Throw of switch.** The distance through which the tongue rails move laterally at the toe of the switch for movement of trains is known as throw of switch. In values in Indian Railways are :

Table 16·13.

Gauge	*Maximum Value*	*Minimum value*
B.G.	48 mm $\left(1\frac{7}{8}''\right)$	44 mm $\left(1\frac{3}{4}''\right)$
M.G.	44 mm $\left(1\frac{3}{4}''\right)$	41 mm $\left(1\frac{5}{8}''\right)$

(2) **Crossings.** The arrangement of rails which is provided to unable the flanges of wheels to cross the rail of other track is called as crossings. The various components of crossings are :

(*a*) **Crossing lead rails.** The heels of tongue rails are connected to the crossing with two rails, one straight and other curved rail. These two rails are called crossing lead rails.

(*b*) **Point rail.** The rail of *V* shaped portion of the crossing *i.e.*, frog which ends at the nose of crossing, is called a point rail.

(*c*) **Splice rail.** The rail of *V* shaped portion of the crossing *i.e.*, frog which ends a little behind the nose of the crossing called splice rail.

(*d*) **Wing rails.** The two bent up rails of the crossing of which are connected to the ends of the crossing lead rails (one straight and other curved) are called wing rails.

The point rail, the slice rail and wing rails formerly all built up into one simple unit of high carbon or manganese steel. But now a days the different rails are built separately and are assembled to make a single unit.

(*e*) **Toe of crossings.** The line joining the joints of the rails of the crossing assembly with the ends of crossing lead rails is called the toe of crossing.

(*f*) **Heel of crossings.** The line which joins the ends of point rails and splice rail of the crossing is called heel of the crossings.

(*g*) **Throat.** The movement space between the two wing rails of a crossing is called the throat of the crossing.

(*h*) **Crossing angle.** The angle between the gauge faces of the point rail and splice rail is called crossing angle (α). The size of the crossing is designated by its crossing angle.

(*i*) **Theoretical nose of crossing (TNC).** The point of outer section of the gauge faces of the point rail and splice rail of a crossing, is called the theoretical nose of crossing. It is slightly away from the actual nose of the crossing.

(*j*) **Actual nose of crossing (ANC).** The end of the point rail in the gap of the crossing is called actual nose of the crossing. The actual nose of crossing (ANC) is generally kept equal to the web thickness of the rail. T.N.C. (theoretical nose of crossing) being knife edged would soon be knocked off, the point rail is therefore cut a little short gets length to form a blunt round end about 15 mm wide. To protect the nose from being knocked off by the jumping of wheels across the gap at the throat, the following precautions are taken :

(*a*) The top of the wing rail is kept 3 to 5 mm higher than that of the nose by means of packing underneath or the top of surface of the nose is planed by that much amount to kept it below the tops of both the wing rails.

(*b*) The gauge is made tight in the front of the points, exact at the heel of the switch and a little easy thereafter upto the nose.

Note : (1) All the measurements are taken from the T.M.C. for designing other points and the turn out.

(2) Distance between ANC and TMC = thickness of the nose × number of crossings (discussed later).

(3) Distance from TMC to elbow of wing wall = Number of crossings × flange way clearance at the nose.

(4) The length of the gap in front of T.N.C. upto throat is 56 cm (1′-10″) for B.G. and 53 cm (1′-9″) for M.G. track.

Check rails. The short pieces of rails which are provided to guide the flange of the wheel of the train on the straight continuous rail while the opposite wheel is jumping over the gap between the wing rails in front of the nose are called as check rails. The length of check rails varies from 244 cm to 610 cm according to the crossing numbers. These are placed so that 2/3 rd of its length is ahead of the crossing nose and is splayed out at each end. Its clearance distance is gradually reduced to that required opposite the nose to enable the wheel flange to be guided smoothly through the flange space. The absence of the check rails, the side ways movement of the flanges might either cause derailment or strike and break the nose.

Technical terms in turn outs (Points and crossings)

(*i*) **Turn out.** Combination of points and crossings in a railway train these are of the following types according to the direction of diversion.

(*a*) **Left hand turn outs.** The turn out which diverts the train to the left.

(*b*) **Right hand turn outs.** The turn out which diverts the train to the right.

(*ii*) **Facing points.** When the train travels from the switch to the frog (*V*-crossing) the points are known as facing points or facing turnouts. The facing points should be avoided in main track as these lead to accident.

(*iii*) **Trailing points.** When a train travels in the direction from the crossing to the switches, the points are known as trailing points or trailing turn outs.

Types of crossings. The types can be classified as under :

(1) **Classification based on the type of angle of the crossing**

(*i*) **Acute angle crossing or *V*-crossing or Frog.** This type of rail crossing is obtained when right hand rail of track crosses a left hand rail of another converging track or vice versa. The angle of crossing is an acute angle. The value of clearance between the wing rail and *V*-portion is usually kept on 47·6 $\left(1\frac{7}{8}''\right)$ mm for B.G. and 44·5 mm $\left(1\frac{3}{4}''\right)$ for M.G. track.

The length of gap between the nose and the throat of crossing (for both gauges) is as under :

$$\text{Gap in gauge face} = \frac{d}{\sin \alpha} \quad \text{...(1)}$$

where d = the narrowest flange way clearance in front of the nose.

and α = angle of crossing.

Note : As the wheels have to be carried over this gap over the length of the wing rail the treads of tyres are made sufficient wide to remain on the wing rail. In practice this gap is larger than that of the theoretical value obtained in the equation (1), because the nose of the crossing in cut-off at some distance short of the actual point of intersection of the gauge faces.

The distance between the T.N.C. and A.N.C. can be calculated as under :

$t \cos \alpha = t.N$ where t = the thickness of the ANC and N is the number of crossing. The distance between ANC and TNC varies from 101·6 mm (4″) to 190·5 mm (7½″) depending on the number of crossings. All measurements are with reference to the T.N.C.

(*ii*) **Obtuse angle or Diamond crossing.** The crossing in which the rails crossed are either right hand or left hand or both the track is called an "obtuse angle crossing". The length of gap *ab* on each gauge face may be calculated from the formula length of gap $ab = d\ (\cot \alpha + \operatorname{cosec} \alpha)$ where d is flange clearance at nose and α is the angle of crossing.

Square crossing. When two tracks of the same or different gauges cross one another at Right angle, the crossing is called as square crossing.

The use of square crossings are avoided due to the following causes—

(*a*) A severe joint is felt at the crossing.

(*b*) Due to heavy impact, there is rapid wear of the crossings and also heavy damage to the rolling stock.

Number of crossing. The acute angle between the gauge faces of the point rail and splice rail of a *V*-crossing, is called the angle of crossing. It is generally designated by a number which is represented by '*N*'.

The number of crossings may be defined as the ratio of the spread (in ft. or in MKS as 30·48 cm) of the crossing and the length of the crossing from the theoretical nose crossing. The value of the number of crossing *i.e.* '*N*' may be determined by one of the following methods :

(*i*) **Cole's method.** $N = \cot \alpha$ (where α is the angle of crossing (standard method in Indian rails)

(*ii*) **Isosceles triangle method.** $N = 1/2 \operatorname{cosec} \alpha/2$ (used in layout of train ways).

(*iii*) **Centre line method.** $N = 1/2 \cot \alpha/2$ (used in USA and UK)

Number of crossings in use are : 1 : 6, 1 in 8½, 1 in 12, 1 in 16 and 1 in 20 (on B.G. and M.G. gauges)

Table 16·14.

Crossing No.	*Rt. angle*	*Isoscates triangle*	*Centre line*
11 in 6	9° 27′ 44″	9° 33′ 37″	9° 31′ 38″
1 in 8½	6° 42′ 35″	6° 44′ 41″	6° 43′ 59″
1 in 12	4° 45′ 49″	4° 46′ 34″	4° 46′ 19″
1 in 16	3° 34′ 35″	3° 34′ 54″	3° 34′ 47″

$$\text{Number of crossing} = \frac{\text{distance of the straight rail from toe to heel in feet}}{\text{sum of spreads at each end equal to 1 foot}} \text{ in FPS}$$

Number of crossings = distance in ft. or a multiple of 30·48 cm from 1 m to a point where spread of the point and splice rail is one foot (or 30·48 cm)

Standard length of crossings in Indian Railways

Gauge	*Number of crossing*	*Length*	
		Feet	*Metres*
B.G.	11 m 16	22′ 11·75″	7·004
B.G.	1 in 12	19′-07″	5·969
B.G.	1 in 8½	15′-9″	4·801
M.G.	1 in 12	15′-9″	4·801

Switches : They are mainly of two types *viz.*, (1) Stub switch and (2) Split switch

(1) **Stub switch.** In this arrangement two small rail lengths *AB* and *CD* of the main train rigidly tied together and kept at a fixed distance apart by a tie rod are hinged to the main track rails *A* and *C*. When these rails are pulled by the rod, the ends *B* and *D* assume the position *B′* and *D′* so as to be in line with the curved rails *B′G* and *D′E* respectively. When these rails are pushed back and ends *B′D′* assume the original position to be in line with the main straight track.

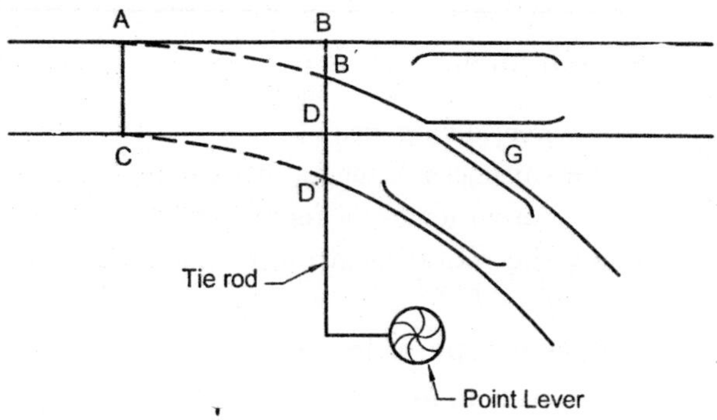

Fig. 16·55. A stub switch.

Split switch. It consists of the following parts :

(*i*) A pair of stock rails

(*ii*) A pair of tongue rails

(*iii*) Heel as distance blocks

(*iv*) Two or three stretcher bars

(*v*) Sliding plate or sliding chair

(*vi*) Switch tee rod

(*vii*) Slopes or studs

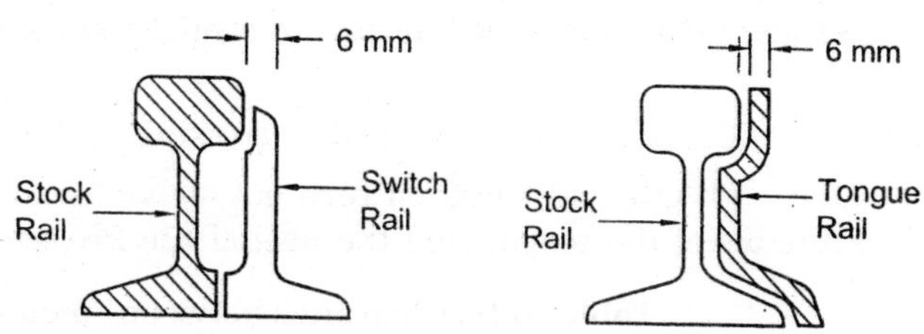

(*a*) Under cut (*b*) Over riding

Fig. 16·56.

The split switches are of two types :

(*i*) Loose heel type

(*ii*) Flexible heel type, flexible or spring switch

Classification of the toe of switches :

(*a*) Under cut switch (*b*) Over riding switch

Length of stock rail and tongue rail. The distance *d* at the heel of the tongue rail between the gauge faces of the stock rail and tongue rail is called heel divergence, heel offset or heel clearance. Its value depends on the flange clearance and the width of rail heel. The usual values of heel divergence are 159 mm, 114 mm, 137 mm to 133 mm $\left(5\frac{3}{8}'' \text{ to } 5\frac{1}{4}''\right)$ for B.G. tracks ; 121 mm to 117 mm $\left(4\frac{3}{4}'' \text{ to } 4\frac{5}{8}''\right)$ for M.G. tracks and 98 mm $\left(3\frac{7}{8}''\right)$ for N.G. tracks.

Table 16·15. Standard length of switches adopted on Indian Railways are as under.

Gauge	*Number of crossings*	*Standard length*		*Remarks*
		feet	*mm*	
B.G.	1 in 16	32′-0″	9755	curved
M.G.	1 in 16	24′-9″	7417	curved
B.G.	1 in 12	21′-0″	6410	straight
M.G.	1 in 12	18′-0″	5485	straight
B.G.	1 in 8½	15′-6″	4725	straight
M.G.	1 in 8½	13′-6″	4115	straight

Switch angle. $\sin \alpha = \frac{1}{x}$

where d = heel divergence

t = thickness of tongue rail at toe

D_1 = actual length of tongue rail

D_2 = theoretical length of tongue rail

$x = D_2 - D_1$

Different type of loads :

(1) **Switch load.** The distance from the springing of the turn out *i.e.*, toe of tongue, to the heel of the switch, measured along the straight stock rail is known as switch load it is denoted by S.L.

(2) **Crossing load.** The distance from the heel of the switch to the theoretical nose of crossing (TNC) measured along the straight stock rail is known as crossing load denoted by C.I.

(3) **Curve load.** The distance from the toe of the tongue to the theoretical nose of crossing (TNC) measured along the straight stock rail is known as curve load and is denoted by C.L.

Curve load = switch load + crossing load or C.L. = S.L. + C.I.

(4) Over all length of turn out – the distance between the end of the stock rail just ahead of the toe of the tongue and the heel of the Projected length of the straight stock rail.

Table 16·16. Clearance between stock and tongue rails at heel of switch

Gauge	*Turn out*		
	1 in 16	*1 in 12*	*1 in 8½*
B.G.	133 mm $\left(5\frac{1}{4}''\right)$	183 mm $\left(5\frac{1}{4}''\right)$	136 mm $\left(5\frac{3}{8}''\right)$
M.G.	117 mm $\left(4\frac{5}{8}''\right)$	117 mm $\left(4\frac{5}{8}''\right)$	120 mm $\left(4\frac{3}{4}''\right)$

Throw of switches

Gauge	*Recommended*	*Minimum*
B.G.	115 mm $\left(4\frac{1}{2}''\right)$	95 mm $\left(3\frac{3}{4}''\right)$
M.G.	100 mm (4″)	80 mm $\left(3\frac{1}{2}''\right)$

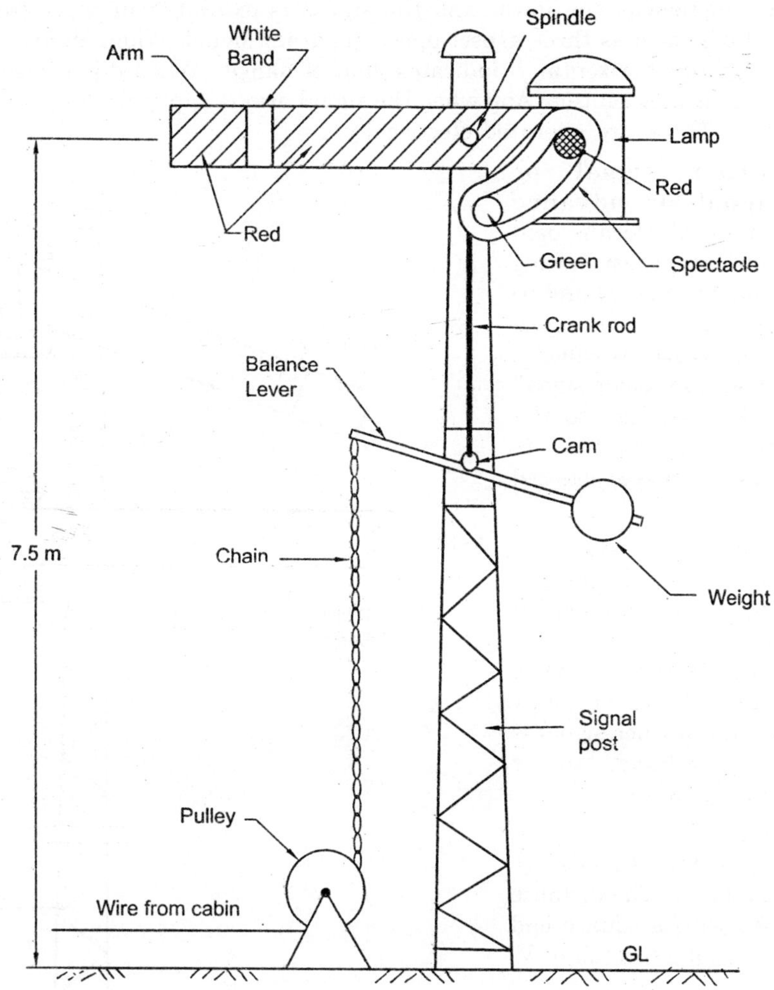

Fig. 16·57. A semaphore signal.

16·12. Signalling. A device for controlling movement of trains.

(*a*) **Stop signals or semaphore type signals.** Main important parts of a semaphore type of signal are :

(1) Signal or vertical tower	(2) Semaphore arm	(3) Lamp for night use
(4) Coloured spaders	(5) Pulley or wire	(6) Cam or fulcrum
(7) Crank rod	(8) Weight of the lever	(9) Signal wire
(10) Chain	(11) Spindle	(12) White bend in semaphore arm

The semaphore signal is operated by pulling the signal wire from the cabin. In case signal wire or any other defect comes in the signal due to which it cannot be operated and its arm remain in 'stop' position indicating any danger.

The semaphore signals are placed on the left side of the direction of train movement and its arm projects to the left of the driver of the train for which it gives an indication. The indicator face of the semaphore arm is painted red with a white vertical band near the end where as opposite face is painted while with a black tend near the end.

On some sections of Indian Railway the arm of the semaphore signal is moved in the upper quadrants instead of the lower and the signal is exhibited in three positions. Such a semaphore signal is known as three aspect upper quadrant signal. When an arm of three aspects upper quadrant signal is horizontal, it indicates 'stop' or danger. When it is moved up through 45° with horizontal it indicates caution. And when the signal arm is kept parallel to the vertical post it indicates 'proceed'. These are operated electrically.

(2) **Warner signal or permissive signal or advance outer signal.** The signal which is used for warning the drivers of fast moving trains to control the train speed and be prepared to stop at the 1st stop signal in case it is still at danger is called a warner signal or advance outer signal. A warner signal is similar to the semaphore signal excepting that its horizontal arm has a *V*-shaped notched at its free end.

When the warner signal is horizontal, it is said to be 'ON' position and it signifies that the signal beyond it is at danger. When the arm is at an angle of 45°, it indicates that the signal head is 'OFF' and the driver may proceed at speed. The warner signal is placed ahead of an ordinary stop or distant semaphore signal.

On some lines arms of warning and the distant signals are fixed on the same tower. The distance signal is provided with a square end and the warning signal a fish tail or *V*-notch.

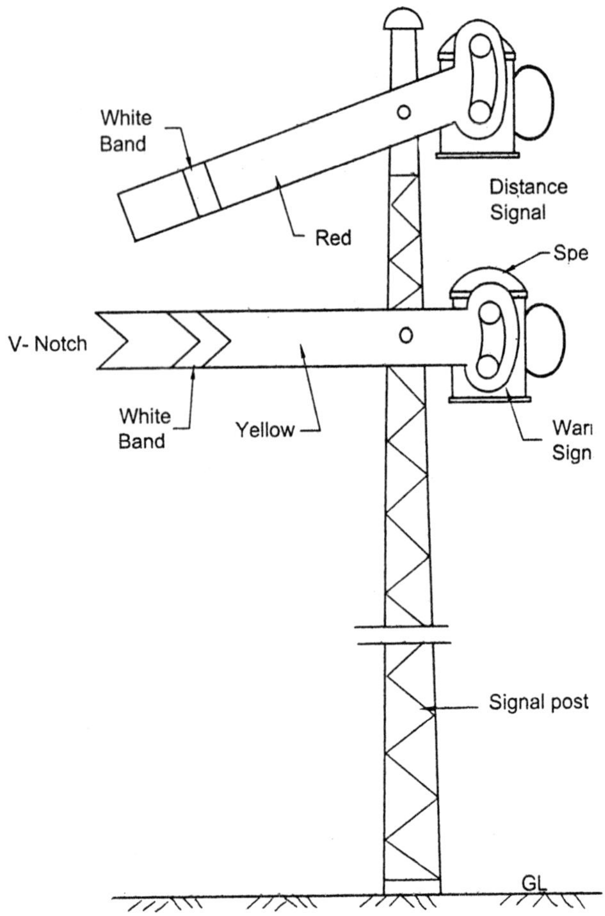

Fig. 16·58. Distant and Warner signal on same tower.

In case fish tailed warning signal is in danger position or 'ON' position and the square end distant signal is in down or in off option, the driver can proceed but cautiously upto the home signal. When both the signals *i.e.*, distant as well as warner are clear, the driver may proceed up to the plateform.

It is customary that the distant signal cannot be lowered unless its home signal head if it is lowered. In case home signal is at line clear and the distant signal is at danger, the driver knows that the section is clear only upto the plateform. For a non stopping train, the distant, home and starter signals should be at the clear position *i.e.*, down. For a stopping train at the station the warner may be at danger, the home signal at clear and the slate at danger.

Coloured light signals. The signals which use a high unevenly beam colour light both during day and night are called coloured light signals. In electrified railways, the semaphore signals are being replaced by coloured light signals that are of two types :

(*a*) Two aspect signal (*b*) Three aspect signal

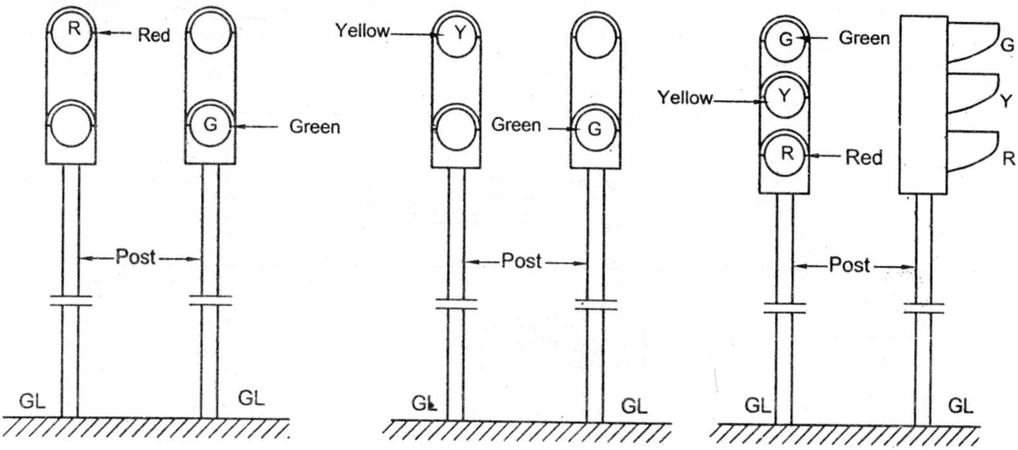

(*a*) Two aspect signals (*b*) Three aspect signal

Fig. 16·59.

(*a*) **Two aspect signals.** These colour signals indicate two colours either red and green or yellow and green. These are shown in the Fig. 16·59 (*a*).

(*b*) **Three aspect signals.** These colour signals indicate three colours *i.e.*, red, yellow and green. A three aspect signal is shown in the Fig. 16·59 (*b*).

Classification of signals according to the locations. These are classified as under :

(*i*) Distance signal or outer signal (*ii*) Home signals

(*i*) **Distance signal or outer signal.** The first signal for the incoming train, which is fixed at a safe braking distance from the home signal is called a distance signal. Its distance from the home signal depends upon the gradient and braking power of the locomotive and should be 580 metres but not less than 400 m. When the outer signal is 'ON' or 'STOP' or 'DANGER' position, the driver must bring the train to stop at a distance of roughly 9 m from the signal and proceed to the Home signal with caution. If the outer signal is in 'OFF' or 'PROCEED' position, the driver can take the train at a speed taking for granted that the Home signal will also be in 'OFF' or 'PROCEED' position, provided the warner is also OFF.

(*ii*) **Home Signal.** The signal which is placed at the farthest, set of switches so as to proceed the cross overs and turn outs is called a Home signal. It is a protecting signal for the railway station.

When home signal is a *V*-stop position, it indicates that the driver must stop the train short of the signal. In the 'Proceed' position the driver can cautiously proceed to enter the station upto the plateform for which home signal is lowered.

Departure signals. The departure signals are :

(*i*) Starter signal (*ii*) Advance starter signal

(*i*) **Starter signal.** The signal which is provided for controlling the movement of trains leaving a plateform is called a starter signal.

It is placed at the forward end of platform beyond the farthest point connection on the lever. No train can leave the plateform unless starter signal is levered. Separate starter signals are provided for each line.

(*ii*) **Advance starter signals.** The signal which is placed beyond the outermost set of the points connected is called starter signal. An advance starter signal is placed at the start of the block section. The block section lies between the advance starter signal of one station to the outer signal after next station. No train can leave the station unless the advance starter is lowered or placed in OFF position.

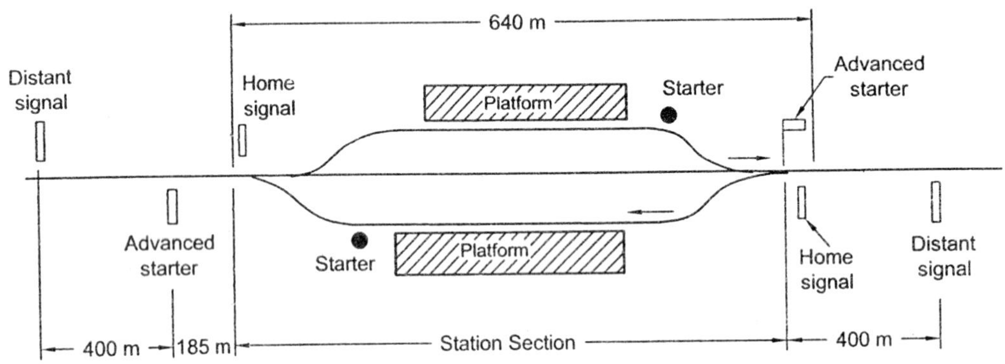

Fig. 16·60. Signal positions of a station yard.

16·13. Technical terms—Railways

Capacity of a railway track. The number of trains that can be run safely on a track per hour is known as, capacity of a railway track.

Rail closer or short rails. A rail piece whose length to less than the length of a standard rail.

S.W.R. (Short welded rails). Welding of 3 rails, 5 rails and 10 rails points are termed as short welded rails.

L.W.R. (Long welded rails). A panel of welding of rails more than 10. In Indian Railways a rail panel longer than 5 rails (6·5 m for B.G., 60 m for M.G. are generally provided).

Roaring rails. Corrugations in the rails which creates a noise when train passes.

Wear of rails. Due to friction between the table top of rail and the moving wheels over them. The rail head gets worn out in course of time is known wear of rails.

Burr. The projections of metal beyond the original section of the rail on the gauge side are called burrs.

Equilibrium cant. The super elevation provided on the basis of equilibrium speed is called equilibrium cantts.

Tube Railways. The underground railways, which are constructed in tunnels at a depth of 25 metres or more are called tube railways.

Hogging. The rails whose ends get defected downward due to battering action of the moving wheels on their ends.

Battering of rails. The hammered down and flattened rail end due to impact of running wheels is called as battered end or crippled end.

Angular break. When the rail breaks completely in an uncleared plane, it is known to have an angular break.

Split web. The web which gets split up in two places is called a split web.

Buckling of rails. The rail track which gets distorted due to prevention of free expansion of rails particularly in hot weather, goes out of its position or alignment. This phenomenon is called as buckling of rails.

Adzing. To cut the sleeper in order to fit the rail for tilting.

Creep. Creep is a longitudinal displacement of a rail.

Tread. The width of conical portion of the wheel.

Cant. Slope of the tilting of the rails which is 1 : 20.

Frog. V-shaped crossing (acute angle) is called as frog.

Rolling stock. Vehicles that ply on railway track.

Sand hump. It is a heap of sand on the dead end of a track to absorb the kinetic energy of the running vehicles.

Versine $= \dfrac{\left(\frac{1}{2}\text{ rail length}\right)^2}{2\text{ rad.}}$. The versine is the amount of bend at the centre of the chord joining the ends of a bent rail.

Derailing switch. It is a switch used for derailing a train. Train passes on a track if the switch is closed and derails when opened.

Blinding of rails on curves. Upto 4° curve the flexibility of the rail material adjusts the curve while on sharper curves bending is necessary.

Rolling stock. Vehicles that ply on the railway track.

Curve resistance. It is the resistance on the outer wheels on a curve.

Throw of the switch. The distance for which toes of the switches move sideways. It is 115 mm (4½″) in B.G.

Switches. (*a*) **Stub switch.** The main line is fixed upto the points *AA*′. The length *AB* and *A*′*B*′ is placed on moving chairs and is connected to a tee rod at points *B* and *B*′ so that their distance may not change. The lengths *AB* and *A*′*B*′ is turned to an arc to make the turn out and is fitted with a level to operate.

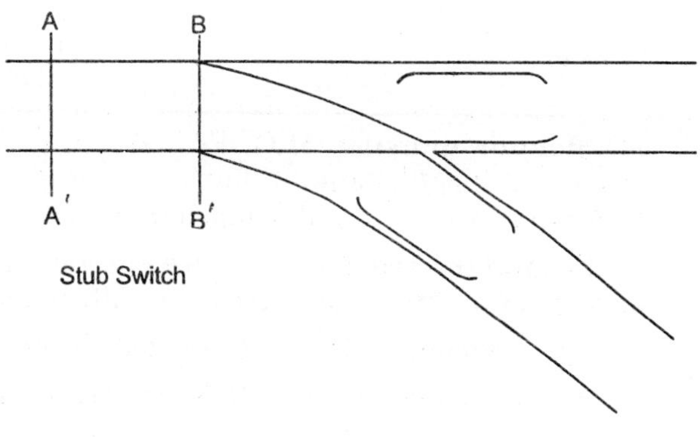

Fig. 16·61. Stub switch

Split switch. One rail of the main track and another of the turn out track is moved laterally and are known as switch rails.

Wharton Safety Switches. Both the main line rails are fixed and of subsidiary lines are movable.

Turn out. One track when bifurcates from another, the assembly of the both at their turning point is known as turn out.

Diamond crossing. When two tracks cross each other at an angle. The crossing point assembly is known as diamond crossing.

Cross over. When two adjacent tracks may be parallel is connected by a diagonal track so that vehicle on one may pass to the other is called a turn over.

Turn Table. It is a bridge which can be rotated in a horizontal plane to reverse direction of locomotives.

The maximum speed of vehicles on a rail track.

$V = 4{\cdot}4\sqrt{R - 70}$, V = Speed (maximum) in km/hr and R = rad. of curve in m.

For non transitioned curves the speed should be 4/5 of the speed given by the above formula. This formula is applicable for B.G. as well as for M.G.

Super elevation. Maximum super elevation : M.G. = 102 mm (4″), B.G. = 165 mm (6½″). Maximum deficiency permissible in cant calculations for the speed of the fastest train on the section : M.G. = 50 mm (2″), B.G. = 76 mm (3″).

16·14. Miscellaneous

Table 16·17. Gauge on Curves

M.G.		*B.G.*	
Curve radius	*Gauge slackness*	*Curve rad.*	*Gauge slackness*
Upto curves of 292 m (955 ft.) rad.	Exact gauge	upto 4° curve	Exact gauge
Below curves of 292 m (955 ft.) and upto 175 m (573 ft.) rad.	6 mm (¼″) slackness	above 4° curve	6 mm (¼″) slackness
Below 175 m and upto 109 m (358′) rad.	13 mm (½″) slackness		

Sleepers

Sleeper size	*M.G.*	*B.G.*
Minimum length	1·83 m (6′-0″)	2·75 m (9′-0″)
Minimum width	0·203 m (8″)	0·25 m (10″)
Minimum depth	0·114 m (4½″)	0·127 m (5″)
For soft wood with bearing plates	adopt sleeper section 0·178 × 0·127 m (7″ × 5″)	adopt sleeper section 230 × ·52 mm (9″ × 6″)

Sleeper density. M.G. Primary tracks : 1430 sleepers/km where traffic density exceeds 2·5 million/km/annum but does not exceed 5 million. 1500 sleepers/km where the traffic density exceeds 5 million/km/annum.

Secondary tracks. 1340 sleepers/km where the traffic density exceeds 1·25 million per km/annum but does not exceed 2·5 million/km per annum (G.T. km/annum)

B.G. upto and including 17 ton axle loads = $n + 1$

B.G. upto and including 18·5 ton axle loads = $n + 2$ n = length of rail in yds.

B.G. upto and including 22·5 ton axle loads = $n + 3$

B.G. upto and including 25·0 ton axle loads = $n + 4$

B.G. upto and including 28·0 ton axle loads = $n + 5$

Ballast section	*MG*	*BG*
Width of ballast at level of foot rail	2·29 m (7′-6″)	3·36 m (11′-0″)
Depth of ballast below sleepers	203 mm (8″)	203 mm (8″)

Rails apparatus details

Table 16·18.

	Section of rail		Axle load including wt. of wheels and axle	
M.G.	37·0 kg/m	(75 lbs/yd)	17·5 tonnes	17·0 tons
	34·5 kg/m	(70 lbs/yd)	15·5 tonnes	15·0 tons
	32·0 kg/m	(65 lbs/yd)	14·0 tonnes	14·0 tons
	30·0 kg/m	(60 lbs/yd)	13·0 tonnes	13·0 tons
	27·5 kg/m	(55 lbs/yd)	11·5 tonnes	11·5 tons
	25·0 kg/m	(50 lbs/yd)	10·5 tonnes	10·5 tons
	22·5 kg/m	(45 lbs/yd)	9·0 tonnes	9·0 tons
	20·0 kg/m	(40 lbs/yd)	8·0 tonnes	8·0 tons
B.G.	115 lbs/yd	28·0 tons		
	100 lbs/yd	25·0 tons		
	90 lbs/yd	22·5 tons		
	85 lbs/yd	20·5 tons		
	80 lbs/yd	18·5 tons		
	75 lbs/yd	17·0 tons		

Heavy clay peat soils and loamy soils may be improved by the following methods :

(*i*) Admixures of different soils
(*ii*) Cement grouting
(*iii*) Lime grouting
(*iv*) Sand piling
(*v*) Concrete mats
(*vi*) Blanketing
(*vii*) Sub-drainage

According to Indian Railways, specification, the width for embankments/ceilings is as under :

Table 16·19. Embankment

	B.G.	*M.G.*	*M.G.*
1. Single lane traffic	610 cm	488 cm	370 cm
2. Double lane traffic	1082 cm	884 cm	732 cm
Cuttings			
1. Single lane traffic	549 cm	427 cm	335 cm
2. Double lane traffic	1021 cm	827 cm	701 cm

Setting out the slope stakes

(*i*) **Grade.** The reduced level of the finished work of the excavation or embankment is called grade.

(*ii*) **Grade stake.** The stake which is driven until the top is attained the same elevation as that of the finished work is called the grade stake.

(*iii*) **Ground staff reading.** The staff reading at a point when a cut or fill is desired.

(*iv*) **Grade staff reading.** The difference between the heights of collimation and the grade elevation.

(*v*) **Cut.** The difference between the grade staff reading and the ground staff reading.

(*vi*) **Fill.** The difference between the ground staff reading and the grade staff reading.

(*vii*) **Slope stakes.** The stakes which are fixed at the intersection of the side slopes and the natural ground on either side of the central stake.

17

Water Supply

17·1. Harmful Constituents in water and their tests

(1) **Presence of organic matter or sewage.** Add four drops of solution of Potassium permanganate in a beaker and shake. If the colour is red, the sample is pure and if it turns yellow the solution contains organic impurities. These are due to decomposition of plants and animals. It may also be due to the manufactures waste or sewage.

Suspended—Vegetable causes colour taste and acidity ; dead animals produces diseases.

Desolved—Vegetable produces bacteria ; dead animals pollute water and produce diseases.

(2) **Presence of lead.** Add six drops of sulphuric acid in a beaker, a white precipitate will be formed. Add one drop of ammonium sulphide and stir. If the precipitate turns to blakish, the presence of lead is evident.

The quantity of lead more than 0·3 to 0·5 ppm (parts per million) by weight makes water poisonous. It must be less than 0·1 ppm and so lead pipes must be avoided.

(3) **Presence of zinc or iron.** Few drops of ferrous cinide of potassium turns the water greenish. If zinc is there and blue if iron.

Presence of iron in excess cause unpleasant taste, decolours clothes, stains glazed sanitary-ware and harmful for blood pressure patients. It can be removed by aeration and washing water through pressure filters and lime softening process. Sedimentation and filtration is followed by aeration.

(4) **Presence of copper.** Eight drops of ammonia mixed in water in a beaker will turn the water blue if copper is present.

(5) **Presence of carbonic acid.** Shake the sample with lime water, it will turn to milky, which disappears on the addition of hydrochloric acid.

(6) **Presence of plants and other impurities and their removal.**

(*i*) **Algae.** It is greenish growth on water surface. It can be controlled by roofing. It must be removed from surface and treated with bleaching powder and chlorine. Aeration of water and passing water from activated carbon beds, taste colour and odour can be removed. About 1/2 to 2 kg of copper sulphate mixed with one million litres of water according to the quantity of algae is used to kill this plant life.

(7) **Fungi.** These plants grow in absence of sun light. This growth can be controlled by treating water with chlorine or copper sulphate.

(8) **Gases in water.** These are found dissolved in water.

Carbon dioxide. Excess of carbon dioxide can be removed by aeration and addition of lime or passing it over lime stone or on marble chips. It causes acidity and corrode the metals.

Hydrogen sulphide. It gives objectionable smell and corrodes the constituents of metal and produce acidity and can be removed by aeration.

Nitrogen. It may be due to organic matter.

Oxygen. It helps in corrosion. It combines with iron and gives a colour. It effects taste and produce acidity.

(9) **Acid and Plumbers solvents.** May be set right by addition of chaulk, lime and sodium silicate.

(10) **Goiter.** It is due to deefficiency of iodine which is necessary in water to some extent.

(11) **Moltted enamel.** If water contains fluorides more than 1·5 ppm a teeth disease in children may cause. Hence fluorides must be 0·5 to 1·0 ppm.

Some other salts are also found dissolved in water in which some are necessary for drinking water while some are harmful.

Physical defects in water. (1) Colour, odour or taste. It is due to dissolved or colloidal organic matter or mineral salts such as iron and manganese oxides etc. Colour can be removed by filtration followed by coagulation. A pale colour is always mean an impure water or a colourless water a pure water. Odour is due to decaying plants in solution, it may also due to dissolved gases. Sedimentation and chlorination helps in colour and odour removal. Animal bone charcoal powder in a solution with water if added (5 to 20 ppm) improves colour odour and taste defficiencies and is applied before sedimentation when the impurities settle down. Chlorination also helps for colour removal. If water is passed through activated charcoal filter, odour and taste can be improved.

(2) **Turbidity.** It is due to finally divided particles of clay, silt and organic matter all in suspension. It is removed by sedimentation with or without co-agulation and filtration.

Physical classification of impurities of water

(1) **Suspended impurities.** Solid particles including clay, algae, fungi and other organic or inorganic matter causing turbidity in suspension, can be removed by sedimentation and filtration.

(2) **Colloidal impurities.** When very fine particles that can not be removed by filter nor are visible by naked eye are known as colloidal impurities. They are due to electrically charged, do not settle. Colour of water is generally due to the presence of these colloidal impurities.

(3) **Dissolved impurities.** Gases, solids and liquids may be dissolved in water. Their concentration can be expressed as ppm and is obtained by weighing the residue after evaporation of the water sample from a filtered sample.

pH value. It is a relative physical indication regarding the acidity or alkalinity of water. pH No. 7 indicates a sample neither alkalinic nor acidic. The value ranges from zero to 14. Value less than 7 is acidic and above as alkalinic. Water below value 7 can be improved by adding a small quantity of soda ash or lime before admitting to the mains. Alkalinic water is tasteful, but too much alkalinity or acidity is not fit for drinking.

Potable water. The water which is satisfactory for drinking, culinary and domestic purposes and meet the requirements necessary for health.

Hard and soft water. Physical classification of hard and soft water.

Soft water. If water mixed with soap show **Lather** in it is known as soft water and if not known as hard water. A soft water if aerated forms a good drinking water.

Hard water. The hardness is due to the presence of salts of calcium and magnesium dissolved in water. The hardness may be temporary which can be removed by boiling. The salts precipitate or stick to the sides of the vessel in a shape of white film. The permanent hardness is due to the presence of the salts of calcium and magnesium. Addition of a little of washing soda (sodium carbonate) makes the water (if hard) milky and forms a precipitate.

Alkalinity or Caustic alkalinity. Some but not all of the compounds those cause alkalinity also causes hardness. Acidity on ther other hand is caused by the presence of mineral acids, free carbon dioxide, sulphates of iron and aluminium etc. in water.

The pH value of water can be measured quickly and automatically with the help of a potentiometer, which measures the electrical potential exerted by hydrogen ions and thus indicating their concentration. It can also be measured with the help of colour indicators (dyes) which are added to water and the colour produced is compared with the standard colours of known pH values. Sets of standard scaled tubes containing coloured waters of known pH values with different indicators are generally kept in the Public Health laboratories for ready references. The indicators generally used for different pH ranges are given in table below :

Table 17·1.

Indicator	*pH range*	*Original colour of indicator dye*	*Final colour produced in water*
Thymol blue	1·2 to 2·8	Red	Yellow
Bromophenol blue	3·0 to 4·6	Yellow	Blue
Methyl orange	2·8 to 4·4	Red	Yellow
Brom cresol green	3·8 to 5·4	Yellow	Blue
Methyl red	4·4 to 6·2	Red	Yellow
Chlorophenol blue	5·4 to 6·8	Yellow	Red
Brown-thymol blue	6·0 to 7·6	Yellow	Blue
Phynol red	6·8 to 8·4	Yellow	Red
Cresol red	7·2 to 8·0	Yellow	Red
Thymol blue	8·0 to 9·6	Yellow	Blue
Phenolphathalein red	8·6 to 10·3	Yellow	Red
Tolyl red	10·0 to 11·6	Red	Yellow

Permissible pH values. For public water supplies attempts should be made to keep the pH as close to 7 as possible. The lower values (*i.e.* acidic water) may cause tuberculosis and corrosion while the higher value *i.e.* alkaline waters may produce incrustation, sediment deposits, difficulties in chlorination, certain psycological effects on human system etc. However the permissible pH values for public supplies may range between 6·6 to 8·5.

pH value of water. The pH value of water indicates the logarithm of reciprocal of hydrogen ion concentration present in water. It is thus an indicator of the acidity or the alkalinity of water.

Since the pH is the log of reciprocal of H^+, the higher values of pH means lower hydrogen ion concentrations and thus represent alkaline solution, where as the lower values of pH means higher hydrogen ion concentration representing acidic solution.

Truely speaking pure water is a balanced combination of positively charged hydrogen ions (H^+) and negatively charged hydroxyl ions $(OH)^-$ in pure or neutral waters, their number is equal. Further it has been found that the product of concentration of H ions and concentration of OH ions in a water solution is constant. This constant has been found to be equal to 10^{-14} moles/litre. Therefore if H ion and OH ion concentrations are equal, virtually each will have a concentration equal to $\sqrt{10^{-14}} = 10^{-7}$ moles per litre. A neutral water will therefore have a pH equal to $\log_{10}\left(\frac{1}{H^+}\right) = \log_{10}\left(\frac{1}{10^{-7}}\right) = \log_{10} 10^7 = 7.$

If an acid is added to the neutral or pure water, the number of hydrogen ions will increase because of the hydrogen contained in the acid. For example if hydrochloric acid is dissolved in water the dissociation becomes

$$H_2O \rightleftarrows H^+ + OH^- \; ; \; HCl \rightleftarrows H^+ + Cl^-$$

Then the net concentration of hydrogen ions will exceed that of hydroxyl ions and will be more than the hydrogen ion concentration of neutral water (*i.e.* 10^{-7}) and thus decreasing the pH values to less than 7 and thereby making the water acidic.

Similarly, if an alkali is dissolved in pure water, the concentration of hydroxyl ions will exceed the hydroxyle ion concentration of neutral water and thus reducing the concentration of hydrogen ions to less than 10 (their product being constant = 10^{-14} moles/litre). For example if Sodium hydroxide is added to water the dissociation will be

$$H_2O \rightleftarrows H^+ + OH^- \; ; \; NaOH \rightleftarrows Na^+ + OH^-$$

The net amount of OH ions present in this alkalene water will therefore be more than that present in a neutral water and thus reducing the hydrogen ion concentration to less than 10^{-7}, and thereby increasing the pH above 7 and making the water alkaline.

Hence if pH of water is more than 7 it will be alkalinic and if it is less than 7 it will be acidic. The maximum acidity will be at zero value of pH and the maximum alkalinity will be at a value of pH equal to 14.

The alkalinity is caused by the presence of bicarbonates of calcium and magnesium, or by carbonates or hydroxides of sodium, potassium, calcium and magnesium. Alkalinity caused by bicarbonates is called carbonate alkalinity, and that caused by hydroxides is called hydrauxide.

Measurements of hardness. (1) **English or Clarks scale.** One gram of hardening salt if dissolved in 70,000 grams (1 gal) of water is taken as one degree hardness or hardness 70 ppm by weight is termed as soft while above it is called as hard. A distilled water is 100 percent soft.

(2) **Metric scale.** One part by weight of the salt dissolved in 1,00,000 parts by weight of water is taken as one degree hardness so as to say that one degree of hardness on English scale is $1^3/_7$ degree in hardness on metric scale.

Water in deep wells is generally hard and in tanks and rivers is generally soft. Soft water has corrosive action on metals, they dissolves lead which is harmful for health. Soft water is tasteless.

Table 17·2

Degree of hardness	*ppm*	*Degree of hardness*	*ppm*
Extremely soft	15	Moderately hard	110
Very soft	30	Hard	150
Soft	45	Very hard	170
Moderately soft	90	Excessive hard	230
		Too hard	250

Softening of hard water

Lime or Clarks process. For every 100 parts of calcium bicarbonate in water 56 parts of unslacked lime is added from which 200 parts of chalk (Calcium Carbonate) is precipitated. It is thoroughly mixed and allowed to stand for 3 to 4 hours for sludge (Precipitate) to settle. Thus sludge is burnt and can be used again as calcium oxide (quick lime). Carbondioxide is again diffused through water or alum is mixed in settling tanks.

Soda or alkali process. Soda ash or caustic soda is added (9·25 ppm) to remove salts of sulphates, nitrates and chlorides of calcium. Rest of the process is the same as lime process.

Lime soda process. It is combination of the above two process and is used when impurities of nitrates, sulphates and chlorides of magnesium is present.

17·2. Purification of water

(1) **Screening.** When the water is trapped from rivers and canals it is screened before its entry to the outlet pipe. The screens are two in series. 1st is bar screens with openings of 25 to 75 mm to exclude all big wood or other floating impurities like leaves and dead animals etc. The other has fine meshes 3 mm to 10 mm opening. Bar screens are fixed in the gate of the plant while fine screens are fitted with the outlet pipe. The velocity of water in screens must not be more than 60 cu.m/sec. The openings of mesh should be twice the area of the outlet pipe.

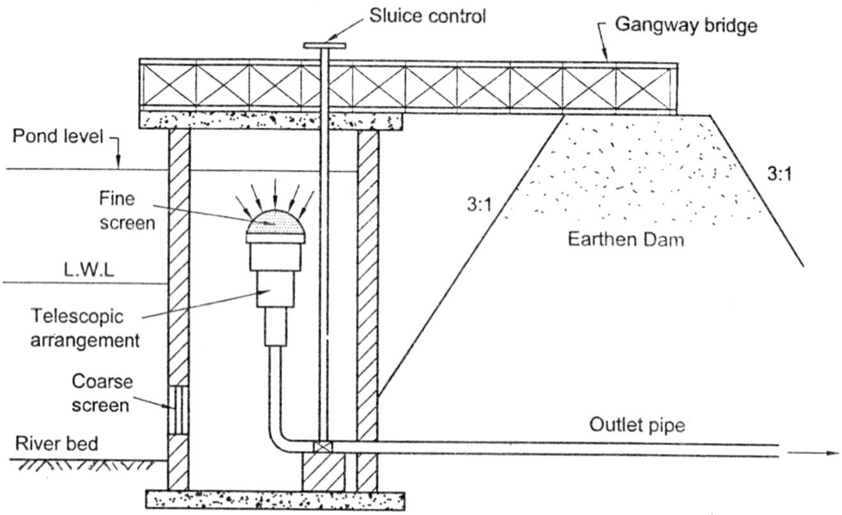

Fig. 17·1. River or reservoir intake.

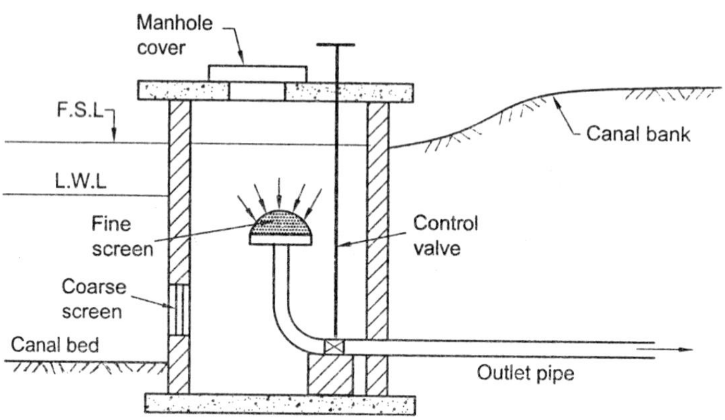

Fig. 17·2. Canal intake.

(2) **Sedimentation.** The raw water obtained from rivers or canals is full of silt and other impurities, hence it is passed through sedimentation tanks. If the silt load is more it is passed in two series of settling tanks. In 1st the heavy load is settled while in the other the finer load is settled. Sedimentation tanks are open or covered in which water is passed either at reduced velocity or is kept still for a day or so. In the sedimentation tank for finer silt water is passed in staggered baffles to reduce velocity where it settles. Two sets of tanks are kept in which one remain in settling condition while the other is in process of cleaning the sediment.

In the figure there are four sets of tanks which remain alternately under operation of cleaning and settling.

Vertical pumps are used when the space is limited. The load is settled down due to the gravity, but to make the process fast some coagulent like aluminium is mixed with water. The detention is 1·5 to 3·0 days, but when coagulation process is used the time reduces to 2 to 4 hours. The length to width ratio of tank are kept 2 : 1 to 4 : 1. The velocity of flow is kept 15 to 30 cm/min. Depth is generally kept 3 to 4·5 metres with 1·8 m minimum to 6 m maximum. The depth of hoppers in vertical flow filters is 4·5 to 6 metres.

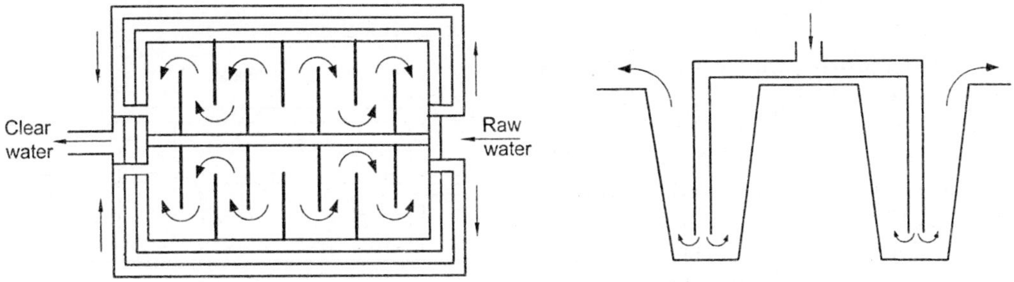

(*a*) Horizontal flow tank. (*b*) Vertical flow tank.

Fig. 17·3.

The tanks may be rectangular or circular in plan. The dia. of circular tanks is limited to 60 m. The load per sq. m of surface area of settling tank should be between 14,000 to 1,95,000 litres/day for granular solids and 40,000 to 1,00,000 for amorphous slow settling solids. For flocculent materials the load per sq. m may be 50,000 to 60,000 litres/day. The slope in bed is kept towards flow.

$$\text{Detension period} = \frac{\text{Capacity of tank}}{\text{Rate of flow of tank}}$$

Table 17·3. Time taken by different soils to settle in 30 cm deep water

Material	*Size in mm*	*Time taken*
Coarse sand	1·00	3 sec
	0·50	6 sec
Fine sand	0·25	10 sec
	0·20	15 sec
	0·10	40 sec
Silt or colloidal matter	0·06	80 sec
	0·05	10 sec
	0·04	2·5 min
	0·02	8·5 min
	0·01	3·5 min
	0·005	2·0 hours
Clay	0·001	57 hours
Bacteria	0·001	35 hours

Design of sedimentation tank

(1) Assess no. of consumers say 30,000.

(2) Take quantity utilized per head say 30 litres/head/day.

(3) Calculate total requirement as above 30,000 × 30 = 9,00,000 litres.

(4) Assume two working tanks and one stand by total 3.

(5) Capacity of each tank $= \frac{9,00,000}{2} = 4,50,000.$

(6) Assume rate of filtration $= 1200$ litres/hr/m^2.

$\therefore$ Area of each sedimentation basin $= \frac{19,000}{1200} = 16 \text{ m}^2$

Assume L/B $= \frac{\text{length}}{\text{breadth}} = 4$ then $4B \times B = 16$ or $B = 2$ m.

So length $= 8$ m and size is 8×2 m.

(3) **Coagulation or Flocculation.** A coagulent is a chemical by the addition of which a heavier precipitate of impurities is formed which helps in settling. The precipitate is known as floc and the process as flocculation. The detension period is known as flocculent period. The coagulation is known as dose. The most common coagulator is alum. It is added after a trial or on the past experience basis. The flocculators or the basins are equipped with mechanical mixing devices operated by paddles. These basins are provided with scrapping arrangements to remove the silted flock. These are called as clarifiers. The speed of flow flocculating chamber is kept 12-15 cu.m/sec. Main coagulents are named below :

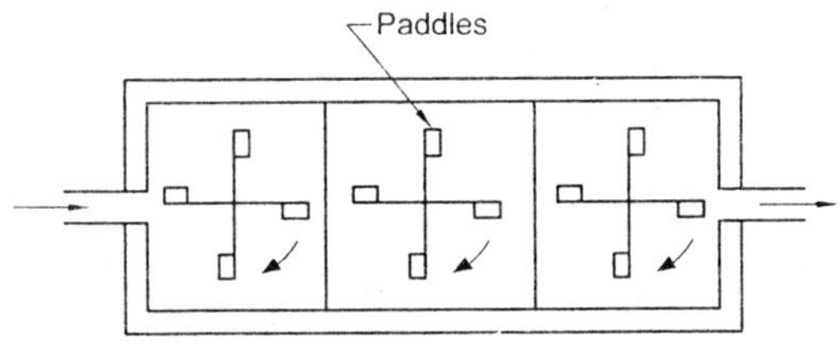

Fig. 17·4.

(1) Aluminium sulphate

(2) Aluminium sulphate + Hydrated lime

(3) Aluminium sulphate + Caustic soda

(4) Aluminium sulphate + Sodium carbonate

(5) Copper sulphate

(6) Copper sulphate + Hydrated lime

(7) Potassium per mangnet + Ferrous sulphate

(8) Ferrous sulphate + Hydrated lime or chlorine

(9) Ferrous sulphate

(10) Ferric chloride

(11) Ferric sulphate

(12) Sodium aluminate

(13) Sodium aluminate + Ferric chloride

(14) Sodium aluminate + Magnesium chloride

(15) Ferric sulphate + Hydrated lime

(16) Sodium aluminate + Aluminium sulphate.

Note : Copper sulphate is used for destroying algae and for removal of unpleasant taste due to vegetable origin.

Ferric coagulants are used for the flocculation of water with pH values between 7 and 8.

Cupric coagulants are suitable for alkaline water.

Mechanical flocculators may be either circular tanks with paddles revolving on a vertical shaft or rectangular tanks with paddles revolving on a horizontal shaft. Water mixed with

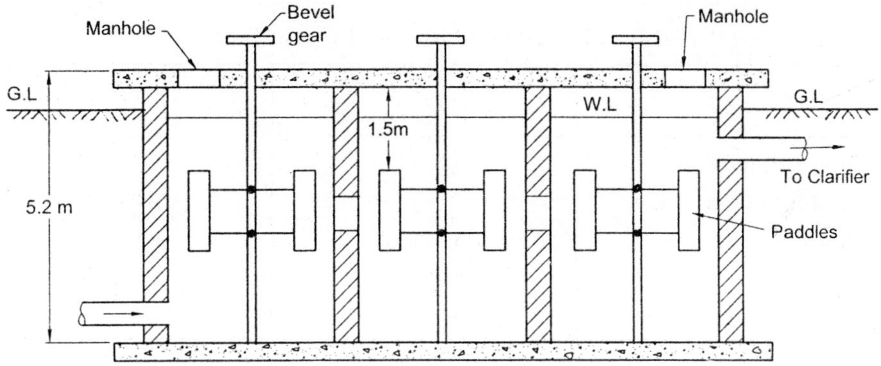

(*a*) Sectional elevation.

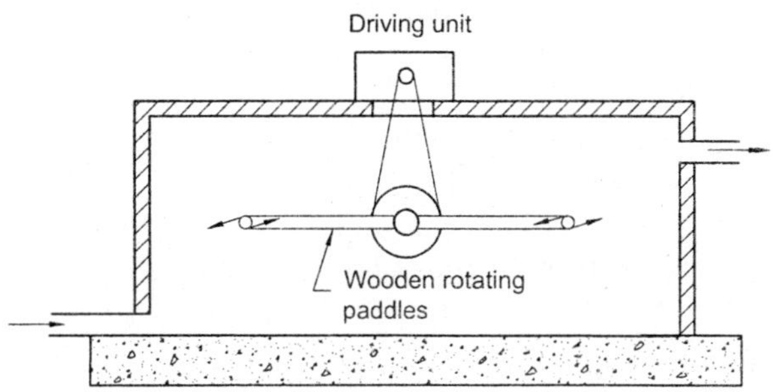

(*b*) Coagulation system.

Fig. 17·5.

chemical (coagulent) enters into one end and leaves at the other end to clarifiers. This induces a spiral flow. The slowly revolving paddles are placed in the path of water and they help in the formation of floc in considerable short time. Velocity of flow is 15 to 30 cm per sec.

Estimate for the quantity of dose. Take equal volume of the water sample in 6 jars having capacity 1 to 2 litres. Mix coagulent in different amounts and shake it with peddles for 5 minutes. The jars are kept on a glass plate form. The speed of the peddles is kept 30 to 40 rpm and then slowed to 20 similarly in all the jars. The floc is allowed to settle for 30 min. and the amount of floe settled in each jar is noted. The dose which gives the maximum amount of floc is taken as a dose for the plant. The coagulent is mixed in the form of solution of known strength.

Accelerators like activated silica is added to the water before or after the coagulator is added. This makes the process efficient and much heavier floc is obtained. Activated silica is a product of partially neutralised alkalinity of the solution of sodium silicate. Some other accelerators are as below :

(1) Bentonite
(2) Certain type of clays
(3) Kiesel gulin or infusorial earth
(4) Powdered activated carbon
(5) Non activated sodium silicate and
(6) Whitings (calcium carbonate)

After flocculation the coagulated water is passed in secondary settling tanks or clarifiers having detension period of 3 to 4 hours where the flocs are removed. The design is the same as for primary sedimentation tanks, only the detention period differs. Bacteria up to 65% is also removed by this process. The floc is removed by scrapers.

Table. 17·4. Normal doses of Coagulents

Coagulent	*pH value range for best coagulation*	*Normal dose mg/lit*
Aluminium sulphate	5·5-80·0	5·15-8·5
Sodium aluminate	—	3·4-34·0
Ferric chloride	5·5-11·0	8·5-51·0
Ferric sulphate	5·5-11·0	8·5-51·0
Ferrous sulphate (copperas)	8·5-11·0	5·1-51·0

(4) **Filtration.** Filtration consists of passing the water over a pervious layer. Suspended collodial and also bacteria is screened out by filters.

The following type of filters are used, the functions of which are clear from the Fig. 17·6. The slope in floor is kept towards flow.

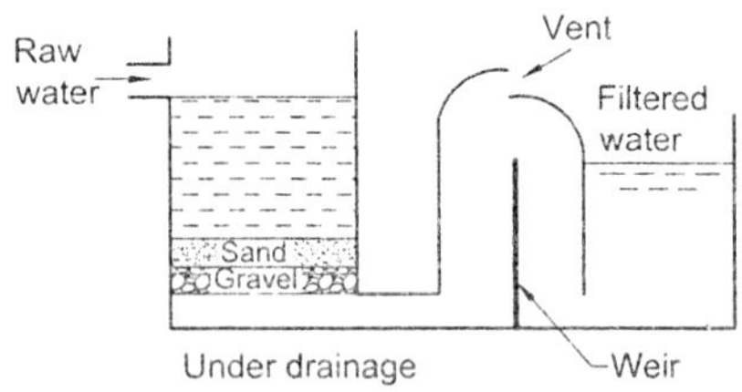

Fig. 17·6.

(1) **Slow sand filter.** The size is about 30-60 × 15-30 × 2·5-3·0 m in which sand is 60 to 90 cm and gravel 30 to 60 cm is provided. The gravel and the sand is graded. The under drains are perforated pipes laid longitudinally and crosswise.

The thickness of the filtering material is taken as below :

1.	Brocken stone or brick bats or gravel	40-65 mm = 10·15 cm
2.	Gravel 20-40 mm or brick bats or gravel	8 to 15 cm
3.	Gravel 3-6 mm or brick bats or gravel	5 to 10 cm
4.	Coarse sand or brick bats or gravel	15 cm
5.	Fine sand or brick bats or gravel	60-90 cm

These filters are required to clean when choked by removing all material. Water from a high tank with a high pressure is also used to clean the filter. Water jets are also used.

(2) **Rapid sand filters or mechanical filters.** In these type of filters the outlet chamber is kept at lower level than the water in the filter and hence a rapid flow is maintained due to a larger head of water. These filters take less time.

(3) **Pressure filters.** In pressure filters water is passed under pressure to increase the rate of water supply.

(5) **Aeration of water.** It improves physical and chemical characteristics of water. Aeration removes carbondioxide and water absorbs more oxygen from air. It is done to remove iron and magnesium from water which is generally found in underground water. Some types of aeration plants are given the figures which are self explanatory.

(6) **Chlorination.** Chlorine has a quick action on organic mater bacteria and algae. Chlorine also eliminates, taste, odour and colour pollutions. It also improves the action of coagulation. Chlorine is given in three forms, (*a*) solid as a bleaching powder for very small supplies. (*b*) As a liquid in the form of sodium hypochloride having 10 to 15 percent by weight of chlorine for water plants installed in small towns. (*c*) As a gas in big plants. The chlorine may be added at any stage of water treatment plant, where considered necessary. Prechlorination before sedimentation improves coagulation and filtration. The dosage should be such that a precipitate of 0·1 to 0·5 ppm goes to the filters.

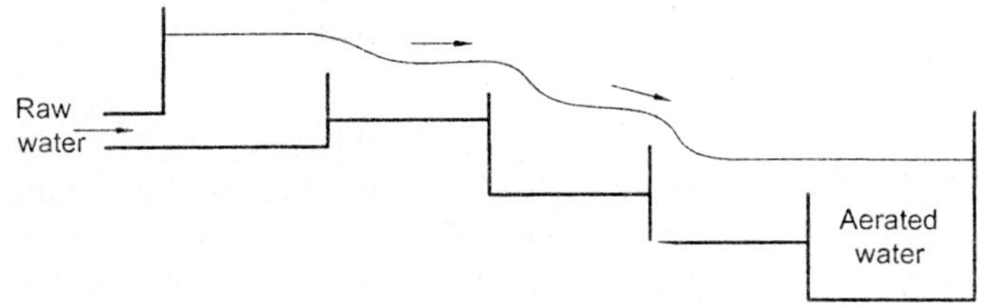

(*a*) Cascade aerator.

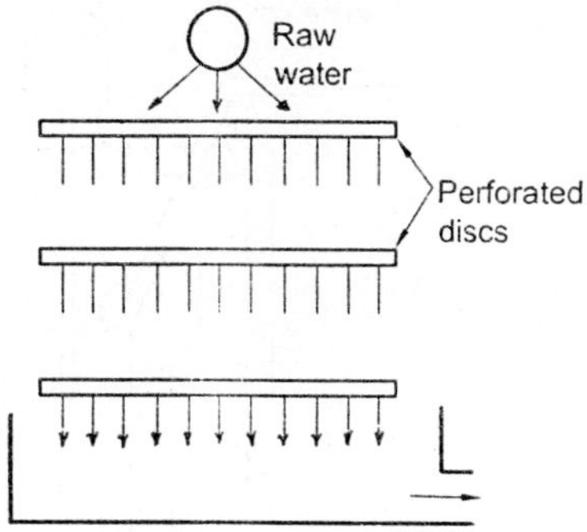

(*b*) Disc aeration.

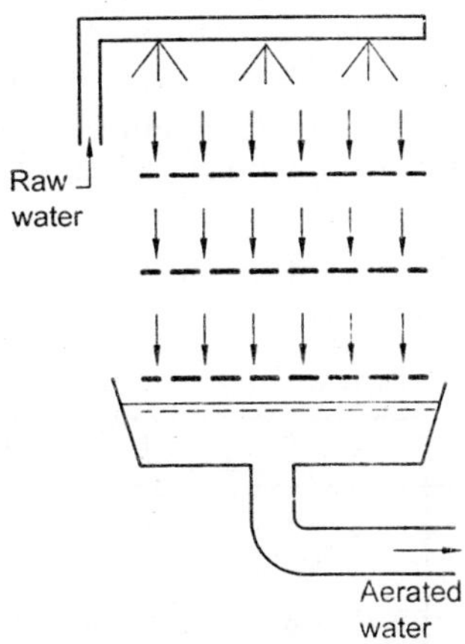

(*c*) Tray aerator.

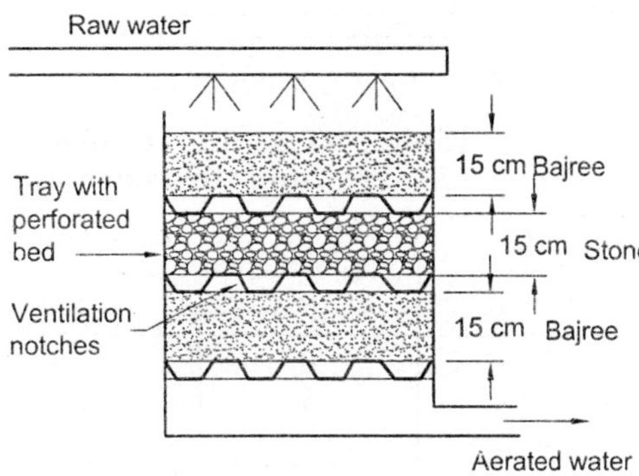

(*d*) Trickling filter aerator.

Fig. 17·7.

Dosage of chlorine. For disinfaction 0·1 to 0·2 ppm is given in underground water and 0·5 to 1·5 ppm for surface water and in highly polluted water it can be given even upto 3·0 ppm. The residual chlorine after the disinfaction of the supply should be 0·1 to 0·2 ppm after 30 min. After chlorination the water should be allowed to settle for about 20 min.

Water treatment flow diagram

Surface water
↓
Pump
↓
Screening
↓ ← Chlorination
Coagulation
↓
Sedimentation
↓ Sludge removal →
Filtration
↓
Chlorination
↓
Storage
↓
Supply

Sub Soil Water
↓
Pump
↓
Softening → Iron removal → Supply

Fig. 17·8. Chlorine mixture.

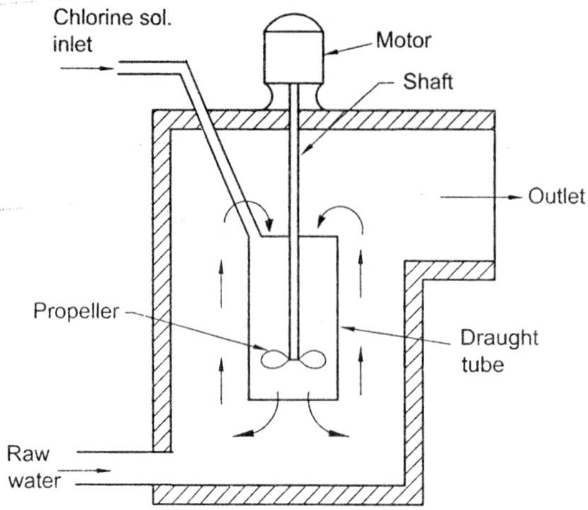

Fig. 17·9. Chlorine mixture.

Chlorine gas steel cylinders having compressed gas in the form of liquids of yellowish green colour is solid in market commercially.

Mixing of chlorine. There are many mixing devices of chlorine operated manually or mechanically. Chlorine is mixed in liquid stage better in water. It is then mixed in a chlorinator. Chlorine gives an acidic taste, pungent odour when mixed which disappears after a short time. It should be handled carefully as it is poisonous. The effect of chlorine finished shortly and ammonia in ratio of 1:4 ($^1/_4$th of Cl_2) is mixed with water before chlorination, which prolongs the effect of chlorine on water.

Table 17·5 (*a*). Relationship between the depth, dia. of the well and the consumption of bleaching powder.

Water depth (m)	*Bleaching powder (g) for wells with diameters*				
	0·5 m	*0·8 m*	*1·0 m*	*1·5 m*	*2·0 m*
1	1·6	4·1	6·4	14·4	25·6
2	3·2	8·2	12·8	28·4	51·2
3	4·8	12·3	19·2	43·2	76·2
4	6·4	16·4	25·6	57·6	102·4
5	8·0	20·5	32·0	72·0	128·0
6	9·6	24·6	38·4	86·4	153·6
7	11·2	28·7	44·8	100·8	179·2
8	12·8	32·8	51·2	115·2	204·8
9	14·4	36·9	57·6	129·6	230·4
10	16·0	41·0	64·0	144·0	265·0

The required chlorine is 2 mg of bleaching powder containing 25% free available chlorine for each litre of treated water

Table 17·5(*b*). Bleaching powder containing 25% chlorine (consumption for different sources of water)

Source of water	*Chlorine requirement mg/lit.*	*Bleaching powder consumption gm/m³*
Rain water	0·5-1·0	2-4
Deep well water	0·5-1·0	2-4
Shallow well water	1·0-1·5	4-6
Spring water	1·5-2·0	6-8
Turbid river water	2·0-2·5	8-10
Pond water (in good environments)	2·0-2·5	8-10
Pond water (poor environments)	2·5-3·0	10-12
Lightly polluted stored water	2·0-2·5	8-10
Heavily polluted stored water	2·5-3·0	10-12

Test for presence of chlorine—Orthotolidin test. One ml or orthotolidin solution is added to 100 ml of the sample of water in a glass tube. The sample must be taken after 10 minutes of the addition of the chlorine dose. If yellow colour forms the presence of chlorine is evident. The deeper is the colour the greater percentage of residual chlorine is there.

Super chlorination. For bacterial purification at some sources of water more chlorine than normal is mixed to kill the bacterial effect.

Plain chlorination. Water from some sources such as springs and streams is pure and chlorine is directly added without any other treatment. This is called as plain chlorination.

Dechlorination. When residual chlorine in water is more than desired, it is dechlorinised by adding sulphurdioxide, sodium bisulphate, ammonia or by aeration of water.

17·3. Requirement of water

1. Domestic requirement of water (IS : 1993)

(1)	Bathing	75 litres per head per day
(2)	Washing of clothes	25 litres per head per day
(3)	Flushing of WCS	45 litres per head per day
(4)	Washing of house	15 litres per head per day
(5)	Washing of utensils	15 litres per head per day
(6)	Cooking	5 litres per head per day
(7)	Drinking	5 litres per head per day
(8)	Lawn watering and gardening	15 litres per head per day
		250 litres (55·0 gallons)

2. Water requirement for Public buildings (IS : 1172)

(1)	(*a*) Factories with no bath rooms	30 litres/capita/day
	(*b*) Factories with bath rooms	45 litres/capita/day
(2)	Hospitals per bed (*a*) upto 100 beds	340 litres/capita/day
	(*b*) above 100 beds	450 litres/capita/day
(3)	Medical quarters and nurses homes	135 litres/capita/day
(4)	Hostels quarters and nurses homes	135 litres/capita/day
(5)	Offices quarters and nurses homes	45 litres/capita/day
(6)	Hotels per bed and nurses homes	180 litres/capita/day
(7)	Restaurants per seat	68 litres/capita/day
(8)	Cinema etc. per seat	135 litres/capita/day
(9)	Schools (*a*) day schools	45·5 litres/capita/day
	(*b*) Boarding schools	135 litres/capita/day
(10)	Gardens and sports ground	315 litres/capita/day
(11)	Animals/vehicles	45 litres/capita/day
(12)	Dwelling houses	70 litres/capita/day

(C) **Water supply requirement for Railway and Bus stations (IS : 1172)**

(*a*)	Junctions with bathing facilities	70 litres/capita/day
	Junctions with no bathing facilities	45 litres/capita/day
(*b*)	Terminous stations with or without bathing facilities	45 litres/capita/day
(*c*)	Intermediate stations with bathing facilities	45 litres/capita/day
	Intermediate stations with no bathing facilities	23 litres/capita/day

(*d*) The no. of persons shall be determined by the average no. of passengers buy the ticket daily at stations. Staff and venders likely to use the facility should be added.

Periods for different parts of a water supply scheme

(1)	Storage of dams	50 years
(2)	Infiltration works	30 years
(3)	Pumping (*i*) Pump house	30 years
	(*ii*) Electric motors & pumps	15 years
(4)	Water treatment units	15 years
(5)	Pipe connection to the severe treatments units and other appurtenances	30 years
(6)	Raw water and clear water conveying units	30 years
(7)	Clear water reservoir at the head works, balancing tanks and service reservoirs lower head or ground level.	15 years
(8)	Distribution system	30 years

Table 17·6. Population densities

Sl. No.	*Type of area*		*No. of persons per hectare*
1.	Residential areas	(*a*) Single family dwellings large lots	10-40
		(*b*) Single family dwellings small lots	40-90
		(*c*) Multiple family dwellings	90-250
		(*d*) Apartments or tanement houses	250-3500 or more
2.	Commercial trade areas		40-75
3.	Industrial areas		10-41
4.	Total exclusive of parks, playgrounds etc.		25-125

(D) **Water requirement for public purposes**

Road watering	140 litres % m^2 of road surface
Sewer flushing	45 litres per head
Irrigation—Road side trees	28,000 litres/km
Public parks and private parks	20-30 litres % m^2
Cattles	45-65 litres per day

(E) **Storage of water for various fittings**

Water closet	180 litres	Lavatory basin	90 litres
Sink	90 litres	Urinal	180 litres
Yard tap	180 litres	Fire fighting requirement	1 lit/head/day

(F) **Water requirement for flushing of buildings**

(1)	Tenements having common conveniences	900 litres/w.c.
(2)	For residential premises other than tenements having common conveniences	270 litres/w.c.
(3)	Factories and workshops and urinals	900 litres/w.c. 180 litres/urinal
(4)	For cinema and public assembly halls and urinals	900 litres/w.c. 350 litres per urinal

(G) **Requirement for domestic and non-domestic needs**

(Manual of water supply, Ministry of works and housing)

(*a*)	For communities with population upto 10,000	70-100 litres
	For communities with population upto 10,000-50,000	100-125 litres
	For communities with population above 50,000	125-200 litres

(H) **Requirement of water in area having well and hand pump facilities** 45 litres/head per day

(I) **Fire demand—** Freeman formula $Q = 1135\left(\frac{P}{5} + 10\right)$

Kuchling formula $Q = 3000\sqrt{P}$

National Board of fire Formula $Q = 4640\sqrt{P\left(1 - 0{\cdot}01\sqrt{P}\right)}$

Buston's Formula $Q = 5{,}663\sqrt{P}$

$$Q = \frac{4360\,R^{0{\cdot}275}}{(t+12)^{0{\cdot}757}}$$

where R = Recurrence interval of fire *i.e.* period of occurrence of fire in years which will be different for residential, commercial and industrial cities. The minimum value as recommended is one year.

t = Duration of fire in minutes, its recommended minimum value is 30 minutes.

For fire occurrence once in 3 years $Q = 146{\cdot}4$ lit/min

Q = Fire demand in litres/min and P = Population in thousands.

Note : This demand is momentary and cannot be taken as a whole in the design.

(J) **Storage of water in buildings for interruptions in supply**

	Type of building	*Per person*	*Storage in litres*
(*a*)	Dwelling houses	per person	70
(*b*)	Hostels	per person	70
(*c*)	Hotels	per person	135
(*d*)	Commercial building with canteens	per person	35
	Commercial building without canteens	per person	45
(*e*)	Restaurants —	per meal	7

(*f*)	Day schools	per head	25
(*g*)	Boarding schools	per resident	90
(*h*)	Nurses home and medical quarters	per resident	135
(*i*)	Tenements having common conveniences		900 litres/w.c.
(*j*)	Residences having common conveniences		270 litres/w.c. and 180 litres for each additional seat in the same flat
(*k*)	Factories and work shops and per urinal		900 litres/w.c. 180 litres
(*l*)	Cinemas, Public assembly halls, etc. and per urinal		900 litres/w.c. 300 litres
(*m*)	Requirement of fire storage		2250 litres/min. for 45 min. with a terminal pressure of 3 kg per cm^2

(K) **For premises occupied as tenements with common conveniences**

(*a*) (*i*) **Ground floor** **Storage :** Nil, provided no downtake fittings are installed

(*ii*) **1st, 2nd, 3rd, 4th and upper floors** **Storage :** 500 litres per tenement

(*b*) **For Premises occupied as flats or blocks**

(*i*) **Ground floor** **Storage :** Nil, provided no downtake fittings are provided

(*ii*) **1st, 2nd, 3rd, 4th and upper floors** **Storage :** 800 litres per tenement

Note: The above storage may be permitted to be installed provided than the total domestic storage calculated on the basis is not less than the storage calculated on the number of downtake fittings as per scale given below :

1. Downtake taps — 70 litres each
2. Showers — 135 litres each
3. Bath tubs — 200 litres each

If the premises are situated at a place higher than the road level in front of premises, storage at ground level should be provided on the same lines as in the 1st floor.

For an average Indian town the requirements of water is as below :

1. Domestic	135 litres/capita/day
2. Industrial	40 litres/capita/day
3. Public use	27 litres/capita/day
4. Fire demand	14 litres/capita/day
5. Loss and wastage	5 litres/capita/day
Total	**221**

Note : Population of town multiplied by 221 litres will give the water requirement, 1·35 to 1·50 times, may be taken as design demand, taking variations in consideration. For meeting the peak demand 2·50 to 3·0 times of the average is taken.

Peak factors

Population etc.	Peak factors
1. (*a*) Upto 50,000	3·0
(*b*) 50,000 to 2,00,000	5·2
(*c*) 2,00,000 and above	2·0
2. For rural areas	3·0

Note : Evidently the peak factor tends to reduce on higher population.

The average value of peak factor is 2·7.

Factors affecting per capita demand. The annual average demand for water (*i.e.* per capita demand) varies considerable on different factors discussed below. The figure generally ranges between 100 to 360 litres/capita/day.

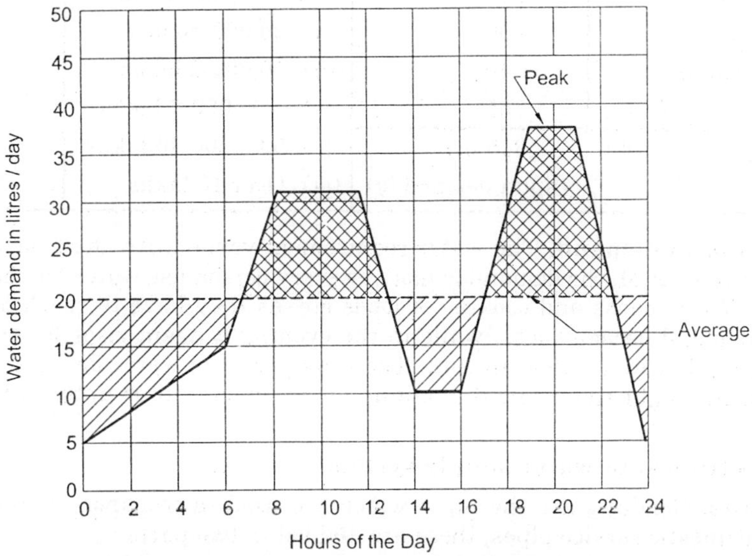

Fig. 17·10. Hourly rate of water consumption.

(*i*) **Size of the city.** The big cities have consumption per capita per day is more than that of smaller cities due to the large requirements and having limited sources of other personal supply of water such as hand pumps and wells etc.

(*ii*) **Climate conditions.** The drier is the climate larger will be the demand of water.

(*iii*) **Types of the peoples and their habits.** The richer and the advanced gentry require more water than the poor and unadvanced people. Richer and advanced people need more water for cleaning and washing etc.

(*iv*) **Industrial or commercial population.** Industries and commercial places require more water for running their plants etc.

(*v*) **System of supply.** If the water will be supplied round the clock the consumption will be higher than that of supplied for limited period.

(*vi*) **Cost of water.** If the rates of water per unit are higher the consumption will be lower.

(*vii*) **Quality of water.** If the water supplied is tasty and free of impurities the consumption will be higher.

(*viii*) **Habits of the people.** If the people are irresponsible they leave the taps open.

(*viii*) **Metering and method of charging.** If the water cost is charged on the basis of units used the consumption will be less than that of the cost is charged on the lump sum or on fixed rates.

(*ix*) **Pressure in distribution pipes.** If the pressure in the pipes are more the consumption will be more as for a certain time the water consumed will be more due to a higher discharge.

Table 17·7.

Per capita demand (q) for an average Indian city		*Variation in per capita demand (q) with population in India*	
Use	*Demand/lit. per head/day*	*Population*	*Per capita demand in litres/day/person*
(*i*) Domestic use	200	(*i*) less than 20,000	110
(*ii*) Industrial use	50	(*ii*) 20,000-50,000	110-150
(*iii*) Commercial use	10	(*iii*) 50,000-2 lakhs	150-240
(*iv*) Wastes and thefts etc.	55	(*iv*) 2,00,000-5 lakhs	240-275
Total	315 per	(*v*) 5,00,000-10 lakhs	275-335
	capita demand (*q*)	(*vi*) Over 10 lakhs	335-360

Variation in demand. The water requirement varies with the time of the day. In the morning 8.00 to 10.00 A.M. the demand is more as every person use water for their daily activities such as use in W.Cs., baths and cooking of foods etc. as they have to reach on their duties. In afternoon the demand becomes less, while in the evening it again rises for the same activities as in the morning, but in a larger amount. The peak period of water demand is as such in 6.30 to 8.30 P.M. In the night the demand is minimum as almost nil or upto 5 litres per head only (Fig. 17·10).

17·4. Conduits (Pipes) in water supply system

Conduits. Conduits are the pipes which are used to transport water supply from the intakes to the domestic service pipes, these are divided in two parts :

(1) Gravity conduits

(2) Pressure conduits.

(1) **Gravity conduits.** Gravity conduits are those in which the water flows under the maximum action of gravity. In such conduits the hydraulic gradient line coincides with the water surface and is parallel to the bed of the conduit. In such conduits water is all along at atmospheric pressure and thus there is no pressure term in Bernoulli's equation. Since the bed of such a conduit follows the gradual slope of the hydraulic gradient line. The **Gravity or grade conduits** can not therefore go upand down with the hill surface or as desired by the existing topography of the area. Hence these are taken on trestles in depression or in tunnels or in deep cuttings in ridges like canals, flumes and aquaduct etc. Alternately they may be carried along zigzag paths like roads etc. causing the increased lengths.

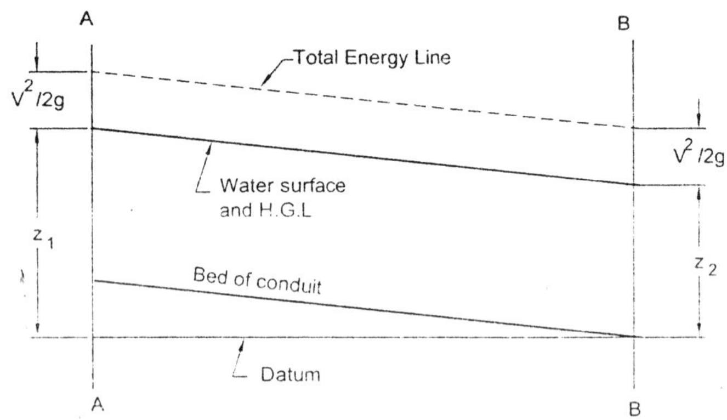

Fig. 17·11. Flow in gravity conduit.

Pressure conduits. Pressure conduits are closed conduits and as such no air can enter into them. The water flows under pressure above the atmospheric pressure. The hydraulic gradient line for such a conduit can be obtained by joining the water surface elevations in the piezometers installed in the conduit at various places. The bed or the invert of the conduit in pressure flow is thus independent of the grade of the hydraulic gradient line which really governs the flow velocities.

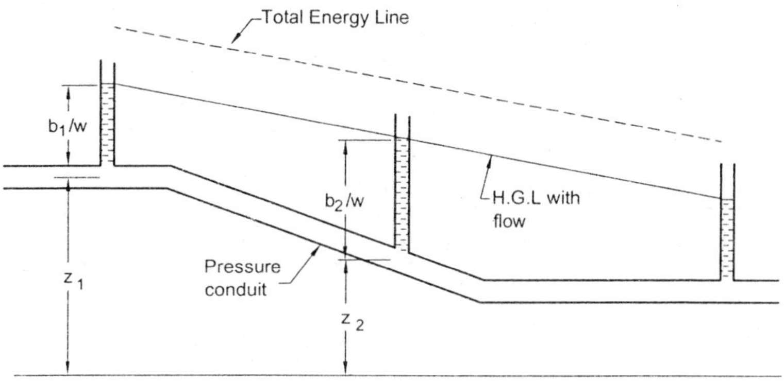

Fig. 17·12. Flow in a pressure conduit.

The pressure conduits can therefore follow the natural availabl ~round surface and can go up and down or can dip beneath valleys or hills, some times even rising above the hydraulic gradient lines and thus requiring lesser length of conduits.

The aquaduct or tunnel sections are generally circular. Due to their circular sections they are generally termed as pressure pipe. When a pressure pipe drops beneath a valley, stream or some other depression is called a **sag** or **depressed pipe** or an **inverted siphon.** Pressure pipes are economical than canals or flumes because they can follow shorter routes. Water goes in conduits in closed conditions hence it is not liable to any pollution.

When going above the hydraulic gradient line a negative pressure is created in such cases and since there is a limit of allowable –ve pressure due to cavitation etc. encroachment upto maximum 8·3 m is generally permitted.

The pressure pipes are generally used in water supply, while the gravity conduits are used in carrying sewage and drainage.

In the conduit going much below the H.G.L. the pressure developed may be so high that the pipe may burst due to this high pressure and there is limitation of going down the H.G.L.

Design of pressure pipes. The hydraulic gradient line (H.G.L.) should be such as to generate velocities which are neither so small as to require large size dia. pipe nor so large as to cause excessive loss of pressure head. The velocities must be non silting and non scouring. These are designed so that the available pressure head bet veen the source and the town is just lost in overcoming the frictional resistance offered to the flow by the pipe wall or surface. Although in addition to the frictional losses other losses such as by the abrupt change in the flow geometry due to change of pipe dia., bends, valves and fittings etc. should be considered. The head loss due to friction etc. which are governed by the following formulae :

(1) Darcy-Weisbach formula — $H_L = \dfrac{f'.L}{d} \cdot \dfrac{V^2}{2g}$

where H_L = Head loss in meters L = length of pipe in meters

V = Mean velocity of flow in pipe in m/sec. g = acceleration due to gravity

$f'*$ = Dimensionless friction factor

*f' generally varying between 0·02 for new smooth pipes to 0·075 for old rough pipes, generally average values of 0·024 is considered for all new pipes.

(2) Mannings formula — $H_L = n^2 . V^2 . \frac{L}{R^{4/3}}$

where, n = Mannings rugosity constant, L and V as above

R = Hydraulic mean depth of pipe = $\left(\frac{A}{P} = \frac{\pi d^2}{\pi d} = \frac{d}{4}\right)$ in metres (d is dia. of pipe)

(3) Hazen-William formula — $V = 0{\cdot}85\ C_H\ R^{0\cdot63} . S^{0\cdot54}$

where, C_H = Coefficient of hydraulic capacity given by table below. The smoother the pipe the greater the value of C_H.

R = Hydraulic mean depth of water in metres = $\left(\frac{d}{A}\right)$ for circular pipes, flowing full.

S = Slope of energy line and V = velocity of flow in pipe in m/sec.

Table 17·8. for value of C_H

Pipe material	*Value of C_H (depending on the smoothness of the pipe material)*
Concrete (regardless of age)	130
Cast iron (New)	130
5 years old	150
20 years old	100
Welded steel (New)	120
Riveted steel (New)	110
Vitrified clay	110
Brick sewers	100
Asbestos cement	140

Note : The carrying capacities decrease with time because with laps of time their surfaces become rough. Hence it is customary to select values of f' and n lower and values of C_H for old pipes is taken less than the new ones.

$$f' = 0{\cdot}04\left[1 + \frac{1}{35d}\right] \text{ for old pipes where } d = \text{dia. of pipe in m.}$$

$$= 0{\cdot}02\left[1 + \frac{1}{35d}\right] \text{ for new pipes}$$

f' is a function of Re (Reynold number) so

(*i*) $f' = \frac{64}{Re}$ for laminar flow upto $Re = 2000$

Relative roughness $\delta = \frac{2e}{d}$

where e = roughness of the pipe ; d = internal dia. of pipe ; $2e$ = absolute roughness of pipe.

(*ii*) Above *Re* 4000 turbulent flow

Nickuradse and others suggested

(*a*) $\frac{1}{\sqrt{f'}} = \left[2 \log_{10} Re\sqrt{f'} - 0.8\right]$ for smooth pipes

(*b*) $\frac{1}{\sqrt{f'}} = \left[2 \log_{10} \frac{d}{2e} + 1.74\right]$ for rough pipes

(*iii*) In the critical zone between Re = 2000 and Re 4000 Clebrook and White gave a formula

$$\frac{1}{\sqrt{f'}} = 1.74 - 2 \log_{10}\left[\frac{2e}{d} + \frac{18.7}{Re\sqrt{f'}}\right] \text{ (values of } 2e \text{ is as below)}$$

Table. 17·9. For the absolute value of 2*e*

Sl. No.	*Material of pipe*	*Values of 2e in mm × 10^{-3}*
1.	Glass, copper, lead or asbestos	1·524
2.	Steel or wrought iron	45·75
3.	Asphalted cast iron	122
4.	Galvanised iron	152
5.	Cast iron	300
6.	Concrete	300-3000
7.	Riveted steel	900-9000

Note : Some engineers represent friction factor by f and others by $4f$ so for avoiding confusion the symbol f' is taken.

For smooth pipes Re = 20,000 to 20,00,000

Stitcher formula $f' = 0.005 + \frac{0.396}{Re^{0.3}}$

$f' = 0.04\left[1 + \frac{1}{35d}\right]$ for old pipes.

(4) **Modified Hazen William's formula**

$$V = \frac{3.83 C_R \left[d^{0.6575} (g \cdot S)^{0.5525}\right]}{\nu^{0.105}}$$

where, C_R = dimensionless coefficient of roughness (values given in table below)

d = pipe dia. g = acc. due to gravity S = friction slope = $\frac{H_L}{L}$

ν = viscoscity of liquid, using ν for water at 20°C = 10^{-6} m/s and g = 9·81 m/s²

The equation reduces to $V = \mathbf{143.534\, C_R\, R^{0.6575}\, S^{0.5525}}$

where R = Hydraulic radius or Hydraulic mean depth = $\frac{A}{P}$, S = friction slope $\frac{H_L}{L}$

S is substituted by $\frac{H_L}{L}$, $R = \frac{d}{A}$ and $V = \frac{Q}{\frac{\pi}{4}d^2}$ for circular conduits.

The above equation yields as

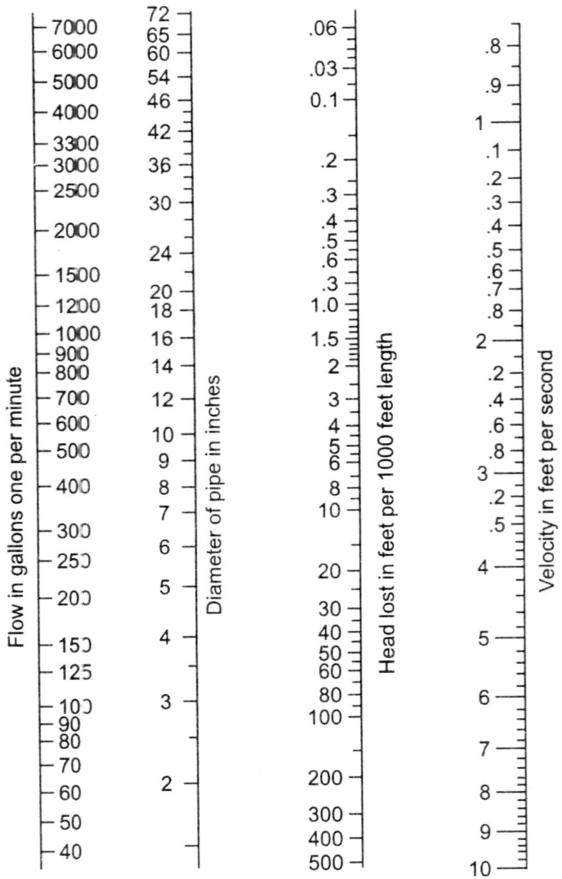

Chart for flow in the water pipes
(Based on Hazen and Williams Formula with $C = 100$)

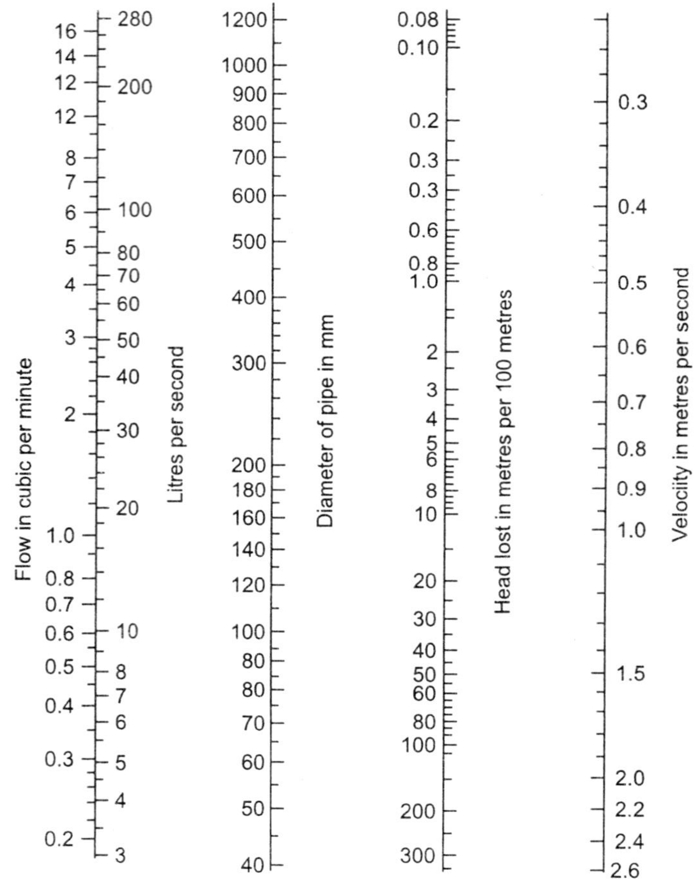

Nomogram for flow in water pipes
(Based on Hazen and Williams Formula with $C = 100$)
Multiplying factor for values of 'C' other than 100

C	*40*	*60*	*80*	*90*	*100*	*110*	*120*	*130*	*140*	
A	5·06	2·50	1·51	1·22	1·00	0·84	0·71	3·62	0·54	Loss of head
B	0·40	0·60	0·80	0·90	1·00	1·10	1·20	1·30	1·40	quality of flow

Fig. 17·13.

$$H_L = \text{Friction head loss} = \frac{L\left(\dfrac{Q}{C_R}\right)^{1\cdot81}}{994{\cdot}62\ d^{4\cdot81}}$$ where d = internal dia. of pipe in m and Q = flow in pipe

Table 17·10. Recommended C_R values in Modified Hazen-William's formula at 20°C

Sl. no.	*Pipe material*	*Dia (mm)*		*Velocity m/s*		*C_R value when new*	*C_R value for design period of 3 years*	
		From	*To*	*From*	*To*			
1.	RCC	100	2000	0·3	1·8	1·0	1·0	
2.	AC	100	600	0·3	6·0	1·0	1·0	
3.	HDPE/PVC	20	100	0·3	1·8	1·0	1·0	
4.	C.I.	100	1000	0·3	1·8	1·0	0·85*	For water with +ve Langelier's index
5.	C.I.	100	1000	0·3	1·8	1·0	0·53*	With –ve Langelier index
6.	Steel	100	2000	0·3	2·1	1·0	0·73*	With –ve Langelier's index
7.	SGSW	100	600	0·3	2·1	1·0	1·0	
8.	G.I.	15	100	0·3	1·5	0·87*	0·74*	With –ve Langelier's index

* These are average C_R values which result as a maximum error of ± 5% in estimation of surface resistance.

Table 17·11. Minor Losses in pipes due to other minor factors

Sl. No.	*Item*	*Loss represented by $K_L - \dfrac{V^2}{2g}$, value of K_L*
1	2	3
(1)	(*i*) Losses in enterance (*ii*) Bell mouth entry	0·04
	(*iii*) Square edge entry	0·5
(2)	Loss at exit	1·0
(3)	Loss due to sudden contraction	0 to 0·5 (varying with dia ratios)
(4)	Loss due to sudden enlargement	0·17 to 1·0 varying with angle between two sides of the tapering sec.
(5)	Losses in fittings and valves	
	(*i*) Standard 90° elbow = 0·9 ;	
	(*ii*) standard tee = 1·8 ;	
	(*iii*) Return bend = 2·2 ;	
	(*iv*) Gate valve half open = 5·6 ;	
	(*v*) Gate valve = 0·2 (wide open) ;	
	(*vi*) Swing check value = 2·5 (wide open)	
	(*vii*) Glove valve = 10·0 (wide open)	
	(*viii*) Angle value = 5·0	
	(*ix*) Meter venturi = 0·3	
	(*x*) Orifice = 1·0	

Flow in parallel pipes. When two pipes are laid in parallel as shown in the Fig. 17·13.

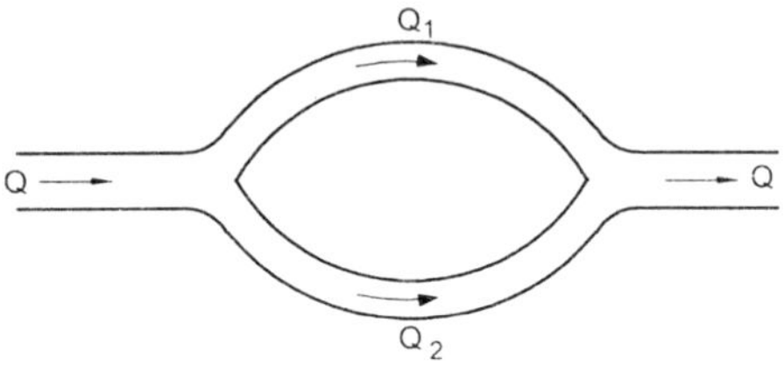

$Q = Q_1 + Q_2$

Fig. 17·13 (*b*).

The loss of head through each pipes will be the same. It is due to the following reasons:

(*i*) In order to increase the capacity of the line pipes are laid in parallel to the earlier one's.

(*ii*) Two or more pipes are sometimes preferred because when one pipe is in repair water can be supplied from the other.

(*iii*) When the single large pipe is not available in market, two or three pipes are replaced in place of a single large pipe.

(*iv*) To accommodate a larger area by two pipes in two different colonies.

If there are several pipes in parallel or in series or in combination of both it is generally convenient to express the head loss in the pipe system by an expression

$$H_L = KQ^x$$

where K depends upon the arrangement of length, dia. and roughness of pipes and x is the factor such as 1·85 in William Hazen's formula and 2 in Darcy-Weisbach and Manning's formulae.

Hydraulic Mean depth of pipes. $m = \dfrac{A}{P}$

where m = hydraulic mean depth ; A = area of the section and P is the wetted perimeter.

In case of pipes $\qquad m = \dfrac{\dfrac{\pi d^2}{4}}{\pi d} = \dfrac{d}{4}.$

Turbulent Flow in pipes. Nikuradse gives the following expression for Turbulents flow,

$$\frac{1}{\sqrt{f'}} = 2\log_{10}\left(Re\sqrt{f'} - 0{\cdot}8 \text{ or } \log_{10} Re = \frac{1}{2\sqrt{f'}} - \log_{10}\sqrt{f'} + 4\right) \text{ for } Re \text{ ranges from 20,000 to 32,00,000.}$$

Prandtl-von Karman equation for laminar flow :

$$fe = \mu\frac{dV}{dy}$$

where μ is the friction coefficient.

Similarly for turbulent flow :

$$fe = \eta\frac{dV}{dy}$$

where η is the eddy viscosity.

Critical velocity. Reynolds determined the critical velocity in a pipe by the following colour filament method. The apparatus consists of a glass tube of uniform bore with a bell mouth entrance inserted horizontally in a supply tank of glass. The tank is filled with calm water. A valve is provided at the outer end of glass tube to regulate the flow. A narrow glass tube with a small container having dye is used to inject a fine thread of coloured liquid of the bell mouthed enterance of glass tube.

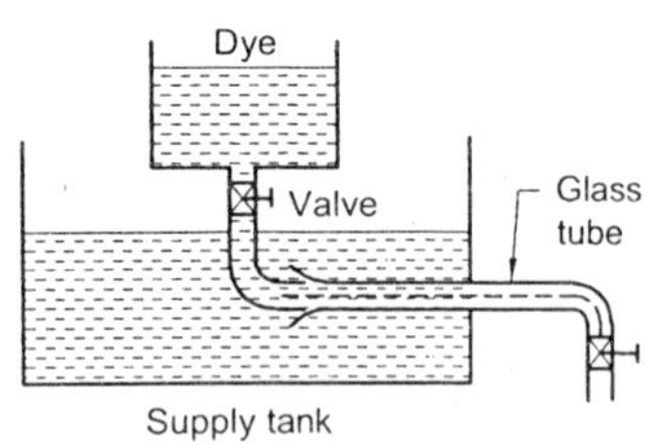

Fig. 17·14.

By regulating the flow with the help of valve, the velocities of water through the glass tube can be altered. The colour filament will remain in a straight line for a low velocity which is laminar flow. With increasing velocity the coloured filament will be waver and become confused which indicates a turbulent velocity. The velocity at which the filament starts diffusing is a laminar or critical velocity. In order to find the velocity of water, the water at critical position is measured in a graduated cylinder for a certain time by which the velocity can be calculated $\left(\frac{Q}{t}\right)$. Velocity meter can also be fixed above the valve to measure the velocity. The valve is remained untouched during the operation of measuring the velocity.

Water hammer in pipes. It is a phenomenon in a pipe line when the flowing water experiences a sudden reduction of velocity by closing the valve suddenly. With the energy or momentum of moving water is suddenly checked giving rise to a series of pressure. Pulsations above and below the normal working pressure. Such pressure pulsations create noise which is known as **knocking**. The sudden rise in pressure is called **hammer blow**. The pipe line or pen stock in power houses may burst if the hammer blow is excessive. The magnitude of pressure rise and fall depends upon the speed at which the valve is closed. The length of the pipe line and the elastic properties of the pipe material as well as that of flowing water. The valve may be closed gradually or instantaneously and the pressure head due to water hammer can be calculated according to the nature of the closure of the valves.

(*a*) **Gradual closure of valve.** The inertia head developed is

$$\text{Inertia head developed} = \frac{p_i}{w} = \frac{\rho}{g} \cdot \frac{v}{t}$$

where h_i = Inertia head or the force of inertia = mass × retardation of velocity

p_i = pressure intensity of inertia force

a = area of cross section of the pipe

l = length of pipe

g = acc. due to gravity

v = velocity of flowing water

t = time of closing of the valve

w = unit wt. of water

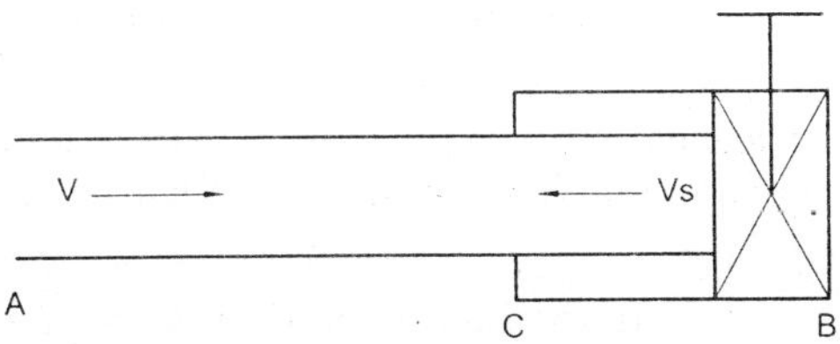

Fig. 17·15.

$$\text{Mass of water contained in pipe} = \frac{wal}{g}$$

$$\text{Rate of retardation of water column} = \frac{v}{t}$$

Force available for producing retardation acting axially = inertia pressure × sec. area

$$= p_i . a$$

Also force $= \text{mass} \times \text{retardation}$

$$\therefore \quad p_i . a = \frac{w.al}{g} . \frac{v}{t}$$

or

$$p_i = \frac{w.lv}{gt}$$

$$\text{Inertia head} = h_i = \frac{p_i}{w} = \frac{l.v}{g.t}$$

(*b*) **Instantaneous closure of valve.** Let the water be flowing with a velocity V and pressure P in the pipe AB (Fig. 17·15) having a valve at its end B. If the valve is suddenly closed, the velocity of water at this point is reduced to zero and there will be rise of pressure at the pipe end B due to inertia of moving water. A wave of inertia prssure will then travel backwards with velocity of sound V_s from B toward C. Consider a moment the wave has reached the point C, then in the portion of pipe AC. The water continues to flow with its original velocity V. However the water in the portion CB is compressed and the pipe dia. is stretched as shown exaggerated in the Fig. 17·15. When the pipe wave reaches the point A or C reaches A, all the water in the pipe is under high pressure and it continues to flow in the pipe backwards from B to A. This causes the pressure to fall. The wave of the falling pressure will then travel from A to B. With a velocity of sound V_S. Thus point C moves from A to B, when it reaches a place as shown in position AB, the water is moving towards A with velocity V and in position BC it is at rest.

Table 17·12. Normal values of water hammer pressures to be adopted in steel and C.I. pipes

Pipe dia. in cm	*Water hammer pressure in kN/m^2*
7·5 to 25	840
30	770
40	700
50	630
60	600
75	500-560
90	530
105 to 150	490

When C reaches B, the water in whole of the pipe length is moving back towards A. This causes the pressure fall to P with which a wave of –ve pressure or wave of rarefaction travel B to A with velocity of sound. When it reaches the end A, the water will start flowing towards B with which the pressure will again rises.

The wave of rising pressure will travel from A to B and so on. Such series of rising pressure and –ve pressure waves will go on following one another indefinitely, but due to friction in the pipe, compressibility of water and pipe material the wave is damped.

In the above equation $h_i = \frac{lv}{gt}$ if $l = 0$ then inertia head $h_i = 0$, but it is seen in practice that the magnitude of h_i is such that it is not possible to measure it, because the moving water in a pipe line of length l can not be brought to rest in time lesser than that it takes a sound wave to travel in water from the valve along the pipe can be brought to rest.

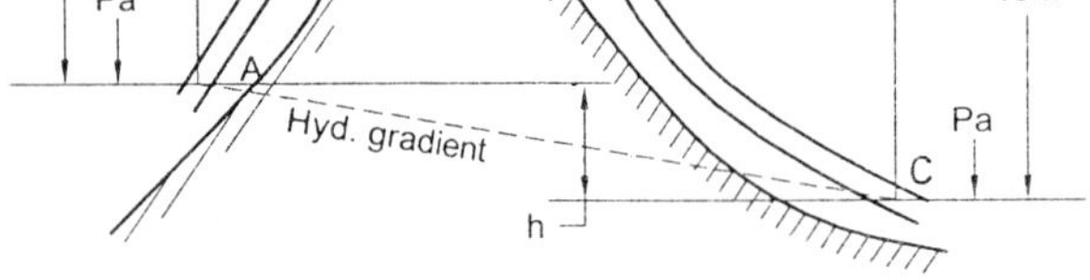

Fig. 17·16. Siphon over a ridge.

Negative pressure in pipes. The condition at which the pipe will flow full of water is that the absolute pressure of summit. Point B (Fig. 17·16) of siphon must not fall below zero. This can be found by applying Bernoulli's theorem between inlet point A and the summit B. If point B has negative absolute pressure, the siphon will not run full as at this point the air will be liberated from water. For this reason the minimum height of summit over the inlet A is $\frac{P_a}{w}$ *i.e.* 10 m of water, provided the pipe has a uniform dia. In practice this height is decreases to about 7·5 m due to separation of air and vapours from water at low pressure.

The above phenomenon of negative pressure can also be explained with the help of hydraulic gradient. The line joining *A* and *C* is the hydraulic gradient. When vacuum is created in the siphon the water is forced upto in the inlet leg *AB* by the atmospheric pressure. In a second line *A′C′* imaginary hydraulic gradient is drawn parallel to and at a vertical distance of *AC* equal to barometer height *i.e.* 10 m of water, the distance of siphon below *A′C′* will represent the absolute pressure at any point. Now the minimum allowable absolute pressure at *B* is zero as stated above, therefore if the summit of pipe rises above the line *A′C′*, the absolute pressure of that point will be negative with which the flow will be interrupted. For practical purpose the imaginary hydraulic gradient *A″C′* should be drawn at a height of 7·5 m above actual hydraulic gradient *AC*.

Starting of siphon. A siphon can be put in action either by exhausting air, thus creating vacuum in it by filling it with water. The air can be exhausted by a vacuum pump. The water in the siphon can be poured through an opening mode at the summit which is only possible by closing the outlets *A* and *C* temporarily.

While in operation the air separates itself from the flowing water and has the tendency to be collected at the bend. An air vessel can be provided to get rid of this difficulty, otherwise there will be an interruption in flow.

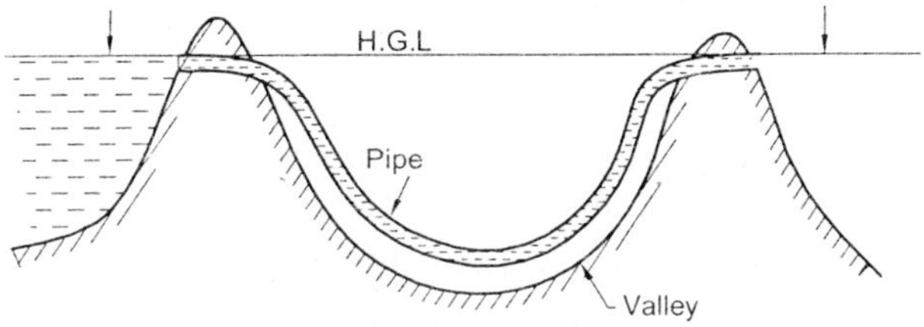

Fig. 17·17. Inverted siphon in a valley.

Inverted siphon in a valley. The hydraulic gradient line in a valley passes above the pipe line and the line is in a heavy pressure. Such pipe lines are called as inverted siphons.

Pipe in series or compound pipe. If pipe line is made up of a several pipes of different diameters d_1, d_2 etc. of corresponding lengths l_1, l_2 etc. connected in series, the difference in water surface levels is equal to the sum of head losses in all the sections.

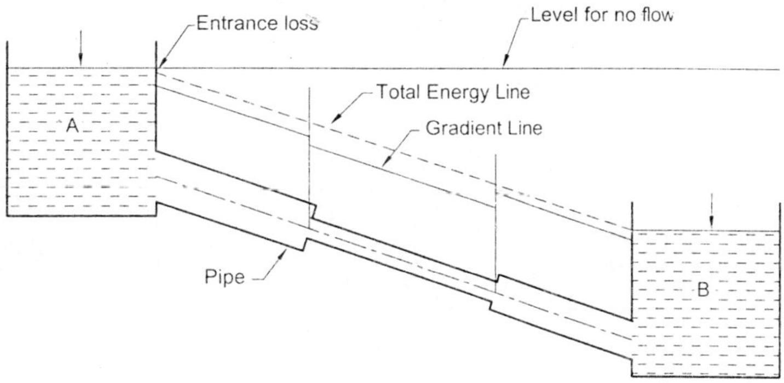

Fig. 17·18. Hydraulic gradient line and total energy line for pipe lines of varying sections.

i.e. H = head loss at enterance + head loss due to friction + head loss due to sudden contraction from pipe (1) to (2) + head loss due to friction in pipe (2) + head loss due to sudden enlargement from pipe (2) to (3) + head loss due to friction in pipe (3) etc. + head loss at exit.

Temperature stress in pipes. Stress = E strain = $E_P \alpha T$ or $f = E_P \alpha T$ (f being stress)

where E_P = Modulus of elasticity of the pipe material

α = Coefficient of expansion of the pipe material

T = Change of temperature in °C

E for water $= 21 \times 10^5$ kN/m^2

E_P for steel $= 21 \times 10^7$ kN/m^2

E_P for cast iron $= 10{\cdot}5 \times 10^7$ kN/m^2

E_P for cement concrete $= 21 \times 10^6$ kN/m^2

Table 17·13. Values of α-for various materials

Sl. No.	*Material*	*Coefficient of linear expansion (α) in mm/°C (20°-100°)*
1.	Steel	$12{\cdot}6 \times 10^{-6}$
2.	Cast iron	$11{\cdot}0 \times 10^{-6}$
3.	Concrete	$9{\cdot}8 \times 10^{-6}$
4.	Copper	$16{\cdot}5 \times 10^{-6}$

Some definitions regarding pressures in pressure pipes

Working Pressure. It is actual pressure (maximum including abnormal conditions such as water hammer etc.) to which the pipe will be subjected during the operation.

Design Pressure. It is the maximum pressure for which the pipe has been designed. It is product of the working pressure and suitable factor of safety to cover abnormal increase in pressure due to unforseen circumstances.

Test Pressure. It is the maximum pressure which the pipe can withstand without any leakage when tested for hydrostratic pressure in accordance with the standard methods of testing.

Various types of pressure pipes.

(1) **Cast iron pipes.** They are sufficiently resistant to corrosion and may last for 100 years or so. They are manufactured in lengths of 3·5 meters upto 6 m or so. Centrifugally cast iron pipes are called **Sand Spun pipes.**

Table. 17·14. Types of cast iron (spun) pipes as per IS 1536—1976

Sl. No.	*Category of pipes in the order of increasing thickness for the same dia.*	*Test pressure in kN/m²*	*Working pressure in kN/m²*
1.	Class LA	3500	1200
2.	Class A	3500	1800
3.	Class B	3500	2000

Nominal dia. available are 80 to 750 mm, their respective thickness for class LA are 7·2 to 18·3 mm.

For class A the thickness are 7·9 to 20·2 mm.

For class B the thickness are 8·6 to 22·0 mm.

Table 17·15(*a*). Test Pressures in Vertically cast iron pipes as per IS : 1537–1976

Sl. No.	*Diameter*	*Test pressure kN/m² using socket and spigot joint*	
		Class A	*Class B*
1.	Upto and including 300 mm	2000	2500
2.	Over 300 mm and upto and including 600 mm	2000	2500
3.	Over 600 mm and upto and including 1000 mm	1500	2000
4.	Over 1000 mm and upto 1500 mm	1000	1500

Table 17·15(b). Centrifugally cast (spun) iron pipes

Nominal dia. of pipe (mm)	*Outside dia. of barrel (mm)*	*Thickness of pipe barrel (wall)*		
		Class LA pipe (mm)	*Class A pipe (mm)*	*Class B pipe (mm)*
80 (3″)	98	7·2	7·9	8·6
100 (4″)	118	7·5	8·3	9·0
125 (5″)	144	7·9	8·7	9·5
150 (6″)	170	8·3	9·2	10·0
200 (8″)	222	9·2	10·1	11·0
250 (10″)	274	10·0	11·0	12·0
300 (12″)	326	10·8	11·9	13·0
350 (14″)	378	11·7	12·8	14·0
400 (16″)	429	12·5	13·8	15·0
450 (18″)	480	13·3	14·7	16·0
500 (20″)	532	14·2	15·6	17·0
600 (24″)	635	15·8	17·4	19·0
700 (28″)	738	17·5	19·3	21·0
750 (30″)	790	18·3	20·2	22·2

Pipes have been classified according to their wall thickness, class *A* pipes have 10% greater thickness than class *LA*, class *B* pipes have 10% greater thickness than class *A* pipes.

Standard length of pipes :

(*A*) Centrifugally cast pipes:

(*i*) Socket and spigot pipes—2, 2·8, 3, 4, 4·88, 5, 5·5 metres

(*ii*) Ditto for flanged pipes (end to end to flange)—3·66, 4, 4·88, 5, 5·5 metres

(*B*) Vertically cast pipes:

(*i*) Socket and spigot pipes—3·66, 4, 4·88, 5, 5·5 metres

(*ii*) Ditto for flanged pipes (end to end of flange)—1 to 3 metres for 80 pipes and 1 to 4 metres for other pipes.

Advantages of C.I. Pipes. The cast iron pipes are moderate in cast, easy to joint, strong and durable, corrosion resistant and have long life upto 100 years.

Disadvantages of C.I. Pipes. Water carrying capacity decreases with time. They can not be used for high pressures, generally not used above 700 kN/m^2, when large they are heavy and uneconomical and break during transportation.

Steel pipes. Steel pipes of varying thickness for with standing different pressures are generally bent and welded (or sometimes riveted). G.T. steel pipes with circumferential corrugations are much more stronger than ordinary steel pipes. They are in large diameters and smaller thickness. They are manufactured from 20 cm to 2 m in diameter and are lighter than C.I. pipes and hence can easily be transported. The various pipe lengths can be connected by riveted or welded joints. Pipes which are exposed to the atmosphere may require expansion joints. They can last for 40 years.

The steel pipes can not withstand high negative pressures.

Table 17·15(c). Data for steel water pipes
Thickness for various diameters and working pressure

Inside dia. of pipe mm	*Wall thickness plate* mm	*Safe work-pressure head of water* m	*Max. safe span* m	*Inside dia. of pipe* mm	*Wall thickness plate* mm	*Safe work-pressure head of water* m	*Max. safe span* m
1	2	3	4	1	2	3	4
600	5	160	10	1200	6	100	12
	6	200	11		8	135	13
	8	275	12		10	165	14
	10	330	13		12	220	15
					14	300	16
750	5	130	10				
	6	160	11	1350	8	120	13
	8	220	12		10	150	14
	10	260	13		12	175	15
	12	350	14		14	200	16
					16	250	17
900	6	130	11	1500	8	110	13
	8	180	13		10	130	14
	10	220	14		12	155	15
	12	300	15		14	180	16
	14	400	16		16	220	18
1050	6	110	12	1800	8	90	14
	8	155	13		10	110	15
	10	185	14		12	130	16
	12	250	15		14	150	17
	14	350	16		16	185	18

Theoretical plate thickness have been rounded off according to the thickness of steel plates manufacatured. The table is good for estimating purposes. Exact thickness can be worked out from using the formula, $t = \dfrac{P \times d}{2 \times S \times F}$.

where t = thickness of pipe wall in kg/sq. cm stress,

P = inter water pressure in kg/sq. cm which causes the hoop stress.

S = Safe working stress per pipe wall material in kg/cm^2 ; may be taken at about 1100 for steel pipes.

F = a factor for efficiency of longitudinal joints. F is usually taken as—

For Single riveted lap joints = 0·60; Double riveted = 0·70;

Triple riveted lap joint = 0·80; For a jack bar joint or seamless pipe = 1·00

Strength for welded joint is taken at 90%.

It is usual to take thickness of wall plate in excess of theoretical to meet the action of corrosion etc.

Corrosion in metal pipes and their protection. The metal pipes (generally cast iron or steel) are attacked and disintegrate by atmosphere and flowing water and are generally rusted. This corrosion can be controlled by the following treatments.

(*i*) **Protective coverings.** The pipe surfaces are coated with coatings of paint, galvanizing, bituminous compounds, cement linings etc. Red lead paint and zinc pigments offer some degree of protections and are often used for painting the exterior of the pipes. Sometimes water proof papers are also rapped round the pipes.

(*ii*) **Selection of proper pipe materials.** The constituents of the materials should be resistant to corrosion. Certain alloys of iron or steel with chromium, copper or nickel have been found to be better than the pure iron or steel.

(*iii*) **Improving quality of water.** The water passing through the pipes should be made as less corrosive as possible. This can be achieved by rising the pH of water by adding alkalinity in the form of lines or powdered chalk or by reducing the dissolved oxygen or carbondioxide by adding certain chemical compounds. Such as sodium hexameta phosphate in small doses of the order of 0·5 to 2 ppm.

(*iv*) **Cathodic protection.** Electrolytic corrosion can be prevented by connecting the pipe with negative terminal of a D.C. generator and connecting its positive terminal with blocks of zinc or magnesium buried in the ground near the pipe.

Cement concrete pipes or RCC pipes. Plain cement concrete pipes can only be made in small sizes (maximum upto 0·6 m in dia.). In order to increase their size they are reinforced with wires of dia. 1 mm to 5 mm. The reinforced pipes are available upto dia. of about 1·8 m. These pipes may either be prepared at site or can be manufactured in factories and then transported to site. They can be manufactured in three different ways.

(*a*) Pipes having bar and mesh reinforcement and concrete is poured as in ordinary cement concrete process.

(*b*) Pipes made by rotating the mould rapidly about the pipe axis. The mould (form) contains concrete and fabricated reinforcement. The centrifugal force throws off the concrete which then spreads the uniform layer over the internal surface of the mould and embed the reinforcement, thus providing a high density water light concrete surface. They are known as centrifugal type.

(*c*) The third type of RCC pipes are made by lining their cylinderical steel shells both internally and externally with rich cement concrete. There are stronger and more water light than the 1st two and are used for larger pressure. They are known as cylinder type. These pipes can be made by centrifugal process also. They are manufactured under the patented name of Hume steel pipes.

RCC pipes are generally made from 1 : 2 : 2 cement concrete ratio with a maximum aggregate size as 6 mm. They are provided longitudinal reinforcement as well as circumferential reinforcement to carry hoop tension and a nominal longitudinal reinforcement equal to 0·25% of the cross-sectional area of concrete. Their thickness may vary from 2·5 cm to 6·5 cm for pipes of diameters varying from 0·1 m to 1·2 m. Such RCC pipes are lengthened by providing end bars of different lengths batting against one another and welding them and finally filling the gap with rich cement concrete so as to provide water light joint. The joints are also joined by providing collors of cement concrete made specially for this purpose suiting the size of the pipes.

Pre-stressed concrete pipes have also come in to the market. In these pipes the permanent internal stresses upto desired extent are deliberately introduced in the steel reinforcement, so as to counteract the stresses, that are likely to come by internal loads when such pipes are subjected to loadings.

Table 17·16. Ordinary RCC pipes as per IS : 458—1988

Category	*Diameter available*	*Test pressure in kN/m²*	*Places where used*
Class P_1	80-1200 mm	200	Used on gravity mains, design pressure not exceeding 2/3 of test pressure
Class P_2	80-600 mm	400	Used on pumping mains, the design pressure not exceeding 1/2 of the test pressure
Class P_3	80-400 mm	600	--do--

The steel cylinder, reinforced cement concrete pipes are manufactured in India as per provisions of IS : 1916—1989 and are available in dia. ranging from 200 mm to 1800 mm. They are used in water mains, sewers, irrigation works etc.

Table 17·17 (*a*). Steel cylinder RCC pipe as per IS : 1916—1989

Category	*Test pressure in kN/m²*	*Working pressure*
Class 1	500	In general working pressure for pumping mains is taken as 50% of the test pressure and for gravity mains is taken as 2/3rd of the test pressure.
Class 2	1000	
Class 3	1500	
Class 4	2000	
Class 5	2500	
Special class	Above 2500, to be specified by users	

The prestressed pipes can be designed for high heads and are manufactured in India as per the provisions of IS : 784—1978. They are available in the diameter ranging from 80 mm to 1800 mm. These pipes are subjected to hydrostatic pressure test as specified in IS : 3597—1985 and the test pressure must be twice the designed pressure.

Advantages of RCC pipes. (*i*) They can resist external compressive loads and do not collapse under nominal vacuums and traffic loads.

(*ii*) They are not corroded from inside by normal potable water and from outside by soils.

(*iii*) They are strong and their useful life is about 75 years.

(*iv*) They can be easily constructed at work sites.

(*v*) Their coefficient of expansion being low and hence is not much effected by hot weather.

(*vi*) The empty pipes do not float in water being heavy.

Disadvantages. (*i*) They can be corroded by surface water having pressure of acids alkalies and sulphur compounds.

(*ii*) They are difficult to repair.

(*iii*) They can not withstand heavy pressure.

(*iv*) Being heavy they are difficult to transport.

(*v*) Their joints are difficult to make them water light and strong.

(*vi*) They can crack due to the shrinkage and hence tends to leak and are porous.

Table 17·17(*b*). Asbestos-cement pipes are classified according to the pressures as follows

Class-1	5 kg/sq. cm.	The maximum working pressure under which each pipe is used shall not exceed half the test pressure for that class of pipe.
Class-2	10 kg/sq. cm.	
Class-3	15 kg/sq. cm.	
Class-4	20 kg/sq. cm.	
Class-5	25 kg/sq. cm.	

Approximate weight and thickness of medium grade G.I. water pipes per meter length

Nominal bore in mm	10	15	20	25	32	40	50	65	80	100
Thickness in mm	2·35	2·65	2·65	3·25	3·25	3·25	3·65	3·65	4·05	4·50
Wt. in kg/meter	0·85	1·21	1·57	2·42	3·11	3·59	5·07	6·49	8·43	12·0

Plastic pipes are classified as 2·5, 4, 6 and 10

Test pressures and allowable working pressure, IS : 3076 and 4985

Class of pipe	*Test pressure*		*Working pressure allowable*	
	kg/sq. cm	*Head in meters*	*kg/sq. cm*	*Head in meters*
2·5	3·75	37·5	1·875	18·75
4	6	60	3·0	30
6	9	90	4·5	45
10	15	150	7·5	75

Polyethylene pipe

Nominal bore in mm	25	32	40	50
Nominal outside dia. (mm)	32	40	48	60

Asbestos pipes. Asbestos, silica and cement are converted under pressure to a dense homogeneous material processing high strength and is called as **asbestos cement.** The **asbestos fibre** which are thoroughly mixed with cement serves as reinforcement. These pipes are generally available in different sizes ranging from 10 to 90 cm in diameter in about 2 to 4 m in lengths. These pipes are generally made in four different grades to withstand pressures of 350 kN/m^2 to 1400 kN/m^2 as per provisions of IS : 1592—1984. These pipes are joined by means of special type of couplings, called as **surplex joints**, which consists of a pipe sleeve and two rubber rings which are compressed between the pipe and the interior of the sleeve (Fig. 17·19).

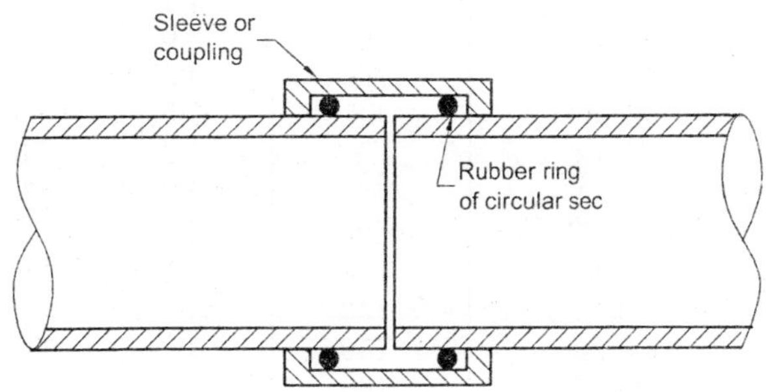

Fig. 17·19.

Advantages of asbestos pipes. (*i*) They are light and easy to transport.

(*ii*) They are highly resistant to corrosion.

(*iii*) Expansion joints are not required as its thermal expansion coefficient is low.

Disadvantages. These pipes are not more stronger and liable to break in even low loads. The rubber joint may deteriorate if exposed to gasoline petroleum products.

Vitrified earthenware pipes. They are not strong and hence are used in unimportant works. They can not be used as pressure pipes and are used only in household drains to pass waste water. The formation of water tight joints are difficult. They are available in short lengths from 6 to 1·2 m. They are painted from outside.

Plastic pipes. Plastic pipes are used widely these days. They are light and hence easy to transport. They can not withstand high temperature exceeding 60°C or so. They can not take loads and liable to crack. The manufacture of low and high density polyethylene pipes for possible water supply is done which is governed by IS : 3076—1985 and IS : 4484—1995 respectively. The unplasticised PVC pipes for potable water are manufactured as per IS : 4985—1988. These pipes are also used widely as rain water pipes. These pipes are available 2 cm to 15 cm diameter in lengths of 3 m to 6 m. These pipes are joined by plastic sockets by a solution paste. Bends and elbows are also available for making turning points.

Pipe Joints

(1) **RCC pipes cement joint** used in drainage pipes.

(2) **Spigot and socket** used in metal pipes of water mains. Spigot and socket are caulked with lead. This joint can adjust temperature expansion and contraction. It has also a capacity to adjust itself for any minor settlement and hence is considered to be a flexible joint. It is not suitable for high pressure hydraulic pipes and are liable to leak.

Table 17·17(c). Approximate quantity of material and labour required for joining cast iron pipes of different diameters per 10 joints

Nominal dia. of pipe	*Lead*	*Spun yarn*	*Fuel wood*	*Kerosine oil*	*Labour*		
					Fitter	*Asstt. fitter*	*Helper*
mm(inch)	*kg*	*kg*	*kg*	*litres*	*No.*	*No.*	*No.*
80(33″)	19	1·0	19	0·4	1	1	2
100(4″)	25	1·8	29	0·5	1	1	2
125(5″)	30	2·0	38	0·8	1·5	1·5	3
150(6″)	38	2·0	43	0·8	1·5	1·5	3
200(8″)	50	3·0	57	0·9	1·75	1·75	3·5
225(9″)	55	3·2	62	1·2	1·75	1·75	3·5
250(10″)	63	3·5	66	1·3	2·0	2·0	4
300(12″)	77	4·8	76	1·5	2·25	2·25	4·5
350(14″)	90	6·0	90	1·7	2·5	2·5	4·5
375(15″)	98	6·7	100	1·8	2·75	2·75	5·5
400(16″)	110	7·5	110	2·0	3	3	6
450(18″)	130	9·5	125	2·8	3·5	3·5	7
500(20″)	150	10·0	130	2·8	4	4	8
525(21″)	160	10·8	140	2·9	4·5	4·5	9
600(24″)	185	12·6	170	3·0	6	6	12
900(28″)	220	13·5	216	3·2	7	7	14
750(30″)	250	14·5	240	3·5	7·5	7·5	15
800(32″)	280	15·3	260	3·8	8	8	16
900(36″)	340	18·8	290	4·5	9	9	18
1000(40″)	410	20·5	350	4·8	10	10	20
1100(44″)	460	24·0	380	5·0	11	11	22
1200(48″)	500	26·0	420	6·0	12	12	24
1500(60″)	660	28·0	500	7·5	14	14	28
1800(72″)	900	31·0	600	8·5	16	16	32

Quantity of lead wool or lead yarn required for different sizes of pipes

Nominal dia. of pipe mm	*Wt. of lead wool per joint kg*	*Depth of lead wool per joint kg*	*Nominal dia. of pipe mm*	*Wt. of lead wool per joint kg*	*Depth of lead wool per joint kg*
80	0·80	19	400	5·70	31
100	0·90	19	450	6·70	32
125	1·25	20	500	8·30	33
150	1·60	23	600	10·0	35
200	2·05	23	700	11·8	36
250	2·95	25	750	13·6	38
300	3·50	25	800	15·4	40
350	4·65	29	900	16·8	40

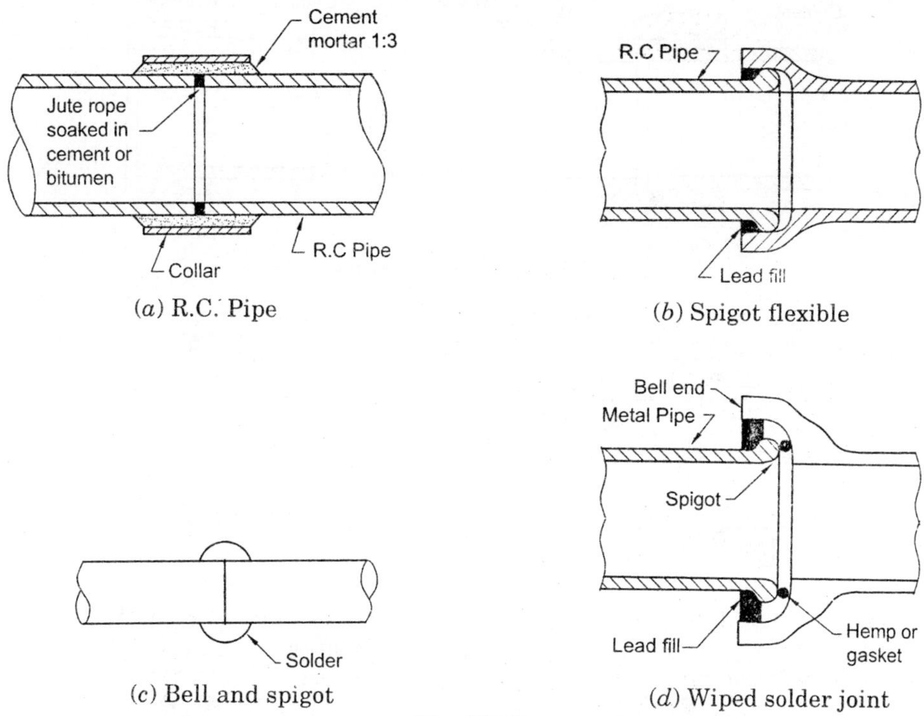

(a) R.C. Pipe (b) Spigot flexible

(c) Bell and spigot (d) Wiped solder joint

Fig. 17·20.

Cement used as a caulking material makes the joint right. Other materials used for caulking are lead wool (under wet conditions) or tarred or asphalted yarn (for sewers).

(3) **Wiped solder joints are used to join lead pipes.** Minimum width of joint is given in the table below :

(4) **Flange joints.** Mechanical or bolted joints. The flanges screwed to pipes (steel) are bolted together. These joints are used in sluice or air valves. A packing also called as gasket or washer is placed between the two flanges. The gasket is made of rubber, leather, compressed fibre board or gatta parcha, smeared with graphite paste or mixure of red and white lead. The thickness of gasket is 1·5 mm for 200 mm pipes and 2·5 to 2 mm for bigger pipes. In cast iron these flanges are casted with the pipe.

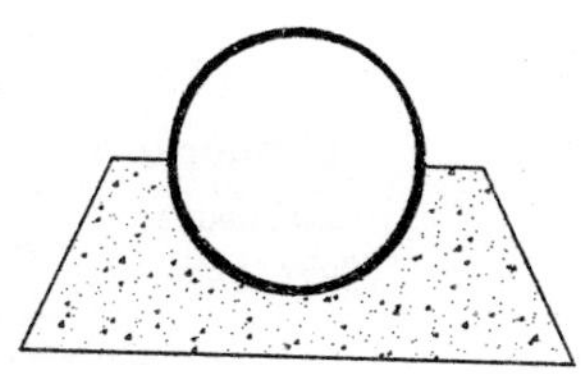
Fig. 17·21. Base of joint.

Base of joints. The base of joints may be of a semi-circular concrete block rested on a firm based trench.

Table 17·18. Minimum width of wiped solder joint

Pipe dia. mm	*15*	*20*	*25*	*40*	*50*	*80*	*100*	*125*	*150*
Joint length mm	*57*	*64*	*70*	*70*	*76*	*76*	*82*	*90*	*90*

Joint of pipe to storage tank. The end of the pipe is bushed and passed through a hole and secured by a backnut both inside and outside of the tank. The pipe end is kept flushed with the face of the inside back nut to save the pipe from corrosion. For joining with copper pipes a connector of non-ferrous metal shall be used having a shoulder to bear on the outside of the tank and secured by a backnut from inside.

Joints in Pipes

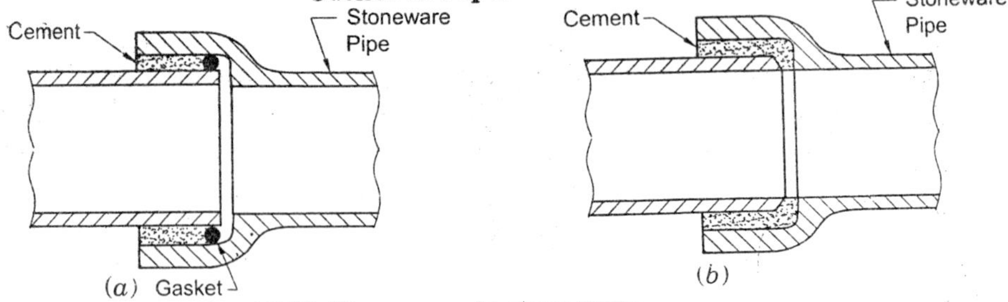

Fig. 17·22. Stone ware to stone ware

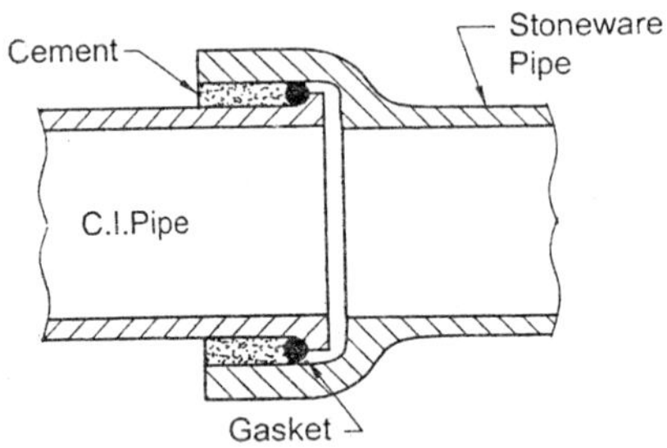

Fig. 17·23. C.I. to stone ware.

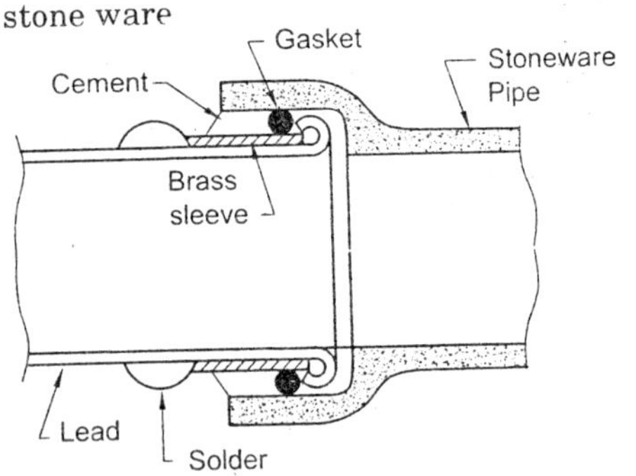

Fig. 17·24. Lead to stone ware.

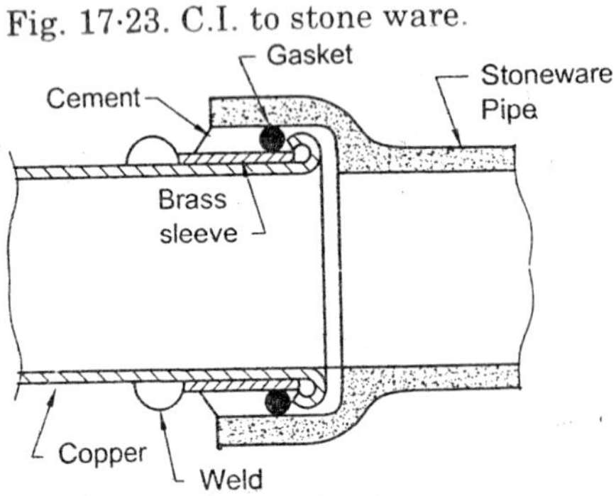

Fig. 17·25. Copper to stone ware

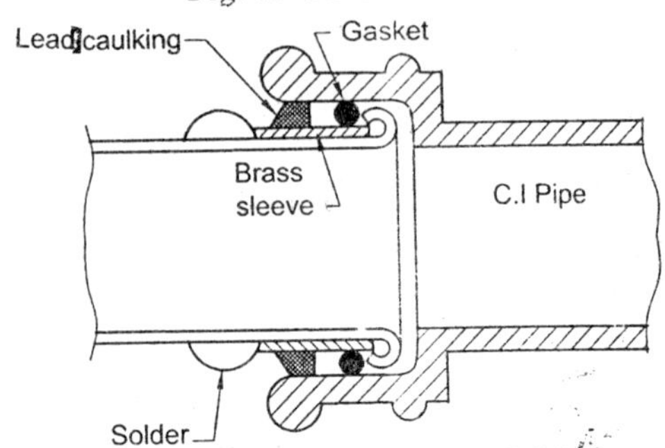

Fig. 17·26. Lead to C.I.

Copper to C.I. : Same as Lead-C.I. except solder joint is replaced by weld.

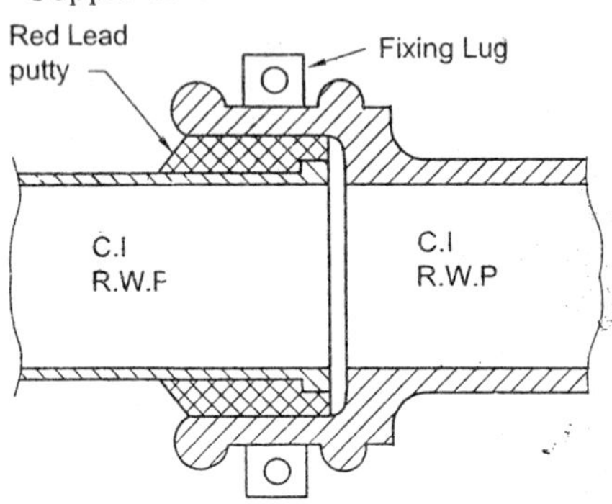

Fig. 17·27. C.I. to C.I. RWP.

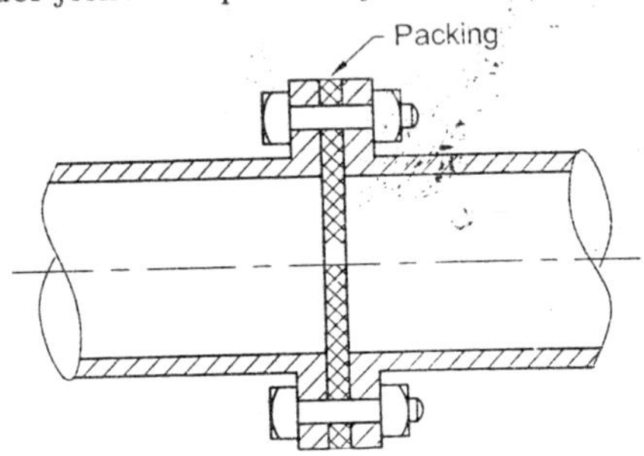

Fig. 17·28. Flange joint.

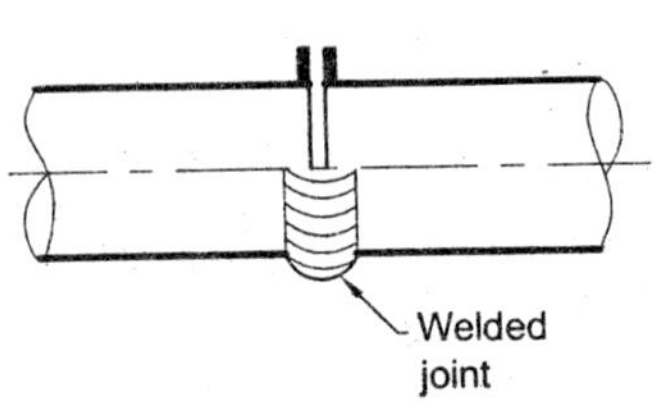

Fig. 17·29. Weld joints.

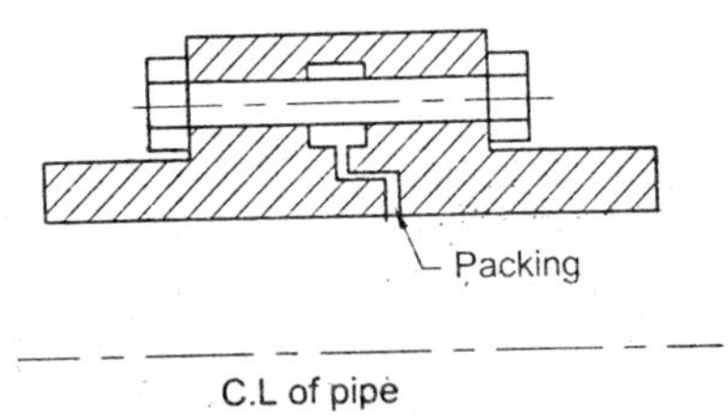

Fig. 17·30. Hydraulic joint

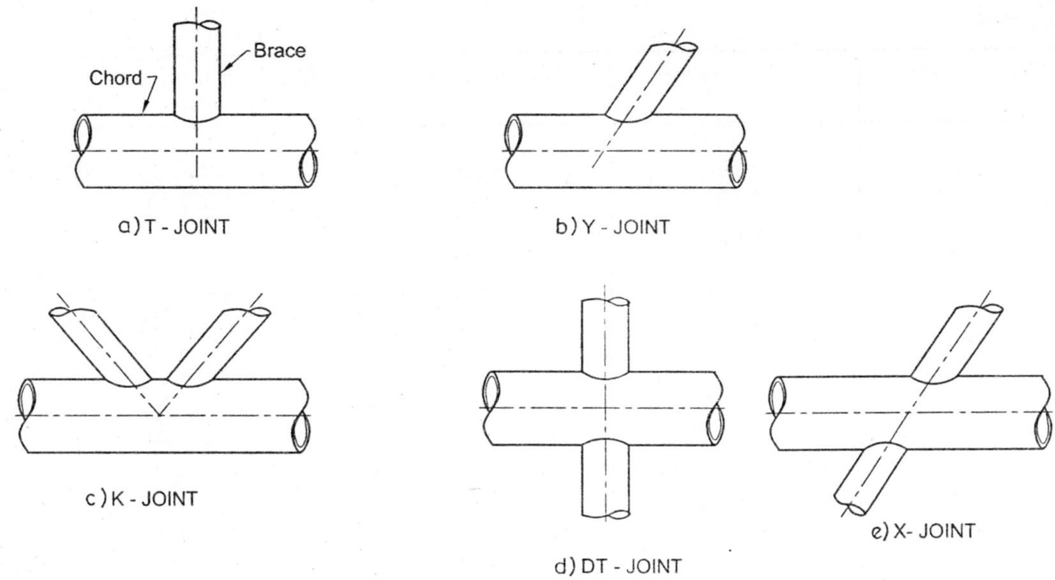

Fig. 17·31. Typical welded joint in pipes.

Fibrous materials. (Packing materials). There may be inorganic or organic, natural or synthetic.

(1) **Asbestos.** It is a mineral fibre of natural origin, can stand at high temperature as in steam pipe joints.

(2) **Glass wool** is a very fine fibre (0·025 mm dia.) prepared by allowing molten glass to drop from a very fine orifice used in packing as a fine resistant.

(3) **Lead wool.** A very finely divided fibre prepared by lead and used as cold packing in place of molten lead in pipe joints in moist situations.

Burlap is a coarse jute, hemp or flux textile used as a water proofing membrane.

Hessian. It is jute fabric.

Rubber. It is plant production.

Cork. It is a light wood.

Gasket is a packing material such as cotton rope, unpregnated with oil or greaze. Flat sheet asbestos compound used for making gas tight joints. Hemp, cotton or jute yarn (impregnated) are used in water and sewer pipe joints as a caulking material.

Natural origin fibres are animal fibres as sheeps wool, camels hair, silk from cocoons or vegetable fibres like cotton, cellulose, flux, hemp, jute, dhak fibre. Vegetable fibres are much less water absorbing and more flexible than animal fibres.

Dhak fibres (locally known as **Bakota**) swells with water, making the joint water tight, used in boats to make the wood joints water tight.

Table 17·19. C.I. Pipes for water supply (Crumps and Burgs Table)

Minimum flow is 2·5 times of the average flow

Pipe dia (mm)	*Cap in cm/min*	*Velocity in m/sec*	*Loss of head due to friction (in m% m length)*
75	0·21 0·209 0·157	0·90 0·75 0·66	23·80 16·40 10·52

Table contd...

Table contd...

Pipe dia (mm)	*Cap in cm/min*	*Velocity in m/sec*	*Loss of head due to friction (in m% m length)*
100	0·444 0·370 0·297	0·90 0·75 0·60	16·11 11·22 7·14
125	0·691 0·580 0·466	0·90 0·75 0·60	11·90 8·33 5·40
150	1·170 1·050 0·983	1·05 0·90 0·75	12·80 9·53 6·45
175	1·590 1·367 1·131	1·05 0·90 0·75	10·41 7·69 5·26
200	2·075 1·790 1·490	1·05 0·90 0·75	8·70 6·45 4·45
225	3·060 2·620 2·240	1·20 1·05 0·90	10·00 7·40 5·40
250	3·680 3·255 2·780	1·20 1·05 0·90	8·33 6·45 4·76
300	5·350 4·700 3·450	1·20 1·05 0·90	6·67 5·13 3·70
350	7·20 6·39 5·45	1·20 1·05 0·90	5·40 4·17 3·30
375	9·40 8·31 7·30	1·35 1·20 1·05	6·25 4·89 3·77
400	10·70 9·53 3·29	1·35 1·20 1·05	5·72 4·54 3·45
450	15·08 13·51 12·00	1·50 1·35 1·20	6·06 4·88 3·85

Table 17·20. Dimensions of concrete pipes (IS : 458—1961)

Internal dia. mm	*Thickness mm*	*Length m*	*Particulars*
80,100,150,250 300 350,400 450	25 30 32 35	1·0	Unreinforced concrete, non pressure pipes for drainage and irrigation use, above ground in shallow trenches. The class of these pipes is NP_1 R.C.C. light duty non pressure pipes for culverts bearing light traffic. The class of these pipes in NP_2.
80,100,150,250 300	25 30	2·0 2·0, 2·5, 3·0	

Table contd...

Table contd...

Internal dia. mm	*Thickness mm*	*Length m*	*Particulars*
350, 400	32	2·0, 3·0	
450, 500	35		
600, 700	40		
800	45		
900	50		
1000	55		
1100	60	2·5, 3·0	
1200	65		
1400	75		
1600	80		
1800	90		
350, 400, 500, 550	75		
600, 700	80		RCC, heavy duty, non pressure pipes for culverts, carrying heavy traffic such as Railways. The class of the pipes is NP_3.
800	90	2·5, 3·0	
900, 1000	100		
1100, 1200	115		
80, 100, 150, 250	25	2·0	RCC pressure pipes tested to a hydraulic pressure of 2·0 kg/sq cm (20 m head) for use on gravity mains. The actual working pressure not exceeding 2/3 of the net pressure. The class of these pipes is P_1.
300	30		
350	32	2·0, 3·0	
400	32		
450, 500	35		
600, 700	40		
800	45	2·5, 3·0	
900	50		
1000	55		
1100	60		
1200	65		
80, 100, 150	25	2·0	RCC pressure pipes tested to a hydraustatic pressure of 4·0/cm^2 (40 m head) for use on pumping mains. The actual working pressure not exceeding half of the test pressure. The class of these loadings is P_2.
250	30		
300	40	2·0, 3·0	
350	45		
400, 450	50		
500	55	2·0, 3·0	
600	65		
80, 100, 150	25	2·0	RCC pressure pipes tested to a hydraustatic pressure of 6·0 kg/cm^2 (60 m head) for use on pumping mains. The actual working pressure not exceeding half of the test pressure. The class of these pipes is P_3.
250	35		
300	45		
350	55	2·0, 3·0	
400	60		

Table 17·21. Dimensions of prestressed pipes (IS : 784—1959)

Internal dia. of pipe in mm	*Length in meters*
80, 100, 125, 150, 250, 300, 350, 400	2·0
450, 500, 600, 700, 800, 900, 1000, 1100, 1200, 1400, 1600, 1800	2·5

Table 17·22. Head in meters to overcome the frictional resistance in 100 m length of different discharges

(This table gives friction head for smooth straight pipes. Allowance for increased resistance to bends etc. should be given)

Discharge in litres/min.	*Internal dia. of pipe in mm*																	
	50	*75*	*100*	*125*	*150*	*175*	*200*	*225*	*250*	*300*	*350*	*375*	*400*	*450*	*500*	*525*	*550*	*600*
45	0·46	0·46																
90	1·61	0·24	0·90															
135	3·45	0·57	0·14															
180	5·40	0·86	0·23	0·10														
225	8·28	1·38	0·34	0·14														
270	11·5	1·84	0·52	0·20	0·90													
337·5	17·8	2·64	0·72	0·28	0·13													
450		4·37	1·15	0·46	0·20	0·10												
675		9·43	2·42	0·86	0·39	0·21	0·10											
900		16·10	4·26	1·56	0·69	0·32	0·17	0·10										
1125			6·44	2·30	0·99	0·40	0·25	0·15	0·10									
1350			9·20	3·16	1·38	0·64	0·36	0·21	0·13									
1575			11·8	4·37	1·84	0·86	0·46	0·28	0·17	0·08								
1800			15·5	5·52	2·42	1·15	0·59	0·34	0·21	0·09								
2025			19·1	6·77	2·88	1·44	0·74	0·43	0·26	0·11								
2250			23·0	8·05	3·45	1·61	0·86	0·52	0·31	0·13								
2700				11·5	4·83	2·18	1·16	0·71	0·44	0·20	0·90	0·08						
3150				15·3	6·32	2·82	1·55	0·98	0·51	0·25	0·13	0·09						
3600				19·5	8·50	3·74	2·00	1·22	0·73	0·32	0·16	0·11	0·09					
4050					11·3	4·60	2·48	1·50	0·43	0·43	0·20	0·14	0·01					
4500					12·5	6·32	3·08	1·84	1·20	0·48	0·24	0·17	0·13					
5400					15·0	8·51	4·37	2·50	1·55	0·67	0·32	0·24	0·17	0·10				
6300						11·3	6·00	3·32	2·00	0·90	0·44	0·32	0·23	0·14				
7200						14·7	7·60	4·32	2·64	1·15	0·56	0·40	0·30	0·16	0·10			
8100						18·4	9·66	5·52	3·40	1·39	0·69	0·49	0·37	0·21	0·14	0·10		
9000							11·3	6·63	4·03	1·75	0·83	0·60	0·44	0·25	0·16	0·13	0·10	
11,250								10·3	6·10	2·11	1·21	0·87	0·67	0·39	0·24	0·20	0·16	0·10
13,500									8·63	3·68	1·75	1·26	0·92	0·54	0·33	0·26	0·22	0·15
15,750									11·3	4·83	2·36	1·66	1·23	0·71	0·45	0·36	0·28	0·20
18,000										6·32	3·00	2·16	1·70	0·91	0·57	0·46	0·36	0·24
20,250										7·82	3·74	2·64	1·93	1·15	0·69	0·56	0·46	0·29
22,500										9·66	4·60	3·28	2·37	1·36	0·83	0·67	0·55	0·36
24,750										11·1	5·40	3·91	2·88	1·63	0·97	0·77	0·63	0·43
27,000											6·44	4·60	3·40	1·93	1·15	0·92	0·75	0·51
31,500											8·62	6·10	5·54	2·56	1·55	1·24	1·00	0·67
36,000											11·3	8·05	5·75	3·34	2·01	1·61	1·27	0·85

Design of water supply pipes

(*a*) Maximum demand period is 6 to 9 A.M. and 5 to 10 P.M. It is presumed that half of the total demand of the day is required during the above six hours while the rest half is needed in the balance 18 hours.

(*b*) The maximum hourly demand can be taken as 2·5 to 3 times the average hourly demand and 3 to 3·75 during summer, which is less in coastal areas.

(*c*) An allowance of one percent is taken for the fire requirements.

(*d*) **Leakage losses.** 10 to 25 percent of the total requirement.

The leakage losses increase with increasing head (pressure) in the proportion of square root of the pressure. A leakage allowance of 4000 to 5000 litres for 24 hours per kilometer for 100 mm dia. pipe may be taken for estimate purposes.

Table showing approximate leakages in litres/hr at a pressure of 7 kg/cm^2 in 1000 m long pipes.

Table 17·23.

Dia of pipe in mm	80	100	150	200	250	300	400	500	600	750	900
Leakage in litres	130	180	240	330	390	440	600	750	900	1100	1400

Size of distribution pipes. Taking above factors in view the discharge likely to pass in the pipe is determined. The size of the pipe line is decided according to the slope of the country and a velocity as recommended is assumed (60 to 120 cm/sec, maximum of 180 cu.m/sec and gradient 1 to 3 per thousand) or as suitable according to the material of the pipe. The dia. of the pipe is located from the table suiting the discharge slope and velocity conditions by trial method.

Following rough guide can be followed:

(*a*) When pipes are connected at each ends to main upto 150 m

Upto 150 m length	50 to 80 mm
Upto 600 m length	100 mm

(*b*)

Dead ends length upto 100 meter	50 to 80 mm
Dead ends length upto 400 meter	100 mm

(*c*) Pipes with fire hydrants both ends connected to main

Lengths upto 150 m	100 mm
Length above 150 m	minimum 150 mm

Size of mains. Discharge through main can be calculated on the following basis:

Trunks less than 5000 population	3·0 times the average hourly dis.
5000 to 50,000	2·5 times the average hourly dis.
Above 50,000	2·0 times the average hourly dis.
Service pipes	1·5 to 2·0 times the average hourly dis.

This can meet with the peak demand. The average hourly discharge should include all factors as leakages, friction and fire requirements.

Velocity in mains. Maximum 3·0 m/sec and minimum 0·61 to 0·75 m/sec. So that it may not be silting. An average of 1·5 m/sec can be taken. High velocity in small mains give more friction. Friction losses varies as a square of the velocity.

Slope of the pipe is decided according to the slope of the country or the type of the material of the pipe and velocity is decided according to the above criteria. The dia. of the pipe then is decided from tables on the basis of above slope velocity and discharge.

A rough guide can also be taken as below:

(*a*) Iron mains fed from one end minimum size 100 mm

Iron mains fed from both ends minimum size 80 mm

Branch iron pipes minimum 50 mm

Pumps are designed on 1·5 times the average requirement. Sedimentation tanks are also designed as above.

Service pipes. The service pipes are connected to the mains by a ferrule cock connection. The maximum size of ferrule is 15 mm for 80 mm main. 20 mm for 100 mm main and 25 mm for 150 mm main.

Table 17·24. Supply from service pipes

Dia. of pipe (mm)	15	20	25	32	40	50
Flow in liters/min.	10	20	30	45	70	110

Loss of head in pipes

(1) Loss of head due to velocity $= \dfrac{V^2}{2g}$ where v = velocity m/sec

(2) Loss of head due to bends $= K\dfrac{V^2}{2g}$, g = acc. due to gravity m/sec/sec

Table 17·25. Values of *K*

Dia. of pipe/radius of bend	0·2	0·4	0·6	0·8	1·0	1·2	1·4	1·6	1·8	2·0
Value of K	0·13	0·14	0·16	0·21	0·29	0·44	0·66	0·98	1·40	1·98

(3) Loss of head due to sudden enlargement $= \dfrac{(V_1 - V_2)^2}{2g}$, V_1 = velocity in smaller pipe

(4) Loss of head due to sudden contraction $= \dfrac{V^2}{4g}$, V_2 = velocity in bigger pipe

(5) Loss of head at entrance of pipe $= \dfrac{V^2}{4g}$

(6) Loss of head at obstruction $= \left(\dfrac{A}{0{\cdot}06(A-a)} - 1\right)^2 \dfrac{V^2}{2g}$

A = Area of pipe, a = area of obstruction.

(7) Loss of head due to friction in pipes $= \dfrac{uflV^2}{d.2g}$

l = length of pipe, f = frictional coefficient, d = dia. of pipe.

"f" for new pipes $= 0{\cdot}005\left(1 + \dfrac{1}{40\,d}\right)$ and for old pipes $= 0{\cdot}01\left(1 + \dfrac{1}{40}d\right)$

(8) Loss of head due to valve and fittings $= K\dfrac{v^2}{2g}$, K = resistance coefficient.

Valves carrying laminar flow. Loss of head is negligible flanged valves and fittings have lower value of *K* than screwed fittings. The values of *K* are given in the table below. The lower limits should be used with flanged valves and fittings, practically with sizes above 10 cm nominal dia.

Table 17·26. Values of *K* in valves and fittings

	Description of valves and fittings			*Value of K*
1.	Inlets and reducers	(*a*) bell mouth		0·04-0·05
		(*b*) square edge		0·07-0·56
2.	Elbows	(*a*) Regular screwed 45° elbow		0·30-0·42
		(*b*) Regular screwed 90° elbow		0·55-0·90
		(*c*) Long rad. flanged 45° elbow		0·18-0·20
		(*d*) Long rad. flanged 90° elbow		0·14-0·23
		(*e*) Regular flanged 90° elbow		0·21-0·30
		(*f*) Long rad. screwed 90° elbow		0·22-0·66
3.	Bends	(*a*) Screwed return bend close pattern		0·75-2·2
		(*b*) Flanged return bend compound of 90° flanged elbow	(*i*) Regular	0·38
			(*ii*) Long rad.	0·25
4.	Inward projecting pipes			0·62-1·0
5.	Valves of	(*a*) Globe valves	(*i*) Composition disc	0·23-5·2
			(*ii*) Bevel seat	6·2-7·2
			(*iii*) Plug disc	7·2-10·3
		(*b*) Gate valves	(*i*) Wedge disc	0·05-0·19
			(*ii*) Double disc	0·08-0·13
		(*c*) Check valves	(*i*) Swing	0·6-2·3
			(*ii*) Horizontal lift	8·0-12·0
			(*iii*) Ball	2·1-3·1
		(*d*) Angle valve		2·1-3·1
		(*e*) γ or blow off valve		2·9
		(*f*) Foot valve		15
6.	Couplings and unions			0·02-0·07
7.	Reducing, bushing and coupling used as reducer			0·05-2·0
8.	Standard screwed tee	(*a*) branch blanked off		0·4
		(*b*) line blanked off	(*i*) flow line to branch	0·85-1·3
			(*ii*) flow branch to line	0·92-2·15
9.	Long radius screwed tee	(*a*) line blanked off	(*i*) flow line to branch	0·37-0·80
			(*ii*) flow branch to line	0·50-0·52

Note : When reducer is used as increaser, loss is upto 40% more than that caused by sudden enlargement.

Table 17·27. Pressure due to water hammer in pipes

Dia. of pipe in cm	8·25	30	40	50	60	75	90	100-150
Pressure in kg/cm²	8·4	7·7	7·0	6·3	6·0	5·6	5·3	4·9

Velocity in pipes. (Also refer hydraulics section : Velocity in pipes)

Chezy's formula $V = c\sqrt{mi}$ m = hydraulic mean depth

i = slope in fraction

$$C = \frac{2g}{f} \text{ where } f = 0{\cdot}01\left(1 + \frac{1}{35d}\right) \text{ for old pipes}$$

$$= 0{\cdot}00\left(1 + \frac{1}{35d}\right) \text{ for new pipes, } d = \text{dia. of pipe.}$$

Table 17·28(*a*). Value of *C* in new pipes

Pipe dia. in cm	1·25	2·5	7·5	15	30	60	90
Value of C	36	44	54	58	60	61	61·5

Crimp and Brugs formula for brick sewer and conduits

$V = 83{\cdot}5\ m^{2/3} i^{2/3}$ in metric units

Hazen and William's formula for pipes and channels

$V = 0{\cdot}85\ cm^{0{\cdot}63}\ i^{0{\cdot}54}$ in metric units

Values of C in Hazen and William's formula

Cast iron new pipes = 130
old 5-12 years = 115
13-20 years = 100
26-35 years = 80
very rough = 60
Rivetted steel pipe new = 110
Medium = 100
W.I. pipe smooth new = 120
Old = 80
AC pipes = 140
Welded steel pipes = 120
Wooden pipes = 120

Masonry
Concrete cement lined pipes 120-140
Brick smooth 100
rough 90
very rough 80
open channels
good masonry 80-100
rough masonry 50-80
earth rough 65-75
earth with gravel 35·6

Note : (1) Coefficient 130 is corresponding to Mannings coefficient $N = 0{\cdot}011$

(2) Increase of head necessary to maintain the same pressure and velocity is old C.I. pipes for values of C.

Table 17·28(*b*).

Values of C	120	110	100	90	80
Percentage increase in head	16	36	63	100	146

For maximum discharge in circular sections

Depth of water = 0·95 dia.
Hydraulic mean depth = 0·286 dia.
Wetted perimeter = 2·60 dia.
= 2·83 depth of water

For maximum discharge wetted perimeter must be minimum.

For maximum velocity in circular pipes

Depth of water = 0·810 dia. ; Hydraulic mean depth = 0·304 dia.

Wetted perimeter = 2·245 dia.

8. Testing of pipe lines for leakage. The following step by step procedure is adopted.

(*i*) The pipe line is tested from section to section. At a time only one particular section lying between two sluice valves is taken up.

(*ii*) The down stream sluice valve is closed and water is admitted into the pipe through the u/s sluice valve. The air valves will be properly operated during fill up of the pipe.

(*iii*) The u/s valve through which water was admitted is closed as to completely isolate the pipe section from the rest of the pipe.

(*iv*) Pressure gauges are then fitted along the length of the pipe sections at suitable intervals (say. 1 km or so) on the crown through holes left for this purpose.

(*v*) The pipe section is then connected to the delivery side of a pump through a small by pass valve and the pump is started so as to develop pressure in the pipe. The operation is continued till the pressure in the ten pipe reaches the designed value which can be read from the pressure gauges fixed on the pipe.

(*vi*) The by-pass valve is then closed and pumping is discontinued.

(*vii*) The pipe is thus kept under pressure for 24 hours and inspected for possible defects, leakages at the joints etc. This completes the 'pressure test'.

The pipe is finally emptied through drain valves and the observed defects (obtained in the test) are rectified. The pipe is again filled and tested till no defect is observed.

The pipes are disinfected by keeping them fill with water and adding chlorine in amounts as to maintain a residue of 50 mg/l (*i.e.* 50 ppm). This residue is maintained for 12 hours and the pipe is emptied and flushed with fresh treated water. This making the pipe ready for carrying potable water to the consumers or to the storage tanks.

Table 17·29(*a*). Velocities and discharges for various dia. and gradient

Inclination		*Pipe diameter*				
		100 mm	*150 mm*	*200 mm*	*250 mm*	*300 mm*
1 : 62	vel. m/sec	0·91	1·2	1·45	1·7	1·9
	dis. m^3/sec	0·444	1·313	2·828	5·123	8·35
1 : 76	vel. m/sec	1·06	1·56	1·3	1·5	1·70
	dis. m^3/sec	0·402	1·186	2·553	4·64	7·528

Table 17·29(*b*). Velocity of water in pipes

Min. velocity in m/sec	0·6	0·9	1·21	1·52	1·82
Dia. of pipe in cum (minimum absolute)	5	10	15	25	40

Table 17·29(*c*). Velocity in water mains

Pipe dia. (mm)	*Velocity m/sec*	*Pipe dia. (mm)*	*Velocity m/sec*
100	0·75-0·91	500	1·40
150	0·81-1·22	650	1·69

Table contd...

Table contd...

Pipe dia. (mm)	*Velocity m/sec*	*Pipe dia. (mm)*	*Velocity m/sec*
200	0·91-1·32	800	1·92
250	0·99-1·52	900	1·95
320	1·09-1·67	1000	2·00
400	1·27-1·03	Service pipes	2·13

Table 17·30. Threads in water pipes (IS)

Internal dia. of pipe inches/mm	*External dia. of pipe inches/mm*	*No. of threads per inch/cm*
¼/6·3	0·656/16·4	19/8
½/12·5	0·825/20·63	14/6
¾/18·8	1·041/26·0	14/6
1·0/25	1·309/32·73	11/4·5
1¼/31·3	1·650/41·25	11/4·5
1½/37·5	1·882/47·05	11/4·5
1¾/43·8	2·116/52·9	11/4·5
2·0/50	2·347/58·68	11/4·5

17·5. Appurtenances in the water supply distribution system

Ferrule. It is a right angled sleeve of brass or gun metal and is fitted to a hole drilled in the water main to which it is screwed down with a plug. Its size usually varies between 10 to 50 mm dia. according to the dimension of the service pipe used. For the connections of more than 50 mm dia. a tee branch connection off the main is used.

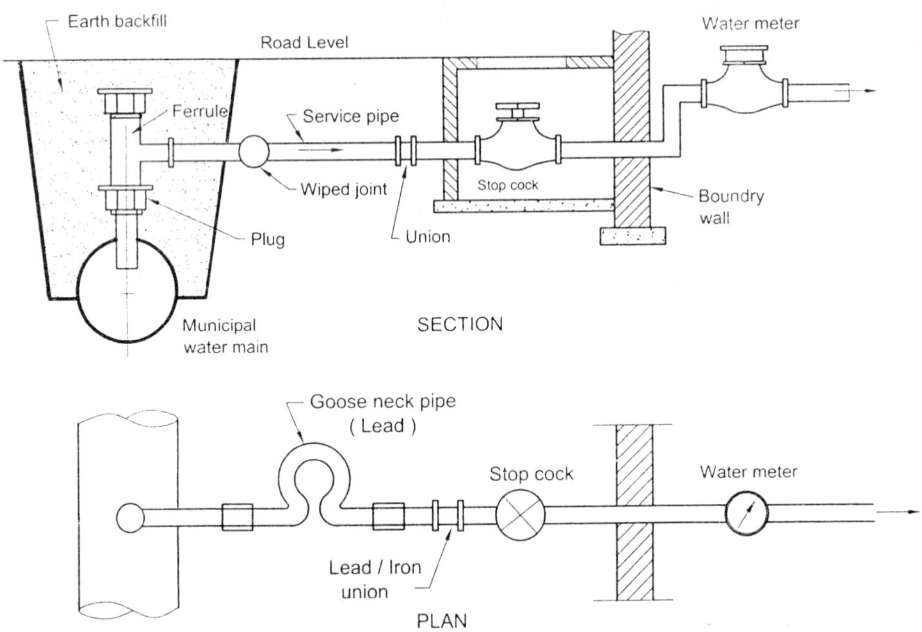

Fig. 17·32. Ferrule connection to main pipe.

Goose neck. It is a small size curved pipe made of a flexible material usually lead and is about 75 cm in length forming a flexible connection between the water main and the service pipe.

Service pipe. It is a galvanised iron pipe of size less than 50 mm dia. It lies in a trench and connects the water supply to the building through a goose neck pipe and ferrule to the main municipal supply pipe.

Stop cock. The stop cock is provided before the water enters the water meter in the house. It is provided just at the point of entry of water to the building so that whole of the water supply used in the building may be metered. By closing of the stop cock the supply of water is closed. It is consealed in a mainhole just adjoining the boundary wall of the building.

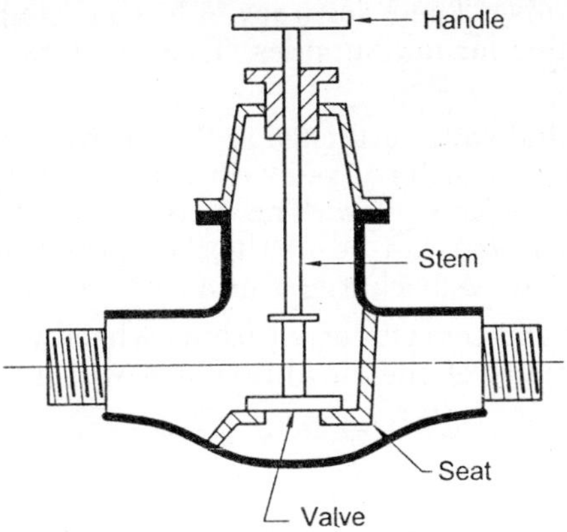

(*a*) Stop cock.

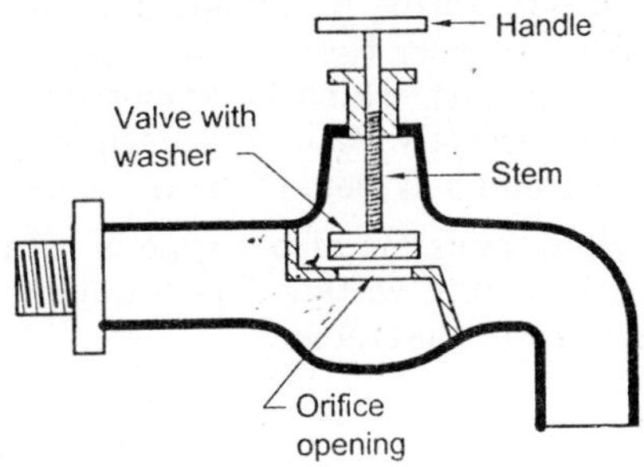

(*b*) Bib cock.

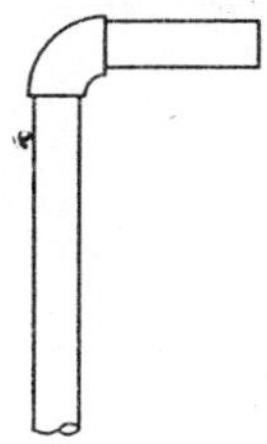

(*c*) Ventilation pipe

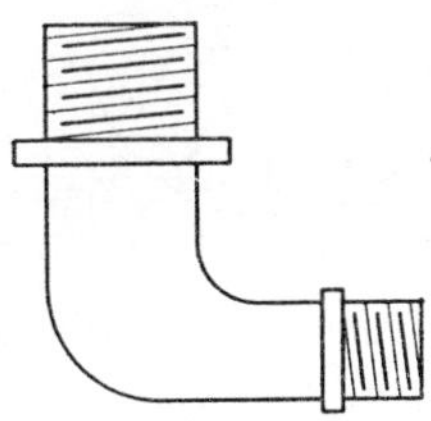

(*d*) Reducing elbow

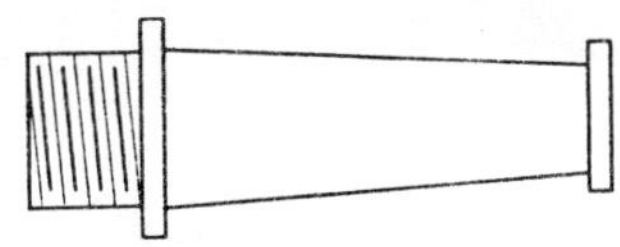

(*e*) Straight reducer

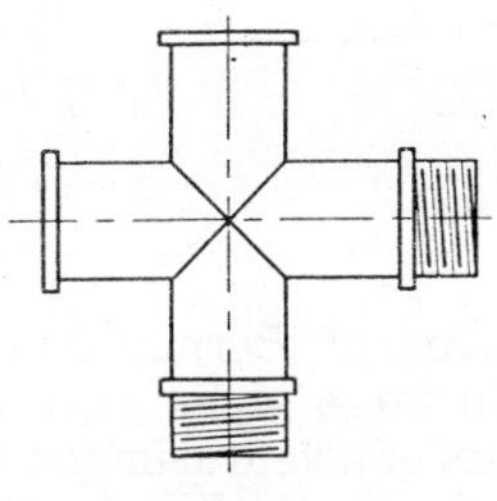

(*f*) Cross

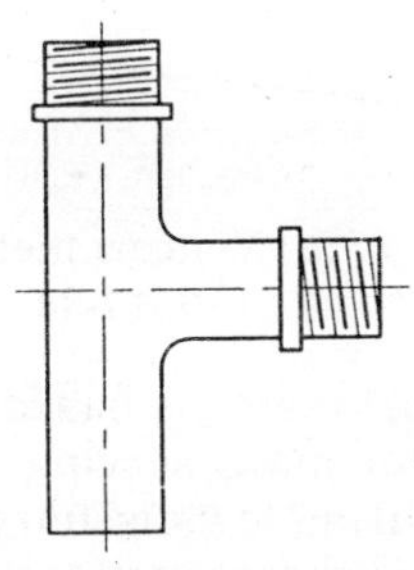

(*g*) Tee

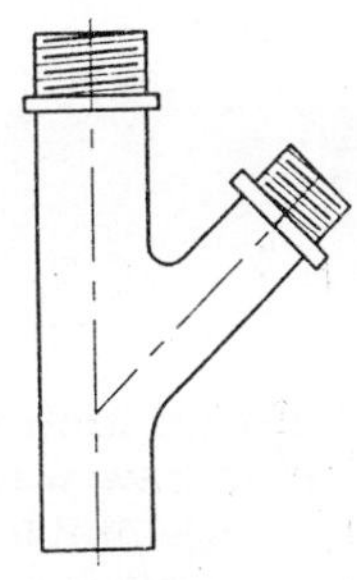

(*h*) Wye

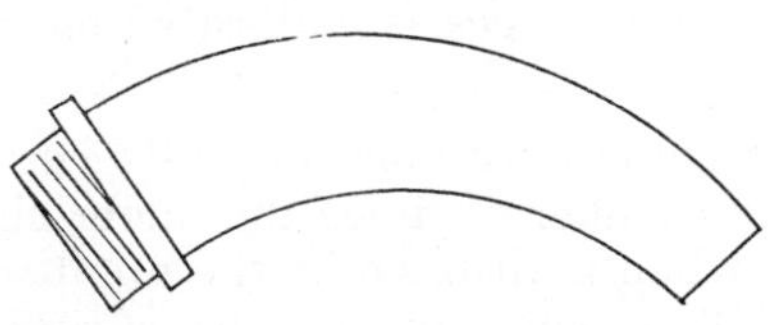

(*i*) Reducing bend with single hub

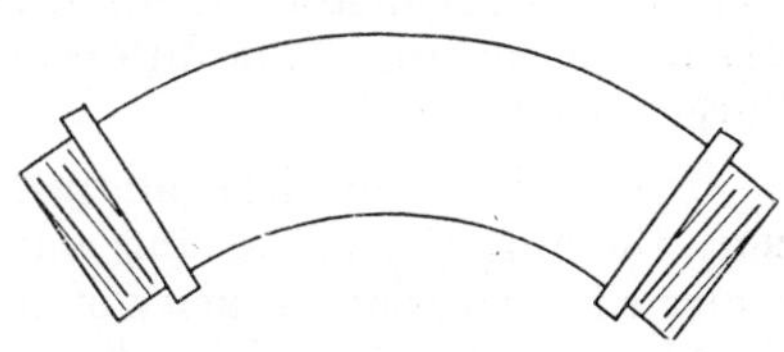

(*j*) A bend with double hub

Fig. 17·33.

Water meter. Water meter measures and records the quantity of water consumed in the building and is fitted into the service pipe with unions, which enables the meter to be changed when necessary. The water meter is fixed in an iron box fitted in a cavity in the boundary wall or in any other secured position. There are two types of meters (*a*) velocity or the inferential meters and (*b*) Positive or the displacement meters.

(*a*) **The velocity of inferentials meter.** In such type of meters the velocity of the flowing water is measured by the meter. The discharge is calculated by multiplying the velocity to the area of section of flow and the meter is calibrated accordingly to give direct discharge automatically. The velocity meters are generally used for high supplies and are not suitable for low domestic supplies. They can work in turbid water also. Their accuracy is less as compared to displacement type of meters and these are not suitable for low supplies. These meters are of two types (*i*) rotary, (*ii*) venturi type.

(*i*) **Rotary meter.** It consists of a number of radial vanes attached to a shaft when water passes through the vanes they rotate and in turn the shaft which is fixed with vanes also rotates with a certain velocity which is proportional to the velocity of flow. The meter can hence be calibrated as to directly read the discharge. This discharge can be further integrated by an integrating device of a system of gears, so as to read the total discharge over a certain period.

A turbine meter is also a type of rotary meter and consists of a turbine wheel which is rotated by the moving water. The number of revolutions of the turbine wheel will give the discharge as in rotary meters.

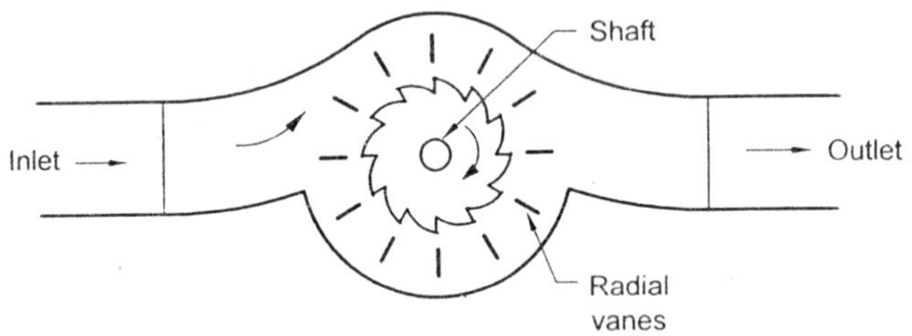

(*a*) Rotary meter.

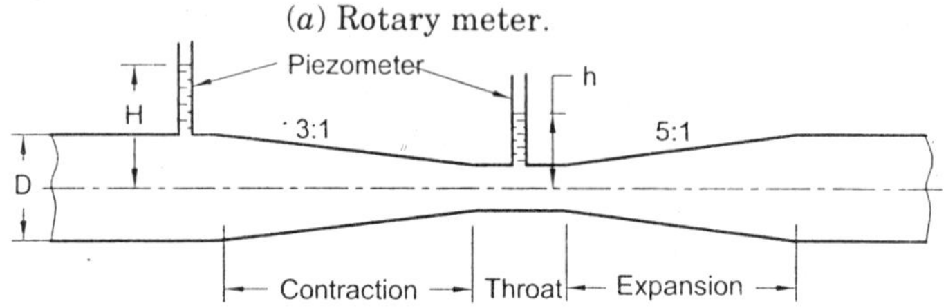

(*b*) Venturi meter.
Fig. 17·34.

(*ii*) **Venturi meter.** A venturi meter is based on the principle of "Bernoulli's equation". It can be used in raw waters and for main serving high flows in large pipes with a nominal head loss. It is not suitable for measuring low discharges. It consists of a venturimeter of normal pipe having contracting, enlarging and throat sections as shown in the figure. When water passes through the venturimeter the difference of level in the two piezometer tubes is proportional to the discharge passing. This difference of level in piezometer tubes is calibrated on a scale as discharge passing.

(*b*) **Positive or displacement meters.** These meters are more accurate because they measure the quantity of passing water by counting the number of times the meter chamber is filled and emptied. The capacity of the meter chamber when multiplied by the number of times it is filled and emptied, will directly give the quantity of flow over a given period of time. Various types of displacement meters are available in the market depending upon the type of motion of the moving part in the meter. The common type of displacement meters are oscillated type, disc type and reciprocated type. The most commonly used is a **discmeter** which is used generally in domestic houses.

Disc water meter. Consists of a disc placed inside a chamber, provided with an inlet and an outlet. The water when enters the chamber oscillates the disc about its centre with a spiral motion. Arrangements are so made that one complete filling and emptying of the chamber gives one revolution to the gears and the meter thus goes on recording the volume of the water passing through it. Such meters are available in sizes 16 to 150 mm in diameter with a measuring capacity of 90 to 4500 litres per minute.

The manufacture of meters are guided by the provisions of IS 779—1994 and that of bulk meters by IS 2373—1981. The maintenance and installations of domestic meters is governed by IS 2401—1973 and their testing by IS : 6784—1996. The precaution in installing such meters is that they must not be located in such position where occurrence of water hammer is possible.

Stop cocks. A stop cock is a screw down type of sluice valve which is used in smaller sized pipes in service connecting for stopping or opening the supply. They are generally provided at the water enterance of each building and also with in the building.

A typical stop cock is as shown in Fig. 17·33(*a*) is a valve body so casted that the water passes through an orifice. When the valve stem is raised. When the valve is closed it rests against the seat, and thereby closing the orifice. They are used widely in the pipes upto 50 mm dia. The function of the valve is self explanatory from the figure itself.

Water taps Bib cocks. Water taps are the types of valves provided at the end of service pipes for withdrawing water at the consumers place. Several types of water taps are available in the market, the most common of them is a bib cock. By rotating the handle of the bib cock, the orifice opening through which water passes, can be increased or decreased, thereby controlling the overflow through the spout. These are available to suit different pipe sizes 10 to 50 mm dia.

The Bib cocks may also be push type which opens with a slight push given vertically upward and closes down automatically due to self weight when the push is removed. Such valves are used in public taps in order to avoid wastage of water from handle type bib cock which may be left open by irresponsible users. A spring may also be provided for automatic closing of the valve when not in use.

The rubber washers when damaged should be replaced as water leaks when these washers are damaged. The rubber or the leather washers are used to make the valve water light.

Service pipe fittings. The following service fittings are generally used in pipes :

Unions. Sockets or pipes for connecting two pipes.

Elbows. Square or round.

Tees. All these pipes can be of one dia. or with the stem of different diameters from the cross pieces.

Crosses. With all four pipes of one diameter or with two pairs of different diameters.

Sockets. Plain or diminishing.

Caps. For closing a pipe end.

Plugs. For closing a socket end.

Backnuts. With long screws to prevent back movement of the socket and leakage.

Nipples. For making junctions when a hole is tapped in a main for a branch pipe.

Flanges. For connections of pipes.

Reducers. It is a joint piece when larger dia. pipe is associated with a smaller dia. pipe.

Reflux valves, check valves, Non-return valves and flap valves. These valves are of many types, which open only in one direction of the flow and automatically close when a burst in the main occurs and then flow reverses its direction. These valves are placed at intervals (say 300 m) in large pumping mains to prevent back pressure in the engine on the rising mains at the foot of long upward inclined lines, in force mains just beyond the pumps to cut off automatically the back flow when the pumps stop running at the bottom of the rising leg of an inverted syphon, and at point where a breakage would mean great loss of water by backward flow such as at the enterance to a reservoir.

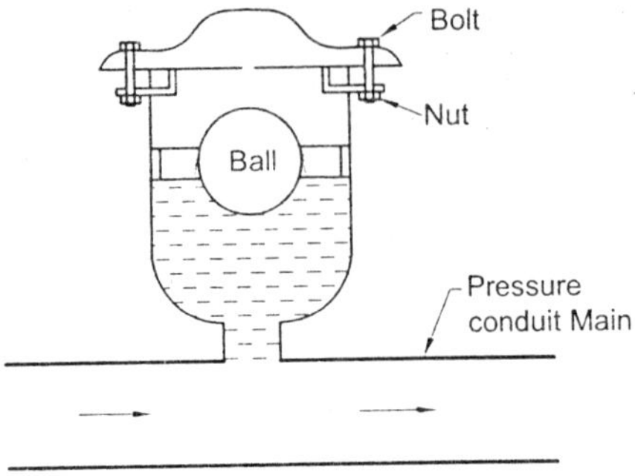

Fig. 17·35. Air relief valve.

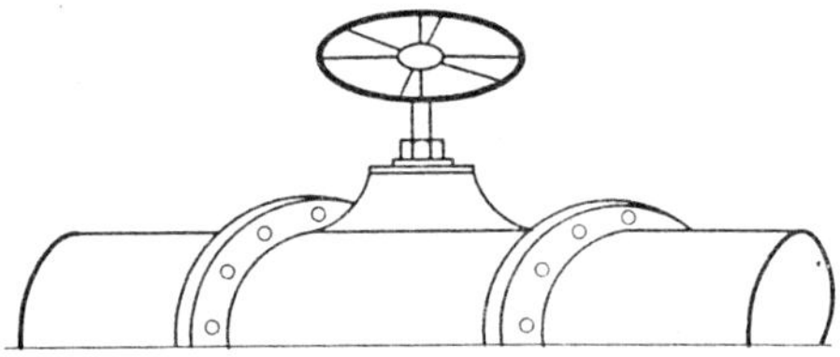

Fig. 17·36. Top view of sluice valve.

Foot valves are similar to reflux valves but are usually placed in a vertical position on the end of suction lines of pumps.

Relief valve must be placed at the pumping statues on the delivery of pipe to save the pumps from damage or strain on any obstruction with consequent water hammer. With two or more pumps discharging into the same main, each of them should be provided with a non-return and an air relief valve.

Air valve or air relief valves. These valves are fixed on trunk and secondary mains at the highest points (wash outs or scour valves are fixed at the lower points between summits) on undulating water mains on long stretches of nearly level mains and at summits of all changes of gradline. Their function is to allow the accumulated air to escape when the pipe is filled and to permit the air to enter when the pipe is emptied. Air and vacuum relief valves are essential on large dia. Steel pipe which would collapse if subjected to a vacuum on the inside.

Such valves need not be fixed on service mains as entrapped air is released through the service pipes when the pipes rise above hydraulic gradient it is useless to fix an air valve.

Air valves consists of a floating ball in a chamber which allows the air to escape and closes as soon as the air is expelled under pressure by water. At some places "double acting" valves are used which have a larger and a small chamber with a ball in each. A large-orifice air valve discharges displaced air when mains are being charged with water, but when air is liable to collect at summits under ordinary conditions of flow, small orifice air valves are required. Single air valves are usually provided on mains of 75 mm dia. and double air valves on mains of 100 mm dia. and above. The usual sizes are—

Size of main in mm	Upto 100	125-200	250-300	400-500	600
Size of air valve in mm	40	50	80	100	150

The most common fault in air valves is the sticking of the ball on its seating, and air valves on important mains should be controlled by sluice valves so that they can be removed without shutting down the main. A short connection with a stop valve should be given at the highest point and a valve on the main lower down. Air valves are usually bolted on to a standard flanged tee. The common practice in respect of placing of air valves on long water mains while ascending or descending is at 400 to 800 meters intervals. A galvanised iron pipe is taken from the top of the main pipe on which an air valve is to be fixed to the side of the road where a suitable site for the valve has been selected. A cock is fixed at its lower end and a screwed plug at the other. The air valve is fixed in a suitable masonry pit for protection and a weep hole is provided for the escape of water which may pass the air valve with the escaping air.

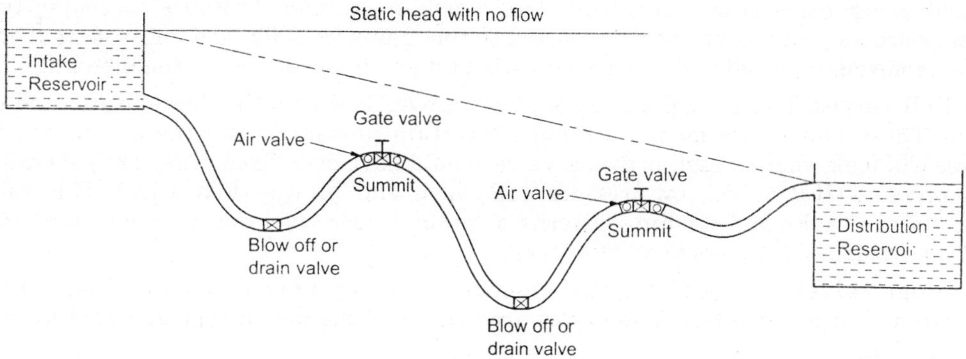

Fig. 17·37. Pressure pipe showing position of gates and valves.

Scour or Blow-off valves. (Also called as wash-out) which are ordinary sluice valves provided at the bottom of all depressions and dead ends to drain out the waste water or sediments collected. Scour valves are usually 80 to 150 mm dia. leading from the main from a flanged tee branch to a ditch with a sluice valve control. They should be fixed in a manner so that the inverts of the outlets branch and the main are at the same level. In small mains a stop cock or even a plug will be sufficient. A combined stop cock and scour valve is frequently used for buildings.

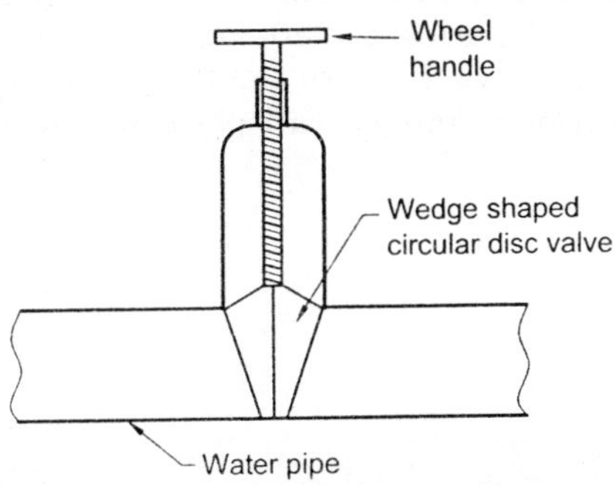

Fig. 17·38. Vertical section of a sluice valve.

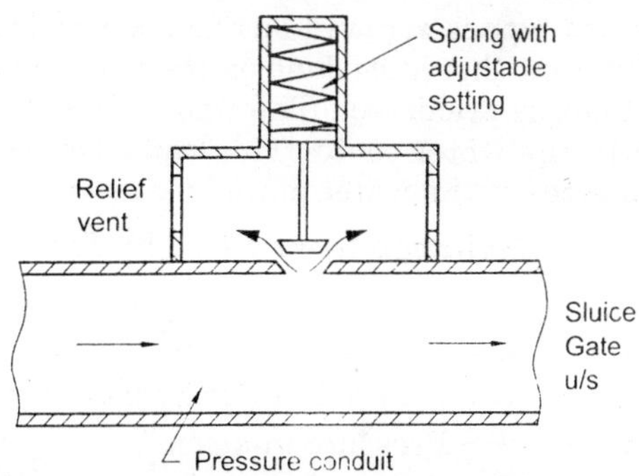

Fig. 17·39. Vertical section of a pressure relief valve in open position

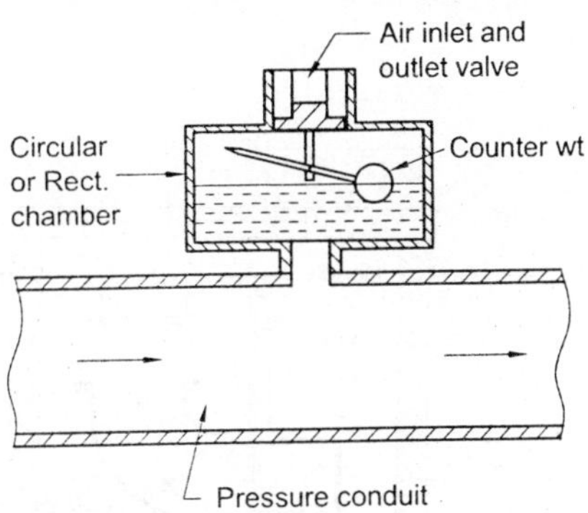

Fig. 17·40. Vertical section of an air valve

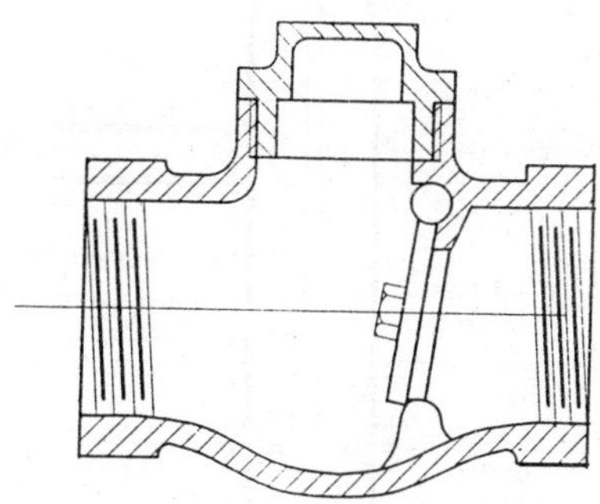

Fig. 17·41.Swing check valve (flap type).

Pressure relief or safety valves. These are some times fixed at the down stream ends of long lengths of mains or where water hammer is likely to occur, to relieve excessive pressure. These are automatic valves that close when pressure becomes excessive on the d/s side. They are heavily weighted spring controlled valves which open under pressure exceeding those for which they are set. Valves are best connected to the mains with flanged joints so that they can be easily removed, repaired and reinserted without disturbing the rest of the pipe line.

Bell valves. These are float operated valves which control the flow of water and prevent overflow. These valves are made suitable for certain pressures and the one meant for low pressures will leak where a high pressure valve should have been fixed. They are generally made for high pressure (H.P. valve), low pressure (L.P. valve) and full way (F.W. valve). H.P. valves are used on storage tanks and flushing cisterns at ground floor level and they will remain closed against a pressure of 7 meters head of water.

Float valves are used on distribution reservoirs or other tanks and filter beds etc. to maintain constant water levels. The valves are usually of the piston type actuated by means of a lever and floats.

Fire hydrants. Fire hydrants may be located at distance apart of about 90 to 120 meters when the buildings are large and close together or built of inflammable material and 100 meters or further apart in open areas. Areas of about 4,000 to 10,000 sq. meters are taken per hydrant accordingly to the density of the population and importance of the locality as regards its protection against fire. Hydrants are provided at all street crossings. Water required for fire fighting for Indian towns has been estimated at one litre per head per day.

The hydrants are of two types, (*i*) Post fire hydrant and (*ii*) Flush fire hydrants.

Post fire or piller hydrants are not much in use now. Such type or flush hydrants are fixed below the road surface having a cast iron cover which is flush with the road surface. A vertical pipe is screwed on the such hydrant when required and hose pipe is fixed on it. Fixing of hydrant should be done on the water main which should be atleast of 80 mm dia. (a size appx. 150 mm is preferred). The flange end of the hydrant should be fixed to the flanged outlet of a tee in the water main. This can also be fixed by main of a flanged tail piece which may be connected to the water main by cast iron special.

Discharge from a fire hydrant

$$Q = 67\, d^2 \sqrt{P}$$

where Q = Discharge in litres/m

d = Internal dia. of hydrant nozzle in cm

and P = Pressure in kg/cm^2

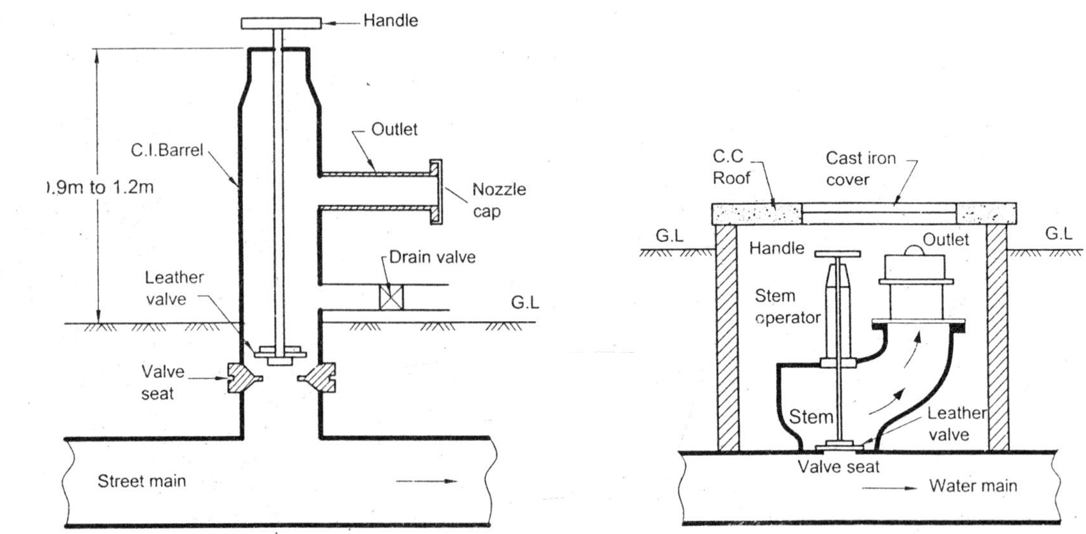

(*a*) Post fire hydrant (*b*) Flush fire hydrant

Fig. 17·42.

Fire hydrants should be of spindle type with 65 mm (2·5") outlet combined with sluice valve and should be located at street intersections. These are 2, 3 or 4 way hydrants common arrangement of hydrants is recommended to be one 115 mm (4·5") connection for fire engine pumper and two 65 mm connections for hose outlet. A minimum flow of 900 litres per minute is necessary through a 30 mm ($1^1/_8$") smooth nozzle with a pressure at the base of the tip of 3 kg/sq cm which is effective to a height of about 21 meters above the ground with a horizontal line not exceeding 18 meters.

Minimum residual pressure heads required for fire hydrants is :

With pumping engine	35 meters
For direct flow single storey buildings	20 meters

Residual pressure heads recommended at the fire hydrants for which provision should be made, if possible, while designing a supply system—

With pumping engines	10·5 to 14 meters
For direct flow	42 to 53 meters

The hydrant should have the following components—

(*i*) One sluice valve, (*ii*) a duck foot bend, (*iii*) a 65 mm male coupling instantaneous (*iv*) C.I. cap permanently secured to the duck foot bend by means of a chain.

The flanged end of the hydrant shall be fixed to the flanged outlet of a tee in the water main by means of bolts, nuts and 3 mm rubber insertion or compressed fibre board 1·5 mm thickness. This can also be fixed by means of flanged rail piece which may be connected to the water main by C.I. specials.

Hydrants are also used for street washing, flushing sewers and watering of gardens etc.

17·6. Distribution system of water supply

Layout of pipe lines (Distribution system)

(1) **Dead end system or tree system.** In mains or other branches, the end is a dead end where a stagnent unused supply is held.

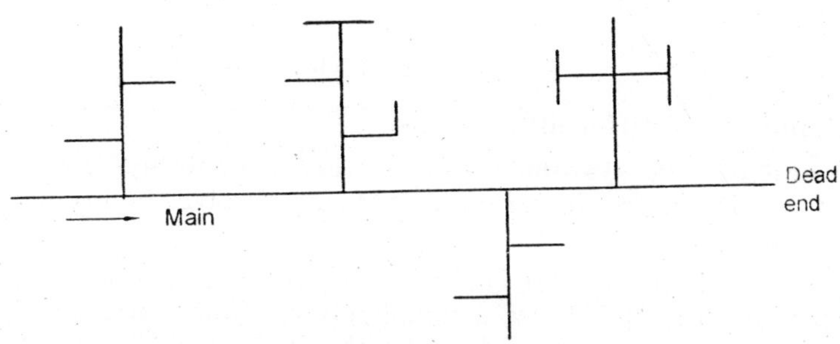

Fig. 17·43.

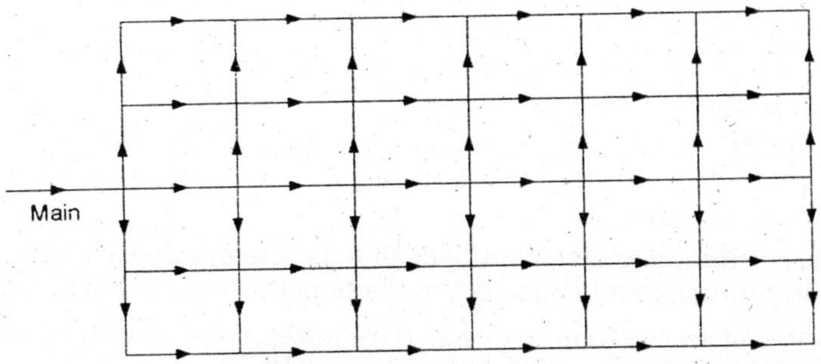

Fig. 17·44.

In dead end system the hole supply is held for any repair in main or in a branch called laterals. There are several dead ends.

(2) **Grid system.** The water is supplied in grids, where there is no dead end. The repair in any grid do not held the supply in other grids. The stop cocks are provided at the beginning of each grid so that it may be closed for any repair. It is also called as interlaced or reticulation system.

(3) **Radial system.** In this system each distinct (area) is supplied with a central main pipe. The rapair stoppage in any arm do not effect the other arms.

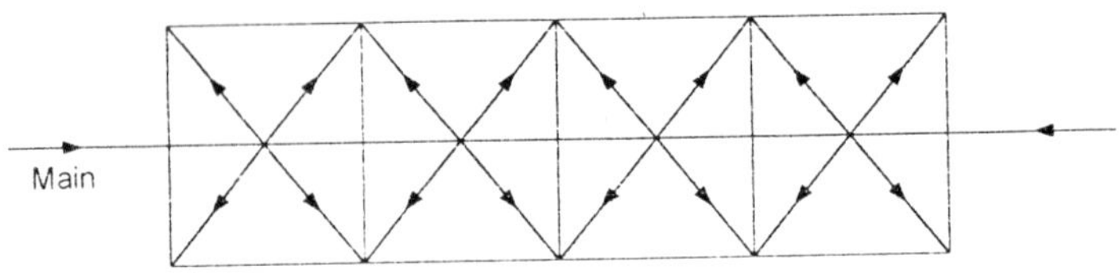

Fig. 17·45.

(4) **Ring system.** The main runs along the periphery of an area and the branches also run with subsidiary rings connected to each other. In this type of system pressure in the pipe does not vary too much.

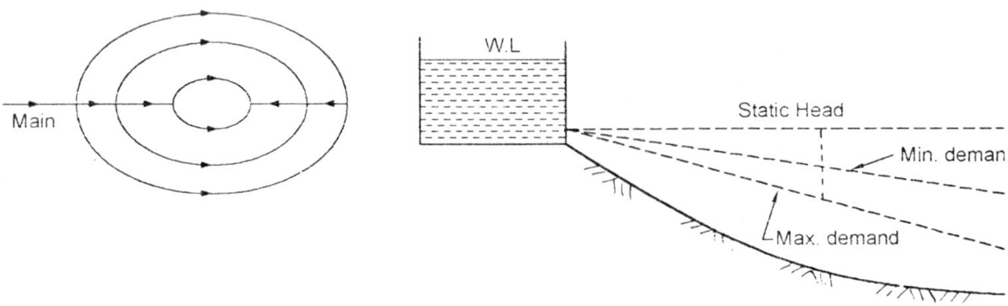

Fig. 17·46.

Merits and demerits of different systems

Dead end or tree system. It is cheap and easy to lay. It can be developed with the growth of the town. It requires lesser number of cut-off valves (sluice valves) and needs shorter lengths of pipe lines.

Since in this method water can reach a particular point only through one route any damage or repair in any pipe line will completely stop the water supply of the area lying on that pipe line causing great inconvenience to the consumers. There are several dead ends in this system, which prevent the free circulation of water. The stale dead end water should therefore be remained periodically the dead and stagnant, water also becomes turbid which is to be removed by scour valves and thus a great amount of water is wasted.

The supplies of water can not be increased at any emergency since there is only one route for the supply. It is used in unplanned cities.

Grid iron system. It is used in planned cities or towns. Water reaches at different places through more than one route. During any repairs the whole area is not suffered as at least some supply will reach from some other route.

Due to the different interconnections, the dead ends are eliminated and therefore water remains in continuous circulations and hence not liable to pollution due to stagnation.

The disadvantages of the system are that it requires more length of pipes and larger number of sluice valves. It is costlier and the design is difficult.

Ring system or circular system. The advantages and disadvantages of this system are more or less the same as grid iron system.

Radial system. The pipe lines can be best laid in a radial method by placing the distribution reservoirs at the centres. This method ensures high pressures and efficient water distribution.

Methods of distribution. (1) Gravitational system (2) Pumping system.

Gravitational system. In this system the water from the high level source is distributed to the consumers at lower level by gravity flow. In the maximum demand the head is increased causing a greater velocity in the pipe while in the lesser demand the head is reduced causing a lower velocity in the supply pipe.

Pumping system. In this system, the treated water is pumped at a constant rate into an elevated distribution reservoir from where it is distributed to the consumers by the gravity method.

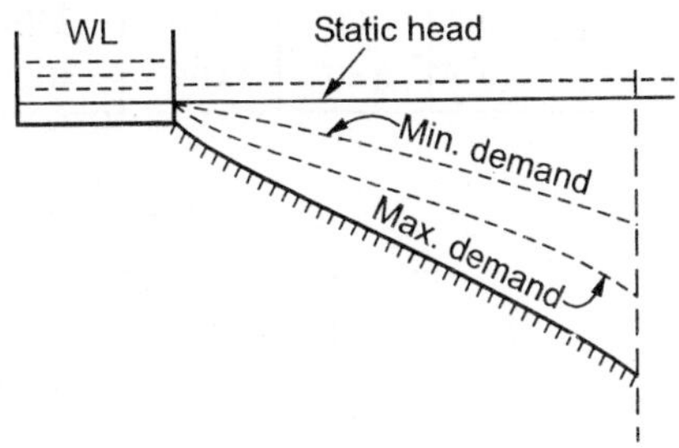

Fig. 17·47.

Table 17·31(*a*). Design of Distribution System
Suggested Internal Diameters of pipes in mm for various length of discharge lines

Discharge in litres/min	*Length of pipe line in metres*									
	15	*30*	*75*	*150*	*250*	*300*	*600*	*900*	*1200*	*1500*
25	25	25	25	25	32	32	32	40	40	40
35	25	32	32	32	40	40	40	50	50	50
45	25	32	32	32	40	40	40	50	50	50
70	32	32	40	40	50	50	50	65	65	80
90	32	40	50	50	65	65	65	80	80	100
135	40	50	50	65	65	80	80	80	100	100
180	50	50	65	65	80	80	80	100	100	125
225	50	50	65	80	80	100	100	100	125	125
270	50	65	65	80	80	100	100	100	125	125
320	65	65	65	80	100	100	125	125	125	125
360	65	65	65	80	100	100	125	125	125	125
450	65	80	80	100	100	100	125	125	125	150
550	80	80	80	100	100	125	125	125	150	150
700	80	100	100	125	125	125	125	150	150	150
900	100	100	100	125	125	125	125	150	150	150
1100	100	100	100	125	125	125	150	150	150	200
1300	100	125	125	125	125	150	150	150	200	200
1800	125	125	150	150	150	200	200	200	250	250
2500	150	150	150	200	200	200	200	250	250	250
3000	150	150	150	200	200	200	250	300	300	300
3500	200	200	200	200	250	250	300	300	350	350
4500	200	200	200	250	250	250	300	300	350	350
5500	200	250	250	250	300	300	350	350	380	400
7000	250	250	250	300	300	350	350	350	400	400
8000	250	250	300	300	350	350	380	400	450	450

Table contd...

Table contd...

Discharge in litres/min	*Length of pipe line in metres*									
	15	*30*	*75*	*150*	*250*	*300*	*600*	*900*	*1200*	*1500*
9000	250	300	300	300	350	350	400	450	450	450
10,000	300	300	300	350	350	380	400	450	450	450
11,000	300	300	300	350	350	380	400	450	450	500
13,000	300	350	350	350	380	400	450	450	500	500
16,000	300	350	350	350	380	400	450	500	600	600
18,000	350	380	400	400	400	500	500	500	600	600

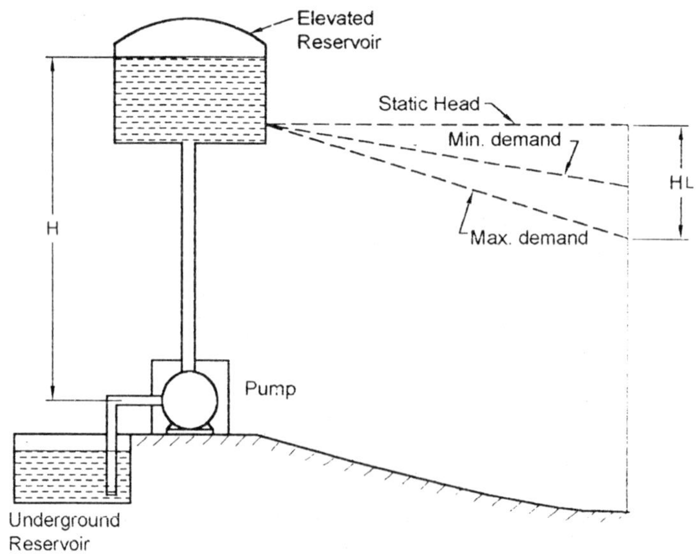

Fig. 17·48.

Technical terms in water supply

(1) **Potable water—**Water which can be used for drinking.

(2) **Feed cistern—**It is a storage vessel, used for supplying cold water to a hot water appliance.

(3) **Direct tap—**It is a tap which is connected to supply pipe and subject to maximum pressure from the water.

(4) **Fittings—**All fittings in the water supply system such as, couplings, flanges, unions, waste with plug, bib cock, stop cock, hydrants, geyser pumping sets, ferrules, bends, elbows, tees, air vent, water cistern etc.

(5) **Flushing cistern—**A cistern with discharge arrangements for flushing a water closet, a sink or a urinal etc.

(6) **Cavitation—**When water is flowing in a machine or turbine and reaches in a low pressure region, the evaporation of water starts and bubbles are formed. These bubbles when strike to the wall of the machine, collapse and causes cavity formation on the walls of the machine. This cavity formation is known as "**cavitation**".

(7) **Residual head or terminal pressure—**It is the pressure available at the tail end of the distribution system.

(8) **Down take up**—A tap connected to a system of piping not subject to water pressure from the water main. They are connected with one head storage tank to supply water.

(9) **Wash-out valve**—A device located at the bottom of the tank for the purpose of cleaning and maintenance etc.

(10) **Air vent**—Air ventilation pipe provided in the pipe fitting, to connect the pipe with atmosphere.

(11) **Float operated valve**—These are ball valves or ball tops and equilibrium valves operated by means of a float.

(12) **Water mains**—It is water supply pipe for public use which is in the administration of water supply authority.

(13) **Floc**—It is the precipitate of impuries settled down in coagulation process of purification of water by the addition of a chemical (alum).

(14) **Flocculation.** It is the coagulation process used in purification of water by adding a chemical (alum) which makes the impurities to settle down as a precipitate.

17·7. Distribution reservoirs (Service reservoirs). Distribution reservoirs store the treated water for supplying water during requirements of public use and in emergencies such as altering fires, break down or repair etc. and also to help in absorbing the hourly fluctuation in the normal water demand. The main types and functions of the reservoirs are :

• **Surface reservoirs.** These reservoirs are constructed on the ground level or underground. The surface reservoirs are constructed on the highest point. of the town so as to supply the water to the city on the gravity flow. Stand pipe reservoir is an example of this type.

• **Underground storage tank (IS : 2065—1963).** The underground storage tanks shall not be used for water for domestic purposes unless following requirements are fulfilled.

(1) The tank shall be atleast 30 cm above the H.F.L. If it is not possible the manhole cover should be raised 30 cm above H.F.L.

(2) The design should be such that it may be drained when necessary and water shall not be allowed to collect on the round about of tank.

(3) Tank should be perfectly water proof.

(4) The inner surface of the tank must be rendered water proof and smooth.

(5) The tank must be provided with a cement concrete cover having a mainhole opening provided with a properly fitted mosquito proof hinged cast iron cover fitted with a leak proof cast iron frame.

(6) No gap shall be allowed to remain around the suction pipe and arrangements shall be provided for proper discharge of spill water from the electric pump by connecting the pump cabin to the water drainer by providing a small hole which will enable the water to flow out.

(7) The flow pipes or vent shafts if provided shall have a wire gauge cover of 1·5 mm mesh, properly screwed tightly to the opening.

• **Elevated reservoir.** Elevated reservoirs are rectangular, circular, elliptical or octagonal in plan and erected on a certain elevation so as to feed the city by gravity. These reservoirs are supported on towers. These reservoirs are of RCC, prestressed concrete or may be of steel. These reservoirs are covered at top by the roof slabs in order to avoid the contamination of water due to dirts, birds, insects etc. Roofs should however be provided with air ventilators, so as to allow free circulation of air. Other accessories in such a reservoir are as follows :

(*i*) Inlet pipe for the entry of water. It is provided at the top above F.R.L.

(*ii*) Outlet pipe connected to on distribution mains for the exit of water and is provided lowest point of the reservoir.

(*iii*) Overflow pipe to discharge the surplus water into a drain by a pipe and is provided at the full reservoir level.

(*iv*) A float, gauge or an indicator for indicating the level of the water in the reservoir and which can be read from outside and is painted on the outside surface of the reservoir.

(*v*) A wash out pipe or a drain pipe to empty the reservoir in emergency or for cleaning purposes and is provided in the bottom of reservoir.

(*vi*) Automatic device to stop pumping when the reservoir is full in order to check the wastage of water.

(*vii*) Ladders to reach to the top of reservoir and then to the bottom of the reservoir inside for inspection.

(*viii*) Manholes for entry in the reservoir for inspection and for cleaning.

(*ix*) Air ventilators for air circulation.

Storage capacity. It must meet the following requirements :

(1) **Balancing storage.** The main function of a reservoir is to balance the fluctuations of demand. It may store the incoming supply when demand is low and then to feed it during the keen demand period when the demand is more than the incoming supply. This balancing storage can be worked out by the **mass curve diagram.**

Mass curve for pumping during limited supply

Mass curve during continuous supply (Total storage $(A + B)$)

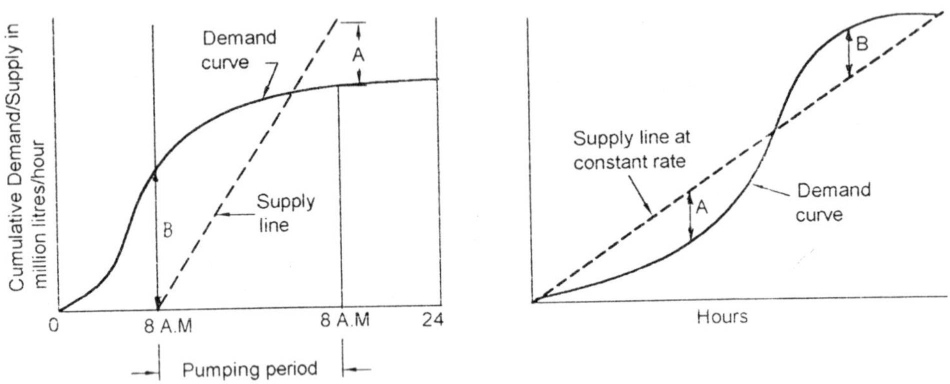

(*a*) (*b*)

Fig. 17·49. Mass diagram for 24 hours pumping.

Mass curve method. A mass curve is the plot of accumulated inflow *i.e.* supply or outflow *i.e.* demand versus time. The mass curve *i.e.* supply line is therefore drawn first and is then superimposed by the demand curve. The amount of balancing storage can then be determined by adding the maximum ordinates between the demand and the supply lines. To draw such diagrams for a particular water supply project, we have to proceed as follows :

(*i*) From the past records, determine the hourly demand for all 24 hours for controlling days (maximum average or minimum demand).

(*ii*) Calculate and plot the cumulative demand against time and then plot the mass curve of demand.

(*iii*) Plot the cumulative supply also against time as shown in the Fig. 17·49.

(*iv*) Read the storage required as the sum of the two maximum ordinates between demand and supply line as shown in the Figs.

(*v*) Repeat the procedure for all the controlling days (maximum average) and determine the maximum storage required for the worst day.

Solution. The cumulative hourly supplies are tabulated for all the 24 hours. The hourly excess of demand as well as the hourly excess of supply (cumulative) are then worked out. The summation of the excess of demand and the maximum of excess of supply will give required storage capacity.

Example. *For a water supply, for a daily requirement of 2,25,000 litres. Design the storage capacity of the reservoir.*

The drawn off pattern is *7·00 AM–8·00 AM 30% of days supply*
8·00 AM–5·00 PM 35% of days supply
5·00 PM–6·30 PM 30% of days supply
6·30 PM–7·00 PM 5% of days supply

The pumping is to be done at a constant rate of 8 litres per day (8 A.M. to 4 P.M.)

The supply line on the mass diagram therefore be a straight line with its slope as $28{\cdot}125 \times 10^3$ litres per hour as shown by the dotted line in the Fig. 17·49.

The given demand pattern is converted into cumulative demand as below :

Table 17·31(*b*).

Period	*Rate of demand*	*Demand in litres col (2) × (2·25 × 10³)*	*Cumulative demand in litres × 10³*
(1)	(2)	(3)	(4)
7·00 AM–8·00 AM	30% of total	$67{\cdot}5 \times 10^3$	67·50
8·00 AM–5·00 PM	35% of total	$78{\cdot}75 \times 10^3$	146·25
5·00 PM–6·30 PM	30% of total	$67{\cdot}5 \times 10^3$	213·74
6·30 PM–7·00 AM	5% of total	$11{\cdot}25 \times 10^3$	225·00

The mass curve of demand is plotted from the data of columns (1) and (4) of the above table and is shown in the Fig. 17·50. The two maximum ordinates *A* and *B* enclosed between the demand and the supply lines are read from the Fig. 17·49.

$$A = 88 \times 10^3 \text{ litres}$$

$$B = 67{\cdot}5 \times 10^3 \text{ litres}$$

Total storage required

$$= 155{\cdot}5 \times 10^3 \text{ litres}$$

Total capacity

$$= 155{\cdot}5 \text{ m}^3$$

$$= 1{,}55{,}500 \text{ litres}$$

Average supply in 8 hours

$$= \frac{225 \times 10^3}{8}$$

$$= 28{\cdot}125 \times 10^3 \text{ litres}$$

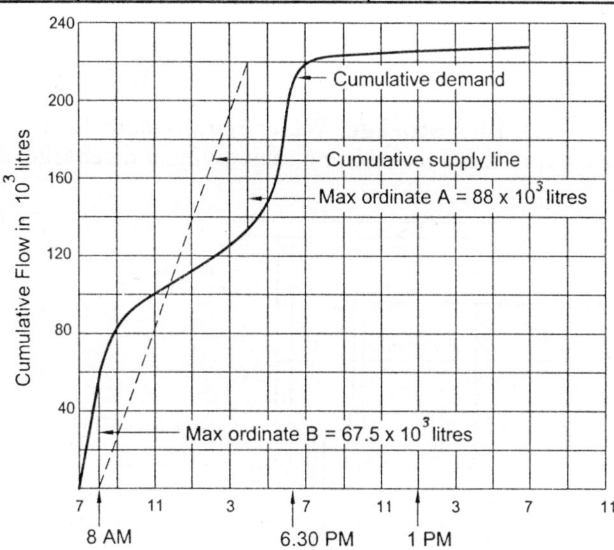

Fig. 17·50.

(2) **Break down storage.** The break down storage or the **emergency storage** is the storage preserved in order to overcome the emergencies caused by the failure of pumps or any other breakdown in supply line. As it is difficult to assess such emergencies hence a lumpsum provision is made for this purpose. It is taken from 25 percent to twice the capacity according to this possibilities of failure.

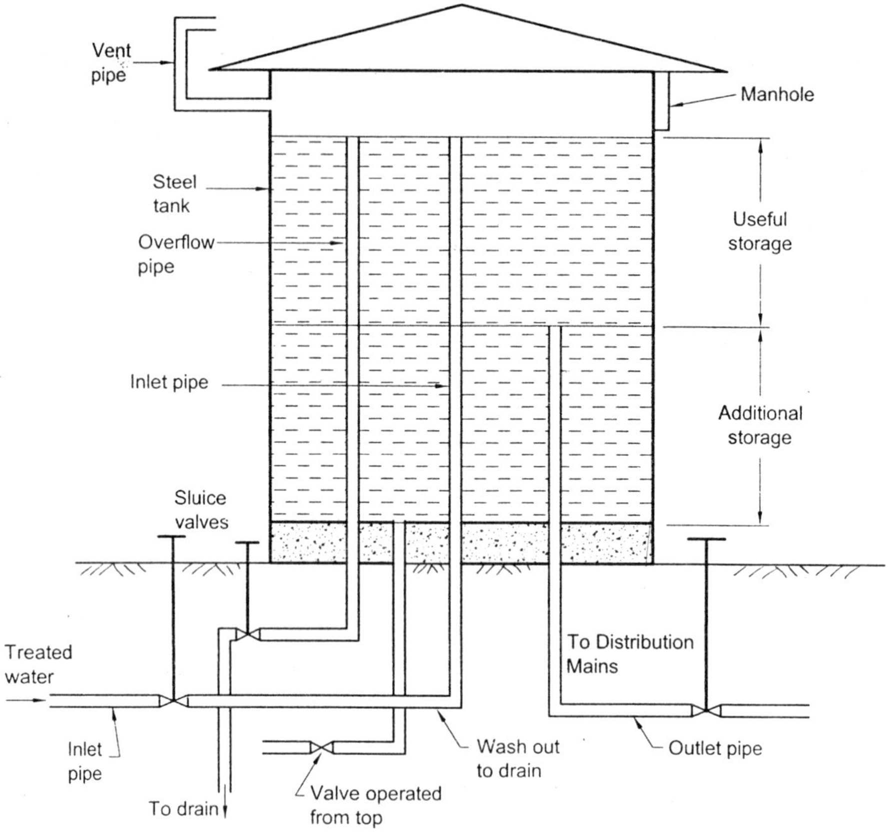

Fig. 17·51. Stand pipe.

(3) **Fire storage.** Water requirement for fire fighting is generally 1 to 5 litres per day per capita. Three jet streams each giving a discharge of about 1100 litres/minute must be thrown on the fire. Thus if a provision for 10 hours of fire fighting per day is desired, the volume of water required to be stored

$$= (3 \times 1100) \times (10 \times 60) \text{ litres/day}$$

$$= 198 \times 10^4 \text{ litres per day}$$

The National Board of under writers of America recommends provision for extinguishing a serious fire of 10 hours at a rate of about 10,000 to 50,000 litres/min. for towns with populations more than 6000 and upto 2 lakhs. For smaller communities with population of 4000, 2000 and 1000 the provision may be made for extinguishing a serious fire of 8, 6 and 4 hours respectively. In India we may store about 1 to 4 litres per capita per day as the necessary fire storage depending upon the importance of the city.

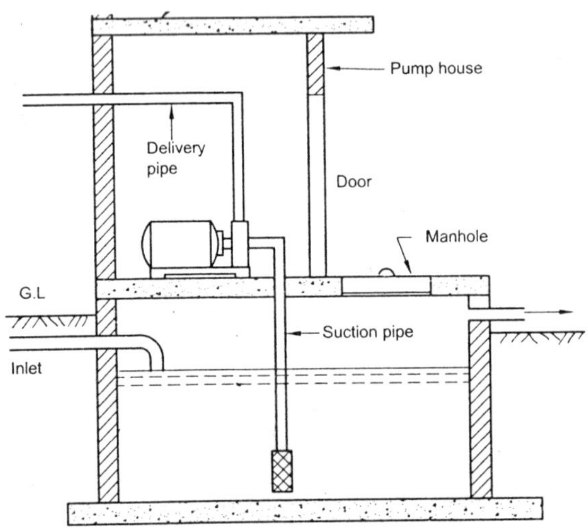

Fig. 17·52. Domestic under ground storage tank.

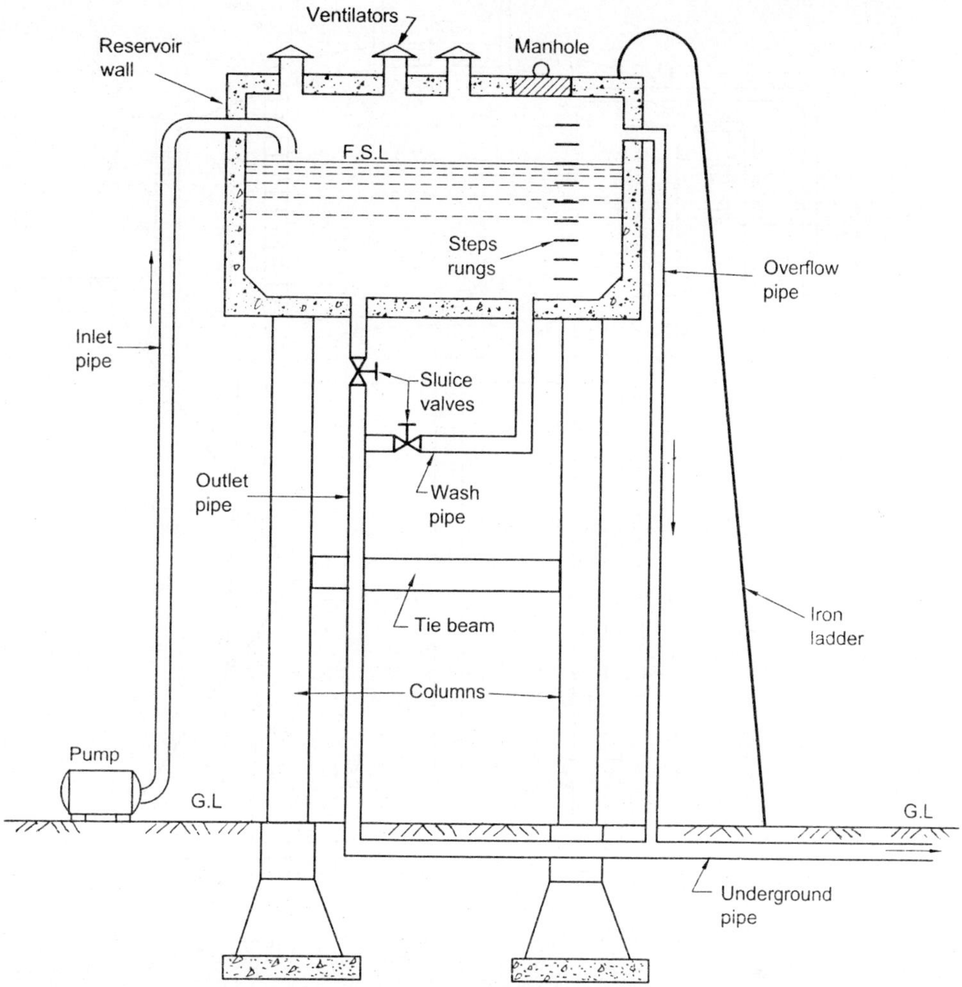

Fig. 17·53. Rectangular over head tank.

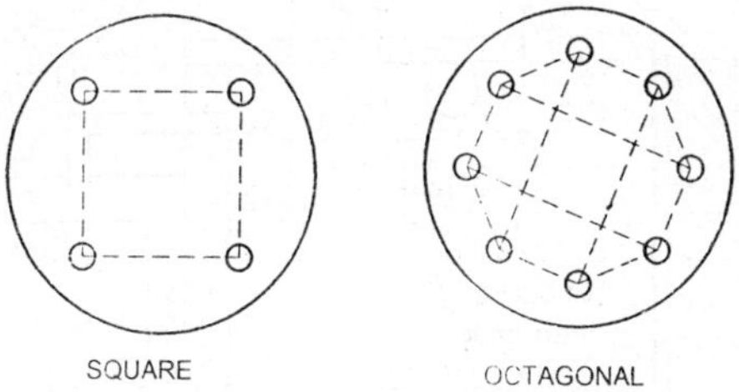

Fig. 17·54. Setting of columns and beams.

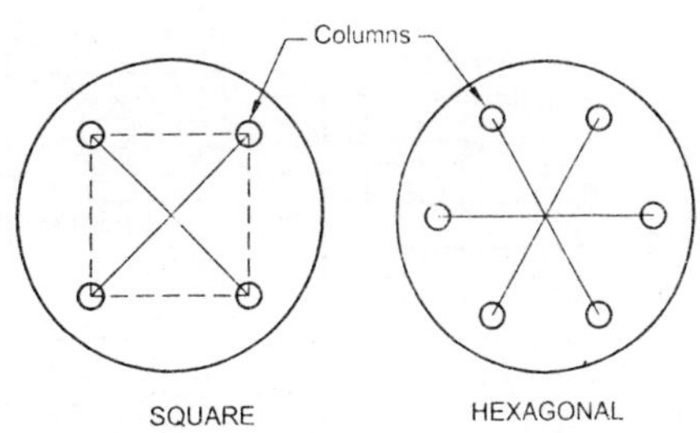

Fig. 17·55. Plan for column's position.

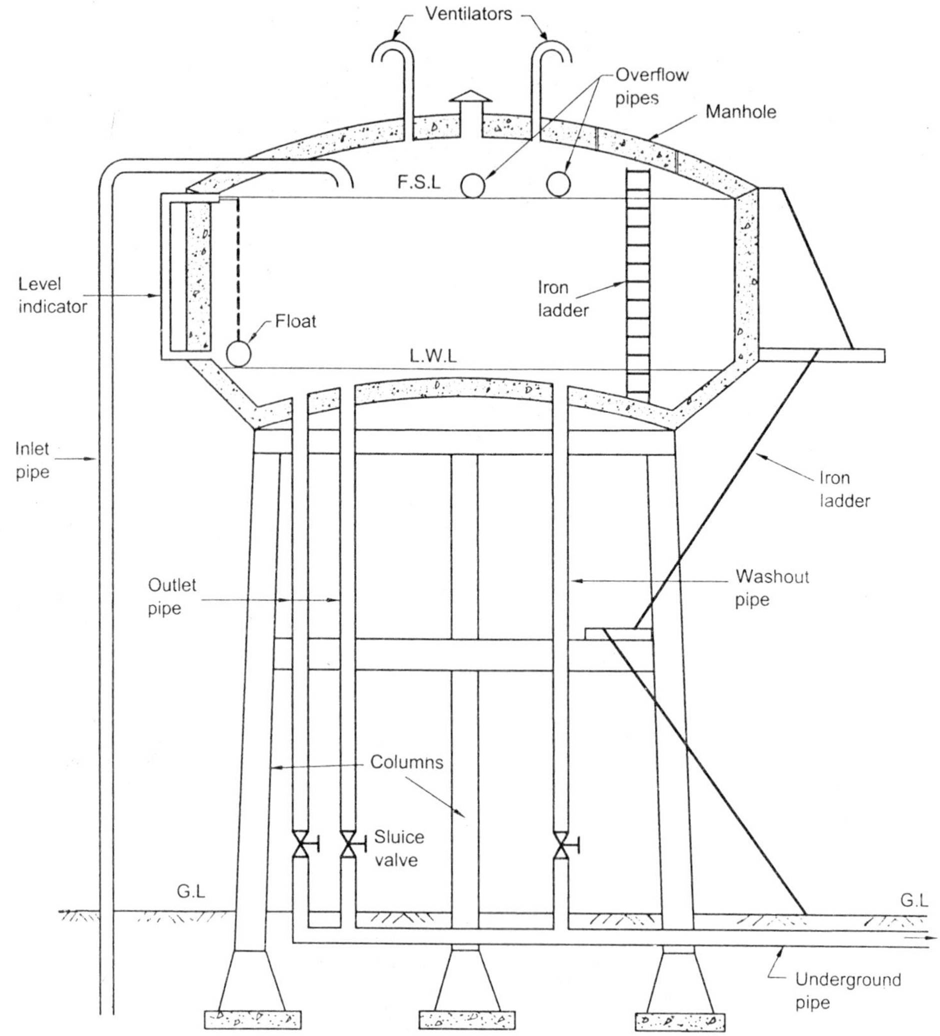

Fig. 17·56. Intz tank.

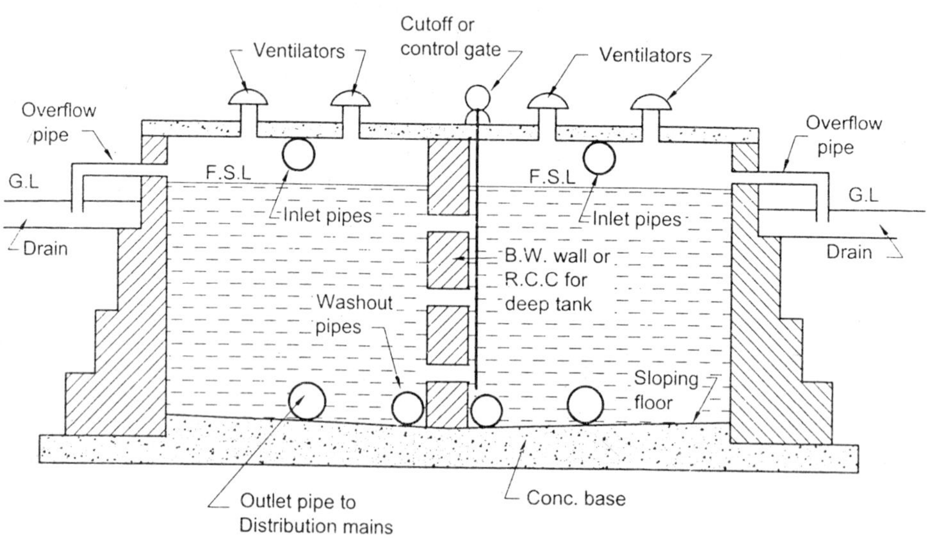

Fig. 17·57. Ground reservoir.

The total storage of the reservoir can be obtained by adding the three *viz.* (*i*) balancing storage + (*ii*) Breakdown storage + (*iii*) Fire storage.

Location of the storage reservoirs (*i*) They should be located in the heart of the city (*ii*) They should be located at the height elevation so as to supply by gravity. (*iii*) They should be located at a place where power and other machines have an clear assess.

Locating the leakage in the distribution pipes. The following methods are used in this connection :

(*i*) By direct observation (*ii*) By using sounding rods

(*iii*) By plotting hydraulic gradient line and (*iv*) By using wash detecting meters.

(*i*) **By direct observation.** Observing wet spots on unpaved surfaces or heavy grass or vegitation on a spot, or emergence of a spring. All such indications give a hint for the leakage of the pipe line. Such leakages are frequent in loamy soils.

(*ii*) **By using sounding rods.** A pointed iron rod is inserted forcely over a pipe line in ground. When it is taken out the wet and muddy point indicates the presence of the leakage. When the rod is inserted a hissing sound can be heart at the top of the rod by the ear which is due to the motion of the water. This sound can be heard by an instrument known as **aquaphone** or a **sonoscope**. The sound hearing must be done during night in a calm atmosphere.

(*iii*) **By plotting hydraulic gradient.** The pressures at various points of a suspected pipe line are measured and a hydraulic gradient line is drawn. An abrupt change or kink in the hydraulic gradient line will indicate a leakage in the pipe.

(*iv*) **By using wash detection meters.** By these meters actually the velocity in the pipe is measured. A high velocity in any low lying area will indicate any leakage. For this test the suspected pipe line is closed at its two ends preferably in night time and the velocity at the suspected point is measured. A velocity in the inflow water indicates a leakage. The meter is provided with a pencil points and a square paper wrapped round a revolving drum so as to automatically register the flow at disposal points. **Deacon's wash water detection meters** are widely used for this purpose as they are quite sensitive and accurate.

Velocities in pipe lines. Efforts are made to achieve the optimum velocities between 0·9 to 1·8 m/sec for pipe diameters varying between 10 cm to 40 cm.

Table 17·32. Optimum velocities in pipes of different sizes

Pipe dia. in cm	*App. velocity in m/sec*
10	0·9
15	1·2
25	1·5
40	1·8

Steel tanks. The following types of tanks are commonly used for storing water :

(1) Stand pipes

(2) Elevated tanks with the spherical segmented or conical bottom

(3) Pressed steel tanks

(1) **Stand pipes.** Stand pipe is a tank, generally cylinderical used for the storage of water, petroleum etc. Its height in most cases, is considerably greater than its diameter. It has a flat

Table 17·33. Design data for small circular RCC water tanks
(RC designers manual—The concrete association of India)

Capacity in 1000 litres	*Inside dia. in metres*	*Depth including free board (m)*	*Thickness of wall and floor (cm)*	*Reinforcement*					
				Wall				*Floor Bars each way*	
				Hor. steel at bottom half depth		*Vertical steel*			
				Bar dia. mm	*Spacing cm*	*Bar dia. mm*	*Spacing cm*	*Bar dia. mm*	*Spacing cm*
2	1·75	1·00	10	10	20	10	20	10	20
3	2·00	1·40	10	10	20	10	20	10	20
5	2·25	1·45	10	10	20	10	20	10	20
7	2·50	1·55	10	10	20	10	20	10	20
9	2·75	1·70	13	10	20	10	20	10	20
14	3·00	2·10	13	10	20	10	20	10	20
23	3·75	2·25	15	10	17	10	20	10	20
34	4·25	2·55	15	10	17	10	20	16	20
45	5·75	2·65	18	12	20	12	30	12	30
90	6·00	3·25	18	12	12	12	20	12	20
Design data for small square RCC tank									
2	1·5 × 1·5	1·00	10·0	6	15	6	15	6	20
3	1·8 × 1·8	1·25	10·0	6	15	6	15	6	20
5	2·0 × 2·0	1·40	10·0	6	15	6	15	6	20
7	2·3 × 2·3	1·50	11·5	10	22	10	22	6	20
9	2·5 × 2·5	1·60	11·5	10	20	10	13	6	20
14	2·8 × 2·8	2·00	13·0	10	18	12	18	6	14
23	3·5 × 3·5	2·10	15·0	10	16	16	10	6	12
34	4·0 × 4·0	2·30	16·6	10	15	16	18	6	10
45	4·2 × 4·2	2·70	18·0	12	20	16	15	6	10

Circular tanks capacity above 100 × 1000 litres

Capacity 1000 litres	*Inside dia. in m*	*Depth of water in m*	*Thickness of wall in cm*	*Hor. hoop reinforcement*			*Vertical reinforcement*	
				Ht. L in meters	*Bar dia. mm*	*Spacing cm*	*Bar dia. mm*	*Spacing cm*
450	11·30	4·5	25·0	1·89	16	14·5	12	14·0
360	10·10	4·5	22·5	1·68	16	15·0	12	15·5
225	8·00	4·5	20·0	1·58	16	17·5	12	17·5
135	6·20	4·5	17·5	1·35	12	11·5	12	18·5
450	12·65	3·5	22·5	1·82	12	12·0	12	15·0
360	11·30	3·5	20·0	1·60	12	12·5	12	16·5
225	8·45	3·5	17·5	1·40	12	13·0	10	15·5
135	6·95	3·5	17·5	1·26	12	15·0	10	16·0
450	13·80	3·0	20·0	1·80	12	14·5	10	16·0
360	12·30	3·0	17·5	1·50	12	15·5	10	18·0
225	9·75	3·0	15·0	1·29	12	15·5	10	15·5
135	7·75	3·0	15·0	1·17	12	17·0	10	18·0
450	15·70	2·5	17·5	2·00	10	13·5	10	13·5
360	13·55	2·5	17·5	1·75	10	14·5	10	15·0
225	10·72	2·5	15·0	1·40	10	15·5	10	16·5
135	8·30	2·5	15·0	1·20	10	16·5	10	18·0

bottom and rests directly on its foundation. The use of stand pipe is very common in industries for storage liquids, where the capacity is more important than pressure. A stand pipe can also be used for municipal water supply provided it is located on an elevated ground and an additional supporting tower is not needed. The term stand pipe is specifically used for those tanks whose height is considerably more than the diameter. If the diameter is comparably to is larger than height, it is called cylinderical tank or reservoir. To prevent the water from becoming a breeding place for mosquitoes, flies etc. a conical cover may be used on top (refer Fig. 17·56 and 17·58).

The following accessories are very commonly rquired for the stand pipe :

Shell manhole. It is a circular mainhole 0·6 m (24″) dia. or an elliptical manhole 18″ × 2″ minimum size located in the first ring of the tank shell. It has a cover hinged to the shell.

Pipe connection. The fitting for the pipe is provided at suitable location near the bottom of the tank. The connecting pipe can be caulked into this fitting.

Overflow. The overflow pipe is provided at suitable elevation to drain the excess water. If the overflow pipe is taken to the ground level, it should be supported at proper intervals with suitable brackets. It should terminate at the top in a weir box. The overflow pipe and the weir box should have a capacity at least equal to the pumping rate.

Outside tank ladder. A tank ladder outside of the tank shell is usually provided near the manhole. The side rails of the ladder should not be less than 2″ × 5/16″. The spacing of the side rails is nearly 14 to 15 inches. The minimum size of the rings is 5/8″ round or square bars spaced at 12″ centre.

Roof ladder. A roof ladder is required on stand pipe roofs which are sloping and one can not walk on these safely.

Roof hatch. A roof door is provided for inspection near the outside tank ladder. The hatch should have minimum opening dimension of 24″. A suitable cover is provided on the hatch.

Vent. In case the tank roof is of light construction, a suitable vent should be provided above the maximum water level which should have a capacity to pass over the maximum possible rate of the water either entering or leaving the tank, so that the dangerous pressure may not be developed. The overflow pipe should not be considered as vent. The vent should pereferably be screwed to prevent the entry of birds etc.

(2) **Elevated tank.** The elevated steel tanks are common for storing municipal water supply. These overcome the low pressure during periods of peak demand and maintain uniform pressure in water distribution system. The various accessories of the elevated steel tanks *i.e.* vent, overflow pipe, roof hatch, revolving ladder, tower ladder, inside ladder, pipe connections etc. have been shown in the Fig. 17·58 with reference to welded steel tanks.

Although the elevated cylinderical tanks are very simple for fabrication. A cylinderical tank is not the most favourable shape for storing liquid. When a rubber bag is filled with a liquid and placed on a table it flattens, where as when filled with compressed air it becomes spherical. When partially filled with liquid and partially with compressed air, it assume the shape of spheroid. These are the forms in which the stresses are minimum. Now a days there has been a tendency to build spheroid shape tanks. For stress analysis a general case of a tank consisting of a surface of revolution about vertical axes will be considered. The tank will be assumed to be supported on a circular ring RR (Fig. 17·58). As the thickness of the shell forming the tank is usually very small as compared to its radii of curvature. The shell can be regarded as a membrane and the tensile or compressive stresses will be uniform over the thickness. Thus there will be no bending moment in the shell.

Design considerations. The steel tanks are mainly designed for water pressure. The supporting structure has to be designed for weight of tank and also the wind pressure. The wind pressure depends upon the location of the tank and its height above the ground level. Reference

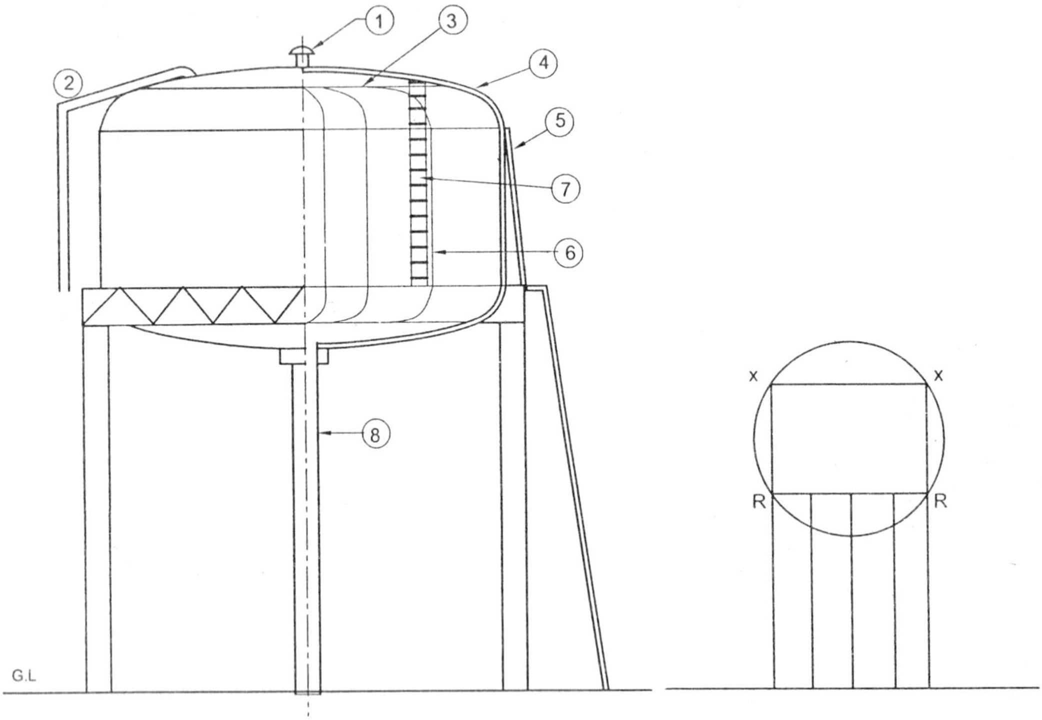

(*a*) (*b*)

1. Screened fixial vent.
2. Stub over flow pipe
3. Roof hatch
4. Stop lug for revolving ladder
5. Revolving type outside ladder
6. Spider
7. Inside ladder
8. Outlet pipe.

Fig. 17·58. Elevated steel tank.

may be made to IS : 875 for wind pressure. The earthquake forces are usually important in the design of supporting structures for tanks due to the higher location of c.g. of load. The intensity of earthquake will depend upon the location of the tank. For areas around Roorkee a horizontal force of 4-6% of the total weight of water can be assumed to act at the c.g. of the water, the higher value being used when tank is on soft soil. If a balcony is provided around a tank a vertical load of 1000 lbs is assumed to be applied at any point on the balcony floor. The tank roof should be designed to take a load of 500 lb at any point.

The allowable tensile stress in structural mild steel plates is assumed as 15000 psi or 1055 kg/cm^2 on the net area. The other stresses are kept the same as IS : 800—1962. The minimum thickness for plates is 5 mm for parts not in contact and 6 mm for parts in contact with water. However a small thickness will be permissible for pressed steel tanks.

The riveted steel tanks, the minimum pitch will be 3 × dia. of rivets and the maximum pitch along caulked edge will be 10 × thickening plate. The minimum distance from the centre of the outer row to plate edge is 1·5 × dia. of rivet. The rivet diameters may be used as given to table below :

Table 17·34.

Plate (mm)	*Rivet dia. (mm)*	*Plate (inch)*	*Rivet dia. in inch*	*Remarks*
5	11	3/16	1/2	
6-8	16	1/4-5/16	5/8	
9-11	19	3/8-7/16	3/4	
12-16	22	1/2-5/8	7/8	
17-19	25	11/16-3/4	1	
20-22	29	13/16-7/8	$1^1/_8$	
over 22	32	over 7/8	$1^1/_4$	

In circumferential joints the same size rivets are used as in vertical joint. For designing the plates for tension, a joint efficiency of about 70% may be assumed to start with, which may be checked after proportioning the plates and rivets.

Supporting Ring Beam. The circular tank with conical or segmented bottom will be supported on a ring beam which is in turn is supported by a number of columns (4 to 8 in number). This beam will be carrying a uniformly distributed load along its length. In addition to B.M. and S.F. this beam will be subjected to torsional moments also which will be zero at the supports and at the mid span. The values of maximum S.F. and coefficients for maximum positive and negative B.M. and torsional moments are given in the table below :

Table 17·35.

No. of supports	*Load on each column*	*Maximum shear*	*m'*	*m*	m_t	*a*
4	*w*/4	*w*/8	−0·03415	+ 0·0176	0·0051	19°-12′
6	*w*/6	*w*/12	−0·01482	+ 0·0075	0·00101	12°-44′
8	*w*/9	*w*/6	− 0·00827	+ 0·00416	0·00063	9°-33′
12	*w*/12	*w*/24	0·00365	+ 0·00190	0·000185	6°-21′

w = Total load on beam

a = angular distance from supports to points of zero moment and maximum m_1

r = rad. of ring beam

m_t = torsional moment, m= moment

The columns may be vertical or slightly slanting.

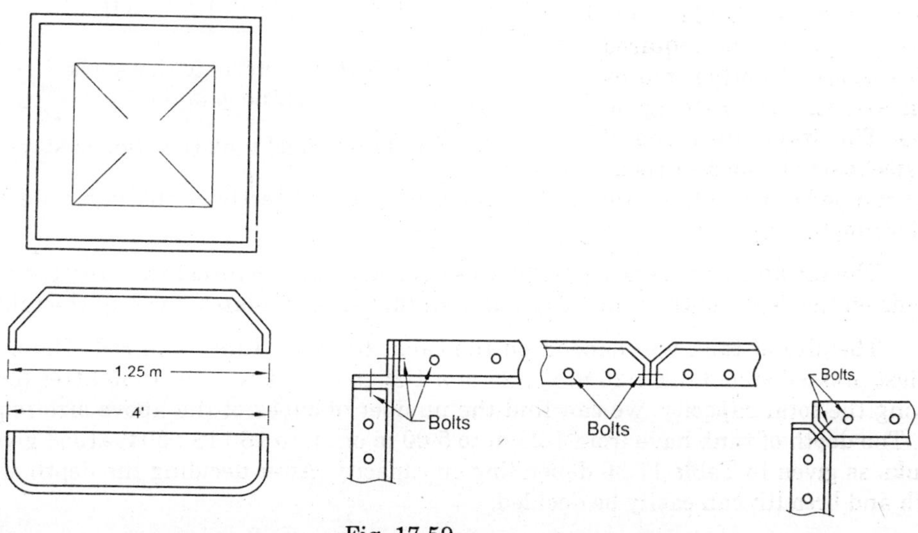

Fig. 17·59.

(3) **Pressed steel tanks.** The pressed steel tanks are usually rectangular and are fabricated by joining together the pressed plates by bolting. The plates are heated uniformly in a furnace and formed into the required shape by pressing. The plates can also be pressed cold. The usual shapes of pressed plates are shown in the Fig. 17·59.

The flanges of the plates can be pressed square or partly square and partly 45° to the face of the plate. The usual size of the plate is 1·25 m × 1·25 m (4′ × 4′). Therefore the dimensions of the tank have to be in multiple of 1·25 × 1·25. The width of the perpendicular portion of flanges, should be sufficient to contact one row of bolts.

For joining the bolts together, the bolts are used because they are easiest to be dismentled. The portion of all bolt holes on all flanges should be kept the same so that the plates are interchangeable. The typical joints are shown in Fig. 17·59(*b*).

A plastic compound is filled in the joints to make them water light. The spacing of the bolts should be limited to 75 mm or 3″ and the dia. of the bolt should not be less than 14 mm (or 9/16″). The tanks can be constructed with all flanges turned out or all flanges turned in. The joints can also be arranged such that the bottom flanges are internal and side flanges are external. The tank with all flanges turned out gives a plane internal surface. The tanks with all flanges turned in or with only bottom flanges turned in are useful if the tank has to be supported on plane floor.

The joints connecting pressed steel plates consists of single line of bolts and can not resist any bending moment. The sides of tanks therefore have to be supported by stags at the junction of two or more plates. Judgement must be exercised in deciding upon the pattern of stags to see that all sides of tank is are stable. A typical arrangement of stags shown in Fig. 17·60. It may be seen that all the corners of plates at the sides have been supported either by stays or by perpendicular side. The stays may not be required at all corners of bottom plates which are directly resting on beams. The stays are made of mild steel bars or rolled sections. These can be bolted to the flanges of the pressed plates directly or through mild steel cleats of equal strength.

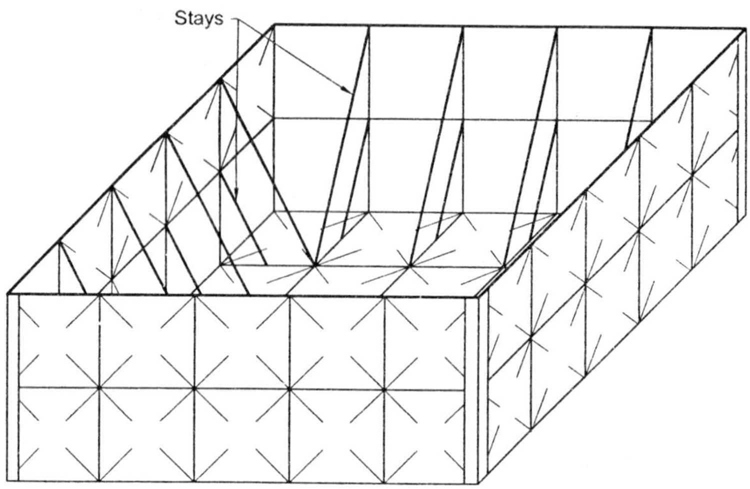

Note : Aleternate tier stays for deep tanks

Fig. 17·60. Steel tank (Position of stays)

The thickness of pressed steel plates depends on the hydrostatic pressure which in turn, depends on the depth of the tank. The required thickness of plates given in the table below :

The size of tank will depend on the capacity of the tank required. The capacity of the smallest pressed steel tank 1·25 m × 1·25 m × 1·25 m (4′ × 4′ × 4′) is 1950 litres (or 400 gallons) knowing the total capacity, we can find the number of cubes of the above size required for the tank. The depth of tank have from 1·25 m to 5·00 m or (4′ to 16′) IS : 804—1958 gives the depths of tanks as given in Table 17·36 depending on capacity. After deciding the depth of the tank the length and breadth can easily be decided.

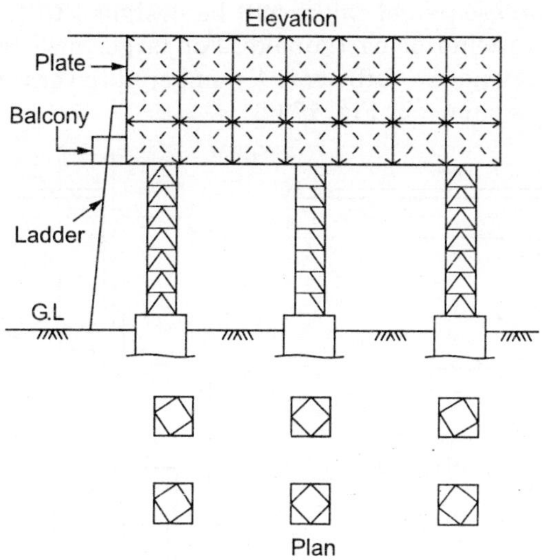

Fig. 17·61. Steel tank tower.

Table 17·36. Thickness of plates

Depth of tank		*Location of plate*	*Thickness of*		*Depth*	*Capacity*
(m)	*(ft.)*		*(mm)*	*(in.)*	*(m)*	*(litres)*
1·25	4	Bottom, sides	5·0	3/16	1·25	1,450-95,550
2·50	8	Bottom and 1st tier of sides	6·0	1/4		
		Top tier of sides	5·0	3/16	2·50	7,800-1,91,100
3·7	12	Bottom and 1st tier of sides	8·0	5/16	3·75	52,650-988,600
		2nd tier of sides	6·0	1/4	5.00	73,200-13,18,200
		Top tier of sides	5·0	3/16		
5·0	16	Bottom and 1st tier of sides	8·0	5/16		
		2nd and 3rd tier of sides	9·0	1/4		
		Top tier of sides	5·0	3/16		

Note : If size of tank is 1·25 × 1·25 × 1·25 m (4′ × 4′ × 4′), the thickness of all five plates could be 3 mm (1/8″).

IS : 804—1950 tests the weight of empty tanks of different capacities. In general the weight of the tank can approximately be calculated by counting the number of pressed steel plates of different sizes and the following unit weights per plate including connections etc.

Table. 17·37. Weights of the pressed steel plates

Pressed steel plate size	*App. weight*
1·25 m × 1·25 m × 3·00 mm ; 4 × 4 × 1/8″	52 kg ; 112 lb.
1·25 m × 1·25 m × 5·00 mm ; 4′ × 4 × 3/16″	86 kg ; 187 lb.
1·25 m × 1·25 m × 6·50 mm ; 4 × 4 × 1/4″	112 kg ; 242 lb.
1·25 m × 1·25 m × 8·00 mm ; 4 × 4 × 5/16″	138 kg ; 300 lb.

The staging for the pressed steel tanks will be designed to take the vertical load and also the horizontal load due to wind or earthquake. For larger size tanks, four typical design will be illustrated. Columns may not be sufficient. A number of towers consisting of four columns braced together may be used as shown in Fig. 17·62.

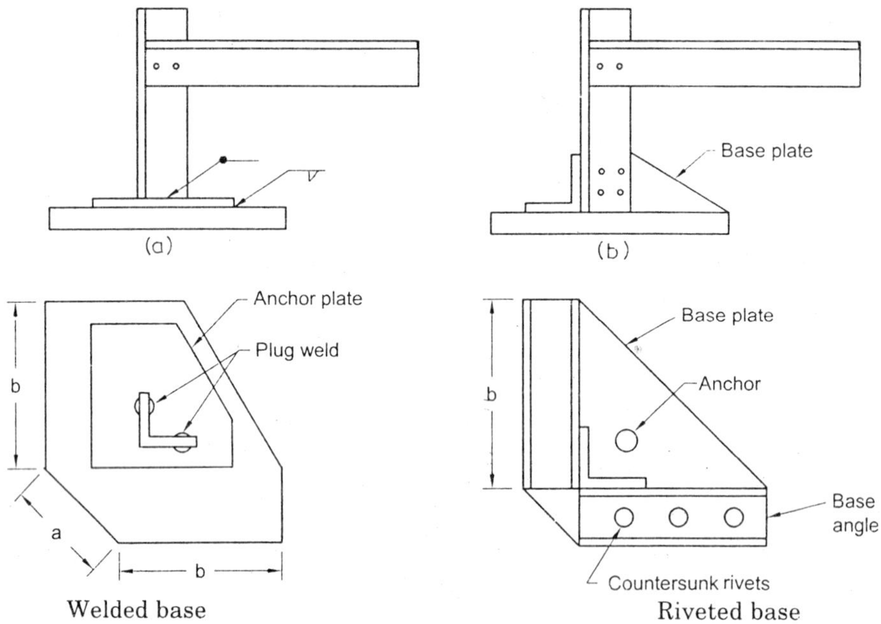

Fig. 17·62

The load from columns will be transferred to the concrete bars through the base plate. If a square or rectangular bar plate is used below an angle section, the c.g. angle of section coinciding with the c.g. of the rectangle plate, the projection of base plate on one side will be larger and the thickness of the plate will have to be larger, the shape of the base plate.

17·7. Water supply system in buildings. The distribution of water in a building from the city mains or other source such as ground water, can be obtained by several piping systems. Each method has its own merits and demerits depending upon the local conditions. The piping systems to be adopted will differ when the main supply is used, when the over head tank supply is used or when the underground tank supply is used, as discussed below.

(1) **Direct supply is used.** In this system water is supplied to all the fixures at all floors of a building directly from the city main, through the house connections as shown in Fig. 17·63. Such a system is however successful only when the water supply is available at adequate pressures round the clock. The minimum pressure available will however, limit the number of floors to which water can be supplied. This system is convenient and cheap to users as it avoids the necessity of storage tanks and pumping sets etc. Even in such a system, separate provision of supplying overhead water to closets and urinals is sometimes made to ensure supply to these fixures in case of accidental low pressure or break down in mains of the city.

(2) **Piping system using overhead tank.** In many cities, the water pressure in the municipal mains is sufficient to make the water reach upto 3 to 4 storeys or higher, but only for a limited period in the mornings and evenings. To meet the water requirement during nonsupply hours, water is stored in overhead tanks placed on the terraces which are filled with a direct connection from the mains. Supply to kitchen is taken from the direct main, while supply to taps for bathing and flushing etc. is taken from the overhead tanks. Such a piping system is shown in Fig. 17·64.

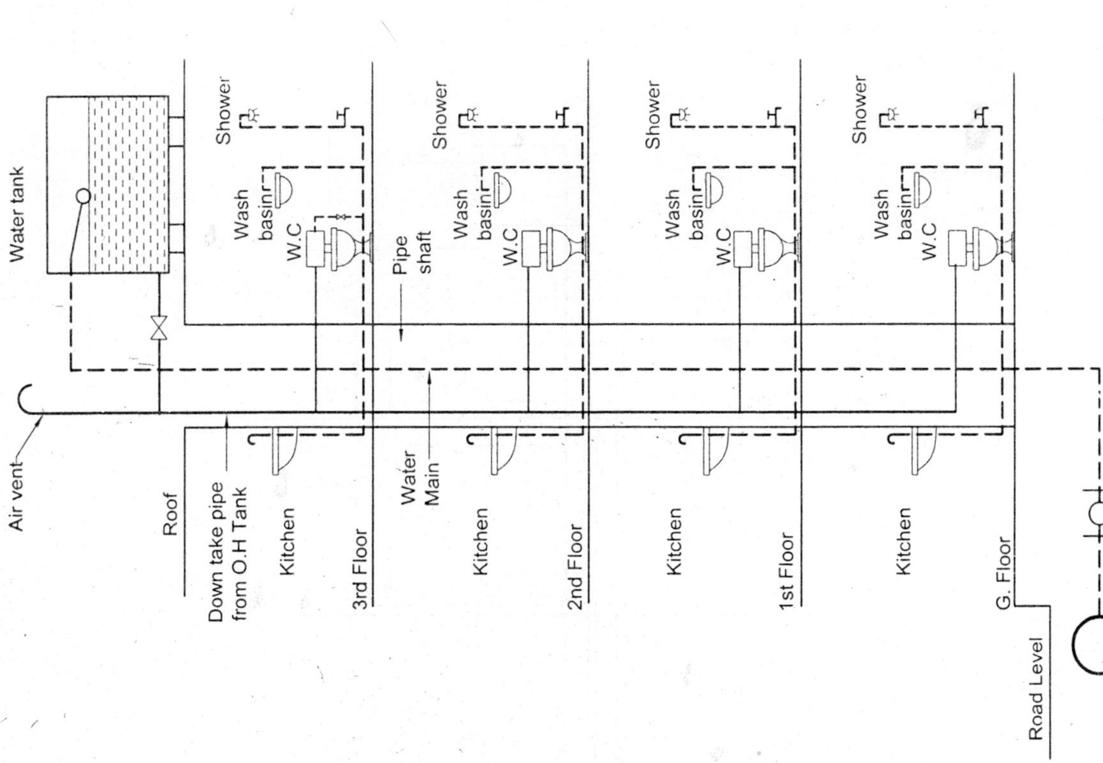

DIRECT SUPPLY WITH OVERHEAD TANK

Fig. 17·64.

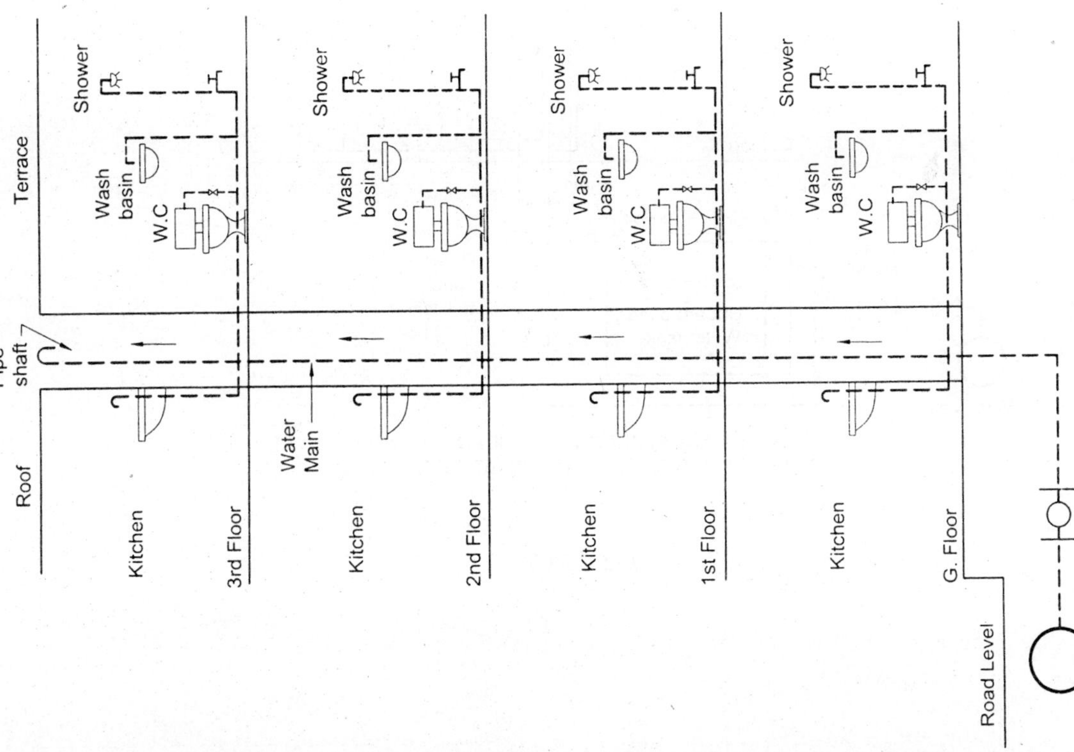

DIRECT SUPPLY TO FIXTURES

Fig. 17·63.

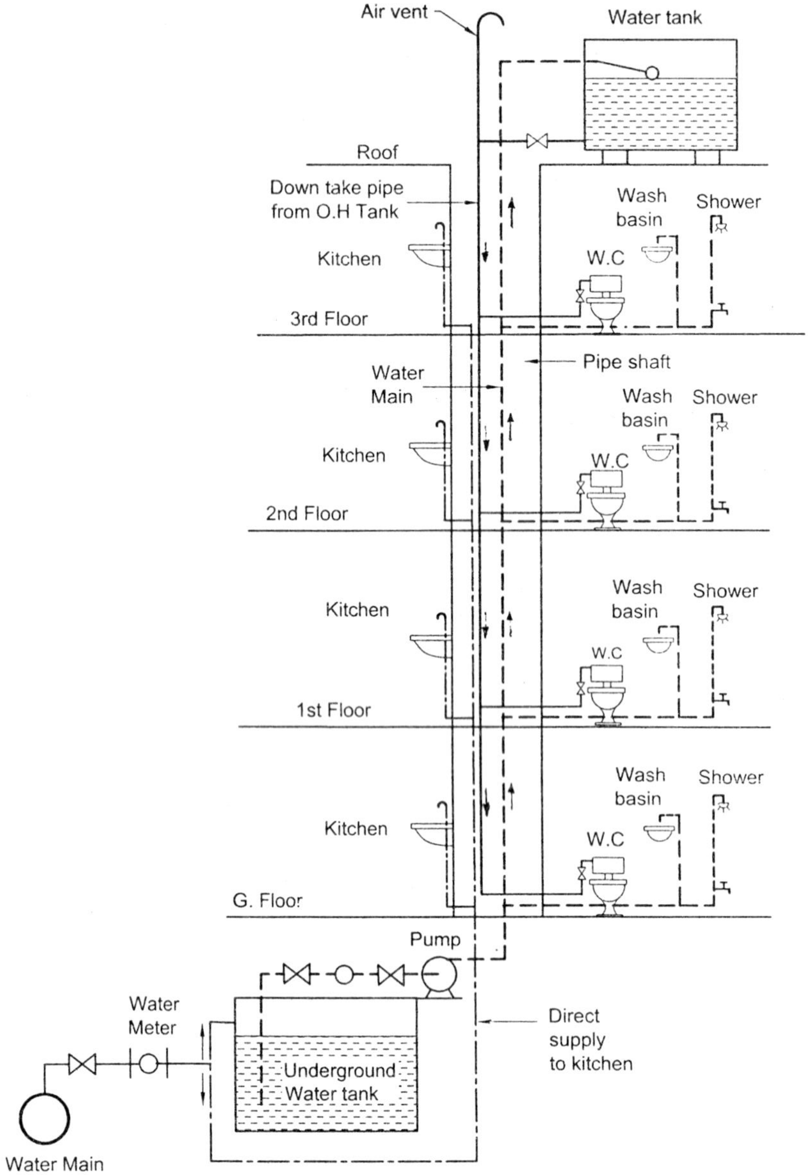

OVERHEAD TANK FEEDED WITH UNDERGROUND TANK WITH PUMP SET AND DIRECT SUPPLY IN KITCHEN

Fig. 17·65.

(3) **Piping system using underground tank supply.** When the municipal water supplies are at low pressure, whether intermittant or continuous, then it becomes necessary to store water in underground tanks (since direct connection of pumps to main is prohibited). The water collected in the underground tank is finally lifted to the overhead tank as mentioned earlier.

Direct supply connection may be made in the lower storeys as to obtain at least some amount of direct supply for draining etc.

(4) **Collecting underground water by lifting with pumps in the overhead storage tanks.** The underground water is lifted by pump and collected in a overhead tank for emergency use. Local hand pumps is also connected with it so that it can be used when electric supply is not available (Fig. 17·66). The overhead tanks may be of masonry or plastic which are available in the market in different capacities.

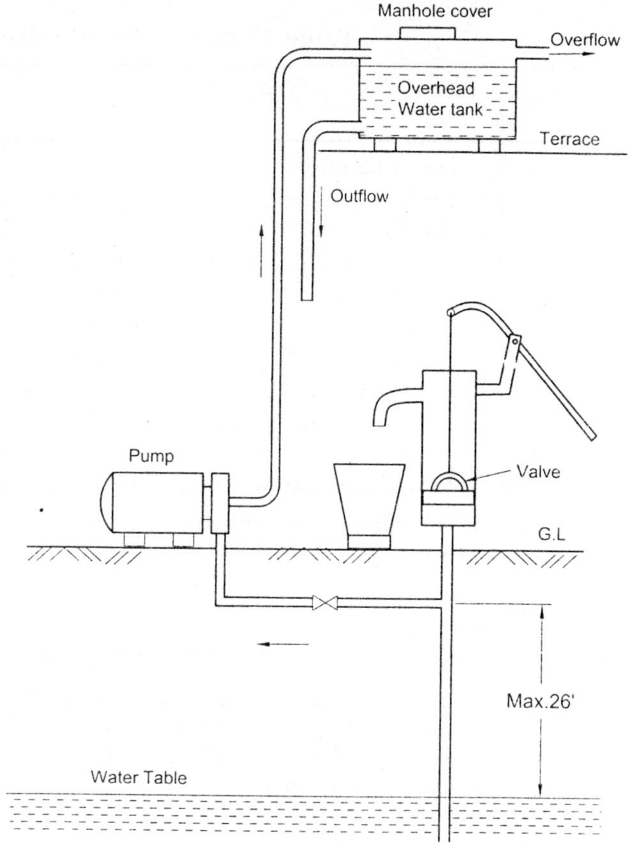

Note : When water table is lower than 26 ft. from the clay of pump, pump is to be lowered down in a trence, so as to maintain a head of less than 26 ft.

Fig. 17·66. Use of underground water supply.

Water demand for a building. The daily water demand of a building will have to be worked out by multiplying per capita demand of the dwellers in the building.

Projected population for different buildings

(*i*) Residence	5 persons per dwelling unit area
(*ii*) Offices	1 person per 10-15 m^2 of plinth area
(*iii*) Schools	Strength of school plus teaching staff
(*iv*) Hotels	Number of beds + staff + requirement of restaurant seats
(*v*) Hostels	Number of beds + 4·5 × (Warden's residence) + staff
(*vi*) Hospitals	Number of beds + staff (residential requirement if any should be added.

Note : 5 to 15% additional population, depending on the usage of the building shall be added for visitors and floating population likely to use the building.

Table 17·38. Water storage required for flushing in buildings

Sl. No.	*Type of building*	*Storage capacity required*
1.	For tenents having common conveniences	900 litres per w.c. (water closet)
2.	For residential premises other than (1) above	270 litres for one w.c. seat and 180 litres for each additional seat in the same flat
3.	For factories and work shops	900 litres per w.c. and 180 litres per urinal seat
4.	For cinema halls, public assembly halls etc.	900 litres per w.c. seat 350 litres per urinal seat

Table 17·39. Storage required for domestic uses

Sl. No.	*Type of building*	*Unit per*	*Unit strength in litres per unit*
1.	Dwelling units	Resident	70
2.	Hostels	Resident	90
3.	Hotels	Resident	135
4.	Commercial buildings without canteens	Head	35
5.	Commercial buildings with canteens	Head	45
6.	Restaurants	Meal	7
7.	Day schools	Head	25
8.	Boarding schools	Resident	90
9.	Nursing homes and medical quarters	Resident	135

Required flow for various water supply fixing and probable simultaneous demand

Table. 17·40. Flow rates and fixture units of various types of water supply fixtures

Sl. No.	*Type of fixture*	*Required flow rate in lit/sec*	*Fixture units assigned each fixture*
(1)	(2)	(3)	(4)
1.	Ablution tap (occasionally used *i.e.* for W.Cs baths etc.)	0·12	1
2.	Ablution tap in (Public places of workshop, common baths etc.)	0·15	3
3.	Bath tubs (supply taps)	0·20	4
4.	Showers with spray heads, individual/common	0·15	2
5.	Showers with 125 mm dia. individual/common	0·20-0·30	4
6.	Wash basins	0·12	1
7.	Surgeon wash basins	0·15	2
8.	Kitchen sinks (domestic)	0·15	2
9.	Kitchen sinks (canteen etc.)	0·15-0·20	1
10.	Drinking fountains (connection to water cooler)	0·10	1
11.	Bidet	0·15	3
12.	Water closet with flushing tank	0·12	1
13.	Water closet with flush valve	1-1·5	8
14.	Urinals automatic/manual flush tank	0·12	1
15.	Urinals, flush valve operated	0·5-1	6

A simple method known as **'Fretwel's formula'** gives the probable simultaneous demand as

$$n = \sqrt{N}$$

where n = Probable number of fixtures likely to be open at the same line.

N = Total number of fixtures in the circuit.

The different types of water supply fixtures are assigned different fixture units and by considering the total loading units, the probable water demand l/sec can be read out using the chart in Fig. 17·67.

Storage tanks in buildings

(*i*) **RCC or masonry tanks.** For small storage brick masonry tanks are made while for larger storage RCC tanks are constructed. These tanks can be built according to the storage size required and the availability of space. Such tanks are made water tight by using water sealing compounds. All outlet and inlet pipes are inserted during construction to avoid joints which becomes a source of leakage.

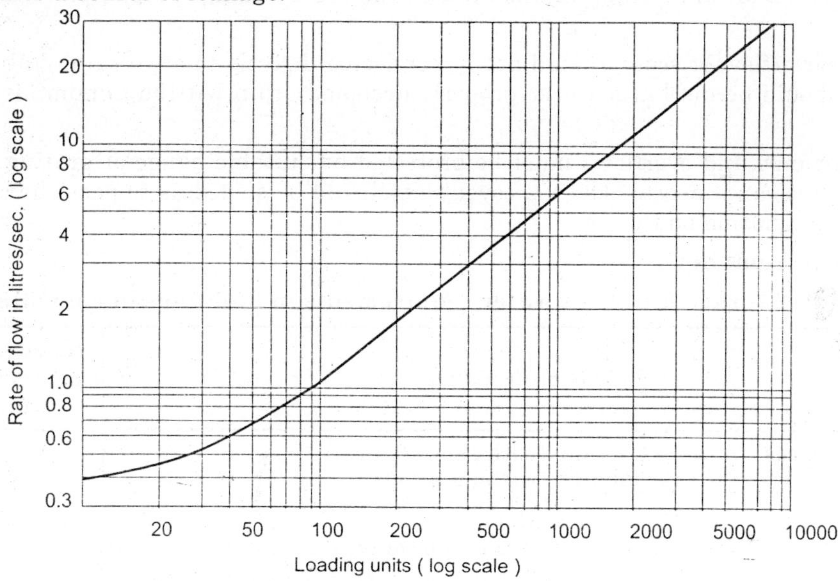

Fig. 17·67. Probable simultaneous demand (log log scale).

(*ii*) **Metal tanks.** Metal tanks are fabricated from mild steel or G.I. sheets. The sheets are welded on angle iron frames for a better support and stability. Mild steel sheets are painted to avoid corrosion. These are light, durable and easy to install and can be shifted to any place when required. They are fabricated upto 1800 litres or 1·8 m^3 in capacity. When the tank of a MS sheet is used for drinking purposes, the paints used must be non-toxic.

Plastic tanks. Plastic tanks are usually made of high density polyethylene (HDPE) or fibre glass reinforced plastic (FRP) or any such strong material. They are available in a variety of shapes and sizes in the market and are light and corrosion resistant. Though they are not immune to ultra violet radiation from sunlight, yet they can be protected by using appropriate gas in coverings. Sintex brand HDPE tank (Fig. 17·68) have now a days is very popular in the market.

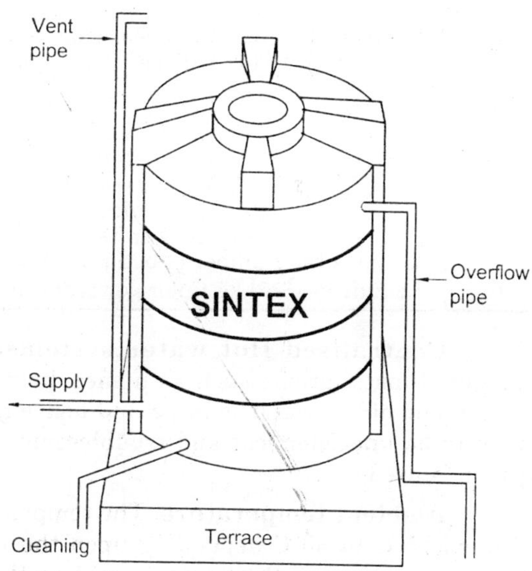

Fig. 17·68. HDPE tank.

The general requirements of a domestic tank

(1) They should be water tight. They should be of a non corrosive and non-toxic materials. They should have a smooth surface inside. These should one manholes or assess holes for repair and cleaning.

(2) They should be provided with a vent pipe for ventilation as well as prevention of negative pressures when water is drawn from the tank. Such negative pressures, may otherwise trigger and collapse if it is weak.

(3) They should have an overflow pipe so as to maintain the water level in the tank.

(4) They should have a scour pipe with a plug at the bottom so that it can be emptied easily. In underground tanks emptying has to be achieved by using the pumping sets provided for boosting.

(5) The overflow or scour should not be connected directly to any drain, gully trap or to any sewer. It should be discharged over properly designed drain with minimum air gap of 75-100 mm.

(6) Vent pipe and overflows must be protected by suitable gauge or grating to prevent entry of mosquitoes and insects. The top cover slab should be sloped as to pass the water away to prevent any stagnation on the top.

Hot Water Requirements

Table 17·41. Average Daily hot water requirements in buildings in cold climates

Sl. No.	*Type of building/use*		*Average daily hot water demand litre / day/head*
1.	Residences	(*a*) Residential (with showers/taps)	45
		(*b*) Residential (with both tubs)	135
2.	Factories	(*a*) Factories (with showers)	90
		(*b*) Factories (ablution taps only)	30-45
3.	Hospitals	(*a*) Beds (Patients, clean up nurses station etc.)	180
		(*b*) Staff doctors and nurses	90
		(*c*) Visitors	10
4.	Hostels	(*a*) Colleges, schools, nurses, hostels etc.	135
		(*b*) Offices, schools, colleges (day use where required)	140
5.	Hotels	(*a*) Rooms with showers	70-90
		(*b*) Rooms with tubs	135
		(*c*) Hotel staff	25-45
		(*d*) Visitors (average 2/room daily)	15
		(*e*) Swimming pools, changing rooms	45
		(*f*) Kitchen/restaurants	5/meal served
	(3 times the number of bed plus 2 times number of seat covers in all restaurants)		
6.	Loundries (3-5) kg linen per room (includes staff uniforms, restaurant linen)		

Centralised Hot water systems. Individual geysers are only useful. For small individual installations such as homes, hostels etc. However in large installations like hotels, the demand of hot water is large and hence installing individual geysers in such buildings may prove to be uneconomical and troublesome. Hence in such situations a centralised hot water system is used.

Ambient temperature. The temperature of the hot water to be supplied is usually kept between 55°C to 80°C depending upon the required uses and climate conditions of the place. The heat required in the boiler to achieve this desired temperature will of course depend upon the temperature of the incoming water which usually vary between 10°C to 20°C even it may be much lower upto 0°C in hilly regions.

Pressure developed during heating system is calculated by the equation :

$$H = \frac{h}{P_w}\left(P_{w2} - P_{w1}\right)$$

where H = Circulating pressure in metre head of water

h = area height in metre between the boiler and the supply point.

P_{w1} = density of hot water at flow temperature t_1 in pipe AB

P_{w2} = density of less hot water at return temperature in pipe DEF

f_w = density of water at 0°C = 1000 kg/m^3

Hot water piping systems. Piping system using natural Thermo-siphonic action.

A simple typical installation of hot water system using an overhead cold storage tank, a centralised boiler at ground level, one hot water main (2) rising vertically up from the boiler, one distribution main (3) as shown in Fig. 17·69. The remotest point *D* of the distribution main is connected back to the boiler by a section pipe *DEF* (4).

In such an installation the circulation of hot water from the main pipe connected to the boiler and the line (1) can occur without the aid of pump by the natural thermo-siphonic action, which occurs due to the difference in the density of water at different temperatures; density being more at lower temperature. **Thermo-siphonic circulation** will take place only when the boiler is placed below the point of supply (3) so that the hottest water from the boiler rises in the main line (2) to the top of the system. Hot water in the rest of the system will have a lower temperature due to loss of heat to the system, and eventually will be heavier, tending to settle at the bottom of the system through the return pipe. This water will then move towards the boiler, from where it again rises after getting reheated. Convection currents is thus generated in the system, which is known as thermo-siphonic action. The overhead tank maintains pressure in the system through a cold feed line (1). The hot water pipe is extended up, as an expansion pipe above the overhead tank.

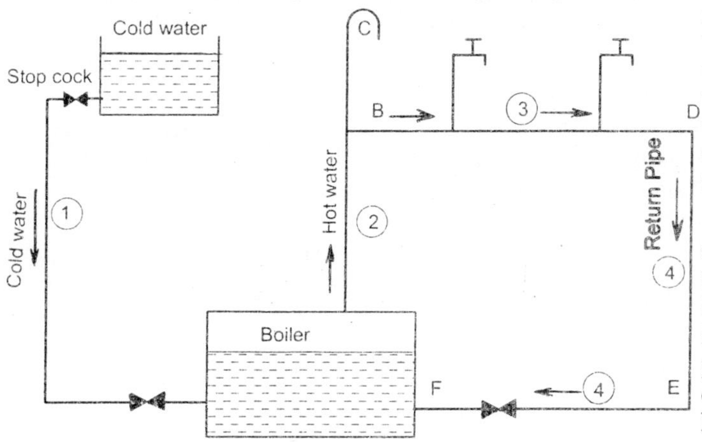

Fig. 17·69. Thermo-siphonic action system of hot water distribution.

Piping system with forced circulation. Since the natural thermo-siphonic circulating pressure is usually low, it becomes necessary in larger installations to generate additional pressure within the system to force the circulation by means of a pump. This helps in using reduced pipe sizes and allows hot water to circulate in all parts of the distribution system for quick draw off of the hot water.

The circulating pumps should however, never be used as booster pumps for increasing the pressure in the hot water lines which infact is provided by the cold water over head tank. When the source of cold water taps as well as in the hot water taps will remain almost the same, which is very much desirable.

Piping layouts. The hot water piping network can be arranged in different ways depending upon the architectural and structural considerations of a building. The most common systems are the following :

(1) Downward system (2) Upward system (3) Reverse circulation system

(1) **Downward system.** In this system (Fig. 17·70), the main vertical hot water line *AB* (pipe marked as (1)) is lifted upto the top floor or to terrace level, where the distribution main (pipe 2) will run over the floor. Single down take pipes (3) are dropped in each shaft to join a common return line *DE* (4) at the lowest level, which is connected to the boiler. A recirculation pump may be attached as shown in figure to improve circulation pressure. For efficient operation, the flow pipe on the top floor must run horizontally at the same level. Any change in its direction in vertical plane should be avoided to prevent air traps. Accessible space is therefore necessary to lay this main pipe (2) on the top floor. When such space on the top floor is not available, this pipe may be laid on the terrace. This system, is simple, efficient and economical.

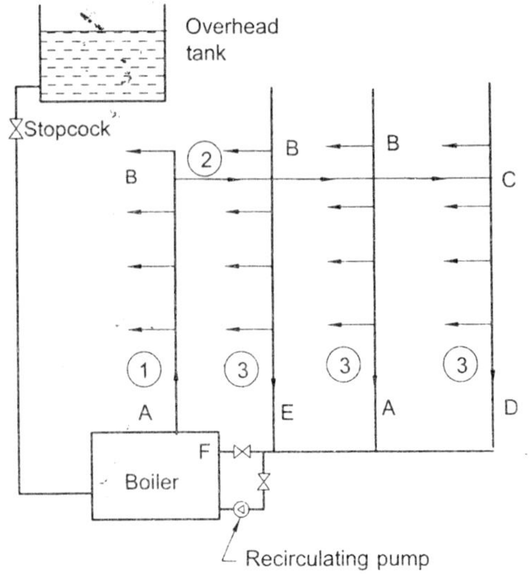

Fig. 17·70. Downward piping system.

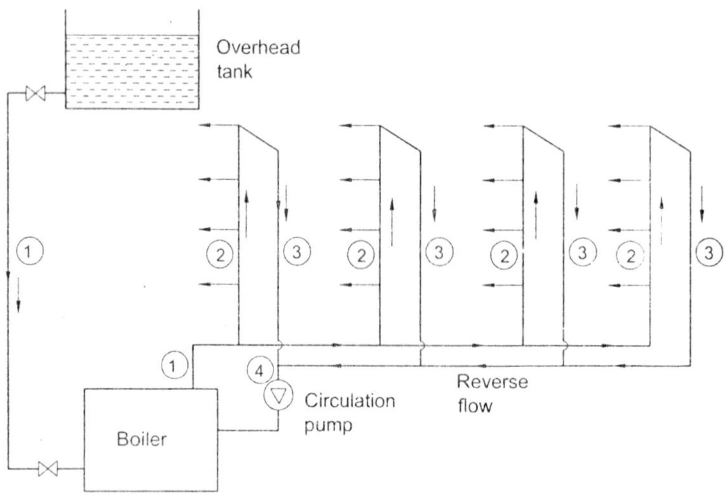

Fig. 17·71. Upfeed piping system.

(2) **Upward system.** In this system (Fig. 17·71) the main flow line (1) and the return line (4) are both laid at the ceiling of the lowest floor like basement roof or on ground floor. Vertical upflow pipes (2) and their corresponding return pipes (3) supply the water to the rooms above. Circulation may occur either at under natural thermo-siphonic action as discussed before.

(3) **Reverse circulation system.** This system (Fig. 17·72) is similar to the upward system except that the return flow occurs in the same direction as that of the main floor pipe (1) till the end of the remotest circuit, from where it returns to the boiler through a separate reverse return line (4).

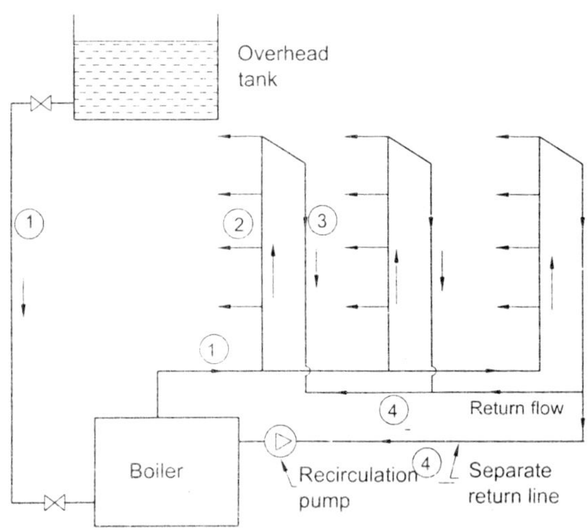

Fig. 17·72. Reverse circulation system.

The system is suitable where the circuits are long and where there is a possibility of the least favourably placed fixtures not getting adequate flow or pressure. A reverse revolution enables closer balancing of pressure in the system.

Geysers

Table 17·42. Limiting values of standing loss in Automatic Geysers

Rate Capacity of geyser in litres	*Maximum permissible energy loss in K.W.H. per day for 45°C difference*	*Rate Capacity of geyser in litres*	*Maximum permissible energy loss in K.W.H. per day for 45°C difference*
0	0·880	50	2·035
10	1·100	70	2·310
15	1·265	100	2·640
25	1·540	140	2·970
35	1·760	200	2·300

Note : The name Geyser is derived from the hot water springs in hills known as Geysers.

Electrical Geysers. These are of two types (*i*) Instantaneous (*ii*) Storage type.

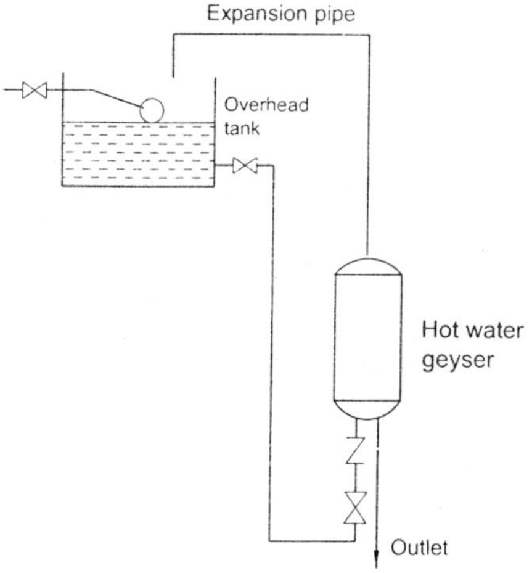

Fig. 17·73. Storage geyser.

(1) **Instantaneous electrical geysers.** A heating element is bounded round a pipe and the bounded pipe is immerged in a bucket of water which is filled with a tap of water. (an electrical immersion rod may also be used) and the electric switch is made on. A precaution is taken that the temperature of water is not tested when the supply is on, it must be checked only after closing the electric supply. The heating element has to be a much higher capacity (wattage) as compared to the one required in a storage heater. An electrical load of 6 kw is found to give water for showering at 3 lit/min. With an electrical load of 3 K.W. will give warm water at a rate of about 1·4 litres/min.

Storage geysers. These geysers are usually of pressure type (Fig. 17·73) which are connected with an assured water supply from a cold cover head storage tank. Such geysers should under no circumstances be connected to the direct main water supply, which may stop and suck back the water from the geyser (inlet may become outlet), if the check valve fails to function, which is normal.

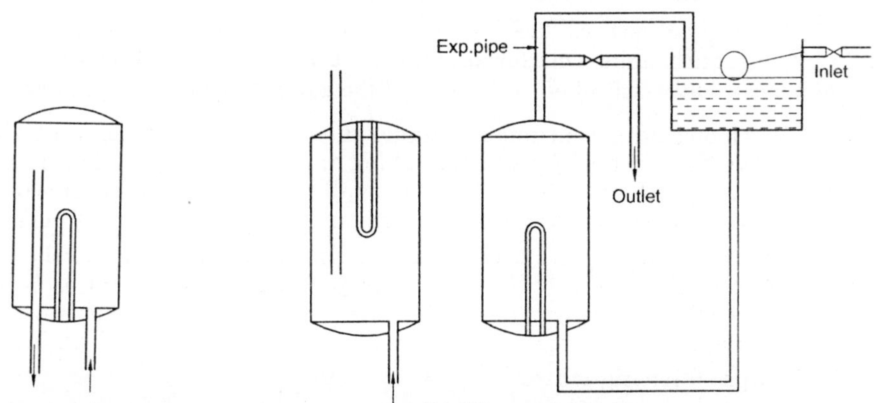

(*a*) Closed water heaters (*b*) Cistern for heater.

Fig. 17·74.

Direct main water supply can however be connected to the **non-pressure type** or open **outlet type of a geyser** Fig. (17·74) in which the outlet is kept open and not provided with any bib cock or stop cock. In such a geyser the well stop cock is opened to draw water from the open outlet. The gyser is open to the atmosphere, hence under no condition of use can this pressure at the surface of water be other than atmosphere.

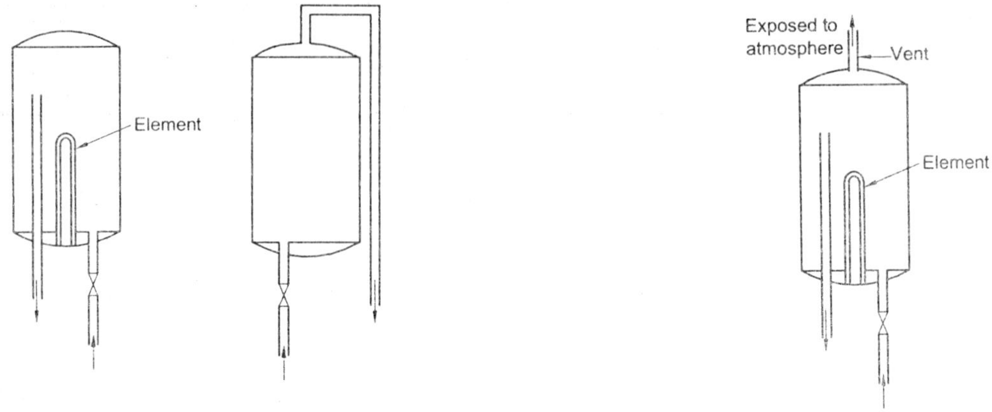

(*a*) Closed unvented open outlet type water heater. (*b*) Vented open outlet type of geysers.

Fig. 17·75.

In all the geysers the inlet pipe is provided at lower end while the supply is taken from the top. Thus when hot water is not being drawn, the supply to such a geyser (either direct or from over head tank) will be closed by closing the inlet stop cock, and hence there will be no water pressure on the geyser. When supply is open, equal amount of hot water will be out of the geyser. There will thus, be no water pressure over acting on the geyser, and hence such a geyser is called a **non-pressure type** of a geyser. Such geysers are manufactured in smaller capacities and are rarely used in modern day life, since it gives only hot water in a bucket and won't allow automatic mixing, cold and hot water. The non-pressure type of geysers though provided with a 'thermostat', does not however require any expansion pipe on vacuum breaker, as are required by the pressure type of geysers. The difference between pressure and non-pressure types of geysers is shown in Figs. above.

Table 17·43.

Rated capacity in litres	6	15	25	35	50	70	100	140	200
Recommended input in kW.	1	1	1	1·5	2	2	3	4	5

Note : Two electrical heating elements are usually provided in dual heater type water heater having two heating units. One towards the top contacting and the other near the bottom, the unit being independently controlled. The shape of the geyser is generally cylinderical.

When operating continuously under the thermostatic control a 2 kW geyser is adequate for small dwellings, requiring 90 litres of hot water storage, smaller sized geysers of 1 kW (15 to 25 litres) can also serve the purpose in small households, but there would have to some time gap between the use of hot water by one person for bath and the next person).

In all storage geysers the cold water enters at the bottom of the geyser tank while the hot water from the top is withdrawn. The withdrawn hot water is infact displaced by the equivalent cold feed entering through the inlet. This keeps the geyser always filled up with water thereby eliminating the danger of the geyser becoming empty and burning of the element.

17·8. Pumps to lifting water

Types of pumps : (1) Rotodynamic pumps and (2) Displacement pumps.

(1) **Rotodynamic pump.** It has a wheel which rotates the water in casing and imparts energy to the water. It has two types :

(*a*) Centrifugal pump and (*b*) Axial flow pumps

(2) **Displacement pump.** It works on the principle of mechanically inducing vacuum in a chamber, thereby drawing in a volume of water which is then mechanically displaced and forced out of the chamber. It has two types :

(*a*) Reciprocating pump and (*b*) Rotary type.

There are also other types of pumps such as (*i*) air lift pumps (*ii*) jet pumps and (*iii*) hydraulic rams etc.

Rotodynamic pumps. Such types of pumps have a wheel which revolves on an axis called as impeller. The shape of an impeller vanes are such that the water flows (*i*) in a direction perpendicular to the axis (radial flow), (*ii*) in a direction perpendicular to the axis as well as in the direction of parallel to the axis (mixed flow) (*iii*) In the direction of the axis (axial flow). The radial and mixed flow pumps are known as **Centrifugal pumps** while the pumps having flow in the direction of axis are known as **axial flow pumps.**

Centrifugal pumps. The centrifugal pumps may be open or closed. The open impeller pump has a hub to which the vanes are attached while close impeller has plates on each side of vanes.

The efficiency of the "open impeller centrifugal pump" is generally much less than that of a closed impeller centrifugal pump". But however since the "open impeller" is less likely to be clogged by debris etc. it is usually adopted for pumping raw water or sewage containing solid and other impurities.

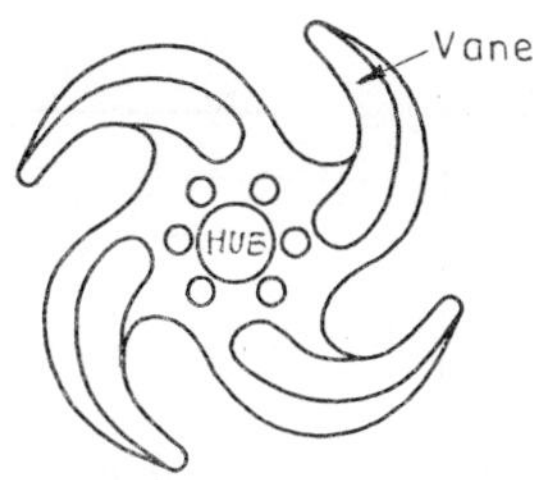

(*a*) Open impeller

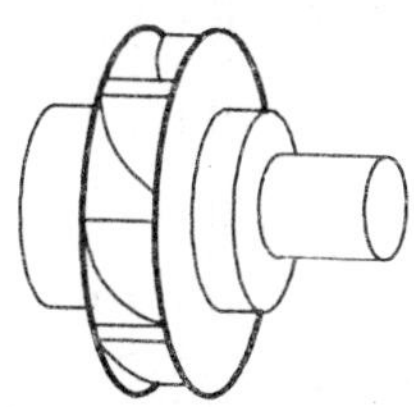

(*b*) Closed impeller

Fig. 17·76.

The casing of a radial flow centrifugal pump may either be of a volute type or of a turbine type.

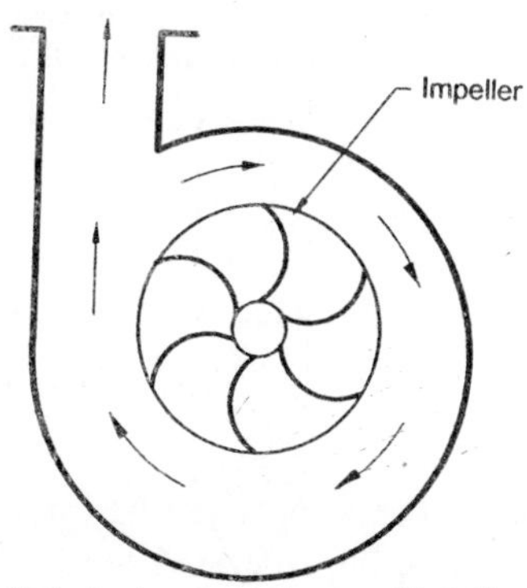

(*a*) Volute type casing radial flow centrifugal pump

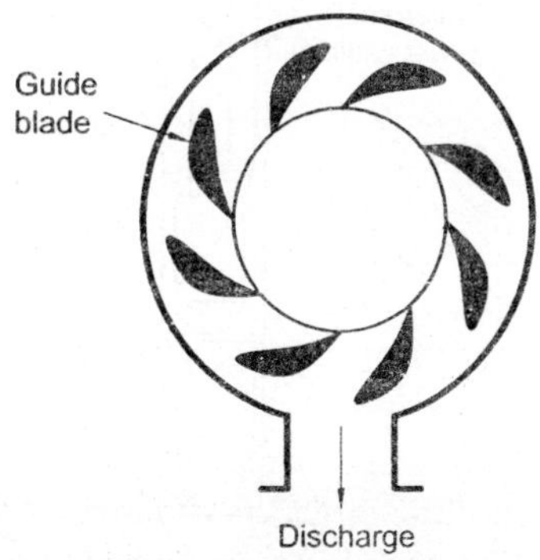

(*b*) Turbine type casing radial flow centrifugal pump

Fig. 17·77.

In volute type pump, the impeller discharges into a gradually expending spiral casing which is designed to produce an equal velocity of flow around the circumference of the impeller and to reduce the velocity of water as it enters the discharge pipe, thus creating the required pressure head, while in a turbine type or diffuser type of pump the impeller is surrounded by stationary guide vanes, which reduces the velocity of water before the water enters the casing, thus connecting the velocity head into pressure head in the casing itself. The casing surrounding the guide vanes is generally circular and concentric with the impeller. The velocity of water is thus almost completely converted into pressure head, resulting in higher efficiency then what is possible in a volute pump.

When only one impeller is used, it is known as single stage pump while when two or more impellers are arranged and placed in such a way that the discharge from one impeller enters the eye of the next impeller, it is called a double or multi stage pump. Such pumps are an used for high lifts. In case of a bore hole pump such type of deep well turbine pump is used. The impellers are installed in a vertical shaft which is suspended and rotated from the prime mover (Motor) placed at the ground surface. The pump bowls are thus kept below the well water line (spring line).

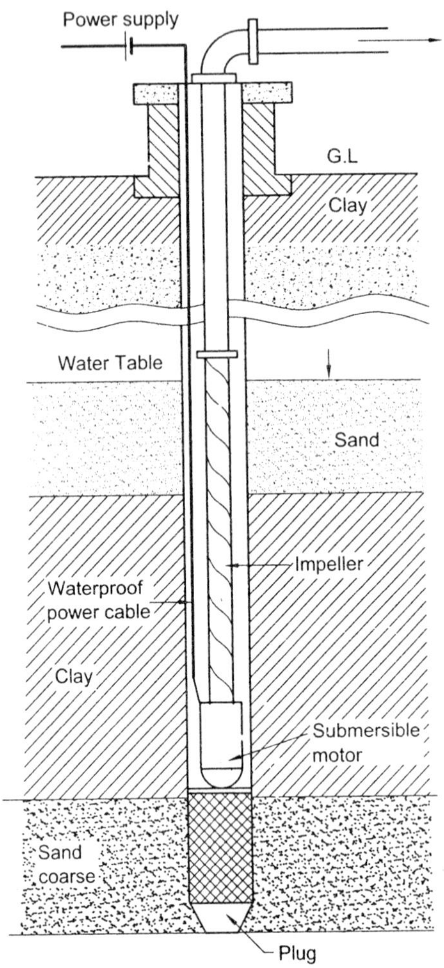

(*a*) Submersible pump

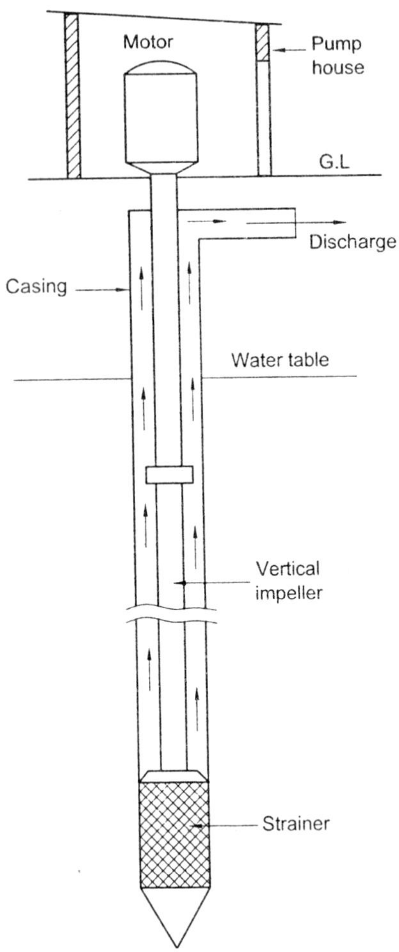

(*b*) Motor at GL

Fig. 17·78. (Turbine type bore hole pump)

Another type of deep well pump called as submersible pump (Fig. 17·78) differs from the usual deep well turbine pump in the sense that the driving motor here is placed below the pump bowels with in the well water level. Thus the driving shaft is completely eliminated and the water rises to the surface through a riser pipe on which the assembly is suspended. The elimination of the driving shaft from the ground surface to the pump, reduces the bearing friction and provides an unobstructed pipe for the delivery of water to the surface. The well water can be prevented from coming in contact with the electrical parts at the motor bearings by enclosing it in oil filled case mercury seal. Now a days the windings are allowed to remain surrounded by water which acts as coolant and bearing lubricants.

Priming of centrifugal pump. A centrifugal pump may have to be primed before it is started. The priming consists in filling the pump casing with water, so that the air trapped in the pump does not hinder its operation to reduce its efficiency.

A pump installed below the water level does not normally require priming although some air may be trapped, is to fill the pump with water from an outside source, while permitting the displaced air to escape through an exhausts valve. Certain pumps are provided with vacuum pumps to remove the air from the casing.

Displacement pumps. (1) Reciprocating pumps and (2) Rotary pumps.

Reciprocating pump. The most common type of reciprocating pump is a hand pump generally used in common houses. In such pumps. In such types of pumps a piston or a plunger reciprocates up and down by hand. The function is simple and is not required here in detail.

These pumps can be used at any depth. Where water table is within 6 m or so the cylinderical machine with valve is kept at the ground level but a foot valve at the lower end of the suction pipes is required to avoid priming. Where the water level in the dug well from which the water is to be lifted is more than 6 m below the ground level, the cylinder is taken upto the water table and the valve is filled within a range of 6 m from the water table. These type of hand pump is a single acting from which the discharge is obtained only on alternate strokes. However double acting pumps are also some times used for better discharge.

Rotary pumps. In rotary type of displacement pumps the rotary motion is used for lifting water instead of reciprocating motion. These are of (*i*) cam type and (*ii*) gear type.

Cam type rotary pump. The rotary motion is obtained by using two cams (Fig. 17·79(*a*)) or two gears (Fig. 17·79(*b*)) which mesh together and rotate in opposite directions. The rotating elements fit the casing closely. The water through the suction pipe is trapped between the cams (or the teeth of gears) and the casing. It is then forced out through the discharge pipe as the cams or the gears rotate. A definite quantity of water depending on the size and shape of the gears or cams is thus raised with each revolution.

These pumps do not need any priming and hence these are used in place of the large centrifugal pumps.

Air lift pumps. Air lift pumps are generally used for pumping water from deep wells for lifts about 60-80 metres. A typical arrangement of an air lift pump is shown in Fig. 17·80. In such a pump compressed air is forced into the well though a small air pipe and is released through a diffuser into the eduction pipe at the bottom of the well as shown. The air rises in small bubbles in the eduction pipes thus forming a mixture of air and water. This resulting mixture of air and water inside the eduction pipe is lighter than water outside the pipe and hence is forced upward by hydrostatic pressure, finally coming out through the outlet at the top. A separator is often placed at the outlet. So as to remove air from water. The reclaimed air is generally cooler than the atmospheric air and can be compressed again more cheaply. Air lift can be used for lifting water upto 150 metres. Their efficiency is low and is of the order of 25 to 50 percent. The effectiveness of an air lift pump is generally measured by a factor called percentage submergence.

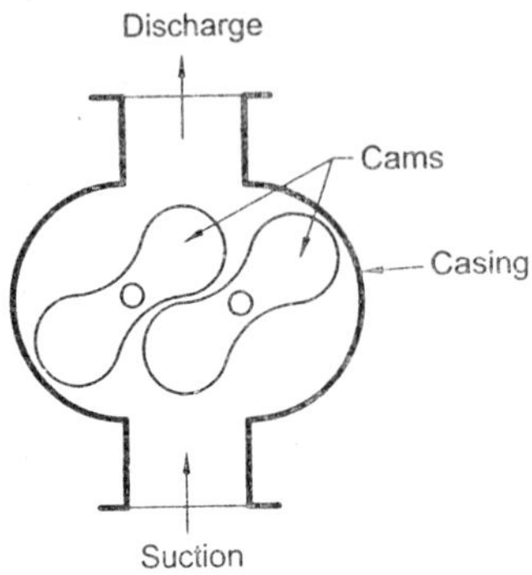

(a) Cam type

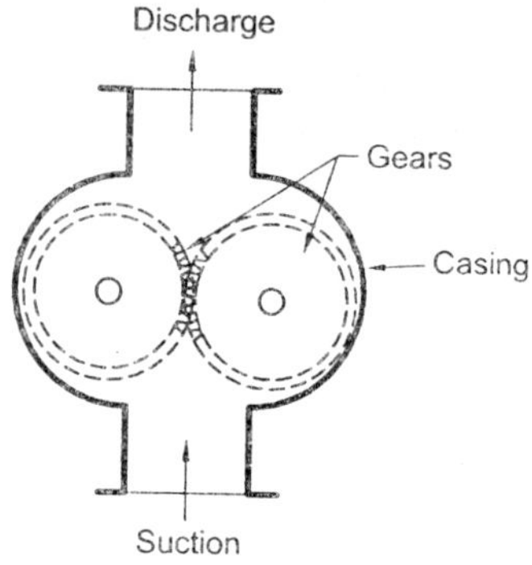

(b) Gear type

Fig. 17·79. Rotary pumps.

Percentage submergence

$$= \frac{\text{Depth of submergence}(D_s) \times 100}{\text{Depth of submergence}(D_s) + \text{effective lift of pump}(H_c)}$$

$$= \frac{D_s \times 100}{D_s + H_c} (D_s + H_c = \text{effective length of eduction pipe})$$

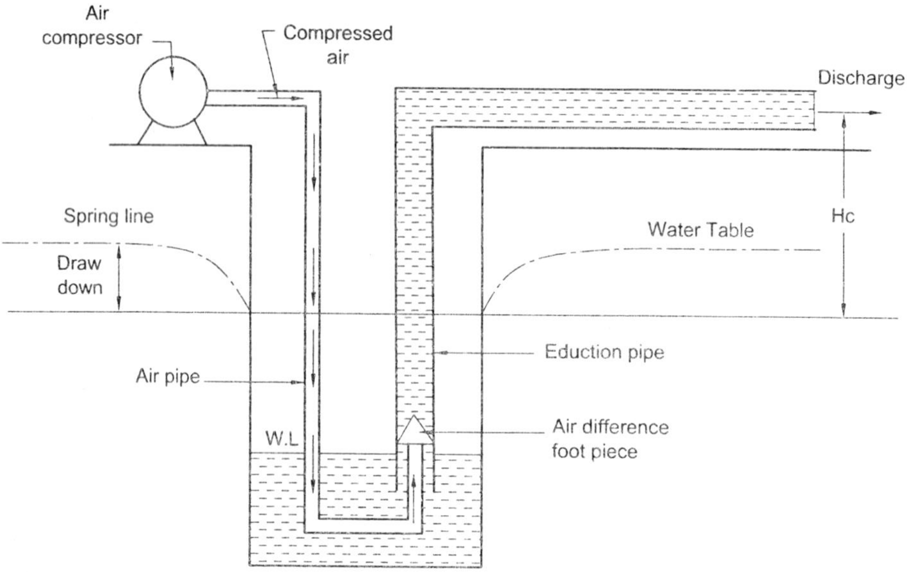

Fig. 17·80. Air lift pump.

Head, Power and efficiency of Pumps

(i) Suction lift (H_s) ; Delivery head (H_d); All the losses (H_L)

$$H = H_s + H_d + H_L$$

The work done by the pump in lifting Q cumecs of water against head H.

$$H = \gamma_w QH \text{ kN m/s } (i.e. \text{ Joules or Watts})$$

where γ_w = unit weight of water in kN/m^3 *i.e.* 9·81 kN/m^3

Q = discharge to be pumped in m^3/sec.

The water H.P. of the pump is as

$$W.H.P. = \frac{\gamma_w QH}{0{\cdot}735} (\because 1\,H.P. = 735 \text{ Watts} = 0{\cdot}735 \text{ kN})$$

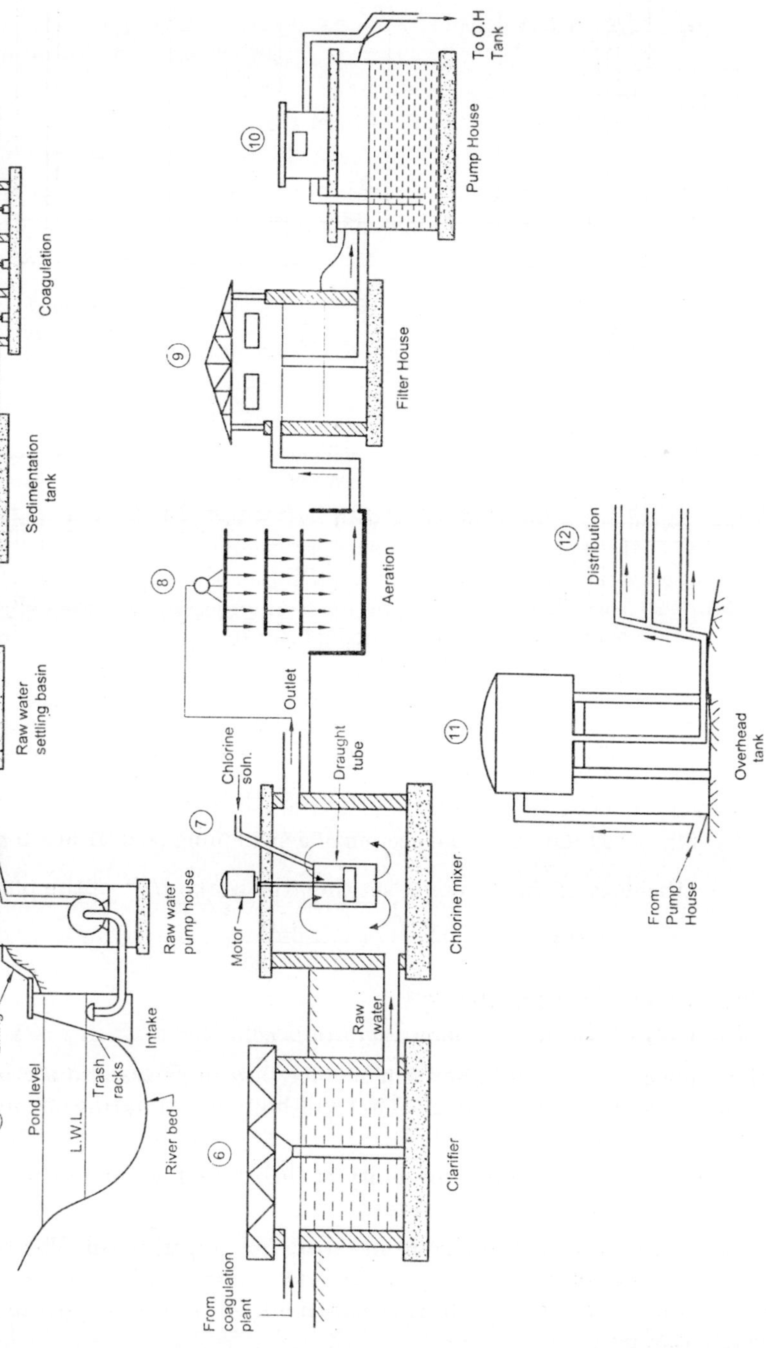

Flow Chart of a Water Supply Plant

Fig. 17·81. Flow of supply system of a town.

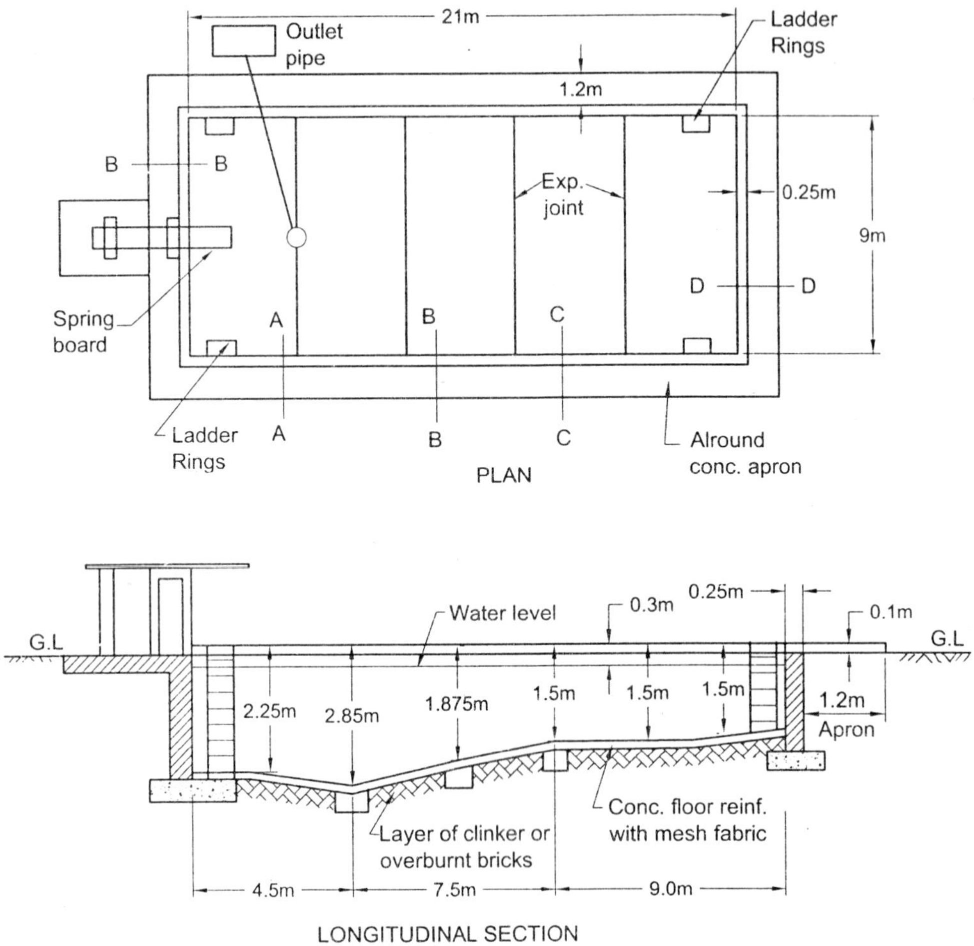

Fig. 17·82. Longitudinal section of a swimming pool 21 m × 9 m

If η is the efficiency of the pumping set then the brake *H.P.* of the pump is

$$B.H.P. = \frac{WHP}{\eta} = \frac{\gamma_w QH}{\eta \times 0.735}$$

17·9. Planning of water supply project

(1) **Collection of data.** The following data is collected :

(*i*) Hydrological data available from surface flow in rivers and streams in vicinity and water rainfall of the area and its pondage. This will help in estimating the availability of water on surface flow sources.

(*ii*) Geology of the area and availability of the ground water in the area. It will help in assessing the availability of the ground water.

(*iii*) **Data of the water requirements and the population.** The requirements of the inhabitants and their way of living. The position and requirement for water of the industries in the area. The requirements of the public institutions for water. It will help to estimate the quantum of water required.

(*iv*) **The position of existing water supply systems and their consumption of water.** It will help in estimating the extra requirement for water on the proposed project.

(*v*) **The data of sanitary conditions and possible sources of pollution.** It will help in estimating the possible pollution or contamination of the water from such sources and which will help in assessing the remedial measures.

(*vi*) **The topography of the area.** It will help in fixing the suitable intake positions and the distribution system afterwards.

(*vii*) The public opinion and their requirements.

(*viii*) Legal position of land and ownerships of different organisations.

(*ix*) Future needs and aspects of development.

(*x*) The analysis of the water available (physical, chemical and biological) which will help to design the treatment required for the water.

(*xi*) The power required to function the scheme after construction and the availability of the power and machinery.

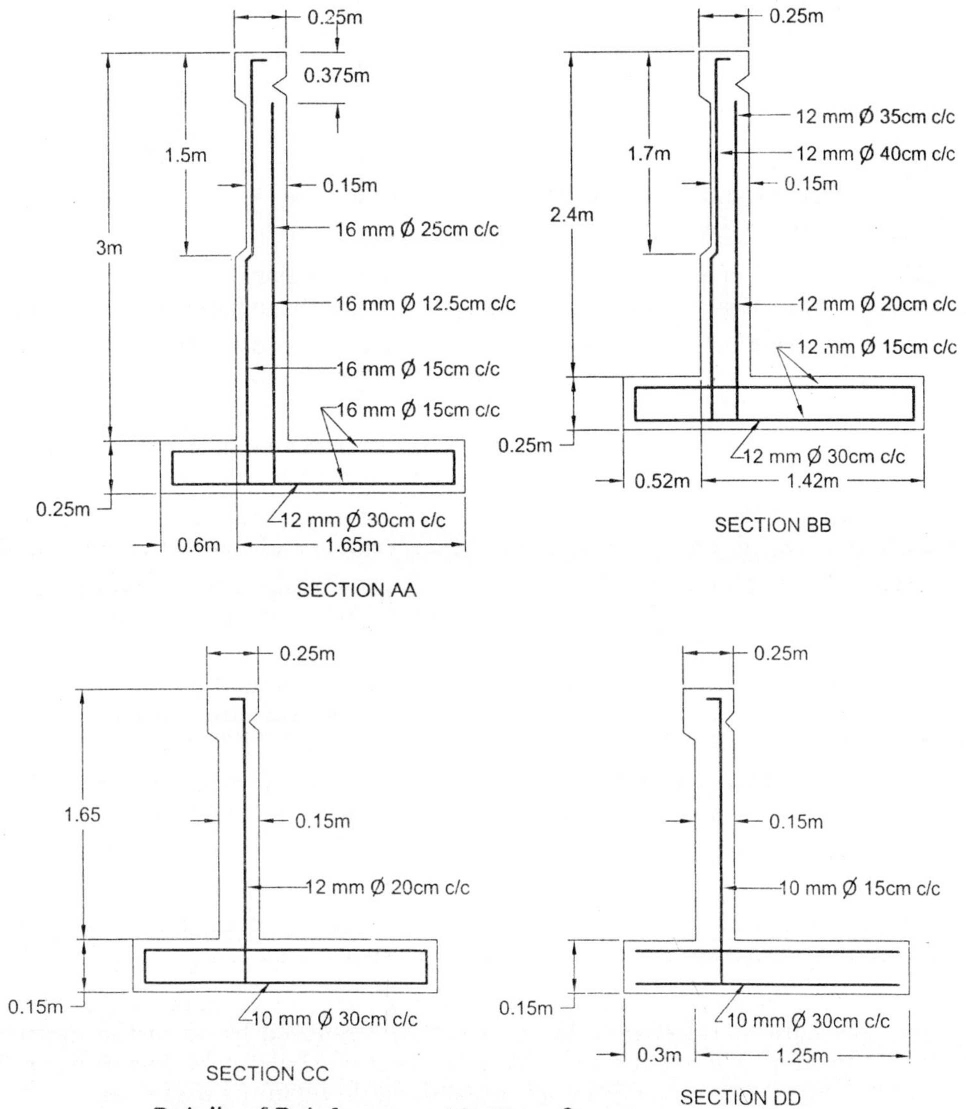

Details of Reinforcement in Floor & Walls

Fig. 17·83. Typical draining of a swimming pool.

Project estimates. After the preliminary investigations, the project estimate of cost is prepared and sent to the competent authority for seeking administrative approval and for the allotment of funds. It will include, the cost of materials, cost of land to be acquired for the project, cost of the machinery and its installations, quarters for the staff and the cost involved for the availability of the power etc.

Table 17·44. Tentative costs of components of water supply schemes

Sl. No.	*Component item*	*Cost of item as percentage of the total*
1.	Pumping stations	18
2.	Reservoirs	6
3.	Treatment plant	10
4.	Supply reserve stocks	9
5.	Distribution system	50
6.	Buildings for housing operational staff etc.	2
7.	Meters and other contingencies	5
	Total	100%

The project report should consist the following points

(1) Necessity of the scheme with reasons and urgency.

(2) **General details of the area.** It must be mentioned regarding topography and the geological conditions of the area. Availability of the surface and sub-surface water available.

(3) **Water requirements. The population of the area and their requirements**— Position of the industries and their requirements. Position and requirements of the public institutions such as schools and hospitals etc.

(4) **Purification of water needed.** The analysis of the available water for the scheme and its physical, chemical and biological analysis should be incorporated in the project.

(5) **Pumping requirements.** The types and horse power of pumps required. The stages and the places where required. The brand by units their operation and operational staff needed.

(6) **Distribution system.** The location and necessity of reservoirs etc. overhead tanks materials for construction. Storage capacity dimensions and sizes of pipes etc. Details of distribution network, their layouts etc.

(7) **Provisions for fire fighting.** General locations of hydrants, their numbers per km length of pipe, their types, the pressure available at the hydrant, the size and numbers of fire scheme to be used etc.

Cost and expenditure. The 1st cost of installing various units of the water works ; the methods of raising funds ; the revenue to be reserved and rates of water charges etc.

Expenditure in maintenance

Engineering economy of the project. Cost benefits ratio consideration.

Summary and conclusions. Review of the whole scheme in brief with reference to overall expected performance and achievements in relation to the aims and goals etc.

A road map of the town should be enclosed showing positions of intakes, lifting pumps, elevated towers, hydrants and distribution pipes etc. The reduced levels of the important controlling points should also be mentioned in order to indicate the gravity flow in pipes. The position of stores for materials and machines etc. are also be shown in the road map.

18

Sewage

18·1. Collection of sewage

Systems of disposal of human waste. There are two ways of disposal of human waste (*i*) Conservancy system (*ii*) Water carriage system.

(*i*) **Conservancy system.** In this system the human waste called as excreta, night-soil etc. and other wash products of society is collected, carried and disposed of manually or on wheel barrows to the disposal points by sweepers. This process is inhygienic as well as inharmonic.

(*ii*) **Water-carried sewerage system.** In this system sewage is carried through underground pipes known as sewers by water. Though this system is more hygienic yet very expensive. This modern system not only helps in removing the domestic, and industrial waste water with human excreta, but also helps in removing storm water drainage. Sewers are the conduits which carry the sweage or human waste to the disposal point.

Estimation of sewage discharge. The quantity of sewage (domestic + industrial) that is likely to enter the municipal sewers under design, should be equal to the quantity of water supplied to the controlling area from the water works. The following additions and subtractions are also required as explained below.

(*i*) Additions due to unaccounted water resources such as private wells and tubewells. Some private industries have their own water supply system which ultimately reaches into the sewers.

(*ii*) **Infiltration water.** In underground water supply system below the water table some underground water enters into the sewers due to faulty pipe lines. If the sewer line is above the water table, the rain water may also reach in the sewer from faults.

(*iii*) Subtraction due to water losses from the pipe lines through leakages.

(*iv*) Water which does not reach in the sewers and is disposed off by soak pits or other sources is spreaded on waste lands.

Design of Sewers

The quantity of sewage that is likely to pass through a sewer (Q') can be easily computed by multiplying per capita production sewage q' by the expected population at the end of the design period. The per capita sewage which is produced (q) in a community, can also be taken as 75 to 80 per cent of the per capita water supplied to the public (q). It is also kept in mind that the future increase in population may also increase per capita water estimate and consequently may increase per capita sewage disposal. This increase as an estimate can be assumed as 5% annually. Waste water from buildings and public complexes can be taken as 0·03 m^3/min % persons. For water consumption per head as 135 litres/day, 70 to 90% of water supplied can be taken as waste water dwellings with no water supply 25 to 45 litres/day/head can be taken.

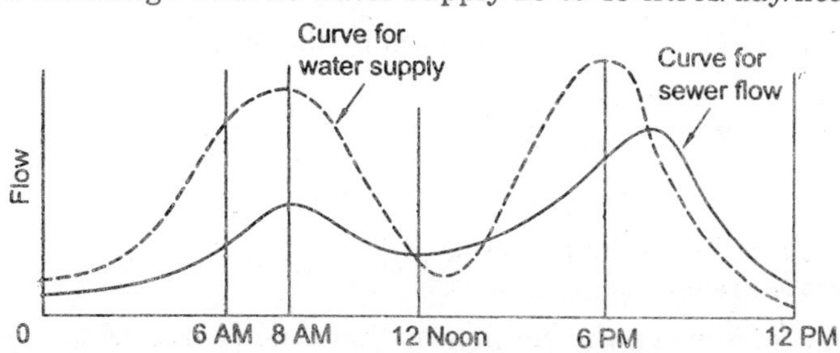

Fig. 18·1. Hourly flow of water supply and sewage.

Table. 18·1. Design periods for different components of a sewage scheme

S. No.	*Type and name of the component structure*	*Special characteristics and reasons for the selected design period*	*Design period in years*
(1)	(2)	(3)	(4)
1.	Lateral sewers, less than 15 cm in dia.	Requirements may change faster in limited area	Full development
2.	Branches, mains and trunk sewers	Difficult and costly to enlarge	40-50
3.	Treatment units	Growth and interest rates being high to moderate	15-20
4.	Pumping plant	The additional pumps can be installed in future, very easily and also within a short notice	5-10

Table. 18·2. Variation in per capita water demand and sewers production with population

Sl. No.	*Population*	*Per capita water demand in litres per day per person*	*Per capita sewerage production in litres / day / capita*
(1)	(2)	(3)	(4)
1.	Less than 20,000	110	90
2.	20,000-50,000	110-150	90-120
3.	50,000-2 lakhs	150-180	120-150
4.	2 lakhs-5 lakhs	180-210	150-170
5.	5 lakhs-10 lakhs	210-240	170-190
6.	Over 10 lakhs	240-270	190-200

Table. 18·3. Hourly variation in sewage flow

Sl. No.	*Types of sewer*	*Ratio of Maximum flow to enrage*
1.	Trunk mains above 1·25 m dia.	1·5
2.	Mains upto 1 m dia.	2·0
3.	Branches upto 0·5 m dia.	3·0
4.	Laterals and small sewers upto 0·25 m in dia.	4·0

The sizes of the sewers can then be designed for carrying the computed maximum hourly flows with sewers running 3/4th fall.

Peak sewage flow ($Q_{max.}$) can be computed by the formula

$$Q_{max} = \frac{18 + \sqrt{P}}{4 + \sqrt{P}} Q_{av}$$

where P = population in thousands.

Minimum daily flow = 2/3 × average daily
(for moderate areas)

In the design of sewers the minimum flow knowledge is also must, as on the low discharges the velocity reduces, causing silting in the sewer. Thus minimum flow in laterals may be lesser than 25% of the average while in mains it may be 50-70 per cent of the average.

Minimum hourly flow = 1/2 minimum daily flow = 1/3 average daily.

Peak drainage discharge. The following rational formula is given by knuckling of America for drains.

$$Q_P = \left(\frac{1}{36}\right) K\, p_c . A$$

where Q_P = Peak rate of run off in cumecs

K = Coefficient of run off.

A = The catchment area contributing to run off at the considered point in hectares.

P_c = Critical rainfall intensity of the design frequency *i.e.*, the rainfall intensity during the critical rainfall duration equal to the time of concentration in cm/hr.

The coefficient of runoff (*K*). It is actually the rate of precipitation to run off and can be said as impervious factor. The value of *K* increases as the imperviousness of the area increases thus tending to make $K = 1$ for perfect impervious area. It is generally taken 0·9 for paved areas to 0·15 for lawns and gardens.

The following table gives the value of *K* for different surfaces.

Table. 18·4. Values of run off coefficient (*K*) for various surfaces

Sl. No.	*Type of surface*	*Value of K*
1.	Water light roof surfaces	0·70-0·95
2.	Asphalt pavement in good order	0·85-0·90
3.	Stone, brick, wood block pavement with cement joints	0·75-0·85
4.	Same as above with uncemented joints	0·50-0·70
5.	Water bond macadam roads	0·25-0·60
6.	Gravel roads and walls	0·15-0·30
7.	Unpaved sheets and vacant lands	0·10-0·30
8.	Parks, lawns, gardens, meadows etc.	0·05-0·25
9.	Wooded lands	0·01-0·20

Table. 18·5. Values of run off coefficient (*K*) for different types of localities

Sl. No.	*Type of locality*	*Average app. population density in persons / hectare*	*Value of (K)*
1.	Extreme suburban areas with 20 to 40% parking and widely detached houses	75-125	0·35
2.	Suburban areas with widelydetachable houses	125-150	0·45-0·55
3.	Areas with 50% attached houses and 50% detached houses	375-500	0·65
4.	Areas closely built up	500-625	0·75
5.	Business areas	more than 625	0·85

The time of concentration for a given storm is divided in two parts :

(*i*) The inlet time or overland flow time is time of equilibrium say T_1

$$T_1 = \left(0{\cdot}885 \frac{L}{H}\right)^{0{\cdot}385}$$

where T_1 = Inlet time in hours

L = Length or overland flow in K metres from the critical point to the mouth of the drain.

H = Total fall of level from the critical point to the mouth of the drain in metres.

L and H can be found from survey plan of the area.

(*ii*) **Channel flow.** or gutter flow time say T_F. It is the time taken by water to flow in the drain channel from the mouth to the considered point.

$$T_f = \frac{\text{Length of the drain}}{\text{Velocity of the drain}}$$

The arial distribution factor or the dispersion factor. The intensity of rainfall in a catchment varies from point to point. The average intensity of rainfall over the catchment as a whole goes on decreasing compared to the point intensity recorded at a particular rain gauge station. Therefore the area distribution factor (dispersion factor) is always applied to the point rainfall for working out the design rainfall intensity.

The following formulae are used for calculating peak discharge for a drain which depends on imperviousness, slope of the land at area of the rain fall.

(1) **Ryve's formula :** $Q_P = C_1 M^{2/3}$

where C_1 varies from 6·8 to 10·1 for south India.

M is the catchment area in sq. km

Q_P = Peak discharge in cumecs.

Values of C_1 in Ryves formula :

Area with in 24 km from the coast	6·8
Areas with in 24 km to 16 km from the coast	8·8
Limited areas near hills	10·1

(2) **Dicken's formula :** $Q_P = CM^3/4$

where Q_P = peak discharge in cumecs

M = catchment area in sq. km.

C = a constant depending upon all the factors which affect the runoff

The value of C depends on nature of catchment and intensity of rainfall. An average value of 11·5 is generally used. For hilly regions it should be increased. The greater will be the rainfall the greater will be the value of C.

Note : The symbol for area used as A when catchment is expressed in hectares and M when catchment is expressed in sq. km.

(3) **Inglis formula :** $Q_P = \dfrac{123\,M}{1\,M + 10{\cdot}4} = 123\sqrt{M}$

Values of denotations are the same as above.

(4) **Nawab Jung Bahadur formula :** $Q_P = C_2 M^{\left[0{\cdot}93 - \left(\frac{1}{14}\right)\log M^1\right]}$

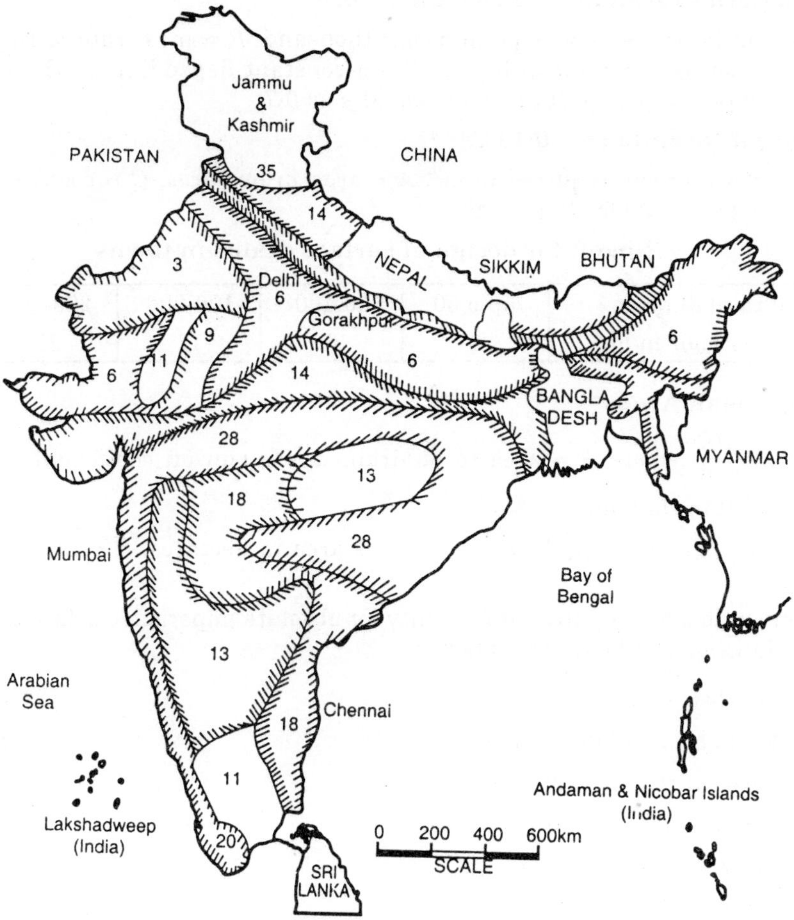

Value of C in Dicken's formula
(Catchment in sq. k.m.)
Fig. 18·2.

The values of C_2 varies 48 to 60. M is the catchment area in acres.

(5) **Burkli Ziegler formula :** $Q_P = \left(\frac{1}{455}\right) K^1 \, PA \sqrt{\frac{S_0}{A}}$. It is the oldest formula

where Q_P = Peak run off in curves

K^1 = Run off coefficient depending on the permeability of the surface having average value of 0·7.

P = The maximum rainfall intensity over the entire area and is usually taken as 2·5 to 7·5 cm/hr.

A = Drainage area in hectares

S_0 = The slope of the ground surface in metres per thousand metres.

(6) **Dredge or Burge's formula :** $Q_P = 19{\cdot}6 \, \frac{M}{L^{2/3}}$

where L is the length of drainage basin in k.m.

(7) **MaMath's formula :** $Q = 23 \cdot 5$ CRA $(S/A)^{1/5}$

where A = area in hectares, S = slope in m per thousand, R = max. rate of rainfall in cm/hour over the whole area, Q = run off in lit/sec, C = a constant depending on the nature of ground with respect to imperviousness. Its value is usually as 0·7.

(8) **Talbot formula :** $a = 0 \cdot 18\ CA^{3/4}$,

where a = sec. of waterway required in m^2, A = area in hectares, C = coefficient varying from 1·0 for mountainous to 0·20 for flat areas.

Run off for design of surface drains in towns

Annual rainfall in cm	upto 50	50-100	100-200	200-300	above 300
Run off per hour in mm	3	6	12	20	25

Urban Small Areas

(*i*) $Q = \dfrac{AIR}{360}$ where A = area to be drained, I = run off coefficient for the area, R = intensity of rainfall in cm/hour.

(*ii*) $Q = 28\ AIR$ where Q is litres/sec, A is area in hectares, R = intensity of rainfall in cm/hour.

The imperviousness coefficient I is unity for absolute imperious surface to zero to absolute pervious one. Its value can be taken as below :

Nature of area	*Value of I*
1. Most density built up areas	0·7 to 0·9
2. Adjacent to well builtup areas	0·5 to 0·7
3. Residential areas with detached houses	0·25 to 0·5
4. Areas with few buildings	0·10 to 0·25
Kuichling's run off coefficients	
1. Water tight roof surface	0·70 to 0·95
2. Asphalt pavements in good order	0·85 to 0·90
3. Stone, brick, wood block pavements with cement joints	0·75 to 0·85
4. Stone, brick, wood block pavements with uncement joints	0·50 to 0·70
5. Macadam roads	0·25 to 0·60
6. Gravel road and walks	0·15 to 0·30
7. Unpaved streets, vacant land	0·10 to 0·30
8. Parks, lawns, gardens and meadows	0·05 to 0·25
9. Wooded land	0·10 to 0·20
Frushling's coefficients	*Value of I*
1. Extreme sub-urban areas with 20 to 40% parking and detached houses	0·35
2. Sub urban areas, with widely detached houses	0·45 to 0·55
3. Areas with 50% attached houses and 58% detached houses	0·65
4. Areas closely built up	0·75
5. Business areas	0·85

(1) **Intensity of Rainfall**

(*i*) $R = \dfrac{760}{t+10}$ for storms having duration between 5 to 20 minutes.

(*ii*) $R = \dfrac{1020}{t+20}$ for storms having duration between 20 and 100 minutes.

where R = intensity of rainfall in mm/hour, t = duration of storm in minutes.

Time of concentration for an area is the time which passes before rain water falling on the remotest point of the area reaches the sewer or the drain.

Design of sewers and drain sections. The drainage of rain water and the disposal of sewage is designed in one combined system and sometimes both are designed and laid separately called as separate sewerage system. The sewers are generally circular or other types of closed sections, while the S.W. drains are rectangular or trapezoidal in sections. Both are provided with a slope which may have a itself cleansing velocity. The design of the sewers (*i.e.* the cross sections and slopes) is almost the same as used in water supply pipes. The main differences are :

(*i*) The water supply pipes carry clean water, while the sewers carry polluted water, the heavy particles of which settle down in the bed of the sewer when the velocity goes down than that of the self cleansing velocity. The polluted water may corrode the sewer material.

(*ii*) The water supply pipes run full with pressure therefore they can be passed on undulating grounds while the sewer pipes run part filled on gravity flow hence can not run on undulating ground but runs on a proper slope upto the point of disposal from where the water is lifted if required by pumps.

Free board in sewers and S.W. drains. As the sewers do not run full, hence an adequate free board must be given above water surface to the soffit of pipe, so that, any increase in the discharge may be adjusted. If the section is inadequate for the discharge and if the discharge increases the sewer will run full and it will then under pressure with a higher velocity than cleansing velocity which may damage and upset the sewer. In case of S.W. drains the section may be designed as an open channel and if discharge increases it can flow over causing no significant loss or damage.

18·6. Values of free board to be adopted for the design of S.W. drains

Peak discharge of the drain in cumecs	*Free board required in metres*
Below 0·3	0·3
0·3 to 1·0	0·4
1·0 to 5	0·5
5 to 10	0·6
10 to 30	0·75
30 to 150	0·90
Over 150	1·0

The section of sewers and S.W. drains are designed as an open channel which is dealt in the "Irrigation" section of this book. A formula as William Hazen's Formula is given as

$$V = 0{\cdot}85\, C_h\, r^{0{\cdot}63} . S^{0{\cdot}54} \qquad \text{All variables are the same.}$$

Table 18·7. The values of C_h for William-Hazen's formula

Sl. No	*Type of pipe material*	*Values of Cu for*	
		New pipes	*Design purposes*
1.	Concrete and R.C.C. pipes	140	110
2.	Cast iron pipes	130	100
3.	Galvanized iron pipes	120	100
4.	Steel pipes with welded joints	140	100
5.	Steel pipe with rivetted joints	110	95
6.	Steel pipes with welded joints lined with cement or bituminous enamel	140	110
7.	Asbestos cement pipes	150	120
8.	Plastic pipes	150	120

Table 18·8. Manning's or Kutter's Rugosity coefficients (*N*)

Sl. No.	*Pipe material*	*Values of n at full depth*	
		Good interior surface	*Fair interior surface*
(1)	(2)	(3)	(4)
1.	Salt glased stoneware pipes	0·12	0·014
2.	Cement concrete pipes	0·013	0·015
3.	Cast iron pipes	0·012	0·013
4.	Brick unglazed sewer and drains	0·013	0·015
5.	Asbestos cement	0·001	0·012
6.	Plastic smooth pipes	0·011	0·011

Table. 18·9 (*a*) Sewer gradient required to generate self cleansing velocities running full in different pipes

Dia. of sewer (mm)	*Gradient 1 in for developing velocity of*		
	0·75 m/sec	*0·90 m/sec*	*1·05 m/sec*
100	90	75	60
150	150	105	78
225	265	180	135
300	385	270	195
375	520	355	265
450	660	460	340
525	820	570	415
600	970	680	500
675	1,100	790	580
750	1,300	910	670
900	1,700	1,200	850
1,950	2,100	1,450	1,050
1,200	2,500	1,700	1,250

Table 18·9 (*b*) Hydraulic mean depth for circular and oval shaped sewers

Types of pipe	*1/3 full*		*1/2 full*		*2/3 full*		*Full*		*Remarks*
	R	*A*	*R*	*A*	*R*	*A*	*R*	*A*	
Circular	0·186 D	0·229 D^2	0·25D	0·393 D^2	0·241 D	0·556 D^2	0·25 D	0·785 D^2	R = hyd. mean depth
Oval	0·206 D	0·285 D^2	0·268 D	0·509 D^2	0·316 D	0·756 D^2	0·299 D^2	1·149 D^2	A = Area, D = dia.

Table 18·9 (*c*) General gradients in branch drains

Diameter (mm)	*Gradient*	*Vel., m/sec.*	*Discharge, m³/min*
100	1 in 80	0·58	0·14
150	1 in 100	0·61	0·33
230	1 in 120	0·79	0·97

Table 18·9 (*d*) Building drains following half full

Diameter, mm	*Gradient*	*Discharge in m³/min*
100	1 in 35	0·18
150	1 in 65	0·42
230	1 in 120	0·93
300	1 in 200	1·66

Table 18·9 (*e*) Cast iron pipes with a velocity of 2·4 m/sec

Diameter (mm)	*Gradient*	*Discharge in m³/min*
100	1 in 3·5	0·59
150	1 in 7·3	1·32
230	1 in 13·8	2·98
300	1 in 20·5	5·3

Table 18·9 (*f*) Pipe sizes for different drainage system

Drainage pipes	minimum 100 m
Soil pipes	minimum 100 m
Waste pipes	minimum 32 to 50 m

Table 18·9 (*g*) Size of Gutters for rain water

Type	*Roof area (m²)*	*Gutter size (mm)*	*Size of down lake pipe (mm)*
Half round	2, 73, 450	100, 110, 100	60, 60, 70
Moulded	50, 90, 144	100 × 75	75, 75, 100
		125 × 100	
		150 × 125	
Ogee	2, 33, 240	100, 110, 150	60, 60, 60

Note : (1) For normal rainfall of 7·5 cm/hr in slope of 1 : 100 is given in roofs.

(2) Down take pipe may be PVC, APWCT.

Shield's expression for self cleansing velocity

$$V_s = C\sqrt{Kd'(G-1)}$$

where C = Chezy's constant which can be equal to $\sqrt{\frac{8g}{d'}}$

d' = dia. of the grain of suspended particles.

The actual value of K for different materials can be determined only by experiments. However the usual value of K for relatively clean in organic and organic materials present in sewage are 0·04 and 0·06 respectively.

Table. 18·10. N.B.O. (National Building Organisation) recommendation for small sewers

Dia. of sewer in mm	*Gradient required to generate self cleansing velocity*	*Velocity generated in the sewer when running half full for which depth, in small Sewers is usually designed*
100	1 in 60	0·58 m/sec
150	1 in 100	0·61 m/sec
225	1 in 120	0·79 m/sec

The variation in value of N at lower depths are considered.

Table. 18·11. Non-scouring limiting velocities in sewers and drains

Sl. No.	*Sewer material*	*Limiting velocity*	*Remarks*
1.	Vitrified tiles and glazed bricks	4·5-5·5 m/sec	Vitrified tiles and glazed bricks are much more resistant to wear as compared to ordinary bricks or concrete. Therefore ordinary brick or concrete. Sewers are some times coated with vitrified tiles lining or glazed bricks.
2.	Cast iron sewers	3·5-4·5 m/sec	
3.	Stone ware sewers	3·0-4·0 m/sec	
4.	Cement concrete sewers	2·5-3·0 m/sec	
5.	Ordinary brick lined sewers	1·5-2·5 m/sec	
6.	Earthen channels	0·6-1·2 m/sec	

Effect of flow variation on velocity in a sewer. The discharge in a sewer varies time to time due to this variation, the depth of water and hence the hydraulic mean depth varies. The flow velocity which is directly depends on $(\text{N.M.D.})^{2/3}$ gets affected time to time. When the flow reduces and the sewer becomes less than half full, it is necessary to check the sewer for maintaining a minimum velocity of about 0·45 m/sec at the time of minimum (hourly) flow (assumed about 1/3rd of average daily flow). The designer should also ensure that a velocity of about 0·9 m/sec is developed at least at the time of maximum flow and preferably during the average flow periods also. It should also be seen to see that at the time of maximum flow, the velocity generated does not exceed the scouring value given in table 18·11. However in flat areas like indo-gangtic planes of North India sewers are designed to develop self cleansing velocity of about 0·9 m/sec at maximum discharge only. This permits flatter of gradients avoiding deep excavations.

If the available ground slope is neither too steep nor too flat. The condition of developing 0·9 m/sec velocity at average flow may be practically possible and economical. In hilly areas of steep slopes, the sewers may be designed to develop such velocities of 0·9 m/sec even at minimum discharge and they may be checked for limiting non scouring velocities at maximum discharge.

Hydraulic characteristics of circular sewers. The circular sections are commonly used in sewers, however sometimes of egg shape or horse shoe shape sewers are also constructed when the circular sewer is running full.

Its hydraulic mean depth $= \dfrac{\pi r^2}{2\pi r} = \dfrac{r}{2} = \dfrac{D}{4}$

Hydraulic mean depth of a circular sewer when running partially full.

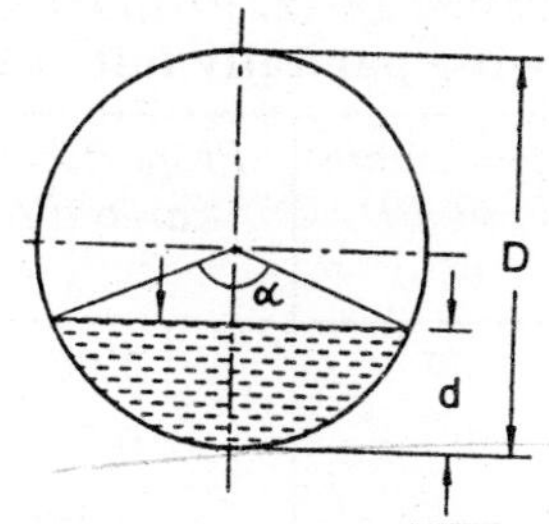

Fig. 18·3. Partially filled circular section.

The depth of partial flow $= d = \left(\dfrac{D}{2} - \dfrac{D}{2}\cos\dfrac{\alpha}{2}\right)$

where α is the angle at centre with the water edges in degrees (See Fig. 18·3)

Proportional depth $= \dfrac{d}{D} = \dfrac{1}{2}\left(1 - \cos\dfrac{\alpha}{2}\right)$

Area of water section for partial flow = a (say)

Then $a = \dfrac{\pi D^2}{4} \cdot \dfrac{\alpha^\circ}{360^\circ} - \dfrac{D}{2}\cos\dfrac{\alpha}{2} \cdot \dfrac{D}{2}\sin\dfrac{\alpha}{2}$

$= \dfrac{\pi D^2}{4}\left[\dfrac{\alpha^\circ}{360^\circ} - \dfrac{\sin\alpha}{2\pi}\right]$ being $\sin\alpha = 2\sin\dfrac{\alpha}{2}\cos\dfrac{\alpha}{2}$

Proportional area $= \dfrac{a}{A} = \left[\dfrac{\alpha}{360} - \dfrac{\sin\alpha}{2\pi}\right]$

Wetted perimeter for partial flow $= P = \pi D . \dfrac{\alpha}{360}$

Proportional perimeter $= \dfrac{D}{P} = \dfrac{\alpha}{360^\circ}$

Hydraulic mean depth (H.M.D) while running part full $= r = \dfrac{a}{P} = \dfrac{D}{4}\left[1 - \dfrac{360^\circ \sin\alpha}{2\pi\alpha}\right]$

Proportional H.M.D. $= \dfrac{r}{R} = \left[1 - \dfrac{360^\circ \sin\alpha}{2\pi\alpha}\right]$

Velocity of flow is given by Mannings formula as V = velocity at partial flow.

$$= \frac{1}{n} r^{2/3}\sqrt{S_0}$$

(Bed slope $S = S_0$ remaining constant whether pipe run full or partial)

∴ Proportional velocity $= \dfrac{v}{V} = \dfrac{N}{n} \dfrac{r^{2/3}}{R^{2/3}}$

(assuming that roughness coefficient does not vary with depth, we have $n = N$)

Proportionate velocity $= \dfrac{v}{V} = \dfrac{r^{2/3}}{R^{2/3}} = \left[1 - \dfrac{360^\circ \sin\alpha}{2\pi\alpha}\right]$

Since discharge is given by av therefore discharge when pipe is running partial

$$= q = av$$

Discharge when pipe is running full = $Q.AV$

Proportionate discharge $= \dfrac{q}{Q} = \dfrac{av}{AV} = \dfrac{a}{A}\cdot\dfrac{v}{V} = \left[\dfrac{\alpha}{360^\circ} - \dfrac{\sin\alpha}{2\pi}\right]\left[1 - \dfrac{360^\circ \sin\alpha}{2\pi\alpha}\right]^{2/3}$

In all above divided equation except α, everything is constant and hence by giving different values to α, all the six proportionate elements can be calculated.

By taking proportionate depth d/D as reference, values of other elements can be found out from the ready made computed values shown in the table below.

Table. 18·12. Proportionate values of Hydraulic elements for circular sewers when flowing partially full (without being corrected for variations of roughness with depth)

Proportionate Depth d/D	*Proportionate area a/A*	*Proportionate wetted perimeter p/P*	*Proportionate H.M.D. r/R*	*Proportionate velocity v/V*	*Proportionate discharged q/Q*
1·00	1·00	1·00	1·00	1·00	1·00
0·9	0·949	0·857	1·192	1·124	1·066
0·80	0·858	0·705	1·217	1·140	0·988
0·70	0·748	0·631	1·185	1·120	0·838
0·60	0·626	0·564	1·110	1·072	0·671
0·50	0·500	0·500	1·000	1·000	0·500
0·40	0·373	0·444	0·857	0·902	0·337
0·30	0·252	0·369	0·684	0·776	0·146
0·20	0·143	0·296	0·482	0·615	0·088
0·10	0·052	0·205	0·254	0·401	0·021
0·00	0·00	0·00	0·00	0·00	0·00

Velocity in Sewer Pipes

(*i*) **Chezy's formula :** $V = C\sqrt{mi}$, V = velocity in m/sec, m = hydraulic mean depth in meter = $r/2$, r = inner radius, i = gradient.

Value of C in Kutter's formula,

$$C = \frac{23 + \dfrac{0{\cdot}0015}{i} + \dfrac{1}{N}}{1 + \left(23 + \dfrac{0{\cdot}00015}{i}\right)\dfrac{N}{\sqrt{m}}}$$ N being coefficient of roughness

Values of N :

(1) Sewers 60 cm or less in dia. = 0·015

(2) Sewers 60 cm or over in dia. = 0·012 (best work)

(3) Sewers 60 cm or over in dia. = 0·013 (ordinary work)

(4) Brick sewers lined with vitrified or reasonable smooth hard burnt bricks and laid with great care with closed joints = 0·014

(5) Brick work under ordinary conditions = 0·015

(6) Brick sewers rough work = 0·017-0·02

(7) Earthen channels = 0·02-0·22

(8) Rough channels with weed growth = 0·0225-0·05

(*ii*) Manning's formula, $V = \left(\frac{1}{N}\right) \times m^{2/3}\, i^{1/2}$

(*iii*) Crimp and Burg's formula : $83{\cdot}5\, m^{1/3}\, i^{1/2}$ (same as Manning's only the value N is 0·012)

(*iv*) William-Hazen's formula for flow in sewer pipes $V = C\, m^{0{\cdot}63}\, i^{0{\cdot}54}$

Value of C — (1) Vitrified clay = 93 (2) Cement concrete = 103
(3) C.I. pipe (new) = 85 (4) C.I. pipe old = 110
(5) Brick work = 5

Sections which give the maximum discharge :

Rectangular section. Depth is half of breadth.

Circular, Semi-circular. The wetted perimeter must be least when velocity is maximum and hydraulic mean depth is also maximum.

Design computation from tables and Nomograms. The mathematical work becomes enormous while designing a sewerage scheme. To reduce the calculation work readymade charts and tables based upon their original formulae are generally prepared to use in design office.

Fig. 18·4 shows a nomogram based on mannings formulae, for sewers running full, using a value of N as 0·013. This nomogram can be used by placing a straight edge rule across any two known variable such as velocity and discharge. If the value of N to be used is different from 0·013 (say for example it is 0·017 ; than the velocity or discharge obtained from this chart for a value of N = 0·013 should be multiplied by a ratio $\frac{0.013}{0.017}\left(i.e. \frac{0.013}{N}\right)$ to obtain the real velocity or discharge produced as N = 0·017. Similarly if the discharge or velocity is given the required parameters can be found by 1st correcting the given discharge or velocity by multiplying of them by $\frac{0.017}{0.013}\left\{i.e. \frac{N}{0.013}\right\}$ and then placing the straight edge rule across the two known values.

Santo-Crimps tables are ready made table based on Crimp and Burge's formula. A simple page of this table is given below :

Table. 18·13. Sample page of Santo-Crimps tables for sewers running full

Sewer dia. in mm	*Grade 1 in 225*		*Grade 1 in 100*	
	Velocity in m/sec	*Discharge in litres/sec*	*Velocity in m/sec*	*Discharge in litres/sec*
100	0·479	3·76	0·560	440·00
150	0·628	11·12	0·942	16·07
200	0·760	23·96	1·140	35·83
250	0·833	43·34	1·324	65·01
300	0·996	70·52	1·494	105·80
375	1·156	127·70	1·735	191·70
450	1·306	208·00	1·960	312·30
525	1·447	313·70	2·170	470·10
600	1·582	448·10	2·373	672·00
750	1·837	812·50	2·754	1219·00
900	2·073	1320·00	3·200	2038·00

(*i*) **Advantages of circular sections.** (1) They can be manufactured easily and conveniently.

(2) It provides the maximum area for a given perim[illegible] and thus provides the maximum hydraulic mean depth when running full or half full and therefore is the most efficient sewer.

(3) It needs the minimum quantity of material in its manufacture and hence is cheaper and economical.

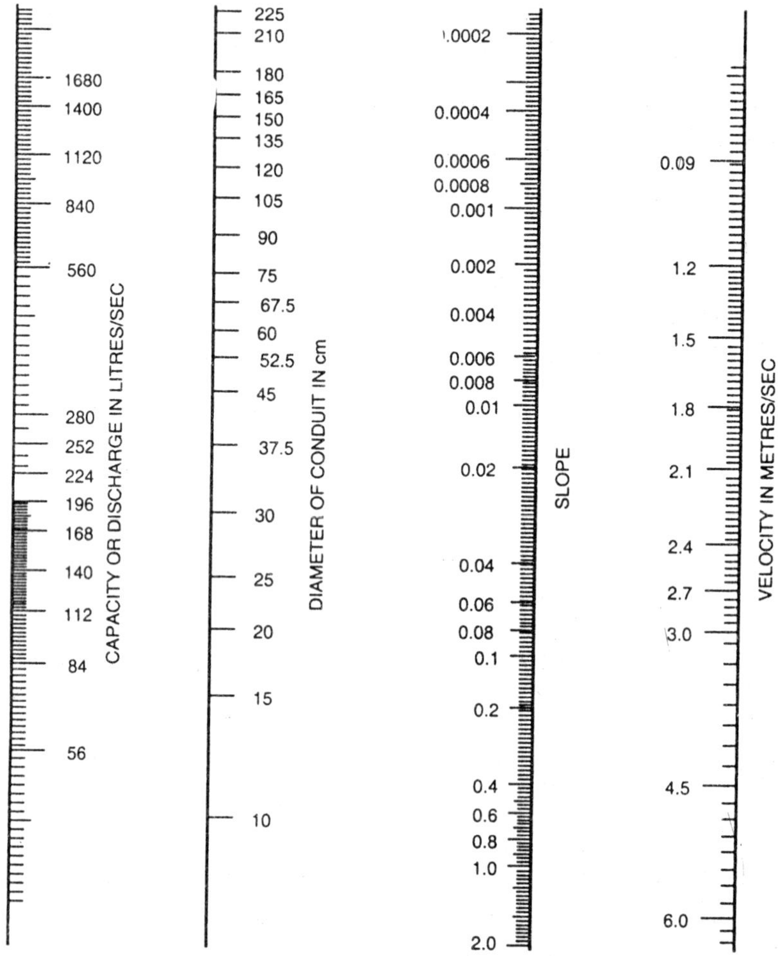

Fig. 18·4. Nanogram based on Manning's formula.

(4) A circular section being of uniform curvature all round, offers less chances of bed deposits.

All the above advantages of circular sewers are only obtained if the section runs at least half full. These merits are lost if the section runs less than half full. The velocity and discharge reduces considerably with the reduction of depth.

The performance of circular section is the best if there is no variation in discharge.

The egg shaped sewers are generally used in combined system. They have the following disadvantages over circular section.

(1) They are difficult to construct.

(2) Since the lower portion contains a lesser section and has to bear the upper higher load of bigger size hence they are less stable.

(3) They are costlier as they require more material for constructions.

Shapes of sewers

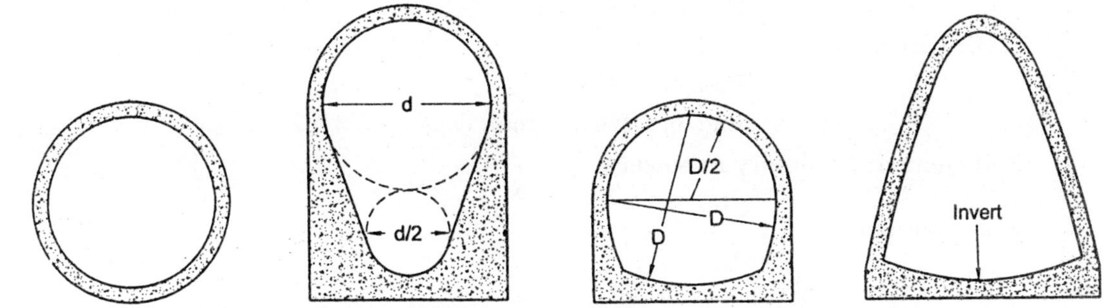

(*a*) Circular sewer widely used

(*b*) Egg-shaped sewer preferable for combined sewers

(*c*) Horse shoe sewer used in large sewers with heavy discharge as in trunk and out fall sewers

(*d*) Parabolic sewer carrying comparative lesser discharges

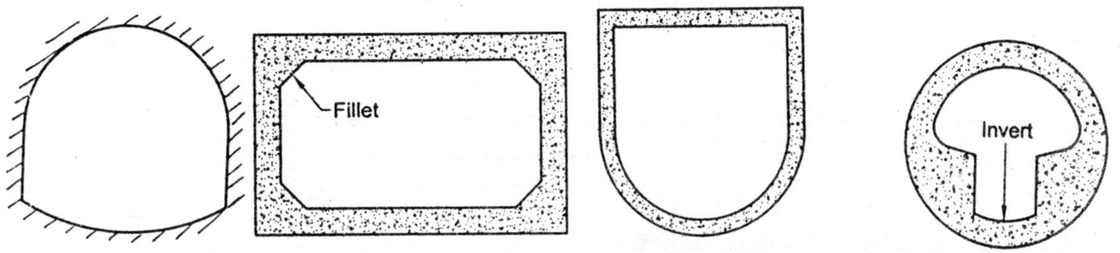

(*e*) Semi-elliptical sewer used in soft soils carry large discharges Dia. generally 1·8 m

(*f*) Rectangular section used in covered rain water drains

(*g*) Semi-circular or flat used in larger sewers in open cuts

(*h*) Basket handle sewer out of date

Fig. 18·5. Shapes of sewers

Suitability of different sections of sewers

(1) **Circular.** It is suitable for separate system of sewage disposal and not for combined system. It is strongest to bear pressure and gives highest velocity when running full or half. It is suitable for constant discharge.

(2) **Elliptical.** It is suitable for variable and low discharges and higher velocities, and hence there is less chances for solid deposits in bed. Max. discharge is at depth of 0·94 and min. at 0·33. They are costlier than circular sections.

(3) **Rectangular.** It is suitable for large discharges. Take good discharge at depth of 0·9 but it is reduced by 30% when full due to sudden increase of wetted perimeter. A *V*-shape curette is provided in bottom for low flows and better cleaning.

(4) **Horse shoe.** It is semi-circular at top and sides sloping with flat bottom. It is better to concrete conduits of power channels.

Properties of different sections of sewers

(1) **Trapezoidal sec.** Hydraulic mean depth = 0·5 depth of water

Area of section = $1{\cdot}828\ d^2$ (d = depth of water)

Wetted perimeter = $3{\cdot}656\ d$

Bottom width = $0{\cdot}828\ d$, side slopes 1·1

(2) **Circular sec.**	Depth of maximum velocity	= 0·81 dia. of pipe
	Depth for maximum discharge	= 0·95 dia. of pipe
(3) **Elliptical sec.**	Rad. of crown	= hyd. mean depth say R
	Rad. of invert	= R^2
	Rad. of sides and total depth	= $3R$

Self cleansing velocity in sewers

Shield Formula : $V = \sqrt{\frac{8\,K}{f}\left(\frac{S - P}{P}\right) \times gd}$

where f = Darcy coeff. friction being ·03 normally

K = Characteristics of solid particles kept in suspension by sewage, its value in m.k.s. varies from 0·06 to 0·04

S = Specific gravity of particle. Its value varies from 1·20 to 2·65.

P = Specific gravity of transporting liquid which is water.

d = Dia. of particle carried in suspension.

Note : The velocity which is essential to keep the particle in suspension works out to be nearly 0·5 m/sec. For design purposes it can be taken as 1 m/sec.

Following self cleansing velocities may be adopted for different types of sewers :

150 to 300 mm dia.—1 m/sec, 300 to 600 mm dia.—0·75 m/sec.

Above 600 mm dia.—0·60 m/sec.

Limiting max. velocities in sewers

(1) Brick sewers = 2·0 to 2·5 m/sec

(2) Stone ware vitrified clay = 3·0 to 3·5 m/sec

(3) Conc. sewers = 2·5 to 3·0 m/sec

(4) Cast iron = 2·5 to 4·0 m/sec

The min. velocity in mains is 0·3 m/sec

Non-scouring velocities in sewers

Stoneware sewers—3 to 4·5 m/sec ; Brick lined—1·5 to 2·4 m/sec

Cement conc.—2·4 m to 3·0 m/sec and Earthen channels—0·6 to 1·2 m per sec.

Table 18·13 (*a*)

Dia of sewer	*Grad. 1 : 1225*		*Grad. 1 in 100*	
in mm	*vel. m/sec*	*Dis. lit/min.*	*Vel. m/sec.*	*Dis. lit/min.*
100	0·4787	3·76	0·56	4·40
150	0·628	11·12	0·942	16·67
200	0·76	23·4	1·14	35·83
250	0·8826	43·34	1·324	65·01
300	0·996	70·52	1·494	105·80
375	1·156	127·1	1·735	191·70
450	1·306	200·0	1·960	312·30
525	1·443	313·3	2·170	470·10
600	1·582	448·1	2·373	672·00
675	1·711	611·2	2·566	918·50
750	1·837	812·5	2·754	1219·00
900	2·073	1320·0	3·200	2038·00

Self cleansing slopes—In upper reaches steeper slopes can be given than in lower.

Inter mural drain	1 : 250	At outfall	1 : 500 to 800
Intercepting drain	1 : 300	(upper reaches)	
	1 : 500	(lower reaches)	

In large drains a slope of more than 1 in 1200 must not be given.

For larger slopes falls should be provided at man holes.

Velocity discharge in circular pipes running part filled.

d = dia. of pipe, V = vel. and Q discharge

Table 18·13 (*b*). To obtain area of pipe, multiply factor in area col. by d^2

Depth of flow	*Area = factor × d^2*	*Proportional V*	*Proportional Q*	*Depth of flow*	*Area = factor × d^2*	*Proportional V*	*Proportional Q*
0·05	0·0147	0·257	0·005	0·55	0·4426	1·034	0·506
0·10	0·0404	0·401	0·021	0·6	0·4920	1·072	0·672
0·15	0·0739	0·517	0·049	0·65	0·5404	1·099	0·756
0·20	0·1118	0·615	0·088	0·7	0·5872	1·120	0·837
0·25	0·1535	0·701	0·137	0·75	0·6318	1·134	0·912
0·30	0·1982	0·776	0·196	0·8	0·6737	1·140	0·977
0·35	0·2450	0·443	0·263	0·85	0·7115	1·137	1·030
0·40	0·3954	0·902	0·337	0·9	0·7445	1·124	1·066
0·45	0·3428	0·954	0·417	0·95	0·7707	1·095	1·075
0·50	0·3927	1·00	0·500	1·00	0·7854	1·000	1·000

(1) Average pipe flowing are quarter of its depth has a velocity 0·72 and discharge 0·14 of when it is running full.

(2) When flowing half its depth it has a velocity 1·0 and discharge 0·50.

(3) Max. velocity of 1·13 occurs when the depth of flow is 0·82 and max. discharge 1·068 when depth of flow is 0·94.

(4) The sewers are designed for 2/3rd of their depth leaving 1/3rd for gases.

(5) The branch drains should join main tangentially or through curves, not at right angle.

18·2. Sewer construction and Appurtenances

The sewers generally run under gravity except for the outfall sewers which carries the treated and pumped sewage into the discharging point and hence flow under pressure. The sewer pipes are generally circular in section, sometimes these are of egg shape, horse shoe, parabolic elliptical or rectangular in shape next to circular egg shaped sewers are preferred.

Forces which act on sewers are (*i*) Internal pressure of sewage, (*ii*) Pressure due to external forces, temperature and flexural stresses. Some section are shown in Fig. 18·5.

Internal pressure. The pressure which is exerted on pipe from inside when these are running full. As such the sewers must also be designed for internal pressure consideration.

Pressure due to external loads. (*a*) This pressure may be due to loose fill of earth over pipes which run in filling. Such pipes may be laid over undistrubed soil. Covered by fills such as in culverts. The external force is likely to come per unit length of pipe as W (say).

$$W = C_P \gamma D^2$$

where C_P = a coefficient whose value depends upon the type of pipe and character of foundation basefill. Typical values of C_P are given in table 18·14.

γ = specific gravity of the fill material.

D = External dia. of the pipe = internal dia. + 2 thickness.

(*b*) For flexible pipes such as steel pipes, burried in the trenches, with compacted sidefill.

$$W = C\gamma BD$$

where C is a coefficient depending on the fill material and the ratio H/B. Typical values are given in the table. (Table 18·15)

Table 18·14.

Type condition	Cover depth / External pipe dia. $= \frac{H}{D}$	*Values of C_P*	
		For rigid pipe	*For flexible pipes*
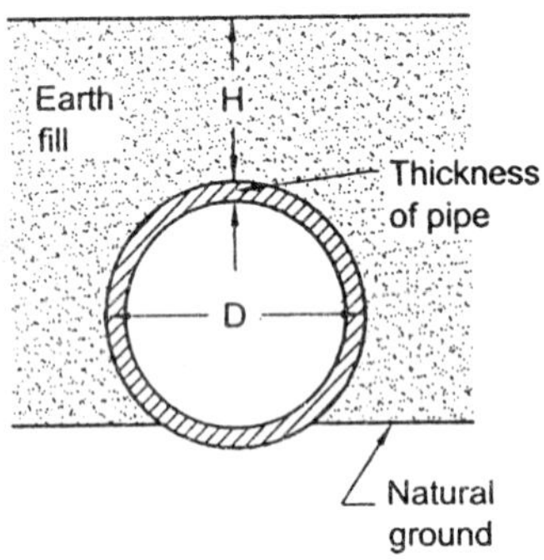	1·0	1·2	1·1
	2·0	2·8	2·6
	3·0	4·7	4·0
	4·0	6·7	5·4
	6·0	11·0	8·2
Fig. 18·6.	8·0	16·0	11·0

(*c*) **For rigid pipes.** Rigid pipes such as concrete, cast iron or vitrified clay etc. burried in trenches and side filled with compacted cohesion less fills be load per unit length of pipe $W = C\gamma \cdot B$. Where $C\gamma$ and B have the same meaning as above.

Table. 18·15. Values of *C* for type (*b*) and (*c*)

Type condition	*Fill material* → *Sp. weight in kg/m³* ↓ *values of A/B*	*Dry sand and gravel 1600*	*Saturated top soil 1600*	*Clay 1920*	*Saturated clay 2080*
		Values of C			
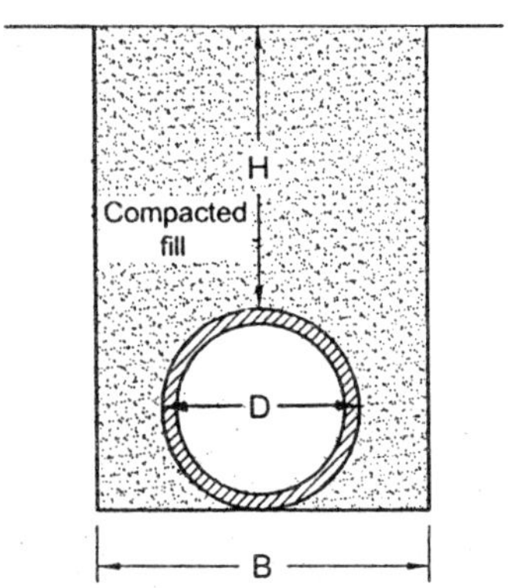	1·0	0·84	0·86	0·88	0·90
	2·0	1·45	1·50	1·55	1·62
	3·0	1·90	2·00	2·10	2·26
	4·0	2·22	2·33	2·49	2·65
	5·0	2·45	2·60	2·80	3·03
	6·0	2·60	2·78	3·04	3·33
	7·0	2·75	2·95	3·23	3·57
	8·0	2·80	3·03	3·37	3·76
	9·0	2·88	3·11	3·48	3·92
	10·0	2·92	3·17	3·58	4·04
	12·0	2·97	3·24	3·68	4·22
Fig. 18·7.	14·0	3·00	3·28	3·75	4·34

Pressure due to temperature stress. When the sewer pipe is laid above the ground, it is subjected to temperature variation. They expand during day and contract during night. This change in length due to temperature change is prevented by friction. Longitudinal stresses are produced in the pipe material, which is calculated as below

$$\text{Elongation} = L\,\alpha\,T \text{ but strain} = \text{elongation per unit length}$$

$$\frac{L\,\alpha\,T}{L} = \alpha T$$

$$\text{stress} = \text{E and strain} = E_P\,\alpha\,T$$

or $$\text{(the stress) } f = E_P\,\alpha\,T$$

where E_P = Modulus of elasticity of the pipe material

α = Coefficient of expansion of pipe material

T = Change of temperature in °C

In open pipes expansion joints are given at a suitable distance apart say 20 to 30 meter.

Flexural stresses. When the pipes run on trestles over ditches or filled earth which may settle. In such cases the pipe acts as a beam with sewage load together with its own load or any other superimposed load if any. Hence such types of sewer pipes are designed as a beam.

Types of sewer pipes. The following types of pipes are used as sewers.

(*i*) **Asbestos cement sewers.** A.C. pipes are constructed by a mixing of asbestos fibre, silica and cement which is converted in a solid homogeneous mass where asbestos fibres works as a reinforcement. Such types of pipes are available in market in dia metres ranging from 10 to 90 cm and are generally 1·8 and 3 m in length. They are weaker than RCC pipes.

(*ii*) **Plain and reinforced cement pipes.** The non pressure RCC pipes are classified according to IS : 458—1988 into the following three classes.

(*a*) **NP_2 pipes.** They are light duty RCC non pressure pipes normally used for drainage and irrigation use and for culverts with light traffic. The thickness of NP_2 pipe vary from 25 mm for 8 cm dia. pipes to 110 mm for 2·2 m dia. pipes.

(*b*) **NP_3 pipes.** They are medium duty non pressure pipes. Normally used for drainage and irrigation use and for culverts for medium traffic. The thickness of these pipes vary from 25 mm for 8 cm dia. pipe to 215 mm for 2·6 m dia pipe.

(*c*) **NP_4 pipes.** They are heavy duty non pressure pipes, normally used as above carrying heavy traffic.

RCC pipes are either moulded or linen (spun) type casted by centrifugal system.

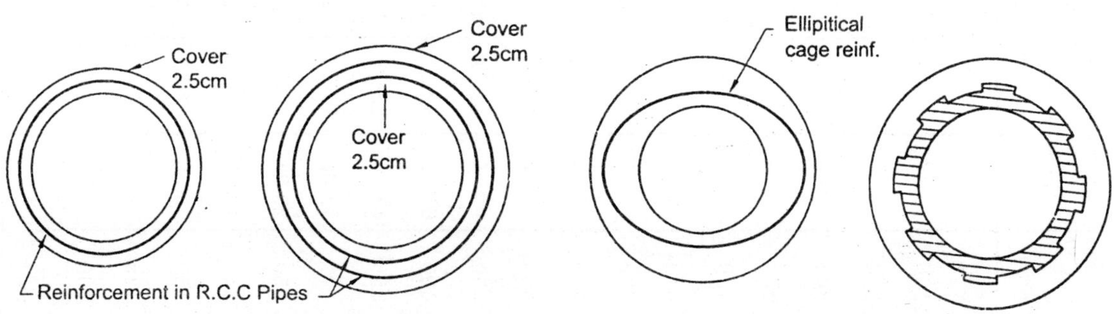

Fig. 18·8. Cement concrete pipe line inside with vitrified clay.

Equivalent pipe sizes

Diameter	*Diameter in mm*															
(*mm*)	75	100	125	150	200	250	300	350	400	450	500	550	600	700	900	1200
1200	—	—	—	—	—	—	—	—	15·59	11·61	8·92	7·03	5·65	3·24	2·03	1·0
1100	—	—	—	—	—	—	—	17·50	12·54	9·34	7·17	5·67	4·55	2·61	1·65	—
1000	—	—	—	—	—	—	20·23	13·47	7·85	7·31	5·64	4·44	3·57	2·05	1·26	—
900	—	—	—	—	—	—	15·58	8·41	7·59	5·63	4·34	3·42	2·73	1·58	1·00	—
825	—	—	—	—	34·55	19·78	12·54	8·52	6·11	4·55	3·44	2·74	2·21	1·27	—	—
750	—	—	—	—	27·00	15·54	9·84	6·54	4·80	3·57	2·76	2·16	1·74	1·00	—	—
675	—	—	—	42·95	16·61	9·96	7·39	5·16	3·70	2·75	2·11	1·67	1·34	—	—	—
600	—	—	50·50	32·00	15·58	8·92	5·65	3·84	2·75	2·05	1·57	1·24	1·00	—	—	—
550	—	70·96	40·10	25·73	12·53	7·17	4·55	3·09	2·16	1·65	1·26	1·00	—	—	—	—
500	—	55·96	32·05	20·29	9·88	5·66	3·58	2·43	1·71	1·30	1·00	—	—	—	—	—
450	—	42·71	24·63	15·08	7·25	4·34	2·75	1·87	1·34	1·00	—	—	—	—	—	—
400	65·77	32·01	18·31	11·60	5·65	3·23	2·05	1·39	1·00	—	—	—	—	—	—	—
350	47·14	22·74	13·15	8·32	4·05	2·32	1·47	1·00	—	—	—	—	—	—	—	—
300	32·05	15·60	8·93	5·63	2·75	1·57	1·00	—	—	—	—	—	—	—	—	—
250	20·21	9·80	5·66	3·38	1·74	1·00	—	—	—	—	—	—	—	—	—	—
200	11·63	5·66	3·24	2·05	1·00	—	—	—	—	—	—	—	—	—	—	—
150	5·66	2·75	1·58	1·00	—	—	—	—	—	—	—	—	—	—	—	—
125	3·58	1·75	1·00	—	—	—	—	—	—	—	—	—	—	—	—	—
100	2·05	1·00	—	—	—	—	—	—	—	—	—	—	—	—	—	—
75	1·00	—	—	—	—	—	—	—	—	—	—	—	—	—	—	—

(*iii*) **Cast iron pipes.** These pipes are structurally strung for with standing greater tensile compression as well as bending stress. They are used in sewer under special circumstances such as :

(*a*) For outfull sewers, for rising mains of pumping stations or for inverted syphons all running under pressure.

(*b*) For sewers to be laid below heavy traffic loads such as those laid below high way or railways.

(*c*) For sewers carried over piers or trestles while crossing ditches.

(*d*) For sewers which are to be 100% leak proof.

Quantity of Cement and Gas kin per joint for RCC pipes with collar jointed with cement mortar 1 : 1

Dia. of pipe mm	*Cement (kg)*	*Gas kin (kg)*	*Dia. of pipe*	*Cement (kg)*	*Gas kin (kg)*
100	2	0·10	600	20	0·12
150	3	0·18	700	24	0·03
250	5	0·29	800	27	0·95
300	7	0·36	900	30	1·08
350	9	0·40	1000	34	1·20
400	12	0·50	1100	37	1·36
450	15	0·55	1200	40	1·85
500	18	0·60			

Cement concrete pipes (classification as per IS : 458)

Class	*Description*	*Conditions where normally used*
NP_1	Unreinforced concrete non pressure pipes	For drainage and irrigation use above ground or in shallow trenches.
NP_2	R.C. light duty, non pressure pipes	For culverts carrying light traffic.
NP_3	R.C. heavy duty, no pressure pipes	For culverts carrying heavy traffic.
NP_4	R.C. heavy duty, no pressure pipes	For culverts carrying very heavy traffic such as railways loadings.
P_1	R.C. pressure pipes tested to a hydrostatic pressure of 2·0 kg/sq. cm (20 m head)	For use on gravity mains. The actual working pressure not exceeding 2/3 of the test pressure.
P_2	R.C. pressure pipes tested to a hydrostatic pressure of 4·0 kg/sq. cm (40 m head)	For use on pumping mains, actual working pressure not exceeding 1/2 of the test pressure.
P_3	R.C. pressure pipes tested to a hydrostatic pressure of 6·0 kg/sq. cm (60 m head)	For use on pumping mains, actual working pressure not exceeding 1/2 of the test pressure.

Hydrostatic test pressure for cast iron centrifugally spun pipes

Class of pipe	*Hydrostatic test pressure at works*	*Max. hydrostatic test pressure after installation*	
	(Socket and spigot pipes)		
	kg/sq. cm	kg/sq. cm	Head of water (m)
L.A.	35	12	120
A	35	18	180
B	35	24	240
	Flanged pipes (upto 300 mm dia.)		
A	35	18	180
B	35	18	240

Hydrostatic Test Pressure for Vertically Cast Iron pipes.

Nominal diameter	*Test pressure in kg/sq. cm*			
	Socket and spigot pipes		*Flanged pipes*	
	Class A	*Class B*	*Class A*	*Class B*
Upto and including 300 mm	20	25	20	25
Over 300 mm upto 600 mm	20	25	15	20
Over 600 mm upto 1000 mm	15	20	10	15
Over 1000 mm to 15,000 mm	10	15	10	10

Diameter of Flanges of cast iron pipes (both centrifugally spun and vertically cast)

Nominal dia. of pipe	80	100	125	150	200	250	300	350	400	450
mm (inch)	(3″)	(4″)	(5″)	(6″)	(8″)	(10″)	(12″)	(14″)	(16″)	(18″)
Dia. of flange (Outside)	200	220	250	285	340	395	445	525	565	615
Nominal dia. of pipe	500	600	700	750	800	900	1000	1100	1200	1500
mm (inch)	20	24	28	30	32	36	40	44	48	60
Dia. of flanged (Outside)	670	780	895	960	1015	1115	1230	1340	1455	1800

inches	3	4	6	9	12	15	18	21	24	27	30	33
mm	76	105	152	229	305	381	457	533	610	686	762	838

(*iv*) **Lead sewers.** The lead pipes are smooth, soft and can be easily bent to take desired shapes. They are available in smaller sizes (3 to 4 cm dia.) and smaller in length and are generally used in toilets. They may be used as a down take pipes of flushing cistern or as waste pipes from stall urinals and wash basins or for geysers connections.

(*v*) **Plastic sewers.** These are used as non pressure pipes. They are weak and break downs even for small hits. They are jointed by a synthetic solution.

(*vi*) **Vitrified clay or stone ware pipes** or **salt glazed sewers.** These pipes are widely used for carrying sewerage and drainage as house connecting as well as in lateral sewers. They are available for 10 to 30 cm in increments of 5 cm and 7·5 cm increments from 36 to 90 cm. They are rarely available larger than 90 cm dia.

These pipes are manufactured from clays and shales of special quality which are first pulverised and mixed with water thoroughly. This is used for casting of pipes in standard sizes at a pressure of about 8·0 kg/cm^2. The moulds are dried in warm air and then burnt in hot kilns. The temperature of the kiln is maintained at about 150°C and then raised to about 700°C and finally upto 1200°C increased slowly. Near the end of burning sodium chloride (common salt) is placed in kiln. The salt vapours in intense heat reacts with clay and forms a thin smooth and hard water proof layer on pipe surface. These pipes are joined by a bell and a spigot flexible compression joint. The sockets for joints are moulded with the pipes while manufacturing in bell and spigot ends in lengths of about 0·9 to 1·2 m. The interior surface of these socket end and the exterior surface of spigot end are not glazed so as to make the joint water tight. The advantages of these pipes are :

(*i*) They are highly resistant to sulphide corrosion and hence is preferred to carry polluted sewage.

(*ii*) The interior being smooth they are hydraulically very efficient.

(*iii*) They are impervious and not allows the leakage of the sewer out.

(*iv*) They are though weak in tension however strong in compression hence they can bear high compression due to traffic and back fill upto 4·5 m. soil cover, if a pipe length remains hanging between joints due to removal of soil from below. They however withstand only very small tensile stresses caused by internal pressure. They are not used for sewers running under pressure.

(*v*) They are cheap and handled and laid adjointed easily.

(*vi*) They are non absorbent and do not absorb water more than 5% of their own weight hence they can be kept immersed in water for 24 hours.

The disadvantages are (*a*) They are heavy bulky and brittle and therefore difficult to transport, hence they are casted in small lengths.

(*b*) Due to shorter lengths the number of joints are numerous.

(*c*) They can not be used as pressure pipes as they are weak in tension.

(*vii*) Brick masonary sewers can be made at desired sections. The mortar used must be rich of the order of about 1 : 2 to 1 : 3 in 1st class bricks.

Note : The joints of pipes are seated over concrete base to avoid any settlement.

Sewer system and required appurtenances

Manholes. Manholes are masonary or RCC chambers constructed at suitable intervals and at the point of control such as curve points, change of slope, bends or any other such point where frequent check is necessary so that the inspection of pipe lines and their clearance may be possible. If the manhole covers are preforated they must act as a ventilation to the sewer.The manholes can also be located at certain intervals even in straight reaches on the changing section of the sewer pipes.

Classification of Manholes. (*i*) Shallow (*ii*) Normal (*iii*) Deep.

(*i*) **Shallow manholes.** They are 0·7 to 0·9 m in depth and are constructed at the start of branch sewers which are not subjected to heavy traffic, hence they have thin cover on their inspection lids.

Table 18·16.
Manhole spacings as per IS : 1742—1960

Size of sewer	*Recommended spacing of manholes on straight reaches of sewers*
Upto 0·3 m dia.	45 m
Upto 0·6 m dia.	75 m
Upto 0·9 m dia.	90 m
Upto 1·2 m dia.	120 m
Upto 1·5 m dia.	250 m
Greater than 1·5 m dia.	300 m

Min. internal dimensions for manhole chambers IS : 1742—1960

Depth	*Minimum size specified*
0·8 m or less	0·75 m × 0·75 m
0·8 m and 2·1 m	1·2 m × 0·9 m
greater than 2·1 m	Circular min. dia. of 1·4 rectangular with min. dimension 1·2 × 0·9 m
Minimum wall thickness upto	
(*a*) 1·5 m depth	20 cm
(*b*) greater than 1·5 m depth	30 cm

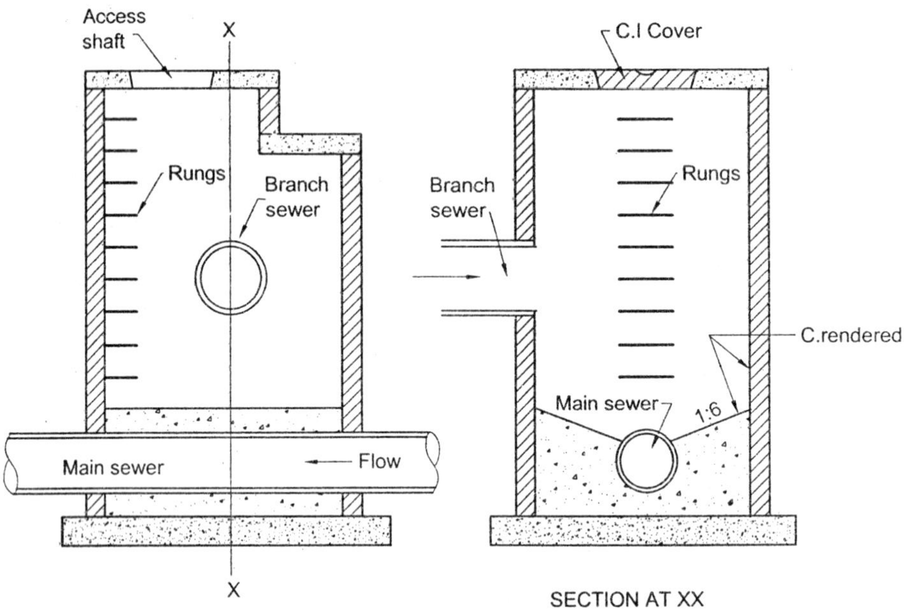

Fig. 18·9. Deep manhole.

(*ii*) **Medium manholes.** They are about 1·5 m in depth and are constructed 1m square or 1·2 m × 1·3 m rectangular shape. Such a manhole is provided with a heavy lid so that it may bear a heavier traffic on its top.

(*iii*) **Deep manholes.** They have depth more than 1·5 m. The section of such manholes is reduced at top by giving an offset as shown in Fig. 18·9.

Rungs are provided for descending into the manholes and the lower portion is kept wider so that a man can work and move easily inside the hole.

The component parts of manhole are :

(*i*) **Access shaft.** The upper portion of a deep manhole is known as access shaft. Its minimum size for a rectangular manhole is about 0·75 × 0·6 m and for a circular mainhole the minimum dia. is about 0·6 × 0·75 m. The depth is taken as per site conditions. The section at upper portion is reduced by providing a R.C. slab or by corbelling an arch.

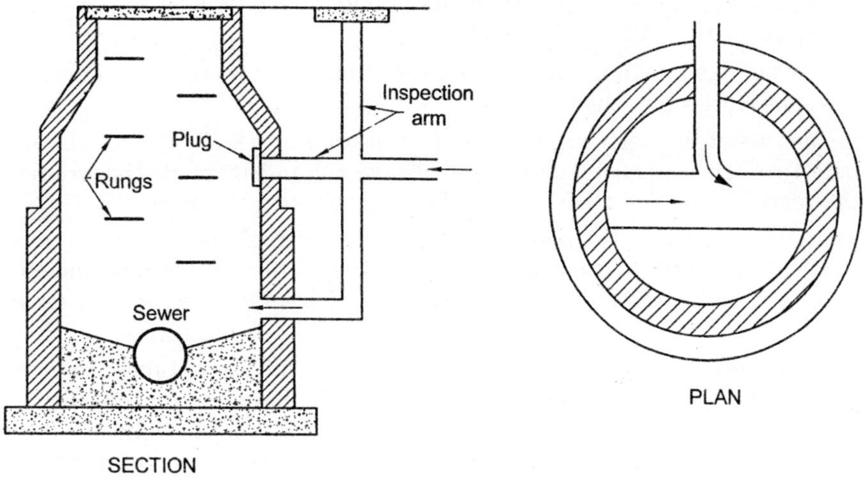

Fig. 18·10.

(*ii*) **Working chamber.** The lower portion in which a man works for inspection or cleaning is known as working chamber. Its minimum size is 1·2 × 0·9 m for rectangular and 1·2 m dia. for circular chamber. The depth must not be less than 1·8 m.

(*iii*) **Benching.** Bottom or invert portion of the manhole, made of concrete. U shaped or semi-circular section is generally provided and the seats are mesh sloping towards it. The concreting is known as benching and facilitates the entry of sewage into the main sewer. If the branch as well as the main sewer meet at the same level at the bottom of the mainhole, channels connected with each other will have to be constructed. Such constructions are made with easy curves.

(*iv*) **The side walls.** The side walls are generally constructed in brick with having thickness to the size of a brick *i.e.* (9″). These walls may also be of stone masonary or may be RCC. For deeper holes the thickness may be increased by giving an offset of quarter of a brick size.

(*v*) **Ladders.** Rungs are provided to descend a worker down into the hole. The rungs may be of 16 mm bars bent in a rectangular shape and are provided staggered at a horizontal distance of about 20 cm and at a vertical distance c/c of about 30 cm. They are U shaped and their legs are embedded into the wall. The staggering is not however necessary. For deeper manholes ladders are provided.

(*vi*) **Cover.** The manhole is provided with a cast iron cover fitted in a cast iron frame. The frame is embedded in the pavement by lugs. The cover may be rectangular or circular. The size of rectangular cover is about 0·6 m × 0·45 m and that of a circular have a dia. of about 0·5 to 0·6 m. The top surface is made rough so as to avoid slipping. An arrow mark is also made on the cover in the direction of flow. The top surface is kept flush with the pavement. To make the cover tight and fit a gasket may also be placed between the lid and frame. The weight of the cover varies from 90 to 270 kg according to the load of the traffic.

Drop manholes. When a branch sewer enters a main sewer manhole by more than 0·5 to 0·6 m above the main sewer. In such cases the branch sewer is not allowed to fall directly in the mainhole over the main sewer, but is brought into it through a down pipe taken from the branch sewer to the bottom of the manhole. If the drop is only a few metres, the down pipe can be kept sloping at 45° to the ground and if the drop is more, a vertical pipe is economical. A manhole in which a vertical pipe such as shown in Fig. 18·10 is used, is called a drop manhole whereas when it is an inclined pipe it is called a "ramp". It is done due to the following reasons :

(*i*) The steep gradient required in the branch sewer to meet the main sewer is avoided causing saving in earth work and high velocities.

(*ii*) The sewage trickling into the manhole from the directly placed branch sewer is likely to fall on persons working in the manhole.

The details of the vertical pipe is shown in the Fig. 18·10. The branch sewer is joined to the manhole through a vertical pipe. The sewage coming through the branch sewer dips in through the vertical pipe and trickles over the main sewer just above.

A plug is provided at the point where branch sewer, if taken straight, intersects the wall of the manhole. The length of the branch sewer between the vertical pipe and the plug is known as inspection arm and can be used for inspecting and cleaning the branch sewer after opening the plug.

Lamp holes. Lamp holes are small openings in the sewer pipes from which a lamp can be inserted. The lamp light is viewed from the u/s and d/s manholes and the idea about a blockage is made by the intensity of the light. If there is an obstruction the light is not seen or if seen it is dim. The vertical shaft may be a pipe of cast iron or concrete. It is jointed to the sewer with a *T*-joint. The cover of the shaft may take the load of traffic. The lamp holes are generally provided at controlling points such as bends and joints etc. The lamp hole may also be used as a flushing device or if its cover is perforated it can be used as a ventilating pipe.

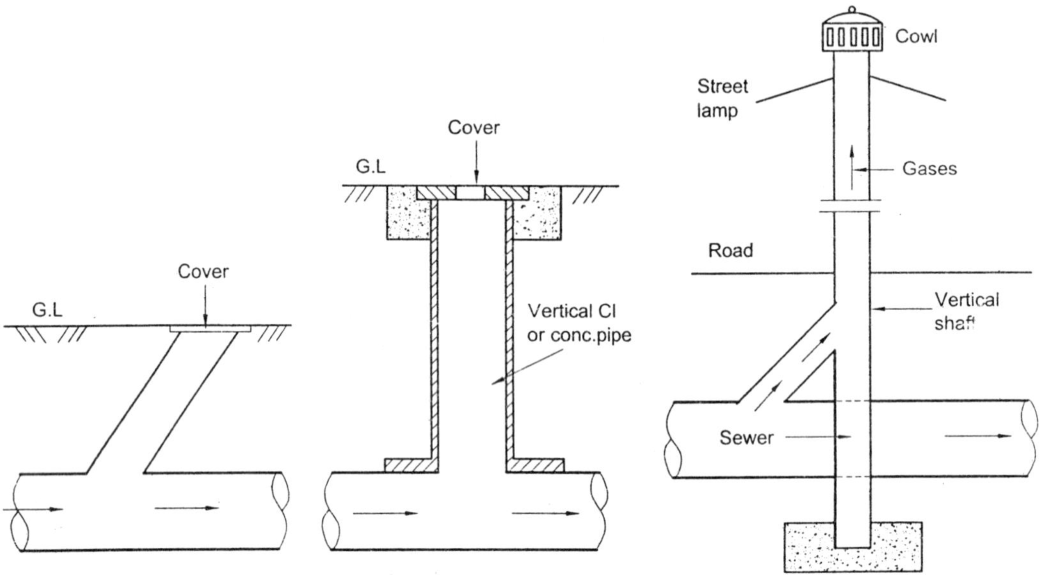

(*a*) Clean out (*b*) Lamp hole (*c*) Ventilation shaft

Fig. 18·11.

Clean outs. These are slanting pipes from the ground to the sewer for the purpose of cleaning the sewers. For its use the cover is removed and a flexible pipe is forced in the clean out pipe to remove any obstacle. For large obstacles a flexible rod is used. Clean outs are generally provided at the upper ends of lateral sewers in place of manholes.

Street inlets or gullies. Inlets are gullies or openings on the road surface at the lowest point mostly by the side of the foot path and are connected to the central or a nearby mainhole by pipes to drain off water. The gullies is known as vertical inlets, if the inlet is vertical by the side of the foot path and as horizontal if top cover of the chamber is fitted with gratings to pass the water. These are provided on the road sides at an interval of 30 × 60 m apart on both sides of the road staggered. (Fig. 18·4)

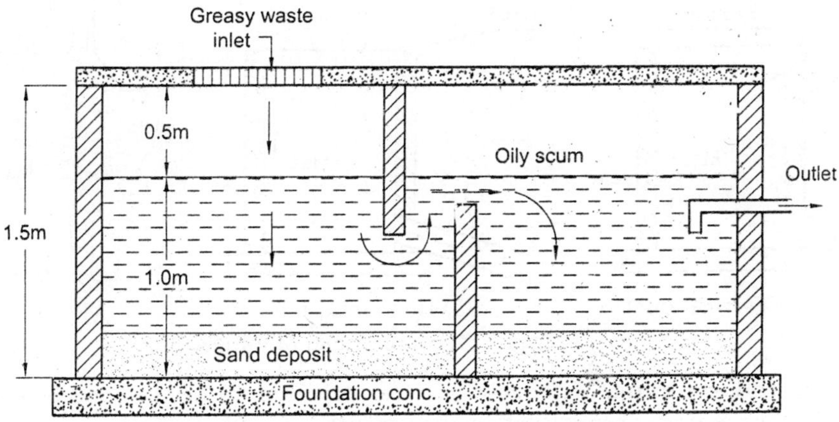

Fig. 18·12. Combined oil grease and sand trap.

Grease and oil traps. As shown in the Fig. 18·12 Grease and oil traps are those trap chambers which are constructed in a sewerage systems to remove oil and grease from the sewage before it enters into the sewer such traps are located near the sources contributing grease and oil to the sewage. They are therefore located at places such as automobile repair centres, garrages and kitchens etc. where the use of grease and oils is done. The function of the grease trap is self explanatory from the Fig. 18·12. The grease scum floats on the top surface of water which can be removed from top covers by spoons.

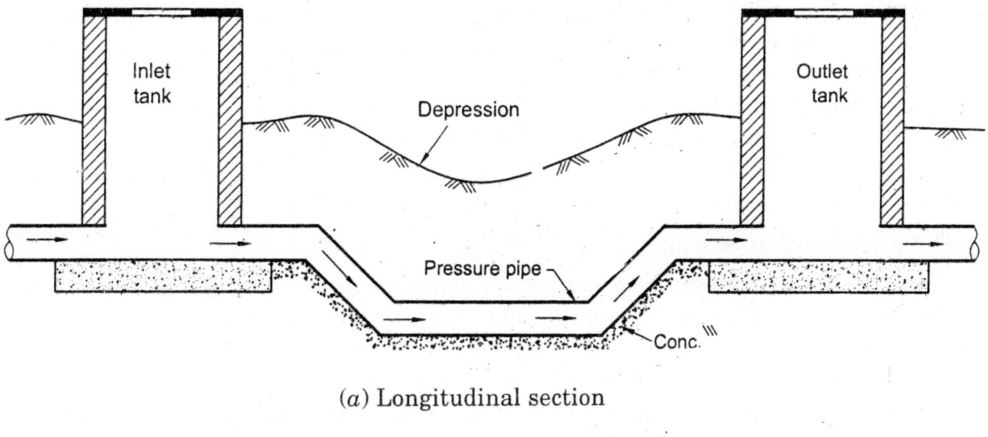

(*a*) Longitudinal section

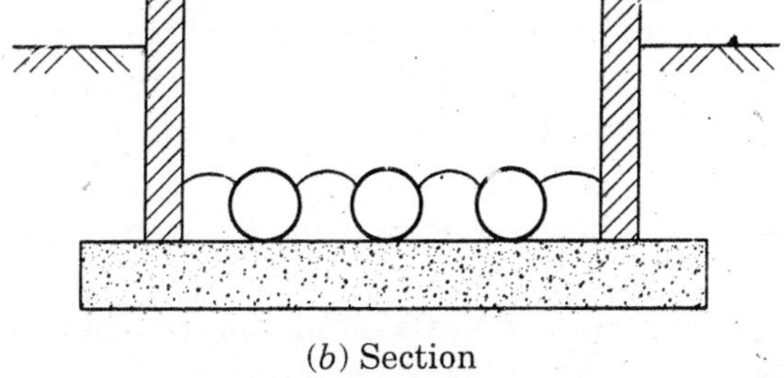

(*b*) Section

Fig. 18·13. Inverted siphon.

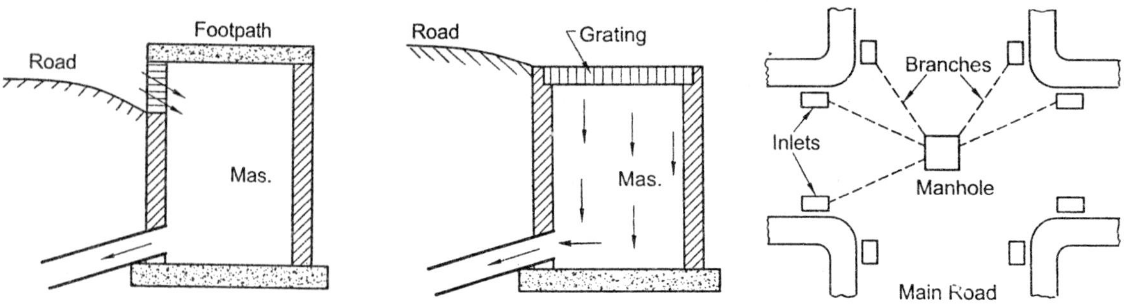

(*a*) Vertical inlet (*b*) Horizontal inlet (*c*) Top layout

Fig. 18·14. Street inlets or gulies.

Inverted syphons. Whenever a sewer pipe has to be dropped below the hydraulic gradient line for passing it beneath of a valley or ditch, a road or railway a construction provided for this purpose is known as inverted system. The water in the syphon passes under pressure. The siphon should therefore be designed to develop a self cleansing velocity of about 0·9 m/sec even during minimum discharge. For this purpose the inverted syphon is usually provided with three conditions laid side by side in plan as shown in Fig. 18·13.

Ventilation of sewers. The sewers must be properly ventilated for the following reasons :

(*i*) To pass out the poisonous sewer gases such as CO_2, CO, methane or hydrogen sulphide etc.

(*ii*) To ensure a continuous flow of sewage inside the sewer. This is achieved by ventilation by keeping the surface of sewerage in contact with free air and thus preventing the air locks in the sewage. A ventilation column is inserted by the side of the road in the ground near a sewer on a concrete foundation so that it may not be loose. This column may be a pipe of concrete or cast iron provided with a cowel at top to pass air. A bit below the road surface this column is connected to the sewer with a pipe to collect air from the sewer. The function and shape of the ventilation column in clear from the Fig. 18·11(*c*).

18·3. Decomposing of sewage

Disposal of sewage. Sewage before being disposed of either in river or on land has generally to be treated so as to make it safe. Screening is the first operation carried out at a sewage treatment plant, and consists of passing the sewage through different types of screens, so as to trap and remove the floating matter, such as pieces of cloth, paper, food, cork, hair fibre and kitchen waist etc. present in sewage. These materials if not removed will choke the pipes and will adversely affect the working of the pumps and other equipments. Thus the main idea of screening is to save the pumps and other equipments from damage due to floating material. The screens are preferably placed before the grit chambers, however if the quality of 'grit' is not of much importance, as in the case of land fillings etc., screens may be placed after the grit chambers. Depending on the size of openings, screens may be classified as coarse, medium and fine screens.

(*i*) **Coarse screens** also known as 'Racks' and the spacing between the bars *i.e.* opening size is about 50 mm or more. These screens help in removing loose floating objects from sewage which may be disposed of by incineration, burial or dumpings. They collect about 6 litres of solids per million litre of sewage.

(*ii*) **Medium screens.** The spacing between bars is about 6 to 40 mm. They ordinarily collect 30 to 90 litres of materials per million litre of sewage. The screenings usually contain some quantity of organic material, which may putrefy and become offensive and must therefore be disposed of by incineration or burial (not dumping).

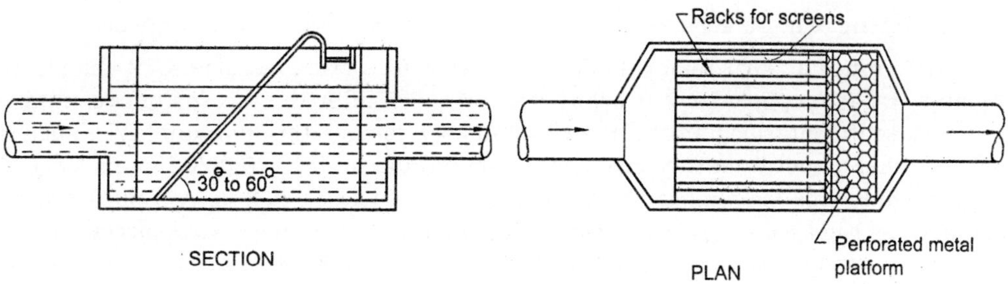

Fig. 18·15. Fixed bar coarse or medium screen.

Rectangular shaped coarse and medium screens are now a days widely used at sewage treatment plants. They are made of steel bars fixed parallel to one another at desired spacings on a rectangular steel frame and are called bar screens. The screens are set in a masonry or RCC chamber called as screen chamber.

The screens are kept inclined 30 to 60° to the direction of flow so as to increase the opening area, and to reduce the flow velocity. The clear openings should have sufficient area so that the velocity through them is not more than 0·8 to 1 m/sec so that the screenings may not pass through the screens.

The material collected on bar screens can be removed either manually or mechanically, by rakes. A rake is a toothed bar. The tooth of the rake is so designed that they fit in between the spacings of the screen bars. The operator fit the rake in the bar openings and pull up the waste towards the perforated platform and dump it on the floor. Slanting screen bars help the operator in dragging the waste.

The screens may be movable and can be removed from position for cleaning them.

(*iii*) **Fine screens.** The fine screens have perforations of 1·5 to 3 mm in size. They remove 20% of the suspended solids from sewage. These screens however clogged frequently and need their cleaning. After these screens the sewage needs considerable less of further treatment. The metal used must be rust proof hence Bronze plates in screens are used. The fine screen may be disc or drum type and operated by motor driven scrapers.

Some times comminutors or shradders are provided with the screens which cut the big solids to about 6 mm size. It eliminates the problem of disposal of large solids.

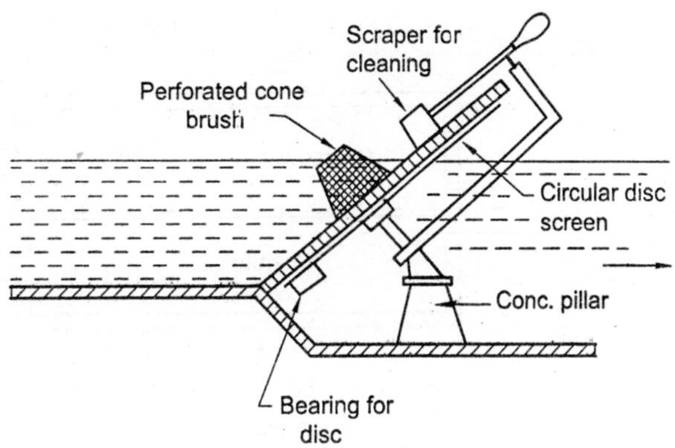

Fig. 18·16. Fine disc screen.

Disposal of screenings (material left on the screens). This material contains 86·9% moisture. It can be disposed off (*i*) By burning (*ii*) By burial (*iii*) By dumping.

(*i*) **Burning.** The screens are 1st dried in the sun and then is burned in the incinerators, similar to those used for burning garbage at a temperature of about 760 to 815°C. The screenings may also be compressed after drying in sun by a hydraulic press.

(*ii*) **Burial.** The process is technically called as composting. The screening are burried in 1 to 1·5 m deep trenches and then covered with 0·3 to 0·45 m porous earth. After some time such screenings can be used as composed manure.

Dumping. The screens are dumped in the low lying areas or in large bodies of water.

Grit removal. Grit removal devices are known as grit chambers. Grit chambers are the sedimentation basins placed either before the screens of after the screens but certainly prior to the primary sedimentation tank. The grit chambers remove the inorganic grit, such as sand, gravel and other mineral matter that has a nominal dia. of 0·15 to 0·20 mm or large. The grit may also include smaller mineral particles that may settle as well as non purgesciple organic matter, such as rags, coffee grounds, vegetables cuttings ash clinker, wood pieces and tea leaves etc. The grit quantity may vary between 0·004 to 0·037 $m^3/1000\ m^3$ of sewage for separate sewage system while it is 0·004 to 0·180 $m^3/1000^3$ for combined sewage system.

It is not at all desirable to remove any organic matter in grit chamber, become no further treatment of removal grit is provided. The grit chamber must hence be designed to scour the lighter organic particles while the heavier grit particles remain settled. The organic material is not allowed to settle in this process, as otherwise the organic matter gets entangled with the inorganic matter causing septicity of sewage and requiring unnecessary labour for disposal or removal.

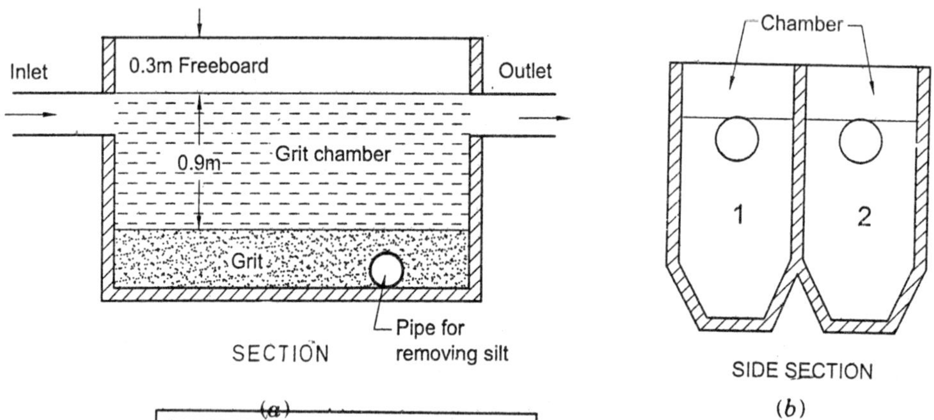

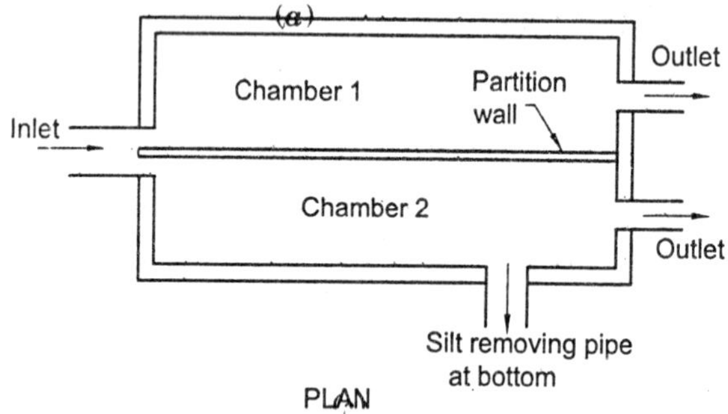

Fig. 18·17. Grit chamber.

The **grit-chambers** are designed to have a constant velocity horizontal flow at varying discharges. The constant velocity is achieved by providing a velocity control section, such as proportional flow weir at the effluent end of a rectangular chamber or a Venturi flume in a parabolic or *V*-shaped chamber.

Tanks for removing oils and grease (Skimming Tanks). Skimming tanks are provided to remove oils and grease from sewage and placed before primary sedimentation tanks. They are used where sewage contains too much grease or oils which include fats, waxes, soaps fatty acids etc. A typical details of a skimming tank is given in Fig. 18·18. The screen may be removed from top.

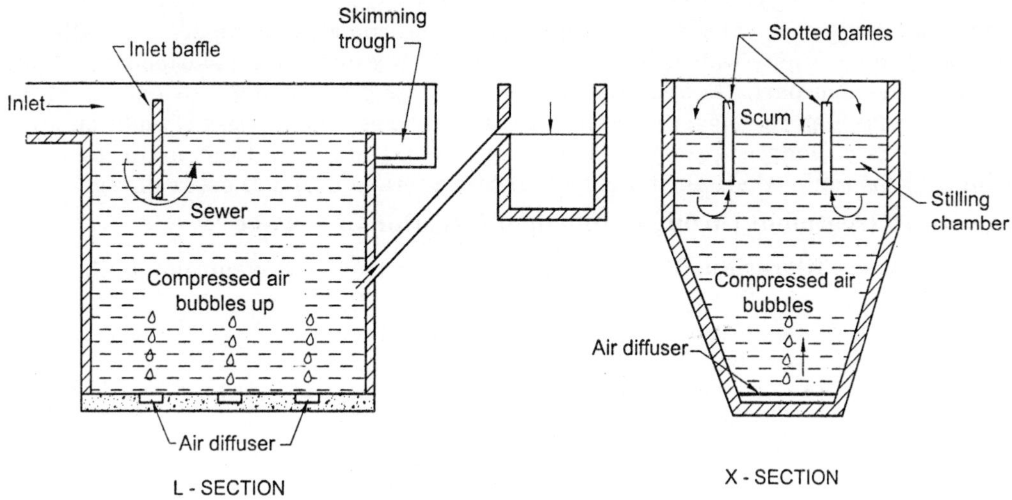

Fig. 18·18. Skimming tank.

The skimming tank consists of a long trough shaped structure divided into two or three lateral compartments by means of vertical slotted baffle walls for a short distance below the sewage surface as shown in Fig. 18·18. The baffle walls help in pushing the rising or coagulated greasy material into the side chambers (called as silting chambers). The rise of oil and grease is brought about by blowing compressed air into the sewage from diffusers placed at the bottom of the tank. The collected greasy materials are removed (skimmed off) either manually or by some mechanical arrangement. It may be disposed either by burning or burial.

Sewage enters the tank at one end, flows through longitudinally and finally goes out through a narrow inclined duct. This is so narrow that the suspended heavier particles are carried up its slope and out of the tank. A detention period of about 3 to 5 minutes is usually sufficient, and the amount of compressed air required is about 300 to 6000 m^3 per million litres of sewage. The surface area required for the tank can be found by the formula.

$$A = 0{\cdot}00622 \frac{q}{V_v}$$

where q = Rate of flow of sewage in m^3/day

V_v = Minimum rising velocity of greasy material to be removed in m/min. = 0·25 m/min. mostly.

Chlorine can be passed with the compressed air which increases the efficiency of the tank four times.

Primary sedimentation. The screens and the grit chambers do remove most of the floating materials like paper, wood, rags, cloths, wood, tree branches etc. and the heavy inorganic settlable solids from the sewage. However a part of the suspended solids which are too heavy to be removed as floating matters and too light to be removed by grit chambers which are designed to remove only the heavy inorganic solids of size more than 0·2 mm and of specific gravity 2·65 are generally removed by the sedimentation tanks. The sedimentation tanks are thus designed to remove a part of the organic matter from the sewage effluent coming out from the grit chambers. It is known as primary sedimentation. (Fig 18·19)

Sedimentation with coagulation. Very fine suspended particles present in waste water, which can not be removed in plain sedimentation, may sometimes be settled by increasing their size by changing them into flocculated particles. For this purpose, certain chemical compounds like ferric chloride from sulphate, alum, chlorinated copper etc. called coagulants are added to the waste waters, which on thorough mixing form a gelatinous precipitate called floc. The fine mud particles and other colloidal matter present in waste waters get absorbed in these flocs, forming the bigger sized flocculated particles. The process of addition and mixing of chemicals is called coagulation. The coagulated sewage is then made to pass through sedimentation tank, where the flocculated particle settle down and get removed.

Secondary treatment through biological filtration of sewage

Sewage filtration. The effluent from the primary sedimentation tank contains about

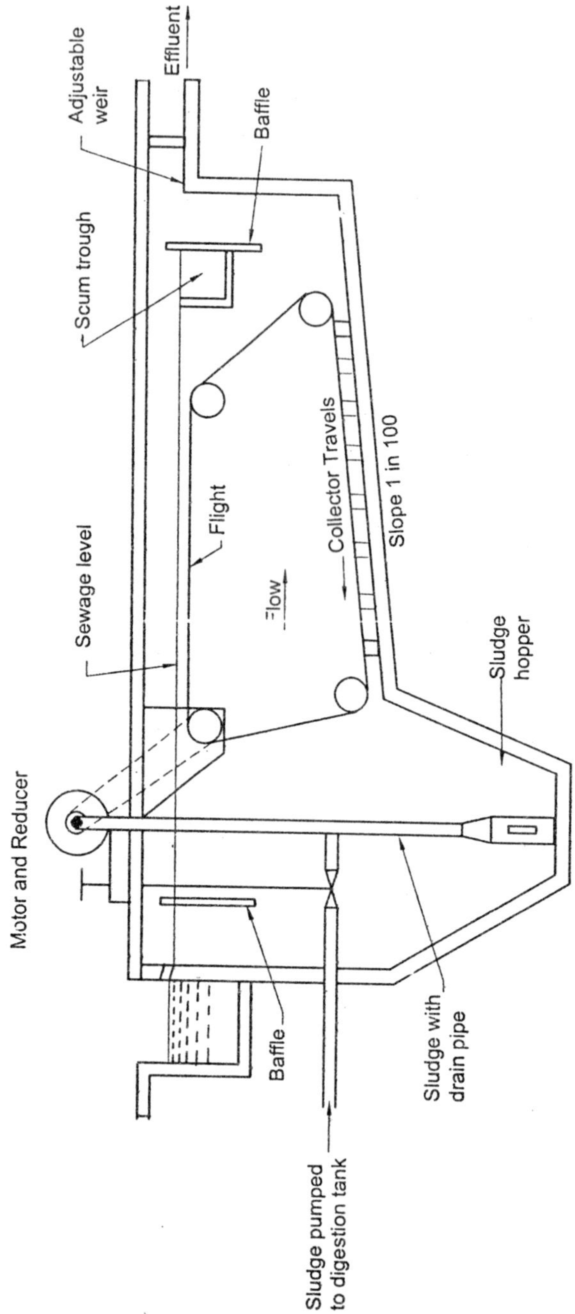

Fig. 18·19. Rectangular sedimentation tank.

60 to 80% of the unstable organic matter which passes the primary sedimentation, without settling these, has to be removed by further treatment. Thus further treatment of sewage, called secondary or biological treatment is carried out by changing the character of the organic matter, and thus converting it into stable forms like nitrates sulphates etc. by oxidation or nitrification.

The character of the sewage may be changed by different methods which are classified as (*i*) Filtration and (*ii*) activated sludge process. These processes help in changing the unstable organic matter into stable forms and thus ensuring their removal when the effluent from these units is settled in secondary sedimentation tanks. All this secondary treatment is done by aerobic bacterial decomposition in the presence of O_2 (air). Thus aerobic decomposition does not produce bad smells which are produced in aerobic decomposition in absence of air (O_2).

The filter units of secondary treatment consists of open beds of coarse aggregates over which the effluent from the primary treatment is sprinkled intermittently. The necessary contact surface for the growth of aerobic bacteria is provided by the aggregates in this bed and the aeration is provided by nature. The effluent from filter units is settled out in secondary clarification. On the other hand an activated sludge treatment unit consists of aeration tanks of long detention period in which the activated sludge mixed with the sedimenting sewage is agitated and aerated. The sludge solids thus kept in suspension will provide the necessary contact surfaces for the growth of aerobic bacteria. The mixed liquor after agitation is silted out in secondary clarifiers. The sludge so sillted in secondary clarifiers is called the activated sludge as it contains a lot of oxygen and is thus biological active. This sludge will be disposed off after digestion. Although a small part of it will be taken to aeration tanks for keeping the activated sludge process continue.

There are various kinds of filters that are commonly used either singly or in combination for giving secondary treatment of sewage. All these filters try to oxidise the unstable organic matter into stable forms, mainly be aerobic decomposition. These filters are as below :

(*a*) Contact beds which are used in very small plants.

(*b*) Trickling filters mostly used these days.

(*c*) Intermittent sand filter used in smaller plants.

(*d*) Miscellaneous types of filters used under special circumstances.

(*a*) **Contact beds for biological filtration.** In contact beds or also known as contact filters sewage is kept in contact with the filtering media for a certain period (known as 1st contact period). The sewage percolates through the filtering media, fine colloidal organic matter is trapped in the racks between the particles of the filtering media. Due to this an organic film is deposited around the particales of the filtering media. A large number of aerobic bacteria is present in the film will carry out the oxidation of the organic matter present in this film by process of aerobic decomposition. In order to make sufficient oxygen available for the growth of aerobic bacteria the filter is left empty *i.e.* without any sewage for a certain period for the 2nd contact period. During this time the process will go on, on the stand by filter. During this idle period the filter will absorb oxygen from the atmosphere and will complete the oxidation process. This makes one cycle of the operation. The stablised atmosphere organic matter in the 1st cycle will be washed away by fresh sewage in the next cycle.

A contact bed consists of a water tight rectangular tank filled with filtering media such as gravel ballast or brick ballast. The size of the media matter is between 20 to 40 mm. The depth varies 1 to 1·8 metres at an average of 1·2 m. These tanks are generally dug below the ground level. In dosing bed a siphon is provided for two or three contact beds. The dosing tank receives the effluent from primary sedimentation tank and feeds to the contact beds turn by turn at regular intervals by the timed siphonic action. Ordinary tanks without siphon is also used which are operated manually by valves. The sewage after percolating from the filtering media is collected at the bottom by a system of suitably laid open joints under drain. This effluent may be taken to the secondary sedimentation.

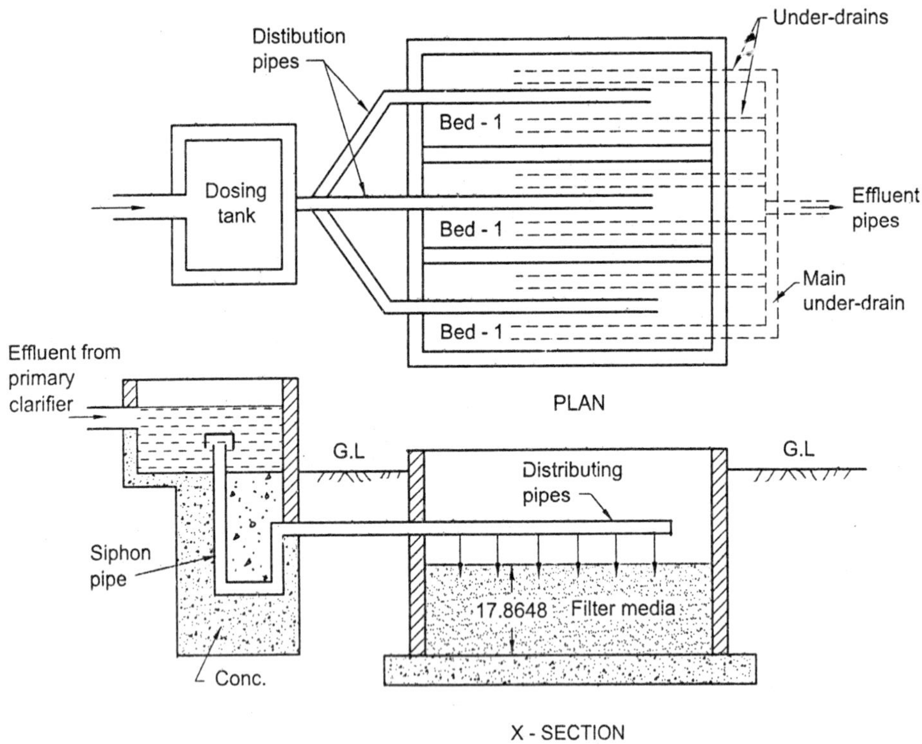

Fig. 18·20. Contact beds.

Intermittent sand filters. These filters are of the same type of construction as contact beds. The only difference is that the filtering media is sand in place of ballast in a thickness of 0·9 to 1·05 m.

Trickling filters for biological filtering of sewage. Trickling filters with their improved forms are being used these days known as **High rate trickling filter** for secondary treatment to sewage. These filters also called as **percolating filters** or **sprinkling filters** consists of tanks of coarser filtering media, over which the sewage is allowed to sprinkle or trickle down, by means of spray nozzles or rotary distributors. The percolating sewage is collected at the bottom of the tank through a well designed under-drainage system. The purification of the sewage is brought about mainly by the aerobic bacteria, which form a bacterial film around the particles of the filtering media. The action due to the mechanical straining of the filter bed is much less. In order to ensure the large scale growth of the aerobic bacteria, sufficient quantity of oxygen is supplied by providing suitable ventilation facilities in the body of the filter and also to some extent by the intermittent functioning of the filter.

The effluent obtained from the filter must be taken to the secondary sedimentation tank for settling out the organic meter, oxidised while passing down the filter. The sewage influent entering the filter must be given pre-treatments including screening and primary sedimentation.

Secondary sedimentation tank or **Humous tanks.** As is pointed out that in the biological filtration a very small percentage of the finally divided organic matter present in sewage is removed, while the majority of this organic matter undergoes a change of character only due to the biological oxidation and nitrification taking place in the filter. Due to this aerobic oxidation and nitrification that takes place in the filter the organic solids are converted into coagulated suspended mass, which is heavier and bulkier and would thus settle down by gravity if allowed to do so in sedimentation tanks. The effluent of the filter is therefore passed through a sedimentation tank called secondary clarifier or secondary settling tank or Humous Tank.

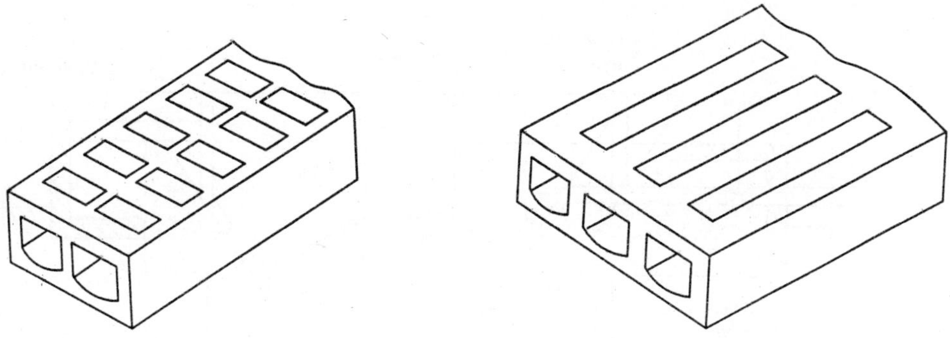

(*a*) Under drain block for standard trickling filler.

(*b*) Under drain block for high rate trickling filler.

Fig. 18·21.

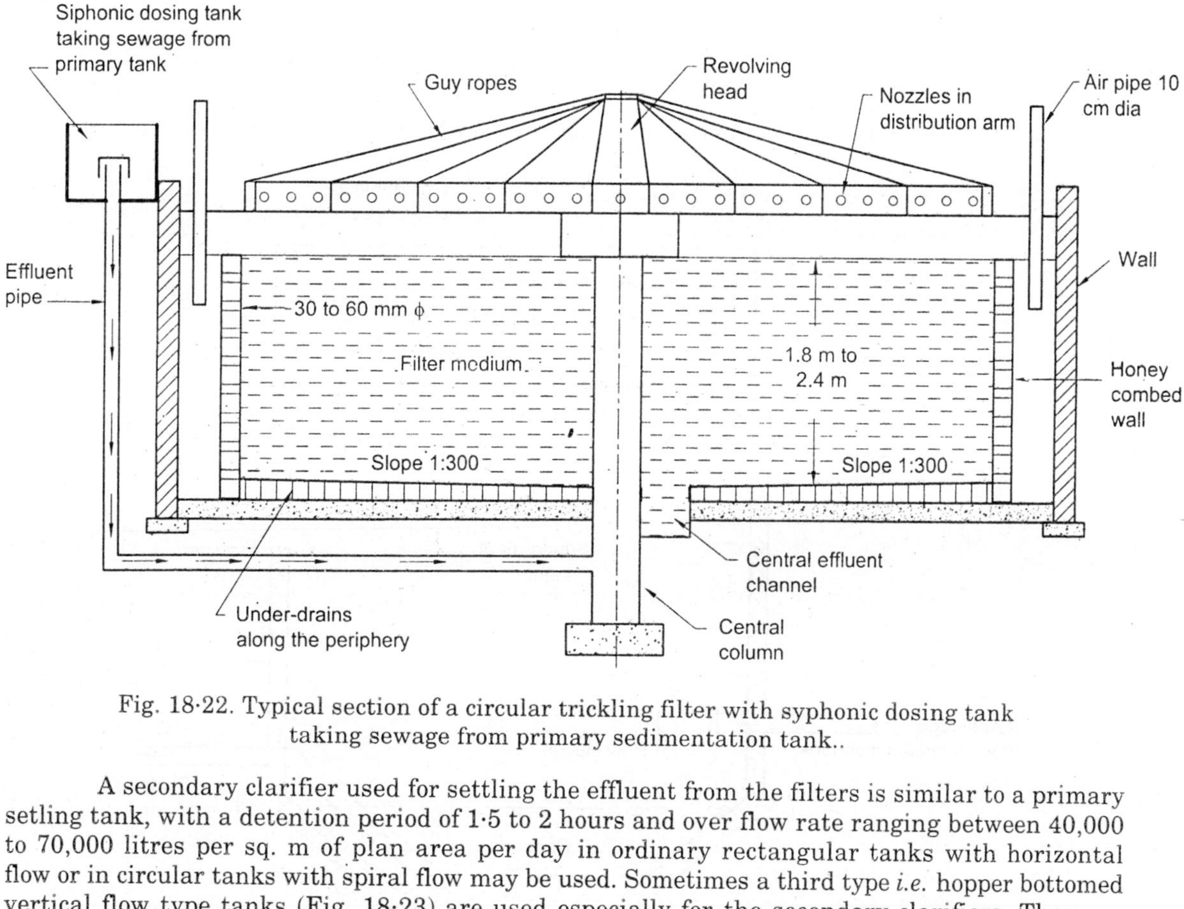

Fig. 18·22. Typical section of a circular trickling filter with syphonic dosing tank taking sewage from primary sedimentation tank..

A secondary clarifier used for settling the effluent from the filters is similar to a primary setling tank, with a detention period of 1·5 to 2 hours and over flow rate ranging between 40,000 to 70,000 litres per sq. m of plan area per day in ordinary rectangular tanks with horizontal flow or in circular tanks with spiral flow may be used. Sometimes a third type *i.e.* hopper bottomed vertical flow type tanks (Fig. 18·23) are used especially for the secondary clarifiers. They are circular tanks with deep conical hoppers with dia. as well as height ranging between 7·5 to 9 m. They are very costly and as such not generally used these days and ordinary rectangular tanks with horizontal flow are generally preferred even for secondary clarification.

The sludge settled at the bottom of the humus tanks should be continuously and rapidly removed and sent to the digestion tanks either directly or through primary clarifiers.

Digestion of sludge. The sludge obtained from primary sedimentation known as **Raw**

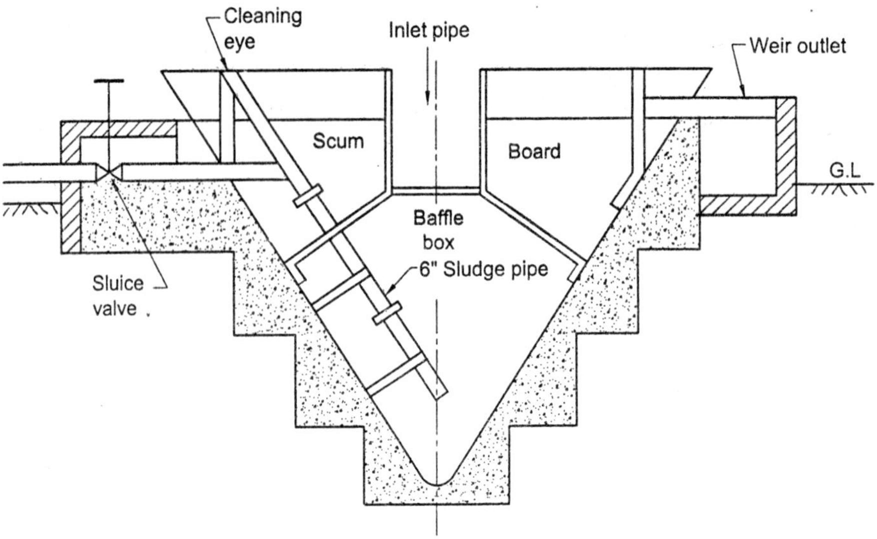

Fig. 18·23. Hopper bottomed conical vertical flow type sedimentation tank.

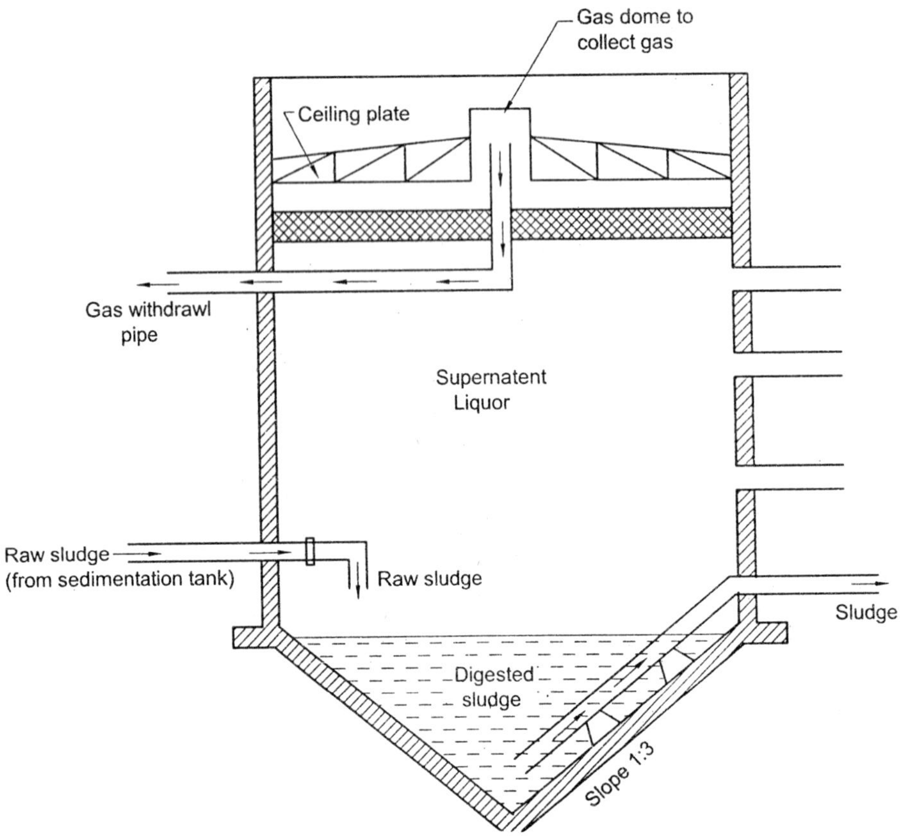

Fig. 18·24. Section of a sludge digestion tank.

sludge and which is obtained from the secondary sedimentation known as **secondary sludge** is odorous, moist and pulversible. Hence the sludge so obtained is stabilised before final disposal.

The sludge obtained from primary sedimentation contains 95% moisture while secondary sludge contains 96 and in case of trickling sedimentation upto 99%. Being moist it is bulky and difficult to handle. Therefore it is dried by special treatments since the water is so tenaciously held in the sludge. 70 to 80% moist sludge becomes viscous and at about 10% moisture content it becomes dry and assumes powder form 99% moisture contains 1 litre of solids in 100 litres of sludge.

Sludge digestion process. If the untreated sludge is disposed of without any treatment it will decompose (organic matter) into putrious and foul gases which create hazardous condition. Therefore it is first of all stabilised by decomposing the organic matter under controlled anaerobic conditions and then disposed of suitably after drying on drying beds etc. The process of stabilising is called the sludge digestion, and the tank where the process is carried out is called the sludge digestion tank. The resulting sludge is a stable humous like solid, tary black in colour with a reduced moisture content.

Sludge digestion tank known as Digestors. It contains a circular RCC tank with hoppered bottom, and having a fixed or a floating type of roof over its top which can raise or drop with the pressure of gas.

The raw sludge is pumped into the tank and when the tank is first put into operation it is feeded with the digested sludge from another tank. A screw pump with an arrangement for circulating the sludge from bottom to top of the tank or vice versa is commonly used for stirring the sludge. Some times power driven mechanical devices may be used for stirring the sludge, although these are not very popular at present. In cold countries the tank may be provided with heating coils or the hot water is circulated.

The gases which are chiefly methane and carbon dioxide are collected in a gas zone in small tanks while remaining other gases are collected separately in gas holders on larger tanks for subsequent use. The digested sludge which settles down to the hoppered bottom of the tank is removed under hydrostatic pressure periodically, once in a week or so. The supernatant liquor lying between the sludge and the scum is removed at suitable elevations, though a number of withdrawal pipes as shown. The supernatant liquor being higher in BOD and suspended solids contents is sent back for treatment along with the raw sewage in the treatment plant. The scum formed at the top surface of the supernatant liquor is brocken by the recirculating flow or through the mechanical rakers called scum breakers.

Table. 18·17. Design capacities of the digestion tanks per capita basis

Sl. No.	*Type of raw sludge to be digested*	*kg of volatile solids present per cu.m. of sludge/month*	*Per capita capacity in cu.m./capita*
1.	Primary sludge	8	0·021
2.	Mixture of primary sludge and secondary sludge from trickling filters (humus filters)	7·36	0·036
3.	Mixture of primary sludge and secondary activated sludge	5·76	0·04
4.	Chemicals coagulated sludge	—	0·056

Drying digested sludge. Sludge drying beds are open beds of land 45 to 60 cm and consisting of about 30 to 40 cm thick graded layers of gravel or crushed stone ballast varying 15 cm at bottom to 1·25 cm at top over which 10 to 15 cm thick layer of coarse sand is laid. Open jointed under drain pipe of 15 cm dia. at 5 to 7 cm c/c spacing are laid below the filled bed (graded ballast to sand layer). A slope of 1 : 100 is given to the bed which is surrounded by boundary walls. The bed is about 15 × 30 m in plan.

The sludge from the digestion tank is brought and spreaded on the beds in a depth of about 20 to 30 cm through distribution troughs having openings of about 15 × 20 cm at a distance of about 2 m or so.

A portion of the moisture is drained through drain while most of it remains in the atmosphere for about 2 week to 2 months depending on the weather condition of bed. A typical drawing of the bed is shown below. A minimum of drying beds are made according to the requirement and some beds are kept idle for rotation.

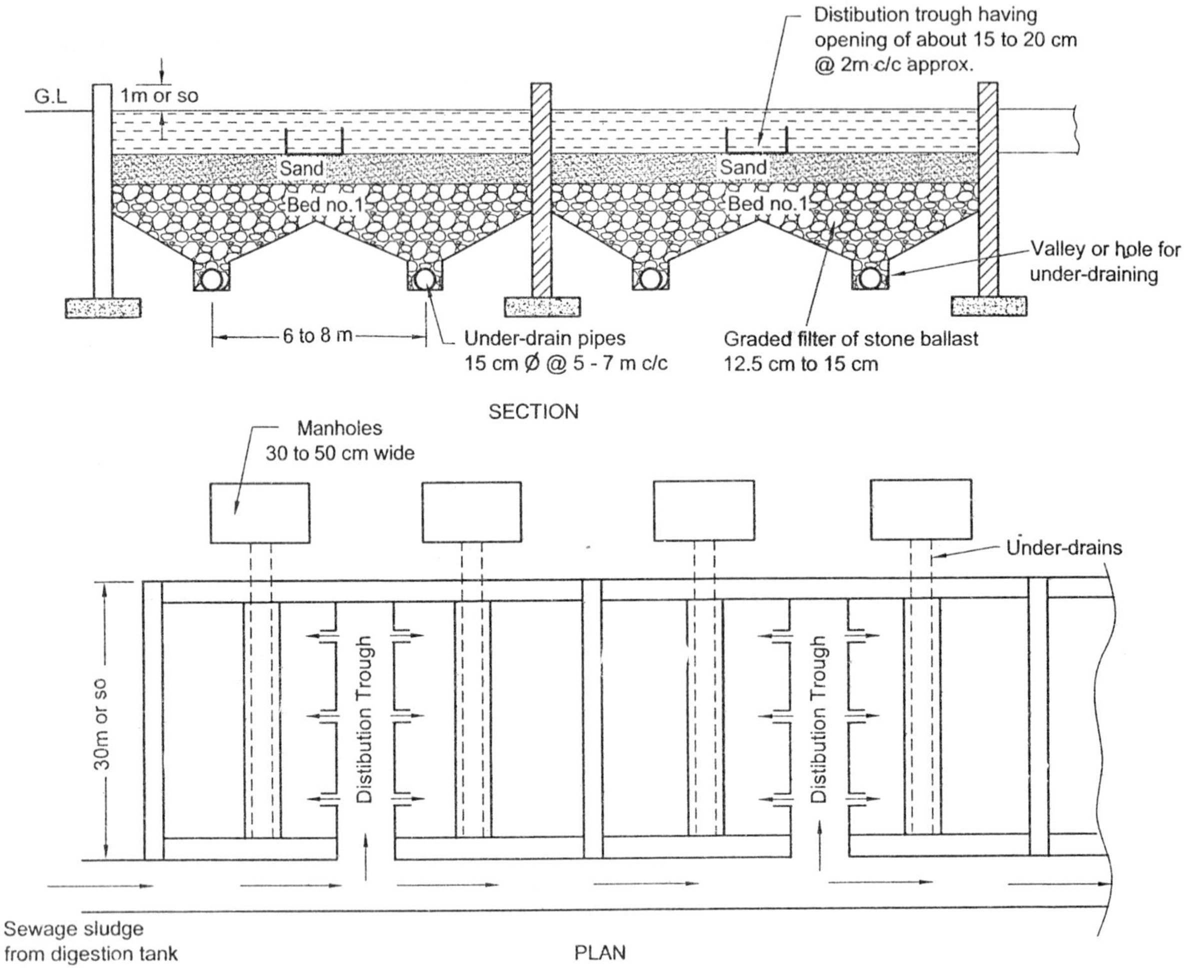

Fig. 18·25. Sludge drying beds.

Table. 18·18. Approximate area of drying beds for different type of sludges

Sl. No.	*Source of sludge*	*Area in m²/capita*	
		Open beds	*Covered beds*
1.	Primary clarifiers	0·1	0·08
2.	Intermittent sand filters	0·1	0·08
3.	Standard rate trickling filters	0·12	0·10
4.	High rate trickling filters	0·15	0·12
5.	Activated sludges	0·18	0·14
6.	Coagulated sludges	0·20	0·15

Use of lagoons for disposal of raw sludges. These are used for disposing of sludge without digestion. In this method the raw sludge is kept at rest in shallow open pond called lagoon. The detention period is 1 to 2 months which may extend upto 6 months. In this process the sludge undergoes to anaerobic digestion thereby gets stabilised. Due to anaerobic decomposition of sludge foul gases will be evolved from a lagoon and hence the lagoons are located away the town and the direction of common winds be such that the smells are not carried towards the towns or habitation.

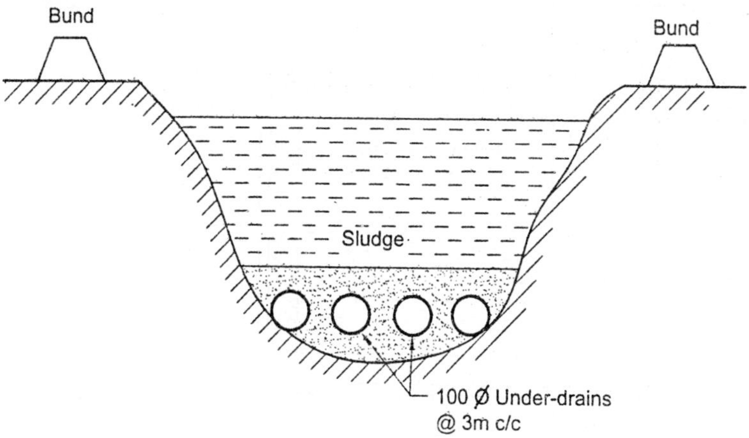

Fig. 18·26.

A shallow pit 0·6 to 1·2 m deep is formed by excavation in the ground. At the bottom of this pit a 15 cm thick layer of ashes or clinker is placed.

Agriculture tile drains of about 10 cm dia. are laid at bottom as under drains at about 3 m c/c. Spoil banks are formed in shape of bends at the both ends from the excavated earth.

After the sludge has been stabilised and the moisture has been drained away or evaporated during the detention in the lagoon, the contents are dugs to about half of their original volume and used as manure.

The method is cheap but it pollutes the environment due to eruption of foul gases which spreads in the area.

Chlorination of the sewage. The sewage can be disinfected by adding chlorine to it as is done for disinfecting the water supply. When chlorine is added to the treated sewage as a final step in its treatment, it is called **Post-chlorination.** This is adopted where an effluent is low in bacterial count, is necessary. The disinfecting action of chlorine will no doubt reduces the bacteria but its oxidising action will also reduce BOD to some extent.

Prochlorination of sewage before it enters the sedimentation tank may help in controlling odours, may prevent flies in trickling filters and may assist in the removal of grease.

Chlorine may sometimes be added to the sewage, both at beginning as well as at the end of the treatment process. It is known as **split-chlorination.**

Septic tank* is a horizontal continuous type of a sedimentation tank with a longer detention period of 12 to 36 hours against a period of 2 hours in an ordinary sedimentation tank with an extra provision of digestion of the settled sludge. Since the digestion of the silted settled sludge is carried out by anaerobic decomposition process, the septic tank unit is generally classified under the units which work on the principle of anaerobic decomposition. Due to anaerobic decomposition foul all are evolved in the tank. Therefore a septic tank is always covered and is provided with a ventilation pipe. A septic tank, receives the sewage directly and removes about 60 to 70% of the same out. Effluent from septic tanks are of foul in nature hence it will have to be disposed off either for sub irrigation or in cess pools (soak pits) or to be treated in trickling filters before disposing it to water courses for irrigation. The sludge settled at the bottom of the septic tank and the greasy oils at the top of sewage as scum are left in the septic tanks for several months. During this period they are decomposed by the anaerobic bacteria to form gases and liquids by the process of digestion. The resultant sludge produced is sufficiently less than that which is produced in ordinary settling tanks due to digestion. The digested sludges is

* For details also refer section 18·6 latter in this chapter.

periodically at intervals of about a year is removed and is taken to nearby sump from where its may be pumped to the ground and is disposed of desirably. The disposal of sludge from the tank must not be detained more than 3 years.

Septic tanks are generally provided in areas where sewers have not been laid and for catering to the sanitary disposal of sewage produced from isolated communities, schools, hospitals and other public institutions.

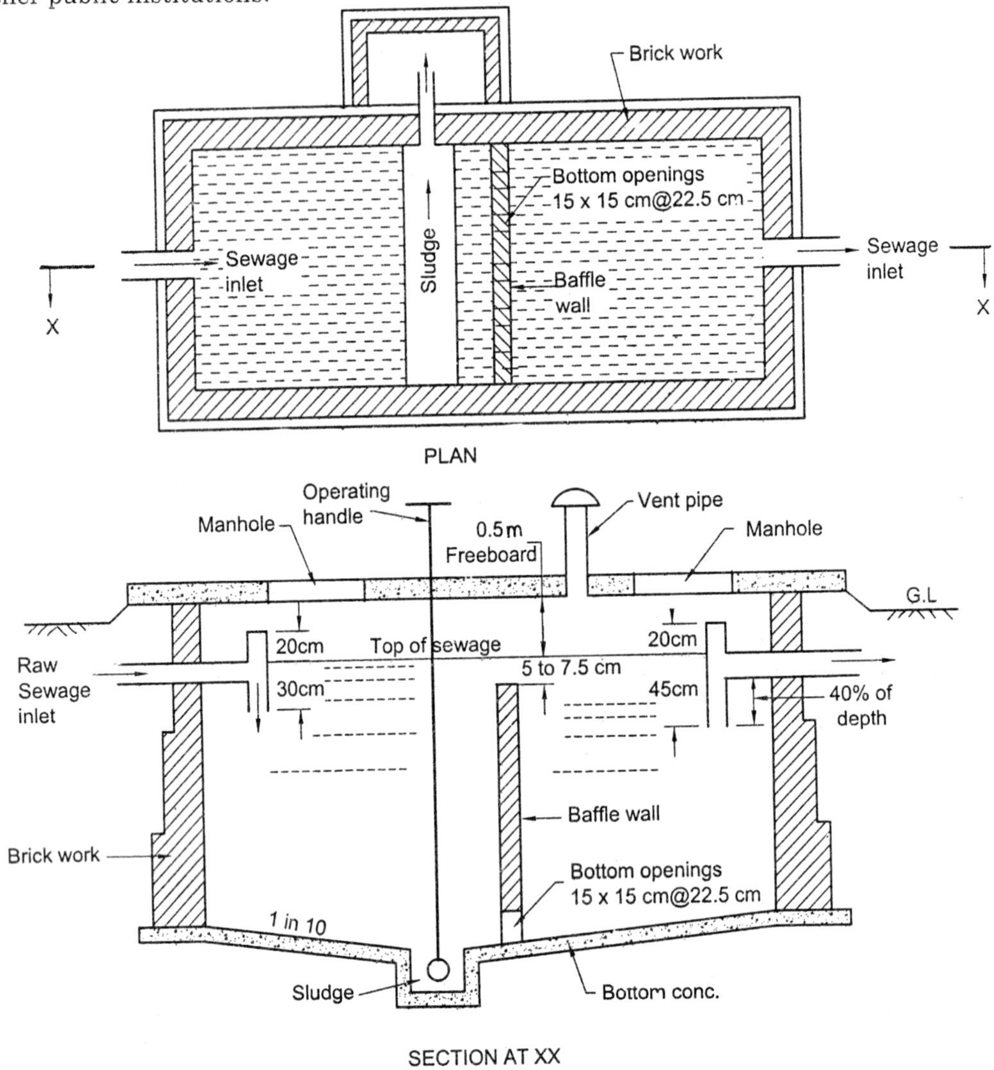

Fig. 18·27. Septic tank*.

Imhoff tanks. Imhoff tank is an improved septic tank in which the incoming sewage is not allowed to get mixed with sludge produced and the outgoing effluent is not allowed to carry with its large amount of organic load, as in the case of septic tanks. In fact it is a two storeyed tank.

The typical type of imhoff tank is shown in Fig. 18·28. It is a double chamber rectangular

* Septic tank is a sedimentation tank for a longer detention period for sludge and is used where public sewers are not laid. The isolated institutional buildings like hospitals, schools, charitable trusts etc. use it for inhouse disposal of sewage.

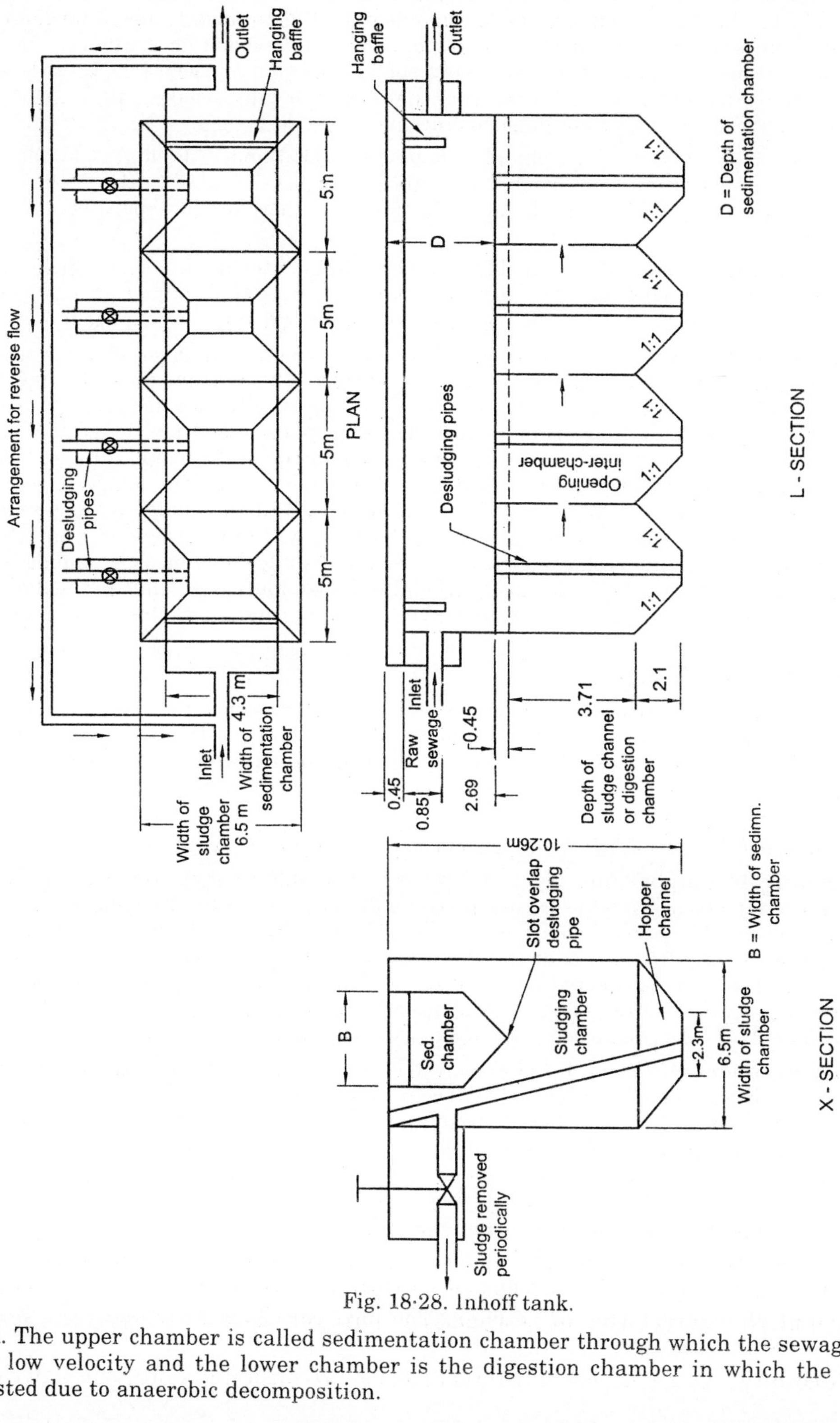

Fig. 18·28. Inhoff tank.

tank. The upper chamber is called sedimentation chamber through which the sewage flows at a very low velocity and the lower chamber is the digestion chamber in which the sludge gets digested due to anaerobic decomposition.

The solids of the slow moving sewage settling down to the bottom of the sedimentation chamber through the sloping bottom sides of the chamber (1 : 1·25) and slide down the digestion chamber through an entrance slot at the lowest point of a sedimentation chamber. The slot (minimum width 15 cm) is trapped or overlapped in such a way that the gases generated in the digestion chamber can not enter the sedimentation chamber, and thus avoiding direct contact of sewage with the foul gases and its consequent pollution.

A gas vent also called as scum chamber is also provided above the digestion chamber and along side of sedimentation chamber to take care of the gas escaping to the surface. The chief gas is methane having a considerable fuel value and may therefore be separately collected for use.

In order to prevent the particles of sludge or scum from entering into the sedimentation chamber from the digestion chamber, the scum or sludge must be maintained at least 45 cm above and below the slots respectively. The free or clear zone is called the neutral zone.

The digestion chamber (*i.e.* the lower chamber) is divided into a number of (three or four) interconnected compartment as shown in the Fig. 18·28. The bottom of each digestion compartment is made up in the form of a inverted cone or hopper with side slopes 1 : 1 so as to concentrate the sludge at the bottom of the hopper. The digested sludge from the bottom of the hoppers is removed periodically (after 1 to 1½ months, depending upon the temperature of sludge) through the cast iron desludging pipes provided in each compartment. The sludge is removed with flow under hydrostatic pressure of 1·2 to 1·8 m. Moreover all the sludge is not removed, and only the bottom layers which are completely digested are withdrawn, leaving some sludge to keep the tank seedes with anaerobic bacteria. The removed sludge may be dried and disposed off in a sanitary manner. Further in order to ensure uniform distribution of solids in the different hoppers, the flow of sewage in the sedimentation compartment *i.e.* above is reversed intermittently.

18·3. Decomposition of Sewage

Decomposition of sewage. Mostly the organic matter present in the sewage is unstable and decomposes through chemical as well as biological actions. The organic matter which is decomposed by bacateria under biological action is called **biodegradable** organic matter. Most of the organic matter present in sewage is biodegradable, and hence undergoes biological decomposition which is divided in two classes.

(*i*) Aerobic decomposition (*ii*) Anaerobic decomposition called putrefaction.

(*i*) **Aerobic decomposition.** If air or oxygen is available freely to the waste water in dissolved form, then the biodegradable organic matter will undergo aerobic decomposition caused by aerobic bacteria as well as by faculative bacteria. These bacteria will then utilise the free oxygen as electron causing thereby oxidising the organic matter to stable and unobjectionable end products. The stable end products like nitrates, CO_2 and sulphates are formed respectively for three forms of matters *i.e.* nitrogenous, carbonaceous and sulphuric matters. Water heat and additing bacteria will also be produced in this biological oxidation.

Anaerobic decomposition. If free dissolved oxygen is not available to the sewage, then anaerobic decomposition called putrefaction will occur. Anaerobic bacteria as well as facultative bacteria-operating anaerobically will then flourish and convert the complex organic matter into simpler organic compounds of nitrogen, carbon and sulphur. These anaerobic bacteria infact, survive by extracting and consuming the bounded molecular oxygen present in compounds like nitrates and sulphates. Gases like ammonia, nitrogen, hydrogen, sulphide, methane etc. are also evolved in the decomposition producing obnoxious odours.

Characteristics of sewage. The quality of sewage can be checked and analysed by sludging and testing its physical, chemical and bacteriological characteristics as discussed below:

Physical characteristics of sewage. The physical characteristics of the sewage together with their tests are given below :

(*i*) **Turbidity.** Sewage is generally turbid having dirty dish water or waste water from baths having other floating matter like foliage, pieces of paper, cigarette ends, match sticks, greases of soaps and, spurt skies etc. The degree of turbidity can be measured and tested by turbidity rods or by turbidimeters as is done for testing raw water supplied.

Colour. The colour of a sewage can be seen by naked eye. If the sewage is fresh its colour will be yellowish, grey or light brown. If the colour is black or dark brown, the sewage is stale and septic. Other colours shows the presence of industrial wastes.

Odour. Fresh sewage is odourless, but within 3 or 4 hours it becomes stale with all oxygen present in sewage being practically exhausted. It then starts offensive odour especially that of hydrogen sulphide gas which has produced by the decomposition of sewage.

Temperature. The temperature of the sewage affects the solubility and biological activity of the bacteria present in sewage temperature also affects the viscosity of sewage which in turn affects the sedimentation of the sewage. The temperature of a normal sewage is slightly higher than water.

Chemical characteristics of the sewage and their testing. The chemical tests of sewage help in indicating the stage of decomposition, its strength and extent and type of treatment required for making it safe to the point of disposal. It includes the following tests :

(*i*) Total solids, suspended solids, and settleable solids

(*ii*) pH value

(*iii*) Chemical content

(*iv*) Nitrogen content

(*v*) Presence of fats, grease and oils

(*vi*) Sulphides, sulphates and H_2S gas

(*vii*) Dissolved oxygen

(*viii*) Chemical oxygen demand (COD)

(*ix*) Biochemical oxygen demand (BOD)

These tests are discussed in brief as below :

(*i*) Sewage normally contain very small quantity of solids in comparison to the huge amount of water which is about 99·9%. It only contains about 0·05% to 0·6% (*i.e.* 500 to 1000 mg (litres) of total. Solids may be in the form of suspended solids, dissolved solids, colloidal solids and settleable solids.

Suspended solids are those solids which floats in the sewage. Dissolved solids remain dissolved in water like salts. Colloidal solids are finally divided solids which remain either in suspension or remain dissolved. Selleable solids are that portion of solid matter which settles out, if sewage is allowed to remain undisturbed for a period of 2 hours.

It has been estimated that about 1000 kg of sewage contain about 0·45 kg of total solids out of which 0·225 kg is in solution, 0·112 kg is in suspension and 0·112 kg is settleable. Both organic and inorganic solids are found in the sewage in the percentages of about 45 and 55% respectively. Inorganic matter consists of minerals and salts like sand, gravel, dissolved salts chlorides and sulphates etc. Organic matter contains (*i*) carbohydrates such as cellulose, cotton, fibre, starch, sugar etc. (*ii*) fats and oils received from kitchens, laundries, garages and shops etc. (*iii*) nitrogenous compounds like proteins and their decomposed products including waste from animal, urea, fatty acids and hydrocarbons etc. The presence of the inorganic material are not harmful and can be removed by mechanical means, while the organic matter creates harmful odour and nuisance. The amount of various kinds of solids can be determined as follows :

(*i*) By **evaporating** the known quantity of the sewage and then weighing the residue left. It will determine the percentage of solids (say S_1).

(*ii*) By **filtration**. A known quantity of the sample is filtered in a filter of 1 mm pores. The dry residue is then weighed (say S_2).

(*iii*) The difference of the two residues as obtained above is dissolved solids plus colloids or filtrated solids (say S_3) so ($S_3 = S_1 - S_2$).

(*iv*) The total suspended solids (S_2) may either be volatile or fixed. For determining their proportion the residue (S_2) is burnt to about 550°C for about 15 to 20 minutes. Loss of weight due to ignition will represent the volatile solids in the sample volume filtered, say it is S_4 (mg/l).

(*v*) The difference $S_2 - S_4 = S_5$ (say will represent unfixed solids.

(*vi*) The quantity of the settleable solids say (S_6) can be determined by the Inhoff cone.

In half cone (Fig. 18·29) is a glass conical graduated vessel of capacity of one litre. The sewage is allowed to stand in the cone for a period of two hours and the quantity of solids settle in the bottom of the cone is directly read (the cone is graduated upto 50 ml). However in order to obtain more reliable amount of settleable solids, the liquid from the cone should be decanted off and the settleable solids collected at the bottom of the cone should be dried and weighed.

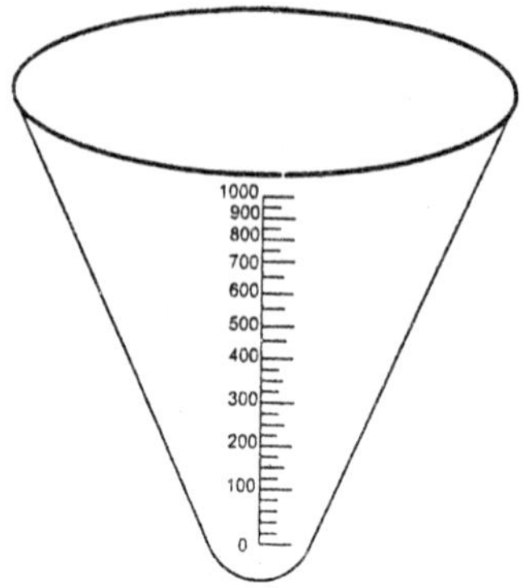

Fig. 18·29. Imhoff cone.

Table 18·19. Quantities of solids present in domestic sewage in mg/l

Type of solid		*Strength (weak)*	*Medium*	*Strong*
Total solids		400	800	1200
Suspended solids	(Total)	100	200	350
	(Volatile)	75	135	210
Settleable		2·5	5	7
Either soluble matters, such as fats oils and greases		6	14	20

pH value. pH value of sewage indicates the negative log of hydrogen ion concentration present in sewage be

$$pH = -\log H^+ \text{ or } H^+ = (10)^{-pH}$$

It is the indication of alkalinity. If the pH value is less than 7, the sewage is acidic and if more it is alkaline. The less is the pH value, the lesser is the alkalinity. It can be measured by a potentiometer.

Chloride content. The chlorides are obtained in kitchen and urinal wastes. The normal chloride content in the domestic waste is 120 mg/l where permissible content is 250 mg/l. Large quantities may be obtained in industrial wastes. The chloride contents can be found by titratun with standard silver nitrate solution using potassium chromate as indicator.

Nitrogen content. The presence of nitrogen in the sample indicates the presence of organic matter in the form of free ammonia called ammonia N, albuminoid nitrogen called as organic N, nitrates and nitrites.

Presence of fats, oils and greases. These are obtained from fats and oils from the discharge of animals and vegetable matter or from the industries like garages, kitchen of hotels and restaurants etc.

Sulphides, sulphates and hydrogen sulphide gas. The determination of sulphide and sulphates in sewage is rarely called for, although their presence reflects aerobic or anaerobic composition.

In anaerobic digestion of sewage, however, the anaerobic and facultative bacteria reduce the sulphur and its compounds into sulphides with evolution of H_2S gas along with methane and carbon dioxide. Thus causing very obnoxious odours. If however the quantity of H_2S in raw sewage is below 1 ppm, obnoxious odours are not felt.

Dissolved oxygen (D.O). The determination of the presence of the dissolved oxygen is very important, because while discharging the treated sewage into some river, it is necessary to ensure at least 4 ppm (D.O.) in it as otherwise, fish are likely to be killed creating nuisance near the vicinity of disposal. To ensure this (D.O.) tests are performed during sewage disposal treatment processes. If the temperature of sewage is more, the D.O. content will be less. The solubility of the oxygen in sewage is 95% of that in distilled water. The D.O. contents in sewage is generally determined by the **Winkler's method** which is an oxidation-reduction process carried out chemically to liberate iodine in amount equivalent to the quantity of dissolved oxygen originally present.

Chemical oxygen demand (COD). The organic matter present in water can be measured in a number of ways. Volatile solids determination being a crude measure of organic matter. Organism is most often assessed in terms of oxygen required to completely oxidise the organic matter to CO_2, H_2O and other oxidised species.

The oxygen required to oxidise the organic matter present in a given waste can be theoretically computed if the organics present in waste water is known. Thus if the chemical formulae and the concentrations of the chemical compounds present in water are known to us, we can easily calculate the **theoretical oxygen demands** of each of these compounds by writing the balanced reaction for the compound with oxygen to produce CO_2, H_2O and oxidised inorganic components.

Total organic carbon. Another important method of expressing organic matter in terms of its carbon content. Carbon is the primary constituent of organic matter and hence the chemical formula of every organic compound will reflect the extent of carbon present in that compound. Known concentrations of each chemical compounds in a given waste water will thus enable us to theoretically calculate the carbon present in that waste water per litre of solution.

Bio-chemical oxygen demand (B.O.D.). The organic matter, infact is of two types *i.e.* (*i*) that which is biologically oxidised *i.e.* oxidised by bacteria and is called **biologically active** or biologically degradable and (*ii*) that which can not be oxidised biologically and is called **biologically inactive.** In fact while testing a waste water we are mainly interested in finding out the amount of biologically active organic matter present in it, where as the C.O.D. test gives us total of biologically active as well as biologically inactive organic matters. Hence further testing is carried out to determine the **biochemical oxygen demand** (B.O.D.) of sewages which directly gives us the amount of **biologically active organic matter** present in sewage. B.O.D. test is discussed as below.

If sufficient oxygen is available in waste water, the useful aerobic bacteria will flourish and cause the aerobic biological decomposition of waste water, which will continue until oxidation is completed. The amount of oxygen consumed in the process is the B.O.D. polluted waters will continue to absorbe oxygen for many months, and it is not practically feasible to determine the ultimate oxygen demand.

Hence the BOD water during 5 days at 20°C is generally taken as the standard demand and is about 68% of the total demand. A 60 days BOD (BOD 10) is about 90% of the total.

The standard 5 day BOD denoted by BODs or simply BOD is determined in the laboratory by mixing or diluting a known volume of a sample of waste water with a known volume of pure water and then calculating the DO of this diluted sample. The diluted sample is then incubated for 5 days at 20°C. The DO of the diluted sample after this period of incubation is again calculated. The difference between the initial DO value and the final D.O. value will indicate the oxygen consumed by the sewage sample in 5 days (used in causing aerobic decomposition of wastes). The BOD in ppm is then calculated by using the equation.

$$\text{BOD or BODs} = \text{DO consumed in the test by the diluted sample} \times \left[\frac{\text{Volume of the diluted sample}}{\text{Volume of the indiluted sewage sample}}\right]$$

The factor on the right hand side in the above equation is **Dilution factor.**

For example 1% diluted sample means. 1 ml of sewage is diluted to make 100 ml of test sample, and hence dilution factor would be 100 as 1 ml has been diluted by 100 times to make 100 ml. Hence the multiplying factor of the right hand side would be 100.

Relative stability may be defined as the ratio of oxygen available in the effluent (as D.O. nitrate or nitrate) to the total oxygen requires to satisfy its first stage BOD demand. It is expressed as percentage of the total oxygen required and can be expressed as

Relative stability, $S_1 = 100\,[1 - (0{\cdot}794)^{t/(20)}]$ or $S = 100[1 - (0{\cdot}630)^{t/(37)}]$

where $t(20)$ and $t(37)$ represent the time in days for a sewage sample to discontinue a standard volume of methane blue solution wherein at 20°C or 37°C respectively.

Collection of sewage samples for physical or chemical tests. The physical and chemical characteristics of sewage vary from top to bottom of sewage depth as well as with times from morning to evening. Therefore samples are taken at a point beneath the surface where the turbulence is thoroughly mixed up the sewage particles. This is called as a **grab sample.** Such samples are taken at regular intervals during a day which are mixed together and the amount utilised from each specimen is proportional to the rate of flow at the time the sample is collected. This sample is taken for testing. The sample is kept cool to prevent biological action from taking place. Preservatives are chloroform, formal dehyde and sulphuric acid which are added in collecting bottles.

18·4. Disposing of sewage. There are two methods of disposing the sewage :

(*a*) Dilution *i.e.* Disposal in water

(*b*) Effluent irrigation or broad irrigation or sewage farming disposal on land.

Disposal dilution. Disposal by dilution is the process to which the treated sewage or the effluent from the sewage treatment plant is discharged into a river, tank or a large body of water. The discharged sewage in due course of time is purified by what is known as "self purification process of natural water". The degree and amount of treatment given to raw sewage before disposing it of into the river in question will not only depend upon the quality of the raw sewage but also upon the self purification capacity of the river and the intended use of water.

Favouring conditions for disposal by dilution :

(*i*) The sewage must be fresh 4 to 5 hours old, and free from floating and settleable solids which are easily removed by primary treatment.

(*ii*) The diluting water has a high dissolved oxygen (D.O.) content.

(*iii*) When diluting, water has not to be used for water supply or for navigation for at least some reasonable distance apart from the point of disposal.

(*iv*) When the flow of diluting waste is favourable to the river flow causing no deposition, nuisance or destruction of aquate life.

(*v*) When the outfall sewer is situated near in natural water source.

The ratio of the quantity of the diluting water to that of the sewage which is known as **dilution factor.**

Table. 18·20. Standards of dilution based on Royal Commission Report

Dilution factor	*Standard of purification required*
Above 500	No treatment is required. Raw sewage can be directly discharged into the volume of dilution water.
300-500	Primary treatment as plain sedimentation should be given to sewage and the effluents should not contain suspended solids more than 150 ppm.

Table contd...

Table contd...

Dilution factor	*Standard of purification required*
150-300	Treatment such as sedimentation, screening and essentially chemical precipitation are required. The sewage effluent should not contain suspended solids more than 600 ppm.
Less than 150	Complete thorough treatment should be given to sewage. The sewage effluent should not contain suspended solids more than 30 ppm and its 5 days BOD at 18·3°C should not exceed 20 ppm.

Dilution in rivers and self purification of natural streams. When sewage is discharged into a natural body of water, the receiving water gets polluted due to waste products present in sewage effluents. This solution is not permanent because the natural activity of purification, such as dilution, sedimentation, oxidation-reduction in sun light etc. go on acting upon the pollution elements and bring back the water into its original condition. This automatic purification of polluted water in due course is called as the "self purification phenomenon". If the self purification is not achieved due to the quantity of the polluted water in too much excess, the river water itself will get polluted in turn it will pollute the sea water.

The various material forces which help in the natural purification are as below :

(1) Physical forces : (*i*) Dilution and dispersion (*ii*) Sedimentation (*iii*) Sun light which acts through bio-chemical reactions.

(*i*) **Dilution and dispersion.** When the putresible organic matter is discharged into a large volume of water contained in the river stream, it gets rapidly dispersed and diluted. The action thus results in diminishing the concentration of organic matter, and thus reduces the potential nuisance of sewage.

$$C_S.Q_S + C_RQ_R = C(Q_S + Q_R)$$

or

$$C = \frac{C_SQ_S + C_RQ_R}{Q_S + Q_R}$$

where sewage of concentration C_S flows at rate Q_S into the river stream with concentration C_R flows at a rate Q_R. The concentration C of the resulting mixture. This equation is applicable separately to concentrations of different impurities such as oxygen content, BOD, suspended sediments and other characteristic contents of sewage.

(*ii*) **Sedimentation.** The settleable solids, if present in sewage effluents will settle down into the bed of the river near the outfall of sewage which helps in the self purification.

(*iii*) **Sun light.** The sun light has a bleaching and stabilising effect of bacteria. It also helps certain micro-organisms to derive energy from it, and convert themselves into food for other forms of life, thus absorbing carbondioxide and releasing oxygen by a process known as **photosynthesis.** The evolution of oxygen in river water due to sun light helps in achieving self purification through oxidation as below :

(*iv*) **Oxidation.** The oxidation of the organic matter present in sewage effluent will stale as soon as sewage outfalls into the river water containing dissolved oxygen. The deficiency of oxygen so created, will be filled up by atmospheric oxygen. The process of oxidation will continue till the organic matter has been completely oxidised.

(*v*) **Reduction.** Reduction occurs due to hydrolysis of organic matter settled at the bottom either chemically or biologically. Anaerobic bacteria will help in splitting the complex organic constituents of sewage into liquids and gases and thus paving the way for their ultimate stabilisation by oxidation.

The various factors on which these natural forces of purification depend are (*a*) temperature (*b*) turbulence (*c*) hydrography such as the velocity and surface expanse of the river (*d*) available dissolved oxygen and the amount and type of organic matter present (*e*) rate of re-aeration etc.

Zones of pollution of river

(*i*) **Zone of degradation.** This zone is just a certain length below the point where the sewage is discharged into the river. The water in this zone becomes dark turbid with formation of sludge deposited at the bottom. D.O. (dissolved oxygen) is reduced to about 40% of the saturation value (Saturation value at 30°C = 7·6 mg/l). Increase in the CO_2 content, in re-oxygeneration.

(*ii*) **Zone of active decomposition.** This zone is marked by heavy pollution. The water becomes greyish and darker than in previous zone. De concentration falls down to zero and anaerobic conditions may set in with the evolution of gases like methane, CO_2, hydrogen sulphide etc. bubbling to the surface with masses of sludge forming an ugly scum layer at the surface.

(*iii*) **Zone of recovery.** In this zone the river tries to recover from its degraded condition to its former appearance. The water becomes clearer and so the algae reappears while fungi decreases. B.O.D. falls down and D.O, contents rises above 40% of the saturation value.

(*iv*) **Zone of clearer water.** In this zone the river attains its original conditions. With DO rising upto the saturation value. Water becomes clear and Game fish (which requires at least 4 to 5 mg/l of D.O.) and usual aquatic life prevails. Some pathogenic organisms may still, however survive and remain present which confirms the fact that "when once a river water has been polluted it will not be safe to drink it unless it is properly treated.".

Disposal of waste water into the sea. Sea water normally contains 20% less oxygen than that contained in fresh water of a river. Moreover sea water normally contains a large amount of dissolved matter. The capacity of sea water to absorb sewage is not as high as that of fresh water of a stream. Moreover sewage solids, when thrown into sea water, chemically react with the dissolved matter of sea water resulting in precipitation of some of the sewage solids getting a milky appearance to sea water and forming sludge banks which are undesirable as they are likely to produce offensive hydrogen sulphide gas by reacting with sulphate rich water of the sea. The oxygen contents of sea water is less than that of fresh water and also its recreation is slower. However, since the sea contains too larger volume of water, most of these de-efficiencies are removed, provided the sewage is taken deep into the sea and away from the coast.

Since specific gravity of sea water is greater than that of sewage water and temperature of sea water is lower than sewage, the lighter and warmer sewage will rise up to the surface when thrown into the sea water. This will result in spreading of the sewage at the top surface of sea in a thin film or 'sleek'.

To prevent the backing up and spreading of sewage on the sea shore, the sewage should be disposed of only during low tides. Large sized tanks may therefore be constructed to hold the sewage during high tides. Provision of a large sized sewer, graded with a non-return valve at the end is also an alternative to hold the sewage during high tides.

Table 18·21. BIS (ISI) standards for waste water effluents to be discharged into marine coasts.

S. No.	*Constituent pollutant contained in the waste water effluent*	*Tolerance limit*
1.	BODs	100 mg/l
2.	COD	250 mg/l
3.	pH value	5·5 to 9·0
4.	Total suspended solids	100 mg/l
5.	Oil and grease	20 mg/l
6.	Flourides (as F)	15 mg/l
7.	Ammoniacal Nitrogen (as N)	50 mg/l

Note : In addition to these major constituents, limits are prescribed for many trace metals and non metals.

Disposal of sewage on land. When there is not any river or a vast mass of water nearby in which the sewage may be disposed off or there is scarcity for water for irrigation, the disposal of the sewage effluent is done on open waste lands. This effluent disposed water may either join the water table by percolating or is collected below by a system of under drains. This water can also be used for irrigation proposed as it contains a lot of fertilising minerals. The sewage effluent before being used as irrigation water must be tested for its serviceability for irrigation so that it may not cause any poisonous effects. This type of irrigation is also known as "broad irrigation".

When raw or partly treated sewage is applied on to the land part of it evaporates and the remaining portion or a part of it percolates into the ground and joins the water table. The effects on the underground must also be checked whether it has a poisonous effects on it. If it has any objectionable effect the disposal of the effluent must be closed. While percolating through the soil the suspended particles present in the sewage are caught in the soil voids. If proper aeration of these voids is maintained, the organic sewage solids caught is these soils get oxidised by aerobic process. Such aeration and aerobic conditions will more likely prevail if the soil is sufficiently permeable such as sands and porous loams. If the land is made of heavy, sticky or fine grained materials such as clays etc. the void spaces will soon get choked up and resulting is non-aeration of these voids. This action will lead to the development of non aeration decomposition of organic matter and develops evolution of foul gases. Moreover excessive clogging may also result in accumulation of sewage water as ponds over the farm land where mosquitoes may breed in large number causing further nuisance. Application too long or too heavy loads of effluent disposal will also create the same situation in the quick formation of an aerobic condition. Hence to reduce this position either the disposal must be pre-treated or must be diluted with water to avoid clogging of the soil voids or pores. If the land irrigated is more porous or sandy the sewage effluent may contain more solids and other wastes and thus requiring lesser treatment as compared to the case where the soil is less porous or sticky.

Table. 18·22. Recommended doses for sewage farming

Type of soil		*Doses of sewage in cubic metres per hectare per day*	
		Raw sewage	*Treated sewage*
Sandy	All depends on the type of crops grown in the area	120-150	220-280
Sandy loam		90-100	170-220
Loam		60-80	110-170
Clayey loam		40-50	60-110
Clayey		30-45	30-60

The Bureau of Indian Standards (BIS) previously known as Indian Standards Institutions (ISI) has vide its code No. 3307—1968 laid down the tolerance limits for various polluting characteristics/constituents of waste water effluents for their discharge on land for irrigation. These standards are based upon the quality of irrigation water required by the crops and thus limit the concentration of pollutants contained in sewage of industry liquid waste which may prove harmful to the crops. The prescribed BIS standards are given in the table below :

Table. 18·23. BIS (ISI) standards of waste water effluent to be discharged on land for irrigation

S. No.	*Characteristics (constituent of effluent waste water)*	*Tolerance limit as per IS : 3307—1965*
1.	BODs	550 mg/l
2.	pH value	5·5-9·0
3.	Total dissolved solids (T.D.S.)	2100 mg/l

Table contd...

Table contd...

S. No.	*Characteristics (constituent of effluent waste water)*	*Tolerance limit as per IS : 3307—1965*
4.	Oil and greases	30 mg/l
5.	Chlorides (as chlorine)	600 mg/l
6.	Boron	2 mg/l
7.	Sulphates	1000 mg/l
8.	Percentage of sodium with respect to total contents of sodium, calcium, Mg or Pt.	60%
9.	Radio active materials	
	(*a*) α-emitters	10^{-9} μC/ml
	(*b*) β-emitters	10^{-8} μC/ml

Table. 18·24. Standards for discharge of polluted effluents on land for irrigation under environment protection Rules, 1986

S. No.	*Characteristics of effluent i.e. pollutant of waste water*	*Standards under environment (Protection) Rules, 1986*
1	2	3
1.	Colour and odour	All efforts should be made to remove colour and unpleasant odour as far as practicable
2.	BODs	100 mg/l
3.	Suspended solids	200 mg/l
4.	pH value	5·5 to 9·0
5.	Oil and grease	10 mg/l
6.	Arsenic (As)	0·2 mg/l
7.	Cynide (as CN)	0·2 mg/l
8.	Radio active materials	
	(*a*) Alpha emitters	10^{-8} μC/ml
	(*b*) Beta emitters	10^{-7} μC/ml
9.	Bio-assay test	90% survival of fish after 96 hours in 100% effluent
10.	**Pesticides**	
	(*i*) Benzene hexachloride	10 μ g/l
	(*ii*) Carbaryl	10 μ g/l
	(*iii*) D.D.T.	10 μ g/l
	(*iv*) Endo sulfass	10 μ g/l
	(*v*) Diamethoate	45 μ g/l
	(*vi*) Peni trothian	10 μ g/l
	(*vii*) Malathion	10 μ g/l
	(*viii*) Phorate	10 μ g/l
	(*ix*) Methyl parathion	10 μ g/l
	(*x*) Dyrethroms	10 μ g/l
	(*xi*) Copper oxychloride	9600 μ g/l
	(*xii*) Copper sulphate	50 μ g/l
	(*xiii*) Phenthorate	10 μ g/l
	(*xiv*) Ziram	1000 μ g/l
	(*xv*) Sulphur	30 μ g/l
	(*xvi*) Paraouat	2300 μ g/l
	(*xvii*) Proponil	7300 μ g/l
	(*xviii*) Nitrogen	7800 μ g/l

Effluent irrigation (Broad irrigation). In this type of irrigation by sewage disposal the chief aim is disposal of effluent while the irrigation is the by-aim.

Sewage farming. In this type of irrigation by sewage the chief aim is farming.

In case of broad irrigation, the raw or treated sewage is discharged on a vacant land, which is provided underneath, with a system of properly laid drains. These under drains usually consists of 15 to 20 cm dia. porous pipes laid open jointed at a spacing of 12 to 30 m. The effluent collected in these drains after getting filtered through the soil pores is generally small as a large quantity gets evaporated and well stabilised and can be easily disposed off into some natural water courses without any treatment.

In case of sewage farming the stress is laid upon the use of sewage effluent for irrigation. In the pre-treatment effort is made to remove the ingradient which may prove to be harmful and toxic to the plants.

Application of the sewage for irrigation. It is almost the same as is done in irrigation system by canals through channel system. The following methods are use in the system of irrigation by sewage water.

(1) **Free flooded.** The treated waste effluent water is passed through channels. A main channel is divided in sub channels in the form of grids. Two grid forms are made are on either side of the main channel. The water is also allowed to pass through the grids where it has a chance to settle the solid waste again. This solid waste is cleaned in one grid form while the other is in function. The top clear water is then passed in the side channel which leads to fields for irrigation.

(2) **Sub surface irrigation.** In this method sewage is supplied directly to the root zone of crops, through a system of properly laid open jointed porous pipes sewage as flows over these pipes percolates through the open joints and is distributed in the surrounding area by action of capillarity.

(3) **Sprinkling or spray irrigation.** In this method sewage is spreaded only the soil through nozzles which are fitted at the tips of pipes carrying sewage, under pressure. The process being costly is not practicable.

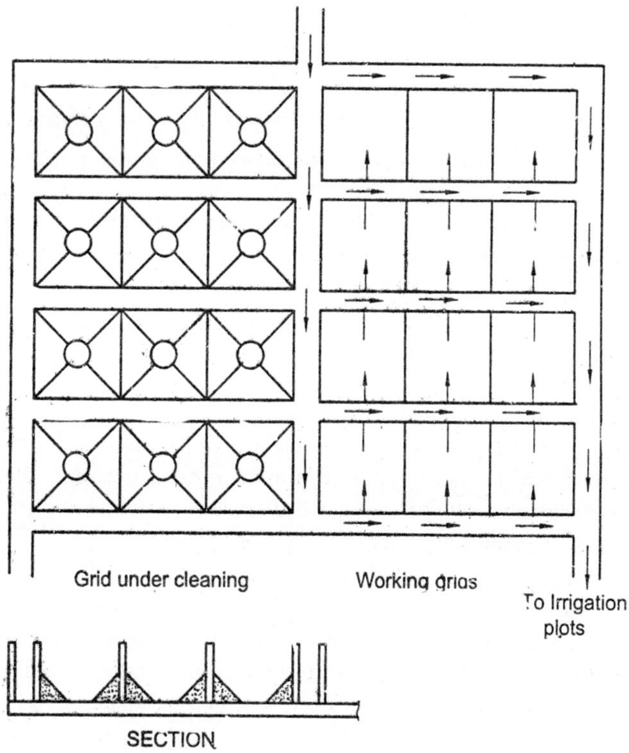

Note : Top clean water is used for irrigation while the bed residue is used as manure.

Fig. 18·30.

Sewage sickness. When sewage passes over a land continuously the soil voids or pores are clogged by the sewage solids entrapped between them. The time taken for clogging of their pores depend on the type of soil and the load present in the effluent. But once these voids are clogged, free circulation of air will be prevented and anaerobic position will develop with in the pores. Due to this the aerobic decomposition of the organic matter will stop and anaerobic decomposition starts. The organic matter will thus be mineralised, but with the evolution of foul gases, like hydrogen, sulphide carbon dioxide and methane. This phenomenon of the soil getting clogged is known as sewage sickness of land concerned.

To check the sewage sickness the following measures are taken :

(*i*) **Primary treatment.** Primary treatment of the sewage must be done such as screening, gritting, sedimentation which helps in reducing the BOD load by 30% or so.

(*ii*) **Choice of land.** The land must be porous or sandy.

(*iii*) **Under drainage of soil.** The land should have a proper drainage such as under drain system with open joints to collect effluent, this will help in minimising the sewage sickness.

(*iv*) **Giving rest to the land.** The land is required to use intermittently by keeping an extra altenative land which may be used turn by turn. During the rest period the land should be thoroughly ploughed and left to dry in sun. So that it gets brocken up and aerated.

(*v*) **Rotation of crops.** This will help in utilising the fertilising elements of sewage and help in aeration of soil.

(*vi*) **Applying shallow depths.** The sewage must not be filled in the area in deep depths and must be filled in shallow depths in the layers.

Pumping in sewage disposal. There are two essential differences between the requirements of a pumping stations in a water supply system and a station in a sewage system.

(*i*) Sewage cannot be stored for short periods of time and the flow is highly variable ; hence in a sewage pumping station provision must be made for pump capacities capable of handling peak flows as they arrive at the station. In order to ensure this two or more pumps and in some cases two sources of power are needed. As against this water can be stored easily for future use and as such water supply pumps may be sized on the basis of average daily or longer use.

(*ii*) Sewage contains coarse solids, both floating and suspended and hence requires special pumps which should not get easily clogged. As against the water does not contain signficant amount of suspended matter and as such no specially designed pumps are required for pumping water. In view of this it can be easily stated that the most important characteristic of a sewage pump is its ability to operate without clogging. The interior of the pump should be easily accessible for cleaning or removal of obstructions. The material of the pump must be resistant to corrosion as a certain type of corrosive materials are present in the sewage.

Sewage pumping mains should not discharge direct into sewer but into a chamber from which it may be directed to sewers. The chamber should be well ventilated. Pumps have been detailed in the chapter of water supply yet there are some special types of pumps suited for lifting sewage and the pumps which are most commonly used are centrifugal pumps which should be of the open impeller or blade less impeller type to avoid chokage. The pumps must be full way able to pass a ball of 75 mm dia. without choking. Such pumps are comparatively low efficiency pump but do away with the necessity of installing screens. It is considered better to screen the sewage and pass it through ordinary pump of high efficiency.

All sewage should however be screened and passed through grit chambers to remove suspended solids before allowing to pass through pumps. Propeller type pump may be used for dealing with storm water flow. The flow pump should be adopted where the volume of sewage to be pumped is large and where the minimum head exceeds about 12 m. The axial flow or propeller type pump should be used where large volume of sewage has to be pumped against a low head.

Vertical spindle centrifugal pump should be preferred. This pump has the advantage of permitting the motor to be placed above the pump but to safeguard against damage to flooding. The space occupied by the set is less than that occupied by a horizontal set of similar capacity and the vertical shaft can be made of any length.

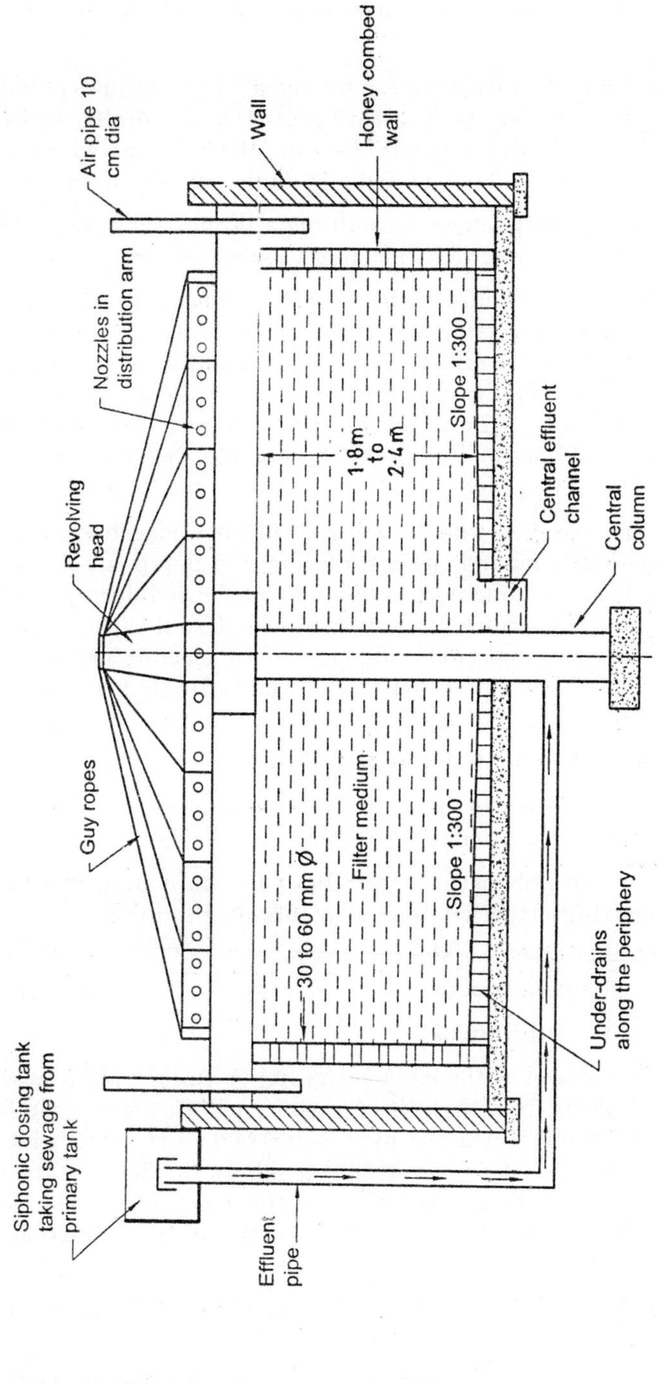

Fig. 18·31. Typical sewage pumping station.

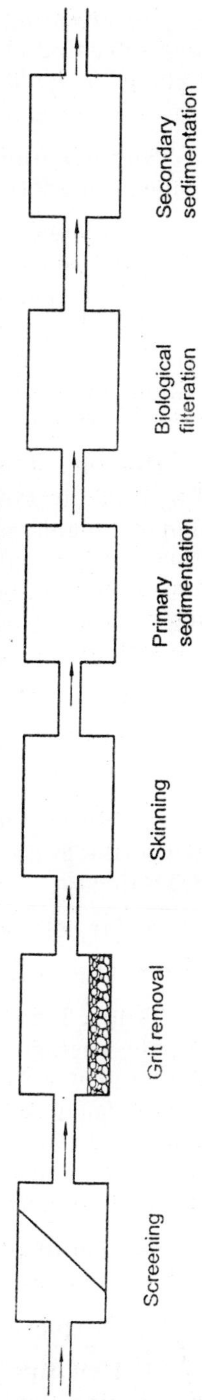

Fig. 18·32. Flow chart of sewage treatment and disposal.

Direct coupled vertical pump is the most economical. The low jointed direct coupled pump set may be preferable where the depth of the installation is 45 m or less. This set is more easily maintained. Except where the current is not available, starting should be automatic by float, pneumatic or electric control.

Reciprocating pumps are less used for pumping sewage as they are susceptible to choking and fine screening of the sewage is necessary. They are particularly suitable for dealing with thick sludge or for pumping against variable heads. Reciprocating pumps which used should preferably be of the plunger type. Turbine pumps are not suitable and also not rotary.

Number and capacity of pumps. (*i*) For small installations there should be two sets each capable of handling an average daily sewage flow in six to eight hours.

(*ii*) For medium installations a minimum of three sets would be necessary, one set average daily flow, one set twice average daily flow, and one set capable of handling three times average daily flow. Some engineers recommend that all the three sets should be of equal capacity, each capable of dealing with half the maximum rate of flow, so that frequent cutting in and out is avoided. The economic diameter of rising main which depends on the velocity at the normal rate of pumping, not the peak rate, should not be less than 100 mm and the velocity of the flow not less than 75 cm and not more than 180 cm/sec.

Pneumatic ejectors are installed where quantities of unserviceable sewage are to be lifted to a high level in isolated locations and the installation of a pump is not justified. They are simple, reliable, easy to maintain and no part is liable to be clogged during working, silent in action, but their efficiency is low, hence are used in small jobs. Usual capacity is 1 to 5 cu.m. for min. in lifts of about 6 m. "Shores" and "wet well" pneumatic ejectors are available in the market. In large installations the detension period of wet well is limited to 15 to 20 min. At small installation it has one hour average flow.

Valves of the pumping mains be located as follows :

(*a*) **Reflux valves.** Immediately above the pump to reduce back surge and water hammer, and should be placed on the horizontal portion on the main.

(*b*) **Sluice valves.** They are provided above reflux valve to enable this to be readily isolated in the event of its requiring attention, also at points on the main where required to isolate sections.

(*c*) **Air release values.** At summits of mains.

18·5. Domestic sanitation and its appliances

Traps. Traps are fittings placed at the ends of the soil or sullage pipes (waste pipe) to prevent the passage of the foul gases from the soil or waste pipes to the outside for which a ventilation pipe is fitted. The function is attained by a water seal in the trap which prevents the entry of foul gases outside. The efficiency of the trap depends on the depth of the water seal. The greater is the depth of water seal the greater effective the seal will be. The depth varies with a minimum of 25 mm to 75 mm. The different type of seals and their function is given in the Fig. 18·30 which are self explanatory.

System of plumbing. The following four types of plumbing systems for drainage are adopted in buildings.

(1) Two pipe system (2) One pipe system (3) Single stack system

(1) **Two pipe system.** In this system of plumbing two sets of vertical pipes are provided, one for draining night soil and the other for draining sludge. The 1st set which carries the night soil with urinal waste are called soil pipes and the pipes which carry the sludge are called as

sludge or waste pipes which carry the waste of bathrooms and of kitchens. The soil pipes are connected to the branch or lateral mains while waste pipes are connected to the branch. Both type of pipes are connected separately to the ventilation or anti siphonage pipes as shown in the Fig. 18·33. This system of plumbing is costly as it needs great number of sanitary pipes.

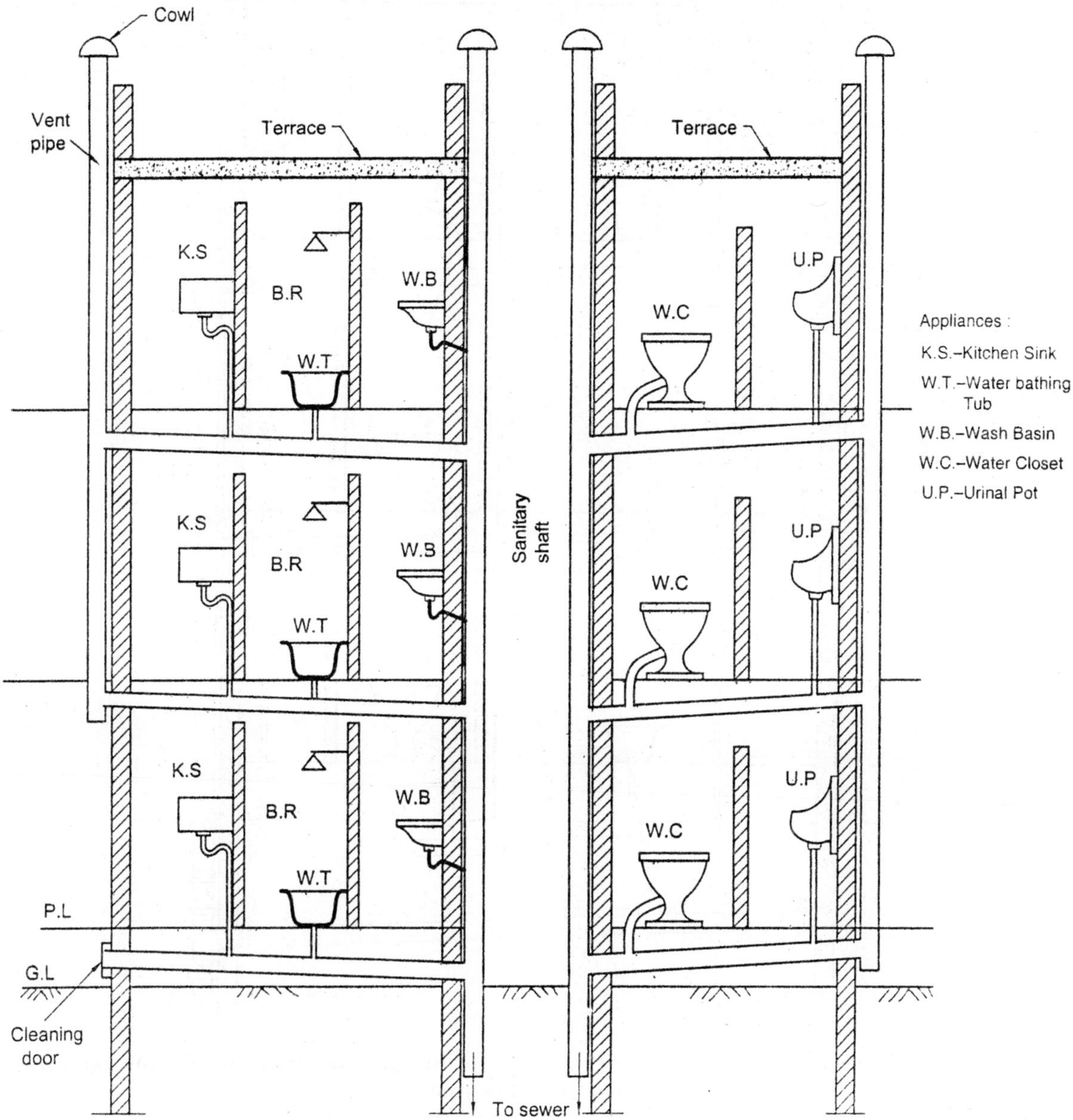

Fig. 18·33. Two pipe system of plumbing.

One pipe system of plumbing. In this system instead of carrying two pipes for night soil and sullage separately only one vertical pipe is provided for the disposal of the both. The main pipe is ventilated in itself by providing cowel at top, and in addition to this a separate pipe is also provided for ventilation.

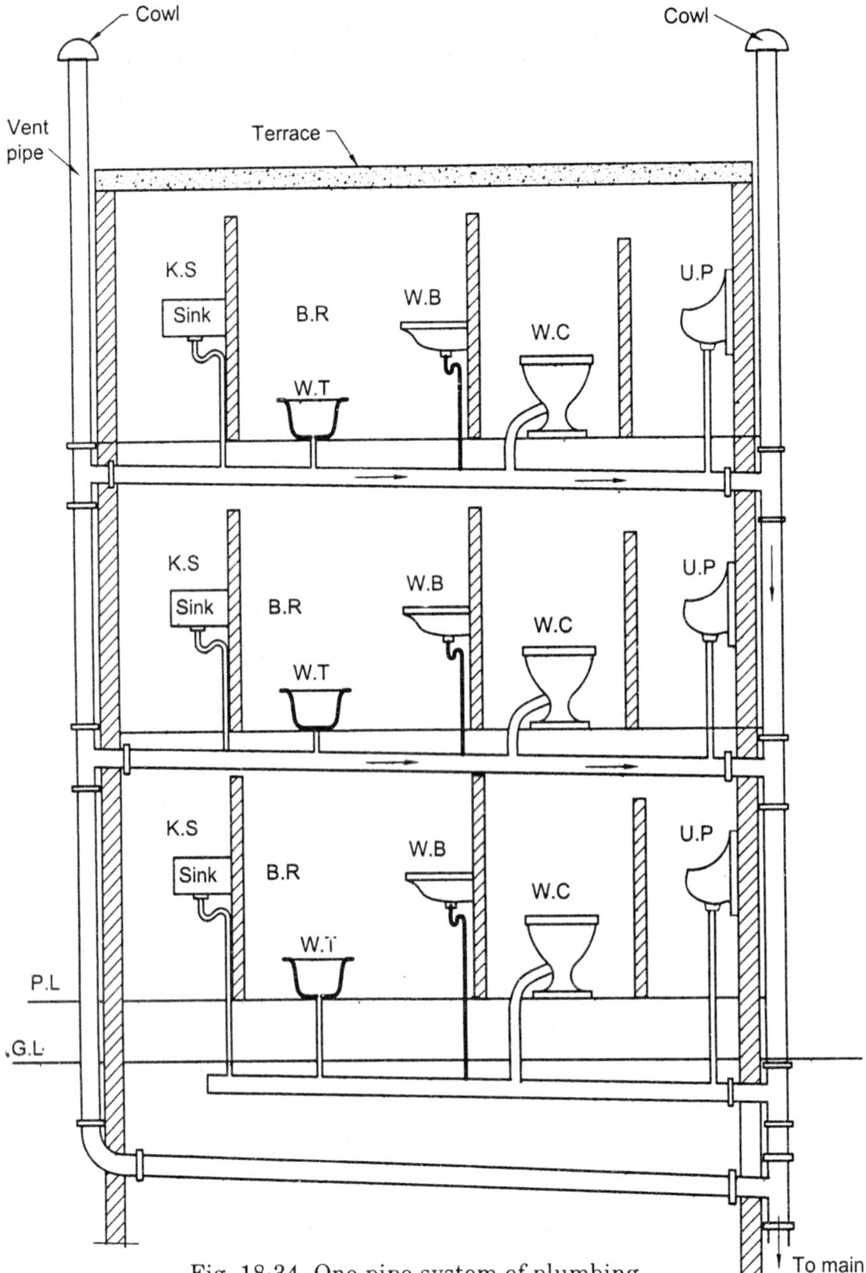

Fig. 18·34. One pipe system of plumbing.

Table 18·25. Recommended gradient and discharge capacity of house sewage pipe (as per IS : 1742-1960)

Dia. of pipe (mm)	*Gradient*	*Discharge in m^3/min (m^3 per day)*
100	1 in 35	0·18 (259)
150	1 in 65	0·42 (605)
230	1 in 120	0·93 (1339)
300	1 in 200	1·66 (2390)

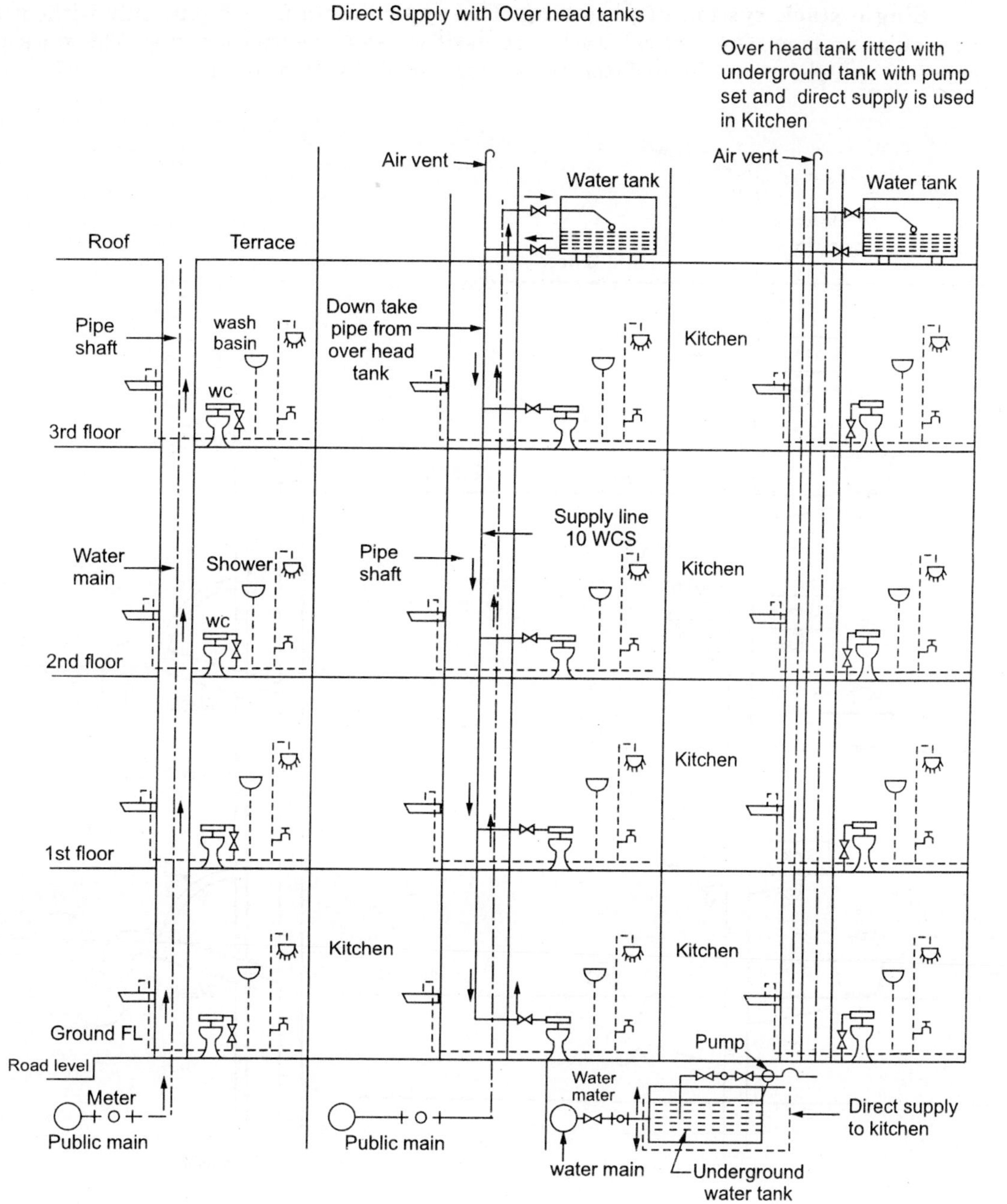
Direct Supply with Over head tanks
Over head tank fitted with underground tank with pump set and direct supply is used in Kitchen
Air vent
Water tank
Air vent
Water tank
Roof
Terrace
Pipe shaft
wash basin
Down take pipe from over head tank
Kitchen
wc
3rd floor
Supply line 10 WCS
Water main
Shower
Pipe shaft
Kitchen
wc
2nd floor
Kitchen
1st floor
Kitchen
Kitchen
Ground FL
Pump
Road level
Meter
Water mater
Direct supply to kitchen
Public main
Public main
water main
Underground water tank

Fig. 18·34-A.

Single stack system of plumbing. This system contains one pipe only without any extra ventilation pipe. The vertical stack pipe itself works as ventilation pipe. The stack pipe extends to 2 m higher than the roof (terrace) and is provided with a cowel.

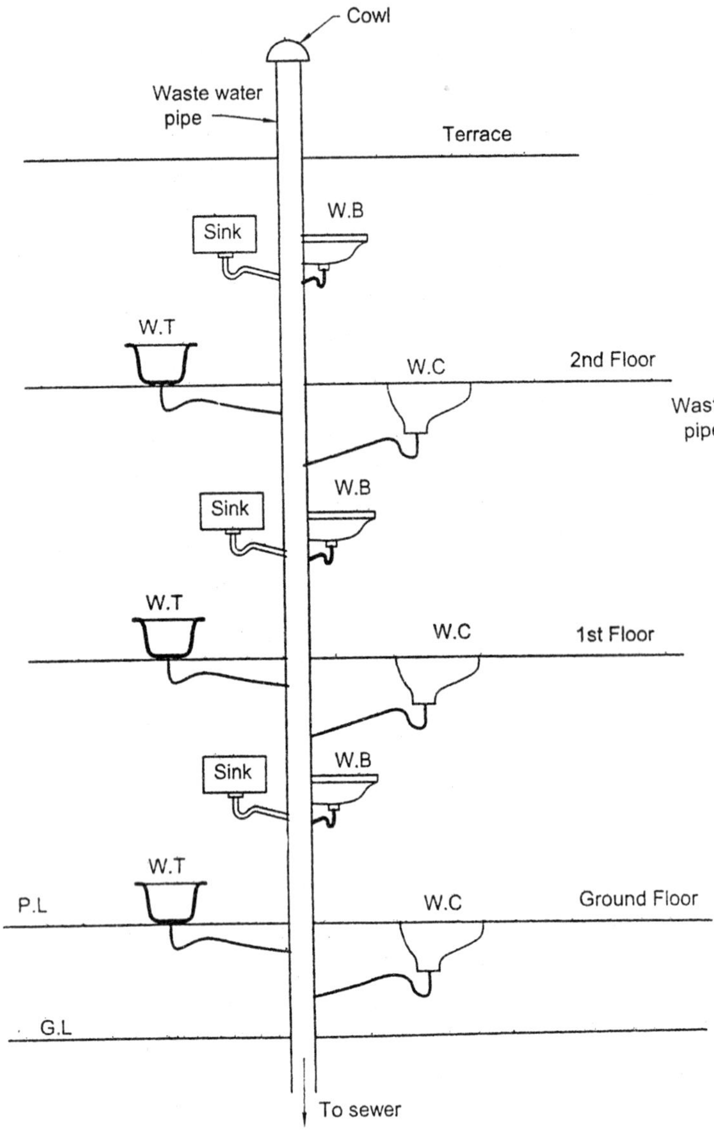

Fig. 18·35. Single stack system of plumbing.

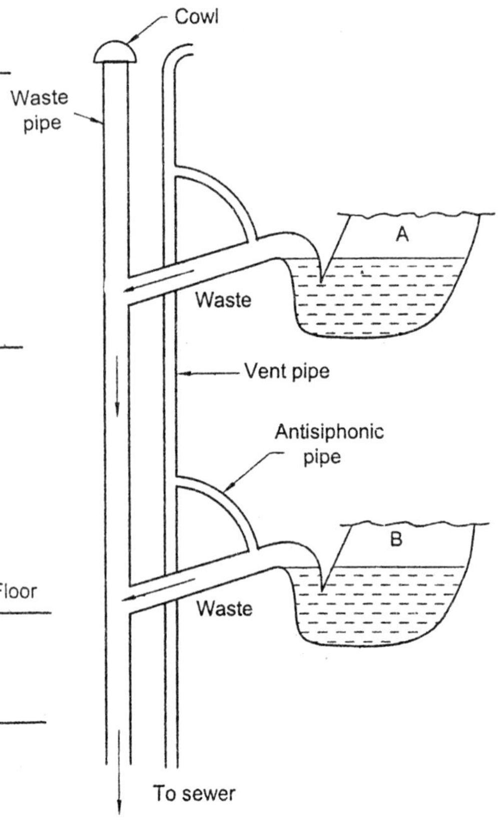

Fig. 18·36. Siphonage and anti-siphonage pipes.

Ventilation of drains and sanitary pipes. The ventilation pipes are provided to

(*i*) Relieve the pressure of foul gases which may otherwise break the water seals of the shallow seat traps.

(*ii*) Prevent breakage of trap's seat by siphonic action and

(*iii*) To dilute the foul gases and to reduce their abnoxious effects.

The ventilation is usually an activity providing a **fresh air inlet**, connected to the house drain through the lower most manhole. Fresh air from the atmosphere enters through this inlet into the manhole and finally goes out through the vent pipes provided in conjunction with soil and waste pipe. This air along with foul gases will finally escape out from the cowel provided at the top of the ventilation pipe at least 2 m above the roof level.

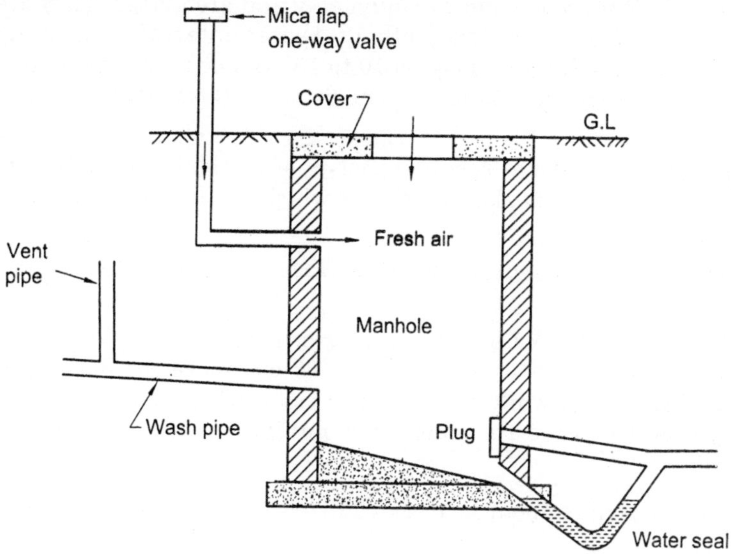

Fig. 18·37. Manhole with intercepting and a fresh air inlet.

A mica **flap valve** is provided at head of the fresh air inlet with slits admitting fresh air, which is so hinged at the top that it easily opens inside to admit fresh air, but it closes with the slightest back pressure of gases from the manhole, to avoid the escape of foul gases in the street or house yard.

Anti siphonage pipes. Water seals of traps provided in multi-storeyed building may some times broken due to siphonic action detailed as below :

When waste water is suddenly discharged from a sanitary frame on the upper floor, it moves down rapidly through the soil or wash pipe and in its movement it may suck some air from the lateral pipe connecting the soil pipe with the fixture at the lower floor. This sucked air causes siphonic action resulting in the flow of water from the trap of the fixture to the soil pipe and thus breaking the water seal. To overcome this difficulty a separate pipe smaller in diameter is attached to the trap, which connects the trap with the ventilation pipe as shown in Fig. 18·36. This pipe is known as anti siphonage pipe it supplies air to the short branch pipe of the lower frame at the time of suction, normally it also acts as a ventilation pipe and it only functions as an anti-siphonage only in case of suction.

Sanitary fittings and other appliances. The appliances generally required are shown in the figures which are self explanatory. Some of which are detailed as below :

Water closets (W.Cs). They are of two types, (*a*) Squatting or Indian type and the other is Pedestal type (European type).

Squatting or Indian type W.C (Fig. 18·39 *a*). It is a porcelain or vitreous China clay pot. having 45 to 63 cm overall length and 45 to 50 cm outer height. The pan is fitted with a *P* or *S* trap. The trap has an opening for fixing the anti-siphonage pipe or ventilation pipe. The pan has a flushing rim to spread the flush water. The excreta must not fall directly into the trap and need to be forced into it and into the soil pipe, by flushing the pan with water released under pressure from the flushing cistern. W.C. requires about 10 litres of water for proper flushing. **To set the W.C. in level of the floor and to accommodate the trap the floor slab is laid about 45 cm below the level of the floor.** The W.C. is fitted a bit above the floor level and is provided with two **foot rests** to sit while using the W.C.

Pedestal or European type W.C. It is provided with wide flushing run and a 50 mm trap. It is one piece construction in which pan and the trap is not separate as is provided in Indian seats. It is provided with an inlet or a supply pipe for connecting to the flushing pipe. The W.C. may be provided with a *P* or *S* type trap, as desired. They are raised from the floor level. (Fig. 18·39 *b* and *c*)

Urinals. The bowl or basin type of urinals are of one piece construction having two fixing holes on each side for fixing on the wall. They are made by China clay and are glazed. They are generally flushed with siphonic action which act automatically at desired interval of time and are generally used in public urinals. The time interval may be 10 to 15 min. or so. At the bottom of the bowl shaped pot an outlet horn is provided for connecting the urinal to the soil pipe through a floor trap. Refer Fig. 18·42.

Stall or slab type of urinals. This urinal system consists of suitable compartments made by raising side walls and the wall in front is glazed, against which the urine is passed by mats.

Flushing cisterns. A flushing cistern is a device which releases water of fixed quantity under pressure to wash or flush the W.C.

High level cisterns. In Indian type of W.Cs high level cisterns are fixed at about 2 m above the floor level, while in pedestal type W.Cs it is fixed about 60 cm above the floor level. These cisterns are generally made of cast iron, while the low level cisterns are made of glazed vitreous ware or of plastic. The high level cisterns are operated by pulling a chain and the later type is operated by turning a handle.

The discharging capacity of a cistern is about 5, 10 or 15 litres. Their norms are guided by the IS : 774-1964.

Bell type of flushing cistern. It consists of a cast iron box of 10 to 15 litres capacity with a central outlet stand pipe covered by a bell shape C.I. vessel. This bell is connected to a chain through a lever arm (refer Fig. 18·40) when the chain is pulled, the bell receives a jerk and splashes some water. The water runs down the pipe, takes away some air with it, which causes a partial vacuum at the top of the bell shaped vessel *i.e.* at the crown. This starts the siphonic action and all the water inside the cistern is sucked rapidly through the large opening near the bore of this bell. This emptying action takes only a few seconds causing a powerful flush in the W.C. The chain should be released immediately to avoid entry of air. (Fig. 18·40)

The cistern is supplied with a ball valve arrangement so that the water inlet gets closed when the cistern is full with water upto the water line, and gets open when it is empty permitting entry of water. It is also provided with an overflow pipe to drain out excess coming water, if the ball cock gets out of order so as to avoid spilling of water over the cistern in the toilet.

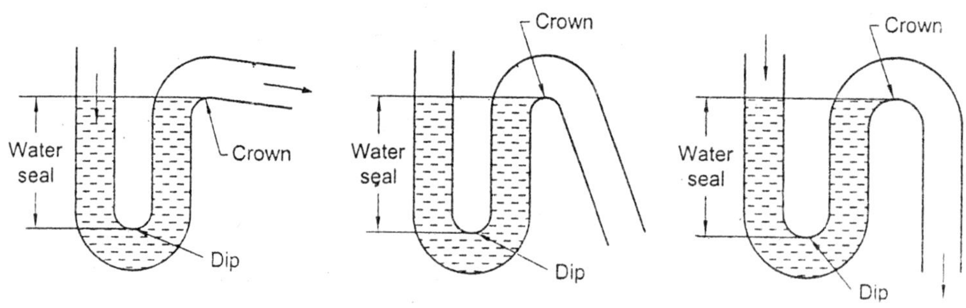

P-trap Q-trap S-trap

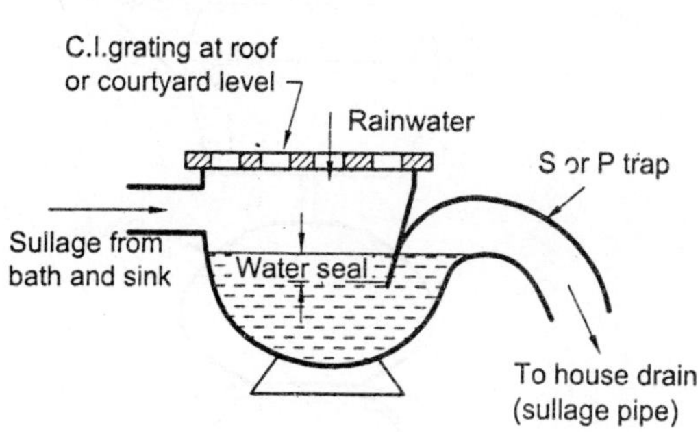

Floor trap

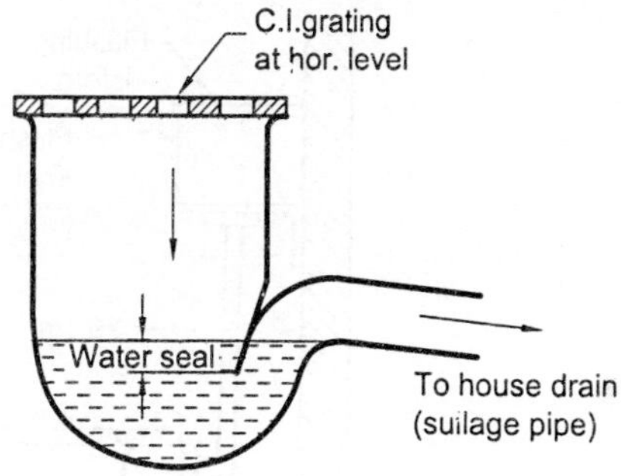

Gulley trap

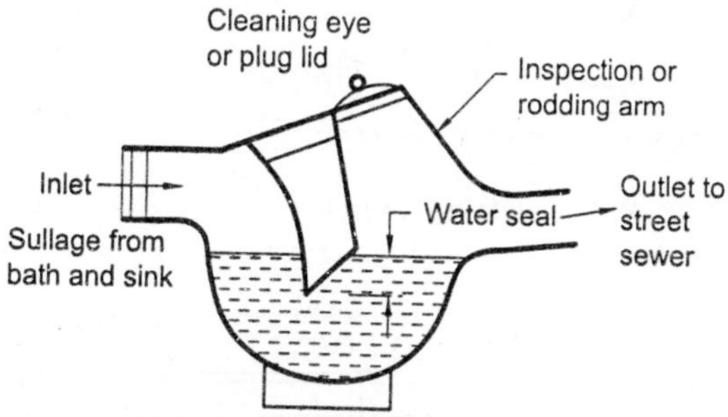

Intercepting trap

Fig. 18·38. Traps.

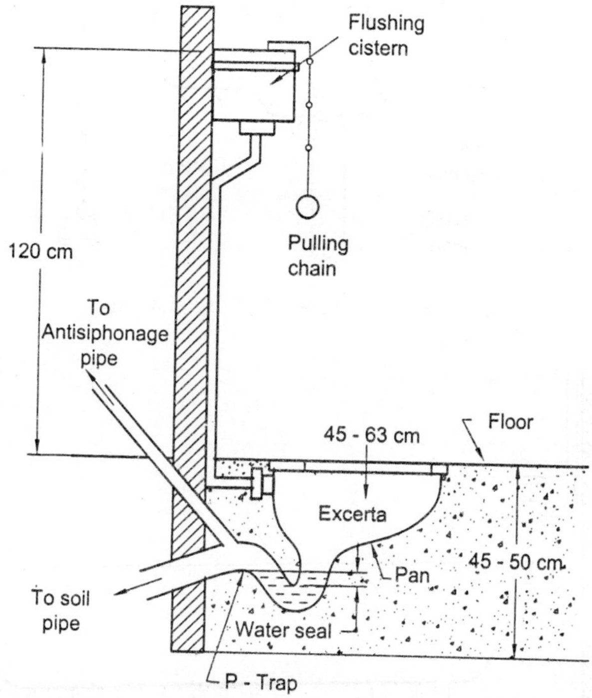

Fig. 18·39 (*a*). Indian type W.C. with flush (squatting type).

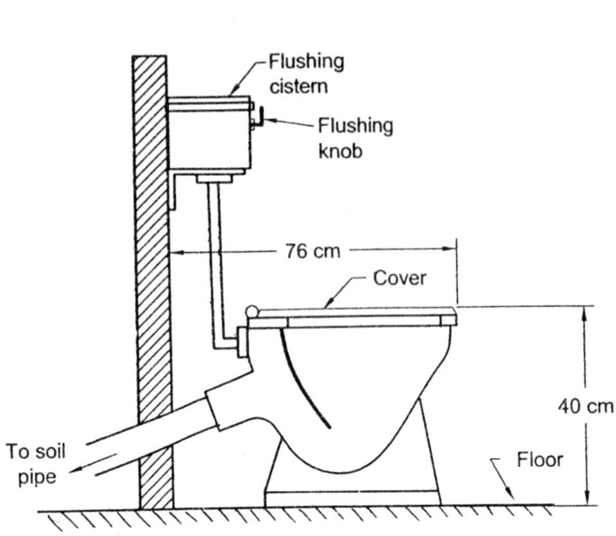

(b) European type W.C. (pedestal type)

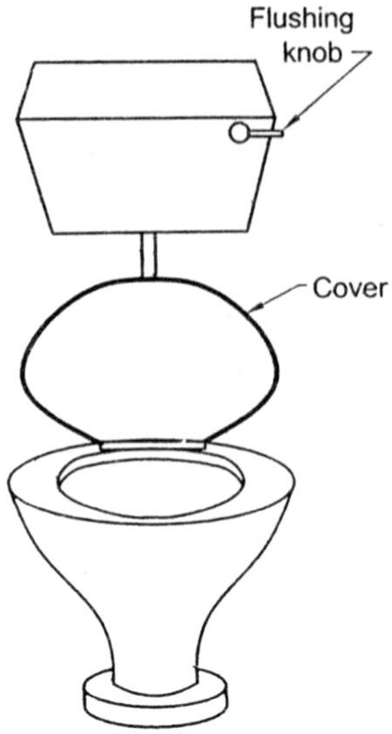

(c) Perspective view.

Fig. 18·39

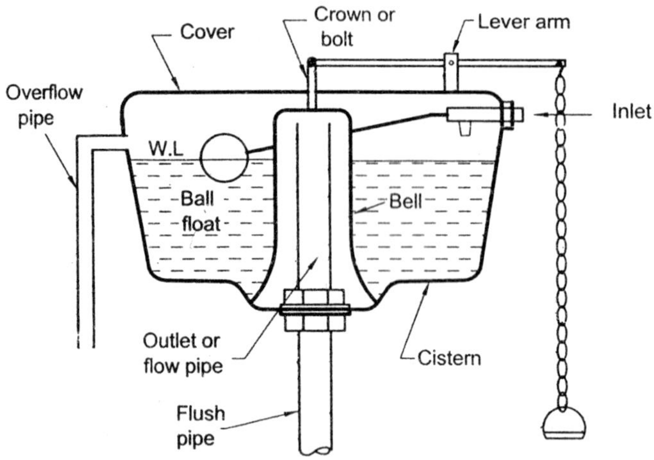

Fig. 18·40. Bell type flushing cistern

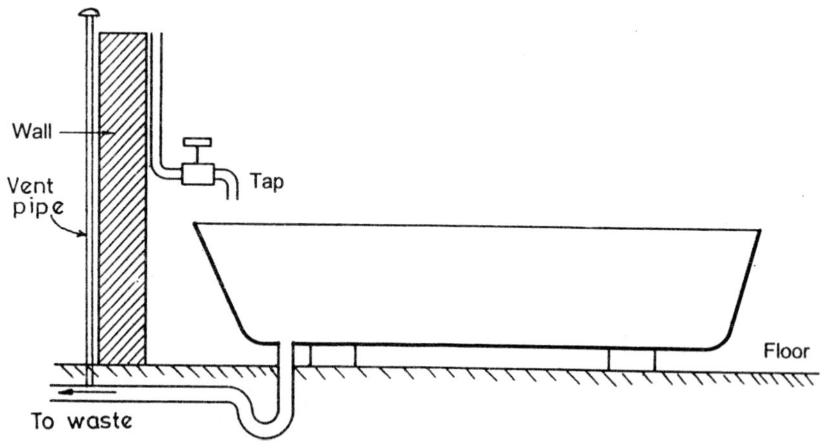

Fig. 18·41. Bathing tub.

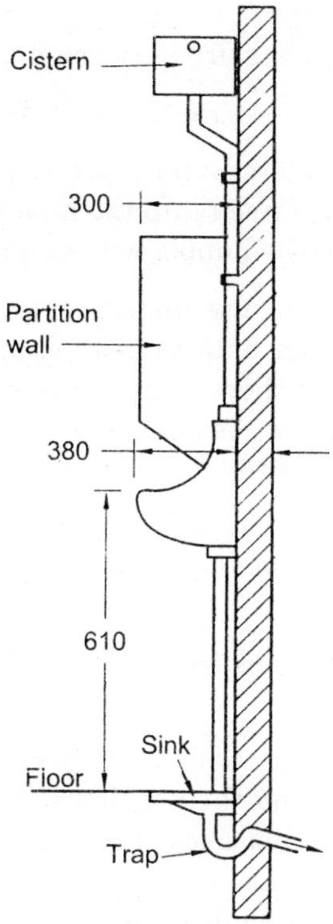

Fig. 18·42. Urinal.

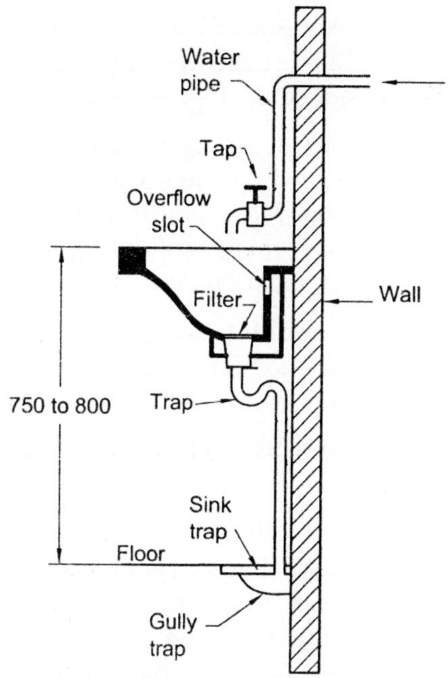

Fig. 18·43. Wash basin.

Commonly adopted sizes of house drains

Soil pipe = 100 mm dia.
Sullage pipe vertical = 75 mm dia.
Sullage pipe horizontal = 32 mm to 50 mm dia.
Vent pipe = 50 mm dia.

Table 18·26 (*a*). Commonly available size of wash basins

Pattern	*Size*
Flat back	660 × 450 mm
	550 × 400 mm
Agnle back	600 × 480 mm
	400 × 400 mm

Table 18·26 (*b*). Usual dimensions of kitchen and laboratory sinks

Type of sink	*Available size*
Kitchen sinks	600 × 450 × 150 mm
	600 × 450 × 250 mm
	750 × 450 × 250 mm
Laboratory sinks	400 × 250 × 150 mm
	450 × 300 × 150 mm
	500 × 350 × 150 mm
	600 × 400 × 200 mm

Testing of house sewage pipes. The following tests are performed :

(*i*) Air test (*ii*) Water test (*iii*) Smoke test

(*i*) **Air test.** This test is done for vertical and underground pipes. The section which is to be checked is plugged at lower and upper ends and air is forced into the pipe with pumps. Soap solutions applied at the junctions. If there is any leakage the bubble will be formed at that spot.

(*ii*) **Water or hydraulic test.** This test is done for the underground pipes. The lower end is plugged while the water is filled from the upper end upto to head of about 1·0 to 1·5 m. The level of the water is watched for about 10 minutes. If there is no depression is observed in the water level, there is no leakage and if this water level goes down is the indication of any leakage which must be located visually and should be rectified.

(*iii*) **Smoke test.** The test is generally done to the vertical or rain water pipes. In this test the smoke is forced into the pipe with blowers. The leakage can be tested by the smell on the leaky joints which can be repaired.

Sulabh Shauchalaya. A low cost alternative for sewage disposal for rural and urban housings.

Due to polluted environment of rural areas the population of villages are being migrated to the towns. As there is no proper provision for laterins and the people have to go to the fields for this purpose which creates chances for several type of diseases. The disposal of excreta is a proper alternative and solution for this. The modern sewage system is costly and can not be utilised in a rural area, hence to overcome this problem a sulabh shauchalaya scheme is started specially for rural areas.

The seat of the sauchalaya has been recommended by the National Environmental Engineering Research Institute Nagpur, Yojna Anusandhan and Karya Sansthan, Lucknow and Indian Standards Institute, Delhi as it is odourless and its maintenance is economical. More over it requires less water for its use. This seat can be constructed by cement concrete, Mosaic, porcelain or reinforced plastic fibres and is known as P.R.A.I. seat. A, P-shaped water trap is fitted in this seat which is made of porcelain, cement concrete or plastic and is connected by pipes with two leaching pits only. One pit is used at a time and for a family of five members can use this pit for five years. When this pit is filled the other pit is opened and connected to the seat. Being closed the excreta of the pit changes in a good manure after two years. This manure is odourless and is not harmful to handle it.

Water trap. There are many types of traps available in the market but the trap which is used in "Sulabh Shauchalaya Seals" has the depth of water seal 12 mm to 20 mm due to which the water required is less. An alternative has also been prepared so that the water used produces such a velocity which helps to wash off the excreta from the trap. Only 1·5 to 2·0 litres water is required to make the excreta to reach to the pit.

The dimension of the shauchalaya. In order that a user may use it in his all positions the dimensions are kept as a minimum of 75 cm × 90 cm, but it requires a great precaution while fitting the seat and its foots. Keeping in mind that a fat and tall man can also use it comfortable its dimensions are kept in 80 cm × 100 cm. Keeping in mind the customary bricks the size is kept a 80 cm × 103 cm.

Materials for construction. Keeping in mind the availability of the materials such as bricks, stone, concrete, ferrow cement, tarcoal, empty drums bamboo mats and hard soil units are proposed for their construction as easily available on the work sites.

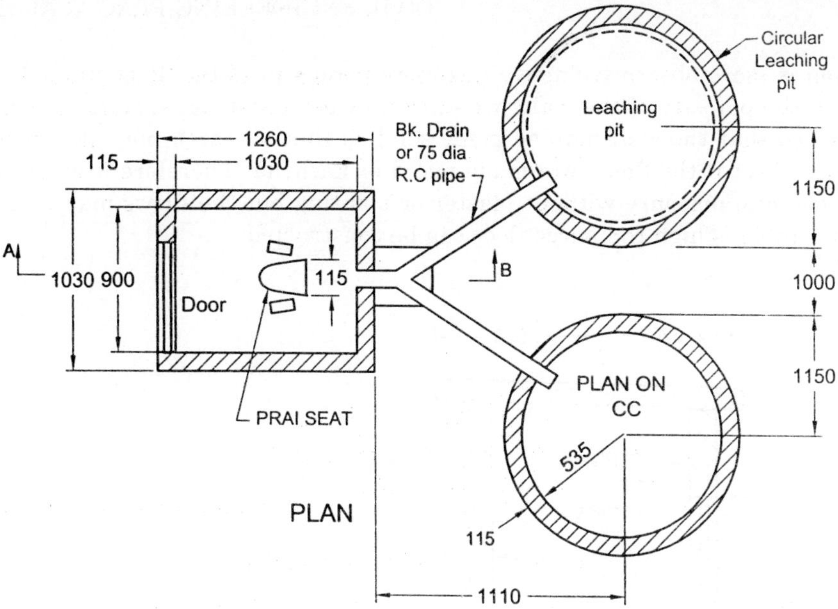

Plan—Circular Leaching Pit

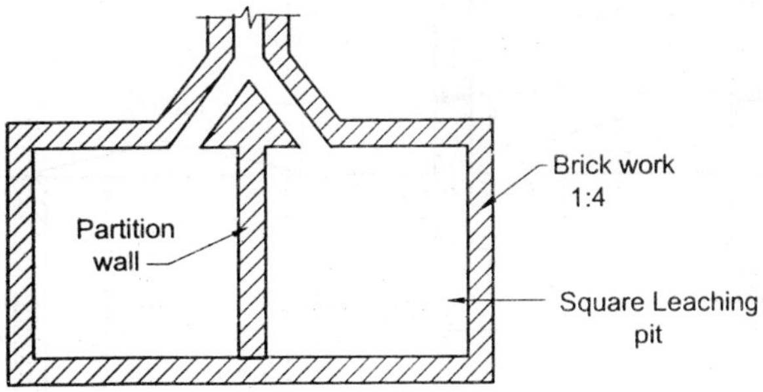

Square Leaching Pit

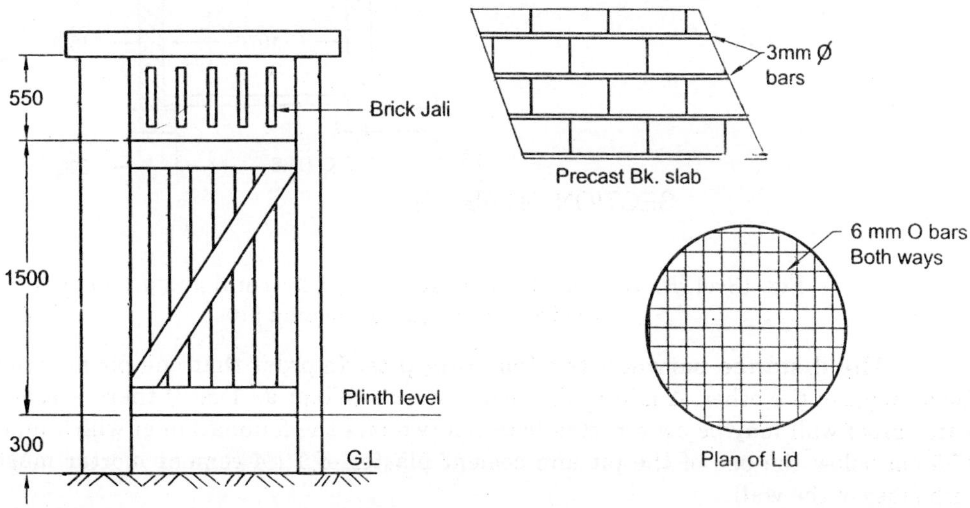

(All dimensions in mm)

Fig. 18·44 (*A*). Sulabh Shauchalaya—A low cost alternative for disposal of sewage of rural and urban houses.

The soil is more absorptive as well as more porous to water. It is studied that there is no difference in the porosity of the walls whether they are constructed solid or honey combing, there it is decided that the wall may be made solid so that no earth may slip in the pits. But there is a major effect if the floors are made pucca or kachcha. Therefore it is decided that the walls may be made in masonry without plaster or pointing but the floors may be kept kachcha and if the water table is high the pucca floor can be constructed.

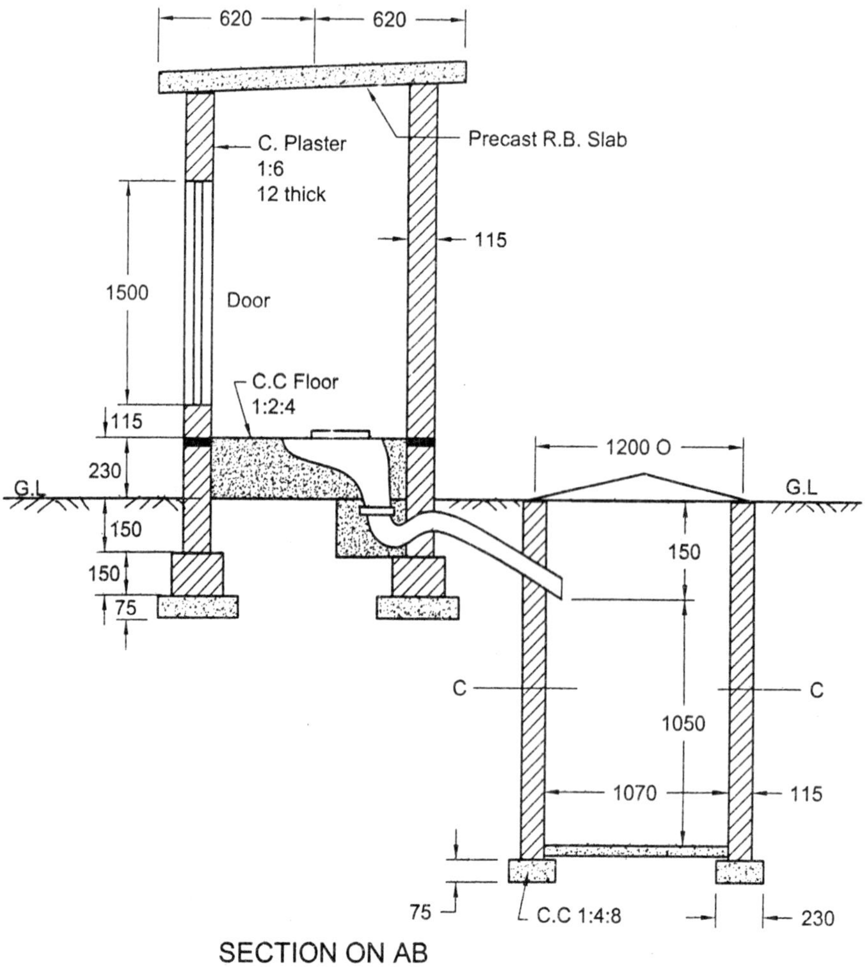

Fig. 18·44 (*B*). Section of sulabh sauchalaya for rural and urban area with circular or square leaching pits.

The distance between the leaching pits. In order that one pit may not affected by the seepage of the other. A minimum clear distance is kept as 1 m. If there is scarcity of land a water proof wall may be constructed between two pits the foundation of which must be at least 37·5 cm below the bed of the pit and cement plaster of 1 : 4 cement mortar must be done on both sides of the wall.

The distance of the leaching pit from the building. The minimum clear distance between the leaching pit and the building must be 85 cm for the areas of clogs and 125 cm for the areas of sandy soil. This is according to the depth of the leaching pit as 150 cm. If this depth is more than the required distance may be considered accordingly.

The volume of the leaching pit. The decomposition of the excreta is occured in the wet position due to which the excreta becomes solid and its volume becomes 17 to 30 litres per user/year. In the sandy soils the decomposition of excreta occurs in less water and the excreta becomes in spungy shape and its volume becomes 45 to 48 litres per user per year. There the volume of the pit is decided to be kept as 44 litre per user per year whose capacity 41·1 m^3. This is sufficient for 4 years for 5 users in case of sandy soil and in case of clay it can be used for six years.

The shape of the leaching pits. There is no difference whether an pit is kept as circular or square. It is decided on basis of experiments. The square may easier to construct. The dia. and depth of a circular pit is kept 1·07 cm and 1·75 respectively and for square pit the side and depth is kept as 0·92 and 1·20 respectively. The pits of above dimensions are suffice for a family of 5 users for 5 years. It is decided on the basis of study keeping in mind all the points.

Cost of the Shauchalaya. According to the market rates in the year 1992 in north India, the total cost of a shauchalaya comes to Rs. 4000 (app.) with room and leaching pits. For other places and time the cost may be computed on the market rate index.

General. The depth of water table must be at least 2 m below the bed of the pit so that the polluted water of the pit may not seep to the underground water as it cause to pollute the underground water.

Table. 18·27. Materials required for the construction of the sauchalaya upto plinth level including square leaching pit.

Building material	*No/quantity*	*Labour*	
Cement	4·5 bags	Skilled	4 Nos.
Sand	0·6 m^3	Unskilled	8 Nos.
1st class bricks	750		
Ballast 12 mm or less (stone)	0·2 m^3		
Brick ballast (40 mm)	0·12 m^3		
5-6 mm for steel bars	8·5 kg		
W.C. including trap	1 set		
Foots	1 pair		
Binding wire	200 gm		
Hooks for lifting soak pit lids of 6-5 mm thick bars	0		

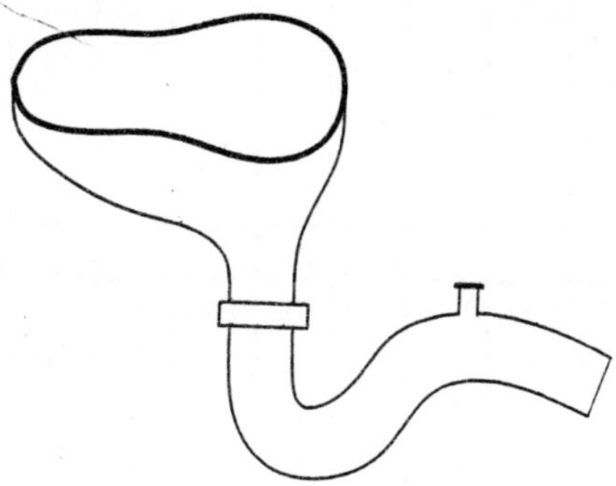

DRAI seat and trap

Industrial or trade wastes. The waste water produced by manufacturing process is of no commercial value. If this waste is of such composition as would damage the sewer or interfere with the treatment processes, then pre-treatment of these wastes is essential before discharge into main sewers or treatment plants. Provision of screens for removing suspended solids and sedimentation tanks or chemical precipitation tanks will be adequate for most of these trade wastes.

Open Drains

Table 18·28. Showing velocity and discharge

A	*R*	*Type*		*Slope 1 in.*													
*cm*²	*cm*			*25*	*50*	*75*	*100*	*150*	*200*	*300*	*400*	*500*	*600*	*700*	*800*	*900*	*1000*
915	3·8	I	*V*	1·89	1·32	1·08	0·95	0·77	0·66	0·54	0·47	0·42	0·38	0·36	0·33	0·31	—
			Q	1·02	0·72	0·59	0·50	0·42	0·35	0·29	0·25	0·23	0·20	0·20	0·18	0·18	—
251	6·4	II	*V*	2·67	1·88	1·54	1·34	1·09	0·94	0·37	0·67	0·59	0·55	0·51	0·47	0·44	0·42
			Q	4·00	2·82	2·30	2·00	1·63	1·41	1·16	0·98	0·89	0·82	0·76	0·71	0·66	0·62
465	8·2	III	*V*	3·16	2·26	1·81	1·58	1·29	1·12	0·91	0·78	0·71	0·64	0·60	0·56	0·52	0·50
			Q	8·77	6·18	5·02	4·38	3·58	3·09	2·54	2·18	2·00	1·78	1·66	1·55	1·114	1·38
706	9·8	IV	*V*	3·56	2·49	2·03	1·77	1·44	1·25	1·02	0·88	0·79	0·72	0·67	0·63	0·58	0·56
			Q	15·0	10·5	8·57	7·44	6·08	5·28	4·30	3·73	3·37	3·04	2·81	2·64	2·42	2·33
1031	11·3	V	*V*	3·59	2·53	2·06	1·80	1·47	1·27	1·04	0·90	0·80	0·73	0·68	0·64	0·59	0·57
			Q	21·9	15·5	12·6	11·0	8·45	7·74	6·33	5·64	4·01	4·47	4·15	3·91	3·63	3·46
1035	12·8	VI	*V*	3·90	2·27	2·25	1·95	1·61	1·38	1·13	0·98	0·87	0·80	0·74	0·70	0·65	0·62
			Q	31·2	22·0	17·9	15·6	12·8	11·0	9·10	7·80	6·97	6·30	5·90	5·56	5·19	4·92

A = Area of flow in cm², *R* = hydraulic radius in cm.,

V = velocity in m/sec, *Q* = Dis. in m³/min

Drain I to IV have smooth cement concrete surface ; Type V and VI are of B.W. plaster over to smooth surface. (Ref. Fig. 18·45).

Dia	*1 :20*		*1 : 25*		*1 : 33·3*		*1 : 40*		*1 : 50*		*1 : 57*		*1 : 67*		*1 : 80*		*1 : 100*	
mm	*V*	*Q*	*V*	*Q*	*V*	*Q*	*V*	*Q*	*V*	*Q*	*V*	*Q*	*V*	*Q*	*V*	*Q*	*V*	*Q*
150	1·69	3·08	1·51	28	1·30	23	1·20	22	1·10	19·5	1·00	18·5	0·92	17	0·84	15·5	0·75	14
200	2·14	70·0	1·91	63	1·66	54	1·51	49	1·35	44	1·27	41	1·17	38	1·07	35	0·96	31
250	2·54	29·0	2·27	116	1·97	100	1·80	92	1·60	82	1·50	76	1·39	71	1·27	66	1·14	58
300	2·92	2·14	2·61	191	2·26	166	2·10	151	1·85	135	1·73	126	1·60	117	1·46	107	1·30	95
375			3·10	353	2·67	305	2·44	280	2·20	250	2·04	233	1·89	216	1·73	197·5	1·54	176
450					3·10	504	2·79	460	2·40	412	2·33	384	2·16	356	1·97	325	1·76	291
525							3·12	700	2·78	625	2·60	535	2·41	540	2·20	493	1·97	442
600									3·10	896	2·86	840	2·65	780	2·42	710	2·16	636
675											3·12	1150	2·90	1076	2·64	980	2·37	826
750													3·12	1430	2·84	1300	2·54	1162
900															3·12	2117	2·83	1900
	1 : 133·3		1 : 2000		1 : 300		1 : 500		1 : 667		1 : 1000		1 : 1333		1 : 2000		1 : 4000	
150	0·65	11·5	0·53	9	0·442	8	0·34	6·2	0·29	5	—	—	—	—	—	—	—	—
200	0·83	27	0·67	22	0·52	16·8	0·42	13·5	0·37	11	0·30	9·5	—	—	—	—	—	—
250	1·13	50	0·79	40	0·62	31·2	0·50	26·0	0·44	22	0·35	17	0·30	15	0·25	12·5	—	—
300	1·34	83	0·93	67	0·71	52	0·51	42·5	0·50	36	0·40	30	0·35	26	0·20	21	—	—
375	1·34	152·5	1·09	125	0·84	95	0·68	78	0·59	67	0·48	55	0·41	47	0·33	38	0·23	26·5
450	1·53	250	1·25	205	0·97	159	0·78	128	0·68	112	0·56	91	0·47	78	0·38	63	0·26	43
525	1·70	380	1·39	310	1·08	241	0·88	197·5	0·75	169	0·62	138	0·53	120	0·43	97	0·30	66
600	1·83	549	1·53	448	1·19	347	0·97	283	0·84	245	0·68	198	0·59	172	0·47	139	0·33	95
675	2·05	759	1·66	618	1·30	480	1·05	390	0·91	336	0·74	278	0·64	235	0·52	192	0·37	133
750	2·20	1008	1·80	823	1·39	636	1·13	520	0·98	450	0·80	364	0·69	316	0·56	255	0·39	177
900	2·50	1650	2·03	1345	1·58	1044	1·29	828	1·12	736	0·90	596	0·78	518	0·63	418	0·44	290

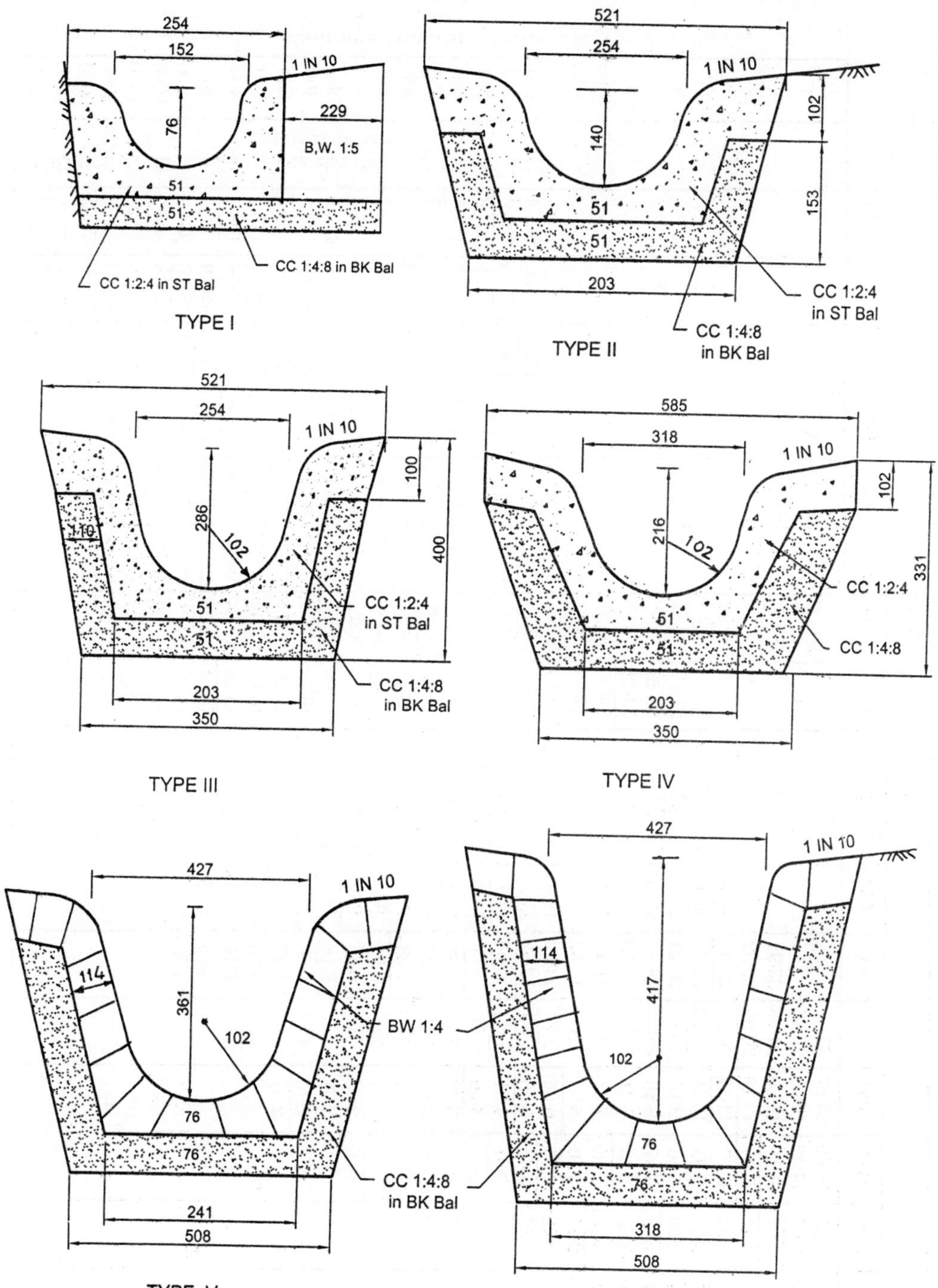

Fig. 18·45

18·6. Septic Tanks

The settleable solid of the sewage that comes from W.C. settles down in the form of a sludge and biological action takes place. The sewage is retained in the septic tank for a day or so

Table 18·29 (b) Flow of Sewage in new clean Asphalted cast iron pipes
(Table giving dicharge in cubic metres per minute flowing full)

Hydraulic Gradient of slope 1 in.	Velocity in metres/sec.	150	200	250	300	350	400	450	500	Velocity	600	700	750	800	900	1000	1100	1200	Velocity in metres/second	Hydraulic Gradient of slope 1 in.
10		3·41	7·55	14·09	23·87	35·46														10
15	3·05	2·80	6·07	11·43	19·09	28·87														15
20		2·39	5·27	9·91	16·36	24·78	35·91													20
30		1·93	4·27	7·96	13·18	20·05	29·32													30
40		1·64	3·64	6·77	11·37	16·82	25·00	34·10												40
50	1·22	1·46	3·20	6·05	10·09	15·23	22·28	30·46	41·37											50
60		1·34	2·96	5·46	9·18	13·87	20·23	27·73	37·28	3·05	61·37									60
70		1·23	2·68	5·07	8·46	12·73	18·41	25·46	34·10		56·83									70
80		1·15	2·52	4·73	7·84	11·87	17·26	23·87	31·82		53·42									80
90		1·09	2·39	4·45	7·32	11·18	16·14	22·28	29·78	2·43	50·00	76·24	93·19							90
100	0·91	1·02	2·25	4·16	6·96	10·59	15·32	21·14	28·41		47·28	70·92	88·69	113·6						100
120		0·24	2·05	3·86	6·36	9·77	14·09	19·55	26·14		43·19	64·55	80·46	105·0	132·3	178·2				120
150		0·84	1·82	3·41	5·68	8·59	12·59	17·05	23·18		38·64	57·73	70·92	93·9	118·2	158·2	204·6	261·4		150
200	0·01	0·72	1·55	2·91	4·91	7·32	10·86	14·77	19·96	1·52	32·50	49·78	60·92	80·01	103·2	136·1	175·0	225·0	3·05	200
250		0·63	1·39	2·61	4·36	6·59	9·77	13·18	17·23		29·55	44·55	54·55	71·37	91·37	122·7	156·4	204·6		250
300			1·26	2·39	3·93	5·41	6·68	11·82	15·91		26·37	39·78	49·10	63·64	81·83	109·6	140·4	181·8	2·43	300
350			1·02	2·16	3·59	5·46	7·96	10·91	14·55	1·22	24·32	36·37	44·55	58·42	74·55	100·9	129·6	163·7		350
400				2·00	3·32	5·09	7·32	10·81	13·18		22·73	34·10	42·03	54·55	69·55	95·01	120·9	153·6		400
450				1·90	3·11	4·86	6·91	9·55	12·73		21·37	31·82	39·55	61·82	65·01	89·10	113·7	145·5		450
500				1·80	2·98	4·55	6·55	9·09	12·27		20·23	30·23	37·50	49·10	61·83	86·37	107·7	136·8		500
550					2·82	4·32	6·18	8·64	11·50		19·09	28·64	35·46	46·14	59·10	79·56	103·2	130·9		550
600					2·70	4·14	5·96	8·18	11·14	0·91	18·18	27·73	33·64	43·87	56·37	75·92	99·10	126·4		600
650					2·57	3·93	5·77	7·80	10·55		17·30	26·14	32·28	42·73	54·32	72·74	95·01	120·5		650
700						3·80	5·50	7·50	10·18		16·64	25·46	30·92	40·46	51·82	69·33	90·47	115·5		700
800						3·55	5·14	7·00	9·50		15·50	23·64	28·87	37·96	48·68	64·10	84·56	108·2	1·52	800
900							4·84	6·59	5·00		14·64	22·28	27·28	35·00	45·69	60·92	79·10	102·7		900
1000							4·55	6·21	8·41		13·82	20·91	25·68	33·41	42·96	57·51	74·10	95·92		1000
1200								5·61	7·68	0·61	12·57	19·09	23·41	30·23	39·19	52·28	67·28	86·83	1·22	1200
1500									6·75		11·27	16·73	20·87	27·05	34·55	46·60	59·78	77·28		1500
2000											9·77	14·55	17·73	23·41	33·00	40·00	51·82	66·60	0·91	2000
3000												11·82	14·50	19·00	24·32	31·81	41·82	53·64		3000
4000														15·91	20·68	27·73	35·46	45·46	0·61	4000
5000																	31·37	40·91		5000

for this action. The undissolved solid sludge settles down in the bottom and is removed periodically. The gas escapes through the vent pipe provided above the surface of scum water. The liquid effluent is further strained through a filter and discharged out. (Fig. 18·46)

The septic tanks are divided in two compartments one is known as the grit chamber while the other as septic tank chamber. (Fig. 18·46)

(*i*) **Grit chamber.** The sewage enters into this compartment through a submerged inlet. This chamber is separated from the septic tank chamber by a baffle wall. The top of which is kept a bit above the scum level in the tank and bottom to the max. depth of solid sludge allowed to accumulate before removal.

(2) **Septic chamber.** The liquid enters in the compartment through the bottom opening below the baffle. The scum formed on the surface prevents the liquid sludge from the direct contact of the air as bacterial action takes place only in the absence of air. The sludge deposited in the bed is removed periodically. This chamber can be divided in two parts, in the 1st part bacterial action takes place, while in the 2nd solidless water collects, which is escaped through an outlet.

Septic tank requirements. (1) The min. area of grit chamber must be 700 cm^2 per user and min. volumetric capacity must be 20 litres per user.

(2) The minimum capacity of the septic tank (Total for both chambers) must be 85 litres per user. For large tanks it may be reduced slightly. The sludge accumulating capacity must be 45 litres per user if the tank is cleaned every year.

(3) The retention period must be 12 hours to 3 days with a normal of one day (24 hours).

(4) The min. width must be 75 cm, min. depth one metre below water level and liquid capacity of one cubic metre, and the ratio of length to width may be 2 : 1.

The masonry of the tank may be of brick work, min. 22·5 cm thick or stone min. 37 cm thick, plastered with 1 : 3 cement sand mortar. The bed must be cement concrete 1 : 2 : 4 in stone grit sloping towards the outlet. The cover may be of RCC slab 50 mm thick provided with suitable circular opening for desludging and inspection. The bed and sides must have water tight smooth surface with cement slurry and water proofing compound.

Table 18·30. Sizes of domestic septic tanks (IS 2470)

No. of users	*Length in metres*	*Width in metres*	*Liquid depth in metres*	*Free board in cm*	*Liquid capacity m^3*	*Cleaning interval*
5	1·5	0·75	1·10	30	1·12	6 months
			1·00		1·20	12 months
			1·05		1·18	24 months
10	2·0	0·9	1·0	30	1·8	6 months
			1·3		1·8	12 months
			2·0		2·52	24 months
15	2·0	0·9	1·0	30	1·8	6 months
			1·3		2·34	12 months
			2·0		3·60	24 months
20	2·3	1·1	1·0	30	2·53	6 months
			1·3		3·30	12 months
			1·8		4·55	24 months
50	4·0	1·4	1·0	30	5·6	6 months
			1·3		7·28	12 months
			2·0		11·2	24 months

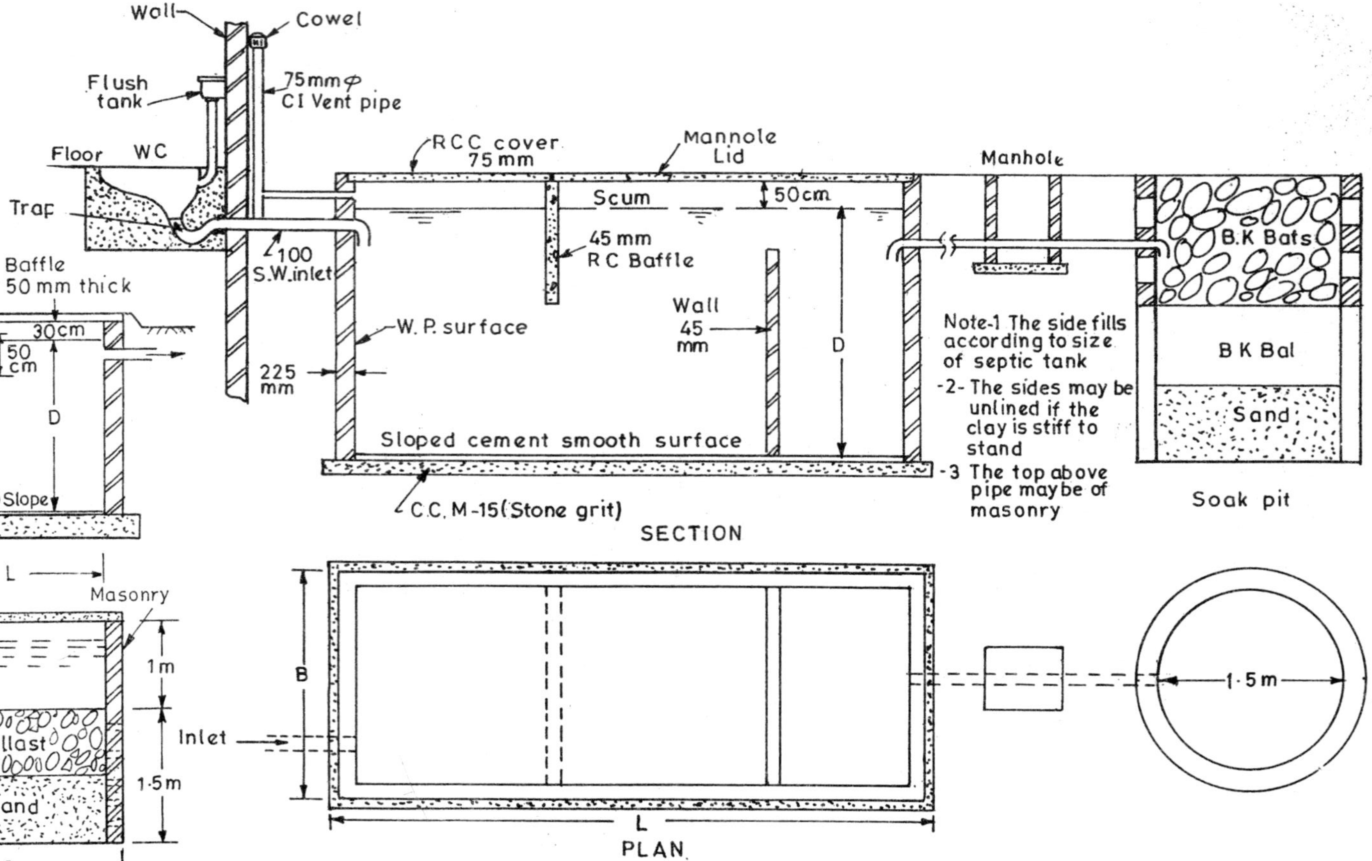

Fig. 18·46 Layout of septic tank.

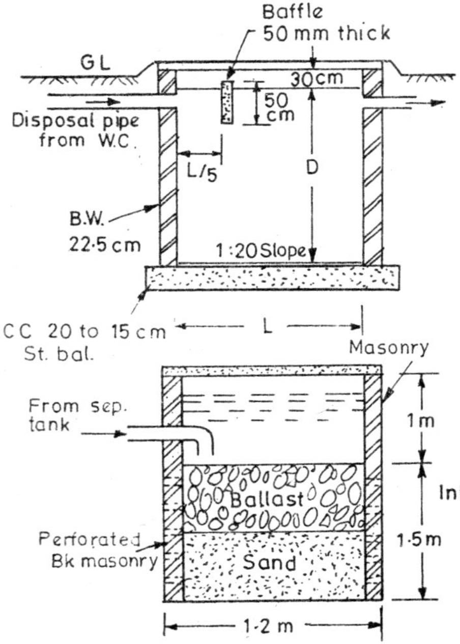

Fig. 18·47. Cess pool.

Septic tank sizes for housing colonies

No. of users	*Length in metres*	*Width in metres*	*Liquid depth for stated interval of sludge with drawal*		*Distance of partition wall from the inlet end*
			Less than 12 months	*Once in two years*	
100	8·0	2·6	1 m	1·04 m	5·3 m
150	10·6	2·7	1 m	1·15 m	7·1 m
200	12·4	3·1	1 m	1·15 m	8·1 m
300	14·6	3·9	1 m	1·15 m	9·7 m

Table 18·31. Septic tanks for Hostel etc.

No. of users	*Length in metres*	*Width in metres*	*Liquid depth for stated interval of sludge withdrawal*		*Distance of partition wall from the inlet*
			12 months	*24 months*	
50	5	1·6	1·3	1·4	3·3
100	5·7	2·1	1·4	1·7	3·8
150	7·7	2·4	1·4	1·7	5·2
200	8·9	2·7	1·4	1·7	6·0
300	10·7	3·3	1·4	1·7	7·2

Ventilation pipe. It is A.C. or C.I. pipe with min. of 50 mm internal dia. provided in the lid of the grit chamber and below the W.C. trap for escaping the gases out. At the top a perforated covered cap known as cowl is provided. The height of the vent pipe is kept at least 2 m when the location of the septic tank is away than 15 m from the existing buildings and 2 m above the top of the building when it is situated less than 15 m from the building.

Sludge disposal. The liquid sludge from the tank is disposed off :

(1) In a nala, sewer, or any other drain flowing nearby to carry off the public waste from dwellings.

(2) By providing following disposal devices :

(*a*) **Soak pit.** A circular pit of at least 90 cm in dia. and one metre deep is excavated. The size and depth is increased according to the size of the tank. The sides of the pit are lined with perforated brick or stone walls or kept without lining if the soil is stiff. The outlet pipe is kept 90 cm below the antimosquito measure. The outside rim of the perforated wall is provided with 15 cm thick sand filter.

The inside of the pit may also be filled with three layers of sand, ballast and brick bats below the outlet pipe. The top circumference of the pit is made with 225 × 225 mm brick work, covered with a concrete or stone top.

(*b*) **Cess pool.** It is a combination of a soak pit and a septic tank having a dia. of 1·2 to 1·5 m and must be away from the building. The upper half is designed as a septic tank with water tight sides having a depth of about 1·0 to 1·5 m. The disposal pipe (not more than 6 m in length) of the septic tank falls in the upper half. The top is covered by a concrete cover. The lower half is made of masonry (perforated) the voids of which are surrounded by a 15 cm thick sand filter. The depth of the lower portion varies from 1·5 to 2·1 m. The absorption area of the pit must be above the water table of the area. The more absorptive is the soil, the less is the time of soaking sometimes the pit is filled with graded filter material as in soak pits. It can be used as a single chamber septic tank. (Fig. 18·47)

Dispersion trench. The liquid sludge from the septic tank is passed in a long trench about 30 to 100 cm deep and wide. The lower half is filled with sand and the upper half with ballast of brick. Open jointed unglazed earthenware pipes passes in between through which sludge water passes and is soaked, when soak pit is not provided. (Fig. 18·47)

18·7. Air pollution

The atmosphere and rivers have self cleaning properties by natural process upto some extent so long as the pollutants discharged by man into the environment is lower than the natural cleaning capacity of atmosphere it remains normal to the man, but when the discharged pollutants exceed the natural cleaning capacity, it becomes pollutant causing hazardous to us.

Natural self cleansing agencies of the nature which help in the self cleaning process are the following :

(*i*) Dispersion

(*ii*) Gravitational settling or without flocculation of particles.

(*iii*) Absorption including wash out and scavenging.

(*iv*) Rainout and

(*v*) Adsorption

(*i*) **Dispersion.** Dispersion of pollutants by winds. In the strick sense it does not remove them from atmosphere but only dilute them. Disperson of smoke of long chimneys only reduces or dilutes it only for the neighbouring areas and does not reduce their long term in desirable effects as a whole to the whole community. Its adverse effects are seen in the distant areas.

(*ii*) **Gravitational settling.** Gravitational settling is the most important natural mechanism under which larger heavy particles from the ambient air settle down on buildings, trees and other objects. This process also helps in removing flocculated particles formed by uniting of smaller particles over larger particles, till flock particles, large and heavy enough to settle out under gravity is formed.

(*iii*) **Absorption.** In the natural absorption process, the gaseous as well as particulate pollutants from the air gets collected in the rain or mist and may settle out with that moisture. This phenomenon takes place below the cloud level when falling rain drops absorb pollutants and is also known as wash out or scavenging. The process however does not help in removing particles smaller than 1 μ mm in size.

(*iv*) **Rain out.** Rain out is the process involving precipitation above the cloud level, when submicron particles present in the atmosphere in the clouds serve as condensation nuclei around which drops of water may form and fall out as rain drops. This phenomena helps in increased rainfall and fog formation in urban areas containing huge quantities of such particles rising high above the cloud level.

(*v*) **Adsorption.** In adsorption, the gaseous, liquid or solid pollutants present in the ambient air are kept attracted generally electro statically by a surface where they are concentrated and retained. Material surfaces such as soils, rocks, leaves, grain, buildings and other objects adsorb and retain pollutants.

In **Dilution system** such as in tall chimneys the smoke is diluted and is spreaded in the larger area by air so that the pollutant is shared by a larger area where such factories are not in existence. Hence by providing the tall chimneys not only the pollutant is removed but also varified.

Measures taken for removing or reducing the pollutants

(*i*) By using better quality of fuel which does not produce smoke.

(*ii*) By replacing automobiles which give smokes by electric motors or engines operated by LPG gas. (Liquid Petroleum gas).

In industries the following mechanical devices are used :

(i) Gravitational settling chambers

(ii) Centrifugal collections including cyclic collectors and dynamic precipitators.

(iii) Wet scrubbers (collectors, including spray lates, wet cyclone scrubbers and venture-scrubbers.

(iv) Electrostatic precipitators and

(v) Fabric filters.

Green revolution. In this revolution the trees and green vegetation is densified in the area which helps for more rain and checking the flow of pollutants and helps to get settled their load near them.

Disposal of sewage must be done after proper treatment. Some devices for mechanical particulation are used.

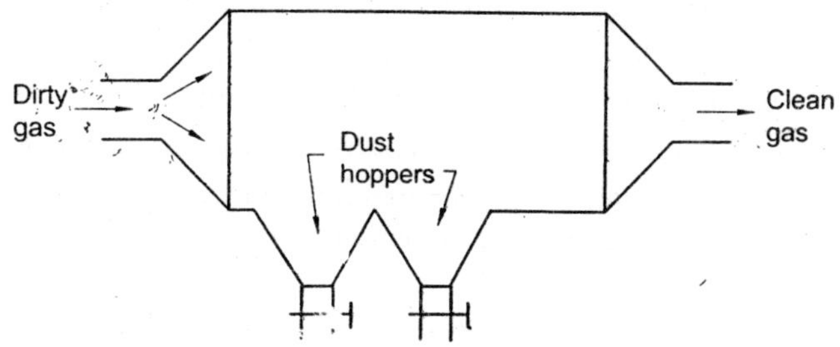

Gravitational chamber

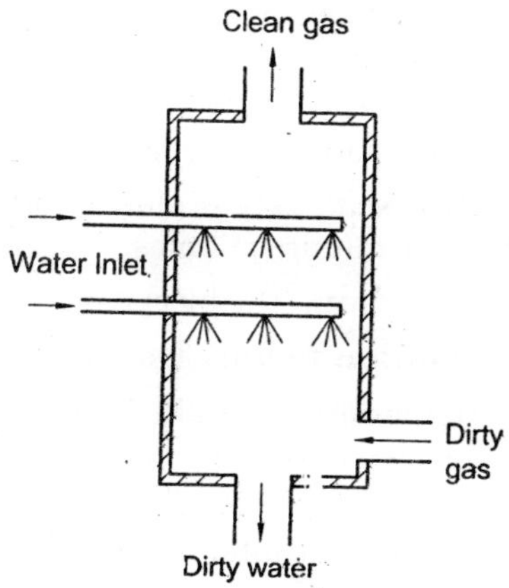

Spray tower (a mechanical device) also used for removing gaseous pollutants

Fig. 18·48.

18·8. Technical Terms

Activated sludge. Sludge settled out of sewage previously treated in the presence of air.

Anti siphon pipe. A ventilating pipe connected to the outlet side of a trap.

Benching. The sloped floor of a manhole both sides to the sewer pipe so that water of a side sewer falling in the slope may go in the sewer and a man can do repair work unit.

Bib tap. A top having horizontal inlet and a bent mouth to discharge water downward.

B.O.D. Biochemical oxygen demand a test indicating the loss of oxygen in the process of decomposition of sewage.

Born sewage. A waste water from stables of animals containing animal waste.

Box union. A device for jointing together two threaded pipes.

Broad irrigation. The disposal of sewage for land farming in which the disposal of sewage is the prime aim and the **farm irrigation** is only an incidental. It is also called as **effluent irrigation.**

Centrifuge. A device in which sludge is dewatered by rapid radition and automatically discharged.

Cess pool. A pit with open joints towards the bottom in which the effluent from a septic tank or other household liquid waste is discharged and from which the liquid reaches upto the surrounding soil or is otherwise removed.

Chase. A continuous recess in a wall floor or ceiling for the purpose of holding pipes and conduits.

Clarification. The process of removing suspended and colloidal matter from a turbid liquid or sewage.

Classified sewage. Device used for the sewage from which suspended matter has been partly or completely removed.

Cleaning eye. An access opening having a removable cover to enable removal of deposits obstructing flow.

Colloids. Finely divided suspended matter which will not settle and the apparently dissolved material which may be transformed into suspended matter by contact with solid surface or precipitate by chemical treatment.

Conservancy system. A system in which right soil is collected in buckets and removed outside on heads.

Cowl. Top which is perforated and fitted at the top of a ventilating pipe so as to check any entry of a substance from top.

Diffuse. A porous plate or other device through which air is forced and enters the sewage in the form of minute pubbles.

Digestion. The biochemical decomposition of original matter in a sewage.

Dilution factor. The ratio of the quantity of the diluted water to that of the sewage.

Dispersion trench. A trench in which open jointed pipes surrounded by coarse aggregate media and overlaid by fine aggregate are laid. The effluent get dispersed through the open joints and is absorbed in the neighbouring soil.

Drop manhole. A manhole provided for connecting a sewer or drain at high level to other at low level.

Drop connection. A branch drain in which the last length of piping of the incoming drain before connection to the sewer is vertical.

Duck foot bend or rest bend. A bend supported in a vertical position by a foot formed at its base.

Farm irrigation. When the main aim is to provide irrigation by the effluent sewage and not the disposal of the effluent which is only incidental.

French drain. A small shallow trench filled with coarse rubble, clinker, or any other similar material.

Free water. The water that moves in a soil under the force of gravity without being retained by the soil.

Garbage. It is a dry waste such as waste paper, sweepings and vegetable pealings. It may be taken as 0·14 kg to 0·24 kg per capita per day.

Gasket. A compressible piece between two flat surfaces bolted together to make them air and water tight.

Gully or Gulley. A receptible of stone ware, concrete cast iron or any other material provided with a grid placed at the side of a road or building to receive drainage from a gutter or channel.

Gulley trap. A trap provided in a drainage system with a water seal to collect waste water from the sculptures, kitchen sink, wash basin, baths and rain water pipes.

Gutter. A surface drain to carry out rain water of streets.

Haunching. Concrete bedding with additional concrete at the sides of the pipe.

Hydro-isobaths. Lines of similar depth of sub soil water table below C.L.

Inert. The lowest point of a sewer, while suffet is the highest point.

Interceptor manhole or interceptor chamber. A manhole incorporating an intercepting trap and providing means of an access thereto and equipped with a fresh air inlet on the u/s side of the trap.

Isoyets. Lines joining the places of equal reinfall on a map.

Kerb inlet. An aperture formed in a kerb to let in surface water from the pavement to a gulley.

Lateral sewer. It is a street sewer into which sewage from house connection pours.

Launching. Concrete inside of pipe with bed concrete.

Liquifactum. The result of the action of bacteria for the decomposition and purification of sewage or waste matter.

Night soil. A mixture of human excreta, urine and personal cleaning materials.

Oakum. Hemp or old hemp rope soaked in oil to make it water proof.

One pipe system. A single soil waste pipe conveys both the soil and the waste directly to the building drain.

Podding eye. An access opening having a removable cover for the obstruction to be cleared by mean of a drain rod.

Puff ventilation. A ventilation provided for waste traps in two pipes system to preserve the water seal.

Putrefaction. The 1st stage of sewage purification by the action of anaerobic bacteria.

Saddle. A fitting made to suit a purpose shaped as to fit over a hole cut in a sewer to form branch connection.

Scum. A greasy deposits over the surface of a sewer or a treatment tank.

Scum board. Also called as baffle wall. A thin partition wall built in a sewage treatment tank to prevent the incoming sewage disturbing the scum.

Sewage. The liquid waste from a community such as water closets, urinals, hospitals and stables etc. excluding storm water. It may also be called as solid sewage.

Sewage sickness. The pores of the land under sewage irrigation when clogged with salts of the effluent and the aeration activity is stopped is known as the sewage sickness.

Shaft. A vertical open space left in buildings to pass sanitary pipes etc. connecting to all floors.

Single stack system. A name given to a simplified one pipe system, wherein all ventilation pipes are omitted. The stack itself is made to provide for all the ventilation requirements by restarting the flow into the stack to certain pre-determined limits.

Sludge. The solid matter deposited at the bottom of a tank during treatment of the sewage which is in a semi solid condition.

Sludge digestion. The bichemical process by which organic matter in sludge is converted into non stable organic matters.

Soak away or soak pit. A pit prepared to receive soil waste and to pass it in the surrounding ground.

Soil pipe. A pipe used to convey liquid waste from water closets and urinals.

Soil waste. The discharge from W.Cs, urinals, sinks, stables or cow sheds and similar appliances.

Spigot. The male part of a spigot and socket joint.

Spigot and socket joint. Joint in which the end of one pipe enters the enlarged end of the next pipe.

Stack. A vertical pipe for conveying the waste water.

Sub irrigation. The irrigation by the settled effluent by means of pipes laid at shallow depths below the surface of the land.

Sullage. Waste water from bathrooms, lavatory basins, kitchen sinks, street and roof wastings etc. which does not contain human excreta.

Sump or wet well. The underground position of a sewage pumping station which resumes the sewage and from which it is drawn by the pumps.

Trap. A fitting or device so designed that a water seal prevents the back passage of air or gas without materially affecting the flow of sewer or waste water through it.

Trunk sewer. Is the main sewer into which all smaller sewers discharge and which in turn discharges at the point of disposal.

Two pipe system. In household dwellings the pipes for conveying the excreta or urinal waste in separate pipes besides the pipe which is provided for conveying the bathrooms waste.

Union. A pipe fitting used for jointing the ends of two pipes, neither of which can be turned.

Vent or ventilating pipe. A pipe provided for circulation of air or to pass foul gases.

Wastepipe. A pipe used to convey liquid waste excluding human excreta. Waste stack is a vertical pipe to convey the waste liquid including human excreta.

Water seal. The depth of water which should be removed from a fully charged trap before air can pass through the trap.

Appendix 18·1. Sanitation requirement for hotels.

Sl. No.	*Fitments*	*For residential*	*For public rooms*		*For non-residential staff*	
			For males	*For females*	*For males*	*For females*
1	2	3	4	5	6	7
1.	Water closet	One per 8 persons, omitting occupants of the room with attached water closet minimum of two in both saxes and lodged	Over per 100 persons upto 400 persons. For over 400 persons add at the rate of one per 250 persons or part thereof.	2 for 100 persons upto 200 persons. Over 200 persons add at the rate of one per 100 persons or part thereof.	One for 1-15 persons. Two for 16-35 persons. Three for 36-65 persons. Four for 66-100 persons.	One for 1-12 persons Two for 13-25 persons Three for 25-40 persons Four for 41-57 persons
2.	Ablution taps	One in each water closet	One in each water closet	One in each water closet.	One in each water closet.	
		One water tap with draining arrangements shall be provided for every 50 persons or part thereof in the vicinity of water closets and urinals.				
3.	Urinals	—	One for 50 persons or part thereof.	—	Nil upto 6 persons 1 for 7 to 20 persons 2 for 21-45 persons 3 for 46-70 persons 4 for 71-100 persons	
4.	Wash basins	One for 10 persons omitting the wash basins installed in the room suites.	One per water closet and urinals provided one per water closet provided.	—	1 for 1-15 2 for 16-35 3 for 36-65 4 for 66-100	1 for 1-12 persons 2 for 13-25 persons 3 for 26-40 persons 4 for 41-57 persons 5 for 58-77 persons 6 for 78-100 persons
5.	Baths	One for 10 persons omitting occupants of the room with bath in the suite.	—	—	—	
6.	Slop sink	One per 30 bed rooms (one per floor min)	—	—	—	
7.	Kitchen sinks	One in each kitchen	One in each kitchen.	One in each kitchen	One in each kitchen	

Note : It may be assumed that the two thirds of the number are for males and one third for females.

Appendix 18·2. Sanitation requirement for educational occupancy.

Sl. No.	Fitments	Nursury schools	Boarding institutions		Other educational institutions	
			For boys	*For girls*	*For boys*	*For girls*
1	2	3	4	5	6	7
1.	Water closet	One for 15 pupils and part thereof.	One for/every 8 pupils or part thereof.	One for/every 5 pupils or part thereof.	One for/every 40 pupils or part thereof	One for/every 25 pupils or part thereof.
2.	Abution taps	One in each water closet.	One in each water closet.	One in each water closet	One in each water closet.	One in each water closet.
		Note :- One water tap with draining arrangements shall be provided for every 50 persons or part thereof in the vicinity of water closets and urinals.				
3.	Urinals	—	One for every 20 pupils or part thereof.	—	One for every 25 pupils or part thereof.	—
4.	Wash basins	One per 15 pupils or part thereof.	One for every 8 pupils or part thereof.	One for every 6 pupils or part thereof.	One per 40 pupils or part thereof.	One per 40 pupils or part thereof.
5.	Baths	One bath sink per 40 pupils	One for every 8 pupils or part thereof	One for every 6 pupils or part thereof.	—	—
6.	Drinking water fountains	One for every 60 pupils or part thereof.	One for every 80 pupils or part thereof.	One for every 50 pupils or part thereof.	One for every 50 pupils or part thereof.	One for every 50 pupils or part thereof.
7.	Cleaners sink	—	One per floor (min.)	One per floor (min.)	One per floor (min.)	One per floor (min.)

Note : It may be assumed that the two thirds of the number are for males and one third for females.

Appendix 18·3. Sanitation requirements for institutional (medical occupancy—Hospitals)

Sl. No.	Fitments	Hospitals for indoor patients ward	Hospitals for outdoor patients		Administration buildings	
			For males	*For females*	*For males*	*For females*
1	2	3	4	5	6	7
1.	Water closet	One for every 8 beds or part thereof	One for every 100 person or part thereof.	One for every 100 persons or part thereof.	One for every 25 persons or part thereof.	One to every 15 persons or part thereof.
2.	Ablution taps	One for each water closet plus one water tap with draining arrangements in the vicinity of water closets and urinals for every 50 beds or part thereof.	One in each water closets.	One in each water closet.	One in each water closets.	One in each water closet.
3.	Wash basins	2 upto 30 beds add one for every additional 30 bed or part thereof.	One for every 25 persons or part thereof.	—	One for every 25 persons or part thereof.	One for every 25 persons or part thereof.
4.	Bath	One bath with shower for every 8 beds or part thereof.	—	—	One on each floor.	One on each floor.
5.	Bed pan washing sinks	One for each ward.		—	—	—
6.	Cleaning sink	One for each ward.				
7.	Kitchen sinks and dish washers (where kitchen is provided)	One for every 50 persons or part thereof	One for each ward			
8.	Urinals	—			Nil upto 6 persons 1 for 7-20 persons 2 for 21-45 persons 3 for 46-70 persons 4 for 71-100 persons From 101 to 200 persons add at the rate of 3% for over 200 persons, add at the rate of 2·5%.	

Appendix 18·4. Sanitation requirements for institutional (medical)occupancy (Staff quarters and hostels)

Sl No.	*Fitments*	*For male staff*	*For female staff*	*Nurses hostel*
1	2	3	4	5
1.	Water closet	One for 4 persons.	One for 4 persons.	One for 4 persons or part thereof.
2.	Ablution taps	One in each water closet.	One in each water closet.	One in each water closet.
		1 water tap with draining arrangements shall be provided for every 50 persons or pat thereof in vicinity of water closets and urinals.		
3.	Wash basins	One for every 8 persons or part thereof.	One for every 8 persons or part thereof.	One for every 8 persons or part thereof.
4.	Bath with shower	One for four persons or part thereof.	One for every 4 persons to part thereof.	One for every 8 persons or part thereof.
5.	Cleaner's sink	One at every floor (min.).	One at every floor (min.).	One at every floor (min.).

Appendix 18·5. Sanitation requirements for governmental or semi-public business occupancy

Sl No.	*Fitments*	*For male personal*	*For female personal*
1	2	3	4
1.	Water closet	One for every 25 persons or part thereof.	One for every 15 persons part thereof.
2.	Ablution taps	One for each water closet	One in each closet.
		One water tap with draining arrangements shall be provided for every 50 persons or part thereof in the vicinity of water closet and urinals.	
3.	Urinals	Nil upto 6 persons 1 for 7-20 persons 2 for 21-45 persons 3 for 46-70 persons 4 for 71-100 persons From 101 to 200 persons add at the rate of 3% For over 200 persons add at the rate of 2·5%	
4.	Wash Basins	One for every 25 persons or part thereof.	
5.	Drinking water fountains	One for every 100 persons with a minimum of one for each other 100	
6.	Baths	One preferably one on each floor.	
7.	Cleaner's sinks	One per floor minimum, preferably in or adjacent to sanitary room.	

Appendix 18·6. Sanitation requirements for assembly buildings (Theatres, Auditoriums and Cinemas)

Sl No.	*Fitments*	*For public*		*For staff*	
		Male	*Female*	*Male*	*Female*
1	2	3	4	5	6
1.	Water closet	1 for 100 persons upto 400 persons For over 400 persons add at the rate of 1 per 250 persons or part thereof.	2 for 100 persons upto 200 persons. For over 200 persons add at the rate of 1 per 100 persons or part thereof.	1 for 1-15 persons. 2 for 16 persons.	1 for 1-12 persons. 2 for 13-25 persons.
2.	Ablution taps	1 in each water closet.	1 in each water closet.	1 in each water closet.	1 in each water closet.
		One water tap with draining arrangements shall be provided for every 50 persons or part thereof in the vicinity of water closet and urinals.			
3.	Urinals	1 for 50 persons or part thereof.	—	Nil upto 6 persons. 1 for 7-20 persons. 2 for 21-45 persons.	
4.	Wash Basins	1 for every 200 persons.	1 for every 200 persons or part thereof.	1 for 1-15 persons. 2 for 16-35 persons.	1 for 1-12 person. 2 for 13-25 persons

Note : It may be assumed that two third of the numbers are males and one third females.

Appendix 18·7. Sanitation requirements for assembly occupancy buildings (Art Galleries, Libraries and Museums)

Sl. No.	*Fitments*	*For public*		*For staff*	
		Male	*Female*	*Male*	*Female*
1	2	3	4	5	6
1.	Water closet	1 per 200 pesons upto 400 persons. For over 400 persons add at the rate of 1 per 250 persons or part thereof.	1 per 100 persons upto 200 persons. For over 200 persons add at the rate of 1 per 100 persons or part thereof.	1 for 1-15 persons. 2 for 16-35 persons.	1 for 1-12 persons. 2 for 13-25 persons.
2.	Ablution taps	1 in each water closet. 1 water tap with draining arrangements shall be provided for every 50 persons or part thereof in the vicinity of water closet and urinals.	1 in each water closet.	1 in each water closet.	1 in each water closet.
3.	Urinals	1 for 50 persons	—	Nil upto 6 persons. 1 for 7-20 persons. 2 for 21-45 persons.	
4.	Wash Basins	1 for every 200 person or part thereof. For over 400 persons add at 1 per 250 persons or part thereof.	1 for every 200 persons or part thereof. For over 200 persons add at 1 per 150 persons or part thereof.	1 for 1-15 persons. 2 for 16-35 persons.	1 for 1-12 persons. 2 for 13-25 persons.
5.	Cleaner's sinks	—	1 per floor minimum.	—	—

Note : It may be assumed that $^{2}/_{3}$rds of the numbers are males and $^{1}/_{3}$rd females.

Appendix 18·8. Sanitation requirements for other buildings.

Sl No.	*Fitments*	*For public*		*For staff*	
		Male	*Female*	*Male*	*Female*
1	2	3	4	5	6
1.	Water closet	1 for 50 seats upto 200 seats. For over 200 seats add as 1 per 100 seats or part thereof.	1 for 50 seats upto 200 seats. For over 200 seats add at 1 per 100 seats or part thereof.	1 for 1-15 persons. 2 for 16-35 persons. 3 for 36-65 persons. 4 for 66-100 persons.	1 for 1-12 persons. 2 for 13-25 persons. 3 for 26-40 persons. 4 for 41-57 persons. 5 for 58-77 persons. 6 for 78-100 persons.
2.	Ablution taps		1 in each water closet.		
		One water tap with draining arrangements shall be provided for every 50 persons or part thereof in the vicinity of water closets and urinals.			
3.	Urinals	1 per 50 seats.		Nil upto 6 persons. 1 for 7-20 persons. 2 for 21-45 persons. 3 for 46-70 persons. 4 for 71-100 persons.	—
4.	Wash Basins	—	1 for every water closet.	—	—
5.	Kitchen sinks	—	1 in each kitchen.	—	—
6.	Service sinks	—	1 in each restaurant.	—	—

Note : It may be assumed that $^2/_3$rds of the numbers are males and $^1/_3$rd females. Min. one drinking water tap at each floor.

Appendix 18·9. Sanitation requirements for shops and commercial offices.

Sl. No.	*Fitments*	*For personal*
1	2	3
1.	Water closet	One for every 25 persons or part thereof exceeding 15 (including employees and customers) for female personnel one per every 15 persons or part thereof exceeding 10.
2.	Drinking water fountain	One for every 100 persons with a min. of one at each floor.
3.	Wash Basins	One for every 25 persons or part thereof.
4.	Urinals	Same as sl. no. 3 or "Table for Govt. or Semi-Business occupancies".
5.	Cleaner's sink	One per floor minimum, preferably in or adjacent to sanitary rooms.

Note : Number of customers for the purpose of the above calculation shall be the average number of persons in the permises for a time interval of one hour during the peak period. For male and female calculation a ratio of 1 : 1 may be assumed.

Appendix 18·10. Sanitation requirements for factories.

Sl. No.	*Fitments*	*For male personnel*	*For female personnel*
1.	Water closet	1 for 1-15 persons. 2 for 16-35 persons. 3 for 36-65 persons. 4 for 66-100 persons. From 101 to 200 persons add at 3%. From over 200 persons add at 2·5%.	1 for 1-12 persons. 2 for 13-25 persons. 3 for 26-40 persons. 4 for 41-57 persons. 5 for 58-77 persons. 6 For 78-100 persons. From 101 to 200 persons add at 5%. From over 200 persons add at 4%.
2.	Ablution taps	1 in each water closet.	1 in each water closet.
		One water tap with draining arrangements shall be provided for every 50 persons or part thereof in the vicinity of water closets and urinals.	
3.	Urinals	Nil upto 6 persons. 1 for 7-20 persons. 2 for 21-45 persons. 3 for 46-70 persons. 4 for 71-100 persons. From 101 to 200 persons add 3%, for over 200 persons add at 2·5%.	—
4.	Wash Basins/taps with draining	1 for every 25 persons or part thereof.	One for every 25 persons or part thereof.
5.	Drinking water fountains	—	One for every 100 persons with a minimum of on each floor.
6.	Baths (preferably showers)	—	As required for particular trades of occupancies.

Appendix 18·11. Sanitation required for residences

Sl. No.	*Fitments*	*Dwelling with individual convenience*	*Dwelling without individual conveniences*
1	2	3	4
1.	Bath rooms	One provided with water tap	One for every two tenements
2.	Water closet	One	One for every two tenements
3.	Sink (or Nahani in the floor)	One	One
4.	Water tap	One	1 with draining arrangements in each tenement. 1 in common bath rooms and common water closet.

Note : When only one water closet is provided in a dwelling, the bath and water closet shall be separately accommodated.

Appendix 18·12. Sanitation requirements for large stations and airports.

Sl. No.	*Place*	*W.C. for males*	*W.C. for females*	*Urinals for males only*
1.	Junction station	3 for 1000 persons	4 for 1st 1000 persons and 1 for every additional 1000 persons.	4 for every 1000 persons and 1 for every additional 1000 persons.
	Intermediate station	1 for every subsequent 1000 persons or part thereof.		
2.	Terminal station & Bus terminal	4 for 1st 1000 persons and one for every subsequent 1000 persons or part thereof.	5 for 1st 1000 persons and 1 for every subsequent 2000 persons or part thereof.	6 for 1st 1000 persons and 1 for every additional at 1000 persons or part thereof.
3.	Domestic Airports	2*	4*	2*
	For 200 persons	5	8	8
	For 400 persons	9	15	12
	For 600 persons	12	20	16
	For 800 persons	16	26	20
	For 1000 persons.	18	29	22
4.	International airports			
	For 200 persons	6	16	8
	For 600 persons	12	20	16
	For 1000 persons	18	29	22

Note : Separate provisions shall be made for staff and workers. Atleast one Indian style closet shall be provided in each toilet. Assume 60 males to 40 females in any area.

(19)

Earthquake Engineering—(Engineering Seismology)

Amongst all natural disasters earth quakes are feared most. This is probably due to the fact that there is no season for earth quake. Floods occur during rainy season. Cyclones on the eastern coast occur during post monsoon period October to March. But earth quake may occur any time during year or at any hour of the day.

19·1. Causes of earth quakes

1. Tectonic earth quakes are one of the most important factors, the cause of which is the motion of earth. The earth moves around itself in one day and around sun in one year. The subject of dynamics tells us that any rotating object generates centrifugal and centripetal force. This acceleration thus generated generates strain in the rock. As the constitution of the earth is not uniform and homogeneous the strain inside the earth is not distributed uniformly. Moreover, the density of the earth is also not uniform. Hence the strain gets concentrated at the weakest region of the rock, usually known as fault. The rock goes on accepting the strain till it is within the elastic limits of the rock. When it goes beyond the elastic limits, the rock yields and earthquake occurs. What happens at the focus cannot be seen or observed by scientists and engineers. As such the theory is mostly conjectural and hypothetical. But the surface manifestation of the fault in the form of ground rupture is the clear observable, measurable post-seismic evidence. Most of the big earthquakes are associated with surface rupture or faulting. Table 19·1 gives details about observed faulting during some earthquakes.

The earthquakes listed in Table 19·1 gives details about faulting during some significant earthquakes. The ruptures seen on the surface of the earth penetrate deep inside the crust and are known as fault. It could be seen that the immediate cause of earthquake was rupture. Sometime earthquakes occur without any observable surface rupture. Under such cases the rupture takes place inside the earth. The energy required for rupturing and the associated magnitude are more or less comparable. Hence faulting appears to be the cause of earthquake.

2. Volcanic earth quakes. The interior of earth goes on hotter and hotter as we go deeper and deeper and its temperature reaches upto the extent that even rocks liquify with high pressure which tries to come up through weaker zones known as a fault in the shape of lava (magma). Due to this sudden erruption earth shakes which causes earth quakes as per reasons given below.

Earth quakes are due to sudden release of accumulated strain energy with in a limited rock mass underneath. Due to disturbance in the equilibrium of the elastic energy the focal region, where the rock of irregulated shape and huge dimensions ruptures is known as hypocentre or '**Focus**'. The localities radially above the focus is known as **epicentre** on the crust of the earth (the upper layer of thickness between 20 km to 70 km) and the distance between epicentre and hypocentre (focus) in km is known as depth of focus or focal depth of the earth quake. The epicentre is a geographical location with latitude and longitude. The distance of a particular place A from the epicentre on earth is known as an epicentral distance.

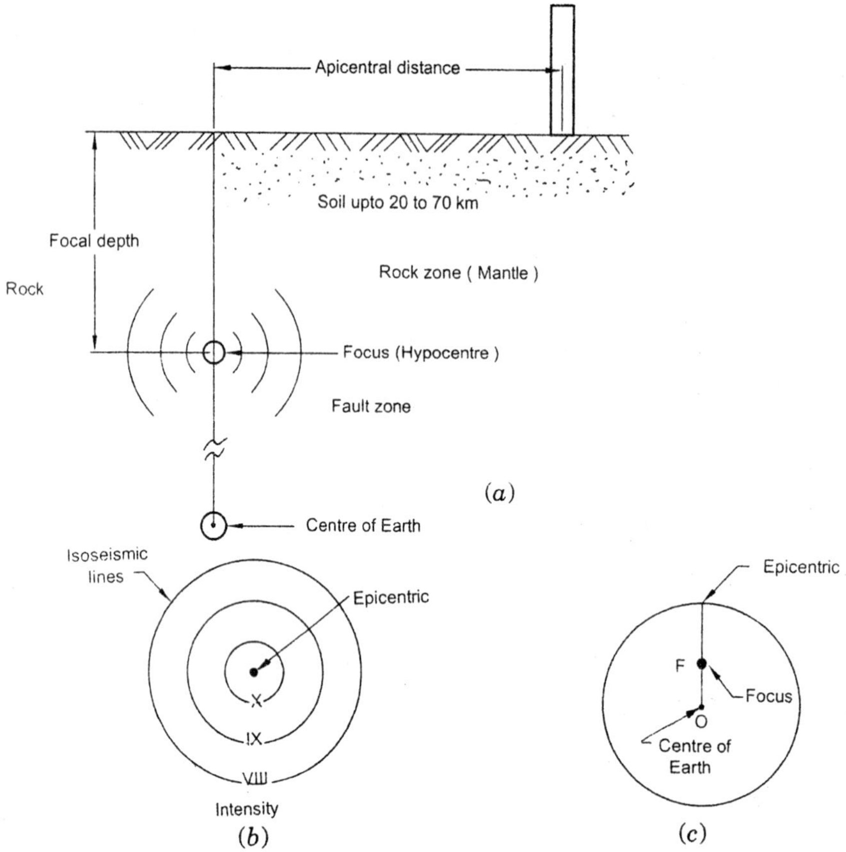

Fig. 19·1

Other details about earth quake are date and time of occurrence, its magnitude and intensity. The sources of energy prior to occurrence of earth quake are due to the above two reasons.

Table 19·1. Earthquakes and associated faulting (some selected examples)

No.	*Date*	*Place*	*Magnitude*	*Fault*
1.	June 16, 1819	Rann of Kutch	8·25	Allabund about 80 km long, downthrow up to 3 m
2.	March 26, 1872	Owen Valley Ca, USA	8·30	Near Alabama Hills, 15 km long, vertical throw up to 7 m, horizontal displacement up to 4·8 m
3.	June 12, 1897	Shillong, Assam	8·70	Chedrang Fault 20 km upthrow 10·5 m
4.	April 18, 1906	San Francisco, Ca, USA	8·30	San Andreas Fault 430 km strike slip up to 6·3 m

Table contd...

Table contd...

No.	*Date*	*Place*	*Magnitude*	*Fault*
5.	March 27, 1964	Alaska, USA	8·50	350 km uplift up to 13.5 m subsidence up to 2·2 m
6.	December 11, 1967	Koyna	6·50	20 km throw up to 1·0 m

3. The concept of Plate Tectonics (Plate Tectonic Theory). The outer shell of the earth has gradually cooled down over geological periods. The process of cooling is still continuing and the interior of the earth are at high temperatures. **The outer shell having cooled faster contracts and becomes small to fit the inner shell.** These results in built up of tensions on the surface of the earth, which leads to storage of strain at a few weak locations, which the seismologists call as fault. Based on this historical development a simple new theory, known as **plate tectonic theory** explains several aspects of earthquake occurrence. The theory assumes that the outer shell can be divided into finite number of rigid plates, which move as units. The interacting plate boundaries are the epicentral areas of current seismic activity. The new material ascends from depths to surface where these plates are moving apart. This is currently happening in Atlantic Ocean region and is known as sea-floor spreading. There are some plates, which are colliding. The Indian Plate has struck the Eurasian Plate and the boundary between these two plates is the great Himalayan Range. This area is seismically active and a large number of earthquakes have taken place here.

19·2. Earthquake damage and intensity

With the above background information it will be useful to know more about the damage observations and the earthquake intensity. The damage potential of any earthquake is dependent not only on magnitude of earthquake but in addition on several factors such as depth of focus, geology of the area, type of construction, time of occurrence of earthquake etc. The magnitude gives in absolute term the amount of energy released during the earthquake. The magnitude of an earthquake is measured on Richter Scale, which is logarithmic in nature. However, the intensity is a descriptive in nature. It tries to quantify the damage. The intensity scale used for damage assessment is MM Scale of intensity. It is always written in Roman Capital numbers. It begins at I, II, III, IV, ..., IX, X, XI and ends at XII. Intensity of any earthquake is highest at the epicentral area and it goes on decreasing with increasing distance from earthquake epicentre. The intensity scale had undergone several revisions during historical times. At present the UNESCO scale is the most popular and the latest, which is described below.

UNESCO Intensity Scale

Before going in details of the scale it is necessary to note some of the details about structures, quantity, building etc.

Types of structures (Buildings)

Structure A : Buildings in fieldstone, rural structures, abode houses, clay houses.

Structure B : Ordinary brick buildings, buildings of large blocks and prefabricated type, half-timbered structures, buildings in natural hewn stone.

Structure C : Reinforced buildings, well built wooden structures.

Definition of Quantity :

Single, few about 5%

Many	about	50%
Most	about	75%

Classification of damage to Buildings

Grade 1 Slight damage	:	Fine cracks in plaster, fall of small pieces of plaster.
Grade 2 Moderate damage	:	Small cracks in walls, fall of fairly large pieces of plaster, pantiles slip off, cracks in chimneys, part of chimney falls down.
Grade 3 Heavy damage	:	Large and deep cracks, fall of chimneys.
Grade 4 Destruction	:	Gaps in walls, part of building may collapse, Separate parts of the building loose their cohesion, walls collapse.
Grade 5 Total damage	:	Total collapse of buildings.

The intensity scale is as described below :

(*i*) **Not noticeable.** The intensity of the vibration is below the limit of sensibility. The tremor is detected and recorded by seismographs only.

(*ii*) **Scarcely noticeable (very slight).** Vibration is felt only by individual person at rest in houses, especially on the upper floors of buildings.

(*iii*) **Weak only partially observed.** A few persons felt the earthquake indoors, outdoors only in most favourable conditions. The vibration is similar to the passing of a light truck. Attentive observers notice a slight swinging of hanging objects, somewhat more intense on upper floors.

(*iv*) **Largely observed.** The earthquake is felt by many persons, outdoors by a few. Here and there people wake up but no one is frightened. The vibration is similar to a passing truck. Windows, doors, and dishes rattle. Floors and walls crack. Furniture begins to shake. Hanging objects swing slightly. Liquids in open vessels are slightly disturbed. The shock is noticeable in standing motor car.

(*v*) **Awakening**

(*a*) The earthquake is felt indoors by all, outdoors by many. Many sleeping persons wake up. A few run outdoors. Animals become uneasy. Buildings tremble throughout. Hanging objects swing considerably. Pictures knock against walls or swing out of place. Occasionally pendulum clocks stop. Unstable objects may be overturned or shifted. Open doors and windows are thrust open and slam back again. Liquids spill in small amounts from well-filled open containers. The sensation of vibration is similar to the falling of a heavy object inside a building.

(*b*) Slight damages in buildings of Type A are possible.

(*c*) Sometime a change in the flow of spring occurs.

(*vi*) **Frightening**

(*a*) Felt by most indoors and outdoors. Many people in building are frightened and run outdoors. A few lose their balance. Animals run out of their stalls. In a few instances, dishes and glassware may break and books fall down. Heavy furniture may possibly move and small steeple bells may ring.

(*b*) Damage of Grade 1 is sustained in single buildings of type B and in many of Type A. Damage in a few buildings of Type A is of Grade 2.

(*c*) In a few cases cracks up to 1 cm in width are possible in wet ground; occasional landslides in mountains, change in the flow of springs and in the water level of wells is observed.

(*vii*) **Damage to Buildings**

(*a*) Most people are frightened and run outdoors. Many find it difficult to stand. Persons driving motor cars notice the vibrations. Large temple or church bells ring.

(*b*) In many buildings of Type C damage of Grade 1 is caused; in many buildings of Type B damage is of Grade 2. Most buildings of Type A suffer damage of Grade 3, a few of Grade 4. In single instance, landslips of roadways on steep slopes, cracks in roads, seam of pipelines damaged; cracks in stone walls.

(*viii*) **Destruction of Buildings**

(*a*) **Fright and panic.** Persons driving motor cars are disturbed. At a few locations branches of tree may break off. Heavy furniture moves or partly overturns of topples. Hanging lamps are damaged in parts.

(*b*) Most buildings of Type C suffer damage of Grade 2, and a few of Grade 3. Most buildings of Type B suffer damage of Grade 3, and most buildings of Type A suffer damage of Grade 4. Occasional breaking of pipe seams. Memorials and monuments move and twist. Tombstones overturn. Stone walls collapse.

(*c*) Small landslips in hollows and unbanked roads on steep slopes; cracks in ground up to width of several centimetres. Water in lakes becomes turbid. New reservoirs come in existence. Dry wells refill and existing wells become dry. In many case change in the flow and level of water occurs.

(*ix*) **General Damage to Buildings**

(*a*) **General panic**. Considerable damage to furniture. Animals run to and fro in confusion and vocalize.

(*b*) Many buildings of Type C suffer damage of Grade 3, a few of Grade 4. Many buildings of Type B show damage of Grade 4; a few of Grade 5. Many buildings of Type A suffer damage of Grade 5. Monuments and columns fall. Considerable damage to reservoirs; underground pipes partly broken. In individual cases railway lines are bent and roadways damaged.

(*c*) Overflow of water on flat land, sand and mud is often observed. Ground cracks to widths of up to 10 cms; on slopes and river banks more than 10 cms; furthermore, a large number of slight cracks in ground; fall of rock, many landslides and earthflows; large waves in water. Dry wells renew their flow and existing wells dry up.

(*x*) **General Destruction of Buildings**

(*a*) Many buildings of Type C suffer damage of Grade 4, a few of Grade 5. Many buildings of Type B show damage of Grade 4; most of Type A have destruction of Grade 5; critical damage to dams and dikes and severe damage to bridges. Railway lines are bent slightly. Underground pipes broken or bent. Road paving and asphalt show waves.

(*b*) In ground cracks up to width of several cms, sometimes up to 1 meter. Broad fissures appear parallel to watercourse. Loose ground slides from steep slopes. Considerable landslides are possible near riverbanks and steep coasts. In coastal area displacement of sand and mud; change of water level in wells; water from canals, lakes, river etc. thrown out. New lakes appear.

(*xi*) **Destruction**

(*a*) Severe damage to well-built buildings, bridges, water dams and railway lines; highway becomes useless; underground pipes destroyed.

(*b*) Ground considerably destroyed by broad cracks and fissures, as well as by movement in vertical and horizontal directions; numerous landslips and falls of rock. The intensity of the earthquake requires special investigations.

(*xii*) **Landscape Change**

(*a*) Practically all structures above and below ground are greatly damaged or destroyed.

(*b*) The surface of the ground is radically changed. Considerable ground cracks with extensive vertical and horizontal movements are observed. Fall of rocks and slumping of riverbanks over wide areas; lakes are dammed; water falls appear, and rivers are deflated. The intensity of the earthquake requires special investigation.

Intensity and earthquake acceleration

The most important factor in earthquake engineering is the level of ground acceleration. Usually for the measurement of ground acceleration during earthquake, Strong Motion Instruments are installed. In absence of such installations, the likely value of acceleration could be worked out from the intensity maps known as isoseismal map. The derived acceleration from such maps is empirical in nature and is somewhat approximate. If the centre of gravity of the object is at a sufficient height compared to the base, then the moment of horizontal component of inertial force around a possible point of overturning on the base rim of the object may also equal or exceed the stabilizing moment, depending on the degree of shaking. Under such conditions the object may overturn after rocking on the base rim. Observations on sliding, rocking, and overturning with measurements of dimensions of the object, its weight and friction, could allow a quantitative estimate of the ground acceleration. This is more useful where no strong motion instruments are installed. There are several empirical relations for this. However, one of the most useful relation is

$$\text{Log } a = I(1/3) - 0{\cdot}5$$

Another relationship between magnitude and intensity given by Gutenberg and Richter is

$$M = 1{\cdot}3 + 0{\cdot}6I \text{ (max)}$$

where a is the acceleration in cm/s^2 and I is the intensity on MM scale, I (max) being maximum intensity. While calculating acceleration, the highest value of intensity should be used. The seismic intensity of VII to VIII will approximately represent a ground acceleration of 0·1 g. These maps and calculations could be used to prepare isoacceleration maps for engineering purposes.

In addition, there is important relationship between rupture length (L) of fault and magnitude (M) as follows :

$$\text{Log } L = 1{\cdot}02M - 5{\cdot}77$$

Guttenberg and Ritcher relation

$\log_{10}E = 9{\cdot}4 + 2{\cdot}14\text{ M} - 0{\cdot}05\,M^2$ where E is energy in Ergs, released by a shock of magnitude M. The table given below gives values of E released by different magnitudes M :

M	*Energy E* (10^{21} ergs)
5	0·0056
6	0·1477
7	5·4200
8	115·9000
8·7	853·1000

The magnitude M is thus a number that indicates the size of the earthquake. The larger is the magnitude of a shock, the greater the area which is effected.

This relationship helps in extracting seismic parameter from field observations.

Seismic waves. The theory of seismic wave propagation consists of rigid mathematical formulations and series of equation. The waves generated during an earthquake are of different types as below.

(1) **Body waves.** The waves generated during an earthquake and where travel through the earth are known as body waves. They are divided in primary and secondary waves.

(2) **Primary waves (P).** These are longitudinal, compressive or rare faction waves. They are always 1st to arrive and recorded.

(3) **Secondary (S) waves.** These are 2nd to arrive and usually have greater amplitude and destructive power than P waves.

(4) **Surface waves.** The waves which travel on the surface of Earth. The propagation of various waves is useful in determining various sub-surface propeties of earth.

Seismic Instruments. In the field of earthquake measurement, the major instrument for measurement and monitoring are seismograph. A seismograph consists of a sensor, galvanometer and recorder. The sensor senses ground vibrations and with the help of lamp and scale arrangement and galvanometer the throw is magnified and recorded on a photosensitive paper. Sometime ink and pen recording is used. There are also arrangement to record it on heat sensitive papers. In the present day advanced electronic instrumentation, various electronic chips are used and it is possible to connect the instrument directly to computer for analysis. The latest version of seismic instrument is micro-earthquake recorder. It is capable of recording earthquake up to magnitude –3 or so.

Strong Motion Instruments. The seismological instruments are continuous type of instruments and run for 24 hour. Basically, it senses displacement. However, for engineering purposes, the value of acceleration is required. For this purpose, the instrument used is known as Strong Motion Accelerograph. This instrument is installed at selected location and it gets triggered only when some level of acceleration is generated. Usually this level is set to 1% of g.

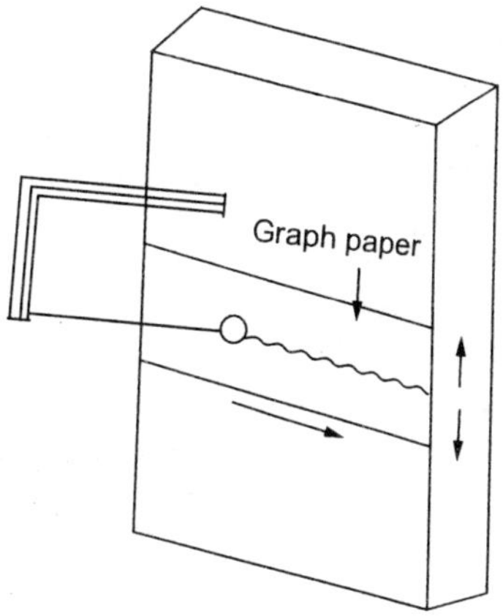

Fig. 19·1A. Seismograph.

19·4. Geology and Foundation Engineering (Remedial measures of Earthquakes)

Preliminary Geological and Geotechnical Investigations (refer soil mechanics Foundation and Bridge Engineering)

Geological and geotechnical conditions at the foundation are important factors in the design of structures. It is, therefore, essential to know accurately the geological conditions at the foundation before the designing of a structure is taken in hand, and geological investigations must be carried out to ascertain them. Numerous cases are on record in which neglect of geological conditions has given rise to all sorts of difficulties and has led to avoidable delays and increasing the cost of the project. On the other hand thorough understanding of geological conditions made possible large economies in the execution of many projects. A large number of failures have occurred in cases of structures founded on soils, weathered rocks (murum), and even on rocks. Thorough geological investigations must, therefore, be carried out before starting work on a project. The cost of geological investigation would be very major and there is no justification for avoiding them on the grounds of economics.

Subsurface exploration. Subsurface exploration is to be carried out by both excavation and core drilling. Both methods have their advantage and limitation and judicious use of both must be made. As rocks, soils and their structures as they actually occur in nature can be observed in the excavation, they give more reliable information. They are, however, practical and economic limitations to depth to which excavation can extend, and information from deeper levels is more conveniently obtained by core drilling. Drilling data can, however, be misinterpreted, particularly if proper surface geological work has not been carried out, and extreme caution is required in using the method.

There are various methods for subsurface exploration. These are described in brief below :

Aerial Photography. For inaccessible and unfamiliar areas air photography may be adopted as an aid in planning for detailed exploration work.

Geophysical Methods. They are grouped as

(*a*) seismic : refraction method, reflection method, velocity sounding method ;

(*b*) electrical ; (*c*) magnetic ; (*d*) gravitational ; and (*e*) sonic.

Shock or seismic waves are created by detonating small charges or by striking a rod or a plate near the surface. The radiating waves are picked up and time of travel from source recorded by detectors known as geophones or seismometers. In seismic method, either refracted or reflected waves are detected. They are used to determine depth to rock or depth of significantly differing soil strata and can be used only velocity of travel in lower layers is significantly greater than the upper ones. This method is usually limited to depths up to 30 m in a single stratum.

Test Pits, Trenches and Open Cuts. Test pits, trenches or any type of open excavation can be carried out manually or by machines. The sides of open cuts need be provided with lateral support with the help of bracings whenever there is a danger of caveins. Applicable in all soils, provide for visual examination of soil strata in their natural conditions, disturbed or undisturbed samples can be conveniently obtained at required depths. Use is usually limited to shallow depths of 3 m to 5 m. For greater depths cost of open excavation and necessary side bracing become uneconomical.

Borings. Principle boring types are auger boring, wash boring, percussion drilling and rotary drilling. Rotary drilling can be used in all types of soils and rocks and can be used to great depths, being increasingly used because of the fast rate of progress in all soil types and rocks. Undisturbed samples can be obtained at desired depth by using suitable samplers.

Load Test

(*a*) Vertical Plate Bearing Test. Vertical plate bearing test is very common. In this method a plate of 30 cm—75 cm of square or circular shape is loaded in increments to obtain load settlement curves. It is used in estimating allowable bearing pressure, co-efficient of elastic uniform compression (when the test is cyclic) and modulus of subgrade reaction.

(*b*) Pressure Meter Test. Generally done in bore hole. Cylindrical probe is inserted in a bore and subject to cylindrical pressure increments and deformations noted. It is useful in all soils particularly in bouldery strata, weathered rock etc. where it is difficult to obtain undisturbed samples for laboratory tests of difficult to rely on in situ tests. Like penetrations tests.

Exploratory Excavation. Test pits, trenches should be excavated according to local conditions. For this purpose instructions contained in IS 4453-1967, 'Exploration by pits, trenches, drifts and shafts' should be followed.

Core Drilling. Core drilling must be carried out by double tube diamond drill method only. Singly tube drilling methods should never be adopted. In the region such as Mumbai, where more soft weak and delicate rocks such tuff, volcanic breccia with tuffacious lava matrix and shale occur, triple tube drilling will be needed to procure the cores which are otherwise not obtainable. Drilling has to be used very carefully taking proper precautions to ensure that drilling data are not misinterpreted. As such surface exploration data about soils and rocks can not be interpreted without knowledge of local geology, drilling should not be undertaken before establishing local geology by means of surface survey of worksite and surrounding areas. For obtaining correct result and correct interpretations about subsurface geological conditions standard procedures laid down and guidelines provided in following IS codes about observations and precautions during drilling should be strictly followed :

1. Code of practice for diamond core drilling, for site investigations — IS : 6926-1973.
2. Guide for core drilling observations — IS : 5313-1969.

3. Code of practice for indexing and storage of drill cores — IS : 4078-1967.

4. Code of practice for presentation of drilling information and core description in foundation investigations — IS : 4464-1967.

Minimum Depth of Drilling. There is no uniform practice about depth up to which exploratory holes should be drilled. Practice followed is to drill about 3 m in hard rock and 5 m in soft rock. With such depths firstly possibility of in situ boulder and major cavities gets ruled out and even if such boulders are present, intensity of pressure below it will be substantially lower.

Foundations

Introduction. A major earthquake produces a strong ground movement in the subsoil. Consequently underground and surface structures supported on groundmass will be induced to move and take dynamic forces. The magnitude of inertia forces are proportional to the acceleration at the depth at which the foundation of the structure is placed. Their action in the foundation structure may be estimated knowing the subsurface behaviour. The general geology of the affected areas is important and the stratigraphy of the upper part of the subsoil comprising the soft sediments where the strong ground motions takes place should be determined.

When the seismic waves coming from the zone of generation hit the inner phase of the firm ground with the unconsolidated sediments, two types of body waves are originated, namely, irrotational and pure shear waves. The irrotational waves travel with high velocity than the shear waves, and for translation require change in volume of the soil. Therefore, in saturated soil they produce high pore pressures and eventually, if the acceleration is high in non-cohesive soil, liquefaction may take place at the ground surface. The shear waves do not produce the volume change in the soil during their propagation ; however, high shear stresses may develop running over the shear strength of the soil. From the above consideration two types of foundation problems may be considered : (*i*) problems induced by irrotational waves ; and (*ii*) problems induced by transverse waves.

Irrotational Seismic Waves. The stability of the foundation in cohesion less fine sediments with very low cohesion may be importantly affected by dilation, or irrotational waves. In a saturated soil the pore pressure originated during a strong ground motion may be high and the shear strength may be completely lost and liquefaction of the soil may take place. The phenomenon is detected at the ground surface boils appearing after the earthquake. Nevertheless, even with small acceleration the shear strength is reduced to a point that the bearing capacity is affected and the foundation supported on the type of soil may suffer partial or total failure. The reduction in bearing capacity of the soil may be approximately investigated by estimating the pore water pressure during the earthquake induced by irrotational waves, propagating from ground to the surface. The high pressure induced by strong earthquake may cause the failure of the structural foundation on firm soils.

Shear Seismic Waves. The transverse or pure shear waves propagate from the interface at the firm ground into unconsolidated sediments producing important shear distortion in the soil mass. Deep foundation and underground installations may be strong stressed when large displacements are obtained by the shear waves. The behaviour of the soil may be estimated with the knowledge of the dynamic shear modulus of elasticity and shear wave velocity. The subsoil behaviour may be calculated from soil profile at the site and dynamic shear modulus of elasticity. Hence, the shear distribution is calculated at the centre of the section and at the edge based on uniform soil reaction. Based on the above it is essential to carry out the subsurface investigation. This will include the determination of effective grain size, the consolidation and the shear strength characteristics, permeability characteristics of the soil as well as the previous stress history.

Liquefaction of Foundation Soils under Earthquake

Introduction. Liquefaction is a phenomenon in which a saturated cohesionless soil looses strength during an earthquake and acquires a degree of mobility sufficient to permit significant movements. When sand is not saturated the earthquake may cause significant compaction and subsidence. Catastrophic failures have occurred by liquefaction of cohesionless soils during recent earthquakes.

Site and Soil Conditions. Because the foundation must be capable of adequately supporting a structure in an economical manner it is imperative that there be proper geotechnical investigations. These geotechnical investigations provide information about the soil types beneath the site and their physical characteristics (strength, compressibility, permeability etc.) The investigation should provide economical and feasible alternatives for the support of the structure. In the seismic environment geotechnical investigations would also need to evaluate behaviour of the supporting soils under earthquake excitation, predict the consequences for the structure and recommend the foundation types.

Not only it is important to investigate the soil conditions, the general site conditions also need deep scrutiny. The investigation should indicate the features near the building area and also distant features. Important nearby site features include water levels, topographical features and the presence of other structures both above and below the ground, for example, the presence of faults, folds, fractures shear zones, cavernous rocks, weak bedding planes, dykes etc. will have influence on the structures.

Soil Liquefaction

Causes of Liquefaction. Soil liquefaction during an earthquake leads to loss of strength and stiffness of soil. This could result in the settlement of the structure, causes land slides, precipitate failures of earth dams, or cause other types of hazards. The soil liquefaction has been observed to occur most often in loose saturated sand deposits. During strong earthquake shaking the loose saturated sand deposits will have a tendency to compact and thus decrease in volume. If these deposits can not drain rapidly, there will be an increase in the pore water pressure. Effective stresses in the sand deposit is equal to the difference between the overburden pressure and the pore water pressure. With increasing oscillations, the pore water pressure can increase to the value of overburden pressure. Since the shear strength of a cohesionless soil is directly proportional to the effective stress, the sand will not have any shear strength, it is now in the liquefied state. Sand boils appearing at the ground surface during an earthquake are evidence that liquefaction has occurred.

Factors Known to Influence Liquefaction

Both laboratory investigations and observations of field performance have shown that the significant factors on which liquefaction potential of a soil deposit depends are : (*i*) Soil type ; (*ii*) Relative density of void ratio ; (*iii*) Initial confining pressure ; (*iv*) Intensity of ground shaking ; and (*v*) Duration of ground shaking.

(*i*) **Soil Type.** In general, fine uniform sands are found to be most susceptible to liquefaction in terms of grain size. It can be stated that soils containing less than 10% fines (silts and clay sizes), D 60 between 0·2 mm to 1 mm, uniformity coefficient U_c between 2 and 5 are most susceptible to liquefaction for given relative density of soil and intensity of earthquake. Thus, uniformly graded materials are more susceptible to liquefaction than well graded material. Also fine sands are more susceptible than gravely soil, silty sands, silts or clays.

(*ii*) **Relative Density or Void Ratio.** The susceptibility of given soil to liquefaction is determined to a high degree by its relative density. In general, it may be said that in cohesionless soils of relative density less than 50%, liquefaction might occur during ground accelerations of approximately 0·1 g, while for relative density greater than 75%, liquefaction is unlikely for most earthquake loadings.

(*iii*) **Initial Confining Pressure.** Laboratory investigations have indicated that for a given initial soil density, the stress required to initiate liquefaction under cyclic load conditions increases with initial confining pressure. It can also be said that liquefaction potential of soil is reduced by an increase in confining pressure.

(*iv*) **and** (*v*) **Intensity and Duration of Ground Shaking.** For a soil in a given condition and under a given confining pressure, the vulnerability to liquefaction during an earthquake depends on the magnitude of the stresses or strains induced in it by earthquake. These in turn are related to the intensity of ground shaking. Duration of ground acceleration also affect the susceptibility to liquefaction, naturally susceptibility increases with increasing duration. The effective duration of earthquake with Richter magnitude greater than 5 and less than 8 can be approximated by,

$$t = 4 + 11\,(M - 5)$$

where t is the effective duration or duration of strong shaking in seconds ; M, magnitude of earthquake on Richter scale.

Increase the value of t as obtained from the above equation, by 50% for earthquake with the Richter magnitude equal to or greater than 8·3.

Liquefaction-Induced Ground Failures and Effects on Structures. If a soil becomes liquefied and losses its shear strength, ground failure may result. If there are structures founded over or near these soil deposits, they may be damaged. Youd has classified ground failures caused by liquefaction into three categories

(*i*) Lateral spreading ;

(*ii*) Flow failures ; and

(*iii*) Loss of bearing capacity

Lateral spreading is a movement of surficial soil layers in a direction parallel to the ground surface, which occurs when three is a loss of shearing strength in a subsurface layer due to liquefaction. Lateral spreading usually occurs on very gentle slopes with a slope of less than 5%. If there is a differential lateral spreading under a structure, there can be sufficient tensile stresses developed in the structure to tear it apart. Flexible buildings have been observed to withstand extensional displacements better than stiff or brittle buildings.

Lateral spreading can have a catastrophic impact upon long, linear buried utilities ('life lines'). Flow failures occur when large zones of soil become liquefied or blocks of unliquefied soils flow over a layer of liquefied soils. Flow slides can develop where the slopes are generally greater than 5%. Liquefaction can also result in loss of bearing capacity usually accompanied by large soil deformations. Structures founded on these soils may settle, tilt or even overturn. Buried structures have even been floated out of the ground. In extreme cases where the thickness of liquefied soils is large tilting or overturning failures can occur. Where the liquefied soil is thin, or where there is relatively thick non-liquefied soil overlaying the liquefied soil deposit, severe tilting or overturning of structures will not occur, but differential vertical settlements can.

Buried structures such as underground tanks may be subjected to excess buoyancy because of increase of pore water pressure associated with the liquefaction. Retaining structures, such as retaining walls port structures, may also be subjected to increase in the lateral pressure should liquefaction occur in the adjacent soils. The formation if sink (when sand boils occur) holes may cause differential settlement or tilting of structures established on shallow foundations.

Of course, the degree to which structures are affected directly or indirectly by liquefaction-caused failures will depend upon how extensive the liquefaction is. If the liquefaction occurs in a thick and a horizontally extensive layer of sand, the effect on structure will be very great. If, in contrast, the liquefaction is associated to very thin and discontinuous layers (lenses) of soils, structures may suffer minimal or even no noticeable damage.

Facing the Liquefaction Problem

If liquefaction is identified as a hazard, there are choices that must be made. For new construction the available choices are :

(*i*) design for liquefaction by modifying the site soil conditions or strengthening the structure ;

(*ii*) abandon or move the project, or ;

(*iii*) accept the risk by proceeding without designing for liquefaction.

Obviously, economics will influence the choice in the major way. Second choice would be dependant on whether there is an alternate site without liquefaction problem.

Data Needed

(*i*) Maximum ground acceleration, a_{max} produced by design earthquake. It is generally given as 0·1 g, 0·2 g etc. The ground acceleration can also be estimated, if earthquake intensity on Modified Mercalli scale is known. Thus log 10 $a_{max} = (lm/3) - 0{\cdot}5$

where a_{max} is the maximum ground acceleration in cm/s^2 ; and lm, modified Mercalli estimated intensity. The above equation is proposed by US Coast and Geodetic Survey. Donovan recommends equation to estimate maximum ground acceleration. This equation is expression for mean of 678 peak acceleration values of Western USA, Japan and New Guinea and represents conservative estimate of mean peak accelerations on sites with 6 m or more of soil overlaying the rock.

$$a_{max} = [1080(e)\ 0{\cdot}5\ M]/(R + 25)\ 132$$

where, M is the magnitude of earthquake on Richter scale ; R, focal distance in km ; a_{max}, maximum ground acceleration in cm/s^2 ; and e, logarithmic base is 2·7183.

Another attenuation relationship based on recent corrected and statistically evaluated data is that of Esteva, who gives the expression for peak ground acceleration as :

$$a_{max} = 5600(e)\ 0{\cdot}8\ M/(R + 40)\ 2\ (\text{for } R > 15)$$

(*ii*) Number of significant stress cycles, N_{sig}, obtained from the knowledge of earthquake magnitude. According to Seed and ldriss (1971), the following relationship given in table below can be assumed.

(*iii*) Subsoil conditions, particularly soil type, density, ground water position, D 50 size, relative density or blow count (N) from Standard Penetration Test.

Table 19·2. N_{sig} against earthquake magnitude

Earthquake magnitude, Richter scale	*Number of significant stress cycle,* N_{sig}
7	10
7·5	20
8	30

Case Histories. In a table below known cases of earthquake with site conditions are given. Also, it is stated whether liquefaction or occurred not. Magnitude of earthquake indicated is as per Richter scale.

Mitigation and Liquefaction Hazard by Site Modification. There are site modification methods, which can reduce susceptibility of the soils beneath a site to liquefaction. These methods are summarized below.

1. Excavation and replacement of liquefiable soils

(*a*) Excavation and engineered compaction of existing soils ;

(*b*) Excavation and engineered compaction of soils improved with additives ; and

(*c*) Excavation of existing soils and replacement with properly compacted and non-liquefiable soils.

2. Densifications of in situ soils

(*a*) Compaction piles ;

(*b*) Vibratory probes ;

(*c*) Vibroflotation ;

(*d*) Compaction grouting ; and

(*e*) Dynamic compaction or impact densification.

3. In situ improvement of the soils by alterations

(*a*) Mixing in situ soils with additives ; and

(*b*) Removing in situ soils by jetting and replacement with no liquefiable soils.

4. Grouting or chemical stabilization.

Mitigation of Liquefaction Hazard by Structural Design. In designing a structure to resist liquefaction one must take into account the deformation of the soil that could occur during liquefaction. This will greatly affect foundation design of the building. Designing for the liquefaction may be accomplished by the use of piles or caissons which rely upon the soil or rock beneath the potentially liquefiable soil layers for supports. Such designs need to take account of possible down drag forces on the piles and caissons because of the settlement of the upper soils. Also, special design for the lateral forces or base shear may be needed because there could be a significant loss of the ability to transfer horizontal forces to the liquefied soils ; this may require use of battered piles or the design of caissons as unsupported columns through the liquefied zones. The foundation system will need to be tied together quite well to resist possible lateral spreading of the soils. Floor slabs on grade could be subject to settlement or differential movement and may have to be structurally supported to minimize the effects of liquefaction.

For structures of low profile and uniform mass distribution, a mat foundation may be feasible. The mat should be able to bridge the local areas of settlement so that the structure can act more or less as a rigid body. Any permanent deformation of the structure could then be corrected by grouting or mud-jacking the structure to its proper level.

Even with a structural solutions to mitigate again liquefaction there will remain some risk that the structure will be damaged and that some remedial work will be needed after the liquefaction event.

Mitigation of Liquefaction Hazard by Drainage. Dewatering systems may reduce potential for liquefaction by removing the water from those layers, which could liquefy. Also the resulting increase in effective overburden pressure will add to the resistance of the soils against liquefaction. If total dewatering of a site is not practical, providing some means of drainage may mitigate the problem. Drainage allows for the rapid dissipation of excess pore pressures in the potentially liquefiable soil layers. If the pore pressures can be relieved quickly, the effective stresses will not be decreased significantly and soil will retain most of its shear strength not allowing liquefaction to occur. Vertical gravel drains placed in a grid pattern may be able to accomplish this. Vibroreplacement also utilizes this principle, as the coarse grained stone column will be very permeable in comparison with the surrounding soils.

Seismic Settlement, Subsidence and Differential Compaction.. Seismic settlement and subsidence are two terms used to describe surface subsidence resulting from compactional densification of granular soil by earthquake induced vibration, which may occur over large areas. Although this phenomenon produces a result which is similar to what occurs from liquefaction, it occur in dry or partially saturated soil or in saturated soils which have good drain, that is, soil that do not liquefy.

During an earthquake a granular soil is subjected to cyclic shear from horizontal and vertical accelerations. In a strong earthquake the horizontal motion can cause densification because of the numerous shear cycles that occur. Whitman and De Pablo have demonstrated that vertical accelerations greater than the acceleration of the gravity are required to cause significant densification of granular soils. However, it has been reported that over 1 m (about 3 feet) of ground subsidence due to densification was experienced in Valdivia, Chile during the 1960 earthquake. It has also been reported that there was ground subsidence on the order of 5 m to 7 m over a very large area in the Mississippi Valley as the result of New Madrid earthquakes of 1811 and 1812.

Foundation of Structures on Rocks. Uptil now foundation problems associated with soils have been discussed. It is general misconception that there will be no problems for foundations on rocks. But there are large number of cases when structures founded on rocks, fresh or moderately weathered, have failed. This problem will be more aggravated in highly seismic areas. The rocks like shales, slates, phylites, tuffs, volcanic breccias with red tachylitic basalt matrix, volcanic breccia with tuff matrix, black, red, green, tachylyte, and the geological structures like fault zones, shear zones, crush zones, folds, limestones with solution cavities, and areas where mining activity is in progress etc. pose a lot of problems for foundations. Some rocks in dry conditions may have adequate strength, but soften with water and loose their strength to a great extent leading to uneven settlement. Difference in the degree of weathering and deterioration in dry and wet condition also leads to settlement of the structures. **Structures constructed on unstable slopes, with slope greater than dip of bed will fail when major shocks occur.** Therefore, during investigations due care must be taken while drilling not only through soils but also through weathered rocks and fresh rocks. All the features of rock like mineral composition, texture, state of preservation of rock masses, *i.e.*, degree of weathering, structure of rock masses like strike, dip, joints, bedding planes laminations, lineation, poliations, plane of schistocity, folds, faults, shear zones, crush zones, tension cracks, dykes, solution cavities and caves, spheroidical weathering, sheeting etc. must be recorded carefully and taken cognizance of while deciding the (SBC), type of foundation during the design of structure, in general and in earthquake prone areas in particular.

Landsliding and Lurching

Landslide. Earthquakes may trigger landslides or other forms of slope instability. Slope failures may occur as a result of development of excess pore pressures which will reduce the shear strength of the soil or cause loss of strength along bedding or joints in the rock materials.

Earthquakes may also cause shallow debris slides in areas with high, steep slopes. These slides can be minor or quite major. The 1970 debris avalanche triggered by the Peruvian earthquake of May 31, 1970 buried the towns of Yungay Ranrahirca, in which 18000 lives were lost. Careful consideration should be given to the structures which are sighted in a location that could directly or indirectly be affected by some form of slope instability. A very careful geotechnical and geological investigation will be needed to determine if such hazards exists and if there are any practical means of mitigation.

Lurching. Lurching means movement of soil or rock masses at the right angles to a cliff or steep slope. Structure founded either in part or whole on such masses may experience significant lateral and vertical deformation.

Earthquake Induced Slope Instability

While scientist are busy analysing the recent major earthquakes, that have occurred in recent years in India, for example, the one at Latur, Uttarkashi and Jabalpur, which have taken a high toll of human life and have also threatened the structures, engineers are, at the same time engaged in research and developmental activity for making safe aseismic structure. Studies carried out after 22nd May 1977 earthquake of Jabalpur have gathered evidences to prove that large scale upliftment of geological terrain takes place near and around epicentre as an immediate effect of seismic activity. This causes maximum damage to human life and structures due to differential upliftment.

Where the earthquakes occur in sparsely populated areas or uninhabited areas, the phenomenon of differential upliftment goes unnoticed as it does not manifests itself immediately through damage to man-made structures but causes damage to stability of the slopes of the hilly mountains and ridges to become seriously unstable. Recent major landslide of Gadhwal regions are in fact connected with the earthquake. They have their genesis in the previous seismic activities that have occurred there.

Fault Rupture. If ground surface rupture due to earthquake faulting were to occur beneath a structure, there would be a significant threat to the integrity of the structure and to its contents and inhabitants. The structure will in all probability be damaged if not a total failure due to differential ground displacement between the two sides of the fault. This displacement will be mostly lateral if the fault is strike slip fault, and mostly vertical if it is a thrust type of fault ; some faults will exhibit a combination of these two types of movement.

Indian Seismicity and Past Earthquakes

Some Great Earthquakes of India

1. 1819 Kutch Earthquake (M8·3)
2. 1905 Kangra Earthquake (M8·0)
3. 1950 Assam Earthquake (M8·7)
4. 1934 Bihar-Nepal Earthquake (M8·4)
5. 1950 Assam Tibet Earthquake (M8·7)
6. 1967 Koyana Earthquake (M6·5)
7. 1988 Bihar-Nepal Earthquake (M6·6)
8. 1991 Uttarkashi Earthquake (M6·6)
9. 1993 Killari (Latur) Earthquake (M6·4)
10. 1997 Jabalpur Earthquake (M6·0)
11. 1999 Chamoli Earthquake (M6·5)
12. 2001 Bhuj (Gujrat) Earthquake (M7·7)

19·5. Indian Standards on Earthquake Engineering. For the safety and stability of the structures following Indian Standard Codes should be followed. They have been formulated by Earthquake Engineering Sectional Committee, of Bureau of Indian Standards.

IS 1893:1984 Criteria for Earthquake Resistant Design of Structures

This standard deals with earthquake resistant design of structures and is applicable to buildings ; elevated structures ; bridges ; dams etc. It also gives a map which divides the country into five seismic zones based on the seismic intensity.

IS 1893:1984 was initially published in 1962 as 'Recommendations for Earthquake Resistant Design of Structures' and then revised in 1966. As a result of additional seismic data collected in India and further knowledge and experience gained the standard was revised in 1970, 1975 and then in 1984.

Consequent to the publication of this standard on account of earthquakes in various parts of the country including that in Uttarkashi and Latur and technological advancement in the field, the sectional committees decided to revise the standard into five parts which deals with different types of structures.

Part 1 : General provisions and buildings

Part 2 : Liquid retaining tanks—elevated and ground supported

Part 3 : Bridges and retaining walls

Part 4 : Industrial structures including stack like structures

Part 5 : Dams and embankments.

Part 1 contains provisions that are general in nature and applicable to all structures. Also, it contains provisions that are specific to buildings only. It covers general principles and design criteria, land combinations, design spectrum, main attributes of buildings, dynamics analysis, apart from seismic zoning map and seismic coefficients of important towns, map showing epicentres, map showing tectonic features and lithological map of India.

Following are the major and important modifications made in this revision :

(*a*) The seismic zone map is revised with only four zones, instead of fire. Erstwhile zone I has been merged to zone II and hence zone I does not appear in the new zoning ; only zones II, III, IV and V do. The Killari area has been included in zone III and necessary modifications made, keeping in view the probabilistic hazard evaluation. The Bellary isolated zone has been removed. The parts of eastern coast area have shown similar hazard to that of the Killari area, the level of zone II has been enhanced to zone III and connected with zone III of Godawari Graben area.

(*b*) This revision adopts the procedure of first calculating the actual force that may be experienced by the structure during the probable maximum earthquake, if its were to remain elastic. Then the concept of response reduction due to ductile deformation or frictional energy dissipation in the cracks are brought into the code explicitly, by introducing the 'response reduction factor' in place of the earlier performance factor.

(*c*) The values of seismic zone factors have been changed ; these now reflect more realistic values of effective peak ground acceleration considering Maximum Considered Earthquake (MCE) and service life of structure in each seismic zone.

(*d*) A clause has been introduced to restrict the use of foundations vulnerable to differential settlements in severe seismic zones.

Here it is worthwhile to mention that it is not intended in this standard to lay down regulation so that no structure shall suffer any damage during earthquake of all magnitudes. It has been endeavoured to ensure that as far as possible structures are able to respond, without structural damage to shocks of moderate intensities and without total collapse to shocks of heavy intensities.

IS 4326:1993 Earthquake Resistant Design and Construction of Buildings—Code of Practice

This standard provides guidance in selection of materials, special features of design and construction for earthquake resistant buildings including masonry construction, timber construction, prefabricated construction etc. In this standard, it is intended to cover the specified features of design and construction for earthquake resistance of building of conventional types. The general principles to be observed in the construction of such earthquake resistant buildings as specified in this standard are lightness, continuity of construction, avoiding/reinforcing projecting and suspended parts, building configuration, strength in various directions, stable foundations, ductility of structure, connection to nonstructural parts and fire safety of structures.

Special construction features like separation of adjoining structures, crumple section, foundation design, roofs and floors and staircases have been elaborated in the standard. It also covers the details pertaining to the type of construction, masonry construction with rectangular masonry units, masonry bearing walls, openings in bearing walls, seismic strengthening arrangements, farming of thin load bearing walls, reinforcing details for hollow block masonry, flooring/ roofing with precast components and timber construction.

IS 13827:1993 Improving Earthquake Resistance of Earthen Buildings—Guidelines

The guidelines covered in this standard deal with the design and construction aspects for improving earthquake resistance of earthen houses, without the use of stabilizers such as lime, cement, asphalt, etc.

The provisions of this standard are applicable for seismic zones III, IV and V. No special provisions are considered necessary in zones I and II. However, considering inherently weak against water and earthquake, earthen buildings should preferably be avoided in flood prone, high rainfall areas and seismic zones IV and V.

It has been recommended that such buildings should be light, single storeyed and of simple rectangular plan. Qualitative tests for the suitability of soil have been suggested.

Guidelines for block or adobe construction, rammed earth construction, seismic strengthening of bearing wall buildings, internal bracing in earthen houses and earthen constructions with wood or cane structure have been elaborated in this standard.

IS 13828:1993 Improving Earthquake Resistance of Low Strength Masonry Building—Guidelines

This standard covers the special features of design and construction for improving earthquake resistance of buildings of low-strength masonry.

The provisions of this standard are applicable in all seismic zones. No special provisions are considered necessary for buildings in seismic zones I and II if cement-sand mortar not leaner than 1.6 is used in masonry and through stones or bonding elements are used in stone walls.

The various provisions of IS 4326:1993 regarding general principles, special construction features, types of construction, categories of buildings and masonry construction with rectangular masonry buildings of low strength dealt with in this standard. There are, however, certain restrictions, exceptions and additional details which are specifically included herein.

IS 13920:1993 Ductile Detailing of Reinforced Concrete Structures Subjected to Seismic Forces—Code of Practice

This standard covers the requirements for designing and detailing of monolithic reinforced concrete buildings so as to give them adequate toughness and ductility to resist severe earthquake shocks without collapse.

The provisions for reinforced concrete construction given in this standard apply specifically to monolithic reinforced concrete construction. Precast and/or prestressed concrete members may be used only if they can provide the same level of ductility as that of a monolithic reinforced concrete construction during or after an earthquake.

Provisions on minimum and maximum reinforcement have been elaborated which includes the requirements for beams at longitudinal reinforcement in beams at joint face, splices and anchorage requirements. Provisions have been included for calculation of design shear force and for detailing of transverse reinforcement in beams.

Material specifications are indicated for lateral force resisting elements of frames. The provisions are also given for detailing of reinforcement in the wall web, boundary elements, coupling beams, around openings, at construction joints, and for the development, splicing and anchorage of reinforcement.

IS 13935:1993, Repair and Seismic Strengthening of Buildings—Guidelines

This standard covers the selection of materials and techniques to be used for repair and seismic strengthening of damaged buildings during earthquakes and retrofitting for upgrading of seismic of existing buildings.

The provisions of this standard are applicable for buildings in seismic zones III to V of IS 1893 : 1984, which are based on damaging seismic intensities VII and more on MSK scales.

The Buildings affected by earthquake may suffer both non-structural and structural damages. This standard lays down guidelines for non-structural/architectural as well as structural repairs, seismic strengthening and seismic retrofitting of existing buildings. Guidelines have been given for selection of materials for repair work such as cement, steel, epoxy mortar, quick setting cement mortar and special techniques such as shotcrete, mechanical anchorage etc. Seismic strengthening techniques for the modification of roofs or floors, inserting new walls, strengthening existing walls, masonry arches, random rubble masonry walls, strengthening long walls, strengthening reinforced concrete members and strengthening of foundations have been elaborated in detail.

IS 6922:1973, Criteria for Safety and Design of Structures Subject to Underground Blasts

This standard deals with the safety of structures during underground blasting and is applicable to normal structures like buildings, elevated structures, bridges, retaining walls, concrete and masonry dams constructed in materials like brickwork, stones masonry and concrete.

As underground blasting operations have become almost a must for excavation purposes, this standard lays down criteria for safety of such structures from cracking and also specifies the effective accelerations for their design in certain cases.

IS 4991:1968, Criteria for Blast Resistant Design of Structures for Explosions above Ground

This standard covers the criteria for design of structures for blast effects of explosions above ground excluding blast effects of nuclear explosions.

IS 4967:1968, Recommendations for Seismic Instrumentation for River Valley Projects

19·6. Earthquake Ground Motion and Codal Provisions

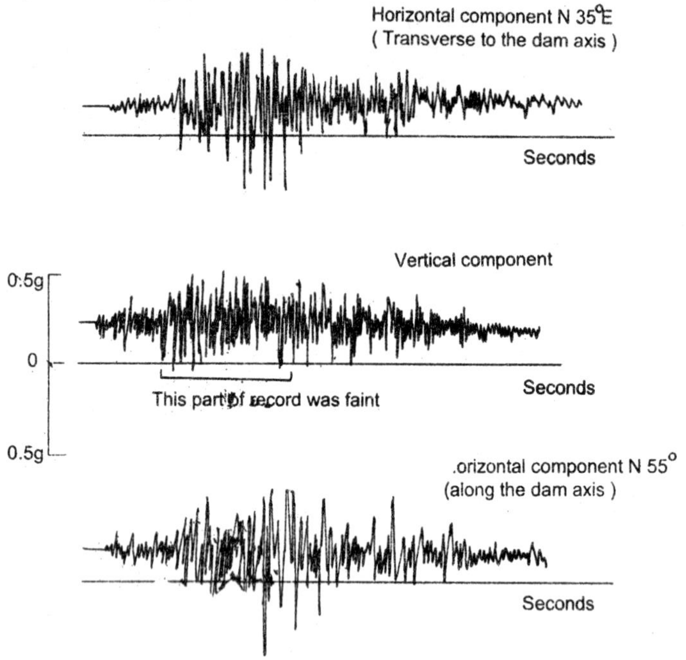

Fig. 19·2 (A) Tracing of the accelerogram for the December 11, 1967 Koyna earthquake.

The principal nucleus of the entire subject of earthquake engineering is strong motion. Till now a large number of accelerograms have been recorded on similar ground conditions. But they are never identical. Each record has its own signature and distinct characteristics. Two records from the same instrument and at the same site on different dates also vary in their characteristics. **Ground acceleration, velocity and displacement (referred to as ground motion) when transmitted through structures, in most of the cases, are amplified.** The amplified motion can produce forces and displacements, which may exceed what those structures, can sustain. Earthquake ground motion is usually measured by strong-motion accelerographs, which records the acceleration of ground at a particular location. The recorded accelerograms after they are corrected for instrumental errors and adjusted for baseline are integrated to obtain the velocity and displacement time histories. The maximum values of the ground motion such as peak ground acceleration, peak ground velocity and peak ground displacement is of significance in engineering analysis and design. These parameters, however, do not by themselves describe the intensity of shaking that structure or equipment experience. There are other factors such as the magnitude of the earthquake, distance from the fault or epicentre, duration of shaking, soil conditions at site, the frequency content of motion which also influence the response of the structure. It is proposed to discuss some of these topics.

Ground motion during an earthquake is measured of the ground

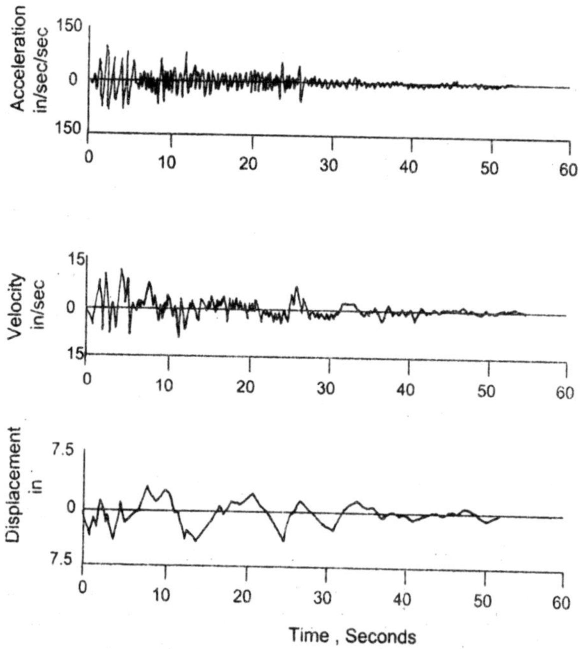

Fig. 19·3. Corrected accelerogram and integrated velocity and displacement time-histories for the SOOE component of El Centro, the Imperial Valley Earthquake of May 18, 1940.

by strong motion accelerographs which record acceleration of the ground in three orthogonal directions, two inhorizontal direction and one in vertical direction. The instrument may be located in free field or may be mounted on a structure. The first strong ground motion in India, recorded during the Koyna earthquake of magnitude 6.5 on December 11, 1967 shown in Fig. 19·2 (*A*). It shows the three components. The highest acceleration recorded at Koyna is 0.67 g. In addition, Fig. 19·3 shows one of the oldest strong motion records from El Centro Valley earthquake of May 18, 1940. It shows the corrected accelero-gram and integrated velocity and displacement time histories. Since the earlier times the accelero-grams are recorded on photo-sensitive films. Due to design and inherent complexities of the instru-ment, a number of corrections were required to be applied to the record. There were base correc-tions. The Earthquake Engineer-ing Research Laboratory of the California Institute of Technology has carried out the digitization, correction, and processing of acce-lerograms in the past. However, at present the instruments are mostly electronic types and the records are available on a computer. These could be integrated accurately to obtain correct velocity and displacement parameters.

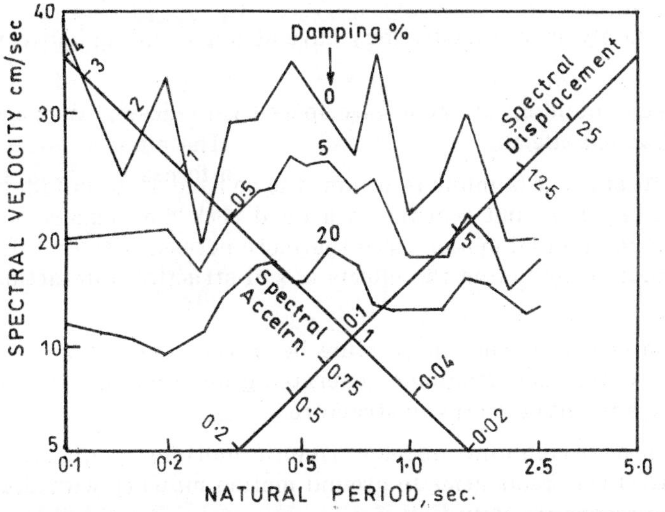

Fig. 19·4. Response spectra for the transverse of December 11, 1967 Koyna earthquake (Krishna *et al*, 1969)

Effective Duration. The other factor, which influences the spectrum, is effective duration. Actual earthquake motions have a concentration of larger and smaller amplitudes at different times and, therefore, the effective and total duration differs. The importance of effective duration of shaking becomes very clear while studying liquefaction of saturated sand deposits. Housner was the first to give the estimates of the effective duration along with peak horizontal acceleration. A simple way to define effective duration is to specify the time during which the ground acceleration must remain above a particular threshold level. The time over which the function reaches its 75% value has been called effective duration. For example, if the threshold value is fixed as 0.10 g, then the duration the value of acceleration is above 75% of 0.10 g will be effective duration.

Rigid Link Analogy. Three dimensional symmetrical buildings frames are idealized as frames placed side by side and connected by rigid links at each floor levels with the assumption that the lateral displacement of frames at each floor level is same.

Moment Resisting Frames. The frame with rigid joints and finite beam stiffness behaves as a moment resisting frame. Moment resisting frame with shear wall or vertical trusses, if any, efficiently transfer the lateral loads from the floor diaphragms to the foundations. In case of buildings where floors/roof are not able to provide diaphragm action, the building frames behave independently and may be analysed frame by frame with tributary masses. Dynamic response of such frames may be obtained considering rotations of beam column joints and axial deformations in columns and floors.

Drift. An earthquake develops inertia forces, *i.e.*, lateral forces in the direction of ground motion and significant undesirable lateral displacements in building, known as drift.

Adequate lateral stiffness in a structure is usually ensured by seismic design codes by limiting the overall lateral displacement and inter-storey displacement. The overall displacement is usually expressed as overall drift index (ODI) which is the ratio of maximum roof displacement to the height of structure and inter-storey drift ISD is ratio of interstorey displacement and storey height. IDI and ISD should not exceed 1.0% to 1.5%.

Coupling of Lateral and Torsional Motions. In irregular building the centre of mass and centre of stiffness of the building do not coincide. This causes eccentricity and hence lateral and torsional motions of the building during earthquake. If the eccentricities are large lateral and torsional motions will be strongly coupled. Accidental eccentricities are considered as follows

(*i*) for natural frequency > 1, eccentricity > 5% of longer plan dimension of the building ; and

(*ii*) for natural frequency > 2, eccentricity > 10% of longer plan dimension of the building. Wherever there are large differences in lateral stiffnesses between adjacent floors, torsion and *P* delta effect need to be considered.

Modal Interaction Effects. Closely spaced modes may have strong coupling between lateral and torsional responses.

As normal modes of an symmetric building are generally spaced very closely, they are characterized by very large modal interaction effects.

Soil-structure Interaction Effects. The building is assumed to be fixed on an infinitely rigid foundation but in reality a building base not resting on a hard rock may experience significant deformations during earthquake ground motion. It is therefore necessary to find the response of building with flexible foundation by taking the effects of soil structure interaction into account in a rigorously way.

Resonance. The foundation natural frequency of building lie in the range of 0.1 s to 3 s. This is also the range of frequency content of earthquake generated ground motion. Hence, the ground motion imparts considerable amount of energy to structure.

Vibration of building consists of a combination of harmonic motions of different frequencies and magnitudes. When any of the frequencies in ground motion matches with that of natural frequency of the building, the resonance occurs.

Resonance is considered as multi-fold increase in response. At resonance, significant damage is observed in a building. Damping reduces the response of building. This reduction is significant at resonance.

Non-linear Response. The acceleration, velocity and displacement vectors contain the additional degree-of-freedom in non-linear response analysis. Mass matrix includes the translational mass and rotational mass terms on the main diagonal. The stiffness matrix includes the incremental stiffness contributions. The damping matrix is represent as a linear combination of the mass and stiffness matrices.

Non-linear response analysis of a building may include response parameters as envelopes and the maximum storey displacement (inter-storey drift), the maximum ductility demand of beams and columns, envelops of maximum plastic rotation and envelops of maximum storey shear.

Ductility. Ductility is the capacity of structure to undergo deformation beyond yield without loosing much of the load carrying capacity. Ductility may be expressed in terms of displacement or rotation or curvature or strains.

Ductility Factor. A measure of the structural ductility is the displacement ductility factor μ defined as $\mu = \delta_{max}/\delta y$ where δ_{max} is the lateral deflection at the ultimate condition and δy is the lateral deflection at yield. Usually these displacements are measured at roof level.

Ductility Reduction Factor. As a structure is subjected to a strong ground motion, initially it responds elastically after yielding, the lateral stiffness of structure reduced, *i.e.*, reduction in stiffness. The reduction in the maximum force from F_{max} is to Fy due to ductility μ is termed as ductility reduction factor R_{μ}.

In structures of natural period less than 0.1 s the ductility does not help in reducing the response. Hence for such structures ductility reduction factor is essentially 1.0.

For structures with natural period higher than 0.5 s the response reduction factor is approximately equal to μ. Therefore, structure with ductility of $\mu = 5$ could be designed to yield at one-fifth the expected maximum linear elastic force.

The buildings with moment resisting frames designed specially for ductility are assigned lower design seismic force than those not specially designed for ductility.

Finally it may be concluded that :

(*i*) A dynamic analysis can take a number of forms but should take account of the irregularities of the structure by modelling its structural and dynamic characteristics, including natural frequencies, mode shapes and damping.

(*ii*) At present because of computer software development the methods for earthquake response analysis of buildings are amenable to good accuracy and the task of earthquake resistant design of buildings can be achieved with high degree of reliability.

19·7. Concepts of Seismic Design and Configuration

Earthquake Hazards

Strong Ground Motion. Seismic waves reaching ground surface cause strong ground motion, which causes buildings/structures to shake in variety of complex ways. Many buildings cannot withstand this movement. Most of the times damages and economic losses caused by earthquakes are due to strong ground motion.

Failure of Foundation Strata. Strong ground motion causes cracking and fissuring of earth, softening, warkening, sinking, settlement of soil surface faults, displacement and liquefaction and landslides.

Tsunamis. These are immense sea waves, travelling across the ocean at very high speed and as high as 15 metres when reach the sea shore. These cause enormous damage in coastal region.

Effects of Earthquakes on Buildings

Ground Motion. The dynamic response of the building to earthquake ground motion induced by seismic waves is the most important cause of damage to the building.

Strong ground motion sets building in motion starting with building foundation and transferring motion through rest of the building. This action is very complex and depends upon complexity of earthquake ground motion.

Complexity of Earthquake Ground Motion. During earthquake, ground vibrates in a complex manner as seismic waves of different frequencies and amplitudes interact with each other.

The complexity is due to three factors :

(*i*) **Source Effects.** The seismic waves generated at the time of fault movement are not of uniform character.

(*ii*) **Path Effects.** The waves are modified by the soil and rock media when they pass through them on their way from earthquake source to building sites.

(*iii*) **Local Site Effects.** When seismic waves reach the building sites, they further undergo modification due to soil below the building.

The characteristics of earthquake ground motions which have the greatest importance for buildings are the duration, amplitude (displacement, velocity and acceleration) and frequency of ground motion. *Frequency is number of complete cycles of vibration of the wave per second.* Actually surface ground motion at the building site is complex superposition of vibrations of different frequencies. At any given site some frequencies are dominant. The distribution of frequencies in ground motion is referred as its frequency content. The response of building is as complex as the ground motion itself. Building also begins to vibrate in a complex manner during earthquake. It also possesses a frequency content. Buildings vibrations tend to centre around a particular frequency which is natural frequency of fundamental frequency. When the frequency contents of the ground motion are centered around the buildings natural frequency the building and the ground motion are in resonance with one another. Resonance tends to amplify building's response and building suffers great damage.

Table 19·3. Behaviour of Buildings. Shorter buildings have higher natural frequency. In other words shorter buildings have less natural period, where period is defined as time building takes for one complete vibration. If f is natural frequency, then natural period $T = 1/f$.

Building height, storey	*Typical natural period, s*
2	0·2
5	0·5
10	1·0
20	2·0
30	3·0

Seismic Structural Configurations. Building's architecture plays a major role in the building's seismic performance. The architectural decisions influencing seismic performance are grouped into three categories.

(*i*) The building configuration—it means geometrical properties of the form of building such as size, shape, proportions of three-dimensional form of building, also location, shape and approximate size of major structural components.

(*ii*) Structurally responsive detailed architectural design—this means architectural details of columns or walls that are detrimental to good seismic design practice.

(*iii*) Hazardous nonstructural components.

Configuration Characteristics and their Effects. For a given ground motion, total inertial force is due to building mass. The size and shape of the building establish its mass. For any building with specific requirements of spaces, inside activities and equipments it contain, a variety of configurations can provide solution. Variables in these configurations affect distribution of inertial forces and thus influence seismic performance. Thus it is necessary to identify configuration variables or irregularities (deviation from regular configuration) that affect the distribution of forces.

Regular configuration is optimum or ideal with respect to dealing forces.

Figure 19·5 shows three structures, employing three typical alternative for lateral resistance, that are seismically ideal. These three have the attributes of

(*a*) Low height to base ratio ;

(*b*) Balanced response ;

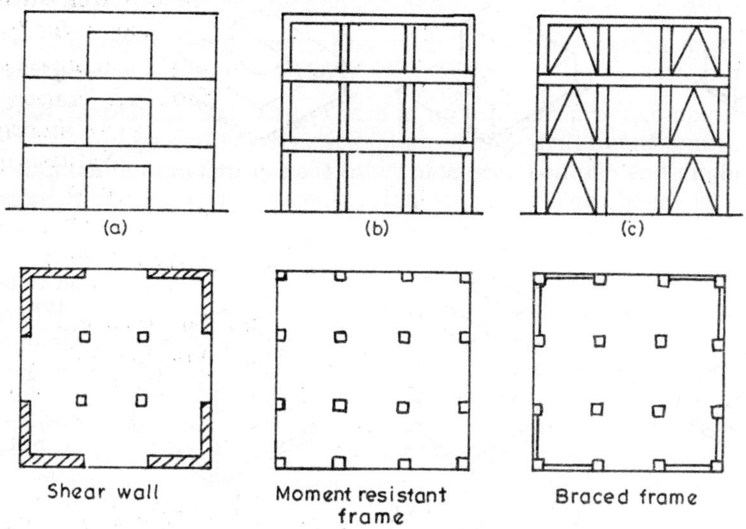

Fig. 19·5. The optimal seismic configurations.

(*c*) Symmetrical plan ;

(*d*) Uniform section and elevation ;

(*e*) Maximum torsional resistance (due to location of shear walls and bracings) ;

(*f*) Short spans ;

(*g*) Direct load paths ; and

(*h*) Uniform floor heights

In last two decades, architectural configurations along with method of construction have changed significantly. Frames have become much more open and irregular. The rugged systems of masonry walls and concrete floors have been replaced by prefabricated elements. Thus, old method of equivalent lateral forces for analysis of ground motion can not be useful for assessment of damage of structure due to earthquake and more rigorous methods of analysis are required to be used.

The list of irregularities considered here are to be avoided for better performance of a building during earthquake.

Irregular Configurations. There can be many irregular structures or framing systems, which need extra analysis and dynamic consideration rather than normal equivalent static force method. These types are illustrated in Fig. 19·6.

Plan Irregularities. In the plans when re-entrant corners are provided and when both projections of the structure beyond re-entrant corner are greater than 15% of the plan dimension they need special consideration. Refer Fig. 19·7.

Diaphragm Discontinuity. Diaphragms with abrupt discontinuity or variation in stiffness, having cutout or open areas greater than 50% of gross enclosed diaphragm area or change in effective diaphragm stiffness of more than 50% percent from one storey to the next can be avoided.

Vertical Structural Irregularities

Stiffness irregularity. Soft storey to be avoided. Soft storey is the one in which the lateral stiffness is less than 70% of that in the storey above or less than 80% of the average stiffness of the three stories above. Refer Fig. 19·8.

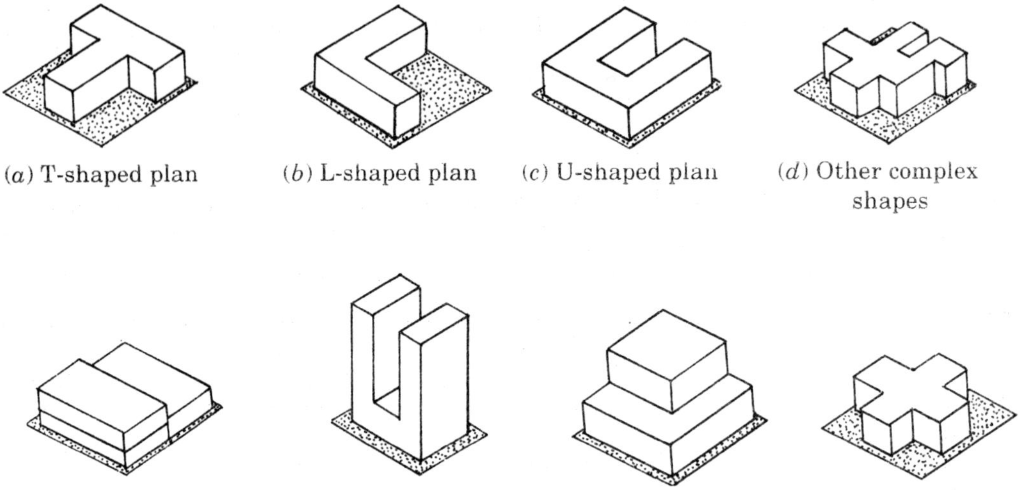

(*a*) T-shaped plan (*b*) L-shaped plan (*c*) U-shaped plan (*d*) Other complex shapes

(*e*) Split levels (*f*) Multiple towers (*g*) Set backs (*h*) Cruciform plan

Fig. 19·6 (*A*).

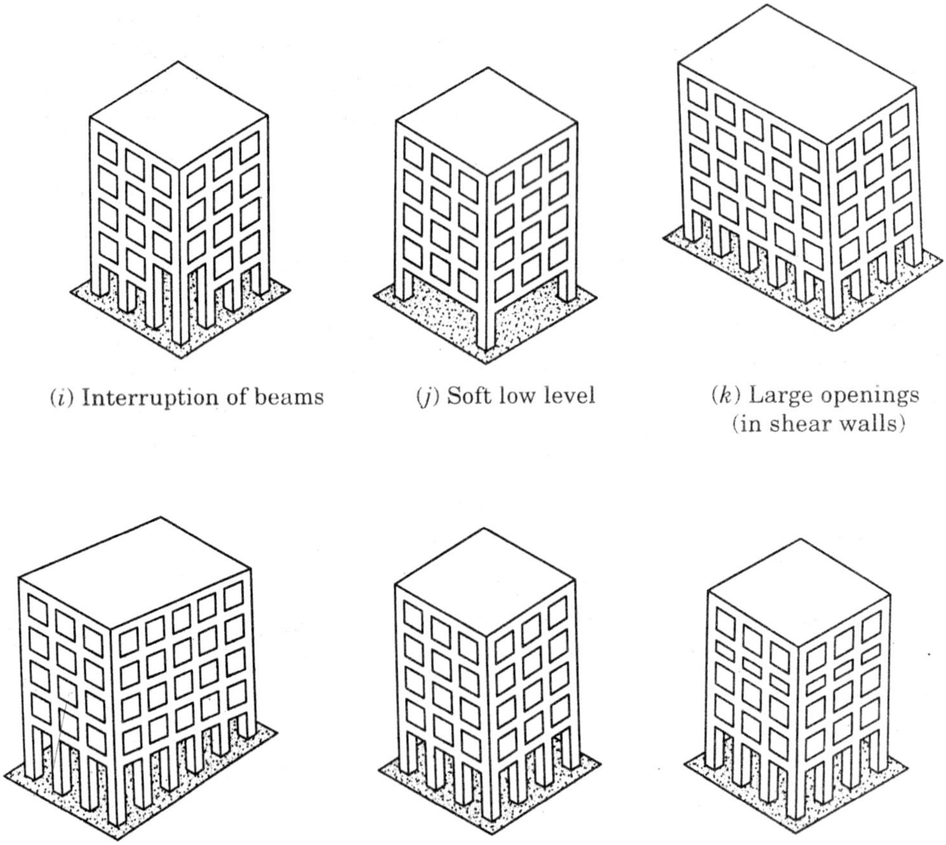

(*i*) Interruption of beams (*j*) Soft low level (*k*) Large openings (in shear walls)

(*l*) Building on hill side (*m*) Unusually high story (*n*) Unusually low story

Fig. 19·6 (*B*).

Extreme Soft Storey. Lateral stiffness is less than 60% of that in storey above or less than 70% of the average stiffness of the three stories above.

Mass Irregularity. When effective mass of any storey is more than 150% of the effective mass of the adjacent storey. A roof lighter than the floor below need not be considered.

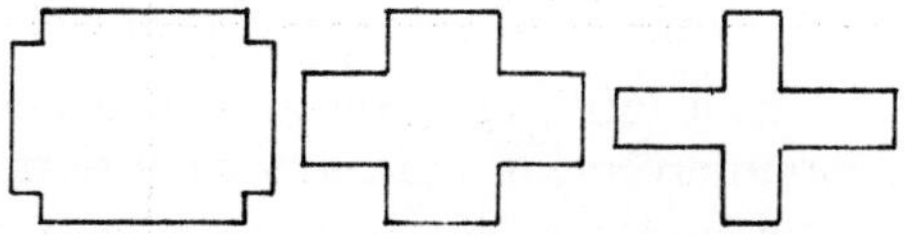

Fig. 19·7. The re-entrant corner plan.

Vertical Geometric Irregularity. Vertical geometric irregularity shall be considered to exist when horizontal dimension of the lateral force resisting system in any storey is more than 130% of that in adjacent storey.

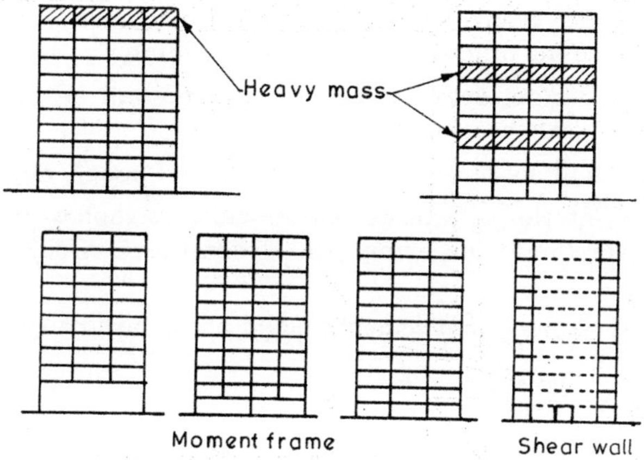

Fig. 19·8. Vertical irregularities.

In Plane Discontinuity in Vertical Lateral Force Resisting Elements. An in plane offset of the lateral force resisting elements greater than the length of those elements or reduction in the stiffness of the resisting element in the storey below.

Weak Storey. The storey lateral strength is less than 80% of that storey above. The storey strength is the total strength of all seismic resisting elements sharing the storey shear for the direction under consideration.

Concepts of Seismic Design and Configurations

Damage of the structure due to the earthquake forces can be reduced if proper structural configuration is used and irregularities in configuration are avoided.

Before starting analysis, following factors shall be included in the basic structural system, to that its performance during earthquake will improve.

(*a*) Earthquake forces is an inertia force and depends on masses and acts through the centre of mass. The centre of mass and centre of rigidity of building shall coincide to avoid undesirable torsional effect.

(*b*) Heavy masses at the higher level shall be avoided.

(*c*) The lateral load-bearing members shall be uniformly distributed.

(*d*) All columns and walls shall be continuous and without offset from roof to foundation.

(*e*) Columns are co-axial.

(*f*) Principal members are without sudden change in section.

(*g*) The parts of the structure are tied together in such a manner that the building is as continuous and monolithic as possible.

(*h*) Infill wall : masonry infill wall changes the behaviour of relatively flexible frames.

If the infilling material is intended to act in combination with the enclosing frame, then proper reinforcement and connection to the enclosing frame are essential.

If of fairly brittle material, namely, glass or hollow brick, and is not expected to contribute significantly to lateral resistance, then it should be effectively isolated from the surrounding frame by gaps or readily crushable/yielding material.

Special attention needs to be given to building on stilts. The stilt storey are becomes a soft one on account of absence of infill walls and creates a plane of weakness resulting in collapse of structure. Modified behaviours of the infilled frames should be considered in analysis.

(*i*) Projecting parts shall be properly reinforced and firmly tied to the main structure.

(*j*) A sufficient distance to prevent their hammering against each other, if not properly tied together, should separate the different portions of a building.

(*k*) Before starting design, detail soil investigation shall be carried out to ascertain required depth of foundation, safe bearing capacity, etc.

(*l*) The foundation shall not be on loose soil, which will liquefy during earthquake.

(*m*) Bearing walls (interior or exterior) are provided to support vertical load only. RCC band shall be provided over the load-bearing wall at lintel level around the periphery of the structure.

(*n*) Governing criteria for reinforcement should not be arbitrary but shall be adequate for earthquake resistance.

(*o*) Low height to base ratio.

(*p*) Symmetrical plan.

(*q*) Short plans.

(*r*) Uniform floor height

(*s*) Uniform section and elevation.

(*t*) Max. torsional resistance due to location of shear walls and bracings.

19·8. Seismic Design and Detailing of Masonry Buildings Including Code Provisions

Behaviour of Brick Masonry. The shear strength of masonry in combined shear and compression is of importance in relation to resistance of buildings to lateral seismic forces.

The formula is to

$$V_{ult} = V_0 + \mu f_{mc}$$

= Shear at zero compression + μ Stress in compression

where value of μ varies between 0.3 and 0.4; V_{ult}, ultimate shear stress ; V_0, shear no compression ; f_{mc}, allowable stress in masonry in compression.

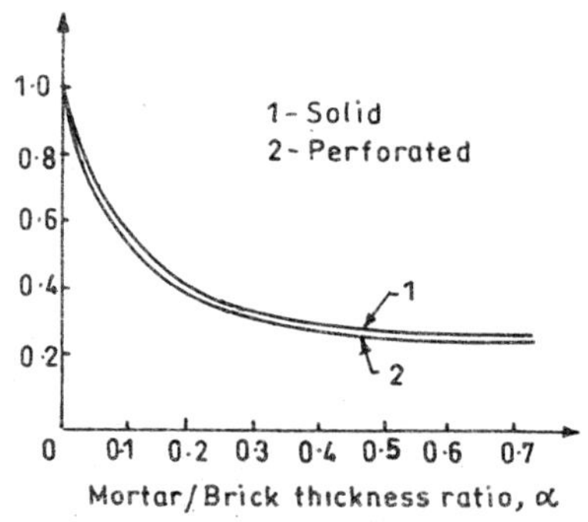

Fig. 19·9. Plot of brickwork prism to brick compressive strength ratio to the ratio of mortar to brick thickness.

The stress-strain relationship in cases of masonry is approximately parabolic and Young's Modulus 'E_m' can be safely assumed as

$$E_m = 700\, f_c$$

where f_c is crushed strength of masonry. This value of E_m could be applicable to upto 75% of the crushing strength.

For estimating long term deformations, a reduced value of E_m should be used by assuming between 1/3 and 1/2 of the value given above.

Behaviour of Reinforced Masonry

Masonry design has been traditionally done by elastic methods and the codes have been drafted with this in mind. The low values of allowable stresses is essentially for code stipulated seismic forces. The codes have taken this approach with a belief that masonry behaviour can be predicted more accurately at service load levels that at ultimate load levels. This is not true. Ultimate load behaviour is insensitive to creep, shrinkage, etc. Hence moments and shear at ultimate strains can be predicted with considerable accuracy. With considerable research carried out on reinforced masonry, it is now possible to design with sufficient reliability, masonry behaviour at ultimate load.

IS 1893 (Draft) gives different response reduction factors 'R' for type of masonry construction.

(*a*) Un-reinforced masonry $R = 4$

(*b*) Reinforced with horizontal band $R = 5$

(*c*) Reinforced vertically and horizontally $R = 6$

The variation in 'R' value between un-reinforced masonry and masonry reinforced horizontally and vertically is four to six. The horizontal seismic force for which structures are designed for the two conditions will be more by 50% in case of unreinforced masonry compaired to reinforcement masonry. This is because the un-reinforced masonry will be brittle and will loose load carrying capacity rapidly as cracks develop. Even with sufficient care taken during construction at the intersection of walls and corners, walls tend to separate at these locations leading to instability of walls loaded with out-of-plane forces. Designing for increased seismic force would not ensure wall stability in moderate to high earthquake occurrence. The stability is suddenly lost with cracking at wall junctions and the structural behaviour changing from box action to individual-wall action. This reduces the overall rigidity (I) of the structure substantially thereby increasing the stresses in the walls leading to collapse.

It is therefore necessary to offset these disadvantages of unreinforced masonry by suitable reinforcing it both vertically and horizontally. The vertical reinforcement acts in sustaining the bending stresses in the walls and giving it the necessary ductility to avoid collapse. Horizontal reinforcement helps in ensuring that walls will be bound together giving Box-action and high rigidity (I value) to the structure. This helps in lower stresses at ultimate loads and hence superior performance.

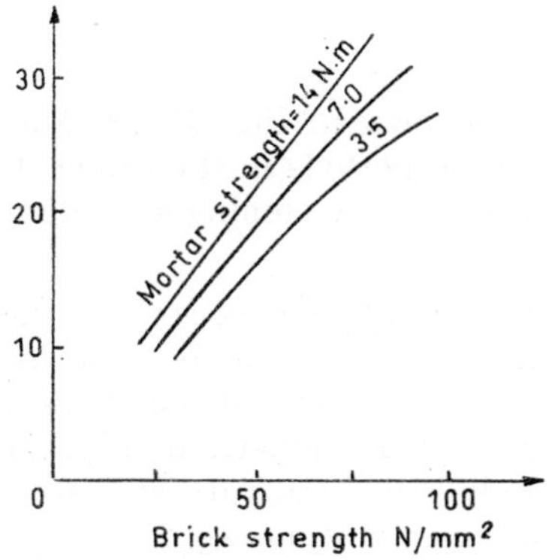

Fig. 19·10. Plots of brick strength against brickwork strength for various mortar strengths.

Codes in USA (UBC 99), Japan, New Zealand recommend only reinforced masonry in case of seismic zones equivalent to III, IV and V stipulated in our code. Looking to the great destruction and loss of life and property in every earthquake, we need to adopt ways of changing our detailing of masonry structures. The methods should be easily adoptable in villages where ground floor structures predominate or in cities where three to four storeys is the norm.

Methods of Reinforcing Masonry. Reinforced masonry designed for seismic resistance will have to be as light weight as possible and should be able to incorporate vertical and horizontal reinforcement during construction easily. Two much systems are described, one for brick masonry and the other for hollow concentrate block masonry.

Bricks Masonry with 'Quetta' Bond. This bond with standard clay bricks was developed and used after a large earthquake in 1935 at Quetta. The courses are shown in Fig. 19·11. The hollows created are grouted with vertical reinforcement. The horizontal reinforcement of 8 mm ϕ is placed in the mortar joints at suitable locations, properly anchored at corners and junctions of walls. This methods can be used for buildings of upto four floors. A building has been built by the author in Delhi with basement ground and one upper floor with reinforced Quetta bond walls. The basement retaining wall in reinforced brick masonry and the first floor has 4 m cantilever wall beams supporting two floors slabs. The structure has performed well for the last 15 years.

Hollow Block Concrete Masonry. The Fig. 19·12 shows typical concrete hollow block masonry having vertical reinforcement placed and grouted in the hollows of the blocks. The horizontal reinforcement is placed in the mortar joints at suitable locations. The centre to centre location is decided on the shear resistance to be generated. The vertical steel should be placed at well corner and junctions as well as at the jambs of windows and door openings.

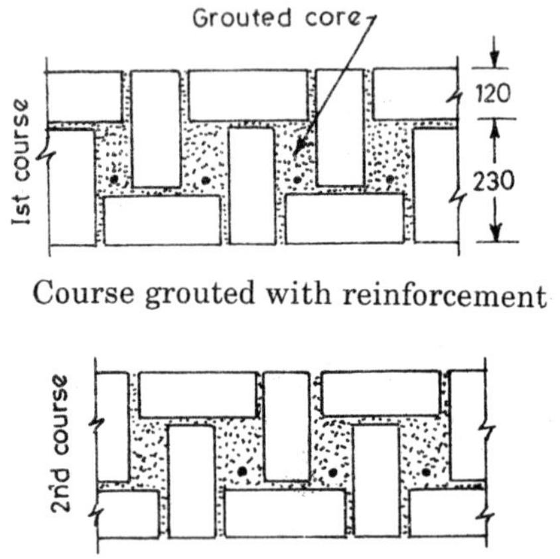

Fig. 19·11. Courses of brickwork for Quetta Bond.

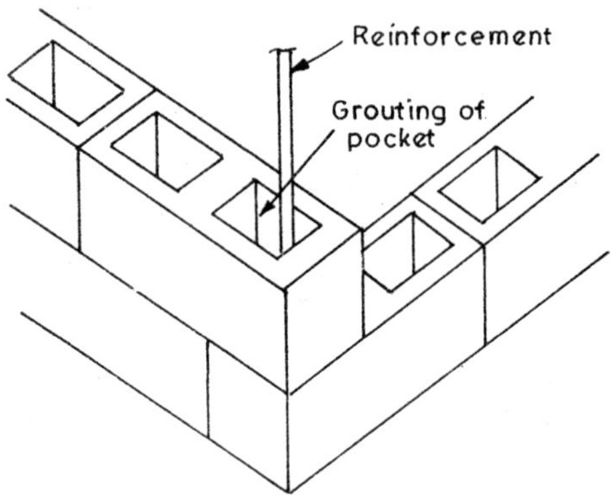

Fig. 19·12. Typical course of concrete hollow block masonry.

Masonry Structures—Seismic Behaviour

A typical smoothed acceleration response spectra is shown in Fig. 19·13. Masonry structures are normally very stiff and generally have fundamental periods in the range of 0.1 s to 0.8 s, thus falling within the frequency range of maximum response. Assuming a 5% damping, peak elastic response of the order of 0.8 g can be anticipated.

Design for such high lateral force levels is not viable economically and seismic coefficients given in most of the codes are reduced from the elastic response levels by a factor of about four This automatically implies a very large ductility demand on the structural members of the masonry as reduced design strength is accompanied by increased inelastic displacements. Consequently it is expected that under design level earthquake, the structure will attain its ultimate strength, and be required to deform in a ductile manner without significant loss of strength.

If design is to be done as per elastic theory, than the structure has to be designed for full lateral force level corresponding to elastic response. This would lead to very costly structure, totally uneconomical in normal circumstances. A more realistic approach, therefore, is to ensure that the ultimate capacity of the structure will be attained. The design has to ensure that materials and structural system adopted will sustain the required ductility without major strength or stiffness degradation.

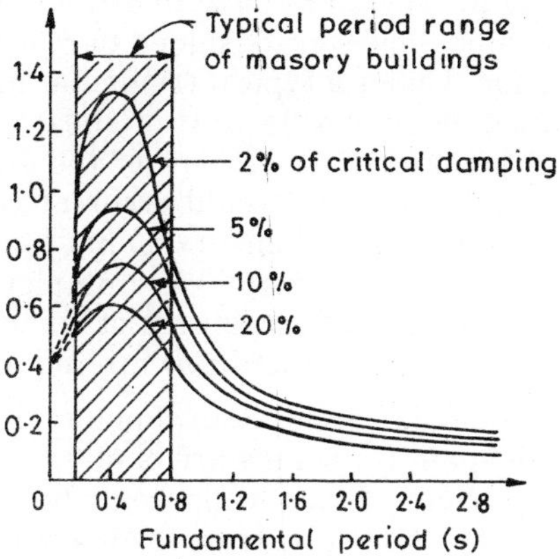

Fig. 19·13. Plot of peak response acceleration against fundamental period showing typical period range of masonry buildings.

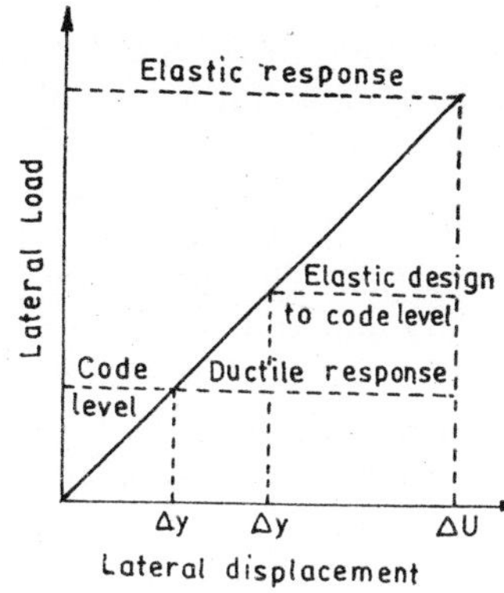

Fig. 19·14.

Structural Forms and Failure Modes

The most important aspect of masonry structure design philosophy is the correct choice of suitable structural form. This will dictate the behaviour of the load carrying elements as well as the location of areas where inelasticity (plastic hinges) take place. These areas can then be designed for the local curvature ductility demand.

Cantilever Shear Walls. To ensure a ductile seismic response, the force should be preferably carried by simple cantilever walls. Wherever two or more of such cantilever walls occur in the same plane, linkage between them should be by flexible floor slabs Fig. 19·15(*a*). This linkage should not be as far as possible with stiff beams. These stiff beams alter the behaviour with large moments and shears generated in them. A flexible connection between walls substantially reduces the moment transfer.

Columns may be used in conjunction with walls to partly carry gravity loads. Openings in the walls should be kept small to ensure that the wall will basically behave as vertical cantilever. The reinforcement provided in the wall should be so detailed that the energy dissipation would occur in properly located plastic hinges at the base of the wall.

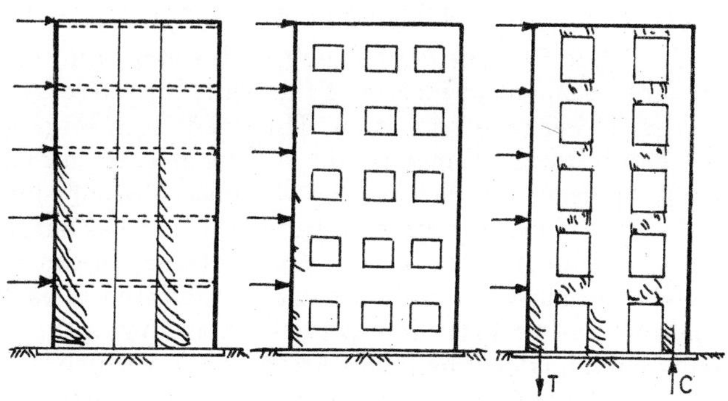

(*a*) Cantilever walls linked by flexible floor slab

(*b*) Coupled walls with pier hinging

(*c*) Coupled walls with spandrel hinging

Fig. 19·15. Masonry structural forms.

Coupled Walls with Pier Hinging. Most of the masonry structure are architecturally designed as load bearing peripheral walls with openings for windows and doors. A typical wall is shown in Fig. 19·15 (*b*). The figure shows the pattern of cracks, mainly in the piers. The ground floor piers will be subjected to large moments and shears. The piers have to exhibit substantial ductility in order to carry design earthquake. They can be, however, designed to resist the force elastically with very little ductility demand on the section. Under a typical triangular distribution of lateral seismic forces, the yield load will be attained when the flexural or shear strength of the lower floor piers is reached. This stage will not bring other members of the structure to yield. With added displacement, deformation of the yielding piers would occur at constant or decreasing lateral force. This would ensure that other structural elements do not reach a stage of inelastic action. The plastic deformation in thus concentrated in the yielding piers. As very large ductility demands are to be met by ductile piers in case of structures of six storeys and above, such construction is only suitable if very low displacement ductilities are required.

Coupled Walls with Spandrel Beams. In particular architectural plans, the windows openings in the walls are of such proportions that the spandrel beams are of sizes which make them relatively weaker than the pier elements. The behaviour of such walls would be like coupled walls with hinges formed in the spandrel beams. Fig. 19·15 (*c*) illustrates this action. Though coupled walls form very efficient systems of carrying horizontal loads, high ductility demand from coupling beams if they are of masonry, can be very unsuitable. However, coupling beam of reinforcement concrete can be suitably designed to form plastic hinges and accommodate high ductility demands. In case of masonry spandrels, rapid strength and stiffness degradation would lead to moment values more like simple linked cantilevers than designed as coupled walls. If the walls are designed to carry moments based on coupled wall action, than the enhanced moments at the base of the wall will exceed the capacity. The consequence would be excessive ductility demand for plastic hinges forming at the base. These issues have to be properly thought out during design.

Masonry Infilled Frames. In large number of structures, masonry walls as infill walls in frames are expected to contribute to the seismic resistance of the system. However, it is not correct to assume that increased rigidity will result in better seismic performance. The rigidity will be increased in frames having infill panels. This may result in shifting of the centre of rigidity which will subject the structure to seismic torsional response. Increase in rigidity will lower the natural period of the structure, correspondingly increasing the seismic forces. One more condition which needs to be guarded against is of partial infill of frames. This happens when infill extends to part of the storey height to create opening for windows. Influence of the infill will be to stiffen the central and one side column causing plastic hinges to form at top of column and top of infill. The consequence will be a substantial increase in the column shears. If the column is not designed for the higher shear force, shear failure of column could be expected.

Basic Concepts of Design. Masonry buildings due to their method of construction and very large moment of inertia of the walls, are necessarily very stiff structures. Consequently it has a short period of vibration. This leads to a large acceleration response. Masonry buildings are 2/3 storeys and hence would fall in the category of buildings with short period. Hence they have to be designed for large force values. Masonry building due to thicker walls has relatively more dead weight compared to frame structures. Larger dead weight also means larger seismic force as seismic force is directly proportional to the weight of the structures. This is inherent deficiency of masonry buildings when subjected to earthquake. One advantage obtained due to numerous mortar brick joints in the masonry is the large energy dissipation that takes place during earthquake. The joints are planes on which movement can take place and the frictional resistance contributes towards internal resistance to horizontal force. This can also be seen as a cause which contributes to improved damping value.

Ductility. If masonry has to show ductility, it should be able to carry loads with large slopes and deflection beyond the yield point. This means that load carrying capacity will be retained without failure, at least for deflections or strains of the order of three to four times that at yield point. Unreinforced masonry is not able to carry load beyond yield and cracking. This leads to sudden collapse also called brittle failure. This behaviour of unreinfored masonry does not cause structural problems in case of gravity loads. The allowable stress values are also with large factor of safety, thus keeping large margins to yield point. However, in the event of a major earthquake, the strains and deflections reach much beyond values at yield and building designed for gravity loads fail with sudden distress. It should also be noted that the '*R*' value in equation for the calculation of seismic force is four for unreinforced masonry ; a 1.5 times higher value than reinforced masonry. Reinforced masonry is a necessity in construction in seismic zones III, IV and V. The reinforcement grouted in the wall is kept uniformly distributed. It can be proved that bundled reinforcement at the end of the wall has the same moment capacity at ultimate strength as that provided by distributed reinforcement through the wall length. All the leading codes of countries with high seismic activities do not permit unreinforced masonry in zones of high seismic activity. The horizontal reinforcement is placed at the suitable height within the mortar course. Different codes stipulate different spacing of reinforcement horizontally and vertically. The normal spacing being about 400 mm—500 mm horizontally and 300 mm—450 mm vertically. The vertical steel by the side of door and window openings is a must.

Planning Considerations. For the overall stability of the structure it is necessary that all the walls must act together forming a box-type unit. The configuration of the walls should be so selected at the time of the planning, and suitably reinforced to act as such. The length and height of walls are also important as long unsupported lengths would lead to wall instability for out of plane forces. The structural walls should have as small openings as possible and they should be symmetrically placed to facilitate a clean load path from top of the wall to foundations. Such a wall will act as a cantilever from foundation to top, sharing load with other structural wall elements. As a very rough guide, the total length of structural wall that should be available to carry seismic forces, is to be more than 200 mm length/m^2 of the plan area. This guideline will help in selecting walls to be designed as elements used for resisting horizontal forces.

There are several other points that should be incorporated at planning stage to ensure sound behaviour.

(*a*) Walls of upper storeys should always be above those of lower storeys. This would avoid change of rigidity between two floors and abrupt change in load path from upper to lower floor.

(*b*) RC beams to be provided as pad beams over walls transferring load evenly from the slab to the wall. This is also a location where vertical steel of the walls crosses and gets anchored with the reinforcement of the slabs. The slabs act as horizontal diaphragms transferring horizontal forces to the walls. It is necessary that this junction be properly detailed.

(*c*) Vertical reinforcement placed at regular intervals and grouted within the masonry wall carries the shear developed due to horizontal forces. It also improves the shear ductility many folds and greatly improves the performance of the wall. The vertical reinforcement is much more effective in resisting shear than the horizontal reinforcement.

(*d*) The junction between walls and the floor system should be detailed in such a way that transfer of horizontal forces through floor diaphragm is ensured. The connection must be able to withstand the forces generated. The connection between walls horizontally as well as vertically should be such as to ensure box action of walls, *ie,* walls must act as rigidly connected structural members and not as individual members. This can be looked at as connection between web and flange of the structural member.

(*e*) The foundation provided for load bearing walls is a strip footing. Normally, this is un-reinforced. In case of earthquake resistant buildings, strips foundations will have to be designed as reinforced strip footing. The footing will have to be very stiff and strong enough to carry differential settlement. This should be carefully investigated as the foundation has rapidly changing bearing capacity, demands differing substantially between adjacent walls and their foundations.

Design of Wall Systems. The wall design can be carried out by two approaches :

(*a*) Allowable stress design ; and (*b*) Limit state design.

Allowable Stress Designs by ATC-3 (1978). This is elastic analysis of the wall and the stresses in the masonry are taken from the code. It also assumes that there is no tension in the section. This may hold true for gravity loads but for seismic forces this is a very questionable assumption.

The compressive load in the column is worked out by the equation.

$$P_a = A_g(0{\cdot}18\, f'_m + 0{\cdot}65\, p_s\, f_s)[1 - [h/40t]^3]$$

where P_a is total load ; A_g, gross area of wall ; f'_m, specified compressive strength of masonry wall (test prism) ; p_s, steel percentage ; f_s, allowable stress in steel ; h, height of wall ; and t, thickness of wall.

The expression in the last bracket gives reduction due slenderness of wall. Permissible compressive stress in the given by

$$Fa = 0{\cdot}2\ f'_m[1 - [h/40t]^3]$$

Limit State Design as per 'Unified Building Code' (UBC). The design of slender wall for out of plane horizontal forces as well as vertical loads is given along with the design wall for shear. The procedure can be used for designing of walls after shear forces and moments acting on individual wall sections are analysed.

Following Conditions are stipulated for carrying out this design procedure

(*i*) Minimum nominal thickness of the wall to be 150 mm.

(*ii*) The ratio of unsupported wall height (h) to nominal wall thickness (t) may no exceed 36 unless the axial stress at the location of maximum movement is equal to or less than 0.04 f'_m.

(*iii*) The minimum reinforcement ratio to wall area shall be 0.0007 in either direction and 0.002 total.

(*iv*) The maximum steel shall not exceed 50% of the balance steel ratio. The maximum steel in each cell shall not exceed 0.03 times the grouted cell area.

(*v*) The principal wall reinforcement in the direction of the span shall not be spliced within the middle third of the span.

(*vi*) The masonry wall at corners and intersecting cross walls shall be effectively anchored to each other.

(*vii*) All grout should have a minimum compressive strength f'_c not less than 13 N/mm^2 nor greater than 25 N/mm^2.

(*viii*) All grouts shall be vibrated with mechanical vibration over the depth of pour.

(*ix*) The specified compressive strength of the masonry f'_m shall not be less than 10 N/mm^2 nor greater than 20 N/mm^2 as determined by the prism tests.

(*x*) Proper inspection should be provided at all stages of construction.

Design Load Factors. The strength required by the masonry wall shall be based on factored loads. The basic load combination for loads due to Dead Load (D), Live Load (L), Wind (W) and Earthquake (E) for required strength (U) are given below.

UBC FACTORS	IS FACTORS
U = 0·75(1·4 D + 1·7 L + 1·87 E)	U = 1·5(DL + LL)
U = 0·75(1·4 D + 1·7 L + 1·7 W)	U = 1·2(DL + LL + EQ/WL)
U = 0·9 D + 1·43 E	U = 1·5(DL + EQ/WL)
U = 0·9 D + 1·3 W	U = 0·9(DL + 1·5 EQ/WL)

Design Assumptions for Nominal Strength

(*i*) The nominal strength of singly reinforced concrete masonry wall cross-sections, subject to combined flexural and axial loads, shall be based on applicable conditions of equilibrium and compatibility of strains. Strains are assumed directly proportional to the distance from the neutral axis.

(*ii*) Maximum strain of extreme masonry compression fibre shall be assumed to be equal to 0.003.

(*iii*) For steel strains less than the steel yield strain, the stress in reinforcement shall be taken as E_s times the steel strain.

(*iv*) The tensile strength of masonry shall be neglected in flexural calculations of strength, except when computing the nominal cracking moment strength.

Design strength

(*a*) The required moment strength M_u, shall be equal to or less than the nominal moment strength. (M_n) multiplied by a strength Reduction Factor (Φ).

$$M_u \leq \Phi M_n$$

Wall Thickness, mm	Reduction Factor
≥ 200	0·80
< 200	0·65

(*b*) Nominal Value of Modulus of Elasticity

$$Em = 750 f'_m$$

(*c*) Nominal Values of Modulus of Elasticity

Type of Wall	N/mm^2
Solid Grouted	$0{\cdot}4 \sqrt{f'_m}$
Partial Grouted	$0{\cdot}27 \sqrt{f'_m}$

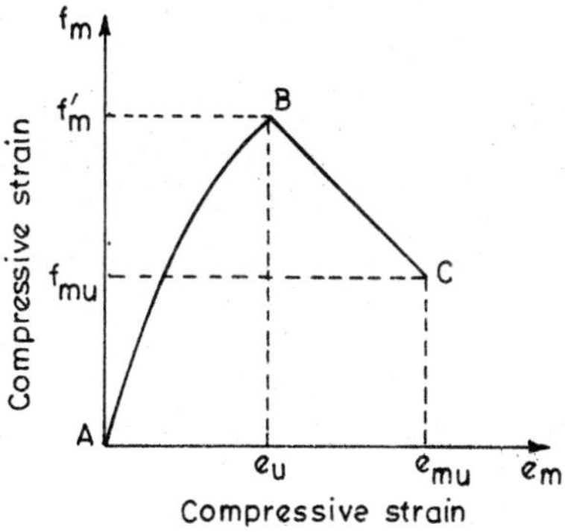

Fig 9·16. Stress-strain behaviour of masonry.

(*d*) Deflection Limited for Unfactored Loads

Wall Thickness, mm	Maximum Deflection, mm
≥ 200	1/150 × *h*
< 200	1/200 × *h*

where *h* is height of wall between supports.

(*e*) Strength-reduction Factor for Cracking Moment Strength

Wall Thickness, mm	Reduction Factor
≥ 200	0·90
< 200	0·75

(*f*) Stress-strain Behaviour of Unconfined Masonry

Maximum allowable strain in masonry can be increased where confinement is provided. Experimental evidence indicate that confinement increases the maximum usable strain and therefore the component curvature ductility Figure 9.

where f'_m is ultimate compressive stress ; E_u, strain corresponding to f'_m. A nominal design value of 0·002 to 0·0025 recommended ; F_{mu}, the minimum usable compressive stress in the strain region defined by strain values greater than the strain at ultimate compressive stress. A value of 0·5 f'_m is recommended ; and E_{mu}, maximum usable unconfined strain. A maximum value of 0·003.

Share Wall Design. Large number of shear walls with different steel percentages and axial load levels have be tested and it is possible to design walls for shear with imparting ductility that will perform well during seismic loading.

The design load factors have been already stipulated which could be used have also.

Design Strength. The design strength provided by the shear wall cross-section in terms of axial force, share and moment shall be computed as the nominal strength multiplied by the strength reduction factor Φ. The shear wall should be proportioned so that the design strength exceeds the required strength.

Only axial load	0·05
Axial plus flexure	0·65
Shear with reinforcement	0·60
Shear by masonry	0·40

Reinforcement in walls

(*a*) Minimum reinforcement shall be 0·0007 of wall section in either direction and 0·002 total.

(*b*) The minimum amount of vertical reinforcement shall not be less than one-half the horizontal reinforcement.

(*c*) Maximum spacing of horizontal reinforcement with in the region gives below shall not exceed three times nominal wall thickness or 600 mm whichever is less.

Axial Strength. Nominal axial strength of shear wall supportly axial loads only given by

$$P_o = 0{\cdot}85\, f'_m\,(A_n - A_s) + f'_y \times A_s$$

Seismic Design and Detailing of Reinforced Cement Concrete Buildings Including Code Provisions

Behaviour of Concrete Members under Earthquake Type Loading

General Objectives of Member Design. A general objective in the design of RC members is to so proportion such elements that they possess adequate stiffness and strength, so that the strength is governed by flexure rather than by shear on bond/anchorage. Code design requirements are framed with the intent of allowing members to develop their flexural or axial load capacity, before shear or bond/anchorage failure occurs. Diagonal reinforcement in conjunction with horizontal and vertical reinforcement, improves performance of RC walls.

Some Results of Analytical Studies on the Behaviour of RC Members under Earthquake. Proper performance means primarily possessing adequate ductility. Quasistatic test is most widely used for this purpose. In terms of this test proper performance requires that the critical region should be capable of sustaining a minimum number of deformation cycles of specified amplitude without significant loss of strength.

Beams. Under earthquake loading beams are most critically stressed at and near their intersection with the supporting columns. Plastic hinging can take place at these critical sections. The design of lateral reinforcement for potential hinging regions in the form of closed hoops or spirals must be done with special attention. The lateral reinforcement in hinging regions of beams is designed to provide.

(*i*) Confinement of the concrete core,

(*ii*) Support for the longitudinal compressive reinforcement against inelastic buckling, and

(*iii*) Resistance in conjunction with the confined concrete against transverse shear.

The level of shear present significantly affects flexural ductility of hinging regions in beams. Use of crossing diagonal or inclined web reinforcement in combination with vertical tiles as shown in Fig. 19·17 can effectively minimise the degradation of stiffness associated with sliding shear.

Columns. Design of earthquake resistant RC moment resisting frame should be such that the plastic hinging occurs in beams rather than in columns. This is referred to as the strong-column, weak-beam concept. This ensures the stability of the frame while undergoing large lateral displacements under earthquake excitations.

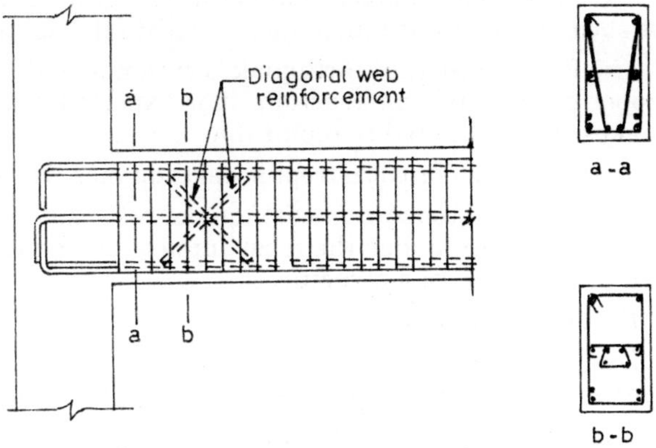

Fig. 19·17. Crossing diagonal web reinforcement in combination with vertical web steel for hinging regions under high shear.

Typical reinforcement at junction of wall and beam.

To safeguard against strain degradation due to hinging in the columns of a frame, codes require lateral rein-forcement for both confinement and shear in the regions of potential plastic hinging. The closely spaced transverse reinforcement in critical regions of columns is intended to provide

(*i*) Confinement for the concrete core,

(*ii*) Lateral support of the longitudinal column reinforcement against buckling, and

(*iii*) Resistance against transverse shear.

The transverse reinforcement can be provided in the form of spirals circular or rectangular hoops.

Beam-Column Joints. Beam-column joints have to be designed so that the connected elements perform properly. This requires that the joints be proportioned and detailed to allow the columns and beams framing into them to develop and maintain their strength as well as stiffness, while undergoing large inelastic deformations. A loss in strength or stiffness in a frame resulting from deterioration in the joints can lead to a substantial increase in lateral displacements of the frame including possible instability due to P-delta effects.

The design of beam-column joints is primarily aimed at

(*i*) Preserving the integrity of the joint so that the strength and deformation capacity of the connected beam and columns can be developed and substantially maintained, and

(*ii*) Preventing significant degradation of the joint stiffness, due to cracking of the joint and loss of bond between concrete and the longitudinal column and beam reinforcement or anchorage failure of beam reinforcement.

Drift in Multi-storey Structures. The maximum horizontal relative displacement (sway) due to earthquake forces between two successive floors is called as drift. It shall not exceed 0·004 times the difference in levels between these floors. The drift limitation is necessary to save elements (non-structural elements) which form an integral part of the structure and to avoid upsetting the occupant's psychology. The building analyzed for seismic forces must be checked for the drift limitation.

Code Provisions for Earthquake Resistant Design

Performance Criterion. The performance criterion implicit in most earthquake code provisions require that a structure be able to

(*i*) Resist earthquakes of minor intensity without damage, a structure would be expected to resist such frequent but minor shocks within its elastic range of stresses.

(*ii*) Resist moderate earthquakes with minor structural and some non-structural damage, with proper design and construction, it is expected that structural damage due to majority of earthquakes will be limited to repairable damage.

(*iii*) Resist major catastrophic earthquakes without collapse.

The principal concern in earthquake resistant design of buildings is to ensure life safety, *ie,* to prevent collapse under the most intense earthquake that may be reasonably expected at the site during the life of a structure.

Principal Design Steps

Design of a RC building in accordance with the equivalent static force procedure found in current seismic codes involves the following principle steps.

(*i*) Determination of design 'earthquake' forces. This includes

(*a*) Calculation of base shear corresponding to the computed or estimated fundamental period of vibration of the structure

(*b*) Distribution of the base shear over the height of the building.

(*ii*) Analysis of the structure under static lateral forces calculated in step (*i*) above as well as under gravity and wind loads, to obtain member design forces. The lateral load analysis can be carried out by using a computer program for frame analysis

(*iii*) Designing members and joints for the most unfavourable combination of gravity and lateral loads. Designing and detailing of members and their connections must ensure ductile behaviour.

The above steps are to be carried out in each principal (plan) direction of the building. Orthogonal effects must be considered for certain building categories, which may be sensitive to torsional oscillations or characterised by significant irregularities.

For these cases, the design should be based on the more severe combination of 100% of the prescribed seismic forces in one direction plus 30% of the forces in the perpendicular direction.

Design and detailing of reinforcement in members and their connections should ensure ductile behaviour and thus allow the structure to sustain without collapse the severe distortions that may occur during a major earthquake. Code provisions intended to ensure adequate ductility in structural elements represent the major difference between the design requirements for conventional, non-earthquake resistant structures and those located in regions of high earthquake risk.

Plastic Hinge Location. It was argued that in order to ensure proper performance of the joint, it is advisable to ensure that stresses remain within elastic limits by proper proportion-

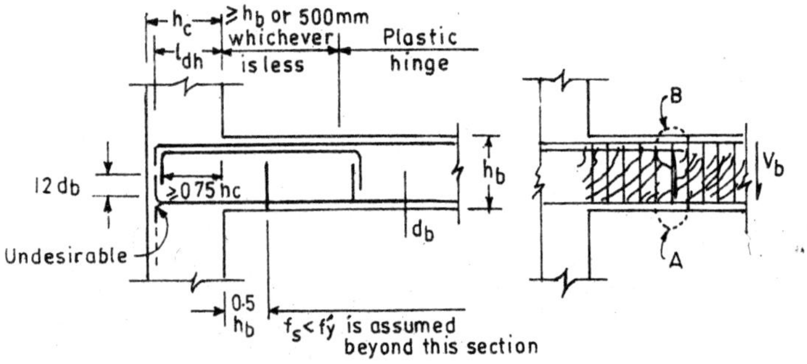

Fig. 19·18. Potential plastic hinge relocated from the face of a column.

ing as well as by providing adequate reinforcement. One way to ensure elastic joint response is to relocate the potential plastic hinge from the face of the column as shown in the Figure 9·18. As shown in the figure, the beam bars may be curtailed so that stresses in the reinforcement may be developed at the critical section of the plastic hinge. Therefore, this section must be sufficient distance away from the face of the column. **A minimum distance of hb or 500 mm** whichever is less is thought appropriate. In view of the unusual nature of shear transfer across the critical section of the plastic hinge region, care must be taken with the detailing of such relocated plastic hinges, Fig. 19·18 (*b*) indicates that the beam shear force *vb*, introduced by diagonal forces *A*, needs to be transformed to the top of the beam at region *B*. This necessitates stirrups extending between these regions, perhaps supplemented by the specially bent top beam bars, to carry the entire shear force.

Design of Beam-column Joint. Beam column joints should be designed so as to avoid failure within the joint. The joint should be strong enough to withstand the yielding of connecting beams or columns.

Shear Resistance. The shear is resisted by compressive strut action in concrete and in the horizontal stirrups (Fig. 19·19). The strength of the diagonal strut controls the joint strength, when the joint shear forces are large and diagonal cracking occurs in the joint core, there are in fact several struts, separated from one another by diagonal cracks. These are subjected to indeter-minable eccentricities and are exposed to transverse tensile strains. In this biaxial state of stress, a considerable reduction of strength occurs. Cyclic loading in the cross-cracked concrete causes repeated opening and closure of the cracks. Since shearing action across the joint is dominant movements parallel to open cracks also occur in the joint core.

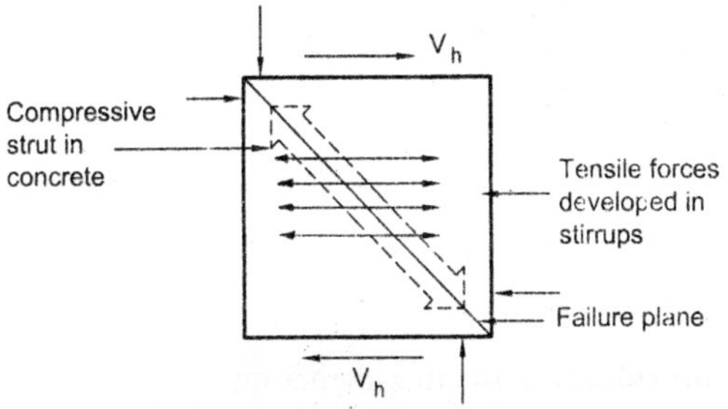

Fig. 19·19. Horizontal shear resistance in beam-column joint.

The joint reinforcement does not play a major role in such situation. Hence, it is necessary to limit the magnitude of horizontal joint shear stress to protect the joint against diagonal crushing. When the cracks become large, the transverse reinforcement yields and process of grinding and progressive splitting due to uneven concrete bearing begins. The transverse reinforcement can resist shear only at this stage.

Bond Stresses. At the interior beam columns joints, high bond stresses may develop where bars may have high tensile stress at one face and a high compressive stress on the other face. Formation of a plastic hinge in the beam may reduce the effective bond.

Internal Beam Column Joints. Considerable distress may be suffered in this area due to following principal mechanisms of failure.

(*i*) Shear within the joint.

(*ii*) Anchorage failure of beam bars anchored in the joint.

(*iii*) Bond failure of beam or column bars passing through the joint.

SOLVED PROBLEM

Design of Interior Joint

(A) Shear analysis of interior beam column joint in *Z*-direction:

Figure 14(*a*) shows forces acting on a typical interior beam-column joint.

Muu = Ultimate moment shared by upper column

= 222.4 kNm

Mul = Ultimate moment shared by lower column

= 231.4 kNm

Therefore, total moment = 453.8 kNm

It is assumed that the beams in the adjoining faces are deformed so that plastic hinges form at their junctions with the columns.

$Mpr1$ = Probable moment strength of beam-1

= 162.4 kNm

$Mpr2$ = Probably moment strength of beam-2

= 291.4 kNm

Total moment = 453.8 kNm

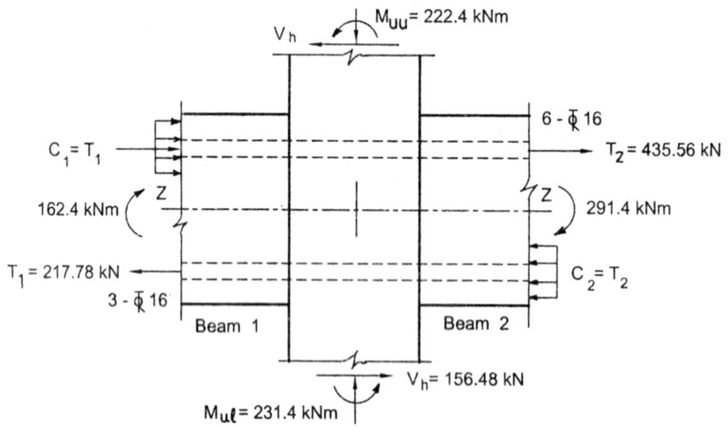

Fig. 19·20. Shear analysis of interior beam-column joint in z-direction.

19·9. Seismic Design and Detailing of Steel Structures

Introduction. For many years, the basic intent of the building code seismic provisions has been to provide buildings with an ability to withstand intense grounds shaking without collapse, but potentially with some significant structural damage.

Damage to Welds Observed Failure Mode. Observation of damage sustained by buildings in the 1994 Northridge earthquake and at Kobe indicated that, contrary to the intended behaviour in many cases, brittle fractures initiated within the connections at very low levels of plastic demand, and in some cases, while the structures remained essentially elastic. Typically, but not always, fractures initiated at the complete joint penetration (CJP) weld between the beam bottom flange and column flange (Fig. 19·22). Once initiated, these fractures progressed along a number of different paths depending on the individual joints conditions.

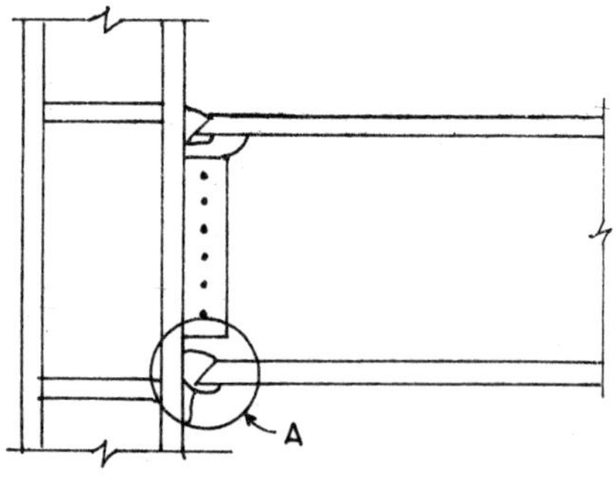

Fig. 19·21. Typical weld connection employed in steel moment-frame construction.

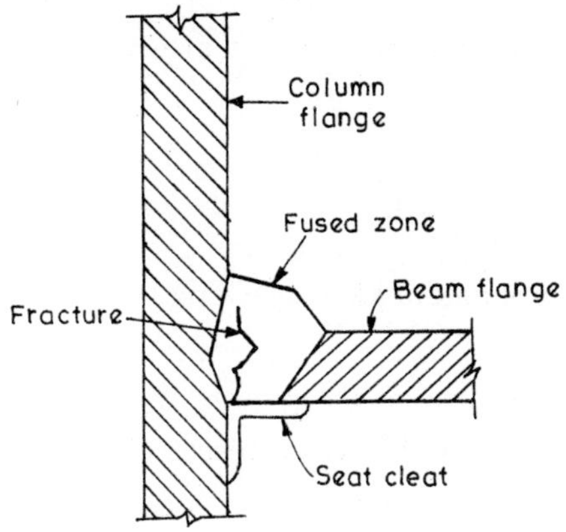

Fig. 19·22. Complete joint penetration weld between beam bottom flange and column flange.

In some cases, the fractures progressed completely through the thickness of the weld, and when fire protective finishes were removed, the fractures were evident as a crack through exposed faces of the weld, or the metal just behind the weld. Other fracture patterns also developed. In some cases, the fracture developed into a crack of the columns flange material behind the CJP weld. In these cases, a portion of the column flange remained bonded to the beam flange, but pulled free from the remainder of the column. This fracture pattern has sometimes been termed a 'divot' or 'nugget' failure.

19·10. Concentrically Braced Frames

Design Philosophy

Concentrically braced frames are frequently used to provide lateral strength and stiffness to low-and-mid-rise buildings to resist wind and earthquake forces. Although some architects favour the less intrusive moment frames, others have found architectural expression in exposing braced frame which the public intuitively associates with seismic safety in some earthquake-prone regions. However, for those frames to provide adequate earthquake resistance, they must be designed for appropriate strength and ductility. This is possible for many of the concentrically braced frame (CBF) configurations shown in Fig. 19·23 but not all, as described in this section.

In a manner consistent with the earthquake resistance design philosophy presented elsewhere in this chapter, modern concentrically braced frames are expected to undergo inelastic response during infrequent yet large earthquake. Specially designed diagonal braces in these frames can sustain plastic deformations and dissipate hysteretic energy in a stable manner through successive cycles of bucking in compression and yielding in tension. The preferred design strategy is, therefore, to ensure that plastic deformations only occur in the braces, leaving the columns, beams, and connections, undamaged, thus allowing the structure to survive strong earthquake without losing gravity-load resistance.

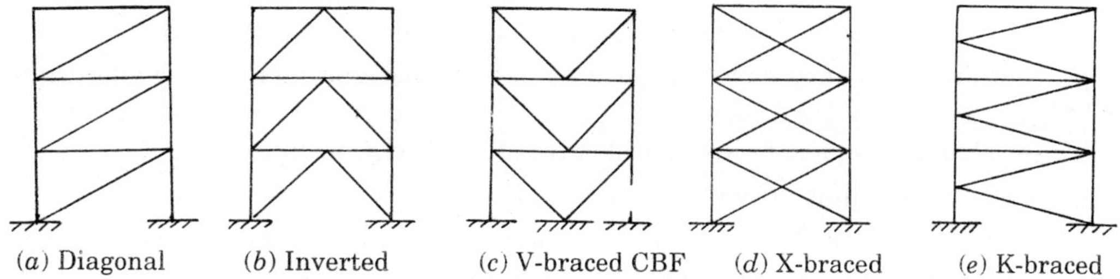

(*a*) Diagonal braced CBF (*b*) Inverted V-braced CBF (*c*) V-braced CBF (*d*) X-braced CBF (*e*) K-braced CBF

Fig. 19·23. Concentrically braced frame configurations.

Appendages to buildings such as masonry parapets, penthouses, roof tanks, claddings, unduly loaded cantilevers (either balconies or beams), very thin size and floating columns generally behave very badly during the severe shocks. The reasons for this are (*i*) they are designed without any ductility, and (*ii*) effects of dynamic by the building to which they are attached may greatly increase the forces applied to them.

19·11. Typical damage to elements subjected to bending, with or without direct force are as under :

— Cracking in the tension zone.

— Diagonal cracking in the core.

— Loss of concrete cover.

— The concrete core breaking into lumps by reversing diagonal cracking.

— Stirrups bursting outwards.

— Buckling of main reinforcement.

— Bond failure, particularly in zones where there are high cyclic stresses in the concrete.

— Direct shear failure of short elements, or those constrained so that only a short length is effectively free.

— Shear cracking the beam-column junction.

— Tearing of slabs at discontinuities, and junctions with stiff vertical elements.

— Diagonal cracking in shear walls, particularly concentrated around openings.

In Ahmedabad following deficiencies in the buildings were observed—

—Majority structure not designed for any lateral forces.

—The column beam junctions assumed as hinge connection

—Missing RCC shear walls in multi-storey buildings

—The structures were lacking in redundancy, *ie,* sufficient number of columns.

—Use of floating columns leading to sudden discontinuity in stiffness.

—Use of small width (150 mm) columns.

—The open parking floor acting as a soft storey.

—Poor connection (inadequate rigid floor diaphragm action) of staircase and RCC lift wall to the rest of structure.

—Structural planning and design not as per good engineering practice such as

—Use of long cantilever,

—Beams cantilevering out from cantilever beams,

—Walls resting directly on slab without any beams,

—Slabs having ly/lx ratio < 1.5 are also designed as one way slab.

—Staircase/inclined slabs designed to rest on floor and mid-landing slab without any beams.

—Columns designed for axial load only without any moments.

—Ductile detailing missing.

—No soil investigation carried out for assessing the strata and bearing capacity

—Structure having small and insufficient frames.

—Irregular/complex shapes of buildings.

—Re-entrant corners unattended.

—Use of inferior quality material and bad construction quality.

—As per NDT reports, strength of concrete of earthquake affected structures found to be substantially low.

The various non-destructive techniques/methods adopted are

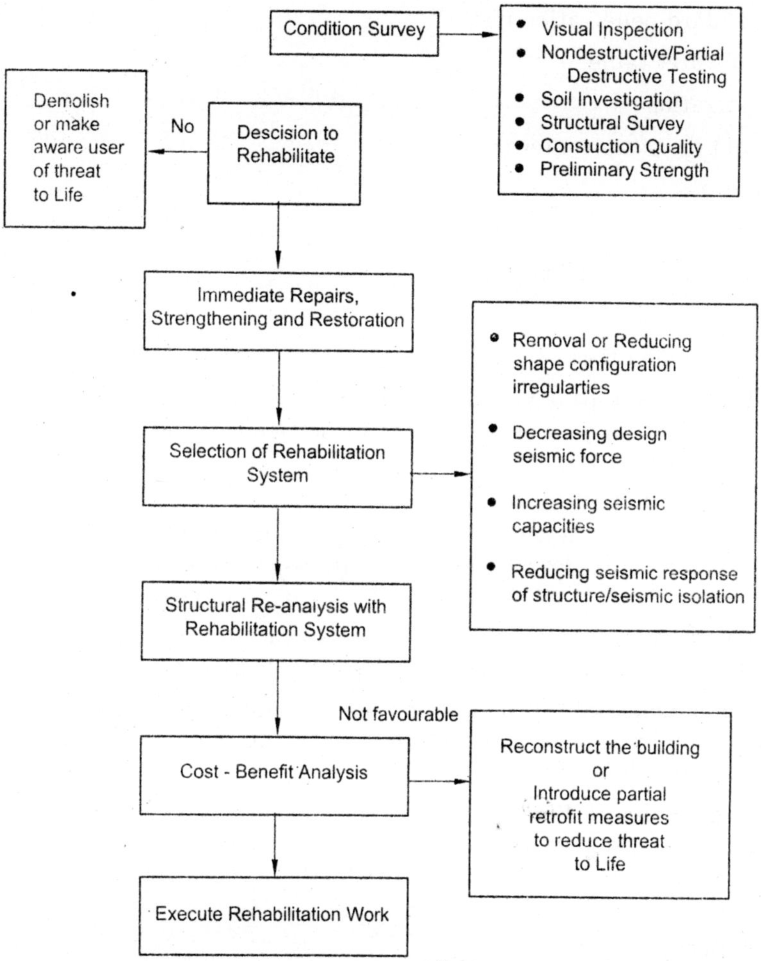

Fig. 19·24. Seismic rehabilitation methodology.

—Tapping by wooden hammers.

—Rebound hammer.

—Ultrasonic pulse velocity test.

—Core extraction.

—Chemical analysis of concrete.

—Carbonation.

—Rebar locator, bar size detector.

—Half-cell potentiometer and resistivity meter for corrosion mapping.

Soil Investigation

A detail geo-technical investigation shall be carried out covering following aspects—

Field Investigation

—Drilling of bore holes.

—Collection of soil samples (disturbed and undisturbed).

—Conducting standard penetration test.

—Noting depth of water table.

Laboratory Investigation

—Bulk density and moisture content.

—Grain size analysis.

—Index properties.

—Shear tests (tri-axial shear test).

—Consolidation test.

—Unconfined compression test.

Foundations. The data of type of foundations, depth of foundation, tie beam connectivity at footing level, evidence of any foundation movement or settlement and deterioration of any concrete element shall be noted.

(*a*) During the violent shaking there is always an increase in the lateral and vertical forces which disturbs the stability of the non-cohesive soils with the result that the buildings do sink down, tilt or ultimately collapse down. This is a clear case of massive foundation failures due to liquefaction.

(*b*) Shear movements may also occur either at the surface or at deep levels which also cause damage to the underground structures which also should be investigate in depth.

(*c*) During the earthquakes elastic displacements also occur which are very critical in the design of piles, underground pipelines, and culvert-type structures. Failure of these do affect the work of post-earthquake rehabilitation works.

Decreasing Design Seismic Force. Since the seismic force is proportional to the mass of the structure, one way to decrease design seismic force, is to reduce the mass of the structure. This technique is generally performed in combination with other type of rehabilitation schemes. The mass can be reduced by :

—Removal of top floors.

—Removal of water tanks, equipments.

—Removal of architectural features such as heavy parapets, balconies, cladding etc. having substantial mass.

—Reducing the live load, by change of use.

In Ahmedabad, one of the multi-storey building is suggested for removal of top two floors. In analysis it was observed, that the columns are not safe to bear gravity loads. In addition to removal of top floors, removal of water tanks from roof is also recommended.

19·12. Increasing Capacity

Addition of Shear Wall. Walls modify a framed structure making it a stiffer resisting system, subjected to smaller lateral displacements, resulting therefore in less non-structural damage. Shear walls are more efficient structural system with better seismic performance.

To locate the structural walls along the perimeter of the structure with a symmetrical layout in both orthogonal directions is undoubtedly the best solution, offering higher resistance to torsion. Generally, shear walls are located along the column axes. The shear walls shall extend for full height of structure. The size of shear wall shall be such that, it shall be capable of resisting 70% to 75% of design force in both the directions.

To give continuity to vertical reinforcement it is necessary to drill holes through the beams or slab, alternatively the beam may be jacketed by wall. The connection to the existing columns is made through steel bar/shear connectors placed inside epoxy filled holes. In some case it is convenient to jacket or surround the columns with reinforced elements increasing the surface contact between the existing column and the new wall for a better transfer of shear force, as well as giving more confinement to column concrete and thereby increasing axial load capacity of the column. It is necessary to carefully prepare the contact surface between walls and columns to ensure a better and composite behaviour, use polymer bonding agent is recommended.

Shear wall solution has proven to be the most effective and economical one.

Addition of infill walls. Masonry infill walls are sometimes added to reinforced concrete frames. The use of infill walls has been shown to control effectively lateral displacement in repaired structure. These infill walls act as a first line of defence of the building. This addition of infill walls especially in **parking floor (soft storey)** improves stiffness of soft storey. In Gujarat earthquake, it has been seen that, columns in parking floor adjoining to the infill wall, suffered less damage compared to the columns in open frame. Infill wall behaviour is similar to structural wall behaviour as long as continuity is provided with beams and columns. In this case column acts as boundary elements.

These walls significantly increase the lateral strength of the existing frame. If proper shear transfer mechanism by way of providing epoxy grouted dowels embedded into the original frames or by fixing welded mesh at junction of masonry and concrete elements, then these infill walls may perform in much better way. Restore infill panels between columns during repair first so as to provide side as shutter for column and beam, and then cast concrete, it helps to transfer shear. When expected shear force is not very large a good quality masonry infill wall may be adopted as retrofitting measure.

It is common practice to treat infill walls as non-structural elements and to ignore the strength and stiffness contributed by them. They normally participate in the behaviour of structure. Un-reinforced brick masonry infills in RC moment resisting frame are observed to make the building stiffer by as much as four times in comparison to the bare RC moment resisting frames. Thus ignoring stiffness of infill walls may lead to calculating higher fundamental period (T) and decrease in the design force. Hence the proposed draft of IS 1893 suggests to use the expression for calculating T as ;

$$T = 0.09\, H/\sqrt{d} \text{ and not as } T = 0.1n$$

Avoid vertical discontinuous infills.

Avoid unsymmetrical placement of infill walls.

Avoid infills over cantilevers.

Avoid partial height infills as they lead to short-column.

Avoid half-brick infills.

Addition of Bracing. Exceptional results have been reported with the use of steel elements forming bracing/trusses in the repair of earthquake damaged structures in Mexico city. In some cases slabs had to be strengthened locally to transmit the lateral forces to the bracing elements or shear walls.

The buildings having re-entrant corners/ducts, especially, 'H' shape buildings, steel bracing in plan is a good solution. Such plan bracing help to provide rigid floor diaphragm action. Many bracing configurations are possible such as X, V, K etc, which allow for openings, entrances, services etc.

The connection of steel braces to the existing concrete elements needs to be carried out with proper system. Welded connections are also used to fix steel braces to the existing concrete elements. In this case collars or steel jackets had to surround the column to be able to weld against these elements. Welding against steel jackets provide a very good alternative because the axial forces generated by steel braces can be carried by the strengthened columns. **Another way, is to bond the plate to the concrete surface with epoxy gout** and use mechanical anchor fasteners to fix the plate to the concrete elements. The bracing elements may be fixed to these plate either by welding or by using friction bolts.

In general, low slenderness ratio of the bracing elements are recommended to make the elements yield in compression rather than buckling. Cable braces have also been used in western countries. These systems are known to buckle elastically under load reversal.

Addition of New Members. Many a times to remove the irregularities in structural layout or to improve redundancy some new elements may be required to be added. Use of bracing in plan, addition of tie beams improves the rigid diaphragm action at cut out locations or release stress concentration at re-entrant corners. Addition of column/beam increases the redundancy. Addition of beams at unconnected locations in frames improves stiffness of moment resisting frames. Newly added shear walls may be required to be properly connected with the existing structure with addition of new elements.

Jacketing/Strengthening of Weak Elements. Jacketing, though increases the capacity of the system and increases its stiffness to some extent, it is not a very efficient to control the flexibility and does not modify significantly the behaviour of framed structure. These structures will continue to be vulnerable to large displacements and to suffer significant non-structural damage. Jacketing provides additional axial, flexural and shear capacity, confinement and ductility.

The jacketing may be in the form of additional RCC section or steel jacketing. The steel jacketing has proven to be the most effective in providing flexural ductility and enhancing shear strength.

The jacketing of columns shall cover even column beam joint. The proper shear connection of old and new concrete with use of bonding agents, shear connectors is essential.

Jacketing the foundation will increasing the shear capacity as well as flexural capacity of footing. Increasing size of the foundation may be required if the footing demand higher area due to lower bearing capacity.

Stiffening Soft Storey. Due to shortage of space in big cities, the local governing bodies force to provide parking facility on the ground floor. Thus, normally all new buildings constructed in last two or three decades have open parking at ground level below the structure. This creates a substantial reduction in stiffness of structure at parking level. It has been observed in the past earthquakes that, around 20% to 30% failures of structures are caused by soft storey.

The effective way of removing stiffness irregularity of soft storey is to introduce shear wall, bracing or infill walls. These walls or bracing shall be extended right up to foundation. The ideal location of these elements is on the exterior of the structure, which improves the torsional capacity also.

Foundation Strengthening. In some of the cases foundation strengthening or addition of new foundation may be required. When the existing foundations are not designed for lateral forces or designed for lower bearing capacity or when load paths are changed due to retrofitting, then structure may generate higher forces at the foundation level. In such cases foundation strengthening may be required. Use of new raft, addition of piles, jacketing, underpinning are the various ways to strengthen the foundations. In some cases foundation beams are provided to tie isolated footings. Foundation strengthening could be difficult due to site conditions and accessibility problems.

19·13. Construction Chemicals. In last two decades, use of construction chemicals has significantly increased. Resins are usually used for injection grouting into cracks. Polymer bond coats are used to bond old and new concrete. Variety of products are available, with different chemical compositions, chemical and mechanical properties, mixing ratios and with filler additives. The user shall have sufficient and proper knowledge, while selecting the proper compatible material. Epoxy resins are most widely used resins. Epoxy resins have much superior properties compared to concrete. They are much higher in compressive, tensile and flexural strength and they have got very good elongation property. Use plasticisers for repair works to facilitate easy placement and compaction.

Following are the general guidelines for using proper grout materials for sealing the cracks.

Table 19·5.

Crack Width	*Description of Grout*
Non-moving cracks	
05-10 mm	Non-shrink cementitious grouts (ready to use) with sand (less than 1.18 mm size)
02-05 mm	Non-shrink cementitous grouts (ready to use) without sand
).2-03 mm	Low viscosity (500 cps) epoxy injection grouts with 5 kg/cm^2 to 7 kg/cm^2 pressure
0.2-1.0 mm	Super low viscosity (less than 200 cps) epoxy injection grouts with 5 kg/cm^2 to 7 kg/cm^2 pressure
0.1-0·2 mm	High molecular weight very low viscosity (2 cps to 5 cps). Resin injection grout with 2 kg/cm^2 pressure
Moving Cracks	
01-05 mm	Flexible epoxy/polyurethane sealant (for non-structural cracks)
01-05 mm	Silicon/polysulphide sealant (for surface gap sealing)

New Retrofitting Techniques—Fibre Wrapping. In recent years Fibre reinforced composites are successfully used for retrofitting of earthquake damaged structures. Advantages of fibre wrapping are it is very easy to execute/apply, other structural elements do not get damaged. Light weight with high strength to weight ratio, good resistant to chemical attack, can be moulded in any form/shape. But presently the cost of these materials is high.

FRC are available in the form of laminates and different thickness and orientation.

FRC can be used in the concrete structures in following forms—

Plate —at a face to improve the tension capacity.

Bars —as a reinforcement in the beams and slabs replacing the steel bars.

Cable —as tendons and post tension members.

Wraps—around concrete members to confine concrete and improve the compressive strength.

Stand alone components—to replace heavier concrete or steel members to reduce self weight and increase capacity of structure.

The use of FRC in seismic retrofitting has been done in Gujarat. The FRC are being used to improve the joint strength and ductility. If the concrete elements is confined using wrapping with FRC then, failure due to tensile cracks can be prevented, further the compressive strength is also increased to much higher level. The FRC is elastic upto failure, thus it increases the ductility of concrete elements to a large extent and upto their failure point.

The comparative material characteristics of steel and FRC is as under—

Table 19·4.

Type of fibre	*Modulus of elasticity, Gpa*	*Tensile strength, Gpa*
Carbon	240-640	2.50-4.00
Aramid	124	3.00-4.00
Glass	65-70	1.70-3.00
Polyester	12-15	2.00-3.00
Steel	210	0.25-0.55

Upgradation of Existing Deficient Structures. It is noticed that, majority of the buildings in India are not designed as per any IS code practices, especially for seismic design and are highly vulnerable to strong seismic ground motions. In city like Mumbai, the building damage due to corrosion attack is extensive. Such buildings though originally designed for seismic forces have now become vulnerable to seismic attack due to loss in strength of concrete and loss of reinforcement. Further all multi-storey buildings constructed before 1993, *ie*, enforcement of ductility code IS 13920, may not be detailed properly for ductility.

Thus it becomes essential to identify such structures and retrofit them, with new code provisions. In first stage assessment and rehabilitation of important structures such as hospitals, schools etc, in all major cities is very much essential to reduce damages and loss of life in future earthquakes. In second stage all multi-storey buildings needs to be retrofitted. The volume of work involved and the fund requirements will be very high, but government will be required to take policy decision in short time.

Earthquake Disaster Mitigation

19·14. Earthquake mechanism. The crust of the earth (the upper layer of thickness between 20 km to 70 km) undergoes changes due to stress which are primarily generated due to the dynamic movement of the earth. As the crust is non-homogeneous, the distribution of the stress is also non-homogeneous. The rock goes on accepting or storing the stress within its elastic limits. When the value exceeds the elastic limit of rock, the excess and stored energy is released and earthquake occurs. Normally the stresses are localized in the vicinity of the weakest portion of the rock, which in geological terms is known as fault.

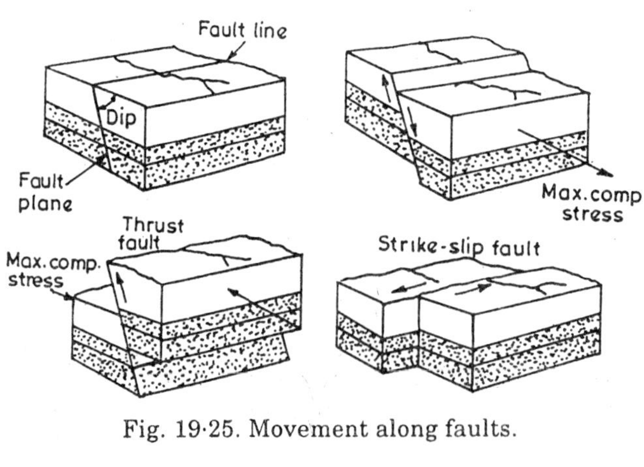

Fig. 19·25. Movement along faults.

Seismological Observatories. The India Meteorological Department has been officially assigned the work of earthquake studies by Government of India. It has about 70 seismological observatories all over the country. In addition, some state governments also run small nets of seismological observatories around some of the irrigation projects such as Koyna (Maharashtra), Sundernagar (Himachal Pradesh), Narmada (Gujarat) etc.

In addition to the above, there are few more observatories by Brahmaputra Board, National Geophysical Research Institute (Hyderabad), Regional Research Laboratory (Jorhat) and some University Departments. But the functioning of these observatories is either for a short time or for specific purpose. These are housed temporarily for specific works. Moreover, the locations also change as per the requirements of the specific work.

Seismological Information. If any information about seismic data, earthquake and allied phenomenon is required, it could be obtained from the following leamed institutes. (*a*) The Director General, India Meteorology Department, Lodi Road, New Delhi—110 003 ; (*b*) The Director, National Geophysical Research Institute, Uppal Road, Hyderabad—500 007 ; (*c*) The Director Regional Research Laboratory, Jorhat ; (*d*) The Director, Shillong Seismological Observatory, India Meteorology Department, Shillong ; and (*e*) The Director General, Geological Survey of India, Kolkata.

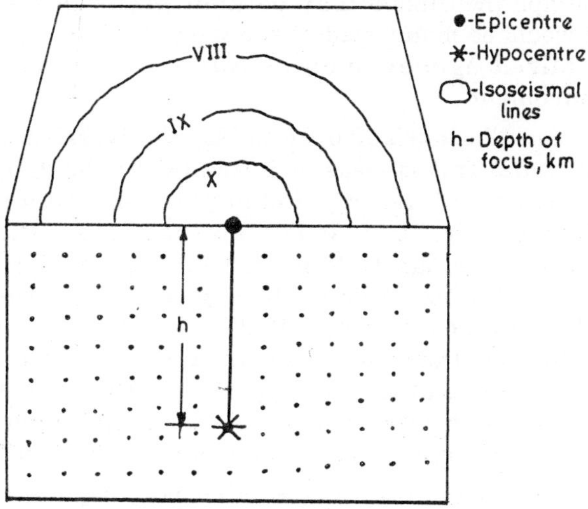

Magnitude of EQ

The strength of EQ is measured by Richter scale, which is logarithmic in nature and it measure the amount of energy released, in ergs

1.	5.0-6.0	~	$10^{19\text{-}20}$	mild
2.	6.1-7.0	~	$10^{21\text{-}22}$	moderate
3.	7.1-8.0	~	$10^{22\text{-}23}$	major
4.	M > 8.0	~	$10^{23\text{-}24}$	severe

Fig. 19·26. Earthquake mechanism.

Seismic Monitoring

(*a*) Keep a map of the area ready on the computer. The GIS (Geographical Information System) maps are extremely useful for this purpose. It has all the information about (*i*) roads ; (*ii*) railway ; (*iii*) crossings ; (*iv*) telephone lines ; (*v*) electric lines ; (*vi*) water lines ; (*vii*) sewer lines ; (*viii*) canals ; (*ix*) residential areas ; (*x*) vital structures such as power house, dams, water tanks, sensitive installations ; (*xi*) communication towers ; (*xii*) airports ; (*xiii*) railway stations ; and (*xiv*) hospitals. Such a map will be helpful in locating various details about damage of the structures and knowing alternate route if one route is blocked.

(*b*) The tilt of land in seismological lexicon is one of the most important seismic precursors. **The land in the vulnerable seismic area either rises up or sinks down, prior to the occurrence of an earthquake. Before the occurrence of the Bihar-Nepal earthquake of 14th January 1934, the land in the epicentral area had come up by about 8.5 m.** Usually the work of measurement of tilt is undertaken by Survey of India (located at Dehra Doon) this is the official agency for such jobs. But this office is too busy. If it is not possible for the Survey of India to undertake the measurement of tilt, a method could be used for this purpose. This method lacks precision. But it provides some useful information about tilt. If there is any change in the tilt then tall structures at the top show the effect. This could be done by taking periodic photos of tall structures (usually more than 15 m high). **Take two photos of the tall structure (chimney, tower multistoried building etc. once in six months in two horizontal directions East-West and North-South directions.** At the time of each photograph the camera **may be kept preferably at the same locations.** If there were any tilt it would be manifested at the top of the **tall structures. If such a tilt is seen then the specialized agency such as Survey of India could rush to the site for precision measurement.**

(*c*) The agricultural colleges/universities keep daily log of average sub-surface temperature. This is measured usually at a depth upto 1 m. This is useful for monitoring the growth of agricultural crop. Obtain this temperature data regularly and plot these readings as shown in the Fig. 19·25. **It is seen that before the occurrence of any medium to major earthquake, (magnitude more than 5.5 on Richter scale) the subsurface temperature starts rising about two to three years before the occurrence of the earthquake. If the graph is as shown in Fig. 19·27 then it should cause concern. Incidentally the graph is for the readings from Uttarkashi region. It could be seen that about two years before the occurrence of the earthquake on 19th October 1991, the sub-surface temperature had amply exhibited the observation that there is a remarkable rise in sub-surface temperature prior to the occurrence of an earthquake.**

(*d*) Small Magnitude Earthquake : If the site is located in seismically active area, then do not get alarmed by large number of small magnitude earthquakes, which are non-destructive. If the occurrences are stray and scattered then there is no reason for disturbance. As a matter of fact if there are periodic occurrences of small magnitude earthquakes, then this is an indication that the stress is being released. Conversely, if there is no occurrence of any earthquake or no felt earthquake for several months, then it should cause some concern. Under such conditions consult a seismologist. If the occurrence of small magnitude earthquakes (usually of magnitude less than 5.0 on Richter scale) goes on increasing rapidly with time then these could be 'foreshocks' of a major seismic event. Under such conditions consult a seismologist for advice.

In addition, there have been a few sites where seismic swarms have been observed. In seismology, **seismic swarms mean occurrence of a large number of micro-earthquake. These earthquakes do not cause any damage.** But in some cases, the swarm indicates that it could be a precursory phenomenon to a big jolt. Prior to the occurrence of the Latur (Killari) earthquake on 30th September 1993, the region was experiencing a large number of micro-earthquake in the form of swarm. The Bhuj earthquake was preceded by a large number of micro-earthquakes at Bhavnagar. These microtremors were sometime accompanied with loud noise. These sounds are known as sub-terrainian noise. Seismic swarm and sub-terrainian noises are more or less of similar character. Balsad (Bulsar) in Gujarat and Khandwa in Madhya Pradesh had experienced seismic swarms in nineties. The number of micro-earthquakes per day were as high as few thousand. There were questions in Parliament and state Assemblies about the seismic activity, which had created panic and fear-psychosis amongst people. Temporary seismological observatories were set up on an emergency basis. At present, Balsad and Khandwa are seismically quite and dormant. These sites need to be watched carefully.

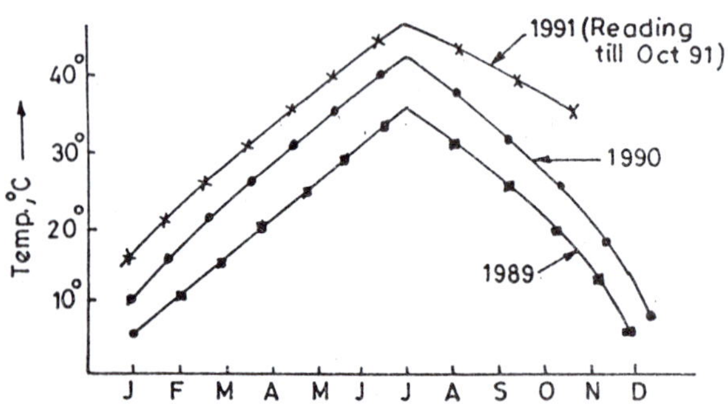

Fig. 19·27. Effect of sub-surface temperature.

Seismically, the nature has been periodically exhibiting precursory indirect evidences in various forms. Sudden depletion or rise (or appearance) of water levels in the wells is one reliable precursory item. A large number of dry wells in Gujarat and Rajasthan were full of water sometime in late December 2000/early 2001. Seismic dormancy is one of the several parameters. The advantage about seismic dormancy is that it does not require any instrument or seismic knowledge. Experience is also very important in understanding seismic dormancy. In 1996, a farmer in Indonesia told that he was highly worried. When enquired about the cause, he told that there is no earthquake for last four months. He further said that the dormant time section is always pregnant with an earthquake.

Seismic Force. Earthquake shock causes vibrations in a structure. The response of a structure depends on its location with respect to distance of wave motion, the distance from epicentre and natural period of vibration of structure. The vibrations in the horizontal directions are most important. The horizontal acceleration is taken 8 to 12 percent of the gravitational force. The general equation is $F = CW$, where F is the shear force at base, C is a constant and W is the total wt. of the building above the base. Thus total force F is distributed over the height of the building, so that the force is given by $P = FC_1$, where $C_1 = \frac{Wh \, . \, h^2}{\Sigma Wh^2}$ where Wh is the wt. of all floors above a level h from base is the weight of floor at h level.

It should be noted that for less important and small structures design is not done as given in code, but certain constructional details such as diagonal bracing in vertical panels of framed structure, strengthening of openings in walls, tombs, corners of sections of walls and provision of continuous bond at lintel level are provided.

For important structures located in highly seismic zones and very tall buildings dynamic analysis is attempted.

IS 4326-1977 has suggested salient features of earthquake resistant construction as below :

(1) Since earthquake force is proportional to mass of structure, the buildings shall be as light as possible.

(2) As far as possible the parts of the building should be tied together so that whole building should act as one unit.

(3) Building should have symmetrical rectangular shape in plan both for mass and rigidity and the centres of mass and rigidity should coincide to avoid eccentric forces.

(4) There should be no projection as far as possible.

(5) There should be proper connection between non-structural parts to structural parts to avoid any damage to the non-structural elements due to deformations of structural elements.

Residential and Commercial Buildings

Single Storyed Buildings. The seismic coefficients for calculatiang horizontal forces shall be given in the table "seismic coefficient for different zones of India".(Appendix 9·1)

Multi Storyed Buildings. The seismic coefficients as obtained in the above table is derived by the formula

$$K = \frac{0{\cdot}35S}{N + 0{\cdot}9(S - 8)}$$

where S = total no. of storeys in the building subject to minimum of 13.

N = No. of storeys above the one under consideration.

Note : The formula is applicable upto S = 30 and K not more than one.

The total horizontal shear at each floor level is equal to the Seismic coefficient multiplied by the Total dead load + Design live load on the floors above the one under considerations.

$$V_1 = \frac{4 \cdot 5}{6 \cdot 0 + 4 \cdot 5}(W_1 + W_2) \qquad V_1 = \text{shear for eleven storeys}$$

$$V_2 = \frac{10 \cdot 5}{15 + 19 \cdot 8}(W_1 + 15W_2) \qquad V_2 = \text{shear for thirty storeys}$$

W_1 = wt. of roof + live load on it.

W_2 = wt. of floor + live load on it and wt. of walls above it. (app. equal for all floors).

Industrial Buildings. Industrial buildings with continuous human occupancy are designed for coefficients given in the Table. Industrial buildings subjected to intermittent human occupancy are designed for 80% of the coefficients given in the table. This reduction is not applied for the buildings in zone V and VI or for buildings for essential services.

For heavy machines on floors special study of the forces should be done.

Miscellaneous. Portions projecting above the road or cantilevered in walls such as chimney shafts, parapets, balconeys, sun shades and chajjas etc. shall be designed for five times the seismic coefficients for which the structure is designed. Compound walls etc. are not required to design for seismic loads.

Terminology for Earthquake Engineering

(1) For the purpose of this standard, the following definitions shall apply which are applicable generally to all structures.

Note : For the definitions of terms pertaining to soil mechanics and soil dynamics references may be made to IS 2809 and IS 2810.

(2) **Closely-spaced modes.** Closely-spaced modes of a structure are those of its natural modes of vibration whose natural frequencies differ from each other by 10 percent or less of the lower frequency.

(3) **Critical Damping.** The damping beyond which the free vibration motion will not be oscillatory.

(4) **Damping.** The effect of internal friction, imperfect elasticity of material, slipping, sliding, etc. in reducing the amplitude of vibration and is expressed as a percentage of critical damping.

(5) **Design acceleration spectrum.** Design acceleration spectrum refers to an average smoothened plot of maximum acceleration as a function of frequency or time period of vibration for a specified damping ratio for earthquake excitations at the base of a single degree of freedom system.

(6) **Design basis earthquake (DBE).** It is the earthquake which can reasonably be expected to occur at least once during the design life of the structure.

(7) **Design horizontal acceleration coefficient (A_{t1}).** It is a horizontal acceleration coefficient that shall be used for design of structures.

(8) **Design lateral force.** It is the horizontal seismic force prescribed by this standard, that shall be used to design a structure.

(9) **Ductility.** Ductility of a structure, or its members, is the capacity to undergo large inelastic deformations without significant loss of strength or stiffness.

(10) **Epicentre.** The geographical point on the surface of earth vertically above the focus of the earthquake.

(11) **Effective Peak Ground Acceleration (EPGA).** It is 0·4 times the 5 percent damped average spectral acceleration between period 0S1 to 0·3s. This shall be taken as Zero Period Acceleration (ZPA).

(12) **Floor response spectra.** Floor response spectra is the response spectra for a time history motion of a floor. This floor motion time history is obtained by an analysis of multi-storey building for appropriate material damping values subjected to specified earthquake motion at the base of structure.

(13) **Focus.** The originating earthquake source of the elastic waves inside the earth which cause shaking of ground due to earthquake.

(14) **Importance factor (*I*).** It is a factor used to obtain the design seismic force depending on the functional use of the structure, characterised by hazardous consequences of its failure, its post-earthquake functional need, historic value, or economic importance.

(15) **Intensity of earthquake.** The intensity of an earthquake at a place is a measure of the strength of shaking during the earthquake, and is indicated by a number according to the modified Mercalli Scale or M.S.K. Scale of seismic intensities (See Annex D).

(16) **Liquefaction.** Liquefaction is a state in saturated coyhensionless soil wherein the effective shear strength is reduced to negligible value for all engineering purpose due to pore pressure caused by vibrations during an earthquake when they approach the total confining pressure. In this condition the soil tends to behave like a fluid mass.

(17) **Lithological features.** The name of the geological formation of the earths crust above bed rock on the basis of such characteristics as colour, structure, mineralogical composition and grain size.

(18) **Magnitude of earthquake (Richter's Magnitude).** The magnitude of earthquake is a number, which is a measure of energy released in an earthquake. It is defined as logarithm to the base 10 oOf the maximum trace amplitude, expressed in microns, which the standard short-period torsion seismometer (with a period o 0·8 s, magnificance 2800 and damping nearly critical) would register due to the earthquake at an epicentral distance of 100 km.

(19) **Maximum Considered Earthquake (MCE).** The most severe earthquake effects considered by this standard.

(20) **Modal mass (M_k).** Modal mass of a structure subjected to horizontal or vertical, as the case may be, ground motion is a part of the total seismic mass of the structure that is effective in mode k of vibration. The modal mass for a given mode has a unique value irrespective of scaling of the mode shape.

(21) **Modal participation factor (P_k).** Modal participation factor of mode k of vibrationis the amount of which mode k contributes to the overall vibration of the structure under horizontal and vertical earthquake ground motions. Since the amplitudes of 95 percent mode shapes can be scaled arbitrarily, the valuye of this factor depends on the scaling used for mode shapes.

(22) **Modes of vibration** (See **Normal mode).**

(23) **Mode shape coefficient (ϕ_{ik}).** When a system is vibrating in normal mode k, at any particular instant of time, the amplitude of mass i expressed as a ratio of the amplitude of one of the masses of the system, is known as mode shape coefficient (ϕ_{ik}).

(24) **Natural period (*T*).** Natural period of a structure is its time period of undamped free vibration.

Fundamental natural period (T_1). It is the first (longest) modal time period of vibration.

Modal natural period (T_k). The modal natural period of mode k is the time period of vibration in mode k.

(25) **Normal mode.** A system is said to be vibrating in a normal mode when all its masses attain maximum values of displacements and rotations simultaneously, and pass through equilibrium positions simultaneously.

(26) **Response reduction factor (*R*).** It is the factor by which the actual base shear force, that would be generated if the structure were to remain elastic during its response to the Design Basis Earthquake (DBE) shaking, shall be reduced to obtain the design lateral force.

(27) **Response spectrum.** The representation of the maximum response of idealized single degree freedom systems having cvertain period and damping, during earthquake ground motion. The maximum response is plotted against the undamped natural period and for various damping values, and can be expressed in terms of maximum absolute acceleration, maximum relative velocity, or maximum relative displacement.

(28) **Seismic mass.** It is the seismic weight divided acceleration due to gravity.

(29) **Seismic weight (*W*).** It is the total dead load plus appropriate amounts of specified imposed load.

(30) **Structural response factors (S_a/g).** It is a factor denoting the acceleration response spectrum of the structure subjected to earthquake ground vibrations, and depends on natural period of vibration and damping of the structure.

(31) **Tectonic features.** The nature of geological formation of the bed rock in the earth's crust revealing regions characterised by structural features, such as dislocation, distortion, faults, folding, thrusts, volcanoes with their age of formation, which are directly involved in the earth movement or quake resulting in the above consequences.

(32) **Time history analysis.** It is an analysis of the dynamic response of the structure at each increment of time, when its base is subjected to a specific ground motion time history.

(33) **Zone factor (*Z*).** It is a factor to obtain the design spectrum depending on the perceived maximum seismic risk characterised by Maximum Considered Earthquake (MCE) in the zone in which the structure is located. The basic zone factors included in this standard are reasonable estimate of effective peak ground acceleration.

(34) **Zero Period Acceleration (ZPA).** It is the value of acceleration response spectrum for period below 0·03 s (frequencies above 33 Hz).

Terminology for Earthquake Engineering of Buildings

(1) For the purpose of earthquake resistant design of buildings in this standard, the following definitions shall apply.

(2) **Base.** It is the level at which inertia forces generated in the structure are transferred to the foundation, which then transfers these forces to the ground.

(3) **Base dimensions (*d*).** Base dimension of the building along a direction is the dimension at its base, in metre, along that direction.

(4) **Centre of mass.** The point through which the resultant of the masses of a system acts. This point corresponds to the centre of gravity of masses of system.

(5) **Centre of stiffness.** The point through which the resultant of the restoring forces of a system acts.

(6) **Design eccentricity (e_{di}).** It is the value of eccentricity to be used at floor i in torsion calculations for design.

(7) **Design seismic base shear (V_B).** It is the total design lateral force at the base of a structure.

(8) **Diaphragm.** It is a horizontal, or nearly horizontal system, which transmits lateral forces to the vertical resisting elements, for example, reinforced concrete floors and horizontal bracing systems.

(9) **Dual system.** Buildings with dual system consist of shear walls (or braced frames) and moment resisting frames such that :

(*a*) The two systems are designed to resist the total design lateral force in proportion to their lateral stiffness considering the interaction of the dual system at all floor levels, and

(*b*) The moment resisting frames are designed to independently resist at least 25 percent of the design base shear.

(10) **Height of floor (h_1).** It is the difference in levels between the base of the building and that of floor *i*.

(11) **Height of structure (h).** It is the different in levels, in metres, between its base and its highest level.

(12) **Horizontal bracing system.** It is a horizontal truss system that serves the same function as a diaphragm.

(13) **Joint.** It is the portion of the column that is common to other members, for example, beams, framing into it.

(14) **Lateral force resisting element.** It is part of the structural system assigned to resist lateral forces.

(15) **Moment-resisting frame.** It is a frame in which members and joints are capable of resisting forces primarily by flexure.

Ordinary moment-resisting frame. It is a moment-resisting frame not meeting special detailing requirements for ductile behaviour.

Special moment-resisting frame. It is a moment-resisting frame specially detailed to provide ductile behvaiour and comply with the requirements given in IS : 4326 or IS 13920 or SP 6(6).

(16) **Number of storeys (n).** Number of storeys of a building is the number of levels above the base. This excludes the basement storeys, where basement walls are connected with the ground floor deck or fitted between the building columns. But, it includes the basement storeys, when they are not so connected.

(17) **Principal axes.** Principal axes of a building are generally two mutually perpendicular horizontal directions in plan of a building along which the geometry of the building is oriented.

(18) **P-D effect.** It is the secondary effect on shears and moments of frame members due to action of the vertical loads, interacting with the lateral displacement of building resulting from seismic forces.

(19) **Shear wall.** It is a wall designed to resist lateral forces acting in its own plane.

(20) **Soft storey.** It is one in which the lateral stiffness is less than 70 percent of that in the storey above or less than 80 percent of the average lateral stiffness of the three storey above.

(21) **Static eccentricity (e_{si}).** It is the distance between centre of mass and centre of rigidity of floor *i*.

(22) **Storey.** It is the space between two adjacent floors.

(23) **Storey drift.** It is the displacement of one level relative to the other level above or below.

(24) **Storey shear (V_1).** It is the sum of design lateral forces at all levels above the storey under consideration.

(25) **Weak storey.** It is one in which the storey lateral strength is less than 80 percent of that in the storey above. The storey lateral strength is the total strength of all seismic force resisting elements shearing the storey shear in the considered direction.

General Principles of Design

(1) **Additions of to existing structure.** The addition to existing structures are to be made as follows :

(*a*) An addition that is structurally independent from an existing structure shall be designed and constructed in accordance with the seismic requirements for new structures.

(*b*) An addition that is not structurally independent from an existing structure shall be designed and constructed such that the entire structure confirms to the seismic force resistance requirement for new structures unless the following three conditions are complied with :

(*i*) The addition shall comply with the requirement for new structures.

(*ii*) The addition shall not increase the seismic forces in any structural elements of the existing structure by more than 5 percent unless the capacity of the element subject to the increased force is still in compliance with the standard and

(*iii*) The addition shall not decrease the seismic resistance of any structural element of the existing structure unless reduced resistance is equal to or greater than that required for new structure.

(2) **Change in occupancy.** When a change of occupancy results in a structure being reclassified to a higher Importance factor (*I*). The structure shall confirm to the seismic requirement new structure with the higher Importance Facator.

(3) Earthquake is not likely to occur simultaneously with wind or maximum flood or maximum sea waves.

(4) In the plaster design of steel structures, the falling load combination shall be accounted for

(*i*) $1{\cdot}7\ (DL + IL)$
(*ii*) $1{\cdot}7\ (DL + EL)$
(*iii*) $1{\cdot}3\ (DL + IL + EL)$

where *DL* is Dead Load
IL is Imposed Load and
EL is Designed Earthquake Load.

(5) In design of RCC and Prestored concrete structures for Limit State Design partial safety factors are :

(*i*) $1{\cdot}5\ (DL + IL)$

(*ii*) $1{\cdot}2\ (DL + IL + EL)$

(*iii*) $1{\cdot}5\ (DL + EL)$

(*iv*) $0{\cdot}9\ (DL \pm 1{\cdot}5\ EL)$

(6) **Design Horizontal Earthquake Loads.** When the lateral load resisting elements are oriental along orthogonal horizontal direction, the structure shall be designed for the effects due to full design earthquake load in one horizontal direction at a time.

(7) When the lateral load resisting elements are not oriental along the orthogonal horizontal directions, the structure shall be designed for the effects due to full design earthquake load in one horizontal direction plus 30 percent of the design earthquake load in the other direction.

(8) **Design vertical earthquake load.** Where effects due to vertical earthquake loads are to be considered, then design vertical forces shall be calculated.

Buildings

(1) To perform well in a earthquakes, a building should possess four man attributes, namely simple and regular configuration and adquate lateral strength, stiffness and ductility. Buildings having simple regular geometry and uniformly disturbuted mass and stiffness in plan

as well as in elevation, suffer much the changes than buildings with irregular configuration. A building should be considered as irregular for the purposes of the standard.

Seismic weight of floors. The seismic weight of each floor is its full dead load plus appropriate amount of imposed load when computing the seismic weight of each floor the weight of columns and walls in any storey shall be equally distributed to the floor above and below the storey.

Seismic weight of building. The seismic weight of whole building is the sum of the seismic weights of all the floor. Any weight supported in between storeys shall be distributed to the floor above and below in inverse proportion to its distance from the floors.

Important factors for different buildings

Sl. No.	*Structure*	*Important factor*
i	Important service and community buildings such as hospitals, schools, monumental structures, emergency buildings like telephone exchange, television stations, radio station, railway station, fire station buildings, large community halls like PVR's/ Cinema halls, assembly halls and subway stations, power stations.	1·5
ii	All other buildings.	1·0

Note (*i*) : The design engineer may choose values of important factors/ greater than above.

(*ii*) : Buildings not cover in sl. no. (*i*) and (*ii*) above may be designed for higher values of I depending on economy.

(*iii*) : This does not apply to temporary structures like excavators, scaffolding of short duration.

Compound walls. Compound walls shall be designed for design horizontal coefficient A_h with important factor $I = 1{\cdot}0$.

19·15. Seismology

Focus. The centre of the earthquake.

Epicentre. The place on the earth surface, located directly over the focus.

Primary (*P*) Waves. These are longitudinal or, compressive or rarefaction waves. They are always 1st to arrive and recorded.

Secondary (*S*) Waves. These are 2nd to arriave and usually have greater amplitude and destruction power than P waves.

Magnitude (*M*). It can be calculated by the following relation given by Guttenberg and Richter.

$\text{Log}_{10}\, E = 9{\cdot}4 + 2{\cdot}14M - 0{\cdot}054\, M^2$ where E is energy in Ergs released by a shock of magnitude M. The table given below gives values of E released by different magnitudes M.

M	*Energy E* (10^{21} ergs)
5	0·0056
6	0·1477
7	5·4200
8	115·9000
8·7	353·1000

The magnitude M is thus a number that indicates the size of the earthquake. The larger the magnitude of a shock. The greater the area which is effected.

Intensity of Earthquake. It is a number which measures the damage at a particular place and thus varies with distance from the centre of shock. A shock of magnitude say 6 may be valid to have the intensity VIII near centre and V at a distance of 60 km from centre. According to modified Mercalli intensity scale 1931, the intensities are classified according to the degree of observed damage from I to XII starting from feeble to severe.

Seismic Coefficient. From Newton's 2nd law of motion. Force is equal to mass of body or structure multiplied by the acceleration.

$F = m \times f = w \times f/g$ where F = earthquake force and w = wt. of structure, f is earthquake acceleration and g is acc. due to gravity.

In above expression $f/g = \alpha$ (say) is known as seismic coeff.

Seismic Zones of India. For purpose of determining the seismic coefficients the country has been divided in seven zones 0 to VI. (Appendix 19·3)

Wind Loads and Seismic Loads are not adopted simultaneously as both are horizontal and similar and such the higher of the two is taken.

Permissible increase in Stresses. Where seismic loads are taken into account the permissible stresses are increased about one 3rd. For prestressed conc. the max. limit is 85 % of its ultimate strength. For steel structures the max. stress in no case exceed the yield stress.

Permissible Decrease in Allowable Bearing Pressure of Soils

Nature of soil	*Permissible decrease in bearing pressure percent*
1. Hard soil having a bearing capacity greater than 45 tonnes/m^2	50
2. Average soils having a bearing capacity gtreater than 20 tonnes/m^2 and equal to or less than 45t/m^2	30
3. Soft soil having a bearing capacity greater than 10t/m^2 and equal to or less than 20t/m^2	0 to 30

Note : When the earthquake forces are inclined and the permissible stresses are increased, the mm factor of safety shall be 2.

Residential and Commercial Buildings

Single Storyed Building. The seismic coefficients for calculating horizontal forces shall be given in the table "seismic coefficients for different zones of India."

Multistoryed Buildings. The seismic coefficients as obtained in the above table is decreased by the formula.

$$K - \frac{0{\cdot}35\,S}{N + 0{\cdot}9(S - 8)}$$

where S = total no. of storeys in the building subject to min. of 13.

N = no. of storeys above the one under consideration.

Note : The formula is applicable upto S = 30 and K not more than one.

The total horizontal shear at each floor level is equal to the seismic coefficient multiplied by the total dead load + design line load on the floors above the one under considerations.

Residential and Commercial Buildings

Single Storyed Building. The seismic coefficients for calculating horizontal forces shall be given in the table "seismic coefficients for different zones of India."

Multistoryed Buildings. The seismic coefficients as obtained in the above table is decreased by the formula.

$$K - \frac{0{\cdot}35\,S}{N + 0{\cdot}9(S - 8)}$$

where S = total no. of storeys in the building subject to min. of 13.

N = no. of storeys above the one under consideration.

Note : The formula is applicable upto $S = 30$ and K not more than one.

The total horizontal shear at each floor level is equal to the seismic coefficient multiplied by the total dead load + design line load on the floors above the one under considerations.

$$V_1 = \frac{4{\cdot}5}{6{\cdot}0 + 4{\cdot}5}(w_1 + 6w_2)\ V_1 = \text{Shear for eleven storeys}$$

$$V_2 = \frac{10{\cdot}5}{15 + 19{\cdot}8}(w_1 + 15w_2)\ V_2 = \text{Shear for thirty storeys.}$$

w_1 = wt. of roof + line load on it.

w_2 = wt. of floor + line load on it and wt. of walls above it.
(app. equal for all floors)

Industrial Buildings. Industrial buildings with continuous human occupancy are designed for coefficients given in the table. Industrial buildings subjected to intermittent human occupancy are designed or 80% of the coefficients given in the table. This reduction is not applied for the buildings in zones V and VI or for buildings for essential services.

For heavy machines on floors special study of the forces should be done.

Miscellaneous. Portions projecting above the road or cantilevered in walls such as chimney shafts, ppts, balconeys, sunshades and chhajjas etc. shallbe designed for fine tunes the seismic coefficients for which the structure is designed. Compound walls etc. are not required to design of seismic loads.

Seismic Coefficient (α)—From Newton's 2nd law of motion. Force is equal to mass of body or structure multiplied by acceleration.

$$F = mf = W \times f/g$$

where F = earthquake force and W = wt. of structure, f is earthquake acceleration and g is acceleration due to gravity.

In above expression f/g = a (say) is known as seismic coefficient.

Seismic Zone	*II*	*III*	*IV*	*V*
Seismic Intensity	Low	Moderate	Severy	V. severy
Z (Zone factor)	0·10	0·16	0·24	0·36

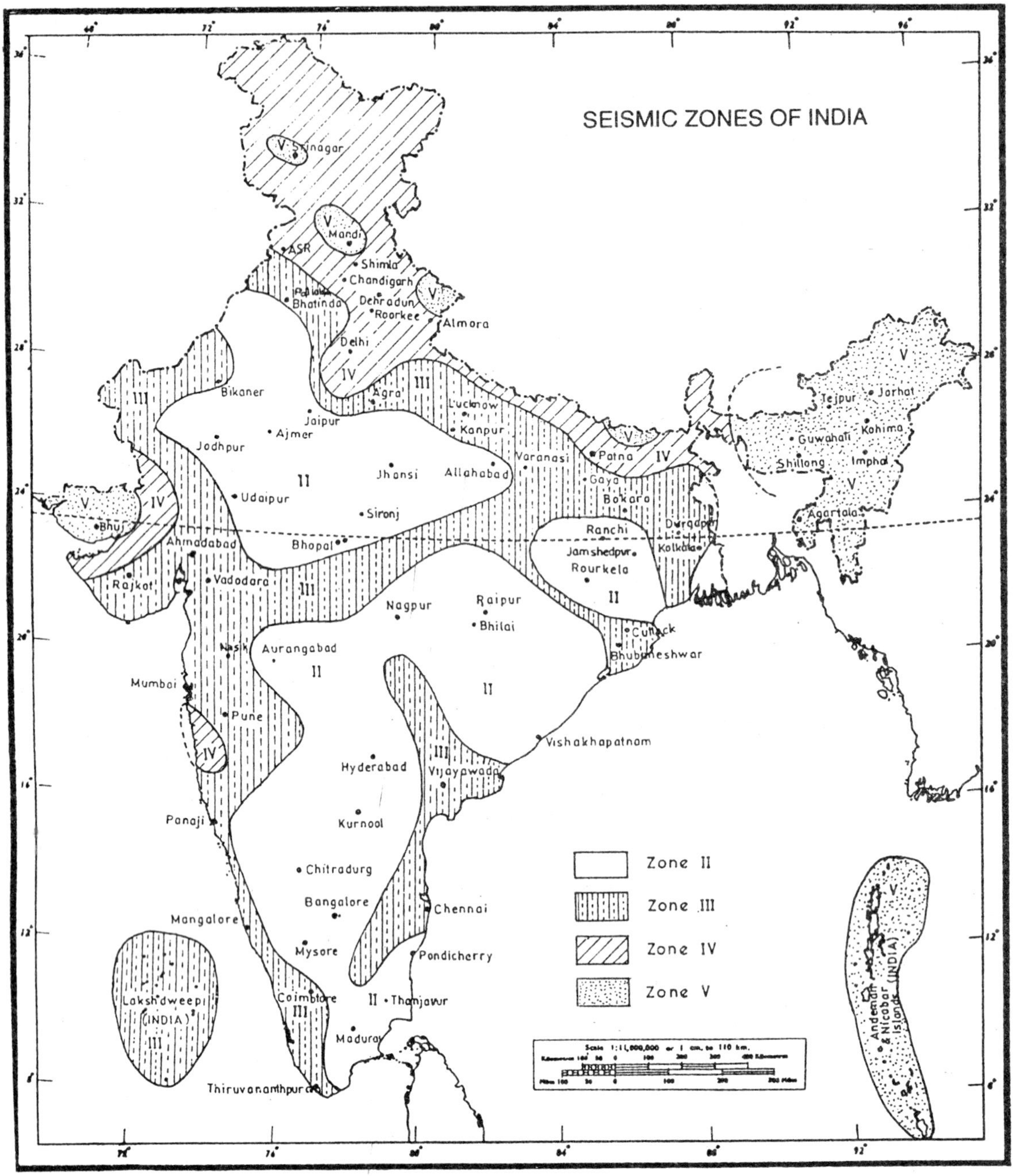
SEISMIC ZONES OF INDIA
Srinagar
Mandi
ASR
Shimla
Chandigarh
Bhatinda
Dehradun
Roorkee
Almora
Delhi
Agra
Bikaner
Jaipur
Ajmer
Jodhpur
Lucknow
Kanpur
Varanasi
Patna
Gaya
Bokaro
Jhansi
Allahabad
Udaipur
Sironj
Bhuj
Ahmadabad
Bhopal
Ranchi
Jamshedpur
Rourkela
Kolkata
Rajkot
Vadodara
Nagpur
Raipur
Bhilai
Cuttack
Bhubaneshwar
Nasik
Aurangabad
Mumbai
Pune
Vishakhapatnam
Hyderabad
Vijayawada
Panaji
Kurnool
Chitradurg
Bangalore
Chennai
Mangalore
Mysore
Pondicherry
Coimbatore
Thanjavur
Madurai
Thiruvananthpuram
Lakshdweep (INDIA)
Tejpur
Jorhat
Guwahati
Kohima
Shillong
Imphal
Agartala
Andaman & Nicobar Islands (INDIA)
Zone II
Zone III
Zone IV
Zone V

Fig. 19·28.

Appendix 19·1. Basic Horizontal Seismic Coefficients for Some Important Towns

Town	*Zone*	*Zone Factor, Z*	*Town*	*Zone*	*Zone Factor, Z*
Agra	III	0·16	Jorhat	V	0·36
Ahmedabad	III	0·16	Kanpur	III	0·16
Ajmer	II	0·10	Kohima	V	0·36
Allahabad	II	0·10	Kolkata	III	0.16
Almora	IV	0·24	Kurnool	II	0·10
Ambala	IV	0·24	Lucknow	III	0·16
Amritsar	IV	0·24	Ludhiana	IV	0·24
Asansol	III	0·16	Madurai	II	0·10
Aurangabad	II	0·10	Mandi	V	0·36
Bahraich	IV	0·24	Mangalore	III	0·16
Bangalore	II	0·10	Monghyr	IV	0·24
Barauni	IV	0·24	Moradabad	IV	0·24
Bareilly	III	0·16	Mumbai	III	0.16
Bhatinda	III	0·16	Mysore	II	0·10
Bhilai	II	0·10	Nagpur	II	0·10
Bhopal	II	0·10	Nainital	IV	0·24
Bhubaneswar	III	0·16	Nasik	III	0·16
Bhuj	V	0·36	Nellore	III	0·16
Bikaner	III	0·16	Panjim	III	0·16
Bokaro	III	0·16	Patiala	III	0·16
Burdwan	III	0·16	Patna	IV	0·24
Calicut	III	0·16	Pilibhit	IV	0·24
Chandigarh	IV	0·24	Pondicherry	II	0·10
Chennai	III	0·16	Pune	III	0·16
Chitradurga	II	0·10	Raipur	II	0·10
Coimbatore	III	0·16	Rajkot	III	0·16
Cuttack	III	0·16	Ranchi	II	0·10
Darbhanga	V	0·36	Roorkee	IV	0·24
Darjeeling	IV	0·24	Rourkela	II	0·10
Dehra Dun	IV	0·24	Sadiya	V	0·36
Delhi	IV	0·24	Simla	IV	0·24
Durgapur	III	0·16	Sironj	II	0·10
Gangtok	IV	0·24	Srinagar	V	0·36
Gauhati	V	0·36	Surat	III	0·16
Gaya	III	0·16	Tezpur	V	0·36
Gorakhpur	IV	0·24	Thanjavur	II	0·10
Hyderabad	II	0·10	Thiruvanthapuram	III	0·16
Imphal	V	0·36	Tiruchirapalli	II	0·10
Jabalpur	III	0·16	Udaipur	II	0·10
Jaipur	II	0·10	Vadodara	III	0·16
Jamshedpur	II	0·10	Varanasi	III	0·16
Jhansi	II	0·10	Vijayawada	III	0·16
Jodhpur	II	0·10	Visakhapatnam	II	0·10

Appendix 19·2. List of Some Damaging Earthquakes in India.

Date	*Epicentre* *Lat(°N)*	*Long(°E)*	*Location*	*Magnitude*
1819 Jun 16	23·6	68·6	Kutch (Gujrat)	8·0
1869 Jan 10	25	93	Near Cachar, Assam	7·5
1885 May 30	34·1	74·6	Sopor, J & K	7·0
1897 Jun 12	25·9	91·0	Shillong Plateau	8·7
1905 Apr 04	32·3	76·3	Kangra, HP	8·0
1918 Jul 08	24·5	91·0	Srimangal, Assam	7·6
1930 Jul 02	25·8	90·2	Dhubri, Assam	7·1
1934 Jan 15	26·6	86·8	Bihar-Nepal Border	8·3
1941 Jun 26	12·4	92·5	Andaman islands	8·1
1943 Oct 23	26·8	94·0	Assam	7·2
1950 Aug 15	28·5	96·7	Arunachal-China border	8·5
1956 Jul 21	23·3	70·0	Anjar, Gujrat	7·0
1967 Dec 10	17·37	73·75	Koyna, Maharashtra	6·5
1975 Jan 19	32·38	78·49	Kinnaur, HP	6·2
1988 Aug 06	25·13	95·15	Manipur-Mayanmar border	6·6
1988 Aug 21	26·72	86·63	Bihar-Nepal border	6·4
1991 Oct 20	30·75	78·86	Uttarkashi, UP hills	6·6
1993 Sep 30	18·07	76·62	Latur-Osmanabad, Maharashtra	6·3
1997 May 22	23·08	80·06	Jabalpur, MP	6·0
1999 Mar 29	30·41	79·42	Chamoli District, Uttranchal hills	6·8

Appendix 19·3

Seismic zones of India—For purpose of determining the seismic coefficients, the country has been divided in seven zones (0 to VI).

Seismic coefficients for different seismic zones of India

Zone No.	*Seismic coefficient* (α)		
	Hard soil	*Average soil*	*Soft soil*
0	0	0	0
I	0	0·01	0·02
II	0·02	0·03	0·04
III	0·04	0·05	0·06
IV	0·05	0·06	0·08
V	0·06	0·08	0·10
VI	0·08	0·10	0·12

Note : 1. Buildings having accommodations of essential services such as hospitals, food grain stores, power stations and water works etc. are designed for 1½ times of the seismic coefficients.

2. Permissible increase in stresses—where seismic loads are taken into account the permissible stresses are increased about one 3rd. For prestressed concrete the max. limit is 85% of its ultimate strength. For steel structures the max. stress in no case to exceed the yield stress.

3. Wind loads and seismic loads are not adopted simultaneously as both are horizontal and similar and such the higher of the two is taken.

Appendix 19·4. Permissible increase in allowable bearing pressure or resistance of soils.

Sl. No.	*Type of soil mainly constituting the foundation*	*Permissible Increase in Allowable Bearing Pressure, Percent*					
		Piles passsing through any soil but resting on soil type I	*Piles not covered under Col. 3*	*Raft foundations*	*Combined or isolated RCC footing with tie beams*	*Isolated RCC footing without tie beams or unreinforced strip foundations*	*Well Foundations*
(1)	(2)	(3)	(4)	(5)	(6)	(7)	(8)
(*i*)	*Type I Rock or Hard Soils*— Well graded gravels and sand gravel mixtures with or without clay binder, and clayey sands poorly graded or sand clay mixtures (GB, CW, SB, SW and SC) having N^* above 30, where N is the standard penetration value.	50	–	50	50	50	50
(*ii*)	*Type II Medium Soils* — All soils with N between 10 and 30 and poorly graded sands or gravelly sands with little or no fines (SP) with $N > 15$	50	25	50	25	25	25
(*iii*)	*Type III Soft Soils* — All soils other than SP with $N < 10$	50	25	50	25	–	25

If any increase in bearing pressure has already been permitted for forces other than seismic forces, the total increase in allowable bearing pressure when seismic force is also included shall not exceed the limits specified above.

Submerged loose sands and soils falling under classification SP with standard penetration values less than the values specified in Note 2 below, the vibrations caused by earthquake may cause liquefaction or excessive total and differential settlements. In important projects this aspect of the problem need be investigated and appropriate methods of compaction or stabilisation adopted to achieve suitable N. Alternatively, deep pile foundation may be provided and taken to depths well into the layer which are not likely to liquefy. Marine clays and other sensitive clays are also known to liquefy due to collapse of soil structure and will need special treatment according to site conditions.

1. The piles should be designed for lateral loads neglecting lateral resistance of soil layers liable to liquefy.
2. Desirable field values of N are as follows :

Zone	*Depth below ground level in metres*	*N Values*	*Remarks*
III, IV and V	Upto 5 ≥ 10	15 25	For values of depth between 5 to 10 m linear interpolation is recommended
II (for important structures only)	Upto 5 ≥ 10	15 20	

Note : When the earthquake forces are inclined and the permissible stresses are increased, the minimum factor of safety shall be 2.

Appendix 19·5. The Modified Mercalli Intensity Scale and corresponding approximate ground accelerations.

Intensity	Description	Ground Acceleration a ($\frac{cm}{sec}$)	$\frac{a}{g}$
I	— Not felt except by a very few under especially favorable circumstances		
II	— Felt only by a few persons at rest especially on upper floors of buildings. Delicately suspended objects may swing.	2, 3	
III	— Felt quite noticeably indoors, especially on upper floors of buildings, but many people do not recognize it as an earthquake. Standing motor cars may rock slightly. Vibration like passing truck. Duration estimated.	4, 5, 6	·005 g
IV	— During the day felt indoors by many, outdoors by few. At night some awakened. Dishes, windows, doors disturbed, walls make creaking sound. Sensation like heavy truck striking building. Standing motor cars rocked noticeably.	7, 8, 9, 10	·01g
V	— Felt by nearly everyone; many awakened. Some dishes, windows, etc., broken a few instances of cracked plaster, unstable objects overturned. Disturbances of trees, poles, and other tall objects sometimes noticed. Pendulum clocks may stop.	20, 30	
VI	— Felt by all; many frightened and run outdoors. Some heavy furniture moved, a few instances of fallen plaster or damaged chimneys. Damage slight.	40, 50, 60	·05g
VII	— Everybody runs outdoors. Damage negligible in buildings of good design and construction; slight to moderate in well-built ordinary structures considerable in poorly built or badly designed structures some, chimneys broken. Noticed by persons driving motor cars.	70, 80, 90, 100	0·1g
VIII	— Damage slight in specially designed structures considerable in ordinary substantial buildings, with partial collapse, great in poorly built structures. Panel walls thrown out of frame structures. Fall of chimneys, factory stacks, columns, monuments, walls. Heavy furniture overturned. Sand and mud ejected in small amounts. Changes in well water. Disturbs persons driving motor cars.	200, 300	
IX	— Damage considerable in specially designed structures; well-designed frame structures thrown out of plumb great in substantial buildings, with partial collapse. Buildings shifted off foundations. Ground cracked conspicuously. Underground pipes broken.	400, 500, 600	0·5
X	— Some well-built, wooden structures destroyed, most masonry and frame structures destroyed with foundations, ground badly cracked. Rails bent. Landslides considerable from river banks and steep slope. Shifted sand and mud. Water splashed over banks.	700, 800, 900, 1000	1·0g
XI	— Few, if any, (masonry) structures remain standing. Bridges destroyed. Broad fissures in ground. Underground pipelines completely out of service. Earth slumps and land slips in soft ground. Rails bent greatly.	2000, 3000	
XII	— Damage total. Waves seen on ground surfaces. Lines of sight and level distorted. Objects thrown upward into the air.	4000, 5000, 6000	5·0g

APPENDIX-I

Design of Steel Structures—General

Design of Tension Members. A member carrying direct tension is called a tie.

$$\text{Failure load} = \text{yield stress} \times \text{Area}$$

$$\text{Working load} = \frac{\text{Failure load}}{\text{Factor of safety}} = \frac{\text{Yield stress}}{\text{Factor of safety}} = \text{Allowable stress} \times \text{Area}$$

To design a tension member when there are holes for rivets or bolts which are 1/16" (1·5 mm) greater in diameter than the diameter of the rivet or bolt, the net effective area is calculated after deducting the area of the hole.

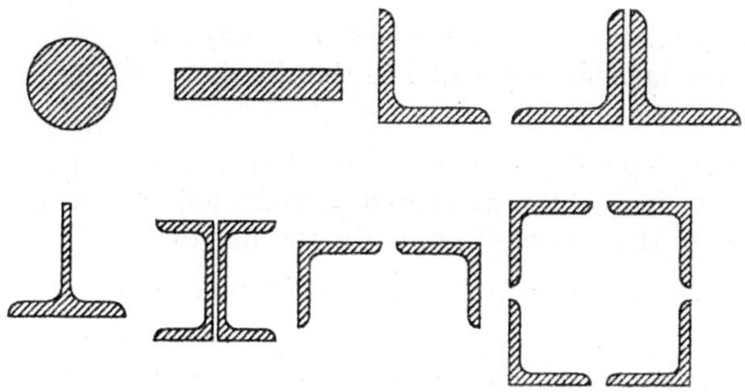

Fig. A·1. Tie sections.

Material	Form	*Allowable stress* kg/cm^2 (*tsi*)	*Yield strength* kg/cm^2 (*tsi*)	*Ultimate strength* kg/cm^2 (*tsi*)	*Factor of safety on*	
					Yield strength	*Ultimate strength*
1. Mild steel confirming to IS : 226 1962	(*a*) Rolled *I*-beaming and channels.	1500 (9·5)	2600 (16·5)	4200-5400 (26·7 – 34·3)	1·73	2·8 to 3·6
	(*b*) Plates, bars, universal beams and columns.					
	(*c*) Upto and including 20 mm (3/4")	1500 (9·5)	2600 (16·5)	4200-5400 (26·7-34·3)	1·73	2·8 to 3·6
	(*d*) Over 20 mm (3/4")	1420 (9·0)	2300 (14·6)	4200-5400 (26·7-34·3)	1·62	2·96 to 3·8
2. High tensile steel (*a*) confirming to IS : 961-1962 H.T. grade	Plates, sections and bars					
	(*i*) Upto 45 mm (1¾")	2125 (13·5)	3500 (22·2)	5800 (36·8)	1·65	2·73

Table contd...

Table contd...

Material	*Form*	*Allowable stress kg/cm²* (*t.si*)	*Yield strength kg/cm²* (*t.si*)	*Ultimate strength kg/cm²* (*t.si*)	*Factor of safety on*	
					Yield strength	*Ultimate strength*
	(*ii*) Over 45 mm (1¾″)	1810 (11·5)	3000 (19·1)	5500 (34·9)	1·66	3·04
(*b*) Confirming to IS : 961-962 H.T.W. grade	Plates sections and bars					
	(*i*) Upto 25 mm (1″)	1970 (12·5)	3500 (22·2)	5500 (34·9)	1·78	2·89
	(*ii*) Over 25 mm (1″)	1730 (11·0)	3400 (21·6)	5200 (33·0)	1·97	3·01

Notes : H.T. = High tensile H.T.W. = High tensile weldable.

Net effective width (b_c) is obtained by deducting from the gross width the sum of the diameters of all the holes in the chain and adding the each gauge space in the chain the quantity $P^2/4g$.

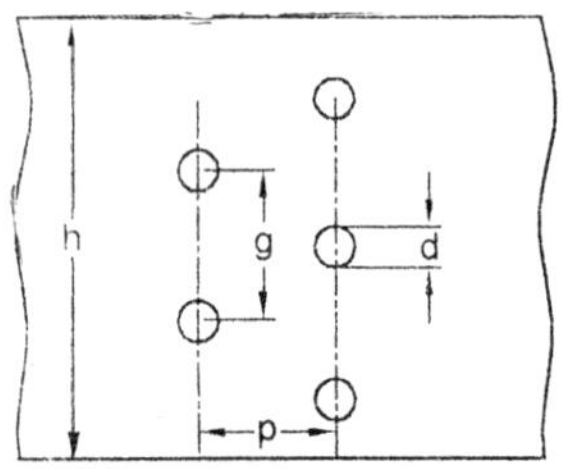

Fig. A·2.

where p = the staggered pitch *i.e.* the space between any two consecutive rivets measured parallel to the direction of stress in the member.

g = gauge *i.e.* the space between the same two consecutive rivets in a chain measured at right angles to the direction of the stress direction in the member.

n = no. of rivet holes and n_1 = no. of zigzag or inclined lines.

Thus for a 5 rivets holes section have effective area $b_c = b - 5\,d + 4\,(P^2/4g)$.

In general $b_c = b - nd + n_1\,(p^2/4g)$.

Effective areas in the case of L_s and T_s etc. An angle or Tee is generally connected to the gusset plate or to any other section by one leg only causing non uniformed stress distribution on the section. Indian Standards Code IS : 800-1962 recommends the following not effective areas for angles and Tees.

(*i*) Single angle in tension, connected by one angle only.

net effective area = $a + k_1\,b$ where a = net sectional area of connected leg.

b = area of the out standing leg.

$$k_1 = \frac{1}{1 + 0{\cdot}35\dfrac{b}{a}}$$

(*ii*) Pair of angles back to back (or a single Tee) in tension connected by only one leg of each angle (or by flange of a Tee) to the same side of the gusset.

Net effective area = $a + k_2\,b$

where, a = net area of the connected legs (or flange of the Tee)

b = area of the outstanding leg or web of the Tee.

$$k_2 = \frac{1}{1 + 0{\cdot}2\dfrac{b}{a}}$$

In order that the two angles act as one member, it is necessary to connect them together along this length by tacking rivets. The maximum spacing of tacking shall be 1·0 m (3′-6″). If tacking rivets or welds are not used, both the angles bend separately and their net effective area should be computed according to the equation, net effective area = $a + k_1 b$.

(*iii*) For double angles or tees, carrying direct tension, placed back to back and connected to both sides of the gusset or to both sides of a rolled section, the area to be taken in computing the mean tensile stress shall be the full gross area less the deductions for the holes, provided the members are connected together along their length by tacking rivets *i.e.* net effective area = gross area – holes. If the tacking rivets are not used, each angle or tee will behave separately. Then the effective section of an angle be calculated by the equation, effective section = $a + k_1 b$ and of tee by the equation effective area = $a + k_2 b$.

Example 1. *A tension member consisting of 4 hS 4 × 4 × 3/8 is connected to the gusset plate by 3/4″ dia rivets as shown in Fig. A·3.*

Find permissible load when

(*a*) angles are tack riveted along *a, b, c* and *d*.

(*b*) angles are tack riveted along *c* and *d* only.

(*c*) angles are tack riveted along *a* and *b* only.

(*d*) no tack riveting is done.

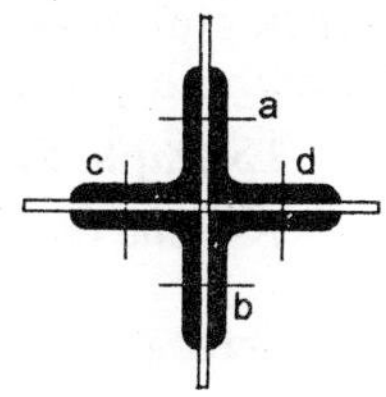

Fig. A·3.

(*a*) **Angles tack riveted along *a, b, c* and *d* (case *iii*).**

Net effective area = Gross area – holes = 4 × 2·86 – 4 × 13/16 × 3/8 = 10·22 sq. in.

Safe permissible load = 10·22 × 9·00 = 91·98 tons (9·00 is the permissible stress).

(*b*) **Angles tack riveted along *c* and *d* only.**

Net effective area = Same as in case (*a*) = 10·22 sq. in.

Safe tensile load = 91·90 tons

(*c*) **Angles tack riveted along *c* and *b* only.** These pair of angles are each connected to the same side of gusset therefore equation given below is used.

Net effected area = $a + k_2 b$

Net area of connected legs = $a = 4\left(4 - \frac{13}{16}\right)\frac{3}{8}$ = 4·78 sq. in.

Area of outstanding legs = $b = \left(4 - \frac{3}{8}\right)\frac{3}{8}$ = 5·44 sq. in.

$$k_2 = \frac{1}{1 + 0{\cdot}2 \times \dfrac{5{\cdot}44}{4{\cdot}78}} = 0{\cdot}815$$

Net effective area = $a + k_2 b$ = 4·78 + 0·815 × 5·44 = 9·22

Safe tensile load = 9·22 × 9 = 83 tons

(*d*) **No tack riveting.** Each angle will be individual. Therefore equation

Net effective area = $a + k_1 b$ is used

Net area of connected legs a = 4(4 – 3/16)(3/8) = 4·78

Area of outstanding legs b = 4(4 – 3/8)3/8

$$k_1 = \frac{1}{1 + 0{\cdot}35 \times \dfrac{5{\cdot}44}{4{\cdot}78}} = 0{\cdot}715$$

Net effective area $= a + k_1 b = 4{\cdot}78 + 0{\cdot}715 \times 5{\cdot}44$
$= 8{\cdot}66$ sq. in.
Safe tensile load $= 8{\cdot}66 \times 9{\cdot}0$ or safe tensile load
$= 78$ tons.

Lug angles. Lug angles are used to reduce the length of the connections (refer Fig. A·4) which shows the use of lug angles with single angle or channel type tension member. Due to the possible deformation of the outstanding leg of the lug angle, the rivets connecting the gusset plate with the lug angle will share less load than the rivets connecting the main member with the gusset plates. The lug angle should be designed to develop a strength not less than 20% in excess of the force in outstanding leg of the main angle.

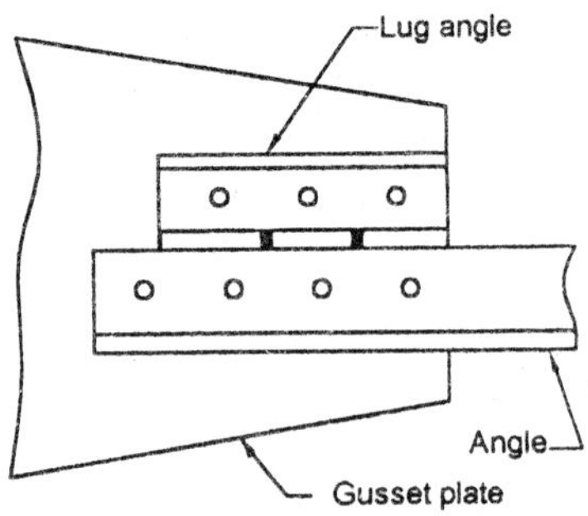

Fig. A·4.

Example 2. *Design a splice to connect 12" × 3/8" plate with 12" × 3/4" plate. The load is 34 tons. Assume one face of each plate is flushed with each other.*

Strength of 3/4" dia rivet (13/16" hole) in double shear $= 2 \times \frac{\pi}{4}\left(\frac{13}{16}\right)^2 \times 6{\cdot}5 = 6{\cdot}71$ tons

in bearing on 3/8" plate $= \frac{13}{16} \times \frac{3}{8} \times 15 = 4{\cdot}58$ toOns

∴ Number of rivets $= \frac{34}{4{\cdot}58} = 7{\cdot}4$ say 8

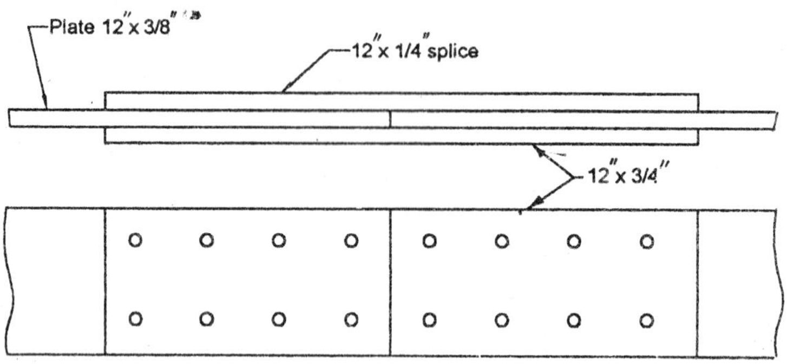

Fig. A·5.

Since the thickness of packing is 3/8" (greater than 1/4"), the no. of rivets to be increased by 12% (2% for each 1/16" of packing above the calculated number). Therefore number of rivets $= 1{\cdot}12 \times 7{\cdot}4 = 8{\cdot}28$ say 9.

The additional number of rivet is to be placed in an extension of the filler.

The area of splice plates may not be checked as it provides an area equal to the area of the main 3/8"plate.

Tension splice. The strength of the splice plates and the rivets connecting to it with the member should at least be equal to the design load of the tension member when splice plate is used to join the sections of different thickness, filler plates are used to make the face in level. The rivets or bolts carrying calculated shear stress through a packing greater than 1/4" (6 mm) thick should be increased above the number required by normal calculations by 2·5 percent for each 5/66" (2·0 mm) thickness of packing. For double shear connections packed on both sides, the number of additional rivets or bolts required should be determined from the thickness of the thicker packing. The additional rivets or bolts may preferably be placed in an extension of the packing.

Calculation for a lug angle. (in a particular case for illustration).

If the rivets will be 3/4″ in nominal diameter, consequently the gross diameter of the rivet will be 13/16″. Gross area of angle be 3·75 sq. in. A minimum of one rivet hole will be deducted.

∴ Net area of angle $= 3{\cdot}75 - (13/16) \times ½ = 3{\cdot}34$ sq. in.

Strength of member $= 3{\cdot}34 \times 9{\cdot}0 = 30{\cdot}1$ tons

Strength of outstanding leg $= \dfrac{3{\cdot}5}{3{\cdot}5 + 4} \times 30{\cdot}1 = 14{\cdot}05$ tons

Strength of connected leg $= 16{\cdot}05$ tons

Required strength of lug angle $= 1{\cdot}2 \times 14{\cdot}05 = 16{\cdot}85$ tons

∴ Net area required $= \dfrac{16{\cdot}85}{9{\cdot}0} = 1{\cdot}87$ sq. in.

Use 4″ × 4″ × 5/16″ angles which will give a net area of 2·40 = 5/16 × 13/16 = 2·15 sq. in

The thickness of gusset can be assumed to be 5/8″.

The strength of rivet in single shear $= \dfrac{\pi}{4}\left(\dfrac{13}{16}\right)^2 \times 6{\cdot}5 = 3{\cdot}36$ tons

In bearing on 1/2″ plate $= 13/16 \times 1/2 \times 15 = 6{\cdot}1$ tons

In bearing on 5/16″ plate $= 13/16 \times 5/16 \times 15 = 3{\cdot}8$ tons

∴ Rivet value for all cases is 3·36 tons

Number of rivets joining (*i*) connected leg with gusset plate $= \dfrac{16{\cdot}05}{3{\cdot}36} = 6$ say

(*ii*) Outstanding leg with lug angle $= 1{\cdot}4 \times \dfrac{14{\cdot}05}{3{\cdot}36} = 7$ say

(*iii*) Lug angle with gusset plate $= 1{\cdot}2 \times \dfrac{14{\cdot}05}{3{\cdot}36} = 6$ say

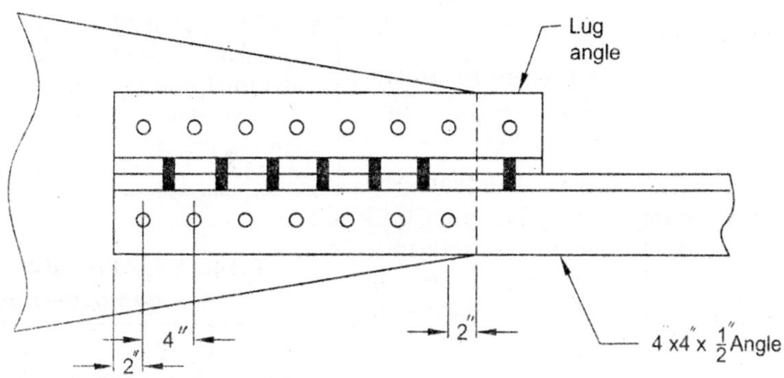

Fig. A·6.

The arrangement is shown in the Fig. A·6.

Note : (1) In threaded bolts the sec. area of bolt must be taken at the root of the thread.

(2) In welded connections, we can adjust the lengths of the welds so that the centre of gravity of the joint lies on the line passing through the centre of gravity of the member.

Compression Members

A structural member carrying axial compression is known as column, post or stanchion. Compression members in roof trusses are called struts.

Design of Compression Member

(1) Assume an allowable stress from the limits on slenderness ratio (l/r) for compressive members for dead and live loads we find that l/r should be between 0 and 180. From the lable of allowable compressive stress, the corresponding allowable stresses are 7·92 *tsi* and 2·13 *tsi* (1250 and 336 kg/cm^2) respectively. For l/r 0 to 180 an average value of the stress equal to 5 *tsi* (800 kg/cm^2) may therefore be assumed to start with. This corresponds to l/r = 110 app. such a value of l/r is quite frequent in the members of roof trusses or single I columns. But for built up shapes of columns or chords of bridge trusses this will be rather high. In such cases a stress of the order of 7 *tsi* may be assumed to start with. l is effective length and r = lease radius of gyration.

(2) Select a trial section for the assumed allowable stress.

(3) Determine the actual allowable stress for the l/r value of the trial section. Find the sectional area as required now.

(4) Compare the required area with that of the trial section.

(5) Repeat the above procedure till the actual required area is slightly smaller or just equal to the area of the trial section.

An example is given to illustrate the procedure. In this example it is assumed that two rivets are used at the end connections which are the least (32 rivets) for reasons of rigidity. In comp-ressive members area due to rivet holes is not deducted.

Example. *Find the sec. of an angle for a strut of 5 ft. effective length carrying a load 25,000 lbs.*

Effective length $l = 5 \times 12$

$= 60$ inch or 5′;

load = 25,000 lbs

= 11·15 tons

Type	*Effective*	*Length l*
1. Effectively held in position at both ends but not restrained in direction	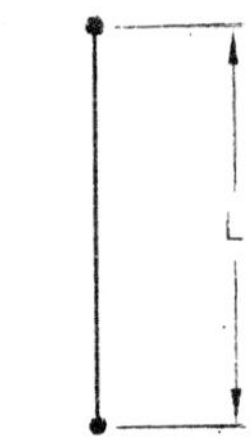	L
2. Effectively held in position at both ends and restrained in direction at one end	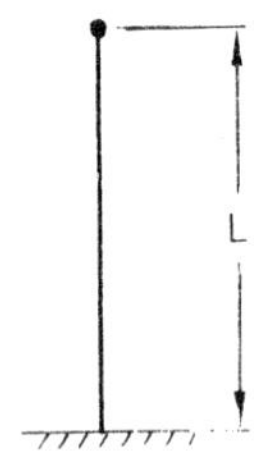	0·85 L
3. Effectively held in position and restrained in direction or both ends	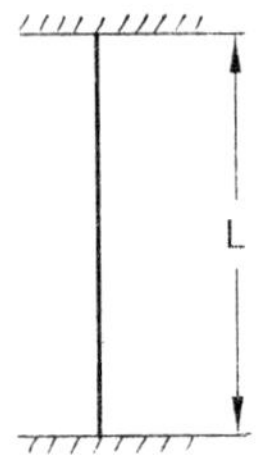	0·67 L
4. Effectively held in position and restrained in direction at one end and free at the other	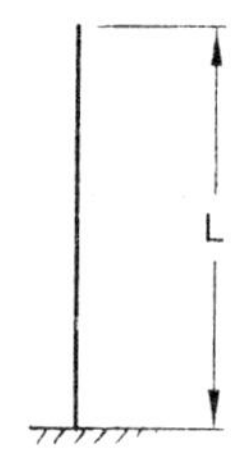	2L

Table A·1. Allowable stresses for axial compression, kg/cm^2

l/r	F_c	l/r	F_c	l/r	F_c	l/r	F_c
0	1250	70	1075	140	531	210	243
10	1246	80	1007	150	474	220	219
20	1239	90	928	160	423	230	199
30	1224	100	840	170	377	240	181
40	1203	110	753	180	336	250	166
50	1172	120	671	190	300	300	109
60	1130	130	597	200	270	350	76

Let allowable stress = 5 *tsi* ;

Area required = 2·23 sq. in

Equal angles having area near about 2·23 sq. in are

3 × 3 × 7/16= 2·43 sq. in area is tried

$\gamma_{min} = 0{\cdot}58$ so $l/r = 60/0{\cdot}58 = 103{\cdot}5$.

$F_c = 809{\cdot}6$ kg/cm² a 5·14 *tsi*

$$\text{Area required} = \frac{11{\cdot}5}{5{\cdot}14} = 2{\cdot}17 \text{ sq. inch. ;}$$

Area provided = 2·43 sq. inch.

Area provided is about 12% in excess of that required. We may try the lower sections.

Try 3 × 3 × 3/8 angle

$r_{min} = 0{\cdot}58$ inch $l/r = 10{\cdot}35$ $F_c = 5{\cdot}14$ *tsi*

Area required = 2·17 sq. inch ; Area provided = 2·11 sq. inch (unsafe)

Hence use 3″ × 3″ × 7/16″ angle.

Example 3. *The continuous principal rafter of a truss is 10 ft. long between intermediate connections. It carries a thrust of 35000 lb. Find a suitable double angle sec. for it. Assuming that there will be at least two rivets.*

$$l = 0{\cdot}7 \times 10 \times 12 = 84 \text{ inch}$$

Let $F_c = 7$ *tsi* Area required $= \dfrac{35000}{7{\cdot}00 \times 2240} = 2{\cdot}23$ sq. inch.

For double angle section, unequal angles with longer legs back to back are more suitable, as by so placing the angle, approximately equal radii of gyration are obtained in the two principal directions. Try 3″ × 2½″ × 5/16″ angles placed as shown in Fig. A·7. Providing $A = 2{\cdot}92$ sq. inch.

Radius of gyration about *xx* for the combination is the same as for one angle.

$r_{xx} = 0{\cdot}93$; Radius of gyration about *yy* by finding the moment of inertia about it.

$$I_{yy} = 2 \times 0{\cdot}87 + 1{\cdot}62\,(0{\cdot}67 + 3/8 \times 1/2)^2 \times 2$$

$$= 1{\cdot}74 + 3{\cdot}12 = 4{\cdot}86 \text{ inch}^4$$

$$r_{yy} = \sqrt{\frac{4{\cdot}86}{2 \times 1{\cdot}62}} = 1{\cdot}225 \text{ inch}$$

$$\therefore \quad r_{min} = 0\text{-}93 \text{ inch} \quad ; \quad l/r_{min} = \frac{7 \times 12}{0{\cdot}93} = 90{\cdot}3$$

$$\therefore \quad F_c = 925{\cdot}4 \text{ kg/cm}^2 \text{ inch } 5{\cdot}88 \textit{ tsi}$$

$$\text{Required } A = \frac{3500}{5{\cdot}88 \times 2240} = 2{\cdot}66 \text{ sq. inch}$$

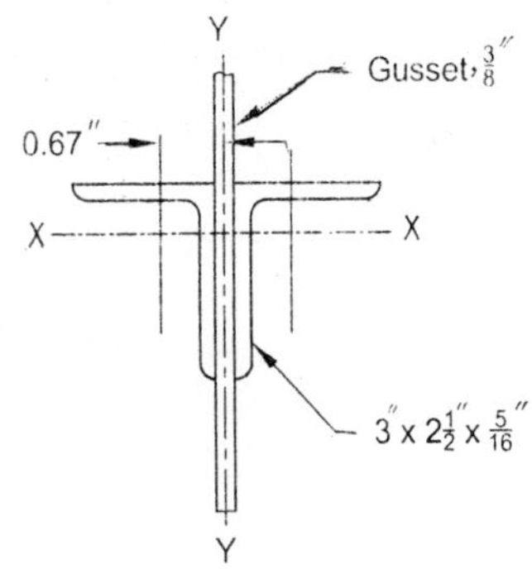

Fig. A·7.

Provided $A = 2 \times 1{\cdot}46 = 2{\cdot}92$ sq. inch (10% excess)

The next choice can now be made of 3″ × 2½″ × ¼″ angles. Because r_{xx} for these is same as before. The area required now is still 2·66. Area provided is 2 × 1·31 = 2·62 sq. inch. This is only 1½% small and can be accepted.

Local Buckling. Compute the compressive strength of an axially loaded column having the section as shown in Fig. A·8, effective length = 11′ (use ISI specifications). For the flanges $b/t = 2{\cdot}0716$. Since the maximum b should be equal to $16t$ *i.e.* 4″. We may consider 1″

length on each flange as removed, both for computing the rad. of gyration and the x-section area. For web b/t = 15(1/4) = 60. This is less than 90 but more than 50 *i.e.* 12·5″ and the central 2·5″ depth be considered ineffective.

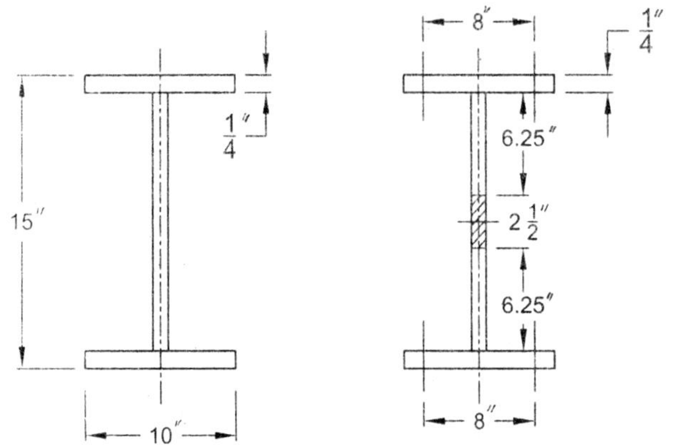

(*a*) Actual area (*b*) Effective area

Fig. A·8.

$$I_y = 12.5\frac{\left(\frac{1}{4}\right)^3}{12} + 2 \times \frac{\frac{1}{4}(8)^3}{12}$$

$$= 21.35 \text{ inch}^4$$

$$A = 2 \times 8 \times ¼ + 12.5 \times ¼ = 7.125\ ;$$

$$r_y = \sqrt{\frac{2.35}{7.125}} = 1.728 \text{ inch}$$

$$l/sy = \frac{11 \times 12}{1.728} = 76.5$$

Allowable compressive stress = 1030·8 kg/cm^2 or 6·55 *tsi* ; A_{eff} = 7·125

Permissible load = 6·55 × 7·125 = 46·6 tons.

It may be noted that same area at the tip of the flanges and of the middle of the web was considered ineffective. These are the positions which will buckle 1st and share less load.

Column Splice. The splicing of a long column can be done at any convenient height preferably about 15 cm to 30 cm above the floor for easy working. The columns may be of the same size or smaller size. The ends should be milled to have a smoother joint. Theoretically for axially loaded column, the splice material will not carry any load but due to wind loads etc. the splices are considered to carry some loads and are designed according to IS : 800—1962. To carry 50% of the direct loads in addition to the moments carried by the members. Care should be taken that the c.g. of the splice should be in the line of the c.g. of the axis of the column.

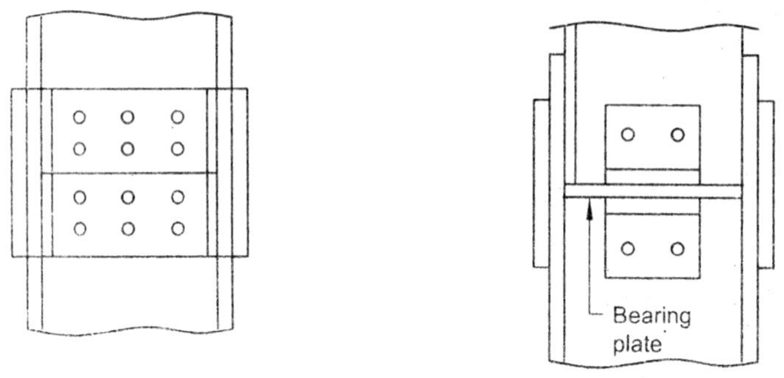

(*a*) (*b*)

Fig. A·9. Riveted splices.

Fig. A·9 shows the typical riveted splices (*a*) members having the same size (*b*) members having different depths, the difference can be covered up by filler plates. A bearing plate should be inserted between the two compressive members to transfer the load.

Welded splices are also very common in these days. Some of the welded splices are shown in the Fig. A·10 and can be used to connect the compressive members of the same dimensions.

Butt welded column splices are more economical than flat welded because they require less welded metal for the given load. Small in equalities in sections can be covered up by intervening filler plates.

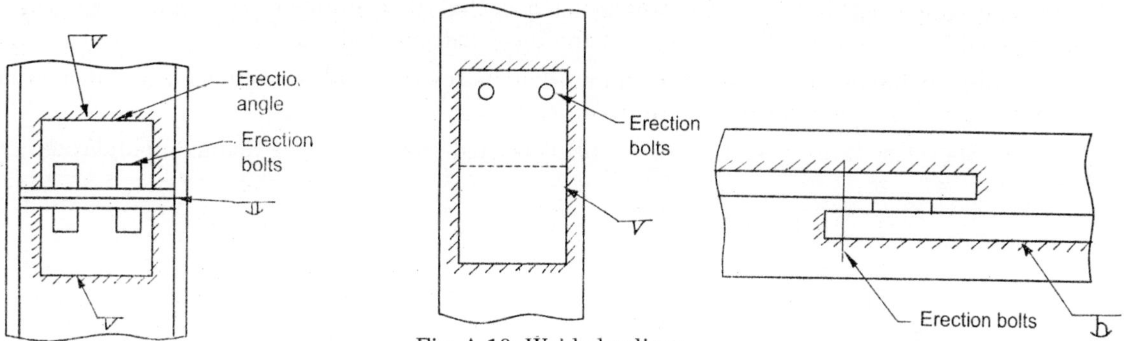

Fig. A·10. Welded splices.

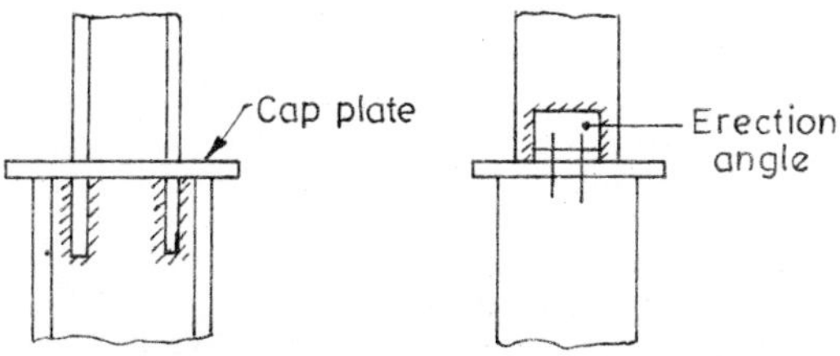

Fig. A·11. Unequal sections.

When the difference in the depths of the sections is such that the flange of upper column. lies within the flange of the lower column, a cap plate is required to transfer the load. The cap plates may be welded in the lower column in the shop and the upper column may be field welded. Erection angle and bolts are used for alignment. The cap plate is designed in bending. When the difference in the depths of the members is large, the cap plate may be reinforced with support stiffners to transfer this load directly to the web of the lower column. This will reduce the bending in the cap plate.

Cased columns. (1) The entire load is taken by the steel section and only stiffeners of the column is increased.

(2) The radius of gyration of the column section about the axis in the plane of its web will be 0·2 (b + 4) in or 0·2 (b + 100) mm where b is the width of the steel flange in inches (or in mm). The radius of gyration about its other axis is taken as that of the uncased section.

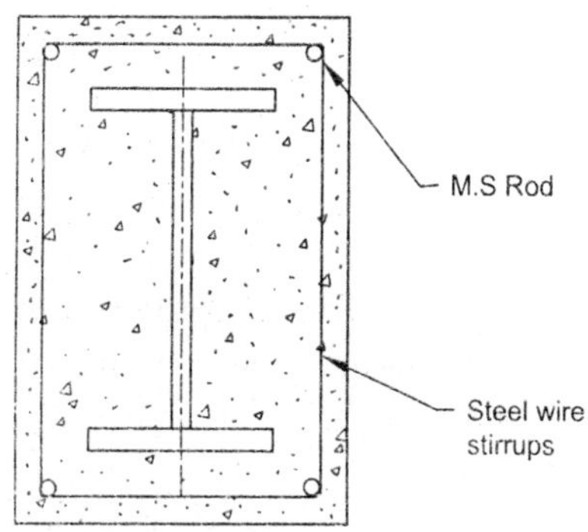

Fig. A·12. Cased columns.

A cased column has to fulfill the following design conditions (IS : 800—1962) :

(1) The member is of symmetrical I-shape of a single I-beam or channels back to back with or without flange plates.

(2) The overall dimensions of the steel section do not exceed 30″ × 18″ (or 750 × 450 mm) over plating where used. The larger dimension being parallel to the web.

(3) The steel column is unpainted and solidly encased in an ordinary dense concrete mix having cube strength not less than 2250 (160 kg/cm^2) at 28 days.

(4) The min. width of solid casing is equal to b + 4 inches (or b + 100 mm) when b is the width of the steel flange in inches or mm.

(5) The surfaces and the edges of the steel column have a concrete cover not less than 2″ (or 50 mm).

(6) The casing is effectively reinforced with steel wires of maximum diameter 3/16″ or 5 mm which must be in the form of stirrups or binding is not more than 6″ (150 mm) pitch so arranged as to pass through the centre of the covering of the edges and outer faces of the

flanges and supported by longitudinal bars not less than 4 in number. The load on the cased column should not be more than 2 times of the designed uncased load.

Column bases. The base of a column distributes the load on column in a wider area. Mainly three types of column bases are used.

(*a*) Slab base (Base plate) (*b*) Gusseted base (*c*) Grillage foundation

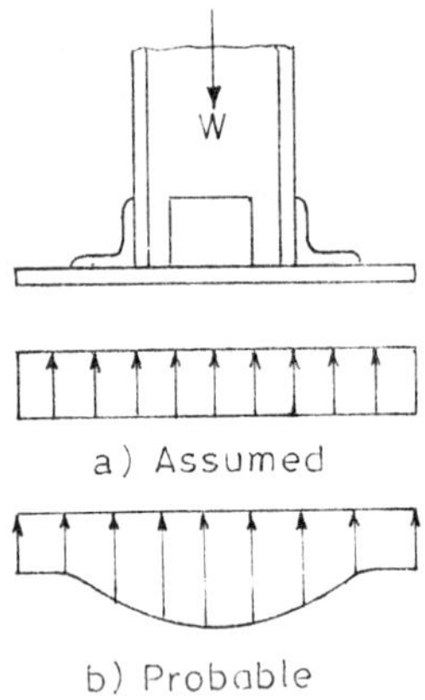

Fig. A·13.

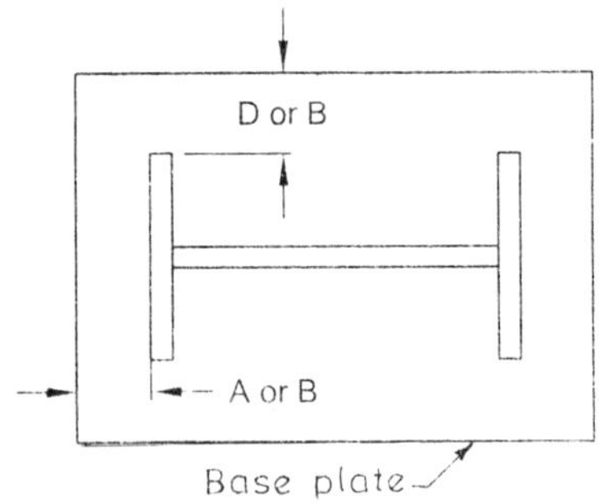

Fig. A·14.

(*a*) **Slab base.** No gusset plate is required. The column section rests on the plate directly by fasteners to retain the parts securely in place to resist all moments and forces other than direct compression, including forces arising due to transit, unloading and erection. The thickness of the base plate is computed by the formula given below (IS : 800—1962) :

$$t = \frac{3w}{F_b}\sqrt{\left(A^2 - \frac{B^2}{4}\right)}$$ where t is the thickness of plate

A = greater projection of the plate beyond column

B = lesser projection of plate beyond column

w = the pressure or loading on the underside of the base

F_b = Permissible bending stress in the slab bases

The permissible bending stress for base plate is 12 *tsi* (1890 kg/cm^2)

For square bases and round column following expression can be used.

$$t = \sqrt{\frac{9w}{16Fb}\cdot\frac{D}{D-d}}$$ where D = side of base, d = dia. of column.

Grillage Footings. Given separately in chapter of Foundations.

Gusset bases. When the end of the column is machined for complete bearing on the base plate, 50% of the axial column load is assumed to be transferred to the base plate by direct bearing and the remaining 50% of axial load will be transferred through the fastenings including gusset plates angle cleats or stiffeners etc.

Where the ends of the column shafts and the gusset plates are not forced for complete bearing, the fastening connecting them to the base plate will be designed to transmit all forces to which the base is subjected.

Circular Pipe or Tube Column. Circular columns have the same radius of gyration about all axes normal to the column section. The tubes for structural purposes are available as below in different dia. d and wall thickness t.

here d = mean diameter of pipe and t is its wall thickness.

The yield stress of ST 40 is the same as mild steel and the design procedure for only this grade of tube will be discussed.

Secant formula for allowable compressive stress,

$$F_c = \frac{f_y/m}{1 + 0{\cdot}15 \text{ sec. } l/r \sqrt{\dfrac{m F_c}{4E}}}$$

This expression has been used only for l/r between 60 and 150. For $l/r = 0$ allowable strain has been taken as $0{\cdot}6\, f_y$. For $l/r = 0$ to 60 linear variation between allowable stress and l/r has been assumed. For $l/r > 150$ the allowable stresses are given by the expression

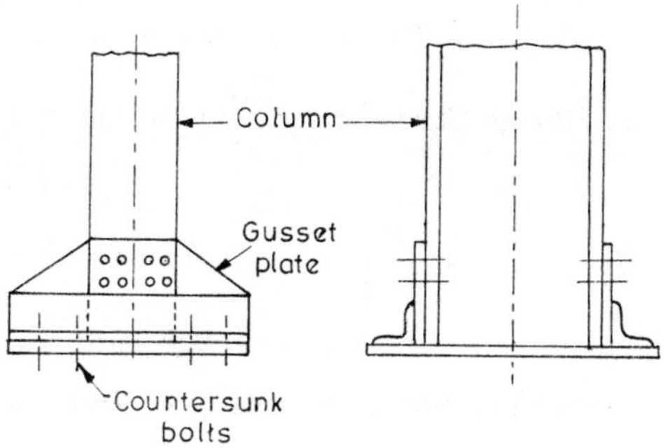

Fig. A·15.

$$Fe = \frac{f_y/m}{1 + 0{\cdot}15 \text{ sec. } l/r \sqrt{\dfrac{m\, Fe}{4E}}} \left(1{\cdot}2 - \frac{1}{750\, r}\right)$$

The radius of allowable stresses are given in table below :

Table A·2. Allowable Axial Stresses in Compressive in Grade ST 40 Tubes

l/r	*Fe kg/cm²*	*Fe, tsi*	*l/r*	*Fe kg/cm²*	*Fe, tsi*
0	1500	9·50	130	638	4·05
10	1448	9·20	140	565	3·59
20	1400	8·89	150	503	3·19
30	1352	8·58	160	443	2·81
40	1303	8·28	170	392	2·49
50	1255	7·97	180	348	2·21
60	1207	7·66	190	311	1·97
70	1155	7·34	200	278	1·77
80	1088	6·91	211	249	1·58
90	1003	6·37	220	225	1·43
100	910	5·78	250	167	1·06
110	813	5·16	300	106	0·67
120	721	4·51	350	71	0·45

To prevent the total buckling of these tubes before failure of tube, the thickness of the tube subject to compressive stress shall not be less than $0{\cdot}865\sqrt[3]{D}$ mm or $1/10\sqrt[3]{D}$ inch where D = outside diameter of tube in inch or mm. Standard sizes of tubes are available.

Design of Steel Beams

Stress in Beams and Permissible Stresses

(*a*) **Bending Stresses :** $f_b = \dfrac{M}{I}.y\ ;\ Z = \dfrac{M}{f_b}$

where f_b = bending stress, M = Moment of resistance, I = Moment of inertia and

y = The distance of the fibre from the neutral axis

z = The section modulus along x-axis

(b) **Shear Stress :** $\frac{FA\bar{y}}{Ib}$ where F = Shear force on the section

I = Moment of inertia

$= \frac{F}{t_w . d}$ b = width of section and f_s = shear stress desired.

where t_w = thickness of web end, d = overall depth of beam.

Allowable Shear Stress (IS : 800—196)

Maximum *Fs* : when depth of web does not exceed 85 times the web thickness and the max. shear stress is calculated from equation $fs = \frac{FA\bar{y}}{Ib}$ it should not exceed 7·0 *tsi* (1100 kg/sq. cm.).

Average *Fs* : For webs whose depth does not exceed 85 times their thickness, the allowable average shearing stress *Fs* is equal to 6 *tsi* (945 kg/sq. cm.) The allowable shear stress may be increased by 33¹/₃% when wind and seismic forces are taken into account. For webs where depth thickness ratio exceeds 85. Stiffeners are necessary and the allowable shear stress depends upon the dimensions of the panel.

(c) **Safe Bearing Stress :** (IS : 800—1962). The permissible bearing stress for steel confirming to IS : 226—1962 in specified as 12 *tsi* (1800 kg/cm^2) for normal and live loads. When the effect of earthquake or wind is also included, the safe bearing stress may be increased by $33^1/_3$%.

(d) **Deflection.** The maximum deflection in beams is given by the following formula :

$$\Delta = K\frac{wL^3}{EI}$$

Δ = Maximum deflection W = Total load on the span

L = Span length E = Young's modulus of elasticity

I = Moment of Inertia

and K is a constant depending upon the distribution of loading and end conditions of the beam.

Allowable Bending Stress

Form		F_{bc}* *tsi*	or F_{bt}# *kg/cm*^{2}
Rolled *I*-beams and channels		10·5	1650
Other sections thickness	≤ 20 mm	10·0	1575
	> 20 mm	9·5	1500
Compound beams : I or channels with cover plates thickness	≤ 20 mm	10·5	1650
	> 20 mm	10·0	1575
Plate girders, plate thickness	≤ 20 mm	10·0	1575
	> 20 mm	9·5	1500
Slab bases and rectangular sections		12·0	1890
circular pins		13·5	2120

* F_{bc} on gross area #F_{bt} on net area

Data for Design Beams

Beam	*km coeff. of max. moment*	*k coeff. of max. def.*	*a/L min.*	*a/L Min. for f = 10·5 tsi*
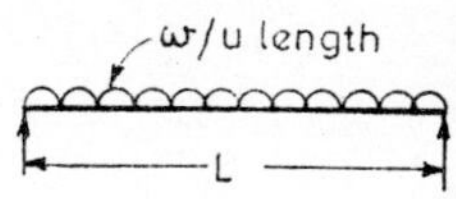	1/8	5/384	67·7 *t/E*	1/18·9
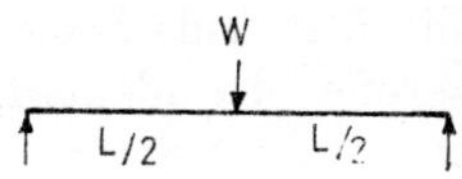	1/4	1/48	54·2 *t/E*	1/23·5
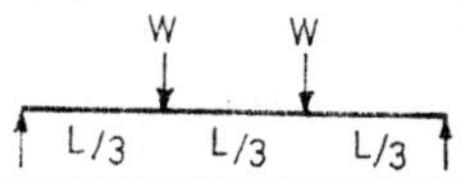	1/3	23/648	69·2 *t/E*	1/18·5
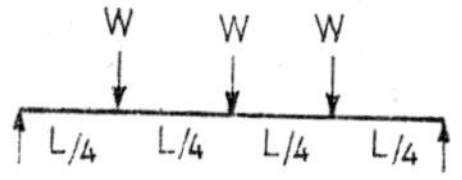	1/2	19/384	64·4 *t/E*	1/19·0
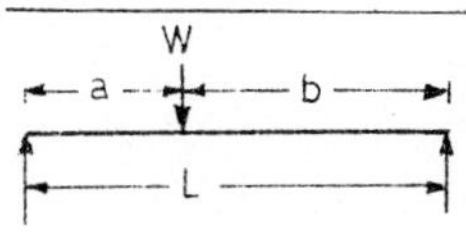	$\frac{ab}{L^2}\;\frac{1}{a\sqrt{3}}$	$\frac{a}{L}\left(1-\frac{ab}{L^2}\right)^{\frac{3}{2}}$		
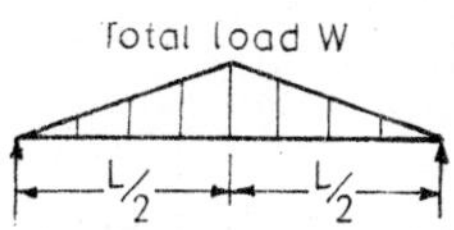	1/6	1/60	65·0 *t/E*	1/19·6
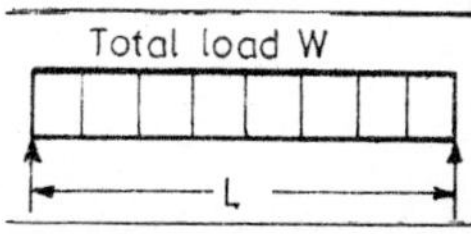	1/2	1/8	81·7 *t/E*	1/15·6
	1	1/3	109 *t/E*	1/11·7
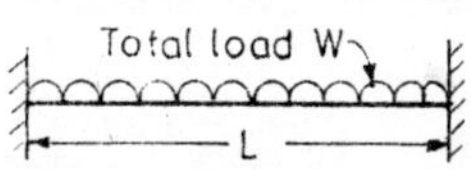	1/12	1/384	20·4 *t/E*	1/62·5
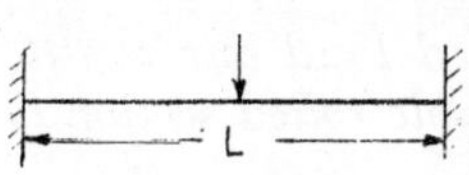	1/8	1/192	27·3 *t/E*	1/46·6
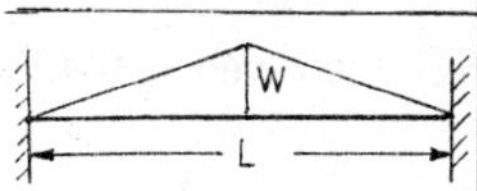	5/48	7/1920	22·7 *t/E*	1/56·1
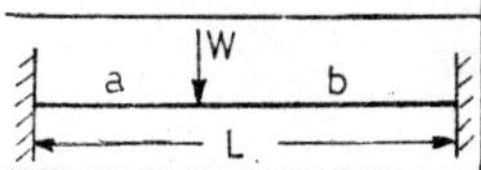	$\frac{ab^2}{L^3}$			

Fig. A·16.

Example 4. *Effective span 25′, uniformly distributed load 1280 lbs/ft. including its own weight. Design the beam according to IS : 800. Flange is held against lateral displacements.*

$$M = \frac{1280 \times 25^2}{8} \times 12 = 1200{,}000 \text{ in lbs} = 356 \text{ in tons } (wl^2/8)$$

$$F = \frac{1280 \times 25}{2} = 1600 \text{ lb} = 7{\cdot}14 \text{ tons } (wl/2)$$

Allowable bending stress $Fb = 10{\cdot}5\ tsi$

Allowable shearing stress $Fs = 6{\cdot}0\ tsi$

Design for Bending stress

$$Z \text{ required} = \frac{536}{10{\cdot}5} = 51{\cdot}1 \text{ inch}^3$$

From steel tables it is found that 14 × 5/2 *I* @ 40 *i.e.* 14″ deep and 25½″ wide *I*-joist weighing 40 lb per ft.) has a section modulus of 53·87 inch^3. This may therefore be adopted, check for shear—For 14 × 5½ *I* @ 40, $t_w = 0{\cdot}37$ so $A_w = 0{\cdot}37 \times 14 = 5{\cdot}18$ inch^2.

$$fs = \frac{7{\cdot}14}{5{\cdot}18} = 1{\cdot}38\ tsi < 6\ tsi \text{ (safe)}$$

Check for deflection $= \Delta = \frac{5}{384} \cdot \frac{wL^3}{EI}$; $w = 1280 \times \frac{25}{2240} = 14{\cdot}28$ tons

I for 14 × 5½ *I* @ 40 = 377·1 inch^4 from steel tables.

$E = 13400\ tsi$

$$\Delta = \frac{5}{384} \cdot \frac{14{\cdot}28 \times (25 \times 12)^3}{13400 \times 377{\cdot}1} = 0{\cdot}993 \text{ inch.}$$

$$\frac{\Delta}{L} = \frac{0{\cdot}993}{25 \times 12} = \frac{1}{302} > \frac{1}{325} \text{ not safe hence revise the section}$$

To reduce the deflection *I* should be increased in the ratio $\frac{325}{302}$.

From the steel tables 15 × 5 @ 14*z* (with *I* = 428·5 inch″, *z* = 57·13 inch^3) may be taken.

Built up Beams (Refer Fig. A·17)

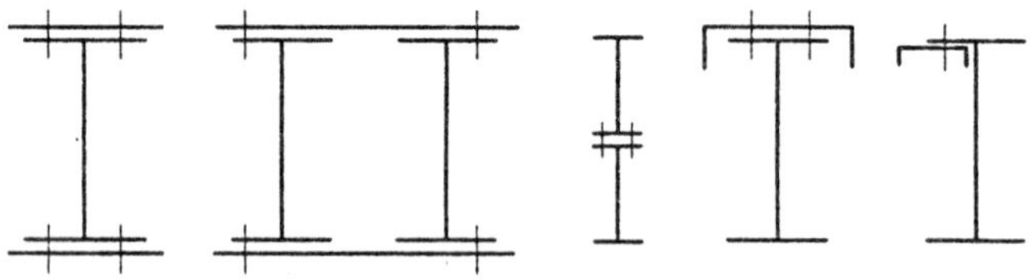

Fig. A·17.

Example 5. (*For composite section)—span 15′, Total distributed load one ton/ft. uniform two concentrated loads of 10 tons each at mid 3rd points. The available rolled section is 15 × 5 I 42. Take* $F_b = 10\ tsi$.

For 15 × 5 *I* 42, *Z* = 57·13 inch^3 *I* = 428·5 inch ; flange thickness = 0·647 inch web = 0·42″ thick.

Flange plates : Maximum $M = \left(\frac{1 \times 15^2}{8} + \frac{10 \times 15}{3}\right) \times 12 = 948$ in tons.

Allowable bending stress given = 10 *tsi*

Required $Z = \frac{940}{10} = 94{\cdot}0 \text{ m}^3 > 57{\cdot}13 \text{ in}^3$. Therefore the flanges are to be reinforced with extra flange plates.

Assuming that the flange plates will be connected to the I beam by 3/4″ diameter rivets provided in two parallel rows in top as well bottom flanges, the I beam section will be reduced by four rivet holes in the flanges, using equation $\frac{Z - Z_1}{d} + A_h = A_s$ (where A_s = area of holes and A_p = Area of plate).

$$A_p = \frac{94{\cdot}0 - 57{\cdot}13}{15} + 2 \times \frac{13}{16} \times 0{\cdot}647 \text{ or } A_p = 3{\cdot}51 \text{ sq. in.}$$

Assuming 1/2″ thick plates, gross width $= \frac{3{\cdot}51}{0{\cdot}5} + 2 \times \frac{13}{6} = 8{\cdot}65$ inch

Try ½″ × 9½″ plates

Check for fibre stress—Gross I = 428·5 + 2 × 9·5 × ½ × 7·75² = 998 m⁴

$$fb = \frac{940}{298} \times 8{\cdot}0 = 7{\cdot}54 \; tsi$$

This beam is safe in compressive stress. To find the maximum tensile stress, the bending stress found above is increased in the ratio of gross area of tension flange to its net area.

$$\therefore \text{ Maximum tensile stress} = 7{\cdot}54 \times \frac{9{\cdot}5 \times \frac{1}{2} + 0{\cdot}647 \times 5}{9{\cdot}5 \times \frac{1}{2} + 0{\cdot}647 \times 5{\cdot}2 \times \frac{13}{16}(0{\cdot}5 + 0{\cdot}647)} = 9{\cdot}83 \; tsi < 10 \; tsi \text{ O.K.}$$

Rivets : Maximum S.F. = 17·5 tons

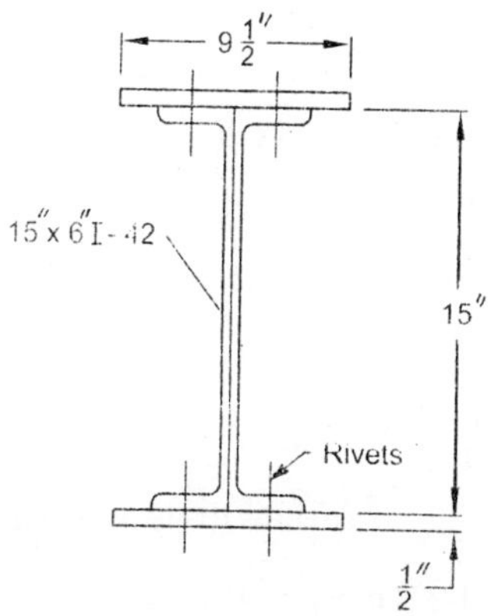

Fig. A·18.

Strength of 3/4″ diameter power driven shop rivet in single shear $= 6{\cdot}5 \times \frac{\pi}{4}\left(\frac{13}{16}\right)^2 = 3{\cdot}36$ tons in bearing on 1/2″ plate $= 15 \times \frac{13}{16} \times 0{\cdot}5 = 6{\cdot}1$ tons.

∴ Rivet value R = 3·36 tons ;

$$p = \frac{4IR}{F_{bt}(d + t)} = \frac{4 \times 998 \times 3{\cdot}36}{17{\cdot}5 \times 9{\cdot}5 \times 0{\cdot}5(15 + 0{\cdot}5)}$$

$$= 10{\cdot}9'' \; (p \text{ is pitch of rivet})$$

From IS : 600—1962 the maximum pitch in compressive flange is $16t$ or 8″ whichever is less. (t is thickness of plate)

Here $16t$ = 16 × ½ = 8″. Hence on the compressive side 8″ pitch may be adopted throughout. The maximum pitch in tension is specified as $24t$ or 12″ whichever is less. This gives maximum pitch of 12″. Since the required pitch is less than the maximum a pitch of 10½″ may be provided near the ends which may be increased to 12″ towards the centre where the shear force decreases.

Design of a Plate Girder. The design of a plate girder can be done by following the example given below :

Example 6. *Design a riveted plate girder to carry a uniform load of 4900 kg/m excluding self weight of the girder. In addition the girder has to support two concentrated loads at the top flange at one-3rd point. Each concentrated load is 40,000 kg. The effective span of the girder is 18 m. Use Indian Standard Specifications.*

Total load on girder = 4900 × 18 + 2 × 40,000 = 168200 kg.

From the equation, $w = \frac{W}{300}$; where w = self weight of girder in kg/m and W is the total load applied to the girder in kg.

$$w = \frac{166200}{300} = 550 \text{ kg/m}$$

assume a load weight of girder = 500 kg per m.

$$\text{Maximum B.M.} \quad M_{max.} = \left[\frac{(4900 + 500)18^2}{8} + 40,000 \times \frac{18}{3}\right] \times 100 = 45940,000 \text{ kg/cm}$$

$$\text{Maximum S.F.} \quad F_{max.} = (4900 + 500)\frac{18}{2} + 40,000 = 88,600 \text{ kg.}$$

Preliminary Design. The girder is assumed to be effectively supported laterally and the allowable bending stresses both in tension and compression will be taken as 1500 kg/cm^2.

$$\text{Economical depth } d = 1{\cdot}1\sqrt{\frac{M}{F_b . t_w}} = 1{\cdot}1\sqrt{\frac{45,940,000}{1500 \times 0{\cdot}6}} = 248 \text{ cm.}$$

The thickness of the web will be kept **the minimum permissible *i.e.* 6 mm. Since the adopted depth should be kept smaller than the value given by the economical depth formula**, we may choose the depth of web as 200 cm. For checking the assumed weight the equation $w = \frac{3M}{F_b . d}$ may be used which gives

$$w = \frac{3 \times 45940000}{200 \times 1500} = 460 \text{ kg/m}$$

which is less than the assumed weight of 500 kg/cm. So reasonable

The B.M. and S.F. diameter for the girder is shown below :

Shear stress$[(\text{S.F.})/(d.t_w)] = \frac{88,600}{200 \times 0{\cdot}6}$ = 739 kg/cm < 945 kg/cm^2 ; **945** being allowable shear stress, IS : 800—1962.

$$\text{Net area for flange required} = \frac{1{\cdot}05\, M}{F_b . d} - \frac{A_w}{8} \quad \left(\textbf{equation } A_f = \frac{1{\cdot}05\, M}{Fb.d} - \frac{A_w}{8}\right)$$

$$= \frac{1{\cdot}05 \times 45,940,000}{1500 \times 200} - \frac{0{\cdot}6 \times 200}{8} = 145{\cdot}1 \text{ sq. cm.}$$

Use the following composition of each flange. The rivets are assumed to be **22 mm diameter** so the **diameter of hole = 23·5 mm.**

Element	*Gross area*	*Deduction for holes*	*Net area*
2 *Ls* I.S.A. 150150 @ 27·2 kg/m	2 × 34·59 = 69·18	4 × 1·2 × 2·35 = 11·33	57·88
2 PIS, 400 mm × 12 mm	2 × 40 × 1·2 = 96·00	2 × 2·4 × 2·35 = 11·30	84·70
	165·18		142·58
Equivalent web area	1/6 × 0·6 × 200 = 20·00		1/8 × 0·6 × 200 =15·00
Total	185·10		157·58

(Equivalent web area = 1/6 t_w for given and 1/8 t_w for net is taken in the flange area).

It is more than 145·1 sq. m. as required hence is adequate.

Checking of Section. The chosen section is shown in the Fig. below :

Moment of inertia of gross section :

	I_0	+	Ay^2	=	I
web	$\frac{0{\cdot}6 \times 200}{12}$		—		400,900
angles	$4 \times 735{\cdot}4$	+	$4 \times 34{\cdot}59\,(100{\cdot}5 - 4{\cdot}14)^2$	=	1293,000
cover plates	$2 \times 40(2{\cdot}4)^3$	+	$2 \times 40 \times 2{\cdot}4(100{\cdot}5 + 1{\cdot}2)^2$	=	1940,000
			Total	=	3,683,000 cm^4

Bending stress on gross area

$$= \frac{45,940,000}{3,683,000} \times 102{\cdot}9$$

$$= 1282 \text{ kg/cm}^2$$

Bending stress on net area,

$$fb = 1282 \times \frac{185{\cdot}18}{157{\cdot}53}$$

$\therefore$ $fb = 1505$ kg/cm^2

(Safe as the allowable tensile stress = 1500 kg/cm^2)

Hence assumed section is O.K.

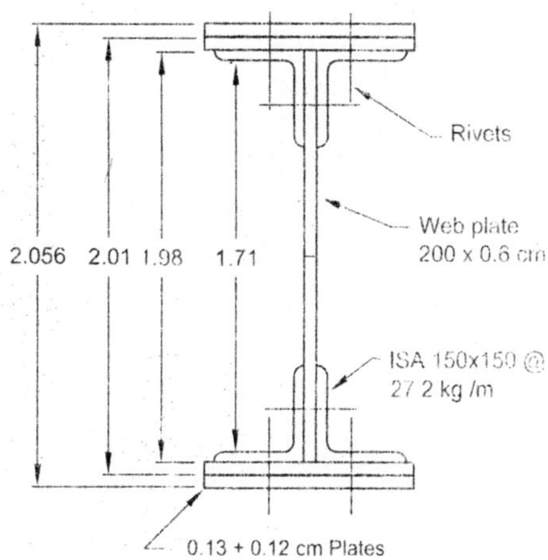

Fig. A·19.

Intermediate Stiffeners

Clear depth of web = 171 cm

$$\frac{d}{t_w} = \frac{171}{0{\cdot}6} = 285$$

As the $\frac{d}{t_w}$ ratio is greater than **250**, both longitudinal and transverse stiffeners will be used. The longitudinal stiffeners will be placed *d/s* from the comp. flange and at the neutral axis of the girder. The clear d' for the web will now be $1/2 \times 171 = 85{\cdot}5$ cm and $\frac{d'}{t_w} = \frac{85{\cdot}5}{0{\cdot}6} = 142{\cdot}5$ (171 cm will be the clear distance of web excluding LS as shown in Fig. A·19)

(*a*) **Vertical Stiffeners.** From the table of shear stresses for an actual shear stress of 739 kg/cm^2 (= 4·7 *tsi*) and $\frac{d'}{t_w} = 142{\cdot}5$ we find the maximum stiffener spacing as 1·5 d'. Thus the spacing of $1{\cdot}5 \times 171/2 = 182{\cdot}2$ is permissible. Since by the condition of the problem, there will be bearing stiffeners at the ends and at the 3rd points *i.e.* 6 metres apart, a spacing of 120 cm may be adopted for the vertical web stiffeners for the sake of uniformity.

For the transverse stiffeners, required moment of inertia.

$I = 1{\cdot}5\, d'^3\, t_w{}^3/c^2$ (The moment of inertia of stiffener angles should not be less than $1{\cdot}5\, d'^3\, t_w{}^3/c^2$)

where c is the stiffener spacing.

$$I = 1{\cdot}5 \times 85{\cdot}5^3 \times 0{\cdot}6^3/120^2 = 14{\cdot}1 \text{ cm}^4$$

Trying an angle sufficient to accommodate 22 mm rivets in the connected leg as ISA 7070 with 6 mm thickness we get

I on face of web = $36{\cdot}8 + 8{\cdot}06 \times 1{\cdot}94^2$ O.K.

These stiffeners will be placed alternatively on each side of the web. No filler will be used and the stiffeners will be joggled over the vertical leg of the flange angle.

Note : ISA 7045, 6 mm would have sufficient but outstanding leg of 70 mm is adopted to make it equal to that of the longitudinal stiffeners in the order to improve the look of the girder.

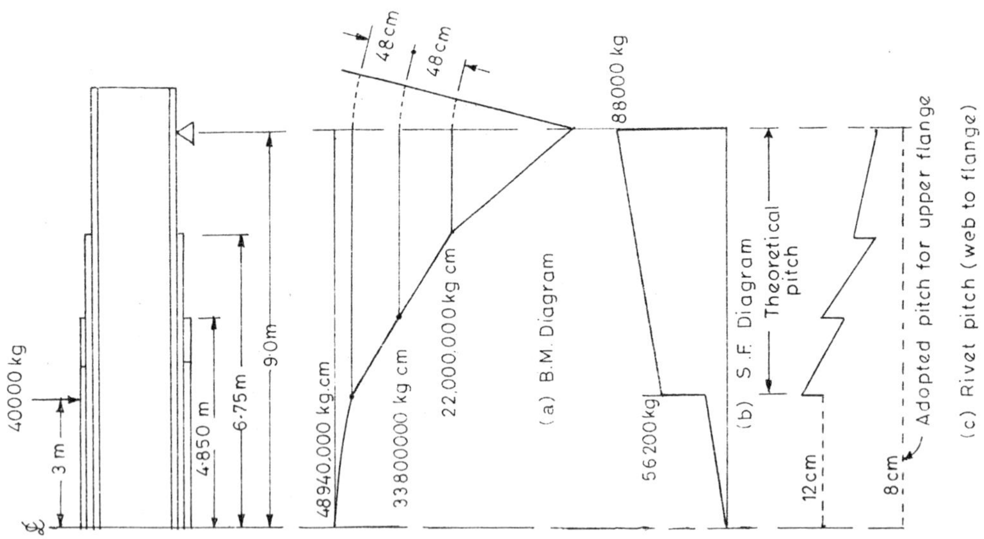

Fig. A·20.

Note : Depth of web = 1/10 to 1/12 of the span (Not rigid). The girders deeper than 1/10th of span and shallower the 1/12th of span can also be used. It also depends on the head room of the girder. After the depth has been decided the width of web can be calculated which must not less than 6 mm. The allowable shear stress = 945 kg/cm^2 (IS : 800—1962) provided d/t_w ratio for the web does not exceed 85. d = clear distance between the flanges.

Table A·3. Allowable Average Shear Stress in Stiffened webs

d'/t_w	*For distance 'C' between Vertical Stiffeners (tsi)*												
	0·33 d'	*0·4 d'*	*0·5 d'*	*0·6 d'*	*0·7 d'*	*0·8 d'*	*0·9 d'*	*d'*	*1·1 d'*	*1·2 d'*	*1·3 d'*	*1·4 d'*	*1·5 d'*
85	6	6	6	6	6	6	6	6	6	6	6	6	6
90	6	6	6	6	6	6	6	6	6	6	6·00	6·00	6·00
100	6	6	6	6	6	6	6	6	6	6	5·95	5·89	5·84
110	6	6	6	6	6	6	6·00	6·00	5·93	5·84	5·76	5·70	5·64
120	6	6	6	6	6	6·00	5·96	5·88	5·76	5·66	5·58	5·51	5·45
130	6	6	6	6	6·00	5·91	5·80	5·72	5·59	5·49	5·39	5·32	5·25
140	6	6	6	6·00	5·91	5·76	5·05	5·56	5·42	5·31	5·21	5·12	5·05
150	6	6	6	5·97	5·78	5·62	5·49	5·40	5·25	5·13	5·02	4·93	4·86
160	6	6	6·00	5·85	5·64	5·47	5·34	5·24	5·08	4·95	4·84	4·74	4·66
170	6	6	5·99	5·73	5·51	5·33	5·19	5·08	4·91	4·77	4·65	4·55	4·46
180	6	6	5·88	5·60	5·37	5·10	5·03	4·92	4·74	4·60	4·47	4·36	4·27
190	6	6	5·77	5·48	5·24	5·04	4·88	—	—	—	—	—	—
200	6	6·00	5·67	5·36	5·10	4·89	4·23	—	—	—	—	—	—
210	6·00	5·93	5·56	5·24	4·97	4·75	—	—	—	—	—	—	—
220	6·00	5·84	5·45	5·15	4·83	4·60	—	—	—	—	—	—	—
230	6·00	5·76	5·35	4·99	4·70	—	—	—	—	—	—	—	—
240	6·00	5·67	5·24	4·87	4·56	—	—	—	—	—	—	—	—

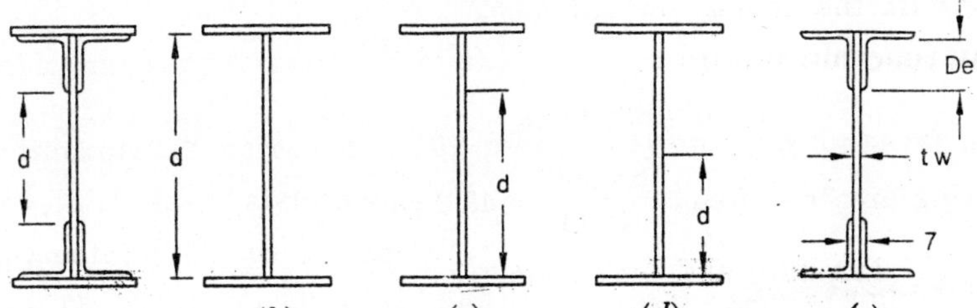

Fig. A·21.

$$d' = D_1 - 2D_2 \text{ or } d' = D_1 - 8\,(T + 7)$$

Shear between angle and web $= \dfrac{t_w^2}{2h} = \dfrac{0{\cdot}6^2}{2} \times 7{\cdot}0 = 0{\cdot}0257$ t/cm

Strength of 22 mm rivet in single shear $= \dfrac{\pi}{4} \times 2{\cdot}35^2 \times 1025 = 4450$ kg

In bearing on 0·6 mm = 2·35 × 0·6 × 2360 = 3350 kg. So rivet value = 3550 kg.

$$\text{Pitch} = \frac{3{\cdot}350}{0{\cdot}0257} = 130 \text{ cm.}$$

Maximum pitch = 32 t = 32 × 0·6 = 19·2 cm. Adopt a pitch of 19 cm.

(*b*) Horizontal stiffeners at $d/5$ depth.

Required $I = 4c_1\, l_w{}^3 = 4 \times 120 \times 0{\cdot}6^3 = 103{\cdot}8$ cm^4.

Try pair of angles ISA 7070, 6 mm thick placed on both sides of web.

I (centre of web) = $2[36{\cdot}8 + 8{\cdot}06\,(1{\cdot}94 + 0{\cdot}03)^2]$

$= 154{\cdot}4$ cm^4 > $103{\cdot}8$ cm^2

Alternatively try ISA 7070, 6 mm thick single angle

I(face of web) $= 57{\cdot}2 + 13{\cdot}02 \times 2{\cdot}10^2 = 114{\cdot}7$ cm^2 > $103{\cdot}8$ cm^4 O.K.

This will be adopted. Rivets may be provided at 19 cm pitch.

(*c*) Horizontal stiffener at mid depth.

Required $I = d'\, t_w^3 = 85{\cdot}5 \times 0{\cdot}6^3 = 18{\cdot}5$ cm^3

Try ISA 7550, 6 mm thick with 75 mm leg connected with the web.

I face of web $= 14{\cdot}3 + 7{\cdot}16 \times 1{\cdot}2^2 = 24{\cdot}6$ cm^4 > $18{\cdot}5$ cm^4

Rivets may be provided at 19 cm pitch.

Bearing Stiffeners. Bearing stiffeners are provided at the concentrated loads and at bearing of the girder.

(*a*) **Bearing stiffener at the concentrated load :**

Load = 40,000 kg

Bearing area required $= \dfrac{40{,}000}{1890} = 21{\cdot}2$ sq. cm^2

Try 2 Nos. ISA 130130 @ 19·7 kg/m. The connected legs of the bearing angles will be chamfered to clear the fillets of flange angles and only the outstanding legs give the required bearing area.

Bearing area = 2(13 − 1·0) 1·0 = 24·0 sq. cm O.K.

Effective length = 0·7 × Actual length = 0·7 (201·2 × 1·2) 139 cm

A length of web (20 × thickness of web on each side of the centre line of stiffener) will be considered with the area of the stiffener.

(*b*) **At reaction points :**

$$\text{Load} = 88600 \text{ kg}$$

$$\text{Bearing area required} = \frac{88,600}{1890} = 45{\cdot}2 \text{ cm}^2$$

Try 4 No. ISA 130130 @ 19·7 kg/metre

$$\text{Bearing area} = (13 - 1{\cdot}0) + 4 = 48{\cdot}0 \text{ cm}^2$$

$$\text{Effective length} = 139 \text{ cm.}$$

Curtailment of cover plates. Refer B.M. diagram which must be drawn to the scale.

The maximum moment occurs at mid of the span and goes on decreasing towards the supports. The cover plates can be curtailed as the moment decreases. The simplest procedure for locating the theoretical points of cut-offs for cover plates is graphical.

Moment of resistance $M_R = (A_f + A_w/6)\ F_b.d_c$ ($A_w/6$ is the equivalent area of web taken for load bearing with flange)

or $\quad M_R = A_a + A_w/6 + A_1 + A_2 + A_3 \,..A_n)$

where A_1 = area of flange and A_a = area of flange angles and A_1, A_2 ... A_n is the areas of different cover plates.

The moment of resistance contributed by various flange plates and angles can be brocken up as follows :

M_R due to 1st plate $= A_1\ F_b.d$

M_R due to 2nd plate $= A_2\ F_b.d$

M_R due to nth plate $= A_n\ F_b.d$

Thus the moment of resistance due to various flange plates is proportional to their areas. To find out the points of curtailment, mark the M_R values with different section combinations of the flange on the y-axis which represents the moments of resistance and then draw lines parallel to the x-axis and mark the points of intersection with the B.M. diameter. The section combination concerned can be curtailed a bit beyond their respective points of intersection with the B.M. diameter.

If the load is uniformly distributed and the B.M. diameter is a parabola then the point of curtailment can be computed analytically within formula $x_r = \dfrac{l}{2}\sqrt{\dfrac{A_1 + A_2 + A_3 - A_r}{Af + \dfrac{A_w}{6}}}$ where x_r is the distance for rth plate.

Total span load $= 12{\cdot}5 \times 9 = 112{\cdot}5$ tonnes

$$\text{Approximately self load of girder} = \frac{W}{300}\ \frac{\text{kg}}{\text{m}} \text{ (as in case of riveted girder)}$$

$$= \frac{112500}{300} = 417 \text{ kg/m}$$

Let the dead weight of the girder be 400 kg/m. The maximum B.M. will occur at any section when the live load is fully acting. For computing the maximum S.F. at any section the load will be assumed to be acting only on one side (the larger side). The maximum B.M. and S.F. diameter are shown in Fig. A·20.

Maximum B.M.= 333 tonnes.meters   Maximum S.F. = 60·2 tonnes

Web. Allowing about 10 cm for the two flanges, try a web of height 100 tons which is commonly available.

Allowable shear stress = 945 kg cm^2 d_w = depth of web

t_w = thickness of web

Thickness of web = $\dfrac{60200}{945 \times 100}$ = 0·646 cm, used 7 mm thick web plate.

Flange. $A_f = \dfrac{M}{f\,8g} - 1/6\,A_w = \dfrac{33,300,000}{1500 \times 104} - \dfrac{1}{6} \times 100 \times 0{\cdot}7$

assuming 4 cm thick flanges, distance between c.g. of two flanges is 104 cm.

or A_f= 218 – 11·67 = 206·33 cm^2

Use a flange plate of size 50 cm × 4·5 inch. Although the beam is laterally supported the flange width should not be less than span/50 *i.e.* 40 cm.

Checking of stresses : Moment of Inertia I

$$= \frac{0{\cdot}7(100)^3}{12} + 2 \times 50 \times 4{\cdot}5(52{\cdot}25)^2$$

$$= 58{\cdot}00 + 1230000$$

$$= 1{\cdot}288{,}300 \text{ cm}^4$$

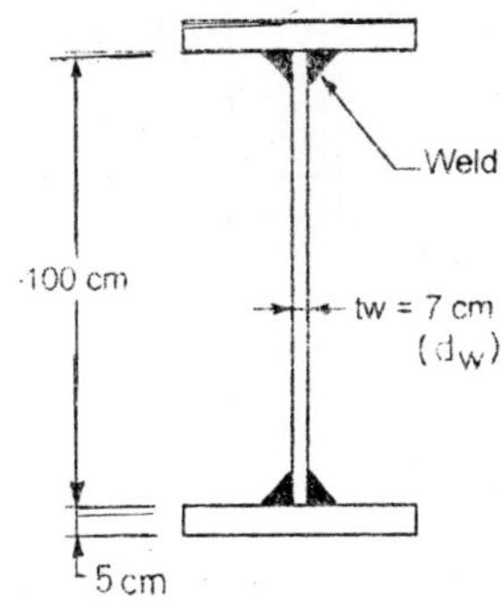

Fig. A·22.

Bearing stress $= \dfrac{33,300,000}{12,88,300} \times 54{\cdot}5$ = 1410 kg/cm^2 (safe)

Intermediate stiffener : For web $\dfrac{d_w}{t_w} = \dfrac{100}{0{\cdot}7} = 143 > 85$

Hence intermediate stiffeners will be required.

Shear stress $= \dfrac{60{\cdot}2 \times 1000}{100 \times 0{\cdot}7}$ = 862 kg/cm^2

From the table A·3 the spacing of transverse stiffeners can be equal to d *i.e.* 100 cm. Although the spacing of vertical stiffeners can be increased as shear stress decreases. It will not be convenient in this problem as the bearing stiffeners will be provided at every 2 metres.

Required I for the stiffener $= 1{\cdot}5\dfrac{d^3 t^3}{c^2} = 1{\cdot}5\dfrac{(100)^3(0{\cdot}7)^3}{(100)^2}$ = 36·5 cm^4

Try 8 cm × 0·6 cm plate on one side

$$I = 0{\cdot}6\ (8)^3 = 102{\cdot}5 \text{ cm}^3$$

S.F. on welds connecting stiffener to web $= \dfrac{t^2}{2h}$ tonnes/cm

$$= \frac{(0{\cdot}7)^2}{2 \times 8} = 0{\cdot}0306 \text{ tonnes/cm}$$

Size of weld $= \dfrac{\cdot 0306}{0{\cdot}7 \times 1{\cdot}025}$ = 0·043 cm (too small)

Use 3 mm intermittent weld with welded length = 7·5 cm

Unwelded length = 7·5 cm.

Bearing Stiffeners

End Stiffener. Load = 60·2 tonnes ; allowable bearing stress = 1890 kg/cm^2

$$\text{Bearing area required} = \frac{62,200}{1850} = 33 \text{ cm}^2$$

The bearing stiffener should extand as nearly as practable to the outer edges of the flanges. Use 18 cm width plates. As *b/t* ratio should not exceed 16, thickness of stiffener should not be less than 1·125 cm say 1·2 cm.

Bearing area = 2 × 16·5 × 1·2 = 35·6 (OK)

To take up the compressive load, a length of web equal to 20 t_w *i.e.* 14 cm will be assumed to be acting with the stiffener. Since one side only 10 cm is available the area shadded in the Fig. A·23 will be considered to take reaction.

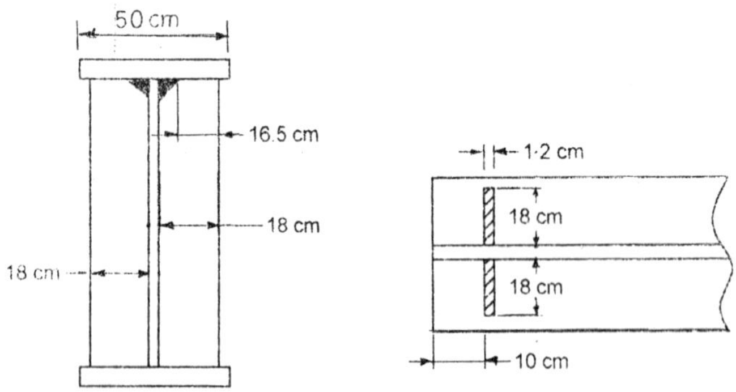

Fig. A·23.

$$I = 1{\cdot}2\frac{(36{\cdot}7)^3}{12} = 4940 \text{ cm}^4$$

$$A = 0{\cdot}7 \times 24 + 36 \times 1{\cdot}2 = 60{\cdot}0 \text{ cm}^2$$

$$r = \sqrt{\frac{4940}{60}} = 9{\cdot}1 \text{ cm}$$

Effective depth

= 0·7 × actual length

= 0·7 × 100 = 70 cm

$$l/r = \frac{70}{9{\cdot}1} = 7{\cdot}7$$

allowable compressive stress = 1247 kg/cm^2 (Table A·4).

$$\text{Area required} = \frac{60,200}{1247} = 48{\cdot}3 \text{ cm}^2 < 60{\cdot}0 \text{ (O.K.)}$$

Length of weld = 2(100 – 1·5) = 197 cm

$$\text{Required strength of weld per cm} = \frac{60200}{197} = 306 \text{ kg/cm}^2$$

$$\text{Size of weld} = \frac{306}{0{\cdot}7 \times 1025} = 0{\cdot}426 \text{ cm or use 5 mm weld.}$$

Table A·4. Allowable Stress for Axial Compression IS : 800—1962

l/r	f_c *kg/cm*^{2}	*l/r*	f_c *kg/cm*^{2}	*l/r*	f_c *kg/cm*^{2}	*l/r*	f_c *kg/cm*^{2}
0	1250	70	1075	140	531	210	243
10	1246	80	1007	150	474	220	219
20	1239	90	928	160	423	236	199
30	1224	100	840	170	377	240	181
40	1203	110	753	180	336	250	166
50	1172	120	671	190	300	300	109
60	1130	130	597	200	270	350	76

(*b*) **Bearing stiffener at concentrated loads.** If the beams *D* and *E* frame into the web of the girder, another bearing stiffener is required. The joint will stiffen the web. In any case, if bearing stiffeners are required. The same size as above will be used because for 18 cm wide stiffener the minimum thickness is 1·2 cm.

Deduction in size of flange plate. The thickness of the flange plate will be reduced in two steps.

With 50 cm × 3·2 cm flange plates.

$$I = \frac{0{\cdot}7(100)^3}{12} + 2 \times 50 \times 3{\cdot}2(51{\cdot}6)^2 = 58{,}300 + 852{,}000 = 918{,}300 \text{ cm}^4$$

$$\text{Moment of resistance} = \frac{90{,}300 \times 1500}{53{\cdot}2} = 25{,}600{,}000 \text{ kg cm} = 256 \text{ tonne-m with } 50 \text{ cm} \times$$

2·0 cm flange plate.

$$I = \frac{0{\cdot}7(100)^3}{12} + 2 \times 50 \times 2{\cdot}00(51)^2 = 58{,}300 + 520{,}000 = 578{,}300 \text{ cm}^4$$

$$\text{Moment of resistance} = \frac{578{,}300 \times 1{,}500}{52} = 16{,}600{,}000 \text{ kg cm} = 166 \text{ cm.}$$

Fig. B.M. & S.F. diagram shows the points where the section of the plate can be reduced. Thickness of flange plate can be reduced to 3·2 cm at 590 cm from the support and to 20 cm at 310 cm from the support.

Attachment of flange to web. Maximum shear at sunction of web and flange

$$= \frac{FA\bar{y}}{I} = 60{,}200 \times 50 \times 4{\cdot}5 \times 52{\cdot}25 = 551 \text{ kg/cm}$$

$$\text{Size of weld} = \frac{551}{2 \times 0{\cdot}7 \times 1025} = 0{\cdot}385 \text{ cm} \text{ ; Minimum size of weld } 6{\cdot}0 \text{ mm}$$

$$\text{Percentage of welded length} = \frac{3{\cdot}95}{6{\cdot}0} \times 100 = 65{\cdot}8\%, \text{ use welded length} = 15 \text{ cm.}$$

Unwelded length = 7·5 cm

The details of welded girder is shear in the adjoining Fig. A·25.

Web Splice. Web carries moment proportional to its share of moment of inertia. Let the web splice be located at 50 cm towards the centre from the point of application of concentrated load. At this section we find,

Total moment, $M = 44{,}080{,}000$ kg.cm.

Total shear, $V = 13500$ kg.

$$I_w = \frac{0{\cdot}6 \times 200^3}{12} = 400{,}000 \text{ cm}^4$$

$$M_w = \frac{4000}{3683000} \times 44080000 = 4800000 \text{ kg.cm}$$

Thus the web splice is to be designed for moment M_w and shear force V. The splice will be designed by using moment plates *A* to carry only moments M_w and shear plates *B* to carry only vertical shear force. The allowable bending stress in the moment plates is equal to the actual bending stress in the plate girder at that level.

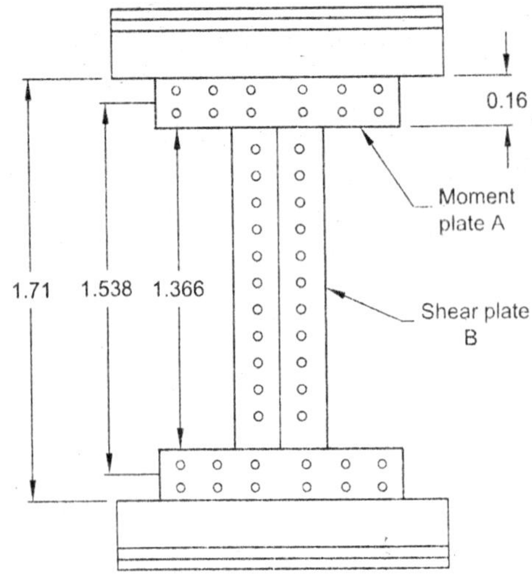

Fig. A·24.

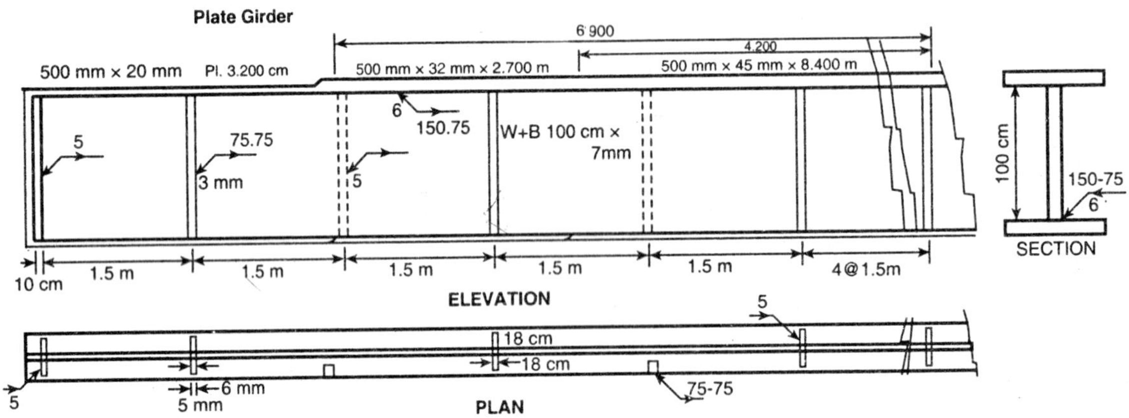

Fig. A·25. Plate girder.

Moment plates. Let 2 rivets be used per vertical line for moment. The width of plate required for 22 mm rivets is 2 × 7·5 say 16 cm. Allowing 6 mm clearance between the flange angles and plates *A*, the lever arm of plate *A* is given as = 171·0 – 1·2 – 16 = 153·8 cm.

$$\text{Force in each plate} = \frac{4800{,}000}{153\cdot8} = 31200 \text{ kg}$$

$$\text{Bending stress at centre of plate } A = \frac{44080000}{3683000} \times \frac{153\cdot8}{2} = 921 \text{ kg/cm}^2$$

$$\text{Net area of plate } A = \frac{31200}{921} = 33\cdot9 \text{ cm}^2$$

$$\text{Thickness} = \frac{33\cdot9}{16 - 2 \times 2\cdot35} = 3\cdot1 \text{ cm}$$

Provide 16 cm × 16 mm plate on both sides of the web.

Number of connecting rivets should be sufficient to develop the strength of plate *A*.

Rivet value of rivet on web = 3350 kg (as earlier)

$$\text{No. of rivets} = \frac{31200}{3350} = 9\cdot3 \text{ say } 10$$

Provides two rows of 5 rivets each on either side of the joint.

Length of these plates will be 10 × 7·5 = 75 cm.

Shear plates. Allowing 6 mm clearance between plate A and B, depth of these plates

$$= 153{\cdot}8 - 16 - 1{\cdot}2 = 136{\cdot}6 \text{ cm}$$

Thickness for shear $= \dfrac{13500}{136{\cdot}6 \times 945} = 0{\cdot}104$ cm, too small

Provide 6 mm thick plates on both sides of the web plate.

No. of rivets $= \dfrac{13500}{3350} - 4{\cdot}03$

Maximum pitch of rivets = 32 t_w = 19·2 cm. Provide single line of rivets on each side of the joint.

Flange Splice. The angles are available in lengths greater than 18 metres and no flange splice should actually be needed. However the process is illustrated as below.

Flange angle splice will be designed at area of the girder is available and the B.M. at that section is 344,300 kg metres.

Area of the flange angle spliced $= 34{\cdot}59 \text{ cm}^2$

∴ Area of splice material $= 1{\cdot}05 \times 34{\cdot}39$ (15% excess area of spliced angle)

$= 32{\cdot}22$ cm

use ISA 130 130 @ 28·9 kg/m giving an area of 36·31 cm^2 (Leg size of this angle is less than the original so that it will not project beyond).

Distance of c.g. of flange angle from N.A. = 85·5 + 10·86

= 96·36 c

Average stress on the flange angle $= My/I$

$$= \frac{34{,}430{,}000}{3683000} \times 96{\cdot}36$$

$= 901$ kg/cm^2 (on gross area)

Force in flange angle = 34·39 × 901 = 31,200 kg

Force in splice angle = 1·05 × 31200 = 32,800 kg

The splice angle will be connected by 22 mm rivets. Rivet valine (in single shear)

= 4450 kg (as before)

No. of rivets $= \dfrac{32{,}800}{4450} = 7{\cdot}4$ or 8 rivets

The corner of the splicing angle will be shaped to get the fillet of the original angle.

Welded Plate Girder. In welded structure the section loss in rivet holes is saved and hence it is stronger than rivetted structures for the same mass. In welded structure web plates are directly welded to flange and no flange angles are used. Box girders are welded girders with two webs. The main design principle is the same as is rivetted girders. The design is illustrated through an example.

Example 7. *Fig. A·26 shows a cross-section of a theatre balcony. The girder A receives the load from the beams D and E and transmits it to the column as which it is supported. The spacing of beams D and E is 2 m c/c and these transfer a dead load of 5 tonnes and a live load of 7·5 tonnes at every 2 m on the girder A. The span of the girder is 20 m. Design a welded plate girder for A. The depth of the girder is limited to 110 cm. Beam D and E and the slab provide the lateral support.*

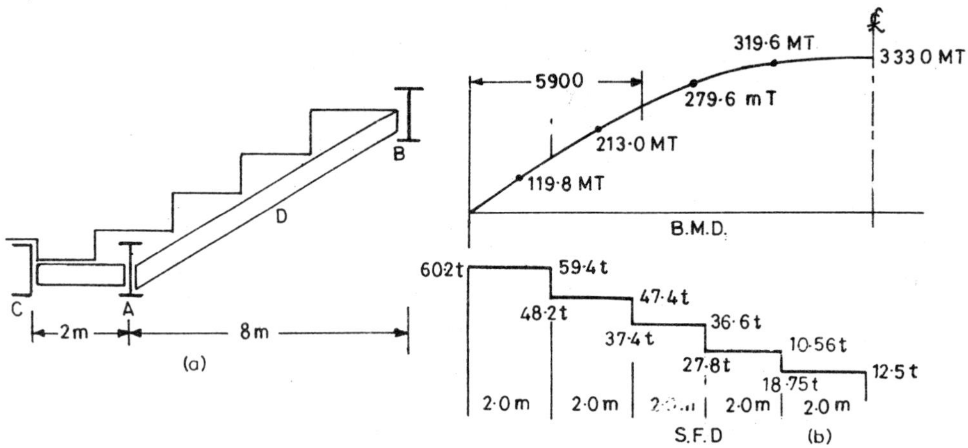

Fig. A·26.

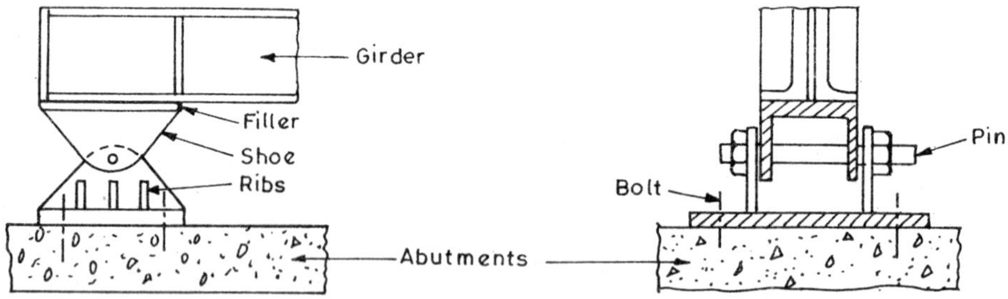

(*a*) (*b*)

Fig. A·27. Rocker bearing.

Rocker Bearings. The typical Rocker Bearings are shown in the Fig. A·27(*a*). The rotation is allowed by insertion of a pin. The shoe transfers the load to the pin by direct bearing. Two or more pins depending upon the magnitude of reactions are used to transfer the load. The vertical plates on the sides completely encircle the pin. This provides the resistance to uplift. The centre plate however, does not completely encircle the pin but contacts it on a surface which is slightly less than half cylinder. For a positive reactions all plates are effective and for uplift only those plates will be effective which completely encircle the pin. The pin will be designed for bearing shear and bending. The thickness of vertical plates and the diameters of the pin can be determined by trial and error only. The thickness of the plate depends on the diameter of the pin, as the thickness multiplied by the diameter of the pin gives the bearing area and the bending moment in the pin depends upon the thickness of the plates. The size of the base plate is determined by the allowable bearing pressure on the supporting masonry.

The addition in the vertical loads, the bearings are subjected in lateral and longitudinal loads also. The increase in vertical loads caused by the lateral and longitudinal loads should be taken into account. The lateral and longitudinal loads may be assumed to act at the level of the pin. There will therefore cause moment about both the areas of the base plate, resulting in additional pressure on masonry. The total vertical pressure should be checked. The wind and the earthquake loads should also be considered.

The base plate is designed in bending to take up the pressure on masonry. The plates of the base plate will act as beam or cantilever depending on the location of the ribs.

The anchor bolts are used to prevent shifting of the bearings under lateral or longitudinal loads and also to resist any unexpected uplift. As the lateral loads are generally accompanied by the vertical loads also, friction is usually sufficient to prevent shifting. The initial lightening of the bolts helps in increasing the friction.

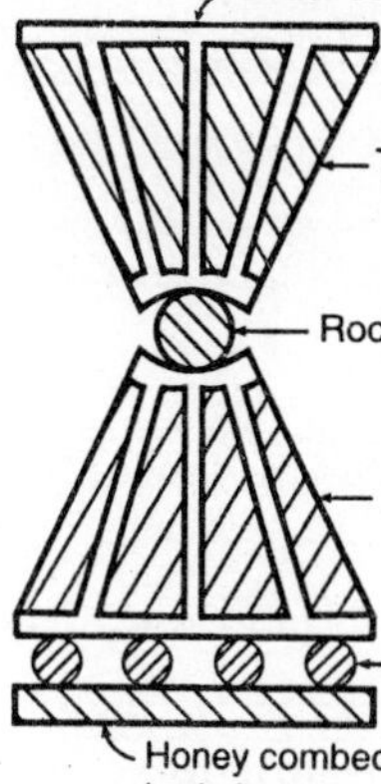

Fig. A·28. Roller bearings.

Roller Bearings. In addition of the functions of the roller bearing, a roller bearing has to perform the function of permitting the longitudinal movement of the girder. The longitudinal movement may be due to stress in the supported chord or flange, temperature changes or shifting of abutment. The extent of horizontal movement is generally specified by the specifications. It can be taken as 3 mm for every 3 m span. Unlike sliding bearings the roller bearings require a small longitudinal force to cause the movement. The rolling friction is taken as 0·03. Rollers are used to allow the movement. The pressure in tons per linear inch on rollers of rolled steel having a maximum tolerance of 0·0 and 0·0015 inch on the diameters should not exceed 0·30*d* where *d* dia. of roller in inches. For cast iron rollers, the allowable loads may be taken 300 *d* pounds per inch length.

In the Fig. A·27 (*b*) in the bearings a single roller is used, which gives both purposes of permitting the rotations and horizontal movement. For heavier loads either a larger diameter roller will be required or a much larger length will be necessary. **To make the bearing more compact a number of rollers are used.** If the rollers are of small size circular rollers are used. For the larger dia. rollers sides are formed so that these may be placed close to each other. Such rollers are called segmented rollers. When two or more rollers are used, the longitudinal movement is permitted very easily, but due to the rotation of the girders, the rollers towards the mid point will be heavily stressed to allow the girder to change slope and to have equal loads on all rollers, we have to use either a rocker or a pin.

To keep the rollers correctly spaced, side bars are used to connect them. Tooth guides may be used for proper movement. A kind of key or tongue may be used to prevent sliding of rollers in the lateral directions.